Baseball

1998 Almanac

A Comprehensive Review Of the 1997 Season, Featuring Statistics and Commentary

Distributed by Simon & Schuster

For additional copies, send $12.95 plus $5.00 shipping and handling to:
Baseball America, P.O. Box 2089, Durham, N.C 27702

Baseball America's 1998 Almanac

PUBLISHED BY
Baseball America Inc.

EDITOR
Allan Simpson

ASSISTANT EDITOR
John Royster

CONTRIBUTING EDITORS
Steve Borelli
Will Lingo
Lacy Lusk
John Manuel

CONTRIBUTING WRITERS
Peter Barrouquere, Mike Berardino, Jim Callis, Pat Caputo, Joe Christensen, Wayne Graczyk, Howard Herman, Sean Kernan, Gary Klein, Andrew Linker, Javier Morales, Tim Pearrell, John Perrotto, Curt Rallo, Gene Sapakoff, George Schroeder, Larry Starks, Susan Wade, Jeff Wilson

PRODUCTION
Jeff Brunk
Valerie Holbert
Casey Mansfield Thomas

STATISTICAL PRODUCTION CONSULTANT
Howe Sportsdata International,
Boston, Mass.

Baseball America

PUBLISHER/Dave Chase
EDITOR/Allan Simpson
MANAGING EDITOR/Will Lingo
PRODUCTION SUPERVISOR/Jeff Brunk
ADVERTISING DIRECTOR/Kris Howard

COVER PHOTO/Ken Griffey by David Seelig

EDITOR'S NOTE

Major league statistics are based on final, unofficial 1997 averages. Minor league statistics are official.

The organization statistics, which begin on page 47, include all players who participated in at least one game during the 1997 season. Pitchers' batting statistics are not included, nor are the pitching statistics of field players who pitched on rare occasions. For players who played with more than one team in the same league, the player's cumulative statistics appear on the line immediately after the player's second-team statistics.

Innings have been rounded off to the nearest full inning.

*Lefthanded batter, pitcher #Switch hitter

Contents

Major Leagues

1997 SEASON

Interleague play, chase for 61 homers hightlight year

BY MIKE BERARDINO

The earth did not quake. The sky did not fall. Civilization as we know it did not come screeching to a halt in 1997.

All of which must have surprised the purists nearly as much as the mere sight of American League teams playing baseball against National League teams. In the middle of June. In the midst of (gasp) the regular season.

The Ballpark at Arlington was the site of the first interleague baseball game in regular-season history. The San Francisco Giants took a 4-3 victory over the Texas Rangers on June 12, setting in motion an experiment that proved, for the most part, wildly popular.

Attendance spiked up 20 percent across the board for the 214 interleague games, spread over two week-long stints–the first in June, the second at the end of August and first few days of September. The booming attendance (33,407 average) included the largest three-game series crowd in Camden Yards history (for the Orioles-Phillies) and a Canada Day Expos-Blue Jays game that spurred the first SkyDome sellout in 26 months and 195 home dates.

The National League came out on top, 117-97, in the head-to-head duels, for which the designated hitter was used in American League parks only.

For the first go-round, Eastern and Central division teams played a total of 15 games against their league counterparts–five series of three games each. The Western divisions played four series of four games each against their counterparts, for a total of 16 interleague games.

And though the bold experiment made for some strange scheduling–two-game series proved maddening to participants and followers alike–in the end it proved more than worthwhile.

The Mets and Yankees dueled memorably in Yankee Stadium. Same for the Cubs and White Sox in Comiskey Park, the Angels and Dodgers in Dodger Stadium, the Athletics and Giants in 3Com Park. Perhaps we didn't really need to see the Brewers clash with the Pirates or the game's two worst pitching staffs, from Oakland and Colorado, square off in (yikes!) Coors Field.

But everyone seemed to have a good time.

"Baseball considers itself the purest sport, but it's probably the most unpure of all sports," said Lou Piniella, manager of the Seattle Mariners, a particularly hot interleague draw. "You have different strike zones in the two leagues. You have a DH in one league and no DH in the other. And the game still doesn't have a commissioner.

"I like the idea of fans in both leagues being able to see the best ballplayers. In the past, fans in both leagues got cheated. They only got to see certain players on television or read about them."

As for the argument that interleague play would detract from the All-Star Game and the World Series, year one found that to be profoundly wrong. Fans were treated to a stirring American League victory in Cleveland in the midsummer classic, while the Fall Classic still featured a matchup of two teams that had never met outside spring training: the Marlins and the Indians. Florida won Game Seven, 3-2, on Edgar Renteria's two-out hit in the bottom of the 11th inning.

FRANK RAGSDALE

Ken Griffey went deep 56 times
Challenged Roger Maris' mark of 61 homers

About the only real mishap wrought by interleague play came when Pirates outfielder Al Martin tried to find the home ballpark of the Minnesota Twins. Martin, on his first visit to the Twin Cities, showed up not at the Metrodome but at the Target Center, home of the NBA's Minnesota Timberwolves.

"It did seem kind of small," Martin said. "I was thinking, 'It's a bandbox. No wonder the ball flies out of here.' "

Divisive Issue

The task of finding divisional homes for 1998 expansion teams in Tampa Bay and Arizona proved quite painful. It nearly sparked a revolution.

For several months major league owners floated a proposal that would shift league affiliations for as many as half of the game's 30 franchises. So-called radical realignment was based on the results of a July survey in which focus groups in Miami, New York,

Cleveland and San Francisco overwhelmingly favored such a plan.

According to the owners, 76 percent of the 801 fans surveyed supported realignment of both leagues for geographical purposes. If that meant putting every Eastern time zone team in the American League and all Mountain and Pacific time zone teams in the National League, so be it.

If that meant hacking up the six-division arrangement just when people were getting used to it and going back to two divisions in each league–while adding a second wild card in each league–the owners were willing to do that too.

Acting commissioner Bud Selig, Red Sox owner John Harrington and other leaders of the realignment push focused on the benefits. Of the 4,000 major league games played each year, 80 percent would have been played in a team's own time zone. Considerable savings in travel costs and the generation of new regional rivalries were cited as selling points as well.

LARRY GOREN

Bud Selig
Interleague stalemate

"You can call it evolution, but nothing lasts forever," said Dodgers broadcaster Vin Scully, an unlikely proponent of realignment. "Back in the days of Nap Lajoie, foul balls weren't strikes. Once upon a time, you had eight teams in two leagues playing 154 games per season. A lot of things have changed over the years. It's time to be practical."

Opponents of radical realignment focused on the loss of tradition, which had kept the leagues distinct and separate for 96 years. They recoiled at the thought of teams like the Cincinnati Reds and Atlanta Braves leaving behind nearly a century of National League history. They scoffed at any plan that would allow four second-place teams into the postseason.

They also quarreled with the notion that such a menacing boulder could be set in motion by two franchises yet to play their first game.

"There's absolutely no truth to the rumor," said NBC broadcaster and avowed purist Bob Costas, "that the Devil Rays will be in the same division as the Minnesota Timberwolves."

Eventually the union chimed in with a reminder that its membership would have to ratify any sweeping change. Taking the DH out of more than a half-dozen AL cities–or worse, eliminating it altogether, as some proposals held–would not endear the plan to Donald Fehr and company.

Controversy boiled over throughout the summer and into the fall as the owners threatened to give back the considerable gains the game had made since ending the work stoppage of 1994-95.

More than 56 percent of the respondents in a Baseball America poll agreed that "realignment is inherently evil."

In the end, a compromise was struck on Oct. 15. Radical realignment was scaled back drastically. Instead of 15 teams changing leagues, there would be just one, Selig's Milwaukee Brewers.

The three-division setup would stay. Arizona's Diamondbacks would report to the National League West (as they wished). The Tampa Bay Devil Rays would head to the AL East, bumping the Tigers into the AL Central. The Royals chose to stay put, enabling the Brewers to then jump to the NL Central and leaving the game with 14 AL teams and 16 in the NL.

Returning to an unbalanced number was the only solution that would keep baseball from having to schedule at least one interleague game every day.

Chasing Roger

Roger Maris' record for single-season home runs withstood its most serious challenge yet.

This assault was double-barreled. Swinging from the left: Ken Griffey. Whaling from the right: Mark McGwire.

Griffey, the Mariners center fielder, hit two homers on Opening Day and stayed hot. He set records for most home runs through April (13) and May (24) and finished June with 29.

Beset by injuries throughout his career, Griffey finally stayed healthy enough to make a serious run at Maris. A monthlong power outage (one homer from June 23-July 24) knocked him off pace, but he nearly made up for that with a scorching September (12 homers).

Griffey reached 52 with 11 games to play and 55 with five to play. He finished with 56 home runs, 12 ahead of his next closest American League challenger, Tino Martinez of the Yankees. Griffey became the

LARRY GOREN

Mark McGwire switches leagues
34 homers for Oakland, 24 homers for St. Louis

fifth AL player since 1990 to hit 50 home runs or more.

Said Mariners teammate Jay Buhner: "When he gets locked in a zone, and I've seen Junior get locked in for a long time, anything's possible."

McGwire, with 58, came even closer to immortality. The hulking Athletics first baseman overcame the breakup of his marriage and persistent trade rumors to reach 34 homers by July 16. A trade to St. Louis reunited him with his old manager, Tony La Russa, but McGwire adjusted slowly to National League pitching.

He endured the second-longest power drought of his career (19 games) before coming to life on Aug. 8. McGwire hit 24 homers the rest of the year, including 15 in September and three in the season's final two days.

Of course, McGwire didn't just hit them, he *really* hit them. Five of the six longest home runs of the season belonged to McGwire.

"He's not human; he doesn't count," said Jose Canseco, McGwire's former Oakland Bash Brother. "Check his blood. Mac's an alien from the future who's come back to show us how to play this game."

Still, he wasn't able to catch Mr. Asterisk. Maris' mark has now stood since 1961, two years longer than Babe Ruth managed to hold the previous record.

LARRY GOREN

Larry Walker
Triple Crown threat

Another record chase, although somewhat less compelling and sustained, involved Ted Williams' 56-year run as the last man to bat .400.

Rockies outfielder Larry Walker carried a .408 mark into July. Padres outfielder Tony Gwynn, Williams' fellow San Diegan and the consensus pick as most likely to match Teddy Ballgame's feat, stayed at the hallowed .400 mark until June 13.

Gwynn, with the help of a special shoe that protected his troublesome heel, finished at .372-17-119 to win his fourth consecutive batting crown and eighth overall.

Walker finished second in batting (.366), first in homers (49) and third in RBIs (130) to evoke memories of Carl Yastrzemski, whose triple crown season of 1967 remains the last of its kind.

"There's no doubt it will happen within the next couple of years," Yastrzemski said of the triple crown, which only 14 major leaguers have accomplished. "There's better hitter's parks now, and there's the expansion thing. And there's a lot of great hitters out there. It's really a great time to be a hitter."

Significant Deals

In many ways the Florida Marlins were the perfect World Series champion.

They spent the winter lavishing $89 million on a handful of high-profile free agents, including Alex Fernandez, Bobby Bonilla and Moises Alou, then signed Gary Sheffield to a six-year, $61 million contract extension in April.

DENIS BANCROFT

World Series MVP Livan Hernandez
Short-lived celebration?

By June, owner Wayne Huizenga, projecting an annual loss of $30 million, announced he was putting the team up for sale. Without a new downtown Miami ballpark featuring a retractable roof and gobs of luxury-box money, the Marlins could not afford the price of competition.

By October, the Marlins were downing the Indians in Game Seven of the World Series, besting by three years the '69 Mets record as the youngest expansion champion.

After the Series, Huizenga announced plans to sell the team to a group led by club president Don Smiley.

"You don't do the game a favor by going to the postseason when you lose $30 million and feel you have to sell the team," Cubs president Andy MacPhail said. "There's something very–what's the word?–wrong about that."

The Marlins' sea of red ink came amid claims from the owners that they had lost a combined $185 million in 1996 and a total of $875 million over a three-year period. That '96 loss was significantly lower than the one for fiscal 1995, when the owners lost $326 million in a season shortened three weeks by the lingering strike.

Still, even as major league owners cried poverty in 1997 they continued throwing obscene riches at their on-field employees.

Albert Belle bolted from the Indians to the White Sox for a record $55 million over five years. That it was hawkish owner Jerry Reinsdorf's signature beside Belle's on the contract only served to heighten the outrage and expedite ratification of a new Basic Agreement.

1997 MAJOR LEAGUE ALL-STAR GAME

Alomar Emerges As Hero In Entertaining Affair

For the second year in a row, a hometown boy made good at the All-Star Game. After Philadelphia-area native Mike Piazza earned MVP honors at Veteran's Stadium in 1996, Sandy Alomar electrified Cleveland's Jacobs Field faithful with a similarly heroic effort.

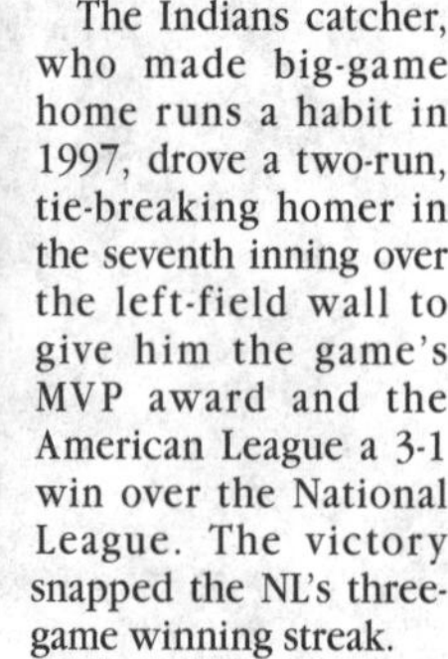

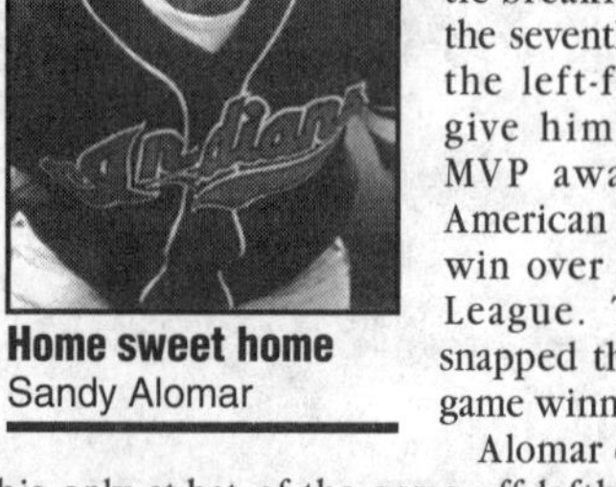

Home sweet home
Sandy Alomar

The Indians catcher, who made big-game home runs a habit in 1997, drove a two-run, tie-breaking homer in the seventh inning over the left-field wall to give him the game's MVP award and the American League a 3-1 win over the National League. The victory snapped the NL's three-game winning streak.

Alomar connected in his only at-bat of the game off lefthander Shawn Estes (Giants), who took the loss. Lefthander Jose Rosado (Royals) picked up the win, even though he gave up the lone NL run in the seventh and worked only one inning. Righthander Mariano Rivera (Yankees) pitched a scoreless ninth for the save.

TOP VOTE GETTERS

AMERICAN LEAGUE

CATCHER: 1. Ivan Rodriguez, Rangers, 1,666,384; 2. Sandy Alomar, Indians, 1,557,431; 3. Dan Wilson, Mariners, 571,336.

FIRST BASE: 1. Tino Martinez, Yankees, 866,722; 2. Jim Thome, Indians, 847,416; 3. Frank Thomas, White Sox, 817,008.

SECOND BASE: 1. Roberto Alomar, Orioles, 1,657,418; 2. Chuck Knoblauch, Twins, 920,774; 3. Joey Cora, Mariners, 766,395.

THIRD BASE: 1. Cal Ripken, Orioles, 2,571,985; 2. Matt Williams, Indians, 1,226,778; 3. Wade Boggs, Yankees, 455,757.

SHORTSTOP: 1. Alex Rodriguez, Mariners, 1,854,758; 2. Omar Vizquel, Indians, 954,822; 3. Derek Jeter, Yankees, 796,619.

OUTFIELD: 1. Ken Griffey, Mariners, 3,514,340; 2. David Justice, Indians, 1,840,716; 3. Brady Anderson, Orioles, 1,197,617; 4. Juan Gonzalez, Rangers, 869,235; 5. Marquis Grissom, Indians, 854,364; 6. Manny Ramirez, Indians, 801,585; 7. Jay Buhner, Mariners, 772,972; 8. Albert Belle, White Sox, 660,019; 9. Bernie Williams, Yankees, 585,380.

NATIONAL LEAGUE

CATCHER: 1. Mike Piazza, Dodgers, 2,626,213; 2. Javier Lopez, Braves, 598,858; 3. Kirt Manwaring, Rockies, 498,930.

FIRST BASE: 1. Jeff Bagwell, Astros, 1,494,752; 2. Andres Galarraga, Rockies, 1,185,850; 3. Fred McGriff, Braves, 1,132,842.

SECOND BASE: 1. Craig Biggio, Astros, 1,161,610; 2. Eric Young, Rockies, 848,510; 3. Ryne Sandberg, Cubs, 735,720.

THIRD BASE: 1. Ken Caminiti, Padres, 1,438,736; 2. Chipper Jones, Braves, 1,102,585; 3. Vinny Castilla, Rockies, 938,960.

SHORTSTOP: 1. Barry Larkin, Reds, 1,160,651; 2. Jeff Blauser, Braves, 971,124; 3. Walt Weiss, Rockies, 671,142.

OUTFIELD: 1. Kenny Lofton, Braves, 2,174,613; 2. Larry Walker, Rockies, 1,732,886; 3. Tony Gwynn, Padres, 1,603,730; 4. Barry Bonds, Giants, 1,559,313; 5. Dante Bichette, Rockies, 924,563; 6. Deion Sanders, Reds, 657,070; 7. Ellis Burks, Rockies, 609,450; 8. Gary Sheffield, Marlins, 588,479; 9. Sammy Sosa, Cubs, 529,407.

ROSTERS

AMERICAN LEAGUE

MANAGER: Joe Torre, Yankees.

PITCHERS: Roger Clemens, Blue Jays; David Cone, Yankees; Jason Dickson, Angels; Pat Hentgen, Blue Jays; **Randy Johnson, Mariners**; Mike Mussina, Orioles; Randy Myers, Orioles; Mariano Rivera, Yankees; Jose Rosado, Royals; Justin Thompson, Tigers.

CATCHERS: Sandy Alomar, Indians; **Ivan Rodriguez, Rangers.**

INFIELDERS: **Roberto Alomar (2b), Orioles**; Jeff Cirillo, Brewers; Joey Cora, Mariners; Nomar Garciaparra, Red Sox; Chuck Knoblauch, Twins; **Edgar Martinez (dh), Mariners**; **Tino Martinez (1b), Yankees**; Mark McGwire, Athletics; **Cal Ripken (3b), Orioles**; **Alex Rodriguez (ss), Mariners**; Frank Thomas, White Sox.

OUTFIELDERS: **Brady Anderson (lf), Orioles**; Albert Belle, White Sox; **Ken Griffey (cf), Mariners**; x-David Justice, Indians; **y-Paul O'Neill (rf), Yankees**; Bernie Williams, Yankees.

NATIONAL LEAGUE

MANAGER: Bobby Cox, Braves.

PITCHERS: Rod Beck, Giants; Kevin Brown, Marlins; Shawn Estes, Giants; Tom Glavine, Braves; Bobby Jones, Mets; Darryl Kile, Astros; **Greg Maddux, Braves**; Pedro Martinez, Expos; Denny Neagle, Braves; Curt Schilling, Phillies.

CATCHERS: Todd Hundley, Mets; Javier Lopez, Braves; **Mike Piazza, Dodgers.**

INFIELDERS: **Jeff Bagwell (1b), Astros**; **Craig Biggio (2b), Astros**; **Jeff Blauser (ss), Braves**; **Ken Caminiti (3b), Padres**; y-Royce Clayton, Cardinals; Andres Galarraga, Rockies; Mark Grace, Cubs; Chipper Jones, Braves; x-Barry Larkin, Reds; Tony Womack, Pirates.

OUTFIELDERS: Moises Alou, Marlins; **Barry Bonds (lf), Giants**; y-Steve Finley, Padres; **Tony Gwynn (dh), Padres**; **Ray Lankford (cf), Cardinals**; x-Kenny Lofton, Braves; **Larry Walker (rf), Rockies.**

Starters in **boldface**. x-injured, did not play. y-injury replacement.

July 8 in Cleveland
American League 3, National League 1

NATIONAL	ab	r	h	bi	AMERICAN	ab	r	h	bi
Biggio 2b	3	0	0	0	Anderson lf-rf	4	0	2	0
Womack 2b	1	0	0	0	Rodriguez ss	3	0	1	0
Gwynn dh	3	0	0	0	Garciaparra ss	1	0	0	0
Galarraga ph-dh	1	0	0	0	Griffey cf	4	0	0	0
Bonds lf	2	0	0	0	T. Martinez 1b	2	0	0	0
Finley lf	1	0	0	0	McGwire 1b	2	0	0	0
Piazza c	1	0	0	0	E. Martinez dh	2	1	2	1
Lopez c	1	1	1	1	Thome dh	1	0	0	0
C. Johnson c	1	0	0	0	O'Neill rf	2	0	0	0
Bagwell 1b	3	0	0	0	Williams lf	0	1	0	0
Grace 1b	1	0	0	0	Ripken 3b	2	0	1	0
Walker rf	1	0	0	0	Cora pr-2b	1	0	0	0
Alou rf	2	0	1	0	Knoblauch 2b	0	0	0	0
Caminiti 3b	2	0	0	0	I. Rodriguez c	2	0	0	0
C. Jones 3b	1	0	0	0	S. Alomar c	1	1	1	2
Lankford cf	2	0	0	0	R. Alomar 2b	2	0	0	0
Blauser ss	2	0	1	0	Cirillo 3b	1	0	0	0
Clayton ss	1	0	0	0					
Totals	**29**	**1**	**3**	**1**	**Totals**	**30**	**3**	**7**	**3**

National	**000 000 100—1**
American	**010 000 20x—3**

LOB—National 5, American 4. **2B**—Anderson. **HR**—Lopez, E. Martinez, S. Alomar. **SB**—Bonds. **CS**—E. Martinez.

National	ip	h	r	er	bb	so	American	ip	h	r	er	bb	so
Maddux	2	2	1	1	0	0	R. Johnson	2	0	0	0	1	2
Schilling	2	2	0	0	0	3	Clemens	1	1	0	0	0	0
Brown	1	1	0	0	0	0	Cone	1	0	0	0	2	0
P. Martinez	1	0	0	0	0	2	Thompson	1	0	0	0	0	1
Estes L	1	1	2	2	1	1	Hentgen	1	0	0	0	0	0
B. Jones	1	1	0	0	0	2	Rosado W	1	2	1	1	1	1
							Myers	1	0	0	0	0	2
							Rivera S	1	0	0	0	0	1

PB—Lopez. **WP**—Schilling, Estes.

Umpires: HP—Larry Barnett; **1B**— Jerry Davis; **2B**—Drew Coble; **3B**—Jeff Kellogg; **LF**—Terry Craft; **RF**—Wally Bell.

T—2:36. **A**—44,916.

Belle struggled through a mediocre season that included a tasteless boycott of the All-Star Game in Cleveland. Of course, Belle initiated his protest after arriving in his former workplace and pocketing the $50,000 bonus, thus preventing potential first-timers like Rusty Greer and Tony Clark the opportunity to have an all-star experience.

Trendsetter
Albert Belle

Reinsdorf struck again in late July when he shipped 30 percent of his pitching staff (Wilson Alvarez, Danny Darwin and closer Roberto Hernandez) to the Giants for a bushel of prospects.

"Anybody who thinks we can catch the Indians is crazy," Reinsdorf said, becoming the first man in baseball history to deem a 3½-game deficit insurmountable.

Later, when the predictable firestorm of public opinion raged, the man who signs Michael Jordan's $35 million annual paycheck shrugged and said the White Sox would have made the same trade had they been five games ahead.

On the field, the players responded by staying in the race until early September. At one point third baseman Robin Ventura, who had rushed through rehab from a gruesome spring-training ankle injury to rejoin the team, had T-shirts printed that read "Chicago Leftovers" on the front and "We Just Might Be Crazy Enough to Win This" on the back.

More palatable were the deals that brought McGwire to St. Louis, John Olerud to the Mets and Jose Cruz Jr. to the Blue Jays.

While Olerud rediscovered his sweet swing after several down years with the Blue Jays and his old team took advantage of the Mariners' desperate search for relief help (swapping Mike Timlin and Paul Spoljaric), McGwire found a home.

After arriving from Oakland at the trade deadline for reliever T.J. Mathews and prospects, the intimidating slugger quickly adjusted to his new league and surroundings.

A potential free agent, McGwire signed a three-year, $28.5 million deal with the Cardinals in September, well below his value on the open market.

"What it all comes down to is, 'Are you happy where you are?' " McGwire said. "It wasn't hard to fall in love with St. Louis. This is what everyone was talking about when I came here . . . It makes me float every time I come to the ballpark and play in front of these fans. I've never been treated this way as a ballplayer."

Meanwhile, the Braves and Indians nearly met in the World Series after a game-jarring trade in late March.

Atlanta shipped outfielders Marquis Grissom and David Justice to Cleveland for center fielder Kenny Lofton and reliever Alan Embree.

The Indians quickly signed Justice and Grissom to contract extensions totaling $53 million for nine years, and rode their improved chemistry to their second World Series appearance in three seasons.

The Braves, having freed up almost $23 million in salary through 1999, used that extra cash to lock up the game's best rotation. Greg Maddux re-upped for $57.5 million over five years, while Tom Glavine, Denny Neagle and John Smoltz also signed on though the turn of the century. Combined, those four pitchers will cost the Braves $130 million through the life of their contracts.

Those weren't the only salaries spiraling to the stratosphere.

Among the more notable signings were Cubs outfielder Sammy Sosa ($10 million a year), Rangers catcher Ivan Rodriguez (five years, $42 million), Blue Jays pitcher Roger Clemens (three years, $24.75 million) and Orioles pitcher Mike Mussina, a bargain at $20.5 million over three years.

Clemens had a sterling season for Toronto, leading the American League in wins (20), ERA (2.05) and strikeouts (292).

Perhaps the extravagant buying would slow if the evidence weren't so overwhelming that overspending pays.

For the second straight season, the top five payrolls produced the final four playoff teams. The Yankees ($67 million), Orioles ($65 million), Indians ($58.7 million), Braves ($58.5 million) and Marlins ($56 million) led the way. Of those, only the Yankees failed to make the League Championship Series.

Payback year
Roger Clemens

More refreshing was the performance of the Pirates. Despite a $9 million payroll that fell well short of the Belle Line, the Pirates managed to chase the Astros to the wire in the NL Central.

Sheffield, another of those individuals who make more than the entire Pirates team, actually sounded a bit embarrassed by the NBA-style figures.

"Am I worth it?" he said after signing the extension. "All I can say is I think the Marlins think so. I can't hold myself accountable for the way things are."

Selling The Family Business

The O'Malleys, perhaps baseball's last royal family, begged out of the insanity with a January announcement they were selling the Dodgers after 47 seasons.

Peter O'Malley, who replaced his father Walter as chairman in 1970, managed to wangle a record $350 million out of Rupert Murdoch's Fox Group by September. That eclipsed the previous franchise sale price record of $172 million, set by Peter Angelos when he bought the Orioles in 1993.

The Fox Group's purchase–which still had to gain formal approval–would include Dodger Stadium and the surrounding Chavez Ravine property as well as the Dodgertown complex in Vero Beach, Fla., and a complex outside Santo Domingo, Dominican

Organization of the Year

Revitalized Tigers rise from scrapheap

They say the major league club is the last thing to go when an organization is neglected. That theory held true when it came to the Tigers.

Detroit was the best team in the major leagues during its 1984 World Series championship season, leading the American League East wire-to-wire and losing just one game during the postseason.

Yet while the Tigers were in the penthouse at the big league level, the foundation of the franchise was already beginning to show signs of trouble.

Detroit had no coaches at any minor league level, just managers and three roving instructors. The scouting staff was understaffed, underpaid and unproductive.

Beginning in the late 1980s, the Tigers realized the errors that they had made and tried to play catch-up, but it was too late. By the time president John McHale Jr. took control of the club in January 1995, the franchise was in ruins.

But in just under two years, through the work of McHale and energetic yet patient employees such general manager Randy Smith and manager Buddy Bell, McHale has built it back up to the top. The Tigers are Baseball America's 1997 Organization of the Year.

When McHale took over, the payroll was high and the talent level low. Interest in the ballclub in Detroit, one of America's great sports towns, was nil. The Tigers were about to hit rock bottom, which came in 1996.

In Bell's first season as manager, the Tigers won 53 games with overpaid veterans and overmatched youngsters, and there seemed to be little help on the way from the minor leagues.

"It was a mess," McHale says. "There were times when I wondered what we had gotten into. The situation was much worse than with an expansion team. There was a lot more to do than just build. But that was part of the challenge, part of the fun and part of the reason I was asked to come here. I don't think I would have been asked to play a role here if everything was perfect."

PREVIOUS WINNERS

1982—Oakland Athletics
1983—New York Mets
1984—New York Mets
1985—Milwaukee Brewers
1986—Milwaukee Brewers
1987—Milwaukee Brewers
1988—Montreal Expos
1989—Texas Rangers
1990—Montreal Expos
1991—Atlanta Braves
1992—Cleveland Indians
1993—Toronto Blue Jays
1994—Kansas City Royals
1995—New York Mets
1996—Atlanta Braves

The Tigers turnaround was as swift as it was stunning.

After the 1996 crash-and-burn, the Tigers fell just four games short of .500 in 1997. Detroit won 79 games, 26 more than the season before.

Not only that, the Tigers' six minor league affiliates went a combined 363-320. The gem of the group was prospect-laden Class A West Michigan, which stormed to a 92-39 regular-season record, earning it the honor of Baseball America's Minor League Team of the Year.

Despite facing a difficult political climate, ground was broken for a new stadium in downtown Detroit in November. It is expected to be ready by Opening Day 2000.

"We're not there yet," Smith says. "Our better arms are still anywhere between A ball and (Triple-A) Toledo. A lot of things went right for us this year. There are going to be some bumps in the road. We expect that, but we're prepared to handle them."

—PAT CAPUTO

Republic.

Aside from spiraling costs, O'Malley was said to have sold the team for tax purposes and to avoid a fight over succession among his three children and his 10 nieces and nephews.

"Family ownership is probably a dying breed," O'Malley said. "It's a high-risk business, as high risk as the oil business. You need a broader base than an individual family to carry through the storms. Groups or corporations are the wave of the future."

"We are very excited with the potential opportunity of carrying on one of the greatest winning traditions in all of sports," said Peter Chernin, chairman of the Fox Group. "The O'Malleys have set the gold standard for franchise ownership, and if we are approved, we will do all in our power to live up to that standard."

Only the Yawkey family, whose involvement with the Red Sox dates to 1933, had a longer uninterrupted run in big league baseball than the O'Malleys.

Murdoch, the swashbuckling Australian media mogul, is worth an estimated $2.8 billion. That's 33 percent more than his avowed enemy, Braves owner and Time Warner vice chairman Ted Turner ($2.1 billion).

While the O'Malleys were getting out, several franchises were positioning themselves for new stadiums. The Astros and Tigers had stadium projects in the works, while the Expos, Padres and Twins were looking for similar projects to get off the ground.

Twins owner Carl Pohlad, in fact, was making serious threats to sell the club to North Carolina-based nursing-home executive Don Beaver if the Minnesota legislature did not build the team a new baseball-only, open-air ballpark to replace the Metrodome.

A series of proposals failed in the state legislature

before Pohlad set Nov. 30 as a deadline. One of those proposals called for the state to purchase 49 percent of the team in exchange for public money toward a new stadium.

Pohlad bought the Twins in 1984 from Calvin Griffith.

Beaver, who owns parts of five minor league teams and owns a minority share of the Pirates, would move the team to Charlotte, N.C., for the 1999 and 2000 seasons, then potentially move to a new stadium in North Carolina's Triad (Greensboro/Winston-Salem/High Point) area in 2001.

No major league team had changed cities in a quarter century. The Washington Senators' move to Arlington, Texas, in 1972 was baseball's last franchise relocation.

Another team that had been for sale, the Blue Jays, was taken off the market by its Belgian beer company owner. A consortium led by Toronto real estate developer Murray Frum had been expected to buy the Blue Jays, but negotiations dragged on until Interbrew SA finally decided in late October not to sell.

Cuban Cash

Salary inflation continued on the international market as well.

The Devil Rays struck first with the April 21 signing of 28-year-old Cuban righthander Rolando Arrojo. His $7 million signing bonus was the third-largest ever given to an amateur and the largest to an international amateur, easily besting the $2.5 million bonus grabbed by countryman Livan Hernandez in 1996.

LARRY GOREN

Hideki Irabu

Arrojo, a 6-foot-4 power pitcher, had defected nine months earlier in Albany, Ga., shortly before he was to compete in the Atlanta Olympics. He was expected to contend for a spot in the Devil Rays' Opening Day rotation.

"It's a dream of all the boys in Cuba to play baseball one day," Arrojo said through an interpreter, "with the best quality players in the major leagues."

Not to be outdone, George Steinbrenner's Yankees responded the following day with the acquisition of another 28-year-old, Japanese righthander Hideki Irabu. The Yankees traded outfielder Ruben Rivera, righthander Rafael Medina and $3 million to the Padres, who had purchased Irabu's rights through a working agreement with the Chiba Lotte Marines, his team in Japan.

Irabu refused to sign with the Padres and through his agent Don Nomura, orchestrated a trade to his favorite team.

Touted by several scouts, including former Rangers pitching coach Tom House, as the Nolan Ryan of Japan, Irabu signed for $12.8 million, including an $8.5 million bonus. After zipping through the minor leagues, Irabu reached the majors shortly after the all-star break.

He started strong but faded to a 5-4, 7.09 season, a victim of poor conditioning, faulty mechanics, decreased velocity and impossible expectations.

"Everything is different," said Irabu, who had struck out 1,111 batters in 1,003 professional innings back home. "The big league hitters are a lot better, a lot more powerful than the Japanese hitters."

Two other Japanese pitchers, though far less heralded, signed in the big leagues. Righthander Shigetoshi Hasegawa signed with the Angels, who paid $1 million to the Orix Blue Wave for his rights. The Mets signed lefty reliever Takashi Kashiwada, whom manager Bobby Valentine had watched while working in Japan. Kashiwada was released after the season.

Niekro Walks In Alone

The increasingly finicky Baseball Writers Association of America saw fit to send just one player to Cooperstown in 1997: Phil Niekro.

Tommy Lasorda

The Veterans Committee again compensated by electing Tommy Lasorda, Nellie Fox and former Negro League shortstop Willie Wells to the Hall of Fame.

Niekro, the ageless knuckleballer, made it on the basis of his 318 career wins, five Gold Gloves and five all-star appearances. The son of a Polish coal miner in Lansing, Ohio, Niekro joined Jesse Haines and Hoyt Wilhelm as the only knuckleballers in the Hall.

"I would have liked to throw a Tom Seaver fastball or a Bob Gibson slider," said Niekro, who was named on 80 percent of the ballots (75 percent is required for election). "But I couldn't do it. I had to do what I did best, and that was throw a knuckleball."

Signed in 1958 out of a Milwaukee Braves tryout camp for $500, Niekro won only 31 games in his 20s but set a big league record with 121 wins after his 40th birthday.

Phil Niekro

Lasorda, 70, managed the Dodgers for two decades before retiring in 1996 after a heart attack. He compiled a record of 1,599-1,439 and led the Dodgers to four National League pennants and two World Series titles ('81 and '88). He liked to say he bled Dodger blue, having spent 43 years in the organization as a pitcher, coach, scout and manager.

"This is the greatest thing that has happened to me in my lifetime," Lasorda said. "The Hall of Fame is eternity. I feel it won't be long before my mother is shaking me to

MAJOR LEAGUE DEBUTS, 1997

AMERICAN LEAGUE

Anaheim Angels	
Mike Bovee, rhp	Sept. 13
Anthony Chavez, rhp	Sept. 2
Shigetoshi Hasegawa, rhp	April 5
Matt Perisho, lhp	May 27

Baltimore Orioles	
Danny Clyburn, of	Sept. 15
David Dellucci, of	June 3
Mike Johnson, rhp	April 6
Melvin Rosario, c	Sept. 11

Boston Red Sox	
Robinson Checo, rhp	Sept. 16
Michael Coleman, of	Sept. 1
Brian Rose, rhp	July 25
Jason Varitek, c	Sept. 24

Chicago White Sox	
Jeff Abbott, of	June 10
Carlos Castillo, rhp	April 2
Chris Clemons, rhp	July 23
Nelson Cruz, rhp	Aug. 1
Scott Eyre, lhp	Aug. 1
Tom Fordham, lhp	Aug. 19
Magglio Ordonez, of	Aug. 29
Mario Valdez, 1b	June 15

Cleveland Indians	
Bruce Aven, of	Aug. 27
Sean Casey, 1b	Sept. 12
Bartolo Colon, rhp	April 4
Steve Kline, rhp	April 2
Richie Sexson, 1b	Sept. 14
Enrique Wilson, 2b	Sept. 24
Jaret Wright, rhp	June 24

Detroit Tigers	
Frank Catalanotto, 2b	Sept. 3
Deivi Cruz, ss	April 1
Roberto Duran, lhp	July 6
Juan Encarnacion, of	Sept. 2
Eddie Gaillard, rhp	Aug. 11
Fernando Hernandez, rhp	April 3
Jimmy Hurst, of	Sept. 10
Bubba Trammell, of	

Kansas City Royals	
Roland DelaMaza, rhp	Sept. 26
Shane Halter, ss	April 6
Jed Hansen, 2b	July 29
Ryan Long, of	July 16
Felix Martinez, ss	Sept. 3
Allen McDill, lhp	May 15
Glendon Rusch, lhp	April 6
Jose Santiago, rhp	June 7
Andy Stewart, 1b	Sept. 6
Larry Sutton, 1b	Aug. 17
Jamie Walker, lhp	April 2

Milwaukee Brewers	
Eddy Diaz, 3b	April 17
Sean Maloney, rhp	April 28
Mike Misuraca, rhp	July 27
Antone Williamson, 1b	May 31
Steve Woodard, rhp	July 28

Minnesota	
Shane Bowers, rhp	July 26
Torii Hunter, of	Aug. 22
Chris Latham, of	April 12
Damian Miller, c	Aug. 10
David Ortiz, 1b	Sept. 2
Todd Ritchie, rhp	April 3
Javier Valentin, c	Sept. 13

New York Yankees	
Homer Bush, 2b	Aug. 16
Ivan Cruz, 1b	July 18
Mike Figga, c	Sept. 16
Hideki Irabu, rhp	July 10
Danny Rios, rhp	May 30

Oakland Athletics	
Mark Bellhorn, 2b	June 10
Ben Grieve, of	Sept. 3
Gary Haught, rhp	July 16

LARRY GOREN

Jose Cruz Jr.

Tim Kubinski, lhp	July 16
Jason McDonald, of	June 5
Brad Rigby, rhp	June 28
Scott Sheldon, 3b	May 18
Miguel Tejada, ss	Aug. 27

Seattle Mariners	
Ken Cloude, rhp	Aug. 9
Jose Cruz, Jr., of	May 31
Giomar Guevara, 2b	Sept. 19
Derek Lowe, rhp	April 26
Dan Rohrmeier, of	Sept. 3

Texas Rangers	
Hanley Frias, ss	June 21
Eric Moody, rhp	Aug. 3
Marc Sagmoen, of	April 15
Julio Santana, rhp	April 6
Fernando Tatis, 3b	July 26

Toronto Blue Jays	
Carlos Almanzar, rhp	Sept. 4
Rich Butler, of	Sept. 6
Chris Carpenter, rhp	May 12
Kelvim Escobar, rhp	June 29
Tom Evans, 3b	Sept. 2

NATIONAL LEAGUE

Atlanta Braves	
Chris Brock, rhp	June 11
Mike Cather, rhp	July 13
Chad Fox, rhp	July 13
John LeRoy, rhp	Sept. 26
Kerry Lightenberg, rhp	Aug. 12
Kevin Millwood, rhp	July 14
Randall Simon, 1b	Sept. 1

Chicago Cubs	
Jeremi Gonzalez, rhp	May 27
Terrell Lowery, of	Sept. 13
Kevin Orie, 3b	April 1
Marc Pisciotta, rhp	June 30
Ramon Tatis, lhp	April 5

Cincinnati Reds	
Aaron Boone, 3b	June 20
Jim Crowell, lhp	Sept. 12
Pokey Reese, ss	April 1
Pete Rose, Jr., 3b	Sept. 1
Brett Tomko, rhp	May 27
Pat Watkins, of	Sept. 9
Scott Winchester, rhp	Sept. 8

Colorado Rockies	
Mike DeJean, rhp	May 2
Todd Helton, 1b	Aug. 2
Bobby Jones, lhp	May 18
John Thomson, rhp	May 11

Florida Marlins	
Antonio Alfonseca, rhp	June 17
Todd Dunwoody, of	May 10
Mark Kotsay, of	July 11
Kirt Ojala, lhp	Aug. 18
Tony Saunders, lhp	April 5
Robby Stanifer, rhp	May 3
Matt Whisenant, lhp	July 4

Houston Astros	
Manuel Barrios, rhp	Sept. 16
Jose Cabrera, rhp	July 15
Oscar Henriquez, rhp	Sept. 7
Richard Hidalgo, of	Sept. 1
Russ Johnson, 3b	April 8
Tom Martin, lhp	April 2
Ken Ramos, of	May 16

Los Angeles Dodgers	
Henry Blanco, c	July 25
Rick Gorecki, rhp	Sept. 10
Mike Judd, rhp	Sept. 28
Paul Konerko, 1b	Sept. 8
Dennis Reyes, lhp	July 13
Adam Riggs, 2b	Aug. 7

Montreal Expos	
Shayne Bennett, rhp	Aug. 22
Rick DeHart, rhp	July 16
Steve Falteisek, rhp	July 22
Brad Fullmer, 1b	Sept. 2
Orlando Cabrera, ss	Sept. 3
Ryan McGuire, 1b	June 5
Everett Stull, rhp	April 14
Mike Thurman, rhp	Sept. 2
Jose Vidro, 3b	June 8

New York Mets	
Steve Bieser, of	April 1
Joe Crawford, lhp	April 7
Shawn Gilbert, 3b	June 2
Takashi Kashiwada, rhp	May 1
Cory Lidle, rhp	May 8
Carlos Mendoza, of	Sept. 3
Kevin Morgan, 2b	June 15

Philadelphia Phillies	
Wayne Gomes, rhp	June 13
Ryan Nye, rhp	June 7
Edgar Ramos, rhp	May 21
Darrin Winston, rhp	Sept. 10

Pittsburgh Pirates	
Adrian Brown, of	May 16
Emil Brown, of	April 3
Lou Collier, ss	June 28
Jose Guillen, of	April 1
Jason Johnson, rhp	Aug. 27
Abraham Nunez, ss	Aug. 27
Kevin Polcovich, ss	May 17
Ricardo Rincon, lhp	April 3
Jeff Wallace, lhp	Aug. 21

St. Louis Cardinals	
Manny Aybar, rhp	Aug. 4
Rigo Beltran, lhp	June 2
Jeff Berblinger, 2b	Sept. 7
Micah Franklin, of	May 13
Bert Green, of	Aug. 2
Mike Gulan, 3b	May 14
Curtis King, rhp	Aug. 1
Sean Lowe, rhp	Aug. 29
Eli Marrero, c	Sept. 3
Tom McGraw, lhp	May 7
Matt Morris, rhp	April 4
Luis Ordaz, ss	Sept. 3
Brady Raggio, rhp	April 15

San Diego Padres	
Will Cunnane, rhp	April 3
Todd Erdos, rhp	June 8
Derrek Lee, 1b	April 28
Joey Long, lhp	April 25
Heath Murray, lhp	May 24
Mandy Romero, c	July 15
Jorge Velandia, ss	June 20

San Francisco Giants	
Keith Foulke, rhp	May 21
Dante Powell, of	April 15

Rookie of the Year

Garciaparra enjoys all-star campaign

In 1997, Nomar Garciaparra's best not only was far more than anyone expected but also one of the best seasons ever by a major league shortstop. Baseball America's 1997 Rookie of the Year is yet another in the long line of prodigies who don't seem to realize that shortstops, at least before they came along, were supposed to speak softly and carry little sticks.

"Sometimes I think he's played here before," Red Sox manager Jimy Williams says. "I don't know who with or when, but he was here before."

Garciaparra, 24, also put together a 30-game hitting streak, which set an American League rookie record and tied the Indians' Sandy Alomar for the longest in the majors in 1997.

"He's all business," Red Sox first baseman Mo Vaughn said. "He'd hit a home run and when he came back to the dugout say, 'That's what I was supposed to do.' When he made a great play, we'd just say, 'That's Nomar. That's what he's supposed to do.'

"His concentration, his will to succeed, his attitude, you can always see it on the field in somebody's eyes. He's got that."

Garciaparra, the Red Sox' first-round pick in 1994, hit .291-13-44 in the first half and was named the Red Sox' representative to the All-Star Game.

The 6-foot, 180-pounder swung at 45 percent of first pitches, more often than any other American League hitter except Ozzie Guillen of the White Sox, but he also hit .385 on those first pitches, helping him hit .306 overall.

He had 209 hits, which set a Red Sox rookie record. He clubbed 30 home runs, 44 doubles and a league-leading 11 triples. His 98 RBIs were the most ever for a leadoff man.

Still, humble Nomar Garciaparra always went to his script when asked about his magical rookie season.

"Stats aren't going to tell me about what I did," Garciaparra said. "I might have gone 0-for-4 but hit the ball on a line all four times. And I might go 4-for-4 and crack my bat all four. What's a better day?

"Did we win or did we lose? That's what interests me. My job is to go out and play hard and do the best I can."

"He's a tough little player," Yankees manager Joe Torre said. "He reminds me of the guys in my time. But little players didn't hit 30 homers in those days."

—ALAN SCHWARZ

Nomar Garciaparra

TOP 20 ROOKIES

Selected by Baseball America

1. Nomar Garciaparra, ss, Red Sox
2. Scott Rolen, 3b, Phillies
3. Matt Morris, rhp, Cardinals
4. Rich Loiselle, rhp, Pirates
5. Andruw Jones, of, Braves
6. Jose Cruz Jr., of, Mariners/Blue Jays
7. Deivi Cruz, ss, Tigers
8. Brett Tomko, rhp, Reds
9. Jose Guillen, of, Pirates
10. Vladimir Guerrero, of, Expos
11. Livan Hernandez, rhp, Marlins
12. Scott Spiezio, 2b, Athletics
13. Jason Dickson, rhp, Angels
14. Mike Cameron, of, White Sox
15. Jaret Wright, rhp, Indians
16. Neifi Perez, ss/2b, Rockies
17. Jeremi Gonzalez, rhp, Cubs
18. Kelvim Escobar, rhp, Blue Jays
19. Chris Holt, rhp, Astros
20. Garrett Stephenson, rhp, Phillies

PREVIOUS WINNERS

1989—Gregg Olson, rhp, Orioles
1990—Sandy Alomar, c, Indians
1991—Jeff Bagwell, 1b, Astros
1992—Pat Listach, ss, Brewers
1993—Mike Piazza, c, Dodgers
1994—Raul Mondesi, of, Dodgers
1995—Hideo Nomo, rhp, Dodgers
1996—Derek Jeter, ss, Yankees

wake up and go to school."

Fox, a standout second baseman for the White Sox, Athletics and Colt .45s, was a 12-time all-star who batted .288 over his 19-year career. Fox, who died in 1975, was the AL MVP in 1959 and won three Gold Gloves. Fellow Hall member Joe Morgan credits Fox with helping break in as a rookie in Houston.

Wells, a slick fielder nicknamed "The Devil," had a career .331 batting average with nine Negro League teams from 1924-49. He became the 14th Negro Leaguer inducted to Cooperstown.

Less fortunate in the voting were Don Sutton and Tony Perez, who came up short despite strong qualifications. Sutton won 324 games, more than any other righthander since the 1920s, but was named on 73.15 percent of the ballots. Perez, a key cog in the Big Red Machine, has more career RBIs than Mike Schmidt and more hits than Ted Williams.

Obituaries

The year also marked the passing of several all-time greats.

Curt Flood was remembered as a baseball martyr after his death on Jan. 20 at age 59 in Los Angeles. Without his courage, the astronomical salaries of today would almost surely be impossible.

The seven-time Gold Glove winner and three-time all-star refused to report to Philadelphia when the Cardinals traded him following the 1969 season. He filed a lawsuit in January 1970 claiming baseball's longstanding reserve clause violated antitrust laws. The suit resulted in a Supreme Court defeat two years later, but it inspired Dave McNally and Andy Messersmith to mount the challenge that led to free agency in 1975.

Flood played in just 13 games after his trade–all for the Washington Senators in 1971–and retired at age 33 with career totals of .295-85-636. Despite his undeniable significance, no current players attended Flood's funeral, and only Don Baylor, Doug DeCinces and Steve Garvey showed up among his contemporaries.

"The principle," Flood once said, "is more important than the cost."

Richie Ashburn's life was far less painful. The former Phillies center fielder died Sept. 9 in New York City, hours after broadcasting a Phillies game from Shea Stadium. He was 70.

The Hall of Fame player went on to spend 35 years in radio and television. He spent five decades as an immensely popular part of Philadelphia's sporting culture. At his wake, 40,000 people stood in line to pay their last respects.

Just as popular in Baltimore was Rex Barney, the scatter-armed Brooklyn Dodgers righthander who would spend his last 20 years as the Orioles' public-address announcer.

His trademark calls of "Give that fan a contract" and "Thank youuuuuu" were as much a part of games at Memorial Stadium and Camden Yards as Earl Weaver and Cal Ripken.

"He had a genuine love for the game," Orioles coach Elrod Hendricks said of Barney, 72. "I hope some of the younger players who had a chance to hear him will have the same passion and love for the game that he had."

Baseball also mourned the passing at age 82 of Johnny Vander Meer, whose consecutive no-hitters in 1938 remain unique in big league lore. As a lefthander for the Cincinnati Reds, Vander Meer beat the Boston Braves 3-0 on June 11. Four days later, in the first-ever night game at Ebbets Field, he blanked the Dodgers 6-0 on no hits to achieve sporting immortality.

His career numbers of 119-121 were ordinary, but at his peak he was unhittable. In 1952, at the end of his playing career, he threw a no-hitter for Tulsa of the Texas League. He went on to manage in the Reds chain before leaving baseball in 1963.

Temporary Insanity

Bud Selig's reign as acting commissioner reached its five-year anniversary on Sept. 9. While the world's slowest search committee continues to hunt for a worthy successor, Selig has now occupied the office longer than four actual baseball commissioners.

"I think Bud has done an incredibly good job navigating baseball through tough times," said former commissioner Peter Ueberroth.

Reinsdorf, who originally persuaded Selig to replace Fay Vincent in the first place, raved about his pal.

"He missed his calling," Reinsdorf said. "He should be the Senate majority leader."

Selig seemed to prove that point with a steady stream of indecipherable non-denials when pressed about his future plans.

"There are a lot of things in life I want to do," Selig said. "As far as I'm concerned, I've made my feelings well known. And I have every confidence that the search committee will reach a successful conclusion . . . It's hard in life to just deal in hypotheticals. So I'm not going to do that."

At least the owners set up a potential line of succession with the August appointment of Paul Beeston to a new MLB post of president and chief operating officer. Beeston, 51, has been described as that rarest of creatures, an accountant with a sense of humor.

New MLB president
Paul Beeston

The first employee hired by the Blue Jays in 1976, Beeston helped build that dynasty before a change in ownership caused him to look elsewhere. Known for his lack of pretension, socks and a blow dryer, the stogie-smoking Beeston seemed a perfect choice to roust baseball from its double-speak doldrums.

"To me, he's always the guy who's having some fun with this," said Rockies owner Jerry McMorris. "Some people get so dour. This game can do that to you. But Paul enjoys it. He enjoys baseball."

Beeston, an avowed supporter of the DH but otherwise likable enough, expressed optimism upon moving to New York.

"I can't tell you I'm not a little nervous," he said. "But I have the confidence to think I can contribute. I don't want to sound trite or Pollyanna-ish, but I think baseball is the best game in the world."

Greg Murphy might be less sanguine. He lasted just 16 months as CEO of the newly created MLB Enterprises before deciding it was time to return to the business world.

Murphy, 48, either resigned or was fired, depending on which tale you trust, during the World Series. Praised for his prior marketing work with General Foods and Entenmanns, where he humanized a giant pitcher of Kool-Aid and popularized the concept of fat-free doughnuts, Murphy preached a fans-first mantra during his tenure.

The first sign of trouble came in January, when the owners killed a 10-year, $325-million deal Murphy had negotiated with Nike.

According to the Associated Press, Murphy "ran afoul of the teams and the staff of the commissioner's office."

Selig, not surprisingly, favored a different spin.

"Greg resigned because he felt it would be the best all the way around," Selig said. "I feel very good about the future of the department. It's something we should have done years ago. At least he got our great marketing experiment off the ground."

Remembering Jackie

In April, baseball honored the 50th anniversary of Jackie Robinson's Brooklyn debut by retiring his No. 42 in perpetuity. Several players currently wearing the number were grandfathered into the plan.

President Clinton and Rachel Robinson, Jackie's

Rachel Robinson, Jackie's widow
Honored by Dodgers on 50th anniversary

widow, were on hand at Shea Stadium for the April 15 celebration of the first player to cross baseball's color barrier. Most other teams held a Jackie Robinson Day at some point to extend the season-long celebration.

"I couldn't have done what Jackie did," said Phillies hitting coach Hal McRae. "No way. I couldn't have lasted two days. In my opinion, he's the only one who could have played the way he did and handled it the way he did."

The anniversary prompted a fresh discussion of baseball's progress in the area of racial equity. The evidence wasn't that encouraging.

Just three black managers were in the big leagues, and none had been hired since Dusty Baker in 1993. The Yankees' Bob Watson remained the game's only black general manager. The Dodgers, Robinson's old team, found themselves with just one African-American on their roster (Wayne Kirby) for the first time since June 1948.

Don Newcombe, the Dodgers community relations director, blasted the team to the Los Angeles Times: "We're reverting right back to where we were 50 years ago," he said.

Coming Back

Heroism was on display in the form of Brett Butler and Eric Davis.

Butler, 40, less than a year removed from a bout with throat cancer, played 105 games for the Dodgers in his 17th big league season. Davis, 35, had colon cancer surgery on June 13, then defied all medical logic by returning to the Orioles lineup on Sept 15.

Davis hit a home run in the playoffs while in the midst of an 18-week chemotherapy cycle. He lost 25 pounds after the surgery, in which doctors removed a baseball-sized tumor from his abdomen as well as one third of his large intestine.

"It's an incredible story," said Pat Gillick, Baltimore's general manager.

"I'm no more courageous than anyone else who battles this," Davis said. "It just so happens that I'm a professional athlete."

Others who fought through serious health problems were Mets righthander Jason Isringhausen (tuberculosis) and his teammate Pete Harnisch, who fought clinical depression after giving up smokeless tobacco. Both pitchers returned late in the season.

Personnel Changes

Things were fairly quiet on the managerial front—at least until Baltimore skipper Davey Johnson resigned under fire, the same day he was named AL Manager of the Year by the BBWAA. Relations between Johnson and Orioles owner Peter Angelos deteriorated after Balimore was eliminated by Cleveland in the AL Championship Series.

The Royals fired Bob Boone at the all-star break and replaced him with Cubs hitting coach Tony Muser. The Reds replaced Ray Knight with 66-year-old Jack McKeon, who had served the team as an adviser for five years. The White Sox chased Terry Bevington after their strange season. And the Blue Jays fired Cito Gaston and hired Cubs Triple-A manager Tim Johnson.

Out in Baltimore
Davey Johnson

Two big front-office names stepped aside as well. The Mets fired GM Joe McIlvaine at midseason when he refused to sacrifice scouting director John Barr. "Father Joe" also refused to carry a cellular phone and ignored some organizational conference calls, which caused the club to replace him with the younger and ostensibly more technology-friendly Steve Phillips.

"He just didn't want to deal with the politics," a friend said of McIlvaine, who helped build the Mets 1986 World Series titlists and crafted a team that contended for a 1997 wild-card into September. "Joe's a baseball purist. He wouldn't change."

Athletics GM Sandy Alderson, the longest-serving GM in the majors, gave that title to longtime assistant Billy Beane after the season. Alderson, the architect of Oakland's American League dynasty (1988-90) stayed on as president. Elsewhere, Dave Montgomery took over as Phillies president, replacing Bill Giles, who remains team chairman.

Notable retirements included future Hall of Famer Ryne Sandberg of the Cubs, classy righthander Dennis Martinez and Rangers DH Mickey Tettleton, whose 245 homers rank eighth-best all-time by a switch-hitter.

Sandberg, 38, finished his career with 282 homers, most in history for a second baseman. He was the 1984 National League MVP and won nine Gold Gloves.

EXPANSION DRAFT

Devil Rays, Diamondbacks select young players, make big trades

Despite their expansion status, the Arizona Diamondbacks and Tampa Bay Devil Rays have the financial resources to sign established major league players and compete quickly. So when the 1997 expansion draft came, they . . . selected a bunch of youngsters.

Both teams met expectations minutes after the draft, trading some of the young players for the likes of Travis Fryman and Fred McGriff. Even the non-expansion teams made trades with each other, including a blockbuster that sent the National League's 1997 Cy Young Award winner, Pedro Martinez, to the Red Sox.

ESPN and ESPN2 covered the draft for seven hours, then left the air just as the fun began. In all, 15 teams made or completed 13 deals involving 32 players.

The draft was held Nov. 18 at the Phoenix Civic Plaza, but the general managers had been in town for their annual meeting the week before, so they had plenty of opportunity to cook up trades.

"We've talked trade or had some scenario with every team during the week, or almost every team," said Devil Rays GM Chuck LaMar.

Before the deals could be consummated, LaMar's team made Marlins lefthander Tony Saunders the No. 1 overall pick in the draft. Saunders, 23, was one of the few recognizable names selected. He went just 4-6, 4.61 during the regular season for Florida, but started two games in the team's post-season run to the World Series championship.

"It's an honor to be the first player picked," Saunders said. "It made me feel like I was doing something right. Somebody wanted me."

The Diamondbacks' top pick, second overall, was lefthander Brian Anderson, who went 4-2, 4.69 for the Indians and made six impressive relief appearances in the postseason.

MORRIS FOSTOFF

A trivia answer for life
Tony Saunders was picked first

Fifty-two of the 70 players selected appeared in the majors in 1997, but none had the stature of those the expansion teams either traded for or signed as free agents before and after the draft. That group included shortstop Jay Bell, third baseman Fryman and outfielder Devon White of the Diamondbacks, and righthander Roberto Hernandez and first baseman McGriff of the Devil Rays.

ARIZONA DIAMONDBACKS

FIRST ROUND

Player, Pos.	Sel. From	Player, Pos.	Sel. From
2. Brian Anderson, lhp	Indians	15. Joel Adamson, lhp	Brewers
3. Jeff Suppan, rhp	Red Sox	17. Ben Ford, rhp	Yankees
5. Gabe Alvarez, 3b*	Padres	19. Yamil Benitez, of	Royals
7. Jorge Fabregas, c	White Sox	21. Neil Weber, lhp	Expos
9. Karim Garcia, of	Dodgers	23. Jason Boyd, rhp	Phillies
11. Edwin Diaz, 2b	Rangers	25. Brent Brede, of	Twins
13. Cory Lidle, rhp	Mets	27. Tony Batista, ss	Athletics

SECOND ROUND

Player, Pos.	Sel. From	Player, Pos.	Sel. From
29. Tom Martin, lhp	Astros	43. Chris Clemons, rhp	White Sox
31. Omar Daal, lhp	Blue Jays	45. David Dellucci, of	Orioles
33. Scott Winchester, rhp*	Reds	47. Damian Miller, c	Twins
35. Clint Sodowsky, rhp	Pirates	49. Hector Carrasco, rhp	Royals
37. Danny Klassen, ss	Brewers	51. Hanley Frias, ss	Rangers
39. Matt Drews, rhp*	Tigers	53. Bob Wolcott, rhp	Mariners
41. Todd Erdos, rhp	Padres	55. Mike Bell, 2b-3b	Angels

THIRD ROUND

Player, Pos.	Sel. From	Player, Pos.	Sel. From
57. Joe Randa, 3b*	Pirates	65. Kelly Stinnett, c	Brewers
59. Jesus Martinez, lhp*	Dodgers	67. Chuck McElroy, lhp*	White Sox
61. Russ Springer, rhp	Astros	69. Marty Janzen, rhp	Blue Jays
63. Bryan Corey, rhp	Tigers		

*Later traded.

TAMPA BAY DEVIL RAYS

FIRST ROUND

Player, Pos.	Sel. From	Player, Pos.	Sel. From
1. Tony Saunders, lhp	Marlins	16. Dmitri Young, 1b*	Cardinals
4. Quinton McCracken, of	Rockies	18. Esteban Yan, rhp	Orioles
6. Bob Abreu, of*	Astros	20. Mike Difelice, c	Cardinals
8. Miguel Cairo, 2b	Cubs	22. Bubba Trammell, of	Tigers
10. Rich Butler, of	Blue Jays	24. Andy Sheets, inf*	Mariners
12. Robert Smith, 3b-ss	Braves	26. Dennis Springer, rhp	Angels
14. Jason Johnson, rhp	Pirates	28. Dan Carlson, rhp	Giants

SECOND ROUND

Player, Pos.	Sel. From	Player, Pos.	Sel. From
30. Brian Boehringer, rhp*	Yankees	44. Kerry Robinson, of	Cardinals
32. Mike Duvall, lhp	Marlins	46. Steve Cox, 1b	Athletics
34. John LeRoy, rhp	Braves	48. Albie Lopez, rhp	Indians
36. Jim Mecir, rhp	Red Sox	50. Jose Paniagua, rhp	Expos
38. Bryan Rekar, rhp	Rockies	52. Carlos Mendoza, of	Mets
40. Rick Gorecki, rhp	Dodgers	54. Ryan Karp, lhp	Phillies
42. Ramon Tatis, lhp	Cubs	56. Santos Hernandez, rhp	Giants

THIRD ROUND

Player, Pos.	Sel. From	Player, Pos.	Sel. From
58. Randy Winn, of	Marlins	66. Luke Wilcox, of	Yankees
60. Terrell Wade, lhp	Braves	68. Herbert Perry, 1b	Indians
62. Aaron Ledesma, ss	Orioles	70. Vaughn Eshelman, lhp	Athletics
64. Brooks Kieschnick, of-1b	Cubs		

WORLD SERIES

Amid adversity, Marlins-Indians play a game for the ages

BY JOHN PERROTTO

Through the first six games, the 93rd World Series ranged from nondescript to dull to comedic to amateurish. And it drew criticism from all directions.

Acting commissioner Bud Selig blasted the pace of games. NBC West Coast president Don Ohlmeyer hoped for a sweep so the network could get higher ratings with its regular prime-time lineup. Columnists throughout the country ripped the quality of play. Baseball purists bristled at the thought of the National League wild-card entry (Florida Marlins) playing a club with the fourth-best record in the American League (Cleveland Indians).

DENIS BANCROFT

A champagne celebration
Marlins players show emotional outpouring after Game Seven triumph

But Game Seven made up for all the bad baseball and negative talk. Quite simply, it was a classic and turned a forgettable World Series into an unforgettable one.

The Marlins rallied from a 2-0 deficit in the seventh inning to beat the Indians 3-2 on shortstop Edgar Renteria's bases-loaded single with two out in the bottom of the 11th inning at Pro Player Stadium in Miami. The neophyte Marlins beating the cursed Indians in the second-longest seventh game in Series history will go down in baseball lore.

In just their fifth year of existence, the Marlins won baseball's biggest prize. No expansion team had ever won it all faster, the New York Mets previously taking eight years to capture the World Series championship in 1969.

"I guess every little boy imagines this might happen at one time," Marlins manager Jim Leyland said. "It's a total fantasy for me. To actually win this thing and the way we won, it's unbelievable."

Unbelievable was a word the Indians used, too. They had their first Series title in 49 years in their grasp and lost their grip.

A two-run single by second baseman Tony Fernandez in the second inning off starter Al Leiter staked the Indians to a 2-0 lead and it appeared ready to stand as the game-winner with 21-year-old righthander Jaret Wright mowing down Florida.

However, third baseman Bobby Bonilla hit a solo home run on Wright's first pitch in the bottom of the seventh inning. The Marlins suddenly had a pulse.

The Indians were still holding a 2-1 lead when they called on closer Jose Mesa to start the ninth inning. Two outs away from nailing down the win, Mesa faltered as rookie second baseman Craig Counsell tied the game with a sacrifice fly.

The Marlins then broke through in the 11th against righthander Charles Nagy, originally scheduled to start Game Seven but scratched in favor of Wright due to his ineffectiveness in the postseason.

Bonilla led off with a single to center. After reserve catcher Gregg Zaun popped out on a bunt attempt, Counsell followed with a grounder in the hole between first and second base. Fernandez, a former Gold Glove shortstop, ranged to his left but the ball rolled under his glove for an error.

Fernandez' miscue put runners on first and third with one out. Jim Eisenreich was intentionally walked to load the bases.

Fernandez, whose 11th-inning homer in Game Six of the American League Championship Series against the Baltimore Orioles propelled the Indians into the Series, looked on his way to redeeming himself when he fielded center fielder Devon White's grounder and threw a strike home to force out Bonilla.

Up to the plate stepped Renteria and that was not a good sign for the Indians. The 21-year-old, overshadowed by higher-profile players on the Marlins roster in his first full major league season, was a big reason why Florida made it to the Series.

Comeback And Heartbreak

The Marlins had 51 come-from-behind wins, including 27 in their last at bat. Renteria alone had won five of the last at-bat games with hits. The last of those came in the ninth inning of Game One of the Marlins' three-game sweep of the San Francisco Giants in the NL Division Series.

Renteria, only the fourth native of Colombia to play in the major leagues, took a first-pitch strike then lined a low curveball back through the box. The ball

WORLD SERIES YEAR-BY-YEAR

Year	Winner	Manager	Loser	Manager	Result	MVP
1903	Boston (AL)	Jimmy Collins	Pittsburgh (NL)	Fred Clarke	5-3	None Selected
1904	NO SERIES					
1905	New York (NL)	John McGraw	Philadelphia (AL)	Connie Mack	4-1	None Selected
1906	Chicago (AL)	Fielder Jones	Chicago (NL)	Frank Chance	4-2	None Selected
1907	Chicago (NL)	Frank Chance	Detroit (AL)	Hugh Jennings	4-0	None Selected
1908	Chicago (NL)	Frank Chance	Detroit (AL)	Hugh Jennings	4-1	None Selected
1909	Pittsburgh (NL)	Fred Clarke	Detroit (AL)	Hugh Jennings	4-3	None Selected
1910	Philadelphia (AL)	Connie Mack	Chicago (NL)	Frank Chance	4-1	None Selected
1911	Philadelphia (AL)	Connie Mack	New York (NL)	John McGraw	4-2	None Selected
1912	Boston (AL)	Jake Stahl	New York (NL)	John McGraw	4-3-1	None Selected
1913	Philadelphia (AL)	Connie Mack	New York (NL)	John McGraw	4-1	None Selected
1914	Boston (NL)	George Stallings	Philadelphia (AL)	Connie Mack	4-0	None Selected
1915	Boston (AL)	Bill Carrigan	Philadelphia (NL)	Pat Moran	4-1	None Selected
1916	Boston (AL)	Bill Carrigan	Brooklyn (NL)	Wilbert Robinson	4-1	None Selected
1917	Chicago (AL)	Pants Rowland	New York (NL)	John McGraw	4-2	None Selected
1918	Boston (AL)	Ed Barrow	Chicago (NL)	Fred Mitchell	4-2	None Selected
1919	Cincinnati (NL)	Pat Moran	Chicago (AL)	Kid Gleason	5-3	None Selected
1920	Cleveland (AL)	Tris Speaker	Brooklyn (NL)	Wilbert Robinson	5-2	None Selected
1921	New York (NL)	John McGraw	New York (AL)	Miller Huggins	5-3	None Selected
1922	New York (NL)	John McGraw	New York (AL)	Miller Huggins	4-0	None Selected
1923	New York (AL)	Miller Huggins	New York (NL)	John McGraw	4-2	None Selected
1924	Washington (AL)	Bucky Harris	New York (NL)	John McGraw	4-3	None Selected
1925	Pittsburgh (NL)	Bill McKechnie	Washington (AL)	Bucky Harris	4-3	None Selected
1926	St. Louis (NL)	Rogers Hornsby	New York (AL)	Miller Huggins	4-3	None Selected
1927	New York (AL)	Miller Huggins	Pittsburgh (NL)	Donie Bush	4-0	None Selected
1928	New York (AL)	Miller Huggins	St. Louis (NL)	Bill McKechnie	4-0	None Selected
1929	Philadelphia (AL)	Connie Mack	Chicago (NL)	Joe McCarthy	4-1	None Selected
1930	Philadelphia (AL)	Connie Mack	St. Louis (NL)	Gabby Street	4-2	None Selected
1931	St. Louis (NL)	Gabby Street	Philadelphia (AL)	Connie Mack	4-3	None Selected
1932	New York (AL)	Joe McCarthy	Chicago (NL)	Charlie Grimm	4-0	None Selected
1933	New York (NL)	Bill Terry	Washington (AL)	Joe Cronin	4-1	None Selected
1934	St. Louis (NL)	Frankie Frisch	Detroit (AL)	Mickey Cochrane	4-3	None Selected
1935	Detroit (AL)	Mickey Cochrane	Chicago (NL)	Charlie Grimm	4-2	None Selected
1936	New York (AL)	Joe McCarthy	New York (NL)	Bill Terry	4-2	None Selected
1937	New York (AL)	Joe McCarthy	New York (NL)	Bill Terry	4-1	None Selected
1938	New York (AL)	Joe McCarthy	Chicago (NL)	Gabby Hartnett	4-0	None Selected
1939	New York (AL)	Joe McCarthy	Cincinnati (NL)	Bill McKechnie	4-0	None Selected
1940	Cincinnati (NL)	Bill McKechnie	Detroit (AL)	Del Baker	4-3	None Selected
1941	New York (AL)	Joe McCarthy	Brooklyn (NL)	Leo Durocher	4-1	None Selected
1942	St. Louis (NL)	Billy Southworth	New York (AL)	Joe McCarthy	4-1	None Selected
1943	New York (AL)	Joe McCarthy	St. Louis (NL)	Billy Southworth	4-1	None Selected
1944	St. Louis (NL)	Billy Southworth	St. Louis (AL)	Luke Sewell	4-2	None Selected
1945	Detroit (AL)	Steve O'Neill	Chicago (NL)	Charlie Grimm	4-3	None Selected
1946	St. Louis (NL)	Eddie Dyer	Boston (AL)	Joe Cronin	4-3	None Selected
1947	New York (AL)	Bucky Harris	Brooklyn (NL)	Burt Shotton	4-3	None Selected
1948	Cleveland (AL)	Lou Boudreau	Boston (NL)	Billy Southworth	4-2	None Selected
1949	New York (AL)	Casey Stengel	Brooklyn (NL)	Burt Shotton	4-1	None Selected
1950	New York (AL)	Casey Stengel	Philadelphia (NL)	Eddie Sawyer	4-0	None Selected

Year	Winner	Manager	Loser	Manager	Result	MVP
1951	New York (AL)	Casey Stengel	New York (NL)	Leo Durocher	4-2	None Selected
1952	New York (AL)	Casey Stengel	Brooklyn (NL)	Chuck Dressen	4-3	None Selected
1953	New York (AL)	Casey Stengel	Brooklyn (NL)	Chuck Dressen	4-2	None Selected
1954	New York (NL)	Leo Durocher	Cleveland (AL)	Al Lopez	4-0	None Selected
1955	Brooklyn (NL)	Walter Alston	New York (AL)	Casey Stengel	4-3	Johnny Podres, p, Brooklyn
1956	New York (AL)	Casey Stengel	Brooklyn (NL)	Walter Alston	4-3	Don Larsen, p, New York
1957	Milwaukee (NL)	Fred Haney	New York (AL)	Casey Stengel	4-3	Lew Burdette, p, Milwaukee
1958	New York (AL)	Casey Stengel	Milwaukee (NL)	Fred Haney	4-3	Bob Turley, p, New York
1959	Los Angeles (NL)	Walter Alston	Chicago (AL)	Al Lopez	4-2	Larry Sherry, p, Los Angeles
1960	Pittsburgh (NL)	Danny Murtaugh	New York (AL)	Casey Stengel	4-3	Bobby Richardson, 2b, New York
1961	New York (AL)	Ralph Houk	Cincinnati (NL)	Fred Hutchinson	4-1	Whitey Ford, p, New York
1962	New York (AL)	Ralph Houk	San Francisco (NL)	Alvin Dark	4-3	Ralph Terry, p, New York
1963	Los Angeles (NL)	Walter Alston	New York (AL)	Ralph Houk	4-0	Sandy Koufax, p, Los Angeles
1964	St. Louis (NL)	Johnny Keene	New York (AL)	Yogi Berra	4-3	Bob Gibson, p, St. Louis
1965	Los Angeles (NL)	Walter Alston	Minnesota (AL)	Sam Mele	4-3	Sandy Koufax, p, Los Angeles
1966	Baltimore (AL)	Hank Bauer	Los Angeles (NL)	Walter Alston	4-0	Frank Robinson, of, Baltimore
1967	St. Louis (NL)	Red Schoendienst	Boston (AL)	Dick Williams	4-3	Bob Gibson, p, St. Louis
1968	Detroit (AL)	Mayo Smith	St. Louis (NL)	Red Schoendienst	4-3	Mickey Lolich, p, Detroit
1969	New York (NL)	Gil Hodges	Baltimore (AL)	Earl Weaver	4-1	Donn Clendenon, 1b, New York
1970	Baltimore (AL)	Earl Weaver	Cincinnati (NL)	Sparky Anderson	4-1	Brooks Robinson, 3b, Baltimore
1971	Pittsburgh (NL)	Danny Murtaugh	Baltimore (AL)	Earl Weaver	4-3	Roberto Clemente, of, Pittsburgh
1972	Oakland (AL)	Dick Williams	Cincinnati (NL)	Sparky Anderson	4-3	Gene Tenace, c, Oakland
1973	Oakland (AL)	Dick Williams	New York (NL)	Yogi Berra	4-3	Reggie Jackson, of, Oakland
1974	Oakland (AL)	Alvin Dark	Los Angeles (NL)	Walter Alston	4-1	Rollie Fingers, p, Oakland
1975	Cincinnati (NL)	Sparky Anderson	Boston (AL)	Darrell Johnson	4-3	Pete Rose, 3b, Cincinnati
1976	Cincinnati (NL)	Sparky Anderson	New York (AL)	Billy Martin	4-0	Johnny Bench, c, Cincinnati
1977	New York (AL)	Billy Martin	Los Angeles (NL)	Tom Lasorda	4-2	Reggie Jackson, of, New York
1978	New York (AL)	Bob Lemon	Los Angeles (NL)	Tom Lasorda	4-2	Bucky Dent, ss, New York
1979	Pittsburgh (NL)	Chuck Tanner	Baltimore (AL)	Earl Weaver	4-3	Willie Stargell, 1b, Pittsburgh
1980	Philadelphia (NL)	Dallas Green	Kansas City (AL)	Jim Frey	4-2	Mike Schmidt, 3b, Philadelphia
1981	Los Angeles (NL)	Tom Lasorda	New York (AL)	Bob Lemon	4-2	Cey/Guerrero/Yeager, Los Angeles
1982	St. Louis (NL)	Whitey Herzog	Milwaukee (AL)	Harvey Kuenn	4-3	Darrell Porter, c, St. Louis
1983	Baltimore (AL)	Joe Altobelli	Philadelphia (NL)	Paul Owens	4-1	Rick Dempsey, c, Baltimore
1984	Detroit (AL)	Sparky Anderson	San Diego (NL)	Dick Williams	4-1	Alan Trammell, ss, Detroit
1985	Kansas City (AL)	Dick Howser	St. Louis (NL)	Whitey Herzog	4-3	Bret Saberhagen, p, Kansas City
1986	New York (NL)	Dave Johnson	Boston (AL)	John McNamara	4-3	Ray Knight, 3b, New York
1987	Minnesota (AL)	Tom Kelly	St. Louis (NL)	Whitey Herzog	4-3	Frank Viola, p, Minnesota
1988	Los Angeles (NL)	Tom Lasorda	Oakland (AL)	Tony La Russa	4-1	Orel Hershiser, p, Los Angeles
1989	Oakland (AL)	Tony La Russa	San Francisco (NL)	Roger Craig	4-0	Dave Stewart, p, Oakland
1990	Cincinnati (NL)	Lou Piniella	Oakland (AL)	Tony La Russa	4-0	Jose Rijo, p, Cincinnati
1991	Minnesota (AL)	Tom Kelly	Atlanta (NL)	Bobby Cox	4-3	Jack Morris, p, Minnesota
1992	Toronto (AL)	Cito Gaston	Atlanta (NL)	Bobby Cox	4-2	Pat Borders, c, Toronto
1993	Toronto (AL)	Cito Gaston	Philadelphia (NL)	Jim Fregosi	4-2	Paul Molitor, dh, Toronto
1994	NO SERIES					
1995	Atlanta (NL)	Bobby Cox	Cleveland (AL)	Mike Hargrove	4-2	Tom Glavine, p, Atlanta
1996	New York (AL)	Joe Torre	Atlanta (NL)	Bobby Cox	4-2	John Wetteland, p, New York
1997	Florida (NL)	Jim Leyland	Cleveland (AL)	Mike Hargrove	4-3	Livan Hernandez, p, Florida

nicked Nagy's glove and carried into center field as Counsell trotted home with the Series-winning run.

"I have been in those situations before so I wasn't nervous," said Renteria, who grew up helping his mother as a fruit and fish vendor in the coastal town of Barranquilla. "I felt relaxed."

His teammates couldn't say the same.

"I was too nervous to watch," said first baseman Jeff Conine, the lone Marlin left from Opening Day of their inaugural 1993 season. "I don't think you can find a better finish than that."

"Yeah, I was a little nervous at times," said Leyland, a chain smoker who looks as if he was born nervous. "But we hadn't given up all year and I felt good because of that. The seventh game of the World Series certainly isn't a time to give up and I knew we wouldn't."

Said Marlins first-base coach Tommy Sandt, "It was a fitting way for us to end this season. All year long, we've been running out on the field at the end of games after a game-winning hit. You kind of knew that's the way it would end."

DENIS BANCROFT

Another game winner
Marlins shortstop Edgar Renteria drives home deciding run

Just as Indians fans had the sinking feeling it would end this way for their team. Nearly five decades of futility conditions the heart to harden, though the Indians gave their fans hope by pulling two upsets in the AL playoffs.

Cleveland won the final two games of the best-of-five Division Series to eliminate the New York Yankees, the defending World Series champions, before similarly upsetting the Orioles.

"I'm very disappointed that we lost. I can't describe how disappointed," said Indians manager Mike Hargrove, enduring the heartbreak of Game Seven on his 48th birthday. "But I told the team how proud I was of them and how hard they played all season long. I'm proud to have been associated with this group. They played a good Series and had a very good postseason.

"We have nothing to be ashamed of or feel sad about. We don't have to feel bad with what we did or where we came from. We played like champions and I wouldn't count us out for next year."

One-Hit Wonder?

The Marlins, though, might be the first team in baseball history to be counted out of a chance to defend their Series title.

Owner Wayne Huizenga spent $7.5 million to lure Leyland away from the Pittsburgh Pirates, $89 million on six free agents (righthanded starter Alex Fernandez, lefthanded reliever Dennis Cook, third baseman Bobby Bonilla, left fielder Moises Alou, reserve outfielders Eisenreich and John Cangelosi) and $79 million contract extensions for right fielder Gary Sheffield and closer Robb Nen.

While the $175-million spending spree netted the Marlins a World Series title, Huizenga claims he lost $34 million in 1997. He put the team up for sale in June and said after the Series he would sell the Marlins to a group led by team president Don Smiley. Huizenga said a $300 million, publicly financed ballpark in Miami would have a better chance of becoming a reality if he wasn't still the team's owner. Smiley's group reportedly wants to cut the payroll by as much as $35 million to under $20 million.

"Who wants to worry about that now?," said reliever Jay Powell, who pitched one scoreless inning for the win in Game Seven. "Next year is next year."

"Do I have regrets about the money we spent? When I sign the paychecks," Huizenga said in the aftermath of the Marlins victory. "But now is not the time to talk about the sale or anything else. It's just time to enjoy the moment. This is a great story, just enjoy that for now."

Actually, the Marlins provided two great stories in the Series in Leyland and rookie righthander Livan Hernandez, voted MVP after winning Games One and Five against Cleveland ace righthander Orel Hershiser. Hernandez was also the MVP as Florida stunned the Atlanta Braves in six games in the National League Championship Series following their sweep of the Giants.

Leyland had never been to the World Series in his 34-year professional career, losing in the NLCS in three straight years from 1990-92 while with Pittsburgh. He never got out of Double-A during seven seasons as a catcher in the Detroit Tigers farm system. He then managed 11 years in the Tigers organization before a four-year stint as the Chicago White Sox third-base coach under Tony La Russa.

Long considered one of the game's best managers, Leyland was so excited about finally shedding the label of not being able to win the big one that he did a victory lap around Pro Player Stadium following Renteria's Series-winning liner.

He then dedicated the victory to baseball's "little guys."

"This is for all those guys managing down in winter ball or instructional league, people who feel like they'll never get the chance to be here," Leyland said.

"I was a flunky backup catcher in Double-A and now I've arrived at the pinnacle of baseball. This gives hope for all those guys. This tells them they just never give up because it could happen to them, too. Dreams do come true."

Unfinished Business

Growing up in Communist-led Cuba, Hernandez never dreamed of pitching in a Series.

"It never ever entered my mind," he said. "It was just something you didn't think about in Cuba."

Sent to the bullpen for the postseason, Hernandez wound up starting when Fernandez suffered a torn rotator cuff in his pitching shoulder during Game Two of the NLCS. Hernandez went 2-0 in the NLCS, including a record 15 strikeouts in a Game Five win over the Braves.

Topping off Hernandez' dream postseason was the arrival of his mother Miriam Carreras at Pro Player Stadium just before the start of Game Seven. Carreras was granted an exit visa from Cuba the previous day.

"It's the happiest day of my life," the 22-year-old said. "My mother's here and we're champions.

"I feel so happy. Last year, there were a lot of things affecting me: the preoccupations with adjusting to the American way of life, the worries about my family and how they were doing. I ate too much, adjusting to the differences in food. I had no friends. I didn't know anyone, really.

"Now I feel comfortable pitching the way I know how to pitch."

Often in this series, the pitchers acted like they had no idea what to do. The teams combined for a Series-record 76 walks, drawing the ire of Selig after the Marlins' 14-11 victory in Game Three included 17 bases on balls and took 4 hours and 12 minutes.

"The Unfinished Symphony had a better chance of finishing before that game," Selig said. "What drives people crazy is when the pitcher's circling the mound, waiting for a message from heaven or something, and the hitter's stepping out.

"Ball one. Ball two. Ball three. It reminds me of my own club," added Selig, owner of the Milwaukee Brewers. "When you have pitchers who can't throw the ball over the plate, and when they do it hits the wall somewhere, you're going to have long games."

Selig's criticism irked both teams. So did remarks made by Ohlmeyer before the Series bemoaning that the lack of large-market teams made for low TV ratings. It did wind up being the second-lowest rated Series ever behind the earthquake-interrupted one between the Oakland Athletics and Giants in 1989.

Finally, in his press conference before Game Five, Leyland erupted.

"All this stuff is making me puke," Leyland said. "I'm sick and tired of hearing about New York and Atlanta and Baltimore. Mike Hargrove said it best: 'They had the same chance that we did.'

"I'm sick of hearing the weak comments about the pitchers and everybody crying because Atlanta, Baltimore and New York aren't here. We beat them. And the Indians beat everybody they had to beat. I get tired of having to apologize because the Florida Marlins and the Cleveland Indians are in the World Series. It's great for baseball."

JOE RIMKUS JR./MIAMI HERALD

Sealing the win
Marlins' Craig Counsell scores game-winning run

Hot And Cold

But it wasn't exactly great baseball for the first six games.

The Series started with a bang at Pro Player Stadium as Alou hit a three-run homer and catcher Charles Johnson followed with a solo shot in the fourth inning off Hershiser, enabling the Marlins to break a 1-1 tie and go on to a 7-4 win.

Hernandez allowed three runs on eight hits in 5⅔ innings for the win while Hershiser gave up seven runs on six hits in 4⅓ innings. Right fielder Manny Ramirez and first baseman Jim Thome homered for Cleveland but the comeback fell short when Nen worked a scoreless ninth for the save.

Catcher Sandy Alomar's two-run homer off Marlins ace Kevin Brown sparked the Indians to a 6-1 win in Game Two. Center fielder Marquis Grissom, MVP of the ALCS, added three hits for the Indians.

The Series then shifted to Jacobs Field in Cleveland and the balmy conditions of South Florida gave way to Arctic-like blasts off Lake Erie. Game time temperatures for the three games at Jacobs Field were 49, 35 (the coldest ever for a World Series game) and 46 with the wind chill falling into single digits in Game Four.

Game Three, won by Florida 14-11, was the ugly one that drew Selig's wrath. Florida trailed 7-3 after five innings but Eisenreich's two-run homer in the sixth and two more Marlins runs in the seventh tied it at 7-7.

Florida then took advantage of errors by Marquis Grissom, Thome and Fernandez to score seven runs in the ninth. Errors allowed the first three runs to score before Sheffield and Bonilla hit consecutive two-run singles. Nen then gave up four runs in the bottom of the ninth before hanging on.

The teams continued to alternate wins the rest of the Series, with Cleveland forcing a seventh game on the strength of Chad Ogea's four-hitter in Game Six, a 4-1 Indians victory.

WORLD SERIES

BOX SCORES

GAME ONE: October 18

Marlins 7, Indians 4

Cleveland	ab	r	h	bi	bb	so	Florida	ab	r	h	bi	bb	so
Roberts 2b	4	1	2	0	1	0	White cf	4	0	0	0	1	1
Vizquel ss	4	0	0	0	0	2	Renteria ss	4	0	0	1	0	0
Ramirez rf	3	1	1	1	2	0	Sheffield rf	2	1	0	0	2	1
Justice lf	4	0	2	1	1	0	Bonilla 3b	3	2	2	0	1	1
Williams 3b	5	0	1	0	0	1	Daulton 1b	2	1	1	0	0	0
Thome 1b	5	1	1	1	0	2	Conine 1b	2	0	1	1	0	0
Alomar c	5	0	1	0	0	2	Alou lf	3	1	1	3	1	1
Grissom cf	3	1	2	0	1	1	Johnson c	3	1	1	1	1	0
Hershiser p	2	0	0	0	0	1	Counsell 2b	3	1	1	0	1	0
Juden p	0	0	0	0	0	0	Hernandez p	2	0	0	0	0	0
Branson ph	1	0	0	0	0	1	Cook p	0	0	0	0	0	0
Plunk p	0	0	0	0	0	0	Powell p	0	0	0	0	0	0
Giles ph	1	0	1	1	0	0	Cangelosi ph	1	0	0	0	0	1
Assenmacher p	0	0	0	0	0	0	Nen p	0	0	0	0	0	0
Totals	37	4	11	4	5	10	**Totals**	29	7	7	6	7	5

Cleveland	**100 011 010—4**
Florida	**001 420 00X—7**

E—Sheffield (1). **DP**—Cleveland 1. **LOB**—Cleveland 12, Florida 6. **2B**—Counsell (1), Roberts 2 (2), Grissom (1), Giles (1). **HR**—Alou (1), Johnson (1), Ramirez (1), Thome (1). **S**—Hernandez, Vizquel.

Cleveland	ip	h	r	er	bb	so	Florida	ip	h	r	er	bb	so
Hershiser L	4⅓	6	7	7	4	2	Hernandez W	5⅔	8	3	3	2	5
Juden	⅔	0	0	0	2	0	Cook	1⅔	0	0	0	1	2
Plunk	2	1	0	0	1	1	Powell	⅔	1	1	1	2	1
Assenmacher	1	0	0	0	0	2	Nen S	1	2	0	0	0	2

WP—Juden.

Umpires: HP—Montague; **1B**—Ford; **2B**—West; **3B**—Kosc; **LF**—Marsh; **RF**—Kaiser.

T—3:19. **A**—67,245.

GAME TWO: October 19

Cleveland 6, Marlins 1

Cleveland	ab	r	h	bi	bb	so	Florida	ab	r	h	bi	bb	so
Roberts 2b	3	0	1	2	0	1	White cf	5	0	2	0	0	1
Fernandez 2b	2	0	2	0	0	0	Renteria ss	4	1	2	0	0	1
Vizquel ss	4	1	2	0	1	0	Sheffield rf	2	0	1	0	1	0
Ramirez rf	5	0	0	0	0	1	Bonilla 3b	4	0	0	0	0	1
Justice lf	3	0	1	1	1	1	Conine 1b	3	0	1	1	0	0
Williams 3b	4	2	2	0	0	0	Daulton ph-1b	1	0	0	0	0	0
Thome 1b	4	0	1	0	0	1	Alou lf	4	0	2	0	0	0
Alomar c	4	2	2	2	0	0	Johnson c	3	0	0	0	0	1
Grissom cf	4	1	3	1	0	0	Zaun ph	1	0	0	0	0	0
Ogea p	2	0	0	0	0	1	Counsell 2b	3	0	0	0	1	0
Jackson p	1	0	0	0	0	0	Brown p	2	0	0	0	0	1
Mesa p	0	0	0	0	0	0	Heredia p	0	0	0	0	0	0
							Eisenreich ph	1	0	0	0	0	0
							Alfonseca p	0	0	0	0	0	0
							Floyd ph	1	0	0	0	0	1
Totals	36	6	14	6	2	5	**Totals**	34	1	8	1	2	6

Cleveland	**100 032 000—6**
Florida	**100 000 000—1**

DP—Cleveland 1, Florida 3. **LOB**—Cleveland 6, Florida 9. **2B**—Vizquel (1), Fernandez (1), Renteria (1), Alou 2 (2), White (1). **HR**—Alomar (1). **CS**—Justice. **S**—Ogea.

Cleveland	ip	h	r	er	bb	so	Florida	ip	h	r	er	bb	so
Ogea W	6⅔	7	1	1	1	4	Brown L	6	10	6	6	2	4
Jackson	1⅓	1	0	0	0	1	Heredia	1	1	0	0	0	1
Mesa	1	0	0	0	1	1	Alfonseca	2	3	0	0	0	0

HBP—Sheffield (by Ogea).

Umpires: HP—Ford; **1B**—West; **2B**—Kosc; **3B**—Marsh; **LF**—Kaiser; **RF**—Montague.

T—2:48. **A**—67,025.

GAME THREE: October 21

Florida 14, Cleveland 11

Florida	ab	r	h	bi	bb	so	Cleveland	ab	r	h	bi	bb	so
White cf	5	0	1	0	1	1	Roberts lf	5	1	1	2	0	1
Renteria ss	4	2	2	1	2	0	Vizquel ss	4	0	0	1	2	1
Sheffield rf	5	2	3	5	1	0	Ramirez rf	5	0	1	1	0	0
Bonilla 3b	5	1	1	2	1	1	Justice dh	3	2	0	0	2	0
Daulton 1b	4	3	2	1	2	0	Williams 3b	5	0	1	1	0	2
Conine 1b	0	0	0	0	0	0	Alomar c	3	2	2	1	1	0
Alou lf	5	0	0	0	0	3	Giles ph	0	1	0	0	1	0
Eisenreich dh	3	1	2	2	0	0	Thome 1b	4	3	2	2	1	1
Abbott dh	1	0	0	0	0	1	Fernandez 2b	4	0	1	1	0	0
Floyd dh	0	1	0	0	1	0	Grissom cf	3	2	2	1	2	0
Johnson c	5	2	3	0	0	0							
Counsell 2b	5	2	2	1	0	2							
Totals	42	14	16	12	8	8	**Totals**	36	11	10	10	9	5

Florida	**101 102 207—14**
Cleveland	**200 320 004—11**

E—Bonilla 2 (2), Leiter (1), Thome (1), Fernandez (1), Grissom (1). **DP**—Florida 1, Cleveland 2. **LOB**—Florida 9, Cleveland 9. **2B**—Sheffield (1), Roberts (3). **HR**—Eisenreich (1), Daulton (1), Sheffield (1), Thome (2). **S**—Roberts. **SF**—Fernandez.

Florida	ip	h	r	er	bb	so	Cleveland	ip	h	r	er	bb	so
Leiter	4⅔	6	7	4	6	3	Nagy	6	6	5	5	4	5
Heredia	2⅓	0	0	0	1	0	Anderson	⅓	1	1	1	0	0
Cook W	1	1	0	0	0	1	Jackson	⅔	2	1	1	1	0
Nen	1	3	4	4	2	1	Assenmacher	⅔	3	0	0	0	1
							Plunk L	⅔	2	4	3	2	1
							Morman	⅓	0	2	0	1	1
							Mesa	⅓	2	1	1	0	0

WP—Mesa.

Umpires: HP—West; **1B**—Kosc; **2B**—Marsh; **3B**—Kaiser; **LF**—Montague; **RF**—Ford.

T—4:12. **A**—44,880.

GAME FOUR: October 22

Cleveland 10, Florida 3

Florida	ab	r	h	bi	bb	so	Cleveland	ab	r	h	bi	bb	so
White cf	4	0	0	0	0	4	Roberts lf	4	0	1	0	0	2
Renteria ss	4	0	1	0	0	0	Giles lf	1	0	1	1	0	0
Sheffield rf	3	0	0	0	1	2	Vizquel ss	5	2	2	0	0	0
Bonilla 3b	4	0	0	0	0	0	Ramirez rf	4	2	1	2	1	1
Daulton 1b	3	2	2	0	1	0	Justice dh	3	2	1	0	2	2
Alou lf	3	1	1	2	1	0	Williams 3b	3	3	3	2	2	0
Eisenreich dh	2	0	2	1	1	0	Alomar c	5	0	3	3	0	0
Arias dh	1	0	0	0	0	0	Thome	4	0	1	0	1	1
Johnson c	4	0	0	0	0	1	Fernandez 2b	5	1	2	1	0	0
Counsell 2b	2	0	0	0	1	0	Grissom cf	4	0	0	0	0	1
Abbott ph	1	0	0	0	0	0							
Totals	31	3	6	3	5	7	**Totals**	38	10	15	9	6	7

Florida	**000 102 000— 3**
Cleveland	**303 001 12X—10**

E—Saunders (1), Renteria (1). **DP**—Cleveland 2. **LOB**—Florida 6, Cleveland 10. **2B**—Daulton (1), Alomar (1), Roberts (4). **HR**—Alou (2), Ramirez (2), Williams (1). **SB**—Counsell (1), Vizquel (1). **CS**—Giles.

Florida	ip	h	r	er	bb	so	Cleveland	ip	h	r	er	bb	so
Saunders L	2	7	6	6	3	2	Wright W	6	5	3	3	5	5
Alfonseca	3	3	0	0	0	4	Anderson	3	1	0	0	0	2
Vosberg	2	3	2	2	2	1							
Powell	1	2	2	2	1	0							

Sanders pitched to five batters in third.

WP—Wright.

Umpires: HP—Kosc; **1B**—Marsh; **2B**—Kaiser; **3B**—Montague; **LF**—Ford; **RF**—West.

T—3:15. **A**—44,877.

GAME FIVE: October 23

Florida 8, Cleveland 7

Florida	ab	r	h	bi	bb	so	Cleveland	ab	r	h	bi	bb	so
White cf	4	0	2	2	1	0	Roberts 2b	3	1	0	0	2	0
Renteria ss	5	0	1	0	0	2	Vizquel ss	4	1	1	0	0	0
Sheffield rf	5	1	2	0	0	0	Ramirez rf	5	0	1	0	0	1
Bonilla 3b	4	1	1	0	1	0	Justice dh	5	0	1	2	0	1
Arias 3b	0	1	0	0	0	0	Williams 3b	3	2	1	0	2	0
Daulton dh	5	1	2	0	0	0	Thome 1b	4	2	2	1	1	0
Alou lf	5	2	3	4	0	1	Alomar c	5	1	2	4	0	0
Conine 1b	5	1	1	0	0	0	Giles lf	1	0	0	0	3	1
Johnson c	5	1	3	2	0	2	Grissom cf	4	0	1	0	0	0
Counsell 2b	2	0	0	0	2	1							
Totals	40	8	15	8	4	6	**Totals**	34	7	9	7	8	3

Florida	**002 004 011—8**
Cleveland	**013 000 003—7**

E—Hernandez (1), Counsell (1). **DP**—Florida 2, Cleveland 1. **LOB**—Florida 9, Cleveland 9. **2B**—Daulton (2), White 2 (3), Bonilla (1). **3B**—Thome (1). **HR**—Alou (3), Alomar (2). **SB**—Alou (1), Daulton (1). **S**—Vizquel.

Florida	ip	h	r	er	bb	so	Cleveland	ip	h	r	er	bb	so
Hernandez W	8	7	6	5	8	2	Hershiser L	5⅔	9	6	6	2	3
Nen S	1	2	1	0	0	1	Morman	0	0	0	0	1	0
							Plunk	⅓	0	0	0	1	1
							Juden	1⅓	2	1	1	0	0
							Assenmacher	⅔	1	0	0	0	1
							Mesa	1	3	1	1	0	1

Morman pitched to one batter in sixth.

WP—Hernandez.

Umpires: HP—Marsh; **1B**—Kaiser; **2B**—Montague; **3B**—Ford; **LF**—West; **RF**—Kosc.

T—3:39. **A**—44,888.

GAME SIX: October 25
Cleveland 4, Florida 1

Cleveland	ab	r	h	bi	bb	so	Florida	ab	r	h	bi	bb	so
Roberts 2b	3	0	1	0	0	1	White cf	5	0	3	0	0	1
Fernandez 2b	1	0	1	0	0	0	Renteria ss	5	0	0	0	0	2
Vizquel ss	4	1	1	0	0	0	Sheffield rf	3	0	0	0	2	0
Ramirez rf	1	0	0	2	1	0	Bonilla 3b	4	0	0	0	0	0
Justice lf	4	0	0	0	0	1	Conine 1b	2	0	0	0	0	0
Williams 3b	4	1	2	0	0	1	Eisenreich 1b	1	0	0	0	1	1
Thome 1b	3	1	0	0	1	2	Alou lf	3	1	1	0	1	0
Alomar c	3	0	0	0	1	1	Johnson c	4	0	2	0	0	0
Grissom cf	3	0	0	0	1	1	Counsell 2b	4	0	1	0	0	1
Ogea p	2	1	2	2	0	0	Brown p	1	0	0	0	0	0
Jackson p	1	0	0	0	0	1	Daulton ph	0	0	0	1	0	0
Assenmacher p	0	0	0	0	0	0	Heredia p	0	0	0	0	0	0
Seitzer ph	1	0	0	0	0	0	Cangelosi ph	1	0	1	0	0	0
Mesa p	0	0	0	0	0	0	Powell p	0	0	0	0	0	0
							Vosberg p	0	0	0	0	0	0
							Floyd ph	1	0	0	0	0	0
Totals	**30**	**4**	**7**	**4**	**4**	**8**	**Totals**	**34**	**1**	**8**	**1**	**4**	**5**

Cleveland	**021 010 000—4**
Florida	**000 010 000—1**

DP—Florida 1. **LOB**—Cleveland 5, Florida 11. **2B**—Vizquel (2), Williams (1), Ogea (1). **3B**—White (1). **SB**—Vizquel 2 (3), White (1). **CS**—Roberts. **SF**—Ramirez 2, Daulton.

Cleveland	ip	h	r	er	bb	so	Florida	ip	h	r	er	bb	so
Ogea W	5	4	1	1	2	1	Brown L	5	5	4	4	3	2
Jackson	2	2	0	0	2	2	Heredia	2	0	0	0	0	4
Assenmacher	1	1	0	0	0	1	Powell	1	2	0	0	0	1
Mesa S	1	1	0	0	0	1	Vosberg	1	0	0	0	1	1

Ogea pitched to one batter in sixth; Powell pitched to one batter in ninth.

Umpires: HP—Kaiser; **1B**—Montague; **2B**—Ford; **3B**—West; **LF**—Kosc; **RF**—Marsh.

T—3:15. **A**—67,498.

GAME SEVEN: October 26
Florida 3, Cleveland 2

Cleveland	ab	r	h	bi	bb	so	Florida	ab	r	h	bi	bb	so
Vizquel ss	5	0	1	0	0	2	White cf	6	0	0	0	0	2
Fernandez 2b	5	0	2	2	0	1	Renteria ss	5	0	3	1	1	0
Ramirez rf	3	0	0	0	2	2	Sheffield rf	4	0	1	0	1	2
Justice lf	5	0	0	0	0	3	Daulton 1b	3	0	0	0	0	0
Williams 3b	2	0	0	0	3	2	Conine 1b	1	0	0	0	0	0
Alomar c	5	0	1	0	0	0	Nen p	0	0	0	0	0	0
Thome 1b	4	1	1	0	1	0	Cangelosi ph	1	0	0	0	0	1
Grissom cf	4	1	1	0	0	1	Powell p	0	0	0	0	0	0
Wright p	2	0	0	0	0	2	Alou lf	5	1	1	0	0	1
Assenmacher p	0	0	0	0	0	0	Bonilla 3b	5	1	2	1	0	2
Jackson p	0	0	0	0	0	0	Johnson c	4	0	1	0	0	2
Anderson p	0	0	0	0	0	0	Zaun pr-c	1	0	0	0	0	0
Giles ph	1	0	0	0	0	0	Counsell 2b	3	1	0	1	1	1
Mesa p	0	0	0	0	0	0	Leiter p	0	0	0	0	2	0
Nagy p	0	0	0	0	0	0	Cook p	0	0	0	0	0	0
							Floyd ph	0	0	0	0	0	0
							Abbott ph	1	0	0	0	0	0
							Alfonseca p	0	0	0	0	0	0
							Heredia p	0	0	0	0	0	0
							Eisenreich 1b	1	0	0	0	1	0
Totals	**36**	**2**	**6**	**2**	**6**	**13**	**Totals**	**40**	**3**	**8**	**3**	**6**	**11**

Cleveland	**002 000 000 00—2**
Florida	**000 000 101 01—3**

E—Ramirez (1), Fernandez (2). **DP**—Cleveland 1, Florida 2. **LOB**—Cleveland 8, Florida 12. **2B**—Renteria (2). **HR**—Bonilla (1). **SB**—Vizquel 2 (5). **S**—Wright. **SF**—Counsell.

Cleveland	ip	h	r	er	bb	so	Florida	ip	h	r	er	bb	so
Wright	6⅓	2	1	1	5	7	Leiter	6	4	2	2	4	7
Assenmacher	⅔	0	0	0	0	1	Cook	1	0	0	0	0	2
Jackson	⅔	0	0	0	0	1	Alfonseca	1⅓	0	0	0	1	1
Anderson	⅓	0	0	0	0	1	Heredia	0	1	0	0	0	0
Mesa	1⅔	4	1	1	0	2	Nen	1⅔	1	0	0	0	3
Nagy L	1	2	1	0	1	0	Powell W	1	0	0	0	1	0

Heredia pitched to one batter in 9th.

Umpires: HP—Montague; **1B**—Ford; **2B**—West; **3B**—Kosc; **LF**—Marsh; **RF**—Kaiser.

T—4:11. **A**—67,204.

COMPOSITE BOX

CLEVELAND

Player, Pos.	AVG	G	AB	R	H	2B	3B	HR	RBI	BB	SO	SB
Chad Ogea, p	.500	2	4	1	2	1	0	0	2	0	1	0
Brian Giles, ph-lf	.500	5	4	1	2	1	0	0	2	4	1	0
Tony Fernandez, 2b	.471	5	17	1	8	1	0	0	4	0	1	0
Matt Williams, 3b	.385	7	26	8	10	1	0	1	3	7	6	0
Sandy Alomar, c	.367	7	30	5	11	1	0	2	10	2	3	0
Marquis Grissom, cf	.360	7	25	5	9	1	0	0	2	4	4	0
Jim Thome, 1b	.286	7	28	8	8	0	1	2	4	5	7	0
Bip Roberts, 2b-lf	.273	6	22	3	6	4	0	0	4	3	5	0
Omar Vizquel, ss	.233	7	30	5	7	2	0	0	1	3	5	5
Dave Justice, lf-dh	.185	7	27	4	5	0	0	0	4	6	8	0
Manny Ramirez, rf	.154	7	26	3	4	0	0	2	6	6	5	0
Jeff Branson, ph	.000	1	1	0	0	0	0	0	0	0	1	0
Kevin Seitzer, ph	.000	1	1	0	0	0	0	0	0	0	0	0
Orel Hershiser, p	.000	1	2	0	0	0	0	0	0	0	1	0
Jaret Wright, p	.000	2	2	0	0	0	0	0	0	0	2	0
Mike Jackson, p	.000	3	2	0	0	0	0	0	0	0	1	0
Totals	**.291**	**7**	**247**	**44**	**72**	**12**	**1**	**7**	**42**	**40**	**51**	**5**

Pitching	W	L	ERA	G	GS	SV	IP	H	R	ER	BB	SO
Paul Assenmacher	0	0	0.00	5	0	0	4	5	0	0	0	6
Alvin Morman	0	0	0.00	2	0	0	0	0	2	0	2	1
Chad Ogea	2	0	1.54	2	2	0	12	11	2	2	3	5
Mike Jackson	0	0	1.93	4	0	0	5	5	1	1	3	4
Brian Anderson	0	0	2.45	3	0	1	4	2	1	1	0	2
Jaret Wright	1	0	2.92	2	2	0	12	7	4	4	10	12
Jeff Juden	0	0	4.50	2	0	0	2	2	1	1	2	0
Jose Mesa	0	0	5.40	5	0	1	5	10	3	3	1	5
Charles Nagy	0	1	6.43	2	1	0	7	8	6	5	5	5
Eric Plunk	0	1	9.00	3	0	0	3	3	4	3	4	3
Orel Hershiser	0	2	11.70	2	2	0	10	15	13	13	6	5
Totals	**3**	**4**	**4.66**	**7**	**7**	**2**	**64**	**68**	**37**	**33**	**36**	**48**

FLORIDA

Player, Pos.	AVG	G	AB	R	H	2B	3B	HR	RBI	BB	SO	SB
Jim Eisenreich, dh-1b	.500	5	8	1	4	0	0	1	3	3	1	0
Darren Daulton, dh-1b	.389	7	18	7	7	2	0	1	2	3	0	1
Charles Johnson, c	.357	7	28	4	10	0	0	1	3	1	6	0
John Cangelosi, ph	.333	3	3	0	1	0	0	0	0	0	2	0
Moises Alou, of	.321	7	28	6	9	2	0	3	9	3	6	1
Gary Sheffield, rf	.292	7	24	4	7	1	0	1	5	8	5	0
Edgar Renteria, ss	.290	7	31	3	9	2	0	0	3	3	5	0
Devon White, cf	.242	7	33	0	8	3	1	0	2	3	10	1
Jeff Conine, 1b	.231	6	13	1	3	0	0	0	2	0	0	0
Bobby Bonilla, 3b	.207	7	29	5	6	1	0	1	3	3	5	0
Craig Counsell, 2b	.182	7	22	4	4	1	0	0	2	6	5	1
Alex Arias, 3b-pr	.000	2	1	1	0	0	0	0	0	0	0	0
Livan Hernandez, p	.000	1	2	0	0	0	0	0	0	0	0	0
Gregg Zaun, c-ph	.000	2	2	0	0	0	0	0	0	0	0	0
Cliff Floyd, dh-ph	.000	4	2	1	0	0	0	0	0	1	1	0
Kurt Abbott, ph	.000	3	3	0	0	0	0	0	0	0	1	0
Kevin Brown, p	.000	2	3	0	0	0	0	0	0	0	1	0
Totals	**.272**	**7**	**250**	**37**	**68**	**12**	**1**	**8**	**34**	**36**	**48**	**4**

Pitcher	W	L	ERA	G	GS	SV	IP	H	R	ER	BB	SO
Antonio Alfonseca	0	0	0.00	3	0	0	6	6	0	0	1	5
Felix Heredia	0	0	0.00	4	0	0	5	2	0	0	1	5
Dennis Cook	1	0	0.00	3	0	0	4	1	0	0	1	5
Al Leiter	0	0	5.06	2	2	0	11	10	9	6	10	10
Livan Hernandez	2	0	5.27	2	2	0	14	15	9	8	10	7
Ed Vosberg	0	0	6.00	2	0	0	3	3	2	2	3	2
Jay Powell	1	0	7.36	4	0	0	4	5	3	3	4	2
Robb Nen	0	0	7.71	4	0	2	5	8	5	4	2	7
Kevin Brown	0	2	8.18	2	2	0	11	15	10	10	5	6
Tony Saunders	0	1	27.00	1	1	0	2	7	6	6	3	2
Totals	**4**	**3**	**5.48**	**7**	**7**	**2**	**64**	**72**	**44**	**39**	**40**	**51**

SCORE BY INNINGS	
Cleveland	**739 374 137 00 — 44**
Florida	**222 638 319 01 — 37**

DP—Cleveland 7, Florida 6. **LOB**—Cleveland 59, Florida 62. **E**—Bonilla 2, Sheffield, Leiter, Thome, Fernandez 2, Grissom, Renteria, Saunders, Counsell, Hernandez, Ramirez. **CS**—Justice, Giles, Roberts. **S**—Vizquel 2, Hernandez, Ogea, Roberts, Wright. **SF**—Fernandez, Ramirez 2, Daulton, Counsell. **WP**—Mesa, Wright.

Umpires—Dale Ford, Ken Kaiser, Greg Kosc, Randy Marsh, Ed Montague, Joe West.

AMERICAN LEAGUE

Indians reshuffle deck and turn table on befuddled Orioles

BY LACY LUSK

After a regular season fall, the Indians bounced back in thrilling style in the postseason.

With four one-run victories over the Orioles, the Indians took the 1997 American League Championship Series in six games. They advanced to their second World Series in three years, and it came after an 86-75 regular season. In each of the two previous campaigns, Cleveland had led the AL in both ERA and batting average. The Tribe had gone a combined 199-106 in that span, sporting the best record in the majors in both seasons.

The Indians went to the Series after some major retooling by general manager John Hart and his staff. In the offseason, left fielder Albert Belle signed a five-year, $55 million contract with the Central Division rival White Sox. Late in spring training, center fielder Kenny Lofton and lefthanded reliever Alan Embree were dealt to the Braves for two new outfielders, David Justice and Marquis Grissom. Cleveland also acquired third baseman Matt Williams in a trade with the Giants, and second baseman Tony Fernandez through free agency.

"Comparing this year's team and last year's team is like comparing apples and oranges," Indians manager Mike Hargrove said early in the 1997 season. "The personality of this year's team is definitely a lot better than last year's. This one is a much more media-friendly team. This is a better defensive team. This team is stronger mentally. And offensively, we're stronger one through nine than we were. Maybe not one through four, but one through nine."

It was Cleveland's ninth-place hitter, Grissom, who turned out to be MVP of the League Championship Series. He hit a series-turning three-run home run in the eighth inning of Game Two at Camden Yards.

LARRY GOREN

Indians stalwart Sandy Alomar
Keyed Cleveland's drive to AL title

JOHN KLEIN

ALCS MVP Marquis Grissom
Series turned on his three-run homer

Grissom also was credited with a steal of home on the game-ending play in the 12th inning of Game Three. On the play, Omar Vizquel attempted a squeeze bunt. Plate umpire John Hirschbeck ruled Grissom safe as he crossed the plate while Orioles catcher Lenny Webster was retrieving the ball. Webster later claimed the ball was tipped and that Vizquel had admitted that to him.

Game Four included a two-run wild pitch that involved Webster behind the plate. Then in Game Six, Mike Mussina's eight innings of one-hit ball were not enough in a 1-0 season-ending loss for Baltimore. The Indians managed only three hits in 11 innings, but the third was a solo home run by Fernandez, who replaced Bip Roberts in the starting lineup after Roberts was hurt in pregame warmups by a Fernandez line drive.

"I don't know that fate's in our corner," Hargrove said. "If it is, we'll take it. I choose to think this ballclub puts itself in position to take advantage of breaks that come its way."

Fernandez and Grissom each hit their crucial home runs off Baltimore reliever Armando Benitez, who was a key part of a bullpen that had the league's best regular season ERA and top closer in Randy Myers (45 saves). In the LCS, that bullpen went 0-4 while Cleveland's was 4-0.

Cleveland reached the ALCS after another dramatic

AMERICAN LEAGUE CHAMPIONS, 1901-1997

	Pennant	Pct.	GA
1901	Chicago	.610	4
1902	Philadelphia	.610	5
1903	Boston	.659	14½
1904	Boston	.617	1½
1905	Philadelphia	.622	2
1906	Chicago	.616	3
1907	Detroit	.613	1½
1908	Detroit	.588	½
1909	Detroit	.645	3½
1910	Philadelphia	.680	14½
1911	Philadelphia	.669	13½
1912	Boston	.691	14
1913	Philadelphia	.627	6½
1914	Philadelphia	.651	8½
1915	Boston	.669	2½
1916	Boston	.591	2
1917	Chicago	.649	9
1918	Boston	.595	2½
1919	Chicago	.629	3½
1920	Cleveland	.636	2
1921	New York	.641	4½
1922	New York	.610	1
1923	New York	.645	16
1924	Washington	.597	2
1925	Washington	.636	8½
1926	New York	.591	3
1927	New York	.714	19
1928	New York	.656	2½
1929	Philadelphia	.693	18
1930	Philadelphia	.662	8

	Pennant	Pct.	GA	MVP
1931	Philadelphia	.704	13½	Lefty Grove, lhp, Philadelphia
1932	New York	.695	13	Jimmie Foxx, 1b, Philadelphia
1933	Washington	.651	7	Jimmie Foxx, 1b, Philadelphia
1934	Detroit	.656	7	Mickey Cochrane, c, Detroit
1935	Detroit	.616	3	Hank Greenberg, 1b, Detroit
1936	New York	.667	19½	Lou Gehrig, 1b, New York
1937	New York	.662	13	Charlie Gehringer, 2b, Detroit
1938	New York	.651	9½	Jimmie Foxx, 1b, Boston
1939	New York	.702	17	Joe DiMaggio, of, New York
1940	Detroit	.584	1	Hank Greenberg, 1b, Detroit
1941	New York	.656	17	Joe DiMaggio, of, New York
1942	New York	.669	9	Joe Gordon, 2b, New York
1943	New York	.636	13½	Spud Chandler, rhp, New York
1944	St. Louis	.578	1	Hal Newhouser, lhp, Detroit
1945	Detroit	.575	1½	Hal Newhouher, lhp, Detroit
1946	Boston	.675	12	Ted Williams, of, Boston
1947	New York	.630	12	Joe DiMaggio, of, New York
1948	Cleveland	.626	1	Lou Boudreau, ss, Cleveland
1949	New York	.630	1	Ted Williams, of, Boston
1950	New York	.636	3	Phil Rizzuto, ss, New York
1951	New York	.636	5	Yogi Berra, c, New York
1952	New York	.617	2	Bobby Shantz, lhp, Philadelphia
1953	New York	.656	8½	Al Rosen, 3b, Cleveland
1954	Cleveland	.721	8	Yogi Berra, c, New York
1955	New York	.623	3	Yogi Berra, c, New York
1956	New York	.630	9	Mickey Mantle, of, New York
1957	New York	.636	8	Mickey Mantle, of, New York
1958	New York	.597	10	Jackie Jensen, of, Boston
1959	Chicago	.610	5	Nellie Fox, 2b, Chicago
1960	New York	.630	8	Roger Maris, of, New York
1961	New York	.673	8	Roger Maris, of, New York
1962	New York	.593	5	Mickey Mantle, of, New York
1963	New York	.646	10½	Elston Howard, c, New York
1964	New York	.611	1	Brooks Robinson, 3b, Baltimore
1965	Minnesota	.630	7	Zoilo Versalles, ss, Minnesota
1966	Baltimore	.606	9	Frank Robinson, of, Baltimore
1967	Boston	.568	1	Carl Yastrzemski, of, Boston
1968	Detroit	.636	12	Denny McLain, rhp, Detroit

	East. Div.	PCT	GA	West. Div.	PCT	GA	Pennant		MVP
1969	Baltimore	.673	19	Minnesota	.599	9	Baltimore	3-0	Harmon Killebrew, 1b-3b, Minnesota
1970	Baltimore	.667	15	Minnesota	.605	9	Baltimore	3-0	Boog Powell, 1b, Baltimore
1971	Baltimore	.639	12	Oakland	.627	16	Baltimore	3-0	Vida Blue, lhp, Oakland
1972	Detroit	.551	½	Oakland	.600	5½	Oakland	3-2	Dick Allen, 1b, Chicago
1973	Baltimore	.599	8	Oakland	.580	6	Oakland	3-2	Reggie Jackson, of, Oakland
1974	Baltimore	.562	2	Oakland	.556	5	Oakland	3-1	Jeff Burroughs, of, Texas
1975	Boston	.594	4½	Oakland	.605	7	Boston	3-0	Fred Lynn, of, Boston
1976	New York	.610	10½	Kansas City	.556	2½	New York	3-2	Thurman Munson, c, New York
1977	New York	.617	2½	Kansas City	.630	8	New York	3-2	Rod Carew, 1b, Minnesota
1978	New York	.613	1	Kansas City	.568	5	New York	3-1	Jim Rice, of, Boston
1979	Baltimore	.642	8	California	.543	3	Baltimore	3-1	Don Baylor, dh, California
1980	New York	.636	3	Kansas City	.599	14	Kansas City	3-0	George Brett, 3b, Kansas City
1981	New York*	.607	2	Oakland**	.587	—	New York	3-0	Rollie Fingers, rhp, Milwaukee
	Milwaukee	.585	1½	Kansas City	.566	1			
1982	Milwaukee	.586	1	California	.574	3	Milwaukee	3-2	Robin Yount, ss, Milwaukee
1983	Baltimore	.605	6	Chicago	.611	20	Baltimore	3-1	Cal Ripken Jr., ss, Baltimore
1984	Detroit	.642	15	Kansas City	.519	3	Detroit	3-0	Willie Hernandez, lhp, Detroit
1985	Toronto	.615	2	Kansas City	.562	1	Kansas City	4-3	Don Mattingly, 1b, New York
1986	Boston	.590	5½	California	.568	5	Boston	4-3	Roger Clemens, rhp, Boston
1987	Detroit	.605	2	Minnesota	.525	2	Minnesota	4-1	George Bell, of, Toronto
1988	Boston	.549	1	Oakland	.642	13	Oakland	4-0	Jose Canseco, of, Oakland
1989	Toronto	.549	2	Oakland	.611	7	Oakland	4-1	Robin Yount, of, Milwaukee
1990	Boston	.543	2	Oakland	.636	9	Oakland	4-0	Rickey Henderson, of, Oakland
1991	Toronto	.562	7	Minnesota	.586	8	Minnesota	4-1	Cal Ripken Jr., ss, Baltimore
1992	Toronto	.593	4	Oakland	.593	6	Toronto	4-2	Dennis Eckersley, rhp, Oakland
1993	Toronto	.586	7	Chicago	.580	8	Toronto	4-2	Frank Thomas, 1b, Chicago

	East Div.	PCT	GA	Central Div.	PCT	GA	West Div.	PCT	GA	MVP
1994	New York	.619	6½	Chicago	.593	1	Texas	.456	1	Frank Thomas, 1b, Chicago
1995	Boston	.597	7	Cleveland#	.694	30	Seattle	.545	1	Mo Vaughn, 1b, Boston
1996	New York@	.568	4	Cleveland	.615	14½	Texas	.556	4	Juan Gonzalez, of, Texas
1997	Baltimore	.605	2	Cleveland†	.534	6	Seattle	.556	6	Ken Griffey, of, Seattle

*Won first half; defeated Milwaukee 3-2 in best-of-5 playoff. **Won first half, defeated Kansas City 3-0 in best-of-5 playoff.
#Won AL pennant, defeating Seattle 4-2. @ Won AL pennant, defeating Baltimore 4-1. † Won AL pennant, defeating Baltimore 4-2

AMERICAN LEAGUE STANDINGS

Page	EAST	W	L	PCT	GB	Manager(s)	General Manager	Attend./Dates	Last Penn.
64	Baltimore Orioles	98	64	.605	—	Dave Johnson	Pat Gillick	3,711,132 (81)	1983
158	New York Yankees*	96	66	.593	2	Joe Torre	Bob Watson	2,580,445 (78)	1996
108	Detroit Tigers	79	83	.488	19	Buddy Bell	Randy Smith	1,365,157 (79)	1984
71	Boston Red Sox	78	84	.481	20	Jimy Williams	Dan Duquette	2,226,136 (80)	1986
226	Toronto Blue Jays	76	86	.469	22	C. Gaston/M. Queen	Gord Ash	2,589,297 (81)	1993
Page	**CENTRAL**	**W**	**L**	**PCT**	**GB**	**Manager(s)**	**General Manager**	**Attend./Dates**	**Last Penn.**
96	Cleveland Indians	86	75	.534	—	Mike Hargrove	John Hart	3,404,750 (80)	1997
78	Chicago White Sox	80	81	.497	6	Terry Bevington	Ron Schueler	1,865,222 (78)	1959
139	Milwaukee Brewers	78	83	.484	8	Phil Garner	Sal Bando	1,444,027 (78)	1982
145	Minnesota Twins	68	94	.420	18½	Tom Kelly	Terry Ryan	1,411,064 (81)	1991
126	Kansas City Royals	67	94	.416	19	B. Boone/T. Muser	Herk Robinson	1,517,638 (77)	1985
Page	**WEST**	**W**	**L**	**PCT**	**GB**	**Manager**	**General Manager**	**Attend./Dates**	**Last Penn.**
210	Seattle Mariners	90	72	.556	—	Lou Piniella	Woody Woodward	3,198,995 (81)	None
48	Anaheim Angels	84	78	.519	6	Terry Collins	Bill Bavasi	1,767,324 (81)	None
220	Texas Rangers	77	85	.475	13	Johnny Oates	Doug Melvin	2,945,228 (80)	None
172	Oakland Athletics	65	97	.401	25	Art Howe	Sandy Alderson	1,261,219 (79)	1990

*Won wild-card playoff berth

NOTE: Team's individual batting, pitching and fielding statistics can be found on page indicated in lefthand column.

home run. Four outs from elimination in Game Four of the Division Series, Sandy Alomar Jr. delivered a game-tying shot off Yankees closer Mariano Rivera. The Indians went on to win the game in the ninth before taking the series in five. Twice in the series, including the final game, 21-year-old righthander Jaret Wright bested 25-year-old Andy Pettitte.

Mussina's Masterpieces

Mussina didn't win a game in the ALCS, yet he had one of the game's best-ever postseasons.

In his first start against the Indians, he set a League Championship Series record with 15 strikeouts. The Orioles, though, lost Game Three in 12 innings. Later in the series, Mussina didn't get a decision in Game Six despite eight shutout innings. Baltimore left 14 runners on base in the 11-inning shutout.

DAVID SEELIG

Orioles ace Mike Mussina
Baltimore failed despite his heroic efforts

"I'm not disappointed for me, I'm disappointed for this team," Mussina said. "It's just unfortunate. We had a great group of guys. We had our chances all day, and it just didn't happen."

MORRIS FOSTOFF

Tino Martinez

Counting his two wins over the Mariners' Randy Johnson in the Division Series, Mussina went 2-0 with a 1.24 ERA in the AL playoffs. He struck out a postseason record 41 hitters in 29 innings, while allowing 11 hits and seven walks.

Mussina also had a dominant start against Cleveland in the regular season. On May 30, he made a bid to become the first Oriole to throw a perfect game. He retired the first 25 batters until Alomar's single in the ninth inning of an eventual one-hitter.

No Repeat

Though the Yankees went 96-66 to show a four-game improvement over their 1996 regular season, they couldn't repeat as World Series champions.

New York was four outs away from creating an Eastern Division rematch in the ALCS. Alomar, though, delivered his game-tying home run off Rivera in Game Four of the Division Series. The Indians added a run in the ninth and went on to win Game Five in Jacobs Field.

Rivera, who had helped the Yankees win the 1996 title as a set-up man for John Wetteland, had an outstanding year as the New York closer. He saved 43 games and had an ERA of 1.88.

First baseman Tino Martinez also had a stellar season, finishing with career highs of 44 home runs and 141 RBIs.

New York finished with the AL's second-best record

AMERICAN LEAGUE YEAR-BY-YEAR BATTING LEADERS

Year	Batting Average		Home Runs		RBIs	
1901	Nap Lajoie, Philadelphia	.422	Nap Lajoie, Philadelphia	14	Nap Lajoie, Philadelphia	125
1902	Ed Delahanty, Wash.	.376	Socks Seybold, Philadelphia	16	Buck Freeman, Boston	121
1903	Nap Lajoie, Cleveland	.355	Buck Freeman, Boston	13	Buck Freeman, Boston	104
1904	Nap Lajoie, Cleveland	.381	Harry Davis, Philadelphia	10	Nap Lajoie, Cleveland	102
1905	Elmer Flick, Cleveland	.306	Harry Davis, Philadelphia	8	Harry Davis, Philadelphia	83
1906	George Stone, St. Louis	.358	Harry Davis, Philadelphia	12	Harry Davis, Philadelphia	96
1907	Ty Cobb, Detroit	.350	Harry Davis, Philadelphia	8	Ty Cobb, Detroit	116
1908	Ty Cobb, Detroit	.324	Sam Crawford, Detroit	7	Ty Cobb, Detroit	101
1909	Ty Cobb, Detroit	.377	Ty Cobb, Detroit	9	Ty Cobb, Detroit	115
1910	Ty Cobb, Detroit	.385	Jake Stahl, Boston	10	Sam Crawford, Detroit	115
1911	TyCobb, Detroit	.420	Frank Baker, Philadelphia	11	Ty Cobb, Detroit	144
1912	Ty Cobb, Detroit	.410	2 tied at	10	Frank Baker, Philadelphia	133
1913	Ty Cobb, Detroit	.390	Frank Baker, Philadelphia	12	Frank Baker, Philadelphia	126
1914	Ty Cobb, Detroit	.368	Frank Baker, Philadelphia	9	Sam Crawford, Detroit	112
1915	Ty Cobb, Detroit	.370	Braggo Roth, Cleveland	7	Sam Crawford, Detroit	116
1916	Tris Speaker, Cleveland	.386	Wally Pipp, New York	12	Wally Pipp, New York	99
1917	Ty Cobb, Detroit	.383	Wally Pipp, New York	9	Bob Veah, Detroit	115
1918	Ty Cobb, Detroit	.382	2 tied at	11	2 tied at	74
1919	Ty Cobb, Detroit	.384	Babe Ruth, Boston	29	Babe Ruth, Boston	112
1920	George Sisler, St. Louis	.407	Babe Ruth, New York	54	Babe Ruth, New York	137
1921	Harry Heilmann, Detroit	.394	Babe Ruth, New York	59	Babe Ruth, New York	171
1922	George Sisler, St. Louis	.420	Kenny Williams, St. Louis	39	Kenny Williams, St. Louis	155
1923	Harry Heilmann, Detroit	.403	Babe Ruth, New York	43	Babe Ruth, New York	131
1924	Babe Ruth, New York	.378	Babe Ruth, New York	46	Goose Goslin, Wash.	129
1925	Harry Heilmann, Detroit	.393	Bob Meusel, New York	33	Bob Meusel, New York	138
1926	Heinie Manush, Detroit	.377	Babe Ruth, New York	47	Babe Ruth, New York	145
1927	Harry Heilmann, Detroit	.398	Babe Ruth, New York	60	Lou Gehrig, New York	175
1928	Goose Goslin, Wash.	.379	Babe Ruth, New York	54	2 tied at	142
1929	Lew Fonseca, Cleveland	.369	Babe Ruth, New York	46	Al Simmons, Philadelphia	157
1930	Al Simmons, Philadelphia	.381	Babe Ruth, New York	49	Lou Gehrig, New York	174
1931	Al Simmons, Philadelphia	.390	2 tied at	46	Lou Gehrig, New York	184
1932	Dale Alexander, Det.-Bos.	.367	Jimmie Foxx, Philadelphia	58	Jimmie Foxx, Philadelphia	169
1933	Jimmie Foxx, Philadelphia	.356	Jimmie Foxx, Philadelphia	48	Jimmie Foxx, Philadelphia	163
1934	Lou Gehrig, New York	.363	Lou Gehrig, New York	49	Lou Gehrig, New York	165
1935	Buddy Myer, Washington	.349	2 tied at	36	Hank Greenberg, Detroit	170
1936	Luke Appling, Chicago	.388	Lou Gehrig, New York	49	Hal Trosky, Cleveland	162
1937	Charlie Gehringer, Detroit	.371	Joe DiMaggio, New York	46	Hank Greenberg, Detroit	183
1938	Jimmie Foxx, Boston	.349	Hank Greenberg, Detroit	58	Jimmie Foxx, Boston	175
1939	Joe DiMaggio, New York	.381	Jimmie Foxx, Boston	35	Ted Williams, Boston	145
1940	Joe DiMaggio, New York	.352	Hank Greenberg, Detroit	41	Hank Greenberg, Detroit	150
1941	Ted Williams, Boston	.406	Ted Williams, Boston	37	Joe DiMaggio, New York	125
1942	Ted Williams, Boston	.356	Ted Williams, Boston	36	Ted Williams, Boston	137
1943	Luke Appling, Chicago	.328	Rudy York, Detroit	34	Rudy York, Detroit	118
1944	Lou Boudreau, Cleve.	.327	Nick Etten, New York	22	Vern Stephens, St. Louis	109
1945	Snuffy Stirnweiss, N.Y.	.309	Vern Stephens, St. Louis	24	Nick Etten, New York	111
1946	Mickey Vernon, Wash.	.352	Hank Greenberg, Detroit	44	Hank Greenberg, Detroit	127
1947	Ted Williams, Boston	.343	Ted Williams, Boston	32	Ted Williams, Boston	114
1948	Ted Williams, Boston	.369	Joe DiMaggio, New York	39	Joe DiMaggio, New York	155
1949	George Kell, Detroit	.343	Ted Williams, Boston	43	2 tied at	159
1950	Billy Goodman, Boston	.354	Al Rosen, Cleveland	37	2 tied at	144
1951	Ferris Fain, Philadelphia	.344	Gus Zernial, Chi.-Phil.	33	Gus Zernial, Chi.-Phil.	129
1952	Ferris Fain, Philadelphia	.327	Larry Doby, Cleveland	32	Al Rosen, Cleveland	105
1953	Mickey Vernon, Wash.	.337	Al Rosen, Cleveland	43	Al Rosen, Cleveland	145
1954	Bobby Avila, Cleveland	.341	Larry Doby, Cleveland	32	Larry Doby, Cleveland	126
1955	Al Kaline, Detroit	.340	Mickey Mantle, New York	37	2 tied at	116
1956	Mickey Mantle, New York	.353	Mickey Mantle, New York	52	Mickey Mantle, New York	130
1957	Ted Williams, Boston	.388	Roy Sievers, Washington	42	Roy Sievers, Washington	114
1958	Ted Williams, Boston	.328	Mickey Mantle, New York	42	Jackie Jensen, Boston	122
1959	Harvey Kuenn, Detroit	.353	2 tied at	42	Jackie Jensen, Boston	112
1960	Pete Runnels, Boston	.320	Mickey Mantle, New York	40	Roger Maris, New York	112
1961	Norm Cash, Detroit	.361	Roger Maris, New York	61	Roger Maris, New York	142
1962	Pete Runnels, Boston	.326	Harmon Killebrew, Minn.	48	Harmon Killebrew, Minn.	126
1963	Carl Yastrzemski, Boston	.321	Harmon Killebrew, Minn.	45	Dick Stuart, Boston	118
1964	Tony Oliva, Minnesota	.323	Harmon Killebrew, Minn.	49	Brooks Robinson, Balt.	118
1965	Tony Oliva, Minnesota	.321	Tony Conigliaro, Boston	32	Rocky Colavito, Cleveland	108
1966	Frank Robinson, Balt.	.316	Frank Robinson, Baltimore	49	Frank Robinson, Baltimore	122
1967	Carl Yastrzemski, Boston	.326	2 tied at	44	Carl Yastrzemski, Boston	121
1968	Carl Yastrzemski, Boston	.301	Frank Howard, Washington	44	Ken Harrelson, Boston	109
1969	Rod Carew, Minnesota	.332	Harmon Killebrew, Minn.	49	Harmon Killebrew, Minn.	140
1970	Alex Johnson, California	.329	Frank Howard, Washington	44	Frank Howard, Washington	126
1971	Tony Oliva, Minnesota	.337	Bill Melton, Chicago	33	Harmon Killebrew, Minn.	119
1972	Rod Carew, Minnesota	.318	Dick Allen, Chicago	37	Dick Allen, Chicago	113
1973	Rod Carew, Minnesota	.350	Reggie Jackson, Oakland	32	Reggie Jackson, Oakland	117
1974	Rod Carew, Minnesota	.364	Dick Allen, Chicago	32	Jeff Burroughs, Texas	118
1975	Rod Carew, Minnesota	.359	2 tied at	36	George Scott, Milwaukee	109
1976	George Brett, Kansas City	.333	Graig Nettles, New York	32	Lee May, Baltimore	109
1977	Rod Carew, Minnesota	.388	Jim Rice, Boston	39	Larry Hisle, Minnesota	119
1978	Rod Carew, Minnesota	.333	Jim Rice, Boston	46	Jim Rice, Boston	139
1979	Fred Lynn, Boston	.333	Gorman Thomas, Mil.	45	Don Baylor, California	139
1980	George Brett, Kansas City	.390	2 tied at	41	Cecil Cooper, Milwaukee	122
1981	Carney Lansford, Boston	.336	4 tied at	22	Eddie Murray, Baltimore	78
1982	Willie Wilson, Kansas City	.332	2 tied at	39	Hal McRae, Kansas City	133
1983	Wade Boggs, Boston	.361	Jim Rice, Boston	39	2 tied at	126
1984	Don Mattingly, New York	.343	Tony Armas, Boston	43	Tony Armas, Boston	123
1985	Wade Boggs, Boston	.368	Darrell Evans, Detroit	40	Don Mattingly, New York	145
1986	Wade Boggs, Boston	.357	Jesse Barfield, Toronto	40	Joe Carter, Cleveland	121
1987	Wade Boggs, Boston	.363	Mark McGwire, Oakland	49	George Bell, Toronto	134
1988	Wade Boggs, Boston	.366	Jose Canseco, Oakland	42	Jose Canseco, Oakland	124
1989	Kirby Puckett, Minn.	.339	Fred McGriff, Toronto	36	Ruben Sierra, Texas	119
1990	George Brett, Kansas City	.329	Cecil Fielder, Detroit	51	Cecil Fielder, Detroit	132
1991	Julio Franco, Texas	.341	2 tied at	44	Cecil Fielder, Detroit	133
1992	Edgar Martinez, Seattle	.343	Juan Gonzalez, Texas	43	Cecil Fielder, Detroit	124
1993	John Olerud, Toronto	.363	Juan Gonzalez, Texas	46	Albert Belle, Cleveland	129
1994	Paul O'Neill, New York	.359	Ken Griffey, Seattle	40	Kirby Puckett, Minnesota	112
1995	Edgar Martinez, Seattle	.356	Albert Belle, Cleveland	50	2 tied at	126
1996	Alex Rodriguez, Seattle	.358	Mark McGwire Oakland	52	Albert Belle, Cleveland	148
1997	Frank Thomas, Chicago	.347	Ken Griffey, Seattle	56	Ken Griffey, Seattle	147

AMERICAN LEAGUE YEAR-BY-YEAR PITCHING LEADERS

Year	Wins		ERA		Strikeouts	
1901	Cy Young, Boston	33	Cy Young, Boston	1.63	Cy Young, Boston	158
1902	Cy Young, Boston	32	Ed Siever, Detroit	1.91	Rube Waddell, Philadelphia	210
1903	Cy Young, Boston	28	Earl Moore, Cleveland	1.77	Rube Waddell, Philadelphia	302
1904	Jack Chesbro, New York	41	Addie Joss, Cleveland	1.59	Rube Waddell, Philadelphia	349
1905	Rube Waddell, Phil.	26	Rube Waddell, Philadelphia	1.48	Rue Waddell, Philadelphia	287
1906	Al Orth, New York	27	Doc White, Chicago	1.52	Rube Waddell, Philadelphia	196
1907	2 tied at	27	Ed Walsh, Chicago	1.60	Rube Waddell, Philadelphia	232
1908	Ed Walsh, Chicago	40	Addie Joss, Cleveland	1.16	Ed Walsh, Chicago	269
1909	George Mullin, Detroit	29	Harry Krause, Philadelphia	1.39	Frank Smith, Chicago	177
1910	Jack Coombs, Phil.	31	Ed Walsh, Chicago	1.27	Walter Johnson, Washington	313
1911	Jack Coombs, Phil.	28	Vean Gregg, Cleveland	1.81	Ed Walsh, Chicago	255
1912	Joe Wood, Boston	34	Walter Johnson, Wash.	1.39	Walter Johnson, Washington	303
1913	Walter Johnson, Wash.	36	Walter Johnson, Wash.	1.14	Walter Johnson, Washington	243
1914	Walter Johnson, Wash.	28	Dutch Leonard, Bos.	1.00	Walter Johnson, Washington	225
1915	Walter Johnson, Wash.	27	Joe Wood, Boston	1.49	Walter Johnson, Washington	203
1916	Walter Johnson, Wash.	25	Babe Ruth, Boston	1.75	Walter Johnson, Washington	228
1917	Ed Cicotte, Chicago	28	Ed Cicotte, Chicago	1.53	Walter Johnson, Washington	188
1918	Walter Johnson, Wash.	23	Walter Johnson, Wash.	1.27	Walter Johnson, Washington	162
1919	Ed Cicotte, Chicago	29	Walter Johnson, Wash.	1.49	Walter Johnson, Washington	147
1920	Jim Bagby, Cleveland	31	Bob Shawkey, New York	2.45	Stan Coveleski, Claveland	133
1921	2 tied at	27	Red Faber, Chicago	2.48	Walter Johnson, Washington	143
1922	Eddie Rommel, Phil.	27	Red Faber, Chicago	2.80	Urban Shocker, St. Louis	149
1923	George Uhle, Cleveland	26	Stan Coveleski, Claveland	2.76	Walter Johnson, Washington	130
1924	Walter Johnson, Wash.	23	Walter Johnson, Wash.	2.72	Walter Johnson, Washington	158
1925	2 tied at	21	Stan Coveleski, Wash.	2.84	Lefty Grove, Philadelphia	116
1926	George Uhle, Claveland	27	Lefty Grove, Philadelphia	2.51	Lefty Grove, Philadelphia	194
1927	2 tied at	22	Wilcy Moore, New York	2.28	Lefty Grove, Philadelphia	174
1928	2 tied at	24	Garland Braxton, Wash.	2.52	Lefty Grove, Philadelphia	183
1929	George Earnshaw, Phil.	24	Lefty Grove, Philadelphia	2.82	Lefty Grove, Philadelphia	170
1930	Lefty Grove, Philadelphia	28	Lefty Grove, Philadelphia	2.54	Lefty Grove, Philadelphia	209
1931	Lefty Grove, Philadelphia	31	Lefty Grove, Philadelphia	2.05	Lefty Grove, Philadelphia	175
1932	General Crowder, Wash.	26	Lefty Grove, Philadelphia	2.84	Red Ruffing, New York	190
1933	2 tied at	24	Monte Pearson, Claveland	2.33	Lefty Gomez, New York	163
1934	Lefty Gomez, New York	26	Lefty Gomez, New York	2.33	Lefty Gomez, New York	158
1935	Wes Ferrell, Boston	25	Lefty Grove, Boston.	2.70	Tommy Bridges, Detroit	163
1936	Tommy Bridges, Detroit	23	Lefty Grove, Boston.	2.81	Tommy Bridges, Detroit	175
1937	Lefty Gomez, New York	21	Lefty Gomez, New York	2.33	Lefty Gomez, New York	194
1938	Red Ruffing, New York	21	Lefty Grove, Philadelphia	3.07	Bob Feller, Cleveland	240
1939	Bob Feller, Cleveland	24	Lefty Grove, Philadelphia	2.54	Bob Feller, Cleveland	246
1940	Bob Feller, Cleveland	27	Bob Feller, Cleveland	2.62	Bob Feller, Cleveland	261
1941	Bob Feller, Cleveland	25	Thornton Lee, Chicago	2.37	Bob Feller, Cleveland	260
1942	Tex Hughson, Boston	22	Ted Lyons, Chicago	2.10	2 tied at	113
1943	2 tied at	20	Spud Chandler, New York	1.64	Allie Reynolds, Cleveland	151
1944	Hal Newhouser, Detroit	29	Dizzy Trout, Detroit	2.12	Hal Newhouser, Detroit	187
1945	Hal Newhouser, Detroit	25	Hal Newhouser, Detroit	1.81	Hal Newhouser, Detroit	212
1946	2 tied at	26	Hal Newhouser, Detroit	1.94	Bob Feller, Cleveland	348
1947	Bob Feller, Cleveland	20	Spud Chandler, New York	2.46	Bob Feller, Cleveland	196
1948	Hal Newhouser, Detroit	21	Gene Bearden, Cleveland	2.43	Bob Feller, Cleveland	164
1949	Mel Parnell, Boston	25	Mel Parnell, Boston	2.78	Virgil Trucks, Detroit	153
1950	Bob Lemon, Cleveland	23	Early Wynn, Cleveland	3.20	Bob Lemon, Cleveland	170
1951	Bob Feller, Cleveland	22	Saul Rogovin, Det.-Chi.	2.78	Vic Raschi, New York	164
1952	Bobby Shantz, Phil.	24	Allie Reynolds, New York	2.07	Allie Reynolds, New York	160
1953	Bob Porterfield, Wash.	22	Eddie Lopat, New York	2.43	Billy Pierce, Chicago	186
1954	2 tied at	23	Mike Garcia, Cleveland	2.64	Bob Turley, Baltimore	185
1955	3 tied at	18	Billy Pierce, Chicago	1.97	Herb Score, Cleveland	245
1956	Frank Lary, Detroit	21	Whitey Ford, New York	2.47	Herb Score, Cleveland	263
1957	2 tied at	20	Bobby Shantz, New York	2.45	Early Wynn, Cleveland	184
1958	Bob Turley, New York	21	Whitey Ford, New York	2.01	Early Wynn, Chicago	179
1959	Early Wynn, Chicago	22	Hoyt Wilhelm, Balt.	2.19	Jim Bunning, Detroit	201
1960	2 tied at	18	Frank Baumann, Chicago	2.68	Jim Bunning, Detroit	201
1961	Whitey Ford, New York	25	Dick Donovan, Washington	2.40	Camilo Pascual, Minnesota	221
1962	Ralph Terry, New York	23	Hank Aguirre, Detroit	2.21	Camilo Pascual, Minnesota	206
1963	Whitey Ford, New York	24	Gary Peters, Chicago	2.33	Camilo Pascual, Minnesota	202
1964	2 tied at	20	Dean Chance, L.A.	1.65	Al Downing, New York	217
1965	Mudcat Grant, Minnesota	21	Sam McDowell, Claveland	2.18	Sam McDowell, Cleveland	325
1966	Jim Kaat, Minnesota	25	Gary Peters, Chicago	1.98	Sam McDowell, Cleveland	225
1967	2 tied at	22	Joel Horlen, Chicago	2.06	Jim Lonborg, Boston	246
1968	Denny McLain, Detroit	31	Luis Tiant, Cleveland	1.60	Sam McDowell, Cleveland	283
1969	Denny McLain, Detroit	24	Dick Bosman, Washington	2.19	Sam McDowell, Cleveland	279
1970	3 tied at	24	Diego Segui, Oakland	2.56	Sam McDowell, Cleveland	304
1971	Mickey Lolich, Detroit	25	Vida Blue, Oakland	1.82	Mickey Lolich, Detroit	308
1972	2 tied at	24	Luis Tiant, Boston	1.91	Nolan Ryan, California	329
1973	Wilbur Wood, Chicago	24	Jim Palmer, Baltimore	2.40	Nolan Ryan, California	383
1974	2 tied at	25	Catfish Hunter, Oakland	2.49	Nolan Ryan, California	367
1975	2 tied at	23	Jim Palmer, Baltimore	2.09	Frank Tanana, California	269
1976	Jim Palmer, Baltimore	22	Mark Fidrych, Detroit	2.34	Nolan Ryan, California	327
1977	3 tied at	20	Frank Tanana, California	2.54	Nolan Ryan, California	341
1978	Ron Guidry, New York	25	Ron Guidry, New York	1.74	Nolan Ryan, California	260
1979	Mike Flanagan, Baltimore	23	Ron Guidry, New York	2.78	Nolan Ryan, California	223
1980	Steve Stone, Baltimore	25	Rudy May, New York	2.47	Len Barker, Cleveland	187
1981	Steve McCatty, Oakland	14	Steve McCatty, Oak.	2.32	Len Barker, Cleveland	127
1982	LaMarr Hoyt, Chicago	19	Rick Sutcliffe, Claveland	2.96	Floyd Bannister, Seattle	209
1983	LaMarr Hoyt, Chicago	21	Rick Honeycutt, Texas	2.42	Jack Morris, Detroit	232
1984	Mike Boddicker, Balt.	20	Mike Boddicker, Balt.	2.79	Mark Langston, Seattle	204
1985	Ron Guidry, New York	22	Dave Stieb, Toronto	2.48	Bert Blyleven, Cleve.-Minn.	206
1986	Roger Clemens, Boston	24	Roger Clemens, Boston	2.48	Mark Langston, Seattle	245
1987	2 tied at	20	Jimmy Key, Toronto	2.76	Mark Langston, Seattle	262
1988	Frank Viola, Minnesota	24	Allan Anderson, Minnesota	2.45	Roger Clemens, Boston	291
1989	Bret Saberhagen, K.C.	23	Bret Saberhagen, K.C.	2.16	Nolan Ryan, Texas	301
1990	Bob Welch, Oakland	27	Roger Clemens, Boston	1.93	Nolan Ryan, Texas	232
1991	2 tied at	20	Roger Clemens, Boston	2.62	Roger Clemens, Boston	241
1992	2 tied at	21	Roger Clemens, Boston	2.41	Randy Johnson, Seattle	241
1993	Jack McDowell, Chicago	22	Kevin Appier, Kansas City	2.56	Randy Johnson, Seattle	308
1994	Jimmy Key, New York	17	Steve Ontiveros, Oakland	2.65	Randy Johnson, Seattle	204
1995	Mike Mussina, Baltimore	19	Randy Johnson, Seattle	2.48	Randy Johnson, Seattle	294
1996	Andy Pettitte, New York	21	Juan Guzman, Toronto	2.93	Roger Clemens, Boston	257
1997	Roger Clemens, Toronto	21	Roger Clemens, Toronto	2.05	Roger Clemens, Toronto	292

and came within two games of Baltimore, which led from wire to wire.

The Yankees' most publicized in-season acquisition, Japanese righthander Hideki Irabu, went 5-4 with a 7.09 ERA. He was not on New York's postseason roster. The Padres, who had Irabu's original rights, traded him to New York with infielder Homer Bush and outfielder Vernon Maxwell for prospects Ruben Rivera and Rafael Medina and $3 million.

Sky-Rocketing

Roger Clemens turned 35 during his first season as a Toronto Blue Jay, but he pitched more like a 25-year-old Clemens. After a 10-13, 3.63 season in his final year with the Red Sox, he won the league's pitching triple crown at 21-7, 2.05 with 292 strikeouts.

LARRY GOREN

Randy Johnson

Seattle's Johnson wasn't far behind in any of those categories. He became the Mariners' first 20-game winner with a relief victory after his last start. Johnson went 20-4, 2.28 with 291 strikeouts.

In 1996, Clemens had tied his own major league record with a 20-strikeout game against the Tigers. But he finished a four-year stretch with a 40-39 record. From 1986-1992, he won at least 17 games each season.

"I am a power pitcher and I can still pitch," Clemens said. "I can't simplify it any more than that. My mechanics are the same as always. Nobody's messed with my mechanics. A big thing is my legs. As long as they're strong, I'm going to be a power pitcher."

Before the season, Clemens signed a three-year, $24.75 million contract with Toronto. Boston general manager Dan Duquette had offered him $20 million over four years.

Despite the strong individual numbers, Clemens' stated goal of playing for a winner didn't pan out. The Blue Jays finished last in the AL East, two games behind Boston.

DAVID SEELIG

Toronto ace Roger Clemens
Won pitcher's version of triple crown

Thanks For The Memories

Manager Cito Gaston, who guided Toronto to its only two World Series crowns in 1992 and 1993, was fired in the last week of the season.

Gaston had managed the Jays since 1989, when he took over a 12-24 team that wound up 89-73 and atop the AL East. He won four division titles, but had no winning seasons since 1993.

Kings Of Swing

Baltimore's hold on the majors' single-season home run record lasted all of one year.

AMERICAN LEAGUE ALL-STARS

Selected by Baseball America

Pos.	Player, Team	B-T	Ht.	Wt.	Age	'97 Salary	AVG	AB	R	H	2B	3B	HR	RBI	SB
C	Ivan Rodriguez, Texas	R-R	5-9	205	25	$6,650,000	.313	597	98	187	34	4	20	77	7
1B	Tino Martinez, New York	L-R	6-2	210	29	4,300,000	.296	594	96	176	31	2	44	141	3
2B	Chuck Knoblauch, Minn.	R-R	5-9	181	29	6,000,000	.291	611	117	178	26	10	9	58	62
3B	John Valentin, Boston	R-R	6-0	185	30	3,750,000	.306	575	95	176	47	5	18	77	7
SS	Nomar Garciaparra, Boston	R-R	6-0	165	24	150,000	.306	684	122	209	44	11	30	98	22
OF	Juan Gonzalez, Texas	R-R	6-3	210	28	7,400,000	.296	533	87	158	24	3	42	131	0
	Ken Griffey, Seattle	R-R	6-3	220	27	7,875,000	.304	608	125	185	34	3	56	147	15
	Paul O'Neill, New York	L-L	6-4	215	34	5,450,000	.324	553	89	179	42	0	21	117	10
DH	Frank Thomas, Chicago	R-R	6-5	257	29	7,150,000	.347	530	110	184	35	0	35	125	1
							W	L	ERA	G	SV	IP	H	BB	SO
P	Roger Clemens, Toronto	R-R	6-4	220	35	8,250,000	21	7	2.05	34	0	264	204	68	292
	Randy Johnson, Seattle	R-L	6-10	225	33	6,275,000	20	4	2.28	30	0	213	147	77	291
	Andy Pettitte, New York	L-L	6-5	235	25	600,000	18	7	2.88	35	0	240	233	65	166
	Brad Radke, Minnesota	R-R	6-2	180	24	400,000	20	10	3.87	35	0	240	238	48	174
RP	Randy Myers, Baltimore	L-L	6-1	210	34	3,700,000	2	3	1.51	61	45	60	47	22	56

Player of the Year: Ken Griffey, of, Seattle. **Pitcher of the Year:** Roger Clemens, rhp, Toronto. **Rookie of the Year:** Nomar Garciaparra, ss, Boston.

Manager of the Year: Phil Garner, Milwaukee. **Executive of the Year:** Randy Smith, Detroit.

In 1997, Seattle eclipsed the Orioles' total of 257. The Mariners hit 264, led by Ken Griffey's 56–the most by any AL player since Roger Maris in 1961.

Maris, Mickey Mantle and the '61 Yankees held the record with 240 until the 1996 season, when the Orioles, Mariners (245) and Athletics (243) all topped that mark.

Despite the power from the lineup and Randy Johnson's left arm, the Mariners were eliminated in the Division Series in four games by Baltimore. Johnson lost twice in that series to Mussina, giving him an 0-4 record against the Orioles for the year. He went 20-2 against the rest of the league.

Tradeoffs

At the July trade deadline, the Mariners and White Sox each made controversial moves. The trades were questioned for two extremely different reasons.

The Mariners parted with prospect Jose Cruz Jr., who had appeared to be the answer in their long search for a left fielder. They sent him to Toronto for relievers Mike Timlin and Paul Spoljaric.

Chicago dealt veteran pitchers Wilson Alvarez, Danny Darwin and Roberto Hernandez to the Giants for six minor leaguers. At the time of the trade, the White Sox were 3½ games behind the eventual division champion Indians. Chicago owner Jerry Reinsdorf said, "Anyone who thinks this White Sox team will catch Cleveland is crazy."

Despite the $55 million contract he gave Belle in the offseason, Reinsdorf chose to trade two players in the last year of their contracts–Alvarez and Hernandez–rather than try to make a run at the division title.

"I've never heard an owner come out and say, 'We have no chance of catching the team in front of us,' " said Darwin, who first came to the major leagues in 1978.

JOHN KLEIN

New Cleveland slugger Dave Justice
Trade worked out well for Indians

As for the Cruz trade, Seattle was making a bid to win its first pennant. The Mariners fell short of that with the four-game loss to Baltimore in the Division Series. Cruz finished the season with 26 home runs in 395 at-bats.

Twins' Killer

Aside from Clemens and Johnson, the only 20-game winner in the AL was Twins righthander Brad Radke.

Radke went 20-10, 3.87 and won 12 straight starts. He became the third pitcher since 1950 to accomplish that feat, and he tied Scott Erickson's Minnesota record for consecutive victories.

Radke entered the season with a lifetime mark of 22-30 and a 4.84 ERA.

"I don't try to analyze anything I'm doing now as opposed to the past," Radke said. "I never really thought about being the anchor of the team. I just wanted to pitch a lot of innings and keep getting better."

AL: BEST TOOLS

A Baseball America survey of American League managers, conducted at midseason 1997, ranked AL players with the best tools:

BEST HITTER
1. Frank Thomas, White Sox
2. Edgar Martinez, Mariners
3. Ken Griffey, Mariners

BEST POWER HITTER
1. Mark McGwire, Athletics
2. Ken Griffey, Mariners
3. Juan Gonzalez, Rangers

BEST BUNTER
1. Roberto Alomar, Orioles
2. Tom Goodwin, Royals
3. Otis Nixon, Blue Jays

BEST HIT-AND-RUN ARTIST
1. Chuck Knoblauch, Twins
2. Jay Bell, Royals
3. Paul Molitor, Twins

BEST BASERUNNER
1. Paul Molitor, Twins
2. Tom Goodwin, Royals
3. Roberto Alomar, Orioles

FASTEST BASERUNNER
1. Tom Goodwin, Royals
2. Brian Hunter, Tigers
3. Otis Nixon, Blue Jays

BEST PITCHER
1. Randy Johnson, Mariners
2. Roger Clemens, Blue Jays
3. Mike Mussina, Orioles

BEST FASTBALL
1. Randy Johnson, Mariners
2. Roger Clemens, Blue Jays
3. Mariano Rivera, Yankees

BEST CURVEBALL
1. Tom Gordon, Red Sox
2. Mike Mussina, Orioles
3. Pat Hentgen, Blue Jays

BEST SLIDER
1. Randy Johnson, Mariners
2. David Cone, Yankees
3. Kevin Appier, Royals

BEST CHANGEUP
1. Jimmy Key, Orioles
2. Mike Mussina, Orioles
3. Doug Jones, Brewers

BEST CONTROL
1. Mike Mussina, Orioles
2. Bob Tewksbury, Twins
3. Roger Clemens, Blue Jays

BEST PICKOFF MOVE
1. Andy Pettitte, Yankees
2. Ed Vosberg, Rangers
3. Jimmy Key, Orioles

BEST RELIEVER
1. Mariano Rivera, Yankees
2. Randy Myers, Orioles
3. John Wetteland, Rangers

BEST DEFENSIVE C
1. Ivan Rodriguez, Rangers
2. Dan Wilson, Mariners
3. Sandy Alomar, Indians

BEST DEFENSIVE 1B
1. Rafael Palmeiro, Orioles
2. Will Clark, Rangers
3. Tino Martinez, Yankees

BEST DEFENSIVE 2B
1. Roberto Alomar, Orioles
2. Chuck Knoblauch, Twins
3. Fernando Vina, Brewers

BEST DEFENSIVE 3B
1. Matt Williams, Indians
2. Cal Ripken, Orioles
3. Jeff Cirillo, Brewers

BEST DEFENSIVE SS
1. Alex Rodriguez, Mariners
2. Mike Bordick, Orioles
3. Omar Vizquel, Indians

BEST INFIELD ARM
1. Alex Rodriguez, Mariners
2. Dave Hollins, Angels
3. Deivi Cruz, Tigers

BEST DEFENSIVE OF
1. Ken Griffey, Mariners
2. Jim Edmonds, Angels
3. Bernie Williams, Yankees

BEST OF ARM
1. Jay Buhner, Mariners
2. Ken Griffey, Mariners
3. Tim Salmon, Angels

MOST EXCITING PLAYER
1. Ken Griffey, Mariners
2. Alex Rodriguez, Mariners
3. Mark McGwire, Athletics

BEST MANAGER
1. Lou Piniella, Mariners
2. Davey Johnson, Orioles
3. Tom Kelly, Twins

Major Leagues

AMERICAN LEAGUE
DEPARTMENT LEADERS

BATTING

GAMES
Cal Ripken, Baltimore 162
Brian Hunter, Detroit 162
Albert Belle, Chicago 161
Tony Clark, Detroit 159
Derek Jeter, New York 159

AT-BATS
Nomar Garciaparra, Boston 684
Brian Hunter, Detroit 658
Derek Jeter, New York 654
Albert Belle, Chicago 634
Ray Durham, Chicago 634

RUNS
Ken Griffey, Seattle 125
Nomar Garciaparra, Boston 122
Chuck Knoblauch, Minnesota 117
Derek Jeter, New York 116
Rusty Greer, Texas 112
Brian Hunter, Detroit 112

HITS
Nomar Garciaparra, Boston 209
Rusty Greer, Texas 193
Derek Jeter, New York 190
Garret Anderson, Anaheim 189
Ivan Rodriguez, Texas 187

TOTAL BASES
Ken Griffey, Seattle 393
Nomar Garciaparra, Boston 365
Tino Martinez, New York 343
Frank Thomas, Chicago 324
Rusty Greer, Texas 319

EXTRA-BASE HITS
Ken Griffey, Seattle 93
Nomar Garciaparra, Boston 85
Tino Martinez, New York 77
Albert Belle, Chicago 76
Carlos Delgado, Toronto 75

SINGLES
Garret Anderson, Angels 142
Derek Jeter, New York 142
Brian Hunter, Detroit 137
Chuck Knoblauch, Minnesota 133
Ray Durham, Chicago 129
Ivan Rodriguez, Texas 129

DOUBLES
John Valentin, Boston 47
Jeff Cirillo, Milwaukee 46
Albert Belle, Chicago 45
Nomar Garciaparra, Boston 44
Paul O'Neill, New York 42
Carlos Delgado, Toronto 42
Rusty Greer, Texas 42

Frank Thomas
.347 average, 125 RBIs

TRIPLES
Nomar Garciaparra, Boston 11
Chuck Knoblauch, Minnesota 10
Johnny Damon, Kansas City 8
Jeromy Burnitz, Milwaukee 8
Derek Jeter, New York 7
Shannon Stewart, Toronto 7
Luis Alicea, Anaheim 7
Brady Anderson, Baltimore 7
Brian Hunter, Detroit 7

HOME RUNS
Ken Griffey, Seattle 56
Tino Martinez, New York 44
Juan Gonzalez, Texas 42
Jim Thome, Cleveland 40
Jay Buhner, Seattle 40

HOME RUN RATIO
(At-Bats per Home Runs)
Ken Griffey, Seattle 10.9
Jim Thome, Cleveland 12.4
Juan Gonzalez, Texas 12.7
Jay Buhner, Seattle 13.5
Tino Martinez, New York 13.5

RUNS BATTED IN
Ken Griffey, Seattle 147
Tino Martinez, New York 141
Juan Gonzalez, Texas 131
Tim Salmon, Anaheim 129
Frank Thomas, Chicago 125

SACRIFICE BUNTS
Omar Vizquel, Cleveland 16
Deivi Cruz, Detroit 14
Mike Bordick, Baltimore 12
Alex Gonzalez, Toronto 11
Tom Goodwin, Texas/Kansas City 11
Ozzie Guillen, Chicago 11
Jeff Reboulet, Baltimore 11

SACRIFICE FLIES
Tino Martinez, New York 13
Ken Griffey, Seattle 12
Jeff King, Kansas City 12
Paul Molitor, Minnesota 12
Travis Fryman, Detroit 11
Tim Salmon, Anaheim 11

HIT BY PITCH
Brady Anderson, Baltimore 19
Chuck Knoblauch, Minnesota 17
Damion Easley, Detroit 16
Pat Meares, Minnesota 16
Jeff Cirillo, Milwaukee 14

WALKS
Jim Thome, Cleveland 120
Jay Buhner, Seattle 119
Edgar Martinez, Seattle 119
Frank Thomas, Chicago 109
Tony Phillips, Anaheim/Chicago 102

INTENTIONAL WALKS
Ken Griffey, Seattle 23
Mo Vaughn, Boston 17
Chili Davis, Kansas City 16
Tino Martinez, New York 14
B.J. Surhoff, Baltimore 14

STRIKEOUTS
Jay Buhner, Seattle 175
Melvin Nieves, Detroit 157
Mo Vaughn, Boston 154
Jim Thome, Cleveland 146
Tony Clark, Detroit 144

TOUGHEST TO STRIKE OUT
(Plate Appearances per SO)
Ozzie Guillen, Chicago 22.0
Gary DiSarcina, Anaheim 20.1
Joey Cora, Seattle 13.2
Omar Vizquel, Cleveland 11.1

JOHN KLEIN

Brian Hunter
74 stolen bases

STOLEN BASES
Brian Hunter, Detroit 74
Chuck Knoblauch, Minnesota 62
Tom Goodwin, Texas/Kansas City 50
Otis Nixon, Toronto 47
Omar Vizquel, Cleveland 43

CAUGHT STEALING
Brian Hunter, Detroit 18
Ray Durham, Chicago 16
Tom Goodwin, Texas/Kansas City 16
Jeromy Burnitz, Milwuakee 13
Damion Easley, Detroit 13
Marquis Grissom, Cleveland 13

GIDP
Albert Belle, Chicago 26
Mike Bordick, Baltimore 23
Jay Buhner, Seattle 23
Edgar Martinez, Seattle 21
John Valentin, Boston 21

HITTING STREAKS
Nomar Garciaparra, Boston 30
Sandy Alomar, Cleveland 30
Albert Belle, Chicago 27
Jason Giambi, Oakland 25

MULTIPLE-HIT GAMES
Nomar Garciaparra, Boston 68
Rusty Greer, Texas 59
Derek Jeter, New York 57
Manny Ramirez, Cleveland 57
Frank Thomas, Chicago 55
Ken Griffey, Seattle 55

SLUGGING PERCENTAGE
Ken Griffey, Seattle .... .646
Frank Thomas, Chicago .... .611
David Justice, Cleveland .... .596
Juan Gonzalez, Texas .... .589
Jim Thome, Cleveland .... .579

ON-BASE PERCENTAGE
Frank Thomas, Chicago .... .456
Edgar Martinez, Seattle .... .456
Jim Thome, Cleveland .... .423
Mo Vaughn, Boston .... .420
David Justice, Cleveland .... .418

PITCHING

WINS
Roger Clemens, Toronto 21
Randy Johnson, Seattle 20
Brad Radke, Minnesota 20
Andy Pettitte, New York 18
Jamie Moyer, Seattle 17

LOSSES
James Baldwin, Chicago 15
Cal Eldred, Milwaukee 15
Tim Wakefield, Boston 15
Jaime Navarro, Chicago 14
Scott Sanders, Seattle/Detroit 14
Woody Williams, Toronto 14

WINNING PERCENTAGE
Randy Johnson, Seattle .... .833
Jamie Moyer, Seattle .... .773
Roger Clemens, Toronto .... .750
Andy Pettitte, New York .... .720
Orel Hershiser, Cleveland .... .700

GAMES
Mike Myers, Detroit 88
Buddy Groom, Oakland 78
Jeff Nelson, New York 77
Paul Quantrill, Toronto 77
Heathcliff Slocumb, Seattle/Boston 76

GAMES STARTED
Pat Hentgen, Toronto 35
Jeff Fassero, Seattle 35
Andy Pettitte, New York 35
Brad Radke, Minnesota 35
Six tied at 34

COMPLETE GAMES
Pat Hentgen, Toronto 9
Roger Clemens, Toronto 9
Randy Johnson, Seattle 5
David Wells, New York 5
Bob Tewksbury, Minnesota 5

SHUTOUTS
Pat Hentgen, Toronto 3
Roger Clemens, Toronto 3
Tim Wakefield, Boston 2
Scott Erickson, Baltimore 2
Omar Olivares, Detroit/Seattle 2
Randy Johnson, Seattle 2
David Wells, New York 2
Bob Tewksbury, Minnesota 2

GAMES FINISHED
Heathcliff Slocumb, Boston/Seattle 61
John Wetteland, Texas 58
Rick Aquilera, Minnesota 57
Randy Myers, Baltimore 57
Mariano Rivera, New York 56

SAVES
Randy Myers, Baltimore 45
Mariano Rivera, New York 43
Doug Jones, Milwaukee 36

Brad Radke
20 wins

MORIS FOSTOFF

Randy Myers
45 saves

Todd Jones, Detroit 31
John Wetteland, Texas 31

INNINGS PITCHED
Pat Hentgen, Toronto 264
Roger Clemens, Toronto 264
Andy Pettitte, New York 240
Brad Radke, Minnesota 240
Kevin Appier, Kansas City 236

HITS ALLOWED
Jaime Navarro, Chicago 267
Pat Hentgen, Toronto 253
Charles Nagy, Cleveland 253
Bobby Witt, Texas 245
Tim Belcher, Kansas City 242

RUNS ALLOWED
Jaime Navarro, Chicago 155
James Baldwin, Chicago 128
Tim Belcher, Kansas City 128
Allen Watson, Anaheim 121
Cal Eldred, Milwaukee 118
Dennis Springer, Anaheim 118

HOME RUNS ALLOWED
Allen Watson, Anaheim 37
Bobby Witt, Texas 33
Jason Dickson, Anaheim 32
Dennis Springer, Anaheim 32
Tim Belcher, Kansas City 31
Cal Eldred, Milwaukee 31
Pat Hentgen, Toronto 31
Woody Williams, Toronto 31

WALKS
Ken Hill, Anaheim/Texas 95
Cal Eldred, Milwaukee 89
Tim Wakefield, Boston 87
David Cone, New York 86
Jeff Fassero, Seattle 84

FEWEST WALKS PER 9 INNINGS
John Burkett, Texas 1.4
Bob Tewksbury, Minnesota 1.7
Brad Radke, Minnesota 1.8
David Wells, New York 1.9
Jamie Moyer, Seattle 2.1

HIT BATSMEN
Tim Wakefield, Boston 16
Aaron Sele, Boston 15
Omar Olivares, Detroit/Seattle 13
Roger Clemens, Toronto 12
Orel Hershiser, Cleveland 11
Darren Oliver, Texas 11

STRIKEOUTS
Roger Clemens, Toronto 292
Randy Johnson, Seattle 291
David Cone, New York 222
Mike Mussina, Baltimore 218
Kevin Appier, Kansas City 196

STRIKEOUTS PER 9 INNINGS
Randy Johnson, Seattle 12.3
David Cone, New York 10.3
Roger Clemens, Toronto 10.0
Mike Mussina, Baltimore 8.7
Chuck Finley, Anaheim 8.5

PICKOFFS
Andy Pettitte, New York 14
Allen Watson, Anaheim 10
Justin Thompson, Detroit 8
Pat Hentgen, Toronto 7
Jimmy Key, Baltimore 7
Kenny Rogers, New York 7

WILD PITCHES
Kevin Appier, Kansas City 14
James Baldwin, Chicago 14
David Cone, New York 14
Jaime Navarro, Chicago 14
Jeff Fassero, Seattle 13

BALKS
James Baldwin, Chicago 3
LaTroy Hawkins, Minnesota 3
Hideki Irabu, New York 3
Paul Spoljaric, Toronto/Seattle 3

OPPONENTS BATTING AVERAGE
Randy Johnson, Seattle .... .194
Roger Clemens, Toronto .... .213
David Cone, New York .... .218
Tom Gordon, Boston .... .226
Justin Thompson, Detroit .... .233

FIELDING

PITCHER
PCT Charles Nagy, Cleveland 1.000
PO Kevin Appier, Kansas City 24
A Charles Nagy, Cleveland 45
E Scott Erickson, Baltimore 6
TC Scott Erickson, Baltimore 66
DP Bob Tewksbury, Minnesota 7

CATCHER
PCT Chris Hoiles, Baltimore 1.000
PO Dan Wilson, Seattle 1051
A Ivan Rodriguez, Texas 75
E Sandy Alomar, Cleveland 12
TC Dan Wilson, Seattle 1129
DP Three tied at 13
PB Two tied at 17

FIRST BASE
PCT Jeff King, Kansas City .... .996
PO Tony Clark, Detroit 1422
A Jeff King, Kansas City 147
E Mo Vaughn, Boston 14
TC Tony Clark, Detroit 1532
DP Jeff King, Kansas City 135

SECOND BASE
PCT Scott Spiezio, Oakland .... .990
PO Joey Cora, Seattle 307
A Chuck Knoblauch, Minn. 425
E Ray Durham, Chicago 18
TC Chuck Knoblauch, Minn. 719
DP Chuck Knoblauch, Minn. 101

THIRD BASE
PCT Travis Fryman, Detroit .... .978
PO Two tied at 126
A Jeff Cirillo, Milwaukee 320
E Dave Hollins, Anaheim 29
TC Jeff Cirillo, Milwaukee 463
DP Jeff Cirillo, Milwaukee 29

SHORTSTOP
PCT Alex Gonzalez, Toronto .... .986
PO Nomar Garciaparra, Boston 249
A Derek Jeter, New York 457
E Alex Rodriguez, Seattle 24
TC Nomar Garciaparra, Boston 720
DP Nomar Garciaparra, Boston 113

OUTFIELD
PCT Jay Buhner, Seattle .... .997
PO Brian Hunter, Detroit 408
A Bob Higginson, Detroit 20
E Rusty Greer, Texas 12
TC Brian Hunter, Detroit 420
DP Two tied at 5

1997 American League Statistics

CLUB BATTING

	AVG	G	AB	R	H	2B	3B	HR	BB	SO	SB
Boston	.291	162	5781	851	1684	373	32	185	514	1044	68
New York	.287	162	5710	891	1636	325	23	161	676	954	99
Cleveland	.286	161	5556	868	1589	301	22	220	617	955	118
Seattle	.280	162	5614	925	1574	312	21	264	626	1110	89
Texas	.274	162	5651	807	1547	311	27	187	500	1116	72
Chicago	.273	161	5491	779	1498	260	28	158	569	901	106
Anaheim	.272	162	5628	829	1531	279	25	161	617	953	126
Minnesota	.270	162	5634	772	1522	305	40	132	495	1121	151
Baltimore	.268	162	5584	812	1498	264	22	196	586	952	63
Kansas City	.264	161	5599	747	1478	256	35	158	561	1061	130
Milwaukee	.260	161	5444	681	1415	294	27	135	494	967	103
Oakland	.260	162	5589	764	1451	274	23	197	642	1181	71
Detroit	.258	162	5481	784	1415	268	32	176	578	1164	161
Toronto	.244	162	5473	654	1333	275	41	147	487	1138	134

CLUB PITCHING

	ERA	G	CG	SHO	SV	IP	H	R	ER	BB	SO
New York	3.84	162	11	10	51	1468	1463	688	626	532	1165
Baltimore	3.91	162	8	10	59	1461	1404	681	635	563	1139
Toronto	3.92	162	19	16	34	1443	1453	694	628	497	1150
Milwaukee	4.22	161	6	8	44	1427	1419	742	670	542	1016
Anaheim	4.52	162	9	5	39	1455	1506	794	730	605	1050
Detroit	4.56	162	13	8	42	1446	1476	790	732	552	982
Texas	4.69	162	8	9	33	1430	1598	823	745	541	925
Kansas City	4.69	161	11	5	29	1443	1530	820	753	531	961
Cleveland	4.73	161	4	3	39	1426	1528	815	749	575	1036
Chicago	4.73	161	6	7	52	1422	1505	833	748	575	961
Seattle	4.78	162	9	8	38	1448	1500	833	769	598	1207
Boston	4.85	162	7	4	40	1452	1569	857	782	611	987
Minnesota	4.99	162	10	4	30	1434	1596	861	795	495	908
Oakland	5.48	162	2	1	38	1445	1734	946	880	642	953

CLUB FIELDING

	PCT	PO	A	E	DP		PCT	PO	A	E	DP
Detroit	.985	4337	1719	92	146	Oakland	.980	4336	1765	122	170
Kansas City	.985	4329	1630	91	168	Texas	.980	4289	1666	121	155
Toronto	.984	4328	1536	94	150	Milwaukee	.980	4282	1655	121	170
Baltimore	.984	4383	1666	97	148	Anaheim	.980	4364	1592	123	140
Minnesota	.983	4302	1694	101	171	Seattle	.979	4343	1572	126	143
New York	.983	4403	1705	104	156	Chicago	.978	4267	1439	127	131
Cleveland	.983	4277	1728	106	159	Boston	.978	4355	1696	135	179

INDIVIDUAL BATTING LEADERS

(Minimum 502 Plate Appearances)

	AVG	G	AB	R	H	2B	3B	HR	RBI	BB	SO	SB
Thomas, Frank, Chicago	.347	146	530	110	184	35	0	35	125	109	69	1
Martinez, Edgar, Seattle	.330	155	542	104	179	35	1	28	108	119	86	2
Justice, David, Cleveland	.329	139	495	84	163	31	1	33	101	80	79	3
Williams, Bernie, New York	.328	129	509	107	167	35	6	21	100	73	80	15
Ramirez, Manny, Cleveland	.328	150	561	99	184	40	0	26	88	79	115	2
O'Neill, Paul, New York	.324	149	553	89	179	42	0	21	117	75	92	10
Greer, Rusty, Texas	.321	157	601	112	193	42	3	26	87	83	87	9
Jefferson, Reggie, Boston	.319	136	489	74	156	33	1	13	67	24	93	1
Vaughn, Mo, Boston	.315	141	527	91	166	24	0	35	96	86	154	2
Rodriguez, Ivan, Texas	.313	150	597	98	187	34	4	20	77	38	89	7

INDIVIDUAL PITCHING LEADERS

(Minimum 162 Innings)

	W	L	ERA	G	GS	CG	SV	IP	H	R	ER	BB	SO
Clemens, Roger, Toronto	21	7	2.05	34	34	9	0	264	204	65	60	68	292
Johnson, Randy, Seattle	20	4	2.28	30	29	5	0	213	147	60	54	77	291
Cone, David, New York	12	6	2.82	29	29	1	0	195	155	67	61	86	222
Pettitte, Andy, New York	18	7	2.88	35	35	4	0	240	233	86	77	65	166
Thompson, Justin, Detroit	15	11	3.02	32	32	4	0	223	188	82	75	66	151
Mussina, Mike, Baltimore	15	8	3.20	33	33	4	0	225	197	87	80	54	218
Appier, Kevin, KC	9	13	3.40	34	34	4	0	236	215	96	89	74	196
Key, Jimmy, Baltimore	16	10	3.43	34	34	1	0	212	210	90	81	82	141
Fassero, Jeff, Seattle	16	9	3.61	35	35	2	0	234	226	108	94	84	189
Hentgen, Pat, Toronto	15	10	3.68	35	35	9	0	264	253	116	108	71	160

AWARD WINNERS

Selected by Baseball Writers Association of America

MVP

Player, Team	1st	2nd	3rd	Total
Ken Griffey, Seattle	28	0	0	392
Tino Martinez, N.Y.	0	24	4	248
Frank Thomas, Chi.	0	3	10	172
Randy Myers, Balt.	0	0	8	128
David Justice, Cleve.	0	0	2	90
Jim Thome, Cleve.	0	0	1	89
Tim Salmon, Anaheim	0	1	1	84
Nomar Garciaparra, Bos.	0	0	0	83
Juan Gonzalez, Texas	0	0	0	66
Roger Clemens, Tor.	0	0	1	56
Randy Johnson, Sea.	0	0	1	42
Paul O'Neill, N.Y.	0	0	0	37
Rafael Palmeiro, Balt.	0	0	0	36
Edgar Martinez, Sea.	0	0	0	22
Sandy Alomar, Cleve.	0	0	0	22
Ivan Rodriguez, Texas	0	0	0	16
Bernie Williams, N.Y.	0	0	0	14
Tony Clark, Detroit	0	0	0	13
Jay Buhner, Seattle	0	0	0	12
Doug Jones, Mil.	0	0	0	5
Arthur Rhodes, Balt.	0	0	0	5
Roberto Alomar, Balt.	0	0	0	4
Rusty Greer, Texas	0	0	0	4
Derek Jeter, N.Y.	0	0	0	3
Mariano Rivera, N.Y.	0	0	0	2
Brad Radke, Minn.	0	0	0	2
Deivi Cruz, Detroit	0	0	0	2
Mo Vaughn, Boston	0	0	0	2
Jeromy Burnitz, Mil.	0	0	0	1

CY YOUNG AWARD

Player, Team	1st	2nd	3rd	Total
Roger Clemens, Tor.	25	3	0	134
Randy Johnson, Sea.	2	21	4	77
Brad Radke, Minn.	0	2	11	17
Randy Myers, Balt.	1	1	6	14
Andy Pettitte, N.Y.	0	1	6	9
Mike Mussina, Balt.	0	0	1	1

ROOKIE OF THE YEAR

Player, Team	1st	2nd	3rd	Total
Nomar Garciaparra, Bos.	28	0	0	140
Jose Cruz Jr., Sea.-Tor.	0	18	7	61
Jason Dickson, Ana.	0	6	9	27
Deivi Cruz, Detroit	0	3	3	12
Jaret Wright, Cleve.	0	1	4	7
Mike Cameron, Chi.	0	0	5	5

MANAGER OF THE YEAR

Manager, Team	1st	2nd	3rd	Total
Davey Johnson, Balt.	10	11	5	88
Buddy Bell, Detroit	4	7	9	50
Phil Garner, Mil.	5	5	2	42
Lou Piniella, Sea.	3	3	6	30
Terry Collins, Ana.	4	1	1	24
Mike Hargrove, Cleve.	2	0	3	13
Joe Torre, New York	0	1	2	5

NOTE: MVP balloting based on 14 points for first-place vote, nine for second, eight for third, etc.; Cy Young Award, Rookie of the Year and Manager of the Year balloting based on five points for first-place vote, three for second and one for third.

GOLD GLOVE AWARDS

Selected by AL managers

C—Ivan Rodriguez, Texas. **1B**—Rafael Palmeiro, Baltimore. **2B**—Chuck Knoblauch, Minnesota. **3B**—Matt Williams, Cleveland. **SS**—Omar Vizquel, Cleveland. **OF**—Ken Griffey, Seattle; Jim Edmonds, Anaheim; Bernie Williams, New York. **P**—Mike Mussina, Baltimore.

AMERICAN LEAGUE

DIVISION SERIES

NEW YORK vs. CLEVELAND

COMPOSITE BOX

NEW YORK

Player, Pos.	AVG	G	AB	R	H	2B	3B	HR	RBI	BB	SO	SB
Mike Stanley, c-dh	.750	2	4	1	3	1	0	0	1	0	1	0
Wade Boggs, 3b	.429	5	7	1	3	0	0	0	2	0	0	0
Paul O'Neill, of	.421	5	19	5	8	2	0	2	7	2	0	0
Derek Jeter, ss	.333	5	21	6	7	1	0	2	2	3	5	1
Charlie Hayes, 3b	.333	5	15	0	5	0	0	0	1	0	2	0
Tino Martinez, 1b	.222	5	18	1	4	1	0	1	4	3	4	0
Tim Raines, of-dh	.211	5	19	4	4	0	0	1	3	3	1	2
Rey Sanchez, 2b	.200	5	15	1	3	1	0	0	1	1	2	0
Chad Curtis, of	.167	4	6	0	1	0	0	0	0	3	1	0
Joe Girardi, c	.133	5	15	2	2	0	0	0	0	1	3	0
Cecil Fielder, dh	.125	2	8	0	1	0	0	0	1	0	3	0
Bernie Williams, of	.117	5	17	3	2	1	0	0	1	4	3	0
Jorge Posada, c	.000	3	0	0	0	0	0	0	0	0	1	0
Andy Fox, pr	.000	2	0	0	0	0	0	0	0	0	0	0
Totals	**.262**	**5**	**164**	**24**	**43**	**7**	**0**	**6**	**23**	**20**	**26**	**3**

Pitcher	W	L	ERA	G	GS	SV	IP	H	R	ER	BB	SO
Brian Boehringer	0	0	0.00	1	0	0	2	1	0	0	1	2
Graeme Lloyd	0	0	0.00	2	0	0	1	0	0	0	0	1
Jeff Nelson	0	0	0.00	4	0	0	4	4	0	0	2	0
Mike Stanton	0	0	0.00	3	0	0	1	1	0	0	1	3
David Wells	1	0	1.00	1	1	0	9	5	1	1	0	1
Dwight Gooden	0	0	1.59	1	1	0	6	5	1	1	3	5
Ramiro Mendoza	1	1	2.45	2	0	0	4	3	1	1	0	2
Mariano Rivera	0	0	4.50	2	0	1	2	2	1	1	0	1
Andy Pettitte	0	2	8.49	2	2	0	12	15	11	11	1	5
David Cone	0	0	16.20	1	1	0	3	7	6	6	2	2
Totals	**2**	**3**	**4.43**	**5**	**5**	**1**	**43**	**43**	**21**	**21**	**10**	**22**

CLEVELAND

Player, Pos.	AVG	G	AB	R	H	2B	3B	HR	RBI	BB	SO	SB
Omar Vizquel, ss	.500	5	18	3	9	0	0	0	1	2	1	4
Sandy Alomar, c	.316	5	19	4	6	1	0	2	5	0	2	0
Bip Roberts, of-2b	.316	5	19	1	6	0	0	0	1	2	2	2
David Justice, dh	.263	5	19	3	5	2	0	1	2	2	3	0
Marquis Grissom, of	.235	5	17	3	4	0	1	0	0	1	2	0
Matt Williams, 3b	.235	5	17	4	4	1	0	1	3	3	3	0
Jim Thome, 1b	.200	4	15	1	3	0	0	0	1	0	5	0
Tony Fernandez, 2b	.182	4	11	0	2	1	0	0	4	0	0	0
Brian Giles, of	.143	3	7	0	1	0	0	0	0	0	1	0
Manny Ramirez, of	.143	5	21	2	3	1	0	0	3	0	3	0
Kevin Seitzer, 1b	.000	1	4	0	0	0	0	0	0	0	0	0
Totals	**.257**	**5**	**167**	**21**	**43**	**6**	**1**	**4**	**20**	**10**	**22**	**6**

Pitcher	W	L	ERA	G	GS	SV	IP	H	R	ER	BB	SO
Mike Jackson	1	0	0.00	4	0	0	4	3	0	0	1	5
Chad Ogea	0	0	1.69	1	0	0	5	2	1	1	0	1
Orel Hershiser	0	0	3.97	2	2	0	11	14	5	5	2	4
Jaret Wright	2	0	3.97	2	2	0	11	11	6	5	7	10
Jose Mesa	0	0	2.70	2	0	1	3	5	1	1	1	2
Paul Assenmacher	0	0	5.40	4	0	0	2	2	2	2	2	2
Charles Nagy	0	1	9.82	1	1	0	4	2	5	4	6	1
Eric Plunk	0	1	27.00	1	0	0	1	4	4	4	0	1
Alvin Morman	0	0	—	1	0	0	0	0	0	0	1	0
Totals	**3**	**2**	**4.64**	**5**	**5**	**1**	**43**	**43**	**24**	**22**	**20**	**26**

SCORE BY INNINGS					
New York	**611**	**536**	**011**	**—**	**24**
Cleveland	**523**	**720**	**011**	**—**	**21**

DP—New York 2, Cleveland 6. **LOB**—New York 37, Cleveland 32. **E**—Hayes 3, Boehringer; Alomar, Ramirez, Wright, Nagy. **S**—Sanchez, Girardi, Roberts, Vizquel 2, Thome. **SF**—Raines, Hayes, Fernandez. **CS**—Grissom, Roberts. **HBP**—M. Williams (by Cone), B. Williams (by Assenmacher), Stanley (by Mesa), Martinez (by Hershiser). **WP**—Cone.

BALTIMORE vs. SEATTLE

COMPOSITE BOX

BALTIMORE

Player, Pos.	AVG	G	AB	R	H	2B	3B	HR	RBI	BB	SO	SB
Cal Ripken, 3b	.438	4	16	1	7	2	0	0	1	2	2	0
Mike Bordick, ss	.400	4	10	4	4	1	0	0	4	4	2	0
Harold Baines, dh	.400	2	5	2	2	0	0	1	1	1	0	0
Geronimo Berroa, of	.385	4	13	4	5	1	0	2	2	2	2	0
Brady Anderson, of	.353	4	17	3	6	1	0	1	4	1	4	1
Roberto Alomar, 2b	.300	4	10	1	3	2	0	0	2	1	1	0
B.J. Surhoff, of	.273	3	11	0	3	1	0	0	2	0	2	0
Rafael Palmeiro, 1b	.250	4	12	2	3	2	0	0	0	0	2	0
Eric Davis, of	.222	3	9	0	2	0	0	0	2	0	5	0
Jeff Reboulet, 2b	.200	2	5	1	1	0	0	1	1	0	2	0
Lenny Webster, c	.167	3	6	1	1	0	0	0	1	1	0	0
Chris Hoiles, c	.143	3	7	1	1	0	0	1	1	2	1	0
Jeffrey Hammonds, of	.100	4	10	3	1	1	0	0	2	2	2	1
Jerome Walton, 1b	.000	2	4	0	0	0	0	0	0	0	2	0
Totals	**.289**	**4**	**135**	**23**	**39**	**11**	**0**	**6**	**23**	**16**	**27**	**2**

Pitcher	W	L	ERA	G	GS	SV	IP	H	R	ER	BB	SO
Arthur Rhodes	0	0	0.00	1	0	0	2	0	0	0	0	4
Randy Myers	0	0	0.00	2	0	1	2	0	0	0	0	5
Jesse Orosco	0	0	0.00	2	0	0	1	1	0	0	0	1
Alan Mills	0	0	0.00	1	0	0	1	1	0	0	0	1
Mike Mussina	2	0	1.93	2	2	0	14	7	3	3	3	16
Armando Benitez	0	0	3.00	3	0	0	3	3	1	1	2	4
Jimmy Key	0	1	3.86	1	1	0	5	8	2	2	0	4
Scott Erickson	1	0	4.05	1	1	0	7	7	3	3	2	6
Terry Mathews	0	0	18.00	1	0	0	1	2	2	2	0	1
Totals	**3**	**1**	**2.75**	**4**	**4**	**1**	**36**	**29**	**11**	**11**	**7**	**42**

SEATTLE

Player, Pos.	AVG	G	AB	R	H	2B	3B	HR	RBI	BB	SO	SB
Rich Amaral, of	.500	2	4	2	2	0	0	0	0	0	1	0
Rob Ducey, of	.500	2	4	0	2	0	0	0	1	0	0	0
Andy Sheets, 3b	.333	2	3	0	1	0	0	0	0	0	2	0
Alex Rodriguez, ss	.313	4	16	1	5	1	0	1	1	0	5	0
Roberto Kelly, of	.308	4	13	1	4	3	0	0	1	0	3	0
Paul Sorrento, 1b	.300	4	10	2	3	1	0	1	1	2	3	0
Jay Buhner, of	.231	4	13	2	3	0	0	2	2	3	6	0
Mike Blowers, 1b	.200	3	5	0	1	0	0	0	0	0	3	0
Edgar Martinez, dh	.188	4	16	2	3	0	0	2	3	0	3	0
Joey Cora, 2b	.176	4	17	1	3	0	0	0	0	0	4	0
Ken Griffey, of	.133	4	15	0	2	0	0	0	2	1	3	2
Brent Gates, 3b	.000	2	4	0	0	0	0	0	0	0	0	0
Dan Wilson, c	.000	4	13	0	0	0	0	0	0	0	9	0
Rick Wilkins, ph	—	1	0	0	0	0	0	0	0	1	0	0
Totals	**.218**	**4**	**133**	**11**	**29**	**5**	**0**	**6**	**11**	**7**	**42**	**2**

Pitcher	W	L	ERA	G	GS	SV	IP	H	R	ER	BB	SO
Norm Charlton	0	0	0.00	2	0	0	2	2	0	0	0	1
Paul Spoljaric	0	0	0.00	2	0	0	2	4	0	0	0	1
Bob Wells	0	0	0.00	1	0	0	1	1	0	0	0	1
Jeff Fassero	1	0	1.13	1	1	0	8	3	1	1	4	3
Heathcliff Slocumb	0	0	4.50	2	0	0	2	3	1	1	1	0
Randy Johnson	0	2	5.54	2	2	0	13	14	8	8	6	16
Jamie Moyer	0	1	5.79	1	1	0	5	5	3	3	1	2
Bobby Ayala	0	0	40.50	1	0	0	1	4	6	6	3	2
Mike Timlin	0	0	54.00	1	0	0	1	3	4	4	1	1
Totals	**1**	**3**	**5.91**	**4**	**4**	**0**	**35**	**39**	**23**	**23**	**16**	**27**

DIAMOND IMAGES

Cleveland defensive whiz Omar Vizquel
Hit .500 in Division Series, .040 in ALCS

SCORE BY INNINGS

Seattle	**211**	**110**	**203**	**— 11**
Baltimore	**211**	**074**	**242**	**— 23**

DP—Seattle 3, Baltimore 1. **LOB**—Seattle 21, Baltimore 25. **E**—Sorrento. **SH**—Alomar, Reboulet. **CS**—Bordick, Davis. **PB**—Webster. **WP**—Key.

CHAMPIONSHIP SERIES

CLEVELAND vs. BALTIMORE

COMPOSITE BOX

CLEVELAND

Player, Pos	AVG	G	AB	R	H	2B	3B	HR	RBI	BB	SO	SB
Tony Fernandez, 2b	.357	5	14	1	5	1	0	1	2	1	2	0
David Justice, dh	.333	6	21	3	7	1	0	0	0	2	4	0
Manny Ramirez, of	.286	6	21	3	6	1	0	2	3	5	5	0
Marquis Grissom, of	.261	6	23	2	6	0	0	1	4	1	9	3
Matt Williams, 3b	.217	6	23	1	5	1	0	0	2	3	7	1
Brian Giles, of	.188	6	16	1	3	3	0	0	0	2	6	0
Bip Roberts, 2b-of	.150	5	20	0	3	1	0	0	0	0	8	1
Sandy Alomar, c	.125	6	24	3	3	0	0	1	4	1	3	0
Jim Thome, 1b	.071	6	14	3	1	0	0	0	0	5	4	0
Omar Vizquel, ss	.040	6	25	1	1	0	0	0	0	2	10	0
Kevin Seitzer, 1b	.000	4	4	0	0	0	0	0	0	1	2	0
Jeff Branson, dh	.000	1	2	0	0	0	0	0	0	0	2	0
Totals	**.193**	**6**	**207**	**18**	**40**	**8**	**0**	**5**	**15**	**23**	**62**	**5**

Pitcher	W	L	ERA	G	GS	SV	IP	H	R	ER	BB	SO
Orel Hershiser	0	0	0.00	1	1	0	7	4	0	0	1	7
Mike Jackson	0	0	0.00	5	0	0	4	1	0	0	1	7
Alvin Morman	0	0	0.00	2	0	0	1	0	0	0	0	1
Jeff Juden	0	0	0.00	3	0	0	1	2	0	0	2	2
Eric Plunk	1	0	0.00	1	0	0	1	1	0	0	0	0
Brian Anderson	1	0	1.42	3	0	0	6	1	1	1	3	7
Charles Nagy	0	0	2.77	2	2	0	13	17	4	4	5	5
Chad Ogea	0	2	3.21	2	2	0	14	12	5	5	5	7
Jose Mesa	1	0	3.38	4	0	2	5	5	2	2	3	5
Paul Assenmacher	1	0	9.00	5	0	0	2	5	2	2	1	3
Jaret Wright	0	0	15.00	1	1	0	3	6	5	5	2	3
Totals	**4**	**2**	**2.95**	**6**	**6**	**2**	**58**	**54**	**19**	**19**	**23**	**47**

BALTIMORE

Player, Pos	AVG	G	AB	R	H	2B	3B	HR	RBI	BB	SO	SB
Brady Anderson, of	.360	6	25	5	9	2	0	2	3	4	4	2
Harold Baines, dh	.353	6	17	1	6	0	0	1	2	2	1	0
Cal Ripken, 3b	.348	6	23	3	8	2	0	1	3	4	6	0
Geronimo Berroa, of-dh	.286	6	21	1	6	2	0	0	3	0	3	0
Rafael Palmeiro, 1b	.280	6	25	3	7	2	0	1	2	0	10	0
Lenny Webster, c	.222	4	9	0	2	0	0	0	0	0	1	0
B.J. Surhoff, of-1b	.200	6	25	1	5	2	0	0	1	2	2	0
Roberto Alomar, 2b	.182	6	22	2	4	0	0	1	2	7	3	0
Mike Bordick, ss	.158	6	19	0	3	1	0	0	2	0	6	0
Eric Davis, of-dh	.154	6	13	1	2	0	0	1	1	1	3	0
Chris Hoiles, c	.143	4	14	1	2	0	0	0	0	2	5	0
Jeffrey Hammonds, of	.000	5	3	0	0	0	0	0	0	1	2	1
Jeff Reboulet, ss	.000	1	2	1	0	0	0	0	0	0	1	0
Totals	**.248**	**6**	**218**	**19**	**54**	**11**	**0**	**7**	**19**	**23**	**47**	**3**

LARRY GOREN

Rookie hotshot Jaret Wright
Beat Yankees twice in Division Series

Pitcher	W	L	ERA	G	GS	SV	IP	H	R	ER	BB	SO
Scott Kamieniecki	1	0	0.00	2	1	0	8	4	0	0	2	5
Arthur Rhodes	0	0	0.00	2	0	0	2	2	0	0	3	2
Jesse Orosco	0	0	0.00	2	0	0	1	0	0	0	1	1
Mike Mussina	0	0	0.60	2	2	0	15	4	1	1	4	25
Jimmy Key	0	0	2.57	2	1	0	7	5	2	2	3	7
Alan Mills	0	1	2.70	3	0	0	3	1	1	1	2	3
Scott Erickson	1	0	4.26	2	2	0	13	15	7	6	1	6
Randy Myers	0	1	5.06	4	0	1	5	6	3	3	3	7
Armando Benitez	0	2	12.00	4	0	0	3	3	4	4	4	6
Totals	**2**	**4**	**2.64**	**6**	**6**	**1**	**58**	**40**	**18**	**17**	**23**	**62**

SCORE BY INNINGS

Cleveland	**220**	**140**	**133**	**011**	**— 18**
Baltimore	**138**	**002**	**104**	**000**	**— 19**

DP—Cleveland 11, Baltimore 4. **LOB**—Cleveland 44, Baltimore 50. **E**—Williams 2, Fernandez, Ramirez, Roberts; R. Alomar 2, Webster 2, By. Anderson. **CS**—Baines. **SH**—Vizquel, Seitzer, Bordick. **HBP**—Fernandez (by Key), Justice (by Key), Vizquel (by Key), Ramirez (by Kamieniecki), Palmeiro (by Nagy). **WP**—Rhodes 2.

NATIONAL LEAGUE

Marlins overcome adversity, topple favored Braves

BY JOHN ROYSTER

It was a long swim against a strong current, but the Fish got where they wanted to go in 1997–the World Series.

Every pennant-winning team overcomes some sort of adversity, but it tends to happen no more often in October than it does in April. The Marlins had a couple of months worth in less than a week, but still managed to upset the two-time defending champion Braves in six games in the National League Championship Series.

"I expected we'd win this series," Marlins manager Jim Leyland said after Game Six. "I had a feeling, and that's what I told the guys before the game. We'd had some adversity, but we were going to overcome it tonight."

But that's getting ahead of the story a bit, because the Marlins' luck actually started out pretty good. All five of their runs were unearned in a 5-3 win over the Braves in Game One in Atlanta. Three of the runs came gift-wrapped in the top of the very first inning, courtesy of an error by first baseman Fred McGriff and a misplay by third baseman Chipper Jones.

That allowed Florida to overcome its first major obstacle, Braves righthander Greg Maddux. He pitched well but lost.

But the Marlins' troubles began even as they were winning. Left fielder Moises Alou, the team leader in RBIs, sprained his wrist. He missed all of Game Two and made only a pinch-hitting appearance in Game Three.

Marlins starter Alex Fernandez showed much-reduced velocity in the second game, and the Braves hammered him for five runs in 2⅔ innings en route to a 7-1 win. And the problem was much worse than just that. An MRI the next morning revealed that Fernandez had a torn right rotator cuff. He was done for the postseason, not to mention all of 1998 as well.

Jim Leyland

When Game Three began in Miami, Florida's players affixed Fernandez' No. 32 to their caps and went out and erased two Atlanta leads to win 5-2. The second tying run scored in the sixth, when Braves right fielder Andruw Jones misplayed Darren Daulton's fly ball into a double.

Two batters later, a legitimate, bases-loaded double by Charles Johnson sealed the deal. Left fielder Ryan Klesko made a headlong, diving attempt to catch the ball near the wall, but all he got for his trouble was a nagging arm injury of his own.

DAVID SEELIG

Rising star Livan Hernandez
NLCS turned on his masterpiece

Livan Hernandez was the winner in relief, but starter Tony Saunders kept the Marlins in the game and made the victory possible. Saunders, a rookie lefthander who in Atlanta ranks right up there with traffic and William Tecumseh Sherman, gave up two runs and four hits in 5⅓ innings.

If Saunders had gotten the win, it would have been his fifth in the major leagues. Three of the other four came against the Braves during the regular season, as he went 4-6 with a 4.61 ERA. The only other team he beat was the lowly Phillies.

Saunders also was the last Marlins pitcher to start an NLCS game when he was supposed to. While he pitched Game Three, scheduled Game Four starter Kevin Brown sat at home with a stomach virus, watching on TV and trying to keep his saltines down.

When Brown couldn't pitch the next day, Leyland's scheduled seven-game rotation of Brown-Fernandez-Saunders-Brown-Al Leiter-Fernandez-Brown became Brown-Fernandez-Saunders-TBA-Leiter-TBA-TBA.

Leyland chose to move Leiter up a day, which didn't work out too well. He gave up four runs in six innings and lost 4-0. Braves lefthander Denny Neagle, a 20-game winner during the regular season, pitched a four-hit shutout in his first postseason start after playing fourth fiddle to Maddux, Tom Glavine and John Smoltz.

For Game Five Leyland turned to Hernandez, an effective starter in the regular season and an effective reliever in two postseason appearances.

As a postseason starter, Hernandez proved only as

NATIONAL LEAGUE CHAMPIONS, 1901-1997

	Pennant	Pct.	GA
1901	Pittsburgh	.647	½
1902	Pittsburgh	.741	27½
1903	Pittsburgh	.650	6½
1904	New York	.693	13
1905	New York	.686	9
1906	Chicago	.763	20
1907	Chicago	.704	17
1908	Chicago	.643	1
1909	Pittsburgh	.724	6½
1910	Chicago	.675	13
1911	New York	.647	7½
1912	New York	.682	10
1913	New York	.664	12½
1914	Boston	.614	10½
1915	Philadelphia	.592	7
1916	Brooklyn	.610	2½
1917	New York	.636	10
1918	Chicago	.651	10½
1919	Cincinnati	.686	9
1920	Brooklyn	.604	7
1921	New York	.614	4
1922	New York	.604	7
1923	New York	.621	4½
1924	New York	.608	1½
1925	Pittsburgh	.621	8½
1926	St. Louis	.578	2
1927	Pittsburgh	.610	1½
1928	St. Louis	.617	2
1929	Chicago	.645	10½
1930	St. Louis	.597	2

	Pennant	Pct.	GA	MVP
1931	St. Louis	.656	13	Frankie Frisch, 2b, St.Louis
1932	Chicago	.584	4	Chuck Klein, of, Philadelphia
1933	New York	.599	5	Carl Hubbell, lhp, New York
1934	St. Louis	.621	2	Dizzy Dean, rhp, St.Louis
1935	Chicago	.649	4	Gabby Hartnett, c, Chicago
1936	New York	.597	5	Carl Hubbell, lhp, New York
1937	New York	.625	3	Joe Medwick, of, St. Louis
1938	Chicago	.586	2	Ernie Lombardi, c, Cincinnati
1939	Cincinnati	.630	4½	Bucky Walters, rhp, Cincinnati
1940	Cincinnati	.654	12	Frank McCormick, 1b, Cincinnati
1941	Brooklyn	.649	2½	Dolf Camilli, 1b, Brooklyn
1942	St. Louis	.688	2	Mort Cooper, rhp, St. Louis
1943	St. Louis	.682	18	Stan Musial, of, St. Louis
1944	St. Louis	.682	14½	Marty Marion, ss, St. Louis
1945	Chicago	.636	3	Phil Cavarretta, 1b, Chicago
1946	St. Louis	.628	2	Stan Musial, 1b, St. Louis
1947	Brooklyn	.610	5	Bob Elliott, 3b, Boston
1948	Boston	.595	6½	Stan Musial, of, St. Louis
1949	Brooklyn	.630	1	Jackie Robinson, 2b, Brooklyn
1950	Philadelphia	.591	2	Jim Konstanty, rhp, Philadelphia
1951	New York	.624	1	Roy Campanella, c, Brooklyn
1952	Brooklyn	.627	4½	Hank Sauer, of, Chicago
1953	Brooklyn	.682	13	Roy Campanella, c, Brooklyn
1954	New York	.630	5	Willie Mays, of, New York
1955	Brooklyn	.641	13½	Roy Campanella, c, Brooklyn
1956	Brooklyn	.604	1	Don Newcombe, rhp, Brooklyn
1957	Milwaukee	.617	8	Hank Aaron, of, Milwaukee
1958	Milwaukee	.597	8	Ernie Banks, ss, Chicago
1959	Los Angeles	.564	2	Ernie Banks, ss, Chicago
1960	Pittsburgh	.617	7	Dick Groat, ss, Pittsburgh
1961	Cincinnati	.604	4	Frank Robinson, of, Cincinnati
1962	San Francisco	.624	1	Maury Wills, ss, Los Angeles
1963	Los Angeles	.611	6	Sandy Koufax, lhp, Los Angeles
1964	St. Louis	.574	1	Ken Boyer, 3b, St. Louis
1965	Los Angeles	.599	2	Willie Mays, of, San Francisco
1966	Los Angeles	.586	1½	Roberto Clemente, of, Pittsburgh
1967	St. Louis	.627	10½	Orlando Cepeda, 1b, St. Louis
1968	St. Louis	.599	9	Bob Gibson, rhp, St. Louis

	East. Div.	PCT	GA	West. Div.	PCT	GA	Pennant		MVP
1969	New York	.617	8	Atlanta	.574	3	New York	3-0	Willie McCovey, 1b, San Francisco
1970	Pittsburgh	.549	5	Cincinnati	.630	14½	Cincinnati	3-0	Johnny Bench, c, Cincinnati
1971	Pittsburgh	.599	7	San Francisco	.556	1	Pittsburgh	3-1	Joe Torre, 3b, St. Louis
1972	Pittsburgh	.619	11	Cincinnati	.617	10½	Cincinnati	3-2	Johnny Bench, c, Cincinnati
1973	New York	.509	1½	Cincinnati	.611	3½	New York	3-2	Pete Rose, of, Cincinnati
1974	Pittsburgh	.543	1½	Los Angeles	.630	4	Los Angeles	3-1	Steve Garvey, 1b, Los Angeles
1975	Pittsburgh	.571	6½	Cincinnati	.667	20	Cincinnati	3-0	Joe Morgan, 2b, Cincinnati
1976	Philadelphia	.623	9	Cincinnati	.630	10	Cincinnati	3-0	Joe Morgan, 2b, Cincinnati
1977	Philadelphia	.623	5	Los Angeles	.605	10	Los Angeles	3-1	George Foster, of, Cincinnati
1978	Philadelphia	.556	1½	Los Angeles	.586	2½	Los Angeles	3-1	Dave Parker, of, Pittsburgh
1979	Pittsburgh	.605	2	Cincinnati	.559	1½	Pittsburgh	3-0	Hernandez, St. Louis; Stargell, Pittsburgh
1980	Philadelphia	.562	1	Houston	.571	1	Philadelphia	3-2	Mike Schmidt, 3b, Philadelphia
1981	Montreal*	.566	½	Los Angeles**	.632	½	Los Angeles	3-2	Mike Schmidt, 3b, Philadelphia
	Philadelphia	.618	1½	Houston	.623	1			
1982	St. Louis	.568	3	Atlanta	.549	1	St. Louis	3-0	Dale Murphy, of, Atlanta
1983	Philadelphia	.556	6	Los Angeles	.562	3	Philadelphia	3-1	Dale Murphy, of, Atlanta
1984	Chicago	.596	6½	San Diego	.568	12	San Diego	3-2	Ryne Sandberg, 2b, Chicago
1985	St. Louis	.623	3	Los Angeles	.586	5½	St. Louis	4-2	Willie McGee, of, St. Louis
1986	New York	.667	21½	Houston	.593	10	New York	4-2	Mike Schmidt, 3b, Philadelphia
1987	St. Louis	.586	3	San Francisco	.556	6	St. Louis	4-3	Andre Dawson, of, Chicago
1988	New York	.625	15	Los Angeles	.584	7	Los Angeles	4-3	Kirk Gibson, of, Los Angeles
1989	Chicago	.571	6	San Francisco	.568	3	San Francisco	4-1	Kevin Mitchell, of, San Francisco
1990	Pittsburgh	.586	4	Cincinnati	.562	5	Cincinnati	4-2	Barry Bonds, of, Pittsburgh
1991	Pittsburgh	.605	14	Atlanta	.580	1	Atlanta	4-3	Terry Pendleton, 3b, Atlanta
1992	Pittsburgh	.593	9	Atlanta	.605	8	Atlanta	4-3	Barry Bonds, of, Pittsburgh
1993	Philadelphia	.599	3	Atlanta	.642	1	Philadelphia	4-2	Barry Bonds, of, San Francisco

East Div.		PCT	GA	Central Div.	PCT	GA	West Div.	PCT	GA	MVP
1994	Montreal	.649	6	Cincinnati	.593	½	Los Angeles	.509	3½	Jeff Bagwell, 1b, Houston
1995	Atlanta#	.625	21	Cincinnati	.590	9	Los Angeles	.542	1	Barry Larkin, ss, Cincinnati
1996	Atlanta@	.593	8	St. Louis	.543	6	San Diego	.562	1	Ken Caminiti, 3b, San Diego
1997	Atlanta†	.623	9	Houston	.519	5	San Francisco	.556	2	Larry Walker, of, Colorado

*Won second half; defeated Philadelphia 3-2 in best-of-5 playoff. **Won first half; defeated Houston 3-2 in best-of-5 playoff.
#Won NL pennant, defeating Cincinnati 4-2. @ Won NL pennant, defeating St. Louis 4-3.
† Florida (wild card) won NL pennant, defeating Atlanta 4-2.

NATIONAL LEAGUE STANDINGS

Page	EAST	W	L	PCT	GB	Manager	General Manager	Attend./Dates	Last Penn.
58	Atlanta Braves	101	61	.623	—	Bobby Cox	John Schuerholz	3,463,988 (81)	1996
114	Florida Marlins*	92	70	.568	9	Jim Leyland	Dave Dombrowski	2,364,387 (80)	1997
165	New York Mets	88	74	.543	13	Bobby Valentine	McIlvaine/Phillips	1,766,174 (78)	1986
151	Montreal Expos	78	84	.481	23	Felipe Alou	Jim Beattie	1,497,609 (81)	None
178	Philadelphia Phillies	68	94	.420	33	Terry Francona	Lee Thomas	1,490,638 (77)	1993
Page	**CENTRAL**	**W**	**L**	**PCT**	**GB**	**Manager(s)**	**General Manager**	**Attend./Dates**	**Last Penn.**
120	Houston Astros	84	78	.519	—	Larry Dierker	Gerry Hunsicker	2,046,811 (81)	None
184	Pittsburgh Pirates	79	83	.488	5	Gene Lamont	Cam Bonifay	1,657,022 (80)	1979
90	Cincinnati Reds	76	86	.469	8	Knight/McKeon	Jim Bowden	1,785,788 (80)	1990
191	St. Louis Cardinals	73	89	.451	11	Tony La Russa	Walt Jocketty	2,658,357 (81)	1987
84	Chicago Cubs	68	94	.420	16	Jim Riggleman	Ed Lynch	2,190,308 (79)	1945
Page	**WEST**	**W**	**L**	**PCT**	**GB**	**Manager**	**General Manager**	**Attend./Dates**	**Last Penn.**
204	San Francisco Giants	90	72	.556	—	Dusty Baker	Brian Sabean	1,690,831 (80)	1989
132	Los Angeles Dodgers	88	74	.543	2	Bill Russell	Fred Claire	3,318,886 (81)	1988
102	Colorado Rockies	83	79	.512	7	Don Baylor	Bob Gebhard	3,888,453 (81)	None
197	San Diego Padres	76	86	.469	14	Bruce Bochy	Kevin Towers	2,089,336 (80)	1984

*Won wild-card playoff berth

NOTE: Team's individual batting, pitching and fielding statistics can be found on page indicated in lefthand column.

effective as Sandy Koufax. He struck out 15, tying the postseason record held by Koufax and matched by the Orioles' Mike Mussina in the American League series just the day before. He gave up three hits in nine innings, and beat an almost-as-brilliant Maddux 2-1.

The Marlins headed back to Atlanta with a 3-2 lead in games and Brown finally ready. Ready to pitch a lot longer than Leyland figured, as it turned out.

With Florida holding a 7-3 lead after six innings, Leyland figured it was a propitious time to take Brown out. But Brown had appeared to strengthen in the fifth and sixth, and expressed that opinion to Leyland with the kind of body language usually reserved for arguments between managers and umpires.

"I told Jim it wasn't about me, but about the team," Brown said. "I told him I had more left to give the team. I said if he wanted to take it on a batter-to-batter basis, and take me out if someone got on base, fine."

Brown stayed, for nine innings. Atlanta went, 7-4.

The Braves' 101-win regular season led only to more postseason frustration, and they complained bitterly about umpire Eric Gregg's ball-strike calls in the Hernandez game. They've qualified for the playoffs every year since their worst-to-first fairy tale in 1991, but won the World Series only in 1995.

Particularly galling for the Braves was the fact that they finished nine games ahead of the wild-card Marlins in the NL East. But they lost eight of 12 games to Florida during the regular season, and couldn't find a way to win the LCS despite outplaying their opponent in many departments. They outhit the Marlins .253-.199, outhomered them 6-1 and their ERA was lower, 2.60-3.57.

But they didn't win in the mistakes-at-bad-times department.

Hernandez was named the series MVP, but it was Brown who completed the swim for the Marlins. Just four days after it was his stomach that was swimming.

MORRIS FOSTOFF

Playoff win not enough
Atlanta's Denny Neagle won 20 games and shut out the Marlins in the NLCS

Closer Than It Looked

Both of the Division Series were sweeps, but the games were close.

The Marlins won the first two games over the Giants in the bottom of the ninth, on RBI singles by shortstop Edgar Renteria in Game One and Alou in Game Two. Alou's grand slam and Fernandez' good pitching gave Florida a 6-2 win in the clincher.

In Game One of the Braves-Astros series, Atlanta managed only two hits but won 2-1. Maddux scattered seven hits in a complete game, and Houston's only run scored on a single by pitcher Darryl Kile.

The Braves routed the Astros in the second game, then rode the three-hit pitching of Smoltz to a 4-1 win in the third. Houston stars Jeff Bagwell and Craig Biggio each went 1-for-12 as the Astros scored five

NATIONAL LEAGUE YEAR-BY-YEAR BATTING LEADERS

Year	Batting Average		Home Runs		RBIs	
1901	Jesse Burkett, St. Louis	.382	Sam Crawford, Cincinnati	16	Honus Wagner, Pittsburgh	126
1902	Ginger Beaumont, Pitt.	.357	Tom Leach, Pittsburgh	6	Honus Wagner, Pittsburgh	91
1903	Honus Wagner, Pitt.	.355	Jim Sheckard, Brooklyn	9	Sam Mertes, New York	104
1904	Honus Wagner, Pitt.	.349	Harry Lumley, Brooklyn	9	Bill Dahlen, New York	80
1905	Cy Seymour, Cincinnati	.377	Fred Odwell, Cincinnati	9	Cy Seymour, Cincinnati	121
1906	Honus Wagner, Pitt.	.339	Tim Jordan, Brooklyn	12	2 tied at	83
1907	Honus Wagner, Pitt.	.350	Dave Brain, Boston	10	Sherry Magee, Philadelphia	85
1908	Honus Wagner, Pitt.	.354	Tim Jordan, Brooklyn	12	Honus Wagner, Pittsburgh	109
1909	Honus Wagner, Pitt.	.339	Red Murray, New York	7	Honus Wagner, Pittsburgh	100
1910	Sherry Magee, Phil.	.331	2 tied at	10	Sherry Magee, Philadelphia	123
1911	Honus Wagner, Pitt.	.334	Wildfire Schulte, Chicago	21	Wildfire Schulte, Chicago	121
1912	Heinie Zimmerman, Chi.	.372	Heinie Zimmerman, Chicago	14	Heinie Zimmerman, Chi.	103
1913	Jake Daubert, Brooklyn	.350	Gavvy Cravath, Philadelphia	19	Gavvy Cravath, Phil.	128
1914	Jake Daubert, Brooklyn	.329	Gavvy Cravath, Philadelphia	19	Sherry Magee, Phil.	103
1915	Larry Doyle, New York	.320	Gavvy Cravath, Philadelphia	24	Gavvy Cravath, Phil.	115
1916	Hal Chase, Cincinnati	.339	2 tied at	12	Heinie Zimmerman, Chi.-N.Y.	83
1917	Edd Roush, Cincinnati	.341	2 tied at	12	Heinie Zimmerman, N.Y.	102
1918	Zack Wheat, Brooklyn	.335	Gavvy Cravath, Philadelphia	8	Sherry Magee, Cincinnati	76
1919	Edd Roush, Cincinnati	.321	Gavvy Cravath, Philadelphia	12	Hy Myers, Brooklyn	73
1920	Rogers Hornsby, St.L	.370	Cy Williams, Philadelphia	15	2 tied at	94
1921	Rogers Hornsby, St.L	.397	George Kelly, New York	23	Rogers Hornsby, St. Louis	126
1922	Rogers Hornsby, St.L	.401	Rogers Hornsby, St. Louis	42	Rogers Hornsby, St. Louis	155
1923	Rogers Hornsby, St.L	.384	Cy Williams, Philadelphia	41	Emil Meusel, New York	125
1924	Rogers Hornsby, St.L	.424	Jack Fournier, Brooklyn	27	George Kelly, New York	136
1925	Rogers Hornsby, St.L	.403	Rogers Hornsby, St. Louis	39	Rogers Hornsby, St. Louis	143
1926	Bubbles Hargrave, Cinc.	.353	Hack Wilson, Chicago	21	Jim Bottomley, St. Louis	120
1927	Paul Waner, Pittsburgh	.380	2 tied at	30	Paul Waner, Pittsburgh	131
1928	Rogers Hornsby, St.L	.370	2 tied at	31	Jim Bottomley, St. Louis	136
1929	Lefty ODoul, Philadelphia	.398	Chuck Klein, Philadelphia	43	Hack Wilson, Chicago	159
1930	Bill Terry, New York	.401	Hack Wilson, Chicago	56	Hack Wilson, Chicago	190
1931	Chick Hafey, St. Louis	.349	Chuck Klein, Philadelphia	31	Chuck Klein, Philadelphia	121
1932	Lefty ODoul, Brooklyn	.368	2 tied at	38	Frank Hurst, Philadelphia	143
1933	Chuck Klein, Philadelphia	.368	Chuck Klein, Philadelphia	28	Chuck Klein, Philadelphia	120
1934	Paul Waner, Pittsburgh	.362	2 tied at	35	Mel Ott, New York	135
1935	Arky Vaughan, Pittsburgh	.385	Wally Berger, Boston	34	Wally Berger, Boston	130
1936	Paul Waner, Pittsburgh	.373	Mel Ott, New York	33	Joe Medwick, St. Louis	138
1937	Joe Medwick, St. Louis	.374	2 tied at	31	Joe Medwick, St. Louis	154
1938	Ernie Lombardi, Cinc.	.342	Mel Ott, New York	36	Joe Medwick, St. Louis	122
1939	Johnny Mize, St. Louis	.349	Johnny Mize, St. Louis	28	Frank McCormick, Cinc.	128
1940	Debs Garms, Pittsburgh	.355	Johnny Mize, St. Louis	43	Johnny Mize, St. Louis	137
1941	Pete Reiser, Brooklyn	.343	Dolf Camilli, Brooklyn	34	Dolf Camilli, Brooklyn	120
1942	Ernie Lombardi, Boston	.330	Mel Ott, New York	30	Johnny Mize, New York	110
1943	Stan Musial, St. Louis	.357	Bill Nicholson, Chicago	29	Bill Nicholson, Chicago	128
1944	Dixie Walker, Brooklyn	.357	Bill Nicholson, Chicago	33	Bill Nicholson, Chicago	122
1945	Phil Cavarretta, Chicago	.355	Tommy Holmes, Boston	28	Dixie Walker, Brooklyn	124
1946	Stan Musial, St. Louis	.365	Ralph Kiner, Pittsburgh	23	Enos Slaughter, St. Louis	130
1947	Harry Walker, St.L-Phil.	.363	2 tied at	51	Johnny Mize, New York	138
1948	Stan Musial, St. Louis	.376	2 tied at	40	Stan Musial, St. Louis	131
1949	Jackie Robinson, Brook.	.342	Ralph Kiner, Pittsburgh	54	Ralph Kiner, Pittsburgh	127
1950	Stan Musial, St. Louis	.346	Ralph Kiner, Pittsburgh	47	Del Ennis, Philadelphia	126
1951	Stan Musial, St. Louis	.355	Ralph Kiner, Pittsburgh	42	Monte Irvin, New York	121
1952	Stan Musial, St. Louis	.336	2 tied at	37	Hank Sauer, Chicago	121
1953	Carl Furillo, Brooklyn	.344	Eddie Mathews, Milwaukee	47	Roy Campanella, Brooklyn	142
1954	Willie Mays, New York	.345	Ted Kluszewski, Cincinnati	49	Ted Kluszewski, Cincinnati	141
1955	Richie Ashburn, Phil.	.338	Willie Mays, New York	51	Duke Snider, Brooklyn	136
1956	Hank Aaron, Milwaukee	.328	Duke Snider, Brooklyn	43	Stan Musial, St. Louis	109
1957	Stan Musial, St. Louis	.351	Hank Aaron, Milwaukee	44	Hank Aaron, Milwaukee	132
1958	Richie Ashburn, Phil.	.350	Ernie Banks, Chicago	47	Ernie Banks, Chicago	129
1959	Hank Aaron, Milwaukee	.355	Eddie Mathews, Milwaukee	46	Ernie Banks, Chicago	143
1960	Dick Groat, Pittsburgh	.325	Ernie Banks, Chicago	41	Hank Aaron, Milwaukee	126
1961	Roberto Clemente, Pitt.	.351	Orlando Cepeda, San Fran.	46	Orlando Cepeda, San Fran.	142
1962	Tommy Davis, L.A.	.346	Willie Mays, San Francisco	49	Tommy Davis, Los Angeles	153
1963	Tommy Davis, L.A.	.326	2 tied at	44	Hank Aaron, Milwaukee	130
1964	Roberto Clemente, Pitt.	.339	Willie Mays, San Francisco	47	Ken Boyer, St. Louis	119
1965	Roberto Clemente, Pitt.	.329	Willie Mays, San Francisco	52	Deron Johnson, Cincinnati	130
1966	Matty Alou, Pittsburgh	.342	Hank Aaron, Atlanta	44	Hank Aaron, Atlanta	127
1967	Roberto Clemente, Pitt.	.357	Hank Aaron, Atlanta	39	Orlando Cepeda, San Fran.	111
1968	Pete Rose, Cincinnati	.335	Willie McCovey, San Fran.	36	Willie McCovey, San Fran.	105
1969	Pete Rose, Cincinnati	.348	Willie McCovey, San Fran.	45	Willie McCovey, San Fran.	126
1970	Rico Carty, Atlanta	.366	Johnny Bench, Cincinnati	45	Johnny Bench, Cincinnati	148
1971	Joe Torre, St. Louis	.363	Willie Stargell, Pittsburgh	48	Joe Torre, St. Louis	137
1972	Billy Williams, Chicago	.333	Johnny Bench, Cincinnati	40	Johnny Bench, Cincinnati	125
1973	Pete Rose, Cincinnati	.338	Willie Stargell, Pittsburgh	44	Willie Stargell, Pittsburgh	119
1974	Ralph Garr, Atlanta	.353	Mike Schmidt, Philadelphia	36	Johnny Bench, Cincinnati	129
1975	Bill Madlock, Chicago	.354	Mike Schmidt, Philadelphia	38	Greg Luzinski, Philadelphia	120
1976	Bill Madlock, Chicago	.339	Mike Schmidt, Philadelphia	38	George Foster, Cincinnati	121
1977	Dave Parker, Pittsburgh	.338	George Foster, Cincinnati	52	George Foster, Cincinnati	149
1978	Dave Parker, Pittsburgh	.334	George Foster, Cincinnati	40	George Foster, Cincinnati	120
1979	Keith Hernandez, St.L	.344	Dave Kingman, Chicago	48	Dave Winfield, San Diego	118
1980	Bill Buckner, Chicago	.324	Mike Schmidt, Philadelphia	48	Mike Schmidt, Philadelphia	121
1981	Bill Madlock, Pittsburgh	.341	Mike Schmidt, Philadelphia	31	Mike Schmidt, Philadelphia	91
1982	Al Oliver, Montreal	.331	Dave Kingman, New York	37	2 tied at	109
1983	Bill Madlock, Pittsburgh	.323	Mike Schmidt, Philadelphia	40	Dale Murphy, Atlanta	121
1984	Tony Gwynn, San Diego	.351	2 tied at	36	2 tied at	106
1985	Willie McGee, St. Louis	.353	Dale Murphy, Atlanta	37	Dave Parker, Cincinnati	125
1986	Tim Raines, Montreal	.334	Mike Schmidt, Philadelphia	37	Mike Schmidt, Philadelphia	119
1987	Tony Gwynn, San Diego	.370	Andre Dawson, Chicago	49	Andre Dawson, Chicago	137
1988	Tony Gwynn, San Diego	.313	Darryl Strawberry, New York	39	Will Clark, San Francisco	109
1989	Tony Gwynn, San Diego	.336	Kevin Mitchell, S.F.	47	Kevin Mitchell, S.F.	125
1990	Willie McGee, St. Louis	.335	Ryne Sandberg, Chicago	40	Matt Williams, S.F.	122
1991	Terry Pendleton, Atlanta	.319	Howard Johnson, New York	38	Howard Johnson, New York	117
1992	Gary Sheffield, S.D.	.330	Fred McGriff, San Diego	35	Darren Daulton, Phil.	109
1993	Andres Galarraga, Colo.	.370	Barry Bonds, San Francisco	46	Barry Bonds, S.F.	123
1994	Tony Gwynn, San Diego	.394	Matt Williams, S.F.	43	Jeff Bagwell, Houston	116
1995	Tony Gwynn, San Diego	.368	Dante Bichette, Colorado	40	Dante Bichette, Colorado	128
1996	Tony Gwynn, San Diego	.353	Andres Galarraga, Colorado	47	Andres Galarraga, Colorado	150
1997	Tony Gwynn, San Diego	.372	Larry Walker, Colorado	49	Andres Galarraga, Colorado	140

NATIONAL LEAGUE YEAR-BY-YEAR PITCHING LEADERS

Year	Wins		ERA		Strikeouts	
1901	Bill Donovan, Brooklyn	25	Jesse Tannehill, Pittsburgh	2.18	Noodles Hahn, Cin.	233
1902	Jack Chesbro, Pittsburgh	28	Jack Taylor, Chicago	1.33	Vic Willis, Boston	226
1903	Joe McGinnity, New York	31	Sam Leever, Pittsburgh	2.06	Christy Mathewson, N.Y.	267
1904	Joe McGinnity, New York	35	Joe McGinnity, New York	1.61	Christy Mathewson, N.Y.	212
1905	Christy Mathewson, N.Y.	32	Christy Mathewson, N.Y.	1.27	Christy Mathewson, N.Y.	206
1906	Joe McGinnity, New York	27	Mordecai Brown, Chicago	1.04	Fred Beebe, Chi.-St.L	171
1907	Christy Mathewson, N.Y.	24	Jack Pfiester, Chicago	1.15	Christy Mathewson, N.Y.	178
1908	Christy Mathewson, N.Y.	37	Christy Mathewson, N.Y.	1.43	Christy Mathewson, N.Y.	259
1909	Mordecai Brown, Chicago	27	Christy Mathewson, N.Y.	1.14	Orval Overall, Chicago	205
1910	Christy Mathewson, N.Y.	27	George McQuillan, Phil.	1.60	Christy Mathewson, N.Y.	190
1911	Grover Alexander, Phil.	28	Christy Mathewson, N.Y.	1.99	Rube Marquard, New York	237
1912	2 tied at	26	Jeff Tesreau, New York	1.96	Grover Alexander, Phil.	195
1913	Tom Seaton, Philadelphia	27	Christy Mathewson, N.Y.	2.06	Tom Seaton, Philadelphia	168
1914	2 tied at	27	Bill Doak, St. Louis.	1.72	Grover Alexander, Phil.	214
1915	Grover Alexander, Phil.	31	Grover Alexander, Phil.	1.22	Grover Alexander, Phil.	241
1916	Grover Alexander, Phil.	33	Grover Alexander, Phil.	1.55	Grover Alexander, Phil.	167
1917	Grover Alexander, Phil.	30	Grover Alexander, Phil.	1.85	Grover Alexander, Phil.	200
1918	Hippo Vaughn, Chicago	22	Hippo Vaughn, Chicago	1.74	Hippo Vaughn, Chicago	148
1919	Jesse Barnes, New York	25	Grover Alexander, Chicago	1.72	Hippo Vaughn, Chicago	141
1920	Grover Alexander, Chicago	27	Grover Alexander, Chicago	1.91	Grover Alexander, Chicago	173
1921	2 tied at	22	Bill Doak, St. Louis	2.58	Burleigh Grimes, Brooklyn	136
1922	Eppa Rixey, Cincinnati	25	Rosy Ryan, New York	3.00	Dazzy Vance, Brooklyn	134
1923	Dolf Luque, Cincinnati	27	Dolf Luque, Cincinnati	1.93	Dazzy Vance, Brooklyn	197
1924	Dazzy Vance, Brooklyn	28	Dazzy Vance, Brooklyn	2.16	Dazzy Vance, Brooklyn	262
1925	Dazzy Vance, Brooklyn	22	Dolf Luque, Cincinnati	2.63	Dazzy Vance, Brooklyn	221
1926	4 tied at	20	Ray Kremer, Pittsburgh	2.61	Dazzy Vance, Brooklyn	140
1927	Charlie Root, Chicago	26	Ray Kremer, Pittsburgh	2.47	Dazzy Vance, Brooklyn	184
1928	2 tied at	25	Dazzy Vance, Brooklyn	2.09	Dazzy Vance, Brooklyn	200
1929	Pat Malone, Chicago	22	Bill Walker, New York	3.08	Pat Malone, Chicago	166
1930	2 tied at	20	Dazzy Vance, Brooklyn	2.61	Bill Hallahan, St. Louis	177
1931	3 tied at	19	Bill Walker, New York	2.26	Bill Hallahan, St. Louis	159
1932	Lon Warneke, Chicago	22	Lon Warneke, Chicago	2.37	Dizzy Dean, St. Louis	191
1933	Carl Hubbell, New York	23	Carl Hubbell, New York	1.66	Dizzy Dean, St. Louis	199
1934	Dizzy Dean, St. Louis	30	Carl Hubbell, New York	2.30	Dizzy Dean, St. Louis	195
1935	Dizzy Dean, St. Louis	28	Cy Blanton, Pittsburgh	2.59	Dizzy Dean, St. Louis	182
1936	Carl Hubbell, New York	26	Carl Hubbell, New York	2.31	Van Lingle Mungo, Brooklyn	238
1937	Carl Hubbell, New York	22	Jim Turner, Boston	2.38	Carl Hubbell, New York	159
1938	Bill Lee, Chicago	22	Bill Lee, Chicago	2.66	Clay Bryant, Chicago	135
1939	Bucky Walters, Cincinnati	27	Bucky Walters, Cincinnati	2.29	2 tied at	137
1940	Bucky Walters, Cincinnati	22	Bucky Walters, Cincinnati	2.48	Kirby Higbe, Philadelphia	137
1941	2 tied at	22	Elmer Riddle, Cincinnati	2.24	Johnny Vander Meer, Cin.	202
1942	Mort Cooper, St. Louis	22	Mort Cooper, St. Louis	1.77	Johnny Vander Meer, Cin.	186
1943	3 tied at	21	Howie Pollet, St. Louis	1.75	Johnny Vander Meer, Cin.	174
1944	Bucky Walters, Cincinnati	23	Ed Heusser, Cincinnati	2.38	Bill Voiselle, New York	161
1945	Red Barrett, Bos.-St.L.	23	Hank Borowy, Chicago	2.14	Preacher Roe, Pittsburgh	148
1946	Howie Pollet, St. Louis	21	Howie Pollet, St. Louis	2.10	John Schmitz, Chicago	135
1947	Ewell Blackwell, Cincinnati	22	Warren Spahn, Boston	2.33	Ewell Blackwell, Cincinnati	193
1948	Johnny Sain, Boston	24	Harry Brecheen, St. Louis	2.24	Harry Brecheen, St. Louis	149
1949	Warren Spahn, Boston	21	Dave Koslo, New York	2.50	Warren Spahn, Boston	151
1950	Warren Spahn, Boston	21	Jim Hearn, St.L.-N.Y.	2.49	Warren Spahn, Boston	191
1951	2 tied at	23	Chet Nichols, Boston	2.88	2 tied at	164
1952	Robin Roberts, Phil.	28	Hoyt Wilhelm, New York	2.43	Warren Spahn, Boston	183
1953	2 tied at	23	Warren Spahn, Milwaukee	2.10	Robin Roberts, Philadelphia	198
1954	Robin Roberts, Phil.	23	John Antonelli, New York	2.29	Robin Roberts, Philadelphia	185
1955	Robin Roberts, Phil.	23	Bob Friend, Pittsburgh	2.84	Sam Jones, Chicago	198
1956	Don Newcombe, Brooklyn	27	Lew Burdette, Milwaukee	2.71	Sam Jones, Chicago	176
1957	Warren Spahn, Milwaukee	21	Johnny Podres, Brooklyn	2.66	Jack Sanford, Philadelphia	188
1958	2 tied	22	Stu Miller, San Francisco	2.47	Sam Jones, St. Louis	225
1959	3 tied at	21	Sam Jones, S.F.	2.82	Don Drysdale, L.A.	242
1960	2 tied at	21	Mike McCormick, S.F.	2.70	Don Drysdale, L.A.	246
1961	2 tied at	21	Warren Spahn, Milwaukee	3.01	Sandy Koufax, L.A.	269
1962	Don Drysdale, Los Angeles	25	Sandy Koufax, L.A.	2.54	Don Drysdale, L.A.	232
1963	2 tied at	25	Sandy Koufax, L.A.	1.88	Sandy Koufax, L.A.	306
1964	Larry Jackson, Chicago	24	Sandy Koufax, L.A.	1.74	Bob Veale, Pittsburgh	250
1965	Sandy Koufax, L.A.	26	Sandy Koufax, L.A.	2.04	Sandy Koufax, Los Angeles	382
1966	Sandy Koufax, L.A.	27	Sandy Koufax, L.A.	1.73	Sandy Koufax, Los Angeles	317
1967	Mike McCormick, S.F.	22	Phil Niekro, Atlanta	1.87	Jim Bunning, Philadelphia	253
1968	Juan Marichal, San Fran.	26	Bob Gibson, St. Louis	1.12	Bob Gibson, St. Louis	268
1969	Tom Seaver, New York	25	Juan Marichal, San Fran.	2.10	Ferguson Jenkins, Chicago	273
1970	2 tied at	23	Tom Seaver, New York	2.81	Tom Seaver, New York	283
1971	Ferguson Jenkins, Chicago	24	Tom Seaver, New York	1.76	Tom Seaver, New York	289
1972	Steve Carlton, Phil.	27	Steve Carlton, Phil.	1.98	Steve Carlton, Phil.	310
1973	Ron Bryant, San Francisco	24	Tom Seaver, New York	2.08	Tom Seaver, New York	251
1974	2 tied at	20	Buzz Capra, Atlanta	2.28	Steve Carlton, Phil.	240
1975	Tom Seaver, New York	23	Randy Jones, San Diego	2.24	Tom Seaver, New York	243
1976	Randy Jones, San Diego	22	John Denny, St. Louis	2.52	Tom Seaver, New York	235
1977	Steve Carlton, Phil.	23	John Candelaria, Pitt.	2.34	Phil Niekro, Atlanta	252
1978	Gaylord Perry, San Diego	21	Craig Swan, New York	2.43	J.R. Richard, Houston	303
1979	2 tied at	21	J.R. Richard, Houston	2.71	J.R. Richard, Houston	313
1980	Steve Carlton, Phil.	24	Don Sutton, Los Angeles	2.21	Steve Carlton, Phil.	286
1981	Tom Seaver, Cincinnati	14	Nolan Ryan, Houston	1.69	Fernando Valenzuela, L.A.	180
1982	Steve Carlton, Phil.	23	Steve Rogers, Montreal	2.40	Steve Carlton, Phil.	286
1983	John Denny, Phil.	19	Atlee Hammaker, S.F.	2.25	Steve Carlton, Phil.	275
1984	Joaquin Andujar, St. Louis	20	Alejandro Pena, L.A.	2.48	Dwight Gooden, New York	276
1985	Dwight Gooden, New York	24	Dwight Gooden, New York	1.53	Dwight Gooden, New York	268
1986	Fernando Valenzuela, L.A.	21	Mike Scott, Houston	2.22	Mike Scott, Houston	306
1987	Rick Sutcliffe, Chicago	18	Nolan Ryan, Houston	2.76	Nolan Ryan, Houston	270
1988	2 tied at	23	Joe Magrane, St. Louis	2.18	Nolan Ryan, Houston	228
1989	Mike Scott, Houston	20	Scott Garrelts, San Fran.	2.28	Jose DeLeon, St. Louis	201
1990	Doug Drabek, Pittsburgh	22	Danny Darwin, Houston	2.21	David Cone, New York	233
1991	2 tied at	20	Dennis Martinez, Mon.	2.39	David Cone, New York	241
1992	2 tied at	20	Bill Swift, San Francisco	2.08	John Smoltz, Atlanta	215
1993	2 tied at	22	Greg Maddux, Atlanta	2.36	Jose Rijo, Cincinnati	227
1994	2 tied at	16	Greg Maddux, Atlanta	1.56	Andy Benes, San Diego	189
1995	Greg Maddux, Atlanta	19	Greg Maddux, Atlanta	1.63	Hideo Nomo, Los Angeles	236
1996	John Smoltz, Atlanta	24	Kevin Brown, Florida	1.89	John Smoltz, Atlanta	276
1997	Denny Neagle, Atlanta	20	Pedro Martinez, Montreal	1.90	Curt Schilling, Philadelphia	319

runs in three games.

Good Pitching, Good Hitting

Just a year after one of the most explosive offensive seasons in history, NL pitchers reasserted themselves somewhat in 1997.

No less than six players waged a spirited battle for the Cy Young Award. Two, the Phillies' Curt Schilling and the Expos' Pedro Martinez, topped 300 strikeouts, something no NL pitcher had done since Mike Scott in 1986.

Neagle was the leading winner with 20 victories, Maddux was his usual dominating self and Martinez had a 1.90 ERA and a .184 batting average against. Schilling went 17-11 for a last-place team. Kile was 19-7, 2.57 and was the closest thing to a playoff hero the Astros had. The Giants' Shawn Estes went 19-5, 3.18.

Pedro Martinez

Still, it's not like the hitters disappeared. Rockies right fielder Larry Walker had a season for the ages, batting .366 with 49 homers, 130 RBIs and 33 stolen bases and doing most of his damage away from hitter-friendly Coors Field.

"He's having a year every player in this game dreams about," said Padres outfielder Tony Gwynn, who won his eight NL batting title and fourth straight. "What more could a guy possibly do?"

Yet Walker wasn't a clear-cut winner as league MVP. Cases were made for teammate Andres Galarraga (.318-41-140), Dodgers catcher Mike Piazza (.362-40-124) and Bagwell (.286-43-135).

Those Lovable Pirates

The Astros won a mediocre NL Central with a hot streak after the all-star break, but it was their closest pursuer, the Pirates, who provided the feel-good story of the year.

MORRIS FOSTOFF

San Diego's Tony Gwynn
Wins eighth batting title

Pittsburgh's umpteenth rebuilding program brought about an almost complete removal of veterans during and after the 1996 season. Even the manager, Leyland, left for greener pastures in Miami.

The Pirates predictably finished below .500, but only four games below. And in the Central, that was enough to keep them in first place some of the time and in the race until the final week.

They did it with a bargain-basement payroll of $9 million and a roster of young no-names. Probably the biggest stars were closer Rich Loiselle, a former Astros farmhand who saved 29 games, and

NATIONAL LEAGUE ALL-STARS

Selected by Baseball America

Pos.	Player, Team	B-T	Ht.	Wt.	Age	'97 Salary	AVG	AB	R	H	2B	3B	HR	RBI	SB
C	Mike Piazza, Los Angeles	R-R	6-3	220	29	$7,000,000	.362	556	104	201	32	1	40	124	5
1B	Jeff Bagwell, Houston	R-R	6-0	195	29	8,015,000	.286	566	109	162	40	2	43	135	31
2B	Craig Biggio, Houston	R-R	5-11	180	31	6,180,000	.309	619	146	191	37	8	22	81	47
3B	Chipper Jones, Atlanta	S-R	6-3	195	25	1,500,000	.295	597	100	176	41	3	21	111	20
SS	Jeff Blauser, Atlanta	R-R	6-1	180	31	3,500,000	.308	519	90	160	31	4	17	70	5
OF	Barry Bonds, San Francisco	L-L	6-1	185	33	8,666,667	.291	532	123	155	26	5	40	101	37
	Tony Gwynn, San Diego	L-L	5-11	210	37	4,000,000	.372	592	97	220	49	2	17	119	12
	Larry Walker, Colorado	L-R	6-2	185	30	5,750,000	.366	568	143	208	46	4	49	130	33
							W	**L**	**ERA**	**G**	**SV**	**IP**	**H**	**BB**	**SO**
P	Darryl Kile, Houston	R-R	6-5	185	28	1,700,000	19	7	2.57	34	0	256	208	94	205
	Greg Maddux, Atlanta	R-R	6-0	175	31	6,500,000	19	4	2.20	33	0	233	200	20	177
	Pedro Martinez, Montreal	R-R	5-11	150	26	3,500,000	17	8	1.90	31	0	241	158	67	305
	Curt Schilling, Philadelphia	R-R	6-4	215	30	3,500,000	17	11	2.97	35	0	254	208	58	319
RP	Rod Beck, San Francisco	R-R	6-1	236	29	2,933,380	7	4	3.47	73	37	70	67	8	53

Player of the Year: Larry Walker, of, Colorado. **Pitcher of the Year:** Pedro Martinez, rhp, Montreal. **Rookie of the Year:** Scott Rolen, 3b, Philadelphia.

Manager of the Year: Dusty Baker, San Francisco. **Executive of the Year:** Brian Sabean, San Francisco.

righthander Francisco Cordova, a Mexican League find who went 11-8, 3.63.

"I guess people are learning our players' names," said manager Gene Lamont, Leyland's hand-picked successor. "Hey, we didn't want these guys to be unknowns or our payroll to be $9 million forever. We want them to show us they're big league players."

That much, they did.

Giants Of Men

The Giants were nearly as surprising as the Pirates, and did them one better by winning the West.

Most observers thought general manager Brian Sabean had taken leave of his senses when, shortly after the '96 season, he traded star third baseman Matt Williams to the Indians for righthanders Julian Tavarez and Joe Roa and infielders Jeff Kent and Jose Vizcaino.

"I am not an idiot," Sabean declared at the time.

Turns out he wasn't. The players from the Williams trade, plus other Sabean acquisitions like first baseman J.T. Snow, infielder Mark Lewis and outfielder Darryl Hamilton, were gamers. The pitching, led by Estes, was better than anyone expected. Barry Bonds overcame a slow start to hit .291 with 40 homers, 101 RBIs and 37 steals.

And then shortly before the July 31 trade deadline, Sabean made the deal of the year. He traded a package of minor leaguers to the White Sox for major league pitchers Wilson Alvarez, Danny Darwin and Roberto Hernandez. He also acquired catcher Brian Johnson in a trade with Detroit. Johnson responded with a couple of critical game-winning home runs down the stretch, including one in the 12th inning that sunk the Dodgers, the Giants' closest pursuers.

Hernandez was by far the most effective, but Alvarez ate innings down the stretch and the trade put the Giants over the top. They eliminated the Dodgers on the final weekend of the season.

Odds And Ends

■ The other deal of the year also occurred just before the July 31 deadline, when the Cardinals acquired first baseman Mark McGwire from the Athletics.

The trade involved considerable risk, because McGwire was eligible for free agency after the season, and the Cardinals gave up promising pitchers Eric Ludwick, T.J. Mathews and Blake Stein. But a warm reception from St. Louis fans—and $32 million over four years—persuaded McGwire to sign with the Cards.

"It makes me float every time I come to the ballpark and play in front of these fans," McGwire said. "I've never been treated this way as a ballplayer."

■ The 1997 season was the final one for Cubs second baseman Ryne Sandberg and Dodgers outfielder Brett Butler, who retired when it was over.

Sandberg had retired before, midway through the 1994 season, and sat out a year before coming back to play two more. He leaves as the all-time leader among second basemen in home runs and fielding percentage, and is a likely Hall of Famer.

Butler probably will be best remembered for battling through throat cancer in his next-to-last season, and returning to play late in the year. His last season was a disappointment, as he warmed the bench while the Dodgers failed to catch the Giants.

■ The Phillies made a change at the top in midseason, when Bill Giles stepped aside as team president in favor of Dave Montgomery. Giles remained as chairman, leading the effort for a new ballpark. Montgomery, who was groomed as Giles' successor for several years, will handle day-to-day operations.

■ The Mets fired general manager Joe McIlvaine in July, even as the team contended for the wild-card playoff spot. Despite the team's resurgence, McIlvaine was the loser in a running dispute with owner Fred Wilpon.

Steve Phillips became the ninth GM in Mets history and at 34 the second-youngest in the big leagues, behind the Tigers' Randy Smith.

■ The Reds fired manager Ray Knight, also in July, after his own running dispute with several players.

Cincinnati surprised everyone by naming Jack

NL: BEST TOOLS

A Baseball America survey of National League managers, conducted at midseason 1997, ranked NL players with the best tools:

BEST HITTER
1. Tony Gwynn, Padres
2. Larry Walker, Rockies
3. Mike Piazza, Dodgers

BEST POWER HITTER
1. Jeff Bagwell, Astros
2. Andres Galarraga, Rockies
3. Barry Bonds, Giants

BEST BUNTER
1. Brett Butler, Dodgers
2. Kenny Lofton, Braves
3. Steve Finley, Padres

BEST HIT-AND-RUN ARTIST
1. Tony Gwynn, Padres
2. Barry Larkin, Reds
3. Craig Biggio, Astros

BEST BASERUNNER
1. Kenny Lofton, Braves
2. Larry Walker, Rockies
3. Barry Larkin, Reds

FASTEST BASERUNNER
1. Deion Sanders, Reds
2. Kenny Lofton, Braves
3. Tony Womack, Pirates

BEST PITCHER
1. Greg Maddux, Braves
2. Pedro Martinez, Expos
3. Kevin Brown, Marlins

BEST FASTBALL
1. Mark Wohlers, Braves
2. Robb Nen, Marlins
3. Pedro Martinez, Expos

BEST CURVEBALL
1. Darryl Kile, Astros
2. Bobby Jones, Mets
3. Pedro Martinez, Expos

BEST SLIDER
1. John Smoltz, Braves
2. Kevin Brown, Marlins
3. Al Leiter, Marlins

BEST CHANGEUP
1. Greg Maddux, Braves
2. Tom Glavine, Braves
3. Pedro Martinez, Expos

BEST CONTROL
1. Greg Maddux, Braves
2. Tom Glavine, Braves
3. Bobby Jones, Mets

BEST PICKOFF MOVE
1. Armando Reynoso, Mets
2. Terry Mulholland, Cubs
3. Jeremi Gonzalez, Cubs

BEST RELIEVER
1. Mark Wohlers, Braves
2. Rod Beck, Giants
3. Billy Wagner, Astros

BEST DEFENSIVE C
1. Charles Johnson, Marlins
2. Brad Ausmus, Astros
3. Todd Hundley, Mets

BEST DEFENSIVE 1B
1. Mark Grace, Cubs
2. Andres Galarraga, Rockies
3. J.T. Snow, Giants

BEST DEFENSIVE 2B
1. Craig Biggio, Astros
2. Mike Lansing, Expos
3. Mark Lemke, Braves

BEST DEFENSIVE 3B
1. Ken Caminiti, Padres
2. Chipper Jones, Braves
3. Edgardo Alfonso, Mets

BEST DEFENSIVE SS
1. Barry Larkin, Reds
2. Mark Grudzielanek, Expos
3. Walt Weiss, Rockies

BEST INFIELD ARM
1. Ken Caminiti, Padres
2. Shawon Dunston, Cubs
3. Edgar Renteria, Marlins

BEST DEFENSIVE OF
1. Kenny Lofton, Braves
2. Barry Bonds, Giants
3. Steve Finley, Padres

BEST OF ARM
1. Raul Mondesi, Dodgers
2. Alex Ochoa, Mets
3. Sammy Sosa, Cubs

MOST EXCITING PLAYER
1. Kenny Lofton, Braves
2. Larry Walker, Rockies
3. Barry Bonds, Giants

BEST MANAGER
1. Jim Leyland, Marlins
2. Bobby Cox, Braves
3. Felipe Alou, Expos

Major Leagues

NATIONAL LEAGUE
DEPARTMENT LEADERS

BATTING

GAMES
Jeff Bagwell, Houston 162
Craig Biggio, Houston 162
Eric Karros, Los Angeles 162
Sammy Sosa, Chicago 162
Todd Zeile, Los Angeles 160

AT-BATS
Mark Grudzielanek, Montreal 649
Sammy Sosa, Chicago 642
Tony Womack, Pittsburgh 641
Eric Karros, Los Angeles 628
Eric Young, Colo./Los Angeles 622

RUNS
Craig Biggio, Houston 146
Larry Walker, Colorado 143
Barry Bonds, San Francisco 123
Andres Galarraga, Colorado 120
Jeff Bagwell, Houston 109

HITS
Tony Gwynn, San Diego 220
Larry Walker, Colorado 208
Mike Piazza, Los Angeles 201
Craig Biggio, Houston 191
Andres Galarraga, Colorado 191
Raul Mondesi, Los Angeles 191

TOTAL BASES
Larry Walker, Colorado 409
Mike Piazza, Los Angeles 355
Andres Galarraga, Colorado 351
Jeff Bagwell, Houston 335
Vinny Castilla, Colorado 335

EXTRA-BASE HITS
Larry Walker, Colorado 99
Jeff Bagwell, Houston 85
Raul Mondesi, Los Angeles 77
Andres Galarraga, Colorado 75
Mike Piazza, Los Angeles 73

SINGLES
Tony Gwynn, San Diego 152
Edgar Renteria, Florida 143
Tony Womack, Pittsburgh 137
Kenny Lofton, Atlanta 133
Mike Piazza, Los Angeles 128

DOUBLES
Mark Grudzielanek, Montreal 54
Tony Gwynn, San Diego 49
Larry Walker, Colorado 46
Mike Lansing, Montreal 45
Raul Mondesi, Los Angeles 42

MORRIS FOSTOFF

Jeff Bagwell
43 homers, 135 RBIs

MEL BAILEY

Andres Galarraga
41 homers, 140 RBIs

TRIPLES
Delino DeShields, St. Louis 14
Neifi Perez, Colorado 10
Wilton Guerrero, Los Angeles 9
Joe Randa, Pittsburgh 9
Tony Womack, Pittsburgh 9

HOME RUNS
Larry Walker, Colorado 49
Jeff Bagwell, Houston 43
Andres Galarraga, Colorado 41
Barry Bonds, San Francisco 40
Vinny Castilla, Colorado 40
Mike Piazza, Los Angeles 40

HOME RUN RATIO
(At-Bats per Home Runs)
Larry Walker, Colorado 11.6
Jeff Bagwell, Houston 13.2
Barry Bonds, San Francisco 13.3
Mike Piazza, Los Angeles 13.9
Todd Hundley, New York 13.9

RUNS BATTED IN
Andres Galarraga, Colorado 140
Jeff Bagwell, Houston 135
Larry Walker, Colorado 130
Mike Piazza, Los Angeles 124
Jeff Kent, San Francisco 121

SACRIFICE BUNTS
Edgar Renteria, Florida 19
Tom Glavine, Atlanta 17
Brett Butler, Los Angeles 15
Rey Ordonez, New York 14
Wilton Guerrero, Los Angeles 13
Jose Vizcaino, San Francisco 13

SACRIFICE FLIES
Bernard Gilkey, New York 12
Tony Gwynn, San Diego 12
Wally Joyner, San Diego 10
Jeff Kent, San Francisco 10
Jeff Blauser, Atlanta 9
Darren Daulton, Philadelphia/Florida 9
Eric Karros, Los Angeles 9

HIT BY PITCH
Craig Biggio, Houston 34
Jason Kendall, Pittsburgh 31
F.P. Santangelo, Montreal 25
Jeff Blauser, Atlanta 20
Andres Galarraga, Colorado 17

WALKS
Barry Bonds, San Francisco 145
Jeff Bagwell, Houston 127
Gary Sheffield, Florida 121
J.T. Snow, San Francisco 96
Ray Lankford, St. Louis 95

INTENTIONAL WALKS
Barry Bonds, San Francisco 34
Jeff Bagwell, Houston 27
Todd Hundley, New York 16
Larry Walker, Colorado 14
J.T. Snow, San Francisco 13

STRIKEOUTS
Sammy Sosa, Chicago 174
Ron Gant, St. Louis 162
Henry Rodriguez, Montreal 149
Andres Galarraga, Colorado 141
Scott Rolen, Philadelphia 138

TOUGHEST TO STRIKE OUT
(Plate Appearances per SO)
Tony Gwynn, San Diego 23.3
Gregg Jefferies, Philadelphia 19.7
Mark Grace, Chicago 14.5
Eric Young, Colorado/Los Angeles 13.3
Doug Glanville, Chicago 11.1

STOLEN BASES
Tony Womack, Pittsburgh 60
Deion Sanders, Cincinnati 56
Delino DeShields, St. Louis 55
Craig Biggio, Houston 47
Eric Young, Colorado/Los Angeles 45

CAUGHT STEALING
Kenny Lofton, Atlanta 20
Raul Mondesi, Los Angeles 15
Edgar Renteria, Florida 15
Delino DeShields, St. Louis 14
Eric Young, Colorado/Los Angeles 14

GIDP
Fred McGriff, Atlanta 22
Butch Huskey, New York 21
Gary Gaetti, St. Louis 20
Royce Clayton, St. Louis 19
Chipper Jones, Atlanta 19
John Olerud, New York 19
Mike Piazza, Los Angeles 19
Rondell White, Montreal 19

HITTING STREAKS
Luis Gonzalez, Houston 23
Vinny Castilla, Colorado 22
Four tied at 20

MULTIPLE-HIT GAMES
Tony Gwynn, San Diego 67
Larry Walker, Colorado 65
Mike Piazza, Los Angeles 62
Craig Biggio, Houston 57

Craig Biggio
146 runs, 34 HBP

Eric Young, Colorado/Los Angeles 54
Chipper Jones, Atlanta 54

SLUGGING PERCENTAGE

Larry Walker, Colorado .... .720
Mike Piazza, Los Angeles .... .638
Jeff Bagwell, Houston .... .592
Andres Galarraga, Colorado .... .585
Ray Lankford, St. Louis .... .585
Barry Bonds, San Francisco .... .585

ON-BASE PERCENTAGE

Larry Walker, Colorado .... .452
Barry Bonds, San Francisco .... .446
Mike Piazza, Los Angeles .... .431
Jeff Bagwell, Houston .... .425
Gary Sheffield, Florida .... .424

PITCHING

WINS

Denny Neagle, Atlanta 20
Shawn Estes, San Francisco 19
Darryl Kile, Houston 19
Greg Maddux, Atlanta 19
Alex Fernandez, Florida 17
Pedro Martinez, Montreal 17
Curt Schilling, Philadelphia 17

LOSSES

Mark Leiter, Philadelphia 17
Steve Cooke, Pittsburgh 15
Jon Lieber, Pittsburgh 14
Terry Mulholland, Chicago/San Fran. .. 13
Carlos Perez, Montreal 13

WINNING PERCENTAGE

Greg Maddux, Atlanta .... .826
Denny Neagle, Atlanta .... .800
Shawn Estes, San Francisco .... .792
Darryl Kile, Houston .... .731
Jeff Juden, Montreal .... .688

GAMES

Julian Tavarez, San Francisco 89
Stan Belinda, Cincinnati 84
Jeff Shaw, Cincinnati 78
Mel Rojas, New York 77
Bob Patterson, Chicago 76
Jerry Spradlin, Philadelphia 76

GAMES STARTED

Curt Schilling, Philadelphia 35
John Smoltz, Atlanta 35
Mike Hampton, Houston 34
Darryl Kile, Houston 34
Denny Neagle, Atlanta 34
Steve Trachsel, Chicago 34

COMPLETE GAMES

Pedro Martinez, Montreal 13
Carlos Perez, Montreal 8
Mike Hampton, Houston 7
Curt Schilling, Philadelphia 7
John Smoltz, Atlanta 7

SHUTOUTS

Carlos Perez, Montreal 5
Pedro Martinez, Montreal 4
Denny Neagle, Atlanta 4
Darryl Kile, Houston 4
Ten tied at 2

GAMES FINISHED

Rod Beck, San Francisco 66
Robb Nen, Florida 65
Jeff Shaw, Cincinnati 62
Ricky Bottalico, Philadelphia 61
Trevor Hoffman, San Diego 59

SAVES

Jeff Shaw, Cincinnati 42
Rod Beck, San Francisco 37
Trevor Hoffman, San Diego 37
Dennis Eckersley, St. Louis 36
John Franco, New York 36

INNINGS PITCHED

John Smoltz, Atlanta 256
Darryl Kile, Houston 256
Curt Schilling, Philadelphia 254
Pedro Martinez, Montreal 241
Tom Glavine, Atlanta 240

DAVID SCHOFIELD

Curt Schilling
17 wins, 319 strikeouts

HITS ALLOWED

John Smoltz, Atlanta 234
Steve Trachsel, Chicago 225
Frank Castillo, Chicago/Colorado 220
Mike Hampton, Houston 217
Mark Leiter, Philadelphia 216

RUNS ALLOWED

Mark Leiter, Philadelphia 132
Frank Castillo, Chicago/Colorado 121
Jamey Wright, Colorado 113
Steve Trachsel, Chicago 110
Carlos Perez, Montreal 109

HOME RUNS ALLOWED

Steve Trachsel, Chicago 32
Mark Gardner, San Francisco 28
Roger Bailey, Colorado 27
Kevin Foster, Chicago 27
Matt Beech, Philadelphia 25
Frank Castillo, Chicago/Colorado 25
Alex Fernandez, Florida 25
Mark Leiter, Philadelphia 25
Curt Schilling, Philadelphia 25

WALKS

Shawn Estes, San Francisco 100
Darryl Kile, Houston 94
Hideo Nomo, Los Angeles 92
Al Leiter, Florida 91
Tom Glavine, Atlanta 79

FEWEST WALKS PER 9 INNINGS

Greg Maddux, Atlanta 0.8
Rick Reed, New York 1.3
Denny Neagle, Atlanta 1.9
Curt Schilling, Philadelphia 2.1
Carlos Perez, Montreal 2.1

HIT BATSMEN

Kevin Brown, Florida 14
Roger Bailey, Colorado 13
Jim Bullinger, Montreal 12
Joey Hamilton, San Diego 12
Al Leiter, Florida 12
Esteban Loaiza, Pittsburgh 12
Todd Stottlemyre, St. Louis 12

STRIKEOUTS

Curt Schilling, Philadelphia 319
Pedro Martinez, Montreal 305
John Smoltz, Atlanta 241
Hideo Nomo, Los Angeles 233
Kevin Brown, Florida 205
Darryl Kile, Houston 205

STRIKEOUTS PER 9 INNINGS

Pedro Martinez, Montreal 11.4
Curt Schilling, Philadelphia 11.3
Hideo Nomo, Los Angeles 10.1
Andy Benes, St. Louis 8.9
John Smoltz, Atlanta 8.5

WILD PITCHES

Mike Remlinger, Cincinnati 12
Mark Leiter, Philadelphia 11
Shawn Estes, San Francisco 10
Hideo Nomo, Los Angeles 10
John Smoltz, Atlanta 10

PICKOFFS

Roger Bailey, Colorado 7
Mike Remlinger, Cincinnati 7
Kirk Rueter, San Francisco 7
Jamey Wright, Colorado 7

BALKS

Hideo Nomo, Los Angeles 4
Pedro Astacio, Los Angeles/Colo. 3
Mark Gardner, San Francisco 3
Esteban Loaiza, Pittsburgh 3
Matt Morris, St. Louis 3
Ricardo Rincon, Pittsburgh 3
Pete Smith, San Diego 3

OPPONENTS BATTING AVERAGE

Pedro Martinez, Montreal .... .184
Chan Ho Park, Los Angeles .... .213
Shawn Estes, San Francisco .... .223
Curt Schilling, Philadelphia .... .224
Darryl Kile, Houston .... .225

FIELDING

PITCHER

PCT	Roger Bailey, Colorado 1.000
PO	Kevin Brown, Florida 36
A	Mike Hampton, Houston 57
E	Matt Morris, St. Louis 5
TC	Kevin Brown, Florida 80
DP	Roger Bailey, Colorado 7

CATCHER

PCT	Charles Johnson, Florida 1.000
PO	Mike Piazza, Los Angeles 1045
A	Jason Kendall, Pittsburgh 103
E	Mike Piazza, Los Angeles 16
TC	Mike Piazza, Los Angeles 1135
DP	Jason Kendall, Pittsburgh 20

FIRST BASE

PCT	Wally Joyner, San Diego ...... .996
PO	Andres Galarraga, Colorado 1458
A	Jeff Bagwell, Houston 137
E	Andres Galarraga, Colorado 15
TC	Andres Galarraga, Colorado 1590
DP	Andres Galarraga, Colorado .. 176

SECOND BASE

PCT	Bret Boone, Cincinnati .... .997
PO	Craig Biggio, Houston 341
A	Craig Biggio, Houston 504
E	Tony Womack, Pittsburgh 20
TC	Craig Biggio, Houston 863
DP	Eric Young, Colo./L.A. 110

THIRD BASE

PCT	Gary Gaetti, St. Louis .... .978
PO	Scott Rolen, Philadelphia 144
A	Vinny Castilla, Colorado 323
E	Todd Zeile, Los Angeles 26
TC	Scott Rolen, Philadelphia 459
DP	Vinny Castilla, Colorado 41

SHORTSTOP

PCT	Rey Ordonez, New York .... .983
PO	Edgar Renterria, Florida 242
A	Royce Clayton, St. Louis 452
E	Mark Grudzielanek, Montreal.... 32
TC	Mark Grudzielanek, Montreal.. 715
DP	Mark Grudzielanek, Montreal.... 99

OUTFIELD

PCT	Rondell White, Montreal .... .992
PO	Rondell White, Montreal 376
A	Bernard Gilkey, New York 17
E	Vladimir Guerrero, Montreal 12
TC	Rondell White, Montreal 385
DP	Larry Walker, Colorado 4

1997 National League Statistics

CLUB BATTING

	AVG	G	AB	R	H	2B	3B	HR	BB	SO	SB
Colorado	.288	162	5603	923	1611	269	40	239	562	1060	137
San Diego	.271	162	5609	795	1519	275	16	152	604	1129	140
Atlanta	.270	162	5528	791	1490	268	37	174	597	1160	108
Los Angeles	.268	162	5544	742	1488	242	33	174	498	1079	131
Chicago	.263	162	5489	687	1444	269	39	127	451	1003	116
New York	.262	162	5524	777	1448	274	28	153	550	1029	97
Pittsburgh	.262	162	5503	725	1440	291	52	129	481	1161	160
Houston	.259	162	5502	777	1427	314	40	133	633	1085	171
Florida	.259	162	5439	740	1410	272	28	136	686	1074	115
San Francisco	.258	162	5485	784	1415	266	37	172	642	1120	121
Montreal	.258	162	5526	691	1423	339	34	172	420	1084	75
Philadelphia	.255	162	5443	668	1390	290	35	116	519	1032	92
St. Louis	.255	162	5524	689	1409	269	39	144	543	1191	164
Cincinnati	.253	162	5484	651	1386	269	27	142	518	1113	190

CLUB PITCHING

	ERA	G	CG	SHO	SV	IP	H	R	ER	BB	SO
Atlanta	3.18	162	21	17	37	1466	1319	581	518	450	1196
Los Angeles	3.62	162	6	6	45	1459	1325	645	587	546	1232
Houston	3.66	162	16	12	37	1459	1379	660	594	511	1138
Florida	3.83	162	12	10	39	1447	1353	669	615	639	1188
St. Louis	3.88	162	5	3	39	1456	1422	708	627	536	1130
New York	3.95	162	7	8	49	1459	1452	709	640	504	982
Montreal	4.13	162	27	14	37	1447	1365	740	665	557	1138
Pittsburgh	4.28	162	6	8	41	1436	1503	760	683	560	1080
San Francisco	4.39	162	5	9	45	1446	1494	793	706	578	1044
Cincinnati	4.41	162	5	8	49	1449	1408	764	710	558	1159
Chicago	4.44	162	6	4	37	1429	1451	759	705	590	1072
Philadelphia	4.85	162	13	7	35	1420	1441	840	765	616	1209
San Diego	4.98	162	5	2	43	1450	1581	891	803	596	1059
Colorado	5.25	162	9	5	38	1433	1697	908	836	566	870

CLUB FIELDING

	PCT	PO	A	E	DP
Colorado	.983	4298	1945	111	202
Cincinnati	.982	4347	1576	106	129
Philadelphia	.982	4261	1547	108	134
Atlanta	.982	4397	1669	114	136
Chicago	.981	4287	1605	112	117
New York	.981	4378	1881	120	165
Florida	.981	4340	1647	116	167
Los Angeles	.981	4378	1561	116	104
St. Louis	.980	4367	1739	123	156
San Francisco	.980	4338	1799	125	157
Houston	.979	4377	1874	131	169
Pittsburgh	.979	4308	1831	131	149
San Diego	.979	4350	1819	132	132
Montreal	.979	4341	1697	132	150

INDIVIDUAL BATTING LEADERS

(Minimum 502 Plate Appearances)

	AVG	G	AB	R	H	2B	3B	HR	RBI	BB	SO	SB
Gwynn, Tony, San Diego	.372	149	592	97	220	49	2	17	119	43	28	12
Walker, Larry, Colorado	.366	153	568	143	208	46	4	49	130	78	90	33
Piazza, Mike, Los Angeles	.362	152	556	104	201	32	1	40	124	69	77	5
Lofton, Kenny, Atlanta	.333	122	493	90	164	20	6	5	48	64	83	27
Joyner, Wally, San Diego	.327	135	455	59	149	29	2	13	83	51	51	3
Grace, Mark, Chicago	.319	151	555	87	177	32	5	13	78	88	45	2
Galarraga, Andres, Colorado	.318	154	600	120	191	31	3	41	140	54	141	15
Alfonzo, Edgardo, New York	.315	151	518	84	163	27	2	10	72	63	56	11
Mondesi, Raul, Los Angeles	.310	159	616	95	191	42	5	30	87	44	105	32
Biggio, Craig, Houston	.309	162	619	146	191	37	8	22	81	84	107	47

INDIVIDUAL PITCHING LEADERS

(Minimum 162 Innings)

	W	L	ERA	G	GS	CG	SV	IP	H	R	ER	BB	SO
Martinez, Pedro, Mon.	17	8	1.90	31	31	13	0	241	158	65	51	67	305
Maddux, Greg, Atlanta	19	4	2.20	33	33	5	0	233	200	58	57	20	177
Kile, Darryl, Houston	19	7	2.57	34	34	6	0	256	208	87	73	94	205
Valdes, Ismael, LA	10	11	2.65	30	30	0	0	197	171	68	58	47	140
Brown, Kevin, Florida	16	8	2.69	33	33	6	0	237	214	77	71	66	205
Reed, Rick, New York	13	9	2.89	33	31	2	0	208	186	76	67	31	113
Glavine, Tom, Atlanta	14	7	2.96	33	33	5	0	240	197	86	79	79	152
Neagle, Denny, Atlanta	20	5	2.97	34	34	4	0	233	204	87	77	49	172
Schilling, Curt, Phil	17	11	2.97	35	35	7	0	254	208	96	84	58	319
Smoltz, John, Atlanta	15	12	3.02	35	35	7	0	256	234	97	86	63	241

AWARD WINNERS

Selected by Baseball Writers Association of America

MVP

Player, Team	1st	2nd	3rd	Total
Larry Walker, Colo.	22	3	3	359
Mike Piazza, L.A.	3	22	2	263
Jeff Bagwell, Houston	3	2	15	233
Craig Biggio, Houston	0	1	3	157
Barry Bonds, S.F.	0	0	1	123
Tony Gwynn, S.D.	0	0	3	113
Andres Galarraga, Colo.	0	0	0	85
Jeff Kent, S.F.	0	0	1	80
Chipper Jones, Atl.	0	0	0	70
Moises Alou, Fla.	0	0	0	60
Charles Johnson, Fla.	0	0	0	22
Greg Maddux, Atl.	0	0	0	16
Edgardo Alfonzo, N.Y.	0	0	0	10
Curt Schilling, Phil.	0	0	0	9
Raul Mondesi, L.A.	0	0	0	8
Pedro Martinez, Mon.	0	0	0	6
Mark McGwire, St.L.	0	0	0	6
Ray Lankford, St.L.	0	0	0	6
Sammy Sosa, Chi.	0	0	0	5
Kevin Young, Pitt.	0	0	0	5
Jeff Blauser, Atl.	0	0	0	4
Vinny Castilla, Colo.	0	0	0	3
Darryl Kile, Houston	0	0	0	3
Rod Beck, S.F.	0	0	0	2
Tony Womack, Pitt.	0	0	0	2
Kenny Lofton, Atl.	0	0	0	1
J.T. Snow, S.F.	0	0	0	1

CY YOUNG AWARD

Player, Team	1st	2nd	3rd	Total
Pedro Martinez, Mon.	25	3	0	134
Greg Maddux, Atl.	3	18	6	75
Denny Neagle, Atl.	0	5	9	24
Curt Schilling, Phil.	0	1	9	12
Darryl Kile, Houston	0	1	4	7

ROOKIE OF THE YEAR

Player, Team	1st	2nd	3rd	Total
Scott Rolen, Phil.	28	0	0	140
Livan Hernandez, Fla.	0	8	1	25
Matt Morris, St. Louis	0	7	4	25
Rich Loiselle, Pitt.	0	4	10	22
Andruw Jones, Atl.	0	4	3	15
Vladimir Guerrero, Mon.	0	1	6	9
Jose Guillen, Pitt.	0	1	1	4
Brett Tomko, Cinc.	0	1	1	4
Jeremi Gonzalez, Chi.	0	1	0	3
xTony Womack, Pitt.	0	1	0	3
Kevin Orie, Chicago	0	0	1	1
Neifi Perez, Colo.	0	0	1	1

x non-qualifier

MANAGER OF THE YEAR

Manager, Team	1st	2nd	3rd	Total
Dusty Baker, S.F.	17	7	4	110
Gene Lamont, Pitt.	10	13	3	92
Larry Dierker, Hous.	1	5	14	34
Bobby Valentine, N.Y.	0	2	1	7
Bobby Cox, Atlanta	0	1	3	6
Terry Francona, Phil.	0	0	2	2
Jim Leyland, Florida	0	0	1	1

GOLD GLOVE AWARDS

Selected by NL managers

C—Charles Johnson, Florida. **1B**—J.T. Snow, San Francisco. **2B**—Craig Biggio, Houston. **3B**—Ken Caminiti, San Diego. **SS**—Rey Ordonez, New York. **OF**—Barry Bonds, San Francisco; Raul Mondesi, Los Angeles; Larry Walker, Colorado. **P**—Greg Maddux, Atlanta.

McKeon as interim manager, then pulled a bigger surprise by keeping him as the permanent manager. McKeon had worked as an adviser to the team for five years, and the interim period was seen as a chance to have him evaluate the players. It turned into more than that.

■ Brown narrowly missed a perfect game in pitching a 9-0 no-hitter on June 10 at San Francisco. Brown still had the perfect game with two outs in the eighth when he hit outfielder Marvin Benard with a pitch.

Brown's pitching opponent, righthander William VanLandingham, carried a no-hitter into the seventh inning, but the Marlins scored seven runs in that frame.

The only other NL no-hitter in 1997 was a combined, 10-inning one by Cordova and Pirates lefthander Ricardo Rincon on July 12. They beat the Astros 3-0. The game also was the Pirates' first sellout, other than Opening Day or the playoffs, since 1977.

■ Mets first baseman John Olerud hit for the cycle on Sept. 11, in a 9-5 win over the Expos in New York. It capped a comeback year for Olerud, who hit .294 with 22 homers and 102 RBIs after seeing his career stall with the Blue Jays.

■ Charles Johnson broke the major league record for consecutive errorless games by a catcher. With his 160th on Sept. 12, he eclipsed the mark of Rick Cerone. Johnson finished the season without an error and only one passed ball.

■ Biggio set a major league record by playing in his 155th game without grounding into a double play.

■ And last but not least, the Reds played a game without recording an assist. On Aug. 20, they got 27 outs against the visiting Rockies on 14 fly balls, 12 strikeouts and one unassisted groundout to first base. Alas, Cincinnati lost 5-3.

GEORGE GOJKOVICH

Pirates highlight
Francisco Cordova led an unsung staff and combined with Ricardo Rincon on a no-hitter

NATIONAL LEAGUE

DIVISION SERIES

ATLANTA vs. HOUSTON

COMPOSITE BOX

ATLANTA

Player, Pos.	AVG	G	AB	R	H	2B	3B	HR	RBI	BB	SO	SB
Greg Colbrunn, ph	1.000	1	1	0	1	0	0	0	2	0	0	0
Tom Glavine, p	.667	1	3	2	2	0	0	0	0	0	0	0
Chipper Jones, 3b	.500	3	8	3	4	0	0	1	2	3	2	1
Danny Bautista, of	.333	3	3	0	1	0	0	0	2	0	1	0
Jeff Blauser, ss	.300	3	10	2	3	0	0	1	4	2	2	0
Javy Lopez, c	.286	2	7	3	2	2	0	0	1	2	1	0
Ryan Klesko, of	.250	3	8	2	2	1	0	1	1	0	2	0
Fred McGriff, 1b	.222	3	9	4	2	0	0	0	1	3	2	0
Michael Tucker, of	.167	2	6	0	1	0	0	0	1	0	1	0
Kenny Lofton, of	.154	3	13	2	2	1	0	0	0	1	2	0
Tony Graffanino, 2b	.000	3	3	0	0	0	0	0	0	2	1	0
Andruw Jones, of	.000	3	5	1	0	0	0	0	1	1	1	0
Keith Lockhart, 2b	.000	2	6	0	0	0	0	0	0	0	1	0
Eddie Perez, c	.000	1	3	0	0	0	0	0	0	0	1	0
Mike Cather, p	.000	1	1	0	0	0	0	0	0	0	1	0
Greg Maddux, p	.000	1	2	0	0	0	0	0	0	1	1	0
John Smoltz, p	.000	1	4	0	0	0	0	0	0	0	1	0
Totals	**.220**	**3**	**92**	**19**	**20**	**4**	**0**	**3**	**15**	**15**	**20**	**1**

Pitcher	W	L	ERA	G	GS	SV	IP	H	R	ER	BB	SO
Mike Cather	0	0	0.00	1	0	0	2	0	0	0	1	2
Mark Wohlers	0	0	0.00	1	0	0	1	1	0	0	0	1
Greg Maddux	1	0	1.00	1	1	0	9	7	1	1	1	6
John Smoltz	1	0	1.00	1	1	0	9	1	1	1	1	11
Tom Glavine	1	0	4.50	1	1	0	6	5	3	3	5	4
Totals	**3**	**0**	**1.67**	**3**	**3**	**0**	**27**	**16**	**5**	**5**	**8**	**24**

HOUSTON

Player, Pos.	AVG	G	AB	R	H	2B	3B	HR	RBI	BB	SO	SB
Darryl Kile, p	1.000	1	2	0	2	0	0	0	1	0	0	0
Tony Eusebio, c	.667	1	3	1	2	0	0	0	0	0	1	1
Mike Hampton, p	.500	1	2	0	1	0	0	0	1	0	0	0
Brad Ausmus, c	.400	2	5	1	2	1	0	0	2	0	1	0
Bob Abreu, of	.333	3	3	0	1	0	0	0	0	0	2	1
Luis Gonzalez, of	.333	3	12	0	4	0	0	0	0	0	1	0
Chuck Carr, of	.250	2	4	1	1	0	0	1	1	1	3	0
Ricky Gutierrez, ss	.125	3	8	0	1	0	0	0	0	2	1	0
Jeff Bagwell, 1b	.083	3	12	0	1	0	0	0	0	1	5	0
Craig Biggio, 2b	.083	3	12	0	1	0	0	0	0	1	0	0
Derek Bell, of	.000	3	13	0	0	0	0	0	0	0	3	0
Sean Berry, 3b	.000	1	1	0	0	0	0	0	0	0	0	0
Richard Hildalgo, of	.000	2	5	1	0	0	0	0	0	1	2	0
Thomas Howard, ph	.000	2	1	0	0	0	0	0	0	1	1	0
Russ Johnson, ph	.000	1	1	0	0	0	0	0	0	0	1	0
Bill Spiers, 3b	.000	3	11	1	0	0	0	0	0	1	2	0
Tony Pena, c	.000	2	0	0	0	0	0	0	0	0	0	0
Shane Reynolds	.000	1	1	0	0	0	0	0	0	0	1	0
Totals	**.167**	**3**	**96**	**5**	**16**	**1**	**0**	**1**	**5**	**8**	**24**	**2**

Pitcher	W	L	ERA	G	GS	SV	IP	H	R	ER	BB	SO
Ramon Garcia	0	0	0.00	2	0	0	1	1	2	0	1	1
Jose Lima	0	0	0.00	1	0	0	1	0	0	0	1	1
Tom Martin	0	0	0.00	2	0	0	1	1	1	0	1	0
Darryl Kile	0	1	2.57	1	1	0	7	2	2	2	2	4
Shane Reynolds	0	1	3.00	1	1	0	6	5	2	2	1	5
Mike Magnante	0	0	4.50	2	0	0	2	4	3	1	0	2
Russ Springer	0	0	5.40	2	0	0	2	2	1	1	1	3
Mike Hampton	0	1	11.57	1	1	0	5	2	6	6	8	2
Billy Wagner	0	0	18.00	1	0	0	1	3	2	2	0	2
Totals	**0**	**3**	**5.04**	**3**	**3**	**0**	**25**	**20**	**19**	**14**	**15**	**20**

SCORE BY INNINGS	
Atlanta	**223 035 130 —19**
Houston	**000 310 100 — 5**

DP—Atlanta 2, Houston 2. **LOB**—Atlanta 14, Houston 18. **E**—C. Jones, Klesko, Lockhart; Bagwell 2, Biggio, Gonzalez. **CS**—Lofton. **SF**—C. Jones. **PB**—Ausmus.

FLORIDA vs SAN FRANCISCO

COMPOSITE BOX

FLORIDA

Player, Pos	AVG	G	AB	R	H	2B	3B	HR	RBI	BB	SO	SB
Alex Arias, ph	1.000	1	1	0	1	0	0	0	1	0	0	0
Gary Sheffield, of	.556	3	9	3	5	1	0	1	1	5	0	1

Player, Pos	AVG	G	AB	R	H	2B	3B	HR	RBI	BB	SO	SB
Craig Counsell, 2b	.400	3	5	0	2	1	0	0	1	1	0	0
Jeff Conine, 1b	.364	3	11	3	4	1	0	0	0	1	0	0
Bobby Bonilla, 3b	.333	3	12	1	4	0	0	1	3	2	1	0
Kurt Abbott, 2b	.250	3	8	0	2	0	0	0	0	0	0	0
Charles Johnson, c	.250	3	8	5	2	1	0	1	2	3	2	0
Moises Alou, of	.214	3	14	1	3	1	0	0	1	0	3	0
Devon White, of	.182	3	11	1	2	0	0	1	4	2	3	0
Edgar Renteria, ss	.154	3	13	1	2	0	0	0	1	2	4	0
John Cangelosi, of	.000	1	1	0	0	0	0	0	0	0	0	0
Jim Eisenreich, ph	.000	2	0	0	0	0	0	0	0	2	0	0
Kevin Brown, p	.000	1	2	0	0	0	0	0	0	0	2	0
John Wehner, pr	.000	1	0	0	0	0	0	0	0	0	0	0
Alex Fernandez, p	.000	1	2	0	0	0	0	0	0	1	1	0
Al Leiter, p	.000	1	1	0	0	0	0	0	0	0	0	0
Livan Hernandez, p	.000	1	0	0	0	0	0	0	0	0	0	0
Totals	**.276**	**3**	**98**	**15**	**27**	**5**	**0**	**4**	**14**	**19**	**16**	**1**

Pitcher	W	L	ERA	G	GS	SV	IP	H	R	ER	BB	SO
Dennis Cook	1	0	0.00	2	0	0	3	0	0	0	1	3
Robb Nen	1	0	0.00	2	0	0	2	1	1	0	2	2
Kevin Brown	0	0	1.29	1	1	0	7	4	1	1	0	5
Livan Hernandez	0	0	2.25	1	0	0	4	3	1	1	0	3
Alex Fernandez	1	0	2.57	1	1	0	7	7	2	2	0	5
Al Leiter	0	0	9.00	1	1	0	4	7	4	4	3	3
Totals	**3**	**0**	**3.00**	**3**	**3**	**0**	**27**	**22**	**9**	**8**	**6**	**21**

SAN FRANCISCO

Player, Pos	AVG	G	AB	R	H	2B	3B	HR	RBI	BB	SO	SB
Mark Lewis, 2b	.600	1	5	0	3	0	0	0	1	0	0	0
Kirk Rueter, p	.500	1	2	0	1	0	0	0	0	0	0	0
Stan Javier, of	.417	3	12	2	5	1	0	0	1	0	2	1
Jeff Kent, 2b-1b	.300	3	10	2	3	0	0	2	2	2	1	0
Barry Bonds, of	.250	3	12	0	3	2	0	0	2	0	3	1
Bill Mueller, 3b	.250	3	12	1	3	0	0	1	1	0	0	0
Jose Vizcaino, ss	.182	3	11	1	2	1	0	0	0	0	5	0
J.T. Snow, 1b	.167	3	6	0	1	0	0	0	0	1	1	0
Brian Johnson, c	.100	3	10	2	1	0	0	1	1	1	4	0
Marvin Benard, ph	.000	2	2	0	0	0	0	0	0	0	1	0
Damon Berryhill, ph	.000	1	1	0	0	0	0	0	0	0	0	0
Darryl Hamilton, of	.000	2	5	1	0	0	0	0	0	0	1	0
Glenallen Hill, of	.000	3	7	0	0	0	0	0	0	2	2	0
Wilson Alvarez, p	.000	1	2	0	0	0	0	0	0	0	0	0
Dante Powell, pr	.000	1	0	0	0	0	0	0	0	0	0	0
Shawn Estes, p	.000	1	1	0	0	0	0	0	0	0	1	0
Totals	**.224**	**3**	**98**	**9**	**22**	**4**	**0**	**4**	**8**	**6**	**21**	**2**

Pitcher	W	L	ERA	G	GS	SV	IP	H	R	ER	BB	SO
Rod Beck	0	0	0.00	1	0	0	1	1	0	0	0	1
Doug Henry	0	0	0.00	1	0	0	2	1	0	0	3	2
Rich Rodriguez	0	0	0.00	2	0	0	1	1	0	0	0	0
Kirk Rueter	0	0	1.29	1	1	0	7	4	1	1	3	5
Julian Tavarez	0	1	4.50	3	0	0	4	4	2	2	2	0
Wilson Alvarez	0	1	6.00	1	1	0	6	6	4	4	4	4
Shawn Estes	0	0	15.00	1	1	0	3	5	5	5	4	3
Roberto Hernandez	0	1	20.25	3	0	0	1	5	3	3	3	1
Totals	**0**	**3**	**5.26**	**3**	**3**	**0**	**25**	**27**	**15**	**15**	**19**	**16**

SCORE BY INNINGS

Florida	**201 205 122 — 15**
San Francisco	**111 201 201 — 9**

DP—Florida 3, San Francisco 4. **LOB**—Florida 28, San Francisco 17. **E**—Renteria 2, Conine, Counsell. **SH**—Counsell, Estes, Vizcaino. **SF**—Bonds. **CS**—Javier, Lewis, Mueller. **HBP**—C. Johnson (by Tavarez).

CHAMPIONSHIP SERIES

ATLANTA vs. FLORIDA

COMPOSITE BOX

FLORIDA

Player, Pos	AVG	G	AB	R	H	2B	3B	HR	RBI	BB	SO	SB
Alex Arias, 3b	1.000	3	1	0	1	0	0	0	0	0	0	0
Craig Counsell, 2b	.429	5	14	0	6	0	0	0	2	3	3	0
Kurt Abbott, 2b	.375	2	8	0	3	1	0	0	0	0	2	0
Bobby Bonilla, 3b	.261	6	23	3	6	1	0	0	4	1	6	0
Darren Daulton, 1b	.250	3	4	1	1	1	0	0	1	1	2	0
Gary Sheffield, of	.235	6	17	6	4	0	0	1	1	7	3	0
Edgar Renteria, ss	.227	6	22	4	5	1	0	0	0	3	6	1
John Cangelosi, of	.200	3	5	0	1	0	0	0	0	1	0	0
Devon White, of	.190	6	21	4	4	1	0	0	1	2	7	1
Charles Johnson, c	.118	6	17	1	2	2	0	0	5	3	8	0
Jeff Conine, 1b	.111	6	18	1	2	0	0	0	1	1	4	0
Moises Alou, of	.067	5	15	0	1	1	0	0	5	1	3	0
Greg Zaun, c	.000	1	0	0	0	0	0	0	0	0	0	0
Alex Fernandez, p	.000	1	1	0	0	0	0	0	0	0	1	0
Al Leiter, p	.000	2	1	0	0	0	0	0	0	0	1	0
Kevin Brown, p	.000	2	6	0	0	0	0	0	0	0	3	0
Tony Saunders, p	.000	1	2	0	0	0	0	0	0	0	2	0
Livan Hernandez, p	.000	2	3	0	0	0	0	0	0	0	1	0
Jim Eisenreich, lf	.000	1	3	0	0	0	0	0	0	0	0	0
Totals	**.199**	**6**	**181**	**20**	**36**	**8**	**0**	**1**	**20**	**23**	**52**	**2**

LARRY GOREN

40-40 man again

But Barry Bonds has yet to win a playoff series

Pitching	W	L	ERA	G	GS	SV	IP	H	R	ER	BB	SO
Ed Vosberg	0	0	0.00	2	0	0	3	2	0	0	1	3
Dennis Cook	0	0	0.00	2	0	0	2	0	0	0	0	2
Robb Nen	0	0	0.00	2	0	2	2	0	0	0	0	1
Jay Powell	0	0	0.00	1	0	0	1	0	0	0	0	0
Livan Hernandez	2	0	0.84	2	1	0	11	5	1	1	2	16
Tony Saunders	0	0	3.38	1	1	0	5	4	2	2	3	3
Kevin Brown	2	0	4.20	2	2	0	15	16	7	7	5	11
Al Leiter	0	1	4.32	2	1	0	8	13	4	4	2	6
Felix Heredia	0	0	5.40	2	0	0	3	3	2	2	2	4
Alex Fernandez	0	1	16.88	1	1	0	3	6	5	5	1	3
Totals	**4**	**2**	**3.57**	**6**	**6**	**2**	**53**	**49**	**21**	**21**	**16**	**49**

ATLANTA

Player, Pos	AVG	G	AB	R	H	2B	3B	HR	RBI	BB	SO	SB
Greg Colbrunn, ph	.667	3	3	0	2	0	0	0	0	0	0	0
Keith Lockhart, 2b	.500	5	16	4	8	1	1	0	3	1	1	0
Andruw Jones, of	.444	5	9	0	4	0	0	0	1	1	1	0
Fred McGriff, 1b	.333	6	21	0	7	1	0	0	4	2	7	0
Tom Glavine, p	.333	2	3	0	1	0	0	0	0	0	2	0
Greg Blauser, ss	.300	6	20	5	6	0	0	1	1	3	6	0
Chipper Jones, of	.292	6	24	5	7	1	0	2	4	2	3	0
Tony Graffanino, 2b	.250	3	8	1	2	1	0	0	0	0	3	0
Danny Bautista, of	.250	2	4	0	1	0	0	0	0	0	0	0
Ryan Klesko, of	.235	5	17	2	4	0	0	2	4	2	3	0
Kenny Lofton, of	.185	6	27	3	5	0	1	0	1	1	7	1
Michael Tucker, of	.100	5	10	1	1	0	0	1	1	3	4	0
Javier Lopez, c	.059	5	17	0	1	1	0	0	2	1	7	0
Eddie Perez, c	.000	2	3	0	0	0	0	0	0	0	0	0
Tommy Gregg, ph	.000	4	4	0	0	0	0	0	0	0	1	0
John Smoltz, p	.000	1	2	0	0	0	0	0	0	0	1	0
Greg Maddux, p	.000	2	3	0	0	0	0	0	0	0	2	0
Denny Neagle, p	.000	2	3	0	0	0	0	0	0	0	1	0
Totals	**.253**	**6**	**194**	**21**	**49**	**5**	**2**	**6**	**21**	**16**	**49**	**1**

Pitching	W	L	ERA	G	GS	SV	IP	H	R	ER	BB	SO
Denny Neagle	1	0	0.00	2	1	0	12	5	0	0	1	9
Kerry Lightenberg	0	0	0.00	2	0	0	3	1	0	0	0	4
Mike Cather	0	0	0.00	4	0	0	3	3	0	0	0	3
Alan Embree	0	0	0.00	1	0	0	1	0	0	0	1	1
Mark Wohlers	0	0	0.00	1	0	0	1	0	0	0	1	1
Greg Maddux	0	2	1.38	2	2	0	13	9	7	2	4	16
Tom Glavine	1	1	5.40	2	2	0	13	13	8	8	11	9
John Smoltz	0	1	7.50	1	1	0	6	5	5	5	5	9
Totals	**2**	**4**	**2.60**	**6**	**6**	**0**	**52**	**36**	**20**	**15**	**23**	**52**

SCORE BY INNINGS

Florida	**802 107 110 — 20**
Atlanta	**634 122 201 — 21**

DP—Florida 4, Atlanta 7. **LOB**—Florida 36, Atlanta 40. **E**—C. Johnson 2, Counsell; Lofton 2, Blauser, McGriff. **SF**—Lopez 2, McGriff. **SH**—K. Brown 2, Conine, Hernandez, C. Johnson; C. Jones, Maddux, Neagle, Glavine 2. **HBP**—Lockhart (by Cook), Renteria (by Neagle), C. Johnson (by Glavine).

Organization Statistics

Anaheim ANGELS

Manager: Terry Collins.

1997 Record: 84-78, .519 (2nd, AL West)

BATTING	AVG	G	AB	R	H	2B	3B	HR	RBI	BB	SO	SB	CS	B	T	HT	WT	DOB	1st Yr	Resides
Alicea, Luis	.253	128	388	59	98	16	7	5	37	69	65	22	8	S	R	5-9	177	7-29-65	1986	Loxahatchie, Fla.
Anderson, Garret	.303	154	624	76	189	36	3	8	92	30	70	10	4	L	L	6-3	190	6-30-72	1990	Granada Hills, Calif.
Arias, George	.333	3	6	1	2	0	0	0	1	0	0	0	0	R	R	5-11	190	3-12-72	1993	Tucson, Ariz.
DiSarcina, Gary	.246	154	549	52	135	28	2	4	47	17	29	7	8	R	R	6-1	178	11-19-67	1988	East Sandwich, Mass.
Edmonds, Jim	.291	133	502	82	146	27	0	26	80	60	80	5	7	L	L	6-1	190	6-27-70	1988	Diamond Bar, Calif.
Eenhoorn, Robert	.350	11	20	2	7	1	0	1	6	0	2	0	0	R	R	6-3	175	2-9-68	1990	Rotterdam, Holland
Encarnacion, Angelo	.412	11	17	2	7	1	0	1	4	0	1	2	0	R	R	5-8	180	4-18-73	1990	Santo Domingo, D.R.
Erstad, Darin	.299	139	539	99	161	34	4	16	77	51	86	23	8	L	L	6-2	195	6-4-74	1995	Jamestown, N.D.
Fabregas, Jorge	.079	21	38	2	3	1	0	0	3	3	3	0	0	L	R	6-3	205	3-13-70	1991	Miami, Fla.
Grebeck, Craig	.270	63	126	12	34	9	0	1	6	18	11	0	1	R	R	5-7	148	12-29-64	1987	Cerritos, Calif.
Greene, Todd	.290	34	124	24	36	6	0	9	24	7	25	2	0	R	R	5-10	195	5-8-71	1993	Martinez, Ga.
Henderson, Rickey	.183	32	115	21	21	3	0	2	7	26	23	16	4	R	L	5-10	195	12-25-58	1976	Oakland, Calif.
Hollins, Dave	.288	149	572	101	165	29	2	16	85	62	124	16	6	S	R	6-1	207	5-25-66	1987	Orchard Park, N.Y.
Howell, Jack	.259	77	174	25	45	7	0	14	34	13	36	1	0	L	R	6-0	201	8-18-61	1983	Tucson, Ariz.
Kreuter, Chad	.234	70	218	19	51	7	1	4	18	21	57	0	2	S	R	6-2	190	8-26-64	1985	Arlington, Texas
2-team (19 Chicago)	.231	89	255	25	59	9	2	5	21	29	66	0	3							
Leyritz, Jim	.276	84	294	47	81	7	0	11	50	37	56	1	1	R	R	6-0	190	12-27-63	1986	Plantation, Fla.
Murray, Eddie	.219	46	160	13	35	7	0	3	15	13	24	1	0	S	R	6-2	220	2-24-56	1973	Canyon Country, Calif.
Palmeiro, Orlando	.216	74	134	19	29.	2	2	0	8	17	11	2	2	L	R	5-11	155	1-19-69	1991	Miami, Fla.
Phillips, Tony	.264	105	405	73	107	28	2	6	48	73	89	9	9	S	R	5-10	175	4-25-59	1978	Scottsdale, Ariz.
2-team (36 Chicago)	.275	141	534	96	147	34	2	8	57	102	118	13	10							
Salmon, Tim	.296	157	582	95	172	28	1	33	129	95	142	9	12	R	R	6-3	220	8-24-68	1989	Phoenix, Ariz.
Turner, Chris	.261	13	23	4	6	1	1	1	2	5	8	0	0	R	R	6-1	190	3-23-69	1991	Bowling Green, Ky.
Velarde, Randy	.000	1	0	0	0	0	0	0	0	0	0	0	0	R	R	6-0	185	11-24-62	1985	Midland, Texas

PITCHING	W	L	ERA	G	GS	CG	SV	IP	H	R	ER	BB	SO	B	T	HT	WT	DOB	1st Yr	Resides
Bovee, Mike	0	0	5.40	3	0	0	0	3	3	2	2	1	5	R	R	5-10	200	8-21-73	1991	Mira Mesa, Calif.
Cadaret, Greg	0	0	3.29	15	0	0	0	14	11	5	5	8	11	L	L	6-3	215	2-27-62	1983	Mesa, Ariz.
Chavez, Anthony	0	0	0.93	7	0	0	0	10	7	1	1	5	10	R	R	5-11	180	10-22-70	1992	Merced, Calif.
DeLucia, Rich	6	4	3.61	33	0	0	3	42	29	18	17	27	42	R	R	6-0	185	10-7-64	1986	Shillington, Pa.
Dickson, Jason	13	9	4.29	33	32	2	0	204	236	111	97	56	115	L	R	6-0	190	3-30-73	1994	Chatham, N.B.
Finley, Chuck	13	6	4.23	25	25	3	0	164	152	79	77	65	155	L	L	6-6	214	11-26-62	1985	Newport Beach, Calif.
Gross, Kevin	2	1	6.75	12	3	0	0	25	30	20	19	20	20	R	R	6-0	185	10-7-64	1986	Shillington, Pa.
Gubicza, Mark	0	1	25.07	2	2	0	0	5	13	13	13	3	5	R	R	6-5	230	8-14-62	1981	Northridge, Calif.
Harris, Pep	5	4	3.62	61	0	0	0	80	82	33	32	38	56	R	R	6-2	185	9-23-72	1991	Lancaster, S.C.
Hasegawa, Shigetoshi	3	7	3.93	50	7	0	0	117	118	60	51	46	83	R	R	5-11	160	8-1-68	1997	Kobe, Japan
Hill, Ken	4	4	3.65	12	12	1	0	79	65	34	32	39	38	R	R	6-2	175	12-14-65	1985	Lynn, Mass.
2-team (19 Texas)	9	12	4.55	31	31	1	0	190	194	103	96	95	106							
Holtz, Mike	3	4	3.32	66	0	0	2	43	38	21	16	15	40	L	L	5-9	172	10-10-72	1994	Ebensburg, Ark.
James, Mike	5	5	4.31	58	0	0	7	63	69	32	30	28	57	R	R	6-3	180	8-15-67	1988	Mary Esther, Fla.
Langston, Mark	2	4	5.85	9	9	0	0	48	61	34	31	29	30	R	L	6-2	184	8-20-60	1981	Anaheim Hills, Calif.
May, Darrell	2	1	5.23	29	2	0	0	52	56	31	30	25	42	L	L	6-2	170	6-13-72	1992	Rogue River, Ore.
McElroy, Chuck	0	0	3.45	13	0	0	0	16	17	7	6	3	18	L	L	6-0	195	10-1-67	1986	Friendswood, Texas
Percival, Troy	5	5	3.46	55	0	0	27	52	40	20	20	22	72	R	R	6-3	200	8-9-69	1990	Moreno Valley, Calif.
Perisho, Matt	0	2	6.00	11	8	0	0	45	59	34	30	28	35	L	L	6-0	190	6-8-75	1993	Chandler, Ariz.
Springer, Dennis	9	9	5.18	32	28	3	0	195	199	118	112	73	75	R	R	5-10	185	2-12-65	1987	Fresno, Calif.
Watson, Allen	12	12	4.93	35	34	0	0	199	220	121	109	73	141	L	L	6-3	195	11-18-70	1991	Middle Village, N.Y.
Williams, Shad	0	0	0.00	1	0	0	0	1	1	0	0	1	0	R	R	6-0	185	3-10-71	1991	Fresno, Calif.

FIELDING

Catcher	PCT	G	PO	A	E	DP	PB
Encarnacion	.940	11	43	4	3	0	0
Fabregas	.989	21	81	5	1	1	0
Greene	1.000	26	153	7	0	2	5
Kreuter	.994	67	431	29	3	1	4
Leyritz	1.000	58	361	40	0	4	9
Turner	1.000	8	26	2	0	0	1

First Base	PCT	G	PO	A	E	DP
Edmonds	1.000	11	84	7	0	5
Erstad	.990	126	1000	64	11	92
Hollins	1.000	14	107	8	0	10
Howell	.962	12	44	6	2	4
Kreuter	.750	2	2	1	1	1
Leyritz	.977	15	79	5	2	17
Turner	1.000	2	7	0	0	1

Second Base	PCT	G	PO	A	E	DP
Alicea	.978	105	218	268	11	58
Eenhoorn	.667	3	1	1	1	0
Grebeck	1.000	26	45	55	0	17
Phillips	.968	43	78	101	6	21

Third Base	PCT	G	PO	A	E	DP
Alicea	.960	12	5	19	1	1
Arias	1.000	1	0	3	0	0
Eenhoorn	.833	5	2	3	1	0
Grebeck	1.000	15	1	2	0	0
Hollins	.922	135	101	241	29	17
Howell	.976	24	14	27	1	4
Phillips	1.000	1	0	1	0	0

Shortstop	PCT	G	PO	A	E	DP
DiSarcina	.977	153	227	421	15	85
Eenhoorn	.900	2	5	4	1	2
Grebeck	.959	20	16	31	2	7

Outfield	PCT	G	PO	A	E	DP
Anderson	.992	148	343	14	3	2
Edmonds	.985	115	311	9	5	2
Erstad	1.000	1	3	0	0	0
Grebeck	1.000	3	6	0	0	0
Henderson	1.000	13	26	0	0	0
Palmeiro	.975	52	78	1	2	0
Phillips	.968	35	59	1	2	0
Salmon	.971	153	352	15	11	5
Turner	1.000	1	1	0	0	0

LARRY GOREN

Tim Salmon

FARM SYSTEM

Director of Player Development: Ken Forsch

Class	Farm Team	League	W	L	Pct.	Finish*	Manager	First Yr
AAA	Vancouver (B.C.) Canadians	Pacific Coast	75	68	.524	5th (10)	Bruce Hines	1993
AA	Midland (Texas) Angels	Texas	64	75	.460	6th (8)	Mitch Seoane	1985
#A	Lake Elsinore (Calif.) Storm	California	61	79	.436	9th (10)	Don Long	1994
A	Cedar Rapids (Iowa) Kernels	Midwest	62	76	.449	12th (14)	Mario Mendoza	1993
A	Boise (Idaho) Hawks	Northwest	51	25	.671	1st (8)	Tom Kotchman	1990
#R	Butte (Mont.) Copper Kings	Pioneer	30	42	.417	7th (8)	Bill Lachemann	1997

*Finish in overall standings (No. of teams in league) #Advanced level

Organization Statistics

ORGANIZATION LEADERS

MAJOR LEAGUERS

BATTING

*AVG	Garret Anderson	.303
R	Dave Hollins	101
H	Garret Anderson	189
TB	Tim Salmon	301
2B	Garret Anderson	36
3B	Luis Alicea	7
HR	Tim Salmon	33
RBI	Tim Salmon	129
BB	Tim Salmon	95
SO	Tim Salmon	142
SB	Darin Erstad	23

PITCHING

W	Two tied at	13
L	Allen Watson	12
#ERA	Pep Harris	3.62
G	Mike Holtz	66
CG	Two tied at	3
SV	Troy Percival	27
IP	Jason Dickson	204
BB	Two tied at	73
SO	Chuck Finley	155

Garret Anderson

MEL BAILEY

Todd Greene

MINOR LEAGUERS

BATTING

*AVG	Todd Greene, Vancouver	.354
R	Rob Sasser, Cedar Rapids	103
H	Norm Hutchins, Lake Elsinore	163
TB	Norm Hutchins, Lake Elsinore	263
2B	Jamie Burke, Vancouver/Midland	45
3B	Jovino Carvajal, Vancouver	20
HR	Chris Norton, Van./Midland/Lake Els.	28
RBI	Frank Bolick, Vancouver/Midland	93
BB	Frank Bolick, Vancouver/Midland	72
SO	Chuck Abbott, Cedar Rapids	170
SB	Jusin Baughman, Lake Elsinore	68

PITCHING

W	Jarrod Washburn, Vancouver/Midland	15
L	Jason Stockstill, Cedar Rapids	14
#ERA	Matt Wise, Boise	3.25
G	Anthony Chavez, Vancouver/Midland	61
CG	Ramon Ortiz, Cedar Rapids	8
SV	Anthony Chavez, Vancouver/Midland	21
IP	Jarrod Washburn, Vancouver/Midland	194
BB	Geoff Edsell, Vancouver	96
SO	Ramon Ortiz, Cedar Rapids	225

*Minimum 250 At-Bats #Minimum 75 Innings

TOP 10 PROSPECTS

LEE SCHMID

Jarrod Washburn

How the Angels Top 10 prospects, as judged by Baseball America prior to the 1997 season, fared in 1997:

Player, Pos.	Club (Class)	AVG	AB	R	H	2B	3B	HR	RBI	SB
2. Todd Greene, c	Anaheim	.290	124	24	36	6	0	9	24	2
	Vancouver (AAA)	.354	260	51	92	22	0	25	75	5
5. Norm Hutchins, of	Lake Elsinore (A)	.289	564	82	163	31	12	15	69	39
6. Rich Stuart, of	Lake Elsinore (A)	.230	165	25	38	11	6	6	33	6
9. Marcus Knight, of	Butte (Rookie)	.294	293	51	86	15	5	8	43	8

Player, Pos.	Club (Class)	W	L	ERA	G	SV	IP	H	BB	SO
1. Jarrod Washburn, lhp	Vancouver (AAA)	0	0	3.60	1	0	5	4	2	6
	Midland (AA)	15	12	4.80	29	0	189	211	65	146
3. Jason Dickson, rhp	Anaheim	13	9	4.29	33	0	204	236	56	115
4. Scott Schoeneweis, lhp	Midland (AA)	7	5	5.96	20	0	113	145	39	94
7. Matt Perisho, lhp	Anaheim	0	2	6.00	11	0	45	59	28	35
	Vancouver (AAA)	4	4	5.33	9	0	52	68	29	47
	Midland (AA)	5	2	2.96	10	0	73	60	26	62
8. Shig. Hasegawa, rhp	Anaheim	3	7	3.93	50	0	117	118	46	83
10. Pete Janicki, rhrp	Vancouver (AAA)	1	4	7.80	42	1	47	48	44	43
	Midland (AA)	0	0	0.00	2	0	2	3	2	2

TM

VANCOUVER — Class AAA

PACIFIC COAST LEAGUE

BATTING	AVG	G	AB	R	H	2B	3B	HR	RBI	BB	SO	SB	CS	B	T	HT	WT	DOB	1st Yr	Resides
Arias, George	.279	105	401	71	112	28	3	11	60	39	51	3	4	R	R	5-11	190	3-12-72	1993	Tucson, Ariz.
Bass, Kevin	.333	4	12	4	4	0	0	1	1	3	2	0	1	S	R	6-0	190	5-12-59	1977	Sugar Land, Texas
Betten, Randy	.279	23	61	9	17	4	0	1	12	7	21	1	1	R	R	5-11	170	7-28-71	1995	Highland, Calif.
Bolick, Frank	.304	102	362	61	110	27	4	16	66	46	70	4	1	S	R	5-10	177	6-28-66	1987	Mt. Carmel, Pa.
Burke, Jamie	.296	8	27	4	8	1	0	0	3	3	2	0	0	R	R	6-0	195	9-24-71	1993	Roseburg, Ore.
Caceres, Edgar	.310	82	258	30	80	13	0	2	37	19	23	6	6	S	R	6-1	170	6-6-64	1984	Barquisimeto, Venez.
Carvajal, Jovino	.285	131	480	80	137	20	20	2	51	21	85	28	9	S	R	6-1	160	9-2-68	1987	La Romana, D.R.
Cruz, Fausto	.288	118	413	52	119	28	1	11	67	18	81	5	8	R	R	5-11	165	1-5-72	1990	Villa Vasquez, D.R.
Eenhoorn, Robert	.308	120	455	77	140	29	5	12	58	25	59	1	4	R	R	6-3	175	2-9-68	1990	Rotterdam, Holland
Greene, Todd	.354	64	260	51	92	22	0	25	75	20	31	5	1	R	R	5-10	195	5-8-71	1993	Martinez, Ga.
Monzon, Jose	.234	17	47	2	11	2	0	0	6	4	8	1	0	R	R	6-1	178	11-8-68	1987	Municipio Vargas, Venez.
Norton, Chris	.200	1	5	1	1	0	0	1	1	0	2	0	0	R	R	6-2	215	9-21-70	1992	Maitland, Fla.
Pritchett, Chris	.279	109	383	60	107	30	3	7	47	42	72	5	3	L	R	6-4	185	1-31-70	1991	Modesto, Calif.
Riley, Marquis	.264	65	242	33	64	6	0	0	8	36	27	27	7	S	R	5-10	170	12-27-70	1992	Ashdown, Ark.
Singleton, Duane	.206	108	383	56	79	17	3	5	36	37	79	15	12	L	R	6-1	170	8-6-72	1990	Staten Island, N.Y.
Thurston, Jerrey	.236	65	195	17	46	3	1	4	19	8	59	3	2	R	R	6-4	200	4-17-72	1990	Longwood, Fla.
Turner, Chris	.370	37	135	26	50	10	0	4	22	14	22	0	0	R	R	6-1	190	3-23-69	1991	Bowling Green, Ky.
White, Derrick	.324	116	414	64	134	35	2	11	65	44	73	11	7	R	R	6-1	215	10-12-69	1991	San Rafael, Calif.
Williams, Reggie	.250	12	40	10	10	3	0	2	5	6	13	3	2	S	R	6-1	180	5-5-66	1988	Laurens, S.C.
Wolff, Mike	.282	91	266	58	75	15	0	21	64	53	75	6	4	R	R	6-1	195	12-19-70	1992	Wilmington, N.C.

PITCHING	W	L	ERA	G	GS	CG	SV	IP	H	R	ER	BB	SO	B	T	HT	WT	DOB	1st Yr	Resides
Bene, Bill	0	1	7.24	19	0	0	0	27	28	25	22	26	29	R	R	6-4	205	11-21-67	1988	Montebello, Calif.
Bovee, Mike	4	3	3.44	12	12	1	0	89	92	38	34	25	71	R	R	5-10	200	8-21-73	1991	Mira Mesa, Calif.
Buckley, Travis	7	11	5.11	32	25	1	1	176	223	116	100	51	119	R	R	6-4	208	6-15-70	1989	Overland Park, Kan.
Cadaret, Greg	0	1	3.14	9	0	0	3	14	11	5	5	4	16	L	L	6-3	215	2-27-62	1983	Mesa, Ariz.
Chavez, Anthony	4	1	2.54	28	0	0	15	28	21	8	8	6	22	R	R	5-11	180	10-22-70	1992	Merced, Calif.
Dunbar, Matt	0	0	27.00	2	0	0	0	2	3	6	6	6	2	L	L	6-0	160	10-15-68	1990	Tallahassee, Fla.
2-team (12 Edmon.)	1	0	6.85	14	1	0	0	24	32	18	18	14	20							
Edsell, Geoff	14	11	5.15	30	29	6	0	183	196	121	105	96	95	L	R	6-2	195	12-10-71	1993	Muncy, Pa.
Ellis, Robert	9	10	5.92	29	23	3	0	149	185	108	98	83	70	R	R	6-5	220	12-15-70	1990	Baton Rouge, La.
Fortugno, Tim	4	2	5.23	34	0	0	0	31	29	21	18	17	36	L	L	6-0	185	4-11-62	1986	Huntington Beach, Calif.
Frey, Steve	3	3	5.01	31	1	0	4	41	45	23	23	21	28	L	L	5-9	170	7-29-63	1983	Newtown, Pa.
Gohr, Greg	5	1	3.80	8	7	0	0	47	51	23	20	14	27	R	R	6-3	205	10-29-67	1989	Campbell, Calif.
Gross, Kevin	1	0	1.64	2	2	0	0	11	7	2	2	0	5	R	R	6-5	215	6-8-61	1981	Claremont, Calif.
Hancock, Ryan	3	3	3.63	39	2	0	2	74	72	37	30	36	60	R	R	6-2	220	11-11-71	1993	Cupertino, Calif.
Janicki, Pete	1	4	7.80	42	0	0	1	47	48	43	41	44	43	R	R	6-4	190	1-26-71	1992	Mesa, Ariz.
Macey, Fausto	1	3	8.10	9	8	0	0	40	47	39	36	32	23	R	R	6-4	185	10-9-75	1994	Santo Domingo, D.R.
May, Darrell	7	5	3.26	13	12	2	0	80	65	31	29	31	62	L	L	6-2	170	6-13-72	1992	Rogue River, Ore.
Perisho, Matt	4	4	5.33	9	9	1	0	52	68	42	31	29	47	L	L	6-0	190	6-8-75	1993	Chandler, Ariz.
Schmidt, Jeff	1	2	5.32	27	0	0	10	22	22	14	13	20	14	R	R	6-5	210	2-21-71	1992	La Crosse, Wis.
Skuse, Nick	0	0	0.00	1	0	0	0	1	0	0	0	0	2	R	R	6-7	240	1-9-72	1994	Los Gatos, Calif.
Springer, Dennis	1	1	3.00	2	2	2	0	15	12	6	5	6	7	R	R	5-10	185	2-12-65	1987	Fresno, Calif.
Washburn, Jarrod	0	0	3.60	1	1	0	0	5	4	2	2	2	6	L	L	6-1	185	8-13-74	1995	Webster, Wis.
Williams, Shad	6	2	3.82	40	10	0	1	99	98	52	42	41	52	R	R	6-0	185	3-10-71	1991	Fresno, Calif.

FIELDING

Catcher	PCT	G	PO	A	E	DP	PB
Burke	.935	4	27	2	2	0	0
Greene	.992	56	313	42	3	4	4
Monzon	.980	17	87	11	2	1	2
Thurston	.977	64	353	30	9	0	10
Turner	.968	14	87	4	3	1	2

First Base	PCT	G	PO	A	E	DP
Bolick	.996	29	208	15	1	22
Caceres	1.000	1	5	2	0	1
Greene	1.000	3	15	1	0	1
Norton	1.000	1	6	0	0	2
Pritchett	.991	79	607	51	6	62
Turner	.991	23	203	11	2	15
White	1.000	11	70	7	0	8
Wolff	.980	8	44	6	1	6

Second Base	PCT	G	PO	A	E	DP
Betten	.940	11	24	23	3	5
Bolick	1.000	2	5	2	0	0
Caceres	.982	55	100	123	4	31
Cruz	.962	81	180	199	15	50
Eenhoorn	1.000	4	4	9	0	0
Williams	1.000	2	5	4	0	1

Third Base	PCT	G	PO	A	E	DP
Arias	.955	99	93	203	14	22
Bolick	1.000	24	12	53	0	6
Burke	.875	3	1	6	1	1
Caceres	.920	19	15	31	4	4
Wolff	.000	1	0	0	0	0

Shortstop	PCT	G	PO	A	E	DP
Arias	1.000	3	3	10	0	2
Caceres	.857	3	3	9	2	1
Cruz	.939	29	45	62	7	11
Eenhoorn	.955	115	153	293	21	56

Outfield	PCT	G	PO	A	E	DP
Bass	1.000	3	3	0	0	0
Betten	1.000	7	10	0	0	0
Carvajal	.958	126	262	9	12	3
Cruz	.923	8	12	0	1	0
Greene	1.000	2	3	0	0	0
Pritchett	.933	9	14	0	1	0
Riley	.995	65	177	4	1	2
Singleton	.978	100	209	15	5	2
Turner	1.000	1	1	0	0	0
White	.979	85	183	7	4	0
Williams	1.000	9	22	1	0	1
Wolff	.944	40	64	4	4	2

MIDLAND — Class AA

TEXAS LEAGUE

BATTING	AVG	G	AB	R	H	2B	3B	HR	RBI	BB	SO	SB	CS	B	T	HT	WT	DOB	1st Yr	Resides
Betten, Randy	.291	57	220	39	64	13	3	3	24	22	45	7	3	R	R	5-11	170	7-28-71	1995	Highland, Calif.
Bilderback, Ty	.227	21	66	7	15	5	0	0	5	6	17	1	3	L	L	6-2	180	10-29-73	1995	Mesa, Ariz.
Bolick, Frank	.330	28	97	26	32	5	1	8	27	26	18	0	0	S	R	5-10	177	6-28-66	1987	Mt. Carmel, Pa.
Burke, Jamie	.329	116	428	77	141	44	3	6	72	40	46	2	3	R	R	6-0	195	9-24-71	1993	Roseburg, Ore.
Buxbaum, Danny	.288	130	514	78	148	42	2	10	70	51	91	1	1	R	R	6-4	217	1-17-73	1995	Alachua, Fla.
Carter, Cale	.167	7	24	3	4	0	0	0	2	3	7	1	0	L	R	5-10	185	9-18-73	1996	Tustin, Calif.
Carter, Michael	.277	15	65	9	18	3	1	0	2	2	8	5	2	R	R	5-9	170	5-5-69	1990	Vicksburg, Miss.
Dalton, Jed	.225	94	360	63	81	18	2	11	48	35	58	7	12	R	R	6-1	190	4-3-73	1995	Omaha, Neb.
Davalillo, David	.250	49	176	21	44	6	2	1	12	6	26	1	2	R	R	5-8	170	8-17-74	1993	Santa Teresa, Venez.
Diaz, Freddie	.267	43	135	21	36	9	0	2	18	18	30	0	0	S	R	5-11	175	9-10-72	1992	El Monte, Calif.
Guiel, Aaron	.329	116	419	91	138	37	7	22	85	59	94	14	10	L	R	5-10	190	10-5-72	1993	Langley, B.C.
Harkrider, Tim	.287	69	251	39	72	12	3	1	24	22	17	1	2	S	R	6-0	180	9-5-71	1993	Carthage, Texas
Hemphill, Bret	.308	78	266	46	82	15	2	10	63	47	56	0	2	S	R	6-3	210	12-17-71	1994	Santa Clara, Calif.

BATTING	AVG	G	AB	R	H	2B	3B	HR	RBI	BB	SO	SB	CS	B	T	HT	WT	DOB	1st Yr	Resides
Herrick, Jason	.252	118	416	60	105	27	4	20	67	34	141	9	6	L	L	6-0	175	7-29-73	1991	Franklin, Wis.
Johnson, Jack	.200	5	15	2	3	2	0	1	3	1	4	0	0	R	R	6-3	205	3-24-70	1991	Chicago, Ill.
Luuloa, Keith	.273	120	421	67	115	29	5	9	59	36	59	7	4	R	R	6-1	175	12-24-74	1994	Kaunakakai, Hawaii
Molina, Ben	.330	29	106	18	35	8	0	6	30	10	7	0	0	R	R	5-11	190	7-20-74	1993	Vega Alta, P.R.
Norton, Chris	.265	58	200	40	53	8	1	16	47	35	57	2	1	R	R	6-2	215	9-21-70	1992	Maitland, Fla.
Ryder, Derek	.231	25	78	4	18	2	0	0	6	2	6	1	0	R	R	6-1	190	3-30-73	1995	Wellingford, Pa.
Singleton, Duane	.309	13	55	15	17	5	1	2	8	6	8	4	0	L	R	6-1	170	8-6-72	1990	Staten Island, N.Y.
White, Derrick	.189	10	37	2	7	2	0	0	3	5	6	1	0	R	R	6-1	215	10-12-69	1991	San Rafael, Calif.
Young, Kevin	.284	103	338	64	96	23	6	6	53	49	40	6	9	R	R	6-0	195	1-22-72	1994	Northville, Mich.

PITCHING	W	L	ERA	G	GS	CG	SV	IP	H	R	ER	BB	SO	B	T	HT	WT	DOB	1st Yr	Resides
Alvarez, Juan	4	1	8.27	24	0	0	0	37	63	42	34	22	27	L	L	6-1	180	8-9-73	1995	Miami, Fla.
Beaumont, Matt	0	2	25.14	4	3	0	0	10	24	27	27	10	11	L	L	6-3	210	4-22-73	1994	Rittman, Ohio
Bene, Bill	0	3	6.31	25	0	0	0	41	42	33	29	40	41	R	R	6-4	205	11-21-67	1988	Montebello, Calif.
Bonanno, Rob	5	10	4.60	21	21	3	0	125	125	83	64	34	64	L	R	6-0	195	1-5-71	1994	Tampa, Fla.
Bovee, Mike	8	2	4.24	20	13	3	0	102	117	53	48	23	61	R	R	5-10	200	8-21-73	1991	Mira Mesa, Calif.
Chavez, Anthony	1	2	4.21	33	1	0	6	47	53	23	22	15	35	R	R	5-11	180	10-22-70	1992	Merced, Calif.
De la Cruz, Fernando	2	5	7.79	13	13	0	0	72	81	70	62	46	44	R	R	6-0	175	1-25-71	1993	La Romana, D.R.
Freehill, Mike	0	7	7.05	35	0	0	10	37	46	33	29	20	32	R	R	6-3	177	6-2-71	1994	Phoenix, Ariz.
Gamez, Robert	7	2	5.10	51	0	0	0	48	62	37	27	20	46	L	L	6-5	185	11-18-68	1988	Newark, Calif.
Harris, Bryan	0	2	11.29	10	1	0	1	18	28	26	23	15	15	L	L	6-2	205	9-11-71	1993	Peachtree City, Ga.
Hook, Chris	1	4	7.07	22	2	0	2	36	41	34	28	19	24	R	R	6-5	195	8-4-68	1989	Florence, Ky.
Janicki, Pete	0	0	0.00	2	0	0	0	2	3	3	0	2	2	R	R	6-4	190	1-26-71	1992	Mesa, Ariz.
Knudsen, Kurt	0	4	8.68	35	4	0	0	57	88	63	55	25	35	R	R	6-3	200	2-20-67	1988	Folsom, Calif.
Macey, Fausto	6	9	8.03	17	17	1	0	96	141	93	86	46	38	R	R	6-4	185	10-9-75	1994	Santo Domingo, D.R.
Perisho, Matt	5	2	2.96	10	10	3	0	73	60	26	24	26	62	L	L	6-0	190	6-8-75	1993	Chandler, Ariz.
Quirico, Rafael	3	3	6.91	20	5	0	0	55	73	47	42	22	37	L	L	6-3	170	9-7-69	1987	Santo Domingo, D.R.
Schoeneweis, Scott	7	5	5.96	20	20	3	0	113	145	84	75	39	94	L	L	6-0	180	10-2-73	1996	Mt. Laurel, N.J.
Skuse, Nick	0	0	6.27	30	0	0	16	33	31	26	23	15	30	R	R	6-7	240	1-9-72	1994	Los Gatos, Calif.
Washburn, Jarrod	15	12	4.80	29	29	5	0	189	211	115	101	65	146	L	L	6-1	185	8-13-74	1995	Webster, Wis.

FIELDING

Catcher	PCT	G	PO	A	E	DP	PB
Burke	.969	26	134	22	5	2	8
Hemphill	.985	67	425	48	7	4	9
Johnson	1.000	5	28	4	0	1	0
Molina	.978	13	74	15	2	3	2
Norton	.963	13	75	3	3	0	9
Ryder	.993	25	125	20	1	3	6

First Base	PCT	G	PO	A	E	DP
Betten	1.000	1	9	0	0	2
Burke	1.000	4	45	2	0	5
Buxbaum	.991	118	1022	92	10	102
Norton	.994	17	170	8	1	14

Second Base	PCT	G	PO	A	E	DP
Betten	.963	6	11	15	1	4
Davalillo	.982	10	30	25	1	10
Diaz	.967	12	21	38	2	7
Guiel	.943	6	12	21	2	3
Luuloa	.965	92	210	260	17	65
Young	.987	17	34	42	1	12

Third Base	PCT	G	PO	A	E	DP
Betten	.930	24	14	66	6	3
Bolick	.872	13	6	28	5	4
Burke	.925	84	64	195	21	20
Buxbaum	1.000	2	2	1	0	1
Davalillo	.931	10	10	17	2	2
Diaz	.977	12	9	34	1	2
Guiel	.875	7	3	18	3	3

Shortstop	PCT	G	PO	A	E	DP
Betten	.957	6	6	16	1	3
Davalillo	.960	28	34	85	5	10
Diaz	.970	15	22	43	2	12
Harkrider	.951	68	98	232	17	48
Luuloa	.941	29	35	77	7	17

Outfield	PCT	G	PO	A	E	DP
Betten	.968	15	30	0	1	0
Bilderback	.978	19	43	1	1	0
Burke	1.000	5	10	1	0	0
C. Carter	1.000	7	12	0	0	0
M. Carter	1.000	15	26	2	0	0
Dalton	.972	93	197	11	6	2
Guiel	.973	63	103	6	3	1
Herrick	.983	116	216	12	4	2
Norton	.833	6	9	1	2	0
Singleton	.960	13	23	1	1	0
White	1.000	2	3	0	0	0
Young	.965	84	103	7	4	1

LAKE ELSINORE — Class A

CALIFORNIA LEAGUE

BATTING	AVG	G	AB	R	H	2B	3B	HR	RBI	BB	SO	SB	CS	B	T	HT	WT	DOB	1st Yr	Resides
Barlok, Todd	.212	49	170	21	36	5	4	1	15	17	51	10	4	R	R	6-4	220	8-8-71	1995	Bristol, Conn.
2-team (44 San Bern.)	.248	93	286	46	71	11	7	6	34	34	83	17	9							
Barnes, Larry	.287	115	446	68	128	32	2	13	71	43	84	3	4	L	L	6-1	195	7-23-74	1995	Bakersfield, Calif.
Baughman, Justin	.274	134	478	71	131	14	3	2	48	40	79	68	15	R	R	5-11	175	8-1-74	1995	Reno, Nev.
Betten, Randy	.345	35	116	18	40	5	2	2	27	16	29	7	5	R	R	5-11	170	7-28-71	1995	Highland, Calif.
Bilderback, Ty	.316	62	209	38	66	13	3	2	30	36	42	11	5	L	L	6-2	180	10-29-73	1995	Mesa, Ariz.
Carter, Cale	.228	25	79	19	18	2	0	1	5	9	15	2	0	L	R	5-10	185	9-18-73	1996	Tustin, Calif.
Curtis, Matt	.330	74	264	58	87	25	8	17	55	25	54	3	1	S	R	6-0	195	8-14-74	1996	Visalia, Calif.
Davalillo, David	.222	37	126	15	28	6	2	0	9	7	33	3	1	R	R	5-8	170	8-17-74	1993	Santa Teresa, Venez.
Dougherty, Jeb	.231	12	26	2	6	0	0	0	1	1	5	3	2	R	R	6-0	180	7-16-75	1997	Yucca Valley, Calif.
Durrington, Trent	.247	123	409	60	101	21	3	3	36	51	90	52	18	S	R	5-10	185	8-27-75	1994	Broadbeach Waters, Australia
Failla, Paul	.228	103	360	43	82	20	1	1	42	55	89	21	10	S	R	6-2	195	12-8-72	1994	Sewickley, Pa.
Geronimo, Cesar	.571	3	7	1	4	0	0	0	2	0	0	0	0	R	R	6-0	180	12-19-75	1995	Santo Domingo, D.R.
Hutchins, Norm	.289	132	564	82	163	31	12	15	69	23	147	39	17	L	L	6-2	185	11-20-75	1994	Greenburgh, N.Y.
McAninch, John	.250	61	188	24	47	12	1	4	21	15	43	1	1	R	R	6-0	205	8-1-73	1995	Oak Harbor, Wash.
Molina, Ben	.282	36	149	18	42	10	2	4	33	7	9	0	1	R	R	5-11	190	7-20-74	1993	Vega Alta, P.R.
Morris, Greg	.288	74	278	38	80	26	1	3	30	29	47	1	3	R	R	6-4	210	1-29-72	1994	Carmichael, Calif.
Murray, Eddie	.500	2	8	1	4	0	0	1	2	0	0	0	0	S	R	6-2	220	2-24-56	1973	Canyon Country, Calif.
Norton, Chris	.275	37	138	34	38	7	2	11	35	22	41	0	1	R	R	6-2	215	9-21-70	1992	Maitland, Fla.
Parker, Allan	.182	8	11	2	2	0	0	1	3	0	3	0	0	R	R	5-11	165	5-27-72	1994	Hernando, Fla.
Ready, Randy	.182	7	22	6	4	1	0	2	4	8	6	0	0	R	R	5-11	180	1-8-60	1980	Cardiff, Calif.
Ryder, Derek	.231	36	91	12	21	5	2	1	13	8	17	1	2	R	R	6-1	190	3-30-73	1995	Wellingford, Pa.
Stuart, Rich	.230	45	165	25	38	11	6	6	33	13	50	6	4	R	R	5-10	175	7-31-76	1994	Arecibo, P.R.
Thurston, Jerrey	.500	2	6	1	3	1	0	0	1	0	2	0	0	R	R	6-4	200	4-17-72	1990	Longwood, Fla.
Turner, Chris	.083	3	12	0	1	0	1	0	1	0	3	0	0	R	R	6-1	190	3-23-69	1991	Bowling Green, Ky.
Urso, Joe	.000	2	1	0	0	0	0	0	0	0	0	0	0	R	R	5-7	160	7-28-70	1992	Tampa, Fla.
Ussery, Brian	.241	10	29	1	7	1	0	0	4	2	11	0	0	S	R	6-0	180	2-25-74	1996	Brandon, Fla.
VanderGriend, Jon	.182	118	402	45	73	17	2	14	45	32	153	19	5	L	R	6-5	220	4-25-72	1995	Lynden, Wash.
Welles, Robby	.000	3	5	0	0	0	0	0	0	1	2	0	0	R	R	6-4	195	8-17-72	1994	Beverly Hills, Calif.

GAMES BY POSITION: C—Curtis 47, McAninch 30, Molina 33, Norton 3, Ryder 35, Thurston 2, Turner 3, Ussery 9. **1B**—Barnes 113, Betten 1, Failla 15, McAninch 15, Morris 1. **2B**—Betten 1, Davalillo 4, Durrington 111, Failla 26, Parker 2, Ready 1. **3B**—Barlok 25, Betten

11, Curtis 5, Davalillo 26, Durrington 1, Failla 19, Morris 57, Parker 3, Ready 1. **SS**—Baughman 129, Betten 1, Davalillo 7, Failla 7, Parker 1. **OF**—Barlok 22, Barnes 1, Betten 17, Bilderback 30, Carter 22, Curtis 8, Dougherty 9, Durrington 6, Failla 29, Geronimo 3, Hutchins 130, Stuart 43, VanderGriend 117, Welles 2.

PITCHING	W	L	ERA	G	GS	CG	SV	IP	H	R	ER	BB	SO	B	T	HT	WT	DOB	1st Yr	Resides
Agosto, Stevenson	5	8	5.32	24	21	1	0	137	155	91	81	50	91	L	L	5-10	175	9-2-75	1994	Rio Grande, P.R.
Alvarez, Juan	4	2	1.40	27	0	0	3	51	33	9	8	13	46	L	L	6-1	180	8-9-73	1995	Miami, Fla.
Beaumont, Matt	0	0	6.75	1	1	0	0	1	2	1	1	1	1	L	L	6-3	210	4-22-73	1994	Rittman, Ohio
Cintron, Jose	2	3	6.11	28	6	0	0	63	76	44	43	22	50	S	R	6-2	185	9-12-75	1993	Yabucoa, P.R.
Cooper, Brian	7	3	3.54	17	17	1	0	117	111	56	46	27	104	R	R	6-1	175	8-19-74	1995	Glendora, Calif.
Deakman, Josh	8	11	4.75	26	25	1	0	165	182	107	87	42	99	R	R	6-5	185	2-25-74	1995	Beaverton, Ore.
De la Cruz, Fernando	2	2	4.54	8	6	0	0	38	36	22	19	17	26	R	R	6-0	175	1-25-71	1993	La Romana, D.R.
Finley, Chuck	0	0	2.00	2	2	0	0	9	5	3	2	4	12	L	L	6-6	214	11-26-62	1985	Newport Beach, Calif.
Freehill, Mike	0	1	1.99	21	0	0	8	23	18	7	5	8	20	R	R	6-3	177	6-2-71	1994	Phoenix, Ariz.
Goedhart, Darrell	0	2	8.44	8	3	0	0	16	29	18	15	11	12	R	R	6-3	210	7-18-70	1989	San Jacinto, Calif.
Gubicza, Mark	0	1	15.75	2	2	0	0	4	12	7	7	1	1	R	R	6-5	230	8-14-62	1981	Northridge, Calif.
Harris, Bryan	5	5	3.98	31	0	0	0	43	35	23	19	23	39	L	L	6-2	205	9-11-71	1993	Peachtree City, Ga.
Henderson, Juan	1	1	10.45	9	0	0	0	10	20	13	12	2	6	R	R	5-10	175	4-17-74	1993	Santo Domingo, D.R.
Hill, Jason	3	7	4.23	54	0	0	15	66	71	43	31	34	73	R	L	5-11	175	4-14-72	1994	Redding, Calif.
Humphreys, Kevin	0	1	3.50	16	0	0	0	18	19	9	7	2	15	R	R	6-0	180	8-21-73	1996	Panama City, Fla.
Johnson, Greg	1	0	3.43	34	0	0	0	45	46	21	17	9	35	L	L	6-0	185	4-28-74	1996	Frostburg, Md.
Knudsen, Kurt	1	2	6.97	7	0	0	3	10	13	9	8	4	10	R	R	6-3	200	2-20-67	1988	Folsom, Calif.
Langston, Mark	0	2	3.21	3	3	0	0	14	11	7	5	2	10	R	L	6-2	184	8-20-60	1981	Anaheim Hills, Calif.
Mayer, Aaron	2	3	7.29	36	0	0	0	58	69	57	47	41	38	R	R	6-6	230	8-13-74	1993	San Ramon, Calif.
Ontiveros, Steve	0	1	27.00	1	1	0	0	0	0	1	1	1	0	R	R	6-0	180	3-5-61	1982	Stafford, Texas
Percival, Troy	0	0	0.00	2	1	0	0	2	1	0	0	0	3	R	R	6-3	200	8-9-69	1990	Moreno Valley, Calif.
Quirico, Rafael	8	4	2.83	14	13	0	0	92	94	43	29	29	74	L	L	6-3	170	9-7-69	1987	Santo Domingo, D.R.
Riggan, Jerrod	2	5	6.07	8	8	0	0	43	60	36	29	16	31	R	R	6-4	185	5-16-74	1996	Brewster, Wash.
Scutero, Brian	0	1	11.25	5	0	0	0	8	16	11	10	6	8	R	R	6-1	190	8-15-73	1995	Winter Park, Fla.
Skuse, Nick	0	0	2.03	17	0	0	0	27	23	13	6	8	40	R	R	6-7	240	1-9-72	1994	Los Gatos, Calif.
Stephens, Jason	7	11	5.40	24	22	1	0	127	149	86	76	42	101	R	R	6-0	180	9-10-75	1996	Springhill, La.
Thurmond, Travis	3	3	2.52	9	9	2	0	61	41	21	17	22	53	R	R	6-3	200	12-8-73	1992	Hillsboro, Ore.

CEDAR RAPIDS — Class A

MIDWEST LEAGUE

BATTING	AVG	G	AB	R	H	2B	3B	HR	RBI	BB	SO	SB	CS	B	T	HT	WT	DOB	1st Yr	Resides
Abbott, Chuck	.231	133	520	86	120	21	5	7	54	62	170	31	12	S	R	6-1	180	1-26-75	1996	Schaumburg, Ill.
Carter, Cale	.221	30	86	18	19	3	0	0	8	8	16	2	1	L	R	5-10	185	9-18-73	1996	Tustin, Calif.
Curtis, Matt	.248	34	113	21	28	8	1	4	18	17	16	0	0	S	R	6-0	195	8-14-74	1996	Visalia, Calif.
Fefee, Theo	.240	110	367	40	88	13	6	3	35	18	90	10	9	L	L	6-3	190	4-26-74	1996	Springfield, Ill.
Garrick, Matt	.221	28	95	11	21	6	1	0	14	12	23	1	0	R	R	6-0	185	8-19-75	1997	Duncanville, Texas
Geronimo, Cesar	.167	17	42	5	7	0	0	0	1	2	10	1	0	R	R	6-0	180	12-19-75	1995	Santo Domingo, D.R.
Gillespie, Eric	.254	122	421	78	107	26	7	18	72	55	80	8	0	L	R	5-10	200	6-6-75	1996	Long Beach, Calif.
Graves, Bryan	.204	68	191	14	39	12	0	1	17	32	32	1	2	R	R	6-0	200	10-8-74	1995	Bogalusa, La.
Guiel, Jeff	.318	41	132	32	42	7	0	10	26	35	28	13	2	L	R	5-11	195	1-12-74	1997	Langley, B.C.
Ham, Kevin	.281	123	441	67	124	26	1	15	73	41	127	9	9	R	R	6-1	195	9-14-74	1993	El Paso, Texas
Monzon, Jose	.225	34	111	12	25	3	0	4	14	12	14	0	0	R	R	6-1	178	11-8-68	1987	Municipio Vargas, Venez.
Murphy, Nate	.221	51	149	21	33	4	2	0	13	19	43	4	2	L	L	6-1	190	4-15-75	1996	Montague, Mass.
Parker, Allan	.250	15	48	4	12	2	0	0	5	3	10	3	3	R	R	5-11	165	5-27-72	1994	Hernando, Fla.
Rodriguez, Juan	.281	111	416	66	117	18	8	12	55	43	106	11	12	S	L	5-10	185	12-16-74	1994	Arecibo, P.R.
Sasser, Rob	.272	134	497	103	135	26	5	17	77	69	92	37	13	R	R	6-4	190	3-6-75	1993	Oakland, Calif.
t'Hoen, E.J.	.203	123	384	41	78	19	3	3	46	31	114	2	3	R	R	6-2	184	11-8-75	1996	Alphen, Holland
Ussery, Brian	.000	1	1	0	0	0	0	0	0	0	0	0	0	S	R	6-0	180	2-25-74	1996	Brandon, Fla.
Vallone, Gar	.236	41	89	13	21	1	0	1	8	18	20	0	2	S	R	6-0	175	5-9-73	1995	Placentia, Calif.
Welles, Robby	.266	20	64	10	17	2	0	2	8	5	18	2	0	R	R	6-4	195	8-17-72	1994	Beverly Hills, Calif.
Wooten, Shawn	.289	108	353	43	102	23	1	15	75	49	71	0	1	R	R	5-11	205	7-24-72	1993	La Verne, Calif.

GAMES BY POSITION: C—Curtis 7, Garrick 23, Gillespie 7, Graves 64, Monzon 32, Wooten 19. **1B**—Curtis 5, Gillespie 101, J. Rodriguez 22, Vallone 5, Welles 11, Wooten 9. **2B**—Abbott 113, t'Hoen 18, Vallone 11. **3B**—Gillespie 12, Parker 1, Sasser 133. **SS**—Abbott 19, Gillespie 2, Parker 13, Sasser 3, t'Hoen 102, Vallone 10. **OF**—Carter 22, Curtis 17, Fefee 99, Garrick 1, Geronimo 13, Graves 1, Guiel 41, Ham 121, Murphy 18, J. Rodriguez 96, Vallone 3, Welles 3.

PITCHING	W	L	ERA	G	GS	CG	SV	IP	H	R	ER	BB	SO	B	T	HT	WT	DOB	1st Yr	Resides
Cintron, Jose	0	0	5.40	2	0	0	0	5	3	3	3	0	4	S	R	6-2	185	9-12-75	1993	Yabucoa, P.R.
Cowsill, Brendon	3	5	4.75	26	0	0	3	36	41	24	19	16	32	R	R	6-3	190	1-7-75	1994	Chula Vista, Calif.
Darrell, Tommy	12	10	4.04	27	26	5	0	192	212	108	86	40	106	R	R	6-6	210	7-21-76	1995	Dunbar, Pa.
De la Cruz, Fernando	0	2	11.48	10	0	0	1	13	19	22	17	14	10	R	R	6-0	175	1-25-71	1993	La Romana, D.R.
Gadway, Chris	0	1	4.56	15	0	0	0	24	23	12	12	9	14	R	R	5-10	175	1-19-74	1997	East Yarmouth, Maine
Greene, Danny	1	1	0.45	24	0	0	12	40	27	7	2	11	42	R	R	6-3	220	2-24-73	1996	Nashua, N.H.
Harriger, Mark	1	6	7.82	12	11	1	0	51	70	50	44	33	50	R	R	6-2	196	4-29-75	1996	Lakewood, Calif.
Henderson, Juan	1	4	9.13	20	7	0	1	45	70	55	46	17	21	R	R	5-10	175	4-17-74	1993	Santo Domingo, D.R.
Humphreys, Kevin	5	1	5.62	30	0	0	2	66	75	45	41	9	40	R	R	6-0	180	8-21-73	1996	Panama City, Fla.
Leyva, Edgar	8	6	4.69	22	21	0	1	121	118	73	63	58	77	R	R	6-1	198	7-27-77	1995	Guasave, Mexico
O'Quinn, Jimmy	0	1	8.22	14	0	0	0	15	17	14	14	11	17	L	L	6-0	190	8-27-73	1995	Jacksonville, Fla.
Ortiz, Ramon	11	10	3.58	27	27	8	0	181	156	78	72	53	225	R	R	6-0	150	5-23-76	1995	Cotui, D.R.
Puffer, Brandon	0	0	2.60	10	0	0	0	17	8	6	5	10	11	R	R	6-3	185	10-5-75	1994	Mission Viejo, Calif.
Riggan, Jerrod	9	8	4.89	19	19	3	0	116	132	70	63	36	65	R	R	6-4	185	5-16-74	1996	Brewster, Wash.
Rodriguez, Hector	1	0	12.19	9	0	0	0	10	14	15	14	13	15	R	R	6-2	225	3-21-75	1996	Caguas, P.R.
Scutero, Brian	0	1	0.87	10	0	0	1	10	14	5	1	6	11	R	R	6-1	190	8-15-73	1995	Winter Park, Fla.
Soriano, Jacobo	1	4	7.75	25	0	0	1	34	43	33	29	23	28	S	R	5-11	175	11-28-74	1992	Los Llanos, D.R.
Stockstill, Jason	7	14	5.38	27	27	1	0	161	167	111	96	86	116	L	L	6-5	200	11-13-76	1995	Villa Park, Calif.
Volkman, Keith	2	2	2.45	38	0	0	5	51	36	18	14	27	43	L	L	6-2	215	1-13-76	1994	Pasadena, Md.

BOISE — Short-Season Class A

NORTHWEST LEAGUE

BATTING	AVG	G	AB	R	H	2B	3B	HR	RBI	BB	SO	SB	CS	B	T	HT	WT	DOB	1st Yr	Resides
Betancourt, Oscar	.286	68	266	47	76	16	1	9	46	30	70	2	2	R	R	6-1	200	7-9-75	1997	San Diego, Calif.

BATTING	AVG	G	AB	R	H	2B	3B	HR	RBI	BB	SO	SB	CS	B	T	HT	WT	DOB	1st Yr	Resides
Castro, Nelson	.294	69	293	74	86	16	1	7	37	38	53	26	6	S	R	5-11	182	6-4-76	1994	Villa Vasquez, D.R.
Child, Casey	.325	68	274	69	89	26	2	11	57	34	47	18	2	R	R	6-2	185	2-11-76	1997	Orem, Utah
Delgado, Ariel	.242	60	207	37	50	10	1	1	22	16	43	6	1	L	L	6-2	205	9-11-76	1994	Carolina, P.R.
Dewey, Jason	.324	68	272	55	88	17	2	13	64	41	70	5	2	R	R	6-2	190	4-18-77	1997	Valrico, Fla.
Dougherty, Jeb	.304	25	92	20	28	5	1	0	8	8	10	3	0	R	R	6-0	180	7-16-75	1997	Yucca Valley, Calif.
Garrick, Matt	.300	5	20	1	6	0	0	0	4	3	2	0	0	R	R	6-0	185	8-19-75	1997	Duncanville, Texas
Geronimo, Cesar	.286	54	192	32	55	11	2	2	29	15	29	3	2	R	R	6-0	180	12-19-75	1995	Santo Domingo, D.R.
Leggett, Adam	.224	62	219	47	49	16	2	1	32	34	54	8	1	S	R	6-0	190	4-3-76	1997	Longview, Texas
Martin, Casey	.337	50	181	30	61	14	0	8	48	23	45	1	0	R	R	6-2	220	12-24-75	1997	Lakewood, Calif.
Medosch, Keith	.220	45	132	25	29	5	0	0	9	26	31	5	3	R	R	5-11	175	1-31-75	1997	St. Petersburg, Fla.
Nunley, Jay	.282	60	216	34	61	16	1	5	39	26	37	5	3	R	R	6-2	200	6-4-75	1997	Jacksonville, Fla.
Peckham, Chris	.257	17	35	7	9	0	0	1	6	10	10	0	0	R	R	5-10	195	9-17-75	1997	West Bridgewater, Mass.
Philip-Guide, Sheldon	.235	19	51	7	12	4	0	0	5	7	16	2	0	R	R	6-0	208	2-17-74	1997	Santa Monica, Calif.
Russoniello, Mike	.000	2	3	1	0	0	0	0	1	0	2	0	0	R	R	6-0	195	5-29-77	1996	Scottsdale, Ariz.
Stewart, Paxton	.333	72	282	59	94	16	2	7	45	41	55	8	5	L	R	6-3	185	5-4-74	1995	New York, N.Y.
Ussery, Brian	.262	15	42	5	11	0	0	0	5	11	11	0	0	S	R	6-0	180	2-25-74	1996	Brandon, Fla.

GAMES BY POSITION: C—Dewey 52, Garrick 4, Martin 14, Russoniello 2, Ussery 11. **1B**—Delgado 10, Martin 12, Stewart 61. **2B**—Leggett 60, Medosch 21. **3B**—Betancourt 68, Medosch 3, Peckham 13. **SS**—Castro 68, Medosch 12. **OF**—Child 64, Delgado 49, Dougherty 24, Geronimo 49, Medosch 9, Nunley 45, Philip-Guide 15, Stewart 6.

PITCHING	W	L	ERA	G	GS	CG	SV	IP	H	R	ER	BB	SO	B	T	HT	WT	DOB	1st Yr	Resides
Anderson, Jason	1	0	19.80	5	0	0	0	5	15	13	11	6	3	R	R	6-3	215	5-16-75	1997	Brooklyn, Mich.
Cummings, Ryan	6	2	3.09	14	13	0	0	70	73	38	24	10	79	R	R	6-3	210	6-3-76	1997	Marietta, Ga.
Dobson, Dwayne	0	0	6.45	12	0	0	0	22	28	17	16	8	17	R	R	6-5	205	2-23-76	1997	Clearwater, Fla.
Donaldson, Bo	3	1	1.21	27	0	0	15	52	31	10	7	20	88	R	R	6-1	200	10-10-73	1997	Philadelphia, Pa.
Fish, Steve	5	2	4.08	24	4	0	0	75	69	41	34	23	79	R	R	6-1	190	10-25-74	1997	Bend, Ore.
Gangemi, Joe	7	2	5.47	16	16	0	0	79	97	56	48	31	61	R	L	6-3	180	5-3-76	1997	Denville, N.J.
Harriger, Mark	3	4	7.94	13	12	0	0	51	51	52	45	36	42	R	R	6-2	196	4-29-75	1996	Lakewood, Calif.
Hughes, Michael	0	2	7.56	11	3	0	0	17	20	16	14	12	18	R	R	6-3	205	9-25-76	1996	Fresno, Calif.
Jones, Greg	2	2	3.62	21	4	0	2	37	35	19	15	19	39	R	R	6-2	190	11-15-76	1997	Seminole, Fla.
Nickle, Doug	0	1	6.41	17	2	0	0	20	27	17	14	8	22	R	R	6-4	210	10-2-74	1997	Sonoma, Calif.
Puffer, Brandon	0	0	2.35	6	0	0	1	15	10	5	4	2	15	R	R	6-3	195	10-5-75	1994	Mission Viejo, Calif.
Rodriguez, Hector	5	1	2.38	25	0	0	2	42	35	16	11	30	55	R	R	6-2	225	3-21-75	1996	Caguas, P.R.
Shields, Scot	7	2	2.94	30	0	0	2	52	45	20	17	24	61	R	R	6-1	175	7-22-75	1997	Fort Lauderdale, Fla.
Snellings, Ryan	1	2	6.37	12	6	0	1	30	44	28	21	11	27	R	L	6-3	200	2-18-77	1997	Seminole, Fla.
Soriano, Jacobo	0	0	6.75	3	0	0	0	4	3	3	3	4	3	S	R	5-11	175	11-28-74	1992	Los Llanos, D.R.
Williams, Kris	2	3	3.43	19	1	0	0	39	47	33	15	14	35	R	R	6-0	195	9-28-76	1997	Westfield, N.J.
Wise, Matt	9	1	3.25	15	15	0	0	83	62	37	30	34	86	R	R	6-4	190	11-18-75	1997	La Verne, Calif.

BUTTE — Rookie

PIONEER LEAGUE

BATTING	AVG	G	AB	R	H	2B	3B	HR	RBI	BB	SO	SB	CS	B	T	HT	WT	DOB	1st Yr	Resides
Adams, Tim	.260	38	131	20	34	4	1	1	17	8	43	0	1	R	R	6-3	225	9-19-74	1997	Colfax, Calif.
Battle, Rohn	.250	2	8	2	2	0	1	0	1	0	3	0	0	R	R	5-9	160	12-19-74	1997	San Diego, Calif.
Brewer, Brad	.239	19	67	14	16	2	0	0	8	14	17	0	2	R	R	5-10	170	11-19-75	1997	Fairfield, Calif.
Collier, Marc	.071	5	14	0	1	0	0	0	0	1	6	0	0	R	R	5-10	170	3-25-78	1996	Hummelstown, Pa.
Condon, Mike	.304	49	181	38	55	12	1	1	19	14	19	4	1	R	R	5-10	180	2-13-74	1997	Brielle, N.J.
DeJesus, Eddie	.297	57	219	38	65	14	1	4	35	23	58	4	4	R	R	6-4	190	1-11-77	1995	Boca Chica, D.R.
Encarnacion, Bien	.259	26	81	11	21	5	0	0	9	2	14	2	2	S	R	5-11	165	2-24-78	1995	Bani, D.R.
Guzman, Elpidio	.302	17	43	12	13	2	1	3	13	5	5	3	0	L	L	6-2	166	2-24-79	1996	Santo Domingo, D.R.
Hagins, Steve	.351	64	268	59	94	20	1	17	56	17	53	13	3	R	R	6-1	205	3-7-75	1997	Aliso Viejo, Calif.
Johnson, Patrick	.250	47	160	31	40	9	0	3	21	24	32	1	1	R	R	6-3	200	4-18-75	1996	Taylorsville, Utah
Knight, Marcus	.294	72	293	51	86	15	5	8	43	44	62	8	3	S	R	5-11	195	9-10-78	1996	Pembroke Pines, Fla.
Lawrence, Mike	.259	69	263	43	68	10	2	2	46	36	40	4	2	R	R	6-5	200	2-18-76	1995	Chico, Calif.
Llanos, Alex	.335	49	179	41	60	9	2	8	43	17	30	3	1	L	R	6-1	185	9-20-76	1995	Carolina, P.R.
Nizov, Alexander	.276	27	87	12	24	5	1	1	8	8	21	1	2	R	R	6-0	162	7-12-74	1993	Nizhny Novgorod, Russia
Philip-Guide, Sheldon	.260	17	50	10	13	2	0	0	2	11	17	3	0	R	R	6-0	208	2-17-74	1997	Santa Monica, Calif.
Pichardo, Gilbert	.217	8	23	7	5	1	0	1	5	5	10	0	1	S	R	6-1	195	1-8-79	1997	Brooklyn, N.Y.
Quittner, Peter	.284	36	134	21	38	2	1	3	13	2	26	3	1	L	R	6-2	190	10-7-74	1997	San Jose, Calif.
Santos, Jose	.229	21	70	11	16	3	0	1	9	9	20	1	1	R	R	6-1	200	11-5-77	1996	San Francisco de Macoris, D.R.
Talbott, Ben	.200	22	65	13	13	1	0	1	13	12	29	0	0	S	R	6-2	215	12-2-74	1997	Haddam, Conn.
Tolentino, Juan	.300	61	213	44	64	16	4	10	53	24	53	21	2	R	R	5-11	175	3-12-76	1995	Bronx, N.Y.

GAMES BY POSITION: C—Hagins 1, Johnson 47, Quittner 8, Santos 21. **1B**—Adams 34, Llanos 4, Quittner 25, Talbott 13. **2B**—Brewer 2, Collier 3, Condon 17, Hagins 1, Llanos 34, Nizov 26. **3B**—Lawrence 69, Llanos 5. **SS**—Brewer 18, Collier 2, Condon 33, Encarnacion 26. **OF**—Battle 2, DeJesus 57, Guzman 17, Knight 70, Philip-Guide 16, Pichardo 7, Tolentino 59.

PITCHING	W	L	ERA	G	GS	CG	SV	IP	H	R	ER	BB	SO	B	T	HT	WT	DOB	1st Yr	Resides
Bane, Jaymie	3	2	5.80	24	0	0	6	40	43	33	26	16	47	R	L	5-11	170	2-19-75	1997	Phoenix, Ariz.
Elias, Javier	0	2	7.09	18	0	0	0	27	47	36	21	16	18	R	R	6-0	177	2-21-79	1997	Mexicali, Mexico
Figueroa, Claudio	1	0	5.79	4	0	0	0	5	7	3	3	2	4	R	R	5-11	200	11-2-78	1997	San Luis Rio Colorado, Mexico
McGuire, Brandon	3	4	9.79	17	2	0	0	34	55	43	37	25	20	S	R	6-4	220	8-10-77	1995	Big Spring, Texas
Miller, Ernie	1	4	8.01	20	2	0	1	39	53	41	35	26	39	L	L	6-5	195	7-19-75	1997	Jackson Heights, N.Y.
Padilla, Charly	0	2	6.62	20	0	0	0	34	44	31	25	12	24	R	R	6-4	180	9-11-78	1996	Urachiche, Venez.
Perozo, Felix	1	6	5.81	14	14	2	0	79	106	63	51	35	54	R	R	6-6	192	3-24-74	1991	Santo Domingo, D.R.
Porter, Aaron	2	2	7.47	13	4	0	0	37	53	34	31	15	25	R	R	6-1	185	2-3-75	1997	Sacramento, Calif.
Ricks, Ronald	5	3	5.23	17	8	2	0	62	80	48	36	22	48	R	R	6-5	225	3-23-75	1997	Tallahassee, Fla.
Rodriguez, Hector	1	0	1.93	2	0	0	0	5	5	1	1	4	7	R	R	6-2	225	3-21-75	1996	Caguas, P.R.
Rojas, Renney	8	4	3.51	15	15	5	0	110	113	54	43	19	65	S	R	6-0	185	11-7-78	1996	Maracaibo, Venez.
Romero, John	0	3	10.07	15	1	0	0	22	33	34	25	22	17	R	R	6-2	175	9-1-75	1995	Sylmar, Calif.
Steele, Brandon	3	4	4.52	13	13	1	0	70	83	53	35	42	55	R	R	6-3	195	8-21-78	1996	Huntington Beach, Calif.
Timmerman, Heath	0	2	6.35	7	6	0	0	17	26	21	12	10	10	R	R	6-2	190	8-29-77	1997	Skiatook, Okla.
Tokarse, Brian	2	4	6.87	8	7	0	0	37	44	33	28	8	34	R	R	6-3	180	2-28-75	1997	Whittier, Calif.
Torrealba, Aquiles	0	0	3.86	2	0	0	0	2	2	1	1	1	3	R	R	6-4	190	9-29-78	1996	San Mateo, Venez.

Arizona DIAMONDBACKS

FARM SYSTEM

Director of Player Development: Mel Didier

Class	Farm Team	League	W	L	Pct.	Finish*	Manager	First Yr
#A	High Desert (Calif.) Mavericks	California	83	57	.593	+1st (10)	Chris Speier	1997
A	South Bend (Ind.) Silver Hawks	Midwest	54	83	.394	14th (14)	Dick Scott	1997
#R	Lethbridge (Alta.) Black Diamonds	Pioneer	39	33	.542	4th (8)	Tommy Jones	1996
R	Phoenix (Ariz.) Diamondbacks	Arizona	27	29	.482	4th (6)	Don Wakamatsu	1996

*Finish in overall standings (No. of teams in league) #Advanced level +Won league championship

ORGANIZATION LEADERS

MINOR LEAGUERS

BATTING

*AVG	Mike Stoner, High Desert	.358
R	Mike Stoner, High Desert	115
H	Mike Stoner, High Desert	203
TB	Mike Stoner, High Desert	356
2B	Mike Stoner, High Desert	44
3B	Garry Maddox, High Desert	12
HR	Two tied at	33
RBI	Mike Stoner, High Desert	142
BB	Stanton Cameron, High Desert	93
SO	Stanton Cameron, High Desert	127
SB	Jason Conti, High Desert/South Bend	31

PITCHING

W	Jeff Sobkoviak, High Desert	14
L	Three tied at	11
#ERA	Chris Michalak, High Desert	2.65
G	Three tied at	50
CG	Five tied at	1
SV	Dave Tuttle, High Desert	19
IP	Jeff Sobkoviak, High Desert	160
BB	Ben Norris, South Bend/Lethbridge	54
SO	Jason Robbins, High Desert/South Bend	153

*Minimum 250 At-Bats #Minimum 75 Innings

JEFF GOLDEN

Travis Lee

TOP 10 PROSPECTS

STEVE MOORE

John Patterson

How the Diamondbacks Top 10 prospects, as judged by Baseball America prior to the 1997 season, fared in 1997:

Player, Pos.	Club (Class)	AVG	AB	R	H	2B	3B	HR	RBI	SB
1. Travis Lee, 1b	Tucson (AAA)	.300	227	42	68	16	2	14	46	2
	High Desert (A)	.363	226	63	82	18	1	18	63	5
7. Mark Osborne, c	High Desert (A)	.190	42	6	8	1	1	1	5	0
	South Bend (A)	.264	333	38	88	25	2	8	51	2
8. Rod Barajas, c	High Desert (A)	.266	199	24	53	11	0	7	30	0

Player, Pos.	Club (Class)	W	L	ERA	G	SV	IP	H	BB	SO
2. John Patterson, rhp	South Bend (A)	1	9	3.23	18	0	78	63	34	95
3. Vladimir Nunez, rhp	High Desert (A)	8	5	5.17	28	0	158	169	40	142
4. Nick Bierbrodt, lhp	South Bend (A)	2	4	4.04	15	0	76	77	37	64
5. Larry Rodriguez, rhp	South Bend (A)	4	11	3.62	19	0	104	102	37	72
6. Brad Penny, rhp	South Bend (A)	10	5	2.73	25	0	119	91	43	116
9. Mike McCutcheon, lhp	South Bend (A)	7	5	3.41	31	1	106	104	49	67
10. Ben Norris, lhp	South Bend (A)	1	8	4.03	14	0	60	69	31	40
	Lethbridge (R)	7	3	4.86	14	0	83	93	23	54

TM

TUCSON — Class AAA

PACIFIC COAST LEAGUE

BATTING	AVG	G	AB	R	H	2B	3B	HR	RBI	BB	SO	SB	CS	B	T	Ht.	Wt.	DOB	1st Yr.	Resides
Lee, Travis	.300	59	227	42	68	16	2	14	46	31	46	2	0	L	L	6-3	205	5-26-75	1993	Olympia, Wash.

For complete Tucson statistics, see page 142.

NEW HAVEN — Class AA

EASTERN LEAGUE

BATTING	AVG	G	AB	R	H	2B	3B	HR	RBI	BB	SO	SB	CS	B	T	Ht.	Wt.	DOB	1st Yr.	Resides
Osborne, Mark	.000	3	5	1	0	0	0	0	0	2	4	0	0	L	R	6-4	204	2-1-78	1996	Sanford, N.C.

For complete New Haven statistics, see page 105.

HIGH DESERT — Class A

CALIFORNIA LEAGUE

BATTING	AVG	G	AB	R	H	2B	3B	HR	RBI	BB	SO	SB	CS	B	T	HT	WT	DOB	1st Yr	Resides
Baltzell, Beau	.100	8	20	3	2	0	0	1	4	3	10	0	0	R	R	5-11	215	8-2-73	1996	Omaha, Neb.
Barajas, Rod	.266	57	199	24	53	11	0	7	30	8	41	0	2	R	R	6-2	220	9-5-75	1996	Norwalk, Calif.
Boughton, Mike	.178	20	45	6	8	3	1	0	2	2	11	1	0	S	R	6-3	170	11-8-74	1996	Double Oak, Texas
Cameron, Stanton	.300	139	514	103	154	31	3	33	113	93	127	1	0	R	R	6-5	195	7-5-69	1987	Powell, Tenn.
Clark, Kevin	.234	13	47	4	11	4	0	1	3	3	13	0	0	R	R	6-1	200	4-30-73	1993	Henderson, Nev.
Conti, Jason	.356	14	59	15	21	5	1	2	8	10	12	1	2	L	R	5-11	175	1-27-75	1996	Cranberry Township, Pa.
Davis, Reggie	.266	44	154	24	41	8	0	8	35	12	26	0	2	R	R	5-10	210	11-2-74	1996	Winston, Ga.
Durkac, Bo	.282	137	510	76	144	27	4	8	71	63	70	1	0	S	R	6-1	205	12-12-72	1996	Kittanning, Pa.
Fick, Chris	.241	17	54	12	13	3	0	2	10	11	12	1	0	L	R	6-2	190	10-4-69	1994	Thousand Oaks, Calif.
Gann, Jamie	.225	91	267	33	60	12	2	6	32	17	71	2	1	R	R	6-1	185	5-1-75	1996	Norman, Okla.
Garcia, Juan	.000	3	3	0	0	0	0	0	0	0	1	0	0	R	R	5-9	160	9-25-78	1996	San Francisco de Macoris, D.R.
Glasser, Scott	.248	57	121	23	30	5	0	1	11	14	19	3	4	R	R	6-1	180	12-9-75	1996	Huntington Beach, Calif.
Goligoski, Jason	.300	123	437	92	131	17	3	3	58	76	91	15	6	L	R	6-1	180	10-2-71	1993	Hamilton, Mont.
Hardy, Brett	.114	12	35	3	4	1	0	0	0	1	14	1	0	L	L	6-0	180	12-22-73	1996	Laguna Beach, Calif.
Hartman, Ron	.292	75	291	43	85	22	0	14	65	30	57	0	2	R	R	6-1	200	12-12-74	1996	Baltimore, Md.
Lee, Travis	.363	61	226	63	82	18	1	18	63	47	36	5	1	L	L	6-3	205	5-26-75	1993	Olympia, Wash.
Maddox, Garry	.306	101	409	89	125	22	12	7	44	52	94	25	8	L	R	6-3	185	10-24-74	1996	Penn Valley, Pa.
Mota, Gary	.252	31	107	23	27	3	0	5	16	15	25	2	3	R	R	6-0	195	10-6-70	1990	La Crescenta, Calif.
Osborne, Mark	.190	15	42	6	8	1	1	1	5	10	14	0	0	L	R	6-4	204	2-1-78	1996	Sanford, N.C.
Panaro, Carmen	.212	51	104	7	22	1	1	0	3	1	31	0	1	L	R	6-0	195	9-21-75	1996	Buffalo, N.Y.
Spivey, Ernest	.273	136	491	88	134	24	6	6	53	69	115	14	9	R	R	6-0	185	1-28-75	1996	Oklahoma City, Okla.
Steverson, Todd	.229	24	83	16	19	4	0	4	15	19	34	0	1	R	R	6-2	185	11-15-71	1992	Inglewood, Calif.
Stoner, Mike	.358	136	567	115	203	44	5	33	142	36	91	6	4	R	R	6-0	200	5-23-73	1996	Simpsonville, Ky.
Wilson, Keith	.230	60	148	22	34	8	0	5	25	14	40	1	0	R	R	6-1	195	12-31-73	1996	Buckeye, Ariz.

GAMES BY POSITION: C—Baltzell 4, Barajas 54, Clark 13, R. Davis 42, Osborne 15, Panaro 51, Wilson 2. **1B**—Barajas 2, Cameron 1, Durkac 69, Glasser 6, Lee 55, Wilson 19. **2B**—Boughton 2, Glasser 11, Spivey 136. **3B**—Durkac 64, Glasser 7, Goligoski 1, Hartman 75, Wilson 3. **SS**—Boughton 15, Glasser 25, Goligoski 121. **OF**—Cameron 105, Conti 14, Fick 5, Gann 89, Garcia 2, Glasser 3, Hardy 3, Maddox 97, Mota 8, Stoner 127, Wilson 7.

PITCHING	W	L	ERA	G	GS	CG	SV	IP	H	R	ER	BB	SO	B	T	HT	WT	DOB	1st Yr	Resides
Backlund, Brett	4	2	3.67	17	0	0	0	34	23	19	14	11	38	R	R	6-0	195	12-16-69	1992	Salem, Ore.
Bedinger, Doug	0	0	40.50	1	0	0	0	1	3	5	3	2	0	R	R	6-2	206	8-22-74	1994	Channahon, Ill.
Bice, Justin	2	0	4.13	4	4	0	0	24	18	12	11	9	22	R	R	6-3	210	4-17-75	1996	Mesa, Ariz.
Crossan, Clay	0	0	6.00	2	1	0	0	6	8	8	4	2	0	R	R	6-1	175	8-30-73	1996	Loomis, Calif.
Davis, Mark	3	1	2.66	16	0	0	0	20	17	6	6	4	28	L	L	6-4	210	10-19-60	1979	Marietta, Ga.
Eden, Bill	1	0	5.23	6	0	0	0	10	7	6	6	8	12	L	L	6-2	205	4-4-73	1994	Franklin, Tenn.
Emerson, Scott	0	0	6.75	3	1	0	0	4	4	4	3	4	6	L	L	6-5	175	12-22-71	1992	Phoenix, Ariz.
Fleming, John	0	0	16.88	1	1	0	0	3	7	5	5	3	1	R	R	6-3	185	1-20-78	1996	Chula Vista, Calif.
Jordan, Jason	2	0	6.14	6	4	0	0	15	16	12	10	13	10	R	R	6-3	220	10-2-72	1994	Wichita, Kan.
Marenghi, Matt	4	3	3.07	38	0	0	2	73	81	38	25	23	45	R	R	6-2	185	1-22-73	1994	Las Vegas, Nev.
Michalak, Chris	3	7	2.65	49	0	0	4	85	76	36	25	31	74	L	L	6-2	195	1-4-71	1993	Lemont, Ill.
Nunez, Vladimir	8	5	5.17	28	28	1	0	158	169	102	91	40	142	R	R	6-5	240	3-15-75	1996	Santo Domingo, D.R.
Oleksik, George	2	2	8.63	17	0	0	0	24	32	28	23	22	13	R	R	6-4	205	4-19-74	1996	McMinnville, Tenn.
Pena, Alex	2	1	6.49	33	3	0	0	69	80	56	50	30	39	R	R	6-0	175	9-9-72	1993	El Paso, Texas
Peters, Don	1	2	1.62	21	0	0	7	33	20	10	6	13	25	R	R	6-0	190	10-7-69	1990	Crestwood, Ill.
Robbins, Jason	7	5	4.42	23	23	1	0	128	125	74	63	42	127	R	R	6-3	195	12-20-72	1993	South Bend, Ind.
Sabel, Erik	11	11	5.32	31	22	0	1	144	174	101	85	40	86	R	R	6-3	186	10-14-74	1996	West Lafayette, Ind.
Sobkoviak, Jeff	14	6	4.28	28	28	0	0	160	167	88	76	37	101	R	R	6-7	225	8-22-71	1992	Iroquois, Ill.
Steed, Rick	6	1	2.79	46	0	0	1	77	58	28	24	31	64	R	R	6-2	185	9-8-70	1989	West Covina, Calif.
Tranbarger, Mark	1	0	4.70	5	0	0	0	8	9	4	4	5	4	R	L	6-2	205	9-17-69	1991	Cincinnati, Ohio
Tuttle, Dave	4	3	2.43	50	0	0	19	63	54	22	17	23	57	R	R	6-3	190	9-29-69	1992	Los Gatos, Calif.
Verplancke, Joe	7	2	5.81	17	17	0	0	74	91	53	48	30	64	R	R	6-2	185	5-11-75	1996	Ontario, Calif.
Zerbe, Chad	1	6	7.43	9	8	0	0	36	61	49	30	15	26	L	L	6-0	190	4-27-72	1991	Tampa, Fla.

SOUTH BEND — Class A

MIDWEST LEAGUE

BATTING	AVG	G	AB	R	H	2B	3B	HR	RBI	BB	SO	SB	CS	B	T	HT	WT	DOB	1st Yr	Resides
Adams, John	.259	60	216	22	56	7	1	10	36	5	71	3	0	R	R	6-5	215	8-10-76	1997	Olathe, Kan.
Allison, Brad	.133	55	166	5	22	3	0	0	9	11	52	1	0	R	R	5-11	220	11-24-73	1996	Cynthiana, Ky.
Bautista, Juan	.130	31	92	12	12	1	1	0	4	6	32	1	0	R	R	6-1	157	7-20-78	1996	San Francisco de Macoris, D.R.
Boughton, Mike	.098	15	51	2	5	2	0	0	2	4	11	0	0	S	R	6-3	170	11-8-74	1996	Double Oak, Texas
Calloway, Ron	.280	9	25	3	7	1	0	0	1	2	8	1	0	L	L	6-1	190	9-6-76	1997	San Jose, Calif.
Conti, Jason	.310	117	458	78	142	22	10	3	43	45	99	30	18	L	R	5-11	175	1-27-75	1996	Cranberry Township, Pa.

BATTING	AVG	G	AB	R	H	2B	3B	HR	RBI	BB	SO	SB	CS	B	T	HT	WT	DOB	1st Yr	Resides
Cuntz, Casey	.272	49	169	19	46	11	0	1	14	27	34	3	4	R	R	6-3	185	2-4-75	1997	Metairie, La.
Gann, Jamie	.167	12	36	4	6	1	0	0	3	1	9	0	1	R	R	6-1	185	5-1-75	1996	Norman, Okla.
Gjerde, Jeff	.202	31	104	9	21	0	0	0	3	12	34	0	1	L	R	6-1	190	1-9-75	1997	Billings, Mont.
Hartman, Ron	.254	53	197	25	50	17	2	3	37	25	35	1	0	R	R	6-1	200	12-12-74	1996	Baltimore, Md.
Hudson, Bert	.147	28	95	5	14	2	0	0	9	5	36	1	2	R	R	5-11	183	10-6-77	1996	Jay, Fla.
Madera, Wil	.248	70	210	22	52	8	4	1	20	16	66	6	3	L	L	6-1	170	4-13-77	1997	Ponce, P.R.
Martin, Jared	.247	34	97	13	24	6	1	0	10	9	30	2	1	S	R	5-10	170	3-3-75	1997	Tallahassee, Fla.
Martinez, Tony	.272	108	404	54	110	21	1	6	62	37	85	1	3	R	R	6-2	185	11-27-73	1996	Fullerton, Calif.
McAffee, Josh	.196	50	168	16	33	9	1	4	17	12	67	0	1	R	R	6-1	210	11-4-77	1996	Rock Springs, Wyo.
Moore, Jason	.143	59	196	21	28	5	0	8	16	19	80	2	2	R	R	6-3	240	7-16-75	1996	Hurricane, W.Va.
Morgan, James	.000	5	6	1	0	0	0	0	0	1	1	0	0	R	R	6-3	215	7-18-74	1997	Marietta, Ga.
Nunez, Jose	.276	108	351	58	97	16	11	1	45	59	67	4	1	R	R	5-9	180	3-4-76	1996	New York, N.Y.
Osborne, Mark	.264	96	333	38	88	25	2	8	51	43	98	2	2	L	R	6-4	204	2-1-78	1996	Sanford, N.C.
Rexrode, Jackie	.282	92	330	60	93	10	5	2	27	55	47	15	5	L	R	5-10	170	9-16-78	1996	Laurel, Md.
Ryan, Rob	.314	121	421	71	132	35	5	8	73	89	58	12	1	L	L	5-11	180	6-24-73	1996	Spokane, Wash.
Sandoval, Jhensy	.264	19	72	9	19	3	0	1	4	2	19	4	3	R	R	6-0	200	9-11-78	1996	Santo Domingo, D.R.
Sweeney, Kevin	.263	68	232	36	61	16	1	4	37	39	56	1	0	L	L	5-11	185	3-30-74	1996	Cheektowaga, N.Y.
Taveras, Jose	.186	15	43	5	8	0	0	1	2	2	11	2	1	R	R	6-3	180	4-3-79	1997	San Francisco de Macoris, D.R.
Valera, Gregori	.185	8	27	2	5	2	0	0	2	0	7	0	0	R	R	6-1	135	1-11-79	1996	Palenque, D.R.

GAMES BY POSITION: C—Allison 48, McAffee 36, Morgan 3, Osborne 58. **1B**—Allison 3, Gjerde 31, Hartman 4, Martinez 42, Moore 51, Osborne 13. **2B**—Martin 26, Nunez 28, Rexrode 92. **3B**—Bautista 5, Hartman 48, Martinez 43, Moore 4, Nunez 40, Taveras 8. **SS**—Bautista 25, Boughton 15, Cuntz 48, Hartman 1, Martin 4, Nunez 43, Taveras 7, Valera 8. **OF**—Adams 57, Calloway 8, Conti 117, Gann 9, Hudson 26, Madera 56, Martinez 17, Ryan 111, Sandoval 19, Sweeney 2.

PITCHING	W	L	ERA	G	GS	CG	SV	IP	H	R	ER	BB	SO	B	T	HT	WT	DOB	1st Yr	Resides
Allison, Brad	0	0	15.88	3	0	0	0	5	13	10	10	2	4	R	R	5-11	220	11-24-73	1996	Cynthiana, Ky.
Andrews, Jeff	1	5	5.24	23	4	0	0	55	52	37	32	27	32	R	R	6-2	175	9-1-74	1997	Beverly, Mass.
Bedinger, Doug	0	1	2.49	11	0	0	1	22	19	6	6	8	26	R	R	6-2	206	8-22-74	1994	Channahon, Ill.
Bell, Matt	2	3	6.75	14	0	0	0	23	27	27	17	9	22	R	R	6-5	210	1-8-78	1996	Joplin, Mo.
Bierbrodt, Nick	2	4	4.04	15	15	0	0	76	77	43	34	37	64	L	L	6-5	180	5-16-78	1996	Long Beach, Calif.
Crews, Jason	4	6	3.18	50	0	0	9	82	78	39	29	27	74	R	R	6-2	200	8-28-73	1996	Plantation, Fla.
Fleming, John	0	0	3.86	5	0	0	0	9	11	6	4	7	5	R	R	6-3	185	1-20-78	1996	Chula Vista, Calif.
Harvell, Pete	4	5	2.90	50	0	0	13	62	50	27	20	36	57	L	L	6-2	190	10-14-71	1993	San Jose, Calif.
Kiess, Barry	3	4	5.12	19	0	0	1	32	29	19	18	19	34	R	R	6-0	180	9-19-73	1997	Los Alamos, N.M.
Lister, Marty	0	0	16.20	3	0	0	0	3	6	6	6	2	1	L	L	6-2	210	6-12-72	1992	Pensacola, Fla.
McCall, Travis	7	6	3.87	25	22	0	0	121	140	74	52	35	86	L	L	5-11	180	12-20-77	1996	Chino Hills, Calif.
McCutcheon, Mike	7	5	3.41	31	17	0	1	106	104	55	40	49	67	L	L	6-0	170	7-5-77	1996	Mauna Loa, Hawaii
Norris, Ben	1	8	4.03	14	13	0	0	60	69	44	27	31	40	S	L	6-3	185	12-6-77	1996	Austin, Texas
Oleksik, George	3	2	2.52	24	0	0	1	50	52	26	14	29	44	R	R	6-4	205	4-19-74	1996	McMinnville, Tenn.
Patterson, John	1	9	3.23	18	18	0	0	78	63	32	28	34	95	R	R	6-6	200	1-30-78	1996	Houston, Texas
Penny, Brad	10	5	2.73	25	25	0	0	119	91	44	36	43	116	R	R	6-4	195	5-24-78	1996	Broken Arrow, Okla.
Peters, Don	0	2	2.93	13	0	0	0	15	19	7	5	4	8	R	R	6-0	190	10-7-69	1990	Crestwood, Ill.
Robbins, Jason	2	0	0.87	5	4	0	0	21	7	2	2	10	26	R	R	6-3	195	12-20-72	1993	South Bend, Ind.
Rodriguez, Larry	4	11	3.62	19	19	1	0	104	102	56	42	37	72	R	R	6-2	195	9-9-74	1996	Isla de Margarita, Venez.
Tranbarger, Mark	2	2	4.14	32	0	0	0	54	56	29	25	27	39	R	L	6-2	205	9-17-69	1991	Cincinnati, Ohio
Vanwormer, Marc	0	5	5.54	39	0	0	1	76	90	63	47	45	56	R	R	6-7	220	8-21-77	1996	Prescott, Ariz.
Verplancke, Joe	1	0	1.93	2	0	0	0	5	3	1	1	3	3	R	R	6-2	185	5-11-75	1996	Ontario, Calif.

LETHBRIDGE — Rookie

PIONEER LEAGUE

BATTING	AVG	G	AB	R	H	2B	3B	HR	RBI	BB	SO	SB	CS	B	T	HT	WT	DOB	1st Yr	Resides
Bautista, Juan	.206	43	136	23	28	3	1	1	14	12	35	4	1	R	R	6-1	157	7-20-78	1996	San Francisco de Macoris, D.R.
Calloway, Ron	.250	43	148	23	37	5	0	0	9	14	29	5	8	L	L	6-1	190	9-6-76	1997	San Jose, Calif.
Cintron, Alex	.333	1	3	0	1	0	0	0	0	0	1	0	0	S	R	6-3	165	12-17-78	1997	Yabucoa, P.R.
Doherty, Steven	.286	53	185	38	53	12	1	5	29	22	28	5	4	L	R	6-0	175	9-30-74	1997	Richmond, B.C.
Fox, Brian	.295	64	220	30	65	9	2	9	44	34	45	1	0	L	R	6-2	200	3-5-77	1997	Lubbock, Texas
Guzman, Julio	.217	22	60	11	13	3	2	1	12	2	23	2	0	R	R	6-3	205	4-28-76	1997	Homestead, Fla.
Hudson, Bert	.256	60	219	28	56	11	0	9	34	19	57	5	3	R	R	5-11	183	10-6-77	1996	Jay, Fla.
Jones, Keith	.257	58	214	27	55	8	1	5	28	15	76	3	3	R	R	6-2	190	1-30-76	1997	Whittier, Calif.
Madera, Wil	.297	33	101	15	30	4	0	3	11	4	29	5	0	L	L	6-1	170	4-13-77	1997	Ponce, P.R.
Martin, Jared	.231	25	78	12	18	3	3	0	5	15	19	1	0	S	R	5-10	170	3-3-75	1997	Tallahassee, Fla.
Martinez, Belvani	.344	25	90	21	31	4	1	6	13	5	13	4	1	R	R	5-11	150	12-14-78	1996	Palenque, D.R.
McAffee, Josh	.198	36	101	26	20	5	2	4	18	13	32	0	1	R	R	6-1	210	11-4-77	1996	Rock Springs, Wyo.
Nunez, Abraham	.167	2	6	2	1	0	0	0	1	1	0	0	0	S	R	6-2	160	5-2-80	1996	Haina, D.R.
Quire, Jeremy	.293	30	58	11	17	5	0	0	7	3	8	0	0	R	R	6-2	205	4-8-75	1997	Anderson, Ind.
Rexrode, Jackie	.337	26	89	29	30	2	2	1	14	29	17	7	3	L	R	5-10	170	9-16-78	1996	Laurel, Md.
Sandoval, Jhensy	.375	40	160	33	60	14	1	8	37	8	36	7	3	R	R	6-0	200	9-11-78	1996	Santo Domingo, D.R.
Steelmon, Wyley	.271	53	166	29	45	5	1	8	26	41	50	3	0	L	R	6-3	225	8-29-75	1997	Enid, Okla.
Sykes, Jamie	.305	58	223	45	68	8	6	4	37	25	40	9	2	R	R	5-11	190	1-14-75	1997	Kankakee, Ill.
Taveras, Jose	.234	67	235	36	55	6	2	8	38	19	65	5	4	R	R	6-3	180	4-3-79	1997	San Francisco de Macoris, D.R.

GAMES BY POSITION: C—Fox 30, Martin 1, McAffee 36, Quire 28. **1B**—Fox 25, K. Jones 30, Steelmon 8, Taveras 17. **2B**—Bautista 1, Doherty 35, Martin 6, Martinez 21, Rexrode 11, Taveras 1. **3B**—Doherty 13, Hudson 1, K. Jones 23, Taveras 42. **SS**—Bautista 41, Cintron 1, Martin 19, Martinez 4, Taveras 12. **OF**—Calloway 40, Guzman 17, Hudson 50, Madera 30, Nunez 2, Sandoval 40, Sykes 55.

PITCHING	W	L	ERA	G	GS	CG	SV	IP	H	R	ER	BB	SO	B	T	HT	WT	DOB	1st Yr	Resides
Anderson, Dallas	0	0	9.00	10	0	0	0	11	10	12	11	11	11	R	R	6-4	210	2-27-74	1996	Taber, Alberta
Andrews, Jeff	3	3	3.26	9	9	1	0	50	55	27	18	10	50	R	R	6-2	175	9-1-74	1997	Beverly, Mass.
Bell, Matt	1	0	0.00	2	0	0	0	4	4	0	0	3	5	R	R	6-5	210	1-8-78	1996	Joplin, Mo.
Bloomer, Chris	5	2	1.76	27	0	0	9	31	19	14	6	9	38	R	R	6-4	215	5-6-75	1997	White Bear Lake, Minn.
Fleming, John	3	6	4.50	12	12	0	0	64	80	37	32	25	32	R	R	6-3	185	1-20-78	1996	Chula Vista, Calif.
Fontanes, Reuben	1	0	9.00	5	0	0	0	6	8	6	6	7	8	R	R	6-3	190	5-6-74	1997	Yuma, Ariz.
Frias, Miguel	0	0	0.00	1	0	0	0	1	2	0	0	0	3	L	L	5-11	165	12-27-77	1996	Santo Domingo, D.R.

PITCHING	W	L	ERA	G	GS	CG	SV	IP	H	R	ER	BB	SO	B	T	HT	WT	DOB	1st Yr	Resides
Harper, David	2	0	6.08	8	0	0	0	13	16	9	9	6	13	R	R	6-3	185	9-14-74	1996	Mansfield, Texas
Haverstick, David	0	1	16.20	1	0	0	0	2	3	3	3	2	1	R	R	6-8	220	6-3-76	1997	Mishawaka, Ind.
Jensen, Jason	4	3	4.97	14	14	0	0	63	73	43	35	23	46	L	L	6-2	175	11-4-75	1997	Portland, Maine
Jones, Charlie	0	3	6.23	16	0	0	0	22	23	21	15	17	18	L	R	6-0	188	2-6-76	1997	Vero Beach, Fla.
Knott, Eric	0	4	2.87	21	3	0	3	47	41	21	15	9	62	L	L	6-1	170	9-23-74	1997	Sebring, Fla.
Martines, Jason	3	3	3.14	22	0	0	0	43	45	15	15	11	34	L	R	6-2	190	1-21-76	1997	Hanover, Mich.
Norris, Ben	7	3	4.86	14	14	0	0	83	93	61	45	23	54	S	L	6-3	185	12-6-77	1996	Austin, Texas
Puorto, Jamie	4	2	2.43	20	6	0	2	59	44	26	16	9	58	L	L	6-3	190	6-21-75	1997	Chicago, Ill.
Rooney, Mike	5	2	5.49	13	13	1	0	62	72	42	38	24	40	R	R	6-1	175	10-6-75	1997	Stony Point, N.Y.
Santa, Jeff	0	0	4.68	18	1	0	0	25	27	19	13	8	28	R	L	6-0	175	11-16-74	1997	Newark, Ohio
Wilson, Jeff	1	1	4.46	22	0	0	0	36	35	22	18	12	49	R	L	6-2	175	5-30-76	1997	Greensboro, N.C.

PHOENIX — Rookie

ARIZONA LEAGUE

BATTING	AVG	G	AB	R	H	2B	3B	HR	RBI	BB	SO	SB	CS	B	T	HT	WT	DOB	1st Yr	Resides
Brooks, Jeff	.225	54	204	22	46	9	0	0	27	12	50	3	1	R	R	6-5	220	9-4-79	1997	Nottingham, Pa.
Cintron, Alex	.197	43	152	23	30	6	1	0	20	21	32	1	4	S	R	6-3	165	12-17-78	1997	Yabucoa, P.R.
Cust, Jack	.306	35	121	26	37	11	1	3	33	31	39	2	0	L	R	6-2	200	1-16-79	1997	Flemington, N.J.
Downing, Lance	.381	55	215	48	82	12	1	2	40	37	26	10	4	L	R	5-11	185	3-9-79	1997	Pine Bluff, Ark.
German, Manuel	.223	34	112	21	25	5	2	1	11	16	36	2	2	R	R	5-11	175	3-19-78	1996	San Cristobal, D.R.
Gordon, Brian	.247	54	219	27	54	18	4	4	46	9	62	8	3	L	R	6-1	180	8-16-78	1997	Round Rock, Texas
Guzman, Julio	.222	12	36	4	8	0	0	1	5	4	11	1	0	R	R	6-3	205	4-28-76	1997	Homestead, Fla.
Lopez, Jose	.265	41	155	17	41	7	2	1	22	7	22	1	4	R	R	5-9	187	12-23-78	1996	San Francisco de Macoris, D.R.
Lopez, Miguel	.267	29	105	14	28	4	2	2	9	8	32	1	0	R	R	5-11	180	10-12-78	1996	La Vega, D.R.
Martinez, Belvani	.321	30	134	25	43	11	2	0	11	3	18	7	2	R	R	5-11	164	12-14-78	1996	Palenque, D.R.
Montilla, Alvin	.185	20	54	4	10	1	0	0	3	7	20	0	0	R	R	5-11	190	9-26-78	1997	Bronx, N.Y.
Morgan, James	.000	4	9	1	0	0	0	0	0	1	4	0	0	R	R	6-3	215	7-18-74	1997	Marietta, Ga.
Moye, Tutu	.203	28	79	10	16	1	0	1	5	14	16	2	1	R	R	6-0	190	9-8-78	1997	Greenville, N.C.
Nunez, Abraham	.305	54	213	52	65	17	4	0	21	26	40	3	3	S	R	6-2	160	5-2-80	1996	Haina, D.R.
Proctor, Jerry	.083	3	12	2	1	0	1	0	0	0	6	1	0	R	R	6-5	200	3-5-78	1996	Pasadena, Calif.
Urquiola, Carlos	.000	2	2	1	0	0	0	0	0	0	1	1	0	L	R	5-8	150	4-22-80	1997	Caracas, Venez.
Weichard, Paul	.183	36	115	27	21	3	1	0	7	30	54	4	3	S	L	5-10	180	11-7-79	1997	Ringwood, Australia

GAMES BY POSITION: C—J. Lopez 33, M. Lopez 22, Morgan 4. **1B**—Downing 53, Guzman 1, Moye 3. **2B**—German 14, Martinez 28, Moye 16. **3B**—Brooks 53, Downing 3, German 1, J. Lopez 2, Moye 4. **SS**—Cintron 43, German 14, Moye 1. **OF**—Cust 34, Gordon 49, Guzman 6, M. Lopez 1, Montilla 17, Nunez 53, Weichard 19.

PITCHING	W	L	ERA	G	GS	CG	SV	IP	H	R	ER	BB	SO	B	T	HT	WT	DOB	1st Yr	Resides
Abeyta, Scott	1	1	3.29	17	0	0	1	27	29	12	10	9	25	L	L	6-0	190	3-14-77	1997	Vallejo, Calif.
Bedinger, Doug	0	0	0.00	1	0	0	0	2	0	0	0	0	5	R	R	6-2	206	8-22-74	1994	Channahon, Ill.
Bell, Matt	3	2	2.88	18	0	0	2	34	31	18	11	16	36	R	R	6-5	210	1-8-78	1996	Joplin, Mo.
Bido, Jose	0	1	27.00	1	1	0	0	1	5	3	3	0	0	R	R	6-3	180	12-20-78	1996	San Francisco de Macoris, D.R.
Boughton, Mike	3	3	3.96	15	1	0	0	39	51	24	17	11	31	S	R	6-3	170	11-8-74	1996	Double Oak, Texas
Cepeda, Wellington	4	0	1.64	15	1	0	0	38	31	16	7	12	32	R	R	6-2	195	11-25-77	1996	Santo Domingo, D.R.
Frias, Miguel	4	2	2.25	21	0	0	8	32	35	11	8	5	38	L	L	5-11	165	12-27-77	1996	Santo Domingo, D.R.
Haverstick, David	2	5	5.56	14	14	0	0	57	71	42	35	20	39	R	R	6-8	220	6-3-76	1997	Mishawaka, Ind.
Jones, Charlie	0	1	7.50	7	0	0	1	12	14	12	10	8	10	L	R	6-0	188	2-6-76	1997	Vero Beach, Fla.
Kohl, Doug	1	2	3.96	14	14	0	0	61	62	33	27	25	46	S	R	6-3	200	7-9-79	1997	Henderson, Nev.
Manzueta, Roberto	0	0	1.54	7	0	0	0	12	6	3	2	2	4	R	R	6-1	170	12-28-78	1996	Cotui, D.R.
Mendoza, Hatuey	1	5	7.58	17	0	0	0	30	29	27	25	25	24	R	R	6-0	160	3-16-80	1997	Santo Domingo, D.R.
Morel, Francis	0	0	18.00	1	0	0	0	1	3	2	2	0	0	R	R	6-5	196	12-22-78	1996	Cabrera, D.R.
Paredes, Vladimir	2	0	3.78	12	0	0	0	17	18	10	7	7	12	L	L	6-0	180	5-11-78	1996	Santo Domingo, D.R.
Royer, Jason	3	0	3.71	13	13	0	0	51	53	29	21	22	40	R	R	6-5	200	7-3-78	1997	Del City, Okla.
Sanchez, Simon	3	5	5.05	14	12	0	0	57	66	45	32	25	44	R	R	6-2	182	3-24-78	1996	San Francisco de Macoris, D.R.
Tate, Seth	0	2	4.76	11	0	0	1	23	25	21	12	11	12	R	R	6-0	185	1-7-77	1997	Wenatchee, Wash.

Atlanta BRAVES

Manager: Bobby Cox.

1997 Record: 101-61, .623 (1st, NL East)

BATTING	AVG	G	AB	R	H	2B	3B	HR	RBI	BB	SO	SB	CS	B	T	HT	WT	DOB	1st Yr	Resides
Bautista, Danny	.243	64	103	14	25	3	2	3	9	5	24	2	0	R	R	5-11	170	5-24-72	1989	Santo Domingo, D.R.
Belliard, Rafael	.211	72	71	9	15	3	0	1	3	1	17	0	1	R	R	5-6	160	10-24-61	1980	Boca Raton, Fla.
Blauser, Jeff	.308	151	519	90	160	31	4	17	70	70	101	5	1	R	R	6-1	180	11-8-65	1984	Alpharetta, Ga.
Colbrunn, Greg	.278	28	54	3	15	3	0	2	9	2	11	0	0	R	R	6-0	200	7-26-69	1988	Weston, Fla.
Giovanola, Ed	.250	14	8	0	2	0	0	0	0	2	1	0	0	L	R	5-10	170	3-4-69	1990	San Jose, Calif.
Graffanino, Tony	.258	104	186	33	48	9	1	8	20	26	46	6	4	R	R	6-1	200	6-6-72	1990	Seneca, S.C.
Gregg, Tommy	.263	13	19	1	5	2	0	0	0	1	2	1	1	L	L	6-1	190	7-29-63	1985	Smyrna, Ga.
Jones, Andruw	.231	153	399	60	92	18	1	18	70	56	107	20	11	R	R	6-1	170	4-23-77	1994	Willemstad, Curacao
Jones, Chipper	.295	157	597	100	176	41	3	21	111	76	88	20	5	S	R	6-3	195	4-24-72	1990	New Smyrna Beach, Fla.
Klesko, Ryan	.261	143	467	67	122	23	6	24	84	48	130	4	4	L	L	6-3	220	6-12-71	1989	Boynton Beach, Fla.
Lemke, Mark	.245	109	351	33	86	17	1	2	26	33	51	2	0	S	R	5-9	167	8-13-65	1983	Atlanta, Ga.
Lockhart, Keith	.279	96	147	25	41	5	3	6	32	14	17	0	0	L	R	5-10	170	11-10-64	1986	Largo, Fla.
Lofton, Kenny	.333	122	493	90	164	20	6	5	48	64	83	27	20	L	L	6-0	180	5-31-67	1988	Tucson, Ariz.
Lopez, Javy	.295	123	414	52	122	28	1	23	68	40	82	1	1	R	R	6-3	185	11-5-70	1988	Ponce, P.R.
McGriff, Fred	.277	152	564	77	156	25	1	22	97	68	112	5	0	L	L	6-3	215	10-31-63	1981	Tampa, Fla.
Mordecai, Mike	.173	61	81	8	14	2	1	0	3	6	16	0	1	R	R	5-11	175	12-13-67	1989	Pinson, Ala.
Myers, Greg	.111	9	9	0	1	0	0	0	1	1	3	0	0	L	R	6-2	215	4-14-66	1984	Riverside, Calif.
Perez, Eddie	.215	73	191	20	41	5	0	6	18	10	35	0	1	R	R	6-1	175	5-4-68	1987	Maracaibo, Venez.
Simon, Randall	.429	13	14	2	6	1	0	0	1	1	2	0	0	L	L	6-0	180	5-26-75	1993	Willemstad, Curacao
Spehr, Tim	.214	8	14	2	3	1	0	1	4	0	4	1	0	R	R	6-2	205	7-2-66	1988	Waco, Texas
Tucker, Michael	.283	138	499	80	141	25	7	14	56	44	116	12	7	L	R	6-2	185	6-25-71	1992	Chase City, Va.

PITCHING	W	L	ERA	G	GS	CG	SV	IP	H	R	ER	BB	SO	B	T	HT	WT	DOB	1st Yr	Resides
Bielecki, Mike	3	7	4.08	50	0	0	2	57	56	33	26	21	60	R	R	6-3	195	7-31-59	1979	Crownsville, Md.
Borowski, Joe	2	2	3.75	20	0	0	0	24	27	11	10	16	6	R	R	6-2	225	5-4-71	1989	Bayonne, N.J.
Brock, Chris	0	0	5.58	7	6	0	0	31	34	23	19	19	16	R	R	6-0	175	2-5-70	1992	Altamonte Springs, Fla.
Byrd, Paul	4	4	5.26	31	4	0	0	53	47	34	31	28	37	R	R	6-1	185	12-3-70	1991	Louisville, Ky.
Cather, Mike	2	4	2.39	35	0	0	0	38	23	12	10	19	29	R	R	6-2	180	12-17-70	1993	Folsom, Calif.
Clontz, Brad	5	1	3.75	51	0	0	1	48	52	24	20	18	42	R	R	6-1	180	4-25-71	1992	Patrick Springs, Va.
Embree, Alan	3	1	2.54	66	0	0	0	46	36	13	13	20	45	L	L	6-2	190	1-23-70	1990	Brush Prairie, Wash.
Fox, Chad	0	1	3.29	30	0	0	0	27	24	12	10	16	28	R	R	6-2	180	9-3-70	1992	Houston, Texas
Glavine, Tom	14	7	2.96	33	33	5	0	240	197	86	79	79	152	L	L	6-1	185	3-25-66	1984	Billerica, Mass.
LeRoy, John	1	0	0.00	1	0	0	0	2	1	0	0	3	3	R	R	6-3	175	4-19-75	1993	Bellevue, Wash.
Ligtenberg, Kerry	1	0	3.00	15	0	0	1	15	12	5	5	4	19	R	R	6-2	185	5-11-71	1994	Cottage Grove, Minn.
Maddux, Greg	19	4	2.20	33	33	5	0	233	200	58	57	20	177	R	R	6-0	175	4-14-66	1984	Las Vegas, Nev.
Millwood, Kevin	5	3	4.03	12	8	0	0	51	55	26	23	21	42	R	R	6-4	205	12-24-74	1993	Bessemer City, N.C.
Neagle, Denny	20	5	2.97	34	34	4	0	233	204	87	77	49	172	L	L	6-2	215	9-13-68	1989	Gambrills, Md.
Smoltz, John	15	12	3.02	35	35	7	0	256	234	97	86	63	241	R	R	6-3	185	5-15-67	1986	Duluth, Ga.
Wade, Terrell	2	3	5.36	12	9	0	0	42	60	31	25	16	35	L	L	6-3	204	1-25-73	1991	Rembert, S.C.
Wohlers, Mark	5	7	3.50	71	0	0	33	69	57	29	27	38	92	R	R	6-4	207	1-23-70	1988	Atlanta, Ga.

FIELDING

Catcher	PCT	G	PO	A	E	DP	PB
Lopez	.993	117	792	56	6	7	9
Myers	1.000	2	11	2	0	0	0
Perez	.988	64	392	23	5	1	2
Spehr	.947	7	32	4	2	0	0

First Base	PCT	G	PO	A	E	DP
Colbrunn	.984	14	54	6	1	3
Graffanino	1.000	1	1	0	0	0
Gregg	1.000	1	3	0	0	0
Klesko	1.000	22	63	3	0	7
McGriff	.990	149	1191	96	13	111
Mordecai	1.000	3	11	2	0	0
Perez	1.000	6	25	1	0	0
Simon	1.000	6	16	2	0	2

Second Base	PCT	G	PO	A	E	DP
Belliard	1.000	7	1	5	0	0
Giovanola	1.000	1	0	2	0	0
Graffanino	.982	75	88	178	5	29
Lemke	.980	104	191	309	10	65
Lockhart	.983	20	22	37	1	9
Mordecai	1.000	4	3	2	0	0

Third Base	PCT	G	PO	A	E	DP
Giovanola	1.000	8	0	3	0	0
Graffanino	1.000	2	1	0	0	0
C. Jones	.955	152	77	241	15	17
Lockhart	.867	11	2	11	2	1
Mordecai	1.000	19	9	11	0	2

Shortstop	PCT	G	PO	A	E	DP
Belliard	.990	53	36	64	1	14
Blauser	.973	149	204	372	16	79
Giovanola	1.000	1	0	1	0	0
Graffanino	1.000	2	0	2	0	0
Mordecai	1.000	4	3	2	0	2

Outfield	PCT	G	PO	A	E	DP
Bautista	.984	57	59	1	1	1
Gregg	1.000	6	2	0	0	0
A. Jones	.977	147	287	14	7	2
C. Jones	1.000	5	6	0	0	0
Klesko	.969	130	182	3	6	0
Lofton	.983	122	290	5	5	1
Mordecai	.000	1	0	0	0	0
Tucker	.980	129	237	6	5	2

MORRIS FOSTOFF

Kenny Lofton

FARM SYSTEM

Director of Player Development: Paul Snyder

Class	Farm Team	League	W	L	Pct.	Finish*	Manager	First Yr
AAA	Richmond (Va.) Braves	International	70	72	.493	6th (10)	Bill Dancy	1966
AA	Greenville (S.C.) Braves	Southern	74	66	.529	+4th (10)	Randy Ingle	1984
#A	Durham (N.C.) Bulls	Carolina	63	76	.453	6th (8)	Paul Runge	1980
A	Macon (Ga.) Braves	South Atlantic	80	60	.571	1st (14)	Brian Snitker	1991
A	Eugene (Ore.) Emeralds	Northwest	31	45	.408	6th (8)	Jim Saul	1995
#R	Danville (Va.) Braves	Appalachian	30	38	.441	7th (10)	Rick Albert	1993
R	Orlando (Fla.) Braves	Gulf Coast	21	38	.356	15th (15)	Frank Howard	1976

*Finish in overall standings (No. of teams in league) # Advanced level +Won league championship.

ORGANIZATION LEADERS

MAJOR LEAGUERS

BATTING

*AVG	Kenny Lofton	.333
R	Chipper Jones	100
H	Chipper Jones	176
TB	Chipper Jones	286
2B	Chipper Jones	41
3B	Michael Tucker	7
HR	Ryan Klesko	24
RBI	Chipper Jones	111
BB	Chipper Jones	76
SO	Ryan Klesko	130
SB	Kenny Lofton	27

PITCHING

W	Denny Neagle	20
L	John Smoltz	12
#ERA	Greg Maddux	2.20
G	Mark Wohlers	71
CG	John Smoltz	7
SV	Mark Wohlers	33
IP	John Smoltz	256
BB	Tom Glavine	79
SO	John Smoltz	241

GEORGE GOJKOVICH

Chipper Jones

JOHN SPEAR

Randall Simon

MINOR LEAGUERS

BATTING

*AVG	Tommy Gregg, Richmond	.332
R	Gabe Whatley, Greenville/Durham	97
H	Randall Simon, Richmond	160
TB	Steve Hacker, Macon	285
2B	Randall Simon, Richmond	45
3B	Brad Tyler, Richmond	10
HR	Steve Hacker, Macon	33
RBI	Steve Hacker, Macon	119
BB	Gabe Whatley, Greenville/Durham	78
SO	Mike Hessman, Macon	167
SB	Tyrone Pendergrass, Macon	70

PITCHING

W	Two tied at	14
L	Two tied at	14
#ERA	Odalis Perez, Macon	1.65
G	Scott Brow, Richmond	61
CG	Larry Luebbers, Richmond	2
SV	David Cortes, Green./Durham/Macon	23
IP	Derrin Ebert, Greenville	176
BB	Dwayne Jacobs, Durham	85
SO	Bruce Chen, Macon	182

*Minimum 250 At-Bats #Minimum 75 Innings

TOP 10 PROSPECTS

BILL SETLIFF

Andruw Jones

How the Braves Top 10 prospects, as judged by Baseball America prior to the 1997 season, fared in 1997:

Player, Pos.	Club (Class)	AVG	AB	R	H	2B	3B	HR	RBI	SB
1. Andruw Jones, of	Atlanta	.231	399	60	92	18	1	18	70	20
4. George Lombard, of	Durham (A)	.264	462	65	122	25	7	14	72	35
5. Wes Helms, 3b	Richmond (AAA)	.191	110	11	21	4	0	3	15	1
	Greenville (AA)	.296	314	50	93	14	1	11	44	3

Player, Pos.	Club (Class)	W	L	ERA	G	SV	IP	H	BB	SO
2. Kevin McGlinchy, rhp	Durham (A)	3	7	4.90	26	0	140	145	39	113
3. Bruce Chen, lhp	Macon (A)	12	7	3.51	28	0	146	120	44	182
6. Jason Marquis, rhp	Macon (A)	14	10	4.38	28	0	142	156	55	121
7. Damian Moss, lhp	Greenville (AA)	6	8	5.35	21	0	113	111	58	116
8. John LeRoy, rhp	Atlanta	1	0	0.00	1	0	2	1	3	3
	Greenville (AA)	5	5	5.03	29	1	98	105	43	84
9. Rob Bell, rhp	Macon (A)	14	7	3.68	27	0	147	144	41	140
10. Jimmy Osting, lhp	Macon (A)	2	3	3.28	15	0	58	54	29	62

RICHMOND — Class AAA

INTERNATIONAL LEAGUE

BATTING	AVG	G	AB	R	H	2B	3B	HR	RBI	BB	SO	SB	CS	B	T	HT	WT	DOB	1st Yr	Resides
Ayrault, Joe	.286	18	56	11	16	2	0	3	5	4	17	0	0	R	R	6-3	190	10-8-71	1990	Sarasota, Fla.
Bautista, Danny	.282	46	170	28	48	10	3	2	28	19	30	1	0	R	R	5-11	170	5-24-72	1989	Santo Domingo, D.R.
Giovanola, Ed	.291	116	395	65	115	23	5	2	46	64	56	2	2	L	R	5-10	170	3-4-69	1990	San Jose, Calif.
Gregg, Tommy	.332	115	385	52	128	36	1	9	54	46	64	3	3	L	L	6-1	190	7-29-63	1985	Smyrna, Ga.
Helms, Wes	.191	32	110	11	21	4	0	3	15	10	34	1	1	R	R	6-4	210	5-12-76	1994	Gastonia, N.C.
Hollins, Damon	.265	134	498	73	132	31	3	20	63	45	84	7	2	R	L	5-11	180	6-12-74	1992	Vallejo, Calif.
Lewis, T.R.	.295	117	363	65	107	20	5	7	58	37	71	8	3	R	R	6-0	180	4-17-71	1989	Jacksonville, Fla.
Malloy, Marty	.285	108	414	66	118	19	5	2	25	41	61	17	7	L	R	5-10	160	7-6-72	1992	Trenton, Fla.
Martinez, Pablo	.257	96	296	32	76	14	1	4	20	26	77	9	11	S	R	5-10	155	6-29-69	1989	San Juan Baron, D.R.
Mordecai, Mike	.311	31	122	23	38	10	0	3	15	9	17	0	1	R	R	5-11	175	12-13-67	1989	Pinson, Ala.
Rodarte, Raul	.242	41	95	13	23	4	0	0	10	10	22	2	2	R	R	5-11	190	4-9-70	1991	Diamond Bar, Calif.
Simon, Randall	.308	133	519	62	160	45	1	14	102	17	76	1	6	L	L	6-0	180	5-26-75	1993	Willemstad, Curacao
Smith, Bobby	.246	100	357	47	88	10	2	12	47	44	109	6	5	R	R	6-3	190	4-10-74	1992	Oakland, Calif.
Spehr, Tim	.192	36	120	13	23	5	0	3	14	12	37	0	0	R	R	6-2	205	7-2-66	1988	Waco, Texas
Tejero, Fausto	.231	76	225	31	52	11	0	6	28	23	41	0	1	R	R	6-2	205	10-26-68	1990	Hialeah, Fla.
Toth, Dave	.196	14	46	6	9	3	0	0	5	4	8	0	0	R	R	6-1	195	12-8-69	1990	West Keansburg, N.J.
Tyler, Brad	.264	129	383	69	101	15	10	18	77	55	110	13	6	L	R	6-2	175	3-3-69	1990	Aurora, Ind.
Valle, Dave	.211	12	38	2	8	0	0	0	2	1	7	0	0	R	R	6-2	220	10-30-60	1978	Renton, Wash.

PITCHING	W	L	ERA	G	GS	CG	SV	IP	H	R	ER	BB	SO	B	T	HT	WT	DOB	1st Yr	Resides
Borowski, Joe	1	2	3.58	21	0	0	2	38	32	16	15	19	34	R	R	6-2	225	5-4-71	1989	Bayonne, N.J.
Brock, Chris	10	6	3.34	20	19	0	0	119	97	50	44	51	83	R	R	6-0	175	2-5-70	1992	Altamonte Springs, Fla.
Brow, Scott	5	9	4.45	61	1	0	18	83	89	48	41	35	62	R	R	6-3	200	3-17-69	1990	Hillsboro, Ore.
Byrd, Paul	2	1	3.18	3	3	0	0	17	14	6	6	1	14	R	R	6-1	185	12-3-70	1991	Louisville, Ky.
Carlyle, Ken	4	1	2.84	16	11	1	0	70	69	26	22	19	48	R	R	6-1	185	9-16-69	1992	Cordova, Tenn.
Cather, Mike	0	0	1.73	13	0	0	3	26	17	6	5	9	22	R	R	6-2	180	12-17-70	1993	Folsom, Calif.
Clontz, Brad	0	0	0.00	16	0	0	6	22	10	1	0	2	24	R	R	6-1	180	4-25-71	1992	Patrick Springs, Va.
Dyer, Mike	2	1	4.87	29	0	0	1	41	42	25	22	24	23	R	R	6-3	200	9-8-66	1986	Fullerton, Calif.
Fox, Chad	1	0	3.70	13	0	0	0	24	24	10	10	14	25	R	R	6-2	180	9-3-70	1992	Houston, Texas
Harrison, Tommy	9	7	4.20	22	22	1	0	122	118	64	57	40	92	R	R	6-2	180	9-30-71	1993	Miamisburg, Ohio
Hartgraves, Dean	7	4	4.48	50	0	0	3	72	76	38	36	39	56	R	L	6-0	185	8-12-66	1987	Central Point, Ore.
Hostetler, Mike	1	2	9.43	5	5	0	0	21	33	23	22	9	14	R	R	6-2	195	6-5-70	1991	Marietta, Ga.
Ligtenberg, Kerry	0	3	4.32	14	0	0	1	25	21	13	12	2	35	R	R	6-2	185	5-11-71	1994	Cottage Grove, Minn.
Luebbers, Larry	3	14	5.38	27	26	2	0	144	180	101	86	44	91	R	R	6-6	190	10-11-69	1990	Florence, Ky.
Millwood, Kevin	7	0	1.93	9	9	1	0	61	38	13	13	16	46	R	R	6-4	205	12-24-74	1993	Bessemer City, N.C.
Rogers, Bryan	1	1	5.17	21	0	0	0	38	45	26	22	16	25	R	R	5-11	170	10-30-67	1988	Hollister, Calif.
Rogers, Kevin	0	2	7.36	10	0	0	0	11	15	11	9	5	9	L	L	6-1	198	8-20-68	1988	Parchman, Miss.
Schutz, Carl	4	6	5.33	27	10	0	0	79	83	56	47	51	66	L	L	5-11	200	8-22-71	1993	Paulina, La.
Thobe, Tom	5	2	4.14	19	10	0	0	72	70	37	33	22	36	R	L	6-5	195	9-3-69	1988	Huntington Beach, Calif.
Woodall, Brad	8	11	5.51	26	26	1	0	149	177	100	91	52	117	S	L	6-0	175	6-25-69	1991	Blythewood, S.C.

FIELDING

Catcher	PCT	G	PO	A	E	DP	PB
Ayrault	.978	18	83	7	2	1	2
Spehr	.983	35	262	36	5	1	2
Tejero	.981	75	471	49	10	9	2
Toth	.974	13	72	2	2	0	1
Valle	.986	12	66	6	1	0	2

First Base	PCT	G	PO	A	E	DP
Gregg	.994	20	148	9	1	15
Simon	.988	127	1063	72	14	115

Second Base	PCT	G	PO	A	E	DP
Malloy	.975	101	195	278	12	67
Martinez	.986	30	62	78	2	20
Mordecai	1.000	11	21	35	0	10
Tyler	.900	4	2	7	1	0

Third Base	PCT	G	PO	A	E	DP
Giovanola	.957	79	51	148	9	21
Helms	.902	32	18	65	9	5
Martinez	.903	28	13	52	7	5
Mordecai	1.000	11	2	17	0	2

Shortstop	PCT	G	PO	A	E	DP
Giovanola	.939	25	28	79	7	13
Martinez	.975	22	30	48	2	11
Mordecai	.938	4	6	9	1	4
Smith	.952	98	161	297	23	59

Outfield	PCT	G	PO	A	E	DP
Bautista	1.000	42	104	4	0	3
Giovanola	1.000	5	8	0	0	0
Gregg	.988	52	82	3	1	2
Hollins	.977	133	319	14	8	2
Lewis	.984	100	179	6	3	1
Rodarte	1.000	19	24	1	0	0
Tyler	.967	109	170	7	6	0

GREENVILLE — Class AA

SOUTHERN LEAGUE

BATTING	AVG	G	AB	R	H	2B	3B	HR	RBI	BB	SO	SB	CS	B	T	HT	WT	DOB	1st Yr	Resides
Ayrault, Joe	.242	13	33	6	8	2	0	2	4	6	8	0	0	R	R	6-3	190	10-8-71	1990	Sarasota, Fla.
Benbow, Lou	.232	117	315	39	73	14	1	9	34	34	80	4	8	R	R	6-0	167	1-12-71	1991	Laguna Hills, Calif.
Brito, Luis	.289	97	336	35	97	12	0	1	36	15	25	4	5	S	R	6-0	155	4-12-71	1989	San Pedro de Macoris, D.R.
Cordero, Edward	.400	3	5	1	2	0	0	0	0	0	1	0	0	R	R	6-0	155	6-6-75	1992	Santo Domingo, D.R.
Eaglin, Mike	.288	126	396	62	114	15	3	5	47	41	66	15	10	R	R	5-10	170	4-25-73	1992	San Pablo, Calif.
Grijak, Kevin	.250	72	240	35	60	12	1	13	48	18	35	0	1	L	R	6-2	195	8-6-70	1991	Sterling Heights, Mich.
Helms, Wes	.296	86	314	50	93	14	1	11	44	33	50	3	4	R	R	6-4	210	5-12-76	1994	Gastonia, N.C.
Hicks, Jamie	.294	8	17	3	5	0	0	1	1	2	3	1	0	R	R	6-2	200	11-15-71	1994	Hermitage, Tenn.
Jimenez, Manny	.291	115	430	59	125	24	2	5	45	22	70	3	10	R	R	5-11	160	7-4-71	1990	Pueblo Nuevo, D.R.
Lewis, Marc	.273	135	512	64	140	17	3	17	67	25	84	21	14	R	R	6-2	175	5-20-75	1994	Decatur, Ala.
Magee, Danny	.273	7	22	1	6	0	0	1	3	1	6	0	1	R	R	6-2	175	11-25-74	1993	Denham Springs, La.
Mahoney, Mike	.228	87	298	46	68	17	0	8	46	28	75	1	0	R	R	6-0	185	12-5-72	1995	Des Moines, Iowa
McBride, Gator	.244	45	127	24	31	5	0	5	15	11	20	0	1	R	R	5-10	170	8-12-73	1993	Hurricane, W.Va.
Monds, Wonderful	.315	27	89	21	28	5	0	8	15	20	23	6	3	R	R	6-3	190	1-11-73	1993	Fort Pierce, Fla.
Norris, Dax	.333	2	9	3	3	0	0	1	3	0	1	0	0	R	R	5-10	190	11-14-73	1996	La Grange, Ga.
Rodarte, Raul	.221	55	172	29	38	8	1	7	22	26	30	10	6	R	R	5-11	190	4-9-70	1991	Diamond Bar, Calif.
Swann, Pedro	.286	124	465	78	133	29	2	24	83	49	75	5	5	L	R	6-0	195	10-27-70	1991	Townsend, Del.
Toth, Dave	.245	58	184	23	45	9	0	7	24	25	35	2	2	R	R	6-1	195	12-8-69	1990	West Keansburg, N.J.
Warner, Mike	.320	91	303	58	97	22	3	7	35	61	61	12	9	L	L	5-10	170	5-9-71	1992	Palm Beach Gardens, Fla.
Whatley, Gabe	.303	95	310	60	94	17	5	15	57	50	42	5	5	L	R	6-0	180	12-29-71	1993	Stone Mountain, Ga.

PITCHING	W	L	ERA	G	GS	CG	SV	IP	H	R	ER	BB	SO	B	T	HT	WT	DOB	1st Yr	Resides
Arnold, Jamie	0	1	11.57	1	1	0	0	5	10	6	6	2	3	R	R	6-2	188	3-24-74	1992	Kissimmee, Fla.
Bowie, Micah	3	2	3.50	8	7	0	0	44	34	19	17	26	41	L	L	6-4	185	11-10-74	1993	Humble, Texas
Briggs, Anthony	6	3	5.44	19	13	0	0	94	91	64	57	43	59	R	R	6-1	162	9-14-73	1994	Manning, S.C.
Brooks, Antone	1	0	4.79	14	0	0	0	21	21	14	11	8	10	L	L	6-0	176	12-20-73	1995	Florence, S.C.
Butler, Adam	5	1	2.57	46	0	0	22	49	40	16	14	15	56	L	L	6-2	225	8-17-73	1995	Burke, Va.
Byrd, Matt	3	2	6.00	28	0	0	0	45	58	31	30	21	38	S	R	6-2	200	5-17-71	1993	Brighton, Mich.
Cather, Mike	5	2	4.34	22	0	0	1	37	37	18	18	7	29	R	R	6-2	180	12-17-70	1993	Folsom, Calif.
Cortes, David	1	0	1.80	3	0	0	0	5	4	1	1	1	7	R	R	5-11	195	10-15-73	1996	El Centro, Calif.
Ebert, Derrin	11	8	4.10	27	25	0	0	176	191	95	80	48	101	R	L	6-3	175	8-21-76	1994	Hesperia, Calif.
Giard, Ken	3	0	1.96	25	0	0	6	37	30	9	8	11	39	R	R	6-3	210	4-2-73	1991	Warwick, R.I.
Harvey, Bryan	1	1	5.18	22	8	0	0	24	23	15	14	16	18	R	R	6-2	212	6-2-63	1985	Catawba, N.C.
Hines, Rich	4	0	6.58	41	0	0	1	67	85	56	49	22	49	L	L	6-1	185	5-20-69	1990	Milton, Fla.
Jacobs, Ryan	1	8	7.21	28	6	0	1	69	84	61	55	43	52	R	L	6-2	175	2-3-74	1992	Winston-Salem, N.C.
King, Ray	5	5	6.85	12	9	0	0	66	85	53	50	24	42	L	L	6-1	221	1-15-74	1995	Ripley, Tenn.
LeRoy, John	5	5	5.03	29	14	0	1	98	105	59	55	43	84	R	R	6-3	175	4-19-75	1993	Bellevue, Wash.
Ligtenberg, Kerry	3	1	2.04	31	0	0	16	35	20	8	8	14	43	R	R	6-2	185	5-11-71	1994	Cottage Grove, Minn.
Millwood, Kevin	3	5	4.11	11	11	0	0	61	59	37	28	24	61	R	R	6-4	205	12-24-74	1993	Bessemer City, N.C.
Moss, Damian	6	8	5.35	21	19	1	0	113	111	73	67	58	116	R	L	6-0	187	11-24-76	1994	Sadler, Australia
Nelson, Erick	0	1	4.50	5	0	0	0	6	9	4	3	4	4	L	L	6-2	185	5-22-72	1997	Bemidji, Minn.
Olszewski, Eric	0	0	6.00	4	0	0	0	6	9	6	4	8	7	L	R	6-3	205	11-4-74	1993	Spring, Texas
Rocker, John	5	6	4.86	22	18	0	0	113	119	69	61	61	96	R	L	6-4	205	10-17-74	1994	Macon, Ga.
Rogers, Bryan	2	3	3.08	19	0	0	1	26	20	11	9	12	14	R	R	5-11	170	10-30-67	1988	Hollister, Calif.
Stewart, Chaad	1	2	8.50	6	3	0	0	18	20	18	17	12	11	L	L	6-4	212	10-8-74	1994	Elgin, Ill.
Wade, Terrell	0	2	4.97	8	6	0	0	13	15	10	7	8	14	L	L	6-3	204	1-25-73	1991	Rembert, S.C.

FIELDING

Catcher	PCT	G	PO	A	E	DP	PB
Ayrault	1.000	11	62	4	0	0	0
Hicks	1.000	2	9	2	0	0	0
Mahoney	.985	85	589	58	10	6	8
Norris	1.000	2	9	1	0	1	0
Toth	.995	47	333	35	2	5	2

First Base	PCT	G	PO	A	E	DP
Benbow	.992	61	357	20	3	35
Grijak	.992	46	323	32	3	27
Hicks	.941	2	16	0	1	2
Jimenez	1.000	1	2	0	0	0
Rodarte	.984	16	115	7	2	12
Toth	.000	1	0	0	0	0
Whatley	.997	51	354	20	1	27

Second Base	PCT	G	PO	A	E	DP
Benbow	1.000	8	4	8	0	3
Brito	.975	31	58	57	3	11
Eaglin	.961	120	237	306	22	58

Third Base	PCT	G	PO	A	E	DP
Benbow	.875	25	20	36	8	4
Helms	.950	86	60	147	11	10
Jimenez	.958	33	16	52	3	6
Magee	.667	5	3	9	6	1
Rodarte	.750	1	0	3	1	0
Whatley	.778	2	1	6	2	0

Shortstop	PCT	G	PO	A	E	DP
Benbow	.948	23	28	45	4	8
Brito	.951	54	69	124	10	27
Cordero	.909	2	4	6	1	0
Jimenez	.943	88	103	228	20	40

Outfield	PCT	G	PO	A	E	DP
Benbow	.000	1	0	0	0	0
Brito	1.000	6	4	0	0	0
Lewis	.982	133	275	4	5	3
McBride	.977	32	39	3	1	0
Monds	.941	27	61	3	4	0
Rodarte	.955	36	61	2	3	1
Swann	.957	94	150	4	7	1
Warner	.962	89	167	10	7	1
Whatley	.978	59	88	3	2	0

DURHAM — Class A

CAROLINA LEAGUE

BATTING	AVG	G	AB	R	H	2B	3B	HR	RBI	BB	SO	SB	CS	B	T	HT	WT	DOB	1st Yr	Resides
Bass, Jayson	.256	75	277	48	71	20	4	4	34	29	57	8	4	S	R	6-0	175	6-2-76	1994	Fayette, Ala.
Cordero, Edward	.224	57	165	19	37	6	0	2	15	15	45	7	4	R	R	6-0	155	6-6-75	1992	Santo Domingo, D.R.
Delgado, Jose	.264	129	492	72	130	27	1	2	45	39	72	8	10	S	R	5-11	155	3-20-75	1993	Carolina, P.R.
DeRosa, Mark	.269	92	346	51	93	11	3	8	37	25	73	6	8	R	R	6-1	185	2-26-75	1996	Carlstadt, N.J.
Foote, Derek	.240	68	217	28	52	10	0	6	33	18	73	0	1	L	R	6-4	235	11-18-74	1994	Smithfield, N.C.
Johnson, Adam	.281	133	502	80	141	39	3	26	92	50	94	18	8	L	L	6-0	185	7-18-75	1996	Naples, Fla.
Lombard, George	.264	131	462	65	122	25	7	14	72	66	145	35	7	L	R	6-0	208	9-14-75	1994	Atlanta, Ga.
Matos, Pascual	.242	117	430	51	104	18	3	18	50	14	122	4	5	R	R	6-2	160	12-23-74	1992	Barahona, D.R.
McBride, Gator	.111	5	18	1	2	1	0	0	1	2	4	1	0	R	R	5-10	170	8-12-73	1993	Hurricane, W.Va.
Norris, Dax	.237	95	338	29	80	19	0	7	45	32	49	2	5	R	R	5-10	190	11-14-73	1996	La Grange, Ga.
Rust, Brian	.258	122	430	67	111	29	2	12	71	43	104	10	4	R	R	6-3	205	8-1-74	1995	Portland, Ore.
Salzano, Jerry	.279	68	226	29	63	20	0	1	24	26	42	6	4	R	R	6-0	175	10-27-74	1992	Trenton, N.J.
Trippy, Joe	.272	120	437	62	119	24	4	4	45	61	76	34	20	L	L	5-10	185	7-31-73	1995	Seattle, Wash.
Utting, Ben	.216	67	148	18	32	5	0	0	5	20	26	6	4	L	R	6-1	160	12-22-75	1993	Melbourne, Australia
Whatley, Gabe	.273	43	154	37	42	16	0	8	30	28	33	9	1	L	R	6-0	180	12-29-71	1993	Stone Mountain, Ga.

GAMES BY POSITION: C—Foote 2, Matos 109, Norris 33. **1B**—Foote 58, Johnson 1, Norris 10, Rust 55, Salzano 14, Utting 8, Whatley 9. **2B**—Cordero 19, Delgado 122, Utting 7. **3B**—Cordero 4, Rust 67, Salzano 51, Utting 23, Whatley 5. **SS**—Cordero 31, DeRosa 91, Utting 24. **OF**—Bass 50, Cordero 4, Johnson 123, Lombard 125, McBride 2, Salzano 3, Trippy 112, Whatley 8.

PITCHING	W	L	ERA	G	GS	CG	SV	IP	H	R	ER	BB	SO	B	T	HT	WT	DOB	1st Yr	Resides
Arnold, Jamie	2	2	5.92	5	5	0	0	24	25	21	16	13	21	R	R	6-2	188	3-24-74	1992	Kissimmee, Fla.
Blanco, Roger	3	3	7.64	36	0	0	0	68	91	64	58	33	33	R	R	6-6	220	8-29-76	1993	La Sabana, Venez.
Bowie, Micah	2	2	3.66	9	6	0	0	39	29	16	16	27	44	L	L	6-4	185	11-10-74	1993	Humble, Texas
Briggs, Anthony	1	2	4.50	17	0	0	3	30	27	16	15	13	25	R	R	6-1	162	9-14-73	1994	Manning, S.C.
Cortes, David	2	0	2.33	19	0	0	8	19	15	5	5	5	16	R	R	5-11	195	10-15-73	1996	El Centro, Calif.
Cruz, Charlie	5	0	3.16	49	0	0	1	85	80	37	30	44	76	L	L	5-10	175	10-22-73	1995	Miami, Fla.
Giard, Ken	2	2	2.33	30	0	0	12	39	28	14	10	35	47	R	R	6-3	210	4-2-73	1991	Warwick, R.I.
Jacobs, Dwayne	4	8	5.01	25	24	1	0	117	112	78	65	85	115	R	R	6-8	195	7-17-76	1994	Jacksonville, Fla.
King, Ray	6	9	5.40	24	6	0	3	72	89	54	43	26	60	L	L	6-1	221	1-15-74	1995	Ripley, Tenn.
McGlinchy, Kevin	3	7	4.90	26	26	0	0	140	145	78	76	39	113	R	R	6-5	220	6-28-77	1996	Malden, Mass.
McLaughlin, Denis	0	1	15.00	11	0	0	0	9	23	20	15	11	4	R	R	6-5	215	11-19-72	1994	Warwick, N.Y.
Nelson, Erick	6	8	4.76	41	1	0	1	70	76	49	37	30	42	L	L	6-2	185	5-22-72	1997	Bemidji, Minn.
Nelson, Joe	10	6	4.76	25	24	0	0	125	114	74	66	61	99	R	R	6-2	180	10-25-74	1996	Alameda, Calif.
Onley, Shawn	5	11	4.92	27	27	0	0	134	158	86	73	59	112	R	R	6-5	190	9-10-74	1996	Mt. Pleasant, Texas
Rocker, John	1	1	4.33	11	1	0	0	35	33	21	17	22	39	R	L	6-4	205	10-17-74	1994	Macon, Ga.
Stewart, Chaad	1	0	2.90	8	5	0	0	31	26	12	10	15	19	L	L	6-4	212	10-8-74	1994	Elgin, Ill.
Villegas, Ismael	2	5	5.07	30	1	0	1	55	60	33	31	32	44	R	R	6-0	177	8-12-76	1995	Caguas, P.R.
Winkelsas, Joseph	1	4	7.11	13	0	0	1	19	24	18	15	11	17	R	R	6-3	188	9-14-73	1996	Buffalo, N.Y.
Zwirchitz, Andy	7	5	4.26	33	13	0	0	108	107	59	51	59	100	R	R	6-1	180	5-3-76	1996	Appleton, Wis.

MACON — Class A

SOUTH ATLANTIC LEAGUE

BATTING	AVG	G	AB	R	H	2B	3B	HR	RBI	BB	SO	SB	CS	B	T	HT	WT	DOB	1st Yr	Resides
Arnold, John	.429	2	7	2	3	0	0	1	1	1	0	0	0	R	R	6-0	215	2-12-75	1996	Albuquerque, N.M.
Borges, Alex	.195	39	118	14	23	2	0	3	14	8	45	1	0	R	R	6-1	185	7-2-74	1996	Miramar, Fla.
Brown, Gavin	.233	66	227	27	53	7	2	3	25	30	40	8	4	R	R	6-4	211	5-12-75	1996	Newport Beach, Calif.
Hacker, Steve	.324	117	460	80	149	35	1	33	119	34	91	1	0	R	R	6-5	240	9-6-74	1995	St. Louis, Mo.
Hessman, Mike	.235	122	459	69	108	25	0	21	74	41	167	0	2	R	R	6-5	220	3-5-78	1996	Westminster, Calif.
Hines, Pooh	.163	32	104	19	17	3	2	0	7	16	29	3	2	R	R	5-11	185	9-13-74	1995	College Park, Ga.
Katz, Jason	.234	74	222	36	52	9	0	6	24	32	41	11	4	S	R	5-10	180	10-7-73	1996	Bayside, N.Y.
Lunar, Fernando	.261	105	380	41	99	26	2	7	37	18	42	0	1	R	R	6-2	205	5-25-77	1994	Anaco, Venez.
Pendergrass, Tyrone	.260	127	489	81	127	16	5	6	37	60	101	70	15	S	R	6-1	174	7-31-76	1995	Hartsville, S.C.
Ross, Jason	.258	112	430	70	111	20	5	9	59	37	121	16	7	R	R	6-4	215	6-10-74	1996	Augusta, Ga.
Scharrer, Jim	.245	121	444	67	109	19	2	20	57	37	136	0	3	R	R	6-4	220	11-5-76	1995	Erie, Pa.
Terhune, Mike	.226	92	328	33	74	11	4	1	28	25	45	8	3	S	R	6-1	185	10-14-75	1996	Pocono Manor, Pa.
Thorpe, A.D.	.249	97	350	52	87	9	1	2	29	42	46	29	17	S	R	5-11	160	6-19-77	1996	Rougemont, N.C.
Williams, Glenn	.266	77	297	52	79	18	2	14	52	24	105	9	6	S	R	6-1	185	7-18-77	1994	Ingleburn, Australia
Wong, Jerrod	.278	118	439	46	122	22	5	15	60	18	92	6	5	L	L	6-3	200	5-29-74	1996	Boise, Idaho

GAMES BY POSITION: C—Arnold 2, Borges 37, Brown 1, Lunar 105. **1B**—Hacker 49, Scharrer 90, Wong 3. **2B**—Borges 1, Hines 20, Katz 34, Terhune 58, Thorpe 38. **3B**—Hessman 116, Katz 6, Terhune 23. **SS**—Terhune 13, Thorpe 58, Williams 74. **OF**—Brown 53, Hines 5, Katz 25, Pendergrass 127, Ross 111, Wong 110.

PITCHING	W	L	ERA	G	GS	CG	SV	IP	H	R	ER	BB	SO	B	T	HT	WT	DOB	1st Yr	Resides
Bauldree, Joe	3	1	4.62	39	2	0	0	60	65	40	31	25	66	R	R	6-6	185	3-23-77	1995	Wake Forest, N.C.
Beasley, Ray	3	4	2.65	49	0	0	8	71	52	28	21	26	102	R	L	5-11	168	1-10-76	1996	Lake City, Fla.
Bell, Rob	14	7	3.68	27	27	1	0	147	144	72	60	41	140	R	R	6-5	225	1-17-77	1995	Marlboro, N.Y.
Blythe, Billy	2	5	5.22	35	1	0	0	59	54	40	34	38	57	R	R	6-2	190	1-25-76	1994	Lexington, Ky.
Chen, Bruce	12	7	3.51	28	28	1	0	146	120	67	57	44	182	S	L	6-2	180	6-19-77	1994	Panama City, Panama
Cortes, David	3	0	0.57	27	0	0	15	31	16	3	2	4	32	R	R	5-11	195	10-15-73	1996	El Centro, Calif.
Koehler, Luther	3	7	4.48	26	7	0	0	62	60	44	31	24	46	L	L	6-8	215	8-10-73	1994	Medford, Ore.
Marquis, Jason	14	10	4.38	28	28	0	0	142	156	78	69	55	121	L	R	6-1	185	8-21-78	1996	Coral Springs, Fla.
Milburn, Robert	4	1	3.34	46	0	0	4	70	71	29	26	23	51	R	L	6-1	195	4-17-74	1996	Springfield, Ky.
Osting, Jimmy	2	3	3.28	15	15	0	0	58	54	28	21	29	62	R	L	6-5	200	4-7-77	1995	Louisville, Ky.
Pacheco, Delvis	1	3	4.05	35	4	0	2	80	77	39	36	23	74	R	R	6-2	180	6-25-78	1995	Maracay, Venez.
Perez, Odalis	4	5	1.65	36	0	0	5	87	67	31	16	27	100	L	L	6-1	175	6-7-78	1994	Las Matas de Farfan, D.R.
Rivera, Luis	2	0	1.29	4	4	0	0	21	13	4	3	7	27	R	R	6-2	145	6-21-78	1995	Chihuahua, Mexico
Shiell, Jason	10	5	2.86	27	24	0	0	129	113	53	41	32	101	R	R	6-0	180	10-19-76	1995	Savannah, Ga.
Winkelsas, Joseph	3	2	2.01	38	0	0	5	63	44	17	14	13	45	R	R	6-3	188	9-14-73	1996	Buffalo, N.Y.

EUGENE — Short-Season Class A

NORTHWEST LEAGUE

BATTING	AVG	G	AB	R	H	2B	3B	HR	RBI	BB	SO	SB	CS	B	T	HT	WT	DOB	1st Yr	Resides
Arnold, John	.245	50	159	25	39	9	1	5	30	28	50	0	1	R	R	6-0	215	2-12-75	1996	Albuquerque, N.M.
Ashley, Steve	.267	4	15	3	4	1	0	0	0	2	3	0	0	R	R	6-0	195	3-21-74	1997	San Mateo, Calif.
Burke, Mark	.305	62	236	37	72	17	0	7	45	36	41	1	1	L	L	6-0	195	6-7-75	1997	Portland, Ore.
Castro, Al	.199	71	226	20	45	8	3	1	23	24	56	7	1	S	R	6-1	160	10-23-79	1996	Valencia, Venez.
Hines, Pooh	.274	69	266	40	73	10	4	3	35	40	52	5	6	R	R	5-11	185	9-13-74	1995	College Park, Ga.
Mortimer, Mark	.305	53	174	25	53	7	2	2	21	16	24	1	1	R	R	6-1	215	9-15-75	1997	Forest Park, Ga.
Pierce, Brett	.278	57	176	23	49	7	1	1	19	22	25	3	3	R	R	5-10	190	5-9-77	1997	Covina, Calif.
Pugh, Josh	.148	30	88	10	13	3	0	0	5	4	23	0	0	R	R	6-0	200	9-10-77	1996	Lexington, Ky.
Sanchez, Manuel	.288	58	229	46	66	6	4	3	27	12	39	14	5	L	R	5-11	160	10-4-76	1994	San Pedro de Macoris, D.R.
Smothers, Stewart	.275	59	233	31	64	11	6	2	27	21	57	12	4	R	R	5-10	180	4-29-76	1997	Los Angeles, Calif.
Spencer, Jeff	.262	67	275	46	72	14	2	12	54	27	83	4	2	R	R	6-3	185	6-25-77	1995	Nar Nar Goon, Australia
Strangfeld, Aaron	.068	11	44	0	3	1	0	0	1	2	13	0	0	S	R	6-1	215	10-27-77	1996	Lemon Grove, Calif.
Strickland, Greg	.284	55	204	33	58	8	3	0	16	14	62	9	2	L	L	5-10	175	11-8-75	1997	McKenzie, Tenn.
Terhune, Mike	.213	14	61	4	13	1	0	0	3	4	6	0	0	S	R	6-1	185	10-14-75	1996	Pocono Manor, Pa.
Wissen, Collin	.204	73	260	40	53	8	1	1	22	23	75	2	2	L	L	5-11	175	10-12-75	1997	Manchaca, Texas

GAMES BY POSITION: C—Arnold 20, Ashley 4, Mortimer 43, Pugh 21. **1B**—Arnold 4, Burke 62, Pierce 1, Strangfeld 11. **2B**—Hines 16, Pierce 1, Sanchez 54, Terhune 7. **3B**—Hines 25, Mortimer 4, Pierce 1, Sanchez 1, Spencer 44, Terhune 7. **SS**—Arnold 1, Castro 69, Hines 2, Pierce 13. **OF**—Hines 18, Mortimer 3, Pierce 35, Pugh 1, Smothers 58, Strickland 52, Wissen 72.

PITCHING	W	L	ERA	G	GS	CG	SV	IP	H	R	ER	BB	SO	B	T	HT	WT	DOB	1st Yr	Resides
Allen, Rodney	1	1	6.28	20	1	0	2	43	56	35	30	27	29	R	R	6-2	210	6-29-74	1996	Lindside, W.Va.
Dishman, Richard	2	2	3.00	19	1	0	3	51	47	19	17	13	60	R	R	6-5	220	4-26-75	1997	Roosevelt Island, N.Y.
Flach, Jason	4	3	2.97	23	0	0	5	39	40	18	13	24	51	R	R	6-0	165	11-25-73	1996	Davenport, Iowa
Greene, Ryan	3	7	4.59	15	15	0	0	84	96	52	43	30	72	R	R	6-4	215	8-6-74	1997	Menlo Park, Calif.
Lagrandeur, Yan	1	1	7.91	21	0	0	0	33	41	34	29	21	35	R	R	6-2	197	9-21-76	1996	Granby, Quebec
Lebejko, David	0	3	6.19	20	0	0	0	32	44	32	22	31	27	R	R	6-2	200	9-2-74	1997	Uncasville, Conn.
Newell, Brett	2	1	2.62	19	0	0	4	34	17	12	10	18	46	R	R	6-0	180	10-25-72	1994	El Segundo, Calif.
Roberts, Mike	7	6	7.08	15	15	0	0	75	104	63	59	33	33	R	R	6-4	220	8-28-75	1997	Wilbraham, Mass.
Schurman, Ryan	4	6	3.23	16	15	0	0	86	75	46	31	43	95	R	R	6-4	195	8-28-76	1995	Tualatin, Ore.
Shumate, Jacob	0	2	10.89	19	0	0	0	21	19	32	25	43	23	R	R	6-1	190	1-22-76	1994	Hartsville, S.C.
Thieme, Richard	5	3	5.81	14	14	0	0	70	92	50	45	39	51	L	L	6-1	216	10-10-75	1997	Lakemont, Ga.
Wise, Jamie	2	0	3.77	22	0	0	2	43	59	34	18	20	31	L	L	6-4	220	3-20-76	1995	Meldrim, Ga.
Wyatt, Ben	0	10	7.02	15	15	0	0	59	88	65	46	42	47	L	L	6-5	205	11-14-76	1995	Little Rock, Ark.

DANVILLE — Rookie

APPALACHIAN LEAGUE

BATTING	AVG	G	AB	R	H	2B	3B	HR	RBI	BB	SO	SB	CS	B	T	HT	WT	DOB	1st Yr	Resides
Allen, Troy	.214	43	131	16	28	5	0	2	12	19	44	1	1	L	R	6-5	225	10-8-75	1997	Reston, Va.

BATTING	AVG	G	AB	R	H	2B	3B	HR	RBI	BB	SO	SB	CS	B	T	HT	WT	DOB	1st Yr	Resides
Ashley, Steve	.162	26	74	7	12	2	0	1	5	5	15	1	0	R	R	6-0	195	3-21-74	1997	San Mateo, Calif.
Brignac, Junior	.244	59	225	47	55	10	0	4	25	29	70	12	4	R	R	6-3	175	2-15-78	1996	Sun Valley, Calif.
Brooks, Anthony	.271	67	229	43	62	12	1	4	24	8	59	15	5	R	R	6-0	190	1-25-77	1996	Pensacola, Fla.
Cameron, Troy	.216	56	208	28	45	5	2	6	24	25	80	1	3	S	R	5-11	180	8-31-78	1997	Plantation, Fla.
Crespo, Jesse	.286	14	42	11	12	0	0	3	7	3	8	0	0	R	R	6-3	200	9-18-77	1996	Camuy, P.R.
Giles, Marcus	.348	55	207	53	72	13	3	8	45	32	47	5	2	R	R	5-8	180	5-18-78	1997	El Cajon, Calif.
Hairston, Jason	.243	52	177	21	43	4	3	6	33	19	42	7	3	R	R	6-2	212	5-3-76	1997	Portland, Ore.
Mortimer, Mark	.077	5	13	1	1	0	0	0	3	4	1	0	0	R	R	6-1	215	9-15-75	1997	Forest Park, Ga.
Torrealba, Steve	.227	44	150	17	34	9	0	2	18	15	27	0	1	R	R	6-0	175	2-24-78	1995	Barquisimeto, Venez.
Villar, Jose	.222	54	203	34	45	10	4	2	16	12	69	16	5	R	R	6-1	170	5-1-79	1996	Santo Domingo, D.R.
Wilson, Travis	.215	61	233	29	50	14	6	0	27	14	60	4	1	R	R	6-2	185	7-10-77	1996	Christchurch, New Zealand
Zapp, A.J.	.338	65	234	34	79	23	2	7	56	35	78	0	1	L	R	6-2	190	4-24-78	1996	Greenwood, Ind.
Zydowsky, John	.232	43	151	19	35	6	0	1	15	20	42	2	4	R	R	5-11	175	4-18-78	1996	Pardeeville, Wis.

GAMES BY POSITION: C—Ashley 26, Hairston 4, Mortimer 5, Torrealba 42. **1B**—Allen 4, Zapp 65. **2B**—Giles 42, Zydowsky 27. **3B**—Wilson 56, Zydowsky 14. **SS**—Brignac 33, Cameron 35. **OF**—Allen 38, Brooks 67, Crespo 13, Hairston 45, Villar 54, Wilson 5.

PITCHING	W	L	ERA	G	GS	CG	SV	IP	H	R	ER	BB	SO	B	T	HT	WT	DOB	1st Yr	Resides
Birrell, Simon	4	3	4.71	13	9	0	0	50	59	36	26	27	25	R	R	6-6	185	10-7-77	1995	Ephrata, Wash.
Brummitt, Travis	0	0	13.05	12	0	0	0	20	34	36	29	16	24	R	R	6-7	225	4-27-76	1997	Knoxville, Tenn.
Canciobello, Anthony	0	0	12.27	3	0	0	0	4	6	6	5	6	4	R	R	6-1	185	8-21-76	1996	Carol City, Fla.
Ciravolo, Jon	4	2	5.06	19	0	0	1	37	48	31	21	13	42	S	R	6-1	190	9-26-75	1997	Kenilworth, N.J.
Dolby, Lawrence	0	0	5.87	3	0	0	0	8	7	5	5	5	6	S	R	6-4	205	9-26-74	1997	Sterling, Va.
Embry, Byron	2	1	1.97	20	1	0	3	32	14	7	7	15	56	R	R	6-2	240	9-5-76	1997	Richmond, Ky.
Fleck, Will	2	3	3.57	23	0	0	6	35	36	17	14	17	56	R	R	6-0	175	8-29-76	1997	Milford, N.J.
Fry, Jeff	1	1	4.12	21	0	0	1	20	19	12	9	20	16	R	L	6-2	215	9-4-74	1997	Tyrone, Pa.
Lee, Garrett	5	5	4.93	14	14	1	0	84	87	57	46	17	72	R	R	6-5	210	8-17-76	1996	Montrose, Calif.
Lewis, Derrick	2	4	6.34	16	9	0	0	50	59	48	35	31	46	R	R	6-5	215	5-7-76	1997	Montgomery, Ala.
Lyons, Tim	0	0	32.40	10	0	0	0	8	14	31	30	19	13	R	R	6-1	170	9-14-74	1997	Mission Viejo, Calif.
Nation, Joey	1	2	2.73	8	8	0	0	26	24	11	8	5	41	L	L	6-2	175	9-28-78	1997	Oklahoma City, Okla.
Quevedo, Ruben	1	5	3.56	13	11	0	0	68	46	37	27	27	78	R	R	6-1	180	1-5-79	1996	Valencia, Venez.
Rivera, Luis	3	1	2.41	9	9	0	0	41	28	15	11	17	57	R	R	6-2	145	6-21-78	1995	Chihuahua, Mexico
Shanklin, Paul	4	3	4.95	17	0	0	3	44	51	27	24	9	44	R	R	6-3	200	2-20-76	1997	Stallings, W.Va.
Taylor, Aaron	1	8	5.53	15	7	0	0	55	65	49	34	31	38	R	R	6-7	205	8-20-77	1996	Hahira, Ga.

ORLANDO — Rookie

GULF COAST LEAGUE

BATTING	AVG	G	AB	R	H	2B	3B	HR	RBI	BB	SO	SB	CS	B	T	HT	WT	DOB	1st Yr	Resides
Aldridge, Cory	.278	46	169	26	47	8	1	3	37	14	37	1	0	L	R	6-0	210	6-13-79	1997	Abilene, Texas
Betemit, Wilson	.212	32	113	12	24	6	1	0	15	9	32	0	0	S	R	6-2	155	7-28-80	1996	Santo Domingo, D.R.
Boscan, Jean	.202	36	104	7	21	5	0	1	12	16	21	0	1	R	R	6-2	160	12-26-79	1996	Maracaibo, Venez.
Burke, Mark	.433	9	30	9	13	3	0	3	7	4	2	1	0	L	L	6-0	195	6-7-75	1997	Portland, Ore.
Crespo, Jesse	.327	16	52	5	17	2	0	1	8	3	5	2	0	R	R	6-3	200	9-18-77	1996	Camuy, P.R.
Ewan, Bry	.307	36	127	9	39	3	1	3	15	12	33	2	2	R	R	6-2	205	8-2-78	1997	Georgetown, Texas
Frawley, Scott	.104	26	77	6	8	0	0	0	2	11	30	0	0	R	R	6-1	205	9-7-77	1997	Orland Hills, Ill.
Furcal, Rafael	.258	50	190	31	49	5	4	1	9	20	21	15	2	S	R	5-10	150	8-24-80	1993	Loma de Cabrera, D.R.
Heffernan, Christian	.174	36	121	7	21	1	1	0	9	6	52	3	3	L	R	6-2	193	6-15-78	1997	London, Ontario
Lehr, Ryan	.300	54	207	30	62	15	2	4	34	9	32	1	0	R	R	5-11	205	2-15-79	1997	La Mesa, Calif.
McLaughlin, Eric	.286	10	21	5	6	1	0	2	6	6	6	0	0	R	R	6-5	225	8-3-78	1996	Dover, Del.
Milton, Prinz	.253	26	83	12	21	5	0	1	8	7	29	1	1	R	R	6-3	225	3-2-79	1997	Gardena, Calif.
Monds, Wonderful	.250	2	4	2	1	0	0	1	1	1	1	0	0	R	R	6-3	190	1-11-73	1993	Fort Pierce, Fla.
Oropeza, Asdrubal	.228	50	167	38	38	8	0	4	22	37	27	3	0	R	R	6-2	170	7-3-80	1996	Barquisimeto, Venez.
Strangfeld, Aaron	.237	11	38	4	9	1	0	1	4	4	10	0	0	S	R	6-1	215	10-27-77	1996	Lemon Grove, Calif.
Velazquez, Juan	.219	30	96	14	21	3	0	0	4	18	26	2	2	S	R	5-11	150	8-22-78	1997	San Lorenzo, P.R.
Ward, Greg	.215	48	163	20	35	7	0	0	10	16	46	0	0	R	R	6-5	215	4-8-78	1996	Avon, Conn.
Wilson, Heath	.193	21	57	7	11	2	0	0	5	13	22	0	1	R	R	6-2	190	8-9-78	1996	Torquay, Australia

GAMES BY POSITION: C—Boscan 35, Ewan 11, Frawley 10, Wilson 5. **1B**—Burke 9, Crespo 4, Ewan 16, Frawley 10, Lehr 1, Strangfeld 11, Wilson 10. **2B**—Furcal 49, Oropeza 8, Velazquez 1. **3B**—Lehr 19, Oropeza 39. **SS**—Betemit 32, Velazquez 26. **OF**—Aldridge 29, Crespo 12, Furcal 1, Heffernan 36, Lehr 28, McLaughlin 1, Milton 23, Monds 2, Velazquez 1, Ward 48, Wilson 3.

PITCHING	W	L	ERA	G	GS	CG	SV	IP	H	R	ER	BB	SO	B	T	HT	WT	DOB	1st Yr	Resides
Arnold, Jamie	1	0	2.84	5	5	0	0	19	13	6	6	6	21	R	R	6-2	188	3-24-74	1992	Kissimmee, Fla.
Bowers, Jason	2	3	9.10	12	0	0	0	30	40	32	30	28	21	L	L	6-1	175	1-12-78	1997	Concord, N.C.
Ceasar, Donald	1	1	7.11	10	0	0	2	19	27	24	15	8	12	R	R	6-6	197	10-25-78	1996	Lake Charles, La.
Colon, Roman	3	4	4.29	14	12	0	0	63	68	47	30	28	44	R	R	6-3	155	8-13-79	1996	Monte Cristi, D.R.
Dolby, Lawrence	1	5	6.43	10	6	0	1	35	41	34	25	16	33	S	R	6-4	205	9-26-74	1997	Sterling, Va.
Harden, Nathan	1	6	5.36	11	9	0	0	47	46	40	28	30	36	R	R	6-2	185	1-13-78	1996	Dripping Springs, Texas
Holzbauer, Joseph	2	2	7.71	15	0	0	1	26	30	25	22	29	22	R	R	6-2	185	3-11-76	1997	Oceanside, Calif.
Lyons, Tim	0	0	0.00	1	0	0	0	1	1	0	0	1	3	R	R	6-1	170	9-14-74	1997	Mission Viejo, Calif.
Phillips, Randy	0	1	4.50	4	0	0	0	4	6	3	2	2	4	L	L	6-2	180	7-21-76	1997	Franklin, Ind.
Porter, Robert	0	1	9.19	7	0	0	0	16	23	20	16	15	20	S	L	6-4	185	2-22-77	1997	McComb, Miss.
Ramirez, Horacio	3	3	2.25	11	8	0	0	44	30	13	11	18	61	L	L	6-1	170	11-24-79	1997	Inglewood, Calif.
Schmidt, Pat	2	3	4.03	12	1	0	0	38	52	29	17	20	23	L	L	6-3	185	4-3-79	1997	Bellefontaine, Ohio
Simpson, Cory	1	3	4.73	12	2	0	1	27	29	20	14	22	27	R	R	6-5	215	2-1-78	1997	Kentwood, La.
Sylvester, Billy	3	4	3.91	12	9	0	0	53	45	25	23	28	58	R	R	6-5	218	10-1-76	1997	Florence, S.C.
Willoughby, Justin	0	2	4.07	13	6	0	1	42	40	24	19	12	45	L	L	6-3	170	4-9-78	1996	Princeton, N.C.

Baltimore ORIOLES

Manager: Davey Johnson.

1997 Record: 98-64, .605 (1st, AL East)

BATTING	AVG	G	AB	R	H	2B	3B	HR	RBI	BB	SO	SB	CS	B	T	HT	WT	DOB	1st Yr	Resides
Alomar, Roberto	.333	112	412	64	137	23	2	14	60	40	43	9	3	S	R	6-0	175	2-5-68	1985	Salinas, P.R.
Anderson, Brady	.288	151	590	97	170	39	7	18	73	84	105	18	12	L	L	6-1	195	1-18-64	1985	Newport Beach, Calif.
Baines, Harold	.291	44	134	15	39	5	0	4	15	14	15	0	0	L	L	6-2	195	3-15-59	1977	St. Michaels, Md.
2-team (93 Chicago)	.301	137	452	55	136	23	0	16	67	55	62	0	1							
Berroa, Geronimo	.260	83	300	48	78	13	0	10	48	40	62	1	2	R	R	6-0	165	3-18-65	1984	New York, N.Y.
2-team (73 Oakland)	.283	156	561	88	159	25	0	26	90	76	120	4	4							
Bordick, Mike	.236	153	509	55	120	19	1	7	46	33	66	0	2	R	R	5-11	170	7-21-65	1986	Winterport, Maine
Clyburn, Danny	.000	2	3	0	0	0	0	0	0	0	2	0	0	R	R	6-3	217	4-6-74	1992	Lancaster, S.C.
Davis, Eric	.304	42	158	29	48	11	0	8	25	14	47	6	0	R	R	6-3	185	5-29-62	1980	Woodland Hills, Calif.
Dellucci, David	.222	17	27	3	6	1	0	1	3	4	7	0	0	L	L	5-10	180	10-31-73	1995	Baton Rouge, La.
Greene, Charlie	.000	5	2	0	0	0	0	0	1	0	1	0	0	R	R	6-1	177	1-23-71	1991	Miami, Fla.
Hammonds, Jeffrey	.264	118	397	71	105	19	3	21	55	32	73	15	1	R	R	6-0	180	3-5-71	1992	Scotch Plains, N.J.
Hoiles, Chris	.259	99	320	45	83	15	0	12	49	51	86	1	0	R	R	6-0	213	3-20-65	1986	Cockeysville, Md.
Incaviglia, Pete	.246	48	138	18	34	4	0	5	12	11	43	0	0	R	R	6-1	225	4-2-64	1986	Collegeville, Texas
Laker, Tim	.000	7	14	0	0	0	0	0	1	2	9	0	0	R	R	6-2	175	11-27-69	1988	Simi Valley, Calif.
Ledesma, Aaron	.352	43	88	24	31	5	1	2	11	13	9	1	0	R	R	6-2	200	6-3-71	1990	Union City, Calif.
Palmeiro, Rafael	.254	158	614	95	156	24	2	38	110	67	109	5	2	L	L	6-0	188	9-24-64	1985	Arlington, Texas
Reboulet, Jeff	.237	99	228	26	54	9	0	4	27	23	44	3	0	R	R	6-0	168	4-30-64	1986	Kettering, Ohio
Ripken, Cal	.270	162	615	79	166	30	0	17	84	56	73	1	0	R	R	6-4	220	8-24-60	1978	Reisterstown, Md.
Rosario, Mel	.000	4	3	0	0	0	0	0	0	0	1	0	0	S	R	6-0	191	5-25-73	1992	Miami, Fla.
Surhoff, B.J.	.284	147	528	80	150	30	4	18	88	49	60	1	1	L	R	6-1	200	8-4-64	1985	Franklin, Wis.
Tarasco, Tony	.205	100	166	26	34	8	1	7	26	25	33	2	2	L	R	6-1	205	12-9-70	1988	Santa Monica, Calif.
Walton, Jerome	.294	26	68	8	20	1	0	3	9	4	10	0	0	R	R	6-1	175	7-8-65	1986	Fairburn, Ga.
Webster, Lenny	.255	98	259	29	66	8	1	7	37	22	46	0	1	R	R	5-9	195	2-10-65	1986	Charlotte, N.C.

PITCHING	W	L	ERA	G	GS	CG	SV	IP	H	R	ER	BB	SO	B	T	HT	WT	DOB	1st Yr	Resides
Benitez, Armando	4	5	2.45	71	0	0	9	73	49	22	20	43	106	R	R	6-4	220	11-3-72	1990	San Pedro de Macoris, D.R.
Boskie, Shawn	6	6	6.43	28	9	0	1	77	95	57	55	26	50	R	R	6-3	205	3-28-67	1986	Reno, Nev.
Coppinger, Rocky	1	1	6.30	5	4	0	0	20	21	14	14	16	22	R	R	6-5	245	3-19-74	1994	El Paso, Texas
Erickson, Scott	16	7	3.69	34	33	3	0	222	218	100	91	61	131	R	R	6-4	225	2-2-68	1989	Sunnyvale, Calif.
Johnson, Mike	0	1	7.94	14	5	0	2	40	52	36	35	16	29	L	R	6-2	175	10-3-75	1993	Edmonton, Alberta
Kamieniecki, Scott	10	6	4.01	30	30	0	0	179	179	83	80	67	109	R	R	6-0	190	4-19-64	1987	Flint, Mich.
Key, Jimmy	16	10	3.43	34	34	1	0	212	210	90	81	82	141	R	L	6-1	185	4-22-61	1982	Tarpon Springs, Fla.
Krivda, Rick	4	2	6.30	10	10	0	0	50	67	36	35	18	29	R	L	6-1	180	1-19-70	1991	McKeesport, Pa.
Mathews, Terry	4	4	4.41	57	0	0	1	63	63	35	31	36	39	L	R	6-2	225	10-5-64	1987	Boyce, La.
Mills, Alan	2	3	4.89	39	0	0	0	39	41	23	21	33	32	S	R	6-1	192	10-18-66	1986	Lakeland, Fla.
Mussina, Mike	15	8	3.20	33	33	4	0	225	197	87	80	54	218	R	R	6-2	185	12-8-68	1990	Montoursville, Pa.
Myers, Randy	2	3	1.51	61	0	0	45	60	47	12	10	22	56	L	L	6-1	210	9-19-62	1982	Vancouver, Wash.
Orosco, Jesse	6	3	2.32	71	0	0	0	50	29	13	13	30	46	R	L	6-2	205	4-21-57	1978	Poway, Calif.
Rhodes, Arthur	10	3	3.02	53	0	0	1	95	75	32	32	26	102	L	L	6-2	204	10-24-69	1988	Sarasota, Fla.
Rodriguez, Nerio	2	1	4.91	6	2	0	0	22	21	15	12	8	11	R	R	6-1	195	3-22-73	1991	San Pedro de Macoris, D.R.
Williams, Brian	0	0	3.00	13	0	0	0	24	20	8	8	18	14	R	R	6-2	195	2-15-69	1990	Cayce, S.C.
Yan, Esteban	0	1	15.83	3	2	0	0	10	20	18	17	7	4	R	R	6-4	180	6-22-74	1991	La Higuera, D.R.

FIELDING

Catcher	PCT	G	PO	A	E	DP	PB
Greene	1.000	4	4	0	0	0	0
Hoiles	1.000	87	602	28	0	4	3
Laker	.966	7	28	0	1	0	0
Rosario	.875	4	7	0	1	0	0
Webster	.995	97	532	36	3	5	4

First Base	PCT	G	PO	A	E	DP
Hoiles	1.000	4	20	3	0	1
Ledesma	1.000	5	30	1	0	4
Palmeiro	.993	155	1305	112	10	124
Surhoff	1.000	3	21	3	0	4
Walton	1.000	5	23	1	0	1

Second Base	PCT	G	PO	A	E	DP
Alomar	.988	109	202	301	6	66
Ledesma	.973	22	32	41	2	8
Reboulet	.977	63	83	130	5	28

Third Base	PCT	G	PO	A	E	DP
Hoiles	.000	1	0	0	0	0
Ledesma	.929	11	5	8	1	1
Reboulet	.875	12	1	6	1	0
Ripken	.949	162	98	313	22	25
Surhoff	1.000	3	0	2	0	1

Shortstop	PCT	G	PO	A	E	DP
Bordick	.980	153	224	424	13	95
Ledesma	1.000	4	1	2	0	0
Reboulet	.979	22	20	27	1	4
Ripken	1.000	3	2	0	0	0

Outfield	PCT	G	PO	A	E	DP
Anderson	.989	124	276	2	3	0
Baines	.000	1	0	0	0	0
Berroa	.959	40	70	1	3	0
Clyburn	.000	1	0	0	0	0
Davis	.975	30	39	0	1	0
Dellucci	1.000	9	20	1	0	0
Hammonds	.980	114	240	4	5	0
Reboulet	1.000	1	2	0	0	0
Surhoff	.992	133	247	11	2	3
Tarasco	.991	81	104	4	1	1
Walton	1.000	19	29	0	0	0

DIAMOND IMAGES

Mike Mussina

FARM SYSTEM

Director of Player Development: Syd Thrift

Class	Farm Team	League	W	L	Pct.	Finish*	Manager(s)	First Yr
AAA	Rochester (N.Y.) Red Wings	International	83	58	.589	+1st (10)	Marv Foley	1961
AA	Bowie (Md.) Baysox	Eastern	75	67	.528	3rd (10)	Joe Ferguson	1993
#A	Frederick (Md.) Keys	Carolina	69	71	.493	4th (8)	Dave Hilton	1989
A	Delmarva (Md.) Shorebirds	South Atlantic	77	65	.542	+3rd (14)	Tom Shields/Tom Trebelhorn	1997
#R	Bluefield (W.Va.) Orioles	Appalachian	40	29	.580	+2nd (10)	Bobby Dickerson	1958
R	Sarasota (Fla.) Orioles	Gulf Coast	27	33	.450	10th (15)	Butch Davis	**1991**

*Finish in overall standings (No. of teams in league) #Advanced level +Won league championship

ORGANIZATION LEADERS

MAJOR LEAGUERS

BATTING

*AVG	Roberto Alomar	.333
R	Brady Anderson	97
H	Brady Anderson	170
TB	Rafael Palmeiro	298
2B	Brady Anderson	39
3B	Brady Anderson	7
HR	Rafael Palmeiro	38
RBI	Rafael Palmeiro	110
BB	Brady Anderson	84
SO	Rafael Palmeiro	109
SB	Brady Anderson	18

PITCHING

W	Two tied at	16
L	Jimmy Key	10
#ERA	Arthur Rhodes	3.02
G	Two tied at	71
CG	Mike Mussina	4
SV	Randy Myers	45
IP	Mike Mussina	225
BB	Jimmy Key	82
SO	Mike Mussina	218

Rafael Palmeiro

JOHN SPEAR

Ryan Minor

MINOR LEAGUERS

BATTING

*AVG	David Dellucci, Bowie	.327
R	Danny Clyburn, Rochester	91
H	Danny Clyburn, Rochester	156
TB	Ryan Minor, Delmarva	266
2B	Ryan Minor, Delmarva	42
3B	Three tied at	8
HR	Calvin Pickering, Delmarva	25
RBI	Jim Foster, Roch./Bowie/Frederick	110
BB	Tim DeCinces, Delmarva	97
SO	Chris Kirgan, Bowie	141
SB	Darrell Dent, Delmarva	60

PITCHING

W	Rick Krivda, Rochester	14
L	Two tied at	11
#ERA	Scott Eibey, Delmarva	1.83
G	Matt Snyder, Bowie	67
CG	Rick Krivda, Rochester	6
SV	Ryan Kohlmeier, Bowie/Delmarva	25
IP	Dan Reed, Frederick	173
BB	Francisco Saneaux, Bowie/Frederick	116
SO	Nerio Rodriguez, Rochester	160

*Minimum 250 At-Bats #Minimum 75 Innings

TOP 10 PROSPECTS

STEVE MOORE

Nerio Rodriguez

How the Orioles Top 10 prospects, as judged by Baseball America prior to the 1997 season, fared in 1997:

Player, Pos.	Club (Class)	AVG	AB	R	H	2B	3B	HR	RBI	SB
3. Eugene Kingsale, of	Bowie (AA)	.413	46	8	19	6	0	0	4	5
	Sarasota (R)	.294	17	2	5	0	0	0	0	1
5. Ryan Minor, 3b	Delmarva (A)	.307	488	83	150	42	1	24	97	7
7. Calvin Pickering,1b	Delmarva (A)	.311	444	88	138	31	1	25	79	6

		W	L	ERA	G	SV	IP	H	BB	SO
1. Nerio Rodriguez, rhp	Baltimore	2	1	4.91	6	0	22	21	8	11
	Rochester (AAA)	11	10	3.90	27	0	168	124	62	160
2. Sidney Ponson, rhp	Bowie (AA)	2	7	5.42	13	0	75	77	32	56
	Sarasota (R)	1	0	0.00	1	0	2	0	0	1
4. Chris Fussell, rhp	Bowie (AA)	1	8	7.11	19	0	82	102	58	71
	Frederick (A)	3	3	3.96	9	0	50	42	31	54
6. Julio Moreno, rhp	Bowie (AA)	9	6	3.83	27	0	139	141	64	106
8. Alvie Shepherd, rhp	Bowie (AA)	10	6	5.33	22	0	106	98	57	80
9. Mark Seaver, rhp	Frederick (A)	3	2	3.05	11	0	62	57	17	68
10. Brian Falkenborg, rhp	Bowie (AA)	0	1	16.20	1	0	2	3	3	0
	Delmarva (A)	7	9	4.46	25	0	127	122	46	107

ROCHESTER — Class AAA

INTERNATIONAL LEAGUE

BATTING	AVG	G	AB	R	H	2B	3B	HR	RBI	BB	SO	SB	CS	B	T	HT	WT	DOB	1st Yr	Resides
Berry, Mike	.299	54	177	23	53	11	3	1	19	13	31	1	1	R	R	5-10	185	8-12-70	1993	Rolling Hills, Calif.
Bullett, Scott	.250	136	512	73	128	24	8	9	58	45	112	19	11	L	L	6-2	190	12-25-68	1988	Martinsburg, W.Va.
Carney, Bartt	.000	4	6	1	0	0	0	0	0	3	2	0	0	S	R	5-11	170	12-16-73	1994	Parnell, Iowa
Clyburn, Danny	.300	137	520	91	156	33	5	20	76	53	107	14	4	R	R	6-3	217	4-6-74	1992	Lancaster, S.C.
Davis, Tommy	.304	119	438	74	133	22	2	15	62	43	90	6	1	R	R	6-1	195	5-21-73	1994	Semmes, Ala.
Forbes, P.J.	.272	116	434	67	118	22	2	8	54	35	42	15	4	R	R	5-10	160	9-22-67	1990	Pittsburg, Kan.
Foster, Jim	.556	3	9	4	5	2	0	0	4	3	0	0	1	R	R	6-4	220	8-18-71	1993	Warwick, R.I.
Fox, Eric	.222	5	18	2	4	1	0	0	0	2	2	0	0	S	L	5-10	180	8-15-63	1986	Paso Robles, Calif.
Frazier, Lou	.248	84	302	40	75	12	4	2	39	36	68	24	6	S	R	6-2	175	1-26-65	1986	St. Louis, Mo.
Gresham, Kris	.107	13	28	1	3	1	0	0	0	2	8	0	0	R	R	6-2	206	8-30-70	1991	Mt. Pleasant, N.C.
Gruber, Kelly	.250	38	144	26	36	9	2	2	23	15	14	1	1	R	R	6-0	185	2-26-62	1980	Austin, Texas
Johns, Keith	.000	1	1	0	0	0	0	0	0	0	0	0	0	R	R	6-1	175	7-19-71	1992	St. Louis, Mo.
Laker, Tim	.259	79	290	45	75	11	1	11	37	34	49	1	2	R	R	6-2	175	11-27-69	1988	Simi Valley, Calif.
Lawrence, Chip	.233	17	43	9	10	0	1	0	7	3	8	1	1	R	R	6-2	182	11-14-74	1996	St. Petersburg, Fla.
Ledesma, Aaron	.325	85	326	40	106	26	1	3	43	35	48	12	2	R	R	6-2	200	6-3-71	1990	Union City, Calif.
Luzinski, Ryan	.208	42	125	12	26	7	1	2	16	19	49	0	1	R	R	6-1	215	8-22-73	1992	Medford, N.J.
Martinez, Eddy	.074	12	27	0	2	1	0	0	3	1	8	0	0	R	R	6-2	150	10-23-77	1995	San Pedro de Macoris, D.R.
Matos, Francisco	.324	101	389	51	126	17	4	4	51	9	42	8	2	R	R	6-1	160	4-8-70	1988	Azua, D.R.
Ojeda, Augie	.234	15	47	5	11	3	1	0	6	8	4	1	2	S	R	5-9	171	12-20-74	1996	South Gate, Calif.
Otanez, Willis	.208	49	168	20	35	9	0	5	25	15	35	0	0	R	R	5-11	150	4-19-73	1990	Las Matas de Cotui, D.R.
Tarasco, Tony	.200	10	35	4	7	0	0	2	6	7	7	0	0	L	R	6-1	205	12-9-70	1988	Santa Monica, Calif.
Tolentino, Jose	.211	20	57	6	12	2	0	1	9	14	11	0	0	L	L	6-1	195	6-3-61	1983	Mexico City, Mexico
Waszgis, B.J.	.260	100	315	61	82	15	1	13	48	56	78	1	1	R	R	6-2	210	8-24-70	1991	Omaha, Neb.
Wawruck, Jim	.271	94	339	47	92	20	3	5	35	34	64	12	6	L	L	5-11	185	4-23-70	1991	Glastonbury, Conn.

PITCHING	W	L	ERA	G	GS	CG	SV	IP	H	R	ER	BB	SO	B	T	HT	WT	DOB	1st Yr	Resides
Bennett, Chris	4	2	3.54	25	0	0	1	41	40	17	16	7	28	R	R	6-6	205	9-8-65	1986	Yreka, Calif.
Carrara, Giovanni	4	2	4.44	8	8	1	0	47	45	23	23	16	48	R	R	6-2	210	3-4-68	1990	Anzoategui, Venez.
Coppinger, Rocky	1	2	5.52	3	3	0	0	15	16	10	9	11	9	R	R	6-5	245	3-19-74	1994	El Paso, Texas
Corbin, Archie	4	3	4.00	43	1	0	5	70	47	32	31	62	66	R	R	6-4	187	12-30-67	1986	Beaumont, Texas
Greer, Ken	0	2	5.79	15	0	0	1	23	30	15	15	5	14	R	R	6-2	215	5-12-67	1988	Hull, Mass.
Haynes, Jimmy	5	4	3.44	16	16	2	0	102	89	49	39	55	113	R	R	6-4	185	9-5-72	1991	La Grange, Ga.
Johns, Doug	3	1	3.74	9	8	2	0	55	57	25	23	13	42	R	L	6-2	185	12-19-67	1990	Plantation, Fla.
Krivda, Rick	14	2	3.39	22	21	6	0	146	122	61	55	34	128	R	L	6-1	180	1-19-70	1991	McKeesport, Pa.
Montgomery, Steve	0	2	12.15	2	1	0	0	7	15	12	9	3	2	R	R	6-7	230	2-21-74	1994	Warren, Ohio
Ramirez, Hector	8	7	4.91	39	9	0	3	103	114	65	56	38	50	R	R	6-3	218	12-15-71	1988	El Seibo, D.R.
Rodriguez, Nerio	11	10	3.90	27	27	1	0	168	124	82	73	62	160	R	R	6-1	195	3-22-73	1991	San Pedro de Macoris, D.R.
Sackinsky, Brian	1	0	5.11	2	2	0	0	12	12	7	7	3	6	R	R	6-4	220	6-22-71	1992	Library, Pa.
Schrenk, Steve	4	7	4.66	25	24	1	0	126	127	73	65	36	99	R	R	6-3	185	11-20-68	1987	Aurora, Ore.
Shouse, Brian	6	2	2.27	54	0	0	9	71	48	21	18	21	81	L	L	5-11	180	9-26-68	1990	Effingham, Ill.
Steph, Rod	3	3	4.25	41	0	0	14	49	49	24	23	12	51	R	R	5-11	185	8-27-69	1991	Plano, Texas
Swift, Billy	0	1	4.91	2	0	0	0	4	2	2	2	3	2	R	R	6-0	191	10-27-61	1985	Paradise Valley, Ariz.
Williams, Brian	4	3	3.89	22	9	0	8	69	68	33	30	23	78	R	R	6-2	195	2-15-69	1990	Cayce, S.C.
Yan, Esteban	11	5	3.10	34	12	0	2	119	107	54	41	37	131	R	R	6-4	180	6-22-74	1991	La Higuera, D.R.

FIELDING

Catcher	PCT	G	PO	A	E	DP	PB
Foster	1.000	1	10	1	0	0	0
Gresham	.985	12	56	8	1	0	0
Laker	.980	33	283	17	6	1	1
Luzinski	.993	35	270	27	2	5	4
Waszgis	.980	70	538	37	12	1	9

First Base	PCT	G	PO	A	E	DP
Davis	.994	116	875	72	6	56
Gruber	.968	8	56	5	2	6
Ledesma	1.000	1	3	1	0	1
Otanez	.977	7	39	3	1	2
Tolentino	.959	12	66	5	3	7
Waszgis	1.000	3	23	2	0	2

Second Base	PCT	G	PO	A	E	DP
Berry	1.000	6	1	6	0	0
Forbes	.979	58	102	131	5	28
Gruber	.963	21	31	48	3	8
Lawrence	.889	2	2	6	1	0
Matos	.975	66	100	135	6	17

Third Base	PCT	G	PO	A	E	DP
Berry	.936	44	33	69	7	4
Forbes	.952	57	43	95	7	4
Lawrence	1.000	4	3	9	0	0
Otanez	.894	44	28	65	11	2

Shortstop	PCT	G	PO	A	E	DP
Forbes	1.000	6	5	11	0	3
Johns	1.000	1	0	1	0	0
Lawrence	.929	9	11	15	2	1
Ledesma	.959	81	118	184	13	39
Martinez	.969	12	6	25	1	4
Matos	.975	28	31	48	2	7
Ojeda	.922	15	24	35	5	6

Outfield	PCT	G	PO	A	E	DP
Bullett	.972	122	232	8	7	2
Carney	1.000	3	7	0	0	0
Clyburn	.961	133	241	5	10	1
Forbes	.000	1	0	0	0	0
Fox	1.000	4	8	0	0	0
Frazier	.981	83	204	6	4	0
Gruber	1.000	6	14	0	0	0
Tarasco	1.000	10	19	1	0	0
Wawruck	.984	64	118	6	2	0

BOWIE — Class AA

EASTERN LEAGUE

BATTING	AVG	G	AB	R	H	2B	3B	HR	RBI	BB	SO	SB	CS	B	T	HT	WT	DOB	1st Yr	Resides
Almonte, Wady	.207	69	222	25	46	7	2	6	25	27	64	2	4	R	R	6-0	180	4-20-75	1993	Higuey, D.R.
Bautista, Juan	.250	21	68	9	17	1	0	0	3	5	17	1	2	R	R	6-1	185	6-24-75	1992	San Pedro de Macoris, D.R.
Berry, Mike	.230	53	204	34	47	10	0	8	30	24	53	1	1	R	R	5-10	185	8-12-70	1993	Rolling Hills, Calif.
Bogle, Bryan	.255	102	384	50	98	17	0	13	58	27	92	3	4	R	R	6-1	205	5-18-73	1994	Merritt Island, Fla.
Carney, Bartt	.269	66	156	27	42	5	0	0	8	31	31	8	5	S	R	5-11	170	12-16-73	1994	Parnell, Iowa
Chavez, Eric	.000	1	0	0	0	0	0	0	0	0	0	0	0	R	R	5-11	212	9-7-70	1992	Carlsbad, N.M.
Clark, Howie	.287	105	314	39	90	16	0	9	37	32	38	2	2	L	R	5-10	171	2-13-74	1992	Huntington Beach, Calif.
Curtis, Kevin	.269	22	67	7	18	6	0	1	13	7	22	1	1	R	R	6-2	210	8-19-72	1993	Upland, Calif.
Daedelow, Craig	.000	1	1	0	0	0	0	0	0	0	1	0	0	R	R	5-11	175	4-3-76	1994	Huntington Beach, Calif.
Dellucci, David	.327	107	385	71	126	29	3	20	55	58	69	11	4	L	L	5-10	180	10-31-73	1995	Baton Rouge, La.
Foster, Jim	.275	63	211	36	58	12	0	7	41	36	31	1	1	R	R	6-4	220	8-18-71	1993	Warwick, R.I.
Frazier, Lou	.233	25	103	20	24	4	2	0	8	21	20	13	1	S	R	6-2	175	1-26-65	1986	St. Louis, Mo.
Garcia, Jesse	.236	141	437	52	103	18	1	5	42	38	71	7	7	R	R	5-9	165	9-24-73	1993	Robstown, Texas
Hoiles, Chris	.143	3	7	1	1	1	0	0	2	3	2	0	0	R	R	6-0	213	3-20-65	1986	Cockeysville, Md.

BATTING	AVG	G	AB	R	H	2B	3B	HR	RBI	BB	SO	SB	CS	B	T	HT	WT	DOB	1st Yr	Resides
Isom, Johnny	.274	135	518	70	142	29	4	20	91	44	121	1	5	R	R	5-11	210	8-9-73	1995	Fort Worth, Texas
Kingsale, Eugene	.413	13	46	8	19	6	0	0	4	5	4	5	1	S	R	6-3	170	8-20-76	1994	Oranjestad, Aruba
Kirgan, Chris	.230	139	504	72	116	25	0	19	71	60	141	0	0	R	R	6-4	235	6-29-73	1994	Littleton, Colo.
Lamb, David	.331	73	269	46	89	20	2	4	38	34	35	0	0	S	R	6-3	175	6-6-75	1993	Newbury Park, Calif.
Lasater, Chris	.250	3	4	0	1	0	0	0	0	0	1	0	0	R	R	5-11	200	11-6-72	1997	Morehead City, N.C.
Lawrence, Chip	.231	7	13	1	3	0	0	0	0	1	3	0	0	R	R	6-2	182	11-14-74	1996	St. Petersburg, Fla.
LeCronier, Jason	.300	6	10	0	3	0	0	0	2	0	4	0	0	L	R	5-11	200	3-30-73	1995	Lake Charles, La.
Luzinski, Ryan	.284	30	81	12	23	4	0	5	15	10	17	3	0	R	R	6-1	215	8-22-73	1992	Medford, N.J.
Martin, Lincoln	.292	12	24	3	7	2	0	0	3	3	2	0	1	S	R	5-10	170	10-20-71	1993	Douglasville, Ga.
Martinez, Eddy	.156	16	45	3	7	3	0	0	1	6	12	2	0	R	R	6-2	150	10-23-77	1995	San Pedro de Macoris, D.R.
Ojeda, Augie	.294	58	204	33	60	9	1	2	23	31	17	7	0	S	R	5-9	171	12-20-74	1996	South Gate, Calif.
Otanez, Willis	.333	19	78	13	26	9	0	3	13	9	19	0	1	R	R	5-11	150	4-19-73	1990	Las Matas de Cotui, D.R.
Paxton, Chris	.136	12	22	1	3	1	0	0	1	1	7	0	0	L	R	6-2	195	12-11-76	1995	Palmdale, Calif.
Rosario, Melvin	.263	123	430	68	113	26	1	12	60	27	106	4	7	S	R	6-0	191	5-25-73	1992	Miami, Fla.

PITCHING	W	L	ERA	G	GS	CG	SV	IP	H	R	ER	BB	SO	B	T	HT	WT	DOB	1st Yr	Resides
Bennett, Chris	2	1	2.89	10	0	0	0	19	15	9	6	11	9	R	R	6-6	205	9-8-65	1986	Yreka, Calif.
Bennett, Joel	6	8	3.18	44	10	0	4	113	89	45	40	40	146	R	R	6-1	161	1-31-70	1991	Kirkwood, N.Y.
Bullard, Jason	7	2	2.62	61	0	0	3	93	84	39	27	39	77	R	R	6-2	185	10-23-68	1991	Sweeny, Texas
Cafaro, Rocco	3	3	5.40	13	6	0	0	48	50	34	29	16	43	R	R	6-0	175	12-2-72	1993	Brandon, Fla.
Clark, Howie	0	0	16.88	2	0	0	0	2	5	5	5	3	3	L	R	5-10	171	2-13-74	1992	Huntington Beach, Calif.
Coppinger, Rocky	1	1	4.80	3	3	0	0	15	15	9	8	3	15	R	R	6-5	245	3-19-74	1994	El Paso, Texas
Curtis, Chris	6	1	3.62	36	6	0	2	87	100	41	35	17	48	R	R	6-2	185	5-8-71	1991	Duncanville, Texas
Dykhoff, Radhames	0	0	8.31	7	0	0	0	9	10	9	8	7	7	L	L	6-0	205	9-27-74	1993	Oranjestad, Aruba
Falkenborg, Brian	0	1	16.20	1	1	0	0	2	3	3	3	3	0	R	R	6-6	187	1-18-78	1996	Redmond, Wash.
Fussell, Chris	1	8	7.11	19	18	0	0	82	102	71	65	58	71	R	R	6-2	185	5-19-76	1994	Oregon, Ohio
Gallaher, Kevin	1	5	4.46	26	1	0	8	42	50	27	21	15	36	L	R	6-3	190	8-1-68	1991	Vienna, Va.
Greer, Ken	1	1	4.08	11	0	0	0	18	17	9	8	3	12	R	R	6-2	215	5-12-67	1988	Hull, Mass.
Hernandez, Francisco	0	0	1.59	6	0	0	0	6	7	1	1	4	2	R	R	6-0	160	12-17-76	1994	San Pedro de Macoris, D.R.
Kirgan, Chris	1	0	6.75	5	0	0	0	4	4	3	3	1	2	R	R	6-4	235	6-29-73	1994	Littleton, Colo.
Kohlmeier, Ryan	0	0	0.00	2	0	0	1	3	0	0	0	2	5	R	R	6-2	195	6-25-77	1996	Cottonwood Falls, Kan.
Lane, Aaron	0	1	7.94	7	0	0	0	6	6	5	5	6	4	L	L	6-1	180	6-2-71	1992	Taylorville, Ill.
Maine, Dalton	0	0	0.00	9	0	0	0	13	4	0	0	6	11	R	R	6-3	185	3-22-72	1995	Framingham, Mass.
Montgomery, Steve	10	5	3.10	24	23	2	0	136	116	56	47	52	127	R	R	6-7	230	2-21-74	1994	Warren, Ohio
Moreno, Julio	9	6	3.83	27	25	1	0	139	141	76	59	64	106	R	R	6-1	145	10-23-75	1994	Los Llanos, D.R.
Osteen, Gavin	1	1	2.05	18	2	0	0	31	20	7	7	11	22	R	L	6-0	195	11-27-69	1989	Bethany Beach, Del.
Parrish, John	1	0	1.80	1	1	0	0	5	3	1	1	2	3	L	L	5-11	165	11-26-77	1996	Lancaster, Pa.
Percibal, Billy	0	1	3.00	1	1	1	0	6	5	2	2	1	5	R	R	6-1	170	2-2-74	1992	San Pedro de Macoris, D.R.
Ponson, Sidney	2	7	5.42	13	13	1	0	75	77	51	45	32	56	R	R	6-1	200	11-2-76	1994	Oranjestad, Aruba
Saneaux, Francisco	0	0	8.56	8	0	0	0	14	8	14	13	32	13	R	R	6-4	180	3-3-74	1991	Santo Domingo, D.R.
Shepherd, Alvie	10	6	5.33	22	19	0	0	106	98	68	63	57	80	R	R	6-7	245	5-12-74	1996	Bellwood, Ill.
Smith, Hut	5	4	4.22	14	13	0	0	81	90	45	38	22	46	S	R	6-3	195	6-8-73	1992	Kannapolis, N.C.
Snyder, Matt	7	5	4.16	67	0	0	19	80	89	48	37	42	68	R	R	5-11	190	7-7-74	1995	Philadelphia, Pa.
Steph, Rod	1	0	1.32	7	0	0	0	14	6	3	2	3	9	R	R	5-11	185	8-27-69	1991	Plano, Texas

FIELDING

Catcher	PCT	G	PO	A	E	DP	PB
Chavez	1.000	1	0	1	0	0	0
Foster	.981	39	284	29	6	4	1
Hoiles	1.000	2	12	0	0	0	0
Lasater	1.000	2	5	0	0	0	3
Luzinski	.985	18	114	16	2	1	4
Paxton	.957	5	19	3	1	0	0
Rosario	.986	92	621	87	10	7	12

First Base	PCT	G	PO	A	E	DP
Clark	1.000	7	8	4	0	1
Curtis	1.000	5	22	1	0	5
Foster	1.000	2	17	0	0	2
Kirgan	.992	139	1228	89	11	111
Paxton	1.000	3	4	0	0	1

Second Base	PCT	G	PO	A	E	DP
Berry	.000	1	0	0	0	0
Clark	.962	20	24	27	2	4
Garcia	.985	134	277	362	10	84
Lamb	.941	4	8	8	1	6
Lawrence	1.000	1	1	0	0	0
Martin	.950	8	7	12	1	0

Third Base	PCT	G	PO	A	E	DP
Berry	.927	52	32	108	11	11
Clark	.882	66	29	106	18	10
Garcia	1.000	1	1	0	0	0
Lamb	.933	29	13	29	3	3
Lawrence	.909	5	4	6	1	0
Luzinski	.000	1	0	0	0	0
Otanez	.955	7	1	20	1	2

Shortstop	PCT	G	PO	A	E	DP
Bautista	.942	21	25	73	6	15
Garcia	.900	10	12	15	3	3
Lamb	.963	46	60	122	7	20
Lawrence	1.000	1	2	1	0	1
Martinez	.943	16	17	49	4	9
Ojeda	.967	58	84	176	9	37

Outfield	PCT	G	PO	A	E	DP
Almonte	.916	68	94	4	9	0
Bogle	.958	95	152	9	7	0
Carney	.971	59	95	4	3	1
Curtis	.667	1	2	0	1	0
Dellucci	.994	91	162	2	1	1
Frazier	.917	25	52	3	5	0
Isom	.975	99	148	5	4	3
Kingsale	.958	12	23	0	1	0
LeCronier	1.000	4	6	0	0	0
Martin	1.000	3	8	0	0	0

FREDERICK — Class A

CAROLINA LEAGUE

BATTING	AVG	G	AB	R	H	2B	3B	HR	RBI	BB	SO	SB	CS	B	T	HT	WT	DOB	1st Yr	Resides
Akins, Carlos	.212	110	335	53	71	16	0	2	30	54	79	14	4	R	R	6-0	180	7-12-74	1995	Oklahoma City, Okla.
Almonte, Wady	.257	57	202	34	52	13	2	10	36	16	59	4	1	R	R	6-0	180	4-20-75	1993	Higuey, D.R.
Bello, Jilberto	.286	2	7	0	2	1	0	0	1	1	2	0	0	R	R	6-3	150	2-26-77	1994	San Pedro de Macoris, D.R.
Bryant, Chris	.274	91	317	53	87	17	1	7	36	47	65	6	3	R	R	6-2	195	12-15-72	1995	Middlesex, N.C.
Carney, Bartt	.000	4	6	2	0	0	0	0	0	2	0	0	0	S	R	5-11	170	12-16-73	1994	Parnell, Iowa
Chavez, Eric	.188	82	272	29	51	16	0	11	34	22	69	1	3	R	R	5-11	212	9-7-70	1992	Carlsbad, N.M.
Diaz, Maikell	.000	7	15	2	0	0	0	0	0	3	3	0	1	R	R	5-10	158	9-29-78	1996	Miranda, Venez.
Foster, Jim	.350	61	200	48	70	12	1	16	65	45	28	8	0	R	R	6-4	220	8-18-71	1993	Warwick, R.I.
Gresham, Kris	.237	43	131	17	31	7	0	3	19	15	30	3	2	R	R	6-2	206	8-30-70	1991	Mt. Pleasant, N.C.
Hendricks, Ryan	.194	77	222	21	43	9	0	6	25	30	71	1	4	L	R	6-3	205	8-3-72	1994	Randallstown, Md.
Kurtz, Tony	.218	81	262	35	57	11	4	3	17	38	90	7	2	L	R	5-10	183	11-2-73	1997	Columbia Heights, Minn.
Lamb, David	.261	70	249	30	65	21	1	2	39	25	32	3	1	S	R	6-3	175	6-6-75	1993	Newbury Park, Calif.
Lanza, Mike	.224	23	67	4	15	4	0	0	5	3	13	1	2	R	R	6-1	170	10-22-73	1994	Port Chester, N.Y.
Lawrence, Chip	.268	57	164	18	44	5	0	2	14	13	19	2	4	R	R	6-2	182	11-14-74	1996	St. Petersburg, Fla.
LeCronier, Jason	.273	117	421	68	115	25	2	19	59	31	112	6	0	L	R	5-11	200	3-30-73	1995	Lake Charles, La.
Luzinski, Ryan	.667	1	3	1	2	0	0	0	0	1	0	0	0	R	R	6-1	215	8-22-73	1992	Medford, N.J.

LARRY GOREN

Baltimore's Geronimo Berroa

DIAMOND IMAGES

Frederick's Jim Foster

BATTING	AVG	G	AB	R	H	2B	3B	HR	RBI	BB	SO	SB	CS	B	T	HT	WT	DOB	1st Yr	Resides
Martin, Lincoln	.194	79	253	42	49	6	5	2	23	33	52	11	2	S	R	5-10	170	10-20-71	1993	Douglasville, Ga.
Martinez, Eddy	.241	54	174	14	42	6	0	1	14	19	43	6	7	R	R	6-2	150	10-23-77	1995	San Pedro de Macoris, D.R.
McKinnis, Leroy	.288	88	319	36	92	24	1	4	39	20	62	3	3	R	R	6-1	185	11-14-72	1993	Irving, Texas
O'Toole, Bobby	.276	12	29	5	8	2	0	1	4	7	4	0	0	R	R	6-0	195	5-19-74	1995	Newton, Mass.
Ojeda, Augie	.344	34	128	25	44	11	1	1	20	18	18	2	5	S	R	5-9	171	12-20-74	1996	South Gate, Calif.
Paxton, Chris	.267	4	15	1	4	0	0	1	1	0	5	0	0	L	R	6-2	195	12-11-76	1995	Palmdale, Calif.
Rivera, Roberto	.226	16	53	8	12	1	0	1	8	3	16	1	1	R	R	6-2	160	11-25-76	1994	La Romana, D.R.
Short, Rick	.319	126	480	73	153	29	1	10	72	38	44	10	7	R	R	6-0	190	12-6-72	1994	South Elgin, Ill.
Walton, Jerome	.211	7	19	1	4	0	0	1	2	5	0	1	1	R	R	6-1	175	7-8-65	1986	Fairburn, Ga.
Wolff, Mike	.252	112	321	50	81	12	0	8	34	45	47	4	4	L	L	6-3	205	2-17-73	1994	Granger, Ind.

GAMES BY POSITION: C—Bello 1, Bryant 3, Chavez 32, Foster 41, Gresham 28, Luzinski 1, McKinnis 35, O'Toole 10, Paxton 4. **1B**—Bryant 2, Chavez 12, Gresham 3, Hendricks 42, McKinnis 8, Walton 1, Wolff 103. **2B**—Bryant 2, Lamb 61, Lawrence 20, Martin 8, Short 63. **3B**—Bryant 71, Chavez 12, Gresham 7, Lamb 3, Lawrence 4, Short 54. **SS**—Bryant 4, Diaz 6, Lamb 7, Lanza 23, Lawrence 31, Martinez 53, Ojeda 34. **OF**—Akins 109, Almonte 47, Bryant 13, Carney 3, Hendricks 2, Kurtz 79, Lawrence 2, LeCronier 105, Martin 61, McKinnis 17, Rivera 15, Walton 5.

PITCHING	W	L	ERA	G	GS	CG	SV	IP	H	R	ER	BB	SO	B	T	HT	WT	DOB	1st Yr	Resides
Dyess, Todd	4	2	3.28	10	10	0	0	47	32	19	17	23	50	R	R	6-3	192	3-20-73	1994	Florence, Miss.
Dykhoff, Radhames	3	3	2.42	31	0	0	5	67	48	19	18	38	98	L	L	6-0	205	9-27-74	1993	Oranjestad, Aruba
Estes, Eric	9	8	3.47	26	25	1	0	148	142	70	57	30	124	R	R	6-4	190	9-4-74	1997	Vancouver, Wash.
Freedberg, Todd	0	0	3.00	1	0	0	0	3	1	1	1	1	3	S	R	5-9	172	1-8-75	1997	North Miami, Fla.
Fussell, Chris	3	3	3.96	9	9	1	0	50	42	23	22	31	54	R	R	6-2	185	5-19-76	1994	Oregon, Ohio
Hernandez, Francisco	4	4	2.31	49	0	0	24	58	51	23	15	21	51	R	R	6-0	160	12-17-76	1994	San Pedro de Macoris, D.R.
Marache, Luis	0	2	10.13	2	2	0	0	8	12	14	9	7	6	L	L	6-4	165	9-4-79	1996	La Romana, D.R.
Markham, Andy	4	0	3.03	20	0	0	1	30	31	13	10	12	22	R	R	6-3	200	11-12-72	1993	Phoenix, Ariz.
McClinton, Pat	0	1	27.00	1	0	0	0	0	1	1	1	2	0	L	L	6-5	210	8-9-71	1993	Louisville, Ky.
Morseman, Bob	0	5	4.81	38	0	0	2	64	61	37	34	46	61	L	L	6-4	190	6-10-74	1995	Westfield, Pa.
Olszewski, Tim	3	1	5.43	34	0	0	1	65	75	48	39	29	41	R	R	6-2	200	2-24-74	1995	Germantown, Wis.
Parrish, John	1	3	6.04	5	5	0	0	22	23	18	15	16	17	L	L	5-11	165	11-26-77	1996	Lancaster, Pa.
Percibal, Billy	1	3	5.74	7	6	0	0	27	28	18	17	18	28	R	R	6-1	170	2-2-74	1992	San Pedro de Macoris, D.R.
Reed, Dan	10	10	4.21	28	27	2	0	173	189	104	81	75	108	R	L	6-4	210	10-20-74	1995	Rochester, Minn.
Rhodes, Joey	7	11	5.45	28	22	0	0	117	130	86	71	61	75	R	R	6-3	205	1-8-75	1994	Hendersonville, N.C.
Rogers, Jason	5	3	5.73	36	5	0	0	71	68	46	45	48	57	L	L	6-6	215	4-5-73	1994	Reno, Nev.
Saneaux, Francisco	2	6	4.50	32	5	0	0	74	56	48	37	84	89	R	R	6-4	180	3-3-74	1991	Santo Domingo, D.R.
Seaver, Mark	3	2	3.05	11	10	0	0	62	57	29	21	17	68	R	R	6-8	240	4-6-75	1996	Hickory, Pa.
Smith, Hut	4	1	3.87	16	11	0	1	79	63	42	34	27	77	S	R	6-3	195	6-8-73	1992	Kannapolis, N.C.
Towers, Josh	6	2	4.86	25	3	0	1	54	74	36	29	18	64	R	R	6-1	150	2-26-77	1996	Port Hueneme, Calif.

DELMARVA — Class A

SOUTH ATLANTIC LEAGUE

BATTING	AVG	G	AB	R	H	2B	3B	HR	RBI	BB	SO	SB	CS	B	T	HT	WT	DOB	1st Yr	Resides
Alley, Chip	.236	82	250	19	59	17	1	3	32	34	45	7	2	S	R	6-3	190	12-20-76	1995	West Palm Beach, Fla.

BATTING	AVG	G	AB	R	H	2B	3B	HR	RBI	BB	SO	SB	CS	B	T	HT	WT	DOB	1st Yr	Resides
Carney, Bartt	.100	14	30	3	3	1	0	0	1	5	10	4	1	S	R	5-11	170	12-16-73	1994	Parnell, Iowa
Casimiro, Carlos	.243	122	457	54	111	21	8	9	51	26	108	20	13	R	R	6-0	155	11-8-76	1994	San Pedro de Macoris, D.R.
Charles, Curtis	.193	95	244	29	47	12	2	3	8	16	104	20	10	R	R	6-1	179	3-15-76	1995	Caracas, Venez.
Chavez, Eric	.224	26	85	10	19	4	0	1	12	10	23	1	0	R	R	5-11	212	9-7-70	1992	Carlsbad, N.M.
Coffie, Evanon	.275	90	305	41	84	14	5	3	48	23	45	19	10	L	R	6-1	170	5-16-77	1995	Curacao, Neth. Antilles
Daedelow, Craig	.267	101	277	37	74	17	1	1	35	24	46	11	5	R	R	5-11	175	4-3-76	1994	Huntington Beach, Calif.
Dent, Darrell	.234	128	441	69	103	17	4	1	37	63	110	60	15	L	L	6-2	172	5-26-77	1995	North Hills, Calif.
DeCinces, Tim	.257	127	416	65	107	20	0	13	70	97	117	3	4	L	R	6-2	195	4-26-74	1996	Newport Beach, Calif.
Figueroa, Frank	.179	7	28	2	5	1	0	0	3	0	8	0	0	R	R	6-6	225	2-9-77	1996	Hialeah, Fla.
Fowler, Maleke	.230	105	339	49	78	9	2	0	18	20	69	36	16	R	R	5-11	180	8-11-75	1996	Baton Rouge, La.
Garavito, Eddy	.000	2	4	0	0	0	0	0	0	0	0	0	0	S	R	5-8	170	12-2-78	1996	Manrreza, D.R.
Hooper, Daren	.000	7	15	1	0	0	0	0	0	1	7	1	0	R	R	6-1	215	5-15-77	1996	Woodside, Calif.
Kurtz, Tony	.244	38	119	13	29	6	4	0	9	11	49	4	0	L	R	5-10	183	11-2-73	1997	Columbia Heights, Minn.
Lasater, Chris	.181	25	72	6	13	5	0	2	11	7	16	0	0	R	R	5-11	200	11-6-72	1997	Morehead City, N.C.
Matos, Luis	.210	36	119	10	25	1	2	0	13	9	21	8	5	R	R	6-1	155	10-30-78	1996	Bayamon, P.R.
Minor, Ryan	.307	134	488	83	150	42	1	24	97	51	102	7	3	R	R	6-7	225	1-5-74	1996	Edmond, Okla.
O'Toole, Bobby	.000	1	0	0	0	0	0	0	0	0	0	0	0	R	R	6-0	195	5-19-74	1995	Newton, Mass.
Paz, Richard	.242	111	389	60	94	14	4	2	48	38	60	15	5	R	R	5-8	130	7-30-77	1994	Los Teques, Venez.
Perez, Richard	.235	27	68	9	16	5	2	0	8	9	21	5	2	R	R	6-0	155	2-18-78	1995	San Pedro de Macoris, D.R.
Pickering, Calvin	.311	122	444	88	138	31	1	25	79	53	139	6	3	L	L	6-3	283	9-29-76	1995	Temple Terrace, Fla.
Rivera, Roberto	.153	17	59	6	9	0	1	2	5	1	20	1	2	R	R	6-2	160	11-25-76	1994	La Romana, D.R.
Stephens, Joel	.224	33	76	14	17	4	0	2	4	12	26	4	1	R	R	6-1	207	3-15-76	1995	Tioga, Pa.

GAMES BY POSITION: C—Alley 72, Chavez 16, DeCinces 53, Lasater 17, O'Toole 1. **1B**—Chavez 5, Daedelow 1, DeCinces 8, Figueroa 7, Lasater 1, Minor 14, Pickering 115. **2B**—Casimiro 115, Daedelow 18, Fowler 2, Paz 20. **3B**—Coffie 7, Daedelow 5, Lasater 1, Minor 113, Paz 24. **SS**—Coffie 79, Daedelow 28, Paz 50. **OF**—Carney 14, Charles 87, Daedelow 18, Dent 127, Fowler 97, Heredia 1, Kurtz 37, Matos 36, Paz 1, Perez 25, Rivera 13, Stephens 29.

PITCHING	W	L	ERA	G	GS	CG	SV	IP	H	R	ER	BB	SO	B	T	HT	WT	DOB	1st Yr	Resides
Achilles, Matt	0	0	9.53	3	0	0	1	6	11	9	6	3	2	R	R	6-3	175	8-18-76	1996	Moline, Ill.
Bauer, Richard	0	0	0.00	1	0	0	1	2	0	0	0	1	2	R	R	6-5	190	1-10-77	1997	Eagle, Idaho
Brown, Derek	0	0	0.00	2	0	0	0	2	2	0	0	1	2	R	R	6-0	170	7-23-76	1994	Hagerstown, Md.
Daedelow, Craig	0	0	0.00	3	0	0	0	2	1	0	0	1	2	R	R	5-11	175	4-3-76	1994	Huntington Beach, Calif.
Dykhoff, Radhames	0	0	0.00	1	0	0	1	3	3	0	0	0	3	L	L	6-0	205	9-27-74	1993	Oranjestad, Aruba
Eibey, Scott	10	4	1.83	47	0	0	7	93	65	25	19	33	82	L	L	6-4	210	1-19-74	1995	Waterloo, Iowa
Falkenborg, Brian	7	9	4.46	25	25	0	0	127	122	73	63	46	107	R	R	6-6	187	1-18-78	1996	Redmond, Wash.
Forbes, Cameron	6	7	3.74	34	17	1	1	130	108	68	54	64	111	R	R	6-2	175	2-28-77	1996	Victoria, Australia
Freedberg, Todd	0	1	3.26	9	0	0	0	19	19	9	7	15	12	S	R	5-9	172	1-8-75	1997	North Miami, Fla.
Hacen, Abraham	7	5	4.25	23	23	0	0	112	95	59	53	58	103	R	R	6-2	175	1-22-76	1993	La Romana, D.R.
Heredia, Maximo	10	5	2.13	37	6	0	1	114	97	29	27	20	73	R	R	6-1	145	9-27-76	1994	San Pedro de Macoris, D.R.
Kohlmeier, Ryan	2	2	2.65	50	0	0	24	75	48	22	22	17	99	R	R	6-2	195	6-25-77	1996	Cottonwood Falls, Kan.
McNatt, Josh	6	2	3.63	28	11	0	1	97	97	48	39	45	73	L	L	6-4	200	7-23-77	1996	Jackson, Tenn.
Molina, Gabe	8	6	2.18	46	0	0	7	91	59	24	22	32	119	R	R	5-11	190	5-3-75	1996	Denver, Colo.
Morseman, Bob	0	1	4.73	7	0	0	0	13	13	11	7	11	18	L	L	6-4	190	6-10-74	1995	Westfield, Pa.
Olszewski, Tim	0	0	3.18	3	0	0	0	6	4	3	2	0	7	R	R	6-2	200	2-24-74	1995	Germantown, Wis.
Paronto, Chad	6	9	4.74	28	23	0	0	127	133	95	67	56	93	R	R	6-5	255	7-28-75	1996	North Haverhill, N.H.
Parrish, John	3	3	3.84	23	10	0	1	73	69	39	31	32	76	L	L	5-11	165	11-26-77	1996	Lancaster, Pa.
Peguero, Americo	11	10	4.87	27	26	1	0	142	152	97	77	53	133	R	R	6-0	140	5-20-77	1995	La Romana, D.R.
Ramagli, Matt	1	1	5.63	4	0	0	0	8	13	6	5	5	6	R	R	6-3	188	4-14-75	1997	Emerson, N.J.
Towers, Josh	0	0	3.44	9	1	0	1	18	18	8	7	2	16	R	R	6-1	150	2-26-77	1996	Port Hueneme, Calif.

BLUEFIELD — Rookie

APPALACHIAN LEAGUE

BATTING	AVG	G	AB	R	H	2B	3B	HR	RBI	BB	SO	SB	CS	B	T	HT	WT	DOB	1st Yr	Resides
Davison, Ashanti	.247	49	162	31	40	10	4	2	25	17	29	8	2	R	R	5-10	170	10-31-78	1996	Stockton, Calif.
Figueroa, Frank	.267	63	243	32	65	14	1	8	41	14	70	4	2	R	R	6-6	225	2-9-77	1996	Hialeah, Fla.
Garavito, Eddy	.303	61	231	47	70	12	3	5	44	21	30	26	9	S	R	5-8	170	12-2-78	1996	Manrreza, D.R.
Hairston, Jerry	.330	59	221	44	73	13	4	2	36	21	29	13	9	R	R	5-10	172	5-29-76	1997	Naperville, Ill.
Haman, Mack	.226	47	133	28	30	6	0	5	17	24	51	6	5	R	R	6-4	205	12-11-75	1997	Newark, Del.
Hooper, Daren	.125	10	32	4	4	1	0	1	4	6	11	0	1	R	R	6-1	215	5-15-77	1996	Woodside, Calif.
Lasater, Chris	.257	11	35	8	9	4	0	2	9	3	6	0	1	R	R	5-11	200	11-6-72	1997	Morehead City, N.C.
Martin, Tommy	.289	40	90	17	26	3	1	1	9	8	31	9	3	R	R	5-10	175	9-12-75	1997	Ypsilanti, Mich.
Matos, Luis	.275	61	240	37	66	7	3	2	35	20	36	26	4	R	R	6-1	155	10-30-78	1996	Bayamon, P.R.
McGee, Thomas	.244	27	86	14	21	5	0	1	8	11	22	2	1	R	R	5-11	190	1-29-75	1997	Rialto, Calif.
Morales, Domingo	.000	4	6	2	0	0	0	0	0	0	0	0	0	R	R	6-0	160	8-15-76	1994	Hato Mayor, D.R.
Pacheco, Juan	.197	47	132	21	26	3	1	1	12	11	32	2	4	R	R	6-0	175	11-4-76	1997	Newark, N.J.
Paxton, Chris	.303	38	109	19	33	8	0	3	22	19	26	0	0	L	R	6-2	195	12-11-76	1995	Palmdale, Calif.
Perez, Richard	.173	20	52	11	9	3	0	0	5	6	17	6	0	R	R	6-0	155	2-18-78	1995	San Pedro de Macoris, D.R.
Rivera, Roberto	.318	50	192	28	61	20	2	3	27	13	43	6	6	R	R	6-2	160	11-25-76	1994	La Romana, D.R.
Stephens, Joel	.167	6	18	3	3	0	0	0	1	2	2	2	1	R	R	6-1	207	3-15-76	1995	Tioga, Pa.
Utting, Andy	.230	51	152	22	35	7	1	4	18	30	41	2	4	S	R	6-1	175	9-9-77	1995	Melbourne, Australia
Van Asselberg, Ricky	.210	27	62	5	13	2	0	1	7	6	9	1	0	L	R	5-11	225	5-24-74	1997	Boyce, La.
Wilson, Cliff	.240	46	129	16	31	2	2	1	14	15	35	3	1	L	R	6-2	198	4-10-77	1997	Lyman, S.C.

GAMES BY POSITION: C—Lasater 5, McGee 16, Paxton 11, Utting 44, Van Asselberg 3. **1B**—Figueroa 63, Lasater 1, McGee 3, Paxton 3, Van Asselberg 3, Wilson 1. **2B**—Garavito 60, Martin 5, Pacheco 9. **3B**—Lasater 1, Martin 20, Pacheco 22, Stephens 1, Wilson 38. **SS**—Hairston 58, Martin 3, Pacheco 16, Wilson 1. **OF**—Davison 44, Haman 38, Hooper 8, Matos 61, McGee 1, Morales 3, Perez 13, Rivera 44, Stephens 5.

PITCHING	W	L	ERA	G	GS	CG	SV	IP	H	R	ER	BB	SO	B	T	HT	WT	DOB	1st Yr	Resides
Achilles, Matt	7	2	3.95	14	13	0	0	73	60	37	32	33	68	R	R	6-3	175	8-18-76	1996	Moline, Ill.
Andrade, Jancy	0	0	2.51	4	4	0	0	14	9	5	4	11	13	R	R	6-2	165	6-29-78	1995	Cumana, Venez.
Bauer, Richard	8	3	2.86	13	13	0	0	72	58	31	23	20	67	R	R	6-5	190	1-10-77	1997	Eagle, Idaho
Bray, Chris	0	0	15.75	3	0	0	0	4	1	7	7	4	5	R	R	6-4	200	10-28-74	1995	Currituck, N.C.
Brown, Derek	2	5	5.01	17	5	1	1	41	44	26	23	13	48	R	R	6-0	170	7-23-76	1994	Hagerstown, Md.

PITCHING	W	L	ERA	G	GS	CG	SV	IP	H	R	ER	BB	SO	B	T	HT	WT	DOB	1st Yr	Resides
Fontaine, Tom	5	1	6.02	21	2	0	0	40	44	31	27	28	50	R	R	5-11	180	3-17-75	1997	Greenville, Pa.
Freedberg, Todd	2	1	1.98	11	1	0	0	27	29	14	6	12	29	S	R	5-9	172	1-8-75	1997	North Miami, Fla.
Halpin, Jeremy	1	0	3.24	15	0	0	0	25	30	14	9	4	22	R	R	6-3	190	11-20-74	1997	Rome, N.Y.
Lee, Chris	2	0	4.06	23	0	0	2	31	24	17	14	14	32	R	R	6-1	235	9-8-75	1997	La Grange, Ga.
Mastrolonardo, David	4	0	1.08	26	0	0	12	33	15	5	4	12	45	R	R	6-4	220	8-23-74	1997	Satellite Beach, Fla.
Murphy, Darren	1	3	5.82	23	1	0	0	39	48	28	25	18	42	L	L	6-3	175	9-13-76	1997	Santee, Calif.
Perez, Norberto	3	5	3.46	10	10	0	0	55	52	29	21	16	58	R	R	6-4	175	10-10-77	1995	El Seibo, D.R.
Phipps, Jeff	0	2	10.80	4	2	0	0	10	12	13	12	8	6	R	R	6-8	225	2-5-75	1996	Blythe, Calif.
Romero, Jordan	1	3	6.51	12	5	0	0	28	31	20	20	17	38	R	R	6-1	170	10-8-76	1997	San Jose, Calif.
Sims, Kenny	1	2	3.06	18	2	0	1	35	30	18	12	22	33	R	R	6-4	187	7-24-75	1996	Hobbs, N.M.
Spurgeon, Jay	1	1	3.34	9	7	0	0	35	35	13	13	14	32	R	R	6-6	225	7-5-76	1997	Madera, Calif.
Stephens, John	2	0	2.25	4	4	0	0	24	17	6	6	5	34	R	R	6-1	175	11-15-79	1996	Berala, Australia
Theodile, Simeon	0	0	21.86	4	0	0	0	7	21	20	17	4	6	R	R	6-2	190	4-15-77	1997	Jeanerette, La.

SARASOTA — Rookie

GULF COAST LEAGUE

BATTING	AVG	G	AB	R	H	2B	3B	HR	RBI	BB	SO	SB	CS	B	T	Ht.	Wt.	DOB	1st Yr.	Resides
Bautista, Juan	.111	3	9	3	1	0	0	0	0	1	2	1	1	R	R	6-1	185	6-24-75	1992	San Pedro de Macoris, D.R.
Bello, Jilberto	.245	33	102	8	25	5	1	0	14	8	29	2	2	R	R	6-3	150	2-26-77	1994	San Pedro de Macoris, D.R.
Bethea, Larry	.164	36	116	6	19	3	2	0	15	11	32	2	1	R	R	6-4	230	10-9-76	1995	Red Springs, N.C.
Carter, Shannon	.195	50	159	22	31	3	2	0	11	12	45	13	5	L	L	6-0	170	3-23-79	1997	El Reno, Okla.
Charles, Curtis	.250	6	20	4	5	1	0	1	3	2	5	0	0	R	R	6-1	179	3-15-76	1995	Caracas, Venez.
Collier, Marc	.183	24	71	10	13	2	0	0	6	10	16	2	0	R	R	5-10	170	3-25-78	1996	Hummelstown, Pa.
Diaz, Maikell	.255	46	137	19	35	5	2	1	15	20	30	18	2	R	R	5-10	158	9-29-78	1996	Miranda, Venez.
Escalante, Jaime	.273	50	143	12	39	9	1	0	17	18	34	0	1	S	R	6-2	210	4-5-77	1997	Federalsburg, Md.
Guzman, Juan	.149	15	47	1	7	1	0	0	4	1	18	0	0	R	R	6-2	160	3-4-78	1995	Los Llanos, D.R.
Hooper, Daren	.323	19	62	7	20	5	1	1	5	9	20	1	1	R	R	6-1	215	5-15-77	1996	Woodside, Calif.
Ide, Antoine	.207	33	92	13	19	0	0	0	6	8	21	12	4	R	R	6-0	170	3-2-79	1997	Portland, Ore.
Kingsale, Eugene	.294	6	17	2	5	0	0	0	0	2	2	1	0	S	R	6-3	170	8-20-76	1994	Oranjestad, Aruba
Kirkpatrick, Michael	.252	38	115	18	29	6	3	1	12	9	22	7	0	L	L	6-0	180	11-12-77	1996	New Castle, Del.
Morales, Domingo	.255	33	98	8	25	4	0	0	6	9	11	5	2	R	R	6-0	160	8-15-76	1994	Hato Mayor, D.R.
Morgan, Todd	.000	9	16	1	0	0	0	0	0	1	11	0	0	R	R	6-1	185	10-8-77	1996	Pompano Beach, Fla.
Ndungidi, Ntema	.185	18	54	10	10	2	1	2	7	12	15	4	0	S	R	6-3	175	3-15-79	1997	Montreal, Quebec
Nolasco, Regino	.224	58	165	17	37	10	0	1	18	21	33	3	7	R	R	6-0	145	7-28-79	1996	San Pedro de Macoris, D.R.
O'Toole, Bobby	.286	6	21	1	6	0	0	1	3	1	5	0	0	R	R	6-0	195	5-19-74	1995	Newton, Mass.
Otanez, Willis	.320	8	25	5	8	2	0	2	3	2	4	0	0	R	R	5-11	150	4-19-73	1990	Las Matas de Cotui, D.R.
Perez, Jesse	.227	35	110	12	25	1	1	0	7	7	39	1	4	S	R	6-4	175	7-19-78	1996	Mayaguez, P.R.
Ramirez, Luis	.237	45	156	24	37	5	5	1	24	12	49	5	2	R	R	6-3	180	9-26-78	1996	Arroyo, P.R.
Werth, Jayson	.295	32	88	16	26	6	0	1	8	22	22	7	1	R	R	6-5	191	5-20-79	1997	Chatham, Ill.
Ziths, DeShawn	.152	17	33	7	5	0	0	0	3	3	16	1	0	R	R	6-2	195	7-29-75	1997	Brooklyn, N.Y.

GAMES BY POSITION: C—Bello 13, Escalante 15, Guzman 15, O'Toole 4, Werth 21. **1B**—Bethea 29, Escalante 27, Ramirez 9, Werth 8. **2B**—Bello 1, Collier 7, Diaz 3, Nolasco 55, Perez 4. **3B**—Collier 6, Escalante 3, Perez 34, Ramirez 26. **SS**—Bautista 3, Collier 13, Diaz 42, Nolasco 3. **OF**—Carter 48, Charles 6, Hooper 19, Ide 29, Kingsale 6, Kirkpatrick 26, Morales 20, Morgan 7, Ndungidi 18, Ramirez 18, Werth 2, Ziths 12.

PITCHING	W	L	ERA	G	GS	CG	SV	IP	H	R	ER	BB	SO	B	T	HT	WT	DOB	1st Yr	Resides
Casteel, Ricky	2	3	2.77	15	9	0	1	65	63	31	20	30	37	R	R	6-2	195	10-29-77	1997	Texarkana, Texas
Coppinger, Rocky	0	0	1.80	3	3	0	0	10	7	3	2	0	13	R	R	6-5	245	3-19-74	1994	El Paso, Texas
Cruz, Charlie	2	2	9.41	15	0	0	1	22	36	23	23	14	7	R	R	6-4	225	2-12-77	1995	Santiago, D.R.
Curtis, Shawn	1	2	4.57	15	4	0	1	41	54	29	21	23	28	R	R	6-2	190	5-26-78	1997	Lexington, Ky.
Douglass, Sean	1	3	6.11	9	1	0	0	18	20	14	12	9	10	R	R	6-6	210	4-28-79	1997	Lancaster, Calif.
Huntsman, Brandon	0	0	0.00	2	0	0	0	5	3	0	0	1	6	R	R	6-4	205	11-19-75	1994	Pleasant Grove, Utah
Jimenez, Ricardo	3	1	3.46	8	6	0	1	39	30	22	15	21	27	R	R	6-0	160	5-23-78	1995	La Higuera, D.R.
Johnson, Jeremiah	2	1	2.84	6	0	0	1	6	4	2	2	4	4	R	R	6-6	210	7-19-77	1996	Litchfield, Mich.
Jones, Sean	0	0	3.00	9	0	0	0	15	18	7	5	7	7	R	R	6-7	180	4-12-78	1997	Hamilton, Ontario
Maine, Dalton	0	0	0.00	2	0	0	1	3	1	0	0	0	4	R	R	6-3	185	3-22-72	1995	Framingham, Mass.
Marache, Luis	4	6	3.14	11	10	1	0	57	48	26	20	17	45	L	L	6-4	165	9-4-79	1996	La Romana, D.R.
Morales, Johnny	3	4	4.23	18	1	0	1	38	40	21	18	12	47	L	L	6-4	205	6-24-77	1997	Glendale, Ariz.
Percibal, Billy	0	0	0.90	4	3	0	0	10	11	1	1	2	12	R	R	6-1	170	2-2-74	1992	San Pedro de Macoris, D.R.
Ponson, Sidney	1	0	0.00	1	0	0	0	2	0	0	0	0	1	R	R	6-1	200	11-2-76	1994	Oranjestad, Aruba
Ratliff, Craig	2	5	2.75	12	12	0	0	59	60	26	18	32	50	R	R	6-7	215	1-19-78	1996	West Van Lear, Ky.
Ryba, Jason	3	4	4.60	14	8	1	1	43	51	33	22	19	30	R	R	6-4	205	10-5-78	1997	Brooklyn Heights, Ohio
Santos, Juan	0	1	1.50	3	0	0	0	6	6	4	1	2	5	R	R	6-2	160	2-23-76	1993	Ramon Santana, D.R.
Stephens, John	3	0	0.82	9	3	0	1	33	15	3	3	9	43	R	R	6-1	175	11-15-79	1996	Berala, Australia
Theodile, Simeon	0	1	1.99	15	0	0	6	23	22	6	5	7	17	R	R	6-2	190	4-15-77	1997	Jeanerette, La.

Boston RED SOX

Manager: Jimy Williams. **1998 Record:** 78-84, .481 (4th, AL East)

BATTING	AVG	G	AB	R	H	2B	3B	HR	RBI	BB	SO	SB	CS	B	T	HT	WT	DOB	1st Yr	Resides
Benjamin, Mike	.233	49	116	12	27	9	1	0	7	4	27	2	3	R	R	6-0	169	11-22-65	1987	Chandler, Ariz.
Bragg, Darren	.257	153	513	65	132	35	2	9	57	61	102	10	6	L	R	5-9	180	9-7-69	1991	Wolcott, Conn.
Coleman, Michael	.167	8	24	2	4	1	0	0	2	0	11	1	0	R	R	5-11	180	8-16-75	1994	Nashville, Tenn.
Cordero, Wil	.281	140	570	82	160	26	3	18	72	31	122	1	3	R	R	6-2	185	10-3-71	1988	Mayaguez, P.R.
Frye, Jeff	.312	127	404	56	126	36	2	3	51	27	44	19	8	R	R	5-9	180	8-31-66	1988	Las Vegas, Nev.
Garciaparra, Nomar	.306	153	684	122	209	44	11	30	98	35	92	22	9	R	R	6-0	165	7-23-73	1994	Whittier, Calif.
Haselman, Bill	.236	67	212	22	50	15	0	6	26	15	44	0	2	R	R	6-3	215	5-25-66	1987	Saratoga, Calif.
Hatteberg, Scott	.277	114	350	46	97	23	1	10	44	40	70	0	1	L	R	6-1	185	12-14-69	1991	Yakima, Wash.
Jefferson, Reggie	.319	136	489	74	156	33	1	13	67	24	93	1	2	L	L	6-4	215	9-25-68	1986	Tallahassee, Fla.
Mack, Shane	.315	60	130	13	41	7	0	3	17	9	24	2	1	R	R	6-0	190	12-7-63	1985	Chanhassen, Minn.
Malave, Jose	.000	4	4	0	0	0	0	0	0	0	2	0	0	R	R	6-2	195	5-31-71	1990	Cumana, Venez.
McKeel, Walt	.000	5	3	0	0	0	0	0	0	0	1	0	0	R	R	6-2	200	1-17-72	1990	Stantonsburg, N.C.
Naehring, Tim	.286	70	259	38	74	18	1	9	40	38	40	1	1	R	R	6-2	200	2-1-67	1988	Cincinnati, Ohio
O'Leary, Troy	.309	146	499	65	154	32	4	15	80	39	70	0	5	L	L	6-0	190	8-4-69	1987	Rialto, Calif.
Pemberton, Rudy	.238	27	63	8	15	2	0	2	10	4	13	0	0	R	R	6-1	185	12-17-69	1987	San Pedro de Macoris, D.R.
Pozo, Arquimedez	.267	4	15	0	4	1	0	0	3	0	5	0	0	R	R	5-10	160	8-24-73	1991	Santo Domingo, D.R.
Pride, Curtis	.500	2	2	1	1	0	0	1	1	0	1	0	0	L	R	5-11	195	12-17-68	1986	Wellington, Fla.
2-team (79 Detroit)	.213	81	164	22	35	4	4	3	20	24	46	6	4							
Stanley, Mike	.300	97	260	45	78	17	0	13	53	39	50	0	1	R	R	6-0	190	6-25-63	1985	Oviedo, Fla.
Tavarez, Jesus	.174	42	69	12	12	3	1	0	9	4	9	0	0	S	R	6-0	170	3-26-71	1990	Santo Domingo, D.R.
Valentin, John	.306	143	575	95	176	47	5	18	77	58	66	7	4	R	R	6-0	185	2-18-67	1988	Braintree, Mass.
Varitek, Jason	1.000	1	1	0	1	0	0	0	0	0	0	0	0	S	R	6-2	210	4-11-72	1995	Longwood, Fla.
Vaughn, Mo	.315	141	527	91	166	24	0	35	96	86	154	2	2	L	R	6-1	230	12-15-67	1989	Braintree, Mass.

PITCHING	W	L	ERA	G	GS	CG	SV	IP	H	R	ER	BB	SO	B	T	HT	WT	DOB	1st Yr	Resides
Avery, Steve	6	7	6.42	22	18	0	0	97	127	76	69	49	51	L	L	6-4	205	4-14-70	1988	Taylor, Mich.
Borland, Toby	0	0	13.50	3	0	0	0	3	6	5	5	7	1	R	R	6-7	175	5-29-69	1989	Quitman, La.
Brandenburg, Mark	0	2	5.49	31	0	0	0	41	49	25	25	16	34	R	R	6-0	170	7-14-70	1992	Humble, Texas
Checo, Robinson	1	1	3.38	5	2	0	0	13	12	5	5	3	14	R	R	6-1	165	9-9-71	1989	Santiago, D.R.
Corsi, Jim	5	3	3.43	52	0	0	2	58	56	26	22	21	40	R	R	6-1	220	9-9-61	1982	Natick, Mass.
Eshelman, Vaughn	3	3	6.33	21	6	0	0	43	58	32	30	17	18	L	L	6-3	205	5-22-69	1991	Houston, Texas
Garces, Rich	0	1	4.61	12	0	0	0	14	14	9	7	9	12	R	R	6-0	230	5-18-71	1988	Maracay, Venez.
Gordon, Tom	6	10	3.74	42	25	2	11	183	155	85	76	78	159	R	R	5-9	180	11-18-67	1986	Avon Park, Fla.
Grundt, Ken	0	0	9.00	2	0	0	0	3	5	3	3	0	0	L	L	6-4	195	8-26-69	1991	Chicago, Ill.
Hammond, Chris	3	4	5.92	29	8	0	1	65	81	45	43	27	48	L	L	6-1	195	1-21-66	1986	Birmingham, Ala.
Henry, Butch	7	3	3.52	36	5	0	6	84	89	36	33	19	51	L	L	6-1	195	10-7-68	1987	El Paso, Texas
Hudson, Joe	3	1	3.53	26	0	0	0	36	39	16	14	14	14	R	R	6-1	180	9-29-70	1992	Medford, N.J.
Lacy, Kerry	1	1	6.11	33	0	0	3	46	60	34	31	22	18	R	R	6-2	195	8-7-72	1991	Higdon, Ala.
Lowe, Derek	0	2	3.38	8	0	0	0	16	15	6	6	3	13	R	R	6-6	170	6-1-73	1991	Dearborn, Mich.
2-team (12 Seattle)	2	6	6.13	20	9	0	0	69	74	49	47	23	52							
Mahay, Ron	3	0	2.52	28	0	0	0	25	19	7	7	11	22	L	L	6-2	185	6-28-71	1991	Crestwood, Ill.
Mahomes, Pat	1	0	8.10	10	0	0	0	10	15	10	9	10	5	R	R	6-4	210	8-9-70	1988	Lindale, Texas
Rose, Brian L.	0	0	12.00	1	1	0	0	3	5	4	4	2	3	R	R	6-3	215	2-13-76	1995	Dartmouth, Mass.
Saberhagen, Bret	0	1	6.58	6	6	0	0	26	30	20	19	10	14	R	R	6-1	200	4-11-64	1983	Babylon, N.Y.
Sele, Aaron	13	12	5.38	33	33	1	0	177	196	115	106	80	122	R	R	6-5	218	6-25-70	1991	Poulsbo, Wash.
Slocumb, Heathcliff	0	5	5.79	49	0	0	17	47	58	32	30	34	36	R	R	6-3	180	6-7-66	1984	Richmond Hill, N.Y.
Suppan, Jeff	7	3	5.69	23	22	0	0	112	140	75	71	36	67	R	R	6-2	210	1-2-75	1993	West Hills, Calif.
Trlicek, Ricky	3	4	4.63	18	0	0	0	23	26	14	12	18	10	R	R	6-3	200	4-26-69	1987	Houston, Texas
Wakefield, Tim	12	15	4.25	35	29	4	0	201	193	109	95	87	151	R	R	6-2	204	8-2-66	1988	Melbourne, Fla.
Wasdin, John	4	6	4.40	53	7	0	0	125	121	68	61	38	84	R	R	6-2	195	8-5-72	1993	Tallahassee, Fla.

FIELDING

Catcher	PCT	G	PO	A	E	DP	PB
Haselman	.983	66	373	40	7	4	17
Hatteberg	.983	106	574	46	11	13	17
McKeel	1.000	4	4	0	0	0	0
Varitek	1.000	1	1	0	0	0	0

First Base	PCT	G	PO	A	E	DP
Benjamin	1.000	4	6	2	0	1
Frye	1.000	1	2	0	0	1
Jefferson	.975	12	74	5	2	9
McKeel	1.000	1	2	0	0	0
Stanley	.996	31	231	18	1	26
Vaughn	.988	131	1088	75	14	117

Second Base	PCT	G	PO	A	E	DP
Benjamin	1.000	5	14	11	0	6
Cordero	1.000	1	0	3	0	0
Frye	.991	80	196	228	4	63
Valentin	.976	79	180	259	11	67

Third Base	PCT	G	PO	A	E	DP
Benjamin	.929	19	13	39	4	4
Bragg	.000	1	0	0	0	0
Frye	.878	18	11	32	6	2
Naehring	.981	68	40	111	3	11
Pozo	.947	4	4	14	1	1
Valentin	.942	64	59	121	11	15

Shortstop	PCT	G	PO	A	E	DP
Benjamin	.958	16	17	29	2	4
Frye	1.000	3	2	2	0	0
Garciaparra	.971	153	249	450	21	113

Outfield	PCT	G	PO	A	E	DP
Bragg	.987	150	364	11	5	3
Coleman	.941	7	16	0	1	0
Cordero	.992	137	248	8	2	4
Frye	.900	13	16	2	2	0
Mack	1.000	45	75	0	0	0
Malave	1.000	4	3	0	0	0
O'Leary	.979	142	267	8	6	0
Pemberton	.949	23	35	2	2	1
Pride	.980	35	49	0	1	0
Tavarez	.980	35	49	1	1	1

LARRY GOREN

Mo Vaughn

FARM SYSTEM

Director of Player Development: Bob Schaefer

Class	Farm Team	League	W	L	Pct.	Finish*	Manager	First Yr
AAA	Pawtucket (R.I.) Red Sox	International	81	60	.574	2nd (10)	Ken Macha	1973
AA	Trenton (N.J.) Thunder	Eastern	71	70	.504	6th (10)	DeMarlo Hale	1995
#A	Sarasota (Fla.) Red Sox	Florida State	63	75	.457	11th (14)	Rob Derksen	1994
A	Michigan Battle Cats	Midwest	70	67	.511	4th (14)	Bill Gardner	1995
A	Lowell (Mass.) Spinners	New York-Penn	38	38	.500	6th (14)	Dick Berardino	1996
R	Fort Myers (Fla.) Red Sox	Gulf Coast	31	28	.525	5th (15)	Luis Aguayo	1993

*Finish in overall standings (No. of teams in league) #Advanced level

ORGANIZATION LEADERS

MAJOR LEAGUERS

BATTING

*AVG	Reggie Jefferson	.319
R	Nomar Garciaparra	122
H	Nomar Garciaparra	209
TB	Nomar Garciaparra	365
2B	John Valentin	47
3B	Nomar Garciaparra	11
HR	Mo Vaughn	35
RBI	Nomar Garciaparra	98
BB	Mo Vaughn	86
SO	Mo Vaughn	154
SB	Nomar Garciaparra	22

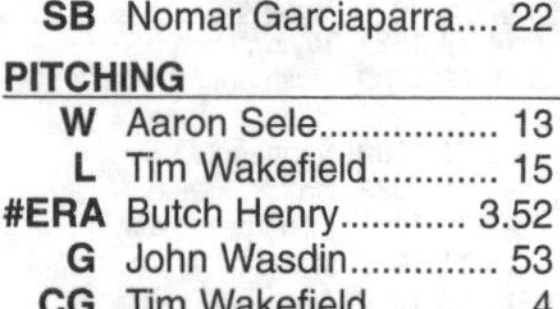

PITCHING

W	Aaron Sele	13
L	Tim Wakefield	15
#ERA	Butch Henry	3.52
G	John Wasdin	53
CG	Tim Wakefield	4
SV	Heathcliff Slocumb	17
IP	Tim Wakefield	201
BB	Tim Wakefield	87
SO	Tom Gordon	159

John Valentin

KEN BABBITT/FUJI FILM

Michael Coleman

MINOR LEAGUERS

BATTING

*AVG	Cole Liniak, Trenton/Sarasota	.309
R	Jim Chamblee, Michigan	112
H	Michael Coleman, Pawtucket/Trenton	152
TB	Michael Coleman, Pawtucket/Trenton	261
2B	Dernell Stenson, Michigan	35
3B	Michael Coleman, Pawtucket/Trenton	10
HR	Adam Hyzdu, Pawtucket	23
RBI	David Gibralter, Trenton	86
BB	Aaron Fuller, Trenton	95
SO	Corey Jenkins, Michigan	129
SB	Aaron Fuller, Trenton	40

PITCHING

W	Brian Rose, Pawtucket	17
L	Two tied at	12
#ERA	Brian Rose, Pawtucket	3.02
G	Germaine Hunter, Michigan	52
CG	Brian Barkley, Trenton	4
SV	Chuck Beale, Michigan	12
IP	Brian Rose, Pawtucket	191
BB	Jared Fernandez, Pawtucket/Trenton	94
SO	Juan Pena, Trenton/Sarasota	167

*Minimum 250 At-Bats #Minimum 75 Innings

TOP 10 PROSPECTS

LARRY GOREN

Nomar Garciaparra

How the Red Sox Top 10 prospects, as judged by Baseball America prior to the 1997 season, fared in 1997:

Player, Pos.	Club (Class)	AVG	AB	R	H	2B	3B	HR	RBI	SB
1. Nomar Garciapara, ss	Boston	.306	684	122	209	44	11	30	98	22
5. Donnie Sadler, 2b	Pawtucket (AAA)	.212	481	74	102	18	2	11	36	20
8. Damian Sapp, c	Injured—Did not play									
10. Cole Laniak, 3b	Trenton (AA)	.280	200	20	56	11	0	2	18	0
	Sarasota (A)	.336	217	32	73	16	0	6	42	1

Player, Pos.	Club (Class)	W	L	ERA	G	SV	IP	H	BB	SO
2. Carl Pavano, rhp	Pawtucket (AAA)	11	6	3.12	23	0	162	148	34	147
3. Brian Rose, rhp	Boston	0	0	12.00	1	0	3	5	0	0
	Pawtucket (AAA)	17	5	3.02	27	0	191	188	46	116
4. Chris Reitsma, rhp	Michigan (A)	4	1	2.90	9	0	50	57	13	41
6. Jeff Suppan, rhp	Boston	7	3	5.69	23	0	112	140	36	67
	Pawtucket (AAA)	5	1	3.71	9	0	61	51	15	40
7. Robinson Checo, rhp	Boston	1	1	3.38	5	0	13	12	3	14
	Pawtucket (AAA)	4	2	3.42	9	0	55	41	16	56
	Trenton (AA)	1	0	2.35	1	0	8	6	1	9
	Sarasota (A)	1	4	5.30	11	0	56	54	27	63
9. Peter Munro, rhp	Trenton (AA)	7	10	4.95	22	0	116	113	47	109

PAWTUCKET — Class AAA

INTERNATIONAL LEAGUE

BATTING	AVG	G	AB	R	H	2B	3B	HR	RBI	BB	SO	SB	CS	B	T	HT	WT	DOB	1st Yr	Resides
Abad, Andy	.273	68	227	28	62	7	0	9	32	36	47	3	2	L	L	6-1	185	8-25-72	1993	Jupiter, Fla.
Allison, Chris	.280	8	25	2	7	2	0	0	1	1	0	0	1	R	R	5-10	165	10-22-71	1994	Rock Island, Ill.
Benjamin, Mike	.248	33	105	12	26	4	1	4	12	8	20	4	1	R	R	6-0	169	11-22-65	1987	Chandler, Ariz.
Bennett, Gary	.214	71	224	16	48	7	1	4	22	18	39	1	1	R	R	6-0	190	4-17-72	1990	Waukegan, Ill.
Borrero, Richie	.255	15	51	4	13	1	0	2	6	1	17	0	1	R	R	6-1	195	1-5-73	1990	Hormigueros, P.R.
Bryant, Pat	.294	9	34	3	10	2	1	0	4	1	11	2	0	R	R	5-11	182	10-27-72	1990	Sherman Oaks, Calif.
Carey, Todd	.216	113	380	35	82	16	0	12	58	34	114	1	2	L	R	6-1	180	8-14-71	1992	Cumberland, R.I.
Coleman, Michael	.319	28	113	27	36	9	2	7	19	12	27	4	2	R	R	5-11	180	8-16-75	1994	Nashville, Tenn.
Correia, Rod	.195	35	128	17	25	4	1	1	15	5	14	3	0	R	R	5-11	185	9-13-67	1988	Rehoboth, Mass.
Dodson, Bo	.295	17	61	8	18	6	0	0	6	5	11	0	0	L	L	6-2	195	12-7-70	1989	West Sacramento, Calif.
Hyzdu, Adam	.276	119	413	77	114	21	1	23	84	72	113	10	6	R	R	6-2	210	12-6-71	1990	Mesa, Ariz.
Malave, Jose	.297	115	427	87	127	24	2	17	70	55	78	12	4	R	R	6-2	195	5-31-71	1990	Cumana, Venez.
McKeel, Walt	.253	66	237	34	60	15	0	6	30	34	39	0	1	R	R	6-2	200	1-17-72	1990	Stantonsburg, N.C.
Merloni, Lou	.297	49	165	24	49	10	0	5	24	15	20	0	2	R	R	5-10	188	4-6-71	1993	Framingham, Mass.
Nixon, Trot	.244	130	475	80	116	18	3	20	61	63	86	11	4	L	L	6-1	195	4-11-74	1993	Wilmington, N.C.
Pozo, Arquimedez	.284	101	377	61	107	18	1	22	70	37	55	4	4	R	R	5-10	160	8-24-73	1991	Santo Domingo, D.R.
Pride, Curtis	.000	1	3	0	0	0	0	0	0	0	2	0	0	L	R	5-11	195	12-17-68	1986	Wellington, Fla.
Rodriguez, Tony	.249	82	285	27	71	12	0	2	19	9	47	5	2	R	R	5-11	165	8-15-70	1991	Cidra, P.R.
Sadler, Donnie	.212	125	481	74	102	18	2	11	36	57	121	20	14	R	R	5-6	165	6-17-75	1994	Valley Mills, Texas
Tavarez, Jesus	.266	59	229	43	61	6	3	3	20	27	31	22	9	S	R	6-0	170	3-26-71	1990	Santo Domingo, D.R.
Varitek, Jason	.197	20	66	6	13	5	0	1	5	8	12	0	0	S	R	6-2	210	4-11-72	1995	Longwood, Fla.
Williams, Juan	.198	27	81	11	16	4	0	3	10	20	35	2	3	L	R	6-0	180	10-9-72	1990	Riverside, Calif.
Woods, Tyrone	.352	29	105	16	37	3	1	9	28	11	35	1	1	R	R	6-1	190	8-19-69	1988	Brooksville, Fla.

PITCHING	W	L	ERA	G	GS	CG	SV	IP	H	R	ER	BB	SO	B	T	HT	WT	DOB	1st Yr	Resides
Avery, Steve	1	0	0.00	1	1	0	0	5	1	0	0	3	1	L	L	6-4	205	4-14-70	1988	Taylor, Mich.
Blais, Mike	1	4	8.31	10	0	0	0	13	10	15	12	10	10	R	R	6-5	226	10-2-71	1993	East Lyme, Conn.
Borland, Toby	2	0	3.99	28	2	0	2	47	50	22	21	25	46	R	R	6-7	175	5-29-69	1989	Quitman, La.
Brandenburg, Mark	2	1	2.41	9	0	0	0	19	13	6	5	3	23	R	R	6-0	170	7-14-70	1992	Humble, Texas
Cain, Tim	3	3	5.93	17	0	0	2	30	34	22	20	12	13	S	R	6-1	180	10-9-69	1990	Piscataway, N.J.
Checo, Robinson	4	2	3.42	9	9	2	0	55	41	22	21	16	56	R	R	6-1	165	9-9-71	1989	Santiago, D.R.
Corsi, Jim	0	0	0.00	2	0	0	1	2	2	0	0	1	3	R	R	6-1	220	9-9-61	1982	Natick, Mass.
Eshelman, Vaughn	3	4	4.86	14	13	0	1	67	63	38	36	22	57	L	L	6-3	205	5-22-69	1991	Houston, Texas
Farrell, Jim	0	0	0.00	1	1	0	0	5	4	0	0	2	6	R	R	6-1	180	11-1-73	1995	Hartville, Ohio
Fernandez, Jared	0	3	5.79	11	11	0	0	61	76	45	39	28	33	R	R	6-2	225	2-2-72	1994	West Valley, Utah
Garces, Rich	2	1	1.45	26	0	0	5	31	24	5	5	13	42	R	R	6-0	230	5-18-71	1988	Maracay, Venez.
Grundt, Ken	4	2	5.32	49	1	0	3	47	59	30	28	22	28	L	L	6-4	195	8-26-69	1991	Chicago, Ill.
Hudson, Joe	2	1	2.25	29	0	0	7	32	25	22	8	23	14	R	R	6-1	180	9-29-70	1992	Medford, N.J.
Lacy, Kerry	5	3	4.73	23	0	0	8	32	36	18	17	11	21	R	R	6-2	195	8-7-72	1991	Higdon, Ala.
Lowe, Derek	4	0	2.37	6	5	0	0	30	23	8	8	11	21	R	R	6-6	170	6-1-73	1991	Dearborn, Mich.
Mahay, Ron	1	0	0.00	2	0	0	0	5	3	0	0	1	6	L	L	6-2	185	6-28-71	1991	Crestwood, Ill.
Mahomes, Pat	5	1	2.84	18	1	0	7	32	22	11	10	17	40	R	R	6-4	210	8-9-70	1988	Lindale, Texas
Meacham, Rusty	3	3	4.78	28	2	0	1	43	54	23	23	15	42	R	R	6-2	175	1-27-68	1988	Palm City, Fla.
Mimbs, Mark	3	8	5.06	15	14	0	0	84	97	58	47	35	81	L	L	6-2	180	2-13-69	1990	Macon, Ga.
Orellano, Rafael	3	5	7.14	16	12	1	0	69	65	58	55	55	46	L	L	6-2	160	4-28-73	1993	Humacao, P.R.
Pavano, Carl	11	6	3.12	23	23	3	0	162	148	62	56	34	147	R	R	6-5	230	1-8-76	1994	Southington, Conn.
Peterson, Dean	0	1	3.00	2	0	0	0	3	2	1	1	1	2	R	R	6-3	200	8-3-72	1993	Cortland, Ohio
Rose, Brian L.	17	5	3.02	27	26	3	0	191	188	74	64	46	116	R	R	6-3	215	2-13-76	1995	Dartmouth, Mass.
Ruffin, Johnny	0	1	4.50	6	1	0	0	14	5	7	7	16	16	R	R	6-3	170	7-29-71	1988	Butler, Ala.
Saberhagen, Bret	0	1	3.27	2	2	0	0	11	11	4	4	1	9	R	R	6-1	200	4-11-64	1983	Babylon, N.Y.
Suppan, Jeff	5	1	3.71	9	9	2	0	61	51	26	25	15	40	R	R	6-2	210	1-2-75	1993	West Hills, Calif.
Valdez, Carlos	0	4	4.69	35	8	0	1	79	73	49	41	46	64	R	R	5-11	165	12-26-71	1990	Nizao, D.R.
Walker, Pete	0	0	5.40	7	0	0	0	12	14	8	7	7	8	R	R	6-2	184	4-8-69	1990	East Lyme, Conn.

FIELDING

Catcher	PCT	G	PO	A	E	DP	PB
Bennett	.985	65	480	33	8	0	1
Borrero	.983	15	107	9	2	0	8
McKeel	.997	48	303	32	1	8	10
Varitek	.993	19	123	10	1	1	3

First Base	PCT	G	PO	A	E	DP
Abad	.984	33	275	25	5	24
Bennett	1.000	6	48	3	0	1
Carey	.993	52	369	31	3	40
Correia	.949	4	34	3	2	5
Dodson	.987	16	141	13	2	12
Malave	.983	17	165	9	3	12
McKeel	.968	20	144	7	5	12
Rodriguez	1.000	2	17	1	0	3
Woods	1.000	2	22	0	0	0

Second Base	PCT	G	PO	A	E	DP
Allison	.970	8	12	20	1	3
Benjamin	1.000	1	0	3	0	0
Carey	.952	13	15	45	3	11
Merloni	.986	33	50	94	2	17
Pozo	1.000	5	5	9	0	1
Rodriguez	.944	9	16	18	2	2
Sadler	.971	78	173	234	12	51

Third Base	PCT	G	PO	A	E	DP
Benjamin	1.000	2	1	2	0	0
Carey	.917	28	17	49	6	1
Correia	1.000	7	7	21	0	3
Merloni	.955	8	6	15	1	0
Pozo	.957	86	61	161	10	8
Rodriguez	.955	21	15	48	3	7

Shortstop	PCT	G	PO	A	E	DP
Benjamin	.962	27	45	81	5	15
Carey	.867	5	6	7	2	2
Correia	.960	20	33	63	4	13
Merloni	.947	7	5	13	1	3
Rodriguez	.973	42	73	105	5	25
Sadler	.985	46	79	120	3	24

Outfield	PCT	G	PO	A	E	DP
Abad	.942	34	48	1	3	0
Bryant	.882	8	15	0	2	0
Coleman	.932	28	53	2	4	0
Correia	.500	1	1	0	1	0
Hyzdu	.978	92	170	10	4	0
Malave	.970	63	94	3	3	2
Nixon	.986	129	268	10	4	4
Pride	1.000	1	2	0	0	0
Sadler	.000	1	0	0	0	0
Tavarez	.978	57	127	7	3	1
Williams	.971	18	33	0	1	0

TRENTON — Class AA

EASTERN LEAGUE

BATTING	AVG	G	AB	R	H	2B	3B	HR	RBI	BB	SO	SB	CS	B	T	HT	WT	DOB	1st Yr	Resides
Abad, Andy	.303	45	165	37	50	13	0	8	24	33	27	2	4	L	L	6-1	185	8-25-72	1993	Jupiter, Fla.
Borrero, Richie	.251	57	203	31	51	12	1	3	23	13	46	2	2	R	R	6-1	195	1-5-73	1990	Hormigueros, P.R.

BATTING	AVG	G	AB	R	H	2B	3B	HR	RBI	BB	SO	SB	CS	B	T	HT	WT	DOB	1st Yr	Resides
Brown, Randy	.256	97	336	51	86	11	4	8	49	38	102	9	7	R	R	5-11	160	5-1-70	1989	Houston, Texas
Bryant, Pat	.288	104	379	73	109	20	3	19	77	60	76	18	7	R	R	5-11	182	10-27-72	1990	Sherman Oaks, Calif.
Coleman, Michael	.301	102	385	56	116	17	8	14	58	41	89	20	7	R	R	5-11	180	8-16-75	1994	Nashville, Tenn.
Correia, Rod	.293	67	249	40	73	18	1	7	33	22	32	4	2	R	R	5-11	185	9-13-67	1988	Rehoboth, Mass.
DePastino, Joe	.254	79	276	51	70	14	1	17	55	32	63	1	2	R	R	6-2	210	9-4-73	1992	Sarasota, Fla.
Derosso, Tony	.216	102	357	50	77	18	1	14	40	26	94	13	1	R	R	6-3	215	11-7-75	1994	Moultrie, Ga.
Epperson, Chad	.333	3	9	2	3	1	0	0	1	0	2	1	0	S	R	6-3	221	3-26-72	1992	Fort Myers, Fla.
Faggett, Ethan	.286	17	56	10	16	2	0	2	8	8	17	2	0	L	L	6-0	190	8-21-74	1992	Burleson, Texas
Fuller, Aaron	.260	128	481	87	125	17	6	6	46	95	84	40	15	S	R	5-10	170	9-7-71	1993	Sacramento, Calif.
Gibralter, David	.274	123	478	70	131	25	1	14	86	44	103	3	5	R	R	6-3	215	6-19-75	1993	Duncanville, Texas
Haselman, Bill	.231	7	26	3	6	1	0	2	3	2	2	0	0	R	R	6-3	215	5-25-66	1987	Saratoga, Calif.
Jackson, Gavin	.272	100	301	46	82	12	0	1	46	48	36	2	6	R	R	5-10	170	7-19-73	1993	Sylvester, Ga.
Liniak, Cole	.280	53	200	20	56	11	0	2	18	17	29	0	1	R	R	6-1	181	8-23-76	1995	San Diego, Calif.
Madonna, Chris	.341	14	41	7	14	3	0	0	6	6	11	2	2	L	R	5-11	190	3-13-73	1994	Smithtown, N.Y.
McKeel, Walt	.160	7	25	0	4	2	0	0	4	1	2	0	0	R	R	6-2	200	1-17-72	1990	Stantonsburg, N.C.
Merloni, Lou	.310	69	255	49	79	17	4	5	37	30	43	3	2	R	R	5-10	188	4-6-71	1993	Framingham, Mass.
Ortiz, Nick	.281	87	288	47	81	17	2	8	53	27	55	3	2	R	R	6-0	165	7-9-73	1991	Cidra, P.R.
Tebbs, Nate	.313	5	16	2	5	0	0	0	0	2	1	0	1	S	R	5-11	175	12-14-72	1993	Salt Lake City, Utah
Williams, Juan	.200	63	200	34	40	5	1	12	30	33	63	0	4	L	R	6-0	180	10-9-72	1990	Riverside, Calif.

PITCHING	W	L	ERA	G	GS	CG	SV	IP	H	R	ER	BB	SO	B	T	HT	WT	DOB	1st Yr	Resides
Barkley, Brian	12	9	4.94	29	29	4	0	179	208	113	98	79	121	L	L	6-2	170	12-8-75	1994	Waco, Texas
Betti, Rich	2	0	6.35	30	0	0	3	40	42	29	28	17	30	R	L	5-11	170	9-16-73	1993	Milford, Mass.
Blais, Mike	2	0	3.32	18	0	0	5	22	26	11	8	12	14	R	R	6-5	226	10-2-71	1993	East Lyme, Conn.
Cannon, Kevan	1	1	2.81	13	0	0	1	16	7	7	5	12	11	L	L	6-3	215	8-24-74	1995	Columbus, Ohio
Cederblad, Brett	0	0	8.68	6	0	0	0	9	12	10	9	2	7	S	R	6-5	195	3-6-73	1995	Parkwood, Australia
Checo, Robinson	1	0	2.35	1	1	0	0	8	6	3	2	1	9	R	R	6-1	165	9-9-71	1989	Santiago, D.R.
Farrell, Jim	12	7	4.37	26	26	0	0	163	173	93	79	57	110	R	R	6-1	180	11-1-73	1995	Hartville, Ohio
Fernandez, Jared	4	6	5.41	21	16	1	0	121	138	90	73	66	73	R	R	6-2	225	2-2-72	1994	West Valley, Utah
Gonzales, Frank	3	1	5.88	14	0	0	2	26	29	18	17	16	14	R	L	6-0	185	3-12-68	1989	La Junta, Colo.
Hale, Chad	0	0	8.31	3	0	0	0	4	5	5	4	5	2	R	L	6-6	245	8-3-71	1994	Thornville, Ohio
Haynes, Heath	1	1	2.36	14	0	0	2	27	26	8	7	8	26	R	R	6-0	175	11-30-68	1991	Wheeling, W.Va.
Hecker, Doug	1	0	2.57	4	0	0	0	7	5	2	2	9	7	R	R	6-4	210	1-21-71	1992	Wantagh, N.Y.
Mahay, Ron	3	3	3.10	17	4	0	5	41	29	16	14	13	47	L	L	6-2	185	6-28-71	1991	Crestwood, Ill.
Munro, Peter	7	10	4.95	22	22	1	0	116	113	76	64	47	109	R	R	6-2	185	6-14-75	1994	Little Neck, N.Y.
Orellano, Rafael	0	1	17.05	2	2	0	0	6	14	12	12	7	5	L	L	6-2	160	4-28-73	1993	Humacao, P.R.
Pena, Juan	5	6	4.73	16	14	0	0	97	98	56	51	31	79	R	R	6-5	210	6-27-77	1995	Hialeah, Fla.
Peterson, Dean	1	3	4.60	33	1	0	5	59	67	30	30	30	48	R	R	6-3	200	8-3-72	1993	Cortland, Ohio
Ramirez, Felix	4	2	5.44	18	3	0	2	41	43	28	25	20	29	L	L	5-11	170	1-7-75	1996	Beverly Hills, Calif.
Rose, Brian K.	2	1	2.84	15	0	0	0	25	23	8	8	10	18	R	R	6-1	195	10-7-72	1994	Potsdam, N.Y.
Saberhagen, Bret	0	0	0.00	2	2	0	0	8	2	0	0	1	9	R	R	6-1	200	4-11-64	1983	Babylon, N.Y.
Smetana, Steve	1	2	2.95	18	0	0	3	21	25	9	7	7	16	L	L	6-0	205	4-14-73	1996	Chardon, Ohio
Tweedlie, Brad	4	6	5.77	41	0	0	5	58	62	41	37	44	30	R	R	6-2	215	12-9-71	1993	Enfield, Conn.
Walker, Pete	0	0	4.05	8	0	0	3	13	14	6	6	7	13	R	R	6-2	184	4-8-69	1990	East Lyme, Conn.
Yennaco, Jay	5	11	6.33	21	21	0	0	122	146	89	86	54	73	R	R	6-2	220	11-17-75	1996	Windham, N.H.

FIELDING

Catcher	PCT	G	PO	A	E	DP	PB
Borrero	.983	56	373	39	7	1	17
DePastino	.988	71	447	45	6	4	7
Epperson	1.000	1	4	0	0	0	0
Haselman	1.000	4	30	2	0	0	0
Madonna	1.000	11	69	5	0	0	1
McKeel	1.000	2	12	0	0	0	1

First Base	PCT	G	PO	A	E	DP
Abad	.989	21	167	14	2	13
Derosso	.985	7	57	9	1	4
Epperson	1.000	1	6	0	0	0
Gibralter	.990	114	942	74	10	86
Madonna	1.000	2	1	0	0	0
McKeel	1.000	1	5	1	0	1

Second Base	PCT	G	PO	A	E	DP
Brown	.944	17	35	50	5	9
Correia	.949	28	43	69	6	15
Fuller	1.000	2	4	6	0	1
Jackson	.981	27	39	67	2	12
Merloni	.981	12	23	28	1	8
Ortiz	.984	63	129	176	5	36
Tebbs	1.000	2	7	3	0	1

Third Base	PCT	G	PO	A	E	DP
Derosso	.876	41	20	72	13	8
Liniak	.929	46	35	82	9	11
Merloni	.948	53	45	102	8	8
Ortiz	.833	4	3	7	2	0
Tebbs	1.000	1	0	1	0	0

Shortstop	PCT	G	PO	A	E	DP
Brown	.945	59	92	149	14	33
Jackson	.947	73	113	175	16	27
Merloni	.000	1	0	0	0	0
Ortiz	.944	12	20	31	3	6
Tebbs	1.000	1	0	3	0	0

Outfield	PCT	G	PO	A	E	DP
Abad	.971	19	33	1	1	0
Brown	1.000	4	3	0	0	0
Bryant	.985	96	197	6	3	2
Coleman	.981	100	259	6	5	1
Correia	1.000	16	27	3	0	0
Derosso	1.000	18	25	1	0	0
Faggett	.950	14	19	0	1	0
Fuller	.976	122	232	11	6	1
Gibralter	.000	1	0	0	0	0
Williams	.990	48	100	4	1	1

SARASOTA — Class A

FLORIDA STATE LEAGUE

BATTING	AVG	G	AB	R	H	2B	3B	HR	RBI	BB	SO	SB	CS	B	T	HT	WT	DOB	1st Yr	Resides
Allison, Chris	.293	109	365	51	107	10	7	2	52	32	28	13	11	R	R	5-10	165	10-22-71	1994	Rock Island, Ill.
Bazzani, Matt	.195	58	169	21	33	5	0	6	18	11	51	4	2	R	R	6-1	205	9-17-73	1994	Foster City, Calif.
Chevalier, Virgil	.208	94	289	31	60	13	1	6	37	19	43	8	7	R	R	6-2	230	10-31-73	1995	Burnt Hills, N.Y.
Choi, Kyung	.232	85	228	26	53	9	1	3	25	23	35	4	3	L	L	6-1	180	5-12-72	1995	Seoul, South Korea
Clark, Kevin	.600	3	5	0	3	0	0	0	1	0	2	0	0	R	R	6-1	200	4-30-73	1993	Henderson, Nev.
Epperson, Chad	.272	107	367	45	100	25	1	8	48	32	95	13	8	S	R	6-3	221	3-26-72	1992	Fort Myers, Fla.
Espinal, Juan	.248	109	322	49	80	20	2	7	45	51	79	4	5	R	R	6-0	207	4-15-75	1992	La Vega, D.R.
Faggett, Ethan	.293	114	410	56	120	19	9	3	46	43	87	23	12	L	L	6-0	190	8-21-74	1992	Burleson, Texas
Fuentes, Javier	.286	47	147	16	42	6	2	2	22	12	19	4	6	R	R	6-1	180	9-27-74	1996	Austin, Texas
Hamilton, Joe	.278	104	317	51	88	17	3	12	52	43	89	14	3	L	R	6-0	185	7-12-74	1992	Rehoboth, Mass.
Hillenbrand, Shea	.295	57	220	25	65	12	0	2	28	7	29	9	8	R	R	6-1	185	7-27-75	1996	Mesa, Ariz.
Liniak, Cole	.336	64	217	32	73	16	0	6	42	22	31	1	2	R	R	6-1	181	8-23-76	1995	San Diego, Calif.
Marino, Larry	.091	4	11	2	1	1	0	0	0	1	2	0	0	R	R	5-10	185	10-11-74	1997	Lutherville, Md.
Marsh, Roy	.230	107	230	47	53	4	4	1	14	23	44	19	8	R	R	5-8	180	11-22-73	1994	Baltimore, Md.
Padilla, Roy	.246	130	463	66	114	16	4	2	38	41	80	24	19	L	L	6-7	230	8-4-75	1993	Panama City, Panama
Patton, Greg	.250	4	16	2	4	1	0	0	1	2	2	0	0	R	R	6-4	190	3-8-72	1993	Springfield, Va.

DAVID SEELIG

Boston's Tom Gordon

DAVID SCHOFIELD

Sarasota's Cole Liniak

BATTING	AVG	G	AB	R	H	2B	3B	HR	RBI	BB	SO	SB	CS	B	T	HT	WT	DOB	1st Yr	Resides
Raifstanger, John	.230	95	256	26	59	8	1	4	28	27	51	7	9	R	R	6-0	190	6-2-73	1994	Great Barrington, Mass.
Sanchez, Orlando	.182	41	99	10	18	3	1	0	9	6	29	2	1	R	R	6-0	160	7-19-78	1996	Sinaloa, Mexico
Tebbs, Nate	.261	111	375	52	98	14	3	5	39	27	65	15	9	S	R	5-11	175	12-14-72	1993	Salt Lake City, Utah

GAMES BY POSITION: C—Bazzani 49, Chevalier 65, Clark 1, Epperson 42, Raifstanger 2. **1B**—Bazzani 1, Chevalier 24, Epperson 30, Espinal 55, Hamilton 3, Hillenbrand 22, Raifstanger 29. **2B**—Allison 106, Fuentes 6, Marino 2, Marsh 1, Raifstanger 16, Sanchez 2, Tebbs 26. **3B**—Bazzani 1, Espinal 41, Hillenbrand 34, Liniak 60, Marino 2, Marsh 1, Raifstanger 3, Sanchez 2, Tebbs 13. **SS**—Espinal 2, Fuentes 39, Patton 4, Raifstanger 1, Sanchez 34, Tebbs 76. **OF**—Bazzani 1, Choi 49, Clark 1, Faggett 111, Hamilton 76, Marsh 92, Padilla 126, Raifstanger 17, Sanchez 1.

PITCHING	W	L	ERA	G	GS	CG	SV	IP	H	R	ER	BB	SO	B	T	HT	WT	DOB	1st Yr	Resides
Armas, Tony	2	1	6.62	3	3	0	0	18	18	13	13	12	9	R	R	6-4	175	4-29-78	1994	Puerto Piritu, Venez.
2-team (9 Tampa)	5	2	4.24	12	12	0	0	64	61	36	30	28	35							
Avery, Steve	0	0	0.00	1	1	0	0	3	2	0	0	1	3	L	L	6-4	205	4-14-70	1988	Taylor, Mich.
Barnes, Keith	2	3	5.57	28	5	0	1	65	72	48	40	38	39	L	L	6-3	189	8-9-74	1992	Hixson, Tenn.
Bosio, Chris	0	0	1.93	1	1	0	0	5	6	2	1	0	5	R	R	6-3	225	4-3-63	1982	Shingle Springs, Calif.
Brandenburg, Mark	0	0	0.00	1	0	0	0	3	3	0	0	0	1	R	R	6-0	170	7-14-70	1992	Humble, Texas
Cannon, Kevan	5	0	4.15	32	0	0	5	43	41	27	20	26	35	L	L	6-3	215	8-24-74	1995	Columbus, Ohio
Checo, Robinson	1	4	5.30	11	11	0	0	56	54	37	33	27	63	R	R	6-1	165	9-9-71	1989	Santiago, D.R.
Crawford, Paxton	4	8	4.55	12	11	2	0	65	69	42	33	27	56	R	R	6-3	190	8-4-77	1995	Morrilton, Ark.
Cressend, Jack	8	11	3.80	28	25	2	0	166	163	98	70	56	149	R	R	6-1	185	5-13-75	1996	Covington, La.
Henry, Butch	0	1	5.40	2	2	0	0	8	8	5	5	0	7	L	L	6-1	195	10-7-68	1987	El Paso, Texas
Hollis, Ron	1	1	2.84	13	0	0	4	19	13	8	6	7	21	L	R	6-3	205	8-13-73	1994	Brighton, Mich.
Iddon, Brent	1	2	4.95	37	2	0	3	56	63	39	31	28	50	R	R	6-2	180	2-4-76	1994	Sydney, Australia
Lyons, Jonathan	3	12	6.05	25	14	0	0	97	125	79	65	45	47	R	R	6-3	205	1-13-75	1996	Olive Branch, Miss.
McMullen, Jerry	2	4	5.23	33	0	0	2	52	61	33	30	28	37	L	L	6-2	190	10-13-73	1995	Redmond, Ore.
Merrill, Ethan	2	0	6.32	12	0	0	1	16	27	11	11	8	8	L	L	6-3	200	4-21-72	1994	South Burlington, Vt.
Pena, Juan	4	6	2.96	13	13	3	0	91	67	39	30	23	88	R	R	6-5	210	6-27-77	1995	Hialeah, Fla.
Ramirez, Felix	2	1	1.53	19	0	0	1	35	39	10	6	12	31	L	L	5-11	170	1-7-75	1996	Beverly Hills, Calif.
Ramsay, Rob	9	9	4.78	23	22	1	0	136	134	90	72	63	115	L	L	6-4	220	12-3-73	1996	Washougal, Wash.
Rose, Brian K.	4	1	3.00	21	0	0	7	33	35	16	11	12	34	R	R	6-1	195	10-7-72	1994	Potsdam, N.Y.
Sekany, Jason	4	4	5.57	10	9	0	0	65	56	43	40	41	32	R	R	6-4	215	7-20-75	1996	Fort Myers, Fla.
Smetana, Steve	0	1	4.71	10	1	0	0	21	25	12	11	7	20	L	L	6-0	205	4-14-73	1996	Chardon, Ohio
Spinelli, Mike	0	4	5.40	5	5	0	0	27	34	22	16	12	11	L	L	6-2	220	10-5-76	1996	Revere, Mass.
Thompson, Chris	5	2	3.69	29	6	0	0	61	68	35	25	29	36	R	R	6-2	195	9-29-72	1996	Elyria, Ohio
Yennaco, Jay	4	0	2.23	7	7	2	0	44	30	12	11	19	41	R	R	6-2	220	11-17-75	1996	Windham, N.H.

MICHIGAN — Class A

MIDWEST LEAGUE

BATTING	AVG	G	AB	R	H	2B	3B	HR	RBI	BB	SO	SB	CS	B	T	HT	WT	DOB	1st Yr	Resides
Ahumada, Alejandro	.250	3	12	1	3	1	1	0	1	0	3	0	0	R	R	6-1	155	1-20-79	1996	Sinaloa, Mexico
Barnes, John	.304	130	490	80	149	19	5	6	73	65	42	19	5	R	R	6-2	205	4-24-76	1996	El Cajon, Calif.
Chamblee, Jim	.300	133	487	112	146	29	5	22	73	53	107	18	4	R	R	6-4	175	5-6-75	1995	Denton, Texas

BATTING	AVG	G	AB	R	H	2B	3B	HR	RBI	BB	SO	SB	CS	B	T	HT	WT	DOB	1st Yr	Resides
DeLeon, Jorge	.271	20	59	10	16	3	0	0	4	0	19	2	0	R	R	6-1	175	9-26-74	1997	Guayama, P.R.
Fuentes, Javier	.169	30	77	10	13	1	1	0	8	7	18	1	1	R	R	6-1	180	9-27-74	1996	Austin, Texas
Hillenbrand, Shea	.290	64	224	28	65	13	3	3	39	9	20	1	3	R	R	6-1	185	7-27-75	1996	Mesa, Ariz.
Jenkins, Corey	.239	111	426	68	102	17	4	18	62	28	129	5	5	R	R	6-2	195	8-25-76	1995	Columbia, S.C.
Johnson, Rontrez	.241	118	411	87	99	10	6	5	40	65	96	29	12	R	R	5-10	160	12-12-76	1995	Marshall, Texas
Kratochvil, Tim	.264	44	129	11	34	4	1	0	19	9	35	0	0	R	R	6-2	220	4-2-74	1996	Mt. Olive, Ill.
Lomasney, Steve	.275	102	324	50	89	27	3	12	51	32	98	3	4	R	R	6-0	185	8-9-77	1995	Peabody, Mass.
LoCurto, Gary	.236	120	419	64	99	27	0	4	63	63	93	8	5	S	R	6-2	200	5-25-78	1996	San Diego, Calif.
Madonna, Chris	.147	16	34	4	5	2	0	0	1	6	9	1	0	L	R	5-11	190	3-13-73	1994	Smithtown, N.Y.
Olmeda, Jose	.191	61	194	24	37	7	0	1	21	11	63	5	0	S	R	6-1	165	7-7-77	1995	Fajardo, P.R.
Ortiz, Asbel	.280	43	143	19	40	8	1	3	6	3	32	1	0	S	R	5-10	155	6-20-76	1994	Cidra, P.R.
Prodanov, Peter	.184	55	141	24	26	5	1	5	21	18	30	1	1	R	R	6-1	200	9-4-73	1995	Princeton, N.J.
Sanchez, Orlando	.180	21	61	3	11	2	1	1	10	9	15	0	0	R	R	6-0	160	7-19-78	1996	Sinaloa, Mexico
Stenson, Dernell	.291	131	471	79	137	35	2	15	80	72	105	6	4	L	L	6-1	215	6-17-78	1996	La Grange, Ga.
Veras, Wilton	.288	131	489	51	141	21	3	8	68	31	51	3	2	R	R	6-1	180	1-19-78	1995	Santo Domingo, D.R.

GAMES BY POSITION: C—Kratochvil 40, Lomasney 94, Madonna 9, Prodanov 12. **1B**—Fuentes 1, Hillenbrand 16, LoCurto 112, Madonna 2, Prodanov 13. **2B**—Ahumada 1, Chamblee 104, DeLeon 1, Fuentes 3, Ortiz 30, Prodanov 4, Sanchez 4. **3B**—Fuentes 1, Hillenbrand 8, Ortiz 1, Prodanov 4, Veras 130. **SS**—Ahumada 2, Chamblee 27, DeLeon 18, Fuentes 25, Olmeda 59, Ortiz 8, Sanchez 16. **OF**—Barnes 113, Jenkins 72, Johnson 109, Kratochvil 1, Ortiz 1, Prodanov 18, Stenson 108.

PITCHING	W	L	ERA	G	GS	CG	SV	IP	H	R	ER	BB	SO	B	T	HT	WT	DOB	1st Yr	Resides
Beale, Chuck	2	7	3.73	39	9	1	12	89	111	58	37	17	86	R	R	6-0	180	3-19-74	1996	Dublin, Ga.
Betancourt, Rafael	0	3	1.95	27	0	0	11	32	26	9	7	2	52	R	R	6-1	187	4-29-75	1994	Cumana, Venez.
Duchscherer, Justin	1	1	5.63	4	4	0	0	24	26	17	15	10	19	R	R	6-3	165	11-19-77	1996	Lubbock, Texas
Festa, Chris	4	5	4.04	37	10	0	0	94	109	50	42	34	53	R	R	6-2	190	9-7-72	1996	Holliston, Mass.
Garrett, Josh	8	10	4.80	22	22	2	0	139	164	94	74	35	64	R	R	6-4	190	1-12-78	1996	Richland, Ind.
Hazlett, Andy	1	0	5.25	2	2	0	0	12	15	7	7	1	12	L	L	6-3	195	8-27-75	1997	Dallas, Ore.
Hunter, Germaine	5	4	3.64	52	0	0	1	72	65	40	29	42	68	R	R	5-11	185	1-9-74	1996	Omaha, Neb.
Kinney, Matt	8	5	3.53	22	22	2	0	117	93	59	46	78	123	R	R	6-4	190	12-16-76	1995	Bangor, Maine
Musgrave, Scott	4	5	5.61	15	11	0	0	79	96	59	49	17	51	L	L	6-2	200	4-24-74	1996	Princeton, N.C.
Partenheimer, Brian	1	1	6.65	17	0	0	0	22	32	16	16	9	16	L	L	6-6	225	4-13-75	1997	Birdseye, Ind.
Prempas, Lyle	2	1	7.79	13	1	0	0	17	27	17	15	20	15	L	L	6-7	205	12-3-74	1993	Westchester, Ill.
Reitsma, Chris	4	1	2.90	9	9	0	0	50	57	23	16	13	41	R	R	6-5	200	12-31-77	1996	Calgary, Alberta
Romboli, Curtis	5	2	3.00	46	1	0	1	69	60	29	23	25	69	L	L	6-0	190	2-7-73	1995	Cape Coral, Fla.
Rose, Brian K.	4	1	1.76	10	0	0	0	15	12	3	3	2	19	R	R	6-1	195	10-7-72	1994	Potsdam, N.Y.
Sekany, Jason	5	6	4.08	16	16	3	0	106	92	55	48	41	103	R	R	6-4	215	7-20-75	1996	Fort Myers, Fla.
Smetana, Steve	2	1	2.35	18	0	0	2	31	23	16	8	12	29	L	L	6-0	205	4-14-73	1996	Chardon, Ohio
Thompson, Chris	0	1	1.15	8	0	0	0	16	11	7	2	1	13	R	R	6-2	195	9-29-72	1996	Elyria, Ohio
Welch, Robb	13	10	4.22	26	26	3	0	154	142	88	72	80	158	R	R	6-4	190	12-30-75	1994	Twin Falls, Idaho
Wimberly, Larry	1	3	6.89	13	4	0	1	31	34	25	24	9	27	L	L	6-2	185	8-22-75	1994	Winter Garden, Fla.

LOWELL — Short-Season Class A

NEW YORK-PENN LEAGUE

BATTING	AVG	G	AB	R	H	2B	3B	HR	RBI	BB	SO	SB	CS	B	T	HT	WT	DOB	1st Yr	Resides
Ahumada, Alejandro	.222	57	203	25	45	4	1	1	13	15	49	5	1	R	R	6-1	155	1-20-79	1996	Sinaloa, Mexico
Alayon, Elvis	.207	32	111	12	23	4	1	1	7	5	16	1	2	L	R	5-11	170	12-14-74	1995	New York, N.Y.
Alevras, Chad	.145	22	55	8	8	2	0	1	5	10	13	1	1	R	R	6-1	190	1-8-75	1997	Littleton, Colo.
DeLeon, Jorge	.333	3	12	1	4	0	0	0	2	0	0	0	0	R	R	6-1	175	9-26-74	1997	Guayama, P.R.
Eckstein, David	.301	68	249	43	75	11	4	4	39	33	29	21	5	R	R	5-9	170	1-20-75	1997	Sanford, Fla.
Fischer, Mark	.330	48	179	25	59	15	1	5	25	15	38	13	2	R	R	6-2	208	4-15-76	1997	Marietta, Ga.
Flores, Jose	.221	37	122	13	27	4	0	1	9	6	36	4	1	S	R	6-3	180	4-24-78	1995	Ciudad Guayana, Venez.
Gancasz, Michael	.210	34	81	10	17	4	0	0	6	13	25	0	0	R	R	6-3	210	5-16-74	1996	Royersford, Pa.
Goodwin, Keith	.228	67	241	23	55	11	0	2	25	14	50	4	0	R	R	6-2	188	2-5-75	1994	Sulphur, La.
Gray, Travis	.198	45	116	18	23	3	0	3	12	21	41	2	1	L	R	6-0	191	6-28-75	1997	Ashville, Ohio
Haas, Danny	.179	9	28	6	5	3	0	0	0	2	8	3	0	L	R	5-11	169	1-4-76	1997	Paducah, Ky.
Howard, Marcus	.208	70	221	38	46	10	1	9	25	29	78	2	5	R	R	6-0	200	10-3-75	1997	Toledo, Ohio
Keaveney, Jeff	.204	51	191	26	39	12	0	7	29	18	58	0	0	R	R	6-5	240	10-7-75	1996	Framingham, Mass.
Kingsbury, Willy	.169	23	77	6	13	4	0	1	5	4	32	0	0	L	R	6-2	218	1-5-74	1996	East Corinth, Vt.
Lebron, Ruben	.305	51	167	25	51	9	1	1	24	6	30	13	3	S	R	5-10	140	8-10-75	1992	San Pedro de Macoris, D.R.
Metzger, Erik	.195	41	128	15	25	7	0	2	21	11	40	0	1	R	R	6-0	205	7-27-74	1996	Brentwood, Tenn.
Olmeda, Jose	.289	54	187	24	54	8	2	4	27	16	42	2	2	S	R	6-1	165	7-7-77	1995	Fajardo, P.R.
Ruecker, Dion	.219	50	160	16	35	6	1	1	11	4	32	0	0	R	R	5-11	180	9-9-73	1996	Vancouver, Wash.

GAMES BY POSITION: C—Alevras 21, Gancasz 34, Kingsbury 5, Metzger 31. **1B**—Gray 20, Keaveney 48, Kingsbury 7, Ruecker 9. **2B**—Ahumada 9, Eckstein 66, Lebron 7, Olmeda 1. **3B**—Ahumada 22, DeLeon 2, Gray 22, Lebron 5, Ruecker 38. **SS**—Ahumada 24, DeLeon 1, Lebron 3, Olmeda 52, Ruecker 2. **OF**—Alayon 31, Fischer 41, Flores 36, Goodwin 65, Haas 4, Howard 65, Lebron 4.

PITCHING	W	L	ERA	G	GS	CG	SV	IP	H	R	ER	BB	SO	B	T	HT	WT	DOB	1st Yr	Resides
Benzing, Skipp	0	1	5.91	2	2	0	0	11	11	8	7	2	6	L	R	6-2	180	11-29-76	1996	Gays Mills, Wis.
Calvert, Klae	1	0	8.36	3	3	0	0	14	16	13	13	3	8	R	R	6-5	180	11-30-76	1996	Gold Coast, Australia
Hayden, Terry	0	6	3.19	16	5	0	0	54	42	21	19	14	52	L	L	6-6	215	6-26-75	1997	Taylor, Mich.
Hazlett, Andy	5	0	1.61	19	3	0	4	50	44	16	9	7	66	L	L	6-3	195	8-27-75	1997	Dallas, Ore.
McCleary, Marty	3	6	3.75	13	13	0	0	62	53	38	26	36	43	R	R	6-4	220	10-26-74	1997	Mansfield, Ohio
Miller, Tom	1	3	2.77	24	0	0	1	39	38	24	12	20	42	L	L	6-1	185	5-18-75	1997	Eagle, Mich.
Montemayor, Humberto	0	1	13.50	1	0	0	0	1	2	1	1	1	0	R	R	6-0	174	10-12-77	1996	Nuevo Leon, Mexico
O'Dette, Rick	5	3	3.47	13	10	1	0	60	64	30	23	28	61	L	L	6-3	180	2-11-76	1997	Tinley Park, Ill.
Parker, Eric	3	0	3.24	23	0	0	1	42	32	20	15	23	41	L	L	5-11	175	1-15-74	1997	Harrisonburg, Va.
Partenheimer, Brian	2	1	0.68	5	0	0	1	13	9	1	1	1	11	L	L	6-6	225	4-13-75	1997	Birdseye, Ind.
Prempas, Lyle	0	0	10.80	3	0	0	0	3	1	4	4	4	2	L	L	6-7	205	12-3-74	1993	Westchester, Ill.
Rayborn, Kenny	2	2	2.74	11	7	0	1	46	39	18	14	15	35	R	R	6-4	210	11-22-74	1997	Purvis, Miss.
Rupp, Michael	0	1	3.55	2	2	0	0	13	8	5	5	3	10	R	R	6-2	175	2-21-78	1996	Spring Valley, Calif.
Saberhagen, Bret	0	0	0.00	1	1	0	0	3	1	0	0	0	2	R	R	6-1	200	4-11-64	1983	Babylon, N.Y.
Santana, Pedro	6	3	4.09	15	15	2	0	88	90	47	40	17	65	R	R	6-3	186	11-22-77	1995	San Pedro de Macoris, D.R.
Taglienti, Jeff	3	4	4.91	17	4	0	6	37	30	22	20	13	34	R	R	6-0	205	11-13-75	1997	Walpole, Mass.

PITCHING	W	L	ERA	G	GS	CG	SV	IP	H	R	ER	BB	SO	B	T	HT	WT	DOB	1st Yr	Resides
Thomas, Joe	4	5	3.84	18	11	0	2	75	71	43	32	19	61	L	L	6-3	225	1-25-75	1997	Kenmore, N.Y.
Villalobos, Noe	3	2	4.25	24	0	0	3	49	58	30	23	13	51	R	R	6-2	170	4-29-76	1996	Mexicali, Mexico

FORT MYERS — Rookie

GULF COAST LEAGUE

BATTING	AVG	G	AB	R	H	2B	3B	HR	RBI	BB	SO	SB	CS	B	T	Ht.	Wt.	DOB	1st Yr.	Resides
Capista, Aaron	.239	38	134	16	32	6	1	0	14	16	17	6	2	S	R	6-2	175	5-31-79	1997	Nashville, Tenn.
Chaidez, Juan	.147	14	34	1	5	0	0	0	2	5	16	0	0	S	R	6-2	205	3-29-77	1996	Miramar, Fla.
Dodson, Bo	.417	12	36	6	15	5	0	1	9	4	5	0	0	L	L	6-2	195	12-7-70	1989	West Sacramento, Calif.
Ferguson, Dwight	.253	33	95	13	24	5	1	0	9	5	33	8	1	L	L	6-1	170	12-9-76	1995	Miami, Fla.
Flores, Jose	.289	29	90	18	26	4	3	1	8	13	20	9	6	S	R	6-3	180	4-24-78	1995	Ciudad Guayana, Venez.
Gray, Travis	.261	8	23	0	6	2	0	0	4	5	4	0	0	L	R	6-0	191	6-28-75	1997	Ashville, Ohio
Haselman, Bill	.125	4	16	2	2	0	0	0	1	0	1	1	0	R	R	6-3	215	5-25-66	1987	Saratoga, Calif.
Leon, Carlos	.246	44	126	18	31	5	3	0	15	14	25	10	3	S	R	5-10	162	8-31-79	1997	Cabimas, Venez.
Marino, Larry	.283	47	145	15	41	7	0	1	19	15	19	0	0	R	R	5-10	185	10-11-74	1997	Lutherville, Md.
McKinley, Michael	.268	22	56	5	15	3	0	0	6	3	8	1	1	R	R	6-0	180	11-30-74	1996	Chandler, Ariz.
Mendoza, Angel	.271	49	170	18	46	6	4	0	17	9	36	13	1	R	R	6-2	165	11-30-78	1996	San Pedro de Macoris, D.R.
Nova, Geraldo	.287	40	122	8	35	5	2	0	17	18	33	1	3	S	R	6-0	168	3-1-78	1995	Santo Domingo, D.R.
Pena, Rodolfo	.306	44	124	7	38	5	1	0	12	10	21	1	2	R	R	6-0	180	3-7-79	1996	Monte Cristi, D.R.
Perez, Alejandro	.272	48	151	19	41	12	3	3	10	8	33	1	2	R	R	6-2	175	3-18-79	1996	Santiago, D.R.
Perini, Mike	.220	39	118	12	26	4	1	0	9	14	33	2	0	L	R	6-2	200	4-27-78	1996	Carlsbad, N.M.
Persails, Mike	.190	10	21	3	4	0	0	1	4	4	5	1	0	R	R	6-3	185	8-27-77	1997	Escondido, Calif.
Rojas, Mo	.286	39	112	16	32	7	3	0	6	7	16	1	1	R	R	5-11	180	11-25-76	1995	Hialeah, Fla.
Santos, Ramon	.183	17	60	8	11	1	0	0	7	7	11	8	3	S	R	5-10	175	8-14-79	1997	Cayey, P.R.
Terni, Chas	.184	27	76	12	14	3	0	0	4	7	23	2	0	R	R	5-10	170	10-1-78	1997	Uncasville, Conn.
Zapata, Wilson	.110	47	109	16	12	2	1	1	8	12	45	3	1	R	R	6-3	175	9-21-78	1996	Santo Domingo, D.R.

GAMES BY POSITION: C—Chaidez 3, Pena 43, Rojas 23. **1B**—Chaidez 11, Dodson 7, Perini 36, Rojas 8, Zapata 8. **2B**—Leon 42, Marino 4, Mendoza 1, Terni 19. **3B**—Gray 7, Marino 40, Nova 19, Terni 1. **SS**—Capista 31, Mendoza 23, Santos 8. **OF**—Ferguson 28, Flores 27, McKinley 18, Mendoza 24, Nova 11, Perez 44, Persails 8, Rojas 1, Zapata 40.

PITCHING	W	L	ERA	G	GS	CG	SV	IP	H	R	ER	BB	SO	B	T	HT	WT	DOB	1st Yr	Resides
Arias, Rafael	3	3	3.96	11	5	2	2	50	65	26	22	7	37	R	R	6-5	168	2-4-77	1994	San Pedro de Macoris, D.R.
Avery, Steve	0	0	1.50	1	1	0	0	6	5	3	1	0	8	L	L	6-4	205	4-14-70	1988	Taylor, Mich.
Becker, Keith	0	1	4.70	5	0	0	0	8	7	5	4	4	7	R	R	6-1	220	8-18-74	1997	Cincinnati, Ohio
Benzing, Skipp	0	3	5.51	6	2	0	1	16	16	16	10	9	17	L	R	6-2	180	11-29-76	1996	Gays Mills, Wis.
Betti, Rich	1	0	1.00	4	0	0	0	9	4	1	1	0	14	R	L	5-11	170	9-16-73	1993	Milford, Mass.
Blais, Mike	1	0	0.00	3	1	0	0	5	2	0	0	0	5	R	R	6-5	226	10-2-71	1993	East Lyme, Conn.
Bosio, Chris	0	0	0.00	2	2	0	0	5	2	0	0	2	4	R	R	6-3	225	4-3-63	1982	Shingle Springs, Calif.
Calvert, Klae	6	0	2.31	12	4	0	1	47	52	16	12	7	37	R	R	6-5	180	11-30-76	1996	Gold Coast, Australia
Cederblad, Brett	0	0	0.00	1	0	0	0	2	0	0	0	1	1	S	R	6-5	195	3-6-73	1995	Parkwood, Australia
Corsi, Jim	1	0	0.00	3	2	0	0	4	2	1	0	0	6	R	R	6-1	220	9-9-61	1982	Natick, Mass.
Curtice, John	2	0	0.79	4	3	0	0	11	6	2	1	5	11	L	L	6-4	210	11-1-79	1997	Chesapeake, Va.
Duchscherer, Justin	2	3	1.81	10	8	0	0	45	34	18	9	17	59	R	R	6-3	165	11-19-77	1996	Lubbock, Texas
Garcia, Luis	1	2	2.87	8	1	0	1	16	12	10	5	10	18	R	R	6-4	176	11-5-78	1996	Tlaquepaque, Mexico
Glaser, Eric	1	2	3.97	7	6	0	0	23	29	13	10	5	22	R	R	6-7	210	1-23-78	1997	Fort Thomas, Ky.
Hayden, Terry	1	0	2.25	3	0	0	0	8	6	2	2	1	8	L	L	6-6	215	6-26-75	1997	Taylor, Mich.
Hecker, Doug	0	0	0.00	1	0	0	0	1	0	0	0	1	1	R	R	6-4	210	1-21-71	1992	Wantagh, N.Y.
Hollis, Ron	0	0	1.29	4	0	0	1	7	7	1	1	0	7	L	R	6-3	205	8-13-73	1994	Brighton, Mich.
Martinez, Mark	4	2	2.64	14	4	0	0	48	35	18	14	18	78	L	L	5-11	175	12-13-77	1997	Lubbock, Texas
Miller, Greg	0	2	3.72	4	4	0	0	10	8	6	4	6	6	R	L	6-5	205	9-30-79	1997	Aurora, Ill.
Miller, Tom	0	1	6.75	1	0	0	0	1	2	1	1	2	3	L	L	6-1	185	5-18-75	1997	Eagle, Mich.
Molina, Primitivo	2	0	0.00	15	0	0	4	20	12	0	0	2	22	R	R	6-2	170	12-10-77	1996	Tijuana, Mexico
Montanez, Jorge	0	1	1.80	5	0	0	0	5	5	2	1	2	1	R	R	6-2	184	6-8-77	1996	Lara, Venez.
Montemayor, Humberto	1	0	4.19	9	0	0	1	19	29	13	9	2	19	R	R	6-0	174	10-12-77	1996	Nuevo Leon, Mexico
O'Dette, Rick	0	1	2.25	3	0	0	0	8	6	3	2	1	6	L	L	6-3	180	2-11-76	1997	Tinley Park, Ill.
Orellano, Rafael	1	0	1.29	2	1	0	0	7	2	1	1	1	9	L	L	6-2	160	4-28-73	1993	Humacao, P.R.
Peterson, Dean	0	0	0.00	2	0	0	1	2	1	0	0	1	1	R	R	6-3	200	8-3-72	1993	Cortland, Ohio
Roller, Adam	1	1	3.18	10	0	0	0	17	7	9	6	14	21	R	R	6-3	208	6-27-78	1997	Lakeland, Fla.
Rupp, Michael	1	4	1.22	11	9	3	0	59	51	23	8	17	56	R	R	6-2	175	2-21-78	1996	Spring Valley, Calif.
Spinelli, Mike	0	2	11.37	3	3	0	0	6	15	16	8	4	15	L	L	6-2	220	10-5-76	1996	Revere, Mass.
Tyrell, Jim	0	0	5.40	3	0	0	0	3	5	3	2	1	6	R	L	5-11	170	10-14-72	1992	Poughkeepsie, N.Y.
Walker, Pete	0	0	0.96	4	3	0	0	9	5	1	1	1	14	R	R	6-2	184	4-8-69	1990	East Lyme, Conn.
Wimberly, Larry	1	0	3.00	1	0	0	0	3	2	1	1	0	1	L	L	6-2	185	8-22-75	1994	Winter Garden, Fla.

Chicago WHITE SOX

Manager: Terry Bevington.

1997 Record: 80-81, .497 (2nd, AL Central)

BATTING	AVG	G	AB	R	H	2B	3B	HR	RBI	BB	SO	SB	CS	B	T	HT	WT	DOB	1st Yr	Resides
Abbott, Jeff	.263	19	38	8	10	1	0	1	2	0	6	0	0	R	L	6-2	190	8-17-72	1994	Atlanta, Ga.
Baines, Harold	.305	93	318	40	97	18	0	12	52	41	47	0	1	L	L	6-2	195	3-15-59	1977	St. Michaels, Md.
Belle, Albert	.274	161	634	90	174	45	1	30	116	53	105	4	4	R	R	6-2	210	8-25-66	1987	Euclid, Ohio
Cameron, Mike	.259	116	379	63	98	18	3	14	55	55	105	23	2	R	R	6-1	170	1-8-73	1991	La Grange, Ga.
Durham, Ray	.271	155	634	106	172	27	5	11	53	61	96	33	16	S	R	5-8	170	11-30-71	1990	Charlotte, N.C.
Fabregas, Jorge	.280	100	322	31	90	10	1	7	48	11	43	1	1	L	R	6-3	205	3-13-70	1991	Miami, Fla.
2-team (21 Anaheim)	.258	121	360	33	93	11	1	7	51	14	46	1	1							
Fonville, Chad	.111	9	9	1	1	0	0	0	1	1	1	2	0	S	R	5-7	155	3-5-71	1992	Midway Park, N.C.
Guillen, Ozzie	.245	142	490	59	120	21	6	4	52	22	24	5	3	L	R	5-11	164	1-20-64	1981	Guarenas, Venez.
Karkovice, Ron	.181	51	138	10	25	3	0	6	18	11	32	0	0	R	R	6-1	215	8-8-63	1982	Orlando, Fla.
Kreuter, Chad	.216	19	37	6	8	2	1	1	3	8	9	0	1	S	R	6-2	190	8-26-64	1985	Arlington, Texas
Lewis, Darren	.234	81	77	15	18	1	0	0	5	11	14	11	4	R	R	6-0	180	8-28-67	1988	Burlingame, Calif.
Machado, Robert	.200	10	15	1	3	0	1	0	2	1	6	0	0	R	R	6-1	150	6-3-73	1991	Caracas, Venez.
Martin, Norberto	.300	71	213	24	64	7	1	2	27	6	31	1	4	S	R	5-10	164	12-10-66	1984	Hato Rey, P.R.
Martinez, Dave	.286	145	504	78	144	16	6	12	55	55	69	12	6	L	L	5-10	175	9-26-64	1983	Safety Harbor, Fla.
Mouton, Lyle	.269	88	242	26	65	9	0	5	23	14	66	4	4	R	R	6-4	240	5-13-69	1991	Lafayette, La.
Norton, Greg	.265	18	34	5	9	2	2	0	1	2	8	0	0	S	R	6-1	182	7-6-72	1993	Walnut Creek, Calif.
Ordonez, Magglio	.319	21	69	12	22	6	0	4	11	2	8	1	2	R	R	5-11	155	1-28-74	1991	Caracas, Venez.
Pena, Tony	.164	31	67	4	11	1	0	0	8	8	13	0	0	R	R	6-0	184	6-4-57	1976	Santiago, D.R.
Phillips, Tony	.310	36	129	23	40	6	0	2	9	29	29	4	1	S	R	5-10	175	4-25-59	1978	Scottsdale, Ariz.
Snopek, Chris	.218	86	298	27	65	15	0	5	35	18	51	3	2	R	R	6-1	185	9-20-70	1992	Cynthiana, Ky.
Thomas, Frank	.347	146	530	110	184	35	0	35	125	109	69	1	1	R	R	6-5	257	5-27-68	1989	Burr Ridge, Ill.
Valdez, Mario	.243	54	115	11	28	7	0	1	13	17	39	1	0	L	R	6-2	190	11-19-74	1994	Hialeah, Fla.
Ventura, Robin	.262	54	183	27	48	10	1	6	26	34	21	0	0	L	R	6-1	185	7-14-67	1989	Santa Maria, Calif.

PITCHING	W	L	ERA	G	GS	CG	SV	IP	H	R	ER	BB	SO	B	T	HT	WT	DOB	1st Yr	Resides
Alvarez, Wilson	9	8	3.03	22	22	2	0	146	126	61	49	55	110	L	L	6-1	235	3-24-70	1987	Maracaibo, Venez.
Baldwin, James	12	15	5.27	32	32	1	0	200	205	128	117	83	140	R	R	6-4	210	7-15-71	1990	Southern Pines, N.C.
Bere, Jason	4	2	4.71	6	6	0	0	29	20	15	15	17	21	R	R	6-3	185	5-26-71	1990	Wilmington, Mass.
Bertotti, Mike	0	0	7.36	9	0	0	0	4	9	3	3	2	4	L	L	6-1	185	1-18-70	1991	Highland Mills, N.Y.
Castillo, Carlos	2	1	4.48	37	2	0	1	66	68	35	33	33	43	R	R	6-2	230	4-21-75	1994	Miami, Fla.
Castillo, Tony	4	4	4.91	64	0	0	4	62	74	48	34	23	42	L	L	5-10	190	3-1-63	1983	Lara, Venez.
Clemons, Chris	0	2	8.53	5	2	0	0	13	19	13	12	11	8	R	R	6-4	220	10-31-72	1994	McGregor, Texas
Cruz, Nelson	0	2	6.49	19	0	0	0	26	29	19	19	9	23	R	R	6-1	160	9-13-72	1990	Puerto Plata, D.R.
Darwin, Danny	4	8	4.13	21	17	1	0	113	130	60	52	31	62	R	R	6-3	202	10-25-55	1976	Valley View, Texas
Darwin, Jeff	0	1	5.27	14	0	0	0	14	17	8	8	7	9	R	R	6-3	180	7-6-69	1989	Gainesville, Texas
Drabek, Doug	12	11	5.74	31	31	0	0	169	170	109	108	69	85	R	R	6-1	185	7-25-62	1983	The Woodlands, Texas
Eyre, Scott	4	4	5.04	11	11	0	0	61	62	36	34	31	36	L	L	6-1	160	5-30-72	1991	Magna, Utah
Fordham, Tom	0	1	6.23	7	1	0	0	17	17	13	12	10	10	L	L	6-2	210	2-20-74	1993	El Cajon, Calif.
Foulke, Keith	3	0	3.45	16	0	0	3	29	28	11	11	5	21	R	R	6-1	195	10-19-72	1994	Huffman, Texas
Hernandez, Roberto	5	1	2.44	46	0	0	27	48	38	15	13	24	47	R	R	6-4	235	11-11-64	1986	Cobo Rojo, P.R.
Karchner, Matt	3	1	2.91	52	0	0	15	53	50	18	17	26	30	R	R	6-4	245	6-28-67	1989	Woodbridge, Va.
Levine, Alan	2	2	6.91	25	0	0	0	27	35	22	21	16	22	L	R	6-3	180	5-22-68	1991	Hanover Park, Ill.
McElroy, Chuck	1	3	3.94	48	0	0	1	59	56	29	26	19	44	L	L	6-0	195	10-1-67	1986	Friendswood, Texas
2-team (13 Anaheim)	1	3	3.84	61	0	0	1	75	73	36	32	22	62							
Navarro, Jaime	9	14	5.79	33	33	2	0	210	267	155	135	73	142	R	R	6-4	225	3-27-67	1987	Orlando, Fla.
Simas, Bill	3	1	4.14	40	0	0	1	41	46	23	19	24	38	L	R	6-3	220	11-28-71	1992	Fresno, Calif.
Sirotka, Mike	3	0	2.25	7	4	0	0	32	36	9	8	5	24	L	L	6-1	190	5-13-71	1993	Houston, Texas
Thomas, Larry	0	0	8.10	5	0	0	0	3	3	3	3	2	0	R	L	6-1	190	10-25-69	1991	Mobile, Ala.

FIELDING

Catcher	PCT	G	PO	A	E	DP	PB
Fabregas	.988	92	519	46	7	8	8
Karkovice	.996	51	261	13	1	1	2
Kreuter	.984	13	57	3	1	0	4
Machado	1.000	10	34	3	0	1	1
Pena	1.000	30	143	8	0	2	5

First Base	PCT	G	PO	A	E	DP
Fabregas	1.000	1	1	0	0	0
Martinez	.979	52	256	24	6	23
Thomas	.986	97	739	49	11	70
Valdez	1.000	47	256	12	0	19

Second Base	PCT	G	PO	A	E	DP
Durham	.974	153	270	395	18	77
Fonville	1.000	2	0	1	0	0
Martin	.975	9	14	25	1	3

Third Base	PCT	G	PO	A	E	DP
Martin	.973	17	9	27	1	2
Norton	.864	11	4	15	3	0
Pena	.000	1	0	0	0	0
Phillips	.950	9	7	12	1	1

	PCT	G	PO	A	E	DP
Snopek	.915	82	56	117	16	11
Valdez	.000	1	0	0	0	0
Ventura	.956	54	53	99	7	11

Shortstop	PCT	G	PO	A	E	DP
Fonville	.800	2	2	2	1	0
Guillen	.974	139	207	348	15	78
Martin	.960	28	27	45	3	11
Snopek	1.000	4	5	8	0	2

Outfield	PCT	G	PO	A	E	DP
Abbott	1.000	10	15	0	0	0
Belle	.972	154	351	1	10	0
Cameron	.985	112	334	5	5	2
Fonville	1.000	3	7	0	0	0
Lewis	1.000	64	90	1	0	1
Martinez	.996	105	229	6	1	3
Mouton	.969	67	126	1	4	0
Ordonez	1.000	19	43	1	0	0
Phillips	.972	28	67	3	2	1

JOHN KLEIN

Frank Thomas

FARM SYSTEM

Director of Player Development: Ken Williams

Class	Farm Team	League	W	L	Pct.	Finish*	Manager(s)	First Yr
AAA	Nashville (Tenn.) Sounds	American Assoc.	74	69	.517	3rd (8)	Tom Spencer	1993
AA	Birmingham (Ala.) Barons	Southern	76	62	.551	2nd (10)	Dave Huppert	1986
#A	Winston-Salem (N.C.) Warthogs	Carolina	63	77	.450	7th (8)	Mike Heath/Mark Haley	1997
A	Hickory (N.C.) Crawdads	South Atlantic	76	64	.543	4th (14)	Chris Cron	1993
#R	Bristol (Va.) White Sox	Appalachian	30	38	.441	7th (10)	Nick Capra	1995
R	Sarasota (Fla.) White Sox	Gulf Coast	26	34	.433	11th (15)	Roly de Armas	1964

*Finish in overall standings (No. of teams in league) #Advanced level

ORGANIZATION LEADERS

MAJOR LEAGUERS

BATTING

*AVG	Frank Thomas	.347
R	Frank Thomas	110
H	Frank Thomas	184
TB	Frank Thomas	324
2B	Albert Belle	45
3B	Two tied at	6
HR	Frank Thomas	35
RBI	Frank Thomas	125
BB	Frank Thomas	109
SO	Two tied at	105
SB	Ray Durham	33

PITCHING

W	Two tied at	12
L	James Baldwin	15
#ERA	Wilson Alvarez	3.03
G	Tony Castillo	64
CG	Two tied at	2
SV	Roberto Hernandez	27
IP	Jaime Navarro	210
BB	James Baldwin	83
SO	Jaime Navarro	142

MORRIS FOSTOFF

Albert Belle

RODGER WOOD

Carlos Lee

MINOR LEAGUERS

BATTING

*AVG	Luis Raven, Birmingham	.336
R	Brian Simmons, Birmingham	108
H	Jeff Inglin, Hickory	179
TB	Carlos Lee, Winston-Salem	282
2B	Carlos Lee, Winston-Salem	50
3B	Three tied at	12
HR	Luis Raven, Birmingham	30
RBI	Luis Raven, Birmingham	112
BB	Mark Johnson, Winston-Salem	106
SO	Juan Thomas, Birm./Win.-Salem	153
SB	Ramon Gomez, Winston-Salem	53

PITCHING

W	Joe Farley, Hickory	14
L	Jason Olsen, Birmingham	14
#ERA	Brian Scott, Hickory	2.16
G	Todd Rizzo, Nashville	54
CG	Three tied at	3
SV	Jeff Darwin, Nashville	22
IP	Joe Farley, Hickory	173
BB	John Ambrose, Winston-Salem	117
SO	Jason Lakman, Hickory	168

*Minimum 250 At-Bats #Minimum 75 Innings

TOP 10 PROSPECTS

LARRY GOREN

Mike Cameron

How the White Sox Top 10 prospects, as judged by Baseball America prior to the 1997 season, fared in 1997:

Player, Pos.	Club (Class)	AVG	AB	R	H	2B	3B	HR	RBI	SB
1. Mike Cameron, of	Chicago	.259	379	63	98	18	3	14	55	23
	Nashville (AAA)	.275	120	21	33	7	3	6	17	4
2. Jeff Abbott, of	Chicago	.263	38	8	10	1	0	1	2	0
	Nashville (AAA)	.327	465	88	152	35	3	11	63	12
3. Jeff Liefer, of	Birmingham (AA)	.238	474	67	113	24	9	15	71	2
4. Greg Norton, ss-3b	Chicago	.265	34	5	9	2	2	0	1	0
	Nashville (AAA)	.275	414	82	114	27	1	26	76	3
6. Josh Paul, c	Birmingham (AA)	.296	115	18	34	5	0	1	16	6
7. Brian Simmons, of	Birmingham (AA)	.262	546	108	143	28	12	15	72	15
8. Mario Valdez, 1b	Chicago	.243	115	11	28	7	0	1	13	1
	Nashville (AAA)	.280	282	44	79	20	1	15	61	1
10. Carlos Lee, 3b	Winston-Salem (A)	.317	546	81	173	50	4	17	82	11

Player, Pos.	Club (Class)	W	L	ERA	G	SV	IP	H	BB	SO
5. Chris Clemons, rhp	Chicago	0	2	8.53	5	0	13	19	11	8
	Nashville (AAA)	5	5	4.55	22	0	125	115	65	70
9. Tom Fordham, lhp	Chicago	0	1	6.23	7	0	17	17	10	10
	Nashville (AAA)	6	7	4.74	21	0	114	113	53	90

NASHVILLE — Class AAA

AMERICAN ASSOCIATION

BATTING	AVG	G	AB	R	H	2B	3B	HR	RBI	BB	SO	SB	CS	B	T	HT	WT	DOB	1st Yr	Resides
Abbott, Jeff	.327	118	465	88	152	35	3	11	63	41	52	12	7	R	L	6-2	190	8-17-72	1994	Atlanta, Ga.
Battle, Allen	.222	11	27	6	6	1	0	2	5	5	7	0	0	R	R	6-0	170	11-29-68	1991	Mount Olive, N.C.
Brady, Doug	.238	106	370	43	88	12	3	7	36	18	47	13	4	S	R	5-11	165	11-23-69	1991	Las Vegas, Nev.
Cameron, Mike	.275	30	120	21	33	7	3	6	17	18	31	4	2	R	R	6-1	170	1-8-73	1991	La Grange, Ga.
Cappuccio, Carmine	.220	55	177	22	39	11	0	4	21	16	24	1	0	L	R	6-3	185	2-1-70	1992	Malden, Mass.
Cotton, John	.269	94	323	45	87	14	3	11	50	24	94	8	2	L	R	6-0	170	10-30-70	1989	Huntsville, Texas
Downs, Brian	.222	7	18	1	4	0	0	0	1	0	5	0	1	R	R	6-2	210	4-10-75	1995	Chino, Calif.
Evans, Jason	.284	65	194	38	55	10	1	1	27	49	45	6	3	S	R	5-11	187	2-11-71	1992	Chatsworth, Calif.
Leius, Scott	.240	30	104	15	25	2	0	7	17	11	6	0	0	R	R	6-3	208	9-24-65	1986	Minnetonka, Minn.
Machado, Robert	.269	84	308	43	83	18	0	8	30	12	61	5	0	R	R	6-1	150	6-3-73	1991	Caracas, Venez.
Menechino, Frankie	.230	37	113	20	26	4	0	4	11	26	31	3	2	R	R	5-9	175	1-7-71	1993	Staten Island, N.Y.
Norton, Greg	.275	114	414	82	114	27	1	26	76	57	101	3	5	S	R	6-1	182	7-6-72	1993	Walnut Creek, Calif.
Ordonez, Magglio	.329	135	523	65	172	29	3	14	90	32	61	14	10	R	R	5-11	155	1-28-74	1991	Caracas, Venez.
Pearson, Eddie	.223	41	148	17	33	4	0	4	16	6	23	1	1	S	R	6-3	225	1-31-74	1992	Mobile, Ala.
Polidor, Wil	.097	9	31	2	3	0	0	0	2	0	4	0	0	S	R	6-1	158	9-23-73	1991	Caracas, Venez.
Schall, Gene	.196	33	112	11	22	0	1	5	17	11	32	1	1	R	R	6-3	190	6-5-70	1991	Willow Grove, Pa.
Snopek, Chris	.233	20	73	8	17	4	0	3	8	7	13	0	0	R	R	6-1	185	9-20-70	1992	Cynthiana, Ky.
Valdez, Mario	.280	81	282	44	79	20	1	15	61	43	77	1	1	L	R	6-2	190	11-19-74	1994	Hialeah, Fla.
Ventura, Robin	.400	5	15	3	6	1	0	2	5	2	1	0	1	L	R	6-1	185	7-14-67	1989	Santa Maria, Calif.
Vinas, Julio	.232	91	314	39	73	12	2	11	41	25	72	4	4	R	R	6-0	200	2-14-73	1991	Hialeah, Fla.
Wilson, Craig	.272	137	453	71	123	20	2	6	42	48	31	4	4	R	R	6-1	190	9-3-70	1992	Phoenix, Ariz.
Wrona, Rick	.246	70	211	22	52	15	0	6	22	3	41	1	1	R	R	6-0	180	12-10-63	1985	Tulsa, Okla.

PITCHING	W	L	ERA	G	GS	CG	SV	IP	H	R	ER	BB	SO	B	T	HT	WT	DOB	1st Yr	Resides
Bere, Jason	1	1	5.59	4	4	0	0	19	23	13	12	7	13	R	R	6-3	185	5-26-71	1990	Wilmington, Mass.
Bertotti, Mike	5	9	5.35	21	20	1	0	108	91	70	64	105	87	L	L	6-1	185	1-18-70	1991	Highland Mills, N.Y.
Castillo, Carlos	0	0	1.50	4	0	0	3	6	4	1	1	0	4	R	R	6-2	230	4-21-75	1994	Miami, Fla.
Clemons, Chris	5	5	4.55	22	21	1	0	125	115	73	63	65	70	R	R	6-4	220	10-31-72	1994	McGregor, Texas
Cruz, Nelson	11	7	5.11	21	20	1	0	123	139	75	70	31	93	R	R	6-1	160	9-13-72	1990	Puerto Plata, D.R.
Darwin, Jeff	4	3	4.53	47	0	0	22	54	60	32	27	24	44	R	R	6-3	180	7-6-69	1989	Gainesville, Texas
Fordham, Tom	6	7	4.74	21	20	2	0	114	113	64	60	53	90	L	L	6-2	210	2-20-74	1993	El Cajon, Calif.
Foulke, Keith	0	0	5.79	1	1	0	0	5	8	3	3	0	4	R	R	6-1	195	10-19-72	1994	Huffman, Texas
Hasselhoff, Derek	1	1	9.82	6	0	0	0	7	9	8	8	7	2	R	R	6-2	185	10-10-73	1995	Pasadena, Md.
Heathcott, Mike	2	3	7.33	17	0	0	0	27	39	23	22	12	23	R	R	6-3	180	5-16-69	1991	Chicago, Ill.
Johnson, Barry	4	1	3.55	14	0	0	2	25	24	10	10	11	10	R	R	6-4	200	8-21-69	1991	Joliet, Ill.
Jones, Stacy	0	0	54.00	1	0	0	0	0	4	3	2	0	0	R	R	6-6	225	5-26-67	1988	Attalla, Ala.
Karchner, Matt	2	1	1.93	13	0	0	3	19	12	5	4	6	11	R	R	6-4	245	6-28-67	1989	Woodbridge, Va.
Keyser, Brian	7	5	2.87	44	9	3	1	119	114	44	38	45	68	R	R	6-1	180	10-31-66	1989	Walnut Creek, Calif.
Levine, Alan	1	1	7.13	26	0	0	2	35	58	32	28	11	29	L	R	6-3	180	5-22-68	1991	Hanover Park, Ill.
Parque, Jim	1	0	4.22	2	2	0	0	11	9	5	5	9	5	L	L	5-10	166	2-8-76	1997	La Crescenta, Calif.
Pratt, Rich	9	8	4.58	29	24	2	0	149	165	89	76	50	71	L	L	6-3	201	5-7-71	1993	East Hartford, Conn.
Rizzo, Todd	4	5	3.57	54	0	0	6	71	63	39	28	33	60	R	L	6-3	220	5-24-71	1992	Aston, Pa.
Sirotka, Mike	7	5	3.28	19	19	1	0	112	115	49	41	22	92	L	L	6-1	190	5-13-71	1993	Houston, Texas
Smith, Chuck	0	3	8.81	20	1	0	0	32	39	33	31	23	29	R	R	6-1	175	10-21-69	1991	Cleveland, Ohio
Thomas, Larry	3	2	3.94	44	1	0	2	48	47	21	21	18	53	R	L	6-1	190	10-25-69	1991	Mobile, Ala.
Woods, Brian	1	2	7.71	14	1	0	0	23	34	24	20	20	22	R	R	6-6	212	6-7-71	1993	West Caldwell, N.J.

FIELDING

Catcher	PCT	G	PO	A	E	DP	PB
Downs	1.000	6	16	1	0	0	0
Machado	.988	72	461	49	6	7	9
Vinas	.986	31	193	15	3	0	1
Wrona	.986	44	243	30	4	1	2

First Base	PCT	G	PO	A	E	DP
Cotton	1.000	2	5	2	0	2
Leius	.980	6	49	1	1	4
Pearson	.993	37	281	16	2	33
Schall	1.000	8	45	5	0	9
Valdez	.991	75	616	44	6	48
Vinas	.986	16	129	8	2	14
Wrona	1.000	12	64	8	0	11

Second Base	PCT	G	PO	A	E	DP
Brady	.983	90	211	200	7	66
Cotton	.952	11	16	24	2	7
Menechino	.949	32	74	74	8	19
Norton	1.000	6	7	9	0	1
Polidor	.974	9	17	21	1	4
Wilson	.982	10	32	24	1	8

Third Base	PCT	G	PO	A	E	DP
Brady	.625	5	1	4	3	0
Cotton	.000	3	0	0	1	0
Leius	.895	13	8	26	4	1
Menechino	.941	4	4	12	1	0
Norton	.896	94	62	189	29	25
Schall	.636	3	2	5	4	0
Snopek	1.000	1	2	1	0	0
Ventura	1.000	4	1	12	0	0
Vinas	.857	6	9	9	3	0
Wilson	1.000	17	12	37	0	2
Wrona	.875	12	4	24	4	3

Shortstop	PCT	G	PO	A	E	DP
Brady	.500	1	0	1	1	0
Norton	.875	18	14	49	9	11
Snopek	.963	18	27	51	3	11
Wilson	.962	113	145	336	19	67

Outfield	PCT	G	PO	A	E	DP
Abbott	1.000	113	237	6	0	0
Battle	1.000	10	9	1	0	0
Brady	.935	15	29	0	2	0
Cameron	.985	29	63	3	1	0
Cappuccio	1.000	38	56	1	0	0
Cotton	.983	63	106	7	2	2
Evans	.992	63	115	6	1	1
Menechino	1.000	1	1	0	0	0
Ordonez	.983	121	278	8	5	0
Wrona	.000	4	0	0	0	0

BIRMINGHAM — Class AA

SOUTHERN LEAGUE

BATTING	AVG	G	AB	R	H	2B	3B	HR	RBI	BB	SO	SB	CS	B	T	HT	WT	DOB	1st Yr	Resides
Alvarez, Clemente	.202	79	242	29	49	10	1	3	23	27	49	0	0	R	R	5-11	180	5-18-68	1987	Anzoategui, Venez.
Bautista, Juan	.239	12	46	6	11	3	0	0	4	3	15	0	1	R	R	6-1	185	6-24-75	1992	San Pedro de Macoris, D.R.
Coolbaugh, Scott	.289	68	235	35	68	18	0	11	50	37	60	0	0	R	R	5-11	195	6-13-66	1987	Seguin, Texas
Cotton, John	.290	33	124	23	36	10	2	7	26	9	33	1	2	L	R	6-0	170	10-30-70	1989	Huntsville, Texas
Evans, Jason	.305	63	223	33	68	16	1	5	25	28	51	2	2	S	R	5-11	187	2-11-71	1992	Chatsworth, Calif.
Fagley, Dan	.368	20	19	1	7	1	0	0	0	0	5	0	0	R	R	5-10	185	12-18-74	1994	Riverton, N.J.
Finn, John	.276	73	246	49	68	15	0	0	27	39	28	13	2	R	R	5-8	168	10-18-67	1989	Oakland, Calif.
Liefer, Jeff	.238	119	474	67	113	24	9	15	71	38	115	2	0	L	R	6-3	195	8-17-74	1996	Upland, Calif.
McKinnon, Sandy	.271	96	332	58	90	20	1	4	31	31	68	13	6	R	R	5-8	175	9-20-73	1993	Nicholls, Ga.
Menechino, Frank	.299	90	318	78	95	28	4	12	60	79	77	7	3	R	R	5-9	175	1-7-71	1993	Staten Island, N.Y.

BATTING	AVG	G	AB	R	H	2B	3B	HR	RBI	BB	SO	SB	CS	B	T	HT	WT	DOB	1st Yr	Resides
Moore, Brandon	.256	125	414	58	106	15	1	1	47	45	48	4	7	R	R	5-11	175	8-23-72	1994	Springville, Ala.
Mouton, Lyle	.182	3	11	1	2	0	0	1	1	1	4	0	0	R	R	6-4	240	5-13-69	1991	Lafayette, La.
Paul, Josh	.296	34	115	18	34	5	0	1	16	12	25	6	2	R	R	6-1	185	5-19-75	1996	Buffalo Grove, Ill.
Pearson, Eddie	.327	95	382	59	125	33	1	5	59	23	50	1	1	S	R	6-3	225	1-31-74	1992	Mobile, Ala.
Polidor, Wil	.269	33	93	11	25	2	1	0	13	1	16	0	2	S	R	6-1	158	9-23-73	1991	Caracas, Venez.
Raven, Luis	.336	117	456	88	153	30	3	30	112	46	126	4	3	R	R	6-4	230	11-19-68	1989	La Guaira, Venez.
Sawkiw, Warren	.286	4	7	1	2	0	0	1	3	0	1	0	0	S	R	5-11	180	1-19-68	1990	Lakeland, Fla.
Simmons, Brian	.262	138	546	108	143	28	12	15	72	88	124	15	12	S	R	6-2	191	9-4-73	1995	McMurray, Pa.
Thomas, Juan	.302	80	311	50	94	16	2	10	55	23	92	1	2	R	R	6-5	240	4-17-72	1991	Ashland, Ky.
Topham, Ryan	.213	17	47	6	10	5	1	0	8	6	15	1	0	L	L	6-3	200	12-17-73	1995	Portage, Mich.
Ventura, Robin	.294	4	17	3	5	1	0	1	2	1	1	0	0	L	R	6-1	185	7-14-67	1989	Santa Maria, Calif.
Wrona, Rick	.252	29	103	11	26	7	1	2	24	3	12	0	0	R	R	6-0	180	12-10-63	1985	Tulsa, Okla.

PITCHING	W	L	ERA	G	GS	CG	SV	IP	H	R	ER	BB	SO	B	T	HT	WT	DOB	1st Yr	Resides
Barcelo, Lorenzo	2	1	4.86	6	6	0	0	33	36	20	18	9	29	R	R	6-4	205	9-10-77	1994	San Pedro de Macoris, D.R.
Beirne, Kevin	6	4	4.92	13	12	0	0	75	76	51	41	41	49	L	R	6-4	210	1-1-74	1995	The Woodlands, Texas
Bere, Jason	0	1	7.71	2	2	0	0	7	8	7	6	2	7	R	R	6-3	185	5-26-71	1990	Wilmington, Mass.
Buteaux, Shane	2	2	4.19	44	0	0	2	73	74	41	34	34	34	R	R	6-3	202	12-28-71	1994	New Iberia, La.
Christman, Scott	2	7	9.05	15	14	0	0	64	100	74	64	38	39	L	L	6-3	190	12-3-71	1993	Vancouver, Wash.
Eyre, Scott	13	5	3.84	22	22	0	0	127	110	61	54	55	127	L	L	6-1	160	5-30-72	1991	Magna, Utah
Hasselhoff, Derek	5	2	2.41	18	0	0	3	34	35	10	9	11	22	R	R	6-2	185	10-10-73	1995	Pasadena, Md.
Heathcott, Mike	3	1	1.83	30	1	0	7	59	50	20	12	25	47	R	R	6-3	180	5-16-69	1991	Chicago, Ill.
Herbert, Russ	13	5	3.63	27	26	3	0	159	136	72	64	80	126	R	R	6-4	200	4-21-72	1994	Mentor, Ohio
Howry, Bobby	0	0	2.84	12	0	0	2	13	16	4	4	3	3	L	R	6-5	215	8-4-73	1994	Glendale, Ariz.
Lundquist, David	0	0	8.78	7	0	0	0	13	26	20	13	5	15	R	R	6-2	200	6-4-73	1993	Carson City, Nev.
Newman, Alan	7	3	2.49	44	0	0	10	72	55	34	20	40	64	L	L	6-6	225	10-2-69	1988	La Habra, Calif.
Nunez, Maximo	0	0	7.64	14	0	0	0	18	19	18	15	13	14	R	R	6-5	165	1-15-73	1991	Villa Mella, D.R.
Olsen, Jason	9	14	4.88	28	27	1	0	160	183	101	87	58	121	R	R	6-4	210	3-16-75	1995	Fairfield, Calif.
Smith, Chuck	2	2	3.16	25	0	0	0	63	63	35	22	27	57	R	R	6-1	175	10-21-69	1991	Cleveland, Ohio
Snyder, John	7	8	4.64	20	20	2	0	114	130	76	59	43	90	R	R	6-3	185	8-16-74	1992	Thousand Oaks, Calif.
Theodile, Robert	2	0	5.49	19	9	0	1	57	72	43	35	35	41	R	R	6-3	190	9-16-72	1992	Jeanerette, La.
Woods, Brian	1	5	6.31	35	0	0	10	46	49	41	32	28	35	R	R	6-6	212	6-7-71	1993	West Caldwell, N.J.
Worrell, Steve	2	2	5.47	18	0	0	1	25	28	16	15	12	21	L	L	6-2	190	11-25-69	1992	Cape May, N.J.

FIELDING

Catcher	PCT	G	PO	A	E	DP	PB
Alvarez	.998	78	500	49	1	5	10
Fagley	.933	20	40	2	3	0	0
Paul	.988	32	221	17	3	0	7
Sawkiw	1.000	1	6	0	0	0	2
Wrona	.987	29	199	28	3	4	4

First Base	PCT	G	PO	A	E	DP
Pearson	.988	89	737	60	10	68
Raven	1.000	4	33	3	0	2
Thomas	.983	47	400	13	7	56

Second Base	PCT	G	PO	A	E	DP
Cotton	.948	24	60	50	6	17
Finn	.982	12	17	37	1	8
Menechino	.972	78	167	211	11	58
Moore	1.000	12	35	27	0	13
Polidor	.941	17	27	37	4	6

Third Base	PCT	G	PO	A	E	DP
Coolbaugh	.960	62	42	124	7	16
Cotton	.556	5	1	4	4	0
Finn	.922	20	9	38	4	4
Menechino	1.000	12	9	26	0	5
Polidor	.696	10	1	15	7	1
Raven	.800	39	19	73	23	4
Ventura	.714	4	2	3	2	0

Shortstop	PCT	G	PO	A	E	DP
Bautista	.912	12	20	32	5	6
Finn	.936	13	17	27	3	4
Moore	.960	112	177	354	22	70
Polidor	.833	8	6	19	5	1

Outfield	PCT	G	PO	A	E	DP
Cotton	1.000	4	5	0	0	0
Evans	.920	61	89	3	8	0
Finn	1.000	15	26	3	0	0
Liefer	.955	106	166	2	8	0
McKinnon	.972	88	170	6	5	1
Mouton	1.000	3	5	0	0	0
Simmons	.985	136	322	7	5	1
Topham	.968	13	30	0	1	0

WINSTON-SALEM — Class A

CAROLINA LEAGUE

BATTING	AVG	G	AB	R	H	2B	3B	HR	RBI	BB	SO	SB	CS	B	T	HT	WT	DOB	1st Yr	Resides
Albert, Rashad	.181	24	72	10	13	1	1	4	9	8	25	3	5	R	R	6-1	165	9-18-75	1994	Fernandina Beach, Fla.
Alvarez, Clemente	.250	2	4	0	1	0	0	0	1	0	2	0	0	R	R	5-11	180	5-18-68	1987	Anzoategui, Venez.
Antczak, Chuck	.143	5	14	0	2	0	0	0	0	0	3	0	0	R	R	6-0	185	10-8-73	1995	Sarasota, Fla.
Baugh, Darren	.225	101	325	41	73	11	4	3	22	27	100	13	3	R	R	6-3	175	9-3-75	1996	San Mateo, Calif.
Boulware, Ben	.256	43	176	24	45	12	2	3	16	7	29	9	8	R	R	5-11	185	2-25-72	1993	Los Gatos, Calif.
Caruso, Mike	.227	28	119	12	27	3	2	0	14	4	8	3	0	S	R	6-1	172	5-27-77	1996	Coral Springs, Fla.
Connacher, Kevin	.288	70	243	32	70	16	2	3	27	28	50	12	8	S	R	5-9	175	4-6-75	1997	Boca Raton, Fla.
Downs, Brian	.260	33	100	13	26	7	1	3	12	8	22	0	0	R	R	6-2	210	4-10-75	1995	Chino, Calif.
Garcia, Luis	.257	130	498	55	128	29	7	13	81	16	93	4	8	R	R	6-3	200	9-22-75	1995	Hermosillo, Mexico
Gomez, Ramon	.277	118	477	78	132	23	12	2	42	42	132	53	21	R	R	6-2	175	10-6-75	1994	San Pedro de Macoris, D.R.
Johnson, Mark	.253	120	375	59	95	27	4	4	46	106	85	4	2	L	R	6-0	185	9-12-75	1994	Warner Robins, Ga.
Lee, Carlos	.317	139	546	81	173	50	4	17	82	36	65	11	5	R	R	6-2	202	6-20-76	1994	Aguadulce, Panama
Manning, Brian	.292	28	106	13	31	6	0	2	12	8	14	1	2	R	R	6-3	200	2-1-75	1996	Hazlet, N.J.
Polidor, Wil	.248	41	149	14	37	7	0	0	11	2	16	6	1	S	R	6-1	158	9-23-73	1991	Caracas, Venez.
Pryor, Pete	.210	124	391	51	82	15	0	8	44	71	97	3	0	L	L	6-4	265	9-3-73	1996	Sacramento, Calif.
Randolph, Ed	.220	72	241	21	53	12	1	4	27	13	68	0	1	S	R	6-2	205	10-17-74	1993	Dallas, Texas
Thomas, Allen	.169	31	77	11	13	4	0	1	11	13	27	1	3	L	L	6-0	190	2-4-74	1996	Morganton, N.C.
Thomas, Juan	.262	45	164	28	43	7	0	13	28	17	61	1	1	R	R	6-5	240	4-17-72	1991	Ashland, Ky.
Topham, Ryan	.238	58	193	26	46	13	2	4	21	24	53	0	2	L	L	6-3	200	12-17-73	1995	Portage, Mich.
Whittaker, Jerry	.271	52	170	24	46	17	2	5	20	14	62	3	1	R	R	6-2	190	11-17-73	1994	Long Beach, Calif.
Wilhelm, Brent	.206	48	155	22	32	8	1	3	26	21	33	1	0	R	R	6-0	185	1-22-73	1995	Independence, Mo.

GAMES BY POSITION: C—Alvarez 2, Antczak 5, Downs 16, Johnson 117, Randolph 8. **1B**—Downs 8, Pryor 99, Randolph 6, J. Thomas 26, Wilhelm 7. **2B**—Baugh 3, Boulware 41, Connacher 68, Polidor 16, Wilhelm 18. **3B**—Baugh 1, Lee 133, Polidor 3, Wilhelm 5. **SS**—Baugh 91, Caruso 26, Polidor 18, Wilhelm 9. **OF**—Albert 22, Baugh 1, Garcia 113, Gomez 113, Manning 22, Randolph 42, A. Thomas 23, Topham 49, Whittaker 46.

PITCHING	W	L	ERA	G	GS	CG	SV	IP	H	R	ER	BB	SO	B	T	HT	WT	DOB	1st Yr	Resides
Ambrose, John	8	13	5.47	27	27	1	0	150	136	102	91	117	137	R	R	6-5	171	11-1-74	1994	St. Petersburg, Fla.
Beirne, Kevin	4	4	3.05	13	13	1	0	83	66	38	28	28	75	L	R	6-4	210	1-1-74	1995	The Woodlands, Texas
Bradford, Chad	3	7	3.95	46	0	0	15	55	51	30	24	25	43	R	R	6-5	205	9-14-74	1996	Jackson, Miss.

PITCHING	W	L	ERA	G	GS	CG	SV	IP	H	R	ER	BB	SO	B	T	HT	WT	DOB	1st Yr	Resides
Chantres, Carlos	9	11	4.70	26	26	2	0	165	152	94	86	71	158	R	R	6-3	175	4-1-76	1994	Miami, Fla.
Dixon, Jim	0	1	4.05	16	0	0	0	33	29	16	15	10	29	R	R	6-3	195	10-7-72	1993	Raton, N.M.
Duncan, Sean	0	1	8.68	6	0	0	0	9	16	12	9	7	9	L	L	6-2	195	6-9-73	1994	Arlington, Texas
Hasselhoff, Derek	3	2	1.56	20	0	0	3	35	22	10	6	15	41	R	R	6-2	185	10-10-73	1995	Pasadena, Md.
Hunt, Jon	0	2	4.35	25	2	0	0	31	32	21	15	14	26	L	L	6-1	190	5-17-74	1995	Ironton, Ohio
Lundquist, David	3	1	6.75	20	6	0	0	48	65	41	36	23	39	R	R	6-2	200	6-4-73	1993	Carson City, Nev.
Mitchell, Kendrick	0	0	4.50	5	0	0	0	6	7	3	3	2	5	R	R	6-4	210	12-6-73	1992	Portland, Ore.
Nunez, Maximo	0	2	1.73	28	0	0	8	52	35	15	10	21	53	R	R	6-5	165	1-15-73	1991	Villa Mella, D.R.
Parque, Jim	7	2	2.77	11	11	0	0	62	29	19	19	23	76	L	L	5-10	166	2-8-76	1997	La Crescenta, Calif.
Roberts, Mark	5	9	4.04	14	14	3	0	91	78	48	41	45	64	R	R	6-2	190	9-29-75	1996	Zephyrhills, Fla.
Ruiz, Rafael	0	1	8.31	10	0	0	0	9	16	10	8	10	9	L	L	6-0	170	2-17-75	1992	Caracas, Venez.
Schmack, Brian	2	5	2.75	42	0	0	6	75	65	32	23	36	71	R	R	6-2	195	12-7-73	1996	Barrington, Ill.
Secoda, Jason	7	4	4.14	29	15	1	2	120	118	67	55	57	85	R	R	6-1	195	9-2-74	1995	Fullerton, Calif.
Theodile, Robert	7	3	2.94	13	12	0	0	83	66	34	27	33	75	R	R	6-3	190	9-16-72	1992	Jeanerette, La.
Vining, Ken	2	2	2.86	5	5	0	0	35	36	17	11	11	38	L	L	5-11	180	12-5-74	1996	Hopkins, S.C.
Virchis, Adam	3	7	4.78	14	9	1	0	58	62	44	31	19	42	R	R	6-3	180	10-15-73	1995	Del Mar, Calif.

HICKORY — Class A

SOUTH ATLANTIC LEAGUE

BATTING	AVG	G	AB	R	H	2B	3B	HR	RBI	BB	SO	SB	CS	B	T	HT	WT	DOB	1st Yr	Resides
Antczak, Chuck	1.000	1	1	0	1	0	0	0	1	0	0	0	0	R	R	6-0	185	10-8-73	1995	Sarasota, Fla.
Christensen, McKay	.280	127	503	95	141	12	12	5	47	52	61	28	20	L	L	5-11	178	8-14-75	1995	Clovis, Calif.
Crede, Joe	.271	113	402	45	109	25	0	5	62	24	83	3	1	R	R	6-3	185	4-26-78	1996	Westphalia, Mo.
Dellaero, Jason	.277	55	191	37	53	10	3	6	29	17	49	3	1	S	R	6-2	195	12-17-76	1997	Bayonet Point, Fla.
Downs, Brian	.232	25	82	8	19	4	0	4	7	3	22	0	0	R	R	6-2	210	4-10-75	1995	Chino, Calif.
Fagley, Dan	.200	9	20	4	4	2	0	0	2	4	9	0	0	R	R	5-10	185	12-18-74	1994	Riverton, N.J.
Fauske, Josh	.235	98	344	56	81	24	0	15	60	38	76	1	0	R	R	6-4	230	3-16-74	1995	Mercer Island, Wash.
Frias, Ovidio	.231	33	108	10	25	3	1	0	11	6	20	1	2	R	R	5-11	165	3-19-77	1995	Santo Domingo, D.R.
Gonzalez, Manuel	.275	116	469	70	129	21	2	11	54	28	78	31	12	S	R	6-2	192	5-30-76	1994	Santo Domingo, D.R.
Heintz, Chris	.284	107	388	57	110	28	1	2	54	28	57	1	3	R	R	6-1	200	8-6-74	1996	Clearwater, Fla.
Hollins, Darontaye	.235	42	115	22	27	9	0	4	13	15	37	3	1	R	R	6-0	200	9-6-74	1995	Roseville, Calif.
Inglin, Jeff	.334	135	536	100	179	34	6	16	102	49	87	31	8	R	R	5-11	185	10-8-75	1996	Petaluma, Calif.
Klee, Chuck	.270	119	400	55	108	18	3	1	48	31	78	5	8	R	R	6-3	175	5-15-77	1995	Lighthouse Point, Fla.
Olson, Dan	.286	98	350	59	100	31	3	9	47	36	120	4	1	L	L	6-2	215	4-14-75	1996	Cape May, N.J.
Rodriguez, Liu	.289	129	450	72	130	21	6	1	62	65	56	12	13	S	R	5-9	170	11-5-76	1995	Caracas, Venez.
Sheppard, Greg	.307	102	342	54	105	27	2	12	62	46	81	4	2	R	R	6-0	190	3-1-75	1996	Palmdale, Calif.
Solano, Angel	.095	11	21	0	2	1	0	0	3	0	7	0	0	R	R	5-11	160	5-9-76	1995	Villa Magdella, D.R.
Thomas, Allen	.082	27	49	4	4	2	0	0	2	4	19	0	1	L	L	6-0	190	2-4-74	1996	Morganton, N.C.

GAMES BY POSITION: C—Antczak 1, Downs 25, Fagley 7, Fauske 78, Heintz 43, Sheppard 6. **1B**—Heintz 69, Klee 8, Olson 5, Sheppard 68. **2B**—Frias 6, Klee 11, Rodriguez 126. **3B**—Crede 112, Frias 20, Klee 14. **SS**—Dellaero 55, Frias 7, Klee 80, Rodriguez 2, Solano 2. **OF**—Christensen 124, Frias 1, Gonzalez 114, Hollins 27, Inglin 88, Olson 63, Sheppard 4, Thomas 20.

PITCHING	W	L	ERA	G	GS	CG	SV	IP	H	R	ER	BB	SO	B	T	HT	WT	DOB	1st Yr	Resides
Bales, Joe	0	0	6.48	11	0	0	1	25	29	19	18	16	28	R	R	6-5	175	9-13-74	1993	Reno, Nev.
Bere, Jason	0	0	6.00	1	1	0	0	3	4	2	2	0	2	R	R	6-3	185	5-26-71	1990	Wilmington, Mass.
Biddle, Rocky	0	1	4.64	13	0	0	1	21	22	18	11	10	25	R	R	6-3	230	5-21-76	1997	Arcadia, Calif.
Buckman, Tom	5	8	5.69	24	19	1	0	112	140	83	71	29	64	R	R	6-6	200	6-28-74	1995	Pembroke Pines, Fla.
Cardona, Steve	4	5	4.33	32	0	0	1	60	62	41	29	16	40	R	R	6-2	190	2-18-74	1996	Stockton, Calif.
Dixon, Jim	1	3	3.63	16	0	0	6	22	17	12	9	7	22	R	R	6-3	195	10-7-72	1993	Raton, N.M.
Farley, Joe	14	6	4.30	28	27	3	0	174	190	94	83	48	94	L	L	6-3	185	9-12-74	1996	Montoursville, Pa.
Garcia, Ariel	0	1	13.50	1	1	0	0	3	6	5	4	2	0	R	R	6-0	158	10-3-75	1993	Panama City, Panama
Hunt, Jon	2	3	4.21	10	9	0	0	47	65	33	22	23	28	L	L	6-1	190	5-17-74	1995	Ironton, Ohio
Iglesias, Mario	8	4	3.41	36	0	0	10	69	64	29	26	26	64	R	R	6-3	195	6-2-74	1996	Castro Valley, Calif.
Irvine, Kirk	3	3	3.39	29	5	0	0	64	80	34	24	18	51	R	R	6-0	185	1-27-75	1996	Chino Hills, Calif.
Kraus, Tim	0	2	4.99	15	0	0	0	31	37	22	17	13	29	L	R	6-1	190	12-26-72	1995	Paoli, Pa.
Lakman, Jason	10	9	3.90	27	27	3	0	155	139	82	67	70	168	R	R	6-4	220	10-17-76	1995	Woodinville, Wash.
Musachio, John	1	0	3.66	11	0	0	1	20	21	8	8	4	19	L	L	6-1	205	12-28-73	1997	La Grange, Ill.
Myette, Aaron	3	1	1.14	5	5	0	0	32	19	6	4	11	27	R	R	6-4	195	9-26-77	1997	Gig Harbor, Wash.
Nichols, James	12	6	4.14	28	27	1	0	159	161	85	73	49	112	R	R	6-4	215	1-22-76	1995	Bear, Del.
Pena, Jesus	5	3	2.22	43	0	0	8	65	55	24	16	19	57	L	L	6-0	170	3-8-75	1993	Santo Domingo, D.R.
Roberts, Mark	0	2	3.68	4	4	0	0	22	23	12	9	9	14	R	R	6-2	190	9-29-75	1996	Zephyrhills, Fla.
Scott, Brian	6	3	2.16	13	13	1	0	83	57	26	20	23	69	R	R	6-3	190	4-29-76	1997	Ramona, Calif.
Tucker, Julien	0	0	3.68	4	0	0	0	7	11	7	3	2	7	L	R	6-7	200	4-19-73	1993	Chateauguay, Quebec
Virchis, Adam	2	3	3.86	15	2	0	1	44	42	20	19	11	34	R	R	6-3	180	10-15-73	1995	Del Mar, Calif.
Whitley, Curtis	0	1	3.65	9	0	0	0	12	11	7	5	5	8	L	L	6-5	240	1-9-74	1997	Goldsboro, N.C.

BRISTOL — Rookie

APPALACHIAN LEAGUE

BATTING	AVG	G	AB	R	H	2B	3B	HR	RBI	BB	SO	SB	CS	B	T	HT	WT	DOB	1st Yr	Resides
Albert, Rashad	.235	4	17	2	4	0	0	1	2	1	7	2	0	R	R	6-1	165	9-18-75	1994	Fernandina Beach, Fla.
Berger, Matt	.289	66	232	51	67	11	1	18	56	40	72	1	0	R	R	6-1	195	10-2-74	1997	Fort Mitchell, Ky.
Caradonna, Brett	.313	22	80	16	25	3	0	1	12	13	16	3	2	L	R	6-1	185	12-3-78	1997	San Diego, Calif.
Fennell, Jason	.284	48	190	39	54	9	0	5	36	18	38	6	3	S	R	6-3	205	11-15-77	1996	Butler, Pa.
Frias, Ovidio	.299	35	117	15	35	7	0	1	20	7	12	3	2	R	R	5-11	165	3-19-77	1995	Santo Domingo, D.R.
Gonzalez, Jose	.306	24	85	10	26	5	1	0	8	8	19	1	1	R	R	5-10	170	9-24-77	1996	Barcelona, Venez.
Hollins, Darontaye	.240	54	196	42	47	10	1	3	18	20	47	21	7	R	R	6-0	200	9-6-74	1995	Roseville, Calif.
Lopes, Omar	.276	49	170	29	47	4	0	3	23	24	22	7	3	R	R	6-0	180	1-3-77	1994	Valencia, Venez.
Lutz, Manuel	.325	65	249	50	81	11	3	13	61	19	71	6	3	L	R	6-2	230	6-14-76	1995	Spring Valley, Calif.
Newkirk, J.J.	.298	48	188	46	56	14	3	7	24	28	29	6	4	L	L	5-10	185	8-1-75	1997	Kinston, N.C.
Nova, Fernando	.266	42	143	29	38	9	1	2	23	14	35	8	3	R	R	6-0	168	2-9-76	1995	San Pedro de Macoris, D.R.
Rapp, Travis	.185	26	81	9	15	4	0	2	12	9	33	0	1	R	R	6-2	210	1-25-75	1997	Sebring, Fla.

BATTING	AVG	G	AB	R	H	2B	3B	HR	RBI	BB	SO	SB	CS	B	T	HT	WT	DOB	1st Yr	Resides
Romero, Marty	.500	2	2	0	1	0	0	0	0	1	1	0	0	L	R	6-1	180	9-13-76	1994	Cape Coral, Fla.
Sutton, Joe	.332	56	190	46	63	18	2	11	43	35	51	7	0	R	R	6-3	225	10-17-74	1996	West Union, W.Va.
Terrell, Jim	.216	47	176	30	38	4	1	1	22	17	40	5	0	L	R	6-2	175	9-8-77	1996	Blue Springs, Mo.
Wallace, Derek	.242	50	186	26	45	12	2	7	29	11	65	8	2	R	R	6-3	195	9-24-76	1996	Monroe, La.

GAMES BY POSITION: C—Rapp 26, Romero 2, Sutton 45. **1B**—Berger 7, Fennell 10, Lutz 52. **2B**—Frias 8, Gonzalez 9, Lopes 8, Terrell 47. **3B**—Berger 59, Frias 6, Gonzalez 2, Lopes 7. **SS**—Frias 21, Gonzalez 14, Lopes 34. **OF**—Albert 4, Caradonna 18, Fennell 3, Hollins 52, Newkirk 45, Nova 40, Wallace 46.

PITCHING	W	L	ERA	G	GS	CG	SV	IP	H	R	ER	BB	SO	B	T	HT	WT	DOB	1st Yr	Resides
Bales, Joe	8	3	4.12	14	14	1	0	83	73	50	38	49	86	R	R	6-5	175	9-13-74	1993	Reno, Nev.
Currens, Tim	0	4	4.88	20	0	0	1	28	29	21	15	13	23	L	R	6-4	195	10-2-75	1997	Bowling Green, Ky.
Daneker, Pat	3	6	6.50	12	12	0	0	64	83	55	46	20	53	R	R	6-3	195	1-14-76	1997	Williamsport, Pa.
Felix, Miguel	2	5	7.51	11	10	0	0	50	78	52	42	22	38	R	R	6-1	155	12-30-76	1995	San Pedro de Macoris, D.R.
Gray, Jason	0	3	18.29	4	3	0	0	10	22	21	21	8	11	R	R	6-2	185	4-28-77	1995	North Lauderdale, Fla.
Hodges, Reid	0	2	5.13	27	0	0	2	26	30	16	15	19	32	R	R	6-3	215	12-25-74	1996	Stone Mountain, Ga.
Izquierdo, Hansel	2	2	4.30	9	2	0	0	23	25	14	11	8	24	R	R	6-2	200	1-2-77	1995	Miami, Fla.
Jacobson, Andrew	1	2	6.98	14	7	0	0	49	57	51	38	46	47	R	R	6-8	210	1-25-76	1997	McRain, Mich.
Kvasnicka, Jay	1	2	6.08	4	4	0	0	24	22	18	16	12	19	R	R	6-4	180	7-21-76	1997	Chicago Heights, Ill.
Lopez, Jose	3	1	7.01	20	0	0	0	44	62	42	34	18	33	S	R	6-2	185	4-16-76	1996	Ridgewood, N.Y.
Meyer, Jake	1	1	2.25	17	0	0	5	20	15	7	5	7	25	R	R	6-1	195	1-7-75	1997	San Diego, Calif.
Myette, Aaron	4	3	3.61	9	8	1	0	47	39	28	19	20	50	R	R	6-4	195	9-26-77	1997	Gig Harbor, Wash.
Reimers, Tom	3	2	6.38	12	4	0	0	42	47	35	30	28	47	R	R	6-2	185	5-27-75	1996	Santa Ana, Calif.
Rodgers, Marcus	0	1	9.43	6	4	0	0	21	35	26	22	16	14	R	R	6-3	225	11-7-76	1996	Saraland, Ala.
Ruiz, Rafael	2	1	4.26	23	0	0	1	38	34	21	18	18	56	L	L	6-0	170	2-17-75	1992	Caracas, Venez.
Williams, Thomas	0	0	13.50	4	0	0	0	5	4	8	7	8	2	R	R	6-1	220	1-30-76	1997	Lake Charles, La.

SARASOTA — Rookie

GULF COAST LEAGUE

BATTING	AVG	G	AB	R	H	2B	3B	HR	RBI	BB	SO	SB	CS	B	T	HT	WT	DOB	1st Yr	Resides
Aceves, Jonathan	.184	30	76	9	14	4	0	0	4	9	18	0	0	R	R	6-2	187	3-7-78	1997	Sonora, Mexico
Borges, Elio	.288	28	80	9	23	6	1	0	15	12	14	4	0	S	R	6-0	180	10-7-77	1997	Hialeah, Fla.
Caradonna, Brett	.276	36	123	15	34	5	3	2	16	11	21	3	0	L	R	6-1	185	12-3-78	1997	San Diego, Calif.
Cochran, Ed	.116	28	69	12	8	1	0	0	5	4	14	2	0	R	R	6-2	185	1-3-78	1996	Arroyo, P.R.
Cordero, Ellery	.259	29	81	12	21	5	1	1	6	5	18	2	1	R	R	5-11	165	5-6-79	1997	Caracas, Venez.
DeArmas, Francisco	.224	17	49	5	11	3	1	0	2	4	12	0	0	R	R	6-1	180	2-11-78	1997	Miami, Fla.
Delgado, Chris	.275	51	189	24	52	12	1	0	19	7	40	0	1	R	R	6-3	215	10-8-77	1997	Pembroke Pines, Fla.
Dellaero, Jason	.200	5	15	1	3	2	0	0	1	1	2	0	0	S	R	6-2	195	12-17-76	1997	Bayonet Point, Fla.
Durham, Chad	.328	49	189	24	62	5	3	1	17	12	17	22	3	R	R	5-8	175	6-23-78	1997	Charlotte, N.C.
Garza, Rolando	.248	36	109	2	27	5	1	0	10	7	22	2	1	R	R	6-3	180	12-14-79	1997	Coachella, Calif.
Hill, Michael	.142	46	134	16	19	3	1	1	15	21	47	5	2	R	R	6-1	186	4-14-75	1997	East Bridgewater, Mass.
Hyde, Brandon	.195	28	77	10	15	4	0	1	14	11	24	0	0	R	R	6-3	210	10-3-73	1997	Santa Rosa, Calif.
Iglesias, Rigoberto	.220	48	159	20	35	8	4	2	20	19	24	2	2	S	R	5-11	180	7-28-75	1997	Miami, Fla.
Medrano, Ricardo	.231	29	91	10	21	4	1	0	8	8	21	2	1	S	R	5-9	165	4-23-78	1996	Maracay, Venez.
Mounts, J.R.	.241	41	145	18	35	5	0	5	22	15	54	9	4	S	R	6-1	190	11-13-78	1997	Key West, Fla.
Paul, Josh	.429	5	14	3	6	0	1	0	0	1	3	1	0	R	R	6-1	185	5-19-75	1996	Buffalo Grove, Ill.
Ramon, Ricardo	.265	38	132	10	35	2	0	0	5	10	16	4	5	L	L	6-0	170	2-2-78	1997	Hialeah, Fla.
Roman, Junior	.250	38	132	18	33	1	0	0	10	6	23	8	4	S	R	5-11	160	8-30-80	1997	Santo Domingo, D.R.
Saenz, Olmedo	1.000	2	1	0	1	1	0	0	0	0	0	0	0	R	R	6-2	185	10-8-70	1990	Chitre Herrera, Panama

GAMES BY POSITION: C—Aceves 27, DeArmas 16, Hyde 21, Paul 5. **1B**—Delgado 51, Hyde 7, Iglesias 5. **2B**—Durham 37, Medrano 24, Roman 1. **3B**—Borges 22, Cordero 26, Garza 11, Medrano 6. **SS**—Borges 3, Dellaero 4, Garza 20, Roman 35. **OF**—Caradonna 31, Cochran 7, Durham 12, Hill 44, Iglesias 42, Mounts 22, Ramon 26, Roman 1.

PITCHING	W	L	ERA	G	GS	CG	SV	IP	H	R	ER	BB	SO	B	T	HT	WT	DOB	1st Yr	Resides
Bere, Jason	0	0	0.00	2	2	0	0	5	2	0	0	0	5	R	R	6-3	185	5-26-71	1990	Wilmington, Mass.
Connolly, Sean	2	1	2.86	15	0	0	3	22	21	12	7	15	17	R	R	6-2	195	1-4-74	1996	East Sandwich, Mass.
Desrosiers, Erik	0	1	3.32	7	6	0	0	22	19	8	8	3	18	R	R	6-4	210	9-21-74	1995	Fountain Hills, Ariz.
Felix, Miguel	0	0	1.50	3	2	0	0	12	10	3	2	2	10	R	R	6-1	155	12-30-76	1995	San Pedro de Macoris, D.R.
Figueroa, Juan	1	4	3.36	11	10	0	0	64	66	31	24	14	43	R	R	6-3	150	6-24-79	1996	Santo Domingo, D.R.
Forti, Gene	4	1	2.91	11	8	0	0	53	42	21	17	30	44	L	L	6-2	210	9-2-77	1996	El Paso, Texas
Frias, Yovany	0	0	3.65	7	0	0	0	12	14	12	5	7	2	R	R	6-3	165	11-15-77	1994	San Pedro de Macoris, D.R.
Garcia, Ariel	2	1	2.57	10	1	0	2	28	23	11	8	11	28	R	R	6-0	158	10-3-75	1993	Panama City, Panama
Gray, Jason	3	2	4.66	10	5	0	0	37	43	20	19	12	34	R	R	6-2	185	4-28-77	1995	North Lauderdale, Fla.
Izquierdo, Hansel	0	0	3.48	5	0	0	0	10	9	4	4	8	15	R	R	6-2	200	1-2-77	1995	Miami, Fla.
Jones, Stacy	0	0	0.00	2	1	0	1	3	2	0	0	0	4	R	R	6-6	225	5-26-67	1988	Attalla, Ala.
Kvasnicka, Jay	2	3	5.45	8	7	0	1	36	43	24	22	6	44	R	R	6-4	180	7-21-76	1997	Chicago Heights, Ill.
Mendoza, Geronimo	2	7	3.67	12	8	0	0	54	51	32	22	28	41	R	R	6-4	160	1-23-78	1995	Santo Domingo, D.R.
Mitchell, Kendrick	0	0	0.00	4	0	0	0	9	3	0	0	6	12	R	R	6-4	210	12-6-73	1992	Portland, Ore.
Perez, Elvis	3	7	4.19	12	8	1	0	58	57	41	27	44	50	L	L	6-2	185	2-9-78	1996	Hialeah, Fla.
Santana, Fausto	3	3	4.05	13	0	0	2	20	16	10	9	9	10	R	R	5-11	175	2-6-78	1996	Puerto Plata, D.R.
Stinson, Kevin	1	2	6.59	10	0	0	0	14	21	10	10	8	12	R	R	6-2	190	1-31-76	1996	Kirkland, Wash.
Tellez, Eloy	0	0	2.25	2	2	0	0	4	2	2	1	3	2	L	R	6-3	215	1-29-76	1996	El Paso, Texas
Whitley, Curtis	1	1	6.23	3	0	0	0	4	7	4	3	2	6	L	L	6-5	240	1-9-74	1997	Goldsboro, N.C.
Williams, Tom	2	1	3.92	11	0	0	2	21	22	16	9	9	15	R	R	6-1	220	1-30-76	1997	Lake Charles, La.

Chicago CUBS

Manager: Jim Riggleman.

1997 Record: 68-94, .420 (5th, NL Central)

BATTING	AVG	G	AB	R	H	2B	3B	HR	RBI	BB	SO	SB	CS	B	T	HT	WT	DOB	1st Yr	Resides
Alexander, Manny	.293	33	99	11	29	3	1	1	7	8	16	2	1	R	R	5-10	165	3-20-71	1988	San Pedro de Macoris, D.R.
2-team (54 New York)	.266	87	248	37	66	12	4	3	22	17	54	13	1							
Brown, Brant	.234	46	137	15	32	7	1	5	15	7	28	2	1	L	L	6-3	220	6-22-71	1992	Porterville, Calif.
Cairo, Miguel	.241	16	29	7	7	1	0	0	1	2	3	0	0	R	R	6-1	160	5-4-74	1991	Anaco, Venez.
Clark, Dave	.301	102	143	19	43	8	0	5	32	19	34	1	0	L	R	6-2	210	9-3-62	1983	Tupelo, Miss.
Dunston, Shawon	.284	114	419	57	119	18	4	9	41	8	64	29	7	R	R	6-1	175	3-21-63	1982	Corona, N.Y.
Glanville, Doug	.300	146	474	79	142	22	5	4	35	24	46	19	11	R	R	6-2	170	8-25-70	1991	Teaneck, N.J.
Grace, Mark	.319	151	555	87	177	32	5	13	78	88	45	2	4	L	L	6-2	190	6-28-64	1986	Pacific Palisades, Calif.
Hansen, Dave	.311	90	151	19	47	8	2	3	21	31	32	1	2	L	R	6-0	195	11-24-68	1986	Laguna Hills, Calif.
Hernandez, Jose	.273	121	183	33	50	8	5	7	26	14	42	2	5	R	R	6-0	180	7-14-69	1987	Vega Alta, P.R.
Houston, Tyler	.260	72	196	15	51	10	0	2	28	9	35	1	0	L	R	6-2	210	1-17-71	1989	Las Vegas, Nev.
Hubbard, Mike	.203	29	64	4	13	0	0	1	2	2	21	0	0	R	R	6-1	180	2-16-71	1992	Madison Heights, Va.
Jennings, Robin	.167	9	18	1	3	1	0	0	2	0	2	0	0	L	L	6-2	200	4-11-72	1992	Miami, Fla.
Johnson, Lance	.303	39	145	17	44	6	2	4	15	9	10	5	2	L	L	5-11	160	7-6-63	1984	Mobile, Ala.
2-team (72 New York)	.307	111	410	60	126	16	8	5	39	42	31	20	12							
Kieschnick, Brooks	.200	39	90	9	18	2	0	4	12	12	21	1	0	L	R	6-4	228	6-6-72	1993	Caldwell, Texas
Lowery, Terrell	.286	9	14	2	4	0	0	0	0	3	3	1	0	R	R	6-3	175	10-25-70	1991	Oakland, Calif.
McRae, Brian	.240	108	417	63	100	27	5	6	28	52	62	14	6	S	R	6-0	185	8-27-67	1985	Bradenton, Fla.
Orie, Kevin	.275	114	364	40	100	23	5	8	44	39	57	2	2	R	R	6-4	215	9-1-72	1993	Pittsburgh, Pa.
Sanchez, Rey	.249	97	205	14	51	9	0	1	12	11	26	4	2	R	R	5-10	180	10-5-67	1986	Charlotte Harbor, Fla.
Sandberg, Ryne	.264	135	447	54	118	26	0	12	64	28	94	7	4	R	R	6-1	175	9-18-59	1978	Phoenix, Ariz.
Servais, Scott	.260	122	385	36	100	21	0	6	45	24	56	0	1	R	R	6-2	195	6-4-67	1989	Coon Valley, Wis.
Sosa, Sammy	.251	162	642	90	161	31	4	36	119	45	174	22	12	R	R	6-0	165	11-12-68	1986	San Pedro de Macoris, D.R.

PITCHING	W	L	ERA	G	GS	CG	SV	IP	H	R	ER	BB	SO	B	T	HT	WT	DOB	1st Yr	Resides
Adams, Terry	2	9	4.62	74	0	0	18	74	91	43	38	40	64	R	R	6-3	180	3-6-73	1991	Semmes, Ala.
Batista, Miguel	0	5	5.70	11	6	0	0	36	36	24	23	24	27	R	R	6-0	160	2-19-71	1988	San Pedro de Macoris, D.R.
Bottenfield, Kent	2	3	3.86	64	0	0	2	84	82	39	36	35	74	R	R	6-2	225	11-14-68	1986	Royal Palm Beach, Fla.
Casian, Larry	0	1	7.45	12	0	0	0	10	16	9	8	2	7	R	L	6-0	173	10-28-65	1987	Salem, Ore.
Castillo, Frank	6	9	5.42	20	19	0	0	98	113	64	59	44	67	R	R	6-1	185	4-1-69	1987	El Paso, Texas
Clark, Mark	6	1	2.86	9	9	2	0	63	55	22	20	12	51	R	R	6-5	225	5-12-68	1988	Bath, Ill.
2-team (23 New York)	14	8	3.82	32	31	3	0	205	213	96	87	59	123							
Foster, Kevin	10	7	4.61	26	25	1	0	146	141	79	75	66	118	R	R	6-1	160	1-13-69	1988	Evanston, Ill.
Gonzalez, Jeremi	11	9	4.25	23	23	1	0	144	126	73	68	69	93	R	R	6-1	180	1-8-75	1992	Maracaibo, Venez.
Morel, Ramon	0	0	4.91	3	0	0	0	4	3	2	2	3	3	R	R	6-2	170	8-15-74	1991	Villa Gonzalez, D.R.
2-team (5 Pittsburgh)	0	0	4.76	8	0	0	0	11	14	6	6	7	7							
Mulholland, Terry	6	12	4.07	25	25	1	0	157	162	79	71	45	74	R	L	6-3	200	3-9-63	1984	Paradise Valley, Ariz.
Myers, Rodney	0	0	6.00	5	1	0	0	9	12	6	6	7	6	R	R	6-1	190	6-26-69	1990	Rockford, Ill.
Patterson, Bob	1	6	3.34	76	0	0	0	59	47	23	22	10	58	R	L	6-2	185	5-16-59	1982	Hickory, N.C.
Pisciotta, Marc	3	1	3.18	24	0	0	0	28	20	10	10	16	21	R	R	6-5	240	8-7-70	1991	Charlotte, N.C.
Rojas, Mel	0	4	4.42	54	0	0	13	59	54	30	29	30	61	R	R	5-11	165	12-10-66	1986	Haina, D.R.
Stevens, Dave	0	2	9.64	10	0	0	0	9	13	11	10	9	13	R	R	6-3	210	3-4-70	1990	La Habra, Calif.
Swartzbaugh, Dave	0	1	9.00	2	2	0	0	8	12	8	8	7	4	R	R	6-2	195	2-11-68	1989	Middletown, Ohio
Tapani, Kevin	9	3	3.39	13	13	1	0	85	77	33	32	23	55	R	R	6-0	175	2-18-64	1986	Eden Prairie, Minn.
Tatis, Ramon	1	1	5.34	56	0	0	0	56	66	36	33	29	33	L	L	6-2	180	1-5-73	1991	Guayubin, D.R.
Telemaco, Amaury	0	3	6.16	10	5	0	0	38	47	26	26	11	29	R	R	6-3	180	1-19-74	1991	La Romana, D.R.
Trachsel, Steve	8	12	4.51	34	34	0	0	201	225	110	101	69	160	R	R	6-3	185	10-31-70	1991	Yorba Linda, Calif.
Wendell, Turk	3	5	4.20	52	0	0	4	60	53	32	28	39	54	S	R	6-2	175	5-19-67	1988	Dalton, Mass.

FIELDING

Catcher	PCT	G	PO	A	E	DP	PB
Houston	.986	41	263	16	4	1	6
Hubbard	.992	20	120	8	1	0	2
Servais	.990	118	735	73	8	9	8

First Base	PCT	G	PO	A	E	DP
Brown	.976	12	78	4	2	7
Grace	.995	148	1202	120	6	93
Hansen	.955	4	19	2	1	4
Hernandez	.857	1	6	0	1	0
Houston	1.000	2	8	2	0	1
Servais	1.000	1	1	0	0	0

Second Base	PCT	G	PO	A	E	DP
Alexander	1.000	4	8	8	0	1
Cairo	1.000	9	15	15	0	5
Hansen	.000	1	0	0	0	0
Hernandez	.969	20	31	31	2	3
Houston	1.000	1	1	1	0	0
Sanchez	.992	32	51	72	1	16
Sandberg	.984	126	204	297	8	58

Third Base	PCT	G	PO	A	E	DP
Alexander	1.000	1	0	1	0	0
Hansen	.922	51	26	45	6	5
Hernandez	.922	47	19	28	4	3
Houston	.963	12	8	18	1	2
Hubbard	.000	1	0	0	0	0
Orie	.971	112	91	212	9	15
Sanchez	.000	1	0	0	0	0

Shortstop	PCT	G	PO	A	E	DP
Alexander	.942	28	30	83	7	11
Cairo	1.000	2	1	3	0	2
Dunston	.970	108	163	227	12	46
Hernandez	.981	21	19	32	1	8
Houston	.000	1	0	0	0	0
Orie	1.000	3	0	1	0	0
Sanchez	.964	63	49	85	5	12

Outfield	PCT	G	PO	A	E	DP
Brown	1.000	27	43	3	0	0
D. Clark	.953	25	39	2	2	0
Glanville	.989	138	247	12	3	3
Hernandez	1.000	6	4	0	0	0
Jennings	1.000	5	5	0	0	0
Johnson	.963	39	79	0	3	0
Kieschnick	.952	27	39	1	2	0
Lowery	1.000	6	7	2	0	1
McRae	.996	107	242	3	1	2
Sosa	.977	161	325	16	8	1

LARRY GOREN

Mark Grace

FARM SYSTEM

Director of Player Development: David Wilder

Class	Farm Team	League	W	L	Pct.	Finish*	Manager	First Yr
AAA	Iowa Cubs	American Assoc.	74	69	.517	3rd (8)	Tim Johnson	1981
AA	Orlando (Fla.) Rays	Southern	63	75	.457	9th (10)	Dave Trembley	1993
#A	Daytona (Fla.) Cubs	Florida State	65	73	.471	10th (14)	Steve Roadcap	1993
A	Rockford (Ill.) Cubbies	Midwest	66	66	.500	9th (14)	Ruben Amaro Sr.	1995
A	Williamsport (Pa.) Cubs	New York-Penn	29	46	.387	12th (14)	Bob Ralston	1994
R	Mesa (Ariz.) Cubs	Arizona	34	20	.630	1st (6)	Terry Kennedy	1997

*Finish in overall standings (No. of teams in league) #Advanced level

ORGANIZATION LEADERS

MAJOR LEAGUERS

BATTING

*AVG	Mark Grace	.319
R	Sammy Sosa	90
H	Mark Grace	177
TB	Sammy Sosa	308
2B	Mark Grace	32
3B	Four tied at	5
HR	Sammy Sosa	36
RBI	Sammy Sosa	119
BB	Mark Grace	88
SO	Sammy Sosa	174
SB	Sammy Sosa	22

PITCHING

W	Jeremi Gonzalez	11
L	Two tied at	12
#ERA	Kevin Tapani	3.39
G	Bob Patterson	76
CG	Mark Clark	2
SV	Terry Adams	18
IP	Steve Trachsel	201
BB	Two tied at	69
SO	Steve Trachsel	160

GEORGE GOJKOVICH

Sammy Sosa

RODGER WOOD

Courtney Duncan

MINOR LEAGUERS

BATTING

*AVG	Elinton Jasco, Daytona	.335
R	Bo Porter, Orlando/Daytona	91
H	Miguel Cairo, Iowa	159
TB	Bo Porter, Orlando/Daytona	230
2B	Miguel Cairo, Iowa	35
3B	Terry Joseph, Orlando	11
HR	Rod McCall, Iowa/Orlando	26
RBI	Scott Vieira, Daytona	80
BB	Jason Maxwell, Orlando	82
SO	Derrick Bly, Rockford/Williamsport	151
SB	Chad Meyers, Rockford	54

PITCHING

W	Phillip Norton, Orlando/Daytona/Rock.	13
L	Javier Martinez, Daytona/Rockford	13
#ERA	Courtney Duncan, Orlando/Daytona	2.11
G	Justin Speier, Iowa/Orlando	58
CG	Phillip Norton, Orlando/Daytona/Rock.	6
SV	Marc Pisciotta, Iowa	22
IP	Jason Ryan, Daytona	170
BB	Kerry Wood, Iowa/Orlando	131
SO	Kerry Wood, Iowa/Orlando	186

*Minimum 250 At-Bats #Minimum 75 Innings

TOP 10 PROSPECTS

STAN DENNY

Kerry Wood

How the Cubs Top 10 prospects, as judged by Baseball America prior to the 1997 season, fared in 1997:

Player, Pos.	Club (Class)	AVG	AB	R	H	2B	3B	HR	RBI	SB
2. Kevin Orie, 3b	Chicago	.275	364	40	100	23	5	8	44	2
	Iowa (AAA)	.375	32	7	12	4	0	1	8	0
	Orlando (AA)	.385	13	3	5	2	0	2	6	0
3. Pat Cline, c	Iowa (AAA)	.221	95	6	21	2	0	3	10	0
	Orlando (AA)	.255	271	39	69	19	0	7	37	2
6. Quincy Carter, of	Rockford (A)	.211	388	61	82	26	2	2	34	17
7. Brooks Kieschnick, of-1b	Chicago	.200	90	9	18	2	0	4	12	1
	Iowa (AAA)	.258	360	57	93	21	0	21	66	0

Player, Pos.	Club (Class)	W	L	ERA	G	SV	IP	H	BB	SO
1. Kerry Wood, rhp	Iowa (AAA)	4	2	4.68	10	0	58	35	52	80
	Orlando (AA)	6	7	4.50	19	0	94	58	79	106
4. Jeremi Gonzalez, rhp	Chicago	11	9	4.25	23	0	144	126	69	93
	Iowa (AAA)	2	2	3.48	10	0	62	47	21	58
5. Chris Gissell, rhp	Rockford (A)	6	11	4.45	26	0	144	155	62	105
8. Steve Rain, rhp	Iowa (AAA)	7	1	5.89	40	1	44	51	34	50
	Orlando (AA)	1	2	3.07	14	4	15	16	8	11
9. Todd Noel, rhp	Mesa (R)	5	1	1.98	12	1	59	39	30	63
10. Kyle Farnsworth, rhp	Daytona (A)	10	10	4.09	28	0	156	178	47	105

IOWA — Class AAA

AMERICAN ASSOCIATION

BATTING	AVG	G	AB	R	H	2B	3B	HR	RBI	BB	SO	SB	CS	B	T	HT	Wt.	DOB	1st Yr	Resides
Brown, Brant	.301	71	256	51	77	19	3	16	51	31	44	6	6	L	L	6-3	220	6-22-71	1992	Porterville, Calif.
Cairo, Miguel	.279	135	569	82	159	35	4	5	46	24	54	40	15	R	R	6-1	160	5-4-74	1991	Anaco, Venez.
Caraballo, Ramon	.211	49	133	16	28	8	0	4	21	18	25	5	2	S	R	5-7	150	5-23-69	1989	Santo Domingo, D.R.
Cholowsky, Dan	.185	36	65	12	12	2	0	1	4	9	17	2	1	R	R	6-0	195	10-30-70	1991	San Jose, Calif.
Cline, Pat	.221	27	95	6	21	2	0	3	10	10	24	0	1	R	R	6-3	220	10-9-74	1993	Bradenton, Fla.
Dalesandro, Mark	.262	115	405	48	106	14	0	8	48	33	51	0	0	R	R	6-0	185	5-14-68	1990	Chicago, Ill.
Dowler, Dee	.230	42	100	14	23	2	0	2	12	10	16	6	1	R	R	5-9	175	7-23-71	1993	Indianapolis, Ind.
Freeman, Ricky	.169	31	77	7	13	0	0	1	4	8	20	1	0	R	R	6-4	205	2-3-72	1994	Houston, Texas
Houston, Tyler	.217	6	23	0	5	2	0	0	4	0	2	0	0	L	R	6-2	210	1-17-71	1989	Las Vegas, Nev.
Hubbard, Mike	.280	50	186	24	52	15	1	6	26	11	23	2	0	R	R	6-1	180	2-16-71	1992	Madison Heights, Va.
Jennings, Robin	.276	126	464	67	128	25	5	20	71	56	73	5	3	L	L	6-2	200	4-11-72	1992	Miami, Fla.
Kieschnick, Brooks	.258	97	360	57	93	21	0	21	66	36	89	0	2	L	R	6-4	228	6-6-72	1993	Caldwell, Texas
Lisanti, Bob	.364	4	11	2	4	0	0	0	1	2	5	0	0	R	R	5-10	180	5-28-73	1996	Chicago, Ill.
Lowery, Terrell	.301	110	386	69	116	28	3	17	71	65	97	9	8	R	R	6-3	175	10-25-70	1991	Oakland, Calif.
McCall, Rod	.284	49	148	26	42	5	0	14	35	22	53	0	0	L	L	6-7	235	11-4-71	1990	Stanton, Calif.
2-team (36 Buffalo)	.263	85	255	38	67	10	0	20	55	30	90	0	0							
McIntosh, Tim	.259	17	54	9	14	3	0	2	8	3	14	0	0	R	R	5-11	195	3-21-65	1986	Herald, Calif.
Molina, Jose	.333	1	3	0	1	0	0	0	0	1	1	0	0	R	R	6-1	180	6-3-75	1993	Vega Alta, P.R.
Nava, Lipso	.266	109	319	37	85	17	1	9	36	22	53	2	3	R	R	6-2	175	11-28-68	1990	Maracaibo, Venez.
Orie, Kevin	.375	9	32	7	12	4	0	1	8	5	5	0	0	R	R	6-4	215	9-1-72	1993	Pittsburgh, Pa.
Pegues, Steve	.375	6	24	3	9	2	0	0	1	0	3	0	0	R	R	6-2	190	5-21-68	1987	Pontotoc, Miss.
Petersen, Chris	.240	119	391	49	94	16	2	3	33	32	89	1	6	S	R	5-10	160	11-6-70	1992	Southington, Conn.
Valdes, Pedro	.284	125	464	65	132	30	1	14	60	48	67	9	2	L	L	6-1	160	6-29-73	1991	Loiza, P.R.
Williams, Harold	.179	9	28	2	5	2	0	1	2	2	8	0	0	L	R	6-4	200	2-14-71	1993	Garyville, La.
Wilson, Brandon	.258	19	62	4	16	2	0	0	3	2	10	3	2	R	R	6-1	175	2-26-69	1990	Owensboro, Ky.
2-team (68 Indy)	.236	87	242	28	57	5	4	1	17	20	48	8	6							

PITCHING	W	L	ERA	G	GS	CG	SV	IP	H	R	ER	BB	SO	B	T	HT	Wt.	DOB	1st Yr	Resides
Batista, Miguel	9	4	4.20	31	14	2	0	122	117	60	57	38	95	R	R	6-0	160	2-19-71	1988	San Pedro de Macoris, D.R.
Fletcher, Paul	10	6	3.56	54	0	0	0	78	63	32	31	39	67	R	R	6-1	185	1-14-67	1988	Ravenswood, W.Va.
Gonzalez, Jeremi	2	2	3.48	10	10	1	0	62	47	27	24	21	58	R	R	6-1	180	1-8-75	1992	Maracaibo, Venez.
Hart, Jason	0	1	18.00	1	0	0	0	1	1	2	2	2	3	R	R	6-0	195	11-14-71	1994	Round Rock, Texas
Heredia, Gil	4	2	3.86	31	1	0	1	47	54	22	20	9	30	R	R	6-1	190	10-26-65	1987	Tucson, Ariz.
Lyons, Curt	0	2	6.37	8	8	0	0	30	35	23	21	21	26	R	R	6-5	228	10-17-74	1992	Richmond, Ky.
Myers, Rodney	7	8	4.09	24	23	1	0	141	140	76	64	38	79	R	R	6-1	190	6-26-69	1990	Rockford, Ill.
Pisciotta, Marc	6	2	2.36	42	0	0	22	46	29	12	12	23	48	R	R	6-5	240	8-7-70	1991	Charlotte, N.C.
Rain, Steve	7	1	5.89	40	0	0	1	44	51	30	29	34	50	R	R	6-6	225	6-2-75	1993	Walnut, Calif.
Ratliff, Jon	1	3	5.57	9	4	0	1	32	30	20	20	7	25	R	R	6-5	200	12-22-71	1993	Clay, N.Y.
Russell, LaGrande	0	3	12.54	7	3	0	0	19	36	26	26	8	3	R	R	6-2	175	8-20-70	1990	Hallsboro, N.C.
Sauveur, Rich	1	3	3.38	39	1	0	2	45	46	19	17	21	37	L	L	6-4	170	11-23-63	1983	Falls Church, Va.
Speier, Justin	2	0	0.00	8	0	0	1	12	5	0	0	1	9	R	R	6-4	195	11-6-73	1995	Scottsdale, Ariz.
Steenstra, Kennie	5	10	3.92	25	25	4	0	161	161	85	70	41	111	R	R	6-5	220	10-13-70	1992	Lynchburg, Mo.
Stevens, Dave	1	1	4.70	6	0	0	1	8	8	4	4	5	8	R	R	6-3	210	3-4-70	1990	La Habra, Calif.
Swartzbaugh, Dave	8	7	2.82	24	20	1	1	134	129	55	42	48	97	R	R	6-2	195	2-11-68	1989	Middletown, Ohio
Tapani, Kevin	0	1	4.00	1	1	1	0	9	5	4	4	1	4	R	R	6-0	175	2-18-64	1986	Eden Prairie, Minn.
Telemaco, Amaury	5	9	4.51	18	18	3	0	114	121	70	57	38	75	R	R	6-3	180	1-19-74	1991	La Romana, D.R.
VanRyn, Ben	2	2	4.59	51	5	0	3	80	88	43	41	25	64	L	L	6-5	195	8-9-71	1990	Kendallville, Ind.
Wood, Kerry	4	2	4.68	10	10	0	0	58	35	35	30	52	80	R	R	6-5	190	6-16-77	1995	Irving, Texas

FIELDING

Catcher	PCT	G	PO	A	E	DP	PB
Cholowsky	.980	14	92	7	2	1	0
Cline	.990	27	188	11	2	0	1
Dalesandro	.991	51	305	19	3	2	3
Houston	1.000	1	4	1	0	0	0
Hubbard	.994	46	310	22	2	6	4
Lisanti	1.000	4	22	2	0	1	2
McIntosh	.969	8	57	6	2	1	1
Molina	1.000	1	3	0	0	0	0

First Base	PCT	G	PO	A	E	DP
Brown	.979	17	128	13	3	11
Dalesandro	.994	19	140	13	1	16
Freeman	1.000	23	192	13	0	18
Kieschnick	.991	63	531	38	5	66
McCall	.995	21	176	8	1	14
McIntosh	.947	2	17	1	1	3
Nava	1.000	6	25	3	0	1
Williams	1.000	1	7	0	0	1

Second Base	PCT	G	PO	A	E	DP
Cairo	.979	105	201	305	11	80
Caraballo	.972	33	60	79	4	18
Petersen	1.000	4	8	8	0	2
Wilson	1.000	3	2	6	0	1

Third Base	PCT	G	PO	A	E	DP
Caraballo	.778	4	3	4	2	0
Cholowsky	1.000	8	2	4	0	1
Dalesandro	1.000	40	19	58	0	3
Houston	.833	4	2	8	2	2
Kieschnick	.875	7	5	16	3	1
Nava	.940	85	52	135	12	18
Orie	.938	6	2	13	1	2
Petersen	1.000	4	4	4	0	0
Wilson	.962	12	8	17	1	2

Shortstop	PCT	G	PO	A	E	DP
Cairo	.934	30	47	81	9	15
Nava	1.000	4	4	7	0	0
Petersen	.973	111	164	341	14	84
Wilson	1.000	3	4	9	0	3

Outfield	PCT	G	PO	A	E	DP
Brown	.987	47	74	0	1	0
Cholowsky	1.000	2	1	1	0	0
Dalesandro	1.000	5	3	0	0	0
Dowler	1.000	31	60	3	0	0
Hubbard	.000	1	0	0	0	0
Jennings	.986	119	197	10	3	3
Kieschnick	1.000	14	26	0	0	0
Lowery	.988	104	244	8	3	1
McIntosh	1.000	2	1	0	0	0
Pegues	.833	4	4	1	1	1
Valdes	.989	116	256	13	3	6

ORLANDO — Class AA

SOUTHERN LEAGUE

BATTING	AVG	G	AB	R	H	2B	3B	HR	RBI	BB	SO	SB	CS	B	T	HT	WT	DOB	1st Yr	Resides
Ballara, Juan	.194	15	31	2	6	0	0	0	2	5	10	2	0	R	R	6-2	150	3-30-72	1990	Santo Domingo, D.R.
Cline, Pat	.255	78	271	39	69	19	0	7	37	27	78	2	2	R	R	6-3	220	10-9-74	1993	Bradenton, Fla.
Cox, Darron	.222	3	9	2	2	1	0	1	4	1	1	0	0	R	R	6-1	205	11-21-67	1989	Norman, Okla.
*Devarez, Cesar	.281	34	96	13	27	4	1	5	17	8	15	1	0	R	R	5-10	175	9-22-69	1988	San Francisco de Macoris, D.R.
Dowler, Dee	.253	52	178	32	45	7	0	3	19	21	23	8	4	R	R	5-9	175	7-23-71	1993	Indianapolis, Ind.
Ellis, Kevin	.255	104	330	41	84	15	4	8	41	25	66	6	1	R	R	6-0	210	11-21-71	1993	Waco, Texas
Font, Franklin	.300	10	20	3	6	0	0	0	2	2	1	0	1	R	R	5-10	175	11-4-77	1995	Caracas, Venez.
Forkerway, Trey	.199	75	166	19	33	6	0	1	10	25	30	4	4	R	R	5-11	175	5-17-71	1993	Abilene, Texas
Freeman, Ricky	.312	81	308	58	96	19	2	16	73	29	51	8	5	R	R	6-4	205	2-3-72	1994	Houston, Texas

BATTING	AVG	G	AB	R	H	2B	3B	HR	RBI	BB	SO	SB	CS	B	T	HT	WT	DOB	1st Yr	Resides
Gazarek, Marty	.331	76	290	55	96	23	0	10	52	20	31	10	3	R	R	6-2	190	6-1-73	1994	North Baltimore, Ohio
Hightower, Vee	.233	87	283	35	66	8	2	6	29	43	66	16	11	S	R	6-5	205	4-26-72	1993	Mount Lebanon, Pa.
Joseph, Terry	.277	134	452	80	125	22	11	11	68	59	87	17	16	R	R	5-9	185	11-20-73	1995	Harvey, La.
Livsey, Shawn	.267	13	30	6	8	2	0	1	2	7	4	2	0	S	R	5-11	180	7-21-73	1991	Chicago, Ill.
Maxwell, Jason	.279	122	409	87	114	22	6	14	58	82	72	12	9	R	R	6-0	175	3-21-72	1993	Lewisburg, Tenn.
McCall, Rod	.300	19	70	11	21	2	0	6	20	10	24	0	0	L	L	6-7	235	11-4-71	1990	Stanton, Calif.
Micucci, Mike	.000	4	6	0	0	0	0	0	0	0	1	0	0	L	R	5-11	185	12-15-72	1994	Emerson, N.J.
Molina, Jose	.172	37	99	10	17	3	0	1	15	12	28	0	1	R	R	6-1	180	6-3-75	1993	Vega Alta, P.R.
Morris, Bobby	.313	4	16	3	5	1	0	0	1	2	3	0	0	L	R	6-0	180	11-22-72	1993	Munster, Ind.
Nelson, Bry	.288	110	382	51	110	33	2	8	58	45	43	5	7	S	R	5-10	170	1-27-74	1994	Crossett, Ark.
Nunez, Raymond	.296	106	351	59	104	13	3	16	65	15	65	1	2	R	R	6-0	150	9-22-72	1990	Manzanillo, D.R.
Orie, Kevin	.385	3	13	3	5	2	0	2	6	2	1	0	0	R	R	6-4	215	9-1-72	1993	Pittsburgh, Pa.
Porter, Bo	.258	8	31	4	8	1	0	1	3	0	11	0	1	R	R	6-1	188	7-5-72	1994	Newark, N.J.
Samuels, Scott	.283	34	127	30	36	7	3	3	17	18	34	5	4	L	R	5-11	190	5-19-71	1992	San Jose, Calif.
Williams, Harold	.352	26	88	13	31	12	0	1	11	6	15	1	1	L	R	6-4	200	2-14-71	1993	Garyville, La.
Wimmer, Chris	.275	102	371	62	102	15	3	2	28	23	37	23	4	R	R	5-11	170	9-25-70	1992	Wichita, Kan.

PITCHING	W	L	ERA	G	GS	CG	SV	IP	H	R	ER	BB	SO	B	T	HT	Wt.	DOB	1st Yr	Resides
Barker, Richie	0	1	3.30	19	0	0	2	30	25	17	11	7	19	R	R	6-2	195	10-29-72	1994	Malden, Mass.
Brown, Darold	0	0	4.20	18	0	0	0	30	28	15	14	18	24	L	L	6-0	175	8-16-73	1993	Atlanta, Ga.
Byrne, Earl	5	5	3.95	32	20	0	0	130	102	62	57	73	128	L	L	6-1	165	7-2-72	1994	Melbourne, Australia
Duncan, Courtney	2	2	3.40	8	8	0	0	45	37	28	17	29	45	L	R	5-11	175	10-9-74	1996	Daphne, Ala.
Garcia, Al	4	4	3.48	12	12	0	0	72	87	39	28	23	27	R	R	6-2	175	6-11-74	1993	Buena Park, Calif.
Hammack, Brandon	0	6	7.29	39	0	0	8	42	58	43	34	28	36	R	R	6-5	240	3-5-73	1995	Amarillo, Texas
Hancock, Lee	0	2	16.62	3	2	0	0	4	12	13	8	4	2	L	L	6-4	215	6-27-67	1988	Saratoga, Calif.
Hart, Jason	0	1	6.62	14	0	0	0	18	20	13	13	2	21	R	R	6-0	195	11-14-71	1994	Round Rock, Texas
Lyons, Curt	0	0	7.50	2	2	0	0	6	6	5	5	2	8	R	R	6-5	228	10-17-74	1992	Richmond, Ky.
McNichol, Brian	7	10	5.81	22	22	0	0	119	153	89	77	42	97	L	L	6-6	210	5-20-74	1995	Woodbridge, Va.
Moten, Scott	0	1	13.50	4	1	0	0	7	9	10	10	6	1	R	R	6-1	198	4-12-72	1992	Bellflower, Calif.
Norton, Phillip	1	0	2.57	2	1	0	0	7	8	2	2	2	7	R	L	6-1	180	2-1-76	1996	Texarkana, Texas
Peterson, Mark	0	2	9.88	9	0	0	0	14	26	15	15	4	8	L	L	5-11	195	11-27-70	1992	Kirkland, Wash.
Pierce, Jeff	0	0	9.87	5	4	0	0	17	28	21	19	7	8	R	R	6-1	200	6-7-69	1991	Staatsburg, N.Y.
Pool, Matt	4	2	4.60	9	8	1	0	47	47	28	24	21	38	S	R	6-6	190	7-8-73	1994	Fresno, Calif.
Rain, Steve	1	2	3.07	14	0	0	4	15	16	7	5	8	11	R	R	6-6	225	6-2-75	1993	Walnut, Calif.
Ratliff, Jon	6	4	4.35	18	15	0	0	101	112	59	49	32	68	R	R	6-5	200	12-22-71	1993	Clay, N.Y.
Ricketts, Chad	0	0	18.00	2	0	0	0	2	7	4	4	2	3	R	R	6-5	195	2-12-75	1995	Thorold, Ontario
Russell, LaGrande	6	4	6.22	25	9	1	0	81	102	66	56	27	43	R	R	6-2	175	8-20-70	1990	Hallsboro, N.C.
Speier, Justin	6	5	4.48	50	0	0	6	78	77	46	39	23	63	R	R	6-4	195	11-6-73	1995	Scottsdale, Ariz.
Stephenson, Brian	0	2	9.64	6	0	0	0	9	10	10	10	5	9	R	R	6-3	205	7-17-73	1994	Fullerton, Calif.
Tapani, Kevin	0	0	4.50	1	1	0	0	4	3	2	2	2	2	R	R	6-0	175	2-18-64	1986	Eden Prairie, Minn.
Telemaco, Amaury	1	0	2.25	1	1	0	0	8	9	2	2	2	6	R	R	6-3	180	1-19-74	1991	La Romana, D.R.
Twiggs, Greg	2	4	4.31	48	1	0	1	63	79	33	30	24	38	L	L	5-10	155	10-15-71	1993	Winter Springs, Fla.
Walker, Wade	2	2	8.64	4	4	0	0	17	19	17	16	13	11	R	R	6-1	190	9-18-71	1993	Gonzales, La.
*White, Rick	5	7	4.71	39	8	0	12	86	93	55	45	22	65	R	R	6-4	215	12-23-68	1990	Springfield, Ohio
Wood, Kerry	6	7	4.50	19	19	0	0	94	58	49	47	79	106	R	R	6-5	190	6-16-77	1995	Irving, Texas
Worrell, Steve	5	2	2.15	26	0	0	1	38	24	9	9	8	33	L	L	6-2	190	11-25-69	1992	Cape May, N.J.
2-team (18 Birm.)	7	4	3.47	44	0	0	2	62	52	25	24	20	54							

*Property of Tampa Bay Devil Rays

FIELDING

Catcher	PCT	G	PO	A	E	DP	PB
Ballara	1.000	14	53	11	0	1	1
Cline	.989	71	416	35	5	1	8
Cox	1.000	3	20	4	0	0	1
Devarez	.985	31	182	20	3	1	1
Ellis	1.000	5	5	1	0	0	1
Micucci	1.000	4	10	0	0	0	0
Molina	.993	36	237	28	2	1	3

First Base	PCT	G	PO	A	E	DP
Ellis	.975	19	144	14	4	9
Freeman	.989	81	718	63	9	67
McCall	.978	15	125	7	3	16
Nunez	.992	23	112	10	1	12
Williams	1.000	16	114	6	0	11

Second Base	PCT	G	PO	A	E	DP
Font	1.000	1	2	1	0	0
Forkerway	.979	40	58	85	3	19
Livsey	.897	9	11	15	3	3
Maxwell	1.000	3	3	7	0	1
Morris	1.000	4	7	9	0	3
Wimmer	.982	97	190	246	8	66

Third Base	PCT	G	PO	A	E	DP
Forkerway	.000	3	0	0	0	0
Nelson	.884	96	50	179	30	13
Nunez	.919	49	23	91	10	9

Shortstop	PCT	G	PO	A	E	DP
Font	1.000	7	7	16	0	4
Forkerway	.963	26	29	50	3	14
Maxwell	.951	118	173	369	28	67
Nelson	.893	6	14	11	3	3

Outfield	PCT	G	PO	A	E	DP
Dowler	.983	52	114	3	2	0
Ellis	.955	54	63	1	3	0
Gazarek	.994	75	145	10	1	2
Hightower	1.000	82	156	2	0	0
Joseph	.972	133	206	3	6	0
Livsey	.000	2	0	0	0	0
Porter	.938	8	13	2	1	0
Samuels	.974	33	70	4	2	0

DAYTONA — Class A

FLORIDA STATE LEAGUE

BATTING	AVG	G	AB	R	H	2B	3B	HR	RBI	BB	SO	SB	CS	B	T	HT	Wt.	DOB	1st Yr	Resides
Barnes, Kelvin	.261	123	433	64	113	26	7	4	51	25	82	22	8	R	R	6-2	183	9-4-74	1994	Battleboro, N.C.
Bentley, Kevin	.228	26	79	12	18	2	1	2	14	8	26	1	2	R	R	6-2	210	9-21-72	1995	Bedford, Texas
Colon, Jose	.210	52	100	11	21	4	1	0	7	8	31	1	2	R	R	6-2	190	1-25-76	1995	Melbourne, Fla.
Font, Franklin	.220	19	59	8	13	2	1	0	2	4	13	2	1	R	R	5-10	175	11-4-77	1995	Caracas, Venez.
Hall, Ronnie	.271	125	450	65	122	23	3	11	78	47	80	21	14	R	R	6-4	195	10-14-75	1993	Tustin, Calif.
Jasco, Elinton	.335	84	281	50	94	10	4	1	22	31	61	32	11	R	R	5-10	150	5-11-75	1993	San Pedro de Macoris, D.R.
Kelley, Erskine	.257	35	113	24	29	6	0	5	19	11	38	2	1	R	R	6-5	210	2-27-71	1992	Freeport, N.Y.
Kennedy, Gus	.261	113	368	63	96	20	0	14	57	46	89	15	8	R	R	5-10	195	12-26-73	1994	Seligman, Ariz.
Lewis, Jeremy	.279	72	233	31	65	15	3	4	30	9	45	2	1	R	R	6-1	186	9-7-72	1996	Cedar Rapids, Iowa
Lewis, Keith	.213	62	94	11	20	4	0	1	10	8	25	1	1	S	R	5-10	175	7-30-74	1996	Alpharetta, Ga.
Manning, Nate	.244	120	454	51	111	29	0	7	54	14	93	5	4	R	R	6-2	200	12-20-73	1996	Keosauqua, Iowa
Micucci, Mike	.250	54	140	15	35	5	0	1	24	12	27	1	4	L	R	5-11	185	12-15-72	1994	Emerson, N.J.
Molina, Jose	.251	55	179	17	45	9	1	0	23	14	25	4	0	R	R	6-1	180	6-3-75	1993	Vega Alta, P.R.
Nieves, Jose	.275	85	331	51	91	20	1	4	42	17	55	16	6	R	R	6-0	153	6-16-75	1992	Guacara, Venez.
Porter, Bo	.307	122	440	87	135	20	6	17	65	61	115	23	13	R	R	6-1	188	7-5-72	1994	Newark, N.J.
Valette, Ramon	.332	106	371	54	123	25	2	6	50	20	49	20	6	R	R	6-1	160	1-20-72	1990	Palenque, D.R.
Vieira, Scott	.275	134	476	84	131	27	3	18	80	70	125	9	7	R	R	5-11	185	8-17-73	1995	San Ramon, Calif.

GAMES BY POSITION: C—J. Lewis 51, Micucci 47, Molina 55. **1B**—Manning 13, Valette 1, Vieira 126. **2B**—Font 1, Jasco 81, K. Lewis 26, Micucci 1, Nieves 18, Porter 1, Valette 20. **3B**—Barnes 55, J. Lewis 1, K. Lewis 32, Manning 69, Valette 27. **SS**—Font 17, Jasco 1, K. Lewis 3, Nieves 65, Valette 61. **OF**—Barnes 23, Bentley 24, Colon 50, Hall 123, Kelley 26, Kennedy 97, Porter 118.

PITCHING	W	L	ERA	G	GS	CG	SV	IP	H	R	ER	BB	SO	B	T	HT	Wt.	DOB	1st Yr	Resides
Barcelo, Marc	3	3	5.48	23	3	0	1	43	45	35	26	27	30	R	R	6-3	210	1-10-72	1993	Tucson, Ariz.
Barker, Richie	2	1	3.35	29	1	0	1	51	49	27	19	15	38	R	R	6-2	195	10-29-72	1994	Malden, Mass.
Birsner, Roark	0	0	4.76	8	0	0	0	11	15	6	6	3	12	R	R	6-4	180	12-2-75	1994	Berlin, N.J.
Bogle, Sean	1	1	6.75	8	0	0	2	7	11	7	5	7	3	R	R	6-2	195	10-3-73	1994	Indianapolis, Ind.
Brown, Darold	2	3	2.79	29	1	0	1	39	33	16	12	20	32	L	L	6-0	175	8-16-73	1993	Atlanta, Ga.
Bryant, Chris	0	1	9.53	8	1	0	0	11	20	12	12	8	10	L	L	6-1	180	8-13-75	1993	Tampa, Fla.
Cannon, Jon	1	0	1.32	2	2	0	0	14	7	2	2	10	13	R	L	6-3	185	1-1-75	1996	Los Altos, Calif.
DeJesus, Javy	3	1	5.17	8	5	0	0	31	32	19	18	12	21	L	L	5-11	198	8-3-71	1992	Beaumont, Texas
DeWitt, Chris	1	8	5.88	38	2	0	3	64	89	55	42	20	42	R	R	6-5	215	3-24-74	1995	Ozark, Mo.
Duncan, Courtney	8	4	1.63	19	19	1	0	122	90	35	22	35	120	L	R	5-11	175	10-9-74	1996	Daphne, Ala.
Farnsworth, Kyle	10	10	4.09	27	27	2	0	156	178	91	71	47	105	R	R	6-4	190	4-14-76	1995	Roswell, Ga.
Faulkner, Neal	3	7	6.83	36	0	0	5	55	65	44	42	19	40	R	R	6-9	230	4-16-75	1994	Montgomery, Ala.
Hammack, Brandon	2	3	2.37	16	0	0	1	19	25	11	5	7	20	R	R	6-5	240	3-5-73	1995	Amarillo, Texas
Hart, Len	1	2	5.79	8	0	0	0	9	10	6	6	7	12	L	L	5-11	185	10-8-73	1996	Oak Ridge, Tenn.
Largusa, Levon	0	0	8.31	14	0	0	0	9	16	11	8	8	5	L	L	5-11	180	5-21-71	1992	San Leandro, Calif.
Markey, Barry	5	7	5.55	22	21	2	0	120	144	81	74	41	67	R	R	6-5	195	7-20-76	1995	St. Petersburg, Fla.
Marshall, Gary	0	0	4.79	22	0	0	6	21	23	13	11	8	23	R	L	6-5	215	9-22-73	1996	La Mesa, Calif.
Martinez, Javier	2	6	5.79	9	9	2	0	51	65	40	33	26	34	R	R	6-2	195	2-5-77	1994	Bayamon, P.R.
McNichol, Brian	2	2	2.31	6	6	0	0	39	32	14	10	10	40	L	L	6-6	210	5-20-74	1995	Woodbridge, Va.
Norton, Phillip	3	2	2.34	7	6	3	0	42	40	11	11	12	44	R	L	6-1	180	2-1-76	1996	Texarkana, Texas
Parotte, Frisco	0	0	0.00	5	0	0	0	5	1	0	0	4	4	R	R	6-3	180	9-10-75	1994	Levittown, P.R.
Ricketts, Chad	3	1	0.44	20	0	0	8	20	13	4	1	6	18	R	R	6-5	195	2-12-75	1995	Thorold, Ontario
Ryan, Jason	9	8	4.44	27	27	5	0	170	168	105	84	55	140	S	R	6-2	180	1-23-76	1994	Bound Brook, N.J.
Tapani, Kevin	0	0	3.86	1	1	0	0	5	5	2	2	2	4	R	R	6-0	175	2-18-64	1986	Eden Prairie, Minn.
Tribe, Byron	0	0	7.32	18	0	0	0	20	21	20	16	22	19	R	R	6-3	195	3-21-75	1996	Katy, Texas
Valette, Ramon	0	0	7.71	3	0	0	0	2	2	2	2	2	1	R	R	6-1	160	1—72	1990	Palenque, D.R.
Winslett, Dax	4	3	6.19	9	7	0	0	36	51	27	25	7	16	R	R	6-1	200	1-1-72	1993	Houston, Texas

ROCKFORD — Class A

MIDWEST LEAGUE

BATTING	AVG	G	AB	R	H	2B	3B	HR	RBI	BB	SO	SB	CS	B	T	HT	Wt.	DOB	1st Yr	Resides
Abreu, Dennis	.321	126	483	71	155	19	3	1	37	45	99	36	26	R	R	6-0	165	4-22-78	1995	Tumero, Venez.
Abreu, Nelson	.240	63	179	27	43	4	5	2	20	19	52	9	6	R	R	6-0	170	8-16-76	1994	Maracay, Venez.
Andersen, Ryan	.264	19	53	2	14	3	0	0	4	6	10	1	0	R	R	6-1	175	7-18-73	1996	Huntington Beach, Calif.
Bly, Derrick	.242	109	392	48	95	19	5	8	43	35	131	6	3	R	R	6-0	205	9-19-74	1996	Tucson, Ariz.
Carter, Quincy	.211	105	388	61	82	26	2	2	34	48	100	17	10	R	R	6-3	200	10-13-77	1996	Elkwood, Ga.
Catlett, David	.250	42	132	21	33	11	3	1	21	17	37	4	2	R	R	6-0	195	4-6-74	1993	Berkeley, Calif.
Colon, Jose	.246	56	195	16	48	14	1	2	28	21	35	1	3	R	R	6-2	190	1-25-76	1995	Melbourne, Fla.
Ellison, Tony	.195	34	118	21	23	5	2	5	13	14	25	1	1	R	R	6-0	195	7-12-74	1995	Grifton, N.C.
Hall, Doug	.290	115	407	49	118	19	2	3	46	33	106	26	13	L	L	6-0	175	12-12-74	1996	Gallatin, Tenn.
Houston, Tyler	.500	2	6	1	3	1	0	0	1	0	0	0	0	L	R	6-2	210	1-17-71	1989	Las Vegas, Nev.
Jefferson, Dave	.200	18	55	7	11	2	1	0	2	3	12	3	1	R	R	6-2	190	6-18-75	1993	Palo Alto, Calif.
Johnson, Gary	.000	1	3	0	0	0	0	0	0	1	1	1	0	R	R	6-3	200	9-6-76	1997	Baldwin Park, Calif.
King, Brad	.250	68	204	31	51	14	1	7	29	19	35	4	4	R	R	6-2	190	12-3-74	1996	Austin, Texas
Lewis, Keith	.171	15	41	5	7	2	0	0	5	3	9	1	0	S	R	5-10	175	7-30-74	1996	Alpharetta, Ga.
Lisanti, Bob	.236	66	182	18	43	8	0	0	21	15	42	1	3	R	R	5-10	180	5-28-73	1996	Chicago, Ill.
Longmire, Marcel	.218	84	266	20	58	7	2	3	21	14	77	6	5	R	R	6-2	205	4-18-78	1996	Vallejo, Calif.
Meyers, Chad	.301	125	439	89	132	28	4	4	58	74	72	54	16	R	R	6-0	180	8-8-75	1996	Papillion, Neb.
Salazar, Juan	.267	54	161	16	43	9	0	3	17	13	36	2	1	S	R	6-4	200	10-31-77	1994	Valencia, Venez.
Smith, Jason	.182	9	33	4	6	0	1	0	3	2	11	1	0	L	R	6-3	190	7-24-77	1997	Nashville, Tenn.
Speed, Dorian	.248	44	157	27	39	7	1	1	18	18	45	18	4	R	R	6-3	190	3-1-74	1995	Tempe, Ariz.
Walker, Ron	.333	4	15	1	5	0	0	1	5	3	2	0	0	R	R	6-2	215	12-29-75	1997	Vincent Town, N.J.
Zuleta, Julio	.288	119	430	59	124	30	5	6	77	35	88	5	5	R	R	6-6	230	3-28-75	1993	Juan Diaz, Panama

GAMES BY POSITION: C—Houston 1, King 62, Lisanti 66, Longmire 2, Salazar 24. **1B**—Bly 7, Catlett 19, Salazar 19, Zuleta 100. **2B**—D. Abreu 39, N. Abreu 1, Lewis 11, Meyers 97. **3B**—N. Abreu 26, Anderson 8, Bly 92, Houston 1, King 1, Meyers 10, Walker 4. **SS**—D. Abreu 95, N. Abreu 33, Anderson 10, Lewis 3, Meyers 1, Smith 9. **OF**—N. Abreu 7, Carter 104, Catlett 9, Colon 56, Ellison 22, Hall 111, Jefferson 17, Longmire 70, Meyers 24, Speed 8.

PITCHING	W	L	ERA	G	GS	CG	SV	IP	H	R	ER	BB	SO	B	T	HT	WT	DOB	1st Yr	Resides
Birsner, Roark	0	2	3.73	18	0	0	2	31	33	19	13	24	33	R	R	6-4	180	12-2-75	1994	Berlin, N.J.
Brookens, Casey	3	2	3.18	28	0	0	3	51	48	20	18	21	51	R	R	6-0	185	11-24-73	1996	Fayetteville, Pa.
Cannon, Jon	9	6	3.13	24	20	1	0	129	110	53	45	50	130	R	L	6-3	185	1-1-75	1996	Los Altos, Calif.
Cedeno, Blas	3	3	2.90	22	0	0	0	40	36	19	13	14	25	R	R	6-0	165	11-15-72	1991	Campo Carabobo, Venez.
Crane, Randy	3	6	5.74	21	12	0	0	74	68	51	47	55	62	R	R	6-2	180	7-4-75	1996	McMinnville, Ore.
Downs, Scott	3	0	1.25	5	5	0	0	36	17	5	5	8	43	L	L	6-2	180	3-17-76	1997	Louisville, Ky.
Espinal, Jose	10	10	4.92	24	24	1	0	121	147	83	66	41	107	R	R	6-1	175	8-31-76	1994	Santo Domingo, D.R.
Gissell, Chris	6	11	4.45	26	24	3	0	144	155	89	71	62	105	R	R	6-4	180	1-4-78	1996	Vancouver, Wash.
Hart, Len	2	1	2.09	27	0	0	0	47	30	11	11	28	55	L	L	5-11	185	10-8-73	1996	Oak Ridge, Tenn.
Kelley, Jason	1	0	4.97	22	0	0	2	29	29	20	16	27	20	R	R	6-1	225	11-14-75	1994	Live Oak, Fla.
Marshall, Gary	4	1	3.82	29	0	0	2	33	34	20	14	17	21	R	L	6-5	215	9-22-73	1996	La Mesa, Calif.
Martinez, Javier	1	7	5.70	17	17	1	0	79	85	61	50	50	70	R	R	6-2	195	2-5-77	1994	Bayamon, P.R.
Norton, Phillip	9	3	3.22	18	18	3	0	109	92	51	39	44	114	R	L	6-1	180	2-1-76	1996	Texarkana, Texas
Polanco, Elvis	2	5	8.60	16	5	0	0	45	66	53	43	36	34	R	R	6-2	164	3-10-78	1994	Puerto Cabello, Venez.
Ricketts, Chad	4	0	2.48	16	0	0	3	29	19	9	8	11	32	R	R	6-5	195	2-12-75	1995	Thorold, Ontario
Rolocut, Brian	0	1	6.16	14	0	0	1	31	43	23	21	15	20	R	R	6-1	195	4-8-74	1993	Gambrills, Md.
Schaffer, Trevor	2	3	2.47	46	0	0	21	47	44	16	13	19	46	R	R	6-3	210	1-13-74	1996	Menlo Park, Calif.
Tapani, Kevin	1	0	0.82	2	2	0	0	11	5	1	1	0	7	R	R	6-0	175	2-18-64	1986	Eden Prairie, Minn.
Teut, Nate	0	1	10.13	2	2	0	0	11	18	12	12	2	6	R	L	6-6	210	3-11-76	1997	Monroe, Iowa
Tribe, Byron	2	2	5.40	13	0	0	0	22	20	14	13	20	30	R	R	6-3	195	3-21-75	1996	Katy, Texas
Ward, Brandon	1	2	11.95	9	3	0	0	20	30	33	27	24	18	R	R	6-5	170	1-21-76	1996	Fontana, Calif.

WILLIAMSPORT — Short-Season Class A

NEW YORK-PENN LEAGUE

BATTING	AVG	G	AB	R	H	2B	3B	HR	RBI	BB	SO	SB	CS	B	T	HT	Wt.	DOB	1st Yr	Resides
Abreu, Nelson	.306	14	49	8	15	1	2	0	3	9	17	6	3	R	R	6-0	170	8-16-76	1994	Maracay, Venez.
Amrhein, Mike	.278	62	237	17	66	11	1	1	31	10	19	0	2	R	R	6-2	220	6-14-75	1997	Oak Park, Ill.
Banks, Tony	.259	37	116	21	30	11	3	2	11	27	23	4	1	L	L	5-11	190	9-21-71	1993	Oakland, Calif.
Bernhardt, Tom	.205	38	122	8	25	3	4	1	8	10	39	2	1	R	R	6-0	195	10-28-74	1997	Miami, Fla.
Bly, Derrick	.149	13	47	2	7	2	0	0	3	5	20	0	0	R	R	6-0	205	9-19-74	1996	Tucson, Ariz.
Connell, Gerry	.281	55	203	25	57	7	6	3	18	20	55	4	3	R	R	6-2	197	7-17-77	1995	Avenel, N.J.
Fereday, Todd	.209	32	115	13	24	5	1	2	11	7	20	4	2	R	R	6-0	190	2-14-75	1997	Oklahoma City, Okla.
Font, Franklin	.311	33	135	13	42	6	2	0	12	7	20	10	4	R	R	5-10	175	11-4-77	1995	Caracas, Venez.
Grubbs, Chris	.204	23	54	5	11	1	0	0	2	11	17	0	0	R	R	6-3	195	12-27-75	1996	Ocoee, Fla.
Hubbard, Jeremy	.125	6	8	0	1	1	0	0	1	0	2	0	0	R	R	5-8	165	8-25-76	1997	Roseburg, Ore.
Jefferies, Daryl	.289	10	38	7	11	2	0	0	2	2	6	1	0	R	R	5-10	172	2-16-74	1996	St. Peters, Mo.
Jimenez, Felipe	.115	10	26	3	3	0	0	0	0	1	8	0	0	R	R	6-3	185	12-22-76	1994	Camatagua, Venez.
Kiefer, Dax	.244	70	234	28	57	5	1	4	18	28	61	7	1	R	R	5-11	185	12-4-73	1996	Deer Park, Texas
Otero, Oscar	.161	19	62	3	10	1	0	0	7	3	10	0	0	R	R	6-1	165	5-28-77	1995	Cayey, P.R.
Pressley, Kasey	.193	44	140	15	27	7	0	3	13	8	56	1	2	L	R	6-4	220	9-5-76	1995	Longwood, Fla.
Ribaudo, Mike	.170	30	88	6	15	2	0	3	8	2	25	1	0	R	R	6-2	175	6-21-75	1995	Sarasota, Fla.
Salazar, Juan	.200	29	105	12	21	6	0	1	11	8	20	1	0	S	R	6-4	200	10-31-77	1994	Valencia, Venez.
Smith, Jason	.288	51	205	25	59	5	2	0	11	10	44	9	2	L	R	6-3	190	7-24-77	1997	Nashville, Tenn.
Stewart, Courteney	.243	54	181	13	44	5	0	0	26	11	50	8	5	R	R	6-2	195	4-10-76	1996	Stone Mountain, Ga.
Walker, Ron	.349	54	189	30	66	10	1	9	39	17	48	0	1	R	R	6-2	215	12-29-75	1997	Vincent Town, N.J.
Watson, Al	.250	45	136	21	34	0	0	0	11	19	21	10	5	S	R	5-8	165	3-9-74	1997	Los Angeles, Calif.

GAMES BY POSITION: C—Amrhein 39, Grubbs 23, Hubbard 6, Ribaudo 19, Salazar 2. **1B**—Amrhein 10, Fereday 5, Otero 8, Pressley 31, Salazar 26. **2B**—Fereday 16, Font 22, Jefferies 3, Watson 38. **3B**—Bly 12, Fereday 6, Jefferies 6, Otero 11, Walker 42. **SS**—Abreu 14, Font 11, Smith 51. **OF**—Banks 21, Bernhardt 23, Connell 55, Jimenez 10, Kiefer 70, Ribaudo 2, Stewart 52, Watson 2.

PITCHING	W	L	ERA	G	GS	CG	SV	IP	H	R	ER	BB	SO	B	T	HT	Wt.	DOB	1st Yr	Resides
Booker, Chris	1	5	3.35	24	3	0	1	46	39	20	17	25	60	R	R	6-3	205	12-9-76	1995	Monroeville, Ala.
Bryant, Chris	0	0	6.75	4	0	0	0	7	13	8	5	5	8	L	L	6-1	180	8-13-75	1993	Tampa, Fla.
Downs, Scott	0	2	2.74	5	5	0	0	23	15	11	7	7	28	L	L	6-2	180	3-17-76	1997	Louisville, Ky.
Fennell, Barry	2	10	6.11	17	10	0	0	66	92	51	45	29	50	R	L	6-4	200	9-30-76	1994	Pennsauken, N.J.
Fisher, Louis	1	3	4.69	11	9	0	0	40	41	27	21	32	31	R	R	6-1	189	10-14-76	1995	Oakland, Calif.
Holobinko, Mike	0	0	3.29	12	0	0	0	14	16	6	5	7	10	L	L	6-2	210	12-4-76	1995	Rahway, N.J.
Kelley, Jason	2	2	7.16	27	0	0	10	28	28	31	22	32	16	R	R	6-1	225	11-14-75	1994	Live Oak, Fla.
Licciardi, Ron	4	1	4.98	17	9	0	0	65	84	41	36	25	56	L	L	6-2	190	3-26-76	1995	Oakdale, Conn.
Magers, Mathew	4	4	3.58	27	0	0	5	50	46	28	20	35	48	L	L	6-0	195	3-31-76	1997	Gaylord, Minn.
Meyers, Mike	0	0	0.00	1	1	0	0	4	3	0	0	1	2	R	R	6-3	215	10-18-77	1997	Tillsonburg, Ontario
Palma, Ricardo	4	7	3.48	14	14	1	0	78	77	36	30	36	47	L	L	6-1	160	9-26-79	1996	Maracay, Venez.
Pitt, Jye	0	1	4.26	4	0	0	0	6	9	11	3	5	9	L	R	6-2	190	2-21-78	1996	Dapto, Australia
Polanco, Elvis	2	5	3.23	15	15	0	0	84	71	45	30	46	64	R	R	6-2	164	3-10-78	1994	Puerto Cabello, Venez.
Santiago, Antonio	3	1	1.55	26	0	0	1	46	41	15	8	21	33	L	L	6-1	185	8-30-76	1994	Carolina, P.R.
Teut, Nate	3	4	2.57	9	9	0	0	49	55	23	14	6	37	R	L	6-6	210	3-11-76	1997	Monroe, Iowa
Vizcaino, Edward	1	1	2.75	11	0	0	0	20	15	13	6	4	14	R	R	6-0	160	4-17-77	1994	Bani, D.R.
Ward, Brandon	2	0	3.86	19	0	0	0	21	11	12	9	24	16	R	R	6-5	170	1-21-76	1996	Fontana, Calif.

MESA — Rookie

ARIZONA LEAGUE

BATTING	AVG	G	AB	R	H	2B	3B	HR	RBI	BB	SO	SB	CS	B	T	HT	Wt.	DOB	1st Yr	Resides
Aldrup, Morey	.192	36	125	13	24	6	0	1	12	8	43	4	3	R	R	5-10	165	12-23-78	1997	Santa Ana, Calif.
Bernhardt, Tom	.267	8	30	11	8	3	1	0	5	6	6	2	1	R	R	6-0	195	10-28-74	1997	Miami, Fla.
De la Cruz, Henry	.138	25	80	11	11	2	0	0	3	16	32	5	3	R	R	6-0	180	8-25-76	1994	Santo Domingo, D.R.
Eaddy, Deon	.281	53	221	43	62	5	1	1	25	18	17	2	3	R	R	5-9	165	9-25-76	1997	Florence, S.C.
Fereday, Todd	.374	24	91	19	34	12	3	1	23	8	14	5	1	R	R	6-0	190	2-14-75	1997	Oklahoma City, Okla.
German, Franklin	.172	35	116	22	20	3	1	1	22	16	40	8	3	R	R	5-10	160	2-28-80	1997	Santo Domingo, D.R.
Hargreaves, Brad	.240	32	104	11	25	2	0	0	12	8	26	1	0	R	R	6-0	180	10-30-77	1997	Cincinnati, Ohio
Jimenez, Felipe	.248	41	137	23	34	3	4	1	22	7	37	17	1	R	R	6-3	185	12-22-76	1994	Camatagua, Venez.
Johnson, Gary	.288	52	198	40	57	14	5	1	31	23	26	9	3	R	R	6-3	200	9-6-76	1997	Baldwin Park, Calif.
Mauck, Matt	.285	40	144	28	41	8	4	1	19	21	46	8	3	L	R	6-3	215	2-12-79	1997	Jasper, Ind.
Payne, Ronald	.279	53	179	28	50	6	1	1	31	37	31	16	10	L	L	6-0	180	1-9-76	1997	Hamlet, N.C.
Ramsey, Brad	.315	51	200	50	63	10	3	8	34	22	33	8	0	R	R	6-4	210	11-7-76	1997	West Monroe, La.
Randolph, Jaisen	.266	53	218	42	58	1	4	0	26	26	45	24	5	R	R	6-0	185	1-19-79	1997	Tampa, Fla.

GAMES BY POSITION: C—Hargreaves 16, Ramsey 41. **1B**—Bernhardt 6, Hargreaves 4, Johnson 45, Mauck 2, Payne 1. **2B**—Aldrup 23, Eaddy 1, Fereday 5, German 29. **3B**—Aldrup 6, Fereday 11, German 5, Mauck 36. **SS**—Aldrup 4, Eaddy 51, Hargreaves 1. **OF**—Aldrup 1, Bernhardt 2, De la Cruz 14, Hargreaves 3, Jimenez 40, Johnson 9, Payne 51, Randolph 52.

PITCHING	W	L	ERA	G	GS	CG	SV	IP	H	R	ER	BB	SO	B	T	HT	WT	DOB	1st Yr	Resides
Acosta, Jhon	1	0	2.53	14	0	0	1	21	27	10	6	6	15	S	R	6-3	180	10-30-79	1996	Maracay, Venez.
Batts, Nathan	2	0	7.45	8	1	0	0	10	11	9	8	10	9	R	L	6-4	190	3-30-78	1997	Mt. Vernon, N.H.
Beltran, Francis	0	1	3.42	16	0	0	1	24	27	18	9	8	17	R	R	6-5	205	7-25-80	1997	Santo Domingo, D.R.
Connell, Brian	3	5	3.76	12	9	0	0	38	46	31	16	29	32	L	L	6-3	203	8-4-77	1996	Clearwater, Fla.
Delano, Michael	0	1	12.41	8	1	0	0	12	22	21	17	9	13	L	L	6-7	190	11-9-77	1997	Las Vegas, Nev.
Garland, Jon	3	2	2.70	10	7	0	0	40	37	14	12	10	39	R	R	6-5	200	9-27-79	1997	Granada Hills, Calif.
Lohse, Kyle	2	2	3.02	12	11	0	0	48	46	22	16	22	49	R	R	6-2	190	10-4-78	1997	Glenn, Calif.
Mallory, Andrew	3	4	4.24	12	10	0	0	51	63	38	24	22	32	R	R	6-2	165	9-25-76	1996	St. Petersburg, Fla.
Medina, Eleazer	0	0	6.23	8	0	0	0	13	17	11	9	17	2	R	R	6-6	190	10-23-79	1996	Maracay, Venez.
Meyers, Mike	3	1	1.41	12	2	0	3	38	34	15	6	13	45	R	R	6-3	215	10-18-77	1997	Tillsonburg, Ontario
Noel, Todd	5	1	1.98	12	11	0	1	59	39	27	13	30	63	R	R	6-4	185	9-28-78	1996	Maurice, La.
Piersoll, Chris	4	0	2.08	15	0	0	2	35	26	12	8	9	41	R	R	6-4	195	9-25-77	1997	Carlsbad, Calif.
Pitt, Jye	3	0	2.66	13	1	0	1	24	14	9	7	17	28	L	R	6-2	190	2-21-78	1996	Dapto, Australia
Powalski, Richard	0	0	1.59	6	0	0	0	11	11	4	2	7	13	L	L	6-10	190	5-9-78	1997	Clearwater, Fla.
Sullivan, Shane	1	2	2.70	21	0	0	9	23	21	11	7	8	22	R	R	6-2	215	12-10-77	1997	Pinon Hills, Calif.
Vracar, Paul	0	1	6.75	7	2	0	0	11	17	11	8	10	9	R	R	6-5	195	12-5-79	1997	Stoney Creek, Ontario
Waldrum, Kevin	1	1	7.36	8	0	0	0	7	10	15	6	13	6	L	R	6-4	200	3-22-79	1997	Weatherford, Texas
Waligora, Tom	3	0	5.16	16	0	0	2	23	25	16	13	15	29	R	R	6-8	230	8-7-76	1997	Richmond, Va.

Cincinnati REDS

Managers: Ray Knight, Jack McKeon. **1997 Record:** 76-86, .469 (3rd, NL Central)

BATTING	AVG	G	AB	R	H	2B	3B	HR	RBI	BB	SO	SB	CS	B	T	HT	WT	DOB	1st Yr	Resides
Boone, Aaron	.245	16	49	5	12	1	0	0	5	2	5	1	0	R	R	6-2	190	3-9-73	1994	Villa Park, Calif.
Boone, Bret	.223	139	443	40	99	25	1	7	46	45	101	5	5	R	R	5-10	180	4-6-69	1990	Villa Park, Calif.
Branson, Jeff	.153	65	98	9	15	3	1	1	5	7	23	1	0	L	R	6-0	180	1-26-67	1989	Millry, Ala.
Fordyce, Brook	.208	47	96	7	20	5	0	1	8	8	15	2	0	R	R	6-1	185	5-7-70	1989	Old Lyme, Conn.
Goodwin, Curtis	.253	85	265	27	67	11	0	1	12	24	53	22	13	L	L	5-11	180	9-30-72	1991	San Leandro, Calif.
Greene, Willie	.253	151	495	62	125	22	1	26	91	78	111	6	0	L	R	5-11	184	9-23-71	1989	Haddock, Ga.
Harris, Lenny	.273	120	238	32	65	13	1	3	28	18	18	4	3	L	R	5-10	205	10-28-64	1983	Miami, Fla.
Jackson, Damian	.222	12	27	6	6	2	1	1	2	4	7	1	1	R	R	5-10	160	8-16-73	1992	Concord, Calif.
Kelly, Mike	.293	73	140	27	41	13	2	6	19	10	30	6	1	R	R	6-4	195	6-2-70	1991	Los Alamitos, Calif.
Larkin, Barry	.317	73	224	34	71	17	3	4	20	47	24	14	3	R	R	6-0	190	4-28-64	1985	Cincinnati, Ohio
Morris, Hal	.276	96	333	42	92	20	1	1	33	23	43	3	1	L	L	6-4	215	4-9-65	1986	Union, Ky.
Nunnally, Jon	.318	65	201	38	64	12	3	13	35	26	51	7	3	L	R	5-10	188	11-9-71	1992	Pelham, N.C.
Oliver, Joe	.258	111	349	28	90	13	0	14	43	25	58	1	3	R	R	6-3	220	7-24-65	1983	Orlando, Fla.
Owens, Eric	.263	27	57	8	15	0	0	0	3	4	11	3	2	R	R	6-1	184	2-3-71	1992	Danville, Va.
Pendleton, Terry	.248	50	113	11	28	9	0	1	17	12	14	2	1	S	R	5-9	195	7-16-60	1982	Duluth, Ga.
Perez, Eduardo	.253	106	297	44	75	18	0	16	52	29	76	5	1	R	R	6-4	215	9-11-69	1991	Santurce, P.R.
Reese, Pokey	.219	128	397	48	87	15	0	4	26	31	82	25	7	R	R	6-0	160	6-10-73	1991	Columbia, S.C.
Rose, Pete	.143	11	14	2	2	0	0	0	0	2	9	0	0	L	R	6-1	180	11-16-69	1989	Cincinnati, Ohio
Sanders, Deion	.273	115	465	53	127	13	7	5	23	34	67	56	13	L	L	6-1	195	8-9-67	1988	Alpharetta, Ga.
Sanders, Reggie	.253	86	312	52	79	19	2	19	56	42	93	13	7	R	R	6-1	180	12-1-67	1988	Cincinnati, Ohio
Sierra, Ruben	.244	25	90	6	22	5	1	2	7	6	21	0	0	S	R	6-1	200	10-6-65	1983	Carolina, P.R.
Stynes, Chris	.348	49	198	31	69	7	1	6	28	11	13	11	2	R	R	5-9	170	1-19-73	1991	Boca Raton, Fla.
Taubensee, Eddie	.268	108	254	26	68	18	0	10	34	22	66	0	1	L	R	6-4	205	10-31-68	1986	Houston, Texas
Timmons, Ozzie	.333	6	9	1	3	1	0	0	0	0	1	0	0	R	R	6-2	205	9-18-70	1991	Tampa, Fla.
Watkins, Pat	.207	17	29	2	6	2	0	0	0	0	5	1	0	R	R	6-2	185	9-2-72	1993	Garner, N.C.

PITCHING	W	L	ERA	G	GS	CG	SV	IP	H	R	ER	BB	SO	B	T	HT	WT	DOB	1st Yr	Resides
Belinda, Stan	1	5	3.71	84	0	0	1	99	84	42	41	33	114	R	R	6-3	215	8-6-66	1985	Alexandria, Pa.
Bones, Ricky	0	1	10.19	9	2	0	0	18	31	22	20	11	8	R	R	6-0	190	4-7-69	1986	Guayama, P.R.
Brantley, Jeff	1	1	3.86	13	0	0	1	12	9	5	5	7	16	R	R	5-10	189	9-5-63	1985	Clinton, Miss.
Burba, Dave	11	10	4.73	30	27	2	0	160	157	88	84	73	131	R	R	6-4	240	7-7-66	1987	Springfield, Ohio
Carrara, Giovanni	0	1	7.84	2	2	0	0	10	14	9	9	6	5	R	R	6-2	210	3-4-68	1990	Anzoategui, Venez.
Carrasco, Hector	1	2	3.68	38	0	0	0	51	51	25	21	25	46	R	R	6-2	175	10-22-69	1988	San Pedro de Macoris, D.R.
Crowell, Jim	0	1	9.95	2	1	0	0	6	12	7	7	5	3	L	L	6-4	220	5-14-74	1995	Valparaiso, Ind.
Eischen, Joey	0	0	6.75	1	0	0	0	1	2	2	1	1	2	L	L	6-1	190	5-25-70	1989	West Covina, Calif.
Graves, Danny	0	0	6.14	10	0	0	0	15	26	14	10	11	7	R	R	5-11	200	8-7-73	1995	Valrico, Fla.
Jarvis, Kevin	0	1	10.13	9	0	0	1	13	21	16	15	7	12	S	R	6-2	200	8-1-69	1991	Lexington, Ky.
Lewis, Richie	0	0	6.35	4	0	0	0	6	4	5	4	3	4	R	R	5-10	175	1-25-66	1987	Losantville, Ind.
Martinez, Pedro	1	1	9.45	8	0	0	0	7	8	9	7	7	4	L	L	6-2	155	11-29-68	1987	Villa Mella, D.R.
Mercker, Kent	8	11	3.92	28	25	0	0	145	135	65	63	62	75	L	L	6-2	195	2-1-68	1986	Dublin, Ohio
Morgan, Mike	9	12	4.78	31	30	1	0	162	165	91	86	49	103	R	R	6-2	222	10-8-59	1978	Ogden, Utah
Remlinger, Mike	8	8	4.14	69	12	2	2	124	100	61	57	60	145	L	L	6-0	195	3-23-66	1987	Plymouth, Mass.
Rodriguez, Felix	0	0	4.30	26	1	0	0	46	48	23	22	28	34	R	R	6-1	190	12-5-72	1990	Monte Cristi, D.R.
Schourek, Pete	5	8	5.42	18	17	0	0	85	78	59	51	38	59	L	L	6-5	195	5-10-69	1987	Falls Church, Va.
Service, Scott	0	0	11.81	4	0	0	0	5	11	7	7	1	3	R	R	6-6	226	2-26-67	1986	Cincinnati, Ohio
Shaw, Jeff	4	2	2.38	78	0	0	42	95	79	26	25	12	74	R	R	6-2	185	7-7-66	1986	Washington Courthouse, Ohio
Smiley, John	9	10	5.23	20	20	0	0	117	139	76	68	31	94	L	L	6-4	215	3-17-65	1983	Trappe, Pa.
Sullivan, Scott	5	3	3.24	59	0	0	1	97	79	36	35	30	96	R	R	6-3	210	3-13-71	1993	Carrollton, Ala.
Tabaka, Jeff	0	0	4.50	3	0	0	0	2	1	1	1	1	1	R	L	6-2	195	1-17-64	1986	Clinton, Ohio
Tomko, Brett	11	7	3.43	22	19	0	0	126	106	50	48	47	95	R	R	6-4	205	4-7-73	1995	Tampa, Fla.
White, Gabe	2	2	4.39	12	6	0	1	41	39	20	20	8	25	L	L	6-2	200	11-20-71	1990	Sebring, Fla.
Winchester, Scott	0	0	6.00	5	0	0	0	6	9	5	4	2	3	R	R	6-2	210	4-20-73	1995	Midland, Mich.

FIELDING

Catcher	PCT	G	PO	A	E	DP	PB
Fordyce	.983	30	162	12	3	1	2
Oliver	.990	106	667	53	7	10	4
Taubensee	.987	64	358	24	5	6	7

First Base	PCT	G	PO	A	E	DP
Greene	1.000	7	47	2	0	2
Harris	.982	11	51	5	1	1
Morris	.990	89	672	52	7	67
Oliver	1.000	4	14	2	0	0
Perez	.996	67	489	35	2	37
Rose	1.000	1	6	0	0	0
Taubensee	1.000	7	42	1	0	4

Second Base	PCT	G	PO	A	E	DP
A. Boone	.000	1	0	0	0	0
B. Boone	.997	136	271	334	2	74
Branson	.930	14	17	23	3	7
Harris	.984	20	26	34	1	6
Jackson	.933	3	7	7	1	1
Owens	.000	2	0	0	0	0
Reese	1.000	8	9	20	0	2
Stynes	1.000	8	10	19	0	2

Third Base	PCT	G	PO	A	E	DP
A. Boone	.917	13	11	22	3	0
Branson	.971	27	12	22	1	4
Greene	.934	103	55	172	16	7
Harris	1.000	13	2	17	0	1
Pendleton	.942	32	14	35	3	1
Perez	1.000	8	6	14	0	1
Reese	1.000	8	2	3	0	0
Rose	.600	2	0	3	2	0
Stynes	1.000	3	1	9	0	1

Shortstop	PCT	G	PO	A	E	DP
Branson	1.000	11	6	11	0	2
Greene	.000	3	0	0	0	0
Jackson	1.000	6	5	14	0	2
Larkin	.980	63	77	171	5	33
Reese	.966	110	171	261	15	56

Outfield	PCT	G	PO	A	E	DP
Goodwin	1.000	71	159	3	0	2
Greene	.987	39	74	1	1	1
Harris	.977	42	41	1	1	0
Kelly	.978	59	88	2	2	0
Nunnally	.984	60	120	3	2	1
Owens	.938	18	15	0	1	0
Perez	1.000	12	11	0	0	0
D. Sanders	.984	113	236	3	4	1
R. Sanders	.974	85	183	4	5	1
Sierra	1.000	24	34	3	0	0
Stynes	.976	38	76	5	2	0
Taubensee	1.000	11	8	1	0	0
Timmons	.000	1	0	0	1	0
Watkins	1.000	15	12	1	0	0

FARM SYSTEM

Director of Player Development: Chief Bender

Class	Farm Team	League	W	L	Pct.	Finish*	Manager	First Yr
AAA	Indianapolis (Ind.) Indians	American Assoc.	85	59	.590	2nd (8)	Dave Miley	1993
AA	Chattanooga (Tenn.) Lookouts	Southern	70	69	.504	6th (10)	Mark Berry	1988
A	Burlington (Iowa) Bees	Midwest	72	68	.514	3rd (14)	Phillip Wellman	1997
A	Charleston (W.Va.) Alley Cats	South Atlantic	76	62	.551	2nd (14)	Barry Lyons	1990
#R	Billings (Mont.) Mustangs	Pioneer	39	32	.549	+2nd (8)	Donnie Scott	1974

*Finish in overall standings (No. of teams in league) #Advanced level +Won league championship

ORGANIZATION LEADERS

MAJOR LEAGUERS

BATTING

*AVG	Hal Morris	.276
R	Willie Greene	62
H	Deion Sanders	127
TB	Willie Greene	227
2B	Bret Boone	25
3B	Deion Sanders	7
HR	Willie Greene	26
RBI	Willie Greene	91
BB	Willie Greene	78
SO	Willie Greene	111
SB	Deion Sanders	56

PITCHING

W	Two tied at	11
L	Mike Morgan	12
#ERA	Jeff Shaw	2.38
G	Stan Belinda	84
CG	Two tied at	2
SV	Jeff Shaw	42
IP	Mike Morgan	162
BB	Dave Burba	73
SO	Mike Remlinger	145

MORRIS FOSTOFF

Willie Greene

JOHN SPEAR

Darron Ingram

MINOR LEAGUERS

BATTING

*AVG	Mike Frank, Billings	.376
R	Brady Clark, Burlington	108
H	Jason Williams, Chatt./Burlington	167
TB	Darron Ingram, Burlington	255
2B	Jason LaRue, Charleston	50
3B	Yuri Sanchez, Burlington	12
HR	Darron Ingram, Burlington	29
RBI	Jason Parsons, Charleston	102
BB	Brady Clark, Burlington	76
SO	Darron Ingram, Burlington	195
SB	Wylie Campbell, Charleston	34

PITCHING

W	Two tied at	14
L	Mark Corey, Charleston	13
#ERA	Scott Williamson, Billings	1.78
G	Tom Doyle, Chattanooga	65
CG	Two tied at	4
SV	Todd Williams, Indy/Chattanooga	33
IP	Scott Klingenbeck, Indianapolis	171
BB	Jay Peterson, Burlington	79
SO	Eddie Priest, Chattanooga/Charleston	133

*Minimum 250 At-Bats #Minimum 75 Innings

TOP 10 PROSPECTS

DAVID SEELIG

Brett Tomko

How the Reds Top 10 prospects, as judged by Baseball America prior to the 1997 season, fared in 1997:

Player, Pos.	Club (Class)	AVG	AB	R	H	2B	3B	HR	RBI	SB
1. Aaron Boone, 3b	Cincinnati	.223	443	40	99	25	1	7	46	5
	Indianapolis (AAA)	.290	476	79	138	30	4	22	75	12
3. Pokey Reese, ss	Cincinnati	.219	397	48	87	15	0	4	26	25
	Indianapolis (AAA)	.236	72	12	17	2	0	4	11	4
5. Chad Mottola, of	Indianapolis (AAA	.289	284	33	82	10	6	7	45	12
	Chattanooga (AA)	.362	174	35	63	9	3	5	32	7
6. Paul Bako, c	Indianapolis (AAA)	.243	321	34	78	14	1	8	43	0
7. Justin Towle, c	Chattanooga (AA)	.309	418	62	129	37	5	11	70	5
9. Jeremy Skeens, of	Billings (R)	.204	49	12	10	0	0	1	9	2
10. Darron Ingram, 1b-of	Burlington (A)	.265	510	74	135	25	4	29	97	8

Player, Pos.	Club (Class)	W	L	ERA	G	SV	IP	H	BB	SO
2. Brett Tomko, rhp	Cincinnati	11	7	3.43	22	0	126	106	47	95
	Indianapolis (AAA)	6	3	2.95	10	0	61	53	9	60
4. *Curt Lyons, rhp	Iowa (AAA)	0	2	6.37	8	0	30	35	21	26
	Orlando (AA)	0	0	7.50	2	0	6	6	2	8
8. Scott Sullivan, rhp	Cincinnati	5	3	3.24	59	1	97	79	30	96
	Indianapolis (AAA)	3	1	1.30	19	2	28	16	4	23

*Traded to Cubs

INDIANAPOLIS — Class AAA

AMERICAN ASSOCIATION

BATTING	AVG	G	AB	R	H	2B	3B	HR	RBI	BB	SO	SB	CS	B	T	HT	WT	DOB	1st Yr.	Resides
Bako, Paul	.243	104	321	34	78	14	1	8	43	34	81	0	5	L	R	6-2	205	6-20-72	1993	Lafayette, La.
Belk, Tim	.290	90	255	37	74	18	1	8	38	26	45	5	3	R	R	6-3	200	4-6-70	1992	Houston, Texas
Boone, Aaron	.290	131	476	79	138	30	4	22	75	40	81	12	4	R	R	6-2	190	3-9-73	1994	Villa Park, Calif.
Boone, Bret	.286	3	7	1	2	1	0	0	1	2	2	1	0	R	R	5-10	180	4-6-69	1990	Villa Park, Calif.
Branson, Jeff	.211	15	57	7	12	3	0	1	4	6	10	0	0	L	R	6-0	180	1-26-67	1989	Millry, Ala.
Fordyce, Brook	.234	12	47	7	11	2	0	2	6	5	6	1	1	R	R	6-1	185	5-7-70	1989	Old Lyme, Conn.
Garcia, Guillermo	.238	55	151	16	36	2	0	10	20	9	46	0	2	R	R	6-3	190	4-4-72	1990	Santo Domingo, D.R.
Goodwin, Curtis	.276	30	116	14	32	4	1	1	7	15	20	11	8	L	L	5-11	180	9-30-72	1991	San Leandro, Calif.
Hall, Billy	.200	10	20	3	4	0	0	0	3	1	6	0	0	S	R	5-9	180	6-17-69	1991	Wichita, Kan.
Hunter, Brian	.281	139	506	74	142	36	4	21	85	42	76	9	6	R	L	6-0	195	3-4-68	1987	Anaheim, Calif.
Jackson, Damian	.268	19	71	12	19	6	1	0	7	10	17	4	1	R	R	5-10	160	8-16-73	1992	Concord, Calif.
2-team (73 Buffalo)	.288	92	337	63	97	18	1	4	20	47	62	24	93							
Johnson, Mark	.000	3	4	0	0	0	0	0	0	2	2	0	1	L	L	6-4	220	10-17-67	1990	Worcester, Mass.
Kelly, Mike	.348	27	92	28	32	8	0	7	18	23	23	7	1	R	R	6-4	195	6-2-70	1991	Los Alamitos, Calif.
Kmak, Joe	.158	16	38	6	6	0	0	1	2	5	6	0	0	R	R	6-0	185	5-3-63	1985	Foster City, Calif.
Maas, Kevin	.224	31	67	14	15	4	0	2	7	25	15	0	0	L	L	6-3	205	1-20-65	1986	Berkeley, Calif.
Magdaleno, Ricky	.206	56	155	20	32	11	0	4	14	16	48	0	1	R	R	6-1	170	7-6-74	1993	Baldwin Park, Calif.
Mitchell, Keith	.265	124	407	72	108	24	1	15	60	72	65	10	4	R	R	5-10	180	8-6-69	1987	San Diego, Calif.
Mottola, Chad	.289	83	284	33	82	10	6	7	45	16	43	12	4	R	R	6-3	215	10-15-71	1992	Pembroke Pines, Fla.
Murray, Glenn	.167	7	12	1	2	1	0	0	0	2	3	0	0	R	R	6-2	200	11-23-70	1989	Manning, S.C.
Oliver, Joe	.333	2	9	1	3	0	0	1	1	0	1	0	0	R	R	6-3	220	7-24-65	1983	Orlando, Fla.
Owens, Eric	.286	104	391	56	112	15	4	11	44	42	55	23	10	R	R	6-1	184	2-3-71	1992	Danville, Va.
Pendleton, Terry	.167	4	12	2	2	0	0	0	2	4	1	0	0	S	R	5-9	195	7-16-60	1982	Duluth, Ga.
Reese, Pokey	.236	17	72	12	17	2	0	4	11	9	12	4	0	R	R	6-0	160	6-10-73	1991	Columbia, S.C.
Rose, Pete	.225	12	40	2	9	2	0	0	1	2	11	0	0	L	R	6-1	180	11-16-69	1989	Cincinnati, Ohio
Sanders, Reggie	.211	5	19	1	4	0	0	0	1	1	6	0	0	R	R	6-1	180	12-1-67	1988	Cincinnati, Ohio
Stynes, Chris	.360	21	86	14	31	8	0	1	17	2	5	4	1	R	R	5-9	170	1-19-73	1991	Boca Raton, Fla.
2-team (82 Omaha)	.285	103	418	67	119	26	1	9	61	21	30	7	2							
Timmons, Ozzie	.253	125	407	46	103	14	1	14	55	60	100	1	4	R	R	6-2	205	9-18-70	1991	Tampa, Fla.
Watkins, Pat	.280	84	325	46	91	14	7	9	35	24	55	13	9	R	R	6-2	185	9-2-72	1993	Garner, N.C.
Wilson, Brandon	.228	68	180	24	41	3	4	1	14	18	38	5	4	R	R	6-1	175	2-26-69	1990	Owensboro, Ky.

PITCHING	W	L	ERA	G	GS	CG	SV	IP	H	R	ER	BB	SO	B	T	HT	WT	DOB	1st Yr.	Resides
Bolton, Rodney	9	8	4.30	28	27	1	0	170	185	96	81	47	108	R	R	6-2	190	9-23-68	1990	Chattanooga, Tenn.
Carrara, Giovanni	12	5	3.51	19	18	2	0	121	111	50	47	51	105	R	R	6-2	210	3-4-68	1990	Anzoategui, Venez.
Carrasco, Hector	0	0	6.23	3	0	0	1	4	5	3	3	3	4	R	R	6-2	175	10-22-69	1988	San Pedro de Macoris, D.R.
Crowell, Jim	1	1	2.75	3	3	1	0	20	19	7	6	8	6	L	L	6-4	220	5-14-74	1995	Valparaiso, Ind.
Eischen, Joey	1	0	1.27	26	5	0	2	43	41	7	6	13	26	L	L	6-1	190	5-25-70	1989	West Covina, Calif.
Graves, Danny	1	0	3.09	11	0	0	5	12	7	4	4	5	5	R	R	5-11	200	8-7-73	1995	Valrico, Fla.
2-team (19 Buffalo)	3	3	3.95	30	3	0	7	55	52	25	24	16	26							
Klingenbeck, Scott	12	8	3.96	27	27	2	0	171	180	85	75	41	119	R	R	6-2	205	2-3-71	1992	Cincinnati, Ohio
Lewis, Richie	0	1	1.52	27	0	0	9	30	22	7	5	7	33	R	R	5-10	175	1-25-66	1987	Losantville, Ind.
Martinez, Pedro	4	3	3.47	28	11	1	0	80	70	37	31	35	36	L	L	6-2	155	11-29-68	1987	Villa Mella, D.R.
Nix, James	3	0	8.82	12	0	0	0	16	18	16	16	16	13	R	R	5-11	175	9-6-70	1992	Burton, Texas
Parris, Steve	2	3	3.57	5	5	1	0	35	26	15	14	11	27	R	R	6-0	190	12-17-67	1989	Joliet, Ill.
Reed, Chris	0	1	5.79	3	3	0	0	14	19	11	9	9	4	R	R	6-3	206	8-25-73	1991	Anaheim, Calif.
Rodriguez, Felix	3	3	1.01	23	0	0	1	27	22	10	3	16	26	R	R	6-1	190	12-5-72	1990	Monte Cristi, D.R.
Salkeld, Roger	4	8	6.75	36	11	0	1	88	91	75	66	60	88	R	R	6-5	215	3-6-71	1989	Saugus, Calif.
Service, Scott	3	2	3.71	33	0	0	15	34	30	15	14	12	53	R	R	6-6	226	2-26-67	1986	Cincinnati, Ohio
Sullivan, Scott	3	1	1.30	19	0	0	2	28	16	4	4	4	23	R	R	6-3	210	3-13-71	1993	Carrollton, Ala.
Tabaka, Jeff	3	2	2.65	58	0	0	3	58	44	19	17	19	68	R	L	6-2	195	1-17-64	1986	Clinton, Ohio
Tomko, Brett	6	3	2.95	10	10	0	0	61	53	21	20	9	60	R	R	6-4	205	4-7-73	1995	Tampa, Fla.
Walker, Mike	9	6	2.98	55	5	0	7	103	80	35	34	46	80	R	R	6-1	195	10-4-66	1986	Brooksville, Fla.
White, Gabe	7	4	2.82	20	19	0	0	118	119	46	37	18	62	L	L	6-2	200	11-20-71	1990	Sebring, Fla.
Williams, Todd	2	0	2.13	12	0	0	2	13	11	4	3	6	11	R	R	6-3	185	2-13-71	1991	East Syracuse, N.Y.
Winchester, Scott	0	0	0.00	4	0	0	0	6	2	0	0	2	2	R	R	6-2	210	4-20-73	1995	Midland, Mich.

FIELDING

Catcher	PCT	G	PO	A	E	DP	PB
Bako	.991	99	622	64	6	10	9
Fordyce	1.000	11	73	8	0	0	2
Garcia	1.000	35	189	6	0	3	8
Kmak	.976	13	71	11	2	0	0
Oliver	1.000	2	21	4	0	0	0

First Base	PCT	G	PO	A	E	DP
Belk	.992	69	462	24	4	43
Garcia	1.000	4	11	0	0	0
Hunter	.988	81	635	52	8	61
Johnson	1.000	3	17	2	0	0
Maas	.975	10	72	5	2	2
Mitchell	1.000	2	8	0	0	0

Second Base	PCT	G	PO	A	E	DP
A. Boone	.900	6	19	8	3	0
B. Boone	1.000	3	6	10	0	2
Garcia	1.000	10	13	18	0	5
Hall	1.000	6	15	15	0	4
Jackson	.967	12	25	33	2	7
Owens	.955	84	157	201	17	35
Reese	1.000	4	10	11	0	2
Stynes	.982	21	47	61	2	17
Wilson	1.000	12	14	28	0	4

Third Base	PCT	G	PO	A	E	DP
Belk	.885	9	10	13	3	1
A. Boone	.943	122	76	241	19	27
Branson	1.000	2	1	2	0	0
Garcia	.909	6	3	7	1	0
Magdaleno	1.000	1	1	1	0	0
Owens	1.000	3	0	1	0	0
Pendleton	1.000	4	3	10	0	0
Rose	.957	10	3	19	1	2
Wilson	.500	4	1	0	1	0

Shortstop	PCT	G	PO	A	E	DP
A. Boone	.949	11	17	20	2	3
Branson	.979	14	17	30	1	7
Jackson	.917	7	11	22	3	5
Magdaleno	.941	54	62	147	13	24
Owens	.863	19	24	39	10	5
Reese	.955	13	33	31	3	5
Wilson	.942	47	58	88	9	21

Outfield	PCT	G	PO	A	E	DP
Goodwin	1.000	30	57	2	0	0
Hunter	.990	58	99	4	1	0
Kelly	.963	25	51	1	2	0
Maas	1.000	1	1	0	0	0
Mitchell	.978	83	169	6	4	4
Mottola	.947	75	136	8	8	3
Murray	1.000	2	4	0	0	0
Owens	1.000	4	3	0	0	0
Sanders	.750	5	6	0	2	0
Timmons	.983	97	172	3	3	1
Watkins	.989	83	170	5	2	1

CHATTANOOGA — Class AA

SOUTHERN LEAGUE

BATTING	AVG	G	AB	R	H	2B	3B	HR	RBI	BB	SO	SB	CS	B	T	HT	WT	DOB	1st Yr.	Resides
Allen, Marlon	.255	62	196	27	50	15	2	4	23	26	39	0	1	R	R	6-6	228	3-28-73	1994	Columbus, Ga.
Broach, Donald	.274	105	402	62	110	15	4	0	31	35	47	12	15	R	R	6-0	185	7-18-71	1993	Cincinnati, Ohio
Coughlin, Kevin	.292	54	168	22	49	7	0	3	15	15	20	0	2	L	L	6-0	175	9-7-70	1989	Clarksburg, Md.
Dismuke, Jamie	.286	36	98	21	28	5	0	4	25	18	10	0	1	L	R	6-1	210	10-17-69	1989	Syracuse, N.Y.
Eddie, Steve	.287	118	394	57	113	25	4	8	49	21	64	3	2	R	R	6-1	185	1-6-71	1993	Storm Lake, Iowa
Garcia, Guillermo	.284	20	74	11	21	1	1	4	19	8	13	0	0	R	R	6-3	190	4-4-72	1990	Santo Domingo, D.R.
Gibralter, Steve	.258	30	97	20	25	9	0	2	12	13	22	0	0	R	R	6-0	170	10-9-72	1990	Duncanville, Texas
Gordon, Keith	.167	4	12	2	2	0	0	1	2	3	7	1	1	R	R	6-1	205	1-22-69	1990	Olney, Md.
Grall, Greg	.250	2	4	0	1	0	0	0	0	0	2	0	0	R	R	6-0	170	1-25-65	1997	Chattanooga, Tenn.
Griffey, Craig	.228	55	180	28	41	5	1	0	15	24	41	8	7	R	R	5-11	175	6-3-71	1991	West Chester, Ohio
2-team (35 Memphis)	.223	90	300	48	67	8	2	0	20	37	63	14	8							
Hall, Billy	.256	58	215	31	55	4	2	3	19	24	35	13	8	S	R	5-9	180	6-17-69	1991	Wichita, Kan.
Kelly, Mike	.350	15	60	14	21	7	0	3	12	3	16	3	2	R	R	6-4	195	6-2-70	1991	Los Alamitos, Calif.
Koelling, Brian	.280	73	279	50	78	9	3	3	22	28	49	18	9	R	R	6-1	185	6-11-69	1991	Cleveland, Ohio
Ladell, Cleveland	.344	14	32	3	11	1	0	0	4	0	3	1	1	R	R	5-11	170	9-19-70	1992	Dallas, Texas
Larson, Brandon	.268	11	41	4	11	5	1	0	6	1	10	0	0	R	R	5-11	190	5-24-76	1997	San Antonio, Texas
Magdaleno, Ricky	.262	61	187	33	49	13	1	8	34	42	51	1	1	R	R	6-1	170	7-6-74	1993	Baldwin Park, Calif.
Mottola, Chad	.362	46	174	35	63	9	3	5	32	16	23	7	1	R	R	6-3	215	10-15-71	1992	Pembroke Pines, Fla.
Murray, Glenn	.283	94	329	66	93	16	2	26	73	56	91	7	5	R	R	6-2	200	11-23-70	1989	Manning, S.C.
Presto, Nick	.226	9	31	2	7	1	0	0	6	2	7	1	0	R	R	5-10	175	7-8-74	1996	Jupiter, Fla.
Price, Corey	.333	1	3	0	1	0	0	0	0	1	1	0	0	S	R	6-0	170	9-18-76	1996	Mt. Pleasant, Texas
Rose, Pete	.308	112	445	75	137	31	0	25	98	34	63	0	1	L	R	6-1	180	11-16-69	1989	Cincinnati, Ohio
Rumfield, Toby	.287	101	331	35	95	22	1	5	38	18	32	0	1	R	R	6-3	190	9-4-72	1991	Belton, Texas
Sanders, Reggie	.545	3	11	3	6	1	1	1	3	1	2	0	0	R	R	6-1	180	12-1-67	1988	Cincinnati, Ohio
Towle, Justin	.309	119	418	62	129	37	5	11	70	55	77	5	5	R	R	6-3	210	2-21-74	1992	Seattle, Wash.
Wagner, Mark	.250	2	4	0	1	0	0	0	1	0	0	0	0	R	R	6-0	175	3-4-54	1997	Ashtabula, Ohio
Watkins, Pat	.350	46	177	35	62	15	1	7	30	15	16	9	3	R	R	6-2	185	9-2-72	1993	Garner, N.C.
Williams, Jason	.310	69	271	38	84	21	1	5	28	18	35	5	5	R	R	5-8	180	12-18-73	1996	Gonzales, La.

PITCHING	W	L	ERA	G	GS	CG	SV	IP	H	R	ER	BB	SO	B	T	HT	WT	DOB	1st Yr.	Resides
Atchley, Justin	4	2	4.70	13	13	1	0	67	75	45	35	14	48	L	L	6-2	205	9-5-73	1995	Sedro Woolley, Wash.
Boggs, Robert	1	3	7.59	9	9	0	0	40	53	36	34	21	35	R	R	6-4	225	8-30-74	1995	Ivydale, W.Va.
Bryant, Adam	1	0	7.00	6	0	0	0	9	15	8	7	1	4	R	R	6-6	225	12-27-71	1994	Levittown, Pa.
Caruthers, Clay	2	4	9.09	9	6	0	0	35	63	36	35	17	30	S	R	6-2	200	11-20-72	1994	North Richland Hills, Texas
Courtright, John	5	7	6.82	20	16	0	0	92	137	79	70	42	42	L	L	6-2	185	5-30-70	1991	Columbus, Ohio
Crowell, Jim	2	1	2.84	3	3	0	0	19	19	6	6	5	14	L	L	6-4	220	5-14-74	1995	Valparaiso, Ind.
Cushman, Dwayne	0	0	16.20	1	0	0	0	2	4	3	3	1	1	R	R	6-0	175	11-27-71	1995	Port Salerno, Fla.
Donnelly, Brendan	6	4	3.27	62	0	0	6	83	71	43	30	37	64	R	R	6-3	200	7-4-71	1992	Albuquerque, N.M.
Doyle, Tom	7	3	3.51	65	0	0	0	67	62	32	26	38	46	L	L	6-3	205	1-20-70	1988	Redondo Beach, Calif.
Eddie, Steve	0	0	12.00	3	0	0	0	3	4	4	4	1	0	R	R	6-1	185	1-6-71	1993	Storm Lake, Iowa
Etler, Todd	0	3	6.57	23	0	0	0	37	38	29	27	24	29	R	R	6-0	205	4-18-74	1992	Villa Hills, Ky.
Gower, Tim	2	0	4.57	24	0	0	0	45	52	24	23	12	28	R	R	6-1	185	9-16-71	1997	Salinas, Calif.
Jean, Domingo	1	1	9.75	10	0	0	1	12	17	20	13	15	9	R	R	6-2	175	1-9-69	1990	San Pedro de Macoris, D.R.
Koppe, Clint	2	5	7.38	13	13	0	0	68	82	58	56	44	33	R	R	6-4	220	8-14-73	1994	Lake Jackson, Texas
LeBlanc, Eric	2	4	5.58	8	8	0	0	50	53	35	31	21	25	L	R	6-1	195	7-6-73	1996	North Troy, Vt.
Lott, Brian	6	7	6.77	25	14	0	0	92	108	76	69	50	62	R	R	6-0	200	5-15-72	1994	Cleveland, Texas
McKenzie, Scott	2	0	5.77	30	0	0	0	53	74	37	34	19	30	R	R	6-0	185	9-30-70	1993	Arlington, Texas
Nix, James	6	1	3.13	28	0	0	0	37	31	15	13	20	32	R	R	5-11	175	9-6-70	1992	Burton, Texas
Parris, Steve	6	2	4.13	14	14	0	0	81	78	44	37	29	68	R	R	6-0	190	12-17-67	1989	Joliet, Ill.
Priest, Eddie	4	6	3.44	14	14	1	0	92	101	39	35	17	63	R	L	6-1	200	4-8-74	1994	Horton, Ala.
Reed, Chris	6	8	5.34	23	23	0	0	130	140	93	77	68	96	R	R	6-3	206	8-25-73	1991	Anaheim, Calif.
Tryon, Eric	0	4	8.31	6	6	0	0	26	35	27	24	16	7	R	L	6-0	195	9-3-75	1997	Terre Haute, Ind.
Williams, Todd	3	3	2.10	48	0	0	31	56	38	16	13	25	45	R	R	6-3	185	2-13-71	1991	East Syracuse, N.Y.
Winchester, Scott	2	1	1.69	9	0	0	3	11	9	4	2	3	3	R	R	6-2	210	4-20-73	1995	Midland, Mich.

FIELDING

Catcher	PCT	G	PO	A	E	DP	PB
Garcia	.988	11	75	7	1	2	0
Rumfield	.988	34	219	23	3	4	3
Towle	.984	96	537	68	10	4	18

First Base	PCT	G	PO	A	E	DP
Allen	.984	57	463	26	8	52
Dismuke	.995	24	190	17	1	16
Eddie	.981	30	193	16	4	17
Garcia	1.000	1	10	0	0	2
Rumfield	.981	40	324	31	7	32
Towle	1.000	5	37	3	0	4

Second Base	PCT	G	PO	A	E	DP
Eddie	1.000	2	1	1	0	0
Garcia	1.000	3	7	8	0	2
Hall	.973	29	59	83	4	16
Koelling	.954	42	80	107	9	28
Presto	1.000	1	3	2	0	0
Price	1.000	1	1	4	0	1
Williams	.988	65	140	180	4	50

Third Base	PCT	G	PO	A	E	DP
Eddie	.933	36	24	73	7	6
Koelling	.778	6	1	6	2	0
Rose	.917	102	81	217	27	31
Rumfield	.750	1	0	3	1	0
Wagner	1.000	1	1	1	0	0

Shortstop	PCT	G	PO	A	E	DP
Eddie	.929	36	51	106	12	26
Garcia	1.000	1	3	4	0	0
Hall	.919	8	16	18	3	5
Koelling	.938	20	31	60	6	13
Larson	.891	11	19	22	5	5
Magdaleno	.941	58	116	171	18	28
Presto	.917	8	8	14	2	2

Outfield	PCT	G	PO	A	E	DP
Broach	.987	99	215	9	3	1
Coughlin	.986	45	68	4	1	0
Eddie	.947	10	18	0	1	0
Gibralter	.972	19	35	0	1	0
Gordon	1.000	4	6	0	0	0
Griffey	.981	52	95	6	2	1
Hall	.962	12	25	0	1	0
Kelly	1.000	15	32	2	0	0
Ladell	1.000	10	22	0	0	0
Mottola	.963	44	74	5	3	0
Murray	.974	75	146	6	4	0
Rumfield	1.000	6	11	2	0	0
Sanders	1.000	3	11	0	0	0
Towle	.000	1	0	0	0	0
Watkins	1.000	43	78	3	0	1

BURLINGTON — Class A

MIDWEST LEAGUE

BATTING	AVG	G	AB	R	H	2B	3B	HR	RBI	BB	SO	SB	CS	B	T	HT	WT	DOB	1st Yr	Resides
Allen, Marlon	.310	69	242	42	75	20	1	12	52	36	61	5	3	R	R	6-6	228	3-28-73	1994	Columbus, Ga.

BATTING	AVG	G	AB	R	H	2B	3B	HR	RBI	BB	SO	SB	CS	B	T	HT	WT	DOB	1st Yr	Resides
Baderdeen, Kevin	.220	39	127	18	28	3	0	3	8	14	61	3	1	R	R	6-2	175	1-12-77	1997	Goshen, Ind.
Boyette, Tony	.273	4	11	1	3	0	0	1	4	1	4	0	0	R	R	6-0	200	12-7-75	1994	Alachua, Fla.
Clark, Brady	.325	126	459	108	149	29	7	11	63	76	71	31	18	R	R	6-2	195	4-18-73	1996	San Diego, Calif.
Craig, Benny	.275	61	240	43	66	16	3	10	45	22	70	6	3	S	R	6-4	210	1-15-75	1997	Santee, Calif.
Davis, James	.292	91	319	37	93	18	1	5	46	17	46	3	0	R	R	6-4	205	4-14-73	1995	Bowling Green, Ky.
Goodhart, Steve	.185	19	54	11	10	3	0	0	4	16	13	3	0	R	R	6-0	170	2-14-73	1995	Heath, Ohio
Hampton, Mike	.241	77	228	52	55	8	3	13	42	47	58	18	4	R	R	6-7	195	1-17-72	1994	Colorado Springs, Colo.
Ingram, Darron	.265	134	510	74	135	25	4	29	97	46	195	8	5	R	R	6-3	225	6-7-76	1994	Lexington, Ky.
Lofton, James	.265	129	483	83	128	18	3	4	45	54	89	20	12	S	R	5-9	170	3-6-74	1993	Los Angeles, Calif.
Presto, Nick	.213	27	94	14	20	7	0	0	8	7	15	3	2	R	R	5-10	175	7-8-74	1996	Jupiter, Fla.
Rojas, Christian	.239	101	348	53	83	17	3	16	56	33	106	7	3	R	R	6-1	170	6-3-75	1994	Santo Domingo, D.R.
Sanchez, Yuri	.255	101	364	66	93	12	12	13	48	35	116	7	3	L	R	6-1	165	11-11-73	1992	Lynn, Mass.
Scott, Tom	.301	50	183	30	55	16	1	6	34	9	57	10	1	R	R	6-0	185	3-29-73	1995	Canby, Ore.
Sharp, Scott	.149	30	87	9	13	2	0	0	10	12	36	0	2	R	R	6-2	200	10-16-72	1994	Sykesville, Md.
Sorg, Jay	.283	112	399	62	113	18	2	13	72	56	65	13	7	L	R	6-3	195	5-10-73	1994	Louisville, Ky.
Valdez, Trovin	.252	33	119	22	30	3	1	0	11	16	28	14	4	R	R	5-10	163	11-18-73	1993	New York, N.Y.
Whitehead, Braxton	.187	36	123	11	23	6	0	0	13	9	27	2	2	R	R	6-2	215	10-20-75	1997	Newton, Miss.
Williams, Jason	.324	68	256	49	83	17	1	7	41	21	40	9	6	R	R	5-8	180	12-18-73	1996	Gonzales, La.

GAMES BY POSITION: C—Boyette 4, Davis 90, Sharp 27, Whitehead 26. **1B**—Allen 51, Hampton 1, Ingram 23, Sorg 64, Whitehead 6. **2B**—Goodhart 19, Lofton 75, Presto 26, Sanchez 1, Williams 23. **3B**—Baderdeen 35, Hampton 16, Lofton 51, Sharp 3, Sorg 43. **SS**—Baderdeen 4, Presto 1, Sanchez 93, Williams 45. **OF**—Clark 117, Craig 40, Hampton 39, Ingram 86, Lofton 3, Rojas 67, Scott 44, Valdez 33.

PITCHING	W	L	ERA	G	GS	CG	SV	IP	H	R	ER	BB	SO	B	T	HT	WT	DOB	1st Yr	Resides
Callahan, Damon	2	2	3.86	11	7	0	0	37	33	17	16	15	29	R	R	6-4	190	12-10-75	1994	Cleveland, Tenn.
Caruthers, Clay	3	7	5.84	17	13	0	0	74	103	63	48	26	44	S	R	6-2	200	11-20-72	1994	North Richland Hills, Texas
Cushman, Dwayne	1	4	3.02	47	0	0	19	51	45	22	17	25	54	R	R	6-0	175	11-27-71	1995	Port Salerno, Fla.
Davis, Lance	4	6	6.59	30	13	0	0	97	121	78	71	55	51	R	L	6-0	165	9-1-76	1995	Polk City, Fla.
Etler, Todd	2	3	2.09	25	0	0	3	43	34	13	10	14	40	R	R	6-0	205	4-18-74	1992	Villa Hills, Ky.
Garcia, Eddy	6	6	5.58	22	6	0	0	69	84	49	43	21	60	R	R	6-2	205	5-31-76	1994	San Cristobal, D.R.
Giuliano, Joe	6	5	4.91	32	15	0	0	114	123	74	62	44	76	R	R	6-2	180	1-1-76	1994	Hamilton, Ohio
Hurst, Doug	2	1	3.13	22	0	0	1	46	44	19	16	18	23	R	R	5-11	195	2-23-76	1997	Pensacola, Fla.
MacRae, Scott	11	4	3.82	27	26	4	0	160	159	76	68	57	89	R	R	6-3	205	8-13-74	1995	Marietta, Ga.
O'Toole, Ryan	1	1	1.93	3	0	0	0	9	9	4	2	3	4	R	R	6-3	190	10-2-75	1997	Irvine, Calif.
Peterson, Jay	14	6	4.48	26	26	0	0	145	139	88	72	79	112	S	R	6-4	185	11-2-75	1994	Commerce City, Colo.
Phillips, Jon	4	5	3.95	37	1	0	0	71	63	33	31	33	66	R	R	6-5	205	1-23-75	1996	Hiram, Ga.
Riedling, John	7	6	5.26	35	16	0	0	103	101	70	60	47	104	R	R	5-11	190	8-29-75	1994	Pompano Beach, Fla.
Sparks, Jeff	2	5	5.72	22	9	0	0	61	61	49	39	39	72	R	R	6-3	210	4-4-72	1995	Houston, Texas
Tryon, Eric	2	0	3.53	7	7	0	0	36	37	15	14	19	25	R	L	6-0	195	9-3-75	1997	Terre Haute, Ind.
Wright, Scott	5	7	3.11	42	1	0	5	84	74	39	29	34	75	R	R	6-2	205	10-15-72	1995	Medford, Wis.

CHARLESTON, W. Va. — Class A

SOUTH ATLANTIC LEAGUE

BATTING	AVG	G	AB	R	H	2B	3B	HR	RBI	BB	SO	SB	CS	B	T	HT	WT	DOB	1st Yr	Resides
Broach, Donald	.300	18	60	15	18	0	0	0	8	11	9	8	1	R	R	6-0	185	7-18-71	1993	Cincinnati, Ohio
Burress, Andy	.207	38	87	12	18	0	0	2	14	4	26	1	0	R	R	6-0	190	7-18-77	1995	McRae, Ga.
Campbell, Wylie	.272	121	453	73	123	18	4	0	36	41	80	34	12	S	R	5-11	170	3-27-75	1996	Grove, Okla.
Claybrook, Steve	.241	95	249	38	60	6	3	1	21	28	68	22	10	L	R	6-0	170	12-30-72	1995	Robstown, Texas
Garrett, Scott	.257	33	101	9	26	4	0	0	14	4	39	1	1	R	R	6-5	225	3-8-74	1996	Denver, N.C.
Goodhart, Steve	.226	81	252	26	57	5	2	1	28	32	66	7	3	R	R	6-0	170	2-14-73	1995	Heath, Ohio
Guthrie, David	.215	73	233	27	50	7	2	3	26	20	75	6	2	S	R	6-2	185	5-21-74	1995	Raleigh, N.C.
Keller, Jeremy	.262	117	386	55	101	19	1	9	66	48	93	3	0	L	R	6-0	190	1-24-74	1996	Rock Hill, S.C.
Larkin, Stephen	.278	129	464	88	129	23	10	13	79	52	83	28	9	L	L	6-0	190	7-24-73	1994	Cincinnati, Ohio
LaRue, Jason	.315	132	473	78	149	50	3	8	81	47	90	14	4	R	R	5-11	195	3-19-74	1995	Spring Branch, Texas
Montgomery, Andre	.190	20	58	6	11	3	0	0	5	2	23	7	2	R	R	5-10	185	6-27-77	1995	Louisville, Ky.
Murphy, Robbie	.184	53	174	19	32	10	0	0	7	7	38	7	2	S	R	5-11	165	3-22-73	1996	Dickson, Tenn.
Newman, Howard	.161	12	31	3	5	1	0	1	4	6	10	2	0	R	R	5-10	190	12-5-75	1997	Riverside, Calif.
O'Hearn, Brandon	.242	65	215	27	52	13	3	6	32	23	69	6	2	R	R	6-3	200	6-24-75	1996	Butler, Ga.
Parsons, Jason	.311	131	460	87	143	34	0	20	102	62	99	5	1	R	R	6-3	220	9-2-72	1995	Laguna Beach, Calif.
Presto, Nick	.287	83	300	57	86	19	2	3	44	26	60	16	2	R	R	5-10	175	7-8-74	1996	Jupiter, Fla.
Price, Corey	.258	22	62	7	16	1	0	0	10	9	16	4	3	S	R	6-0	170	9-18-76	1996	Mt. Pleasant, Texas
Scott, Tom	.250	60	212	27	53	14	2	8	28	17	82	6	6	R	R	6-0	185	3-29-73	1995	Canby, Ore.
Tidwell, David	.264	65	258	40	68	8	3	2	26	25	47	15	9	R	R	5-9	170	1-17-75	1997	Grenada, Miss.

GAMES BY POSITION: C—Burress 4, Garrett 30, LaRue 106, Newman 11. **1B**—Keller 22, Larkin 32, LaRue 7, O'Hearn 1, Parsons 89. **2B**—Campbell 15, Goodhart 80, Montgomery 15, Presto 20, Price 13. **3B**—Campbell 95, Keller 40, LaRue 5, Presto 10, Price 1. **SS**—Campbell 11, Guthrie 73, Presto 54, Price 4. **OF**—Broach 17, Burress 11, Claybrook 84, Larkin 100, LaRue 1, Murphy 50, O'Hearn 61, Scott 60, Tidwell 64.

PITCHING	W	L	ERA	G	GS	CG	SV	IP	H	R	ER	BB	SO	B	T	HT	WT	DOB	1st Yr	Resides
Acevedo, Jose	3	3	3.92	15	8	0	0	57	61	29	25	9	34	R	R	6-0	185	12-18-77	1997	Santiago, D.R.
Altman, Gene	1	4	7.79	17	1	0	0	32	45	31	28	10	35	R	R	6-7	209	9-1-78	1996	Lynchburg, S.C.
Arminio, Sam	2	3	3.80	46	2	0	6	90	113	45	38	20	58	R	R	6-2	200	9-23-72	1997	Hamilton, Ohio
Averette, Robert	2	2	7.86	11	3	0	1	26	42	28	23	12	20	R	R	6-2	185	9-30-76	1997	Sylacauga, Ala.
Boggs, Robert	1	1	7.34	15	1	0	0	34	44	30	28	20	25	R	R	6-4	225	8-30-74	1995	Ivydale, W.Va.
Carlyle, Buddy	14	5	2.77	23	23	4	0	143	130	51	44	27	111	S	R	6-2	175	12-21-77	1996	Bellevue, Neb.
Corey, Mark	8	13	4.57	26	26	1	0	136	169	87	69	42	97	R	R	6-3	210	11-16-74	1995	Austin, Pa.
Danner, Andy	1	2	2.66	22	0	0	2	44	38	23	13	15	35	R	R	6-0	195	7-23-75	1997	Springfield, Ill.
Garcia, Eddy	1	1	7.88	6	0	0	0	16	16	16	14	5	10	R	R	6-2	205	5-31-76	1994	San Cristobal, D.R.
Giron, Roberto	1	1	8.64	7	0	0	0	8	14	8	8	6	5	R	R	6-2	175	3-24-76	1994	Villa Mella, D.R.
Gower, Tim	4	2	2.68	35	0	0	13	37	31	13	11	9	30	R	R	6-1	185	9-16-71	1997	Salinas, Calif.
Holliday, Hugh	0	0	2.40	14	0	0	1	15	10	4	4	6	15	L	L	6-2	220	1-16-73	1997	Easley, S.C.
Koppe, Clint	0	1	7.57	23	1	0	4	27	38	23	23	10	23	R	R	6-4	220	8-14-73	1994	Lake Jackson, Texas
LeBlanc, Eric	10	7	3.36	24	13	2	1	107	98	51	40	29	77	L	R	6-1	195	7-6-73	1996	North Troy, Vt.
Mallard, Randi	3	3	3.83	13	12	0	0	56	51	25	24	23	61	R	R	6-1	185	8-11-75	1996	Tampa, Fla.

PITCHING	W	L	ERA	G	GS	CG	SV	IP	H	R	ER	BB	SO	B	T	HT	WT	DOB	1st Yr	Resides
Needham, Kevin	4	3	4.81	35	11	0	2	79	93	58	42	28	51	L	L	6-0	190	1-30-75	1996	Burlington, Ontario
Priest, Eddie	5	3	3.62	14	14	0	0	77	79	38	31	10	70	R	L	6-1	200	4-8-74	1994	Horton, Ala.
Rose, Ted	11	6	2.51	38	13	2	4	129	108	44	36	27	132	L	R	6-1	180	8-23-73	1996	St. Clairsville, Ohio
Shepard, David	5	2	4.95	18	10	0	3	67	82	46	37	17	45	R	R	6-1	190	2-6-74	1996	Hormel, N.Y.

BILLINGS — Rookie

PIONEER LEAGUE

BATTING	AVG	G	AB	R	H	2B	3B	HR	RBI	BB	SO	SB	CS	B	T	HT	WT	DOB	1st Yr	Resides
Armenta, Jason	.237	44	97	17	23	5	0	0	5	7	27	2	2	L	L	5-10	180	10-31-76	1997	San Diego, Calif.
Burress, Andy	.304	27	102	13	31	7	0	5	18	6	20	1	1	R	R	6-0	190	7-18-77	1995	McRae, Ga.
Caceres, Wilmy	.263	15	38	10	10	2	0	0	9	2	3	1	1	S	R	6-0	170	10-2-78	1997	Santo Domingo, D.R.
Dawkins, Travis	.241	70	253	47	61	5	0	4	37	30	38	16	6	R	R	6-1	180	5-12-79	1997	Chappells, S.C.
Frank, Mike	.376	69	266	62	100	22	6	10	62	35	24	18	8	L	L	6-2	185	1-14-75	1997	Escondido, Calif.
Markray, Thad	.143	46	119	11	17	3	0	0	5	15	44	3	0	R	R	6-3	215	9-20-79	1997	Springhill, La.
Montgomery, Andre	.314	51	207	43	65	18	2	4	31	15	47	6	4	R	R	5-10	185	6-27-77	1995	Louisville, Ky.
Newman, Howard	.295	17	44	7	13	3	0	1	7	0	14	0	0	R	R	5-10	190	12-5-75	1997	Riverside, Calif.
Oliver, John	.091	6	11	1	1	0	0	0	0	1	3	0	0	R	R	6-3	200	5-14-78	1996	Dallas, Pa.
Pascual, Edison	.071	10	14	2	1	0	0	0	0	2	5	0	0	L	L	6-3	198	9-10-76	1994	Santo Domingo, D.R.
Price, Corey	.267	19	60	11	16	1	0	0	8	7	14	0	1	S	R	6-0	170	9-18-76	1996	Mt. Pleasant, Texas
Rios, Fernando	.333	41	153	19	51	8	1	0	18	11	22	1	5	R	R	6-2	180	12-15-78	1997	Glendale, Calif.
Rivera, Francisco	.239	26	46	4	11	2	0	1	5	6	13	0	0	L	R	6-2	195	10-4-79	1996	El Tejar, Mexico
Sanchez, Toby	.219	62	178	37	39	5	0	5	35	39	76	4	6	R	R	6-1	230	6-27-75	1997	Tustin, Calif.
Skeens, Jeremy	.204	23	49	12	10	0	0	1	9	12	15	2	0	R	R	6-2	175	11-13-77	1996	Middletown, Ohio
Solano, Manny	.224	42	98	14	22	3	1	1	9	9	15	0	3	R	R	5-11	185	5-17-78	1995	Villa Mella, D.R.
Suarez, Marc	.347	64	219	42	76	17	0	9	37	33	51	2	1	R	R	6-4	235	1-18-76	1997	Miami, Fla.
Welsh, Eric	.315	67	260	41	82	13	2	11	54	18	38	2	4	L	L	6-3	200	9-17-76	1997	Lockport, Ill.
Wise, DeWayne	.313	62	268	53	84	13	9	7	41	9	47	18	8	L	L	6-1	170	2-24-78	1997	Chapin, S.C.

GAMES BY POSITION: C—Burress 1, Newman 13, Rivera 13, Suarez 62. **1B**—Pascual 5, Sanchez 26, Welsh 48. **2B**—Caceres 10, Montgomery 46, Price 19, Solano 7. **3B**—Caceres 1, Markray 44, Montgomery 7, Sanchez 11, Solano 31. **SS**—Caceres 4, Dawkins 70, Solano 2. **OF**—Armenta 37, Burress 7, Frank 69, Oliver 3, Rios 41, Skeens 23, Solano 1, Wise 62.

PITCHING	W	L	ERA	G	GS	CG	SV	IP	H	R	ER	BB	SO	B	T	HT	WT	DOB	1st Yr	Resides
Altman, Gene	3	2	7.83	20	5	0	3	33	48	36	29	19	34	R	R	6-7	209	9-1-78	1996	Lynchburg, S.C.
Averette, Robert	0	0	0.00	2	1	0	0	3	3	0	0	1	3	R	R	6-2	185	9-30-76	1997	Sylacauga, Ala.
Brewer, Clint	3	5	3.29	22	0	0	4	41	33	21	15	20	37	R	R	6-3	185	11-22-78	1997	Dibble, Okla.
Brown, Zay	0	0	5.73	8	0	0	0	11	22	14	7	9	12	R	R	6-1	175	1-5-79	1997	Warrenville, S.C.
Caddell, Carl	1	1	0.93	4	1	0	0	10	7	1	1	3	5	L	L	6-3	185	10-13-75	1996	Fort Worth, Texas
Haring, Brett	0	2	4.63	14	0	0	0	23	30	14	12	9	16	R	L	5-11	180	2-7-75	1997	Coleman, Mich.
Harris, Josh	4	6	4.02	14	14	0	0	85	103	51	38	26	56	R	R	6-3	230	10-23-77	1996	Canyon Lake, Texas
Hurst, Doug	0	0	4.50	1	0	0	0	2	2	1	1	1	2	R	R	5-11	195	2-23-76	1997	Pensacola, Fla.
Levy, Tye	1	0	3.60	18	2	0	0	30	32	14	12	9	32	L	L	6-4	185	4-20-78	1997	Alexandria, Pa.
Merrell, Philip	2	6	4.33	14	14	0	0	73	72	51	35	27	62	R	R	6-4	200	3-11-78	1996	Nampa, Idaho
O'Toole, Ryan	1	0	2.37	11	1	0	1	19	20	12	5	7	6	R	R	6-3	190	10-2-75	1997	Irvine, Calif.
Robinson, Dustin	6	2	3.68	16	9	2	4	73	91	38	30	6	48	R	R	6-6	215	9-13-75	1997	Chandler, Okla.
Roundtree, Monte	1	2	5.06	13	5	0	1	37	37	38	21	33	40	L	L	6-4	165	2-7-78	1997	Greenville, N.C.
Runk, David	0	0	8.10	10	0	0	0	13	13	14	12	16	8	R	R	6-3	190	9-1-78	1997	Broad Top, Pa.
Stumbo, Wes	3	2	4.19	15	2	0	1	34	33	21	16	22	40	R	R	6-6	230	2-19-76	1997	Lexington, Ky.
Timm, Dan	4	1	4.66	20	4	0	4	39	47	24	20	26	36	S	R	6-2	165	4-2-76	1997	Glen Ellyn, Ill.
Whitesides, John	2	1	7.36	9	0	0	0	11	16	14	9	7	10	R	R	6-4	200	3-2-78	1997	Sarasota, Fla.
Williamson, Scott	8	2	1.78	13	13	2	0	86	66	25	17	23	101	R	R	6-1	185	2-17-76	1997	Friendswood, Texas

Cleveland INDIANS

Manager: Mike Hargrove.

1997 Record: 86-75, .534 (1st, AL Central)

BATTING	AVG	G	AB	R	H	2B	3B	HR	RBI	BB	SO	SB	CS	B	T	HT	WT	DOB	1st Yr	Resides
Alomar, Sandy	.324	125	451	63	146	37	0	21	83	19	48	0	2	R	R	6-5	215	6-18-66	1984	Westlake, Ohio
Aven, Bruce	.211	13	19	4	4	1	0	0	2	1	5	0	1	R	R	5-9	180	3-4-72	1994	Orange, Texas
Borders, Pat	.296	55	159	17	47	7	1	4	15	9	27	0	2	R	R	6-2	195	5-14-63	1982	Lake Wales, Fla.
Branson, Jeff	.264	29	72	5	19	4	0	2	7	7	17	0	2	L	R	6-0	180	1-26-67	1989	Millry, Ala.
Candaele, Casey	.308	14	26	5	8	1	0	0	4	1	1	1	0	S	R	5-9	165	1-12-61	1983	San Luis Obispo, Calif.
Casey, Sean	.200	6	10	1	2	0	0	0	1	1	2	0	0	L	R	6-4	215	7-2-74	1995	Pittsburgh, Pa.
Curtis, Chad	.207	22	29	8	6	1	0	3	5	7	10	0	0	R	R	5-10	175	11-6-68	1989	Middleville, Mich.
Diaz, Einar	.143	5	7	1	1	1	0	0	1	0	2	0	0	R	R	5-10	165	12-28-72	1991	Chiriqui, Panama
Fernandez, Tony	.286	120	409	55	117	21	1	11	44	22	47	6	6	S	R	6-2	175	6-30-62	1980	Santo Domingo, D.R.
Franco, Julio	.284	78	289	46	82	13	1	3	25	38	75	8	5	R	R	6-1	188	8-23-61	1978	San Pedro de Macoris, D.R.
Giles, Brian	.268	130	377	62	101	15	3	17	61	63	50	13	3	L	L	5-11	195	1-20-71	1989	El Cajon, Calif.
Grissom, Marquis	.262	144	558	74	146	27	6	12	66	43	89	22	13	R	R	5-11	192	4-17-67	1988	Red Oak, Ga.
Hubbard, Trenidad	.250	7	12	3	3	1	0	0	0	1	3	2	0	R	R	5-8	180	5-11-66	1986	Houston, Texas
Jackson, Damian	.111	8	9	2	1	0	0	0	0	0	1	1	0	R	R	5-10	160	8-16-73	1992	Concord, Calif.
Justice, David	.329	139	495	84	163	31	1	33	101	80	79	3	5	L	L	6-3	200	4-14-66	1985	Atlanta, Ga.
Manto, Jeff	.267	16	30	3	8	3	0	2	7	1	10	0	0	R	R	6-3	210	8-23-64	1985	Bristol, Pa.
Mitchell, Kevin	.153	20	59	7	9	1	0	4	11	9	11	1	0	R	R	5-11	210	1-13-62	1981	Chula Vista, Calif.
Ramirez, Manny	.328	150	561	99	184	40	0	26	88	79	115	2	3	R	R	6-0	190	5-30-72	1991	Brooklyn, N.Y.
Roberts, Bip	.271	23	85	19	23	3	0	3	8	7	14	3	0	S	R	5-7	160	10-27-63	1982	Las Vegas, Nev.
2-team (97 K.C.)	.302	120	431	63	130	20	2	4	44	28	67	18	3							
Seitzer, Kevin	.268	64	198	27	53	14	0	2	24	18	25	0	0	R	R	5-11	190	3-26-62	1983	Overland Park, Kan.
Sexson, Richie	.273	5	11	1	3	0	0	0	0	0	2	0	0	R	R	6-6	206	12-29-74	1993	Brush Prairie, Wash.
Thome, Jim	.286	147	496	104	142	25	0	40	102	120	146	1	1	L	R	6-4	220	8-27-70	1989	Peoria, Ill.
Vizquel, Omar	.280	153	565	89	158	23	6	5	49	57	58	43	12	S	R	5-9	165	4-24-67	1984	Caracas, Venez.
Williams, Matt	.263	151	596	86	157	32	3	32	105	34	108	12	4	R	R	6-2	205	11-28-65	1986	Scottsdale, Ariz.
Wilson, Enrique	.333	5	15	2	5	0	0	0	1	0	2	0	0	S	R	5-11	160	7-27-75	1992	Santo Domingo, D.R.

PITCHING	W	L	ERA	G	GS	CG	SV	IP	H	R	ER	BB	SO	B	T	HT	WT	DOB	1st Yr	Resides
Anderson, Brian	4	2	4.69	8	8	0	0	48	55	28	25	11	22	S	L	6-1	180	4-26-72	1993	Geneva, Ohio
Assenmacher, Paul	5	0	2.94	75	0	0	4	49	43	17	16	15	53	L	L	6-3	195	12-10-60	1983	Stone Mountain, Ga.
Clark, Terry	0	3	6.15	4	4	0	0	26	29	21	18	13	13	R	R	6-2	196	10-10-60	1979	Fontana, Calif.
Colon, Bartolo	4	7	5.65	19	17	1	0	94	107	66	59	45	66	R	R	6-0	185	5-24-75	1994	Puerto Plata, D.R.
Graves, Danny	0	0	4.76	5	0	0	0	11	15	8	6	9	4	R	R	5-11	200	8-7-73	1995	Valrico, Fla.
Hershiser, Orel	14	6	4.47	32	32	1	0	195	199	105	97	69	107	R	R	6-3	193	9-16-58	1979	Pasadena, Calif.
Jackson, Mike	2	5	3.24	71	0	0	15	75	59	33	27	29	74	R	R	6-2	223	12-22-64	1984	Spring, Texas
Jacome, Jason	2	0	5.27	21	4	0	0	43	45	26	25	15	24	L	L	6-0	180	11-24-70	1991	Tucson, Ariz.
2-team (7 K.C.)	2	0	5.84	28	4	0	0	49	58	33	32	20	27							
Juden, Jeff	0	1	5.46	8	5	0	0	31	32	21	19	15	29	R	R	6-7	245	1-19-71	1989	Salem, Mass.
Kline, Steve	3	1	5.81	20	1	0	0	26	42	19	17	13	17	S	L	6-2	200	8-22-72	1993	Winfield, Pa.
Lopez, Albie	3	7	6.93	37	6	0	0	77	101	61	59	40	63	R	R	6-2	205	8-18-71	1991	Mesa, Ariz.
McDowell, Jack	3	3	5.09	8	6	0	0	41	44	25	23	18	38	R	R	6-5	185	1-16-66	1987	Chicago, Ill.
Mesa, Jose	4	4	2.40	66	0	0	16	82	83	28	22	28	69	R	R	6-3	225	5-22-66	1982	Westlake, Ohio
Morman, Alvin	0	0	5.89	34	0	0	2	18	19	13	12	14	13	R	L	6-3	210	1-6-69	1991	Rockingham, N.C.
Nagy, Charles	15	11	4.28	34	34	1	0	227	253	115	108	77	149	L	R	6-3	200	5-5-67	1989	Westlake, Ohio
Ogea, Chad	8	9	4.99	21	21	1	0	126	139	79	70	47	80	R	R	6-2	200	11-9-70	1991	Lake Charles, La.
Plunk, Eric	4	5	4.66	55	0	0	0	66	62	37	34	36	66	R	R	6-6	220	9-3-63	1981	Riverside, Calif.
Shuey, Paul	4	2	6.20	40	0	0	2	45	52	31	31	28	46	R	R	6-3	215	9-16-70	1992	Raleigh, N.C.
Smiley, John	2	4	5.54	6	6	0	0	37	45	23	23	10	26	L	L	6-4	215	3-17-65	1983	Trappe, Pa.
Weathers, Dave	1	2	7.56	9	1	0	0	17	23	14	14	8	14	R	R	6-3	205	9-25-69	1988	Loretto, Tenn.
2-team (10 New York)	1	3	8.42	19	1	0	0	26	38	24	24	15	18							
Wright, Jaret	8	3	4.38	16	16	0	0	90	81	45	44	35	63	R	R	6-2	220	12-29-75	1994	Anaheim, Calif.

FIELDING

Catcher	PCT	G	PO	A	E	DP	PB
Alomar	.985	119	743	40	12	8	3
Borders	1.000	53	312	19	0	2	5
Diaz	.955	5	18	3	1	0	0

First Base	PCT	G	PO	A	E	DP
Casey	1.000	1	2	0	0	0
Franco	1.000	1	1	0	0	0
Manto	1.000	6	35	1	0	4
Seitzer	1.000	19	146	13	0	17
Sexson	1.000	2	11	1	0	0
Thome	.993	145	1233	95	10	123

Second Base	PCT	G	PO	A	E	DP
Branson	.986	19	21	51	1	10
Candaele	1.000	9	10	25	0	4
Fernandez	.981	109	207	296	10	59
Franco	.983	35	69	107	3	23
D. Jackson	.000	1	0	0	0	0
Roberts	.932	13	24	31	4	9
Wilson	1.000	1	1	3	0	0

Third Base	PCT	G	PO	A	E	DP
Branson	1.000	6	2	8	0	2
Candaele	.000	1	0	0	0	0
Manto	1.000	7	0	4	0	0
Roberts	1.000	10	3	12	0	1
Seitzer	.885	13	3	20	3	0
Williams	.970	151	89	301	12	21

Shortstop	PCT	G	PO	A	E	DP
Branson	1.000	2	0	1	0	0
Fernandez	.974	10	12	26	1	7
Jackson	1.000	5	7	7	0	2
Vizquel	.985	152	245	428	10	98
Wilson	.941	4	6	10	1	4

Outfield	PCT	G	PO	A	E	DP
Aven	1.000	13	15	1	0	0
Curtis	1.000	19	20	0	0	0
Giles	.972	115	201	7	6	1
Grissom	.992	144	356	7	3	3
Hubbard	1.000	6	3	0	0	0
Justice	.984	78	120	3	2	0
Manto	.000	1	0	0	0	0
Mitchell	.000	1	0	0	1	0
Ramirez	.975	146	259	10	7	2
Roberts	1.000	10	13	2	0	1

FARM SYSTEM

Director of Player Development: Mark Shapiro

Class	Farm Team	League	W	L	Pct.	Finish*	Manager	First Yr
AAA	Buffalo (N.Y.) Bisons	American Assoc.	87	57	.604	+1st (8)	Brian Graham	1995
AA	Akron (Ohio) Aeros	Eastern	51	90	.362	10th (10)	Jeff Datz	1997
#A	Kinston (N.C.) Indians	Carolina	87	53	.621	1st (8)	Joel Skinner	1987
A	Columbus (Ga.) RedStixx	South Atlantic	62	76	.449	12th (14)	Jack Mull	1991
A	Watertown (N.Y.) Indians	New York-Penn	39	36	.520	5th (14)	Ted Kubiak	1989
R	Burlington (N.C.) Indians	Appalachian	32	36	.471	6th (10)	Harry Spilman	1986

*Finish in overall standings (No. of teams in league) #Advanced level + Won league championship

ORGANIZATION LEADERS

MAJOR LEAGUERS

BATTING

*AVG	Dave Justice	.329
R	Jim Thome	104
H	Manny Ramirez	184
TB	Manny Ramirez	302
2B	Manny Ramirez	40
3B	Two tied at	6
HR	Jim Thome	40
RBI	Matt Williams	105
BB	Jim Thome	120
SO	Jim Thome	146
SB	Omar Vizquel	43

PITCHING

W	Charles Nagy	15
L	Charles Nagy	11
#ERA	Jose Mesa	2.40
G	Paul Assenmacher	75
CG	Four tied at	1
SV	Jose Mesa	16
IP	Charles Nagy	227
BB	Charles Nagy	77
SO	Charles Nagy	149

Jim Thome

KEN BABBITT

Russ Branyan

MINOR LEAGUERS

BATTING

*AVG	Sean Casey, Buffalo/Akron	.380
R	Scott Morgan, Akron/Kinston	97
H	David Miller, Akron	153
TB	Russ Branyan, Akron/Kinston	269
2B	Scott Morgan, Akron/Kinston	35
3B	David Miller, Akron	9
HR	Russ Branyan, Akron/Kinston	39
RBI	Russ Branyan, Akron/Kinston	105
BB	Danny Peoples, Kinston	84
SO	Russ Branyan, Akron/Kinston	150
SB	Joe Kilburg, Kinston/Burlington	30

PITCHING

W	Frankie Sanders, Kinston	11
L	Mike Bacsik, Columbus	14
#ERA	Jim Crowell, Akron/Kinston	2.65
G	Marc Deschenes, Kinston/Columbus	60
CG	Maximo de la Rosa, Buffalo/Akron	5
SV	Scott Winchester, Akron/Kinston	30
IP	Jason Rakers, Akron/Kinston	151
BB	Teddy Warrecker, Akron/Kinston	80
SO	Jason Rakers, Akron/Kinston	139

*Minimum 250 At-Bats #Minimum 75 Innings

TOP 10 PROSPECTS

STAN DENNY

Bartolo Colon

How the Indians Top 10 prospects, as judged by Baseball America prior to the 1997 season, fared in 1997:

Player, Pos.	Club (Class)	AVG	AB	R	H	2B	3B	HR	RBI	SB
4. Enrique Wilson, ss-2b	Cleveland	.333	15	2	5	0	0	0	1	0
	Buffalo (AAA)	.306	451	78	138	20	3	11	39	9
5. Russ Branyan, 3b	Akron (AA)	.234	137	26	32	4	0	12	30	0
	Kinston (A)	.290	297	59	86	26	2	27	75	3
6. Richie Sexson, 1b	Cleveland	.273	11	1	3	0	0	0	0	0
	Buffalo (AA)	.260	434	57	113	20	2	31	88	5
8. Sean Casey, 1b	Cleveland	.200	10	1	2	0	0	0	1	0
	Buffalo (AAA)	.361	72	12	26	7	0	5	18	0
	Akron (AA)	.386	241	38	93	19	1	10	66	0
9. Einar Diaz, c	Cleveland	.143	7	1	1	1	0	0	1	0
	Buffalo (AAA)	.256	336	40	86	18	2	3	31	2
10. *Damian Jackson, ss	Cleveland	.111	9	2	1	0	0	0	0	1
	Cincinnati	.222	27	6	6	2	1	1	2	1
	Buffalo (AAA)	.293	266	51	78	12	0	4	13	20
	Indianapolis (AAA)	.268	71	12	19	6	1	0	7	4
		W	**L**	**ERA**	**G**	**SV**	**IP**	**H**	**BB**	**SO**
1. Bartolo Colon, rhp	Cleveland	4	7	5.65	19	0	94	107	45	66
	Buffalo (AAA)	7	1	2.22	10	0	57	45	23	54
2. Jaret Wright, rhp	Cleveland	8	3	4.38	16	0	90	81	35	63
	Buffalo (AAA)	4	1	1.80	7	0	45	30	19	47
	Akron (AA)	3	3	3.67	8	0	54	43	23	59
3. Willie Martinez, rhp	Kinston (A)	8	2	3.09	23	0	137	125	42	120
7. *Danny Graves, rhp	Cleveland	0	0	4.76	5	0	11	15	9	4
	Cincinnati	0	0	6.14	10	0	15	26	11	7
	Indianapolis (AAA)	1	0	3.09	11	5	12	7	5	5
	Buffalo (AAA)	2	3	4.19	19	2	43	45	11	21

*Traded to Cincinnati

Organization Statistics

BUFFALO — Class AAA

AMERICAN ASSOCIATION

BATTING	AVG	G	AB	R	H	2B	3B	HR	RBI	BB	SO	SB	CS	B	T	HT	WT	DOB	1st Yr	Resides
Aven, Bruce	.287	121	432	69	124	27	3	17	77	50	99	10	3	R	R	5-9	180	3-4-72	1994	Orange, Texas
Brewer, Rod	.161	10	31	3	5	1	0	2	5	8	9	0	0	L	L	6-3	208	2-24-66	1987	Zellwood, Fla.
Busch, Mike	.181	51	166	24	30	4	0	12	29	22	68	0	0	R	R	6-5	241	7-7-68	1990	Donahue, Iowa
Candaele, Casey	.228	79	311	39	71	21	0	7	38	31	43	1	6	S	R	5-9	165	1-12-61	1983	San Luis Obispo, Calif.
Casey, Sean	.361	20	72	12	26	7	0	5	18	9	11	0	0	L	R	6-4	215	7-2-74	1995	Pittsburgh, Pa.
Curtis, Randy	.270	41	111	14	30	7	0	5	15	14	22	1	1	L	L	5-10	180	1-16-71	1991	Norco, Calif.
Diaz, Einar	.256	109	336	40	86	18	2	3	31	18	34	2	6	R	R	5-10	165	12-28-72	1991	Chiriqui, Panama
Hubbard, Trenidad	.312	103	375	71	117	22	1	16	60	57	52	26	10	R	R	5-8	180	5-11-66	1986	Houston, Texas
Jackson, Damian	.293	73	266	51	78	12	0	4	13	37	45	20	8	R	R	5-10	160	8-16-73	1992	Concord, Calif.
Listach, Pat	.260	25	73	3	19	1	1	0	2	12	10	6	3	S	R	5-9	170	9-12-67	1988	Spring, Texas
Lovullo, Torey	.227	97	321	40	73	18	0	12	40	51	64	0	5	S	R	6-0	185	7-25-65	1987	Northridge, Calif.
Manto, Jeff	.321	54	187	37	60	11	0	20	54	31	43	0	2	R	R	6-3	210	8-23-64	1985	Bristol, Pa.
McCall, Rod	.234	36	107	12	25	5	0	6	20	9	37	0	0	L	L	6-7	235	11-4-71	1990	Stanton, Calif.
Norman, Les	.259	118	428	71	111	20	1	17	56	43	80	7	6	R	R	6-1	185	2-25-69	1991	Greenfield, Ill.
Ramirez, Alex	.286	119	416	59	119	19	8	11	44	24	95	10	5	R	R	5-11	176	10-3-74	1991	Miranda, Venez.
Scutaro, Marcos	.263	21	57	8	15	3	0	1	6	6	8	0	1	R	R	5-10	170	10-30-75	1995	San Felipe, Venez.
Sexson, Richie	.260	115	434	57	113	20	2	31	88	27	87	5	1	R	R	6-6	206	12-29-74	1993	Brush Prairie, Wash.
Soliz, Steve	.192	62	151	12	29	5	0	1	13	10	40	0	1	R	R	5-10	180	1-27-71	1993	Oxnard, Calif.
Thomas, Greg	.077	11	13	1	1	1	0	0	2	3	6	0	0	L	L	6-3	200	7-19-72	1993	Orlando, Fla.
Thompson, Ryan	.242	24	66	10	16	0	0	1	6	5	16	2	0	R	R	6-3	200	11-4-67	1987	Edesville, Md.
Wilson, Enrique	.306	118	451	78	138	20	3	11	39	42	41	9	8	S	R	5-11	160	7-27-75	1992	Santo Domingo, D.R.

PITCHING	W	L	ERA	G	GS	CG	SV	IP	H	R	ER	BB	SO	B	T	HT	WT	DOB	1st Yr	Resides
Anderson, Brian	7	1	3.05	15	15	1	0	86	78	33	29	15	60	S	L	6-1	180	4-26-72	1993	Geneva, Ohio
Barfield, John	0	1	27.00	1	0	0	0	1	3	3	3	0	1	L	L	6-1	195	10-15-64	1986	Pine Bluff, Ark.
Blomdahl, Ben	7	8	4.76	29	13	1	0	104	110	64	55	31	60	R	R	6-2	185	12-30-70	1991	Riverside, Calif.
Cabrera, Jose	3	0	1.20	5	0	0	0	15	8	2	2	7	11	R	R	6-0	197	3-24-72	1991	Santiago, D.R.
Cadaret, Greg	2	2	4.86	29	1	0	4	50	46	31	27	35	49	L	L	6-3	215	2-27-62	1983	Mesa, Ariz.
Clark, Terry	7	3	2.85	25	10	4	3	95	86	34	30	30	63	R	R	6-2	196	10-10-60	1979	Fontana, Calif.
Colon, Bart	7	1	2.22	10	10	1	0	57	45	15	14	23	54	R	R	6-0	185	5-24-75	1994	Puerto Plata, D.R.
Delamaza, Roland	9	4	2.90	34	14	2	2	115	104	42	37	43	73	R	R	6-2	195	11-11-71	1993	Arleta, Calif.
De la Rosa, Maximo	2	2	6.49	15	4	0	0	43	43	34	31	33	31	R	R	5-11	170	7-12-71	1990	Villa Mella, D.R.
Dougherty, Tony	2	0	3.77	18	0	0	2	29	31	17	12	18	21	R	R	6-2	205	4-12-73	1994	Slippery Rock, Pa.
Driskill, Travis	8	7	4.65	29	24	1	0	147	159	86	76	60	102	R	R	6-0	185	8-1-71	1993	Austin, Texas
Graves, Danny	2	3	4.19	19	3	0	2	43	45	21	20	11	21	R	R	5-11	200	8-7-73	1995	Valrico, Fla.
Ilsley, Blaise	0	0	2.19	9	0	0	0	12	12	3	3	1	7	L	L	6-1	185	4-9-64	1985	Alpena, Mich.
Jacome, Jason	3	1	3.16	7	7	1	0	37	41	14	13	10	23	L	L	6-0	180	11-24-70	1991	Tucson, Ariz.
Kirkreit, Daron	1	0	0.00	1	1	1	0	7	3	0	0	1	2	R	R	6-6	225	8-7-72	1993	Norco, Calif.
Kline, Steve	3	3	4.03	20	4	0	1	51	53	26	23	13	41	S	L	6-2	200	8-22-72	1993	Winfield, Pa.
Lopez, Albie	1	0	0.00	7	0	0	1	11	6	0	0	2	13	R	R	6-2	205	8-18-71	1991	Mesa, Ariz.
Matthews, Mike	0	2	7.71	5	5	0	0	21	32	19	18	10	17	L	L	6-2	175	10-24-73	1992	Woodbridge, Va.
Miranda, Angel	0	2	10.03	9	0	0	0	12	20	14	13	5	9	L	L	6-1	195	11-9-69	1987	Arecibo, P.R.
Montgomery, Steve	1	2	5.63	7	0	0	1	8	12	6	5	3	5	R	R	6-4	200	12-25-70	1992	Corona Del Mar, Calif.
Moore, Marcus	5	3	2.54	10	10	3	0	71	54	26	20	31	72	S	R	6-5	204	11-2-70	1989	Oakland, Calif.
Morman, Alvin	0	0	0.00	3	0	0	0	3	2	0	0	0	3	R	L	6-3	210	1-6-69	1991	Rockingham, N.C.
2-team (8 N.O.)	0	1	3.38	11	0	0	0	13	13	5	5	2	17							
Ogea, Chad	1	1	4.29	4	4	0	0	21	24	10	10	6	11	R	R	6-2	200	11-9-70	1991	Lake Charles, La.
Rakers, Jason	1	0	0.00	1	1	0	0	7	5	0	0	1	3	R	R	6-2	197	6-29-73	1995	Pittsburgh, Pa.
Scott, Darryl	5	6	2.88	48	0	0	12	66	52	24	21	28	29	R	R	6-1	185	8-6-68	1990	Prior Lake, Minn.
Sexton, Jeff	2	1	5.32	15	0	0	0	24	17	14	14	12	15	R	R	6-2	190	10-4-71	1993	Indianola, Okla.
Shuey, Paul	0	0	3.60	2	0	0	0	5	4	2	2	4	6	R	R	6-3	215	9-16-70	1992	Raleigh, N.C.
Weathers, David	4	3	3.15	11	11	2	0	69	71	37	24	17	51	R	R	6-3	205	9-25-69	1988	Loretto, Tenn.
Whitten, Casey	0	0	0.00	2	0	0	0	1	1	0	0	0	0	L	L	6-0	175	5-23-72	1993	Terre Haute, Ind.
Wright, Jaret	4	1	1.80	7	7	1	0	45	30	16	9	19	47	R	R	6-2	220	12-29-75	1994	Anaheim, Calif.

FIELDING

Catcher	PCT	G	PO	A	E	DP	PB
Candaele	.000	2	0	0	0	0	0
Diaz	.975	105	650	60	18	8	3
Soliz	.974	60	276	24	8	2	5

First Base	PCT	G	PO	A	E	DP
Brewer	.947	2	18	0	1	1
Busch	.991	13	104	6	1	13
Casey	1.000	2	17	1	0	1
Lovullo	1.000	3	16	1	0	1
Manto	1.000	5	43	0	0	9
McCall	1.000	10	74	3	0	5
Norman	1.000	3	17	1	0	4
Sexson	.996	110	922	77	4	105
Thomas	1.000	2	6	0	0	1

Second Base	PCT	G	PO	A	E	DP
Candaele	.980	55	95	155	5	35
Jackson	.968	6	13	17	1	5
Listach	1.000	2	1	4	0	1
Lovullo	.967	28	50	67	4	22
Scutaro	1.000	12	18	27	0	10
Wilson	.970	51	117	143	8	31

Third Base	PCT	G	PO	A	E	DP
Busch	.857	5	5	7	2	2
Candaele	.899	26	24	47	8	3
Diaz	.909	3	3	7	1	1
Hubbard	.967	11	8	21	1	3
Listach	1.000	5	1	6	0	1
Lovullo	.958	66	49	134	8	13
Manto	.918	28	13	54	6	9
Scutaro	.889	7	6	10	2	1
Wilson	1.000	2	2	4	0	1

Shortstop	PCT	G	PO	A	E	DP
Candaele	1.000	1	0	1	0	0
Jackson	.940	66	113	229	22	53
Listach	.929	12	20	32	4	6
Lovullo	1.000	1	0	1	0	1
Scutaro	.900	2	3	6	1	2
Wilson	.959	64	99	185	12	45

Outfield	PCT	G	PO	A	E	DP
Aven	.991	108	219	3	2	1
Brewer	.500	1	1	0	1	0
Curtis	1.000	27	48	1	0	0
Hubbard	.996	89	228	5	1	2
Jackson	1.000	1	2	0	0	0
Listach	1.000	6	12	0	0	0
Manto	1.000	2	3	0	0	0
Norman	.995	107	206	6	1	1
Ramirez	.946	99	167	8	10	3
Thompson	.955	15	20	1	1	0

AKRON — Class AA

EASTERN LEAGUE

BATTING	AVG	G	AB	R	H	2B	3B	HR	RBI	BB	SO	SB	CS	B	T	HT	WT	DOB	1st Yr	Resides
Betts, Todd	.246	128	439	65	108	25	1	20	69	73	97	1	3	L	R	6-0	190	6-24-73	1993	Scarborough, Ontario
Betzsold, Jim	.265	118	434	76	115	21	5	19	79	60	119	4	5	R	R	6-3	210	8-7-72	1994	Orange, Calif.
Branyan, Russell	.234	41	137	26	32	4	0	12	30	28	56	0	0	L	R	6-3	195	12-19-75	1994	Warner Robins, Ga.

BATTING	AVG	G	AB	R	H	2B	3B	HR	RBI	BB	SO	SB	CS	B	T	HT	WT	DOB	1st Yr	Resides
Casey, Sean	.386	62	241	38	93	19	1	10	66	23	34	0	1	L	R	6-4	215	7-2-74	1995	Pittsburgh, Pa.
Claudio, Patricio	.212	17	33	6	7	1	0	0	6	3	14	2	2	R	R	6-0	173	4-12-72	1991	Santiago, D.R.
Curtis, Chad	.389	4	18	5	7	1	0	3	6	0	3	0	1	R	R	5-10	175	11-6-68	1989	Middleville, Mich.
Curtis, Randy	.237	29	93	19	22	3	0	5	15	22	27	2	3	L	L	5-10	180	1-16-71	1991	Norco, Calif.
Glass, Chip	.259	113	394	74	102	17	4	5	37	56	61	16	10	L	L	5-11	180	6-24-71	1994	Ukiah, Calif.
Gross, Rafael	.286	19	49	7	14	4	0	0	2	2	13	3	3	R	R	5-11	185	8-15-74	1993	Santo Domingo, D.R.
Harriss, Robin	.267	49	146	24	39	8	0	1	17	20	36	0	1	R	R	6-1	205	8-7-71	1994	San Angelo, Texas
Mercedes, Guillermo	.208	97	288	37	60	7	1	0	27	28	38	2	3	S	R	5-11	155	1-17-74	1991	La Romana, D.R.
Miller, David	.301	134	509	84	153	27	9	4	61	48	77	22	11	L	L	6-4	200	12-9-73	1996	Wyndmoor, Pa.
Morgan, Scott	.174	21	69	11	12	3	0	2	6	8	20	1	0	R	R	6-7	230	7-19-73	1995	Lompoc, Calif.
Morris, Bobby	.252	42	119	17	30	9	1	1	15	22	21	1	2	L	R	6-0	180	11-22-72	1993	Munster, Ind.
Moyle, Mike	.231	104	342	56	79	15	0	16	53	53	71	3	0	R	R	6-2	200	9-8-71	1992	Dianella, Australia
Mulligan, Sean	.429	2	7	1	3	1	0	0	1	1	0	0	0	R	R	6-2	205	4-25-70	1991	Diamond Bar, Calif.
Neal, Mike	.282	126	457	77	129	24	2	17	69	55	103	8	7	R	R	6-1	180	11-5-71	1993	Hammond, La.
Perry, Chan	.315	119	476	74	150	34	2	20	96	28	61	3	3	R	R	6-2	200	9-13-72	1994	Mayo, Fla.
Riggs, Kevin	.225	53	178	34	40	9	0	1	20	34	35	3	1	L	R	5-11	190	2-3-69	1990	East Hartford, Conn.
Thomas, Greg	.244	67	242	27	59	13	2	7	42	29	50	2	1	L	L	6-3	200	7-19-72	1993	Orlando, Fla.

PITCHING	W	L	ERA	G	GS	CG	SV	IP	H	R	ER	BB	SO	B	T	HT	WT	DOB	1st Yr	Resides
Badorek, Mike	1	2	6.12	4	4	1	0	25	40	22	17	6	15	R	R	6-5	230	5-15-69	1991	Mt. Zion, Ill.
Baker, Scott	2	1	3.42	4	4	1	0	26	25	11	10	4	12	S	L	6-2	175	5-18-70	1990	Henderson, Nev.
Bennett, Erik	2	3	4.81	11	1	0	0	24	26	13	13	9	20	R	R	6-2	205	9-13-68	1989	Yreka, Calif.
Briscoe, John	0	1	3.94	33	0	0	5	32	41	19	14	12	28	R	R	6-3	195	9-22-67	1988	Richardson, Texas
Calmus, Lance	1	1	6.10	5	1	0	0	10	6	7	7	9	10	R	R	6-5	225	1-19-73	1996	Oklahoma City, Okla.
Camp, Jared	2	8	6.19	12	12	1	0	64	79	49	44	26	39	R	R	6-1	195	5-4-75	1995	Huntington, W.Va.
Carter, John	1	2	10.30	10	0	0	0	25	32	30	29	22	10	R	R	6-1	195	2-16-72	1991	Chicago, Ill.
2-team (9 Bing.)	1	2	9.00	19	0	0	0	39	51	45	39	26	24							
Crowell, Jim	1	0	4.50	3	3	0	0	18	13	12	9	11	7	L	L	6-4	220	5-14-74	1995	Valparaiso, Ind.
De la Rosa, Maximo	4	9	4.44	17	13	5	0	97	112	63	48	32	70	R	R	5-11	170	7-12-71	1990	Villa Mella, D.R.
Dougherty, Tony	0	2	2.54	28	0	0	8	39	31	11	11	19	31	R	R	6-2	205	4-12-73	1994	Slippery Rock, Pa.
Gordon, Mike	1	2	4.15	6	6	0	0	30	37	28	14	14	16	L	R	6-2	195	11-30-72	1992	Quincy, Fla.
Granata, Chris	1	0	7.20	4	0	0	0	5	8	5	4	4	3	R	R	6-0	205	2-26-72	1994	Columbus, Ohio
Gray, Dennis	0	2	12.27	10	0	0	0	7	13	10	10	9	5	L	L	6-6	225	12-24-69	1991	Banning, Calif.
Kirkreit, Daron	8	9	5.20	26	20	1	0	118	131	96	68	69	83	R	R	6-6	225	8-7-72	1993	Norco, Calif.
Lopez, Albie	0	0	0.00	1	0	0	0	1	2	0	0	0	2	R	R	6-2	205	8-18-71	1991	Mesa, Ariz.
Martinez, Johnny	1	8	4.96	32	0	0	2	49	63	32	27	26	31	R	R	6-3	168	11-25-72	1991	Guayabin, D.R.
Matthews, Mike	6	8	3.82	19	19	3	0	113	116	62	48	57	69	L	L	6-2	175	10-24-73	1992	Woodbridge, Va.
Mesa, Rafael	0	1	4.21	14	0	0	0	26	36	13	12	9	7	R	R	6-4	175	10-9-73	1991	Azua, D.R.
Montoya, Wilmer	0	0	11.57	2	0	0	0	2	4	3	3	2	2	R	R	5-10	165	3-15-74	1993	Carabobo, Venez.
Moore, Marcus	3	5	4.94	13	10	1	0	71	84	50	39	32	63	S	R	6-5	204	11-2-70	1989	Oakland, Calif.
Najera, Noe	4	8	6.06	25	14	1	0	85	96	63	57	40	50	L	L	6-2	190	12-9-70	1992	Norwalk, Calif.
Perez, Julio	1	0	5.63	9	0	0	1	24	27	16	15	13	23	R	R	6-1	163	5-18-74	1993	San Cristobal, D.R.
Rakers, Jason	1	4	4.39	7	7	1	0	41	36	21	20	11	31	R	R	6-2	197	6-29-73	1995	Pittsburgh, Pa.
Sexton, Jeff	2	0	4.75	16	3	0	1	47	55	27	25	15	38	R	R	6-2	190	10-4-71	1993	Indianola, Okla.
Shuey, Paul	0	0	3.38	3	0	0	0	8	10	3	3	0	9	R	R	6-3	215	9-16-70	1992	Raleigh, N.C.
Vaught, Jay	2	3	5.22	29	4	0	1	71	65	43	41	40	56	L	R	6-1	185	12-21-71	1994	Deer Park, Texas
Warrecker, Teddy	1	5	11.53	10	7	0	0	32	44	50	41	40	25	L	R	6-6	215	10-1-72	1994	Santa Barbara, Calif.
Weber, Lenny	1	0	15.43	6	0	0	0	9	22	17	16	9	8	R	R	6-1	180	8-6-72	1994	Jeanerette, La.
Wertz, Bill	1	0	9.61	11	1	0	0	20	32	24	21	12	7	R	R	6-6	220	1-15-67	1989	Cleveland, Ohio
Whitten, Casey	1	3	5.87	4	4	0	0	15	20	12	10	11	14	L	L	6-0	175	5-23-72	1993	Terre Haute, Ind.
Winchester, Scott	0	0	3.86	6	0	0	1	7	8	3	3	2	8	R	R	6-2	210	4-20-73	1995	Midland, Mich.
Wright, Jaret	3	3	3.67	8	8	1	0	54	43	26	22	23	59	R	R	6-2	220	12-29-75	1994	Anaheim, Calif.

FIELDING

Catcher	PCT	G	PO	A	E	DP	PB
Harriss	.991	47	294	29	3	2	3
Moyle	.993	99	592	80	5	10	17
Mulligan	1.000	2	11	0	0	0	0

First Base	PCT	G	PO	A	E	DP
Betts	.900	2	8	1	1	0
Casey	.988	52	405	22	5	35
Miller	1.000	2	15	1	0	0
Perry	.994	56	427	34	3	32
Thomas	.963	39	296	19	12	25

Second Base	PCT	G	PO	A	E	DP
Gross	1.000	6	15	8	0	5
Morris	.927	32	69	84	12	11
Neal	.967	72	167	158	11	34
Riggs	.916	40	79	73	14	18

Third Base	PCT	G	PO	A	E	DP
Betts	.904	94	75	178	27	17
Branyan	.921	39	31	98	11	7
Gross	.889	3	0	8	1	0
Neal	.947	9	5	13	1	0
Perry	1.000	1	1	2	0	0

Shortstop	PCT	G	PO	A	E	DP
Gross	.769	3	3	7	3	2
Mercedes	.963	97	161	283	17	42
Neal	.923	49	78	127	17	23

Outfield	PCT	G	PO	A	E	DP
Betzsold	.960	117	197	17	9	1
Claudio	1.000	12	25	0	0	0
C. Curtis	1.000	4	5	2	0	0
R. Curtis	.923	21	47	1	4	0
Glass	.962	101	191	11	8	1
Gross	1.000	5	14	0	0	0
Harriss	1.000	2	1	0	0	0
Miller	.980	132	230	9	5	0
Morgan	.976	21	37	4	1	1
Perry	1.000	14	31	2	0	0
Thomas	.958	13	23	0	1	0

KINSTON — Class A

CAROLINA LEAGUE

BATTING	AVG	G	AB	R	H	2B	3B	HR	RBI	BB	SO	SB	CS	B	T	HT	WT	DOB	1st Yr	Resides
Betances, Junior	.278	74	230	34	64	10	2	4	26	24	34	8	4	R	R	5-10	170	5-26-73	1991	La Vega, D.R.
Branyan, Russell	.290	83	297	59	86	26	2	27	75	52	94	3	1	L	R	6-3	195	12-19-75	1994	Warner Robins, Ga.
Budzinski, Mark	.286	68	241	43	69	13	3	7	39	48	61	6	4	L	L	6-2	175	8-26-73	1995	Severna Park, Md.
Claudio, Patricio	.303	24	89	14	27	5	0	1	9	2	16	1	2	R	R	6-0	173	4-12-72	1991	Santiago, D.R.
Evans, Pat	.203	26	69	5	14	3	0	0	2	8	21	0	1	S	R	5-10	175	12-5-72	1994	San Ramon, Calif.
Gonzalez, Richard	.254	44	142	17	36	6	0	2	17	13	25	0	0	R	R	6-0	185	11-13-74	1995	Miami, Fla.
Gross, Rafael	.267	73	266	53	71	20	0	9	36	30	68	17	10	R	R	5-11	185	8-15-74	1993	Santo Domingo, D.R.
Hayes, Heath	.254	103	378	54	96	22	0	24	59	40	107	2	3	R	R	6-3	195	2-29-72	1994	Citrus Heights, Calif.
Huelsmann, Mike	.246	90	289	50	71	9	4	2	19	48	56	12	4	S	R	5-11	165	11-21-74	1996	St. Louis, Mo.
Jorgensen, Tim	.284	91	334	49	95	19	2	18	65	28	47	0	1	L	R	6-3	200	11-30-72	1995	Depere, Wis.
Kilburg, Joe	.233	9	30	5	7	2	0	1	5	5	6	1	0	L	R	5-11	180	12-20-75	1997	Bay Village, Ohio
McDonald, John	.259	130	541	77	140	27	3	5	53	51	75	6	5	R	R	5-11	175	9-24-74	1996	East Lyme, Conn.
Morgan, Scott	.315	95	368	86	116	32	3	23	67	47	87	4	2	R	R	6-7	230	7-19-73	1995	Lompoc, Calif.
Morris, Bobby	.156	10	32	6	5	1	0	2	10	4	6	0	0	L	R	6-0	180	11-22-72	1993	Munster, Ind.
Motley, Mel	.211	7	19	3	4	1	0	1	1	0	5	0	0	R	R	6-4	195	2-5-74	1996	Riverside, Calif.

BATTING	AVG	G	AB	R	H	2B	3B	HR	RBI	BB	SO	SB	CS	B	T	HT	WT	DOB	1st Yr	Resides
Peoples, Danny	.249	121	409	82	102	21	1	34	84	84	145	8	1	R	R	6-1	207	1-20-75	1996	Round Rock, Texas
Petke, Jonathan	.168	41	101	8	17	6	0	0	10	9	24	0	1	R	R	6-1	195	1-14-73	1996	Mission Viejo, Calif.
Scutaro, Marcos	.272	97	378	58	103	17	6	10	59	35	72	23	7	R	R	5-10	170	10-30-75	1995	San Felipe, Venez.
Stumberger, Darren	.283	133	502	72	142	30	0	15	79	60	88	1	0	R	R	6-3	205	4-11-73	1994	Boca Raton, Fla.

GAMES BY POSITION: C—Evans 15, Gonzalez 41, Hayes 91. **1B**—Hayes 3, Jorgensen 5, Morris 1, Petke 2, Stumberger 133. **2B**—Betances 44, Gross 1, Jorgensen 11, Kilburg 8, Morris 9, Scutaro 74. **3B**—Betances 12, Branyan 69, Gross 4, Hayes 2, Jorgensen 40, Scutaro 19. **SS**—Betances 14, McDonald 130. **OF**—Budzinski 65, Claudio 15, Gross 66, Huelsmann 87, Kilburg 2, Morgan 86, Motley 7, Peoples 76, Petke 40.

PITCHING	W	L	ERA	G	GS	CG	SV	IP	H	R	ER	BB	SO	B	T	HT	WT	DOB	1st Yr	Resides
Atkins, Ross	8	4	3.62	27	16	0	0	117	98	53	47	62	84	R	R	6-3	195	8-7-73	1995	Coral Gables, Fla.
Caldwell, David	2	1	4.33	9	3	0	0	27	31	16	13	10	16	L	L	6-3	190	11-14-74	1994	Brooklyn, N.Y.
Camp, Jared	5	4	3.79	13	12	0	0	74	57	36	31	20	64	R	R	6-1	195	5-4-75	1995	Huntington, W.Va.
Crowell, Jim	9	4	2.37	17	17	0	0	114	96	41	30	26	94	L	L	6-4	220	5-14-74	1995	Valparaiso, Ind.
Deschenes, Marc	2	0	0.81	20	0	0	10	22	9	2	2	4	39	R	R	6-0	175	1-6-73	1995	Dracut, Mass.
Edwards, Jon	6	4	6.60	33	0	0	2	61	65	48	45	38	55	R	R	6-0	175	6-15-73	1995	Milton-Freewater, Ore.
Garza, Alberto	1	0	3.38	1	1	0	0	8	5	3	3	4	4	R	R	6-3	195	5-25-77	1996	Wapato, Wash.
Granata, Chris	0	1	10.02	9	1	0	1	21	30	23	23	7	11	R	R	6-0	205	2-26-72	1994	Columbus, Ohio
Granger, Greg	4	6	4.40	18	0	0	0	31	39	17	15	18	18	R	R	6-5	200	3-7-73	1993	Ellettsville, Ind.
Horgan, Joe	1	2	7.27	4	2	0	0	17	23	15	14	9	9	L	L	6-1	200	6-7-77	1996	Rancho Cordova, Calif.
Horn, Keith	0	0	9.60	9	0	0	1	15	20	16	16	8	11	R	R	5-11	185	5-17-74	1995	Pine Bluff, Ark.
Koeman, Matt	1	1	7.63	7	0	0	0	15	20	14	13	4	12	R	R	6-3	200	10-13-73	1996	Manhattan, Kan.
Martinez, Johnny	1	2	2.21	9	0	0	1	20	16	5	5	6	14	R	R	6-3	168	11-25-72	1991	Guayabin, D.R.
Martinez, Willie	8	2	3.09	23	23	1	0	137	125	61	47	42	120	R	R	6-2	165	1-4-78	1995	Barquisimeto, Venez.
Mays, Jarrod	7	5	4.13	20	19	0	0	100	94	53	46	42	64	R	R	6-4	190	10-8-74	1996	El Dorado Springs, Mo.
Merrick, Brett	0	1	1.08	8	0	0	1	8	7	4	1	5	3	L	L	6-0	180	5-30-74	1995	Lynwood, Wash.
Perez, Julio	6	1	4.84	27	0	0	0	48	58	35	26	17	35	R	R	6-1	163	5-18-74	1993	San Cristobal, D.R.
Rakers, Jason	8	5	3.07	17	17	2	0	103	93	41	35	18	105	R	R	6-2	197	6-29-73	1995	Pittsburgh, Pa.
Riske, David	4	4	2.25	39	0	0	2	72	58	22	18	33	90	R	R	6-2	175	10-23-76	1996	Kent, Wash.
Sanders, Frankie	11	5	4.06	25	25	2	0	146	130	72	66	66	127	R	R	5-11	165	8-27-75	1995	Sarasota, Fla.
Warrecker, Teddy	1	0	5.18	6	4	0	0	24	19	14	14	20	26	L	R	6-6	215	10-1-72	1994	Santa Barbara, Calif.
Winchester, Scott	2	1	1.47	34	0	0	29	37	21	6	6	11	45	R	R	6-2	210	4-20-73	1995	Midland, Mich.

COLUMBUS — Class A

SOUTH ATLANTIC LEAGUE

BATTING	AVG	G	AB	R	H	2B	3B	HR	RBI	BB	SO	SB	CS	B	T	HT	WT	DOB	1st Yr	Resides
Bruce, Robert	.248	69	234	42	58	8	1	11	36	33	69	6	0	R	R	6-5	225	11-13-74	1996	River Forest, Ill.
Evans, Pat	.181	32	83	13	15	3	1	0	6	17	19	0	2	S	R	5-10	175	12-5-72	1994	San Ramon, Calif.
Fowler, Ben	.183	19	60	5	11	1	0	1	7	2	26	1	0	S	R	6-4	185	1-21-77	1995	Alpharetta, Ga.
Glavine, Mike	.239	114	397	62	95	16	0	28	75	80	127	0	1	L	L	6-3	210	1-24-73	1995	Billerica, Mass.
Kent, Troy	.274	117	463	61	127	22	6	14	71	31	91	13	4	R	R	6-1	200	9-11-73	1996	Palo Alto, Calif.
Konrady, Dennis	.301	107	365	60	110	23	3	2	43	62	60	15	7	L	R	5-11	185	9-21-74	1996	Eugene, Ore.
Landstad, Rob	.224	96	331	41	74	12	7	13	56	27	91	5	3	L	R	6-0	230	4-17-73	1996	Canora, Saskatchewan
Melendez, Jorge	.233	57	146	15	34	9	1	0	12	11	37	0	0	R	R	6-0	170	3-18-74	1992	Cementerio, Venez.
Motley, Mel	.217	28	92	18	20	4	1	3	10	14	29	4	2	R	R	6-4	195	2-5-74	1996	Riverside, Calif.
Perez, Edwin	.278	52	187	30	52	10	1	5	24	17	41	2	2	R	R	5-10	165	5-10-75	1993	Navarrete, D.R.
Rodriquez, Gary	.257	116	482	73	124	12	5	1	37	46	94	22	8	L	R	5-11	165	7-17-76	1996	Keller, Texas
Sharpe, Grant	.130	33	108	10	14	4	0	2	9	15	46	0	0	L	R	6-4	215	12-4-77	1996	Laurel, Miss.
Smith, Casey	.333	13	36	6	12	0	0	1	3	8	15	0	0	L	R	6-3	200	5-7-77	1996	Carrollton, Texas
Taylor, Adam	.187	47	123	14	23	3	3	1	16	24	66	1	0	R	R	5-11	195	3-14-74	1996	Albuquerque, N.M.
Valera, Willy	.267	117	431	47	115	15	6	8	40	20	91	8	4	R	R	6-0	155	7-23-75	1993	San Cristobal, D.R.
Whitaker, Chad	.273	109	432	48	118	25	2	12	72	23	144	3	0	L	R	6-2	190	9-16-76	1995	Fort Lauderdale, Fla.
Whitlock, Brian	.263	92	327	56	86	14	7	11	41	28	92	5	4	R	R	6-1	180	9-16-74	1996	Sarasota, Fla.
Williams, Jewell	.188	113	399	57	75	20	3	10	40	33	140	14	6	R	R	6-2	185	6-25-77	1995	Las Vegas, Nev.

GAMES BY POSITION: C—Evans 31, Fowler 16, Landstad 2, Melendez 57, Smith 13, Taylor 45. **1B**—Bruce 38, Glavine 71, Kent 27, Sharpe 11. **2B**—Kent 91, Konrady 8, Perez 23, Whitlock 24. **3B**—Bruce 9, Konrady 72, Perez 13, Whitlock 55. **SS**—Konrady 27, Perez 3, Valera 116. **OF**—Landstad 58, Motley 24, Rodriquez 116, Whitaker 107, Whitlock 10, Williams 110.

PITCHING	W	L	ERA	G	GS	CG	SV	IP	H	R	ER	BB	SO	B	T	HT	WT	DOB	1st Yr	Resides
Bacsik, Mike	4	14	5.44	28	28	0	0	139	163	94	84	47	100	L	L	6-3	190	11-11-77	1996	Duncanville, Texas
Brammer, J.D.	6	10	7.02	28	23	0	1	117	132	102	91	50	105	R	R	6-4	235	1-30-75	1996	West Logan, W.Va.
Caldwell, David	2	1	4.18	5	5	0	0	24	25	13	11	4	22	L	L	6-3	190	11-14-74	1994	Brooklyn, N.Y.
Calmus, Lance	1	5	5.83	23	15	0	0	88	94	64	57	41	78	R	R	6-5	225	1-19-73	1996	Oklahoma City, Okla.
Deschenes, Marc	2	2	1.90	40	0	0	19	43	31	11	9	21	69	R	R	6-0	175	1-6-73	1995	Dracut, Mass.
DePaula, Sean	4	5	5.20	29	1	0	0	71	71	56	41	43	75	R	R	6-4	215	11-7-73	1996	Derry, N.H.
Feliz, Bienvenido	3	0	2.28	6	4	0	0	28	21	7	7	8	20	R	R	6-0	175	6-4-77	1994	Santo Domingo, D.R.
Garza, Alberto	8	3	3.13	18	18	2	0	95	72	34	33	32	107	R	R	6-3	195	5-25-77	1996	Wapato, Wash.
Granger, Greg	2	0	0.82	5	0	0	0	11	8	3	1	3	6	R	R	6-5	200	3-7-73	1993	Ellettsville, Ind.
Hamilton, Jimmy	5	7	4.46	22	22	0	0	123	123	68	61	66	137	R	L	6-3	185	8-1-75	1996	Weyers Cave, W.Va.
Harrison, Scott	0	1	21.00	1	1	0	0	3	8	7	7	1	1	R	R	6-3	195	7-3-77	1995	Pinole, Calif.
Koeman, Matt	4	5	2.62	34	0	0	2	58	38	17	17	23	63	R	R	6-3	200	10-13-73	1996	Manhattan, Kan.
Mackey, Jason	2	8	5.01	18	17	0	0	93	86	61	52	45	69	L	L	6-2	185	4-8-74	1993	Kelso, Wash.
Martinez, Dennis	0	2	23.40	6	0	0	0	5	7	13	13	8	2	S	R	6-3	170	11-16-73	1995	Miami, Fla.
Merrick, Brett	2	2	4.94	23	0	0	0	31	29	24	17	21	25	L	L	6-0	180	5-30-74	1995	Lynwood, Wash.
Minter, Matt	5	3	4.26	30	0	0	2	57	57	29	27	18	49	L	L	6-0	185	2-22-73	1996	Bellaire, Texas
Negrette, Richard	2	1	4.46	16	0	0	1	36	24	23	18	16	21	S	R	6-2	175	3-6-76	1994	Maracaibo, Venez.
Reichow, Robert	3	2	3.39	20	2	0	2	61	54	32	23	11	50	R	R	6-5	220	10-10-73	1996	Temperance, Mich.
Roberson, Charles	0	0	4.50	1	0	0	0	2	1	1	1	1	2	R	R	6-1	210	9-18-74	1996	Seattle, Wash.
Spiegel, Mike	0	0	3.60	2	2	0	0	10	6	4	4	5	6	L	L	6-5	200	11-24-75	1996	Carmichael, Calif.
Taylor, Mark	1	1	7.50	20	0	0	0	30	37	29	25	26	28	L	L	6-3	185	10-30-74	1996	St. Petersburg, Fla.
Wagner, Ken	6	4	4.96	47	0	0	11	85	80	50	47	37	92	R	R	6-4	218	8-3-74	1995	West Palm Beach, Fla.

WATERTOWN — Short-Season Class A

NEW YORK-PENN LEAGUE

BATTING	AVG	G	AB	R	H	2B	3B	HR	RBI	BB	SO	SB	CS	B	T	HT	WT	DOB	1st Yr	Resides
Allison, Cody	.265	51	181	25	48	10	0	1	23	20	34	7	3	L	R	6-1	200	8-8-74	1996	Odessa, Texas

BATTING	AVG	G	AB	R	H	2B	3B	HR	RBI	BB	SO	SB	CS	B	T	HT	WT	DOB	1st Yr	Resides
Alvarez, Carlos	.300	22	80	15	24	5	0	6	17	2	21	3	2	R	R	6-0	170	4-28-76	1995	Bachayuero, Venez.
Bender, Heath	.231	62	186	19	43	6	0	2	20	10	38	1	1	L	L	6-4	230	4-16-75	1997	Rock Island, Ill.
Benefield, Brian	.287	69	265	47	76	9	1	4	19	49	40	23	7	R	R	6-0	181	8-12-76	1997	Carrollton, Texas
Fitzgerald, Jason	.196	34	112	11	22	8	0	1	13	17	31	2	0	L	L	6-1	190	9-16-75	1997	Belle Chasse, La.
Haley, Ryan	.000	12	13	4	0	0	0	0	0	2	4	1	1	L	R	6-1	185	11-21-75	1997	Chandler, Okla.
Hernandez, Jesus	.222	16	45	4	10	4	0	0	3	6	10	1	0	L	L	6-2	170	6-6-77	1994	Laguna Salada, D.R.
Miner, Tony	.274	49	164	26	45	8	1	4	23	15	30	1	2	R	R	6-2	205	2-15-75	1997	Portland, Maine
Mohr, Dustan	.291	74	275	52	80	20	2	7	53	31	76	3	6	R	R	6-2	210	6-19-76	1997	Hattiesburg, Miss.
Mota, Cristian	.238	75	311	51	74	21	2	2	33	18	67	13	4	S	R	5-11	165	3-31-76	1994	San Pedro de Macoris, D.R.
Rodriguez, Aurelio	.305	51	203	34	62	11	1	2	22	16	32	5	1	R	R	5-10	165	12-10-73	1996	Los Mochis, Mexico
Rosa, Erick	.188	28	85	6	16	2	1	0	7	7	22	0	2	R	R	5-11	185	3-5-75	1997	Rio Piedras, P.R.
Russell, Jake	.000	2	2	0	0	0	0	0	0	0	0	0	0	R	R	5-11	190	3-2-74	1994	Salina, Okla.
Stanton, Rob	.270	55	189	21	51	11	4	5	34	20	72	4	2	R	R	6-5	225	4-18-75	1996	Winter Park, Fla.
Taylor, Adam	.221	50	149	27	33	8	2	7	33	25	54	1	0	R	R	5-11	195	3-14-74	1996	Albuquerque, N.M.
Tiller, Brad	.245	29	98	15	24	6	0	2	10	12	25	6	2	R	R	5-10	165	11-21-75	1994	Inez, Ky.
Upshaw, Ryan	.242	41	132	26	32	7	1	3	21	27	31	3	0	R	R	6-0	200	1-21-75	1997	Humble, Texas

GAMES BY POSITION: C—Allison 3, Rosa 28, Taylor 48. **1B**—Allison 19, Bender 61, Miner 3, Mota 1, Rodriguez 1. **2B**—Benefield 69, Haley 3, Rodriguez 4. **3B**—Miner 44, Mota 20, Rodriguez 15, Russell 2. **SS**—Haley 1, Mota 50, Tiller 25. **OF**—Alvarez 22, Fitzgerald 33, Haley 1, Hernandez 14, Mohr 74, Mota 5, Stanton 47, Upshaw 40.

PITCHING	W	L	ERA	G	GS	CG	SV	IP	H	R	ER	BB	SO	B	T	HT	WT	DOB	1st Yr	Resides
Alvarez, Danny	0	0	13.50	3	0	0	0	3	9	6	5	0	2	R	R	6-2	185	4-14-76	1997	Miami, Fla.
Baez, Miguel	0	1	1.93	3	0	0	1	5	5	2	1	1	6	R	R	5-11	160	9-24-77	1995	San Cristobal, D.R.
Brown, Jamie	10	2	3.08	13	13	1	0	73	66	35	25	15	57	R	R	6-2	205	3-31-77	1997	Collinsville, Miss.
Cali, Joe	1	0	9.00	2	0	0	0	3	4	3	3	0	3	R	R	5-11	185	4-8-75	1997	Naples, Fla.
DePaula, Sean	1	1	2.84	9	0	0	0	19	21	6	6	8	17	R	R	6-4	215	11-7-73	1996	Derry, N.H.
Drew, Tim	0	0	1.93	1	1	0	0	5	4	1	1	3	9	R	R	6-1	195	8-31-78	1997	Hahira, Ga.
Erwin, David	3	1	5.25	18	2	0	1	36	36	24	21	23	36	R	R	6-3	210	3-19-75	1997	Brighton, Tenn.
Fuduric, Tony	0	1	8.22	2	2	0	0	8	8	8	7	5	2	R	R	6-3	185	9-6-74	1993	Huntsburg, Ohio
Garff, Jeff	3	0	2.81	6	4	0	0	26	31	12	8	7	18	R	R	6-4	195	12-3-75	1995	Bountiful, Utah
Horgan, Joe	0	1	6.10	15	4	0	0	38	48	31	26	18	31	L	L	6-1	200	6-7-77	1996	Rancho Cordova, Calif.
Hughes, Mike	5	3	3.51	13	13	2	0	77	69	37	30	25	80	L	L	6-1	192	12-5-75	1997	East Meadow, N.Y.
McNally, Andrew	2	3	2.87	23	0	0	8	31	23	10	10	13	37	L	R	6-0	185	12-3-73	1997	Honolulu, Hawaii
Minter, Matt	0	0	4.70	7	0	0	0	8	6	4	4	5	12	L	L	6-0	185	2-22-73	1996	Bellaire, Texas
Negrette, Richard	2	3	3.66	17	0	0	1	39	25	17	16	29	30	S	R	6-2	175	3-6-76	1994	Maracaibo, Venez.
Pelton, Brad	1	5	5.10	9	9	0	0	48	54	31	27	18	29	R	R	6-3	202	8-4-74	1995	Pensacola, Fla.
Roberson, Charles	3	1	3.09	18	2	0	2	44	39	18	15	17	35	R	R	6-1	210	9-18-74	1996	Seattle, Wash.
Swinburnson, Tyler	3	2	4.62	25	0	0	5	39	40	26	20	24	38	R	R	6-4	200	8-5-75	1997	Blaine, Wash.
Taylor, Mark	3	7	4.67	15	13	1	0	71	68	45	37	45	58	L	L	6-3	185	10-30-74	1996	St. Petersburg, Fla.
Vael, Rob	1	4	4.62	12	12	1	0	62	63	38	32	30	47	R	R	6-3	200	1-8-76	1997	Tacoma, Wash.
Vasquez, Antonio	1	1	6.75	3	0	0	0	8	13	7	6	6	6	R	R	5-11	165	1-17-77	1996	Porlamar, Venez.

BURLINGTON — Rookie

APPALACHIAN LEAGUE

BATTING	AVG	G	AB	R	H	2B	3B	HR	RBI	BB	SO	SB	CS	B	T	HT	WT	DOB	1st Yr	Resides
Bosch, Bryon	.067	13	30	1	2	1	0	0	0	1	17	0	0	R	R	6-2	205	9-25-77	1996	Seattle, Wash.
Cruz, Edgar	.211	46	171	18	36	7	0	5	29	14	54	0	1	R	R	6-3	195	8-12-78	1997	Juncos, P.R.
Dampeer, Kelly	.255	53	212	37	54	19	0	3	24	15	32	9	3	R	R	5-11	190	1-25-75	1997	Roanoke, Va.
Edwards, Michael	.288	60	236	50	68	16	2	4	41	38	53	10	5	R	R	6-1	185	11-24-76	1995	Mechanicsburg, Pa.
Haley, Ryan	.250	8	24	4	6	1	0	0	2	1	5	2	0	L	R	6-1	185	11-21-75	1997	Chandler, Okla.
Hamilton, Jonathan	.243	64	247	50	60	11	3	4	20	51	69	25	5	L	L	6-1	195	10-23-77	1997	San Ramon, Calif.
Harding, Todd	.177	24	79	8	14	1	1	1	4	4	33	3	2	R	R	6-0	180	9-14-77	1997	Eugene, Ore.
Hernandez, Jesus	.302	50	192	37	58	12	0	7	40	25	36	7	2	L	L	6-2	170	6-6-77	1994	Laguna Salada, D.R.
Kilburg, Joe	.335	52	182	59	61	8	7	3	30	39	46	29	5	L	R	5-11	180	12-20-75	1997	Bay Village, Ohio
Lugo, Ursino	.271	13	48	8	13	2	0	0	5	5	7	9	4	S	R	6-0	158	11-9-74	1993	Bani, D.R.
Messner, Jake	.251	49	179	28	45	10	0	9	26	8	47	7	3	L	L	6-0	192	5-18-77	1995	Sacramento, Calif.
Russell, Jake	.256	27	86	20	22	2	0	3	17	14	21	0	0	R	R	5-11	190	3-2-74	1994	Salina, Okla.
Sharpe, Grant	.253	64	245	29	62	12	1	10	51	29	86	0	0	L	R	6-4	215	12-4-77	1996	Laurel, Miss.
Smith, Casey	.351	19	77	8	27	2	0	2	9	3	22	1	0	R	R	6-3	200	5-7-77	1996	Carrollton, Texas
Taveras, Frank	.263	56	194	29	51	10	3	2	34	16	56	11	8	L	R	6-1	158	9-6-75	1993	Santiago, D.R.
Ventura, Frankie	.256	35	117	17	30	6	1	0	18	13	26	3	3	R	R	6-1	180	6-4-77	1995	Santo Domingo, D.R.

GAMES BY POSITION: C—Bosch 11, Cruz 38, Russell 15, Smith 11. **1B**—Edwards 3, Russell 5, Sharpe 61, Taveras 3. **2B**—Dampeer 31, Haley 3, Harding 1, Kilburg 35. **3B**—Dampeer 5, Edwards 46, Harding 18. **SS**—Dampeer 12, Edwards 1, Haley 2, Kilburg 2, Taveras 54. **OF**—Edwards 1, Hamilton 64, Hernandez 48, Kilburg 10, Lugo 13, Messner 45, Ventura 27.

PITCHING	W	L	ERA	G	GS	CG	SV	IP	H	R	ER	BB	SO	B	T	HT	WT	DOB	1st Yr	Resides
Alvarez, Danny	0	2	6.75	3	1	0	0	7	10	6	5	4	6	R	R	6-2	185	4-14-76	1997	Miami, Fla.
Aracena, Juan	1	4	4.89	19	0	0	2	39	45	32	21	16	31	R	R	6-0	150	12-17-76	1994	La Vega, D.R.
Baez, Miguel	1	3	2.15	19	0	0	2	29	21	17	7	14	33	R	R	5-11	160	9-24-77	1995	San Cristobal, D.R.
Cali, Joe	1	2	11.07	14	0	0	0	20	37	36	25	20	24	R	R	5-11	185	4-8-75	1997	Naples, Fla.
Drew, Tim	0	1	6.17	4	4	0	0	12	16	15	8	4	14	R	R	6-1	195	8-31-78	1997	Hahira, Ga.
Garff, Jeff	1	1	4.50	5	0	0	1	8	9	4	4	2	9	R	R	6-4	195	12-3-75	1995	Bountiful, Utah
Granadillo, Adel	6	4	5.44	15	4	0	0	48	55	30	29	23	44	R	R	6-0	165	8-29-78	1996	Maracaibo, Venez.
Harrison, Scott	3	5	3.71	12	12	0	0	63	62	37	26	24	50	R	R	6-3	195	7-3-77	1995	Pinole, Calif.
Layne, Roger	1	4	3.62	11	11	0	0	60	55	39	24	21	52	R	R	6-3	185	6-27-77	1996	Whitwell, Tenn.
Malloy, Pat	0	1	6.83	17	0	0	1	29	35	24	22	14	26	R	R	6-3	215	5-19-76	1997	Philadelphia, Pa.
McDermott, Ryan	3	3	6.49	8	8	0	0	35	45	29	25	25	22	R	R	6-9	225	6-28-78	1996	Alamogordo, N.M.
Perez, Sam	1	1	5.96	16	1	0	0	23	26	19	15	10	14	L	L	6-2	160	7-19-76	1994	Boca Chica, D.R.
Pugmire, Rob	1	2	3.92	14	14	0	0	67	72	42	29	29	62	R	R	6-3	205	9-5-78	1997	Snohomish, Wash.
Silva, Troy	1	1	3.54	20	0	0	3	41	35	22	16	18	50	R	R	6-2	205	10-15-75	1997	Atascadero, Calif.
Turnbow, Mark	8	2	2.78	13	13	0	0	74	49	25	23	18	53	R	R	6-3	205	11-26-78	1997	Saltillo, Tenn.
Vasquez, Antonio	2	0	2.81	12	0	0	1	26	23	13	8	13	20	R	R	5-11	165	1-17-77	1996	Porlamar, Venez.
Wheeler, Johnnie	2	0	2.08	6	0	0	0	13	10	3	3	6	12	L	L	6-3	175	12-24-77	1997	Bristow, Okla.

Colorado ROCKIES

Manager: Don Baylor.

1997 Record: 83-79, .512 (3rd, NL West)

BATTING	AVG	G	AB	R	H	2B	3B	HR	RBI	BB	SO	SB	CS	B	T	HT	WT	DOB	1st Yr	Resides
Bates, Jason	.240	62	121	17	29	10	0	3	11	15	27	0	1	S	R	5-11	170	1-5-71	1992	Norwalk, Calif.
Bichette, Dante	.308	151	561	81	173	31	2	26	118	30	90	6	5	R	R	6-3	235	11-18-63	1984	Palm Beach Gardens, Fla.
Burks, Ellis	.290	119	424	91	123	19	2	32	82	47	75	7	2	R	R	6-2	205	9-11-64	1983	Denver, Colo.
Castilla, Vinny	.304	159	612	94	186	25	2	40	113	44	108	2	4	R	R	6-1	185	7-4-67	1990	Oaxaca, Mexico
Coles, Darnell	.318	21	22	1	7	1	0	1	2	0	6	0	0	R	R	6-1	185	6-2-62	1991	Safety Harbor, Fla.
Counsell, Craig	.000	1	0	0	0	0	0	0	0	0	0	0	0	L	R	6-0	177	8-21-70	1992	Whitefish Bay, Wis.
Echevarria, Angel	.250	15	20	4	5	2	0	0	0	2	5	0	0	R	R	6-4	215	5-25-71	1992	Bridgeport, Conn.
Galarraga, Andres	.318	154	600	120	191	31	3	41	140	54	141	15	8	R	R	6-3	245	6-18-61	1979	Caracas, Venez.
Gonzales, Rene	.500	2	2	0	1	0	0	0	1	0	0	0	0	R	R	6-3	215	9-3-61	1982	Newport Beach, Calif.
Helton, Todd	.280	35	93	13	26	2	1	5	11	8	11	0	1	L	L	6-2	195	8-20-73	1995	Powell, Tenn.
Manwaring, Kirt	.226	104	337	22	76	6	4	1	27	30	78	1	5	R	R	5-11	203	7-15-65	1986	Scottsdale, Ariz.
McCracken, Quinton	.292	147	325	69	95	11	1	3	36	42	62	28	11	S	R	5-8	170	3-16-70	1992	Southport, N.C.
Perez, Neifi	.291	83	313	46	91	13	10	5	31	21	43	4	3	S	R	6-0	175	6-2-75	1993	Villa Mella, D.R.
Pulliam, Harvey	.284	59	67	15	19	3	0	3	9	5	15	0	1	R	R	6-0	205	10-20-67	1986	San Francisco, Calif.
Raabe, Brian	.333	2	3	0	1	0	0	0	0	0	1	0	0	R	R	5-9	170	11-5-67	1990	Blaine, Minn.
Reed, Jeff	.297	90	256	43	76	10	0	17	47	35	55	2	1	L	R	6-2	190	11-12-62	1980	Elizabethton, Tenn.
Vander Wal, John	.174	76	92	7	16	2	0	1	11	10	33	1	1	L	L	6-1	180	4-29-66	1987	Hudsonville, Mich.
Walker, Larry	.366	153	568	143	208	46	4	49	130	78	90	33	8	L	R	6-2	185	12-1-66	1985	Maple Ridge, B.C.
Weiss, Walt	.270	121	393	52	106	23	5	4	38	66	56	5	2	S	R	6-0	178	11-28-63	1985	Danville, Calif.
Young, Eric	.282	118	468	78	132	29	6	6	45	57	37	32	12	R	R	5-9	180	5-18-67	1989	New Brunswick, N.J.

PITCHING	W	L	ERA	G	GS	CG	SV	IP	H	R	ER	BB	SO	B	T	HT	WT	DOB	1st Yr	Resides
Astacio, Pedro	5	1	4.25	7	7	0	0	49	49	23	23	14	51	R	R	6-2	195	11-28-69	1988	Miami, Fla.
2-team (26 L.A.)	12	10	4.14	33	31	2	0	202	200	98	93	61	166							
Bailey, Roger	9	10	4.29	29	29	5	0	191	210	103	91	70	84	R	R	6-1	180	10-3-70	1992	Tallahassee, Fla.
Beckett, Robbie	0	0	5.40	2	0	0	0	2	1	1	1	1	2	R	L	6-5	235	7-16-72	1990	Austin, Texas
Burke, John	2	5	6.56	17	9	0	0	59	83	46	43	26	39	R	R	6-4	220	2-9-70	1992	Highlands Ranch, Colo.
Castillo, Frank	6	3	5.42	14	14	0	0	86	107	57	52	25	59	R	R	6-1	185	4-1-69	1987	El Paso, Texas
2-team (20 Chicago)	12	12	5.42	34	33	0	0	184	220	121	111	69	126							
DeJean, Mike	5	0	3.99	55	0	0	2	68	74	34	30	24	38	R	R	6-2	205	9-28-70	1992	Denham Springs, La.
DiPoto, Jerry	5	3	4.70	74	0	0	16	96	108	56	50	33	74	R	R	6-2	200	5-24-68	1989	North Olmstead, Ohio
Holmes, Darren	9	2	5.34	42	6	0	3	89	113	58	53	36	70	R	R	6-0	199	4-25-66	1984	Fletcher, N.C.
Hutton, Mark	0	1	7.11	8	1	0	0	13	22	10	10	7	10	R	R	6-6	225	2-6-70	1989	Adelaide, Australia
2-team (32 Florida)	3	2	4.48	40	1	0	0	60	72	34	30	26	39							
Jones, Bobby	1	1	8.38	4	4	0	0	19	30	18	18	12	5	R	L	6-0	175	4-11-72	1992	Rutherford, N.J.
Leskanic, Curt	4	0	5.55	55	0	0	2	58	59	36	36	24	53	R	R	6-0	180	4-2-68	1990	Pineville, La.
McCurry, Jeff	1	4	4.43	33	0	0	0	41	43	22	20	20	19	R	R	6-7	210	1-21-70	1991	Houston, Texas
Minchey, Nate	0	0	13.50	2	0	0	0	2	5	3	3	1	1	R	R	6-7	225	8-31-69	1987	San Antonio, Texas
Munoz, Mike	3	3	4.53	64	0	0	2	46	52	25	23	13	26	L	L	6-2	190	7-12-65	1986	West Covina, Calif.
Reed, Steve	4	6	4.04	63	0	0	6	62	49	28	28	27	43	R	R	6-2	195	3-11-66	1988	Lewiston, Idaho
Rekar, Bryan	1	0	5.79	2	2	0	0	9	11	7	6	6	4	R	R	6-3	205	6-3-72	1993	Orland Park, Ill.
Ritz, Kevin	6	8	5.87	18	18	1	0	107	142	72	70	46	56	R	R	6-4	220	6-8-65	1986	Cambridge, Ohio
Ruffin, Bruce	0	2	5.32	23	0	0	7	22	18	15	13	18	31	S	L	6-2	213	10-4-63	1985	Austin, Texas
Scott, Tim	0	0	10.13	3	0	0	0	3	5	3	3	2	2	R	R	6-2	205	11-16-66	1984	Hanford, Calif.
2-team (14 San Diego)	1	1	8.14	17	0	0	0	21	30	20	19	7	16							
Swift, Billy	4	6	6.34	14	13	0	0	65	85	57	46	26	29	R	R	6-0	191	10-27-61	1985	Paradise Valley, Ariz.
Thompson, Mark	3	3	7.89	6	6	0	0	30	40	27	26	13	9	R	R	6-2	205	4-7-71	1992	Russellville, Ky.
Thomson, John	7	9	4.71	27	27	2	0	166	193	94	87	51	106	R	R	6-3	175	10-1-73	1993	Sulphur, La.
Wright, Jamey	8	12	6.25	26	26	1	0	150	198	113	104	71	59	R	R	6-6	205	12-24-74	1993	Moore, Okla.

FIELDING

Catcher	PCT	G	PO	A	E	DP	PB
Manwaring	.994	100	488	40	3	7	3
Reed	.987	78	428	37	6	8	2

First Base	PCT	G	PO	A	E	DP
Galarraga	.991	154	1458	117	15	176
Helton	1.000	8	68	10	0	7
VanderWal	1.000	5	26	0	0	2
Walker	1.000	3	22	2	0	3

Second Base	PCT	G	PO	A	E	DP
Bates	1.000	22	27	25	0	12
Perez	.992	41	105	130	2	39
Raabe	1.000	1	0	4	0	0
Young	.978	117	258	414	15	93

Third Base	PCT	G	PO	A	E	DP
Bates	1.000	6	2	6	0	0
Castilla	.954	157	112	323	21	41
Coles	1.000	3	0	3	0	0
Gonzales	.000	1	0	0	0	0
Perez	.857	2	2	4	1	0

Shortstop	PCT	G	PO	A	E	DP
Bates	.945	16	15	37	3	12
Perez	.975	45	78	153	6	34
Weiss	.983	119	191	372	10	88

Outfield	PCT	G	PO	A	E	DP
Bichette	.987	139	225	4	3	1
Burks	.982	112	207	6	4	1
Coles	.000	2	0	0	0	0
Echevarria	1.000	7	4	1	0	0
Helton	1.000	15	16	2	0	0
McCracken	.980	132	195	5	4	3
Pulliam	.962	33	23	2	1	0
VanderWal	.923	9	12	0	1	0
Walker	.992	151	232	12	2	4

MEL BAILEY

Larry Walker

FARM SYSTEM

Director of Player Development: Dick Balderson

Class	Farm Team	League	W	L	Pct.	Finish*	Manager	First Yr
AAA	Colo. Springs (Colo.) Sky Sox	Pacific Coast	76	64	.543	3rd (10)	Paul Zuvella	1993
AA	New Haven (Conn.) Ravens	Eastern	64	78	.451	9th (10)	Bill Hayes	1994
#A	Salem (Va.) Avalanche	Carolina	63	75	.457	5th (8)	Bill McGuire	1995
A	Asheville (N.C.) Tourists	South Atlantic	62	76	.449	12th (14)	Ron Gideon	1994
A	Portland (Ore.) Rockies	Northwest	44	32	.579	+3rd (8)	Jim Eppard	1995
R	Chandler (Ariz.) Rockies	Arizona	21	34	.382	6th (6)	Tim Blackwell	1992

*Finish in overall standings (No. of teams in league) #Advanced level +Won league championship

ORGANIZATION LEADERS

MAJOR LEAGUERS

BATTING

*AVG	Larry Walker .... .366
R	Larry Walker 143
H	Larry Walker 208
TB	Larry Walker 409
2B	Larry Walker 46
3B	Neifi Perez................. 10
HR	Larry Walker 49
RBI	Andres Galarraga.... 140
BB	Larry Walker 78
SO	Andres Galarraga.... 141
SB	Larry Walker 33

PITCHING

W	Two tied at.................... 9
L	Jamey Wright 12
#ERA	Roger Bailey........... 4.29
G	Jerry DiPoto............... 74
CG	Roger Bailey................ 5
SV	Jerry DiPoto............... 16
IP	Roger Bailey............ 191
BB	Jamey Wright 71
SO	John Thomson......... 106

MEL BAILEY

Andres Galarraga

JOHN SPEAR

Nate Minchey

MINOR LEAGUERS

BATTING

*AVG	Neifi Perez, Colorado Springs .... .363
R	Derrick Gibson, Colo. Spr./New Haven .. 105
H	Derrick Gibson, Colo. Spr./New Haven .. 179
TB	Derrick Gibson, Colo. Spr./New Haven .. 292
2B	Tom Quinlan, Colorado Springs 36
3B	Edgard Velazquez, Colorado Springs .. 10
HR	Derrick Gibson, Colo. Spr./New Haven 26
RBI	Tom Quinlan, Colorado Springs 113
BB	Chris Sexton, Colo. Spr./New Haven 78
SO	Tal Light, New Haven/Salem 180
SB	Bernard Hutchison, Asheville 81

PITCHING

W	Nate Minchey, Colorado Springs 15
L	Two tied at 14
#ERA	Mike Vavrek, New Haven/Salem........ 2.43
G	Heath Bost, New Haven/Salem 53
CG	Mike Saipe, Colo. Spr./New Haven 5
SV	Heath Bost, New Haven/Salem 23
IP	Mike Saipe, Colo. Spr./New Haven 197
BB	Steve Shoemaker, Colo. Spr./NH/Salem .. 95
SO	Steve Shoemaker, Colo. Spr./NH/Salem 214

*Minimum 250 At-Bats #Minimum 75 Innings

TOP 10 PROSPECTS

LARRY GOREN

Todd Helton

How the Rockies Top 10 prospects, as judged by Baseball America prior to the 1997 season, fared in 1997:

Player, Pos.	Club (Class)	AVG	AB	R	H	2B	3B	HR	RBI	SB
1. Todd Helton, 1b	Colorado	.280	93	13	26	2	1	5	11	0
	Colo. Springs (AAA)	.352	392	87	138	31	2	16	88	3
2. Neifi Perez, ss	Colorado	.291	313	46	91	13	10	5	31	4
	Colo. Springs (AAA)	.363	303	68	110	24	3	8	46	8
3. Derrick Gibson, of	Colo. Springs (AAA)	.423	78	14	33	7	0	3	12	0
	New Haven (AA)	.317	461	91	146	24	2	23	75	20
4. Ben Petrick, c	Salem (A)	.248	412	68	102	23	3	15	56	30
5. Edgard Velazquez, of	Colo. Springs (AAA)	.281	438	70	123	24	10	17	73	6
		W	L	ERA	G	SV	IP	H	BB	SO
6. Jake Westbrook, rhp	Asheville (A)	14	11	4.29	28	0	170	176	55	92
7. Shawn Chacon, rhp	Asheville (A)	11	7	3.89	28	0	162	155	63	149
8. Doug Million, lhp	New Haven (AA)	0	5	9.23	10	0	40	64	36	19
	Salem (A)	5	9	5.12	18	0	97	104	55	58
9. John Thomson, rhp	Colorado	7	9	4.71	27	0	166	193	51	106
	Colo. Springs (AAA)	4	2	3.43	7	0	42	36	14	49
10. Mike Kusiewicz, lhp	New Haven (AA)	2	4	6.35	10	0	28	41	10	11
	Salem (Carolina)	8	6	2.52	19	0	118	99	32	107

TM

COLORADO SPRINGS — Class AAA

PACIFIC COAST LEAGUE

BATTING	AVG	G	AB	R	H	2B	3B	HR	RBI	BB	SO	SB	CS	B	T	HT	WT	DOB	1st Yr	Resides
Barry, Jeff	.300	81	273	46	82	13	3	13	70	30	45	5	0	S	R	6-0	200	9-22-68	1990	San Diego, Calif.
Bates, Jason	.237	35	135	21	32	6	1	3	18	13	36	1	3	S	R	5-11	170	1-5-71	1992	Norwalk, Calif.
Boston, D.J.	.333	2	6	1	2	0	0	0	0	0	3	0	0	L	L	6-7	230	9-6-71	1991	Cincinnati, Ohio
Cholowsky, Dan	.333	26	84	17	28	6	0	5	19	15	21	1	1	R	R	6-0	195	10-30-70	1991	San Jose, Calif.
Counsell, Craig	.335	96	376	77	126	31	6	5	63	45	38	12	2	L	R	6-0	177	8-21-70	1992	Whitefish Bay, Wis.
Echevarria, Angel	.322	77	295	59	95	24	0	13	80	28	47	6	2	R	R	6-4	215	5-25-71	1992	Bridgeport, Conn.
Gibson, Derrick	.423	21	78	14	33	7	0	3	12	5	9	0	2	R	R	6-2	238	2-5-75	1993	Winter Haven, Fla.
Gonzales, Rene	.297	85	296	48	88	20	1	3	39	37	43	2	4	R	R	6-3	215	9-3-61	1982	Newport Beach, Calif.
2-team (13 L.V.)	.283	98	339	50	96	21	1	3	42	43	49	2	4							
Gubanich, Creighton	.191	14	47	4	9	1	0	3	6	4	18	0	0	R	R	6-4	220	3-27-72	1991	Phoenixville, Pa.
3-team (43 Edm./24 Tuc.)	.310	81	277	40	86	19	0	15	57	19	79	1	2							
Hall, Billy	.255	13	51	6	13	0	2	0	6	3	11	3	1	S	R	5-9	180	6-17-69	1991	Wichita, Kan.
Helton, Todd	.352	99	392	87	138	31	2	16	88	61	68	3	1	L	L	6-2	195	8-20-73	1995	Powell, Tenn.
Howitt, Dann	.332	102	316	57	105	29	0	14	62	32	71	2	2	L	R	6-5	205	2-13-64	1986	Medford, Ore.
Huson, Jeff	.350	9	20	3	7	3	0	1	5	2	2	0	0	L	R	6-3	180	8-15-64	1986	Bedford, Texas
Jones, Terry	.270	92	363	70	98	14	4	1	25	25	49	36	6	R	R	5-10	160	2-15-71	1993	Pinson, Ala.
Owens, Jayhawk	.260	95	289	57	75	17	0	10	34	55	98	4	1	R	R	6-0	200	2-10-69	1990	Sardinia, Ohio
Perez, Neifi	.363	68	303	68	110	24	3	8	46	17	27	8	2	S	R	6-0	175	6-2-75	1993	Villa Mella, D.R.
Pulliam, Harvey	.401	40	137	44	55	10	2	12	43	21	19	1	0	R	R	6-0	205	10-20-67	1986	San Francisco, Calif.
Quinlan, Tom	.285	134	509	85	145	36	2	23	113	50	117	1	1	R	R	6-3	210	3-27-68	1987	Maplewood, Minn.
Sexton, Chris	.268	33	112	18	30	3	1	1	8	16	21	1	1	R	R	5-11	180	8-3-71	1993	Cincinnati, Ohio
Shumpert, Terry	.297	10	37	8	11	3	0	1	2	2	7	0	0	R	R	5-11	185	8-16-66	1987	Paducah, Ky.
2-team (32 L.V.)	.288	42	146	26	42	11	1	2	18	11	27	3	0							
Strittmatter, Mark	.246	45	114	16	28	8	0	2	12	11	21	0	1	R	R	6-1	200	4-4-69	1992	Ridgewood, N.J.
Vander Wal, John	.408	25	103	29	42	12	1	3	19	11	28	1	1	L	L	6-1	180	4-29-66	1987	Hudsonville, Mich.
Velazquez, Edgard	.281	120	438	70	123	24	10	17	73	34	119	6	3	R	R	6-0	170	12-15-75	1993	Guaynabo, P.R.

PITCHING	W	L	ERA	G	GS	CG	SV	IP	H	R	ER	BB	SO	B	T	HT	WT	DOB	1st Yr	Resides
Ausanio, Joe	0	0	29.45	3	0	0	0	4	14	13	12	3	3	R	R	6-1	205	12-9-65	1988	Kingston, N.Y.
Beckett, Robbie	1	3	6.79	45	1	0	1	54	61	49	41	47	67	R	L	6-5	235	7-16-72	1990	Austin, Texas
Bost, Heath	0	1	21.00	2	0	0	0	3	10	8	7	1	3	R	R	6-4	200	10-13-74	1995	Taylorsville, N.C.
Bourgeois, Steve	9	7	5.99	33	18	2	0	122	154	96	81	66	86	R	R	6-1	220	8-4-72	1993	Paulina, La.
Burke, John	1	2	5.82	3	3	0	0	17	23	14	11	14	15	R	R	6-4	220	2-9-70	1992	Highlands Ranch, Colo.
DeJean, Mike	0	1	5.40	10	0	0	4	10	17	6	6	7	9	R	R	6-2	205	9-28-70	1992	Denham Springs, La.
Farmer, Mike	5	5	6.75	18	8	0	0	55	70	42	41	18	29	S	L	6-1	200	7-3-68	1990	Gary, Ind.
Henderson, Ryan	1	1	12.46	6	1	0	0	13	20	18	18	9	12	R	R	6-1	190	9-30-69	1992	Dana Point, Calif.
2-team (13 Albuq.)	2	4	8.90	19	1	0	0	30	40	32	30	23	29							
Hope, John	4	3	7.22	43	9	0	0	100	115	85	80	65	67	R	R	6-3	206	12-21-70	1989	Fort Lauderdale, Fla.
Jones, Bobby	7	11	5.14	25	21	0	0	133	135	89	76	71	104	R	L	6-0	175	4-11-72	1992	Rutherford, N.J.
Kramer, Tom	3	2	5.23	51	0	0	11	62	57	42	36	40	56	R	R	6-0	205	1-9-68	1987	St. Bernard, Ohio
Lee, Mark	1	2	6.28	48	0	0	3	67	93	49	47	21	63	L	L	6-3	195	7-20-64	1985	Colorado Springs, Colo.
Leskanic, Curt	0	0	3.79	10	3	0	2	19	11	9	8	18	20	R	R	6-0	180	4-2-68	1990	Pineville, La.
McCurry, Jeff	1	1	5.09	16	0	0	3	18	17	12	10	6	13	R	R	6-7	210	1-21-70	1991	Houston, Texas
Minchey, Nate	15	6	4.51	27	21	3	0	158	172	87	79	53	107	R	R	6-7	225	8-31-69	1987	San Antonio, Texas
Moore, Joel	3	1	7.76	5	5	0	0	27	47	26	23	12	20	L	R	6-2	200	8-13-72	1993	Elgin, Ill.
Rekar, Bryan	10	9	5.46	28	25	0	0	145	169	96	88	39	116	R	R	6-3	205	6-3-72	1993	Orland Park, Ill.
Ruffin, Bruce	0	0	3.38	2	0	0	0	3	1	1	1	0	2	S	L	6-2	213	10-4-63	1985	Austin, Texas
Saipe, Mike	4	3	5.52	10	10	1	0	60	74	42	37	24	40	R	R	6-1	190	9-10-73	1994	San Diego, Calif.
Scott, Tim	0	0	1.23	12	0	0	3	15	7	2	2	3	18	R	R	6-2	205	11-16-66	1984	Hanford, Calif.
Shoemaker, Steve	1	1	8.41	5	4	0	0	20	23	19	19	17	27	L	R	6-1	195	2-3-73	1994	Phoenixville, Pa.
Stidham, Phil	5	2	9.91	26	0	0	0	36	55	43	40	26	20	R	R	6-0	180	11-18-68	1991	Tulsa, Okla.
Swift, Billy	0	1	12.00	1	1	0	0	3	4	4	4	3	4	R	R	6-0	191	10-27-61	1985	Paradise Valley, Ariz.
Thompson, Mark	0	0	12.00	1	1	0	0	3	6	4	4	1	1	R	R	6-2	205	4-7-71	1992	Russellville, Ky.
Thomson, John	4	2	3.43	7	7	0	0	42	36	18	16	14	49	R	R	6-3	175	10-1-73	1993	Sulphur, La.
Wright, Jamey	1	0	1.64	2	2	0	0	11	9	3	2	5	11	R	R	6-6	205	12-24-74	1993	Moore, Okla.

FIELDING

Catcher	PCT	G	PO	A	E	DP	PB
Cholowsky	.987	20	142	12	2	3	3
Gubanich	.970	13	89	8	3	2	2
Owens	.988	82	529	52	7	6	5
Strittmatter	.996	44	241	15	1	2	2

First Base	PCT	G	PO	A	E	DP
Boston	1.000	1	3	1	0	0
Cholowsky	1.000	2	10	0	0	0
Echevarria	1.000	4	29	3	0	1
Gonzales	.973	22	167	13	5	23
Helton	.986	78	585	61	9	78
Howitt	.990	25	179	17	2	23
Vanderwal	.976	18	153	10	4	16

Second Base	PCT	G	PO	A	E	DP
Bates	.980	10	19	30	1	10
Counsell	.980	90	204	239	9	69
Gonzales	.961	34	58	114	7	22
Hall	.920	6	10	13	2	3
Huson	1.000	3	2	4	0	2
Shumpert	.929	3	3	10	1	2

Third Base	PCT	G	PO	A	E	DP
Cholowsky	1.000	1	1	1	0	0
Gonzales	.857	9	2	10	2	1
Howitt	.000	1	0	0	0	0
Huson	1.000	4	3	4	0	0
Owens	.000	1	0	0	0	0
Quinlan	.960	131	91	269	15	30
Shumpert	.500	1	0	1	1	0

Shortstop	PCT	G	PO	A	E	DP
Bates	.955	25	41	65	5	20
Counsell	1.000	6	9	21	0	5
Gonzales	.914	10	13	19	3	7
Perez	.975	67	119	198	8	56
Sexton	.966	32	57	87	5	20
Shumpert	.824	5	5	9	3	3

Outfield	PCT	G	PO	A	E	DP
Barry	1.000	70	130	11	0	1
Echevarria	.991	63	106	6	1	0
Gibson	.968	18	30	0	1	0
Hall	.938	7	15	0	1	0
Helton	1.000	22	37	3	0	0
Howitt	1.000	20	29	2	0	1
Jones	.993	87	139	11	1	3
Owens	1.000	11	16	0	0	0
Pulliam	.957	32	44	0	2	0
Shumpert	.000	1	0	0	0	0
Vanderwal	1.000	4	5	0	0	0
Velazquez	.974	114	208	13	6	5

NEW HAVEN — Class AA

EASTERN LEAGUE

BATTING	AVG	G	AB	R	H	2B	3B	HR	RBI	BB	SO	SB	CS	B	T	HT	WT	DOB	1st Yr	Resides
Barry, Jeff	.219	40	146	21	32	4	0	5	12	4	34	3	2	S	R	6-0	200	9-22-68	1990	San Diego, Calif.
Barthol, Blake	.243	109	325	42	79	12	2	6	39	31	76	5	3	R	R	6-0	200	4-7-73	1995	Emmaus, Pa.

BATTING	AVG	G	AB	R	H	2B	3B	HR	RBI	BB	SO	SB	CS	B	T	HT	WT	DOB	1st Yr	Resides
Bernhardt, Steve	.213	101	315	35	67	14	0	6	38	27	46	2	2	R	R	6-0	180	10-9-70	1993	Timonium, Md.
Boston, D.J.	.287	83	293	53	84	14	2	7	49	49	63	1	5	L	L	6-7	230	9-6-71	1991	Cincinnati, Ohio
Curtis, Kevin	.273	105	362	58	99	24	0	17	69	34	82	0	2	R	R	6-2	210	8-19-72	1993	Upland, Calif.
2-team (22 Bowie)	.273	127	429	65	117	30	0	18	82	41	104	1	3							
Feuerstein, Dave	.260	26	104	8	27	4	3	0	10	7	20	2	1	R	R	6-2	200	7-19-73	1995	Scarsdale, N.Y.
Garcia, Vicente	.155	22	58	9	9	2	0	2	11	12	19	0	1	R	R	6-0	170	2-14-75	1993	Maracaibo, Venez.
Gibson, Derrick	.317	119	461	91	146	24	2	23	75	36	100	20	13	R	R	6-2	238	2-5-75	1993	Winter Haven, Fla.
Giudice, John	.250	63	216	26	54	8	2	5	30	16	49	5	1	R	R	6-1	205	6-19-71	1993	New Britain, Conn.
Grunewald, Keith	.242	103	310	41	75	11	1	0	24	25	78	7	3	S	R	6-1	185	10-15-71	1993	Marietta, Ga.
Hall, Billy	.220	17	59	8	13	2	1	1	7	7	10	7	1	S	R	5-9	180	6-17-69	1991	Wichita, Kan.
Holdren, Nate	.183	25	82	9	15	2	0	4	9	3	28	0	2	R	R	6-4	240	12-8-71	1993	Richland, Wash.
Jarrett, Link	.303	88	261	19	79	9	1	1	27	18	30	2	2	S	R	5-10	165	1-26-72	1994	Tallahassee, Fla.
Lewis, Anthony	.228	51	167	32	38	9	0	12	36	13	39	1	1	L	L	5-11	205	2-2-71	1989	Las Vegas, Nev.
Light, Tal	.241	25	83	10	20	6	0	5	11	5	36	0	1	R	R	6-3	205	11-28-73	1995	Lumberton, Texas
Newstrom, Doug	.266	95	244	29	65	10	1	1	43	39	32	9	5	L	R	6-1	195	9-18-71	1993	Goodyear, Ariz.
*Osborne, Mark	.000	3	5	1	0	0	0	0	0	2	4	0	0	L	R	6-4	204	2-1-78	1996	Sanford, N.C.
Pledger, Kinnis	.254	61	201	35	51	10	2	10	26	30	53	2	2	L	R	6-4	215	7-17-68	1987	Benton, Ark.
Sexton, Chris	.297	98	360	65	107	22	4	1	38	62	37	8	16	R	R	5-11	180	8-3-71	1993	Cincinnati, Ohio
Shumpert, Terry	.235	5	17	2	4	0	0	1	1	0	2	0	0	R	R	5-11	185	8-16-66	1987	Paducah, Ky.
Taylor, Jamie	.325	104	329	43	107	17	1	8	41	35	49	2	3	L	R	6-2	220	10-10-70	1992	Bloomingdale, Ohio
Wells, Forry	.224	39	98	16	22	4	0	2	7	21	37	1	2	L	R	6-4	205	3-21-71	1994	Belleville, Ill.

PITCHING	W	L	ERA	G	GS	CG	SV	IP	H	R	ER	BB	SO	B	T	HT	WT	DOB	1st Yr	Resides
Bost, Heath	2	2	3.56	38	0	0	20	43	44	18	17	10	45	R	R	6-4	200	10-13-74	1995	Taylorsville, N.C.
Brownson, Mark	10	9	4.19	29	29	2	0	185	172	101	86	55	170	L	R	6-2	175	6-17-75	1994	Wellington, Fla.
Byrd, Matt	1	3	5.01	10	3	0	0	23	22	15	13	12	17	S	R	6-2	200	5-17-71	1993	Brighton, Mich.
DeJean, Mike	0	1	6.00	2	0	0	0	3	3	2	2	2	2	R	R	6-2	205	9-28-70	1992	Denham Springs, La.
Hackman, Luther	0	6	7.82	10	10	0	0	51	58	49	44	34	34	R	R	6-4	195	10-10-74	1994	Columbus, Miss.
Haynes, Heath	0	0	1.13	5	0	0	0	8	7	1	1	1	8	R	R	6-0	175	11-30-68	1991	Wheeling, W.Va.
Henderson, Ryan	2	5	4.80	24	4	0	0	51	54	29	27	27	46	R	R	6-1	190	9-30-69	1992	Dana Point, Calif.
Kammerer, James	0	0	3.60	1	1	0	0	5	3	2	2	3	1	L	L	6-3	205	7-21-73	1995	Winona, Minn.
Kusiewicz, Mike	2	4	6.35	10	4	0	0	28	41	28	20	10	11	R	L	6-2	185	11-1-76	1995	Nepean, Ontario
Macca, Chris	0	4	7.77	46	0	0	9	44	47	40	38	55	29	R	R	6-2	185	11-14-74	1995	Plant City, Fla.
Million, Doug	0	5	9.23	10	10	0	0	40	64	46	41	36	19	L	L	6-4	175	10-13-75	1994	Sarasota, Fla.
Moore, Joel	6	4	3.84	19	12	1	0	77	77	38	33	35	47	L	R	6-2	200	8-13-72	1993	Elgin, Ill.
Norman, Scott	1	5	6.75	29	0	0	1	41	58	38	31	15	21	R	R	6-0	195	9-1-72	1993	Sarasota, Fla.
Peever, Lloyd	5	5	5.50	20	10	0	0	74	70	49	45	24	46	R	R	5-11	185	9-15-71	1992	Stonewall, Okla.
Pool, Matt	3	5	4.28	29	1	0	0	48	57	36	23	16	23	S	R	6-6	190	7-8-73	1994	Fresno, Calif.
Price, Tom	1	3	3.16	48	1	0	0	57	55	25	20	21	48	L	L	6-0	190	3-19-72	1994	Edwardsville, Ill.
Saipe, Mike	8	5	3.10	19	19	4	0	137	127	57	47	29	123	R	R	6-1	190	9-10-73	1994	San Diego, Calif.
Shoemaker, Steve	6	4	3.02	14	14	1	0	95	64	36	32	53	111	L	R	6-1	195	2-3-73	1994	Phoenixville, Pa.
Stidham, Phil	0	0	3.72	8	0	0	1	10	10	4	4	8	7	R	R	6-0	180	11-18-68	1991	Tulsa, Okla.
Vavrek, Mike	12	3	2.57	17	17	2	0	123	94	38	35	34	101	L	L	6-2	185	4-23-74	1995	Glendale Heights, Ill.
Watkins, Scott	2	0	3.52	13	0	0	0	15	9	6	6	3	8	L	L	6-3	180	5-15-70	1992	Sand Springs, Okla.
Zolecki, Mike	3	5	5.08	16	7	1	0	57	64	38	32	32	32	R	R	6-2	195	12-6-71	1993	South Milwaukee, Wis.

*Property of Arizona Diamondbacks

FIELDING

Catcher	PCT	G	PO	A	E	DP	PB
Barthol	.984	107	671	71	12	5	13
Newstrom	.985	52	296	36	5	3	3

First Base	PCT	G	PO	A	E	DP
Barry	.971	6	57	10	2	5
Boston	.990	81	665	59	7	77
Curtis	.984	12	105	15	2	18
Grunewald	.986	18	130	7	2	12
Holdren	.960	20	161	9	7	16
Newstrom	1.000	11	83	14	0	8
Taylor	1.000	1	1	0	0	0

Second Base	PCT	G	PO	A	E	DP
Bernhardt	.974	80	177	199	10	59
Garcia	.988	21	44	35	1	15
Grunewald	.992	29	47	75	1	17
Hall	.930	11	9	31	3	4
Jarrett	1.000	11	29	19	0	6
Shumpert	1.000	4	8	17	0	7

Third Base	PCT	G	PO	A	E	DP
Bernhardt	.750	3	0	3	1	0
Grunewald	.855	25	7	40	8	6
Jarrett	1.000	4	0	3	0	0
Light	.816	24	14	57	16	4
Taylor	.955	98	60	218	13	20

Shortstop	PCT	G	PO	A	E	DP
Grunewald	.906	11	14	34	5	8
Hall	1.000	1	1	2	0	0
Jarrett	.982	64	80	189	5	46
Sexton	.961	72	120	199	13	45

Outfield	PCT	G	PO	A	E	DP
Barry	.943	30	65	1	4	0
Curtis	.970	80	126	4	4	1
Feuerstein	1.000	24	53	2	0	1
Gibson	.947	115	188	8	11	0
Giudice	.969	58	123	4	4	0
Hall	.000	1	0	0	0	0
Lewis	.978	28	45	0	1	0
Pledger	.990	55	95	3	1	0
Sexton	.983	26	58	1	1	0
Wells	.912	24	26	5	3	0

SALEM — Class A

CAROLINA LEAGUE

BATTING	AVG	G	AB	R	H	2B	3B	HR	RBI	BB	SO	SB	CS	B	T	HT	WT	DOB	1st Yr	Resides
Bair, Rod	.273	16	44	5	12	3	0	0	6	0	6	2	0	R	R	5-11	190	10-29-74	1996	Tempe, Ariz.
Bryant, Clint	.227	52	185	15	42	9	0	2	18	14	36	4	4	R	R	6-0	180	8-29-73	1996	Kingsville, Texas
Clifford, John	.235	17	34	3	8	0	0	0	3	1	7	0	1	R	R	6-1	185	8-18-73	1995	Shrewsbury, Mass.
Drizos, Justin	.185	57	151	13	28	7	1	5	19	15	56	1	1	L	L	6-2	200	12-8-73	1995	Irvine, Calif.
Duverge, Salvador	.186	42	113	9	21	5	0	0	9	9	32	1	4	R	R	6-0	165	5-14-76	1994	San Cristobal, D.R.
Elam, Brett	.200	6	15	0	3	0	0	0	0	1	1	0	2	R	R	6-0	170	8-1-72	1995	Council Bluffs, Iowa
Feuerstein, Dave	.232	94	327	47	76	13	3	1	34	21	45	20	6	R	R	6-2	200	7-19-73	1995	Scarsdale, N.Y.
Gambill, Chad	.247	124	450	61	111	18	2	11	73	37	125	6	11	R	R	6-2	190	11-27-74	1993	Clearwater, Fla.
Garcia, Vicente	.257	98	319	49	82	22	1	4	37	44	51	11	5	R	R	6-0	170	2-14-75	1993	Maracaibo, Venez.
Houser, Kyle	.217	110	383	36	83	18	1	0	28	33	61	11	8	R	R	6-0	150	1-21-75	1993	Dallas, Texas
Jarrett, Link	.160	9	25	1	4	0	0	0	1	1	5	0	0	S	R	5-10	165	1-26-72	1994	Tallahassee, Fla.
Keck, Brian	.281	48	121	22	34	4	0	0	11	11	21	17	3	R	R	6-3	185	1-15-74	1996	Dodge City, Kan.
Light, Tal	.265	104	373	57	99	19	2	15	65	59	144	0	1	R	R	6-3	205	11-28-73	1995	Lumberton, Texas
Marnell, Dean	.192	17	52	4	10	2	0	0	7	3	1	0	0	R	R	5-11	185	1-9-76	1996	Footscray, Australia
Neubart, Garrett	.256	133	527	66	135	23	3	0	34	39	90	50	18	R	R	5-10	160	11-7-73	1995	Livingston, N.J.
Pena, Elvis	.222	93	279	41	62	9	2	1	30	37	53	16	6	S	R	5-11	155	9-15-76	1994	Santo Domingo, D.R.

BATTING	AVG	G	AB	R	H	2B	3B	HR	RBI	BB	SO	SB	CS	B	T	HT	WT	DOB	1st Yr	Resides
Petrick, Ben	.248	121	412	68	102	23	3	15	56	62	100	30	11	R	R	6-0	195	4-7-77	1996	Hillsboro, Ore.
Taylor, Jamie	.263	23	80	13	21	4	1	1	9	13	27	2	2	L	R	6-2	220	10-10-70	1992	Bloomingdale, Ohio
Vidal, Carlos	.239	80	226	20	54	21	0	6	30	19	54	1	2	R	R	5-10	188	4-21-75	1995	Virginia Gardens, Fla.
Wells, Forry	.299	93	321	58	96	27	3	11	52	48	64	19	7	L	R	6-4	205	3-21-71	1994	Belleville, Ill.

GAMES BY POSITION: C—Petrick 107, Vidal 41. **1B**—Clifford 10, Drizos 53, Light 14, Taylor 7, Wells 70. **2B**—Elam 2, Garcia 97, Jarrett 5, Pena 38. **3B**—Bryant 39, Elam 3, Jarrett 2, Keck 28, Light 53, Pena 19, Taylor 6. **SS**—Bryant 1, Elam 2, Houser 110, Jarrett 1, Keck 2, Pena 29. **OF**—Bair 5, Drizos 1, Duverge 41, Feuerstein 91, Gambill 123, Keck 7, Marnell 17, Neubart 132, Wells 14.

PITCHING	W	L	ERA	G	GS	CG	SV	IP	H	R	ER	BB	SO	B	T	HT	WT	DOB	1st Yr	Resides
Bevel, Bobby	4	7	4.64	50	0	0	3	66	69	37	34	17	57	L	L	5-10	180	10-10-73	1995	West Plains, Mo.
Bost, Heath	1	0	2.40	13	0	0	3	15	9	4	4	2	9	R	R	6-4	200	10-13-74	1995	Taylorsville, N.C.
Colmenares, Luis	6	1	3.92	32	3	0	2	67	60	34	29	30	70	R	R	5-11	189	11-25-76	1994	Valencia, Venez.
Dietrich, Jason	3	2	3.26	21	0	0	2	30	15	11	11	16	38	R	R	5-11	190	11-15-72	1994	Garden Grove, Calif.
Gonzalez, Lariel	5	0	2.53	44	0	0	8	57	42	19	16	23	79	R	R	6-4	180	5-25-76	1994	San Cristobal, D.R.
Hackman, Luther	1	4	5.80	15	15	2	0	81	99	60	52	37	59	R	R	6-4	195	10-10-74	1994	Columbus, Miss.
Kammerer, James	0	0	2.87	6	1	0	0	16	10	5	5	3	12	L	L	6-3	205	7-21-73	1995	Winona, Minn.
Kusiewicz, Mike	8	6	2.52	19	18	1	0	118	99	44	33	32	107	R	L	6-2	185	11-1-76	1995	Nepean, Ontario
Leskanic, Curt	0	0	3.86	2	1	0	0	2	5	2	1	1	3	R	R	6-0	180	4-2-68	1990	Pineville, La.
Martin, Chandler	1	5	3.97	16	5	0	1	45	46	25	20	25	30	R	R	6-1	180	10-23-73	1995	Salem, Ore.
Million, Doug	5	9	5.12	18	17	1	0	97	104	59	55	55	58	L	L	6-4	175	10-13-75	1994	Sarasota, Fla.
Murphy, Sean	1	3	4.58	15	0	0	0	20	21	16	10	12	11	R	R	6-1	180	12-7-72	1995	Hays, Kan.
Norman, Scott	0	1	3.96	18	0	0	1	25	29	12	11	8	13	R	R	6-0	195	9-1-72	1993	Sarasota, Fla.
Peever, Lloyd	0	0	3.27	4	1	0	0	11	13	6	4	3	10	R	R	5-11	185	9-15-71	1992	Stonewall, Okla.
Randall, Scott	9	10	3.84	27	26	2	0	176	167	93	75	66	128	R	R	6-3	178	10-29-75	1995	Goleta, Calif.
Schroeffel, Scott	1	4	8.16	16	3	0	0	29	34	27	26	17	24	S	R	6-0	190	12-30-73	1996	Wexford, Pa.
Shoemaker, Steve	3	3	2.77	9	9	1	0	52	31	21	16	25	76	L	R	6-1	195	2-3-73	1994	Phoenixville, Pa.
Stepka, Tom	11	14	4.15	28	28	4	0	182	205	100	84	28	120	R	R	6-2	185	11-29-75	1996	Williamsville, N.Y.
Swift, Billy	0	1	6.75	1	1	0	0	4	4	3	3	0	1	R	R	6-0	191	10-27-61	1985	Paradise Valley, Ariz.
Vavrek, Mike	2	2	2.15	10	9	0	0	63	55	21	15	18	48	L	L	6-2	185	4-23-74	1995	Glendale Heights, Ill.
Wright, Jamey	0	1	9.00	1	1	0	0	1	1	1	1	1	1	R	R	6-6	205	12-24-74	1993	Moore, Okla.
Zolecki, Mike	2	2	2.65	22	0	0	6	34	22	10	10	11	31	R	R	6-2	195	12-6-71	1993	South Milwaukee, Wis.

ASHEVILLE — Class A

SOUTH ATLANTIC LEAGUE

BATTING	AVG	G	AB	R	H	2B	3B	HR	RBI	BB	SO	SB	CS	B	T	HT	WT	DOB	1st Yr	Resides
Alamo, Efrain	.232	34	125	17	29	9	0	1	14	6	49	2	3	R	R	6-2	190	10-5-76	1994	Canovanas, P.R.
Anderson, Blake	.267	73	247	30	66	9	2	7	31	32	50	2	5	S	R	6-0	195	9-22-73	1996	Dallas, Texas
Anthony, Brian	.257	83	296	41	76	17	1	12	49	23	75	4	4	L	R	6-2	218	10-22-73	1996	Walnut Creek, Calif.
Arias, Rogelio	.239	72	251	23	60	4	0	2	19	10	21	4	2	R	R	6-0	165	6-9-76	1993	Santo Domingo, D.R.
Bair, Rod	.281	91	356	50	100	20	1	8	51	13	51	9	6	R	R	5-11	190	10-29-74	1996	Tempe, Ariz.
Bryant, Clint	.268	63	220	30	59	12	0	2	25	19	62	9	3	R	R	6-0	180	8-29-73	1996	Kingsville, Texas
Duverge, Salvador	.223	28	94	7	21	3	1	2	8	13	23	4	1	R	R	6-0	165	5-14-76	1994	San Cristobal, D.R.
Elam, Brett	.243	96	337	44	82	12	1	2	30	35	58	8	5	R	R	6-0	170	8-1-72	1995	Council Bluffs, Iowa
Gordon, Gary	.199	79	231	34	46	5	1	0	18	32	73	21	10	R	R	5-10	190	12-13-76	1995	Willington, N.J.
Hamlin, Mark	.290	134	497	79	144	31	0	18	74	55	107	6	3	R	R	6-3	220	2-9-74	1996	Augusta, Ga.
Hutchison, Bernard	.232	108	419	59	97	10	2	0	30	35	91	81	18	R	R	5-10	160	5-2-74	1996	Tallassee, Ala.
Keck, Brian	.234	37	124	8	29	3	0	0	8	9	22	5	2	R	R	6-3	185	1-15-74	1996	Dodge City, Kan.
Lindsey, John	.236	110	399	54	94	20	2	12	67	29	110	3	2	R	R	6-3	215	1-30-77	1995	Hattiesburg, Miss.
Livingston, Doug	.263	128	468	53	123	30	3	3	61	45	82	8	5	R	R	5-8	160	4-9-74	1996	Thonotosassa, Fla.
Myers, Aaron	.075	12	40	3	3	1	0	0	3	4	8	0	0	R	R	6-1	200	5-14-76	1994	Santa Maria, Calif.
Rodriguez, Chris	.000	2	4	0	0	0	0	0	0	0	1	0	0	R	R	6-2	190	5-10-76	1996	Modesto, Calif.
Whitley, Matt	.232	129	461	67	107	21	0	1	43	77	57	14	9	R	R	6-0	170	3-29-72	1995	Knoxville, Tenn.

GAMES BY POSITION: C—Anderson 69, Arias 72, Rodriguez 2. **1B**—Anthony 60, Elam 1, Lindsey 84. **2B**—Elam 3, Livingston 121, Whitley 17. **3B**—Bryant 50, Elam 48, Keck 31, Myers 12. **SS**—Elam 32, Keck 3, Whitley 106. **OF**—Alamo 31, Bair 87, Duverge 28, Gordon 60, Hamlin 113, Hutchison 100.

PITCHING	W	L	ERA	G	GS	CG	SV	IP	H	R	ER	BB	SO	B	T	HT	WT	DOB	1st Yr	Resides
Brueggemann, Dean	2	8	4.25	34	12	0	3	110	116	62	52	44	99	L	L	6-4	195	3-11-76	1996	Smithton, Ill.
Chacon, Shawn	11	7	3.89	28	27	1	0	162	155	80	70	63	149	R	R	6-3	195	12-23-77	1996	Greeley, Colo.
Christman, Tim	7	3	3.41	29	0	0	3	63	55	32	24	18	87	L	L	6-2	180	3-31-75	1996	Oneonta, N.Y.
D'Alessandro, Marc	0	2	5.62	29	0	0	1	66	87	47	41	19	46	L	L	6-2	195	7-23-75	1994	Ocean, N.J.
Emiliano, Jamie	0	1	5.85	18	0	0	0	20	24	15	13	12	20	R	R	5-10	210	8-2-74	1995	Andrews, Texas
Kammerer, James	0	2	2.82	12	3	1	0	38	37	15	12	20	27	L	L	6-3	205	7-21-73	1995	Winona, Minn.
Lee, David	4	8	4.08	51	0	0	22	53	61	30	24	23	59	R	R	6-2	200	3-12-73	1995	Pittsburgh, Pa.
Mahlberg, John	0	0	5.03	12	0	0	2	20	29	15	11	8	16	R	R	6-2	197	10-2-76	1995	Coquille, Ore.
Matcuk, Steve	5	12	4.45	28	27	3	1	160	157	86	79	55	100	R	R	6-2	185	4-8-76	1996	Pasadena, Md.
Nicholson, John	8	9	3.78	25	25	0	0	136	128	70	57	36	115	S	R	6-4	205	12-6-77	1996	Houston, Texas
Rivera, Alvin	0	1	0.00	1	1	0	0	2	2	1	0	4	0	R	R	6-2	205	8-30-78	1996	Yabucoa, P.R.
Romine, Jason	4	2	4.02	28	0	0	1	47	45	23	21	14	53	R	R	6-5	215	4-11-75	1995	Omak, Wash.
Schroeffel, Scott	2	3	3.74	19	2	0	0	46	31	23	19	20	40	S	R	6-0	190	12-30-73	1996	Wexford, Pa.
Slamka, John	1	3	3.75	26	2	0	0	58	61	31	24	27	48	R	L	6-3	190	4-2-74	1994	Phoenix, Ariz.
Thompson, Mark	0	2	2.70	4	4	0	0	13	11	5	4	5	9	R	R	6-2	205	4-7-71	1992	Russellville, Ky.
Walls, Doug	4	2	2.96	10	9	0	0	52	50	23	17	22	62	L	R	6-3	200	3-21-74	1993	Union, Ohio
Westbrook, Jake	14	11	4.29	28	27	3	0	170	176	93	81	55	92	R	R	6-3	180	9-29-77	1996	Danielsville, Ga.

PORTLAND — Short-Season Class A

NORTHWEST LEAGUE

BATTING	AVG	G	AB	R	H	2B	3B	HR	RBI	BB	SO	SB	CS	B	T	HT	WT	DOB	1st Yr	Resides
Alamo, Efrain	.216	69	255	27	55	13	2	2	33	22	88	12	4	R	R	6-2	190	10-5-76	1994	Canovanas, P.R.
Alviso, Jerome	.319	69	270	48	86	15	3	2	45	19	46	12	5	S	R	6-1	180	9-4-75	1997	Livermore, Calif.
Clark, John	.204	17	54	8	11	3	1	0	3	9	16	0	0	R	R	6-4	205	10-17-76	1995	Cibolo, Texas
Clifford, John	.059	6	17	2	1	0	0	0	1	0	3	0	2	R	R	6-1	185	8-18-73	1995	Shrewsbury, Mass.

BATTING	AVG	G	AB	R	H	2B	3B	HR	RBI	BB	SO	SB	CS	B	T	HT	WT	DOB	1st Yr	Resides
Folmar, Ryan	.180	19	61	8	11	5	0	1	9	9	19	2	1	L	R	5-11	205	11-8-74	1997	Chambersburg, Pa.
Franklin, Jason	.237	63	211	37	50	13	1	6	37	37	60	4	1	R	R	6-1	200	12-20-76	1997	Winter Haven, Fla.
Gonzales, Jose	.241	48	166	18	40	9	0	3	16	25	30	1	1	R	R	6-0	205	4-25-75	1997	Lubbock, Texas
Jackson, Jeremy	.284	68	289	45	82	12	4	1	26	20	70	13	4	L	R	6-2	195	5-9-76	1997	Moline, Ill.
Johns, Michael	.232	62	220	28	51	4	3	3	27	11	66	2	2	R	R	6-2	190	8-26-75	1997	Fernandina Beach, Fla.
Kirkpatrick, Brian	.286	2	7	1	2	0	0	0	0	0	3	0	0	R	R	6-3	195	9-7-76	1995	King City, Calif.
Marnell, Dean	.300	19	70	13	21	1	0	0	9	7	8	1	1	R	R	5-11	185	1-9-76	1996	Footscray, Australia
Mitchell, Andres	.230	69	265	57	61	5	6	4	20	36	102	21	8	R	R	6-1	185	5-26-76	1996	Brentwood, Tenn.
Petersen, Mike	.235	13	51	8	12	2	0	0	5	4	12	0	1	R	R	6-4	190	10-15-76	1996	Missouri City, Texas
Rodriguez, Chris	.264	23	72	7	19	1	1	0	4	6	12	0	1	R	R	6-2	190	5-10-76	1996	Modesto, Calif.
Schwartzbauer, Whitey	.256	50	156	22	40	7	2	3	29	37	47	2	2	L	R	6-1	185	5-4-77	1996	White Bear Lake, Minn.
Sears, Todd	.270	55	200	37	54	13	1	2	29	41	49	2	0	L	R	6-6	205	10-23-75	1997	Ankeny, Iowa
Zweifel, Kent	.288	57	198	28	57	14	2	4	44	29	50	7	2	R	R	6-3	210	3-21-77	1996	Klamath Falls, Ore.

GAMES BY POSITION: C—Folmar 12, Gonzales 47, Rodriguez 20. **1B**—Clifford 3, Kirkpatrick 1, Petersen 11, Schwartzbauer 1, Sears 55, Zweifel 8. **2B**—Alviso 43, Clark 9, Franklin 3, Johns 23, Schwartzbauer 1. **3B**—Franklin 43, Kirkpatrick 1, Mitchell 2, Schwartzbauer 31. **SS**—Alviso 26, Clark 8, Johns 38, Mitchell 6. **OF**—Alamo 68, Clifford 1, Jackson 67, Marnell 16, Mitchell 63, Zweifel 19.

PITCHING	W	L	ERA	G	GS	CG	SV	IP	H	R	ER	BB	SO	B	T	HT	WT	DOB	1st Yr	Resides
Barber, Andrew	6	1	2.48	22	0	0	1	33	23	10	9	18	39	R	R	6-1	195	5-23-73	1996	Loveland, Colo.
Johnson, David	0	1	3.24	18	0	0	5	17	10	8	6	20	21	R	R	6-3	220	10-6-74	1997	Baxter Springs, Kan.
Kalinowski, Josh	0	1	2.41	6	6	0	0	19	15	6	5	10	27	L	L	6-2	190	12-12-76	1997	Casper, Wyo.
Kennedy, Ryan	0	0	12.27	6	0	0	0	7	10	10	10	4	5	R	R	6-4	215	10-29-75	1996	Shubuta, Miss.
Kringen, Jake	6	5	3.46	15	15	1	0	83	84	40	32	20	72	L	L	6-2	215	6-25-76	1997	Elma, Wash.
Mahlberg, John	2	4	6.65	18	7	0	0	46	69	47	34	14	31	R	R	6-2	197	10-2-76	1995	Coquille, Ore.
Miller, Justin	4	2	2.14	14	11	0	0	67	68	26	16	20	54	R	R	6-2	200	8-27-77	1997	Torrance, Calif.
Petrosian, Ara	3	1	2.40	29	0	0	13	45	42	18	12	14	37	R	R	6-4	225	3-3-75	1997	Fountain Valley, Calif.
Price, Chris	3	1	6.06	26	0	0	1	33	41	25	22	5	22	R	R	6-4	225	12-5-74	1997	Roswell, N.M.
Rivera, Alvin	3	0	4.99	13	6	0	0	40	41	23	22	13	19	R	R	6-2	205	8-30-78	1996	Yabucoa, P.R.
Rosa, Cristy	4	2	5.56	21	0	0	1	44	54	32	27	14	35	R	R	6-1	165	10-5-77	1995	Guanica, P.R.
Schmidt, Donnie	4	2	4.97	22	0	0	2	42	47	24	23	23	32	R	R	6-1	175	2-18-75	1996	Sherwood, Ore.
Sebring, Jeff	2	0	3.20	13	0	0	0	25	28	10	9	8	27	L	L	6-2	185	11-6-74	1996	Boone, Iowa
Seifert, Ryan	1	7	4.84	16	15	0	0	74	89	49	40	31	52	R	R	6-5	215	8-14-75	1997	Chaska, Minn.
Thompson, Travis	5	5	4.50	18	11	0	0	74	88	51	37	16	51	R	R	6-4	190	1-10-75	1996	Greenfield, Wis.
Walls, Doug	1	0	1.23	5	5	0	0	22	19	3	3	10	23	L	R	6-3	200	3-21-74	1993	Union, Ohio

CHANDLER — Rookie

ARIZONA LEAGUE

BATTING	AVG	G	AB	R	H	2B	3B	HR	RBI	BB	SO	SB	CS	B	T	HT	WT	DOB	1st Yr	Resides
Castro, Juan	.171	33	129	13	22	4	1	3	13	5	42	3	3	R	R	6-1	205	4-21-77	1996	Turmero, Venez.
Encarnacion, Bernaldo	.261	43	142	27	37	9	0	3	23	19	37	2	1	R	R	6-2	205	2-8-78	1996	Santo Domingo, D.R.
Figgins, Chone	.280	54	214	41	60	5	6	1	23	35	51	30	13	S	R	5-8	155	1-22-78	1997	Brandon, Fla.
Folmar, Ryan	.304	11	46	5	14	6	0	0	7	3	2	0	2	L	R	5-11	205	11-8-74	1997	Chambersburg, Pa.
Kirkpatrick, Brian	.254	45	173	23	44	5	1	3	25	9	28	2	1	R	R	6-3	195	9-7-76	1995	King City, Calif.
Landaeta, Luis	.291	38	148	25	43	6	3	0	13	7	9	4	3	L	L	6-0	180	3-4-77	1996	Valencia, Venez.
Lina, Donald	.232	30	95	15	22	1	1	0	8	7	28	8	2	R	R	6-1	177	6-25-78	1995	Santo Domingo, D.R.
Mahoney, Ricardo	.282	32	124	15	35	3	0	0	17	6	20	8	6	R	R	6-2	190	10-13-78	1996	Panama City, Panama
Nunez, Jose	.365	52	208	31	76	17	3	3	32	19	31	12	2	R	R	6-1	167	10-7-78	1996	Santo Domingo, D.R.
Petersen, Mike	.220	33	118	18	26	7	1	0	13	7	20	2	2	R	R	6-4	190	10-15-76	1996	Missouri City, Texas
Rosario, Carlos	.284	46	169	29	48	7	0	1	18	10	22	14	3	S	L	5-11	190	5-10-77	1996	Santo Domingo, D.R.
Sanchez, Agustin	.271	36	118	15	32	2	1	0	15	15	24	15	0	S	R	6-0	160	2-2-79	1997	Yauco, P.R.
Smith, Sam	.235	52	200	27	47	9	2	1	18	24	38	6	1	R	R	6-1	180	3-21-79	1997	Jasper, Texas
Sosa, Jorge	.140	29	93	13	13	1	2	0	6	13	36	6	0	S	R	6-2	177	4-28-78	1995	Santo Domingo, D.R.

GAMES BY POSITION: C—Castro 29, Folmar 2, Mahoney 26. **1B**—Folmar 1, Kirkpatrick 40, Lina 1, Mahoney 2, Petersen 17. **2B**—Lina 16, Nunez 42. **3B**—Kirkpatrick 7, Lina 5, Smith 48. **SS**—Figgins 51, Lina 8. **OF**—Encarnacion 38, Landaeta 32, Petersen 11, Rosario 41, Sanchez 34, Sosa 26.

PITCHING	W	L	ERA	G	GS	CG	SV	IP	H	R	ER	BB	SO	B	T	HT	WT	DOB	1st Yr	Resides
Barboza, Carlos	1	1	4.03	16	0	0	1	29	29	23	13	25	18	R	R	6-1	188	2-21-78	1996	Maracaibo, Venez.
Cook, Aaron	1	3	3.13	9	8	0	0	46	48	27	16	17	35	R	R	6-3	175	2-8-79	1997	Loveland, Ohio
Gonzalez, Armando	1	3	2.57	13	4	0	0	42	33	27	12	13	33	R	R	6-1	195	10-12-77	1997	Pico Rivera, Calif.
Iannacone, Steve	1	2	4.19	11	0	0	1	19	24	11	9	14	13	R	R	6-6	220	10-5-77	1997	Sicklerville, N.J.
Kidd, Jake	5	0	1.62	19	0	0	3	39	37	14	7	10	27	R	R	6-6	180	2-11-78	1997	Hesperia, Calif.
Labitzke, Jesse	0	1	10.27	12	4	0	0	24	41	33	27	21	22	L	L	6-5	220	11-23-77	1996	Laramie, Wyo.
Little, Rodney	3	1	7.36	15	1	0	0	26	29	26	21	19	21	R	R	6-3	176	8-14-78	1997	Combs, Ky.
Little, Roger	2	1	5.45	14	4	0	1	33	30	24	20	23	31	R	R	6-3	180	8-14-78	1997	Combs, Ky.
Lora, Edison	0	0	6.75	11	0	0	0	21	31	20	16	9	8	R	R	6-5	200	5-12-78	1995	Santo Domingo, D.R.
Mangum, Mark	4	6	4.80	14	14	0	0	66	67	45	35	38	77	R	R	6-2	165	8-24-78	1997	Kingwood, Texas
Medina, Jaime	1	1	7.20	10	0	0	0	15	19	17	12	10	8	R	R	5-11	165	4-5-80	1996	El Guayabo, Venez.
Price, Ryan	2	7	3.51	14	14	0	0	77	69	49	30	28	98	R	R	6-3	190	1-31-78	1997	Roswell, N.M.
Vargas, Derrick	0	3	6.03	11	7	0	0	31	40	33	21	23	28	L	L	6-4	204	5-13-77	1997	Newark, Calif.
Woodard, Brad	1	5	2.73	19	0	0	6	30	33	25	9	7	30	R	R	6-2	190	10-16-77	1997	San Mateo, Fla.

Detroit TIGERS

Manager: Buddy Bell.

1997 Record: 79-83, .488 (3rd, AL East)

BATTING	AVG	G	AB	R	H	2B	3B	HR	RBI	BB	SO	SB	CS	B	T	HT	WT	DOB	1st Yr	Resides
Bartee, Kimera	.200	12	5	4	1	0	0	0	0	2	2	3	1	S	R	6-0	180	7-21-72	1993	Omaha, Neb.
Casanova, Raul	.243	101	304	27	74	10	1	5	24	26	48	1	1	R	R	6-0	192	8-24-72	1990	Ponce, P.R.
Catalanotto, Frank	.308	13	26	2	8	2	0	0	3	3	7	0	0	L	R	6-0	170	4-27-74	1992	Smithtown, N.Y.
Clark, Tony	.276	159	580	105	160	28	3	32	117	93	144	1	3	S	R	6-8	240	6-15-72	1990	El Cajon, Calif.
Coleman, Vince	.071	6	14	0	1	0	0	0	0	1	3	0	0	S	R	6-1	185	9-22-61	1982	St. Louis, Mo.
Cruz, Deivi	.241	147	436	35	105	26	0	2	40	14	55	3	6	R	R	6-0	175	6-11-75	1993	Bani, D.R.
Easley, Damion	.264	151	527	97	139	37	3	22	72	68	102	28	13	R	R	5-11	155	11-11-69	1989	Glendale, Ariz.
Encarnacion, Juan	.212	11	33	3	7	1	1	1	5	3	12	3	1	R	R	6-2	160	3-8-76	1993	Las Matas de Farfan, D.R.
Fryman, Travis	.274	154	595	90	163	27	3	22	102	46	113	16	3	R	R	6-1	194	3-25-69	1987	Cantonment, Fla.
Hall, Joe	.500	2	4	1	2	1	0	0	3	0	0	0	0	R	R	6-0	180	3-6-66	1988	Paducah, Ky.
Hamelin, Bob	.270	110	318	47	86	15	0	18	52	48	72	2	1	L	L	6-0	235	11-29-67	1988	Charlotte, N.C.
Higginson, Bob	.299	146	546	94	163	30	5	27	101	70	85	12	7	L	R	5-11	180	8-18-70	1992	Philadelphia, Pa.
Hunter, Brian	.269	162	658	112	177	29	7	4	45	66	121	74	18	R	R	6-4	180	3-5-71	1989	Vancouver, Wash.
Hurst, Jimmy	.176	13	17	1	3	1	0	1	1	2	6	0	0	R	R	6-6	225	3-1-72	1991	Tuscaloosa, Ala.
Jensen, Marcus	.182	8	11	1	2	0	0	0	1	1	5	0	0	S	R	6-4	195	12-14-72	1990	Oakland, Calif.
Johnson, Brian	.237	45	139	13	33	6	1	2	18	5	19	1	0	R	R	6-2	210	1-8-68	1989	Oakland, Calif.
Miller, Orlando	.234	50	111	13	26	7	1	2	10	5	24	1	0	R	R	6-1	180	1-13-69	1988	Estafeta El Dorado, Panama
Nevin, Phil	.235	93	251	32	59	16	1	9	35	25	68	0	1	R	R	6-2	185	1-19-71	1992	Placentia, Calif.
Nieves, Melvin	.228	116	359	46	82	18	1	20	64	39	157	1	7	S	R	6-2	186	12-28-71	1988	Bayamon, P.R.
Pride, Curtis	.210	79	162	21	34	4	4	2	19	24	45	6	4	L	R	5-11	195	12-17-68	1986	Wellington, Fla.
Reed, Jody	.196	52	112	6	22	2	0	0	8	10	15	3	2	R	R	5-9	165	7-26-62	1984	Tampa, Fla.
Trammell, Bubba	.228	44	123	14	28	5	0	4	13	15	35	3	1	R	R	6-2	205	11-6-71	1994	Knoxville, Tenn.
Walbeck, Matt	.277	47	137	18	38	3	0	3	10	12	19	3	3	S	R	5-11	188	10-2-69	1987	Sacramento, Calif.

PITCHING	W	L	ERA	G	GS	CG	SV	IP	H	R	ER	BB	SO	B	T	HT	WT	DOB	1st Yr	Resides
Bautista, Jose	2	2	6.69	21	0	0	0	40	55	32	30	12	19	R	R	6-2	207	7-25-64	1981	Cooper City, Fla.
Blair, Willie	16	8	4.17	29	27	2	0	175	186	85	81	46	90	R	R	6-1	185	12-18-65	1986	Lexington, Ky.
Brocail, Doug	3	4	3.23	61	4	0	2	78	74	31	28	36	60	L	R	6-5	190	5-16-67	1986	Lamar, Colo.
Cummings, John	2	0	5.47	19	0	0	0	25	32	22	15	14	8	L	L	6-3	200	5-10-69	1990	Laguna Niguel, Calif.
Dishman, Glenn	1	2	5.28	7	4	0	0	29	30	18	17	8	20	R	L	6-1	195	11-5-70	1993	Fremont, Calif.
Duran, Roberto	0	0	7.59	13	0	0	0	11	7	9	9	15	11	L	L	6-0	190	3-6-73	1990	Moca, D.R.
Gaillard, Eddie	1	0	5.31	16	0	0	1	20	16	12	12	10	12	R	R	6-1	180	8-13-70	1993	West Palm Beach, Fla.
Hernandez, Fernando	0	0	40.50	2	0	0	0	1	5	6	6	3	2	R	R	6-2	185	6-16-71	1990	Santiago, D.R.
Jarvis, Kevin	0	3	5.40	17	3	0	0	42	55	28	25	14	27	S	R	6-2	200	8-1-69	1991	Lexington, Ky.
2-team (6 Minnesota)	0	3	7.08	23	5	0	0	55	78	46	43	22	36							
Jones, Todd	5	4	3.09	68	0	0	31	70	60	29	24	35	70	L	R	6-3	200	4-24-68	1989	Pell City, Ala.
Keagle, Greg	3	5	6.55	11	10	0	0	45	58	33	33	18	33	R	R	6-2	185	6-28-71	1993	Horseheads, N.Y.
Lira, Felipe	5	7	5.77	20	15	1	0	92	101	61	59	45	64	R	R	6-0	170	4-26-72	1990	Miranda, Venez.
Miceli, Danny	3	2	5.01	71	0	0	3	83	77	49	46	38	79	R	R	5-11	205	9-9-70	1990	Orlando, Fla.
Moehler, Brian	11	12	4.67	31	31	2	0	175	198	97	91	61	97	R	R	6-3	195	12-31-71	1993	Rockingham, N.C.
Myers, Mike	0	4	5.70	88	0	0	2	54	58	36	34	25	50	L	L	6-3	197	6-26-69	1990	Wheeling, Ill.
Olivares, Omar	5	6	4.70	19	19	3	0	115	110	68	60	53	74	R	R	6-1	183	7-6-67	1987	San German, P.R.
Pugh, Tim	1	1	5.00	2	2	0	0	9	6	5	5	5	4	R	R	6-6	225	1-26-67	1989	Florence, Ky.
Sager, A.J.	3	4	4.18	38	1	0	3	84	81	43	39	24	53	R	R	6-4	220	3-3-65	1988	Kirkersville, Ohio
Sanders, Scott	3	8	5.33	14	14	1	0	74	79	44	44	24	58	R	R	6-4	220	3-25-69	1990	Thibodaux, La.
2-team (33 Seattle)	6	14	5.86	47	20	1	2	140	152	92	91	62	120							
Thompson, Justin	15	11	3.02	32	32	4	0	223	188	82	75	66	151	L	L	6-3	175	3-8-73	1991	Spring, Texas

FIELDING

Catcher	PCT	G	PO	A	E	DP	PB
Casanova	.985	92	543	38	9	6	8
Jensen	.964	8	26	1	1	0	0
Johnson	.987	43	217	9	3	2	0
Nevin	1.000	1	1	0	0	0	0
Walbeck	.988	44	240	15	3	2	3

First Base	PCT	G	PO	A	E	DP
Clark	.993	158	1422	100	10	131
Hamelin	1.000	7	29	1	0	1
Miller	1.000	3	6	0	0	0
Nevin	.958	7	22	1	1	0

Second Base	PCT	G	PO	A	E	DP
Catalanotto	1.000	6	7	9	0	0
Easley	.981	137	235	389	12	82
Reed	.987	41	49	107	2	18

Third Base	PCT	G	PO	A	E	DP
Fryman	.978	153	126	312	10	21
Miller	.889	4	1	7	1	0
Nevin	1.000	17	6	13	0	1

Shortstop	PCT	G	PO	A	E	DP
Cruz	.979	147	192	420	13	94
Easley	1.000	21	9	16	0	0
Miller	.979	31	30	64	2	18

Outfield	PCT	G	PO	A	E	DP
Bartee	1.000	6	3	0	0	0
Coleman	1.000	3	3	0	0	0
Encarnacion	1.000	10	22	0	0	0
Hall	1.000	1	1	0	0	0
Higginson	.972	143	287	20	9	5
Hunter	.990	162	408	8	4	0
Hurst	1.000	12	12	0	0	0
Nevin	.986	40	65	4	1	2
Nieves	.979	99	187	4	4	1
Trammell	1.000	28	52	1	0	0

DIAMOND IMAGES

Justin Thompson

FARM SYSTEM

Assistant General Manager/Minor Leagues: Steve Lubratich

Class	Farm Team	League	W	L	Pct.	Finish*	Manager(s)	First Yr
AAA	Toledo (Ohio) Mud Hens	International	68	73	.482	7th (10)	Glenn Ezell/Gene Roof	1987
AA	Jacksonville (Fla.) Suns	Southern	66	73	.475	8th (10)	Dave Anderson	1995
#A	Lakeland (Fla.) Tigers	Florida State	81	57	.587	2nd (14)	Mark Meleski	1960
A	West Michigan Whitecaps	Midwest	92	39	.702	1st (14)	Bruce Fields	1997
A	Jamestown (N.Y.) Jammers	New York-Penn	25	49	.338	14th (15)	Dwight Lowry/Matt Martin	1994
R	Lakeland (Fla.) Tigers	Gulf Coast	31	29	.517	7th (15)	Kevin Bradshaw	1995

*Finish in overall standings (No. of teams in league) #Advanced level

ORGANIZATION LEADERS

MAJOR LEAGUERS

BATTING

*AVG	Bob Higginson	.299
R	Brian Hunter	112
H	Brian Hunter	177
TB	Tony Clark	290
2B	Damion Easley	37
3B	Brian Hunter	7
HR	Tony Clark	32
RBI	Tony Clark	117
BB	Tony Clark	93
SO	Melvin Nieves	157
SB	Brian Hunter	74

PITCHING

W	Willie Blair	16
L	Brian Moehler	12
#ERA	Justin Thompson	3.02
G	Mike Myers	88
CG	Justin Thompson	4
SV	Todd Jones	31
IP	Justin Thompson	223
BB	Justin Thompson	66
SO	Justin Thompson	151

Tony Clark

RODGER WOOD

Juan Encarnacion

MINOR LEAGUERS

BATTING

*AVG	Robert Fick, West Michigan	.341
R	Robert Fick, West Michigan	100
H	Juan Encarnacion, Jacksonville	159
TB	Juan Encarnacion, Jacksonville	276
2B	Robert Fick, West Michigan	50
3B	Santiago Perez, Lakeland	12
HR	Bubba Trammell, Toledo	28
RBI	Alejandro Freire, Lakeland	92
BB	Scott Sollmann, West Michigan	79
SO	Kimera Bartee, Toledo	154
SB	Scott Sollmann, West Michigan	40

PITCHING

W	Two tied at	15
L	Willis Roberts, Jacksonville	15
#ERA	Craig Quintal, West Michigan	1.96
G	Rick Greene, Toledo	57
CG	Brian Powell, Lakeland	8
SV	Francisco Cordero, West Michigan	35
IP	Brian Powell, Lakeland	183
BB	Mike Drumright, Toledo/Jacksonville	104
SO	Greg Keagle, Toledo	140

*Minimum 250 At-Bats #Minimum 75 Innings

TOP 10 PROSPECTS

STEVE MOORE

Mike Drumright

How the Tigers Top 10 prospects, as judged by Baseball America prior to the 1997 season, fared in 1997:

Player, Pos.	Club (Class)	AVG	AB	R	H	2B	3B	HR	RBI	SB
3. Bubba Trammell, of	Detroit	.228	123	14	28	5	0	4	13	3
	Toledo (AAA)	.251	319	56	80	15	1	28	75	2
4. Raul Casanova, c	Detroit	.243	304	27	74	10	1	5	24	1
	Toledo (AAA)	.195	41	1	8	0	0	1	3	0
6. Juan Encarnacion, of	Detroit	.212	33	3	7	1	1	1	5	3
	Jacksonville (AA)	.323	493	91	159	31	4	26	90	17
8. Richard Almanzar, 2b	Jacksonville (AA)	.243	387	55	94	20	2	5	35	20
10. Gabe Kapler, of	Lakeland (A)	.295	519	87	153	40	6	19	87	8

Player, Pos.	Club (Class)	W	L	ERA	G	SV	IP	H	BB	SO
1. Mike Drumright, rhp	Toledo (AAA)	5	10	5.06	23	0	133	134	91	115
	Jacksonville (AA)	1	1	1.57	5	0	29	16	13	24
2. Seth Greisinger, rhp	Jacksonville (AA)	10	6	5.20	28	0	159	194	53	105
5. Willis Roberts, rhp	Jacksonville (AA)	6	15	6.28	26	0	149	181	64	86
7. Dave Borkowski, rhp	West Michigan (A)	15	3	3.46	25	0	164	143	31	104
9. Matt Drews, rhp	Toledo (AAA)	0	2	6.60	3	0	15	14	14	7
	Jacksonville (AA)	8	11	5.49	24	0	144	160	50	85

TOLEDO — Class AAA

INTERNATIONAL LEAGUE

BATTING	AVG	G	AB	R	H	2B	3B	HR	RBI	BB	SO	SB	CS	B	T	HT	WT	DOB	1st Yr	Resides
Barker, Glen	.191	21	47	9	9	1	0	1	3	5	15	6	2	R	R	5-10	180	5-10-71	1993	Albany, N.Y.
Bartee, Kimera	.218	136	501	67	109	13	7	3	33	52	154	33	9	S	R	6-0	180	7-21-72	1993	Omaha, Neb.
Bream, Scott	.231	30	91	11	21	1	0	0	0	13	31	0	1	S	R	6-1	170	11-4-70	1989	Omaha, Neb.
Casanova, Raul	.195	12	41	1	8	0	0	1	3	3	8	0	0	R	R	6-0	192	8-24-72	1990	Ponce, P.R.
Catalanotto, Frank	.300	134	500	75	150	32	3	16	68	47	80	12	11	L	R	6-0	170	4-27-74	1992	Smithtown, N.Y.
Hajek, Dave	.217	72	253	27	55	14	2	4	32	21	18	0	2	R	R	5-10	165	10-14-67	1990	Colorado Springs, Colo.
Hall, Joe	.251	75	271	35	68	18	2	6	30	22	48	2	1	R	R	6-0	180	3-6-66	1988	Paducah, Ky.
Hamelin, Bob	.242	27	91	14	22	7	0	6	24	27	24	0	0	L	L	6-0	235	11-29-67	1988	Charlotte, N.C.
Hare, Shawn	.180	23	61	9	11	4	0	1	6	18	25	0	0	L	L	6-1	200	3-26-67	1989	Lakeland, Fla.
Holbert, Ray	.242	109	372	43	90	18	7	7	37	32	109	16	7	R	R	6-0	165	9-25-70	1988	Moreno Valley, Calif.
Hurst, Jimmy	.271	110	377	51	102	11	3	18	58	47	115	14	5	R	R	6-6	225	3-1-72	1991	Tuscaloosa, Ala.
Hyers, Tim	.274	121	424	61	116	22	3	12	55	41	65	1	2	L	L	6-1	180	10-3-71	1990	Covington, Ga.
Jensen, Marcus	.175	24	80	5	14	5	0	0	9	9	25	0	0	S	R	6-4	195	12-14-72	1990	Oakland, Calif.
Johnson, Brian	.143	7	21	0	3	2	0	0	1	0	2	0	0	R	R	6-2	210	1-8-68	1989	Oakland, Calif.
Komminsk, Brad	.667	1	3	0	2	1	0	0	0	0	0	0	0	R	R	6-2	205	4-4-61	1979	Lima, Ohio
Makarewicz, Scott	.235	100	340	34	80	15	1	7	38	14	68	0	5	R	R	6-0	200	3-1-67	1989	Grand Rapids, Mich.
Miller, Orlando	.267	8	30	3	8	1	0	1	5	2	5	2	1	R	R	6-1	180	1-13-69	1988	Estafeta El Dorado, Panama
Mitchell, Tony	.186	22	70	7	13	2	0	2	9	16	19	1	1	S	R	6-4	225	10-14-70	1989	Detroit, Mich.
Nevin, Phil	.158	5	19	1	3	0	0	1	3	2	9	0	0	R	R	6-2	185	1-19-71	1992	Placentia, Calif.
Rodriguez, Adam	.200	29	70	4	14	2	0	1	3	3	17	0	1	R	R	5-10	195	3-16-71	1993	Tucson, Ariz.
Rodriguez, Steve	.233	107	425	57	99	30	1	4	38	26	58	18	5	R	R	5-9	170	11-29-70	1992	Las Vegas, Nev.
Smith, Ira	.243	39	148	19	36	8	0	1	13	11	29	0	1	R	R	5-11	185	8-4-67	1990	Chestertown, Md.
Trammell, Bubba	.251	90	319	56	80	15	1	28	75	38	91	2	2	R	R	6-2	205	11-6-71	1994	Knoxville, Tenn.
Walbeck, Matt	.305	17	59	6	18	2	1	1	8	4	15	0	0	S	R	5-11	188	10-2-69	1987	Sacramento, Calif.

PITCHING	W	L	ERA	G	GS	CG	SV	IP	H	R	ER	BB	SO	B	T	HT	WT	DOB	1st Yr	Resides
Barnes, Brian	7	10	6.71	32	18	0	0	115	143	100	86	57	86	L	L	5-9	170	3-25-67	1989	Smyrna, Ga.
Blair, Willie	0	0	0.00	1	1	0	0	7	1	1	0	2	4	R	R	6-1	185	12-18-65	1986	Lexington, Ky.
Crow, Dean	3	0	7.85	18	0	0	2	18	26	16	16	10	10	R	R	6-5	212	8-21-72	1993	Houston, Texas
Cummings, John	2	1	2.76	19	0	0	0	16	13	6	5	6	7	L	L	6-3	200	5-10-69	1990	Laguna Niguel, Calif.
Dace, Derek	0	0	3.60	5	0	0	0	10	13	8	4	6	6	L	L	6-7	200	4-9-75	1994	Sullivan, Mo.
Dishman, Glenn	7	6	3.87	21	18	1	1	114	112	53	49	32	77	R	L	6-1	195	11-5-70	1993	Fremont, Calif.
Drews, Matt	0	2	6.60	3	3	0	0	15	14	11	11	14	7	R	R	6-8	205	8-29-74	1994	Sarasota, Fla.
Drumright, Mike	5	10	5.06	23	23	0	0	133	134	78	75	91	115	L	R	6-4	210	4-19-74	1995	Valley Center, Kan.
Fermin, Ramon	4	2	4.93	41	8	0	0	80	103	53	44	33	46	R	R	6-3	180	11-25-72	1990	San Francisco de Macoris, D.R.
Gaillard, Eddie	1	4	4.25	55	0	0	28	53	52	27	25	24	54	R	R	6-1	180	8-13-70	1993	West Palm Beach, Fla.
Gallaher, Kevin	1	1	4.74	9	0	0	0	19	16	12	10	17	13	L	R	6-3	190	8-1-68	1991	Vienna, Va.
Goldsmith, Gary	0	0	4.50	1	0	0	0	2	2	1	1	0	1	R	R	6-2	205	7-4-71	1993	Alamogordo, N.M.
Greene, Rick	6	8	2.83	57	0	0	1	70	49	29	22	32	51	R	R	6-5	200	1-2-71	1992	Miami, Fla.
Harriger, Denny	11	8	3.99	27	27	2	0	167	159	87	74	63	109	R	R	5-11	185	7-21-69	1987	Ford City, Pa.
Hernandez, Fernando	6	5	4.11	55	1	0	4	77	71	44	35	51	98	R	R	6-2	185	6-16-71	1990	Santiago, D.R.
Jarvis, Kevin	0	1	6.75	2	2	0	0	8	7	6	6	4	5	S	R	6-2	200	8-1-69	1991	Lexington, Ky.
Keagle, Greg	11	7	3.81	23	23	3	0	151	136	68	64	61	140	R	R	6-2	185	6-28-71	1993	Horseheads, N.Y.
Pugh, Tim	3	5	4.29	19	17	0	0	109	115	60	52	28	97	R	R	6-6	225	1-26-67	1989	Florence, Ky.
Rosengren, John	1	3	3.99	54	0	0	2	56	44	29	25	49	53	L	L	6-4	190	8-10-72	1992	Rye, N.Y.

FIELDING

Catcher	PCT	G	PO	A	E	DP	PB
Casanova	.977	12	77	8	2	0	1
Jensen	.994	22	149	6	1	2	0
Johnson	1.000	5	38	4	0	0	1
Makarewicz	.991	88	624	59	6	9	4
A. Rodriguez	.975	12	73	4	2	0	0
Walbeck	.955	10	55	9	3	0	2

First Base	PCT	G	PO	A	E	DP
Bream	1.000	3	26	1	0	2
Hall	.988	11	74	10	1	1
Hamelin	.984	14	121	5	2	12
Hyers	.990	113	879	94	10	80
Nevin	1.000	3	19	3	0	4
A. Rodriguez	.946	5	33	2	2	3

Second Base	PCT	G	PO	A	E	DP
Bream	.962	17	31	45	3	4
Catalanotto	.984	96	152	276	7	51
Hajek	1.000	9	17	19	0	3
S. Rodriguez	.991	21	42	63	1	14

Third Base	PCT	G	PO	A	E	DP
Catalanotto	.890	36	14	75	11	3
Hajek	.899	53	33	83	13	11
Holbert	.947	6	4	14	1	0
Hyers	.000	1	0	0	0	0
Nevin	1.000	1	0	1	0	0
A. Rodriguez	1.000	1	0	2	0	0
S. Rodriguez	.917	48	19	80	9	7

Shortstop	PCT	G	PO	A	E	DP
Bream	.897	9	16	19	4	4
Holbert	.952	104	183	288	24	58
Miller	.957	7	10	12	1	1
S. Rodriguez	.933	24	42	55	7	13

Outfield	PCT	G	PO	A	E	DP
Barker	1.000	17	24	1	0	0
Bartee	.997	135	336	4	1	1
Bream	.000	1	0	0	0	0
Catalanotto	1.000	2	2	0	0	0
Hall	1.000	38	61	5	0	1
Hare	1.000	12	15	1	0	1
Hurst	.962	106	210	18	9	3
Hyers	.933	11	13	1	1	0
Mitchell	.967	18	27	2	1	1
S. Rodriguez	1.000	5	5	2	0	0
Smith	1.000	16	33	0	0	0
Trammell	.972	75	103	3	3	1

JACKSONVILLE — Class AA

SOUTHERN LEAGUE

BATTING	AVG	G	AB	R	H	2B	3B	HR	RBI	BB	SO	SB	CS	B	T	HT	WT	DOB	1st Yr	Resides
Almanzar, Richard	.243	103	387	55	94	20	2	5	35	37	43	20	6	R	R	5-10	155	4-3-76	1993	San Francisco de Macoris, D.R.
Barker, Glen	.280	69	257	47	72	8	4	6	29	29	72	17	8	R	R	5-10	180	5-10-71	1993	Albany, N.Y.
Bream, Scott	.273	19	55	12	15	1	0	2	3	14	12	1	0	S	R	6-1	170	11-4-70	1989	Omaha, Neb.
Bruno, Julio	.265	120	438	51	116	22	3	6	57	38	70	6	3	R	R	5-11	190	10-15-72	1990	Puerto Plata, D.R.
Conner, Decomba	.208	47	154	22	32	6	3	4	17	30	45	5	1	R	R	5-10	184	7-17-73	1994	Mooresville, N.C.
Encarnacion, Juan	.323	131	493	91	159	31	4	26	90	43	86	17	3	R	R	6-2	160	3-8-76	1993	Las Matas de Farfan, D.R.
Garcia, Luis	.268	126	456	55	122	19	1	5	48	10	59	3	2	R	R	6-0	174	5-20-75	1993	San Francisco de Macoris, D.R.
Hurst, Jimmy	.471	5	17	5	8	2	0	2	6	3	6	0	0	R	R	6-6	225	3-1-72	1991	Tuscaloosa, Ala.
Ibarra, Jesse	.283	115	441	73	125	24	1	25	91	55	85	3	2	S	R	6-3	195	7-12-72	1994	El Monte, Calif.
Johnson, Earl	.226	36	146	24	33	3	1	2	13	9	19	7	1	R	R	5-9	163	10-3-71	1991	Detroit, Mich.
2-team (78 Mobile)	.245	114	453	76	111	14	4	3	35	30	75	42	14							

BATTING	AVG	G	AB	R	H	2B	3B	HR	RBI	BB	SO	SB	CS	B	T	HT	WT	DOB	1st Yr	Resides
Lackey, Steve	.077	5	13	1	1	0	0	0	0	0	1	1	0	R	R	5-11	165	9-25-74	1992	Riverside, Calif.
Lidle, Kevin	.151	59	186	18	28	7	0	1	16	17	77	0	0	R	R	5-11	170	3-22-72	1992	West Covina, Calif.
Marine, Del	.238	99	328	45	78	22	1	12	43	48	92	0	1	R	R	6-0	205	10-18-71	1992	Woodland Hills, Calif.
Marquez, Jesus	.267	114	465	56	124	24	4	12	74	22	77	9	5	L	L	6-0	175	3-12-73	1990	Caracas, Venez.
Miller, Orlando	.364	3	11	2	4	1	0	1	3	1	1	0	0	R	R	6-1	180	1-13-69	1988	Estafeta El Dorado, Panama
Roberts, David	.296	105	415	76	123	24	2	4	41	45	62	23	5	L	L	5-10	172	5-31-72	1994	Oceanside, Calif.
Rodriguez, Adam	.200	2	5	0	1	0	0	0	0	2	0	0	0	R	R	5-10	195	3-16-71	1993	Tucson, Ariz.
Schmidt, Tom	.258	82	291	37	75	17	1	9	44	29	81	2	0	R	R	6-3	200	2-12-73	1992	Perry Hall, Md.
Smith, Ira	.308	53	172	29	53	14	2	5	20	35	30	1	1	R	R	5-11	185	8-4-67	1990	Chestertown, Md.

PITCHING	W	L	ERA	G	GS	CG	SV	IP	H	R	ER	BB	SO	B	T	HT	WT	DOB	1st Yr	Resides
Corey, Bryan	3	8	4.76	52	0	0	9	68	74	42	36	21	37	R	R	6-1	170	10-21-73	1993	Newbury Park, Calif.
Drews, Matt	8	11	5.49	24	24	4	0	144	160	109	88	50	85	R	R	6-8	205	8-29-74	1994	Sarasota, Fla.
Drumright, Mike	1	1	1.57	5	5	0	0	29	16	7	5	13	24	L	R	6-4	210	4-19-74	1995	Valley Center, Kan.
Duran, Roberto	4	2	2.37	50	0	0	16	61	41	19	16	39	95	L	L	6-0	190	3-6-73	1990	Moca, D.R.
Gallaher, Kevin	4	3	6.47	10	10	2	0	57	70	45	41	32	33	L	R	6-3	190	8-1-68	1991	Vienna, Va.
Gentile, Scott	1	5	5.23	43	0	0	2	64	69	41	37	21	52	R	R	5-11	210	12-21-70	1992	Berlin, Conn.
Goldsmith, Gary	4	5	4.07	31	8	1	1	97	97	48	44	30	45	R	R	6-2	205	7-4-71	1993	Alamogordo, N.M.
Greisinger, Seth	10	6	5.20	28	28	1	0	159	194	103	92	53	105	R	R	6-4	190	7-29-75	1996	Falls Church, Va.
Marrero, Kenny	4	3	2.94	37	0	0	0	64	45	32	21	37	60	R	R	6-3	208	5-13-70	1991	Dorado, P.R.
Melendez, Dave	6	4	5.33	12	11	2	0	73	77	47	43	24	55	S	R	6-0	168	6-25-76	1996	Caguas, P.R.
Reed, Brandon	11	9	4.55	27	27	2	0	176	190	100	89	54	90	R	R	6-4	185	12-18-74	1994	Lapeer, Mich.
Roberts, Willis	6	15	6.28	26	26	2	0	149	181	120	104	64	86	R	R	6-3	175	6-19-75	1992	San Cristobal, D.R.
Santana, Marino	4	1	3.28	39	0	0	1	74	55	28	27	43	98	R	R	6-1	188	5-10-72	1990	Boca Chica, D.R.
Schroeder, Chad	0	0	0.00	2	0	0	0	4	1	0	0	1	4	R	R	6-3	200	9-21-73	1996	Elgin, Ill.

FIELDING

Catcher	PCT	G	PO	A	E	DP	PB
Lidle	.980	58	336	51	8	8	7
Marine	.984	85	550	59	10	6	17
Rodriguez	1.000	2	10	0	0	0	0

First Base	PCT	G	PO	A	E	DP
Ibarra	.985	109	925	104	16	90
Marine	.975	13	105	11	3	12
Schmidt	.974	21	176	11	5	24

Second Base	PCT	G	PO	A	E	DP
Almanzar	.969	103	237	292	17	85
Bream	.983	12	20	38	1	13
Bruno	.957	26	53	59	5	15
Lackey	.929	4	8	18	2	2
Schmidt	.750	2	1	2	1	0

Third Base	PCT	G	PO	A	E	DP
Bream	1.000	2	1	1	0	0
Bruno	.935	91	51	207	18	16
Marine	1.000	2	1	2	0	1
Schmidt	.948	48	25	103	7	9

Shortstop	PCT	G	PO	A	E	DP
Bream	1.000	5	6	9	0	1
Garcia	.948	125	176	370	30	74
Miller	.846	3	3	8	2	1
Schmidt	.882	9	8	22	4	4

Outfield	PCT	G	PO	A	E	DP
Barker	.988	64	154	6	2	2
Bruno	.000	1	0	0	0	0
Conner	.960	47	96	1	4	0
Encarnacion	.987	112	208	12	3	3
Hurst	1.000	3	3	0	0	0
Johnson	.986	29	69	4	1	2
Lidle	.000	1	0	0	0	0
Marquez	.965	106	182	11	7	1
Roberts	.954	34	82	1	4	1
Smith	.980	29	48	2	1	0

LAKELAND — Class A

FLORIDA STATE LEAGUE

BATTING	AVG	G	AB	R	H	2B	3B	HR	RBI	BB	SO	SB	CS	B	T	HT	WT	DOB	1st Yr	Resides
Airoso, Kurt	.194	22	62	12	12	1	2	0	7	11	23	0	0	R	R	6-2	190	2-12-75	1996	Tulare, Calif.
Balfe, Ryan	.269	86	312	40	84	13	2	13	48	24	75	1	1	S	R	6-1	180	11-11-75	1994	Cornwall, N.Y.
Barker, Glen	.316	13	57	9	18	4	0	1	11	4	17	7	1	R	R	5-10	180	5-10-71	1993	Albany, N.Y.
Bass, Jayson	.258	108	376	58	97	18	4	13	53	41	130	17	7	L	L	6-3	212	6-22-74	1993	Seattle, Wash.
Bautista, Rayner	.167	6	12	1	2	0	0	0	0	0	2	0	0	R	R	5-11	155	8-17-79	1996	Nizao, D.R.
Bream, Scott	.216	11	37	5	8	1	1	0	6	3	11	0	0	S	R	6-1	170	11-4-70	1989	Omaha, Neb.
Cardona, Javier	.289	85	284	28	82	15	0	7	38	25	51	1	3	R	R	6-0	185	9-15-75	1994	Dorado, P.R.
Conner, Decomba	.318	56	201	35	64	7	4	7	29	21	47	9	2	R	R	5-10	184	7-17-73	1994	Mooresville, N.C.
Freeman, Sean	.226	13	53	3	12	0	0	1	5	3	12	0	0	L	L	6-3	205	9-10-71	1994	Andover, Ohio
Freire, Alejandro	.323	130	477	85	154	30	2	24	92	50	84	13	4	R	R	6-1	170	8-23-74	1992	Caracas, Venez.
Fuller, Brian	.217	45	129	13	28	2	1	2	18	7	26	0	0	R	R	6-2	205	11-5-72	1995	Plover, Wis.
Hernaiz, Juan	.279	118	438	58	122	13	6	12	56	22	107	29	13	R	R	5-11	185	2-15-75	1992	Carolina, P.R.
Kapler, Gabe	.295	137	519	87	153	40	6	19	87	54	68	8	6	R	R	6-1	190	7-31-75	1995	Reseda, Calif.
Lackey, Steve	.223	71	247	24	55	14	0	0	22	10	58	5	4	R	R	5-11	165	9-25-74	1992	Riverside, Calif.
Lindstrom, David	.207	76	213	25	44	8	0	3	14	24	25	1	0	R	R	5-10	185	8-6-74	1996	Brooklyn Park, Minn.
Macias, Jose	.267	122	424	54	113	18	2	2	21	52	33	10	14	R	R	5-10	173	1-25-74	1992	Panama City, Panama
Miller, Orlando	.190	5	21	1	4	1	1	0	0	1	4	0	0	R	R	6-1	180	1-13-69	1988	Estafeta El Dorado, Panama
Nevin, Phil	.556	3	9	3	5	1	0	1	4	3	2	0	0	R	R	6-2	185	1-19-71	1992	Placentia, Calif.
Perez, Santiago	.274	111	445	66	122	20	12	4	46	20	98	21	9	S	R	6-2	150	12-30-75	1993	Santo Domingo, D.R.
Salzano, Jerry	.222	40	135	20	30	4	1	2	8	22	27	1	1	R	R	6-0	175	10-27-74	1992	Trenton, N.J.
Villalobos, Carlos	.252	39	147	19	37	5	0	1	15	11	25	0	1	R	R	6-0	170	4-5-74	1993	Cartagena, Colombia
Walbeck, Matt	.500	4	10	4	5	1	0	0	3	4	1	0	1	S	R	5-11	188	10-2-69	1987	Sacramento, Calif.

GAMES BY POSITION: C—Cardona 80, Fuller 18, Lindstrom 53, Walbeck 3. **1B**—Freire 124, Lindstrom 19, Nevin 1, Salzano 1, Villalobos 1. **2B**—Bautista 3, Bream 4, Lackey 18, Macias 120. **3B**—Balfe 75, Bream 5, Lackey 26, Nevin 1, Salzano 11, Villalobos 28. **SS**—Bautista 3, Bream 1, Lackey 28, Miller 3, Perez 109. **OF**—Airoso 16, Barker 13, Bass 86, Conner 56, Hernaiz 104, Kapler 137, Macias 1, Salzano 6.

PITCHING	W	L	ERA	G	GS	CG	SV	IP	H	R	ER	BB	SO	B	T	HT	WT	DOB	1st Yr	Resides
Alvord, Aaron	0	0	2.89	5	0	0	0	9	9	3	3	2	4	R	R	6-1	180	6-21-77	1996	Canton, Kan.
Bailey, Ben	4	4	3.87	15	14	1	0	93	102	49	40	24	61	R	R	6-2	220	8-31-74	1995	Howe, Ind.
Bauer, Chris	3	2	4.63	19	0	0	2	35	43	31	18	11	19	R	R	6-1	185	12-28-73	1996	Tulsa, Okla.
Bettencourt, Justin	7	10	4.14	25	25	1	0	143	143	78	66	68	112	L	L	6-2	198	12-19-73	1994	Capitola, Calif.
Dace, Derek	0	0	3.86	2	0	0	0	2	2	1	1	1	0	L	L	6-7	200	4-9-75	1994	Sullivan, Mo.
Darwin, David	10	1	2.50	12	12	1	0	83	70	23	23	18	41	L	L	6-0	185	12-19-73	1996	Durham, N.C.
Dinyar, Eric	0	0	5.63	15	0	0	1	16	9	10	10	22	12	R	R	6-6	210	8-13-73	1994	Johnstown, Pa.
Durkovic, Peter	6	4	2.47	40	0	0	10	66	50	21	18	14	53	L	L	6-4	215	7-9-73	1995	Flushing, N.Y.
Kimsey, Keith	2	5	5.04	26	12	0	1	80	92	57	45	42	42	R	R	6-7	200	8-15-72	1991	Lakeland, Fla.
Malenfant, David	0	0	15.00	6	0	0	0	6	18	12	10	7	3	R	R	6-3	205	4-30-75	1996	Flint, Mich.
Melendez, Dave	8	4	1.76	15	15	2	0	102	70	28	20	32	79	S	R	6-0	168	6-25-76	1996	Caguas, P.R.

PITCHING	W	L	ERA	G	GS	CG	SV	IP	H	R	ER	BB	SO	B	T	HT	WT	DOB	1st Yr	Resides
Oakley, Matt	1	2	5.98	27	0	0	0	44	54	35	29	26	34	R	R	6-2	225	7-12-73	1995	Raleigh, N.C.
Patino, Leonardo	6	4	2.63	40	3	0	8	72	61	25	21	20	75	L	L	6-2	190	11-24-73	1994	Cali, Colombia
Powell, Brian	13	9	2.50	27	27	8	0	183	153	70	51	35	122	R	R	6-2	205	10-10-73	1995	Bainbridge, Ga.
Santos, Victor	10	5	3.23	26	26	4	0	145	136	74	52	59	108	R	R	6-3	175	10-2-76	1995	Clifton, N.J.
Schroeder, Chad	0	3	4.76	12	1	0	0	23	25	14	12	8	8	R	R	6-3	200	9-21-73	1996	Elgin, Ill.
Smith, Keilan	9	2	2.57	40	3	0	7	77	65	23	22	27	46	R	R	6-4	175	12-20-73	1992	Memphis, Tenn.
Sobik, Trad	0	1	40.50	2	0	0	0	1	4	3	3	3	1	R	R	6-2	175	1-29-76	1994	Palm Harbor, Fla.
Zamarripa, Mark	2	1	8.03	11	0	0	1	12	16	12	11	11	9	R	R	6-0	180	7-28-74	1996	Los Angeles, Calif.

WEST MICHIGAN — Class A

MIDWEST LEAGUE

BATTING	AVG	G	AB	R	H	2B	3B	HR	RBI	BB	SO	SB	CS	B	T	HT	WT	DOB	1st Yr	Resides
Airoso, Kurt	.297	14	37	6	11	5	0	0	2	6	15	0	0	R	R	6-2	190	2-12-75	1996	Tulare, Calif.
Capellan, Rene	.287	100	383	61	110	26	4	4	48	25	60	7	9	R	R	5-11	160	4-24-78	1995	Santo Domingo, D.R.
Cedeno, Jesus	.270	110	429	42	116	24	3	8	63	18	77	13	5	R	R	5-11	160	6-24-76	1994	Santo Domingo, D.R.
Dubose, Brian	.268	105	358	72	96	12	7	15	79	66	87	17	2	L	R	6-3	208	5-17-71	1990	Detroit, Mich.
Fick, Robert	.341	122	463	100	158	50	3	16	90	75	74	13	4	L	R	6-1	195	3-15-74	1996	Thousand Oaks, Calif.
Landry, Jacques	.274	103	369	51	101	18	5	16	52	21	99	15	3	R	R	6-3	205	8-15-73	1996	La Marque, Texas
Lemonis, Chris	.304	48	158	27	48	10	1	3	30	9	31	2	5	L	R	5-11	185	8-21-73	1995	New York, N.Y.
Mitchell, Derek	.198	110	353	47	70	14	2	1	31	50	91	11	8	R	R	6-1	180	3-9-75	1996	Gurnee, Ill.
Ozarowski, Richard	.216	36	134	14	29	7	1	0	13	8	35	2	1	S	R	5-9	175	10-19-74	1997	Boca Raton, Fla.
Santana, Pedro	.261	74	287	36	75	10	6	3	28	14	55	20	3	R	R	5-11	160	9-21-76	1995	San Pedro de Macoris, D.R.
Sollmann, Scott	.313	121	460	89	144	13	4	0	33	79	81	40	14	L	L	5-9	167	5-2-75	1996	Cincinnati, Ohio
Sosa, Franklin	.256	57	195	24	50	4	0	0	16	10	24	2	3	R	R	5-11	170	2-27-76	1994	Los Llanos, D.R.
Stevenson, Chad	.220	72	259	32	57	10	1	7	32	20	77	2	4	R	R	6-4	215	2-3-76	1994	Henderson, Nev.
Wakeland, Chris	.285	111	414	64	118	38	2	7	75	43	120	20	6	L	L	6-0	190	6-15-74	1996	St. Helens, Ore.
Zapata, Alexis	.223	64	206	33	46	8	3	6	27	11	54	4	0	R	R	6-3	190	5-20-77	1996	Bronx, N.Y.

GAMES BY POSITION: C—Fick 9, Sosa 57, Stevenson 70. **1B**—Dubose 33, Fick 96, Landry 4. **2B**—Capellan 77, Ozarowski 11, Santana 45. **3B**—Capellan 3, Fick 3, Landry 92, Lemonis 26, Ozarowski 20. **SS**—Mitchell 110, Ozarowski 4, Santana 19. **OF**—Airoso 10, Capellan 1, Cedeno 109, Ozarowski 1, Sollmann 119, Wakeland 111, Zapata 51.

PITCHING	W	L	ERA	G	GS	CG	SV	IP	H	R	ER	BB	SO	B	T	HT	WT	DOB	1st Yr	Resides
Bauer, Chris	0	2	4.07	18	0	0	1	24	30	15	11	10	11	R	R	6-1	185	12-28-73	1996	Tulsa, Okla.
Blair, Willie	0	0	0.00	1	1	0	0	5	1	0	0	0	7	R	R	6-1	185	12-18-65	1986	Lexington, Ky.
Borkowski, Dave	15	3	3.46	25	25	4	0	164	143	79	63	31	104	R	R	6-1	200	2-7-77	1995	Sterling Heights, Mich.
Bruner, Clayton	15	3	2.38	24	24	3	0	166	134	52	44	48	135	R	R	6-3	190	10-16-76	1995	Weatherford, Okla.
Cordero, Francisco	6	1	0.99	50	0	0	35	54	36	13	6	15	67	R	R	6-2	170	8-11-77	1994	Santo Domingo, D.R.
Dace, Derek	1	0	0.72	10	2	0	2	25	23	2	2	4	24	L	L	6-7	200	4-9-75	1994	Sullivan, Mo.
Darwin, David	1	0	0.89	21	4	0	3	40	23	7	4	20	31	L	L	6-0	185	12-19-73	1996	Durham, N.C.
Foran, John	2	2	3.71	29	0	0	1	53	51	27	22	29	45	R	R	6-1	185	10-22-73	1995	Alford, Fla.
Garcia, Apostol	7	2	3.02	33	5	0	1	66	48	26	22	31	52	S	R	6-0	155	8-3-76	1994	Las Matas de Farfan, D.R.
Martinez, Romulo	6	4	2.39	36	0	0	2	79	73	28	21	21	51	R	R	6-1	170	12-5-76	1994	Santiago, D.R.
Quintal, Craig	11	6	1.96	23	23	3	0	156	133	48	34	31	88	R	R	6-0	200	1-21-75	1996	New Orleans, La.
Romo, Greg	12	6	3.54	24	24	0	0	140	128	65	55	51	124	L	R	6-3	175	5-14-75	1995	Wasco, Calif.
Schroeder, Chad	2	3	3.71	18	0	0	0	27	22	14	11	16	24	R	R	6-3	200	9-21-73	1996	Elgin, Ill.
Spear, Russell	11	6	2.96	23	23	1	0	140	126	63	46	61	112	R	R	6-3	190	8-30-77	1995	Albanvale, Australia
Zamarripa, Mark	3	1	2.12	20	0	0	2	30	13	17	7	18	41	R	R	6-0	180	7-28-74	1996	Los Angeles, Calif.

JAMESTOWN — Short-Season Class A

NEW YORK-PENN LEAGUE

BATTING	AVG	G	AB	R	H	2B	3B	HR	RBI	BB	SO	SB	CS	B	T	HT	WT	DOB	1st Yr	Resides
Aybar, Ramon	.200	40	125	20	25	0	0	0	13	13	32	5	2	L	R	5-9	150	5-10-76	1994	Bani, D.R.
Grimmett, Ryan	.324	17	68	14	22	5	1	2	9	11	9	11	2	R	R	5-10	165	3-4-75	1997	Cincinnati, Ohio
Hervey, Brennan	.243	58	222	24	54	10	0	4	29	17	62	1	2	S	R	6-5	230	4-26-75	1997	St. Petersburg, Fla.
Jacomino, Mandy	.301	62	229	32	69	9	0	4	26	24	44	0	1	L	R	6-2	210	6-1-74	1997	Miami, Fla.
Lauterhahn, Dan	.247	53	186	18	46	7	0	1	14	14	39	2	4	R	R	6-1	175	4-23-76	1997	Wallington, N.J.
Lignitz, Jeremiah	.280	41	150	16	42	7	1	2	27	9	47	0	2	L	R	6-2	210	5-18-77	1995	Lakeland, Fla.
McKinney, Antonio	.155	35	116	12	18	6	1	0	3	10	41	3	1	R	R	5-10	175	1-2-78	1996	Portland, Ore.
Meran, Jorge	.175	51	183	21	32	11	0	4	15	11	50	2	1	R	R	6-0	175	2-14-75	1991	Santo Domingo, D.R.
Ozarowski, Richard	.286	7	28	5	8	2	1	0	2	1	8	0	0	S	R	5-9	175	10-19-74	1997	Boca Raton, Fla.
Parker, Clark	.080	9	25	1	2	0	0	0	0	2	7	0	1	S	R	5-9	170	9-26-75	1997	Beverly Hills, Calif.
Pedersoli, Bernie	.162	32	105	11	17	2	0	0	6	7	28	1	0	R	R	6-0	170	12-20-74	1997	Park Forest, Ill.
Rios, Brian	.263	45	167	23	44	6	1	4	23	14	22	3	0	R	R	6-3	190	7-15-74	1996	Corona, Calif.
Schaffer, Jacob	.293	55	215	39	63	14	4	6	26	21	35	5	2	R	R	5-10	170	3-28-75	1997	Bloomington, Minn.
Schesser, Heath	.284	67	271	30	77	12	2	3	39	21	40	3	2	R	R	6-1	180	1-17-76	1997	Manhattan, Kan.
Steele, Alex	.311	72	257	51	80	15	4	14	43	37	61	6	3	R	R	6-3	225	12-9-75	1997	Harrington Park, N.J.
Whitner, Keith	.237	46	156	19	37	5	2	0	12	7	40	0	0	R	R	6-3	195	9-26-75	1996	Marietta, Ga.

GAMES BY POSITION: C—Lignitz 9, Meran 46, Pedersoli 25. **1B**—Hervey 56, Lignitz 19. **2B**—Aybar 13, Lauterhahn 39, Parker 4, Schaffer 6, Schesser 16. **3B**—Rios 45, Schaffer 2, Schesser 29. **SS**—Lauterhahn 11, Schaffer 42, Schesser 21. **OF**—Aybar 16, Grimmett 17, Jacomino 44, McKinney 33, Ozarowski 6, Parker 2, Steele 71, Whitner 40.

PITCHING	W	L	ERA	G	GS	CG	SV	IP	H	R	ER	BB	SO	B	T	HT	WT	DOB	1st Yr	Resides
Alkire, John	0	3	8.51	9	7	1	0	37	61	42	35	14	33	R	R	6-5	190	4-29-75	1997	San Jose, Calif.
Beck, Matt	1	0	6.91	17	0	0	0	29	41	30	22	9	17	R	R	6-2	195	8-10-75	1997	Cowden, Ill.
Diebolt, Mike	3	6	4.30	15	13	0	0	82	87	50	39	38	63	R	L	6-0	195	11-2-74	1997	Mayfield Village, Ohio
Greene, Joel	4	1	2.40	20	0	0	1	30	26	14	8	19	22	L	L	6-2	185	5-18-76	1997	Portland, Ore.
Guilmet, John	0	6	5.26	17	6	0	1	50	68	44	29	10	29	R	R	6-6	205	5-22-75	1997	North Andover, Mass.
Howard, Jason	4	3	5.24	13	1	0	0	22	21	22	13	14	21	R	R	6-4	205	6-18-75	1997	Kokomo, Ind.
Johnson, Craig	3	10	4.43	14	14	3	0	83	88	59	41	10	66	R	R	6-3	200	11-8-75	1997	Tuftonboro, N.H.
Keller, Kris	0	2	8.67	16	0	0	0	27	37	33	26	20	18	R	R	6-2	220	3-1-78	1996	Atlantic Beach, Fla.
Mear, Richard	1	1	12.54	8	0	0	0	9	6	18	13	28	7	L	L	6-3	218	6-30-76	1994	Rowland Heights, Calif.

PITCHING	W	L	ERA	G	GS	CG	SV	IP	H	R	ER	BB	SO	B	T	HT	WT	DOB	1st Yr	Resides
Mobley, Kevin	2	1	3.16	18	0	0	0	26	27	10	9	11	24	R	R	6-7	245	1-26-75	1997	Vidalia, Ga.
Persails, Mark	3	7	5.74	15	14	2	0	85	103	64	54	33	56	R	R	6-3	185	10-25-75	1995	Vassar, Mich.
Ramirez, Jose	3	4	3.90	15	15	1	0	95	84	49	41	38	75	L	L	6-1	170	9-1-75	1994	Santo Domingo, D.R.
Santamaria, Juan	0	2	9.49	8	4	0	0	25	28	29	26	18	11	R	R	6-1	165	5-6-77	1995	Santo Domingo, D.R.
Snyder, William	1	3	2.17	25	0	0	9	29	19	8	7	20	42	R	R	6-0	190	1-29-75	1997	Martville, N.Y.

LAKELAND — Rookie

GULF COAST LEAGUE

BATTING	AVG	G	AB	R	H	2B	3B	HR	RBI	BB	SO	SB	CS	B	T	HT	WT	DOB	1st Yr	Resides
Airoso, Kurt	.000	4	10	1	0	0	0	0	0	3	3	0	0	R	R	6-2	190	2-12-75	1996	Tulare, Calif.
Alvarez, Julio	.167	6	18	1	3	0	0	0	0	2	5	0	0	S	R	6-0	160	3-2-79	1996	Santiago, D.R.
Alvarez, Nelson	.247	34	85	21	21	3	0	1	10	12	16	4	3	R	R	6-0	175	9-27-78	1997	Haverstraw, N.Y.
Balfe, Ryan	.571	2	7	2	4	0	0	1	1	1	1	0	0	S	R	6-1	180	11-11-75	1994	Cornwall, N.Y.
Bautista, Rayner	.299	49	164	33	49	11	2	1	17	11	33	7	1	R	R	5-11	155	8-17-79	1996	Nizao, D.R.
Boone, Matt	.204	48	152	13	31	11	0	0	15	13	37	2	1	R	R	6-2	175	7-18-79	1997	Orlando, Fla.
Hasbun, Andy	.231	21	52	7	12	2	0	0	5	8	9	2	0	R	R	5-9	180	3-11-78	1997	New York, N.Y.
Hazelton, Justin	.257	35	105	21	27	3	2	2	17	25	36	3	1	R	R	6-2	180	7-9-78	1996	Philipsburg, Pa.
Lara, Balmes	.238	43	151	26	36	4	3	6	29	20	51	0	3	R	R	6-3	180	6-19-78	1995	Santo Domingo, D.R.
Linares, Rodney	.228	25	57	5	13	0	1	0	10	6	23	0	2	R	R	5-11	180	8-7-77	1997	Brooklyn, N.Y.
McKinney, Antonio	.246	18	65	16	16	3	0	3	12	10	13	5	2	R	R	5-10	175	1-2-78	1996	Portland, Ore.
Mora, Juan	.348	43	155	26	54	9	5	4	31	18	43	9	2	L	L	5-11	170	11-26-77	1996	Bayamon, P.R.
Parker, Chris	.161	31	87	6	14	1	0	0	7	10	33	0	1	R	R	6-2	185	8-16-79	1997	Thousand Oaks, Calif.
Pender, Darrell	.178	37	101	16	18	2	0	0	4	9	38	11	0	R	R	5-10	170	1-14-79	1997	Miami, Fla.
Peniche, Fray	.264	35	106	19	28	4	0	0	9	14	16	7	3	R	R	6-2	185	11-2-76	1995	Santo Domingo, D.R.
Reyes, Deurys	.257	38	113	24	29	8	1	1	14	25	32	7	1	L	L	5-11	155	8-8-79	1996	Santo Domingo, D.R.
Rivera, Michael	.286	47	154	34	44	9	2	10	36	18	25	0	0	R	R	6-2	195	9-8-76	1997	Bayamon, P.R.
Runnells, T.J.	.226	48	159	19	36	5	1	0	23	17	28	7	1	R	R	5-10	160	2-15-78	1997	Greeley, Colo.
Sassanella, Jeremy	.221	32	113	12	25	4	0	1	17	5	24	3	0	S	R	6-1	225	10-21-78	1997	Auburn, Ind.
Schaffer, Jake	.333	6	21	5	7	1	1	0	4	5	2	0	0	R	R	5-10	170	3-28-75	1997	Bloomington, Minn.
St. Pierre, Maxim	.244	20	41	3	10	1	0	0	3	3	8	2	0	R	R	6-0	175	4-17-80	1997	Montreal, Quebec

GAMES BY POSITION: C—J. Alvarez 2, N. Alvarez 19, Parker 18, Rivera 27, Sassanella 3, St. Pierre 15. **1B**—Hazelton 1, Lara 5, Peniche 32, Rivera 3, Sassanella 25. **2B**—J. Alvarez 2, Hasbun 1, Linares 13, Runnells 48. **3B**—J. Alvarez 1, Balfe 1, Boone 48, Hasbun 3, Linares 14, Schaffer 5. **SS**—Bautista 49, Hasbun 17, Schaffer 1. **OF**—Airoso 3, Hazelton 31, Lara 35, McKinney 18, Mora 41, Pender 33, Reyes 37.

PITCHING	W	L	ERA	G	GS	CG	SV	IP	H	R	ER	BB	SO	B	T	HT	WT	DOB	1st Yr	Resides
Alvord, Aaron	0	3	4.30	9	5	0	0	29	36	28	14	13	24	R	R	6-1	180	6-21-77	1996	Canton, Kan.
Castillo, Jose	4	5	3.25	12	10	1	0	55	50	28	20	7	47	R	R	6-2	170	6-12-77	1994	Santo Domingo, D.R.
Dinyar, Eric	0	0	19.64	7	0	0	0	4	4	9	8	9	1	R	R	6-6	210	8-13-73	1994	Johnstown, Pa.
Johnston, Bruce	1	1	4.00	18	2	0	0	36	37	22	16	11	29	R	R	6-2	195	10-23-76	1996	West Bayshore, N.Y.
Loux, Shane	4	1	0.84	10	9	1	0	43	19	7	4	10	33	R	R	6-2	210	8-31-79	1997	Gilbert, Ariz.
Malenfant, David	0	0	27.00	1	0	0	0	1	1	2	2	2	1	R	R	6-3	205	4-30-75	1996	Flint, Mich.
Mercado, Hector	3	3	3.79	15	5	0	0	40	45	23	17	12	32	R	R	6-4	180	1-11-77	1996	Arecibo, P.R.
Reed, Aaron	2	2	2.66	13	0	0	0	24	18	7	7	6	24	R	R	6-3	180	12-4-77	1996	Eagleby, Australia
Rivera, Homero	4	4	4.94	15	9	0	0	51	67	36	28	10	47	R	L	5-10	160	8-13-78	1995	Nizao, D.R.
Rivera, Raul	2	1	2.73	15	2	0	2	30	20	15	9	21	36	R	R	6-1	200	10-4-76	1997	Brooklyn, N.Y.
Roberts, Rick	2	2	4.24	11	10	0	0	34	35	22	16	19	40	L	L	6-1	180	5-20-79	1997	Summer Hill, Pa.
Rosario, Rafael	1	1	3.22	22	0	0	0	36	37	19	13	18	28	R	R	6-1	170	12-29-76	1995	El Seibo, D.R.
Rosario, Reynaldo	2	2	3.94	21	0	0	4	32	32	15	14	13	39	R	R	6-4	175	5-5-77	1994	Santo Domingo, D.R.
Santana, Alfredo	3	3	3.44	19	0	0	3	37	37	20	14	11	20	R	R	6-2	180	12-24-77	1995	San Cristobal, D.R.
Webb, Alan	3	1	3.74	9	8	0	0	34	27	17	14	11	46	L	L	6-0	175	9-26-79	1997	Las Vegas, Nev.
Zamarripa, Mark	0	0	6.48	4	0	0	1	8	6	6	6	6	11	R	R	6-0	180	7-28-74	1996	Los Angeles, Calif.

Florida MARLINS

Manager: Jim Leyland.

1997 Record: 92-70, .568 (2nd, NL East)

BATTING	AVG	G	AB	R	H	2B	3B	HR	RBI	BB	SO	SB	CS	B	T	HT	WT	DOB	1st Yr	Resides
Abbott, Kurt	.274	94	252	35	69	18	2	6	30	14	68	3	1	R	R	6-0	170	6-2-69	1989	St. Petersburg, Fla.
Alou, Moises	.292	150	538	88	157	29	5	23	115	70	85	9	5	R	R	6-3	195	7-3-66	1986	Redwood City, Calif.
Arias, Alex	.247	74	93	13	23	2	0	1	11	12	12	0	1	R	R	6-3	185	11-20-67	1987	New York, N.Y.
Bonilla, Bobby	.297	153	562	77	167	39	3	17	96	73	94	6	6	S	R	6-3	240	2-23-63	1981	Bradenton, Fla.
Booty, Josh	.600	4	5	2	3	0	0	0	1	1	1	0	0	R	R	6-3	210	4-29-75	1994	Shreveport, La.
Cangelosi, John	.245	103	192	28	47	8	0	1	12	19	33	5	1	S	L	5-8	160	3-10-63	1982	Chicago, Ill.
Castillo, Luis	.240	75	263	27	63	8	0	0	8	27	53	16	10	S	R	5-11	146	9-12-75	1993	San Pedro de Macoris, D.R.
Conine, Jeff	.242	151	405	46	98	13	1	17	61	57	89	2	0	R	R	6-1	220	6-27-66	1988	Rialto, Calif.
Counsell, Craig	.299	51	164	20	49	9	2	1	16	18	17	1	1	L	R	6-0	177	8-21-70	1992	Whitefish Bay, Wis.
2-team (1 Colorado)	.299	52	164	20	49	9	2	1	16	18	17	1	1							
Daulton, Darren	.262	52	126	22	33	8	2	3	21	22	17	2	1	L	R	6-2	201	1-3-62	1980	Safety Harbor, Fla.
2-team (84 Phil.)	.263	136	395	68	104	21	8	14	63	76	74	6	1							
Dunwoody, Todd	.260	19	50	7	13	2	2	2	7	7	21	2	0	L	L	6-2	185	4-11-75	1993	West Lafayette, Ind.
Eisenreich, Jim	.280	120	293	36	82	19	1	2	34	30	28	0	0	L	L	5-11	200	4-18-59	1980	Blue Springs, Mo.
Floyd, Cliff	.234	61	137	23	32	9	1	6	19	24	33	6	2	L	R	6-4	220	12-5-72	1991	Markham, Ill.
Johnson, Charles	.250	124	416	43	104	26	1	19	63	60	109	0	2	R	R	6-2	215	7-20-71	1992	Fort Pierce, Fla.
Kotsay, Mark	.192	14	52	5	10	1	1	0	4	4	7	3	0	L	L	6-0	180	12-2-75	1996	Pembroke Pines, Fla.
McMillon, Billy	.111	13	18	0	2	1	0	0	1	0	7	0	0	L	L	5-11	172	11-17-71	1993	Sumter, S.C.
Milliard, Ralph	.200	8	30	2	6	0	0	0	2	3	3	1	1	R	R	5-10	160	12-30-73	1993	Soest, Neth. Antilles
Morman, Russ	.286	4	7	3	2	1	0	1	2	0	2	1	0	R	R	6-4	215	4-28-62	1983	Blue Springs, Mo.
Natal, Bob	.500	4	4	2	2	1	0	1	3	2	0	0	0	R	R	5-11	190	11-13-65	1987	Chula Vista, Calif.
Renteria, Edgar	.277	154	617	90	171	21	3	4	52	45	108	32	15	R	R	6-1	172	8-7-75	1992	Barranquilla, Colombia
Sheffield, Gary	.250	135	444	86	111	22	1	21	71	121	79	11	7	R	R	5-11	190	11-18-68	1986	St. Petersburg, Fla.
Wehner, John	.278	44	36	8	10	2	0	0	2	2	5	1	0	R	R	6-3	205	6-29-67	1988	Pittsburgh, Pa.
White, Devon	.245	74	265	37	65	13	1	6	34	32	65	13	5	S	R	6-2	178	12-29-62	1981	Mesa, Ariz.
Zaun, Gregg	.301	58	143	21	43	10	2	2	20	26	18	1	0	S	R	5-10	170	4-14-71	1989	Glendale, Calif.

PITCHING	W	L	ERA	G	GS	CG	SV	IP	H	R	ER	BB	SO	B	T	HT	WT	DOB	1st Yr	Resides
Alfonseca, Antonio	1	3	4.91	17	0	0	0	26	36	16	14	10	19	R	R	6-4	160	4-16-72	1990	La Romana, D.R.
Brown, Kevin	16	8	2.69	33	33	6	0	237	214	77	71	66	205	R	R	6-4	195	3-14-65	1986	Macon, Ga.
Cook, Dennis	1	2	3.90	59	0	0	0	62	64	28	27	28	63	L	L	6-3	190	10-4-62	1985	Austin, Texas
Fernandez, Alex	17	12	3.59	32	32	5	0	221	193	93	88	69	183	R	R	6-0	195	8-13-69	1990	Hialeah, Fla.
Helling, Rick	2	6	4.38	31	8	0	0	76	61	38	37	48	53	R	R	6-3	215	12-15-70	1992	West Fargo, N.D.
Heredia, Felix	5	3	4.29	56	0	0	0	57	53	30	27	30	54	L	L	6-0	160	6-18-76	1993	Barahona, D.R.
Hernandez, Livan	9	3	3.18	17	17	0	0	96	81	39	34	38	72	R	R	6-2	220	2-20-75	1996	Miami, Fla.
Hutton, Mark	3	1	3.78	32	0	0	0	48	50	24	20	19	29	R	R	6-6	225	2-6-70	1989	Adelaide, Australia
Leiter, Al	11	9	4.34	27	27	0	0	151	133	78	73	91	132	L	L	6-1	190	10-23-65	1984	Plantation, Fla.
Miller, Kurt	0	1	9.82	7	0	0	0	7	12	8	8	7	7	R	R	6-5	200	8-24-72	1990	Bakersfield, Calif.
Nen, Robb	9	3	3.89	73	0	0	35	74	72	35	32	40	81	R	R	6-4	190	11-28-69	1987	Seal Beach, Calif.
Ojala, Kirt	1	2	3.14	7	5	0	0	29	28	10	10	18	19	L	L	6-2	200	12-24-68	1990	Portage, Mich.
Pall, Donn	0	0	3.86	2	0	0	0	2	3	1	1	1	0	R	R	6-1	180	1-11-62	1985	Bloomingdale, Ill.
Powell, Jay	7	2	3.28	74	0	0	2	80	71	35	29	30	65	R	R	6-4	220	1-9-72	1993	Collinsville, Tenn.
Rapp, Pat	4	6	4.47	19	19	1	0	109	121	59	54	51	64	R	R	6-3	210	7-13-67	1989	Sulphur, La.
Saunders, Tony	4	6	4.61	22	21	0	0	111	99	62	57	64	102	L	L	6-1	189	4-29-74	1992	Ellicott City, Md.
Stanifer, Robby	1	2	4.60	36	0	0	1	45	43	23	23	16	28	R	R	6-2	195	3-10-72	1994	Easley, S.C.
Vosberg, Ed	1	1	3.75	17	0	0	1	12	15	7	5	6	8	L	L	6-1	190	9-28-61	1983	Tucson, Ariz.
Whisenant, Matt	0	0	16.88	4	0	0	0	3	4	6	5	6	4	L	L	6-3	215	6-8-71	1990	La Canada, Calif.

FIELDING

Catcher	PCT	G	PO	A	E	DP	PB
Johnson	1.000	123	901	73	0	17	1
Natal	1.000	4	16	0	0	0	0
Zaun	.978	50	327	24	8	2	6

First Base	PCT	G	PO	A	E	DP
Bonilla	1.000	2	2	0	0	0
Conine	.992	145	897	104	8	101
Daulton	.984	39	229	17	4	22
Eisenreich	.993	29	136	11	1	15
Floyd	.974	9	36	1	1	5
Morman	1.000	1	3	0	0	0
Zaun	1.000	1	2	1	0	1

Second Base	PCT	G	PO	A	E	DP
Abbott	.969	54	101	116	7	21
Castillo	.971	70	129	177	9	44
Counsell	.989	51	124	149	3	37
Milliard	1.000	8	14	32	0	9

Third Base	PCT	G	PO	A	E	DP
Abbott	.750	4	2	1	1	0
Arias	.971	37	13	20	1	3
Bonilla	.938	149	105	225	22	29
Booty	.857	4	1	5	1	1
Wehner	1.000	6	1	3	0	0

Shortstop	PCT	G	PO	A	E	DP
Abbott	1.000	7	10	19	0	6
Arias	.969	11	13	18	1	7
Renteria	.975	153	242	415	17	95

Outfield	PCT	G	PO	A	E	DP
Abbott	1.000	10	13	0	0	0
Alou	.988	150	248	4	3	1
Cangelosi	1.000	58	84	1	0	0
Conine	.000	1	0	0	0	0
Daulton	.000	3	0	0	0	0
Dunwoody	.929	14	26	0	2	0
Eisenreich	.987	55	75	2	1	1
Floyd	.970	38	60	4	2	2
Kotsay	1.000	14	31	2	0	1
McMillon	1.000	2	4	0	0	0
Morman	1.000	2	0	1	0	0
Sheffield	.980	132	226	14	5	1
Wehner	1.000	27	13	0	0	0
White	.987	71	152	4	2	1

MORRIS FOSTOFF

Kevin Brown

FARM SYSTEM

Director of Player Development: John Boles

Class	Farm Team	League	W	L	Pct.	Finish*	Manager	First Yr
AAA	Charlotte (N.C.) Knights	International	76	65	.539	4th (10)	Carlos Tosca	1995
AA	Portland (Maine) Sea Dogs	Eastern	79	63	.556	2nd (10)	Fredi Gonzalez	1994
#A	Brevard County (Fla.) Manatees	Florida State	62	76	.449	12th (14)	Lorenzo Bundy	1994
A	Kane County (Ill.) Cougars	Midwest	70	68	.507	5th (14)	Lynn Jones	1993
A	Utica (N.Y.) Blue Sox	New York-Penn	36	38	.486	7th (14)	Juan Bustabad	1996
R	Melbourne (Fla.) Marlins	Gulf Coast	31	28	.525	5th (15)	Jon Deeble	1992

*Finish in overall standings (No. of teams in league) #Advanced level

ORGANIZATION LEADERS

MAJOR LEAGUERS

BATTING

*AVG	Bobby Bonilla	.297
R	Edgar Renteria	90
H	Edgar Renteria	171
TB	Moises Alou	265
2B	Bobby Bonilla	39
3B	Moises Alou	5
HR	Moises Alou	23
RBI	Moises Alou	115
BB	Gary Sheffield	121
SO	Charles Johnson	109
SB	Edgar Renteria	32

PITCHING

W	Alex Fernandez	17
L	Alex Fernandez	12
#ERA	Kevin Brown	2.69
G	Jay Powell	74
CG	Kevin Brown	6
SV	Robb Nen	35
IP	Kevin Brown	237
BB	Al Leiter	91
SO	Kevin Brown	205

Moises Alou

MORRIS FOSTOFF

Mark Kotsay

MINOR LEAGUERS

BATTING

*AVG	Raul Franco, Utica	.350
R	Mark Kotsay, Portland	103
H	Kevin Millar, Portland	175
TB	Kevin Millar, Portland	309
2B	Brian Daubach, Charlotte	40
3B	Randy Winn, Portland/Brevard County	8
HR	Russ Morman, Charlotte	33
RBI	Kevin Millar, Portland	131
BB	Tyrone Horne, Kane County	104
SO	Josh Booty, Portland	166
SB	Randy Winn, Portland/Brevard County	51

PITCHING

W	Reid Cornelius, Charlotte/Portland	17
L	Shannon Stephens, Brevard County	13
#ERA	Mike Duvall, Portland/Brevard County	1.67
G	Gabe Gonzalez, Charlotte/Portland	66
CG	Two tied at	4
SV	Mike Duvall, Portland/Brevard County	24
IP	Brian Meadows, Portland	176
BB	Andy Larkin, Charlotte	76
SO	Brent Billingsley, Kane County	175

*Minimum 250 At-Bats #Minimum 75 Innings

TOP 10 PROSPECTS

DIAMOND IMAGES

Alex Gonzalez

How the Marlins Top 10 prospects, as judged by Baseball America prior to the 1997 season, fared in 1997:

Player, Pos.	Club (Class)	AVG	AB	R	H	2B	3B	HR	RBI	SB
2. Alex Gonzalez, ss	Portland (AA)	.254	449	69	114	16	4	19	65	4
3. Mark Kotsay, of	Florida	.192	52	5	10	1	1	0	4	3
	Portland (AA)	.306	438	103	134	27	2	20	77	17
4. Todd Dunwoody, of	Florida	.260	50	7	13	2	2	2	7	2
	Charlotte (AAA)	.262	401	74	105	16	7	23	62	25
8. Jaime Jones, of	Brevard County (A)	.271	373	63	101	27	4	10	60	6
9. Nate Rolison, 1b	Brevard County (A)	.256	473	59	121	22	0	16	65	3
		W	L	ERA	G	SV	IP	H	BB	SO
1. Felix Heredia, lhp	Florida	5	3	4.29	56	0	57	53	30	54
5. Livan Hernandez, rhp	Florida	9	3	3.18	17	0	96	81	38	72
	Charlotte (AAA)	5	3	3.98	14	0	81	76	38	58
	Portland (AA)	0	0	2.25	1	0	4	2	7	2
6. Andy Larkin, rhp	Charlotte (AAA)	6	11	6.05	28	0	144	166	76	103
7. *Dustin Hermanson, rhp	Montreal	8	8	3.69	32	0	158	134	66	136
10. Ryan Dempster, rhp	Brevard County (A)	10	9	4.90	28	0	165	190	46	131

*Traded to Expos

CHARLOTTE — Class AAA

INTERNATIONAL LEAGUE

BATTING	AVG	G	AB	R	H	2B	3B	HR	RBI	BB	SO	SB	CS	B	T	HT	WT	DOB	1st Yr	Resides
Berg, Dave	.295	117	424	76	125	26	6	9	47	55	71	16	7	R	R	5-11	185	9-3-70	1993	Roseville, Calif.
Castillo, Luis	.354	37	130	25	46	5	0	0	5	16	22	8	6	S	R	5-11	146	9-12-75	1993	San Pedro de Macoris, D.R.
Clapinski, Chris	.262	110	340	62	89	24	2	12	52	48	64	14	2	S	R	6-0	165	8-20-71	1992	Rancho Mirage, Calif.
Cole, Alex	.210	39	105	20	22	5	0	2	7	18	20	4	1	L	L	6-2	183	8-17-65	1985	St. Petersburg, Fla.
Daubach, Brian	.278	136	461	66	128	40	2	21	93	65	126	1	8	L	R	6-1	201	2-11-72	1990	Belleville, Ill.
Delgado, Alex	.211	14	38	1	8	1	0	0	6	3	7	0	0	R	R	6-0	160	1-11-71	1988	Palmarejo, Venez.
Dunwoody, Todd	.262	107	401	74	105	16	7	23	62	39	129	25	3	L	L	6-2	185	4-11-75	1993	West Lafayette, Ind.
Floyd, Cliff	.366	39	131	27	48	10	0	9	33	10	29	7	2	L	R	6-4	220	12-5-72	1991	Markham, Ill.
Kmak, Joe	.237	36	93	7	22	6	1	0	12	11	28	1	0	R	R	6-0	185	5-3-63	1985	Foster City, Calif.
Kuilan, Hector	.103	14	39	3	4	0	0	0	3	2	8	0	0	R	R	5-11	190	4-3-76	1994	Vega Alta, P.R.
Lucca, Lou	.284	96	292	40	83	22	1	18	51	22	56	5	4	R	R	5-11	210	10-13-70	1992	South San Francisco, Calif.
McMillon, Billy	.279	57	204	34	57	18	0	8	26	32	51	8	0	L	L	5-11	172	11-17-71	1993	Sumter, S.C.
Milliard, Ralph	.265	33	132	19	35	5	1	4	18	9	21	5	3	R	R	5-10	160	12-30-73	1993	Soest, Neth. Antilles
Morman, Russ	.319	117	395	82	126	17	2	33	99	58	89	3	2	R	R	6-4	215	4-28-62	1983	Blue Springs, Mo.
Natal, Rob	.267	78	251	34	67	17	2	11	49	19	37	2	2	R	R	5-11	190	11-13-65	1987	Chula Vista, Calif.
Olmeda, Jose	.207	83	242	24	50	11	1	1	29	21	41	3	2	S	R	5-9	155	6-20-68	1989	Gurabo, P.R.
Redmond, Mike	.213	22	61	8	13	5	1	1	2	1	10	0	1	R	R	6-0	190	5-5-71	1993	Spokane, Wash.
Rodriguez, Maximo	.048	7	21	2	1	0	0	0	0	1	7	0	0	R	R	6-0	170	11-18-73	1993	La Romana, D.R.
Sheff, Chris	.255	120	322	54	82	23	1	11	43	43	76	16	4	R	R	6-3	210	2-4-71	1992	Laguna Hills, Calif.
Torres, Tony	.279	29	68	9	19	3	0	1	8	7	26	3	2	R	R	5-9	165	6-1-70	1992	San Pablo, Calif.
Wehner, John	.280	31	93	16	26	5	0	3	11	6	18	3	1	R	R	6-3	205	6-29-67	1988	Pittsburgh, Pa.
Wilson, Pookie	.253	60	146	27	37	6	1	2	13	17	26	1	2	L	L	5-10	180	10-24-70	1992	Sylacauga, Ala.

PITCHING	W	L	ERA	G	GS	CG	SV	IP	H	R	ER	BB	SO	B	T	HT	WT	DOB	1st Yr	Resides
Alfonseca, Antonio	7	2	4.32	46	0	0	7	58	58	34	28	20	45	R	R	6-4	160	4-16-72	1990	La Romana, D.R.
Castro, Tony	0	0	4.91	2	0	0	0	4	2	2	2	2	1	R	R	6-2	175	7-9-71	1989	Phoenix, Ariz.
Chergey, Dan	3	1	3.14	27	4	0	6	43	37	18	15	9	40	R	R	6-2	195	1-29-71	1993	Thousand Oaks, Calif.
Cornelius, Reid	12	5	5.10	22	22	1	0	131	134	82	74	43	80	R	R	6-0	190	6-2-70	1989	Thomasville, Ala.
Darensbourg, Vic	4	2	4.38	27	0	0	2	25	22	12	12	15	21	L	L	5-10	165	11-13-70	1992	Los Angeles, Calif.
Gonzalez, Gabe	2	2	2.74	37	1	0	3	43	38	15	13	14	24	S	L	6-1	160	5-24-72	1995	Long Beach, Calif.
Harvey, Bryan	0	0	0.00	2	0	0	0	1	0	0	0	0	0	R	R	6-2	212	6-2-63	1985	Catawba, N.C.
Hernandez, Livan	5	3	3.98	14	14	0	0	81	76	39	36	38	58	R	R	6-2	220	2-20-75	1996	Miami, Fla.
Hurst, Bill	1	2	7.76	27	0	0	3	29	39	27	25	22	15	R	R	6-7	220	4-28-70	1990	Miami, Fla.
Juelsgaard, Jarod	1	3	6.04	21	6	0	0	51	65	41	34	39	31	R	R	6-3	190	6-27-68	1991	Elk Horn, Iowa
Larkin, Andy	6	11	6.05	28	27	3	0	144	166	109	97	76	103	R	R	6-4	181	6-27-74	1992	Medford, Ore.
Mendoza, Reynol	7	8	5.49	46	17	0	9	115	134	79	70	57	93	R	R	6-0	215	10-27-70	1992	San Antonio, Texas
Mercado, Hector	0	1	9.00	1	1	0	0	5	5	5	5	5	1	L	L	6-3	205	4-29-74	1992	Dorado, P.R.
Miller, Kurt	2	1	3.58	21	0	0	0	28	25	12	11	22	31	R	R	6-5	200	8-24-72	1990	Bakersfield, Calif.
Norris, Joe	0	0	11.81	9	1	0	0	16	23	22	21	13	10	R	R	6-4	215	11-29-70	1989	Oswego, S.C.
Ojala, Kirt	8	7	3.50	25	24	0	0	149	148	74	58	55	119	L	L	6-2	200	12-24-68	1990	Portage, Mich.
Pall, Donn	4	7	3.39	59	0	0	8	80	82	40	30	11	70	R	R	6-1	180	1-11-62	1985	Bloomingdale, Ill.
Press, Gregg	0	0	4.50	1	1	0	0	6	5	3	3	4	2	R	R	6-3	200	9-21-71	1994	Santa Cruz, Calif.
Saunders, Tony	1	0	2.77	3	3	0	0	13	9	4	4	6	9	L	L	6-1	189	4-29-74	1992	Ellicott City, Md.
Seelbach, Chris	5	0	6.26	16	6	0	0	50	58	36	35	34	50	R	R	6-4	180	12-18-72	1991	Lufkin, Texas
Stanifer, Robby	4	0	4.88	22	0	0	5	28	34	16	15	7	25	R	R	6-2	195	3-10-72	1994	Easley, S.C.
Ward, Bryan	2	9	6.93	15	14	2	0	75	102	62	58	30	48	L	L	6-2	210	1-28-72	1993	Mt. Holly, N.J.
Whisenant, Matt	2	1	7.20	16	0	0	0	15	16	12	12	12	19	L	L	6-3	215	6-8-71	1990	La Canada, Calif.

FIELDING

Catcher	PCT	G	PO	A	E	DP	PB
Delgado	.990	14	88	11	1	1	2
Kmak	.985	33	187	13	3	1	4
Kuilan	.988	14	76	9	1	2	2
Natal	.991	72	396	34	4	4	8
Redmond	.985	20	119	13	2	1	1
Rodriguez	.981	6	49	3	1	0	0

First Base	PCT	G	PO	A	E	DP
Daubach	.991	101	870	62	8	92
Floyd	.971	3	32	1	1	7
Kmak	.000	1	0	0	0	0
Morman	.986	50	339	26	5	35
Wehner	1.000	2	8	0	0	1

Second Base	PCT	G	PO	A	E	DP
Berg	1.000	2	1	2	0	0
Castillo	.970	36	66	97	5	24
Clapinski	.969	40	89	96	6	27
Milliard	.994	32	71	91	1	33
Olmeda	.981	23	46	55	2	16
Torres	1.000	19	24	44	0	13
Wehner	1.000	1	0	2	0	0

Third Base	PCT	G	PO	A	E	DP
Berg	1.000	1	0	4	0	2
Clapinski	.969	24	17	45	2	3
Kmak	1.000	1	0	1	0	0
Lucca	.946	91	43	201	14	15
Olmeda	.918	21	13	54	6	10
Wehner	.975	14	8	31	1	5

Shortstop	PCT	G	PO	A	E	DP
Berg	.954	108	135	318	22	70
Clapinski	.971	32	42	93	4	19
Olmeda	.857	1	4	2	1	1

Outfield	PCT	G	PO	A	E	DP
Clapinski	.000	1	0	0	0	0
Cole	.980	34	46	2	1	1
Dunwoody	.992	105	231	5	2	1
Floyd	1.000	36	47	4	0	0
McMillon	.978	57	84	5	2	0
Morman	1.000	41	59	3	0	0
Natal	1.000	1	5	0	0	0
Olmeda	.982	28	52	4	1	0
Sheff	1.000	105	154	5	0	0
Wehner	.941	13	16	0	1	0
Wilson	1.000	47	75	2	0	1

PORTLAND — Class AA

EASTERN LEAGUE

BATTING	AVG	G	AB	R	H	2B	3B	HR	RBI	BB	SO	SB	CS	B	T	HT	WT	DOB	1st Yr	Resides
Booty, Josh	.210	122	448	42	94	19	2	20	69	27	166	2	2	R	R	6-3	210	4-29-75	1994	Shreveport, La.
Cook, Hayward	.295	69	166	37	49	13	0	5	21	13	44	2	5	R	R	5-10	195	6-24-72	1994	San Jose, Calif.
Gonzalez, Alex	.254	133	449	69	114	16	4	19	65	27	83	4	7	R	R	6-0	150	2-15-77	1994	Turmero, Venez.
Hastings, Lionel	.344	93	279	55	96	21	0	10	35	39	53	6	3	R	R	5-9	175	1-26-73	1994	Orange, Calif.
Jackson, Ryan	.312	134	491	87	153	28	4	26	98	51	85	2	5	L	L	6-2	195	11-15-71	1994	Sarasota, Fla.
Koeyers, Ramsey	.259	83	286	37	74	14	1	12	50	15	67	0	3	R	R	6-1	187	8-7-74	1991	Brievengst, Neth. Antilles
Kotsay, Mark	.306	114	438	103	134	27	2	20	77	75	65	17	5	L	L	6-0	180	12-2-75	1996	Pembroke Pines, Fla.
Millar, Kevin	.342	135	511	94	175	34	2	32	131	66	53	2	3	R	R	6-1	195	9-24-71	1993	Encino, Calif.
Milliard, Ralph	.275	19	69	13	19	1	2	0	5	7	8	3	2	R	R	5-10	160	12-30-73	1993	Soest, Neth. Antilles
Reeves, Glenn	.351	66	222	53	78	14	2	6	35	39	43	9	4	R	R	6-0	175	1-19-74	1993	Glen Waverly, Australia

BATTING	AVG	G	AB	R	H	2B	3B	HR	RBI	BB	SO	SB	CS	B	T	HT	WT	DOB	1st Yr	Resides
Rodriguez, Victor	.277	113	401	63	111	18	4	3	38	30	43	13	7	R	R	6-2	175	10-25-76	1994	Guayama, P.R.
Roskos, John	.308	123	451	66	139	31	1	24	84	50	81	4	6	R	R	5-11	198	11-19-74	1993	Rio Rancho, N.M.
Torres, Tony	.260	29	50	12	13	2	1	2	4	8	15	2	3	R	R	5-9	165	6-1-70	1992	San Pablo, Calif.
Wilson, Pookie	.252	45	115	15	29	6	0	3	14	11	15	2	3	L	L	5-10	180	10-24-70	1992	Sylacauga, Ala.
Winn, Randy	.292	96	384	66	112	15	6	8	36	42	92	35	20	S	R	6-2	175	6-9-74	1995	Danville, Calif.

PITCHING	W	L	ERA	G	GS	CG	SV	IP	H	R	ER	BB	SO	B	T	HT	WT	DOB	1st Yr	Resides
Burgus, Travis	4	3	6.75	16	9	0	0	52	63	47	39	26	29	L	L	6-2	185	11-6-72	1995	Mission Viejo, Calif.
Castro, Tony	1	2	4.58	27	0	0	0	39	47	21	20	17	21	R	R	6-2	175	7-9-71	1989	Phoenix, Ariz.
Chavez, Carlos	2	1	5.26	30	0	0	1	39	35	23	23	16	32	R	R	6-1	200	8-25-72	1992	El Paso, Texas
Chergey, Dan	2	0	3.23	32	0	0	7	39	30	14	14	7	44	R	R	6-2	195	1-29-71	1993	Thousand Oaks, Calif.
Cornelius, Reid	5	0	2.73	6	6	0	0	33	32	11	10	17	24	R	R	6-0	190	6-2-70	1989	Thomasville, Ala.
Duvall, Mike	4	6	1.84	45	0	0	18	68	63	20	14	20	49	R	L	6-0	185	10-11-74	1995	Morgantown, W.Va.
Gonzalez, Gabe	3	2	2.11	29	0	0	3	43	43	12	10	5	28	S	L	6-1	160	5-24-72	1995	Long Beach, Calif.
Gonzalez, Juan	0	1	6.75	17	0	0	0	29	32	25	22	10	21	R	R	6-1	188	1-28-75	1992	Bani, D.R.
Haynes, Heath	4	0	3.79	28	0	0	1	38	36	16	16	7	39	R	R	6-0	175	11-30-68	1991	Wheeling, W.Va.
3-team (14 Tren./5 N.H.)	5	1	2.97	47	0	0	3	73	69	25	24	16	73							
Hernandez, Livan	0	0	2.25	1	1	0	0	4	2	1	1	7	2	R	R	6-2	220	2-20-75	1996	Miami, Fla.
Hurst, Bill	0	0	0.00	2	0	0	0	2	1	0	0	0	2	R	R	6-7	220	4-28-70	1990	Miami, Fla.
Jacobsen, Joe	5	5	5.09	47	1	0	11	58	76	44	33	23	48	R	R	6-3	225	12-26-71	1992	Clovis, Calif.
Mantei, Matt	1	0	6.75	5	0	0	0	4	1	3	3	8	7	R	R	6-1	181	7-7-73	1991	Sawyer, Mich.
Meadows, Brian	9	7	4.61	29	29	4	0	176	204	99	90	48	115	R	R	6-4	210	11-21-75	1994	Troy, Ala.
Mercado, Hector	11	3	3.96	31	17	1	0	130	129	66	57	54	125	L	L	6-3	205	4-29-74	1992	Dorado, P.R.
Mix, Greg	7	7	4.73	30	13	0	0	103	121	70	54	32	74	R	R	6-4	210	8-21-71	1993	Albuquerque, N.M.
Norris, Joe	2	0	6.75	9	0	0	0	12	11	9	9	5	14	R	R	6-4	215	11-29-70	1989	Oswego, S.C.
Parisi, Mike	1	3	7.08	9	9	0	0	41	56	36	32	14	27	R	R	6-3	195	6-18-73	1994	Arcadia, Calif.
Press, Gregg	7	11	4.98	28	25	1	0	145	178	101	80	41	93	R	R	6-3	200	9-21-71	1994	Santa Cruz, Calif.
Rector, Bobby	2	2	4.81	6	6	0	0	34	45	20	18	11	23	R	R	6-1	170	9-24-74	1994	Imperial Beach, Calif.
Saunders, Tony	0	0	9.00	1	1	0	0	2	3	2	2	1	3	L	L	6-1	189	4-29-74	1992	Ellicott City, Md.
Townsend, Dave	3	7	4.87	15	13	1	0	78	86	49	42	36	30	R	R	6-3	230	8-2-74	1996	Canton, Miss.
Ward, Bryan	6	3	3.91	12	12	0	0	76	71	39	33	19	69	L	L	6-2	210	1-28-72	1993	Mt. Holly, N.J.

FIELDING

Catcher	PCT	G	PO	A	E	DP	PB
Hastings	.000	1	0	0	0	0	0
Koeyers	.988	75	450	42	6	4	17
Roskos	.984	73	469	27	8	2	8

First Base	PCT	G	PO	A	E	DP
Hastings	.500	1	1	0	1	0
Jackson	.979	8	44	3	1	5
Millar	.990	122	1140	93	13	116
Roskos	1.000	18	161	10	0	19
Wilson	1.000	1	1	0	0	1

Second Base	PCT	G	PO	A	E	DP
Hastings	.975	43	79	120	5	29
Milliard	.989	19	37	53	1	10
Rodriguez	.978	87	178	220	9	62
Torres	1.000	9	12	13	0	2

Third Base	PCT	G	PO	A	E	DP
Booty	.934	113	75	262	24	38
Hastings	.938	26	17	58	5	5
Millar	.895	13	6	28	4	1

Shortstop	PCT	G	PO	A	E	DP
Gonzalez	.943	133	192	423	37	87
Hastings	.917	14	9	35	4	3
Rodriguez	1.000	1	0	1	0	0
Torres	.781	6	10	15	7	6

Outfield	PCT	G	PO	A	E	DP
Cook	.955	50	59	5	3	1
Hastings	1.000	9	4	0	0	0
Jackson	.979	103	183	6	4	3
Kotsay	.992	113	230	12	2	4
Reeves	.989	61	84	3	1	1
Wilson	.933	34	40	2	3	0
Winn	.979	93	182	6	4	0

BREVARD COUNTY — Class A

FLORIDA STATE LEAGUE

BATTING	AVG	G	AB	R	H	2B	3B	HR	RBI	BB	SO	SB	CS	B	T	HT	WT	DOB	1st Yr	Resides
Bautista, Jorge	.000	10	15	2	0	0	0	0	1	1	7	0	0	R	R	5-9	165	7-12-76	1995	San Cristobal, D.R.
Braughler, Matt	.240	26	75	5	18	2	0	1	10	6	17	0	0	L	R	6-2	200	5-12-73	1996	Morehead, Ky.
Brown, Roosevelt	.246	33	114	8	28	7	1	1	12	7	31	0	3	L	R	5-10	190	8-3-75	1993	Vicksburg, Miss.
Camilo, Jose	.235	107	371	53	87	12	2	8	51	46	62	20	9	L	L	5-11	175	9-28-76	1994	Trujillo Alto, P.R.
Darden, Tony	.286	107	392	50	112	32	4	6	48	32	72	7	3	R	R	6-0	170	5-29-74	1994	Gilmer, Texas
Fagley, Dan	.214	6	14	3	3	1	0	0	1	1	6	0	0	R	R	5-10	185	12-18-74	1994	Riverton, N.J.
Foster, Quincy	.247	61	186	25	46	8	2	1	11	14	47	12	4	L	R	6-2	175	10-30-74	1996	Hendersonville, N.C.
Funaro, Joe	.319	125	470	67	150	16	6	4	53	49	65	9	5	R	R	5-9	170	3-20-73	1995	Hamden, Conn.
Garcia, Amaury	.288	124	479	77	138	30	2	7	44	49	97	45	11	R	R	5-10	160	5-20-75	1993	Santo Domingo, D.R.
Goodell, Steve	.270	117	381	48	103	18	2	11	61	60	67	1	1	R	R	6-3	196	4-23-75	1995	Danville, Calif.
Harvey, Aaron	.270	115	455	65	123	17	6	6	47	30	78	30	15	L	R	5-10	180	6-11-73	1994	Donvale, Australia
Jones, Jaime	.271	95	373	63	101	27	4	10	60	44	86	6	1	L	L	6-3	190	8-2-76	1995	Melbourne, Fla.
Kuilan, Hector	.226	77	265	18	60	16	0	0	25	7	41	0	1	R	R	5-11	190	4-3-76	1994	Vega Alta, P.R.
McCartney, Sommer	.245	16	53	3	13	2	0	1	12	3	19	0	0	R	R	6-0	200	8-2-72	1994	San Jose, Calif.
Redmond, Mike	.000	5	17	2	0	0	0	0	0	2	2	0	0	R	R	6-0	190	5-5-71	1993	Spokane, Wash.
Reynoso, Ismael	.000	2	3	0	0	0	0	0	0	1	2	0	0	R	R	5-10	165	6-17-78	1995	La Romana, D.R.
Rodriguez, Maximo	.203	42	118	14	24	4	2	2	10	10	30	0	1	R	R	6-0	170	11-18-73	1993	La Romana, D.R.
Rolison, Nate	.256	122	473	59	121	22	0	16	65	38	143	3	1	L	R	6-5	225	3-27-77	1995	Petal, Miss.
Schifano, Tony	.000	1	1	0	0	0	0	0	0	0	1	0	0	R	R	6-1	175	11-11-74	1997	Anaheim Hills, Calif.
Treanor, Matt	.214	23	70	11	15	4	1	0	3	12	14	0	0	R	R	6-1	188	3-3-76	1994	Anaheim, Calif.
White, Walter	.202	54	163	18	33	8	0	1	15	14	41	0	0	R	R	6-0	180	12-12-71	1994	Rohnert Park, Calif.
Winn, Randy	.315	36	143	26	45	8	2	0	15	16	28	16	8	S	R	6-2	175	6-9-74	1995	Danville, Calif.

GAMES BY POSITION: C—Braughler 15, Fagley 3, Kuilan 77, McCartney 1, Rodriguez 29, Treanor 22. **1B**—Braughler 2, Camilo 1, Goodell 20, Redmond 1, Rodriguez 1, Rolison 115, White 3. **2B**—Darden 6, Garcia 124, White 15. **3B**—Bautista 9, Braughler 1, Darden 90, Goodell 36, White 18. **SS**—Darden 7, Funaro 112, Goodell 4, Reynoso 2, Schifano 1, White 21. **OF**—Brown 31, Camilo 86, Darden 4, Foster 60, Funaro 1, Goodell 54, Harvey 94, Jones 61, Winn 36.

PITCHING	W	L	ERA	G	GS	CG	SV	IP	H	R	ER	BB	SO	B	T	HT	WT	DOB	1st Yr	Resides
Alejo, Nigel	1	0	2.13	7	0	0	0	13	8	4	3	1	11	R	R	6-0	171	1-12-75	1993	Palo Negro, Venez.
Caravelli, Mike	3	5	4.70	40	0	0	3	61	81	44	32	12	35	R	L	6-2	200	7-27-72	1995	Santa Monica, Calif.
Castro, Tony	1	0	5.76	14	0	0	1	25	29	18	16	7	16	R	R	6-2	175	7-9-71	1989	Phoenix, Ariz.
Collins, Ed	2	3	5.16	26	1	0	2	45	49	33	26	24	29	R	R	6-3	225	8-26-76	1994	Union, N.J.
Danner, Adam	1	1	7.43	17	0	0	0	27	50	28	22	11	14	R	R	6-3	210	8-1-74	1997	Tampa, Fla.
Dempster, Ryan	10	9	4.90	28	26	2	0	165	190	100	90	46	131	R	R	6-2	195	5-3-77	1995	Gibsons, B.C.

PITCHING	W	L	ERA	G	GS	CG	SV	IP	H	R	ER	BB	SO	B	T	HT	WT	DOB	1st Yr	Resides
DeWitt, Scott	4	10	4.16	25	24	0	0	132	145	80	61	51	121	R	L	6-4	200	10-6-74	1995	Springfield, Ore.
Duvall, Mike	1	0	0.73	11	0	0	6	12	7	1	1	3	9	R	L	6-0	185	10-11-74	1995	Morgantown, W.Va.
Ehlers, Corey	0	0	2.38	6	0	0	0	11	9	3	3	3	3	R	R	6-3	190	8-22-73	1997	Floresville, Texas
Getz, Rod	9	12	3.23	27	26	4	0	164	166	84	59	39	92	R	R	6-5	180	2-17-76	1995	Lawrenceburg, Ind.
Gonzalez, Juan	3	2	2.39	26	0	0	6	38	32	13	10	7	28	R	R	6-1	188	1-28-75	1992	Bani, D.R.
Harvey, Bryan	0	1	4.91	4	4	0	0	11	11	9	6	1	11	R	R	6-2	212	6-2-63	1985	Catawba, N.C.
Hurtado, Victor	4	7	4.89	17	16	2	0	92	102	54	50	34	58	R	R	6-1	155	6-14-77	1994	Santo Domingo, D.R.
Mantei, Matt	0	0	6.00	4	0	0	0	6	4	4	4	6	11	R	R	6-1	181	7-7-73	1991	Sawyer, Mich.
Miles, Chad	3	4	4.50	42	0	0	5	64	63	46	32	31	59	S	L	6-3	195	2-26-73	1994	Renton, Wash.
Miller, Kurt	0	0	1.80	2	2	0	0	5	6	1	1	2	7	R	R	6-5	200	8-24-72	1990	Bakersfield, Calif.
Miranda, Walter	2	3	5.19	10	9	0	0	35	45	32	20	26	15	R	R	6-4	190	1-6-75	1992	Cartagena, Colombia
Morris, Alex	0	0	0.00	2	0	0	0	3	1	1	0	0	2	L	R	6-4	220	12-31-76	1996	Austin, Texas
Pailthorpe, Bob	6	4	4.86	35	3	0	1	74	88	50	40	24	53	R	R	6-1	210	12-6-72	1995	Fremont, Calif.
Santiago, Derek	3	2	4.45	10	1	0	0	28	20	14	14	19	17	R	R	6-1	155	10-10-75	1995	Aurora, Ill.
Santoro, Gary	0	0	3.38	20	0	0	2	27	32	11	10	3	14	R	R	6-3	205	12-15-72	1995	Watertown, Conn.
Stephens, Shannon	8	13	4.81	27	25	2	0	150	162	93	80	34	90	R	R	6-2	205	8-28-73	1995	Grover Beach, Calif.
Whisenant, Matt	0	0	8.10	2	1	0	0	3	3	3	3	3	4	L	L	6-3	215	6-8-71	1990	La Canada, Calif.
Zaleski, Kevin	1	0	0.00	3	0	0	0	4	3	0	0	0	3	R	R	6-2	215	8-18-73	1996	Glendale Heights, Ill.

KANE COUNTY — Class A

MIDWEST LEAGUE

BATTING	AVG	G	AB	R	H	2B	3B	HR	RBI	BB	SO	SB	CS	B	T	HT	WT	DOB	1st Yr	Resides
Agnoly, Earl	.210	34	100	9	21	0	1	2	10	6	23	3	1	R	R	6-0	170	11-18-75	1993	Colon, Panama
Alaimo, Jason	.244	36	90	7	22	5	0	2	10	5	25	1	2	R	R	5-8	200	7-31-75	1996	Holbrook, N.Y.
Aversa, Joe	.202	63	203	17	41	3	2	0	17	30	58	3	1	S	R	5-10	155	5-20-68	1990	Huntington Beach, Calif.
Bautista, Jorge	.149	20	67	9	10	3	0	0	7	5	18	2	2	R	R	5-9	165	7-12-76	1995	San Cristobal, D.R.
Brown, Roosevelt	.237	61	211	29	50	7	1	4	30	22	52	5	4	L	R	5-10	190	8-3-75	1993	Vicksburg, Miss.
Clark, Chris	.170	21	47	7	8	3	0	0	2	6	12	2	1	R	R	6-3	195	11-7-73	1997	Smackover, Ark.
Garrett, Jason	.275	128	476	72	131	28	3	5	68	35	101	3	2	R	R	6-2	180	6-10-73	1995	Austin, Texas
Glozier, Larry	.176	55	159	21	28	5	0	0	16	16	29	2	2	R	R	5-10	180	9-2-73	1996	Chicago, Ill.
Heinrichs, Jon	.268	60	235	35	63	12	2	1	36	19	34	8	5	R	R	6-0	185	11-18-74	1997	La Mesa, Calif.
Horne, Tyrone	.306	133	468	89	143	24	2	21	91	104	88	18	7	L	R	5-10	185	11-2-70	1989	Troy, N.C.
Jones, Jay	.295	64	210	20	62	6	0	4	31	8	29	0	2	L	R	6-0	195	10-24-74	1996	Trussville, Ala.
Kleinz, Larry	.242	107	364	50	88	16	1	11	44	48	63	1	2	R	R	6-1	195	3-3-74	1996	Hamilton Square, N.J.
Melconian, Alex	.100	3	10	0	1	0	0	0	0	1	2	0	0	R	R	5-10	190	3-18-75	1997	Berwyn, Pa.
Podsednik, Scott	.277	135	531	80	147	23	4	3	49	60	72	28	11	L	L	6-0	170	3-18-76	1994	West, Texas
Ramirez, Julio	.255	99	376	70	96	18	7	14	53	37	122	41	6	S	R	5-11	160	8-10-77	1994	Santo Domingo, D.R.
Reynoso, Ismael	.132	34	91	4	12	0	0	0	10	8	21	1	2	R	R	5-10	165	6-17-78	1995	La Romana, D.R.
Robertson, Ryan	.285	116	376	64	107	22	1	11	71	85	69	0	3	L	R	6-4	210	9-30-72	1996	Port Neches, Texas
Rupcich, Larry	.216	33	111	13	24	1	0	0	8	17	21	2	0	L	R	6-0	185	1-2-75	1997	Fresno, Calif.
Venghaus, Jeff	.236	128	416	71	98	20	3	0	43	86	105	17	11	S	R	6-0	185	9-17-74	1996	Spring, Texas

GAMES BY POSITION: C—Alaimo 33, Jones 23, Robertson 98. **1B**—Agnoly 9, Garrett 123, Jones 10. **2B**—Aversa 1, Glozier 12, Rupcich 6, Venghaus 125. **3B**—Bautista 20, Glozier 3, Kleinz 106, Rupcich 12. **SS**—Aversa 62, Glozier 41, Reynoso 34, Rupcich 16. **OF**—Agnoly 20, Brown 59, Clark 19, Heinrichs 60, Horne 34, Melconian 3, Podsednik 133, Ramirez 99, Venghaus 5.

PITCHING	W	L	ERA	G	GS	CG	SV	IP	H	R	ER	BB	SO	B	T	HT	WT	DOB	1st Yr	Resides
Almonte, Hector	0	1	3.86	8	1	0	1	14	11	6	6	6	10	R	R	6-0	170	10-17-75	1993	Santo Domingo, D.R.
Billingsley, Brent	14	7	3.01	26	26	3	0	171	146	67	57	50	175	L	L	6-2	200	4-19-75	1996	Chino Hills, Calif.
Cames, Aaron	8	10	3.91	26	26	3	0	150	143	67	65	43	157	R	R	6-1	192	11-21-75	1996	Woodland, Calif.
Danner, Adam	1	4	4.12	10	0	0	0	20	26	12	9	8	16	R	R	6-3	210	8-1-74	1997	Tampa, Fla.
Duncan, Geoff	7	2	4.07	44	2	0	1	86	85	46	39	30	96	R	R	6-2	175	4-1-75	1996	Duluth, Ga.
Johannsen, Jeff	0	0	7.15	7	0	0	0	11	13	10	9	7	10	L	L	6-3	200	6-10-73	1996	Eldridge, Iowa
Knotts, Gary	1	5	13.05	7	7	0	0	20	33	34	29	17	19	R	R	6-4	200	2-12-77	1996	Decatur, Ala.
Lara, Nelson	1	2	3.99	29	0	0	3	38	37	20	17	14	43	R	R	6-4	165	7-15-78	1995	Santo Domingo, D.R.
Leese, Brandon	3	1	3.83	7	6	0	0	42	27	18	18	18	32	R	R	6-4	190	10-8-75	1996	Lincolnshire, Ill.
Levan, Matt	2	3	3.09	11	9	0	0	44	44	16	15	16	45	L	L	6-3	180	6-24-75	1996	Coatesville, Pa.
McClaskey, Tim	2	1	3.16	18	2	0	1	37	29	18	13	8	38	R	R	6-1	170	1-11-76	1996	Wilton, Iowa
Morris, Alex	4	0	5.34	19	0	0	0	32	39	24	19	19	22	L	R	6-4	220	12-31-76	1996	Austin, Texas
Rector, Bobby	1	0	0.86	3	3	1	0	21	11	2	2	4	24	R	R	6-1	170	9-24-74	1994	Imperial Beach, Calif.
Richards, Mark	1	1	2.38	18	0	0	1	34	34	13	9	7	27	R	R	6-6	220	6-19-74	1997	Tipp City, Ohio
Rodgers, Bobby	8	10	3.86	27	27	2	0	166	154	81	71	61	138	R	R	6-3	225	7-22-74	1996	St. Charles, Mo.
Sanchez, Martin	3	5	4.50	51	0	0	22	54	40	31	27	32	57	R	R	6-2	175	1-19-77	1994	Santo Domingo, D.R.
Santiago, Derek	1	6	8.02	12	8	0	0	46	72	46	41	18	30	R	R	6-1	155	10-10-75	1995	Aurora, Ill.
Townsend, Dave	5	1	2.40	12	11	1	0	64	54	20	17	16	51	R	R	6-3	230	8-2-74	1996	Canton, Miss.
Widerski, Jon	2	4	5.71	17	10	0	0	65	76	46	41	30	45	R	R	6-4	190	5-17-77	1995	Minneapolis, Minn.
Wyckoff, Travis	4	2	2.68	40	0	0	0	50	50	23	15	22	36	S	L	6-0	180	9-30-73	1996	Wichita, Kan.
Zaleski, Kevin	2	3	5.47	21	0	0	0	25	37	20	15	12	19	R	R	6-2	215	8-18-73	1996	Glendale Heights, Ill.

UTICA — Short-Season Class A

NEW YORK-PENN LEAGUE

BATTING	AVG	G	AB	R	H	2B	3B	HR	RBI	BB	SO	SB	CS	B	T	HT	WT	DOB	1st Yr	Resides
Bautista, Jorge	.244	58	201	19	49	10	1	3	27	25	55	5	3	R	R	5-9	165	7-12-76	1995	San Cristobal, D.R.
Clark, Chris	.063	6	16	1	1	1	0	0	1	2	8	0	0	R	R	6-3	195	11-7-73	1997	Smackover, Ark.
Donaldson, Rhodney	.264	70	269	49	71	3	2	1	16	37	42	21	6	L	R	5-11	170	4-9-74	1997	Cairo, Ga.
Erickson, Matt	.328	69	238	44	78	10	0	5	44	48	36	9	3	L	R	5-11	190	7-30-75	1997	Appleton, Wis.
Franco, Raul	.352	72	293	41	103	19	0	3	38	17	24	10	4	R	R	5-11	150	1-14-76	1994	San Pedro de Macoris, D.R.
Gload, Ross	.261	68	245	28	64	15	2	3	43	28	57	1	1	L	L	6-2	195	4-5-76	1997	East Hampton, N.Y.
Green, Kevin	.238	10	21	2	5	0	0	0	2	4	6	2	0	R	R	6-1	190	8-9-75	1997	Rome, N.Y.
Harper, Brandon	.257	47	152	27	39	7	2	2	22	19	32	1	1	R	R	6-4	200	4-29-76	1997	Hobbs, N.M.
Hunter, Travis	.226	19	53	3	12	4	0	0	4	4	12	0	0	R	R	6-2	230	9-3-79	1997	Airmount, N.Y.
Maduro, Remy	.217	49	157	16	34	5	3	0	12	15	27	2	5	L	R	6-1	176	9-18-76	1996	Hoofddorp, Netherlands

BATTING	AVG	G	AB	R	H	2B	3B	HR	RBI	BB	SO	SB	CS	B	T	HT	WT	DOB	1st Yr	Resides
Melconian, Alex	.279	62	215	37	60	6	2	2	22	18	48	6	6	R	R	5-10	190	3-18-75	1997	Berwyn, Pa.
Polonia, Israel	.173	37	110	13	19	7	0	1	8	15	51	1	1	R	R	6-0	160	10-10-77	1995	San Pedro de Macoris, D.R.
Reese, Nate	.205	13	44	5	9	2	0	0	5	2	14	0	0	R	R	5-11	215	10-17-74	1997	Shawnee Mission, Kan.
Schifano, Tony	.261	48	153	26	40	7	0	1	14	11	28	5	5	R	R	6-1	175	11-11-74	1997	Anaheim Hills, Calif.
Schnabel, Matt	.191	67	225	23	43	6	0	2	22	37	46	5	4	L	R	6-0	195	8-29-74	1997	Englewood, Colo.

GAMES BY POSITION: C—Harper 46, Melconian 19, Reese 11. **1B**—Bautista 14, Gload 63. **2B**—Erickson 5, Franco 67, Schifano 5. **3B**—Bautista 12, Erickson 61, Schifano 2. **SS**—Polonia 37, Schifano 42. **OF**—Clark 5, Donaldson 68, Green 10, Hunter 1, Maduro 40, Melconian 41, Schifano 1, Schnabel 65.

PITCHING	W	L	ERA	G	GS	CG	SV	IP	H	R	ER	BB	SO	B	T	HT	WT	DOB	1st Yr	Resides
Bair, Andy	1	6	6.32	12	12	0	0	53	54	42	37	17	32	L	L	6-5	255	1-27-77	1995	Manchester, Md.
Borges, Reece	7	5	4.80	15	15	2	0	81	92	54	43	28	58	R	R	6-3	195	4-4-76	1997	Reno, Nev.
Casey, Shaw	0	2	12.00	9	0	0	0	12	28	21	16	8	11	R	R	6-2	190	3-27-75	1996	Las Vegas, Nev.
Doan, Zachary	2	2	5.65	13	0	0	1	29	34	18	18	13	22	R	R	6-3	195	8-4-75	1997	Hoffman Estates, Ill.
Ehlers, Corey	1	0	1.47	9	0	0	1	18	16	3	3	1	16	R	R	6-3	190	8-22-73	1997	Floresville, Texas
Fowler, Blair	2	2	4.00	18	1	0	0	36	40	23	16	9	29	R	R	6-2	185	6-25-75	1997	Everett, Wash.
Gagliano, Steve	0	1	9.82	1	1	0	0	4	6	4	4	3	6	R	R	6-4	185	8-4-77	1996	Rolling Meadows, Ill.
Henderson, Scott	5	1	2.27	15	1	0	4	40	28	11	10	7	51	R	R	6-3	195	2-27-75	1997	Villa Park, Calif.
Knotts, Gary	3	5	3.62	12	12	1	0	70	70	34	28	27	65	R	R	6-4	200	2-12-77	1996	Decatur, Ala.
Levan, Matt	0	0	6.75	1	1	0	0	4	5	3	3	1	6	L	L	6-3	180	6-24-75	1996	Coatesville, Pa.
Lima, Cory	3	1	2.03	17	2	0	1	40	31	11	9	11	40	R	R	6-4	180	3-16-75	1997	Stone Mountain, Ga.
Marriott, Mike	1	2	5.52	7	7	0	0	29	31	25	18	14	21	R	R	6-3	195	3-12-77	1995	Spring, Texas
McClaskey, Tim	1	0	0.00	1	0	0	0	5	1	0	0	0	8	R	R	6-1	170	1-11-76	1996	Wilton, Iowa
Putnicki, Billy	3	4	2.47	21	0	0	4	44	44	17	12	10	33	R	R	6-3	205	12-21-73	1997	San Antonio, Texas
Richards, Mark	0	0	0.00	2	0	0	0	2	1	0	0	0	3	R	R	6-6	220	6-19-74	1997	Tipp City, Ohio
Rizzo, Nick	4	1	2.36	15	10	0	1	69	64	30	18	12	54	R	R	6-0	180	1-23-74	1997	Bellmawr, N.J.
Tejera, Michael	3	3	3.76	12	12	0	0	69	65	36	29	11	67	L	L	5-9	175	10-18-76	1995	Miami, Fla.
Williams, Henry	0	3	7.66	18	0	0	2	25	38	24	21	18	26	R	R	5-11	180	3-12-75	1997	Blackwood, N.J.

MELBOURNE — Rookie

GULF COAST LEAGUE

BATTING	AVG	G	AB	R	H	2B	3B	HR	RBI	BB	SO	SB	CS	B	T	HT	WT	DOB	1st Yr	Resides
Abreu, Miguel	.213	37	94	10	20	2	1	0	6	4	28	2	2	R	R	6-1	160	8-15-78	1994	San Pedro de Macoris, D.R.
Aguila, Chris	.217	46	157	12	34	7	0	1	17	21	49	2	1	R	R	5-11	190	2-23-79	1997	Reno, Nev.
Bailey, Jeff	.143	5	7	0	1	0	0	0	0	1	2	0	0	R	R	6-2	195	11-19-78	1997	Kelso, Wash.
Conway, Scott	.000	2	4	0	0	0	0	0	1	1	1	0	0	L	L	6-4	200	10-18-78	1996	Mt. Laurel, N.J.
Feliz, Joselyn	.294	34	102	9	30	4	0	0	9	6	17	0	1	R	R	6-2	200	6-2-76	1994	Santo Domingo, D.R.
Harper, Brandon	.000	2	6	0	0	0	0	0	1	0	1	0	0	R	R	6-4	200	4-29-76	1997	Hobbs, N.M.
Jackson, Quantaa	.230	41	126	17	29	8	0	2	13	8	52	6	1	R	R	6-2	215	10-19-77	1996	Wharton, Texas
Medrano, Jesus	.279	40	111	20	31	4	0	0	16	19	18	16	3	R	R	6-0	165	9-11-78	1997	La Puente, Calif.
Mejia, Renato	.229	35	109	15	25	9	0	1	8	14	27	2	1	R	R	6-1	160	1-2-77	1994	Hato Mayor, D.R.
Morales, Stephen	.210	20	62	7	13	1	0	2	13	6	10	1	1	S	R	5-11	180	5-4-78	1996	Mayaguez, P.R.
Pass, Patrick	.222	19	45	7	10	1	0	1	8	10	16	3	1	R	R	6-1	202	12-31-77	1996	Tucker, Ga.
Pimentel, Eddie	.256	44	133	23	34	7	2	0	17	10	39	8	3	S	R	6-3	155	12-25-77	1994	San Francisco de Macoris, D.R.
Redmond, Mike	.345	16	55	7	19	3	0	0	5	9	5	2	0	R	R	6-0	190	5-5-71	1993	Spokane, Wash.
Reed, Brian	.199	48	166	22	33	3	2	0	10	27	48	16	5	R	R	5-9	170	3-3-78	1997	Henderson, Nev.
Reese, Nate	.241	11	29	3	7	1	0	0	3	3	9	0	1	R	R	5-11	215	10-17-74	1997	Shawnee Mission, Kan.
Reynoso, Ismael	.284	48	162	19	46	11	0	2	19	23	30	8	2	R	R	5-10	165	6-17-78	1995	La Romana, D.R.
Roneberg, Brett	.265	53	185	25	49	11	2	0	13	28	35	6	5	L	L	6-1	183	2-5-79	1996	Cairns, Australia
Walker, Javon	.106	16	47	7	5	0	0	0	1	8	21	0	0	R	R	6-4	205	10-14-78	1997	Lafayette, La.
Washington, Cory	.224	27	76	14	17	3	2	1	10	12	19	3	1	R	R	5-11	175	12-23-77	1996	Fayetteville, N.C.
Washington, Kelley	.107	35	103	8	11	0	1	0	6	10	32	2	1	R	R	6-2	180	8-21-79	1997	Stephens City, Va.

GAMES BY POSITION: C—Feliz 32, Harper 2, Morales 20, Reese 11. **1B**—Conway 1, Mejia 8, Pass 1, Roneberg 53. **2B**—Medrano 38, Reynoso 8, C. Washington 14, K. Washington 3. **3B**—Aguila 45, Feliz 2, Reynoso 13. **SS**—Reynoso 29, K. Washington 33. **OF**—Abreu 27, Bailey 1, Jackson 19, Mejia 23, Pass 15, Pimentel 37, Reed 42, Walker 15, C. Washington 12.

PITCHING	W	L	ERA	G	GS	CG	SV	IP	H	R	ER	BB	SO	B	T	HT	WT	DOB	1st Yr	Resides
Akin, Aaron	0	0	2.31	4	4	0	0	12	13	5	3	3	5	R	R	6-2	190	6-13-77	1997	Pembroke Pines, Fla.
Almonte, Hector	2	0	0.76	8	0	0	3	24	12	3	2	6	25	R	R	6-0	170	10-17-75	1993	Santo Domingo, D.R.
Blanco, Pablo	2	5	4.06	11	9	1	0	51	41	31	23	36	44	R	R	6-2	170	1-15-78	1995	Santo Domingo, D.R.
Doan, Zachary	0	0	0.00	1	0	0	0	2	1	0	0	1	1	R	R	6-3	195	8-4-75	1997	Hoffman Estates, Ill.
Ehlers, Corey	0	1	4.70	2	2	0	0	8	11	6	4	0	5	R	R	6-3	190	8-22-73	1997	Floresville, Texas
Farizo, Brad	3	6	3.71	11	11	2	0	61	55	34	25	21	52	R	R	6-4	175	11-3-78	1996	Marrero, La.
Gagliano, Steve	3	4	3.70	12	12	1	0	56	56	28	23	16	50	R	R	6-4	185	8-4-77	1996	Rolling Meadows, Ill.
Garvin, Robert	4	3	1.62	14	0	0	1	33	28	20	6	4	27	R	R	6-2	165	3-14-79	1997	Charleston, S.C.
Lopez, Gustavo	0	3	4.13	7	6	1	0	33	33	20	15	10	25	R	R	6-0	175	12-12-78	1996	Santiago, D.R.
Minaya, Pedro	3	1	1.88	12	6	0	0	38	30	14	8	15	39	R	R	6-3	160	7-30-77	1994	Santo Domingo, D.R.
Moore, Chris	3	2	2.65	10	9	1	0	54	39	23	16	29	40	R	R	6-3	175	8-3-78	1996	Hazel Crest, Ill.
Neal, Blaine	4	1	3.63	10	0	0	1	22	24	11	9	11	19	L	R	6-5	205	4-6-78	1996	Port Ritchie, Fla.
Pidgeon, Matt	2	1	4.56	16	0	0	4	26	25	21	13	15	21	R	R	6-4	200	6-25-77	1997	Eureka, Calif.
Shields, Drew	3	1	5.93	10	0	0	0	30	42	24	20	10	27	R	R	6-4	190	9-9-78	1997	Tucson, Ariz.
Thomas, Gaige	2	0	3.52	12	0	0	0	23	18	16	9	17	30	S	R	6-1	185	2-28-79	1997	Brenham, Texas

Houston ASTROS

Manager: Larry Dierker.

1997 Record: 84-78, .519 (1st, NL Central)

BATTING	AVG	G	AB	R	H	2B	3B	HR	RBI	BB	SO	SB	CS	B	T	HT	WT	DOB	1st Yr	Resides
Abreu, Bob	.250	59	188	22	47	10	2	3	26	21	48	7	2	L	R	6-0	160	3-11-74	1991	Turmero, Venez.
Ausmus, Brad	.266	130	425	45	113	25	1	4	44	38	78	14	6	R	R	5-11	185	4-14-69	1988	Cheshire, Conn.
Bagwell, Jeff	.286	162	566	109	162	40	2	43	135	127	122	31	10	R	R	6-0	195	5-27-68	1989	Houston, Texas
Bell, Derek	.276	129	493	67	136	29	3	15	71	40	94	15	7	R	R	6-2	200	12-11-68	1987	Tampa, Fla.
Berry, Sean	.256	96	301	37	77	24	1	8	43	25	53	1	5	R	R	5-11	210	3-22-66	1986	Rolling Hills Estates, Calif.
Biggio, Craig	.309	162	619	146	191	37	8	22	81	84	107	47	10	R	R	5-11	180	12-14-65	1987	Houston, Texas
Bogar, Tim	.249	97	241	30	60	14	4	4	30	24	42	4	1	R	R	6-2	198	10-28-66	1987	Kankakee, Ill.
Carr, Chuck	.276	63	192	34	53	11	2	4	17	15	37	11	5	S	R	5-10	165	8-10-68	1986	Tucson, Ariz.
Eusebio, Tony	.274	60	164	12	45	2	0	1	18	19	27	0	1	R	R	6-2	180	4-27-67	1985	Kissimmee, Fla.
Gonzalez, Luis	.258	152	550	78	142	31	2	10	68	71	67	10	7	L	R	6-2	180	9-3-67	1988	Houston, Texas
Gutierrez, Ricky	.261	102	303	33	79	14	4	3	34	21	50	5	2	R	R	6-1	175	5-23-70	1988	Miami, Fla.
Hidalgo, Richard	.306	19	62	8	19	5	0	2	6	4	18	1	0	R	R	6-2	175	7-2-75	1991	Guarenas, Venez.
Howard, Thomas	.247	107	255	24	63	16	1	3	22	26	48	1	2	S	R	6-2	205	12-11-64	1986	Elk Grove, Calif.
Johnson, Russ	.300	21	60	7	18	1	0	2	9	6	14	1	1	R	R	5-10	185	2-22-73	1994	Baton Rouge, La.
Knorr, Randy	.375	4	8	1	3	0	0	1	1	0	2	0	0	R	R	6-2	212	11-12-68	1986	Covina, Calif.
Listach, Pat	.182	52	132	13	24	2	2	0	6	11	24	4	2	S	R	5-9	170	9-12-67	1988	Spring, Texas
Montgomery, Ray	.235	29	68	8	16	4	1	0	4	5	18	0	0	R	R	6-3	195	8-8-69	1990	Bronxville, N.Y.
Mouton, James	.211	86	180	24	38	9	1	3	23	18	30	9	7	R	R	5-9	175	12-29-68	1991	Sacramento, Calif.
Pena, Tony	.211	9	19	2	4	3	0	0	2	2	3	0	0	R	R	6-0	184	6-4-57	1976	Santiago, D.R.
Phillips, J.R.	.133	13	15	2	2	0	0	1	4	0	7	0	0	L	L	6-1	185	4-29-70	1988	Moreno Valley, Calif.
Ramos, Ken	.000	14	12	0	0	0	0	0	1	2	0	0	0	L	L	6-1	185	6-8-67	1989	Pueblo, Colo.
Rivera, Luis	.231	7	13	2	3	0	1	0	3	1	6	0	0	R	R	5-10	172	1-3-64	1982	Cidra, P.R.
Spiers, Bill	.320	132	291	51	93	27	4	4	48	61	42	10	5	L	R	6-2	190	6-5-66	1987	Elloree, S.C.

PITCHING	W	L	ERA	G	GS	CG	SV	IP	H	R	ER	BB	SO	B	T	HT	WT	DOB	1st Yr	Resides
Barrios, Manuel	0	0	12.00	2	0	0	0	3	6	4	4	3	3	R	R	6-0	145	9-21-74	1993	Cabecera, Panama
Cabrera, Jose	0	0	1.17	12	0	0	0	15	6	2	2	6	18	R	R	6-0	197	3-24-72	1991	Santiago, D.R.
Fernandez, Sid	1	0	3.60	1	1	0	0	5	4	2	2	2	3	L	L	6-1	220	10-12-62	1981	Honolulu, Hawaii
Garcia, Ramon	9	8	3.69	42	20	1	1	159	155	71	65	52	120	R	R	6-2	200	12-9-69	1987	Guanare, Venez.
Greene, Tommy	0	1	7.00	2	2	0	0	9	10	7	7	5	11	R	R	6-5	225	4-6-67	1985	Richmond, Va.
Hampton, Mike	15	10	3.83	34	34	7	0	223	217	105	95	77	139	R	L	5-10	180	9-9-72	1990	Homosassa, Fla.
Henriquez, Oscar	0	1	4.50	4	0	0	0	4	2	2	2	3	3	R	R	6-4	175	1-28-74	1991	La Guaira, Venez.
Holt, Chris	8	12	3.52	33	32	0	0	210	211	98	82	61	95	R	R	6-4	205	9-18-71	1992	Dallas, Texas
Hudek, John	1	3	5.98	40	0	0	4	41	38	27	27	33	36	S	R	6-1	200	8-8-66	1988	Tampa, Fla.
Kile, Darryl	19	7	2.57	34	34	6	0	256	208	87	73	94	205	R	R	6-5	185	12-2-68	1988	Corona, Calif.
Lima, Jose	1	6	5.28	52	1	0	2	75	79	45	44	16	63	R	R	6-2	170	9-30-72	1989	Santiago, D.R.
Magnante, Mike	3	1	2.27	40	0	0	1	48	39	16	12	11	43	L	L	6-1	190	6-17-65	1988	Burbank, Calif.
Martin, Tom	5	3	2.09	55	0	0	2	56	52	13	13	23	36	L	L	6-1	185	5-21-70	1989	Panama City, Fla.
Minor, Blas	1	0	4.50	11	0	0	1	12	13	7	6	5	6	R	R	6-3	200	3-20-66	1988	Gilbert, Ariz.
Reynolds, Shane	9	10	4.23	30	30	2	0	181	189	92	85	47	152	R	R	6-3	210	3-26-68	1989	Houston, Texas
Springer, Russ	3	3	4.23	54	0	0	3	55	48	28	26	27	74	R	R	6-4	195	11-7-68	1989	Pollack, La.
Wagner, Billy	7	8	2.85	62	0	0	23	66	49	23	21	30	106	L	L	5-10	180	7-25-71	1993	Tannersville, Va.
Wall, Donne	2	5	6.26	8	8	0	0	42	53	31	29	16	25	R	R	6-1	180	7-11-67	1989	Festus, Mo.

FIELDING

Catcher	PCT	G	PO	A	E	DP	PB
Ausmus	.992	129	807	73	7	16	6
Eusebio	.987	43	297	16	4	4	1
Knorr	1.000	3	12	1	0	0	0
Pena	1.000	8	48	6	0	1	0

First Base	PCT	G	PO	A	E	DP
Bagwell	.993	159	1404	137	11	140
Bogar	.000	1	0	0	0	0
Gonzalez	1.000	1	3	0	0	1
Knorr	1.000	2	7	2	0	1
Phillips	1.000	3	6	0	0	1
Spiers	1.000	8	32	1	0	5

Second Base	PCT	G	PO	A	E	DP
Biggio	.979	160	341	504	18	108
Gutierrez	1.000	9	9	3	0	2
Johnson	1.000	3	9	2	0	1
Rivera	1.000	1	3	1	0	0
Spiers	1.000	4	3	13	0	3

Third Base	PCT	G	PO	A	E	DP
Berry	.921	85	47	140	16	11
Bogar	.955	14	7	14	1	2
Gutierrez	1.000	22	10	35	0	3
Johnson	.963	14	4	22	1	2
Spiers	.935	84	44	129	12	12

Shortstop	PCT	G	PO	A	E	DP
Bogar	.985	80	103	215	5	53
Gutierrez	.967	64	85	153	8	35
Listach	.951	31	26	71	5	12
Rivera	.875	6	6	8	2	4
Spiers	.932	28	25	57	6	12

Outfield	PCT	G	PO	A	E	DP
Abreu	.978	53	84	4	2	1
Bell	.967	125	226	5	8	2
Carr	.966	59	111	3	4	1
Gonzalez	.982	146	263	10	5	2
Hidalgo	1.000	19	28	0	0	0
Howard	1.000	62	107	5	0	1
Listach	.900	6	9	0	1	0
Montgomery	1.000	18	25	2	0	1
Mouton	1.000	61	86	1	0	1
Phillips	1.000	3	3	0	0	0
Ramos	.000	2	0	0	0	0

GEORGE GOJKOVICH

Darryl Kile

FARM SYSTEM

Director of Player Development: Jim Duquette

Class	Farm Team	League	W	L	Pct.	Finish*	Manager(s)	First Yr
AAA	New Orleans (La.) Zephyrs	American Assoc.	74	70	.514	5th (8)	Swisher/Galante	1997
AA	Jackson (Miss.) Generals	Texas	66	73	.475	5th (8)	Gary Allenson	1991
#A	Kissimmee (Fla.) Cobras	Florida State	71	66	.518	4th (14)	John Tamargo	1985
A	Quad City (Iowa) River Bandits	Midwest	59	75	.440	13th (14)	Manny Acta	1993
A	Auburn (N.Y.) Doubledays	New York-Penn	29	47	.382	13th (14)	Mike Rojas	1982
R	Kissimmee (Fla.) Astros	Gulf Coast	24	36	.400	13th (15)	Julio Linares	1977

*Finish in overall standings (No. of teams in league) #Advanced level

ORGANIZATION LEADERS

MAJOR LEAGUERS

BATTING

*AVG Bill Spiers .... .320
R Craig Biggio 146
H Craig Biggio 191
TB Jeff Bagwell 335
2B Jeff Bagwell 40
3B Craig Biggio 8
HR Jeff Bagwell 43
RBI Jeff Bagwell 135
BB Jeff Bagwell 127
SO Jeff Bagwell 122
SB Craig Biggio 47

PITCHING

W Darryl Kile 19
L Chris Holt 12
#ERA Darryl Kile 2.57
G Billy Wagner 62
CG Mike Hampton 7
SV Billy Wagner 23
IP Darryl Kile 256
BB Darryl Kile 94
SO Darryl Kile 205

Billy Wagner

ROBERT GURGANUS

Daryle Ward

MINOR LEAGUERS

BATTING

*AVG Daryle Ward, New Orleans/Jackson .. .334
R Julio Lugo, Kissimmee 89
H Daryle Ward, New Orleans/Jackson .. 156
TB Daryle Ward, New Orleans/Jackson .. 245
2B Richard Hidalgo, New Orleans 37
3B Julio Lugo, Kissimmee 14
HR Two tied at 21
RBI Daryle Ward, New Orleans/Jackson 97
BB Russ Johnson, New Orleans 66
SO Kevin Burns, Quad City 114
SB Julio Lugo, Kissimmee 35

PITCHING

W Wade Miller, Kissimmee/Quad City 15
L Jason Green, Kissimmee/Quad City 15
#ERA Wade Miller, Kissimmee/Quad City 2.38
G Oscar Henriquez, New Orleans 60
CG Wade Miller, Kissimmee/Quad City 6
SV Mike Diorio, Jackson/Kissimmee 20
IP Scott Elarton, New Orleans/Jackson .. 187
BB Gabe Garcia, Quad City 75
SO Scott Elarton, New Orleans/Jackson .. 191

*Minimum 250 At-Bats #Minimum 75 Innings

TOP 10 PROSPECTS

STEVE MOORE

Richard Hidalgo

How the Astros Top 10 prospects, as judged by Baseball America prior to the 1997 season, fared in 1997:

Player, Pos.	Club (Class)	AVG	AB	R	H	2B	3B	HR	RBI	SB
1. Richard Hidalgo, of	Houston	.306	62	8	19	5	0	2	6	1
	New Orleans (AAA)	.279	526	74	147	37	5	11	78	6
2. Carlos Guillen, ss	New Orleans (AAA)	.308	13	3	4	1	0	0	0	0
	Jackson (AA)	.254	390	47	99	16	1	10	39	6
3. Bob Abreu, of	Houston	.250	188	22	47	10	2	3	26	7
	New Orleans (AAA)	.268	194	25	52	9	4	2	22	7
	Jackson (AA)	.167	12	2	2	1	0	0	0	0
4. Russ Johnson, ss	Houston	.300	60	7	18	1	0	2	9	1
	New Orleans (AAA)	.276	445	72	123	16	6	4	49	7
7. Jhonny Perez, ss	Jackson (AA)	.253	154	16	39	7	0	3	17	4
	Kissimmee (A)	.264	273	40	72	16	5	3	22	8
9. Daryle Ward, 1b	New Orleans (AAA)	.378	45	4	17	1	0	2	7	0
	Jackson (AA)	.329	422	72	139	25	0	19	90	4

Player, Pos.	Club (Class)	W	L	ERA	G	SV	IP	H	BB	SO
5. Oscar Henriquez, rhp	Houston	0	1	4.50	4	0	4	2	3	3
	New Orleans (AAA)	4	5	2.80	60	12	74	65	27	80
6. Chris Holt, rhp	Houston	8	12	3.52	33	0	210	211	61	95
8. Scott Elarton, rhp	New Orleans (AAA)	4	4	5.33	9	0	54	51	17	50
	Jackson (AA)	7	4	3.24	20	0	133	103	47	141
10. Mark Johnson, rhp	Kissimmee (A)	8	9	3.07	26	0	155	150	39	127

NEW ORLEANS — Class AAA

AMERICAN ASSOCIATION

BATTING	AVG	G	AB	R	H	2B	3B	HR	RBI	BB	SO	SB	CS	B	T	HT	WT	DOB	1st Yr	Resides
Abreu, Bob	.268	47	194	25	52	9	4	2	22	21	49	7	4	L	R	6-0	160	3-11-74	1991	Turmero, Venez.
Bell, Derek	.154	5	13	0	2	0	0	0	1	1	1	1	0	R	R	6-2	200	12-11-68	1987	Tampa, Fla.
Berry, Sean	.333	3	9	1	3	0	0	0	0	3	3	0	0	R	R	5-11	210	3-22-66	1986	Rolling Hills Estates, Calif.
Bridges, Kary	.172	23	64	6	11	1	2	0	3	5	9	1	0	L	R	5-10	165	10-27-71	1993	Hattiesburg, Miss.
Carr, Chuck	.246	19	65	8	16	1	0	0	3	8	14	5	3	S	R	5-10	165	8-10-68	1986	Tucson, Ariz.
Christopherson, Eric	.190	9	21	3	4	0	0	0	0	4	7	0	0	R	R	6-1	190	4-25-69	1990	Westminster, Calif.
Colon, Dennis	.270	129	400	49	108	23	1	6	64	42	48	2	2	L	R	5-10	165	8-4-73	1991	Manati, P.R.
Flora, Kevin	.257	31	109	14	28	1	3	2	14	16	25	8	2	R	R	6-0	185	6-10-69	1987	Chandler, Ariz.
Grebeck, Brian	.126	68	103	15	13	1	0	0	8	21	17	1	0	R	R	5-7	160	8-31-67	1990	Cerritos, Calif.
Guillen, Carlos	.308	3	13	3	4	1	0	0	0	0	4	0	0	S	R	6-0	150	9-30-75	1993	Aragua, Venez.
Gutierrez, Ricky	.185	7	27	2	5	1	0	0	4	2	4	0	1	R	R	6-1	175	5-23-70	1988	Miami, Fla.
Haney, Todd	.282	115	454	63	128	25	0	2	63	43	50	5	2	R	R	5-9	165	7-30-65	1987	Waco, Texas
Hidalgo, Richard	.279	134	526	74	147	37	5	11	78	35	57	6	10	R	R	6-2	175	7-2-75	1991	Guarenas, Venez.
Johnson, Russ	.276	122	445	72	123	16	6	4	49	66	78	7	4	R	R	5-10	185	2-22-73	1994	Baton Rouge, La.
Knorr, Randy	.238	72	244	22	58	10	0	5	27	22	38	0	0	R	R	6-2	212	11-12-68	1986	Covina, Calif.
Maas, Kevin	.218	55	193	24	42	19	1	5	27	23	41	0	0	L	L	6-3	205	1-20-65	1986	Berkeley, Calif.
2-team (31 Indy)	.219	86	260	38	57	23	1	7	34	48	56	0	0							
McNabb, Buck	.158	11	19	2	3	0	1	0	0	1	6	0	0	L	R	6-0	180	1-17-73	1991	Fort Walton Beach, Fla.
Meluskey, Mitch	.250	51	172	22	43	7	0	3	21	25	38	0	0	S	R	6-0	185	9-18-73	1992	Yakima, Wash.
Montgomery, Ray	.288	20	73	17	21	5	0	6	13	11	15	1	1	R	R	6-3	195	8-8-69	1990	Bronxville, N.Y.
Mora, Melvin	.257	119	370	55	95	15	3	2	38	47	52	7	7	R	R	5-10	160	2-2-72	1991	Naquanqua, Venez.
Phillips, J.R.	.290	104	411	59	119	28	0	21	71	39	112	0	1	L	L	6-1	185	4-29-70	1988	Moreno Valley, Calif.
Probst, Alan	.223	46	112	8	25	6	0	2	10	9	27	0	0	R	R	6-4	205	10-24-70	1992	Avis, Pa.
Ramos, Ken	.289	92	253	32	73	9	1	0	22	45	15	2	7	L	L	6-1	185	6-8-67	1989	Pueblo, Colo.
Rivera, Luis	.238	124	382	46	91	23	4	3	45	34	51	5	4	R	R	5-10	172	1-3-64	1982	Cidra, P.R.
Robles, Oscar	.333	2	3	0	1	0	0	0	0	1	1	0	0	L	R	5-11	155	4-9-76	1994	San Diego, Calif.
Saylor, Jamie	.000	2	0	0	0	0	0	0	0	0	0	0	0	L	R	5-11	185	9-11-74	1993	Garland, Texas
Ward, Daryle	.375	14	48	4	18	1	0	2	8	7	7	0	0	L	L	6-2	230	6-27-75	1994	Riverside, Calif.

PITCHING	W	L	ERA	G	GS	CG	SV	IP	H	R	ER	BB	SO	B	T	HT	WT	DOB	1st Yr	Resides
Barrios, Manuel	4	8	3.27	57	0	0	0	83	70	32	30	34	77	R	R	6-0	145	9-21-74	1993	Cabecera, Panama
Cabrera, Jose	2	2	2.54	31	0	0	0	46	31	13	13	13	48	R	R	6-0	197	3-24-72	1991	Santiago, D.R.
2-team (5 Buffalo)	5	2	2.21	36	0	0	0	61	39	15	15	20	59							
Elarton, Scott	4	4	5.33	9	9	0	0	54	51	36	32	17	50	R	R	6-8	225	2-23-76	1994	Lamar, Colo.
Fernandez, Sid	0	1	4.32	2	2	0	0	8	7	4	4	3	7	L	L	6-1	220	10-12-62	1981	Honolulu, Hawaii
Gardiner, Mike	2	1	8.13	11	4	0	0	31	43	32	28	14	24	R	R	6-0	200	10-19-65	1987	Canton, Mass.
Greene, Tommy	5	3	3.38	13	13	0	0	75	59	30	28	25	75	R	R	6-5	225	4-6-67	1985	Richmond, Va.
Gutierrez, Jim	0	1	3.27	7	0	0	0	11	11	4	4	2	8	R	R	6-2	190	11-28-70	1989	Burlington, Wash.
Halama, John	13	3	2.58	26	24	1	0	171	150	57	49	32	126	L	L	6-5	195	2-22-72	1994	Brooklyn, N.Y.
Henriquez, Oscar	4	5	2.80	60	0	0	12	74	65	28	23	27	80	R	R	6-4	175	1-28-74	1991	La Guaira, Venez.
Hudek, John	0	0	0.44	19	0	0	7	21	3	1	1	3	26	S	R	6-1	200	8-8-66	1988	Tampa, Fla.
Magnante, Mike	2	3	4.50	17	0	0	1	24	31	14	12	5	23	L	L	6-1	190	6-17-65	1988	Burbank, Calif.
Manzanillo, Josias	0	0	4.40	11	0	0	0	14	17	7	7	6	11	R	R	6-0	190	10-16-67	1983	Hyde Park, Mass.
Miller, Trever	6	7	3.30	29	27	2	0	164	177	71	60	54	99	R	L	6-3	175	5-29-73	1991	Louisville, Ky.
Mimbs, Mark	1	2	4.36	22	3	0	1	33	36	19	16	9	26	L	L	6-2	180	2-13-69	1990	Macon, Ga.
Minor, Blas	3	3	2.27	23	0	0	6	32	20	8	8	9	27	R	R	6-3	200	3-20-66	1988	Gilbert, Ariz.
Mlicki, Doug	4	3	3.60	14	3	0	0	30	27	12	12	10	18	R	R	6-3	175	4-23-71	1992	Dublin, Ohio
Morman, Alvin	0	1	4.50	8	0	0	0	10	11	5	5	2	14	R	L	6-3	210	1-6-69	1991	Rockingham, N.C.
Mounce, Tony	0	0	1.93	1	1	0	0	5	2	1	1	6	6	L	L	6-2	185	2-8-75	1994	Kennewick, Wash.
Nitkowski, C.J.	8	10	3.98	28	28	1	0	174	183	82	77	56	141	L	L	6-2	185	3-9-73	1994	Milford, Pa.
Patrick, Bronswell	6	5	3.22	30	12	1	0	101	108	45	36	30	88	R	R	6-1	205	9-16-70	1988	Greenville, N.C.
Reynolds, Shane	1	0	0.00	1	1	0	0	5	3	0	0	1	6	R	R	6-3	210	3-26-68	1989	Houston, Texas
Small, Mark	1	1	5.79	7	0	0	0	9	11	9	6	3	7	R	R	6-3	205	11-12-67	1989	Seattle, Wash.
Wall, Donne	8	7	3.85	17	17	1	0	110	109	49	47	24	84	R	R	6-1	180	7-11-67	1989	Festus, Mo.

FIELDING

Catcher	PCT	G	PO	A	E	DP	PB
Christopherson	1.000	6	46	2	0	0	0
Knorr	.984	72	502	54	9	7	5
Meluskey	.989	49	323	26	4	6	4
Probst	.996	35	210	16	1	2	2

First Base	PCT	G	PO	A	E	DP
Colon	.990	97	806	71	9	58
Maas	.987	11	72	4	1	9
Phillips	.989	49	329	31	4	38
Ward	.976	9	75	6	2	9

Second Base	PCT	G	PO	A	E	DP
Bridges	.936	16	35	38	5	13
Grebeck	1.000	10	13	8	0	5
Haney	.990	115	213	259	5	64
Mora	1.000	9	17	19	0	5
Rivera	.800	1	1	3	1	0
Robles	1.000	1	0	2	0	0

Third Base	PCT	G	PO	A	E	DP
Berry	1.000	3	0	6	0	0
Grebeck	.941	13	3	29	2	1
Haney	1.000	1	0	1	0	0
Johnson	.932	106	60	230	21	17
Mora	.888	34	17	54	9	3
Rivera	.875	5	3	11	2	1
Saylor	.000	2	0	0	0	0

Shortstop	PCT	G	PO	A	E	DP
Grebeck	.947	22	22	49	4	9
Guillen	1.000	3	5	6	0	1
Gutierrez	.971	7	12	21	1	3
Johnson	1.000	18	26	39	0	8
Mora	.667	2	2	2	2	0
Rivera	.973	106	144	352	14	70

Outfield	PCT	G	PO	A	E	DP
Abreu	.990	47	99	4	1	0
Bell	1.000	5	10	0	0	0
Carr	1.000	18	35	1	0	0
Flora	1.000	28	45	2	0	0
Hidalgo	.968	127	261	15	9	3
Maas	1.000	16	17	0	0	0
McNabb	1.000	2	4	0	0	0
Montgomery	.971	13	33	0	1	0
Mora	1.000	80	125	5	0	1
Phillips	.967	63	82	5	3	0
Ramos	.993	79	129	4	1	0

JACKSON — Class AA

TEXAS LEAGUE

BATTING	AVG	G	AB	R	H	2B	3B	HR	RBI	BB	SO	SB	CS	B	T	HT	WT	DOB	1st Yr	Resides
Abreu, Bob	.167	3	12	2	2	1	0	0	0	1	5	0	0	L	R	6-0	160	3-11-74	1991	Turmero, Venez.
Flora, Kevin	.000	1	5	0	0	0	0	0	0	0	3	0	0	R	R	6-0	185	6-10-69	1987	Chandler, Ariz.
Forkner, Tim	.261	116	398	52	104	23	1	7	46	60	68	4	0	L	R	5-11	180	3-28-73	1993	Greeley, Colo.
Gonzalez, Jimmy	.254	97	342	49	87	18	0	14	58	37	91	2	1	R	R	6-3	210	3-8-73	1991	Hartford, Conn.

BATTING	AVG	G	AB	R	H	2B	3B	HR	RBI	BB	SO	SB	CS	B	T	HT	WT	DOB	1st Yr	Resides
Guillen, Carlos	.254	115	390	47	99	16	1	10	39	38	78	6	5	S	R	6-0	150	9-30-75	1993	Aragua, Venez.
Hernandez, Carlos	.292	92	363	62	106	12	1	4	33	33	59	17	8	R	R	5-9	160	12-12-75	1993	Caracas, Venez.
Lopez, Pedro	.295	27	88	9	26	5	0	2	13	4	16	0	1	R	R	6-0	160	3-29-69	1988	Vega Baja, P.R.
Martin, James	.274	39	117	15	32	4	1	7	22	16	42	8	4	L	R	6-1	210	12-10-70	1992	Eufaula, Okla.
McNabb, Buck	.258	112	395	65	102	16	2	1	30	42	58	10	9	L	R	6-0	180	1-17-73	1991	Fort Walton Beach, Fla.
Meluskey, Mitch	.340	73	241	49	82	18	0	14	46	31	39	1	3	S	R	6-0	185	9-18-73	1992	Yakima, Wash.
Miller, Ryan	.200	20	55	6	11	0	2	1	8	5	10	1	0	R	R	6-0	175	10-22-72	1994	Tulare, Calif.
Mitchell, Donovan	.256	128	477	64	122	17	6	5	44	61	48	22	11	L	R	5-9	175	11-27-69	1992	White Plains, N.Y.
Perez, Jhonny	.253	48	154	16	39	7	0	3	17	12	26	4	3	R	R	5-10	150	10-23-76	1994	Santo Domingo, D.R.
Peterson, Nate	.301	49	143	19	43	11	0	4	24	17	21	2	2	L	R	6-2	185	7-12-71	1993	Melbourne, Australia
Probst, Alan	.333	8	24	2	8	2	0	1	7	3	7	0	0	R	R	6-4	205	10-24-70	1992	Avis, Pa.
Robinson, Hassan	.174	9	23	3	4	1	0	0	1	0	2	0	0	R	R	6-3	180	9-22-72	1994	Queens, N.Y.
Rodriguez, Noel	.235	33	85	12	20	3	0	4	17	11	18	0	2	R	R	6-3	180	12-5-73	1991	Yabucoa, P.R.
Sanchez, Victor	.211	69	175	22	37	4	0	8	35	23	42	1	2	R	R	5-11	175	12-20-71	1994	Stockton, Calif.
Saylor, Jamie	.254	63	205	24	52	12	3	5	21	19	43	3	2	L	R	5-11	185	9-11-74	1993	Garland, Texas
Trammell, Gary	.264	110	314	38	83	10	1	2	28	24	53	0	4	L	R	6-0	180	10-16-72	1993	Garland, Texas
Ward, Daryle	.329	114	422	72	139	25	0	19	90	46	68	4	2	L	L	6-2	230	6-27-75	1994	Riverside, Calif.

PITCHING	W	L	ERA	G	GS	CG	SV	IP	H	R	ER	BB	SO	B	T	HT	WT	DOB	1st Yr	Resides
Blanco, Alberto	1	0	2.57	1	1	0	0	7	5	2	2	3	4	L	L	6-1	170	6-27-76	1993	Miranda, Venez.
Creek, Ryan	10	5	4.11	19	19	0	0	105	95	57	48	74	88	R	R	6-1	180	9-24-72	1993	Martinsburg, W.Va.
DeClue, Jon	0	2	12.96	9	0	0	0	8	13	13	12	11	7	R	L	6-2	198	9-17-70	1994	Apopka, Fla.
Diorio, Mike	1	3	9.53	8	0	0	1	11	18	17	12	6	9	R	R	6-1	170	3-1-73	1993	Pueblo, Colo.
Elarton, Scott	7	4	3.24	20	20	2	0	133	103	57	48	47	141	R	R	6-8	225	2-23-76	1994	Lamar, Colo.
Grzanich, Mike	7	6	4.96	38	13	0	12	102	114	68	56	46	73	R	R	6-1	180	8-24-72	1992	Champaign, Ill.
Gutierrez, Jim	4	4	2.93	52	3	0	5	89	96	33	29	23	51	R	R	6-2	190	11-28-70	1989	Burlington, Wash.
Haas, David	1	1	5.03	13	0	0	0	20	23	14	11	4	5	R	R	6-1	200	10-19-65	1988	Wichita, Kansas
Humphrey, Rich	0	1	32.40	3	0	0	0	2	7	9	6	3	0	R	R	6-1	185	6-24-71	1993	Lakeland, Fla.
Kester, Tim	4	6	5.23	47	4	0	2	83	107	53	48	26	50	R	R	6-4	185	12-1-71	1993	Coral Springs, Fla.
Lock, Dan	2	2	6.15	35	0	0	0	34	43	29	23	17	20	R	L	6-5	210	3-27-73	1994	Brighton, Mich.
Lopez, Johann	6	8	4.38	35	19	0	1	134	131	79	65	57	109	R	R	6-2	170	4-4-75	1992	Agua Negra, Venez.
Mlicki, Doug	4	4	5.36	9	9	0	0	49	69	36	29	20	35	R	R	6-3	175	4-23-71	1992	Dublin, Ohio
Mounce, Tony	8	9	5.03	25	25	1	0	145	165	91	81	66	116	L	L	6-2	185	2-8-75	1994	Kennewick, Wash.
O'Malley, Paul	0	2	6.45	28	0	0	0	45	53	32	32	21	25	R	R	6-3	180	12-20-72	1994	Skokie, Ill.
Peterson, Mark	0	0	5.40	6	0	0	0	5	7	3	3	2	6	L	L	5-11	195	11-27-70	1992	Kirkland, Wash.
Ramos, Edgar	0	2	4.82	4	3	0	0	19	24	12	10	7	12	R	R	6-4	170	3-6-75	1992	Cumana, Venez.
Rumer, Tim	1	2	3.63	7	6	0	0	35	32	21	14	10	31	L	L	6-3	205	8-8-69	1990	Princeton, N.J.
Sikorski, Brian	5	5	4.63	17	17	0	0	93	91	55	48	31	74	R	R	6-1	190	7-27-74	1995	Roseville, Mich.
Small, Mark	3	4	3.14	37	0	0	9	43	46	20	15	19	40	R	R	6-3	205	11-12-67	1989	Seattle, Wash.
Springer, Russ	0	0	9.00	1	0	0	0	1	2	1	1	0	2	R	R	6-4	195	11-7-68	1989	Pollack, La.
Walter, Mike	2	3	3.63	34	0	0	7	45	38	20	18	30	41	R	R	6-1	190	10-23-74	1993	San Diego, Calif.

FIELDING

Catcher	PCT	G	PO	A	E	DP	PB
Gonzalez	.974	71	471	53	14	4	4
Lopez	.985	9	61	6	1	0	1
Meluskey	.985	54	356	43	6	5	4
Probst	1.000	7	36	11	0	2	0
Sanchez	.979	9	40	7	1	0	2

First Base	PCT	G	PO	A	E	DP
Forkner	1.000	4	15	2	0	3
Gonzalez	.965	12	75	7	3	6
Lopez	.992	16	120	4	1	15
Sanchez	1.000	10	61	2	0	6
Ward	.988	108	951	76	12	84

Second Base	PCT	G	PO	A	E	DP
Forkner	.000	1	0	0	0	0
Hernandez	.983	91	187	269	8	56
Miller	.988	18	34	48	1	10
Mitchell	.971	9	15	19	1	4
Perez	1.000	2	3	7	0	3
Saylor	.956	26	50	58	5	11

Third Base	PCT	G	PO	A	E	DP
Forkner	.906	110	56	195	26	16
Lopez	.000	1	0	0	0	0
Mitchell	1.000	2	1	1	0	0
Perez	.941	8	4	12	1	1
Sanchez	.867	12	6	20	4	1
Saylor	.902	20	7	48	6	2

Shortstop	PCT	G	PO	A	E	DP
Guillen	.932	109	169	313	35	68
Mitchell	.907	10	17	32	5	4
Perez	.904	11	13	34	5	8
Saylor	.909	15	18	42	6	9

Outfield	PCT	G	PO	A	E	DP
Abreu	1.000	3	1	0	0	0
Flora	1.000	1	2	0	0	0
Martin	.979	25	42	4	1	1
McNabb	.957	106	211	12	10	2
Mitchell	.973	109	205	9	6	0
Perez	.970	25	31	1	1	0
Peterson	.986	42	70	3	1	1
Robinson	1.000	7	9	0	0	0
Rodriguez	1.000	19	26	2	0	0
Sanchez	.971	21	33	0	1	0
Saylor	1.000	5	3	0	0	0
Trammell	.946	98	134	6	8	0

KISSIMMEE — Class A

FLORIDA STATE LEAGUE

BATTING	AVG	G	AB	R	H	2B	3B	HR	RBI	BB	SO	SB	CS	B	T	HT	WT	DOB	1st Yr	Resides
Adams, Jason	.211	31	95	9	20	6	0	0	9	11	13	0	0	R	R	6-1	180	6-22-73	1995	Rose Hill, Kan.
Alexander, Chad	.271	129	469	67	127	31	6	4	46	56	91	11	8	R	R	6-0	190	5-22-74	1995	Lufkin, Texas
Amezcua, Adan	.400	9	20	3	8	3	0	0	5	3	3	0	0	R	R	6-1	180	3-9-74	1993	Mazatlan, Mexico
Berkman, Lance	.293	53	184	31	54	10	0	12	35	37	38	2	1	S	L	6-1	205	2-10-76	1997	New Braunfels, Texas
Bovender, Andy	.215	52	177	16	38	8	1	3	16	16	56	3	0	R	R	6-3	190	4-10-73	1995	Charlotte, N.C.
Bowers, R.J.	.206	10	34	3	7	1	0	0	3	5	7	0	0	R	R	6-1	210	2-10-74	1992	West Middlesex, Pa.
Castro, Ramon	.280	115	410	53	115	22	1	8	65	53	73	1	0	R	R	6-3	195	3-1-76	1994	Vega Baja, P.R.
Chapman, Scott	.286	2	7	1	2	0	0	0	0	0	3	0	0	R	R	6-3	205	1-30-78	1995	Albany, Ohio
Coe, Ryan	.217	52	161	21	35	6	0	3	19	14	36	0	1	R	R	5-10	200	1-16-73	1995	East Ridge, Tenn.
Dallimore, Brian	.000	1	3	0	0	0	0	0	0	0	2	0	0	R	R	6-1	185	11-15-73	1996	Las Vegas, Nev.
Deshazer, Jeremy	.200	2	5	2	1	0	0	0	0	2	2	0	0	S	R	5-10	175	8-18-76	1995	Kirkland, Wash.
Duffy, James	.146	19	41	1	6	1	0	0	4	4	9	0	2	R	R	6-2	195	7-18-74	1997	Andover, N.J.
Escalona, Felix	.222	3	9	6	2	0	0	0	0	1	2	0	0	R	R	6-0	170	3-12-79	1996	Puerto Cabello, Venez.
Gonzalez, Jimmy	.341	12	44	7	15	6	2	2	6	1	9	0	0	R	R	6-3	210	3-8-73	1991	Hartford, Conn.
Johnson, Ric	.280	121	453	47	127	11	4	1	40	21	67	21	8	R	R	6-2	185	3-18-74	1995	Chicago, Ill.
Lopez, Pedro	.203	25	69	7	14	4	1	0	8	4	11	0	1	R	R	6-0	160	3-29-69	1988	Vega Baja, P.R.
Lugo, Julio	.267	125	505	89	135	22	14	7	61	46	99	35	8	R	R	5-11	155	11-16-75	1995	Brooklyn, N.Y.
Mansavage, Jay	.273	9	33	4	9	0	1	1	1	2	6	2	0	S	R	6-1	185	7-11-75	1996	Riverwoods, Ill.
Mendez, Donaldo	.188	5	16	0	3	0	0	0	0	1	4	1	1	R	R	6-1	155	6-7-78	1996	Barquisimeto, Venez.
Miller, Ryan	.265	13	34	5	9	0	0	0	1	5	3	1	0	R	R	6-0	175	10-22-72	1994	Tulare, Calif.
2-team (61 St. Lucie)	.256	74	227	32	58	12	1	2	29	16	41	6	5							

BATTING	AVG	G	AB	R	H	2B	3B	HR	RBI	BB	SO	SB	CS	B	T	HT	WT	DOB	1st Yr	Resides
Owens, Billy	.283	96	381	51	108	18	2	10	60	18	68	4	2	S	R	6-1	210	4-12-71	1992	Fresno, Calif.
Perez, Jhonny	.264	69	273	40	72	16	5	3	22	12	38	8	6	R	R	5-10	150	10-23-76	1994	Santo Domingo, D.R.
Robinson, Hassan	.252	35	115	12	29	4	0	0	12	3	14	3	3	R	R	6-3	180	9-22-72	1994	Queens, N.Y.
Robles, Oscar	.225	66	236	39	53	4	0	0	21	43	28	0	1	L	R	5-11	155	4-9-76	1994	San Diego, Calif.
Rodriguez, Noel	.316	65	228	26	72	15	1	4	36	23	24	1	5	R	R	6-3	180	12-5-73	1991	Yabucoa, P.R.
Ross, Tony	.256	74	215	30	55	6	3	1	19	18	40	11	7	R	R	5-11	175	5-11-75	1992	Kansas City, Mo.
Samboy, Nelson	.316	48	190	20	60	9	2	1	13	7	34	9	6	R	R	5-10	155	9-4-76	1994	Pedernales, D.R.
Truby, Chris	.246	57	199	23	49	11	0	2	29	8	40	8	3	R	R	6-2	185	12-9-73	1993	Mukilteo, Wash.
Wheeler, Mike	.417	8	12	2	5	0	0	0	2	1	3	1	0	R	R	6-1	180	10-25-77	1996	Cincinnati, Ohio

GAMES BY POSITION: C—Amezcua 7, Castro 104, Chapman 2, Coe 9, Gonzalez 5, Lopez 24. **1B**—Bovender 4, Coe 27, Duffy 17, Gonzalez 8, Owens 84, Rodriguez 9, Ross 1, Truby 5. **2B**—Adams 4, Dallimore 1, Escalona 3, Lugo 9, Mansavage 4, Miller 6, Perez 4, Robles 65, Samboy 48, Truby 1. **3B**—Adams 23, Alexander 1, Bovender 48, Coe 6, Lugo 1, Mansavage 4, Miller 7, Truby 54, Wheeler 5. **SS**—Adams 6, Lugo 114, Mendez 5, Miller 1, Perez 12, Truby 2. **OF**—Alexander 128, Berkman 44, Bowers 10, Deshazer 2, Duffy 2, Johnson 121, Perez 6, Robinson 32, Rodriguez 14, Ross 60.

PITCHING	W	L	ERA	G	GS	CG	SV	IP	H	R	ER	BB	SO	B	T	HT	WT	DOB	1st Yr	Resides
Barksdale, Shane	0	0	0.00	3	0	0	0	5	5	2	0	2	3	L	R	6-4	195	9-6-76	1994	Gallant, Ala.
Blanco, Alberto	7	4	2.83	19	19	1	0	114	83	45	36	45	95	L	L	6-1	170	6-27-76	1993	Miranda, Venez.
DeClue, Jon	2	0	1.80	7	0	0	0	15	10	4	3	9	13	R	L	6-2	198	9-17-70	1994	Apopka, Fla.
Diorio, Mike	3	2	2.97	36	0	0	19	39	33	15	13	10	30	R	R	6-1	170	3-1-73	1993	Pueblo, Colo.
Garcia, Freddy	10	8	2.56	27	27	5	0	179	165	63	51	49	131	R	R	6-3	180	10-6-76	1994	Miranda, Venez.
Green, Jason	0	3	5.19	8	0	0	0	9	11	12	5	10	3	R	R	6-4	190	6-5-75	1994	Port Hope, Ontario
Hale, Chad	2	4	4.82	46	0	0	7	52	56	30	28	11	46	R	L	6-6	245	8-3-71	1994	Thornville, Ohio
Hall, Billy	0	0	3.86	6	0	0	0	7	7	5	3	5	5	R	R	6-0	200	9-4-73	1994	Mannford, Okla.
Johnson, Mark	8	9	3.07	26	26	3	0	155	150	67	53	39	127	R	R	6-3	215	5-2-75	1996	Houston, Texas
Lock, Dan	0	2	2.67	17	0	0	1	27	28	17	8	11	23	R	L	6-5	210	3-27-73	1994	Brighton, Mich.
Loiz, Niuman	1	1	3.82	11	3	1	0	33	37	19	14	8	19	R	R	6-4	170	12-12-73	1991	Caracas, Venez.
Miller, Wade	10	2	1.80	14	14	4	0	100	79	28	20	14	76	R	R	6-2	185	9-13-76	1996	Topton, Pa.
Mlicki, Doug	0	0	0.00	1	1	0	0	4	4	0	0	0	2	R	R	6-3	175	4-23-71	1992	Dublin, Ohio
O'Malley, Paul	2	2	2.80	24	0	0	5	35	24	12	11	19	20	R	R	6-3	180	12-20-72	1994	Skokie, Ill.
Root, Derek	4	14	4.19	26	22	2	0	129	131	76	60	42	68	L	L	6-5	190	5-26-75	1993	Lakewood, Ohio
Sikorski, Brian	8	2	3.06	11	11	0	0	68	64	29	23	16	46	R	R	6-1	190	7-27-74	1995	Roseville, Mich.
Smith, Eric	2	2	4.41	32	6	0	1	80	84	44	39	29	59	R	R	6-0	185	5-17-74	1995	Garden City, Kan.
Stachler, Eric	4	4	4.13	48	0	0	4	65	76	38	30	21	43	R	R	6-3	215	4-18-73	1995	Coldwater, Ohio
Steinmetz, Earl	0	0	12.00	4	0	0	0	6	8	8	8	3	4	R	R	6-3	175	5-17-71	1989	San Antonio, Texas
Tucker, Julien	8	7	5.22	33	8	0	0	69	79	48	40	42	49	L	R	6-7	200	4-19-73	1993	Chateauguay, Quebec

QUAD CITY — Class A

MIDWEST LEAGUE

BATTING	AVG	G	AB	R	H	2B	3B	HR	RBI	BB	SO	SB	CS	B	T	HT	WT	DOB	1st Yr	Resides
Alleyne, Roberto	.260	63	215	24	56	10	0	5	30	12	55	1	3	R	R	6-4	195	5-15-77	1994	Panama City, Panama
Barr, Tucker	.207	93	309	42	64	10	1	10	36	39	91	0	2	R	R	6-1	205	5-26-75	1996	Atlanta, Ga.
Bovender, Andy	.218	15	55	10	12	3	0	1	8	2	15	1	0	R	R	6-3	190	4-10-73	1995	Charlotte, N.C.
Burns, Kevin	.270	131	477	72	129	28	1	20	86	53	114	1	2	L	L	6-5	210	9-9-75	1995	El Dorado, Ark.
Chavera, Arnie	.262	80	263	35	69	14	1	14	44	36	69	2	0	L	R	5-10	195	9-24-73	1996	Arlington, Texas
Dallimore, Brian	.260	130	492	80	128	23	3	6	48	38	76	24	8	R	R	6-1	185	11-15-73	1996	Las Vegas, Nev.
Duffy, James	.250	12	44	4	11	3	0	0	7	3	9	0	0	R	R	6-2	195	7-18-74	1997	Andover, N.J.
Farraez, Jesus	.219	80	228	30	50	6	1	5	24	19	61	9	8	R	R	6-1	180	10-18-72	1994	La Virginia, Venez.
Hyers, Matt	.248	81	270	32	67	8	3	0	18	25	46	7	6	L	R	5-11	170	8-8-75	1996	Covington, Ga.
Mejia, Marlon	.241	21	54	4	13	1	0	0	2	3	7	0	0	R	R	6-1	175	11-17-74	1995	Jersey City, N.J.
Miles, Aaron	.262	97	370	55	97	13	2	1	35	30	45	18	11	S	R	5-9	160	12-15-76	1995	Antioch, Calif.
Pratt, Wes	.257	124	435	65	112	26	0	12	51	35	56	10	5	R	R	6-3	180	3-5-73	1994	North East, Md.
Reeder, Jim	.244	92	312	35	76	12	2	2	21	20	29	2	4	L	R	6-1	200	3-18-75	1996	Evanston, Ill.
Roche, Marlon	.219	72	233	30	51	5	1	3	36	21	57	7	3	R	R	6-1	172	4-11-75	1992	Caracas, Venez.
Rose, Mike	.256	79	234	22	60	6	1	3	27	28	62	3	1	S	R	6-1	190	8-25-76	1995	Elk Grove, Calif.
Samboy, Nelson	.353	14	51	2	18	3	0	0	8	2	8	1	1	R	R	5-10	155	9-4-76	1994	Pedernales, D.R.
Saylor, Jamie	.246	20	61	10	15	5	0	0	2	11	16	3	2	L	R	5-11	185	9-11-74	1993	Garland, Texas
Truby, Chris	.280	68	268	34	75	14	1	7	46	22	32	13	4	R	R	6-2	185	12-9-73	1993	Mukilteo, Wash.

GAMES BY POSITION: C—Barr 66, Rose 71. **1B**—Alleyne 1, Burns 129, Chavera 5, Duffy 1, Mejia 1. **2B**—Dallimore 24, Hyers 23, Mejia 3, Miles 82, Samboy 9. **3B**—Bovender 14, Dallimore 35, Mejia 17, Samboy 4, Saylor 1, Truby 67. **SS**—Dallimore 68, Hyers 52, Saylor 19. **OF**—Alleyne 59, Chavera 23, Duffy 5, Farraez 79, Pratt 118, Reeder 81, Roche 68.

PITCHING	W	L	ERA	G	GS	CG	SV	IP	H	R	ER	BB	SO	B	T	HT	WT	DOB	1st Yr	Resides
Barksdale, Shane	0	0	7.30	8	0	0	1	12	22	12	10	5	8	L	R	6-4	195	9-6-76	1994	Gallant, Ala.
Braswell, Bryan	6	6	3.79	19	19	1	0	116	107	70	49	32	118	L	L	6-1	195	6-30-75	1996	Springboro, Ohio
Duncan, Sean	6	0	2.89	34	0	0	3	47	39	19	15	15	46	L	L	6-2	195	6-9-73	1994	Arlington, Texas
Garcia, Gabe	5	14	4.40	26	25	2	0	149	153	86	73	75	112	R	R	6-2	200	3-15-77	1996	Union City, Calif.
Green, Jason	7	12	4.58	23	22	1	0	126	126	79	64	53	96	R	R	6-4	190	6-5-75	1994	Port Hope, Ontario
Hecht, Brian	0	0	2.16	5	0	0	1	8	4	3	2	2	5	R	R	6-4	205	7-28-75	1997	Arlington Heights, Ill.
Loiz, Niuman	2	5	4.87	18	9	0	0	65	63	37	35	29	49	R	R	6-4	170	12-12-73	1991	Caracas, Venez.
Lynch, Jim	3	3	4.63	37	0	0	1	58	44	37	30	46	68	R	R	6-4	195	12-12-75	1994	Evansville, Ind.
Maldonado, Esteban	4	4	3.54	39	4	0	9	69	51	38	27	32	56	R	R	6-4	210	8-3-75	1996	Carolina, P.R.
McCarter, Jason	1	0	4.82	5	0	0	0	9	10	7	5	9	7	R	R	6-3	196	9-26-76	1995	Watsonville, Calif.
McFerrin, Chris	1	3	5.79	37	0	0	3	56	55	42	36	49	47	L	R	6-5	175	6-30-76	1995	Fresno, Calif.
McKnight, Tony	4	9	4.68	20	20	0	0	115	116	71	60	55	92	L	R	6-5	205	6-29-77	1995	Texarkana, Ark.
Miller, Wade	5	3	3.36	10	8	2	0	59	45	27	22	10	50	R	R	6-2	185	9-13-76	1996	Topton, Pa.
Rijo, Jose	3	6	4.40	35	0	0	2	59	63	43	29	27	41	R	R	6-1	150	5-4-76	1993	La Romana, D.R.
Robertson, Jeromie	11	8	4.07	26	25	2	1	146	151	86	66	56	135	L	L	6-1	178	3-30-77	1996	Exeter, Calif.
Yanez, Luis	1	2	4.81	27	2	0	7	39	46	25	21	14	33	R	R	6-2	187	12-1-77	1995	Anzoategui, Venez.

AUBURN — Short-Season Class A

NEW YORK-PENN LEAGUE

BATTING	AVG	G	AB	R	H	2B	3B	HR	RBI	BB	SO	SB	CS	B	T	HT	WT	DOB	1st Yr	Resides
Cathey, Joe	.268	70	269	36	72	7	3	0	13	30	56	13	6	S	R	5-11	175	3-2-76	1997	Spring, Texas

BATTING	AVG	G	AB	R	H	2B	3B	HR	RBI	BB	SO	SB	CS	B	T	HT	WT	DOB	1st Yr	Resides
Chapman, Scott	.327	53	205	32	67	11	0	6	39	6	23	1	2	R	R	6-3	205	1-30-78	1995	Albany, Ohio
Cole, Eric	.275	71	222	29	61	20	3	8	34	19	46	4	4	R	R	6-1	180	11-15-75	1995	Lancaster, Calif.
Cutshall, Pat	.297	76	273	54	81	23	1	8	34	31	23	5	6	R	R	5-9	175	10-29-74	1997	Beaver Falls, Pa.
Duffy, James	.276	48	185	28	51	9	1	9	25	14	47	4	4	R	R	6-2	195	7-18-74	1997	Andover, N.J.
Dunn, Ryan	.183	60	142	16	26	9	2	2	15	26	58	2	1	L	R	6-2	195	7-4-76	1997	Arlington, Texas
Lawler, Scott	.236	39	106	16	25	3	0	3	10	9	35	2	0	R	R	6-4	220	10-25-74	1997	Norristown, Pa.
Logan, Kyle	.292	71	260	27	76	16	4	0	29	20	60	5	10	L	R	5-11	195	7-11-75	1997	Hattiesburg, Miss.
Mansavage, Jay	.325	10	40	7	13	3	1	0	2	5	2	1	1	S	R	6-1	185	7-11-75	1996	Riverwoods, Ill.
McNeal, Aaron	.250	12	40	5	10	3	0	0	3	4	10	1	0	R	R	6-3	220	4-28-78	1996	Castro Valley, Calif.
Mejia, Marlon	.304	9	23	5	7	1	0	0	2	2	5	1	1	R	R	6-1	175	11-17-74	1995	Jersey City, N.J.
Murray, Doug	.165	34	79	4	13	1	0	0	5	8	18	0	1	L	R	6-3	215	10-9-74	1996	Orland Park, Ill.
Robinson, Joe	.227	39	75	6	17	1	1	0	3	4	30	1	2	R	R	5-10	170	4-13-75	1997	Burlington, Iowa
Terry, Tony	.178	53	157	14	28	0	1	2	17	11	56	3	4	S	R	6-1	185	8-2-75	1994	Abbeville, S.C.
Thomas, J.J.	.265	66	211	29	56	15	0	3	31	30	72	4	6	R	R	6-4	215	9-18-75	1997	Marietta, Ga.
Wesson, Barry	.260	58	208	24	54	7	3	3	26	10	45	8	4	R	R	6-2	195	4-6-77	1995	Glen Allan, Miss.

GAMES BY POSITION: C—Chapman 51, Lawler 2, Murray 33. **1B**—Cole 2, Duffy 31, Lawler 2, McNeal 10, Thomas 41. **2B**—Cathey 12, Cutshall 34, Mansavage 10, Mejia 5, Robinson 32. **3B**—Cole 57, Cutshall 27, Duffy 1, Mejia 1. **SS**—Cathey 59, Cutshall 20, Robinson 1. **OF**—Duffy 24, Dunn 49, Logan 68, Murray 1, Terry 47, Thomas 5, Wesson 57.

PITCHING	W	L	ERA	G	GS	CG	SV	IP	H	R	ER	BB	SO	B	T	HT	WT	DOB	1st Yr	Resides
Barksdale, Shane	3	3	5.55	22	1	0	0	36	49	28	22	12	22	L	R	6-4	195	9-6-76	1994	Gallant, Ala.
Hecht, Brian	2	2	1.69	26	0	0	11	37	35	10	7	8	35	R	R	6-4	205	7-28-75	1997	Arlington Heights, Ill.
Huber, John	0	4	6.50	4	4	1	0	18	27	20	13	5	5	R	R	6-3	200	4-18-78	1996	West Chester, Ohio
Ireland, Eric	5	7	3.70	16	16	2	0	107	111	55	44	21	78	R	R	6-1	165	3-11-77	1996	Long Beach, Calif.
Love, Farley	0	0	0.00	3	0	0	1	3	1	0	0	1	2	R	R	6-6	200	4-21-73	1993	Eight Mile, Ala.
McCarter, Jason	0	0	3.74	16	0	0	0	22	23	12	9	17	20	R	R	6-3	196	9-26-76	1995	Watsonville, Calif.
Medina, Tomas	0	0	8.46	15	0	0	0	22	33	24	21	21	19	R	R	6-2	165	4-12-75	1994	Lara, Venez.
Mercedes, Carlos	2	4	4.47	28	1	0	2	44	47	26	22	19	43	R	R	6-0	175	3-29-76	1994	El Seibo, D.R.
Messman, Joe	1	2	3.21	25	0	0	1	28	26	13	10	21	31	R	R	6-2	175	7-29-75	1997	Parkdale, Ore.
Oswalt, Roy	2	4	4.53	9	9	1	0	52	50	29	26	15	44	R	R	6-0	170	8-29-77	1997	Weir, Miss.
Pascarella, Josh	0	0	3.00	1	1	0	0	6	8	5	2	1	2	R	R	6-0	175	11-11-76	1996	San Diego, Calif.
Santana, Johan	0	0	2.25	1	1	0	0	4	1	1	1	6	5	L	L	6-0	155	3-13-79	1996	Tovar, Venez.
Shearn, Tom	4	6	3.50	14	14	2	0	82	79	42	32	26	59	R	R	6-5	200	8-28-77	1996	Columbus, Ohio
Thomas, Don	6	4	4.53	15	15	1	0	87	93	50	44	21	72	L	L	6-2	175	12-20-75	1997	Hephzibah, Ga.
Wallace, Jim	3	8	7.13	14	14	0	0	66	98	64	52	37	47	R	R	6-4	195	10-13-75	1997	Wantagh, N.Y.
Whiteman, Trevor	1	3	4.21	30	0	0	0	36	36	26	17	18	50	L	L	6-2	195	1-28-73	1997	Rancho Cucamonga, Calif.

KISSIMMEE — Rookie

GULF COAST LEAGUE

BATTING	AVG	G	AB	R	H	2B	3B	HR	RBI	BB	SO	SB	CS	B	T	HT	WT	DOB	1st Yr	Resides
Alfaro, Jason	.265	34	102	8	27	5	0	2	13	8	14	6	0	R	R	5-10	189	11-29-77	1997	Fort Worth, Texas
Alleyne, Roberto	.385	3	13	1	5	1	1	0	3	1	0	3	0	R	R	6-4	195	5-15-77	1994	Panama City, Panama
Byrd, Brandon	.192	45	146	12	28	5	0	5	18	14	49	2	2	R	R	6-5	225	5-22-78	1996	Montgomery, Ala.
Bystrowski, Rob	.226	51	177	28	40	8	0	3	22	22	47	5	6	R	R	6-1	210	9-27-76	1997	Fair Oaks, Calif.
Colson, Julian	.100	7	10	1	1	1	0	0	0	1	4	0	0	R	R	5-11	190	5-24-77	1996	Lutz, Fla.
Cook, Josh	.222	4	9	0	2	1	0	0	1	1	3	0	0	R	R	6-0	215	9-30-75	1997	Plainville, Ill.
De la Espada, Miguel	.204	49	162	20	33	7	0	3	14	9	45	8	2	R	R	6-4	204	7-8-76	1994	Colon, Panama
Deshazer, Jeremy	.250	46	164	23	41	11	2	1	18	11	23	3	4	S	R	5-10	175	8-18-76	1995	Kirkland, Wash.
Escalona, Felix	.206	51	189	27	39	9	0	1	9	20	49	11	3	R	R	6-0	170	3-12-79	1996	Puerto Cabello, Venez.
Fatheree, Danny	.237	21	38	4	9	1	0	0	3	3	0	0	1	R	R	5-11	232	8-25-78	1997	Grand Prairie, Texas
Flora, Kevin	.200	3	10	1	2	0	0	0	0	0	1	0	0	R	R	6-0	185	6-10-69	1987	Chandler, Ariz.
Hahn, Camron	.194	31	72	8	14	2	0	1	7	7	22	1	1	R	R	6-2	200	12-20-78	1997	Louisville, Ky.
Hill, Jason	.208	8	24	7	5	0	0	0	5	5	5	3	0	R	R	5-11	205	2-25-75	1996	Rimforest, Calif.
Lawler, Scott	.500	1	4	2	2	1	0	0	2	1	0	0	0	R	R	6-4	220	10-25-74	1997	Norristown, Pa.
McNeal, Aaron	.293	46	164	22	48	12	0	3	26	11	28	0	5	R	R	6-3	220	4-28-78	1996	Castro Valley, Calif.
Mendez, Donaldo	.193	48	150	16	29	4	0	1	13	13	32	9	6	R	R	6-1	155	6-7-78	1996	Barquisimeto, Venez.
Nicley, Dru	.119	26	59	5	7	0	0	0	3	4	30	0	0	R	R	6-3	195	6-29-78	1996	Burley, Idaho
Ochoa, Javier	.198	30	81	7	16	2	1	0	14	7	13	1	1	R	R	5-11	160	1-8-79	1996	Maracay, Venez.
Samboy, Nelson	.400	2	5	1	2	0	0	0	1	1	0	0	0	R	R	5-10	155	9-4-76	1994	Pedernales, D.R.
Vasquez, Alejandro	.269	53	186	30	50	9	1	2	20	18	23	8	3	L	L	5-11	175	7-5-77	1995	San Pedro de Macoris, D.R.
Wheeler, Mike	.208	41	130	13	27	4	1	1	6	8	41	5	3	R	R	6-1	180	10-25-77	1996	Cincinnati, Ohio

GAMES BY POSITION: C—Cook 3, Fatheree 17, Hahn 28, Hill 2, Ochoa 30. **1B**—Byrd 27, McNeal 35. **2B**—Alfaro 5, Escalona 50, Samboy 1, Wheeler 7. **3B**—Alfaro 16, Escalona 1, Mendez 1, Nicley 24, Samboy 1, Wheeler 29. **SS**—Alfaro 13, Mendez 47, Wheeler 5. **OF**—Alleyne 2, Bystrowski 51, Colson 4, De la Espada 48, Deshazer 33, Flora 2, Vasquez 49.

PITCHING	W	L	ERA	G	GS	CG	SV	IP	H	R	ER	BB	SO	B	T	HT	WT	DOB	1st Yr	Resides
Alfaro, Jason	1	0	1.50	4	0	0	0	6	5	2	1	3	6	R	R	5-10	189	11—77	1997	Fort Worth, Texas
Blackmore, John	4	2	7.75	15	4	0	0	38	35	40	33	42	32	R	R	6-3	190	11-5-77	1996	Plainville, Conn.
Blanco, Alberto	0	0	0.00	2	2	0	0	5	1	0	0	1	11	L	L	6-1	170	6-27-76	1993	Miranda, Venez.
Bogeajis, Dan	1	1	5.23	7	0	0	1	10	14	6	6	4	6	R	R	6-2	210	10-17-77	1997	Altamonte Springs, Fla.
Celta, Nicolas	0	1	6.59	8	0	0	1	14	14	13	10	9	16	L	L	6-0	160	8-15-77	1994	Maracay, Venez.
Centeno, Juan	1	5	3.46	7	6	1	0	26	21	18	10	6	17	R	R	6-2	180	2-24-78	1996	Provincia, Panama
Corominas, Mike	1	1	4.58	8	2	0	0	20	31	16	10	4	8	L	L	6-2	190	10-31-74	1995	Glendora, Calif.
Hall, Billy	2	5	2.68	7	7	0	0	37	39	17	11	9	26	R	R	6-0	200	9-4-73	1994	Mannford, Okla.
Hamulack, Tim	1	1	4.20	23	0	0	9	45	56	31	21	18	38	R	L	6-4	225	11-14-76	1996	Edgewood, Md.
Jaime, Wilson	2	0	4.66	18	0	0	0	37	37	25	19	29	43	R	R	6-1	160	2-26-75	1992	Santo Domingo, D.R.
Janssen, Mike	0	1	9.36	13	0	0	1	25	28	27	26	23	20	R	R	6-2	200	1-9-77	1997	Phoenix, Ariz.
Love, Farley	0	0	0.00	2	0	0	0	3	1	0	0	2	7	R	R	6-6	200	4-21-73	1993	Eight Mile, Ala.
Oswalt, Roy	1	1	0.64	5	5	0	0	28	25	7	2	7	28	R	R	6-0	170	8-29-77	1997	Weir, Miss.
Pascarella, Josh	2	2	2.55	10	6	1	1	42	37	19	12	15	33	R	R	6-0	175	11-11-76	1996	San Diego, Calif.
Peguero, Darwin	0	4	5.57	9	8	0	0	32	30	26	20	23	36	S	L	6-0	165	12-5-78	1996	Hato Mayor, D.R.
Rodriguez, Wilfredo	8	2	3.04	12	12	1	0	68	54	30	23	32	71	L	L	6-3	180	3-20-79	1996	Bolivar, Venez.
Santana, Johan	0	4	7.93	9	5	1	0	36	49	36	32	18	25	L	L	6-0	155	3-13-79	1996	Tovar, Venez.
Sullivan, Peter	0	6	9.51	14	3	0	0	24	39	35	25	26	14	R	R	6-5	225	9-10-74	1997	Coral Gables, Fla.

Kansas City ROYALS

Managers: Bob Boone, Tony Muser. **1997 Record:** 67-94, .416 (5th, AL Central)

BATTING	AVG	G	AB	R	H	2B	3B	HR	RBI	BB	SO	SB	CS	B	T	HT	WT	DOB	1st Yr	Resides
Bell, Jay	.291	153	573	89	167	28	3	21	92	71	101	10	6	R	R	6-1	175	12-11-65	1984	Valrico, Fla.
Benitez, Yamil	.267	53	191	22	51	7	1	8	21	10	49	2	2	R	R	6-2	180	10-5-72	1990	San Juan, P.R.
Cooper, Scott	.201	75	159	12	32	6	1	3	15	17	32	1	1	L	R	6-3	205	10-13-67	1986	St. Charles, Mo.
Damon, Johnny	.275	146	472	70	130	12	8	8	48	42	70	16	10	L	L	6-0	175	11-5-73	1992	Orlando, Fla.
Davis, Chili	.279	140	477	71	133	20	0	30	90	85	96	6	3	S	R	6-3	217	1-17-60	1978	Scottsdale, Ariz.
Dye, Jermaine	.236	75	263	26	62	14	0	7	22	17	51	2	1	R	R	6-0	195	1-28-74	1993	Vacaville, Calif.
Fasano, Sal	.211	13	38	4	8	2	0	1	1	1	12	0	0	R	R	6-2	220	8-10-71	1993	Hanover Park, Ill.
Goodwin, Tom	.272	97	367	51	100	13	4	2	22	19	51	34	10	L	R	6-1	165	7-27-68	1989	Fresno, Calif.
Halter, Shane	.276	74	123	16	34	5	1	2	10	10	28	4	3	R	R	5-10	160	11-8-69	1991	Papillion, Neb.
Hansen, Jed	.309	34	94	11	29	6	1	1	14	13	29	3	2	R	R	6-1	195	8-19-72	1994	Olympia, Wash.
Howard, David	.241	80	162	24	39	8	1	1	13	10	31	2	2	S	R	6-0	175	2-26-67	1987	Sarasota, Fla.
King, Jeff	.238	155	543	84	129	30	1	28	112	89	96	16	5	R	R	6-1	180	12-26-64	1986	Wexford, Pa.
Long, Ryan	.222	6	9	2	2	0	0	0	2	0	3	0	0	R	R	6-2	185	2-3-73	1991	Houston, Texas
Macfarlane, Mike	.237	82	257	34	61	14	2	8	35	24	47	0	2	R	R	6-1	205	4-12-64	1985	Overland Park, Kan.
Martinez, Felix	.226	16	31	3	7	1	1	0	3	6	8	0	0	S	R	6-0	168	5-18-74	1993	Nagua, D.R.
Myers, Rod	.257	31	101	14	26	7	0	2	9	17	22	4	0	L	L	6-0	190	1-14-73	1991	Conroe, Texas
Nunnally, Jon	.241	13	29	8	7	0	1	1	4	5	7	0	0	L	R	5-10	188	11-9-71	1992	Pelham, N.C.
Offerman, Jose	.297	106	424	59	126	23	6	2	39	41	64	9	10	S	R	6-0	160	11-8-68	1988	San Pedro de Macoris, D.R.
Palmer, Dean	.278	49	187	23	52	10	1	9	31	15	50	1	2	R	R	6-2	195	12-27-68	1986	Tallahassee, Fla.
2-team (94 Texas)	.256	143	542	70	139	31	1	23	86	41	134	2	2							
Paquette, Craig	.230	77	252	26	58	15	1	8	33	10	57	2	2	R	R	6-0	190	3-28-69	1989	Garden Grove, Calif.
Roberts, Bip	.309	97	346	44	107	17	2	1	36	21	53	15	3	S	R	5-7	160	10-27-63	1982	Las Vegas, Nev.
Spehr, Tim	.171	17	35	3	6	0	0	1	2	2	12	0	0	R	R	6-2	205	7-2-66	1988	Waco, Texas
Stewart, Andy	.250	5	8	1	2	1	0	0	0	0	0	0	0	R	R	5-11	205	12-5-70	1990	Oshawa, Ontario
Sutton, Larry	.290	27	69	9	20	2	0	2	8	5	12	0	0	L	L	5-11	175	5-14-70	1992	Temecula, Calif.
Sweeney, Mike	.242	84	240	30	58	8	0	7	31	17	33	3	2	R	R	6-1	195	7-22-73	1991	Ontario, Calif.
Vitiello, Joe	.238	51	130	11	31	6	0	5	18	14	37	0	0	R	R	6-2	215	4-11-70	1991	Stoneham, Mass.

PITCHING	W	L	ERA	G	GS	CG	SV	IP	H	R	ER	BB	SO	B	T	HT	WT	DOB	1st Yr	Resides
Appier, Kevin	9	13	3.40	34	34	4	0	236	215	96	89	74	196	R	R	6-2	195	12-6-67	1987	Overland Park, Kan.
Belcher, Tim	13	12	5.02	32	32	3	0	213	242	128	119	70	113	R	R	6-3	220	10-19-61	1984	Mt. Gilead, Ohio
Bevil, Brian	1	2	6.61	18	0	0	1	16	16	13	12	9	13	R	R	6-3	190	9-5-71	1991	Houston, Texas
Bones, Ricky	4	7	5.97	21	11	1	0	78	102	59	52	25	36	R	R	6-0	190	4-7-69	1986	Guayama, P.R.
Carrasco, Hector	1	6	5.45	28	0	0	0	35	29	21	21	16	30	R	R	6-2	175	10-22-69	1988	San Pedro de Macoris, D.R.
Casian, Larry	0	2	5.06	32	0	0	0	27	32	15	15	6	16	R	L	6-0	173	10-28-65	1987	Salem, Ore.
Converse, Jim	0	0	3.60	3	0	0	0	5	4	2	2	5	3	L	R	5-9	180	8-17-71	1990	Citrus Heights, Calif.
Delamaza, Roland	0	0	4.50	1	0	0	0	2	1	1	1	1	1	R	R	6-2	195	11-11-71	1993	Arleta, Calif.
Haney, Chris	1	2	4.38	8	3	0	0	25	29	16	12	5	16	L	L	6-3	195	11-16-68	1990	Barboursville, Va.
Jacome, Jason	0	0	9.45	7	0	0	0	7	13	7	7	5	3	L	L	6-0	180	11-24-70	1991	Tucson, Ariz.
McDill, Allen	0	0	13.50	3	0	0	0	4	3	6	6	8	2	L	L	6-1	160	8-23-71	1992	Hot Springs, Ark.
Montgomery, Jeff	1	4	3.49	55	0	0	14	59	53	24	23	18	48	R	R	5-11	180	1-7-62	1983	Leawood, Kan.
Olson, Gregg	4	3	3.02	34	0	0	1	42	39	18	14	17	28	R	R	6-4	212	10-11-66	1988	Reisterstown, Md.
2-team (11 Minnesota)	4	3	5.58	45	0	0	1	50	58	35	31	28	34							
Perez, Mike	2	0	3.54	16	0	0	0	20	15	8	8	8	17	R	R	6-0	187	10-19-64	1986	Yauco, P.R.
Pichardo, Hipolito	3	5	4.22	47	0	0	11	49	51	24	23	24	34	R	R	6-1	185	8-22-69	1988	Esperanza, D.R.
Pittsley, Jim	5	8	5.46	21	21	0	0	112	120	72	68	54	52	R	R	6-7	215	4-3-74	1992	Dubois, Pa.
Rosado, Jose	9	12	4.69	33	33	2	0	203	208	117	106	73	129	L	L	6-0	175	11-9-74	1994	Dorado, P.R.
Rusch, Glendon	6	9	5.50	30	27	1	0	170	206	111	104	52	116	L	L	6-2	170	11-7-74	1993	Seattle, Wash.
Santiago, Jose	0	0	1.93	4	0	0	0	5	7	2	1	2	1	R	R	6-3	200	11-5-74	1994	Loiza, P.R.
Service, Scott	0	3	4.76	12	0	0	0	17	17	9	9	5	19	R	R	6-6	226	2-26-67	1986	Cincinnati, Ohio
Veres, Randy	4	0	3.31	24	0	0	1	35	36	17	13	7	28	R	R	6-3	187	11-25-65	1985	Rancho Cordova, Calif.
Walker, Jamie	3	3	5.44	50	0	0	0	43	46	28	26	20	24	L	L	6-2	190	7-1-71	1992	Clarksville, Tenn.
Whisenant, Matt	1	0	2.84	24	0	0	0	19	15	7	6	12	16	L	L	6-3	215	6-8-71	1990	La Canada, Calif.
Williams, Mike	0	2	6.43	10	0	0	1	14	20	11	10	8	10	R	R	6-2	190	7-29-69	1990	Newport, Va.
Williams, Mitch	0	1	10.80	7	0	0	0	7	11	8	8	7	10	L	L	6-4	200	11-17-64	1982	Hico, Texas

FIELDING

Catcher	PCT	G	PO	A	E	DP	PB
Fasano	.982	12	53	3	1	2	2
Macfarlane	.991	81	439	20	4	3	9
Spehr	1.000	17	78	7	0	1	0
Stewart	1.000	4	10	1	0	0	0
Sweeney	.993	76	425	31	3	13	3

First Base	PCT	G	PO	A	E	DP
Cooper	1.000	8	27	1	0	4
King	.996	150	1217	147	5	135
Sutton	1.000	12	92	8	0	11
Vitiello	1.000	1	8	0	0	1

Second Base	PCT	G	PO	A	E	DP
Halter	1.000	18	16	22	0	5
Hansen	.993	31	56	77	1	16
Howard	.973	34	65	81	4	25
Offerman	.981	101	201	254	9	64

Third Base	PCT	G	PO	A	E	DP
Bell	1.000	4	2	7	0	3
Cooper	1.000	39	21	54	0	4
Halter	1.000	12	1	4	0	0
Howard	.867	7	3	10	2	1
Palmer	.924	48	27	82	9	8
Paquette	.935	72	45	129	12	15

Shortstop	PCT	G	PO	A	E	DP
Bell	.985	149	227	443	10	102
Halter	.957	5	9	13	1	3
Howard	.955	9	6	15	1	5
Martinez	.975	12	17	22	1	7

Outfield	PCT	G	PO	A	E	DP
Benitez	.965	52	111	0	4	0
Damon	.988	136	322	5	4	3
Dye	.966	75	164	7	6	3
Goodwin	.996	96	232	3	1	0
Halter	1.000	32	37	1	0	0
Howard	1.000	23	22	3	0	0
Long	1.000	5	8	0	0	0
Myers	.982	26	55	1	1	0
Nunnally	1.000	9	12	0	0	0
Paquette	1.000	4	6	1	0	1
Roberts	.981	84	146	5	3	0
Sutton	.000	1	0	0	0	0
Vitiello	.980	28	48	0	1	0

FARM SYSTEM

Director of Player Development: Bob Hegman

Class	Farm Team	League	W	L	Pct.	Finish*	Manager	First Yr
AAA	Omaha (Neb.) Royals	American Assoc.	61	83	.424	8th (8)	Mike Jirschele	1969
AA	Wichita (Kan.) Wranglers	Texas	64	76	.457	7th (8)	Ron Johnson	1995
#A	Wilmington (Del.) Blue Rocks	Carolina	62	78	.443	8th (8)	John Mizerock	1993
A	Lansing (Mich.) Lugnuts	Midwest	69	68	.504	+6th (14)	Bob Herold	1996
A	Spokane (Wash.) Indians	Northwest	45	31	.592	2nd (8)	Jeff Garber	1995
R	Fort Myers (Fla.) Royals	Gulf Coast	36	24	.600	3rd (15)	Al Pedrique	1993

*Finish in overall standings (No. of teams in league) #Advanced level +Won league championship

ORGANIZATION LEADERS

MAJOR LEAGUERS

BATTING

*AVG	Jose Offerman	.297
R	Jay Bell	89
H	Jay Bell	167
TB	Jay Bell	264
2B	Jeff King	30
3B	Johnny Damon	8
HR	Chili Davis	30
RBI	Jeff King	112
BB	Jeff King	89
SO	Jay Bell	101
SB	Tom Goodwin	34

PITCHING

W	Tim Belcher	13
L	Kevin Appier	13
#ERA	Kevin Appier	3.40
G	Jeff Montomery	55
CG	Kevin Appier	4
SV	Jeff Montgomery	14
IP	Kevin Appier	236
BB	Kevin Appier	74
SO	Kevin Appier	196

Chili Davis

MEL BAILEY

Carlos Mendez

MINOR LEAGUERS

BATTING

*AVG	Tony Miranda, Lansing	.341
R	Kenderick Moore, Lansing	105
H	Carlos Mendez, Wichita	165
TB	Carlos Mendez, Wichita	235
2B	Tony Miranda, Lansing	35
3B	Kenderick Moore, Lansing	8
HR	Clyde Pough, Omaha	22
RBI	Kit Pellow, Wichita/Lansing	93
BB	Two tied at	67
SO	Gary Coffee, Wilmington	157
SB	Jeremy Carr, Omaha/Wichita	51

PITCHING

W	Allen Sanders, Lansing	12
L	Two tied at	12
#ERA	Tim Grieve, Wichita/Wilmington	2.62
G	Stephen Prihoda, Wichita	70
CG	Brian Harrison, Omaha	4
SV	Scott Service, Omaha	24
IP	Brian Harrison, Omaha	178
BB	Two tied at	63
SO	Orber Moreno, Lansing	128

*Minimum 250 At-Bats #Minimum 75 Innings

TOP 10 PROSPECTS

STEVE MOORE

Glendon Rusch

How the Royals Top 10 prospects, as judged by Baseball America prior to the 1997 season, fared in 1997:

Player, Pos.	Club (Class)	AVG	AB	R	H	2B	3B	HR	RBI	SB
2. Carlos Beltran, of	Wilmington (A)	.229	419	57	96	15	4	11	46	17
6. Roderick Myers, of	Kansas City	.257	101	14	26	7	0	2	9	4
	Omaha (AAA)	.252	143	21	36	10	0	2	10	6
	Wichita (AA)	.313	16	3	5	2	0	0	3	0
7. Felix Martinez, ss	Kansas City	.226	31	3	7	1	1	0	3	0
	Omaha (AAA)	.254	410	55	104	19	4	2	36	21
8. Jed Hansen, 2b	Kansas City	.309	94	11	29	6	1	1	14	3
	Omaha (AAA)	.268	380	43	102	20	2	11	44	8
9. Dermal Brown, of	Spokane (A)	.326	298	67	97	20	6	13	73	17

Player, Pos.	Club (Class)	W	L	ERA	G	SV	IP	H	BB	SO
1. Glendon Rusch, lhp	Kansas City	6	9	5.50	30	0	170	206	52	116
	Omaha (AAA)	0	1	4.50	1	0	6	7	1	2
3. Jim Pittsley, rhp	Kansas City	5	8	5.46	21	0	112	120	54	52
	Omaha (AAA)	1	2	4.42	7	0	39	36	20	30
4. Brian Bevil, rhp	Kansas City	1	2	6.61	18	1	16	16	9	13
	Omaha (AAA)	2	1	4.38	26	1	39	34	22	47
	Witchita (AA)	0	0	5.63	4	0	8	11	4	10
5. Jaime Bluma, rhp	Injured—Did not play									
10. Blaine Mull, rhp	Wichita (AA)	1	2	6.65	8	0	45	66	23	16
	Wilmington (A)	8	6	3.56	19	0	111	126	33	64

OMAHA — Class AAA

AMERICAN ASSOCIATION

BATTING	AVG	G	AB	R	H	2B	3B	HR	RBI	BB	SO	SB	CS	B	T	HT	WT	DOB	1st Yr	Resides
Benitez, Yamil	.295	92	329	61	97	14	1	21	71	24	82	12	3	R	R	6-2	180	10-5-72	1990	San Juan, P.R.
Brooks, Ramy	.000	3	9	0	0	0	0	0	0	0	4	0	0	R	R	6-2	180	4-12-70	1990	Blanchard, Okla.
Carr, Jeremy	.267	35	120	17	32	3	2	2	9	15	17	12	3	R	R	5-10	170	3-30-71	1993	Boise, Idaho
Dye, Jermaine	.306	39	144	21	44	6	0	10	25	9	25	0	2	R	R	6-0	195	1-28-74	1993	Vacaville, Calif.
Fasano, Sal	.164	49	152	17	25	7	0	4	14	12	53	0	0	R	R	6-2	220	8-10-71	1993	Hanover Park, Ill.
Halter, Shane	.265	14	49	10	13	1	1	2	9	6	10	0	0	R	R	5-10	160	11-8-69	1991	Papillion, Neb.
Hansen, Jed	.268	114	380	43	102	20	2	11	44	32	78	8	1	R	R	6-1	195	8-19-72	1994	Olympia, Wash.
Hatcher, Chris	.230	68	222	34	51	9	0	11	24	17	68	0	1	R	R	6-3	220	1-7-69	1990	Carter Lake, Iowa
Long, Ryan	.265	113	411	48	109	26	0	19	56	18	98	2	4	R	R	6-2	185	2-3-73	1991	Houston, Texas
Lopez, Mendy	.231	17	52	6	12	2	0	1	6	8	21	0	0	R	R	6-2	165	10-15-74	1992	Santo Domingo, D.R.
Martinez, Felix	.254	112	410	55	104	19	4	2	36	29	86	21	11	S	R	6-0	168	5-18-74	1993	Nagua, D.R.
Medrano, Tony	.203	17	59	10	12	0	0	4	9	4	5	0	1	R	R	5-11	155	12-8-74	1993	Long Beach, Calif.
Merchant, Mark	.000	2	5	0	0	0	0	0	0	0	4	0	0	S	R	6-2	185	1-23-69	1987	Chuluota, Fla.
Myers, Rod	.254	38	142	21	36	10	0	2	10	15	37	6	4	L	L	6-0	190	1-14-73	1991	Conroe, Texas
Nunnally, Jon	.278	68	230	35	64	11	1	15	33	39	67	8	3	L	R	5-10	188	11-9-71	1992	Pelham, N.C.
Ortiz, Hector	.190	21	63	7	12	3	0	0	3	13	15	0	0	R	R	6-0	178	10-14-69	1988	Canovanas, P.R.
Paquette, Craig	.308	23	91	9	28	6	0	3	20	6	26	0	2	R	R	6-0	190	3-28-69	1989	Garden Grove, Calif.
Pough, Pork Chop	.252	124	433	63	109	20	1	22	59	53	113	0	1	R	R	6-0	173	12-25-69	1988	Avon Park, Fla.
Seitzer, Brad	.190	21	63	4	12	3	0	0	4	5	10	0	0	R	R	6-2	195	2-2-70	1991	Memphis, Tenn.
Sisco, Steve	.261	54	188	23	49	8	0	3	12	8	34	2	1	R	R	5-9	180	12-2-69	1992	Thousand Oaks, Calif.
Stewart, Andy	.274	86	288	38	79	10	1	6	24	18	43	1	1	R	R	5-11	205	12-5-70	1990	Oshawa, Ontario
Stynes, Chris	.265	82	332	53	88	18	1	8	44	19	25	3	1	R	R	5-9	170	1-19-73	1991	Boca Raton, Fla.
Sutton, Larry	.300	106	380	61	114	27	1	19	72	61	57	0	0	L	L	5-11	175	5-14-70	1992	Temecula, Calif.
Sweeney, Mike	.236	40	144	22	34	8	1	10	29	18	20	0	2	R	R	6-1	195	7-22-73	1991	Ontario, Calif.
Vitiello, Joe	.214	13	42	5	9	1	0	3	9	5	16	0	0	R	R	6-2	215	4-11-70	1991	Stoneham, Mass.

PITCHING	W	L	ERA	G	GS	CG	SV	IP	H	R	ER	BB	SO	B	T	HT	WT	DOB	1st Yr	Resides
Bevil, Brian	2	1	4.38	26	3	0	1	39	34	22	19	22	47	R	R	6-3	190	9-5-71	1991	Houston, Texas
Brewington, Jamie	2	2	8.31	7	4	0	0	22	21	21	20	13	20	R	R	6-4	180	9-28-71	1992	Greenville, N.C.
Converse, Jim	2	1	6.75	6	3	0	0	17	18	13	13	9	13	L	R	5-9	180	8-17-71	1990	Citrus Heights, Calif.
Flury, Pat	1	0	6.08	18	0	0	0	27	29	18	18	16	24	R	R	6-2	205	3-14-73	1993	Sparks, Nev.
Grimsley, Jason	1	5	6.68	7	6	0	0	31	36	26	23	29	22	R	R	6-3	180	8-7-67	1985	Cleveland, Texas
Haney, Chris	1	0	3.79	4	3	0	0	19	16	12	8	6	7	L	L	6-3	195	11-16-68	1990	Barboursville, Va.
Harrison, Brian	10	12	5.05	30	29	4	0	178	208	114	100	55	83	R	R	6-1	175	12-18-68	1992	Bryan, Texas
Huisman, Rick	1	5	3.62	37	1	0	2	60	59	29	24	35	57	R	R	6-3	200	5-17-69	1990	Bensenville, Ill.
Johns, Doug	1	5	7.56	9	6	1	0	42	58	36	35	11	24	R	L	6-2	185	12-19-67	1990	Plantation, Fla.
McDill, Allen	5	2	5.88	23	6	0	2	64	80	42	42	26	51	L	L	6-1	160	8-23-71	1992	Hot Springs, Ark.
Montgomery, Jeff	0	0	0.00	2	0	0	0	2	1	0	0	1	2	R	R	5-11	180	1-7-62	1983	Leawood, Kan.
Olsen, Steve	4	5	5.76	22	13	0	0	84	96	67	54	48	43	R	R	6-4	225	11-2-69	1991	La Grange, Ky.
Olson, Gregg	3	1	3.31	9	5	0	0	35	30	13	13	10	20	R	R	6-4	212	10-11-66	1988	Reisterstown, Md.
Patterson, Ken	2	2	4.11	22	0	0	4	31	34	17	14	10	28	L	L	6-4	222	7-8-64	1985	McGregor, Texas
Pennington, Brad	2	1	4.32	35	1	0	0	50	41	28	24	41	48	L	L	6-6	215	4-14-69	1989	Salem, Ind.
Perez, Mike	4	1	4.71	34	0	0	8	36	38	22	19	18	29	R	R	6-0	187	10-19-64	1986	Yauco, P.R.
Pichardo, Hipolito	0	0	5.79	5	1	0	1	5	5	3	3	3	3	R	R	6-1	185	8-22-69	1988	Esperanza, D.R.
Pittsley, Jim	1	2	4.42	7	7	0	0	39	36	21	19	20	30	R	R	6-7	215	4-3-74	1992	Dubois, Pa.
Ray, Ken	5	12	6.37	25	21	2	0	113	131	86	80	63	96	R	R	6-2	160	11-27-74	1993	Roswell, Ga.
Rusch, Glendon	0	1	4.50	1	1	0	0	6	7	3	3	1	2	L	L	6-2	170	11-7-74	1993	Seattle, Wash.
Seanez, Rudy	2	5	6.51	28	3	0	0	47	53	42	34	25	46	R	R	5-10	185	10-20-68	1986	El Centro, Calif.
Service, Scott	0	0	0.00	16	0	0	9	15	9	0	0	4	16	R	R	6-6	226	2-26-67	1986	Cincinnati, Ohio
2-team (33 Indy)	3	2	2.59	49	0	0	24	49	39	15	14	16	69							
Smith, Toby	1	3	7.84	17	0	0	3	21	24	19	18	15	11	R	R	6-6	225	11-16-71	1993	Guthrie, Okla.
Toth, Robert	5	2	2.75	15	7	0	0	52	50	18	16	19	30	R	R	6-2	180	7-30-72	1990	Cypress, Calif.
Van Poppel, Todd	1	5	8.03	11	6	0	0	37	50	36	33	24	27	R	R	6-5	210	12-9-71	1990	Arlington, Texas
Veres, Randy	1	1	6.60	11	1	0	0	15	15	11	11	5	19	R	R	6-3	187	11-25-65	1985	Rancho Cordova, Calif.
Watkins, Scott	0	0	6.46	9	0	0	0	15	19	13	11	6	15	L	L	6-3	180	5-15-70	1992	Sand Springs, Okla.
Williams, Mike	3	6	4.22	20	11	1	5	79	71	41	37	38	68	R	R	6-2	190	7-29-69	1990	Newport, Va.
Williams, Mitch	0	0	2.08	3	0	0	0	9	6	2	2	5	8	L	L	6-4	200	11-17-64	1982	Hico, Texas
Zimmerman, Mike	1	3	10.59	7	6	0	0	26	41	32	31	20	17	R	R	6-0	180	2-6-69	1990	Brooklyn, N.Y.

FIELDING

Catcher	PCT	G	PO	A	E	DP	PB
Brooks	1.000	1	1	0	0	0	0
Fasano	.988	47	296	34	4	4	7
Ortiz	.978	21	130	6	3	1	0
Stewart	.994	49	285	26	2	6	4
Sweeney	.996	33	229	15	1	2	4

First Base	PCT	G	PO	A	E	DP
Pough	.992	16	114	13	1	13
Sisco	.960	3	23	1	1	4
Stewart	.991	27	189	32	2	19
Sutton	.994	102	839	54	5	103

Second Base	PCT	G	PO	A	E	DP
Halter	.933	4	9	5	1	3
Hansen	.960	85	164	243	17	69
Medrano	.941	10	25	23	3	3
Sisco	.973	30	46	63	3	17
Stynes	.977	23	41	43	2	19

Third Base	PCT	G	PO	A	E	DP
Halter	.667	5	1	1	1	0
Hansen	1.000	3	2	5	0	2
Lopez	.898	17	15	38	6	5
Paquette	.953	19	12	29	2	3
Pough	.909	69	41	138	18	20
Seitzer	.885	20	16	30	6	3
Sisco	.913	6	9	12	2	3
Stynes	.875	15	8	34	6	4

Shortstop	PCT	G	PO	A	E	DP
Halter	1.000	4	2	8	0	3
Hansen	.950	27	39	75	6	16
Martinez	.931	112	175	312	36	81
Medrano	1.000	8	18	19	0	5

Outfield	PCT	G	PO	A	E	DP
Benitez	.963	89	150	6	6	1
Carr	.983	33	57	2	1	2
Dye	1.000	29	41	2	0	0
Halter	1.000	5	10	0	0	0
Hatcher	.921	39	56	2	5	0
Long	.956	104	186	9	9	1
Merchant	1.000	1	1	0	0	0
Myers	.989	38	89	3	1	1
Nunnally	.963	66	173	8	7	2
Sisco	.957	19	22	0	1	0
Stewart	1.000	4	3	0	0	0
Stynes	.965	23	52	3	2	0
Vitiello	1.000	1	1	0	0	0

WICHITA — Class AA

TEXAS LEAGUE

BATTING	AVG	G	AB	R	H	2B	3B	HR	RBI	BB	SO	SB	CS	B	T	HT	WT	DOB	1st Yr	Resides
Brooks, Ramy	.229	56	140	19	32	5	0	4	16	19	45	2	2	R	R	6-2	180	4-12-70	1990	Blanchard, Okla.

BATTING	AVG	G	AB	R	H	2B	3B	HR	RBI	BB	SO	SB	CS	B	T	HT	WT	DOB	1st Yr	Resides
Byington, Jimmie	.235	92	196	30	46	8	0	2	16	15	39	5	6	R	R	6-0	170	8-22-73	1993	Tulsa, Okla.
Carr, Jeremy	.306	91	340	76	104	19	1	8	40	50	53	39	8	R	R	5-10	170	3-30-71	1993	Boise, Idaho
DeBerry, Joe	.244	30	82	9	20	5	0	1	5	10	20	3	0	L	L	6-2	195	6-30-70	1991	Colorado Springs, Colo.
Diaz, Lino	.284	92	289	36	82	26	3	2	51	23	27	3	6	R	R	5-11	182	7-22-70	1993	Altoona, Pa.
Fasano, Sal	.237	40	131	27	31	5	0	13	27	20	35	0	2	R	R	6-2	220	8-10-71	1993	Hanover Park, Ill.
Giambi, Jeremy	.321	74	268	50	86	15	1	11	52	44	47	4	4	L	L	6-0	185	9-30-74	1996	Covina, Calif.
Gonzalez, Raul	.285	129	452	66	129	30	4	13	74	36	52	12	8	R	R	5-8	175	12-27-73	1991	Villa Carolina, P.R.
Hatcher, Chris	.262	11	42	7	11	0	0	5	7	4	16	1	0	R	R	6-3	220	1-7-69	1990	Carter Lake, Iowa
Lopez, Mendy	.232	101	357	56	83	16	3	5	42	36	70	7	5	R	R	6-2	165	10-15-74	1992	Santo Domingo, D.R.
McNally, Sean	.245	18	53	9	13	4	0	0	2	11	12	1	2	R	R	6-4	205	12-14-72	1994	Rye, N.Y.
Medrano, Tony	.246	108	349	45	86	9	1	4	42	26	32	8	2	R	R	5-11	155	12-8-74	1993	Long Beach, Calif.
Mendez, Carlos	.325	129	507	72	165	32	1	12	90	19	43	4	7	R	R	6-1	195	6-18-74	1991	Caracas, Venez.
Merchant, Mark	.340	49	147	27	50	9	0	9	38	23	35	0	1	S	R	6-2	185	1-23-69	1987	Chuluota, Fla.
Myers, Rod	.313	4	16	3	5	2	0	0	3	3	3	0	1	L	L	6-0	190	1-14-73	1991	Conroe, Texas
Nunez, Sergio	.277	34	137	18	38	1	1	1	11	6	17	12	3	R	R	5-11	155	1-3-75	1992	Santo Domingo, D.R.
Ortiz, Hector	.250	59	180	20	45	3	0	1	25	21	15	1	2	R	R	6-0	178	10-14-69	1988	Canovanas, P.R.
Pellow, Kit	.249	68	241	40	60	12	1	10	41	21	72	5	2	R	R	6-1	200	8-28-73	1996	Galena, Mo.
Pledger, Kinnis	.081	12	37	3	3	1	1	0	0	5	14	0	0	L	R	6-4	215	7-17-68	1987	Benton, Ark.
Quinn, Mark	.375	26	96	26	36	13	0	2	19	15	19	1	1	R	R	6-1	185	5-21-74	1995	West Covina, Calif.
Shirley, Al	.271	81	240	31	65	10	1	4	25	21	92	9	7	R	R	6-1	209	10-18-73	1991	Danville, Va.
Sisco, Steve	.286	55	182	34	52	8	2	3	24	24	29	3	1	R	R	5-9	180	12-2-69	1992	Thousand Oaks, Calif.
Smith, Matt	.227	52	176	19	40	7	1	1	15	13	37	1	0	L	L	6-4	215	6-2-76	1994	Grants Pass, Ore.

PITCHING	W	L	ERA	G	GS	CG	SV	IP	H	R	ER	BB	SO	B	T	HT	WT	DOB	1st Yr	Resides
Bevil, Brian	0	0	5.63	4	2	0	0	8	11	8	5	4	10	R	R	6-3	190	9-5-71	1991	Houston, Texas
Brewington, Jamie	2	5	6.71	10	10	0	0	51	68	43	38	28	31	R	R	6-4	180	9-28-71	1992	Greenville, N.C.
Brixey, Dusty	0	4	6.98	5	3	0	0	19	23	15	15	9	5	R	R	6-4	190	10-16-73	1993	Jay, Okla.
Calero, Enrique	11	9	4.44	23	22	2	0	128	120	78	63	44	100	R	R	6-2	175	1-9-75	1996	Rio Piedras, P.R.
Evans, Bart	1	2	4.59	32	0	0	6	33	45	20	17	8	28	R	R	6-1	190	12-30-70	1992	Ozark, Mo.
Flury, Pat	8	3	3.56	42	0	0	5	48	47	26	19	18	47	R	R	6-2	205	3-14-73	1993	Sparks, Nev.
Gamboa, Javier	0	3	8.69	6	6	0	0	29	49	30	28	8	16	R	R	6-1	185	3-17-74	1994	Paso Robles, Calif.
Grieve, Tim	3	1	3.38	17	0	0	1	37	30	15	14	21	36	R	R	6-0	180	8-17-71	1994	Arlington, Texas
Grundy, Phil	9	11	5.70	28	24	2	0	156	194	108	99	53	117	R	R	6-2	195	9-8-72	1993	Somerset, Ky.
Haney, Chris	0	1	2.70	2	2	0	0	7	5	3	2	0	2	L	L	6-3	195	11-16-68	1990	Barboursville, Va.
McDill, Allen	0	1	3.12	16	0	0	3	17	18	7	6	7	14	L	L	6-1	160	8-23-71	1992	Hot Springs, Ark.
Morvay, Joe	1	2	10.94	9	2	0	0	26	39	32	32	7	13	L	L	6-4	210	2-8-71	1993	Boardman, Ohio
Mull, Blaine	1	2	6.65	8	8	0	0	45	66	41	33	23	16	R	R	6-4	186	8-14-76	1994	Morganton, N.C.
Olsen, Steve	2	0	0.00	3	2	0	0	15	11	1	0	2	7	R	R	6-4	225	11-2-69	1991	La Grange, Ky.
Pennington, Brad	0	0	0.75	12	0	0	3	12	7	1	1	8	14	L	L	6-6	215	4-14-69	1989	Salem, Ind.
Prihoda, Stephen	0	3	3.24	70	0	0	10	89	87	34	32	40	68	R	L	6-6	220	12-7-72	1995	Weimar, Texas
Rawitzer, Kevin	5	1	5.75	44	9	0	0	97	125	68	62	44	75	L	L	5-10	185	2-28-71	1993	Danville, Calif.
Saier, Matt	7	5	4.90	17	17	0	0	101	112	66	55	48	53	R	R	6-2	192	1-29-73	1995	Bradenton, Fla.
Santiago, Jose	2	1	4.00	22	0	0	3	27	32	13	12	8	12	R	R	6-3	200	11-5-74	1994	Loiza, P.R.
Smith, Toby	2	3	4.91	8	8	0	0	44	49	30	24	11	29	R	R	6-6	225	11-16-71	1993	Guthrie, Okla.
Telgheder, Jim	4	7	6.28	28	12	0	0	86	104	66	60	30	47	R	R	6-3	210	3-22-71	1993	Slate Hill, N.Y.
Toth, Robert	4	8	5.82	20	9	1	0	68	82	47	44	26	47	R	R	6-2	180	7-30-72	1990	Cypress, Calif.
Walker, Jamie	0	1	9.45	5	0	0	0	7	6	8	7	5	6	L	L	6-2	190	7-1-71	1992	Clarksville, Tenn.
Wolff, Bryan	1	1	6.52	12	0	0	1	10	18	7	7	5	8	R	R	6-1	195	3-16-72	1993	St. Louis, Mo.
Zimmerman, Mike	1	2	3.67	11	4	0	0	27	21	14	11	17	11	R	R	6-0	180	2-6-69	1990	Brooklyn, N.Y.

FIELDING

Catcher	PCT	G	PO	A	E	DP	PB
Brooks	.979	47	244	30	6	1	5
Fasano	.983	39	217	21	4	4	5
Mendez	.979	8	42	4	1	0	0
Ortiz	.962	59	340	40	15	0	3

First Base	PCT	G	PO	A	E	DP
Byington	1.000	1	2	1	0	0
Diaz	.982	9	49	6	1	6
Fasano	1.000	2	15	0	0	0
Giambi	.000	1	0	0	0	0
Mendez	.990	84	738	67	8	67
Merchant	1.000	1	4	0	0	0
Smith	.988	51	448	37	6	41

Second Base	PCT	G	PO	A	E	DP
Byington	.973	17	32	40	2	8
Diaz	1.000	6	14	11	0	4
Medrano	.982	70	129	190	6	40
Nunez	.943	33	56	93	9	16
Sisco	.993	27	50	83	1	18

Third Base	PCT	G	PO	A	E	DP
Diaz	.912	45	22	82	10	8
McNally	.891	16	17	24	5	3
Pellow	.898	65	51	161	24	13
Sisco	.917	18	9	35	4	2

Shortstop	PCT	G	PO	A	E	DP
Byington	.886	9	11	20	4	5
Diaz	.857	1	4	2	1	1
Lopez	.961	101	193	296	20	59
Medrano	.945	34	56	100	9	24
Sisco	.000	1	0	0	0	0

Outfield	PCT	G	PO	A	E	DP
Byington	1.000	59	75	2	0	1
Carr	.972	91	161	10	5	0
DeBerry	.950	18	19	0	1	0
Diaz	.000	3	0	0	0	0
Giambi	.975	57	117	2	3	0
Gonzalez	.926	101	167	9	14	2
Hatcher	.900	6	9	0	1	0
McNally	1.000	1	1	0	0	0
Mendez	1.000	3	4	0	0	0
Merchant	1.000	11	24	0	0	0
Myers	1.000	4	8	0	0	0
Pledger	1.000	8	9	1	0	0
Quinn	.972	26	35	0	1	0
Shirley	.948	71	104	6	6	1
Sisco	1.000	11	7	0	0	0

WILMINGTON — Class A

CAROLINA LEAGUE

BATTING	AVG	G	AB	R	H	2B	3B	HR	RBI	BB	SO	SB	CS	B	T	HT	WT	DOB	1st Yr	Resides
Beltran, Carlos	.229	120	419	57	96	15	4	11	46	46	96	17	7	S	R	6-1	175	4-24-77	1995	Manati, P.R.
Bronson, Ben	.175	34	57	9	10	3	0	0	4	11	17	2	2	L	R	5-10	175	9-9-72	1996	Houston, Texas
Cepeda, Jose	.282	28	71	9	20	0	0	0	3	12	10	1	0	R	R	6-0	185	8-1-74	1995	Fajardo, P.R.
Coffee, Gary	.222	120	427	58	95	11	1	11	56	55	157	6	4	R	R	6-3	235	3-13-75	1994	Atlanta, Ga.
Delaney, Donovan	.235	124	434	53	102	25	4	5	60	24	112	15	7	R	R	5-11	200	3-24-74	1994	Haughton, La.
Escamilla, Roman	.251	57	167	19	42	7	0	1	21	28	30	0	6	R	R	6-0	193	1-21-74	1996	Corpus Christi, Texas
Escandon, Emiliano	.273	80	238	40	65	9	3	2	32	57	54	9	4	S	R	5-10	170	11-6-74	1995	Ontario, Calif.
Evans, Michael	.227	108	352	55	80	14	1	17	55	54	97	3	2	L	R	6-0	190	8-7-72	1993	Houston, Texas
Febles, Carlos	.237	122	438	78	104	27	6	3	29	51	95	49	11	R	R	5-11	165	5-24-76	1994	La Romana, D.R.
Hallmark, Pat	.300	27	100	22	30	5	0	2	11	12	16	8	3	R	R	6-0	170	12-31-73	1995	Houston, Texas
Longueira, Tony	.241	62	195	27	47	7	0	2	23	21	34	2	3	R	R	6-0	170	9-24-74	1995	Pembroke Pines, Fla.
McNally, Sean	.266	95	323	51	86	22	2	17	68	40	98	2	1	R	R	6-4	205	12-14-72	1994	Rye, N.Y.
Pitts, Rick	.216	15	37	6	8	1	0	2	5	3	14	3	1	R	R	6-1	180	3-13-76	1994	Seattle, Wash.

BATTING	AVG	G	AB	R	H	2B	3B	HR	RBI	BB	SO	SB	CS	B	T	HT	WT	DOB	1st Yr	Resides
Prieto, Alejandro	.215	129	437	52	94	13	3	3	38	41	59	20	8	R	R	5-11	150	6-19-76	1993	Caracas, Venez.
Quinn, Mark	.308	87	299	51	92	22	3	16	71	42	47	3	2	R	R	6-1	185	5-21-74	1995	West Covina, Calif.
Rocha, Juan	.256	97	340	43	87	16	1	10	42	27	67	6	3	R	R	5-11	175	9-8-73	1994	Santa Fe Springs, Calif.
Treanor, Matt	.198	80	257	22	51	6	1	5	25	25	59	1	6	R	R	6-1	188	3-3-76	1994	Anaheim, Calif.

GAMES BY POSITION: C—Escamilla 45, Evans 3, Hallmark 23, Treanor 80. **1B**—Coffee 119, Evans 27, McNally 1. **2B**—Cepeda 1, Escandon 17, Febles 120, Longueira 20. **3B**—Cepeda 27, Escandon 27, Hallmark 1, Longueira 17, McNally 86. **SS**—Escandon 9, Longueira 16, McNally 3, Prieto 129. **OF**—Beltran 119, Bronson 32, Delaney 121, Evans 37, Hallmark 5, Pitts 14, Quinn 64, Rocha 61.

PITCHING	W	L	ERA	G	GS	CG	SV	IP	H	R	ER	BB	SO	B	T	HT	WT	DOB	1st Yr	Resides
Anderson, Eric	1	2	4.89	14	6	0	0	39	37	25	21	16	11	R	R	6-1	190	10-20-74	1993	Blue Springs, Mo.
Bernal, Manuel	6	8	4.33	45	3	0	8	98	108	51	47	27	55	R	R	6-2	163	4-29-74	1994	Los Mochis, Mexico
Brewer, Ryan	5	4	3.34	47	0	0	7	105	100	41	39	29	93	L	R	6-2	180	10-31-73	1996	Lubbock, Texas
Brixey, Dusty	0	4	3.83	24	0	0	1	42	49	29	18	22	22	R	R	6-4	190	10-16-73	1993	Jay, Okla.
Byrdak, Tim	4	3	3.51	22	2	0	3	41	34	17	16	12	47	L	L	5-11	170	10-31-73	1994	Oak Forest, Ill.
Chapman, Jake	8	9	3.85	27	26	0	0	154	163	83	66	59	122	R	L	6-1	180	1-11-74	1996	Rensselaer, Ind.
Evans, Bart	0	1	6.53	16	2	0	0	21	22	18	15	15	22	R	R	6-1	190	12-30-70	1992	Ozark, Mo.
Grieve, Tim	4	1	1.88	26	0	0	7	38	24	11	8	20	34	R	R	6-0	180	8-17-71	1994	Arlington, Texas
Hodges, Kevin	8	11	4.48	28	20	0	1	125	150	78	62	44	63	R	R	6-4	200	6-24-73	1991	Spring, Texas
Mull, Blaine	8	6	3.56	19	19	0	0	111	126	55	44	33	64	R	R	6-4	186	8-14-76	1994	Morganton, N.C.
Mullen, Scott	4	4	4.55	11	11	0	0	59	64	35	30	26	43	R	L	6-2	185	1-17-75	1996	Beaufort, S.C.
Paredes, Carlos	5	9	6.19	23	21	0	0	112	130	90	77	49	93	R	R	6-0	170	5-10-76	1995	Sabana de la Mar, D.R.
Phillips, Marc	0	3	5.19	40	0	0	1	61	72	39	35	23	44	L	L	6-2	195	5-30-72	1994	Waynesboro, Va.
Robbins, Michael	0	0	7.18	20	0	0	0	31	41	26	25	14	24	L	L	6-1	190	2-7-74	1995	Oakland, Calif.
Saier, Matt	2	2	1.69	9	9	0	0	43	31	11	8	15	47	R	R	6-2	192	1-29-73	1995	Bradenton, Fla.
Santiago, Jose	1	1	4.91	4	0	0	2	4	3	3	2	1	1	R	R	6-3	200	11-5-74	1994	Loiza, P.R.
Thorn, Todd	6	10	5.16	27	21	1	0	133	163	89	76	30	71	L	L	6-1	175	11-4-76	1995	Stratford, Ontario

LANSING — Class A

MIDWEST LEAGUE

BATTING	AVG	G	AB	R	H	2B	3B	HR	RBI	BB	SO	SB	CS	B	T	HT	WT	DOB	1st Yr	Resides
Amado, Jose	.342	61	234	49	80	25	1	4	45	24	18	10	2	R	R	6-1	194	1-1-75	1994	San Cristobal, Venez.
Berger, Brandon	.293	107	393	64	115	22	6	12	73	42	79	13	1	R	R	6-0	205	2-21-75	1996	Fort Mitchell, Ky.
Blosser, Doug	.214	38	103	13	22	3	0	3	17	20	29	0	0	L	R	6-3	225	10-1-76	1995	Sarasota, Fla.
Cepeda, Jose	.279	89	326	40	91	17	1	2	35	42	35	4	2	R	R	6-0	185	8-1-74	1995	Fajardo, P.R.
Doezie, Troy	.157	19	51	3	8	2	0	0	1	2	14	0	0	R	R	6-2	210	9-6-73	1992	Sandy, Utah
Giambi, Jeremy	.336	31	116	33	39	11	1	5	21	23	16	5	1	L	L	6-0	185	9-30-74	1996	Covina, Calif.
Griffis, Cade	.300	10	30	4	9	3	0	0	5	4	8	2	1	L	R	5-11	200	7-9-74	1997	Burkburnett, Texas
Hallmark, Pat	.284	88	306	49	87	13	6	0	39	28	43	22	5	R	R	6-0	170	12-31-73	1995	Houston, Texas
Layne, Jason	.276	98	337	54	93	22	3	9	68	54	85	0	0	L	R	6-2	215	5-17-73	1996	Tyler, Texas
LeBron, Juan	.212	35	113	12	24	7	0	3	20	0	32	0	0	R	R	6-4	195	6-7-77	1995	Arroyo, P.R.
Medrano, Steve	.221	97	321	35	71	7	5	0	29	34	39	10	5	S	R	6-0	160	10-8-77	1996	La Puente, Calif.
Miranda, Tony	.341	104	387	85	132	35	5	5	72	54	62	11	10	R	R	5-10	175	5-23-73	1995	Lynwood, Calif.
Montas, Ricardo	.300	4	10	0	3	0	0	0	1	0	2	0	0	R	R	6-2	180	3-9-77	1994	Santo Domingo, D.R.
Moore, Kenderick	.285	112	456	105	130	16	8	6	42	45	78	43	14	R	R	5-10	175	5-17-73	1996	Ardmore, Okla.
Pellow, Kit	.297	65	256	39	76	17	2	11	52	24	74	2	0	R	R	6-1	200	8-28-73	1996	Galena, Mo.
Pitts, Rick	.155	35	58	7	9	3	1	0	6	8	16	2	0	R	R	6-1	180	3-13-76	1994	Seattle, Wash.
Radcliff, Vic	.269	81	253	40	68	25	3	3	33	19	56	3	0	R	R	5-10	180	9-23-76	1995	Belvedere, S.C.
Robles, Juan	.207	51	145	11	30	6	1	2	17	14	40	1	2	R	R	5-10	190	3-17-72	1994	Hermosillo, Mexico
Schafer, Brett	.191	21	47	16	9	3	1	0	6	15	8	3	0	R	R	5-11	175	7-3-73	1995	Malibu, Calif.
Smith, Matt	.278	62	227	33	63	4	3	4	33	21	45	4	2	L	L	6-4	215	6-2-76	1994	Grants Pass, Ore.
Taft, Brett	.249	85	269	41	67	21	0	4	30	47	60	5	4	R	R	5-7	170	11-9-73	1996	Hueytown, Ala.
Ullery, David	.159	18	44	5	7	1	2	1	10	13	16	0	0	L	R	6-3	225	12-16-74	1997	Brazil, Ind.
Williams, Micah	.333	65	249	34	83	13	3	0	30	9	34	22	3	R	R	6-1	185	1-30-75	1997	Phoenix, Ariz.

GAMES BY POSITION: C—Doezie 17, Griffis 10, Hallmark 62, Robles 48, Ullery 18. **1B**—Amado 12, Blosser 7, Layne 56, Miranda 2, Montas 1, Pellow 18, Smith 54. **2B**—Cepeda 43, Montas 1, Moore 57, Schafer 4, Taft 47. **3B**—Amado 27, Cepeda 37, Layne 17, Miranda 5, Montas 2, Pellow 51, Radcliff 1, Schafer 6. **SS**—Cepeda 10, Medrano 95, Taft 41. **OF**—Berger 87, Giambi 17, Hallmark 20, Layne 1, LeBron 31, Miranda 73, Moore 57, Pitts 25, Radcliff 68, Schafer 9, Williams 63.

PITCHING	W	L	ERA	G	GS	CG	SV	IP	H	R	ER	BB	SO	B	T	HT	WT	DOB	1st Yr	Resides
Baird, Brandon	10	7	3.01	55	0	0	7	78	74	31	26	28	83	L	L	5-11	175	9-18-73	1996	Enid, Okla.
Boring, Richard	0	2	20.25	3	0	0	0	3	6	6	6	4	2	R	R	6-6	210	7-23-75	1996	Nacogdoches, Texas
Durbin, Chad	5	8	4.79	26	26	0	0	145	157	85	77	53	116	R	R	6-2	177	12-3-77	1996	Baton Rouge, La.
Gonzalez, Edwin	3	5	3.65	11	11	0	0	69	67	32	28	15	58	R	R	5-11	184	8-13-77	1995	Santo Domingo, D.R.
Gooding, Jason	0	1	5.79	1	1	0	0	5	6	5	3	1	3	R	L	5-11	190	7-29-74	1997	Cambridge, Ontario
Hueston, Stephen	2	2	7.44	34	7	0	0	71	95	65	59	49	42	R	R	6-0	195	9-25-73	1996	Pacifica, Calif.
Lineweaver, Aaron	7	1	3.33	21	9	0	0	84	89	38	31	28	73	R	R	6-1	200	7-26-73	1996	Denton, Texas
Meady, Todd	0	1	4.85	4	2	0	0	13	25	10	7	6	5	R	R	6-4	216	9-13-76	1995	Middlebury, Conn.
Moreno, Orber	4	8	4.81	27	25	0	0	138	150	83	74	45	128	R	R	6-1	140	4-27-77	1994	Los Autos, Venez.
Mullen, Scott	5	2	3.70	16	16	0	0	92	90	46	38	31	78	R	L	6-2	185	1-17-75	1996	Beaufort, S.C.
Myers, Taylor	1	1	9.26	8	2	0	1	23	29	24	24	13	19	R	R	6-0	170	11-8-77	1996	Henderson, Nev.
Paredes, Carlos	0	1	9.00	5	0	0	0	7	8	7	7	8	9	R	R	6-0	170	5-10-76	1995	Sabana de la Mar, D.R.
Penny, Tony	4	1	5.21	22	2	0	0	38	46	30	22	15	25	R	R	6-4	168	3-23-76	1995	Newberry, S.C.
Rodriguez, Chad	5	3	4.01	48	0	0	12	61	66	29	27	11	48	R	R	6-2	210	10-16-73	1996	Topeka, Kan.
Sanders, Allen	12	7	3.78	32	18	2	2	140	143	72	59	32	79	R	R	6-3	195	4-15-75	1995	Deer Park, Texas
Santiago, Jose	1	0	2.08	9	0	0	1	13	10	6	3	6	8	R	R	6-3	200	11-5-74	1994	Loiza, P.R.
Simontacchi, Jason	3	7	6.97	29	1	0	2	61	93	56	47	15	38	R	R	6-2	185	11-13-73	1996	Sunnyvale, Calif.
Stein, Ethan	6	10	4.69	39	10	1	2	125	150	83	65	24	72	R	R	6-6	210	11-11-74	1996	Cary, N.C.
Williamson, Jeremy	1	1	4.22	8	7	0	0	32	31	22	15	16	24	L	L	6-3	190	8-19-74	1995	Sumrall, Miss.

SPOKANE — Short-Season Class A

NORTHWEST LEAGUE

BATTING	AVG	G	AB	R	H	2B	3B	HR	RBI	BB	SO	SB	CS	B	T	HT	WT	DOB	1st Yr	Resides
Bautista, Francisco	.278	29	36	11	10	3	1	0	2	5	14	4	1	R	R	6-1	175	4-22-76	1994	El Seibo, D.R.

BATTING	AVG	G	AB	R	H	2B	3B	HR	RBI	BB	SO	SB	CS	B	T	HT	WT	DOB	1st Yr	Resides
Blosser, Doug	.296	65	213	43	63	14	1	12	50	47	61	2	1	L	R	6-3	225	10-1-76	1995	Sarasota, Fla.
Brambilla, Mike	.226	36	115	16	26	5	1	4	21	12	34	1	2	R	R	6-3	210	5-7-76	1996	Brea, Calif.
Brown, Bobby	.059	14	17	1	1	0	0	0	1	2	9	0	0	R	R	5-11	185	5-24-74	1997	Santa Maria, Calif.
Brown, Dermal	.326	73	298	67	97	20	6	13	73	38	65	17	4	L	R	6-1	210	3-27-78	1996	Newburgh, N.Y.
Caruso, Joe	.299	57	194	48	58	12	3	5	36	29	30	10	4	R	R	5-9	187	12-30-74	1997	Lock Haven, Pa.
Dillon, Joe	.214	19	70	6	15	3	0	2	6	5	13	1	0	R	R	6-2	205	8-2-75	1997	Santa Rosa, Calif.
Griffis, Cade	.107	24	28	1	3	0	0	0	2	5	13	0	0	L	R	5-11	200	7-9-74	1997	Burkburnett, Texas
Hill, Jeremy	.283	60	187	35	53	12	1	3	29	25	53	1	0	R	R	6-0	190	8-8-77	1996	Dallas, Texas
LeBron, Juan	.306	69	288	49	88	27	1	7	45	17	74	8	4	R	R	6-4	195	6-7-77	1995	Arroyo, P.R.
Ligons, Merrell	.224	44	143	25	32	2	0	2	11	32	54	12	2	S	R	5-10	165	6-22-77	1996	Compton, Calif.
Metzler, Rod	.228	62	224	37	51	5	5	3	31	18	48	9	2	S	R	5-11	185	11-19-74	1997	Zionsville, Ind.
Montas, Ricardo	.300	66	217	42	65	5	3	2	20	35	39	5	3	R	R	6-2	180	3-9-77	1994	Santo Domingo, D.R.
Pagan, Carlos	.279	26	68	13	19	2	0	1	10	4	13	0	0	R	R	5-9	195	11-2-75	1997	Vega Baja, P.R.
Petru, Rich	.273	33	99	25	27	5	2	3	17	11	15	2	1	R	R	5-11	180	6-3-75	1997	Houston, Texas
Taylor, Kirk	.254	23	59	9	15	3	1	3	13	8	14	1	0	R	R	6-0	190	10-27-74	1997	Murrysville, Pa.
Tomlinson, Goefrey	.338	58	210	49	71	16	0	4	28	32	20	19	1	L	L	6-1	187	8-19-76	1997	Fort Worth, Texas
Ullery, David	.217	12	23	1	5	0	0	1	4	5	5	0	0	L	R	6-3	225	12-16-74	1997	Brazil, Ind.
Willis, Dave	.286	65	252	36	72	15	3	5	36	11	54	5	2	R	R	6-5	240	7-18-74	1997	Arcadia, Calif.

GAMES BY POSITION: C—Griffis 4, Hill 60, Pagan 25, Ullery 6. **1B**—Blosser 35, Brambilla 10, Montas 3, Willis 44. **2B**—Caruso 51, Metzler 30, Montas 1, Petru 5. **3B**—Griffis 5, Metzler 6, Montas 56, Petru 1, Willis 28. **SS**—Ligons 44, Montas 13, Petru 29. **OF**—Bautista 12, B. Brown 10, D. Brown 70, Griffis 1, LeBron 65, Metzler 24, Taylor 21, Tomlinson 55.

PITCHING	W	L	ERA	G	GS	CG	SV	IP	H	R	ER	BB	SO	B	T	HT	WT	DOB	1st Yr	Resides
Alexander, Jordy	7	3	4.59	16	12	0	1	86	82	59	44	18	83	R	L	6-0	180	5-6-77	1996	Burnaby, B.C.
Boring, Richard	2	1	3.20	26	0	0	7	25	32	15	9	7	17	R	R	6-6	210	7-23-75	1996	Nacogdoches, Texas
Burton, Jamie	0	0	1.29	7	0	0	0	7	4	2	1	5	9	R	L	6-5	198	5-28-75	1995	Central Point, Ore.
Carter, Aaron	2	1	2.06	24	0	0	2	35	23	12	8	27	52	R	R	6-2	190	12-19-74	1997	Adkins, Texas
Fitzpatrick, Ken	2	1	4.24	12	0	0	0	17	15	8	8	6	26	R	R	6-7	245	8-25-74	1992	Bell Gardens, Calif.
Gilfillan, Jason	2	1	5.06	16	0	0	0	16	16	13	9	16	22	R	R	6-6	215	8-31-76	1997	Blacksburg, S.C.
Gooding, Jason	4	0	2.26	11	11	0	0	56	44	16	14	11	58	R	L	5-11	190	7-29-74	1997	Cambridge, Ontario
Key, Scott	3	3	3.23	25	1	0	3	70	55	33	25	31	66	R	R	5-11	162	10-4-76	1995	Cantonment, Fla.
Lamber, Justin	1	1	4.28	25	0	0	4	27	24	14	13	20	40	R	L	6-0	210	5-22-76	1997	Hackensack, N.J.
Meady, Todd	2	3	3.72	21	4	0	0	65	68	38	27	18	39	R	R	6-4	216	9-13-76	1995	Middlebury, Conn.
Pederson, Justin	5	3	3.44	15	13	0	0	65	61	34	25	24	84	R	R	6-1	190	9-5-74	1997	Chippewa Falls, Wis.
Quigley, Don	4	2	5.40	22	1	0	0	45	56	35	27	21	21	R	R	6-0	185	11-17-74	1996	Fremont, Calif.
Reichert, Dan	3	4	2.84	9	9	0	0	38	40	25	12	16	39	R	R	6-3	175	7-12-76	1997	Turlock, Calif.
Roeder, Jason	2	1	7.23	9	0	0	0	19	29	20	15	6	14	R	R	6-2	210	2-26-74	1996	Seymour, Ind.
Thurman, Corey	1	2	5.16	5	5	0	0	23	23	19	13	13	24	R	R	6-2	215	11-5-78	1996	Warren, Mich.
Wilson, Kris	5	3	4.52	15	15	0	0	74	101	50	37	21	72	R	R	6-4	225	8-6-76	1997	Palm Harbor, Fla.
Yanz, Eric	0	2	12.18	8	5	0	0	17	28	27	23	12	17	R	R	6-3	210	11-2-74	1997	Golden, Colo.

FORT MYERS — Rookie

GULF COAST LEAGUE

BATTING	AVG	G	AB	R	H	2B	3B	HR	RBI	BB	SO	SB	CS	B	T	HT	WT	DOB	1st Yr	Resides
Benes, Richard	.205	34	39	15	8	0	1	0	1	3	11	3	1	S	R	5-8	155	2-20-78	1996	Bronx, N.Y.
Brito, Alen	.250	11	24	3	6	0	0	0	3	1	7	1	0	R	R	5-11	156	4-10-77	1997	Miami Beach, Fla.
Brito, Juan	.314	25	70	14	22	4	0	3	15	5	5	0	0	R	R	5-11	185	11-7-79	1996	Santiago Rodriguez, D.R.
Calderon, Henry	.245	43	139	17	34	5	3	1	15	10	31	3	1	R	R	6-1	170	8-3-77	1996	Santo Domingo, D.R.
Dasher, Melvin	.201	49	154	20	31	8	0	1	10	11	47	3	1	R	R	6-2	195	9-9-76	1995	Palatka, Fla.
Diaz, Christian	.200	9	15	3	3	1	0	0	2	1	3	0	0	R	R	5-11	207	1-7-78	1997	Brandon, Fla.
Garcia, Rafael	.252	37	115	19	29	1	0	0	10	11	33	9	4	R	R	6-1	190	10-24-79	1996	Nagua, D.R.
Gomez, Erick	.320	50	169	18	54	16	0	3	29	16	36	0	0	L	R	6-2	240	1-21-76	1997	Wrightwood, Calif.
Graham, Tarik	.143	28	42	10	6	0	1	0	4	20	25	1	2	R	L	5-11	185	8-11-79	1997	Orlando, Fla.
Herrera, Pedro	.297	36	101	15	30	2	0	0	7	7	22	2	1	R	R	6-1	169	5-24-79	1996	Santo Domingo, D.R.
McDonald, Ryan	.281	26	57	9	16	1	1	1	9	10	8	1	0	L	R	5-10	190	9-9-75	1997	Issaquah, Wash.
Nunez, Jose	.207	52	174	22	36	8	4	3	22	21	53	2	0	R	R	6-1	175	1-31-77	1995	Salcedo, D.R.
Nunez, Sergio	.286	5	14	4	4	0	1	0	1	0	2	2	0	R	R	5-11	155	1-3-75	1992	Santo Domingo, D.R.
Petru, Rich	.000	1	1	0	0	0	0	0	1	0	0	0	0	R	R	5-11	180	6-3-75	1997	Houston, Texas
Ramirez, Juan	.203	46	133	11	27	5	0	2	14	6	18	0	1	R	R	6-3	190	7-14-77	1995	La Vega, D.R.
Ruiz, Willy	.360	54	197	33	71	4	0	0	14	9	19	20	11	R	R	5-11	150	10-15-78	1996	Nagua, D.R.
Taveras, Jose	.327	57	205	46	67	14	4	7	39	24	42	14	4	R	R	6-0	160	12-17-76	1994	Nagua, D.R.
Tillis, Cameron	.225	34	102	14	23	2	2	1	12	12	28	4	1	S	R	6-2	205	2-25-77	1997	Opp, Ala.
Torres, Rafael	.306	44	160	20	49	2	0	3	33	7	16	2	1	R	R	6-0	187	10-7-78	1996	Santo Domingo, D.R.
Woods, James	.000	2	5	0	0	0	0	0	0	1	5	0	0	S	R	6-1	185	5-10-78	1997	Muskegon, Mich.

GAMES BY POSITION: C—A. Brito 3, J. Brito 23, Diaz 4, Herrera 36, Woods 2. **1B**—Diaz 1, Gomez 13, J. Nunez 11, Ramirez 43. **2B**—Benes 15, Garcia 3, McDonald 7, S. Nunez 4, Ruiz 43. **3B**—Calderon 21, Diaz 2, Garcia 2, J. Nunez 40, Petru 1, Ramirez 1. **SS**—A. Brito 3, Calderon 22, Garcia 30, Ruiz 9. **OF**—Dasher 47, Graham 23, J. Nunez 1, Taveras 57, Tillis 23, Torres 43.

PITCHING	W	L	ERA	G	GS	CG	SV	IP	H	R	ER	BB	SO	B	T	HT	WT	DOB	1st Yr	Resides
Affeldt, Jeremy	2	0	4.50	10	9	0	0	40	34	24	20	21	36	L	L	6-4	185	6-6-79	1997	Medical Lake, Wash.
Budsky, Pavel	2	1	5.23	6	0	0	0	10	17	6	6	1	7	R	R	6-6	217	10-30-75	1996	Prague, Czech Republic
Crutchley, Rickey	1	1	2.41	11	1	0	0	19	14	6	5	14	19	R	L	6-0	160	11-7-78	1997	Acworth, Ga.
Douglass, Ryan	5	1	3.05	12	9	1	0	56	66	21	19	12	35	R	R	6-3	200	12-3-78	1997	Pittsburgh, Pa.
Gamboa, Javier	0	0	1.13	2	2	0	0	8	4	1	1	1	7	R	R	6-1	185	3-17-74	1994	Paso Robles, Calif.
Gonzalez, Edwin	2	1	1.93	3	3	1	0	19	16	8	4	3	12	R	R	5-11	184	8-13-77	1995	Santo Domingo, D.R.
Kyzar, Cory	0	0	2.45	3	0	0	0	4	2	2	1	0	3	R	R	6-1	190	9-4-77	1996	Ellisville, Miss.
Mancha, Tony	2	6	3.28	13	7	0	2	49	53	28	18	11	47	S	R	6-2	205	10-9-78	1997	Las Cruces, N.M.
Martinez, Carlos	1	0	1.97	14	1	1	4	32	24	8	7	14	19	L	L	5-11	155	7-29-78	1996	Santo Domingo, D.R.
Medrano, Juan	1	3	4.55	15	2	0	1	30	33	21	15	9	17	R	R	6-3	183	12-30-78	1996	Monte Cristi, D.R.
Myers, Taylor	5	4	2.41	11	10	2	0	60	48	21	16	20	48	R	R	6-0	170	11-8-77	1996	Henderson, Nev.
Solano, Francisco	4	1	3.81	12	7	1	0	50	53	25	21	9	30	R	R	5-11	179	7-14-79	1996	Santo Domingo, D.R.
Thurman, Corey	2	1	2.38	8	8	1	0	34	28	12	9	22	42	R	R	6-2	215	11-5-78	1996	Warren, Mich.
Torres, Michael	1	1	3.53	15	0	0	1	36	32	19	14	12	27	R	R	5-11	180	1-11-78	1996	Fontana, Calif.
Vanderhorst, Francisco	8	4	2.72	18	1	0	2	43	35	20	13	17	34	R	R	5-11	174	4-6-78	1995	Samana, D.R.
Walsh, Steven	0	0	4.91	4	0	0	0	4	2	3	2	4	1	R	R	6-6	210	3-11-78	1997	Ottawa, Ontario

Los Angeles DODGERS

Manager: Bill Russell.

1997 Record: 88-74, .543 (2nd, NL West)

BATTING	AVG	G	AB	R	H	2B	3B	HR	RBI	BB	SO	SB	CS	B	T	HT	WT	DOB	1st Yr	Resides
Anthony, Eric	.243	47	74	8	18	3	2	2	5	12	18	2	0	L	L	6-2	195	11-8-67	1986	Houston, Texas
Ashley, Billy	.244	71	131	12	32	7	0	6	19	8	46	0	0	R	R	6-7	230	7-11-70	1988	Belleville, Mich.
Blanco, Henry	.400	3	5	1	2	0	0	1	1	0	1	0	0	R	R	5-11	168	8-29-71	1990	Guarenas, Venez.
Butler, Brett	.283	105	343	52	97	8	3	0	18	42	40	15	10	L	L	5-10	160	6-15-57	1979	Atlanta, Ga.
Castro, Juan	.147	40	75	3	11	3	1	0	4	7	20	0	0	R	R	5-10	163	6-20-72	1991	Los Mochis, Mexico
Cedeno, Roger	.273	80	194	31	53	10	2	3	17	25	44	9	1	S	R	6-1	165	8-16-74	1992	Valencia, Venez.
Cromer, Tripp	.291	28	86	8	25	3	0	4	20	6	16	0	1	R	R	6-2	160	11-21-67	1989	Lexington, S.C.
Fonville, Chad	.143	9	14	1	2	0	0	0	1	2	3	0	1	S	R	5-7	155	3-5-71	1992	Midway Park, N.C.
Gagne, Greg	.251	144	514	49	129	20	3	9	57	31	120	2	5	R	R	5-11	180	11-12-61	1979	Rehoboth, Mass.
Garcia, Karim	.128	15	39	5	5	0	0	1	8	6	14	0	0	L	L	6-0	172	10-29-75	1993	Obregon, Mexico
Guerrero, Wilton	.291	111	357	39	104	10	9	4	32	8	52	6	5	S	R	5-11	145	10-24-74	1992	Nizao, D.R.
Hale, Chip	.083	14	12	0	1	0	0	0	0	2	4	0	0	L	R	5-10	175	12-2-64	1987	Tucson, Ariz.
Hollandsworth, Todd	.247	106	296	39	73	20	2	4	31	17	60	5	5	L	L	6-2	193	4-20-73	1991	San Ramon, Calif.
Ingram, Garey	.444	12	9	2	4	0	0	0	1	1	3	1	0	R	R	5-11	185	7-25-70	1990	Columbus, Ga.
Karros, Eric	.266	162	628	86	167	28	0	31	104	61	116	15	7	R	R	6-4	222	11-4-67	1988	Manhattan Beach, Calif.
Kirby, Wayne	.169	46	65	6	11	2	0	0	4	10	12	0	0	L	R	5-10	185	1-22-64	1983	Yorktown, Va.
Konerko, Paul	.143	6	7	0	1	0	0	0	0	1	2	0	0	R	R	6-3	210	3-5-76	1994	Paradise Valley, Ariz.
Lewis, Darren	.299	26	77	7	23	3	1	1	10	6	17	3	2	R	R	6-0	180	8-28-67	1988	Burlingame, Calif.
Liriano, Nelson	.227	76	88	10	20	6	0	1	11	6	12	0	0	S	R	5-10	178	6-3-64	1983	Puerto Plata, D.R.
Mondesi, Raul	.310	159	616	95	191	42	5	30	87	44	105	32	15	R	R	5-11	210	3-12-71	1988	New York, N.Y.
Murray, Eddie	.286	9	7	0	2	0	0	0	3	2	2	0	0	S	R	6-2	220	2-24-56	1973	Canyon Country, Calif.
Nixon, Otis	.274	42	175	30	48	6	2	1	18	13	24	12	2	S	R	6-2	180	1-9-59	1979	Alpharetta, Ga.
Piazza, Mike	.362	152	556	104	201	32	1	40	124	69	77	5	1	R	R	6-3	200	9-4-68	1989	Manhattan Beach, Calif.
Prince, Tom	.220	47	100	17	22	5	0	3	14	5	15	0	0	R	R	5-11	185	8-13-64	1984	Bradenton, Fla.
Riggs, Adam	.200	9	20	3	4	1	0	0	1	4	3	1	0	R	R	6-0	190	10-4-72	1994	Andover, N.J.
Williams, Eddie	.143	8	7	0	1	0	0	0	1	1	1	0	0	R	R	6-0	175	11-1-64	1983	La Mesa, Calif.
Young, Eric	.273	37	154	28	42	4	2	2	16	14	17	13	2	R	R	5-9	180	5-18-67	1989	New Brunswick, N.J.
2-team (118 Colorado)	.280	155	622	106	174	33	8	8	61	71	54	45	14							
Zeile, Todd	.268	160	575	89	154	17	0	31	90	85	112	8	7	R	R	6-1	185	9-9-65	1986	Valencia, Calif.

PITCHING	W	L	ERA	G	GS	CG	SV	IP	H	R	ER	BB	SO	B	T	HT	WT	DOB	1st Yr	Resides
Astacio, Pedro	7	9	4.10	26	24	2	0	154	151	75	70	47	115	R	R	6-2	195	11-28-69	1988	Miami, Fla.
Candiotti, Tom	10	7	3.60	41	18	0	0	135	128	60	54	40	89	R	R	6-2	220	8-31-57	1979	Concord, Calif.
Dreifort, Darren	5	2	2.86	48	0	0	4	63	45	21	20	34	63	R	R	6-2	205	5-18-72	1994	Wichita, Kan.
Gorecki, Rick	1	0	15.00	4	1	0	0	6	9	10	10	6	6	R	R	6-3	167	8-27-73	1991	Oak Forest, Ill.
Guthrie, Mark	1	4	5.32	62	0	0	1	69	71	44	41	30	42	R	L	6-4	205	9-22-65	1987	Bradenton, Fla.
Hall, Darren	3	2	2.30	63	0	0	2	55	58	15	14	26	39	R	R	6-3	205	7-14-64	1986	Irving, Texas
Harkey, Mike	1	0	4.30	10	0	0	0	15	12	8	7	5	6	R	R	6-5	235	10-25-66	1987	Chino Hills, Calif.
Judd, Mike	0	0	0.00	1	0	0	0	3	4	0	0	0	4	R	R	6-2	200	6-30-75	1995	La Mesa, Calif.
Martinez, Ramon	10	5	3.64	22	22	1	0	134	123	64	54	68	120	S	R	6-4	173	3-22-68	1985	Santo Domingo, D.R.
Nomo, Hideo	14	12	4.25	33	33	1	0	207	193	104	98	92	233	R	R	6-2	210	8-31-68	1995	Kobe, Japan
Osuna, Antonio	3	4	2.19	48	0	0	0	62	46	15	15	19	68	R	R	5-11	160	4-12-73	1991	Juan Jose Rios, Mexico
Park, Chan Ho	14	8	3.38	32	29	2	0	192	149	80	72	70	166	R	R	6-2	185	6-30-73	1994	Kong Ju City, Korea
Radinsky, Scott	5	1	2.89	75	0	0	3	62	54	22	20	21	44	L	L	6-3	204	3-3-68	1986	Simi Valley, Calif.
Reyes, Dennis	2	3	3.83	14	5	0	0	47	51	21	20	18	36	L	L	6-3	220	4-19-77	1994	Higuera de Zaragoza, Mexico
Valdes, Ismael	10	11	2.65	30	30	0	0	197	171	68	58	47	140	R	R	6-3	207	8-21-73	1991	Victoria, Mexico
Worrell, Todd	2	6	5.28	65	0	0	35	60	60	38	35	23	61	R	R	6-5	200	9-28-59	1982	St. Louis, Mo.

FIELDING

Catcher	PCT	G	PO	A	E	DP	PB
Piazza	.986	139	1045	74	16	10	10
Prince	.996	45	221	25	1	5	1

First Base	PCT	G	PO	A	E	DP
Blanco	1.000	1	5	0	0	0
Karros	.992	162	1317	121	11	88
Konerko	1.000	1	3	0	0	1
Liriano	1.000	2	5	1	0	0

Second Base	PCT	G	PO	A	E	DP
Castro	.977	14	15	28	1	4
Cromer	.968	17	24	36	2	7
Fonville	.833	3	0	5	1	0
Guerrero	.989	90	140	221	4	24
Liriano	.949	17	14	23	2	6
Riggs	1.000	8	6	19	0	3
Young	.979	37	60	79	3	17

Third Base	PCT	G	PO	A	E	DP
Blanco	.000	1	0	0	0	0
Castro	1.000	3	2	3	0	0
Cromer	.000	1	0	0	0	0
Hale	1.000	2	1	0	0	0
Konerko	.000	1	0	0	0	0
Liriano	.000	1	0	0	0	0
Zeile	.931	160	105	248	26	27

Shortstop	PCT	G	PO	A	E	DP
Castro	1.000	22	19	34	0	6
Cromer	.980	10	23	25	1	4
Gagne	.971	143	175	357	16	54
Guerrero	1.000	5	8	10	0	2
Liriano	.000	1	0	0	0	0

Outfield	PCT	G	PO	A	E	DP
Anthony	.966	21	26	2	1	1
Ashley	.911	35	39	2	4	0
Butler	1.000	91	163	4	0	2
Cedeno	.987	71	148	1	2	0
Garcia	1.000	12	13	0	0	0
Hollandsworth	.984	99	185	2	3	0
Ingram	1.000	7	4	0	0	0
Kirby	1.000	26	36	1	0	0
Lewis	.980	25	49	1	1	0
Mondesi	.989	159	338	10	4	0
Nixon	.990	42	97	1	1	0

LARRY GOREN

Raul Mondesi

FARM SYSTEM

Director of Player Development: Charlie Blaney

Class	Farm Team	League	W	L	Pct.	Finish*	Manager(s)	First Yr
AAA	Albuquerque (N.M.) Dukes	Pacific Coast	62	79	.440	8th (10)	Glenn Hoffman	1963
AA	San Antonio (Texas) Missions	Texas	84	55	.604	+1st (8)	Ron Roenicke	1977
#A	San Bernardino (Calif.) Spirit	California	68	72	.486	7th (10)	Del Crandall/Dino Ebel	1995
#A	Vero Beach (Fla.) Dodgers	Florida State	70	67	.511	7th (14)	John Shoemaker	1980
A	Savannah (Ga.) Sand Gnats	South Atlantic	63	77	.450	11th (14)	John Shelby	1996
A	Yakima (Wash.) Bears	Northwest	23	53	.303	8th (8)	Joe Vavra	1988
#R	Great Falls (Mont.) Dodgers	Pioneer	40	32	.556	1st (8)	Mickey Hatcher	1984

*Finish in overall standings (No. of teams in league) #Advanced level +Won league championship

ORGANIZATION LEADERS

MAJOR LEAGUERS

BATTING

*AVG	Mike Piazza	.362
R	Mike Piazza	104
H	Mike Piazza	201
TB	Mike Piazza	355
2B	Raul Mondesi	42
3B	Wilton Guerrero	9
HR	Mike Piazza	40
RBI	Mike Piazza	124
BB	Todd Zeile	85
SO	Greg Gagne	120
SB	Raul Mondesi	32

PITCHING

W	Two tied at	14
L	Hideo Nomo	12
#ERA	Ismael Valdez	2.65
G	Scott Radinsky	75
CG	Chan Ho Park	2
SV	Todd Worrell	35
IP	Hideo Nomo	207
BB	Hideo Nomo	92
SO	Hideo Nomo	233

GEORGE GOJKOVICH

Hideo Nomo

MORRIS FOSTOFF

Paul Konerko

MINOR LEAGUERS

BATTING

*AVG	Eddie Williams, Albuquerque	.366
R	Eric Stuckenschneider, Vero Beach	100
H	J.P. Roberge, San Antonio	166
TB	Paul Konerko, Albuquerque	300
2B	Cliff Anderson, San Bernardino	40
3B	Two tied at	13
HR	Paul Konerko, Albuquerque	37
RBI	Paul Konerko, Albuquerque	127
BB	Eric Stuckenschneider, Vero Beach	101
SO	Juan Diaz, Vero Beach/Savannah	156
SB	Mike Metcalfe, San Bernardino	67

PITCHING

W	Two tied at	14
L	Three tied at	12
#ERA	C.D. Stover, Great Falls	2.56
G	Dan Ricabal, Vero Beach	75
CG	Three tied at	3
SV	Dan Ricabal, Vero Beach	28
IP	Mike Judd, San Antonio/Vero Beach	166
BB	Kevin Pincavitch, San Bernardino	112
SO	Mike Judd, San Antonio/Vero Beach	169

*Minimum 250 At-Bats #Minimum 75 Innings

TOP 10 PROSPECTS

LARRY GOREN

Karim Garcia

How the Dodgers Top 10 prospects, as judged by Baseball America prior to the 1997 season, fared in 1997:

Player, Pos.	Club (Class)	AVG	AB	R	H	2B	3B	HR	RBI	SB
1. Paul Konerko, 3b	Los Angeles	.143	7	0	1	0	0	0	0	0
	Albuquerque (AAA)	.323	483	97	156	31	1	37	127	2
2. Karim Garcia, of	Los Angeles	.128	39	5	5	0	0	1	8	0
	Albuquerque (AAA)	.305	262	53	80	17	6	20	66	11
3. Adrian Beltre, 3b	Vero Beach (A)	.317	435	95	138	24	2	26	104	25
4. Wilton Guerrero, 2b	Los Angeles	.291	357	39	104	10	9	4	32	6
	Albuquerque (AAA)	.400	45	9	18	0	1	0	5	3
6. Damian Rolls, 3b	Savannah (A)	.211	475	57	100	17	5	5	47	11
8. Alex Cora, ss	San Antonio (AA)	.234	448	52	105	20	4	3	48	12
9. Adam Riggs, 2b	Los Angeles	.200	20	3	4	1	0	0	1	1
	Albuquerque (AAA)	.304	227	59	69	8	3	13	28	12
10. Omar Moreno, of		Did not play								

Player, Pos.	Club (Class)	W	L	ERA	G	SV	IP	H	BB	SO
5. Onan Masaoka, lhp	Vero Beach (A)	6	8	3.87	28	1	149	113	55	132
7. Ted Lilly, lhp	San Bernardino (A)	7	8	2.81	23	0	135	116	32	158

ALBUQUERQUE — Class AAA

PACIFIC COAST LEAGUE

BATTING	AVG	G	AB	R	H	2B	3B	HR	RBI	BB	SO	SB	CS	B	T	HT	WT	DOB	1st Yr.	Resides
Anthony, Eric	.343	27	105	18	36	6	1	7	27	11	28	2	3	L	L	6-2	195	11-8-67	1986	Houston, Texas
Battle, Howard	.237	50	139	14	33	3	2	3	16	6	23	1	2	R	R	6-0	197	3-25-72	1990	Ocean Springs, Miss.
Blanco, Henry	.313	91	294	38	92	20	1	6	47	37	63	7	4	R	R	5-11	168	8-29-71	1990	Guarenas, Venez.
Castro, Juan	.307	27	101	11	31	5	2	2	11	4	20	1	0	R	R	5-10	163	6-20-72	1991	Los Mochis, Mexico
Cedeno, Roger	.354	29	113	21	40	4	4	2	9	22	16	5	5	S	R	6-1	165	8-16-74	1992	Valencia, Venez.
Cromer, Tripp	.321	43	140	25	45	8	6	5	24	14	34	4	1	R	R	6-2	160	11-21-67	1989	Lexington, S.C.
Demetral, Chris	.250	12	24	1	6	2	0	1	1	6	3	0	1	L	R	5-11	175	12-8-69	1991	Sterling Heights, Mich.
Fonville, Chad	.218	102	371	49	81	5	2	0	22	30	39	23	10	S	R	5-7	155	3-5-71	1992	Midway Park, N.C.
Garcia, Karim	.305	71	262	53	80	17	6	20	66	23	70	11	5	L	L	6-0	172	10-29-75	1993	Obregon, Mexico
Guerrero, Wilton	.400	10	45	9	18	0	1	0	5	2	3	3	0	S	R	5-11	145	10-24-74	1992	Nizao, D.R.
Hale, Chip	.267	88	247	43	66	16	0	2	30	58	26	3	3	L	R	5-10	175	12-2-64	1987	Tucson, Ariz.
Hollandsworth, Todd	.429	13	56	13	24	4	3	1	14	4	4	2	3	L	L	6-2	193	4-20-73	1991	San Ramon, Calif.
Huckaby, Ken	.199	69	201	14	40	5	1	0	18	9	36	1	0	R	R	6-1	205	1-27-71	1991	Philadelphia, Pa.
Kirby, Wayne	.335	68	269	57	90	16	5	10	43	26	33	18	5	L	R	5-10	185	1-22-64	1983	Yorktown, Va.
Konerko, Paul	.323	130	483	97	156	31	1	37	127	64	61	2	3	R	R	6-3	210	3-5-76	1994	Paradise Valley, Ariz.
Marrero, Oreste	.262	96	263	38	69	20	0	9	42	24	70	1	1	L	L	6-0	205	10-31-69	1987	Bayamon, P.R.
Maurer, Ron	.275	114	349	61	96	21	4	8	50	39	59	3	3	R	R	6-1	185	6-10-68	1990	Beachwood, N.J.
Murray, Eddie	.308	9	26	4	8	1	0	2	9	3	3	0	0	S	R	6-2	220	2-24-56	1973	Canyon Country, Calif.
Parker, Rick	.272	49	151	33	41	7	3	6	21	10	26	6	0	R	R	6-0	185	3-20-63	1985	Independence, Mo.
Pennyfeather, Will	.254	115	402	59	102	21	4	17	54	26	73	11	11	R	R	6-2	215	5-25-68	1988	Perth Amboy, N.J.
Riggs, Adam	.304	57	227	59	69	8	3	13	28	29	39	12	2	R	R	6-0	190	10-4-72	1994	Andover, N.J.
Spearman, Vernon	.217	30	92	13	20	3	1	0	8	14	11	5	1	L	L	5-10	160	12-17-69	1991	Union City, Calif.
Steed, Dave	.213	25	47	8	10	4	0	1	4	4	19	0	0	R	R	6-1	205	2-25-73	1993	Starkville, Miss.
Williams, Eddie	.366	76	279	73	102	17	0	29	76	37	45	0	2	R	R	6-0	175	11-1-64	1983	La Mesa, Calif.

PITCHING	W	L	ERA	G	GS	CG	SV	IP	H	R	ER	BB	SO	B	T	HT	WT	DOB	1st Yr	Resides
Ahearne, Pat	2	4	4.90	20	8	0	0	61	82	43	33	20	44	R	R	6-3	195	12-10-69	1992	Atascadero, Calif.
Anderson, Mike	0	0	10.80	6	0	0	1	10	18	12	12	1	9	R	R	6-3	205	7-30-66	1988	Georgetown, Texas
Brown, Alvin	4	6	6.13	12	11	1	0	62	74	50	42	35	43	R	R	6-1	200	9-2-70	1989	Los Angeles, Calif.
Brunson, Will	1	1	6.49	27	0	0	0	26	39	19	19	10	25	L	L	6-4	185	3-20-70	1992	DeSoto, Texas
Dreifort, Darren	0	0	1.59	2	2	0	0	6	2	1	1	1	3	R	R	6-2	205	5-18-72	1994	Wichita, Kan.
Dressendorfer, Kirk	0	2	4.50	7	7	0	0	30	43	18	15	10	14	R	R	5-11	180	4-8-69	1990	Pearland, Texas
Elvira, Narciso	0	0	16.88	4	0	0	0	3	5	6	5	3	4	L	L	5-10	160	10-29-67	1986	Veracruz, Mexico
Garcia, Jose	3	3	5.12	33	0	0	0	46	57	27	26	14	44	R	R	6-3	146	6-12-72	1991	Monte Cristi, D.R.
Harkey, Mike	2	2	2.10	47	0	0	15	56	50	14	13	11	57	R	R	6-5	235	10-25-66	1987	Chino Hills, Calif.
Henderson, Ryan	1	3	6.23	13	0	0	0	17	20	14	12	14	17	R	R	6-1	190	9-30-69	1992	Dana Point, Calif.
Herges, Matt	0	8	8.89	31	12	0	0	85	120	92	84	46	61	L	R	6-0	200	4-1-70	1992	Champaign, Ill.
Hubbs, Dan	6	4	3.90	62	3	0	3	95	103	45	41	38	87	R	R	6-2	200	1-23-71	1993	Renton, Wash.
Kubenka, Jeff	0	2	8.59	8	0	0	2	7	11	9	7	2	10	R	L	6-0	195	8-24-74	1996	Schulenburg, Texas
Martinez, Jesus	7	1	6.21	26	12	0	0	84	112	64	58	52	80	L	L	6-2	145	3-13-74	1991	Santo Domingo, D.R.
Munoz, Bobby	0	3	4.35	18	0	0	0	31	43	17	15	15	20	R	R	6-7	237	3-3-68	1989	Hialeah, Fla.
2-team (17 Las Vegas)	0	5	6.71	35	1	0	0	54	73	43	40	26	33							
Osuna, Antonio	1	1	1.93	13	0	0	6	14	9	3	3	4	26	R	R	5-11	160	4-12-73	1991	Juan Jose Rios, Mexico
Pyc, Dave	12	12	5.33	31	23	3	1	152	181	104	90	50	106	L	L	6-3	235	2-11-71	1992	Depew, N.Y.
Rath, Gary	7	11	6.05	24	24	0	0	132	177	107	89	49	100	L	L	6-2	185	1-10-73	1994	Long Beach, Miss.
Reyes, Dennis	6	3	5.65	10	10	1	0	57	70	40	36	33	45	L	L	6-3	220	4-19-77	1994	Higuera de Zaragoza, Mexico
Roach, Petie	0	5	5.29	31	0	0	1	49	56	31	29	27	33	L	L	6-2	180	9-19-70	1992	Redding, Calif.
Treadwell, Jody	10	5	5.12	27	21	2	1	128	143	80	73	54	108	R	R	6-0	190	12-14-68	1990	Jacksonville, Fla.
Weaver, Eric	0	3	6.42	21	8	0	0	69	101	53	49	38	54	R	R	6-5	230	8-4-73	1991	Illiopolis, Ill.

FIELDING

Catcher	PCT	G	PO	A	E	DP	PB
Blanco	.995	83	568	64	3	11	10
Huckaby	.975	63	359	25	10	2	7
Steed	.989	19	86	8	1	0	0

First Base	PCT	G	PO	A	E	DP
Anthony	1.000	1	1	0	0	0
Battle	1.000	1	6	0	0	3
Blanco	1.000	7	39	4	0	5
Hale	.995	49	379	32	2	40
Konerko	.982	29	206	15	4	17
Marrero	.986	32	195	18	3	24
Maurer	1.000	16	100	5	0	8
Murray	.966	7	56	1	2	7
Parker	1.000	1	5	0	0	0
Williams	.996	31	232	15	1	25

Second Base	PCT	G	PO	A	E	DP
Castro	1.000	3	6	13	0	2
Demetral	1.000	7	14	26	0	7
Fonville	.963	30	53	77	5	17
Guerrero	.952	4	8	12	1	2
Hale	.990	27	40	56	1	21
Konerko	1.000	1	3	3	0	1
Maurer	.991	26	47	59	1	13
Parker	.862	8	8	17	4	2
Riggs	.973	56	129	162	8	35

Third Base	PCT	G	PO	A	E	DP
Battle	.892	33	23	51	9	3
Hale	1.000	7	4	11	0	3
Konerko	.925	105	48	198	20	21
Maurer	1.000	9	4	17	0	1
Parker	1.000	1	1	0	0	0
Riggs	1.000	1	1	0	0	0
Steed	.000	1	0	0	0	0
Williams	.000	1	0	0	0	0

Shortstop	PCT	G	PO	A	E	DP
Battle	1.000	2	2	1	0	0
Castro	.915	24	27	70	9	15
Cromer	.966	42	65	106	6	23
Fonville	.935	26	31	70	7	10
Guerrero	.895	7	8	26	4	7
Maurer	.949	59	79	184	14	45
Parker	1.000	4	4	3	0	0

Outfield	PCT	G	PO	A	E	DP
Ahearne	.000	1	0	0	0	0
Anthony	.968	23	29	1	1	0
Battle	.000	2	0	0	0	0
Blanco	.000	1	0	0	0	0
Cedeno	.964	29	53	1	2	0
Demetral	.000	1	0	0	0	0
Fonville	.968	49	89	2	3	2
Garcia	.952	64	97	3	5	0
Hale	1.000	2	4	0	0	0
Harkey	.000	1	0	0	0	0
Hollandsworth	1.000	13	32	1	0	0
Kirby	.967	66	138	9	5	2
Marrero	.884	41	36	2	5	0
Maurer	1.000	5	3	1	0	0
Parker	.946	33	34	1	2	0
Pennyfeather	.960	111	207	8	9	1
Riggs	1.000	1	1	0	0	0
Spearman	.976	26	36	5	1	1

SAN ANTONIO — Class AA

TEXAS LEAGUE

BATTING	AVG	G	AB	R	H	2B	3B	HR	RBI	BB	SO	SB	CS	B	T	HT	WT	DOB	1st Yr	Resides
Battle, Howard	.242	16	33	2	8	1	0	0	1	0	7	0	0	R	R	6-0	197	3-25-72	1990	Ocean Springs, Miss.
Cooney, Kyle	.290	72	252	39	73	16	2	8	49	7	44	4	2	R	R	6-2	200	3-31-73	1994	Meriden, Conn.
Cora, Alex	.234	127	448	52	105	20	4	3	48	25	60	12	9	L	R	6-0	180	10-18-75	1996	Miami, Fla.

BATTING	AVG	G	AB	R	H	2B	3B	HR	RBI	BB	SO	SB	CS	B	T	HT	WT	DOB	1st Yr	Resides
Davis, Eddie	.209	74	206	30	43	8	2	11	34	15	69	2	3	R	R	6-0	202	12-22-72	1993	New Orleans, La.
Durkin, Chris	.272	38	125	18	34	11	0	4	18	13	33	8	2	L	L	6-6	247	8-12-70	1991	Youngstown, Ohio
Gibbs, Kevin	.335	101	358	89	120	21	6	2	34	72	48	49	19	S	R	6-2	182	4-3-74	1995	Davidsonville, Miss.
Ingram, Garey	.299	92	348	68	104	28	7	12	52	37	50	16	6	R	R	5-11	185	7-25-70	1990	Columbus, Ga.
Johnson, Keith	.268	96	298	43	80	9	3	9	52	17	48	7	6	R	R	5-11	190	4-17-71	1992	Stockton, Calif.
Kirkpatrick, Jay	.260	62	215	22	56	9	0	8	42	8	53	0	1	L	R	6-4	220	7-10-69	1991	Tallahassee, Fla.
LoDuca, Paul	.327	105	385	63	126	28	2	7	69	46	27	16	8	R	R	5-10	193	4-12-72	1993	Phoenix, Ariz.
Melendez, Dan	.256	87	258	40	66	19	1	2	24	44	42	4	2	L	L	6-4	195	1-4-71	1992	Los Angeles, Calif.
Richardson, Brian	.297	134	488	73	145	23	13	13	90	42	99	3	6	R	R	6-2	190	8-31-75	1992	Diamond Bar, Calif.
Richardson, Scott	.283	91	300	49	85	15	1	7	38	46	52	6	5	R	R	6-1	175	2-19-71	1992	Rialto, Calif.
Roberge, J.P.	.322	134	516	94	166	26	4	17	105	39	70	18	9	R	R	6-0	180	9-12-72	1994	Arcadia, Calif.
Romero, Willie	.324	30	108	22	35	8	1	1	16	15	11	7	4	R	R	5-11	158	8-5-74	1991	Candelaria, Venez.
Spearman, Vernon	.279	41	136	31	38	3	3	1	7	19	25	9	3	L	L	5-10	160	12-17-69	1991	Union City, Calif.
Wingate, Ervan	.000	1	3	0	0	0	0	0	0	2	1	0	0	R	R	6-0	185	2-4-74	1992	Redlands, Calif.

PITCHING	W	L	ERA	G	GS	CG	SV	IP	H	R	ER	BB	SO	B	T	HT	WT	DOB	1st Yr	Resides
Ahearne, Pat	4	5	4.50	14	14	3	0	84	109	48	42	13	45	R	R	6-3	195	12-10-69	1992	Atascadero, Calif.
Anderson, Mike	4	2	6.33	19	2	0	0	43	47	31	30	13	30	R	R	6-3	205	7-30-66	1988	Georgetown, Texas
Bland, Nate	3	2	7.02	10	8	0	0	41	47	34	32	24	30	L	L	6-5	195	12-27-74	1993	Birmingham, Ala.
Brown, Alvin	6	5	3.74	16	16	2	0	96	83	48	40	33	67	R	R	6-1	200	9-2-70	1989	Los Angeles, Calif.
Brunson, Will	5	5	3.47	17	11	2	0	73	68	30	28	13	71	L	L	6-4	185	3-20-70	1992	DeSoto, Texas
Flores, Ignacio	10	7	3.25	27	18	0	1	133	125	59	48	39	102	R	R	6-2	188	5-8-75	1995	La Paz, Mexico
Garcia, Jose	3	1	3.15	10	0	0	1	20	19	8	7	4	14	R	R	6-3	146	6-12-72	1991	Monte Cristi, D.R.
Gorecki, Rick	4	2	1.39	7	7	0	0	45	26	8	7	15	33	R	R	6-3	167	8-27-73	1991	Oak Forest, Ill.
Herges, Matt	0	1	8.80	4	3	0	0	15	22	15	15	10	12	L	R	6-0	200	4-1-70	1992	Champaign, Ill.
Iglesias, Mike	6	2	3.64	42	0	0	8	59	51	25	24	26	55	R	R	6-5	215	11-9-72	1991	Castro Valley, Calif.
Judd, Mike	4	2	2.73	12	12	0	0	79	69	27	24	33	65	R	R	6-2	200	6-30-75	1995	La Mesa, Calif.
Kubenka, Jeff	3	0	0.70	19	0	0	4	26	10	2	2	6	38	R	L	6-0	195	8-24-74	1996	Schulenburg, Texas
Lagarde, Joe	4	4	3.76	53	0	0	17	69	68	34	29	31	65	R	R	5-9	180	1-17-75	1993	Washington, D.C.
Linares, Rich	2	1	7.23	18	0	0	0	24	37	21	19	6	11	R	R	5-11	200	8-31-72	1992	Long Beach, Calif.
Neal, Billy	2	4	6.10	25	0	0	0	31	35	25	21	16	12	R	R	6-0	201	9-20-71	1995	Scottsdale, Ariz.
Reyes, Dennis	8	1	3.02	12	12	1	0	80	79	33	27	28	66	L	L	6-3	220	4-19-77	1994	Higuera de Zaragoza, Mexico
Roach, Petie	7	4	3.73	13	13	1	0	82	76	39	34	35	56	L	L	6-2	180	9-19-70	1992	Redding, Calif.
Stone, Ricky	0	3	5.47	25	5	0	3	53	63	33	32	30	46	R	R	6-2	173	2-28-75	1994	Hamilton, Ohio
Urbina, Dan	0	0	3.86	9	0	0	0	14	19	8	6	13	6	R	R	6-0	195	11-13-74	1992	La Urbina, Venez.
Watts, Brandon	0	0	9.00	1	0	0	0	1	2	1	1	0	2	L	L	6-3	190	9-13-72	1991	Ruston, La.
Weaver, Eric	7	2	3.61	13	13	2	0	85	80	43	34	38	60	R	R	6-5	230	8-4-73	1991	Illiopolis, Ill.
Williams, Jeff	2	1	5.40	5	5	0	0	28	30	17	17	7	14	R	L	6-0	185	6-6-72	1996	Page, Australia

FIELDING

Catcher	PCT	G	PO	A	E	DP	PB
Cooney	.983	53	325	26	6	2	6
Kirkpatrick	1.000	3	9	2	0	0	0
LoDuca	.990	88	576	84	7	7	9
Roberge	1.000	1	1	0	0	0	0

First Base	PCT	G	PO	A	E	DP
Battle	1.000	4	46	1	0	3
Cooney	1.000	1	3	0	0	0
Kirkpatrick	.989	29	244	24	3	17
LoDuca	1.000	7	60	7	0	2
Melendez	.985	72	614	45	10	53
B. Richardson	.946	6	32	3	2	3
S. Richardson	1.000	2	5	0	0	1

	PCT	G	PO	A	E	DP
Roberge	.993	33	257	11	2	31

Second Base	PCT	G	PO	A	E	DP
Ingram	.962	69	118	186	12	27
Johnson	.970	36	63	99	5	22
Roberge	.979	39	71	117	4	21
Wingate	1.000	1	2	2	0	0

Third Base	PCT	G	PO	A	E	DP
Battle	1.000	1	0	2	0	0
Ingram	.900	5	3	6	1	0
Johnson	.765	8	2	11	4	0
B. Richardson	.946	130	62	268	19	19

Shortstop	PCT	G	PO	A	E	DP
Cora	.968	127	197	412	20	88
Johnson	.931	13	14	40	4	5
Roberge	.500	1	2	0	2	0

Outfield	PCT	G	PO	A	E	DP
Davis	.965	68	104	7	4	0
Durkin	.961	31	67	6	3	1
Gibbs	.982	98	215	2	4	1
Ingram	1.000	18	33	0	0	0
Johnson	.974	27	36	1	1	0
S. Richardson	.967	83	115	2	4	0
Roberge	1.000	49	70	8	0	1
Romero	1.000	24	37	2	0	0
Spearman	.975	39	73	4	2	1

SAN BERNARDINO — Class A

CALIFORNIA LEAGUE

BATTING	AVG	G	AB	R	H	2B	3B	HR	RBI	BB	SO	SB	CS	B	T	HT	WT	DOB	1st Yr	Resides
Anderson, Cliff	.273	132	458	77	125	40	5	21	79	31	137	3	11	L	R	5-8	165	7-4-70	1992	Kodiak, Alaska
Avila, Rolo	.290	134	507	94	147	25	3	6	47	63	63	52	24	R	R	5-8	170	8-10-73	1994	Paramount, Calif.
Barlok, Todd	.302	44	116	25	35	6	3	5	19	17	32	7	5	R	R	6-4	220	8-8-71	1995	Bristol, Conn.
Bergeron, Peter	.250	2	8	1	2	0	0	0	1	0	2	2	0	L	R	6-1	185	11-9-77	1996	Greenfield, Mass.
Brown, Jason	.255	30	102	15	26	10	0	0	13	3	26	0	3	R	R	6-2	205	5-22-74	1997	Rolling Hills Estates, Calif.
Davis, Glenn	.246	64	228	44	56	16	0	9	36	46	77	7	3	S	L	6-1	200	11-25-75	1997	Aston, Pa.
Durkin, Chris	.167	3	12	1	2	0	0	0	0	0	4	0	0	L	L	6-6	247	8-12-70	1991	Youngstown, Ohio
Faircloth, Kevin	.226	63	159	28	36	9	1	2	16	6	49	10	4	R	R	6-2	170	6-6-73	1994	Winston-Salem, N.C.
Hollandsworth, Todd	.250	2	8	1	2	0	1	0	2	1	2	0	0	L	L	6-2	193	4-20-73	1991	San Ramon, Calif.
Horton, Conan	.100	14	30	3	3	0	0	0	0	2	10	0	1	S	R	6-1	220	6-10-74	1997	Sacramento, Calif.
Jones, Jack	.227	123	388	53	88	21	3	11	52	40	112	10	7	R	R	5-11	165	11-7-74	1996	Modesto, Calif.
Leach, Nick	.367	16	60	11	22	6	1	4	12	5	11	0	1	L	R	6-1	190	12-7-77	1996	Madera, Calif.
Malave, Joshua	.250	1	4	0	1	0	0	0	0	0	0	0	0	R	R	6-0	196	3-22-75	1995	Fort Lauderdale, Fla.
McCarty, Matt	.087	12	23	5	2	0	0	0	1	5	5	3	0	R	R	6-0	172	2-2-76	1995	Crawfordsville, Ind.
Metcalfe, Mike	.283	132	519	83	147	28	7	3	47	55	79	67	32	R	R	5-10	175	1-2-73	1994	Orlando, Fla.
Mikesell, Steve	.000	2	1	0	0	0	0	0	0	1	0	0	0	R	R	6-1	220	8-13-73	1996	Covina, Calif.
Mota, Tony	.240	111	420	53	101	14	13	4	49	30	97	11	8	S	R	6-1	200	10-31-77	1996	Miami, Fla.
Owen, Andy	.269	112	357	46	96	30	5	10	49	26	77	11	13	L	L	5-10	180	7-12-73	1995	Escondido, Calif.
Pena, Angel	.276	86	322	53	89	22	4	16	64	32	84	3	5	R	R	6-0	220	2-16-75	1993	San Pedro de Macoris, D.R.
Proctor, Murph	.304	107	381	66	116	33	2	13	70	65	66	1	7	S	L	6-1	190	6-12-69	1991	Carmel, Calif.
Sankey, Brian	.257	55	179	21	46	10	1	2	22	16	28	3	10	L	L	6-1	195	6-12-74	1996	Orleans, Mass.
Snow, Casey	.197	43	132	10	26	5	3	1	10	4	35	2	3	S	R	5-10	185	12-8-74	1996	Canoga Park, Calif.
Weekley, Jason	.281	101	313	58	88	15	5	16	59	41	102	3	6	R	R	6-3	190	8-20-73	1996	Hercules, Calif.

GAMES BY POSITION: C—Brown 29, Horton 9, Malave 1, Mikesell 2, Pena 81, Snow 29. **1B**—Davis 58, Faircloth 9, Horton 1, Leach 4, McCarty 1, Owen 2, Proctor 27, Sankey 51. **2B**—Anderson 3, Barlok 1, Faircloth 15, Metcalfe 129. **3B**—Anderson 127, Barlok 20,

Faircloth 7, McCarty 1, Weekley 1. **SS**—Anderson 1, Faircloth 27, Jones 122. **OF**—Anderson 2, Avila 134, Barlok 2, Bergeron 2, Durkin 3, Hollandsworth 2, McCarty 8, Mota 110, Owen 98, Weekley 85.

PITCHING	W	L	ERA	G	GS	CG	SV	IP	H	R	ER	BB	SO	B	T	HT	WT	DOB	1st Yr	Resides
Anderson, Mike	1	0	4.00	4	0	0	0	9	7	5	4	5	13	R	R	6-3	205	7-30-66	1988	Georgetown, Texas
Ashworth, Kym	0	3	6.46	9	5	0	0	31	34	27	22	24	26	L	L	6-2	175	7-31-76	1993	Para Hills West, Australia
Backowski, Lance	0	0	13.50	4	0	0	0	6	10	11	9	9	3	R	R	6-0	180	6-8-75	1995	Fresno, Calif.
Cervantes, Peter	0	0	0.00	1	0	0	0	1	1	0	0	0	0	L	R	6-3	195	10-13-74	1995	Los Angeles, Calif.
Davis, John	0	2	7.83	17	4	0	0	44	50	48	38	34	44	R	R	6-4	218	8-31-73	1995	Swainsboro, Ga.
Deskins, Casey	6	5	5.07	37	6	1	2	98	110	56	55	34	65	R	L	6-3	220	4-5-72	1993	Yakima, Wash.
Franklin, Wayne	0	0	0.00	1	0	0	0	2	2	0	0	0	1	L	L	6-2	195	3-9-74	1996	North East, Md.
Gorecki, Rick	2	3	3.88	14	14	0	0	51	38	22	22	32	58	R	R	6-3	167	8-27-73	1991	Oak Forest, Ill.
Kramer, Matthew	0	0	5.94	10	0	0	0	17	18	12	11	16	16	R	R	6-2	210	4-4-76	1996	Simi Valley, Calif.
Kubenka, Jeff	5	1	0.92	34	0	0	19	39	24	4	4	11	62	R	L	6-0	195	8-24-74	1996	Schulenburg, Texas
Lilly, Ted	7	8	2.81	23	21	2	0	135	116	52	42	32	158	L	L	6-1	180	1-4-76	1996	Fresno, Calif.
Linares, Rich	1	0	3.41	26	0	0	10	29	36	11	11	7	33	R	R	5-11	200	8-31-72	1992	Long Beach, Calif.
Martinez, Ramon	0	1	1.15	4	4	0	0	16	10	2	2	4	16	R	R	5-10	155	2-27-79	1996	Monte Cristi, D.R.
Mayo, Blake	1	1	5.16	20	0	0	0	30	36	18	17	17	29	R	R	6-2	210	12-18-72	1996	Gadsden, Ala.
McNeely, Mitch	1	3	7.55	18	0	0	0	39	61	36	33	20	28	L	L	6-6	190	2-14-74	1995	New Albany, Miss.
Mitchell, Dean	0	0	0.00	1	0	0	0	1	0	0	0	1	1	R	R	5-11	175	3-19-74	1996	Waco, Texas
Neal, Billy	0	5	4.24	24	0	0	1	47	50	30	22	17	31	R	R	6-0	201	9-20-71	1995	Scottsdale, Ariz.
Ochsenfeld, Chris	1	1	5.87	13	0	0	1	15	18	13	10	14	12	L	L	6-2	210	8-21-76	1994	Hampton, Va.
Paluk, Jeff	1	3	7.57	28	0	0	0	44	63	39	37	25	38	R	R	6-4	215	9-28-72	1994	Plymouth, Mich.
Pearsall, J.J.	14	11	4.54	31	28	0	0	161	145	91	81	93	112	L	L	6-2	202	9-9-73	1995	Burnt Hills, N.Y.
Pincavitch, Kevin	6	9	6.78	28	27	0	0	135	135	128	102	112	130	R	R	5-11	180	7-5-70	1992	Greensboro, Pa.
Stone, Ricky	3	3	3.35	8	8	0	0	54	40	22	20	10	40	R	R	6-2	173	2-28-75	1994	Hamilton, Ohio
Thompson, Frank	5	2	5.69	39	0	0	2	55	58	39	35	35	40	R	R	6-1	190	4-10-73	1996	Daytona Beach, Fla.
Urbina, Dan	3	2	2.57	13	2	0	0	35	26	14	10	22	33	R	R	6-0	195	11-13-74	1992	La Urbina, Venez.
Warrecker, Teddy	1	5	7.76	10	3	0	0	29	29	28	25	20	36	L	R	6-6	215	10-1-72	1994	Santa Barbara, Calif.
Williams, Jeff	10	4	3.10	18	18	0	0	116	101	52	40	34	72	R	L	6-0	185	6-6-72	1996	Page, Australia

VERO BEACH — Class A

FLORIDA STATE LEAGUE

BATTING	AVG	G	AB	R	H	2B	3B	HR	RBI	BB	SO	SB	CS	B	T	HT	WT	DOB	1st Yr	Resides
Beltre, Adrian	.317	123	435	95	138	24	2	26	104	67	66	25	9	R	R	5-11	200	4-7-78	1994	Santo Domingo, D.R.
Dandridge, Brad	.260	112	388	45	101	21	1	8	65	33	42	4	6	R	R	6-0	190	11-29-71	1993	Santa Maria, Calif.
Demetral, Chris	.277	86	278	52	77	13	3	12	45	48	40	5	2	L	R	5-11	175	12-8-69	1991	Sterling Heights, Mich.
Diaz, Jose	.250	1	4	0	1	0	0	0	0	0	3	0	0	R	R	6-0	175	4-13-80	1996	San Pedro de Macoris, D.R.
Diaz, Juan	.667	1	3	2	2	0	0	1	3	0	1	0	0	R	R	6-2	228	2-19-76	1996	Santo Domingo, D.R.
Gil, Geronimo	.249	66	213	30	53	13	1	6	24	15	41	3	0	R	R	6-2	195	8-7-75	1996	Domicilio Conocid, Mexico
Harkrider, Kip	.282	33	103	18	29	5	0	0	14	5	13	2	1	L	R	5-11	175	9-16-75	1997	Carthage, Texas
Manfredi, Joel	.000	6	3	1	0	0	0	0	0	0	0	0	0	R	R	6-2	205	2-24-76	1995	Stockton, Calif.
Marshall, Monte	.269	18	26	4	7	1	0	0	2	1	4	0	0	S	R	5-7	155	12-6-73	1996	Meridian, Miss.
Morimoto, Ken	.176	34	85	13	15	1	0	0	5	11	29	11	1	R	R	6-1	163	9-22-74	1995	Eleele, Hawaii
Nelson, Charles	.281	113	417	73	117	12	1	6	42	50	62	53	16	L	L	5-10	180	8-11-71	1994	Perham, Minn.
Pimentel, Jose	.259	110	344	56	89	13	1	5	40	17	67	41	19	R	R	6-0	160	12-3-74	1993	San Cristobal, D.R.
Roney, Chad	.171	18	35	0	6	3	0	0	2	2	7	0	0	R	R	6-0	180	9-3-74	1996	Fort Myers, Fla.
Sell, Chip	.284	111	342	50	97	21	7	7	46	29	67	25	8	L	R	6-2	195	6-19-71	1994	Woodburn, Ore.
Sosa, Juan	.220	92	250	32	55	5	2	5	29	14	39	20	8	R	R	6-1	175	8-19-75	1993	San Francisco de Macoris, D.R.
Sotelo, Danilo	.196	23	56	13	11	1	0	2	11	10	17	1	1	R	R	5-8	160	3-25-75	1996	Managua, Nicaragua
Stuckenschneider, Eric	.279	131	452	100	126	25	3	6	45	101	79	40	11	R	R	6-0	190	8-24-71	1994	Freeburg, Mo.
Tucker, Jon	.291	121	422	59	123	27	0	13	78	35	85	5	3	L	L	6-4	200	12-17-76	1995	Northridge, Calif.
Wilson, Steve	.210	84	233	21	49	14	1	3	21	11	63	4	0	R	R	5-11	200	6-12-74	1996	Marietta, Ga.
Wingate, Ervan	.228	84	224	26	51	12	1	3	24	27	51	3	2	R	R	6-0	185	2-4-74	1992	Redlands, Calif.
Yard, Bruce	.309	71	236	37	73	14	1	4	44	24	19	3	2	L	R	6-0	175	10-17-71	1993	McIntyre, Pa.

GAMES BY POSITION: C—Dandridge 5, Gil 63, Manfredi 5, Roney 13, Wilson 84. **1B**—Dandridge 26, Ju. Diaz 1, Sell 1, Tucker 113, Wingate 12. **2B**—Demetral 80, Marshall 11, Morimoto 2, Sosa 32, Sotelo 22, Wingate 14. **3B**—Beltre 121, Dandridge 1, Sosa 10, Wingate 22. **SS**—Harkrider 33, Morimoto 1, Sosa 48, Sotelo 1, Wingate 4, Yard 65. **OF**—Beltre 1, Dandridge 20, Nelson 99, Pimentel 99, Sell 105, Stuckenschneider 117, Wingate 6.

PITCHING	W	L	ERA	G	GS	CG	SV	IP	H	R	ER	BB	SO	B	T	HT	WT	DOB	1st Yr	Resides
Babineaux, Darrin	7	3	4.41	18	12	0	0	82	82	46	40	32	63	R	R	6-4	210	7-10-74	1995	Rayne, La.
Bland, Nate	7	7	3.38	17	14	0	0	83	85	35	31	38	67	L	L	6-5	195	12-27-74	1993	Birmingham, Ala.
Chambers, Scott	5	5	3.30	56	2	0	6	85	67	40	31	48	89	L	L	5-10	175	7-10-75	1995	Benton, Ky.
Correa, Ed	0	0	3.18	5	1	0	0	6	2	3	2	3	7	R	R	6-2	215	4-29-66	1993	Carolina, P.R.
Correa, Ramser	2	3	1.77	9	9	0	0	46	45	19	9	18	31	R	R	6-5	225	11-13-70	1987	Carolina, P.R.
Davis, John	3	5	5.40	11	10	0	0	50	50	38	30	26	39	R	R	6-4	218	8-31-73	1995	Swainsboro, Ga.
Dollar, Toby	0	0	0.00	1	0	0	0	1	1	0	0	0	2	R	R	6-3	215	12-27-74	1996	Graham, Texas
Feliciano, Pedro	0	0	4.50	1	0	0	0	2	3	1	1	0	1	L	L	5-11	165	8-25-76	1995	Dorado, P.R.
Flores, Pedro	0	0	5.79	3	0	0	0	5	10	6	3	4	1	L	L	6-0	205	3-30-77	1996	Baldwin Park, Calif.
Foster, Kris	6	3	5.32	17	17	2	0	90	97	69	53	44	77	R	R	6-1	200	8-30-74	1993	Lehigh Acres, Fla.
Garcia, Miguel	10	3	3.73	45	5	1	0	111	110	53	46	36	105	R	R	6-2	205	2-15-75	1992	Santiago, D.R.
Judd, Mike	6	5	3.53	14	14	1	0	87	67	37	34	39	104	R	R	6-2	200	6-30-75	1995	La Mesa, Calif.
Keppen, Jeff	2	3	3.93	32	8	0	0	69	61	37	30	43	54	R	R	6-2	190	1-31-74	1995	Lawrenceville, Ga.
Masaoka, Onan	6	8	3.87	28	24	2	1	149	113	72	64	55	132	R	L	6-0	188	10-27-77	1995	Hilo, Hawaii
McDonald, Matt	8	8	3.72	57	3	0	0	109	93	53	45	67	123	L	L	6-4	200	6-10-74	1994	Princeton, Ill.
McNeely, Mitch	1	1	5.33	14	1	0	2	27	36	18	16	7	15	L	L	6-6	190	2-14-74	1995	New Albany, Miss.
Nakashima, Tony	1	0	10.91	10	0	0	0	16	23	19	19	11	17	L	L	5-9	160	3-17-78	1995	Sao Paulo, Brazil
Ricabal, Dan	4	5	4.25	75	0	0	28	85	78	44	40	39	79	R	R	6-1	185	7-8-72	1994	Rosemead, Calif.
Spykstra, Dave	2	6	5.91	25	14	0	0	70	79	54	46	51	48	R	R	6-2	200	8-26-73	1992	Denver, Colo.
Urbina, Dan	0	2	8.68	3	3	0	0	9	11	9	9	5	10	R	R	6-0	195	11-13-74	1992	La Urbina, Venez.

SAVANNAH — Class A

SOUTH ATLANTIC LEAGUE

BATTING	AVG	G	AB	R	H	2B	3B	HR	RBI	BB	SO	SB	CS	B	T	HT	WT	DOB	1st Yr	Resides
Bergeron, Peter	.280	131	492	89	138	18	5	5	36	67	110	32	21	L	R	6-1	185	11-9-77	1996	Greenfield, Mass.
Bramlett, Jeff	.187	102	326	49	61	11	6	14	42	49	122	2	1	R	R	6-0	200	4-27-76	1995	Cleveland, Tenn.
Brown, Eric	.242	61	211	26	51	10	3	7	22	17	74	12	1	R	R	6-1	205	2-28-77	1995	LaPlace, La.
Cuevas, Trent	.233	90	313	42	73	10	3	10	41	13	59	3	1	R	R	5-11	175	12-25-76	1995	Placentia, Calif.
Diaz, Juan	.230	127	460	63	106	24	2	25	83	48	155	2	2	R	R	6-2	228	2-19-76	1996	Santo Domingo, D.R.
Flores, Eric	.077	6	13	0	1	0	0	0	0	4	7	0	0	R	R	6-3	190	7-7-76	1995	Oxnard, Calif.
Foulks, Brian	.105	20	57	2	6	2	0	1	3	2	21	1	1	R	R	6-3	205	12-26-73	1996	Lexington, S.C.
Glassey, Josh	.184	73	207	17	38	5	0	0	20	35	72	3	1	L	R	6-1	190	5-6-77	1996	Del Mar, Calif.
Harkrider, Kip	.183	18	71	8	13	0	0	0	4	2	6	0	0	L	R	5-11	175	9-16-75	1997	Carthage, Texas
Illig, Brett	.203	51	158	16	32	4	0	2	11	20	49	1	3	R	R	6-3	195	9-4-77	1995	Phoenixville, Pa.
Leach, Nick	.267	37	131	14	35	6	0	0	13	14	23	1	2	L	R	6-1	190	12-7-77	1996	Madera, Calif.
Malave, Joshua	.252	58	206	23	52	11	1	9	32	4	54	2	1	R	R	6-0	196	3-22-75	1995	Fort Lauderdale, Fla.
Martinez, Luis	.231	75	294	26	68	7	3	2	23	5	48	1	0	R	R	5-8	150	10-29-76	1996	Monterrey, Mexico
Meyer, Travis	.289	13	45	4	13	2	0	0	2	1	6	1	1	R	R	6-0	205	9-18-73	1995	Westerville, Ohio
Morrison, Scott	.233	61	219	30	51	13	3	4	34	17	45	4	1	R	R	6-0	180	9-24-72	1996	Galveston, Texas
Prokopec, Luke	.232	61	164	11	38	7	3	2	20	12	49	3	1	L	R	6-0	180	2-23-78	1995	Renmark, Australia
Riley, Cash	.207	27	87	6	18	3	3	0	3	3	27	4	2	R	R	6-2	190	6-4-77	1996	Irving, Texas
Rolls, Damian	.211	130	475	57	100	17	5	5	47	38	83	11	3	R	R	6-2	205	9-15-77	1996	Kansas City, Kan.
Sankey, Brian	.267	63	210	25	56	11	0	5	27	24	37	5	2	L	L	6-1	195	6-12-74	1996	Orleans, Mass.
Stearns, Randy	.226	94	301	41	68	10	3	2	18	31	96	21	14	L	R	6-0	190	10-22-74	1996	Bloomer, Wis.
Warren, Lance	.240	11	25	5	6	1	1	0	1	3	5	2	0	L	R	6-3	185	8-14-78	1997	Richmond Hill, Ga.
Zaun, Brian	.238	13	42	6	10	2	1	1	6	1	16	0	0	R	R	6-2	195	5-14-74	1996	Maple Grove, Minn.

GAMES BY POSITION: C—Flores 3, Glassey 73, Malave 56, Meyer 13. **1B**—Bramlett 16, Diaz 70, Leach 26, Sankey 32. **2B**—Cuevas 57, Martinez 74, Morrison 15. **3B**—Bramlett 1, Cuevas 2, Malave 1, Rolls 130, Zaun 9. **SS**—Cuevas 32, Harkrider 18, Illig 51, Morrison 45. **OF**—Bergeron 131, Bramlett 56, Brown 58, Foulks 17, Prokopec 47, Riley 26, Sankey 11, Stearns 90.

PITCHING	W	L	ERA	G	GS	CG	SV	IP	H	R	ER	BB	SO	B	T	HT	WT	DOB	1st Yr	Resides
Allen, Craig	0	1	7.53	10	0	0	2	14	13	14	12	13	14	R	R	6-3	200	12-22-72	1996	Franklin, Ky.
Bourbakis, Michael	0	6	7.82	23	13	0	0	59	70	57	51	39	47	R	R	6-3	195	11-19-76	1995	Brooklyn, N.Y.
Cervantes, Peter	8	8	3.84	21	20	1	0	103	113	48	44	22	84	L	R	6-3	195	10-13-74	1995	Los Angeles, Calif.
Dollar, Toby	7	2	2.60	20	8	3	1	90	78	33	26	12	67	R	R	6-3	215	12-27-74	1996	Graham, Texas
Feliciano, Pedro	3	7	2.64	36	9	1	4	106	90	45	31	39	94	L	L	5-11	165	8-25-76	1995	Dorado, P.R.
Franklin, Wayne	5	3	3.18	28	7	1	2	82	79	41	29	35	58	L	L	6-2	195	3-9-74	1996	North East, Md.
Garrett, Hal	0	3	8.44	8	1	0	0	16	21	15	15	7	13	R	R	6-1	160	4-27-75	1993	Mt. Juliet, Tenn.
Jacobson, Brian	1	4	4.04	23	0	0	3	36	36	24	16	10	35	S	L	6-0	190	10-12-74	1996	Perris, Calif.
Kramer, Matthew	6	4	5.85	23	8	0	0	65	62	49	42	31	62	R	R	6-2	210	4-4-76	1996	Simi Valley, Calif.
Mitchell, Dean	11	5	2.88	52	7	1	16	122	110	50	39	25	118	R	R	5-11	175	3-19-74	1996	Waco, Texas
O'Shaughnessy, Jay	6	12	4.44	27	24	0	0	116	87	64	57	83	150	R	R	6-3	220	8-14-74	1995	Belmont, Mass.
Paluk, Brian	3	8	5.78	27	20	1	0	118	141	82	76	35	61	R	R	6-6	225	10-5-75	1996	Plymouth, Mich.
Prokopec, Luke	3	1	4.07	13	6	0	0	42	37	21	19	12	45	L	R	6-0	180	2-23-78	1995	Renmark, Australia
Romero, Alejandro	0	1	10.38	5	0	0	0	4	12	10	5	1	5	R	R	5-11	193	8-17-77	1996	Hermosillo, Mexico
Sanchez, Mike	1	5	4.68	40	0	0	0	75	72	43	39	32	74	R	R	6-3	175	11-23-75	1995	Riverside, Calif.
Simon, Benjamin	7	5	3.09	18	17	2	0	93	84	35	32	27	93	R	R	6-1	198	11-12-74	1996	Berlin Heights, Ohio
Soto, Seferino	2	2	3.79	26	0	0	3	55	57	29	23	28	59	R	R	6-1	175	8-26-75	1995	Escondido, Calif.

YAKIMA — Short-Season Class A

NORTHWEST LEAGUE

BATTING	AVG	G	AB	R	H	2B	3B	HR	RBI	BB	SO	SB	CS	B	T	HT	WT	DOB	1st Yr	Resides
Allen, Shane	.000	12	26	2	0	0	0	0	0	5	13	1	0	R	R	5-11	165	4-25-79	1997	Glenns Ferry, Idaho
Balbuena, Mike	.208	15	48	2	10	1	1	0	4	3	15	1	0	S	R	6-0	175	12-24-78	1997	Key West, Fla.
Bell, Ricky	.258	66	264	42	68	15	1	2	24	15	52	9	0	R	R	6-2	180	4-5-79	1997	Cincinnati, Ohio
Brown, Jason	.203	18	59	6	12	0	0	1	5	6	13	0	0	R	R	6-2	205	5-22-74	1997	Rolling Hills Estates, Calif.
Flores, Eric	.221	33	104	17	23	5	2	6	17	10	48	1	1	R	R	6-3	190	7-7-76	1995	Oxnard, Calif.
Goudie, Jaime	.239	56	230	33	55	10	6	0	16	16	38	21	5	R	R	5-10	170	3-8-79	1997	Columbus, Ga.
Hernandez, John	.182	29	77	7	14	3	0	1	8	9	22	1	1	R	R	6-2	190	9-1-79	1997	La Puente, Calif.
Horton, Conan	.333	1	3	0	1	1	0	0	0	0	0	0	0	S	R	6-1	220	6-10-74	1997	Sacramento, Calif.
Illig, Brett	.000	1	2	0	0	0	0	0	0	0	2	0	0	R	R	6-3	195	9-4-77	1995	Phoenixville, Pa.
King, Willie	.219	50	155	14	34	4	1	4	20	27	43	1	1	L	R	6-1	195	5-31-78	1996	Brooklyn, N.Y.
Leach, Nick	.313	54	192	33	60	18	1	7	47	32	37	5	0	L	R	6-1	190	12-7-77	1996	Madera, Calif.
McCrotty, Will	.200	43	135	12	27	2	0	1	10	9	19	2	0	R	R	6-2	195	6-23-79	1997	Russellville, Ark.
Newton, Kimani	.269	56	201	34	54	7	1	3	14	23	63	20	6	R	R	6-1	195	6-16-79	1996	Christiansted, Virgin Islands
Paterson, Joe	.231	47	156	13	36	12	1	0	15	5	51	2	2	R	R	6-1	195	12-22-78	1997	Ontario, Calif.
Peoples, Derrick	.229	47	144	14	33	7	2	0	16	13	44	7	0	S	R	6-2	190	2-6-78	1996	Denton, Texas
Phoenix, Wynter	.253	56	186	29	47	14	2	3	17	23	36	11	4	L	L	6-2	205	12-7-74	1996	El Cajon, Calif.
Riley, Cash	.265	65	253	36	67	12	7	7	43	21	77	14	3	R	R	6-2	190	6-4-77	1996	Irving, Texas
Saitta, Rich	.311	44	183	37	57	13	2	1	15	14	27	6	2	R	R	5-10	170	7-28-75	1996	Marlboro, N.J.
Slater, Wayne	.235	29	68	11	16	3	0	1	7	11	11	2	0	L	L	6-1	187	8-26-75	1997	Brooklyn, N.Y.
Warren, Lance	.400	2	5	0	2	0	0	0	1	1	1	0	0	L	R	6-3	185	8-14-78	1997	Richmond Hill, Ga.
Zaun, Brian	.312	46	186	23	58	12	1	1	37	8	45	3	1	R	R	6-2	195	5-14-74	1996	Maple Grove, Minn.

GAMES BY POSITION: C—Brown 18, Flores 11, Hernandez 17, Horton 1, McCrotty 41, Warren 2. **1B**—Hernandez 1, King 35, Leach 45, Zaun 1. **2B**—Allen 4, Goudie 51, Saitta 24. **3B**—Balbuena 15, Flores 9, Saitta 12, Zaun 44. **SS**—Bell 66, Flores 9, Illig 1, Saitta 2. **OF**—Flores 2, Newton 55, Paterson 37, Peoples 37, Phoenix 49, Riley 57, Slater 14.

PITCHING	W	L	ERA	G	GS	CG	SV	IP	H	R	ER	BB	SO	B	T	HT	WT	DOB	1st Yr	Resides
Ashworth, Kym	0	1	3.63	4	4	0	0	17	13	7	7	10	15	L	L	6-2	175	7-31-76	1993	Para Hills West, Australia
Backowski, Lance	2	12	6.40	15	15	1	0	72	85	72	51	53	61	R	R	6-0	180	6-8-75	1995	Fresno, Calif.
Bloomfield, Shane	0	0	0.00	1	0	0	0	1	1	0	0	0	0	R	R	6-1	190	4-7-73	1997	Provo, Utah
Burnside, Adrian	6	3	4.93	15	13	0	0	66	67	53	36	49	66	R	L	6-4	168	3-15-77	1996	Alice Springs, Australia
Everly, Bill	2	3	3.41	28	1	0	3	58	48	26	22	33	63	R	R	6-1	175	6-15-75	1997	Carmichaels, Pa.

PITCHING	W	L	ERA	G	GS	CG	SV	IP	H	R	ER	BB	SO	B	T	HT	WT	DOB	1st Yr	Resides
Graham, Kyle	0	3	3.88	21	3	0	0	46	46	28	20	26	52	L	L	6-0	195	12-15-75	1996	Moss Point, Miss.
Hannah, Neal	2	7	5.57	22	2	0	0	63	84	57	39	27	44	R	R	6-2	206	4-1-75	1996	Bremen, Ga.
Husted, Brent	1	5	6.98	10	6	0	0	30	45	32	23	11	22	R	R	6-3	198	3-30-76	1997	San Jose, Calif.
Karabinus, Chris	0	0	15.00	2	0	0	0	3	6	7	5	1	5	R	L	6-3	220	5-31-75	1996	Baltimore, Md.
Maestas, Mickey	1	4	6.61	21	3	0	0	48	65	44	35	30	50	R	R	6-3	195	8-24-75	1996	Key Largo, Fla.
Montgomery, Matt	2	2	2.44	11	9	0	0	55	48	23	15	17	38	R	R	6-4	210	5-13-76	1997	Anaheim, Calif.
Moon, Jared	2	2	5.79	11	6	0	0	37	45	29	24	17	32	R	R	6-5	200	3-2-79	1997	Redondo Beach, Calif.
Ochsenfeld, Chris	2	0	2.08	12	0	0	3	22	13	6	5	13	18	L	L	6-2	210	8-21-76	1994	Hampton, Va.
Parker, Beau	0	8	9.35	15	12	0	0	51	63	59	53	32	44	R	R	6-4	185	6-7-79	1997	Vancouver, Wash.
Rawls, Mike	0	2	5.21	22	2	0	2	38	38	27	22	28	27	L	L	6-0	195	9-1-74	1997	Pensacola, Fla.
Schmalz, Darin	3	1	5.13	22	0	0	1	33	45	27	19	12	29	R	R	6-0	182	7-30-74	1997	Barrington, Ill.
Verigood, Steve	0	0	5.35	21	0	0	0	34	46	26	20	13	33	R	L	6-6	195	4-13-76	1997	Columbia, S.C.

GREAT FALLS — Rookie

PIONEER LEAGUE

BATTING	AVG	G	AB	R	H	2B	3B	HR	RBI	BB	SO	SB	CS	B	T	HT	WT	DOB	1st Yr	Resides
Allen, Jake	.000	1	1	0	0	0	0	0	0	0	1	0	0	R	R	6-3	210	10-24-77	1997	Harrisburg, Ill.
Allen, Luke	.345	67	258	50	89	12	6	7	40	19	53	12	11	L	R	6-2	208	8-4-78	1993	Covington, Ga.
Allen, Shane	.194	24	31	5	6	0	0	0	2	1	14	0	0	R	R	5-11	165	4-25-79	1997	Glenns Ferry, Idaho
Auterson, Jeff	.173	60	156	28	27	8	1	3	17	21	58	6	6	R	R	6-2	190	2-22-78	1996	Riverside, Calif.
Balbuena, Mike	.151	18	53	5	8	1	0	0	4	2	3	1	1	S	R	6-0	175	12-24-78	1997	Key West, Fla.
Cripps, Bobby	.310	47	145	19	45	6	5	4	25	7	26	4	4	L	R	6-2	200	5-9-77	1996	Powell River, B.C.
Dean, Aaron	.330	60	179	28	59	14	1	4	27	13	41	4	4	L	L	6-2	200	11-21-76	1997	Newhall, Calif.
Dempsey, Nicholas	.000	6	8	0	0	0	0	0	0	1	2	0	0	R	R	6-5	225	12-15-78	1997	Johannesburg, South Africa
Falcon, Edwin	.241	50	133	20	32	6	1	5	22	15	39	0	1	R	R	6-1	225	8-28-78	1996	Bayamon, P.R.
Gallo, Ismael	.251	61	199	31	50	9	5	1	34	16	14	4	3	L	R	5-11	165	1-14-77	1997	Ontario, Calif.
Gomera, Rafael	.258	59	209	36	54	11	3	6	29	16	67	13	5	R	R	6-1	172	9-28-77	1994	San Cristobal, D.R.
Hilliker, Tracey	.212	38	99	14	21	2	0	2	10	5	29	3	2	R	R	6-3	245	8-24-77	1996	Cypress, Calif.
Kelleher, Pat	.290	57	145	22	42	8	0	0	10	19	27	6	10	L	R	6-1	185	10-27-76	1997	Paradise Valley, Ariz.
Marshall, Monte	.288	58	184	29	53	8	3	0	21	8	34	12	6	S	R	5-7	155	12-6-73	1996	Meridian, Miss.
Moreta, Ramon	.336	68	265	45	89	6	2	1	20	18	38	29	17	R	R	5-11	175	9-5-75	1994	La Romana, D.R.
Richey, Mikal	.215	32	65	10	14	0	1	1	10	1	29	1	1	R	R	6-0	192	8-3-78	1996	Decatur, Ga.
Saitta, Rich	.241	16	58	4	14	3	0	0	4	2	9	0	1	R	R	5-10	170	7-28-75	1996	Marlboro, N.J.
Snow, Casey	.321	17	53	5	17	3	0	2	9	8	10	2	0	S	R	5-10	185	12-8-74	1996	Canoga Park, Calif.
Torres, Bernie	.251	57	175	23	44	4	3	1	23	12	27	6	4	R	R	5-7	160	9-26-79	1996	Lara, Venez.
Warren, Lance	.200	3	5	0	1	0	0	0	0	1	3	0	0	L	R	6-3	185	8-14-78	1997	Richmond Hill, Ga.
Zamora, Pete	.200	29	20	2	4	0	0	0	0	2	3	0	0	L	L	6-3	185	8-13-75	1997	Mission Viejo, Calif.

GAMES BY POSITION: C—Cripps 46, Falcon 3, Hilliker 24, Snow 15. **1B**—Dean 58, Dempsey 2, Falcon 35, Zamora 2. **2B**—S. Allen 16, Gallo 26, Marshall 41, Saitta 7, Torres 5. **3B**—L. Allen 63, Balbuena 12, Saitta 3. **SS**—Gallo 28, Marshall 1, Torres 52. **OF**—L. Allen 2, S. Allen 1, Auterson 56, Gallo 1, Gomera 58, Kelleher 43, Moreta 67, Richey 21, Saitta 7, Warren 1.

PITCHING	W	L	ERA	G	GS	CG	SV	IP	H	R	ER	BB	SO	B	T	HT	WT	DOB	1st Yr	Resides
Alvarez, Victor	4	1	3.35	12	8	0	0	48	49	30	18	17	50	R	R	5-10	150	11-8-76	1997	Culiacan, Mexico
Baker, Jason	0	0	5.87	9	0	0	1	15	24	10	10	12	22	R	L	6-0	200	12-31-73	1995	Rome, N.Y.
Bornyk, Matt	0	3	5.79	13	2	0	1	23	21	16	15	15	29	R	R	6-2	210	1-31-79	1997	Victoria, B.C.
Correa, Elvis	3	0	1.61	21	0	0	0	28	20	8	5	8	38	R	R	6-1	185	11-10-78	1996	Milwaukee, Wis.
Dotel, Melido	3	7	8.08	14	11	0	0	42	59	54	38	39	26	R	R	6-3	210	4-20-77	1994	San Cristobal, D.R.
Flores, Pedro	2	1	3.55	22	0	0	1	38	36	18	15	27	51	L	L	6-0	205	3-30-77	1996	Baldwin Park, Calif.
Galvez, Randy	3	1	3.64	16	1	0	0	30	29	14	12	10	29	R	R	6-3	180	7-26-78	1995	Guasave, Mexico
Hannah, Neal	1	0	6.75	2	0	0	0	3	2	2	2	3	3	R	R	6-2	206	4-1-75	1996	Bremen, Ga.
Hernandez, Pedro	5	5	4.76	15	14	0	1	76	98	44	40	12	50	R	R	6-2	195	6-5-76	1994	Monte Cristi, D.R.
Montgomery, Matt	1	1	3.91	4	4	0	0	23	24	11	10	3	6	R	R	6-4	210	5-13-76	1997	Anaheim, Calif.
Regalado, Maximo	2	1	1.96	9	6	0	0	37	27	12	8	21	24	R	R	6-1	198	11-18-76	1994	Los Limones, D.R.
Reyes, Nate	3	3	2.51	24	0	0	8	29	26	9	8	15	30	L	L	5-10	160	11-19-78	1996	Guaymas, Mexico
Romero, Alejandro	2	1	4.01	25	0	0	0	43	50	28	19	11	27	R	R	5-11	193	8-17-77	1996	Hermosillo, Mexico
Stover, C.D.	7	2	2.56	12	12	1	0	77	71	36	22	14	61	R	R	6-5	225	12-8-75	1996	Citrus Heights, Calif.
Taczy, Craig	2	1	4.02	18	4	0	3	54	65	29	24	15	44	L	L	6-6	225	4-15-77	1995	Crestwood, Ill.
Zamora, Pete	2	5	2.58	13	10	1	2	70	59	27	20	30	73	L	L	6-3	185	8-13-75	1997	Mission Viejo, Calif.

Milwaukee BREWERS

Organization Statistics

Manager: Phil Garner.

1997 Record: 78-83, .484 (3rd, AL Central)

BATTING	AVG	G	AB	R	H	2B	3B	HR	RBI	BB	SO	SB	CS	B	T	HT	WT	DOB	1st Yr	Resides
Banks, Brian	.206	28	68	9	14	1	0	1	8	6	17	0	1	S	R	6-3	200	9-28-70	1993	Mesa, Ariz.
Burnitz, Jeromy	.281	153	494	85	139	37	8	27	85	75	111	20	13	L	R	6-0	190	4-14-69	1990	Key Largo, Fla.
Carr, Chuck	.130	26	46	3	6	3	0	0	0	2	11	1	0	S	R	5-10	165	8-10-68	1986	Tucson, Ariz.
Cirillo, Jeff	.288	154	580	74	167	46	2	10	82	60	74	4	3	R	R	6-2	180	9-23-69	1991	Van Nuys, Calif.
Diaz, Eddy	.220	16	50	4	11	2	1	0	7	1	5	0	0	R	R	5-10	160	9-29-71	1990	Barquisimeto, Venez.
Dunn, Todd	.229	44	118	17	27	5	0	3	9	2	39	3	0	R	R	6-5	220	7-29-70	1993	Jacksonville, Fla.
Franco, Julio	.241	42	141	22	34	3	0	4	19	31	41	7	1	R	R	6-1	188	8-23-61	1978	San Pedro de Macoris, D.R.
2-team (78 Cleveland)	.270	120	430	68	116	16	1	7	44	69	116	15	6							
Huson, Jeff	.203	84	143	12	29	3	0	0	11	5	15	3	0	L	R	6-3	180	8-15-64	1986	Bedford, Texas
Jackson, Darrin	.272	26	81	7	22	7	0	2	15	2	10	2	1	R	R	6-0	186	8-22-63	1981	Mesa, Ariz.
2-team (49 Minnesota)	.261	75	211	26	55	9	1	5	36	6	31	4	1							
Jaha, John	.247	46	162	25	40	7	0	11	26	25	40	1	0	R	R	6-1	205	5-27-66	1985	Portland, Ore.
Levis, Jesse	.285	99	200	19	57	7	0	1	19	24	17	1	0	L	R	5-9	180	4-14-68	1989	Philadelphia, Pa.
Loretta, Mark	.287	132	418	56	120	17	5	5	47	47	60	5	5	R	R	6-0	175	8-14-71	1993	Laguna Niguel, Calif.
Matheny, Mike	.244	123	320	29	78	16	1	4	32	17	68	0	1	R	R	6-3	205	9-22-70	1991	Reynoldsburg, Ohio
Mieske, Matt	.249	84	253	39	63	15	3	5	21	19	50	1	0	R	R	6-0	185	2-13-68	1990	Livonia, Mich.
Newfield, Marc	.229	50	157	14	36	8	0	1	18	14	27	0	0	R	R	6-4	205	10-19-72	1990	Huntington Beach, Calif.
Nilsson, Dave	.278	156	554	71	154	33	0	20	81	65	88	2	3	L	R	6-3	215	12-14-69	1987	Everton Hills, Australia
Stinnett, Kelly	.250	30	36	2	9	4	0	0	3	3	9	0	0	R	R	5-11	195	2-14-70	1990	Lawton, Okla.
Unroe, Tim	.250	32	16	3	4	1	0	2	5	2	9	2	0	R	R	6-3	200	10-7-70	1992	Round Lake Beach, Ill.
Valentin, Jose	.253	136	494	58	125	23	1	17	58	39	109	19	8	S	R	5-10	175	10-12-69	1987	Manati, P.R.
Vina, Fernando	.275	79	324	37	89	12	2	4	28	12	23	8	7	L	R	5-9	170	4-16-69	1990	Sacramento, Calif.
Voigt, Jack	.245	72	151	20	37	9	2	8	22	19	36	1	2	R	R	6-1	175	5-17-66	1987	Venice, Fla.
Williams, Gerald	.253	155	566	73	143	32	2	10	41	19	90	23	9	R	R	6-2	185	8-10-66	1987	LaPlace, La
Williamson, Antone	.204	24	54	2	11	3	0	0	6	4	8	0	1	L	R	6-1	195	7-18-73	1994	Torrance, Calif.

PITCHING	W	L	ERA	G	GS	CG	SV	IP	H	R	ER	BB	SO	B	T	HT	WT	DOB	1st Yr	Resides
Adamson, Joel	5	3	3.54	30	6	0	0	76	78	36	30	19	56	L	L	6-4	180	7-2-71	1990	Lakewood, Calif.
D'Amico, Jeff	9	7	4.71	23	23	1	0	136	139	81	71	43	94	R	R	6-7	250	12-27-75	1993	Pinellas Park, Fla.
Davis, Mark	0	0	5.51	19	0	0	0	16	21	10	10	5	14	L	L	6-4	210	10-19-60	1979	Marietta, Ga.
Eldred, Cal	13	15	4.99	34	34	1	0	202	207	118	112	89	122	R	R	6-4	235	11-24-67	1989	Center Point, Iowa
Fetters, Mike	1	5	3.45	51	0	0	6	70	62	30	27	33	62	R	R	6-4	215	12-19-64	1986	Gilbert, Ariz.
Florie, Bryce	4	4	4.32	32	8	0	0	75	74	43	36	42	53	R	R	6-0	170	5-21-70	1988	Hanahan, S.C.
Hansell, Greg	0	0	9.64	3	0	0	0	5	5	5	5	1	5	R	R	6-5	215	3-12-71	1989	Gig Harbor, Wash.
Harnisch, Pete	1	1	5.14	4	3	0	0	14	13	9	8	12	10	R	R	6-0	207	9-23-66	1987	Commack, N.Y.
Jones, Doug	6	6	2.02	75	0	0	36	80	62	20	18	9	82	R	R	6-2	195	6-24-57	1978	Tucson, Ariz.
Karl, Scott	10	13	4.47	32	32	1	0	193	212	103	96	67	119	L	L	6-2	195	8-9-71	1992	Carlsbad, Calif.
Maloney, Sean	0	0	5.14	3	0	0	0	7	7	4	4	2	5	R	R	6-7	210	5-25-71	1993	North Kingstown, R.I.
McAndrew, Jamie	1	1	8.38	5	4	0	0	19	24	19	18	23	8	R	R	6-2	190	9-2-67	1989	Fort Myers, Fla.
McDonald, Ben	8	7	4.06	21	21	1	0	133	120	68	60	36	110	R	R	6-7	210	11-24-67	1989	Denham Springs, La.
Mercedes, Jose	7	10	3.79	29	23	2	0	159	146	76	67	53	80	R	R	6-1	180	3-5-71	1990	Las Palmillas, D.R.
Miranda, Angel	0	0	3.86	10	0	0	0	14	17	6	6	9	8	L	L	6-1	195	11-9-69	1987	Arecibo, P.R.
Misuraca, Mike	0	0	11.32	5	0	0	0	10	15	13	13	7	10	R	R	6-0	188	8-21-68	1989	Covina, Calif.
Reyes, Alberto	1	2	5.46	19	0	0	1	30	32	19	18	9	28	R	R	6-0	165	4-10-71	1988	Santo Domingo, D.R.
Villone, Ron	1	0	3.42	50	0	0	0	53	54	23	20	36	40	L	L	6-3	235	1-16-70	1992	Bergenfield, N.J.
Wagner, Paul	1	0	9.00	2	0	0	0	2	3	2	2	0	0	R	R	6-1	202	11-14-67	1989	Germantown, Wis.
Wickman, Bob	7	6	2.73	74	0	0	1	96	89	32	29	41	78	R	R	6-1	220	2-6-69	1990	Abrams, Wis.
Woodard, Steve	3	3	5.15	7	7	0	0	37	39	25	21	6	32	L	R	6-4	225	5-15-75	1994	Hartselle, Ala.

FIELDING

Catcher	PCT	G	PO	A	E	DP	PB
Levis	.994	78	296	19	2	1	4
Matheny	.993	121	697	58	5	6	7
Stinnett	.989	25	81	5	1	1	0

First Base	PCT	G	PO	A	E	DP
Banks	.929	5	9	4	1	0
Franco	.992	13	108	11	1	20
Huson	1.000	21	66	2	0	5
Jaha	.992	27	220	14	2	26
Loretta	.987	19	150	7	2	10
Matheny	.000	2	0	0	0	0
Nilsson	.991	74	610	38	6	71
Unroe	.969	23	57	6	2	5
Voigt	1.000	19	82	3	0	15
Williamson	.977	14	82	4	2	6

Second Base	PCT	G	PO	A	E	DP
Diaz	1.000	14	27	35	0	10
Huson	.989	32	38	49	1	10
Loretta	.980	63	125	170	6	52
Unroe	.000	1	0	0	0	0
Vina	.982	77	149	227	7	53

Third Base	PCT	G	PO	A	E	DP
Banks	1.000	1	2	3	0	0
Cirillo	.963	150	126	320	17	29
Diaz	.000	1	0	0	0	0
Huson	.000	2	0	0	0	0
Loretta	.962	15	9	16	1	3
Unroe	1.000	2	1	3	0	1
Voigt	1.000	6	1	2	0	0

Shortstop	PCT	G	PO	A	E	DP
Diaz	.000	1	0	0	0	0
Loretta	.957	44	50	84	6	23
Valentin	.967	134	208	383	20	86

Outfield	PCT	G	PO	A	E	DP
Banks	.950	15	19	0	1	0
Burnitz	.975	149	256	13	7	3
Carr	1.000	23	25	1	0	0
Dunn	.909	27	39	1	4	0
Huson	1.000	9	5	1	0	1
Jackson	1.000	26	55	2	0	1
Mieske	.962	74	121	6	5	0
Newfield	.977	28	43	0	1	0
Nilsson	1.000	22	31	1	0	0
Unroe	1.000	2	1	0	0	0
Voigt	.985	40	61	5	1	0
Williams	.992	154	357	11	3	4

FARM SYSTEM

Director of Player Development: Cecil Cooper

Class	Farm Team	League	W	L	Pct.	Finish*	Manager(s)	First Yr
AAA	Tucson (Ariz.) Toros	Pacific Coast	64	78	.451	7th (10)	Tim Ireland/Bob Mariano	1997
AA	El Paso (Texas) Diablos	Texas	74	66	.529	3rd (8)	Dave Machemer	1981
#A	Stockton (Calif.) Ports	California	70	70	.500	6th (10)	Greg Mahlberg	1979
A	Beloit (Wis.) Snappers	Midwest	60	73	.451	11th (14)	Luis Salazar	1982
#R	Helena (Mont.) Brewers	Pioneer	37	34	.521	5th (8)	Alex Morales	1985
#R	Ogden (Utah) Raptors	Pioneer	36	35	.507	6th (8)	Bernie Moncallo	1996

*Finish in overall standings (No. of teams in league) #Advanced level

ORGANIZATION LEADERS

MAJOR LEAGUERS

BATTING

*AVG	Jeff Cirillo	.288
R	Jeromy Burnitz	85
H	Jeff Cirillo	167
TB	Jeromy Burnitz	273
2B	Jeff Cirillo	46
3B	Jeromy Burnitz	8
HR	Jeromy Burnitz	27
RBI	Jeromy Burnitz	85
BB	Jeromy Burnitz	75
SO	Jeromy Burnitz	111
SB	Gerald Williams	23

PITCHING

W	Cal Eldred	13
L	Cal Eldred	15
#ERA	Doug Jones	2.02
G	Doug Jones	75
CG	Jose Mercedes	2
SV	Doug Jones	36
IP	Cal Eldred	202
BB	Cal Eldred	89
SO	Cal Eldred	122

Jeromy Burnitz

LARRY GOREN

Kevin Barker

MINOR LEAGUERS

BATTING

*AVG	Mike Kinkade, El Paso	.385
R	Two tied at	112
H	Mike Kinkade, El Paso	180
TB	Mike Kinkade, El Paso	275
2B	Darrell Nicholas, El Paso	47
3B	Chad Green, Stockton	14
HR	Kevin Barker, El Paso/Stockton	23
RBI	Mike Kinkade, El Paso	109
BB	Ronnie Belliard, Tucson	61
SO	Jermaine Swinton, Stockton	152
SB	Greg Martinez, Tucson/El Paso	39

PITCHING

W	Travis Smith, El Paso	16
L	Al Hawkins, Beloit/Ogden	12
#ERA	Jay Akin, Beloit/Helena	2.39
G	Jeff Huber, Tucson/El Paso	59
CG	Steve Woodard, Tucson/El Paso	6
SV	Greg Mullins, El Paso/Stockton	32
IP	Travis Smith, El Paso	184
BB	Jeff Ware, Tucson	80
SO	Brian Passini, Stockton/Beloit	150

*Minimum 250 At-Bats #Minimum 75 Innings

TOP 10 PROSPECTS

LARRY GOREN

Valerio de los Santos

How the Brewers Top 10 prospects, as judged by Baseball America prior to the 1997 season, fared in 1997:

Player, Pos.	Club (Class)	AVG	AB	R	H	2B	3B	HR	RBI	SB
2. Geoff Jenkins, of	Tucson (AAA)	.236	347	44	82	24	3	10	56	0
3. Chad Green, of	Stockton (A)	.250	513	78	128	26	14	2	43	37
4. Todd Dunn, of	Milwaukee	.229	118	17	27	5	0	3	9	3
	Tucson (AAA)	.304	332	66	101	31	4	18	66	5
5. Ron Belliard, 2b	Tucson (AAA)	.282	443	80	125	35	4	4	55	10
6. Antone Williamson, 1b	Milwaukee	.204	54	2	11	3	0	0	6	0
	Tucson (AAA)	.286	304	53	87	20	5	5	41	3
9. Danny Klassen, ss	El Paso (AA)	.331	519	112	172	30	6	14	81	16
10. Brian Banks, c-of	Milwaukee	.206	68	9	14	1	0	1	8	0
	Tucson (AAA)	.296	378	53	112	26	3	10	63	7

Player, Pos.	Club (Class)	W	L	ERA	G	SV	IP	H	BB	SO
1. Valerio de los Santos, lhp	El Paso (AA)	6	10	5.75	26	2	114	146	38	61
7. Sean Maloney, rhp	Milwaukee	0	0	5.14	3	0	7	7	2	5
	Tucson (AAA)	0	2	4.82	15	5	19	24	3	21
8. Mike Pasqualicchio, lhp	Stockton (A)	1	10	6.43	17	1	85	93	44	58

TM

TUCSON — Class AAA

PACIFIC COAST LEAGUE

BATTING	AVG	G	AB	R	H	2B	3B	HR	RBI	BB	SO	SB	CS	B	T	HT	WT	DOB	1st Yr	Resides
Andreopoulos, Alex	.400	10	15	3	6	1	0	0	1	0	1	0	0	L	R	5-10	190	8-19-72	1995	Toronto, Ontario
Banks, Brian	.296	98	378	53	112	26	3	10	63	35	83	7	3	S	R	6-3	200	9-28-70	1993	Mesa, Ariz.
Belliard, Ronnie	.282	118	443	80	125	35	4	4	55	61	69	10	7	R	R	5-9	176	4-7-75	1994	Miami, Fla.
Brown, Jarvis	.265	112	385	65	102	21	3	6	35	52	84	14	6	R	R	5-7	170	3-26-67	1986	Mt. Zion, Ill.
Diaz, Eddy	.329	94	356	65	117	24	3	9	70	26	25	0	1	R	R	5-10	160	9-29-71	1990	Barquisimeto, Venez.
Dunn, Todd	.304	93	332	66	101	31	4	18	66	39	83	5	5	R	R	6-5	220	7-29-70	1993	Jacksonville, Fla.
Felix, Lauro	.319	19	47	7	15	5	0	1	5	5	15	0	0	R	R	5-9	160	6-24-70	1992	El Paso, Texas
Gubanich, Creighton	.341	24	85	13	29	5	0	5	17	1	19	1	0	R	R	6-4	220	3-27-72	1991	Phoenixville, Pa.
Hughes, Bobby	.310	89	290	43	90	29	2	7	51	24	46	0	0	R	R	6-4	220	3-10-71	1992	North Hollywood, Calif.
Iapoce, Anthony	.333	7	21	5	7	4	0	0	3	1	4	0	0	S	L	5-10	178	8-23-73	1994	Ridgewood, N.Y.
Jenkins, Geoff	.236	93	347	44	82	24	3	10	56	33	87	0	2	L	R	6-1	205	7-21-74	1995	Stateline, Nev.
Johns, Keith	.264	112	333	45	88	21	3	5	36	43	61	4	2	R	R	6-1	175	7-19-71	1992	St. Louis, Mo.
Kellner, Frank	.287	67	230	31	66	14	4	0	25	16	38	2	1	S	R	5-11	175	1-5-67	1990	Tucson, Ariz.
*Lee, Travis	.300	59	227	42	68	16	2	14	46	31	46	2	0	L	L	6-3	205	5-26-75	1993	Olympia, Wash.
Martinez, Greg	.417	3	12	2	5	2	0	0	3	0	1	0	0	S	R	5-10	168	1-27-72	1993	Las Vegas, Nev.
Newfield, Marc	.323	8	31	4	10	1	0	1	3	4	6	0	0	R	R	6-4	205	10-19-72	1990	Huntington Beach, Calif.
Seitzer, Brad	.316	62	234	50	74	13	3	9	42	22	33	0	1	R	R	6-2	195	2-2-70	1991	Memphis, Tenn.
Stinnett, Kelly	.321	64	209	50	67	15	3	10	43	42	46	1	1	R	R	5-11	195	2-14-70	1990	Lawton, Okla.
Unroe, Tim	.291	63	234	45	68	17	1	9	46	9	62	3	3	R	R	6-3	200	10-7-70	1992	Round Lake Beach, Ill.
Vina, Fernando	.474	6	19	3	9	3	0	1	5	3	1	0	1	L	R	5-9	170	4-16-69	1990	Sacramento, Calif.
Voigt, Jack	.272	66	235	36	64	20	0	5	40	43	57	4	3	R	R	6-1	175	5-17-66	1987	Venice, Fla.
Wachter, Derek	.289	46	142	24	41	12	0	2	28	18	28	2	2	R	R	6-2	195	8-28-70	1991	Miller Place, N.Y.
Williamson, Antone	.286	83	304	53	87	20	5	5	41	49	41	3	1	L	R	6-1	195	7-18-73	1994	Torrance, Calif.

PITCHING	W	L	ERA	G	GS	CG	SV	IP	H	R	ER	BB	SO	B	T	HT	WT	DOB	1st Yr	Resides
Adamson, Joel	2	1	4.36	6	6	0	0	33	38	16	16	8	24	L	L	6-4	180	7-2-71	1990	Lakewood, Calif.
Bolton, Tom	3	4	6.00	15	7	0	0	57	75	42	38	20	42	L	L	6-3	185	5-6-62	1980	Smyrna, Tenn.
2-team (8 Calgary)	5	10	6.92	23	15	0	0	95	142	80	73	32	71							
Bones, Ricky	5	0	2.79	8	7	0	0	42	40	18	13	8	22	R	R	6-0	190	4-7-69	1986	Guayama, P.R.
Brewington, Jamie	1	3	10.18	6	5	0	0	20	33	26	23	17	13	R	R	6-4	180	9-28-71	1992	Greenville, N.C.
Browne, Byron	0	1	5.23	3	3	0	0	10	13	9	6	8	7	R	R	6-7	200	8-8-70	1991	Phoenix, Ariz.
Davis, Mark	0	2	3.57	17	0	0	2	23	19	9	9	12	19	L	L	6-4	210	10-19-60	1979	Marietta, Ga.
Fetters, Mike	0	0	10.80	2	0	0	0	2	1	2	2	1	0	R	R	6-4	215	12-19-64	1986	Gilbert, Ariz.
Gardner, Scott	1	0	3.00	1	1	0	0	6	6	2	2	3	6	S	R	6-5	225	9-30-71	1990	Fenton, Mich.
Grimsley, Jason	5	10	5.70	36	10	0	4	85	96	70	54	43	65	R	R	6-3	180	8-7-67	1985	Cleveland, Texas
Grott, Matt	3	1	4.79	55	0	0	4	88	94	57	47	33	58	L	L	6-1	205	12-5-67	1989	Glendale, Ariz.
Hansell, Greg	2	3	4.64	40	9	0	2	87	99	52	45	27	76	R	R	6-5	215	3-12-71	1989	Gig Harbor, Wash.
Huber, Jeff	3	7	4.74	40	2	0	5	63	67	36	33	22	37	R	L	6-4	220	12-17-70	1990	Scottsdale, Ariz.
Maloney, Sean	0	2	4.82	15	0	0	5	19	24	10	10	3	21	R	R	6-7	210	5-25-71	1993	North Kingstown, R.I.
McAndrew, Jamie	7	8	6.79	22	21	0	0	109	132	87	82	65	63	R	R	6-2	190	9-2-67	1989	Fort Myers, Fla.
Minor, Blas	2	2	4.03	12	3	0	1	29	36	21	13	15	21	R	R	6-3	200	3-20-66	1988	Gilbert, Ariz.
Misuraca, Mike	8	7	4.98	33	10	0	1	108	119	68	60	39	62	R	R	6-0	188	8-21-68	1989	Covina, Calif.
Montoya, Norm	6	10	6.25	27	24	0	0	131	175	100	91	38	75	L	L	6-1	190	9-24-70	1990	Newark, Calif.
Pace, Scotty	0	0	1.59	2	0	0	0	6	6	2	1	4	2	L	L	6-4	210	9-16-71	1994	Cieba, P.R.
Phillips, Tony	3	2	5.59	29	1	0	0	58	67	43	36	21	32	R	R	6-4	195	6-9-69	1991	Hattiesburg, Miss.
Reyes, Alberto	2	4	5.02	38	0	0	7	57	52	39	32	34	70	R	R	6-0	165	4-10-71	1988	Santo Domingo, D.R.
Roberson, Sid	0	2	11.45	10	4	0	0	22	47	29	28	14	8	L	L	5-9	170	9-7-71	1992	Orange Park, Fla.
Rodriguez, Frankie	3	1	4.40	12	6	1	0	47	53	25	23	19	41	R	R	5-9	170	1-6-73	1992	Brea, Calif.
Sadler, Al	1	0	1.50	1	1	0	0	6	7	1	1	4	1	R	R	6-6	192	2-10-72	1992	Conyers, Ga.
Tyler, Josh	0	0	0.00	1	0	0	0	1	0	0	0	0	0	R	R	6-1	185	9-6-73	1994	Green Lane, Pa.
VanEgmond, Tim	1	0	9.00	1	0	0	0	1	3	1	1	0	0	R	R	6-2	185	5-31-69	1991	Senoia, Ga.
Ware, Jeff	5	8	6.71	25	21	0	0	106	127	98	79	80	69	R	R	6-3	190	11-11-70	1991	Virginia Beach, Va.
Woodard, Steve	1	0	0.00	1	1	0	0	7	3	0	0	1	6	L	R	6-4	225	5-15-75	1994	Hartselle, Ala.

*Property of Arizona Diamondbacks

FIELDING

Catcher	PCT	G	PO	A	E	DP	PB
Andreopoulos	1.000	7	16	1	0	0	0
Banks	.984	13	56	5	1	2	1
Gubanich	.950	15	81	14	5	1	3
Hughes	.977	80	455	45	12	5	11
Stinnett	.993	45	255	34	2	3	3

First Base	PCT	G	PO	A	E	DP
Gubanich	1.000	2	14	1	0	2
Kellner	.991	13	107	7	1	11
Lee	.995	39	379	32	2	33
Seitzer	1.000	23	208	24	0	28
Stinnett	1.000	1	1	0	0	0
Voigt	.982	9	51	5	1	8
Wachter	1.000	3	24	4	0	3
Williamson	.985	63	543	40	9	52

Second Base	PCT	G	PO	A	E	DP
Belliard	.961	114	229	358	24	92
Diaz	.933	6	3	11	1	2
Felix	.929	12	21	31	4	8
Kellner	.967	10	14	15	1	2
Seitzer	.833	2	2	3	1	1
Unroe	1.000	8	12	11	0	5
Vina	.923	6	8	16	2	5
Voigt	1.000	1	0	1	0	0

Third Base	PCT	G	PO	A	E	DP
Diaz	.948	69	31	153	10	17
Felix	1.000	4	1	6	0	0
Gubanich	.000	1	0	0	0	0
Hughes	1.000	1	0	3	0	0
Kellner	.938	12	7	23	2	5
Seitzer	.932	24	15	53	5	4
Unroe	.931	35	20	75	7	9
Voigt	.667	6	0	2	1	0
Williamson	.848	13	7	21	5	1

Shortstop	PCT	G	PO	A	E	DP
Belliard	.882	7	4	11	2	3
Diaz	.926	14	15	35	4	12
Felix	1.000	3	2	5	0	0
Jenkins	.000	1	0	0	0	0
Johns	.941	108	154	308	29	66
Kellner	.942	33	40	91	8	22
Seitzer	.000	1	0	0	0	0
Unroe	1.000	1	0	1	0	0

Outfield	PCT	G	PO	A	E	DP
Banks	.986	78	138	8	2	0
Brown	.966	107	218	12	8	3
Diaz	.900	5	9	0	1	0
Dunn	.961	88	143	4	6	0
Felix	1.000	1	1	0	0	0
Iapoce	1.000	7	18	0	0	0
Jenkins	.961	72	115	7	5	1
Lee	.750	2	3	0	1	0
Martinez	1.000	3	4	0	0	0
Unroe	1.000	21	33	5	0	1
Voigt	1.000	40	61	2	0	1
Wachter	.958	39	65	3	3	0

EL PASO — Class AA

TEXAS LEAGUE

BATTING	AVG	G	AB	R	H	2B	3B	HR	RBI	BB	SO	SB	CS	B	T	HT	WT	DOB	1st Yr	Resides
Andreopoulos, Alex	.154	7	26	1	4	1	0	0	3	1	2	0	0	L	R	5-10	190	8-19-72	1995	Toronto, Ontario
Barker, Kevin	.277	65	238	37	66	15	6	10	63	28	40	3	3	L	L	6-3	205	7-26-75	1996	Mendota, Va.
Dobrolsky, Bill	.264	102	303	44	80	23	0	5	45	38	63	1	3	R	R	6-2	205	3-16-70	1991	Orwigsburg, Pa.
Felix, Lauro	.258	49	128	27	33	9	2	1	17	20	24	1	2	R	R	5-9	160	6-24-70	1992	El Paso, Texas
Groppuso, Mike	.345	29	87	15	30	6	2	8	23	10	19	1	1	R	R	6-3	195	3-9-70	1991	Lake Katrine, N.Y.
Kinkade, Mike	.385	125	468	112	180	35	12	12	109	52	66	17	4	R	R	6-1	210	5-6-73	1995	Pullman, Wash.
Klassen, Danny	.331	135	519	112	172	30	6	14	81	48	104	16	9	R	R	6-0	175	9-22-75	1993	Port St. Lucie, Fla.
Krause, Scott	.361	125	474	97	171	33	11	16	88	20	108	13	4	R	R	6-1	195	8-16-73	1994	Willowick, Ohio
Landry, Todd	.315	106	346	43	109	24	3	7	69	15	52	5	5	R	L	6-4	215	8-21-72	1993	Donaldsonville, La.
Lopez, Mickey	.300	134	483	79	145	21	10	3	58	48	60	20	10	S	R	5-9	165	11-17-73	1995	Miami, Fla.
Martinez, Greg	.291	95	381	75	111	10	10	1	29	32	55	39	7	S	R	5-10	168	1-27-72	1993	Las Vegas, Nev.
Nicholas, Darrell	.315	127	518	79	163	47	5	14	68	27	116	17	6	R	R	6-0	180	5-26-72	1994	Garyville, La.
O'Neal, Troy	.287	40	122	18	35	1	0	1	11	4	29	0	0	R	R	5-11	190	4-24-72	1995	Newark, Del.
Perez, Richard	.300	14	30	5	9	2	1	0	4	5	1	0	0	R	R	6-2	175	1-30-73	1991	Lara, Venez.
Rennhack, Mike	.276	106	369	59	102	28	7	9	64	38	81	4	3	S	R	6-3	190	8-25-74	1992	Orlando, Fla.
Rogue, Francisco	.125	13	24	3	3	1	0	0	1	1	5	0	0	R	R	6-2	170	11-22-75	1993	Santo Domingo, D.R.
Wachter, Derek	.306	13	49	8	15	0	0	1	8	4	7	0	1	R	R	6-2	195	8-28-70	1991	Miller Place, N.Y.
Williams, Drew	.237	71	257	36	61	14	1	9	36	19	49	2	1	L	R	5-11	200	3-27-72	1994	Jacksonville, Fla.

PITCHING	W	L	ERA	G	GS	CG	SV	IP	H	R	ER	BB	SO	B	T	HT	WT	DOB	1st Yr	Resides
Beck, Greg	1	5	6.52	18	6	0	0	48	75	46	35	15	37	R	R	6-4	215	10-21-72	1994	Fort Myers, Fla.
Browne, Byron	0	1	7.50	1	1	0	0	6	8	5	5	3	3	R	R	6-7	200	8-8-70	1991	Phoenix, Ariz.
Dawsey, Jason	2	2	6.81	8	7	0	0	38	50	30	29	23	14	L	L	5-8	165	5-27-74	1995	Lexington, S.C.
De los Santos, Valerio	6	10	5.75	26	16	1	2	114	146	83	73	38	61	L	L	6-4	185	10-6-75	1993	San Joaquin, D.R.
Estrada, Horacio	8	10	4.74	29	23	1	1	154	174	93	81	70	127	L	L	6-1	185	10-19-75	1992	Valencia, Venez.
Fieldbinder, Mick	2	3	5.73	6	6	0	0	38	55	32	24	12	20	R	R	6-4	200	10-2-73	1996	Rochester, Ill.
Gardner, Scott	7	8	5.10	29	22	1	0	139	166	93	79	56	89	S	R	6-5	225	9-30-71	1990	Fenton, Mich.
Huber, Jeff	3	1	3.46	19	0	0	1	26	35	14	10	11	20	R	L	6-4	220	12-17-70	1990	Scottsdale, Ariz.
Huntsman, Scott	4	4	7.20	42	0	0	3	55	76	56	44	21	37	R	R	6-2	230	10-28-72	1994	Zanesville, Ohio
Mullins, Greg	1	1	2.70	25	0	0	13	23	19	8	7	11	21	L	L	6-0	160	12-13-71	1995	Palatka, Fla.
Pace, Scotty	0	5	5.92	41	2	0	0	65	86	52	43	31	38	L	L	6-4	210	9-16-71	1994	Cieba, P.R.
Rodriguez, Frankie	2	2	3.40	31	0	0	4	50	46	23	19	13	40	R	R	5-9	170	1-6-73	1992	Brea, Calif.
Rossiter, Mike	1	0	2.61	8	0	0	0	21	22	6	6	8	11	R	R	6-6	230	6-20-73	1991	Burbank, Calif.
Sadler, Al	6	6	6.62	35	9	0	4	67	102	59	49	28	58	R	R	6-6	192	2-10-72	1992	Conyers, Ga.
Smith, Travis	16	3	4.15	28	28	5	0	184	210	106	85	58	107	R	R	5-10	170	11-7-72	1995	Bend, Ore.
Wagner, Joe	1	2	9.32	19	1	0	1	28	32	35	29	32	19	R	R	6-1	195	12-8-71	1993	Janesville, Wis.
Woodard, Steve	14	3	3.17	19	19	6	0	136	136	56	48	25	97	L	R	6-4	225	5-15-75	1994	Hartselle, Ala.

FIELDING

Catcher	PCT	G	PO	A	E	DP	PB
Andreopoulos	1.000	7	34	5	0	0	4
Dobrolsky	.989	101	585	64	7	9	15
O'Neal	.962	40	166	39	8	6	4
Rogue	.980	13	43	5	1	0	0

First Base	PCT	G	PO	A	E	DP
Barker	.982	49	455	30	9	44
Groppuso	1.000	1	11	0	0	0
Krause	1.000	1	1	0	0	0
Landry	.996	63	510	42	2	52
Williams	.986	36	332	26	5	35

Second Base	PCT	G	PO	A	E	DP
Felix	.964	11	21	33	2	8
Lopez	.976	131	290	397	17	110
Perez	1.000	2	2	4	0	1

Third Base	PCT	G	PO	A	E	DP
Dobrolsky	1.000	1	1	5	0	1
Felix	.887	17	11	36	6	7
Groppuso	.979	16	5	41	1	4
Kinkade	.845	106	79	249	60	17
Perez	.905	8	3	16	2	0

Shortstop	PCT	G	PO	A	E	DP
Felix	.932	9	19	22	3	6
Groppuso	1.000	1	2	2	0	2
Klassen	.920	131	177	399	50	79
Perez	.800	3	1	3	1	1

Outfield	PCT	G	PO	A	E	DP
Felix	1.000	4	2	0	0	0
Groppuso	.000	2	0	0	0	0
Krause	.967	119	195	13	7	3
Landry	1.000	18	20	4	0	0
Martinez	.995	95	193	13	1	4
Nicholas	.963	118	220	11	9	2
Rennhack	.981	72	97	6	2	0
Wachter	1.000	11	18	2	0	0
Williams	.000	1	0	0	0	0

STOCKTON — Class A

CALIFORNIA LEAGUE

BATTING	AVG	G	AB	R	H	2B	3B	HR	RBI	BB	SO	SB	CS	B	T	HT	WT	DOB	1st Yr	Resides
Barker, Kevin	.303	70	267	47	81	20	5	13	45	25	60	4	3	L	L	6-3	205	7-26-75	1996	Mendota, Va.
Cancel, Robinson	.280	64	211	25	59	11	0	1	16	13	40	9	3	R	R	5-11	195	5-4-76	1994	Lajas, P.R.
Elliott, David	.195	25	82	8	16	5	1	1	8	12	18	1	1	R	R	6-2	192	8-10-73	1995	Gladstone, Mich.
Fernandez, Antonio	.235	118	412	46	97	24	0	4	49	35	83	2	4	R	R	6-0	195	5-24-73	1994	Tucson, Ariz.
Green, Chad	.250	127	513	78	128	26	14	2	43	37	138	37	16	S	R	5-10	185	6-28-75	1996	Cincinnati, Ohio
Guerrero, Sergio	.220	76	241	23	53	6	1	0	25	14	31	1	6	R	R	5-9	180	12-22-74	1995	McAllen, Texas
Iapoce, Anthony	.266	99	387	48	103	13	4	1	27	30	71	22	12	S	L	5-10	178	8-23-73	1994	Ridgewood, N.Y.
Kominek, Toby	.300	128	476	83	143	28	7	15	72	50	107	22	14	R	R	6-2	205	6-13-73	1995	Erie, Mich.
Macalutas, Jon	.268	42	164	18	44	10	2	4	35	9	13	2	2	R	R	6-0	190	8-21-74	1996	Stockton, Calif.
O'Neal, Troy	.467	4	15	0	7	1	0	0	3	0	1	0	0	R	R	5-11	190	4-24-72	1995	Newark, Del.
Perez, Richard	.265	35	102	3	27	5	0	0	13	8	18	0	6	R	R	6-2	175	1-30-73	1991	Lara, Venez.
Phair, Kelly	.258	121	415	48	107	21	2	1	31	42	84	6	10	R	R	6-2	185	6-2-73	1995	Cincinnati, Ohio
Rodriguez, Miguel	.275	95	346	41	95	16	2	8	35	17	68	16	5	R	R	6-1	205	5-14-75	1993	El Seibo, D.R.
Swinton, Jermaine	.222	93	352	41	78	14	2	12	41	32	152	2	5	R	R	6-4	250	10-9-72	1990	Brooklyn, N.Y.
Tyler, Josh	.310	114	416	63	129	28	4	4	46	20	54	21	7	R	R	6-1	185	9-6-73	1994	Green Lane, Pa.
Vina, Fernando	.444	3	9	2	4	0	1	0	3	0	0	0	2	L	R	5-9	170	4-16-69	1990	Sacramento, Calif.
Wachter, Derek	.311	49	177	21	55	7	3	3	28	26	24	2	4	R	R	6-2	195	8-28-70	1991	Miller Place, N.Y.
Williams, Drew	.257	48	175	27	45	16	0	3	23	22	37	4	1	L	R	5-11	200	3-27-72	1994	Jacksonville, Fla.

GAMES BY POSITION: C—Cancel 62, O'Neal 4, Rodriguez 75, Tyler 4, Williams 2. **1B**—Barker 61, Macalutas 21, Swinton 20, Williams 44. **2B**—Guerrero 76, Perez 5, Tyler 70, Vina 3. **3B**—Fernandez 118, Perez 13, Tyler 18. **SS**—Perez 19, Phair 121, Tyler 10. **OF**—Cancel 1, Elliott 23, Green 126, Iapoce 93, Kominek 127, Swinton 7, Tyler 20, Wachter 34.

PITCHING	W	L	ERA	G	GS	CG	SV	IP	H	R	ER	BB	SO	B	T	HT	WT	DOB	1st Yr	Resides
Arias, Wagner	2	6	6.13	20	14	0	0	87	89	63	59	64	74	R	R	6-1	180	11-22-74	1992	Bani, D.R.
Beck, Greg	4	4	2.45	27	1	0	0	55	33	16	15	23	46	R	R	6-4	215	10-21-72	1994	Fort Myers, Fla.
Berninger, Darren	3	2	4.35	18	0	0	1	31	33	20	15	17	20	R	R	6-3	225	1-4-73	1995	Baton Rouge, La.
Bishop, Josh	2	3	8.51	11	8	0	0	37	56	38	35	24	39	R	R	6-4	180	7-16-74	1995	Sedalia, Mo.
Blyleven, Todd	1	0	0.00	1	0	0	0	3	2	0	0	0	4	R	R	6-5	230	9-27-72	1993	Villa Park, Calif.
Browne, Byron	1	3	3.58	8	7	0	0	28	22	12	11	22	24	R	R	6-7	200	8-8-70	1991	Phoenix, Ariz.
Cana, Nelson	6	1	3.44	44	0	0	1	92	91	46	35	34	69	L	L	6-2	190	7-17-75	1993	Cumana, Venez.
Chavez, Carlos	0	0	5.40	4	0	0	0	3	5	2	2	0	5	R	R	6-1	200	8-25-72	1992	El Paso, Texas
Fieldbinder, Mick	11	6	2.83	21	21	4	0	143	141	58	45	38	68	R	R	6-4	200	10-2-73	1996	Rochester, Ill.
Hardwick, Bubba	8	6	4.66	31	18	1	0	133	138	75	69	51	80	L	L	5-10	170	1-18-72	1992	Lakeland, Fla.
Hecker, Doug	0	1	4.24	12	0	0	0	17	12	9	8	8	11	R	R	6-4	210	1-21-71	1992	Wantagh, N.Y.
Helmer, Chad	2	0	3.09	7	0	0	1	12	12	4	4	4	10	R	R	6-4	195	9-12-75	1997	Ruskin, Fla.
Hommel, Brian	7	2	3.15	55	0	0	14	71	45	25	25	39	76	L	L	5-10	170	10-26-72	1995	Indianapolis, Ind.
Ishee, Gabe	2	3	6.57	21	3	0	0	49	55	38	36	29	52	R	R	6-2	175	8-14-74	1995	Biloxi, Miss.
Konieczki, Dom	1	1	2.77	12	0	0	1	13	11	5	4	10	16	R	L	6-1	170	6-16-69	1991	Lehigh Acres, Fla.
Miranda, Angel	0	0	0.00	1	1	0	0	2	0	0	0	2	2	L	L	6-1	195	11-9-69	1987	Arecibo, P.R.
Mullins, Greg	0	2	2.18	30	0	0	19	33	22	9	8	12	52	L	L	6-0	160	12-13-71	1995	Palatka, Fla.
Pasqualicchio, Mike	1	10	6.43	17	15	1	1	85	93	67	61	44	58	R	L	6-1	205	8-17-74	1995	Astoria, N.Y.
Passini, Brian	1	5	4.76	8	8	1	0	45	40	28	24	21	34	L	L	6-3	195	1-24-75	1996	Hennepin, Ill.
Rossiter, Mike	8	1	2.72	34	8	0	0	86	83	31	26	27	79	R	R	6-6	230	6-20-73	1991	Burbank, Calif.
Wagner, Joe	3	5	6.72	14	14	0	0	72	83	61	54	44	36	R	R	6-1	195	12-8-71	1993	Janesville, Wis.
Wunsch, Kelly	7	9	3.46	24	22	2	0	143	141	65	55	62	98	L	L	6-5	192	7-12-72	1993	Houston, Texas

BELOIT — Class A

MIDWEST LEAGUE

BATTING	AVG	G	AB	R	H	2B	3B	HR	RBI	BB	SO	SB	CS	B	T	HT	WT	DOB	1st Yr	Resides
Alfano, Jeff	.231	37	121	14	28	3	2	2	16	9	32	3	1	R	R	6-3	190	8-16-76	1996	Visalia, Calif.
Bearden, Doug	.221	56	163	15	36	3	1	0	14	2	37	1	1	R	R	6-2	170	9-11-75	1994	Lexington, S.C.
Cancel, Robinson	.300	17	50	9	15	3	0	0	4	7	9	0	2	R	R	5-11	195	5-4-76	1994	Lajas, P.R.
Elliott, David	.277	76	267	44	74	12	2	12	48	30	60	13	7	R	R	6-2	192	8-10-73	1995	Gladstone, Mich.
Faurot, Adam	.238	100	298	38	71	11	1	1	19	17	56	9	11	R	R	5-11	170	8-7-74	1996	Blountstown, Fla.
Fink, Marc	.148	10	27	4	4	0	0	2	3	6	10	0	0	L	L	6-3	230	7-27-76	1994	Jackson, N.J.
Klimek, Josh	.266	121	443	62	118	31	3	12	66	39	56	4	8	L	R	6-1	175	2-2-74	1996	St. Louis, Mo.
Lopiccolo, Jamie	.332	112	410	72	136	27	3	17	80	38	76	5	6	R	R	6-3	200	5-18-73	1995	Sterling Heights, Mich.
Macalutas, Jon	.313	59	211	45	66	13	1	10	36	24	19	6	5	R	R	6-0	190	8-21-74	1996	Stockton, Calif.
Martinez, David E.	.216	30	88	10	19	1	1	0	5	5	33	1	3	R	R	6-0	165	4-28-76	1993	Santo Domingo, D.R.
Moore, Donnie	.223	47	157	19	35	3	0	0	11	13	53	8	4	R	R	6-2	184	6-12-76	1995	Dallastown, Pa.
Peters, Tony	.235	113	375	50	88	16	6	9	43	31	110	21	7	R	R	6-2	210	10-28-74	1995	Mesa, Ariz.
Rogue, Francisco	.170	17	53	1	9	2	0	0	7	4	7	0	0	R	R	6-2	170	11-22-75	1993	Santo Domingo, D.R.
Schaub, Greg	.226	108	394	35	89	18	4	8	45	17	90	5	3	R	R	6-1	185	3-30-77	1995	Oxford, Pa.
Suero, Ignacio	.226	85	297	32	67	14	1	7	41	14	49	1	3	R	R	5-11	190	7-19-73	1994	Villa Blanca, D.R.
Valentin, Jose	.500	2	6	3	3	1	0	0	1	2	1	0	0	S	R	5-10	175	10-12-69	1987	Manati, P.R.
Walther, Chris	.300	113	437	55	131	25	4	0	38	28	41	5	7	R	R	6-2	200	8-28-76	1995	Odessa, Fla.
Washam, Jason	.283	88	276	44	78	15	3	8	46	33	31	4	2	R	R	6-1	190	8-18-74	1996	Lincoln, Ill.
Wetmore, Mike	.253	114	407	67	103	20	2	2	27	48	83	9	10	S	R	5-9	170	6-16-75	1996	Coupeville, Wash.

GAMES BY POSITION: C—Alfano 32, Cancel 16, Peters 4, Rogue 17, Suero 70, Washam 2. **1B**—Fink 1, Lopiccolo 3, Macalutas 43, Peters 2, Walther 48, Washam 53. **2B**—Faurot 46, Martinez 16, Wetmore 89. **3B**—Faurot 6, Klimek 111, Martinez 3, Walther 24. **SS**—Bearden 55, Faurot 51, Klimek 7, Martinez 9, Valentin 2, Wetmore 28. **OF**—Elliott 75, Faurot 3, Lopiccolo 33, Macalutas 4, Moore 44, Peters 107, Schaub 107, Walther 52.

PITCHING	W	L	ERA	G	GS	CG	SV	IP	H	R	ER	BB	SO	B	T	HT	WT	DOB	1st Yr	Resides
Akin, Jay	1	5	3.17	9	9	0	0	48	52	32	17	11	25	L	L	6-2	200	7-9-74	1997	Memphis, Tenn.
Barnes, Larry	3	6	5.73	13	13	0	0	66	61	47	42	47	58	S	R	6-5	230	8-11-76	1994	Jacksonville, Fla.
Bishop, Josh	5	7	5.99	21	11	1	1	80	79	62	53	34	61	R	R	6-4	180	7-16-74	1995	Sedalia, Mo.
Collins, Ed	0	0	10.80	2	0	0	0	2	3	3	2	3	3	R	R	6-3	225	8-26-76	1994	Union, N.J.
D'Amico, Jeff	0	0	0.00	1	1	0	0	3	0	0	0	1	7	R	R	6-7	250	12-27-75	1993	Pinellas Park, Fla.
Fulcher, John	0	4	4.06	34	0	0	0	51	56	33	23	25	43	L	L	6-3	190	9-18-74	1996	Manassas, Va.
Garcia, Jose	6	11	4.00	27	26	2	0	155	145	89	69	70	126	R	R	6-4	215	4-29-78	1996	Las Vegas, Nev.
Gnirk, Mark	3	2	3.87	38	0	0	1	77	95	46	33	18	63	R	R	6-3	195	8-21-74	1996	Phoenix, Ariz.
Gutierrez, Alfredo	4	3	4.19	19	6	0	0	62	64	38	29	22	35	R	R	6-1	190	3-22-76	1994	Riverside, Calif.
Hawkins, Al	1	4	10.58	6	6	0	0	25	46	33	29	12	17	R	R	6-2	210	1-1-78	1996	Elizabeth, N.J.
Ishee, Gabe	3	1	3.77	13	0	0	1	29	20	12	12	18	24	R	R	6-2	175	8-14-74	1995	Biloxi, Miss.
Levrault, Allen	3	10	5.28	24	24	1	0	131	141	89	77	40	112	R	R	6-3	238	8-15-77	1996	Westport, Mass.
Norris, Mac	1	1	8.62	4	4	0	0	16	20	18	15	13	10	R	R	6-7	218	3-19-76	1995	Mesa, Ariz.
O'Reilly, John	9	2	3.64	36	7	0	2	101	95	51	41	43	106	R	R	6-3	200	8-11-74	1996	Oakland, N.J.
Paredes, Roberto	5	4	2.86	46	0	0	15	50	36	19	16	33	49	R	R	6-3	170	10-16-73	1993	Santo Domingo, D.R.
Passini, Brian	9	5	3.22	19	19	1	0	123	114	48	44	35	116	L	L	6-3	195	1-24-75	1996	Hennepin, Ill.
Tank, Travis	6	3	3.87	41	0	0	1	79	80	42	34	33	45	R	R	6-2	220	3-27-75	1996	Sheboygan Falls, Wis.
Watson, Mark	0	3	6.68	8	7	0	0	32	40	33	24	20	33	R	L	6-4	215	1-23-74	1996	Atlanta, Ga.
Zapata, Juan	1	2	6.86	12	0	0	0	21	26	20	16	9	14	R	R	6-2	205	9-3-75	1993	Rio Arriba, D.R.

HELENA — Rookie

PIONEER LEAGUE

BATTING	AVG	G	AB	R	H	2B	3B	HR	RBI	BB	SO	SB	CS	B	T	HT	WT	DOB	1st Yr	Resides
Beatriz, Ramy	.267	55	187	35	50	12	3	4	27	24	43	9	7	L	L	5-11	180	1-15-79	1996	San Pedro de Macoris, D.R.
Bunkley, Antuan	.381	70	270	52	103	23	0	17	67	32	37	2	4	R	R	6-1	205	9-20-75	1994	West Palm Beach, Fla.
Caiazzo, Nick	.269	63	234	31	63	15	1	3	37	16	34	2	0	R	R	6-4	215	5-17-75	1997	Portland, Maine
Castillo, Alex	.214	5	14	0	3	2	0	0	0	1	5	0	0	R	R	6-2	180	1-11-78	1995	San Pedro de Macoris, D.R.
Fernandez, Ramon	.265	54	196	36	52	8	1	4	28	19	53	2	1	R	R	6-0	185	9-21-77	1996	Cayey, P.R.
Guillen, Jose	.216	25	51	6	11	0	0	1	6	9	17	4	2	S	R	6-0	156	8-10-79	1996	Santo Domingo, D.R.
Kirby, Scott	.262	68	248	65	65	10	1	11	47	53	65	8	6	R	R	6-2	190	7-18-77	1996	Destin, Fla.

BATTING	AVG	G	AB	R	H	2B	3B	HR	RBI	BB	SO	SB	CS	B	T	HT	WT	DOB	1st Yr	Resides
Kraus, Jake	.399	51	183	35	73	17	1	6	48	28	11	5	4	R	R	6-4	240	10-13-73	1997	Malone, Wis.
2-team (18 Ogden)	.390	69	246	51	96	22	1	10	69	38	15	8	4							
Moon, Brian	.282	49	170	15	48	5	0	0	22	8	23	2	1	S	R	6-0	190	7-15-77	1997	Mansfield, Ga.
Patten, Chris	.276	41	163	25	45	6	2	0	16	12	33	4	2	R	R	6-1	180	12-8-78	1997	Tempe, Ariz.
2-team (8 Ogden)	.270	49	189	27	51	6	2	0	19	15	38	4	3							
Patterson, Marty	.237	51	169	24	40	9	0	3	23	13	56	4	2	R	R	6-2	200	12-24-74	1997	Lexington, Mich.
Pearson, Ryan	.209	44	134	17	28	5	1	2	14	9	33	2	3	S	R	6-2	215	8-11-74	1997	Troy, Ala.
Rojas, Eliezer	.268	47	149	26	40	3	0	1	16	8	19	5	2	R	R	5-10	170	1-14-79	1996	Santo Domingo, D.R.
Sanchez, Wellington	.271	61	236	46	64	13	0	2	20	14	47	10	7	R	R	6-0	162	5-27-77	1995	Nigua, D.R.
Warren, Tommy	.278	33	97	21	27	3	0	0	8	20	30	4	3	S	R	6-4	170	11-1-79	1997	Monrovia, Calif.

GAMES BY POSITION: C—Caiazzo 11, Moon 48, Patterson 20. **1B**—Bunkley 26, Caiazzo 4, Castillo 4, Kraus 39, Patterson 5. **2B**—Bunkley 1, Guillen 21, Patten 21, Rojas 45. **3B**—Kirby 66, Patten 7. **SS**—Guillen 3, Patten 12, Sanchez 60. **OF**—Beatriz 53, Caiazzo 50, Fernandez 54, Patten 3, Patterson 10, Pearson 41, Warren 33.

PITCHING	W	L	ERA	G	GS	CG	SV	IP	H	R	ER	BB	SO	B	T	HT	WT	DOB	1st Yr	Resides
Akin, Jay	2	0	1.00	5	5	1	0	27	16	5	3	5	19	L	L	6-2	200	7-9-74	1997	Memphis, Tenn.
Cavanagh, Andrew	2	1	4.29	18	2	0	3	36	32	22	17	18	37	R	R	6-3	210	5-3-77	1997	Dunwoody, Ga.
Childers, Jason	1	1	3.31	10	0	0	2	16	14	9	6	7	25	S	R	6-0	165	1-13-75	1997	Augusta, Ga.
Childers, Matt	1	4	6.20	14	10	0	1	61	81	49	42	24	19	R	R	6-5	190	12-3-78	1997	Augusta, Ga.
Guzman, Jonathan	2	1	2.61	19	1	0	1	31	32	23	9	20	21	L	L	6-2	216	8-26-77	1995	Toa Baja, P.R.
Helmer, Chad	0	2	2.08	14	0	0	2	30	27	12	7	9	33	R	R	6-4	195	9-12-75	1997	Ruskin, Fla.
Incantalupo, Todd	5	4	5.12	14	11	0	0	65	76	48	37	24	51	L	L	6-2	185	5-18-76	1997	Norwalk, Conn.
Johnston, Doug	6	2	4.36	13	13	0	0	74	64	39	36	34	66	R	R	6-5	180	3-16-78	1996	Omaha, Neb.
Jones, Chauncey	0	0	9.53	5	0	0	0	6	8	6	6	7	7	R	R	6-1	195	9-15-75	1997	Council Bluffs, Iowa
Kendall, Phil	3	4	5.45	14	14	0	0	76	84	55	46	37	73	R	R	6-4	208	8-22-77	1996	Jasper, Ind.
Leshay, Maney	1	0	18.56	5	2	0	0	5	11	12	11	10	5	R	R	6-1	190	3-15-73	1996	Tequesta, Fla.
Mallette, Brian	6	2	4.33	23	0	0	5	35	33	19	17	20	58	R	R	6-0	185	1-19-75	1997	Glenwood, Ga.
Martinez, Francisco	0	2	5.61	16	0	0	0	26	30	26	16	18	20	R	R	6-1	165	2-6-78	1995	Santo Domingo, D.R.
Miller, Jim	5	7	5.99	16	13	1	0	71	88	56	47	24	51	S	R	6-7	195	8-1-75	1997	Des Plaines, Ill.
Myers, Rob	1	3	9.43	18	0	0	0	28	43	42	29	24	24	R	R	6-1	185	8-24-76	1997	Loganville, Pa.
Priebe, Kevin	2	1	1.61	19	0	0	6	28	24	7	5	9	25	R	L	6-2	225	1-1-75	1997	North Fond du Lac, Wis.

OGDEN — Rookie

PIONEER LEAGUE

BATTING	AVG	G	AB	R	H	2B	3B	HR	RBI	BB	SO	SB	CS	B	T	HT	WT	DOB	1st Yr	Resides
Alfano, Jeff	.360	46	175	39	63	12	4	7	29	17	31	9	4	R	R	6-3	190	8-16-76	1996	Visalia, Calif.
Baez, Juan	.289	52	128	19	37	7	0	3	21	15	45	2	2	R	R	6-0	173	12-23-77	1994	Villa Mella, D.R.
Candela, Frank	.267	25	75	9	20	0	1	1	10	4	17	3	1	R	R	5-8	175	7-26-78	1997	Peabody, Mass.
Darula, Bobby	.332	69	262	61	87	26	4	6	52	42	23	11	2	L	R	5-10	175	10-29-74	1996	Greenwich, Conn.
Deardorff, Jeff	.275	63	222	33	61	17	3	2	27	24	74	2	2	R	R	6-3	205	8-14-78	1997	Clermont, Fla.
Guthrie, Kendal	.276	63	239	38	66	19	1	1	34	20	57	4	5	R	R	6-1	195	11-29-75	1997	Flower Mound, Texas
Jacobsen, Bucky	.328	67	238	57	78	17	2	8	52	41	44	6	6	R	R	6-4	220	8-30-75	1997	Hermiston, Ore.
James, Brandon	.285	72	267	51	76	14	2	10	58	29	79	8	3	L	R	6-2	215	3-26-75	1997	Carmichael, Calif.
Kraus, Jake	.365	18	63	16	23	5	0	4	21	10	4	3	0	R	R	6-4	240	10-13-73	1997	Malone, Wis.
Mathis, Jared	.279	54	197	30	55	14	0	0	29	6	20	7	3	R	R	5-10	175	8-8-75	1997	Port Orange, Fla.
Morrow, Alvin	.250	2	4	1	1	0	0	0	1	1	2	0	0	R	R	6-4	240	4-28-78	1997	Kirkwood, Mo.
Osilka, Garret	.255	64	231	41	59	9	2	0	19	32	50	10	4	R	R	6-1	180	9-14-77	1996	Jacksonville, Fla.
Patten, Chris	.231	8	26	2	6	0	0	0	3	3	5	0	1	R	R	6-1	180	12-8-78	1997	Tempe, Ariz.
Riggio, Robert	.178	29	73	13	13	2	0	0	10	7	9	0	0	R	R	6-1	195	9-12-75	1997	New York, N.Y.
Rowan, Chris	.251	55	211	46	53	10	3	9	34	27	65	2	5	R	R	6-1	175	3-18-79	1997	Mt. Vernon, N.Y.
Tucent, Fransisco	.248	42	117	22	29	4	0	0	16	9	23	2	0	S	R	6-2	155	6-16-77	1994	Villa Mella, D.R.

GAMES BY POSITION: C—Alfano 23, Darula 41, Guthrie 10, Mathis 7. **1B**—Alfano 3, Darula 2, Guthrie 41, James 6, Kraus 18, Riggio 7. **2B**—Mathis 2, Osilka 2, Patten 4, Riggio 5, Rowan 39, Tucent 36. **3B**—Deardorff 63, Osilka 1, Patten 4, Riggio 11, Tucent 2. **SS**—Mathis 6, Osilka 61, Patten 1, Rowan 13, Tucent 1. **OF**—Baez 50, Candela 23, Jacobsen 62, James 66, Mathis 41, Morrow 1, Tucent 3.

PITCHING	W	L	ERA	G	GS	CG	SV	IP	H	R	ER	BB	SO	B	T	HT	WT	DOB	1st Yr	Resides
Arroyo, Joel	0	1	10.89	16	0	0	0	21	33	37	25	21	18	R	R	6-0	208	7-16-76	1997	Ponce, P.R.
Byrd, Ben	3	1	4.46	18	0	0	1	38	42	27	19	13	35	R	R	6-0	195	10-31-75	1997	Taylorsville, Utah
Eye, Jake	0	0	0.00	1	1	0	0	3	2	1	0	1	2	R	R	6-1	220	12-28-74	1997	Windham, Ohio
Gooda, David	3	2	5.69	16	5	0	0	62	78	49	39	20	62	L	L	6-3	196	8-17-76	1995	Brisbane, Australia
Hawkins, Al	2	8	5.89	14	14	0	0	81	113	74	53	24	47	R	R	6-2	210	1-1-78	1996	Elizabeth, N.J.
Jones, Chauncey	0	1	5.79	9	0	0	0	9	10	7	6	11	10	R	R	6-1	195	9-15-75	1997	Council Bluffs, Iowa
2-team (5 Helena)	0	1	7.20	14	0	0	0	15	18	13	12	18	17							
Kirst, Mark	4	4	5.00	16	10	0	0	67	88	49	37	14	56	R	R	6-4	200	5-23-75	1997	Green Bay, Wis.
Lee, Derek	4	4	3.87	14	13	0	0	74	89	49	32	20	71	L	L	6-4	185	8-20-74	1997	Fort Worth, Texas
Peterson, Kyle	0	0	0.87	3	3	0	0	10	5	2	1	4	11	R	R	6-3	220	4-9-76	1997	Elkhorn, Neb.
Pozo, Jason	0	0	21.00	2	0	0	0	3	7	7	7	3	2	R	R	6-4	205	11-15-75	1997	Palm Harbor, Fla.
Schubmehl, Brian	4	3	5.40	19	0	0	4	30	32	23	18	15	38	R	R	6-1	185	11-3-74	1997	Wayland, N.Y.
Sokol, Trad	2	0	4.19	17	0	0	3	39	44	18	18	16	43	R	L	6-1	185	5-12-77	1997	Charleston, W.Va.
Stewart, Paul	5	6	5.31	15	15	1	0	81	88	59	48	30	82	R	R	6-6	220	10-21-78	1996	Raleigh, N.C.
Watson, Mark	4	3	4.15	10	10	1	0	48	44	26	22	19	49	R	L	6-4	215	1-23-74	1996	Atlanta, Ga.
Wooten, Shane	4	1	5.29	18	0	0	1	34	43	33	20	14	27	S	L	6-0	170	3-14-75	1997	Goodlettsville, Tenn.
Zapata, Juan	2	1	1.23	8	0	0	2	22	11	5	3	13	19	R	R	6-2	205	9-3-75	1993	Rio Arriba, D.R.

Minnesota TWINS

Manager: Tom Kelly.

1997 Record: 68-94, .420 (4th, AL Central)

BATTING	AVG	G	AB	R	H	2B	3B	HR	RBI	BB	SO	SB	CS	B	T	HT	WT	DOB	1st Yr	Resides
Becker, Rich	.264	132	443	61	117	22	3	10	45	62	130	17	5	L	L	5-10	180	2-1-72	1990	Cape Coral, Fla.
Brede, Brent	.274	61	190	25	52	11	1	3	21	21	38	7	2	L	L	6-4	190	9-13-71	1990	Trenton, Ill.
Colbrunn, Greg	.281	70	217	24	61	14	0	5	26	8	38	1	2	R	R	6-0	200	7-26-69	1988	Weston, Fla.
Coomer, Ron	.298	140	523	63	156	30	2	13	85	22	91	4	3	R	R	5-11	195	11-18-66	1987	Crest Hill, Ill.
Cordova, Marty	.246	103	378	44	93	18	4	15	51	30	92	5	3	R	R	6-0	190	7-10-69	1989	Henderson, Nev.
Hocking, Denny	.257	115	253	28	65	12	4	2	25	18	51	3	5	S	R	5-10	174	4-2-70	1990	Torrance, Calif.
Hunter, Torii	.000	1	0	0	0	0	0	0	0	0	0	0	0	R	R	6-2	205	7-18-75	1993	Pine Bluff, Ark.
Jackson, Darrin	.254	49	130	19	33	2	1	3	21	4	21	2	0	R	R	6-0	186	8-22-63	1981	Mesa, Ariz.
Kelly, Roberto	.287	75	247	39	71	19	2	5	37	17	50	7	4	R	R	6-2	202	10-1-64	1982	Panama City, Panama
Knoblauch, Chuck	.291	156	611	117	178	26	10	9	58	84	84	62	10	R	R	5-9	181	7-7-68	1989	Houston, Texas
Latham, Chris	.182	15	22	4	4	1	0	0	1	0	8	0	0	S	R	6-0	188	5-26-73	1991	Las Vegas, Nev.
Lawton, Matt	.248	142	460	74	114	29	3	14	60	76	81	7	4	L	R	5-9	180	11-3-71	1991	Lyman, Miss.
Meares, Pat	.276	134	439	63	121	23	3	10	60	18	86	7	7	R	R	6-0	180	9-6-68	1990	Wichita, Kan.
Miller, Damian	.273	25	66	5	18	1	0	2	13	2	12	0	0	R	R	6-2	190	10-13-69	1990	West Salem, Wis.
Molitor, Paul	.305	135	538	63	164	32	4	10	89	45	73	11	4	R	R	6-0	185	8-22-56	1977	Edina, Minn.
Myers, Greg	.267	62	165	24	44	11	1	5	28	16	29	0	0	L	R	6-2	215	4-14-66	1984	Riverside, Calif.
Ortiz, David	.327	15	49	10	16	3	0	1	6	2	19	0	0	L	L	6-4	230	11-18-75	1993	Haina, D.R.
Stahoviak, Scott	.229	91	275	33	63	17	0	10	33	24	73	5	2	L	R	6-5	222	3-6-70	1991	Grayslake, Ill.
Steinbach, Terry	.248	122	447	60	111	27	1	12	54	35	106	6	1	R	R	6-1	175	3-2-62	1983	Plymouth, Minn.
Valentin, Javier	.286	4	7	1	2	0	0	0	0	0	3	0	0	S	R	5-10	191	9-19-75	1993	Manati, P.R.
Walker, Todd	.237	52	156	15	37	7	1	3	16	11	30	7	0	L	R	6-0	180	5-25-73	1994	Bossier City, La.

PITCHING	W	L	ERA	G	GS	CG	SV	IP	H	R	ER	BB	SO	B	T	HT	WT	DOB	1st Yr	Resides
Aguilera, Rick	5	4	3.82	61	0	0	26	68	65	29	29	22	68	R	R	6-5	203	12-31-61	1983	Chanhassen, Minn.
Aldred, Scott	2	10	7.68	17	15	0	0	77	102	66	66	28	33	L	L	6-4	195	6-12-68	1987	Lakeland, Fla.
Bowers, Shane	0	3	8.05	5	5	0	0	19	27	20	17	8	7	R	R	6-6	215	7-27-71	1993	Covina, Calif.
Guardado, Eddie	0	4	3.91	69	0	0	1	46	45	23	20	17	54	R	L	6-0	187	10-2-70	1991	Stockton, Calif.
Hawkins, LaTroy	6	12	5.84	20	20	0	0	103	134	71	67	47	58	R	R	6-5	195	12-21-72	1991	Gary, Ind.
Jarvis, Kevin	0	0	12.46	6	2	0	0	13	23	18	18	8	9	S	R	6-2	200	8-1-69	1991	Lexington, Ky.
Miller, Travis	1	5	7.63	13	7	0	0	48	64	49	41	23	26	R	L	6-3	205	11-2-72	1994	West Manchester, Ohio
Naulty, Dan	1	1	5.87	29	0	0	1	31	29	20	20	10	23	R	R	6-6	211	1-6-70	1992	Huntington Beach, Calif.
Olson, Gregg	0	0	18.36	11	0	0	0	8	19	17	17	11	6	R	R	6-4	212	10-11-66	1988	Reisterstown, Md.
Radke, Brad	20	10	3.87	35	35	4	0	240	238	114	103	48	174	R	R	6-2	180	10-27-72	1991	Tampa, Fla.
Ritchie, Todd	2	3	4.58	42	0	0	0	75	87	41	38	28	44	R	R	6-3	205	11-7-71	1990	Duncanville, Texas
Robertson, Rich	8	12	5.69	31	26	0	0	147	169	105	93	70	69	L	L	6-4	175	9-15-68	1990	Waller, Texas
Rodriguez, Frank	3	6	4.62	43	15	0	0	142	147	82	73	60	65	R	R	6-0	175	12-11-72	1991	Brooklyn, N.Y.
Serafini, Dan	2	1	3.42	6	4	1	0	26	27	11	10	11	15	S	L	6-1	185	1-25-74	1992	San Bruno, Calif.
Stevens, Dave	1	3	9.00	6	6	0	0	23	41	23	23	17	16	R	R	6-3	210	3-4-70	1990	La Habra, Calif.
Swindell, Greg	7	4	3.58	65	1	0	1	116	102	46	46	25	75	R	L	6-3	225	1-2-65	1986	Houston, Texas
Tewksbury, Bob	8	13	4.22	26	26	5	0	169	200	83	79	31	92	R	R	6-4	200	11-30-60	1981	Penacook, N.H.
Trombley, Mike	2	3	4.37	67	0	0	1	82	77	43	40	31	74	R	R	6-2	200	4-14-67	1989	Fort Myers, Fla.

FIELDING

Catcher	PCT	G	PO	A	E	DP	PB
D. Miller	1.000	20	85	3	0	1	3
Myers	.986	38	196	11	3	2	2
Steinbach	.993	116	654	51	5	4	9
Valentin	1.000	4	11	2	0	0	0

First Base	PCT	G	PO	A	E	DP
Brede	.992	15	121	9	1	9
Colbrunn	.988	64	475	35	6	60
Coomer	1.000	9	40	5	0	5
Hocking	1.000	1	1	0	0	0
Molitor	.991	12	99	7	1	6
Ortiz	.989	11	84	10	1	10
Stahoviak	.990	81	607	58	7	67
Steinbach	.750	2	3	0	1	0

Second Base	PCT	G	PO	A	E	DP
Hocking	1.000	15	13	16	0	5
Knoblauch	.985	154	283	425	11	101
Walker	.964	8	11	16	1	5

Third Base	PCT	G	PO	A	E	DP
Coomer	.966	119	66	216	10	20
Hocking	1.000	39	14	32	0	2
Walker	.969	40	24	70	3	4

Shortstop	PCT	G	PO	A	E	DP
Hocking	.975	44	61	96	4	28
Knoblauch	.833	1	2	3	1	1
Meares	.969	134	211	415	20	93

Outfield	PCT	G	PO	A	E	DP
Becker	.985	128	319	5	5	0
Brede	.957	42	67	0	3	0
Coomer	.950	7	17	2	1	2
Cordova	.991	101	217	12	2	2
Hocking	1.000	20	35	2	0	1
Jackson	.990	44	93	4	1	1
Kelly	1.000	59	101	1	0	0
Latham	.917	10	11	0	1	0
Lawton	.976	138	278	9	7	3

LARRY GOREN

Brad Radke

FARM SYSTEM

Director of Player Development: Jim Rantz

Class	Farm Team	League	W	L	Pct.	Finish*	Manager	First Yr
AAA	Salt Lake (Utah) Buzz	Pacific Coast	72	71	.503	6th (10)	Phil Roof	1994
AA	New Britain (Conn.) Rock Cats	Eastern	70	72	.493	7th (10)	Al Newman	1995
#A	Fort Myers (Fla.) Miracle	Florida State	81	58	.583	3rd (14)	John Russell	1993
A	Fort Wayne (Ind.) Wizards	Midwest	68	67	.504	6th (14)	Mike Boulanger	1993
#R	Elizabethton (Tenn.) Twins	Appalachian	38	30	.559	4th (10)	Jose Marzan	1974
R	Fort Myers (Fla.) Twins	Gulf Coast	28	32	.467	8th (15)	Steve Liddle	1989

*Finish in overall standings (No. of teams in league) #Advanced level

ORGANIZATION LEADERS

MAJOR LEAGUERS

BATTING

*AVG	Paul Molitor	.305
R	Chuck Knoblauch	117
H	Chuck Knoblauch	178
TB	Chuck Knoblauch	251
2B	Paul Molitor	32
3B	Chuck Knoblauch	10
HR	Marty Cordova	15
RBI	Paul Molitor	89
BB	Chuck Knoblauch	84
SO	Rich Becker	130
SB	Chuck Knoblauch	62

PITCHING

W	Brad Radke	20
L	Bob Tewksbury	13
#ERA	Greg Swindell	3.58
G	Eddie Guardado	69
CG	Bob Tewksbury	5
SV	Rick Aguilera	26
IP	Brad Radke	240
BB	Rich Robertson	70
SO	Brad Radke	174

MEL BAILEY

Paul Molitor

MEL BAILEY

David Ortiz

MINOR LEAGUERS

BATTING

*AVG	Brent Brede, Salt Lake	.354
R	Ryan Radmanovich, Salt Lake	92
H	David Ortiz, Salt Lake/N.B./Ft. Myers	171
TB	David Ortiz, Salt Lake/N.B./Ft. Myers	306
2B	David Ortiz, Salt Lake/N.B./Ft. Myers	38
3B	Mitch Simons, Salt Lake	10
HR	Chad Rupp, Salt Lake	32
RBI	David Ortiz, Salt Lake/N.B./Ft. Myers	124
BB	Doug Mientkiewicz, New Britain	98
SO	David Ortiz, Salt Lake/N.B./Ft. Myers	142
SB	Anthony Felston, Fort Wayne	45

PITCHING

W	Three tied at	13
L	Mark Redman, Salt Lake	15
#ERA	Chris Garza, Fort Wayne	2.08
G	Two tied at	60
CG	Two tied at	4
SV	Two tied at	17
IP	David Hooten, Fort Wayne	166
BB	Mark Redman, Salt Lake	80
SO	Jason Bell, New Britain	142

*Minimum 250 At-Bats #Minimum 75 Innings

TOP 10 PROSPECTS

DIAMOND IMAGES

Todd Walker

How the Twins Top 10 prospects, as judged by Baseball America prior to the 1997 season, fared in 1997:

Player, Pos.	Club (Class)	AVG	AB	R	H	2B	3B	HR	RBI	SB
1. Todd Walker, 3b	Minnesota	.237	156	15	37	7	1	3	16	7
	Salt Lake (AAA)	.345	322	69	111	20	1	11	53	5
2. Luis Rivas, ss	Fort Wayne (A)	.239	419	61	100	20	6	1	30	28
3. Torii Hunter, of	Minnesota	.000	0	0	0	0	0	0	0	0
	New Britain (AA)	.231	471	57	109	22	2	8	56	8
4. Javier Valentin, c	Minnesota	.286	7	1	2	0	0	0	0	0
	New Britain (AA)	.243	370	41	90	17	0	8	50	2
7. Jacque Jones, of	Fort Myers (A)	.297	539	84	160	33	6	15	82	24
10. A.J. Pierzynski, c	Fort Myers (A)	.279	412	49	115	23	1	9	64	2
		W	**L**	**ERA**	**G**	**SV**	**IP**	**H**	**BB**	**SO**
5. Dan Serafini, lhp	Minnesota	2	1	3.42	6	0	26	27	11	15
	Salt Lake (AAA)	9	7	4.97	28	0	152	166	55	118
6. Todd Ritchie, rhp	Minnesota	2	3	4.58	42	0	74	87	28	44
8. Travis Miller, lhp	Minnesota	1	5	7.63	13	0	48	64	23	26
	Salt Lake (AAA)	10	6	4.73	21	0	126	140	57	86
9. Mark Redman, lhp	Salt Lake (AAA)	8	15	6.31	29	1	158	204	80	125

SALT LAKE CITY — Class AAA

PACIFIC COAST LEAGUE

BATTING	AVG	G	AB	R	H	2B	3B	HR	RBI	BB	SO	SB	CS	B	T	HT	WT	DOB	1st Yr	Resides
Alvarez, Rafael	.271	17	48	10	13	1	1	0	5	6	9	5	0	L	L	5-11	165	1-22-77	1994	Valencia, Venez.
Baez, Kevin	.274	112	383	38	105	25	3	5	54	29	74	3	4	R	R	6-0	170	1-10-67	1988	Brooklyn, N.Y.
Brede, Brent	.354	84	328	82	116	27	4	9	76	47	62	4	2	L	L	6-4	190	9-13-71	1990	Trenton, Ill.
Castellano, Pedro	.358	43	165	29	59	9	1	7	36	20	31	0	1	R	R	6-1	195	3-11-70	1988	Lara, Venez.
Cordova, Marty	.375	6	24	5	9	4	0	1	4	2	3	1	0	R	R	6-0	190	7-10-69	1989	Henderson, Nev.
Durant, Mike	.206	66	223	33	46	13	1	8	36	21	42	4	1	R	R	6-2	198	9-14-69	1991	Columbus, Ohio
Ferguson, Jeff	.282	65	241	51	68	19	2	8	35	24	48	4	2	R	R	5-10	175	6-18-73	1994	Placentia, Calif.
Horn, Jeff	.333	23	78	16	26	6	0	1	13	11	22	0	0	R	R	6-1	197	8-23-70	1992	Las Vegas, Nev.
Jackson, Darrin	.300	19	80	14	24	3	3	1	12	5	17	3	0	R	R	6-0	186	8-22-63	1981	Mesa, Ariz.
Johnson, J.J.	.146	26	82	6	12	1	1	0	5	4	24	2	2	R	R	6-0	195	8-31-73	1991	Pine Plains, N.Y.
Latham, Chris	.309	118	492	78	152	22	5	8	58	58	110	21	19	S	R	6-0	188	5-26-73	1991	Las Vegas, Nev.
Miller, Damian	.338	85	314	48	106	19	3	11	82	29	62	6	1	R	R	6-2	190	10-13-69	1990	West Salem, Wis.
Ogden, Jamie	.286	97	367	67	105	18	5	14	53	35	99	14	3	L	L	6-5	233	1-19-72	1990	White Bear Lake, Minn.
Ortiz, David	.214	10	42	5	9	1	0	4	10	2	11	0	1	L	L	6-4	230	11-18-75	1993	Haina, D.R.
Radmanovich, Ryan	.264	133	485	92	128	25	4	28	78	67	138	11	4	L	R	6-2	185	8-9-71	1993	Calgary, Alberta
Rupp, Chad	.272	117	426	77	116	19	7	32	94	49	112	2	1	R	R	6-2	215	9-30-71	1993	Charlotte, N.C.
Shave, Jon	.329	103	395	75	130	27	3	7	60	39	62	6	6	R	R	6-0	180	11-4-67	1990	Fernandina Beach, Fla.
Simons, Mitch	.299	115	462	87	138	34	10	5	59	47	48	26	5	R	R	5-9	170	12-13-68	1991	Midwest City, Okla.
Smith, Jeff	.250	7	12	2	3	2	0	0	2	1	3	0	0	L	R	6-3	211	6-17-74	1996	Naples, Fla.
Stahoviak, Scott	.214	8	28	5	6	0	0	2	10	5	8	0	0	L	R	6-5	222	3-6-70	1991	Grayslake, Ill.
Walker, Todd	.345	83	322	69	111	20	1	11	53	46	49	5	5	L	R	6-0	180	5-25-73	1994	Bossier City, La.

PITCHING	W	L	ERA	G	GS	CG	SV	IP	H	R	ER	BB	SO	B	T	HT	WT	DOB	1st Yr	Resides
Aldred, Scott	3	3	7.03	7	7	0	0	40	56	39	31	16	23	L	L	6-4	195	6-12-68	1987	Lakeland, Fla.
Baptist, Travis	4	1	2.08	7	6	1	0	48	47	16	11	9	28	L	L	6-0	190	12-30-71	1990	Aloha, Ore.
Bowers, Shane	6	2	4.79	9	9	1	0	56	64	35	30	14	46	R	R	6-6	215	7-27-71	1993	Covina, Calif.
Dreyer, Steve	1	0	7.36	27	0	0	2	44	65	38	36	10	34	R	R	6-3	180	11-19-69	1990	Cedar Falls, Iowa
Duncan, Chip	0	0	7.94	5	1	0	0	11	17	13	10	3	16	R	R	5-11	185	6-27-65	1987	Fort Myers, Fla.
Gandarillas, Gus	1	0	3.18	11	2	0	2	23	22	8	8	6	13	R	R	6-0	180	7-19-71	1992	Hialeah, Fla.
Hawkins, LaTroy	9	4	5.45	14	13	2	0	76	100	53	46	16	53	R	R	6-5	195	12-21-72	1991	Gary, Ind.
Klingenbeck, Scott	0	0	1.29	1	1	0	0	7	6	1	1	0	6	R	R	6-2	205	2-3-71	1992	Cincinnati, Ohio
Legault, Kevin	1	3	7.52	16	0	0	0	26	39	24	22	7	18	R	R	6-1	185	3-5-71	1992	Watervliet, N.Y.
Linebarger, Keith	4	6	6.63	41	7	0	5	98	135	79	72	42	59	R	R	6-6	220	5-11-71	1992	Ringgold, Ga.
Looney, Brian	0	2	2.19	17	0	0	1	25	20	7	6	10	21	L	L	5-10	180	9-26-69	1991	Cheshire, Conn.
Miller, Travis	10	6	4.73	21	21	0	0	126	140	73	66	57	86	R	L	6-3	205	11-2-72	1994	West Manchester, Ohio
Naulty, Dan	0	1	11.37	6	0	0	0	6	11	10	8	2	5	R	R	6-6	211	1-6-70	1992	Huntington Beach, Calif.
Niedermaier, Brad	2	1	5.88	16	0	0	0	26	29	22	17	13	20	R	R	6-3	205	2-9-73	1995	Niles, Ill.
Ohme, Kevin	2	5	5.62	56	0	0	11	74	70	49	46	34	45	L	L	6-1	175	4-13-71	1993	Brandon, Fla.
Parra, Jose	2	8	6.03	50	4	0	8	94	126	73	63	30	61	R	R	5-11	160	11-28-72	1990	Santiago, D.R.
Rath, Fred	0	1	1.64	10	0	0	3	11	11	2	2	2	11	R	R	6-3	205	1-5-73	1995	Tampa, Fla.
Redman, Mark	8	15	6.31	29	28	0	1	158	204	123	111	80	125	L	L	6-5	220	1-5-74	1995	Fort Myers, Fla.
Roberts, Brett	1	3	6.90	24	6	0	1	59	89	51	45	33	33	R	R	6-7	225	3-24-70	1991	South Webster, Ohio
Serafini, Dan	9	7	4.97	28	24	2	0	152	166	87	84	55	118	S	L	6-1	185	1-25-74	1992	San Bruno, Calif.
Stevens, Dave	9	3	4.30	16	14	1	0	90	93	52	43	31	71	R	R	6-3	210	3-4-70	1990	La Habra, Calif.

FIELDING

Catcher	PCT	G	PO	A	E	DP	PB
Durant	1.000	51	326	23	0	4	4
Horn	.993	23	129	5	1	0	1
Miller	.988	70	445	35	6	8	2
Smith	1.000	6	23	4	0	0	0

First Base	PCT	G	PO	A	E	DP
Brede	.990	39	374	25	4	50
Ferguson	1.000	1	1	0	0	0
Ogden	.995	23	195	10	1	27
Ortiz	1.000	8	71	2	0	7
Rupp	.995	63	563	33	3	58
Shave	.988	10	77	7	1	5
Stahoviak	1.000	7	72	7	0	5

Second Base	PCT	G	PO	A	E	DP
Castellano	1.000	1	1	0	0	0
Ferguson	.958	56	92	183	12	45
Shave	.986	16	26	42	1	9
Simons	.986	75	168	242	6	69

Third Base	PCT	G	PO	A	E	DP
Castellano	.981	38	22	80	2	6
Ferguson	.750	5	1	8	3	3
Radmanovich	.000	1	0	0	0	0
Rupp	.826	7	5	14	4	2
Shave	.946	22	14	56	4	5
Walker	.901	74	44	174	24	20

Shortstop	PCT	G	PO	A	E	DP
Baez	.957	109	164	345	23	74
Castellano	.000	1	0	0	0	0
Ferguson	.778	4	3	11	4	3
Shave	.933	26	42	84	9	17
Simons	.985	13	26	39	1	12

Outfield	PCT	G	PO	A	E	DP
Alvarez	.920	15	22	1	2	0
Brede	.961	42	71	2	3	0
Cordova	.750	2	3	0	1	0
Jackson	1.000	18	26	2	0	1
Johnson	.958	26	22	1	1	0
Latham	.961	118	262	6	11	1
Ogden	1.000	71	129	9	0	0
Radmanovich	.963	130	226	7	9	3
Shave	1.000	16	32	3	0	0
Simons	1.000	7	10	0	0	0

NEW BRITAIN — Class AA

EASTERN LEAGUE

BATTING	AVG	G	AB	R	H	2B	3B	HR	RBI	BB	SO	SB	CS	B	T	HT	WT	DOB	1st Yr	Resides
Allen, Chad	.252	30	115	20	29	9	1	4	18	9	21	2	0	R	R	6-1	190	2-6-75	1996	DeSoto, Texas
Alvarez, Rafael	.255	16	47	5	12	0	0	2	7	5	9	1	4	L	L	5-11	165	1-22-77	1994	Valencia, Venez.
Brown, Armann	.152	14	46	4	7	3	0	0	1	9	13	1	2	R	R	6-1	163	9-10-72	1992	Houston, Texas
Ferguson, Jeff	.244	36	135	19	33	4	0	1	21	12	31	1	1	R	R	5-10	175	6-18-73	1994	Placentia, Calif.
Fortin, Troy	.234	12	47	11	11	2	0	0	4	3	7	0	0	R	R	5-11	200	2-24-75	1993	Lundar, Manitoba
Fraser, Joe	.239	79	238	33	57	11	1	1	16	29	50	11	6	R	R	6-1	200	8-23-74	1995	Westminster, Calif.
Gunderson, Shane	.256	33	117	17	30	7	3	2	10	19	31	7	2	R	R	6-0	205	10-16-73	1995	Faribault, Minn.
Horn, Jeff	.255	56	184	17	47	10	0	4	26	19	24	2	4	R	R	6-1	197	8-23-70	1992	Las Vegas, Nev.
Hunter, Torii	.231	127	471	57	109	22	2	8	56	47	94	8	8	R	R	6-2	205	7-18-75	1993	Pine Bluff, Ark.
Johnson, J.J.	.236	103	356	60	84	11	3	3	42	38	94	13	1	R	R	6-0	195	8-31-73	1991	Pine Plains, N.Y.
Koskie, Corey	.286	131	437	88	125	26	6	23	79	90	106	9	5	L	R	6-3	215	6-28-73	1994	Dugald, Manitoba
Lane, Ryan	.259	128	444	63	115	26	2	5	56	43	79	18	7	R	R	6-1	185	7-6-74	1993	Bellefontaine, Ohio
Legree, Keith	.242	113	343	46	83	19	2	9	58	56	70	10	4	L	R	6-2	195	12-26-71	1991	Statesboro, Ga.

BATTING	AVG	G	AB	R	H	2B	3B	HR	RBI	BB	SO	SB	CS	B	T	HT	WT	DOB	1st Yr	Resides
Mientkiewicz, Doug	.255	132	467	87	119	28	2	15	61	98	67	21	8	L	R	6-2	190	6-19-74	1995	Miami, Fla.
Moriarty, Mike	.221	135	421	60	93	22	5	6	48	53	68	12	5	R	R	6-0	169	3-8-74	1995	Clayton, N.J.
Ortiz, David	.322	69	258	40	83	22	2	14	56	21	78	2	6	L	L	6-4	230	11-18-75	1993	Haina, D.R.
Schaeffer, Jon	.207	10	29	1	6	2	0	0	4	2	7	1	1	R	R	6-1	205	1-20-76	1997	Tarzana, Calif.
Smith, Jeff	.222	5	18	1	4	1	0	0	3	2	4	0	0	L	R	6-3	211	6-17-74	1996	Naples, Fla.
Valentin, Javier	.243	102	370	41	90	17	0	8	50	30	61	2	3	S	R	5-10	191	9-19-75	1993	Manati, P.R.

PITCHING	W	L	ERA	G	GS	CG	SV	IP	H	R	ER	BB	SO	B	T	HT	WT	DOB	1st Yr	Resides
Baptist, Travis	5	6	3.41	36	3	0	0	61	49	27	23	26	50	L	L	6-0	190	12-30-71	1990	Aloha, Ore.
Barcelo, Marc	0	1	8.61	7	4	0	1	23	27	22	22	28	9	R	R	6-3	210	1-10-72	1993	Tucson, Ariz.
Bell, Jason	11	9	3.39	28	28	3	0	165	163	71	62	64	142	R	R	6-3	208	9-30-74	1995	Orlando, Fla.
Bowers, Shane	7	2	3.41	14	13	1	0	71	65	29	27	22	59	R	R	6-6	215	7-27-71	1993	Covina, Calif.
Carrasco, Troy	4	4	4.96	31	3	0	1	65	69	53	36	44	46	S	L	5-11	172	1-27-75	1993	Tampa, Fla.
Cobb, Trevor	6	4	3.43	19	13	3	1	94	77	41	36	39	68	L	L	6-2	185	7-13-73	1992	Marysville, Wash.
Cumberland, Chris	1	0	3.18	1	1	0	0	6	5	2	2	2	2	R	L	6-1	185	1-15-73	1993	Safety Harbor, Fla.
Gandarillas, Gus	2	4	4.70	17	7	1	0	61	67	34	32	15	29	R	R	6-0	180	7-19-71	1992	Hialeah, Fla.
Gourdin, Tom	2	2	5.31	49	0	0	15	61	62	36	36	29	32	R	R	6-3	205	5-24-73	1992	Murray, Utah
Harris, Jeff	2	1	2.34	28	0	0	3	42	30	15	11	16	44	R	R	6-1	190	7-4-74	1995	San Pablo, Calif.
Legault, Kevin	5	1	4.50	40	1	0	3	70	74	37	35	26	40	R	R	6-1	185	3-5-71	1992	Watervliet, N.Y.
Linebarger, Keith	0	1	7.20	1	1	0	0	5	5	4	4	3	1	R	R	6-6	220	5-11-71	1992	Ringgold, Ga.
Mahaffey, Alan	1	2	3.57	13	1	0	1	23	19	11	9	10	29	L	L	6-3	200	2-2-74	1995	Springfield, Mo.
Morse, Paul	3	11	5.98	37	17	0	1	111	124	91	74	70	75	R	R	6-2	185	2-27-73	1995	Danville, Ky.
Mott, Tom	0	0	0.00	1	0	0	0	1	2	0	0	0	0	R	R	6-3	222	10-9-73	1994	San Luis Obispo, Calif.
Perez, David	0	1	6.75	1	1	0	0	4	5	3	3	1	3	R	R	5-11	170	5-23-68	1989	San Antonio, Texas
Perkins, Dan	7	10	4.91	24	24	2	0	145	158	94	79	53	114	R	R	6-2	184	3-15-75	1993	Miami, Fla.
Rath, Fred	3	3	2.68	33	0	0	12	50	43	17	15	13	33	R	R	6-3	205	1-5-73	1995	Tampa, Fla.
Rushing, Will	1	2	3.97	3	2	0	0	11	14	5	5	3	9	L	L	6-3	193	11-8-72	1995	Statesboro, Ga.
Sampson, Benj	10	6	4.19	25	20	0	0	118	112	56	55	49	92	R	L	6-0	197	4-27-75	1993	Bondurant, Iowa
Trinidad, Hector	0	2	6.33	6	3	0	0	21	26	18	15	8	11	R	R	6-2	190	9-8-73	1991	Whittier, Calif.

FIELDING

Catcher	PCT	G	PO	A	E	DP	PB
Fortin	1.000	8	50	13	0	2	2
Horn	.996	43	239	38	1	1	10
Schaeffer	.985	10	57	10	1	0	1
Smith	.956	5	42	1	2	0	0
Valentin	.991	85	513	65	5	8	12

First Base	PCT	G	PO	A	E	DP
Fortin	1.000	2	17	0	0	2
Fraser	1.000	1	1	0	0	0
Horn	.938	2	13	2	1	3
Mientkiewicz	.995	106	963	59	5	98
Ortiz	.990	33	268	16	3	32

Second Base	PCT	G	PO	A	E	DP
Ferguson	.875	8	6	15	3	1
Fraser	.952	14	33	26	3	13
Lane	.975	126	245	372	16	94

Third Base	PCT	G	PO	A	E	DP
Ferguson	1.000	5	3	3	0	0
Fraser	.917	16	12	21	3	4
Koskie	.933	125	72	234	22	14
Valentin	.750	1	3	0	1	0

Shortstop	PCT	G	PO	A	E	DP
Ferguson	.833	3	7	3	2	0
Fraser	1.000	6	7	8	0	0
Lane	1.000	1	1	2	0	0
Moriarty	.973	135	210	475	19	114

Outfield	PCT	G	PO	A	E	DP
Allen	.973	29	35	1	1	0
Alvarez	1.000	16	29	2	0	0
Brown	.944	13	17	0	1	0
Fraser	.955	23	21	0	1	0
Gunderson	.985	33	63	2	1	1
Hunter	.974	124	252	7	7	4
Johnson	.977	94	168	5	4	2
Legree	.963	97	176	8	7	1
Mientkiewicz	1.000	16	26	4	0	1

FORT MYERS — Class A

FLORIDA STATE LEAGUE

BATTING	AVG	G	AB	R	H	2B	3B	HR	RBI	BB	SO	SB	CS	B	T	HT	WT	DOB	1st Yr	Resides
Allen, Chad	.309	105	401	66	124	18	4	3	45	40	51	27	15	R	R	6-1	190	2-6-75	1996	DeSoto, Texas
Alvarez, Rafael	.270	47	122	13	33	9	1	1	15	17	27	6	2	L	L	5-11	165	1-22-77	1994	Valencia, Venez.
Cey, Dan	.284	127	521	84	148	34	5	7	60	34	85	23	9	R	R	6-1	175	11-8-75	1996	Woodland Hills, Calif.
Cranford, Joe	.200	112	355	39	71	9	1	1	22	21	90	4	6	R	R	6-1	180	2-10-75	1996	Macon, Ga.
Fortin, Troy	.295	111	383	58	113	20	0	13	59	34	37	1	2	R	R	5-11	200	2-24-75	1993	Lundar, Manitoba
Garcia, Carlos	.136	69	147	11	20	3	0	0	2	11	31	8	6	R	R	5-11	165	5-21-76	1993	Coraballeda, Venez.
Gunderson, Shane	.280	14	50	5	14	4	0	0	5	7	8	3	1	R	R	6-0	205	10-16-73	1995	Faribault, Minn.
Johnson, Travis	.242	73	227	29	55	16	1	7	36	30	77	2	1	L	R	6-0	210	11-23-73	1995	Monticello, Minn.
Jones, Jacque	.297	131	539	84	160	33	6	15	82	33	110	24	12	L	L	5-10	175	4-25-75	1996	San Diego, Calif.
Kelly, Roberto	.364	4	11	2	4	0	0	1	3	4	1	0	0	R	R	6-2	202	10-1-64	1982	Panama City, Panama
Mucker, Kelcey	.239	114	389	43	93	26	3	3	48	33	80	1	5	L	R	6-4	235	2-17-75	1993	Lawrenceburg, Ind.
Ortiz, David	.331	61	239	45	79	15	0	13	58	22	53	2	1	L	L	6-4	230	11-18-75	1993	Haina, D.R.
Paez, Israel	.253	135	478	56	121	11	1	1	39	35	66	26	16	S	R	5-10	182	12-23-76	1994	Carabobo, Venez.
Pierzynski, A.J.	.279	118	412	49	115	23	1	9	64	16	59	2	1	L	R	6-3	202	12-30-76	1994	Orlando, Fla.
Roper, Chad	.203	66	148	19	30	3	0	3	9	22	23	1	0	R	R	6-1	212	3-29-74	1992	Belton, S.C.
Smith, Jeff	.281	49	121	17	34	5	0	4	26	12	18	0	2	L	R	6-3	211	6-17-74	1996	Naples, Fla.
Vaughn, Lateef	.269	36	93	15	25	2	0	0	8	6	18	2	0	R	R	5-9	170	10-1-75	1997	Long Beach, Calif.

GAMES BY POSITION: C—Fortin 22, Pierzynski 105, Smith 18. **1B**— Fortin 72, Gunderson 1, Johnson 1, Ortiz 59, Pierzynski 2, Smith 8. **2B**—Cey 14, Cranford 100, Garcia 4, Paez 33, Vaughn 1. **3B**—Cranford 3, Fortin 1, Garcia 1, Paez 99, Roper 39. **SS**—Cey 68, Garcia 52, Paez 2, Vaughn 34. **OF**—Allen 105, Alvarez 29, Cranford 1, Garcia 1, Gunderson 13, Johnson 36, Jones 131, Kelly 4, Mucker 103.

PITCHING	W	L	ERA	G	GS	CG	SV	IP	H	R	ER	BB	SO	B	T	HT	WT	DOB	1st Yr	Resides
Carrasco, Troy	3	3	5.37	12	8	0	0	55	61	37	33	18	36	S	L	5-11	172	1-27-75	1993	Tampa, Fla.
Chapman, Walker	6	5	5.80	27	14	0	1	90	121	64	58	32	65	R	R	6-3	219	2-25-76	1994	Frostburg, Md.
Cobb, Trevor	7	0	2.97	15	7	1	0	61	49	29	20	16	48	L	L	6-2	185	7-13-73	1992	Marysville, Wash.
Fidge, Darren	0	3	6.34	24	0	0	0	38	44	29	27	20	25	R	R	6-2	194	11-12-74	1992	Adelaide, Australia
Gillian, Charlie	1	1	2.30	10	0	0	0	16	10	5	4	5	11	R	R	6-2	196	5-29-74	1996	Beckley, W.Va.
Haigler, Phil	11	9	2.84	25	25	4	0	158	172	57	50	32	80	R	R	6-3	220	6-13-74	1996	Pascagoula, Miss.
Harris, Jeff	2	4	2.14	24	0	0	1	42	30	11	10	15	32	R	R	6-1	190	7-4-74	1995	San Pablo, Calif.
LaRosa, Tom	8	6	4.31	25	23	3	0	136	120	73	65	66	118	R	R	5-10	180	6-28-75	1996	Henderson, Nev.
Lincoln, Mike	13	4	2.28	20	20	1	0	134	130	41	34	25	75	R	R	6-2	200	4-10-75	1996	Citrus Heights, Calif.
Mahaffey, Alan	1	2	4.10	38	0	0	1	48	46	27	22	8	55	L	L	6-3	200	2-2-74	1995	Springfield, Mo.
Mott, Tom	2	0	3.19	14	0	0	0	31	25	13	11	12	23	R	R	6-3	222	10-9-73	1994	San Luis Obispo, Calif.
Niedermaier, Brad	2	3	1.47	32	0	0	17	37	27	15	6	12	47	R	R	6-3	205	2-9-73	1995	Niles, Ill.
Radlosky, Rob	9	5	2.59	23	22	3	0	128	87	42	37	37	109	R	R	6-2	200	1-7-74	1994	Lantana, Fla.

PITCHING	W	L	ERA	G	GS	CG	SV	IP	H	R	ER	BB	SO	B	T	HT	WT	DOB	1st Yr	Resides
Rath, Fred	4	0	1.64	17	0	0	2	22	18	4	4	3	22	R	R	6-3	205	1-5-73	1995	Tampa, Fla.
Richardson, Kasey	1	3	4.46	7	7	0	0	34	35	23	17	18	17	L	L	6-4	180	8-27-76	1994	Huntington, Md.
Romero, Juan	1	1	4.38	7	1	0	0	12	11	6	6	4	9	S	L	5-11	195	6-4-76	1997	San Juan, P.R.
Roper, Chad	1	2	2.72	27	1	0	0	39	32	20	12	13	27	R	R	6-1	212	3-29-74	1992	Belton, S.C.
Rushing, Will	1	5	7.51	12	7	0	0	38	54	41	32	22	34	L	L	6-3	193	11-8-72	1995	Statesboro, Ga.
Splittorff, Jamie	0	0	9.53	2	2	0	0	6	11	6	6	1	3	L	R	6-3	185	10-12-73	1995	Blue Springs, Mo.
Stentz, Brent	7	2	2.47	49	1	0	17	69	53	20	19	24	70	R	R	6-5	225	7-24-75	1995	Brooksville, Fla.
Trinidad, Hector	1	0	0.00	2	1	0	0	8	2	0	0	1	5	R	R	6-2	190	9-8-73	1991	Whittier, Calif.

FORT WAYNE — Class A

MIDWEST LEAGUE

BATTING	AVG	G	AB	R	H	2B	3B	HR	RBI	BB	SO	SB	CS	B	T	HT	WT	DOB	1st Yr	Resides
Bolivar, Papo	.262	91	324	30	85	12	6	7	42	11	82	18	9	R	R	5-10	168	10-18-78	1996	Catia La Mar, Venez.
Buchman, Tom	.143	13	42	7	6	1	0	0	5	4	14	0	0	R	R	5-11	205	12-4-74	1996	Lenexa, Kan.
Davidson, Cleatus	.255	124	478	80	122	16	8	6	52	52	100	39	9	S	R	5-10	160	11-1-76	1994	Lake Wales, Fla.
Felston, Anthony	.278	94	338	63	94	10	2	2	29	55	53	45	15	L	L	5-9	170	11-26-74	1996	Leland, Miss.
Gunderson, Shane	.267	13	45	3	12	1	0	0	7	3	3	1	1	R	R	6-0	205	10-16-73	1995	Faribault, Minn.
Huls, Steve	.190	56	158	20	30	7	0	0	16	12	37	2	1	S	R	6-1	170	10-11-74	1996	Cold Spring, Minn.
Johnson, Heath	.209	22	67	10	14	4	0	3	11	13	29	0	1	L	R	6-3	210	8-25-76	1994	Lakefield, Minn.
Knauss, Tom	.190	14	58	3	11	1	0	1	7	6	18	1	0	R	R	6-2	218	6-16-74	1992	Arlington Heights, Ill.
Lopez, Henry	.245	87	327	43	80	13	4	5	29	29	76	10	9	R	R	5-11	185	3-20-78	1996	El Portal, D.R.
Lorenzo, Juan	.143	4	7	0	1	0	0	0	0	0	1	0	0	S	R	6-0	155	6-10-78	1995	San Cristobal, D.R.
Meyer, Brad	.300	12	20	5	6	1	1	0	3	4	6	1	0	L	R	6-0	165	10-23-75	1997	Bloomington, Minn.
Moeller, Chad	.289	108	384	58	111	18	3	9	39	48	76	11	8	R	R	6-3	210	2-18-75	1996	Upland, Calif.
Moss, Rick	.278	133	508	76	141	28	4	3	77	61	57	3	3	L	R	6-0	185	9-18-75	1996	Lockport, Ill.
Patterson, Jacob	.215	121	469	61	101	16	2	20	80	38	131	11	2	L	L	6-0	239	8-1-73	1993	Golden, Colo.
Peterman, Tommy	.293	113	417	46	122	22	0	7	57	28	69	0	4	L	L	6-0	215	5-21-75	1996	Marietta, Ga.
Poepard, Scott	.233	36	103	16	24	9	0	1	8	10	30	3	1	S	R	6-2	195	8-26-74	1997	Forest Lake, Minn.
Prada, Nelson	.245	29	98	8	24	5	0	3	11	3	22	0	1	R	R	6-0	185	2-22-76	1995	Barquisimeto, Venez.
Reyes, Freddy	.261	85	306	37	80	19	2	8	45	12	79	0	0	R	R	6-1	214	4-8-76	1995	Lafayette, Ind.
Rivas, Luis	.239	121	419	61	100	20	6	1	30	33	90	28	18	R	R	5-10	155	8-30-79	1996	La Guaira, Venez.

GAMES BY POSITION: C—Buchman 5, Moeller 107, Prada 29. **1B**—Patterson 57, Peterman 31, Reyes 52. **2B**—Davidson 121, Huls 17, Lorenzo 1. **3B**—Huls 18, Lorenzo 1, Moss 119. **SS**—Huls 16, Lorenzo 2, Rivas 119. **OF**—Bolivar 90, Davidson 1, Felston 91, Gunderson 13, Huls 1, Johnson 22, Knauss 14, Lopez 87, Meyer 10, Moss 3, Peterman 60, Poepard 34.

PITCHING	W	L	ERA	G	GS	CG	SV	IP	H	R	ER	BB	SO	B	T	HT	WT	DOB	1st Yr	Resides
Bauder, Mike	6	4	3.72	40	10	0	0	104	94	51	43	33	96	L	L	5-10	160	5-13-75	1996	Las Vegas, Nev.
Carnes, Matt	0	1	9.00	1	1	0	0	4	2	4	4	5	3	R	R	6-3	210	8-18-75	1997	Miami, Okla.
Clark, Greg	0	1	4.41	6	1	0	0	16	16	9	8	8	7	R	R	6-4	194	8-19-77	1995	Sydney, Australia
Dose, Gary	1	4	4.70	45	4	0	3	67	52	44	35	61	73	R	R	6-0	184	8-22-73	1996	Elgin, Minn.
Fidge, Darren	2	2	2.84	8	0	0	0	13	15	4	4	4	8	R	R	6-2	194	11-12-74	1992	Adelaide, Australia
Gandy, Josh	2	4	5.40	8	5	0	0	20	25	19	12	12	14	R	L	6-2	200	10-12-75	1997	Ringgold, Ga.
Garza, Chris	5	2	1.99	60	0	0	15	95	67	28	21	38	90	L	L	5-11	185	7-23-75	1996	Los Angeles, Calif.
Gillian, Charlie	0	0	3.16	22	0	0	3	26	21	11	9	13	24	R	R	6-2	196	5-29-74	1996	Beckley, W.Va.
Hooten, David	11	8	2.61	28	27	2	0	166	134	57	48	54	138	R	R	6-0	175	5-8-75	1996	Atlanta, Texas
Lindberg, Fred	0	0	3.65	5	0	0	0	12	16	5	5	5	8	L	L	6-6	215	11-19-73	1996	Dianella, Australia
Loonam, Rick	3	2	5.66	34	1	0	0	49	63	36	31	33	35	R	R	6-4	215	11-7-75	1996	Lakewood, Colo.
Lynch, Ryan	2	2	3.15	15	2	0	0	34	38	20	12	10	39	L	L	6-4	225	8-10-74	1996	Solano Beach, Calif.
Malko, Bryan	4	4	3.78	14	13	0	0	64	68	29	27	22	59	R	R	6-3	185	1-23-77	1995	Piscataway, N.J.
McBride, Rodney	3	4	6.31	31	0	0	0	46	57	40	32	32	54	R	R	6-1	205	11-15-74	1994	Memphis, Tenn.
Opipari, Mario	6	7	3.44	53	2	0	8	71	71	45	27	24	61	S	R	6-0	185	1-24-75	1996	Henderson, Nev.
Richardson, Kasey	7	5	3.07	19	19	1	0	114	100	47	39	46	84	L	L	6-4	180	8-27-76	1994	Huntington, Md.
Spiers, Corey	5	9	4.86	24	23	0	0	120	154	83	65	33	94	L	L	6-1	195	6-19-75	1996	Houston, Texas
Tanksley, Scott	0	1	4.05	5	0	0	0	7	4	5	3	4	2	S	R	5-11	185	11-1-73	1995	Kemp, Texas
Yeskie, Nate	11	7	4.84	27	27	2	0	165	190	99	89	41	111	R	R	6-2	195	8-13-74	1996	Carson City, Nev.

ELIZABETHTON — Rookie

APPALACHIAN LEAGUE

BATTING	AVG	G	AB	R	H	2B	3B	HR	RBI	BB	SO	SB	CS	B	T	HT	WT	DOB	1st Yr	Resides
Ayuso, Julio	.224	39	107	13	24	8	0	1	12	17	39	0	1	R	R	6-3	180	6-23-77	1995	Carolina, P.R.
Borrego, Ramon	.280	55	211	43	59	12	0	4	34	26	44	7	5	S	R	5-7	150	6-7-78	1996	Mariara, Venez.
Jaworowski, Aaron	.292	64	264	46	77	18	0	13	66	14	65	1	0	L	R	6-2	205	8-7-75	1997	Ellisville, Ohio
Kennedy, Brian	.293	55	191	26	56	9	0	1	25	22	43	3	4	L	R	6-1	190	8-9-77	1996	Lafayette, Ind.
Lorenzo, Juan	.300	52	210	41	63	10	2	7	34	12	38	4	2	S	R	6-0	155	6-10-78	1995	San Cristobal, D.R.
McHenry, Joe	.321	51	168	40	54	6	0	6	31	22	48	5	3	L	R	6-1	175	5-24-76	1995	Murfreesboro, Tenn.
Melson, Bryant	.263	28	80	18	21	3	1	0	9	7	22	1	0	R	R	6-1	200	3-19-75	1997	Orlando, Fla.
Orndorff, Dave	.368	55	228	62	84	15	1	11	42	22	25	18	4	R	R	5-10	175	8-10-77	1995	Shippensburg, Pa.
Pagan, Felix	.291	59	227	48	66	18	1	9	41	31	59	4	1	R	R	5-11	180	6-12-75	1997	Bayamon, P.R.
Pena, Francisco	.260	37	131	21	34	4	1	6	25	14	27	0	0	R	R	6-1	194	8-22-76	1994	Santo Domingo, D.R.
Ryan, Mike	.300	62	220	44	66	10	0	3	29	38	39	2	2	L	R	6-0	175	7-6-77	1996	Indiana, Pa.
Schaeffer, Jon	.333	48	165	35	55	13	0	6	34	33	32	0	1	R	R	6-1	205	1-20-76	1997	Tarzana, Calif.
Smith, Marcus	.228	44	145	22	33	1	2	5	15	12	32	4	2	L	R	6-0	180	6-7-76	1996	Hammond, Ind.
Vaughn, Lateef	.300	10	40	10	12	3	0	0	5	3	5	1	1	R	R	5-9	170	10-1-75	1997	Long Beach, Calif.

GAMES BY POSITION: C—McHenry 1, Melson 22, Pena 28, Schaeffer 26. **1B**—Jaworowski 64, Pagan 8, Schaeffer 1. **2B**—Borrego 35 Orndorff 29, Pagan 8. **3B**—Lorenzo 3, Pagan 16, Ryan 56. **SS**—Borrego 17, Lorenzo 46, Vaughn 10. **OF**—Ayuso 32, Borrego 2, Kennedy 50, McHenry 46, Melson 1, Orndorff 16, Pagan 28, Schaeffer 7, Smith 42.

PITCHING	W	L	ERA	G	GS	CG	SV	IP	H	R	ER	BB	SO	B	T	HT	WT	DOB	1st Yr	Resides
Carnes, Matt	3	0	3.08	8	7	1	0	38	33	17	13	5	42	R	R	6-3	210	8-18-75	1997	Miami, Okla.
Clark, Greg	1	0	5.08	16	0	0	0	28	34	21	16	8	22	R	R	6-4	194	8-19-77	1995	Sydney, Australia
Cosgrove, Michael	1	1	4.76	12	1	0	2	23	25	16	12	6	31	R	R	6-2	180	2-14-76	1997	Downey, Calif.

PITCHING	W	L	ERA	G	GS	CG	SV	IP	H	R	ER	BB	SO	B	T	HT	WT	DOB	1st Yr	Resides
Davies, Bob	0	1	40.50	1	1	0	0	1	2	3	3	3	1	R	R	6-0	195	4-2-76	1997	Warren, Ohio
Espina, Rendy	0	3	7.94	6	3	0	0	17	25	21	15	9	15	L	L	6-0	180	5-11-78	1995	Cabimas, Venez.
Gandy, Josh	3	0	5.91	8	6	0	0	35	36	26	23	19	47	R	L	6-2	200	10-12-75	1997	Ringgold, Ga.
Gholar, Antonio	2	2	6.04	24	0	0	2	45	49	41	30	32	50	R	R	6-2	195	3-13-74	1996	Bassfield, Miss.
Jurgena, Matt	2	4	5.06	23	5	0	4	43	46	28	24	18	57	R	R	6-3	185	12-12-75	1997	Hastings, Neb.
Lunney, Barry	1	3	9.00	22	0	0	1	25	30	26	25	22	21	L	L	6-2	190	9-11-74	1997	Fort Smith, Ark.
Marshall, Lee	5	3	3.86	14	14	1	0	84	93	56	36	16	41	R	R	6-5	205	9-25-76	1995	Ariton, Ala.
Miller, Aaron	2	1	6.30	23	0	0	0	30	25	25	21	25	43	R	L	6-3	235	7-31-76	1997	Middletown, Del.
Myers, Rob	0	1	15.43	3	0	0	0	5	9	11	8	11	6	R	R	6-3	205	6-22-76	1997	Frederica, Del.
Perez, Pablo	10	0	3.52	17	10	0	0	79	79	37	31	12	69	R	R	6-0	170	8-27-73	1991	Queens, N.Y.
Rincon, Juan	0	1	3.86	2	1	0	0	9	11	4	4	3	7	R	R	5-11	175	1-23-79	1996	Maracaibo, Venez.
Romero, Juan	3	2	4.88	18	0	0	3	24	27	16	13	7	29	S	L	5-11	195	6-4-76	1997	San Juan, P.R.
Thomas, Ben	2	4	7.43	7	7	0	0	27	37	25	22	12	28	L	L	6-3	190	10-6-75	1997	Rapid City, S.D.
Thomas, Brad	3	4	4.48	14	13	0	0	70	78	43	35	21	53	L	L	6-3	192	10-12-77	1996	Seven Hills, Australia

FORT MYERS — Rookie

GULF COAST LEAGUE

BATTING	AVG	G	AB	R	H	2B	3B	HR	RBI	BB	SO	SB	CS	B	T	HT	WT	DOB	1st Yr	Resides
Almonte, Claudio	.287	57	188	19	54	7	2	1	25	12	36	16	5	R	R	6-0	172	8-2-78	1996	Santo Domingo, D.R.
Alvarez, Jimmy	.249	52	185	25	46	5	4	0	14	21	46	12	5	R	R	5-10	168	10-4-79	1997	Santo Domingo, D.R.
Bautista, Jose	.107	14	28	2	3	0	0	0	0	8	9	2	2	S	R	5-10	150	6-6-79	1997	Bonao, D.R.
Brosam, Eric	.241	44	141	13	34	3	2	0	9	14	31	3	0	L	R	6-1	200	12-4-77	1996	Redwood Falls, Minn.
Franklin, Toby	.091	3	11	1	1	0	0	0	0	0	6	0	0	L	R	6-1	185	9-21-76	1997	Fort Pierce, Fla.
Harrison, Jamal	.246	39	126	12	31	6	1	0	17	15	22	5	3	R	R	6-4	207	7-15-77	1995	Palo Alto, Calif.
McCorvey, Ken	.291	42	134	19	39	6	1	3	11	5	24	10	6	R	R	6-2	185	3-16-79	1997	Pensacola, Fla.
Meyer, Brad	.256	16	39	6	10	1	1	0	4	6	5	0	0	L	R	6-0	165	10-23-75	1997	Bloomington, Minn.
Nanita, Emmanuel	.258	22	62	4	16	2	0	0	2	5	14	2	0	R	R	6-2	178	12-25-79	1997	Santo Domingo, D.R.
Smith, Marcus	.071	6	14	0	1	0	0	0	1	3	8	1	0	L	R	6-0	180	6-7-76	1996	Hammond, Ind.
Southward, DeShawn	.260	57	154	24	40	2	0	0	6	29	43	14	4	R	R	5-11	180	5-16-78	1997	Dade City, Fla.
Stevens, Nate	.241	47	170	23	41	3	0	1	17	9	21	9	2	S	R	5-10	155	9-18-78	1997	Keystone Heights, Fla.
Sutton, Bruce	.240	35	96	13	23	5	0	0	4	13	31	1	2	R	R	6-3	180	8-2-76	1997	Ada, Okla.
Torres, Franklin	.258	48	155	18	40	7	1	1	18	17	31	7	3	R	R	5-9	170	9-10-79	1996	Santiago, D.R.
Torres, Gabriel	.257	45	152	17	39	5	1	0	16	19	21	18	3	R	R	6-0	185	3-20-78	1996	Acarigua, Venez.
Valerio, Denny	.182	28	44	8	8	2	0	0	1	4	13	6	1	R	R	5-11	160	4-16-79	1997	Santiago, D.R.
Vilorio, Leonel	.195	50	169	8	33	6	0	0	6	6	31	3	4	R	R	6-1	180	3-10-78	1996	Santo Domingo, D.R.
Wade, Chip	.167	33	102	8	17	2	0	1	14	13	26	1	1	R	R	6-1	205	3-15-75	1997	Pensacola, Fla.

GAMES BY POSITION: C—Nanita 6, G. Torres 41, Wade 22. **1B**—Brosam 39, Harrison 31. **2B**—Bautista 1, Stevens 41, F. Torres 25. **3B**—F. Torres 12, Valerio 2, Vilorio 49, Wade 9. **SS**—Alvarez 51, Bautista 12, Stevens 7, F. Torres 1. **OF**—Almonte 50, Franklin 3, Harrison 4, McCorvey 35, Meyer 14, Smith 6, Southward 55, Sutton 30, Valerio 16, Vilorio 5.

PITCHING	W	L	ERA	G	GS	CG	SV	IP	H	R	ER	BB	SO	B	T	HT	WT	DOB	1st Yr	Resides
Balfour, Grant	2	4	3.76	13	12	0	0	67	73	31	28	20	43	R	R	6-2	190	12-30-77	1997	Glenwood, Australia
Espina, Rendy	2	2	1.30	8	7	0	0	35	24	11	5	6	34	L	L	6-0	180	5-11-78	1995	Cabimas, Venez.
Fitts, Brian	4	2	2.83	10	3	0	0	29	29	15	9	6	31	R	R	6-2	175	7-25-76	1997	Gallatin, Tenn.
Flock, Rick	2	1	2.89	12	0	0	0	19	21	9	6	6	17	R	R	6-2	190	6-19-78	1997	Fort Myers, Fla.
Jacobs, Jake	1	1	0.29	23	0	0	10	31	16	7	1	11	55	R	R	6-6	230	3-28-78	1996	Pensacola, Fla.
Melson, Nate	0	4	5.63	12	7	0	0	38	52	35	24	22	29	R	R	6-5	215	10-28-78	1997	Rogers, Ark.
Moylan, Peter	4	2	4.05	12	7	0	0	40	46	21	18	10	40	R	R	6-0	200	12-2-78	1996	Lesmurdie, Australia
Mundine, John	1	1	1.69	15	0	0	0	32	20	7	6	9	32	S	R	5-11	175	9-6-77	1996	Luling, Texas
Myers, Rob	1	1	0.63	9	0	0	0	14	5	2	1	5	13	R	R	6-3	205	6-22-76	1997	Frederica, Del.
Naulty, Dan	0	0	2.25	2	2	0	0	4	2	1	1	3	3	R	R	6-6	211	1-6-70	1992	Huntington Beach, Calif.
Rincon, Juan	3	3	2.95	11	10	1	0	58	55	21	19	24	46	R	R	5-11	175	1-23-79	1996	Maracaibo, Venez.
Sheets, Matt	2	2	2.38	15	5	0	2	53	49	17	14	10	24	R	R	6-2	200	9-16-77	1996	Grand Rapids, Mich.
Splittorff, Jamie	0	1	2.08	2	0	0	0	4	2	1	1	4	6	L	R	6-3	185	10-12-73	1995	Blue Springs, Mo.
Stenger, Pat	0	2	4.54	15	2	0	0	36	41	21	18	10	22	R	R	6-6	205	10-7-78	1997	Mentor, Ohio
Sturdy, Tim	1	1	0.75	9	2	1	0	24	12	4	2	6	14	R	R	6-1	170	10-8-78	1997	Albuquerque, N.M.
Tanksley, Scott	0	2	2.08	4	0	0	0	9	5	2	2	1	7	S	R	5-11	185	11-1-73	1995	Kemp, Texas
Vallis, Jamie	5	3	4.76	14	3	0	0	34	30	20	18	14	34	R	L	6-6	180	5-22-77	1996	Bedford, N.S.

Montreal EXPOS

Manager: Felipe Alou.

1997 Record: 78-84, .481 (4th, NL East)

BATTING	AVG	G	AB	R	H	2B	3B	HR	RBI	BB	SO	SB	CS	B	T	HT	WT	DOB	1st Yr	Resides
Andrews, Shane	.203	18	64	10	13	3	0	4	9	3	20	0	0	R	R	6-1	205	8-28-71	1990	Carlsbad, N.M.
Cabrera, Orlando	.222	16	18	4	4	0	0	0	2	1	3	1	2	R	R	5-11	165	3-2-74	1994	Cartagena, Colombia
Chavez, Raul	.269	13	26	0	7	0	0	0	2	0	5	1	0	R	R	5-11	175	3-18-73	1990	Valencia, Venez.
Fletcher, Darrin	.277	96	310	39	86	20	1	17	55	17	35	1	1	L	R	6-2	195	10-3-66	1987	Fithian, Ill.
Fullmer, Brad	.300	19	40	4	12	2	0	3	8	2	7	0	0	L	R	6-1	185	1-17-75	1994	Chatsworth, Calif.
Grudzielanek, Mark	.273	156	649	76	177	54	3	4	51	23	76	25	9	R	R	6-1	170	6-30-70	1991	El Paso, Texas
Guerrero, Vladimir	.302	90	325	44	98	22	2	11	40	19	39	3	4	R	R	6-2	158	2-9-76	1993	Nizao, D.R.
Lansing, Mike	.281	144	572	86	161	45	2	20	70	45	92	11	5	R	R	6-0	175	4-3-68	1990	Casper, Wyo.
McGuire, Ryan	.256	84	199	22	51	15	2	3	17	19	34	1	4	L	L	6-1	195	11-23-71	1993	Woodland Hills, Calif.
Meulens, Hensley	.292	16	24	6	7	1	0	2	6	4	10	0	1	R	R	6-3	212	6-23-67	1986	Willemstad, Curacao
Obando, Sherman	.128	41	47	3	6	1	0	2	9	6	14	0	0	R	R	6-4	215	1-23-70	1988	Changuinola, Panama
Orsulak, Joe	.227	106	150	13	34	12	1	1	7	18	17	0	1	L	L	6-1	203	5-31-62	1981	Cockeysville, Md.
Rodriguez, Henry	.244	132	476	55	116	28	3	26	83	42	149	3	3	L	L	6-1	210	11-8-67	1986	New York, N.Y.
Santangelo, F.P.	.249	130	350	56	87	19	5	5	31	50	73	8	5	S	R	5-10	165	10-24-67	1989	El Dorado Hills, Calif.
Segui, David	.307	125	459	75	141	22	3	21	68	57	66	1	0	S	L	6-1	202	7-19-66	1988	Kansas City, Kan.
Stankiewicz, Andy	.224	76	107	11	24	9	0	1	5	4	22	1	1	R	R	5-9	165	8-10-64	1986	La Habra, Calif.
Strange, Doug	.257	118	327	40	84	16	2	12	47	36	76	0	2	S	R	6-2	170	4-13-64	1985	Scottsdale, Ariz.
Vidro, Jose	.249	67	169	19	42	12	1	2	17	11	20	1	0	S	R	5-11	175	8-27-74	1992	Sabana Grande, P.R.
White, Rondell	.270	151	592	84	160	29	5	28	82	31	111	16	8	R	R	6-1	193	2-23-72	1990	Gray, Ga.
Widger, Chris	.234	91	278	30	65	20	3	7	37	22	59	2	0	R	R	6-3	195	5-21-71	1992	Pennsville, N.J.

PITCHING	W	L	ERA	G	GS	CG	SV	IP	H	R	ER	BB	SO	B	T	HT	WT	DOB	1st Yr	Resides
Bennett, Shayne	0	1	3.18	16	0	0	0	23	21	9	8	9	8	R	R	6-5	200	4-10-72	1993	Worongary, Australia
Bullinger, Jim	7	12	5.56	36	25	2	0	155	165	106	96	74	87	R	R	6-2	180	8-21-65	1986	Sarasota, Fla.
Cormier, Rheal	0	1	33.75	1	1	0	0	1	4	5	5	1	0	L	L	5-10	185	4-23-67	1989	Saint John, N.B.
Daal, Omar	1	2	9.79	33	0	0	1	30	48	35	33	15	16	L	L	6-3	185	3-1-72	1990	Valencia, Venez.
DeHart, Rick	2	1	5.52	23	0	0	0	29	33	21	18	14	29	R	L	6-1	180	3-21-70	1992	Topeka, Kan.
Falteisek, Steve	0	0	3.38	5	0	0	0	8	8	4	3	3	2	R	R	6-2	200	1-28-72	1992	Floral Park, N.Y.
Hermanson, Dustin	8	8	3.69	32	28	1	0	158	134	68	65	66	136	R	R	6-3	195	12-21-72	1994	Springfield, Ohio
Johnson, Mike	2	5	5.94	11	11	0	0	50	54	34	33	21	28	L	R	6-2	175	10-3-75	1993	Edmonton, Alberta
Juden, Jeff	11	5	4.22	22	22	3	0	130	125	64	61	57	107	R	R	6-7	245	1-19-71	1989	Salem, Mass.
Kline, Steve	1	3	6.15	26	0	0	0	26	31	18	18	10	20	S	L	6-2	200	8-22-72	1993	Winfield, Pa.
Martinez, Pedro	17	8	1.90	31	31	13	0	241	158	65	51	67	305	R	R	5-11	150	7-25-71	1988	Santo Domingo, D.R.
Paniagua, Jose	1	2	12.00	9	3	0	0	18	29	24	24	16	8	R	R	6-1	160	8-20-73	1991	Santo Domingo, D.R.
Perez, Carlos	12	13	3.88	33	32	8	0	207	206	109	89	48	110	L	L	6-3	200	4-14-71	1990	San Cristobal, D.R.
Smith, Lee	0	1	5.82	25	0	0	5	22	28	16	14	8	15	R	R	6-6	269	12-4-57	1975	Castor, La.
Stull, Everett	0	1	16.20	3	0	0	0	3	7	7	6	4	2	R	R	6-3	195	8-24-71	1992	Stone Mountain, Ga.
Telford, Anthony	4	6	3.24	65	0	0	1	89	77	34	32	33	61	R	R	6-0	175	3-6-66	1987	Pinellas Park, Fla.
Thurman, Mike	1	0	5.40	5	2	0	0	12	8	9	7	4	8	R	R	6-5	190	7-22-73	1994	Philomath, Ore.
Torres, Salomon	0	0	7.25	12	0	0	0	22	25	19	18	12	11	R	R	5-11	150	3-11-72	1990	San Pedro de Macoris, D.R.
Urbina, Ugueth	5	8	3.78	63	0	0	27	64	52	29	27	29	84	R	R	6-2	170	2-15-74	1991	Caracas, Venez.
Valdes, Marc	4	4	3.13	48	7	0	2	95	84	36	33	39	54	R	R	6-0	170	12-20-71	1993	Tampa, Fla.
Veres, Dave	2	3	3.48	53	0	0	1	62	68	28	24	27	47	R	R	6-2	195	10-19-66	1986	Gresham, Ore.

FIELDING

Catcher	PCT	G	PO	A	E	DP	PB
Chavez	1.000	13	47	8	0	1	1
Fletcher	.994	83	606	26	4	4	4
Widger	.981	85	516	40	11	2	8

First Base	PCT	G	PO	A	E	DP
Fullmer	.982	8	49	7	1	6
McGuire	1.000	30	157	16	0	20
Meulens	1.000	3	9	0	0	1
Orsulak	.992	15	112	10	1	4
Rodriguez	1.000	3	22	2	0	2
Segui	.995	125	1035	88	6	104
Strange	1.000	1	2	1	0	1

Second Base	PCT	G	PO	A	E	DP
Cabrera	1.000	4	10	9	0	2
Lansing	.987	144	279	395	9	95
Santangelo	1.000	7	5	6	0	2
Stankiewicz	.957	25	19	47	3	9
Strange	1.000	3	6	5	0	1
Vidro	.938	5	5	10	1	1

Third Base	PCT	G	PO	A	E	DP
Andrews	.895	18	11	40	6	6
Santangelo	.954	32	17	45	3	0
Stankiewicz	1.000	3	1	2	0	1
Strange	.947	105	62	170	13	13
Vidro	.958	36	20	49	3	6

Shortstop	PCT	G	PO	A	E	DP
Cabrera	.875	6	1	6	1	1
Grudzielanek	.955	156	237	446	32	99
Santangelo	1.000	1	0	1	0	0
Stankiewicz	1.000	14	13	19	0	4

Outfield	PCT	G	PO	A	E	DP
Fullmer	.500	2	1	0	1	0
Guerrero	.929	85	148	10	12	3
McGuire	.960	44	69	3	3	1
Meulens	1.000	8	6	0	0	0
Obando	1.000	15	11	0	0	0
Orsulak	1.000	63	41	3	0	0
Rodriguez	.985	126	198	4	3	1
Santangelo	1.000	99	153	4	0	2
Strange	.000	2	0	0	0	0
White	.992	151	376	6	3	3

JOHN KLEIN

Pedro Martinez

FARM SYSTEM

Director of Player Development: David Littlefield

Class	Farm Team	League	W	L	Pct.	Finish*	Manager	First Yr
AAA	Ottawa (Ontario) Lynx	International	54	86	.386	10th (10)	Pat Kelly	1993
AA	Harrisburg (Pa.) Senators	Eastern	86	56	.606	+1st (10)	Rick Sofield	1991
#A	West Palm Beach (Fla.) Expos	Florida State	69	66	.511	6th (14)	Doug Sisson	1969
A	Cape Fear (N.C.) Crocs	South Atlantic	66	74	.471	9th (14)	Phil Stephenson	1997
A	Vermont Expos	New York-Penn	35	41	.461	11th (14)	Kevin Higgins	1994
R	West Palm Beach (Fla.) Expos	Gulf Coast	25	35	.417	12th (15)	Luis Dorante	1986

*Finish in overall standings (No. of teams in league) #Advanced level +Won league championship

ORGANIZATION LEADERS

MAJOR LEAGUERS

BATTING

*AVG	David Segui	.307
R	Mike Lansing	86
H	Mark Grudzielanek	177
TB	Rondell White	283
2B	Mark Grudzielanek	54
3B	Two tied at	5
HR	Rondell White	28
RBI	Henry Rodriguez	83
BB	David Segui	57
SO	Henry Rodriguez	149
SB	Mark Grudzielanek	25

PITCHING

W	Pedro Martinez	17
L	Carlos Perez	13
#ERA	Pedro Martinez	1.90
G	Anthony Telford	65
CG	Pedro Martinez	13
SV	Ugueth Urbina	27
IP	Pedro Martinez	241
BB	Jim Bullinger	74
SO	Pedro Martinez	305

Mark Grudzielanek

JOHN SPEAR

Ben Fleetham

MINOR LEAGUERS

BATTING

*AVG	Talmadge Nunnari, Cape Fear/Vermont	.325
R	Orlando Cabrera, Ottawa/Harr./WPB	107
H	Orlando Cabrera, Ottawa/Harr./WPB	150
TB	Brad Fullmer, Ottawa/Harrisburg	239
2B	Jason Camilli, WPB/Cape Fear	38
3B	Wes Denning, Cape Fear	10
HR	Israel Alcantara, Harrisburg	27
RBI	Darond Stovall, Ottawa/Harrisburg	87
BB	Jon Saffer, Ottawa	76
SO	Chris Schwab, WPB/Cape Fear	152
SB	Orlando Cabrera, Ottawa/Harr./WPB	47

PITCHING

W	Keith Evans, WPB/Cape Fear	14
L	Giovanny Lara, Cape Fear	12
#ERA	Matt Blank, Vermont	1.69
G	Ben Fleetham, Ottawa/Harrisburg	58
CG	Keith Evans, WPB/Cape Fear	5
SV	Ben Fleetham, Ottawa/Harrisburg	31
IP	Keith Evans, WPB/Cape Fear	182
BB	Neil Weber, Ottawa/Harrisburg	91
SO	Neil Weber, Ottawa/Harrisburg	148

*Minimum 250 At-Bats #Minimum 75 Innings

TOP 10 PROSPECTS

GEORGE GOJKOVICH

Vladimir Guerrero

How the Expos Top 10 prospects, as judged by Baseball America prior to the 1997 season, fared in 1997:

Player, Pos.	Club (Class)	AVG	AB	R	H	2B	3B	HR	RBI	SB
1. Vladimir Guerrero, of	Montreal	.302	325	44	96	22	2	11	40	3
2. Hiram Bocachica, ss	Harrisburg (AA)	.278	443	82	123	19	3	11	35	29
3. Brad Fullmer, 1b-of	Montreal	.300	40	4	12	2	0	3	8	0
	Ottawa (AAA)	.297	91	13	27	7	0	3	17	1
	Harrisburg (AA)	.311	357	60	111	24	2	19	62	6
4. Michael Barrett, c	West Palm Beach (A)	.284	423	52	120	30	0	8	61	7
7. Milton Bradley, of	Vermont (A)	.300	200	29	60	7	5	3	30	7
	West Palm Beach (R)	.200	25	6	5	2	0	1	2	2

Player, Pos.	Club (Class)	W	L	ERA	G	SV	IP	H	BB	SO
5. Jason Baker, rhp	West Palm Beach (A)	3	4	6.00	15	0	72	90	31	47
	West Palm Beach (R)	0	0	0.00	2	0	7	4	3	8
6. Javier Vazquez, rhp	Harrisburg (AA)	4	0	1.07	6	0	42	15	12	47
	West Palm Beach (A)	6	3	2.16	19	0	113	98	28	100
8. Neil Weber, lhp	Ottawa (AAA)	2	5	7.94	9	0	40	46	40	27
	Harrisburg (AA)	7	6	3.83	18	0	113	93	51	121
9. Mike Thurman, rhp	Montreal	1	0	5.40	5	0	12	8	4	8
	Ottawa (AAA)	1	3	5.49	4	0	20	17	9	15
	Harrisburg (AA)	9	6	3.81	20	0	116	102	30	85
10. Everett Stull, rhp	Montreal	0	1	16.20	3	0	3	7	4	2
	Ottawa (AAA)	8	10	5.82	27	0	159	166	86	130

OTTAWA — Class AAA

INTERNATIONAL LEAGUE

BATTING	AVG	G	AB	R	H	2B	3B	HR	RBI	BB	SO	SB	CS	B	T	HT	WT	DOB	1st Yr	Resides
Andrews, Shane	.250	3	12	3	3	0	0	1	1	1	0	0	0	R	R	6-1	205	8-28-71	1990	Carlsbad, N.M.
Blum, Geoff	.248	118	407	59	101	21	2	3	35	52	73	14	6	S	R	6-3	193	4-26-73	1994	Chino, Calif.
Cabrera, Jolbert	.283	68	191	28	54	10	4	0	12	11	31	15	5	R	R	6-0	177	12-8-72	1991	Cartagena, Colombia
Cabrera, Orlando	.262	31	122	17	32	5	2	2	14	7	16	8	1	R	R	5-11	165	3-2-74	1994	Cartagena, Colombia
Chavez, Raul	.245	92	310	31	76	17	0	4	46	18	42	1	3	R	R	5-11	175	3-18-73	1990	Valencia, Venez.
Fullmer, Brad	.297	24	91	13	27	7	0	3	17	3	10	1	1	L	R	6-1	185	1-17-75	1994	Chatsworth, Calif.
Lott, Billy	.222	32	108	12	24	5	0	2	18	8	22	1	1	R	R	6-4	210	8-16-70	1989	Petal, Miss.
Lovullo, Torey	.141	28	64	6	9	3	0	0	6	6	13	0	0	S	R	6-0	185	7-25-65	1987	Northridge, Calif.
Lukachyk, Rob	.248	82	286	39	71	16	1	12	39	32	69	18	5	L	R	6-0	185	7-24-68	1987	Sarasota, Fla.
McGuire, Ryan	.299	50	184	37	55	11	1	3	15	36	29	5	2	L	L	6-1	195	11-23-71	1993	Woodland Hills, Calif.
Meulens, Hensley	.274	121	423	81	116	20	2	24	75	62	119	19	5	R	R	6-3	212	6-23-67	1986	Willemstad, Curacao
Morales, Francisco	.111	7	18	2	2	0	1	1	4	1	6	0	0	R	R	6-3	180	1-31-73	1991	San Pedro de Macoris, D.R.
Obando, Sherman	.238	7	21	5	5	0	0	3	8	5	7	0	0	R	R	6-4	215	1-23-70	1988	Changuinola, Panama
Pegues, Steve	.300	66	190	19	57	12	1	3	28	9	29	4	4	R	R	6-2	190	5-21-68	1987	Pontotoc, Miss.
Rossy, Rico	.251	117	375	56	94	23	0	10	52	37	64	5	0	R	R	5-10	175	2-16-64	1985	Bayamon, P.R.
Saffer, Jon	.267	134	483	81	129	20	9	15	60	76	74	13	6	L	R	6-2	200	7-6-73	1992	Tucson, Ariz.
Samuels, Scott	.345	20	55	6	19	3	0	1	7	7	12	2	0	L	R	5-11	190	5-19-71	1992	San Jose, Calif.
Schu, Rick	.190	8	21	3	4	1	0	1	3	0	4	0	0	R	R	6-0	185	1-26-62	1981	Carmichael, Calif.
Seitzer, Brad	.250	18	56	4	14	1	0	1	7	8	11	1	2	R	R	6-2	195	2-2-70	1991	Memphis, Tenn.
Siddall, Joe	.274	57	164	18	45	12	1	1	16	21	42	1	2	R	R	6-1	197	10-25-67	1988	Windsor, Ontario
Stovall, DaRond	.243	98	342	40	83	23	2	4	48	31	114	10	13	S	L	6-1	185	1-3-73	1991	East St. Louis, Ill.
Strange, Doug	.429	2	7	3	3	1	0	0	0	1	1	0	0	S	R	6-2	170	4-13-64	1985	Scottsdale, Ariz.
Thurman, Gary	.212	43	104	16	22	4	1	0	5	18	28	8	4	R	R	5-10	180	11-12-64	1983	Indianapolis, Ind.
2-team (23 Norfolk)	.228	66	184	23	42	8	1	0	17	29	44	12	5							
Valrie, Kerry	.221	34	113	12	25	6	3	3	20	4	22	3	4	R	R	5-10	195	10-31-68	1990	Loxley, Ala.
Vidro, Jose	.323	73	279	40	90	17	0	13	47	22	40	2	0	S	R	5-11	175	8-27-74	1992	Sabana Grande, P.R.

PITCHING	W	L	ERA	G	GS	CG	SV	IP	H	R	ER	BB	SO	B	T	HT	WT	DOB	1st Yr	Resides
Alvarez, Tavo	4	8	4.82	37	13	0	0	106	123	61	57	42	86	R	R	6-3	183	11-25-71	1990	Obregon, Mexico
Aucoin, Derek	0	1	22.74	8	0	0	0	6	5	16	16	21	5	R	R	6-7	226	3-27-70	1989	Boisbriand, Quebec
Baxter, Bob	0	0	12.79	4	0	0	0	6	11	10	9	3	4	R	L	6-1	180	2-17-69	1990	Norwood, Mass.
Bennett, Shayne	1	2	1.57	25	0	0	14	34	23	8	6	21	29	R	R	6-5	200	4-10-72	1993	Worongary, Australia
Bullinger, Kirk	3	4	1.71	22	0	0	5	32	17	7	6	10	15	R	R	6-2	170	10-28-69	1992	Hammond, La.
Bunch, Melvin	4	4	6.35	16	14	0	0	78	102	63	55	45	58	R	R	6-1	165	11-4-71	1992	Texarkana, Texas
Daal, Omar	0	1	5.63	2	2	0	0	8	10	6	5	1	9	L	L	6-3	185	3-1-72	1990	Valencia, Venez.
Dedrick, Jim	0	1	7.07	8	0	0	0	14	15	12	11	13	14	S	R	6-0	185	4-4-68	1990	Everett, Wash.
DeHart, Rick	0	4	4.00	43	0	0	2	63	60	33	28	22	57	R	L	6-1	180	3-21-70	1992	Topeka, Kan.
Dixon, Tim	1	1	9.64	5	0	0	0	9	12	10	10	5	8	L	L	6-2	215	2-26-72	1995	San Jose, Calif.
Falteisek, Steve	6	9	3.96	22	22	1	0	125	135	67	55	54	56	R	R	6-2	200	1-28-72	1992	Floral Park, N.Y.
Fleetham, Ben	1	2	2.00	9	0	0	1	9	2	3	2	10	14	R	R	6-1	205	8-3-72	1994	Minneapolis, Minn.
Henderson, Rod	5	9	4.95	26	20	2	1	124	136	72	68	49	103	R	R	6-4	195	3-11-71	1992	Glasgow, Ky.
Heredia, Gil	0	4	4.70	28	0	0	0	44	50	29	23	9	41	R	R	6-1	190	10-26-65	1987	Tucson, Ariz.
Paniagua, Jose	8	10	4.64	22	22	1	0	138	164	79	71	44	87	R	R	6-1	160	8-20-73	1991	Santo Domingo, D.R.
Pulido, Carlos	5	2	5.42	44	5	0	0	76	84	47	46	25	44	L	L	6-0	182	8-5-71	1989	Caracas, Venez.
Ricci, Chuck	2	2	4.67	22	0	0	0	27	22	16	14	25	27	R	R	6-2	180	11-20-68	1987	Laurel, Md.
Schmidt, Curt	0	3	6.61	31	0	0	5	31	44	24	23	22	18	R	R	6-6	223	3-16-70	1992	Miles City, Mont.
Stull, Everett	8	10	5.82	27	27	1	0	159	166	110	103	86	130	R	R	6-3	195	8-24-71	1992	Stone Mountain, Ga.
Thurman, Mike	1	3	5.49	4	4	0	0	20	17	13	12	9	15	R	R	6-5	190	7-22-73	1994	Philomath, Ore.
Torres, Salomon	0	0	5.40	2	1	0	0	5	7	5	3	2	2	R	R	5-11	150	3-11-72	1990	San Pedro de Macoris, D.R.
Urbani, Tom	3	1	2.61	30	1	0	0	41	37	13	12	12	25	L	L	6-1	190	1-21-68	1990	Santa Cruz, Calif.
Weber, Neil	2	5	7.94	9	9	0	0	40	46	46	35	40	27	L	L	6-5	205	12-6-72	1993	Irvine, Calif.

FIELDING

Catcher	PCT	G	PO	A	E	DP	PB
Chavez	.978	89	593	77	15	9	9
Morales	1.000	5	31	4	0	1	0
Siddall	.987	56	278	32	4	2	5

First Base	PCT	G	PO	A	E	DP
Fullmer	.995	19	172	12	1	17
Lukachyk	.995	24	192	13	1	22
McGuire	.996	50	421	52	2	36
Meulens	.980	38	320	21	7	32
Schu	1.000	1	8	1	0	1
Seitzer	.992	15	112	14	1	11

Second Base	PCT	G	PO	A	E	DP
Blum	.975	70	156	197	9	50
J. Cabrera	1.000	7	20	19	0	1
O. Cabrera	1.000	10	18	27	0	6
Lovullo	1.000	14	31	35	0	6
Rossy	.947	24	38	52	5	16
Vidro	.958	21	40	52	4	14

Third Base	PCT	G	PO	A	E	DP
Andrews	1.000	3	2	4	0	1
Blum	1.000	6	7	8	0	1
J. Cabrera	.962	46	23	102	5	8
Lovullo	1.000	1	0	7	0	0
Meulens	.916	45	29	91	11	11
Schu	1.000	4	1	5	0	0
Seitzer	.800	2	0	8	2	1
Strange	1.000	1	2	3	0	0
Vidro	.972	47	30	109	4	11

Shortstop	PCT	G	PO	A	E	DP
Blum	.952	35	60	100	8	18
J. Cabrera	.867	4	8	5	2	1
O. Cabrera	.969	22	27	67	3	14
Rossy	.959	85	116	236	15	53

Outfield	PCT	G	PO	A	E	DP
J. Cabrera	1.000	1	0	1	0	0
Fullmer	1.000	1	1	0	0	0
Lott	1.000	29	52	2	0	0
Lukachyk	.971	54	93	7	3	1
Meulens	.949	18	35	2	2	1
Obando	1.000	1	3	0	0	0
Pegues	.938	31	40	5	3	0
Saffer	.968	125	226	15	8	8
Samuels	1.000	17	24	2	0	0
Stovall	.965	96	181	10	7	4
Thurman	.983	40	57	1	1	0
Valrie	.973	30	67	4	2	1

HARRISBURG — Class AA

EASTERN LEAGUE

BATTING	AVG	G	AB	R	H	2B	3B	HR	RBI	BB	SO	SB	CS	B	T	HT	WT	DOB	1st Yr	Resides
Alcantara, Israel	.282	89	301	48	85	9	2	27	68	29	84	4	5	R	R	6-2	165	5-6-73	1991	Santo Domingo, D.R.
Bady, Ed	.210	97	267	36	56	8	4	1	22	21	62	15	5	S	R	5-11	170	2-5-73	1994	Queens, N.Y.
Bocachica, Hiram	.278	119	443	82	123	19	3	11	35	41	98	29	12	R	R	5-11	165	3-4-76	1994	Bayamon, P.R.
Brinkley, Josh	.315	22	54	8	17	2	0	2	6	1	12	0	1	R	R	5-10	175	8-5-73	1993	Raleigh, N.C.
Cabrera, Jolbert	.251	48	171	28	43	9	0	2	11	28	28	5	4	R	R	6-0	177	12-8-72	1991	Cartagena, Colombia
Cabrera, Orlando	.308	35	133	34	41	13	2	5	20	15	18	7	2	R	R	5-11	165	3-2-74	1994	Cartagena, Colombia

BATTING	AVG	G	AB	R	H	2B	3B	HR	RBI	BB	SO	SB	CS	B	T	HT	WT	DOB	1st Yr	Resides
Campos, Jesus	.308	82	286	33	88	12	1	5	36	8	24	6	8	R	R	5-9	145	10-12-73	1991	San Pedro de Macoris, D.R.
Carvajal, Jhonny	.259	116	378	36	98	12	1	1	31	27	66	10	7	R	R	5-10	165	7-24-74	1993	Barcelona, Venez.
Coquillette, Trace	.259	81	293	46	76	17	3	10	51	25	40	9	4	R	R	5-11	165	6-4-74	1993	Orangevale, Calif.
Fernandez, Jose	.229	29	96	10	22	3	1	4	11	11	28	2	0	R	R	6-2	210	11-2-74	1993	Santiago, D.R.
Fullmer, Brad	.311	94	357	60	111	24	2	19	62	30	25	6	4	L	R	6-1	185	1-17-75	1994	Chatsworth, Calif.
Haas, Matt	.211	8	19	2	4	1	0	1	4	4	2	1	0	L	R	6-1	175	2-1-72	1994	Paducah, Ky.
Henley, Bob	.304	79	280	41	85	19	0	12	49	32	40	5	1	R	R	6-2	190	1-30-73	1993	Grand Bay, Ala.
Lukachyk, Rob	.275	42	153	26	42	6	3	7	26	11	26	5	3	L	R	6-0	185	7-24-68	1987	Sarasota, Fla.
Morales, Francisco	.204	16	49	5	10	1	0	2	4	3	22	0	0	R	R	6-3	180	1-31-73	1991	San Pedro de Macoris, D.R.
Ortiz, Bo	.223	60	188	24	42	2	3	7	21	12	25	5	0	R	R	5-11	170	4-4-70	1991	Hartford, Conn.
Pachot, John	.279	94	323	40	90	23	3	7	50	22	42	6	6	R	R	6-2	168	11-11-74	1993	Ponce, P.R.
Peterson, Nate	.243	52	140	17	34	4	2	4	18	17	27	1	0	L	R	6-2	185	7-12-71	1993	Melbourne, Australia
Post, Dave	.263	48	156	26	41	10	0	3	18	24	24	5	1	R	R	5-11	170	9-3-73	1992	Kingston, N.Y.
Samuels, Scott	.296	64	223	32	66	19	1	5	32	34	43	13	4	L	R	5-11	190	5-19-71	1992	San Jose, Calif.
Stovall, DaRond	.284	45	169	29	48	4	1	9	39	23	30	4	0	S	L	6-1	185	1-3-73	1991	East St. Louis, Ill.
Stowers, Chris	.288	19	59	9	17	4	2	0	5	5	11	3	1	L	L	6-3	195	8-18-74	1996	Marietta, Ga.
Valdez, Trovin	.310	13	42	8	13	2	0	0	4	4	9	2	1	R	R	5-10	163	11-18-73	1993	New York, N.Y.

PITCHING	W	L	ERA	G	GS	CG	SV	IP	H	R	ER	BB	SO	B	T	HT	WT	DOB	1st Yr	Resides
Bennett, Shayne	4	2	4.40	23	1	0	2	47	47	28	23	20	38	R	R	6-5	200	4-10-72	1993	Worongary, Australia
Benz, Jake	4	1	2.33	23	0	0	2	39	39	12	10	20	36	L	L	5-9	162	2-27-72	1994	Pleasant Hill, Calif.
Bullinger, Kirk	3	0	2.67	21	0	0	6	27	22	9	8	6	21	R	R	6-2	170	10-28-69	1992	Hammond, La.
Bunch, Mel	3	3	4.20	9	9	0	0	49	45	27	23	22	50	R	R	6-1	165	11-4-71	1992	Texarkana, Texas
Cole, Jason	2	3	3.57	37	0	0	0	58	52	31	23	19	31	R	R	6-3	198	9-8-72	1994	Coventry, R.I.
DaSilva, Fernando	0	3	13.83	12	0	0	0	14	21	23	21	10	11	R	R	6-2	194	9-6-71	1991	Brossard, Quebec
Dedrick, Jim	2	1	2.79	15	0	0	1	19	18	8	6	8	17	S	R	6-0	185	4-4-68	1990	Everett, Wash.
Dixon, Tim	5	2	3.38	37	2	0	0	69	66	34	26	24	75	L	L	6-2	215	2-26-72	1995	San Jose, Calif.
Fleetham, Ben	2	1	3.04	49	0	0	30	50	28	21	17	33	69	R	R	6-1	205	8-3-72	1994	Minneapolis, Minn.
Forster, Scott	3	6	2.27	17	15	0	0	79	77	45	20	48	71	R	L	6-1	194	10-27-71	1994	Flourtown, Pa.
Martinez, Ramiro	4	4	3.69	37	3	0	1	76	64	36	31	33	69	L	L	6-2	185	1-28-72	1992	Los Angeles, Calif.
McCommon, Jason	6	3	5.01	29	8	0	0	83	81	50	46	39	58	R	R	6-0	190	8-9-71	1994	Memphis, Tenn.
Mitchell, Scott	1	0	3.63	4	3	0	0	17	11	7	7	3	13	R	R	5-11	170	3-19-73	1995	Citrus Heights, Calif.
Moore, Trey	11	6	4.15	27	27	2	0	163	152	91	75	66	137	L	L	6-1	200	10-2-72	1994	Southlake, Texas
Phelps, Tom	10	6	4.71	18	18	0	0	101	115	68	53	39	86	L	L	6-3	192	3-4-74	1993	Tampa, Fla.
Smart, J.D.	6	3	3.69	12	12	0	0	71	75	34	29	24	43	R	R	6-2	185	11-12-73	1995	Austin, Texas
Stevenson, Rodney	0	0	3.86	4	0	0	0	7	9	5	3	5	6	R	R	6-2	210	3-21-74	1996	Columbus, Ga.
Thurman, Mike	9	6	3.81	20	20	1	0	116	102	54	49	30	85	R	R	6-5	190	7-22-73	1994	Philomath, Ore.
Vazquez, Javier	4	0	1.07	6	6	1	0	42	15	5	5	12	47	R	R	6-2	175	6-25-76	1994	Ponce, P.R.
Weber, Neil	7	6	3.83	18	18	1	0	113	93	56	48	51	121	L	L	6-5	205	12-6-72	1993	Irvine, Calif.
Young, Tim	0	0	0.00	1	0	0	0	2	1	0	0	0	3	L	L	5-9	170	10-15-73	1996	Bristol, Fla.

FIELDING

Catcher	PCT	G	PO	A	E	DP
Brinkley	1.000	4	6	0	0	0
Henley	.995	75	574	77	3	6
Morales	1.000	14	95	6	0	0
Pachot	.972	64	437	44	14	3

First Base	PCT	G	PO	A	E	DP
Alcantara	.979	30	222	11	5	14
Brinkley	1.000	1	8	0	0	1
Fernandez	1.000	3	23	2	0	1
Fullmer	.991	68	507	41	5	39
Haas	1.000	1	12	1	0	0
Pachot	.991	26	195	25	2	15
Peterson	.983	11	53	6	1	6
Post	.973	11	60	12	2	4

Second Base	PCT	G	PO	A	E	DP
Bocachica	.963	28	64	67	5	9
J. Cabrera	.968	26	71	50	4	12
O. Cabrera	1.000	1	4	2	0	1
Carvajal	.938	19	40	36	5	8
Coquillette	.957	56	105	137	11	21
Post	.976	19	40	40	2	9

Third Base	PCT	G	PO	A	E	DP
Alcantara	.877	41	31	69	14	4
Brinkley	.815	14	4	18	5	2
Carvajal	.933	58	37	88	9	4
Coquillette	.896	16	11	32	5	0
Fernandez	.887	22	18	29	6	1
Haas	1.000	2	1	3	0	0
Pachot	.786	6	2	9	3	2
Post	.667	2	1	3	2	0

Shortstop	PCT	G	PO	A	E	DP
Bocachica	.876	57	71	119	27	18
Brinkley	1.000	1	0	2	0	0
J. Cabrera	.904	17	21	26	5	8
O. Cabrera	.964	34	53	81	5	15
Carvajal	.946	42	54	105	9	17

Outfield	PCT	G	PO	A	E	DP
Alcantara	1.000	1	1	0	0	0
Bady	.951	89	149	5	8	1
Brinkley	1.000	1	0	1	0	0
J. Cabrera	1.000	6	6	0	0	0
Campos	.974	81	176	11	5	1
Carvajal	.000	1	0	0	0	0
Fullmer	.969	18	31	0	1	0
Haas	1.000	2	3	0	0	0
Lukachyk	.970	38	60	4	2	0
Ortiz	.990	54	95	3	1	0
Peterson	.980	36	47	1	1	0
Post	1.000	4	2	1	0	0
Samuels	.976	64	116	4	3	1
Stovall	.990	44	93	3	1	1
Stowers	.929	18	37	2	3	1
Valdez	.846	11	9	2	2	0

WEST PALM BEACH — Class A

FLORIDA STATE LEAGUE

BATTING	AVG	G	AB	R	H	2B	3B	HR	RBI	BB	SO	SB	CS	B	T	HT	WT	DOB	1st Yr	Resides
Adolfo, Carlos	.225	120	448	62	101	15	2	11	50	38	91	9	18	R	R	5-11	160	4-20-76	1994	Santo Domingo, D.R.
Andrews, Shane	.176	5	17	2	3	2	0	1	5	2	7	0	1	R	R	6-1	205	8-28-71	1990	Carlsbad, N.M.
Barrett, Michael	.284	119	423	52	120	30	0	8	61	36	49	7	4	R	R	6-3	185	10-22-76	1995	West Palm Beach, Fla.
Bess, Johnny	.145	23	62	2	9	0	0	0	2	3	21	1	1	S	R	6-1	190	4-6-70	1992	Grand Junction, Colo.
Bravo, Danny	.162	15	37	3	6	1	1	0	0	2	5	0	0	S	R	5-11	175	5-27-77	1996	Maracaibo, Venez.
Brinkley, Josh	.260	69	227	24	59	12	2	3	20	9	44	3	1	R	R	5-10	175	8-5-73	1993	Raleigh, N.C.
Brown, Nate	.225	15	40	7	9	1	0	1	5	3	16	2	0	L	L	6-5	225	2-3-71	1993	Berkeley, Calif.
Bustos, Saul	.264	39	106	10	28	5	1	0	12	6	23	1	3	R	R	5-11	170	9-30-72	1994	Odessa, Texas
Byrd, Tony	.111	6	18	2	2	0	0	0	1	4	5	1	0	S	R	5-11	190	11-13-70	1992	Atlanta, Ga.
Cabrera, Orlando	.276	69	279	56	77	19	2	5	26	27	33	32	12	R	R	5-11	165	3-2-74	1994	Cartagena, Colombia
Camilli, Jason	.128	15	47	1	6	3	0	0	1	2	12	0	1	R	R	6-0	178	10-18-75	1994	Phoenix, Ariz.
Campos, Jesus	.190	28	84	11	16	3	1	0	7	1	9	0	1	R	R	5-9	145	10-12-73	1991	San Pedro de Macoris, D.R.
Carroll, Jamey	.243	121	407	56	99	19	1	0	38	43	48	17	11	R	R	5-11	165	2-18-75	1996	Evansville, Ind.
Coquillette, Trace	.319	53	188	34	60	18	2	8	33	27	27	8	7	R	R	5-11	165	6-4-74	1993	Orangevale, Calif.
De la Rosa, Tomas	.222	4	9	1	2	0	0	0	0	2	3	2	0	R	R	5-10	155	1-28-78	1996	La Victoria, D.R.
Fernandez, Jose	.309	97	350	49	108	21	3	9	58	37	76	22	14	R	R	6-2	210	11-2-74	1993	Santiago, D.R.
Guerrero, Vladimir	.400	3	10	0	4	2	0	0	2	1	0	1	0	R	R	6-2	158	2-9-76	1993	Nizao, D.R.
Haas, Matt	.234	72	201	17	47	5	1	1	16	24	34	7	3	L	R	6-1	175	2-1-72	1994	Paducah, Ky.

GEORGE GOJKOVICH

Montreal's Rondell White

MORRIS FOSTOFF

West Palm Beach's Michael Barrett

BATTING	AVG	G	AB	R	H	2B	3B	HR	RBI	BB	SO	SB	CS	B	T	HT	WT	DOB	1st Yr	Resides
Hall, Noah	.000	1	1	0	0	0	0	0	0	0	1	0	0	R	R	5-11	200	6-9-77	1996	Aptos, Calif.
Leidens, Enrique	.143	4	7	1	1	0	0	0	0	0	1	0	0	R	R	5-11	165	2-6-78	1995	Aragua, Venez.
Meulens, Hensley	.250	1	4	0	1	1	0	0	0	0	2	0	0	R	R	6-3	212	6-23-67	1986	Willemstad, Curacao
Morales, Francisco	.283	45	127	15	36	7	1	4	13	10	37	0	2	R	R	6-3	180	1-31-73	1991	San Pedro de Macoris, D.R.
Ovalles, Homy	.000	2	1	2	0	0	0	0	0	0	0	0	0	R	R	5-10	160	7-6-76	1994	Caracas, Venez.
Quero, Pedro	.000	1	2	0	0	0	0	0	0	0	0	0	0	R	R	6-4	190	11-17-77	1995	Caracas, Venez.
Rivera, Luis	.000	1	1	0	0	0	0	0	0	0	0	0	0	R	R	6-3	185	12-21-77	1996	Bayamon, P.R.
Rodriques, Cecil	.146	15	41	9	6	1	0	1	3	3	14	2	0	R	R	6-0	175	9-3-71	1991	Fort Pierce, Fla.
Schwab, Chris	.188	58	207	22	39	7	0	9	28	22	82	3	1	R	L	6-3	215	7-25-74	1993	Eagan, Minn.
Seguignol, Fernando	.254	124	456	70	116	27	5	18	83	30	129	5	5	S	R	6-5	179	1-19-75	1993	Panama City, Panama
Stowers, Chris	.273	111	414	56	113	15	5	4	30	30	77	19	14	L	L	6-3	195	8-18-74	1996	Marietta, Ga.
Valdez, Trovin	.234	55	188	19	44	4	3	2	14	10	24	12	6	R	R	5-10	163	11-18-73	1993	New York, N.Y.

GAMES BY POSITION: C—Barrett 96, Bess 14, Haas 2, Morales 26. **1B**—Bravo 1, Brown 8, Fernandez 2, Haas 16, Seguignol 115. **2B**—Bravo 12, Brinkley 18, Bustos 23, Cabrera 3, Camilli 5, Carroll 36, Coquillette 44, Leidens 4, Ovalles 2. **3B**—Andrews 2, Bravo 1, Brinkley 31, Bustos 14, Carroll 1, Coquillette 1, Fernandez 92, Meulens 1. **SS**—Bustos 3, Cabrera 61, Camilli 10, Carroll 59, De la Rosa 4. **OF**—Adolfo 117, Bess 1, Bravo 1, Brinkley 16, Brown 7, Bustos 1, Byrd 5, Campos 28, Coquillette 1, Guerrero 3, Haas 30, Rodriques 13, Schwab 44, Seguignol 4, Stowers 109, Valdez 53.

PITCHING	W	L	ERA	G	GS	CG	SV	IP	H	R	ER	BB	SO	B	T	HT	WT	DOB	1st Yr	Resides
Aucoin, Derek	0	0	7.58	17	0	0	0	19	13	17	16	27	21	R	R	6-7	226	3-27-70	1989	Boisbriand, Quebec
Baker, Jason	3	4	6.00	15	14	1	0	72	90	55	48	31	47	R	R	6-4	195	11-21-74	1993	Midland, Texas
Bell, Mike	5	4	3.10	41	3	0	4	81	60	30	28	27	56	L	L	6-2	195	10-14-72	1995	Sarasota, Fla.
Benz, Jake	0	2	2.63	14	0	0	0	24	18	9	7	6	28	L	L	5-9	162	2-27-72	1994	Pleasant Hill, Calif.
Bullinger, Kirk	2	0	0.00	2	0	0	0	4	3	0	0	0	7	R	R	6-2	170	10-28-69	1992	Hammond, La.
Civit, Xavier	3	0	1.64	4	0	0	0	11	5	2	2	4	9	R	R	6-2	175	5-17-73	1993	Barcelona, Spain
Cole, Jason	2	1	2.37	11	0	0	2	19	21	7	5	4	8	R	R	6-3	198	9-8-72	1994	Coventry, R.I.
DaSilva, Fernando	8	5	5.28	30	4	0	0	60	73	38	35	12	59	R	R	6-2	194	9-6-71	1991	Brossard, Quebec
Durocher, Jayson	6	4	3.83	25	17	0	0	87	84	58	37	39	71	R	R	6-3	195	8-18-74	1993	Scottsdale, Ariz.
Evans, Keith	2	4	4.33	7	7	2	0	44	42	23	21	11	20	R	R	6-5	200	11-2-75	1996	Woodland Hills, Calif.
Handy, Russell	0	0	22.50	2	0	0	0	2	6	6	5	1	1	R	R	6-4	200	8-4-74	1993	Bakersfield, Calif.
Julio, Jorge	0	0	0.00	1	0	0	0	0	2	1	1	0	0	R	R	6-1	190	3-3-79	1996	Caracas, Venez.
Leslie, Sean	0	0	27.00	1	0	0	0	1	2	2	2	1	0	R	L	6-2	212	12-15-73	1996	Willits, Calif.
Loubier, Scott	0	0	12.60	4	0	0	0	5	10	7	7	2	3	R	R	6-1	200	4-9-74	1997	Boca Raton, Fla.
Marquez, Robert	1	1	2.57	21	0	0	6	28	28	12	8	3	22	R	R	6-0	180	4-21-73	1995	Houston, Texas
Mattes, Troy	6	9	4.94	20	16	2	1	102	123	61	56	20	61	R	R	6-7	185	8-26-75	1994	Sarasota, Fla.
Mitchell, Scott	5	3	2.57	39	3	0	3	74	61	21	21	18	56	R	R	5-11	170	3-19-73	1995	Citrus Heights, Calif.
Moraga, David	1	4	4.91	13	7	0	0	48	50	27	26	18	37	L	L	6-0	184	7-8-75	1994	Suisun City, Calif.
Orta, Juan	0	0	0.00	1	0	0	0	1	2	0	0	0	0	R	R	6-2	175	4-13-78	1995	Maracay, Venez.
Paniagua, Jose	1	0	0.00	2	2	0	0	10	5	0	0	2	11	R	R	6-1	160	8-20-73	1991	Santo Domingo, D.R.
Parker, Christian	0	1	3.32	3	3	0	0	19	22	7	7	5	10	R	R	6-1	200	7-3-75	1996	Albuquerque, N.M.
Powell, Jeremy	9	10	3.02	26	26	1	0	155	162	75	52	62	121	R	R	6-5	230	6-18-76	1994	Sacramento, Calif.
Rivera, Marco	0	1	22.50	2	0	0	0	2	4	5	5	2	1	L	L	5-11	160	2-28-77	1996	Arecibo, P.R.
Sasaki, Junichi	0	0	0.00	1	0	0	0	0	1	0	0	0	0	R	R	6-4	185	8-7-74	1996	Chiba, Japan

PITCHING	W	L	ERA	G	GS	CG	SV	IP	H	R	ER	BB	SO	B	T	HT	WT	DOB	1st Yr	Resides
Smart, J.D.	5	4	3.26	17	13	1	1	102	105	45	37	21	65	R	R	6-2	185	11-12-73	1995	Austin, Texas
Stevenson, Rodney	3	3	1.78	26	0	0	2	35	31	13	7	16	39	R	R	6-2	210	3-21-74	1996	Columbus, Ga.
Vazquez, Javier	6	3	2.16	19	19	1	0	113	98	40	27	28	100	R	R	6-2	175	6-25-76	1994	Ponce, P.R.
Wagner, Matt	0	0	54.00	1	1	0	0	1	4	4	4	1	0	R	R	6-5	215	4-4-72	1994	Cedar Falls, Iowa
Weidert, Chris	0	1	0.00	4	0	0	0	6	5	1	0	3	7	R	R	6-3	210	4-3-74	1994	Emporia, Kan.
Westover, Richard	0	0	15.00	3	0	0	0	3	10	7	5	2	2	R	R	6-3	210	10-28-74	1996	Brooklyn, N.Y.
Woodring, Jason	1	1	2.76	16	0	0	5	16	12	6	5	5	8	R	R	6-3	190	4-2-74	1993	Trinidad, Colo.
Young, Tim	0	0	0.57	11	0	0	5	16	8	1	1	4	13	L	L	5-9	170	10-15-73	1996	Bristol, Fla.

CAPE FEAR — Class A

SOUTH ATLANTIC LEAGUE

BATTING	AVG	G	AB	R	H	2B	3B	HR	RBI	BB	SO	SB	CS	B	T	HT	WT	DOB	1st Yr	Resides
Blakeney, Mo	.265	17	49	10	13	1	0	4	7	3	12	3	1	R	R	5-10	185	1-17-73	1995	Kannapolis, N.C.
Blandford, Paul	.289	113	398	63	115	23	4	5	40	40	50	20	13	R	R	5-10	175	3-29-74	1996	Elk Grove, Calif.
Bravo, Danny	.269	73	253	28	68	9	1	3	34	9	31	3	4	S	R	5-11	175	5-27-77	1996	Maracaibo, Venez.
Camilli, Jason	.298	98	396	57	118	35	2	3	43	31	64	22	11	R	R	6-0	178	10-18-75	1994	Phoenix, Ariz.
Chatman, Karl	.233	121	443	65	103	19	6	6	50	41	131	26	4	R	R	6-1	190	1-17-75	1996	Nacogdoches, Texas
Denning, Wes	.248	137	557	77	138	24	10	5	50	31	97	34	13	L	R	5-11	180	12-30-72	1995	St. Paul, Minn.
Jefferson, Dave	.195	28	87	12	17	1	0	2	6	7	14	6	2	R	R	6-2	190	6-18-75	1993	Palo Alto, Calif.
MacKay, Tripp	.238	68	189	25	45	6	1	0	12	29	20	5	9	S	R	5-10	170	8-15-73	1996	Mt. Pleasant, Texas
Nunnari, Talmadge	.371	9	35	8	13	1	1	1	6	1	5	2	0	L	L	6-1	205	4-9-75	1997	Pensacola, Fla.
Olsen, D.C.	.256	51	160	18	41	9	2	5	29	9	37	2	1	R	R	6-0	220	5-3-72	1995	Oakhurst, Calif.
Oropeza, Willie	.233	78	270	28	63	9	0	7	32	8	46	1	2	R	R	6-1	175	10-16-75	1994	La Guaira, Venez.
Pond, Simon	.270	118	444	48	120	11	0	3	47	37	46	12	8	L	R	6-1	175	10-27-76	1994	North Vancouver, B.C.
Rigoli, David	.188	17	48	5	9	2	1	0	3	8	6	1	0	R	R	6-0	180	10-28-75	1996	Grosseso, Italy
Schneider, Brian	.252	113	381	46	96	20	1	4	49	53	45	3	6	L	R	6-1	180	11-26-76	1995	Cherryville, Pa.
Schwab, Chris	.268	54	209	29	56	19	2	11	42	26	70	3	3	R	L	6-3	215	7-25-74	1993	Eagan, Minn.
Streicher, Robert	.111	15	45	0	5	0	0	0	4	6	10	0	0	R	R	6-1	225	4-8-74	1997	Boca Raton, Fla.
Tracy, Andrew	.300	59	210	31	63	9	2	8	43	21	47	6	1	L	R	6-3	220	12-11-73	1996	Bowling Green, Ohio
Ware, Jeremy	.263	138	529	84	139	32	5	16	77	43	114	32	7	R	R	6-1	190	10-23-75	1995	Guelph, Ontario
White, John	.000	3	9	0	0	0	0	0	1	1	3	0	0	R	R	6-3	225	1-21-75	1997	Jacksonville, Fla.

GAMES BY POSITION: C—Blandford 1, Olsen 7, Oropeza 18, Schneider 108, Streicher 13, White 3. **1B**—Nunnari 8, Olsen 21, Oropeza 51, Pond 16, Tracy 52. **2B**—Blandford 101, Bravo 7, MacKay 36. **3B**—Blandford 2, Bravo 24, MacKay 1, Oropeza 7, Pond 100, Rigoli 12. **SS**—Bravo 29, Camilli 94, MacKay 19. **OF**—Blakeney 12, Blandford 3, Chatman 116, Denning 133, Jefferson 22, MacKay 3, Schwab 15, Ware 130.

PITCHING	W	L	ERA	G	GS	CG	SV	IP	H	R	ER	BB	SO	B	T	HT	WT	DOB	1st Yr	Resides
Civit, Xavier	4	3	3.55	39	0	0	3	63	59	28	25	18	60	R	R	6-2	175	5-17-73	1993	Barcelona, Spain
Evans, Keith	12	7	2.61	21	21	3	0	138	113	56	40	18	102	R	R	6-5	200	11-2-75	1996	Woodland Hills, Calif.
Fortune, Peter	1	1	7.66	12	0	0	0	22	23	19	19	20	21	L	L	6-2	190	3-4-75	1995	Valley Cottage, N.Y.
Handy, Russell	1	0	5.00	19	1	0	0	27	20	22	15	29	22	R	R	6-4	200	8-4-74	1993	Bakersfield, Calif.
Lara, Giovanny	9	12	4.55	28	27	1	0	170	199	107	86	45	100	R	R	6-2	163	9-20-75	1993	San Cristobal, D.R.
Leslie, Sean	0	5	5.02	34	1	0	0	61	75	40	34	27	42	R	L	6-2	212	12-15-73	1996	Willits, Calif.
Loubier, Scott	1	1	2.89	10	2	0	0	28	19	9	9	12	20	R	R	6-1	200	4-9-74	1997	Boca Raton, Fla.
Marquez, Robert	0	0	2.95	12	0	0	2	18	15	6	6	12	18	R	R	6-0	180	4-21-73	1995	Houston, Texas
Matz, Brian	4	6	4.39	44	5	1	0	96	102	54	47	41	64	L	L	6-1	195	9-23-74	1996	Towson, Md.
Mota, Guillermo	5	10	4.36	25	23	0	0	126	135	65	61	33	112	R	R	6-5	185	7-25-73	1991	San Pedro de Macoris, D.R.
Parker, Christian	11	10	3.12	25	25	0	0	153	146	72	53	49	106	R	R	6-1	200	7-3-75	1996	Albuquerque, N.M.
Quezada, Edward	8	6	4.27	30	19	0	2	141	143	73	67	31	87	R	R	6-2	150	1-15-75	1993	Nizao, D.R.
Saylor, Ryan	2	1	4.30	10	0	0	1	15	17	9	7	9	19	L	R	5-10	175	5-20-75	1997	Greenville, Ohio
Stevenson, Rodney	1	1	0.53	16	0	0	5	17	7	3	1	6	20	R	R	6-2	210	3-21-74	1996	Columbus, Ga.
Strickland, Scott	0	1	6.35	3	1	0	1	6	8	7	4	1	8	R	R	5-11	180	4-26-76	1997	Spring, Texas
Turman, Jimmy	5	7	4.18	19	15	1	0	88	84	45	41	35	72	R	R	6-10	210	11-10-75	1996	Gordo, Ala.
Van Gilder, Ryan	1	2	3.18	4	0	0	0	6	8	3	2	4	8	R	R	6-0	175	12-1-75	1997	Watertown, S.D.
Young, Tim	1	1	1.50	45	0	0	18	54	33	12	9	15	66	L	L	5-9	170	10-15-73	1996	Bristol, Fla.

VERMONT — Short-Season Class A

NEW YORK-PENN LEAGUE

BATTING	AVG	G	AB	R	H	2B	3B	HR	RBI	BB	SO	SB	CS	B	T	HT	WT	DOB	1st Yr	Resides
Bagley, Sean	.182	39	121	17	22	2	0	1	9	9	36	7	3	R	R	6-3	195	6-20-76	1994	Gig Harbor, Wash.
Blakeney, Mo	.284	32	116	9	33	3	2	3	11	8	25	4	4	R	R	5-10	185	1-17-73	1995	Kannapolis, N.C.
Bradley, Milton	.300	50	200	29	60	7	5	3	30	17	34	7	7	S	R	6-0	170	4-15-78	1996	Long Beach, Calif.
Burkhart, Lance	.168	38	143	15	24	6	1	0	12	17	40	3	3	R	R	5-9	190	12-16-74	1997	Florissant, Mo.
De la Rosa, Tomas	.266	69	271	46	72	14	6	2	40	32	47	19	6	R	R	5-10	155	1-28-78	1996	La Victoria, D.R.
Forbes, Kevin	.200	30	100	13	20	1	0	0	8	5	22	8	1	R	R	5-11	200	2-17-76	1997	Marina, Calif.
Hall, Noah	.274	73	266	43	73	12	8	2	45	45	48	22	5	R	R	5-11	200	6-9-77	1996	Aptos, Calif.
Hernandez, Rafeal	.234	22	77	8	18	1	0	1	5	4	18	0	2	R	R	5-10	155	9-23-75	1995	San Pedro de Macoris, D.R.
James, Kenny	.233	71	301	61	70	4	5	2	23	13	52	37	4	S	R	6-0	198	10-9-76	1995	Sebring, Fla.
Mateo, Henry	.246	67	228	32	56	9	3	1	31	30	44	21	11	S	R	5-11	170	10-14-76	1995	Santurce, P.R.
Nunnari, Talmadge	.318	62	236	30	75	11	3	4	42	31	37	6	3	L	L	6-1	205	4-9-75	1997	Pensacola, Fla.
Ovalles, Homy	.214	29	84	6	18	4	0	1	12	9	23	3	2	R	R	5-10	160	7-6-76	1994	Caracas, Venez.
Quero, Pedro	.275	13	40	2	11	1	0	0	3	3	14	1	0	R	R	6-4	190	11-17-77	1995	Caracas, Venez.
Reding, Josh	.167	8	24	2	4	2	1	0	0	3	11	0	0	R	R	6-2	165	3-7-77	1997	Anaheim, Calif.
Rivera, Luis	.252	40	135	17	34	12	2	0	13	10	37	1	1	R	R	6-2	205	4-3-75	1997	Miami, Fla.
Zech, Scott	.265	63	204	31	54	11	0	1	20	27	36	17	7	R	R	5-11	175	6-6-74	1997	Boca Raton, Fla.

GAMES BY POSITION: C—Bagley 28, Burkhart 15, Rivera 36. **1B**—Bagley 6, Nunnari 61, Quero 13. **2B**—Mateo 64, Ovalles 6, Zech 6. **3B**—Burkhart 8, Hernandez 2, Ovalles 14, Reding 4, Zech 50. **SS**—De la Rosa 69, Ovalles 5, Reding 1, Zech 2. **OF**—Bagley 3, Blakeney 26, Bradley 50, Forbes 20, Hall 60, Hernandez 7, James 70.

PITCHING	W	L	ERA	G	GS	CG	SV	IP	H	R	ER	BB	SO	B	T	HT	WT	DOB	1st Yr	Resides
Becks, Ryan	2	8	5.83	15	15	1	0	79	92	61	51	33	57	L	L	6-3	185	4-7-76	1997	San Jose, Calif.

PITCHING	W	L	ERA	G	GS	CG	SV	IP	H	R	ER	BB	SO	B	T	HT	WT	DOB	1st Yr	Resides
Blank, Matt	6	4	1.69	16	15	2	0	96	74	26	18	14	84	L	L	6-2	200	4-5-76	1997	Arlington, Texas
Daniels, Ronney	0	0	3.60	3	0	0	0	5	5	2	2	2	1	R	L	6-3	210	9-17-76	1995	Lake Wales, Fla.
Fraser, Joe	0	3	6.11	10	3	0	0	18	22	21	12	17	7	R	R	6-1	195	10-23-77	1996	Anaheim, Calif.
Lanzetta, Tobin	1	4	5.61	23	5	0	1	43	60	36	27	8	43	R	R	6-2	185	7-31-75	1997	Tucson, Ariz.
Loubier, Scott	3	2	3.08	7	6	0	0	38	32	16	13	10	29	R	R	6-1	200	4-9-74	1997	Boca Raton, Fla.
Lynde, Jerry	0	2	9.24	12	2	0	0	13	17	17	13	18	12	R	R	6-4	205	4-10-75	1997	Northfield, Vt.
Martin, Trey	1	0	6.20	11	0	0	0	25	30	19	17	7	13	R	R	6-2	175	10-2-76	1995	Phoenix, Ariz.
Perez, Julio	0	1	5.68	3	1	0	0	6	12	8	4	2	5	R	R	6-2	170	8-6-78	1997	Miami, Fla.
Plummer, Ray	4	3	5.26	28	0	0	0	39	39	28	23	17	28	L	L	5-11	190	11-1-75	1997	San Diego, Calif.
Rahilly, Michael	2	0	2.30	9	0	0	1	16	9	4	4	4	18	R	R	6-6	230	12-3-76	1996	Cape Coral, Fla.
Sadler, Carl	2	2	4.21	7	6	0	0	36	33	20	17	23	27	L	L	6-2	180	10-11-76	1996	Perry, Fla.
Salyers, Jeremy	3	4	5.00	16	14	0	0	77	87	53	43	31	32	R	R	6-3	205	1-31-76	1996	Pound, Va.
Sasaki, Junichi	1	0	3.24	11	0	0	1	17	14	7	6	4	19	R	R	6-4	185	8-7-74	1996	Chiba, Japan
Saylor, Ryan	3	0	2.37	16	0	0	2	19	17	7	5	8	29	L	R	5-10	175	5-20-75	1997	Greenville, Ohio
Sparks, Eric	0	4	4.29	28	0	0	2	42	34	22	20	26	46	S	L	6-1	210	6-2-74	1996	Hoosick Falls, N.Y.
Strickland, Scott	5	2	3.82	15	9	1	0	61	56	27	26	20	69	R	R	5-11	180	4-26-76	1997	Spring, Texas
Van Gilder, Ryan	2	1	2.61	19	0	0	8	21	17	9	6	9	19	R	R	6-0	175	12-1-75	1997	Watertown, S.D.
Westover, Richard	0	1	15.12	7	0	0	0	8	19	18	14	6	8	R	R	6-3	210	10-28-74	1996	Brooklyn, N.Y.

WEST PALM BEACH — Rookie

GULF COAST LEAGUE

BATTING	AVG	G	AB	R	H	2B	3B	HR	RBI	BB	SO	SB	CS	B	T	HT	WT	DOB	1st Yr	Resides
Ackerman, Scott	.239	43	142	17	34	6	1	2	18	14	26	3	4	R	R	6-2	195	4-23-79	1997	Oregon City, Ore.
Bradley, Milton	.200	9	25	6	5	2	0	1	2	4	4	2	2	S	R	6-0	170	4-15-78	1996	Long Beach, Calif.
Caracciolo, Anthony	.199	40	156	17	31	4	0	1	10	14	35	16	9	R	R	6-1	180	7-12-79	1997	Henderson, Nev.
DeJesus, Wilmer	.294	13	34	5	10	1	0	0	5	4	6	0	1	R	R	6-1	190	8-10-77	1995	Caracas, Venez.
Edge, Michael	.139	50	144	17	20	1	0	0	4	28	42	20	1	R	R	6-0	180	8-13-79	1997	Winnabow, N.C.
Forbes, Kevin	.234	22	77	8	18	3	3	1	10	8	26	1	2	R	R	5-11	200	2-17-76	1997	Marina, Calif.
Hernandez, Rafeal	.378	29	82	17	31	10	0	3	20	9	12	0	2	R	R	5-10	155	9-23-75	1995	San Pedro de Macoris, D.R.
Hodges, Scott	.235	57	196	26	46	13	2	2	23	23	47	2	2	L	R	6-0	185	12-26-78	1997	Lexington, Ky.
Hoshina, Koji	.322	19	59	8	19	0	0	0	5	4	7	1	0	S	R	5-10	165	10-19-79	1996	Tokyo, Japan
Leidens, Enrique	.317	19	41	6	13	5	0	0	3	3	9	2	2	R	R	5-11	165	2-6-78	1995	Aragua, Venez.
Myers, Tootie	.230	54	217	26	50	9	2	0	13	11	58	24	8	R	R	5-11	165	9-8-78	1997	Petal, Miss.
Pittman, Thomas	.152	15	46	7	7	2	0	0	2	6	9	0	0	R	R	6-4	270	11-2-79	1997	Garyville, La.
Quero, Pedro	.311	56	190	28	59	14	4	1	21	12	31	6	0	R	R	6-4	190	11-17-77	1995	Caracas, Venez.
Reding, Josh	.255	56	196	34	50	11	1	2	19	22	31	14	3	R	R	6-2	165	3-7-77	1997	Anaheim, Calif.
Rivera, Luis	.206	50	165	15	34	7	1	0	7	13	34	0	0	R	R	6-2	205	4-3-75	1997	Miami, Fla.
Tancred, Lachlan	.231	22	52	4	12	3	0	0	4	10	8	1	4	R	R	5-11	177	6-4-78	1997	Castle Hill, Australia

GAMES BY POSITION: C—Ackerman 29, DeJesus 11, Leidens 1, Rivera 22. **1B**—DeJesus 2, Hernandez 3, Hodges 18, Pittman 12, Quero 17, Rivera 15. **2B**—Caracciolo 8, Hoshina 8, Leidens 14, Myers 31, Reding 1. **3B**—Caracciolo 21, Hernandez 5, Hodges 35. **SS**—Caracciolo 5, Hoshina 9, Leidens 1, Reding 46. **OF**—Bradley 9, Edge 50, Forbes 22, Hernandez 21, Hodges 1, Hoshina 1, Myers 18, Quero 42, Tancred 21.

PITCHING	W	L	ERA	G	GS	CG	SV	IP	H	R	ER	BB	SO	B	T	HT	WT	DOB	1st Yr	Resides
Andujar, Jesse	1	2	7.99	17	0	0	2	24	27	25	21	30	18	R	R	6-1	175	7-23-79	1996	San Pedro de Macoris, D.R.
Arthurs, Shane	0	3	9.82	8	7	0	0	26	37	31	28	14	12	R	R	6-5	185	8-30-79	1997	Oklahoma City, Okla.
Baker, Jason	0	0	0.00	2	2	0	0	7	4	0	0	3	8	R	R	6-4	195	11-21-74	1993	Midland, Texas
Bridges, Donnie	0	2	6.30	5	2	0	0	10	14	9	7	5	6	R	R	6-4	195	12-10-78	1997	Purvis, Miss.
Daniels, Ronney	0	0	0.00	8	0	0	0	12	2	0	0	5	7	R	L	6-3	210	9-17-76	1995	Lake Wales, Fla.
Fraser, Joe	0	1	2.89	3	1	0	0	9	8	3	3	6	9	R	R	6-1	195	10-23-77	1996	Anaheim, Calif.
Fretwell, Joseph	2	0	3.94	8	0	0	1	16	19	8	7	2	14	S	R	6-4	175	5-24-77	1997	Oakland Park, Fla.
Julio, Jorge	5	6	3.58	15	8	0	1	55	57	25	22	21	42	R	R	6-1	190	3-3-79	1996	Caracas, Venez.
Lopez, Carlos	2	4	3.38	14	6	0	0	43	47	28	16	14	24	R	R	6-2	190	9-26-79	1996	Maracaibo, Venez.
Orta, Juan	0	4	3.10	19	0	0	4	29	27	12	10	7	12	R	R	6-2	175	4-13-78	1995	Maracay, Venez.
Perez, Julio	3	2	2.88	10	9	0	0	50	38	18	16	13	38	R	R	6-2	170	8-6-78	1997	Miami, Fla.
Rahilly, Michael	4	0	3.18	12	0	0	2	28	25	11	10	7	19	R	R	6-6	230	12-3-76	1996	Cape Coral, Fla.
Rivera, Marco	1	4	2.25	19	0	0	0	28	28	10	7	6	17	L	L	5-11	160	2-28-77	1996	Arecibo, P.R.
Rodriguez, Cristobol	3	3	1.65	13	10	0	1	55	45	15	10	16	61	R	R	6-2	190	1-27-79	1996	Chichiriviche, Venez.
Sadler, Carl	0	2	4.35	9	3	0	0	21	26	11	10	5	14	L	L	6-2	180	10-11-76	1996	Perry, Fla.
Sasaki, Junichi	1	0	0.52	11	0	0	2	17	15	2	1	3	13	R	R	6-4	185	8-7-74	1996	Chiba, Japan
Stowe, Chris	2	1	3.23	9	9	0	0	39	32	19	14	20	36	R	R	6-3	175	6-8-79	1997	Fredericksburg, Va.
Tetz, Kris	0	0	4.15	3	0	0	0	4	2	2	2	3	5	R	R	6-5	220	9-3-78	1997	Lodi, Calif.
Tucker, T.J.	1	0	1.93	3	2	0	0	5	5	1	1	1	11	R	R	6-3	245	8-20-78	1997	New Port Richey, Fla.

New York YANKEES

Manager: Joe Torre. **1997 Record:** 96-66, .593 (2nd, AL East)

BATTING	AVG	G	AB	R	H	2B	3B	HR	RBI	BB	SO	SB	CS	B	T	HT	WT	DOB	1st Yr	Resides
Boggs, Wade	.292	104	353	55	103	23	1	4	28	48	38	0	1	L	R	6-2	197	6-15-58	1976	Tampa, Fla.
Bush, Homer	.364	10	11	2	4	0	0	0	3	0	0	0	0	R	R	5-11	180	11-11-72	1991	East St. Louis, Ill.
Cruz, Ivan	.250	11	20	0	5	1	0	0	3	2	4	0	0	L	L	6-3	210	5-3-68	1989	Fajardo, P.R.
Curtis, Chad	.291	93	320	51	93	21	1	12	50	36	49	12	6	R	R	5-10	175	11-6-68	1989	Middleville, Mich.
2-team (22 Cleveland)	.284	115	349	59	99	22	1	15	55	43	59	12	6							
Duncan, Mariano	.244	50	172	16	42	8	0	1	13	6	39	2	1	R	R	6-0	185	3-13-63	1982	Miami, Fla.
Fielder, Cecil	.260	98	361	40	94	15	0	13	61	51	87	0	0	R	R	6-3	250	9-21-63	1982	Grosse Point Farms, Mich.
Figga, Mike	.000	2	4	0	0	0	0	0	0	0	3	0	0	R	R	6-0	200	7-31-70	1990	Tampa, Fla.
Fox, Andy	.226	22	31	13	7	1	0	0	1	7	9	2	1	L	R	6-4	185	1-12-71	1989	Sacramento, Calif.
Girardi, Joe	.264	112	398	38	105	23	1	1	50	26	53	2	3	R	R	5-11	195	10-14-64	1986	Lake Forest, Ill.
Hayes, Charlie	.258	100	353	39	91	16	0	11	53	40	66	3	2	R	R	6-0	224	5-29-65	1983	Hattiesburg, Miss.
Incaviglia, Pete	.250	5	16	1	4	0	0	0	0	0	3	0	0	R	R	6-1	225	4-2-64	1986	Collegeville, Texas
2-team (48 Baltimore)	.247	53	154	19	38	4	0	5	12	11	46	0	0							
Jeter, Derek	.291	159	654	116	190	31	7	10	70	74	125	23	12	R	R	6-3	175	6-26-74	1992	Kalamazoo, Mich.
Kelly, Pat	.242	67	120	25	29	6	1	2	10	14	37	8	1	R	R	6-0	180	10-14-67	1988	Bangor, Pa.
Martinez, Tino	.296	158	594	96	176	31	2	44	141	75	75	3	1	L	R	6-2	210	12-7-67	1989	Tampa, Fla.
O'Neill, Paul	.324	149	553	89	179	42	0	21	117	75	92	10	7	L	L	6-4	215	2-25-63	1981	Cincinnati, Ohio
Posada, Jorge	.250	60	188	29	47	12	0	6	25	30	33	1	2	S	R	6-0	167	8-17-71	1991	Rio Piedras, P.R.
Pose, Scott	.218	54	87	19	19	2	1	0	5	9	11	3	1	L	R	5-11	165	2-11-67	1989	West Des Moines, Iowa
Raines, Tim	.321	74	271	56	87	20	2	4	38	41	34	8	5	S	R	5-8	185	9-16-59	1977	Heathrow, Fla.
Sanchez, Rey	.312	38	138	21	43	12	0	1	15	5	21	0	4	R	R	5-10	180	10-5-67	1986	Charlotte Harbor , Fla.
Sojo, Luis	.307	77	215	27	66	6	1	2	25	16	14	3	1	R	R	5-11	174	1-3-66	1987	Barquisimeto, Venez.
Stanley, Mike	.287	28	87	16	25	8	0	3	12	15	22	0	0	R	R	6-0	190	6-25-63	1985	Oviedo, Fla.
2-team (97 Boston)	.297	125	347	61	103	25	0	16	65	54	72	0	1							
Strawberry, Darryl	.103	11	29	1	3	1	0	0	2	3	9	0	0	L	L	6-6	215	3-12-62	1980	Glendale, Calif.
Whiten, Mark	.265	69	215	34	57	11	0	5	24	30	47	4	2	S	R	6-3	215	11-25-66	1986	Pensacola, Fla.
Williams, Bernie	.328	129	509	107	167	35	6	21	100	73	80	15	8	S	R	6-2	196	9-13-68	1986	Vega Alta, P.R.

PITCHING	W	L	ERA	G	GS	CG	SV	IP	H	R	ER	BB	SO	B	T	HT	WT	DOB	1st Yr	Resides
Banks, Willie	3	0	1.93	5	1	0	0	14	9	3	3	6	8	R	R	6-1	202	2-27-69	1987	Jersey City, N.J.
Boehringer, Brian	3	2	2.63	34	0	0	0	48	39	16	14	32	53	S	R	6-2	180	1-8-69	1991	Fenton, Mo.
Borowski, Joe	0	1	9.00	1	0	0	0	2	2	2	2	4	2	R	R	6-2	225	5-4-71	1989	Bayonne, N.J.
Cone, David	12	6	2.82	29	29	1	0	195	155	67	61	86	222	L	R	6-1	190	1-2-63	1981	Leawood, Kan.
Gooden, Dwight	9	5	4.91	20	19	0	0	106	116	61	58	53	66	R	R	6-2	210	11-16-64	1982	St. Petersburg, Fla.
Irabu, Hideki	5	4	7.09	13	9	0	0	53	69	47	42	20	56	R	R	6-3	225	5-5-69	1997	Chiba, Japan
Lloyd, Graeme	1	1	3.31	46	0	0	1	49	55	24	18	20	26	L	L	6-7	230	4-9-67	1988	Gnarwarre, Australia
Mecir, Jim	0	4	5.88	25	0	0	0	34	36	23	22	10	25	R	R	6-1	195	5-16-70	1991	St. James, N.Y.
Mendoza, Ramiro	8	6	4.24	39	15	0	2	134	157	67	63	28	82	R	R	6-2	154	6-15-72	1992	Los Santos, Panama
Nelson, Jeff	3	7	2.86	77	0	0	2	79	53	32	25	37	81	R	R	6-8	225	11-17-66	1984	Baltimore, Md.
Pettitte, Andy	18	7	2.88	35	35	4	0	240	233	86	77	65	166	L	L	6-5	220	6-15-72	1991	Deer Park, Texas
Rios, Dan	0	0	19.29	2	0	0	0	2	9	5	5	2	1	R	R	6-2	208	11-11-72	1993	Hialeah, Fla.
Rivera, Mariano	6	4	1.88	66	0	0	43	72	65	17	15	20	68	R	R	6-4	168	11-29-69	1990	Puerto Caimito, Panama
Rogers, Kenny	6	7	5.65	31	22	1	0	145	161	100	91	62	78	L	L	6-1	205	11-10-64	1982	Arlington, Texas
Stanton, Mike	6	1	2.57	64	0	0	3	67	50	19	19	34	70	L	L	6-1	190	6-2-67	1987	Houston, Texas
Weathers, David	0	1	10.00	10	0	0	0	9	15	10	10	7	4	R	R	6-3	205	9-25-69	1988	Loretto, Tenn.
Wells, David	16	10	4.21	32	32	5	0	218	239	109	102	45	156	L	L	6-4	225	5-20-63	1982	Palm Harbor, Fla.

FIELDING

Catcher	PCT	G	PO	A	E	DP	PB
Figga	1.000	1	6	0	0	0	0
Girardi	.994	111	829	55	5	11	11
Posada	.992	60	367	23	3	3	8
Stanley	.982	15	53	3	1	0	2

First Base	PCT	G	PO	A	E	DP
Cruz	1.000	3	7	0	0	0
Fielder	1.000	8	59	6	0	8
Martinez	.994	150	1302	105	8	123
O'Neill	1.000	2	1	0	0	0
Sojo	1.000	2	4	0	0	1
Stanley	1.000	12	71	3	0	8

Second Base	PCT	G	PO	A	E	DP
Bush	.913	8	8	13	2	2
Duncan	.976	41	65	99	4	20
Fox	1.000	5	9	13	0	4
Hayes	1.000	5	2	1	0	1
Kelly	.981	48	63	92	3	26
Sanchez	.976	37	63	101	4	21
Sojo	.982	72	121	147	5	35

Third Base	PCT	G	PO	A	E	DP
Boggs	.978	76	42	140	4	15
Fox	1.000	11	5	13	0	1
Hayes	.947	98	65	168	13	19
Sojo	1.000	3	1	2	0	0

Shortstop	PCT	G	PO	A	E	DP
Fox	1.000	2	3	3	0	2
Jeter	.975	159	243	457	18	87
Sanchez	1.000	6	3	9	0	1
Sojo	1.000	4	5	4	0	3

Outfield	PCT	G	PO	A	E	DP
Cruz	1.000	1	1	0	0	0
Curtis	.978	92	168	6	4	1
Fox	.750	2	2	1	1	0
Incaviglia	.952	18	20	0	1	0
O'Neill	.984	146	292	7	5	0
Pose	1.000	45	44	2	0	1
Raines	.988	57	79	1	1	0
Strawberry	1.000	4	5	0	0	0
Whiten	.954	57	102	2	5	0
Williams	.993	128	270	2	2	1

DAVID SEELIG

Tino Martinez

FARM SYSTEM

Director of Player Development: Mark Newman

Class	Farm Team	League	W	L	Pct.	Finish*	Manager	First Yr
AAA	Columbus (Ohio) Clippers	International	79	63	.556	3rd (10)	Stump Merrill	1979
AA	Norwich (Conn.) Navigators	Eastern	73	69	.514	5th (10)	Trey Hillman	1995
#A	Tampa (Fla.) Yankees	Florida State	70	66	.515	5th (14)	Lee Mazzilli	1994
A	Greensboro (N.C.) Bats	South Atlantic	75	65	.536	6th (14)	Tom Nieto	1990
A	Oneonta (N.C.) Yankees	New York-Penn	49	25	.662	1st (14)	Joe Arnold	1967
R	Tampa (Fla.) Yankees	Gulf Coast	40	20	.667	2nd (15)	Ken Dominguez	1980

*Finish in overall standings (No. of teams in league) #Advanced level

ORGANIZATION LEADERS

MAJOR LEAGUERS

BATTING

*AVG	Bernie Williams	.328
R	Derek Jeter	116
H	Derek Jeter	190
TB	Tino Martinez	343
2B	Paul O'Neill	42
3B	Derek Jeter	7
HR	Tino Martinez	44
RBI	Tino Martinez	141
BB	Two tied at	75
SO	Derek Jeter	125
SB	Derek Jeter	23

PITCHING

W	Andy Pettitte	18
L	David Wells	10
#ERA	David Cone	2.82
G	Jeff Nelson	77
CG	David Wells	5
SV	Mariano Rivera	43
IP	Andy Pettitte	240
BB	David Cone	86
SO	David Cone	222

MEL BAILEY

Mariano Rivera

JOHN SPEAR

Ivan Cruz

MINOR LEAGUERS

BATTING

*AVG	Gabby Martinez, Nor./GCL Yankees	.322
R	Two tied at	96
H	Brian Buchanan, Columbus/Norwich	162
TB	Mike Lowell, Columbus/Norwich	278
2B	Ivan Cruz, Columbus	35
3B	Donzell McDonald, Tampa	8
HR	Two tied at	30
RBI	Ivan Cruz, Columbus	95
BB	Tom Wilson, Columbus/Norwich	87
SO	Rod Smith, Greensboro	148
SB	Vick Brown, Tampa	55

PITCHING

W	Two tied at	14
L	Two tied at	11
#ERA	Zach Day, Oneonta	2.15
G	Dale Polley, Columbus	62
CG	Julio Rangel, Greensboro	4
SV	Craig Dingman, Tampa/Greensboro	25
IP	Luis De los Santos, Nor./Tampa/G'boro	175
BB	Jason Coble, Greensboro	96
SO	Eric Milton, Norwich/Tampa	162

*Minimum 250 At-Bats #Minimum 75 Innings

TOP 10 PROSPECTS

MEL BAILEY

Ruben Rivera

How the Yankees Top 10 prospects, as judged by Baseball America prior to the 1997 season, fared in 1997:

Player, Pos.	Club (Class)	AVG	AB	R	H	2B	3B	HR	RBI	SB
1. *Ruben Rivera, of	San Diego	.250	20	2	5	1	0	0	1	2
	Las Vegas (AAA)	.250	48	6	12	5	1	1	6	1
	Rancho Cuca. (A)	.174	23	6	4	1	0	1	3	1
2. Ricky Ledee, of	Columbus (AAA)	.306	170	38	52	12	1	10	39	4
3. Jackson Melian, of	Tampa (R)	.263	213	32	56	11	2	3	36	9
7. Cristian Guzman, ss	Greensboro (A)	.273	495	68	135	21	4	4	52	23

		W	L	ERA	G	SV	IP	H	BB	SO
4. *Rafael Medina, rhp	Las Vegas (AAA)	4	5	7.56	13	0	67	90	39	50
	Rancho Cuca. (A)	2	0	2.00	3	0	18	13	5	14
5. Katsuhiro Maeda, rhp	Norwich (AA)	8	10	4.56	25	0	124	117	62	76
6. Eric Milton, lhp	Norwich (AA)	6	3	3.13	14	0	78	59	36	67
	Tampa (A)	8	3	3.09	14	0	93	78	14	95
8. Jason Coble, lhp	Greensboro (A)	2	11	4.94	24	0	120	93	96	99
9. Danny Rios, rhp	New York	0	0	19.29	2	0	2	9	2	1
	Columbus (AAA)	7	4	3.08	58	3	85	73	31	53
10. #Tony Armas Jr., rhp	Greensboro (A)	5	2	1.05	9	0	52	36	13	64
	Sarasota (A)	5	2	4.24	12	0	64	61	28	35

*Traded to Padres #Traded to Red Sox

COLUMBUS — Class AAA

INTERNATIONAL LEAGUE

BATTING	AVG	G	AB	R	H	2B	3B	HR	RBI	BB	SO	SB	CS	B	T	HT	WT	DOB	1st Yr	Resides
Barker, Tim	.279	65	208	36	58	10	2	5	30	32	41	14	6	R	R	6-0	175	6-30-68	1989	Salisbury, Md.
Bellinger, Clay	.274	111	416	55	114	31	3	12	59	34	74	10	4	R	R	6-3	195	11-18-68	1989	Oneonta, N.Y.
Brown, Ron	.182	10	33	4	6	0	1	0	1	2	3	1	0	R	R	6-3	185	1-17-70	1993	Tampa, Fla.
Buchanan, Brian	.279	18	61	8	17	1	0	4	7	4	11	2	1	R	R	6-4	220	7-21-73	1994	Clifton, Va.
Bush, Homer	.247	74	275	36	68	10	3	2	26	25	56	12	7	R	R	5-11	180	11-11-72	1991	East St. Louis, Ill.
Carpenter, Bubba	.280	85	271	47	76	12	4	6	39	48	46	4	8	L	L	6-1	185	7-23-68	1991	Winslow, Ark.
Cruz, Ivan	.300	116	417	69	125	35	1	24	95	65	78	4	5	L	L	6-3	210	5-3-68	1989	Fajardo, P.R.
Delvecchio, Nick	.179	31	95	16	17	1	1	4	10	17	39	1	0	L	R	6-5	203	1-23-70	1992	Natick, Mass.
Figga, Mike	.244	110	390	48	95	14	4	12	54	18	104	3	3	R	R	6-0	200	7-31-70	1990	Tampa, Fla.
Fox, Andy	.274	95	318	66	87	11	4	6	33	54	64	28	11	L	R	6-4	185	1-12-71	1989	Sacramento, Calif.
Hare, Shawn	.208	11	24	3	5	1	0	0	2	4	9	0	0	L	L	6-1	200	3-26-67	1989	Lakeland, Fla.
2-team (23 Toledo)	.188	34	85	12	16	5	0	1	8	22	34	0	0							
Howard, Matt	.312	122	478	90	149	28	7	6	67	54	33	22	7	R	R	5-10	170	9-22-67	1989	San Diego, Calif.
Incaviglia, Pete	.308	3	13	1	4	1	0	0	2	0	4	0	0	R	R	6-1	225	4-2-64	1986	Collegeville, Texas
Jimenez, D'Angelo	.143	2	7	1	1	0	0	0	1	0	1	0	0	S	R	6-0	160	12-21-77	1995	Santo Domingo, D.R.
Kelly, Pat	.341	11	44	8	15	4	0	2	6	4	6	1	1	R	R	6-0	180	10-14-67	1988	Bangor, Pa.
Ledee, Ricky	.306	43	170	38	52	12	1	10	39	21	49	4	0	L	L	6-2	160	11-22-73	1990	Salinas, P.R.
Long, R.D.	.184	19	49	6	9	2	0	2	6	2	18	2	0	S	R	6-1	183	4-2-71	1992	Penfield, N.Y.
Lowell, Mike	.276	57	210	36	58	13	1	15	45	23	34	2	4	R	R	6-4	195	2-24-74	1995	Coral Gables, Fla.
Luke, Matt	.228	87	337	42	77	19	3	8	45	29	64	0	3	L	L	6-5	225	2-26-71	1992	Brea, Calif.
Pose, Scott	.308	57	227	50	70	10	7	2	32	32	29	13	5	L	R	5-11	165	2-11-67	1989	West Des Moines, Iowa
Raines, Tim	.154	4	13	1	2	0	0	0	0	3	2	0	0	S	R	5-8	185	9-16-59	1977	Heathrow, Fla.
Ronan, Marc	.276	55	156	16	43	12	0	1	19	27	24	1	3	L	R	6-2	190	9-19-69	1990	Tallahassee, Fla.
Russo, Paul	.136	9	22	3	3	0	0	2	4	5	6	0	0	R	R	5-11	215	8-26-69	1990	Tampa, Fla.
Spencer, Shane	.241	125	452	78	109	34	4	30	86	71	105	0	2	R	R	5-11	182	2-20-72	1990	El Cajon, Calif.
Strawberry, Darryl	.289	11	38	8	11	3	0	6	19	8	10	0	0	L	L	6-6	215	3-12-62	1980	Glendale, Calif.
Troilo, Jason	.136	8	22	1	3	2	0	0	1	4	9	0	0	R	R	6-1	195	9-7-72	1994	Avondale, Pa.
Wilson, Tom	.000	1	3	0	0	0	0	0	0	1	0	0	0	R	R	6-3	185	12-19-70	1991	Yorba Linda, Calif.

PITCHING	W	L	ERA	G	GS	CG	SV	IP	H	R	ER	BB	SO	B	T	HT	WT	DOB	1st Yr	Resides
Alberro, Jose	0	1	3.38	1	1	1	0	8	5	4	3	1	6	R	R	6-2	190	6-29-69	1991	Bajadero, P.R.
Arocha, Rene	1	0	1.86	4	1	0	0	10	7	2	2	2	10	R	R	6-0	180	2-24-66	1992	Miami, Fla.
Banks, Willie	14	5	4.27	33	24	1	3	154	164	87	73	45	130	R	R	6-1	202	2-27-69	1987	Jersey City, N.J.
Bowen, Ryan	0	1	9.00	2	2	0	0	10	15	10	10	5	7	R	R	6-0	185	2-10-68	1987	Houston, Texas
Buddie, Mike	6	6	2.64	53	0	0	2	75	85	24	22	25	67	R	R	6-3	210	12-12-70	1992	Berea, Ohio
Converse, Jim	0	2	3.32	10	1	0	1	19	22	8	7	11	13	L	R	5-9	180	8-17-71	1990	Citrus Heights, Calif.
Edenfield, Ken	1	0	6.92	9	0	0	0	13	23	19	10	8	11	R	R	6-1	165	3-18-67	1990	Knoxville, Tenn.
Eiland, Dave	4	2	6.64	13	11	0	0	62	80	47	46	14	43	R	R	6-3	205	7-5-66	1987	Dade City, Fla.
Gardiner, Mike	5	4	3.92	14	13	1	0	85	83	40	37	24	65	R	R	6-0	200	10-19-65	1987	Canton, Mass.
Gooden, Dwight	1	1	3.75	2	2	0	0	12	7	5	5	4	10	R	R	6-2	210	11-16-64	1982	St. Petersburg, Fla.
Irabu, Hideki	2	0	1.67	4	4	1	0	27	19	7	5	5	28	R	R	6-3	225	5-5-69	1997	Chiba, Japan
Jerzembeck, Mike	7	5	3.59	20	20	2	0	130	125	55	52	37	118	R	R	6-1	185	5-18-72	1993	Queens, N.Y.
Lankford, Frank	7	4	2.69	15	13	1	0	94	84	33	28	22	40	R	R	6-2	190	3-26-71	1993	Atlanta, Ga.
Lomon, Kevin	1	1	6.28	3	3	0	0	14	21	12	10	7	14	R	R	6-1	195	11-20-71	1991	Cameron, Okla.
Mecir, Jim	1	1	1.00	24	0	0	11	27	14	4	3	6	34	R	R	6-1	195	5-16-70	1991	St. James, N.Y.
Mendoza, Ramiro	0	0	5.68	1	1	0	0	6	7	6	4	1	4	R	R	6-2	154	6-15-72	1992	Los Santos, Panama
Pavlas, Dave	1	3	4.62	26	0	0	12	25	33	14	13	4	34	R	R	6-7	195	8-12-62	1985	Phoenix, Ariz.
Polley, Dale	2	2	3.75	62	0	0	2	48	47	20	20	20	49	R	L	6-0	165	8-9-65	1987	Frankfort, Ky.
Reyes, Carlos	0	0	18.00	1	1	0	0	2	5	4	4	0	2	S	R	6-1	190	4-19-69	1991	Macon, Ga.
Ricken, Ray	11	7	5.54	26	26	0	0	153	172	104	94	81	99	R	R	6-5	225	8-11-73	1994	Warren, Mich.
Rios, Dan	7	4	3.08	58	0	0	3	85	73	37	29	31	53	R	R	6-2	208	11-11-72	1993	Hialeah, Fla.
Rose, Scott	2	2	3.70	26	0	0	11	24	24	11	10	6	13	R	R	6-3	200	5-12-70	1990	Tampa, Fla.
Rumer, Tim	4	7	6.16	17	12	1	0	69	79	54	47	41	46	L	L	6-3	205	8-8-69	1990	Princeton, N.J.
Urso, Sal	0	3	4.73	24	2	0	0	46	59	29	24	19	44	R	L	5-11	195	1-19-72	1990	Tampa, Fla.
Weathers, David	2	2	3.19	5	5	1	0	37	35	18	13	7	35	R	R	6-3	205	9-25-69	1988	Loretto, Tenn.

FIELDING

Catcher	PCT	G	PO	A	E	DP	PB
Figga	.986	102	706	62	11	6	12
Ronan	.990	48	249	36	3	3	5
Russo	.000	1	0	0	0	0	1
Troilo	1.000	4	26	6	0	1	1
Wilson	1.000	1	8	0	0	0	0

First Base	PCT	G	PO	A	E	DP
Bellinger	1.000	9	65	2	0	7
Cruz	.992	114	974	83	8	89
Hare	.944	5	30	4	2	4
Luke	.989	18	157	15	2	14
Ronan	1.000	3	18	2	0	4

Second Base	PCT	G	PO	A	E	DP
Barker	.985	31	54	74	2	16
Bellinger	1.000	3	8	8	0	1
Bush	.978	74	153	253	9	62
Fox	.982	22	46	66	2	13
Howard	1.000	5	6	13	0	2
Kelly	1.000	10	15	39	0	6

Third Base	PCT	G	PO	A	E	DP
Bellinger	.918	48	28	84	10	9
Fox	.934	49	26	101	9	6
Long	.700	8	2	5	3	1
Lowell	.954	43	31	73	5	5
Russo	1.000	1	1	2	0	0
Spencer	1.000	2	1	2	0	0
Troilo	.750	2	1	2	1	0

Shortstop	PCT	G	PO	A	E	DP
Barker	.778	3	2	5	2	2
Bellinger	.945	11	13	39	3	2
Fox	.964	17	30	51	3	9
Howard	.989	110	154	293	5	69
Jimenez	.833	2	2	8	2	0
Lowell	.833	3	5	10	3	3

Outfield	PCT	G	PO	A	E	DP
Banks	.000	1	0	0	1	0
Barker	1.000	19	40	3	0	1
Bellinger	.975	37	73	4	2	0
Brown	1.000	10	16	0	0	0
Buchanan	.947	12	17	1	1	0
Carpenter	.994	79	164	6	1	3
Delvecchio	1.000	3	3	0	0	0
Fox	1.000	6	9	0	0	0
Hare	1.000	4	7	1	0	0
Incaviglia	1.000	3	7	1	0	0
Ledee	.966	34	56	0	2	0
Luke	.983	63	106	8	2	0
Pose	.992	56	113	6	1	2
Raines	1.000	4	4	0	0	0
Spencer	.980	109	188	5	4	0

NORWICH — Class AA

EASTERN LEAGUE

BATTING	AVG	G	AB	R	H	2B	3B	HR	RBI	BB	SO	SB	CS	B	T	HT	WT	DOB	1st Yr	Resides
Ashby, Chris	.249	136	457	92	114	20	1	24	82	80	95	10	7	R	R	6-3	185	12-15-74	1993	Boca Raton, Fla.

JOHN KLEIN

New York's Derek Jeter

DIAMOND IMAGES

Norwich's Luke Wilcox

BATTING	AVG	G	AB	R	H	2B	3B	HR	RBI	BB	SO	SB	CS	B	T	HT	WT	DOB	1st Yr	Resides
Bierek, Kurt	.271	133	473	77	128	32	2	18	78	56	89	4	4	L	R	6-4	200	9-13-72	1993	Hillsboro, Ore.
Brown, Randy	.217	19	60	10	13	2	0	3	8	9	22	2	1	R	R	5-11	160	5-1-70	1989	Houston, Texas
2-team (97 Trenton)	.250	116	396	61	99	13	4	11	57	47	124	11	8							
Brown, Ron	.287	100	362	47	104	17	3	5	50	35	59	5	7	R	R	6-3	185	1-17-70	1993	Tampa, Fla.
Buchanan, Brian	.309	116	470	75	145	25	2	10	69	32	85	11	9	R	R	6-4	220	7-21-73	1994	Clifton, Va.
Dennis, Les	.333	10	30	4	10	1	0	0	2	5	11	1	1	R	R	6-0	175	6-3-73	1995	West Linn, Ore.
Donato, Dan	.275	96	349	44	96	16	1	5	43	26	44	7	4	L	R	6-1	205	11-15-72	1995	Dedham, Mass.
Dukart, Derek	.344	9	32	4	11	2	0	0	5	3	4	0	0	L	R	6-4	205	8-17-71	1994	Lincoln, Neb.
Fithian, Grant	.281	79	253	38	71	16	1	8	51	41	52	1	1	R	R	6-0	192	11-20-71	1994	Rockwall, Texas
Gomez, Rudy	.300	102	393	65	118	18	7	5	52	61	64	11	7	R	R	5-11	180	9-14-74	1996	Miami, Fla.
Hawkins, Kraig	.261	51	188	36	49	6	1	0	16	26	37	12	2	R	R	6-2	170	12-4-71	1992	Lake Charles, La.
Hinds, Rob	.244	51	119	15	29	4	1	0	12	12	31	1	1	R	R	6-1	180	4-26-71	1992	Cerritos, Calif.
Lobaton, Jose	.193	68	197	16	38	6	0	1	15	12	60	2	3	R	R	5-11	154	3-29-74	1992	Acarigua, Venez.
Long, R.D.	.281	34	89	18	25	5	1	2	17	13	21	5	3	S	R	6-1	183	4-2-71	1992	Penfield, N.Y.
Lowell, Mike	.344	78	285	60	98	17	0	15	47	48	30	2	1	R	R	6-4	195	2-24-74	1995	Coral Gables, Fla.
Martinez, Gabby	.321	77	312	49	100	12	5	6	54	11	44	21	6	R	R	6-2	170	1-7-74	1992	Santurce, P.R.
Raines, Tim	.286	2	7	0	2	1	0	0	2	0	2	0	0	S	R	5-8	185	9-16-59	1977	Heathrow, Fla.
Ramirez, Angel	.000	2	1	0	0	0	0	0	0	0	1	0	0	R	R	5-10	166	1-24-73	1991	Azua, D.R.
Smith, Sloan	.200	2	5	1	1	0	0	0	1	2	2	0	0	S	R	6-4	215	11-29-72	1993	Evanston, Ill.
Strawberry, Darryl	.000	1	2	0	0	0	0	0	0	0	1	0	0	L	L	6-6	215	3-12-62	1980	Glendale, Calif.
Wilcox, Luke	.277	74	300	45	83	13	1	6	34	18	36	13	3	L	R	6-4	190	11-15-73	1995	St. John's, Mich.
Wilson, Tom	.296	124	419	88	124	21	4	21	80	86	126	1	4	R	R	6-3	185	12-19-70	1991	Yorba Linda, Calif.

PITCHING	W	L	ERA	G	GS	CG	SV	IP	H	R	ER	BB	SO	B	T	HT	WT	DOB	1st Yr	Resides
Beverlin, Jason	1	0	7.78	25	0	0	0	42	50	38	36	24	42	L	R	6-5	230	11-27-73	1994	Waynesville, N.C.
Buddie, Mike	0	0	0.00	1	0	0	0	1	0	0	0	0	3	R	R	6-3	210	12-12-70	1992	Berea, Ohio
Croghan, Andy	2	1	5.72	42	1	0	4	68	72	48	43	36	85	R	R	6-5	205	10-26-69	1991	Yorba Linda, Calif.
Cumberland, Chris	11	10	4.02	25	25	3	0	155	188	100	69	59	81	R	L	6-1	185	1-15-73	1993	Safety Harbor, Fla.
De los Santos, Luis	1	1	2.52	4	4	0	0	25	23	9	7	7	15	R	R	6-2	187	11-1-77	1995	San Pedro de Macoris, D.R.
De la Cruz, Francisco	0	1	3.24	2	2	0	0	8	8	3	3	7	0	R	R	6-2	175	7-9-73	1991	La Romana, D.R.
Ford, Ben	4	3	4.22	28	0	0	1	43	35	28	20	19	38	R	R	6-7	200	8-15-75	1994	Cedar Rapids, Iowa
Gooden, Dwight	3	0	3.00	3	3	0	0	18	13	6	6	5	14	R	R	6-2	210	11-16-64	1982	St. Petersburg, Fla.
Henthorne, Kevin	2	1	3.31	33	6	0	2	73	72	32	27	14	64	S	R	6-2	182	12-9-69	1994	La Crosse, Wis.
Hubbard, Mark	0	0	15.43	2	0	0	0	2	6	4	4	1	0	L	L	6-2	190	2-2-70	1991	Dover, Fla.
Irabu, Hideki	1	1	4.50	2	2	0	0	10	13	5	5	0	9	R	R	6-3	225	5-5-69	1997	Chiba, Japan
Jerzembeck, Mike	2	1	1.71	8	8	0	0	42	21	10	8	16	42	R	R	6-1	185	5-18-72	1993	Queens, N.Y.
Lankford, Frank	4	2	2.90	11	11	2	0	68	58	28	22	15	39	R	R	6-2	190	3-26-71	1993	Atlanta, Ga.
Lomon, Kevin	9	7	3.21	18	18	2	0	115	104	51	41	50	117	R	R	6-1	195	11-20-71	1991	Cameron, Okla.
Maeda, Katsuhiro	8	10	4.56	25	21	1	0	124	117	75	63	62	76	R	R	6-2	215	6-23-71	1996	Los Angeles, Calif.
Milton, Eric	6	3	3.13	14	14	1	0	78	59	29	27	36	67	L	L	6-3	200	8-4-75	1996	Bellefonte, Pa.
Mitchell, Larry	9	9	3.49	57	0	0	0	95	98	45	37	37	99	R	R	6-1	200	10-16-71	1992	Charlottesville, Va.
Resz, Greg	5	4	4.70	25	13	0	0	90	94	59	47	43	75	L	R	6-5	215	12-25-71	1993	Springfield, Mo.
Ricken, Ray	0	2	6.75	2	2	0	0	11	12	8	8	5	13	R	R	6-5	225	8-11-73	1994	Warren, Mich.
Rose, Scott	0	2	2.67	21	0	0	4	30	34	17	9	8	20	R	R	6-3	200	5-12-70	1990	Tampa, Fla.
Schlomann, Brett	1	4	7.85	10	10	0	0	47	66	43	41	17	36	R	R	6-1	185	7-31-74	1994	Collinsville, Okla.
Tessmer, Jay	3	6	5.31	55	0	0	17	63	78	41	37	24	51	R	R	6-3	190	12-26-72	1995	Meadville, Pa.
Urso, Sal	1	1	1.26	7	2	0	1	14	14	2	2	5	13	R	L	5-11	195	1-19-72	1990	Tampa, Fla.

FIELDING

Catcher	PCT	G	PO	A	E	DP	PB
Fithian	.988	45	298	42	4	0	7
Wilson	.991	103	694	80	7	5	13

First Base	PCT	G	PO	A	E	DP
Ashby	.983	117	994	75	19	92
Bierek	.991	27	209	17	2	14
Donato	1.000	1	14	0	0	1
Fithian	1.000	2	2	0	0	0
Wilson	1.000	2	13	1	0	1

Second Base	PCT	G	PO	A	E	DP
Gomez	.979	92	177	244	9	48
Hinds	.922	21	28	31	5	4
Lobaton	.983	15	19	40	1	10
Long	.893	14	22	28	6	8
Martinez	.929	19	34	57	7	17

Third Base	PCT	G	PO	A	E	DP
Bierek	.800	3	2	6	2	0
Randy Brown	.800	1	0	4	1	0
Donato	.937	63	37	127	11	6
Dukart	.875	7	6	8	2	0
Fithian	.500	2	0	1	1	0
Gomez	.950	9	3	16	1	1
Long	.000	1	0	0	0	0
Lowell	.923	65	48	120	14	10
Wilson	.750	1	0	3	1	0

Shortstop	PCT	G	PO	A	E	DP
Randy Brown	.987	18	30	45	1	8
Dennis	.917	8	13	31	4	7
Donato	.000	1	0	0	0	0
Dukart	.833	2	2	3	1	0
Gomez	.933	5	4	10	1	1
Lobaton	.955	51	68	100	8	26
Long	.898	16	16	37	6	6
Lowell	.957	7	9	13	1	2
Martinez	.956	53	65	152	10	33

Outfield	PCT	G	PO	A	E	DP
Bierek	.952	93	157	3	8	0
Ron Brown	.960	96	160	7	7	0
Buchanan	.962	114	192	11	8	1
Donato	.000	1	0	0	0	0
Hawkins	.983	50	112	1	2	0
Henthorne	1.000	1	1	0	0	0
Hinds	.923	9	12	0	1	0
Lobaton	.000	1	0	0	0	0
Raines	1.000	2	2	0	0	0
Ramirez	1.000	2	3	0	0	0
Rose	.000	1	0	0	0	0
Smith	.800	2	4	0	1	0
Strawberry	.000	1	0	0	0	0
Wilcox	.980	72	141	6	3	1

TAMPA — Class A

FLORIDA STATE LEAGUE

BATTING	AVG	G	AB	R	H	2B	3B	HR	RBI	BB	SO	SB	CS	B	T	HT	WT	DOB	1st Yr	Resides
August, Brian	.209	23	67	5	14	4	0	1	11	5	14	0	2	R	R	6-2	185	3-7-76	1997	Newark, Del.
Brown, Ron	.059	5	17	1	1	0	1	0	3	2	4	1	1	R	R	6-3	185	1-17-70	1993	Tampa, Fla.
Brown, Vick	.292	123	463	77	135	19	4	2	42	38	78	55	13	R	R	6-1	165	11-14-72	1993	Cypress, Fla.
Cruz, Alain	.111	10	27	3	3	2	0	0	2	2	13	0	0	R	R	5-11	185	7-3-75	1996	Hialeah, Fla.
Dennis, Les	.260	85	177	24	46	4	0	0	17	16	36	1	6	R	R	6-0	175	6-3-73	1995	West Linn, Ore.
Dukart, Derek	.273	37	110	10	30	2	0	1	10	8	9	1	1	L	R	6-4	205	8-17-71	1994	Lincoln, Neb.
Emmons, Scott	.178	51	118	19	21	5	0	2	14	9	28	0	0	R	R	6-4	205	12-25-73	1995	Norco, Calif.
Guzman, Cristian	.286	4	14	4	4	0	0	0	1	1	1	0	1	S	R	6-0	150	3-21-78	1995	Santo Domingo, D.R.
Hawkins, Kraig	.300	9	30	2	9	1	0	0	4	8	2	3	2	R	R	6-2	170	12-4-71	1992	Lake Charles, La.
Jimenez, D'Angelo	.281	94	352	52	99	14	6	6	48	50	50	8	14	S	R	6-0	160	12-21-77	1995	Santo Domingo, D.R.
Kane, Ryan	.224	95	303	36	68	8	2	5	20	37	66	1	1	R	R	6-4	210	1-25-74	1995	Acton, Mass.
Keel, David	.267	92	300	50	80	15	0	16	48	39	57	9	3	L	R	6-3	205	7-23-72	1992	Toney, Ala.
Kofler, Eric	.232	39	151	12	35	8	1	2	22	5	25	0	4	L	L	6-1	170	2-11-76	1994	Palm Harbor, Fla.
Lobaton, Jose	.130	7	23	0	3	0	0	0	5	2	6	0	0	R	R	5-11	154	3-29-74	1992	Acarigua, Venez.
McDonald, Donzell	.296	77	297	69	88	23	8	3	23	48	75	39	18	S	R	6-0	165	2-20-75	1995	Tampa, Fla.
Morenz, Shea	.236	117	403	43	95	14	1	7	44	18	101	2	3	L	R	6-2	205	1-22-74	1995	San Angelo, Texas
Raines, Tim	.343	11	35	8	12	0	0	2	5	11	1	1	0	S	R	5-8	185	9-16-59	1977	Heathrow, Fla.
Rowson, James	.060	25	50	2	3	2	0	0	4	4	29	2	1	R	R	5-11	190	9-12-76	1995	Mt. Vernon, N.Y.
Samuel, Cody	.232	92	323	39	75	15	3	16	61	32	121	2	0	R	R	6-1	210	4-10-74	1992	Redondo Beach, Calif.
Shumpert, Derek	.260	44	169	24	44	6	1	1	6	20	49	6	8	R	R	6-2	185	9-30-75	1993	St. Louis, Mo.
Smith, Sloan	.220	65	186	32	41	9	1	4	23	33	64	2	4	S	R	6-4	215	11-29-72	1993	Evanston, Ill.
Strawberry, Darryl	.438	4	16	2	7	1	0	0	4	1	3	0	0	L	L	6-6	215	3-12-62	1980	Glendale, Calif.
Torres, Jaime	.294	115	408	48	120	28	0	10	56	28	30	0	2	R	R	6-0	176	3-12-73	1992	Aragua, Venez.
Troilo, Jason	.333	3	9	0	3	0	0	0	0	1	5	0	0	R	R	6-1	195	9-7-72	1994	Avondale, Pa.
Twombley, Dennis	.333	4	9	1	3	0	0	0	0	0	4	1	0	R	R	6-2	218	6-8-75	1996	San Diego, Calif.
Wilcox, Luke	.300	12	40	7	12	4	0	0	4	7	6	1	1	L	R	6-4	190	11-15-73	1995	St. John's, Mich.
Yedo, Carlos	.242	131	446	51	108	26	1	13	54	46	126	1	0	L	L	6-4	210	2-24-74	1994	Miami, Fla.

GAMES BY POSITION: C—Cruz 1, Emmons 49, Rowson 1, Torres 104, Troilo 3, Twombley 4. **1B**—Dukart 3, Emmons 1, Samuel 12, Torres 2, Yedo 130. **2B**—August 6, R. Brown 5, V. Brown 122, Dennis 8, Lobaton 2. **3B**—August 13, Cruz 6, Dennis 28, Dukart 24, Kane 91, Lobaton 5. **SS**—August 3, V. Brown 1, Dennis 43, Guzman 4, Jimenez 93. **OF**—Hawkins 9, Keel 53, Kofler 39, McDonald 77, Morenz 116, Raines 7, Rowson 18, Shumpert 43, Smith 59, Wilcox 12.

PITCHING	W	L	ERA	G	GS	CG	SV	IP	H	R	ER	BB	SO	B	T	HT	WT	DOB	1st Yr	Resides
Armas, Tony	3	1	3.33	9	9	0	0	46	43	23	17	16	26	R	R	6-4	175	4-29-78	1994	Puerto Piritu, Venez.
Becker, Tom	2	1	5.02	25	0	0	0	43	45	29	24	26	26	R	R	6-3	205	1-13-75	1994	Adelaide, Australia
Beverlin, Jason	1	3	4.79	7	6	0	0	41	37	26	22	13	24	L	R	6-5	230	11-27-73	1994	Waynesville, N.C.
Boehringer, Brian	0	1	5.00	3	3	0	0	9	9	5	5	5	8	S	R	6-2	180	1-8-69	1991	Fenton, Mo.
Bowen, Ryan	0	2	4.02	4	4	0	0	16	17	7	7	5	15	R	R	6-0	185	2-10-68	1987	Houston, Texas
Brown, Charlie	4	3	4.76	28	0	0	0	40	44	24	21	25	26	R	R	6-3	178	9-13-73	1992	Fort Pierce, Fla.
De los Santos, Luis	5	0	2.34	10	10	0	0	62	49	19	16	8	39	R	R	6-2	187	11-1-77	1995	San Pedro de Macoris, D.R.
De la Cruz, Francisco	0	2	6.87	8	8	0	0	37	39	30	28	29	22	R	R	6-2	175	7-9-73	1991	La Romana, D.R.
Dingman, Craig	0	4	5.24	19	0	0	6	22	15	14	13	14	26	R	R	6-4	190	3-12-74	1994	Wichita, Kan.
Dudeck, Dave	0	0	3.00	5	0	0	0	9	9	3	3	2	5	R	R	6-2	210	8-24-72	1994	Bridgewater, N.J.
Eiland, Dave	1	0	3.75	3	3	0	0	12	11	5	5	0	11	R	R	6-3	205	7-5-66	1987	Dade City, Fla.
Einerston, Darrell	5	4	2.15	45	0	0	6	71	63	24	17	19	55	R	R	6-2	190	9-4-72	1995	Tampa, Fla.
Ford, Ben	4	0	1.93	32	0	0	18	37	27	8	8	14	37	R	R	6-7	200	8-15-75	1994	Cedar Rapids, Iowa
Irabu, Hideki	1	0	0.00	2	2	0	0	9	4	0	0	0	12	R	R	6-3	225	5-5-69	1997	Chiba, Japan
Lail, Denny	3	5	3.90	44	1	0	1	62	67	38	27	23	40	R	R	6-0	185	9-10-74	1995	Taylorsville, N.C.
Mairena, Oswaldo	0	0	4.15	3	0	0	0	4	6	2	2	0	6	L	L	5-11	165	7-30-75	1996	Chinandega, Nicaragua
Milton, Eric	8	3	3.09	14	14	1	0	93	78	35	32	14	95	L	L	6-3	200	8-4-75	1996	Bellefonte, Pa.
Phillips, Ben	8	11	4.41	25	25	0	0	137	135	83	67	79	97	R	R	6-3	195	7-28-75	1996	Sheridan, Wyo.
Randolph, Stephen	4	7	3.87	34	13	1	1	95	74	55	41	63	108	L	L	6-3	185	5-1-74	1995	Austin, Texas
Resz, Greg	1	0	3.18	1	1	0	0	6	5	2	2	2	5	L	R	6-5	215	12-25-71	1993	Springfield, Mo.
Robbins, Jake	1	1	5.06	3	3	0	0	16	18	14	9	10	5	R	R	6-5	195	5-23-76	1994	Charlotte, N.C.
Schlomann, Brett	8	4	3.65	19	18	1	0	118	129	55	48	29	86	R	R	6-1	185	7-31-74	1994	Collinsville, Okla.
Shelby, Anthony	4	3	2.60	48	0	0	2	69	68	23	20	16	57	L	L	6-3	200	12-11-73	1993	Sarasota, Fla.
Smith, Sloan	0	0	0.00	5	0	0	0	8	4	0	0	5	3	S	R	6-4	215	11-29-72	1993	Evanston, Ill.
Spence, Cam	1	2	2.37	15	5	0	0	49	42	16	13	10	31	R	R	6-2	195	10-11-74	1996	Lithonia, Ga.
St. Pierre, Bob	3	5	3.86	27	3	0	1	51	66	27	22	18	37	R	R	6-1	190	4-11-74	1995	Huntington, Md.
Verdin, Cesar	3	4	5.40	8	8	0	0	43	41	27	26	13	37	L	L	6-3	210	11-11-76	1995	San Diego, Calif.

GREENSBORO — Class A

SOUTH ATLANTIC LEAGUE

BATTING	AVG	G	AB	R	H	2B	3B	HR	RBI	BB	SO	SB	CS	B	T	HT	WT	DOB	1st Yr	Resides
Antrim, Pat	.225	68	173	23	39	3	0	0	13	7	40	3	2	S	R	6-2	170	8-18-73	1995	Dana Point, Calif.
Aylor, Brian	.160	61	181	25	29	7	4	9	28	16	90	3	0	L	L	6-2	200	4-6-74	1996	Midwest City, Okla.
Baksh, Ray	.167	4	6	1	1	0	0	0	2	0	2	0	0	R	R	6-3	210	2-6-75	1997	Monroe, N.Y.
Butler, Garrett	.194	82	237	31	46	14	1	1	14	11	58	11	5	S	R	6-2	165	5-20-76	1994	Miami, Fla.
Emmons, Scott	.286	3	7	1	2	1	0	0	0	1	1	0	0	R	R	6-4	205	12-25-73	1995	Norco, Calif.
Guzman, Cristian	.273	124	495	68	135	21	4	4	52	17	105	23	12	S	R	6-0	150	3-21-78	1995	Santo Domingo, D.R.
Huffman, Ryan	.125	4	8	0	1	0	0	0	0	2	3	0	1	R	R	6-2	215	8-7-73	1996	Cleburne, Texas
Johnson, Nick	.273	127	433	77	118	23	1	16	75	76	99	16	3	L	L	6-3	195	9-19-78	1996	Sacramento, Calif.
Keech, Erik	.250	26	72	5	18	1	0	2	9	3	15	0	0	L	R	6-2	195	9-7-74	1995	Sarasota, Fla.
Kofler, Eric	.275	73	262	23	72	17	2	5	39	7	54	3	2	L	L	6-1	170	2-11-76	1994	Palm Harbor, Fla.
Leon, Donny	.254	137	516	45	131	32	1	12	74	15	106	6	4	S	R	6-2	180	5-7-76	1995	Ponce, P.R.
Munson, Mike	.000	1	0	0	0	0	0	0	0	0	0	0	0	R	R	5-9	200	7-29-75	1995	Canton, Ohio
Pinto, Rene	.286	35	105	20	30	9	1	2	10	3	34	0	0	R	R	6-0	195	7-17-77	1994	Palo Negra, Venez.
Rowson, James	.286	8	21	1	6	1	0	0	2	5	8	0	0	R	R	5-11	190	9-12-76	1995	Mt. Vernon, N.Y.
Saffer, Jeff	.206	90	267	40	55	13	1	12	39	35	79	0	3	R	R	6-4	220	6-30-75	1995	Tucson, Ariz.
Seabol, Scott	.265	48	136	11	36	12	2	2	15	9	26	3	1	R	R	6-4	200	5-17-75	1996	McKeesport, Pa.
Shumpert, Derek	.301	86	322	49	97	22	6	6	39	27	91	12	6	R	R	6-2	185	9-30-75	1993	St. Louis, Mo.
Smith, Rod	.248	137	528	96	131	25	6	13	50	69	148	54	20	S	R	6-0	185	9-2-75	1994	Lexington, Ky.
Staubach, Jeff	.000	1	4	0	0	0	0	0	0	0	1	0	0	R	R	6-0	215	12-28-74	1997	Dallas, Texas
Thames, Marcus	.313	4	16	2	5	1	0	0	2	0	3	1	0	R	R	6-2	205	3-6-77	1997	Louisville, Miss.
Twombley, Dennis	.194	15	36	4	7	0	0	1	2	3	12	0	0	R	R	6-2	218	6-8-75	1996	San Diego, Calif.
Valencia, Victor	.221	107	353	42	78	12	1	13	43	43	116	2	1	R	R	6-2	185	5-30-77	1994	Maracay, Venez.
Velazquez, Jose	.280	137	489	77	137	19	3	9	62	42	71	10	8	L	L	6-3	205	8-24-75	1994	Guayama, P.R.

GAMES BY POSITION: C—Emmons 3, Keech 12, Munson 1, Pinto 28, Twombley 8, Valencia 100. **1B**—Baksh 4, Huffman 1, Johnson 126, Saffer 7, Velazquez 14. **2B**—Antrim 13, Smith 134. **3B**—Antrim 5, Leon 136, Seabol 10. **SS**—Antrim 24, Guzman 122, Seabol 2. **OF**—Antrim 12, Aylor 59, Butler 74, Huffman 1, Keech 1, Kofler 62, Rowson 8, Saffer 12, Seabol 17, Shumpert 86, Thames 4, Velazquez 115.

PITCHING	W	L	ERA	G	GS	CG	SV	IP	H	R	ER	BB	SO	B	T	HT	WT	DOB	1st Yr	Resides
Armas, Tony	5	2	1.05	9	9	2	0	52	36	13	6	13	64	R	R	6-4	175	4-29-78	1994	Puerto Piritu, Venez.
Brand, Scott	2	0	3.43	8	0	0	1	21	21	8	8	5	22	R	R	6-3	200	1-1-76	1995	Lubbock, Texas
Coble, Jason	2	11	4.94	24	23	1	0	120	93	84	66	96	99	R	L	6-3	185	2-28-78	1996	Fayetteville, Tenn.
De los Santos, Luis	5	6	3.05	14	14	1	0	89	91	45	30	13	62	R	R	6-2	187	11-1-77	1995	San Pedro de Macoris, D.R.
De la Cruz, Francisco	5	4	3.30	13	13	1	0	85	71	41	31	36	75	R	R	6-2	175	7-9-73	1991	La Romana, D.R.
Dingman, Craig	2	0	1.91	30	0	0	19	33	19	7	7	12	41	R	R	6-4	190	3-12-74	1994	Wichita, Kan.
Dudeck, Dave	3	4	3.60	25	1	0	0	50	48	29	20	16	43	R	R	6-2	210	8-24-72	1994	Bridgewater, N.J.
Ellison, Jason	1	0	4.85	9	0	0	1	13	16	10	7	3	11	R	R	6-4	180	7-24-75	1996	Buffalo, Texas
Krall, Eric	2	2	3.86	15	1	0	0	35	37	23	15	14	26	L	L	6-4	215	2-27-74	1996	Apopka, Fla.
Mairena, Oswaldo	6	1	2.54	49	0	0	8	60	43	24	17	16	75	L	L	5-11	165	7-30-75	1996	Chinandega, Nicaragua
Mota, Daniel	2	0	1.82	20	0	0	1	30	17	6	6	11	30	R	R	6-0	170	10-9-75	1994	Santo Domingo, D.R.
Obando, Omar	5	7	4.65	45	0	0	7	60	61	36	31	26	41	R	R	6-2	180	3-23-77	1996	Chinandega, Nicaragua
Olivier, Rich	8	5	4.13	35	13	0	2	107	111	61	49	51	79	R	R	6-0	155	11-22-74	1992	Santo Domingo, D.R.
Parotte, Frisco	1	1	4.19	18	0	0	2	39	48	27	18	14	28	R	R	6-3	180	9-10-75	1994	Levittown, P.R.
Rangel, Julio	12	9	3.57	26	26	4	0	164	147	80	65	49	122	R	R	6-3	190	9-28-75	1994	Panama City, Panama
Robbins, Jake	6	4	5.77	20	19	0	0	101	114	81	65	55	72	R	R	6-5	195	5-23-76	1994	Charlotte, N.C.
Schaffner, Eric	5	2	3.45	28	7	0	0	78	73	35	30	23	73	R	R	6-4	190	10-19-74	1994	Keizer, Ore.
Spence, Cam	2	2	3.38	8	7	0	0	48	43	23	18	10	35	R	R	6-2	195	10-11-74	1996	Lithonia, Ga.
Taylor, Brien	1	4	14.33	8	7	0	0	27	31	47	43	52	20	L	L	6-4	215	12-26-71	1991	Beaufort, N.C.
Verdin, Cesar	0	1	1.80	1	1	0	0	5	5	3	1	1	8	L	L	6-3	210	11-11-76	1995	San Diego, Calif.

ONEONTA — Short-Season Class A

NEW YORK-PENN LEAGUE

BATTING	AVG	G	AB	R	H	2B	3B	HR	RBI	BB	SO	SB	CS	B	T	HT	WT	DOB	1st Yr	Resides
Bronikowski, Bill	.000	1	2	0	0	0	0	0	0	0	2	0	0	R	R	6-3	200	2-5-75	1997	Toledo, Ohio
Butler, Allen	.280	68	214	40	60	11	4	3	30	46	57	4	3	L	R	6-3	190	1-22-75	1996	Clinchport, Va.
Carey, Orlando	.248	71	238	40	59	4	4	2	17	23	59	20	6	R	R	6-1	185	2-25-76	1996	Gallatin, Tenn.
Chambliss, Russ	.132	29	53	4	7	1	0	0	2	4	24	4	0	L	R	6-3	190	6-12-75	1997	Briarcliff Manor, N.Y.
Darjean, John	.291	58	189	30	55	4	3	0	13	8	36	27	11	R	R	6-1	175	4-3-76	1997	Baton Rouge, La.
Halper, Jason	.063	11	16	0	1	0	0	0	3	0	4	0	0	S	R	5-10	175	5-5-75	1997	Livingston, N.J.
Harrell, Ken	.167	11	24	1	4	1	0	0	2	2	8	5	0	R	R	6-0	193	1-29-75	1997	Alamogordo, N.M.
Jones, Aaron	.241	63	166	25	40	8	2	0	17	43	40	4	6	L	L	6-4	205	9-7-75	1997	Newport, Mich.
Kane, Kevin	.125	4	8	1	1	0	0	0	0	1	4	0	1	R	R	5-10	160	11-27-73	1996	Tampa, Fla.
Keech, Erik	.270	12	37	3	10	1	0	0	5	0	9	0	0	L	R	6-2	195	9-7-74	1995	Sarasota, Fla.
Kidd, Scott	.263	74	281	38	74	14	3	5	45	18	62	7	2	R	R	5-10	180	1-15-74	1997	Cupertino, Calif.
Maxwell, Vernon	.196	50	148	14	29	6	2	0	22	13	49	7	2	R	R	6-3	195	10-22-76	1996	Midwest City, Okla.
Mirizzi, Marc	.261	74	245	40	64	5	1	1	33	38	36	12	7	S	R	6-1	190	6-17-75	1997	Los Gatos, Calif.
Morris, Jeremy	.280	68	239	44	67	19	1	2	28	29	47	10	3	R	R	6-3	225	10-7-74	1993	Quincy, Fla.
Phillips, Blaine	.109	31	46	6	5	0	1	0	1	5	12	1	0	R	R	6-1	200	6-28-73	1996	Sheridan, Wyo.
Pinto, Rene	.289	52	187	31	54	8	2	4	29	11	37	1	3	R	R	6-0	195	7-17-77	1994	Palo Negra, Venez.
Purkiss, Matt	.277	65	213	31	59	14	0	6	41	21	53	0	2	L	R	6-3	230	7-15-75	1997	Visalia, Calif.
Rowson, James	.195	12	41	8	8	2	2	0	4	4	17	1	0	R	R	5-11	190	9-12-76	1995	Mt. Vernon, N.Y.
Twombley, Dennis	.243	15	37	3	9	1	0	1	7	10	12	0	1	R	R	6-2	218	6-8-75	1996	San Diego, Calif.

GAMES BY POSITION: C—Harrell 4, Keech 12, Phillips 29, Pinto 36, Twombley 15. **1B**—Jones 26, Morris 1, Purkiss 54. **2B**—Kane 4, Kidd 73. **3B**—Butler 66, Morris 15. **SS**—Butler 1, Kidd 1, Mirizzi 74. **OF**—Butler 1, Carey 70, Chambliss 19, Darjean 47, Halper 7, Harrell 5, Jones 2, Maxwell 43, Morris 51, Purkiss 1, Rowson.

PITCHING	W	L	ERA	G	GS	CG	SV	IP	H	R	ER	BB	SO	B	T	HT	WT	DOB	1st Yr	Resides
Bradley, Ryan	3	1	1.35	14	0	0	1	27	22	5	4	5	22	R	R	6-4	220	10-26-75	1997	Chino Hills, Calif.
Brand, Scott	4	3	7.32	10	2	0	0	20	24	17	16	8	18	R	R	6-3	200	1-1-76	1995	Lubbock, Texas
Carpenter, Justin	3	1	4.60	24	0	0	0	29	32	17	15	20	36	R	R	6-4	215	1-18-77	1997	Prague, Okla.

PITCHING	W	L	ERA	G	GS	CG	SV	IP	H	R	ER	BB	SO	B	T	HT	WT	DOB	1st Yr	Resides
Choate, Randy	5	1	1.73	10	10	0	0	62	49	12	12	12	61	L	L	6-3	180	9-5-75	1997	Tallahassee, Fla.
Day, Zach	7	2	2.15	14	14	0	0	92	82	26	22	23	92	R	R	6-4	185	6-15-78	1996	West Harrison, Ind.
Ellison, Jason	0	1	1.74	11	0	0	0	21	19	6	4	4	19	R	R	6-4	180	7-24-75	1996	Buffalo, Texas
Flores, Randy	4	4	3.25	13	13	2	0	75	64	32	27	23	70	L	L	6-0	185	7-31-75	1997	Pico Rivera, Calif.
Henry, Jason	5	4	2.56	12	12	0	0	63	61	27	18	23	57	R	R	6-7	260	11-9-76	1997	Gurnee, Ill.
Koch, Jack	0	0	0.00	1	0	0	0	2	1	0	0	1	2	R	R	6-3	220	8-29-76	1997	Kissimmee, Fla.
McBride, Jason	0	0	0.00	2	0	0	0	3	1	1	0	3	2	R	R	6-1	175	2-10-76	1996	Pace, Fla.
Mota, Daniel	1	0	2.22	27	0	0	17	28	21	8	7	16	40	R	R	6-0	170	10-9-75	1994	Santo Domingo, D.R.
Schnautz, Brad	0	1	9.39	4	0	0	0	8	16	14	8	2	9	L	L	6-4	190	4-6-76	1996	Bryan, Texas
Smith, Andy	3	2	2.93	26	0	0	1	40	30	13	13	13	55	L	R	6-5	245	9-13-75	1997	Defiance, Ohio
Tisone, Jason	1	0	6.39	18	0	0	2	31	42	27	22	13	27	R	R	6-2	210	10-1-74	1997	Levittown, Pa.
Wallace, Chris	2	1	3.63	10	2	0	0	22	22	13	9	8	13	R	R	6-2	210	5-5-76	1997	Marion, Ohio
White, Samuel	5	2	4.47	17	8	0	0	52	52	32	26	30	43	R	R	6-3	198	2-6-74	1997	Lumberton, Texas
Wiggins, Scott	6	2	2.56	13	13	1	0	63	58	25	18	22	44	L	L	6-3	205	3-24-76	1997	Newport, Ky.

TAMPA — Rookie

GULF COAST LEAGUE

BATTING	AVG	G	AB	R	H	2B	3B	HR	RBI	BB	SO	SB	CS	B	T	HT	WT	DOB	1st Yr	Resides
Almonte, Erick	.283	52	180	32	51	4	4	3	31	21	27	8	2	R	R	6-2	180	2-1-78	1996	Santo Domingo, D.R.
August, Brian	.277	17	47	8	13	2	2	3	7	5	7	0	1	R	R	6-2	185	3-7-76	1997	Newark, Del.
Beltres, Manuel	.223	29	103	13	23	1	0	0	11	13	27	9	4	S	R	5-11	140	7-15-77	1995	Santo Domingo, D.R.
Brown, Richard	.367	10	30	7	11	3	0	0	3	5	6	0	0	L	L	6-1	190	4-28-77	1996	Plantation, Fla.
Canaguacan, Oscar	.313	7	16	3	5	1	0	0	2	2	3	1	0	S	R	5-11	160	5-8-80	1997	Aragua, Venez.
Candelaria, Vidal	.263	35	114	12	30	3	0	0	16	8	28	3	0	L	R	6-0	170	5-9-78	1996	Manati, P.R.
Cruz, Alain	.000	1	1	0	0	0	0	0	0	0	1	0	0	R	R	5-11	185	7-3-75	1996	Hialeah, Fla.
Fuentes, Omar	.211	32	90	8	19	5	0	0	11	11	16	0	1	R	R	6-1	175	4-6-80	1996	Maracay, Venez.
Ledee, Ricky	.333	7	21	3	7	1	0	0	2	2	4	0	0	L	L	6-2	160	11-22-73	1990	Salinas, P.R.
Martinez, Gabby	.400	2	5	3	2	0	0	1	2	1	0	2	0	R	R	6-2	170	1-7-74	1992	Santurce, P.R.
Mateo, Victor	.269	26	93	18	25	3	0	0	10	6	14	4	0	S	R	6-0	170	11-23-76	1995	Santo Domingo, D.R.
Meier, Bob	.400	5	5	1	2	0	0	0	0	1	2	0	0	R	R	6-0	170	9-5-78	1996	Cinnaminson, N.J.
Melian, Jackson	.263	57	213	32	56	11	2	3	36	20	52	9	1	R	R	6-2	185	1-7-80	1996	Barcelona, Venez.
Olivares, Teuris	.261	38	153	33	40	4	7	0	17	14	40	7	2	R	R	6-0	164	12-15-78	1996	San Francisco de Macoris, D.R.
Ortiz, Miguel	.228	36	123	19	28	6	1	1	12	5	31	4	2	R	R	6-1	175	2-19-79	1996	Villa de Cura, Venez.
Preciado, Victor	.251	54	187	21	47	9	5	3	29	15	37	6	1	S	R	6-4	205	9-3-76	1995	David Chirriqui, Panama
Raines, Tim	.250	1	4	0	1	0	0	0	2	1	1	0	0	S	R	5-8	185	9-16-59	1977	Heathrow, Fla.
Rodriguez, John	.299	46	157	31	47	10	2	3	23	30	32	7	0	L	L	6-0	185	1-20-78	1997	New York, N.Y.
Thames, Marcus	.344	57	195	51	67	17	4	7	36	16	26	6	4	R	R	6-2	205	3-6-77	1997	Louisville, Miss.
Valdez, Angel	.260	41	100	19	26	1	2	1	10	13	21	6	0	R	R	6-2	178	5-22-78	1996	Santo Domingo, D.R.
Washington, Dion	.303	52	165	35	50	10	1	3	33	36	39	2	0	R	R	6-3	225	12-21-76	1997	Las Vegas, Nev.

GAMES BY POSITION: C—Candelaria 35, Cruz 1, Fuentes 31, Meier 3. **1B**—Preciado 54, Valdez 11. **2B**—August 12, Beltres 3, Canaguacan 3, Martinez 2, Mateo 19, Ortiz 27. **3B**—Almonte 51, August 3, Beltres 2, Ortiz 7. **SS**—August 1, Beltres 20, Canaguacan 2, Mateo 2, Olivares 38, Ortiz 1. **OF**—Brown 5, Ledee 1, Melian 53, Raines 1, Rodriguez 36, Thames 55, Valdez 26, Washington 27.

PITCHING	W	L	ERA	G	GS	CG	SV	IP	H	R	ER	BB	SO	B	T	HT	WT	DOB	1st Yr	Resides
Acosta, Alberto	1	1	3.28	9	3	0	0	25	24	14	9	10	11	R	R	6-4	170	8-25-77	1996	Colon, Panama
Blevins, Jeremy	5	3	2.43	11	9	0	0	56	50	27	15	23	46	R	R	6-3	195	10-5-77	1995	Bluff City, Tenn.
Boehringer, Brian	0	0	0.00	1	1	0	0	2	1	0	0	0	2	S	R	6-2	180	1-8-69	1991	Fenton, Mo.
Converse, Jim	0	0	1.93	3	3	0	0	5	5	1	1	1	8	L	R	5-9	180	8-17-71	1990	Citrus Heights, Calif.
Coriolan, Roberto	4	0	3.50	10	0	0	0	18	19	14	7	10	10	R	R	6-0	190	3-27-77	1994	Santo Domingo, D.R.
Cremer, Richard	4	2	3.96	10	9	1	0	39	30	24	17	25	47	L	L	6-4	180	4-19-77	1996	West Frankfort, Ill.
Cubillan, Darwin	0	0	0.00	1	1	0	0	2	1	0	0	1	2	R	R	6-2	170	11-15-74	1994	Maracay, Venez.
Eavenson, Samuel	1	1	6.75	10	0	0	0	13	18	10	10	8	11	R	R	6-3	185	3-6-78	1997	Loganville, Ga.
Eiland, Dave	0	1	9.00	2	1	0	0	7	12	8	7	0	5	R	R	6-3	205	7-5-66	1987	Dade City, Fla.
Hollins, Jessie	2	0	12.00	4	1	0	0	6	13	8	8	8	5	R	R	6-3	200	1-27-70	1989	Willis, Texas
Klein, Cody	1	0	0.51	10	0	0	1	18	13	1	1	9	17	L	L	6-2	205	2-4-79	1997	Andrews, Texas
Knowles, Michael	2	2	4.85	9	8	0	0	39	41	30	21	14	24	R	R	6-5	210	7-15-79	1997	Daytona Beach, Fla.
Koch, Jack	0	0	16.20	2	0	0	0	2	6	3	3	2	0	R	R	6-3	220	8-29-76	1997	Kissimmee, Fla.
Langston, David	2	1	3.60	11	0	0	0	20	19	11	8	9	11	R	R	6-5	215	12-11-78	1997	Ringgold, Ga.
Mejia, Luis	1	2	1.14	13	0	0	2	24	8	4	3	9	31	R	R	6-2	155	3-16-77	1995	Santo Domingo, D.R.
Padua, Geraldo	8	0	2.92	11	8	1	0	62	46	24	20	8	36	R	R	6-2	165	2-9-77	1995	Santo Domingo, D.R.
Paraqueima, Jesus	0	1	8.44	3	0	0	0	5	14	11	5	0	2	R	R	6-4	185	2-24-78	1996	El Tigre, Venez.
Reith, Brian	4	2	2.86	12	11	1	0	63	70	28	20	14	40	R	R	6-5	190	2-28-78	1996	Fort Wayne, Ind.
Rodriguez, Jorge	0	3	4.91	17	0	0	4	26	31	19	14	8	12	R	R	6-2	170	10-11-76	1996	Penuelas, P.R.
Valle, Yoiset	1	1	0.45	11	0	0	0	20	8	1	1	4	20	L	L	6-3	200	6-9-78	1996	Miami Lakes, Fla.
Verdin, Cesar	1	0	1.50	3	3	0	0	12	5	2	2	2	17	L	L	6-3	210	11-11-76	1995	San Diego, Calif.
Williams, Bradford	1	0	5.75	11	2	0	0	20	16	19	13	19	27	L	L	6-5	205	11-26-76	1995	Tucson, Ariz.
Wood, Stanton	2	0	2.45	17	0	0	8	26	18	7	7	7	21	R	R	6-2	185	12-5-76	1997	Hawthorne, Calif.

New York METS

Manager: Bobby Valentine. **1997 Record:** 88-74, .543 (3rd, NL East)

BATTING	AVG	G	AB	R	H	2B	3B	HR	RBI	BB	SO	SB	CS	B	T	HT	WT	DOB	1st Yr	Resides
Alexander, Manny	.248	54	149	26	37	9	3	2	15	9	38	11	0	R	R	5-10	165	3-20-71	1988	San Pedro de Macoris, D.R.
Alfonzo, Edgardo	.315	151	518	84	163	27	2	10	72	63	56	11	6	R	R	5-11	185	8-11-73	1991	Caracas, Venez.
Baerga, Carlos	.281	133	467	53	131	25	1	9	52	20	54	2	6	S	R	5-11	200	11-4-68	1986	West Lake, Ohio
Bieser, Steve	.246	47	69	16	17	3	0	0	4	7	20	2	3	L	R	5-10	170	8-4-67	1989	St. Genevieve, Mo.
Castillo, Alberto	.203	35	59	3	12	1	0	0	7	9	16	0	1	R	R	6-0	184	2-10-70	1987	Las Matas, D.R.
Everett, Carl	.248	142	443	58	110	28	3	14	57	32	102	17	9	S	R	6-0	190	6-3-71	1990	Tampa, Fla.
Franco, Matt	.276	112	163	21	45	5	0	5	21	13	23	1	0	L	R	6-3	195	8-19-69	1987	Thousand Oaks, Calif.
Gilbert, Shawn	.136	29	22	3	3	0	0	1	1	1	8	1	0	R	R	5-9	170	3-12-65	1987	Glendale, Ariz.
Gilkey, Bernard	.249	145	518	85	129	31	1	18	78	70	111	7	11	R	R	6-0	170	9-24-66	1985	St. Louis, Mo.
Hardtke, Jason	.268	30	56	9	15	2	0	2	8	4	6	1	1	S	R	5-10	175	9-15-71	1990	San Jose, Calif.
Hundley, Todd	.273	132	417	78	114	21	2	30	86	83	116	2	3	S	R	5-11	185	5-27-69	1987	Port St. Lucie, Fla.
Huskey, Butch	.287	142	471	61	135	26	2	24	81	25	84	8	5	R	R	6-3	240	11-10-71	1989	Lawton, Okla.
Johnson, Lance	.309	72	265	43	82	10	6	1	24	33	21	15	10	L	L	5-11	160	7-6-63	1984	Mobile, Ala.
Lopez, Luis	.270	78	178	19	48	12	1	1	19	12	42	2	4	S	R	5-11	175	9-4-70	1988	Cidra, P.R.
McRae, Brian	.248	45	145	23	36	5	2	5	15	13	22	3	4	S	R	6-0	185	8-27-67	1985	Bradenton, Fla.
2-team (92 Chicago)	.242	153	562	86	136	32	7	11	43	65	84	17	10							
Mendoza, Carlos	.250	15	12	6	3	0	0	0	1	4	2	0	0	L	L	5-11	160	11-4-74	1994	Bolivar, Venez.
Morgan, Kevin	.000	1	1	0	0	0	0	0	0	0	0	0	0	R	R	6-1	170	3-3-70	1991	Duson, La.
Ochoa, Alex	.244	113	238	31	58	14	1	3	22	18	32	3	4	R	R	6-0	185	3-29-72	1991	Miami Lakes, Fla.
Olerud, John	.294	154	524	90	154	34	1	22	102	85	67	0	0	L	L	6-5	218	8-5-68	1989	Bellevue, Wash.
Ordonez, Rey	.216	120	356	35	77	5	3	1	33	18	36	11	5	R	R	5-9	159	1-11-72	1993	Miami, Fla.
Petagine, Roberto	.067	12	15	2	1	0	0	0	2	3	6	0	0	L	L	6-1	172	6-2-71	1990	Caracas, Venez.
Pratt, Todd	.283	39	106	12	30	6	0	2	19	13	32	0	1	R	R	6-3	195	2-9-67	1985	Boca Raton, Fla.
Thurman, Gary	.167	11	6	0	1	0	0	0	0	0	0	0	1	R	R	5-10	180	11-12-64	1983	Indianapolis, Ind.
Tomberlin, Andy	.286	6	7	0	2	0	0	0	0	1	3	0	0	L	L	5-11	160	11-7-66	1986	Monroe, N.C.

PITCHING	W	L	ERA	G	GS	CG	SV	IP	H	R	ER	BB	SO	B	T	HT	WT	DOB	1st Yr	Resides
Acevedo, Juan	3	1	3.59	25	2	0	0	48	52	24	19	22	33	R	R	6-2	195	5-5-70	1992	Carpentersville, Ill.
Bohanon, Brian	6	4	3.82	19	14	0	0	94	95	49	40	34	66	L	L	6-3	220	8-1-68	1987	Houston, Texas
Borland, Toby	0	1	6.08	13	0	0	1	13	11	9	9	14	7	R	R	6-7	175	5-29-69	1989	Quitman, La.
Clark, Mark	8	7	4.25	23	22	1	0	142	158	74	67	47	72	R	R	6-5	225	5-12-68	1988	Bath, Ill.
Crawford, Joe	4	3	3.30	19	2	0	0	46	36	18	17	13	25	L	L	6-3	225	5-2-70	1991	Hillsboro, Ohio
Franco, John	5	3	2.55	59	0	0	36	60	49	18	17	20	53	L	L	5-10	185	9-17-60	1981	Brooklyn, N.Y.
Harnisch, Pete	0	1	8.06	6	5	0	0	26	35	24	23	11	12	R	R	6-0	207	9-23-66	1987	Commack, N.Y.
Isringhausen, Jason	2	2	7.58	6	6	0	0	30	40	27	25	22	25	R	R	6-3	196	9-7-72	1992	Brighton, Ill.
Jones, Bobby	15	9	3.63	30	30	2	0	193	177	88	78	63	125	R	R	6-4	205	2-10-70	1991	Kerman, Calif.
Jordan, Ricardo	1	2	5.33	22	0	0	0	27	31	17	16	15	19	L	L	5-11	165	6-27-70	1990	Delray Beach, Fla.
Kashiwada, Takashi	3	1	4.31	35	0	0	0	31	35	15	15	18	19	L	L	5-11	165	5-14-71	1997	Tokyo, Japan
Lidle, Cory	7	2	3.53	54	2	0	2	82	86	38	32	20	54	R	R	6-0	175	3-22-72	1991	West Covina, Calif.
Manuel, Barry	0	1	5.26	19	0	0	0	26	35	18	15	13	21	R	R	5-11	185	8-12-65	1987	Mamou, La.
McMichael, Greg	7	10	2.98	73	0	0	7	88	73	34	29	27	81	R	R	6-3	215	12-1-66	1988	Alpharetta, Ga.
Mlicki, Dave	8	12	4.00	32	32	1	0	194	194	89	86	76	157	R	R	6-4	190	6-8-68	1990	Galloway, Ohio
Perez, Yorkis	0	1	8.31	9	0	0	0	9	15	8	8	4	7	L	L	6-0	160	9-30-67	1983	Haina, D.R.
Reed, Rick	13	9	2.89	33	31	2	0	208	186	76	67	31	113	R	R	6-0	200	8-16-64	1986	Huntington, W.Va.
Reynoso, Armando	6	3	4.53	16	16	1	0	91	95	47	46	29	47	R	R	6-0	196	5-1-66	1989	Jalisco, Mexico
Rojas, Mel	0	2	5.13	23	0	0	2	26	24	17	15	6	32	R	R	5-11	165	12-10-66	1986	Haina, D.R.
2-team (54 Chicago)	0	6	4.64	77	0	0	15	85	78	47	44	36	93							
Trlicek, Ricky	0	0	8.00	9	0	0	0	9	10	9	8	5	4	R	R	6-3	200	4-26-69	1987	Houston, Texas
Wendell, Turk	0	0	4.96	13	0	0	1	16	15	10	9	14	10	S	R	6-2	175	5-19-67	1988	Dalton, Mass.
2-team (52 Chicago)	3	5	4.36	65	0	0	5	76	68	42	37	53	64							

FIELDING

Catcher	PCT	G	PO	A	E	DP	PB
Bieser	1.000	2	2	0	0	0	0
Castillo	.987	34	142	8	2	0	2
Hundley	.987	122	678	54	10	6	7
Pratt	.990	36	186	22	2	3	1

First Base	PCT	G	PO	A	E	DP
Franco	1.000	13	50	4	0	5
Huskey	.990	22	182	10	2	19
Olerud	.995	146	1292	120	7	125
Petagine	1.000	6	9	3	0	0

Second Base	PCT	G	PO	A	E	DP
Alexander	.979	31	28	64	2	17
Alfonzo	1.000	3	4	6	0	0
Baerga	.978	131	244	371	14	88
Gilbert	.875	8	6	1	1	1
Hardtke	.981	21	25	26	1	7
Lopez	.961	20	34	40	3	8

Third Base	PCT	G	PO	A	E	DP
Alfonzo	.967	143	82	269	12	29
Franco	.937	39	11	48	4	6
Gilbert	1.000	3	1	3	0	0
Hardtke	.000	1	0	0	0	0
Huskey	.848	15	17	22	7	3
Lopez	.944	4	4	13	1	1
Morgan	1.000	1	0	1	0	0

Shortstop	PCT	G	PO	A	E	DP
Alexander	.980	26	31	65	2	10
Alfonzo	1.000	12	12	15	0	3
Gilbert	1.000	6	4	4	0	0
Lopez	.966	45	41	103	5	21
Ordonez	.983	118	171	355	9	71

Outfield	PCT	G	PO	A	E	DP
Bieser	1.000	21	30	2	0	0
Everett	.971	128	226	8	7	3
Franco	.000	1	0	0	0	0
Gilbert	.000	1	0	0	0	0
Gilkey	.989	136	251	17	3	2
Huskey	.968	92	178	6	6	1
Johnson	.975	66	152	4	4	2
McRae	.957	41	65	1	3	0
Mendoza	1.000	3	5	0	0	0
Ochoa	.982	88	104	7	2	1
Petagine	1.000	1	1	0	0	0
Thurman	1.000	7	4	0	0	0
Tomberlin	1.000	2	2	0	0	0

FARM SYSTEM

Director of Player Development: Jack Zduriencik

Class	Farm Team	League	W	L	Pct.	Finish*	Manager(s)	First Yr
AAA	Norfolk (Va.) Tides	International	75	67	.528	5th (10)	Rick Dempsey	1969
AA	Binghamton (N.Y.) Mets	Eastern	66	76	.465	8th (10)	Rick Sweet	1992
#A	St. Lucie (Fla.) Mets	Florida State	54	81	.400	14th (14)	John Gibbons	1988
A	Capital City (S.C.) Bombers	South Atlantic	77	63	.550	2nd (14)	Doug Mansolino/John Stephenson	1983
A	Pittsfield (N.Y.) Mets	New York-Penn	42	32	.568	4th (14)	Doug Davis	1989
#R	Kingsport (Tenn.) Mets	Appalachian	37	31	.544	5th (10)	Ken Berry	1980
R	Port St. Lucie (Fla.) Mets	Gulf Coast	42	18	.700	+1st (15)	Mickey Brantley/Doug Flynn	1988

*Finish in overall standings (No. of teams in league) #Advanced level +Won league championship

ORGANIZATION LEADERS

MAJOR LEAGUERS

BATTING

*AVG	Edgardo Alfonzo	.315
R	John Olerud	90
H	Edgardo Alfonzo	163
TB	John Olerud	256
2B	John Olerud	34
3B	Lance Johnson	6
HR	Todd Hundley	30
RBI	John Olerud	102
BB	John Olerud	85
SO	Todd Hundley	116
SB	Carl Everett	17

PITCHING

W	Bobby Jones	15
L	Dave Mlicki	12
#ERA	Rick Reed	2.89
G	Greg McMichael	73
CG	Two tied at	2
SV	John Franco	36
IP	Rick Reed	208
BB	Dave Mlicki	76
SO	Dave Mlicki	157

MORRIS FOSTOFF

Todd Hundley

KEN BABBITT

Fletcher Bates

MINOR LEAGUERS

BATTING

*AVG	Carlos Mendoza, Nor./Binghamton	.350
R	Fletcher Bates, Binghamton/St. Lucie	93
H	Daniel Ramirez, Capital City	146
TB	Two tied at	267
2B	Fletcher Bates, Binghamton/St. Lucie	33
3B	Fletcher Bates, Binghamton/St. Lucie	13
HR	Matt Raleigh, Binghamton	37
RBI	Roberto Petagine, Norfolk	100
BB	Roberto Petagine, Norolk	85
SO	Matt Raleigh, Binghamton	169
SB	Daniel Ramirez, Capital City	51

PITCHING

W	Jesus Sanchez, Binghamton	13
L	Brett Herbison, Capital City	14
#ERA	Scott Comer, Pittsfield	1.74
G	Rich Turrentine, Binghamton	61
CG	Kyle Kessel, Capital City	5
SV	Mike Welch, Norfolk	20
IP	Kyle Kessel, Capital City	169
BB	Two tied at	81
SO	Jesus Sanchez, Binghamton	176

*Minimum 250 At-Bats #Minimum 75 Innings

TOP 10 PROSPECTS

JOHN KLEIN

Jay Payton

How the Mets Top 10 prospects, as judged by Baseball America prior to the 1997 season, fared in 1997:

Player, Pos.	Club (Class)	AVG	AB	R	H	2B	3B	HR	RBI	SB
1. Jay Payton, of		Injured—Did not play								
2. Terrence Long, of	St. Lucie (A)	.251	470	52	118	29	7	8	61	24
6. Corey Erickson, 3b-2b	St. Lucie (A)	.201	134	10	27	3	0	3	11	0
	Capital City (A)	.214	173	18	37	11	2	2	16	3
8. Preston Wilson, of	Binghamton (AA)	.286	259	37	74	12	1	19	47	7
	St. Lucie (A)	.245	245	32	60	12	1	11	48	3
9. Pee Wee Lopez, c	St. Lucie (A)	.248	375	40	93	19	0	3	30	3

Player, Pos.	Club (Class)	W	L	ERA	G	SV	IP	H	BB	SO
3. Arnold Gooch, rhp	Binghamton (AA)	10	12	5.09	27	0	161	179	76	98
4. Grant Roberts, rhp	Capital City (A)	11	3	2.36	22	0	130	98	44	122
5. Derek Wallace, rhp	Norfolk (AAA)	0	1	9.00	1	0	1	2	1	0
7. Brett Herbison, rhp	Capital City (A)	7	14	3.99	28	0	160	166	63	146
10. Octavio Dotel, rhp	Binghamton (AA)	3	4	5.98	12	0	56	66	38	40
	St. Lucie (A)	5	2	2.52	9	0	50	44	23	39
	Port St. Lucie (R)	0	0	0.96	3	1	9	9	2	7

NORFOLK — Class AAA

INTERNATIONAL LEAGUE

BATTING	AVG	G	AB	R	H	2B	3B	HR	RBI	BB	SO	SB	CS	B	T	HT	WT	DOB	1st Yr	Resides
Agbayani, Benny	.310	127	468	90	145	24	2	11	51	67	106	29	14	R	R	5-11	175	12-28-71	1993	Aiea, Hawaii
Azuaje, Jesus	.306	22	49	11	15	3	0	1	6	7	8	1	0	R	R	5-10	170	1-16-73	1992	Bolivar, Venez.
Bieser, Steve	.164	41	122	6	20	5	0	0	4	9	20	4	3	L	R	5-10	170	8-4-67	1989	St. Genevieve, Mo.
Castillo, Alberto	.217	34	83	4	18	1	0	1	8	17	16	1	0	R	R	6-0	184	2-10-70	1987	Las Matas, D.R.
Chamberlain, Wes	.274	97	336	33	92	16	2	7	50	24	58	7	2	R	R	6-2	219	4-13-66	1987	Chicago, Ill.
Diaz, Alex	.077	7	26	0	2	1	0	0	1	2	3	0	0	S	R	5-11	180	10-5-68	1987	San Sebastian, P.R.
Espinosa, Ramon	.338	27	77	7	26	3	1	0	8	2	10	2	1	R	R	6-0	175	2-7-72	1990	San Pedro de Macoris, D.R.
Franco, Matt	.269	7	26	5	7	2	0	0	0	2	2	0	0	L	R	6-3	195	8-19-69	1987	Thousand Oaks, Calif.
Geisler, Phil	.256	109	336	28	86	24	0	9	57	24	90	2	5	L	L	6-3	200	10-23-69	1991	Springfield, Ore.
Gilbert, Shawn	.264	78	288	53	76	13	1	8	33	43	64	16	4	R	R	5-9	170	3-12-65	1987	Glendale, Ariz.
Greene, Charlie	.206	76	238	27	49	7	0	8	28	9	54	1	0	R	R	6-1	177	1-23-71	1991	Miami, Fla.
Hardtke, Jason	.276	97	388	46	107	23	3	11	45	40	54	3	6	S	R	5-10	175	9-15-71	1990	San Jose, Calif.
Jaime, Angel	.192	16	26	3	5	1	0	0	5	0	7	0	1	R	R	6-0	160	3-6-73	1992	Santo Domingo, D.R.
Lopez, Jose	.333	2	6	1	2	0	0	0	0	0	2	0	0	R	R	6-1	175	8-4-75	1994	Santiago, D.R.
Lopez, Luis	.330	48	203	32	67	12	1	4	19	9	29	2	6	S	R	5-11	175	9-4-70	1988	Cidra, P.R.
Martin, James	.250	37	104	10	26	4	2	3	18	8	44	5	2	L	R	6-1	210	12-10-70	1992	Eufaula, Okla.
McClain, Scott	.280	127	429	71	120	29	2	21	64	64	93	1	3	R	R	6-3	209	5-19-72	1990	Glendale, Ariz.
Mendoza, Carlos	.143	10	35	3	5	0	1	0	0	3	4	1	0	L	L	5-11	160	11-4-74	1994	Bolivar, Venez.
Moore, Michael	.241	34	83	10	20	4	0	2	6	9	33	1	0	R	R	6-4	200	3-7-71	1992	Beverly Hills, Calif.
Morgan, Kevin	.273	71	256	34	70	11	1	2	20	27	26	6	5	R	R	6-1	170	3-3-70	1991	Duson, La.
Petagine, Roberto	.317	129	441	90	140	32	1	31	100	85	92	0	1	L	L	6-1	172	6-2-71	1990	Caracas, Venez.
Pratt, Todd	.301	59	206	42	62	8	3	9	34	26	48	1	2	R	R	6-3	195	2-9-67	1985	Boca Raton, Fla.
Pye, Eddie	.083	3	12	3	1	0	0	0	0	4	2	0	0	R	R	5-10	170	2-13-67	1988	Columbia, Tenn.
Saunders, Chris	.249	68	173	24	43	9	0	0	24	37	37	2	2	R	R	6-1	203	7-19-70	1992	Clovis, Calif.
Seefried, Tate	.229	33	96	11	22	6	1	3	13	13	31	2	0	L	R	6-4	180	4-22-72	1990	El Segundo, Calif.
Thurman, Gary	.250	23	80	7	20	4	0	0	12	11	16	4	1	R	R	5-10	180	11-12-64	1983	Indianapolis, Ind.

PITCHING	W	L	ERA	G	GS	CG	SV	IP	H	R	ER	BB	SO	B	T	HT	WT	DOB	1st Yr	Resides
Acevedo, Juan	6	6	3.86	18	18	1	0	117	111	55	50	34	99	R	R	6-2	195	5-5-70	1992	Carpentersville, Ill.
Bohanon, Brian	9	3	2.63	15	14	4	0	96	88	37	28	32	84	L	L	6-3	220	8-1-68	1987	Houston, Texas
Crawford, Joe	8	2	3.52	16	16	0	0	100	109	45	39	31	72	L	L	6-3	225	5-2-70	1991	Hillsboro, Ohio
Dougherty, Jim	10	1	1.45	49	0	0	4	62	45	11	10	43	59	R	R	6-0	210	3-8-68	1991	Kitty Hawk, N.C.
Edmondson, Brian	4	3	2.90	31	4	0	1	68	62	27	22	37	65	R	R	6-2	165	1-29-73	1991	Riverside, Calif.
Harnisch, Pete	1	1	5.40	3	3	0	0	17	16	12	10	10	16	R	R	6-0	207	9-23-66	1987	Commack, N.Y.
Isringhausen, Jason	0	2	4.05	3	3	0	0	20	20	10	9	8	17	R	R	6-3	196	9-7-72	1992	Brighton, Ill.
Jordan, Ricardo	0	1	2.79	34	0	0	1	29	20	11	9	24	34	L	L	5-11	165	6-27-70	1990	Delray Beach, Fla.
Kashiwada, Takashi	0	1	4.73	14	0	0	0	13	11	9	7	5	12	L	L	5-11	165	5-14-71	1997	Tokyo, Japan
Lidle, Cory	4	2	3.64	7	7	1	0	42	46	20	17	10	34	R	R	6-0	175	3-22-72	1991	West Covina, Calif.
Manuel, Barry	2	5	4.87	19	8	0	0	61	60	36	33	21	52	R	R	5-11	185	8-12-65	1987	Mamou, La.
Myers, Jimmy	2	4	1.83	45	0	0	2	69	57	23	14	33	31	R	R	6-1	185	4-28-69	1987	Crowder, Okla.
Perez, Yorkis	1	0	3.48	17	0	0	3	21	22	9	8	7	24	L	L	6-0	160	9-30-67	1983	Haina, D.R.
Pulsipher, Bill	0	5	7.81	8	5	0	0	28	23	29	24	38	18	L	L	6-3	200	10-9-73	1991	Clifton, Va.
Roberts, Chris	0	4	2.89	7	6	0	0	37	38	17	12	17	21	R	L	5-10	185	6-25-71	1992	Middleburg, Fla.
Sauerbeck, Scott	1	0	3.60	1	1	0	0	5	3	2	2	4	4	R	L	6-3	190	11-9-71	1994	Cincinnati, Ohio
Seanez, Rudy	1	0	4.05	9	0	0	0	13	12	8	6	11	17	R	R	5-10	185	10-20-68	1986	El Centro, Calif.
Shepherd, Keith	8	8	4.37	19	18	0	0	107	119	61	52	55	78	R	R	6-2	197	1-21-68	1986	Wabash, Ind.
Tam, Jeff	7	5	4.67	40	11	0	6	112	137	72	58	14	67	R	R	6-1	185	8-19-70	1993	Tallahassee, Fla.
Wallace, Derek	0	1	9.00	1	0	0	0	1	2	2	1	1	0	R	R	6-3	200	9-1-71	1992	Oxnard, Calif.
Welch, Mike	2	2	3.66	46	0	0	20	52	53	21	21	16	35	L	R	6-2	207	8-25-72	1993	Nashua, N.H.
Withem, Shannon	9	10	4.34	29	27	1	0	156	167	85	75	48	109	R	R	6-3	185	9-21-72	1990	Ypsilanti, Mich.
Yarnall, Ed	0	1	14.40	1	1	0	0	5	11	8	8	7	2	L	L	6-4	220	12-4-75	1996	Coral Springs, Fla.

FIELDING

Catcher	PCT	G	PO	A	E	DP	PB
Bieser	.909	2	8	2	1	0	0
Castillo	.973	33	197	16	6	4	4
Greene	.985	75	475	49	8	8	5
Pratt	.988	48	317	24	4	4	4

First Base	PCT	G	PO	A	E	DP
Franco	1.000	2	11	3	0	1
Martin	1.000	1	1	0	0	0
McClain	.985	8	58	8	1	7
Petagine	.990	116	1002	68	11	117
Saunders	1.000	5	31	3	0	4
Seefried	1.000	21	158	11	0	21

Second Base	PCT	G	PO	A	E	DP
Azuaje	.940	11	22	25	3	6
Bieser	1.000	3	4	7	0	0
Gilbert	.921	8	13	22	3	7
Hardtke	.981	95	187	319	10	76
Jaime	1.000	1	2	2	0	1
L. Lopez	.974	8	14	24	1	7
Morgan	.968	22	27	63	3	11
Pye	1.000	1	2	2	0	0

Third Base	PCT	G	PO	A	E	DP
Azuaje	1.000	8	1	15	0	1
Bieser	.500	2	0	1	1	0
Franco	.000	1	0	0	0	0
Gilbert	1.000	7	1	14	0	3
J. Lopez	.900	2	2	7	1	1
McClain	.949	92	64	194	14	19
Saunders	.926	37	19	56	6	7
Seefried	.846	8	0	11	2	1

Shortstop	PCT	G	PO	A	E	DP
Gilbert	.939	38	60	95	10	29
L. Lopez	.927	40	65	99	13	31
McClain	.964	22	39	68	4	15
Morgan	.945	50	73	150	13	32
Pye	1.000	1	1	4	0	0

Outfield	PCT	G	PO	A	E	DP
Agbayani	.978	120	207	12	5	1
Bieser	.935	21	29	0	2	0
Castillo	.000	1	0	0	1	0
Chamberlain	.942	61	75	6	5	0
Diaz	.923	6	10	2	1	0
Espinosa	1.000	23	31	1	0	0
Franco	1.000	3	2	1	0	0
Geisler	.994	93	171	6	1	3
Gilbert	.946	31	50	3	3	1
Jaime	1.000	9	10	2	0	1
Martin	1.000	23	39	3	0	0
Mendoza	1.000	9	17	0	0	0
Moore	.957	26	45	0	2	0
Petagine	1.000	16	21	0	0	0
Thurman	.981	23	51	2	1	0

BINGHAMTON — Class AA

EASTERN LEAGUE

BATTING	AVG	G	AB	R	H	2B	3B	HR	RBI	BB	SO	SB	CS	B	T	HT	WT	DOB	1st Yr	Resides
Azuaje, Jesus	.278	100	331	50	92	15	1	6	37	45	42	11	9	R	R	5-10	170	1-16-73	1992	Bolivar, Venez.
Bates, Fletcher	.257	68	245	44	63	14	2	12	34	26	71	9	3	S	R	6-1	193	3-24-74	1994	Wilmington, N.C.
Espinosa, Ramon	.271	67	255	32	69	7	1	11	37	13	39	10	1	R	R	6-0	175	2-7-72	1990	San Pedro de Macoris, D.R.

BATTING	AVG	G	AB	R	H	2B	3B	HR	RBI	BB	SO	SB	CS	B	T	HT	WT	DOB	1st Yr	Resides
Grifol, Pedro	.200	61	200	15	40	6	0	3	15	9	29	1	1	R	R	6-1	205	11-28-69	1991	Miami, Fla.
Hardtke, Jason	.385	6	26	3	10	2	0	1	4	2	2	0	0	S	R	5-10	175	9-15-71	1990	San Jose, Calif.
Hunter, Scott	.256	80	289	45	74	12	2	10	31	25	52	24	9	R	R	6-1	195	12-17-75	1994	Philadelphia, Pa.
Knowles, Eric	.236	51	157	16	37	10	0	3	22	16	34	7	0	R	R	6-0	190	10-21-73	1991	Miami, Fla.
Lopez, Jose	.246	66	207	31	51	10	1	11	26	13	63	4	2	R	R	6-1	175	8-4-75	1994	Santiago, D.R.
Mahalik, John	.217	74	189	19	41	12	0	1	18	11	39	2	3	R	R	6-2	190	7-28-71	1993	Irving, Texas
Maness, Dwight	.189	74	259	33	49	13	3	5	31	24	73	4	4	R	R	6-3	180	4-3-74	1992	New Castle, Del.
Martin, James	.233	36	90	17	21	2	0	8	14	16	37	6	4	L	R	6-1	210	12-10-70	1992	Eufaula, Okla.
Mendoza, Carlos	.382	59	228	36	87	12	2	1	13	14	25	14	12	L	L	5-11	160	11-4-74	1994	Bolivar, Venez.
Moore, Michael	.300	50	130	19	39	11	1	2	13	18	47	7	3	R	R	6-4	200	3-7-71	1992	Beverly Hills, Calif.
Morales, Elvin	.250	1	4	0	1	0	0	0	0	0	1	0	0	R	R	6-0	170	8-15-75	1993	San Pedro de Macoris, D.R.
Morgan, Kevin	.194	51	191	16	37	7	0	1	10	19	25	11	2	R	R	6-1	170	3-3-70	1991	Duson, La.
Parra, Franklin	.200	5	15	2	3	1	0	0	1	0	5	0	0	S	R	6-0	165	7-8-71	1989	Puerto Plata, D.R.
Polanco, Enohel	.300	82	263	34	79	13	4	3	32	17	59	7	5	R	R	5-11	140	8-11-75	1992	Puerto Plata, D.R.
Raleigh, Matt	.196	122	398	71	78	15	0	37	74	79	169	0	2	R	R	5-11	205	7-18-70	1992	Swanton, Vt.
Roberts, Chris	.077	23	26	2	2	1	0	1	5	1	10	0	0	R	L	5-10	185	6—71	1992	Middleburg, Fla.
Saunders, Chris	.324	30	111	16	36	13	0	3	22	12	20	3	1	R	R	6-1	203	7-19-70	1992	Clovis, Calif.
Seefried, Tate	.313	96	335	59	105	16	0	29	79	54	99	9	4	L	R	6-4	180	4-22-72	1990	El Segundo, Calif.
Wilson, Preston	.286	70	259	37	74	12	1	19	47	21	71	7	1	R	R	6-2	193	7-19-74	1992	Eastover, S.C.
Wilson, Vance	.276	92	322	46	89	17	0	15	40	20	46	2	5	R	R	5-11	190	3-17-73	1994	Mesa, Ariz.
Zorrilla, Julio	.125	7	24	2	3	1	0	0	0	0	5	0	0	S	R	5-11	156	2-20-75	1993	San Pedro de Macoris, D.R.

PITCHING	W	L	ERA	G	GS	CG	SV	IP	H	R	ER	BB	SO	B	T	HT	WT	DOB	1st Yr	Resides
Arroyo, Luis	0	0	3.07	7	0	0	0	15	14	6	5	6	9	L	L	6-0	175	9-29-73	1992	Arecibo, P.R.
Carpenter, Brian	0	1	9.00	17	0	0	0	23	37	23	23	12	22	R	R	6-0	225	3-3-71	1992	Marble Falls, Texas
Carter, John	0	0	6.59	9	0	0	0	14	19	15	10	4	14	R	R	6-1	195	2-16-72	1991	Chicago, Ill.
Dotel, Octavio	3	4	5.98	12	12	0	0	56	66	50	37	38	40	R	R	6-5	160	11-25-73	1993	Santo Domingo, D.R.
Edmondson, Brian	2	0	1.23	14	0	0	3	22	17	4	3	7	18	R	R	6-2	165	1-29-73	1991	Riverside, Calif.
Fesh, Sean	3	1	3.25	45	0	0	4	55	60	26	20	24	37	L	L	6-2	165	11-3-72	1991	Bethel, Conn.
Figueroa, Nelson	5	11	4.34	33	22	0	0	143	137	76	69	68	116	S	R	6-1	165	5-18-74	1995	Brooklyn, N.Y.
Gooch, Arnold	10	12	5.09	27	27	4	0	161	179	106	91	76	98	R	R	6-2	195	11-12-76	1994	Levittown, Pa.
Guerra, Mark	4	8	3.23	48	7	1	7	95	96	46	34	30	74	R	R	6-2	185	11-4-71	1994	Grand Ridge, Fla.
Howard, Chris	0	0	1.15	13	0	0	1	16	6	2	2	7	16	R	L	6-0	185	11-18-65	1986	Nahant, Mass.
Mahalik, John	0	0	0.00	3	0	0	0	3	0	0	0	1	4	R	R	6-2	190	7-28-71	1993	Irving, Texas
Perez, Yorkis	2	1	0.66	12	3	0	0	27	15	4	2	12	39	L	L	6-0	160	9-30-67	1983	Haina, D.R.
Pierson, Jason	2	2	7.88	13	0	0	0	16	33	22	14	7	7	R	L	6-0	190	1-6-71	1992	Berwyn, Pa.
Pulsipher, Bill	0	0	1.42	10	0	0	0	13	11	3	2	7	12	L	L	6-3	200	10-9-73	1991	Clifton, Va.
Roberts, Chris	5	8	4.96	19	19	1	0	105	103	69	58	33	66	R	L	5-10	185	6-25-71	1992	Middleburg, Fla.
Roque, Rafael	1	1	6.84	16	0	0	0	26	35	26	20	17	23	L	L	6-4	186	1-1-72	1991	Santo Domingo, D.R.
Sanchez, Jesus	13	10	4.30	26	26	3	0	165	146	87	79	61	176	L	L	5-10	153	10-11-74	1992	Nizao, D.R.
Sauerbeck, Scott	8	9	4.93	27	20	2	0	131	144	89	72	50	88	R	L	6-3	190	11-9-71	1994	Cincinnati, Ohio
Short, Barry	2	0	2.61	6	0	0	0	10	9	3	3	4	6	R	R	6-3	182	12-15-73	1994	Mansfield, Mo.
Tolar, Kevin	1	1	5.12	22	0	0	0	32	38	20	18	22	26	R	L	6-3	225	1-28-71	1989	Panama City, Fla.
Turrentine, Rich	2	4	5.23	61	0	0	13	62	66	38	36	54	58	R	R	6-0	175	5-21-71	1989	Texarkana, Ark.
Vasquez, Leoner	0	1	10.13	1	1	0	0	5	7	6	6	2	2	L	L	6-4	190	7-1-73	1996	La Romana, D.R.
Yarnall, Ed	3	2	3.06	5	5	0	0	32	20	11	11	11	32	L	L	6-4	220	12-4-75	1996	Coral Springs, Fla.

FIELDING

Catcher	PCT	G	PO	A	E	DP	PB
Grifol	.977	55	383	47	10	5	7
Mahalik	1.000	1	3	0	0	0	1
Morales	1.000	1	7	0	0	0	0
V. Wilson	.984	91	604	69	11	4	13

First Base	PCT	G	PO	A	E	DP
Grifol	1.000	1	3	0	0	1
Mahalik	1.000	8	30	2	0	3
Martin	.962	3	24	1	1	1
Raleigh	.983	45	374	25	7	43
Saunders	.971	3	31	3	1	2
Seefried	.984	91	830	55	14	83

Second Base	PCT	G	PO	A	E	DP
Azuaje	.981	92	178	239	8	64
Hardtke	1.000	6	13	20	0	3
Knowles	.944	10	19	32	3	6
Mahalik	.976	27	43	80	3	18
Morgan	.986	13	37	35	1	14
Parra	.600	2	1	2	2	0
Seefried	.000	1	0	0	0	0
Zorrilla	.967	6	12	17	1	4

Third Base	PCT	G	PO	A	E	DP
Azuaje	1.000	6	3	8	0	1
Knowles	.904	19	8	39	5	2
Lopez	.903	32	15	69	9	6
Mahalik	.968	21	6	24	1	5
Parra	1.000	2	0	4	0	1
Raleigh	.939	56	28	110	9	10
Saunders	.986	25	11	57	1	3
Seefried	1.000	1	1	0	0	0
P. Wilson	.000	1	0	0	0	0

Shortstop	PCT	G	PO	A	E	DP
Knowles	.880	21	31	42	10	12
Mahalik	.911	11	12	29	4	6
Morgan	.943	39	75	139	13	28
Parra	.667	1	0	2	1	1
Polanco	.939	81	119	250	24	56

Outfield	PCT	G	PO	A	E	DP
Bates	.963	62	96	7	4	0
Espinosa	.939	62	86	6	6	0
Hunter	.991	77	109	7	1	0
Mahalik	1.000	1	2	1	0	0
Maness	.993	72	140	2	1	0
Martin	.968	25	29	1	1	0
Mendoza	.988	46	79	5	1	0
Moore	.953	43	57	4	3	1
Raleigh	.000	2	0	0	0	0
Roberts	.000	1	0	0	0	0
P. Wilson	.952	65	116	3	6	0

ST. LUCIE — Class A

FLORIDA STATE LEAGUE

BATTING	AVG	G	AB	R	H	2B	3B	HR	RBI	BB	SO	SB	CS	B	T	HT	WT	DOB	1st Yr	Resides
Alexander, Manny	.250	1	4	0	1	0	0	0	0	0	1	0	0	R	R	5-10	165	3-20-71	1988	San Pedro de Macoris, D.R.
Bates, Fletcher	.300	70	253	49	76	19	11	11	38	33	66	7	6	S	R	6-1	193	3-24-74	1994	Wilmington, N.C.
Bennett, Ryan	.000	2	2	0	0	0	0	0	0	0	2	0	0	R	R	6-0	195	7-26-74	1996	Waukegan, Ill.
Brooks, Eddie	.193	41	119	12	23	3	0	2	9	10	39	1	3	R	R	6-1	175	11-23-72	1994	Lexington, Ky.
Engle, Beau	.192	28	78	3	15	6	0	1	3	5	22	1	1	R	R	6-1	180	11-9-74	1994	Altus, Okla.
Erickson, Corey	.201	46	134	10	27	3	0	3	11	22	43	0	2	R	R	5-11	185	1-10-77	1995	Springfield, Ill.
Gainey, Bryon	.240	117	405	33	97	22	0	13	51	18	133	0	2	L	R	6-5	209	1-23-76	1994	Mobile, Ala.
Gargiulo, Mike	.224	19	49	4	11	0	0	1	5	2	10	0	0	L	R	6-1	175	1-22-75	1993	Harrisburg, Pa.
Jaime, Angel	.240	80	258	25	62	9	0	3	27	29	43	15	4	R	R	6-0	160	3-6-73	1992	Santo Domingo, D.R.
Knowles, Eric	.167	24	84	8	14	5	0	1	10	7	16	3	1	R	R	6-0	190	10-21-73	1991	Miami, Fla.
Lambert, Clark	.000	2	2	0	0	0	0	0	0	0	0	0	0	R	R	6-0	185	5-9-75	1997	Lewisburg, Tenn.
Long, Terrence	.251	126	470	52	118	29	7	8	61	40	102	24	8	L	L	6-1	179	2-29-76	1994	Millbrook, Ala.
Lopez, Jose	.195	23	87	14	17	3	1	4	13	3	25	2	0	R	R	6-1	175	8-4-75	1994	Santiago, D.R.
Lopez, Pee Wee	.248	113	375	40	93	19	0	3	30	39	56	3	2	R	R	6-0	195	10-22-76	1996	Miami, Fla.

BATTING	AVG	G	AB	R	H	2B	3B	HR	RBI	BB	SO	SB	CS	B	T	HT	WT	DOB	1st Yr	Resides
Maness, Dwight	.296	45	179	29	53	9	2	3	19	12	29	12	6	R	R	6-3	180	4-3-74	1992	New Castle, Del.
Martinez, Rafael	.196	66	204	24	40	11	2	1	13	15	54	0	1	L	L	6-3	185	8-24-75	1992	Santo Domingo, D.R.
Miller, Ryan	.254	61	193	27	49	12	1	2	28	11	38	5	5	R	R	6-0	175	10-22-72	1994	Tulare, Calif.
Morales, Eric	.238	38	101	12	24	7	0	0	6	14	24	1	2	S	R	5-11	171	9-26-73	1992	Moca, P.R.
Mulvehill, Brandon	.000	2	6	0	0	0	0	0	0	0	2	0	0	R	R	6-2	180	2-24-78	1996	Pell City, Ala.
Parra, Franklin	.261	56	199	23	52	10	3	2	25	22	33	11	5	S	R	6-0	165	7-8-71	1989	Puerto Plata, D.R.
Parsons, Jeff	.209	45	134	13	28	0	0	0	5	18	31	7	6	R	R	5-10	160	11-16-73	1995	Shawnee, Okla.
Polanco, Enohel	.252	43	131	20	33	9	1	0	12	10	33	2	5	R	R	5-11	140	8-11-75	1992	Puerto Plata, D.R.
Sanderson, David	.228	97	267	41	61	8	2	0	14	54	76	11	3	L	L	6-3	185	10-2-72	1994	Fulton, Mo.
Tomberlin, Andy	.000	1	3	0	0	0	0	0	1	1	2	0	0	L	L	5-11	160	11-7-66	1986	Monroe, N.C.
Wilson, Preston	.245	63	245	32	60	12	1	11	48	8	66	3	4	R	R	6-2	193	7-19-74	1992	Eastover, S.C.
Zorrilla, Julio	.251	118	418	41	105	18	3	1	31	26	50	14	12	S	R	5-11	156	2-20-75	1993	San Pedro de Macoris, D.R.

GAMES BY POSITION: C—Bennett 1, Engle 8, Gargiulo 12, Lambert 2, P. Lopez 95, Morales 35. **1B**—Brooks 4, Gainey 79, Knowles 1, Martinez 59. **2B**—Brooks 9, Knowles 4, Miller 14, Parra 2, Parsons 3, Zorrilla 116. **3B**—Brooks 21, Erickson 44, Jaime 3, Knowles 11, J. Lopez 3, P. Lopez 12, Miller 22, Parsons 34. **SS**—Alexander 1, Brooks 8, Jaime 9, Knowles 9, Miller 25, Parra 51, Parsons 2, Polanco 43. **OF**—Bates 63, Jaime 61, Long 117, Maness 41, Martinez 1, Mulvehill 2, Parsons 7, Sanderson 67, Wilson 61.

PITCHING	W	L	ERA	G	GS	CG	SV	IP	H	R	ER	BB	SO	B	T	HT	WT	DOB	1st Yr	Resides
Arroyo, Luis	3	3	2.09	36	2	0	0	56	37	21	13	23	57	L	L	6-0	175	9-29-73	1992	Arecibo, P.R.
Brittan, Corey	3	5	3.58	51	1	0	3	78	91	35	31	21	57	R	R	6-6	197	2-23-75	1996	Scott City, Kan.
Coronado, Osvaldo	0	0	4.32	5	0	0	0	8	9	7	4	4	4	R	R	6-2	185	12-30-73	1992	Puerto Plata, D.R.
Dotel, Octavio	5	2	2.52	9	8	1	0	50	44	18	14	23	39	R	R	6-5	160	11-25-73	1993	Santo Domingo, D.R.
Gulin, Lindsay	0	3	9.23	9	6	0	0	26	36	31	27	21	11	L	L	6-3	160	11-22-76	1995	Issaquah, Wash.
Harnisch, Pete	1	0	3.00	2	2	0	0	12	5	5	4	4	7	R	R	6-0	207	9-23-66	1987	Commack, N.Y.
Howard, Chris	1	1	7.15	10	0	0	1	11	12	9	9	6	10	R	L	6-0	185	11-18-65	1986	Nahant, Mass.
Howatt, Jeff	1	2	4.31	39	0	0	2	65	78	41	31	20	41	R	R	6-6	225	1-30-74	1995	Augusta, Ga.
Isringhausen, Jason	1	0	0.00	2	2	0	0	12	8	1	0	5	15	R	R	6-3	196	9-7-72	1992	Brighton, Ill.
Larson, Toby	0	1	7.20	4	0	0	0	5	9	6	4	1	3	R	R	6-3	210	2-22-73	1994	Olympia, Wash.
Lisio, Joseph	2	6	4.56	48	0	0	16	47	48	27	24	19	42	R	R	6-2	205	8-5-73	1994	West Hempstead, N.Y.
McEntire, Ethan	0	1	6.17	3	3	0	0	12	16	9	8	7	8	L	L	6-1	195	7-19-75	1993	Clarkesville, Ga.
Murray, Dan	12	10	3.45	30	24	4	0	156	150	75	60	55	91	R	R	6-1	185	11-21-73	1995	Garden Grove, Calif.
Olson, Phillip	3	3	3.30	47	0	0	1	71	74	32	26	26	57	R	R	6-3	225	10-24-73	1995	Palmetto, Fla.
Pierson, Jason	0	1	2.30	7	1	0	0	16	13	4	4	2	6	R	L	6-0	190	1-6-71	1992	Berwyn, Pa.
Pulsipher, Bill	1	4	5.89	12	7	0	0	37	29	27	24	35	35	L	L	6-3	200	10-9-73	1991	Clifton, Va.
Reynoso, Armando	1	1	2.70	2	2	0	0	10	9	3	3	1	6	R	R	6-0	196	5-1-66	1989	Jalisco, Mexico
Roque, Rafael	2	10	4.29	17	13	1	0	78	81	42	37	25	54	L	L	6-4	186	1-1-72	1991	Santo Domingo, D.R.
Stewart, Scott	5	10	4.01	22	18	4	0	123	114	62	55	18	64	R	L	6-2	200	8-14-75	1994	Stanley, N.C.
Tolar, Kevin	0	0	2.03	9	0	0	1	13	9	3	3	6	8	R	L	6-3	225	1-28-71	1989	Panama City, Fla.
Trumpour, Andy	8	10	4.11	27	27	0	0	145	159	75	66	57	86	R	R	6-4	185	10-22-73	1992	Anaheim, Calif.
Wallace, Derek	0	0	6.43	5	0	0	0	7	7	6	5	2	8	R	R	6-3	200	9-1-71	1992	Oxnard, Calif.
Wilson, Paul	0	0	2.57	1	1	0	0	7	6	2	2	0	6	R	R	6-5	235	3-28-73	1994	Orlando, Fla.
Yarnall, Ed	5	8	2.48	18	18	2	0	105	93	33	29	30	114	L	L	6-4	220	12-4-75	1996	Coral Springs, Fla.

CAPITAL CITY — Class A

SOUTH ATLANTIC LEAGUE

BATTING	AVG	G	AB	R	H	2B	3B	HR	RBI	BB	SO	SB	CS	B	T	HT	WT	DOB	1st Yr	Resides
Bennett, Ryan	.190	19	42	6	8	1	0	0	3	5	15	0	0	R	R	6-0	195	7-26-74	1996	Waukegan, Ill.
Bishop, Tim	.204	14	49	4	10	2	0	0	2	6	16	7	2	R	R	6-0	168	5-25-74	1994	Valparaiso, Ind.
Chancey, Bailey	.247	30	85	12	21	0	0	0	7	13	19	5	2	S	R	5-8	160	8-25-74	1996	Millbrook, Ala.
Edmondson, Tracy	.191	50	131	16	25	6	1	1	12	16	38	1	1	R	R	6-0	165	6-10-75	1995	Riverside, Calif.
Engle, Beau	.300	6	10	0	3	0	0	0	2	2	3	0	0	R	R	6-1	180	11-9-74	1994	Altus, Okla.
Erickson, Corey	.214	49	173	18	37	11	2	2	16	11	49	3	1	R	R	5-11	185	1-10-77	1995	Springfield, Ill.
Espada, Angel	.324	30	102	17	33	6	0	0	7	9	9	8	4	R	R	5-9	150	8-15-75	1994	Salinas, P.R.
Haltiwanger, Garrick	.261	125	441	59	115	19	2	14	73	45	107	20	7	R	L	6-2	190	3-3-75	1996	Irmo, S.C.
Huff, Brent	.253	99	363	49	92	20	5	7	41	19	78	11	3	R	R	6-1	185	8-1-75	1996	Chandler, Ind.
Jaroncyk, Ryan	.174	29	86	5	15	1	2	0	7	11	25	4	4	S	R	6-0	160	3-26-77	1995	Escondido, Calif.
Martinez, Rafael	.268	44	149	20	40	7	2	5	25	17	44	10	2	L	L	6-3	185	8-24-75	1992	Santo Domingo, D.R.
McCarthy, Kevin	.194	31	98	6	19	1	0	1	9	8	21	1	1	L	L	6-4	198	7-5-76	1994	Pittsburgh, Pa.
Parsons, Jeff	.270	52	152	25	41	2	0	0	11	26	41	16	2	R	R	5-10	160	11-16-73	1995	Shawnee, Okla.
Penalver, Juan	.273	9	22	1	6	1	0	0	1	3	3	0	1	R	R	6-1	175	7-15-75	1994	Maturin, Venez.
Perez, Jersen	.667	2	6	3	4	3	0	0	2	0	0	1	0	R	R	5-8	175	1-20-76	1996	Lynn, Mass.
Ramirez, Daniel	.305	130	478	82	146	24	4	1	42	44	104	51	25	R	R	6-0	175	2-22-74	1992	San Pedro de Macoris, D.R.
Rijo-Berger, Jose	.229	17	48	4	11	2	0	0	1	6	12	2	1	S	R	5-10	190	2-28-75	1997	Everett, Wash.
Simpson, Jeramie	.241	10	29	4	7	0	1	0	2	1	15	1	1	L	R	5-10	160	11-28-74	1994	Edmond, Okla.
Soriano, Carlos	.208	101	318	37	66	14	0	4	41	24	52	5	2	R	R	6-0	165	10-24-74	1992	San Pedro de Macoris, D.R.
Stanton, Thomas	.189	60	190	29	36	10	0	7	31	24	79	0	1	S	R	6-1	200	2-3-76	1996	Middleburg, Fla.
Tamargo, John	.249	113	393	44	98	17	2	1	47	45	72	13	7	S	R	5-10	165	5-3-75	1996	Tampa, Fla.
Tessmar, Tim	.244	120	430	53	105	14	4	8	55	36	93	10	3	L	L	6-3	185	1-22-74	1995	Rochester Hills, Mich.
Valera, Yohanny	.191	94	293	32	56	14	0	8	33	21	101	2	0	R	R	6-1	170	8-17-76	1993	San Cristobal, D.R.
Vickers, Randy	.171	72	245	22	42	10	1	10	26	9	99	1	4	R	R	6-3	200	7-21-75	1994	West Covina, Calif.
Zamora, Junior	.250	36	124	16	31	5	0	8	19	10	29	0	1	R	R	6-2	168	5-3-76	1994	San Pedro de Macoris, D.R.

GAMES BY POSITION: C—Bennett 18, Engle 4, Stanton 43, Valera 89. **1B**—Edmondson 1, Martinez 17, Tessmar 103, Vickers 24. **2B**—Edmondson 11, Erickson 46, Espada 30, Parsons 8, Penalver 8, Perez 2, Soriano 31, Tamargo 21. **3B**—Edmondson 22, Erickson 3, Parsons 4, Penalver 2, Soriano 65, Vickers 25, Zamora 36. **SS**—Edmondson 15, Jaroncyk 29, Parsons 17, Perez 1, Tamargo 84. **OF**—Bishop 14, Chancey 18, Edmondson 3, Haltiwanger 113, Huff 83, Martinez 18, McCarthy 27, Parsons 13, Ramirez 125, Rijo-Berger 15, Simpson 10.

PITCHING	W	L	ERA	G	GS	CG	SV	IP	H	R	ER	BB	SO	B	T	HT	WT	DOB	1st Yr	Resides
Arteaga, Juan	1	0	0.00	1	1	0	0	6	3	0	0	0	4	L	L	6-3	220	8-2-74	1997	Miami, Fla.
Beebe, Hans	0	0	9.95	6	0	0	0	13	21	15	14	6	6	L	L	6-4	175	4-30-75	1994	Berlin, N.J.
Coronado, Osvaldo	2	4	2.64	26	0	0	0	48	42	18	14	15	42	R	R	6-2	185	12-30-73	1992	Puerto Plata, D.R.
Cutchins, Todd	0	1	5.40	3	1	0	0	7	7	4	4	5	6	R	L	6-0	190	7-14-75	1996	Westlake, La.
Gonzalez, Dicky	1	4	4.94	10	7	1	0	47	50	28	26	15	49	R	R	5-11	155	10-21-78	1996	Bayamon, P.R.
Gulin, Lindsay	8	1	2.91	17	15	1	0	99	77	37	32	60	118	L	L	6-3	160	11-22-76	1995	Issaquah, Wash.

PITCHING	W	L	ERA	G	GS	CG	SV	IP	H	R	ER	BB	SO	B	T	HT	WT	DOB	1st Yr	Resides
Hafer, Jeff	6	5	2.99	37	2	0	7	69	59	29	23	21	74	R	R	6-1	175	10-27-74	1996	Springfield, Va.
Herbison, Brett	7	14	3.99	28	27	2	0	160	166	86	71	63	146	R	R	6-5	175	6-13-77	1995	Elgin, Ill.
Kessel, Kyle	11	11	2.72	27	27	5	0	169	131	63	51	53	151	R	L	6-0	160	6-2-76	1994	Mundelein, Ill.
Lyons, Mike	6	2	1.86	44	0	0	14	58	40	15	12	20	55	R	R	6-3	205	5-20-75	1996	Altamonte Springs, Fla.
McCrary, Scott	3	2	0.96	13	0	0	0	28	20	4	3	5	24	R	R	6-4	205	1-8-74	1997	Vacaville, Calif.
Ojeda, Erick	0	2	5.79	7	0	0	0	14	14	10	9	4	13	L	L	5-10	177	10-15-75	1993	Valencia, Venez.
Presley, Kirk	0	1	10.80	2	0	0	0	3	5	4	4	0	5	R	R	6-3	195	4-17-75	1994	Tupelo, Miss.
Pumphrey, Kenny	12	6	3.10	27	27	3	0	166	137	70	57	72	133	R	R	6-6	195	9-10-76	1994	Glen Burnie, Md.
Roberts, Grant	11	3	2.36	22	22	2	0	130	98	37	34	44	122	R	R	6-3	187	9-13-77	1995	El Cajon, Calif.
Santamaria, Bill	2	1	3.33	14	0	0	0	24	22	11	9	16	18	R	R	6-2	223	1-6-76	1994	Lakewood, N.J.
Splawn, Matt	0	0	0.93	7	0	0	0	10	7	4	1	1	10	L	R	6-1	190	1-2-73	1996	Waxahachie, Texas
Vasquez, Leoner	4	5	5.14	22	8	0	1	56	63	37	32	22	49	L	L	6-4	190	7-1-73	1996	La Romana, D.R.
Villafuerte, Brandon	3	1	2.38	47	3	0	7	76	58	23	20	33	88	R	R	5-11	165	12-17-75	1995	Morgan Hill, Calif.

PITTSFIELD — Short-Season Class A

NEW YORK-PENN LEAGUE

BATTING	AVG	G	AB	R	H	2B	3B	HR	RBI	BB	SO	SB	CS	B	T	HT	WT	DOB	1st Yr	Resides
Bruce, Maurice	.348	29	115	26	40	7	3	4	14	11	23	12	2	R	R	5-10	180	5-1-75	1996	Kansas City, Mo.
Copeland, Brandon	.256	27	90	24	23	6	0	1	7	13	30	0	0	R	R	6-0	205	3-31-77	1996	Kansas City, Mo.
Espada, Angel	.305	20	82	15	25	1	0	0	7	5	5	7	3	R	R	5-9	150	8-15-75	1994	Salinas, P.R.
Johnson, Tom	.234	57	209	28	49	15	0	5	38	14	51	12	3	R	R	6-5	210	1-25-76	1996	Elizabeth, N.J.
McCarthy, Kevin	.204	57	201	20	41	9	2	0	20	14	55	4	2	L	L	6-4	198	7-5-76	1994	Pittsburgh, Pa.
McCladdie, Tony	.236	52	178	30	42	9	1	0	22	25	30	11	4	R	R	5-10	185	10-11-75	1996	Martinez, Ga.
Miller, Kenny	.226	26	93	16	21	3	0	0	14	6	13	4	1	R	R	5-11	170	6-25-76	1997	Joliet, Ill.
Moreno, Juan	.289	71	287	35	83	17	4	2	41	12	60	19	6	R	R	6-2	165	3-19-76	1995	Monte Plata, D.R.
Nolte, Bruce	.230	47	161	22	37	3	4	0	18	11	37	4	0	R	R	6-0	160	4-4-74	1993	Pennsauken, N.J.
Patton, Cory	.211	56	199	27	42	2	3	1	18	14	51	16	1	R	R	6-2	185	10-18-75	1996	Harrisburg, Ill.
Phillips, Jason	.206	48	155	15	32	9	0	2	17	13	24	4	0	R	R	6-1	180	9-27-76	1997	El Cajon, Calif.
Rijo-Berger, Jose	.296	36	135	20	40	5	0	0	9	19	11	7	2	S	R	5-10	190	2-28-75	1997	Everett, Wash.
Roach, Jason	.213	64	235	26	50	11	0	6	28	8	70	0	0	R	R	6-4	200	4-20-76	1997	Kinston, N.C.
Rodriguez, Sammy	.245	36	110	15	27	6	2	5	20	21	33	2	1	R	R	5-10	180	8-20-75	1995	New York, N.Y.
Santiago, Jorge	.255	48	145	16	37	3	1	0	17	8	24	5	3	R	R	5-10	160	7-20-75	1997	Commack, N.Y.
Valentine, Anthony	.177	17	62	8	11	2	0	0	3	4	19	0	0	R	R	5-10	180	1-15-75	1997	Darien, Conn.

GAMES BY POSITION: C—Phillips 46, Rodriguez 30. **1B**—McCarthy 33, Nolte 5, Roach 27, Valentine 17. **2B**—Bruce 24, Espada 18, McCladdie 8, Moreno 1, Nolte 16, Santiago 15. **3B**—McCladdie 29, Nolte 17, Roach 35, Santiago 1. **SS**—Bruce 5, Miller 26, Nolte 12, Santiago 35. **OF**—Bruce 1, Copeland 24, Johnson 55, McCarthy 18, Moreno 49, Patton 48, Rijo-Berger 32, Roach 1.

PITCHING	W	L	ERA	G	GS	CG	SV	IP	H	R	ER	BB	SO	B	T	HT	WT	DOB	1st Yr	Resides
Arteaga, J.D.	4	2	2.67	12	3	0	0	30	32	15	9	4	29	L	L	6-3	220	8-2-74	1997	Miami, Fla.
Barry, Shawn	2	3	1.73	22	0	0	0	26	14	6	5	10	35	L	L	6-3	210	7-15-74	1997	Colchester, Conn.
Beebe, Hans	6	6	3.90	15	15	3	0	90	90	49	39	22	71	L	L	6-4	175	4-30-75	1994	Berlin, N.J.
Burnett, Allan	3	1	4.70	9	9	0	0	44	28	26	23	35	48	R	R	6-5	204	1-3-77	1995	North Little Rock, Ark.
Cammack, Eric	0	1	0.86	23	0	0	8	31	9	4	3	14	32	R	R	6-1	180	8-14-75	1997	Port Neches, Texas
Comer, Scott	7	1	1.74	14	14	1	0	93	71	25	18	12	98	L	L	6-5	195	6-23-77	1996	Klamath Falls, Ore.
Davis, Mike	1	2	3.34	24	1	0	4	35	31	17	13	16	20	R	R	5-11	180	8-30-75	1996	Rocky Face, Ga.
Estrella, Leoncio	7	6	3.03	15	15	0	0	92	91	48	31	27	55	R	R	6-1	165	2-20-75	1994	Puerto Plata, D.R.
Gaskill, Derek	3	2	2.58	21	3	0	0	45	41	23	13	5	39	R	R	6-6	190	5-6-74	1992	Portsmouth, Va.
Lohrman, David	1	2	2.91	22	0	0	4	34	25	18	11	12	42	R	R	6-6	205	9-16-75	1997	East Amherst, N.Y.
Mangieri, John	0	0	20.25	2	0	0	0	1	3	3	3	0	0	R	R	6-2	200	9-24-76	1997	Howard Beach, N.Y.
Poupart, Melvin	0	0	2.70	8	1	0	0	10	10	8	3	14	9	R	R	6-0	193	7-1-75	1994	Humacao, P.R.
Pyrtle, Joe	3	2	0.75	23	0	0	4	36	13	7	3	8	44	R	R	6-1	200	11-21-73	1995	Wilmington, N.C.
Queen, Mike	5	4	3.24	13	13	1	0	75	86	33	27	13	63	L	L	6-4	205	12-5-77	1996	Gravette, Ark.
Walker, Tyler	0	0	13.50	1	0	0	0	1	2	2	1	1	1	R	R	6-3	260	5-15-76	1997	Ross, Calif.

KINGSPORT — Rookie

APPALACHIAN LEAGUE

BATTING	AVG	G	AB	R	H	2B	3B	HR	RBI	BB	SO	SB	CS	B	T	HT	WT	DOB	1st Yr	Resides
Bowring, Jason	.248	61	218	32	54	10	1	6	35	12	43	8	3	R	R	6-1	190	5-10-77	1997	San Bernardino, Calif.
Brett, Jason	.271	49	170	25	46	3	3	0	18	20	42	6	2	R	R	6-0	171	4-28-77	1997	Perry, Ga.
Bruce, Maurice	.367	34	128	35	47	8	3	3	21	16	20	14	4	R	R	5-10	180	5-1-75	1996	Kansas City, Mo.
Burns, Patrick	.246	60	224	32	55	11	3	0	30	17	67	7	4	S	L	6-1	190	9-16-77	1996	Denton, Texas
Chavez, Endy	.301	19	73	16	22	4	0	0	4	13	10	5	2	L	L	5-11	170	2-7-78	1996	Tobuyito, Venez.
Cook, Josh	.150	9	20	0	3	0	0	0	2	5	10	0	1	R	R	6-0	215	9-30-75	1997	Plainville, Ill.
Copeland, Brandon	.338	41	148	31	50	10	1	7	37	23	33	6	3	R	R	6-0	205	3-31-77	1996	Kansas City, Mo.
Durick, Chad	.302	31	126	23	38	13	0	5	25	7	35	1	0	R	R	6-0	175	12-28-76	1996	Port St. Lucie, Fla.
Escobar, Alex	.194	10	36	6	7	3	0	0	3	3	8	1	0	R	R	6-1	170	9-6-78	1996	Valencia, Venez.
Johnson, Anthony	.333	15	45	10	15	3	0	3	9	9	17	1	1	R	R	6-3	210	2-17-73	1995	Neptune, N.J.
McGrath, Sean	.256	26	78	18	20	4	0	0	6	7	26	4	4	R	R	6-0	194	4-4-76	1997	North Adams, Mass.
Nunez, Jose	.000	2	6	1	0	0	0	0	0	0	2	0	0	R	R	5-10	155	10-3-76	1996	Miami, Fla.
Penalver, Juan	.317	51	180	37	57	8	1	2	28	32	32	7	6	R	R	6-1	175	7-15-75	1994	Maturin, Venez.
Perez, Jersen	.267	65	258	45	69	10	2	3	29	7	41	12	7	R	R	5-8	175	1-20-76	1996	Lynn, Mass.
Ramos, Kelly	.224	50	170	25	38	3	1	7	32	17	33	2	3	S	R	6-0	168	10-15-76	1994	San Pedro de Macoris, D.R.
Rodriguez, Mark	.149	26	87	12	13	1	0	3	14	8	25	0	0	R	R	5-11	215	2-4-74	1996	Miami, Fla.
Smith, Shane	.221	37	113	15	25	7	0	3	13	15	22	2	1	R	R	6-3	220	5-18-75	1997	Knoxville, Tenn.
Stratton, Robert	.249	63	245	51	61	11	5	15	50	19	94	11	6	R	R	6-2	220	10-7-77	1996	Santa Barbara, Calif.

GAMES BY POSITION: C—Cook 5, Ramos 45, Smith 25. **1B**—Bruce 1, Burns 49, Durick 8, Rodriguez 8, Smith 3. **2B**—Bowring 14, Brett 28, Bruce 6, McGrath 7, Penalver 9, Perez 7. **3B**—Bowring 15, Durick 3, McGrath 11, Penalver 38, Perez 2, Rodriguez 4. **SS**—Brett 8, McGrath 2, Nunez 1, Penalver 5, Perez 52. **OF**—Bowring 28, Brett 3, Bruce 23, Burns 8, Chavez 18, Copeland 40, Durick 14, Escobar 10, Johnson 8, Stratton 63.

PITCHING	W	L	ERA	G	GS	CG	SV	IP	H	R	ER	BB	SO	B	T	HT	WT	DOB	1st Yr	Resides
Borkowski, Robert	2	0	16.88	5	0	0	2	5	13	10	10	2	5	R	R	6-2	190	11-10-76	1994	Wilmington, Del.

PITCHING	W	L	ERA	G	GS	CG	SV	IP	H	R	ER	BB	SO	B	T	HT	WT	DOB	1st Yr	Resides
Bowring, Jason	0	0	9.00	2	0	0	0	4	7	4	4	1	4	R	R	6-1	190	5-10-77	1997	San Bernardino, Calif.
Corcoran, Tim	2	0	4.24	7	0	0	0	17	12	10	8	8	14	R	R	6-2	180	4-15-78	1997	Slaughter, La.
Cox, Robert	1	2	4.71	21	0	0	2	42	49	25	22	16	24	R	R	6-1	176	11-11-75	1994	Culver City, Calif.
De la Cruz, Ynocencio	2	3	6.61	6	6	0	0	31	46	30	23	8	31	R	R	6-2	158	2-28-77	1994	Puerta Plata, D.R.
Durick, Chad	1	1	1.17	6	0	0	0	7	3	2	1	3	11	R	R	6-0	175	12—76	1996	Port St. Lucie, Fla.
Enloe, Mark	1	1	6.45	15	4	0	0	45	57	37	32	21	36	L	L	6-3	200	2-5-77	1995	Cleveland, Texas
Garmon, Adam	2	2	7.71	18	5	0	3	42	50	43	36	21	39	R	R	6-4	200	8-5-77	1996	St. Augustine, Fla.
Gonzalez, Dicky	3	6	4.36	12	12	1	0	66	70	38	32	10	76	R	R	5-11	155	10-21-78	1996	Bayamon, P.R.
Hamilton, Randy	5	3	2.53	21	0	0	4	46	38	18	13	15	44	L	L	6-3	190	1-1-76	1997	Independence, Ky.
Lovingood, Ray	6	3	5.86	13	13	0	0	63	80	48	41	30	65	L	L	6-6	190	4-8-78	1996	Riceville, Tenn.
Maberry, Mark	2	2	1.80	22	0	0	5	35	36	14	7	13	51	R	R	6-3	205	7-31-74	1997	Cookeville, Tenn.
Mattson, John	1	0	4.63	6	4	0	0	23	25	12	12	5	25	R	R	6-4	205	10-1-76	1997	Port Orchard, Wash.
Montada, Joaquin	3	2	6.90	13	11	0	0	60	78	55	46	22	52	R	R	6-2	178	8-19-77	1997	Hialeah, Fla.
Payne, Tony	3	0	5.26	10	0	0	0	26	31	17	15	14	28	R	L	6-1	180	10-11-77	1996	Panama City, Fla.
Santana, Humberto	3	6	5.28	13	13	1	0	77	87	51	45	16	71	L	L	5-11	175	3-10-77	1995	Provincia Espaill, D.R.
Smith, Shane	0	0	13.50	2	0	0	0	2	1	4	3	3	2	R	R	6-3	220	5—75	1997	Knoxville, Tenn.

PORT ST. LUCIE — Rookie

GULF COAST LEAGUE

BATTING	AVG	G	AB	R	H	2B	3B	HR	RBI	BB	SO	SB	CS	B	T	HT	WT	DOB	1st Yr	Resides
Cardona, Luis	.143	2	7	0	1	0	0	0	2	0	1	0	0	R	R	6-1	198	9-14-77	1995	San Sebastian, P.R.
Chavez, Endy	.277	33	119	26	33	6	3	0	15	20	10	1	2	L	L	5-11	170	2-7-78	1996	Tobuyito, Venez.
Davila, Angel	.231	5	13	4	3	0	1	0	1	5	1	0	0	R	R	5-9	155	5-1-75	1996	Guena Diac, P.R.
De la Cruz, Ruddi	.171	38	129	16	22	3	1	0	6	8	25	3	2	R	R	6-0	155	11-2-79	1996	San Pedro de Macoris, D.R.
Durick, Chad	.318	25	88	13	28	10	1	3	24	2	15	3	1	R	R	6-0	175	12-28-76	1996	Port St. Lucie, Fla.
Escobar, Alex	.247	26	73	12	18	4	1	1	11	10	17	0	0	R	R	6-1	170	9-6-78	1996	Valencia, Venez.
Fafard, Mathias	.159	23	69	11	11	3	2	0	2	11	17	1	0	R	R	6-1	185	12-21-76	1997	Cocoa, Fla.
Hill, Bobby	.292	41	144	27	42	9	2	3	24	17	37	3	5	L	R	5-10	160	6-25-79	1997	Waldo, Fla.
Jenkins, Brian	.349	36	109	17	38	6	1	1	15	4	16	1	1	R	R	5-11	185	10-11-78	1997	Port St. Joe, Fla.
Lambert, Clark	.228	35	114	12	26	5	0	0	11	12	18	0	0	R	R	6-0	185	5-9-75	1997	Lewisburg, Tenn.
Martinez, Andres	.240	31	96	18	23	8	4	0	7	9	33	1	1	R	R	6-1	160	11-30-76	1994	Santo Domingo, D.R.
Meadows, Mike	.291	43	134	28	39	12	2	3	22	16	35	0	0	R	R	6-1	175	10-19-78	1996	Sanford, Fla.
Mulvehill, Brandon	.260	49	169	20	44	7	0	1	19	13	30	7	2	R	R	6-2	180	2-24-78	1996	Pell City, Ala.
Nunez, Jose	.333	5	15	3	5	1	0	0	2	1	4	0	1	R	R	5-10	155	10-3-76	1996	Miami, Fla.
Proctor, Mark	.267	16	45	7	12	3	0	0	3	3	14	1	1	R	R	6-3	180	9-14-79	1997	Fredericksburg, Va.
Prosper, Gerard	.283	39	120	26	34	8	3	0	13	30	22	7	5	L	L	5-11	175	2-10-78	1997	Ocean Reef, Australia
Rains, Nick	.220	30	100	11	22	4	1	0	8	7	39	4	1	R	R	6-1	180	8-12-78	1997	Fort Pierce, Fla.
Shuck, Jason	.274	25	73	10	20	6	1	0	8	12	13	2	1	R	R	5-11	160	1-29-78	1997	Mansfield, Ark.
Tomberlin, Andy	.318	7	22	6	7	0	0	2	7	3	7	1	0	L	L	5-11	160	11-7-66	1986	Monroe, N.C.
Valentine, Anthony	.326	30	92	19	30	7	1	0	14	15	12	3	0	R	R	5-10	180	1-15-75	1997	Darien, Conn.
Yancy, Michael	.252	38	131	22	33	3	4	1	20	12	26	5	2	R	R	5-11	185	3-26-79	1997	San Diego, Calif.

GAMES BY POSITION: C—Cardona 2, Jenkins 30, Lambert 34, Valentine 2. **1B**—Durick 15, Meadows 27, Mulvehill 2, Rains 1, Valentine 22. **2B**—Hill 17, Martinez 13, Nunez 5, Proctor 5, Shuck 23. **3B**—Davila 3, Durick 6, Fafard 21, Martinez 16, Meadows 8, Proctor 10, Valentine 1. **SS**—De la Cruz 38, Escobar 1, Hill 20, Shuck 1. **OF**—Chavez 33, Escobar 19, Mulvehill 39, Prosper 36, Rains 25, Tomberlin 2, Yancy 34.

PITCHING	W	L	ERA	G	GS	CG	SV	IP	H	R	ER	BB	SO	B	T	HT	WT	DOB	1st Yr	Resides
Burnett, Allan	0	1	3.18	3	2	0	0	11	8	8	4	8	15	R	R	6-5	204	1-3-77	1995	North Little Rock, Ark.
Chivers, Jason	1	0	5.25	11	0	0	1	12	10	7	7	11	14	L	L	6-6	230	12-19-78	1993	Lancaster, Calif.
Corcoran, Tim	3	0	3.00	10	0	0	3	21	16	8	7	15	20	R	R	6-2	180	4-15-78	1997	Slaughter, La.
De la Cruz, Ynocencio	3	3	1.15	6	5	0	0	39	31	12	5	3	42	R	R	6-2	158	2-28-77	1994	Puerta Plata, D.R.
Dotel, Octavio	0	0	0.96	3	2	0	1	9	9	1	1	2	7	R	R	6-5	160	11-25-73	1993	Santo Domingo, D.R.
Dougherty, James	6	1	1.93	11	8	0	0	51	42	18	11	13	51	L	L	6-4	210	3-4-78	1996	Voorhees, N.J.
Encarnacion, Orlando	4	2	2.45	13	0	0	1	22	23	8	6	5	27	R	R	6-0	200	3-1-79	1997	Bronx, N.Y.
Goetz, Geoff	0	2	2.73	8	6	0	1	26	23	11	8	18	28	L	L	6-1	175	4-3-79	1997	Lutz, Fla.
Gomez, Rafael	0	0	0.90	4	2	0	0	10	9	2	1	2	6	R	R	6-1	178	9-8-77	1995	San Pedro de Macoris, D.R.
Gorman, Pat	1	1	1.80	11	0	0	5	15	10	3	3	4	13	R	R	6-2	205	8-16-77	1997	Valley Cottage, N.Y.
Harnisch, Pete	0	0	12.00	1	1	0	0	3	7	4	4	0	5	R	R	6-0	207	9-23-66	1987	Commack, N.Y.
Howard, Chris	0	1	5.14	4	2	0	0	7	7	4	4	2	11	R	L	6-0	185	11-18-65	1986	Nahant, Mass.
Isringhausen, Jason	1	0	1.93	1	0	0	0	5	2	1	1	1	7	R	R	6-3	196	9-7-72	1992	Brighton, Ill.
Larson, Toby	1	0	2.25	2	1	0	0	4	4	1	1	0	4	R	R	6-3	210	2-22-73	1994	Olympia, Wash.
Lowe, Matt	2	0	1.13	5	0	0	1	8	4	1	1	9	15	R	R	6-4	210	4-3-79	1997	Walhalla, S.C.
Maness, Nick	3	2	3.02	11	6	0	0	45	52	25	15	20	54	R	R	6-4	185	10-17-78	1997	Robbins, N.C.
Mangieri, John	2	0	7.08	13	0	0	1	20	28	16	16	14	15	R	R	6-2	200	9-24-76	1997	Howard Beach, N.Y.
McCrary, Scott	1	0	0.00	5	0	0	2	9	5	3	0	2	15	R	R	6-4	205	1-8-74	1997	Vacaville, Calif.
Mikkola, Shaun	5	0	1.17	14	4	0	0	38	25	11	5	16	23	R	R	6-2	185	8-3-79	1997	Largo, Fla.
Pierson, Jason	0	0	0.00	1	0	0	0	2	0	0	0	1	3	R	L	6-0	190	1-6-71	1992	Berwyn, Pa.
Pulsipher, Bill	0	0	1.80	2	2	0	0	5	3	1	1	1	4	L	L	6-3	200	10-9-73	1991	Clifton, Va.
Sordo, Fernando	3	1	3.58	11	3	0	0	28	26	12	11	7	12	L	R	6-4	185	1-30-77	1997	Boca Raton, Fla.
Suggs, Willie	5	3	2.49	10	8	1	0	51	34	21	14	22	32	R	R	6-3	180	8-25-78	1996	Mt. Vernon, Ill.
Walker, Tyler	0	0	1.00	5	0	0	3	9	8	1	1	2	9	R	R	6-3	260	5-15-76	1997	Ross, Calif.
Wallace, Derek	0	1	3.38	8	5	0	0	8	6	3	3	1	9	R	R	6-3	200	9-1-71	1992	Oxnard, Calif.
Wilson, Paul	1	0	1.45	4	3	0	1	19	14	7	3	4	18	R	R	6-5	235	3-28-73	1994	Orlando, Fla.

Oakland ATHLETICS

Manager: Art Howe.

1997 Record: 65-97, .401 (4th, AL West)

BATTING	AVG	G	AB	R	H	2B	3B	HR	RBI	BB	SO	SB	CS	B	T	HT	WT	DOB	1st Yr	Resides
Batista, Tony	.202	68	188	22	38	10	1	4	18	14	31	2	2	R	R	6-0	180	12-9-73	1992	Mao Valverde, D.R.
Bellhorn, Mark	.228	68	224	33	51	9	1	6	19	32	70	7	1	S	R	6-1	195	8-23-74	1995	Oviedo, Fla.
Berroa, Geronimo	.310	73	261	40	81	12	0	16	42	36	58	3	2	R	R	6-0	165	3-18-65	1984	New York, N.Y.
Bournigal, Rafael	.279	79	222	29	62	9	0	1	20	16	19	2	1	R	R	5-11	165	5-12-66	1987	Santo Domingo, D.R.
Brito, Tilson	.283	17	46	8	13	2	1	2	6	1	10	0	0	R	R	6-0	170	5-28-72	1990	Los Trinitarios, D.R.
2-team (49 Toronto)	.238	66	172	17	41	5	1	2	14	10	38	1	0							
Brosius, Scott	.203	129	479	59	97	20	1	11	41	34	102	9	4	R	R	6-1	190	8-15-66	1987	McMinnville, Ore.
Canseco, Jose	.235	108	388	56	91	19	0	23	74	51	122	8	2	R	R	6-3	185	7-2-64	1982	Miami, Fla.
Giambi, Jason	.293	142	519	66	152	41	2	20	81	55	89	0	1	L	R	6-2	200	1-8-71	1992	Covina, Calif.
Grieve, Ben	.312	24	93	12	29	6	0	3	24	13	25	0	0	L	R	6-4	220	5-4-76	1994	Arlington, Texas
Lennon, Patrick	.293	56	116	14	34	6	1	1	14	15	35	0	1	R	R	6-2	200	4-27-68	1986	Whiteville, N.C.
Lesher, Brian	.229	46	131	17	30	4	1	4	16	9	30	4	1	R	L	6-5	205	3-5-71	1992	Newark, Del.
Magadan, Dave	.303	128	271	38	82	10	1	4	30	50	40	1	0	L	R	6-3	200	9-30-62	1983	Tampa, Fla.
Mashore, Damon	.247	92	279	55	69	10	2	3	18	50	82	5	4	R	R	5-11	195	10-31-69	1991	Concord, Calif.
Mayne, Brent	.289	85	256	29	74	12	0	6	22	18	33	1	0	L	R	6-1	190	4-19-68	1989	Costa Mesa, Calif.
McDonald, Jason	.263	78	236	47	62	11	4	4	14	36	49	13	8	S	R	5-8	175	3-20-72	1993	Elk Grove, Calif.
McGwire, Mark	.284	105	366	48	104	24	0	34	81	58	98	1	0	R	R	6-5	225	10-1-63	1984	Claremont, Calif.
Molina, Izzy	.198	48	111	6	22	3	1	3	7	3	17	0	0	R	R	6-0	200	6-3-71	1990	Miami, Fla.
Sheldon, Scott	.250	13	24	2	6	0	0	1	2	1	6	0	0	R	R	6-3	185	11-28-68	1991	Houston, Texas
Spiezio, Scott	.243	147	538	58	131	28	4	14	65	44	75	9	3	S	R	6-2	205	9-21-72	1993	Morris, Ill.
Stairs, Matt	.298	133	352	62	105	19	0	27	73	50	60	3	2	L	R	5-9	175	2-27-69	1989	Stanley, N.B.
Tejada, Miguel	.202	26	99	10	20	3	2	2	10	2	22	2	0	R	R	5-11	180	5-25-76	1994	Bani, D.R.
Williams, George	.289	76	201	30	58	9	1	3	22	35	46	0	1	S	R	5-10	190	4-22-69	1991	La Crosse, Wis.
Young, Ernie	.223	71	175	22	39	7	0	5	15	19	57	1	3	R	R	6-1	190	7-8-69	1990	Chicago, Ill.

PITCHING	W	L	ERA	G	GS	CG	SV	IP	H	R	ER	BB	SO	B	T	HT	WT	DOB	1st Yr	Resides
Acre, Mark	2	0	5.74	15	0	0	0	16	21	10	10	8	12	R	R	6-8	235	9-16-68	1991	Corning, Calif.
Adams, Willie	3	5	8.18	13	12	0	0	58	73	53	53	32	37	R	R	6-7	215	10-8-72	1993	La Mirada, Calif.
Brewer, Billy	0	0	13.50	3	0	0	0	2	4	3	3	2	1	L	L	6-1	175	4-15-68	1990	Waco, Texas
Groom, Buddy	2	2	5.15	78	0	0	3	65	75	38	37	24	45	L	L	6-2	200	7-10-65	1987	Red Oak, Texas
Haught, Gary	0	0	7.15	6	0	0	0	11	12	9	9	6	11	S	R	6-1	190	9-29-70	1992	Choctaw, Okla.
Haynes, Jimmy	3	6	4.42	13	13	0	0	73	74	38	36	40	65	R	R	6-4	185	9-5-72	1991	La Grange, Ga.
Johnson, Dane	4	1	4.53	38	0	0	2	46	49	28	23	31	43	R	R	6-5	205	2-10-63	1993	Miami, Fla.
Johnstone, John	0	0	2.84	5	0	0	0	6	7	2	2	7	4	R	R	6-3	195	11-25-68	1987	Jacksonville, Fla.
Karsay, Steve	3	12	5.77	24	24	0	0	133	166	92	85	47	92	R	R	6-3	210	3-24-72	1990	Tempe, Ariz.
Kubinski, Tim	0	0	5.68	11	0	0	0	13	12	9	8	6	10	L	L	6-4	205	1-20-72	1993	San Luis Obispo, Calif.
Lewis, Richie	2	0	9.64	14	0	0	0	19	24	21	20	15	12	R	R	5-10	175	1-25-66	1987	Losantville, Ind.
Lorraine, Andrew	3	1	6.37	12	6	0	0	30	45	22	21	15	18	L	L	6-3	195	8-11-72	1993	Valencia, Calif.
Ludwick, Eric	1	4	8.25	6	5	0	0	24	32	24	22	16	14	R	R	6-5	210	12-14-71	1993	Las Vegas, Nev.
Mathews, T.J.	6	2	4.40	24	0	0	3	29	34	18	14	12	24	R	R	6-2	200	1-19-70	1992	Henderson, Nev.
Mohler, Mike	1	10	5.13	62	10	0	1	102	116	65	58	54	66	R	L	6-2	195	7-26-68	1990	Gonzales, La.
Montgomery, Steve	0	1	9.95	4	0	0	0	6	10	7	7	8	1	R	R	6-4	200	12-25-70	1992	Corona Del Mar, Calif.
Oquist, Mike	4	6	5.02	19	17	1	0	108	111	62	60	43	72	R	R	6-2	170	5-30-68	1989	La Junta, Colo.
Prieto, Ariel	6	8	5.04	22	22	0	0	125	155	84	70	70	90	R	R	6-3	220	10-22-66	1995	Naples, Fla.
Reyes, Carlos	3	4	5.82	37	6	0	0	77	101	52	50	25	43	S	R	6-1	190	4-19-69	1991	Macon, Ga.
Rigby, Brad	1	7	4.87	14	14	0	0	78	92	44	42	22	34	R	R	6-6	203	5-14-73	1994	Longwood, Fla.
Small, Aaron	9	5	4.28	71	0	0	4	97	109	50	46	40	57	R	R	6-5	200	11-23-71	1989	Victorville, Calif.
Taylor, Billy	3	4	3.82	72	0	0	23	73	70	32	31	36	66	R	R	6-8	200	10-16-61	1980	Thomasville, Ga.
Telgheder, Dave	4	6	6.06	20	19	0	0	101	134	71	68	35	55	R	R	6-3	212	11-11-66	1989	Slate Hill, N.Y.
Wengert, Don	5	11	6.04	49	12	1	2	134	177	96	90	41	68	R	R	6-3	205	11-6-69	1992	Sioux City, Iowa
Witasick, Jay	0	0	5.73	8	0	0	0	11	14	7	7	6	8	R	R	6-4	205	8-28-72	1993	Bel Air, Md.
Wojciechowski, Steve	0	2	7.84	2	2	0	0	10	17	9	9	1	5	L	L	6-2	185	7-29-70	1991	Calumet City, Ill.

FIELDING

Catcher	PCT	G	PO	A	E	DP	PB
Mayne	.996	83	419	36	2	5	1
Molina	.992	48	218	17	2	1	3
Williams	.984	67	337	27	6	3	1

First Base	PCT	G	PO	A	E	DP
Giambi	.989	51	399	39	5	49
Lesher	1.000	3	21	2	0	3
Magadan	1.000	30	123	11	0	15
McGwire	.994	101	884	60	6	88
Stairs	.958	7	20	3	1	2

Second Base	PCT	G	PO	A	E	DP
Batista	1.000	1	2	4	0	0
Bellhorn	.960	17	41	56	4	16
Bournigal	1.000	7	1	7	0	0
Brito	1.000	2	3	8	0	5
Sheldon	1.000	1	1	2	0	1
Spiezio	.990	146	280	415	7	93

Third Base	PCT	G	PO	A	E	DP
Batista	1.000	4	3	1	0	0
Bellhorn	.951	40	31	66	5	8
Brito	.920	10	8	15	2	2
Brosius	.977	107	92	205	7	23
Magadan	.940	49	25	54	5	7
Sheldon	.000	1	0	0	0	0
Spiezio	.000	1	0	0	0	0

Shortstop	PCT	G	PO	A	E	DP
Batista	.970	61	91	169	8	38
Bellhorn	1.000	1	0	1	0	0
Bournigal	.980	74	99	192	6	40
Brito	1.000	6	5	8	0	1
Brosius	.970	30	25	39	2	8
Sheldon	.939	12	15	16	2	4
Tejada	.969	26	54	69	4	18

Outfield	PCT	G	PO	A	E	DP
Berroa	.986	43	71	1	1	0
Brosius	.964	22	25	2	1	0
Canseco	.938	44	74	2	5	0
Giambi	.982	68	102	5	2	1
Grieve	1.000	24	39	1	0	1
Lennon	.948	36	55	0	3	0
Lesher	.958	32	66	3	3	1
Mashore	.991	89	203	10	2	3
McDonald	.969	74	151	3	5	1
Stairs	.977	89	122	6	3	0
Young	.972	66	135	4	4	0

FARM SYSTEM

Director of Player Development: Keith Lieppman

Class	Farm Team	League	W	L	Pct.	Finish*	Manager	First Yr
AAA	Edmonton (Alta.) Trappers	Pacific Coast	80	64	.556	+2nd (10)	Gary Jones	1995
AA	Huntsville (Ala.) Stars	Southern	77	62	.554	1st (10)	Mike Quade	1985
#A	Modesto (Calif.) A's	California	74	67	.525	4th (10)	Jeffrey Leonard	1975
#A	Visalia (Calif.) Oaks	California	71	69	.507	5th (10)	Tony DeFrancesco	1997
A	Southern Oregon Timberjacks	Northwest	41	35	.539	4th (8)	John Kuehl	1979
R	Scottsdale (Ariz.) Athletics	Arizona	29	27	.518	3rd (6)	Juan Navarrete	1988

*Finish in overall standings (No. of teams in league) #Advanced level +Won league championship

ORGANIZATION LEADERS

MAJOR LEAGUERS

BATTING

*AVG	Geronimo Berroa	.310
R	Jason Giambi	66
H	Jason Giambi	152
TB	Jason Giambi	257
2B	Jason Giambi	41
3B	Two tied at	4
HR	Mark McGwire	34
RBI	Two tied at	81
BB	Mark McGwire	58
SO	Jose Canseco	122
SB	Jason McDonald	13

PITCHING

W	Aaron Small	9
L	Steve Karsay	12
#ERA	Aaron Small	4.28
G	Buddy Groom	78
CG	Two tied at	1
SV	Billy Taylor	23
IP	Don Wengert	134
BB	Ariel Prieto	70
SO	Steve Karsay	92

MEL BAILEY

Jason Giambi

MEL BAILEY

Ben Grieve

MINOR LEAGUERS

BATTING

*AVG	Ben Grieve, Edmonton/Huntsville	.350
R	Mike Neill, Edmonton/Huntsville	132
H	D.T. Cromer, Huntsville	176
TB	Ben Grieve, Edmonton/Huntsville	307
2B	T.R. Marcinczyk, Modesto	41
3B	Ryan Christenson, Edm./Hunt./Visalia	13
HR	Ben Grieve, Edmonton/Huntsville	31
RBI	Ben Grieve, Edmonton/Huntsville	136
BB	Ryan Christenson, Edm./Hunt./Visalia	105
SO	Jose Castro, Edm./Hunts./Modesto	129
SB	Josue Espada, Visalia	46

PITCHING

W	Two tied at	12
L	Chris Nichting, Edmonton	13
#ERA	Brett Laxton, Visalia	2.99
G	Todd Weinberg, Huntsville/Visalia	58
CG	Two tied at	3
SV	Todd Weinberg, Huntsville/Visalia	23
IP	Bill King, Huntsville	176
BB	Stacy Hollins, Edmonton/Huntsville	75
SO	Kevin Gregg, Visalia	136

*Minimum 250 At-Bats #Minimum 75 Innings

TOP 10 PROSPECTS

MEL BAILEY

Miguel Tejada

How the Athletics Top 10 prospects, as judged by Baseball America prior to the 1997 season, fared in 1997:

Player, Pos.	Club (Class)	AVG	AB	R	H	2B	3B	HR	RBI	SB
1. Miguel Tejada, ss	Oakland	.202	99	10	20	3	2	2	10	2
	Huntsville (AA)	.275	502	85	138	20	3	22	97	15
2. Ben Grieve, of	Oakland	.312	93	12	29	6	0	3	24	0
	Edmonton (AAA)	.426	108	27	46	11	1	7	28	0
	Huntsvile (AA)	.328	372	100	122	29	2	24	108	5
3. Eric Chavez, 3b	Visalia (A)	.271	520	67	141	30	3	18	100	13
6. Steve Cox, 1b	Edmonton (AAA)	.274	467	84	128	34	1	15	93	1
7. Mark Bellhorn, 2b	Oakland	.228	224	33	51	9	1	6	19	7
	Edmonton (AAA)	.328	241	54	79	18	3	11	46	6
9. Scott Spiezio, 2b	Oakland	.243	538	58	131	28	4	14	65	9
10. Danny Ardoin, c	Huntsville (AA)	.231	208	26	48	10	1	4	23	2
	Visalia (A)	.234	145	16	34	7	1	3	19	0

Player, Pos.	Club (Class)	W	L	ERA	G	SV	IP	H	BB	SO
4. Brad Rigby, rhp	Oakland	1	7	4.87	14	0	78	92	22	34
	Edmonton (AAA)	8	4	4.37	15	0	82	95	26	49
5. Jay Witasick, rhp	Oakland	0	0	5.73	8	0	11	14	6	8
	Edmonton (AAA)	3	2	4.28	13	0	27	25	15	17
	Modesto (A)	0	1	4.15	9	1	17	16	5	29
8. Jamey Price, rhp	Edmonton (AAA)	2	0	1.64	2	0	11	9	1	10
	Huntsville (AA)	9	3	5.30	20	0	110	153	38	80

EDMONTON — Class AAA

PACIFIC COAST LEAGUE

BATTING	AVG	G	AB	R	H	2B	3B	HR	RBI	BB	SO	SB	CS	B	T	HT	WT	DOB	1st Yr	Resides
Batista, Tony	.315	33	124	25	39	10	1	3	21	17	18	2	2	R	R	6-0	180	12-9-73	1992	Mao Valverde, D.R.
Bellhorn, Mark	.328	70	241	54	79	18	3	11	46	64	59	6	6	S	R	6-1	195	8-23-74	1995	Oviedo, Fla.
Castro, Jose	.167	2	6	0	1	0	0	0	0	1	2	0	1	S	R	5-10	165	10-15-74	1994	Villa Vasquez, D.R.
Christenson, Ryan	.286	16	49	12	14	2	2	2	5	11	11	2	0	R	R	5-11	175	3-28-74	1995	Apple Valley, Calif.
Cox, Steve	.274	131	467	84	128	34	1	15	93	88	90	1	3	L	L	6-4	225	10-31-74	1992	Strathmore, Calif.
Garrison, Webster	.289	125	429	70	124	24	2	15	80	57	91	5	3	R	R	5-11	170	8-24-65	1984	Marrero, La.
Grieve, Ben	.426	27	108	27	46	11	1	7	28	12	16	0	1	L	R	6-4	220	5-4-76	1994	Arlington, Texas
Gubanich, Creighton	.331	43	145	23	48	13	0	7	34	14	42	0	2	R	R	6-4	220	3-27-72	1991	Phoenixville, Pa.
Herrera, Jose	.297	122	421	64	125	21	2	4	41	42	64	7	5	L	L	6-0	164	8-30-72	1991	Santo Domingo, D.R.
Hinch, A.J.	.376	39	125	23	47	7	0	4	24	20	13	2	0	R	R	6-1	195	5-15-74	1996	Midwest City, Okla.
Lennon, Patrick	.343	39	134	28	46	7	0	9	35	22	34	0	0	R	R	6-2	200	4-27-68	1986	Whiteville, N.C.
Lesher, Brian	.323	110	415	85	134	27	5	21	78	64	86	14	3	R	L	6-5	205	3-5-71	1992	Newark, Del.
Martins, Eric	.280	27	82	17	23	7	1	1	8	11	19	0	0	R	R	5-10	175	11-19-72	1994	Rowland Heights, Calif.
Mayne, Brent	.000	2	3	0	0	0	0	0	0	0	1	0	0	L	R	6-1	190	4-19-68	1989	Costa Mesa, Calif.
McDonald, Jason	.264	79	276	74	73	14	6	4	30	74	58	31	9	S	R	5-8	175	3-20-72	1993	Elk Grove, Calif.
Molina, Izzy	.261	61	218	33	57	11	3	6	34	12	27	2	0	R	R	6-0	200	6-3-71	1990	Miami, Fla.
Morales, Willie	.291	56	179	23	52	12	0	5	35	11	27	0	2	R	R	5-10	182	9-7-72	1993	Tucson, Ariz.
Neill, Mike	.190	7	21	3	4	0	0	0	3	7	7	1	1	L	L	6-2	200	4-27-70	1991	Seaford, Del.
Sheldon, Scott	.315	118	422	89	133	39	6	19	77	59	104	5	2	R	R	6-3	185	11-28-68	1991	Houston, Texas
Smith, Demond	.219	42	151	22	33	3	4	5	22	23	31	10	3	S	R	5-11	170	11-6-72	1990	Rialto, Calif.
Williams, George	.000	3	7	0	0	0	0	0	0	1	1	0	0	S	R	5-10	190	4-22-69	1991	La Crosse, Wis.
Wood, Jason	.321	130	505	83	162	35	7	19	87	45	74	2	4	R	R	6-1	170	12-16-69	1991	Fresno, Calif.
Young, Ernie	.323	54	195	39	63	10	0	9	45	37	46	5	2	R	R	6-1	190	7-8-69	1990	Chicago, Ill.

PITCHING	W	L	ERA	G	GS	CG	SV	IP	H	R	ER	BB	SO	B	T	HT	WT	DOB	1st Yr	Resides
Acre, Mark	3	4	4.15	43	0	0	11	48	48	27	22	20	46	R	R	6-8	235	9-16-68	1991	Corning, Calif.
Adams, Willie	5	4	6.45	13	12	0	0	75	105	57	54	19	58	R	R	6-7	215	10-8-72	1993	La Mirada, Calif.
Boever, Joe	6	3	4.96	17	3	0	1	45	53	26	25	4	26	R	R	6-1	200	10-4-60	1982	Palm Harbor, Fla.
2-team (36 Calgary)	10	8	4.99	53	3	0	9	92	112	54	51	23	81							
Brewer, Billy	0	0	5.63	7	1	0	1	8	8	5	5	6	11	L	L	6-1	175	4-15-68	1990	Waco, Texas
Burrows, Terry	2	2	5.67	13	0	0	0	27	35	18	17	15	24	L	L	6-1	185	11-28-68	1990	Lake Charles, La.
2-team (31 Las Vegas)	3	7	6.08	44	1	0	2	61	79	42	41	34	50							
Chouinard, Bobby	6	6	6.03	25	21	1	0	100	129	80	67	26	58	R	R	6-1	188	5-1-72	1990	Forest Grove, Ore.
D'Amico, Jeff	1	2	8.22	10	7	0	1	31	42	29	28	6	19	R	R	6-3	200	11-9-74	1993	Redmond, Wash.
Daspit, Jamie	0	1	5.87	3	0	0	0	8	9	5	5	2	2	R	R	6-7	210	8-10-69	1990	Sacramento, Calif.
2-team (10 Las Vegas)	0	2	6.83	13	2	0	0	28	31	22	21	9	14							
Dunbar, Matt	1	0	4.98	12	1	0	0	22	29	12	12	8	18	L	L	6-0	160	10-15-68	1990	Tallahassee, Fla.
Haught, Gary	1	1	3.59	30	2	0	11	43	37	20	17	13	35	S	R	6-1	190	9-29-70	1992	Choctaw, Okla.
Haynes, Jimmy	0	2	4.85	5	5	0	0	30	36	22	16	11	24	R	R	6-4	185	9-5-72	1991	La Grange, Ga.
Hollins, Stacy	0	0	10.13	1	1	0	0	3	5	4	3	3	2	R	R	6-3	195	7-31-72	1992	Willis, Texas
Jimenez, Miguel	0	2	11.15	7	2	0	1	15	29	19	19	11	11	R	R	6-2	205	8-19-69	1991	New York, N.Y.
Johnson, Dane	1	1	5.63	14	0	0	6	16	17	11	10	8	13	R	R	6-5	205	2-10-63	1993	Miami, Fla.
Kjos, Ryan	0	1	36.00	1	0	0	0	2	6	8	8	3	2	R	R	6-5	230	3-4-73	1995	Hopkins, Minn.
Kubinski, Tim	4	4	4.50	47	0	0	7	76	64	39	38	34	53	L	L	6-4	205	1-20-72	1993	San Luis Obispo, Calif.
Lewis, Richie	1	1	5.85	11	1	0	1	20	24	13	13	14	25	R	R	5-10	175	1-25-66	1987	Losantville, Ind.
Lorraine, Andrew	8	6	4.74	23	20	2	0	118	143	72	62	34	75	L	L	6-3	195	8-11-72	1993	Valencia, Calif.
Ludwick, Eric	1	1	3.32	6	3	0	0	19	22	7	7	4	20	R	R	6-5	210	12-14-71	1993	Las Vegas, Nev.
Montgomery, Steve	2	1	5.79	30	0	0	3	47	61	30	30	17	38	R	R	6-4	200	12-25-70	1992	Corona Del Mar, Calif.
Nichting, Chris	7	13	7.76	33	24	3	1	131	170	120	113	46	90	R	R	6-1	205	5-13-66	1988	Cincinnati, Ohio
Oquist, Mike	6	1	3.25	9	9	1	0	53	57	23	19	16	37	R	R	6-2	170	5-30-68	1989	La Junta, Colo.
Phillips, Tony	1	0	5.09	11	1	0	0	23	28	13	13	6	14	R	R	6-4	195	6-9-69	1991	Hattiesburg, Miss.
2-team (29 Tucson)	4	2	5.44	40	2	0	0	81	95	56	49	27	46							
Price, Jamey	2	0	1.64	2	1	0	0	11	9	3	2	1	10	L	R	6-7	205	2-11-72	1996	Pine Bluff, Ark.
Prieto, Ariel	0	0	1.50	2	2	0	0	6	4	1	1	1	7	R	R	6-3	220	10-22-66	1995	Naples, Fla.
Reyes, Carlos	2	0	3.48	5	4	1	0	31	30	14	12	3	23	S	R	6-1	190	4-19-69	1991	Macon, Ga.
Ricci, Chuck	0	0	16.88	4	0	0	0	5	10	10	10	6	5	R	R	6-2	180	11-20-68	1987	Laurel, Md.
Rigby, Brad	8	4	4.37	15	15	0	0	82	95	49	40	26	49	R	R	6-6	203	5-14-73	1994	Longwood, Fla.
Small, Aaron	1	0	0.00	1	1	0	0	5	1	0	0	0	4	R	R	6-5	200	11-23-71	1989	Victorville, Calif.
Witasick, Jay	3	2	4.28	13	1	0	0	27	25	13	13	15	17	R	R	6-4	205	8-28-72	1993	Bel Air, Md.
Wojciechowski, Steve	8	2	3.84	26	7	0	1	66	68	33	28	23	49	L	L	6-2	185	7-29-70	1991	Calumet City, Ill.

FIELDING

Catcher	PCT	G	PO	A	E	DP	PB
Gubanich	.991	29	194	17	2	3	8
Hinch	.986	31	197	7	3	3	1
Mayne	1.000	1	5	0	0	0	0
Molina	.995	55	330	32	2	6	6
Morales	.976	32	153	7	4	1	2
Williams	1.000	2	8	1	0	0	0

First Base	PCT	G	PO	A	E	DP
Cox	.991	128	1043	70	10	104
Garrison	1.000	12	85	3	0	6
Lesher	1.000	7	35	0	0	4
Morales	1.000	3	25	1	0	4

Second Base	PCT	G	PO	A	E	DP
Bellhorn	.970	42	74	118	6	24
Castro	.923	2	3	9	1	1
Garrison	.988	58	105	132	3	35
Martins	.959	19	29	42	3	8
Sheldon	.992	31	43	85	1	21

Third Base	PCT	G	PO	A	E	DP
Bellhorn	1.000	5	1	9	0	1
Garrison	.933	23	16	40	4	1
Morales	1.000	5	3	5	0	1
Wood	.954	117	88	222	15	30

Shortstop	PCT	G	PO	A	E	DP
Batista	.952	32	40	78	6	16
Bellhorn	.928	23	30	60	7	11
Sheldon	.970	81	96	228	10	44
Wood	.966	11	15	42	2	7

Outfield	PCT	G	PO	A	E	DP
Christenson	1.000	16	42	1	0	1
Garrison	.967	20	29	0	1	0
Grieve	.964	27	51	2	2	1
Herrera	.965	114	210	9	8	1
Hinch	1.000	3	4	0	0	0
Lennon	1.000	10	13	1	0	0
Lesher	.970	99	185	6	6	2
McDonald	.975	78	187	10	5	3
Neill	.857	5	6	0	1	0
Smith	.958	29	67	2	3	0
Young	.991	43	100	5	1	2

HUNTSVILLE — Class AA

SOUTHERN LEAGUE

BATTING	AVG	G	AB	R	H	2B	3B	HR	RBI	BB	SO	SB	CS	B	T	HT	WT	DOB	1st Yr	Resides
Ardoin, Danny	.231	57	208	26	48	10	1	4	23	17	38	2	3	R	R	6-0	195	7-8-74	1995	Ville Platte, La.

BATTING	AVG	G	AB	R	H	2B	3B	HR	RBI	BB	SO	SB	CS	B	T	HT	WT	DOB	1st Yr	Resides
Castro, Jose	.385	5	13	4	5	0	0	0	0	4	2	0	0	S	R	5-10	165	10-15-74	1994	Villa Vasquez, D.R.
Christenson, Ryan	.367	29	120	39	44	9	3	2	18	24	23	5	4	R	R	5-11	175	3-28-74	1995	Apple Valley, Calif.
Coolbaugh, Mike	.308	139	559	100	172	37	2	30	132	52	105	8	3	R	R	6-1	190	6-5-72	1990	San Antonio, Texas
Cromer, D.T.	.323	134	545	100	176	40	6	15	121	60	102	12	7	L	L	6-2	205	3-19-71	1992	Murrells Inlet, S.C.
DeBoer, Rob	.243	91	288	55	70	16	1	18	48	60	111	8	5	R	R	5-10	205	2-4-71	1994	Omaha, Neb.
Grieve, Ben	.328	100	372	100	122	29	2	24	108	81	75	5	1	L	R	6-4	220	5-4-76	1994	Arlington, Texas
Hernandez, Ramon	.193	44	161	27	31	3	0	4	24	18	23	0	0	R	R	6-0	170	5-20-76	1994	Caracas, Venez.
Hughes, Troy	.209	72	258	37	54	12	0	5	33	23	50	2	1	R	R	6-4	212	1-3-71	1989	Mt. Vernon, Ill.
Martins, Eric	.259	61	205	33	53	10	3	3	31	23	31	2	1	R	R	5-10	175	11-19-72	1994	Rowland Heights, Calif.
Morales, Willie	.272	36	136	19	37	11	0	3	24	17	24	1	0	R	R	5-10	182	9-7-72	1993	Tucson, Ariz.
Neill, Mike	.340	122	486	129	165	30	2	14	80	72	113	16	7	L	L	6-2	200	4-27-70	1991	Seaford, Del.
Newhan, David	.316	57	212	40	67	13	2	5	35	28	59	5	5	L	R	5-11	180	9-7-73	1995	Yorba Linda, Calif.
Ramirez, Roberto	.318	19	66	7	21	4	0	0	6	0	16	2	0	R	R	6-2	180	3-18-70	1989	Phoenix, Ariz.
Smith, Demond	.279	87	323	79	90	20	6	8	39	65	76	31	9	S	R	5-11	170	11-6-72	1990	Rialto, Calif.
Tejada, Miguel	.275	128	502	85	138	20	3	22	97	50	99	15	11	R	R	5-11	180	5-25-76	1994	Bani, D.R.
Walker, Dane	.241	106	361	62	87	17	3	7	52	68	87	7	2	L	R	5-10	180	11-16-69	1991	Lake Oswego, Ore.

PITCHING	W	L	ERA	G	GS	CG	SV	IP	H	R	ER	BB	SO	B	T	HT	WT	DOB	1st Yr	Resides
Baez, Benito	2	4	9.14	15	7	0	0	42	64	47	43	22	27	L	L	6-0	180	5-6-77	1994	Bonao, D.R.
Baxter, Bob	1	1	11.57	6	0	0	0	5	15	10	6	3	3	R	L	6-1	180	2-17-69	1990	Norwood, Mass.
Bennett, Bob	4	3	7.17	23	1	0	1	43	64	38	34	15	32	R	R	6-4	205	12-30-70	1992	Rapid City, S.D.
Bradley, Bert	0	0	0.00	1	0	0	0	1	0	0	0	0	0	R	R	6-1	190	12-23-56	1997	Mattoon, Ill.
Bussa, Todd	2	1	4.22	19	0	0	7	21	20	13	10	12	27	R	R	5-11	170	12-13-72	1991	Palm Beach Gardens, Fla.
Connelly, Steve	3	3	3.75	43	0	0	7	70	74	33	29	20	49	R	R	6-3	210	4-27-74	1995	Long Beach, Calif.
Dale, Carl	6	4	5.38	20	16	0	0	85	95	61	51	43	57	R	R	6-2	215	12-7-72	1994	Algood, Tenn.
Dunbar, Matt	1	0	5.40	5	0	0	0	5	8	3	3	1	7	L	L	6-0	160	10-15-68	1990	Tallahassee, Fla.
Haught, Gary	0	1	5.59	6	0	0	0	10	15	6	6	2	6	S	R	6-1	190	9-29-70	1992	Choctaw, Okla.
Hollins, Stacy	5	4	5.37	32	17	0	2	114	110	77	68	72	68	R	R	6-3	195	7-31-72	1992	Willis, Texas
Jimenez, Miguel	7	6	5.86	24	18	1	0	101	127	83	66	50	64	R	R	6-2	205	8-19-69	1991	New York, N.Y.
King, Bill	9	7	4.19	28	27	1	0	176	216	99	82	28	103	R	R	6-5	225	2-18-73	1994	Chipley, Fla.
Manning, Derek	1	2	5.93	21	0	0	2	44	57	31	29	12	27	L	L	6-4	220	7-21-70	1993	Wilmington, N.C.
Maurer, Mike	8	7	3.83	52	5	0	2	85	86	48	36	31	61	R	R	6-2	195	7-4-72	1994	Burnsville, Minn.
Nelson, Chris	9	3	4.97	20	15	1	0	100	116	60	55	25	71	R	R	6-3	180	1-26-73	1995	San Diego, Calif.
Phoenix, Steve	0	3	5.80	29	0	0	9	36	43	25	23	11	25	R	R	6-3	183	1-31-68	1990	El Cajon, Calif.
Price, Jamey	9	3	5.30	20	20	0	0	110	153	71	65	38	80	L	R	6-7	205	2-11-72	1996	Pine Bluff, Ark.
Rajotte, Jason	2	6	4.40	55	0	0	3	57	67	35	28	29	35	L	L	6-0	185	12-15-72	1993	West Warwick, R.I.
Rivette, Scott	3	1	6.69	7	6	0	0	39	52	29	29	19	33	S	R	6-2	200	2-8-74	1995	Upland, Calif.
Stein, Blake	3	2	5.71	7	7	0	0	35	36	24	22	20	25	R	R	6-7	210	8-3-73	1994	Folsom, La.
Wagner, Bret	0	0	20.25	3	0	0	0	3	7	11	6	6	3	L	L	6-0	190	4-17-73	1994	New Cumberland, Pa.
Weinberg, Todd	2	1	2.33	20	0	0	3	27	18	12	7	17	24	R	L	6-3	225	6-13-72	1993	Somerset, Mass.

FIELDING

Catcher	PCT	G	PO	A	E	DP	
Ardoin	.972	51	301	43	10	6	8
DeBoer	.979	42	205	24	5	3	2
Hernandez	.996	34	238	23	1	1	0
Morales	.991	17	102	10	1	2	2

First Base	PCT	G	PO	A	E	DP
Cromer	.986	131	1167	100	18	129
Hernandez	1.000	4	34	2	0	2
Morales	.980	5	43	7	1	6

Second Base	PCT	G	PO	A	E	DP
Castro	.000	1	0	0	0	0
Coolbaugh	1.000	1	1	1	0	0
Martins	.967	57	126	168	10	46
Newhan	.934	48	96	129	16	27
Walker	.932	39	74	104	13	28

Third Base	PCT	G	PO	A	E	DP
Ardoin	1.000	3	1	2	0	0
Coolbaugh	.943	131	94	302	24	35
Hernandez	1.000	2	2	2	0	0
Martins	.000	1	0	0	1	0
Walker	.842	8	5	11	3	1

Shortstop	PCT	G	PO	A	E	DP
Castro	.913	5	4	17	2	6
Coolbaugh	.950	8	11	27	2	5
Tejada	.948	128	229	423	36	97

Outfield	PCT	G	PO	A	E	DP
Christenson	.988	29	81	1	1	0
Cromer	1.000	1	2	1	0	0
DeBoer	.714	4	5	0	2	0
Grieve	.961	98	193	6	8	2
Hughes	.974	50	67	9	2	2
Neill	.982	119	212	12	4	2
Ramirez	.935	17	25	4	2	1
Smith	.971	84	167	2	5	0
Walker	1.000	29	38	6	0	0

MODESTO — Class A

CALIFORNIA LEAGUE

BATTING	AVG	G	AB	R	H	2B	3B	HR	RBI	BB	SO	SB	CS	B	T	HT	WT	DOB	1st Yr	Resides
Bournigal, Rafael	.238	7	21	0	5	1	0	0	2	3	2	0	0	R	R	5-11	165	5-12-66	1987	Santo Domingo, D.R.
Bowles, Justin	.327	107	394	66	129	39	9	7	51	56	85	6	3	L	L	6-0	195	8-20-73	1996	Lake Jackson, Texas
Brito, Tilson	.333	4	9	3	3	1	0	1	3	2	1	0	0	R	R	6-0	170	5-28-72	1990	Los Trinitarios, D.R.
Brosius, Scott	.333	2	3	1	1	0	0	0	1	1	0	0	0	R	R	6-1	190	8-15-66	1987	McMinnville, Ore.
Castro, Jose	.212	112	368	67	78	17	4	5	28	58	125	27	13	S	R	5-10	165	10-15-74	1994	Villa Vasquez, D.R.
Dilone, Juan	.225	97	325	54	73	15	6	19	51	44	112	7	1	S	R	6-1	188	5-10-73	1990	Higuey, D.R.
Encarnacion, Mario	.297	111	364	70	108	17	9	18	78	42	121	14	11	R	R	6-2	187	9-24-77	1994	Bani, D.R.
Figueroa, Jose	.182	7	11	2	2	0	0	1	3	4	3	1	0	R	R	6-1	200	12-25-77	1995	Santo Domingo, D.R.
Hinch, A.J.	.309	95	333	70	103	25	3	20	73	42	68	8	3	R	R	6-1	195	5-15-74	1996	Midwest City, Okla.
Jones, Tim	.239	119	309	45	74	18	3	8	47	46	120	8	3	L	R	6-0	208	9-13-77	1995	Buena Park, Calif.
Lara, Edward	.000	2	0	0	0	0	0	0	0	0	0	0	0	S	R	5-9	145	10-30-75	1993	Bani, D.R.
Lennon, Patrick	.188	5	16	3	3	1	0	1	4	3	5	0	0	R	R	6-2	200	4-27-68	1986	Whiteville, N.C.
Marcinczyk, T.R.	.276	133	463	89	128	41	2	23	91	71	107	4	4	R	R	6-2	195	10-11-73	1996	Plainville, Conn.
McKay, Cody	.249	125	390	47	97	20	1	7	50	46	69	4	2	L	R	6-0	190	1-11-74	1996	Scottsdale, Ariz.
Ortiz, Jose	.245	128	497	92	122	25	7	16	58	60	107	22	14	R	R	5-11	160	6-13-77	1996	Cotui, D.R.
Paulino, Arturo	.207	88	217	26	45	12	0	2	22	17	70	1	5	R	R	5-11	170	7-18-74	1993	San Cristobal, D.R.
Penix, Troy	.225	58	160	12	36	8	0	3	18	10	40	0	0	L	L	6-4	230	8-25-71	1992	Stockton, Calif.
Polanco, Juan	.234	68	137	19	32	3	2	6	19	21	39	7	2	R	R	6-0	190	1-6-75	1993	Bani, D.R.
Soriano, Jose	.228	124	360	51	82	13	3	5	44	37	95	28	11	R	R	6-0	165	4-4-74	1992	Bani, D.R.
Valenti, Jon	.293	105	283	43	83	17	1	5	43	39	55	0	3	R	R	6-1	195	11-26-73	1994	Bakersfield, Calif.
Williams, George	.318	13	44	8	14	4	0	1	6	7	14	0	1	S	R	5-10	190	4-22-69	1991	La Crosse, Wis.

GAMES BY POSITION: C—Figueroa 5, Hinch 86, McKay 59, Valenti 4, Williams 8. **1B**—Dilone 20, Hinch 1, Marcinczyk 100, Penix 34, Valenti 20. **2B**—Castro 109, Lara 2, Ortiz 6, Paulino 40, Valenti 3. **3B**—Brosius 2, Castro 1, Marcinczyk 20, McKay 64, Paulino 12, Polanco 1, Valenti 74. **SS**—Bournigal 5, Brito 4, Castro 1, Ortiz 116, Paulino 27, Valenti 1. **OF**— Bowles 102, Dilone 24, Encarnacion 92, Jones 100,

Lennon 1, Marcinczyk 1, Polanco 50, Soriano 116, Valenti 9.

PITCHING	W	L	ERA	G	GS	CG	SV	IP	H	R	ER	BB	SO	B	T	HT	WT	DOB	1st Yr	Resides
Bennett, Tom	6	9	5.71	25	24	0	0	112	118	84	71	73	116	R	R	6-4	180	5-13-76	1995	Alameda, Calif.
Bussa, Todd	5	4	1.75	30	0	0	8	46	34	15	9	16	61	R	R	5-11	170	12-13-72	1991	Palm Beach Gardens, Fla.
D'Amico, Jeff	7	3	3.80	20	13	0	1	97	115	57	41	34	89	R	R	6-3	200	11-9-74	1993	Redmond, Wash.
Della Ratta, Pete	6	7	3.33	45	0	0	3	84	73	45	31	31	81	R	R	6-4	220	2-14-74	1996	Gulf Breeze, Fla.
Enochs, Chris	3	0	2.78	10	9	0	0	45	51	20	14	12	45	R	R	6-3	225	10-11-75	1997	Newell, W.Va.
Gogolin, Al	0	0	18.00	4	0	0	0	4	9	8	8	2	3	R	R	6-5	215	1-14-72	1994	Marietta, Ga.
Gunther, Kevin	7	2	3.38	42	0	0	17	53	53	24	20	11	43	R	R	6-0	200	2-6-73	1995	Yelm, Wash.
Hause, Brendan	0	0	3.86	2	0	0	0	5	6	2	2	1	1	L	L	6-1	185	10-21-74	1992	San Diego, Calif.
Kjos, Ryan	2	2	3.82	34	0	0	0	61	57	38	26	30	73	R	R	6-5	230	3-4-73	1995	Hopkins, Minn.
Lagattuta, Rico	0	0	9.00	3	0	0	0	1	3	1	1	3	1	L	L	6-2	205	1-14-74	1996	Thousand Oaks, Calif.
Leyva, Julian	4	9	4.92	28	19	0	2	139	148	99	76	38	90	L	R	6-0	218	2-11-78	1996	Riverside, Calif.
Manwiller, Tim	1	1	3.05	7	0	0	0	21	21	8	7	7	18	R	R	6-2	205	9-5-74	1997	Annville, Pa.
Nelson, Chris	3	3	3.83	8	8	0	0	47	55	23	20	7	53	R	R	6-3	180	1-26-73	1995	San Diego, Calif.
Niles, Randy	4	0	2.60	7	5	0	0	35	32	13	10	9	20	R	R	6-2	200	8-28-75	1997	Key West, Fla.
Noriega, Ray	5	8	4.04	28	28	0	0	156	161	101	70	69	119	R	L	5-10	175	3-28-74	1996	Tucson, Ariz.
Oquist, Mike	0	0	4.91	2	2	0	0	4	5	2	2	1	5	R	R	6-2	170	5-30-68	1989	La Junta, Colo.
Rivette, Scott	9	9	3.57	20	20	3	0	126	147	65	50	31	96	S	R	6-2	200	2-8-74	1995	Upland, Calif.
Robertson, Doug	0	0	.00	1	0	0	0	1	1	0	0	0	0	R	R	6-0	205	10-17-74	1996	Bath, Ill.
Telgheder, David	0	0	3.38	2	2	0	0	5	3	2	2	2	4	R	R	6-3	212	11-11-66	1989	Slate Hill, N.Y.
Vizcaino, Luis	0	3	13.19	7	0	0	0	14	24	24	21	13	15	R	R	6-1	180	6-1-77	1995	Bani, D.R.
Wallace, Flint	10	4	3.73	35	8	0	1	99	105	53	41	34	59	R	R	6-1	185	7-21-74	1996	Clyde, Texas
Winkleman, Greg	2	2	5.70	39	1	0	0	60	71	44	38	37	54	L	L	5-10	170	9-7-73	1996	Santa Rosa, Calif.
Witasick, Jay	0	1	4.15	9	2	0	1	17	16	9	8	5	29	R	R	6-4	205	8-28-72	1993	Bel Air, Md.

VISALIA — Class A

CALIFORNIA LEAGUE

BATTING	AVG	G	AB	R	H	2B	3B	HR	RBI	BB	SO	SB	CS	B	T	HT	WT	DOB	1st Yr	Resides
Ardoin, Danny	.234	43	145	16	34	7	1	3	19	21	39	0	1	R	R	6-0	195	7-8-74	1995	Ville Platte, La.
Boston, D.J.	.224	14	49	7	11	3	0	1	4	5	13	0	0	L	L	6-7	230	9-6-71	1991	Cincinnati, Ohio
Byers, MacGregor	.226	18	53	8	12	5	1	0	9	6	15	2	1	R	R	6-0	185	7-22-74	1996	Houston, Texas
Cesar, Dionys	.239	97	285	60	68	16	2	1	11	43	79	10	12	S	R	5-10	167	9-27-76	1994	Santo Domingo, D.R.
Chavez, Eric	.271	134	520	67	141	30	3	18	100	37	91	13	7	L	R	6-1	190	12-7-77	1996	San Diego, Calif.
Christenson, Ryan	.292	83	308	69	90	18	8	13	54	70	72	20	11	R	R	5-11	175	3-28-74	1995	Apple Valley, Calif.
DaVanon, Jeff	.255	119	408	70	104	17	3	6	38	81	101	23	14	S	R	6-0	185	12-8-73	1995	Del Mar, Calif.
Espada, Josue	.274	118	445	90	122	7	3	3	39	72	69	46	17	R	R	5-10	175	8-30-75	1996	Carolina, P.R.
Filchner, Duane	.257	126	432	59	111	30	3	11	55	66	76	6	3	L	L	6-1	185	2-28-73	1995	Radford, Va.
Hernandez, Ramon	.361	86	332	57	120	21	2	15	85	35	47	2	4	R	R	6-0	170	5-20-76	1994	Caracas, Venez.
Koerner, Mike	.188	32	85	13	16	3	2	2	12	8	27	2	3	L	L	6-0	195	3-28-76	1997	Turnersville, N.J.
Lara, Edward	.222	13	45	10	10	4	0	1	3	4	9	1	1	S	R	5-9	145	10-30-75	1993	Bani, D.R.
Mensik, Todd	.200	15	45	3	9	1	0	1	6	6	11	0	0	L	L	6-2	195	2-27-75	1996	Orland Park, Ill.
Miranda, Alex	.174	11	23	2	4	1	1	0	4	3	9	0	1	L	L	6-2	205	5-14-72	1994	Miami, Fla.
Newhan, David	.278	67	241	52	67	15	2	7	48	44	58	9	3	L	R	5-11	180	9-7-73	1995	Yorba Linda, Calif.
Penix, Troy	.208	49	154	13	32	7	0	5	23	9	46	0	2	L	L	6-4	230	8-25-71	1992	Stockton, Calif.
2-team (58 Modesto)	.217	107	314	25	68	15	0	8	41	19	86	0	2							
Ramirez, Roberto	.298	63	242	28	72	12	1	3	29	19	46	4	3	R	R	6-2	180	3-18-70	1989	Phoenix, Ariz.
Rauer, Troy	.221	90	299	37	66	14	3	7	31	25	100	5	5	R	R	6-4	225	11-18-72	1995	Scottsdale, Ariz.
Slemmer, Dave	.280	115	404	70	113	25	1	10	64	44	83	11	3	R	R	6-0	187	3-29-73	1995	Edwardsville, Ill.
Vaz, Roberto	.356	19	73	9	26	5	0	3	13	8	10	2	5	L	L	5-9	195	3-15-75	1997	Tuscaloosa, Ala.
Ventura, Wilfredo	.196	62	184	23	36	5	0	6	23	9	64	1	0	R	R	5-11	210	10-11-76	1993	Santo Domingo, D.R.

GAMES BY POSITION: C—Ardoin 41, Hernandez 80, Ventura 33. **1B**—Ardoin 3, Boston 14, Byers 4, Hernandez 2, Mensik 13, Miranda 11, Penix 43, Slemmer 72, Ventura 13. **2B**—Cesar 52, Lara 10, Newhan 60, Slemmer 38. **3B**—Ardoin 1, Cesar 14, Chavez 118, Lara 1, Slemmer 11. **SS**—Cesar 28, Espada 117, Lara 3. **OF**—Ardoin 1, Byers 10, Cesar 2, Christenson 81, DaVanon 107, Filchner 56, Koerner 31, Ramirez 61, Rauer 80, Slemmer 1, Vaz 19.

PITCHING	W	L	ERA	G	GS	CG	SV	IP	H	R	ER	BB	SO	B	T	HT	WT	DOB	1st Yr	Resides
Abbott, Todd	11	10	5.93	31	20	0	0	121	146	100	80	63	70	R	R	6-4	200	9-13-73	1995	Fayetteville, Ark.
Abreu, Oscar	0	1	14.66	5	2	0	0	12	19	23	19	10	14	R	R	6-1	208	2-21-76	1994	Santo Domingo, D.R.
Baez, Benito	5	5	3.54	16	15	1	0	97	83	40	38	28	87	L	L	6-0	180	5-6-77	1994	Bonao, D.R.
Blumenstock, Brad	0	0	13.89	9	0	0	0	12	22	18	18	11	3	R	R	6-6	225	2-19-75	1996	Marion, Ill.
Brewer, Billy	0	0	0.00	2	2	0	0	3	1	1	0	4	5	L	L	6-1	175	4-15-68	1990	Waco, Texas
DuBose, Eric	1	3	7.04	10	9	0	0	38	43	37	30	28	39	L	L	6-3	215	5-15-76	1997	Nashville, Tenn.
Gregg, Kevin	6	8	5.70	25	24	0	0	115	116	81	73	74	136	R	R	6-6	205	6-20-78	1996	Corvallis, Ore.
Harville, Chad	0	0	5.79	14	0	0	0	19	25	14	12	13	24	R	R	5-9	180	9-16-76	1997	Savannah, Tenn.
Holmes, Mike	2	1	3.81	16	0	0	3	28	28	13	12	4	20	R	R	6-2	200	10-11-75	1997	Greensboro, N.C.
Kazmirski, Robert	1	1	16.62	5	0	0	1	4	11	9	8	5	6	R	R	6-3	200	6-24-72	1995	Agoura Hills, Calif.
Kern, Brian	3	0	7.60	23	0	0	1	34	42	38	29	28	39	R	R	6-0	185	5-11-74	1996	Ewing, Ill.
Laxton, Brett	11	5	2.99	29	22	0	0	139	141	62	46	50	121	L	R	6-2	205	10-5-73	1996	Denham Springs, La.
Mlodik, Kevin	8	9	5.44	35	19	0	0	129	164	86	78	42	91	R	R	6-1	205	8-21-74	1995	Rosholt, Wis.
Morrison, Chris	3	3	3.84	48	0	0	2	80	92	46	34	39	43	R	R	6-0	195	4-3-72	1995	Auburn, Ala.
O'Dell, Jake	8	5	4.54	27	27	1	0	151	159	86	76	47	117	R	R	6-1	205	9-22-73	1996	Round Rock, Texas
Paulino, Jose	3	2	4.54	39	0	0	2	83	89	48	42	32	67	R	R	6-4	180	1-2-77	1994	San Cristobal, D.R.
Perez, Juan	3	6	2.78	53	0	0	8	65	47	30	20	24	66	L	L	6-0	178	3-28-73	1992	La Romana, D.R.
Petcka, Joe	0	1	23.63	4	0	0	0	3	8	8	7	6	1	R	R	6-3	195	10-20-70	1992	Clintonville, Wis.
Smith, Andy	3	7	3.82	42	0	0	1	71	77	40	30	39	67	R	R	6-5	220	1-29-75	1993	Kannapolis, N.C.
Weinberg, Todd	3	2	4.26	38	0	0	20	38	33	23	18	22	39	R	L	6-3	225	6-13-72	1993	Somerset, Mass.

SOUTHERN OREGON — Short-Season Class A

NORTHWEST LEAGUE

BATTING	AVG	G	AB	R	H	2B	3B	HR	RBI	BB	SO	SB	CS	B	T	HT	WT	DOB	1st Yr	Resides
Camilo, Juan	.231	4	13	0	3	0	0	0	2	1	4	0	1	L	R	6-0	203	6-24-78	1996	Santo Domingo, D.R.

BATTING	AVG	G	AB	R	H	2B	3B	HR	RBI	BB	SO	SB	CS	B	T	HT	WT	DOB	1st Yr	Resides
Clifton, Rodney	.270	69	256	66	69	13	5	5	31	54	76	14	3	R	R	6-2	190	11-7-76	1996	Elgin, Ill.
Farris, Ed	.267	66	255	33	68	19	2	5	56	22	76	4	1	L	R	6-0	210	6-3-74	1997	Harrison, Ohio
Figueroa, Jose	.237	41	131	16	31	8	1	2	16	11	40	3	0	R	R	6-1	200	12-25-77	1995	Santo Domingo, D.R.
Flores, Javier	.331	45	160	25	53	11	3	1	25	17	22	2	1	R	R	6-0	185	12-20-75	1997	Broken Arrow, Okla.
Goris, Braulio	.067	5	15	3	1	1	0	0	0	4	11	0	0	L	L	6-3	207	10-5-76	1995	New York, N.Y.
Gorrie, Brad	.302	59	205	48	62	11	2	3	29	28	50	19	3	R	R	5-9	180	1-25-75	1997	Northboro, Mass.
Haynes, Nathan	.280	24	82	18	23	1	1	0	9	26	21	19	3	L	L	5-10	170	9-7-79	1997	Hercules, Calif.
Hernandez, Victor	.149	43	121	14	18	5	1	0	18	12	43	5	0	R	R	6-0	167	2-28-77	1995	Ciales, P.R.
Koerner, Mike	.340	24	106	21	36	12	1	2	19	11	30	7	3	L	L	6-0	195	3-28-76	1997	Turnersville, N.J.
Lara, Edward	.274	65	252	45	69	12	5	2	43	32	28	25	7	S	R	5-9	145	10-30-75	1993	Bani, D.R.
Martinez, Hipolito	.324	65	222	45	72	13	4	9	44	34	65	3	2	R	R	6-1	200	1-30-77	1994	Bani, D.R.
Piatt, Adam	.292	57	216	63	63	9	1	13	35	35	58	19	4	R	R	6-2	195	2-8-76	1997	Fort Myers, Fla.
Robinson, Adam	.272	68	250	41	68	13	2	3	27	28	68	13	11	R	R	6-0	190	6-28-75	1997	Long Valley, N.J.
Sosa, Nick	.230	62	196	29	45	7	2	2	26	55	80	0	3	R	R	6-3	205	7-18-77	1996	Longwood, Fla.
Spiezio, Scott	.556	2	9	1	5	0	0	0	2	2	1	0	0	S	R	6-2	205	9-21-72	1993	Morris, Ill.
Tegland, Ron	.231	37	108	17	25	6	1	3	19	8	37	0	1	R	R	6-2	223	10-18-73	1996	Oxnard, Calif.
Vaz, Roberto	.321	22	78	11	25	6	0	3	15	7	4	5	3	L	L	5-9	195	3-15-75	1997	Tuscaloosa, Ala.

GAMES BY POSITION: C—Figueroa 36, Flores 36, Tegland 18. **1B**—Farris 34, Piatt 1, Sosa 47. **2B**—Gorrie 20, Hernandez 6, Lara 25, Robinson 34, Spiezio 1. **3B**—Flores 3, Goris 1, Gorrie 15, Hernandez 8, Lara 1, Piatt 50, Tegland 3. **SS**—Gorrie 8, Lara 40, Robinson 37. **OF**—Camilo 4, Clifton 69, Farris 9, Gorrie 14, Haynes 22, Hernandez 28, Koerner 24, Martinez 62, Tegland 9, Vaz 13.

PITCHING	W	L	ERA	G	GS	CG	SV	IP	H	R	ER	BB	SO	B	T	HT	WT	DOB	1st Yr	Resides
Abreu, Oscar	2	2	8.31	20	0	0	1	26	26	28	24	25	47	R	R	6-1	208	2-21-76	1994	Santo Domingo, D.R.
Anderson, Jason	3	3	4.99	14	9	0	0	52	63	38	29	19	38	L	L	6-2	185	4-6-76	1997	Salem, Va.
Blumenstock, Brad	0	4	9.33	19	7	0	0	45	61	51	47	30	28	R	R	6-6	225	2-19-75	1996	Marion, Ill.
DuBose, Eric	1	0	0.00	3	1	0	0	10	5	0	0	6	15	L	L	6-3	215	5-15-76	1997	Nashville, Tenn.
Enochs, Chris	0	0	3.48	3	3	0	0	10	12	4	4	2	10	R	R	6-3	225	10-11-75	1997	Newell, W.Va.
Faust, Jason	5	0	2.91	16	2	0	2	46	37	22	15	25	62	R	L	6-0	175	7-14-75	1997	Belleville, Ill.
Gallagher, Bryan	0	1	3.86	2	0	0	0	2	1	2	1	3	3	L	L	6-2	195	10-7-76	1996	Klamath Falls, Ore.
Glaze, Randy	1	2	4.21	21	1	0	1	36	30	21	17	21	38	R	R	6-4	195	2-11-74	1996	Carthage, Texas
Gorrell, Chris	5	3	4.65	18	10	1	0	72	86	50	37	28	60	R	R	6-2	188	1-27-76	1996	Las Vegas, Nev.
Harville, Chad	1	0	0.00	3	0	0	0	5	3	0	0	3	6	R	R	5-9	180	9-16-76	1997	Savannah, Tenn.
Holmes, Mike	2	0	2.51	7	0	0	0	14	14	8	4	4	16	R	R	6-2	200	10-11-75	1997	Greensboro, N.C.
Hudson, Tim	3	1	2.51	8	4	0	0	29	12	8	8	15	37	R	R	6-0	160	7-14-75	1997	Salem, Ala.
Jensen, Jared	4	2	3.71	23	0	0	6	27	27	13	11	8	34	R	R	6-1	190	3-6-74	1997	Provo, Utah
Jones, Marcus	3	3	4.50	14	10	0	0	56	58	37	28	22	49	R	R	6-5	235	3-29-75	1997	Yorba Linda, Calif.
Kimball, Andy	3	2	3.62	13	7	0	0	55	37	29	22	17	75	R	R	6-0	190	8-23-75	1997	Oshkosh, Wis.
Knickerbocker, Tom	1	0	2.81	4	4	0	0	16	20	7	5	6	18	L	L	6-4	230	7-15-75	1995	Prarie du Chien, Wis.
Lagattuta, Rico	2	1	4.97	16	0	0	2	29	35	21	16	14	17	L	L	6-2	205	1-14-74	1996	Thousand Oaks, Calif.
Manwiller, Tim	2	0	1.86	12	3	0	2	29	19	8	6	10	30	R	R	6-2	205	9-5-74	1997	Annville, Pa.
Montero, Agus	0	0	6.75	2	0	0	0	3	4	2	2	3	1	R	R	6-2	206	8-26-77	1995	San Pedro de Macoris, D.R.
Niles, Randy	0	1	1.99	7	4	0	0	23	14	12	5	12	15	R	R	6-2	200	8-28-75	1997	Key West, Fla.
Nina, Elvin	1	3	5.23	18	2	0	1	31	36	24	18	18	26	S	R	6-1	175	11-25-75	1997	East Orange, N.J.
Vizcaino, Luis	1	6	7.93	22	5	0	0	48	62	51	42	27	42	R	R	6-1	180	6-1-77	1995	Bani, D.R.
Wagner, Denny	1	1	15.43	10	4	0	0	14	29	27	24	14	11	R	R	6-0	205	11-8-76	1997	Castlewood, Va.
Waites, David	0	0	6.75	1	0	0	0	1	3	1	1	2	0	R	R	6-3	220	2-2-76	1997	Fritch, Texas

SCOTTSDALE — Rookie

ARIZONA LEAGUE

BATTING	AVG	G	AB	R	H	2B	3B	HR	RBI	BB	SO	SB	CS	B	T	HT	WT	DOB	1st Yr	Resides
Basabe, Jesus	.313	55	201	51	63	11	4	11	43	40	76	6	2	R	R	6-2	175	5-14-77	1995	Bobures, Venez.
Camilo, Juan	.346	50	191	48	66	11	5	8	47	41	41	12	2	L	R	6-0	203	6-24-78	1996	Santo Domingo, D.R.
Cochrane, Chris	.000	2	8	0	0	0	0	0	1	0	1	0	0	R	R	6-3	215	12-21-72	1994	South Plainfield, N.J.
Cosme, Caonabo	.215	37	130	28	28	6	1	1	17	19	28	7	1	R	R	6-2	190	3-18-79	1996	La Vega, D.R.
Davis, Monty	.329	47	173	34	57	12	0	5	34	25	25	5	2	R	R	6-1	195	12-25-77	1996	Vernon, B.C.
Declet, Miguel	.300	13	30	7	9	2	0	0	4	2	6	2	0	R	R	6-3	185	9-9-79	1997	Caguas, P.R.
Haynes, Nathan	.278	17	54	8	15	1	0	0	6	7	9	5	1	L	L	5-10	170	9-7-79	1997	Hercules, Calif.
Luderer, Brian	.268	39	123	21	33	4	0	3	26	17	12	3	4	R	R	5-11	170	8-19-78	1996	Tarzana, Calif.
Nova, Kelvin	.244	33	123	19	30	1	3	1	20	19	27	18	4	S	R	5-11	175	6-15-77	1994	Bani, D.R.
Nunez, Jose	.282	51	181	39	51	10	3	6	42	47	47	2	2	R	R	6-0	208	11-12-76	1995	Bonao, D.R.
Pimentel, Hector	.211	41	123	17	26	2	0	0	13	21	21	4	1	R	R	6-1	180	2-23-79	1996	Bani, D.R.
Porter, Jamie	.253	33	95	23	24	11	1	1	11	11	31	5	1	R	R	6-1	195	5-16-76	1997	Bothell, Wash.
Rosario, Omar	.241	56	216	48	52	9	3	0	28	38	51	40	3	L	L	6-1	170	1-14-78	1996	Santo Domingo, D.R.
Thomas, Gary	.228	28	92	17	21	2	2	1	7	9	25	6	2	R	R	5-7	175	9-6-79	1997	Houma, La.
Yoshida, Kota	.238	48	181	47	43	8	1	0	22	36	39	22	6	S	R	5-10	160	12-24-77	1997	Tokyo, Japan

GAMES BY POSITION: C—Camilo 1, Luderer 35, Nunez 29. **1B**—Camilo 2, Cosme 1, Davis 12, Luderer 2, Nunez 3, Pimentel 2, Rosario 40. **2B**—Davis 20, Nova 14, Thomas 1, Yoshida 27. **3B**—Cosme 4, Davis 8, Nova 17, Pimentel 34. **SS**—Cosme 34, Declet 12, Yoshida 21. **OF**—Basabe 52, Camilo 47, Haynes 13, Pimentel 2, Porter 26, Rosario 17, Thomas 27.

PITCHING	W	L	ERA	G	GS	CG	SV	IP	H	R	ER	BB	SO	B	T	HT	WT	DOB	1st Yr	Resides
Corniel, Henry	2	1	6.46	20	0	0	3	30	42	27	22	11	25	R	R	6-0	180	6-18-77	1994	San Pedro de Macoris, D.R.
Crawford, Jeremy	1	3	6.75	15	0	0	2	23	29	19	17	14	20	L	L	6-0	165	12-24-78	1997	Chatham, Ill.
Gallagher, Bryan	1	3	2.94	17	0	0	2	34	29	14	11	10	27	L	L	6-2	195	10-7-76	1996	Klamath Falls, Ore.
Garcia, Bryan	4	2	5.67	15	7	0	0	46	50	36	29	34	45	R	R	6-3	165	6-21-78	1996	Quartz Hill, Calif.
Garcia, Expeddy	1	3	7.82	8	1	0	0	13	20	13	11	7	9	L	L	6-2	180	2-28-77	1994	Santo Domingo, D.R.
Hause, Brendan	3	1	3.86	6	0	0	0	12	13	7	5	1	11	L	L	6-1	185	10-21-74	1992	San Diego, Calif.
Jacobs, Frankey	0	2	7.12	15	3	0	0	37	52	37	29	17	22	R	R	6-6	190	1-15-78	1997	Durham, N.C.
Meeks, Eric	1	2	5.35	15	3	0	1	39	40	30	23	26	24	R	R	6-4	216	4-12-79	1997	Orlando, Fla.
Mercedes, Jose	5	1	5.53	14	12	0	0	57	68	43	35	30	35	R	R	6-4	185	4-12-77	1994	San Pedro de Macoris, D.R.
Montero, Agus	3	2	3.59	14	13	0	0	73	72	38	29	31	88	R	R	6-2	206	8-26-77	1995	San Pedro de Macoris, D.R.
Nix, Wayne	1	3	5.85	15	4	0	0	32	32	28	21	29	32	R	R	6-5	210	9-16-76	1995	North Hills, Calif.
Pena, Juan	6	2	2.91	14	13	0	0	65	54	38	21	33	67	L	L	6-3	193	6-4-79	1996	Santo Domingo, D.R.
Waites, David	1	2	3.09	21	0	0	5	23	24	14	8	11	35	R	R	6-3	220	2-2-76	1997	Fritch, Texas

Philadelphia PHILLIES

Manager: Terry Francona.

1997 Record: 68-94, .420 (5th, NL East)

BATTING	AVG	G	AB	R	H	2B	3B	HR	RBI	BB	SO	SB	CS	B	T	HT	WT	DOB	1st Yr	Resides
Amaro, Ruben	.234	117	175	18	41	6	1	2	21	21	24	1	1	S	R	5-10	175	2-12-65	1987	Philadelphia, Pa.
Barron, Tony	.286	57	189	22	54	12	1	4	24	12	38	0	1	R	R	6-0	185	8-17-66	1987	Tacoma, Wash.
Brogna, Rico	.252	148	543	68	137	36	1	20	81	33	116	12	3	L	L	6-2	200	4-18-70	1988	Watertown, Conn.
Butler, Rob	.292	43	89	10	26	9	1	0	13	5	8	1	0	L	L	5-11	185	4-10-70	1991	Toronto, Ontario
Cummings, Midre	.303	63	208	24	63	16	4	1	23	23	30	2	3	L	R	6-0	196	10-14-71	1990	St. Croix, Virgin Islands
2-team (52 Pittsburgh)	.264	115	314	35	83	22	6	4	31	31	56	2	3							
Daulton, Darren	.264	84	269	46	71	13	6	11	42	54	57	4	0	L	R	6-2	201	1-3-62	1980	Safety Harbor, Fla.
Estalella, Bobby	.345	13	29	9	10	1	0	4	9	7	7	0	0	R	R	6-1	200	8-23-74	1993	Pembroke Pines, Fla.
Hudler, Rex	.221	50	122	17	27	4	0	5	10	6	28	1	0	R	R	6-2	180	9-2-60	1978	Fresno, Calif.
Jefferies, Gregg	.256	130	476	68	122	25	3	11	48	53	27	12	6	S	R	5-10	185	8-1-67	1985	Millbrae, Calif.
Jordan, Kevin	.266	84	177	19	47	8	0	6	30	3	26	0	1	R	R	6-1	185	10-9-69	1990	San Francisco, Calif.
Lieberthal, Mike	.246	134	455	59	112	27	1	20	77	44	76	3	4	R	R	6-0	170	1-18-72	1990	Westlake Village, Calif.
Magee, Wendell	.200	38	115	7	23	4	0	1	9	9	20	1	4	R	R	6-0	225	8-3-72	1994	Hattiesburg, Miss.
May, Derrick	.228	83	149	8	34	5	1	1	13	8	26	4	1	L	R	6-4	200	7-14-68	1986	Newark, Del.
McMillon, Billy	.292	24	72	10	21	4	1	2	13	6	17	2	1	L	L	5-11	172	11-17-71	1993	Sumter, S.C.
2-team (13 Florida)	.256	37	90	10	23	5	1	2	14	6	24	2	1							
Morandini, Mickey	.295	150	553	83	163	40	2	1	39	62	91	16	13	L	R	5-11	171	4-22-66	1989	Valparaiso, Ind.
Otero, Ricky	.252	50	151	20	38	6	2	0	3	19	15	0	3	S	L	5-7	150	4-15-72	1991	Vega Baja, P.R.
Parent, Mark	.150	39	113	4	17	3	0	0	8	7	39	0	1	R	R	6-5	225	9-16-61	1979	San Diego, Calif.
Relaford, Desi	.184	15	38	3	7	1	2	0	6	5	6	3	0	S	R	5-8	155	9-16-73	1991	Jacksonville, Fla.
Robertson, Mike	.211	22	38	3	8	2	1	0	4	0	6	1	0	L	L	6-0	180	10-9-70	1991	Placentia, Calif.
Rolen, Scott	.283	156	561	93	159	35	3	21	92	76	138	16	6	R	R	6-4	210	4-4-75	1993	Jasper, Ind.
Sefcik, Kevin	.269	61	119	11	32	3	0	2	6	4	9	1	2	R	R	5-10	175	2-10-71	1993	Tinley Park, Ill.
Stocker, Kevin	.266	149	504	51	134	23	5	4	40	51	91	11	6	S	R	6-1	175	2-13-70	1991	Spokane, Wash.
Tartabull, Danny	.000	3	7	2	0	0	0	0	0	4	4	0	0	R	R	6-1	210	10-30-62	1980	Malibu, Calif.

PITCHING	W	L	ERA	G	GS	CG	SV	IP	H	R	ER	BB	SO	B	T	HT	WT	DOB	1st Yr	Resides
Beech, Matt	4	9	5.07	24	24	0	0	137	147	81	77	57	120	L	L	6-2	190	1-20-72	1994	San Antonio, Texas
Blazier, Ron	1	1	5.03	36	0	0	0	54	62	31	30	21	42	R	R	6-6	215	7-30-71	1990	Bellwood, Pa.
Bottalico, Ricky	2	5	3.65	69	0	0	34	74	68	31	30	42	89	L	R	6-1	190	8-26-69	1991	Newington, Conn.
Brewer, Billy	1	2	3.27	25	0	0	0	22	15	8	8	11	16	L	L	6-1	175	4-15-68	1990	Waco, Texas
Gomes, Wayne	5	1	5.27	37	0	0	0	43	45	26	25	24	24	R	R	6-0	215	1-15-73	1993	Hampton, Va.
Grace, Mike	3	2	3.46	6	6	1	0	39	32	16	15	10	26	R	R	6-4	210	6-20-70	1991	Joliet, Ill.
Green, Tyler	4	4	4.93	14	14	0	0	77	72	50	42	45	58	R	R	6-5	185	2-18-70	1991	Englewood, Colo.
Harris, Reggie	1	3	5.30	50	0	0	0	54	55	33	32	43	45	R	R	6-1	190	8-12-68	1987	Waynesboro, Va.
Karp, Ryan	1	1	5.40	15	1	0	0	15	12	12	9	9	18	L	L	6-4	205	4-5-70	1992	Coral Gables, Fla.
Leiter, Mark	10	17	5.67	31	31	3	0	183	216	132	115	64	148	R	R	6-3	210	4-13-63	1983	West Caldwell, N.J.
Maduro, Calvin	3	7	7.23	15	13	0	0	71	83	59	57	41	31	R	R	6-0	175	9-5-74	1992	Santa Cruz, Aruba
Mimbs, Mike	0	3	7.53	17	1	0	0	29	31	27	24	27	29	L	L	6-2	182	2-13-69	1990	Macon, Ga.
Munoz, Bobby	1	5	8.91	8	7	0	0	33	47	35	33	15	20	R	R	6-7	237	3-3-68	1989	Hialeah, Fla.
Nye, Ryan	0	2	8.25	4	2	0	0	12	20	11	11	9	7	R	R	6-2	195	6-24-73	1994	Cameron, Okla.
Plantenberg, Erik	0	0	4.91	35	0	0	0	26	25	14	14	12	12	L	L	6-1	180	10-30-68	1990	Bellevue, Wash.
Portugal, Mark	0	2	4.61	3	3	0	0	14	17	8	7	5	2	R	R	6-0	190	10-30-62	1981	Missouri City, Texas
Ramos, Edgar	0	2	5.14	4	2	0	0	14	15	9	8	6	4	R	R	6-4	170	3-6-75	1992	Cumana, Venez.
Ruffcorn, Scott	0	3	7.71	18	4	0	0	40	42	40	34	36	33	R	R	6-4	215	12-29-69	1991	Austin, Texas
Ryan, Ken	1	0	9.58	22	0	0	0	21	31	23	22	13	10	R	R	6-3	215	10-24-68	1986	Attleboro, Mass.
Schilling, Curt	17	11	2.97	35	35	7	0	254	208	96	84	58	319	R	R	6-4	215	11-14-66	1986	Marlton, N.J.
Spradlin, Jerry	4	8	4.74	76	0	0	1	82	86	45	43	27	67	S	R	6-7	240	6-14-67	1988	Anaheim, Calif.
Stephenson, Garrett	8	6	3.15	20	18	2	0	117	104	45	41	38	81	R	R	6-4	185	1-2-72	1992	Kimberly, Md.
Winston, Darrin	2	0	5.25	7	1	0	0	12	8	8	7	3	8	R	L	6-0	195	7-6-66	1988	Fords, N.J.

FIELDING

Catcher	PCT	G	PO	A	E	DP	PB
Estalella	1.000	11	49	3	0	0	1
Lieberthal	.988	129	934	73	12	8	12
Parent	.996	38	225	21	1	2	3

First Base	PCT	G	PO	A	E	DP
Amaro	1.000	1	4	0	0	1
Brogna	.994	145	1053	119	7	100
Daulton	1.000	3	29	0	0	0
Jordan	.987	25	148	9	2	12
Robertson	1.000	5	20	1	0	1

Second Base	PCT	G	PO	A	E	DP
Hudler	.952	6	11	9	1	2
Jordan	.882	6	4	11	2	1
Morandini	.990	146	254	350	6	87
Sefcik	.961	22	29	45	3	6

Third Base	PCT	G	PO	A	E	DP
Jordan	.889	12	5	11	2	0
Rolen	.948	155	144	291	24	30
Sefcik	1.000	4	2	3	0	1

Shortstop	PCT	G	PO	A	E	DP
Morandini	.000	1	0	0	0	0
Relaford	.977	12	12	31	1	3
Sefcik	.957	10	8	14	1	2
Stocker	.981	147	190	376	11	74

Outfield	PCT	G	PO	A	E	DP
Amaro	.987	72	75	2	1	0
Barron	.983	53	111	3	2	1
Butler	1.000	25	33	3	0	2
Cummings	.991	54	113	1	1	0
Daulton	.979	70	133	6	3	1
Hudler	.962	35	50	1	2	0
Jefferies	.986	124	211	5	3	2
Magee	.960	38	95	2	4	1
May	.961	56	69	4	3	1
McMillon	.957	21	42	2	2	0
Otero	1.000	42	95	4	0	1
Robertson	1.000	5	8	0	0	0
Tartabull	1.000	3	2	0	0	0

DAVID SCHOFIELD

Curt Schilling

FARM SYSTEM

Director of Player Development: Del Unser

Class	Farm Team	League	W	L	Pct.	Finish*	Manager	First Yr
AAA	Scranton/W-B (Pa.) Red Barons	International	66	76	.465	8th (10)	Marc Bombard	1989
AA	Reading (Pa.) Phillies	Eastern	74	68	.521	4th (10)	Al LeBoeuf	1967
#A	Clearwater (Fla.) Phillies	Florida State	70	68	.507	8th (14)	Roy Majtyka	1985
A	Piedmont (N.C.) Boll Weevils	South Atlantic	70	72	.493	8th (14)	Ken Oberkfell	1995
A	Batavia (N.Y.) Clippers	New York-Penn	47	27	.635	3rd (14)	Greg Legg	1988
#R	Martinsville (Va.) Phillies	Appalachian	29	39	.426	9th (10)	Kelly Heath	1988

*Finish in overall standings (No. of teams in league) #Advanced level

ORGANIZATION LEADERS

MAJOR LEAGUERS

BATTING

*AVG	Mickey Morandini	.295
R	Scott Rolen	93
H	Mickey Morandini	163
TB	Scott Rolen	263
2B	Mickey Morandini	40
3B	Darren Daulton	6
HR	Scott Rolen	21
RBI	Scott Rolen	92
BB	Scott Rolen	76
SO	Scott Rolen	138
SB	Two tied at	16

PITCHING

W	Curt Schilling	17
L	Mark Leiter	17
#ERA	Curt Schilling	2.97
G	Jerry Spradlin	76
CG	Curt Schilling	7
SV	Ricky Bottalico	34
IP	Curt Schilling	254
BB	Mark Leiter	64
SO	Curt Schilling	319

Ricky Bottalico

DAVID SCHOFIELD

Ryan Brannan

MINOR LEAGUERS

BATTING

*AVG	Tony Barron, Scranton/Wilkes-Barre	.328
R	Jimmy Rollins, Piedmont	94
H	Jimmy Rollins, Piedmont	151
TB	Dan Held, Reading	260
2B	Two tied at	37
3B	Jeff Key, Clearwater	11
HR	Dan Held, Reading	26
RBI	Jeff Key, Clearwater	87
BB	Jon Zuber, Scranton/Wilkes-Barre	79
SO	Brad Crede, Piedmont	145
SB	Jimmy Rollins, Piedmont	46

PITCHING

W	Kris Stevens, Clearwater/Piedmont	12
L	Three tied at	13
#ERA	Derek Adair, Batavia	2.11
G	Ryan Brannan, Reading/Clearwater	66
CG	Three tied at	4
SV	Ryan Brannan, Reading/Clearwater	30
IP	Carlton Loewer, Scranton/WB	184
BB	Rob Burger, Clearwater	93
SO	Evan Thomas, Reading/Clearwater	172

*Minimum 250 At-Bats #Minimum 75 Innings

TOP 10 PROSPECTS

DAVID SEELIG

Scott Rolen

How the Phillies Top 10 prospects, as judged by Baseball America prior to the 1997 season, fared in 1997:

Player, Pos.	Club (Class)	AVG	AB	R	H	2B	3B	HR	RBI	SB
1. Scott Rolen, 3b	Philadelphia	.283	561	93	159	35	3	21	92	16
2. Bobby Estalella, c	Philadelphia	.345	29	9	10	1	0	4	9	0
	Scranton (AAA)	.233	433	63	101	32	0	16	65	3
4. Reggie Taylor, of	Clearwater (A)	.244	545	73	133	18	6	12	47	40
6. Marlon Anderson, 2b	Reading (AA)	.266	553	88	147	18	6	10	62	27
10. Steve Carver, 1b-of	Reading (AA)	.262	282	41	74	11	3	15	43	2
		W	**L**	**ERA**	**G**	**SV**	**IP**	**H**	**BB**	**SO**
3. Dave Coggin, rhp	Clearwater (A)	11	8	4.70	27	0	155	160	86	110
5. Adam Eaton, rhp	Piedmont (A)	5	6	4.16	14	0	71	81	30	57
7. Ryan Brannan, rhp	Reading (AA)	4	2	3.10	45	20	52	52	20	39
	Clearwater (A)	0	0	0.33	21	10	27	20	8	25
8. Carlton Loewer, rhp	Scranton (AAA)	5	13	4.60	29	0	184	198	50	152
9. Rob Burger, rhp	Clearwater (A)	11	9	3.59	28	0	161	131	93	154

SCRANTON/WILKES-BARRE — Class AAA

INTERNATIONAL LEAGUE

BATTING	AVG	G	AB	R	H	2B	3B	HR	RBI	BB	SO	SB	CS	B	T	HT	WT	DOB	1st Yr	Resides
Amador, Manuel	.343	23	70	12	24	5	0	1	9	6	11	0	0	S	R	6-0	165	11-21-75	1993	Santo Domingo, D.R.
Angeli, Doug	.224	78	241	24	54	11	2	2	19	27	53	0	3	R	R	5-11	183	1-7-71	1993	Springfield, Ill.
Barron, Tony	.328	92	329	51	108	21	4	18	78	27	64	3	4	R	R	6-0	185	8-17-66	1987	Tacoma, Wash.
Bowers, Brent	.255	39	110	15	28	2	0	3	7	8	28	1	1	L	R	6-3	200	5-2-71	1989	Bridgeview, Ill.
Burton, Darren	.249	70	253	34	63	16	3	8	39	19	40	3	0	S	R	6-1	185	9-16-72	1990	Somerset, Ky.
Butler, Rob	.282	21	71	8	20	4	0	0	9	1	9	0	0	L	L	5-11	185	4-10-70	1991	Toronto, Ontario
Doster, David	.315	108	410	70	129	32	2	16	79	30	60	5	5	R	R	5-10	185	10-8-70	1993	New Haven, Ind.
Estalella, Bobby	.233	123	433	63	101	32	0	16	65	56	109	3	0	R	R	6-1	200	8-23-74	1993	Pembroke Pines, Fla.
Flores, Jose	.250	71	204	32	51	14	1	1	18	28	51	3	1	R	R	5-11	160	6-26-73	1994	New York, N.Y.
Fox, Eric	.285	87	246	39	70	16	3	3	26	19	48	2	3	S	L	5-10	180	8-15-63	1986	Paso Robles, Calif.
2-team (5 Rochester)	.280	92	264	41	74	17	3	3	26	21	50	2	3							
Hudler, Rex	.333	3	9	0	3	0	0	0	0	0	0	0	0	R	R	6-2	180	9-2-60	1978	Fresno, Calif.
Jordan, Kevin	.300	7	30	5	9	2	2	0	2	2	6	2	0	R	R	6-1	185	10-9-69	1990	San Francisco, Calif.
Magee, Wendell	.245	83	294	39	72	20	1	10	39	30	56	4	7	R	R	6-0	225	8-3-72	1994	Hattiesburg, Miss.
McMillon, Billy	.293	26	92	18	27	8	1	4	21	12	24	2	0	L	L	5-11	172	11-17-71	1993	Sumter, S.C.
2-team (57 Charlotte)	.284	83	296	52	84	26	1	12	47	44	75	10	0							
Millan, Adan	.500	1	2	0	1	0	0	0	1	1	0	0	0	R	R	6-0	195	3-26-72	1994	Montebello, Calif.
Northeimer, Jamie	.154	4	13	1	2	0	0	0	1	1	6	0	0	R	R	5-10	174	7-5-72	1994	Sacramento, Calif.
Otero, Ricky	.331	38	160	24	53	10	5	1	15	13	13	5	4	S	L	5-7	150	4-15-72	1991	Vega Baja, P.R.
Relaford, Desi	.267	131	517	82	138	34	4	9	53	43	77	29	8	S	R	5-8	155	9-16-73	1991	Jacksonville, Fla.
Robertson, Mike	.298	121	416	61	124	17	3	12	72	58	67	0	2	L	L	6-0	180	10-9-70	1991	Placentia, Calif.
Sefcik, Kevin	.333	29	123	19	41	11	2	1	7	9	11	5	1	R	R	5-10	175	2-10-71	1993	Tinley Park, Ill.
Wedge, Eric	.256	47	129	25	33	8	1	7	36	22	40	0	0	R	R	6-3	215	1-27-68	1989	Fort Wayne, Ind.
Zuber, Jon	.315	126	435	85	137	37	2	6	64	79	53	3	4	L	L	6-1	175	12-10-69	1992	Moraga, Calif.

PITCHING	W	L	ERA	G	GS	CG	SV	IP	H	R	ER	BB	SO	B	T	HT	WT	DOB	1st Yr	Resides
Beech, Matt	3	1	5.70	5	5	1	0	30	24	20	19	10	38	L	L	6-2	190	1-20-72	1994	San Antonio, Texas
Blazier, Ron	0	3	3.68	11	0	0	1	15	17	9	6	3	10	R	R	6-6	215	7-30-71	1990	Bellwood, Pa.
Brewer, Billy	2	1	3.00	11	0	0	1	9	10	7	3	5	9	L	L	6-1	175	4-15-68	1990	Waco, Texas
Fiore, Tony	3	5	3.86	9	9	1	0	61	60	34	26	26	56	R	R	6-4	200	10-12-71	1992	Chicago, Ill.
Fortugno, Tim	0	1	6.62	19	0	0	3	18	21	13	13	8	15	L	L	6-0	185	4-11-62	1986	Huntington Beach, Calif.
Gomes, Wayne	3	1	2.37	26	0	0	7	38	31	11	10	24	36	R	R	6-0	215	1-15-73	1993	Hampton, Va.
Grace, Mike	5	6	4.56	12	12	4	0	75	84	43	38	27	55	R	R	6-4	210	6-20-70	1991	Joliet, Ill.
Green, Tyler	4	8	6.10	12	12	3	0	72	80	54	49	29	40	R	R	6-5	185	2-18-70	1991	Englewood, Colo.
Hawblitzel, Ryan	6	9	4.99	34	15	1	2	115	132	65	64	33	80	R	R	6-2	170	4-30-71	1990	Lake Worth, Fla.
Heflin, Bronson	1	1	2.28	35	0	0	13	43	29	17	11	25	36	R	R	6-3	195	8-29-71	1994	Clarksville, Tenn.
Holman, Craig	3	1	4.64	48	0	0	3	76	100	44	39	27	75	S	R	6-2	200	3-13-69	1991	Attalla, Ala.
Karp, Ryan	4	3	4.19	32	5	0	1	73	72	35	34	42	55	L	L	6-4	205	4-5-70	1992	Coral Gables, Fla.
Loewer, Carlton	5	13	4.60	29	29	4	0	184	198	120	94	50	152	S	R	6-6	220	9-24-73	1995	Eunice, La.
Maduro, Calvin	6	4	4.99	13	13	2	0	79	71	48	44	57	53	R	R	6-0	175	9-5-74	1992	Santa Cruz, Aruba
Mimbs, Mike	4	2	5.98	11	8	1	0	44	52	33	29	20	41	L	L	6-2	182	2-13-69	1990	Macon, Ga.
Nye, Ryan	4	10	5.52	17	17	0	0	109	117	70	67	32	85	R	R	6-2	195	6-24-73	1994	Cameron, Okla.
Plantenberg, Erik	0	2	7.53	18	0	0	0	14	22	12	12	9	12	L	L	6-1	180	10-30-68	1990	Bellevue, Wash.
Ruffcorn, Scott	2	0	1.16	5	5	2	0	31	22	6	4	10	20	R	R	6-4	215	12-29-69	1991	Austin, Texas
Ryan, Ken	1	0	4.50	3	0	0	1	4	5	2	2	3	3	R	R	6-3	215	10-24-68	1986	Attleboro, Mass.
Stephenson, Garrett	3	1	5.90	7	3	0	0	29	27	19	19	12	27	R	R	6-4	185	1-2-72	1992	Kimberly, Md.
Winston, Darrin	7	4	3.43	39	9	1	0	89	74	38	34	36	66	R	L	6-0	195	7-6-66	1988	Fords, N.J.

FIELDING

Catcher	PCT	G	PO	A	E	DP	PB
Estalella	.986	117	844	71	13	9	7
Millan	1.000	1	5	1	0	0	0
Northeimer	1.000	4	26	2	0	0	0
Wedge	.985	21	121	8	2	1	1

First Base	PCT	G	PO	A	E	DP
Jordan	1.000	1	17	0	0	2
Robertson	.987	120	951	97	14	82
Wedge	.895	4	16	1	2	1
Zuber	.995	23	189	15	1	19

Second Base	PCT	G	PO	A	E	DP
Angeli	.963	20	29	50	3	14
Doster	.979	74	123	200	7	37
Flores	.987	33	65	92	2	19
Hudler	1.000	1	1	5	0	1
Jordan	1.000	3	5	11	0	2
Sefcik	.973	16	33	40	2	8

Third Base	PCT	G	PO	A	E	DP
Amador	.895	20	14	37	6	3
Angeli	.867	46	23	94	18	6
Doster	.917	34	29	48	7	5
Flores	.897	30	25	45	8	4
Jordan	.889	4	1	7	1	0
Sefcik	.879	13	14	15	4	0

Shortstop	PCT	G	PO	A	E	DP
Angeli	.976	11	10	31	1	3
Flores	.938	7	3	12	1	0
Relaford	.942	130	180	373	34	81

Outfield	PCT	G	PO	A	E	DP
Angeli	1.000	2	3	0	0	0
Barron	.963	70	102	3	4	1
Bowers	.964	20	25	2	1	0
Burton	.980	63	138	9	3	0
Butler	1.000	15	23	1	0	0
Fox	.990	50	98	2	1	1
Magee	.983	80	167	3	3	0
McMillon	1.000	24	49	3	0	0
Otero	.979	38	90	5	2	0
Robertson	.000	1	0	0	0	0
Sefcik	1.000	1	4	1	0	0
Zuber	1.000	77	111	3	0	0

READING — Class AA

EASTERN LEAGUE

BATTING	AVG	G	AB	R	H	2B	3B	HR	RBI	BB	SO	SB	CS	B	T	HT	WT	DOB	1st Yr	Resides
Amador, Manuel	.243	63	169	17	41	9	1	2	22	20	29	0	0	S	R	6-0	165	11-21-75	1993	Santo Domingo, D.R.
Anderson, Marlon	.266	137	553	88	147	18	6	10	62	42	77	27	15	L	R	5-10	190	1-3-74	1995	Prattville, Ala.
Angeli, Doug	.223	42	148	25	33	5	1	5	19	16	28	1	2	R	R	5-11	183	1-7-71	1993	Springfield, Ill.
Burton, Darren	.315	45	184	23	58	11	3	8	34	9	39	1	1	S	R	6-1	185	9-16-72	1990	Somerset, Ky.
Carver, Steve	.262	79	282	41	74	11	3	15	43	36	69	2	2	L	R	6-3	215	9-27-72	1995	Jacksonville, Fla.
Costello, Brian	.194	16	36	6	7	2	1	1	5	2	12	0	1	R	R	6-1	195	10-4-74	1993	Orlando, Fla.
Dawkins, Walter	.239	106	331	48	79	13	1	8	40	35	90	4	5	R	R	5-10	190	8-6-72	1995	Moraga, Calif.
Guiliano, Matt	.226	119	367	38	83	15	3	7	37	34	99	7	6	R	R	5-7	175	6-7-72	1994	Ronkonkoma, N.Y.
Held, Dan	.272	138	525	80	143	31	4	26	86	42	116	1	3	R	R	6-0	200	10-7-70	1993	Neosho, Wis.
Hudler, Rex	.348	6	23	5	8	2	0	1	5	1	2	0	0	R	R	6-2	180	9-2-60	1978	Fresno, Calif.
Huff, Larry	.264	124	425	58	112	21	3	5	41	36	57	24	7	R	R	6-0	175	1-24-72	1994	Las Vegas, Nev.

BATTING	AVG	G	AB	R	H	2B	3B	HR	RBI	BB	SO	SB	CS	B	T	HT	WT	DOB	1st Yr	Resides
Millan, Adan	.244	95	266	43	65	10	0	9	43	44	52	0	0	R	R	6-0	195	3-26-72	1994	Montebello, Calif.
Northeimer, Jamie	.200	44	100	14	20	6	0	1	16	25	22	0	0	R	R	5-10	174	7-5-72	1994	Sacramento, Calif.
Pagano, Scott	.274	117	468	77	128	16	3	3	44	48	62	17	13	S	R	5-11	175	4-26-71	1992	Dania, Fla.
Royster, Aaron	.257	112	412	59	106	18	5	15	62	53	104	2	3	R	R	6-1	220	11-30-72	1994	Chicago, Ill.
Tremie, Chris	.203	97	295	20	60	11	1	2	31	36	61	0	5	R	R	6-0	200	10-17-69	1992	Houston, Texas
Wesemann, Jason	.182	7	11	4	2	0	0	0	1	2	2	0	0	R	R	6-0	180	3-29-74	1996	Watertown, Wis.

PITCHING	W	L	ERA	G	GS	CG	SV	IP	H	R	ER	BB	SO	B	T	HT	WT	DOB	1st Yr	Resides
Barbao, Joe	2	3	5.23	52	0	0	2	76	101	53	44	28	33	R	R	6-1	190	4-18-72	1994	Crown Point, Ind.
Boyd, Jason	10	6	4.82	48	7	0	0	116	113	65	62	64	98	R	R	6-2	165	2-23-73	1994	Edwardsville, Ill.
Brannan, Ryan	4	2	3.10	45	0	0	20	52	52	18	18	20	39	R	R	6-3	210	4-27-75	1996	Huntington Beach, Calif.
Censale, Silvio	9	4	4.36	20	20	0	0	107	88	58	52	56	102	L	L	6-2	195	11-21-71	1993	Lodi, N.J.
Costa, Tony	7	12	5.24	28	28	2	0	165	174	111	96	72	110	R	R	6-4	210	12-19-70	1992	Lemoore, Calif.
Dodd, Robert	9	4	3.25	63	0	0	8	80	61	29	29	21	94	L	L	6-3	195	3-14-73	1994	Plano, Texas
Fiore, Tony	8	3	3.01	17	16	0	0	105	89	47	35	40	64	R	R	6-4	200	10-12-71	1992	Chicago, Ill.
Foster, Mark	2	2	6.35	9	0	0	1	17	20	16	12	8	9	L	L	6-1	200	12-24-71	1993	Severn, Md.
Grace, Mike	1	3	5.75	4	4	0	0	20	28	17	13	6	10	R	R	6-4	210	6-20-70	1991	Joliet, Ill.
Guiliano, Matt	0	0	49.50	2	0	0	0	2	5	11	11	6	0	R	R	5-7	175	6-7-72	1994	Ronkonkoma, N.Y.
Hunter, Rich	6	11	4.69	29	28	1	0	163	191	100	85	60	104	R	R	6-1	180	9-25-74	1993	Temecula, Calif.
Manning, Len	3	1	5.34	28	7	0	0	62	66	40	37	46	41	L	L	6-2	195	12-30-71	1994	New Brighton, Minn.
Ryan, Ken	0	0	0.00	2	2	0	0	2	1	0	0	1	0	R	R	6-3	215	10-24-68	1986	Attleboro, Mass.
Thomas, Evan	3	6	4.12	15	15	0	0	83	98	51	38	32	83	R	R	5-10	175	6-14-74	1996	Pembroke Pines, Fla.
Troutman, Keith	6	5	3.77	57	3	0	7	107	94	48	45	34	103	R	R	6-1	200	5-29-73	1992	Candler, N.C.
Westbrook, Destry	0	2	8.20	26	3	0	4	45	70	49	41	22	38	R	R	6-1	195	12-13-70	1992	Montrose, Colo.
Whiteman, Greg	4	4	4.05	9	9	0	0	53	57	27	24	21	31	L	L	6-2	185	6-12-73	1994	Wileyford, W.Va.

FIELDING

Catcher	PCT	G	PO	A	E	DP	PB
Millan	.981	42	236	26	5	1	11
Northeimer	.969	22	113	14	4	1	5
Tremie	.995	97	650	84	4	6	5

First Base	PCT	G	PO	A	E	DP
Guiliano	1.000	2	2	0	0	0
Held	.994	130	1123	76	7	89
Millan	.984	20	116	7	2	16
Northeimer	1.000	1	1	0	0	0

Second Base	PCT	G	PO	A	E	DP
Anderson	.961	137	323	396	29	87
Hudler	.000	1	0	0	0	0
Huff	1.000	8	13	19	0	5

Third Base	PCT	G	PO	A	E	DP
Amador	.889	32	22	42	8	3
Guiliano	.940	18	5	42	3	5
Held	.933	5	4	10	1	1
Huff	.930	98	62	202	20	17
Wesemann	1.000	6	2	7	0	1

Shortstop	PCT	G	PO	A	E	DP
Angeli	.966	41	55	116	6	19
Guiliano	.960	95	120	266	16	49
Huff	1.000	11	15	23	0	4

Outfield	PCT	G	PO	A	E	DP
Burton	.972	45	98	7	3	0
Carver	.943	74	116	0	7	0
Costello	.926	9	23	2	2	0
Dawkins	.972	86	134	4	4	0
Hudler	1.000	4	4	1	0	0
Huff	1.000	6	9	0	0	0
Pagano	.975	115	302	13	8	4
Royster	.975	105	153	4	4	0
Wesemann	.000	1	0	0	0	0

CLEARWATER — Class A

FLORIDA STATE LEAGUE

BATTING	AVG	G	AB	R	H	2B	3B	HR	RBI	BB	SO	SB	CS	B	T	HT	WT	DOB	1st Yr	Resides
Cornelius, Jonathon	.141	33	71	4	10	1	0	1	4	3	29	2	0	R	R	6-1	195	11-30-73	1995	Covina, Calif.
Costello, Brian	.241	87	282	37	68	11	2	10	43	15	73	8	3	R	R	6-1	195	10-4-74	1993	Orlando, Fla.
Crane, Todd	.143	2	7	0	1	1	0	0	1	0	1	0	0	R	R	6-1	185	7-2-73	1995	Roswell, Ga.
Elliott, Zach	.263	129	448	65	118	21	3	4	45	46	63	7	6	R	R	6-0	180	9-1-73	1995	Tustin, Calif.
Francia, David	.280	21	75	5	21	3	1	0	10	6	7	5	2	L	L	5-11	175	4-16-75	1996	Mobile, Ala.
Haws, Scott	.203	39	123	5	25	1	0	0	5	11	13	0	0	L	R	6-0	190	1-11-72	1992	Fairless Hills, Pa.
Hudler, Rex	.324	9	34	8	11	2	1	3	6	0	8	1	0	R	R	6-2	180	9-2-60	1978	Fresno, Calif.
Key, Jeff	.282	136	522	85	147	37	11	17	87	29	112	15	9	L	R	6-1	200	11-22-74	1993	Covington, Ga.
Knupfer, Jason	.258	108	365	56	94	15	0	1	40	49	70	5	6	R	R	6-0	180	9-21-74	1996	Redwood City, Calif.
Marsters, Brandon	.184	44	141	10	26	3	0	0	18	15	26	1	0	R	R	5-10	195	3-14-75	1996	Sarasota, Fla.
McMullen, Jon	.195	21	77	7	15	3	0	0	8	5	19	0	0	L	R	6-0	240	11-30-73	1992	Ventura, Calif.
Mejia, Juan	.179	26	78	9	14	0	1	0	6	6	16	3	1	R	R	6-0	150	11-22-75	1994	San Pedro de Macoris, D.R.
Millan, Adan	.291	13	55	7	16	3	1	1	8	5	8	1	0	R	R	6-0	195	3-26-72	1994	Montebello, Calif.
Nichols, Kevin	.000	4	12	0	0	0	0	0	0	0	2	0	0	R	R	6-0	195	4-16-73	1996	Southport, Fla.
Northeimer, Jamie	.254	20	71	13	18	6	0	3	8	9	13	0	0	R	R	5-10	174	7-5-72	1994	Sacramento, Calif.
Pierce, Kirk	.265	24	68	9	18	1	1	1	5	3	13	0	0	R	R	6-3	200	5-26-73	1995	Murrieta, Calif.
Raynor, Mark	.235	136	469	54	110	12	2	3	45	60	58	8	6	R	R	6-0	180	4-1-73	1995	Williamston, N.C.
Rivero, Eddie	.288	132	455	61	131	30	2	15	74	49	107	1	2	L	L	6-0	190	7-14-73	1996	Miami, Fla.
Shores, Scott	.268	27	97	20	26	7	0	3	7	11	23	6	3	R	R	6-1	190	2-4-72	1994	Phoenix, Ariz.
Snusz, Chris	.200	36	105	12	21	7	0	0	3	2	22	0	0	R	R	6-0	195	11-8-72	1995	Buffalo, N.Y.
Taylor, Greg	.193	32	83	7	16	4	0	0	6	11	16	0	2	R	R	6-0	170	10-30-73	1996	Fort Wayne, Ind.
Taylor, Reggie	.244	134	545	73	133	18	6	12	47	30	130	40	23	L	R	6-1	180	1-12-77	1995	Newberry, S.C.
Torti, Mike	.220	70	232	29	51	12	1	4	27	26	57	1	0	R	R	5-11	190	8-29-74	1996	Carrollton, Texas
Wesemann, Jason	.159	38	88	7	14	1	0	0	4	10	20	1	0	R	R	6-0	180	3-29-74	1996	Watertown, Wis.

GAMES BY POSITION: C—Haws 27, Marsters 44, Millan 4, Northeimer 18, Pierce 22, Snusz 36. **1B**—Elliott 81, Haws 8, Knupfer 1, McMullen 21, Millan 8, Rivero 16, Torti 14. **2B**—Elliott 9, Hudler 2, Knupfer 99, Mejia 23, G. Taylor 12. **3B**—Elliott 47, Knupfer 10, Nichols 4, G. Taylor 3, Torti 52, Wesemann 37. **SS**—Knupfer 2, Mejia 2, Raynor 136, G. Taylor 1. **OF**—Cornelius 17, Costello 82, Crane 2, Elliott 1, Francia 21, Hudler 3, Key 102, Rivero 53, Shores 22, G. Taylor 2, R. Taylor 132.

PITCHING	W	L	ERA	G	GS	CG	SV	IP	H	R	ER	BB	SO	B	T	HT	WT	DOB	1st Yr	Resides
Aguiar, Doug	0	1	6.75	1	1	0	0	4	4	3	3	1	2	R	R	6-0	160	2-20-77	1995	Zulia, Venez.
Barnett, Marty	5	6	3.69	17	15	1	0	98	102	50	40	29	62	R	R	6-3	210	3-10-74	1995	Harlan, Iowa
Beech, Matt	0	0	0.00	1	1	0	0	6	1	1	0	4	9	L	L	6-2	190	1-20-72	1994	San Antonio, Texas
Blazier, Ron	2	3	2.93	15	0	0	3	31	24	11	10	8	45	R	R	6-6	215	7-30-71	1990	Bellwood, Pa.
Brannan, Ryan	0	0	0.33	21	0	0	10	27	20	2	1	8	25	R	R	6-3	210	4-27-75	1996	Huntington Beach, Calif.
Burger, Rob	11	9	3.59	28	27	1	0	161	131	79	64	93	154	R	R	6-1	190	3-25-76	1994	Willow Street, Pa.
Coggin, David	11	8	4.70	27	27	3	0	155	160	96	81	86	110	R	R	6-4	195	10-30-76	1995	Upland, Calif.
Davis, Jason	2	1	1.49	24	0	0	2	42	31	11	7	17	36	L	L	6-3	185	8-15-74	1996	Winters, Calif.
Estavil, Mauricio	1	0	3.92	9	2	0	0	21	23	11	9	13	6	L	L	6-0	185	6-27-72	1994	Calabasas, Calif.

PITCHING	W	L	ERA	G	GS	CG	SV	IP	H	R	ER	BB	SO	B	T	HT	WT	DOB	1st Yr	Resides
Kershner, Jason	5	10	3.90	22	16	0	1	99	113	49	43	21	51	L	L	6-2	160	12-19-76	1995	Scottsdale, Ariz.
Knoll, Randy	1	2	4.45	5	5	0	0	30	33	18	15	7	20	R	R	6-4	190	3-21-77	1995	Riverside, Calif.
Manning, Len	0	0	0.00	5	0	0	0	6	2	0	0	0	7	L	L	6-2	195	12-30-71	1994	New Brighton, Minn.
Mejia, Javier	6	3	3.09	52	0	0	7	64	68	22	22	24	54	R	R	6-0	190	7-28-74	1996	Los Angeles, Calif.
Nyari, Pete	0	4	2.70	31	0	0	5	43	29	20	13	21	35	R	R	5-11	200	9-4-71	1994	Erie, Pa.
Ramos, Edgar	0	0	3.60	2	2	0	0	5	3	3	2	2	3	R	R	6-4	170	3-6-75	1992	Cumana, Venez.
Shumaker, Anthony	5	4	2.13	61	0	0	9	72	64	22	17	17	77	L	L	6-5	223	5-14-73	1995	Kokomo, Ind.
Stevens, Kris	6	3	4.56	13	13	0	0	71	80	42	36	30	53	R	L	6-2	188	9-19-77	1996	Fontana, Calif.
Stumpf, Brian	0	0	5.92	17	0	0	0	24	31	18	16	9	23	L	R	6-3	200	5-22-72	1994	Springfield, Pa.
Thomas, Evan	5	5	2.44	13	12	2	0	85	68	30	23	23	89	R	R	5-10	175	6-14-74	1996	Pembroke Pines, Fla.
Vandemark, John	2	1	2.88	14	0	0	0	25	21	11	8	12	22	L	L	6-1	205	9-28-71	1990	Lockport, N.Y.
Whiteman, Greg	3	3	4.59	11	11	0	0	51	57	30	26	26	32	L	L	6-2	185	6-12-73	1994	Wileyford, W.Va.
Yeager, Gary	5	5	6.11	39	6	0	0	74	91	55	50	25	42	R	R	6-1	190	11-6-73	1995	Pottsville, Pa.

PIEDMONT — Class A

SOUTH ATLANTIC LEAGUE

BATTING	AVG	G	AB	R	H	2B	3B	HR	RBI	BB	SO	SB	CS	B	T	HT	WT	DOB	1st Yr	Resides
Batts, Rodney	.224	24	67	8	15	3	1	1	7	11	19	1	1	R	R	5-10	170	10-13-73	1996	Columbus, Miss.
Clark, Kirby	.175	42	143	18	25	8	0	0	10	10	50	0	1	L	R	6-0	200	10-6-73	1996	Toomsuba, Miss.
Cooley, Shannon	.266	90	304	35	81	16	1	1	28	10	57	5	4	L	R	6-1	170	6-24-74	1996	Hickory, Miss.
Crane, Todd	.290	80	314	50	91	13	0	5	35	30	57	26	6	R	R	6-1	185	7-2-73	1995	Roswell, Ga.
Crawford, Marty	.226	108	389	37	88	15	1	4	51	30	51	3	1	L	R	5-7	175	2-19-74	1996	Grand Prairie, Texas
Crede, Brad	.214	110	402	52	86	18	1	10	47	32	145	0	3	R	R	6-5	200	8-15-74	1996	Westphalia, Mo.
Edwards, Lamont	.249	106	386	48	96	16	3	2	53	29	68	18	7	R	R	6-2	200	8-6-73	1996	Clinton, N.C.
Francia, David	.300	112	424	72	127	24	7	9	65	25	61	39	12	L	L	5-11	175	4-16-75	1996	Mobile, Ala.
Kiil, Skip	.226	82	261	48	59	15	3	7	34	35	74	13	2	R	R	6-0	185	4-10-74	1996	Milpitas, Calif.
Marsters, Brandon	.203	61	212	25	43	8	0	2	20	22	51	0	0	R	R	5-10	195	3-14-75	1996	Sarasota, Fla.
Mejia, Juan	.250	36	112	15	28	6	2	0	12	0	32	7	0	R	R	6-0	150	11-22-75	1994	San Pedro de Macoris, D.R.
Nichols, Kevin	.293	81	321	21	94	16	2	5	46	9	46	1	1	R	R	6-0	195	4-16-73	1996	Southport, Fla.
Oliveros, Leonardo	.171	38	129	6	22	3	0	0	5	5	18	0	0	S	R	5-10	185	12-1-75	1994	Maturin, Venez.
Rollins, Jimmy	.270	139	560	94	151	22	8	6	59	52	80	46	6	S	R	5-9	165	11-27-78	1996	Alameda, Calif.
Taylor, Greg	.278	41	115	15	32	7	1	0	14	15	11	1	2	R	R	6-0	170	10-30-73	1996	Fort Wayne, Ind.
Thompson, Nick	.258	58	225	32	58	8	3	3	21	8	33	1	1	R	R	6-0	190	8-23-74	1996	Dunwoody, Ga.
Torti, Mike	.250	49	176	19	44	12	1	6	31	28	47	1	0	R	R	5-11	190	8-29-74	1996	Carrollton, Texas
Wesemann, Jason	.250	44	104	16	26	1	1	1	12	8	23	1	0	R	R	6-0	180	3-29-74	1996	Watertown, Wis.
Williams, Errick	.206	37	136	12	28	5	0	1	6	9	44	10	4	R	R	6-0	215	5-21-77	1995	Austin, Texas

GAMES BY POSITION: C—Clark 16, Marsters 61, Oliveros 26, Thompson 42. **1B**—Clark 1, Crede 109, Nichols 9, Torti 26, Wesemann 1. **2B**—Batts 3, Edwards 106, Mejia 3, Taylor 33. **3B**—Batts 14, Mejia 21, Nichols 56, Taylor 6, Torti 23, Wesemann 42. **SS**—Mejia 5, Rollins 138, Taylor 1, Wesemann 1. **OF**—Batts 3, Clark 6, Cooley 77, Crane 80, Crawford 30, Francia 110, Kiil 80, Thompson 17, Williams 37.

PITCHING	W	L	ERA	G	GS	CG	SV	IP	H	R	ER	BB	SO	B	T	HT	WT	DOB	1st Yr	Resides
Allen, Brandon	11	8	3.54	25	24	4	0	153	153	78	60	38	91	L	L	5-10	180	9-1-74	1996	Littleton, Colo.
Barnett, Marty	2	1	3.16	6	6	0	0	37	34	16	13	11	28	R	R	6-3	210	3-10-74	1995	Harlan, Iowa
Davis, Jason	1	0	0.61	17	0	0	1	29	10	3	2	6	34	L	L	6-3	185	8-15-74	1996	Winters, Calif.
Eaton, Adam	5	6	4.16	14	14	0	0	71	81	38	33	30	57	R	R	6-2	180	11-23-77	1996	Snohomish, Wash.
Jacquez, Tom	2	4	4.97	8	8	0	0	42	45	29	23	13	26	L	L	6-1	195	12-29-75	1997	Stockton, Calif.
Kawabata, Kyle	9	5	1.44	44	0	0	16	63	45	14	10	13	75	R	R	6-0	195	1-2-74	1995	Kailua, Hawaii
Key, Calvin	0	0	3.77	3	1	0	0	14	19	6	6	2	9	R	R	6-4	210	10-17-74	1997	Jacksonville, Ark.
Martinez, Caleb	5	10	4.66	20	19	0	0	110	117	70	57	38	89	L	L	6-2	190	2-10-77	1993	Hialeah, Fla.
Mendes, Jaime	4	5	4.45	42	2	0	0	85	103	48	42	20	47	R	R	5-10	185	4-6-73	1995	Las Cruces, N.M.
Miller, Brian	1	2	4.94	29	7	0	1	75	91	44	41	24	63	R	R	6-0	200	1-26-73	1995	Two Rivers, Wis.
Mitchell, Courtney	7	4	2.41	47	0	0	3	78	60	25	21	19	68	S	L	5-9	178	11-20-72	1994	Garyville, La.
Quintana, Urbano	0	0	18.47	3	0	0	0	6	12	13	13	3	2	R	R	6-0	160	2-9-75	1993	Esperanza Mao, D.R.
Rutherford, Mark	1	4	2.47	9	9	0	0	58	42	17	16	9	47	R	R	6-2	195	11-9-74	1997	Livonia, Mich.
Sikes, Jason	4	5	5.63	27	11	0	0	96	124	67	60	31	63	R	R	6-5	225	6-17-76	1994	Perry, Ga.
Stevens, Kris	6	4	2.22	14	14	3	0	89	66	30	22	31	72	R	L	6-2	188	9-19-77	1996	Fontana, Calif.
Tilton, Ira	7	13	4.78	28	27	3	0	153	171	100	81	50	103	R	R	6-4	185	10-27-74	1996	Indianapolis, Ind.
Tober, Dave	5	1	3.42	46	0	0	10	82	65	34	31	25	55	R	R	5-9	175	5-11-74	1996	Warwick, R.I.

BATAVIA — Short-Season Class A

NEW YORK-PENN LEAGUE

BATTING	AVG	G	AB	R	H	2B	3B	HR	RBI	BB	SO	SB	CS	B	T	HT	WT	DOB	1st Yr	Resides
Burnham, Gary	.325	73	289	44	94	22	4	5	45	30	47	3	1	L	L	5-10	210	10-13-74	1997	South Windsor, Conn.
Collins, Francis	.267	63	206	35	55	5	2	0	16	23	46	16	4	L	L	5-10	185	3-8-74	1997	San Francisco, Calif.
Dominique, Andy	.278	72	277	52	77	17	0	14	48	26	60	4	1	R	R	6-0	205	10-30-75	1997	Granada Hills, Calif.
Estrada, Johnny	.314	58	223	28	70	17	2	6	43	9	15	0	0	S	R	5-11	190	6-27-76	1997	Fresno, Calif.
Fajardo, Alejandro	.270	52	200	35	54	7	4	2	29	7	34	9	2	R	R	6-0	175	2-6-76	1995	Moca, D.R.
Fitzpatrick, Eddie	.143	25	63	5	9	0	0	0	7	2	23	0	0	R	R	6-2	200	2-21-75	1997	Henderson, Tenn.
Fritz, Jim	.267	35	90	10	24	8	1	1	13	14	25	4	1	R	R	6-0	210	6-2-75	1997	Aloha, Ore.
Harris, Brian	.311	51	148	31	46	7	1	0	19	31	27	11	6	S	R	5-10	180	4-28-75	1997	Carmel, Ind.
Johnson, Jason	.294	60	238	40	70	11	5	0	28	17	26	20	7	R	R	6-1	155	8-21-77	1996	Montclair, Calif.
Kurilla, Kevin	.239	60	209	27	50	7	1	5	36	17	59	7	1	R	R	6-4	193	2-21-75	1997	Mt. Wolf, Pa.
McNamara, Rusty	.312	72	295	55	92	17	0	6	54	15	33	3	3	R	R	5-8	185	1-23-75	1997	Riverside, Calif.
Terrell, Jeff	.220	52	159	20	35	4	1	0	17	16	38	3	1	L	R	6-1	175	10-22-74	1997	Blue Springs, Mo.
Thompson, Nick	.200	4	15	4	3	2	0	0	4	3	3	0	0	R	R	6-0	190	8-23-74	1996	Dunwoody, Ga.
Worthy, Thomas	.241	56	141	28	34	3	0	1	9	15	36	9	3	R	R	5-11	165	1-21-77	1996	Attalla, Ala.

GAMES BY POSITION: C—Estrada 51, Fitzpatrick 23, Fritz 7, Thompson 4. **1B**—Burnham 12, Dominique 63, Estrada 1, Fritz 2, Kurilla 1. **2B**—Harris 28, McNamara 8, Terrell 45. **3B**—Fritz 20, McNamara 61. **SS**—Harris 16, Kurilla 57, Terrell 2. **OF**—Burnham 27, Collins 61, Fajardo 51, Johnson 60, Worthy 47.

PITCHING	W	L	ERA	G	GS	CG	SV	IP	H	R	ER	BB	SO	B	T	HT	WT	DOB	1st Yr	Resides
Adair, Derek	7	3	2.11	13	12	1	0	77	71	29	18	4	53	R	R	6-4	188	8-25-75	1997	Albertson, N.Y.

PITCHING	W	L	ERA	G	GS	CG	SV	IP	H	R	ER	BB	SO	B	T	HT	WT	DOB	1st Yr	Resides
Aguiar, Doug	1	0	3.57	7	3	0	0	23	24	15	9	15	15	R	R	6-0	160	2-20-77	1995	Zulia, Venez.
Black, Brett	3	0	1.32	28	0	0	15	41	23	7	6	2	66	R	R	6-0	210	10-3-74	1997	Apopka, Fla.
Cotton, Joseph	7	4	2.99	15	15	0	0	96	90	38	32	29	74	R	R	6-2	190	3-25-75	1996	Uniontown, Ohio
Driscoll, Pat	0	0	3.72	11	0	0	0	10	14	5	4	4	10	L	L	6-0	185	2-11-75	1997	Omaha, Neb.
Eason, Clay	0	1	092	20	0	0	1	29	16	6	3	11	29	R	R	5-11	180	9-28-75	1997	Dunn, N.C.
Fenus, Justin	3	5	4.45	15	7	0	0	55	54	34	27	30	26	R	R	6-3	195	5-19-75	1996	Mountain View, Wyo.
Frush, Jimmy	6	1	2.85	26	0	0	1	41	34	14	13	6	37	R	R	6-4	195	1-22-75	1997	Abilene, Texas
Jacquez, Tom	2	1	2.42	4	4	0	0	22	20	6	6	2	20	L	L	6-1	195	12-29-75	1997	Stockton, Calif.
Manbeck, Mark	1	2	4.76	5	5	0	0	28	36	16	15	4	27	R	R	6-2	190	9-18-74	1997	Round Rock, Texas
Mondello, Peter	0	1	3.71	27	0	0	0	34	32	20	14	17	41	R	R	6-4	180	12-18-74	1997	Port Arthur, Texas
Quintana, Urbano	1	0	2.16	6	0	0	0	8	9	5	2	1	5	R	R	6-0	160	2-9-75	1993	Esperanza Mao, D.R.
Rutherford, Mark	2	1	0.75	3	2	0	0	12	10	5	1	3	11	R	R	6-2	195	11-9-74	1997	Livonia, Mich.
Shipp, Kevin	5	3	2.83	13	7	0	0	48	44	17	15	6	41	R	R	5-11	190	2-8-75	1997	Baton Rouge, La.
Shockley, Keith	1	3	6.82	27	2	0	2	32	48	30	24	6	10	R	L	6-4	190	10-25-76	1996	Wichita, Kan.
Wolf, Randy	4	0	1.58	7	7	0	0	40	29	8	7	8	53	L	L	6-0	195	8-22-76	1997	West Hills, Calif.
Zawatski, Geoff	4	2	5.04	15	10	0	0	55	87	41	31	8	33	R	R	6-4	190	12-6-73	1997	Mechanicsburg, Pa.

MARTINSVILLE — Rookie

APPALACHIAN LEAGUE

BATTING	AVG	G	AB	R	H	2B	3B	HR	RBI	BB	SO	SB	CS	B	T	HT	WT	DOB	1st Yr	Resides
Beverly, Shomari	.256	34	125	13	32	5	0	2	13	5	37	9	5	R	R	6-0	165	2-16-78	1997	Alameda, Calif.
Bonilla, Elin	.207	36	121	16	25	4	2	2	20	6	46	1	1	R	R	6-0	180	12-7-77	1996	La Vega, D.R.
Bushman, Jonathan	.211	12	19	3	4	1	0	0	0	0	8	0	0	R	R	5-10	165	10-13-78	1997	St. Louis, Mo.
Caines, Franklyn	.274	53	197	26	54	12	0	4	30	17	58	6	0	R	R	6-2	170	1-5-77	1994	San Pedro de Macoris, D.R.
Casillas, Uriel	.268	60	220	42	59	12	1	1	26	23	29	5	3	R	R	5-11	160	8-22-75	1997	Downey, Calif.
Cody, Ryan	.237	26	76	9	18	4	0	1	8	8	21	0	1	R	R	6-1	190	6-13-78	1997	Vancouver, Wash.
Collier, Lamonte	.252	62	222	49	56	7	2	2	23	47	50	14	9	R	R	5-9	185	4-1-75	1997	St. Louis, Mo.
Duncan, Carlos	.260	54	204	38	53	8	4	13	33	14	62	11	5	R	R	6-1	155	6-30-77	1995	San Pedro de Macoris, D.R.
Giron, Alejandro	.302	54	202	26	61	15	1	1	27	11	40	6	5	R	R	6-2	170	4-26-79	1996	Santo Domingo, D.R.
Johnson, Duane	.139	35	79	9	11	0	0	0	3	5	35	5	2	R	R	6-0	185	11-19-78	1997	Reno, Nev.
Marchant, Nick	.093	23	75	3	7	0	0	0	3	3	32	2	0	R	R	6-2	205	7-2-78	1997	Boise, Idaho
Norrell, Troy	.192	36	120	17	23	6	0	5	18	15	55	4	3	R	R	6-0	190	10-25-76	1997	Lake Jackson, Texas
Rojas, Alejandro	.180	15	50	4	9	1	0	0	0	1	18	1	2	S	R	5-9	145	3-2-78	1996	La Vega, D.R.
Romans, Billy	.176	19	68	7	12	4	0	0	3	3	16	3	2	R	R	6-1	185	9-9-75	1997	Cocoa, Fla.
Schlicher, B.J.	.295	58	217	33	64	16	0	5	34	28	59	2	3	S	R	6-4	210	11-7-77	1996	Crawfordsville, Ind.
Valdez, Jerry	.272	34	125	21	34	7	0	1	11	7	27	0	2	R	R	5-11	195	6-6-74	1997	El Paso, Texas
Van Iten, Bob	.309	55	204	29	63	9	0	5	35	5	27	3	2	L	R	6-2	170	7-1-77	1996	Independence, Mo.

GAMES BY POSITION: C—Cody 13, Norrell 23, Valdez 21, Van Iten 15. **1B**—Caines 3, Schlicher 53, Van Iten 16. **2B**—Casillas 45, Collier 11, Rojas 14. **3B**—Caines 5, Casillas 5, Collier 43, Romans 18. **SS**—Casillas 13, Collier 3, Duncan 54, Romans 1. **OF**—Beverly 30, Bonilla 36, Bushman 8, Caines 44, Collier 5, Giron 54, Johnson 26, Marchant 19, Van Iten 1.

PITCHING	W	L	ERA	G	GS	CG	SV	IP	H	R	ER	BB	SO	B	T	HT	WT	DOB	1st Yr	Resides
Albaugh, Chad	1	2	5.79	20	0	0	1	33	38	27	21	15	27	R	R	6-2	215	12-26-74	1997	Johnstown, Pa.
Cook, Steven	0	0	5.00	7	0	0	0	9	11	6	5	7	8	R	R	6-3	225	9-20-75	1997	Blair, Neb.
Driscoll, Pat	2	2	2.57	8	0	0	0	14	12	4	4	4	17	L	L	6-0	185	2-11-75	1997	Omaha, Neb.
Hootselle, Jeff	3	3	5.05	14	12	1	0	66	62	43	37	28	69	R	L	6-5	195	10-31-75	1997	Alpharetta, Ga.
Humphries, Chris	1	0	8.38	5	0	0	0	10	14	14	9	8	7	R	R	6-4	220	3-5-74	1997	Las Vegas, Nev.
Key, Calvin	5	2	4.83	14	6	0	0	50	56	35	27	13	53	R	R	6-4	210	10-17-74	1997	Jacksonville, Ark.
Manbeck, Mark	3	1	2.22	9	9	0	0	57	51	16	14	3	64	R	R	6-2	190	9-18-74	1997	Round Rock, Texas
Martinez, Caleb	1	3	3.69	7	7	0	0	39	37	21	16	18	27	L	L	6-2	190	2-10-77	1993	Hialeah, Fla.
Molta, Salvatore	0	2	9.53	13	0	0	0	17	25	18	18	13	12	R	R	6-2	195	10-28-77	1996	Wallington, N.J.
Montero, Francisco	3	5	4.09	14	14	0	0	77	79	49	35	22	47	R	R	6-2	170	1-6-76	1994	Barahona, D.R.
Ramos, Fernando	2	3	2.05	24	0	0	9	26	13	8	6	12	25	R	R	6-1	169	5-3-76	1994	Moca, D.R.
Reyes, Arquimedes	4	1	2.31	20	0	0	0	39	32	17	10	15	39	R	R	5-11	160	9-26-78	1996	Sabana Perdida, D.R.
Serrano, Elio	1	5	5.93	21	0	0	1	41	46	34	27	16	40	R	R	6-3	180	12-4-78	1996	Carabobo, Venez.
Silva, Carlos	2	2	5.15	11	11	0	0	58	66	46	33	14	31	R	R	6-4	198	4-23-79	1996	Guayana, Venez.
Turnbow, Derrick	1	3	7.40	7	7	0	0	24	34	29	20	16	7	R	R	6-3	180	1-25-78	1997	Franklin, Tenn.
Walker, Adam	0	5	6.28	21	2	0	2	29	32	28	20	11	30	L	L	6-6	210	5-28-76	1997	Albuquerque, N.M.

Pittsburgh PIRATES

Manager: Gene Lamont. **1997 Record:** 79-83, .488 (2nd, NL Central)

BATTING	AVG	G	AB	R	H	2B	3B	HR	RBI	BB	SO	SB	CS	B	T	HT	WT	DOB	1st Yr	Resides
Allensworth, Jermaine	.255	108	369	55	94	18	2	3	43	44	79	14	7	R	R	5-11	180	1-11-72	1993	Anderson, Ind.
Brown, Adrian	.190	48	147	17	28	6	0	1	10	13	18	8	4	S	R	6-0	185	2-7-74	1992	Summit, Miss.
Brown, Emil	.179	66	95	16	17	2	1	2	6	10	32	5	1	R	R	6-2	200	12-29-74	1994	Chicago, Ill.
Collier, Lou	.135	18	37	3	5	0	0	0	3	1	11	1	0	R	R	5-10	170	8-21-73	1993	Chicago, Ill.
Cummings, Midre	.189	52	106	11	20	6	2	3	8	8	26	0	0	L	R	6-0	196	10-14-71	1990	St. Croix, V.I.
Dunston, Shawon	.394	18	71	14	28	4	1	5	16	0	11	3	1	R	R	6-1	175	3-21-63	1982	Corona, N.Y.
2-team (114 Chicago)	.300	132	490	71	147	22	5	14	57	8	75	32	8							
Elster, Kevin	.225	39	138	14	31	6	2	7	25	21	39	0	2	R	R	6-2	200	8-3-64	1984	Huntington Beach, Calif.
Garcia, Freddy	.150	20	40	4	6	1	0	3	5	2	17	0	0	R	R	6-2	186	8-1-72	1991	La Romana, D.R.
Guillen, Jose	.267	143	498	58	133	20	5	14	70	17	88	1	2	R	R	5-11	165	5-17-76	1993	San Cristobal, D.R.
Johnson, Mark	.215	78	219	30	47	10	0	4	29	43	78	1	1	L	L	6-4	220	10-17-67	1990	Worcester, Mass.
Kendall, Jason	.294	144	486	71	143	36	4	8	49	49	53	18	6	R	R	6-0	170	6-26-74	1992	Torrance, Calif.
Martin, Al	.291	113	423	64	123	24	7	13	59	45	83	23	7	L	L	6-2	210	11-24-67	1985	Scottsdale, Ariz.
Nunez, Abraham	.225	19	40	3	9	2	2	0	6	3	10	1	0	S	R	5-11	160	3-16-76	1994	Santo Domingo, D.R.
Osik, Keith	.257	49	105	10	27	9	1	0	7	9	21	0	1	R	R	6-0	195	10-22-68	1990	Rocky Point, N.Y.
Polcovich, Kevin	.273	84	245	37	67	16	1	4	21	21	45	2	2	R	R	5-9	165	6-28-70	1992	Auburn, N.Y.
Randa, Joe	.302	126	443	58	134	27	9	7	60	41	64	4	2	R	R	5-11	190	12-18-69	1991	Delafield, Wis.
Smith, Mark	.285	71	193	29	55	13	1	9	35	28	36	3	1	R	R	6-3	205	5-7-70	1991	Arcadia, Calif.
Sveum, Dale	.261	126	306	30	80	20	1	12	47	27	81	0	3	S	R	6-3	185	11-23-63	1982	Glendale, Ariz.
Ward, Turner	.353	71	167	33	59	16	1	7	33	18	17	4	1	S	R	6-2	182	4-11-65	1986	Saraland, Ala.
Williams, Eddie	.247	30	89	12	22	5	0	3	11	10	24	1	0	R	R	6-0	175	11-1-64	1983	La Mesa, Calif.
2-team (8 L.A.)	.240	38	96	12	23	5	0	3	12	11	25	1	0							
Womack, Tony	.278	155	641	85	178	26	9	6	50	43	109	60	7	L	R	5-9	153	9-25-69	1991	Chatham, Va.
Young, Kevin	.300	97	333	59	100	18	3	18	74	16	89	11	2	R	R	6-2	219	6-16-69	1990	Kansas City, Kan.

PITCHING	W	L	ERA	G	GS	CG	SV	IP	H	R	ER	BB	SO	B	T	HT	WT	DOB	1st Yr	Resides
Christiansen, Jason	3	0	2.94	39	0	0	0	34	37	11	11	17	37	R	L	6-5	235	9-21-69	1991	Elkhorn, Neb.
Cooke, Steve	9	15	4.30	32	32	0	0	167	184	95	80	77	109	R	L	6-6	220	1-14-70	1990	Tigard, Ore.
Cordova, Francisco	11	8	3.63	29	29	2	0	179	175	80	72	49	121	R	R	5-11	163	4-26-72	1996	Veracruz, Mexico
Dessens, Elmer	0	0	0.00	3	0	0	0	3	2	0	0	0	2	R	R	6-0	190	1-13-72	1993	Hermosillo, Mexico
Ericks, John	1	0	1.93	10	0	0	6	9	7	3	2	4	6	R	R	6-7	220	9-16-67	1988	Tinley Park, Ill.
Granger, Jeff	0	0	18.00	9	0	0	0	5	10	10	10	8	4	R	L	6-4	200	12-16-71	1993	Orange, Texas
Johnson, Jason	0	0	6.00	3	0	0	0	6	10	4	4	1	3	R	R	6-6	220	10-27-73	1992	Burlington, Ky.
Lieber, Jon	11	14	4.49	33	32	1	0	188	193	102	94	51	160	L	R	6-3	205	4-2-70	1992	Council Bluffs, Iowa
Loaiza, Esteban	11	11	4.13	33	32	1	0	196	214	99	90	56	122	R	R	6-2	172	12-31-71	1991	Imperial Beach, Calif.
Loiselle, Rich	1	5	3.10	72	0	0	29	73	76	29	25	24	66	R	R	6-5	225	1-12-72	1991	Oshkosh, Wis.
Morel, Ramon	0	0	4.70	5	0	0	0	8	11	4	4	4	4	R	R	6-2	170	8-15-74	1991	Villa Gonzalez, D.R.
Peters, Chris	2	2	4.58	31	1	0	0	37	38	23	19	21	17	L	L	6-1	170	1-28-72	1993	McMurray, Pa.
Rincon, Ricardo	4	8	3.45	62	0	0	4	60	51	26	23	24	71	L	L	6-0	190	4-13-70	1997	Veracruz, Mexico
Ruebel, Matt	3	2	6.32	44	0	0	0	63	77	50	44	27	50	L	L	6-2	180	10-16-69	1991	Ames, Iowa
Schmidt, Jason	10	9	4.60	32	32	2	0	188	193	106	96	76	136	R	R	6-5	185	1-29-73	1991	Kelso, Wash.
Silva, Jose	2	1	5.94	11	4	0	0	36	52	26	24	16	30	R	R	6-5	210	12-19-73	1991	San Diego, Calif.
Sodowsky, Clint	2	2	3.63	45	0	0	0	52	49	22	21	34	51	L	R	6-3	180	7-13-72	1991	Ponca City, Okla.
Wagner, Paul	0	0	3.94	14	0	0	0	16	17	7	7	13	9	R	R	6-1	202	11-14-67	1989	Germantown, Wis.
Wainhouse, David	0	1	8.04	25	0	0	0	28	34	28	25	17	21	L	R	6-2	185	11-7-67	1989	Mercer Island, Wash.
Wallace, Jeff	0	0	0.75	11	0	0	0	12	8	2	1	8	14	L	L	6-2	237	4-12-76	1995	Minerva, Ohio
Wilkins, Marc	9	5	3.69	70	0	0	2	76	65	33	31	33	47	R	R	5-11	215	10-21-70	1992	Mansfield, Ohio

FIELDING

Catcher	PCT	G	PO	A	E	DP	PB
Kendall	.990	142	952	103	11	20	7
Osik	.989	32	160	13	2	3	4

First Base	PCT	G	PO	A	E	DP
Garcia	1.000	2	14	0	0	2
Johnson	.992	63	542	44	5	48
Osik	1.000	1	2	0	0	0
Smith	1.000	9	58	5	0	1
Sveum	1.000	21	105	5	0	10
Williams	.991	26	202	8	2	18
Young	.997	77	620	50	2	47

Second Base	PCT	G	PO	A	E	DP
Nunez	1.000	9	5	12	0	0
Osik	1.000	4	1	1	0	0
Polcovich	1.000	2	4	0	0	1
Randa	1.000	13	25	41	0	6
Sveum	.889	2	3	5	1	1
Womack	.974	152	335	429	20	83

Third Base	PCT	G	PO	A	E	DP
Garcia	.842	10	7	9	3	1
Osik	.000	1	0	0	0	0
Polcovich	.000	1	0	0	0	0
Randa	.937	120	66	247	21	24
Sveum	.941	47	17	78	6	4
Young	.885	12	7	16	3	2

Shortstop	PCT	G	PO	A	E	DP
Collier	1.000	18	9	36	0	7
Dunston	.965	18	28	55	3	8
Elster	.994	39	54	123	1	22
Nunez	1.000	12	9	25	0	5
Polcovich	.969	80	121	248	12	38
Sveum	.988	28	29	54	1	14
Womack	1.000	4	0	1	0	0

Outfield	PCT	G	PO	A	E	DP
Allensworth	.980	104	189	5	4	1
A. Brown	.987	38	74	3	1	1
E. Brown	.948	42	53	2	3	1
Cummings	1.000	25	37	1	0	0
Dunston	1.000	7	16	0	0	0
Guillen	.963	136	226	9	9	3
Martin	.957	110	125	8	6	1
Smith	1.000	42	53	4	0	0
Ward	1.000	54	71	2	0	0
Young	1.000	11	17	0	0	0

GEORGE GOJKOVICH

Kevin Young

FARM SYSTEM

Director of Player Development: Paul Tinnell

Class	Farm Team	League	W	L	Pct.	Finish*	Manager(s)	First Yr
AAA	Calgary (Alberta) Cannons	Pacific Coast	60	78	.435	9th (10)	Trent Jewett	1995
AA	Carolina (N.C.) Mudcats	Southern	55	82	.401	10th (10)	Hill/Banister	1991
#A	Lynchburg (Va.) Hillcats	Carolina	82	58	.586	+2nd (8)	Banister/Richardson	1995
A	Augusta (Ga.) GreenJackets	South Atlantic	71	71	.500	7th (14)	Richardson/Little	1988
A	Erie (Pa.) SeaWolves	New York-Penn	50	26	.658	2nd (14)	Marty Brown	1995
R	Bradenton (Fla.) Pirates	Gulf Coast	27	32	.458	9th (15)	Woody Huyke	1967

*Finish in overall standings (No. of teams in league) #Advanced level +Won league championship

ORGANIZATION LEADERS

MAJOR LEAGUERS

BATTING

*AVG	Joe Randa	.302
R	Tony Womack	85
H	Tony Womack	178
TB	Tony Womack	240
2B	Jason Kendall	36
3B	Two tied at	9
HR	Kevin Young	18
RBI	Kevin Young	74
BB	Jason Kendall	49
SO	Tony Womack	109
SB	Tony Womack	60

PITCHING

W	Three tied at	11
L	Steve Cooke	15
#ERA	Francisco Cordova	3.63
G	Rich Loiselle	72
CG	Two tied at	2
SV	Rich Loiselle	29
IP	Esteban Loaiza	196
BB	Steve Cooke	77
SO	Jon Lieber	160

MEL BAILEY

Rich Loiselle

RODGER WOOD

Aramis Ramirez

MINOR LEAGUERS

BATTING

*AVG	Manny Martinez, Calgary	.331
R	Chance Sanford, Calgary/Carolina	88
H	Alex Hernandez, Lynchburg	151
TB	Aramis Ramirez, Lynchburg	249
2B	Two tied at	37
3B	Chance Sanford, Calgary/Carolina	11
HR	Aramis Ramirez, Lynchburg	29
RBI	Aramis Ramirez, Lynchburg	114
BB	Aramis Ramirez, Lynchburg	80
SO	Alex Hernandez, Lynchburg	140
SB	Terrance Freeman, Erie/GCL Pirates	47

PITCHING

W	Three tied at	12
L	Jeff Kelly, Carolina	11
#ERA	Kris Lambert, Erie	2.33
G	David Daniels, Carolina/Augusta	54
CG	Jason Phillips, Carolina/Lynchburg	4
SV	David Daniels, Carolina/Augusta	22
IP	Two tied at	170
BB	Jeff Kelly, Carolina	85
SO	Jason Phillips, Carolina/Lynchburg	162

*Minimum 250 At-Bats #Minimum 75 Innings

TOP 10 PROSPECTS

JIM McLEAN

Kris Benson

How the Pirates Top 10 prospects, as judged by Baseball America prior to the 1997 season, fared in 1997:

Player, Pos.	Club (Class)	AVG	AB	R	H	2B	3B	HR	RBI	SB
2. Chad Hermansen, ss	Carolina (AA)	.275	487	87	134	31	4	20	70	18
3. Aramis Ramirez, 3b	Lynchburg (A)	.278	482	85	134	24	2	29	114	5
4. Jose Guillen, of	Pittsburgh	.267	498	58	133	20	5	14	70	1
5. Ron Wright, 1b	Calgary (AAA)	.304	336	50	102	31	0	16	63	0
6. Abraham Nunez, ss	Pittsburgh	.225	40	3	9	2	2	0	6	1
	Carolina (AA)	.329	198	31	65	6	1	1	14	10
	Lynchburg (A)	.260	304	45	79	9	4	3	32	29
8. Lou Collier, ss	Pittsburgh	.135	37	3	5	0	0	0	3	1
	Calgary (AAA)	.330	397	65	131	31	5	1	48	12
10. Charles Peterson, of	Carolina (AA)	.251	442	59	111	26	4	7	68	20

		W	L	ERA	G	SV	IP	H	BB	SO
1. Kris Benson, rhp	Carolina (AA)	3	5	4.98	14	0	69	81	32	66
	Lynchburg (A)	5	2	2.58	10	0	59	49	13	72
7. Jimmy Anderson, lhp	Calgary (AAA)	7	6	5.68	21	0	103	124	64	71
	Carolina (AA)	2	1	1.46	4	0	25	16	9	23
9. Elvin Hernandez, rhp	Carolina (AA)	2	7	5.73	17	0	93	104	26	66
	Lynchburg (A)	0	0	1.80	3	1	5	4	1	5

CALGARY — Class AAA

PACIFIC COAST LEAGUE

BATTING	AVG	G	AB	R	H	2B	3B	HR	RBI	BB	SO	SB	CS	B	T	HT	WT	DOB	1st Yr	Resides
Allensworth, Jermaine	.400	5	20	5	8	3	1	0	1	2	4	1	1	R	R	5-11	180	1-11-72	1993	Anderson, Ind.
Beasley, Tony	.273	75	220	36	60	7	5	1	28	25	23	11	6	R	R	5-8	165	12-5-66	1989	Bowling Green, Va.
Bridges, Kary	.263	33	95	9	25	4	0	0	6	7	6	1	0	L	R	5-10	165	10-27-71	1993	Hattiesburg, Miss.
Brown, Adrian	.319	62	248	53	79	10	1	1	19	27	38	20	4	S	R	6-0	185	2-7-74	1992	Summit, Miss.
Chamberlain, Wes	.317	18	60	7	19	4	0	2	9	0	14	1	0	R	R	6-2	219	4-13-66	1987	Chicago, Ill.
Collier, Lou	.330	112	397	65	131	31	5	1	48	37	47	12	7	R	R	5-10	170	8-21-73	1993	Chicago, Ill.
Cromer, Brandon	.232	68	228	30	53	15	2	8	36	19	46	3	1	L	R	6-2	175	1-25-74	1992	Lexington, S.C.
Edge, Tim	.235	62	187	23	44	13	2	3	22	13	50	0	2	R	R	6-0	210	10-26-68	1990	Snellville, Ga.
Garcia, Freddy	.240	35	121	21	29	6	0	5	17	9	20	0	0	R	R	6-2	186	8-1-72	1991	La Romana, D.R.
Hazlett, Steve	.298	37	94	18	28	12	2	3	15	12	19	1	0	R	R	5-11	190	3-30-70	1991	Longmont, Colo.
Johnson, Mark	.339	34	115	28	39	11	1	6	16	22	28	4	2	L	L	6-4	220	10-17-67	1990	Worcester, Mass.
Lott, Billy	.314	71	239	45	75	18	0	15	55	35	56	6	0	R	R	6-4	210	8-16-70	1989	Petal, Miss.
Martinez, Manny	.331	109	420	78	139	34	1	16	66	33	80	17	9	R	R	6-2	169	10-3-70	1988	San Pedro de Macoris, D.R.
Marx, Tim	.250	90	300	42	75	18	2	3	40	23	42	9	1	R	R	6-2	190	11-27-68	1991	Evansville, Ind.
Polcovich, Kevin	.306	17	62	7	19	4	0	1	9	1	7	0	0	R	R	5-9	165	6-28-70	1992	Auburn, N.Y.
Randa, Joe	.364	3	11	4	4	1	0	1	4	3	4	0	0	R	R	5-11	190	12-18-69	1991	Delafield, Wis.
Sanford, Chance	.292	89	325	58	95	27	9	6	60	39	82	9	7	L	R	5-10	165	6-2-72	1992	Houston, Texas
Secrist, Reed	.264	40	121	19	32	7	3	5	18	14	32	0	1	L	R	6-1	205	5-7-70	1992	Farmington, Utah
Smith, Mark	.372	39	137	37	51	14	1	14	42	21	15	2	1	R	R	6-3	205	5-7-70	1991	Arcadia, Calif.
Staton, T.J.	.236	65	199	30	47	14	0	2	22	22	51	3	3	L	L	6-3	200	2-17-75	1993	Elyria, Ohio
Thobe, Steve	.255	34	102	16	26	8	0	5	14	15	25	2	1	R	R	6-7	230	5-26-72	1994	Huntington Beach, Calif.
Tolentino, Jose	.308	88	305	52	94	24	0	16	69	31	49	2	5	L	L	6-1	195	6-3-61	1983	Mexico City, Mexico
Ward, Turner	.340	59	209	44	71	18	3	9	44	24	26	7	1	S	R	6-2	182	4-11-65	1986	Saraland, Ala.
Wright, Ron	.304	91	336	50	102	31	0	16	63	24	81	0	2	R	R	6-0	215	1-21-76	1994	Kennewick, Wash.

PITCHING	W	L	ERA	G	GS	CG	SV	IP	H	R	ER	BB	SO	B	T	HT	WT	DOB	1st Yr	Resides
Anderson, Jimmy	7	6	5.68	21	21	0	0	103	124	78	65	64	71	L	L	6-1	180	1-22-76	1994	Chesapeake, Va.
Beatty, Blaine	1	2	23.63	3	2	0	0	5	18	14	14	3	2	L	L	6-2	190	4-25-64	1986	Victoria, Texas
Boever, Joe	4	5	5.01	36	0	0	8	47	59	28	26	19	55	R	R	6-1	200	10-4-60	1982	Palm Harbor, Fla.
Bolton, Tom	2	6	8.29	8	8	0	0	38	67	38	35	12	29	L	L	6-3	185	5-6-62	1980	Smyrna, Tenn.
Briscoe, John	0	1	12.27	4	0	0	0	7	18	11	10	2	7	R	R	6-3	195	9-22-67	1988	Richardson, Texas
Carter, John	1	2	14.57	15	2	0	0	25	45	41	41	27	18	R	R	6-1	195	2-16-72	1991	Chicago, Ill.
Crawford, Carlos	1	5	5.94	9	9	0	0	50	60	43	33	19	26	R	R	6-1	185	10-4-71	1990	Charlotte, N.C.
Ericks, John	0	0	12.86	6	0	0	0	7	14	11	10	1	10	R	R	6-7	220	9-16-67	1988	Tinley Park, Ill.
Gonzales, Frank	1	0	7.26	25	0	0	1	31	43	25	25	9	24	R	L	6-0	185	3-12-68	1989	La Junta, Colo.
Granger, Jeff	1	7	5.55	30	12	0	1	83	111	63	51	33	68	R	L	6-4	200	12-16-71	1993	Orange, Texas
Greer, Ken	0	3	8.46	15	0	0	0	22	33	22	21	7	16	R	R	6-2	215	5-12-67	1988	Hull, Mass.
Halperin, Mike	1	0	6.43	15	4	0	0	28	44	24	20	24	18	L	L	5-10	170	9-8-73	1994	Naples, Fla.
Johnson, Barry	5	2	4.13	34	1	0	1	57	55	30	26	23	51	R	R	6-4	200	8-21-69	1991	Joliet, Ill.
Lawrence, Sean	8	9	4.21	26	26	2	0	143	154	83	67	57	116	L	L	6-4	215	9-2-70	1992	Hillside, Ill.
Morel, Ramon	6	7	5.75	27	18	0	0	102	131	71	65	42	72	R	R	6-2	170	8-15-74	1991	Villa Gonzalez, D.R.
Peters, Chris	2	4	4.38	14	9	0	1	51	52	32	25	30	55	L	L	6-1	170	1-28-72	1993	McMurray, Pa.
Pett, Jose	0	3	9.64	3	3	0	0	14	25	15	15	8	8	R	R	6-6	190	1-8-76	1992	Sao Paulo, Brazil
Schmidt, Curt	2	3	4.26	25	0	0	7	32	43	19	15	14	30	R	R	6-6	223	3-16-70	1992	Miles City, Mont.
Shaw, Curtis	0	3	5.23	21	0	0	2	31	31	26	18	18	23	L	L	6-2	205	8-16-69	1990	Lawrence, Kan.
Shepherd, Keith	0	1	7.64	10	1	0	0	18	23	16	15	14	16	R	R	6-2	197	1-21-68	1986	Wabash, Ind.
Silva, Jose	5	1	3.41	17	11	0	0	66	74	27	25	22	54	R	R	6-5	210	12-19-73	1991	San Diego, Calif.
Sodowsky, Clint	0	1	6.59	8	0	0	1	14	19	10	10	6	9	L	R	6-3	180	7-13-72	1991	Ponca City, Okla.
Taylor, Scott	5	4	2.39	40	0	0	4	75	65	27	20	18	52	R	R	6-3	200	10-3-66	1989	Wichita, Kan.
2-team (2 Las Vegas)	5	4	2.59	42	0	0	4	76	69	29	22	19	53							
Wainhouse, David	2	0	5.92	25	0	0	1	38	46	25	25	13	24	L	R	6-2	185	11-7-67	1989	Mercer Island, Wash.
Wilson, Gary	6	3	5.87	21	11	0	0	84	115	59	55	22	54	R	R	6-3	180	1-1-70	1992	Arcata, Calif.

FIELDING

Catcher	PCT	G	PO	A	E	DP	PB
Edge	.984	53	327	34	6	8	8
Marx	.989	82	564	40	7	6	8
Secrist	.985	12	61	4	1	1	1

First Base	PCT	G	PO	A	E	DP
Johnson	1.000	22	181	25	0	14
Secrist	.980	8	44	4	1	3
Thobe	.960	2	22	2	1	3
Tolentino	.991	40	311	16	3	31
Ward	1.000	2	5	1	0	0
Wright	.995	78	610	44	3	67

Second Base	PCT	G	PO	A	E	DP
Beasley	.960	57	105	158	11	37
Bridges	.985	16	32	33	1	8
Collier	.931	27	59	63	9	15
Cromer	.978	28	51	85	3	13
Hazlett	.938	6	11	19	2	2
Sanford	.985	15	28	38	1	10

Third Base	PCT	G	PO	A	E	DP
Bridges	.857	2	1	5	1	2
Cromer	.857	5	1	5	1	0
Edge	.000	1	0	0	0	0
Garcia	.855	33	18	53	12	1
Randa	.900	3	2	7	1	1
Sanford	.924	70	38	132	14	11
Secrist	.889	13	9	23	4	2
Thobe	.859	23	19	42	10	8

Shortstop	PCT	G	PO	A	E	DP
Beasley	1.000	6	2	12	0	3
Collier	.938	83	128	252	25	46
Cromer	.955	33	43	106	7	19
Polcovich	.930	16	27	53	6	11
Sanford	.964	5	8	19	1	4

Outfield	PCT	G	PO	A	E	DP
Allensworth	1.000	5	8	0	0	0
Beasley	.800	6	4	0	1	0
Bridges	1.000	1	4	0	0	0
Brown	.993	60	130	3	1	1
Chamberlain	.789	9	13	2	4	1
Hazlett	1.000	21	15	0	0	0
Johnson	1.000	3	2	0	0	0
Lott	.990	65	94	6	1	0
Martinez	.976	102	196	7	5	2
Marx	.000	1	0	0	0	0
Secrist	1.000	4	3	0	0	0
Smith	.982	33	55	1	1	1
Staton	.988	61	78	3	1	0
Thobe	.667	1	2	0	1	0
Tolentino	1.000	20	32	0	0	0
Ward	.967	53	82	5	3	1

CAROLINA — Class AA

SOUTHERN LEAGUE

BATTING	AVG	G	AB	R	H	2B	3B	HR	RBI	BB	SO	SB	CS	B	T	HT	WT	DOB	1st Yr	Resides
Asche, Mike	.214	15	42	2	9	1	1	0	2	4	6	0	0	R	R	6-2	190	2-13-72	1994	Kearney, Neb.
Beasley, Tony	.274	31	117	15	32	5	0	0	12	7	16	2	1	R	R	5-8	165	12-5-66	1989	Bowling Green, Va.
Bonifay, Ken	.176	22	68	11	12	4	1	1	7	17	23	1	0	L	R	6-1	185	9-1-70	1991	Kingsport, Tenn.

BATTING	AVG	G	AB	R	H	2B	3B	HR	RBI	BB	SO	SB	CS	B	T	HT	WT	DOB	1st Yr	Resides
Bridges, Kary	.336	66	283	43	95	17	1	3	29	9	10	9	5	L	R	5-10	165	10-27-71	1993	Hattiesburg, Miss.
Brown, Adrian	.303	37	145	29	44	4	4	2	15	18	12	9	5	S	R	6-0	185	2-7-74	1992	Summit, Miss.
Conger, Jeff	.196	58	138	15	27	5	1	3	12	19	53	4	0	L	L	6-0	185	8-6-71	1990	Charlotte, N.C.
Cromer, Brandon	.228	55	193	23	44	12	4	4	14	29	50	1	5	L	R	6-2	175	1-25-74	1992	Lexington, S.C.
Espinosa, Ramon	.278	19	72	10	20	2	1	1	10	3	15	0	2	R	R	6-0	175	2-7-72	1990	San Pedro de Macoris, D.R.
Garcia, Freddy	.291	73	282	47	82	17	4	19	57	18	56	0	1	R	R	6-2	186	8-1-72	1991	La Romana, D.R.
Hanel, Marcus	.237	56	173	15	41	5	0	2	12	9	39	0	0	R	R	6-4	205	10-19-71	1989	Racine, Wis.
Hazlett, Steve	.235	45	153	22	36	7	3	2	17	14	31	1	6	R	R	5-11	190	3-30-70	1991	Longmont, Colo.
Hermansen, Chad	.275	129	487	87	134	31	4	20	70	69	136	18	6	R	R	6-2	185	9-10-77	1995	Henderson, Nev.
Holifield, Rick	.216	51	185	27	40	12	5	5	23	14	59	8	3	L	L	6-2	165	3-25-70	1988	Montclair, Calif.
Jordan, Ricky	.314	52	188	25	59	9	2	7	33	8	25	0	0	R	R	6-3	205	5-26-65	1983	Gold River, Calif.
Martin, Al	.111	3	9	0	1	0	0	0	0	0	0	0	0	L	L	6-2	210	11-24-67	1985	Scottsdale, Ariz.
Mendez, Sergio	.233	49	146	17	34	10	1	2	12	6	33	1	1	R	R	6-2	180	10-12-73	1992	Santo Domingo, D.R.
Mitchell, Tony	.091	4	11	0	1	0	0	0	1	1	4	0	0	S	R	6-4	225	10-14-70	1989	Detroit, Mich.
Miyake, Chris	.000	5	9	1	0	0	0	0	0	0	4	0	0	R	R	6-2	185	5-18-74	1995	San Gabriel, Calif.
Nunez, Abraham	.328	47	198	31	65	6	1	1	14	20	28	10	5	S	R	5-11	160	3-16-76	1994	Santo Domingo, D.R.
Peterson, Charles	.251	126	442	59	111	26	4	7	68	40	105	20	11	R	R	6-3	200	5-8-74	1993	Laurens, S.C.
Polcovich, Kevin	.320	17	50	13	16	5	0	3	7	10	4	4	2	R	R	5-9	165	6-28-70	1992	Auburn, N.Y.
Sanders, Tracy	.271	116	376	77	102	23	1	21	78	74	88	7	6	L	R	6-0	206	7-26-69	1990	Dallas, N.C.
Sanford, Chance	.262	44	149	30	39	10	2	9	36	20	39	3	1	L	R	5-10	165	6-2-72	1992	Houston, Texas
Smith, Mark	.417	3	12	5	5	1	0	3	4	0	1	0	0	R	R	6-3	205	5-7-70	1991	Arcadia, Calif.
Staton, T.J.	.290	58	207	33	60	11	2	6	33	12	60	8	4	L	L	6-3	200	2-17-75	1993	Elyria, Ohio
Sweet, Jon	.245	82	273	22	67	15	1	1	27	15	20	1	1	L	R	6-0	183	11-10-71	1994	Columbus, Ohio
Thobe, Steve	.293	53	181	21	53	10	0	7	32	13	52	4	1	R	R	6-7	230	5-26-72	1994	Huntington Beach, Calif.
Whitmore, Darrell	.333	2	9	1	3	2	0	0	2	0	2	0	0	L	R	6-1	210	11-18-68	1990	Front Royal, Va.

PITCHING	W	L	ERA	G	GS	CG	SV	IP	H	R	ER	BB	SO	B	T	HT	WT	DOB	1st Yr	Resides
Anderson, Jimmy	2	1	1.46	4	4	0	0	25	16	6	4	9	23	L	L	6-1	180	1-22-76	1994	Chesapeake, Va.
Beatty, Blaine	0	5	5.38	19	9	0	0	82	104	61	49	27	41	L	L	6-2	190	4-25-64	1986	Victoria, Texas
Benson, Kris	3	5	4.98	14	14	0	0	69	81	49	38	32	66	R	R	6-4	190	11-7-74	1996	Marietta, Ga.
Brown, Michael	0	0	18.00	1	0	0	0	2	5	5	4	1	2	L	L	6-7	245	11-4-71	1989	Vacaville, Calif.
Carter, John	0	0	54.00	1	0	0	0	1	4	6	6	2	0	R	R	6-1	195	2-16-72	1991	Chicago, Ill.
Chaves, Rafael	0	2	8.59	5	0	0	0	7	12	8	7	4	6	R	R	6-0	195	11-1-68	1986	Isabela, P.R.
Christiansen, Jason	0	1	4.20	8	1	0	1	15	17	7	7	5	25	R	L	6-5	235	9-21-69	1991	Elkhorn, Neb.
Cook, O.J.	0	0	20.25	1	0	0	0	1	5	3	3	1	2	R	R	6-3	195	12-13-76	1995	Bethlehem, Pa.
Crawford, Carlos	3	2	4.19	29	3	0	4	62	62	34	29	25	39	R	R	6-1	185	10-4-71	1990	Charlotte, N.C.
Davis, Kane	0	3	3.77	6	6	0	0	29	22	17	12	16	23	R	R	6-3	180	6-25-75	1993	Reedy, W.Va.
Dillinger, John	6	4	6.00	23	11	0	0	81	88	66	54	52	64	R	R	6-6	230	8-28-73	1992	Connellsville, Pa.
Fredrickson, Scott	0	3	6.08	19	0	0	1	24	22	21	16	19	17	R	R	6-3	215	8-19-67	1990	San Antonio, Texas
Freitas, Mike	1	0	13.50	6	0	0	1	5	8	8	8	4	2	R	R	6-1	160	9-22-69	1989	Sacramento, Calif.
Garrett, Hal	1	2	8.78	6	0	0	0	13	19	14	13	6	7	R	R	6-1	160	4-27-75	1993	Mt. Juliet, Tenn.
Halperin, Mike	6	7	3.87	17	17	0	0	93	102	54	40	40	66	L	L	5-10	170	9-8-73	1994	Naples, Fla.
Hernandez, Elvin	2	7	5.73	17	17	0	0	93	104	67	59	26	66	R	R	6-1	165	8-20-77	1994	Laguna Salada Monte, D.R.
Johnson, Jason	3	3	4.08	9	9	1	0	57	56	31	26	16	63	R	R	6-6	220	10-27-73	1992	Burlington, Ky.
Kelly, Jeff	6	11	4.65	31	19	0	0	128	134	79	66	85	83	L	L	6-6	215	1-11-75	1994	Staten Island, N.Y.
Konuszewski, Dennis	1	0	4.43	15	0	0	0	22	20	12	11	15	21	R	R	6-3	210	2-4-71	1992	Bridgeport, Mich.
Maskivish, Joe	0	1	6.19	15	0	0	0	16	20	11	11	4	7	R	R	6-4	180	8-14-71	1994	Shadyside, Ohio
Mathews, Del	5	2	3.04	21	1	0	1	50	53	25	17	20	51	L	L	6-3	200	10-31-74	1993	Fernandina Beach, Fla.
Paugh, Rick	0	0	5.63	5	0	0	0	8	8	5	5	1	3	L	L	6-1	190	2-6-72	1994	Bridgeport, W.Va.
Pett, Jose	4	4	3.51	14	14	0	0	74	76	37	29	25	39	R	R	6-6	190	1-8-76	1992	Sao Paulo, Brazil
Phillips, Jason	1	2	2.32	4	4	2	0	31	21	8	8	9	22	R	R	6-6	215	3-22-74	1992	Muncy, Pa.
Pickford, Kevin	1	2	7.36	21	1	0	1	29	48	29	24	15	24	L	L	6-3	200	3-12-75	1993	Fresno, Calif.
Ryan, Matt	4	3	2.22	48	0	0	14	53	32	18	13	21	43	R	R	6-5	190	3-20-72	1993	Memphis, Tenn.
Shaw, Curtis	1	1	2.81	27	0	0	0	42	30	23	13	28	46	L	L	6-2	205	8-16-69	1990	Lawrence, Kan.
Wagner, Paul	0	1	10.13	12	3	0	0	16	25	20	18	16	20	R	R	6-1	202	11-14-67	1989	Germantown, Wis.
Wallace, Jeff	4	8	5.40	38	0	0	3	43	43	37	26	36	39	L	L	6-2	237	4-12-76	1995	Minerva, Ohio
Williams, Jeff	0	0	10.80	3	0	0	0	3	6	5	4	4	3	R	R	6-4	230	4-16-69	1990	Grand Prairie, Texas
Wilson, Gary	1	2	5.65	7	4	0	1	29	34	19	18	5	19	R	R	6-3	180	1-1-70	1992	Arcata, Calif.

FIELDING

Catcher	PCT	G	PO	A	E	DP	PB
Hanel	.984	51	326	39	6	2	2
Mendez	1.000	22	137	10	0	0	4
Sweet	.995	75	505	46	3	7	5

First Base	PCT	G	PO	A	E	DP
Asche	1.000	2	14	1	0	0
Bonifay	1.000	10	105	2	0	5
Garcia	1.000	6	41	3	0	6
Hanel	.846	2	10	1	2	1
Jordan	.996	24	211	13	1	19
Mendez	.985	17	125	6	2	7
Sanders	.992	65	553	35	5	58
Sweet	.000	1	0	0	0	0
Thobe	.982	22	196	18	4	16

Second Base	PCT	G	PO	A	E	DP
Asche	1.000	3	6	8	0	1
Beasley	.949	12	29	45	4	6
Bridges	.953	65	123	180	15	55
Cromer	.983	11	29	28	1	7
Hazlett	1.000	2	2	0	0	0
Hermansen	.913	22	39	45	8	10
Miyake	1.000	1	2	1	0	0
Polcovich	.846	4	3	8	2	0
Sanford	.984	23	53	71	2	10
Sweet	.000	1	0	0	0	0

Third Base	PCT	G	PO	A	E	DP
Asche	.684	4	2	11	6	0
Beasley	.900	7	7	11	2	1
Bonifay	.949	11	11	26	2	0
Garcia	.903	68	52	152	22	12
Polcovich	.906	11	7	22	3	1
Sanford	.905	19	5	52	6	4
Sweet	.000	1	0	0	0	0
Thobe	.888	26	20	59	10	6

Shortstop	PCT	G	PO	A	E	DP
Beasley	.955	11	14	28	2	5
Bridges	1.000	1	0	1	0	0
Cromer	.948	44	65	137	11	34
Hazlett	.800	1	2	2	1	1
Hermansen	.839	33	43	77	23	14
Miyake	1.000	2	3	5	0	0
Nunez	.949	47	76	129	11	25
Polcovich	1.000	2	2	3	0	1

Outfield	PCT	G	PO	A	E	DP
Asche	1.000	3	2	0	0	0
Brown	.956	37	63	2	3	1
Conger	.984	39	57	6	1	1
Espinosa	.950	17	19	0	1	0
Hazlett	1.000	38	59	6	0	0
Hermansen	.935	59	112	3	8	0
Holifield	.972	50	100	3	3	2
Martin	1.000	3	2	0	0	0
Mitchell	.800	3	4	0	1	0
Peterson	.967	116	186	17	7	6
Sanders	.881	27	50	2	7	1
Smith	.800	3	4	0	1	0
Staton	.965	50	79	4	3	1

LYNCHBURG — Class A

CAROLINA LEAGUE

BATTING	AVG	G	AB	R	H	2B	3B	HR	RBI	BB	SO	SB	CS	B	T	HT	WT	DOB	1st Yr	Resides
Antigua, Nilson	.243	46	148	18	36	5	0	1	17	5	24	2	2	R	R	6-2	175	12-14-75	1993	Monte Plata, D.R.
Asche, Mike	.306	107	409	70	125	34	4	11	70	41	77	33	3	R	R	6-2	190	2-13-72	1994	Kearney, Neb.
Conger, Jeff	.213	24	61	12	13	3	2	1	5	6	18	2	1	L	L	6-0	185	8-6-71	1990	Charlotte, N.C.
Davis, Albert	.167	18	60	9	10	2	0	1	3	7	13	2	1	R	R	5-9	175	10-5-76	1994	Alcoa, Tenn.
Farris, Mark	.232	116	367	40	85	17	3	4	39	26	71	4	1	L	R	6-3	190	2-9-75	1994	Angleton, Texas
Figueroa, Luis	.281	26	89	12	25	5	0	0	2	7	6	1	2	S	R	5-9	158	2-16-74	1997	Vega Alta, P.R.
Germosen, Julio	.167	3	6	0	1	0	0	0	0	1	2	0	0	R	R	6-0	150	9-28-76	1994	Santo Domingo, D.R.
Hernandez, Alex	.290	131	520	75	151	37	4	5	68	27	140	13	8	L	L	6-4	190	5-28-77	1995	Levittown, P.R.
Kelley, Erskine	.214	39	112	19	24	8	2	4	16	9	31	1	2	R	R	6-5	210	2-27-71	1992	Freeport, N.Y.
Long, Garrett	.207	9	29	1	6	3	0	1	5	3	10	0	0	R	R	6-3	195	10-5-76	1995	Houston, Texas
Mendez, Sergio	.141	17	64	5	9	2	0	2	6	1	18	0	1	R	R	6-2	180	10-12-73	1992	Santo Domingo, D.R.
Miyake, Chris	.250	79	288	40	72	14	1	2	20	28	57	3	2	R	R	6-2	185	5-18-74	1995	San Gabriel, Calif.
Nunez, Abraham	.260	78	304	45	79	9	4	3	32	23	47	29	14	S	R	5-11	160	3-16-76	1994	Santo Domingo, D.R.
Ramirez, Aramis	.278	137	482	85	134	24	2	29	114	80	103	5	3	R	R	6-1	176	6-25-78	1995	Santo Domingo, D.R.
Redman, Tike	.251	125	415	55	104	18	5	4	45	45	82	21	8	L	L	5-11	160	3-10-77	1996	Duncanville, Ala.
Reyes, Jose	.000	2	5	0	0	0	0	0	0	0	2	0	0	R	R	6-1	188	5-1-73	1993	Villa Vazquez, D.R.
Rice, Charles	.211	33	95	10	20	2	1	2	13	10	28	2	0	L	R	6-2	220	8-31-75	1993	Birmingham, Ala.
Robinson, Tony	.295	77	254	40	75	16	3	2	33	28	37	12	6	R	R	6-0	185	6-11-76	1994	Diamond Bar, Calif.
Swafford, Derek	.250	38	112	16	28	5	0	0	5	25	28	8	3	L	R	5-10	175	1-21-75	1993	Ventura, Calif.
Thobe, Steve	.148	12	27	1	4	1	0	0	2	1	10	1	0	R	R	6-7	230	5-26-72	1994	Huntington Beach, Calif.
Turlais, John	.167	14	30	2	5	1	0	1	5	5	9	0	1	L	R	6-3	200	12-30-73	1992	Flora, Ill.
Walker, Morgan	.270	29	89	15	24	6	0	3	8	6	19	0	0	R	L	6-3	215	8-7-74	1996	Missouri City, Texas
Walker, Shon	.261	100	303	59	79	15	6	15	48	77	131	2	3	L	L	6-1	182	6-9-74	1992	Cynthiana, Ky.
Wilson, Craig	.264	117	401	54	106	26	1	19	69	39	98	6	5	R	R	6-2	195	11-30-76	1995	Huntington Beach, Calif.

GAMES BY POSITION: C—Antigua 46, Reyes 2, Rice 1, Turlais 5, Wilson 98. **1B**—Farris 107, Long 4, Mendez 13, Redman 1, Thobe 6, M. Walker 21, S. Walker 8. **2B**—Asche 14, Figueroa 23, Miyake 19, Robinson 74, Swafford 34. **3B**—Asche 6, Farris 6, Miyake 1, Ramirez 131, Thobe 4. **SS**—Figueroa 6, Germosen 3, Miyake 59, Nunez 78, Robinson 5. **OF**—Asche 89, Conger 21, Davis 16, Hernandez 130, Kelley 37, Long 2, Redman 124, Rice 3, S. Walker 22.

PITCHING	W	L	ERA	G	GS	CG	SV	IP	H	R	ER	BB	SO	B	T	HT	WT	DOB	1st Yr	Resides
Ah Yat, Paul	5	1	1.31	6	6	3	0	48	37	8	7	4	38	R	L	6-1	196	10-13-73	1996	Honolulu, Hawaii
Arroyo, Bronson	12	4	3.31	24	24	3	0	160	154	69	59	33	121	R	R	6-5	165	2-24-77	1995	Brooksville, Fla.
Ayers, Mike	5	4	5.00	39	0	0	4	63	54	38	35	44	62	L	L	5-10	190	12-23-73	1996	Cincinnati, Ohio
Benson, Kris	5	2	2.58	10	10	0	0	59	49	20	17	13	72	R	R	6-4	190	11-7-74	1996	Marietta, Ga.
Bullock, Derek	2	0	4.81	15	2	0	0	34	27	20	18	21	34	R	R	6-2	186	2-24-73	1995	Las Vegas, Nev.
Corn, Chris	3	4	3.20	28	1	0	2	65	54	30	23	23	66	R	R	6-2	170	10-4-71	1994	Louisville, Ky.
Daniels, David	1	1	1.80	10	0	0	4	10	6	2	2	1	6	R	R	6-2	185	7-25-73	1996	Nashville, Tenn.
Garrett, Hal	2	5	4.82	29	5	0	5	56	56	36	30	22	45	R	R	6-1	160	4-27-75	1993	Mt. Juliet, Tenn.
Haynie, Jason	2	5	3.25	13	13	1	0	83	68	42	30	23	69	L	L	6-0	190	3-29-74	1996	St. Petersburg Beach, Fla.
Hernandez, Elvin	0	0	1.80	3	0	0	1	5	4	1	1	1	5	R	R	6-1	165	8-20-77	1994	Laguna Salada Monte, D.R.
Johnson, Jason	8	4	3.71	17	17	0	0	99	98	43	41	30	92	R	R	6-6	220	10-27-73	1992	Burlington, Ky.
Martin, Jeff	8	10	5.77	24	21	0	0	115	139	86	74	48	101	R	R	6-1	199	1-25-74	1995	Las Vegas, Nev.
Maskivish, Joe	2	0	2.97	32	0	0	17	33	31	12	11	13	24	R	R	6-4	180	8-14-71	1994	Shadyside, Ohio
Mathews, Del	2	5	3.51	18	5	0	1	49	48	25	19	13	48	L	L	6-3	200	10-31-74	1993	Fernandina Beach, Fla.
Mattson, Craig	0	0	6.23	4	0	0	1	4	6	3	3	2	3	R	R	6-4	205	11-25-73	1993	Belvidere, Ill.
McDade, Neal	2	0	2.89	3	3	0	0	19	16	8	6	6	15	R	R	6-3	165	6-16-76	1996	Orange Park, Fla.
O'Connor, Brian	2	1	3.46	11	0	0	2	13	11	5	5	6	14	L	L	6-2	175	1-4-77	1995	Cincinnati, Ohio
Paugh, Rick	0	2	7.85	24	0	0	5	18	18	17	16	11	18	L	L	6-1	190	2-6-72	1994	Bridgeport, W.Va.
Phillips, Jason	11	6	3.76	23	23	2	0	139	129	66	58	35	140	R	R	6-6	215	3-22-74	1992	Muncy, Pa.
Pickford, Kevin	3	4	3.56	14	10	0	1	73	72	31	29	11	50	L	L	6-3	200	3-12-75	1993	Fresno, Calif.
Temple, Jason	2	0	4.14	28	0	0	1	37	39	21	17	24	34	R	R	6-1	185	11-8-74	1993	Woodhaven, Mich.
Wallace, Jeff	5	0	1.65	9	0	0	1	16	9	3	3	10	13	L	L	6-2	237	4-12-76	1995	Minerva, Ohio
Young, Danny	0	0	5.92	15	0	0	0	24	27	17	16	14	22	R	L	6-5	180	11-3-71	1991	Woodbury, Tenn.

AUGUSTA — Class A

SOUTH ATLANTIC LEAGUE

BATTING	AVG	G	AB	R	H	2B	3B	HR	RBI	BB	SO	SB	CS	B	T	HT	WT	DOB	1st Yr	Resides
Bellenger, Butch	.167	4	12	1	2	1	0	0	0	1	4	0	0	R	R	6-0	200	11-4-73	1996	Lyndhurst, N.J.
Benjamin, Al	.143	5	14	2	2	0	0	0	1	0	3	1	0	R	R	6-1	190	9-9-77	1996	Houston, Texas
Davis, Albert	.240	77	279	51	67	13	3	6	40	49	67	27	8	R	R	5-9	175	10-5-76	1994	Alcoa, Tenn.
Edwards, Randy	.067	6	15	2	1	0	0	0	0	4	2	0	0	R	R	6-1	193	9-18-73	1992	Pomona, Calif.
Evans, Lee	.194	54	186	19	36	9	2	2	23	14	52	6	3	S	R	6-1	185	7-20-77	1996	Northport, Ala.
Figueroa, Luis	.226	71	248	38	56	8	0	0	21	35	29	22	6	S	R	5-9	158	2-16-74	1997	Vega Alta, P.R.
Hundt, Bo	.246	111	407	56	100	21	2	6	42	24	109	18	7	S	R	6-0	200	4-21-75	1996	Bremen, Ind.
Johnson, Jason	.228	20	57	9	13	1	0	1	7	12	17	4	0	R	R	6-2	190	2-1-76	1994	Vallejo, Calif.
Long, Garrett	.300	83	280	50	84	10	2	7	41	61	78	5	2	R	R	6-3	195	10-5-76	1995	Houston, Texas
Lorenzana, Luis	.236	92	288	36	68	11	1	0	20	31	66	4	5	R	R	6-0	170	11-9-78	1996	San Diego, Calif.
May, Freddy	.235	107	358	51	84	13	7	4	33	43	84	16	18	L	L	6-2	190	1-24-76	1995	Seattle, Wash.
May, Scott	.250	19	44	5	11	3	0	0	2	3	8	1	2	L	R	5-11	185	6-1-73	1996	Bradenton, Fla.
Pena, Alex	.244	111	356	34	87	12	2	5	40	18	81	11	10	R	R	6-2	175	9-9-77	1995	Ensanche Luperon, D.R.
Pointer, Corey	.190	84	248	38	47	9	0	7	26	26	116	23	3	R	R	6-2	205	9-2-75	1994	Waxahachie, Texas
Rice, Charles	.250	51	156	24	39	6	1	10	30	16	37	3	1	L	R	6-2	220	8-31-75	1993	Birmingham, Ala.
Rivera, Carlos	.272	120	415	52	113	16	5	9	65	19	82	4	1	L	L	6-1	200	6-10-78	1996	Rio Grande, P.R.
Robinson, Tony	.210	18	62	11	13	4	1	0	8	5	6	3	2	R	R	6-0	185	6-11-76	1994	Diamond Bar, Calif.
Schreiber, Stan	.214	115	345	51	74	10	1	1	26	65	83	40	11	R	R	5-10	175	9-8-75	1994	Appleton, Wis.
Shipp, Skip	.252	81	254	29	64	15	2	0	23	26	53	12	5	R	R	6-2	205	1-12-76	1995	Acworth, Ga.
Springfield, Bo	.242	12	33	7	8	0	0	0	2	7	5	5	1	L	R	5-10	173	1-25-76	1994	Denison, Texas
Swafford, Derek	.217	21	69	12	15	2	0	1	9	8	20	6	2	L	R	5-10	175	1-21-75	1993	Ventura, Calif.
Turlais, John	.292	33	106	8	31	5	0	4	18	10	20	2	1	L	R	6-3	200	12-30-73	1992	Flora, Ill.

BATTING	AVG	G	AB	R	H	2B	3B	HR	RBI	BB	SO	SB	CS	B	T	HT	WT	DOB	1st Yr	Resides
Walker, Morgan	.275	76	295	40	81	17	2	14	64	17	70	3	2	R	L	6-3	215	8-7-74	1996	Missouri City, Texas
Whipple, Boomer	.222	40	108	16	24	7	0	0	13	23	19	2	1	R	R	6-0	185	2-9-73	1995	Lincolnshire, Ill.

GAMES BY POSITION: C—Evans 41, S. May 11, Pointer 6, Shipp 71, Turlais 26. **1B**—Long 34, Rivera 97, Shipp 2, Turlais 1, Walker 17, Whipple 3. **2B**—Bellenger 1, Figueroa 3, Lorenzana 41, Schreiber 82, Swafford 20, Whipple 5. **3B**—Bellenger 2, Evans 1, Hundt 102, Long 1, Lorenzana 1, S. May 3, Schreiber 22, Whipple 32. **SS**—Figueroa 68, Lorenzana 52, Robinson 18, Schreiber 10. **OF**—Benjamin 5, Davis 74, Edwards 1, Hundt 12, Johnson 18, Long 28, F. May 105, S. May 2, Pena 107, Pointer 72, Rice 35, Rivera 1, Schreiber 1, Springfield 9.

PITCHING	W	L	ERA	G	GS	CG	SV	IP	H	R	ER	BB	SO	B	T	HT	WT	DOB	1st Yr	Resides
Ah Yat, Paul	5	1	2.90	29	9	0	0	90	82	34	29	16	119	R	L	6-1	196	10-13-73	1996	Honolulu, Hawaii
Alvarado, Carlos	6	5	3.27	29	20	0	0	113	114	58	41	45	109	R	R	6-4	195	1-24-78	1995	Arecibo, P.R.
Bacci, Anthony	1	3	4.76	6	6	1	0	28	31	20	15	14	24	L	L	6-2	180	8-16-75	1997	Woodstock, Ill.
Bravo, Franklin	0	0	2.35	7	3	0	0	15	12	9	4	5	14	R	R	6-2	170	12-24-78	1996	Santo Domingo, D.R.
Brooks, Wyatt	5	3	3.14	16	4	0	1	52	49	26	18	18	49	R	L	6-1	165	12-13-73	1996	Tallahassee, Fla.
Bullock, Derek	2	4	4.54	8	6	0	0	34	32	21	17	8	30	R	R	6-2	186	2-24-73	1995	Las Vegas, Nev.
Campbell, Tedde	2	1	3.86	5	0	0	1	5	6	3	2	2	4	R	R	6-0	190	7-27-72	1995	Blairsville, Pa.
Chaney, Michael	8	7	3.52	31	14	0	0	125	129	58	49	28	95	S	L	6-3	200	10-3-74	1996	Westchester, Ohio
Daniels, David	6	3	2.62	44	0	0	18	55	51	22	16	13	51	R	R	6-2	185	7-25-73	1996	Nashville, Tenn.
Duff, Matt	0	1	1.50	2	1	0	0	6	6	1	1	2	6	R	R	6-1	205	10-6-74	1997	Alligator, Miss.
Elmore, Jason	2	1	10.20	10	1	0	0	15	17	17	17	14	15	R	R	6-5	245	5-31-74	1996	Lucama, N.C.
Farson, Bryan	0	0	3.60	7	0	0	0	10	5	6	4	8	7	L	L	6-2	198	7-22-72	1994	Massillon, Ohio
Finol, Ricardo	1	2	6.65	11	0	0	0	22	21	17	16	13	16	S	R	6-0	170	5-10-74	1996	San Francisco, Venez.
Fisher, Ryan	0	1	14.85	4	1	0	0	7	15	11	11	3	5	L	L	6-2	190	4-26-74	1995	Luck, Wis.
France, Aaron	7	4	3.52	26	17	1	0	107	98	48	42	44	89	L	R	6-3	175	4-17-74	1994	Anaheim, Calif.
Gonzalez, Michael	1	1	1.86	4	3	0	0	19	11	5	4	8	22	R	L	6-2	210	5-23-78	1997	Pasadena, Texas
Gresko, Michael	1	0	3.60	1	1	0	0	5	7	2	2	3	3	L	L	6-8	200	10-27-76	1996	Trenton, N.J.
Halla, Ryan	1	1	1.75	32	0	0	8	46	26	10	9	10	51	S	R	6-4	250	10-3-73	1997	Birmingham, Ala.
Haynie, Jason	6	5	3.43	14	14	1	0	87	77	39	33	24	81	L	L	6-0	190	3-29-74	1996	St. Petersburg Beach, Fla.
Hlodan, George	1	2	5.58	12	6	0	1	40	40	31	25	15	33	R	R	6-0	170	6-25-76	1996	Elizabeth, Pa.
Kelly, John	0	0	27.00	1	0	0	0	1	4	2	2	0	2	R	R	6-0	180	12-13-72	1994	Leominster, Mass.
McDade, Neal	10	4	2.80	36	12	0	3	112	105	42	35	24	104	R	R	6-3	165	6-16-76	1996	Orange Park, Fla.
O'Connor, Brian	2	7	4.41	25	14	0	0	86	90	54	42	39	91	L	L	6-2	175	1-4-77	1995	Cincinnati, Ohio
Ojeda, Erick	3	6	4.57	37	0	0	1	61	63	36	31	16	53	L	L	5-10	177	10-15-75	1993	Valencia, Venez.
2-team (7 Cap. City)	3	8	4.80	44	0	0	1	75	77	46	40	20	66							
Paugh, Rick	1	2	2.43	24	0	0	8	30	24	9	8	7	40	L	L	6-1	190	2-6-72	1994	Bridgeport, W.Va.
Prater, Andy	0	0	10.95	6	3	0	0	12	21	16	15	6	9	R	R	6-3	175	9-27-77	1996	Florissant, Mo.
Siciliano, Jess	0	0	4.66	11	0	0	1	19	22	12	10	5	9	R	R	6-2	190	8-31-76	1996	East White Plains, N.Y.
Temple, Jason	0	4	5.54	11	5	0	0	37	46	29	23	22	38	R	R	6-1	185	11-8-74	1993	Woodhaven, Mich.
Young, Danny	0	2	9.82	3	2	0	0	7	16	15	8	2	5	R	L	6-5	180	11-3-71	1991	Woodbury, Tenn.

ERIE — Short-Season Class A

NEW YORK-PENN LEAGUE

BATTING	AVG	G	AB	R	H	2B	3B	HR	RBI	BB	SO	SB	CS	B	T	HT	WT	DOB	1st Yr	Resides
Austin, Peter	.154	5	13	1	2	0	0	0	1	1	4	0	0	R	R	6-2	195	11-6-74	1997	Flowood, Miss.
Brooks, Ali	.000	6	11	3	0	0	0	0	0	2	2	1	0	R	R	5-8	160	5-14-76	1996	Oakland, Calif.
Burns, Xavier	.274	63	226	33	62	13	2	7	27	18	62	4	4	R	R	5-11	185	5-8-75	1996	Chicago, Ill.
Clark, Chris	.256	28	90	14	23	4	0	3	12	6	13	0	0	R	R	5-10	180	8-20-75	1997	Cohoes, N.Y.
Cleto, Ambioris	.182	8	22	0	4	0	0	0	2	3	11	0	3	R	R	6-0	160	1-5-80	1996	Santo Domingo, D.R.
Davis, J.J.	.077	4	13	1	1	0	0	0	0	0	4	0	0	R	R	6-6	230	10-25-78	1997	Pomona, Calif.
DeHaan, Korwin	.239	58	205	43	49	8	6	1	18	38	43	14	9	L	R	6-2	185	7-16-76	1997	Pella, Iowa
Diaz, Diogenes	.179	10	28	4	5	3	0	0	4	4	12	0	0	R	R	6-0	190	10-10-78	1996	Villa Mella, D.R.
Elliott, Dawan	.250	57	172	14	43	13	0	2	18	9	32	1	1	L	L	6-3	200	7-30-76	1995	Long Branch, N.J.
Evans, Lee	.298	40	141	20	42	6	0	5	16	11	30	1	2	S	R	6-1	185	7-20-77	1996	Northport, Ala.
Freeman, Terrance	.313	63	217	56	68	9	2	2	19	38	38	46	11	S	R	5-10	170	1-24-75	1995	Brandon, Fla.
Germosen, Julio	.200	42	115	21	23	3	3	3	16	7	34	2	3	R	R	6-0	150	9-28-76	1994	Santo Domingo, D.R.
Haad, Yamid	.290	43	155	27	45	7	3	1	19	7	27	3	3	R	R	6-2	165	9-2-77	1995	Cartagena, Colombia
Haverbusch, Kevin	.311	67	241	37	75	15	2	10	55	13	37	4	4	R	R	6-3	185	6-16-76	1997	Massapequa, N.Y.
Johnson, Jason	.320	28	103	19	33	7	1	2	19	11	21	2	2	R	R	6-2	190	2-1-76	1994	Vallejo, Calif.
Lankford, Derrick	.308	58	195	36	60	11	3	10	55	33	57	2	0	L	R	6-4	220	9-21-74	1997	Harrison, Tenn.
Lara, Felix	.248	50	165	24	41	8	1	1	16	17	55	8	8	L	L	6-0	170	10-30-77	1995	San Cristobal, D.R.
Mackowiak, Robert	.286	61	203	26	58	14	2	1	25	21	47	1	7	L	R	5-10	165	6-20-76	1996	Schererville, Ind.
Maxwell, Keith	.209	42	134	23	28	3	1	6	24	10	38	1	1	R	R	6-1	205	4-18-75	1997	Bristol, Fla.
Pointer, Corey	.116	18	43	5	5	0	0	2	7	3	22	3	1	R	R	6-2	205	9-2-75	1994	Waxahachie, Texas
Reyes, Jose	.152	10	33	3	5	0	0	1	3	2	6	0	0	R	R	6-1	188	5-1-73	1993	Villa Vazquez, D.R.

GAMES BY POSITION: C—Diaz 6, Evans 30, Haad 38, Mackowiak 1, Reyes 6. **1B**—Lankford 49, Mackowiak 1, Maxwell 30, Reyes 4. **2B**—Brooks 4, Freeman 60, Germosen 20, Johnson 1, Mackowiak 3. **3B**—Burns 61, Germosen 2, Haverbusch 1, Mackowiak 16. **SS**—Brooks 2, Cleto 8, Freeman 2, Germosen 21, Haverbusch 55. **OF**—Austin 5, Clark 25, DeHaan 54, Elliott 45, Haverbusch 1, Johnson 19, Lara 48, Mackowiak 40, Pointer 18.

PITCHING	W	L	ERA	G	GS	CG	SV	IP	H	R	ER	BB	SO	B	T	HT	WT	DOB	1st Yr	Resides
Bacci, Anthony	8	3	2.56	15	14	0	0	84	68	34	24	36	50	L	L	6-2	180	8-16-75	1997	Woodstock, Ill.
Bausher, Andy	4	3	3.88	15	10	0	1	65	62	32	28	19	44	R	L	6-3	192	8-17-76	1997	Bethelsville, Pa.
Combs, Chris	2	1	0.73	21	0	0	9	25	13	2	2	3	36	L	R	6-8	230	5-19-75	1997	Raleigh, N.C.
Cook, O.J.	5	2	2.08	34	0	0	10	39	37	14	9	20	43	R	R	6-3	195	12-13-76	1995	Bethlehem, Pa.
Fisher, Ryan	0	0	5.79	2	2	0	0	9	11	7	6	2	6	L	L	6-2	190	4-26-74	1995	Luck, Wis.
Gresko, Michael	1	2	7.66	7	5	0	0	25	29	26	21	17	14	L	L	6-8	200	10-27-76	1996	Trenton, N.J.
Guy, Brad	5	1	1.88	25	0	0	1	53	37	12	11	7	53	R	R	6-2	180	10-25-75	1997	Eureka, Calif.
Guzman, Wilson	1	2	5.06	5	5	0	0	27	26	20	15	6	25	L	L	5-11	160	7-14-77	1995	Monte Cristi, D.R.
Hlodan, George	1	0	6.15	15	1	1	2	34	39	24	23	11	21	R	R	6-0	170	6-25-76	1996	Elizabeth, Pa.
Lambert, Kris	11	2	2.33	15	14	0	0	81	59	28	21	21	94	L	L	5-10	175	11-23-73	1997	Houston, Texas
Luttig, Chris	1	2	3.32	11	0	0	0	19	18	12	7	8	16	L	L	6-0	210	2-19-76	1997	Roscoe, Ill.
McConnell, Sam	2	2	5.06	17	10	0	0	59	56	38	33	24	45	L	L	6-5	204	12-31-75	1997	Fairfield, Ohio
Prater, Andy	3	2	4.40	15	14	0	0	74	82	37	36	26	40	R	R	6-3	175	9-27-77	1996	Florissant, Mo.

PITCHING	W	L	ERA	G	GS	CG	SV	IP	H	R	ER	BB	SO	B	T	HT	WT	DOB	1st Yr	Resides
Siciliano, Jess	2	0	4.24	16	0	0	3	23	22	16	11	10	20	R	R	6-2	190	8-31-76	1996	East White Plains, N.Y.
Stabile, Paul	4	4	2.72	22	0	0	1	43	32	17	13	16	50	L	L	6-0	203	1-16-76	1997	Staten Island, N.Y.
Vogt, Robert	0	0	10.80	1	1	0	0	3	3	4	4	4	0	L	L	6-6	200	10-19-78	1996	Brandon, Fla.

BRADENTON — Rookie

GULF COAST LEAGUE

BATTING	AVG	G	AB	R	H	2B	3B	HR	RBI	BB	SO	SB	CS	B	T	HT	WT	DOB	1st Yr	Resides
Adorno, Wilson	.179	15	39	7	7	0	0	0	4	4	12	0	0	S	R	5-11	180	12-3-77	1996	Vega Alta, P.R.
Austin, Peter	.245	17	53	3	13	2	0	0	6	4	10	2	3	R	R	6-2	195	11-6-74	1997	Flowood, Miss.
Benjamin, Al	.322	39	152	18	49	14	2	2	21	4	26	7	1	R	R	6-1	190	9-9-77	1996	Houston, Texas
Cleto, Ambioris	.188	35	101	9	19	4	0	1	3	15	27	1	7	R	R	6-0	160	1-5-80	1996	Santo Domingo, D.R.
Davis, J.J.	.255	45	165	19	42	10	2	1	18	14	44	0	0	R	R	6-6	230	10-25-78	1997	Pomona, Calif.
De la Cruz, Raul	.239	28	92	6	22	0	1	2	11	3	25	5	0	R	R	5-11	175	6-5-77	1995	Santo Domingo, D.R.
Diaz, Diogenes	.288	34	111	19	32	7	0	4	20	9	30	0	0	R	R	6-0	190	10-10-78	1996	Villa Mella, D.R.
Edwards, Randy	.455	4	11	3	5	3	0	0	1	5	4	0	0	R	R	6-1	193	9-18-73	1992	Pomona, Calif.
Freeman, Terrance	.455	3	11	1	5	0	0	0	4	2	1	1	1	S	R	5-10	170	1-24-75	1995	Brandon, Fla.
Gutierrez, Victor	.237	43	156	28	37	1	1	1	12	20	27	10	3	R	R	5-11	170	12-23-77	1995	Santo Domingo, D.R.
Holifield, Rick	.333	4	15	2	5	1	0	1	3	2	3	1	0	L	L	6-2	165	3-25-70	1988	Montclair, Calif.
Jones, Andrew	.220	29	91	9	20	1	0	0	6	11	21	3	4	R	R	6-3	190	10-27-78	1997	Phoenix, Ariz.
Jordan, Yustin	.269	30	93	15	25	6	0	0	7	14	24	3	1	R	R	6-3	200	8-15-78	1996	Monticello, Ark.
Kaplan, Brett	.053	19	57	5	3	1	0	0	4	3	20	0	0	R	R	6-5	220	6-8-75	1997	Miami, Fla.
Mejias, Oliver	.293	44	157	20	46	12	1	0	9	7	26	8	7	S	R	6-1	180	9-21-76	1995	Caracas, Venez.
Nicolas, Jose	.241	40	141	17	34	6	3	0	11	13	44	3	2	R	R	6-3	210	1-1-79	1997	Miami, Fla.
Pascual, Edison	.429	5	21	1	9	2	0	0	1	0	3	1	0	L	L	6-3	198	9-10-76	1994	Santo Domingo, D.R.
Reyes, Jose	.344	12	32	4	11	2	1	0	4	1	5	1	0	R	R	6-1	188	5-1-73	1993	Villa Vazquez, D.R.
Rockow, Jeremy	.233	23	73	7	17	5	0	3	15	7	18	0	2	L	L	6-3	180	10-25-77	1996	North Fort Myers, Fla.
Sevillano, Jose	.000	1	1	0	0	0	0	0	0	0	0	0	0	S	R	6-2	215	8-12-75	1996	Vega Alta, P.R.
Swafford, Derek	.200	1	5	1	1	0	0	1	1	0	0	0	0	L	R	5-10	175	1-21-75	1993	Ventura, Calif.
Tolbert, William	.245	31	94	10	23	3	0	0	7	12	23	1	1	L	R	6-4	245	1-20-75	1997	Hendersonville, N.C.
Viera, Rob	.200	10	20	2	4	3	0	0	1	1	5	0	1	R	R	6-2	215	4-19-73	1996	Bradenton, Fla.
Washington, Rico	.245	28	98	12	24	6	0	1	11	4	13	1	0	L	R	5-10	170	5-30-78	1997	Gray, Ga.
Washington, Maurice	.202	31	94	8	19	2	1	0	7	11	34	1	1	R	R	6-1	195	5-22-79	1997	Las Vegas, Nev.

GAMES BY POSITION: C—Adorno 14, Diaz 33, Reyes 12, Viera 6. **1B**—De la Cruz 8, Kaplan 18, Pascual 5, Rockow 3, Tolbert 31. **2B**—Freeman 2, Gutierrez 17, Mejias 38, Swafford 1, R. Washington 3. **3B**—Adorno 1, Gutierrez 1, Jordan 30, Mejias 2, R. Washington 24, M. Washington 2. **SS**—Cleto 34, Gutierrez 25, Sevillano 1, R. Washington 1. **OF**—Austin 17, Benjamin 24, Davis 23, De la Cruz 15, Edwards 3, Freeman 1, Holifield 4, Jones 25, Mejias 1, Nicolas 34, Rockow 13, M. Washington 25.

PITCHING	W	L	ERA	G	GS	CG	SV	IP	H	R	ER	BB	SO	B	T	HT	WT	DOB	1st Yr	Resides
Alvarado, David	1	6	3.80	12	6	0	0	47	51	32	20	23	34	R	R	6-3	170	4-29-78	1995	Falcon, Venez.
Beatty, Blaine	1	0	1.52	4	3	1	0	24	23	8	4	2	14	L	L	6-2	190	4-25-64	1986	Victoria, Texas
Bravo, Franklin	0	1	8.00	4	4	0	0	9	16	10	8	5	5	R	R	6-2	170	12-24-78	1996	Santo Domingo, D.R.
Brown, Michael	0	0	4.15	2	0	0	0	4	3	2	2	3	6	L	L	6-7	245	11-4-71	1989	Vacaville, Calif.
Ericks, John	0	0	3.46	9	8	0	0	13	5	5	5	5	18	R	R	6-7	220	9-16-67	1988	Tinley Park, Ill.
Farson, Bryan	0	0	7.63	8	0	0	0	15	19	15	13	12	9	L	L	6-2	198	7-22-72	1994	Massillon, Ohio
Finol, Ricardo	1	1	3.15	6	1	0	1	20	19	13	7	4	10	S	R	6-0	170	5-10-74	1996	San Francisco, Venez.
Gaerte, Travis	1	2	2.73	18	0	0	2	30	26	19	9	10	22	R	R	6-3	180	10-21-76	1995	Fremont, Ind.
Gomez, Ricardo	0	2	6.16	5	4	0	0	19	20	17	13	17	11	R	R	6-2	165	6-14-78	1995	Puerto Plata, D.R.
Gonzalez, Michael	2	0	2.48	7	3	0	0	29	21	9	8	8	33	R	L	6-2	210	5-23-78	1997	Pasadena, Texas
Grabow, John	2	7	4.57	11	8	0	0	45	57	32	23	14	28	L	L	6-2	185	11-4-78	1997	San Gabriel, Calif.
Gresko, Michael	1	1	5.12	6	2	0	1	19	22	11	11	3	21	L	L	6-8	200	10-27-76	1996	Trenton, N.J.
Guzman, Wilson	4	1	2.90	9	8	0	0	40	43	15	13	8	48	L	L	5-11	160	7-14-77	1995	Monte Cristi, D.R.
Hlodan, George	3	0	0.49	3	3	2	0	18	12	1	1	4	12	R	R	6-0	170	6-25-76	1996	Elizabeth, Pa.
Hohenstein, Andrew	1	1	8.38	3	2	0	0	10	11	10	9	6	4	R	R	6-4	210	9-27-77	1996	Riverside, Calif.
Luttig, Chris	1	1	2.49	12	0	0	3	22	23	9	6	9	21	L	L	6-0	210	2-19-76	1997	Roscoe, Ill.
Morel, Jose	2	0	2.93	7	0	0	0	15	11	5	5	6	10	R	L	6-0	185	8-21-75	1992	Monte Cristi, D.R.
Morrobel, Juan	1	0	0.00	3	0	0	0	8	7	1	0	2	4	L	L	6-0	180	9-14-77	1995	Santo Domingo, D.R.
Parkerson, Michael	2	3	4.28	14	0	0	3	27	27	15	13	10	25	R	L	6-2	185	4-26-79	1997	Columbus, Ga.
Quiros, Misael	2	4	3.65	13	3	0	0	37	42	20	15	14	24	R	R	6-1	165	8-11-76	1994	Santo Domingo, D.R.
Raino, Brian	0	0	40.50	1	0	0	0	1	3	3	3	1	2	R	R	6-1	170	2-4-74	1997	Dunkirk, Md.
Viera, Rob	0	0	0.00	4	0	0	0	5	3	0	0	1	2	R	R	6-2	215	4-19-73	1996	Bradenton, Fla.
Vogt, Robert	2	2	3.97	12	4	0	0	34	23	17	15	19	40	L	L	6-6	200	10-19-78	1996	Brandon, Fla.

St. Louis CARDINALS

Manager: Tony La Russa.

1997 Record: 73-89, .451 (4th, NL Central)

BATTING	AVG	G	AB	R	H	2B	3B	HR	RBI	BB	SO	SB	CS	B	T	HT	WT	DOB	1st Yr	Resides
Bell, David	.211	66	142	9	30	7	2	1	12	10	28	1	0	R	R	5-10	170	9-14-72	1990	Cincinnati, Ohio
Berblinger, Jeff	.000	7	5	1	0	0	0	0	0	0	1	0	0	R	R	6-0	190	11-19-70	1993	Goddard, Kan.
Clayton, Royce	.266	154	576	75	153	39	5	9	61	33	109	30	10	R	R	6-0	183	1-2-70	1988	Inglewood, Calif.
DeShields, Delino	.295	150	572	92	169	26	14	11	58	55	72	55	14	L	R	6-1	175	1-15-69	1987	West Palm Beach, Fla.
Difelice, Mike	.238	93	260	16	62	10	1	4	30	19	61	1	1	R	R	6-2	205	5-28-69	1991	Knoxville, Tenn.
Franklin, Micah	.324	17	34	6	11	0	0	2	2	3	10	0	0	S	R	6-0	195	4-25-72	1990	San Francisco, Calif.
Gaetti, Gary	.251	148	502	63	126	24	1	17	69	36	88	7	3	R	R	6-0	200	8-19-58	1979	Raleigh, N.C.
Gallego, Mike	.163	27	43	6	7	2	0	0	1	1	6	0	0	R	R	5-8	160	10-31-60	1981	Yorba Linda, Calif.
Gant, Ron	.229	139	502	68	115	21	4	17	62	58	162	14	6	R	R	6-0	200	3-2-65	1983	Smyrna, Ga.
Green, Bert	.097	20	31	5	3	0	0	0	1	2	5	0	0	S	R	5-10	170	6-9-74	1993	Florissant, Mo.
Gulan, Mike	.000	5	9	2	0	0	0	0	1	1	5	0	0	R	R	6-1	190	12-18-70	1992	Steubenville, Ohio
Jordan, Brian	.234	47	145	17	34	5	0	0	10	10	21	6	1	R	R	6-1	205	3-29-67	1988	Baltimore, Md.
Lampkin, Tom	.245	108	229	28	56	8	1	7	22	28	30	2	1	L	R	5-11	183	3-4-64	1986	Boring, Ore.
Lankford, Ray	.295	133	465	94	137	36	3	31	98	95	125	21	11	L	L	5-11	180	6-5-67	1987	Modesto, Calif.
Livingstone, Scott	.171	42	41	3	7	1	0	0	3	1	10	1	0	L	R	6-0	198	7-15-65	1988	Southlake, Texas
2-team (23 San Diego)	.164	65	67	4	11	2	0	0	6	3	11	1	0							
Mabry, John	.284	116	388	40	110	19	0	5	36	39	77	0	1	L	R	6-4	195	10-17-70	1991	Warwick, Md.
Marrero, Eli	.244	17	45	4	11	2	0	2	7	2	13	4	0	R	R	6-1	180	11-17-73	1993	Miami, Fla.
McGee, Willie	.300	122	300	29	90	19	4	3	38	22	59	8	2	S	R	6-1	185	11-2-58	1977	Hercules, Calif.
McGwire, Mark	.253	51	174	38	44	3	0	24	42	43	61	2	0	R	R	6-5	225	10-1-63	1984	Claremont, Calif.
Mejia, Roberto	.071	7	14	0	1	1	0	0	2	0	5	0	0	R	R	5-11	160	4-14-72	1989	Hato Mayor, D.R.
Ordaz, Luis	.273	12	22	3	6	1	0	0	1	1	2	3	0	R	R	5-11	170	8-12-75	1993	Maracaibo, Venez.
Pagnozzi, Tom	.220	25	50	4	11	3	0	1	8	1	7	0	0	R	R	6-1	190	7-30-62	1983	Tucson, Ariz.
Plantier, Phil	.257	42	113	13	29	8	0	5	18	11	27	0	3	L	R	5-11	195	1-27-69	1987	San Diego, Calif.
2-team (10 San Diego)	.248	52	121	13	30	8	0	5	18	13	30	0	3							
Scarsone, Steve	.100	5	10	0	1	0	0	0	0	2	5	1	0	R	R	6-2	170	4-11-66	1986	Anaheim, Calif.
Sheaffer, Danny	.250	76	132	10	33	5	0	0	11	8	17	1	0	R	R	6-0	190	8-21-61	1981	Winston-Salem, N.C.
Sweeney, Mark	.213	44	61	5	13	3	0	0	4	9	14	0	1	L	L	6-1	195	10-26-69	1991	Holliston, Mass.
Young, Dmitri	.258	110	333	38	86	14	3	5	34	38	63	6	5	S	R	6-2	215	10-11-73	1991	Camarillo, Calif.

PITCHING	W	L	ERA	G	GS	CG	SV	IP	H	R	ER	BB	SO	B	T	HT	WT	DOB	1st Yr	Resides
Aybar, Manny	2	4	4.24	12	12	0	0	68	66	33	32	29	41	R	R	6-1	165	10-5-74	1991	Bani, D.R.
Batchelor, Rich	1	1	4.50	10	0	0	0	16	21	12	8	7	8	R	R	6-1	195	4-8-67	1990	Hartsville, S.C.
Bautista, Jose	0	0	6.57	11	0	0	0	12	15	10	9	2	4	R	R	6-2	207	7-25-64	1981	Cooper City, Fla.
Beltran, Rigo	1	2	3.48	35	4	0	1	54	47	25	21	17	50	L	L	5-11	185	11-13-69	1991	San Diego, Calif.
Benes, Alan	9	9	2.89	23	23	2	0	162	128	60	52	68	160	R	R	6-5	215	1-21-72	1993	Lake Forest, Ill.
Benes, Andy	10	7	3.10	26	26	0	0	177	149	64	61	61	175	R	R	6-6	238	8-20-67	1989	Poway, Calif.
Busby, Mike	0	2	8.79	3	3	0	0	14	24	14	14	4	6	R	R	6-4	215	12-27-72	1991	Glendale, Ariz.
Eckersley, Dennis	1	5	3.91	57	0	0	36	53	49	24	23	8	45	R	R	6-2	195	10-3-54	1972	Sudbury, Mass.
Fossas, Tony	2	7	3.83	71	0	0	0	52	62	32	22	26	41	L	L	6-0	187	9-23-57	1979	Fort Lauderdale, Fla.
Frascatore, John	5	2	2.48	59	0	0	0	80	74	25	22	33	58	R	R	6-1	200	2-4-70	1991	Oceanside, N.Y.
Honeycutt, Rick	0	0	13.50	2	0	0	0	2	5	3	3	1	2	L	L	6-1	192	6-29-54	1976	La Habra Heights, Calif.
Jackson, Danny	1	2	7.71	4	4	0	0	19	26	17	16	8	13	R	L	6-0	205	1-5-62	1982	Lincolnshire, Ill.
King, Curtis	4	2	2.76	30	0	0	0	29	38	14	9	11	13	R	R	6-5	205	10-25-70	1994	Conshohocken, Pa.
Lowe, Sean	0	2	9.35	6	4	0	0	17	27	21	18	10	8	R	R	6-2	205	3-29-71	1992	Mesquite, Texas
Ludwick, Eric	0	1	9.45	5	0	0	0	7	12	7	7	6	7	R	R	6-5	210	12-14-71	1993	Las Vegas, Nev.
Mathews, T.J.	4	4	2.15	40	0	0	0	46	41	14	11	18	46	R	R	6-2	200	1-19-70	1992	Henderson, Nev.
McGraw, Tom	0	0	0.00	2	0	0	0	2	2	0	0	1	0	L	L	6-2	195	12-8-67	1990	Yacolt, Wash.
Morris, Matt	12	9	3.19	33	33	3	0	217	208	88	77	69	149	R	R	6-5	210	8-9-74	1995	Montgomery, N.Y.
Osborne, Donovan	3	7	4.93	14	14	0	0	80	84	46	44	23	51	L	L	6-2	195	6-21-69	1990	Carson City, Nev.
Painter, Lance	1	1	4.76	14	0	0	0	17	13	9	9	8	11	L	L	6-1	195	7-21-67	1990	Milwaukee, Wis.
Petkovsek, Mark	4	7	5.06	55	2	0	2	96	109	61	54	31	51	R	R	6-0	185	11-18-65	1987	Beaumont, Texas
Raggio, Brady	1	2	6.89	15	4	0	0	31	44	24	24	16	21	R	R	6-4	210	9-17-72	1992	Danville, Calif.
Stottlemyre, Todd	12	9	3.88	28	28	0	0	181	155	86	78	65	160	L	R	6-3	195	5-20-65	1986	Yakima, Wash.
Valenzuela, Fernando	0	4	5.56	5	5	0	0	23	22	19	14	14	10	L	L	5-11	202	11-1-60	1978	Los Angeles, Calif.
2-team (13 San Diego)	2	12	4.96	18	18	1	0	89	106	61	49	46	61							

FIELDING

Catcher	PCT	G	PO	A	E	DP
Difelice	.991	91	586	64	6	10
Lampkin	.989	86	413	37	5	6
Marrero	.969	17	82	12	3	2
Pagnozzi	1.000	13	57	2	0	0
Sheaffer	1.000	9	19	1	0	0

First Base	PCT	G	PO	A	E	DP
Difelice	1.000	1	1	0	0	0
Gaetti	1.000	20	61	6	0	8
Livingstone	1.000	2	16	1	0	1
Mabry	.997	49	346	22	1	33
McGwire	.998	50	438	34	1	40
Pagnozzi	1.000	2	6	0	0	1
Sweeney	1.000	4	8	1	0	2
Young	.985	74	601	45	10	50

Second Base	PCT	G	PO	A	E	DP
Bell	.973	23	35	37	2	7
Berblinger	1.000	4	4	4	0	2
DeShields	.972	147	272	398	19	93
Gallego	.962	11	9	16	1	3
Livingstone	1.000	1	0	3	0	0
Mejia	.900	3	3	6	1	3
Scarsone	1.000	2	4	2	0	0
Sheaffer	1.000	3	3	3	0	2

Third Base	PCT	G	PO	A	E	DP
Bell	.913	35	10	32	4	1
Gaetti	.978	132	72	244	7	24
Gallego	1.000	7	1	7	0	0
Gulan	1.000	3	1	1	0	1
Livingstone	1.000	2	0	1	0	0
Mabry	.000	1	0	0	0	0
Pagnozzi	.000	1	0	0	0	0
Scarsone	.000	1	0	0	0	0
Sheaffer	.957	30	8	36	2	2

Shortstop	PCT	G	PO	A	E	DP
Bell	.947	13	10	26	2	4
Clayton	.973	153	228	452	19	93
Gallego	1.000	10	5	18	0	3
Ordaz	.963	11	9	17	1	4

Outfield	PCT	G	PO	A	E	DP
Franklin	1.000	13	13	0	0	0
Gant	.977	128	247	4	6	1
Green	.952	19	19	1	1	0
Jordan	1.000	44	82	2	0	0
Lankford	.971	131	293	4	9	2
Livingstone	.000	1	0	0	0	0
Mabry	1.000	78	109	8	0	1
McGee	.981	81	99	6	2	3
Mejia	.000	1	0	0	0	0
Plantier	.981	32	52	1	1	0
Scarsone	.000	2	0	0	0	0
Sheaffer	1.000	22	13	0	0	0
Sweeney	1.000	25	23	0	0	0
Young	.933	17	40	2	3	0

FARM SYSTEM

Director of Player Development: Mike Jorgensen

Class	Farm Team	League	W	L	Pct.	Finish*	Manager	First Yr
AAA	Louisville (Ky.) Redbirds	American Assoc.	58	85	.406	8th (8)	Gaylen Pitts	1982
AA	Arkansas Travelers	Texas	68	72	.486	4th (8)	Rick Mahler	1966
#A	Prince William (Va.) Cannons	Carolina	69	70	.496	3rd (8)	Roy Silver	1997
A	Peoria (Ill.) Chiefs	Midwest	70	69	.504	8th (14)	Joe Cunningham	1995
A	New Jersey Cardinals	New York-Penn	35	39	.473	8th (14)	Jeff Shireman	1994
R	Johnson City (Tenn.) Cardinals	Appalachian	23	45	.338	10th (10)	Steve Turco	1975

*Finish in overall standings (No. of teams in league) #Advanced level

ORGANIZATION LEADERS

MAJOR LEAGUERS

BATTING

*AVG	Willie McGee .... .300
R	Ray Lankford 94
H	Delino DeShields..... 169
TB	Ray Lankford 272
2B	Royce Clayton 39
3B	Delino DeShields....... 14
HR	Ray Lankford 31
RBI	Ray Lankford 98
BB	Ray Lankford 95
SO	Ron Gant 162
SB	Delino DeShields....... 55

PITCHING

W	Two tied at................. 12
L	Three tied at 9
#ERA	John Frascatore 2.48
G	Tony Fossas 71
CG	Matt Morris 3
SV	Dennis Eckersley....... 36
IP	Matt Morris 217
BB	Matt Morris 69
SO	Andy Benes............. 175

Delino DeShields

JOHN SPEAR

Cliff Politte

MINOR LEAGUERS

BATTING

*AVG	Adam Kennedy, Pr. Will./New Jersey.... .325
R	Three tied at 81
H	Kerry Robinson, Louisville/Arkansas .. 169
TB	Nate Dishington, Prince William.......... 238
2B	Brent Butler, Peoria 37
3B	Juan Munoz, Arkansas/Prince William 9
HR	Joe Freitas, Peoria 33
RBI	Nate Dishington, Prince William.......... 106
BB	Nate Dishington, Prince William............ 81
SO	Chris Haas, Prince William/Peoria 182
SB	Kerry Robinson, Louisville/Arkansas 40

PITCHING

W	Cliff Politte, Arkansas/Prince William 15
L	Mark Nussbeck, Peoria 12
#ERA	Matt Jarvis, Arkansas 1.91
G	Keith Glauber, Louisville/Arkansas........ 65
CG	Manuel Aybar, Louisville.......................... 3
SV	Armando Almanza, Prince William 36
IP	Clint Weibl, Prince William 163
BB	Corey Avrard, Prince William/Peoria .. 113
SO	Corey Avrard, Prince William/Peoria .. 144

*Minimum 250 At-Bats #Minimum 75 Innings

TOP 10 PROSPECTS

DAVID SEELIG

Matt Morris

How the Cardinals Top 10 prospects, as judged by Baseball America prior to the 1997 season, fared in 1997:

Player, Pos.	Club (Class)	AVG	AB	R	H	2B	3B	HR	RBI	SB
2. Dmitri Young, 1b	St. Louis	.258	333	38	86	14	3	5	34	6
	Louisville (AAA)	.277	83	10	23	7	0	4	14	1
4. Eli Marrero, c	St. Louis	.244	45	4	11	2	0	2	7	4
	Louisville (AAA)	.273	395	60	108	21	7	20	68	4
6. Brent Butler, ss	Peoria (A)	.306	480	81	147	37	2	15	71	6
8. Jason Woolf, ss	Prince William (A)	.247	251	59	62	11	3	6	18	26
10. Luis Ordaz, ss	St. Louis	.273	22	3	6	1	0	0	1	3
	Arkansas (AA)	.287	390	44	112	20	6	4	58	11

Player, Pos.	Club (Class)	W	L	ERA	G	SV	IP	H	BB	SO
1. Matt Morris, rhp	St. Louis	12	9	3.19	33	0	217	208	69	149
3. Braden Looper, rhp	Arkansas (AA)	1	4	5.91	19	5	21	24	7	20
	Prince William (A)	3	6	4.48	12	0	64	71	25	58
5. Manuel Aybar, rhp	St. Louis	2	4	4.24	12	0	68	66	29	41
	Louisville (AAA)	5	8	3.48	22	0	137	131	45	114
7. *Eric Ludwick, rhp	St. Louis	0	1	9.45	5	0	7	12	6	7
	Oakland	1	4	8.25	6	0	24	32	16	14
	Louisville (AAA)	6	8	2.93	24	4	80	67	26	85
	Edmonton (AAA)	1	1	3.32	6	0	19	22	4	20
9. *Blake Stein, rhp	Arkansas (AA)	8	7	4.24	22	0	134	128	49	114
	Huntsville (AA)	3	2	5.71	7	0	35	36	20	25

*Traded to Athletics

LOUISVILLE — Class AAA

AMERICAN ASSOCIATION

BATTING	AVG	G	AB	R	H	2B	3B	HR	RBI	BB	SO	SB	CS	B	T	HT	WT	DOB	1st Yr	Resides
Bell, David	.227	6	22	3	5	0	0	1	4	0	6	0	0	R	R	5-10	170	9-14-72	1990	Cincinnati, Ohio
Berblinger, Jeff	.263	133	513	63	135	19	7	11	58	55	98	24	12	R	R	6-0	190	11-19-70	1993	Goddard, Kan.
Bradshaw, Terry	.249	130	453	79	113	17	6	8	43	61	79	26	10	L	R	6-0	180	2-3-69	1990	Zuni, Va.
Costo, Tim	.303	121	400	52	121	26	2	14	54	41	72	4	4	R	R	6-5	230	2-16-69	1990	Glen Ellyn, Ill.
Coughlin, Kevin	.257	12	35	2	9	1	0	0	2	1	7	0	1	L	L	6-0	175	9-7-70	1989	Clarksburg, Md.
Difelice, Mike	.250	1	4	1	1	0	0	1	1	0	1	0	0	R	R	6-2	205	5-28-69	1991	Knoxville, Tenn.
Franklin, Micah	.221	99	326	49	72	14	1	12	48	51	74	2	0	S	R	6-0	195	4-25-72	1990	San Francisco, Calif.
Gallego, Mike	.278	6	18	0	5	1	0	0	1	3	5	1	1	R	R	5-8	160	10-31-60	1981	Yorba Linda, Calif.
Giannelli, Ray	.221	39	95	12	21	4	0	3	12	17	18	0	0	L	R	6-0	195	2-5-66	1988	Lindenhurst, N.Y.
Green, Bert	.254	52	209	26	53	11	2	3	13	22	55	10	7	S	R	5-10	170	6-9-74	1993	Florissant, Mo.
Gulan, Mike	.267	116	412	50	110	20	6	14	61	28	121	5	2	R	R	6-1	190	12-18-70	1992	Steubenville, Ohio
Holbert, Aaron	.255	93	314	32	80	14	3	4	32	15	56	9	5	R	R	6-0	160	1-9-73	1990	Long Beach, Calif.
Jordan, Brian	.150	6	20	1	3	0	0	0	2	1	2	0	1	R	R	6-1	205	3-29-67	1988	Baltimore, Md.
Koslofski, Kevin	.211	106	285	37	60	14	3	9	27	43	78	1	9	L	R	5-8	175	9-24-66	1984	Maroa, Ill.
Livingstone, Scott	.360	9	25	4	9	1	0	0	2	2	3	0	0	L	R	6-0	198	7-15-65	1988	Southlake, Texas
Marrero, Eli	.273	112	395	60	108	21	7	20	68	25	53	4	4	R	R	6-1	180	11-17-73	1993	Miami, Fla.
Mejia, Roberto	.333	6	21	3	7	1	0	1	2	0	4	0	2	R	R	5-11	160	4-14-72	1989	Hato Mayor, D.R.
Nevers, Tom	.233	71	227	22	53	9	0	8	27	12	48	1	3	R	R	6-1	175	9-13-71	1990	Edina, Minn.
Pagnozzi, Tom	.000	3	5	0	0	0	0	0	0	0	1	0	0	R	R	6-1	190	7-30-62	1983	Tucson, Ariz.
Plantier, Phil	.258	9	31	6	8	3	0	1	10	6	3	0	0	L	R	5-11	195	1-27-69	1987	San Diego, Calif.
Robinson, Kerry	.111	2	9	0	1	0	0	0	0	0	1	0	0	L	L	6-0	175	10-3-73	1994	St. Louis, Mo.
Rupp, Brian	.275	59	189	17	52	7	2	0	16	19	36	1	1	R	R	6-5	185	9-20-71	1992	Florissant, Mo.
Scarsone, Steve	.154	10	26	5	4	0	0	1	3	7	10	0	0	R	R	6-2	170	4-11-66	1986	Anaheim, Calif.
Stefanski, Mike	.305	57	197	26	60	10	0	6	22	12	20	0	1	R	R	6-2	190	9-12-69	1991	Redford, Mich.
Warner, Ron	.232	101	276	43	64	16	0	7	30	42	45	4	1	R	R	6-3	185	12-2-68	1991	Redlands, Calif.
Wimmer, Chris	.167	5	12	0	2	0	0	0	1	0	1	0	0	R	R	5-11	170	9-25-70	1992	Wichita, Kan.
Young, Dmitri	.274	24	84	10	23	7	0	4	14	13	15	1	1	S	R	6-2	215	10-11-73	1991	Camarillo, Calif.

PITCHING	W	L	ERA	G	GS	CG	SV	IP	H	R	ER	BB	SO	B	T	HT	WT	DOB	1st Yr	Resides
Arrandale, Matt	2	6	3.67	56	1	0	1	83	84	38	34	38	32	R	R	6-0	165	12-14-70	1993	St. Louis, Mo.
Aybar, Manny	5	8	3.48	22	22	3	0	137	131	60	53	45	114	R	R	6-1	165	10-5-74	1991	Bani, D.R.
Badorek, Mike	0	0	18.00	1	0	0	0	2	4	4	4	2	3	R	R	6-5	230	5-15-69	1991	Mt. Zion, Ill.
Barber, Brian	4	8	6.90	18	18	0	0	93	111	80	71	44	74	R	R	6-1	172	3-4-73	1991	Orlando, Fla.
Batchelor, Rich	0	2	4.50	12	0	0	5	14	18	9	7	6	10	R	R	6-1	195	4-8-67	1990	Hartsville, S.C.
Bautista, Jose	2	0	0.00	11	0	0	0	17	3	0	0	2	11	R	R	6-2	207	7-25-64	1981	Cooper City, Fla.
Beltran, Rigo	5	2	2.32	9	8	1	0	54	45	17	14	21	46	L	L	5-11	185	11-13-69	1991	San Diego, Calif.
Benes, Andy	0	0	1.80	1	1	0	0	5	3	1	1	1	5	R	R	6-6	238	8-20-67	1989	Poway, Calif.
Busby, Mike	4	8	4.61	15	14	1	0	94	95	49	48	30	65	R	R	6-4	215	12-27-72	1991	Glendale, Ariz.
Carpenter, Brian	0	0	4.32	4	0	0	1	8	11	4	4	5	9	R	R	6-0	225	3-3-71	1992	Marble Falls, Texas
Croushore, Rick	1	2	2.47	14	6	0	1	44	37	14	12	13	41	R	R	6-4	210	8-7-70	1993	Houston, Texas
Detmers, Kris	3	3	7.20	10	5	0	0	35	43	28	28	17	22	S	L	6-5	215	6-22-74	1994	Nokomis, Ill.
Glauber, Keith	1	3	5.17	15	0	0	5	16	18	14	9	4	14	R	R	6-2	190	1-18-72	1994	Morganville, N.J.
Heiserman, Rick	0	0	4.50	1	0	0	0	2	2	1	1	1	0	R	R	6-7	220	2-22-73	1994	Omaha, Neb.
Jackson, Danny	1	0	1.80	4	4	0	0	25	20	6	5	8	14	R	L	6-0	205	1-5-62	1982	Lincolnshire, Ill.
King, Curtis	2	1	2.05	16	0	0	3	22	19	5	5	6	9	R	R	6-5	205	10-25-70	1994	Conshohocken, Pa.
Lowe, Sean	6	10	4.37	26	23	1	1	132	142	74	64	53	117	R	R	6-2	205	3-29-71	1992	Mesquite, Texas
Ludwick, Eric	6	8	2.93	24	11	1	4	80	67	31	26	26	85	R	R	6-5	210	12-14-71	1993	Las Vegas, Nev.
Matranga, Jeff	3	3	5.57	37	0	0	0	53	75	34	33	13	30	R	R	6-2	170	12-14-70	1992	Lakeside, Calif.
Maxcy, Brian	2	2	3.76	30	0	0	9	38	36	18	16	24	22	R	R	6-1	170	5-4-71	1992	Amory, Miss.
McGraw, Tom	1	4	5.33	45	0	0	0	49	55	34	29	26	39	L	L	6-2	195	12-8-67	1990	Yacolt, Wash.
Osborne, Donovan	0	1	4.73	3	3	0	0	13	13	7	7	5	13	L	L	6-2	195	6-21-69	1990	Carson City, Nev.
Painter, Lance	1	0	5.23	18	2	0	0	21	18	14	12	4	22	L	L	6-1	195	7-21-67	1990	Milwaukee, Wis.
Raggio, Brady	8	11	4.17	22	22	2	0	138	145	68	64	32	91	R	R	6-4	210	9-17-72	1992	Danville, Calif.
Wiegandt, Scott	1	3	4.45	40	3	0	0	65	57	34	32	36	55	L	L	5-11	180	12-9-67	1989	Louisville, Ky.

FIELDING

Catcher	PCT	G	PO	A	E	DP	PB
Difelice	1.000	1	3	1	0	0	0
Marrero	.991	100	675	68	7	8	5
Pagnozzi	1.000	3	8	3	0	1	0
Stefanski	.978	47	271	34	7	2	0

First Base	PCT	G	PO	A	E	DP
Costo	.995	88	752	54	4	68
Giannelli	.970	4	29	3	1	2
Gulan	1.000	1	5	0	0	0
Livingstone	.971	4	31	3	1	3
Rupp	.996	25	213	9	1	20
Stefanski	.982	8	47	9	1	8
Warner	.989	23	166	14	2	23
Young	1.000	5	36	1	0	1

Second Base	PCT	G	PO	A	E	DP
Bell	1.000	2	5	3	0	1
Berblinger	.981	128	258	362	12	93
Holbert	.957	4	14	8	1	2
Mejia	1.000	3	8	3	0	0
Nevers	1.000	3	9	10	0	3
Scarsone	.957	4	11	11	1	2
Warner	1.000	3	2	3	0	0
Wimmer	1.000	3	2	4	0	0

Third Base	PCT	G	PO	A	E	DP
Bell	1.000	2	0	4	0	1
Gulan	.948	107	73	221	16	22
Mejia	.857	3	1	5	1	0
Nevers	1.000	8	9	10	0	2
Rupp	.875	13	8	13	3	1
Scarsone	1.000	4	2	9	0	0
Warner	.950	20	11	27	2	4
Wimmer	1.000	1	1	1	0	0

Shortstop	PCT	G	PO	A	E	DP
Bell	.800	1	1	3	1	1
Gallego	.955	6	8	13	1	1
Holbert	.934	81	115	253	26	52
Nevers	.963	57	72	162	9	36
Warner	.941	9	10	22	2	3

Outfield	PCT	G	PO	A	E	DP
Berblinger	.000	1	0	0	0	0
Bradshaw	.990	122	187	5	2	0
Coughlin	1.000	12	17	0	0	0
Franklin	.978	94	128	7	3	1
Giannelli	1.000	14	28	0	0	0
Green	.993	52	138	7	1	4
Gulan	.000	1	0	0	0	0
Jordan	1.000	4	6	0	0	0
Koslofski	.985	99	195	8	3	3
Nevers	1.000	2	2	0	0	0
Plantier	1.000	7	7	0	0	0
Robinson	1.000	2	3	0	0	0
Rupp	1.000	13	21	0	0	0
Warner	.976	32	40	1	1	0
Young	.967	19	28	1	1	0

ARKANSAS — Class AA

TEXAS LEAGUE

BATTING	AVG	G	AB	R	H	2B	3B	HR	RBI	BB	SO	SB	CS	B	T	HT	WT	DOB	1st Yr	Resides
Almond, Greg	.203	69	158	23	32	4	1	0	16	29	38	0	0	R	R	6-0	195	4-14-71	1993	Panama City, Fla.
Bell, David	.219	9	32	3	7	2	0	1	3	2	2	1	0	R	R	5-10	170	9-14-72	1990	Cincinnati, Ohio
Coughlin, Kevin	.300	26	90	15	27	6	1	1	8	9	12	0	0	L	L	6-0	175	9-7-70	1989	Clarksburg, Md.
Dalton, Dee	.228	116	360	52	82	16	0	4	43	38	66	2	5	R	R	5-11	170	6-17-72	1993	Roanoke, Va.
Difelice, Mike	.333	1	3	0	1	1	0	0	0	1	0	0	0	R	R	6-2	205	5-28-69	1991	Knoxville, Tenn.
Green, Bert	.307	76	251	45	77	14	4	2	29	36	48	11	5	S	R	5-10	170	6-9-74	1993	Florissant, Mo.
Kleiner, Stacy	.255	16	55	7	14	4	2	1	10	2	14	0	0	R	R	6-0	185	1-12-75	1996	Las Vegas, Nev.
Lariviere, Jason	.274	118	372	50	102	24	5	6	60	33	69	4	3	R	R	5-10	180	9-30-73	1995	Biddeford, Maine
Matvey, Mike	.221	57	136	16	30	4	0	1	9	21	33	1	1	R	R	6-0	180	10-10-71	1993	Charlotte, N.C.
McDonald, Keith	.240	79	233	32	56	16	0	5	30	31	56	0	1	R	R	6-2	215	2-8-73	1994	Yorba Linda, Calif.
McEwing, Joe	.259	103	263	33	68	6	3	4	35	19	39	2	4	R	R	5-10	170	10-19-72	1992	Bristol, Pa.
Munoz, Juan	.279	58	215	28	60	9	2	6	31	16	26	6	10	L	L	5-9	170	3-27-74	1995	Miami, Fla.
Ordaz, Luis	.287	115	390	44	112	20	6	4	58	22	39	11	10	R	R	5-11	170	8-12-75	1993	Maracaibo, Venez.
Ozorio, Yudith	.208	84	144	23	30	2	1	0	9	12	44	6	2	S	R	5-11	155	1-1-75	1991	La Romana, D.R.
Pagnozzi, Tom	.317	21	63	8	20	0	0	5	17	4	8	0	0	R	R	6-1	190	7-30-62	1983	Tucson, Ariz.
Pecorilli, Aldo	.360	31	111	21	40	10	0	4	22	7	15	2	3	R	R	5-11	185	9-12-70	1992	Sterling Heights, Mich.
Polanco, Placido	.291	129	508	71	148	16	3	2	51	29	51	19	5	R	R	5-10	168	10-10-75	1994	Miami, Fla.
Richard, Chris	.269	113	390	62	105	24	3	11	58	60	59	6	4	L	L	6-2	185	6-7-74	1995	San Diego, Calif.
Robinson, Kerry	.321	135	523	80	168	16	3	2	62	54	64	40	23	L	L	6-0	175	10-3-73	1994	St. Louis, Mo.
Rupp, Brian	.295	36	122	18	36	9	0	1	15	13	16	0	3	R	R	6-5	185	9-20-71	1992	Florissant, Mo.
Stefanski, Mike	.250	1	4	1	1	0	1	0	0	0	0	0	0	R	R	6-2	190	9-12-69	1991	Redford, Mich.

PITCHING	W	L	ERA	G	GS	CG	SV	IP	H	R	ER	BB	SO	B	T	HT	WT	DOB	1st Yr	Resides
Barber, Brian	0	1	10.47	3	3	0	0	16	28	19	19	5	15	R	R	6-1	172	3-4-73	1991	Orlando, Fla.
Benes, Andy	1	0	1.29	1	1	0	0	7	2	1	1	2	6	R	R	6-6	238	8-20-67	1989	Poway, Calif.
Chavarria, David	3	6	4.50	28	14	0	2	90	85	56	45	41	62	L	R	6-7	195	5-19-73	1991	Burnaby, B.C.
Croushore, Rick	7	5	4.18	17	16	1	0	93	111	52	43	37	67	R	R	6-4	210	8-7-70	1993	Houston, Texas
Detmers, Kris	5	7	5.77	15	15	0	0	78	99	54	50	27	44	S	L	6-5	215	6-22-74	1994	Nokomis, Ill.
Garcia, Frank	1	3	6.63	28	0	0	0	38	43	38	28	24	25	R	R	5-11	170	3-5-74	1994	Azua, D.R.
Glauber, Keith	5	7	2.75	50	0	0	3	59	48	22	18	25	53	R	R	6-2	190	1-18-72	1994	Morganville, N.J.
Heiserman, Rick	5	8	4.17	34	20	1	4	132	151	73	61	36	90	R	R	6-7	220	2-22-73	1994	Omaha, Neb.
Jarvis, Matt	8	5	1.91	50	4	0	2	80	70	24	17	45	52	R	L	6-4	185	2-22-72	1991	Albuquerque, N.M.
King, Curtis	2	3	4.46	32	0	0	16	36	38	19	18	10	29	R	R	6-5	205	10-25-70	1994	Conshohocken, Pa.
Logan, Marcus	11	7	4.12	27	25	1	0	153	152	75	70	64	101	R	R	6-0	170	5-8-72	1994	Evanston, Ill.
Looper, Braden	1	4	5.91	19	0	0	5	21	24	14	14	7	20	R	R	6-5	225	10-28-74	1996	Arlington, Texas
Lovingier, Kevin	4	3	2.54	59	0	0	3	74	68	27	21	26	82	L	L	6-1	190	8-29-71	1994	Mission Viejo, Calif.
Politte, Cliff	4	1	2.15	6	6	0	0	38	35	15	9	9	26	R	R	5-11	185	2-27-74	1995	St. Louis, Mo.
Pote, Lou	0	0	1.54	7	3	0	0	23	15	10	4	8	21	R	R	6-3	190	8-27-71	1991	Chicago, Ill.
Stein, Blake	8	7	4.24	22	22	1	0	134	128	67	63	49	114	R	R	6-7	210	8-3-73	1994	Folsom, La.
Westbrook, Destry	0	2	2.74	14	0	0	0	23	16	11	7	17	16	R	R	6-1	195	12-13-70	1992	Montrose, Colo.
Windham, Mike	3	3	5.48	29	11	1	0	89	107	61	54	37	44	R	R	6-1	185	3-8-72	1993	West Palm Beach, Fla.

FIELDING

Catcher	PCT	G	PO	A	E	DP	PB
Almond	.986	68	332	20	5	2	7
Difelice	1.000	1	6	2	0	0	0
Kleiner	.983	10	57	1	1	0	1
McDonald	.988	68	384	29	5	6	9
McEwing	1.000	1	1	0	0	0	0
Pagnozzi	.986	14	68	4	1	1	1
Pecorilli	1.000	10	55	7	0	1	5
Stefanski	1.000	1	4	1	0	0	0

First Base	PCT	G	PO	A	E	DP
Coughlin	1.000	1	9	0	0	1
Dalton	1.000	1	3	0	0	1
Lariviere	.988	18	152	14	2	14
McEwing	1.000	2	24	0	0	3
Pecorilli	.980	13	88	10	2	12
Richard	.990	104	921	68	10	103
Rupp	1.000	9	42	3	0	7

Second Base	PCT	G	PO	A	E	DP
Bell	1.000	1	0	5	0	0
Dalton	.952	5	4	16	1	5
Kleiner	1.000	4	6	11	0	3
Matvey	1.000	6	9	9	0	1
McEwing	1.000	5	9	10	0	2
Polanco	.979	128	240	425	14	110

Third Base	PCT	G	PO	A	E	DP
Bell	.929	8	3	10	1	0
Dalton	.939	70	51	134	12	14
Kleiner	1.000	4	2	4	0	1
Matvey	.943	46	22	77	6	11
McEwing	1.000	2	2	3	0	1
Pecorilli	1.000	1	0	3	0	0
Rupp	.947	31	20	51	4	7

Shortstop	PCT	G	PO	A	E	DP
Dalton	.964	39	55	105	6	30
Matvey	1.000	3	0	3	0	0
McEwing	.000	1	0	0	0	0
Ordaz	.935	111	149	327	33	79

Outfield	PCT	G	PO	A	E	DP
Almond	.000	2	0	0	0	0
Coughlin	1.000	18	25	2	0	1
Green	.994	75	170	8	1	1
Lariviere	.991	62	103	5	1	0
McEwing	.982	62	98	11	2	1
Munoz	1.000	55	107	11	0	3
Ozorio	.982	45	53	3	1	0
Richard	1.000	3	3	0	0	0
Robinson	.966	129	193	6	7	1

PRINCE WILLIAM — Class A

CAROLINA LEAGUE

BATTING	AVG	G	AB	R	H	2B	3B	HR	RBI	BB	SO	SB	CS	B	T	HT	WT	DOB	1st Yr	Resides
Almond, Greg	.327	18	52	5	17	7	0	1	2	5	11	1	2	R	R	6-0	195	4-14-71	1993	Panama City, Fla.
Ametller, Jesus	.270	60	215	26	58	10	2	3	26	15	12	3	1	L	R	5-8	175	7-25-74	1997	San Jose, Costa Rica
Clapp, Stubby	.318	78	267	51	85	21	6	4	46	52	41	9	4	S	R	5-8	175	2-24-73	1996	Windsor, Ontario
Dishington, Nate	.272	133	448	75	122	20	6	28	106	81	121	8	5	L	R	6-3	210	1-8-75	1993	Glendale, Calif.
Falciglia, Tony	.197	64	147	16	29	8	0	2	17	9	31	1	1	R	R	5-11	185	9-29-72	1995	Bronx, N.Y.
Farley, Cordell	.261	61	211	34	55	9	3	3	32	15	46	24	7	R	R	6-0	185	3-29-73	1996	Blackstone, Va.
Garcia, Ossie	.239	104	247	38	59	12	3	0	20	25	41	10	5	R	R	6-1	180	10-14-73	1993	Hialeah, Fla.
Haas, Chris	.238	100	361	58	86	10	2	14	54	42	144	1	1	L	R	6-2	210	10-15-76	1995	Paducah, Ky.
Hall, Andy	.193	23	83	13	16	1	2	1	7	10	22	4	1	S	R	6-0	175	4-29-74	1995	San Luis Obispo, Calif.
Jimenez, Ruben	.146	17	41	5	6	1	0	0	1	6	7	2	0	S	R	5-11	155	8-18-75	1993	San Pedro de Macoris, D.R.
Kennedy, Adam	.312	35	154	24	48	9	3	1	27	6	17	4	3	L	R	6-1	180	1-10-76	1997	Riverside, Calif.
Kleiner, Stacy	.313	91	310	37	97	22	4	4	32	28	69	1	1	R	R	6-0	185	1-12-75	1996	Las Vegas, Nev.
Lankford, Ray	.308	4	13	3	4	1	0	0	4	4	5	1	1	L	L	5-11	180	6-5-67	1987	Modesto, Calif.
Matvey, Mike	.228	32	123	22	28	12	0	3	22	15	28	1	0	R	R	6-0	180	10-10-71	1993	Charlotte, N.C.

BATTING	AVG	G	AB	R	H	2B	3B	HR	RBI	BB	SO	SB	CS	B	T	HT	WT	DOB	1st Yr	Resides
Mazurek, Brian	.281	97	324	39	91	17	1	9	47	21	53	0	2	L	L	6-1	195	4-17-74	1996	Matteson, Ill.
McHugh, Ryan	.265	116	442	68	117	27	2	8	61	32	117	4	7	R	R	6-6	215	7-29-73	1995	Lakeland, Fla.
McNally, Shawn	.217	47	138	12	30	7	1	0	18	27	22	3	2	R	R	6-2	215	1-29-73	1995	Winder, Ga.
Mejia, Miguel	.213	39	136	17	29	2	0	0	9	10	25	7	8	R	R	6-1	155	3-25-75	1992	San Pedro de Macoris, D.R.
Munoz, Juan	.313	66	256	41	80	16	7	4	48	19	25	3	1	L	L	5-9	170	3-27-74	1995	Miami, Fla.
Ortega, William	.229	73	249	23	57	14	0	0	15	21	42	1	2	R	R	6-4	205	7-24-75	1997	San Jose, Costa Rica
Schmidt, Dave	.195	82	231	23	45	9	0	0	19	28	66	2	2	L	R	6-1	195	10-11-73	1996	Spokane, Wash.
Woolf, Jason	.247	70	251	59	62	11	3	6	18	55	75	26	5	S	R	6-1	170	6-6-77	1995	Miami, Fla.

GAMES BY POSITION: C—Almond 16, Falciglia 48, Kleiner 24, McNally 1, Schmidt 82, Woolf 1. **1B**—Dishington 100, Mazurek 46, McNally 5. **2B**—Ametller 52, Clapp 42, Hall 22, Jimenez 2, Kleiner 33. **3B**—Haas 97, Kleiner 22, Matvey 14, McNally 10. **SS**—Garcia 3, Jimenez 12, Kennedy 35, Kleiner 10, Matvey 19, Woolf 70. **OF**—Almond 1, Clapp 34, Dishington 4, Farley 58, Garcia 97, Lankford 2, McHugh 83, McNally 31, Mejia 38, Munoz 64, Ortega 56.

PITCHING	W	L	ERA	G	GS	CG	SV	IP	H	R	ER	BB	SO	B	T	HT	WT	DOB	1st Yr	Resides
Almanza, Armando	2	3	1.67	58	0	0	36	65	38	18	12	32	83	L	L	6-3	205	10-26-72	1993	El Paso, Texas
Avrard, Corey	0	3	5.36	8	8	0	0	40	30	28	24	44	50	R	R	6-3	185	12-6-76	1994	Metairie, La.
Barber, Brian	1	1	4.09	2	2	0	0	11	10	5	5	5	13	R	R	6-1	172	3-4-73	1991	Orlando, Fla.
Benes, Adam	3	3	6.27	33	5	0	0	70	92	54	49	29	44	L	R	6-2	195	3-12-73	1995	Evansville, Ind.
Benes, Andy	0	0	0.00	1	1	0	0	5	3	1	0	1	9	R	R	6-6	238	8-20-67	1989	Poway, Calif.
Conway, Keith	1	0	2.79	15	0	0	0	19	18	6	6	8	22	R	L	6-2	200	5-8-73	1993	Philadelphia, Pa.
Donnelly, Rob	5	0	3.51	37	0	0	0	51	44	33	20	26	54	R	R	6-0	180	9-27-73	1995	Fresno, Calif.
Franks, Lance	1	0	2.08	2	0	0	0	4	3	1	1	1	4	R	R	5-11	180	8-20-75	1997	Russellville, Ark.
Garcia, Frank	2	2	9.00	18	0	0	0	24	36	30	24	12	14	R	R	5-11	170	3-5-74	1994	Azua, D.R.
Hall, Yates	6	7	4.77	26	21	0	0	109	89	70	58	94	75	R	R	6-2	190	3-29-73	1994	Front Royal, Va.
Jimenez, Jose	9	7	3.09	24	24	2	0	146	128	73	50	42	81	R	R	6-3	170	7-7-73	1992	San Pedro de Macoris, D.R.
Kown, John	2	6	6.92	20	10	0	0	66	83	60	51	25	32	R	R	6-5	215	12-15-72	1995	Marietta, Ga.
Looper, Braden	3	6	4.48	12	12	0	0	64	71	38	32	25	58	R	R	6-5	225	10-28-74	1996	Arlington, Texas
McNeill, Kevin	2	6	4.96	55	1	0	1	69	66	43	38	28	58	R	L	6-4	210	12-22-70	1994	Waller, Texas
Nestor, Joe	3	7	3.87	58	0	0	3	77	77	39	33	29	63	R	R	5-10	190	9-29-73	1996	Springhill, Fla.
Politte, Cliff	11	1	2.24	19	19	0	0	120	89	37	30	31	118	R	R	5-11	185	2-27-74	1995	St. Louis, Mo.
Reed, Steve	2	2	4.31	7	7	0	0	40	45	24	19	12	25	R	R	6-2	205	9-24-75	1994	Juno Beach, Fla.
Weibl, Clint	12	11	4.64	29	29	0	0	163	185	90	84	62	135	R	R	6-3	180	3-17-75	1996	Dawson, Pa.
Welch, Travis	4	5	4.88	58	0	0	2	79	82	48	43	53	69	R	R	6-0	202	1-30-74	1993	Loomis, Calif.

PEORIA — Class A

MIDWEST LEAGUE

BATTING	AVG	G	AB	R	H	2B	3B	HR	RBI	BB	SO	SB	CS	B	T	HT	WT	DOB	1st Yr	Resides
Abell, Antonio	.160	13	25	4	4	0	0	0	2	4	12	2	2	R	R	5-10	175	1-13-75	1994	Ekron, Ky.
Britt, Bryan	.225	123	413	58	93	23	1	16	59	39	104	5	3	R	R	6-2	220	4-16-75	1996	Wilmington, N.C.
Butler, Brent	.306	129	480	81	147	37	2	15	71	63	69	6	4	R	R	6-0	180	2-11-78	1996	Laurinburg, N.C.
Cameron, Ken	.260	105	323	51	84	20	4	2	27	35	50	21	8	L	L	6-0	185	3-1-73	1995	Tigard, Ore.
Deck, Billy	.269	114	383	51	103	30	0	3	53	51	89	2	5	L	L	6-0	180	9-16-76	1995	Summerville, S.C.
Freitas, Joe	.250	122	436	78	109	16	1	33	86	58	148	6	1	R	R	6-3	195	8-2-73	1995	Hanford, Calif.
Gargiulo, Jimmy	.239	96	305	39	73	14	0	2	29	31	54	1	3	R	R	6-1	190	12-20-75	1996	North Lauderdale, Fla.
Haas, Chris	.313	36	115	23	36	11	0	5	22	22	38	3	0	L	R	6-2	210	10-15-76	1995	Paducah, Ky.
Harris, Rodger	.228	85	250	30	57	7	5	1	15	19	62	12	6	S	R	5-9	165	8-30-75	1995	Hanford, Calif.
Hogan, Todd	.247	112	449	57	111	18	3	6	37	26	104	28	16	R	R	6-2	180	9-18-75	1996	Dublin, Ga.
Leon, Jose	.231	118	399	50	92	21	2	20	54	32	122	6	5	R	R	6-0	160	12-8-76	1994	Cayey, P.R.
McClendon, Travis	.214	6	14	1	3	0	0	0	2	3	4	0	0	R	R	5-11	185	10-22-72	1995	Cottonwood, Ariz.
McNeal, Pepe	.246	56	142	18	35	9	0	5	25	18	32	0	1	R	R	6-3	205	8-11-75	1994	Thonotosassa, Fla.
Rivera, Miguel	.149	49	114	8	17	0	1	0	13	7	20	1	2	R	R	5-10	175	4-14-74	1994	Racine, Wis.
Saturria, Luis	.274	122	445	81	122	19	5	11	51	44	95	23	10	R	R	6-2	165	7-21-76	1994	Boca Chica, D.R.
Schmidt, Todd	.000	1	0	1	0	0	0	0	0	1	0	0	0	S	R	6-3	225	10-12-74	1997	New Haven, Mo.
Tanner, Paul	.233	104	318	31	74	19	3	1	33	19	76	9	3	R	R	6-0	175	9-11-74	1996	Albuquerque, N.M.

GAMES BY POSITION: C—Gargiulo 95, McClendon 5, McNeal 54. **1B**—Britt 71, Deck 79, Leon 1. **2B**—Harris 51, Rivera 22, Schmidt 1, Tanner 85. **3B**—Haas 26, Leon 107, Rivera 17, Tanner 4. **SS**—Butler 129, Rivera 7, Tanner 16. **OF**—Abell 11, Britt 1, Cameron 96, Deck 31, Freitas 52, Harris 29, Hogan 112, Leon 2, Rivera 1, Saturria 115, Tanner 1.

PITCHING	W	L	ERA	G	GS	CG	SV	IP	H	R	ER	BB	SO	B	T	HT	WT	DOB	1st Yr	Resides
Avrard, Corey	4	5	6.36	20	20	0	0	93	97	76	66	69	94	R	R	6-3	185	12-6-76	1994	Metairie, La.
Crafton, Kevin	7	2	1.96	50	0	0	29	55	40	16	12	18	59	R	R	6-1	185	5-10-74	1996	Russellville, Ark.
Dewitt, Matt	9	9	4.09	27	27	1	0	158	152	84	72	57	121	R	R	6-4	220	9-4-77	1995	Las Vegas, Nev.
DeLeon, Jose	11	3	5.01	60	0	0	8	74	79	46	41	35	76	R	R	6-3	152	10-2-76	1994	Azua, D.R.
Gallagher, Keith	2	1	5.79	31	1	0	0	56	68	45	36	29	43	R	R	6-2	200	11-17-73	1996	Orlando, Fla.
Karnuth, Jason	0	3	6.65	4	4	0	0	23	29	19	17	7	12	R	R	6-2	190	5-15-76	1997	Glen Ellyn, Ill.
Montgomery, Greg	2	8	8.53	40	11	0	1	82	103	89	78	69	68	R	R	6-2	200	5-19-75	1996	Greenbrier, Ark.
Nussbeck, Mark	8	12	4.58	27	27	2	0	151	181	92	77	56	132	L	R	6-4	180	5-25-74	1996	Kansas City, Mo.
Onofrei, Tim	5	5	4.78	42	9	0	0	98	111	66	52	45	69	L	R	6-2	195	11-1-74	1996	Vancouver, Wash.
Reames, Jay	6	9	3.98	27	24	2	0	133	132	77	59	86	83	R	R	6-1	205	10-31-74	1996	Seneca, S.C.
Reed, Steve	4	3	5.95	38	6	0	0	76	107	56	50	16	64	R	R	6-2	205	9-24-75	1994	Juno Beach, Fla.
Riegert, Tim	4	2	3.11	55	0	0	0	75	79	35	26	31	69	L	L	6-0	180	6-29-74	1996	Orlando, Fla.
Villafana, Jose	5	3	2.82	10	10	1	0	61	59	22	19	26	28	R	R	6-3	195	4-22-74	1995	Sylmar, Calif.
West, Adam	3	4	3.02	62	0	0	0	66	46	23	22	33	83	L	L	6-1	185	10-10-73	1994	Thousand Oaks, Calif.

NEW JERSEY — Short-Season Class A

NEW YORK-PENN LEAGUE

BATTING	AVG	G	AB	R	H	2B	3B	HR	RBI	BB	SO	SB	CS	B	T	HT	WT	DOB	1st Yr	Resides
Abell, Antonio	.225	10	40	11	9	0	0	1	4	3	16	1	1	R	R	5-10	175	1-13-75	1994	Ekron, Ky.
Bevins, Andy	.272	65	235	35	64	9	5	9	44	18	66	2	1	R	R	6-3	215	10-10-75	1997	Sacramento, Calif.
Chabot, Kevin	.154	12	39	2	6	0	0	1	4	1	14	0	0	L	R	6-0	210	5-5-74	1997	Orlando, Fla.
Farley, Cordell	.368	6	19	6	7	0	0	0	1	2	6	1	0	R	R	6-0	185	3-29-73	1996	Blackstone, Va.
Gentry, Aaron	.249	64	225	30	56	8	6	3	32	20	58	4	7	R	R	6-2	185	5-22-75	1997	Tulsa, Okla.

BATTING	AVG	G	AB	R	H	2B	3B	HR	RBI	BB	SO	SB	CS	B	T	HT	WT	DOB	1st Yr	Resides
Gick, Brady	.216	32	102	9	22	4	0	1	20	8	8	0	1	L	R	6-0	195	7-16-73	1997	Cincinnati, Ohio
Kennedy, Adam	.342	29	114	20	39	6	3	0	19	13	10	9	1	L	R	6-1	180	1-10-76	1997	Riverside, Calif.
Kim, David	.278	58	205	38	57	16	2	5	35	17	39	5	2	R	R	6-0	200	4-2-76	1997	Cherry Hill, N.J.
Lee, Jason	.239	60	226	34	54	10	0	5	37	21	69	8	2	L	R	6-1	185	4-22-77	1995	Burlington, Iowa
Maier, Taber	.213	50	155	19	33	9	1	2	22	20	30	6	2	R	R	6-0	180	2-24-75	1997	Santa Clara, Calif.
Martine, Chris	.211	47	142	22	30	5	0	0	12	22	37	0	0	R	R	6-2	190	7-10-75	1997	Cherry Hill, N.J.
Macrory, Rob	.306	67	248	52	76	9	2	1	26	18	27	23	3	R	R	6-1	165	2-18-75	1997	Montgomery, Ala.
Mejia, Miguel	.331	30	124	22	41	8	1	0	14	6	27	11	3	R	R	6-1	155	3-25-75	1992	San Pedro de Macoris, D.R.
Quaccia, Luke	.230	60	204	27	47	5	0	5	23	15	52	2	3	L	R	6-6	220	2-27-75	1997	Oakdale, Calif.
Schmidt, Todd	.211	15	38	2	8	2	0	0	2	6	12	0	1	S	R	6-3	225	10-12-74	1997	New Haven, Mo.
Speckhardt, Mike	.185	51	135	15	25	5	1	0	6	12	39	3	5	R	R	6-1	200	7-22-75	1997	South Fallsburg, N.Y.
Vazquez, Roberto	.122	19	49	3	6	1	0	1	4	4	13	0	0	R	R	6-0	175	5-5-76	1997	San Lorenzo, P.R.
Wilson, Scott	.248	44	141	28	35	9	1	6	21	24	36	0	2	R	R	6-2	200	1-11-75	1997	Carlsbad, Calif.

GAMES BY POSITION: C—Gick 28, Martine 47, Schmidt 6. **1B**—Chabot 7, Quaccia 60, Wilson 14. **2B**—Gentry 1, Maier 7, Macrory 66, Vazquez 5. **3B**—Gentry 49, Maier 2, Vazquez 6, Wilson 18. **SS**—Gentry 13, Kennedy 26, Maier 37, Vazquez 1. **OF**—Abell 10, Bevins 43, Farley 5, Kim 45, Lee 59, Mejia 30, Speckhardt 44.

PITCHING	W	L	ERA	G	GS	CG	SV	IP	H	R	ER	BB	SO	B	T	HT	WT	DOB	1st Yr	Resides
Arnold, Neal	0	2	3.93	23	0	0	0	37	35	21	16	9	27	R	R	6-5	230	5-21-75	1997	Kearney, Neb.
Brunette, Justin	1	0	7.94	6	0	0	0	6	13	6	5	0	6	L	L	6-1	200	10-7-75	1997	Huntington Beach, Calif.
Coogan, Patrick	2	5	3.70	10	10	0	0	56	56	27	23	14	37	R	R	6-3	185	9-12-75	1997	Baton Rouge, La.
Geis, John	0	0	3.00	3	0	0	0	3	2	1	1	3	3	L	L	6-2	191	12-21-73	1996	Central Square, N.Y.
Heffernan, Greg	0	2	2.57	26	0	0	9	28	23	9	8	7	31	R	R	6-2	180	9-18-74	1996	Guelph, Ontario
Huffaker, Mike	1	4	2.40	33	0	0	1	45	40	17	12	16	36	R	R	6-2	215	8-10-75	1997	Florence, Ala.
Jerue, Tristan	5	4	3.52	13	13	0	0	72	73	35	28	21	55	R	R	6-1	185	12-12-75	1997	Westfield, Mass.
Karnuth, Jason	4	1	1.86	7	7	0	0	39	33	8	8	9	23	R	R	6-2	190	5-15-76	1997	Glen Ellyn, Ill.
Levey, Joshua	1	3	5.35	18	3	0	0	34	31	21	20	14	25	R	R	6-2	185	10-29-74	1997	St. Louis, Mo.
McDougal, Mike	4	4	2.49	13	11	2	0	69	62	24	19	9	63	L	R	6-4	210	3-22-75	1994	Las Vegas, Nev.
Navarro, Jason	1	6	6.85	10	10	1	0	45	60	40	34	22	41	L	L	6-4	225	7-5-75	1997	Lilburn, Ga.
Rosario, Ruben	5	5	4.28	14	14	1	0	74	64	42	35	37	66	R	R	6-3	150	1-26-75	1993	Boca Chica, D.R.
Stechschulte, Gene	1	1	3.22	30	0	0	1	36	45	16	13	16	28	R	R	6-5	210	8-12-73	1996	Kalida, Ohio
Villafana, Jose	4	0	2.63	5	5	0	0	27	20	10	8	9	20	R	R	6-3	195	4-22-74	1995	Sylmar, Calif.
Wingerd, Josh	4	1	6.43	20	1	0	0	28	43	23	20	6	20	R	R	6-0	185	7-3-75	1997	Hood River, Ore.
Woodward, Finley	2	1	3.34	29	0	0	1	32	30	14	12	10	39	R	R	5-11	200	8-15-75	1997	Molino, Fla.

JOHNSON CITY — Rookie

APPALACHIAN LEAGUE

BATTING	AVG	G	AB	R	H	2B	3B	HR	RBI	BB	SO	SB	CS	B	T	HT	WT	DOB	1st Yr	Resides
Alfonso, Eliezer	.275	38	120	15	33	11	1	2	15	7	34	0	1	R	R	6-0	165	2-7-79	1996	Puerto la Cruz, Venez.
Araujo, Danilo	.251	54	187	33	47	7	3	1	24	32	42	8	7	R	R	5-10	160	1-17-77	1995	Peravia, D.R.
Darr, Ryan	.297	54	192	35	57	22	2	10	33	27	55	0	0	R	R	6-1	180	10-28-77	1996	Corona, Calif.
Davis, Tim	.059	13	34	4	2	0	0	0	0	1	12	2	0	R	R	6-0	180	1-16-78	1997	Pearson, Ga.
Diaz, Miguel	.283	59	223	33	63	17	1	4	28	7	32	1	3	R	R	5-11	160	9-29-77	1995	San Pedro de Macoris, D.R.
Eckelman, Alex	.321	49	165	30	53	13	1	7	27	10	23	3	1	R	R	5-11	187	7-16-74	1997	St. Louis, Mo.
Feramisco, Derek	.342	53	184	34	63	12	3	6	36	16	37	8	2	R	R	6-5	195	11-7-74	1997	Clovis, Calif.
Folkers, Brandon	.293	53	150	20	44	8	2	3	20	25	62	3	2	L	L	6-2	180	8-29-75	1997	St. Petersburg, Fla.
Gooden, Carl	.234	43	107	17	25	5	0	4	12	16	38	7	2	R	R	6-1	190	11-25-78	1997	Houston, Texas
Kalcounos, Andy	.130	9	23	4	3	1	0	0	2	7	10	0	0	R	R	6-3	210	8-17-75	1997	Silver Spring, Md.
Ledbetter, Blake	.119	16	42	2	5	1	0	0	2	0	15	0	0	R	R	6-2	210	3-9-77	1997	Bertrand, Mo.
Llibre, Brian	.267	33	105	17	28	10	0	4	22	7	25	1	1	R	R	6-4	201	9-16-77	1995	West Covina, Calif.
McIntyre, Remer	.187	39	107	11	20	3	2	0	3	7	38	0	2	R	R	5-10	180	11-23-78	1997	Tampa, Fla.
Ozuna, Pablo	.323	56	232	40	75	13	1	5	24	10	24	23	5	R	R	6-0	160	8-25-78	1996	Santo Domingo, D.R.
Rodriguez, Miguel	.105	8	19	1	2	0	0	0	0	0	8	0	0	R	R	5-10	170	5-18-77	1995	El Seibo, D.R.
Secoda, Joe	.251	52	187	21	47	5	0	3	16	17	56	4	3	R	R	6-1	190	11-19-77	1997	Fullerton, Calif.
Torres, Reynaldo	.140	34	107	4	15	1	0	1	4	6	58	0	0	R	R	6-5	235	3-14-79	1997	Guanica, P.R.
Williams, Jovany	.246	41	142	25	35	10	1	7	23	2	29	2	1	R	R	6-2	165	1-29-77	1994	San Pedro de Macoris, D.R.

GAMES BY POSITION: C—Alfonso 24, Ledbetter 5, Llibre 11, Williams 39. **1B**—Folkers 47, Llibre 6, Torres 27. **2B**—Araujo 51, Eckelman 14, Secoda 6. **3B**—Darr 52, Eckelman 11, Kalcounos 9, Secoda 3. **SS**—Darr 1, Eckelman 17, Ozuna 56, Secoda 1. **OF**—Davis 13, Diaz 57, Eckelman 4, Feramisco 26, Folkers 4, Gooden 39, McIntyre 36, Rodriguez 1, Secoda 45.

PITCHING	W	L	ERA	G	GS	CG	SV	IP	H	R	ER	BB	SO	B	T	HT	WT	DOB	1st Yr	Resides
Folkers, Brandon	0	0	4.15	4	0	0	0	4	8	2	2	0	6	L	L	6-2	180	8-29-75	1997	St. Petersburg, Fla.
Franks, Lance	0	0	1.17	26	0	0	12	31	16	4	4	7	40	R	R	5-11	180	8-20-75	1997	Russellville, Ark.
Garcia, Wilson	0	2	6.66	25	3	0	0	49	78	59	36	21	44	R	R	6-1	174	7-27-79	1997	Azua, D.R.
Geis, John	3	4	3.98	30	0	0	0	41	44	27	18	15	57	L	L	6-2	191	12-21-73	1996	Central Square, N.Y.
Gooden, Derek	2	2	3.72	31	0	0	1	36	41	22	15	21	48	R	R	6-0	175	6-26-75	1997	Adel, Ga.
Guzman, Toribio	1	7	8.44	13	13	0	0	64	91	75	60	26	49	R	R	6-3	165	7-6-76	1994	Peravia, D.R.
Hogge, Shawn	0	1	5.11	3	3	0	0	12	16	9	7	6	10	R	R	5-11	190	11-29-77	1996	Las Vegas, Nev.
Hopson, Craig	1	3	9.93	15	4	0	0	29	44	43	32	32	23	R	R	6-1	195	2-20-79	1997	Rockford, Ill.
Lambert, Jeremy	1	1	9.19	27	0	0	1	32	46	42	33	37	29	R	R	6-1	192	1-10-79	1997	Kearns, Utah
Lanfranco, Otoniel	2	8	7.64	14	14	0	0	68	85	60	58	31	69	R	R	6-0	160	7-17-76	1996	Cotui, D.R.
Miller, Matt	2	2	7.88	20	3	0	0	40	62	43	35	16	32	R	R	6-0	180	6-22-74	1997	Greensburg, Ind.
Norris, Stephen	4	7	5.90	14	14	0	0	72	84	64	47	42	72	L	L	6-1	185	2-1-76	1996	Fort Worth, Texas
Ortega, Franklin	3	4	7.30	18	7	1	0	49	62	46	40	39	46	R	R	5-11	160	12-2-73	1991	San Pedro de Macoris, D.R.
Rodriguez, Jose	0	0	4.05	4	0	0	0	7	4	3	3	3	8	L	L	6-1	205	12-18-74	1997	Cayey, P.R.
Rojas, Francisco	1	1	5.40	6	0	0	0	10	11	8	6	8	9	R	R	5-10	163	7-2-76	1995	Santo Domingo, D.R.
Tuttle, John	2	3	7.88	7	7	0	0	32	35	30	28	15	24	L	R	6-3	185	11-9-77	1996	San Marino, Calif.

San Diego PADRES

Manager: Bruce Bochy.

1997 Record: 76-86, .469 (4th, NL West)

BATTING	AVG	G	AB	R	H	2B	3B	HR	RBI	BB	SO	SB	CS	B	T	HT	WT	DOB	1st Yr	Resides
Arias, George	.227	11	22	2	5	1	0	0	2	0	1	0	0	R	R	5-11	190	3-12-72	1993	Tucson, Ariz.
Beamon, Trey	.277	43	65	5	18	3	0	0	7	2	17	1	2	L	R	6-3	195	2-11-74	1992	Dallas, Texas
Caminiti, Ken	.290	137	486	92	141	28	0	26	90	80	118	11	2	S	R	6-0	200	4-21-63	1985	Richmond, Texas
Cianfrocco, Archi	.245	89	220	25	54	12	0	4	26	25	80	7	1	R	R	6-5	200	10-6-66	1987	Rome, N.Y.
Finley, Steve	.261	143	560	101	146	26	5	28	92	43	92	15	3	L	L	6-2	180	3-12-65	1987	Houston, Texas
Flaherty, John	.273	129	439	38	120	21	1	9	46	33	62	4	4	R	R	6-1	202	10-21-67	1988	West Nyack, N.Y.
Gomez, Chris	.253	150	522	62	132	19	2	5	54	53	114	5	8	R	R	6-1	183	6-16-71	1992	Lakewood, Calif.
Gwynn, Tony	.372	149	592	97	220	49	2	17	119	43	28	12	5	L	L	5-11	210	5-9-60	1981	San Diego, Calif.
Henderson, Rickey	.274	88	288	63	79	11	0	6	27	71	62	29	4	R	L	5-10	195	12-25-58	1976	Oakland, Calif.
Hernandez, Carlos	.313	50	134	15	42	7	1	3	14	3	27	0	2	R	R	5-11	185	5-24-67	1985	Caracas, Venez.
Jones, Chris	.243	92	152	24	37	9	0	7	25	16	45	7	2	R	R	6-2	205	11-16-65	1984	Cedar Rapids, Iowa
Joyner, Wally	.327	135	455	59	149	29	2	13	83	51	51	3	5	L	L	6-2	200	6-16-62	1983	Lee's Summit, Mo.
Lee, Derrek	.259	22	54	9	14	3	0	1	4	9	24	0	0	R	R	6-5	220	9-6-75	1993	Folsom, Calif.
Livingstone, Scott	.154	23	26	1	4	1	0	0	3	2	1	0	0	L	R	6-0	198	7-15-65	1988	Southlake, Texas
Plantier, Phil	.125	10	8	0	1	0	0	0	0	2	3	0	0	L	R	5-11	195	1-27-69	1987	San Diego, Calif.
Rivera, Ruben	.250	17	20	2	5	1	0	0	1	2	9	2	1	R	R	6-3	190	11-14-73	1992	Chorrera, Panama
Romero, Mandy	.208	21	48	7	10	0	0	2	4	2	18	1	0	S	R	5-11	196	10-19-67	1988	Miami, Fla.
Shipley, Craig	.273	63	139	22	38	9	0	5	19	7	20	1	1	R	R	6-0	168	1-7-63	1984	Jupiter, Fla.
Shumpert, Terry	.273	13	33	4	9	3	0	1	6	3	4	0	0	R	R	5-11	185	8-16-66	1987	Paducah, Ky.
Slaught, Don	.000	20	20	2	0	0	0	0	0	5	4	0	0	R	R	6-1	190	9-11-58	1980	Arlington, Texas
Sweeney, Mark	.320	71	103	11	33	4	0	2	19	11	18	2	2	L	L	6-1	195	10-26-69	1991	Holliston, Mass.
2-team (44 St. Louis)	.280	115	164	16	46	7	0	2	23	20	32	2	3							
Vaughn, Greg	.216	120	361	60	78	10	0	18	57	56	110	7	4	R	R	6-0	205	7-3-65	1986	Elk Grove, Calif.
Velandia, Jorge	.103	14	29	0	3	2	0	0	0	1	7	0	0	R	R	5-9	160	1-12-75	1992	Caracas, Venez.
Veras, Quilvio	.265	145	539	74	143	23	1	3	45	72	84	33	12	S	R	5-8	168	4-3-71	1990	Santo Domingo, D.R.

PITCHING	W	L	ERA	G	GS	CG	SV	IP	H	R	ER	BB	SO	B	T	HT	WT	DOB	1st Yr	Resides
Ashby, Andy	9	11	4.13	30	30	2	0	201	207	108	92	49	144	R	R	6-5	180	7-11-67	1986	Kansas City, Mo.
Batchelor, Rich	2	0	7.82	13	0	0	0	13	19	11	11	7	10	R	R	6-1	195	4-8-67	1990	Hartsville, S.C.
2-team (10 St. Louis)	3	1	5.97	23	0	0	0	29	40	23	19	14	18							
Bergman, Sean	2	4	6.09	44	9	0	0	99	126	72	67	38	74	R	R	6-4	205	4-11-70	1991	Joliet, Ill.
Bochtler, Doug	3	6	4.77	54	0	0	2	60	51	35	32	50	46	R	R	6-3	200	7-5-70	1989	West Palm Beach, Fla.
Bruske, Jim	4	1	3.63	28	0	0	0	45	37	22	18	25	32	R	R	6-1	185	10-7-64	1986	Palmdale, Calif.
Burrows, Terry	0	2	10.45	13	0	0	0	10	12	13	12	8	8	L	L	6-1	185	11-28-68	1990	Lake Charles, La.
Cunnane, Will	6	3	5.81	54	8	0	0	91	114	69	59	49	79	R	R	6-2	165	4-24-74	1993	Congers, N.Y.
Erdos, Todd	2	0	5.27	11	0	0	0	14	17	9	8	4	13	R	R	6-1	205	11-21-73	1992	Meadville, Pa.
Hamilton, Joey	12	7	4.25	31	29	1	0	193	199	100	91	69	124	R	R	6-4	220	9-9-70	1991	Statesboro, Ga.
Hitchcock, Sterling	10	11	5.20	32	28	1	0	161	172	102	93	55	106	L	L	6-1	195	4-29-71	1989	Seffner, Fla.
Hoffman, Trevor	6	4	2.66	70	0	0	37	81	59	25	24	24	111	R	R	6-0	195	10-13-67	1989	Williamsville, N.Y.
Jackson, Danny	1	7	7.53	13	9	0	0	49	72	47	41	20	19	R	L	6-0	205	1-5-62	1982	Lincolnshire, Ill.
2-team (4 St. Louis)	2	9	7.58	17	13	0	0	68	98	64	57	28	32							
Kroon, Marc	0	1	7.15	12	0	0	0	11	14	9	9	5	12	S	R	6-2	175	4-2-73	1991	Phoenix, Ariz.
Long, Joey	0	0	8.18	10	0	0	0	11	17	11	10	8	8	R	L	6-2	215	7-15-70	1991	Rosewood, Ohio
Menhart, Paul	2	3	4.70	9	8	0	0	44	42	23	23	13	22	R	R	6-2	190	3-25-69	1990	Conyers, Ga.
Murray, Heath	1	2	6.75	17	3	0	0	33	50	25	25	21	16	L	L	6-4	205	4-19-73	1994	Troy, Ohio
Scott, Tim	1	1	7.85	14	0	0	0	18	25	17	16	5	14	R	R	6-2	205	11-16-66	1984	Hanford, Calif.
Smith, Pete	7	6	4.81	37	15	0	1	118	120	66	63	52	68	R	R	6-2	200	2-27-66	1984	Smyrna, Ga.
Valenzuela, Fernando	2	8	4.75	13	13	1	0	66	84	42	35	32	51	L	L	5-11	202	11-1-60	1978	Los Angeles, Calif.
Veras, Dario	2	1	5.11	23	0	0	0	25	28	18	14	12	21	R	R	6-2	165	3-13-73	1991	Villa Vasquez, D.R.
Worrell, Tim	4	8	5.16	60	10	0	3	106	116	67	61	50	81	R	R	6-4	215	7-5-67	1990	Arcadia, Calif.

FIELDING

Catcher	PCT	G	PO	A	E	DP
Flaherty	.987	124	753	65	11	13
Hernandez	.989	44	234	26	3	1
Romero	1.000	19	96	8	0	0
Slaught	1.000	6	15	3	0	0

First Base	PCT	G	PO	A	E	DP
Cianfrocco	.983	39	219	19	4	16
Hernandez	1.000	4	5	3	0	0
Joyner	.996	131	1027	89	4	82
Lee	1.000	21	131	13	0	12
Shipley	.933	4	28	0	2	0
Sweeney	.964	7	24	3	1	4

Second Base	PCT	G	PO	A	E	DP
Cianfrocco	1.000	12	15	23	0	7
Shipley	.984	16	24	36	1	8
Shumpert	.973	7	21	15	1	4
Velandia	.929	5	7	6	1	1
Veras	.984	142	276	407	11	65

Third Base	PCT	G	PO	A	E	DP
Arias	.941	8	4	12	1	0
Caminiti	.941	133	90	291	24	20
Cianfrocco	.978	38	24	67	2	4
Livingstone	.750	3	1	5	2	0
Shipley	.000	2	0	0	0	0
Shumpert	.750	2	1	2	1	0
Velandia	.833	3	0	5	1	0

Shortstop	PCT	G	PO	A	E	DP
Cianfrocco	.909	5	3	7	1	0
Gomez	.978	150	226	433	15	79
Shipley	.947	21	17	37	3	5
Velandia	.941	6	4	12	1	4

Outfield	PCT	G	PO	A	E	DP
Beamon	.909	20	17	3	2	0
Cianfrocco	1.000	2	1	0	0	0
Finley	.989	140	338	10	4	3
Gwynn	.983	143	218	8	4	3
Henderson	.959	78	160	4	7	1
Jones	.951	61	73	4	4	1
Plantier	1.000	3	3	0	0	0
Rivera	1.000	7	13	0	0	0
Shumpert	1.000	3	1	0	0	0
Sweeney	.944	20	17	0	1	0
Vaughn	.994	94	153	7	1	0

FARM SYSTEM

Director of Player Development: Jim Skaalen

Class	Farm Team	League	W	L	Pct.	Finish*	Manager	First Yr
AAA	Las Vegas (Nev.) Stars	Pacific Coast	56	85	.397	10th (10)	Jerry Royster	1983
AA	Mobile (Ala.) BayBears	Southern	69	68	.504	5th (10)	Mike Ramsey	1997
#A	Rancho Cuca. (Calif.) Quakes	California	77	63	.550	2nd (10)	Mike Basso	1993
A	Clinton (Iowa) Lumber Kings	Midwest	65	71	.478	10th (14)	Tom LeVasseur	1995
#R	Idaho Falls (Idaho) Braves	Pioneer	39	32	.549	2nd (8)	Don Werner	1995
R	Peoria (Ariz.) Padres	Arizona	25	30	.455	5th (6)	Randy Whisler	1988

*Finish in overall standings (No. of teams in league) #Advanced level

ORGANIZATION LEADERS

MAJOR LEAGUERS

BATTING

*AVG	Tony Gwynn	.372
R	Steve Finley	101
H	Tony Gwynn	220
TB	Tony Gwynn	324
2B	Tony Gwynn	49
3B	Steve Finley	5
HR	Steve Finley	28
RBI	Tony Gwynn	119
BB	Ken Caminitii	80
SO	Ken Caminiti	118
SB	Quilvio Veras	33

PITCHING

W	Joey Hamilton	12
L	Two tied at	11
#ERA	Trevor Hoffman	2.66
G	Trevor Hoffman	70
CG	Andy Ashby	2
SV	Trevor Hoffman	37
IP	Andy Ashby	201
BB	Joey Hamilton	69
SO	Andy Ashby	144

MORRIS FOSTOFF

Trevor Hoffman

Matt Clement

MINOR LEAGUERS

BATTING

*AVG	Mike Mitchell, Rancho Cucamonga	.350
R	Mike Darr, Rancho Cucamonga	104
H	Mike Darr, Rancho Cucamonga	179
TB	Mike Darr, Rancho Cucamonga	278
2B	Mike Mitchell, Rancho Cucamonga	36
3B	Three tied at	11
HR	Three tied at	17
RBI	Mike Mitchell, Rancho Cucamonga	106
BB	Brian McClure, Clinton	90
SO	Rodney Lindsey, Clinton	161
SB	Rodney Lindsey, Clinton	70

PITCHING

W	Eric Newman, Rancho Cucamonga	13
L	Brad Kaufman, Las Vegas/Mobile	18
#ERA	Matt Clement, Mobile/Rancho Cuca.	2.05
G	James Sak, Rancho Cucamonga	57
CG	Domingo Guzman, Rancho Cuca./Clinton	5
SV	Two tied at	27
IP	Matt Clement, Mobile/Rancho Cuca.	189
BB	Brad Kaufman, Las Vegas/Mobile	81
SO	Matt Clement, Mobile/Rancho Cuca.	2 01

*Minimum 250 At-Bats #Minimum 75 Innings

TOP 10 PROSPECTS

FRANK RAGSDALE

Derrek Lee

How the Padres Top 10 prospects, as judged by Baseball America prior to the 1997 season, fared in 1997:

Player, Pos.	Club (Class)	AVG	AB	R	H	2B	3B	HR	RBI	SB
1. Derrek Lee, 1b	San Diego	.259	54	9	14	3	0	1	4	0
	Las Vegas (AAA)	.325	468	85	152	29	2	13	64	17
2. Juan Melo, ss	Las Vegas (AAA)	.271	48	6	13	4	0	1	6	0
	Mobile (AA)	.287	456	52	131	22	2	7	67	7
3. Ben Davis, c	Rancho Cucamonga (A)	.278	474	67	132	30	1	17	76	3
4. Gabe Alvarez, 3b	Mobile (AA)	.300	427	71	128	28	2	14	78	1
7. *Vernon Maxwell, of	Oneonta (A)	.196	148	14	29	6	2	0	22	7
8. Matt Halloran, ss	Clinton (A)	.201	154	19	31	7	0	1	22	9
		W	L	ERA	G	SV	IP	H	BB	SO
5. Heath Murray, lhp	San Diego	1	2	6.75	17	0	33	50	21	16
	Las Vegas (AAA)	6	8	5.45	19	0	109	142	41	99
6. Todd Erdos, rhp	San Diego	2	0	5.27	11	0	14	17	4	13
	Mobile (AA)	1	4	3.36	55	27	59	45	22	49
9. Matt Clement, rhp	Mobile (AA)	6	5	2.56	13	0	88	83	32	92
	Rancho Cucamonga (A)	6	3	1.60	14	0	101	74	31	109
10. Marc Kroon, rhp	San Diego	0	1	7.15	12	0	11	14	5	12
	Las Vegas (AAA)	1	3	4.54	46	15	42	34	22	53

*Traded to Yankees

PACIFIC COAST LEAGUE

BATTING	AVG	G	AB	R	H	2B	3B	HR	RBI	BB	SO	SB	CS	B	T	HT	WT	DOB	1st Yr	Resides
Arias, George	.333	10	30	4	10	4	1	1	5	3	8	0	0	R	R	5-11	190	3-12-72	1993	Tucson, Ariz.
2-team (105 Van.)	.283	115	431	75	122	32	4	12	65	42	59	3	4							
Beamon, Trey	.328	90	329	64	108	19	4	5	49	48	58	14	6	L	R	6-3	195	2-11-74	1992	Dallas, Texas
Briggs, Stoney	.269	119	435	58	117	21	5	11	57	28	122	18	12	R	R	6-3	215	12-26-71	1991	Seaford, Del.
Brown, Ray	.257	41	140	12	36	13	0	2	15	11	28	1	0	L	R	6-2	205	7-30-72	1994	Redding, Calif.
Bush, Homer	.277	38	155	25	43	10	1	3	14	7	40	5	1	R	R	5-11	180	11-11-72	1991	East St. Louis, Ill.
Colbert, Craig	1.000	2	2	0	2	1	0	0	0	0	0	0	0	R	R	6-0	214	2-13-65	1986	Pearland, Texas
Dascenzo, Doug	.277	109	433	61	120	23	4	9	45	45	42	16	8	S	L	5-8	160	6-30-64	1985	La Belle, Pa.
Encarnacion, Angelo	.245	79	253	27	62	12	1	3	23	15	32	1	5	R	R	5-8	180	4-18-73	1990	Santo Domingo, D.R.
Gonzales, Rene	.186	13	43	2	8	1	0	0	3	6	6	0	0	R	R	6-3	215	9-3-61	1982	Newport Beach, Calif.
Hajek, Dave	.340	41	156	25	53	14	1	0	25	14	6	7	2	R	R	5-10	165	10-14-67	1990	Colorado Springs, Colo.
Helfand, Eric	.315	80	238	31	75	21	1	6	33	28	47	1	1	L	R	6-0	210	3-25-69	1990	San Diego, Calif.
Hernandez, Carlos	.400	3	10	1	4	0	0	1	5	1	3	0	0	R	R	5-11	185	5-24-67	1985	Caracas, Venez.
Joyner, Wally	.250	3	8	1	2	0	0	0	1	0	1	0	0	L	L	6-2	200	6-16-62	1983	Lee's Summit, Mo.
Keefe, Jamie	.190	42	58	10	11	2	2	1	6	10	24	0	1	R	R	5-11	180	8-29-73	1992	Rochester, N.H.
Lee, Derek	.294	75	231	22	68	16	1	5	35	32	35	4	1	L	R	6-1	200	7-28-66	1988	Reston, Va.
Lee, Derrek	.324	125	472	86	153	29	2	13	64	60	116	17	3	R	R	6-5	220	9-6-75	1993	Folsom, Calif.
Melo, Juan	.271	12	48	6	13	4	0	1	6	1	10	0	0	S	R	6-3	185	11-5-76	1994	Bani, D.R.
Plantier, Phil	.429	15	56	13	24	6	0	5	9	4	8	1	1	L	R	5-11	195	1-27-69	1987	San Diego, Calif.
Poe, Charles	.261	54	180	28	47	9	3	8	34	22	32	1	2	R	R	6-0	185	11-9-71	1990	West Covina, Calif.
Rivera, Ruben	.250	12	48	6	12	5	1	1	6	1	20	1	0	R	R	6-3	190	11-14-73	1992	Chorrera, Panama
Romero, Mandy	.308	33	91	19	28	4	1	3	13	11	19	0	0	S	R	5-11	196	10-19-67	1988	Miami, Fla.
Scarsone, Steve	.231	82	251	37	58	13	1	11	35	38	78	2	2	R	R	6-2	170	4-11-66	1986	Anaheim, Calif.
Shipley, Craig	.316	6	19	0	6	3	0	0	1	0	5	0	0	R	R	6-0	168	1-7-63	1984	Jupiter, Fla.
Shumpert, Terry	.284	32	109	18	31	8	1	1	16	9	20	3	0	R	R	5-11	185	8-16-66	1987	Paducah, Ky.
Tatum, Jim	.317	44	161	21	51	12	1	9	25	8	39	1	2	R	R	6-2	200	10-9-67	1985	Lakeside, Calif.
Tredaway, Chad	.257	116	409	58	105	23	1	7	50	34	63	6	4	S	R	6-0	193	6-18-72	1992	Mission, Texas
Velandia, Jorge	.272	114	405	46	110	15	2	3	35	29	62	13	3	R	R	5-9	160	1-12-75	1992	Caracas, Venez.

PITCHING	W	L	ERA	G	GS	CG	SV	IP	H	R	ER	BB	SO	B	T	HT	WT	DOB	1st Yr	Resides
Baron, Jim	0	0	11.25	4	0	0	0	4	8	5	5	3	3	L	L	6-3	230	2-22-74	1992	Humble, Texas
Batchelor, Rich	3	0	6.43	15	0	0	0	21	23	15	15	8	19	R	R	6-1	195	4-8-67	1990	Hartsville, S.C.
Berumen, Andres	2	0	5.45	18	1	0	0	33	49	26	20	16	35	R	R	6-1	205	4-5-71	1989	Banning, Calif.
Boze, Marshall	0	7	7.62	14	8	0	0	52	68	51	44	29	44	R	R	6-1	212	5-23-71	1990	Springfield, Ill.
Bruske, Jim	5	4	4.90	16	9	0	0	68	73	41	37	22	67	R	R	6-1	185	10-7-64	1986	Palmdale, Calif.
Burrows, Terry	1	5	6.42	31	1	0	2	34	44	24	24	19	26	L	L	6-1	185	11-28-68	1990	Lake Charles, La.
Castillo, Marino	6	5	5.14	30	19	0	0	126	146	88	72	43	102	R	R	6-0	168	3-17-71	1990	Boca Chica, D.R.
Daspit, Jamie	0	1	7.20	10	2	0	0	20	22	17	16	7	12	R	R	6-7	210	8-10-69	1990	Sacramento, Calif.
Drahman, Brian	2	1	6.33	33	0	0	1	43	51	32	30	28	39	R	R	6-3	231	11-7-66	1986	Fort Lauderdale, Fla.
Hancock, Ryan	0	0	12.60	4	0	0	0	5	9	7	7	4	3	R	R	6-2	220	11-11-71	1993	Cupertino, Calif.
2-team (39 Van.)	3	3	4.20	43	2	0	2	79	81	44	37	40	63							
Hook, Chris	0	7	8.79	19	8	0	0	56	80	64	55	49	35	R	R	6-5	195	8-4-68	1989	Florence, Ky.
Kaufman, Brad	0	5	8.07	6	6	0	0	32	40	37	29	15	19	R	R	6-2	210	4-26-72	1993	Traer, Iowa
Kroon, Marc	1	3	4.54	46	0	0	15	42	34	22	21	22	53	S	R	6-2	175	4-2-73	1991	Phoenix, Ariz.
Long, Joey	0	0	4.82	16	0	0	0	19	17	10	10	12	13	R	L	6-2	215	7-15-70	1991	Rosewood, Ohio
Maddux, Mike	0	2	5.63	3	3	0	0	16	23	11	10	9	13	L	R	6-2	188	8-27-61	1982	Las Vegas, Nev.
2-team (1 Tacoma)	0	2	4.29	4	4	0	0	21	24	11	10	11	18							
Medina, Rafael	4	5	7.56	13	13	0	0	67	90	60	56	39	50	R	R	6-3	194	2-15-75	1993	Panama City, Panama
Menhart, Paul	0	7	5.97	11	11	1	0	66	78	46	44	21	44	R	R	6-2	190	3-25-69	1990	Conyers, Ga.
2-team (15 Tacoma)	4	14	6.06	26	21	1	1	128	154	92	86	55	95							
Mintz, Steve	5	2	8.05	27	0	0	5	35	50	31	31	17	28	L	R	5-11	190	11-24-68	1990	Leland, N.C.
Munoz, Bobby	0	2	9.93	17	1	0	0	23	30	26	25	11	13	R	R	6-7	237	3-3-68	1989	Hialeah, Fla.
Murray, Heath	6	8	5.45	19	19	2	0	109	142	72	66	41	99	L	L	6-4	205	4-19-73	1994	Troy, Ohio
Scanlan, Bob	3	1	3.53	36	1	0	1	51	51	24	20	17	20	R	R	6-8	215	8-9-66	1984	Beverly Hills, Calif.
Schmitt, Todd	5	2	5.03	48	0	0	4	54	55	34	30	38	59	R	R	6-2	170	2-12-70	1992	Clinton Township, Mich.
Smith, Pete	3	2	4.28	6	6	0	0	34	38	16	16	6	24	R	R	6-2	200	2-27-66	1984	Smyrna, Ga.
Spencer, Stan	3	2	3.75	8	8	0	0	48	48	23	20	18	47	R	R	6-3	195	8-2-68	1991	Battleground, Wash.
Taylor, Kerry	7	9	4.31	22	22	3	0	144	150	84	69	55	103	R	R	6-3	200	1-25-71	1989	Roseau, Minn.
Taylor, Scott	0	0	18.00	2	0	0	0	1	4	2	2	1	1	R	R	6-3	200	10-3-66	1989	Wichita, Kan.
Veras, Dario	0	2	5.02	12	0	0	2	14	14	8	8	6	13	R	R	6-2	165	3-13-73	1991	Villa Vazquez, D.R.
Zancanaro, Dave	0	3	15.53	3	3	0	0	13	27	24	23	8	9	S	L	6-1	180	1-8-69	1990	Carmichael, Calif.

FIELDING

Catcher	PCT	G	PO	A	E	DP	PB
Encarnacion	.983	69	453	61	9	6	9
Helfand	.987	65	434	30	6	3	10
Hernandez	1.000	3	15	2	0	0	0
Romero	.983	20	112	6	2	2	3

First Base	PCT	G	PO	A	E	DP
Brown	1.000	12	92	3	0	9
Joyner	1.000	3	16	1	0	0
Derrek Lee	.992	124	1069	111	9	108
Rivera	1.000	1	1	0	0	0
Romero	1.000	4	32	1	0	5
Scarsone	1.000	4	30	2	0	1
Tatum	.960	4	22	2	1	3

Second Base	PCT	G	PO	A	E	DP
Bush	.978	36	73	103	4	25
Hajek	.989	39	64	121	2	24
Keefe	.882	6	3	12	2	2
Scarsone	.990	42	70	131	2	22
Shipley	1.000	1	2	1	0	0
Shumpert	.925	9	15	22	3	4
Tredaway	.939	23	39	54	6	14

Third Base	PCT	G	PO	A	E	DP
Arias	.913	9	6	15	2	1
Gonzales	.935	12	4	25	2	2
Romero	.667	5	1	1	1	0
Scarsone	.873	24	9	39	7	4
Shipley	1.000	1	0	1	0	0
Shumpert	1.000	14	9	21	0	2
Tatum	1.000	8	7	9	0	0
Tredaway	.924	89	66	141	17	26

Shortstop	PCT	G	PO	A	E	DP
Keefe	.875	1	6	1	1	1
Melo	.936	12	11	33	3	7
Scarsone	.929	12	15	37	4	11
Shipley	1.000	2	1	3	0	0
Shumpert	.966	9	13	15	1	5
Velandia	.961	113	170	347	21	69

Outfield	PCT	G	PO	A	E	DP
Beamon	.967	77	111	7	4	1
Briggs	.932	110	181	10	14	2
Brown	.938	27	30	0	2	0
Dascenzo	.992	105	238	6	2	0
Encarnacion	.667	5	2	0	1	0
Keefe	.952	11	20	0	1	0
Derek Lee	1.000	37	46	8	0	2
Plantier	1.000	9	17	2	0	0
Poe	1.000	43	63	4	0	0
Scarsone	1.000	1	2	0	0	0
Shipley	1.000	1	1	0	0	0
Tatum	1.000	30	27	2	0	0

LARRY GOREN

San Diego's Tony Gwynn

LARRY GOREN

Rancho Cucamonga's Ben Davis

MOBILE — Class AA

SOUTHERN LEAGUE

BATTING	AVG	G	AB	R	H	2B	3B	HR	RBI	BB	SO	SB	CS	B	T	HT	WT	DOB	1st Yr	Resides
Allen, Dusty	.253	131	475	85	120	28	4	17	75	81	116	1	4	R	R	6-4	215	8-9-72	1995	Oklahoma City, Okla.
Alvarez, Gabe	.300	114	427	71	128	28	2	14	78	51	64	1	1	R	R	6-1	185	3-6-74	1995	El Monte, Calif.
Bowie, Jim	.241	32	54	4	13	2	0	1	10	10	5	0	0	L	L	6-0	200	2-17-65	1986	Suisun City, Calif.
Brinkley, Darryl	.307	55	215	41	66	14	1	5	33	26	30	10	9	R	R	5-11	205	12-23-68	1994	Stamford, Conn.
Brown, Ray	.352	57	179	28	63	16	0	4	30	33	33	1	0	L	R	6-2	205	7-30-72	1994	Redding, Calif.
Finley, Steve	.500	1	4	1	2	0	0	1	2	1	2	0	0	L	L	6-2	180	3-12-65	1987	Houston, Texas
Gama, Rick	.288	88	295	56	85	16	2	6	43	51	41	9	3	R	R	5-10	180	4-27-73	1995	Mexico City, Mexico
Gonzalez, Wikleman	.273	47	143	15	39	7	1	4	25	10	12	1	1	R	R	5-11	175	5-17-74	1992	Palo Negro, Venez.
Guiel, Aaron	.385	8	26	9	10	2	0	1	9	5	4	1	0	L	R	5-10	190	10-5-72	1993	Langley, B.C.
Hills, Rich	.250	71	216	37	54	12	1	5	30	25	34	2	0	R	R	6-0	195	7-28-73	1995	Springdale, Ark.
Johnson, Earl	.254	78	307	52	78	11	3	1	22	21	56	35	13	R	R	5-9	163	10-3-71	1991	Detroit, Mich.
Keefe, Jamie	.268	16	41	4	11	2	1	0	3	5	12	2	1	R	R	5-11	180	8-29-73	1992	Rochester, N.H.
Killeen, Tim	.202	66	168	23	34	8	1	5	21	53	60	0	1	L	R	6-0	195	7-26-70	1992	Phoenix, Ariz.
LaRocca, Greg	.267	76	300	44	80	16	2	3	31	26	46	8	3	R	R	5-11	185	11-10-72	1994	Bedford, N.H.
Mashore, Justin	.238	90	281	53	67	10	5	11	41	32	70	11	8	R	R	5-9	190	2-14-72	1991	Concord, Calif.
Matthews, Gary	.244	28	90	14	22	4	1	2	12	15	29	3	1	S	R	6-3	185	8-25-74	1994	Canoga Park, Calif.
Melo, Juan	.287	113	456	52	131	22	2	7	67	29	90	7	9	S	R	6-3	185	11-5-76	1994	Bani, D.R.
Poe, Charles	.311	53	193	30	60	7	4	3	35	11	43	5	1	R	R	6-0	185	11-9-71	1990	West Covina, Calif.
Powers, John	.250	14	48	8	12	0	0	1	8	8	9	2	0	L	R	5-9	165	6-2-74	1996	Scottsdale, Ariz.
Prieto, Chris	.320	109	388	80	124	22	9	2	58	59	55	26	6	L	L	5-11	180	8-24-72	1993	Carmel, Calif.
Romero, Mandy	.320	61	222	50	71	22	0	13	52	38	31	0	1	S	R	5-11	196	10-19-67	1988	Miami, Fla.
Schwenke, Matt	.000	1	1	0	0	0	0	0	0	0	0	0	0	S	R	6-2	210	8-12-72	1993	Loomis, Calif.
Tredaway, Chad	.083	4	12	2	1	0	0	0	0	2	1	0	0	S	R	6-0	193	6-18-72	1992	Mission, Texas

PITCHING	W	L	ERA	G	GS	CG	SV	IP	H	R	ER	BB	SO	B	T	HT	WT	DOB	1st Yr	Resides
Anderson, Bill	0	0	1.86	7	0	0	0	10	8	3	2	6	6	R	R	6-0	190	9-23-71	1994	Queensbury, N.Y.
Baron, Jim	2	4	4.54	19	1	0	0	34	35	21	17	13	30	L	L	6-3	230	2-22-74	1992	Humble, Texas
Castillo, Marino	0	1	4.32	8	0	0	1	8	14	4	4	5	10	R	R	6-0	168	3-17-71	1990	Boca Chica, D.R.
Clayton, Craig	0	0	0.00	3	0	0	0	2	1	0	0	3	2	R	R	6-0	185	11-29-70	1991	Anaheim, Calif.
Clement, Matt	6	5	2.56	13	13	1	0	88	83	37	25	32	92	R	R	6-3	190	8-12-74	1994	Butler, Pa.
Dixon, Bubba	7	2	3.45	56	0	0	1	76	67	31	29	37	88	R	L	5-10	165	1-7-72	1994	Lucedale, Miss.
Erdos, Todd	1	4	3.36	55	0	0	27	59	45	22	22	22	49	R	R	6-1	205	11-21-73	1992	Meadville, Pa.
Kaufman, Brad	5	13	6.18	22	22	1	0	125	138	97	86	66	103	R	R	6-2	210	4-26-72	1993	Traer, Iowa
Runyan, Sean	5	2	2.34	40	1	0	1	62	54	25	16	28	52	L	L	6-3	200	6-21-74	1992	Urbandale, Iowa
Skrmetta, Matt	2	3	5.23	21	0	0	1	33	32	21	19	21	30	S	R	6-3	220	11-6-72	1993	Satellite Beach, Fla.
Smith, Cam	3	5	7.03	26	15	0	1	79	85	70	62	73	88	R	R	6-3	190	9-20-73	1993	Selkirk, N.Y.
Taylor, Kerry	2	1	4.85	5	5	0	0	26	27	14	14	13	30	R	R	6-3	200	1-25-71	1989	Roseau, Minn.
Tollberg, Brian	6	3	3.72	31	13	1	0	123	123	60	51	24	108	R	R	6-3	195	9-16-72	1994	Bradenton, Fla.
VanDeWeg, Ryan	9	8	5.43	27	27	2	0	159	198	105	96	55	81	R	R	6-0	180	2-24-74	1995	West Olive, Mich.
Veras, Dario	0	0	9.00	5	2	0	0	5	8	5	5	3	5	R	R	6-2	165	3-13-73	1991	Villa Vazquez, D.R.

PITCHING	W	L	ERA	G	GS	CG	SV	IP	H	R	ER	BB	SO	B	T	HT	WT	DOB	1st Yr	Resides
Walters, Brett	10	7	4.47	31	19	0	0	145	169	85	72	30	98	R	R	6-0	185	9-30-74	1994	Bateman, Australia
Wolff, Bryan	1	2	4.80	20	0	0	0	30	34	18	16	19	37	R	R	6-1	195	3-16-72	1993	St. Louis, Mo.
Zancanaro, Dave	10	8	4.44	27	19	3	1	134	140	69	66	57	66	S	L	6-1	180	1-8-69	1990	Carmichael, Calif.

FIELDING

Catcher	PCT	G	PO	A	E	DP	PB
Gonzalez	.989	41	250	24	3	0	6
Killeen	.982	53	313	20	6	4	2
Romero	.987	57	436	33	6	2	7

First Base	PCT	G	PO	A	E	DP
Allen	.980	76	585	53	13	43
Bowie	1.000	7	36	2	0	3
Brown	.974	35	287	18	8	23
Hills	.995	23	187	19	1	29
Killeen	1.000	6	30	2	0	1

Second Base	PCT	G	PO	A	E	DP
Gama	.978	68	138	127	6	25
Hills	.944	4	9	8	1	2
Keefe	1.000	2	0	2	0	0
LaRocca	.990	68	132	164	3	38
Powers	1.000	2	3	5	0	1
Tredaway	1.000	2	7	6	0	2

Third Base	PCT	G	PO	A	E	DP
Alvarez	.892	107	65	200	32	17
Hills	.923	13	5	31	3	2
Keefe	1.000	2	0	5	0	1
LaRocca	1.000	1	1	2	0	0
Mashore	.833	7	4	11	3	0
Powers	.935	12	7	22	2	1
Tredaway	1.000	2	2	0	0	0

Shortstop	PCT	G	PO	A	E	DP
Alvarez	.933	4	5	9	1	4
Hills	.967	19	27	62	3	5
LaRocca	.970	7	8	24	1	5
Melo	.946	112	182	307	28	61

Outfield	PCT	G	PO	A	E	DP
Allen	.971	56	66	1	2	0
Brinkley	.946	50	68	2	4	0
Brown	.800	8	12	0	3	0
Guiel	1.000	8	8	0	0	0
Hills	.857	8	11	1	2	0
Johnson	.985	76	189	8	3	2
Keefe	1.000	8	13	3	0	2
Killeen	1.000	2	2	0	0	0
Mashore	.985	64	120	11	2	3
Matthews	.960	26	45	3	2	1
Poe	.961	31	47	2	2	0
Prieto	.991	98	212	11	2	3

RANCHO CUCAMONGA — Class A

CALIFORNIA LEAGUE

BATTING	AVG	G	AB	R	H	2B	3B	HR	RBI	BB	SO	SB	CS	B	T	HT	WT	DOB	1st Yr	Resides
Chavez, Steven	.197	88	274	34	54	17	0	5	30	28	77	1	0	L	R	5-11	190	7-30-75	1995	Carlsbad, N.M.
Darr, Mike	.344	134	521	104	179	32	11	15	94	57	90	23	7	L	R	6-3	205	3-21-76	1994	Corona, Calif.
Davis, Ben	.278	122	474	67	132	30	1	17	76	28	107	3	1	S	R	6-4	205	3-10-77	1995	Aston, Pa.
Finley, Steve	.286	4	14	3	4	0	0	2	3	3	2	1	0	L	L	6-2	180	3-12-65	1987	Houston, Texas
Gama, Rick	.252	25	115	17	29	9	0	2	12	6	12	4	2	R	R	5-10	180	4-27-73	1995	Mexico City, Mexico
Gonzalez, Santos	.111	6	18	3	2	0	0	0	1	1	7	0	1	S	R	5-11	170	6-25-77	1994	Bani, D.R.
Gonzalez, Wikleman	.300	33	110	18	33	9	1	5	26	7	25	1	1	R	R	5-11	175	5-17-74	1992	Palo Negro, Venez.
Hernandez, Carlos	.250	1	4	0	1	0	0	0	0	0	1	0	0	R	R	5-11	185	5-24-67	1985	Caracas, Venez.
Hills, Rich	.273	40	128	19	35	8	1	0	15	18	31	1	1	R	R	6-0	195	7-28-73	1995	Springdale, Ark.
Kent, Robbie	.247	81	295	35	73	18	0	4	32	22	65	0	2	R	R	5-10	185	1-8-74	1996	Evansville, Ind.
Livingstone, Scott	.250	3	8	2	2	0	0	0	0	3	0	0	1	L	R	6-0	198	7-15-65	1988	Southlake, Texas
Matthews, Gary	.302	69	268	66	81	15	4	8	40	49	57	10	4	S	R	6-3	185	8-25-74	1994	Canoga Park, Calif.
Mitchell, Mike	.350	109	440	78	154	36	1	17	106	35	83	2	0	L	R	6-3	205	4-5-73	1994	Camarillo, Calif.
Moore, Vince	.234	100	325	43	76	23	1	9	38	30	118	13	3	L	L	6-1	190	9-22-71	1991	Houston, Texas
Nicholson, Kevin	.323	17	65	7	21	5	0	1	9	4	15	2	1	S	R	5-10	190	3-29-76	1997	Surrey, B.C.
Plantier, Phil	.235	4	17	1	4	1	1	0	3	0	1	1	0	L	R	5-11	195	1-27-69	1987	San Diego, Calif.
Powers, John	.254	107	402	77	102	28	5	10	44	63	90	7	8	L	R	5-9	165	6-2-74	1996	Scottsdale, Ariz.
Prieto, Chris	.280	22	82	21	23	4	0	4	12	19	16	4	3	L	L	5-11	180	8-24-72	1993	Carmel, Calif.
Prieto, Rick	.292	68	281	47	82	12	3	5	31	44	45	11	6	S	R	5-10	175	8-24-72	1993	Carmel, Calif.
Reynoso, Ben	.192	120	407	48	78	13	2	1	35	41	92	6	2	R	R	5-9	165	9-12-74	1996	Visalia, Calif.
Rivera, Ruben	.174	6	23	6	4	1	0	1	3	3	9	1	0	R	R	6-3	190	11-14-73	1992	Chorrera, Panama
Schwenke, Matt	.202	69	242	27	49	9	2	4	30	19	67	4	0	S	R	6-2	210	8-12-72	1993	Loomis, Calif.
Shockey, Greg	.339	103	401	60	136	28	4	14	78	36	67	0	2	L	L	6-1	190	4-11-70	1992	Huntington Beach, Calif.

GAMES BY POSITION: C—Davis 110, W. Gonzalez 15, Hernandez 1, Schwenke 19. **1B**—Davis 1, Hills 5, Kent 2, Mitchell 108, Reynoso 1, Schwenke 29. **2B**—Gama 22, S. Gonzalez 2, Hills 1, Kent 22, Powers 98, Reynoso 1. **3B**—Chavez 76, Hills 20, Kent 53, Powers 5, Reynoso 1. **SS**—S. Gonzalez 1, W. Gonzalez 1, Hills 12, Kent 3, Nicholson 14, Reynoso 117. **OF**—Darr 132, Finley 1, Kent 1, Matthews 68, Moore 87, Plantier 4, Powers 2, C. Prieto 20, R. Prieto 68, Shockey 52.

PITCHING	W	L	ERA	G	GS	CG	SV	IP	H	R	ER	BB	SO	B	T	HT	WT	DOB	1st Yr	Resides
Agosto, Stevenson	2	0	2.86	3	3	1	0	22	18	7	7	6	18	L	L	5-10	175	9-2-75	1994	Rio Grande, P.R.
2-team (24 Lake Els.)	7	8	4.98	27	24	2	0	159	173	98	88	56	109							
Anderson, Bill	8	4	4.01	29	14	0	1	101	78	53	45	51	118	R	R	6-0	190	9-23-71	1994	Queensbury, N.Y.
Baron, Jim	1	7	3.38	14	14	0	0	85	89	50	32	28	64	L	L	6-3	230	2-22-74	1992	Humble, Texas
Cairncross, Cameron	1	3	5.63	40	0	0	1	64	81	46	40	15	70	L	L	6-2	212	5-11-72	1991	Cairns, Australia
Carmody, Brian	0	1	8.59	4	3	0	0	15	18	16	14	15	7	L	L	6-3	195	7-1-75	1996	San Jose, Calif.
Clayton, Craig	2	1	6.57	10	0	0	1	12	14	10	9	5	15	R	R	6-0	185	11-29-70	1991	Anaheim, Calif.
Clement, Matt	6	3	1.60	14	14	2	0	101	74	30	18	31	109	R	R	6-3	190	8-12-74	1994	Butler, Pa.
Davis, Keith	8	10	5.74	35	14	0	0	125	141	92	80	65	103	R	R	6-2	210	11-1-72	1994	Vacherie, La.
Drumheller, Al	5	6	4.56	38	6	0	1	81	76	48	41	37	107	R	L	6-0	185	7-31-71	1993	Shenandoah, Pa.
Ervin, Kent	0	0	6.00	2	0	0	0	3	3	2	2	2	0	R	R	6-3	195	1-12-74	1996	Littleton, Colo.
Fesh, Sean	0	1	11.57	4	0	0	0	5	10	7	6	3	5	L	L	6-2	165	11-3-72	1991	Bethel, Conn.
Guzman, Domingo	3	2	5.45	6	6	0	0	38	42	23	23	16	39	R	R	6-3	198	4-5-75	1994	San Cristobal, D.R.
Henderson, Kenny	1	2	4.38	7	7	0	0	25	17	14	12	17	26	R	R	6-5	195	2-14-73	1995	Marco Island, Fla.
Hoff, Steve	4	5	6.24	14	13	0	0	66	73	56	46	48	59	L	L	6-4	205	7-1-77	1996	San Bruno, Calif.
Kolb, Brandon	3	2	3.00	10	10	0	0	63	60	29	21	22	49	R	R	6-1	190	11-20-73	1995	Lubbock, Texas
Medina, Rafael	2	0	2.00	3	3	0	0	18	13	4	4	5	14	R	R	6-3	194	2-15-75	1993	Panama City, Panama
Middlebrook, Jason	0	2	4.03	6	6	0	0	22	29	15	10	12	18	R	R	6-3	200	6-26-75	1996	Grass Lake, Mich.
Narcisse, Tyrone	2	0	3.41	22	0	0	0	34	21	13	13	22	38	R	R	6-5	205	2-4-72	1990	Port Arthur, Texas
Nash, Damon	0	0	0.00	1	0	0	0	0	1	1	1	2	0	L	R	6-2	200	3-7-76	1995	Texarkana, Ark.
Newman, Eric	13	6	4.15	35	15	0	0	124	104	64	57	73	141	R	R	6-4	220	8-27-72	1995	Fremont, Calif.
Remington, Jake	2	1	7.45	6	0	0	0	10	12	9	8	3	9	R	R	6-4	175	8-26-75	1994	Broken Arrow, Okla.
Sak, James	6	3	2.93	57	3	0	27	71	42	28	23	30	113	R	R	6-1	195	8-18-73	1995	Chicago, Ill.
Skrmetta, Matt	0	1	1.59	17	0	0	0	28	27	7	5	10	36	S	R	6-3	220	11-6-72	1993	Satellite Beach, Fla.
Spencer, Stan	3	1	3.35	7	7	0	0	40	37	18	15	5	46	R	R	6-3	195	8-2-68	1991	Battleground, Wash.
Torres, Luis	2	2	4.34	31	0	0	2	56	53	30	27	24	46	R	R	6-2	228	1-13-76	1994	Manati, P.R.
Veras, Dario	0	0	6.00	2	0	0	1	3	3	3	2	1	3	R	R	6-2	165	3-13-73	1991	Villa Vazquez, D.R.
Wolff, Bryan	3	0	1.62	9	2	0	1	33	19	6	6	6	39	R	R	6-1	195	3-16-72	1993	St. Louis, Mo.

CLINTON — Class A

MIDWEST LEAGUE

BATTING	AVG	G	AB	R	H	2B	3B	HR	RBI	BB	SO	SB	CS	B	T	HT	WT	DOB	1st Yr	Resides
Amerson, Gordon	.235	34	102	13	24	7	3	0	16	25	31	6	2	L	L	6-1	185	10-10-76	1994	San Bernardino, Calif.
Carmona, Cesarin	.252	65	234	33	59	7	2	11	32	14	69	15	5	S	R	5-11	180	12-20-76	1994	Bani, D.R.
Cronin, Shane	.239	69	230	21	55	1	1	5	33	25	37	4	0	R	R	6-1	210	2-26-76	1996	Renton, Wash.
Cross, Adam	.226	59	155	22	35	5	2	0	16	14	28	9	7	R	R	6-1	180	8-22-73	1995	Bluff City, Tenn.
Davis, Josh	.189	60	180	13	34	5	1	0	18	13	45	4	3	R	R	6-0	180	6-13-76	1994	Locust Grove, Okla.
Dunn, Nathan	.268	104	399	58	107	22	7	7	48	54	112	8	11	R	R	6-0	190	10-17-74	1996	Pell City, Ala.
Halloran, Matt	.201	46	154	19	31	7	0	1	22	8	37	9	3	R	R	6-2	185	3-3-78	1996	Niceville, Fla.
Lindsey, Rodney	.213	130	502	80	107	15	8	6	49	62	161	70	23	R	R	5-8	175	1-28-76	1994	Opelika, Ala.
Loyd, Brian	.274	73	259	35	71	10	0	2	33	25	41	6	4	R	R	6-2	195	12-3-73	1996	Yorba Linda, Calif.
McClure, Brian	.276	118	416	75	115	18	11	4	55	90	64	12	11	L	R	6-0	170	1-15-74	1996	Champaign, Ill.
Nieves, Wilbert	.218	18	55	6	12	1	1	1	7	6	10	2	1	R	R	5-10	160	9-25-77	1996	Santurce, P.R.
Paciorek, Pete	.234	126	435	70	102	19	11	7	52	70	113	10	4	S	L	6-3	195	5-19-76	1995	San Gabriel, Calif.
Parent, Jerry	.260	87	304	37	79	13	1	0	38	50	75	5	4	L	R	6-2	210	12-7-73	1995	Assonet, Mass.
Pernell, Brandon	.282	95	340	63	96	26	3	12	41	44	77	15	5	R	R	6-2	180	4-11-77	1995	Torrance, Calif.
Ruotsinoja, Jacob	.186	54	188	19	35	10	0	1	16	24	51	2	2	L	R	6-2	195	11-11-76	1996	Seminole, Fla.
Rutherford, Daryl	.220	21	59	9	13	3	0	1	5	4	19	2	1	R	R	6-0	175	10-30-75	1995	Columbia, S.C.
Sanchez, Marcos	.291	63	206	42	60	6	5	4	39	42	53	9	4	S	R	6-0	190	9-25-74	1992	Santo Domingo, D.R.
Seal, Scott	.254	29	114	20	29	6	0	5	23	10	37	2	1	L	L	6-1	205	8-16-75	1997	Irvine, Calif.
Thrower, Jake	.254	19	63	8	16	3	0	0	12	13	15	1	3	S	R	5-11	165	11-19-75	1997	Yuma, Ariz.
Watkins, Sean	.148	10	27	1	4	0	0	1	2	9	10	0	2	L	L	6-4	210	10-6-74	1995	Peoria Heights, Ill.

GAMES BY POSITION: C—Davis 52, Loyd 60, Nieves 18, Sanchez 22. **1B**—Dunn 7, Paciorek 125, Watkins 8. **2B**—Cross 23, Davis 1, Dunn 7, McClure 116. **3B**—Cronin 55, Cross 6, Dunn 77, Thrower 4. **SS**—Carmona 64, Cross 14, Dunn 2, Halloran 46, Thrower 13. **OF**—Amerson 34, Cross 1, Lindsey 129, Paciorek 3, Parent 80, Pernell 91, Ruotsinoja 34, Rutherford 15, Sanchez 2, Seal 29.

PITCHING	W	L	ERA	G	GS	CG	SV	IP	H	R	ER	BB	SO	B	T	HT	WT	DOB	1st Yr	Resides
Carmody, Brian	0	0	1.56	8	1	0	1	17	14	7	3	8	19	L	L	6-3	195	7-1-75	1996	San Jose, Calif.
Clark, Chris	5	5	4.15	32	11	0	3	89	89	50	41	46	91	R	R	6-1	180	10-29-74	1994	Aurora, Colo.
Guzman, Domingo	4	5	3.19	12	12	5	0	79	66	36	28	25	91	R	R	6-3	198	4-5-75	1994	San Cristobal, D.R.
Hite, Kevin	5	5	3.31	38	4	1	1	87	86	38	32	11	85	R	R	6-1	155	7-23-74	1996	Hermitage, Tenn.
Hoff, Steve	7	1	2.71	12	12	1	0	76	72	28	23	18	78	L	L	6-4	205	7-1-77	1996	San Bruno, Calif.
Lopez, Rodrigo	6	8	3.18	37	14	2	9	122	103	49	43	42	123	R	R	5-11	170	12-14-75	1995	Thalnepantla, Mexico
Maurer, Dave	0	4	2.88	25	0	0	3	34	24	15	11	15	43	R	L	6-2	205	2-23-75	1997	Burnsville, Minn.
Middlebrook, Jason	6	4	3.98	14	14	2	0	81	76	46	36	39	86	R	R	6-3	200	6-26-75	1996	Grass Lake, Mich.
Nash, Damon	1	1	3.86	4	0	0	0	7	5	3	3	5	6	L	R	6-2	200	3-7-76	1995	Texarkana, Ark.
Neiman, Josh	0	0	12.91	5	0	0	0	8	16	11	11	4	5	R	R	6-4	210	10-19-74	1994	Durango, Colo.
Parent, Jerry	0	0	0.00	2	0	0	0	2	0	0	0	2	1	L	R	6-2	210	12-7-73	1995	Assonet, Mass.
Perry, Tim	1	0	4.32	6	0	0	0	8	9	7	4	10	13	R	R	6-0	190	8-17-77	1996	Carlsbad, N.M.
Serrano, Wascar	0	1	6.00	1	1	1	0	6	6	5	4	2	2	R	R	6-2	178	7-2-78	1995	Bani, D.R.
Sullivan, Brendan	7	5	3.90	47	0	0	6	62	55	33	27	34	54	R	R	6-3	190	12-15-74	1996	Washington, D.C.
Szymborski, Tom	5	7	3.88	22	22	1	0	135	141	67	58	46	74	R	R	6-3	210	3-7-75	1996	Chicago, Ill.
Torres, Luis	1	0	1.17	5	0	0	0	8	3	5	1	9	8	R	R	6-2	228	1-13-76	1994	Manati, P.R.
Viegas, Randy	1	1	2.70	18	0	0	2	27	18	11	8	24	21	L	L	6-2	175	8-22-75	1994	Roseville, Calif.
Walker, Kevin	6	10	4.88	19	19	3	0	111	133	80	60	37	80	L	L	6-4	190	9-20-76	1995	Glen Rose, Texas
Witte, Dominic	1	4	3.58	40	1	0	1	65	77	44	26	10	55	R	R	6-0	200	11-25-73	1996	Richmond, Ind.
Workman, Widd	9	10	4.94	25	25	1	0	144	161	91	79	72	107	R	R	6-1	195	5-23-74	1996	Gilbert, Ariz.

IDAHO FALLS — Rookie

PIONEER LEAGUE

BATTING	AVG	G	AB	R	H	2B	3B	HR	RBI	BB	SO	SB	CS	B	T	HT	WT	DOB	1st Yr	Resides
Brown, Kent	.270	36	126	22	34	4	0	0	19	22	29	10	7	L	L	6-2	195	6-1-74	1997	Burlington, Iowa
Burford, Kevin	.207	7	29	2	6	0	1	1	3	1	5	0	0	L	L	6-0	190	11-7-77	1997	Westminster, Calif.
Cronin, Shane	.336	32	128	21	43	10	1	2	24	11	18	0	4	R	R	6-1	210	2-26-76	1996	Renton, Wash.
Dallin, Spencer	.000	1	1	0	0	0	0	0	0	0	1	0	0	R	R	5-8	150	4-13-78	1997	Rialto, Calif.
DeMarco, Joey	.280	32	125	21	35	5	1	1	20	16	14	9	3	S	R	5-9	160	10-1-75	1997	Coral Springs, Fla.
Dunham, Trey	.400	1	5	0	2	0	0	0	0	0	2	0	0	L	R	6-1	185	9-8-77	1996	Shattuck, Okla.
Gonzalez, Santos	.297	46	192	41	57	9	6	5	34	19	44	17	7	S	R	5-11	170	6-25-77	1994	Bani, D.R.
Horsman, Brent	.305	52	213	36	65	9	2	1	24	10	35	9	2	L	R	6-3	175	7-31-76	1997	Fairfield, Calif.
Hunter, Johnny	.269	21	67	19	18	4	0	4	15	12	24	1	0	R	R	6-1	190	6-14-75	1997	Mansfield, Texas
Jergenson, Brian	.260	54	196	34	51	8	1	2	32	23	49	6	1	L	L	6-3	215	7-30-74	1997	La Crescent, Minn.
Langdon, Trajan	.189	22	90	11	17	7	0	2	10	11	36	0	1	R	R	6-4	190	5-13-76	1994	Anchorage, Alaska
Lawrence, Tony	.267	56	210	40	56	8	2	7	36	34	48	7	3	R	R	6-1	205	3-7-75	1997	Monroe, La.
McDaniel, Ryan	.189	22	74	5	14	4	1	1	7	7	31	0	1	R	R	6-0	180	3-18-75	1997	Ft. Worth, Texas
Rakers, Jason	.200	5	20	3	4	1	0	0	3	3	5	0	0	L	R	6-0	190	8-28-75	1997	Trenton, Ill.
Rodriguez, John	.296	32	115	17	34	5	0	0	11	10	26	1	4	R	R	6-0	180	11-25-75	1995	Corpus Christi, Texas
Ruotsinoja, Jacob	.303	31	109	20	33	10	1	2	17	29	21	5	0	L	R	6-2	195	11-11-76	1996	Seminole, Fla.
Rutherford, Daryl	.375	15	64	13	24	4	3	0	10	3	9	8	1	R	R	6-0	175	10-30-75	1995	Columbia, S.C.
Ryden, Karl	.263	57	198	48	52	6	3	1	19	45	38	9	6	R	R	5-11	185	5-7-77	1997	League City, Texas
Seal, Scott	.358	30	120	18	43	8	3	3	30	22	24	0	3	L	L	6-1	205	8-16-75	1997	Irvine, Calif.
Snellgrove, Clay	.345	66	281	52	97	19	7	2	48	18	39	3	2	R	R	6-0	180	11-22-74	1997	Lafayette, Ind.
Thrower, Jake	.340	35	141	37	48	10	4	3	28	31	16	10	1	S	R	5-11	165	11-19-75	1997	Yuma, Ariz.
Zucha, Jason	.208	13	48	5	10	1	1	0	5	3	10	0	0	R	R	6-3	205	4-15-76	1997	Corpus Christi, Texas

GAMES BY POSITION: C—Dunham 1, Lawrence 41, McDaniel 21, Zucha 11. **1B**—Cronin 12, Jergenson 53, Lawrence 3, Ryden 2, Seal 7. **2B**—Dallin 1, DeMarco 10, Gonzalez 13, McDaniel 1, Rodriguez 5, Snellgrove 39, Thrower 6. **3B**—Cronin 18, DeMarco 8, Gonzalez 1, Langdon 19, Rodriguez 24, Snellgrove 1, Thrower 4. **SS**—DeMarco 10, Gonzalez 26, Snellgrove 19, Thrower 18. **OF**—Brown 35, Burford 7, Horsman 47, Hunter 9, Lawrence 1, Ruotsinoja 31, Rutherford 14, Ryden 53, Seal 22, Thrower 1.

PITCHING	W	L	ERA	G	GS	CG	SV	IP	H	R	ER	BB	SO	B	T	HT	WT	DOB	1st Yr	Resides
Camp, Shawn	2	1	5.51	30	0	0	12	33	41	22	20	14	41	R	R	6-1	190	11-18-75	1997	Fairfax, Va.
Ervin, Kent	5	6	5.33	16	14	1	0	83	107	57	49	26	59	R	R	6-3	195	1-12-74	1996	Littleton, Colo.
Guttormson, Ricky	3	2	6.43	18	2	0	3	28	34	25	20	11	19	R	R	6-2	185	1-11-77	1997	Anacortes, Wash.
Herndon, Junior	0	0	0.00	1	1	0	0	5	5	0	0	1	3	R	R	6-1	180	9-11-78	1997	Craig, Colo.

PITCHING	W	L	ERA	G	GS	CG	SV	IP	H	R	ER	BB	SO	B	T	HT	WT	DOB	1st Yr	Resides
Herrera, Misael	0	1	11.30	6	3	0	0	14	25	22	18	8	8	R	R	6-0	165	3-15-77	1995	Bani, D.R.
Hunter, Johnny	0	0	1.69	4	0	0	1	5	4	1	1	2	0	R	R	6-1	190	6-14-75	1997	Mansfield, Texas
Naff, Todd	3	3	5.45	24	0	0	1	38	43	31	23	25	29	R	R	6-3	215	3-22-75	1997	Bertram, Texas
Nash, Damon	3	2	6.60	14	10	0	0	60	79	48	44	29	65	L	R	6-2	200	3-7-76	1995	Texarkana, Ark.
Oiseth, Jon	3	1	4.39	18	0	0	1	27	22	15	13	13	27	R	L	6-3	190	10-31-74	1997	Savage, Minn.
Perry, Tim	5	3	5.40	15	14	1	0	78	84	52	47	38	84	R	R	6-0	190	8-17-77	1996	Carlsbad, N.M.
Ryan, Pat	2	1	4.77	14	10	0	0	60	64	42	32	17	47	R	R	6-3	200	11-29-74	1997	DeLand, Fla.
Sellers, Justin	5	1	5.56	24	0	0	4	44	58	28	27	9	32	R	R	6-4	210	2-22-77	1996	Vancouver, Wash.
Serrano, Wascar	0	1	11.88	2	2	0	0	8	13	12	11	4	13	R	R	6-2	178	7-2-78	1995	Bani, D.R.
Smith, Josh	2	2	10.13	26	0	0	0	27	35	33	30	31	24	L	L	5-11	185	8-26-77	1995	Houston, Texas
Viator, Dustin	2	2	5.01	23	5	0	1	50	57	34	28	24	42	R	R	6-3	192	7-12-75	1997	New Iberia, La.
Viegas, Randy	1	1	2.35	5	0	0	0	8	2	4	2	11	12	L	L	6-2	175	8-22-75	1994	Roseville, Calif.
Wasinger, Mark	0	0	3.00	1	0	0	0	3	2	2	1	2	1	R	R	6-0	165	8-4-61	1982	Duluth, Ga.
Werner, Don	0	1	108.0	1	1	0	0	1	10	12	12	2	0	R	R	6-1	185	3-8-53	1971	Arlington, Texas
Young, Doug	3	4	5.58	15	10	0	1	60	69	41	37	27	44	R	R	6-2	190	1-23-76	1997	Roseville, Calif.

PEORIA — Rookie

ARIZONA LEAGUE

BATTING	AVG	G	AB	R	H	2B	3B	HR	RBI	BB	SO	SB	CS	B	T	HT	WT	DOB	1st Yr	Resides
Burford, Kevin	.389	47	167	42	65	15	2	4	50	49	25	12	5	L	L	6-0	190	11-7-77	1997	Westminster, Calif.
Cosentino, Tony	.274	33	106	11	29	3	1	1	14	18	20	1	0	R	R	6-0	195	12-7-78	1997	Torrance, Calif.
Curry, Jesse	.234	39	145	17	34	9	1	2	21	19	62	1	1	L	L	6-4	205	10-25-78	1997	Gresham, Ore.
DeMarco, Joey	.154	7	26	7	4	2	0	0	2	5	6	1	0	S	R	5-9	160	10-1-75	1997	Coral Springs, Fla.
Dunaway, Jason	.260	44	177	30	46	14	0	0	21	19	38	8	2	R	R	6-1	177	1-12-77	1997	Durango, Colo.
Dunham, Trey	.317	35	139	20	44	13	1	2	32	17	42	0	2	L	R	6-1	185	9-8-77	1996	Shattuck, Okla.
Garcia, Alex	.269	21	78	10	21	3	0	1	10	9	14	1	1	R	R	5-11	165	4-14-79	1996	Haina, D.R.
Garcia, Sandro	.214	28	103	22	22	8	2	0	16	16	10	4	0	R	R	5-10	180	11-22-77	1996	Deerfield Beach, Fla.
Gonzalez, Franklin	.273	24	99	12	27	4	0	1	9	5	22	7	4	R	R	6-1	160	7-4-77	1995	Bani, D.R.
Guerrero, Joel	.264	41	140	25	37	2	1	0	10	28	35	22	5	S	R	5-9	160	7-7-78	1996	Santo Domingo, D.R.
Hemmings, Brandon	.202	28	104	18	21	8	2	1	11	8	33	4	0	R	R	6-4	197	5-6-77	1997	Columbus, Ga.
Hunter, Andrew	.273	5	22	3	6	1	1	0	4	2	5	0	0	R	R	6-2	200	12-28-76	1995	Mansfield, Texas
Mashore, Justin	.269	7	26	4	7	3	0	0	3	5	13	1	1	R	R	5-9	190	2-14-72	1991	Concord, Calif.
Minor, Damon	.295	42	146	46	43	2	2	0	18	52	36	12	10	L	L	5-8	175	1-9-75	1997	Kent, Wash.
Motley, Brittan	.240	39	150	27	36	4	2	0	14	10	38	9	5	S	R	6-2	180	10-18-78	1997	Kansas City, Mo.
Nicholson, Kevin	.265	7	34	7	9	1	0	2	8	2	5	0	2	S	R	5-10	190	3-29-76	1997	Surrey, B.C.
Nieves, Wilbert	.296	8	27	2	8	2	0	0	2	5	5	1	0	R	R	5-10	160	9-25-77	1996	Santurce, P.R.
Sawai, Ryosuke	.100	3	10	3	1	0	0	0	1	4	3	1	0	R	R	5-10	170	3-9-78	1997	Saitama, Japan
Soto, Luis	.286	35	140	20	40	12	1	4	32	15	33	0	2	R	R	6-1	194	9-7-78	1995	Bani, D.R.
Tripp, Terry	.130	28	100	9	13	0	0	0	2	8	19	0	1	R	R	6-0	160	12-8-74	1997	Harrisburg, Ill.

GAMES BY POSITION: C—Cosentino 26, Dunham 7, Soto 26. **1B**—Cosentino 1, Curry 39, Dunham 17. **2B**—DeMarco 4, Dunaway 4, A. Garcia 1, S. Garcia 7, Guerrero 36, Tripp 8. **3B**—DeMarco 1, Dunaway 1, A. Garcia 20, S. Garcia 18, Guerrero 1, Sawai 3, Tripp 12. **SS**—DeMarco 1, Dunaway 39, Nicholson 7, Tripp 10. **OF**—Burford 35, Dunham 1, Gonzalez 24, Guerrero 2, Hemmings 24, Hunter 3, Mashore 2, Minor 41, Motley 37, Nieves 3.

PITCHING	W	L	ERA	G	GS	CG	SV	IP	H	R	ER	BB	SO	B	T	HT	WT	DOB	1st Yr	Resides
Darr, Jerry	4	6	6.49	14	13	0	0	60	67	59	43	33	62	R	R	6-2	190	2-26-79	1997	Benton, Ark.
Diaz, Antonio	1	1	3.00	22	0	0	4	39	45	22	13	4	41	R	R	5-11	160	1-28-79	1997	Juncos, P.R.
Gonzalez, Francisco	4	4	5.48	26	2	0	2	48	55	36	29	26	40	R	R	6-4	190	3-21-78	1996	Arecibo, P.R.
Guttormson, Ricky	1	1	4.91	5	0	0	1	11	17	11	6	4	19	R	R	6-2	185	1-11-77	1997	Anacortes, Wash.
Herndon, Junior	3	2	4.42	14	14	0	0	77	80	51	38	32	65	R	R	6-1	180	9-11-78	1997	Craig, Colo.
Herrera, Misael	1	2	8.05	11	0	0	1	19	27	19	17	10	15	R	R	6-0	165	3-15-77	1995	Bani, D.R.
Hohenstein, Andrew	0	0	6.94	9	0	0	0	12	15	9	9	8	13	R	R	6-4	210	9-27-77	1996	Riverside, Calif.
Howard, Ben	1	4	7.45	13	12	0	0	54	54	53	45	63	59	R	R	6-2	190	1-15-79	1997	Jackson, Tenn.
Iida, Masashi	0	2	11.25	11	1	0	0	20	25	29	25	18	11	R	R	5-10	170	5-19-77	1997	Saitama, Japan
Jones, Travis	4	3	3.04	21	2	0	0	53	53	28	18	23	51	L	L	6-3	190	12-3-77	1996	Asher, Okla.
Parent, Jerry	0	0	4.26	5	0	0	0	6	6	3	3	1	7	L	R	6-2	210	12-7-73	1995	Assonet, Mass.
Precinal, Huilberto	0	2	21.00	13	0	0	0	15	27	37	35	34	11	R	R	6-6	190	9-8-77	1995	Bani, D.R.
Serrano, Wascar	6	3	3.18	12	11	0	1	71	60	43	25	22	75	R	R	6-2	178	7-2-78	1995	Bani, D.R.

San Francisco GIANTS

Manager: Dusty Baker.

1997 Record: 90-72, .556 (1st, NL West)

BATTING	AVG	G	AB	R	H	2B	3B	HR	RBI	BB	SO	SB	CS	B	T	HT	WT	DOB	1st Yr	Resides
Aurilia, Rich	.275	46	102	16	28	8	0	5	19	8	15	1	1	R	R	6-0	170	9-2-71	1992	Hazlet, N.J.
Benard, Marvin	.228	84	114	13	26	4	0	1	13	13	29	3	1	L	L	5-10	180	1-20-71	1992	Cudahy, Calif.
Berryhill, Damon	.257	73	167	17	43	8	0	3	23	20	29	0	0	S	R	6-0	205	12-3-63	1984	Laguna Niguel, Calif.
Bonds, Barry	.291	159	532	123	155	26	5	40	101	145	87	37	8	L	L	6-1	185	7-24-64	1985	Murrieta, Calif.
Cruz, Jacob	.160	16	25	3	4	1	0	0	3	3	4	0	0	L	L	6-0	175	1-28-73	1994	Oxnard, Calif.
Delgado, Wilson	.143	8	7	1	1	1	0	0	0	0	2	0	0	S	R	5-11	165	7-15-75	1993	Santo Domingo, D.R.
Hamilton, Darryl	.270	125	460	78	124	23	3	5	43	61	61	15	10	L	R	6-1	180	12-3-64	1986	Sugar Land, Texas
Hill, Glenallen	.261	128	398	47	104	28	4	11	64	19	87	7	4	R	R	6-2	210	3-22-65	1983	Boca Raton, Fla.
Javier, Stan	.286	142	440	69	126	16	4	8	50	56	70	25	3	S	R	6-0	185	1-9-64	1981	Santo Domingo, D.R.
Jensen, Marcus	.149	30	74	5	11	2	0	1	3	7	23	0	0	S	R	6-4	195	12-14-72	1990	Oakland, Calif.
Johnson, Brian	.279	56	179	19	50	7	2	11	27	14	26	0	1	R	R	6-2	210	1-8-68	1989	Oakland, Calif.
Kent, Jeff	.250	155	580	90	145	38	2	29	121	48	133	11	3	R	R	6-1	185	3-7-68	1989	Huntington Beach, Calif.
Lewis, Mark	.267	118	341	50	91	14	6	10	42	23	62	3	2	R	R	6-1	190	11-30-69	1988	Hamilton, Ohio
Mirabelli, Doug	.143	6	7	0	1	0	0	0	0	1	3	0	0	R	R	6-1	205	10-18-70	1992	Las Vegas, Nev.
Mueller, Bill	.292	128	390	51	114	26	3	7	44	48	71	4	3	S	R	5-11	173	3-17-71	1993	Maryland Heights, Mo.
Powell, Dante	.308	27	39	8	12	1	0	1	3	4	11	1	1	R	R	6-2	185	8-25-73	1994	Long Beach, Calif.
Snow, J.T.	.281	157	531	81	149	36	1	28	104	96	124	6	4	S	L	6-2	202	2-26-68	1989	Corona Del Mar, Calif.
Vizcaino, Jose	.266	151	568	77	151	19	7	5	50	48	87	8	8	S	R	6-1	180	3-26-68	1987	El Cajon, Calif.
Wilkins, Rick	.195	66	190	18	37	5	0	6	23	17	65	0	0	L	R	6-2	210	6-4-67	1987	Jacksonville, Fla.

PITCHING	W	L	ERA	G	GS	CG	SV	IP	H	R	ER	BB	SO	B	T	HT	WT	DOB	1st Yr	Resides
Alvarez, Wilson	4	3	4.48	11	11	0	0	66	54	36	33	36	69	L	L	6-1	235	3-24-70	1987	Maracaibo, Venez.
Arocha, Rene	0	0	11.32	6	0	0	0	10	17	14	13	5	7	R	R	6-0	180	2-24-66	1992	Miami, Fla.
Bailey, Cory	0	1	8.38	7	0	0	0	10	15	9	9	4	5	R	R	6-1	210	1-24-71	1991	Marion, Ill.
Beck, Rod	7	4	3.47	73	0	0	37	70	67	31	27	8	53	R	R	6-1	236	8-3-68	1986	Scottsdale, Ariz.
Carlson, Dan	0	0	7.63	6	0	0	0	15	20	14	13	8	14	R	R	6-1	185	1-26-70	1990	Portland, Ore.
Creek, Doug	1	2	6.75	3	3	0	0	13	12	12	10	14	14	L	L	5-10	205	3-1-69	1991	Martinsburg, W.Va.
Darwin, Danny	1	3	4.91	10	7	0	0	44	51	26	24	14	30	R	R	6-3	202	10-25-55	1976	Valley View, Texas
DeLucia, Rich	0	0	10.80	3	0	0	0	2	6	3	2	0	2	R	R	6-0	185	10-7-64	1986	Shillington, Pa.
Estes, Shawn	19	5	3.18	32	32	3	0	201	162	80	71	100	181	R	L	6-2	200	2-28-73	1991	Gardnerville, Nev.
Fernandez, Osvaldo	3	4	4.95	11	11	0	0	56	74	39	31	15	31	R	R	6-2	190	11-4-68	1996	Santo Domingo, D.R.
Foulke, Keith	1	5	8.26	11	8	0	0	45	60	41	41	18	33	R	R	6-1	195	10-19-72	1994	Huffman, Texas
Gardner, Mark	12	9	4.29	30	30	2	0	180	188	92	86	57	136	R	R	6-1	190	3-1-62	1985	Fresno, Calif.
Henry, Doug	4	5	4.71	75	0	0	3	71	70	45	37	41	69	R	R	6-4	205	12-10-63	1986	Hartland, Wis.
Hernandez, Roberto	5	2	2.48	28	0	0	4	33	29	9	9	14	35	R	R	6-4	235	11-11-64	1986	Cobo Rojo, P.R.
Johnstone, John	0	0	3.38	13	0	0	0	19	15	7	7	7	15	R	R	6-3	195	11-25-68	1987	Jacksonville, Fla.
Mulholland, Terry	0	1	5.16	15	2	0	0	30	28	21	17	6	25	R	L	6-3	200	3-9-63	1984	Paradise Valley, Ariz.
2-team (25 Chicago)	6	13	4.24	40	27	1	0	187	190	100	88	51	99							
Poole, Jim	3	1	7.11	63	0	0	0	49	73	44	39	25	26	L	L	6-2	203	4-28-66	1988	Ellicott City, Md.
Rapp, Pat	1	2	6.00	8	6	0	0	33	37	24	22	21	28	R	R	6-3	210	7-13-67	1989	Sulphur, La.
2-team (19 Florida)	5	8	4.83	27	25	1	0	142	158	83	76	72	92							
Roa, Joe	2	5	5.21	28	3	0	0	66	86	40	38	20	34	R	R	6-1	194	10-11-71	1989	Hazel Park, Mich.
Rodriguez, Rich	4	3	3.17	71	0	0	1	65	65	24	23	21	32	L	L	5-11	200	3-1-63	1984	Knoxville, Tenn.
Rueter, Kirk	13	6	3.45	32	32	0	0	191	194	83	73	51	115	L	L	6-3	190	12-1-70	1991	Hoyleton, Ill.
Tavarez, Julian	6	4	3.87	89	0	0	0	88	91	43	38	34	38	R	R	6-2	165	5-22-73	1990	Santiago, D.R.
VanLandingham, William	4	7	4.96	18	17	0	0	89	80	56	49	59	52	R	R	6-2	210	7-16-70	1991	Franklin, Tenn.

FIELDING

Catcher	PCT	G	PO	A	E	DP	PB
Berryhill	.990	51	288	24	3	2	4
Jensen	.983	28	106	10	2	1	2
Johnson	.995	55	344	24	2	5	2
Mirabelli	1.000	6	16	0	0	0	0
Wilkins	.986	57	326	37	5	5	1

First Base	PCT	G	PO	A	E	DP
Berryhill	1.000	1	5	0	0	1
Javier	.955	3	21	0	1	2
Johnson	1.000	2	8	0	0	0
Kent	1.000	13	80	4	0	6
Snow	.995	156	1308	108	7	133

Second Base	PCT	G	PO	A	E	DP
Delgado	1.000	3	1	3	0	1
Kent	.979	148	325	425	16	104
Lewis	.940	29	40	54	6	14
Vizcaino	1.000	5	4	4	0	0

Third Base	PCT	G	PO	A	E	DP
Lewis	.945	69	34	103	8	10
Mueller	.956	122	85	218	14	18

Shortstop	PCT	G	PO	A	E	DP
Aurilia	.979	36	47	91	3	19
Delgado	1.000	1	1	0	0	0
Vizcaino	.976	147	202	446	16	94

Outfield	PCT	G	PO	A	E	DP
Benard	.967	36	27	2	1	0
Bonds	.984	159	289	10	5	0
Cruz	.933	11	12	2	1	1
Hamilton	.980	118	243	1	5	0
Hill	.947	97	158	2	9	0
Javier	.977	130	258	2	6	2
Powell	1.000	22	27	0	0	0

JOHN KLEIN

Shawn Estes

FARM SYSTEM

Director of Player Development: Dick Tidrow

Class	Farm Team	League	W	L	Pct.	Finish*	Manager(s)	First Yr
AAA	Phoenix (Ariz.) Firebirds	Pacific Coast	88	55	.615	1st (10)	Ron Wotus	1966
AA	Shreveport (La.) Captains	Texas	76	62	.551	2nd (8)	Carlos Lezcano	1979
#A	San Jose (Calif.) Giants	California	60	80	.429	10th (10)	Frank Cacciatore	1988
#A	Bakersfield (Calif.) Blaze	California	62	78	.443	8th (10)	Glenn Tufts/Keith Bodie	1997
A	Salem-Keizer (Ore.) Volcanoes	Northwest	40	36	.526	5th (8)	Shane Turner	1997

*Finish in overall standings (No. of teams in league) #Advanced level

ORGANIZATION LEADERS

MAJOR LEAGUERS

BATTING

*AVG	Bill Mueller	.292
R	Barry Bonds	123
H	Barry Bonds	155
TB	Barry Bonds	311
2B	Jeff Kent	38
3B	Jose Vizcaino	7
HR	Barry Bonds	40
RBI	Jeff Kent	121
BB	Barry Bonds	145
SO	Jeff Kent	133
SB	Barry Bonds	37

PITCHING

W	Shawn Estes	19
L	Mark Gardner	9
#ERA	Shawn Estes	3.18
G	Julian Tavarez	89
CG	Shawn Estes	3
SV	Rod Beck	37
IP	Shawn Estes	201
BB	Shawn Estes	100
SO	Shawn Estes	181

MORRIS FOSTOFF
Jeff Kent

JOHN SPEAR
Jacob Cruz

MINOR LEAGUERS

BATTING

*AVG	Jacob Cruz, Phoenix	.361
R	Tim Garland, San Jose	106
H	Jacob Cruz, Phoenix	178
TB	Damon Minor, Bakersfield	283
2B	Jacob Cruz, Phoenix	45
3B	Mike Caruso, San Jose	11
HR	Mike Glendenning, Bakersfield	33
RBI	Keith Williams, Phoenix/Shreveport	106
BB	Damon Minor, Bakersfield	87
SO	Mike Glendenning, Bakersfield	150
SB	Tim Garland, San Jose	65

PITCHING

W	Two tied at	13
L	Manuel Bermudez, Bakersfield	14
#ERA	Troy Brohawn, Shreveport	2.56
G	Ricky Pickett, Phoenix	62
CG	Manuel Bermudez, Bakersfield	3
SV	Mick Pageler, Bakersfield	29
IP	Troy Brohawn, Shreveport	169
BB	Two tied at	83
SO	Jason Brester, San Jose	172

*Minimum 250 At-Bats #Minimum 75 Innings

TOP 10 PROSPECTS

LEE SCHMID
Joe Fontenot

How the Giants Top 10 prospects, as judged by Baseball America prior to the 1997 season, fared in 1997:

Player, Pos.	Club (Class)	AVG	AB	R	H	2B	3B	HR	RBI	SB
2. Dante Powell, of	San Francisco	.308	39	8	12	1	0	1	3	1
	Phoenix (AAA)	.241	452	91	109	24	4	11	42	34
3. *Mike Caruso, ss	San Jose (A)	.333	441	76	147	24	11	2	50	11
	Winston-Salem (A)	.227	119	12	27	3	2	0	14	3
8. Jacob Cruz, of	San Francisco	.160	25	3	4	1	0	0	3	0
	Phoenix (AAA)	.361	493	97	178	45	3	12	94	18

Player, Pos.	Club (Class)	W	L	ERA	G	SV	IP	H	BB	SO
1. Joe Fontenot, rhp	Shreveport (AA)	10	11	5.53	26	0	151	171	65	103
4. Mike Villano, rhp	Phoenix (AAA)	5	3	4.16	13	0	71	75	27	41
	Shreveport (AA)	3	1	6.29	30	2	34	41	20	26
5. Russ Ortiz, rhrp	Phoenix (AAA)	4	3	5.51	14	0	85	96	34	70
	Shreveport (AA)	2	3	4.13	12	0	57	52	37	50
6. Steve Soderstrom, rhp	Phoenix (AAA)	4	8	6.52	31	1	106	143	53	80
7. Darin Blood, rhp	Shreveport (AA)	8	10	4.33	27	0	156	152	83	90
9. Jason Brester, lhp	San Jose (A)	9	9	4.24	26	0	142	164	52	172
10. *Keith Foulke, rhp	San Francisco	1	5	8.26	11	0	45	60	18	33
	Chicago, AL	3	0	3.45	16	3	29	28	5	21
	Phoenix (AAA)	5	4	4.50	12	0	76	79	15	54
	Nashville (AAA)	0	0	5.79	1	0	5	8	0	4

*Traded to White Sox

PHOENIX — Class AAA

PACIFIC COAST LEAGUE

BATTING	AVG	G	AB	R	H	2B	3B	HR	RBI	BB	SO	SB	CS	B	T	HT	WT	DOB	1st Yr	Resides
Aurilia, Rich	.294	8	34	9	10	2	0	1	5	5	4	2	1	R	R	6-0	170	9-2-71	1992	Hazlet, N.J.
Ball, Jeff	.321	126	470	90	151	38	3	18	103	58	84	10	4	R	R	5-10	185	4-17-69	1990	Merced, Calif.
Benard, Marvin	.333	17	60	14	20	5	0	0	5	11	9	4	3	L	L	5-10	180	1-20-71	1992	Cudahy, Calif.
Berryhill, Damon	.385	4	13	0	5	0	0	0	1	2	1	0	0	S	R	6-0	205	12-3-63	1984	Laguna Niguel, Calif.
Bonds Jr., Bobby	.000	1	1	0	0	0	0	0	0	0	0	0	0	R	R	6-4	180	3-7-70	1992	Tampa, Fla.
Canizaro, Jay	.198	23	81	12	16	7	0	2	12	9	24	2	2	R	R	5-10	175	7-4-73	1993	Orange, Texas
Cruz, Jacob	.361	127	493	97	178	45	3	12	95	64	64	18	3	L	L	6-0	175	1-28-73	1994	Oxnard, Calif.
Delgado, Wilson	.288	119	416	47	120	22	4	9	59	24	70	9	3	S	R	5-11	165	7-15-75	1993	Santo Domingo, D.R.
Florez, Tim	.301	114	402	57	121	24	4	7	61	32	68	6	3	R	R	5-10	170	7-23-69	1991	Goleta, Calif.
Hamilton, Darryl	.286	3	14	1	4	1	0	1	2	0	2	0	0	L	R	6-1	180	12-3-64	1986	Sugar Land, Texas
Jones, Dax	.255	93	271	48	69	7	5	3	28	39	39	9	10	R	R	6-0	170	8-4-70	1991	Waukegan, Ill.
Kennedy, Darryl	.173	32	98	10	17	4	0	0	8	6	13	1	1	R	R	5-10	170	1-23-69	1991	Davenport, Fla.
Martinez, Ramon	.281	18	57	6	16	2	0	1	7	5	9	1	0	R	R	6-1	170	10-10-72	1993	Toa Alta, P.R.
Mayes, Craig	.095	7	21	2	2	1	0	0	0	1	5	0	0	L	R	5-10	195	5-8-70	1992	Washington, Mich.
McCarty, Dave	.353	121	434	85	153	27	5	22	92	49	75	9	4	R	L	6-5	207	11-23-69	1991	Houston, Texas
Mirabelli, Doug	.265	100	332	49	88	23	2	8	48	58	69	1	2	R	R	6-1	205	10-18-70	1992	Las Vegas, Nev.
Powell, Dante	.241	108	452	91	109	24	4	11	42	52	105	34	10	R	R	6-2	185	8-25-73	1994	Long Beach, Calif.
Roberson, Kevin	.287	109	349	60	100	19	5	14	67	37	98	9	5	S	R	6-4	210	1-29-68	1988	Decatur, Ill.
Rowland, Rich	.237	19	59	10	14	5	0	2	13	7	13	0	0	R	R	6-1	215	2-25-64	1988	Lakeland, Fla.
Unrat, Chris	.500	1	2	0	1	0	0	0	0	1	0	0	0	L	R	6-1	205	3-28-71	1993	Kirkland, Quebec
Williams, Keith	.200	3	5	0	1	0	0	0	0	0	2	0	0	R	R	6-0	190	4-21-72	1993	Bedford, Pa.
Wilson, Desi	.344	121	451	76	155	27	6	7	53	44	73	16	3	L	L	6-7	230	5-9-68	1991	Glen Cove, N.Y.
Woods, Ken	1.000	1	1	0	1	0	0	0	1	0	0	0	0	R	R	5-10	173	8-2-70	1992	Los Angeles, Calif.
Zosky, Eddie	.278	86	241	38	67	10	4	9	45	16	38	3	3	R	R	6-0	175	2-10-68	1989	Whittier, Calif.

PITCHING	W	L	ERA	G	GS	CG	SV	IP	H	R	ER	BB	SO	B	T	HT	WT	DOB	1st Yr	Resides
Arocha, Rene	7	3	4.76	18	18	1	0	112	121	59	59	27	68	R	R	6-0	180	2-24-66	1992	Miami, Fla.
Bailey, Cory	4	0	1.56	13	0	0	3	17	16	4	3	6	14	R	R	6-1	210	1-24-71	1991	Marion, Ill.
Carlson, Dan	13	3	3.88	29	14	0	3	109	102	53	47	36	108	R	R	6-1	185	1-26-70	1990	Portland, Ore.
Corps, Edwin	2	1	5.68	7	2	0	0	19	26	14	12	8	8	R	R	5-11	180	11-3-72	1994	Carolina, P.R.
Creek, Doug	8	6	4.93	25	23	2	0	130	140	76	71	66	137	L	L	5-10	205	3-1-69	1991	Martinsburg, W.Va.
Fernandez, Osvaldo	0	0	3.00	2	2	0	0	12	10	5	4	3	4	R	R	6-2	190	11-4-68	1996	Santo Domingo, D.R.
Foulke, Keith	5	4	4.50	12	12	0	0	76	79	38	38	15	54	R	R	6-1	195	10-19-72	1994	Huffman, Texas
Frontera, Chad	2	0	6.20	5	5	0	0	25	32	19	17	9	13	R	R	6-2	195	11-22-72	1994	Brooklyn, N.Y.
Hancock, Lee	0	1	6.10	7	0	0	0	10	23	7	7	4	9	L	L	6-4	215	6-27-67	1988	Saratoga, Calif.
Hartvigson, Chad	2	2	5.37	17	4	0	0	54	63	34	32	17	52	L	L	6-2	195	12-15-70	1994	Kirkland, Wash.
Johnstone, John	0	3	4.03	38	0	0	24	38	34	17	17	15	30	R	R	6-3	195	11-25-68	1987	Jacksonville, Fla.
Ortiz, Russ	4	3	5.51	14	14	0	0	85	96	57	52	34	70	R	R	6-1	200	6-5-74	1995	Norman, Okla.
Peterson, Mark	0	0	7.36	3	0	0	0	4	6	4	3	1	2	L	L	5-11	195	11-27-70	1992	Kirkland, Wash.
Phillips, Randy	5	4	3.04	21	3	0	0	47	44	20	16	18	27	R	R	6-3	210	3-18-71	1992	Pine Bluff, Ark.
Pickett, Ricky	3	3	3.19	61	0	0	12	68	52	27	24	49	85	L	L	6-0	185	1-19-70	1992	Fort Worth, Texas
Purdy, Shawn	10	3	4.37	56	0	0	2	82	103	45	40	33	42	R	R	6-0	205	7-30-68	1991	St. Cloud, Fla.
Rapp, Pat	2	0	3.60	3	3	0	0	15	16	6	6	9	6	R	R	6-3	210	7-13-67	1989	Sulphur, La.
Roa, Joe	3	1	4.75	6	5	0	0	36	43	21	19	11	16	R	R	6-1	194	10-11-71	1989	Hazel Park, Mich.
Soderstrom, Steve	4	8	6.47	31	15	0	1	106	141	81	76	52	78	R	R	6-3	215	4-3-72	1994	Turlock, Calif.
Taulbee, Andy	2	2	7.52	19	6	0	0	41	64	41	34	14	20	R	R	6-4	210	10-5-72	1994	Tucker, Ga.
Vanderweele, Doug	6	4	4.59	36	2	0	1	69	99	38	35	18	35	R	R	6-3	200	3-18-70	1991	Las Vegas, Nev.
VanLandingham, William	1	1	9.00	4	4	0	0	17	20	19	17	21	7	R	R	6-2	210	7-16-70	1991	Franklin, Tenn.
Villano, Mike	5	3	4.16	13	11	0	0	71	75	36	33	27	41	R	R	6-1	200	8-10-71	1994	Bay City, Mich.

FIELDING

Catcher	PCT	G	PO	A	E	DP	PB
Berryhill	1.000	3	14	1	0	0	0
Kennedy	.980	30	182	12	4	0	0
Mayes	1.000	5	23	3	0	0	0
Mirabelli	.994	99	629	47	4	6	2
Rowland	1.000	16	115	6	0	0	2
Unrat	.500	1	2	0	2	0	0

First Base	PCT	G	PO	A	E	DP
Ball	.963	3	20	6	1	2
McCarty	.995	75	561	53	3	71
Wilson	.991	75	592	43	6	74

Second Base	PCT	G	PO	A	E	DP
Ball	.857	2	3	3	1	0
Canizaro	.969	15	25	37	2	7
Delgado	1.000	5	11	15	0	3
Florez	.982	105	189	313	9	92
Martinez	.957	14	25	41	3	11
Zosky	.952	16	33	27	3	7

Third Base	PCT	G	PO	A	E	DP
Ball	.938	107	46	166	14	13
Canizaro	1.000	6	7	9	0	1
Florez	.778	3	1	6	2	1
Kennedy	1.000	2	2	2	0	0
Woods	000	1	0	0	0	0
Zosky	.953	42	16	65	4	13

Shortstop	PCT	G	PO	A	E	DP
Aurilia	1.000	8	14	22	0	8
Delgado	.967	114	197	332	18	86
Florez	1.000	4	4	10	0	1
Martinez	1.000	2	1	3	0	0
Zosky	.966	30	44	69	4	18

Outfield	PCT	G	PO	A	E	DP
Benard	.966	17	26	2	1	0
Bonds	000	1	0	0	0	0
Cruz	.970	117	239	16	8	4
Hamilton	1.000	3	6	0	0	0
Jones	.968	81	146	6	5	2
McCarty	1.000	1	2	0	0	0
Powell	.986	108	266	7	4	1
Roberson	.980	92	139	7	3	0
Williams	000	1	0	0	0	0
Wilson	.960	38	66	6	3	1

SHREVEPORT — Class AA

TEXAS LEAGUE

BATTING	AVG	G	AB	R	H	2B	3B	HR	RBI	BB	SO	SB	CS	B	T	HT	WT	DOB	1st Yr	Resides
Bess, Johnny	.143	12	28	1	4	3	0	0	6	3	5	0	0	S	R	6-1	190	4-6-70	1992	Grand Junction, Colo.
Canizaro, Jay	.256	50	176	36	45	9	0	11	38	26	44	2	2	R	R	5-10	175	7-4-73	1993	Orange, Texas
Fick, Chris	.000	4	5	1	0	0	0	0	0	1	4	0	0	L	R	6-2	190	10-4-69	1994	Thousand Oaks, Calif.
Guzman, Edwards	.284	118	380	52	108	15	4	3	42	33	57	3	1	L	R	5-11	192	9-11-76	1996	Naranjito, P.R.
Kennedy, Darryl	.268	22	71	11	19	4	0	2	10	6	8	0	0	R	R	5-10	170	1-23-69	1991	Davenport, Fla.
King, Brett	.216	79	194	28	42	6	1	6	20	30	55	4	5	R	R	6-1	190	7-20-72	1993	Apopka, Fla.
Martinez, Ramon	.319	105	404	72	129	32	4	5	54	40	48	4	5	R	R	6-1	170	10-10-72	1993	Toa Alta, P.R.
Mayes, Craig	.273	86	293	27	80	8	5	2	38	14	29	1	0	L	R	5-10	195	5-8-70	1992	Washington, Mich.
Murray, Calvin	.272	122	419	83	114	25	3	10	56	66	73	52	6	R	R	5-11	185	7-30-71	1992	Dallas, Texas

DAVID SEELIG

San Francisco's Barry Bonds

LEE SCHMID

Shreveport's Darin Blood

BATTING	AVG	G	AB	R	H	2B	3B	HR	RBI	BB	SO	SB	CS	B	T	HT	WT	DOB	1st Yr	Resides
Ramirez, Peto	.177	41	113	8	20	6	0	1	9	7	37	0	0	R	R	6-2	200	9-10-72	1991	Ensenada, P.R.
Rios, Armando	.289	127	461	86	133	30	6	14	79	63	85	17	7	L	L	5-9	178	9-13-71	1994	Carolina, P.R.
Sbrocco, Jon	.262	97	271	32	71	15	3	2	27	40	21	7	8	L	R	5-10	165	1-5-71	1993	Willoughby Hills, Ohio
Simonton, Benji	.256	116	387	73	99	15	2	20	79	81	120	7	5	R	R	6-1	225	5-12-72	1992	Tempe, Ariz.
Singleton, Chris	.317	126	464	85	147	26	10	9	61	22	50	27	11	L	L	6-2	195	8-15-72	1993	Hercules, Calif.
Unrat, Chris	.333	6	12	2	4	1	0	0	4	1	0	0	0	L	R	6-1	205	3-28-71	1993	Kirkland, Quebec
2-team (19 Tulsa)	.238	25	63	6	15	4	0	0	11	17	7	0	0							
Williams, Keith	.320	131	493	83	158	37	7	22	106	46	94	3	0	R	R	6-0	190	4-21-72	1993	Bedford, Pa.
Woods, Ken	.300	104	293	41	88	14	2	2	32	28	40	6	4	R	R	5-10	173	8-2-70	1992	Los Angeles, Calif.

PITCHING	W	L	ERA	G	GS	CG	SV	IP	H	R	ER	BB	SO	B	T	HT	WT	DOB	1st Yr	Resides
Barcelo, Lorenzo	2	0	4.02	5	5	0	0	31	30	19	14	8	20	R	R	6-4	205	9-10-77	1994	San Pedro de Macoris, D.R.
Blood, Darin	8	10	4.33	27	27	0	0	156	152	89	75	83	90	S	R	6-2	205	8-31-74	1995	Veradale, Wash.
Brohawn, Troy	13	5	2.56	26	26	1	0	169	148	57	48	64	98	L	L	6-1	190	1-14-73	1994	Woolford, Md.
Corps, Edwin	5	3	4.35	43	1	0	6	72	66	38	35	35	24	R	R	5-11	180	11-3-72	1994	Carolina, P.R.
Fontenot, Joe	10	11	5.53	26	26	1	0	151	171	105	93	65	103	R	R	6-2	185	3-20-77	1995	Scott, La.
Frontera, Chad	4	4	5.86	15	15	0	0	71	78	48	46	31	42	R	R	6-2	195	11-22-72	1994	Brooklyn, N.Y.
Fultz, Aaron	6	3	2.83	49	0	0	1	70	65	30	22	19	60	L	L	6-0	196	9-4-73	1992	Northport, Ala.
Hartvigson, Chad	1	0	3.55	4	1	1	0	13	11	8	5	5	9	L	L	6-2	195	12-15-70	1994	Kirkland, Wash.
Hernandez, Santos	1	1	2.30	11	0	0	6	16	13	4	4	3	14	R	R	6-1	172	11-3-72	1994	Chiriqui, Panama
Howry, Bob	6	3	4.91	48	0	0	22	55	58	35	30	21	43	L	R	6-5	215	8-4-73	1994	Glendale, Ariz.
Martin, Jeff	0	2	4.26	26	0	0	1	38	33	20	18	15	24	R	R	6-2	195	3-28-73	1991	Renton, Wash.
Myers, Jason	1	0	0.75	7	0	0	0	12	14	7	1	0	12	L	L	6-4	200	9-19-73	1993	Butte Falls, Ore.
Oropesa, Eddie	7	7	3.92	43	9	1	0	124	122	58	54	64	65	L	L	6-2	200	11-23-71	1993	Miami, Fla.
Ortiz, Russ	2	3	4.13	12	12	0	0	57	52	28	26	37	50	R	R	6-1	200	6-5-74	1995	Norman, Okla.
Phillips, Randy	2	0	2.66	11	0	0	1	20	17	6	6	3	8	R	R	6-3	210	3-18-71	1992	Pine Bluff, Ark.
Schramm, Carl	1	0	6.43	3	1	0	0	7	10	6	5	0	5	R	R	6-4	200	6-10-70	1991	Crete, Ill.
Taulbee, Andy	4	8	5.17	14	14	1	0	85	104	59	49	32	46	R	R	6-4	210	10-5-72	1994	Tucker, Ga.
Thurmond, Travis	0	1	6.00	2	1	0	0	6	10	9	4	9	4	R	R	6-3	200	12-8-73	1992	Hillsboro, Ore.
Villano, Mike	3	1	6.29	30	0	0	2	34	41	25	24	20	26	R	R	6-1	200	8-10-71	1994	Bay City, Mich.

FIELDING

Catcher	PCT	G	PO	A	E	DP	PB
Bess	.987	12	65	10	1	0	1
Kennedy	.951	18	104	12	6	4	0
Mayes	.986	84	363	54	6	2	11
Ramirez	.975	35	208	22	6	3	10
Unrat	1.000	5	12	1	0	1	1

First Base	PCT	G	PO	A	E	DP
King	1.000	5	23	1	0	4
Ramirez	1.000	2	1	0	0	0
Simonton	.991	113	1079	77	11	110
Williams	.989	11	81	5	1	5
Woods	1.000	14	136	11	0	12

Second Base	PCT	G	PO	A	E	DP
Canizaro	.974	38	63	85	4	22
King	.985	23	26	41	1	9
Sbrocco	.955	65	124	175	14	47
Woods	.978	33	57	78	3	18

Third Base	PCT	G	PO	A	E	DP
Canizaro	.947	7	3	15	1	0
Guzman	.935	113	73	199	19	17
King	1.000	24	9	39	0	0
Woods	.809	14	7	31	9	2

Shortstop	PCT	G	PO	A	E	DP
Canizaro	.974	8	14	24	1	5
King	.902	22	30	62	10	15
Martinez	.968	104	167	370	18	80
Woods	.940	15	21	42	4	8

Outfield	PCT	G	PO	A	E	DP
Fick	.667	1	2	0	1	0
King	.000	1	0	0	0	0
Murray	.978	107	214	9	5	4
Rios	.972	115	191	17	6	3
Sbrocco	1.000	1	2	0	0	0
Singleton	.974	119	253	11	7	4
Williams	.972	85	163	9	5	2
Woods	1.000	3	2	0	0	0

BAKERSFIELD — Class A

CALIFORNIA LEAGUE

BATTING	AVG	G	AB	R	H	2B	3B	HR	RBI	BB	SO	SB	CS	B	T	HT	WT	DOB	1st Yr	Resides
Baeza, Art	.258	86	310	51	80	18	3	16	60	18	73	2	3	R	R	6-2	195	3-31-74	1996	West Covina, Calif.
Campusano, Carlos	.199	61	191	17	38	8	3	1	15	7	49	2	0	R	R	5-11	155	9-2-75	1994	Palave, D.R.
Cooper, Tim	.223	38	112	15	25	5	0	2	18	24	38	2	2	R	R	6-3	190	3-10-71	1989	Sacramento, Calif.
Delgado, Reymundo	.265	50	166	21	44	8	1	5	29	15	27	3	4	L	L	5-11	200	12-29-75	1996	Rio Piedras, P.R.
Faircloth, Chad	.260	19	73	8	19	5	0	1	7	6	22	1	0	L	R	6-0	180	4-25-75	1997	Winston-Salem, N.C.
Felix, Pedro	.272	135	515	59	140	25	4	14	56	23	90	5	7	R	R	6-1	180	4-27-77	1994	Azua, D.R.
Glendenning, Mike	.258	134	503	95	130	27	0	33	100	63	150	1	4	R	R	6-0	210	8-26-76	1996	West Hills, Calif.
Guse, Bryan	.253	26	87	7	22	3	0	1	6	12	16	0	1	L	R	5-11	185	9-21-74	1997	New Brighton, Minn.
Manning, Brian	.282	105	394	56	111	21	3	8	41	34	74	6	5	R	R	6-3	200	2-1-75	1996	Hazlet, N.J.
Marval, Raul	.256	115	437	41	112	15	3	2	42	11	66	8	6	R	R	6-0	170	12-13-75	1993	Cabodare, Venez.
Minor, Damon	.289	140	532	98	154	34	1	31	99	87	143	2	1	L	L	6-7	230	1-5-74	1996	Edmond, Okla.
Pernalete, Marco	.270	17	37	6	10	0	0	0	2	2	7	0	1	S	R	6-0	152	10-12-78	1996	Barquisimeto, Venez.
Rand, Ian	.232	29	82	9	19	4	0	1	7	4	28	2	2	R	R	6-4	200	1-30-77	1995	La Mesa, Calif.
Torrealba, Yorvit	.274	119	446	52	122	15	3	4	40	31	58	4	2	R	R	5-11	180	7-19-78	1995	Guarenas, Venez.
Twist, Jeff	.137	18	51	4	7	2	0	0	1	4	18	0	0	R	R	6-3	220	6-17-73	1994	Bakersfield, Calif.
Van Rossum, Chris	.261	125	441	72	115	17	5	2	40	57	98	9	12	L	L	6-2	180	2-15-74	1996	Turlock, Calif.
Watson, Jon	.259	119	448	67	116	22	2	2	36	30	66	14	10	R	R	6-0	185	12-18-73	1995	Pompton Lakes, N.J.

GAMES BY POSITION: C—Guse 17, Torrealba 114, Twist 17. **1B**—Baeza 9, Cooper 2, Minor 129. **2B**—Marval 26, Pernalete 14, Watson 109. **3B**—Cooper 4, Felix 135, Pernalete 1, Watson 1. **SS**—Campusano 56, Marval 90. **OF**—Baeza 3, Cooper 6, Delgado 14, Faircloth 18, Glendenning 132, Manning 105, Pernalete 1, Rand 26, Van Rossum 124, Watson 6.

PITCHING	W	L	ERA	G	GS	CG	SV	IP	H	R	ER	BB	SO	B	T	HT	WT	DOB	1st Yr	Resides
Bermudez, Manuel	8	8	4.90	19	18	1	0	112	121	69	61	41	71	R	R	6-1	180	12-15-76	1995	Antioch, Calif.
2-team (9 San Jose)	10	14	5.42	28	27	3	0	156	182	104	94	63	98							
Carlson, Dan	0	0	0.00	2	2	0	0	6	3	0	0	1	7							
Crabtree, Robby	7	7	5.13	45	9	1	1	112	124	77	64	59	116	R	R	6-1	185	1-26-70	1990	Portland, Ore.
Gomez, Dennys	0	4	7.22	32	2	0	1	57	61	52	46	34	50	R	R	6-1	165	11-25-72	1996	Anaheim, Calif.
Grote, Jason	12	8	3.45	25	25	0	0	156	156	77	60	59	116	S	R	6-0	195	6-21-71	1994	Miami, Fla.
Hartvigson, Chad	1	1	3.00	5	4	0	0	27	22	9	9	5	22	R	R	6-0	180	4-13-75	1994	Gresham, Ore.
Hutzler, Jeff	2	7	5.30	47	3	1	1	88	92	59	52	41	70	L	L	6-2	195	12-15-70	1994	Kirkland, Wash.
Jensen, Ryan	0	0	13.50	1	1	0	0	1	3	2	2	0	2	R	R	6-6	220	12-5-72	1995	San Antonio, Texas
Keith, Jeff	1	2	5.73	37	0	0	0	44	45	29	28	32	35	R	R	6-0	205	9-17-75	1996	West Valley, Utah
Knoll, Brian	3	6	5.69	49	0	0	2	68	88	50	43	35	56	L	L	6-1	205	6-1-72	1994	Troy, N.Y.
Larreal, Guillermo	2	0	6.12	32	0	0	1	50	63	40	34	14	37	R	R	6-3	200	8-4-73	1995	Corona, Calif.
Malloy, Bill	7	9	4.79	29	29	0	0	167	184	106	89	83	124	R	R	6-1	175	2-3-76	1995	Maracaibo, Venez.
Myers, Jason	4	3	6.42	10	9	0	0	48	64	43	34	14	32	R	R	6-2	210	5-22-75	1996	Piscataway, N.J.
Pageler, Mick	2	5	4.68	61	0	0	29	65	69	39	34	26	68	L	L	6-4	200	9-19-73	1993	Butte Falls, Ore.
Rector, Bobby	2	4	4.10	8	8	0	0	48	52	27	22	12	32	R	R	6-2	205	4-30-76	1996	Mesa, Ariz.
Rice, Nathan	2	0	1.96	8	1	0	0	18	13	4	4	9	9	R	R	6-1	170	9-24-74	1994	Imperial Beach, Calif.
Riley, Michael	1	2	8.41	6	4	0	0	20	25	20	19	8	17	L	L	6-5	200	4-19-74	1997	Visalia, Calif.
Wells, Matt	8	12	4.45	29	25	0	0	144	154	87	71	81	109	L	L	6-2	165	1-2-75	1996	Seaford, Del.
														R	R	6-3	210	5-25-75	1996	Quincy, Calif.

SAN JOSE — Class A

CALIFORNIA LEAGUE

BATTING	AVG	G	AB	R	H	2B	3B	HR	RBI	BB	SO	SB	CS	B	T	HT	WT	DOB	1st Yr	Resides
Alguacil, Jose	.207	122	392	53	81	15	2	7	42	32	98	13	13	S	R	6-2	175	8-9-72	1991	Caracas, Venez.
Bess, Johnny	.239	44	155	29	37	9	1	5	26	15	41	4	2	S	R	6-1	190	4-6-70	1992	Grand Junction, Colo.
Blanco, Dany	.164	33	73	8	12	2	1	0	4	4	25	0	0	R	R	6-0	170	11-4-75	1994	San Felix, Venez.
Bonds Jr., Bobby	.317	79	268	46	85	12	3	5	44	48	55	17	10	R	R	6-4	180	3-7-70	1992	Tampa, Fla.
Caruso, Mike	.333	108	441	76	147	24	11	2	50	38	19	11	16	S	R	6-1	172	5-27-77	1996	Coral Springs, Fla.
Chiaramonte, Giuseppe	.229	64	223	29	51	11	1	12	44	25	58	0	0	R	R	6-0	200	2-19-76	1997	Santa Cruz, Calif.
Corujo, Rey	.202	30	94	10	19	6	1	2	11	10	19	0	0	R	R	5-11	185	10-19-71	1995	Bayamon, P.R.
Denbow, Don	.248	107	339	58	84	20	1	10	50	86	138	19	12	R	R	6-4	215	4-30-73	1993	Corsicana, Texas
Ehmann, Kurt	.238	50	147	15	35	0	0	1	13	20	33	3	2	R	R	6-1	185	8-18-70	1992	Ukiah, Calif.
Fuentes, Joel	.200	5	5	1	1	0	0	0	1	2	2	0	1	S	R	6-0	178	5-27-76	1997	Cayey, P.R.
Garland, Tim	.298	135	577	106	172	28	9	3	39	34	88	65	15	R	R	6-0	185	7-15-68	1989	Danville, Va.
Gulseth, Mark	.317	95	325	47	103	25	3	10	58	46	49	1	0	L	R	6-4	200	11-12-71	1993	Callaway, Minn.
Melendez, Angel	.207	62	203	16	42	11	2	3	15	14	58	0	1	R	R	6-1	192	10-21-75	1996	Caguas, P.R.
Morales, Alex	.217	29	83	8	18	2	0	0	6	4	28	4	5	R	R	6-0	190	2-15-74	1995	Palm Beach Gardens, Fla.
Mosier, Mark	.262	25	84	8	22	2	0	1	13	10	13	1	0	R	R	6-0	205	6-13-74	1997	Salina, Kan.
Mota, Pedro	.161	13	31	2	5	1	0	0	2	1	13	1	1	L	L	6-1	165	2-28-78	1995	San Pedro de Macoris, D.R.
Poor, Jeff	.186	52	118	11	22	7	0	0	14	28	18	0	0	R	R	6-1	200	5-23-74	1994	El Segundo, Calif.
Prospero, Ted	.262	29	65	6	17	2	1	2	11	3	23	1	0	R	R	5-11	170	2-12-77	1995	San Pedro de Macoris, D.R.
Ramirez, Peto	.267	43	135	17	36	7	0	7	26	15	31	0	0	R	R	6-2	200	9-10-72	1991	Ensenada, P.R.
Rodriguez, Guillermo	.148	13	27	2	4	3	1	0	2	0	9	0	0	R	R	5-11	190	5-15-78	1996	Barquisimeto, Venez.
Unrat, Chris	.244	59	160	18	39	9	0	3	19	30	38	0	1	L	R	6-1	205	3-28-71	1993	Kirkland, Quebec
Wilson, Todd	.345	130	502	66	173	35	3	5	88	32	60	7	3	R	R	6-3	210	11-20-69	1994	San Diego, Calif.
Zuniga, Tony	.183	97	289	24	53	10	0	1	32	33	48	3	3	R	R	6-0	185	1-13-75	1996	Santa Ana, Calif.

GAMES BY POSITION: C—Bess 22, Chiaramonte 56, Poor 34, Ramirez 41, Rodriguez 1, Unrat 4. **1B**—Alguacil 2, Gulseth 84, Poor 3, Ramirez 1, Rodriguez 10, Unrat 16, Wilson 48. **2B**—Alguacil 44, Ehmann 4, Fuentes 3, Mosier 1, Prospero 15, Zuniga 95. **3B**—Alguacil 47, Ehmann 32, Mosier 24, Prospero 6, Wilson 57. **SS**—Alguacil 32, Caruso 106, Ehmann 1, Prospero 4, Wilson 4. **OF**—Alguacil 2, Bess 7, Blanco 27, Bonds 27, Corujo 27, Denbow 103, Ehmann 7, Garland 133, Melendez 60, Morales 27, Mota 9, Prospero 1, Unrat 2, Wilson 27.

PITCHING	W	L	ERA	G	GS	CG	SV	IP	H	R	ER	BB	SO	B	T	HT	WT	DOB	1st Yr	Resides
Andra, Jeff	1	4	6.98	6	6	0	0	30	36	25	23	11	29	L	L	6-5	210	9-9-75	1997	Lenexa, Kan.
Bailey, Philip	0	9	7.35	25	10	0	0	60	70	54	49	33	42	L	L	6-1	185	10-4-73	1995	Benton, Ark.
Barcelo, Lorenzo	5	4	3.94	16	16	1	0	89	91	45	39	30	89	R	R	6-4	205	9-10-77	1994	San Pedro de Macoris, D.R.
Bermudez, Manuel	2	6	6.75	9	9	2	0	44	61	35	33	22	27	R	R	6-1	180	12-15-76	1995	Antioch, Calif.
Brester, Jason	9	9	4.24	26	26	0	0	142	164	80	67	52	172	L	L	6-3	190	12-7-76	1995	Burlington, Wash.

PITCHING	W	L	ERA	G	GS	CG	SV	IP	H	R	ER	BB	SO	B	T	HT	WT	DOB	1st Yr	Resides
Castillo, Alberto	2	2	5.61	18	1	0	0	34	41	26	21	15	30	L	L	6-3	205	7-5-75	1994	New Port Richey, Fla.
Estrella, Luis	5	5	3.39	42	0	0	2	77	84	39	29	25	59	R	R	6-2	215	10-7-74	1996	Santa Ana, Calif.
Hernandez, Santos	2	6	3.47	47	0	0	15	57	51	26	22	14	87	R	R	6-1	172	11-3-72	1994	Chiriqui, Panama
Leese, Brandon	7	5	3.05	19	19	0	0	112	99	44	38	46	99	R	R	6-4	190	10-8-75	1996	Lincolnshire, Ill.
Linebrink, Scott	2	1	3.18	6	6	0	0	28	29	11	10	10	40	R	R	6-3	185	8-4-76	1997	Austin, Texas
Martin, Jeff	0	4	5.40	20	0	0	6	27	36	18	16	11	25	R	R	6-2	195	3-28-73	1991	Renton, Wash.
McMullen, Mike	6	4	2.67	56	0	0	7	91	85	37	27	33	71	R	R	6-6	210	10-13-73	1993	Granada Hills, Calif.
Rogers, Kevin	0	0	2.76	8	8	0	0	29	29	9	9	6	27	L	L	6-1	198	8-20-68	1988	Parchman, Miss.
Schramm, Carl	4	4	4.94	36	4	0	0	93	103	54	51	33	75	R	R	6-4	200	6-10-70	1991	Crete, Ill.
Stoops, Jim	2	5	5.20	50	0	0	4	92	92	56	53	45	114	R	R	6-2	180	6-30-72	1995	Somerset, N.J.
Takahashi, Kurt	1	1	5.95	10	0	0	1	20	20	17	13	8	21	R	R	6-4	215	2-22-74	1995	Clovis, Calif.
Thurmond, Travis	3	5	5.68	12	12	0	0	70	83	53	44	28	61	R	R	6-3	200	12-8-73	1992	Hillsboro, Ore.
2-team (9 Lake Els.)	6	8	4.21	21	21	2	0	130	124	74	61	50	114							
Vining, Ken	9	6	4.21	23	23	1	0	137	140	77	64	60	142	L	L	5-11	180	12-5-74	1996	Hopkins, S.C.

SALEM-KEIZER — Short-Season Class A

NORTHWEST LEAGUE

BATTING	AVG	G	AB	R	H	2B	3B	HR	RBI	BB	SO	SB	CS	B	T	HT	WT	DOB	1st Yr	Resides
Ankrum, C.J.	.266	74	263	44	70	14	1	5	64	49	44	6	5	L	L	6-1	185	12-11-75	1997	San Jose, Calif.
Baeza, Art	.313	6	16	5	5	1	0	2	5	2	3	0	0	R	R	6-2	195	3-31-74	1996	West Covina, Calif.
Byas, Mike	.276	71	290	68	80	9	1	0	16	48	44	51	9	S	R	6-0	165	4-21-76	1997	Chesterfield, Mo.
Casper, Brett	.223	61	229	31	51	14	1	7	34	31	86	17	3	R	R	6-3	215	11-24-75	1997	Omaha, Neb.
Faircloth, Chad	.284	31	102	13	29	5	2	0	13	14	30	2	0	L	R	6-0	180	4-25-75	1997	Winston-Salem, N.C.
Flaherty, Tim	.227	32	110	16	25	6	0	4	17	15	44	1	0	R	R	6-4	215	7-11-76	1997	Williamstown, Mass.
Fuentes, Joel	.218	20	55	7	12	2	0	0	2	17	12	1	1	S	R	6-0	178	5-27-76	1997	Cayey, P.R.
Greene, Clay	.225	33	89	11	20	4	1	0	5	7	19	21	3	R	R	6-0	185	11-10-74	1997	Cleveland, Tenn.
Kenna, David	.198	64	242	23	48	8	2	7	33	17	86	1	1	L	R	6-0	200	3-16-78	1996	North Fort Myers, Fla.
Lopez, Luis	.000	1	4	0	0	0	0	0	1	0	1	0	0	R	R	6-3	195	4-13-78	1995	San Felipe, Venez.
Mendoza, Carlos	.208	33	106	10	22	0	0	0	6	11	19	6	0	S	R	6-1	160	11-27-79	1996	Barquisimeto, Venez.
Mosier, Mark	.306	19	62	10	19	2	0	0	7	9	13	0	2	R	R	6-0	205	6-13-74	1997	Salina, Kan.
Oquendo, Nelvin	.200	4	5	1	1	0	0	0	0	1	2	0	0	R	R	6-1	170	8-14-79	1996	Corazon de Jesus, Venez.
Otero, William	.238	46	147	22	35	9	3	0	12	17	32	2	1	R	R	5-11	175	9-30-76	1997	Bayamon, P.R.
Priess, Matt	.273	46	172	22	47	8	2	3	31	12	30	0	1	R	R	6-2	190	11-24-74	1997	Brea, Calif.
Rodriguez, Guillermo	.231	11	39	3	9	3	0	0	3	5	12	0	1	R	R	5-11	190	5-15-78	1996	Barquisimeto, Venez.
Valderrama, Carlos	.319	41	138	21	44	7	3	3	28	12	29	22	0	R	R	6-0	170	11-30-77	1995	Maracaibo, Venez.
Wells, Zachary	.284	62	218	47	62	9	2	10	43	48	57	3	1	R	R	6-4	205	2-23-77	1997	Clayton, Calif.
Young, Travis	.334	76	320	80	107	11	6	1	34	30	50	40	8	R	R	6-1	185	9-8-74	1997	Albuquerque, N.M.

GAMES BY POSITION: C—Baeza 1, Flaherty 28, Kenna 3, Priess 42, Rodriguez 9. **1B**—Ankrum 73, Faircloth 4, Mosier 1, Rodriguez 1. **2B**—Greene 1, Young 76. **3B**—Baeza 4, Faircloth 12, Kenna 32, Mosier 16, Oquendo 3, Otero 19. **SS**—Baeza 2, Fuentes 20, Mendoza 33, Otero 28. **OF**—Byas 71, Casper 61, Faircloth 15, Greene 27, Valderrama 20, Wells 42.

PITCHING	W	L	ERA	G	GS	CG	SV	IP	H	R	ER	BB	SO	B	T	HT	x	DOB	1st Yr	Resides
Andra, Jeff	3	1	2.03	8	8	0	0	44	39	21	10	10	58	L	L	6-5	210	9-9-75	1997	Lenexa, Kan.
Austin, Shawn	1	1	1.06	13	0	0	0	17	12	7	2	6	18	R	L	6-0	205	3-30-74	1997	Largo, Fla.
Clark, Richard	0	2	7.50	6	0	0	0	6	6	6	5	7	5	R	R	5-10	160	11-1-77	1997	Clearwater, Fla.
DeAbreu, Milton	0	0	14.09	7	0	0	0	8	17	12	12	6	8	R	R	6-2	175	3-10-78	1996	Barquisimeto, Venez.
Farley, Joe	0	1	4.50	10	0	0	0	14	6	7	7	16	17	S	L	6-8	210	4-23-79	1997	Olympia, Wash.
Hutchings, Mark	1	0	8.56	11	0	0	0	14	24	15	13	8	5	R	R	6-4	200	9-18-76	1997	Farmington, Mo.
Jensen, Ryan	7	3	5.15	16	16	0	0	80	87	55	46	32	67	R	R	6-0	205	9-17-75	1996	West Valley, Utah
Johnson, Eric	0	0	11.88	10	0	0	0	8	7	12	11	18	8	R	R	6-4	195	9-12-77	1997	Newberg, Ore.
Joseph, Kevin	3	5	5.40	17	6	0	1	45	44	35	27	26	45	R	R	6-4	200	8-1-76	1997	Dallas, Texas
Larreal, Guillermo	1	2	5.51	13	0	0	1	16	23	12	10	3	16	R	R	6-1	175	2-3-76	1995	Maracaibo, Venez.
Linebrink, Scott	0	0	4.50	3	3	0	0	10	7	5	5	6	6	R	R	6-3	185	8-4-76	1997	Austin, Texas
Malerich, Will	2	1	3.04	21	0	0	0	27	26	14	9	21	43	L	L	5-11	180	10-25-75	1997	Alexandria, Va.
Nathan, Joe	2	1	2.47	18	5	0	2	62	53	22	17	26	44	R	R	6-4	195	11-22-74	1995	Circleville, N.Y.
Nielsen, Tom	1	1	4.82	7	0	0	0	9	10	5	5	4	12	R	L	6-2	170	7-28-76	1997	Coram, N.Y.
Olivo, Gary	0	0	24.00	3	0	0	0	3	4	11	8	6	3	L	L	6-1	195	5-22-74	1994	Santo Domingo, D.R.
Pohl, Jeff	5	4	4.65	18	8	0	0	72	88	51	37	20	47	R	R	6-4	215	3-1-76	1996	St. Charles, Mo.
Rice, Nathan	1	2	5.40	13	0	0	0	18	22	13	11	7	26	L	L	6-5	200	4-19-74	1997	Visalia, Calif.
Riley, Michael	9	2	3.46	15	15	1	0	88	76	39	34	28	96	L	L	6-2	165	1-2-75	1996	Seaford, Del.
Takahashi, Kurt	0	1	3.71	10	1	0	0	17	22	9	7	8	19	R	R	6-4	215	2-22-74	1995	Clovis, Calif.
Travis, Jesse	0	1	2.45	28	0	0	16	29	24	9	8	12	19	R	R	6-2	190	11-4-74	1997	Seattle, Wash.
Verdugo, Jason	4	8	4.83	16	14	0	0	78	85	48	42	25	82	R	R	6-2	195	3-28-75	1997	Winkleman, Ariz.

Seattle MARINERS

Manager: Lou Piniella.

1997 Record: 90-72, .556 (1st, AL West)

BATTING	AVG	G	AB	R	H	2B	3B	HR	RBI	BB	SO	SB	CS	B	T	HT	WT	DOB	1st Yr	Resides
Amaral, Rich	.284	89	190	34	54	5	0	1	21	10	34	12	8	R	R	6-0	175	4-1-62	1983	Seattle, Wash.
Blowers, Mike	.293	68	150	22	44	5	0	5	20	21	33	0	0	R	R	6-2	210	4-24-65	1986	Tacoma, Wash.
Buhner, Jay	.243	157	540	104	131	18	2	40	109	119	175	0	0	R	R	6-3	210	8-13-64	1984	League City, Texas
Cora, Joey	.300	149	574	105	172	40	4	11	54	53	49	6	7	S	R	5-8	155	5-14-65	1985	Caguas, P.R.
Cruz, Jose	.268	49	183	28	49	12	1	12	34	13	45	1	0	S	R	6-0	200	4-19-74	1995	Houston, Texas
Davis, Russ	.271	119	420	57	114	29	1	20	63	27	100	6	2	R	R	6-0	170	9-13-69	1988	Hueytown, Ala.
Ducey, Rob	.287	76	143	25	41	15	2	5	10	6	31	3	3	L	R	6-2	180	5-24-65	1984	Palm Harbor, Fla.
Espinoza, Alvaro	.181	33	72	3	13	1	0	0	7	2	12	1	1	R	R	6-0	190	2-19-62	1979	Bergenfield, N.J.
Gates, Brent	.238	65	151	18	36	8	0	3	20	14	21	0	0	S	R	6-1	180	3-14-70	1991	Grandville, Mich.
Griffey, Ken	.304	157	608	125	185	34	3	56	147	76	121	15	4	L	L	6-3	205	11-21-69	1987	Renton, Wash.
Guevara, Giomar	.000	5	4	0	0	0	0	0	0	0	2	1	0	R	R	5-9	158	10-23-72	1991	Guarenas, Venez.
Ibanez, Raul	.154	11	26	3	4	0	1	1	4	0	6	0	0	L	R	6-2	210	6-2-72	1992	Miami, Fla.
Kelly, Roberto	.298	30	121	19	36	7	0	7	22	5	17	2	1	R	R	6-2	202	10-1-64	1982	Panama City, Panama
2-team (75 Minnesota)	.291	105	368	58	107	26	2	12	59	22	67	9	5							
Martinez, Edgar	.330	155	542	104	179	35	1	28	108	119	86	2	4	R	R	5-11	190	1-2-63	1983	Kirkland, Wash.
Marzano, John	.287	39	87	7	25	3	0	1	10	7	15	0	0	R	R	5-11	195	2-14-63	1985	Philadelphia, Pa.
Raabe, Brian	.000	2	3	0	0	0	0	0	0	1	2	0	0	R	R	5-9	170	11-5-67	1990	Blaine, Minn.
Rodriguez, Alex	.300	141	587	100	176	40	3	23	84	41	99	29	6	R	R	6-2	190	7-27-75	1994	Miami, Fla.
Rohrmeier, Dan	.333	7	9	4	3	0	0	0	2	2	4	0	0	R	R	6-0	185	9-27-65	1987	Woodridge, Ill.
Sheets, Andy	.247	32	89	18	22	3	0	4	9	7	34	2	0	R	R	6-2	180	11-19-71	1992	St. Amant, La.
Sorrento, Paul	.269	146	457	68	123	19	0	31	80	51	112	0	2	L	R	6-2	220	11-17-65	1986	Peabody, Mass.
Tinsley, Lee	.197	49	122	12	24	6	2	0	6	11	34	2	0	S	R	5-10	180	3-4-69	1987	Shelbyville, Ky.
Wilkins, Rick	.250	5	12	2	3	1	0	1	4	1	2	0	0	L	R	6-2	210	6-4-67	1987	Jacksonville, Fla.
Wilson, Dan	.270	146	508	66	137	31	1	15	74	39	72	7	2	R	R	6-3	190	3-25-69	1990	St. Louis Park, Ill.

PITCHING	W	L	ERA	G	GS	CG	SV	IP	H	R	ER	BB	SO	B	T	HT	WT	DOB	1st Yr	Resides
Ayala, Bobby	10	5	3.82	71	0	0	8	97	91	45	41	41	92	R	R	6-3	200	7-8-69	1988	Oxnard, Calif.
Carmona, Rafael	0	0	3.18	4	0	0	0	6	3	3	2	2	6	L	R	6-2	185	10-2-72	1993	Comerio, P.R.
Charlton, Norm	3	8	7.27	71	0	0	14	69	89	59	56	47	55	S	L	6-3	205	1-6-63	1984	Jamaica Beach, Texas
Cloude, Ken	4	2	5.12	10	9	0	0	51	41	32	29	26	46	R	R	6-1	200	1-9-75	1994	Baltimore, Md.
Davis, Tim	0	0	6.75	2	0	0	0	7	6	5	5	4	10	L	L	5-11	165	7-14-70	1992	Bristol, Fla.
Fassero, Jeff	16	9	3.61	35	35	2	0	234	226	108	94	84	189	L	L	6-1	180	1-5-63	1984	Springfield, Ill.
Holzemer, Mark	0	0	6.00	14	0	0	1	9	9	6	6	8	7	L	L	6-0	165	8-20-69	1988	Littleton, Colo.
Hurtado, Edwin	1	2	9.00	13	1	0	0	19	25	19	19	15	10	R	R	6-2	215	2-1-70	1991	Naguaonagua, Venez.
Johnson, Randy	20	4	2.28	30	29	5	0	213	147	60	54	77	291	R	L	6-10	225	9-10-63	1985	Bellevue, Wash.
Lira, Felipe	0	4	9.16	8	3	0	0	19	31	21	19	10	9	R	R	6-0	170	4-26-72	1990	Miranda, Venez.
2-team (20 Detroit)	5	11	6.34	28	18	1	0	111	132	82	78	55	73							
Lowe, Derek	2	4	6.96	12	9	0	0	53	59	43	41	20	39	R	R	6-6	170	6-1-73	1991	Dearborn, Mich.
Maddux, Mike	1	0	10.13	6	0	0	0	11	20	12	12	8	7	L	R	6-2	188	8-27-61	1982	Las Vegas, Nev.
Manzanillo, Josias	0	1	5.40	16	0	0	0	18	19	13	11	17	18	R	R	6-0	190	10-16-67	1983	Hyde Park, Mass.
Martinez, Dennis	1	5	7.71	9	9	0	0	49	65	46	42	29	17	R	R	6-1	183	5-14-55	1974	Miami, Fla.
McCarthy, Greg	1	1	5.46	37	0	0	0	30	26	21	18	16	34	L	L	6-2	193	10-30-68	1987	Shelton, Conn.
Moyer, Jamie	17	5	3.86	30	30	2	0	189	187	82	81	43	113	L	L	6-0	170	11-18-62	1984	Granger, Ill.
Olivares, Omar	1	4	5.49	13	12	0	0	62	81	41	38	28	29	R	R	6-1	183	7-6-67	1987	San German, P.R.
2-team (19 Detroit)	6	10	4.97	32	31	3	0	177	191	109	98	81	103							
Sanders, Scott	3	6	6.47	33	6	0	2	65	73	48	47	38	62	R	R	6-4	220	3-25-69	1990	Thibodaux, La.
Slocumb, Heathcliff	0	4	4.13	27	0	0	10	28	26	13	13	15	28	R	R	6-3	180	6-7-66	1984	Richmond Hill, N.Y.
2-team (49 Boston)	0	9	5.16	76	0	0	27	75	84	45	43	49	64							
Spoljaric, Paul	0	0	4.76	20	0	0	0	23	24	13	12	15	27	L	L	6-3	205	9-24-70	1990	Kelowna, B.C.
2-team (37 Toronto)	0	3	3.69	57	0	0	3	71	61	30	29	36	70							
Timlin, Mike	3	2	3.86	26	0	0	1	26	28	13	11	5	9	R	R	6-4	210	3-10-66	1987	Midland, Texas
2-team (38 Toronto)	6	4	3.22	64	0	0	10	73	69	30	26	20	45							
Torres, Salomon	0	0	27.00	2	0	0	0	3	7	10	10	3	0	R	R	5-11	150	3-11-72	1990	San Pedro de Macoris, D.R.
Wells, Bob	2	0	5.75	46	1	0	2	67	88	49	43	18	51	R	R	6-0	180	11-1-66	1989	Cowiche, Wash.
Wolcott, Bob	5	6	6.03	19	18	0	0	100	129	71	67	29	58	R	R	6-0	190	9-8-73	1992	Medford, Ore.

FIELDING

Catcher	PCT	G	PO	A	E	DP
Marzano	.976	37	191	13	5	4
Wilkins	1.000	3	9	1	0	0
Wilson	.995	144	1051	72	6	13

First Base	PCT	G	PO	A	E	DP
Amaral	1.000	14	27	5	0	3
Blowers	.990	49	263	25	3	27
Gates	.000	1	0	0	0	0
Martinez	.986	7	68	4	1	5
Rohrmeier	1.000	3	6	1	0	0
Sorrento	.996	139	929	86	4	89

Second Base	PCT	G	PO	A	E	DP
Amaral	.927	11	14	24	3	5
Cora	.973	142	307	310	17	81
Espinoza	.978	14	21	23	1	9
Gates	.977	21	13	30	1	4
Guevara	.875	2	2	5	1	0
Raabe	000	1	0	0	0	0
Sheets	1.000	2	2	2	0	0

Third Base	PCT	G	PO	A	E	DP
Amaral	.000	1	0	0	0	0
Blowers	.929	10	3	10	1	1
Davis	.939	117	56	219	18	24
Espinoza	.000	1	0	0	0	0
Gates	.934	32	10	47	4	4
Martinez	.000	1	0	0	0	0
Raabe	1.000	2	1	1	0	0
Sheets	.872	21	8	33	6	4

Shortstop	PCT	G	PO	A	E	DP
Amaral	.000	1	0	0	0	0
Espinoza	.965	17	21	34	2	5
Gates	1.000	5	2	5	0	2
Guevara	1.000	1	0	1	0	0
Rodriguez	.962	140	209	394	24	83
Sheets	.939	9	4	27	2	1

Outfield	PCT	G	PO	A	E	DP
Amaral	1.000	52	62	0	0	0
Blowers	1.000	6	5	0	0	0
Buhner	.997	154	295	5	1	3
Cruz	.966	49	83	1	3	0
Ducey	.986	69	66	3	1	1
Gates	1.000	1	1	0	0	0
Griffey	.985	153	388	9	6	3
Ibanez	1.000	8	9	0	0	0
Kelly	1.000	29	53	1	0	0
Tinsley	1.000	41	68	2	0	2

FARM SYSTEM

Director of Player Development: Larry Beinfest

Class	Farm Team	League	W	L	Pct.	Finish*	Manager	First Yr
AAA	Tacoma (Wash.) Rainiers	Pacific Coast	75	66	.532	4th (10)	Dave Myers	1995
AA	Memphis (Tenn.) Chicks	Southern	67	72	.482	7th (10)	Dave Brundage	1997
#A	Lancaster (Calif.) Jethawks	California	75	66	.532	3rd (10)	Rick Burleson	1996
A	Wisconsin Timber Rattlers	Midwest	76	63	.547	2nd (14)	Gary Varsho	1993
A	Everett (Wash.) Aquasox	Northwest	29	47	.382	7th (8)	Orlando Gomez	1995
R	Peoria (Ariz.) Mariners	Arizona	30	26	.536	2nd (6)	Darrin Garner	1988

*Finish in overall standings (No. of teams in league) #Advanced level

ORGANIZATION LEADERS

MAJOR LEAGUERS

BATTING

*AVG	Edgar Martinez	.330
R	Ken Griffey	125
H	Ken Griffey	185
TB	Ken Griffey	393
2B	Two tied at	40
3B	Joey Cora	4
HR	Ken Griffey	56
RBI	Ken Griffey	147
BB	Two tied at	119
SO	Jay Buhner	175
SB	Alex Rodriguez	29

PITCHING

W	Randy Johnson	20
L	Jeff Fassero	9
#ERA	Randy Johnson	2.28
G	Two tied at	71
CG	Randy Johnson	5
SV	Norm Charlton	14
IP	Jeff Fassero	234
BB	Jeff Fassero	84
SO	Randy Johnson	291

MEL BAILEY

Alex Rodriguez

Brian Raabe

MINOR LEAGUERS

BATTING

*AVG	Brian Raabe, Tacoma	.352
R	Brian Raabe, Tacoma	101
H	Brian Raabe, Tacoma	191
TB	Dan Rohrmeier, Tacoma	290
2B	Dan Rohrmeier, Tacoma	43
3B	Joe Mathis, Lancaster	15
HR	Dan Rohrmeier, Tacoma	33
RBI	Dan Rohrmeier, Tacoma	120
BB	Two tied at	78
SO	Jason Regan, Lancaster/Wisconsin	134
SB	Tarrik Brock, Lancaster	40

PITCHING

W	Joe Mays, Lancaster/Wisconsin	16
L	Justin Kaye, Wisconsin	12
#ERA	Kyle Kennison, Wisconsin	2.13
G	John Thompson, Memphis/Lancaster	48
CG	Two tied at	5
SV	Two tied at	18
IP	Joe Mays, Lancaster/Wisconsin	178
BB	Justin Kaye, Wisconsin	104
SO	Joe Mays, Lancaster/Wisconsin	161

*Minimum 250 At-Bats #Minimum 75 Innings

TOP 10 PROSPECTS

LARRY GOREN

Jose Cruz Jr.

How the Mariners Top 10 prospects, as judged by Baseball America prior to the 1997 season, fared in 1997:

Player, Pos.	Club (Class)	AVG	AB	R	H	2B	3B	HR	RBI	SB
1. *Jose Cruz Jr., of	Seattle	.268	183	28	49	12	1	12	34	1
	Toronto	.231	212	31	49	7	0	14	34	6
	Tacoma (AAA)	.268	190	33	51	16	2	6	30	3
4. Raul Ibanez, of-1b	Seattle	.154	26	3	4	0	1	1	4	0
	Tacoma (AAA)	.304	438	84	133	30	5	15	84	7
5. ^Jason Varitek, c	Boston	1.000	1	0	1	0	0	0	0	0
	Tacoma (AAA)	.254	307	54	78	13	0	15	48	0
	Pawtucket (AAA)	.197	66	6	13	5	0	1	5	0
8. Giomar Guevara, ss-2b	Seattle	.000	4	0	0	0	0	0	0	1
	Tacoma (AAA)	.244	176	29	43	5	1	2	13	3
	Memphis (AA)	.263	228	30	60	10	4	4	28	5
10. Marcus Sturdivant, of	Memphis (AA)	.271	432	71	117	18	5	2	35	21

Player, Pos.	Club (Class)	W	L	ERA	G	SV	IP	H	BB	SO
2. Ken Cloude, rhp	Seattle	4	2	5.12	10	0	51	41	26	46
	Memphis (AA)	11	7	3.87	22	0	133	131	48	124
3. @Dean Crow, rhp	Tacoma (AAA)	4	2	4.78	33	7	43	56	19	36
	Toledo (AAA)	3	0	7.85	18	2	18	26	10	10
6. Greg Wooten, rhp	Memphis (AA)	11	10	4.47	26	0	155	166	59	98
7. Jeff Farnsworth, rhp	Lancaster (A)	1	1	6.97	5	0	21	24	8	18
9. Mac Suzuki, rhp	Tacoma (AAA)	4	9	5.94	32	0	83	79	64	63

*Traded to Blue Jays ^Traded to Red Sox @Traded to Tigers

TM

TACOMA — Class AAA

PACIFIC COAST LEAGUE

BATTING	AVG	G	AB	R	H	2B	3B	HR	RBI	BB	SO	SB	CS	B	T	HT	WT	DOB	1st Yr	Resides
Bonnici, Jim	.250	1	4	0	1	0	0	0	1	1	1	0	0	R	R	6-4	230	1-21-72	1991	Ortonville, Mich.
Castro, Jose	.000	2	1	0	0	0	0	0	0	0	0	0	0	L	L	5-11	192	12-19-75	1993	Los Minas, D.R.
Christian, Eddie	.319	35	135	16	43	5	1	1	9	14	24	3	2	S	L	5-11	180	8-26-71	1992	Richmond, Calif.
Cruz, Jose	.268	50	190	33	51	16	2	6	30	34	44	3	0	S	R	6-0	200	4-19-74	1995	Houston, Texas
Decker, Steve	.297	99	350	44	104	25	1	10	52	22	37	0	0	R	R	6-3	205	10-25-65	1988	Keizer, Ore.
Ducey, Rob	.324	23	74	8	24	8	0	0	11	8	15	0	0	L	R	6-2	180	5-24-65	1984	Palm Harbor, Fla.
Espinoza, Alvaro	.333	4	12	1	4	0	0	0	1	2	1	0	0	R	R	6-0	190	2-19-62	1979	Bergenfield, N.J.
Gates, Brent	.455	7	33	7	15	3	0	0	6	4	2	0	0	S	R	6-1	180	3-14-70	1991	Grandville, Mich.
Gipson, Charles	.314	11	35	5	11	2	0	0	5	4	3	0	1	R	R	6-0	188	12-16-72	1992	Orange, Calif.
Griffey, Craig	.333	3	3	1	1	0	1	0	0	0	0	0	1	R	R	5-11	175	6-3-71	1991	Westchester, Ohio
Guevara, Giomar	.244	54	176	29	43	5	1	2	13	5	39	3	7	R	R	5-9	158	10-23-72	1991	Guarenas, Venez.
Haney, Todd	.353	4	17	3	6	4	0	0	2	2	2	0	0	R	R	5-9	165	7-30-65	1987	Waco, Texas
Ibanez, Raul	.304	111	438	84	133	30	5	15	84	32	75	7	5	L	R	6-2	210	6-2-72	1992	Miami, Fla.
Leach, Jalal	.308	115	415	56	128	26	3	9	55	32	74	6	6	L	L	6-2	200	3-14-69	1990	Novato, Calif.
Millette, Joe	.211	46	123	12	26	2	1	0	5	8	23	1	1	R	R	6-1	175	8-12-66	1989	Lafayette, Calif.
Monahan, Shane	.294	21	85	15	25	4	0	2	12	5	21	5	1	L	R	6-1	200	8-12-74	1995	Marietta, Ga.
Raabe, Brian	.352	135	543	101	191	35	4	14	80	38	20	1	6	R	R	5-9	170	11-5-67	1990	Blaine, Minn.
Reimer, Kevin	.345	46	168	21	58	18	0	3	21	12	22	0	3	L	R	6-2	230	6-28-64	1985	Enderby, B.C.
Rohrmeier, Dan	.297	125	471	86	140	43	4	33	120	45	81	1	0	R	R	6-0	185	9-27-65	1987	Woodridge, Ill.
Sealy, Scot	.273	18	55	8	15	3	0	3	10	5	13	0	1	R	R	6-4	225	2-10-71	1992	Saraland, Ala.
Sheets, Andy	.259	113	401	57	104	23	0	14	53	46	97	7	2	R	R	6-2	180	11-19-71	1992	St. Amant, La.
Silvestre, Juan	.250	8	28	5	7	3	0	0	0	2	9	0	0	R	R	5-11	198	1-10-78	1994	San Pedro de Macoris, D.R.
Tinsley, Lee	.181	31	105	15	19	2	1	2	7	12	34	1	4	S	R	5-10	180	3-4-69	1987	Shelbyville, Ky.
Torres, Paul	.301	59	209	24	63	19	0	5	22	14	31	1	0	R	R	6-3	210	10-19-70	1989	San Lorenzo, Calif.
Varitek, Jason	.254	87	307	54	78	13	0	15	48	34	71	0	1	S	R	6-2	210	4-11-72	1995	Longwood, Fla.
Wilkins, Rick	.338	17	68	16	23	8	0	1	14	8	12	0	0	L	R	6-2	210	6-4-67	1987	Jacksonville, Fla.
Zinter, Alan	.287	110	404	69	116	19	4	20	70	64	113	3	1	S	R	6-2	190	5-19-68	1989	El Paso, Texas

PITCHING	W	L	ERA	G	GS	CG	SV	IP	H	R	ER	BB	SO	B	T	HT	WT	DOB	1st Yr	Resides
Abbott, Paul	8	4	4.13	17	14	3	0	94	80	48	43	29	117	R	R	6-3	195	9-15-67	1985	Fullerton, Calif.
Berumen, Andres	7	4	4.69	16	15	0	0	81	78	45	42	48	79	R	R	6-1	205	4-5-71	1989	Banning, Calif.
2-team (18 Las Vegas)	9	4	4.91	34	16	0	0	114	127	71	62	64	114							
Carmona, Rafael	2	5	3.79	32	5	0	4	59	52	31	25	35	56	L	R	6-2	185	10-2-72	1993	Comerio, P.R.
Crow, Dean	4	2	4.78	33	0	0	7	43	56	25	23	19	36	R	R	6-5	212	8-21-72	1993	Houston, Texas
Davis, Tim	1	0	3.60	1	1	0	0	5	4	2	2	3	5	L	L	5-11	165	7-14-70	1992	Bristol, Fla.
Franklin, Ryan	5	5	4.18	14	14	0	0	90	97	48	42	24	59	R	R	6-3	160	3-5-73	1993	Spiro, Okla.
Gajkowski, Steve	5	3	3.87	44	3	0	2	93	100	43	40	24	48	R	R	6-2	200	12-30-69	1990	Bellevue, Wash.
Harikkala, Tim	6	8	6.43	21	21	0	0	113	160	93	81	50	86	R	R	6-2	185	7-15-71	1992	Lake Worth, Fla.
Holdridge, David	1	1	2.96	15	0	0	1	24	21	9	8	13	24	R	R	6-3	195	2-5-69	1988	Huntington Beach, Calif.
Holzemer, Mark	1	0	2.20	37	0	0	13	41	32	10	10	10	38	L	L	6-0	165	8-20-69	1988	Littleton, Colo.
Hurtado, Edwin	10	6	3.88	20	20	5	0	132	139	60	57	37	100	R	R	6-2	215	2-1-70	1991	Naguaonagua, Venez.
Lira, Felipe	2	0	3.43	3	3	0	0	21	21	8	8	5	17	R	R	6-0	170	4-26-72	1990	Miranda, Venez.
Lowe, Derek	3	4	3.45	10	9	1	0	57	53	26	22	20	49	R	R	6-6	170	6-1-73	1991	Dearborn, Mich.
Maddux, Mike	0	0	0.00	1	1	0	0	5	1	0	0	2	5	L	R	6-2	188	8-27-61	1982	Las Vegas, Nev.
Manzanillo, Josias	0	0	6.43	11	0	0	1	14	16	10	10	8	15	R	R	6-0	190	10-16-67	1983	Hyde Park, Mass.
Manzanillo, Ravelo	2	1	6.52	18	0	0	1	29	34	22	21	22	25	L	L	5-10	190	10-17-63	1981	San Pedro de Macoris, D.R.
McCarthy, Greg	2	1	3.27	22	0	0	3	22	21	8	8	16	34	L	L	6-2	193	10-30-68	1987	Shelton, Conn.
Menhart, Paul	4	7	6.16	15	10	0	1	61	76	46	42	34	51	R	R	6-2	190	3-25-69	1990	Conyers, Ga.
Moyer, Jamie	1	0	0.00	1	1	0	0	5	1	0	0	0	6	L	L	6-0	170	11-18-62	1984	Granger, Ill.
Pacheco, Alex	0	2	8.78	15	2	0	0	28	45	27	27	15	21	R	R	6-3	170	7-19-73	1990	Caracas, Venez.
Smith, Ryan	1	0	0.00	1	1	0	0	5	4	0	0	1	2	R	R	6-3	215	11-11-71	1991	Toledo, Ohio
Suzuki, Mac	4	9	5.94	32	10	0	0	83	79	60	55	64	63	R	R	6-4	195	5-31-75	1992	Kobe, Japan
Witte, Trey	5	1	5.29	32	4	0	0	66	82	49	39	26	52	R	R	6-1	190	1-15-70	1991	Houston, Texas
Wolcott, Bob	1	3	5.11	7	7	0	0	37	40	23	21	7	29	R	R	6-0	190	9-8-73	1992	Medford, Ore.

FIELDING

Catcher	PCT	G	PO	A	E	DP	PB
Decker	.997	44	306	21	1	2	5
Sealy	.971	6	34	0	1	0	1
Varitek	.995	81	613	49	3	6	12
Wilkins	.988	11	75	4	1	0	1
Zinter	1.000	2	11	0	0	0	0

First Base	PCT	G	PO	A	E	DP
Bonnici	.889	1	8	0	1	0
Decker	1.000	9	76	7	0	9
Reimer	.990	15	97	4	1	13
Rohrmeier	.991	40	315	27	3	39
Sealy	1.000	8	57	4	0	8
Torres	1.000	1	9	0	0	2
Wilkins	1.000	1	7	0	0	1
Zinter	.990	72	565	48	6	61

Second Base	PCT	G	PO	A	E	DP
Espinoza	1.000	2	3	4	0	1
Gates	.889	4	4	4	1	0
Gipson	.750	1	1	2	1	1
Guevara	.959	42	86	102	8	27
Millette	1.000	7	8	17	0	4
Raabe	.988	92	163	248	5	62
Sheets	1.000	4	4	11	0	3
Torres	1.000	1	5	2	0	1

Third Base	PCT	G	PO	A	E	DP
Decker	.921	24	18	40	5	2
Espinoza	1.000	1	1	0	0	0
Gipson	.917	7	8	14	2	2
Haney	1.000	2	4	5	0	1
Millette	.949	19	5	32	2	4
Raabe	.976	46	28	92	3	14
Sheets	1.000	2	0	5	0	1
Torres	.926	47	21	66	7	3
Zinter	.875	8	1	20	3	1

Shortstop	PCT	G	PO	A	E	DP
Espinoza	.333	1	1	0	2	0
Gates	.824	4	6	8	3	3
Gipson	.000	1	0	0	0	0
Guevara	.935	12	16	27	3	5
Haney	1.000	1	0	4	0	0
Millette	.956	19	35	52	4	14
Sheets	.973	107	170	298	13	69

Outfield	PCT	G	PO	A	E	DP
Castro	1.000	2	1	0	0	0
Christian	.985	31	65	2	1	2
Cruz	1.000	48	70	3	0	1
Ducey	.940	23	44	3	3	1
Gipson	1.000	3	6	0	0	0
Griffey	1.000	2	4	0	0	0
Haney	1.000	1	1	0	0	0
Ibanez	.976	110	192	12	5	1
Leach	.977	101	205	8	5	1
Monahan	.961	21	46	3	2	1
Reimer	1.000	2	1	0	0	0
Rohrmeier	.979	64	89	4	2	0
Silvestre	.750	7	9	0	3	0
Tinsley	.917	23	32	1	3	1
Torres	1.000	5	8	1	0	0

MEMPHIS — Class AA

SOUTHERN LEAGUE

BATTING	AVG	G	AB	R	H	2B	3B	HR	RBI	BB	SO	SB	CS	B	T	HT	WT	DOB	1st Yr	Resides
Christian, Eddie	.336	68	238	50	80	20	0	4	39	36	24	8	3	S	L	5-11	180	8-26-71	1992	Richmond, Calif.

BATTING	AVG	G	AB	R	H	2B	3B	HR	RBI	BB	SO	SB	CS	B	T	HT	WT	DOB	1st Yr	Resides
Cook, Jason	.216	53	162	23	35	7	0	0	19	21	24	2	1	R	R	6-0	180	12-9-71	1993	Atlanta, Ga.
Correa, Miguel	.260	68	250	33	65	13	0	6	31	16	49	2	2	S	R	6-2	165	9-10-71	1990	Arroyo, P.R.
Dean, Chris	.253	67	237	24	60	11	5	3	18	25	37	3	5	S	R	5-10	178	1-3-74	1994	Hayward, Calif.
Gipson, Charles	.247	88	320	56	79	9	4	1	28	34	71	31	6	R	R	6-0	188	12-16-72	1992	Orange, Calif.
Griffey, Craig	.217	35	120	20	26	3	1	0	5	13	22	6	1	R	R	5-11	175	6-3-71	1991	Westchester, Ohio
Guevara, Giomar	.263	65	228	30	60	10	4	4	28	20	42	5	5	R	R	5-9	158	10-23-72	1991	Guarenas, Venez.
Jorgensen, Randy	.291	129	477	66	139	28	3	11	70	38	58	1	2	L	L	6-2	200	4-3-72	1993	Snohomish, Wash.
Lanza, Mike	.250	21	56	8	14	2	0	0	6	4	13	2	0	R	R	6-1	170	10-22-73	1994	Port Chester, N.Y.
Maynard, Scott	.158	14	38	3	6	0	0	0	3	1	12	0	0	R	R	6-1	215	8-28-77	1995	Laguna Niguel, Calif.
Millette, Joe	.304	57	191	36	58	11	1	3	22	14	35	2	5	R	R	6-1	175	8-12-66	1989	Lafayette, Calif.
Monahan, Shane	.302	107	401	52	121	24	6	12	76	30	100	14	7	L	R	6-1	200	8-12-74	1995	Marietta, Ga.
Saunders, Doug	.259	73	232	33	60	15	0	2	28	46	44	0	3	R	R	6-0	172	12-13-69	1988	Port St. Lucie, Fla.
Sealy, Scot	.238	45	143	17	34	9	0	6	20	15	33	1	2	R	R	6-4	225	2-10-71	1992	Saraland, Ala.
Seitzer, Brad	.329	17	70	14	23	8	1	2	13	6	13	1	0	R	R	6-2	195	2-2-70	1991	Memphis, Tenn.
Smith, Scott	.249	123	453	58	113	19	2	14	67	44	132	4	7	R	R	6-3	215	10-14-71	1994	Coppell, Texas
Sturdivant, Marcus	.271	112	432	71	117	18	5	2	35	63	61	21	17	L	L	5-10	150	10-29-73	1992	Oakboro, N.C.
Thompson, Karl	.230	42	148	18	34	10	0	4	21	11	25	2	0	R	R	6-0	180	12-30-73	1995	Diamond Bar, Calif.
Torres, Paul	.344	62	218	40	75	8	3	6	55	38	30	3	1	R	R	6-3	210	10-19-70	1989	San Lorenzo, Calif.
Wathan, Dusty	.268	49	149	20	40	4	1	4	19	19	28	1	1	S	R	6-5	215	8-22-73	1994	Blue Springs, Mo.

PITCHING	W	L	ERA	G	GS	CG	SV	IP	H	R	ER	BB	SO	B	T	HT	WT	DOB	1st Yr	Resides
Apana, Matt	3	9	5.83	17	16	1	0	80	78	59	52	47	45	R	R	6-0	195	1-16-71	1993	Honolulu, Hawaii
Beck, Chris	0	0	1.93	5	1	0	0	9	8	3	2	10	2	R	R	6-3	205	6-11-72	1994	Garden Grove, Calif.
Brosnan, Jason	2	3	2.53	40	0	0	5	53	44	16	15	11	62	L	L	6-1	190	1-26-68	1989	San Leandro, Calif.
Cloude, Ken	11	7	3.87	22	22	3	0	133	131	62	57	48	124	R	R	6-1	200	1-9-75	1994	Baltimore, Md.
Fernandez, Osvaldo	0	0	2.08	1	1	0	0	4	2	1	1	4	4	L	L	6-2	193	4-15-70	1994	San Fernando, Calif.
Franklin, Ryan	4	2	3.03	11	8	2	0	59	45	22	20	14	49	R	R	6-3	160	3-5-73	1993	Spiro, Okla.
Harikkala, Tim	3	1	3.74	5	5	1	0	34	39	18	14	4	26	R	R	6-2	185	7-15-71	1992	Lake Worth, Fla.
Hinchliffe, Brett	10	10	4.45	24	24	5	0	146	159	81	72	45	107	R	R	6-4	205	7-21-74	1992	Detroit, Mich.
Holdridge, David	0	3	3.34	30	0	0	17	35	31	14	13	17	37	R	R	6-3	195	2-5-69	1988	Huntington Beach, Calif.
Luce, Rob	5	2	3.93	13	13	1	0	76	90	40	33	14	41	S	R	6-0	168	7-19-74	1996	Rescue, Calif.
Manzanillo, Josias	0	0	3.00	2	0	0	0	3	1	1	1	0	6	R	R	6-0	190	10-16-67	1983	Hyde Park, Mass.
Montane, Ivan	0	8	7.53	22	12	0	0	72	83	70	60	51	63	R	R	6-2	195	6-3-73	1992	Miami, Fla.
Pacheco, Alex	1	1	3.75	9	0	0	0	12	7	5	5	9	13	R	R	6-3	170	7-19-73	1990	Caracas, Venez.
Rivera, Rafael	0	0	2.57	6	0	0	0	7	7	3	2	7	8	R	R	6-0	190	12-13-75	1996	Vega Baja, P.R.
Simmons, Scott	8	4	3.28	40	7	0	1	91	77	40	33	40	85	R	L	6-2	200	8-15-69	1991	St. Charles, Mo.
Smith, Roy	0	0	10.38	4	0	0	0	4	6	5	5	1	6	R	R	6-7	210	5-18-76	1994	Pinellas Park, Fla.
Smith, Ryan	3	6	5.60	41	4	0	1	80	97	53	50	22	50	R	R	6-3	215	11-11-71	1991	Toledo, Ohio
Thompson, John	3	2	4.62	45	0	0	4	60	59	33	31	48	44	R	R	6-2	200	1-18-73	1992	Spokane, Wash.
Whiteside, Sean	3	4	5.34	36	0	0	0	57	57	40	34	35	40	L	L	6-4	190	4-19-71	1992	Cordele, Ga.
Wooten, Greg	11	10	4.47	26	26	0	0	155	166	91	77	59	98	R	R	6-7	210	3-30-74	1996	Vancouver, Wash.

FIELDING

Catcher	PCT	G	PO	A	E	DP	PB
Maynard	1.000	14	64	8	0	1	4
Sealy	.991	41	295	19	3	2	7
Thompson	.981	42	283	26	6	5	3
Wathan	.987	48	290	23	4	4	7

First Base	PCT	G	PO	A	E	DP
Jorgensen	.990	120	998	78	11	106
Saunders	.987	9	70	5	1	11
Seitzer	1.000	5	28	1	0	4
Torres	1.000	9	73	7	0	8

Second Base	PCT	G	PO	A	E	DP
Cook	.976	31	59	62	3	20
Dean	.955	65	142	176	15	57
Gipson	.936	17	41	47	6	12
Millette	1.000	9	28	25	0	5
Saunders	1.000	20	32	55	0	12

Third Base	PCT	G	PO	A	E	DP
Cook	.922	21	9	38	4	1
Gipson	.934	30	23	62	6	8
Lanza	.880	11	6	16	3	1
Millette	1.000	3	0	1	0	0
Saunders	.954	24	17	45	3	4
Seitzer	1.000	9	4	21	0	2
Smith	.500	1	0	1	1	0
Torres	.900	51	36	99	15	8

Shortstop	PCT	G	PO	A	E	DP
Cook	1.000	2	5	7	0	2
Gipson	.931	30	49	100	11	22
Guevara	.958	64	80	217	13	55
Lanza	1.000	1	2	2	0	1
Millette	.962	44	57	121	7	25
Saunders	1.000	1	4	4	0	1

Outfield	PCT	G	PO	A	E	DP
Christian	1.000	26	38	1	0	0
Correa	.969	53	89	6	3	1
Gipson	1.000	11	30	2	0	0
Griffey	.979	31	44	2	1	1
Monahan	.980	92	139	10	3	1
Smith	.974	105	173	15	5	1
Sturdivant	.983	106	231	6	4	0

LANCASTER — Class A

CALIFORNIA LEAGUE

BATTING	AVG	G	AB	R	H	2B	3B	HR	RBI	BB	SO	SB	CS	B	T	HT	WT	DOB	1st Yr	Resides
Brock, Tarrik	.269	132	402	88	108	21	12	7	47	78	106	40	8	L	L	6-3	170	12-25-73	1991	Hawthorne, Calif.
Buhner, Shawn	.257	111	397	66	102	22	1	11	53	49	126	4	1	R	R	6-2	205	8-29-72	1994	League City, Texas
Clifford, Jim	.232	122	453	73	105	20	3	25	82	60	109	0	6	L	L	6-2	225	3-23-70	1992	Seattle, Wash.
Connors, Greg	.243	10	37	5	9	2	0	1	5	4	10	0	1	R	R	6-2	185	8-22-74	1996	Smithtown, N.Y.
Correa, Miguel	.329	51	213	46	70	21	4	15	47	17	43	3	7	S	R	6-2	165	9-10-71	1990	Arroyo, P.R.
Cruz, Cirilo	.270	43	152	22	41	10	1	1	25	24	33	0	3	R	R	6-0	185	5-29-75	1995	Arroyo, P.R.
Dean, Chris	.335	68	263	59	88	23	5	8	38	41	51	15	10	S	R	5-10	178	1-3-74	1994	Hayward, Calif.
Donati, John	.000	4	14	0	0	0	0	0	0	0	4	0	0	R	R	6-1	200	5-4-73	1991	Concord, Calif.
Horner, Jim	.258	45	163	26	42	6	0	9	27	16	48	2	0	R	R	6-0	210	11-11-73	1996	Twin Falls, Idaho
Kim, Yuni	.242	89	289	52	70	12	6	15	58	28	93	3	1	R	R	6-2	220	5-12-71	1997	Uwajima, Japan
Martin, Mike	.236	34	110	17	26	5	0	1	16	25	15	1	1	L	R	6-1	175	2-19-73	1995	Tallahassee, Fla.
Mathis, Joe	.283	134	562	94	159	28	15	14	82	38	94	25	16	L	R	5-10	180	8-10-74	1993	Johnston, S.C.
Molina, Luis	.229	105	328	47	75	11	4	7	46	26	63	0	5	R	R	6-0	185	3-22-74	1993	Panama City, Panama
Ramirez, Joel	.280	91	328	41	92	26	4	2	39	12	51	1	3	R	R	5-10	155	8-17-73	1994	Miami, Fla.
Regan, Jason	.281	69	260	50	73	20	2	22	54	45	79	2	2	R	R	5-10	170	6-30-76	1996	Belton, Texas
Skeels, David	.278	59	180	26	50	7	1	0	21	9	40	0	2	R	R	6-2	195	6-23-73	1996	Thousand Oaks, Calif.
Thompson, Karl	.273	6	22	5	6	2	0	0	1	3	5	0	0	R	R	6-0	180	12-30-73	1995	Diamond Bar, Calif.
Tinoco, Luis	.163	12	43	9	7	2	0	2	5	5	12	0	1	R	R	6-2	200	7-24-74	1992	Maracaibo, Venez.
Villalobos, Carlos	.341	86	296	71	101	22	2	11	53	60	42	4	6	R	R	6-0	170	4-5-74	1993	Cartagena, Colombia
Wathan, Dusty	.297	56	202	27	60	17	0	4	35	21	51	0	1	S	R	6-5	215	8-22-73	1994	Blue Springs, Mo.
Watts, Josh	.220	56	159	18	35	5	0	6	25	23	71	1	3	L	R	6-1	205	3-24-75	1993	Glendale, Ariz.

GAMES BY POSITION: C—Connors 2, Horner 37, Martin 8, Skeels 52, Thompson 4, Wathan 52. **1B**—Buhner 64, Clifford 71, Cruz 15, Donati 1, Martin 1, Wathan 1. **2B**—Dean 65, Ramirez 40, Regan 45. **3B**—Cruz 27, Martin 26, Ramirez 2, Regan 27, Villalobos 73. **SS**—Molina 101, Ramirez 50. **OF**—Brock 131, Buhner 7, Connors 8, Correa 49, Cruz 6, Horner 2, Kim 70, Mathis 134, Regan 1, Villalobos 5, Watts 52.

PITCHING	W	L	ERA	G	GS	CG	SV	IP	H	R	ER	BB	SO	B	T	HT	WT	DOB	1st Yr	Resides
Apana, Matt	1	1	5.40	3	3	0	0	12	13	7	7	8	7	R	R	6-0	195	1-16-71	1993	Honolulu, Hawaii
Beck, Chris	1	4	9.00	8	7	0	0	33	53	37	33	15	23	R	R	6-3	205	6-11-72	1994	Garden Grove, Calif.
Bond, Jason	5	7	3.76	36	9	0	2	110	99	54	46	45	123	R	R	6-3	205	6-11-72	1994	Garden Grove, Calif.
Bonilla, Denys	9	6	2.84	40	0	0	6	76	67	29	24	18	92	L	L	5-11	175	11-11-74	1996	Scottsdale, Ariz.
Brea, Lesli	0	0	13.50	1	0	0	0	2	5	5	3	1	1	L	L	6-1	204	3-15-74	1992	Santo Domingo, D.R.
Christianson, Robby	0	1	7.20	6	0	0	0	10	15	12	8	4	4	R	R	5-10	170	10-12-78	1996	Jersey City, N.J.
Farnsworth, Jeff	1	1	6.97	5	5	0	0	21	24	20	16	8	18	R	R	6-2	180	8-29-75	1996	Riverside, Calif.
Gryboski, Kevin	0	7	9.89	21	15	0	0	67	113	82	74	26	41	R	R	6-2	190	10-6-75	1996	Pensacola, Fla.
Gutierrez, Javier	1	1	6.40	14	8	0	0	52	60	39	37	36	51	R	R	6-5	220	11-15-73	1995	Plains, Pa.
Luce, Rob	10	1	2.81	14	14	0	0	86	100	43	27	24	57	R	R	6-2	205	8-26-74	1994	Guanta, Venez.
Marte, Damaso	8	8	4.13	25	25	2	0	139	144	75	64	62	127	S	R	6-0	168	7-19-74	1996	Rescue, Calif.
Mays, Joe	7	4	4.86	15	15	1	0	96	108	55	52	34	82	L	L	6-2	194	2-14-74	1993	Santo Domingo, D.R.
Montane, Ivan	1	2	5.29	6	6	0	0	32	40	25	19	13	34	S	R	6-1	160	12-10-75	1995	Bradenton, Fla.
Morgan, Eric	4	3	5.42	24	13	0	0	90	98	59	54	56	56	R	R	6-2	195	6-3-73	1992	Miami, Fla.
Rivera, Rafael	1	3	3.51	24	1	0	3	49	47	27	19	17	46	R	R	6-0	190	10-24-72	1994	Cocoa, Fla.
Scheffer, Aaron	11	3	5.44	37	3	0	4	93	93	58	56	42	103	R	R	6-0	190	12-13-75	1996	Vega Baja, P.R.
Spencer, Sean	2	3	1.64	39	0	0	18	60	41	12	11	15	72	L	R	6-1	190	8-15-75	1994	Westland, Mich.
Stark, Denny	1	1	3.24	3	3	0	0	17	13	7	6	10	17	L	L	5-11	185	5-29-75	1996	Port Orchard, Wash.
Sweeney, Brian	6	3	3.80	40	0	0	1	85	83	39	36	21	73	R	R	6-2	210	10-27-74	1996	Edgerton, Ohio
Thompson, John	1	0	2.25	3	0	0	0	4	4	1	1	2	3	R	R	6-2	185	6-13-74	1996	Yonkers, N.Y.
Victery, Joe	5	4	4.84	28	14	0	0	102	98	70	55	53	86	R	R	6-2	200	1-18-73	1992	Spokane, Wash.
Westfall, Allan	0	3	6.16	15	0	0	3	19	23	17	13	8	14	R	R	6-2	205	4-26-75	1996	Ninnekah, Okla.

WISCONSIN — Class A

MIDWEST LEAGUE

BATTING	AVG	G	AB	R	H	2B	3B	HR	RBI	BB	SO	SB	CS	B	T	HT	WT	DOB	1st Yr	Resides
Burrows, Mike	.249	102	389	55	97	24	8	12	54	21	91	17	14	L	L	6-4	180	1-19-76	1994	American Fork, Utah
Castro, Jose	.242	64	248	29	60	12	1	1	19	13	50	3	4	L	L	5-11	192	12-19-75	1993	Los Minas, D.R.
Cruz, Cirilo	.299	69	241	26	72	12	1	0	19	21	50	1	6	R	R	6-0	185	5-29-75	1995	Arroyo, P.R.
Espino, Fernando	.250	3	8	2	2	0	0	2	5	2	2	0	0	R	R	6-0	165	11-26-76	1994	La Vega, D.R.
Figueroa, Luis	.286	125	482	56	138	27	2	3	60	33	21	3	3	R	R	5-11	177	3-2-77	1995	Carolina, P.R.
Harrison, Adonis	.318	125	412	61	131	26	6	7	62	55	74	25	18	L	R	5-9	165	9-28-76	1995	Pasadena, Calif.
Horner, Jim	.248	47	161	19	40	10	1	5	24	17	53	0	1	R	R	6-0	210	11-11-73	1996	Twin Falls, Idaho
Liverziani, Claudio	.254	108	346	73	88	22	4	5	31	68	93	11	4	L	R	6-0	185	3-4-75	1996	Novara, Italy
Maldonado, Carlos	.190	97	316	15	60	8	2	0	25	17	33	2	3	R	R	6-2	195	1-3-79	1996	Maracaibo, Venez.
Marchiano, Mike	.111	3	9	1	1	0	0	0	0	1	0	0	0	R	R	6-0	195	2-3-75	1997	Oak Ridge, N.J.
Martinez, Victor	.200	30	95	9	19	2	1	0	6	4	19	3	3	R	R	5-11	180	3-12-78	1996	New York, N.Y.
Myers, Mickey	.200	20	55	4	11	3	1	1	4	3	18	0	1	L	R	6-1	198	11-19-74	1997	Gaithersburg, Md.
Regan, Jason	.254	51	177	31	45	14	1	9	23	23	55	2	0	R	R	5-10	170	6-30-76	1996	Belton, Texas
Sachse, Matt	.268	110	373	37	100	21	3	6	51	26	110	5	3	L	L	6-4	205	6-29-76	1995	Spokane, Wash.
Steinmann, Scott	.213	72	225	26	48	7	0	0	20	24	60	5	3	L	R	6-2	185	7-17-73	1996	Cincinnati, Ohio
Stewart, Keith	.143	4	14	0	2	1	0	0	2	0	2	0	0	L	R	6-0	170	9-26-73	1995	Clay City, Ky.
Valera, Ramon	.176	13	34	6	6	2	0	0	2	4	6	1	4	S	R	5-11	160	8-21-75	1994	Haina, D.R.
Vazquez, Ramon	.269	131	479	79	129	25	5	8	49	78	93	16	10	L	R	5-11	170	8-21-76	1995	Cayey, P.R.
Watts, Josh	.278	51	162	37	45	10	2	8	24	33	55	3	7	L	R	6-1	205	3-24-75	1993	Glendale, Ariz.
Zachmann, Rob	.260	107	358	59	93	24	1	12	61	37	87	5	6	R	R	6-1	205	8-13-73	1996	Oakdale, N.Y.

GAMES BY POSITION: C—Horner 25, Maldonado 97, Myers 1, Steinmann 28. **1B**—Cruz 18, Martinez 1, Regan 5, Steinmann 30, Zachmann 96. **2B**—Cruz 5, Harrison 119, Martinez 6, Regan 17, Steinmann 1, Valera 4. **3B**—Cruz 1, Figueroa 115, Martinez 13, Regan 10, Steinmann 6, Valera 3. **SS**—Cruz 1, Martinez 3, Regan 7, Steinmann 2, Valera 6, Vazquez 131. **OF**—Burrows 102, Castro 63, Cruz 18, Espino 2, Horner 1, Liverziani 75, Marchiano 3, Martinez 4, Regan 9, Sachse 107, Steinmann 7, Stewart 4, Watts 44.

PITCHING	W	L	ERA	G	GS	CG	SV	IP	H	R	ER	BB	SO	B	T	HT	WT	DOB	1st Yr	Resides
Ayala, Julio	11	3	3.67	36	9	0	0	103	114	47	42	30	81	L	L	6-3	203	4-20-75	1996	Guaynabo, P.R.
Derenches, Albert	3	2	4.53	29	0	0	2	44	46	36	22	25	50	S	L	6-3	190	8-17-76	1995	Tampa, Fla.
Fitzgerald, Brian	3	1	1.94	41	0	0	10	70	63	16	15	19	68	L	L	5-11	175	12-26-74	1996	Woodbridge, Va.
Fuentes, Brian	6	7	3.56	22	22	0	0	119	84	52	47	59	153	L	L	6-4	220	8-9-75	1996	Merced, Calif.
Gonzalez, Jose	2	2	2.77	8	7	0	0	39	35	15	12	15	43	R	R	5-11	194	3-4-77	1994	Maracaibo, Venez.
Gutierrez, Javier	2	3	2.83	13	3	0	0	35	29	13	11	19	36	R	R	6-2	205	8-26-74	1994	Guanta, Venez.
Jacobs, Russell	4	2	4.44	21	9	0	1	77	62	41	38	58	76	R	R	6-6	225	1-2-75	1994	Winter Haven, Fla.
Kaye, Justin	8	12	7.30	28	26	0	0	127	129	113	103	104	115	R	R	6-4	185	6-9-76	1995	Las Vegas, Nev.
Kennison, Kyle	2	3	2.13	40	0	0	6	80	54	24	19	38	112	R	R	6-2	220	8-10-72	1996	Oxford, Maine
Koehler, Russ	3	2	4.47	23	0	0	2	48	50	30	24	15	33	R	R	6-5	215	10-5-74	1995	Medford, Ore.
Mays, Joe	9	3	2.09	13	13	1	0	82	62	20	19	23	79	S	R	6-1	160	12-10-75	1995	Bradenton, Fla.
Meche, Gil	0	2	3.00	2	2	0	0	12	12	5	4	4	14	R	R	6-3	190	9-8-78	1996	Scott, La.
Palki, Jeromy	9	3	2.78	44	0	0	8	65	50	22	20	18	75	R	R	6-0	195	4-14-76	1995	Oakland, Ore.
Smith, Roy	3	4	5.59	18	11	0	0	66	81	50	41	31	38	R	R	6-7	210	5-18-76	1994	Pinellas Park, Fla.
Stark, Denny	6	3	1.97	16	15	1	0	91	52	27	20	33	105	R	R	6-2	210	10-27-74	1996	Edgerton, Ohio
Westfall, Allan	0	2	3.62	18	0	0	3	32	26	14	13	20	41	R	R	5-11	190	5-15-75	1996	Deltona, Fla.
Weymouth, Marty	5	7	5.06	23	19	0	0	110	116	75	62	33	83	R	R	6-3	190	8-6-77	1995	Romeo, Mich.
Zimmerman, Jordan	0	1	5.82	3	3	0	0	17	18	11	11	10	18	R	L	6-0	200	4-28-75	1995	Brenham, Texas

EVERETT — Short-Season Class A

NORTHWEST LEAGUE

BATTING	AVG	G	AB	R	H	2B	3B	HR	RBI	BB	SO	SB	CS	B	T	Ht.	Wt.	DOB	1st Yr.	Resides
Alcala, Juan	.152	9	33	3	5	1	0	0	1	1	15	1	0	R	R	6-2	170	4-15-78	1995	San Pedro de Macoris, D.R.
Clark, Jermaine	.337	59	199	42	67	13	2	3	29	34	31	22	3	L	R	5-10	175	9-29-76	1997	Vacaville, Calif.
Connors, Greg	.291	54	230	41	67	18	1	6	43	16	44	6	2	R	R	6-2	185	8-22-74	1996	Smithtown, N.Y.

BATTING	AVG	G	AB	R	H	2B	3B	HR	RBI	BB	SO	SB	CS	B	T	HT	WT	DOB	1st Yr	Resides
Eady, Gerald	.234	67	248	32	58	11	2	3	33	22	89	13	4	R	R	6-2	195	10-25-75	1996	Jacksonville, Fla.
Espino, Fernando	.336	64	256	48	86	17	3	6	36	33	44	9	4	R	R	6-0	165	11-26-76	1994	La Vega, D.R.
Hargrove, Harvey	.271	69	258	40	70	21	5	4	34	30	74	8	2	R	R	5-11	175	10-9-75	1997	Upper Marlboro, Md.
Johnson, Duan	.251	46	171	31	43	4	3	0	14	12	26	10	1	R	R	6-1	205	2-23-76	1995	St. Pauls, N.C.
Kokinda, Steve	.286	34	98	18	28	3	1	2	14	15	27	1	1	L	R	6-3	190	8-21-74	1996	West Palm Beach, Fla.
Marchiano, Mike	.292	63	257	52	75	20	0	15	64	22	42	6	4	R	R	6-0	195	2-3-75	1997	Oak Ridge, N.J.
Martinez, Victor	.241	20	58	10	14	2	1	0	9	8	16	0	1	R	R	5-11	180	3-12-78	1996	New York, N.Y.
Maynard, Scott	.221	24	86	11	19	3	0	2	13	5	30	3	0	R	R	6-1	215	8-28-77	1995	Laguna Niguel, Calif.
Myers, Mickey	.143	4	7	1	1	0	0	0	0	0	2	0	0	L	R	6-1	198	11-19-74	1997	Gaithersburg, Md.
Nelson, Brian	.270	13	37	5	10	2	0	0	3	3	15	0	0	R	R	6-1	185	5-11-76	1996	Sarasota, Fla.
Silvestre, Juan	.315	14	54	9	17	3	1	3	9	4	19	1	0	R	R	5-11	198	1-10-78	1994	San Pedro de Macoris, D.R.
Smith, Brian	.232	33	95	9	22	3	1	1	7	12	29	6	4	S	R	5-9	155	4-29-77	1996	El Cajon, Calif.
Soverel, Bret	.111	13	36	1	4	0	0	1	3	3	13	1	1	R	R	6-3	220	9-12-75	1997	Palm City, Fla.
Stewart, Keith	.268	38	127	19	34	3	2	1	11	16	46	15	3	L	R	6-0	170	9-26-73	1995	Clay City, Ky.
Underwood, Jake	.103	12	29	4	3	0	0	0	3	3	9	0	0	R	R	6-0	195	8-29-78	1997	Hillsboro, Ore.
Valera, Ramon	.317	58	221	43	70	12	3	2	23	37	65	24	6	S	R	5-11	160	8-21-75	1994	Haina, D.R.
Williams, Patrick D.	.267	64	255	38	68	7	0	12	48	19	93	1	0	R	R	6-2	205	10-3-77	1996	Nacogdoches, Texas

GAMES BY POSITION: C—Alcala 9, Connors 21, Maynard 12, Nelson 10, Underwood 9, Williams 23. **1B**—Connors 31, Hargrove 1, Johnson 17, Kokinda 18, Maynard 9, Williams 10. **2B**—Clark 55, Hargrove 3, Martinez 5, Smith 21, Valera 1. **3B**—Clark 1, Hargrove 44, Johnson 32, Martinez 12, Smith 3. **SS**—Hargrove 17, Martinez 2, Smith 2, Valera 56. **OF**—Connors 2, Eady 67, Espino 61, Hargrove 7, Johnson 1, Kokinda 1, Marchiano 47, Silvestre 14, Smith 2, Soverel 4, Stewart 37, Underwood 3.

PITCHING	W	L	ERA	G	GS	CG	SV	IP	H	R	ER	BB	SO	B	T	HT	WT	DOB	1st Yr	Resides
Bello, Emerson	2	4	4.03	22	3	0	1	45	52	27	20	15	65	R	R	5-10	180	10-4-77	1995	Maracaibo, Venez.
Brea, Lesli	2	4	7.99	23	0	0	3	33	34	29	29	29	49	R	R	5-10	170	10-12-78	1996	Jersey City, N.J.
Christianson, Robby	2	2	5.66	20	2	0	0	41	48	31	26	23	46	R	R	6-2	180	8-29-75	1996	Riverside, Calif.
Chrysler, Clint	3	0	0.79	18	0	0	2	23	11	3	2	7	25	L	L	6-0	190	11-4-75	1997	St. Petersburg, Fla.
DeJesus, Tony	2	6	5.89	14	14	0	0	63	68	51	41	48	53	R	L	6-2	185	5-14-78	1996	Havelock, N.C.
Dunham, Pat	0	3	4.13	17	0	0	3	28	26	19	13	12	39	R	R	6-5	200	3-16-76	1997	Portage, Mich.
Gonzalez, Jose	1	3	1.76	6	6	0	0	31	35	20	6	19	38	R	R	5-11	194	3-4-77	1994	Maracaibo, Venez.
Gutierrez, Javier	0	1	9.82	1	1	0	0	4	4	4	4	5	4	R	R	6-2	205	8-26-74	1994	Guanta, Venez.
Kawahara, Orin	0	1	4.76	23	0	0	0	45	50	29	24	33	52	R	R	6-2	195	11-10-77	1996	Haliimaile, Hawaii
Lira, Felipe	1	0	3.60	1	1	0	0	5	6	3	2	2	9	R	R	6-0	170	4-26-72	1990	Miranda, Venez.
Matos, Josue	0	0	2.08	2	0	0	0	4	5	2	1	2	6	R	R	6-4	190	3-15-78	1997	Cabo Rojo, P.R.
Mears, Chris	3	5	5.34	12	12	0	0	62	82	47	37	20	47	R	R	6-4	180	1-20-78	1996	Victoria, B.C.
Meche, Gil	3	4	3.98	12	12	1	0	75	75	40	33	24	62	R	R	6-3	190	9-8-78	1996	Scott, La.
Noe, Matthew	0	1	2.72	23	0	0	1	36	38	20	11	18	35	L	L	6-5	225	11-20-76	1996	Highland, Calif.
Nogowski, Brandon	4	5	6.64	16	9	0	0	60	67	67	44	57	60	L	L	6-0	172	5-13-76	1995	Phoenix, Ariz.
Parker, Brandon	0	0	9.00	2	1	0	0	3	7	3	3	0	5	R	R	6-1	200	12-9-75	1997	Long Beach, Miss.
Pineiro, Joel	4	2	5.33	18	6	0	2	49	54	33	29	18	59	R	R	5-11	180	9-25-78	1997	Orlando, Fla.
Simpson, Allan	0	3	6.84	16	0	0	0	26	26	23	20	24	26	R	R	6-4	185	8-26-77	1997	Las Vegas, Nev.
Zimmerman, Jordan	2	3	4.15	11	9	0	0	39	37	27	18	23	54	R	L	6-0	200	4-28-75	1995	Brenham, Texas

PEORIA — Rookie

ARIZONA LEAGUE

BATTING	AVG	G	AB	R	H	2B	3B	HR	RBI	BB	SO	SB	CS	B	T	HT	WT	DOB	1st Yr	Resides
Alcala, Juan	.228	29	92	15	21	5	0	1	7	7	26	0	0	R	R	6-2	170	4-15-78	1995	San Pedro de Macoris, D.R.
Carroll, Mark	.306	36	121	15	37	4	0	0	26	27	30	3	1	R	R	6-0	185	10-19-78	1996	Athens, N.Y.
Estrella, Gorky	.250	54	188	40	47	6	0	6	34	41	57	6	4	R	R	6-1	205	6-11-77	1996	New York, N.Y.
Garcia, Cip	.205	41	156	29	32	9	1	2	21	19	43	3	1	R	R	6-0	205	10-23-78	1997	Rio Rancho, N.M.
Haynes, Larry	.206	45	136	26	28	6	2	3	13	20	66	10	3	R	R	5-11	175	8-31-77	1997	West Covina, Calif.
Moreno, Jose	.363	51	190	56	69	12	0	0	36	25	18	31	10	R	R	5-11	168	8-9-77	1995	San Pedro de Macoris, D.R.
Nielsen, Bret	.245	48	163	23	40	8	2	2	29	30	64	10	3	L	R	6-2	190	8-25-78	1997	El Cajon, Calif.
Pacheco, Domingo	.305	26	105	16	32	4	4	0	12	2	17	6	3	S	R	6-2	190	11-8-78	1996	Santo Domingo, D.R.
Parker, Hubert	.317	38	123	23	39	6	0	0	17	26	21	5	2	S	R	5-10	170	6-14-79	1997	Rialto, Calif.
Pinson, Brian	.200	32	100	16	20	3	1	1	7	9	20	6	1	L	R	5-8	160	6-12-78	1996	Bremerton, Wash.
Rosario, Felix	.270	26	63	15	17	0	2	0	4	7	20	6	5	S	R	5-10	155	9-13-79	1996	San Pedro de Macoris, D.R.
Silvestre, Juan	.341	34	135	32	46	11	3	7	36	15	31	4	2	R	R	5-11	198	1-10-78	1994	San Pedro de Macoris, D.R.
Soriano, Rafael	.269	38	119	19	32	3	2	0	12	14	31	7	4	R	R	6-2	175	12-19-79	1996	San Pedro de Macoris, D.R.
Tolbert, Ernest	.368	5	19	1	7	0	0	0	3	0	7	0	0	R	R	6-1	210	1-29-76	1995	San Diego, Calif.
Underwood, Jake	.319	22	69	10	22	4	2	0	11	7	16	0	2	R	R	6-0	195	8-29-78	1997	Hillsboro, Ore.
Williams, Patrick J.	.305	47	177	28	54	9	1	0	27	15	43	17	2	R	R	6-3	170	5-7-77	1997	Rockdale, Texas

GAMES BY POSITION: C—Alcala 20, Carroll 22, Garcia 12, Underwood 8. **1B**—Estrella 20, Garcia 19, Parker 1, Soriano 21, Underwood 3. **2B**—Moreno 4, Parker 24, Pinson 23, Rosario 17. **3B**—Estrella 34, Moreno 1, Pacheco 23, Parker 1. **SS**—Moreno 44, Pacheco 3, Parker 11, Rosario 1. **OF**—Haynes 45, Nielsen 46, Rosario 1, Silvestre 31, Soriano 17, Williams 45.

PITCHING	W	L	ERA	G	GS	CG	SV	IP	H	R	ER	BB	SO	B	T	HT	WT	DOB	1st Yr	Resides
Abbott, Paul	0	0	0.93	3	3	0	0	10	0	2	1	7	13	R	R	6-3	195	9-15-67	1985	Fullerton, Calif.
Cueto, Jose	1	3	6.00	17	0	0	1	27	40	24	18	9	28	R	R	6-0	168	11-11-76	1994	Cartagena, Colombia
Delgado, Danny	0	0	5.19	6	0	0	0	9	11	5	5	7	8	R	R	6-2	180	2-10-78	1997	Miami Lakes, Fla.
Duprey, Peter	4	2	1.45	15	0	0	2	43	29	10	7	20	55	R	L	6-3	225	11-26-78	1997	Ocala, Fla.
Garey, Daniel	2	2	5.91	7	7	0	0	35	46	28	23	7	16	R	R	6-2	220	10-22-77	1996	St. Joseph, Mich.
Hearns, Shane	6	2	1.70	21	0	0	2	37	30	20	7	22	42	R	R	6-1	195	9-29-75	1995	Lambertville, Mich.
Ishimaru, Taisuke	1	1	10.57	7	0	0	0	8	3	10	9	16	5	R	R	6-1	155	9-18-77	1996	Tokyo, Japan
Jimenez, Mario	3	1	6.27	7	6	0	0	33	44	32	23	19	18	R	R	6-5	175	11-25-78	1996	San Pedro de Macoris, D.R.
Mateo, Julio	3	1	3.30	13	6	0	1	60	45	32	22	23	54	R	R	5-11	188	8-22-79	1996	Bani, D.R.
Matos, Josue	1	0	4.17	14	1	0	1	45	48	27	21	6	50	R	R	6-4	190	3-15-78	1997	Cabo Rojo, P.R.
Newton, Geronimo	0	0	0.00	4	0	0	3	4	0	0	0	0	6	L	L	6-0	165	12-31-73	1992	Christiansted, V.I.
Pineiro, Joel	1	0	0.00	1	0	0	0	3	1	0	0	0	4	R	R	5-11	180	9-25-78	1997	Orlando, Fla.
Prouty, Scott	0	1	18.00	3	0	0	0	5	11	10	10	9	3	R	R	6-3	190	12-22-78	1997	Marquette Heights, Ill.
Rincones, Gabriel	5	4	3.82	13	11	1	0	68	60	37	29	36	67	R	R	6-2	200	2-5-77	1995	Guacara, Venez.
Torres, Melqui	2	6	6.59	13	10	0	1	55	60	53	40	38	42	R	R	6-1	165	5-27-77	1996	San Pedro de Macoris, D.R.
Walton, Sam	1	3	5.84	13	12	0	0	49	54	49	32	46	46	L	L	6-4	200	12-1-78	1997	Dallas, Texas

Tampa Bay DEVIL RAYS

FARM SYSTEM

Director of Player Development: Bill Livesey

Class	Farm Team	League	W	L	Pct.	Finish*	Manager	First Yr
#A	St. Petersburg (Fla.) Devil Rays	Florida State	81	56	.591	+1st (14)	Bill Evers	1997
A	Charleston (S.C.) Riverdogs	South Atlantic	60	82	.423	14th (14)	Scott Fletcher	1997
A	Hudson Valley (N.Y.) Renegades	New York Penn	35	40	.467	9th (14)	Julio Garcia	1996
#R	Princeton (W.Va.) Devil Rays	Appalachian	39	30	.565	3rd (10)	Charlie Montoyo	1997
R	St. Petersburg (Fla.) Devil Rays	Gulf Coast	25	35	.417	12th (15)	Bobby Ramos	1996

*Finish in overall standings (No. of teams in league) #Advanced level +Won league championship

ORGANIZATION LEADERS

ROBERT GURGANUS

Alex Sanchez

MINOR LEAGUERS

BATTING

*AVG	Greg Blosser, Okla. City/St. Petersburg	.308
R	Two tied at	73
H	Alex Sanchez, Charleston	155
TB	Greg Blosser, Okla. City/St. Petersburg	211
2B	Two tied at	34
3B	Michael DeCelle, Charleston/Hud. Valley	8
HR	Greg Blosser, Okla. City/St. Petersburg	24
RBI	Two tied at	70
BB	Tyler Bain, Charleston	66
SO	Brian Becker, Charleston	120
SB	Alex Sanchez, Charleston	92

PITCHING

W	James Manias, St. Petersburg	13
L	Everard Griffiths, Charleston	13
#ERA	Pablo Ortega, Charleston	2.86
G	John Daniels, St. Petersburg	55
CG	Rolando Arrojo, St. Petersburg	4
SV	John Daniels, St. Petersburg	29
IP	Pablo Ortega, Charleston	189
BB	Cedrick Bowers, Charleston	78
SO	Cedrick Bowers, Charleston	164

*Minimum 250 At-Bats #Minimum 75 Innings

TOP 10 PROSPECTS

MEL BAILEY

Matt White

How the Devil Rays Top 10 prospects, as judged by Baseball America prior to the 1997 season, fared in 1997:

Player, Pos.	Club (Class)	AVG	AB	R	H	2B	3B	HR	RBI	SB
3. Doug Johnson, 3b	Princeton (R)	.201	139	19	28	7	2	4	19	2
4. Paul Wilder, of	Princeton (R)	.206	155	25	32	6	2	6	23	3
6. Alex Sanchez, of	Charleston (A)	.289	537	73	155	15	6	0	34	92
7. Hernando Arredondo, 3b	Charleston (A)	.235	17	0	4	1	0	0	0	0
	Hudson Valley (A)	.275	200	24	55	14	1	1	27	1
10. Eddy de los Santos, ss	Charleston (A)	.234	432	46	101	11	2	2	40	8

Player, Pos.	Club (Class)	W	L	ERA	G	SV	IP	H	BB	SO
1. Matt White, rhp	Hudson Valley (A)	4	6	4.07	15	0	84	78	29	82
2. Bobby Seay, lhp	Charleston (A)	3	4	4.55	13	0	61	56	37	64
5. Pablo Ortega, rhp	Charleston (A)	12	10	2.86	29	0	189	173	30	142
8. Ed Kofler, rhp	Princeton (R)	5	6	5.57	13	0	63	63	28	66
9. Cedrick Bowers, lhp	Charleston (A)	8	10	3.21	28	0	157	119	78	164

OKLAHOMA CITY — Class AAA

AMERICAN ASSOCIATION

BATTING	AVG	G	AB	R	H	2B	3B	HR	RBI	BB	SO	SB	CS	B	T	HT	WT	DOB	1st Yr	Resides
Blosser, Greg	.303	54	178	33	54	11	1	12	27	27	46	6	2	L	L	6-3	205	6-26-71	1989	Sarasota, Fla.

For complete Oklahoma City statistics, see page 221.

ORLANDO — Class AA

SOUTHERN LEAGUE

BATTING	AVG	G	AB	R	H	2B	3B	HR	RBI	BB	SO	SB	CS	B	T	HT	WT	DOB	1st Yr	Resides
Devarez, Cesar	.281	34	96	13	27	4	1	5	17	8	15	1	0	R	R	5-10	175	9-22-69	1988	San Francisco de Macoris, D.R.

PITCHING	W	L	ERA	G	GS	CG	SV	IP	H	R	ER	BB	SO	B	T	HT	WT	DOB	1st Yr	Resides
White, Rick	5	7	4.71	39	8	0	12	86	93	55	45	22	65	R	R	6-4	215	12-23-68	1990	Springfield, Ohio

For complete Orlando statistics, see page 85.

ST. PETERSBURG — Class A

FLORIDA STATE LEAGUE

BATTING	AVG	G	AB	R	H	2B	3B	HR	RBI	BB	SO	SB	CS	B	T	HT	WT	DOB	1st Yr	Resides
Blosser, Greg	.312	52	189	40	59	9	2	12	32	35	42	7	9	L	L	6-3	205	6-26-71	1989	Sarasota, Fla.
Buccheri, Jim	.245	58	204	29	50	9	0	0	13	27	20	25	7	R	R	5-11	165	11-12-68	1988	Fountain Valley, Calif.
Carroll, Doug	.248	73	222	17	55	14	2	2	31	13	25	0	2	L	R	6-2	195	8-31-73	1994	Holliston, Mass.
Carter, Bart	.182	6	11	3	2	0	0	0	1	2	3	0	0	R	R	6-3	220	6-1-76	1997	Prentiss, Miss.
Colina, Roberto	.248	96	351	48	87	13	3	5	49	45	40	4	5	L	L	6-0	200	1-29-71	1997	San Jose, Costa Rica
Corps, Erick	.240	39	121	16	29	5	1	0	14	23	29	0	2	S	R	6-0	180	9-6-74	1992	Carolina, P.R.
Fraraccio, Dan	.296	129	463	67	137	34	3	1	63	53	50	7	7	R	R	5-11	175	9-18-70	1992	Bradenton, Fla.
Garcia, Neil	.226	75	195	33	44	10	2	0	21	31	20	2	3	S	R	6-0	185	4-6-73	1994	Tustin, Calif.
King, Andre	.193	48	114	16	22	2	1	1	11	10	29	8	3	R	R	6-1	190	11-26-73	1993	Fort Lauderdale, Fla.
Martin, Chris	.260	105	393	72	102	20	0	9	49	62	66	23	7	R	R	6-1	170	1-25-68	1990	Los Angeles, Calif.
McCain, Marcus	.284	84	306	47	87	13	3	0	36	10	30	19	7	R	R	5-7	150	3-3-74	1996	Long Beach, Calif.
Morrow, Nick	.269	108	379	51	102	23	5	11	53	43	78	20	7	R	R	5-11	180	4-17-72	1994	Lexington, Ky.
Patel, Manny	.267	129	505	66	135	17	7	4	54	61	51	24	15	L	R	5-10	165	4-22-72	1993	Tampa, Fla.
Pomierski, Joe	.265	119	422	64	112	25	5	11	49	43	78	4	3	L	R	6-2	192	4-15-74	1992	Biloxi, Miss.
Romano, Scott	.298	99	359	54	107	25	1	7	67	42	55	5	3	R	R	6-1	185	8-3-71	1989	Tampa, Fla.
Sandberg, Jared	.333	2	3	1	1	0	0	0	2	2	2	0	0	R	R	6-3	185	3-2-78	1996	Olympia, Wash.
Stricklin, Scott	.259	85	243	28	63	6	0	0	29	52	32	0	3	L	R	5-11	180	2-17-72	1993	The Plains, Ohio
Suplee, Ray	.077	4	13	0	1	0	0	0	0	0	5	0	0	R	R	6-3	200	12-15-70	1992	Sarasota, Fla.
Voita, Sam	.250	14	24	3	6	2	0	1	6	5	6	0	0	S	R	6-1	200	5-16-74	1996	Calabasas, Calif.

GAMES BY POSITION: C—Carter 1, Garcia 59, Stricklin 85, Voita 9. **1B**—Colina 96, Fraraccio 17, Garcia 2, Pomierski 30. **2B**—Corps 8, Fraraccio 4, Garcia 1, Patel 127, Sandberg 2. **3B**—Corps 1, Fraraccio 53, Garcia 3, Pomierski 5, Romano 80. **SS**—Corps 17, Fraraccio 19, Martin 102, Patel 2. **OF**—Blosser 44, Buccheri 46, Carroll 45, Corps 1, Fraraccio 14, Garcia 1, King 40, McCain 82, Morrow 107, Pomierski 56, Suplee 2.

PITCHING	W	L	ERA	G	GS	CG	SV	IP	H	R	ER	BB	SO	B	T	HT	WT	DOB	1st Yr	Resides
Aquino, Julio	3	5	2.85	50	0	0	1	60	53	21	19	8	39	R	R	6-1	173	12-12-72	1991	Estorga de Guerra, D.R.
Arrojo, Rolando	5	6	3.43	16	16	4	0	89	73	40	34	13	73	R	R	6-4	210	7-18-68	1997	San Jose, Costa Rica
Berry, Jason	4	2	4.99	35	0	0	4	49	65	32	27	11	40	R	R	6-4	220	4-2-74	1993	Brockton, Mass.
Cafaro, Rocco	2	2	1.99	19	2	0	0	41	35	10	9	5	28	R	R	6-0	175	12-2-72	1993	Brandon, Fla.
Cain, Travis	1	4	5.06	9	8	0	0	43	44	33	24	30	21	L	R	6-3	185	8-10-75	1993	Anderson, S.C.
Callaway, Mickey	11	7	3.22	28	28	3	0	171	162	74	61	39	109	R	R	6-2	190	5-13-75	1996	Germantown, Tenn.
Carroll, David	4	1	1.78	47	0	0	0	51	50	15	10	20	34	R	L	6-3	205	7-23-72	1993	Fairfax, Va.
Daniels, John	4	4	2.64	55	0	0	29	61	53	24	18	14	72	S	R	6-3	185	2-7-74	1993	Little Chute, Wis.
Harvey, Terry	3	2	7.71	18	3	0	0	35	39	33	30	26	15	R	R	6-1	180	1-29-73	1995	Dacula, Ga.
Kaufman, John	9	5	3.37	26	26	2	0	150	138	62	56	66	121	L	L	5-10	170	10-23-74	1996	Tampa, Fla.
Kimbrell, Mike	0	0	7.71	3	0	0	0	9	10	8	8	7	7	L	L	6-3	215	2-20-74	1996	Greenwell Springs, La.
Manias, James	13	5	3.78	28	28	2	0	171	163	84	72	40	119	L	L	6-4	190	10-21-74	1996	Florham Park, N.J.
Pujals, Denis	9	4	4.43	24	24	2	0	140	156	74	69	27	69	R	R	6-4	215	2-5-73	1996	Miami, Fla.
Rama, Shelby	0	0	18.00	1	0	0	0	1	1	2	2	1	1	R	R	6-6	210	1-22-72	1993	Phoenix, Ariz.
Viano, Jake	3	4	3.15	31	2	0	1	60	62	23	21	18	68	R	R	5-11	180	9-4-73	1993	Long Beach, Calif.
Williams, Matt	9	5	2.97	43	0	0	1	64	57	26	21	24	50	S	L	6-0	185	4-12-71	1992	Virginia Beach, Va.
Ybarra, Jamie	1	0	5.06	3	0	0	0	5	8	3	3	0	3	R	R	6-0	164	6-17-71	1994	San Jose, Calif.

CHARLESTON, S.C. — Class A

SOUTH ATLANTIC LEAGUE

BATTING	AVG	G	AB	R	H	2B	3B	HR	RBI	BB	SO	SB	CS	B	T	HT	WT	DOB	1st Yr	Resides
Anderson, Chris	.188	68	223	27	42	17	0	4	28	13	87	3	1	R	R	6-5	215	9-29-74	1996	Guthrie, Okla.
Arredondo, Hernando	.235	6	17	0	4	1	0	0	0	0	0	0	0	R	R	6-1	195	11-23-77	1996	Guaymas, Mexico
Bain, Tyler	.242	118	429	56	104	17	2	3	42	66	79	33	19	L	R	6-1	185	10-11-74	1996	Greeley, Colo.
Barner, Doug	.222	93	302	35	67	17	1	7	40	43	87	1	3	R	R	6-0	195	12-1-74	1996	Paris, Tenn.
Becker, Brian	.235	135	494	55	116	31	2	11	70	53	120	12	1	R	R	6-7	220	5-26-75	1996	Tempe, Ariz.
Corps, Erick	.229	57	188	28	43	9	0	1	22	42	49	14	6	S	R	6-0	180	9-6-74	1992	Carolina, P.R.
DeCelle, Michael	.223	48	157	23	35	7	1	1	17	21	39	8	8	L	R	6-2	205	7-10-74	1996	Citrus Heights, Calif.
De los Santos, Eddy	.234	127	432	46	101	11	2	2	40	20	101	8	9	R	R	6-2	165	2-24-78	1996	Santo Domingo, D.R.
Kastelic, Matt	.301	50	183	19	55	10	1	0	14	18	19	13	10	L	L	6-1	185	1-7-74	1996	Orange, Calif.
King, Mike	.196	60	199	16	39	7	0	3	16	7	36	6	1	R	R	5-11	175	8-6-73	1996	Columbus, Ohio
McCain, Marcus	.222	9	18	8	4	0	0	0	3	2	0	7	1	R	R	5-7	150	3-3-74	1996	Long Beach, Calif.
McKinnon, Tom	.228	108	412	52	94	19	4	11	53	26	100	13	7	L	R	6-5	185	5-16-73	1991	Lakewood, Calif.
Owens-Bragg, Luke	.226	53	164	29	37	6	0	1	14	21	37	14	2	S	R	5-11	170	6-6-74	1996	Orangevale, Calif.
Quatraro, Matt	.299	78	294	35	88	18	2	7	42	18	55	15	5	R	R	6-2	205	11-14-73	1996	East Selkirk, N.Y.
Salinas, Hector	.276	90	322	33	89	19	3	4	44	24	52	4	6	R	R	6-1	190	6-29-75	1996	Corpus Christi, Texas

BATTING	AVG	G	AB	R	H	2B	3B	HR	RBI	BB	SO	SB	CS	B	T	HT	WT	DOB	1st Yr	Resides
Sanchez, Alex	.289	131	537	73	155	15	6	0	34	37	72	92	40	L	L	5-10	179	8-26-76	1996	Miami, Fla.
Suriel, Miguel	.153	26	85	7	13	2	0	0	4	5	9	1	0	R	R	6-0	165	11-15-76	1994	Palmirito, D.R.
Vazquez, Manny	.233	61	176	20	41	6	1	0	11	17	26	9	6	L	L	6-1	187	2-13-75	1996	Miami, Fla.
Verrall, Jared	.167	8	30	1	5	1	0	1	4	0	9	2	0	R	R	6-4	230	4-19-74	1996	Burlington, Wash.

GAMES BY POSITION: C—Anderson 60, Quatraro 47, Salinas 22, Suriel 19. **1B**—Becker 132, King 7, Quatraro 5, Salinas 1, Suriel 1. **2B**—Bain 115, Owens-Bragg 31. **3B**—Arredondo 6, Barner 79, Corps 53, Owens-Bragg 8, Suriel 2. **SS**—Corps 3, de los Santos 127, Owens-Bragg 13. **OF**—Anderson 4, DeCelle 47, Kastelic 50, King 44, McCain 5, McKinnon 41, Owens-Bragg 1, Salinas 62, Sanchez 131, Suriel 1, Vazquez 52, Verrall 3.

PITCHING	W	L	ERA	G	GS	CG	SV	IP	H	R	ER	BB	SO	B	T	HT	WT	DOB	1st Yr	Resides
Benesh, Ed	4	4	1.95	46	0	0	15	51	44	16	11	14	39	R	R	6-2	185	12-18-74	1996	Chicago Heights, Ill.
Berry, Jason	1	1	5.40	8	0	0	0	10	11	10	6	1	2	R	R	6-4	220	4-2-74	1993	Brockton, Mass.
Bogle, Sean	3	0	1.98	20	0	0	0	36	24	11	8	17	38	R	R	6-2	195	10-3-73	1994	Indianapolis, Ind.
Bowers, Cedrick	8	10	3.21	28	28	0	0	157	119	74	56	78	164	R	L	6-2	210	2-10-78	1996	Chiefland, Fla.
Brown, Elliot	5	8	4.32	33	16	0	3	119	117	73	57	45	86	S	R	6-3	185	6-7-75	1996	Metairie, La.
Brown, Trent	3	1	2.02	33	0	0	1	49	36	12	11	7	43	L	L	6-3	220	2-4-76	1996	San Manuel, Ariz.
Enders, Trevor	4	3	1.88	44	0	0	2	67	55	18	14	17	73	R	L	6-1	205	12-22-74	1996	Houston, Texas
Griffiths, Everard	6	13	4.24	30	21	0	1	140	138	87	66	31	107	R	R	6-3	190	9-11-73	1996	North Miami, Fla.
Hale, Mark	1	2	2.93	18	0	0	4	31	26	12	10	10	39	R	R	6-4	220	8-31-75	1996	Carefree, Ariz.
Hill, T.J.	0	0	4.50	7	0	0	0	16	15	10	8	8	15	R	R	6-2	220	7-15-75	1996	London, Ohio
Kimbrell, Mike	0	0	0.00	1	0	0	0	3	0	0	0	1	4	L	L	6-3	215	2-20-74	1996	Greenwell Springs, La.
Leon, Scott	6	12	3.17	27	25	1	0	156	151	70	55	41	109	R	R	6-4	180	9-8-74	1996	Topeka, Kan.
Madison, Scott	0	1	4.50	2	0	0	0	4	7	6	2	2	4	L	L	6-2	190	9-12-74	1996	Latham, N.Y.
Manon, Julio	3	5	4.47	27	9	0	0	89	95	53	44	22	98	R	R	6-1	183	7-10-73	1992	Boca Chica, D.R.
Ortega, Pablo	12	10	2.86	29	29	3	0	189	173	87	60	30	142	S	R	6-2	170	11-7-76	1993	Nuevo Laredo, Mexico
Rolocut, Brian	0	1	7.27	10	1	0	0	17	23	20	14	7	14	R	R	6-1	195	4-8-74	1993	Gambrills, Md.
Seay, Bobby	3	4	4.55	13	13	0	0	61	56	35	31	37	64	L	L	6-2	190	6-20-78	1996	Sarasota, Fla.
Whitson, Eric	1	7	4.10	30	0	0	1	48	46	23	22	13	47	S	R	6-0	180	8-15-72	1995	Weaverville, N.C.

HUDSON VALLEY — Short-Season Class A

NEW YORK-PENN LEAGUE

BATTING	AVG	G	AB	R	H	2B	3B	HR	RBI	BB	SO	SB	CS	B	T	HT	WT	DOB	1st Yr	Resides
Arredondo, Hernando	.275	50	200	24	55	14	1	1	27	15	44	1	3	R	R	6-1	195	11-23-77	1996	Guaymas, Mexico
Carr, Dustin	.288	74	281	46	81	12	2	5	47	42	42	4	2	R	R	6-0	190	6-7-75	1997	Mt. Vernon, Texas
Carter, Bart	.214	10	28	2	6	1	0	0	2	1	7	0	0	R	R	6-3	220	6-1-76	1997	Prentiss, Miss.
Clark, Jason	.231	62	216	25	50	12	2	1	28	8	47	10	3	L	L	6-3	190	12-23-74	1997	Riverside, Calif.
Cota, Humberto	.222	3	9	0	2	0	0	0	2	0	1	0	0	R	R	6-0	175	2-7-79	1996	San Luis Rio Colorado, Mexico
DeCelle, Michael	.259	73	270	41	70	18	7	3	28	25	69	3	4	L	R	6-2	205	7-10-74	1996	Citrus Heights, Calif.
Drizos, Justin	.215	43	149	23	32	8	1	5	26	21	39	0	0	L	L	6-2	200	12-8-73	1995	Irvine, Calif.
Hall, Toby	.250	55	200	25	50	3	0	1	27	13	33	0	0	R	R	6-3	205	10-21-75	1997	Placerville, Calif.
Joffrion, Jack	.240	73	258	41	62	13	2	9	37	13	61	2	1	R	R	5-11	170	9-19-75	1997	Seabrook, Texas
Lopez-Cao, Mike	.295	14	44	6	13	3	0	1	7	3	10	2	0	L	R	5-6	180	8-14-75	1997	Miami, Fla.
Miller, Travis	.167	37	120	16	20	7	0	0	7	6	44	1	2	R	R	6-2	195	7-26-75	1997	Arlington, Texas
Pandolfini, Ryan	.238	40	130	12	31	4	1	0	9	13	28	2	4	L	R	6-1	195	3-2-76	1997	Hamilton Square, N.J.
Pigott, Anthony	.000	1	4	0	0	0	0	0	1	0	1	0	0	R	R	6-1	195	6-13-76	1997	Wilmington, N.C.
Scioneaux, Damian	.300	70	273	48	82	13	4	0	23	31	45	22	10	L	R	5-8	165	6-4-75	1997	Kenner, La.
Spear, Chad	.298	18	57	13	17	5	1	2	13	8	13	1	0	R	R	6-1	200	2-13-76	1997	Buda, Texas
Verrall, Jared	.138	7	29	4	4	1	0	1	4	0	14	0	0	R	R	6-4	230	4-19-74	1996	Burlington, Wash.
Voita, Sam	.291	32	117	19	34	10	0	1	16	11	20	2	1	S	R	6-1	200	5-16-74	1996	Calabasas, Calif.
Ware, Ryan	.204	44	147	18	30	6	2	0	13	14	40	7	1	R	R	5-11	180	2-6-76	1997	Houston, Texas

GAMES BY POSITION: C—Carter 1, Cota 3, Hall 31, Lopez-Cao 6, Spear 18, Voita 22. **1B**—Arredondo 1, Carter 3, Drizos 43, Pandolfini 31, Voita 1, Ware 1. **2B**—Carr 71, Ware 5. **3B**—Arredondo 49, Ware 30. **SS**—Joffrion 73, Ware 2. **OF**—Clark 60, DeCelle 71, Miller 28, Pigott 1, Scioneaux 70, Verrall 2.

PITCHING	W	L	ERA	G	GS	CG	SV	IP	H	R	ER	BB	SO	B	T	HT	WT	DOB	1st Yr	Resides
Bass, Randall	6	1	3.18	17	3	0	0	45	34	22	16	27	31	L	L	6-3	220	10-1-75	1997	Bolivar, Mo.
Belitz, Todd	4	5	3.53	15	15	0	0	74	65	41	29	18	78	L	L	6-1	218	10-23-75	1997	Huntington Beach, Calif.
Bergan, Thomas	0	5	6.35	27	0	0	0	40	48	34	28	20	32	R	R	6-1	205	9-21-73	1996	Granite Falls, Wash.
Cummins, Jon	1	0	6.43	21	1	0	0	35	37	30	25	32	35	R	R	6-3	210	12-9-75	1997	Frankfort, Ky.
Gonzalez, Ignacio	1	5	2.35	26	0	0	0	38	35	16	10	16	40	R	R	6-1	170	6-2-75	1997	Robstown, Texas
Hill, T.J.	2	2	5.00	11	11	0	0	45	53	36	25	22	31	R	R	6-2	220	7-15-75	1996	London, Ohio
Jimenez, Jason	3	0	0.28	19	0	0	0	32	16	5	1	10	31	R	L	6-2	210	1-10-76	1997	Elk Grove, Calif.
Kimbrell, Mike	1	3	4.54	26	0	0	2	40	34	32	20	18	43	L	L	6-3	215	2-20-74	1996	Greenwell Springs, La.
Madison, Scott	6	4	3.74	15	15	1	0	87	87	43	36	28	54	L	L	6-2	190	9-12-74	1996	Latham, N.Y.
Regalado, Frank	0	0	2.08	5	0	0	0	4	5	1	1	0	3	R	R	6-1	205	12-15-76	1997	Gualluvin, D.R.
Reyes, Eddy	0	2	2.76	31	0	0	14	33	24	12	10	18	29	R	R	6-4	200	4-24-76	1997	Miami, Fla.
Stutz, Shawn	1	0	8.10	6	0	0	1	13	16	21	12	21	9	R	R	6-3	185	6-23-75	1996	Pembroke Pines, Fla.
Wheeler, Dan	6	7	3.00	15	15	0	0	84	75	38	28	17	81	R	R	6-3	215	12-10-77	1997	Warwick, R.I.
White, Matt	4	6	4.07	15	15	0	0	84	78	44	38	29	82	R	R	6-5	215	8-13-78	1996	South Pasadena, Fla.

PRINCETON — Rookie

APPALACHIAN LEAGUE

BATTING	AVG	G	AB	R	H	2B	3B	HR	RBI	BB	SO	SB	CS	B	T	HT	WT	DOB	1st Yr	Resides
Arias, Jeison	.167	5	18	5	3	0	0	0	0	1	5	0	0	R	R	6-1	195	9-27-78	1996	San Jose de Ocoa, D.R.
Benavidez, Eric	.311	52	206	50	64	12	4	0	27	11	25	14	5	R	R	5-9	170	3-2-76	1997	Midland, Texas
Berns, Robert	.327	64	245	53	80	34	1	9	61	34	44	2	4	R	L	6-1	200	10-18-74	1997	San Jose, Calif.
Cruz, Andres	.231	3	13	3	3	1	0	0	4	0	2	0	1	R	R	5-11	174	6-11-77	1995	Salinas, P.R.
Cruz, Luis	.282	18	78	16	22	2	0	3	14	5	16	2	2	R	R	6-0	180	1-21-77	1997	Santo Domingo, D.R.
Garcia, Sandy	.255	58	216	38	55	14	2	4	28	11	75	13	2	R	R	5-11	180	2-19-79	1997	Bani, D.R.
Guzman, Martin	.324	21	74	22	24	7	1	3	15	10	20	2	0	R	R	5-11	200	4-23-77	1997	Santo Domingo, D.R.
Hoover, Paul	.303	66	251	55	76	16	4	4	37	20	37	7	4	R	R	6-1	200	4-14-76	1997	Steubenville, Ohio
Johnson, Doug	.201	34	139	19	28	7	2	4	19	8	56	2	0	R	R	6-3	195	10-27-77	1996	Gainesville, Fla.

BATTING	AVG	G	AB	R	H	2B	3B	HR	RBI	BB	SO	SB	CS	B	T	HT	WT	DOB	1st Yr	Resides
Lopez-Cao, Mike	.226	17	53	7	12	0	1	1	7	5	8	0	0	L	R	5-6	180	8-14-75	1997	Miami, Fla.
McGehee, Mike	.215	33	107	16	23	5	0	4	9	20	33	2	0	S	R	6-2	195	10-15-75	1994	Phoenix, Ariz.
Neuberger, Scott	.276	67	254	46	70	11	2	9	53	30	59	7	1	R	R	6-3	210	8-14-77	1997	Millersville, Md.
Pigott, Anthony	.232	46	151	20	35	4	1	0	14	8	34	2	1	R	R	6-1	195	6-13-76	1997	Wilmington, N.C.
Sandberg, Jared	.302	67	268	61	81	15	5	17	68	42	94	12	3	R	R	6-3	185	3-2-78	1996	Olympia, Wash.
Spear, Chad	.176	9	17	8	3	1	0	0	3	4	6	0	0	R	R	6-1	200	2-13-76	1997	Buda, Texas
Suriel, Miguel	.272	58	202	40	55	3	2	9	38	21	29	2	2	R	R	6-0	165	11-15-76	1994	Palmirito, D.R.
Wilder, Paul	.206	44	155	25	32	6	2	6	23	33	63	3	2	L	R	6-4	230	1-9-78	1996	Raleigh, N.C.

GAMES BY POSITION: C—A. Cruz 1, Guzman 5, Lopez-Cao 15, McGehee 6, Spear 7, Suriel 45. **1B**—Berns 52, McGehee 20, Spear 1, Suriel 1. **2B**—Benavidez 11, A. Cruz 1, L. Cruz 17, Sandberg 40. **3B**—Benavidez 11, Johnson 33, Pigott 1, Sandberg 18, Suriel 10. **SS**—Benavidez 6, L. Cruz 1, Hoover 65. **OF**—Arias 4, Benavidez 17, Garcia 57, Neuberger 65, Pigott 44, Suriel 2, Wilder 34.

PITCHING	W	L	ERA	G	GS	CG	SV	IP	H	R	ER	BB	SO	B	T	HT	WT	DOB	1st Yr	Resides
Box, John	4	1	2.35	25	0	0	3	38	29	15	10	10	53	R	L	6-3	180	4-30-75	1996	Houston, Texas
Carter, Chris	2	0	3.31	26	0	0	2	35	40	16	13	5	24	R	R	6-4	192	5-15-74	1997	Ogden, Utah
Carter, Roger	5	2	4.61	13	13	0	0	57	61	36	29	17	50	R	R	6-2	200	8-17-78	1997	Fort Gibson, Okla.
DeLeon, Julio	1	1	5.26	11	0	0	0	26	26	21	15	10	15	R	R	6-5	198	11-19-75	1994	Santo Domingo, D.R.
James, Delvin	4	4	4.94	20	5	0	0	58	71	57	32	24	46	R	R	6-3	215	1-3-78	1996	Nacogdoches, Texas
Kofler, Ed	5	6	5.57	13	13	0	0	63	63	46	39	28	66	R	R	6-2	165	12-23-77	1996	Palm Harbor, Fla.
Mason, Chris	2	1	3.64	19	1	0	1	42	43	17	17	5	45	R	R	6-2	165	11-26-74	1997	Millbrook, Ala.
McDermott, Toby	0	0	2.25	17	0	0	0	24	16	9	6	11	23	L	L	6-2	200	9-25-75	1997	Federal Way, Wash.
Phelps, Travis	4	3	4.88	14	13	1	0	63	73	42	34	23	60	R	R	6-2	170	7-25-77	1997	Rocky Comfort, Mo.
Pruett, Matt	3	2	4.38	24	0	0	4	25	26	19	12	10	22	R	R	6-0	180	11-23-74	1997	Woodward, Okla.
Reynolds, Chris	1	0	5.49	12	0	0	0	20	21	13	12	6	18	R	R	6-4	195	2-16-76	1997	Irving, Texas
Roberts, Marquis	2	0	4.91	3	3	0	0	18	20	10	10	4	15	L	L	5-11	180	8-29-79	1997	Fresno, Calif.
Seberino, Ronni	4	4	3.17	14	14	0	0	65	71	39	23	28	57	L	L	6-1	177	5-27-79	1996	San Pedro de Macoris, D.R.
Wright, Chris	2	4	7.27	14	7	0	0	43	62	39	35	20	35	R	R	6-2	195	6-6-77	1997	Dale, Okla.
Zambrano, Victor	0	2	1.82	20	0	0	0	30	18	13	6	9	36	R	R	6-1	170	8-6-74	1994	Los Teques, Venez.

ST. PETERSBURG — Rookie

GULF COAST LEAGUE

BATTING	AVG	G	AB	R	H	2B	3B	HR	RBI	BB	SO	SB	CS	B	T	HT	WT	DOB	1st Yr	Resides
Arias, Jeison	.190	39	126	14	24	4	4	2	10	16	41	7	4	R	R	6-1	195	9-27-78	1996	San Jose de Ocoa, D.R.
Batista, Angel	.205	37	117	14	24	4	0	0	11	9	35	2	2	L	L	6-3	190	1-14-80	1996	Santo Domingo, D.R.
Colina, Roberto	.000	1	2	0	0	0	0	0	0	1	0	0	0	L	L	6-0	200	1-29-71	1997	San Jose, Costa Rica
Cota, Humberto	.241	44	133	14	32	6	1	2	20	17	27	3	1	R	R	6-0	175	2-7-79	1996	San Luis Rio Colorado, Mexico
Cruz, Andres	.277	28	83	7	23	4	1	0	6	6	16	3	2	R	R	5-11	174	6-11-77	1995	Salinas, P.R.
Cruz, Luis	.362	34	116	25	42	8	2	4	20	16	26	17	4	R	R	6-0	180	1-21-77	1997	Santo Domingo, D.R.
Devarez, Cesar	.000	4	6	0	0	0	0	0	0	4	2	0	0	R	R	5-10	175	9-22-69	1988	San Francisco de Macoris, D.R.
Guerrero, Francisco	.210	34	100	10	21	4	1	0	6	5	24	5	2	R	R	6-2	190	8-28-79	1996	Santo Domingo, D.R.
Guerrero, Jason	.111	28	72	3	8	1	0	0	3	11	22	2	0	R	R	6-2	175	1-27-79	1997	Pittsburg, Calif.
Gunner, Chie	.285	46	144	18	41	3	3	2	23	22	34	3	2	L	R	6-2	183	7-22-78	1996	Grandview, Mo.
Guzman, Martin	.263	18	38	10	10	1	1	1	6	11	7	3	1	R	R	5-11	200	4-23-77	1997	Santo Domingo, D.R.
Kelly, Kenny	.212	27	99	21	21	2	1	2	7	11	24	6	3	R	R	6-3	180	1-26-79	1997	Plant City, Fla.
LaForest, Pierre-Luc	.262	34	107	21	28	7	2	3	21	10	18	4	3	L	R	6-1	190	1-27-78	1995	Gatineau, Quebec
LeBron, Hector	.255	40	98	7	25	4	0	0	19	13	16	2	1	L	R	6-3	225	7-22-77	1997	Catano, P.R.
Little, Josh	.206	28	63	8	13	0	1	0	4	6	22	1	2	L	L	6-2	180	5-12-79	1997	Taylorsville, N.C.
Mann, Derek	.286	50	168	34	48	2	1	1	17	29	24	8	11	L	R	6-0	165	3-8-78	1996	Midland, Ga.
Myles, Dion	.091	5	11	0	1	0	0	0	1	2	5	1	0	R	R	6-2	190	8-18-77	1996	Brooklyn, N.Y.
Pena, Jose	.126	36	87	12	11	3	1	1	3	12	41	0	0	R	R	6-1	180	8-25-78	1996	Santo Domingo, D.R.
Ramirez, Edgar	.227	42	128	15	29	8	1	0	8	22	31	2	2	R	R	6-2	165	8-7-79	1996	San Pedro de Macoris, D.R.
Vazquez, Carlos	.257	46	152	22	39	12	0	1	17	9	28	2	0	R	R	6-3	190	1-10-79	1997	Ponce, P.R.

GAMES BY POSITION: C—Cota 42, A. Cruz 4, Devarez 2, Guzman 10, Vazquez 16. **1B**—A. Cruz 9, LeBron 39, Vazquez 26. **2B**—L. Cruz 26, Mann 29, Pena 10, Ramirez 1. **3B**—A. Cruz 1, L. Cruz 2, LaForest 33, Pena 21, Ramirez 10. **SS**—L. Cruz 1, J. Guerrero 25, Mann 7, Pena 1, Ramirez 32. **OF**—Arias 34, Batista 35, F. Guerrero 34, J. Guerrero 3, Gunner 40, Kelly 26, Little 21, Myles 5.

PITCHING	W	L	ERA	G	GS	CG	SV	IP	H	R	ER	BB	SO	B	T	HT	WT	DOB	1st Yr	Resides
Cafaro, Rocco	0	0	1.64	4	4	0	0	11	9	2	2	2	8	R	R	6-3	175	8-8-75	1996	Seymour, Conn.
Cain, Travis	1	2	6.00	4	0	0	0	6	8	6	4	4	6	L	R	6-3	185	8-10-75	1993	Anderson, S.C.
Davis, Casey	0	1	4.88	13	2	0	0	24	13	15	13	24	26	L	L	6-8	195	10-14-78	1997	Ashland, Ky.
Deckard, Ed	0	1	7.27	4	2	0	0	9	15	13	7	5	3	R	R	6-5	190	11-23-77	1996	Springfield, Mo.
DeLeon, Julio	0	1	2.89	9	0	0	0	19	18	7	6	5	10	R	R	6-5	198	11-19-75	1994	Santo Domingo, D.R.
Harvey, Terry	2	0	3.75	5	0	0	0	12	5	6	5	5	11	R	R	6-1	180	1-29-72	1995	Dacula, Ga.
Ledden, Ryan	1	0	6.35	8	0	0	0	11	11	9	8	16	4	R	R	6-4	195	10-19-77	1997	Lilburn, Ga.
McCormick, Terry	2	5	4.60	10	9	0	0	43	37	26	22	24	41	L	L	6-1	170	10-14-78	1997	Tampa, Fla.
Pegueros, Radhame	1	1	8.74	3	2	0	0	11	19	11	11	3	9	R	R	6-0	160	4-15-78	1996	San Pedro de Macoris, D.R.
Petique, Marino	2	2	4.15	22	0	0	3	39	48	21	18	11	38	R	R	6-1	185	12-15-75	1997	El Seibo, D.R.
Price, Kevin	3	3	2.77	15	4	0	0	39	31	16	12	17	29	R	R	6-9	180	3-7-79	1997	Riverton, Utah
Regalado, Frank	2	3	1.76	18	1	0	3	31	31	15	6	11	31	R	R	6-1	205	12-15-76	1997	Gualluvin, D.R.
Reynolds, Chris	0	1	5.02	8	0	0	2	14	12	9	8	4	16	R	R	6-4	195	2-16-76	1997	Irving, Texas
Roberts, Marquis	6	1	0.51	12	10	0	0	53	27	8	3	19	68	L	L	5-11	180	8-29-79	1997	Fresno, Calif.
Rolocut, Brian	1	0	0.00	3	0	0	0	7	5	0	0	1	10	R	R	6-1	195	4-8-74	1993	Gambrills, Md.
Standridge, Jason	0	6	3.59	13	13	0	0	58	56	30	23	13	55	R	R	6-4	205	11-9-78	1997	Birmingham, Ala.
Stutz, Shawn	0	0	4.50	2	0	0	0	4	3	2	2	1	2	R	R	6-3	185	6-23-75	1996	Pembroke Pines, Fla.
Wright, Barrett	2	5	3.47	13	11	0	0	49	40	27	19	22	33	R	R	6-3	200	1-5-79	1997	Charlotte, N.C.
Wright, Jason	1	2	6.75	14	1	0	0	24	27	21	18	18	31	R	R	6-6	210	9-30-76	1995	Martinsville, Ind.
Young, Spencer	1	1	4.13	14	1	0	1	24	20	14	11	9	27	R	R	6-2	180	8-19-77	1996	Cottonwood, Ariz.
Zambrano, Victor	0	0	0.00	2	0	0	0	3	1	0	0	0	2	R	R	6-1	170	8-6-74	1994	Los Teques, Venez.

Texas RANGERS

Manager: Johnny Oates. **1997 Record:** 77-85, .475 (3rd, AL West)

BATTING	AVG	G	AB	R	H	2B	3B	HR	RBI	BB	SO	SB	CS	B	T	HT	WT	DOB	1st Yr	Resides
Brown, Kevin	.400	4	5	1	2	0	0	1	1	0	0	0	0	R	R	6-2	200	4-21-73	1994	Winslow, Ind.
Buford, Damon	.224	122	366	49	82	18	0	8	39	30	83	18	7	R	R	5-10	170	6-12-70	1990	Sherman Oaks, Calif.
Cedeno, Domingo	.282	113	365	49	103	19	6	4	36	27	77	3	3	S	R	6-1	170	11-4-68	1988	La Romana, D.R.
Clark, Will	.326	110	393	56	128	29	1	12	51	49	62	0	0	L	L	6-1	196	3-13-64	1985	New Orleans, La.
Devereaux, Mike	.208	29	72	8	15	3	0	0	7	7	10	1	0	R	R	6-0	195	4-10-63	1985	Tampa, Fla.
Diaz, Alex	.222	28	90	8	20	4	0	2	12	5	13	1	1	S	R	5-11	180	10-5-68	1987	San Sebastian, P.R.
Frias, Hanley	.192	14	26	4	5	1	0	0	1	1	4	0	0	S	R	6-0	160	12-5-73	1991	Villa Altagracia, D.R.
Gil, Benji	.224	110	317	35	71	13	2	5	31	17	96	1	2	R	R	6-2	180	10-6-72	1991	San Diego, Calif.
Gonzalez, Juan	.296	133	533	87	158	24	3	42	131	33	107	0	0	R	R	6-3	210	10-16-69	1986	Vega Baja, P.R.
Goodwin, Tom	.237	53	207	39	49	13	2	0	17	25	37	16	6	L	R	6-1	165	7-27-68	1989	Fresno, Calif.
2-team (97 K.C.)	.260	150	574	90	149	26	6	2	39	44	88	50	16							
Greer, Rusty	.321	157	601	112	193	42	3	26	87	83	87	9	5	L	L	6-0	190	1-21-69	1990	Albertville, Ala.
Leyritz, Jim	.282	37	85	11	24	4	0	0	14	23	22	1	0	R	R	6-0	190	12-27-63	1986	Plantation, Fla.
2-team (84 Anaheim)	.277	121	379	58	105	11	0	11	64	60	78	2	1							
McLemore, Mark	.261	89	349	47	91	17	2	1	25	40	54	7	5	S	R	5-11	207	10-4-64	1982	Gilbert, Ariz.
Mercedes, Henry	.213	23	47	4	10	4	0	0	4	6	25	0	0	R	R	5-11	185	7-23-69	1988	Santo Domingo, D.R.
Newson, Warren	.213	81	169	23	36	10	1	10	23	31	53	3	0	L	L	5-7	202	7-3-64	1986	Newnan, Ga.
Palmer, Dean	.245	94	355	47	87	21	0	14	55	26	84	1	0	R	R	6-2	195	12-27-68	1986	Tallahassee, Fla.
Ripken, Billy	.276	71	203	18	56	9	1	3	24	9	32	0	1	R	R	6-1	188	12-16-64	1982	Cockeysville, Md.
Rodriguez, Ivan	.313	150	597	98	187	34	4	20	77	38	89	7	3	R	R	5-9	205	11-30-71	1989	Vega Baja, P.R.
Sagmoen, Marc	.140	21	43	2	6	2	0	1	4	2	13	0	0	L	L	5-11	180	4-6-71	1993	Seattle, Wash.
Silvestri, Dave	.000	2	4	0	0	0	0	0	0	0	1	0	0	R	R	6-0	180	9-29-67	1989	St. Louis, Mo.
Simms, Mike	.252	59	111	13	28	8	0	5	22	8	27	0	1	R	R	6-4	185	1-12-67	1985	Houston, Texas
Stevens, Lee	.300	137	426	58	128	24	2	21	74	23	83	1	3	L	L	6-4	205	7-10-67	1986	Wichita, Kan.
Tatis, Fernando	.256	60	223	29	57	9	0	8	29	14	42	3	0	S	R	6-1	175	1-1-75	1993	San Pedro de Macoris, D.R.
Tettleton, Mickey	.091	17	44	5	4	1	0	3	4	3	12	0	0	S	R	6-2	212	9-16-60	1981	Farmington Hills, Mich.

PITCHING	W	L	ERA	G	GS	CG	SV	IP	H	R	ER	BB	SO	B	T	HT	WT	DOB	1st Yr	Resides
Alberro, Jose	0	3	7.94	10	4	0	0	28	37	33	25	17	11	R	R	6-2	190	6-29-69	1991	Bajadero, P.R.
Bailes, Scott	1	0	2.86	24	0	0	0	22	18	9	7	10	14	L	L	6-2	171	12-18-62	1982	Springfield, Mo.
Burkett, John	9	12	4.56	30	30	2	0	189	240	106	96	30	139	R	R	6-3	205	11-28-64	1983	Scottsdale, Ariz.
Clark, Terry	1	4	5.87	9	5	0	0	31	41	20	20	10	11	R	R	6-2	196	10-10-60	1979	Fontana, Calif.
2-team (4 Cleveland)	1	7	6.00	13	9	0	0	57	70	41	38	23	24							
Eversgerd, Bryan	0	2	20.25	3	0	0	0	1	5	3	3	3	2	R	L	6-1	185	2-11-69	1989	Centralia, Ill.
Gunderson, Eric	2	1	3.26	60	0	0	1	50	45	19	18	15	31	R	L	6-0	195	3-29-66	1987	Portland, Ore.
Helling, Rick	3	3	4.58	10	8	0	0	55	47	29	28	21	46	R	R	6-3	215	12-15-70	1992	West Fargo, N.D.
Heredia, Wilson	1	0	3.20	10	0	0	0	20	14	9	7	16	8	R	R	6-0	165	3-30-72	1990	San Pedro de Macoris, D.R.
Hernandez, Xavier	0	4	4.56	44	0	0	0	49	51	27	25	22	36	L	R	6-2	185	8-16-65	1986	Missouri City, Texas
Hill, Ken	5	8	5.19	19	19	0	0	111	129	69	64	56	68	R	R	6-2	175	12-14-65	1985	Lynn, Mass.
Moody, Eric	0	1	4.26	10	1	0	0	19	26	10	9	2	12	R	R	6-6	185	1-6-71	1993	Williamston, S.C.
Oliver, Darren	13	12	4.20	32	32	3	0	201	213	111	94	82	104	R	L	6-0	170	10-6-70	1988	Rio Linda, Calif.
Patterson, Danny	10	6	3.42	54	0	0	1	71	70	29	27	23	69	R	R	6-0	168	2-17-71	1990	Rosemead, Calif.
Pavlik, Roger	3	5	4.37	11	11	0	0	58	59	29	28	31	35	R	R	6-2	220	10-4-67	1987	Houston, Texas
Santana, Julio	4	6	6.75	30	14	0	0	104	141	86	78	49	64	R	R	6-0	175	1-20-73	1990	San Pedro de Macoris, D.R.
Sturtze, Tanyon	1	1	8.27	9	5	0	0	33	45	30	30	18	18	R	R	6-5	190	10-12-70	1990	Worcester, Mass.
Vosberg, Ed	1	2	4.61	42	0	0	0	41	44	23	21	15	29	L	L	6-1	190	9-28-61	1983	Tucson, Ariz.
Wetteland, John	7	2	1.94	61	0	0	31	65	43	18	14	21	63	R	R	6-2	195	8-21-66	1985	Monroe, La.
Whiteside, Matt	4	1	5.08	42	1	0	0	73	85	45	41	26	44	R	R	6-0	185	8-8-67	1990	Charleston, Mo.
Witt, Bobby	12	12	4.82	34	32	3	0	209	245	118	112	74	121	R	R	6-2	205	5-11-64	1985	Colleyville, Texas

FIELDING

Catcher	PCT	G	PO	A	E	DP
Brown	.900	4	9	0	1	0
Leyritz	.984	11	56	5	1	0
Mercedes	.988	23	78	4	1	2
Rodriguez	.992	143	821	75	7	11

First Base	PCT	G	PO	A	E	DP
Clark	.996	100	880	62	4	86
Diaz	1.000	1	2	0	0	0
Leyritz	1.000	9	60	2	0	4
Ripken	1.000	9	34	4	0	4
Sagmoen	1.000	1	1	0	0	0
Simms	.933	2	13	1	1	2
Stevens	.994	62	456	33	3	45

Second Base	PCT	G	PO	A	E	DP
Cedeno	.960	65	100	162	11	28
Diaz	1.000	1	4	1	0	0
Frias	1.000	1	0	2	0	0
McLemore	.980	89	148	254	8	60
Ripken	.983	25	40	78	2	18

Third Base	PCT	G	PO	A	E	DP
Cedeno	1.000	3	2	6	0	2
Palmer	.959	93	72	162	10	10
Ripken	1.000	13	4	12	0	2
Silvestri	.000	1	0	0	0	0
Tatis	.951	60	45	90	7	5

Shortstop	PCT	G	PO	A	E	DP
Cedeno	.957	43	44	91	6	28
Frias	1.000	12	12	11	0	2
Gil	.963	106	163	328	19	71
Ripken	.971	31	38	64	3	15
Silvestri	1.000	1	0	2	0	0

Outfield	PCT	G	PO	A	E	DP
Buford	.990	117	282	7	3	4
Devereaux	1.000	28	40	0	0	0
Diaz	.980	23	48	2	1	0
Gonzalez	.971	64	128	6	4	1
Goodwin	.986	51	138	3	2	0
Greer	.965	153	318	9	12	0
McLemore	.000	1	0	0	0	0
Newson	.949	58	93	1	5	0
Sagmoen	1.000	17	24	0	0	0
Simms	.958	19	23	0	1	0
Stevens	1.000	22	30	0	0	0

DAVID SEELIG

Juan Gonzalez

FARM SYSTEM

Director of Player Development: Reid Nichols

Class	Farm Team	League	W	L	Pct.	Finish*	Manager	First Yr
AAA	Oklahoma City 89ers	American Assoc.	61	82	.427	6th (8)	Greg Biagini	1983
AA	Tulsa (Okla.) Drillers	Texas	61	78	.439	8th (8)	Bobby Jones	1977
#A	Charlotte (Fla.) Rangers	Florida State	68	71	.489	9th (14)	Butch Wynegar	1987
#R	Pulaski (Va.) Rangers	Appalachian	43	25	.632	1st (10)	Julio Cruz	1997
R	Port Charlotte (Fla.) Rangers	Gulf Coast	34	26	.567	4th (14)	James Bryd	1973

*Finish in overall standings (No. of teams in league) #Advanced level

ORGANIZATION LEADERS

MAJOR LEAGUERS

BATTING

*AVG	Will Clark	.326
R	Rusty Greer	112
H	Rusty Greer	193
TB	Rusty Greer	319
2B	Rusty Greer	42
3B	Domingo Cedeno	6
HR	Juan Gonzalez	42
RBI	Juan Gonzalez	131
BB	Rusty Greer	83
SO	Juan Gonzalez	107
SB	Don Buford	18

PITCHING

W	Darren Oliver	13
L	Three tied at	12
#ERA	Darren Oliver	4.20
G	John Wetteland	61
CG	Two tied at	3
SV	John Wetteland	31
IP	Bobby Witt	209
BB	Darren Oliver	82
SO	John Burkett	139

Rusty Greer

RODGER WOOD

Fernando Tatis

MINOR LEAGUERS

BATTING

*AVG	Fernando Tatis, Tulsa	.314
R	Andy Barkett, Tulsa	82
H	Warren Morris, Okla. City/Charlotte	158
TB	Bubba Smith, Oklahoma City	244
2B	Andrew Vessel, Tulsa	35
3B	Warren Morris, Okla. City/Charlotte	9
HR	Bubba Smith, Oklahoma City	27
RBI	Bubba Smith, Oklahoma City	94
BB	Mike Murphy, Oklahoma City/Tulsa	73
SO	Bubba Smith, Oklahoma City	139
SB	Hanley Frias, Oklahoma City	35

PITCHING

W	Corey Lee, Charlotte	15
L	Dan Smith, Oklahoma City/Tulsa	15
#ERA	Trey Poland, Pulaski	2.00
G	Mike Venafro, Tulsa/Charlotte	46
CG	Corey Lee, Charlotte	6
SV	Cory Bailey, Oklahoma City	15
IP	Brandon Knight, Tulsa/Charlotte	183
BB	Danny Kolb, Tulsa/Charlotte	73
SO	Brandon Knight, Tulsa/Charlotte	175

*Minimum 250 At-Bats #Minimum 75 Innings

TOP 10 PROSPECTS

MORRIS FOSTOFF

Dan Kolb

How the Rangers Top 10 prospects, as judged by Baseball America prior to the 1997 season, fared in 1997:

Player, Pos.	Club (Class)	AVG	AB	R	H	2B	3B	HR	RBI	SB
2. Fernando Tatis, 3b	Texas	.256	223	29	57	9	0	8	29	3
	Tulsa (AA)	.314	382	73	120	26	1	24	61	17
4. Edwin Diaz, 2b	Texas	.222	90	8	20	4	0	2	12	1
	Okla. City (AAA)	.105	76	7	8	3	1	1	4	2
	Tulsa (AA)	.275	440	65	121	31	1	15	46	6
5. Ruben Mateo, of	Charlotte (A)	.314	385	63	121	23	8	12	67	20
7. Jorge Carrion, p-dh	Pulaski (Rookie)	.198	111	19	22	7	0	1	10	8
8. Kevin Brown, c	Texas	.400	5	1	2	0	0	1	1	0
	Okla. City (AAA)	.241	403	56	97	18	2	19	50	2
9. Mike Bell, 3b	Okla. City (AAA)	.235	328	35	77	18	2	5	38	4
	Tulsa (AA)	.285	123	17	35	11	0	8	23	0

Player, Pos.	Club (Class)	W	L	ERA	G	SV	IP	H	BB	SO
1. Danny Kolb, rhp	Tulsa (AA)	0	2	4.76	2	0	11	7	11	6
	Charlotte (A)	4	10	4.87	24	0	133	146	62	83
3. Jonathan Johnson, rhp	Okla. City (AAA)	1	8	7.29	13	1	58	83	29	33
	Tulsa (AA)	5	4	3.52	10	0	72	70	15	47
6. Danny Patterson, rhp	Texas	10	6	3.42	54	1	71	70	23	69
	Tulsa (AA)	0	0	4.50	2	0	2	5	0	0
7. Jorge Carrion, rhp	Pulaski (Rookie)	5	5	4.74	13	0	76	75	44	78
10. Corey Lee, lhp	Charlotte (A)	15	5	3.47	23	0	161	132	60	147

OKLAHOMA CITY — Class AAA

AMERICAN ASSOCIATION

BATTING	AVG	G	AB	R	H	2B	3B	HR	RBI	BB	SO	SB	CS	B	T	HT	WT	DOB	1st Yr	Resides
Anthony, Eric	.444	9	36	3	16	2	0	2	9	2	7	0	0	L	L	6-2	195	11-8-67	1986	Houston, Texas
Bell, Mike	.235	93	328	35	77	18	2	5	38	29	78	4	2	R	R	6-2	185	12-7-74	1993	Cincinnati, Ohio
*Blosser, Greg	.303	54	178	33	54	11	1	12	27	27	46	6	2	L	L	6-3	205	6-26-71	1989	Sarasota, Fla.
Brown, Kevin	.241	116	403	56	97	18	2	19	50	38	111	2	2	R	R	6-2	200	4-21-73	1994	Winslow, Ind.
Castleberry, Kevin	.270	40	111	14	30	6	1	1	9	9	21	1	2	L	R	5-10	170	4-22-68	1989	Midwest City, Okla.
Cedeno, Domingo	.357	6	28	0	10	2	0	0	2	0	6	0	1	S	R	6-1	170	11-4-68	1988	La Romana, D.R.
Diaz, Alex	.286	105	426	65	122	25	2	12	49	33	53	26	7	S	R	5-11	180	10-5-68	1987	San Sebastian, P.R.
Diaz, Edwin	.110	20	73	6	8	3	1	1	4	2	27	1	1	R	R	5-11	170	1-15-75	1993	Vega Alta, P.R.
Estrada, Osmani	.226	92	288	22	65	9	0	1	20	20	37	7	2	R	R	5-8	180	1-23-69	1993	Woodland Hills, Calif.
Frias, Hanley	.264	132	484	64	128	17	4	5	46	56	72	35	15	S	R	6-0	160	12-5-73	1991	Villa Altagracia, D.R.
Little, Mark	.263	121	415	72	109	23	4	15	45	39	100	21	9	R	R	6-0	200	7-11-72	1994	Edwardsville, Ill.
McLemore, Mark	.100	3	10	0	1	0	0	0	1	1	1	1	0	S	R	5-11	207	10-4-64	1982	Gilbert, Ariz.
Mercedes, Henry	.246	16	57	6	14	3	0	1	4	9	12	0	0	R	R	5-11	185	7-23-69	1988	Santo Domingo, D.R.
Morris, Warren	.219	8	32	3	7	1	0	1	3	3	5	0	0	L	R	5-10	175	1-11-74	1996	Alexandria, La.
Murphy, Mike	.329	73	243	37	80	13	5	5	25	38	66	14	5	R	R	6-2	185	1-23-72	1990	Albuquerque, N.M.
O'Neill, Doug	.194	11	31	2	6	3	0	0	1	3	10	1	1	R	R	5-10	200	6-29-70	1991	Campbell, Calif.
Ortiz, Luis	.305	22	82	9	25	5	0	1	11	5	7	1	1	R	R	6-0	195	5-25-70	1991	Santo Domingo, D.R.
Sagmoen, Marc	.263	111	418	47	110	32	6	5	44	26	95	4	3	L	L	5-11	180	4-6-71	1993	Seattle, Wash.
Silvestri, Dave	.240	124	467	54	112	25	3	17	68	55	104	4	6	R	R	6-0	180	9-29-67	1989	St. Louis, Mo.
Simms, Mike	.385	10	39	7	15	4	0	3	8	6	8	0	0	R	R	6-4	185	1-12-67	1985	Houston, Texas
Smith, Bubba	.255	140	514	60	131	30	1	27	94	53	139	2	2	R	R	6-2	225	12-18-69	1991	Riverside, Calif.
Tackett, Jeff	.273	64	209	23	57	15	0	5	19	26	49	4	1	R	R	6-2	206	12-1-65	1984	Cockeysville, Md.
Tettleton, Mickey	.444	4	9	4	4	1	0	0	0	6	1	0	0	S	R	6-2	212	9-16-60	1981	Farmington Hills, Mich.

PITCHING	W	L	ERA	G	GS	CG	SV	IP	H	R	ER	BB	SO	B	T	HT	WT	DOB	1st Yr	Resides
Alberro, Jose	5	6	4.22	16	16	1	0	92	90	48	43	29	59	R	R	6-2	190	6-29-69	1991	Bajadero, P.R.
Bailes, Scott	2	3	3.98	44	0	0	4	43	46	22	19	13	37	L	L	6-2	171	12-18-62	1982	Springfield, Mo.
Bailey, Cory	3	4	3.40	42	0	0	15	50	49	20	19	23	38	R	R	6-1	210	1-24-71	1991	Marion, Ill.
Brower, Jim	2	1	7.23	4	3	0	0	19	30	17	15	8	7	R	R	6-2	205	12-29-72	1994	Minnetonka, Minn.
Buckles, Bucky	0	0	0.77	5	0	0	0	12	12	3	1	4	5	R	R	6-1	190	6-19-73	1994	Victorville, Calif.
Burgos, John	2	0	2.57	7	3	0	0	28	27	8	8	8	15	L	L	5-11	170	8-2-67	1986	Humacao, P.R.
Burkett, John	1	0	3.60	1	1	0	0	5	6	2	2	2	3	R	R	6-3	205	11-28-64	1983	Scottsdale, Ariz.
Davis, Clint	6	1	3.20	40	1	0	0	70	55	28	25	46	53	R	R	6-3	205	9-26-69	1991	Irving, Texas
Dedrick, Jim	0	0	5.91	8	0	0	3	11	16	7	7	10	2	S	R	6-0	185	4-4-68	1990	Everett, Wash.
Eversgerd, Bryan	1	3	4.24	26	7	0	0	76	91	48	36	24	43	R	L	6-1	185	2-11-69	1989	Centralia, Ill.
Gross, Kevin	2	3	4.83	6	6	0	0	32	35	18	17	6	26	R	R	6-5	215	6-8-61	1981	Claremont, Calif.
Hartvigson, Chad	2	2	6.66	14	1	0	2	26	35	21	19	9	22	L	L	6-2	195	12-15-70	1994	Kirkland, Wash.
Heredia, Wilson	7	12	4.97	27	26	2	0	168	167	106	93	70	113	R	R	6-0	165	3-30-72	1990	San Pedro de Macoris, D.R.
Johnson, Jonathan	1	8	7.29	13	12	1	1	58	83	54	47	29	33	R	R	6-0	180	7-16-74	1995	Ocala, Fla.
Kell, Rob	1	0	8.86	11	2	0	0	21	30	24	21	16	20	R	L	6-2	200	9-21-70	1993	Hatfield, Pa.
Manning, David	1	3	4.40	5	5	1	0	29	33	17	14	9	15	R	R	6-3	205	8-14-71	1992	Lantana, Fla.
Miranda, Angel	0	1	16.88	2	0	0	0	3	4	5	5	1	2	L	L	6-1	195	11-9-69	1987	Arecibo, P.R.
2-team (9 Buffalo)	0	3	11.30	11	0	0	0	14	24	19	18	6	11							
Moody, Eric	5	6	3.46	35	10	1	1	112	114	49	43	21	72	R	R	6-6	185	1-6-71	1993	Williamston, S.C.
Pavlik, Roger	0	0	0.00	1	1	0	0	6	2	0	0	0	4	R	R	6-2	220	10-4-67	1987	Houston, Texas
Powell, John	0	0	4.50	1	0	0	0	4	5	2	2	1	2	R	R	5-10	180	4-7-71	1994	Snellville, Ga.
Santana, Julio	0	0	15.00	1	1	0	0	3	9	6	5	2	1	R	R	6-0	175	1-20-73	1990	San Pedro de Macoris, D.R.
Smith, Dan	3	14	5.64	23	23	3	0	129	154	88	81	42	67	L	L	6-5	190	8-20-69	1990	Apple Valley, Minn.
Sturtze, Tanyon	8	6	5.10	25	19	1	0	115	133	76	65	47	79	R	R	6-5	190	10-12-70	1990	Worcester, Mass.
Urbani, Tom	3	2	4.19	21	3	0	1	43	53	21	20	13	21	L	L	6-1	190	1-21-68	1990	Santa Cruz, Calif.
Warren, Brian	5	5	3.62	41	0	0	6	70	73	30	28	22	39	R	R	6-1	165	4-26-67	1990	Bridgewater, Mass.
Whiteside, Matt	1	1	3.54	10	1	0	1	28	30	14	11	13	11	R	R	6-0	185	8-8-67	1990	Charleston, Mo.
York, Mike	0	1	8.10	4	2	0	0	10	12	9	9	12	1	R	R	6-1	180	9-6-64	1983	Justice, Ill.

*Property of Tampa Bay Devil Rays

FIELDING

Catcher	PCT	G	PO	A	E	DP	PB
Brown	.991	95	529	47	5	10	5
Mercedes	.989	14	78	13	1	3	1
Tackett	.985	39	238	31	4	6	3

First Base	PCT	G	PO	A	E	DP
Anthony	1.000	2	14	1	0	1
Bell	.923	5	12	0	1	3
Brown	1.000	15	111	15	0	7
Little	1.000	1	2	0	0	0
Ortiz	.989	9	85	2	1	6
Sagmoen	.963	13	92	12	4	11
Silvestri	.985	13	124	11	2	20
Smith	.994	83	729	46	5	72
Tackett	1.000	16	130	6	0	10

Second Base	PCT	G	PO	A	E	DP
Bell	.957	47	88	112	9	25
Castleberry	1.000	4	8	9	0	3
Cedeno	1.000	6	13	20	0	6
A. Diaz	.939	21	36	41	5	12
E. Diaz	.934	17	37	48	6	12
Estrada	.990	43	94	111	2	27
McLemore	1.000	2	2	3	0	1
Morris	1.000	8	17	31	0	7
Murphy	1.000	1	0	1	0	0
Silvestri	.986	12	36	34	1	13

Third Base	PCT	G	PO	A	E	DP
Bell	.914	35	28	78	10	13
Castleberry	.000	1	0	0	0	0
Estrada	.957	22	12	32	2	7
Ortiz	.750	5	0	6	2	0
Silvestri	.940	88	52	216	17	19
Tackett	1.000	2	2	3	0	0

Shortstop	PCT	G	PO	A	E	DP
A. Diaz	1.000	1	0	2	0	0
Estrada	.971	16	22	46	2	10
Frias	.947	129	176	414	33	81
Silvestri	.667	1	2	2	2	1

Outfield	PCT	G	PO	A	E	DP
Anthony	1.000	5	4	1	0	0
*Blosser	.979	29	44	2	1	0
Castleberry	1.000	30	56	5	0	0
A. Diaz	.968	81	144	9	5	2
Estrada	.973	14	35	1	1	0
Little	.973	116	280	9	8	1
Murphy	1.000	70	139	5	0	2
O'Neill	1.000	10	16	0	0	0
Sagmoen	.986	99	205	9	3	2
Silvestri	1.000	1	1	0	0	0
Simms	1.000	7	17	1	0	0

TULSA — Class AA

TEXAS LEAGUE

BATTING	AVG	G	AB	R	H	2B	3B	HR	RBI	BB	SO	SB	CS	B	T	HT	WT	DOB	1st Yr	Resides
Barkett, Andy	.299	130	471	82	141	34	8	8	65	63	86	1	3	L	L	6-1	205	9-5-74	1995	Raleigh, N.C.
Bell, Mike	.285	33	123	17	35	11	0	8	23	15	28	0	1	R	R	6-2	185	12-7-74	1993	Cincinnati, Ohio

MORRIS FOSTOFF

Texas catcher Ivan Rodriguez

RODGER WOOD

Charlotte catcher Cesar King

BATTING	AVG	G	AB	R	H	2B	3B	HR	RBI	BB	SO	SB	CS	B	T	HT	WT	DOB	1st Yr	Resides
Blair, Brian	.262	86	260	46	68	9	3	4	28	49	64	11	2	L	L	6-0	180	4-9-72	1993	Belton, Texas
Bokemeier, Matt	.231	105	394	51	91	18	3	5	43	37	73	1	6	S	R	6-2	190	8-7-72	1994	Fresno, Calif.
Burton, Essex	.206	17	63	8	13	2	1	0	2	3	7	3	2	R	R	5-9	155	5-16-69	1991	San Diego, Calif.
Cedeno, Domingo	.444	2	9	0	4	0	1	0	0	0	3	0	0	S	R	6-1	170	11-4-68	1988	La Romana, D.R.
Charles, Frank	.230	95	335	38	77	18	2	9	49	24	81	2	2	R	R	6-4	210	2-23-69	1991	Anaheim, Calif.
Christopherson, Eric	.244	39	123	26	30	9	0	6	34	25	22	1	1	R	R	6-1	190	4-25-69	1990	Westminster, Calif.
Collier, Dan	.257	115	389	60	100	20	0	26	79	44	134	1	2	R	R	6-3	200	8-13-70	1991	Ozark, Ala.
Cossins, Tim	.296	36	108	11	32	5	1	4	17	8	24	2	0	R	R	6-1	192	3-31-70	1993	Windsor, Calif.
Diaz, Edwin	.275	105	440	65	121	31	1	15	46	33	102	6	9	R	R	5-11	170	1-15-75	1993	Vega Alta, P.R.
King, Cesar	.356	14	45	6	16	1	0	1	8	5	3	0	1	R	R	6-0	175	2-28-78	1994	La Romana, D.R.
Morillo, Cesar	.264	84	288	38	76	18	1	1	23	28	53	0	4	S	R	5-11	180	7-21-73	1990	Eugene, Ore.
Murphy, Mike	.256	46	156	30	40	10	1	4	19	35	45	6	3	R	R	6-2	185	1-23-72	1990	Albuquerque, N.M.
Newson, Warren	.143	2	7	1	1	0	0	1	2	2	1	0	0	L	L	5-7	202	7-3-64	1986	Newnan, Ga.
O'Neill, Doug	.277	118	412	69	114	21	0	20	64	49	122	12	4	R	R	5-10	200	6-29-70	1991	Campbell, Calif.
Richards, Rowan	.286	11	35	5	10	1	0	0	5	5	9	0	0	R	R	6-0	195	5-17-74	1996	Bloomfield, N.J.
Tatis, Fernando	.314	102	382	73	120	26	1	24	61	46	72	17	8	S	R	6-1	175	1-1-75	1993	San Pedro de Macoris, D.R.
Tettleton, Mickey	.182	3	11	4	2	0	0	1	2	4	2	0	0	S	R	6-2	212	9-16-60	1981	Farmington Hills, Mich.
Unrat, Chris	.216	19	51	4	11	3	0	0	7	16	7	0	0	L	R	6-1	205	3-28-71	1993	Kirkland, Quebec
Vessel, Andrew	.261	138	517	78	135	35	1	12	75	41	87	3	1	R	R	6-3	205	3-11-75	1993	Richmond, Calif.

PITCHING	W	L	ERA	G	GS	CG	SV	IP	H	R	ER	BB	SO	B	T	HT	WT	DOB	1st Yr	Resides
Brower, Jim	5	12	5.21	23	23	1	0	140	156	99	81	42	103	R	R	6-2	205	12-29-72	1994	Minnetonka, Minn.
Buckles, Bucky	2	2	7.00	34	0	0	1	45	59	38	35	20	29	R	R	6-1	190	6-19-73	1994	Victorville, Calif.
Davis, Jeff	4	6	3.65	11	11	2	0	69	76	41	28	17	25	R	R	6-0	170	9-20-72	1993	Somerset, Mass.
Dedrick, Jim	1	0	2.35	12	0	0	0	23	26	9	6	9	16	S	R	6-0	185	4-4-68	1990	Everett, Wash.
Eddy, Chris	4	0	3.18	41	0	0	5	51	48	24	18	24	45	L	L	6-3	200	11-27-69	1992	Duncanville, Texas
Farrar, Terry	1	2	4.95	6	3	0	1	20	18	12	11	15	16	S	L	6-1	180	9-10-69	1991	St. Louis, Mo.
Glynn, Ryan	1	1	3.38	3	3	0	0	21	21	9	8	10	18	R	R	6-3	200	11-1-74	1995	Portsmouth, Va.
Hill, Ken	0	0	0.00	1	1	0	0	5	2	0	0	1	3	R	R	6-2	175	12-14-65	1985	Lynn, Mass.
Johnson, Jonathan	5	4	3.52	10	10	4	0	72	70	35	28	15	47	R	R	6-0	180	7-16-74	1995	Ocala, Fla.
Kell, Rob	0	2	5.88	28	2	0	1	41	60	32	27	14	35	R	L	6-2	200	9-21-70	1993	Hatfield, Pa.
Knight, Brandon	6	4	4.50	14	14	2	0	90	83	52	45	35	84	L	R	6-0	170	10-1-75	1995	Oxnard, Calif.
Kojima, Keiichi	1	8	8.83	13	10	0	0	53	83	55	52	18	40	L	L	6-0	185	7-1-68	1996	Kawasaki, Japan
Kolb, Danny	0	2	4.76	2	2	0	0	11	7	7	6	11	6	R	R	6-4	190	3-29-75	1995	Sterling, Ill.
Manning, David	4	7	4.88	13	12	1	0	76	77	46	41	27	55	R	R	6-3	205	8-14-71	1992	Lantana, Fla.
Moody, Ritchie	2	4	5.88	30	0	0	0	49	52	41	32	41	38	L	L	6-1	185	2-22-71	1992	Brookville, Ohio
Moore, Bobby	4	6	5.35	35	7	0	2	72	74	50	43	34	41	R	R	6-5	217	3-27-73	1995	Spokane, Wash.
Patterson, Danny	0	0	4.50	2	2	0	0	2	5	4	1	0	0	R	R	6-0	168	2-17-71	1990	Rosemead, Calif.
Pavlik, Roger	0	0	3.60	1	1	0	0	5	3	2	2	2	4	R	R	6-2	220	10-4-67	1987	Houston, Texas
Powell, John	4	3	2.56	43	0	0	5	63	54	22	18	23	56	R	R	5-10	180	4-7-71	1994	Snellville, Ga.
Silva, Ted	13	10	4.09	26	25	4	0	172	178	88	78	42	121	R	R	6-0	170	8-4-74	1995	Redondo Beach, Calif.
Smith, Dan	1	1	3.64	5	5	0	0	30	25	18	12	15	27	L	L	6-5	190	8-20-69	1990	Apple Valley, Minn.
Van Poppel, Todd	3	3	5.06	7	7	0	0	43	53	27	24	15	26	R	R	6-5	210	12-9-71	1990	Arlington, Texas
Venafro, Mike	0	1	3.45	11	0	0	1	16	13	12	6	12	13	L	L	5-10	170	8-2-73	1995	Chantilly, Va.
York, Mike	0	0	5.06	1	1	0	0	5	7	3	3	2	2	R	R	6-1	180	9-6-64	1983	Justice, Ill.

FIELDING

Catcher	PCT	G	PO	A	E	DP	PB
Charles	.975	59	339	46	10	0	9
Christopherson	.977	37	237	19	6	0	2
Cossins	.979	35	206	22	5	0	11
King	.969	13	85	8	3	3	1
Unrat	1.000	1	6	0	0	0	0

First Base	PCT	G	PO	A	E	DP
Barkett	.988	130	1114	76	15	92
Blair	1.000	2	6	2	0	0
Charles	.984	11	56	4	1	5
Morillo	.946	4	34	1	2	2

Second Base	PCT	G	PO	A	E	DP
Bokemeier	.667	1	1	1	1	0
Burton	.915	16	27	38	6	3
Diaz	.962	105	170	312	19	58
Morillo	.955	20	25	60	4	11

Third Base	PCT	G	PO	A	E	DP
Bell	.902	33	28	55	9	2
Bokemeier	1.000	1	3	0	0	0
Charles	1.000	1	0	1	0	0
Morillo	1.000	9	5	16	0	0
Tatis	.921	100	53	193	21	15

Shortstop	PCT	G	PO	A	E	DP
Bokemeier	.931	97	145	248	29	45
Cedeno	.923	2	3	9	1	3
Morillo	.943	43	65	118	11	31

Outfield	PCT	G	PO	A	E	DP
Blair	.981	71	154	4	3	1
Charles	.000	1	0	0	0	0
Collier	.969	51	91	4	3	0
Morillo	.000	3	0	0	0	0
Murphy	.991	44	108	2	1	0
O'Neill	.973	111	246	3	7	0
Richards	1.000	11	18	3	0	0
Vessel	.967	133	225	9	8	1

CHARLOTTE — Class A

FLORIDA STATE LEAGUE

BATTING	AVG	G	AB	R	H	2B	3B	HR	RBI	BB	SO	SB	CS	B	T	HT	WT	DOB	1st Yr	Resides
Acevedo, Luis	.000	1	3	0	0	0	0	0	0	0	2	0	0	R	R	5-11	180	11-19-77	1996	Isabela, P.R.
Baker, Derek	.344	8	32	2	11	1	0	1	5	1	7	0	0	L	R	6-2	220	10-5-75	1996	Tustin, Calif.
Brumbaugh, Cliff	.261	139	522	78	136	27	4	15	70	47	99	13	11	R	R	6-2	205	4-21-74	1995	New Castle, Del.
Dransfeldt, Kelly	.227	135	466	64	106	20	7	6	58	42	115	25	16	R	R	6-2	195	4-16-75	1996	Morris, Ill.
Ellis, John	.000	1	2	0	0	0	0	0	0	0	1	0	0	R	R	6-1	195	8-4-75	1996	Niantic, Conn.
Gallagher, Shawn	.141	27	99	7	14	4	0	0	8	5	35	0	0	R	R	6-0	187	11-8-76	1995	Lakeland, Fla.
Goodwin, Joe	.238	61	185	18	44	9	1	2	22	20	18	2	2	R	R	5-10	170	4-19-74	1995	New Windsor, Md.
Gorecki, Ryan	.273	101	388	52	106	13	2	0	24	28	12	6	7	L	R	5-9	160	7-18-73	1995	East Rockaway, N.Y.
King, Cesar	.296	91	307	51	91	14	4	6	37	35	58	8	6	R	R	6-0	175	2-28-78	1994	La Romana, D.R.
Mateo, Ruben	.314	99	385	63	121	23	8	12	67	22	55	20	5	R	R	6-0	170	2-10-78	1995	San Cristobal, D.R.
McLemore, Mark	.571	2	7	1	4	1	0	0	3	2	1	1	1	S	R	5-11	207	10-4-64	1982	Gilbert, Ariz.
Monroe, Craig	.235	92	328	54	77	23	1	7	41	44	80	24	1	R	R	6-2	195	2-27-77	1995	Texarkana, Texas
Montero, Jose	.000	1	0	0	0	0	0	0	0	0	0	0	0	R	R	6-2	190	9-14-78	1996	Lara, Venez.
Morris, Warren	.306	128	494	78	151	27	9	12	75	62	100	16	5	L	R	5-10	175	1-11-74	1996	Alexandria, La.
Myers, Adrian	.247	90	287	40	71	7	4	0	21	36	73	18	15	R	R	5-10	175	5-10-75	1996	Bassfield, Miss.
Nunez, Juan	.197	21	61	7	12	1	1	0	6	8	18	5	7	S	R	5-10	165	1-11-77	1994	Esperanza, D.R.
Parra, Jose	.115	15	26	3	3	0	0	0	1	3	14	0	2	S	R	6-0	155	4-23-77	1994	Santiago, D.R.
Richards, Rowan	.264	60	178	18	47	12	1	3	26	22	54	5	2	R	R	6-0	195	5-17-74	1996	Bloomfield, N.J.
Santos, Jose	.000	2	6	0	0	0	0	0	0	0	4	0	0	R	R	5-11	165	3-1-78	1995	Santiago, D.R.
Schramm, Kevin	.225	88	284	37	64	18	0	6	45	33	80	5	1	R	R	6-2	210	7-24-74	1996	Arcadia, Calif.
Warriax, Brandon	.000	1	4	0	0	0	0	0	0	0	1	0	0	R	R	6-0	165	6-23-79	1997	Maxton, N.C.
Watkins, Sean	.222	21	72	5	16	3	1	0	10	6	25	0	0	L	L	6-4	210	10-6-74	1995	Peoria Heights, Ill.
Zywica, Mike	.258	126	462	75	119	25	5	12	64	50	116	19	19	R	R	6-4	190	9-14-75	1996	Richton Park, Ill.

GAMES BY POSITION: C—Brumbaugh 1, Ellis 1, Goodwin 61, King 85, Montero 1. **1B**—Brumbaugh 8, Gallagher 27, Schramm 82, Watkins 20, Zywica 7. **2B**—Brumbaugh 2, Gorecki 36, McLemore 2, Morris 99, Parra 1, Santos 2. **3B**—Brumbaugh 128, Dransfeldt 3, Goodwin 1, Gorecki 7, King 1, Morris 2, Parra 1, Schramm 3. **SS**—Acevedo 1, Brumbaugh 1, Dransfeldt 133, Parra 10, Warriax 1. **OF**—Mateo 91, Monroe 90, Myers 73, Nunez 21, Richards 40, Zywica 113.

PITCHING	W	L	ERA	G	GS	CG	SV	IP	H	R	ER	BB	SO	B	T	HT	WT	DOB	1st Yr	Resides
Cook, Derrick	5	2	2.30	8	8	2	0	59	54	21	15	15	35	R	R	6-3	198	8-6-75	1996	Staunton, Va.
Davis, Doug	5	3	3.10	9	8	1	0	49	29	19	17	33	52	R	L	6-3	185	9-21-75	1996	Austin, Texas
Dellamano, Anthony	2	3	12.31	15	0	0	4	23	23	33	31	29	15	R	R	6-5	205	8-17-74	1996	Davis, Calif.
Dickey, R.A.	1	4	6.94	8	6	0	0	35	51	32	27	12	32	R	R	6-1	205	10-29-74	1996	Nashville, Tenn.
Glynn, Ryan	8	7	4.97	23	22	5	1	134	148	81	74	44	96	R	R	6-3	200	11-1-74	1995	Portsmouth, Va.
Hower, Dan	0	1	4.50	2	0	0	0	2	2	1	1	2	0	L	L	6-1	190	2-19-73	1994	Omaha, Neb.
Knight, Brandon	7	4	2.23	14	12	3	0	93	82	33	23	22	91	L	R	6-0	170	10-1-75	1995	Oxnard, Calif.
Kojima, Keiichi	0	1	1.73	11	0	0	4	26	24	5	5	5	25	L	L	6-0	185	7-1-68	1996	Kawasaki, Japan
Kolb, Danny	4	10	4.87	24	23	3	0	133	146	91	72	62	83	R	R	6-4	190	3-29-75	1995	Sterling, Ill.
Lee, Corey	15	5	3.47	23	23	6	0	161	132	66	62	60	147	S	L	6-2	180	12-26-74	1996	Clayton, N.C.
Manning, David	0	0	1.50	1	1	0	0	6	4	1	1	4	4	R	R	6-3	205	8-14-71	1992	Lantana, Fla.
Marsonek, Sam	0	2	7.56	2	2	0	0	8	14	10	7	2	7	R	R	6-6	225	7-10-78	1996	Tampa, Fla.
Martinez, Jose	3	1	3.75	26	0	0	2	58	52	25	24	13	48	R	R	6-0	165	2-4-75	1995	Santiago, D.R.
McHugh, Mike	0	1	7.62	18	0	0	0	26	32	25	22	27	23	L	L	5-11	180	4-9-73	1995	Pittsburgh, Pa.
Mota, Henry	2	5	5.23	31	3	0	2	74	84	51	43	29	45	R	R	5-11	170	5-13-78	1995	Santo Domingo, D.R.
Mudd, Scott	0	1	4.91	4	0	0	0	4	5	2	2	4	3	R	R	6-0	195	10-12-72	1995	Louisville, Ky.
Ovalles, Bonelly	2	2	5.87	14	0	0	2	23	26	20	15	15	16	R	R	5-11	164	7-30-78	1995	Santiago, D.R.
Smith, Dan	8	10	4.43	26	25	2	0	161	169	93	79	66	113	R	R	6-2	175	9-15-75	1993	Girard, Kan.
Smith, Ottis	2	3	3.94	27	0	0	5	48	34	21	21	27	34	R	L	6-1	160	1-28-71	1990	Fond du Lac, Wis.
Van Poppel, Todd	0	4	4.04	6	6	2	0	36	36	19	16	10	33	R	R	6-5	210	12-9-71	1990	Arlington, Texas
Venafro, Mike	4	2	3.43	35	0	0	10	45	51	17	17	21	35	L	L	5-10	170	8-2-73	1995	Chantilly, Va.

PULASKI — Rookie

APPALACHIAN LEAGUE

BATTING	AVG	G	AB	R	H	2B	3B	HR	RBI	BB	SO	SB	CS	B	T	HT	WT	DOB	1st Yr	Resides
Carrion, Jorge	.198	43	111	19	22	7	0	1	10	12	26	8	0	R	R	6-1	175	12-10-76	1996	Brooklyn, N.Y.
Castro, Martires	.256	53	211	33	54	13	1	3	27	23	53	7	2	S	R	6-1	160	10-3-77	1995	La Romana, D.R.
De la Rosa, Miguel	.172	22	58	9	10	1	0	3	8	7	28	1	1	R	R	6-0	170	10-29-76	1994	Santo Domingo, D.R.
Ellis, John	.289	37	128	19	37	6	2	1	21	8	22	1	1	R	R	6-1	195	8-4-75	1996	Niantic, Conn.
Fisher, Anthony	.193	30	109	23	21	5	2	2	13	14	43	6	2	R	R	6-1	180	1-18-75	1996	Oakdale, Minn.
Gallagher, Shawn	.322	50	199	41	64	13	3	15	52	10	49	2	0	R	R	6-0	187	11-8-76	1995	Lakeland, Fla.
Grabowski, Jason	.293	50	174	36	51	14	0	4	24	40	32	6	1	L	R	6-3	200	5-24-76	1997	Clinton, Conn.
Jaramillo, Francisco	.295	46	156	26	46	14	0	4	22	25	44	8	4	R	R	5-11	170	11-28-74	1996	Franksville, Wis.
Lamb, Mike	.335	60	233	59	78	19	3	9	47	31	18	7	2	S	R	6-1	185	8-9-75	1997	Valinda, Calif.

BATTING	AVG	G	AB	R	H	2B	3B	HR	RBI	BB	SO	SB	CS	B	T	HT	WT	DOB	1st Yr	Resides
Lina, Estivinson	.176	14	51	5	9	1	0	1	4	5	19	1	0	R	R	6-1	186	10-19-76	1994	Santo Domingo, D.R.
Majcherek, Matt	.194	24	62	11	12	1	0	0	2	15	17	5	0	R	R	5-10	170	11-9-74	1996	Chicago, Ill.
Nunez, Juan	.189	37	122	19	23	1	3	2	14	21	39	21	4	S	R	5-10	165	1-11-77	1994	Esperanza, D.R.
Parra, Jose	.161	51	161	18	26	3	1	1	19	26	44	8	3	S	R	6-0	155	4-23-77	1994	Santiago, D.R.
Pena, Jose	.333	51	204	45	68	14	3	3	31	12	40	17	6	R	R	6-2	175	10-13-76	1994	Santiago, D.R.
Piniella, Juan	.270	33	126	20	34	4	3	1	17	8	22	9	4	R	R	5-10	160	3-13-78	1996	Stafford, Va.
Sergio, Tom	.327	58	226	57	74	14	4	9	40	38	42	25	6	L	R	5-9	175	6-27-75	1997	Norristown, Pa.

GAMES BY POSITION: C—Ellis 27, Grabowski 43, Lina 3. **1B**—De la Rosa 3, Ellis 1, Gallagher 50, Jaramillo 13, Lina 3, Majcherek 6. **2B**—Jaramillo 4, Majcherek 10, Parra 1, Sergio 55. **3B**—Jaramillo 5, Lamb 58, Majcherek 2, Parra 3. **SS**—Jaramillo 21, Majcherek 2, Parra 46. **OF**—Castro 50, De la Rosa 18, Fisher 30, Jaramillo 4, Lina 1, Nunez 34, Pena 46, Piniella 33.

PITCHING	W	L	ERA	G	GS	CG	SV	IP	H	R	ER	BB	SO	B	T	HT	WT	DOB	1st Yr	Resides
Bond, Aaron	5	2	2.45	14	14	0	0	77	56	29	21	22	64	R	R	6-2	230	12-2-76	1997	Las Vegas, Nev.
Carrion, Jorge	5	5	4.74	13	13	0	0	76	75	64	40	44	78	R	R	6-1	175	12-10-76	1996	Brooklyn, N.Y.
Cook, Derrick	2	2	3.74	6	6	0	0	34	32	15	14	12	32	R	R	6-3	198	8-6-75	1996	Staunton, Va.
DeYoung, Dan	4	1	1.91	19	8	1	3	61	52	16	13	12	69	R	R	6-0	210	3-24-76	1997	Libson, Iowa
Elder, David	2	2	1.95	20	0	0	6	32	18	8	7	12	57	R	R	6-0	180	9-23-75	1997	Pensacola, Fla.
Fleming, Emar	1	1	2.12	23	1	0	3	51	36	16	12	16	75	R	R	6-3	210	10-14-76	1996	Baltimore, Md.
Guzman, Ambiorix	3	1	2.27	10	2	0	2	36	40	10	9	3	26	R	R	6-2	160	5-20-78	1995	Santiago, D.R.
Kertis, John	2	0	2.95	14	0	0	0	21	14	9	7	11	22	S	R	6-2	200	3-19-75	1996	Miami, Fla.
Marsonek, Sam	7	3	5.02	12	11	0	0	72	90	57	40	20	65	R	R	6-6	225	7-10-78	1996	Tampa, Fla.
Ovalles, Bonelly	3	4	4.91	26	0	0	1	33	27	23	18	15	39	R	R	5-11	164	7-30-78	1995	Santiago, D.R.
Poland, Trey	7	3	2.00	13	13	3	0	85	57	29	19	18	106	L	L	6-1	190	4-23-75	1997	Shreveport, La.
Smith, Ryan	2	1	8.87	15	0	0	0	22	41	33	22	14	30	L	L	6-4	215	9-4-74	1996	Ramona, Calif.

PORT CHARLOTTE — Rookie

GULF COAST LEAGUE

BATTING	AVG	G	AB	R	H	2B	3B	HR	RBI	BB	SO	SB	CS	B	T	HT	WT	DOB	1st Yr	Resides
Acevedo, Luis	.181	51	155	16	28	3	0	1	7	13	46	8	3	R	R	5-11	180	11-19-77	1996	Isabela, P.R.
Baker, Derek	.364	12	44	7	16	4	0	2	7	2	10	0	1	L	R	6-2	220	10-5-75	1996	Tustin, Calif.
Castillo, Geramel	.237	44	139	20	33	2	3	2	10	4	33	11	2	S	R	6-1	160	10-3-77	1994	La Romana, D.R.
Cordero, Willy	.227	26	66	6	15	2	0	0	8	8	12	7	2	R	R	6-1	155	8-20-78	1995	San Cristobal, D.R.
Cruz, Geronimo	.243	27	70	6	17	3	2	0	6	10	23	4	2	S	L	6-0	177	11-15-77	1997	New York, N.Y.
Fernandez, Winston	.310	18	58	10	18	5	1	0	2	7	14	7	2	L	L	5-8	150	10-9-77	1995	Santo Domingo, D.R.
Fisher, Anthony	.314	22	70	11	22	5	1	1	12	15	17	4	1	R	R	6-1	180	1-18-75	1996	Oakdale, Minn.
Garcia, Douglas	.261	35	119	11	31	6	0	0	12	2	21	4	3	L	L	6-1	165	4-25-79	1996	Barquisimeto, Venez.
Hafner, Travis	.286	55	189	38	54	14	0	5	24	24	45	7	2	L	R	6-3	215	6-3-77	1997	Sykeston, N.D.
Harris, Kevin	.163	32	98	10	16	1	1	0	8	3	31	11	2	R	R	6-2	220	3-27-78	1997	Tampa, Fla.
Infante, Danny	.304	41	148	18	45	7	0	2	24	5	34	7	2	R	R	6-0	175	4-2-78	1995	Santiago, D.R.
Montero, Jose	.393	15	28	5	11	0	1	1	6	9	5	2	0	R	R	6-2	190	9-14-78	1996	Lara, Venez.
Romano, Jason	.257	34	109	27	28	5	3	2	11	13	19	13	4	R	R	6-0	185	6-24-79	1997	Tampa, Fla.
Santos, Jose	.269	28	93	17	25	5	1	1	10	21	30	12	1	R	R	5-11	165	3-1-78	1995	Santiago, D.R.
Taveras, Luis	.241	37	83	10	20	3	0	1	10	9	21	1	0	R	R	5-10	165	8-1-77	1995	Santiago, D.R.
Torres, Jason	.220	31	82	13	18	5	3	0	17	8	10	1	2	L	R	5-10	170	12-11-78	1997	Vero Beach, Fla.
Vazquez, Alex	.100	4	10	2	1	1	0	0	0	3	3	1	0	R	R	6-0	170	3-6-77	1997	Woodbridge, Va.
Warriax, Brandon	.217	47	166	21	36	5	2	0	14	13	47	6	3	R	R	6-0	165	6-23-79	1997	Maxton, N.C.
Wright, Corey	.248	43	145	19	36	2	3	0	11	22	25	14	11	L	L	5-11	165	11-26-79	1997	La Puente, Calif.

GAMES BY POSITION: C—Montero 13, Taveras 33, Torres 29. **1B**—Acevedo 7, Hafner 35, Infante 20, Montero 1. **2B**—Acevedo 13, Castillo 4, Cordero 17, Infante 1, Santos 24, Warriax 7. **3B**—Acevedo 14, Infante 20, Romano 29. **SS**—Acevedo 17, Cordero 9, Warriax 38. **OF**—Castillo 40, Cruz 25, Fernandez 17, Fisher 4, Garcia 32, Hafner 10, Harris 27, Vazquez 4, Wright 39.

PITCHING	W	L	ERA	G	GS	CG	SV	IP	H	R	ER	BB	SO	B	T	HT	WT	DOB	1st Yr	Resides
Benoit, Joaquin	3	3	2.05	10	10	1	0	44	40	14	10	11	38	R	R	6-3	160	7-26-78	1996	Santiago, D.R.
Brazoban, Melvin	1	3	4.20	14	0	0	2	30	28	16	14	14	36	R	R	6-3	165	1-20-77	1994	Santo Domingo, D.R.
Davis, Doug	3	1	1.71	4	4	0	0	21	14	5	4	15	27	R	L	6-3	185	9-21-75	1996	Austin, Texas
Diaz, Billy	2	3	5.02	9	9	1	0	43	49	28	24	7	31	R	R	6-3	180	11-25-79	1997	Vega Alta, P.R.
Figueroa, Carlos	0	0	3.18	5	1	0	1	6	7	2	2	2	9	L	L	6-1	190	10-5-78	1997	Carolina, P.R.
Guzman, Ambiorix	2	0	0.00	5	2	0	1	15	10	1	0	2	15	R	R	6-2	160	5-20-78	1995	Santiago, D.R.
Lundberg, David	1	1	0.84	14	1	0	5	32	13	4	3	11	32	S	R	6-1	185	5-4-77	1997	San Diego, Calif.
Pavlik, Roger	0	0	1.29	2	2	0	0	7	8	1	1	0	5	R	R	6-2	220	10-4-67	1987	Houston, Texas
Quintero, Jose	4	4	3.64	12	9	0	1	59	49	29	24	26	45	L	L	6-3	185	6-13-80	1997	Maracaibo, Venez.
Ridenour, Jeff	3	1	2.56	12	0	0	2	32	26	10	9	14	30	R	R	6-3	190	7-22-76	1997	Granite City, Ill.
Rios, Romualdo	1	2	5.72	10	2	0	1	28	31	24	18	15	31	S	R	6-0	150	2-5-80	1996	Maracaibo, Venez.
Rojas, Cesar	2	0	2.21	10	0	0	3	20	20	8	5	2	15	R	R	6-1	160	5-9-76	1994	San Pedro de Macoris, D.R.
Shourds, Anthony	3	1	1.05	13	1	0	1	34	25	7	4	5	24	R	R	6-3	185	10-9-76	1996	Meriden, Conn.
Siegel, Justin	0	1	1.17	4	0	0	1	8	6	5	1	6	6	L	L	6-0	170	9-3-75	1996	Marina del Rey, Calif.
Silva, Doug	5	4	3.77	11	9	1	0	62	69	34	26	18	46	R	R	6-3	190	7-8-79	1996	Miranda, Venez.
Tynan, Chris	4	2	2.93	11	10	1	0	58	46	27	19	23	39	R	R	6-2	170	11-15-78	1997	Vancouver, Wash.

Toronto BLUE JAYS

Managers: Cito Gaston, Mel Queen. **1997 Record:** 76-86, .469 (5th, AL East)

BATTING	AVG	G	AB	R	H	2B	3B	HR	RBI	BB	SO	SB	CS	B	T	HT	WT	DOB	1st Yr	Resides
Brito, Tilson	.222	49	126	9	28	3	0	0	8	9	28	1	0	R	R	6-0	170	5-28-72	1990	Los Trinitarios, D.R.
Brumfield, Jacob	.207	58	174	22	36	5	1	2	20	14	31	4	4	R	R	6-0	180	5-27-65	1983	Atlanta, Ga.
Butler, Rich	.286	7	14	3	4	1	0	0	2	2	3	0	1	L	R	6-1	180	5-1-73	1991	East York, Ontario
Carter, Joe	.234	157	612	76	143	30	4	21	102	40	105	8	2	R	R	6-3	215	3-7-60	1981	Leawood, Kan.
Crespo, Felipe	.286	12	28	3	8	0	1	1	5	2	4	0	0	S	R	5-11	190	3-5-73	1991	Caguas, P.R.
Cruz, Jose	.231	55	212	31	49	7	0	14	34	28	72	6	2	S	R	6-0	200	4-19-74	1995	Houston, Texas
2-team (49 Seattle)	.248	104	395	59	98	19	1	26	68	41	117	7	2							
Delgado, Carlos	.262	153	519	79	136	42	3	30	91	64	133	0	3	L	R	6-3	206	6-25-72	1989	Aguadilla, P.R.
Duncan, Mariano	.228	39	167	20	38	6	0	0	12	6	39	4	2	R	R	6-0	185	3-13-63	1982	Miami, Fla.
2-team (50 New York)	.236	89	339	36	80	14	0	1	25	12	78	6	3							
Evans, Tom	.289	12	38	7	11	2	0	1	2	2	10	0	1	R	R	6-1	180	7-9-74	1992	Kirkland, Wash.
Garcia, Carlos	.220	103	350	29	77	18	2	3	23	15	60	11	3	R	R	6-1	193	10-15-67	1987	Lancaster, N.Y.
Gonzalez, Alex	.239	126	426	46	102	23	2	12	35	34	94	15	6	R	R	6-0	182	4-8-73	1991	Miami, Fla.
Green, Shawn	.287	135	429	57	123	22	4	16	53	36	99	14	3	L	L	6-4	180	11-10-72	1992	Santa Ana, Calif.
Martinez, Sandy	.000	3	2	1	0	0	0	0	0	1	1	0	0	L	R	6-2	200	10-3-72	1990	Villa Mella, D.R.
Merced, Orlando	.266	98	368	45	98	23	2	9	40	47	62	7	3	L	R	5-11	170	11-2-66	1985	Ocala, Fla.
Mosquera, Julio	.250	3	8	0	2	1	0	0	0	0	2	0	0	R	R	6-0	165	1-29-72	1991	Panama City, Panama
Nixon, Otis	.262	103	401	54	105	12	1	1	26	52	54	47	10	S	R	6-2	180	1-9-59	1979	Alpharetta, Ga.
O'Brien, Charlie	.218	69	225	22	49	15	1	4	27	22	45	0	2	R	R	6-2	205	5-1-61	1982	Tulsa, Okla.
Perez, Robert	.192	37	78	4	15	4	1	2	6	0	16	0	0	R	R	6-3	195	6-4-69	1990	Bolivar, Venez.
Perez, Tomas	.195	40	123	9	24	3	2	0	9	11	28	1	1	S	R	5-11	165	12-29-73	1991	Santo Domingo, D.R.
Samuel, Juan	.284	45	95	13	27	5	4	3	15	10	28	5	3	R	R	5-11	180	12-9-60	1980	Santo Domingo, D.R.
Santiago, Benito	.243	97	341	31	83	10	0	13	42	17	80	1	0	R	R	6-1	182	3-9-65	1983	La Jolla, Calif.
Sierra, Ruben	.208	14	48	4	10	0	2	1	5	3	13	0	0	S	R	6-1	200	10-6-65	1983	Carolina, P.R.
Sprague, Ed	.228	138	504	63	115	29	4	14	48	51	102	0	1	R	R	6-2	215	7-25-67	1989	Lodi, Calif.
Stewart, Shannon	.286	44	168	25	48	13	7	0	22	19	24	10	3	R	R	6-1	185	2-25-74	1992	Miami, Fla.

PITCHING	W	L	ERA	G	GS	CG	SV	IP	H	R	ER	BB	SO	B	T	HT	WT	DOB	1st Yr	Resides
Almanzar, Carlos	0	1	2.70	4	0	0	0	3	1	1	1	1	4	R	R	6-2	166	11-6-73	1991	Santo Domingo, D.R.
Andujar, Luis	0	6	6.48	17	8	0	0	50	76	45	36	21	28	R	R	6-2	175	11-22-72	1991	Bani, D.R.
Carpenter, Chris	3	7	5.09	14	13	1	0	81	108	55	46	37	55	R	R	6-6	220	4-27-75	1994	Raymond, N.H.
Clemens, Roger	21	7	2.05	34	34	9	0	264	204	65	60	68	292	R	R	6-4	220	8-4-62	1983	Houston, Texas
Crabtree, Tim	3	3	7.08	37	0	0	2	41	65	32	32	17	26	R	R	6-4	205	10-13-69	1992	Jackson, Mich.
Daal, Omar	1	1	4.00	9	3	0	0	27	34	13	12	6	28	L	L	6-3	185	3-1-72	1990	Valencia, Venez.
Escobar, Kelvim	3	2	2.90	27	0	0	14	31	28	12	10	19	36	R	R	6-1	195	4-11-76	1992	La Guaira, Venez.
Flener, Huck	0	1	9.87	8	1	0	0	17	40	19	19	6	9	S	L	5-11	180	2-25-69	1990	Fairfield, Calif.
Guzman, Juan	3	6	4.95	13	13	0	0	60	48	42	33	31	52	R	R	5-11	190	10-28-66	1985	Mano Guayabo, D.R.
Hanson, Erik	0	0	7.80	3	2	0	0	15	15	13	13	6	18	R	R	6-6	215	5-18-65	1986	Kirkland, Wash.
Hentgen, Pat	15	10	3.68	35	35	9	0	264	253	116	108	71	160	R	R	6-2	200	11-13-68	1986	Fraser, Mich.
Janzen, Marty	2	1	3.60	12	0	0	0	25	23	11	10	13	17	R	R	6-3	197	5-31-73	1991	Gainesville, Fla.
Person, Robert	5	10	5.61	23	22	0	0	128	125	86	80	60	99	R	R	5-11	180	1-8-69	1989	St. Louis, Mo.
Plesac, Dan	2	4	3.58	73	0	0	1	50	47	22	20	19	61	L	L	6-5	215	2-4-62	1983	Hales Corners, Wis.
Quantrill, Paul	6	7	1.94	77	0	0	5	88	103	25	19	17	56	L	R	6-1	185	11-3-68	1989	Cobourg, Ontario
Risley, Bill	0	1	8.31	3	0	0	0	4	3	4	4	2	2	R	R	6-2	210	5-29-67	1987	Farmington, N.M.
Robinson, Ken	0	0	2.70	3	0	0	0	3	1	1	1	1	4	R	R	5-9	175	11-3-69	1991	Akron, Ohio
Spoljaric, Paul	0	3	3.19	37	0	0	3	48	37	17	17	21	43	L	L	6-3	205	9-24-70	1990	Kelowna, B.C.
Timlin, Mike	3	2	2.87	38	0	0	9	47	41	17	15	15	36	R	R	6-4	210	3-10-66	1987	Midland, Texas
Williams, Woody	9	14	4.35	31	31	0	0	195	201	98	94	66	124	R	R	6-0	190	8-19-66	1988	Houston, Texas

FIELDING

Catcher	PCT	G	PO	A	E	DP
Martinez	.933	3	12	2	1	0
Mosquera	1.000	3	11	1	0	0
O'Brien	.995	69	543	41	3	8
Santiago	.997	95	621	40	2	10

First Base	PCT	G	PO	A	E	DP
Carter	.997	42	325	22	1	24
Delgado	.988	119	962	67	12	98
Merced	1.000	1	3	0	0	0
Samuel	1.000	7	21	1	0	4

Second Base	PCT	G	PO	A	E	DP
Brito	.989	25	28	65	1	14
Crespo	1.000	1	1	3	0	0
Duncan	.984	39	74	111	3	24
Garcia	.981	96	168	253	8	50
T. Perez	.960	8	15	33	2	3
Samuel	1.000	4	7	6	0	1

Third Base	PCT	G	PO	A	E	DP
Brito	1.000	17	12	14	0	3
Crespo	.933	7	8	6	1	1
Evans	.917	12	9	24	3	1
Garcia	.000	4	0	0	0	0
Samuel	1.000	9	3	6	0	2
Sprague	.945	129	106	202	18	19

Shortstop	PCT	G	PO	A	E	DP
Brito	.929	8	13	13	2	6
Garcia	.750	5	3	3	2	1
Gonzalez	.986	125	209	341	8	77
T. Perez	.993	32	43	91	1	22

Outfield	PCT	G	PO	A	E	DP
Brumfield	1.000	47	87	6	0	1
Butler	1.000	3	5	0	0	0
Carter	.972	51	104	1	3	0
Cruz	.981	55	98	3	2	1
Duncan	.889	6	7	1	1	0
Green	.984	91	173	6	3	3
Merced	.985	96	190	10	3	4
Nixon	.996	102	254	1	1	0
R. Perez	1.000	25	35	0	0	0
Samuel	1.000	2	3	0	0	0
Sierra	.929	7	13	0	1	0
Stewart	.980	41	97	1	2	0

JOHN KLEIN

Roger Clemens

FARM SYSTEM

Director of Player Development: Karl Kuehl

Class	Farm Team	League	W	L	Pct.	Finish*	Manager	First Yr
AAA	Syracuse (N.Y.) Chiefs	International	55	87	.387	9th (10)	Garth Iorg	1978
AA	Knoxville (Tenn.) Smokies	Southern	75	63	.543	3rd (10)	Omar Malave	1980
#A	Dunedin (Fla.) Blue Jays	Florida State	57	82	.410	13th (14)	Dennis Holmberg	1987
A	Hagerstown (Md.) Suns	South Atlantic	65	73	.471	10th (14)	J.J. Cannon	1993
A	St. Catharines (Ont.) Stompers	New York-Penn	35	40	.467	9th (14)	Rocket Wheeler	1986
R	Medicine Hat (Alta.) Blue Jays	Pioneer	26	46	.361	8th (8)	Marty Pevey	1978

*Finish in overall standings (No. of teams in league) #Advanced level

ORGANIZATION LEADERS

MAJOR LEAGUERS

BATTING

*AVG	Shawn Green	.287
R	Carlos Delgado	79
H	Joe Carter	143
TB	Carlos Delgado	274
2B	Carlos Delgado	42
3B	Shannon Stewert	7
HR	Carlos Delgado	30
RBI	Joe Carter	102
BB	Carlos Delgado	64
SO	Carlos Delgado	133
SB	Otis Nixon	47

PITCHING

W	Roger Clemens	21
L	Woody Williams	14
#ERA	Paul Quantrill	1.94
G	Paul Quantrill	77
CG	Two tied at	9
SV	Kelvim Escobar	14
IP	Two tied at	264
BB	Pat Hentgen	71
SO	Roger Clemens	292

Carlos Delgado

RODGER WOOD

Clint Lawrence

MINOR LEAGUERS

BATTING

*AVG	Luis Lopez, Hagerstown	.358
R	Luis Lopez, Hagerstown	96
H	Luis Lopez, Hagerstown	180
TB	Rich Butler, Syracuse	281
2B	Luis Lopez, Hagerstown	47
3B	Rich Butler, Syracuse	9
HR	Kevin Witt, Knoxville	30
RBI	Luis Lopez, Hagerstown	99
BB	Mike Whitlock, Dunedin	69
SO	Mike Whitlock, Dunedin	132
SB	Anton French, Dunedin	35

PITCHING

W	Clint Lawrence, Hagerstown	13
L	Gary Glover, Hagerstown	17
#ERA	Woody Heath, St. Catharines	2.42
G	Mark Lukasiewicz, Syracuse/Knoxville	57
CG	Three tied at	3
SV	Ken Robinson, Syracuse	17
IP	Gary Glover, Hagerstown	174
BB	Derek Brandow, Syracuse	91
SO	Two tied at	155

*Minimum 250 At-Bats #Minimum 75 Innings

TOP 10 PROSPECTS

Roy Halladay

How the Blue Jays Top 10 prospects, as judged by Baseball America prior to the 1997 season, fared in 1997:

Player, Pos.	Club (Class)	AVG	AB	R	H	2B	3B	HR	RBI	SB
3. Shannon Stewart, of	Toronto	.286	168	25	48	13	7	0	22	10
	Syracuse (AAA)	.346	208	41	72	13	1	5	24	9
6. Kevin Witt, 1b-3b	Knoxville (AA)	.289	501	76	145	27	4	30	91	1
7. Anthony Sanders, of	Knoxville (AA)	.266	429	68	114	20	4	26	69	20
	Dunedin (A)	.200	5	0	1	1	0	0	1	0
9. Ryan Jones, 1b	Syracuse (AAA)	.138	123	8	17	5	1	3	16	0
	Knoxville (AA)	.256	328	41	84	19	3	12	51	0
10. Tom Evans, 3b	Toronto	.289	38	7	11	2	0	1	2	0
	Syracuse (AAA)	.263	376	60	99	17	1	15	65	1
	Dunedin (A)	.262	42	8	11	2	0	2	4	0

Player, Pos.	Club (Class)	W	L	ERA	G	SV	IP	H	BB	SO
1. Roy Halladay, rhp	Syracuse (AAA)	7	10	4.58	22	0	126	132	53	64
	Knoxville (AA)	2	3	5.40	7	0	37	46	11	30
2. Chris Carpenter, rhp	Toronto	3	7	5.09	14	0	81	108	37	55
	Syracuse (AAA)	4	9	4.50	19	0	120	113	53	97
4. Kelvim Escobar, rhp	Toronto	3	2	2.90	27	14	31	28	19	36
	Knoxville (AA)	2	1	3.70	5	0	24	20	16	31
	Dunedin (A)	0	1	3.75	3	0	12	16	3	16
5. Bill Koch, rhp	Dunedin (A)	0	1	2.08	3	0	22	27	3	20
8. Joe Young, rhp	Knoxville (AA)	5	4	4.42	19	0	59	52	40	62

SYRACUSE — Class AAA

INTERNATIONAL LEAGUE

BATTING	AVG	G	AB	R	H	2B	3B	HR	RBI	BB	SO	SB	CS	B	T	HT	WT	DOB	1st Yr	Resides
Aldrete, Mike	.297	27	74	8	22	5	0	0	8	17	15	0	0	L	L	5-11	180	1-29-61	1983	Monterey, Calif.
Aude, Rich	.283	100	350	48	99	23	2	15	59	26	88	3	0	R	R	6-5	220	7-13-71	1989	Chatsworth, Calif.
Brito, Jorge	.233	8	30	3	7	3	0	2	4	3	10	1	0	R	R	6-1	188	6-22-66	1986	Athens, Ala.
Butler, Rich	.300	137	537	93	161	30	9	24	87	60	107	20	7	L	R	6-1	180	5-1-73	1991	East York, Ontario
Cradle, Rickey	.120	11	25	4	3	0	0	1	3	2	9	0	1	R	R	6-2	180	6-20-73	1991	Cerritos, Calif.
Crespo, Felipe	.259	80	290	53	75	12	0	12	26	46	38	7	7	S	R	5-11	190	3-5-73	1991	Caguas, P.R.
De la Cruz, Lorenzo	.219	39	128	11	28	4	0	5	13	6	35	1	2	R	R	6-1	199	9-5-71	1991	Santo Domingo, D.R.
Evans, Tom	.263	107	376	60	99	17	1	15	65	53	104	1	2	R	R	6-1	180	7-9-74	1992	Kirkland, Wash.
Giannelli, Ray	.175	38	80	9	14	4	0	0	8	18	20	1	1	L	R	6-0	195	2-5-66	1988	Lindenhurst, N.Y.
Henry, Santiago	.241	44	116	15	28	5	1	2	16	2	21	5	1	R	R	5-11	156	7-27-72	1991	San Pedro de Macoris, D.R.
Jones, Ryan	.138	41	123	8	17	5	1	3	16	15	28	0	2	R	R	6-3	220	11-5-74	1993	Irvine, Calif.
Manto, Jeff	.205	40	132	18	27	5	1	3	11	22	30	1	2	R	R	6-3	210	8-23-64	1985	Bristol, Pa.
Martinez, Sandy	.224	96	322	28	72	12	1	4	29	27	76	7	2	L	R	6-2	200	10-3-72	1990	Villa Mella, D.R.
Melhuse, Adam	.237	38	118	7	28	5	1	2	9	12	18	1	1	S	R	6-2	185	3-27-72	1993	Stockton, Calif.
Mosquera, Julio	.229	10	35	5	8	1	0	0	1	2	5	0	0	R	R	6-0	165	1-29-72	1991	Panama City, Panama
Mummau, Rob	.255	103	333	47	85	17	2	8	40	35	60	2	3	R	R	5-11	180	8-21-71	1993	Manheim, Pa.
Patzke, Jeff	.285	96	316	38	90	25	2	2	29	51	66	0	3	S	R	6-0	170	11-19-73	1992	Klamath Falls, Ore.
Perez, Tomas	.224	89	303	32	68	13	0	1	20	37	67	3	4	S	R	5-11	165	12-29-73	1991	Santo Domingo, D.R.
Ramirez, Angel	.174	7	23	4	4	1	0	0	0	0	7	0	0	R	R	5-10	166	1-24-73	1991	Azua, D.R.
Roberts, Lonell	.156	77	173	17	27	4	0	3	10	19	50	6	7	S	R	6-0	172	6-7-71	1989	Bloomington, Calif.
Rodriguez, Luis	.000	3	2	0	0	0	0	0	0	0	2	0	0	R	R	5-9	160	1-3-74	1991	Tampa, Fla.
Sierra, Ruben	.219	8	32	5	7	2	0	1	5	2	6	0	0	S	R	6-1	200	10-6-65	1983	Carolina, P.R.
Soriano, Fred	.114	17	44	3	5	1	1	0	4	1	7	2	0	S	R	5-9	160	8-5-74	1992	Bani, D.R.
Stewart, Shannon	.346	58	208	41	72	13	1	5	24	36	26	9	6	R	R	6-1	185	2-25-74	1992	Miami, Fla.
Thompson, Ryan	.288	83	330	37	95	23	1	16	58	21	59	4	3	R	R	6-3	200	11-4-67	1987	Edesville, Md.
Whitmore, Darrell	.256	58	195	23	50	15	0	4	21	24	54	7	4	L	R	6-1	210	11-18-68	1990	Front Royal, Va.

PITCHING	W	L	ERA	G	GS	CG	SV	IP	H	R	ER	BB	SO	B	T	HT	WT	DOB	1st Yr	Resides
Almanzar, Carlos	5	1	1.41	32	0	0	3	51	30	9	8	8	47	R	R	6-2	166	11-6-73	1991	Santo Domingo, D.R.
Andujar, Luis	1	6	5.54	13	5	1	1	39	37	25	24	14	29	R	R	6-2	175	11-22-72	1991	Bani, D.R.
Bogott, Kurt	1	3	7.89	16	0	0	0	22	23	20	19	15	16	L	L	6-4	195	9-30-72	1993	Sterling, Ill.
Brandow, Derek	7	11	5.41	31	25	1	0	143	161	103	86	91	120	R	R	6-1	200	1-25-70	1992	London, Ontario
Brown, Chad	0	3	6.34	22	0	0	0	38	41	32	27	26	26	L	L	6-0	185	12-9-71	1992	Gastonia, N.C.
Cain, Tim	0	2	5.32	13	1	0	0	22	26	13	13	14	14	S	R	6-1	180	10-9-69	1990	Piscataway, N.J.
2-team (17 Pawtucket)	3	5	5.68	30	1	0	2	52	60	35	33	26	27							
Carpenter, Chris	4	9	4.50	19	19	3	0	120	113	64	60	53	97	R	R	6-6	220	4-27-75	1994	Raymond, N.H.
Crabtree, Tim	0	0	9.82	3	0	0	1	4	7	4	4	1	3	R	R	6-4	205	10-13-69	1992	Jackson, Mich.
Czajkowski, Jim	0	2	3.18	16	0	0	0	23	21	11	8	14	13	R	R	6-4	215	12-18-63	1986	Cary, N.C.
Daal, Omar	3	0	0.53	5	5	1	0	34	18	2	2	10	29	L	L	6-3	185	3-1-72	1990	Valencia, Venez.
2-team (2 Ottawa)	3	1	1.51	7	7	1	0	42	28	8	7	11	38							
Doman, Roger	1	2	7.59	8	0	0	0	11	11	9	9	6	8	R	R	6-5	185	1-26-73	1991	Cassville, Mo.
Flener, Huck	6	6	4.14	20	20	1	0	124	126	71	57	43	58	S	L	5-11	180	2-25-69	1990	Fairfield, Calif.
Freeman, Marvin	0	0	9.00	1	0	0	0	1	1	1	1	1	0	R	R	6-7	222	4-10-63	1984	Country Club Hills, Ill.
Halladay, Roy	7	10	4.58	22	22	2	0	126	132	74	64	53	64	R	R	6-6	200	5-14-77	1995	Arvada, Colo.
Janzen, Marty	0	5	7.20	22	9	0	1	65	76	58	52	36	56	R	R	6-3	197	5-31-73	1991	Gainesville, Fla.
Lukasiewicz, Mark	2	3	5.17	30	0	0	0	31	37	22	18	13	31	L	L	6-5	230	3-8-73	1994	Secaucus, N.J.
Person, Robert	1	0	0.00	1	1	0	0	7	4	1	0	2	5	R	R	5-11	180	1-8-69	1989	St. Louis, Mo.
Rhine, Kendall	0	0	9.00	1	0	0	0	2	2	2	2	3	0	R	R	6-7	215	11-27-70	1992	Lilburn, Ga.
Risley, Bill	1	2	8.22	11	1	0	0	15	19	15	14	10	20	R	R	6-2	210	5-29-67	1987	Farmington, N.M.
Robinson, Ken	7	7	2.56	56	0	0	17	81	44	24	23	36	96	R	R	5-9	175	11-3-69	1991	Akron, Ohio
Romano, Mike	2	4	4.25	40	12	0	0	108	100	56	51	74	83	R	R	6-2	195	3-3-72	1993	Chalmette, La.
Sievert, Mark	0	0	3.38	1	1	0	0	5	5	3	2	2	5	L	R	6-4	180	2-16-73	1991	Janesville, Wis.
Sinclair, Steve	0	0	6.00	6	0	0	0	9	11	6	6	3	9	L	L	6-2	172	8-2-71	1991	Victoria, B.C.
Smith, Brian	7	11	5.37	31	21	0	0	137	169	89	82	51	73	R	R	5-11	185	7-19-72	1994	Salisbury, N.C.

FIELDING

Catcher	PCT	G	PO	A	E	DP	PB
Brito	.969	8	58	5	2	1	0
Martinez	.986	92	588	50	9	8	4
Melhuse	.991	36	211	20	2	3	2
Mosquera	.984	10	55	5	1	0	0
Mummau	1.000	1	0	1	0	0	0
Rodriguez	1.000	3	6	0	0	0	0

First Base	PCT	G	PO	A	E	DP
Aldrete	.989	22	173	10	2	18
Aude	.984	68	587	34	10	78
Crespo	.976	19	151	11	4	16
Giannelli	1.000	6	25	1	0	2
Jones	.991	40	333	16	3	43
Manto	1.000	2	13	4	0	2

Second Base	PCT	G	PO	A	E	DP
Crespo	.962	28	47	78	5	20
Henry	.949	8	16	21	2	6
Melhuse	1.000	1	1	3	0	1
Mummau	.977	35	68	103	4	23
Patzke	.975	78	153	238	10	74
Roberts	.000	1	0	0	0	0
Soriano	.875	2	2	5	1	1

Third Base	PCT	G	PO	A	E	DP
Butler	.000	1	0	0	0	0
Crespo	1.000	3	2	10	0	1
Evans	.964	104	83	242	12	27
Manto	.947	7	3	15	1	2
Mummau	1.000	30	18	55	0	3
Patzke	1.000	1	2	2	0	1
Roberts	1.000	1	2	2	0	0

Shortstop	PCT	G	PO	A	E	DP
Henry	.928	32	57	84	11	24
Mummau	.887	17	25	38	8	10
Perez	.973	89	158	274	12	78
Soriano	.947	14	19	35	3	8

Outfield	PCT	G	PO	A	E	DP
Aldrete	1.000	2	3	0	0	0
Aude	1.000	2	3	0	0	0
Butler	.968	135	236	8	8	4
Cradle	1.000	7	9	1	0	0
Crespo	.944	30	47	4	3	2
De la Cruz	1.000	9	16	2	0	0
Manto	1.000	5	7	0	0	0
Melhuse	.000	1	0	0	0	0
Mummau	.952	16	20	0	1	0
Ramirez	.727	7	8	0	3	0
Roberts	.966	67	83	3	3	0
Sierra	.923	8	10	2	1	1
Stewart	.983	55	115	1	2	0
Thompson	.992	76	117	4	1	0
Whitmore	.986	39	69	1	1	0

KNOXVILLE — Class AA

SOUTHERN LEAGUE

BATTING	AVG	G	AB	R	H	2B	3B	HR	RBI	BB	SO	SB	CS	B	T	HT	WT	DOB	1st Yr	Resides
Adriana, Sharnol	.236	99	314	50	74	11	1	6	39	47	66	9	7	R	R	6-1	185	11-13-70	1991	Willemstad, Neth. Ant.
Candelaria, Ben	.294	120	472	81	139	32	5	15	67	42	89	4	3	L	R	5-11	167	1-29-75	1992	Hatillo, P.R.
Cradle, Rickey	.214	84	257	50	55	16	1	10	34	41	67	5	6	R	R	6-2	180	6-20-73	1991	Cerritos, Calif.

BATTING	AVG	G	AB	R	H	2B	3B	HR	RBI	BB	SO	SB	CS	B	T	HT	WT	DOB	1st Yr	Resides
Curl, John	.207	10	29	0	6	1	0	0	1	3	6	0	0	L	R	6-3	205	11-10-72	1995	Logansport, Ind.
De la Cruz, Lorenzo	.336	39	146	32	49	7	2	7	26	14	38	2	2	R	R	6-1	199	9-5-71	1991	Santo Domingo, D.R.
Diaz, Cesar	.200	7	15	2	3	1	0	1	3	5	2	0	0	R	R	6-3	185	7-12-74	1990	Maracay, Venez.
Freel, Ryan	.202	33	94	18	19	1	1	0	4	19	13	5	3	R	R	5-10	175	3-8-76	1995	Jacksonville, Fla.
French, Anton	.333	2	6	2	2	0	1	0	1	0	2	0	0	S	R	5-10	175	7-25-75	1993	St. Louis, Mo.
Henry, Santiago	.291	52	196	25	57	10	1	5	26	4	35	3	2	R	R	5-11	156	7-27-72	1991	San Pedro de Macoris, D.R.
Jones, Ryan	.256	86	328	41	84	19	3	12	51	27	63	0	1	R	R	6-3	220	11-5-74	1993	Irvine, Calif.
Melhuse, Adam	.230	31	87	14	20	3	0	3	10	19	19	0	0	S	R	6-2	185	3-27-72	1993	Stockton, Calif.
Morgan, Dave	.273	21	44	6	12	2	0	0	4	10	14	0	0	R	R	6-4	215	11-19-71	1993	Needham, Mass.
Mosquera, Julio	.291	87	309	47	90	23	1	5	50	22	56	3	4	R	R	6-0	165	1-29-72	1991	Panama City, Panama
Ramirez, Angel	.309	85	369	55	114	24	7	5	37	10	48	11	6	R	R	5-10	166	1-24-73	1991	Azua, D.R.
Roberts, Lonell	.190	7	21	5	4	0	1	0	0	2	3	0	2	S	R	6-0	172	6-7-71	1989	Bloomington, Calif.
Rodriguez, Luis	.269	24	78	6	21	3	1	0	6	3	20	0	1	R	R	5-9	160	1-3-74	1991	Tampa, Fla.
Sanders, Anthony	.266	111	429	68	114	20	4	26	69	44	121	20	12	R	R	6-2	180	3-2-74	1993	Tucson, Ariz.
Skett, Will	.273	30	110	18	30	6	1	3	15	4	31	4	4	R	R	5-11	190	5-22-74	1996	Encino, Calif.
Solano, Fausto	.265	115	378	52	100	24	4	10	56	37	47	8	14	R	R	5-9	144	6-19-74	1992	Santo Domingo, D.R.
Soriano, Fred	.059	7	17	3	1	0	0	0	0	3	4	1	1	S	R	5-9	160	8-5-74	1992	Bani, D.R.
Strange, Mike	.095	12	21	1	2	0	1	0	0	3	4	0	0	R	R	6-0	172	4-21-74	1994	Melbourne, Fla.
Thompson, Andy	.286	124	448	75	128	25	3	15	71	63	76	0	5	R	R	6-3	210	10-8-75	1995	Sun Prairie, Wis.
Witt, Kevin	.289	127	501	76	145	27	4	30	91	44	109	1	0	L	R	6-4	185	1-5-76	1994	Jacksonville, Fla.

PITCHING	W	L	ERA	G	GS	CG	SV	IP	H	R	ER	BB	SO	B	T	HT	WT	DOB	1st Yr	Resides
Almanzar, Carlos	1	1	4.91	21	0	0	8	26	30	14	14	5	25	R	R	6-2	166	11-6-73	1991	Santo Domingo, D.R.
Bogott, Kurt	2	1	3.90	35	1	0	2	65	66	32	28	25	77	L	L	6-4	195	9-30-72	1993	Sterling, Ill.
Brown, Chad	6	4	3.72	32	0	0	4	56	46	25	23	16	40	L	L	6-0	185	12-9-71	1992	Gastonia, N.C.
Czajkowski, Jim	2	2	6.47	25	0	0	5	32	43	27	23	11	33	R	R	6-4	215	12-18-63	1986	Cary, N.C.
Davey, Tom	6	7	5.83	20	16	0	0	93	108	65	60	50	72	R	R	6-7	215	9-11-73	1994	Canton, Mich.
Doman, Roger	7	3	3.67	48	1	0	4	101	99	46	41	29	71	R	R	6-5	185	1-26-73	1991	Cassville, Mo.
Escobar, Kelvim	2	1	3.70	5	5	1	0	24	20	13	10	16	31	R	R	6-1	195	4-11-76	1992	La Guaira, Venez.
Folkers, Ken	1	0	0.00	1	0	0	0	4	1	0	0	0	4	R	R	6-3	205	10-11-74	1997	Naperville, Ill.
Freeman, Chris	3	3	2.48	47	2	0	8	83	71	32	23	36	86	R	R	6-4	205	8-27-72	1994	Knoxville, Tenn.
Gordon, Mike	2	3	5.33	33	6	0	2	73	91	46	43	40	64	L	R	6-2	195	11-30-72	1992	Quincy, Fla.
Graterol, Beiker	2	1	5.40	3	3	0	0	17	24	12	10	9	11	R	R	6-2	164	11-9-74	1993	Barquisimeto, Venez.
Halladay, Roy	2	3	5.40	7	7	0	0	37	46	26	22	11	30	R	R	6-6	200	5-14-77	1995	Arvada, Colo.
Harris, D.J.	1	1	1.64	2	2	0	0	11	6	2	2	6	8	R	R	5-10	190	4-11-71	1993	Las Vegas, Nev.
Jarvis, Jason	0	2	9.78	4	4	1	0	19	28	24	21	9	11	R	R	6-1	170	10-27-73	1994	West Bountiful, Utah
Lowe, Benny	3	1	5.54	18	0	0	0	26	33	21	16	14	29	L	L	5-10	185	6-13-74	1994	Key West, Fla.
Lukasiewicz, Mark	2	0	3.65	27	0	0	7	37	26	17	15	14	43	L	L	6-5	230	3-8-73	1994	Secaucus, N.J.
McBride, Chris	4	4	3.71	10	10	0	0	61	61	30	25	14	33	L	R	6-5	210	10-13-73	1994	Leland, N.C.
Meiners, Doug	9	5	5.43	23	23	3	0	123	161	85	74	31	81	R	R	6-8	190	5-16-74	1992	Staten Island, N.Y.
Meinershagen, Adam	0	0	3.71	7	7	0	0	17	16	8	7	6	7	R	R	6-4	190	7-25-73	1991	St. Louis, Mo.
Rhine, Kendall	0	0	10.32	8	0	0	0	11	13	13	13	15	6	R	R	6-7	215	11-27-70	1992	Lilburn, Ga.
Smith, Brian	0	0	0.00	1	0	0	0	1	0	0	0	1	1	R	R	5-11	185	7-19-72	1994	Salisbury, N.C.
Stevenson, Jason	12	9	4.27	26	26	2	0	150	166	88	71	43	101	R	R	6-3	180	8-11-74	1994	Phenix City, Ala.
Veniard, Jay	3	8	5.85	17	15	2	0	75	97	59	49	37	54	L	L	6-4	215	8-16-74	1995	Jacksonville, Fla.
Young, Joe	5	4	4.42	19	11	0	0	59	52	38	29	40	62	R	R	6-4	205	4-28-75	1993	Fort McMurray, Alberta

FIELDING

Catcher	PCT	G	PO	A	E	DP	PB
Diaz	1.000	5	26	1	0	0	0
Melhuse	.992	18	114	18	1	3	4
Morgan	.984	16	118	9	2	2	2
Mosquera	.989	86	587	56	7	6	4
Rodriguez	.983	24	153	19	3	2	4

First Base	PCT	G	PO	A	E	DP
Adriana	.963	7	49	3	2	6
Jones	.985	62	546	26	9	44
Melhuse	.982	8	48	6	1	1
Morgan	1.000	3	14	2	0	2
Witt	.992	66	529	60	5	43

Second Base	PCT	G	PO	A	E	DP
Adriana	.955	79	157	223	18	45
Henry	.947	35	87	108	11	25
Fa. Solano	.987	23	30	44	1	10
Fr. Soriano	.947	4	12	6	1	1
Strange	.971	8	15	19	1	2

Third Base	PCT	G	PO	A	E	DP
Adriana	.900	5	1	8	1	0
Thompson	.898	104	72	202	31	9
Witt	.885	34	19	58	10	9

Shortstop	PCT	G	PO	A	E	DP
Freel	.913	33	44	92	13	17
Henry	.938	17	27	63	6	9
Fa. Solano	.950	93	151	267	22	53
Fr. Soriano	.900	2	5	4	1	1
Strange	1.000	1	0	3	0	0
Witt	.000	2	0	0	0	0

Outfield	PCT	G	PO	A	E	DP
Candelaria	.974	102	174	13	5	1
Cradle	.982	73	104	5	2	0
Curl	1.000	1	2	0	0	0
De La Cruz	.957	11	20	2	1	0
French	1.000	2	1	0	0	0
Melhuse	1.000	5	10	2	0	0
Ramirez	.954	82	131	15	7	5
Roberts	.941	7	16	0	1	0
Sanders	.983	109	224	7	4	3
Skett	.977	30	40	2	1	0
Witt	1.000	4	5	0	0	0

DUNEDIN — Class A

FLORIDA STATE LEAGUE

BATTING	AVG	G	AB	R	H	2B	3B	HR	RBI	BB	SO	SB	CS	B	T	HT	WT	DOB	1st Yr	Resides
Blake, Casey	.238	129	449	56	107	21	0	7	39	48	91	19	9	R	R	6-2	195	8-23-73	1996	Indianola, Iowa
Brumfield, Jacob	.160	6	25	2	4	0	0	0	2	0	6	1	1	R	R	6-0	180	5-27-65	1983	Atlanta, Ga.
Curl, John	.255	74	231	36	59	14	0	15	48	24	53	3	2	L	R	6-3	205	11-10-72	1995	Logansport, Ind.
Diaz, Cesar	.290	108	379	50	110	23	1	12	56	36	108	4	7	R	R	6-3	185	7-12-74	1990	Maracay, Venez.
Evans, Tom	.262	15	42	8	11	2	0	2	4	11	10	0	0	R	R	6-1	180	7-9-74	1992	Kirkland, Wash.
Freel, Ryan	.282	61	181	42	51	8	2	3	17	46	28	24	5	R	R	5-10	175	3-8-76	1995	Jacksonville, Fla.
French, Anton	.222	78	261	34	58	5	3	3	17	25	51	35	15	S	R	5-10	175	7-25-75	1993	St. Louis, Mo.
Hayes, Chris	.230	60	139	20	32	5	1	2	20	15	27	2	1	R	R	6-2	190	12-23-73	1995	Jacksonville, Fla.
Koehler, Jason	.000	1	1	1	0	0	0	0	0	1	0	0	0	R	R	6-0	220	9-15-74	1996	Blandon, Pa.
Langaigne, Selwyn	.189	42	90	9	17	3	0	1	7	10	26	4	1	L	L	6-0	185	3-22-76	1994	Las Acaias, Venez.
Morgan, Dave	.208	20	53	8	11	1	0	2	7	6	11	2	2	R	R	6-4	215	11-19-71	1993	Needham, Mass.
Peck, Tom	.190	50	105	12	20	4	1	0	4	14	21	0	1	L	R	6-1	160	7-2-74	1995	Coral Gables, Fla.
Peeples, Mike	.256	129	477	73	122	29	2	2	42	54	83	26	16	R	R	5-11	160	9-3-76	1994	Green Cove Springs, Fla.
Rivers, Jonathan	.269	132	457	62	123	21	3	13	75	53	107	24	8	R	R	6-2	200	8-17-74	1992	Tallassee, Ala.
Sanders, Anthony	.200	1	5	0	1	1	0	0	1	1	1	0	0	R	R	6-2	180	3-2-74	1993	Tucson, Ariz.
Skett, Will	.269	98	361	63	97	22	3	19	71	45	100	12	7	R	R	5-11	190	5-22-74	1996	Encino, Calif.
Soriano, Fred	.308	26	78	18	24	5	1	2	12	8	17	3	0	S	R	5-9	160	8-5-74	1992	Bani, D.R.
Stone, Craig	.235	113	404	56	95	28	1	14	59	25	109	1	2	R	R	6-2	190	7-12-75	1993	Quakers Hill, Australia

BATTING	AVG	G	AB	R	H	2B	3B	HR	RBI	BB	SO	SB	CS	B	T	HT	WT	DOB	1st Yr	Resides
Strange, Mike	.264	48	106	15	28	5	1	0	7	14	39	1	1	R	R	6-0	172	4-21-74	1994	Melbourne, Fla.
Whitlock, Mike	.193	107	322	41	62	14	0	11	48	69	132	1	1	L	R	6-3	200	12-14-76	1995	Oakland, Calif.
Willis, Symmion	.220	56	164	18	36	5	1	2	16	10	37	2	1	R	R	6-4	215	11-27-72	1996	Atlanta, Ga.
Woodward, Chris	.293	91	314	38	92	13	4	1	38	52	52	4	8	R	R	6-0	160	6-27-76	1995	Duarte, Calif.

GAMES BY POSITION: C—Diaz 96, Koehler 1, Morgan 13, Stone 43. **1B**—Curl 23, Hayes 11, Stone 39, Whitlock 86. **2B**—Freel 7, Peeples 124, Skett 3, Soriano 3, Strange 15. **3B**—Blake 121, Evans 4, Freel 4, Hayes 6, Skett 1, Soriano 2, Stone 6, Strange 6. **SS**—Blake 1, Freel 27, Soriano 18, Strange 15, Woodward 89. **OF**—Brumfield 6, Curl 3, Freel 18, French 75, Hayes 32, Langaigne 41, Peck 26, Peeples 1, Rivers 130, Sanders 1, Skett 95, Willis 52.

PITCHING	W	L	ERA	G	GS	CG	SV	IP	H	R	ER	BB	SO	B	T	HT	WT	DOB	1st Yr	Resides
Adkins, Tim	1	1	4.71	39	0	0	3	50	52	43	26	58	55	L	L	6-0	195	5-12-74	1992	Huntington, W.Va.
Bowles, Brian	0	2	7.53	7	1	0	0	14	20	14	12	7	9	R	R	6-5	205	8-18-76	1995	Manhattan Beach, Calif.
Brackeen, Colin	0	2	3.60	6	0	0	0	10	13	4	4	3	11	L	L	6-0	200	3-8-75	1997	Arden Hills, Minn.
Bradford, Josh	8	8	4.99	28	23	2	0	159	173	104	88	65	92	R	R	6-5	185	4-19-74	1996	Cincinnati, Ohio
Crowther, John	1	2	5.88	19	0	0	0	26	36	23	17	15	30	R	R	6-5	231	9-23-73	1994	Savannah, Ga.
Davey, Tom	1	3	4.31	7	6	0	0	40	44	21	19	15	36	R	R	6-7	215	9-11-73	1994	Canton, Mich.
Escobar, Kelvim	0	1	3.75	3	2	0	0	12	16	9	5	3	16	R	R	6-1	195	4-11-76	1992	La Guaira, Venez.
Gomez, Miguel	4	3	4.93	21	0	0	2	35	41	26	19	10	30	R	R	6-3	170	5-31-74	1992	Panama City, Panama
Graterol, Beiker	4	7	4.22	17	10	1	1	81	86	46	38	26	54	R	R	6-2	164	11-9-74	1993	Barquisimeto, Venez.
Guzman, Juan	0	0	0.00	2	2	0	0	4	3	0	0	1	3	R	R	5-11	190	10-28-66	1985	Mano Guayabo, D.R.
Hanson, Erik	0	0	1.29	2	2	0	0	7	7	5	1	1	5	R	R	6-6	215	5-18-65	1986	Kirkland, Wash.
Harris, D.J.	8	4	3.22	42	3	0	5	78	64	41	28	45	66	R	R	5-10	190	4-11-71	1993	Las Vegas, Nev.
Hartshorn, Ty	5	13	4.44	26	24	2	0	160	197	102	79	40	101	R	R	6-5	190	8-3-74	1993	Lamar, Colo.
Jarvis, Jason	6	11	5.19	35	7	0	1	85	92	64	49	47	70	R	R	6-1	170	10-27-73	1994	West Bountiful, Utah
Koch, Bill	0	1	2.08	3	3	0	0	22	27	10	5	3	20	R	R	6-3	210	12-14-74	1996	Clearwater, Fla.
Lee, Jeremy	8	9	4.64	28	22	0	1	153	179	95	79	54	90	R	R	6-8	235	10-20-74	1993	Galesburg, Ill.
Lowe, Benny	2	1	1.84	13	0	0	5	15	7	3	3	3	19	L	L	5-10	185	6-13-74	1994	Key West, Fla.
Mann, Jim	1	0	6.00	12	0	0	0	18	27	12	12	6	13	R	R	6-3	225	11-17-74	1994	Holbrook, Mass.
McBride, Chris	3	0	6.10	10	4	0	0	31	44	25	21	17	25	L	R	6-5	210	10-13-73	1994	Leland, N.C.
McClellan, Sean	0	0	10.80	3	0	0	0	3	5	4	4	5	4	R	R	6-2	215	4-26-73	1996	Seminole, Fla.
Meinershagen, Adam	0	1	5.00	3	2	0	0	9	12	5	5	1	4	R	R	6-4	190	7-25-73	1991	St. Louis, Mo.
Paige, Carey	1	3	3.02	12	9	0	1	45	36	21	15	22	39	R	R	6-3	175	3-2-74	1992	Abilene, Texas
Rhine, Kendall	0	0	12.46	4	0	0	0	4	9	7	6	4	2	R	R	6-7	215	11-27-70	1992	Lilburn, Ga.
Risley, Bill	0	2	4.50	8	6	0	0	12	9	9	6	3	11	R	R	6-2	210	5-29-67	1987	Farmington, N.M.
Sievert, Mark	1	0	3.27	3	2	0	0	11	10	5	4	5	7	L	R	6-4	180	2-16-73	1991	Janesville, Wis.
Sinclair, Steve	2	5	2.90	43	0	0	3	68	63	36	22	26	66	L	L	6-2	172	8-2-71	1991	Victoria, B.C.
Spoljaric, Paul	0	0	1.69	4	3	0	0	11	10	3	2	2	10	L	L	6-3	205	9-24-70	1990	Kelowna, B.C.
Veniard, Jay	1	3	1.88	10	8	0	0	53	49	23	11	35	32	L	L	6-4	215	8-16-74	1995	Jacksonville, Fla.

HAGERSTOWN — Class A

SOUTH ATLANTIC LEAGUE

BATTING	AVG	G	AB	R	H	2B	3B	HR	RBI	BB	SO	SB	CS	B	T	HT	WT	DOB	1st Yr	Resides
Abernathy, Brent	.309	99	379	69	117	27	2	1	26	30	32	22	13	R	R	6-1	185	9-23-77	1996	Marietta, Ga.
Baston, Stan	.212	19	66	8	14	2	1	0	9	8	17	3	1	R	R	6-2	180	2-12-77	1996	Tallahassee, Fla.
Giles, Tim	.334	112	380	54	127	32	0	12	56	46	95	2	2	L	R	6-3	215	9-12-75	1996	Gambrills, Md.
Hampton, Robby	.211	100	337	32	71	22	1	9	34	23	124	9	3	R	R	6-3	200	2-21-76	1994	Mount Pleasant, Texas
Johnson, Damon	.325	84	302	44	98	21	5	10	55	13	65	11	6	R	R	6-1	195	8-22-75	1993	Crossett, Ark.
Kehoe, John	.172	14	58	9	10	3	1	0	4	4	19	2	0	R	R	6-0	185	1-9-73	1995	South Bend, Ind.
Koehler, Jason	.203	26	69	7	14	0	0	3	12	3	19	1	3	R	R	6-0	220	9-15-74	1996	Blandon, Pa.
Lawrence, Joe	.229	116	446	63	102	24	1	8	38	49	107	10	12	R	R	6-2	190	2-13-77	1996	Lake Charles, La.
Lopez, Luis	.358	136	503	96	180	47	4	11	99	60	45	5	8	R	R	6-0	200	10-5-73	1996	Spring Hill, Fla.
Maloney, Jeff	.258	101	395	49	102	19	2	7	38	23	98	19	9	R	R	6-4	190	11-27-76	1995	Basking Ridge, N.J.
Phelps, Josh	.210	68	233	26	49	9	1	7	24	15	72	3	2	R	R	6-3	195	5-12-78	1996	Rathdrum, Idaho
Rodriguez, Luis	.266	27	94	13	25	6	0	2	14	2	20	3	0	R	R	5-9	160	1-3-74	1991	Tampa, Fla.
Rodriguez, Mike	.228	43	123	17	28	3	0	0	12	18	25	0	2	R	R	5-11	185	4-1-75	1996	Stephenville, Texas
Shatley, Andy	.242	117	401	51	97	28	0	12	46	17	114	6	3	R	R	6-3	185	1-23-76	1994	Jonesboro, Ark.
Soriano, Fred	.242	38	120	18	29	9	0	0	6	5	27	8	2	S	R	5-9	160	8-5-74	1992	Bani, D.R.
Stromsborg, Ryan	.288	56	184	22	53	10	0	4	24	13	37	5	1	R	R	6-3	185	12-19-74	1996	Encino, Calif.
Tucci, Peter	.264	127	466	60	123	28	5	10	75	35	95	9	5	R	R	6-2	205	10-8-75	1996	Norwalk, Conn.
Willis, Symmion	.246	25	61	6	15	3	0	0	11	7	21	0	1	R	R	6-4	215	11-27-72	1996	Atlanta, Ga.

GAMES BY POSITION: C—Koehler 26, Phelps 66, L. Rodriguez 25, M. Rodriguez 31. **1B**—Giles 51, Lopez 87, Shatley 4. **2B**—Abernathy 99, Baston 4, Kehoe 14, Shatley 3, Soriano 17, Stromsborg 12. **3B**—Baston 10, Lopez 7, L. Rodriguez 2, Shatley 107, Soriano 8, Stromsborg 12. **SS**—Lawrence 115, Shatley 7, Soriano 10, Stromsborg 8. **OF**—Baston 3, Hampton 98, Johnson 81, Maloney 95, M. Rodriguez 5, Stromsborg 23, Tucci 108, Willis 15.

PITCHING	W	L	ERA	G	GS	CG	SV	IP	H	R	ER	BB	SO	B	T	HT	WT	DOB	1st Yr	Resides
Andrews, Clayton	7	7	4.55	28	15	0	0	115	120	70	58	47	112	R	L	6-0	175	5-15-78	1996	Largo, Fla.
Bale, John	7	7	4.30	25	25	0	0	140	130	83	67	63	155	L	L	6-4	195	5-22-74	1996	Crestview, Fla.
Bleazard, David	5	0	3.32	10	10	0	0	60	52	25	22	20	58	R	R	6-0	175	3-7-74	1996	Tooele, Utah
Bowles, Brian	1	0	6.97	4	0	0	0	10	14	10	8	5	9	R	R	6-5	205	8-18-76	1995	Manhattan Beach, Calif.
Charbonneau, Marc	1	1	9.28	6	1	0	0	11	18	14	11	7	13	R	L	6-3	185	9-29-75	1995	Ottawa, Ontario
Davenport, Joe	4	6	3.68	37	0	0	10	51	43	26	21	24	43	R	R	6-5	225	3-24-76	1994	Santee, Calif.
Delgado, Ernie	5	10	5.23	32	17	0	1	134	163	96	78	56	103	R	R	6-2	190	7-21-75	1993	Tucson, Ariz.
Eversgerd, Randy	0	0	4.50	5	0	0	0	8	13	4	4	2	2	R	R	6-0	180	8-28-76	1997	Centralia, Ill.
Folkers, Ken	0	0	0.00	5	0	0	0	6	3	0	0	2	4	R	R	6-3	205	10-11-74	1997	Naperville, Ill.
Glover, Gary	6	17	3.73	28	28	3	0	174	165	94	72	58	155	R	R	6-5	200	12-3-76	1994	DeLand, Fla.
Gomez, Miguel	1	1	8.04	12	0	0	0	16	27	19	14	9	17	R	R	6-3	170	5-31-74	1992	Panama City, Panama
Graterol, Beiker	1	0	0.00	4	0	0	2	11	7	1	0	3	12	R	R	6-2	164	11-9-74	1993	Barquisimeto, Venez.
Hibbard, Billy	0	0	5.19	11	0	0	0	17	23	10	10	3	13	R	R	6-3	198	6-24-76	1994	Orlando, Fla.
Lachapelle, Yan	7	7	3.26	26	15	1	3	119	73	54	43	74	115	R	R	5-10	190	10-26-75	1996	Gatineau, Quebec
Lawrence, Clint	13	10	3.54	27	27	1	0	170	179	76	67	40	149	L	L	6-4	200	10-19-76	1995	Oakville, Ontario
Lowe, Benny	0	0	0.00	2	0	0	0	2	3	3	0	0	4	L	L	5-10	185	6-13-74	1994	Key West, Fla.
Mann, Jim	0	1	5.06	19	0	0	4	27	35	18	15	11	30	R	R	6-3	225	11-17-74	1994	Holbrook, Mass.
McClellan, Sean	3	2	1.66	35	0	0	11	65	49	21	12	26	80	R	R	6-2	215	4-26-73	1996	Seminole, Fla.
Volkert, Oreste	4	4	3.68	34	0	0	1	51	42	22	21	22	45	R	R	6-6	187	1-16-75	1993	La Habra, Calif.

ST. CATHARINES — Short-Season Class A

NEW YORK-PENN LEAGUE

BATTING	AVG	G	AB	R	H	2B	3B	HR	RBI	BB	SO	SB	CS	B	T	HT	WT	DOB	1st Yr	Resides
Albaral, Randy	.225	56	218	39	49	5	1	0	23	20	27	14	3	R	R	6-2	180	2-27-77	1996	River Ridge, La.
Bagley, Lorenzo	.264	58	197	25	52	10	1	5	21	12	55	3	4	R	R	5-9	225	12-30-75	1996	Citra, Fla.
Barnett, Brian	.230	45	122	18	28	9	1	0	8	22	36	3	3	R	R	5-10	175	5-15-76	1997	McMinnville, Ore.
Baston, Stan	.161	44	137	10	22	2	0	0	14	11	32	1	3	R	R	6-2	180	2-12-77	1996	Tallahassee, Fla.
Chiaffredo, Paul	.239	48	163	20	39	8	1	2	15	9	42	5	2	R	R	6-2	195	5-30-76	1997	San Jose, Calif.
Cripps, Bobby	.125	14	40	4	5	0	1	1	3	4	11	0	0	L	R	6-2	200	5-9-77	1996	Powell River, B.C.
Izturis, Cesar	.190	70	231	32	44	3	0	1	11	15	27	6	3	S	R	5-9	155	2-10-80	1997	Lara, Venez.
Koehler, Jason	.231	10	39	4	9	4	0	1	7	4	11	0	1	R	R	6-0	220	9-15-74	1996	Blandon, Pa.
Langaigne, Selwyn	.320	74	266	50	85	15	4	1	39	48	46	19	9	L	L	6-0	185	3-22-76	1994	Las Acaias, Venez.
Medina, Robert	.228	34	123	18	28	5	1	2	16	7	32	1	0	R	R	6-2	193	4-25-76	1995	Caguas, P.R.
Nieves, Juan	.230	64	243	29	56	14	0	2	30	7	41	3	5	R	R	6-3	170	3-29-77	1996	Carabobo, Venez.
Rodriguez, Mike	.286	2	7	0	2	1	0	0	1	0	1	0	0	R	R	5-11	185	4-1-75	1996	Stephenville, Texas
Sencion, Pablo	.220	51	173	18	38	7	0	8	36	24	47	0	0	S	R	6-1	188	12-12-75	1994	Santo Domingo, D.R.
Wells, Vernon	.307	66	264	52	81	20	1	10	31	30	44	8	6	R	R	6-1	195	12-8-78	1997	Arlington, Texas
Young, Michael	.308	74	276	49	85	18	3	9	48	33	59	9	5	R	R	6-0	175	10-19-76	1997	Covina, Calif.

GAMES BY POSITION: C—Chiaffredo 45, Cripps 9, Koehler 2, Medina 20, Rodriguez 2. **1B**—Chiaffredo 1, Koehler 6, Langaigne 63, Medina 4, Sencion 4. **2B**—Barnett 5, Baston 5, Izturis 40, Young 28. **3B**—Barnett 10, Baston 23, Nieves 2, Sencion 45. **SS**—Barnett 1, Izturis 30, Young 44. **OF**—Albaral 55, Bagley 38, Barnett 5, Baston 7, Langaigne 13, Nieves 57, Wells 61.

PITCHING	W	L	ERA	G	GS	CG	SV	IP	H	R	ER	BB	SO	B	T	HT	WT	DOB	1st Yr	Resides
Bowles, Brian	5	8	5.03	16	16	0	0	79	76	53	44	35	64	R	R	6-5	205	8-18-76	1995	Manhattan Beach, Calif.
Burchart, Kyle	3	4	4.78	14	14	0	0	70	75	49	37	23	56	R	R	6-5	190	8-18-76	1995	Tulsa, Okla.
Casey, Joe	7	4	4.36	14	11	0	1	64	59	42	31	23	43	R	R	6-0	185	1-25-79	1997	Honeybrook, Pa.
Charbonneau, Marc	0	1	7.20	6	0	0	1	10	9	9	8	4	15	R	L	6-3	185	9-29-75	1995	Ottawa, Ontario
Coco, Pascual	1	4	4.89	10	8	0	0	46	48	32	25	16	44	R	R	6-1	160	9-24-77	1995	Santo Domingo, D.R.
Crabtree, Tim	0	0	3.00	2	1	0	0	3	3	2	1	0	3	R	R	6-4	205	10-13-69	1992	Jackson, Mich.
Curtis, Mark	1	0	4.76	4	0	0	0	6	6	4	3	5	5	R	L	6-4	190	12-1-77	1997	St. Albert, Alberta
Eversgerd, Randy	0	1	2.66	13	0	0	0	24	30	16	7	5	34	R	R	6-0	180	8-28-76	1997	Centralia, Ill.
Folkers, Ken	1	0	3.03	14	0	0	0	30	27	16	10	7	28	R	R	6-3	205	10-11-74	1997	Naperville, Ill.
Heath, Woody	7	4	2.42	15	12	0	0	78	63	29	21	19	72	R	R	6-0	170	8-19-76	1997	Issaquah, Wash.
Huff, Tim	1	1	5.34	15	0	0	0	32	38	20	19	13	20	L	L	6-0	170	12-28-74	1997	Phoenix, Ariz.
Huggins, David	0	3	3.28	27	2	0	11	36	33	18	13	15	42	R	R	6-5	190	12-19-75	1997	Chester, Texas
Lacefield, Tim	2	0	4.99	25	0	0	2	40	52	26	22	5	33	R	R	6-3	175	9-8-75	1997	Searcy, Ark.
Markwell, Diegomar	1	6	4.99	16	11	0	0	49	50	35	27	40	33	L	L	6-2	165	8-8-80	1997	Curacao, Neth. Ant.
Seabury, Jaron	2	0	4.50	8	0	0	4	8	7	4	4	6	11	R	R	6-4	215	1-31-76	1995	Mt. Vernon, Wash.
Weimer, Matt	2	2	3.57	23	0	0	0	35	35	21	14	4	22	R	R	6-2	190	11-21-74	1997	Annapolis, Md.
Woodards, Orlando	2	2	5.15	21	0	0	2	37	41	23	21	24	32	R	R	6-2	190	1-2-78	1997	Sacramento, Calif.

MEDICINE HAT — Rookie

PIONEER LEAGUE

BATTING	AVG	G	AB	R	H	2B	3B	HR	RBI	BB	SO	SB	CS	B	T	HT	WT	DOB	1st Yr	Resides
Adams, Lawrence	.179	47	117	9	21	7	0	1	13	11	44	1	3	R	R	6-5	215	2-18-77	1997	Fairburn, Ga.
Barrett, Andrew	.233	43	103	4	24	3	0	0	14	6	30	1	1	L	R	6-0	175	7-12-79	1997	Tacoma, Wash.
Bejarano, Brian	.290	53	193	26	56	8	0	6	29	18	38	1	3	R	R	6-2	200	1-29-75	1995	Laveen, Ariz.
Bernhardt, Josephang	.176	60	199	20	35	2	0	1	13	8	55	3	2	R	R	6-1	165	9-22-80	1996	San Pedro de Macoris, D.R.
Brown, Billy	.287	70	272	63	78	16	4	8	39	36	66	22	4	R	R	6-0	195	3-9-76	1997	Plantation, Fla.
Fortin, Blaine	.329	55	164	21	54	5	0	7	26	5	12	1	3	R	R	6-2	205	8-1-77	1995	Lundar, Manitoba
Hubbel, Travis	.160	42	119	10	19	3	1	0	10	10	43	1	2	R	R	6-1	185	6-27-79	1997	Edmonton, Alberta
Landingham, James	.302	21	43	10	13	3	1	0	3	3	5	3	3	L	L	5-11	205	4-17-77	1997	Homestead, Fla.
Morillo, Luis	.314	8	35	5	11	3	0	0	4	4	6	6	1	L	L	5-11	155	1-13-78	1996	Santo Domingo, D.R.
Morrison, Greg	.448	69	241	63	108	16	3	23	88	14	29	2	3	L	L	6-1	205	2-23-76	1995	Medicine Hat, Alberta
Ortiz, Carlos	.200	31	70	5	14	2	0	0	4	6	17	0	0	R	R	6-4	225	8-7-79	1997	Anaheim, Calif.
Perez, Angelo	.238	70	269	37	64	15	5	6	33	19	62	8	3	R	R	6-1	168	11-14-76	1994	La Romana, D.R.
Rodriguez, Felipe	.253	54	190	48	48	7	0	0	12	29	38	18	6	L	R	5-11	155	2-7-77	1994	Santo Domingo, D.R.
Umbria, Jose	.175	49	126	4	22	2	0	0	15	6	24	2	1	R	R	6-2	205	1-20-78	1996	Barquisimeto, Venez.
Watley, Clarence	.303	10	33	3	10	2	0	0	6	4	13	3	0	S	R	5-11	182	1-28-78	1997	Stone Mountain, Ga.
Zeber, Ryan	.198	43	101	11	20	2	0	1	7	12	26	1	2	R	R	6-2	190	5-24-78	1996	Tustin, Calif.
Zepeda, Jesse	.264	64	216	39	57	14	1	1	23	42	29	6	5	S	R	5-10	165	5-4-74	1996	Santa Maria, Calif.

GAMES BY POSITION: C—Fortin 25, Ortiz 1, Umbria 44, Zeber 28, Zepeda 1. **1B**—Barrett 1, Bejarano 20, Fortin 5, Landingham 1, Morrison 45, Ortiz 24. **2B**—Rodriguez 52, Zeber 4, Zepeda 24. **3B**—Barrett 2, Bejarano 20, Hubbel 37, Ortiz 1, Umbria 3, Watley 3, Zeber 1, Zepeda 24. **SS**—Barrett 8, Bernhardt 60, Zepeda 14. **OF**—Adams 33, Barrett 25, Bejarano 1, Brown 50, Fortin 1, Landingham 14, Morillo 8, Morrison 23, Perez 70, Rodriguez 1, Watley 8, Zeber 5, Zepeda 8.

PITCHING	W	L	ERA	G	GS	CG	SV	IP	H	R	ER	BB	SO	B	T	HT	WT	DOB	1st Yr	Resides
Barrera, Iran	3	1	5.79	17	0	0	0	19	27	22	12	7	15	R	R	5-9	200	3-12-74	1997	Avenal, Calif.
Barrett, Scott	0	6	5.53	19	8	0	0	54	69	42	33	16	46	R	R	6-2	202	3-26-75	1997	Athens, Texas
Bost, Ronald	0	2	7.71	14	0	0	0	16	22	20	14	17	17	L	L	6-2	175	7-24-79	1997	Harrisburg, N.C.
Brackeen, Colin	1	1	1.40	18	0	0	5	19	11	4	3	8	20	L	L	6-0	200	3-8-75	1997	Arden Hills, Minn.
Goure, Sam	2	6	4.71	15	15	1	0	80	99	61	42	20	68	S	L	6-2	185	4-17-78	1996	Pueblo, Colo.
Gourlay, Matthew	2	6	5.72	14	14	1	0	68	72	56	43	28	35	R	R	6-5	200	6-26-79	1996	Cheltenham, Australia
Hueda, Alejandro	1	4	5.71	16	8	0	0	52	59	41	33	28	32	R	R	6-1	180	2-28-76	1996	San Jose, Costa Rica
Keathley, Davan	3	4	6.48	20	0	0	0	25	24	24	18	20	19	R	L	6-4	198	4-9-78	1996	Modesto, Calif.
Lancaster, Roger	1	2	4.82	18	0	0	1	28	33	20	15	15	18	R	R	6-0	201	10-10-74	1997	Spring, Texas
Lynch, Pat	3	3	5.26	12	11	0	0	50	64	40	29	24	34	R	R	6-3	195	6-27-78	1996	Milton, Ontario
McClellan, Matt	2	5	6.92	14	6	0	0	39	50	36	30	24	43	R	R	6-7	205	8-13-76	1997	Toledo, Ohio
Needle, Chad	0	1	2.70	10	0	0	0	17	17	6	5	5	17	R	R	6-5	225	5-17-79	1996	Perth, Australia
Rodriguez, Franklin	0	0	10.24	7	0	0	0	10	22	13	11	7	9	R	L	6-2	185	10-21-76	1994	Bugaba, Panama
Satterfield, Jeremy	0	1	8.46	16	0	0	0	22	29	29	21	27	26	R	R	6-3	200	12-2-75	1996	Santa Barbara, Calif.
Seale, Dustin	0	1	2.30	10	0	0	0	16	21	8	4	3	24	L	L	6-1	170	12-2-77	1997	Safford, Ariz.
Sneed, John	6	1	1.29	15	10	2	0	70	42	19	10	20	79	L	R	6-6	235	6-30-76	1997	Houston, Texas
Salley, Anthony	2	2	4.46	24	0	0	1	36	32	27	18	24	28	L	L	6-0	185	9-23-75	1997	Swansea, S.C.

Minor Leagues

New agreement, record attendance have minors on verge of another golden era

BY WILL LINGO

The off-the-field events didn't draw a whole lot of attention in 1997, but they may have contributed to the most important season in minor league baseball since the current system was established in the early 1960s.

The minor league boom apparently has legs. Just a year earlier, it appeared that the best years of the current surge might have passed. Attendance had leveled off and talk from the majors was about how the current minor league system needed to change to save money.

In 1997, though, attendance reached its greatest level since the 1940s. Triple-A was energized by realignment into two leagues for 1998. And the minors agreed to a new 10-year Professional Baseball Agreement with the majors.

That's quite a summer. And it bodes well for the future of the minor leagues. While it would have been easy to ride the waves of fans coming into ballparks in the 1990s, minor league leaders keep looking for ways to do things better.

Easily the most significant event was the signing of the PBA. After all the cutback talk, the majors eventually were convinced that the current arrangement is good for them. It develops players, of course, but it also develops baseball fans. The majors might finally understand that.

"The PBA is important for the moment and for the long-term health of the industry," National Association president Mike Moore said.

While the PBA was a big achievement, it was expected to get worked out during the summer. Triple-A realignment was much more of a surprise.

Mike Moore

Moore said some teams were reluctant even to consider realignment. He pushed it because he wanted to at least make an honest effort to find out if it was feasible.

"We quickly found out that it could make sense, and then it fell together real fast," he said. "A lot of people were surprised when it was announced because they hadn't heard much talk about it."

Add to that another attendance surge brought on by the latest wave of new ballparks, and it's a good time to be in charge of the minor leagues. But more could be ahead, including possible Double-A realignment.

ORGANIZATION STANDINGS

	—1997—			1996	1995	1994
	W	L	Pct.	Pct.	Pct.	Pct.
New York-AL (6)	386	308	.556	.525	.507	.512
Cincinnati (5)	342	290	.541	.485	.569	.539
Baltimore (6)	371	323	.535	.503	.479	.515
Oakland (6)	372	324	.534	.536	.507	.556
Detroit (6)	363	320	.531	.501	.521	.454
Minnesota (6)	357	330	.520	.520	.514	.502
New York-NL (7)	393	368	.516	574	.536	.509
Boston (6)	354	338	.512	.503	.493	.485
Florida (6)	354	338	.512	.464	.495	.496
San Francisco (5)	326	311	.512	.527	.514	.497
Seattle (6)	352	340	.509	.487	.469	.518
Cleveland (6)	358	348	.507	.542	.544	.521
Philadelphia (6)	356	350	.504	.493	.533	.475
Arizona (4)	203	202	.501	.547	—	—
Chicago-AL (6)	345	344	.501	.430	.473	.524
Pittsburgh (6)	345	347	.499	.486	.499	.430
Tampa Bay (5)	240	243	.497	.466	—	—
Milwaukee (6)	342	356	.490	.524	.550	.544
Chicago-NL (6)	331	349	.487	.499	.546	.446
San Diego (6)	331	350	.486	.530	.456	.458
Texas (5)	267	282	.486	.501	.429	.450
Los Angeles (7)	410	435	.485	.494	.512	.514
Anaheim (6)	343	365	.484	.483	.566	.507
Kansas City (6)	337	360	.484	.521	.535	.589
Atlanta (7)	369	395	.483	.465	.453	.485
Montreal (6)	335	358	.483	.539	.462	.529
Colorado (6)	330	359	.479	.478	.510	.477
Houston (6)	323	367	.468	.493	.515	.501
St. Louis (6)	323	380	.459	.501	.479	.542
Toronto (6)	313	391	.445	.487	.453	.498

Number of farm teams in parentheses

Negotiations Go Smoothly

They said the negotiations would be quiet and cordial. They said the alterations to the Professional Baseball Agreement would not be radical. They said neither side would have to make major sacrifices. They said the changes they agreed to would ensure the long-term stability of the minors. They said it all could be wrapped up by June.

Amazingly, major league and minor league negotiators came through on all those promises in negotiating the new PBA, which gained easy approval by major league and minor league owners in June.

No major changes were made in the new PBA, the document that governs the relationship between the majors and minors. Going into the negotiations, many in the minors feared the big leaguers would try to cut teams or whole leagues.

The major leagues will save money by getting the minor leagues to pay for umpire development and some equipment. But the minors get a guarantee of stability for that money.

CLASSIFICATION ALL-STARS

Selected by Baseball America

*League leader

TRIPLE-A

Pos.	Player, Team	AVG	AB	R	H	2B	3B	HR	RBI	BB	SO	SB
C	Todd Greene, Vancouver (Pacific Coast)	.354	260	51	92	22	0	25	75	20	31	5
1B	Todd Helton, Colorado Springs (Pacifc Coast)	.352	392	87	138	31	2	16	88	61	68	3
2B	Brian Raabe, Tacoma (Pacific Coast)	.352	*543	*101	*191	35	4	14	80	38	20	1
3B	Paul Konerko, Albuquerque (Pacific Coast)	.323	483	97	156	31	1	*37	*127	64	61	2
SS	Neifi Perez, Colorado Springs (Pacific Coast)	.363	303	68	110	24	3	8	46	17	27	8
OF	Jeff Abbott, Nashville (Amer. Association)	.327	465	*88	152	35	3	11	63	41	52	12
OF	Jacob Cruz, Phoenix (Pacific Coast)	*.361	493	97	178	*45	3	12	94	64	64	18
OF	Magglio Ordonez, Nashville (Amer. Association)	*.329	523	65	*172	29	3	14	90	32	61	14
DH	Dan Rohrmeier, Tacoma (Pacific Coast)	.297	471	86	140	43	4	33	120	45	81	1

Pos.	Player, Team	W	L	ERA	G	GS	CG	Sv	IP	H	BB	SO
P	John Halama, New Orleans (Amer. Association)	*13	3	*2.58	26	24	1	0	171	150	32	126
P	Rick Krivda, Rochester (International)	14	2	3.39	22	21	*6	0	146	122	34	128
P	Carl Pavano, Pawtucket (International)	11	6	3.12	23	23	3	0	162	148	34	147
P	Marc Pisciotta, Iowa (Amer. Association)	6	2	2.36	42	0	0	22	46	29	23	48
P	Brian Rose, Pawtucket (International)	*17	5	*3.02	27	26	3	0	*191	188	46	116

Player of the Year: Paul Konerko, 3b, Albuquerque. **Manager of the Year:** Gary Jones, Edmonton (Pacific Coast).

DOUBLE-A

Pos.	Player, Team	AVG	AB	R	H	2B	3B	HR	RBI	BB	SO	SB
C	Justin Towle, Chattanooga (Southern)	.309	418	62	129	37	5	11	70	55	77	5
1B	Kevin Millar, Portland (Eastern)	*.342	511	94	*175	*34	2	32	*131	66	53	2
2B	Placido Polanco, Arkansas (Texas)	.291	508	71	148	16	3	2	51	29	51	19
3B	Fernando Tatis, Tulsa (Texas)	.314	382	73	120	26	1	24	61	46	72	17
SS	Miguel Tejada, Huntsville (Southern)	.275	502	85	138	20	3	22	97	59	99	15
OF	Juan Encarnacion, Jacksonville (Southern)	.323	493	91	159	31	4	26	90	43	86	17
OF	Ben Grieve, Huntsville (Southern)	.328	372	100	122	29	2	24	108	81	75	5
OF	Mark Kotsay, Portland (Eastern)	.306	438	*103	134	27	2	20	77	75	65	17
DH	Mike Kinkade, El Paso (Texas)	*.385	468	*112	*180	35	12	12	*109	52	66	17

Pos.	Player, Team	W	L	ERA	G	GS	CG	Sv	IP	H	BB	SO
P	Troy Brohawn, Shreveport (Texas)	13	5	*2.56	26	26	1	0	169	148	64	98
P	Scott Elarton, Jackson (Texas)	7	4	3.24	20	20	2	0	133	103	47	141
P	Scott Eyre, Birmingham (Southern)	*13	5	3.84	22	22	0	0	127	110	55	127
P	Mike Vavrek, New Haven (Eastern)	12	3	*2.57	17	17	2	0	123	94	34	101
P	Steve Woodard, El Paso (Texas)	14	3	3.17	19	19	*6	0	136	136	25	97

Player of the Year: Ben Grieve, Huntsville. **Player of the Year:** Ron Roenicke, San Antonio (Texas).

CLASS A

Pos.	Player, Team	AVG	AB	R	H	2B	3B	HR	RBI	BB	SO	SB
C	Ramon Hernandez, Visalia (California)	*.361	332	57	120	21	2	15	85	35	47	2
1B	Travis Lee, High Desert (California)	.363	226	63	82	18	1	18	63	47	36	5
2B	Warren Morris, Charlotte (Florida State)	.306	494	78	151	27	9	12	75	62	100	16
3B	Adrian Beltre, Vero Beach (Florida State)	.317	435	95	138	24	2	*26	*104	67	66	25
SS	Brent Butler, Peoria (Midwest)	.306	480	81	147	37	2	15	71	63	69	6
OF	Mike Darr, Rancho Cucamonga (California)	.344	521	104	179	32	11	15	94	57	90	23
OF	Gabe Kapler, Lakeland (Florida State)	.295	519	87	153	*40	6	19	87	54	68	8
OF	Mike Stoner, High Desert (California)	.358	567	*115	*203	*44	5	*33	*142	36	91	6
DH	Robert Fick, West Michigan (Midwest)	*.341	463	100	*158	*50	3	16	90	75	74	13

Pos.	Player, Team	W	L	ERA	G	GS	CG	Sv	IP	H	BB	SO
P	Clay Bruner, West Michigan (Midwest)	*15	3	2.38	24	24	3	0	166	134	48	135
P	Francisco Cordero, West Michigan (Midwest)	6	1	0.99	50	0	0	*35	54	36	15	67
P	Corey Lee, Charlotte (Florida State)	*15	5	3.47	23	23	6	0	161	132	60	147
P	Cliff Politte, Prince William (Carolina)	11	1	2.24	19	19	0	0	120	89	31	118
P	Grant Roberts, Capital City (South Atlantic)	11	3	2.36	22	22	2	0	130	98	44	122

Player of the Year: Adrian Beltre, Vero Beach. **Player of the Year:** Bruce Fields, West Michigan.

SHORT SEASON

Pos.	Player, Team	AVG	AB	R	H	2B	3B	HR	RBI	BB	SO	SB
C	Jason Dewey, Boise (Northwest)	.324	272	55	88	17	2	13	64	41	70	5
1B	Robert Berns, Princeton (Appalachian)	.327	245	53	80	*34	1	9	61	34	44	2
2B	Travis Young, Salem (Northwest)	.334	*320	*80	*107	11	6	1	34	30	50	40
3B	Luke Allen, Great Falls (Pioneer)	.345	258	50	89	12	6	7	40	19	53	12
SS	Kevin Haverbusch, Erie (New York-Penn)	.312	237	37	74	15	2	10	*55	13	37	4
OF	Dermal Brown, Spokane (Northwest)	.326	298	67	97	20	6	13	*73	38	65	17
OF	Mike Frank, Billings (Pioneer)	.376	266	62	100	22	6	10	62	35	24	18
OF	Alex Steele, Jamestown (New York-Penn)	.311	257	51	80	15	4	*14	43	37	61	6
DH	Greg Morrison, Medicine Hat (Pioneer)	*.448	241	63	*108	16	3	*23	*88	14	29	2

Pos.	Player, Team	W	L	ERA	G	GS	CG	Sv	IP	H	BB	SO
P	Brett Black, Batavia (New York-Penn)	3	0	1.32	28	0	0	15	41	23	2	66
P	Scott Comer, Pittsfield (New York-Penn)	7	1	1.74	14	14	1	0	93	71	12	*98
P	Bo Donaldson, Boise (Northwest)	3	1	1.21	27	0	0	15	52	31	20	88
P	Kris Lambert, Erie (New York-Penn)	*11	2	2.33	15	14	0	0	81	59	21	94
P	Scott Williamson, Billings (Pioneer)	*8	2	1.78	13	13	2	0	86	66	23	*101

Player of the Year: Dermal Brown, Spokane. **Player of the Year:** Marty Brown, Erie.

MINOR LEAGUE ALL-STARS

Selected by Baseball America

Pos.	Player, Team	AVG	AB	R	H	2B	3B	HR	RBI	BB	SO	SB
C	A.J. Hinch, Modesto/Edmonton	.328	458	93	150	32	3	24	97	62	81	10
1B	Travis Lee, High Desert/Tucson	.331	453	105	150	34	3	32	109	78	82	7
2B	Brian Raabe, Tacoma	.352	543	101	191	35	4	14	80	38	20	1
3B	Paul Konerko, Albuquerque	.323	483	97	156	31	1	37	127	64	61	2
SS	Miguel Tejada, Huntsville	.275	502	85	138	20	3	22	97	59	99	15
OF	Juan Encarnacion, Jacksonville	.323	493	91	159	31	4	26	90	43	86	17
OF	Ben Grieve, Huntsville/Edmonton	.350	480	127	168	40	3	31	136	93	91	5
OF	Mike Stoner, High Desert	.358	567	115	203	44	5	33	142	36	91	6
DH	Kevin Millar, Portland	.342	511	94	175	34	2	32	131	66	53	2

Pos.	Player, Team	W	L	ERA	G	GS	CG	Sv	IP	H	BB	SO
P	Matt Clement, Rancho Cucamonga/Mobile	12	8	2.05	27	27	3	0	189	157	63	201
P	Francisco Cordero, West Michigan	6	1	0.99	50	0	0	35	54	36	15	67
P	Cliff Politte, Prince William/Arkansas	15	2	2.22	25	25	0	0	158	124	40	144
P	Brian Rose, Pawtucket	17	5	3.02	27	26	3	0	191	188	46	116
P	Steve Woodard, El Paso	14	3	3.17	19	19	6	0	136	136	25	97

Player of the Year: Paul Konerko, Albuquerque. **Manager of the Year:** Gary Jones, Edmonton.

The new PBA extension is supposed to last through the 2007 season, with possible early terminations by either side after the 2003 season or subsequent seasons.

The PBA that ran through the 1997 season had a similar clause, and both sides planned to use it as early as 1994 before the strike and subsequent fallout caused them to let the agreement run its full course.

During the length of the new PBA, the major leagues committed to keeping all existing player-development contracts in place (including the new Double-A and Triple-A expansion teams).

That's the security the minor leagues sought going into the negotiations. The new PBA didn't clear up the hazy future of the Rookie-level Arizona and Gulf Coast leagues. Those teams are owned and operated by major league organizations and bring in no money, so they are not included among the 160 guaranteed player-development contracts.

The minor leagues found that security comes with a price, though.

The biggest new expense will be umpire development, which costs the major leagues about $4.75 million a year now. The program, established in 1964, recruits, trains and evaluates umpires, moving them through the minors much like players.

Real Realignment

In the most sweeping change of the minor league landscape in years, Triple-A baseball will be reduced to two leagues for 1998.

The International League will add four teams and continue as a 14-team league. But the American Association and Pacific Coast League as they were known are gone.

The 10-team Pacific Coast League will move intact to a new 16-team league that will retain the PCL name. The American Association has been torn apart, with some teams going to the International League and some going to the new league.

Triple-A owners approved the change at meetings before the Triple-A all-star game in Des Moines in July.

"I think the driving force for most of the members in the American Association was simply the opportunity to play a greater number of opponents," said AA president Branch Rickey, who was elected president of the new PCL. "We see the reconfiguration of baseball formats and schedules in the major leagues, and we think there are some similar benefits to be gained at the minor league level."

Another possible benefit of the realignment is the resumption of the Junior World Series. There hasn't been a postseason series between Triple-A leagues since 1991, and the three-league alignment made arranging such a series difficult.

"Hopefully that will be one of the main positive outgrowths of this change," International League president Randy Mobley said.

The new International League will include the 10 current members of the league; Buffalo, Indianapolis and Louisville from the American Association; and the expansion team in Durham, N.C.

The new 16-team Pacific Coast League will include the 10 teams from the old PCL; Iowa, Nashville, New Orleans, Oklahoma City and Omaha from the AA; and the expansion team in Memphis.

Double-A Surprise

If you had Altoona, Pa., in your Double-A expansion office pool, you probably made a lot of money.

Altoona–yes, Altoona–was approved by the Double-A expansion committee in October to get one of the franchises that will begin play in the Eastern League in 1999.

The city in southwest Pennsylvania has little previous baseball history. Its most recent claim to baseball fame, such as it is, was the Altoona Rail Kings, the most successful franchise in the independent Heartland League.

Before that team got started in 1996, the city hadn't had professional baseball since 1931, when the Altoona Engineers played in the Class C Middle Atlantic League for about six weeks before moving to Beaver Falls, Pa.

And when the Double-A expansion process got under way, Altoona was nowhere to be found. Bigger cities, with supposedly solid financial plans, led the way.

It looked like the process was wrapped up nicely at the Winter Meetings in December 1996, when the expansion committee announced that Erie, Pa., and Springfield, Mass., would receive the new franchises.

Minor League Player of the Year

Konerko puts on finishing touch in Triple-A

Paul Konerko

Anyone who watched Paul Konerko play for Triple-A Albuquerque in 1997 would say that his time has arrived.

The 6-foot-3, 205-pound infielder hit .323 with 37 homers and 127 RBIs and drew rave reviews from every manager, scout and fan who watched him tear up the Pacific Coast League.

Baseball America's 1997 Minor League Player of the Year is a rare combination of youthful strength and veteran maturity. All at the ripe old age of 21.

"We've had some great young players come through our system the last few years," Dodgers farm director Charlie Blaney said. "But I don't think anyone had the approach to hitting that Paul has at this age."

Konerko seems to have mastered the mechanics of hitting long ago. But his drive to get better with every plate appearance gives him an unsurpassed approach at the plate, and his determination shows.

Even after two-and-a-half promising seasons in the organization, even after jaw-dropping displays of power on the way up, Konerko never seemed to let it get to him.

Konerko has been called a natural-born hitter almost from the day he signed with the Dodgers, who picked him in the first round of the 1994 draft. And though his numbers seem to prove it, others say it's a misnomer.

"People say 'natural-born hitter,' but they don't see the work that he puts in to get better," says second baseman Adam Riggs, who has played and roomed with Konerko at every step through the Dodgers farm system. "I'm not talking about taking a million swings. I'm talking about mental approach.

"Every year he's gotten better. I mean tremendously better. Each year he comes back to spring training he's a different guy. He's always head and shoulders above what he was the year before."

That kind of history should serve Konerko well in 1998, when he tries for the first time to win a major league job out of spring training. It will probably be at first or third base, the positions he's learned after being drafted as a catcher.

"I can't worry about stuff I can't control, like whether there's a job open," Konerko says. "All I can do is keep working to become the best ballplayer I can be in every phase of the game. The rest will take care of itself."

Konerko took care of the PCL in 1997. After the first four games, his average never went lower than .319, and that was in the final week of the season.

"The good thing is, there is no one—the media, the Dodgers or whoever—that's going to put any more expectations on me than I already put on myself," Konerko says. "All I know is, I'm playing third and I've played first. I've gotten better from when I started but I still need to get better. People look at my offensive numbers, but I'm not the hitter I want to be yet.

"There's still a lot of work to be done."

—GARY KLEIN

PREVIOUS WINNERS

1981—Mike Marshall, 1b, Albuquerque (Dodgers)
1982—Ron Kittle, of, Edmonton (White Sox)
1983—Dwight Gooden, rhp, Lynchburg (Mets)
1984—Mike Bielecki, rhp, Hawaii (Pirates)
1985—Jose Canseco, of, Huntsville/Tacoma (Athletics)
1986—Gregg Jefferies, ss, Columbia/Lynchburg/Jackson (Mets)
1987—Gregg Jefferies, ss, Jackson/Tidewater
1988—Tom Gordon, rhp, Appleton/Memphis/Omaha (Royals)
1989—Sandy Alomar, c, Las Vegas (Padres)
1990—Frank Thomas, 1b, Birmingham (White Sox)
1991—Derek Bell, of, Syracuse (Blue Jays)
1992—Tim Salmon, of, Edmonton (Angels)
1993—Manny Ramirez, of, Canton/Charlotte (Indians)
1994—Derek Jeter, ss, Tampa/Albany/Columbus (Yankees)
1995—Andruw Jones, of, Macon (Braves)
1996—Andruw Jones, of, Durham/Greenville/Richmond

Erie worked out fine. The city's existing ballpark, which opened in 1996 for a New York-Penn League franchise, already meets Double-A standards. In fact, Erie ended up being the only city with all its ducks in a row out of all the contestants.

Springfield had its franchise taken away when the public money for its new ballpark didn't come through and the prospective owner, Martin Stone, abandoned ship. That threw the whole process back open.

Altoona came along, with Pennsylvania businessmen Tate DeWeese and Mark Thomas and Altoona native Robert Lozinak as the prospective owners. Lozinak also owns the PCL's Albuquerque Dukes.

When the Double-A expansion committee met in Las Vegas in 1997, to consider Altoona's bid, the city had almost $16 million in public money already in hand. The Pennsylvania legislature approved a $10.8 million bond, and congressmen from Pennsylvania secured another $5 million in federal money.

In addition, Altoona was going to build its 6,000-seat stadium on county-owned land, which would allow it to start construction right away.

Triple-A Expansion Finalized

Triple-A expansion also was finalized after a long

search for a second city.

Durham, N.C., had been approved for one of the new franchises in 1996, but other candidates had come and gone.

Triple-A officials finally settled on Memphis, which was losing its Southern League franchise anyway. Owner David Hersh wanted to move the Chicks to Jackson, Tenn., after he failed in efforts to get a new ballpark in Memphis.

So in 1998, Memphis will have a Pacific Coast League franchise and will play in Tim McCarver Stadium. The team also won the affiliation with the St. Louis Cardinals, who had been in Louisville since 1982.

The Memphis Redbirds, owned by local businessman Dean Jernigan, were able to get a new ballpark, though. The new downtown stadium is expected to be ready for the 1999 season.

The Durham Triple-A franchise will retain the Durham Bulls name and will play in the International League. The franchise will be affiliated with the Devil Rays, who also will own a piece of the team.

The Carolina League franchise that's affiliated with the Braves will move to a new ballpark in Myrtle Beach, S.C., but that park won't be ready until 1999.

So for the 1998 season, the team will play in Danville, Va., the home of the Braves' affiliate in the Appalachian League. The team will be known as the Danville 97s and will share the ballpark with the Danville Braves.

One other move necessitated by major league expansion was still surrounded by uncertainty.

The Fresno Grizzlies received official approval from the National Association at the September meeting of the PCL in Las Vegas. The league had to find a new city because the Diamondbacks are taking over Phoenix.

"We're glad to get that out of the way so we can move on to other things," team president John Carbray said.

Manager of the Year

Edmonton's Jones excels in face of adversity

RODGER WOOD

Gary Jones

In 1987, Gary Jones was a Triple-A infielder in the Athletics organization, trying to no avail to reach the major leagues. But after toiling in Triple-A with the A's as a manager, his hard work paid off when he was named to the big league coaching staff for the 1998 season.

In his third year as skipper of the Pacific Coast League's Edmonton Trappers, Jones added to his impressive managing resume when he was named Baseball America's 1997 Minor League Manager of the Year.

"With my playing experience, I do think I can relate to a lot of guys in Triple-A," said Jones, 36. "A lot of guys get frustrated when they don't get called up if they're playing well, but I was there. You can't let them get frustrated.

"They have to believe in you and your philosophy and be willing to do the work, or it won't matter what you do. It won't work."

In 1997, Jones didn't often know what players he would have to work with, almost on a daily basis. The Trappers made an astonishing 94 player moves during the season, all the more amazing considering Edmonton's remote location from both Double-A Huntsville and Oakland.

"He never complained once about all the player moves," A's assistant general manager Billy Beane said. "His attitude always was, 'We'll be fine. We'll figure something out.'

"Triple-A is the most difficult level to manage, because you've got such a blend of personalities. You had prospects like Ben Grieve and A.J. Hinch, while at the same time you've got guys who have been in the big leagues for two or three years. It can be difficult in the clubhouse."

Jones invariably figured problems out, leading Edmonton to an 80-64 overall record and a second straight PCL title. He did that despite one stretch when player callups and a death in the family of outfielder Ernie Young left him with 10 position players.

During the season's final week, more callups left Jones with nine position players. He was forced to move prized catching prospect Hinch to left field for the last five games of the year.

"It was tough, but it was fun," Jones said. "I looked at it as a challenge. The guys tend to pull together in those kinds of situations. You have to go about your business and get through it. That's something as a player you can't control."

—JOHN MANUEL

PREVIOUS WINNERS

1981—Ed Nottle, Tacoma (Athletics)
1982—Eddie Haas, Richmond (Braves)
1983—Bill Dancy, Reading (Phillies)
1984—Sam Perlozzo, Jackson (Mets)
1985—Jim Lefebvre, Phoenix (Giants)
1986—Brad Fischer, Huntsville (Athletics)
1987—Dave Trembley, Harrisburg (Pirates)
1988—Joe Sparks, Indianapolis (Expos)
1989—Buck Showalter, Albany (Yankees)
1990—Kevin Kennedy, Albuquerque (Dodgers)
1991—Butch Hobson, Pawtucket (Red Sox)
1992—Grady Little, Greenville (Braves)
1993—Terry Francona, Birmingham (White Sox)
1994—Tim Ireland, El Paso (Brewers)
1995—Marc Bombard, Indianapolis (Reds)
1996—Carlos Tosca, Portland (Marlins)

DEPARTMENT LEADERS

Minor Leagues

*Full-season teams only

TEAM

WINS

West Michigan (Midwest) 92
Phoenix (Pacific Coast) 88
Buffalo (American Association) 87
Kinston (Carolina) 87
Harrisburg (Eastern) 86

LONGEST WINNING STREAK

Indianapolis (American Association).... 14
Cubs (Arizona) 14
Portland (Eastern) 12
High Desert (California) 11
Kinston (Carolina) 11
Bluefield (Appalachian) 11

LOSSES

Akron (Eastern) 90
Syracuse (International) 87
Ottawa (International) 86
Las Vegas (Pacific Coast) 85
Louisville (American Association) 85

LONGEST LOSING STREAK

San Bernardino (California) 13
Butte (Pioneer) 13
Colorado Springs (Pacific Coast) 11
Rockford (Midwest) 11
Auburn (New York-Penn) 11

BATTING AVERAGE*

El Paso (Texas) .... .309
Colorado Springs (Pacific Coast) ..... .305
Edmonton (Pacific Coast) .... .303
Salt Lake (Pacific Coast) .... .297
Tacoma (Pacific Coast) .... .295

RUNS

Huntsville (Southern) 942
Colorado Springs (Pacific Coast) 924
High Desert (California) 890
Salt Lake (Pacific Coast) 889
Edmonton (Pacific Coast) 878

HOME RUNS

Portland (Eastern)................................ 191
Kinston (Carolina) 185
Binghamton (Eastern) 182
Buffalo (American Association) 182
Albuquerque (Pacific Coast) 182

STOLEN BASES

Charleston S.C. (South Atlantic) 255
Lake Elsinore (California) 250
Vero Beach (Florida State) 245
Delmarva (South Atlantic) 232
Augusta (South Atlantic) 218

ROBERT GURGANUS

El Paso's Mike Kinkade
Led minors at .385

EARNED RUN AVERAGE*

West Michigan (Midwest) 2.67
Capital City (South Atlantic) 3.17
Kissimmee (Florida State) 3.36
Macon (South Atlantic) 3.39
Lakeland (Florida State) 3.43

STRIKEOUTS

Rancho Cucamonga (California) 1292
Wisconsin (Midwest) 1220
San Jose (California) 1210
Macon (South Atlantic) 1206
Augusta (South Atlantic) 1174

FIELDING AVERAGE*

Columbus (International) .... .980
Iowa (American Association) .... .979
New Orleans (American Association) .978
Tacoma (Pacific Coast) .... .978
Louisville (American Association) .... .977
New Britain (Eastern) .... .977
Charlotte (International) .... .977
Phoenix (Pacific Coast) .... .977
Colorado Springs (Pacific Coast) ..... .977
Edmonton (Pacific Coast) .... .977

INDIVIDUAL BATTING

BATTING AVERAGE

(Minimum 388 Plate Appearances)

Mike Kinkade, El Paso .... .385
Scott Krause, El Paso .... .361
Jacob Cruz, Phoenix .... .361
Luis Lopez, Hagerstown .... .358
Mike Stoner, High Desert .... .358
Dave McCarty, Phoenix .... .353
Brian Raabe, Tacoma .... .352
Todd Helton, Colorado Springs .... .352
Mike Mitchell, Rancho Cucamonga .350
Ben Grieve, Edmonton/Huntsville .... .350

RUNS

Mike Neill, Edmonton/Huntsville 132
Ben Grieve, Edmonton/Huntsville 127
Ryan Christenson, Edm./Hunt./Visalia.. 120
Mike Stoner, High Desert 115
Jim Chamblee, Michigan 112
Danny Klassen, El Paso 112
Mike Kinkade, El Paso 112

HITS

Mike Stoner, High Desert 203
Brian Raabe, Tacoma 191
Mike Kinkade, El Paso 180
Luis Lopez, Hagerstown 180
Jeff Inglin, Hickory 179
Mike Darr, Rancho Cucamonga 179
Derrick Gibson, Colo.Spr./New Haven 179

TOP HITTING STREAKS

Robert Fick, West Michigan 32
Lance Downing, AZL Diamondbacks .. 32
Jeremy Carr, Wichita 31
Ricky Otero, Scranton/Wilkes-Barre .. 25
Jacob Cruz, Phoenix 25

MOST HITS, ONE GAME

Matt Howard, Columbus (IL) 6
Jason Wood, Edmonton 6
Todd Walker, Salt Lake 6
Frank Kellner, Tucson 6
Terry Jones, Colorado Springs 6
Jason Williams, Chattanooga 6
Mike Darr, Rancho Cucamonga 6
Ronnie Hall, Daytona 6
Andy Bevins, New Jersey 6
Pablo Ozuna, Johnson City 6
Juan Silvestre, AZL Mariners 6
Monty Davis, AZL Athletics 6

TOTAL BASES

Mike Stoner, High Desert 355

MEL BAILEY

High Desert's Mike Stoner
Leader in hits, total bases, RBIs

Kevin Millar, Portland (EL) 309
Ben Grieve, Edmonton/Huntsville 307
David Ortiz, Salt Lake/NB/Ft. Myers 306
Mike Coolbaugh, Huntsville 303

EXTRA-BASE HITS

Mike Stoner, High Desert 82
Dan Rohrmeier, Tacoma 80
Ben Grieve, Edmonton/Huntsville 74
Carlos Lee, Winston-Salem 71
Russell Branyan, Akron/Kinston 71
David Ortiz, Salt Lake/NB/Ft. Myers .. 71

DOUBLES

Carlos Lee, Winston-Salem 50
Robert Fick, West Michigan 50
Jason LaRue, Charleston, W.Va. 50
Darrell Nicholas, El Paso 47
Luis Lopez, Hagerstown 47

TRIPLES

Jovino Carvajal, Vancouver 20
Joe Mathis, Lancaster 15
Chad Green, Stockton 14
Julio Lugo, Kissimmee 14
Ryan Christenson, Edm./Hunt./Visalia .. 13
Brian Richardson, San Antonio 13
Tony Mota, San Bernardino 13
Fletcher Bates, Binghamton/St. Lucie 13
Mike Caruso, Win.-Salem/San Jose .. 13

HOME RUNS

Russell Branyan, Akron/Kinston 39
Paul Konerko, Albuquerque 37
Matt Raleigh, Binghamton 37
Danny Peoples, Kinston 34
Dan Rohrmeier, Tacoma 33
Russ Morman, Charlotte 33
Steve Hacker, Macon 33
Stanton Cameron, High Desert 33
Joe Freitas, Peoria 33
Mike Glendenning, Bakersfield 33
Mike Stoner, High Desert 33

RUNS BATTED IN

Mike Stoner, High Desert 142
Ben Grieve, Edmonton/Huntsville 136
Mike Coolbaugh, Huntsville 132
Kevin Millar, Portland 131
Paul Konerko, Albuquerque 127

MOST RBIs, ONE GAME

Chris Norton, Lake Elsinore 9
Monty Davis, AZL Athletics 9

STOLEN BASES

Alex Sanchez, Charleston, S.C. 92

Bernard Hutchison, Asheville 81
Tyrone Pendergrass, Macon 70
Rodney Lindsey, Clinton 70
Justin Baughman, Lake Elsinore 68

CAUGHT STEALING

Alex Sanchez, Charleston, S.C. 40
Mike Metcalfe, San Bernardino 32
Randy Winn, Portland (EL)/Brevard 28
Dennis Abreu, Rockford 26
Daniel Ramirez, Capital City 25

HIT BY PITCHES

Toby Kominek, Stockton 24
James Clifford, Lancaster 22
Will Skett, Knoxville/Dunedin 20
Brian Dallimore, Kissimmee 20
Cliff Anderson, San Bernardino 20
Trace Coquillette, Harrisburg/WP 20
David Francia, Clearwater 20

BASE ON BALLS

Mark Johnson, Winston-Salem 106
Frankie Menechino, Nashville/Birm. .. 105
Ryan Christenson, Edm./Hunt./Visalia 105
Tyrone Horne, Kane County 104
Eric Stuckenschneider, Vero Beach 101

STRIKEOUTS

Darron Ingram, Burlington (MWL) 195
Chris Haas, Prince William/Peoria 182
Tal Light, New Haven/Salem 180
Chuck Abbott, Cedar Rapids 170
Matt Raleigh, Binghamton 169

SACRIFICE FLIES

Adam Johnson, Durham 16
Fernando Seguignol, W. Palm Beach 14
Mike Lowell, Columbus/Norwich 11
Ramon Hernandez, Hunt./Modesto 11
Ramon Castro, Kissimmee 11
Adrian Beltre, Vero Beach 11
Mike Stoner, High Desert 11

SACRIFICE BUNTS

Jesse Garcia, Bowie 24
Brandon Moore, Birmingham 21
Juan Rodriguez, Cedar Rapids 18
Ben Reynoso, Rancho Cucamonga 18
Trent Durrington, Lake Elsinore 17

SLUGGING PERCENTAGE

Ben Grieve, Edmonton/Huntsville ..... .640
Travis Lee, Tucson/High Desert .... .631
Mike Stoner, High Desert .... .628
Russ Morman, Charlotte (IL) .... .623
Paul Konerko, Albuquerque .... .621

ON-BASE PERCENTAGE

Ben Grieve, Edmonton/Huntsville ..... .461
Mike Kinkade, El Paso .... .455
Kevin Gibbs, San Antonio .... .451
R. Christenson, Edm./Huntsville/Visalia .437
Jim Foster, Roch./Bowie/Frederick .. .435
Aaron Guiel, Midland/Mobile .... .435

BATTING AVERAGE*
By Position
(Minimum 400 Plate Appearances)

CATCHER

A.J. Hinch, Edmonton/Visalia .... .328
Paul LoDuca, San Antonio .... .327
Jim Foster, Roch./Bowie/Frederick .. .317
Jason LaRue, Charleston, W.Va. ..... .315
Justin Towle, Chattanooga .... .309

FIRST BASEMEN

Luis Lopez, Hagerstown .... .358
David McCarty, Phoenix .... .353
Todd Helton, Colorado Springs ...... .352
Mike Mitchell, Rancho Cucamonga .350
Desi Wilson, Phoenix .... .344

SECOND BASEMEN

Brian Raabe, Tacoma .... .352
Craig Counsell, Colorado Springs ..... .335
Adonis Harrison, Wisconsin .... .318
Jason Williams, Chatt./Burlington ..... .317
David Doster, Scranton/Wilkes-Barre .315

JOHN SPEAR

Pawtucket's Brian Rose
Led minors with 17 wins

THIRD BASEMEN

Mike Kinkade, El Paso .... .385
Paul Konerko, Albuquerque .... .323
Jason Wood, Edmonton .... .321
Jeff Ball, Phoenix .... .321
Carlos Lee, Winston-Salem .... .317
Adrian Beltre, Vero Beach .... .317

SHORTSTOPS

Danny Klassen, El Paso .... .331
Lou Collier, Calgary .... .330
Dennis Abreu, Rockford .... .321
Joe Funaro, Brevard County .... .319
Ramon Martinez, Phoenix/Shreve. .. .315

OUTFIELDERS

Jacon Cruz, Phoenix .... .361
Scott Krause, El Paso .... .361
Mike Stoner, High Desert .... .358
Ben Grieve, Edmonton/Huntsville .. .350
Mike Darr, Rancho Cucamonga ...... .344

INDIVIDUAL PITCHING

EARNED RUN AVERAGE
(Minimum 112 Innings)

Javier Vazquez, Harrisburg/WPB 1.86
Craig Quintal, West Michigan 1.96
David Darwin, Lakeland/West Mich. 1.98
Matt Clement, Mobile/Rancho Cuca. .. 2.05
Courtney Duncan, Orlando/Daytona 2.11
Maximo Heredia, Delmarva 2.13
Cliff Politte, Arkansas/Pr. William 2.22
Mike Lincoln, Fort Myers 2.28
Paul Ah Yat, Lynchburg/Augusta 2.35
Grant Roberts, Capital City 2.36

WINS

Brian Rose, Pawticket 17
Reid Cornelius, Charlotte/Portland 17
Travis Smith, El Paso 16
Joe Mays, Lancaster/Wisconsin 16
Giovanni Carrara, Indy/Rochester 16

LOSSES

Brad Kaufman, Las Vegas/Mobile 18
Gary Glover, Hagerstown 17
Willis Roberts, Jacksonville 15
Mark Redman, Salt Lake 15
Dan Smith, Okla. City/Tulsa 15
Jason Green, Kissimmee/Quad City .. 15

GAMES

Dan Ricabal, Vero Beach 75
Stephen Prihoda, Wichta 70
Matt Snyder, Bowie 67
Ryan Brannan, Reading/Clearwater .. 66
Gabe Gonzalez, Charlotte/Portland 66

COMPLETE GAMES

Ramon Ortiz, Cedar Rapids 8
Brian Powell, Lakeland 8
Rick Krivda, Rochester 6
Geoff Edsell, Vancouver 6
Steve Woodard, Tucson/El Paso 6
Corey Lee, Charlotte (FSL) 6
Phil Norton, Orl./Daytona/Rockford 6
Wade Miller, Kissimmee/Quad City 6

SAVES

Armando Almanza, Prince William 36
Francisco Cordero, West Michigan 35
Scott Winchester, Indy/Akron/Kinston 33
Todd Williams, Indy/Chattanooga 33
Greg Mullins, El Paso/Stockton 32

INNINGS PITCHED

Mike Saipe, Colo. Springs/NH 197
Jarrod Washburn, Vancouver/Mid. .. 194
Tommy Darrell, Cedar Rapids 192
Mike Bovee, Vancouver/Midland 191
Brian Rose, Pawtucket 191

BASE ON BALLS

Kerry Wood, Iowa/Orlando 131
John Ambrose, Winston-Salem 117
Francisco Saneaux, Bowie/Frederick 116
Corey Avrard, Pr. William/Peoria 113
Kevin Pincavitch, San Bernardino 112

STRIKEOUTS

Ramon Ortiz, Cedar Rapids 225
Stephen Shoemaker, CS/NH/Salem 214
Matt Clement, Mobile/Rancho Cuca. 201
Scott Elarton, New Orleans/Jackson 191
Kerry Wood, Iowa/Orlando 186
Bruce Chen, Macon 182
Ken Vining, Win.-Salem/San Jose 180
Jesus Sanchez, Binghamton 176
Brandon Knight, Tulsa/Charlotte 175
Brent Billingsley, Kane County 175

STRIKEOUTS/9 INNINGS*
(Starters)

Jay O'Shaughnessy, Savannah 11.67
Brian Fuentes, Wisconsin 11.60
Stephen Shoemaker, CS/NH/Salem 11.49
Ramon Ortiz, Cedar Rapids 11.19
Bruce Chen, Macon 11.19

STRIKEOUTS/9 INNINGS*
(Relievers)

Marc Deschenes, Kinston/Col. 14.95
James Sak, Rancho Cucamonga .. 14.39
Roberto Duran, Jacksonville 14.09
Jeff Kubenka, Alb./San An./SB 13.75
Ray Beasley, Macon 12.87

BATTING AVERAGE AGAINST*
(Starters)

Denny Stark, Lancaster/Wisconsin .. .172
Kerry Wood, Iowa/Orlando .... .181
Rob Radlosky, Fort Myers .... .190
Alberto Blanco, Jackson/Kissimmee .200
Javier Vazquez, Harrisburg/WPB ..... .200

BATTING AVERAGE AGAINST*
(Relievers)

Ben Fleetham, Ottawa/Harrisburg .. .146
Ken Robinson, Syracuse .... .158
Matt Ryan, Carolina .... .167
Tim Young, Harr./WPB/Cape Fear .. .168
Jason Davis, Clearwater/Piedmont .. .168

MOST STRIKEOUTS IN ONE GAME

Jason Lakman, Hickory 16
Stephen Shoemaker, Salem 16
Matt Wise, Boise 15
Brian Powell, Lakeland 15
Lorenzo Barcelo, San Jose 15
Bryan Braswell, Quad City 15
Mike Vavrek, New Haven 15

INDIVIDUAL FIELDING

MOST ERRORS

Mike Kinkade, 3b, El Paso 60
Luis Rivas, ss, Fort Wayne 58
Kit Pellow, 3b, Wichita/Lansing 57
Jose Ortiz, ss, Modesto 55
Jose Olmeda, ss, Michigan/Lowell 52

Unfortunately, other things proved to be sticky indeed. After giving conditional approval, the Fresno city council later voted down a stadium financing plan

The Grizzlies will replace Phoenix in the PCL, though the actual mechanics of that shift are a good bit more complicated. Fresno technically purchased the Tucson franchise, and the Phoenix franchise is moving to Tucson.

The net effect is that Fresno is in and will be affiliated with the Giants, and Tucson is in and will be affiliated with the Diamondbacks. Tucson also will change its name from the Toros to the Sidewinders.

The affiliation, in fact, was the least of the Fresno group's worries. The group thought it had a deal with the city to issue a $28 million bond to build a downtown ballpark with at least 12,500 seats.

When that deal was voted down, the Fresno group wasn't sure what would come next. The Grizzlies definitely will play at Beiden Field on the campus of Fresno State University for 1998.

"The doors are not closed, but we must at the same time walk through other doors that are open to us," the Fresno Diamond Group said in a statement.

Tending To Attendance

For the fourth year in a row, attendance in the American minor leagues went past 30 million, with most leagues posting solid gains after several stagnant years.

Overall attendance for the 15 minor leagues was 31,707,761, an average of 3,466 fans a game. That's a 2.6 percent increase over 1996, when 30.9 million fans turned out.

The jump represents another boost after the minor league boom seemed to be leveling off. The increase in attendance from 1995 to '96, for instance, was insignificant, as 30.7 million fans came to minor league games in '95.

The National Association trumpeted the news as even more encouraging, but it includes the Mexican League in its attendance figures. After a disastrous 1996 caused by the country's economic problems, the Mexican League bounced back with nearly 3 million fans in 1997, an increase of almost 25 percent.

With Mexico, the overall attendance increase for National Association leagues was 4.2 percent, to 34.7 million. But even without it the news is still mostly good.

All but three leagues showed at least slight increases, and some leagues improved significantly. And it's important to put these numbers in historical context. We're in the midst of the greatest run of minor league success since the late 1940s.

That's the last time attendance figures like these were posted, with the record being in 1949, when 39,782,717 fans watched 448 teams in 59 leagues. The latest boom crested 30 million (if you include Mexico) in 1993. Just 10 years ago, attendance was 20.2 million.

In Triple-A, both the American Association and International League had increases of about 5 percent. The Pacific Coast League lost more than 6 percent, to about 3.2 million fans, after a 1 percent increase in 1996.

The news in Double-A was much more encouraging than in 1996, when all three leagues lost fans. Two of three leagues made up for those losses in 1997. The Texas League continues its downward trend, with the average crowd dropping almost 5 percent and overall attendance down by more than 7 percent.

But the Eastern League jumped by 8 percent, with the Akron Aeros replacing the Canton-Akron Indians and setting a league attendance record with 473,232 fans. The Southern League was boosted by the Mobile BayBears replacing the Port City Roosters and had an overall increase of more than 10 percent. The move of

Team of the Year

West Michigan dominates Midwest on field and at gate

On Opening Day 1997, the West Michigan Whitecaps beat the Wisconsin Timber Rattlers 1-0. First baseman Robert Fick nailed a solo home run, righthander Clay Bruner pitched six no-hit innings and the bullpen held the lead before 8,535 fans.

Other Midwest League teams got used to seeing that pattern all season.

Dominant pitching, clutch hitting and seemingly as many fans as the parent Tigers drew helped West Michigan roll through the Class A Midwest League's regular season.

Though Lansing eliminated them in two games in the opening round of the playoffs, no minor league team was stronger than the Whitecaps. They finished 92-39, 20 games better than the next-closest Midwest League team. They led the league in ERA (2.67) by more than a run, and they were second in hitting (.273).

West Michigan also drew 536,029 fans, more than every Class A and Double-A team and all but three Triple-A clubs. It's hard to argue with that sort of success, so the Whitecaps are Baseball America's 1997 Minor League Team of the Year.

"This was by far the best team we've ever had, and also the youngest team we've ever had," West Michigan general manager Scott Lane said. "I think everyone was surprised."

West Michigan had switched affiliations after the 1996 season from the Athletics to the Tigers.

The Whitecaps are accustomed to success. They won the league title in 1996, and have made the playoffs all four years of their existence.

"When you have A-ball kids playing in front of crowds of 8,000 a night, it tends to improve their play a bit," said Whitecaps manager Bruce Fields, the league's manager of the year.

—STEPHEN BORELLI

PREVIOUS WINNERS

1993—Harrisburg/Eastern (Expos)
1994—Wilmington/Carolina (Royals)
1995—Norfolk/International (Mets)
1996—Edmonton/Pacific Coast (Athletics)

the Memphis Chicks to Jackson, Tenn., should further increase attendance in 1998.

The big winner in Class A was the California League, which increased attendance by 10 percent to go over 2 million for the first time. The continual building and renovating of ballparks has had Cal League attendance surging for several years.

The Midwest League presents an interesting case. After years of new franchises in big markets, including a double-digit percentage increase in 1996, the league was off by 6 percent in both average and overall attendance in 1997.

After drawing 3.17 million fans in 1996, the league dropped below 3 million again, to 2.95 million. And three franchises–West Michigan, Lansing and Kane County–account for about half of that amount.

The league is the most extreme example of the rich and poor of the minors. New franchises such as West Michigan draw 500,000 fans a year, while older, smaller operations such as Clinton draw 50,000.

Around the Minors

■ Rickey was selected as president of the new PCL at the new league's first formal meeting in Denver in August. As president of the American Association, he was the natural choice. PCL president Bill Cutler had already announced that he would retire after this season, after being in the job since 1979.

■ The annual major league and minor league affiliation mating dance was mercifully quiet following the 1997 season.

That's because most player-development contracts run for two-year increments and expire in even-numbered years. The few changes for 1998 will be at the top.

Several Triple-A teams will have new affiliates, including Louisville, which picked up the Brewers after the Cardinals left for Memphis.

The Brewers left Tucson, where the team desperately wanted to be affiliated with the Diamondbacks.

The new Durham franchise will be affiliated with the Devil Rays, and the Giants will be in Fresno.

The Pirates and White Sox haggled over which franchise would be in Calgary and which would be in Nashville. The Pirates eventually won out. The White Sox had to settle for Calgary.

Double-A saw one change, with the Mariners moving to Orlando for a season, and the Cubs leaving Orlando to affiliate with the West Tenn Diamond Jaxx, the franchise that used to be in Memphis.

Orlando is owned by the Devil Rays, who will take over the affiliation in 1999. The major league expansion franchises won't have Double-A affiliates in 1998.

■ George Shinn found a buyer for his Charlotte Knights (International) in a deal that could have implications beyond the minor leagues.

Shinn will sell the Knights to Beaver Sports Enterprises of Hickory, N.C. The group already owns the Hickory Crawdads (South Atlantic), Knoxville Smokies (Southern) and Winston-Salem Warthogs (Carolina) and owns a minority share of the New Orleans Zephyrs (American Association). Don Beaver, the president of the group, also is a minority owner of the Pirates.

Perhaps more important, though, Beaver was leading an effort to bring major league baseball to North Carolina, specifically to the Greensboro/Winston-Salem area.

Beaver has said that if a big league team comes to the state, he would like to have its minor league affiliates in or near the Carolinas. With Charlotte, he's close to that goal already, though the Winston-Salem franchise likely would have to move.

Beyond that, Charlotte's home park, Knights Castle, seats 10,000 and was built so that it could easily be expanded for a major league team.

If Beaver was able to buy a team such as the Minnesota Twins and move it, he could quickly assemble a big league-quality park in a short time. That would give his team a temporary home while waiting for a new park.

■ A Royals minor league pitcher was suspended and demoted after a mysterious incident in which he beaned a fan in Durham, N.C., but then went into a game and picked up a save.

Righthander Jose Santiago was suspended for a month and fined $300 after the incident. He was demoted from high Class A Wilmington to low Class A Lansing when he returned, though he made a brief appearance in the big leagues later in the season.

Carolina League president John Hopkins said he could find no record of a similar incident in minor league history. It occurred in the ninth inning of a game between the Wilmington Blue Rocks and Durham Bulls. According to witnesses, Santiago, 22, stepped off the bullpen bench to warm up and threw a ball at someone in the stands who had been shouting insults.

The ball missed its intended target and hit Richard Clancy of Durham, who was in front of the people who were shouting. No one on the field, including the umpires, saw what happened.

So while Clancy was getting medical treatment, Santiago took the mound. He retired the side and picked up the save in Wilmington's 8-6 win.

■ Rather than the joy of beginning a minor league season, members of the Capital City Bombers had to deal with the death of one of their teammates, out-

MINOR ADJUSTMENTS

Several clubs will have new affiliations for the 1998 season.

TRIPLE-A	League	1996	1997
Calgary	Pacific Coast	Pirates	White Sox
*Durham	International	—	Devil Rays
Louisville	International	Cardinals	Brewers
*Memphis	Pacific Coast	—	Cardinals
Nashville	Pacific Coast	White Sox	Pirates
Tucson	Pacific Coast	Brewers	D'backs
DOUBLE-A			
#Memphis	Southern	Mariners	Cubs
Orlando	Southern	Cubs	Mariners
CLASS A			
Savannah	South Atlantic	Dodgers	Rangers

*Expansion team

#Franchise moved from Memphis to Jackson, Tenn. (West Tenn) for 1998.

In addition, the former Phoenix Pacific Coast League franchise will relocate to Fresno for 1998, and the former Durham, N.C., Carolina League franchise will play one season in Danville, Va., before moving to Myrtle Beach, S.C., in 1999.

MINOR LEAGUES BEST TOOLS

Full season leagues only

	American Association AAA	International League AAA	Pacific Coast League AAA	Eastern League AA	Southern League AA	Texas League AA	California League A	Carolina League A	Florida State League A	Midwest League A	South Atlantic League A
Batting Prospect	Maggio Ordonez Nashville	Todd Dunwoody Charlotte	Paul Konerko Albuquerque	Mike Lowell Norwich	Juan Encarnacion Jacksonville	Daryle Ward Jackson	Travis Lee High Desert	Russell Branyon Kinston	Adrian Beltre Vero Beach	Robert Fick West Michigan	Luis Lopez Hagerstown
Power Hitter	Bubba Smith Oklahoma City	Ivan Cruz Columbus	Todd Greene Vancouver	Derrick Gibson New Haven	Ben Grieve Huntsville	Daryle Ward Jackson	Travis Lee High Desert	Russell Branyon Kinston	Adrian Beltre Vero Beach	Darron Ingram Burlington	Ryan Minor Delmarva
Base Runner	Damian Jackson Buffalo	Andy Fox Columbus	Jason McDonald Edmonton	Mark Kotsay Portland	Earl Johnson Mobile	Jeremy Carr Wichita	Gary Matthews Rancho Cuca.	Carlos Febles Wilmington	Donzell McDonald Tampa	Rod Lindsey Clinton	Ty. Pendergrass Macon
Fastest Runner	Damian Jackson Buffalo	Kimera Bartee Toledo	Terry Jones Colorado Springs	Randy Winn Portland	Earl Johnson Mobile	Bert Green Arkansas	Chad Green Stockton	Jason Woolf Prince William	Donzell McDonald Tampa	Rod Lindsey Clinton	Alex Sanchez Charleston, S.C.
Pitching Prospect	Brett Tomko Indianapolis	Carl Pavano Pawtucket	Brad Rigby Edmonton	Jaret Wright Akron	Kerry Wood Orlando	Dennis Reyes San Antonio	Matt Clement Rancho Cuca.	Kris Benson Lynchburg	Eric Milton Tampa	Denny Stark Wisconsin	Grant Roberts Capital City
Fastball	Oscar Henriquez New Orleans	Roy Halladay Syracuse	Jose Silva Calgary	Jaret Wright Akron	Kerry Wood Orlando	Braden Looper Arkansas	Matt Clement Rancho Cuca.	Steve Shoemaker Salem	Mike Judd Vero Beach	Francisco Cordero West Michigan	Jason Marquis Macon
Breaking Pitch	Amaury Telemaco Iowa	Jimmy Haynes Rochester	Brad Rigby Edmonton	Mike Saipe New Haven	Brett Hinchliffe Memphis	Ryan Creek Jackson	Jeff Kubenka San Bernardino	Kris Benson Lynchburg	Alberto Blanco Kissimmee	Ramon Ortiz Cedar Rapids	Rob Bell Macon
Control	John Halama New Orleans	Rick Krivda Rochester	Derek Lowe Tacoma	Mike Saipe New Haven	Bill King Huntsville	Steve Woodard El Paso	Ted Lilly San Bernardino	Cliff Politte Prince William	Courtney Duncan Daytona	Craig Quintal West Michigan	Keith Evans Cape Fear
Reliever	Mark Pisciotta Iowa	Eddie Gaillard Toledo	John Johnstone Phoenix	Ryan Brannan Reading	Todd Williams Chattanooga	Bobby Howry Shreveport	Jeff Kubenka San Bernardino	Scott Winchester Kinston	Ben Ford Tampa	Francisco Cordero West Michigan	Odalis Perez Macon
Defensive Catcher	Eli Marrero Louisville	Charlie Greene Norfolk	Henry Blanco Albuquerque	Bob Henley Harrisburg	Mike Mahoney Greenville	Paul LoDuca San Antonio	Ben Davis Rancho Cuca.	Matt Turner Wilmington	Cesar King Charlotte	Chad Moeller Fort Wayne	Fernando Lunar Macon
Defensive First Baseman	Larry Sutton Omaha	Mike Robertson Scranton	Todd Helton Colo. Springs	Dan Held Reading	Randy Jorgensen Memphis	Todd Landry El Paso	Travis Lee High Desert	Darren Stumberger Kinston	Rafael Martinez St. Lucie	Robert Fick West Michigan	Nick Johnson Greensboro
Defensive Second Baseman	Enrique Wilson Buffalo	Donnie Sadler Pawtucket	Craig Counsell Colorado Springs	Jessie Garcia Bowie	Richie Almanzar Jacksonville	Placido Polanco Arkansas	Mike Metcalfe San Bernardino	Carlos Febles Wilmington	Trace Coquillette West Palm Beach	Rene Capellan West Michigan	Liu Rodriguez Hickory
Defensive Third Baseman	Aaron Boone Indianapolis	Scott McClain Norfolk	George Arias Vancouver	Josh Booty Portland	Julio Bruno Jacksonville	Fernando Tatis Tulsa	Eric Chavez Visalia	Carlos Lee Winston-Salem	Adrian Beltre Vero Beach	Rob Sasser Cedar Rapids	Ryan Minor Delmarva
Defensive Shortstop	Damian Jackson Buffalo	Desi Relaford Scranton	Neifi Perez Colo. Springs	Alex Gonzalez Portland	Miguel Tejada Huntsville	Alex Cora San Antonio	Kelly Phair Stockton	Abraham Nunez Lynchburg	Santiago Perez Lakeland	Luis Rivas Fort Wayne	Nick Presto Charleston, W.Va.
Infield Arm	Felix Martinez Omaha	Desi Relaford Scranton	Neifi Perez Colo. Springs	Josh Booty Portland	Wes Helms Greenville	Fernando Tatis Tulsa	Jose Ortiz Modesto	Abraham Nunez Lynchburg	Adrian Beltre Vero Beach	Luis Rivas Fort Wayne	Ryan Minor Delmarva
Defensive Outfield	Terrell Lowery Iowa	Kimera Bartee Toledo	Karim Garcia Albuquerque	Michael Coleman Trenton	Demond Smith Huntsville	Kevin Gibbs San Antonio	Gary Matthews Rancho Cuca.	Carlos Beltran Wilmington	Reggie Taylor Clearwater	Jason Conti South Bend	Alex Sanchez Charleston, S.C.
Outfield Arm	Richard Hidalgo New Orleans	Jimmy Hurst Toledo	Jose Herrera Edmonton	Wady Almonte Bowie	Juan Encarnacion Jacksonville	Armando Rios Shreveport	Gary Matthews Rancho Cuca.	Donovan Delaney Wilmington	Ruben Mateo Charlotte	Julio Ramirez Kane County	Alex Sanchez Charleston, S.C.
Most Exciting Player	Damian Jackson Buffalo	Todd Dunwoody Charlotte	Travis Lee Tucson	Mark Kotsay Portland	Juan Encarnacion Jacksonville	Bert Green Arkansas	Travis Lee High Desert	Russell Branyon Kinston	Adrian Beltre Vero Beach	Brent Butler Peoria	Alex Sanchez Charleston, S.C.
Umpire Prospect	Paul Schrieber	Kerwin Danley	Ron Barnes	Mike Vanvleet	Willie Rodriguez	Dan Iassogna	Pat Riley	Jay Klemm	Webb Turner	Damien Beal	Robert Daly
Managerial Prospect	Tim Johnson Iowa	Rick Dempsey Norfolk	Paul Zuvella Colo. Springs	Fredi Gonzalez Portland	Mark Berry Chattanooga	Dave Machemer El Paso	Mike Basso Rancho Cuca.	John Mizerock Wilmington	John Gibbons St. Lucie	Bruce Fields West Michigan	Tom Nieto Greensboro

Selected at midseason 1997 by minor league managers in consultation with Baseball America.

Freitas Awards

Baltimore affiliates highlight 1997 winners

The 1997 Bob Freitas Awards combined some of the best new minor league franchises with some of those that have been keeping minor league baseball moving for years.

The Freitas Awards annually recognize long-term success by minor league franchises at the Triple-A, Double-A, Class A and short-season levels. They are named for the longtime minor league operator, promoter and ambassador who died in 1989.

Rochester, the winner in Triple-A, is one of the oldest franchises in all of professional baseball and has operated continuously since 1895–the longest continuous run by a minor league club. Another tribute to its long-term stability is its affiliation with the Orioles, which has lasted since 1961–second only to another Baltimore affiliate, Bluefield (Appalachian). The franchise saw a resurgence in 1997 with a new ballpark, Frontier Field.

The Double-A winner, Bowie, is another Baltimore-affiliated club. It is the flagship franchise of Maryland Baseball, the group led by Peter Kirk that also owns the Frederick (Carolina) and Delmarva (South Atlantic) franchises. Bowie has been one of the Eastern League's best franchises since it moved into Prince George's Stadium in 1994.

Another successful new franchise, Rancho Cucamonga, won the award in its first year of eligibility (as did Bowie). A franchise must operate for five seasons before it is eligible. Rancho is one of the best draws in the minor leagues, annually leading the California League and among the top 10 in all of the minors.

The short-season winner is a salute to another franchise that has stood the test of time. Oneonta has been in the New York-Penn League since 1966, and it has spent all but that first season as an affiliate of the Yankees.

PREVIOUS WINNERS

Triple-A

1989—Columbus (International)
1990—Pawtucket (International)
1991—Buffalo (American Assoc.)
1992—Iowa (American Assoc.)
1993—Richmond (International)
1994—Norfolk (International)
1995—Albuquerque (Pacific Coast)
1996—Indianapolis (Amer. Assoc.)

Double-A

1989—El Paso (Texas)
1990—Arkansas (Texas)
1991—Reading (Eastern)
1992—Tulsa (Texas)
1993—Harrisburg (Eastern)
1994—San Antonio (Texas)
1995—Midland (Texas)
1996—Carolina (Southern)

Class A

1989—Durham (Carolina)
1990—San Jose (California)
1991—Asheville (South Atlantic)
1992—Springfield (Midwest)
1993—South Bend (Midwest)
1994—Kinston (Carolina)
1995—Kane County (Midwest)
1996—Wisconsin (Midwest)

Short-Season

1989—Eugene (Northwest)
1990—Salt Lake City (Pioneer)
1991—Spokane (Northwest)
1992—Boise (Northwest)
1993—Billings (Pioneer)
1994—Everett (Northwest)
1995—Great Falls (Pioneer)
1996—Bluefield (Appalachian)

fielder Tim Bishop.

Bishop, 20, was hit by a car while checking a blown tire late on April 18. The Bombers had returned to Columbia, S.C., from a road trip, and Bishop and teammate Randy Vickers were on their way home.

Bishop was driving his 1991 Eagle Talon west on Interstate 126 when a tire blew. The car spun but didn't hit anything and stopped pointing north, blocking the far left lane and the lane next to it.

Bishop and Vickers got out of the car to check the damage, but Bishop went back to turn on his headlights and hazard lights. As Bishop did that, a westbound Pontiac hit Bishop's car.

The collision threw Bishop over the median wall and onto the eastbound lanes of the interstate. Bishop was hit again by at least one car.

The next day's game against the Cape Fear Crocs was canceled. Bombers players wore Bishop's No. 4 on arm patches for the rest of the season.

In the wake of the death, manager Doug Mansolino and his staff were fired by the Mets. There was some evidence that players had been drinking on the bus on the way to Columbia, and an autopsy showed Bishop had alcohol in his system when he died. Mets officials determined that the staff had not sufficiently investigated the claims of drinking.

■ The Tigers organization and their Jamestown affiliate in the New York-Penn League were struck by tragedy twice in 1997.

First, Dwight Lowry, a member of Detroit's 1984 World Series championship team, died July 10 after collapsing outside his home.

Lowry, 39, was the manager at Jamestown and was taking out the trash at his home after a game against Batavia. He collapsed and was pronounced dead a short time later at a local hospital. Though no cause of death was immediately released, Lowry had a history of heart problems.

"He's going to be hard to replace, not only in baseball, but as a person," Tigers farm director Dave Miller said. "He was just so fair with his players and other people. Just a fine individual."

Then pitcher Mike Diebolt died Sept. 5 in a car accident in suburban Cleveland.

Diebolt, drafted by the Tigers in the seventh round in June out of the University of Minnesota, was on his way back home in Mayfield Village, Ohio, when he apparently had a seizure that caused the accident. He was 22.

"This is tragic news for everyone in the Detroit Tigers organization," general manager Randy Smith said. "We are all very shocked and saddened, but at this time our thoughts and prayers are with Mike's family."

Diebolt found out he had diabetes four years ago and had a hard time managing it until his senior season at Minnesota. When he did, he put together a 7-4, 3.99 season in which he had 110 strikeouts to break Dave Winfield's single-season school record.

Jamestown's season had ended the night before, and Diebolt had returned to his home in Mayfield Village. A lefthander, he was 3-6, 4.30 in 15 appearances for the Jammers.

AMERICAN ASSOCIATION

League's flagship Buffalo franchise enjoys fitting goodbye

BY PETER BARROUQUERE

The Buffalo Bisons believe in cutting it close.

Sean Casey's home run in the top of the 10th inning gave the Bisons a 5-4 victory over the Iowa Cubs and their first American Association championship in 13 seasons in the league.

The homer enabled the Bisons, who will move to the International League in 1998 as part of a Triple-A realignment, to complete a sweep of the best-of-five championship series.

Casey's homer came on a 1-1 fastball from reliever Justin Speier, who had not given up a run in 11 games with Iowa. It erased the Bisons' disappointment over losses in the finals in 1991, '92 and '95.

"I was almost in a dream world," Casey said. "I wanted to get around the bases and get in the dugout. I was so excited, but we knew we had three outs to go."

David Weathers, who pitched in the World Series clincher for the Yankees in 1996, nailed down the championship for the Bisons with a scoreless 10th.

Infielder Torey Lovullo, who caught the last out of the championship game, earned MVP honors in the finals. He went 4-for-11 in the championship series, 11-for-26 in the postseason.

Buffalo's semifinal series with Indianapolis went the full five games, and the same teams had a close regular-season race in the Eastern Division, with Buffalo winning by two games. The other division race was even closer. New Orleans played one more game than Iowa, lost it and finished half a game behind. Iowa proved it was no fluke, though, sweeping the Zephyrs in the semifinals.

The league's final season produced historic performances.

New Orleans outfielder J.R. Phillips became the first player in the league to hit home runs in four straight at-bats, accomplishing the feat in the second game of a doubleheader July 2 at Omaha.

"Matty (manager Matt Galante) made me angry by giving me a day off," Phillips, who sat out the first game, said laughing. "I guess I had to take it out on somebody."

Buffalo's Bartolo Colon pitched a complete-game no-hitter against New Orleans on June 20. Colon completed his no-hitter by getting Brian Grebeck on a soft fly toward right.

After playing its first four seasons in 4,700-seat Privateer Park, New Orleans moved into 10,000-seat Zephyr Field and contributed heavily to the fifth-best overall attendance in league history (3,669,203).

The Zephyrs, who drew 180,485 in 1996, packed in 507,164, an improvement of 326,679. Despite falling off by 129,337, Buffalo led with 696,193.

The Zephyrs had a new affiliation to go with their new ballpark. They joined the Astros organization, swapping their Brewers affiliation with Tucson of the Pacific Coast League. New Orleans also changed managers during the season: Galante came aboard when Steve Swisher resigned in the first week.

JOHN SPEAR

Out of nowhere
Magglio Ordonez

Nashville's Magglio Ordonez and New Orleans' John Halama came out of nowhere to lead the league in hitting and pitching.

Ordonez, who had batted .263 at Double-A Birmingham the year before, hit .329 to hold off teammate Jeff Abbott (.327) for the batting title.

"From day one, he hit," Sounds manager Tom Spencer said of Ordonez. "And he kept hitting. He's probably the surprise player in the league."

The most surprised player was probably Halama, a lefthander who went 9-10 for Texas League champion Jackson in 1996. He went 13-3 and led the American Association in wins and ERA (2.58).

"I didn't think I was going to be here at all," Halama said. "I'm very surprised. I didn't plan on having this much success at all."

STANDINGS

Page	EAST	W	L	PCT	GB	Manager	Attendance/Dates	Last Penn.
98	Buffalo Bisons (Indians)	87	57	.604	—	Brian Graham	696,193 (60)	1997
92	Indianapolis Indians (Reds)	85	59	.590	2	Dave Miley	618,095 (67)	1994
80	Nashville Sounds (White Sox)	74	69	.517	12½	Tom Spencer	269,186 (67)	None
193	Louisville Redbirds (Cardinals)	58	85	.406	28½	Gaylen Pitts	408,550 (67)	1995
Page	**WEST**	**W**	**L**	**PCT**	**GB**	**Manager(s)**	**Attendance/Dates**	**Last Penn.**
86	Iowa Cubs (Cubs)	74	69	.517	—	Tim Johnson	403,040 (67)	1993
122	New Orleans Zephyrs (Astros)	74	70	.514	½	Steve Swisher/Matt Galante	507,164 (71)	None
222	Oklahoma City 89ers (Rangers)	61	82	.427	13	Greg Biagini	325,582 (66)	1996
128	Omaha Royals (Royals)	61	83	.424	13½	Mike Jirschele	449,753 (67)	1990

PLAYOFFS—Semifinals: Iowa defeated New Orleans 3-0, and Buffalo defeated Indianapolis 3-2, in best-of-5 series. **Finals:** Buffalo defeated Iowa 3-0, in best-of-5 series.

NOTE: Team's individual batting and pitching statistics can be found on page indicated in lefthand column.

1997 American Association Statistics

CLUB BATTING

	AVG	G	AB	R	H	2B	3B	HR	BB	SO	SB
Nashville	.269	143	4797	706	1292	246	23	153	454	859	81
Buffalo	.268	144	4804	711	1286	242	21	182	509	910	99
Iowa	.265	143	4779	666	1265	254	21	150	453	893	91
Indianapolis	.264	144	4758	669	1257	233	35	150	515	928	122
Oklahoma City	.262	143	4881	622	1278	266	32	138	486	1055	134
Omaha	.261	144	4738	663	1235	232	16	178	434	1014	75
New Orleans	.258	144	4855	639	1253	242	32	77	536	814	58
Louisville	.253	143	4724	611	1195	220	39	130	479	953	93

CLUB PITCHING

	ERA	G	CG	SHO	SV	IP	H	R	ER	BB	SO
New Orleans	3.45	144	6	12	27	1287	1231	560	494	387	1073
Indianapolis	3.56	144	8	12	48	1249	1171	567	495	438	959
Buffalo	3.66	144	18	9	28	1256	1197	593	510	469	900
Iowa	4.11	143	13	11	33	1242	1201	645	567	472	969
Louisville	4.24	143	9	3	30	1243	1260	651	586	465	944
Nashville	4.64	143	11	4	41	1233	1287	718	636	554	881
Oklahoma City	4.67	143	10	8	34	1266	1398	746	657	483	794
Omaha	5.36	144	8	7	35	1216	1316	807	724	598	906

CLUB FIELDING

	PCT	PO	A	E	DP
Iowa	.979	3726	1468	109	146
New Orleans	.978	3861	1586	122	134
Louisville	.977	3729	1537	122	137
Indianapolis	.973	3747	1416	141	120
Buffalo	.973	3767	1520	145	152
Oklahoma City	.973	3797	1613	149	149
Nashville	.972	3700	1525	149	129
Omaha	.967	3647	1421	172	163

INDIVIDUAL BATTING LEADERS

(Minimum 389 Plate Appearances)

	AVG	G	AB	R	H	2B	3B	HR	RBI	BB	SO	SB
Ordonez, Magglio, Nashville	.329	135	523	65	172	29	3	14	90	32	61	14
Abbott, Jeff, Nashville	.327	118	465	88	152	35	3	11	63	41	52	12
Hubbard, Trenidad, Buffalo	.312	103	375	71	117	22	1	16	60	57	52	26
Wilson, Enrique, Buffalo	.306	118	451	78	138	20	3	11	39	42	41	9
Costo, Tim, Louisville	.303	121	400	52	121	26	2	14	54	41	72	4
Lowery, Terrell, Iowa	.301	110	386	69	116	28	3	17	71	65	97	9
Sutton, Larry, Omaha	.300	106	380	61	114	27	1	19	72	61	57	0
Boone, Aaron, Indianapolis	.290	131	476	79	138	30	4	22	75	40	81	12
Phillips, J.R., New Orleans	.290	104	411	59	119	28	0	21	71	39	112	0
Jackson, Damian, Buffalo-Indy	.288	92	337	63	97	18	1	4	20	47	62	24

INDIVIDUAL PITCHING LEADERS

(Minimum 115 Innings)

	W	L	ERA	G	GS	CG	SV	IP	H	R	ER	BB	SO
Halama, John, New Orleans	13	3	2.58	26	24	1	0	171	150	57	49	32	126
Swartzbaugh, Dave, Iowa	8	7	2.82	24	20	1	1	134	129	55	42	48	97
White, Gabe, Indianapolis	7	4	2.82	20	19	0	0	118	119	46	37	18	62
Keyser, Brian, Nashville	7	5	2.87	44	9	3	1	119	114	44	38	45	68
DelaMaza, Roland, Buffalo	9	4	2.90	34	14	2	2	115	104	42	37	43	73
Miller, Trever, New Orleans	6	7	3.30	29	27	2	0	164	177	71	60	54	99
Aybar, Manny, Louisville	5	8	3.48	22	22	3	0	137	131	60	53	45	114
Carrara, Giovanni, Indy	12	5	3.51	19	18	2	0	121	111	50	47	51	105
Steenstra, Kennie, Iowa	5	10	3.92	25	25	4	0	161	161	85	70	41	111
Klingenbeck, Scott, Indy	12	8	3.96	27	27	2	0	171	180	85	75	41	119

ALL-STAR TEAM

C—Eli Marrero, Lousville. **1B**—Richie Sexson, Buffalo. **2B**—Miguel Cairo, Iowa. **3B**—Aaron Boone, Indianapolis. **SS**—Damian Jackson, Buffalo-Indianapolis. **OF**—Jeff Abbott, Nashville; Bruce Aven, Buffalo; Maggilo Ordonez, Nashville. **DH**—Bubba Smith, Oklahoma City. **LHP**—John Halama, New Orleans. **RHP**—Giovanni Carrara, Indianapolis. **RP**—Mark Pisciotta, Iowa.

Most Valuable Player—Magglio Ordonez, Nashville. **Rookie of the Year**—Magglio Ordonez, Nashville. **Manager of the Year**—Dave Miley, Indianapolis.

TOP 10 PROSPECTS

1. Kerry Wood, rhp, Iowa; **2.** Eli Marrero, c, Louisville; **3.** Richard Hidalgo, of, New Orleans; **4.** Damian Jackson, ss, Buffalo-Indianapolis; **5.** Oscar Henriquez, rhp, New Orleans; **6.** Magglio Ordonez, of, Nashville; **7.** Aaron Boone, 3b, Indianapolis; **8.** Richie Sexson, 1b, Buffalo; **9.** Hanley Frias, ss, Oklahoma City; **10.** John Halama, lhp, New Orleans.

DEPT. LEADERS

BATTING

G	Bubba Smith, Oklahoma City	140
AB	Miguel Cairo, Iowa	569
R	Jeff Abbott, Nashville	88
H	Magglio Ordonez, Nashville	172
TB	Brian Hunter, Indianapolis	249
	Magglio Ordonez, Nashville	249
XBH	Brian Hunter, Indianapolis	61
2B	Richard Hidalgo, New Orleans	37
3B	Alex Ramirez, Buffalo	8
HR	Richie Sexson, Buffalo	31
RBI	Bubba Smith, Oklahoma City	94
SH	Craig Wilson, Nashville	12
SF	Magglio Ordonez, Nashville	9
BB	Keith Mitchell, Indianapolis	72
IBB	Dennis Colon, New Orleans	6
HBP	Bruce Aven, Buffalo	11
	Melvin Mora, New Orleans	11
SO	Bubba Smith, Oklahoma City	139
SB	Miguel Cairo, Iowa	40
CS	Miguel Cairo, Iowa	15
	Hanley Frias, Oklahoma City	15
GIDP	Alex Diaz, Oklahoma City	19
	Craig Wilson, Nashville	19
OB%	Trenidad Hubbard, Buffalo	401
SL%	Greg Norton, Nashville	534

PITCHING

G	Oscar Henriquez, New Orleans	60
GS	Brian Harrison, Omaha	29
CG	Three tied at	4
ShO	Three tied at	2
GF	Scott Service, Omaha	42
SV	Scott Service, Omaha	24
W	John Halama, New Orleans	13
L	Dan Smith, Oklahoma City	14
IP	Brian Harrison, Omaha	178
H	Brian Harrison, Omaha	208
R	Brian Harrison, Omaha	114
ER	Brian Harrison, Omaha	100
HR	Scott Klingenbeck, Indianapolis	23
HB	Brian Harrison, Omaha	10
	Sean Lowe, Louisville	10
BB	Mike Bertotti, Nashville	105
SO	C.J. Nitkowski, New Orleans	141
WP	Rodney Bolton, Indianapolis	16
BK	Rich Pratt, Nashville	7

FIELDING

C	**AVG**	Kevin Brown, Okla. City	.991
	PO	Eli Marrero, Louisville	675
	A	Eli Marrero, Louisville	68
	E	Einar Diaz, Buffalo	18
	DP	Paul Bako, Indianapolis	10
		Kevin Brown, Okla. City	10
	PB	Pual Bako, Indianapolis	9
		Robert Machado, Nashville	9
1B	**AVG**	Richie Sexson, Buffalo	.996
	PO	Richie Sexson, Buffalo	922
	A	Richie Sexson, Buffalo	77
	E	Dennis Colon, New Orleans	9
	DP	Richie Sexson, Buffalo	105
2B	**AVG**	Todd Haney, New Orleans	.990
	PO	Jeff Berblinger, Louisville	258
	A	Jeff Berblinger, Louisville	362
	E	Jed Hansen, Omaha	17
		Eric Owens, Indianapolis	17
	DP	Jeff Berblinger, Louisville	93
3B	**AVG**	Mike Gulan, Louisville	.948
	PO	Aaron Boone, Indianapolis	76
	A	Aaron Boone, Indianapolis	241
	E	Greg Norton, Nashville	29
	DP	Aaron Boone, Indianapolis	27
SS	**AVG**	Chris Petersen, Iowa	.973
	PO	Hanley Frias, Okla. City	175
		Felix Martinez, Omaha	175
	A	Hanley Frias, Okla. City	409
	E	Felix Martinez, Omaha	36
	DP	Chris Petersen, Iowa	84
OF	**AVG**	Jeff Abbott, Nashville	1.000
	PO	Mark Little, Oklahoma City	280
	A	Richard Hidalgo, N.O.	15
	E	Alex Ramirez, Buffalo	10
	DP	Pedro Valdes, Iowa	6

INTERNATIONAL LEAGUE

Rochester gives manager Marv Foley unique distinction

BY TIM PEARRELL

Marv Foley grounded out to second to complete Mike Witt's perfect game on Sept. 30, 1984. That was Foley's last major league at-bat and his historical footnote.

Now he'll have something more significant.

Foley became the first manager to win championships in all three Triple-A leagues when Rochester beat Columbus in five games to capture the International League Governors' Cup. The title, Rochester's IL-record 10th, came in the first season of Frontier Field.

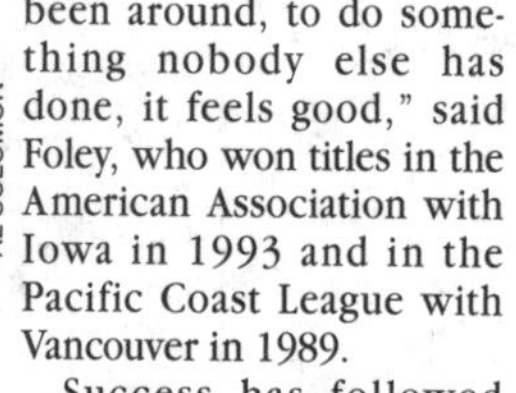

AL SOLOMON

Terrific Tide
Roberto Petagine

Eleven other managers, including Walter Alston and Casey Stengel, won titles in two Triple-A leagues.

"As long as baseball's been around, to do something nobody else has done, it feels good," said Foley, who won titles in the American Association with Iowa in 1993 and in the Pacific Coast League with Vancouver in 1989.

Success has followed Foley as a manager. In seven Triple-A seasons, he has had four first-place clubs. In 10 seasons overall, he has guided seven clubs to the playoffs.

Rochester used a pitching staff that included Rick Krivda (14-2, 3.39), Esteban Yan (11-5, 3.10), Nerio Rodriguez (11-10, 3.90) and Brian Shouse (6-2, 2.27), and an unheralded lineup to forge the league's most consistent team. Foley described his club as "blue collar, hard-working, intense."

The Red Wings' 23-6 July served as a springboard to a league-best 83-58 record, two games ahead of Pawtucket in the Eastern Division. The Red Wings won their best-of-five semifinal series in four games.

Columbus, which spent much of the season chasing Norfolk in the West, finished 79-63 and 2½ games ahead of Charlotte. The Knights caught the fading Tides for second place in the final two weeks. The Clippers disposed of the Knights in four games in their best-of-five semifinal series.

Foley was named manager of the year as the Red Wings reversed the outcome of the Governors' Cup final in 1996, when Columbus swept Rochester in three games.

The MVP award went to Norfolk first baseman Roberto Petagine, who finished second in home runs (31) and RBIs (100), and fourth in average (.317). He was among the top three in six other categories.

Pawtucket righthander Brian Rose, the top winner and ERA leader (17-5, 3.02), was named most valuable pitcher and rookie of the year.

Other highlights:

■ Toledo's Bubba Trammell became the sixth player in league history and the first since 1977 to hit four home runs in a game when he belted a quartet against Richmond on Aug. 9.

■ Scranton/Wilkes-Barre outfielder Ricky Otero had a 25-game hitting streak that actually stretched to 139 days because of a hand injury and two promotions to Philadelphia. That was still 11 games shy of the IL record.

■ There was one managerial change during the season. Gene Roof, the parent Tigers' outfield instructor, took over the Toledo club when Glenn Ezell left to have abdominal surgery.

■ With Triple-A consolidating into two leagues in 1998, the IL will take on four new teams, swelling enrollment to 14. Joining up in the wake of Triple-A expansion and restructuring will be Buffalo, Durham, Indianapolis and Louisville. At least one of the current teams will have new owners. Charlotte owner George Shinn sold the Knights to Beaver Sports Properties Inc. Ottawa owner Howard Darwin also put his club on the market.

STANDINGS

Page	EAST	W	L	PCT	GB	Manager	Attendance/Dates	Last Penn.
66	Rochester Red Wings (Orioles)	83	58	.589	—	Marv Foley	512,570 (66)	1997
73	Pawtucket Red Sox (Red Sox)	81	60	.574	2	Ken Macha	474,557 (69)	1984
180	Scranton/W-B Red Barons (Phillies)	66	76	.465	17½	Marc Bombard	441,413 (65)	None
228	Syracuse SkyChiefs (Blue Jays)	55	87	.387	28½	Garth Iorg	400,804 (67)	1976
153	Ottawa Lynx (Expos)	54	86	.386	28½	Pat Kelly	266,568 (64)	1995
Page	**WEST**	**W**	**L**	**PCT**	**GB**	**Manager(s)**	**Attendance/Dates**	**Last Penn.**
160	Columbus Clippers (Yankees)	79	63	.556	—	Stump Merrill	507,810 (66)	1996
116	Charlotte Knights (Marlins)	76	65	.539	2½	Carlos Tosca	318,102 (67)	1993
167	Norfolk Tides (Mets)	75	67	.528	4	Rick Dempsey	507,328 (66)	1985
60	Richmond Braves (Braves)	70	72	.493	9	Bill Dancy	512,727 (68)	1994
110	Toledo Mud Hens (Tigers)	68	73	.482	10½	Glenn Ezell/Gene Roof	325,532 (67)	1967

PLAYOFFS—Semifinals: Rochester defeated Pawtucket 3-1, and Columbus defeated Charlotte 3-1, in best-of-5 series. **Finals:** Rochester defeated Columbus 3-2, in best-of-5 series.

NOTE: Team's individual batting and pitching statistics can be found on page indicated in lefthand column.

1997 International League Statistics

CLUB BATTING

	AVG	G	AB	R	H	2B	3B	HR	BB	SO	SB
Scranton/W-B	.277	142	4714	715	1304	303	36	118	496	867	70
Rochester	.273	141	4750	702	1295	248	39	103	485	879	116
Richmond	.271	142	4735	680	1284	266	36	110	472	963	70
Columbus	.268	142	4751	768	1274	266	46	159	587	920	124
Charlotte	.268	141	4529	720	1214	268	28	169	508	1013	125
Norfolk	.267	142	4727	659	1260	245	21	131	544	993	91
Ottawa	.260	140	4530	636	1177	240	30	112	483	915	131
Pawtucket	.256	141	4692	692	1200	212	19	161	529	974	105
Syracuse	.254	142	4695	617	1191	245	24	128	537	1008	81
Toledo	.245	141	4615	596	1132	224	31	121	453	1030	107

CLUB PITCHING

	ERA	G	CG	SHO	SV	IP	H	R	ER	BB	SO
Norfolk	3.76	142	7	9	37	1232	1238	616	515	509	952
Rochester	3.93	141	13	13	43	1226	1112	605	535	441	1108
Pawtucket	4.07	141	11	7	38	1242	1198	636	562	491	991
Columbus	4.16	142	9	9	45	1235	1288	654	571	426	975
Richmond	4.33	142	6	10	34	1234	1252	671	594	470	922
Toledo	4.41	141	6	10	38	1223	1211	689	600	581	979
Scranton/W-B	4.59	142	20	7	32	1209	1248	700	617	488	964
Syracuse	4.71	142	9	11	23	1219	1218	720	638	582	902
Charlotte	4.95	141	6	4	43	1190	1278	744	655	535	895
Ottawa	5.03	140	5	5	28	1197	1288	750	669	571	874

CLUB FIELDING

	PCT	PO	A	E	DP
Columbus	.980	3704	1534	106	131
Charlotte	.977	3570	1521	118	145
Pawtucket	.976	3727	1471	126	120
Rochester	.975	3678	1268	127	84
Syracuse	.975	3656	1549	136	176
Richmond	.974	3702	1509	138	138
Ottawa	.974	3592	1570	140	139
Toledo	.973	3669	1468	145	116
Norfolk	.971	3697	1574	156	166
Scranton/W-B	.971	3626	1424	150	118

INDIVIDUAL BATTING LEADERS

(Minimum 383 Plate Appearances)

	AVG	G	AB	R	H	2B	3B	HR	RBI	BB	SO	SB
Gregg, Tommy, Richmond	.332	115	385	52	128	36	1	9	54	46	64	3
Matos, Francisco, Rochester	.324	101	389	51	126	17	4	4	51	9	42	8
Morman, Russ, Charlotte	.319	117	395	82	126	17	2	33	99	58	89	3
Petagine, Roberto, Norfolk	.317	129	441	90	140	32	1	31	100	85	92	0
Zuber, Jon, Scranton	.315	126	435	85	137	37	2	6	64	79	53	3
Doster, David, Scranton	.315	108	410	70	129	32	2	16	79	30	60	5
Howard, Matt, Columbus	.312	122	478	90	149	28	7	6	67	54	33	22
Agbayani, Benny, Norfolk	.310	127	468	90	145	24	2	11	51	67	106	29
Simon, Randall, Richmond	.308	133	519	62	160	45	1	14	102	17	76	1
Davis, Tommy, Rochester	.304	119	438	74	133	22	2	15	62	43	90	6

INDIVIDUAL PITCHING LEADERS

(Minimum 114 Innings)

	W	L	ERA	G	GS	CG	SV	IP	H	R	ER	BB	SO
Rose, Brian, Pawtucket	17	5	3.02	27	26	3	0	191	188	74	64	46	116
Yan, Esteban, Rochester	11	5	3.10	34	12	0	2	119	107	54	41	37	131
Pavano, Carl, Pawtucket	11	6	3.12	23	23	3	0	162	148	62	56	34	147
Brock, Chris, Richmond	10	6	3.34	20	19	0	0	119	97	50	44	51	83
Krivda, Rick, Rochester	14	2	3.39	22	21	6	0	146	122	61	55	34	128
Ojala, Kirt, Charlotte	8	7	3.50	25	24	0	0	149	148	74	58	55	119
Jerzembeck, Mike, Col.	7	5	3.59	20	20	2	0	130	125	55	52	37	118
Keagle, Greg, Toledo	11	7	3.81	23	23	3	0	151	136	68	64	61	140
Acevedo, Juan, Norfolk	6	6	3.86	18	18	1	0	117	111	55	50	34	99
Dishman, Glenn, Toledo	7	6	3.87	21	18	1	1	114	112	53	49	32	77

ALL-STAR TEAM

C—Bobby Estalella, Scranton/Wilkes-Barre. **1B**—Roberto Petagine, Norfolk. **2B**—Frank Catalanotto, Toledo. **3B**—Arquimedez Pozo, Pawtucket. **SS**—Matt Howard, Columbus. **OF**—Tony Barron, Scranton/Wilkes-Barre; Danny Clyburn, Rochester; Todd Dunwoody, Charlotte. **DH**—Russ Morman, Charlotte. **Util**—Randall Simon, Richmond. **SP**—Brian Rose, Pawtucket. **RP**—Eddie Gaillard, Toledo.

Most Valuable Player—Roberto Petagine, Norfolk. **Most Valuable Pitcher**—Brian Rose, Pawtucket. **Rookie of the Year**—Brian Rose, Pawtucket. **Manager of the Year**—Marv Foley, Rochester.

TOP 10 PROSPECTS

1. Carl Pavano, rhp, Pawtucket; **2.** Brian Rose, rhp, Pawtucket; **3.** Kevin Millwood, rhp, Richmond; **4.** Todd Dunwoody, of, Charlotte; **5.** Roy Halladay, rhp, Syracuse; **6.** Ricky Ledee, of, Columbus; **7.** Randall Simon, 1b, Richmond; **8.** Bubba Trammell, of, Toledo; **9.** Shannon Stewart, of, Syracuse; **10.** Chris Carpenter, rhp, Syracuse.

DEPT. LEADERS

BATTING

G	Rich Butler, Syracuse	137
	Danny Clyburn, Rochester	137
AB	Rich Butler, Syracuse	537
R	Rich Butler, Syracuse	93
H	Rich Butler, Syracuse	161
TB	Rich Butler, Syracuse	281
XBH	Shane Spencer, Columbus	68
2B	Randall Simon, Richmond	45
3B	Brad Tyler, Richmond	10
HR	Russ Morman, Charlotte	33
RBI	Randall Simon, Richmond	102
SH	Tomas Perez, Syracuse	14
SF	Brian Daubach, Charlotte	10
BB	Roberto Petagine, Norfolk	85
IBB	Russ Morman, Charlotte	11
HBP	Tony Barron, Scranton/W-B	12
SO	Kimera Bartee, Toledo	154
SB	Kimera Bartee, Toledo	33
CS	Benny Agbayani, Norfolk	14
	Donnie Sadler, Pawtucket	14
GIDP	Damon Hollins, Richmond	18
	Randall Simon, Richmond	18
OB%	Roberto Petagine, Norfolk	.430
SL%	Russ Morman, Charlotte	.623

PITCHING

G	Dale Polley, Columbus	62
GS	Carlton Loewer, Scranton/W-B	29
CG	Rick Krivda, Rochester	6
ShO	Rick Krivda, Rochester	3
GF	Scott Brow, Richmond	50
SV	Eddie Gaillard, Toledo	28
W	Brian Rose, Pawtucket	17
L	Larry Luebbers, Richmond	14
IP	Brian Rose, Pawtucket	191
H	Carlton Loewer, Scranton/W-B	198
R	Carlton Loewer, Scranton/W-B	120
ER	Everett Stull, Ottawa	103
HR	Everett Stull, Ottawa	25
HB	Andy Larkin, Charlotte	15
BB	Derek Brandow, Syracuse	91
	Mike Drumright, Toledo	91
SO	Nerio Rodriguez, Rochester	160
WP	Ray Ricken, Columbus	16
BK	Three tied at	4

FIELDING

C	AVG	Scott Makarewicz, Toledo	.991
	PO	Bobby Estalella, Scranton	844
	A	Raul Chavez, Ottawa	77
	E	Raul Chavez, Ottawa	15
	DP	Four tied at	9
	PB	Mike Figga, Columbus	12
1B	AVG	Tommy Davis, Rochester	.994
	PO	Randall Simon, Richmond	1063
	A	Mike Robertson, Scranton	97
	E	Mike Robertson, Scranton	14
		Randall Simon, Richmond	14
	DP	Roberto Petagine, Norfolk	117
2B	AVG	Frank Catalanotto, Toledo	.984
	PO	Marty Malloy, Richmond	195
	A	Jason Hardtke, Norfolk	319
	E	Marty Malloy, Richmond	12
		Donnie Sadler, Pawtucket	12
	DP	Jason Hardtke, Norfolk	76
3B	AVG	Tom Evans, Syracuse	.964
	PO	Tom Evans, Syracuse	83
	A	Tom Evans, Syracuse	242
	E	Doug Angeli, Scranton	18
	DP	Tom Evans, Syracuse	27
SS	AVG	Matt Howard, Columbus	.989
	PO	Ray Holbert, Toledo	183
	A	Desi Relaford, Scranton	373
	E	Desi Relaford, Scranton	34
	DP	Desi Relaford, Scranton	81
OF	AVG	Chris Sheff, Charlotte	1.000
	PO	Kimera Bartee, Toledo	336
	A	Jimmy Hurst, Toledo	18
	E	Danny Clyburn, Rochester	10
	DP	Jon Saffer, Ottawa	8

PACIFIC COAST LEAGUE

Edmonton wins again, delivers parting shot to Phoenix

BY JAVIER MORALES

Though Edmonton wrecked the storybook ending of the Phoenix franchise in the Pacific Coast League, the Trappers created a feel-good finish of their own in 1997.

Edmonton became only the third team in the last 25 years to win consecutive PCL titles. The Trappers, who again beat the Firebirds in the championship series, will attempt in 1998 to become the first team to threepeat since Albuquerque in 1980-82.

Phoenix, which won its last title in 1977, is out of opportunities. With the expansion Diamondbacks set to start in 1998, the Firebirds left Phoenix for Fresno, ending their 39-year existence in the Valley of the Sun.

"Not only is it the end of a season, but a lot of people that you have worked with and have touched you . . . go their own way," Phoenix manager Ron Wotus said.

Entering the championship series, Phoenix was favored to take the trophy with it to Fresno. The Firebirds had the best overall record at 88-55, and coasted to a double-digit lead in the Southern Division second-half standings.

All-around star
Jacob Cruz

Edmonton had the second-best record at 80-64, but the Trappers barely made the postseason. They finished a half-game behind Vancouver in the first half, and beat Tacoma by a half-game in the second half. Only 11 players remained from the Opening Day roster.

"It's probably been the most satisfying year as far as the players are concerned, because the odds were against them," said Edmonton manager Gary Jones, the winningest manager in the franchise's 17-year history and Baseball America's Minor League Manager of the Year. "Nobody really gave them a chance, but they got it done."

Edmonton and Phoenix both swept their semifinal playoff series in three games, Edmonton over Vancouver and Phoenix over Colorado Springs.

Phoenix' Jacob Cruz was named league MVP after leading in the diverse categories of doubles, on-base percentage and outfield assists.

Albuquerque infielder Paul Konerko, Baseball America's Minor League Player of the Year, led the PCL in home runs (37) and RBIs (127). A September callup, he batted .323 with the Dukes.

Bill Cutler's retirement as PCL president after 18 years on the job and more than 40 years in baseball signaled the beginning of change in the league. Branch Rickey, president of the American Association, was selected to replace Cutler. He takes over as the league expands because of realignment.

New Orleans, Nashville, Iowa and Omaha, all formerly of the American Association, will join the league in 1998.

For the second straight year, attendance decreased league-wide, including Edmonton, which went from a club record of 463,684 in 1996 to 409,383. Attendance in the PCL has dropped from 3,513,867 in 1995 to 3,464,779 in 1996 to 3,168,864 in 1997.

STANDINGS: SPLIT SEASON

FIRST HALF					SECOND HALF				
NORTH	W	L	PCT	GB	NORTH	W	L	PCT	GB
Vancouver	39	32	.549	—	Edmonton	41	31	.569	—
Edmonton	39	33	.542	½	Tacoma	40	31	.563	½
Tacoma	35	35	.500	3½	Salt Lake	38	33	.535	2½
Salt Lake	34	38	.472	5½	Vancouver	36	36	.500	5
Calgary	29	38	.433	8	Calgary	31	40	.437	9½
SOUTH	W	L	PCT	GB	SOUTH	W	L	PCT	GB
Colo. Springs	45	23	.662	—	Phoenix	49	22	.690	—
Phoenix	39	33	.542	8	Las Vegas	31	39	.443	17½
Albuquerque	33	36	.478	12½	Colo. Springs	31	41	.431	18½
Tucson	34	38	.472	13	Tucson	30	40	.429	18½
Las Vegas	25	46	.352	21½	Albuquerque	29	43	.403	20½

PLAYOFFS—Semifinals: Edmonton defeated Vancouver 3-0, and Phoenix defeated Colorado Springs 3-0, in best-of-5 series. **Finals:** Edmonton defeated Phoenix 3-1, in best-of-5 series.

STANDINGS: OVERALL

Page		W	L	PCT	GB	Manager(s)	Attendance/Dates	Last Penn.
206	Phoenix Firebirds (Giants)	88	55	.615	—	Ron Wotus	209,698 (69)	1977
174	Edmonton Trappers (Athletics)	80	64	.556	8½	Gary Jones	432,504 (66)	1997
104	Colorado Springs Sky Sox (Rockies)	76	64	.543	10½	Paul Zuvella	216,716 (64)	1995
212	Tacoma Rainiers (Mariners)	75	66	.532	12	Dave Myers	305,281 (67)	1978
50	Vancouver Canadians (Angels)	75	68	.524	13	Bruce Hines	303,148 (64)	1989
147	Salt Lake Buzz (Twins)	72	71	.503	16	Phil Roof	578,107 (70)	1979
141	Tucson Toros (Brewers)	64	78	.451	23½	Tim Ireland/Bob Mariano	285,817 (68)	1993
134	Albuquerque Dukes (Dodgers)	62	79	.440	25	Glenn Hoffman	307,760 (67)	1994
186	Calgary Cannons (Pirates)	60	78	.435	25½	Trent Jewett	291,918 (62)	None
199	Las Vegas Stars (Padres)	56	85	.397	31	Jerry Royster	313,128 (70)	1988

NOTE: Team's individual batting and pitching statistics can be found on page indicated in lefthand column.

1997 Pacific Coast League Statistics

CLUB BATTING

	AVG	G	AB	R	H	2B	3B	HR	BB	SO	SB
Colorado Springs	.305	140	4937	924	1506	326	39	160	527	986	93
Edmonton	.303	144	4733	878	1433	305	44	166	692	922	95
Salt Lake	.297	143	4998	889	1482	295	54	162	547	1034	117
Tacoma	.295	141	4853	770	1430	316	28	155	453	864	42
Calgary	.294	138	4677	787	1375	340	38	139	465	888	111
Phoenix	.294	143	4918	816	1445	296	46	127	530	928	134
Tucson	.292	142	4911	829	1433	359	43	131	557	936	58
Vancouver	.288	143	4839	766	1396	293	42	136	445	855	124
Albuquerque	.286	141	4815	820	1379	246	51	182	505	853	121
Las Vegas	.282	141	4888	686	1376	290	34	110	473	971	113

CLUB PITCHING

	ERA	G	CG	SHO	SV	IP	H	R	ER	BB	SO
Tacoma	4.65	141	9	8	33	1211	1294	694	626	512	1017
Phoenix	4.77	143	3	3	46	1242	1405	721	658	493	926
Vancouver	4.91	143	16	6	37	1237	1331	767	675	591	836
Edmonton	5.35	144	8	7	45	1193	1400	783	709	402	866
Salt Lake	5.44	143	7	5	34	1251	1511	855	757	472	893
Tucson	5.47	142	1	4	31	1229	1444	869	748	541	843
Albuquerque	5.53	141	7	6	30	1221	1518	849	751	527	992
Calgary	5.66	138	2	1	27	1174	1479	844	738	507	909
Las Vegas	5.89	141	6	3	30	1230	1467	902	806	565	993
Colorado Springs	5.91	140	6	3	27	1203	1406	881	791	584	962

CLUB FIELDING

	PCT	PO	A	E	DP
Tacoma	.978	3634	1402	114	145
Phoenix	.977	3725	1490	121	156
Colo. Springs	.977	3609	1468	118	158
Edmonton	.977	3579	1401	119	132
Las Vegas	.973	3690	1552	145	139

	PCT	PO	A	E	DP
Vancouver	.973	3711	1407	144	129
Salt Lake	.972	3753	1632	156	163
Albuquerque	.969	3663	1578	167	144
Calgary	.968	3521	1495	165	132
Tucson	.967	3688	1653	183	157

INDIVIDUAL BATTING LEADERS

(Minimum 389 Plate Appearances)

	AVG	G	AB	R	H	2B	3B	HR	RBI	BB	SO	SB
Cruz, Jacob, Phoenix	.361	127	493	97	178	45	3	12	95	64	64	18
McCarty, Dave, Phoenix	.353	121	434	85	153	27	5	22	92	49	75	9
Helton, Todd, Colo. Spr.	.352	99	392	87	138	31	2	16	88	61	68	3
Raabe, Brian, Tacoma	.352	135	543	101	191	35	4	14	80	38	20	1
Wilson, Desi, Phoenix	.344	121	451	76	155	27	6	7	53	44	73	16
Counsell, Craig, Colo. Spr.	.335	96	376	77	126	31	6	5	63	45	38	12
Martinez, Manny, Calgary	.331	109	420	78	139	34	1	16	66	33	80	17
Collier, Lou, Calgary	.330	112	397	65	131	31	5	1	48	37	47	12
Shave, Jon, Salt Lake	.329	103	395	75	130	27	3	7	60	39	62	6
Diaz, Eddy, Tucson	.329	94	356	65	117	24	3	9	70	26	25	0

INDIVIDUAL PITCHING LEADERS

(Minimum 115 Innings)

	W	L	ERA	G	GS	CG	SV	IP	H	R	ER	BB	SO
Hurtado, Edwin, Tacoma	10	6	3.88	20	20	5	0	132	139	60	57	37	100
Lawrence, Sean, Calgary	8	9	4.21	26	26	2	0	143	154	83	67	57	116
Taylor, Kerry, Las Vegas	7	9	4.31	22	22	3	0	144	150	84	69	55	103
Minchey, Nate, Colo. Spr.	15	6	4.51	27	21	3	0	158	172	87	79	53	107
Miller, Travis, Salt Lake	10	6	4.73	21	21	0	0	126	140	73	66	57	86
Lorraine, Andrew, Edmonton	8	6	4.74	23	20	2	0	118	143	72	62	34	75
Creek, Doug, Phoenix	8	6	4.93	25	23	2	0	130	140	76	71	66	137
Serafini, Dan, Salt Lake	9	7	4.97	28	24	2	0	152	166	87	84	55	118
Buckley, Travis, Vancouver	7	11	5.11	32	25	1	1	176	223	116	100	51	119
Treadwell, Jody, Albuquerque	10	5	5.12	27	21	2	1	128	143	80	73	54	108

ALL-STAR TEAM

C—Todd Greene, Vancouver. **1B**—Todd Helton, Colorado Springs. **2B**—Brian Raabe, Tacoma. **3B**—Paul Konerko, Albuquerque. **SS**—Neifi Perez, Colorado Springs. **OF**—Jacob Cruz, Phoenix; Manny Martinez, Calgary; Ryan Radmanovich, Salt Lake. **DH**—Dan Rohrmeier, Tacoma. **LHP**—Doug Creek, Phoenix. **RHP**—Dan Carlson, Phoenix. **RP**—John Johnstone, Phoenix.

Most Valuable Player—Paul Konerko, Albuquerque. **Manager of the Year**—Ron Wotus, Phoenix.

TOP 10 PROSPECTS

1. Paul Konerko, 3b-1b, Albuquerque; **2.** Jose Cruz Jr., of, Tacoma; **3.** Neifi Perez, ss, Colorado Springs; **4.** Travis Lee, 1b, Tucson; **5.** Todd Helton, 1b, Colorado Springs; **6.** Todd Greene, c, Vancouver; **7.** Todd Walker, 3b, Salt Lake; **8.** Karim Garcia, of, Albuquerque; **9.** Derrek Lee, 1b, Las Vegas; **10.** Jacob Cruz, of, Phoenix.

DEPT. LEADERS

BATTING

G	Brian Raabe, Tacoma	135
AB	Brian Raabe, Tacoma	543
R	Brian Raabe, Tacoma	101
H	Brian Raabe, Tacoma	191
TB	Paul Konerko, Albuquerque	300
XBH	Dan Rohrmeier, Tacoma	80
2B	Jacob Cruz, Phoenix	45
3B	Jovino Carvajal, Vancouver	20
HR	Paul Konerko, Albuquerque	37
RBI	Paul Konerko, Albuquerque	127
SH	Edgar Caceres, Vancouver	12
	Robert Eenhoorn, Vancouver	12
SF	Steve Cox, Edmonton	9
	Brian Raabe, Tacoma	9
BB	Steve Cox, Edmonton	88
IBB	Jacob Cruz, Phoenix	9
	Alan Zinter, Tacoma	9
HBP	Brian Raabe, Tacoma	16
SO	Ryan Radmanovich, Salt Lake	138
SB	Terry Jones, Colorado Springs	36
CS	Chris Latham, Salt Lake	19
GIDP	Jason Wood, Edmonton	21
OB%	Jacob Cruz, Phoenix	.434
SL%	Paul Konerko, Albuquerque	.621

PITCHING

G	Dan Hubbs, Albuquerque	62
	Ricky Pickett, Phoenix	62
GS	Geoff Edsell, Vancouver	29
CG	Geoff Edsell, Vancouver	6
ShO	Edwin Hurtado, Tacoma	3
GF	Joe Boever, Edmonton	36
SV	John Johnstone, Phoenix	24
W	Nate Minchey, Colorado Springs	15
L	Mark Redman, Salt Lake	15
IP	Geoff Edsell, Vancouver	183
H	Travis Buckley, Vancouver	223
R	Mark Redman, Salt Lake	123
ER	Chris Nichting, Edmonton	113
HR	Travis Buckley, Vancouver	25
HB	Geoff Edsell, Vancouver	12
	Bobby Jones, Colorado Springs	12
BB	Geoff Edsell, Vancouver	96
SO	Doug Creek, Phoenix	137
WP	Jason Grimsley, Tucson	20
BK	Jimmy Anderson, Calgary	4
	Jamie McAndrew, Tucson	4

FIELDING

C	**AVG**	Jason Varitek, Tacoma	.995
	PO	Doug Mirabelli, Phoenix	629
	A	Henry Blanco, Albuquerque	64
	E	Bobby Hughes, Tucson	12
	DP	Henry Blanco, Albuquerque	11
	PB	Creighton Gubanich, CS/Edm.	13
1B	**AVG**	Derrek Lee, Las Vegas	.992
	PO	Derrek Lee, Las Vegas	1059
	A	Derrek Lee, Las Vegas	107
	E	Steve Cox, Edmonton	10
	DP	Derrek Lee, Las Vegas	107
2B	**AVG**	Tim Florez, Phoenix	.982
	PO	Ronnie Belliard, Tucson	229
	A	Ronnie Belliard, Tucson	357
	E	Ronnie Belliard, Tucson	24
	DP	Ronnie Belliard, Tucson	92
		Tim Florez, Phoenix	92
3B	**AVG**	Tom Quinlan, Col. Springs	.960
	PO	George Arias, Van./LV	99
	A	Tom Quinlan, Col. Springs	269
	E	Todd Walker, Salt Lake	24
	DP	Tom Quinlan, Col. Springs	30
		Jason Wood, Edmonton	30
SS	**AVG**	Andy Sheets, Tacoma	.973
	PO	Wilson Delgado, Phoenix	197
	A	Jorge Velandia, Las Vegas	347
	E	Keith Johns, Tucson	29
	DP	Wilson Delgado, Phoenix	86
OF	**AVG**	Doug Dascenzo, LV	.992
	PO	Dante Powell, Phoenix	266
	A	Jacob Cruz, Phoenix	16
	E	Stoney Briggs, Las Vegas	14
	DP	Edgard Velazquez, Col. Springs	5

EASTERN LEAGUE

Harrisburg wins another title, New Britain wins respect

BY ANDREW LINKER

Some things never seem to change: The Harrisburg Senators reached the Eastern League playoffs, and won again.

Some things do change: The league's languishing franchise in New Britain did not have its season effectively end by Memorial Day.

While the Senators of 1997 became the first team to successfully defend their EL title since the Albany-Colonie Yankees in 1989, the Rock Cats kept New Britain in the playoff race until the final weekend of the regular season.

That the Rock Cats were competitive indeed was news, especially considering the franchise had gone six full seasons without so much as a winning month.

"I did talk about that as a motivator," Rock Cats manager Al Newman said. "I told them that we have a chance to do something in New Britain that hasn't been done in a while."

They did it by shaking off a 0-9 start to post a winning month in May—their first winning month since August 1990, when the then-parent Red Sox traded New Britain third baseman Jeff Bagwell to the Astros for reliever Larry Andersen.

"It's been a while since New Britain has had a chance to even think about making the playoffs," Newman said.

Playoffs are all the Senators have thought of since the Expos moved their Double-A affiliate to Harrisburg in 1991.

The seventh season of the affiliation ended with Harrisburg's fifth trip to the finals and third title since 1993. For the second straight year, the Senators beat Portland in four games of the best-of-five finals. Harrisburg defeated Bowie and Portland beat Norwich in the semifinals, with both series going the full five games.

The league's most consistent player was Portland first baseman Kevin Millar, who came within five home runs of becoming the fifth triple crown winner in the EL's 75 seasons.

As it was, Millar led the league in batting, RBIs, hits, doubles, extra-base hits and on-base percentage. He was second in home runs, runs and slugging percentage.

Millar's 131 RBIs were seven shy of the league record, set in 1962 by Binghamton's Ken Harrelson.

The league's most manic player was Binghamton third baseman Matt Raleigh, who led the EL with 37 homers while batting only .196 with 169 strikeouts.

The homers were the most in the league since Buffalo's Rick Lancellotti tied the EL record with 41 in 1979. The strikeouts broke the record of 165 set by Allentown's Ezell King in 1965.

STEWART SMITH

Model of consistency
Kevin Millar

Harrisburg's Israel Alcantara homered in a league-record six straight games, putting together a power surge from July 14-19 that fell one game shy of the all-time record in the minors.

Portland became the first team in league history with five players hitting 20 or more homers, led by Millar's 32 and followed by Ryan Jackson (26), John Roskos (24), Mark Kotsay (20) and Josh Booty (20).

Again the EL had a franchise relocation, as Akron replaced Canton to give the league at least one move in 13 of the last 15 seasons.

This move ended in the record books as the Aeros attracted 473,232 fans to $30 million-plus Canal Park, breaking the league record set in 1995 by Bowie.

Equally impressive was Trenton again filling Waterfront Park beyond capacity. The Thunder averaged standing-room-only crowds of 6,567 for their 6,300-seat ballpark, marking the third straight season they have played before 100-percent capacity crowds.

STANDINGS

Page	NORTH	W	L	PCT	GB	Manager	Attendance/Dates	Last Penn.
116	Portland Sea Dogs (Marlins)	79	63	.556	—	Fredi Gonzalez	397,117 (69)	None
160	Norwich Navigators (Yankees)	73	69	.514	6	Trey Hillman	244,246 (63)	None
147	New Britain Rock Cats (Twins)	70	72	.493	9	Al Newman	151,718 (63)	1983
167	Binghamton Mets (Mets)	66	76	.465	13	Rick Sweet	200,513 (69)	1994
104	New Haven Ravens (Rockies)	64	78	.451	15	Bill Hayes	232,101 (66)	None
Page	**SOUTH**	**W**	**L**	**PCT**	**GB**	**Manager**	**Attendance/Dates**	**Last Penn.**
154	Harrisburg Senators (Expos)	86	56	.606	—	Rick Sofield	242,431 (65)	1997
66	Bowie Baysox (Orioles)	75	67	.528	11	Joe Ferguson	409,285 (69)	None
180	Reading Phillies (Phillies)	74	68	.521	12	Al LeBoeuf	398,182 (68)	1995
73	Trenton Thunder (Red Sox)	71	70	.504	14½	DeMarlo Hale	446,527 (68)	None
98	Akron Aeros (Indians)	51	90	.362	34½	Jeff Datz	473,232 (67)	None

PLAYOFFS—Semifinals: Portland defeated Norwich 3-2, and Harrisburg defeated Bowie 3-2 in best-of-5 series. **Finals:** Harrisburg defeated Portland 3-1, in best-of-5 series.

NOTE: Team's individual batting and pitching statistics can be found on page indicated in lefthand column.

1997 Eastern League Statistics

CLUB BATTING

	AVG	G	AB	R	H	2B	3B	HR	BB	SO	SB
Portland	.288	142	4890	824	1407	262	31	191	510	971	103
Norwich	.283	142	4806	784	1359	234	30	129	576	917	109
Harrisburg	.270	142	4721	692	1274	227	35	145	431	829	143
Trenton	.270	141	4726	766	1274	236	33	142	578	977	125
Akron	.268	141	4671	758	1254	245	28	143	593	936	73
Bowie	.267	142	4809	701	1283	260	16	134	540	1001	72
New Haven	.262	142	4637	663	1216	211	22	119	482	957	77
Binghamton	.257	142	4662	654	1197	223	18	182	464	1097	139
Reading	.250	142	4721	658	1182	201	35	119	493	965	86
New Britain	.250	142	4543	670	1137	242	29	105	585	914	121

CLUB PITCHING

	ERA	G	CG	SHO	SV	IP	H	R	ER	BB	SO
Harrisburg	3.78	142	5	8	42	1244	1135	644	522	513	1087
Norwich	4.14	142	9	11	29	1222	1235	681	562	490	999
Bowie	4.14	142	5	5	37	1251	1215	681	576	553	1029
New Britain	4.32	142	10	6	38	1210	1196	666	581	521	888
New Haven	4.43	142	11	9	31	1215	1200	696	598	515	949
Portland	4.49	142	7	5	41	1245	1365	728	621	426	919
Binghamton	4.51	142	11	8	28	1228	1258	732	615	553	983
Reading	4.60	142	3	4	42	1257	1309	741	643	538	959
Trenton	4.92	141	6	5	36	1229	1313	760	672	555	900
Akron	5.26	141	16	5	19	1197	1357	841	700	588	851

CLUB FIELDING

	PCT	PO	A	E	DP
New Britain	.977	3629	1575	123	153
Trenton	.974	3688	1433	139	115
Reading	.972	3772	1547	155	115
Bowie	.971	3752	1545	156	131
New Haven	.971	3644	1564	155	144

	PCT	PO	A	E	DP
Portland	.971	3735	1637	162	155
Norwich	.966	3667	1514	181	115
Binghamton	.966	3683	1627	189	146
Akron	.963	3591	1488	194	105
Harrisburg	.963	3731	1365	195	89

INDIVIDUAL BATTING LEADERS

(Minimum 383 Plate Appearances)

	AVG	G	AB	R	H	2B	3B	HR	RBI	BB	SO	SB
Millar, Kevin, Portland	.342	135	511	94	175	34	2	32	131	66	53	2
Dellucci, David, Bowie	.327	107	385	71	126	29	3	20	55	58	69	11
Gibson, Derrick, New Haven	.317	119	461	91	146	24	2	23	75	36	100	20
Perry, Chan, Akron	.315	119	476	74	150	34	2	20	96	28	61	3
Seefried, Tate, Binghamton	.313	96	335	59	105	16	0	29	79	54	99	9
Jackson, Ryan, Portland	.312	134	491	87	153	28	4	26	98	51	85	2
Fullmer, Brad, Harrisburg	.311	94	357	60	111	24	2	19	62	30	25	6
Buchanan, Brian, Norwich	.309	116	470	75	145	25	2	10	69	32	85	11
Roskos, John, Portland	.308	123	451	66	139	31	1	24	84	50	81	4
Kotsay, Mark, Portland	.306	114	438	103	134	27	2	20	77	75	65	17

INDIVIDUAL PITCHING LEADERS

(Minimum 114 Innings)

	W	L	ERA	G	GS	CG	SV	IP	H	R	ER	BB	SO
Vavrek, Mike, New Haven	12	3	2.57	17	17	2	0	123	94	38	35	34	101
Saipe, Mike, New Haven	8	5	3.10	19	19	4	0	137	127	57	47	29	123
Montgomery, Steve, Bowie	10	5	3.10	24	23	2	0	136	116	56	47	52	127
Lomon, Kevin, Norwich	9	7	3.21	18	18	2	0	115	104	51	41	50	117
Bell, Jason, New Britain	11	9	3.39	28	28	3	0	165	163	71	62	64	142
Thurman, Mike, Harrisburg	9	6	3.81	20	20	1	0	116	102	54	49	30	85
Moreno, Julio, Bowie	9	6	3.83	27	25	1	0	139	141	76	59	64	106
Mercado, Hector, Port.	11	3	3.96	31	17	1	0	130	129	66	57	54	125
Cumberland, Chris, Nor.-NB	12	10	3.99	26	26	3	0	160	193	102	71	61	83
Moore, Trey, Harrisburg	11	6	4.15	27	27	2	0	163	152	91	75	66	137

ALL-STAR TEAM

C—Bob Henley, Harrisburg. **1B**—Kevin Millar, Portland. **2B**—Rudy Gomez, Norwich. **3B**—Corey Koskie, New Britain. **SS**—Alex Gonzalez, Portland. **OF**—David Dellucci, Bowie; Derrick Gibson, New Haven; Mark Kotsay, Portland. **DH**—Chan Perry, Akron. **Util**—Lionel Hastings, Portland. **LHS**—Jesus Sanchez, Binghamton; Mike Vavrek, New Haven. **RHS**—Steve Montgomery, Bowie; Mike Saipe, New Haven. **RP**—Ben Fleetham, Harrisburg.

Most Valuable Player—Kevin Millar, Portland.

TOP 10 PROSPECTS

1. Mark Kotsay, of, Portland; **2.** Derrick Gibson, of, New Haven; **3.** Jaret Wright, rhp, Akron; **4.** Alex Gonzalez, ss, Portland; **5.** Preston Wilson, of, Binghamton; **6.** David Ortiz, 1b, New Britain; **7.** Michael Coleman, of, Trenton; **8.** Orlando Cabrera, ss, Harrisburg; **9.** Mike Lowell, 3b, Norwich; **10.** Russ Branyan, 3b, Akron.

DEPT. LEADERS

BATTING

G	Jesse Garcia, Bowie	141
AB	Marlon Anderson, Reading	553
R	Mark Kotsay, Portland	103
H	Kevin Millar, Portland	175
TB	Kevin Millar, Portland	309
XBH	Kevin Millar, Portland	68
2B	Kevin Millar, Portland	34
	Chan Perry, Akron	34
3B	David Miller, Akron	9
HR	Matt Raleigh, Binghamton	37
RBI	Kevin Millar, Portland	131
SH	Jesse Garcia, Bowie	24
SF	Three tied at	7
BB	Doug Mientkiewicz, NB	98
IBB	Corey Koskie, New Britain	10
	Tate Seefried, Binghamton	10
HBP	Dan Held, Reading	18
SO	Matt Raleigh, Binghamton	169
SB	Aaron Fuller, Trenton	40
CS	Randy Winn, Portland	20
GIDP	Mike Moyle, Akron	17
	John Roskos, Portland	17
OB%	Kevin Millar, Portland	.423
SL%	Tate Seefried, Binghamton	.621

PITCHING

G	Matt Snyder, Bowie	67
GS	Three tied at	29
CG	Maximo de la Rosa, Akron	5
ShO	Trey Moore, Harrisburg	2
	Mike Saipe, New Haven	2
GF	Jay Tessmer, Norwich	49
SV	Ben Fleetham, Harrisburg	30
W	Jesus Sanchez, Binghamton	13
L	Tony Costa, Reading	12
	Arnold Gooch, Binghamton	12
IP	Mark Brownson, New Haven	185
H	Brian Barkley, Trenton	208
R	Brian Barkley, Trenton	113
ER	Brian Barkley, Trenton	98
HR	Jesus Sanchez, Binghamton	25
HB	Mark Brownson, New Haven	14
BB	Brian Barkley, Trenton	79
SO	Jesus Sanchez, Binghamton	176
WP	Greg Resz, Norwich	17
	Rich Turrentine, Binghamton	17
BK	Five tied at	4

FIELDING

C	AVG	Bob Henley, Harrisburg	.995
	PO	Tom Wilson, Norwich	694
	A	Mel Rosario, Bowie	87
	E	John Pachot, Harrisburg	14
	DP	Mike Moyle, Akron	10
	PB	Three tied at	17
1B	AVG	Doug Mientkiewicz, NB	.995
	PO	Chris Kirgan, Bowie	1228
	A	Kevin Millar, Portland	93
	E	Chris Ashby, Norwich	19
	DP	Kevin Millar, Portland	116
2B	AVG	Jesse Garcia, Bowie	.985
	PO	Marlon Anderson, Reading	323
	A	Marlon Anderson, Reading	396
	E	Marlon Anderson, Reading	29
	DP	Ryan Lane, New Britain	94
3B	AVG	Jamie Taylor, New Haven	.955
	PO	Todd Betts, Akron	75
		Josh Booty, Portland	75
	A	Josh Booty, Portland	262
	E	Todd Betts, Akron	27
	DP	Josh Booty, Portland	38
SS	AVG	Mike Moriarty, New Britain	.973
	PO	Mike Moriarty, New Britain	210
	A	Mike Moriarty, New Britain	475
	E	Alex Gonzalez, Portland	37
	DP	Mike Moriarty, New Britain	114
OF	AVG	Mark Kotsay, Portland	.992
	PO	Scott Pagano, Reading	302
	A	Jim Betzsold, Akron	17
	E	Derrick Gibson, New Haven	11
	DP	Three tied at	4

SOUTHERN LEAGUE

Huntsville dominates regular season, falls to Greenville

BY LARRY STARKS

The 1997 season will be known as the year the Huntsville Stars hit it big.

The Stars had arguably the most successful season in the Southern League since the Greenville Braves won 100 games in 1992.

They set club records in almost every offensive category, had three players reach 100 RBIs and had a fourth player who was widely considered the most exciting in the league. About the only thing the Stars didn't get was the championship ring. They lost in the title round to Greenville in the deciding fifth game.

Huntsville catalyst
Mike Neill

Otherwise, it was a season to remember. The team finished with a .286 batting average, the league's best since Huntsville's .289 average in 1986. And Mike Coolbaugh, D.T. Cromer and league MVP Ben Grieve combined for 361 RBIs, the most productive trio in the league's history.

The Stars also had 164 home runs, and broke league records for runs (942) and RBIs (867).

But the Stars were more than just big guys. Shortstop Miguel Tejada, 21, hit .275 with 22 homers and 97 RBIs. He made 36 errors, but showed wizardry at his position.

Greenville had a quiet, injury-filled season until the playoffs. The Braves went 34-36 in the first half, and by the time anyone noticed them, they had won the title.

On three different occasions, the Braves had seven players on the disabled list. Management had to look up the rules on the maximum number of players it could put on the DL. The Braves made 60 roster moves during the season, and five in the playoffs.

More than that, the Braves were virtually starless. They had only one position player, third baseman Wes Helms considered among the Braves' top prospects.

But league manager of the year Randy Ingle led them to a 40-30 record in the second half. They followed up by beating Knoxville in four games of a best-of-five semifinal series, while Huntsville was eliminating Mobile in five games.

The biggest individual season may have belonged to Jacksonville Suns outfielder Juan Encarnacion. The 21-year-old had a breakthrough year, hitting .323 with 26 homers after hitting .240 for Class A Lakeland in 1996.

The season also will be known as the year the league lost one of its oldest cities, Memphis. The Chicks played their final game before heading 80 miles east to Jackson, Tenn., where they will play in 1998 in a 6,200-seat, $8 million stadium.

The Chicks struggled on the field and at the gate. They averaged less than 2,000 fans a game, the league's lowest and the franchise's worst in 10 years.

The season also marked the debut of the Mobile BayBears, the Double-A affiliate of the San Diego Padres. They opened to the largest attendance in the league, averaging more than 4,700 a game.

The move of the Padres affiliate to Mobile didn't slow their first-half dominance. The BayBears became the third straight Padres SL affiliate to win the Western Division first-half title.

STANDINGS: SPLIT SEASON

FIRST HALF

EAST	W	L	PCT	GB
Knoxville	41	27	.603	—
Jacksonville	34	35	.493	7½
Greenville	34	36	.486	8
Carolina	26	42	.382	15
Orlando	25	44	.362	16½
WEST	**W**	**L**	**PCT**	**GB**
Mobile	39	29	.574	—
Memphis	37	32	.536	2½
Chattanooga	37	32	.536	2½
Birmingham	36	32	.529	3
Huntsville	35	35	.500	5

SECOND HALF

EAST	W	L	PCT	GB
Greenville	40	30	.571	—
Orlando	38	31	.551	1½
Knoxville	34	36	.486	6
Jacksonville	32	38	.457	8
Carolina	29	40	.420	10½
WEST	**W**	**L**	**PCT**	**GB**
Huntsville	42	27	.609	—
Birmingham	40	30	.571	2½
Chattanooga	33	37	.471	9½
Mobile	30	39	.435	12
Memphis	30	40	.429	12½

PLAYOFFS—Semifinals: Greenville defeated Knoxville 3-1, and Huntsville defeated Mobile 3-2, in best-of-5 series. **Finals:** Greenville defeated Huntsville 3-2, in best-of-5 series.

STANDINGS: OVERALL

Page		W	L	PCT	GB	Manager(s)	Attendance/Dates	Last Penn.
175	Huntsville Stars (Athletics)	77	62	.554	—	Mike Quade	285,580 (66)	1994
80	Birmingham Barons (White Sox)	76	62	.551	½	Dave Huppert	302,144 (68)	1993
228	Knoxville Smokies (Blue Jays)	75	63	.543	1½	Omar Malave	138,389 (66)	1978
60	Greenville Braves (Braves)	74	66	.529	3½	Randy Ingle	254,049 (68)	1997
200	Mobile BayBears (Padres)	69	68	.504	7	Mike Ramsey	332,639 (69)	1990
93	Chattanooga Lookouts (Reds)	70	69	.504	7	Mark Berry	228,391 (65)	1988
212	Memphis Chicks (Mariners)	67	72	.482	10	Dave Brundage	113,183 (58)	None
110	Jacksonville Suns (Tigers)	66	73	.475	11	Dave Anderson	238,238 (68)	1996
86	Orlando Rays (Cubs)	63	75	.457	13½	Dave Trembley	147,241 (64)	1991
186	Carolina Mudcats (Pirates)	55	82	.401	21	Marc Hill/Jeff Banister	265,219 (66)	1995

NOTE: Team's individual batting and pitching statistics can be found on page indicated in lefthand column.

1997 Southern League Statistics

CLUB BATTING

	AVG	G	AB	R	H	2B	3B	HR	BB	SO	SB
Huntsville	.286	139	4818	942	1380	281	34	164	664	1036	121
Chattanooga	.284	139	4766	744	1354	274	33	128	484	826	94
Birmingham	.279	139	4761	793	1330	287	40	124	540	1015	70
Mobile	.277	137	4676	768	1297	255	39	108	596	887	126
Greenville	.273	140	4701	711	1283	225	22	147	478	832	92
Knoxville	.272	139	4669	727	1269	255	42	153	466	933	76
Orlando	.272	138	4570	733	1242	244	37	123	500	846	123
Memphis	.272	139	4563	672	1239	229	36	84	495	853	109
Jacksonville	.267	139	4730	699	1263	245	29	127	467	918	115
Carolina	.264	137	4745	688	1255	253	44	129	456	1024	112

CLUB PITCHING

	ERA	G	CG	SHO	SV	IP	H	R	ER	BB	SO
Memphis	4.43	139	13	8	28	1171	1187	657	577	486	910
Birmingham	4.49	139	6	8	36	1211	1266	744	604	559	941
Mobile	4.52	137	8	3	33	1198	1261	687	602	507	975
Knoxville	4.60	139	9	6	40	1202	1307	723	615	480	980
Jacksonville	4.75	139	14	7	29	1219	1270	741	643	482	869
Carolina	4.77	137	3	3	27	1205	1281	786	639	569	933
Greenville	4.89	140	1	4	49	1228	1283	755	667	531	994
Orlando	4.91	138	2	9	34	1184	1255	759	646	515	927
Huntsville	5.16	139	3	1	36	1209	1443	816	693	477	827
Chattanooga	5.26	139	2	2	41	1205	1359	809	704	540	814

CLUB FIELDING

	PCT	PO	A	E	DP
Orlando	.973	3552	1481	140	120
Memphis	.972	3513	1473	141	147
Greenville	.969	3685	1426	161	111
Mobile	.969	3593	1391	158	112
Chattanooga	.969	3616	1491	164	133
Jacksonville	.968	3656	1566	170	145
Birmingham	.967	3633	1443	174	134
Huntsville	.966	3627	1602	184	157
Knoxville	.965	3607	1502	186	116
Carolina	.960	3615	1515	211	125

INDIVIDUAL BATTING LEADERS

(Minimum 378 Plate Appearances)

	AVG	G	AB	R	H	2B	3B	HR	RBI	BB	SO	SB
Neill, Mike, Huntsville	.340	122	486	129	165	30	2	14	80	72	113	16
Raven, Luis, Birmingham	.336	117	456	88	153	30	3	30	112	46	126	4
Grieve, Ben, Huntsville	.328	100	372	100	122	29	2	24	108	81	75	5
Pearson, Eddie, Birmingham	.327	95	382	59	125	33	1	5	59	23	50	1
Cromer, D.T., Huntsville	.323	134	545	100	176	40	6	15	121	60	102	12
Encarnacion, Juan, Jack.	.323	131	493	91	159	31	4	26	90	43	86	17
Prieto, Chris, Mobile	.320	109	388	80	124	22	9	2	58	59	55	26
Ramirez, Angel, Knoxville	.309	85	369	55	114	24	7	5	37	10	48	11
Towle, Justin, Chattanooga	.309	119	418	62	129	37	5	11	70	55	77	5
Rose, Pete, Chattanooga	.308	112	445	75	137	31	0	25	98	34	63	0
Coolbaugh, Mike, Huntsville	.308	139	559	100	172	37	2	30	132	52	105	8

INDIVIDUAL PITCHING LEADERS

(Minimum 112 Innings)

	W	L	ERA	G	GS	CG	SV	IP	H	R	ER	BB	SO
Herbert, Russ, Birmingham	13	5	3.63	27	26	3	0	159	136	72	64	80	126
Tollberg, Brian, Mobile	6	3	3.72	31	13	1	0	123	123	60	51	24	108
Eyre, Scott, Birmingham	13	5	3.84	22	22	0	0	127	110	61	54	55	127
Cloude, Ken, Memphis	11	7	3.87	22	22	3	0	133	131	62	57	48	124
Byrne, Earl, Orlando	5	5	3.95	32	20	0	0	130	102	62	57	73	128
Ebert, Derrin, Greenville	11	8	4.10	27	25	0	0	176	191	95	80	48	101
King, Bill, Huntsville	9	7	4.19	28	27	1	0	176	216	99	82	28	103
Stevenson, Jason, Knoxville	12	9	4.27	26	26	2	0	150	166	88	71	43	101
Zancanaro, Dave, Mobile	10	8	4.44	27	19	3	1	134	140	69	66	57	66
Hinchliffe, Brett, Memphis	10	10	4.45	24	24	5	0	146	159	81	72	45	107

ALL-STAR TEAM

C—Justin Towle, Chattanooga. **1B**—D.T. Cromer, Huntsville. **2B**—Frank Menechino, Birmingham. **3B**—Mike Coolbaugh, Huntsville. **SS**—Miguel Tejada, Huntsville. **OF**—Juan Encarnacion, Jacksonville; Ben Grieve, Huntsville; Mike Neill, Huntsville; Chris Prieto, Mobile; Anthony Sanders, Knoxville. **DH**—Luis Raven, Birmingham. **Util**—Kevin Witt, Knoxville. **LHP**—Scott Eyre, Birmingham. **RHP**—Ken Cloude, Memphis.

Most Valuable Player—Ben Grieve, Huntsville. **Most Outstanding Pitcher**—Scott Eyre, Birmingham. **Manager of the Year**—Randy Ingle, Greenville. **Hustler of the Year**—Brian Simmons, Birmingham.

TOP 10 PROSPECTS

1. Miguel Tejada, ss, Huntsville; **2.** Ben Grieve, of, Huntsville; **3.** Juan Encarnacion, of, Jacksonville; **4.** Kerry Wood, rhp, Orlando; **5.** Chad Hermansen, 2b-of, Carolina; **6.** Kris Benson, rhp, Carolina; **7.** Ken Cloude, rhp, Memphis; **8.** Juan Melo, ss, Mobile; **9.** Kelvim Escobar, rhp, Knoxville; **10.** Kevin Witt, 1b, Knoxville.

DEPT. LEADERS

BATTING

G	Mike Coolbaugh, Huntsville	139
AB	Mike Coolbaugh, Huntsville	559
R	Mike Neill, Huntsville	129
H	D.T. Cromer, Huntsville	176
TB	Mike Coolbaugh, Huntsville	303
XBH	Mike Coolbaugh, Huntsville	69
2B	D.T. Cromer, Huntsville	40
3B	Brian Simmons, Birmingham	12
HR	Three tied at	30
RBI	Mike Coolbaugh, Huntsville	132
SH	Brandon Moore, Birmingham	21
SF	Jason Maxwell, Orlando	9
BB	Brian Simmons, Birmingham	88
IBB	Luis Raven, Birmingham	7
	Kevin Witt, Knoxville	7
HBP	Juan Encarnacion, Jacksonville	19
SO	Chad Hermansen, Carolina	136
SB	Earl Johnson, Mobile/Jack.	42
CS	Marcus Sturdivant, Memphis	17
GIDP	Gabe Alvarez, Mobile	21
OB%	Ben Grieve, Huntsville	.455
SL%	Luis Raven, Birmingham	.612

PITCHING

G	Tom Doyle, Chattanooga	65
GS	Seth Greisinger, Jacksonville	28
CG	Brett Hinchliffe, Memphis	5
ShO	Three tied at	2
GF	Todd Erdos, Mobile	50
SV	Todd Williams, Chattanooga	31
W	Scott Eyre, Birmingham	13
	Russ Herbert, Birmingham	13
L	Willis Roberts, Jacksonville	15
IP	Bill King, Huntsville	176
	Brandon Reed, Jacksonville	176
H	Bill King, Huntsville	216
R	Willis Roberts, Jacksonville	120
ER	Willis Roberts, Jacksonville	104
HR	Seth Greisinger, Jacksonville	29
HB	Matt Drews, Jacksonville	16
BB	Jeff Kelly, Carolina	85
SO	Earl Byrne, Orlando	128
WP	John Rocker, Greenville	17
BK	Earl Byrne, Orlando	7

FIELDING

C	AVG	Clemente Alvarez, Bir.	.998
	PO	Mike Mahoney, Greenville	589
	A	Justin Towle, Chattanooga	68
	E	Four tied at	10
	DP	Kevin Lidle, Jacksonville	8
	PB	Justin Towle, Chattanooga	18
1B	AVG	Randy Jorgensen, Memphis	.990
	PO	D.T. Cromer, Huntsville	1167
	A	Jesse Ibarra, Jacksonville	104
	E	D.T. Cromer, Huntsville	18
	DP	D.T. Cromer, Huntsville	129
2B	AVG	Chris Wimmer, Orlando	.982
	PO	Richard Almanzar, Jack.	237
		Mike Eaglin, Greenville	237
	A	Mike Eaglin, Greenville	306
	E	Mike Eaglin, Greenville	22
	DP	Richard Almanzar, Jack.	85
3B	AVG	Mike Coolbaugh, Huntsville	.943
	PO	Mike Coolbaugh, Huntsville	94
	A	Mike Coolbaugh, Huntsville	302
	E	Gabe Alvarez, Mobile	32
	DP	Mike Coolbaugh, Huntsville	35
SS	AVG	Brandon Moore, Birmingham	.960
	PO	Miguel Tejada, Huntsville	229
	A	Miguel Tejada, Huntsville	423
	E	Miguel Tejada, Huntsville	36
	DP	Miguel Tejada, Huntsville	97
OF	AVG	Chris Prieto, Mobile	.991
	PO	Brian Simmons, Birmingham	322
	A	Charles Peterson, Carolina	17
	E	Four tied at	8
	DP	Charles Peterson, Carolina	6

TEXAS LEAGUE

Missions prevail in series featuring drama, low scores

BY GEORGE SCHROEDER

If you wanted drama, the 1997 Texas League playoffs were chock full. The two best teams produced five shutouts in seven games.

San Antonio and Shreveport each swept the two half-season championships, thus eliminating the need for a first round of playoffs. But the TL championship series compensated.

After blowing a 3-0 series lead, San Antonio won its first league championship since 1964, a drought that spanned six major league affiliations. Fittingly, the final victory was a 2-0 pitching gem.

"You go up 3-0 on a team and I think you get a little flat," Missions outfielder Kevin Gibbs said. "After it got to 3-2, we started to feel the heat a little. But we felt from start to finish we had the best team, and we were able to prove it."

MEL BAILEY

Starter who finishes
Steve Woodard

Led by a dominant pitching staff, the Missions ran away with the Western Division first-half title. Four starters were promoted, but the Missions regrouped late and overtook El Paso for the second-half crown.

A veteran Shreveport club won both halves on the last day. The Captains edged Arkansas by half a game for the Eastern Division's first-half crown, then beat Tulsa for the second-half title.

San Antonio held Shreveport to one run in winning the first three games, all in San Antonio. The Missions pitched two straight shutouts, then won the third game 2-1 on J.P. Roberge's ninth-inning home run.

When the scene shifted to Shreveport, the Captains reversed the roles, winning Games Four, Five and Six with two shutouts and an eighth-inning rally. But San Antonio won Game Seven when lefthander Will Brunson and righthander Jeff Kubenka combined for another shutout.

STANDINGS: SPLIT SEASON

FIRST HALF					SECOND HALF				
EAST	W	L	PCT	GB	EAST	W	L	PCT	GB
Shreveport	37	30	.552	—	Shreveport	39	32	.549	—
Arkansas	37	31	.544	½	Tulsa	38	34	.528	1½
Jackson	32	36	.471	5½	Jackson	34	37	.479	5
Tulsa	23	44	.338	14	Arkansas	31	41	.431	8½
WEST	W	L	PCT	GB	WEST	W	L	PCT	GB
San Antonio	44	23	.657	—	San Antonio	40	32	.556	—
El Paso	35	33	.515	9½	El Paso	39	33	.542	1
Midland	32	35	.478	12	Wichita	34	38	.472	6
Wichita	30	38	.441	14½	Midland	32	40	.444	8

PLAYOFFS—Finals: San Antonio defeated Shreveport 4-3, in best-of-7 series.

El Paso righthander Steve Woodard went 14-3 and pitched six complete games in 19 starts. He finished the season in the majors with the Brewers, going 3-3 in seven starts.

Tulsa outfielder Dan Collier broke a league record and tied a minor league record in mid-June when he hit home runs in seven straight games. Earlier, Jackson first baseman Daryle Ward had tied the old league record by homering in six straight games.

The Texas League experienced a 5 percent drop in average attendance, and a 7.2 percent drop overall. Seven of the league's eight teams drew fewer fans.

But TL president Tom Kayser blamed most of the decline on poor weather. The league lost 38 dates to rain or snow.

Kayser contended the actual attendance drop would have been 1-3 percent if not for the weather, but noted attendance was down 15 percent from the TL's best year, 1994, when 2,108,405 fans clicked through turnstiles.

A year after he sold his team, Jim Paul left the ballpark.

Paul, who turned the El Paso Diablos into a winner with his innovative promotional and marketing schemes, continued to function as the Diablos president and CEO in 1997 after selling the club to Diamond Sports Inc.

But Paul ended a 24-year run with the Diablos when he was named athletic director at New Mexico State University in nearby Las Cruces.

STANDINGS: OVERALL

Page		W	L	PCT	GB	Manager(s)	Attendance/Dates	Last Penn.
142	El Paso Diablos (Brewers)	76	63	.547	—	Dave Machemer	302,894 (68)	1994
222	Tulsa Drillers (Rangers)	75	64	.540	1	Bobby Jones	333,019 (66)	1988
206	Shreveport Captains (Giants)	73	66	.525	3	Carlos Lezcano	164,922 (64)	1995
128	Wichita Wranglers (Royals)	70	70	.500	6½	Ron Johnson	152,205 (60)	1992
122	Jackson Generals (Astros)	70	70	.500	6½	Dave Engle	160,587 (67)	1996
134	San Antonio Missions (Dodgers)	69	70	.496	7	John Shelby	336,542 (63)	None
194	Arkansas Travelers (Cardinals)	67	73	.479	9½	Rick Mahler	195,935 (58)	1989
50	Midland Angels (Angels)	58	82	.414	18½	Mitch Seoane	185,532 (65)	1975

NOTE: Team's individual batting and pitching statistics can be found on page indicated in lefthand column.

1997 Texas League Statistics

CLUB BATTING

	AVG	G	AB	R	H	2B	3B	HR	BB	SO	SB
El Paso	.309	140	4822	851	1489	300	76	111	410	881	139
San Antonio	.283	139	4548	736	1289	245	49	105	452	773	161
Midland	.282	139	4687	792	1324	315	43	134	515	841	70
Shreveport	.278	138	4610	735	1282	249	47	111	518	821	133
Wichita	.275	140	4658	723	1282	240	21	111	465	824	121
Arkansas	.271	140	4565	643	1238	208	35	61	447	753	111
Tulsa	.268	139	4619	712	1237	272	24	149	532	1025	66
Jackson	.266	139	4583	638	1220	210	18	112	488	844	85

CLUB PITCHING

	ERA	G	CG	SHO	SV	IP	H	R	ER	BB	SO
San Antonio	3.97	139	11	11	34	1183	1166	592	522	438	901
Arkansas	4.09	140	5	9	35	1184	1221	639	539	469	868
Shreveport	4.23	138	5	7	39	1188	1195	651	558	514	743
Jackson	4.54	139	3	0	37	1206	1282	722	608	523	939
Tulsa	4.64	139	14	5	16	1175	1252	727	606	445	850
El Paso	4.99	140	14	7	29	1195	1439	797	663	455	800
Wichita	5.15	140	5	3	32	1190	1370	781	681	477	815
Midland	6.04	139	18	2	35	1192	1436	921	801	506	846

CLUB FIELDING

	PCT	PO	A	E	DP
San Antonio	.976	3550	1578	127	122
Arkansas	.976	3553	1535	127	157
Shreveport	.972	3563	1623	151	149
Midland	.968	3576	1634	175	141
Jackson	.966	3617	1523	183	128
Tulsa	.965	3525	1462	179	104
Wichita	.965	3570	1524	186	129
El Paso	.962	3585	1668	207	148

INDIVIDUAL BATTING LEADERS

(Minimum 378 Plate Appearances)

	AVG	G	AB	R	H	2B	3B	HR	RBI	BB	SO	SB
Kinkade, Mike, El Paso	.385	125	468	112	180	35	12	12	109	52	66	17
Krause, Scott, El Paso	.361	125	474	97	171	33	11	16	88	20	108	13
Gibbs, Kevin, San Antonio	.335	101	358	89	120	21	6	2	34	72	48	49
Klassen, Danny, El Paso	.331	135	519	112	172	30	6	14	81	48	104	16
Burke, Jamie, Midland	.329	116	428	77	141	44	3	6	72	40	46	2
Ward, Daryle, Jackson	.329	114	422	72	139	25	0	19	90	46	68	4
Guiel, Aaron, Midland	.329	116	419	91	138	37	7	22	85	59	94	14
LoDuca, Paul, San Antonio	.327	105	385	63	126	28	2	7	69	46	27	16
Mendez, Carlos, Wicihta	.325	129	507	72	165	32	1	12	90	19	43	4
Roberge, J.P., San Antonio	.322	134	516	94	166	26	4	17	105	39	70	18

INDIVIDUAL PITCHING LEADERS

(Minimum 112 Innings)

	W	L	ERA	G	GS	CG	SV	IP	H	R	ER	BB	SO
Brohawn, Troy, Shreveport	13	5	2.56	26	26	1	0	169	148	57	48	64	98
Woodard, Steve, El Paso	14	3	3.17	19	19	6	0	136	136	56	48	25	97
Elarton, Scott, Jackson	7	4	3.24	20	20	2	0	133	103	57	48	47	141
Flores, Ignacio, San Antonio	10	7	3.25	27	18	0	1	133	125	59	48	39	102
Oropesa, Eddie, Shreveport	7	7	3.92	43	9	1	0	124	122	58	54	64	65
Silva, Ted, Tulsa	13	10	4.09	26	25	4	0	172	178	88	78	42	121
Logan, Marcus, Arkansas	11	7	4.12	27	25	1	0	153	152	75	70	64	101
Smith, Travis, El Paso	16	3	4.15	28	28	5	0	184	210	106	85	58	107
Heiserman, Rick, Arkansas	5	8	4.17	34	20	1	4	132	151	73	61	36	90
Stein, Blake, Arkansas	8	7	4.24	22	22	1	0	134	128	67	63	49	114

ALL-STAR TEAM

C—Paul LoDuca, San Antonio. **1B**—Daryle Ward, Jackson. **2B**—Placido Polanco, Arkansas. **3B**—Mike Kinkade, El Paso; Fernando Tatis, Tulsa. **SS**—Danny Klassen, El Paso. **OF**—Kevin Gibbs, San Antonio; Scott Krause, El Paso; Kerry Robinson, Arkansas; Keith Williams, Shreveport. **DH**—Dan Collier, Tulsa. **SP**—Troy Brohawn, Shreveport; Enrique Calero, Wichita; Scott Elarton, Jackson; Travis Smith, El Paso; Steve Woodard, El Paso. **RP**—Bob Howry, Shreveport.

Player of the Year—Mike Kinkade, El Paso. **Pitcher of the Year**—Steve Woodard, El Paso. **Manager of the Year**—Ron Roenicke, San Antonio.

TOP 10 PROSPECTS

1. Fernando Tatis, 3b, Tulsa; **2.** Scott Elarton, rhp, Jackson; **3.** Daryle Ward, 1b, Jackson; **4.** Dennis Reyes, lhp, San Antonio; **5.** Steve Woodard, rhp, El Paso; **6.** Matt Perisho, lhp, Midland; **7.** Joe Fontenot, rhp, Shreveport; **8.** Mike Kinkade, 3b, El Paso; **9.** Curtis King, rhp, Arkansas; **10.** Kevin Gibbs, of, San Antonio.

DEPT. LEADERS

BATTING

G	Andrew Vessel, Tulsa	138
AB	Kerry Robinson, Arkansas	523
R	Mike Kinkade, El Paso	112
	Danny Klassen, El Paso	112
H	Mike Kinkade, El Paso	180
TB	Mike Kinkade, El Paso	275
	Keith Williams, Shreveport	275
XBH	Three tied at	66
2B	Darrell Nicholas, El Paso	47
3B	Brian Richardson, San Antonio	13
HR	Dan Collier, Tulsa	26
RBI	Mike Kinkade, El Paso	109
SH	Donovan Mitchell, Jackson	12
SF	Chris Singleton, Shreveport	9
BB	Benji Simonton, Shreveport	81
IBB	Ten tied at	4
HBP	Aaron Guiel, Midland	18
SO	Jason Herrick, Midland	141
SB	Calvin Murray, Shreveport	52
CS	Kerry Robinson, Arkansas	23
GIDP	Carlos Mendez, Wichita	19
	Luis Ordaz, Arkansas	19
OB%	Mike Kinkade, El Paso	.455
SL%	Aaron Guiel, Midland	.609

PITCHING

G	Stephen Prihoda, Wichita	70
GS	Jarrod Washburn, Midland	29
CG	Steve Woodard, El Paso	6
ShO	Thirteen tied at	1
GF	Bob Howry, Shreveport	39
SV	Bob Howry, Shreveport	22
W	Travis Smith, El Paso	16
L	Jim Brower, Tulsa	12
	Jarrod Washburn, Midland	12
IP	Jarrod Washburn, Midland	189
H	Jarrod Washburn, Midland	211
R	Jarrod Washburn, Midland	115
ER	Jarrod Washburn, Midland	101
HR	Jarrod Washburn, Midland	23
HB	Joe Fontenot, Shreveport	12
BB	Darin Blood, Shreveport	83
SO	Jarrod Washburn, Midland	146
WP	Scott Gardner, El Paso	17
BK	Eddie Oropesa, Shreveport	6

FIELDING

C	AVG	Paul LoDuca, San Antonio	.990
	PO	Bill Dobrolsky, El Paso	585
	A	Paul LoDuca, San Antonio	84
	E	Hector Ortiz, Wichita	15
	DP	Bill Dobrolsky, El Paso	9
	PB	Bill Dobrolsky, El Paso	15
1B	AVG	Danny Buxbaum, Midland	.991
	PO	Andy Barkett, Tulsa	1114
	A	Danny Buxbaum, Midland	92
	E	Andy Barkett, Tulsa	15
	DP	Benji Simonton, Shreveport	110
2B	AVG	Placido Polanco, Arkansas	.979
	PO	Mickey Lopez, El Paso	290
	A	Placido Polanco, Arkansas	425
	E	Edwin Diaz, Tulsa	19
	DP	Mickey Lopez, El Paso	110
		Placido Polanco, Arkansas	110
3B	AVG	Brian Richardson, San Ant.	.945
	PO	Mike Kinkade, El Paso	79
	A	Brian Richardson, San Ant.	267
	E	Mike Kinkade, El Paso	60
	DP	Jamie Burke, Midland	20
SS	AVG	Alex Cora, San Antonio	.968
	PO	Alex Cora, San Antonio	197
	A	Alex Cora, San Antonio	412
	E	Danny Klassen, El Paso	50
	DP	Alex Cora, San Antonio	88
OF	AVG	Greg Martinez, El Paso	.995
	PO	Chris Singleton, Shreveport	253
	A	Armando Rios, Shreveport	17
	E	Raul Gonzalez, Wichita	14
	DP	Three tied at	4

CALIFORNIA LEAGUE

Expansion Diamondbacks have their first title already

BY JOE CHRISTENSEN

Most of them were castoffs. Baseball's throwaways.

The 1997 High Desert Mavericks were a collection of a few Diamondbacks prospects and several other players who had been released or traded by other organizations.

In the end, they dominated their way to the California League championship, winning all six playoff games after finishing with a league-best record of 83-57.

MEL BAILEY

Too good to stay
Ramon Hernanadez

In its first year as an Arizona affiliate, High Desert won the organization's first championship.

"Sure it's special," said Diamondbacks general manager Joe Garagiola Jr., the night the Mavericks completed a three-game sweep of San Bernardino for the title. "This is a special group of guys. Every one of these guys is a good story."

With High Desert trailing 2-0 in Game Three, Stanton Cameron, a 28-year-old player-coach, hit a three-run homer in the sixth inning that held up for a 3-2 victory.

"It's something you dream about as a little kid," said Cameron, who was released by the Royals in 1996. Cameron tied High Desert teammate Mike Stoner and Bakersfield's Mike Glendenning for the league lead with 33 home runs.

Stoner, who batted .358 with 33 homers and 142 RBIs, was a near-unanimous choice as league MVP. The 24-year-old outfielder was also named the league's rookie of the year.

The Diamondbacks didn't have a team above Class A, so it was tough for Mavericks to earn promotions. The exceptions were first baseman Travis Lee, the league's top prospect, and Mark Davis, the 1989 National League Cy Young Award winner. The Diamondbacks loaned both of them to the Brewers so they could play at Triple-A Tucson.

Lee batted .363 with 18 homers before leaving for Tucson prior to the all-star break.

Another top prospect, Visalia catcher Ramon Hernandez, earned a promotion after an outstanding start. He batted .361 with 15 homers and 85 RBIs before leaving for Double-A Huntsville.

San Bernardino won the first-half Freeway Division title and tied for last place in the second half. Manager Del Crandall resigned in the middle of a 13-game losing streak, saying he wasn't having fun anymore. Coach Dino Ebel took over, and the Stampede knocked off Visalia and Rancho Cucamonga to get to the championship series.

The league again broke its attendance record, drawing 2,061,889 fans, as San Bernardino played its first full season in its new stadium. The 1997 season marked the first time since 1982 that every Cal League team had a full affiliation with a major league club.

There were no affiliation changes or franchise relocations expected for 1998. It could be the first year since 1974 that every Cal League franchise has the same affiliation and location as the year before.

STANDINGS: SPLIT SEASON

FIRST HALF					SECOND HALF				
VALLEY	**W**	**L**	**PCT**	**GB**	**VALLEY**	**W**	**L**	**PCT**	**GB**
Stockton	40	30	.571	—	High Desert	45	25	.643	—
High Desert	38	32	.543	2	Modesto	42	29	.592	3½
Lancaster	33	37	.471	7	Lancaster	42	29	.592	3½
Modesto	32	38	.457	8	Stockton	30	40	.429	15
San Jose	30	40	.429	10	San Jose	30	40	.429	15
FREEWAY	**W**	**L**	**PCT**	**GB**	**FREEWAY**	**W**	**L**	**PCT**	**GB**
San Bernardino	40	30	.571	—	R. Cucamonga	39	31	.557	—
R. Cucamonga	38	32	.543	2	Visalia	36	34	.514	3
Visalia	35	35	.500	5	Bakersfield	31	39	.443	8
Lake Elsinore	33	37	.471	7	San Bernardino	28	42	.400	11
Bakersfield	31	39	.443	9	Lake Elsinore	28	42	.400	11

PLAYOFFS—First Round: San Bernardino defeated Visalia 2-0, and Lancaster defeated Stockton 2-1, in best-of-3 series. **Semifinals:** San Bernardino defeated Rancho Cucamonga 3-2 and High Desert defeated Lancaster 3-0, in best-of-5 series. **Finals:** High Desert defeated San Bernardino 3-0, in best-of-5 series.

STANDINGS: OVERALL

Page		W	L	PCT	GB	Manager(s)	Attendance/Dates	Last Penn.
55	High Desert Mavericks (D'backs)	83	57	.593	—	Chris Speier	157,605 (68)	1997
201	Rancho Cucamonga Quakes (Padres)	77	63	.550	6	Mike Basso	404,525 (70)	1994
213	Lancaster JetHawks (Mariners)	75	66	.532	8½	Rick Burleson	298,465 (70)	None
176	Modesto A's (Athletics)	74	67	.525	9½	Jeffrey Leonard	140,861 (65)	1984
176	Visalia Oaks (Athletics)	71	69	.507	12	Tony DeFrancesco	80,078 (70)	1978
142	Stockton Ports (Brewers)	70	70	.500	13	Greg Mahlberg	101,254 (68)	1992
135	San Bernardino Stampede (Dodgers)	68	72	.486	15	Del Crandall/Dino Ebel	273,739 (70)	1995
208	Bakersfield Blaze (Giants)	62	78	.443	21	Glenn Tufts/Keith Bodie	117,818 (70)	1989
51	Lake Elsinore Storm (Angels)	61	79	.436	22	Don Long	341,393 (70)	1996
208	San Jose Giants (Giants)	60	80	.429	23	Frank Cacciatore	146,151 (69)	1979

NOTE: Team's individual batting and pitching statistics can be found on page indicated in lefthand column.

1997 California League Statistics

CLUB BATTING

	AVG	G	AB	R	H	2B	3B	HR	BB	SO	SB
High Desert	.286	140	4933	890	1411	274	40	165	606	1055	79
R. Cucamonga	.276	140	4914	783	1354	298	37	124	516	1077	95
Lancaster	.271	141	4873	842	1319	282	60	161	584	1146	101
Stockton	.267	140	4762	622	1272	251	48	72	393	1000	151
San Bernardino	.266	140	4727	748	1256	290	57	123	489	1098	195
San Jose	.266	140	4736	656	1258	241	40	79	530	964	150
Visalia	.265	140	4772	763	1264	246	36	116	615	1065	157
Lake Elsinore	.263	140	4759	703	1250	265	57	104	460	1105	250
Bakersfield	.262	140	4825	678	1264	229	28	123	428	1023	61
Modesto	.259	141	4704	769	1218	277	50	148	609	1238	137

CLUB PITCHING

	ERA	G	CG	SHO	SV	IP	H	R	ER	BB	SO
R. Cucamonga	4.08	140	3	12	35	1247	1156	683	566	556	1292
Modesto	4.14	141	3	4	33	1234	1309	737	568	466	1076
Stockton	4.28	140	9	9	38	1243	1207	672	591	576	953
San Jose	4.44	140	4	8	35	1232	1314	706	608	483	1210
High Desert	4.52	140	2	5	34	1251	1300	766	629	438	984
Lake Elsinore	4.53	140	6	4	29	1248	1327	758	628	437	998
San Bernardino	4.74	140	3	9	35	1239	1218	760	652	630	1097
Lancaster	4.74	141	3	4	37	1256	1341	773	661	518	1130
Visalia	4.89	140	2	3	38	1244	1355	809	676	572	1058
Bakersfield	4.90	140	3	10	35	1234	1339	790	671	554	973

CLUB FIELDING

	PCT	PO	A	E	DP
Stockton	.973	3730	1567	148	125
San Bern.	.970	3716	1519	163	112
Bakersfield	.969	3701	1742	175	160
R. Cuca.	.969	3741	1425	168	107
Lancaster	.968	3767	1446	171	113
High Desert	.967	3753	1616	183	104
San Jose	.967	3695	1494	179	116
Lake Elsinore	.967	3745	1609	185	106
Visalia	.963	3732	1584	207	92
Modesto	.958	3701	1534	227	135

INDIVIDUAL BATTING LEADERS

(Minimum 378 Plate Appearances)

	AVG	G	AB	R	H	2B	3B	HR	RBI	BB	SO	SB
Hernandez, Ramon, Visalia	.361	86	332	57	120	21	2	15	85	35	47	2
Stoner, Mike, High Desert	.358	136	567	115	203	44	5	33	142	36	91	6
Mitchell, Mike, RC	.350	109	440	78	154	36	1	17	106	35	83	2
Wilson, Todd, San Jose	.345	130	502	66	173	35	3	5	88	32	60	7
Darr, Mike, Rancho Cuca.	.344	134	521	104	179	32	11	15	94	57	90	23
Shockey, Greg, Rancho Cuca.	.339	103	401	60	136	28	4	14	78	36	67	0
Caruso, Mike, San Jose	.333	108	441	76	147	24	11	2	50	38	19	11
Bowles, Justin, Modesto	.327	107	394	66	129	39	9	7	51	56	85	6
Tyler, Josh, Stockton	.310	114	416	63	129	28	4	4	46	20	54	21
Hinch, A.J., Modesto	.309	95	333	70	103	25	3	20	73	42	68	8

INDIVIDUAL PITCHING LEADERS

(Minimum 112 Innings)

	W	L	ERA	G	GS	CG	SV	IP	H	R	ER	BB	SO
Lilly, Ted, San Bernardino	7	8	2.81	23	21	2	0	135	116	52	42	32	158
Fieldbinder, Mick, Stockton	11	6	2.83	21	21	4	0	143	141	58	45	38	68
Laxton, Brett, Visalia	11	5	2.99	29	22	0	0	139	141	62	46	50	121
Leese, Brandon, San Jose	7	5	3.05	19	19	0	0	112	99	44	38	46	99
Williams, Jeff, San Bern.	10	4	3.10	18	18	0	0	116	101	52	40	34	72
Grote, Jason, Bakersfield	12	8	3.45	25	25	0	0	156	156	77	60	59	116
Wunsch, Kelly, Stockton	7	9	3.46	24	22	2	0	143	141	65	55	62	98
Cooper, Brian, Lake Els.	7	3	3.54	17	17	1	0	117	111	56	46	27	104
Rivette, Scott, Modesto	9	9	3.57	20	20	3	0	126	147	65	50	31	96
Noriega, Ray, Modesto	5	8	4.04	28	28	0	0	156	161	101	70	69	119

ALL-STAR TEAM

C—Ramon Hernandez, Visalia. **1B**—Travis Lee, High Desert. **2B**—Mike Metcalfe, San Bernardino. **3B**—Eric Chavez, Visalia. **SS**—Mike Caruso, San Jose. **OF**—Justin Bowles, Modesto; Stanton Cameron, High Desert; Mike Darr, Rancho Cucamonga; Mike Glendenning, Bakersfield; Mike Stoner, High Desert. **DH**—Mike Mitchell, Rancho Cucamonga. **LHP**—Ted Lilly, San Bernardino. **RHP**—Matt Clement, Rancho Cucamonga; Mick Fieldbinder, Stockton. **RP**—James Sak, Rancho Cucamonga.

Most Valuable Player—Mike Stoner, High Desert. **Pitcher of the Year**—Ted Lilly, San Bernardino. **Rookie of the Year**—Mike Stoner, High Desert. **Manager of the Year**—Chris Speier, High Desert.

TOP 10 PROSPECTS

1. Travis Lee, 1b, High Desert; **2.** Matt Clement, rhp, Rancho Cucamonga; **3.** Ramon Hernandez, c, Visalia; **4.** Ben Davis, c, Rancho Cucamonga; **5.** A.J. Hinch, c, Modesto; **6.** Ted Lilly, lhp, San Bernardino; **7.** Eric Chavez, 3b, Visalia; **8.** Vladimir Nunez, rhp, High Desert; **9.** Mike Caruso, ss, San Jose; **10.** Norm Hutchins, of, Lake Elsinore.

DEPT. LEADERS

BATTING

G	Damon Minor, Bakersfield	140
AB	Tim Garland, San Jose	577
R	Mike Stoner, High Desert	115
H	Mike Stoner, High Desert	203
TB	Mike Stoner, High Desert	356
XBH	Mike Stoner, High Desert	82
2B	Mike Stoner, High Desert	44
3B	Joe Mathis, Lancaster	15
HR	Three tied at	33
RBI	Mike Stoner, High Desert	142
SH	Ben Reynoso, Rancho Cuc.	18
SF	Mike Stoner, High Desert	11
BB	Stanton Cameron, High Desert	93
IBB	Damon Minor, Bakersfield	8
HBP	Toby Kominek, Stockton	24
SO	Jon VanderGriend, Lake Elsin.	153
SB	Justin Baughman, Lake Elsin.	68
CS	Mike Metcalfe, San Bernardino	32
GIDP	Todd Wilson, San Jose	23
OB%	Ramon Hernandez, Visalia	.427
SL%	Mike Stoner, High Desert	.628

PITCHING

G	Mick Pageler, Bakersfield	61
GS	Bill Malloy, Bakersfield	29
CG	Mick Fieldbinder, Stockton	4
ShO	Kelly Wunsch, Stockton	2
	Stevenson Agosto, Rancho Cuc.	2
GF	Mick Pageler, Bakersfield	53
SV	Mick Pageler, Bakersfield	29
W	J.J. Pearsall, San Bernardino	14
	Jeff Sobkoviak, High Desert	14
L	Manuel Bermudez, S.J./Bak.	14
IP	Bill Malloy, Bakersfield	167
H	Bill Malloy, Bakersfield	184
R	Kevin Pincavitch, San Bern.	128
ER	Kevin Pincavitch, San Bern.	102
HR	Vladimir Nunez, High Desert	36
HB	Kevin Pincavitch, San Bern.	19
BB	Kevin Pincavitch, San Bern.	112
SO	Jason Brester, San Jose	172
WP	Kevin Gregg, Visalia	28
BK	Manuel Bermudez, S.J./Bak.	10

FIELDING

C	AVG	A.J. Hinch, Modesto	.996
	PO	Ben Davis, Rancho Cuca.	992
	A	Yorvit Torrealba, Bak.	119
	E	Ramon Hernandez, Visalia	16
	DP	Yorvit Torrealba, Bak.	10
	PB	Angel Pena, San Bern.	31
1B	AVG	Larry Barnes, Lake Els.	.993
	PO	Damon Minor, Bakersfield	1261
	A	Damon Minor, Bakersfield	88
	E	Damon Minor, Bakersfield	22
	DP	Damon Minor, Bakersfield	127
2B	AVG	Mike Metcalfe, San Bern.	.979
	PO	Mike Metcalfe, San Bern.	228
	A	Ernest Spivey, High Desert	394
	E	Ernest Spivey, High Desert	33
	DP	Jon Watson, Bakersfield	80
3B	AVG	Pedro Felix, Bakersfield	.950
	PO	Pedro Felix, Bakersfield	112
	A	Pedro Felix, Bakersfield	322
	E	Eric Chavez, Visalia	32
	DP	Pedro Felix, Bakersfield	39
SS	AVG	Kelly Phair, Stockton	.969
	PO	Justin Baughman, Lake Els.	239
	A	Justin Baughman, Lake Els.	403
	E	Jose Ortiz, Modesto	53
	DP	Jose Ortiz, Modesto	80
OF	AVG	Toby Kominek, Stockton	.996
	PO	Chad Green, Stockton	291
	A	Jeff DaVanon, Visalia	17
	E	Norm Hutchins, Lake Els.	13
		Jon VanderGriend, Lake Els.	13
	DP	Tim Garland, San Jose	6
		Jose Soriano, Modesto	6

CAROLINA LEAGUE

Durham, league's flagship city, moves up to Triple-A

BY JOHN MANUEL

Attention, Carolina League franchises: Durham has left the building.

The league will go on but won't be the same without the Bulls, far and away the league's most recognizable franchise.

Durham spent its last season in the Carolina League in 1997, and will move on to the Triple-A International League in 1998 as an affiliate of the Tampa Bay Devil Rays.

"We feel that we have a strong league, and Durham provided a presence and an aura to it," league president John Hopkins said. "They have been a major contributor to that strength, so we'll miss them."

JOHN SPEAR

Fierce Hillcat
Aramis Ramirez

The Braves' Class A affiliate in the Carolina League will have a new home in Myrtle Beach, S.C., after a season in Danville, Va.

In their swan song, the Bulls were barely competitive but led the league in attendance for the third straight year at Durham Bulls Athletic Park, averaging 5,612 fans a game.

At the other end of the attendance ladder were the Lynchburg Hillcats, who averaged 1,652 fans a game. The Hillcats were at the other end of the spectrum from the Bulls on the field as well.

Lynchburg was one of just two clubs with a winning overall record. Kinston was the other, and the two teams met in the championship series. The Hillcats came away with the Mills Cup, winning the series three games to one.

While the Hillcats' strength was their young prospects, such as righthander Bronson Arroyo, outfielder Alex Hernandez and third baseman Aramis Ramirez, the hero of the championship series was 24-year-old righthander David Daniels.

Daniels earned four saves in the postseason, with the biggest one coming in Game Four of the title series. Daniels got the season's final two outs with the bases loaded, saving a 3-2 win and the championship.

Lynchburg lost its manager, Jeff Banister, at midseason. Banister was promoted to Double-A Carolina and replaced by Jeff Richardson, who started the year at Class A Augusta of the South Atlantic League.

Richardson inherited Ramirez, who overcame a sluggish start to earn the league's MVP award and was voted the league's No. 3 prospect. Just 19, Ramirez led the league in home runs and RBIs and finished the season hitting .278 after hitting .180 over the first six weeks.

Kinston slugged its way to titles in both halves in the Southern Division with 185 homers.

Outfielder Danny Peoples, the Indians' first-round pick in 1996, led the team with 34 homers. Third baseman Russell Branyan, voted the league's top prospect, clubbed 27 in 297 at-bats before being promoted to Double-A Akron.

Lynchburg swept Frederick in the playoffs' only semifinal series.

The franchise will move into a new ballpark in Myrtle Beach in 1999 after one season as the Danville 97s. The 97s will share Dan Daniel Park with Danville's Appalachian League franchise.

Part of Durham's sendoff included hosting the second Carolina League-California League all-star game. After an embarrassing tie in the first installment in 1996, the Cal League got the win in 1997, 6-5.

STANDINGS: SPLIT SEASON

FIRST HALF

NORTH	W	L	PCT	GB
Frederick	45	25	.643	—
Lynchburg	40	30	.571	5
Wilmington	34	36	.486	11
Prince William	30	39	.435	14½
SOUTH	**W**	**L**	**PCT**	**GB**
Kinston	46	24	.657	—
Durham	30	39	.435	15½
Salem	27	41	.397	18
Winston-Salem	26	44	.371	20

SECOND HALF

NORTH	W	L	PCT	GB
Lynchburg	42	28	.600	—
Prince William	39	31	.557	3
Wilmington	28	42	.400	14
Frederick	24	46	.343	18
SOUTH	**W**	**L**	**PCT**	**GB**
Kinston	41	29	.586	—
Winston-Salem	37	33	.529	4
Salem	36	34	.514	5
Durham	33	37	.471	8

PLAYOFFS—Semifinals: Lynchburg defeated Frederick 2-0, in best-of-5 series. **Finals:** Lynchburg defeated Kinston 3-1, in best-of-5 series.

STANDINGS: OVERALL

Page		W	L	PCT	GB	Managers	Attendance/Dates	Last Penn.
99	Kinston Indians (Indians)	87	53	.621	—	Joel Skinner	151,953 (64)	1995
188	Lynchburg Hillcats (Pirates)	82	58	.586	5	Jeff Banister/Jeff Richardson	112,363 (68)	1997
194	Prince William Cannons (Cardinals)	69	70	.496	17½	Roy Silver	214,037 (66)	1989
67	Frederick Keys (Orioles)	69	71	.493	18	Dave Hilton	274,894 (67)	1990
105	Salem Avalanche (Rockies)	63	75	.457	23	Bill McGuire	188,023 (65)	1987
61	Durham Bulls (Braves)	63	76	.453	23½	Paul Runge	381,589 (68)	1967
81	Winston-Salem Warthogs (White Sox)	63	77	.450	24	Mike Heath/Mark Haley	156,285 (68)	1993
129	Wilmington Blue Rocks (Royals)	62	78	.443	25	John Mizerock	326,201 (67)	1996

NOTE: Team's individual batting and pitching statistics can be found on page indicated in lefthand column.

1997 Carolina League Statistics

CLUB BATTING

	AVG	G	AB	R	H	2B	3B	HR	BB	SO	SB
Kinston	.268	140	4715	775	1265	270	26	185	588	1037	92
Lynchburg	.260	140	4670	683	1215	253	38	110	500	1061	147
Prince William	.260	139	4700	689	1221	246	45	91	526	1020	116
Durham	.258	139	4642	657	1199	270	27	112	468	1015	154
Frederick	.256	140	4665	670	1194	248	19	111	534	964	94
Winston-Salem	.254	140	4595	615	1168	268	45	92	465	1045	128
Salem	.244	138	4439	588	1084	227	22	72	467	980	191
Wilmington	.242	140	4591	652	1109	203	29	107	549	1062	147

CLUB PITCHING

	ERA	G	CG	SHO	SV	IP	H	R	ER	BB	SO
Kinston	3.80	140	5	8	47	1219	1114	597	514	470	1046
Lynchburg	3.84	140	9	7	45	1225	1154	607	523	410	1093
Salem	3.89	138	11	12	26	1190	1143	612	515	431	985
Winston-Salem	4.03	140	9	5	34	1198	1081	653	537	567	1075
Prince William	4.26	139	2	7	42	1224	1189	698	579	559	1007
Frederick	4.30	140	4	7	35	1220	1195	706	583	605	1096
Wilmington	4.36	140	1	9	30	1216	1317	701	589	435	856
Durham	4.79	139	1	3	30	1219	1262	755	649	620	1026

CLUB FIELDING

	PCT	PO	A	E	DP		PCT	PO	A	E	DP
Kinston	.975	3656	1508	131	143	Frederick	.967	3661	1461	177	117
Salem	.972	3571	1491	145	103	Win-Salem	.964	3595	1397	188	91
Lynchburg	.970	3674	1539	159	120	Prince William	.964	3672	1428	193	100
Durham	.967	3656	1461	174	96	Wilmington	.962	3649	1698	212	153

INDIVIDUAL BATTING LEADERS

(Minimum 378 Plate Appearances)

	AVG	G	AB	R	H	2B	3B	HR	RBI	BB	SO	SB
Short, Rick, Frederick	.319	126	480	73	153	29	1	10	72	38	44	10
Lee, Carlos, Winston-Salem	.317	139	546	81	173	50	4	17	82	36	65	11
Morgan, Scott, Kinston	.315	95	368	86	116	32	3	23	67	47	87	4
Asche, Mike, Lynchburg	.306	107	409	70	125	34	4	11	70	41	77	33
Wells, Forry, Salem	.299	93	321	58	96	27	3	11	52	48	64	19
Hernandez, Alex, Lynch.	.290	131	520	75	151	37	4	5	68	27	140	13
Stumberger, Darren, Kinston	.283	133	502	72	142	30	0	15	79	60	88	1
Johnson, Adam, Durham	.281	133	502	80	141	39	3	26	92	50	94	18
Ramirez, Aramis, Lynchburg	.278	137	482	85	134	24	2	29	114	80	103	5
Gomez, Ramon, Win.-Salem	.277	118	477	78	132	23	12	2	42	42	132	53

INDIVIDUAL PITCHING LEADERS

(Minimum 112 Innings)

	W	L	ERA	G	GS	CG	SV	IP	H	R	ER	BB	SO
Politte, Cliff, Pr. William	11	1	2.24	19	19	0	0	120	89	37	30	31	118
Crowell, Jim, Kinston	9	4	2.37	17	17	0	0	114	96	41	30	26	94
Kusiewicz, Mike, Salem	8	6	2.52	19	18	1	0	118	99	44	33	32	107
Martinez, Willie, Kinston	8	2	3.09	23	23	1	0	137	125	61	47	42	120
Jimenez, Jose, Pr. William	9	7	3.09	24	24	2	0	146	128	73	50	42	81
Arroyo, Bronson, Lynch.	12	4	3.31	24	24	3	0	160	154	69	59	33	121
Estes, Eric, Frederick	9	8	3.47	26	25	1	0	148	142	70	57	30	124
Atkins, Ross, Kinston	8	4	3.62	27	16	0	0	117	98	53	47	62	84
Phillips, Jason, Lynch.	11	6	3.76	23	23	2	0	139	129	66	58	35	140
Randall, Scott, Salem	9	10	3.84	27	26	2	0	176	167	93	75	66	128

ALL-STAR TEAM

C—Heath Hayes, Kinston; Ben Petrick, Salem. **1B**—Nate Dishington, Prince William. **2B**—Rick Short, Frederick. **3B**—Aramis Ramirez, Lynchburg. **SS**—John McDonald, Kinston. **OF**—Adam Johnson, Durham; Scott Morgan, Kinston; Danny Peoples, Kinston. **DH**—Russ Branyan, Kinston. **Util**—Carlos Lee, Winston-Salem; Mark Quinn, Wilmington. **SP**—Cliff Politte, Prince William. **RP**—Armando Almanza, Prince William.

Most Valuable Player—Aramis Ramirez, Lynchburg. **Pitcher of the Year**—Cliff Politte, Prince William. **Manager of the Year**—Joel Skinner, Kinston.

TOP 10 PROSPECTS

1. Russ Branyan, 3b, Kinston; **2.** Kris Benson, rhp, Lynchburg; **3.** Aramis Ramirez, 3b, Lynchburg; **4.** Braden Looper, rhp, Prince William; **5.** Abraham Nunez, ss, Lynchburg; **6.** Carlos Lee, 3b, Winston-Salem; **7.** Ben Petrick, c, Salem; **8.** George Lombard, of, Durham; **9.** Willie Martinez, rhp, Kinston; **10.** Bronson Arroyo, rhp, Lynchburg.

DEPT. LEADERS

BATTING

G	Carlos Lee, Winston-Salem	139
AB	Carlos Lee, Winston-Salem	546
R	Scott Morgan, Kinston	86
H	Carlos Lee, Winston-Salem	173
TB	Carlos Lee, Winston-Salem	282
XBH	Carlos Lee, Winston-Salem	71
2B	Carlos Lee, Winston-Salem	50
3B	Ramon Gomez, Winston-Salem	12
HR	Danny Peoples, Kinston	34
RBI	Aramis Ramirez, Lynchburg	114
SH	Elvis Pena, Salem	14
SF	Adam Johnson, Durham	16
BB	Mark Johnson, Winston-Salem	106
IBB	Nate Dishington, Prince William	11
HBP	Craig Wilson, Lynchburg	15
SO	Gary Coffee, Wilmington	157
SB	Ramon Gomez, Winston-Salem	53
CS	Ramon Gomez, Winston-Salem	21
GIDP	Rick Short, Frederick	20
OB%	Mark Johnson, Winson-Sal.	.420
SL%	Scott Morgan, Kinston	.606

PITCHING

G	Three tied at	58
GS	Clint Weibl, Prince William	29
CG	Tom Stepka, Salem	4
ShO	Tom Stepka, Salem	3
GF	Armando Almanza, Pr. William	47
SV	Armando Almanza, Pr. William	36
W	Bronson Arroyo, Lynchburg	12
	Clint Weibl, Prince William	12
L	Tom Stepka, Salem	14
IP	Tom Stepka, Salem	182
H	Tom Stepka, Salem	205
R	Dan Reed, Frederick	104
ER	John Ambrose, Winston-Salem	91
HR	Tom Stepka, Salem	25
HB	Jarrod Mays, Kinston	13
BB	John Ambrose, Winston-Salem	117
SO	Carlos Chantres, Win.-Salem	158
WP	Francisco Saneaux, Frederick	24
BK	John Ambrose, Winston-Salem	5
	Todd Thorn, Wilmington	5

FIELDING

C	AVG	Mark Johnson, Win-Salem	.989
	PO	Mark Johnson, Win-Salem	899
	A	Pascual Matos, Durham	109
	E	Pascual Matos, Durham	13
	DP	Mark Johnson, Win-Salem	8
		Pascual Matos, Durham	8
	PB	Pascual Matos, Durham	26
1B	AVG	Darren Stumberger, Kin.	.994
	PO	Darren Stumberger, Kin.	1137
	A	Darren Stumberger, Kin.	108
	E	Gary Coffee, Wilmington	23
	DP	Gary Coffee, Wilmington	125
		Darren Stumberger, Kin.	125
2B	AVG	Vicente Garcia, Salem	.970
	PO	Jose Delgado, Durham	223
	A	Carlos Febles, Wilmington	355
	E	Carlos Febles, Wilmington	23
	DP	Carlos Febles, Wilmington	85
3B	AVG	Chris Haas, Prince William	.935
	PO	Carlos Lee, Winston-Salem	93
	A	Aramis Ramirez, Lynchburg	265
	E	Aramis Ramirez, Lynchburg	39
	DP	Sean McNally, Wilmington	24
SS	AVG	John McDonald, Kinston	.961
	PO	John McDonald, Kinston	209
	A	John McDonald, Kinston	413
	E	Alejandro Prieto, Wilmington	37
	DP	John McDonald, Kinston	105
OF	AVG	Carlos Akins, Frederick	.990
	PO	George Lombard, Durham	270
	A	Alex Hernandez, Lynch	15
	E	Ramon Gomez, Winston-Salem	14
	DP	Jerry Whittaker, Winston-Salem	4

FLORIDA STATE LEAGUE

Artful Dodger Adrian Beltre dominates league all season

BY SEAN KERNAN

Years from now, the 1997 Florida State League season may be remembered as the summer of Beltre–Dodgers prospect Adrian Beltre.

The Vero Beach third baseman, 19, was the star of the league, battling for the triple crown with league highs of 26 home runs and 104 RBIs to go with a fourth-best average of .317.

"There was no room for advancement, and he actually benefited from playing the whole year here," said Vero Beach manager John Shoemaker, who also watched the Dominican in 1996 when he was the South Atlantic League's top prospect. "He was able to show he could be consistent even when teams tried to make adjustments. He became a more patient, better hitter."

JOHN SPEAR

Vero Beach belter
Adrian Beltre

The Dodgers weren't in a rush to move the 5-foot-11, 203-pound hitter who was a unanimous choice as the league's top prospect and MVP. His tools–all but speed are well above average–make him the typical "can't-miss" prospect.

The St. Petersburg Devil Rays gave the expansion organization its first title, winning the championship series three games to two over Vero Beach.

The Devil Rays got a 5-1 decision in Game Five, played at Al Lang Stadium in St. Petersburg. First baseman Roberto Colina, who batted .360 with three homers and a postseason-high eight RBIs, and center fielder Jim Buccheri each knocked in two runs.

Righthander Mickey Callaway went 5⅓ innings for the win, striking out five Dodgers.

The Devil Rays won the Western Division in the first half and knocked out the Lakeland Tigers, winners of the second half, in two games, 15-5 and 3-0.

The highest team in the Devil Rays' two-year-old farm system, St. Pete boasted an experienced club. Four players were on Triple-A rosters in 1996 and, counting the 1997 season, 17 of the 24 players on its postseason roster had four years or more of professional experience.

"The front office did a great job of building a team that could be competitive right away," said St. Pete manager Bill Evers during a champagne-spraying celebration on the Al Lang Stadium field. "It was our job to go out and do it, and these guys deserve credit."

The Dodgers defeated the Kissimmee Cobras, an Astros farm club, 2-1 in a three-game set to decide the FSL East winner.

STANDINGS: SPLIT SEASON

FIRST HALF

EAST	W	L	PCT	GB
Vero Beach	38	31	.551	—
West Palm	34	34	.500	3½
Brevard County	33	35	.485	4½
St. Lucie	28	39	.418	9
Daytona	29	41	.414	9½
Kissimmee	28	40	.412	9½
WEST	**W**	**L**	**PCT**	**GB**
St. Petersburg	42	26	.618	—
Tampa	41	26	.612	½
Fort Myers	41	28	.594	1½
Lakeland	38	32	.543	5
Sarasota	34	34	.500	8
Dunedin	32	38	.457	11
Clearwater	31	38	.449	11½
Charlotte	31	38	.449	11½

SECOND HALF

EAST	W	L	PCT	GB
Kissimmee	43	26	.623	—
Daytona	36	32	.529	6½
West Palm	35	32	.522	7
Vero Beach	32	36	.471	10½
Brevard County	29	41	.414	14½
St. Lucie	26	42	.382	16½
WEST	**W**	**L**	**PCT**	**GB**
Lakeland	43	25	.632	—
Fort Myers	40	30	.571	4
St. Petersburg	39	30	.565	4½
Clearwater	39	30	.565	4½
Charlotte	37	33	.529	7
Tampa	29	40	.420	14½
Sarasota	29	41	.414	15
Dunedin	25	44	.362	18½

PLAYOFFS—Semifinals: Vero Beach defeated Kissimmee 2-1, and St. Petersburg defeated Lakeland 2-0, in best-of-3 series. **Finals:** St. Petersburg defeated Vero Beach 3-2, in best-of-5 series.

STANDINGS: OVERALL

Page		W	L	PCT	GB	Manager	Attendance/Dates	Last Penn.
217	St. Petersburg Devil Rays (Devil Rays)	81	56	.591	—	Bill Evers	154,670 (67)	1997
111	Lakeland Tigers (Tigers)	81	57	.587	½	Mark Meleski	21,198 (61)	1992
148	Fort Myers Miracle (Twins)	81	58	.583	1	John Russell	88,266 (65)	1985
123	Kissimmee Cobras (Astros)	71	66	.518	10	John Tamargo	37,989 (64)	None
162	Tampa Yankees (Yankees)	70	66	.515	10½	Lee Mazzilli	149,191 (64)	1994
154	West Palm Beach Expos (Expos)	69	66	.511	11	Doug Sisson	51,747 (61)	1991
136	Vero Beach Dodgers (Dodgers)	70	67	.511	11	John Shoemaker	59,511 (62)	1990
181	Clearwater Phillies (Phillies)	70	68	.507	11½	Roy Majtyka	97,687 (64)	1993
224	Charlotte Rangers (Rangers)	68	71	.489	14	Butch Wynegar	69,072 (67)	1989
87	Daytona Cubs (Cubs)	65	73	.471	16½	Steve Roadcap	86,704 (62)	1995
74	Sarasota Red Sox (Red Sox)	63	75	.457	18½	Rob Derksen	69,813 (65)	1963
117	Brevard County Manatees (Marlins)	62	76	.449	19½	Lorenzo Bundy	132,608 (66)	None
229	Dunedin Blue Jays (Blue Jays)	57	82	.410	25	Dennis Holmberg	54,544 (65)	None
168	St. Lucie Mets (Mets)	54	81	.400	26	John Gibbons	60,210 (62)	1996

NOTE: Team's individual batting and pitching statistics can be found on page indicated in lefthand column.

1997 Florida State League Statistics

CLUB BATTING

	AVG	G	AB	R	H	2B	3B	HR	BB	SO	SB
Daytona	.274	138	4601	698	1262	247	33	95	405	979	177
Lakeland	.271	138	4608	650	1251	216	44	112	412	926	123
Vero Beach	.268	137	4551	728	1220	225	24	107	500	796	245
Fort Myers	.267	139	4636	635	1239	231	23	81	377	834	132
Kissimmee	.266	137	4618	615	1230	214	43	62	415	823	122
St. Petersburg	.266	137	4517	655	1201	227	35	64	559	661	148
Brevard County	.263	138	4632	617	1220	234	34	75	442	956	149
Sarasota	.260	138	4506	608	1171	199	39	69	422	861	164
Charlotte	.259	139	4598	653	1193	228	48	82	466	968	167
Tampa	.255	136	4543	621	1159	210	29	91	471	1003	136
West Palm Beach	.253	135	4402	583	1112	218	30	85	372	870	154
Dunedin	.250	139	4644	662	1160	229	24	111	567	1109	168
Clearwater	.245	138	4503	583	1104	199	32	78	401	906	105
St. Lucie	.241	135	4400	512	1059	214	34	70	399	996	122

CLUB PITCHING

	ERA	G	CG	SHO	SV	IP	H	R	ER	BB	SO
Kissimmee	3.36	137	16	15	36	1192	1134	562	445	385	862
Lakeland	3.43	138	17	9	30	1193	1122	569	454	430	829
Fort Myers	3.53	139	12	16	39	1204	1138	563	473	384	911
St. Petersburg	3.63	137	13	8	36	1201	1169	564	484	349	869
Clearwater	3.66	138	7	7	37	1194	1156	584	486	476	957
Tampa	3.69	136	3	5	35	1207	1145	594	495	458	939
West Palm Beach	3.71	135	8	13	29	1159	1162	583	478	376	883
St. Lucie	3.77	135	12	11	24	1152	1137	574	483	411	829
Vero Beach	4.19	137	6	11	37	1178	1113	653	549	566	1064
Dunedin	4.29	139	5	4	22	1216	1332	760	580	522	921
Charlotte	4.30	139	24	7	30	1203	1198	666	574	502	937
Daytona	4.33	138	15	3	28	1174	1250	696	565	440	913
Brevard County	4.38	138	10	11	26	1198	1312	731	583	388	835
Sarasota	4.41	138	10	5	24	1185	1213	721	580	521	939

CLUB FIELDING

	PCT	PO	A	E	DP
St. Petersburg	.972	3602	1363	141	95
Charlotte	.969	3608	1450	160	130
Fort Myers	.969	3612	1490	163	115
Tampa	.969	3621	1530	166	110
Vero Beach	.969	3535	1335	157	111
Clearwater	.968	3581	1522	168	110
Kissimmee	.968	3576	1581	172	110
Lakeland	.966	3578	1550	178	109
Brevard	.966	3593	1529	180	123
West Palm	.965	3478	1412	175	94
St. Lucie	.963	3455	1492	190	109
Dunedin	.960	3648	1584	220	107
Sarasota	.959	3554	1340	207	108
Daytona	.959	3521	1456	214	97

INDIVIDUAL BATTING LEADERS

(Minimum 378 Plate Appearances)

	AVG	G	AB	R	H	2B	3B	HR	RBI	BB	SO	SB
Valette, Ramon, Daytona	.332	106	371	54	123	25	2	6	50	20	49	20
Freire, Alejandro, Lakeland	.323	130	477	85	154	30	2	24	92	50	84	13
Funaro, Joe, Brevard	.319	125	470	67	150	16	6	4	53	49	65	9
Beltre, Adrian, Vero Beach	.317	123	435	95	138	24	2	26	104	67	66	25
Mateo, Ruben, Charlotte	.314	99	385	63	121	23	8	12	67	22	55	20
Allen, Chad, Fort Myers	.309	105	401	66	124	18	4	3	45	40	51	27
Fernandez, Jose, West Palm	.309	97	350	49	108	21	3	9	58	37	76	22
Porter, Bo, Daytona	.307	122	440	87	135	20	6	17	65	61	115	23
Morris, Warren, Charlotte	.306	128	494	78	151	27	9	12	75	62	100	16
Romano, Scott, St. Pete	.298	99	359	54	107	25	1	7	67	42	55	5

INDIVIDUAL PITCHING LEADERS

(Minimum 112 Innings)

	W	L	ERA	G	GS	CG	SV	IP	H	R	ER	BB	SO
Duncan, Courtney, Daytona	8	4	1.63	19	19	1	0	122	90	35	22	35	120
Vazquez, Javier, West Palm	6	3	2.16	19	19	1	0	113	98	40	27	28	100
Lincoln, Mike, Fort Myers	13	4	2.28	20	20	1	0	134	130	41	34	25	75
Powell, Brian, Lakeland	13	9	2.50	27	27	8	0	183	153	70	51	35	122
Garcia, Freddy, Kissimmee	10	8	2.56	27	27	5	0	179	165	63	51	49	131
Radlosky, Rob, Fort Myers	9	5	2.59	23	22	3	0	128	87	42	37	37	109
Blanco, Alberto, Kissimmee	7	4	2.83	19	19	1	0	114	83	45	36	45	95
Haigler, Phil, Fort Myers	11	9	2.84	25	25	4	0	158	172	57	50	32	80

ALL-STAR TEAM

C—Ramon Castro, Kissimmee; Cesar King, Charlotte. **1B**—Alejandro Freire, Lakeland. **2B**—Warren Morris, Charlotte. **3B**—Adrian Beltre, Vero Beach. **SS**—Joe Funaro, Brevard County. **OF**—Jacque Jones, Fort Myers; Gabe Kapler, Lakeland; Bo Porter, Daytona. **DH**—Jaime Torres, Tampa. **Util**—Ruben Mateo, Charlotte; Ramon Valette, Daytona. **LHP**—Corey Lee, Charlotte; Ed Yarnall, St. Lucie. **RHP**—Courtney Duncan, Daytona; Brian Powell, Lakeland. **RP**—John Daniels, St. Petersburg; Dan Ricabal, Vero Beach.

Most Valuable Player—Adrian Beltre, Vero Beach. **Manager of the Year**—Mark Meleski, Lakeland.

TOP 10 PROSPECTS

1. Adrian Beltre, 3b, Vero Beach; **2.** Ruben Mateo, of, Charlotte; **3.** Eric Milton, lhp, Tampa; **4.** David Ortiz, 1b, Fort Myers; **5.** Corey Lee, lhp, Charlotte; **6.** Jacque Jones, of, Fort Myers; **7.** Carlos King, c, Charlotte; **8.** Lance Berkman, of, Kissimmee; **9.** Michael Barrett, c, West Palm Beach; **10.** Courtney Duncan, rhp, Daytona.

DEPT. LEADERS

BATTING

G	Cliff Brumbaugh, Charlotte	139
AB	Reggie Taylor, Clearwater	545
R	Eric Stuckenschneider, VB	100
H	Jacque Jones, Fort Myers	160
TB	Gabe Kapler, Lakeland	262
XBH	Gabe Kapler, Lakeland	65
	Jeff Key, Clearwater	65
2B	Gabe Kapler, Lakeland	40
3B	Julio Lugo, Kissimmee	14
HR	Adrian Beltre, Vero Beach	26
RBI	Adrian Beltre, Vero Beach	104
SH	Julio Zorrilla, St. Lucie	16
SF	Fernando Seguignol, WPB	14
BB	Eric Stuckenschneider, VB	101
IBB	Adrian Beltre, Vero Beach	12
HBP	Will Skett, Dunedin	19
SO	Nate Rolison, Brevard County	143
SB	Vick Brown, Tampa	55
CS	Reggie Taylor, Clearwater	23
GIDP	Israel Paez, Fort Myers	18
OB%	Eric Stuckenschneider, VB	.419
SL%	Adrian Beltre, Vero Beach	.561

PITCHING

G	Dan Ricabal, Vero Beach	75
GS	Three tied at	28
CG	Brian Powell, Lakeland	8
ShO	Ten tied at	2
GF	Dan Ricabal, Vero Beach	71
SV	John Daniels, St. Petersburg	29
W	Corey Lee, Charlotte	15
L	Derek Root, Kissimmee	14
IP	Brian Powell, Lakeland	183
H	Ty Hartshorn, Dunedin	197
R	Jay Ryan, Daytona	105
ER	Ryan Dempster, Brev. County	90
HR	Jay Ryan, Daytona	22
HB	Shannon Stephens, BC	14
BB	Rob Burger, Clearwater	93
SO	Rob Burger, Clearwater	154
WP	David Coggin, Clearwater	24
BK	Three tied at	7

FIELDING

C	AVG	Ramon Castro, Kissimmee	.992
	PO	Jaime Torres, Tampa	700
	A	Jaime Torres, Tampa	109
	E	Three tied at	13
	DP	Cesar King, Charlotte	10
	PB	Hector Kuilan, Brev. County	32
1B	AVG	Jon Tucker, Vero Beach	.991
	PO	Carlos Yedo, Tampa	1116
	A	Fernando Seguignol, WPB	91
		Carlos Yedo, Tampa	91
	E	Carlos Yedo, Tampa	21
	DP	Nate Rolison, BC	89
2B	AVG	Jose Macias, Lakeland	.989
	PO	Jose Macias, Lakeland	255
	A	Jose Macias, Lakeland	349
	E	Michael Peeples, Dunedin	23
	DP	Julio Zorrilla, St. Lucie	74
3B	AVG	Cliff Brumbaugh, Charlotte	.958
	PO	Casey Blake, Dunedin	98
	A	Cliff Brumbaugh, Charlotte	271
	E	Casey Blake, Dunedin	39
	DP	Adrian Beltre, Vero Beach	26
SS	AVG	Chris Martin, St. Pete	.958
	PO	Kelly Dransfeldt, Charlotte	227
	A	Mark Raynor, Clearwater	419
	E	Julio Lugo, Kissimmee	40
	DP	Kelly Dransfeldt, Charlotte	85
OF	AVG	Aaron Harvey, BC	.994
	PO	Roy Padilla, Sarasota	327
	A	Reggie Taylor, Clearwater	19
	E	Ronnie Hall, Daytona	13
	DP	Craig Monroe, Charlotte	5
		Mike Zywica, Charlotte	5

MIDWEST LEAGUE

Lansing rights itself in the nick of time, wins league title

BY CURT RALLO

It's a good thing Lansing manager Bob Herold is a Christian. A person of lesser conviction may have lost faith amid the turbulent ride that Herold and the Lugnuts took during the 1997 Midwest League season.

The ride turned out to have a heavenly finish, as the Lugnuts won the league championship. Lansing, which was 69-68 overall in the regular season, defeated Kane County three games to two in the championship series.

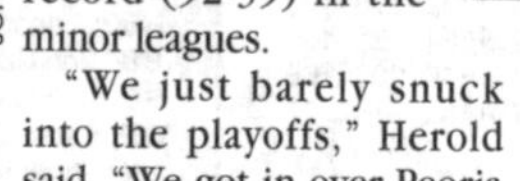

JOHN SPEAR

Batting titlist, barely
Robert Fick

Lansing beat Michigan and Fort Wayne on the way to the title round. Fort Wayne upset heavily favored West Michigan with a two-game sweep in the first round. West Michigan entered the playoffs with the best record (92-39) in the minor leagues.

"We just barely snuck into the playoffs," Herold said. "We got in over Peoria by 17 thousandths of a percentage point. It was too close for comfort."

Longshot was a kind term for the Lugnuts, losers of eight of their last 12 games in the regular season. But they turned in an incredible run in the playoffs.

They won the final two games on Kane County's home field. In the last game, Lansing erased a 4-0 Kane County lead and sweated out a 90-minute power outage before celebrating with a 9-7 victory.

While Lansing owned the postseason, West Michigan was untouchable in the regular season. The Whitecaps had a winning percentage of .702, the best in the MWL since Appleton's 1978 team went 97-40 (.708). It was the best record in the minors since Modesto (California) went 96-40 in 1994.

Excitement in the regular season wasn't limited to team success. In the battle for the batting title, West Michigan's Robert Fick won by .00017 over Lansing's Tony Miranda. The title was decided on the last day of the season, when the two met head-to-head. Fick was pulled from the game when it was calculated that he had won the title even if Miranda got a hit.

Changes are in store for the Midwest League. The sale of the Rockford franchise to Sherrie Myers, wife of Lansing owner Tom Dickson, was approved. Myers planned to move the team to Dayton, Ohio, for the 1999 season. The nearby Cincinnati Reds are expected to be the parent club.

STANDINGS: SPLIT SEASON

FIRST HALF

EAST	W	L	PCT	GB
West Michigan	46	17	.730	—
Michigan	38	31	.551	11
Lansing	34	34	.500	14½
Fort Wayne	32	33	.492	15
South Bend	30	43	.358	24
CENTRAL	**W**	**L**	**PCT**	**GB**
Wisconsin	40	29	.580	—
Rockford	32	32	.500	5½
Beloit	32	32	.500	5½
Peoria	34	35	.493	6
Kane County	33	37	.471	7½
WEST	**W**	**L**	**PCT**	**GB**
Burlington	39	31	.557	—
Clinton	33	34	.493	4½
Quad City	26	38	.406	10
Cedar Rapids	26	43	.377	12½

SECOND HALF

EAST	W	L	PCT	GB
West Michigan	46	22	.676	—
Fort Wayne	36	34	.514	11
Lansing	35	34	.507	11½
Michigan	32	36	.471	14
South Bend	30	40	.429	17
CENTRAL	**W**	**L**	**PCT**	**GB**
Kane County	37	31	.544	—
Wisconsin	36	34	.514	2
Peoria	36	34	.514	2
Rockford	34	34	.500	3
Beloit	28	41	.406	9½
WEST	**W**	**L**	**PCT**	**GB**
Cedar Rapids	36	33	.522	—
Quad City	33	37	.471	3½
Burlington	33	37	.471	3½
Clinton	32	37	.464	4

PLAYOFFS—First Round: Cedar Rapids defeated Burlington 2-0, Kane County defeated Wisconsin 2-0, Fort Wayne defeated West Michigan 2-0, Lansing defeated Michigan 2-1, in best-of-3 series. **Semifinals:** Lansing defeated Fort Wayne 2-0, Kane County defeated Cedar Rapids 2-0, in best-of-3 series. **Finals:** Lansing defeated Kane County 3-2, in best-of-5 series.

STANDINGS: OVERALL

Page		W	L	PCT	GB	Manager	Attendance/Dates	Last Penn.
112	West Michigan Whitecaps (Tigers)	92	39	.702	—	Bruce Fields	536,029 (67)	1996
214	Wisconsin Timber Rattlers (Mariners)	76	63	.547	20	Gary Varsho	227,104 (67)	1984
93	Burlington Bees (Reds)	72	68	.514	24 ½	Phillip Wellman	52,152 (61)	1977
75	Michigan Battle Cats (Red Sox)	70	67	.511	25	Billy Gardner Jr.	126,947 (60)	None
118	Kane County Cougars (Marlins)	70	68	.507	25 ½	Lynn Jones	436,505 (66)	None
149	Fort Wayne Wizards (Twins)	68	67	.504	26	Mike Boulanger	230,210 (69)	None
130	Lansing Lugnuts (Royals)	69	68	.504	26	Bob Herold	523,443 (67)	1997
195	Peoria Chiefs (Cardinals)	70	69	.504	26	Joe Cunningham	148,585 (63)	None
88	Rockford Cubbies (Cubs)	66	66	.500	26 ½	Ruben Amaro	86,716 (61)	None
202	Clinton Lumber Kings (Padres)	65	71	.478	29 ½	Tom LeVasseur	50,597 (64)	1991
143	Beloit Snappers (Brewers)	60	73	.451	33	Luis Salazar	81,564 (63)	1995
52	Cedar Rapids Kernels (Angels)	62	76	.449	33 ½	Mario Mendoza	124,629 (64)	1994
124	Quad City River Bandits (Astros)	59	75	.440	34 ½	Manny Acta	130,932 (60)	1990
55	South Bend Silver Hawks (Diamondbacks)	54	83	.394	41	Dick Scott	197,864 (63)	1993

NOTE: Team's individual batting and pitching statistics can be found on page indicated in lefthand column.

1997 Midwest League Statistics

CLUB BATTING

	AVG	G	AB	R	H	2B	3B	HR	BB	SO	SB
Lansing	.278	137	4731	772	1316	276	52	74	542	889	162
West Michigan	.273	131	4505	698	1229	249	42	86	455	980	168
Burlington	.270	140	4646	785	1255	238	42	143	527	1158	162
Michigan	.264	137	4591	725	1212	231	37	103	481	965	103
Beloit	.261	133	4480	619	1170	218	34	90	367	853	95
Rockford	.261	132	4339	594	1133	228	38	49	438	1025	197
Wisconsin	.259	139	4585	625	1187	250	39	79	480	972	102
Fort Wayne	.255	135	4568	627	1164	203	38	76	422	973	173
Kane County	.254	138	4541	667	1152	196	27	78	598	944	137
Quad City	.252	134	4371	586	1103	190	17	89	399	848	102
Peoria	.252	139	4611	662	1160	244	27	120	472	1079	125
South Bend	.251	137	4499	591	1131	223	45	61	526	1113	92
Cedar Rapids	.251	138	4520	685	1135	220	40	112	531	1080	135
Clinton	.245	136	4422	644	1084	184	56	68	602	1085	191

CLUB PITCHING

	ERA	G	CG	SHO	SV	IP	H	R	ER	BB	SO
West Michigan	2.67	131	11	13	47	1169	984	456	347	386	916
South Bend	3.76	137	1	6	27	1179	1158	653	493	524	972
Clinton	3.83	136	17	5	26	1168	1154	626	497	459	1042
Wisconsin	3.87	139	2	13	32	1218	1084	612	524	555	1220
Fort Wayne	3.88	135	5	12	29	1196	1191	638	516	480	1003
Kane County	4.03	138	10	10	29	1192	1164	620	534	439	1090
Michigan	4.10	137	11	5	28	1168	1195	672	533	448	1018
Rockford	4.31	132	9	9	34	1142	1133	665	547	572	1031
Quad City	4.31	134	8	4	28	1135	1095	682	544	509	963
Burlington	4.49	140	4	2	28	1200	1230	709	598	529	924
Beloit	4.50	133	5	5	21	1151	1173	715	576	487	947
Lansing	4.64	137	3	5	27	1197	1335	730	618	400	910
Peoria	4.69	139	6	10	38	1203	1284	746	627	578	1001
Cedar Rapids	4.89	138	18	7	27	1189	1251	756	646	474	927

CLUB FIELDING

	PCT	PO	A	E	DP
Kane County	.969	3576	1463	159	115
Cedar Rapids	.967	3567	1552	174	138
Burlington	.967	3599	1482	176	134
Wisconsin	.967	3653	1454	177	111
Lansing	.966	3591	1456	176	120
Fort Wayne	.965	3587	1635	187	145
West Michigan	.965	3508	1550	182	126
Peoria	.962	3608	1436	198	123
Beloit	.962	3454	1426	192	128
Quad City	.959	3404	1381	203	104
Rockford	.958	3426	1403	210	122
Clinton	.958	3505	1493	220	104
South Bend	.958	3536	1505	223	121
Michigan	.957	3504	1389	218	117

INDIVIDUAL BATTING LEADERS

(Minimum 378 Plate Appearances)

	AVG	G	AB	R	H	2B	3B	HR	RBI	BB	SO	SB
Fick, Robert, West Michigan	.341	122	463	100	158	50	3	16	90	75	74	13
Miranda, Tony, Lansing	.341	104	387	85	132	35	5	5	72	54	62	11
Lopiccolo, Jamie, Beloit	.332	112	410	72	136	27	3	17	80	38	76	5
Clark, Brady, Burlington	.325	126	459	108	149	29	7	11	63	76	71	31
Abreu, Dennis, Rockford	.321	126	483	71	155	19	3	1	37	45	99	36
Harrison, Adonis, Wisconsin	.318	125	412	61	131	26	6	7	62	55	74	25
Ryan, Rob, South Bend	.314	121	421	71	132	35	5	8	73	89	58	12
Sollmann, Scott, West Mich.	.313	121	460	89	144	13	4	0	33	79	81	40
Conti, Jason, South Bend	.310	117	458	78	142	22	10	3	43	45	99	30
Butler, Brent, Peoria	.306	129	480	81	147	37	2	15	71	63	69	6
Horne, Tyrone, Kane County	.306	133	468	89	143	24	2	21	91	104	88	18

INDIVIDUAL PITCHING LEADERS

(Minimum 112 Innings)

	W	L	ERA	G	GS	CG	SV	IP	H	R	ER	BB	SO
Quintal, Craig, West Mich.	11	6	1.96	23	23	3	0	156	133	48	34	31	88
Bruner, Clay, West Mich.	15	3	2.38	24	24	3	0	166	134	52	44	48	135
Hooten, David, Fort Wayne	11	8	2.61	28	27	2	0	166	134	57	48	54	138
Penny, Brad, South Bend	10	5	2.73	25	25	0	0	119	91	44	36	43	116
Spear, Russell, West Mich.	11	6	2.96	23	23	1	0	140	126	63	46	61	112
Billingsley, Brent, KC	14	7	3.01	26	26	3	0	171	146	67	57	50	175
Richardson, Kasey, FW	7	5	3.07	19	19	1	0	114	100	47	39	46	84
Cannon, Jon, Rockford	9	6	3.13	24	20	1	0	129	110	53	45	50	130

ALL-STAR TEAM

C—Chad Moeller, Fort Wayne. **1B**—Robert Fick, West Michigan. **2B**—Jim Chamblee, Michigan. **3B**—Jose Leon, Peoria. **SS**—Brent Butler, Peoria. **OF**—Brady Clark, Burlington; Jason Conti, South Bend; Julio Ramirez, Kane County. **DH**—Tyrone Home, Kane County. **LHP**—Phillip Norton, Rockford. **RHP**—Dave Borkowski, West Michigan. **LRP**—Chris Garza, Fort Wayne. **RRP**—Francisco Cordero, West Michigan.

Most Valuable Player—Robert Fick, West Michigan. **Manager of the Year**—Bruce Fields, West Michigan.

TOP 10 PROSPECTS

1. Francisco Cordero, rhp, West Michigan; **2.** Brent Butler, ss, Peoria; **3.** John Patterson, rhp, South Bend; **4.** Luis Rivas, ss, Fort Wayne; **5.** Ramon Ortiz, rhp, Cedar Rapids; **6.** Julio Ramirez, of, Kane County; **7.** Denny Stark, rhp, Wisconsin; **8.** Nick Bierbrodt, lhp, South Bend; **9.** Dave Borkowski, rhp, West Michigan; **10.** Dernell Stenson, of, Michigan.

DEPT. LEADERS

BATTING

G	Scott Podsednik, Kane County	135
AB	Scott Podsednik, Kane County	531
R	Jim Chamblee, Michigan	112
H	Robert Fick, West Michigan	158
TB	Robert Fick, West Michigan	262
XBH	Robert Fick, West Michigan	69
2B	Robert Fick, West Michigan	50
3B	Yuri Sanchez, Burlington	12
HR	Joe Freitas, Peoria	33
RBI	Darron Ingram, Burlington	97
SH	Juan Rodriguez, Cedar Rapids	18
SF	Jason Garrett, Kane County	9
BB	Tyrone Horne, Kane County	104
IBB	Tyrone Horne, Kane County	18
HBP	Brian Dallimore, Quad City	20
SO	Darron Ingram, Burlington	195
SB	Rodney Lindsey, Clinton	70
CS	Dennis Abreu, Rockford	26
GIDP	Brian Dallimore, Quad City	19
	Wilton Veras, Michigan	19
OB%	Tyrone Horne, Kane County	.434
SL%	Robert Fick, West Michigan	.566

PITCHING

G	Adam West, Peoria	62
GS	Seven tied at	27
CG	Ramon Ortiz, Cedar Rapids	8
ShO	Ramon Ortiz, Cedar Rapids	4
GF	Francisco Cordero, W. Michigan	47
SV	Francisco Cordero, W. Michigan	35
W	David Borkowski, W. Michigan	15
	Clayton Bruner, West Michigan	15
L	Gabe Garcia, Quad City	14
	Jason Stockstill, Cedar Rapids	14
IP	Tommy Darrell, Cedar Rapids	192
H	Tommy Darrell, Cedar Rapids	212
R	Justin Kaye, Wisconsin	113
ER	Justin Kaye, Wisconsin	103
HR	Jason Stockstill, Cedar Rapids	25
HB	Robb Welch, Michigan	17
BB	Justin Kaye, Wisconsin	104
SO	Ramon Ortiz, Cedar Rapids	225
WP	Greg Montgomery, Peoria	27
BK	Allen Levrault, Beloit	12

FIELDING

C	**AVG**	Ryan Robertson, KC	.991
	PO	Carlos Maldonado, Wis.	857
	A	Carlos Maldonado, Wis.	105
	E	Chad Moeller, Fort Wayne	15
	DP	Brad King, Rockford	11
	PB	Jim Gargiulo, Peoria	19
1B	**AVG**	Rob Zachmann, Wis.	.996
	PO	Pete Paciorek, Clinton	1148
	A	Jason Garrett, Kane County	76
	E	Kevin Burns, Quad City	20
	DP	Kevin Burns, Quad City	94
2B	**AVG**	Brian McClure, Clinton	.978
	PO	Cleatus Davidson, FW	271
	A	Cleatus Davidson, FW	405
	E	Adonis Harrison, Wis.	26
	DP	Cleatus Davidson, FW	98
3B	**AVG**	Wilton Veras, Michigan	.944
	PO	Rob Sasser, Cedar Rapids	104
	A	Rob Sasser, Cedar Rapids	303
	E	Three tied at	31
	DP	Wilton Veras, Michigan	29
SS	**AVG**	Derek Mitchell, W. Michigan	.959
	PO	Brent Butler, Peoria	220
	A	Luis Rivas, Fort Wayne	394
	E	Luis Rivas, Fort Wayne	58
	DP	Luis Rivas, Fort Wayne	92
OF	**AVG**	Doug Hall, Rockford	.991
	PO	Brady Clark, Burlington	265
	A	Luis Saturria, Peoria	24
	E	Dernell Stenson, Michigan	14
	DP	Jason Conti, South Bend	6
		Tony Peters, Beloit	6

SOUTH ATLANTIC LEAGUE

Fledgling Shorebirds fly to championship over Greensboro

BY GENE SAPAKOFF

Neither rain, nor sleet, nor playing second fiddle during the regular season could keep the Delmarva Shorebirds from winning a South Atlantic League title in just their second season in Salisbury, Md.

The Charleston, W.Va., Alley Cats finished first in the Northern Division in both halves of the 1977 season, but Delmarva made the most of a wild-card opportunity. The Shorebirds swept Greensboro 2-0 in a best-of-three championship series after knocking off Hickory and Charleston in the playoffs. The final game in Greensboro took three days to complete because of back-to-back rainouts.

RODGER WOOD

Back from exile
Luis Lopez

First baseman Calvin Pickering's two-run homer, his third of the playoffs, sparked Delmarva in the first inning of an 8-1 win in the last game. Right-hander Maximo Heredia struck out eight over 6⅓ innings to improve to 3-0 in the playoffs.

That the Capital City Bombers made it to the playoffs by winning the second-half Central Division title was remarkable after a tragic and trying first half of the season. Bombers outfielder Tim Bishop died in a highway accident on April 18 in Columbia, S.C., when he and teammate Randy Vickers were returning home after a road trip.

Capital City manager Doug Mansolino and coach Tim Leiper later were dismissed, reportedly after Mets management discovered there had been drinking on board the Bombers' bus the night of Bishop's death. As if that wasn't enough, shortstop Ryan Jaroncyk, the Mets' first-round draft pick in 1995, abruptly retired.

Hagerstown first baseman Luis Lopez hit .358 to win the batting title. Not bad for a guy who spent a year working in a Myrtle Beach, S.C., children's clothing store after he wasn't drafted. Lopez drove to Florida to solicit tryouts, finally getting one from the Blue Jays.

Fans in Charleston, S.C., went from watching baseball in one of the worst minor league facilities, College Park, to perhaps the best in Class A. The eight luxury boxes at Joseph P. Riley Jr. Park overlook the Ashley River, and the architects designed the place to look like a mini-Camden Yards. The RiverDogs set a Charleston minor league record by drawing 231,006 fans.

STANDINGS: SPLIT SEASON

FIRST HALF

NORTH	W	L	PCT	GB
Charleston, W.Va.	39	30	.565	—
Delmarva	40	31	.563	—
Cape Fear	36	34	.514	3½
Hagerstown	31	38	.449	8
CENTRAL	**W**	**L**	**PCT**	**GB**
Greensboro	39	29	.574	—
Hickory	39	31	.557	1
Piedmont	36	35	.507	4½
Capital City	34	35	.493	5½
Charleston, S.C.	31	39	.443	9
Asheville	27	42	.391	12½
SOUTH	**W**	**L**	**PCT**	**GB**
Macon	42	28	.600	—
Augusta	34	37	.479	8½
Columbus	31	39	.443	11
Savannah	30	41	.423	12½

SECOND HALF

NORTH	W	L	PCT	GB
Charleston, W.Va.	37	32	.536	—
Delmarva	37	34	.521	1
Hagerstown	34	35	.493	3
Cape Fear	30	40	.429	7½
CENTRAL	**W**	**L**	**PCT**	**GB**
Capital City	43	28	.606	—
Hickory	37	33	.529	5½
Asheville	35	34	.507	7
Greensboro	36	36	.500	7½
Piedmont	34	37	.479	9
Charleston, S.C.	29	43	.403	14½
SOUTH	**W**	**L**	**PCT**	**GB**
Macon	38	32	.543	—
Augusta	37	34	.521	1½
Savannah	33	36	.478	4½
Columbus	31	37	.456	6

PLAYOFFS—First Round: Delmarva defeated Hickory 2-0, Greensboro defeated Capital City 2-0, Macon defeated Augusta 2-1, Charleston W.Va. defeated Cape Fear 2-0, in best-of-3 series. **Semifinals:** Greensboro defeated Macon 2-0, Delmarva defeated Charleston W.Va. 2-1, in best-of-3 series. **Finals:** Delmarva defeated Greensboro 2-0, in best-of-3 series.

STANDINGS: OVERALL

Page		W	L	PCT	GB	Manager(s)	Attendance/Dates	Last Penn.
62	Macon Braves (Braves)	80	60	.571	—	Brian Snitker	129,723 (69)	None
94	Charleston, W.Va., Alley Cats (Reds)	76	62	.551	3	Barry Lyons	88,378 (62)	1990
169	Capital City Bombers (Mets)	77	63	.550	3	Doug Mansolino/John Stephenson	135,670 (60)	1991
82	Hickory Crawdads (White Sox)	76	64	.543	4	Chris Cron	196,394 (68)	None
68	Delmarva Shorebirds (Orioles)	77	65	.542	4	Tommy Shields/Tom Trebelhorn	324,412 66)	1997
163	Greensboro Bats (Yankees)	75	65	.536	5	Tom Nieto	146,987 (63)	1982
188	Augusta GreenJackets (Pirates)	71	71	.500	10	Jeff Richardson/Scott Little	152,270 (67)	1989
182	Piedmont Boll Weevils (Phillies)	70	72	.493	11	Ken Oberkfell	114,646 (63)	None
155	Cape Fear Crocs (Expos)	66	74	.471	14	Phil Stephenson	69,873 (66)	None
230	Hagerstown Suns (Blue Jays)	65	73	.471	14	J.J. Cannon	115,011 (66)	None
137	Savannah Sand Gnats (Dodgers)	63	77	.450	17	John Shelby	125,729 (64)	1996
100	Columbus RedStixx (Indians)	62	76	.449	17	Jack Mull	119,646 (64)	None
106	Asheville Tourists (Rockies)	62	76	.449	17	Ron Gideon	143,351 (68)	1984
217	Charleston, S.C., RiverDogs (Devil Rays)	60	82	.423	21	Scott Fletcher	231,006 (70)	None

NOTE: Team's individual batting and pitching statistics can be found on page indicated in lefthand column.

1997 South Atlantic League Statistics

CLUB BATTING

	AVG	G	AB	R	H	2B	3B	HR	BB	SO	SB
Hickory	.278	140	4771	748	1327	272	39	91	446	940	127
Hagerstown	.272	138	4617	644	1254	293	23	96	371	1032	118
Charleston, W.Va.	.264	138	4533	695	1198	235	35	77	465	1074	192
Cape Fear	.259	140	4712	634	1222	230	38	83	404	848	181
Macon	.255	140	4757	689	1213	222	31	141	423	1101	162
Greensboro	.252	141	4667	641	1174	233	33	107	391	1162	147
Delmarva	.250	142	4729	668	1182	241	38	91	510	1148	232
Piedmont	.250	142	4786	624	1195	216	35	63	369	967	173
Asheville	.249	139	4569	599	1136	207	14	70	437	940	180
Columbus	.248	138	4696	658	1163	201	47	123	491	1278	99
Charleston, S.C.	.243	142	4662	563	1132	213	25	56	433	977	255
Augusta	.242	142	4635	642	1120	193	31	77	517	1111	218
Capital City	.239	140	4457	564	1067	190	26	77	411	1124	172
Savannah	.229	140	4507	560	1034	174	42	94	410	1164	111

CLUB PITCHING

	ERA	G	CG	SHO	SV	IP	H	R	ER	BB	SO
Capital City	3.17	140	14	19	29	1182	1020	495	416	455	1113
Macon	3.39	140	2	14	39	1226	1106	573	462	411	1206
Charleston, S.C.	3.44	142	4	9	27	1243	1136	617	475	381	1088
Delmarva	3.62	142	2	12	46	1261	1129	625	507	495	1139
Cape Fear	3.81	140	6	8	32	1231	1208	630	522	405	947
Augusta	3.82	142	3	9	42	1250	1225	656	531	417	1174
Piedmont	3.85	142	10	10	31	1242	1238	632	531	363	929
Greensboro	3.92	141	9	7	41	1216	1125	683	530	516	1026
Hickory	3.95	140	9	3	29	1230	1255	669	540	411	962
Hagerstown	3.96	138	5	8	32	1187	1159	646	523	472	1119
Asheville	4.06	139	8	5	33	1215	1225	651	549	445	1022
Charleston, W.Va.	4.07	138	9	6	37	1183	1262	650	535	325	934
Savannah	4.19	140	10	6	31	1195	1162	660	556	451	1079
Columbus	4.78	138	2	8	38	1213	1167	742	645	531	1128

CLUB FIELDING

	PCT	PO	A	E	DP
Capital City	.972	3545	1504	144	96
Piedmont	.969	3727	1626	173	104
Asheville	.967	3645	1608	177	115
Cape Fear	.967	3693	1588	183	101
Char., W.Va.	.966	3548	1440	175	113
Delmarva	.965	3783	1504	190	112
Columbus	.965	3639	1421	182	99
Savannah	.964	3586	1418	185	99
Augusta	.963	3749	1479	203	100
Hagerstown	.963	3562	1371	192	96
Hickory	.962	3689	1509	207	125
Macon	.961	3679	1376	205	105
Greensboro	.959	3648	1528	220	115
Char., S.C.	.959	3729	1531	225	94

INDIVIDUAL BATTING LEADERS

(Minimum 383 Plate Appearances)

	AVG	G	AB	R	H	2B	3B	HR	RBI	BB	SO	SB
Lopez, Luis, Hagerstown	.358	136	503	96	180	47	4	11	99	60	45	5
Giles, Tim, Hagerstown	.334	112	380	54	127	32	0	12	56	46	95	2
Inglin, Jeff, Hickory	.334	135	536	100	179	34	6	16	102	49	87	31
Hacker, Steve, Macon	.324	117	460	80	149	35	1	33	119	34	91	1
LaRue, Jason, Char., W.Va.	.315	132	473	78	149	50	3	8	81	47	90	14
Parsons, Jason, Char., W.Va.	.311	131	460	87	143	34	0	20	102	62	99	5
Pickering, Calvin, Delmarva	.311	122	444	88	138	31	1	25	79	53	139	6
Abernathy, Brent, Hagerstown	.309	99	379	69	117	27	2	1	26	30	32	22
Minor, Ryan, Delmarva	.307	134	488	83	150	42	1	24	97	51	102	7
Sheppard, Greg, Hickory	.307	102	342	54	105	27	2	12	62	46	81	4

INDIVIDUAL PITCHING LEADERS

(Minimum 114 Innings)

	W	L	ERA	G	GS	CG	SV	IP	H	R	ER	BB	SO
Heredia, Maximo, Delmarva	10	5	2.13	37	6	0	1	114	97	29	27	20	73
Roberts, Grant, Cap. City	11	3	2.36	22	22	2	0	130	98	37	34	44	122
Rose, Ted, Char., W.Va.	11	6	2.51	38	13	2	4	129	108	44	36	27	132
Evans, Keith, Cape Fear	12	7	2.61	21	21	3	0	138	113	56	40	18	102
Kessel, Kyle, Capital City	11	11	2.72	27	27	5	0	169	131	63	51	53	151
Carlyle, Buddy, Char., W.Va.	14	5	2.77	23	23	4	0	143	130	51	44	27	111
Shiell, Jason, Macon	10	5	2.86	27	24	0	0	129	113	53	41	32	101
Ortega, Pablo, Char., S.C.	12	10	2.86	29	29	3	0	189	173	87	60	30	142

ALL-STAR TEAM

C—Jason LaRue, Charleston, W.Va. **1B**—Luis Lopez, Hagerstown. **2B**—Brent Abernathy, Hagerstown. **3B**—Ryan Minor, Delmarva. **SS**—Jimmy Rollins, Piedmont. **OF**—Mark Hamlin, Asheville; Jeff Inglin, Hickory; Alex Sanchez, Charleston, S.C. **DH**—Steve Hacker, Macon. **Util**—McKay Christensen, Hickory; Jason Parsons, Charleston, W.Va. **LHP**—Bruce Chen, Macon. **RHP**—Grant Roberts, Capital City.

Most Valuable Player—Luis Lopez, Hagerstown. **Most Outstanding Pitcher**—Grant Roberts, Capital City. **Manager of the Year**—Brian Snitker, Macon.

TOP 10 PROSPECTS

1. Ryan Minor, 3b, Delmarva; **2.** Grant Roberts, rhp, Capital City; **3.** Bruce Chen, lhp, Macon; **4.** Odalis Perez, lhp, Macon; **5.** Jason Marquis, rhp, Macon; **6.** Alex Sanchez, of, Charleston, S.C.; **7.** Shawn Chacon, rhp, Asheville; **8.** Jake Westbrook, rhp, Asheville; **9.** Buddy Carlyle, rhp, Charleston, W.Va.; **10.** Jimmy Rollins, ss, Piedmont.

DEPT. LEADERS

BATTING

G	Jimmy Rollins, Piedmont	139
AB	Jimmy Rollins, Piedmont	560
R	Jeff Inglin, Hickory	100
H	Luis Lopez, Hagerstown	180
TB	Steve Hacker, Macon	285
XBH	Steve Hacker, Macon	69
2B	Jason LaRue, Charleston W.Va.	50
3B	McKay Christensen, Hickory	12
HR	Steve Hacker, Macon	33
RBI	Steve Hacker, Macon	119
SH	Bernard Hutchison, Asheville	16
SF	Three tied at	9
BB	Tim DeCinces, Delmarva	97
IBB	Steve Hacker, Macon	7
HBP	David Francia, Piedmont	19
SO	Mike Hessman, Macon	167
SB	Alex Sanchez, Charleston S.C.	92
CS	Alex Sanchez, Charleston S.C.	40
GIDP	Simon Pond, Cape Fear	22
OB%	Luis Lopez, Hagerstown	.430
SL%	Steve Hacker, Macon	.620

PITCHING

G	Dean Mitchell, Savannah	52
GS	Pablo Ortega, Charleston, S.C.	29
CG	Kyle Kessel, Capital City	5
ShO	Kris Stevens, Piedmont	3
GF	David Lee, Asheville	49
SV	Ryan Kohlmeier, Delmarva	24
W	Five tied at	14
L	Gary Glover, Hagerstown	17
IP	Pablo Ortega, Charleston S.C.	189
H	Giovanny Lara, Cape Fear	199
R	Giovanny Lara, Cape Fear	107
ER	J.D. Brammer, Columbus	91
HR	Bruce Chen, Macon	19
HB	Kenny Pumphrey, Capital City	20
BB	Jason Coble, Greensboro	96
SO	Bruce Chen, Macon	182
WP	Jason Lakman, Hickory	24
BK	Gene Altman, Charleston W.Va.	6

FIELDING

C	AVG	Skip Shipp, Augusta	.989
	PO	Fernando Lunar, Macon	888
	A	Fernando Lunar, Macon	135
	E	Victor Valencia, Greensboro	24
	DP	Brandon Marsters, Piedmont	8
	PB	Josh Fauske, Hickory	26
		Chris Heintz, Hickory	26
1B	AVG	Carlos Rivera, Augusta	.993
	PO	Nick Johnson, Greensboro	1176
	A	Brian Becker, Char. S.C.	106
	E	Calvin Pickering, Delmarva	27
	DP	Nick Johnson, Greensboro	99
2B	AVG	Liu Rodriguez, Hickory	.989
	PO	Rod Smith, Greensboro	244
	A	Rod Smith, Greensboro	387
	E	Rod Smith, Greensboro	33
	DP	Rod Smith, Greensboro	79
3B	AVG	Simon Pond, Cape Fear	.925
	PO	Damian Rolls, Savannah	110
	A	Damian Rolls, Savannah	246
	E	Donny Leon, Greensboro	40
	DP	Joe Crede, Hickory	23
SS	AVG	Jimmy Rollins, Piedmont	.960
	PO	Jimmy Rollins, Piedmont	201
	A	Jimmy Rollins, Piedmont	421
	E	Eddy de los Santos, C-SC	42
	DP	Cristian Guzman, G'boro	68
OF	AVG	Maleke Fowler, Delmarva	.994
	PO	McKay Christensen, Hick.	280
	A	Manuel Gonzalez, Hickory	22
	E	Corey Pointer, Augusta	12
	DP	Rod Bair, Asheville	5
		Alex Pena, Augusta	5

NEW YORK PENN LEAGUE

Pittsfield ends run of near-misses with city's second title

BY HOWARD HERMAN

The 1997 Pittsfield Mets did something only one other team in the long history of Pittsfield minor league baseball had done—win a league championship.

The 1965 Pittsfield Red Sox won the Eastern League championship. The '97 Mets won the New York-Penn League title by taking two of three games from the Batavia Clippers.

Since Pittsfield joined the league in 1989, the Mets have won four division titles and made the playoffs as a wild card once, but had never won the league championship.

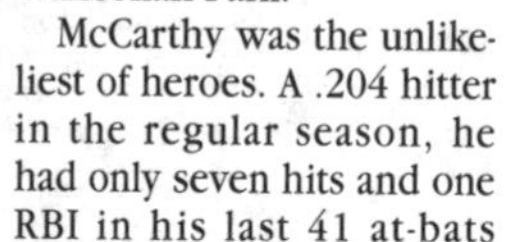

RICH ABEL

Powerful shortstop
Kevin Haverbusch

First baseman Kevin McCarthy's pinch-hit single with the bases loaded and two out in the ninth inning scored pinch-runner Bruce Nolte from third base to give the Mets a 3-2 win in Game Three at Pittsfield's Wahconah Park.

McCarthy was the unlikeliest of heroes. A .204 hitter in the regular season, he had only seven hits and one RBI in his last 41 at-bats before delivering the hit that made a winner of reliever Joe Pyrtle.

"I've had my chances," McCarthy said. "(Manager Doug Davis) put me up in the last two playoff games in clutch situations, and I wasn't able to come through. Thank God I got the big one."

The McNamara Division champion Mets swept Stedler Division champion Erie 2-0 in the semifinals, while wild-card Batavia swept Pinckney Division champion Oneonta.

Pittsfield won the opener of the championship series 9-3 in Batavia, but lost Game Two at Wahconah Park 4-0.

The top prospect in the league had a big bank book and a very bright future. Righthander Matt White, he of the $10.2 million bonus from the Devil Rays, started the year 0-5 at Hudson Valley, then rebounded to finish at 4-6.

The Jamestown team was touched by tragedy all season. On July 9, manager Dwight Lowry collapsed and died at his home shortly after a game. He was replaced by Matt Martin. Two days after the season, pitcher Mike Diebolt was killed in an auto accident. Several relatives of players and front-office people also passed away during the season.

Erie's Kevin Haverbusch batted .311 with 10 homers and a league-leading 55 RBIs, a rare achievement for a shortstop. Teammate Derrick Lankford, a first baseman, also had 55.

For the third straight year, the league set an attendance record. And the Erie SeaWolves set a league record for one team, also for the third time.

A total of 1,234,367 fans clicked through the league's turnstiles, bettering the 1996 figure by more than 30,000.

The SeaWolves, who will join the Double-A Eastern League in 1999, drew 196,212, almost 10,000 more than the previous year.

Most of the 14 clubs experienced increases in attendance. Other major increases were by Pittsfield (up 19,402) and Lowell (up 10,876). On the downside, signifigant decreases were recorded at Jamestown (down 6,828) and Williamsport (down 6,628).

STANDINGS

Page	McNAMARA	W	L	PCT	GB	Manager	Attendance/Dates	Last Penn.
170	Pittsfield Mets (Mets)	42	32	.568	—	Doug Davis	82,935 (35)	1997
76	Lowell Spinners (Red Sox)	38	38	.500	5	Dick Berardino	106,862 (35)	None
195	New Jersey Cardinals (Cardinals)	35	39	.473	7	Jeff Shireman	171,244 (38)	1994
218	Hudson Valley Renegades (Devil Rays)	35	40	.467	7½	Julio Garcia	161,771 (38)	None
156	Vermont Expos (Expos)	35	41	.461	8	Kevin Higgins	91,694 (37)	1996
Page	**PINCKNEY**	**W**	**L**	**PCT**	**GB**	**Manager**	**Attendance/Dates**	**Last Penn.**
163	Oneonta Yankees (Yankees)	49	25	.662	—	Joe Arnold	53,447 (34)	1990
100	Watertown Indians (Indians)	39	36	.520	10½	Ted Kubiak	36,359 (34)	1995
118	Utica Blue Sox (Marlins)	36	38	.486	13	Juan Bustabad	52,185 (34)	1983
89	Williamsport Cubs (Cubs)	29	46	.387	20½	Bobby Ralston	58,795 (36)	None
124	Auburn Doubledays (Astros)	29	47	.382	21	Mike Rojas	51,260 (36)	1973
Page	**STEDLER**	**W**	**L**	**PCT**	**GB**	**Manager(s)**	**Attendance/Dates**	**Last Penn.**
189	Erie SeaWolves (Pirates)	50	26	.658	—	Marty Brown	196,212 (38)	1957
182	Batavia Clippers (Phillies)	47	27	.635	2	Greg Legg	41,192 (35)	1963
231	St. Catharines Stompers (Blue Jays)	35	40	.467	14½	Rocket Wheeler	53,520 (37)	1986
112	Jamestown Jammers (Tigers)	25	49	.338	24	Dwight Lowry/Matt Martin	51,775 (33)	1991

PLAYOFFS—Semifinals: Batavia defeated Oneonta 2-0, and Pittsfield defeated Erie 2-0, in best-of-3 series. **Finals:** Pittsfield defeated Batavia 2-1, in best-of-3 series.

NOTE: Team's individual batting and pitching statistics can be found on page indicated in lefthand column.

1997 New York-Penn League Statistics

CLUB BATTING

	AVG	G	AB	R	H	2B	3B	HR	BB	SO	SB
Batavia	.279	74	2553	414	713	127	21	40	225	472	89
Erie	.266	76	2525	410	672	124	26	57	254	595	93
Auburn	.263	76	2503	332	658	129	20	44	230	586	55
Utica	.262	74	2392	334	627	102	12	23	282	486	68
Watertown	.257	75	2491	383	640	136	15	46	277	588	74
Oneonta	.254	74	2384	359	606	99	25	24	276	568	103
Jamestown	.254	74	2503	336	636	111	17	44	219	565	42
Vermont	.253	76	2546	361	644	100	36	21	263	524	156
Hudson Valley	.252	75	2532	363	639	130	23	30	224	558	57
New Jersey	.252	74	2441	375	615	106	22	40	230	559	75
Williamsport	.251	75	2490	275	625	91	23	29	215	581	68
St. Catharines	.249	75	2499	368	623	121	14	42	246	511	72
Pittsfield	.244	74	2457	343	600	108	20	26	198	536	107
Lowell	.239	76	2529	334	604	117	12	43	222	618	71

CLUB PITCHING

	ERA	G	CG	SHO	SV	IP	H	R	ER	BB	SO
Pittsfield	2.82	74	5	3	20	644	546	284	202	193	586
Oneonta	3.11	74	3	8	21	638	596	275	221	226	610
Batavia	3.14	74	1	9	19	651	641	296	227	156	551
Lowell	3.58	76	3	5	19	659	609	341	262	219	590
Erie	3.58	76	1	7	27	663	595	323	264	230	558
New Jersey	3.74	74	4	5	12	629	630	314	262	202	520
Hudson Valley	3.84	75	1	4	17	655	610	379	279	277	579
Williamsport	3.86	75	1	4	17	646	656	378	277	340	529
Utica	4.12	74	3	4	14	629	653	359	288	192	549
Watertown	4.20	75	5	3	18	643	632	361	300	292	553
St. Catharines	4.27	75	0	1	21	645	652	399	306	244	558
Vermont	4.39	76	4	1	15	659	669	401	321	259	546
Auburn	4.45	76	7	5	15	651	717	405	322	249	534
Jamestown	5.20	74	7	2	11	628	696	472	363	282	484

CLUB FIELDING

	PCT	PO	A	E	DP
Oneonta	.967	1915	809	94	69
New Jersey	.965	1888	822	97	69
Batavia	.963	1953	765	104	64
Watertown	.958	1928	832	122	71
Utica	.958	1888	799	119	56
Auburn	.956	1952	819	129	73
Lowell	.954	1976	729	131	55
St. Catharines	.952	1936	777	136	73
Williamsport	.952	1939	870	143	59
Erie	.952	1990	760	140	69
Hudson Valley	.952	1964	764	139	39
Vermont	.950	1976	764	144	55
Jamestown	.949	1883	819	145	73
Pittsfield	.949	1933	751	145	53

INDIVIDUAL BATTING LEADERS

(Minimum 205 Plate Appearances)

	AVG	G	AB	R	H	2B	3B	HR	RBI	BB	SO	SB
Franco, Raul, Utica	.352	72	293	41	103	19	0	3	38	17	24	10
Walker, Ron, Williamsport	.349	54	189	30	66	10	1	9	39	17	48	0
Erickson, Matt, Utica	.328	69	238	44	78	10	0	5	44	48	36	9
Chapman, Scott, Auburn	.327	53	205	32	67	11	0	6	39	6	23	1
Burnham, Gary, Batavia	.325	73	289	44	94	22	4	5	45	30	47	3
Langaigne, Selwyn, StC	.320	74	266	50	85	15	4	1	39	48	46	19
Nunnari, Talmadge, Vermont	.318	62	236	30	75	11	3	4	42	31	37	6
Estrada, Johnny, Batavia	.314	58	223	28	70	17	2	6	43	9	15	0
Freeman, Terrance, Erie	.313	63	217	56	68	9	2	2	19	38	38	46
McNamara, Rusty, Batavia	.312	72	295	55	92	17	0	6	54	15	33	3

INDIVIDUAL PITCHING LEADERS

(Minimum 61 Innings)

	W	L	ERA	G	GS	CG	SV	IP	H	R	ER	BB	SO
Blank, Matt, Vermont	6	4	1.69	16	15	2	0	96	74	26	18	14	84
Choate, Randy, Oneonta	5	1	1.73	10	10	0	0	62	49	12	12	12	61
Comer, Scott, Pittsfield	7	1	1.74	14	14	1	0	93	71	25	18	12	98
Adair, Derek, Batavia	7	3	2.11	13	12	1	0	77	71	29	18	4	53
Day, Zach, Oneonta	7	2	2.15	14	14	0	0	92	82	26	22	23	92
Lambert, Kris, Erie	11	2	2.33	15	14	0	0	81	59	28	21	21	94
Rizzo, Nick, Utica	4	1	2.36	15	10	0	1	69	64	30	18	12	54
Heath, Woody, StC	7	4	2.42	15	12	0	0	78	63	29	21	19	72
McDougal, Mike, NJ	4	4	2.49	13	11	2	0	69	62	24	19	9	63

ALL-STAR TEAM

C—Scott Chapman, Auburn; Johnny Estrada, Batavia. **1B**—Andy Dominique, Batavia. **2B**—Raul Franco, Utica. **3B**—Ron Walker, Williamsport. **SS**—Kevin Haverbusch, Erie. **OF**—Alex Steele, Jamestown; Dustan Mohr, Watertown; Vernon Wells, St. Catharines; Andy Burress, New Jersey. **DH**—Gary Burnham, Batavia. **Util**—Rusty McNamara, Batavia. **RHP**—Zach Day, Oneonta; Derek Adair, Batavia. **LHP**—Kris Lambert, Erie; Scott Comer, Pittsfield.

Most Valuable Player—Kevin Haverbusch, Erie. **Manager of the Year**—Marty Brown, Erie.

TOP 10 PROSPECTS

1. Matt White, rhp, Hudson Valley; **2.** Vernon Wells, of, St. Catharines; **3.** Alex Steele, of, Jamestown; **4.** Adam Kennedy, ss, New Jersey; **5.** Scott Comer, lhp, Pittsfield; **6.** Kris Lambert, lhp, Erie; **7.** Kevin Haverbusch, ss, Erie; **8.** Miguel Mejia, of, New Jersey; **9.** Randy Wolf, lhp, Batavia; **10.** Raul Franco, 2b, Utica.

DEPT. LEADERS

BATTING

G	Pat Cutshall, Auburn	76
AB	Cristian Mota, Watertown	311
R	Kenny James, Vermont	61
H	Raul Franco, Utica	103
TB	Alex Steele, Jamestown	145
XBH	Alex Steele, Jamestown	33
2B	Pat Cutshall, Auburn	23
3B	Noah Hall, Vermont	8
HR	Alex Steele, Jamestown	14
	Andy Dominique, Batavia	14
RBI	Kevin Haverbusch, Erie	55
	Derrick Lankford, Erie	55
SH	Three tied at	8
SF	Four tied at	6
BB	Brian Benefield, Watertown	49
IBB	Ron Walker, Williamsport	7
HBP	Alex Melconian, Utica	15
SO	Marcus Howard, Lowell	78
SB	Terrance Freeman, Erie	46
CS	Three tied at	11
GIDP	Scott Chapman, Auburn	14
OB%	Matt Erickson, Utica	.455
SL%	Alex Steele, Jamestown	.564

PITCHING

G	O.J. Cook, Erie	34
GS	Brian Bowles, St. Catharines	16
	Eric Ireland, Auburn	16
CG	Craig Johnson, Jamestown	3
ShO	Mike McDougal, New Jersey	2
	Tom Shearn, Auburn	2
GF	Eddy Reyes, Hudson Valley	29
SV	Daniel Mota, Oneonta	17
W	Kris Lambert, Erie	11
L	Barry Fennell, Williamsport	10
	Craig Johnson, Jamestown	10
IP	Eric Ireland, Auburn	107
H	Eric Ireland, Auburn	111
R	Mark Persails, Jamestown	64
	Jim Wallace, Auburn	64
ER	Mark Persails, Jamestown	54
HR	Mike Diebolt, Jamestown	12
HB	Eric Ireland, Auburn	12
BB	Elvis Polanco, Williamsport	46
SO	Scott Comer, Pittsfield	98
WP	Kyle Burchart, St. Catharines	20
BK	Scott Madison, Hudson Valley	6

FIELDING

C	AVG	Johnny Estrada, Batavia	1.000
	PO	Johnny Estrada, Batavia	391
	A	Jorge Meran, Jamestown	55
	E	Two tied at	12
	DP	Chris Martine, New Jersey	8
	PB	Two tied at	15
1B	AVG	Matt Purkiss, Oneonta	.992
	PO	Ross Gload, Utica	546
	A	Selwyn Langaigne, St. Cath.	53
	E	Ross Gload, Utica	16
	DP	Selwyn Langaigne, St. Cath.	58
2B	AVG	David Eckstein, Lowell	.971
	PO	Dustin Carr, Hudson Valley	142
	A	Scott Kidd, Oneonta	231
	E	Dustin Carr, Hudson Valley	24
	DP	Scott Kidd, Oneonta	52
3B	AVG	Matt Erickson, Utica	.942
	PO	Eric Cole, Auburn	49
	A	Matt Erickson, Utica	140
	E	Eric Cole, Auburn	30
	DP	Eric Cole, Auburn	13
SS	AVG	Joseph Cathey, Auburn	.962
	PO	Marc Mirizzi, Oneonta	120
	A	Marc Mirizzi, Oneonta	232
	E	Jack Joffrion, Hudson Valley	33
	DP	Marc Mirizzi, Oneonta	49
OF	AVG	Dustan Mohr, Watertown	.994
	PO	Dustan Mohr, Watertown	140
	A	Dustan Mohr, Watertown	16
	E	Marcus Howard, Lowell	12
		Stephen Logan, Auburn	12
	DP	Two tied at	3

NORTHWEST LEAGUE

Pupil conquers former teacher in championship series

BY SUSAN WADE

Tom Kotchman might be too good for his own good.

His Boise Hawks made him the most successful manager in Northwest League history in 1997, winning the Northern Division at 51-25. But among his Angels organization alumni is Jim Eppard, who won a Pacific Coast League batting title in 1987 while playing for Kotchman at Triple-A Edmonton.

Eppard parlayed Kotchman's instruction into an NWL championship for the Portland Rockies, as they rallied from a two-game deficit to defeat Boise 3-2 in the newly expanded best-of-five championship series.

MEL BAILEY

No more football
Dermal Brown

"There was no pressure on us after the first two games. All Boise had to do was win one," said Eppard, who was selected manager of the year. "I don't think anybody expected us to do it. But Justin Miller (the league ERA leader at 2.14) made it very clear from the beginning of the third game that we were not interested in going home."

Miller struck out seven in eight innings as the Rockies used a 2-1 victory in Boise to gain momentum. Portland combined early run production and Boise mistakes to win the final two games 6-0 and 4-2.

The Rockies lost their final three regular season games, but won the Southern Division title by three games over a skilled Southern Oregon team that had its best finish (41-35) since 1989.

Kotchman passed Cliff Ditto as the winningest manager as Boise posted the second-best record in franchise history. Kotchman, who has brought four league and six division championships to Boise in his eight-year NWL career, has a 370-237 record.

The Hawks led the league in hits (804) and runs (550), as well as batting average (.290).

Perhaps more emotional for Kotchman than watching the Hawks languish in their final three playoff chances was the team farewell to outfielder Jay Nunley. The .282 hitter, who punctuated his short career with a 2-for-4 final performance, was forced to retire with a heart condition.

"I told them all, 'Don't ever take life for granted,' " said Kotchman, who refers to his players as family. "If you're going to play baseball, play it the right way and play it hard. Life is no dress rehearsal."

Boise's only real threat in the Northern Division was Spokane, which missed the playoffs despite registering the league's second-best record (45-31). The Indians finished six games behind the Hawks.

Spokane made its mark with a pitching staff that had the lowest team ERA (4.02), and a talented outfield.

Goefrey Tomlinson, Dermal Brown and Juan LeBron formed a peculiar outfield trio: Tomlinson, a Jamaican cricket player relatively new to baseball; Brown, a first-round draft choice who passed up a football scholarship to the University of Maryland literally at the last minute; and LeBron, a 1995 first-round pick who continues to show promise.

Brown led the NWL in hitting for most of the season, finished as the leader in RBIs (73) and slugging percentage (.564) and was named MVP.

Tomlinson steadily improved and won the batting title at .338, one point higher than Boise's Casey Martin and Everett's Jermaine Clark. LeBron had the most doubles (27) and showed off his above-average arm in right field, joining Brown on the all-star team.

Everett produced home run champion Mike Marchiano, but the AquaSox never recovered from a 10-game losing streak and fell out of the race early. So did 1996's finalists, Yakima and Eugene. Marchiano, the 1997 NCAA Division I batting titlist at Fordham University, hit 15 home runs.

Salem-Keizer celebrated its move from Bellingham by featuring NWL leaders in saves (Jesse Travis, 16), strikeouts (Mike Riley, 96), stolen bases (Mike Byas, 51), hits (Travis Young, 107) and runs (Young, 80).

STANDINGS

Page	NORTH	W	L	PCT	GB	Manager	Attendance/Dates	Last Penn.
52	Boise Hawks (Angels)	51	25	.566	—	Tom Kotchman	154,819 (38)	1995
130	Spokane Indians (Royals)	45	31	.487	6	Jeff Garber	185,304 (38)	1990
214	Everett AquaSox (Mariners)	29	47	.440	22	Orlando Gomez	79,918 (37)	1985
137	Yakima Bears (Dodgers)	23	53	.526	28	Joe Vavra	80,003 (38)	1996
Page	**SOUTH**	**W**	**L**	**PCT**	**GB**	**Manager**	**Attendance/Dates**	**Last Penn.**
106	Portland Rockies (Rockies)	44	32	.579	—	Jim Eppard	213,242 (38)	1997
176	Southern Oregon Timberjacks (A's)	41	35	.539	3	John Kuehl	68,757 (36)	1983
209	Salem-Keizer Volcanoes (Giants)	40	36	.526	4	Shane Turner	136,836 (37)	1992
62	Eugene Emeralds (Braves)	31	45	.408	13	Jim Saul	135,926 (38)	1980

PLAYOFFS—Finals: Portland defeated Boise 3-2, in best-of-5 series.

NOTE: Team's individual batting and pitching statistics can be found on page indicated in lefthand column.

1997 Northwest League Statistics

CLUB BATTING

	AVG	G	AB	R	H	2B	3B	HR	BB	SO	SB
Boise	.290	76	2777	550	804	172	15	65	363	585	92
Spokane	.281	76	2741	514	771	149	28	70	341	628	97
Everett	.276	76	2755	457	761	143	25	61	295	729	127
Southern Oregon	.275	76	2675	496	736	147	31	53	387	714	138
Salem-Keizer	.263	76	2607	434	686	112	24	42	345	613	173
Eugene	.256	76	2649	383	677	111	27	37	275	610	58
Portland	.255	76	2562	394	653	117	26	31	312	681	80
Yakima	.252	76	2678	365	674	139	28	38	251	658	107

CLUB PITCHING

	ERA	G	CG	SHO	SV	IP	H	R	ER	BB	SO
Spokane	4.02	76	0	2	17	685	701	420	306	272	683
Portland	4.12	76	1	3	23	670	728	382	307	240	547
Boise	4.27	76	0	0	23	693	692	421	329	292	730
Salem-Keizer	4.35	76	1	1	20	667	682	408	322	295	644
Southern Oregon	4.85	76	1	2	15	679	694	464	366	334	678
Everett	4.88	76	1	3	12	673	726	480	365	380	735
Eugene	5.24	76	0	3	16	672	781	495	391	384	602
Yakima	5.29	76	1	0	9	674	758	523	396	372	599

CLUB FIELDING

	PCT	PO	A	E	DP		PCT	PO	A	E	DP
Portland	.959	2011	821	122	73	Eugene	.949	2015	842	152	65
Boise	.953	2079	865	144	47	So. Oregon	.949	2038	905	158	64
Salem-Keizer	.951	2000	737	142	65	Yakima	.944	2021	853	171	72
Spokane	.950	2055	830	153	56	Everett	.942	2018	769	173	53

INDIVIDUAL BATTING LEADERS

(Minimum 205 Plate Appearances)

	AVG	G	AB	R	H	2B	3B	HR	RBI	BB	SO	SB
Tomlinson, Goefrey, Spokane	.338	58	210	49	71	16	0	4	28	32	20	19
Martin, Casey, Boise	.337	50	181	30	61	14	0	8	48	23	45	1
Clark, Jermaine, Everett	.337	59	199	42	67	13	2	3	29	34	31	22
Espino, Fernando, Everett	.336	64	256	48	86	17	3	6	36	33	44	9
Young, Travis, Salem	.334	76	320	80	107	11	6	1	34	30	50	40
Stewart, Paxton, Boise	.333	72	282	59	94	16	2	7	45	41	55	8
Brown, Dermal, Spokane	.326	73	298	67	97	20	6	13	73	38	65	17
Child, Casey, Boise	.325	68	274	69	89	26	2	11	57	34	47	18
Martinez, Hipolito, SO	.324	65	222	45	72	13	4	9	44	34	65	3
Dewey, Jason, Boise	.324	68	272	55	88	17	2	13	64	41	70	5

INDIVIDUAL PITCHING LEADERS

(Minimum 61 Innings)

	W	L	ERA	G	GS	CG	SV	IP	H	R	ER	BB	SO
Miller, Justin, Portland	4	2	2.14	14	11	0	0	67	68	26	16	20	54
Nathan, Joe, Salem	2	1	2.47	18	5	0	2	62	53	22	17	26	44
Cummings, Ryan, Boise	6	2	3.09	14	13	0	0	70	73	38	24	10	79
Key, Scott, Spokane	3	3	3.23	25	1	0	3	70	55	33	25	31	66
Schurman, Ryan, Eugene	4	6	3.23	16	15	0	0	86	75	46	31	43	95
Wise, Matt, Boise	9	1	3.25	15	15	0	0	83	62	37	30	34	86
Pederson, Justin, Spokane	5	3	3.44	15	13	0	0	65	61	34	25	24	84
Kringen, Jake, Portland	6	5	3.46	15	15	1	0	83	84	40	32	20	72
Riley, Mike, Salem	9	2	3.46	15	15	1	0	88	76	39	34	28	96
Meady, Todd, Spokane	2	3	3.72	21	4	0	0	65	68	38	27	18	39

ALL-STAR TEAM

C—Jason Dewey, Boise. **1B**—Mark Burke, Eugene; Nick Leach, Yakima. **2B**—Travis Young, Salem-Keizer. **3B**—Adam Piatt, Southern Oregon. **SS**—Nelson Castro, Boise. **OF**—Dermal Brown, Spokane; Casey Child, Boise; Juan LeBron, Spokane. **DH**—Mike Marchiano, Everett. **LHP**—Mike Riley, Salem-Keizer. **RHP**—Matt Wise, Boise. **LRP**—Clint Chrysler, Everett. **RRP**—Ara Petrosian, Portland.

Most Valuable Player—Dermal Brown, Spokane. **Manager of the Year**—Jim Eppard, Portland.

TOP 10 PROSPECTS

1. Dermal Brown, of, Spokane; **2.** Gil Meche, rhp, Everett; **3.** Nelson Castro, ss, Boise; **4.** Jason Dewey, c, Boise; **5.** Nick Leach, 1b, Yakima; **6.** Juan LeBron, of, Spokane; **7.** Adam Piatt, 3b, Southern Oregon; **8.** Mike Byas, of, Salem; **9.** Nathan Haynes, of, Southern Oregon; **10.** Greg Jones, rhp, Boise.

DEPT. LEADERS

BATTING

G	Travis Young, Salem-Keizer	76
AB	Travis Young, Salem-Keizer	320
R	Travis Young, Salem-Keizer	80
H	Travis Young, Salem-Keizer	107
TB	Dermal Brown, Spokane	168
XBH	Dermal Brown, Spokane	39
	Casey Child, Spokane	39
2B	Juan LeBron, Spokane	27
3B	Cash Riley, Yakima	7
HR	Mike Marchiano, Everett	15
RBI	Dermal Brown, Spokane	73
SH	Joe Caruso, Spokane	8
SF	C.J. Ankrum, Salem-Keizer	7
BB	Nick Sosa, Southern Oregon	55
IBB	Todd Sears, Portland	7
HBP	C.J. Ankrum, Salem-Keizer	11
SO	Andres Mitchell, Portland	102
SB	Michael Byas, Salem-Keizer	51
CS	Adam Robinson, So. Oregon	11
GIDP	Gerald Eady, Everett	10
OB%	Goefrey Tomlinson, Spokane	.440
SL%	Dermal Brown, Spokane	.564

PITCHING

G	Scot Shields, Boise	30
GS	Joe Gangemi, Boise	16
	Ryan Jensen, Salem-Keizer	16
CG	Five tied at	1
ShO	Jake Kringen, Portland	1
GF	Jesse Travis, Salem-Keizer	27
SV	Jesse Travis, Salem-Keizer	16
W	Matt Wise, Boise	9
	Michael Riley, Salem-Keizer	9
L	Lance Backowski, Yakima	12
IP	Michael Riley, Salem-Keizer	88
H	Mike Roberts, Eugene	104
R	Lance Backowski, Yakima	72
ER	Mike Roberts, Eugene	59
HR	Three tied at	10
HB	Lance Backowski, Yakima	10
BB	Brandon Nogowski, Everett	57
SO	Michael Riley, Salem-Keizer	96
WP	Mark Harriger, Boise	15
BK	Ryan Greene, Eugene	6

FIELDING

C	AVG	Mark Mortimer, Eugene	.992
	PO	Jason Dewey, Boise	483
	A	Jeremy Hill, Spokane	60
	E	Jose Figueroa, SO	14
	DP	Three tied at	3
	PB	Jeremy Hill, Spokane	29
1B	AVG	Mark Burke, Eugene	.993
	PO	C.J. Ankrum, Salem	609
	A	C.J. Ankrum, Salem	49
	E	Doug Blosser, Spokane	11
	DP	C.J. Ankrum, Salem	53
2B	AVG	Jaime Goudie, Yakima	.971
	PO	Travis Young, Salem	173
	A	Travis Young, Salem	193
	E	Manuel Sanchez, Eugene	19
	DP	Travis Young, Salem	43
3B	AVG	Ricardo Montas, Spokane	.884
	PO	Oscar Betancourt, Boise	37
	A	Oscar Betancourt, Boise	142
	E	Oscar Betancourt, Boise	26
	DP	Brian Zaun, Yakima	13
SS	AVG	Nelson Castro, Boise	.923
	PO	Ramon Valera, Everett	109
	A	Al Castro, Eugene	219
	E	Ramon Valera, Everett	42
	DP	Ricky Bell, Yakima	36
		Al Castro, Eugene	36
OF	AVG	Michael Byas, Salem	.980
	PO	Michael Byas, Salem	140
	A	Efrain Alamo, Portland	11
	E	Cash Riley, Yakima	11
	DP	Juan LeBron, Spokane	4

APPALACHIAN LEAGUE

Bluefield wins league championship, local bragging rights

BY STEPHEN BORELLI

The Bluefield Orioles beat the Pulaski Rangers two games to none for their second straight Appalachian League championship, but first they had to settle an old score.

The Orioles finished the regular season tied for first place in the Eastern Division with the Princeton Devil Rays, their West Virginia rival 10 miles away. The rivalry is even more natural because Bluefield president George McGonagle and Princeton president Dewey Russell, both former city council members, were elected vice mayors of their respective towns during the 1997 season.

A Ray with sting
Jared Sandberg

The Orioles upheld their civic duty by beating Princeton 5-4 in 10 innings in a one-game playoff. Bluefield then rode that momentum to 8-0 and 4-2 wins over Pulaski to take the title.

Orioles righthander Jordan Romero, who struggled at 1-3, 6.51 during the regular season, beat Pulaski in the opener with a four-hit shutout that included 12 strikeouts. Shortstop Jerry Hairston went 3-for-5 and scored two runs.

Righthander Matt Achilles (7-2, 3.95) got the win in the clincher.

The Orioles' surge capped an Appy League season of much-appreciated consistency.

Because the league left Huntington, W.Va., before the 1996 season, nine clubs had to handle an odd schedule. That included doubleheaders in which clubs played one game at home and one on the road against different teams.

"Ernie Banks' quote, 'Let's play two,' I don't think he had that in mind," said Danville Braves general manager Scott Rittenhouse.

Pulaski's re-entry into the league solved those problems. The town last had an Appy League team in 1992, and rejoined when the Texas Rangers needed an affiliate and the Appy League needed a team. Because the Rangers didn't have a low Class A club, Pulaski fielded an unusually experienced lineup.

Danville righthander Luis Rivera (3-1, 2.41) was the league's top prospect.

The Appy League featured several first-round draft picks, including Burlington righthander Tim Drew (fourth overall) and Bristol righthander Aaron Myette (ninth) from 1997, and Danville first baseman A.J. Zapp (fifth) and Kingsport outfielder Robert Stratton (eighth) from 1996.

Drew, younger brother of College Player of the Year J.D. Drew, went 0-1, 6.17 in four starts, but struck out 14 and walked only four in 12 innings. He signed late with the Indians for $1.6 million.

"He has excellent velocity and a better breaking ball than I was led to believe," said Joe Mikulik, Drew's manager at Burlington. "He also had great composure."

Another 1996 first-round pick, Princeton outfielder Paul Wilder, didn't impress Appy League pitchers. Wilder gazed for a while at his long home run in the eighth inning off Burlington's Troy Silva in an 8-0 Princeton win. Righty Antonio Vasquez then hit Wilder with a pitch in the top of the ninth. A bench-clearing brawl ensued and Wilder, who hit .206 for the season, got the heftiest fine and was suspended for five games.

The most feared hitter in the league was a 16th-round 1996 pick, Princeton second baseman Jared Sandberg. A nephew of Cubs second baseman Ryne Sandberg, he led the league in RBIs, total bases–and intentional walks.

Princeton second baseman Robert Berns set Appy League single-season records with 34 doubles and 44 extra-base hits. The doubles total also was a record for a National Association short-season league.

STANDINGS

Page	EAST	W	L	PCT	GB	Manager	Attendance/Dates	Last Penn.
69	Bluefield Orioles (Orioles)	40	29	.580	—	Bobby Dickerson	43,300 (32)	1997
218	Princeton Devil Rays (Devil Rays)	39	30	.565	1	Charlie Montoyo	36,481 (32)	1994
101	Burlington Indians (Indians)	32	38	.471	7½	Harry Spilman	46,915 (34)	1993
62	Danville Braves (Braves)	30	29	.441	9½	Rick Albert	75,745 (34)	None
183	Martinsville Phillies (Phillies)	29	47	.426	10½	Kelly Heath	39,947 (34)	None
Page	**WEST**	**W**	**L**	**PCT**	**GB**	**Manager**	**Attendance/Dates**	**Last Penn.**
224	Pulaski Rangers (Rangers)	43	25	.632	—	Julio Cruz	23,898 (33)	None
149	Elizabethton Twins (Twins)	38	30	.559	5	Jose Marzan	17,397 (32)	1990
170	Kingsport Mets (Mets)	37	31	.544	6	Ken Berry	48,396 (33)	1995
82	Bristol Sox (White Sox)	30	38	.441	13	Nick Capra	25,105 (30)	1985
196	Johnson City Cardinals (Cardinals)	23	45	.338	20	Steve Turco	43,300 (32)	1976

PLAYOFFS—Bluefield defeated Princeton in one-game tiebreaker playoff. **Finals:** Bluefield defeated Pulaski 2-0, in best-of-3 series.
NOTE: Team's individual batting and pitching statistics can be found on page indicated in lefthand column.

1997 Appalachian League Statistics

CLUB BATTING

	AVG	G	AB	R	H	2B	3B	HR	BB	SO	SB
Elizabethton	.295	68	2387	469	704	130	8	72	273	518	50
Bristol	.279	68	2302	440	642	121	15	75	265	558	84
Princeton	.272	69	2447	484	666	138	27	73	263	606	70
Pulaski	.270	68	2331	440	629	130	25	59	295	538	132
Kingsport	.267	68	2327	414	621	109	20	57	230	560	87
Johnson City	.265	68	2326	346	617	139	17	57	197	598	62
Bluefield	.265	69	2325	389	615	120	22	42	247	520	116
Burlington	.262	68	2320	403	609	120	18	53	276	611	116
Martinsville	.252	68	2324	345	585	111	10	42	198	620	72
Danville	.252	68	2277	360	573	113	21	46	240	642	64

CLUB PITCHING

	ERA	G	CG	SHO	SV	IP	H	R	ER	BB	SO
Pulaski	3.33	68	4	4	15	601	538	309	222	199	663
Bluefield	4.20	69	1	4	16	596	564	337	278	255	628
Princeton	4.34	69	1	4	10	607	640	392	293	210	565
Burlington	4.40	68	0	5	10	592	605	393	290	261	522
Martinsville	4.62	68	1	3	13	588	608	395	302	215	503
Elizabethton	5.11	68	2	3	12	583	639	416	331	229	562
Danville	5.13	68	1	3	14	584	601	428	333	275	621
Kingsport	5.31	68	2	1	16	592	683	418	350	208	578
Bristol	5.90	68	2	4	9	574	655	465	377	312	560
Johnson City	6.59	68	1	0	14	578	728	537	424	320	569

CLUB FIELDING

	PCT	PO	A	E	DP
Bluefield	.958	1787	641	106	48
Burlington	.953	1776	790	126	58
Princeton	.953	1821	760	127	48
Kingsport	.951	1776	713	129	56
Pulaski	.948	1802	673	137	45
Elizabethton	.947	1748	710	138	56
Bristol	.944	1722	685	144	57
Martinsville	.943	1765	754	151	57
Johnson City	.941	1735	643	148	52
Danville	.939	1751	638	155	43

INDIVIDUAL BATTING LEADERS

(Minimum 184 Plate Appearances)

	AVG	G	AB	R	H	2B	3B	HR	RBI	BB	SO	SB
Orndorff, Dave, Elizabethton	.368	55	228	62	84	15	1	11	42	22	25	18
Giles, Marcus, Danville	.348	55	207	53	72	13	3	8	45	32	47	5
Feramisco, Derek, JC	.342	53	184	34	63	12	3	6	36	16	37	8
Zapp, A.J., Danville	.338	65	234	34	79	23	2	7	56	35	78	0
Kilburg, Joe, Burlington	.335	52	182	59	61	8	7	3	30	39	46	29
Lamb, Mike, Pulaski	.335	60	233	59	78	19	3	9	47	31	18	7
Pena, Jose, Pulaski	.333	51	204	45	68	14	3	3	31	12	40	17
Schaeffer, Jon, Elizabethton	.333	48	165	35	55	13	0	6	34	33	32	0
Sutton, Joe, Bristol	.332	56	190	46	63	18	2	11	43	35	51	7
Hairston, Jerry, Bluefield	.330	59	221	44	73	13	4	2	36	21	29	13

INDIVIDUAL PITCHING LEADERS

(Minimum 54 Innings)

	W	L	ERA	G	GS	CG	SV	IP	H	R	ER	BB	SO
DeYoung, Dan, Pulaski	4	1	1.91	19	8	1	3	61	52	16	13	12	69
Poland, Trey, Pulaski	7	3	2.00	13	13	3	0	85	57	29	19	18	106
Manbeck, Mark, Mar.	3	1	2.22	9	9	0	0	57	51	16	14	3	64
Bond, Aaron, Pulaski	5	2	2.45	14	14	0	0	77	56	29	21	22	64
Turnbow, Mark, Burlington	8	2	2.78	13	13	0	0	74	49	25	23	18	53
Bauer, Richard, Bluefield	8	3	2.86	13	13	0	0	72	58	31	23	20	67
Seberino, Ronni, Princeton	4	4	3.17	14	14	0	0	65	71	39	23	28	57
Perez, Norberto, Bluefield	3	5	3.46	10	10	0	0	55	52	29	21	16	58
Perez, Pablo, Elizabethton	10	0	3.52	17	10	0	0	79	79	37	31	12	69
Quevedo, Ruben, Danville	1	5	3.56	13	11	0	0	68	46	37	27	27	78

ALL-STAR TEAM

C—Joe Sutton, Bristol. **1B**—Robert Berns, Princeton. **2B**—Jared Sandberg, Princeton. **3B**—Matt Berger, Bristol. **SS**—Pablo Ozuna, Johnson City. **OF**—Brandon Copeland, Kingsport; Derek Feramisco, Johnson City; Robert Stratton, Kingsport. **DH**—David Orndorff, Elizabethton. **Util**—Joe Kilburg, Burlington; Joe McHenry, Elizabethton. **LHP**—Trey Poland, Pulaski. **RHP**—Dan DeYoung, Pulaski. **RP**—David Mastrolonardo, Bluefield.

Most Valuable Player—Jared Sandberg, Princeton. **Pitcher of the Year**—Trey Poland, Pulaski. **Manager of the Year**—Julio Cruz, Pulaski.

TOP 10 PROSPECTS

1. Luis Rivera, rhp, Danville; **2.** Dan DeYoung, rhp, Pulaski; **3.** Tim Drew, rhp, Burlington; **4.** Jared Sandberg, 2b-3b, Princeton; **5.** A. J. Zapp, 1b, Danville; **6.** Trey Poland, lhp, Pulaski; **7.** Brandon Copeland, of, Kingsport; **8.** Robert Stratton, of, Kingsport; **9.** Aaron Myette, rhp, Bristol; **10.** Jerry Hairston, ss, Bluefield.

DEPT. LEADERS

BATTING

G	Three tied at	67
AB	Jared Sandberg, Princeton	268
R	Dave Orndorff, Elizabethton	62
H	Dave Orndorff, Elizabethton	84
TB	Jared Sandberg, Princeton	157
XBH	Robert Berns, Princeton	44
2B	Robert Berns, Princeton	34
3B	Joe Kilburg, Burlington	7
HR	Matt Berger, Bristol	18
RBI	Jared Sandberg, Princeton	68
SH	Jason Brett, Kingsport	6
	Pablo Ozuna, Johnson City	6
SF	Eddy Garavito, Bluefield	7
BB	Jonathan Hamilton, Burlington	51
IBB	Jared Sanberg, Princeton	5
HBP	Uriel Casillas, Martinsville	12
SO	Jared Sandberg, Princeton	94
	Robert Stratton, Kingsport	94
SB	Joe Kilburg, Burlington	29
CS	Three tied at	9
GIDP	Omar Lopes, Bristol	9
OB%	Joe Kilburg, Burlington	.465
SL%	Shawn Gallagher, Pulaski	.643

PITCHING

G	Derek Gooden, Johnson City	31
GS	Eight tied at	14
CG	Trey Poland, Pulaski	3
ShO	Trey Poland, Pulaski	2
GF	Lance Franks, Johnson City	23
SV	Lance Franks, Johnson City	12
	David Mastrolonardo, Bluefield	12
W	Pablo Perez, Elizabethton	10
L	Otoniel Lanfranco, Johnson City	8
	Aaron Taylor, Danville	8
IP	Trey Poland, Pulaski	85
H	Lee Marshall, Elizabethton	93
R	Toribio Guzman, Johnson City	75
ER	Toribio Guzman, Johnson City	60
HR	Otoniel Lanfranco, Johnson City	14
HB	Tim Lyons, Danville	12
BB	Joe Bales, Bristol	49
SO	Trey Poland, Pulaski	106
WP	Tim Lyons, Danville	24
BK	Toribio Guzman, Johnson City	6

FIELDING

C	AVG	Miguel Suriel, Princeton	.983
	PO	Steve Torrealba, Danville	398
	A	Joe Sutton, Bristol	61
	E	Steve Torrealba, Danville	18
	DP	John Ellis, Pulaski	5
	PB	Edgar Cruz, Burlington	20
1B	AVG	Franky Figueroa, Bluefield	.989
	PO	Grant Sharpe, Burlington	547
	A	Robert Berns, Princeton	52
	E	Three tied at	12
	DP	Grant Sharpe, Burlington	51
2B	AVG	Eddy Garavito, Bluefield	.956
	PO	Eddy Garavito, Bluefield	97
	A	Tom Sergio, Pulaski	151
	E	Jim Terrell, Bristol	17
	DP	Uriel Casillas, Martinsville	31
3B	AVG	Michael Edwards, Bur.	.890
	PO	Matt Berger, Bristol	52
	A	Michael Edwards, Bur.	130
	E	Mike Ryan, Elizabethton	28
	DP	Michael Edwards, Bur.	13
SS	AVG	Jerry Hairston, Bluefield	.949
	PO	Paul Hoover, Princeton	111
	A	Paul Hoover, Princeton	199
	E	Paul Hoover, Princeton	33
		Frank Taveras, Burlington	33
	DP	Paul Hoover, Princeton	35
OF	AVG	Joe Secoda, Johnson City	.990
	PO	Luis Matos, Bluefield	125
	A	Scott Neuberger, Princeton	11
	E	Martires Castro, Pulaski	10
	DP	Four tied at	2

PIONEER LEAGUE

Reds prospects, return of Scott give Billings top billing

BY STEPHEN BORELLI

While the Billings Mustangs swept through the Pioneer League playoffs in 1997, the real celebrating may come a few years down the road.

More specifically, it may come several hundred miles southeast in Cincinnati. With five of the league's Top 10 Prospects, the Mustangs gave hope to a Reds organization that's thin in talent at the upper levels.

But first, they took care of business in a 2-0 sweep of the Great Falls Dodgers in the league's best-of-three championship series. Righthander Josh Harris pitched a three-hit shutout for a 4-0 Billings victory in the opener, and Mustangs DH Andy Burress hit a home run in the final game, a 4-3 Billings win.

Burress batted .533 in the postseason. Billings also swept the Idaho Falls Braves in two games in the division series.

Red tide
Mike Frank

The Mustangs, who went 39-32 overall during the regular season, bounced back from an uncustomary 23-49 record in 1996. They won consecutive league titles from 1992-94 under manager Donnie Scott, and it was Scott who led them to their latest triumph.

Scott left his job as Cincinnati's minor league field coordinator to take over for former major leaguer Derrel Thomas, whom the Reds fired before he ever managed a game for Billings.

Scott, who has been the Reds' field coordinator since 1995, inherited quite a team.

Shortstop Travis Dawkins, the league's No. 2-rated prospect, hit .241 with 16 stolen bases. No. 3 DeWayne Wise hit .313 with seven homers and 18 steals, and ran down just about everything in center field. No. 5 Mike Frank, another outfielder, hit .376-10-62 with 18 steals.

No. 7 Scott Williamson (8-2, 1.78), a righthander, and No. 9 Monte Roundtree (1-2, 5.06), a lefty, gave the pitching staff a boost.

All five players were drafted in 1997 by Cincinnati in the first 10 rounds.

Lethbridge outfielder Jhensy Sandoval (.375-8-37, nine steals) edged out Dawkins as the top prospect. Most league mangers thought Sandoval was a five-tool player, and Helena Brewers manager Alex Morales was their best spokesman. "Sandoval can do anything and everything," Morales said.

Medicine Hat first baseman-outfielder Greg Morrison had a memorable season in his hometown. Morrison, whom the Dodgers released after the 1996 season, took home MVP honors by winning a triple crown. He won the batting title with a .448 average and set league single-season records for home runs (23) and RBIs (88).

Attendance went up about 200 people a game in Medicine Hat, thanks largely to all the family and friends Morrison brought in.

"When you're more at home, you're more relaxed," said Morrison, who had been helping out coaching his former high school team before Medicine Hat general manager Chris McKenna found him. "I don't put pressure on myself anymore. It's funny. When you don't count on baseball, you get an opportunity to jump back into the game."

The Butte Copper Kings were the only Pioneer League team to switch afiliations for 1997, moving from the Devil Rays to the Angels.

STANDINGS: SPLIT SEASON

FIRST HALF

NORTH	W	L	PCT	GB
Great Falls	21	15	.583	—
Medicine Hat	17	19	.472	4
Lethbridge	17	19	.472	4
Helena	16	20	.444	5
SOUTH	**W**	**L**	**PCT**	**GB**
Ogden	21	15	.583	—
Billings	21	15	.583	—
Idaho Falls	18	18	.500	3
Butte	13	23	.361	8

SECOND HALF

NORTH	W	L	PCT	GB
Lethbridge	22	14	.611	—
Helena	21	14	.600	½
Great Falls	19	17	.528	3
Medicine Hat	9	27	.250	13
SOUTH	**W**	**L**	**PCT**	**GB**
Idaho Falls	21	15	.583	—
Billings	18	17	.514	2½
Butte	17	19	.472	4
Ogden	16	20	.444	5

PLAYOFFS—Semifinals: Great Falls defeated Lethbridge 2-0, and Billings defeated Idaho Falls 2-0, in best-of-3 series. **Finals:** Billings defeated Great Falls 2-0, in best-of-3 series.

STANDINGS: OVERALL

Page		W	L	PCT	GB	Manager	Attendance/Dates	Last Penn.
138	Great Falls Dodgers (Dodgers)	40	32	.556	—	Mickey Hatcher	58,595 (35)	1990
202	Idaho Falls Braves (Padres)	39	32	.549	½	Don Werner	56,039 (34)	1974
95	Billings Mustangs (Reds)	39	32	.549	½	Donnie Scott	97,708 (35)	1997
56	Lethbridge Black Diamonds (Diamondbacks)	39	33	.542	1	Tommy Jones	46,909 (34)	1980
143	Helena Brewers (Brewers)	37	34	.521	2½	Alex Morales	35,161 (32)	1981
144	Ogden Raptors (Brewers)	36	35	.507	3½	Bernie Moncallo	101,256 (36)	None
53	Butte Copper Kings (Angels)	30	42	.417	10	Bill Lachemann	32,854 (34)	1981
231	Medicine Hat Blue Jays (Blue Jays)	26	46	.361	24	Marty Pevey	46,770 (34)	1982

NOTE: Team's individual batting and pitching statistics can be found on page indicated in lefthand column.

1997 Pioneer League Statistics

CLUB BATTING

	AVG	G	AB	R	H	2B	3B	HR	BB	SO	SB
Idaho Falls	.291	72	2552	465	743	132	37	37	330	524	95
Ogden	.288	72	2528	478	727	156	22	51	287	548	69
Billings	.287	71	2482	446	713	127	21	59	257	516	76
Butte	.286	72	2549	478	728	132	21	64	276	558	71
Helena	.285	71	2501	434	712	131	10	54	266	506	63
Lethbridge	.274	72	2492	439	683	107	25	72	281	603	66
Great Falls	.274	72	2441	376	669	101	31	37	188	527	103
Medicine Hat	.262	72	2492	378	654	110	15	54	233	538	79

CLUB PITCHING

	ERA	G	CG	SHO	SV	IP	H	R	ER	BB	SO
Great Falls	3.77	72	2	5	17	635	660	348	266	252	563
Billings	4.03	71	4	3	18	624	675	389	279	264	548
Lethbridge	4.22	72	2	3	14	624	652	379	293	209	550
Helena	4.87	71	2	2	20	617	664	430	334	292	536
Medicine Hat	4.95	72	4	1	7	621	696	469	342	294	530
Ogden	5.05	72	2	1	11	623	732	468	350	238	573
Idaho Falls	5.92	72	2	2	24	632	756	482	416	294	550
Butte	5.93	72	10	1	7	620	794	529	409	275	470

CLUB FIELDING

	PCT	PO	A	E	DP		PCT	PO	A	E	DP
Idaho Falls	.957	1896	823	123	65	Helena	.948	1850	791	145	59
Great Falls	.952	1905	826	138	73	Billings	.943	1871	751	158	57
Ogden	.950	1870	784	141	57	Butte	.942	1861	854	168	70
Lethbridge	.949	1873	846	146	62	Medicine Hat	.938	1863	777	174	61

INDIVIDUAL BATTING LEADERS

(Minimum 194 Plate Appearances)

	AVG	G	AB	R	H	2B	3B	HR	RBI	BB	SO	SB
Morrison, Greg, Med. Hat	.448	69	241	63	108	16	3	23	88	14	29	2
Kraus, Jake, Helena/Ogden	.390	69	246	51	96	22	1	10	69	38	15	8
Bunkley, Antuan, Helena	.381	70	270	52	103	23	0	17	67	32	37	2
Frank, Mike, Billings	.376	69	266	62	100	22	6	10	62	35	24	18
Alfano, Jeff, Ogden	.360	46	175	39	63	12	4	7	29	17	31	9
Hagins, Steve, Butte	.351	64	268	59	94	20	1	17	56	17	53	13
Suarez, Marc, Billings	.347	64	219	42	76	17	0	9	37	33	51	2
Snellgrove, Clay, IF	.345	66	281	52	97	19	7	2	48	18	39	3
Allen, Luke, Great Falls	.345	67	258	50	89	12	6	7	40	19	53	12
Moreta, Ramon, Great Falls	.336	68	265	45	89	6	2	1	20	18	38	29

INDIVIDUAL PITCHING LEADERS

(Minimum 58 Innings)

	W	L	ERA	G	GS	CG	SV	IP	H	R	ER	BB	SO
Sneed, John, Med. Hat	6	1	1.29	15	10	2	0	70	42	19	10	20	79
Williamson, Scott, Billings	8	2	1.78	13	13	2	0	86	66	25	17	23	101
Puorto, Jamie, Lethbridge	4	2	2.43	20	6	0	2	59	44	26	16	9	58
Stover, C.D., Great Falls	7	2	2.56	12	12	1	0	77	71	36	22	14	61
Zamora, Pete, Great Falls	2	5	2.58	13	10	1	2	70	59	27	20	30	73
Rojas, Renney, Butte	8	4	3.51	15	15	5	0	110	113	54	43	19	65
Robinson, Dustin, Billings	6	2	3.68	16	9	2	4	73	91	38	30	6	48
Lee, Derek, Ogden	4	4	3.87	14	13	0	0	74	89	49	32	20	71
Harris, Josh, Billings	4	6	4.02	14	14	0	0	85	103	51	38	26	56
Merrell, Philip, Billings	2	6	4.33	14	14	0	0	73	72	51	35	27	62

ALL-STAR TEAM

C—Bobby Darula, Ogden. **1B**—Jake Kraus, Helena/Ogden. **2B**—Clay Snellgrove, Idaho Falls. **3B**—Luke Allen, Great Falls. **SS**—Travis Dawkins, Billings. **OF**—Greg Morrison, Medicine Hat; Mike Frank, Billings; Dewayne Wise, Billings. **DH**—Antuan Bunkley, Helena. **LHP**—Derek Lee, Ogden; Craig Taczy, Great Falls. **RHP**—Scott Williamson, Billings. **RP**—Shawn Camp, Idaho Falls.

Most Valuable Player—Greg Morrison, Medicine Hat. **Manager of the Year**—Don Werner, Idaho Falls.

TOP 10 PROSPECTS

1. Jhensy Sandoval, of, Lethbridge; **2.** Travis Dawkins, ss, Billings; **3.** DeWayne Wise, of, Billings; **4.** Kyle Peterson, rhp, Ogden; **5.** Mike Frank, of, Billings; **6.** Luke Allen, 3b, Great Falls; **7.** Scott Williamson, rhp, Billings; **8.** Ramon Moreta, of, Great Falls; **9.** Monte Roundtree, lhp, Billings; **10.** John Sneed, rhp, Medicine Hat.

DEPT. LEADERS

BATTING

G	Marcus Knight, Butte	72
AB	Marcus Knight, Butte	293
R	Scott Kirby, Helena	65
H	Greg Morrison, Medicine Hat	108
TB	Greg Morrison, Medicine Hat	199
XBH	Greg Morrison, Medicine Hat	42
2B	Bobby Darula, Ogden	25
3B	DeWayne Wise, Billings	9
HR	Greg Morrison, Medicine Hat	23
RBI	Greg Morrison, Medicine Hat	88
SH	Monte Marshall, Great Falls	6
	Ramon Moreta, Great Falls	6
SF	Three tied at	6
BB	Scott Kirby, Helena	53
IBB	Antuan Bunkley, Helena	5
	Mike Frank, Billings	5
HBP	Jake Kraus, Ogden/Helena	12
SO	Brandon James, Ogden	78
SB	Ramon Moreta, Great Falls	29
CS	Ramon Moreta, Great Falls	17
GIDP	Jake Kraus, Ogden/Helena	12
OB%	Jake Kraus, Ogden/Helena	.487
SL%	Greg Morrison, Medicine Hat	.826

PITCHING

G	Shawn Camp, Idaho Falls	30
GS	Three tied at	15
CG	Renney Rojas, Butte	5
ShO	Four tied at	1
GF	Shawn Camp, Idaho Falls	24
SV	Shawn Camp, Idaho Falls	12
W	Renney Rojas, Butte	8
	Scott Williamson, Billings	8
L	Al Hawkins, Ogden	8
IP	Renney Rojas, Butte	110
H	Al Hawkins, Ogden	113
	Renney Rojas, Butte	113
R	Al Hawkins, Ogden	74
ER	Al Hawkins, Ogden	53
HR	Paul Stewart, Ogden	13
HB	Mark Kirst, Ogden	10
BB	Brandon Steele, Butte	42
SO	Scott Williamson, Billings	101
WP	Three tied at	12
BK	Victor Alvarez, Great Falls	3
	Franklin Rodriguez, Med. Hat	3

FIELDING

C	**AVG**	Josh McAffee, Lethbridge	.996
	PO	Marc Suarez, Billings	439
	A	Marc Suarez, Billings	64
	E	Marc Suarez, Billings	14
	DP	Brian Moon, Helena	5
	PB	Marc Suarez, Billings	21
1B	**AVG**	Brian Jergenson, IF	.983
	PO	Jake Kraus, Ogden/Hel.	492
	A	Brian Jergenson, IF	41
	E	Edwin Falcon, Great Falls	10
	DP	Jake Kraus, Ogden/Helena	41
2B	**AVG**	Felipe Rodriguez, MH	.929
	PO	Felipe Rodriguez, MH	104
	A	Clay Snellgrove, IF	126
	E	Andre Montgomery, Billings	17
		Felipe Rodriguez, MH	17
	DP	Elieser Rojas, Helena	28
3B	**AVG**	Mike Lawrence, Butte	.935
	PO	Mike Lawrence, Butte	52
	A	Mike Lawrence, Butte	163
	E	Scott Kirby, Helena	37
	DP	Mike Lawrence, Butte	20
SS	**AVG**	Bernie Torres, Great Falls	.942
	PO	Travis Dawkins, Billings	118
	A	Travis Dawkins, Billings	216
	E	Josephang Bernhardt, MH	39
	DP	Wellington Sanchez, Hel.	37
OF	**AVG**	Karl Ryden, Idaho Falls	.989
	PO	Mike Frank, Billings	118
		DeWayne Wise, Billings	118
	A	Mike Frank, Billings	11
	E	DeWayne Wise, Billings	13
	DP	Rafael Gomera, Great Falls	4

ARIZONA LEAGUE

Change of leagues doesn't change Cubs' winning results

BY STEPHEN BORELLI

The Cubs changed their Rookie-level affiliate in 1997, moving from the Gulf Coast League to the Arizona League. And they picked up right where they left off.

After the Angels moved their Rookie-level team from Arizona to Butte of the Pioneer League, the Cubs stepped into the void and won the Arizona League championship by five games over the Mariners. They all but clinched the title with a 14-game winning streak from July 28 to Aug. 9, tying the minor league high for the year. The Cubs had won the GCL's Southwest Division in 1996.

JOHN SPEAR

Healthy numbers
Todd Noel

But wins aside, the AZL Cubs also succeeded at what is the real purpose of the Arizona League, a complex-based league played at spring training sites in and around the Phoenix area. They showcased two of the league's top three prospects, as determined by a poll of managers.

No. 1 prospect Todd Noel pitched only four innings in 1996 in the GCL, the result of a growth plate problem in his pitching arm. Noel, the Cubs' first-round pick in 1996, made up for lost time, going 5-1 with a league-leading 1.96 ERA.

A righthander, he located his 96-mph fastball well and showed a good mix of pitches as he struck out 63 and walked 30 in 59 innings.

"He's a real bulldog," said Cubs manager Terry Kennedy, the former major league catcher. "He really bears down on hitters."

Noel shares a lot in common with righthander Jon Garland, his teammate and the league's No. 3 prospect. Both signed for big bonuses, as the Cubs gave Noel $900,000 and Garland, their first-round pick in 1997, $1.325 million. Both are around 6-foot-5 and 200 pounds, have low- to mid-90s fastballs, as well as similar composure and deliveries.

The defending champion Padres also had two of the Arizona League's top prospects in outfielder Kevin Burford (No. 2) and righthander Wascar Serrano (No. 5). Burford, San Diego's 15th-round pick in the 1997 draft, led the league with a .389 average and 50 RBIs and was selected the league's most valuable player.

Athletics second baseman Monty Davis had one of the best single-game performances in the minors in 1997, when he went 6-for-7 with three homers and nine RBIs against the Padres. His hits and RBIs tied him for the best one-game marks in the minors.

Diamondbacks first baseman Lance Downing, the league's second-ranked hitter at .381, had a league record 32-game hitting streak from July 7 to Aug. 15, tying him for the minor league high. He went 54-for-123 (.439) during the streak.

STANDINGS

Page		Complex Site	W	L	PCT	GB	Manager(s)	Last Penn.
89	Cubs	Mesa	34	20	.630	—	Terry Kennedy	1997
215	Mariners	Peoria	30	26	.536	5	Darrin Garner	None
177	Athletics	Scottsdale	29	27	.518	6	Juan Navarrete	1995
57	Diamondbacks	Phoenix	27	29	.482	8	Brian Butterfield/Don Wakamatsu	None
203	Padres	Peoria	25	30	.455	9½	Randy Whisler	1996
107	Rockies	Chandler	21	34	.382	13½	Tim Blackwell	None

PLAYOFFS—None.

NOTE: Team's individual batting and pitching statistics can be found on page indicated in lefthand column.

1997 Arizona League Statistics

CLUB BATTING

	AVG	G	AB	R	H	2B	3B	HR	BB	SO	SB
Mariners	.278	56	1956	364	543	90	20	22	264	510	114
Athletics	.269	56	1931	407	520	91	23	37	332	442	137
Padres	.265	55	1939	335	513	106	16	18	296	464	85
Rockies	.263	56	1977	297	519	82	21	15	179	388	112
Cubs	.262	55	1886	345	495	75	27	16	222	410	109
Diamondbacks	.262	56	1937	324	507	105	21	15	226	469	47

CLUB PITCHING

	ERA	G	CG	SHO	SV	IP	H	R	ER	BB	SO
Cubs	3.43	55	0	4	20	488	493	294	186	255	464
Diamondbacks	4.17	56	0	1	13	494	530	309	229	200	399
Rockies	4.50	56	0	0	12	499	532	376	250	258	449
Mariners	4.60	56	1	1	11	492	485	344	252	268	458
Athletics	4.87	56	0	1	13	484	526	349	262	260	441
Padres	5.61	55	0	0	9	487	531	400	304	278	472

CLUB FIELDING

	PCT	PO	A	E	DP
Mariners	.949	1476	594	111	40
Diamondbacks	.944	1483	616	124	43
Athletics	.942	1453	594	126	44
Cubs	.941	1464	530	126	51
Rockies	.929	1497	641	163	56
Padres	.926	1462	590	165	55

INDIVIDUAL BATTING LEADERS

(Minimum 151 Plate Appearances)

	AVG	G	AB	R	H	2B	3B	HR	RBI	BB	SO	SB
Burford, Kevin, Padres	.389	47	167	42	65	15	2	4	50	49	25	12
Downing, Lance, D'backs	.381	55	215	48	82	12	1	2	40	37	26	10
Nunez, Jose, Rockies	.365	52	208	31	76	17	3	3	32	19	31	12
Moreno, Jose, Mariners	.363	51	190	56	69	12	0	0	36	25	18	31
Camilo, Juan, Athletics	.346	50	191	48	66	11	5	8	47	41	41	12
Silvestre, Juan, Mariners	.341	34	135	32	46	11	3	7	36	15	31	4
Davis, Monty, Athletics	.329	47	173	34	57	12	0	5	34	25	25	5
Parker, Hubert, Mariners	.317	38	123	23	39	6	0	0	17	26	21	5
Dunham, Traylon, Padres	.317	35	139	20	44	13	1	2	32	17	42	0
Ramsey, Brad, Cubs	.315	51	200	50	63	10	3	8	34	22	33	8

INDIVIDUAL PITCHING LEADERS

(Minimum 45 Innings)

	W	L	ERA	G	GS	CG	SV	IP	H	R	ER	BB	SO
Noel, Todd, Cubs	5	1	1.98	12	11	0	1	59	39	27	13	30	63
Pena, Juan, Athletics	6	2	2.91	14	13	0	0	65	54	38	21	33	67
Lohse, Kyle, Cubs	2	2	3.02	12	11	0	0	48	46	22	16	22	49
Jones, Travis, Padres	4	3	3.04	21	2	0	0	53	53	28	18	23	51
Cook, Aaron, Rockies	1	3	3.13	9	8	0	0	46	48	27	16	17	35
Serrano, Wascar, Padres	6	3	3.18	12	11	0	1	71	60	43	25	22	75
Mateo, Julio, Mariners	3	1	3.30	13	6	0	1	60	45	32	22	23	54
Price, Ryan, Rockies	2	7	3.51	14	14	0	0	77	69	49	30	28	98
Montero, Agus, Athletics	3	2	3.59	14	13	0	0	73	72	38	29	31	88
Royer, Jason, D'backs	3	0	3.71	13	13	0	0	51	53	29	21	22	40

ALL-STAR TEAM

C—Brad Ramsey, Cubs. **1B**—Lance Downing, Diamondbacks. **2B**—Jose Nunez, Rockies. **3B**—Todd Fereday, Cubs. **SS**—Jose Moreno, Mariners. **OF**—Jesus Basabe, Athletics; Kevin Burford, Padres; Juan Camilo, Athletics. **DH**—Juan Silvestre, Mariners. **LHP**—Travis Jones, Padres. **RHP**—Todd Noel, Cubs. **LRP**—Miguel Frias, Diamondbacks. **RRP**—Jake Kidd, Rockies; Shane Sullivan, Cubs.

Most Valuable Player—Kevin Burford, Padres. **Manager of the Year**—Terry Kennedy, Cubs.

TOP 10 PROSPECTS

1. Todd Noel, rhp, Cubs; **2.** Kevin Burford, of, Padres; **3.** Jon Garland, rhp, Cubs; **4.** Jose Nunez, 2b, Rockies; **5.** Wascar Serrano, rhp, Padres; **6.** Jesus Basabe, of, Athletics; **7.** Mark Mangum, rhp, Rockies; **8.** Juan Camilo, of, Athletics; **9.** Brad Ramsey, c, Cubs; **10.** Jose Moreno, ss, Mariners.

DEPT. LEADERS

BATTING

G	Omar Rosario, Athletics	56
AB	Deon Eaddy, Cubs	221
R	Jose Moreno, Mariners	56
H	Lance Downing, Diamondbacks	82
TB	Jesus Basabe, Athletics	115
XBH	Jesus Basabe, Athletics	26
	Brian Gordon, Diamondbacks	26
2B	Brian Gordon, Diamondbacks	18
3B	Chone Figgins, Rockies	6
HR	Jesus Basabe, Athletics	11
RBI	Kevin Burford, Padres	50
SH	Larry Haynes, Mariners	6
SF	Ronald Payne, Cubs	6
BB	Damon Minor, Padres	52
IBB	Jose Nunez, Rockies	2
HBP	Gary Johnson, Cubs	14
SO	Jesus Basabe, Athletics	76
SB	Omar Rosario, Athletics	40
CS	Chone Figgins, Rockies	12
GIDP	Five tied at	6
OB%	Kevin Burford, Padres	.524
SL%	Juan Silvestre, Mariners	.622

PITCHING

G	Francisco Gonzalez, Padres	26
GS	Four tied at	14
CG	Gabriel Rincones, Mariners	1
ShO		0
GF	Shane Sullivan, Cubs	20
SV	Shane Sullivan, Cubs	9
W	Three tied at	6
L	Ryan Price, Rockies	7
IP	Harry Herndon, Padres	77
H	Harry Herndon, Padres	80
R	Jerry Darr, Padres	59
ER	Ben Howard, Padres	45
HR	Doug Kohl, Diamondbacks	5
HB	Melqui Torres, Mariners	11
BB	Ben Howard, Padres	63
SO	Ryan Price, Rockies	98
WP	Ben Howard, Padres	19
	Sam Walton, Mariners	19
BK	Agus Montero, Athletics	9

FIELDING

C	**AVG**	Brad Ramsey, Cubs	.990
	PO	Brad Ramsey, Cubs	358
	A	Jose Lopez, Diamondbacks	41
	E	Luis Soto, Padres	19
	DP	Brad Ramsey, Cubs	6
	PB	Juan Castro, Rockies	16
1B	**AVG**	Gary Johnson, Cubs	.995
	PO	Lance Downing, D'backs	500
	A	Lance Downing, D'backs	28
	E	Jesse Curry, Padres	17
	DP	Jesse Curry, Padres	40
2B	**AVG**	Jose Nunez, Rockies	.928
	PO	Jose Nunez, Rockies	75
	A	Jose Nunez, Rockies	119
	E	Jose Nunez, Rockies	15
	DP	Jose Nunez, Rockies	24
3B	**AVG**	Sam Smith, Rockies	.838
	PO	Sam Smith, Rockies	34
	A	Sam Smith, Rockies	85
	E	Jeff Brooks, Diamondbacks	26
	DP	JeffBrooks, Diamondbacks	12
SS	**AVG**	Jose Moreno, Mariners	.945
	PO	Deon Eaddy, Cubs	97
	A	Chone Figgins, Rockies	162
	E	Chone Figgins, Rockies	40
	DP	Chone Figgins, Rockies	35
OF	**AVG**	Abraham Nunez, D'backs	.991
	PO	Abraham Nunez, D'backs	94
	A	Abraham Nunez, D'backs	12
	E	Brian Gordon, Diamondbacks	8
	DP	Jaisen Randolph, Cubs	4

GULF COAST LEAGUE

Mets' Goetz clinches two championships in one year

BY STEPHEN BORELLI

Again, Geoff Goetz proved he can win the big game.

Though the Gulf Coast League Mets lefthander didn't have a victory during the regular season, he threw seven solid innings to beat the Rangers 8-3 for the 1997 GCL championship.

This is the same Goetz who wrapped up a Florida Class 4-A title in May for Tampa Jesuit High, shaking off flu symptoms to pitch a five-hit, 7-1 win over Dade City's Pasco High.

Overlooked in draft
Marquis Roberts

Goetz, who went 0-2, 2.73 in eight appearances for the GCL Mets during the regular season after signing a $1.7 million contract as New York's first-round draft pick, allowed one earned run over seven innings in the second part of a two-game sweep of the Rangers. Righthander Willie Suggs pitched no-hit ball for seven innings and righthander Tyler Walker, the Mets' second-round pick, got the save as the Mets beat the Rangers 2-0 in the opener.

The major league Mets lost two of three games in the long-awaited Subway Series with the Yankees, but the GCL Mets took the Battle of the Complexes down south. First baseman Mike Meadows' home run with two out in the bottom of the ninth lifted the Mets over the Yanks' GCL team 1-0 in a one-game semifinal. Lefthander James Dougherty and righties Matthew Lowe and Pat Gorman combined for a one-hitter.

Goetz was one of seven 1997 first-round picks making their professional debuts in the GCL. Only outfielder Brett Caradonna, a supplemental first-round pick of the White Sox, made the managers' Top 10 Prospects list, at No. 9.

Lefthander Marquis Roberts, the Devil Rays' fifth-round pick, ranked No. 1. Roberts went 6-1, 0.51 in 12 starts and led the league in ERA. He allowed only 27 hits in 53 innings.

"To me, he was the Jesse James of the draft–he was a steal," Devil Rays manager Bobby Ramos said. "With the way he pitched here, he should have been the first pick. He has everything you look for in a pitcher. He has command of three quality pitches, goes after it hard and has exceptional poise. He really handles adversity well."

Yankees outfielder Jackson Melian, a 17-year-old Venezuelan whom the Yankees signed to a $1.6 million bonus in July 1996, was No. 5 on the list. Melian hit .263 with nine stolen bases in his pro debut.

Before the season, the Cubs changed their complex-level affiliate, moving from the GCL to the Arizona League. That meant the GCL had to move from four divisions to three to accommodate 15 teams.

The winners of the four-team Eastern and Northern divisions met in a one-game playoff, as did the top two finishers in the seven-team Western Division. The Mets took the East, the Yankees the North and the second-place Rangers knocked off the Royals in the West to advance to the finals.

STANDINGS

Page	EAST	Complex Site	W	L	PCT	GB	Manager(s)	Last Penn.
171	Mets	Port St. Lucie	42	18	.700	—	Mickey Brantley/Doug Flynn	1997
119	Marlins	Melbourne	31	28	.525	10½	Jon Deeble	None
157	Expos	West Palm Beach	25	35	.417	17	Luis Dorante	1991
63	Braves	Orlando	21	38	.356	20½	Frank Howard	1964
Page	**NORTH**	**Complex Site**	**W**	**L**	**PCT**	**GB**	**Manager**	**Last Penn.**
164	Yankees	Tampa	40	20	.667	—	Ken Dominguez	1996
113	Tigers	Lakeland	31	29	.517	9	Kevin Bradshaw	None
219	Devil Rays	St. Petersburg	25	35	.417	15	Bobby Ramos	None
125	Astros	Kissimmee	24	36	.400	16	Julio Linares	1994
Page	**WEST**	**Complex Site**	**W**	**L**	**PCT**	**GB**	**Manager**	**Last Penn.**
131	Royals	Fort Myers	36	24	.600	—	Al Pedrique	1992
225	Rangers	Port Charlotte	34	26	.567	2	James Byrd	1993
77	Red Sox	Fort Myers	31	28	.525	4½	Luis Aguayo	None
150	Twins	Fort Myers	28	32	.467	8	Steve Liddle	None
190	Pirates	Bradenton	27	32	.458	8½	Woody Huyke	None
70	Orioles	Sarasota	27	33	.450	9	Butch Davis	None
83	White Sox	Sarasota	26	34	.433	10	Roly de Armas	1977

PLAYOFFS—Semifinals: Mets defeated Yankees and Rangers defeated Royals in one-game series. **Finals:** Mets defeated Rangers 2-0, in best-of-3 series.

NOTE: Team's individual batting and pitching statistics can be found on page indicated in lefthand column.

1997 Gulf Coast League Statistics

CLUB BATTING

	AVG	G	AB	R	H	2B	3B	HR	BB	SO	SB
Yankees	.275	60	2002	349	550	91	30	28	225	414	74
Royals	.269	60	1916	293	516	73	17	25	175	411	67
Mets	.264	60	1862	308	491	105	28	15	210	392	43
Rangers	.251	60	1872	267	470	78	21	18	191	446	120
Red Sox	.251	59	1818	213	456	82	23	8	176	404	68
Pirates	.251	59	1883	226	472	91	12	17	166	445	49
Tigers	.249	60	1916	310	477	81	18	30	235	476	69
White Sox	.244	60	1865	218	455	76	18	13	163	390	66
Braves	.244	58	1819	244	443	75	10	25	206	432	31
Twins	.242	60	1970	220	476	62	13	7	199	418	110
Expos	.241	59	1822	241	439	91	14	13	185	385	92
Devil Rays	.238	60	1850	255	440	73	20	19	232	443	71
Marlins	.233	59	1779	225	414	75	10	10	220	459	77
Orioles	.230	60	1856	226	427	70	19	12	201	481	85
Astros	.225	60	1895	236	427	83	6	23	165	429	65

CLUB PITCHING

	ERA	G	CG	SHO	SV	IP	H	R	ER	BB	SO
Mets	2.50	60	1	8	21	479	406	189	133	183	462
Red Sox	2.56	59	5	5	12	484	437	213	138	146	522
Rangers	2.93	60	4	7	18	500	441	215	163	171	429
Twins	2.95	60	2	7	12	527	482	225	173	168	450
Royals	3.12	60	7	9	10	493	461	225	171	170	385
Marlins	3.34	59	6	5	9	473	428	256	176	194	410
Yankees	3.40	60	3	5	15	507	468	266	192	191	405
Orioles	3.41	60	2	5	15	496	489	251	188	210	394
Expos	3.50	59	0	4	13	479	462	231	186	181	366
Devil Rays	3.62	60	0	4	9	491	436	258	198	214	460
White Sox	3.64	60	1	1	11	488	473	261	197	217	412
Tigers	3.70	60	2	5	10	496	474	278	204	180	459
Pirates	3.77	59	3	4	10	493	489	273	207	189	403
Astros	4.71	60	4	4	13	499	516	348	261	272	438
Braves	5.02	58	0	0	6	463	491	342	258	263	430

CLUB FIELDING

	PCT	PO	A	E	DP
Twins	.963	1581	758	91	48
Orioles	.961	1489	628	86	58
Yankees	.961	1522	620	88	49
Royals	.959	1479	659	91	51
Expos	.958	1436	583	88	34
Devil Rays	.956	1474	555	94	47
Mets	.956	1438	611	95	37
Marlins	.955	1420	633	97	30
Rangers	.954	1500	631	103	53
Pirates	.951	1480	632	108	37
White Sox	.951	1463	611	108	53
Tigers	.948	1487	606	114	33
Astros	.947	1496	594	118	60
Red Sox	.946	1452	588	117	56
Braves	.943	1388	514	114	48

INDIVIDUAL BATTING LEADERS

(Minimum 162 Plate Appearances)

	AVG	G	AB	R	H	2B	3B	HR	RBI	BB	SO	SB
Ruiz, Willy, Royals	.360	54	197	33	71	4	0	0	14	9	19	20
Mora, Juan, Tigers	.348	43	155	26	54	9	5	4	31	18	43	9
Thames, Marcus, Yankees	.344	57	195	51	67	17	4	7	36	16	26	6
Durham, Chad, White Sox	.328	49	189	24	62	5	3	1	17	12	17	22
Taveras, Jose, Royals	.327	57	205	46	67	14	4	7	39	24	42	14
Gomez, Erick, Royals	.320	50	169	18	54	16	0	3	29	16	36	0
Quero, Pdero,, Expos	.311	56	190	28	59	14	4	1	21	12	31	6
Torres, Rafael, Royals	.306	44	160	20	49	2	0	3	33	7	16	2
Washington, Dion, Yankees	.303	52	165	35	50	10	1	3	33	36	39	2
Lehr, Ryan, Braves	.300	54	207	30	62	15	2	4	34	9	32	1

INDIVIDUAL PITCHING LEADERS

(Minimum 48 Innings)

	W	L	ERA	G	GS	CG	SV	IP	H	R	ER	BB	SO
Roberts, Marquis, DRays	6	1	0.51	12	10	0	0	53	27	8	3	19	68
Rupp, Michael, Red Sox	1	4	1.22	11	9	3	0	59	51	23	8	17	56
Rodriguez, Cristobol, Expos	3	3	1.65	13	10	0	1	55	45	15	10	16	61
Dougherty, James, Mets	6	1	1.93	11	8	0	0	51	42	18	11	13	51
Sheets, Matt, Twins	2	2	2.38	15	5	0	2	53	49	17	14	10	24
Myers, Taylor, Royals	5	4	2.41	11	10	2	0	60	48	21	16	20	48
Blevins, Jeremy, Yankees	5	3	2.43	11	9	0	0	56	50	27	15	23	46
Suggs, Willie, Marlins	5	3	2.49	10	8	1	0	51	34	21	14	22	32

ALL-STAR TEAM

C—Michael Rivera, Tigers. **1B**—Travis Hafner, Rangers. **2B**—Willy Ruiz, Royals. **3B**—Erick Almonte, Yankees. **SS**—Rayner Bautista, Tigers. **OF**—Juan Mora, Tigers; Jose Taveras, Royals; Marcus Thames, Yankees. **SP**—Marquis Roberts, Devil Rays. **RP**—Jake Jacobs, Twins.

TOP 10 PROSPECTS

1. Marquis Roberts, lhp, Devil Rays; **2.** Jose Taveras, of, Royals; **3.** Chris Moore, rhp, Marlins; **4.** Erick Almonte, 3b, Yankees; **5.** Luis Cruz, 2b, Devil Rays; **6.** Jackson Melian, of, Yankees; **7.** Alex Escobar, of, Mets; **8.** Joaquin Benoit, rhp, Rangers; **9.** Brett Caradonna, of, White Sox; **10.** Roy Oswalt, rhp, Astros.

DEPT. LEADERS

BATTING

G	Regino Nolasco, Orioles	58
AB	Tootie Myers, Expos	217
R	Marcus Thames, Yankees	51
H	Willy Ruiz, Royals	71
TB	Marcus Thames, Yankees	113
XBH	Marcus Thames, Yankees	28
2B	Marcus Thames, Yankees	17
3B	Teuris Olivares, Yankees	7
HR	Michael Rivera, Tigers	10
RBI	Jose Taveras, Royals	39
SH	Pedro Herrera, Royals	6
SF	Regino Nolasco, Orioles	6
BB	Asdrubal Oropeza, Braves	37
IBB	Five tied at	2
HBP	Bobby Hill, Mets	7
SO	Tootie Myers, Expos	58
SB	Tootie Myers, Expos	24
CS	Three tied at	11
GIDP	Juan Ramirez, Royals	11
OB%	Dion Washington, Yankees	.440
SL%	Marcus Thames, Yankees	.579

PITCHING

G	Three tied at	23
GS	Jason Standridge, Devil Rays	13
CG	Michael Rupp, Red Sox	3
ShO	George Hlodan, Pirates	2
	Taylor Myers, Royals	2
GF	Jake Jacobs, Twins	20
SV	Jake Jacobs, Twins	10
W	Three tied at	8
L	Three tied at	7
IP	Wilfredo Rodriguez, Astros	68
H	Grant Balfour, Twins	73
R	Roman Colon, Braves	47
ER	John Blackmore, Astros	33
HR	Chris Stowe, Expos	5
	Geraldo Padua, Yankees	5
HB	John Blackmore, Astros	9
BB	Elvis Perez, White Sox	44
SO	Mark Martinez, Red Sox	78
WP	John Blackmore, Astros	17
BK	Four tied at	6

FIELDING

C	AVG	Clark Lambert, Mets	.993
	PO	Rodolfo Pena, Red Sox	348
	A	Gabriel Torres, Twins	62
	E	Pedro Herrera, Royals	9
	DP	Three tied at	4
	PB	Jean Boscan, Braves	13
1B	AVG	Brett Roneberg, Marlins	.994
	PO	Brett Roneberg, Marlins	481
	A	Juan Ramirez, Royals	29
		Brett Roneberg, Marlins	29
	E	Chris Delgado, White Sox	12
	DP	Victor Preciado, Yankees	38
2B	AVG	Tony Stevens, Twins	.977
	PO	Rafael Furcal, Braves	122
	A	Felix Escalona, Astros	127
		Regino Nolasco, Orioles	127
	E	Chad Durham, White Sox	11
		Tootie Myers, Expos	11
	DP	Felix Escalona, Astros	37
3B	AVG	Jose Nunez, Royals	.944
	PO	Erick Almonte, Yankees	53
	A	Matt Boone, Tigers	95
	E	Matt Boone, Tigers	23
	DP	Larry Marino, Red Sox	10
SS	AVG	Maikell Diaz, Orioles	.978
	PO	Jimmy Alvarez, Twins	78
	A	Jimmy Alvarez, Twins	178
	E	Wilson Betemit, Braves	20
	DP	Jimmy Alvarez, Twins	33
OF	AVG	Melvin Dasher, Royals	1.000
	PO	Jackson Melian, Yankees	110
	A	DeShawn Southward, Twins	9
	E	Michael Edge, Expos	7
		Alejandro Vasquez, Astros	7
	DP	DeShawn Southward, Twins	3

Independent Leagues

Independent leagues face uncertain future, but enjoy year of prosperity, growth in 1997

BY WILL LINGO

For the first time since the independent baseball renaissance in 1993, the 1997 season brought no new leagues, no new dreams of independent success.

The year could have brought the end of one or two more independent leagues, however. At least a couple of leagues struggled to complete their seasons, and it wasn't at all clear that they would return for 1998.

Since the Northern League and Frontier League started a resurgence of independent baseball with their debuts in 1993, at least two new leagues have started up each season.

Most haven't survived. The Atlantic Coast, Golden State, Great Central, Mid-America, North Atlantic and North Central leagues will end up as nothing more than footnotes in baseball history.

A few, such as the Northern League, have thrived, finding success at the gate and in sending players on to Organized Baseball.

That trend continued in 1997, with a few successful leagues getting overshadowed by the majority of leagues that were trying just to survive.

The North Atlantic League, after losing several franchises but trying to make it to the line for Opening Day, announced that it was suspending operations for 1997 before the season started.

Toward the end of the season, the league announced plans to return in 1998, but it still wasn't clear where the franchises would be or whether the league could find a place in a crowded northeastern baseball landscape.

In addition to numerous major league and minor league teams in the region, the region already had another independent league, the Northeast League, that has struggled but survived through three seasons.

Now comes the possible addition of the Atlantic League, which has big names and big money and has been preparing for Opening Day 1998 for more than two years. It's not entirely clear whether the Atlantic League will get off the ground, but with so much competition that makes it even less likely that the North Atlantic League will return.

The Big South League was crippled by the defection of its best franchises to the Heartland League, leaving it with just four teams. Only three were viable, and the entire league drew 75,000 fans for its 60-game schedule. The league vowed a return to health in 1998.

The Prairie League also had its share of trouble, with one franchise, Moose Jaw, failing midway through the season, and another, Aberdeen, getting its franchise suspended briefly.

After the season, league founder Dave Ferguson resigned, saying the league's finances were unsettled enough that he didn't want to deal with the problems any longer.

Eight independent leagues were around at the end of 1997, a number close to what some longtime operators predicted as the number of leagues that could survive for the long term. With the leagues trying to get started and the leagues trying to stay alive, that number should remain about the same.

LINDA CULLEN

Flood of talent?
More top players could follow J.D. Drew

One possibility of explosive growth was on the horizon, though. J.D. Drew, the second overall pick in the 1997 draft by the Phillies, signed with the Northern League's St. Paul Saints when contract negotiations with the Phillies went nowhere.

Drew argued in a grievance that he should become a free agent before the 1998 draft because he had already signed and played under a professional contract. That grievance was pending, but if an arbitrator ruled in Drew's favor, it could result in a flood of players to independent leagues for bargaining leverage.

Then again, finding players has never been a problem for independent leagues. It's finding the ballparks and fans that allow operators to pay the players that's the sticking point. And until more lucrative markets are discovered, the number of successful independent leagues will remain limited.

FRONTIER LEAGUE

In their first season as part of the five-year old Frontier League, the Canton Crocodiles rallied from a slow start to win the league title in 1997. The Crocs swept Evansville 2-0 in the best-of-three championship series.

The Crocs, who replaced the defunct Zanesville Greys, clinched a playoff berth by going 25-15 in the second half, earning the right to take on Johnstown in the Eastern Division playoffs. Canton swept the Steal

Player of the Year

Change of scenery gives Dukes' Meggers new lease on life

When veteran outfielder Mike Meggers was traded to the Duluth-Superior Dukes from the Winnipeg Goldeyes midway through the 1997 Northern League season, it raised more than a few eyebrows.

But after he batted .305 with 32 homers and 99 RBIs overall and led the Dukes to their first Northern League championship over his former team, Meggers' selection as Baseball America's Independent League Player of the Year was no surprise.

Mike Meggers

Winnipeg was in first place for most of the first half and was the most talented team in the league–with or without Meggers. But to trade the player who led the league in home runs, RBIs and slugging percentage while batting more than .300 seemed too bold a move not to have repercussions later.

The Dukes beat St. Paul in the first round of the playoffs and met Winnipeg in the championship series, where Meggers supplied four home runs and eight RBIs.

It's doubtful the Duluth-Superior team that started the season 4-17 would have won its division, let alone the league, without Meggers' production.

Meggers led the league with 50 extra-base hits and was third with 77 runs and a .645 slugging percentage. He also struck out in Dave Kingman proportions, breaking the Northern League single-season record with 102.

Meggers, the NAIA's all-time single season home run record holder with 36 in 1992, spent four years in the Reds organization before being released in 1996. He joined the Northern League's Madison Black Wolf midway through the first half of 1996, and hit .298 with 14 homers.

C—Kevin Tahan, Alexandria (Texas-Louisiana), .330-9-51.

1B—Terry Lee, Winnipeg (Northern), .358-20-78. **2B**—Jorge Alvarez, Amarillo (Texas-Louisiana), .395-5-68. **3B**—Andy Tarpley, Reno (Western), .404-15-82. **SS**—Tim Howard, Amarillo (Texas-Louisiana), .352-7-51.

OF—J.D. Drew, St. Paul (Northern), .341-18-50; Mike Meggers, Winnipeg/Duluth-Superior (Northern), .305-32-99; Bryan Warner, Rio Grande (Texas-Louisiana), .392-25-94.

DH—Todd Takayoshi, Reno (Western), .407-11-88.

P—Gene Caruso, Fargo-Moorhead (Northern), 11-5, 3.11; John Dopson, Tennessee (Heartland), 10-2, 1.78; Rick Forney, Winnipeg (Northern), 11-4, 3.66; Mike Smith, Mission Viejo (Western), 10-4, 2.95; Jeff Zimmerman, Winnipeg (Northern), 9-2, 2.82.

with easy 6-2 and 7-2 victories before meeting Evansville in the championship.

The Otters finished last in the first half of the Western Division with a 17-23 record but rebounded to take the second half with a 29-10 mark. They defeated Richmond two games to one in the West playoff.

For the second consecutive year, Richmond first baseman Morgan Burkhart was the league's most valuable player. He hit .323 with 24 homers and 74 RBIs and broke the league record for home runs, total bases (186) and runs scored (76).

Burkhardt also set a league record when he hit three homers in one game. The feat was even more impressive because Morgan did his work in a rain-shortened five-inning contest.

The Frontier League has had more than 20 former players sign with major league organizations, including 10 players who signed in 1997 alone.

Evansville, which has led the league in attendance for three consecutive seasons, drew a league-record 91,018 fans in 1997.

There are plans to expand the league, including the revival of the dormant Zanesville franchise which would move to the St. Louis suburb of O'Fallon before the 1999 season.

STANDINGS

FIRST HALF

EASTERN DIVISION	W	L	PCT	GB
Johnstown Steal	25	15	.625	—
Chillicothe Paints	20	20	.500	5
Canton Crocodiles	20	20	.500	5
Ohio Valley Redcoats	10	30	.250	15
WESTERN DIVISION	**W**	**L**	**PCT**	**GB**
xRichmond Roosters	25	15	.625	—
Springfield Capitals	25	15	.550	3
Kalamazoo Kodiaks	18	22	.450	7
Evansville Otters	17	23	.425	8

x-won first half in playoff

SECOND HALF

EASTERN DIVISION	W	L	PCT	GB
Canton Crocodiles	25	15	.625	—
Johnstown Steal	22	18	.550	3
Chililicothe Paints	21	18	.538	3½
Ohio Valley Redcoats	11	29	.275	14
WESTERN DIVISION	**W**	**L**	**PCT**	**GB**
Evansville Otters	29	10	.744	—
Richmond Roosters	18	22	.450	11½
Springfield Capitals	17	22	.436	12
Kalamazoo Kodiaks	15	24	.385	14

PLAYOFFS: Semifinals—Canton defeated Johnstown 2-0, and Evansville defeated Richmond 2-1, in best-of-3 series. **Finals**—Canton defeated Evansville 2-0 in best-of-3 series.

MANAGERS: Canton—Mike Burton. Chillicothe—Roger Hanners. Evansville—Greg Tagert. Johnstown—Henry Manning. Kalamazoo—John Pacella. Ohio Valley—Pete Berrios. Richmond—John Cate, Bill Richardson. Springfield—Mal Fichman.

ATTENDANCE: Evansville 91,018; Canton 75,503; Johnstown 59,768; Chillicothe 56,070; Kalamazoo 55,421; Richmond 46,178; Springfield 44,219; Ohio Valley 18,224.

ALL-STAR TEAM: C—Jeff Ucello, Johnstown. **1B**—Mitch House, Chillicothe. **2B**—Don DeDonatis, Kalamazoo. **3B**—Mike Garner, Kalamazoo. **SS**—Keith Habig, Richmond. **OF**—Jackie Jempson, Chillicothe; Danny Johnson, Canton; Joe Ronca, Springfield. **DH**—Morgan Burkhart, Richmond. **SP**—Mike Arner, Canton; Kevin Gieras, Johnstown; Jeff Montfort, Richmond. **RP**—Randy Bromley, Johnstown.

Most Valuable Player: Morgan Burkhart, Richmond. **Most Valuable Pitcher:** Mike Arner, Canton. **Manager of the Year:** Mike Burton, Canton.

INDIVIDUAL BATTING LEADERS

(Minimum 216 Plate Appearances)

	AVG	AB	R	H	2B	3B	HR	RBI	SB
Habig, Keith, Richmond	.353	295	68	104	18	2	9	51	8
Ronca, Joe, Spring	.341	293	54	100	23	6	17	72	4
Herman, Josh, OV	.339	218	22	74	12	0	4	31	3
Johnson, Danny, Canton	.337	291	67	98	17	4	4	38	33
Williams, Rod, Canton	.332	274	43	91	19	3	4	50	10
Aspeslet, Preston, John/Can	.332	208	40	69	10	0	2	39	11
Wisely, Mike, Kalamazoo	.331	323	52	107	18	5	2	39	18
Garner, Mike, Kalamazoo	.330	261	36	86	15	2	11	56	1
DeDonatis, Don, Kalamazoo	.328	314	64	103	20	3	1	34	65
Bryant, Matt, Canton	.326	224	40	73	15	1	5	53	5

INDIVIDUAL PITCHING LEADERS

(Minimum 64 Innings)

	W	L	ERA	G	SV	IP	H	BB	SO
Arner, Mike, Canton	6	2	2.28	12	0	79	76	30	58
Duff, Matt, Springfield	7	4	2.71	14	0	80	70	27	76
Spears, Bob, Chillicothe	8	6	3.05	16	0	112	102	30	92
Schlee, Jeremy, Evan	6	2	3.09	33	1	64	65	27	50
Schultz, Eric, Canton	6	2	3.14	11	1	66	64	20	63
Nelson, Ron, Richmond	7	3	3.40	13	0	85	83	19	53
Neese, Josh, Springfield	8	1	3.51	18	0	108	97	38	84
Slattery, Alex, Kalamazoo	5	3	3.56	25	1	73	64	50	48
Perri, Tista, Evansville	7	2	3.62	16	0	82	87	21	41
Jacobson, Kelton, Kal	6	4	3.67	15	0	101	100	61	67

CANTON

BATTING	AVG	AB	R	H	2B	3B	HR	RBI	SB
Aspeslet, Preston, of	.349	106	20	37	6	0	1	19	7
Briller, Chris, 1b-3b	.314	287	61	90	23	5	1	53	21
Bryant, Matt, ss	.326	224	40	73	15	1	5	53	5
Bumpers, Mike, 3b	.143	7	1	1	0	0	0	1	0
Burnwell, J.P., c	.000	2	0	0	0	0	0	0	0
English, Keith, ss-3b	.310	58	10	18	1	1	1	13	5
Fernandez, Danny, 1b-dh	.240	171	24	41	9	0	3	30	4
Hunt, Joe, of	.291	103	17	30	1	0	0	11	17
Johnson, Danny, of	.337	291	67	98	17	4	4	38	33
Johnson, Randall, 3b	.182	11	1	2	0	0	0	1	0
Klam, Jason, 2b-of	.304	276	63	84	24	1	9	65	25
LaGreca, Paul, of	.188	32	4	6	1	0	1	6	1
2-team (32 Johnstown)	.232	142	17	33	8	2	3	24	2
Larkin, Garrett, of-2b	.259	201	36	52	10	3	3	28	3
Laskovy, Eric, of	.000	6	0	0	0	0	0	0	0
Mitrovitch, Steve, c	.278	252	48	70	12	1	10	38	5
Munson, Mike, c	.200	25	3	5	2	0	0	2	0
Pegg, Rob, c	.244	82	17	20	2	0	0	9	3
Sachs, Brent, 3b-ss	.293	287	49	84	13	3	5	50	28
Satinoff, Evan, 2b-ss	.121	33	3	4	0	0	0	1	1
2-team (10 Johnstown)	.231	52	9	12	1	0	0	4	1
Schroeder, Bryan, of	.048	21	2	1	1	0	0	1	2
Williams, Rod, of	.332	274	43	91	19	3	4	50	10
Young, Steve, 2b	.176	34	5	6	1	0	0	5	1

PITCHING	W	L	ERA	G	SV	IP	H	BB	SO
Arner, Mike	6	2	2.28	12	0	79	76	30	58
Bawlson, Jeff	0	1	11.25	3	0	4	8	3	2
Bowen, Mitch	0	3	13.50	4	0	13	27	12	8
Briller, Chris	0	0	2.25	3	1	4	2	1	8
Cingel, Jim	0	0	10.24	9	0	10	10	17	6
Crawford, Danny	6	3	4.23	20	1	79	84	20	50
Eannacony, Tony	3	3	6.60	23	0	44	53	28	21
Foster, Cliff	4	2	3.99	13	0	70	63	32	48
Havens, Chris	2	0	5.89	14	4	18	22	9	15
Hill, Chris	4	3	2.53	33	8	46	41	22	36
Klemyk, Jim	4	1	3.80	14	0	47	51	22	24
Knollin, Chris	0	0	0.00	1	0	1	1	2	0
Lapka, Rick	2	3	4.91	9	0	51	47	27	52
Maxwell, Clark	1	2	5.88	6	0	34	38	17	28
Miller, Brent	3	1	2.43	7	0	30	25	19	27
Mueller, Travis	0	4	8.07	13	0	32	39	30	15
Prenzlin, Gregg	2	1	0.79	8	1	11	7	5	5
Reed, Waylon	0	0	8.00	5	0	9	16	8	8
Scheffler, Craig	2	4	6.88	9	0	34	42	19	13
Schultz, Eric	6	2	3.14	11	1	66	64	20	63
Snowden, Chad	0	0	5.56	10	0	11	15	9	6

CHILLICOTHE

BATTING	AVG	AB	R	H	2B	3B	HR	RBI	SB
Acosta, Eddie, ss	.000	9	2	0	0	0	0	0	2
Anderson, Patrick, c-of	.307	205	25	63	13	0	3	29	2
Benyo, Jason, 2b	.283	290	49	82	16	1	2	32	9
Busse, Sean, of	.227	22	1	5	1	0	0	2	0
Clinger, Jon, ss	.246	191	31	47	6	1	3	22	5
Collins, Danny, of	.270	115	18	31	7	1	3	18	1
Fluck, Jesse, 3b-ss	.303	231	37	70	14	1	3	37	17
Graham, Jason, of	.349	146	41	51	7	2	3	17	12
Helms, Telly, dh	.288	208	38	60	13	1	1	26	3
House, Mitch, 1b-3b	.319	260	57	83	20	1	15	62	5
Itzoe, Josh, of	.280	214	32	60	9	0	3	21	3
Jackson, Matt, c	.500	6	1	3	0	0	0	0	0
Jempson, Jackie, of	.270	282	46	76	17	2	17	64	5
Jones, Bobby, of	.299	87	18	26	3	1	4	11	1
Keifer, Greg, of	.300	10	3	3	0	0	0	0	0
Lake, Tim, ss-2b	.500	26	4	13	1	0	0	8	2
Mannino, Brian, 1b	.295	146	22	43	8	1	4	28	0
McQuiniff, Jason, 3b	.288	66	7	19	0	0	0	8	1
Plackemeier, Brad, c	.287	181	27	52	15	0	5	30	1
Pound, Joe, dh	.158	19	1	3	2	0	0	0	0

PITCHING	W	L	ERA	G	SV	IP	H	BB	SO
Bowen, Luther	0	0	9.00	2	0	1	1	3	2
Gardner, Nathan	2	2	4.76	29	8	28	33	20	21
Heineman, Rick	5	4	3.73	17	0	99	101	48	75
Horton, Aaron	1	3	4.05	20	0	40	49	26	32
Lawson, Vince	0	0	4.02	24	1	31	39	22	36
McAninch, Sam	7	4	4.32	16	0	92	106	47	64
Montgomery, Joe	5	7	2.81	31	3	58	57	34	50
Murphy, Chris	1	2	6.14	9	1	37	39	16	33
Mycheck, Andy	4	0	1.75	14	0	26	19	14	24
Palisin, Matt	4	3	6.75	20	0	31	30	19	22
2-team (5 Ohio Valley)	4	6	6.79	25	0	57	66	29	35
Smith, Greg	1	1	9.00	4	0	14	19	4	7
Spears, Bob	8	6	3.05	16	0	112	102	31	92
Taylor, Paul	0	0	6.14	11	0	15	12	10	14
White, Bert	0	2	6.98	9	0	30	44	12	15
Wise, William	3	4	6.81	16	1	71	88	41	52

EVANSVILLE

BATTING	AVG	AB	R	H	2B	3B	HR	RBI	SB
Beyna, Terry, 3b	.290	272	55	79	8	2	2	31	12
Brownlee, Ryan, 2b-of	.297	195	38	58	5	1	0	25	19
Cano, Matt, of-3b	.310	245	43	76	11	1	1	38	4
Caston, Bernard, of	.321	209	44	67	10	3	2	34	34
Dapprich, Scott, 2b	.231	13	4	3	1	0	0	2	0
Davenport, Shane, 1b	.292	257	32	75	20	0	8	45	2
Edwards, Hal, 2b	.226	31	1	7	1	0	0	3	0
Green, Steve, 3b	.300	10	1	3	1	0	0	2	0
Griggs, Rod, of	.167	54	8	9	1	0	0	3	9
Imrisek, Jason, c	.318	192	33	61	13	2	7	37	6
Joseph, Eric, of-2b	.302	129	33	39	8	5	1	19	17
Kass, Mike, of	.282	39	6	11	1	2	1	4	1
Luna, Rich, 2b	.262	187	27	49	10	0	1	21	4
Motzer, Marc, ss	.228	237	33	54	7	3	1	39	12
Neal, Jeff, 1b	.200	10	1	2	0	0	0	0	0
Perry, Bob, 1b-of	.237	135	22	32	6	0	2	16	5
Pethel, Pat, of	.253	99	13	25	2	1	1	9	9
Platz, Larry, c	.270	122	21	33	6	0	2	21	1
Robinson, David, of	.322	233	58	75	17	7	7	50	22
Tavares, John, 2b	.333	3	2	1	0	0	0	0	0

PITCHING	W	L	ERA	G	SV	IP	H	BB	SO
Cordle, Jeff	1	0	0.00	1	0	0	2	1	0
DeConge, Maurice	4	2	3.86	32	4	47	44	21	38
Estep, Rich	2	0	4.82	20	0	28	31	16	28
Garcia, Paco	0	2	40.50	3	0	1	5	3	0
Garola, Rob	3	3	5.22	16	0	79	82	28	60
Kass, Mike	0	3	5.47	10	0	26	23	30	28
Leystra, Jeff	3	4	4.86	12	2	46	46	15	51
Murphy, Rob	3	0	4.06	37	1	44	54	14	32
Niemeier, Todd	3	2	4.87	16	1	44	52	13	35
Perri, Tista	7	2	3.62	16	0	82	87	21	41
Pollak, Dave	3	2	4.76	15	1	79	84	20	65
Rodgers, Mike	3	6	7.51	19	0	62	86	27	39
Scheer, Greg	6	3	1.85	33	10	39	22	21	46
Schlee, Jeremy	6	2	3.09	33	1	64	65	27	50
Smith, Jarod	0	0	9.00	1	0	6	8	0	3
Stephens, Jon	0	0	0.00	2	0	2	2	1	1
Tipton, Shawn	2	2	3.95	8	0	41	37	11	16

JOHNSTOWN

BATTING	AVG	AB	R	H	2B	3B	HR	RBI	SB
Aspeslet, Preston, of	.314	102	20	32	4	0	1	20	4
2-team (30 Canton)	.332	208	40	69	10	0	2	39	11
Berliner, Seth, ss	.295	183	46	54	11	1	4	25	6
2-team (26 Richmond)	.276	261	54	72	14	1	4	30	7
Bolden, Gerald, of	.323	93	19	30	8	1	0	8	3
Conlan, Ed, 1b	.277	119	15	33	8	0	4	24	0
Crothers, K.C., 3b-1b	.286	252	56	72	16	1	9	58	2

BATTING	AVG	AB	R	H	2B	3B	HR	RBI	SB
Dorsey, Jason, of	.318	132	23	42	7	4	4	31	9
English, Keith, of-3b	.241	79	12	19	3	0	2	12	3
2-team (19 Canton)	.270	137	22	37	4	1	3	25	8
Fischer, Carlos, 2b	.211	57	11	12	1	0	0	3	1
Froschauer, Trevor, c	.318	22	5	7	1	0	1	6	0
Gauthier, Derek, 2b	.302	275	57	83	26	3	12	75	3
Glenn, Brandon, of	.307	202	41	62	4	2	1	21	12
Johnson, Eric, of	.143	21	6	3	1	0	0	3	1
2-team (4 Springfield)	.148	27	6	4	1	0	0	4	1
Kalcounos, Andy, 1b	.310	71	18	22	3	1	3	17	3
Kott, Ross, 1b	.159	69	6	11	3	0	0	5	0
LaGreca, Paul, of	.245	110	13	27	7	2	2	18	1
Mack, Anthony, 3b	.248	137	27	34	11	1	5	22	1
Moore, Mike, of	.277	224	38	62	12	0	4	39	2
Murphy, Quinn, of-ss	.245	163	23	40	8	2	0	11	2
Satcho, Rick, c	.203	64	6	13	3	0	1	7	0
Satinoff, Evan, 2b	.421	19	6	8	1	0	0	3	0
Soriano, Juan, ss	.216	74	16	16	2	1	1	5	0
Uccello, Jeff, c	.271	221	37	60	12	2	2	34	2
Yates, Chucky, 2b-of	.000	10	2	0	0	0	0	1	1

PITCHING	W	L	ERA	G	SV	IP	H	BB	SO
Abbott, Jim	5	5	4.03	15	0	83	83	26	70
Bromley, Randy	3	1	2.11	33	13	38	30	25	31
Brown, Trevor	0	0	3.31	9	0	16	14	12	12
Burkindine, Larry	1	1	5.40	4	0	15	12	16	10
Garcia, David	2	0	6.97	9	0	10	19	3	9
Gieras, Kevin	9	3	3.71	17	0	95	93	43	93
Hogan, Sean	0	2	8.71	4	0	21	36	5	15
Irving, Jamie	5	4	4.64	24	1	78	76	30	48
Lavender, Scott	2	1	12.41	6	0	12	23	9	7
Magrini, Paul	8	5	4.33	16	0	100	107	36	85
Masching, Bill	1	0	3.68	5	0	22	24	11	20
Moore, Mike	0	0	2.57	5	1	7	6	1	6
Pashley, Brian	0	1	4.93	28	3	38	52	17	27
Sauget, Rich	5	6	5.44	33	1	50	56	17	49
Schroeder, Chris	2	0	4.91	22	0	29	40	16	24
Smith, Greg	1	0	12.15	7	0	7	13	4	4
2-team (4 Chillicothe)	2	1	10.02	11	0	21	32	8	11
Sneeringer, Daniel	3	4	5.47	13	0	53	57	30	28
Stensler, Brian	0	0	9.00	10	0	16	32	8	9

KALAMAZOO

BATTING	AVG	AB	R	H	2B	3B	HR	RBI	SB
Balint, Rob, c	.279	61	9	17	4	0	1	11	1
Chase, Allen, dh-3b	.284	102	17	29	4	0	3	13	6
2-team (10 Ohio Valley)	.269	130	20	35	5	0	4	14	8
Colon, Frank, dh-c	.000	5	0	0	0	0	0	0	0
2-team (4 Ohio Valley)	.067	15	1	1	0	0	0	2	0
Colson, Julian, of	.208	24	2	5	1	1	0	3	0
Danford, LeeRoy, dh	.240	50	6	12	1	0	0	5	0
DeDonatis, Don, 2b	.328	314	64	103	20	3	1	34	65
Dilello, Tony, 3b	.000	2	0	0	0	0	0	0	0
Dwyer, Ryan, 1b	.000	12	1	0	0	0	0	0	0
Garner, Mike, 3b	.330	261	36	86	15	2	11	56	1
Goodman, Herbert, of	.242	281	48	68	11	1	12	41	20
Grijalva, Mike, dh-3b	.240	25	2	6	1	0	1	1	0
Higgins, Bert, ss	.239	230	22	55	0	1	0	27	12
Johnson, Jace, of	.261	180	23	47	8	1	2	13	8
Mason, Lamont, ss	.421	19	9	8	1	0	0	2	1
Oglesby, Luke, of	.209	110	19	23	2	1	0	13	13
Rudolph, Greg, ss-2b	.220	50	5	11	2	0	1	6	0
Sienko, Ryan, c	.235	179	18	42	9	1	7	29	2
Siponmaa, Ryan, c	.238	80	10	19	3	0	1	9	2
Snyder, Joe, dh-of	.273	22	3	6	1	0	0	3	0
Sullivan, John, of-1b	.247	186	26	46	8	2	2	25	4
Wiseley, Mike, of	.331	323	52	107	18	5	2	39	18
Zerbe, Mike, 1b	.309	220	35	68	23	0	9	34	3

PITCHING	W	L	ERA	G	SV	IP	H	BB	SO
Collins, Richard	6	5	4.41	13	0	84	87	26	45
Davis, Jon	2	1	5.59	17	0	29	33	19	26
Giron, Roberto	1	0	3.28	15	0	25	20	9	14
Holst, Bob	0	0	8.44	3	0	5	5	9	6
Jacobson, Kelton	6	4	3.67	15	0	101	100	61	67
Kapla, Scott	2	2	6.16	8	0	31	49	4	17
McKitrick, Brian	0	0	18.00	2	0	1	3	1	0
Mercer, Chip	0	3	5.23	19	2	21	29	3	8
Mitchell, Chris	0	1	47.25	2	0	1	4	5	1
Podjan, Jimmy	0	1	5.63	8	0	40	51	25	22
Rhodes, Scott	0	3	7.86	5	0	26	40	14	15
Robinson, Jason	4	8	6.24	19	0	118	148	47	80
Scott, Ron	2	5	6.33	28	9	27	29	27	22
Slattery, Alex	5	3	3.56	25	1	73	64	50	48
Vest, Norman	1	2	4.96	18	0	49	52	35	20
Vitale, Anthony	4	6	6.06	26	0	62	76	35	34

PITCHING	W	L	ERA	G	SV	IP	H	BB	SO
Wade, Travis	0	2	30.86	2	0	2	7	4	0

OHIO VALLEY

BATTING	AVG	AB	R	H	2B	3B	HR	RBI	SB
Berman, Jeff, 2b	.248	250	29	62	2	1	1	20	5
Bosch, John, dh-of	.203	69	7	14	2	1	1	12	0
Burks, Donny, ss	.252	238	39	60	7	1	0	23	10
Chase, Allen, of	.214	28	3	6	1	0	1	1	2
Close, Bart, of	.255	145	20	37	9	0	7	22	0
Colon, Frank, c	.100	10	1	1	0	0	0	2	0
Connelly, Brendan, c	.189	37	2	7	1	0	0	2	0
Crawley, Dwayne, of	.319	94	12	30	4	1	0	17	4
Cunningham, Todd, of-1b	.282	195	35	55	8	0	5	27	20
Dansky, Mike, of-2b	.250	32	5	8	0	1	0	5	1
Davenport, Damon, of	.197	157	30	31	6	0	1	10	14
Fatzinger, Darrell, 1b	.308	286	51	88	29	0	14	60	2
Feld, Charles, 3b	.228	92	13	21	1	0	5	11	0
Gordan, Joe, of	.265	102	9	27	7	2	0	10	4
Herman, Josh, c	.339	218	22	74	12	0	4	31	3
Inclan, Alex, of	.000	2	0	0	0	0	0	0	0
Jersey, Brian, of	.271	218	33	59	17	3	5	26	2
Johnson, John, of	.182	11	2	2	0	0	0	0	0
Manuelian, Jon, 1b	.235	34	5	8	4	0	1	6	1
McIver, Rob, 2b-3b	.221	77	12	17	4	0	5	13	1
Mondi, Mark, of	.139	36	5	5	0	0	0	2	1
Moore, Jason, c	.179	112	20	20	4	0	5	20	1
Shelton, Barry, 3b-of	.232	228	32	53	13	0	9	30	2

PITCHING	W	L	ERA	G	SV	IP	H	BB	SO
Anderson, Todd	2	4	5.29	26	4	32	45	13	25
Beach, Scott	1	4	5.36	21	0	81	87	59	54
Blandford, T.J.	4	1	6.71	25	1	60	78	41	48
Bowen, Luther	0	0	20.25	1	0	1	1	3	3
2-team (2 Chillicothe)	0	0	15.43	3	0	2	2	6	5
Burkindine, Larry	0	3	15.26	3	0	8	11	12	4
2-team (4 Johnstown)	1	4	8.74	7	0	23	23	28	14
Cordle, Jeff	0	1	9.24	12	0	13	17	17	5
2-team (1 Evansville)	1	1	9.00	13	0	13	19	18	5
Dobbins, Lance	0	4	12.64	5	0	16	14	26	11
Economou, Sean	6	2	4.97	13	0	54	61	28	35
Fox, Ryan	2	9	6.65	20	1	88	121	20	51
Garsky, Brian	0	1	9.00	2	0	6	8	8	7
Gerland, Greg	1	4	5.56	25	2	44	47	23	41
Hall, Brad	0	1	19.89	3	0	6	18	4	3
Hancock, Stewart	1	9	8.24	25	0	83	109	47	51
Johnson, Matt	1	1	2.77	2	0	13	7	8	14
Krevonick, E.C.	0	0	9.15	7	0	20	34	6	10
Morris, Chad	1	1	6.43	5	0	21	28	4	26
Morris, Gary	0	1	13.50	4	0	6	13	6	5
Palisin, Matt	0	3	6.84	5	0	26	36	10	13
Saweczko, Pete	0	1	13.50	1	0	5	8	5	7
Simmons, Carlos	2	3	4.30	7	0	46	38	24	41
Sutton, Ray	0	3	12.34	3	0	12	19	7	11
Tittrington, Scott	0	3	5.40	22	1	40	57	27	26

RICHMOND

BATTING	AVG	AB	R	H	2B	3B	HR	RBI	SB
Berliner, Seth, ss	.231	78	8	18	3	0	0	5	1
Bolden, Gerald, of-c	.194	139	31	27	5	0	3	18	3
2-team (23 Johnstown)	.246	232	50	57	13	1	3	26	6
Britt, Shane, of	.319	273	57	87	9	6	2	33	21
Buczkowski, Matt, c	.150	20	2	3	0	0	0	2	0
Buirley, Matt, c	.257	191	29	49	7	2	7	29	2
Burkhart, Morgan, dh-1b	.323	285	76	92	22	0	24	74	8
Christy, Jack, of	.000	7	1	0	0	0	0	0	0
DeFrancesco, Alex, 2b	.000	3	0	0	0	0	0	0	0
Eckleman, Alex, ss	.500	12	1	6	1	1	1	5	0
Fitzmorris, Matt, of	.298	168	32	50	13	4	0	24	11
Forsee, Matt, of	.188	16	2	3	0	0	2	3	0
Fowler, Jared, c-of	.216	51	7	11	1	0	0	3	0
Frank, Gary, 2b	.200	5	2	1	0	0	0	0	0
Garcia, Frankie, c	.222	27	4	6	2	0	0	1	1
Habig, Keith, ss-2b	.353	295	68	104	18	2	9	51	8
Hall, Bryan, of	.273	11	1	3	0	0	0	0	0
Holt, Kevin, 1b	.301	249	33	75	13	1	9	55	2
Jefferies, Daryl, 2b	.268	56	6	15	3	1	0	6	4
Lopez, Mark, of	.310	71	11	22	5	1	1	12	2
Pass, Joe, 2b-of	.325	280	44	91	13	1	1	38	4
Riordan, Fran, of	.224	98	15	22	5	2	2	13	2
Ruckman, Steve, 3b	.285	298	44	85	16	2	6	53	13
Spencer, Glen, of-3b	.265	98	11	26	3	0	1	10	2

PITCHING	W	L	ERA	G	SV	IP	H	BB	SO
Bentley, Brian	0	0	18.90	4	0	3	8	2	5
Castrop, Casey	3	3	1.99	30	8	32	24	9	36
Childress, Jason	0	0	0.00	1	0	1	3	0	1
Fowler, Jared	0	0	4.08	9	0	18	19	10	14

	W	L	ERA	G	SV	IP	H	BB	SO
Hahn, Steve	5	2	3.33	31	4	49	46	34	55
Hart, Derek	5	7	6.09	15	0	89	97	41	86
Hartman, Darren	0	1	3.38	4	0	21	26	5	20
Hess, Christian	3	7	5.87	17	0	80	82	46	53
Hussar, Dan	5	1	3.53	30	3	59	59	28	45
Ioviero, Neil	0	1	4.09	3	0	11	10	10	7
Justiniano, Rene	1	0	6.32	4	0	16	18	13	7
McHugh, Pete	0	0	7.71	4	0	7	10	6	4
Miller, Roy	1	2	5.14	10	1	28	31	14	27
Montfort, Jeff	8	6	3.68	16	0	103	102	67	117
Nelson, Ron	7	3	3.40	13	0	85	83	19	53
Parle, Justin	0	0	2.84	5	0	6	10	0	3
Phillips, Jamil	0	0	0.00	2	0	4	0	4	2
Urbanski, John	0	0	3.38	1	0	5	6	1	6
Westergard, Darren	0	0	47.25	1	0	1	6	2	1
Williams, Larry	5	3	3.76	11	0	69	60	32	89

SPRINGFIELD

BATTING	AVG	AB	R	H	2B	3B	HR	RBI	SB
Buckholz, A.J., 2b	.302	202	40	61	11	0	5	25	5
Bush, Darren, of	.288	278	47	80	15	3	7	45	2
Cicero, Frank, c	.233	86	15	20	5	1	1	9	2
Cruz, Paul, of	.345	165	45	57	9	3	8	27	9
Flowers, Travis, 1b-3b	.313	115	23	36	6	1	1	22	0
Gillis, Ed, 2b	.086	35	5	3	1	0	0	2	0
Harris, James, 3b	.307	293	62	90	21	0	14	62	1
Johnson, Eric, 1b-of	.167	6	0	1	0	0	0	1	0
Johnson, Kevin, 1b	.264	129	25	34	11	0	6	23	1
Kaczmar, Scott, of	.265	181	28	48	12	2	8	36	1
Lake, Matt, 1b	.208	96	20	20	6	0	5	18	0
McDonald, Ryan, 2b	.368	38	11	14	2	0	1	7	1
McSparin, Paul, c	.229	70	9	16	3	1	2	7	0
Moore, Baker, 2b-ss	.147	34	5	5	0	0	0	1	0
Murphy, Quinn, ss	.236	72	14	17	1	0	1	6	6
2-team (48 Johnstown)	.243	235	37	57	9	2	1	17	8
Ramos, Tony, ss	.293	181	27	53	8	3	0	27	2
Reed, Curtis, of	.176	17	3	3	0	0	1	1	1
Ronca, Joe, dh-of	.341	293	54	100	23	6	17	72	4
Snyder, Jeff, of	.241	203	32	49	8	0	2	24	8
Taylor, Sammy, of	.294	17	4	5	1	0	0	3	1
Thomas, Nathan, 1b	.286	49	5	14	1	1	0	6	1
Viera, Rob, c	.235	102	13	24	6	1	2	16	0
Walker, Rod, ss	.208	24	1	5	2	0	0	5	1

PITCHING	W	L	ERA	G	SV	IP	H	BB	SO
Abell, Joe	0	0	5.06	3	0	5	7	4	6
Brown, Mike	4	3	4.44	13	0	73	80	27	50
Denly, Greg	0	0	4.15	4	0	4	6	3	4
Duff, Matt	7	4	2.71	14	0	80	70	27	76
Hoffman, J.R.	1	2	3.99	31	2	29	29	14	16
House, Sean	8	6	4.78	19	0	111	137	28	74
Johnson, Matt	0	1	54.00	1	0	1	4	3	1
Neese, Josh	8	1	3.51	18	0	108	97	38	84
Ophus, Josh	3	3	6.05	26	3	39	49	24	35
Pavlovich, Tony	3	5	4.15	30	4	43	52	19	44
Rowland, Thad	1	4	4.11	24	1	61	74	23	43
Seiler, Chris	4	5	5.50	21	1	75	83	29	61
Smith, Brian	1	0	10.13	5	0	8	15	5	6
Smith, Matt	2	3	2.98	27	3	51	52	31	42

NORTHERN LEAGUE

The Duluth-Superior Dukes surprised everyone in 1997 by defeating perennial powerhouses St. Paul and Winnipeg to win their first Northern League championship.

The Dukes struggled to a 4-17 start but turned it around in the second half to finish 22-20, earning the right to face first-half winner St. Paul in the divisional playoffs. They were stretched to five games by St. Paul in the semifinals and five games by Winnipeg in the final.

Dukes pitcher Allen Halley shut down the Goldeyes in the first and last contests of the five-game championship set to earn the series MVP award. He defeated Winnipeg 6-2 in Game One and 3-2 in Game Five.

Duluth's march to the title marked the only time a team other than St. Paul or Winnipeg captured the crown since the league's return to the field in 1993.

To add to Duluth's unusual good fortune, Mike Meggers (.305-32-99) was the league's player of the year and Baseball America's Independent League Player of the Year. His 32 home runs set a league record, as did his 102 strikeouts. His trade from Winnipeg to Duluth at the start of the second half gave the Dukes the boost they needed to make their run at the title.

The Northern League once again stood above the other independent leagues in exposure, attendance and credibility in the eyes of Organized Baseball.

Ila Borders

St. Paul, by far the best independent league draw with 240,514 fans on the year, made its usual headlines by signing lefthander Ila Borders, who became the first woman to pitch in a professional game.

Borders was later traded to Duluth. She was used sparingly by both teams, finishing the year with a 7.53 ERA in 14 innings of work.

The Saints made more big news when they signed former Florida State University standout J.D. Drew. The 21-year-old outfielder was the second overall pick in the draft by the Phillies but came to St. Paul when the teams couldn't come to terms on a signing bonus.

Drew became the league's rookie of the year after hitting .341 with 18 homers and 50 RBIs for the Saints.

Former Winnipeg righthander Mike Cather also made a mark, becoming one of the most reliable middle relievers in the Braves' bullpen after he was called up from Atlanta's Triple-A Richmond affiliate after the all-star break.

STANDINGS

FIRST HALF

EAST DIVISION	W	L	PCT	GB
St. Paul Saints	24	18	.571	—
Thunder Bay Whiskey Jacks	18	24	.429	6
Duluth-Superior Dukes	17	24	.415	6½
Madison Balck Wolf	15	27	.357	9
WEST DIVISION	**W**	**L**	**PCT**	**GB**
Winnipeg Goldeyes	29	12	.707	—
Sioux City Explorers	28	14	.667	1½
Fargo-Moorhead RedHawks	21	21	.500	8½
Sioux Falls Canaries	15	27	.357	14½

SECOND HALF

EASTERN DIVISION	W	L	PCT	GB
Duluth-Superior Dukes	22	20	.524	—
St. Paul Saints	21	21	.500	1
Madison Black Wolf	19	23	.452	3
Thunder Bay Whiskey Jacks	18	24	.429	4
WESTERN DIVISION	**W**	**L**	**PCT**	**GB**
Fargo-Moorhead RedHawks	26	16	.619	—
Winnipeg Goldeyes	24	18	.571	2
Sioux City Explorers	22	20	.524	4
Sioux Falls Canaries	16	26	.381	10

PLAYOFFS: Semifinals—Duluth-Superior defeated St. Paul 3-2, and Winnipeg defeated Fargo-Moorhead 3-2, in best-of-5 series. **Finals**—Duluth-Superior defeated Winnipeg 3-2 in best-of-5 series.

MANAGERS: Duluth-Superior—George Mitterwald. Fargo-Moorhead—Doug Simunic. Madison—Wayne Krenchicki. St. Paul—Marty Scott. Sioux City—Ed Nottle. Sioux Falls—Tommy Thompson, Ken Medlock, Harry Stavrenos. Thunder Bay—Jay Ward. Winnipeg—Hal Lanier.

ATTENDANCE: St. Paul 240,514; Fargo-Moorhead 179,880; Winnipeg 171,240; Sioux City 134,580; Sioux Falls 104,546; Duluth-Superior 69,772; Madison 64,485; Thunder Bay 62,496.

ALL-STAR TEAM: C—Chris Coste, Fargo-Moorhead. **1B**—Terry Lee, Winnipeg. **2B**—Brian Duva, Winnipeg. **3B**—Jason Shanahan, Duluth-Superior. **SS**—John Dorman, Winnipeg. **OF**—Scott Bryant, St. Paul; Nolan Lane, Sioux City; Mike Meggers, Duluth-Superior. **DH**—Darryl Motley, Fargo-Moorhead. **LHP**—Gene Caruso, Fargo-Moorhead. **RHP**—Rick Forney, Winnipeg.

Player of the Year: Mike Meggers, Duluth-Superior. **Rookie of the Year:** J.D. Drew, St. Paul. **Rookie Pitcher of the Year:** Jeff Zimmerman, Winnipeg. **Manager of the Year:** George Mitterwald, Duluth-Superior.

INDIVIDUAL BATTING LEADERS

(Minimum 227 Plate Appearances)

	AVG	AB	R	H	2B	3B	HR	RBI	SB
Lee, Terry, Winnipeg	.358	313	88	112	22	2	20	78	2
Lewis, Danny, TB	.358	288	54	103	16	0	24	67	1
Smith, Dwight, St. Paul	.352	264	53	93	22	1	9	52	10
Duva, Brian, Winnipeg	.332	334	82	111	22	3	4	42	55
Shanahan, Jason, D-S	.331	308	51	102	21	1	14	70	4
Lane, Nolan, SC	.320	334	71	107	23	7	17	74	36
Weaver, Scott, Madison	.320	303	48	97	16	2	3	46	18
Akers, Chad, Fargo	.318	368	75	117	14	6	4	43	27
Motley, Darryl, Fargo	.317	309	70	98	22	0	22	70	4
Pinoni, Scott, Sargo	.314	325	63	102	19	2	20	92	1

INDIVIDUAL PITCHING LEADERS

(Minimum 67 Innings)

	W	L	ERA	G	SV	IP	H	BB	SO
Zimmerman, Jeff, Winnipeg	9	2	2.82	18	0	118	94	35	140
Caruso, Gene, Fargo	11	5	3.11	19	0	133	107	53	132
Badorek, Mike, Madison	6	5	3.15	13	0	100	92	22	63
Aragon, Angel, SF	4	3	3.18	33	3	68	77	27	43
Forney, Rick, Winnipeg	11	4	3.66	17	0	113	113	39	106
Boynewicz, Jim, TB	9	4	3.83	20	0	141	140	44	96
Quinn, Aaron, TB	3	4	3.90	37	2	67	68	29	70
Post, Bobby, SC	9	3	3.92	21	0	129	135	16	58
McGarity, Jeremy, D-S	8	5	3.93	21	0	153	171	45	142
Jersild, Aaron, SC	11	3	3.97	20	0	122	126	41	90

DULUTH-SUPERIOR

BATTING	AVG	AB	R	H	2B	3B	HR	RBI	SB
Arnold, Ken, ss	.270	259	43	70	10	1	2	24	13
Barsoom, Alan, 2b	.186	113	12	21	3	0	1	10	2
Briley, Greg, of	.280	279	44	78	13	2	2	27	23
Cardenas, Johnny, c	.298	242	30	72	12	2	6	39	0
Clark, Jerald, dh-of	.200	35	6	7	1	0	1	7	0
Cooney, Jim, dh	.160	25	1	4	1	0	0	4	0
Cora, Manny, ss	.321	53	5	17	3	0	0	10	0
DiPace, Danny, of	.176	17	1	3	1	0	0	0	0
English, Keith, 2b-3b	.091	11	0	1	0	0	0	2	0
Jensen, Jeff, 1b	.291	309	54	90	19	3	7	39	7
Johnson, Anthony, dh-of	.300	333	63	100	19	5	7	57	12
Meggers, Mike, dh-of	.319	166	39	53	7	1	16	42	3
2-team (40 Winnipeg)	.305	338	77	103	17	1	32	99	8
Mitterwald, Bryan, dh-c	.246	211	33	52	6	0	9	30	0
Porter, Kedric, of	.264	106	14	28	2	0	1	8	6
Rodriguez, Ryan, 2b	.304	184	28	56	14	1	1	21	4
Shanahan, Jason, 3b	.331	308	51	102	21	1	14	70	4
Texidor, Jose, of	.299	261	40	78	10	1	4	31	4

PITCHING	W	L	ERA	G	SV	IP	H	BB	SO
Alazaus, Shawn	0	0	162.00	1	0	0	3	2	1
Austin, Swan	0	1	7.00	3	0	9	13	3	5
Borders, Ila	0	0	7.56	8	0	8	13	5	6
2-team (7 St. Paul)	0	0	7.53	15	0	14	24	9	11
Collett, Andy	0	0	22.50	2	0	2	6	2	2
Giron, Emiliano	3	3	2.72	39	10	53	38	29	70
Glick, David	3	4	4.44	25	0	75	89	23	56
Halley, Allen	4	4	5.18	19	0	92	96	42	110
Lance, David	0	0	14.49	7	0	14	31	7	11
Maddock, Steve	0	0	11.05	4	0	7	11	7	7
Marchesano, Mike	1	0	13.50	4	0	4	9	5	2
McGarity, Jeremy	8	5	3.93	21	0	153	171	45	142
Nuttle, Jamison	6	4	1.90	38	2	66	52	41	80
Scheid, Rich	1	4	6.21	5	0	29	35	14	21
Shaver, Tony	10	8	5.55	22	0	110	122	70	55
Tomlin, Randy	3	10	6.31	16	0	77	107	29	59
Weaver, Andy	0	1	8.78	17	0	27	45	20	16
Yeomans, Jesse	0	0	4.50	6	0	8	8	2	3

FARGO-MOORHEAD

BATTING	AVG	AB	R	H	2B	3B	HR	RBI	SB
Akers, Chad, ss	.318	368	75	117	14	6	4	43	27
Bardin, Brad, c	.292	24	2	7	3	0	0	5	0
2-team (21 Sioux Falls)	.237	93	5	22	5	1	0	10	0
Bloomer, Jason, of	.217	60	13	13	1	1	1	9	3
Castro, Ernest, of	.221	86	13	19	5	0	2	10	0
Coste, Chris, c-3b	.312	337	45	105	22	0	12	50	7
Deak, Darrell, 1b	.269	67	12	18	3	0	6	18	1
Foss, Dan, of	.368	19	2	7	0	0	0	2	0
Hughes, Troy, of	.267	165	28	44	10	2	8	41	8
Knott, John, 3b-of	.313	307	59	96	13	1	10	52	30
Lantigua, Eddie, of	.245	49	6	12	1	0	2	9	0
2-team (23 Sioux Falls)	.260	123	18	32	5	0	5	24	3
Motley, Darryl, dh	.317	309	70	98	22	0	22	70	4
Ottavinia, Paul, of	.333	168	45	56	16	3	0	22	12
Pacitti, Gregg, of	.273	11	1	3	0	0	0	3	1
Powell, Chris, of	.293	92	17	27	5	1	2	9	8
Ross, Jackie, of	.304	263	45	80	16	2	6	34	3
Trahan, Mike, 2b	.277	303	38	84	17	4	5	38	7
Traxler, Brian, 1b	.298	178	29	53	12	0	3	37	1
Vogel, Mike, 1b	.256	160	23	41	11	0	2	21	0
Weaver, Scott, of	.226	31	4	7	0	0	0	6	1
Wick, Chad, of	.000	2	0	0	0	0	0	0	0

PITCHING	W	L	ERA	G	SV	IP	H	BB	SO
Baumann, Craig	1	1	3.52	6	0	8	5	7	10
Bittiger, Jeff	1	2	6.41	5	0	20	32	8	15
Bryant, Chris	0	0	14.04	8	0	8	18	7	11
Caruso, Gene	11	5	3.11	19	0	133	107	53	132
Clancy, Blake	0	0	29.70	3	0	3	6	5	1
Dillon, Jay	0	0	12.60	3	0	5	9	1	3
Ford, Jack	3	3	8.25	14	0	36	53	27	27
Isom, Jeff	7	6	5.10	16	0	101	103	64	93
Jeckell, Matt	0	0	3.65	6	0	12	11	7	5
Lukas, Stephen	1	3	5.26	34	7	50	49	20	49
Lyman, Chuck	0	0	9.53	19	0	17	16	21	20
Merrill, Tajah	0	0	9.00	1	0	2	4	1	0
Nelson, Barry	0	2	1.71	18	12	21	14	3	22
Paull, Kalam	0	0	7.62	15	1	26	36	18	15
Roberts, Brett	5	2	3.53	8	0	43	40	12	41
Runion, Tony	1	1	3.80	11	1	21	25	5	22
Salvevold, Greg	5	5	6.20	19	0	74	85	44	47
Schmidt, George	4	0	2.23	24	0	48	43	16	39
Smith, Tim	8	7	5.32	19	0	107	104	68	82

MADISON

BATTING	AVG	AB	R	H	2B	3B	HR	RBI	SB
Baxter, Duke, 3b-2b	.289	135	24	39	8	2	1	15	2
Bowers, R.J., of	.220	109	14	24	7	1	1	6	2
Busse, Sean, 3b	.091	11	0	1	0	0	0	0	0
Castro, Ernest, of	.233	73	6	17	6	0	1	8	0
2-team (23 Fargo)	.226	159	19	36	11	0	3	18	0
Cole, Alex, of	.339	112	20	38	6	1	2	21	6
Connell, Lino, 2b	.308	344	65	106	26	6	6	45	10
Dattola, Kevin, of	.207	58	8	12	1	0	0	1	4
2-team (61 St. Paul)	.265	275	46	73	13	1	4	28	15
Everson, Darin, c-1b	.291	309	62	90	26	0	17	74	5
Hamlin, Jonas, 1b	.238	286	43	68	20	0	15	40	5
Marabella, Tony, of-3b	.249	285	40	71	9	0	8	37	8
Marsh, Tom, of	.275	80	16	22	3	0	3	8	2
Mosher, Willie, 3b	.074	27	3	2	0	0	0	1	1
Peguero, Jose, 3b	.298	124	16	37	9	5	3	19	7
Piacenti, Neil, c	.257	105	11	27	14	0	1	11	1
Smith, Sean, c	.286	119	11	34	3	1	2	21	1
Vopata, Nate, ss	.237	308	48	73	10	9	10	48	12
Walton, Kevin, of	.217	115	10	25	2	1	0	9	2
Weaver, Scott, of	.331	272	44	90	16	2	3	40	17
2-team (9 Fargo)	.320	303	48	97	16	2	3	46	18

PITCHING	W	L	ERA	G	SV	IP	H	BB	SO
Badorek, Mike	6	5	3.15	13	0	100	92	22	63
Baumann, Craig	0	1	10.05	9	0	14	16	11	11
2-team (6 Fargo)	1	2	7.77	15	0	22	21	18	21
Berthelot, Eric	0	0	12.06	12	0	16	31	7	10
Brewer, Nevin	0	2	5.63	7	4	8	12	6	5
2-team (23 Winnipeg)	1	6	4.18	30	10	32	41	21	25
Etheridge, Roger	6	8	5.53	20	0	112	125	61	86
Gunderson, Trent	0	0	8.22	5	0	8	9	11	7
Hoyman, Adam	0	0	7.15	4	0	11	19	5	2
Johnson, Jason	0	1	21.60	2	0	5	13	4	4
Niemeier, Todd	1	0	7.88	8	0	8	11	4	4
Painich, Joey	3	5	4.57	14	0	61	72	25	30
Renko, Steve	8	10	4.05	21	0	160	159	36	110
Salamon, John	3	4	6.75	26	7	37	37	22	42

PITCHING	W	L	ERA	G	SV	IP	H	BB	SO
Wagner, Matt	1	3	5.44	21	1	45	46	21	32
2-team (2 Sioux Falls)	1	3	5.48	23	1	48	49	24	33
Weber, Lenny	2	4	5.91	28	1	43	47	29	28
Wilstead, Judd	2	6	7.39	17	0	67	83	51	36
Wise, Andy	2	1	5.66	6	0	35	42	9	21
2-team (18 Winnipeg)	6	2	5.18	24	1	75	84	16	53

ST. PAUL

BATTING	AVG	AB	R	H	2B	3B	HR	RBI	SB
Almonte, Dan, ss	.233	43	10	10	2	0	1	8	5
Bryant, Scott, of-3b	.304	345	63	105	30	1	17	73	2
Dattola, Kevin, of	.281	217	38	61	12	1	4	27	11
Delaney, Sean, c	.248	258	35	64	13	0	4	32	4
Dionne, Stephane, c	.263	19	2	5	1	0	1	4	0
Drew, J.D., of	.341	170	51	58	6	1	18	50	5
Evans, Chris, dh-of	.300	250	38	75	12	3	7	43	1
Kennedy, David, 1b	.293	328	61	96	24	0	19	80	2
McInnes, Chris, 3b-2b	.293	280	56	82	12	5	5	43	21
Peltier, Dan, of	.288	73	16	21	5	1	1	9	0
Robbins, Lance, ss	.203	251	41	51	13	0	1	27	3
Rogers, Lamarr, 2b-of	.301	286	55	86	21	3	2	39	20
Santos, Ray, 3b	.288	59	8	17	2	1	1	4	0
Senjem, Guye, c	.000	5	1	0	0	0	0	0	0
Smith, Dwight, of-dh	.352	264	53	93	22	1	9	52	10
Smith, Rob, 3b	.263	38	5	10	2	0	2	7	0

PITCHING	W	L	ERA	G	SV	IP	H	BB	SO
Alkire, Jeff	0	0	6.00	2	0	3	2	1	3
Borders, Ila	0	0	7.50	7	0	6	11	4	5
Dettmer, John	8	9	4.22	19	0	11	126	43	62
Glinatsis, George	3	6	5.02	14	0	81	102	23	52
Kenady, Jake	2	3	3.00	39	4	63	51	56	78
Lapka, Rick	1	0	9.45	13	0	13	19	10	10
McRoberts, Brian	1	1	4.57	16	0	22	20	11	24
Miller, Brent	1	0	4.60	8	0	16	21	11	12
Miller, Joe	5	4	4.58	36	3	75	78	43	58
Paul, Andy	8	6	6.16	18	0	104	120	48	91
Peterman, Ernie	6	3	6.11	19	0	84	93	52	52
Prado, Jose	7	3	5.07	19	0	108	122	47	70
Schlutt, Jason	1	3	6.15	27	12	26	28	15	26
Sullivan, Brian	2	0	4.50	6	0	10	10	8	4

SIOUX CITY

BATTING	AVG	AB	R	H	2B	3B	HR	RBI	SB
Ahrendt, Jay, c-1b	.100	10	1	1	0	0	0	1	0
Cannaday, Aaron, c	.269	249	31	67	17	0	5	43	3
Chiprez, Chris, of	.000	5	5	0	0	0	0	0	1
Cox, Angelo, of	.254	284	59	72	10	4	7	37	31
Flores, Freddy, 2b-3b	.118	17	3	2	0	0	0	0	2
Garner, Kevin, dh	.300	253	64	76	15	0	27	73	0
Grevengoed, Jayson, 3b	.174	23	5	4	1	0	0	0	0
Harrell, Ken, of	.400	5	2	2	0	0	0	0	0
Kliner, Josh, 2b	.237	299	47	71	17	3	5	31	7
Kopacz, Derek, 3b	.295	275	53	81	14	4	12	44	13
Lane, Nolan, of	.320	334	71	107	23	7	17	74	36
Matos, Julius, ss	.266	353	64	94	12	3	6	44	8
Miranda, Jose, of	.271	85	15	23	3	1	2	12	0
Perez, Danny, of	.305	315	70	96	21	2	4	45	14
Petru, Rich, ss-3b	.167	12	1	2	0	0	0	0	1
Pinoni, Scott, 1b	.314	325	63	102	19	2	20	92	1
Slayton, Shane, c	.250	72	11	18	2	0	1	7	0
Vogel, Mike, c	.235	51	3	12	2	0	0	3	0

PITCHER	W	L	ERA	G	SV	IP	H	BB	SO
Aguilar, Alonzo	5	1	4.83	24	0	41	38	32	23
Barron, Mark	1	0	5.66	11	0	21	29	10	11
Brooks, Wes	8	7	4.91	21	0	125	144	32	64
Cerbone, Marc	2	2	4.99	28	1	40	41	25	27
Grife, Rich	5	6	2.98	41	1	63	48	31	42
Jersild, Aaron	11	3	3.97	20	0	122	126	41	90
Porzio, Mike	2	2	4.26	27	0	61	75	27	63
Post, Bobby	9	3	3.92	21	0	129	135	16	58
Shoemaker, Steve	7	7	4.84	19	0	115	147	32	77
Turner, Matt	0	3	5.31	37	16	39	48	16	54

SIOUX FALLS

BATTING	AVG	AB	R	H	2B	3B	HR	RBI	SB
Arnold, John, of	.247	77	7	19	3	1	1	5	0
Bardin, Brad, c	.217	69	3	15	2	1	0	5	0
Berrios, Harry, dh-of	.282	294	41	83	14	1	14	61	7
Buckley, Reagan, of	.097	31	3	3	0	0	0	0	0
Campaniello, Ed, 3b-of	.125	8	2	1	0	0	0	2	0
Castillo, Benny, of	.269	104	19	28	7	0	2	12	3
Cruz, Paul, of	.194	31	7	6	1	1	0	5	0
Dumas, Mike, 2b-of	.261	329	61	86	7	2	0	34	35
Erwin, Mat, c	.203	69	4	14	2	0	0	11	0
Giuffre, Guy, c	.192	73	9	14	3	0	1	3	0
Glenn, Brandon, of	.000	1	0	0	0	0	0	0	0
Grijalva, Mike, of-3b	.174	46	2	8	1	1	1	5	0
Gutfeld, Marc, ss	.282	238	31	67	8	2	0	16	2
Guzman, Ismail, of	.105	19	3	2	0	0	0	2	1
Hearn, Sean, of	.289	180	30	52	11	0	9	28	6
2-team (26 Thunder Bay)	.283	276	47	78	14	0	14	44	9
Heidemann, Mike, 1b	.218	110	13	24	7	0	3	18	0
Kimbler, Doug, ss	.179	84	9	15	7	0	0	13	2
Lantigua, Eddie, dh	.270	74	12	20	4	0	3	15	3
Murphy, Sean, 2b	.343	67	19	23	7	1	1	14	6
Neff, Marty, of	.140	43	3	6	1	0	2	7	0
Powell, Chris, of	.301	103	24	31	4	4	4	15	12
2-team (24 Fargo)	.297	195	41	58	9	5	6	24	20
Reid, Derek, of	.250	156	20	39	9	0	2	27	9
Taniguchi, Hiro, c	.188	16	2	3	0	0	0	1	0
Traxler, Brian, 1b	.313	134	16	42	10	0	3	21	1
2-team (42 Fargo)	.304	312	45	95	22	0	6	58	2
Tsoukalas, John, 3b	.300	300	44	90	19	0	2	34	6
Vogel, Mike, c	.258	89	15	23	4	0	2	11	3
Young, Gerald, of	.212	146	16	31	8	0	1	10	4

PITCHING	W	L	ERA	G	SV	IP	H	BB	SO
Aragon, Angel	4	3	3.18	33	3	68	77	27	43
Chavez, Carlos	0	2	6.00	10	0	15	19	4	15
Grant, Brian	1	4	9.40	10	0	30	39	15	14
Guetterman, Lee	3	7	4.50	13	0	76	89	10	33
Howe, Steve	1	1	1.98	12	1	14	8	2	17
Hyde, Rich	8	6	5.33	20	0	108	134	37	86
Jarolimek, J.J.	1	1	5.49	15	1	39	50	19	21
Mosman, Marc	2	6	4.79	19	0	98	99	47	61
Pack, Steve	0	3	6.68	8	0	34	52	8	18
Pearson, Terry	2	3	4.16	41	1	63	85	30	46
Poeck, Chad	1	4	5.14	16	0	77	84	33	70
Runion, Tony	7	2	4.01	26	2	34	36	12	26
2-team (11 Fargo)	8	3	3.93	37	3	55	61	17	48
Sollecito, Gabe	0	4	7.62	13	1	13	19	8	9
Steen, Troy	0	1	11.25	4	0	4	9	3	3
Wagner, Matt	0	0	6.00	2	0	3	3	3	1
Wanke, Chuck	0	1	4.02	8	0	16	10	3	13
Yoder, Ben	1	5	7.21	16	0	49	69	26	29

THUNDER BAY

BATTING	AVG	AB	R	H	2B	3B	HR	RBI	SB
Buckley, Reagan, c-of	.178	45	5	8	2	1	1	1	2
2-team (12 Sioux Falls)	.145	76	8	11	2	1	1	1	2
Castillo, Benny, of	.333	195	37	65	11	0	7	26	2
2-team (26 Sioux Falls)	.311	299	56	93	18	0	9	38	5
Ellison, Tony, of	.333	141	20	47	11	2	5	23	3
Francois, Manny, 2b	.290	69	8	20	10	0	0	3	3
Hearn, Sean, of	.271	96	17	26	3	0	5	16	3
Jenkins, Dee, 2b	.269	160	28	43	13	2	7	20	2
Jones, Bryan, 2b	.063	16	0	1	0	0	0	1	1
Kessick, Chris, c	.250	28	2	7	1	0	0	2	0
Lewis, Danny, dh	.358	288	54	103	16	0	24	67	1
Mercado, Julio, of	.195	41	5	8	1	0	0	4	5
Meyer, Travis, c	.190	100	10	19	5	0	1	8	1
Pacitti, Gregg, of	.283	145	22	41	12	2	4	14	0
2-team (5 Fargo)	.282	156	23	44	12	2	4	17	1
Patton, Josh, 3b-1b	.235	187	20	44	13	1	5	36	0
Peguero, Jose, 3b-2b	.367	49	8	18	3	0	0	3	4
2-team (32 Madison)	.318	173	24	55	12	5	3	22	11
Ricard, Toby, 3b	.278	252	32	70	17	3	3	31	2
Sawyer, Chris, of	.269	309	48	83	23	2	9	42	14
See, Larry, 1b	.282	319	43	90	13	0	19	69	2
Sturges, Brian, c	.172	87	5	15	2	0	0	6	1
Thornhill, Chad, ss	.284	320	52	91	11	0	0	17	2

PITCHING	W	L	ERA	G	SV	IP	H	BB	SO
Barnes, Jon	0	0	4.50	1	0	2	2	2	1
Bock, Jeff	4	3	5.02	14	0	72	87	34	44
Boynewicz, Jim	9	4	3.83	20	0	141	140	44	96
Danielson, Bobby	2	4	6.47	15	0	56	79	27	42
Duffy, John	2	2	4.66	16	0	19	25	8	14
Evans, Brandon	2	3	4.29	15	0	65	65	35	46
Gast, John	0	4	9.47	8	0	19	31	9	8
Grant, Brian	0	1	14.21	2	0	6	11	4	4
2-team (10 Sioux Falls)	1	5	10.25	12	0	36	50	19	18
Hart, Jason	4	4	4.35	36	16	41	40	23	58
Jesperson, Bob	4	7	7.42	23	0	70	96	30	53
Loaiza, Sabino	0	1	6.48	4	0	17	20	5	13
Merrill, Tajah	1	2	7.59	8	0	21	32	14	16
2-team (1 Fargo)	1	2	7.71	9	0	23	36	15	16

PITCHING	W	L	ERA	G	SV	IP	H	BB	SO
Noffke, Andy	1	5	8.84	15	0	39	60	26	15
Perusek, Bill	0	0	3.48	10	0	21	15	31	16
Quinn, Aaron	3	4	3.90	37	2	67	68	29	70
Rogers, Paul	1	1	7.85	25	0	39	58	20	25
Smyth, Ken	2	2	8.14	13	0	24	35	15	23
2-team (13 Winnipeg)	2	2	7.65	26	0	40	52	24	42
Tilmon, Pat	1	1	5.14	3	0	14	19	3	10

WINNIPEG

PLAYER	AVG	AB	R	H	2B	3B	HR	RBI	SB
Dorman, John, ss	.310	268	50	83	11	4	8	56	15
Duva, Brian, 2b	.332	334	82	111	22	3	4	42	55
Gordon, Jeff, c	.243	37	1	9	1	0	0	3	0
Hernandez, Kiki, c	.478	23	2	11	4	0	1	4	0
Hickey, Mike, 3b	.306	255	48	78	19	1	7	46	22
Kokinda, Chris, of	.278	334	73	93	19	2	6	56	10
Lee, Terry, 1b	.358	313	88	112	22	2	20	78	2
Martin, C.J., of	.307	283	60	87	13	2	12	53	15
Meggers, Mike, dh	.291	172	38	50	10	0	16	57	5
Mitchell, Tony, dh	.316	155	31	49	6	0	8	32	0
Peckham, Chris, 3b	.125	8	1	1	0	0	0	1	0
Pegues, Steve, dh	.400	10	1	4	0	0	0	6	0
Prater, Andrew, c	.262	42	5	11	2	0	0	7	0
Ratliff, Darryl, of	.222	45	9	10	2	0	1	7	4
Reams, Derek, c	.243	235	37	57	16	1	10	41	2
Towner, Kyle, of	.265	181	38	48	6	2	1	16	18
Watts, Brent, of-3b	.267	285	48	76	14	4	5	45	8

PITCHING	W	L	ERA	G	SV	IP	H	BB	SO
Bailey, Mike	5	3	4.43	23	1	81	76	47	89
Brewer, Nevin	1	4	3.70	23	6	24	29	15	20
Carpenter, Brian	2	4	4.66	12	2	48	54	19	36
Forney, Rick	11	4	3.66	17	0	113	113	39	106
Guehne, Dan	1	2	4.21	34	4	26	25	14	35
McHugh, Pete	0	0	21.00	2	0	3	9	3	1
Pedraza, Rod	8	5	5.49	18	0	121	147	18	93
Salamon, John	3	1	5.93	12	2	14	14	8	14
2-team (26 Madison)	6	5	6.53	38	9	51	51	30	56
Smyth, Ken	0	0	6.89	13	0	16	17	9	19
Sparks, Jeff	1	1	4.15	7	0	13	11	10	20
Wiebe, Jeff	0	0	10.16	17	0	28	47	20	19
Williams, Larry	2	1	6.75	7	0	7	9	3	6
Wise, Andy	4	1	4.76	18	1	40	42	7	32
Ybarra, Jamie	6	2	4.52	16	0	92	79	62	92
Zimmerman, Jeff	9	2	2.82	18	0	118	94	35	140

TEXAS-LOUISIANA LEAGUE

Two of the previous year's most disappointing teams battled it out for the Texas-Louisiana League title in 1997, with Alexandria topping Amarillo three games to one in the championship series.

The Aces, who earned a playoff berth by finishing a game in front of Amarillo in the second half, scored 38 runs in four games. They took a two games to none lead by outscoring Amarillo17-5, then closed out the series with a 12-8 victory.

Amarillo, which finished 54-32, drew the most fans in the league for the second straight season, though their 109,407 total was a 15,000 dropoff from a year earlier. Each of the league's six teams suffered decreases in attendance except Tyler, which drew 71,435, up 13,000, and Lubbock which drew 83,488, up 2,200.

Despite a drop in attendance, the league could expand in the years to come. Larger markets such as Austin and Fort Worth in Texas and Lafayette, La., were being scouted by league officials for future franchises.

Rio Grande's Bryan Warner and Tyler's Chris Cassels shared player of the year honors and shared the league record for extra-base hits: 57 apiece.

Warner hit .392 with 25 homers and 94 RBIs, while Cassels hit .333. His 29 homers set a new league record.

STANDINGS

FIRST HALF	W	L	PCT	GB
Amarillo Dillas	28	14	.667	—
Tyler Wildcatters	22	21	.512	6½
Lubbock Crickets	21	22	.488	7½
Alexandria Aces	21	22	.488	7½
Rio Grande Valley WhiteWings	19	25	.432	10
Abilene Prairie Dogs	18	25	.419	10½
SECOND HALF	**W**	**L**	**PCT**	**GB**
Alexandria Aces	27	17	.614	—
Amarillo Dillas	26	18	.591	1
Tyler Wildcatters	25	19	.568	2
Rio Grande Valley WhiteWings	20	24	.455	7
Abilene Prairie Dogs	18	26	.409	9
Lubbock Crickets	16	28	.364	11

PLAYOFFS: Finals—Alexandria defeated Amarillo 3-1 in best of 5 series.

MANAGERS: Abilene—Barry Jones. Alexandria—Stan Cilburn. Amarillo—Glenn Wilson. Lubbock—Glenn Sullivan. Rio Grande Valley—Mike Brumley. Tyler—Darrell Evans.

ATTENDANCE: Amarillo 109,407; Lubbock 83,488; Alexandria 73,892; Rio Grande Valley 75,639; Tyler 71,435; Abilene 65,489.

ALL-STAR TEAM: C—Kevin Tahan, Alexandria. **1B**—John O'Brien, Alexandria. **2B**—Jorge Alvarez, Amarillo. **3B**—Kyle Shade, Alexandria. **SS**—Tim Howard, Amarillo. **OF**—Sean Collins, Tyler; Lonnie Maclin, Amarillo; Bryan Warner, Rio Grande. **DH**—Chris Cassels, Tyler. **Util**—Mike Hardge, Lubbock. **SP**—Daren Brown, Lubbock; Ray Davis, Tyler; Ryan Thomas, Amarillo; Ryan Whitaker, Rio Grande. **RP**—George Preston, Abilene.

Co-Most Valuable Players: Chris Cassels, Tyler; Bryan Warner, Rio Grande. **Co-Most Valuable Pitcher:** Daren Brown, Amarillo; Ray Davis, Tyler. **Rookie of the Year:** Pat Koerner, Rio Grande.

INDIVIDUAL BATTING LEADERS

(Minimum 238 Plate Appearances)

	AVG	AB	R	H	2B	3B	HR	RBI	SB
Alvarez, Jorge, Amarillo	.395	263	60	104	23	5	5	68	21
Warner, Bryan, Rio Grande	.392	339	75	133	28	4	25	94	8
Maclin, Lonnie, Amarillo	.375	312	65	117	19	9	4	58	22
Collins, Sean, Tyler	.374	353	91	132	25	3	13	51	36
McClure, Jason, Abilene	.373	276	61	103	16	2	4	54	20
Ramirez, J.D., Lubbock	.371	240	45	89	26	3	6	47	3
Davis, Jay, Rio Grande	.357	333	68	119	22	2	15	62	33
Shade, Kyle, Alexandria	.354	353	68	125	34	4	8	53	1
Ford, Curt, Amarillo	.353	221	48	78	8	2	4	35	15
Howard, Tim, Amarillo	.352	298	80	105	17	5	7	51	36

INDIVIDUAL PITCHING LEADERS

(Minimum 70 Innings)

	W	L	ERA	G	SV	IP	H	BB	SO
Davis, Ray, Tyler	7	5	2.89	15	0	97	86	31	76
DeJesus, Javy, Alex	5	5	3.63	15	1	97	110	33	70
Farrow, Jason, Tyler	8	4	3.65	38	4	81	85	40	83
Maberry, Louis, Amar/Abi	4	3	3.93	28	0	71	66	53	59
Thomas, Ryan, Amarillo	11	1	4.13	23	0	94	93	29	43
Boebert, Michael, Amarillo	10	7	4.18	27	2	123	131	60	94
Kermode, Al, Amarillo	10	3	4.27	21	0	133	171	25	69
Baine, David, Lubbock	5	5	4.39	22	1	92	100	49	61
Brown, Daren, Amarillo	12	6	4.73	24	3	154	184	50	130
Bicknell, Greg, Lubbock	9	9	4.81	19	0	137	145	56	71

ABILENE

BATTING	AVG	AB	R	H	2B	3B	HR	RBI	SB
Andrews, Jay, of	.311	318	51	99	25	4	8	64	22
Benner, Brian, of	.300	100	17	30	3	1	3	10	6
Bethea, Scott, 2b	.308	289	55	89	10	1	0	26	22
Contreras, Efrain, of	.286	280	43	80	11	2	7	41	5
Gagliano, Manny, 3b	.317	246	36	78	15	1	7	49	4
Gumbs, Lincoln, 2b	.143	14	0	2	1	0	0	0	1
Hughes, Shawn, c	.309	272	46	84	17	2	5	46	5
Hyde, Jerod, 1b-of	.257	109	20	28	8	0	3	24	4
Keith, Jason, ss	.284	306	54	87	13	6	4	42	21
Kiraly, Jeff, 1b	.259	116	17	30	5	0	2	8	4
McClure, Jason, of	.373	276	61	103	16	2	4	54	20
Monroe, Darryl, of	.338	216	50	73	8	5	10	39	25
Motes, Jeff, 3b-2b	.289	211	39	61	10	2	2	28	5
Roberts, Mike, of	.000	2	0	0	0	0	0	0	0
Sandoval, David, 3b	.245	53	6	13	3	1	0	10	2
2-team (63 Amarillo)	.262	229	40	60	15	2	1	28	12

	AVG	AB	R	H	2B	3B	HR	RBI	SB
Takahashi, Barry, p	.221	77	4	17	1	0	0	7	0
Vallarelli, Mike, 1b-c	.276	145	16	40	9	1	1	22	1

PITCHING	W	L	ERA	G	SV	IP	H	BB	SO
Baack, John	3	7	6.38	23	1	92	128	47	38
Borg, Kevin	0	1	10.80	4	0	15	17	21	7
Conger, Bryan	1	3	8.19	12	0	30	44	18	13
Conkle, Troy Dean	7	3	6.44	23	2	88	129	24	53
Glore, Jamie	2	1	2.19	6	0	25	22	13	4
Gongora, Chris	0	2	7.59	10	0	11	11	13	2
Hampton, Mark	8	5	6.72	34	0	71	92	41	45
Hirsch, Troy	2	4	9.46	15	0	46	67	32	30
Johnson, Jay	0	1	27.00	2	0	2	5	6	2
Keling, Korey	0	5	8.10	10	0	53	71	40	22
Lott, Hank	0	4	8.74	8	0	34	41	35	12
Maberry, Louis	4	3	3.54	24	0	61	56	43	53
Matulevich, Jeff	2	0	11.12	9	3	11	19	4	12
2-team (28 Amarillo)	4	2	5.79	37	8	47	56	17	52
Mercer, Chip	0	0	4.30	9	0	15	20	11	7
Preston, George	3	2	4.36	37	10	66	58	44	66
Takahashi, Barry	1	2	6.00	23	1	42	62	21	13
Thomas, Royal	3	9	6.78	14	0	78	118	28	44

ALEXANDRIA

BATTING	AVG	AB	R	H	2B	3B	HR	RBI	SB
Amons, Joshua, 3b	.091	22	5	2	1	0	0	1	0
Cole, Marvin, 2b	.316	354	60	112	21	3	7	58	14
Delafield, Wil, of	.315	314	56	99	23	7	4	50	3
DeLeon, Robert, ss	.277	332	58	92	19	4	12	60	10
Hewes, Robert, 3b-2b	.321	53	19	17	1	3	1	6	0
Matos, Malvin, dh-of	.267	255	44	68	14	1	15	55	7
O'Brien, John, 1b	.314	318	63	100	22	0	24	90	0
Rothe, Ryan, of	.303	244	58	74	15	2	1	29	14
Shade, Kyle, 3b	.354	353	68	125	34	4	8	53	1
Tahan, Kevin, c-dh	.330	273	58	90	23	1	9	51	6
Turco, Frank, of	.327	361	81	118	33	6	8	73	13
White, Darrin, c-dh	.246	171	31	42	13	0	4	23	3

PITCHING	W	L	ERA	G	SV	IP	H	BB	SO
DeJesus, Javi	5	5	3.63	15	1	97	110	33	70
Hartman, Kelly	2	2	8.00	8	0	18	27	10	10
2-team (10 Tyler)	3	3	6.60	18	0	30	42	15	17
Jones, Mike	6	6	6.00	23	0	123	157	56	47
Mack, Tony	9	4	4.99	21	0	144	177	54	74
Moran, Eric	9	6	4.72	43	7	69	82	30	54
Parks, Tommy	0	1	9.64	2	0	5	9	5	1
Pickich, Jeff	1	2	9.87	5	0	17	35	12	7
Ramirez, Luis	7	7	4.50	36	2	68	69	26	52
Reeder, Russell	2	1	5.53	7	0	41	55	8	31
Wiley, Chad	0	0	13.50	4	0	7	11	4	3
Young, Ty	0	1	7.45	18	0	39	53	33	14
Youngblood, Todd	7	5	5.28	18	0	116	134	64	102

AMARILLO

BATTING	AVG	AB	R	H	2B	3B	HR	RBI	SB
Alvarez, Jorge, 2b	.395	263	60	104	23	5	5	68	21
Braddy, Junior, of	.317	249	51	79	19	2	11	57	12
2-team (10 Lubbock)	.297	283	54	84	21	2	11	63	13
Brewer, Rod, 1b	.320	294	73	94	18	2	18	73	18
Busse, Sean, of-1b	.250	8	0	2	0	0	0	1	0
Cook, Jeff, of	.290	193	34	56	6	2	0	27	16
Dubrule, Tim, 3b	.229	48	8	11	0	1	0	2	6
Ford, Curt, of-dh	.353	221	48	78	8	2	4	35	15
Goff, Jerry, c	.294	265	52	78	16	0	16	64	10
Hook, Kenny, ss-2b	.267	120	15	32	1	1	0	14	5
Howard, Tim, ss-of	.352	298	80	105	17	5	7	51	36
Kline, Jason, 2b-ss	.182	11	0	2	0	0	0	1	0
Llanos, Bobby, 3b-of	.324	188	36	61	7	1	5	37	3
Maclin, Lonnie, of	.375	312	65	117	19	9	4	58	22
Reyes, Javier, c	.194	72	8	14	2	0	0	3	0
Sandoval, David, 3b-2b	.267	176	34	47	12	1	1	18	10
Wilson, Michael, of	.315	197	43	62	13	6	0	17	17

PITCHER	W	L	ERA	G	SV	IP	H	BB	SO
Beach, Scott	0	1	12.00	2	0	6	14	4	6
Boebert, Michael	10	7	4.18	27	2	123	131	60	94
Brewer, Rod	1	0	2.70	7	0	7	3	3	6
Brown, Daren	12	6	4.73	24	3	154	184	50	130
Cortinas, Roque	1	1	9.26	7	0	12	18	6	7
Hitt, Chris	0	2	8.44	3	0	11	11	9	6
Kermode, Al	10	3	4.27	21	0	133	171	25	69
Maberry, Louis	0	0	6.30	4	0	10	10	10	6
2-team (24 Abilene)	4	3	3.93	28	0	71	66	53	59
Matulevich, Jeff	2	2	4.08	28	5	35	37	13	40
Resendez, Oscar	5	4	6.43	38	2	77	100	60	61
Scarcello, Brian	1	4	8.12	16	0	48	86	15	23
Shoemaker, John	1	1	5.06	3	0	11	17	3	2
Thomas, Ryan	11	1	4.13	23	0	94	93	29	43
Wright, Adam	1	1	11.25	12	0	24	38	19	3

LUBBOCK

PLAYER	AVG	AB	R	H	2B	3B	HR	RBI	SB
Braddy, Junior, dh-of	.147	34	3	5	2	0	0	6	1
Davis, Brad, of	.175	57	5	10	1	0	3	9	2
Gennaro, Brad, of	.343	268	51	92	23	4	4	54	4
Hardge, Mike, of-3b	.339	360	75	122	27	4	8	54	22
Harris, Donald, of	.319	307	50	98	19	4	12	64	15
Hayes, Darren, 1b	.000	8	0	0	0	0	0	0	0
Jones, Sy, of-c	.271	210	33	57	7	0	4	28	7
King, Mitch, c	.295	78	17	23	8	0	0	17	5
Lowery, David, 2b	.281	299	56	84	12	2	2	33	46
Mason, Lamont, ss	.221	68	8	15	5	0	0	9	2
Monell, Johnny, dh	.293	133	24	39	7	0	0	20	1
Petrulis, Paul, ss	.333	186	36	62	10	1	2	23	6
Ramirez, J.D., 3b	.371	240	45	89	26	3	6	47	3
Skeels, Andy, c	.276	254	40	70	12	3	4	35	8
Sullivan, Drue, 1b	.265	279	37	74	10	1	2	33	10
Vaughn, Derek, of	.271	144	22	39	9	0	1	20	10
Wilson, Bryan, ss	.143	14	3	2	1	0	0	1	0

PITCHING	W	L	ERA	G	SV	IP	H	BB	SO
Baine, David	5	5	4.39	22	1	92	100	49	61
Beltran, Alonso	4	4	5.19	18	0	101	115	45	66
Bicknell, Greg	9	9	4.81	19	0	137	145	56	71
Clayton, Royal	2	1	1.69	12	3	16	12	8	7
DeLeon, Eduardo	1	2	5.40	14	1	23	28	14	13
Escamilla, Jaime	1	5	7.69	20	0	53	77	33	30
Felix, Ruben	2	3	9.75	25	3	36	54	27	21
Frush, Jimmy	0	1	7.94	2	0	6	7	1	5
Guerrero, Jose	2	1	4.40	13	1	45	41	30	26
Harrison, Brian	0	2	4.22	10	2	11	15	13	10
Hollinger, Adrian	2	4	9.68	17	1	31	54	19	18
Madigan, Brian	4	6	5.98	22	0	99	142	42	34
McKinley, Greg	4	3	6.03	17	1	31	39	15	17
Ortiz, Steve	0	1	8.56	7	1	14	18	9	4
Peck, Jeff	1	2	5.71	7	0	17	22	10	6
2-team (9 Rio Grande)	3	5	5.71	16	0	65	82	34	30
Robinson, Lance	1	1	7.56	14	0	25	35	3	13
Rushworth, Jim	0	0	18.00	1	0	1	3	1	1

RIO GRANDE VALLEY

BATTING	AVG	AB	R	H	2B	3B	HR	RBI	SB
Acosta, Xavier, 2b	.188	85	5	16	4	0	0	5	1
Cantu, Mike, dh-1b	.302	235	30	71	14	0	12	45	0
Clark, Kevin, c-1b	.284	250	50	71	15	0	10	45	3
Cox, Chuck, c	.254	240	25	61	8	1	5	24	2
Davis, Jay, of	.357	333	68	119	22	2	15	62	33
Groppuso, Mike, 3b	.336	134	36	45	7	0	10	30	6
Hobbie, Matt, of	.328	320	64	105	15	5	13	54	18
Johnson, Jace, 2b	.239	67	7	16	1	0	1	7	0
Kellner, Frank, ss	.267	45	13	12	4	2	2	8	1
Koerner, Pat, 3b-1b	.292	219	39	64	7	2	9	44	7
Martinez, Joey, 2b-3b	.293	317	62	93	18	2	2	26	21
McAlvain, 1b	.200	40	4	8	1	0	1	6	0
Olivares, Jess, ss	.289	194	33	56	9	0	3	22	4
Pileski, Mark, ss-2b	.282	177	29	50	13	1	4	22	2
Vaughn, Derek, of	.357	56	17	20	5	1	5	16	7
2-team (41 Lubbock)	.295	200	39	59	14	1	6	36	17
Warner, Bryan, of	.392	339	75	133	28	4	25	94	8

PITCHING	W	L	ERA	G	SV	IP	H	BB	SO
Emerson, Scott	2	2	6.04	16	0	22	21	28	17
Fox, Michael	3	7	8.33	16	0	63	84	37	29
Konieczki, Dom	1	1	2.35	24	4	31	23	18	23
MacNaught, Colin	1	0	9.27	22	0	33	48	21	11
Marquardt, Scott	7	6	5.11	19	0	113	126	35	79
Paris, Dave	0	0	4.38	13	0	25	24	7	15
Peck, Jeff	2	3	5.70	9	0	47	60	24	24
Ruch, Rob	2	5	7.45	17	0	64	83	51	42
Stutz, Joseph	3	6	4.37	39	0	60	65	24	49
Tijerina, Tano	2	7	8.38	27	8	58	81	34	39
Trevino, Kiki	3	3	6.23	18	0	56	62	28	24
Whitaker, Ryan	11	6	5.70	20	0	137	184	41	78
Williams, Greg	1	2	9.68	11	3	18	27	11	7
Zimmerman, Mike	1	1	1.69	3	0	16	13	5	9

TYLER

BATTING	AVG	AB	R	H	2B	3B	HR	RBI	SB
Cassels, Chris, dh-1b	.334	308	79	103	28	0	29	87	4
Cedeno, Ramon, of	.321	340	64	109	19	0	21	71	15
Collins, Sean, of-2b	.374	353	91	132	25	3	13	51	36
DiPace, Danny, of	.287	115	22	33	6	0	5	24	4
Emmons, Steve, 1b	.256	39	2	10	2	2	0	3	1

	AVG	AB	R	H	2B	3B	HR	RBI	SB
Frank, Gary, 2b	.190	21	5	4	1	0	0	1	0
Gafford, Cory, c	.226	133	15	30	8	0	1	14	1
Guerrero, Rafael, of-1b	.285	281	41	80	12	3	4	35	8
Gumbs, Lincoln, 3b-2b	.300	30	9	9	0	0	0	1	4
2-team (5 Abilene)	.250	44	9	11	1	0	0	1	5
Henderson, Derek, 3b	.286	322	47	92	24	0	9	67	6
Johnson, Jack, c-1b	.272	250	35	68	18	0	4	37	5
Perez, Carlos, of-1b	.304	303	67	92	19	0	9	57	3
Pichardo, Sandy, 2b-ss	.239	314	52	75	7	6	10	47	15
Smiga, Jason, ss	.320	228	45	73	9	0	0	20	27

PITCHING	W	L	ERA	G	SV	IP	H	BB	SO
Benavidez, Michael	0	0	12.91	4	0	8	11	10	3
Bowen, Luther	1	0	6.75	2	0	4	6	2	3
Caridad, Ron	0	2	6.75	4	0	15	22	5	9
Codrington, John	1	1	5.88	19	0	41	51	27	22
Coleman, Billy	0	0	0.00	1	0	1	1	2	0
Davis, Ray	7	5	2.89	15	0	97	86	31	76
Farrow, Jason	8	4	3.65	37	4	81	85	40	83
Gomez, Javier	3	7	6.17	22	0	101	139	33	52
Hartman, Kelly	1	1	4.50	10	0	12	15	5	7
Hollins, Jessie	0	0	3.18	4	0	6	5	7	7
Johnson, Jack	0	0	8.76	7	1	12	17	3	6
Kitchen, Ron	6	4	5.02	37	5	61	82	24	30
Knox, Kerry	3	2	3.93	8	0	53	67	10	30
Maddock, Steve	0	2	8.00	7	0	18	23	16	17
Martin, Aaron	0	0	0.00	3	0	4	3	1	4
Martin, Jerry	4	2	6.53	14	0	30	29	19	25
Norris, Joe	4	2	4.44	13	0	51	53	16	44
Nunez, Clemente	2	3	8.16	9	0	43	74	15	21
Ortiz, Steve	6	5	5.24	20	0	93	108	34	67
2-team (7 Lubbock)	6	6	5.67	27	1	106	126	43	71
Steinmetz, Earl	2	0	2.22	4	0	28	24	11	18

WESTERN LEAGUE

The Chico Heat blazed a trail to the 1997 Western League title by defeating the Reno Chukars three games to one in their first season in the league.

Sonoma County won both halves in the Southern Division, but Chico made the playoffs because of its second-best overall record. The Heat, managed by ex-big league skipper Bill Plummer, finished with only a .500 record in the regular season, 11 games behind the Crushers.

Buck Rodgers

Sonoma then lost to Chico in the divisional playoffs two games to one, while Reno gained the right to meet the Heat for the championship by beating Grays Harbor in the Northern Division playoffs.

Not only did the Heat win the league in their first year of existance, but they also drew 116,311 fans, best in the league and 85,000 more fans than Palm Springs–the team Chico replaced. Mission Viejo also was new to the league in 1997, replacing two-time league champion Long Beach. The Vigilantes were managed by Buck Rodgers, former California Angels manager.

Reno's Todd Takayoshi was named the league's player of the year for hitting .407 with 11 homers and 88 RBIs as the Chukars' DH. Mission Viejo's Mike Smith was selected as the pitcher of the year with a 10-4 record and 2.95 ERA.

STANDINGS

FIRST HALF

NORTHERN DIVISION	W	L	PCT	GB
Reno Chukars	30	15	.667	—
Grays Harbor Gulls	24	21	.533	6
Tri-City Posse	18	27	.400	12
Bend Bandits	17	28	.378	13
SOUTHERN DIVISION	**W**	**L**	**PCT**	**GB**
Sonoma County Crushers	29	16	.644	—
Salinas Peppers	23	22	.511	6
Chico Heat	21	24	.467	8
Mission Viejo Vigilantes	18	27	.400	11

SECOND HALF

NORTHERN DIVISION	W	L	PCT	GB
Reno Chukars	25	20	.556	—
Grays Harbor Gulls	25	20	.556	—
Bend Bandits	22	23	.489	3
Tri-City Posse	16	29	.356	9
SOUTHERN DIVISION	**W**	**L**	**PCT**	**GB**
Sonoma County Crushers	27	18	.600	—
Chico Heat	24	21	.533	3
Mission Viejo Vigilantes	21	24	.467	6
Salinas Peppers	20	25	.444	7

PLAYOFFS: Semifinals—Reno defeated Grays Harbor 2-1, and Chico defeated Sonoma County 2-1, in best-of-3 series. **Finals**—Chico defeated Reno 3-1 in best-of-5 series.

MANAGERS: Bend—Al Gallagher. Chico—Bill Plummer. Grays Harbor—Charley Kerfeld. Mission Viejo—Buck Rodgers. Reno—Butch Hughes. Salinas—Steve Hendricks. Sonoma County—Dick Dietz. Tri-City—Jamie Nelson.

ATTENDANCE: Chico 116,311; Tri-City 109,101; Mission Viejo 92,960; Sonoma County 91,692; Grays Harbor 56,090; Salinas 55,749; Reno 49,294; Bend 46,487.

ALL-STAR TEAM: C—Jon Fuller, Sonoma County. **1B**—David Mowry, Sonoma County. **2B**—Chris Grubb, Grays Harbor. **3B**—Andy Tarpley, Reno. **SS**—John Casey, Sonoma County. **OF**—Mark Charbonnet, Bend; Corey Paul, Chico; Sam Taylor, Mission Viejo. **DH**—Todd Takayoshi, Reno. **P**—Brian Doughty, Reno; Kris Frank, Sonoma County; Eric Miller, Sonoma County; Mike Smith, Mission Viejo; Chris White, Bend.

Player of the Year: Todd Takayoshi, Reno. **Pitcher of the Year:** Mike Smith, Mission Viejo. **Manager of the Year:** Dick Dietz, Sonoma County.

INDIVIDUAL BATTING LEADERS
(Minimum 243 Plate Appearances)

	AVG	AB	R	H	2B	3B	HR	RBI	SB
Takayoshi, Todd, Reno	.407	337	88	137	28	1	11	88	0
Tarpley, Andy, Reno	.404	317	92	128	28	5	15	82	9
Jenkins, Brett, Reno	.400	240	59	96	21	2	17	55	1
Charbonnet, Mark, Bend	.361	319	54	115	20	1	15	58	14
Barberie, Bret, MV	.347	274	46	95	18	2	11	40	5
Pridy, Todd, Sonoma	.342	295	57	101	16	1	22	70	1
Ellis, Paul, Reno	.337	300	70	101	22	0	16	75	0
Francisco, David, Reno	.336	357	74	120	14	1	14	62	21
Sanchez, David, GH	.335	331	60	111	21	6	7	50	8
Hosey, Steve, Salinas	.331	257	53	85	24	1	18	63	14

INDIVIDUAL PITCHING LEADERS
(Minimum 72 Innings)

	W	L	ERA	G	SV	IP	H	BB	SO
Frank, Kris, Sonoma	8	2	2.48	39	4	73	57	39	92
Smith, Mike, MV	10	4	2.95	19	0	125	98	42	109
Niebla, Ruben, TC	8	6	3.05	20	0	112	108	36	76
Burlingame, Ben, Bend	6	10	3.20	20	0	132	120	27	127
Novoa, Rafael, Chico	11	3	3.69	25	0	117	120	57	58
Anderson, Paul, MV	6	8	3.81	19	0	132	149	23	102
White, Chris, Bend	10	6	3.84	22	0	136	130	52	119
Navarro, Scott, Chico	8	8	4.00	21	0	119	137	36	84
Hernandez, Jeremy, TC	6	7	4.12	32	1	109	111	29	98
Kotes, Chris, GH	5	4	4.15	16	0	89	88	39	66

BEND

BATTING	AVG	AB	R	H	2B	3B	HR	RBI	SB
Brennan, Ryan, of	.250	172	27	43	3	3	1	14	12
Charbonnet, Mark, of	.361	319	54	115	20	1	15	58	14
Cole, Mike, 1b-of	.236	148	28	35	9	3	4	13	8
Conley, Brian, 3b-ss	.274	350	52	96	21	4	6	45	10

BATTING	AVG	AB	R	H	2B	3B	HR	RBI	SB
Duncan, Andres, ss	.241	266	40	64	11	1	5	35	33
Grice, Dan, of-2b	.266	139	26	37	1	1	0	14	5
Harmer, Frank, c	.163	43	3	7	1	1	0	0	0
McGowan, Marcus, of	.230	248	51	57	10	5	4	23	27
Mota, Gary, of	.389	72	14	28	5	0	2	14	2
Nadeau, Mike, 2b	.327	309	58	101	22	5	2	48	12
Neff, Marty, 1b-of	.241	158	20	38	8	1	6	23	1
Nelson, D.G., c-of	.291	158	23	46	11	1	1	27	3
Nunez, Bernie, dh	.307	313	48	96	20	1	16	72	2
Schula, Kevin, 1b	.190	79	8	15	3	0	3	14	0
Shrum, Dennis, 1b-p	.194	72	4	14	0	0	1	4	1
Taylor, Matt, 3b	.143	35	2	5	1	0	0	0	0
Val, Carter, c	.244	197	18	48	11	0	1	21	1
Wieczorek, Ted, 3b-1b	.231	39	2	9	3	0	0	2	0

PITCHING	W	L	ERA	G	SV	IP	H	BB	SO
Boan, Butch	0	3	8.10	3	0	13	20	10	5
Burlingame, Ben	6	10	3.20	20	0	132	120	27	127
Darley, Ned	2	2	4.69	38	7	40	40	29	55
Deremer, Brent	3	4	4.76	17	0	45	58	15	30
Englehart, Scott	0	0	6.94	6	0	12	15	6	10
Graham, Rich	1	2	5.59	14	3	19	26	12	13
2-team (27 Grays Harbor)	1	7	5.89	41	10	44	52	23	32
Highsmith, Brian	0	2	6.00	5	0	9	12	4	3
Lynn, John	2	1	7.91	42	1	47	74	22	24
Mendez, John	0	0	18.56	7	0	5	13	5	5
Peck, John	1	4	6.48	14	0	67	81	34	28
Plooy, Eric	4	4	4.91	26	0	44	53	19	32
Reardon, Kevin	3	3	5.54	9	0	39	50	15	25
Shrum, Dennis	2	6	6.12	14	0	68	82	21	45
Stoecklin, Tony	2	2	5.34	51	6	56	70	30	52
White, Chris	10	6	3.84	22	0	136	130	52	119
Zubiri, Jon	3	2	2.63	11	0	55	51	35	23

CHICO

BATTING	AVG	AB	R	H	2B	3B	HR	RBI	SB
Arntzen, Brian, c	.201	294	34	59	13	0	4	32	0
Butterfield, Chris, dh	.140	57	11	8	3	0	1	8	0
Coats, John, 3b	.236	174	31	41	8	0	8	31	8
2-team (39 Tri-City)	.239	306	44	73	13	1	10	54	18
Cooper, Tim, ss	.294	160	26	47	7	2	7	27	4
2-team (17 Salinas)	.281	221	36	62	10	2	8	33	9
Davis, Matt, 2b-3b	.304	342	73	104	20	1	9	49	6
Funderburk, Levi, 1b-dh	.294	177	23	52	11	0	5	26	1
Gonzalez, Tony, 3b-2b	.290	93	23	27	6	0	2	7	0
Hagge, Kirk, 2b	.167	12	2	2	0	0	0	1	0
Hairston, Tim, of	.231	26	1	6	1	0	0	2	1
Hansen, Terrel, of-1b	.321	224	52	72	13	0	22	60	0
Hawkins, Wes, of	.266	312	52	83	14	4	10	58	10
Kaitfors, Josh, of	.176	34	5	6	1	0	0	3	2
Lazerus, Erik, ss	.245	163	29	40	5	0	1	15	1
Palmer, Nate, c	.267	60	7	16	7	1	0	3	0
Paul, Corey, of	.348	184	48	64	11	4	6	41	15
Reese, Mat, of	.200	165	13	33	8	2	1	23	3
Rhein, Jeff, of	.267	202	37	54	8	6	4	21	27
Serrano, Nestor, 3b	.213	47	3	10	2	0	0	5	0
Shamburg, Ken, 1b-dh	.315	349	74	110	21	1	21	73	2
Smith, Dean, 2b	.226	31	2	7	1	0	0	2	0
Wisler, Brian, of	.429	42	9	18	1	4	3	15	0

PITCHING	W	L	ERA	G	SV	IP	H	BB	SO
Angerhofer, Chad	0	0	10.80	4	0	8	11	5	2
Bryant, Adam	3	4	2.05	43	2	61	54	21	69
Dawley, Joey	1	4	4.35	41	14	41	42	18	51
Guilfoyle, Mike	1	2	5.91	39	0	35	44	17	34
Hayselden, Bobby	0	0	9.64	9	0	14	24	7	8
Hernandez, Jeremy	3	4	4.82	18	1	47	56	14	38
Magre, Pete	3	4	6.16	39	0	73	79	33	65
Montgomery, Josh	4	7	5.79	30	0	73	81	32	77
Navarro, Scott	8	8	4.00	21	0	119	137	36	84
Novoa, Rafael	11	3	3.69	25	0	117	120	57	58
Quijada, Ed	6	4	4.43	21	1	81	91	41	51
Runyan, Paul	5	5	4.96	22	0	120	132	46	62
Van Mierlo, Brad	0	0	0.00	1	0	2	2	1	1

GRAYS HARBOR

BATTING	AVG	AB	R	H	2B	3B	HR	RBI	SB
Coats, Nathan, c	.350	20	2	7	2	0	1	3	0
2-team (11 Tri-City)	.279	43	5	12	4	0	1	5	0
Dietz, Steve, ss	.278	234	35	65	8	2	1	31	4
Gonzalez, Rex, dh-of	.203	148	15	30	11	0	0	15	0
Grubb, Chris, ss-2b	.302	338	59	102	16	2	5	39	7
Kingston, Mark, c	.286	294	54	84	18	1	9	42	1
Koerick, Tom, c	.083	36	2	3	0	0	1	8	0
McDonnell, Tim, 3b	.264	273	37	72	16	0	2	34	1
Mealing, Al, of	.296	338	63	100	17	5	9	53	22
Moultrie, Pat, of	.180	89	16	16	5	0	1	8	3
Nations, Joel, 2b	.282	220	37	62	16	0	4	38	0
O'Connor, Pat, 3b	.247	73	11	18	2	0	0	11	1
Rendina, Mike, 1b	.272	312	61	85	10	1	24	74	2
Sanchez, David, of	.335	331	60	111	21	6	7	50	8
Takayama, Gon, of	.133	15	2	2	1	0	0	1	1
Vallero, Rich, c	.284	67	11	19	3	0	0	9	2
2-team (11 Tri-City)	.248	101	14	25	3	0	0	13	2
Warner, Randy, of	.305	331	54	101	21	5	13	65	8

PITCHING	W	L	ERA	G	SV	IP	H	BB	SO
Basteyns, Brian	4	3	5.30	19	0	70	90	44	53
Charley, Tandy	4	1	4.68	34	0	67	79	31	47
Goedhart, Darrell	5	3	4.50	10	0	74	81	21	54
Graham, Rich	0	5	6.12	27	7	25	26	11	19
Hoy, Wayne	5	6	4.21	24	1	88	91	26	61
Kerfeld, Charley	0	0	0.00	1	0	0	0	1	1
Kotes, Chris	5	4	4.15	16	0	89	88	39	66
Lancaster, Les	1	1	3.46	4	0	26	28	3	15
Marquez, Marco	0	0	7.45	9	1	10	10	6	8
Martineau, Brian	7	1	4.18	45	11	56	53	18	53
Nakayama, Masayuki	1	2	7.80	3	0	15	21	10	12
Peterson, Mark	0	2	4.96	17	1	16	19	5	22
2-team (2 Sonoma)	0	3	6.15	19	1	26	34	8	30
Plooy, Eric	2	0	4.74	19	0	19	23	10	14
2-team (26 Bend)	6	4	4.86	45	0	63	76	29	46
Reid, Rayon	6	5	5.38	16	0	100	107	45	71
Walania, Al	8	8	5.28	19	0	107	133	31	61
Warren, Jason	1	0	10.38	7	0	9	14	8	4
Wise, George	0	0	2.66	16	1	24	22	9	21

MISSION VIEJO

BATTING	AVG	AB	R	H	2B	3B	HR	RBI	SB
Ashbach, Chris, 2b-ss	.244	135	15	33	4	0	0	9	3
Barberie, Bret, 3b-2b	.347	274	46	95	18	2	11	40	5
Briones, Chris, dh	.224	134	11	30	9	0	3	21	1
Brooks, Eric, c	.299	154	13	46	11	0	2	21	1
Burke, Alan, of	.318	355	50	113	23	0	17	77	1
Cowell, Mike, c	.214	168	26	36	3	0	0	18	5
Drinkwater, Sean, ss-3b	.257	304	39	78	10	1	6	36	5
Marquez, Matt, 2b-ss	.088	34	2	3	0	0	0	0	0
Martin, Dustin, of	.220	50	13	11	1	1	0	1	1
Mosher, Willie, 3b-2b	.304	168	37	51	10	2	7	20	6
Moutrey, Mike, of-ss	.249	177	22	44	9	0	0	13	15
Nichols, Carl, c-1b	.288	257	41	74	19	1	6	36	1
O'Connor, Pat, of	.226	53	8	12	3	0	0	1	1
3-team (16 Salinas/26 GH)	.254	177	28	45	7	0	0	19	7
Parker, Corey, 1b	.280	286	40	80	14	0	11	47	1
Pullman, Duke, c	.500	2	0	1	0	0	0	0	0
Reese, Mat, of	.167	24	2	4	2	0	0	4	0
2-team (43 Chico)	.196	189	15	37	10	2	1	27	3
Smiley, Reuben, of	.254	134	24	34	7	1	3	13	8
Stare, Lonny, of	.236	55	6	13	5	0	1	5	1
Taylor, Sam, of	.306	337	60	103	16	1	21	58	9
Zepeda, Jesse, ss	.500	4	2	2	1	0	0	0	0

PITCHING	W	L	ERA	G	SV	IP	H	BB	SO
Anderson, Paul	6	8	3.81	19	0	132	149	23	102
Beck, Dion	0	0	7.71	3	0	2	3	1	3
Boucher, Mike	0	0	3.95	8	0	14	14	8	8
Ceterko, Steve	1	6	5.14	28	5	42	43	28	47
Draeger, Mark	3	2	5.95	11	0	56	74	24	31
Ehler, Dan	5	8	6.06	22	0	101	108	40	79
Gingrich, Josh	0	1	3.52	15	0	23	22	9	19
Homan, John	3	4	4.28	30	1	95	98	30	45
Jones, Donny	0	0	18.69	5	0	4	8	3	0
Kishita, Kirt	3	5	4.18	34	12	47	46	16	33
Magdaleno, Aaron	2	2	7.96	27	2	32	42	31	22
Marquez, Marco	0	1	6.55	4	0	11	12	7	3
2-team (9 Grays Harbor)	0	1	6.97	13	1	21	22	13	11
Rushford, Jim	0	0	12.00	8	0	6	11	7	6
Singleton, Scott	5	10	6.81	18	0	78	104	39	45
Smith, Mike	10	4	2.95	19	0	125	98	42	109
Tranberg, Mark	1	0	5.17	5	0	16	16	10	16

RENO

BATTING	AVG	AB	R	H	2B	3B	HR	RBI	SB
Brissey, Jason, 2b-3b	.249	249	40	62	20	1	4	46	11
Caropresso, Dustin, c-dh	.216	102	15	22	8	1	5	14	1
Ellis, Paul, c	.337	300	70	101	22	0	16	75	0
Flikke, Sean, dh-of	.367	49	11	18	3	1	0	9	3
Francisco, David, of	.336	357	74	120	14	1	14	62	21

	AVG	AB	R	H	2B	3B	HR	RBI	SB
Hagy, Gary, ss-3b	.295	325	54	96	16	3	4	50	7
Jenkins, Brett, of-dh	.400	240	59	96	21	2	17	55	1
Miller, Roy, 3b	.256	78	21	20	5	0	4	22	1
Pfeifer, Scott, of	.305	325	69	99	20	3	8	44	32
Roberts, John, of	.268	328	74	88	21	5	17	74	22
Takayoshi, Todd, 1b-dh	.407	337	88	137	28	1	11	88	0
Tarpley, Andy, 3b-1b	.404	317	92	128	28	5	15	82	9
Zuniga, Dave, 2b-ss	.264	284	55	75	8	1	0	35	8

PITCHING	W	L	ERA	G	SV	IP	H	BB	SO
Adge, Jason	4	3	5.77	24	1	73	90	36	59
Ayrault, Bob	1	3	5.54	31	9	37	38	13	43
Baker, Derek	5	3	6.53	15	0	73	86	37	63
Bedinger, Doug	3	0	5.28	16	1	31	37	13	35
Bendik, Josh	5	3	4.27	26	5	59	57	38	46
Blackburn, Christian	2	0	6.26	12	1	23	28	15	13
2-team (4 Sonoma)	2	2	6.86	16	1	41	58	25	27
Brewer, Brian	2	4	6.99	6	0	28	42	17	23
Carl, Todd	9	6	6.40	20	0	124	156	58	73
Doughty, Brian	11	3	4.68	19	0	131	180	30	83
Enard, Tony	2	1	5.68	26	5	70	76	46	59
Hartley, Mike	5	5	5.70	13	0	71	87	21	38
Sick, Dave	0	0	7.30	6	0	12	14	6	9
White, Darell	5	4	7.69	10	0	50	59	39	34
2-team (9 Salinas)	5	4	8.06	19	0	64	76	53	47
Winslett, Dax	1	0	5.00	2	0	9	11	5	5

SALINAS

BATTING	AVG	AB	R	H	2B	3B	HR	RBI	SB
Arrollado, Courtney, ss	.195	174	15	34	6	2	2	21	3
Bugg, Jason, 3b-2b	.263	160	30	42	13	1	2	21	1
Comeaux, Eddie, of	.292	366	61	107	11	2	2	22	43
Constantino, Kraig, 1b	.318	314	44	100	12	2	11	50	11
Cooper, Tim, ss-3b	.246	61	10	15	3	0	1	6	5
Gonzalez, Tony, 2b-3b	.331	154	24	51	13	0	4	19	0
2-team (24 Chico)	.316	247	47	78	19	0	6	26	0
Hosey, Steve, of	.331	257	53	85	24	1	18	63	14
Johnson, James, of	.206	63	6	13	3	1	0	6	5
Kernan, Phil, dh-of	.257	148	20	38	10	3	4	17	4
Kooiman, Brian, 3b	.293	181	25	53	10	1	10	45	6
Norman, Kenny, of	.282	308	43	87	12	3	6	37	24
O'Connor, Pat, 2b	.294	51	9	15	2	0	0	7	5
Prieto, Rick, 2b	.357	98	14	35	6	2	1	10	15
Samples, Todd, of	.375	16	2	6	2	0	1	3	1
Shepherd, Bodie, c	.320	241	36	77	17	1	7	39	4
Swope, Joe, ss-2b	.247	174	28	43	6	0	0	15	8
Walker, Joe, dh-c	.223	247	44	55	15	0	9	38	1
Waller, Derric, of	.213	89	10	19	4	0	1	12	1

PITCHING	W	L	ERA	G	SV	IP	H	BB	SO
Arellano, Carlos	1	4	3.02	16	0	45	51	14	22
Arola, Bruce	3	3	2.56	40	1	63	56	20	72
Auchard, Dan	1	1	4.24	17	0	17	19	10	10
Binversie, Brian	0	0	16.88	3	0	5	19	4	5
Carrasco, Carlos	10	8	4.75	19	0	116	126	49	64
Deremer, Scott	8	9	4.52	22	0	129	147	47	63
Fahs, Derek	2	5	3.46	31	8	68	70	17	89
Pollard, Craig	1	0	10.13	8	0	5	5	5	2
2-team (11 Sonoma)	2	0	6.46	19	0	15	14	16	10
Ritchie, Wally	9	5	4.56	21	0	136	163	47	66
Scarpitti, Jeff	0	6	8.13	10	0	31	47	12	23
Sollecito, Gabe	4	1	1.39	24	5	32	23	9	37
Trimarco, Mike	3	4	5.29	26	0	102	138	38	61
Weese, Dean	0	0	0.00	1	0	0	4	0	0
White, Darell	0	0	9.45	9	0	13	17	14	13
Winchester, Marty	1	1	6.75	5	0	20	23	16	16
Zankich, Chris	0	0	19.80	2	0	5	11	5	6

SONOMA COUNTY

BATTING	AVG	AB	R	H	2B	3B	HR	RBI	SB
Casey, John, ss	.299	375	80	112	23	3	0	32	4
Fuller, Jon, c	.304	309	52	94	19	1	11	61	1
Hopgood, Scott, 2b-3b	.222	81	12	18	1	1	1	9	1
Lippitt, Mickey, c	.235	34	7	8	0	0	1	5	1
Masterson, Carter, of	.287	334	62	96	19	3	16	71	6
Mowry, David, 1b-dh	.325	360	69	117	22	0	23	82	2
Pridy, Todd, dh-1b	.342	295	57	101	16	1	22	70	1
Sherwood, Bob, c	.000	6	0	0	0	0	0	0	0
Simonton, Cy, of	.245	200	30	49	7	0	1	21	1
Stinson, Ryan, of	.282	216	29	61	5	2	2	34	13
Wallace, Tim, 2b	.286	332	71	95	16	3	1	39	16
Washington, Kyle, of	.296	314	65	93	12	1	20	73	11
White, Eric, 3b	.305	334	53	102	22	1	6	50	8

PITCHING	W	L	ERA	G	SV	IP	H	BB	SO
Blackburn, Christian	0	2	7.64	4	0	18	30	10	14
Coscia, Tony	7	4	4.50	18	0	118	120	38	125
Frank, Kris	8	2	2.48	39	4	73	57	39	92
Genke, Todd	12	4	4.18	24	0	108	124	36	87
Lake, Kevin	7	3	4.22	16	0	96	102	46	63
Miller, Eric	4	2	2.84	40	22	51	38	8	66
Patton, John	8	5	5.20	18	0	116	124	52	109
Peterson, Mark	0	1	8.10	2	0	10	15	3	8
Pollard, Craig	1	0	4.50	11	0	10	9	11	8
Smith, Brook	3	1	4.54	21	1	42	39	31	36
Soldate, John	0	2	3.42	14	1	24	19	10	26
Warembourg, Scott	2	3	8.66	19	1	44	59	36	26
Zerbe, Chad	4	5	5.42	14	0	90	117	36	52

TRI-CITY

BATTING	AVG	AB	R	H	2B	3B	HR	RBI	SB
Booker, Kevin, dh-of	.255	278	40	71	11	1	6	32	18
Cardona, Ruben, 2b	.312	311	43	97	14	1	0	24	21
Coats, John, 3b	.242	132	13	32	5	1	2	23	10
Coats, Nathan, c	.217	23	3	5	2	0	0	2	0
Coppes, Paul, c	.224	85	11	19	5	0	0	6	0
Esquibel, Steve, of	.173	75	11	13	4	0	3	8	2
Koonce, Graham, 1b	.287	286	46	82	15	3	3	34	13
Minici, Jason, of	.209	220	21	46	4	3	0	20	6
Perozo, Ed, dh-3b	.224	58	5	13	3	0	1	7	1
Rutz, Ryan, ss	.244	311	39	76	9	1	1	30	16
Scott, Shawn, of	.289	346	43	100	20	4	4	49	22
Seidel, Ryan, of	.256	324	38	83	13	2	1	35	25
Serrano, Nestor, 3b	.299	147	15	44	11	0	5	21	4
Vallero, Rich, c	.176	34	3	6	0	0	0	4	0
Vicens, Jason, 3b-ss	.301	133	23	40	4	0	0	14	3
Whatley, Brian, c	.211	194	21	41	6	0	2	26	10

PITCHING	W	L	ERA	G	SV	IP	H	BB	SO
Ewen, Jared	2	9	5.96	22	0	83	105	51	76
Gogos, Keith	3	6	4.76	23	0	87	112	34	50
Grebe, Brett	2	3	2.89	37	13	44	36	9	50
Hernandez, Jeremy	3	3	3.59	14	0	63	55	15	60
2-team (18 Chico)	6	7	4.12	32	1	109	111	29	98
Hook, Jeff	0	1	5.97	8	0	32	43	16	20
Moreland, Tyler	0	0	6.75	4	0	7	14	4	1
Niebla, Ruben	8	6	3.05	20	0	112	108	36	76
Ramirez, Leo	1	5	4.85	27	4	39	39	7	42
Rolish, Chad	6	9	4.86	19	0	111	123	49	63
Salcedo, Jose	3	9	4.75	17	0	95	95	27	86
Thomas, Jeff	3	2	4.96	38	2	62	60	39	50
Valenzuela, Derek	3	3	4.27	32	2	53	51	39	41

BIG SOUTH LEAGUE

The Greenville Bluesmen rolled to their second straight Big South title in 1997, posting a 20-6 second-half record and then defeating the Meridian Brakemen three games to none in the league championship series. Ken Krahenbuhl tossed a six-hit, 10-0 shutout for Greenville in the clincher.

Despite the highs of another championship for Greenville, the Big South League drew less than 100,000 fans in 1997. The league moved down to four teams after the defection of three Tennessee teams following the inaugural 1996 campaign.

The Clarksville Coyotes, Tennessee Tomahawks and Columbia Mules all departed for the Heartland League, which left Meridian, Miss., and Greenville, Miss., as the only original teams. Pine Bluff, Ark., didn't field a club but Tupelo, Miss., and the Tullahoma, Tenn., Walkers joined to make it a four-team league.

Tullahoma, however, ran into financial difficulties and was taken over by the league, which forced the team to play all of its games on the road. The financial collapse and subsequent takeover occurred just two weeks into the season.

President Jim Caldwell said the league was looking to move the franchise to Carrolton, Ga. for the 1998 season and possibly adding new franchises.

STANDINGS

FIRST HALF	W	L	PCT	GB
Meridian Brakemen	23	12	.657	—
Tupelo Tornado	19	11	.633	1½
Greenville Bluesmen	19	14	.576	3
Tennessee Walkers	4	28	.125	17½
SECOND HALF	**W**	**L**	**PCT**	**GB**
Greenville Bluesmen	20	6	.769	—
Tupelo Tornado	21	7	.750	1
Meridian Brakemen	9	17	.346	11
Tennessee Walkers	4	24	.143	17

PLAYOFFS: Finals—Greenville defeated Meridian 3-0 in best-of-5 series.

MANAGERS: Greenville—Jim Darrington. Meridian—Jose Santiago. Tennessee—Jeff McCall. Tupelo—Steve Dillard.

ATTENDANCE: Tupelo 32,762; Greenville 17,022; Meridian 15,806; Tennessee 9,956.

INDIVIDUAL BATTING LEADERS

(Minimum 189 Plate Appearances)

	AVG	AB	R	H	2B	3B	HR	RBI	SB
Williams, Jerrone, Tupelo	**.371**	151	**49**	56	12	3	**11**	47	16
#Santiago, Arnold, Meridian	.371	167	39	62	6	0	9	**53**	13
Cheek, Shawn, Meridian	.362	221	48	**80**	**19**	4	8	39	7
Harrelson, Richie, Tupelo	.358	204	31	73	18	0	4	42	3
Capellan, Carlos, Green	.344	215	25	74	8	1	0	24	6
Gardner, Willie, Tupelo	.309	191	42	59	11	2	7	49	10
Echols, Mandell, Meridian	.301	183	33	55	13	1	4	24	11
Gabriel, Denio, Green	.290	231	46	67	6	**5**	1	24	**40**
Murphy, Sean, Green	.289	201	35	58	12	**5**	2	26	16
Edwards, Jerome, Green	.282	170	27	48	6	2	1	27	14
Cole, Popeye, Greenville	.276	185	34	51	5	0	4	28	7
Chism, Chism, Tupelo	.273	172	43	47	9	0	2	14	8
Mackin, Jeff, Tupelo	.268	209	29	56	11	1	2	38	0
Dolias, Steve, Tupelo	.260	131	32	34	2	0	0	19	3

INDIVIDUAL PITCHING LEADERS

(Minimum 56 Innings)

	W	L	ERA	G	SV	IP	H	BB	SO
#Cupit, Wayne, Tupelo	1	2	2.08	27	**13**	26	18	15	28
Miller, Matt, Greenville	**12**	3	**2.26**	15	0	107	76	49	**129**
Krahenbuhl, Ken, Green	8	5	2.65	14	0	112	102	45	106
Lancaster, Les, Tupelo	8	2	2.90	12	0	81	73	19	72
Davidson, Tim, Green	8	4	3.06	15	0	94	83	33	83
Allison, Steve, Tupelo	7	3	3.26	12	0	77	59	51	84
Reeder, Russell, Meridian	4	3	3.70	19	3	73	74	25	66
Ramsey, Brian, Tupelo	7	1	3.98	13	0	84	85	28	35
Ocasio, Mark, Meridian	8	7	4.14	21	1	91	95	51	66
Moore, Ashley, Tupelo	6	3	4.99	15	0	61	65	34	41
Shannon, Chad, Tenn	2	9	5.70	15	0	84	105	35	58

HEARTLAND LEAGUE

The Tennessee Tomahawks posted an astounding 33-1 record in the second half of the 1997 Heartland League season but couldn't survive the divisional playoffs. The Columbia Mules won a hard-fought series, two games to one, to move into the championship round.

The Mules took the first game 4-2, dropped the second 4-1 and came back in game three with a 4-3 win to end the Tomahawks' impressive run. The Tomahawks went 22-14 in the first half, and 55-15 overall.

Columbia went on to win the league title by defeating the Anderson Lawmen three games to one.

The Mules ended the regular season 37-31, a similar mark to their 1996 record of 39-31 as part of the Big South League. The Heartland League blossomed from four teams in 1996 to eight in 1997 with the addition of three franchises from the Big South and one (Altoona) from the North Atlantic League.

With the new teams came a slight increase in the average attendance figures. Tennessee led the way in overall attendance with 51,106 fans.

Will County's Angel Santiago led the league with a .372 average and 95 hits and Tennessee hurler John Dopson, an ex-big leaguer, went 10-2 with a 1.78 ERA over 81 innings.

STANDINGS

FIRST HALF

NORTH	W	L	PCT	GB
Altoona Rail Kings	22	14	.611	—
Will County Cheetahs	18	17	.514	3½
Anderson Lawmen	13	21	.382	8
Lafayette Leopards	13	22	.371	8½
SOUTH	**W**	**L**	**PCT**	**GB**
Tennessee Tomahawks	22	14	.611	—
Columbia Mules	20	15	.571	1½
Dubois County Dragons	16	18	.471	5
Clarksville Coyotes	16	19	.457	5½

SECOND HALF

NORTH	W	L	PCT	GB
Anderson Lawmen	19	16	.543	—
Lafayette Leopards	18	18	.500	1½
Altoona Rail Kings	14	22	.389	5½
WIill County Cheetahs	13	22	.371	6
SOUTH	**W**	**L**	**PCT**	**GB**
Tennessee Tomahawks	33	1	.971	—
Columbia Mules	18	16	.529	15
Clarksville Coyotes	16	20	.444	18
Dubois County Dragons	10	26	.278	24

PLAYOFFS: Semifinals—Columbia defeated Tennessee 2-1, and Anderson defeated Altoona 2-0, in best-of-3 series. **Finals**—Columbia defeated Anderson 3-1 in best-of-5 series.

MANAGERS: Altoona—Michael Richmond. Anderson—David Edwards. Clarksville—Jeff Bibb. Columbia—Steve Howard. Dubois County—Jeff Pinney. Lafayette—Brad Cohen. Tennessee—Jeff Gamble. Will County—Gerry Clarke.

ATTENDANCE: Tennessee, 51,106; Dubois County, 43,481; Altoona, 30,632; Clarksville, 30,877; Columbia, 22,253; Lafayette, 14,909; Will County, 11,119; Anderson, 7,134.

INDIVIDUAL BATTING LEADERS

(Minimum 192 Plate Appearances)

	AVG	AB	R	H	2B	3B	HR	RBI	SB
Santiago, Angel, WC	**.374**	254	49	**95**	16	0	9	44	1
Burroughs, Eric, Altoona	.349	238	48	83	9	4	5	44	15
Overton, Chad, DC	.349	241	43	84	22	3	7	45	5
Allen, Donald, Altoona	.342	257	56	88	5	2	1	20	19
Bailey, Heath, Anderson	.341	217	42	74	14	3	5	28	22
Baker, Jason, Tennessee	.333	282	**58**	94	22	**6**	4	51	14
Michael, Jeff, Tennessee	.333	282	**58**	94	20	2	9	49	25
Harris, Eric, Columbia	.326	264	44	86	**28**	0	11	52	0
Donato, Jude, Altoona	.322	273	48	88	18	2	2	44	12
Wisler, Brian, Clarksville	.318	223	36	71	15	1	7	39	5
Southard, Scott, Tenn	.316	228	31	72	12	0	7	32	2
Satkowski, Larry, Laf	.312	189	33	59	14	1	4	34	4
Tobey, Ryan, Clarksville	.311	180	31	56	11	4	1	27	2
Kinchen, Jason, Lafayette	.309	194	30	60	8	0	12	36	0
Jackson, Jeff, WC	.303	244	53	74	15	0	13	40	**26**
Preston, Doyle, Tenn	.302	245	48	74	17	3	8	50	1
Pallissard, Andy, WC	.301	196	31	59	11	3	2	32	2
Beddies, Jordan, Col.	.297	185	32	55	10	1	7	29	21
Love, Claude, Altoona	.296	253	53	75	8	1	4	31	10
McKnight, Jeff, Columbia	.294	170	27	50	12	1	1	36	1
Cruz, Brian, Anderson	.293	181	30	53	7	2	9	28	5
Tiller, Tim, Columbia	.288	219	34	63	7	0	0	17	9
Nasin, Shawn, Clark	.287	268	**58**	77	16	1	2	27	16
#Mendoza, Alonzo, Tenn.	.282	238	55	67	14	0	12	**60**	6
#Underwood, Curtis, Tenn.	.258	248	45	64	12	0	**15**	53	1

INDIVIDUAL PITCHING LEADERS

(Minimum 58 Innings)

	W	L	ERA	G	SV	IP	H	BB	SO
Dopson, John, Tenn	10	2	**1.78**	13	0	81	58	15	69
Mitchell, John, Columbia	5	4	2.27	10	0	63	58	7	25
Piddington, Brian, And	8	2	2.32	16	3	93	88	16	89

Sepeda, Jamie, Tenn	10	4	2.39	16	1	113	103	26	106
Hedrick, Keith, Columbia	9	2	2.54	13	0	85	73	24	46
Cook, Jake, Lafayette	4	7	2.69	13	0	80	83	35	55
Mianowski, George, Tenn	**11**	1	2.70	14	1	87	65	24	100
Oestreich, John, Tenn	9	4	2.88	16	1	100	88	43	**120**
Westergard, Darren, And	4	3	2.95	11	0	58	37	40	56
Lovett, George, Clark	5	6	2.99	15	0	90	81	36	57
Huguet, Jose, Altoona	8	3	3.01	15	0	99	92	29	55
Bowman, Steve, Tenn	5	1	3.17	14	0	71	72	36	37
Taulman, Jason, Laf	8	2	3.21	16	0	101	112	24	45
Riggs, Dustin, Anderson	6	5	3.58	15	0	98	106	41	63
Stark, Zac, Columbia	5	8	3.62	15	0	99	93	26	75
Lewis, Ryan, Anderson	2	6	3.84	19	0	59	52	26	38
Bennett, Jason, Lafayette	6	5	3.87	15	0	86	111	18	57
Robell, Kevin, DC	3	5	3.91	14	0	74	60	45	62
Byron, Andy, Clarksville	8	2	4.14	18	0	91	89	30	50
Baum, Chris, Altoona	4	6	4.42	14	0	90	94	49	55
Ceballos, Juan, WC	7	6	4.47	16	0	117	130	37	59

NORTHEAST LEAGUE

The Elmira Pioneers won the 1997 league title by sweeping Waterbury and defending champion Albany in a pair of best-of-three series.

The Pioneers finished 43-38 overall, an impressive turnaround from 1996's 34-45 record. It was the first championship for Elmira since the old Pioneers of the New York-Penn League won the title in 1976.

Elmira second baseman Warren Sawkiw hit .467 in the four playoff games and provided the game-winning home run in the final contest, a 3-2 victory.

The league welcomed three new teams in the Allentown Ambassadors, Massachusetts Mad Dogs and Catskill Cougars to give the league eight teams. Massachusetts and Catskill joined after the North Atlantic League folded prior to the 1997 season, while the Rhode Island franchise folded.

The owners of the Allentown franchise spent more than $1 million in renovations to transform Bicentennial Park, a high school stadium that had an all-dirt infield and chain-link fence, into an adequate facility for professional baseball. The Ambassadors drew a third-best 69,537 fans.

STANDINGS

FIRST HALF

NORTH	W	L	PCT	GB
Albany Diamond Dogs	27	15	.643	—
Massachusetts Mad Dogs	22	20	.524	5
Adirondack Lumberjacks	22	20	.524	5
Bangor Blue Ox	19	23	.452	8
SOUTH	**W**	**L**	**PCT**	**GB**
Elmira Pioneers	24	18	.571	—
Waterbury Spirit	22	20	.524	2
Allentown Ambassadors	18	24	.429	6
Catskill Cougars	14	28	.333	10

SECOND HALF

NORTH	W	L	PCT	GB
Massachusetts Mad Dogs	23	17	.575	—
Albany Diamond Dogs	24	18	.571	—
Adirondack Lumberjacks	23	18	.561	½
Bangor Blue Ox	21	20	.512	2½
SOUTH	**W**	**L**	**PCT**	**GB**
Waterbury Spirit	24	17	.585	—
Allentown Ambassadors	21	19	.525	2½
Elmira Pioneers	20	20	.500	3½
Catskill Cougars	7	34	.171	17

PLAYOFFS: Semifinals—Elmira defeated Waterbury 2-0, and Albany defeated Massachusetts 2-1, in best-of-3 series. **Finals:** Elmira defeated Albany 2-0 in best-of-3.

MANAGERS: Adirondack—Dave Holt. Albany—John Wockenfuss. Allentown—Ed Ott. Bangor—Roger LaFrancois. Catskill—Edgar Perez. Elmira—Dan Shwam. Massachusetts—George Scott. Waterbury—Stan Huff.

ATTENDANCE: Albany, 72,985; Massachusetts, 72,681; Allentown, 69,537; Adirondack, 56,955; Elmira, 52,372; Catskill, 39,896; Bangor, 35,591; Waterbury, 32,893.

ALL STAR TEAM: C—Alex Sutherland, Adirondack. **1B**—Ron Lockett, Albany. **2B**—Felix DeLeon, Albany. **3B**—Felix Colon, Massachusetts. **SS**—Danny Mangual, Elmira. **OF**—Kelly Kingston, Adirondack; Rafael Mercado, Albany; Brandon Naples, Allentown. **DH**—Jon Mueller, Albany. **LHP**—Andy Carter, Allentown. **RHP**—Kory Kosek, Adirondack. **RP**—Grant Sullivan, Albany.

Player of the Year: Tom Russin, Waterbury. **Pitcher of the Year:** Gardner O'Flynn, Massachusetts. **Manager of the Year:** John Wockenfuss, Albany.

INDIVIDUAL BATTING LEADERS

(Minimum 221 Plate Appearances)

	AVG	AB	R	H	2B	3B	HR	RBI	SB
Sutherland, Alex, Adir	**.373**	236	42	88	13	1	9	48	6
Colon, Felix, Mass	.357	300	50	107	21	0	10	64	5
DeLeon, Felix, Albany	.356	320	55	**114**	16	2	2	28	13
Hage, Tom, Allentown	.348	302	44	105	17	1	4	43	2
Pagana, Mike, Waterbury	.339	271	49	92	15	6	1	30	20
Mercado, Rafael, Albany	.333	285	47	95	21	4	12	62	0
Demetral, Scott, Allentown	.329	301	46	99	15	0	0	30	1
Naples, Brandon, Allen	.328	268	53	88	15	8	2	35	33
Russin, Tom, Waterbury	.324	318	55	103	**30**	4	8	**75**	2
Keene, Andre, Mass	.322	301	**64**	97	21	2	11	64	8
Sellers, Rick, Elmira	.317	252	37	80	9	0	11	41	0
Miller, Mike, Waterbury	.315	324	62	102	18	6	9	58	5
Hine, Steve, Bangor	.306	324	53	99	16	3	2	51	7
Mueller, Jon, Albany	.306	288	**64**	88	17	0	**20**	74	1
Landrum, Tito, Elmira	.303	287	43	87	19	1	11	48	16
Gerteisen, Aaron, Elmira	.302	252	37	76	19	3	3	37	12
Lockett, Ron, Albany	.298	275	51	82	16	3	7	41	19
Madden, Joey, Waterbury	.298	346	60	103	13	**11**	1	39	**34**
White, Chad, Bangor	.292	274	52	80	11	5	4	41	24
Walker, Hugh, Bangor	.292	312	58	91	13	5	15	51	20
Lewis, Joe, Adirondack	.291	268	45	78	10	1	0	21	6
Mariano, Joe, Albany	.289	228	31	66	10	1	1	24	2
Kingston, Kelly, Adir	.287	321	63	92	18	6	13	41	20
Phillips, Steve, Allentown	.286	255	42	73	19	6	13	53	3
Mitchell, Ed, Cat.-Mass	.286	259	44	74	11	2	1	30	9
Morrow, Tim, Bangor	.283	321	55	91	18	1	14	49	1
Davila, Vic, Adirondack	.283	311	52	88	17	6	3	44	13
Reams, Ron, Adirondack	.281	295	35	83	17	2	3	36	14
Jemison, Andrw, Catskill	.281	292	47	82	16	4	7	42	6
Tirpack, Ken, Albany	.280	325	49	91	23	1	11	66	0
Sawkiw, Warren, Elmira	.280	300	42	84	20	1	1	24	7
Giardi, Mike, Mass	.279	297	54	83	23	5	8	46	6
Doucette, Darren, Adir	.279	219	31	61	15	1	14	36	1
Duross, Gabe, Bangor	.278	252	21	70	13	1	5	48	1

INDIVIDUAL PITCHING LEADERS

(Minimum 66 Innings)

	W	L	ERA	G	SV	IP	H	BB	SO
#Bauer, Chuck, Albany	3	2	1.36	28	**17**	33	19	14	38
Merrill, Ethan, Adirondack	7	4	**2.27**	17	1	83	90	16	40
O'Flynn, Gardner, Mass	**13**	4	2.85	20	1	139	144	38	90
Ponte, Ed, Waterbury	5	6	2.86	15	0	110	97	23	99
Ward, Chad, Adirondack	10	6	2.91	28	0	105	110	24	94
Kosek, Kory, Adirondack	10	4	2.95	23	1	137	136	29	126
Miller, David, Elmira	8	1	3.05	14	0	91	82	33	53
Wegmann, Tom, Elmira	9	6	3.09	16	0	105	110	19	100
Cronemeyer, Mike, Allen	8	3	3.14	15	0	95	94	8	74
Hartmann, Pete, Bangor	8	6	3.46	17	0	120	120	55	118
Carter, Andy, Allentown	8	3	3.46	13	0	91	85	28	81
Frazier, Ron, Waterbury	12	4	3.54	16	0	119	122	21	90
Murphy, Jay, Mass	8	5	3.58	22	1	148	158	40	**131**
Runion, Jeff, Waterbury	5	4	3.60	12	0	70	74	23	68
Christmas, Mo, Bangor	6	4	3.64	14	0	82	95	24	51
Fleming, Dave, Water	5	3	3.64	16	0	101	110	26	69
Williams, Juan, Adir.-Alb	9	0	3.93	16	0	73	74	33	69
Boucher, Denis, Adir	5	7	4.00	18	0	99	121	32	48
Jones, Jeff, Allentown	4	4	4.23	14	0	83	91	24	49
Swanson, Dave, Water	7	7	4.41	16	0	112	129	36	79
Hasler, Jerry, Albany	5	1	4.41	30	5	69	70	16	64
Turnier, Aaron, Elmira	5	7	4.44	17	0	99	118	33	60
Lucey, Tim, Mass	5	5	4.52	20	0	68	77	36	45
Broome, John, Elmira	3	9	4.67	16	0	98	114	27	54
Tsamis, George, Bangor	5	6	4.96	15	0	74	88	18	34

PRAIRIE LEAGUE

The Minot Mallards went 5-0 in the 1997 Prairie League playoffs, including a three-game sweep of Regina in the finals, to win their second straight championship. They defeated Southern Minny in the divisional playoffs and Regina in the championship series.

The team's success on the field went against its troubles at the gate. Minot drew only 24,984 fans, symbolic of the league's poor attendance all season. The league also had to withstand some tense moments when the Moose Jaw Diamond Dogs ceased operations after the players, whose pay was overdue, refused to go on a 10-day road trip.

Although other teams offered to put up meal money and housing for the players while on the road, the Diamond Dogs were not guaranteed payment. They refused to play and the franchise folded. Some players went home while others put their hopes in the dispersal draft.

The Aberdeen Pheasants also had problems after the league shut down the franchise for not paying its $15,000 annual dues. Aberdeen's front office asserted that the dues had been paid, but the Pheasants missed two games while the dispute went unresolved. The franchise was then reinstated.

Regina's Randy Kapano was named the most valuable player for hitting .383 with a league-leading 23 homers and 72 RBIs. Saskatoon's Ernesto Nieves was named the pitcher of the year for posting a league-best 10 wins and 2.45 ERA.

STANDINGS

FIRST HALF	W	L	PCT	GB
Regina Cyclones	23	13	.639	—
Saskatoon Stallions	18	18	.500	5
Moose Jaw Diamond Dogs	16	20	.444	7
West Man Wranglers	8	26	.235	14
SOUTH	**W**	**L**	**PCT**	**GB**
Southern Minny Stars	21	14	.600	—
Grand Forks Varmints	19	15	.559	1½
Aberdeen Pheasants	19	17	.528	2½
Minot Mallards	17	18	.486	4
SECOND HALF				
NORTH	**W**	**L**	**PCT**	**GB**
Saskatoon Stallions	20	10	.667	—
Regina Cyclones	16	14	.533	4
West Man Wranglers	8	19	.296	10½
*Moose Jaw Diamond Dogs	0	5	.000	7½
SOUTH	**W**	**L**	**PCT**	**GB**
Minot Mallards	26	10	.722	—
Southern Minny Stars	21	10	.677	2½
Grand Forks Varmints	14	19	.424	10½
Aberdeen Pheasants	8	26	.235	17

*Team ceased operation

PLAYOFFS: Semifinals—Regina defeated Saskatoon 2-1, and Minot defeated Southern Minny 2-0, in best-of-3 series. **Finals**—Minot defeated Regina 3-0 in best-of-5 series.

MANAGERS: Aberdeen—Bob Flori. Grand Forks—Mike Verdi. Minot—Mitch Zwolensky. Moose Jaw—Scotty Douglas. Regina—Tommy Griffith. Saskatoon—Keith Smitt. Southern Minny—Kevin Graber. West Man—Mike Willoughby.

ATTENDANCE: Regina 47,299; Grand Forks 38,097; Aberdeen 32,748; Saskatoon 28,288; Minot 24,984; Southern Minny 20,868; Moose Jaw 14,428; West Man 7,119.

ALL-STAR TEAM: C—Cory Reeder, Minot. **1B**—James Wambach, Grand Forks. **2B**—Doug Kimbler, Southern Minny. **3B**—Randy Kapano, Regina. **SS**—Brian Giles, Saskatoon. **OF**—Brian Cornelius, Moose Jaw/Saskatoon; Andre Johnson, Saskatoon; Tom Smith, Aberdeen. **DH**—Ed Gerald, Southern Minny. **SP**—Ernesto Nieves, Saskatoon. **RP**—Thomas Taylor, Regina.

Most Valuable Player: Randy Kapano, Regina. **Pitcher of the Year:** Ernesto Nieves, Saskatoon. **Manager of the Year:** Kevin Graber, Southern Minny.

INDIVIDUAL BATTING LEADERS

(Minimum 216 Plate Appearances)

	AVG	AB	R	H	2B	3B	HR	RBI	SB
Kopriva, Dan, GF/MJ	**.384**	224	53	86	14	0	9	34	16
Kapano, Randy, Regina	.383	201	**68**	77	10	2	**23**	72	5
Hoshikawa, Hirohide, Reg	.368	190	52	70	11	1	12	51	11
Patterson, Jarrod, Regina	.363	240	52	87	**24**	2	7	50	7
Robinson, Darryl, Minot	.362	221	35	80	10	2	3	40	3
Giles, Brian, AM-Sask	.360	175	46	63	14	1	6	28	5
Johnson, Andre, Sask	.358	243	67	87	16	0	22	71	20
Smith, Tom, Aberdeen	.350	277	49	97	10	**3**	15	58	3
Powell, Gordon, Regina	.348	282	67	**98**	**24**	2	9	45	32
Halpern, Dan, Saskatoon	.333	252	42	84	13	2	2	42	3
Collum, Gary, Minot	.332	283	56	94	14	2	7	37	25
Wambach, James, GF	.332	238	46	79	14	0	14	54	6
McDonald, Ashanti, Minot	.331	269	50	89	14	2	5	35	11
Cornelius, Brian, MJ-Sask	.331	245	44	81	10	0	11	52	9
Dour, Craig, Aberdeen	.322	211	38	68	17	0	7	38	11
Green, Dario, SM	.318	239	46	76	11	**3**	2	29	29
Gerald, Dwayne, SM	.318	258	43	82	14	2	13	50	5
McKamie, Sean, SM	.314	264	63	83	11	2	5	27	12
Olmstead, Reed, Regina	.310	242	42	75	11	0	10	52	4
Tovar, Edgar, Aberdeen	.308	292	48	90	7	1	4	36	6
Hoffner, Jamie, GF	.307	274	44	84	13	1	3	35	4
Smith, Luke, Aberdeen	.299	271	55	81	14	1	14	55	4
Gerald, Eddie, SM	.291	244	55	71	12	0	18	**76**	16
Larrequi, Ed, Aberdeen	.289	273	30	79	15	0	5	43	1
Bill Dunn, GF-Regina	.288	243	57	70	13	**3**	9	38	**34**
Spicer, Shane, WM	.287	181	37	52	5	1	3	18	18
Rios, Eduardo, Saskatoon	.286	283	58	81	21	2	7	30	2
Billingsley, Kyle, Sask	.284	236	33	67	15	1	3	33	1
Cafferty, Jim, Regina	.282	195	40	55	12	1	2	24	5
Griffith, Tommy, Regina	.282	277	60	78	18	2	4	40	21
Sutter, Brian, SM	.281	210	34	59	7	0	2	25	1
Grevengoed, Jayson, Reg	.280	214	53	60	19	**3**	15	55	5

INDIVIDUAL PITCHING LEADERS

(Minimum 64 Innings)

	W	L	ERA	G	SV	IP	H	BB	SO
#Nelson, Brian, Sask	1	1	1.75	29	**16**	36	17	14	48
Newman, Damon, Minot	7	2	**2.09**	15	0	103	92	33	84
Nieves, Ernesto, Sask	**10**	1	2.45	15	0	84	73	21	63
Berenguer, Juan, SM	8	3	3.09	13	0	82	82	20	55
Fletschock, Justin, SM	9	2	3.19	16	0	102	94	35	63
Kelly, John, Minot	6	3	3.26	14	0	97	81	39	**103**
Wagner, Rick, WM	3	1	3.41	15	0	74	70	23	52
Hogan, Dennis, SM	8	4	3.56	18	1	86	61	48	49
Sontag, Alan, Saskatoon	7	5	3.95	14	0	96	103	25	70
Gaiko, Rob, Grand Forks	9	4	4.13	35	5	72	87	21	54
Shanahan, Chris, Minot	7	2	4.15	16	2	80	80	20	64
Foshie, Joshua, WM	2	5	4.17	12	1	69	72	30	55
Magee, Bo, Regina	4	6	4.29	16	0	84	77	41	101
Brown, Cory, Aberdeen	5	6	4.56	15	0	105	116	43	89
Gogolewski, Chris, SM	7	5	4.60	16	0	86	103	39	50
Reyes, Jose, Aberdeen	8	7	4.91	16	0	106	104	45	82

Statistics in **boldface** indicate league leader

#League leader but non-qualifier

Foreign Leagues

MEXICAN LEAGUE

Tigers beat Red Devils to win battle of Mexico City

BY JOHN ROYSTER

It was a bittersweet year for the Mexico City Tigers in 1997, but one in which they'll be remembered as the best team in the Mexican League.

The Tigers won their first 10 games, took the first-half title in the Central Zone with a late 13-game winning streak, then lost in the second half to the Mexico City Red Devils, who went 83-38 overall.

On the rebound
Ty Gainey

But they beat the Reds when it counted–four times in five games in the best-of-seven league championship series–to win their first league title since 1992.

Along the way, the Tigers lost their owner. Alejo Peralta, 80, who founded the franchise in 1955, died April 8 in Mexico City. Peralta also had served as the league's commissioner, and was instrumental in the establishment of the two successive Mexican academies for young players. The current one, opened near Monterrey in 1995, is named for him.

The Tigers pitched shutouts in the first and fourth games of the championship series. Righthander Scott Lewis went eight innings and Enrique Couoh finished Game One, a 7-0 win. Ernesto Barraza threw a complete-game two-hitter in winning Game Four 9-0.

Lewis also won the deciding game 7-4 as the Red Devils lost in the finals for the third straight year. The Monterrey Sultans had beaten them in both 1995 and '96.

Tigers third baseman Ivan Montalvo was named MVP of the final series after batting .389 with a homer and nine RBIs. Montalvo also tied a league record with 11 straight hits in late April, including a 5-for-5 effort in an 11-inning game against the Red Devils. He shares the record with Espino (1980), Daniel Garcia (1982) and Willie Aikens (1986).

First baseman Alex Cabrera led the Tigers in 14 postseason games by hitting .482 with five homers and 23 RBIs. Lewis went 4-0 with a 1.58 ERA.

The Tigers, who had a staff ERA of 2.12 in postseason play, won their semifinal playoff series over Tabasco in five games, while the Red Devils eliminated Quintana Roo in six. Overall, the Tigers went 12-2 in the playoffs.

Two-time defending champion Monterrey fell in the quarterfinals, in six games to Quintana Roo. The other first-round series were all sweeps, with the Reds beating Reynosa, the Tigers beating Poza Rica and Tabasco beating Monclova.

Oaxaca infielder Nelson Barrera broke the league's career record for RBIs when he drove in No. 1,574 on April 22. Barrera, 39 and in his 21st season, produced the record-breaking run with a hit off Tabasco righthander Gaudencio Aguirre in Oaxaca. Barrera finished the year with 1,639 career RBIs.

The old record of 1,573 was held by Hector Espino, perhaps the most revered player in league history. Espino, 58, lived only 4½ months after seeing the record fall. He died of a heart attack Sept. 7 in Monterrey.

Espino, a first baseman, played for 24 seasons in the league and won five batting titles. He still holds the record for career home runs with 453. The stadium in Hermosillo, home of the Orange Growers of the winter Mexican Pacific League, is named for him.

Saltillo reliever Roberto Osuna broke the league record for appearances with 75. Osuna, the brother of Los Angeles Dodgers reliever Antonio Osuna, eclipsed the record of the late Aurelio "Senor Smoke" Lopez, who went on to a distinguished major league career after appearing in 73 games for the Red Devils in 1977.

Red Devils outfielder Ty Gainey led the league in both home runs (25) and RBIs (108). Gainey, arguably the top import player in the league in the 1990s, bounced back from a subpar 1996 that saw him miss three months with stomach problems. He won a triple crown in '95.

STANDINGS

CENTRAL ZONE	W	L	PCT	GB
Mexico City Reds (15)	83	38	.686	—
Mexico City Tigers (15)	77	40	.658	4
Poza Rica Oilers (13)	67	52	.563	15
Oaxaca Warriors (12)	53	69	.434	30½
Aguascalientes Railroadmen (11)	46	73	.387	36
NORTH ZONE	**W**	**L**	**PCT**	**GB**
Monterrey Sultans (15)	68	52	.567	—
Monclova Steelers (13.5)	65	56	.537	3½
Reynosa Broncos (13.5)	60	57	.513	6½
Saltillo Sarape Makers (12)	55	64	.462	12½
Laredo Owls (12)	55	64	.462	12½
Union Laguna Cotton Pickers (10)	48	70	.407	19
SOUTH ZONE	**W**	**L**	**PCT**	**GB**
Tabasco Olmecas (14.5)	67	52	.563	—
Quintana Roo Lobsters (15)	61	56	.521	5
Yucatan Lions (13.5)	54	64	.458	12½
Campeche Pirates (12)	46	64	.418	16½
Minatitlan Colts (11)	42	76	.356	24½

NOTE: League played a split-season schedule. Points were awarded on basis of finish in each half (8 for first, 7 for second, 6.5 for third, 6 for fourth, 5.5 for fifth, 5 for sixth) to determine playoff pairings.

PLAYOFFS—Quarterfinals: Quintana Roo defeated Monterrey 4-2, Mexico City Red Devils defeated Reynosa 4-0, Mexico City Tigers defeated Poza Rica 4-0, and Tabasco defeated Monclova 4-0, in best-of-7 series. Semifinals—Mexico City Tigers defeated Tabasco 4-1, and Mexico City Reds defeated Quintana Roo 4-2, in best-of-7 series. Finals—Mexico City Tigers defeated Mexico City Red Devils 4-1, in best-of-7 series.

REGULAR-SEASON ATTENDANCE: Mexico City Red Devils 465,313; Mexico City Tigers 439,141; Monterrey 430,274; Monclova 356,885; Yucatan 194,966; Reynosa 135,886; Tabasco 131,612; Poza Rica 125,237; Oaxaca 118,838; Quintana Roo 102,612; Campeche 95,993; Laredo 89,662; Union Laguna 89,128; Saltillo 77,675; Aguascalientes 66,810; Minititlan 64,373.

INDIVIDUAL BATTING LEADERS

(Minimum 329 Plate Appearances)

	AVG	AB	R	H	2B	3B	HR	RBI	SB
Garcia, Cornelio, Monterrey	**.382**	448	86	**171**	24	8	1	34	22
Polonia, Luis, Tigers	.377	408	105	154	29	5	7	59	**48**
Magallanes, Ever, Mont.	.359	334	47	120	17	2	3	46	3
Gainey, Ty, Reds	.353	399	97	141	18	2	**25**	**108**	8
Salas, Heriberto, UL	.349	338	59	118	16	4	2	32	3
Woods, Tyrone, Minatitlan	.342	304	58	104	20	2	18	73	0
Alvarez, Hector, Oaxaca	.341	317	50	108	20	5	2	52	3
Carter, Michael, Laredo	.341	454	69	155	27	5	1	33	41
Stark, Matt, Yucatan	.337	362	53	122	23	0	7	57	2
Arredondo, Luis, Yucatan	.337	481	79	162	16	11	4	49	31
Garcia, Omar, Poza Rica	.336	434	57	146	25	7	0	65	4
Mendez, Roberto, Oaxaca	.328	357	67	117	21	4	8	69	13
Michel, Domingo, Cam.	.327	343	64	112	13	2	8	54	8
Sherman, Darrell, Rey.	.327	355	72	116	17	7	0	16	19
Zazueta, Juan, UL	.327	333	47	109	15	2	0	24	3
Clark, Tim, Saltillo	.326	386	59	126	30	4	14	78	2
Carrillo, Matias, Tigers	.326	417	83	136	22	3	20	102	6
Felix, Junior, Yucatan	.323	356	53	115	16	4	10	77	3
Gonzalez, Jesus, Cam.	.323	402	63	130	21	2	14	55	7
Fernandez, Daniel, Reds	.319	442	**107**	141	18	5	1	39	24
Deak, Darrel, Oaxaca	.319	304	45	97	27	0	3	48	9
Peguero, Julio, QR	.318	450	67	143	20	7	5	58	16
Tellez Alonso, Reynosa	.317	445	55	141	27	6	13	67	2
Paez, Raul, Reynosa	.315	305	30	96	13	5	4	57	5
Cabrera, Alex, Tigers	.314	395	52	124	28	5	23	84	6
Azocar, Oscar, Poza Rica	.312	452	62	141	**35**	3	8	85	8
Fentanes, Oscar, Tabasco	.312	426	41	133	20	5	1	48	6
Barrera, Nelson, Oaxaca	.310	445	57	138	30	1	11	82	5
Martinez, Ray, Reds	.307	296	63	91	20	0	1	49	3
Lydy, Scott, Reds	.306	458	93	140	30	5	18	107	20
Flores, Miguel, Monterrey	.305	334	51	102	23	3	5	41	15
Felder, Mike, Monclova	.305	305	50	93	13	7	5	32	12
Gastelum, Sergio, Tigers	.305	331	48	101	15	0	4	45	7
Montalvo, Ivan, Tigers	.304	365	53	111	28	8	5	63	2
Sanchez, Gerardo, Laredo	.303	462	59	140	20	2	9	74	6
Aganza, Ruben, Monclova	.302	430	53	130	28	1	11	75	4
Munoz, Jose, Tabasco	.301	438	59	132	20	1	2	40	14
Velazquez, Guillermo, Mont.	.301	286	40	86	15	1	12	57	1
Estrada, Hector, Monclova	.298	352	30	105	19	1	4	50	1
Munoz, Noe, Reds	.298	309	42	92	16	1	2	52	2
Diaz, Luis, Laredo	.296	291	34	86	14	0	4	36	1
Esquer, Ramon, Reynosa	.296	416	66	123	13	6	2	39	5
Gonzalez, Denio, Tab.	.295	258	48	76	9	0	16	52	1
Rodriguez, Fernando, UL	.295	397	42	117	22	2	8	75	0
Villegas, Fernando, Sal.	.294	401	61	118	4	9	0	49	2
Vizcarra, Roberto, Aguas.	.294	449	54	132	17	2	8	44	15
Jimenez, Eduardo, Reds	.291	333	78	97	17	1	22	91	2
Leyva, German, Yucatan	.289	401	43	116	17	4	0	40	7
Chance, Tony, Monclova	.288	399	76	115	20	4	23	78	5
Verdugo, Vicente, Reds	.288	385	47	111	13	1	2	54	3
Cox, Darron, Tigers	.287	352	47	101	19	4	3	46	1
Diaz, Remigio, Monterrey	.287	408	57	117	13	0	4	42	22
#Valle, Jorge, UL	.247	381	45	94	11	**13**	2	35	4

(Other Select Players)

	AVG	AB	R	H	2B	3B	HR	RBI	SB
Ratliff, Darryl, UL	.382	110	19	42	3	2	0	17	2
Brinkley, Darrell, Reds	.340	50	13	17	1	0	3	8	4
Valrie, Kerry, Oaxaca	.335	254	56	85	18	3	1	23	7
Howell, Pat, Reds	.318	198	31	63	4	4	0	18	11
Zambrano, Roberto, QR	.311	103	19	32	6	0	6	14	0
Cookson, Brent, Laredo	.301	93	17	28	3	1	8	16	1
Villanueva, Hector, QR	.300	180	26	54	12	0	6	29	1
Denson, Drew, Monclova	.291	182	39	53	8	0	9	35	0
Monell, Johnny, QR	.291	206	31	60	9	1	1	22	3
Reyes, Gilberto, Minatitlan	.291	127	10	37	4	0	1	12	0
Magallanes, Bobby, Reds	.286	49	10	14	3	0	0	7	1
Alfonso, Edgar, Tabasco	.282	394	48	111	25	1	3	53	2
Jimenez, Houston, Reds	.276	246	47	68	9	2	6	31	3
Mack, Quinn, Saltillo	.276	399	58	110	19	4	0	55	16
McGriff, Terry, Laredo	.271	140	13	38	8	0	1	14	1
Delima, Rafael, Poza Rica	.269	324	51	87	13	5	1	29	16
Jose, Felix, Tabasco	.269	308	54	83	16	1	10	41	8
Gonzalez, Jose, Aguas.	.265	313	44	83	11	3	7	38	12
Wright, George, Aguas.	.260	334	56	87	12	1	6	52	9
Worthington, Craig, Mont.	.259	85	10	22	4	0	1	12	0
Williams, Reggie, Mont.	.257	218	23	56	13	2	1	20	10
Williams, Harold, PR	.254	177	8	45	14	0	3	25	0
Dominguez, David, QR	.242	186	29	45	10	0	5	20	1
Jones, Ron, Tabasco	.232	112	10	26	2	1	3	17	0
Wong, Julian, Campeche	.230	248	32	57	15	0	1	23	2
Johnson, Roy, Campeche	.219	32	3	7	2	0	1	6	0
Scott, Gary, QR	.120	25	4	3	0	1	0	0	0

INDIVIDUAL PITCHING LEADERS

(Minimum 98 Innings)

	W	L	ERA	G	SV	IP	H	BB	SO
Lopez, Emigdio, Tab.	15	5	**1.91**	24	4	183	155	47	74
Osuna, Roberto, Saltillo	4	2	1.92	75	0	98	88	27	60
Valdez, Efrain, QR	14	7	2.07	24	5	187	149	54	75
Purata, Julio, Reynosa	**16**	8	2.18	25	3	190	155	74	98
Aguirre, Gaudencio, Tab.	12	4	2.30	28	3	133	118	37	59
Hernandez, Martin, QR	14	4	2.41	24	3	172	147	55	83
Tejeda, Felix, Poza Rica	13	6	2.42	23	2	141	137	24	34
Hernandez, Jose, Lar.	13	8	2.44	23	4	155	149	44	65
Perez, David, Monterrey	8	5	2.45	23	2	140	122	52	61
Lara, Hugo, Poza Rica	13	4	2.50	26	5	158	151	29	69
Osuna, Ricardo, Tabasco	13	8	2.51	25	0	169	147	51	89
Mora, Eleazar, Poza Rica	**16**	3	2.59	27	0	153	128	40	56
Lara, Jorge, Saltillo	10	6	2.64	38	0	133	125	39	79
Gonzalez, Arturo, Mont.	8	6	2.68	21	0	128	132	29	53
Mattson, Rob, Aguas.	11	14	2.87	27	1	191	181	49	73
Adam, David, Tigers	13	5	2.89	24	0	153	137	53	84
Rios, Jesus, Monclova	12	5	2.90	24	0	168	139	57	**121**
Rodriguez, Salvador, Yuc.	7	5	2.91	17	0	105	101	44	42
Campos, Francisco, Cam.	9	10	2.92	25	0	179	144	67	70
Barraza, Ernesto, Tigers	9	5	2.96	19	0	113	107	64	55
Ruiz, Cecilio, Tabasco	9	6	2.98	21	0	130	136	28	50
Pimentel, Roberto, Sal.	7	5	3.08	36	0	117	125	44	46
Acosta, Aaron, Monclova	9	8	3.09	22	0	137	143	60	82
Huerta, Luis, Laredo	9	7	3.13	25	0	150	165	46	63
Garcia, Francisco, Reds	14	6	3.19	27	0	141	136	85	78
Turgeon, David, Reynosa	9	6	3.19	18	0	118	122	31	68
Rojo, Oscar, Campeche	2	6	3.22	30	1	103	111	42	43
Alvarez, Juan, Tabasco	7	12	3.27	27	1	146	147	53	66
Diaz, Rafael, Monterrey	7	6	3.34	21	0	116	100	69	69
Couch, Enrique, Tigers	8	6	3.39	41	1	127	128	49	58
#Marquez, Isidro, Tigers	8	2	3.41	51	**30**	63	61	29	30

(Other Select Players)

	W	L	ERA	G	SV	IP	H	BB	SO
Schullstrom, Eric, Mont.	3	1	0.31	29	2	29	19	13	39
Zimmerman, Mike, Cam.	1	1	1.69	12	2	16	11	15	11
Dennis, Gray, UL	0	1	1.88	15	6	24	15	10	21
Green, Otis, Reds	3	2	1.97	34	0	46	35	26	39
Barfield, John, Laredo	5	2	2.35	45	21	61	55	20	18
Lewis, Scott, Tigers	6	3	2.47	13	0	87	93	12	36
Metoyer, Tony, Reynosa	8	4	2.53	52	29	82	60	44	62
Hurst, Jonathan, Aguas.	1	4	3.08	32	1	38	32	20	25
Elvira, Narciso, Mont.	0	0	3.44	6	0	18	17	10	8
Orozco, Jaime, Minatitlan	12	9	3.54	26	0	160	177	31	65
#Dessens, Elmer, Reds	**16**	5	3.56	26	0	159	156	51	61
Duncan, Chip, Oaxaca	6	8	3.59	23	0	138	122	68	87
Palacios, Vicente, Mont.	11	4	3.59	23	0	148	143	51	120
Leftwich, Phil, Laredo	6	7	3.64	19	0	111	121	39	80
Powell, Dennis, Mont.	4	7	3.72	53	17	56	55	26	46
Esquer, Mercedez, Mont.	13	3	3.78	23	0	129	135	62	58
Williams, Jeff, Saltillo	8	10	4.15	22	0	130	128	66	47
Kelly, Richard, Reynosa	4	9	4.26	19	0	95	101	50	51
Baker, Scott, UL	7	7	4.35	29	0	110	131	43	55
York, Mike, Union Laguna	10	6	4.59	19	1	100	101	74	68
Revenig, Todd, UL	4	0	5.51	26	4	33	36	8	16
Scanlan, Bob, Reds	1	2	5.93	12	1	14	25	11	4
Fajardo, Hector, Monclova	2	3	6.23	7	0	35	33	20	14

Statsitics in **boldface** indicate league leader
# Indicates league leader but non-qualifier

JAPANESE LEAGUE

Swallows beat Lions, continue odd year championship

BY WAYNE GRACZYK

The Yakult Swallows of Tokyo, falling into a pattern of winning the Japan Series every other year, followed championships in 1993 and 1995 by taking it all again in 1997.

They beat the Seibu Lions 4-1 in the best-of-seven Japan Series. The Swallows rebounded from a fourth-place '96 finish in the six-team Central League to another pennant.

Yakult was led by all-star catcher and cleanup hitter Atsuya Furuta, who drove in 86 runs while recording the league's third-best batting average (.322) and playing all 137 games behind the plate (including two ties). Furuta was named MVP for both the Central League and the Japan Series.

The Series win over the Pacific League's Lions capped a year that saw the number of scheduled games increased from 130 to 135, the opening of two new domed stadiums and a failed attempt to have an American umpire work in smoothly.

WAYNE GRACZYK

Fourth title in row
Ichiro Suzuki

The Osaka Dome (capacity 48,000) and Nagoya Dome (capacity 40,500) opened in March and became the homes of the Kintetsu Buffaloes and Chunichi Dragons, respectively. The two fixed-dome structures brought the number of all-weather stadiums to four in Japan, joining the Tokyo Dome (Yomiuri Giants and Nippon Ham Fighters) and the retractable Fukuoka Dome (Fukuoka Daiei Hawks).

After a two-year umpire exchange that saw American and Japanese umps work in each other's countries in spring training, Japan's Central League sought to directly internationalize its staff by hiring Triple-A arbiter Mike DiMuro.

The experiment ended abruptly and unsuccessfully on June 9, when DiMuro resigned and was recalled by Major League Baseball. The league had failed to back him after his ejection of Chunichi Dragons player Yasuaki Taihoh in a June 5 game. DiMuro tossed out Taihoh after the player had argued a called strike, and the umpire was shoved by a gang of Dragons players and coaches that included manager Senichi Hoshino.

The expanded schedule helped the Pacific League establish a new single-season attendance record, drawing 10,012,500 fans, up from 8,770,000 in 1996. Most of that was gained by Kintetsu's move into the Osaka Dome, where attendance more than doubled from 915,000 to 1,866,000.

The extra five games didn't produce a 20-game winner or a 40-home run hitter. Dragons lefthander Masahiro Yamamoto led both leagues with an 18-7 record. Righthanders Fumiya Nishiguchi of the Lions and Hideo Koike of the Buffaloes led the Pacific League with 15 wins each. Nishiguchi, 15-5, 3.12 with a league-leading 192 strikeouts, was named Pacific League MVP.

Foreigners led the home run derby in both leagues. American Dwayne Hosey, a former Red Sox outfielder, hit 38 dingers for the Swallows in the CL. Canadian Nigel Wilson, the No. 1 pick of the Marlins in the 1992 expansion draft and the Nippon Ham DH in 1997, hit 37 in the PL. Wilson's total included a record-tying four in one game.

Former Dodgers and Indians farmhand Luis Lopez, the Hiroshima Carp first baseman, led the CL in RBIs for the second straight year, with 112. Hawks infielder Hiroki Kokubo led the PL with 114 RBIs

Orix BlueWave phenom Ichiro Suzuki won his fourth straight PL batting title with a .345 average. Outfielder Takanori Suzuki (no relation) of the Yokohama BayStars hit .335 in the CL.

Including umpire DiMuro and Chiba Lotte Marines third-base coach Lenn Sakata, 51 foreigners participated in Japan pro baseball, a record which will probably be broken in 1998. The limit will be raised to allow four non-Japanese at a time on each club, up from three in 1997. Of the four, two must be pitchers and two may be position players. There's no limit to foreigners on Japanese farm teams.

Among other former major leaguers who enjoyed productive seasons were Yokohama second baseman Bobby Rose, who hit .328 as the second-leading Central League hitter, and Chunichi third baseman Leo Gomez, who hit .315 with 31 home runs.

Kintetsu first baseman Phil Clark was the runner-up to Ichiro in the PL batting race with a .331 average. He also had 23 home runs and 93 RBIs.

Clark's teammate Tuffy Rhodes, an outfielder, batted .307 with 22 homers and 102 RBIs and was selected to the all-star team. For the Pacific League champion Lions, DH Domingo Martinez hit .305 with 31 homers and 108 RBIs.

CENTRAL LEAGUE

STANDINGS

	W	L	PCT	T	GB
Yakult Swallows	83	52	.615	2	—
Yokohama BayStars	72	63	.533	0	11
Hiroshima Carp	66	69	.489	0	17
Yomiuri Giants	63	72	.467	0	20
Hanshin Tigers	62	73	.459	1	21
Chunichi Dragons	59	76	.437	1	24

INDIVIDUAL BATTING LEADERS
(Minimum 350 Plate Appearances)

	AVG	AB	R	H	2B	3B	HR	RBI	SB
Suzuki, Takanori, BayStars	**.335**	478	76	160	30	4	21	83	11
Rose, Bobby, BayStars	.328	463	70	152	30	7	18	99	3
Furuta, Atsuya, Swallows	.322	509	74	164	32	2	9	86	9
Lopez, Luis, Carp	.320	532	80	**170**	**37**	0	30	**112**	0

Player	AVG	AB	R	H	2B	3B	HR	RBI	SB
Ishii, Takuro, BayStars	.319	521	95	166	23	1	10	44	23
Gomez, Leo, Dragons	.315	483	84	152	23	1	31	81	2
Komada, Norihiro, BayStars	.308	507	57	156	31	2	12	86	2
Iida, Tetsuya, Swallows	.306	421	62	129	15	7	3	37	26
Shimizu, Takayuki, Giants	.304	381	50	116	12	3	12	36	7
Maeda, Tomonari, Carp	.304	382	55	116	23	1	15	68	1
Kanemoto, Tomoaki, Carp	.301	465	77	140	17	2	33	82	13
Wada, Yutaka, Tigers	.300	390	51	117	17	5	2	26	2
Matsui, Hideki, Giants	.298	484	93	144	18	0	37	103	9
Haru, Toshio, BayStars	.295	502	89	148	22	3	8	41	16
Hiratsuka, Katsuhiro, Tigers	.293	484	51	142	22	0	17	68	0
Hosey, Dwayne, Swallows	.289	498	101	144	32	3	**38**	100	20
Kawai, Masahiro, Giants	.288	416	68	120	21	2	6	25	2
Miyamoto, Shinya, Swallows	.282	387	44	109	15	3	1	33	16
Hirosawa, Katsumi, Giants	.280	428	56	120	13	1	22	67	2
Nomura, Kenjiro, Carp	.280	540	81	151	25	0	13	52	26
Ikeyama, Takahiro, Swallows	.276	439	65	121	26	3	18	79	11
Ogata, Koichi, Carp	.271	528	**103**	143	26	5	17	57	**49**
Tatsunami, Kazuyoshi, Dragons	.269	495	77	133	24	3	14	55	8
Masuda, Daisuke, Dragons	.269	402	54	108	15	**8**	2	24	11
Inaba, Atsunori, Swallows	.267	439	71	117	24	4	21	65	9
Kuji, Teruyoshi, Tigers	.257	393	55	101	11	2	3	20	8
Yamazaki, Takeshi, Dragons	.257	421	45	108	19	2	19	54	0
Powell, Alonzo, Dragons	.253	379	36	96	13	1	14	56	0
Eto, Akira, Carp	.252	393	78	99	12	3	28	76	3

(Other Foriegn Players)

Player	AVG	AB	R	H	2B	3B	HR	RBI	SB
Tatum, Jim, Swallows	.309	139	27	43	7	0	13	25	4
Perez, Timoniel, Carp	.245	139	17	34	4	2	3	15	2
Coles, Darnell, Tigers	.242	231	28	56	16	0	7	28	0
De los Santos, Luis, Giants	.237	114	7	27	6	1	0	14	0
Greenwell, Mike, Tigers	.231	26	2	6	1	1	0	5	9
Selby, Bill, BayStars	.228	171	19	39	4	1	5	17	3
Hiatt, Phil, Tigers	.204	206	26	42	7	3	11	30	3
Castellano, Pedro, Giants	.197	122	8	24	8	1	4	23	0
Secrist, Reed, Tigers	.192	52	4	10	4	0	0	4	0
Ortiz, Luis, Swallows	.172	29	3	5	1	1	0	7	0
Soriano, Alfonso, Carp	.118	17	2	2	0	0	0	0	0

INDIVIDUAL PITCHING LEADERS

(Minimum 133 Innings)

Player	W	L	ERA	G	SV	IP	H	BB	SO
#Sasaki, Kazuhiro, BayStars	3	0	0.90	49	**38**	60	38	17	63
#Sun, Dong Yol, Dragons	1	1	1.28	43	**38**	63	36	12	69
Ono, Yuktaka, Carp	9	6	**2.85**	23	0	136	121	47	80
Yamamoto, Masahiro, Dragons	**18**	7	2.92	29	1	207	174	57	**159**
Tabata, Kazuya, Swallows	15	5	2.96	26	0	170	160	43	83
Yoshii, Masato, Swallows	13	6	2.99	28	0	174	149	48	104
Takeuchi, Yoshiya, Tigers	8	6	3.01	38	0	140	126	60	75
Galvez, Balvino, Giants	12	12	3.32	27	0	193	165	48	118
Kawamura, Takeo, BayStars	10	7	3.32	26	0	152	113	49	147
Miura, Daisuke, BayStars	10	3	3.35	26	0	142	113	51	129
Makibara, Hiromi, Giants	12	9	3.46	25	0	151	140	36	115
Yufune, Toshiro, Tigers	10	6	3.56	27	0	137	152	53	76
Yabu, Keiichi, Tigers	10	12	3.59	29	0	183	172	62	111
Sawazaki, Toshikazu, Carp	12	8	3.74	38	0	156	162	47	106
Kuwata, Masumi, Giants	10	7	3.77	26	0	141	127	37	104
Nomura, Hiroki, BayStars	10	8	3.89	25	0	143	153	43	94

(Other Foreign Players)

Player	W	L	ERA	G	SV	IP	H	BB	SO
Hillman, Eric, Giants	0	1	3.00	2	0	6	8	2	3
Perdomo, Felix, Carp	2	2	4.03	17	0	29	26	13	18
Mahomes, Pat, BayStars	3	4	4.82	11	0	53	54	25	42
Bross, Terry, Swallows	7	8	4.99	23	0	115	129	56	89
Pavlas, Dave, Giants	0	0	6.00	7	4	6	10	4	4
MacDonald, Bob, Tigers	0	1	7.36	9	0	7	7	4	9

PACIFIC LEAGUE

STANDINGS

Team	W	L	PCT	T	GB
Seibu Lions	76	56	.576	3	—
Orix Blue Wave	71	61	.538	3	5
Kintetsu Buffaloes	68	63	.519	4	7½
Nippon Ham Fighters	63	71	.470	1	14
Fukuoka Daiei Hawks	63	71	.470	1	14
Chiba Lotte Marines	57	76	.429	2	19½

INDIVIDUAL BATTING LEADERS

(Minimum 350 Plate Appearances)

Nigel Wilson **Dwayne Hosey**

Player	AVG	AB	R	H	2B	3B	HR	RBI	SB
Suzuki, Ichiro, Blue Wave	**.345**	536	**94**	**185**	31	4	17	91	39
Clark, Phil, Buffaloes	.331	526	61	174	27	0	23	93	1
Suzuki, Ken, Lions	.312	471	72	147	34	3	19	94	2
Matsui, Kazuo, Lions	.309	576	91	178	23	**13**	7	63	**62**
Jojima, Kenji, Hawks	.308	432	49	133	24	2	15	68	6
Rhodes, Tuffy, Buffaloes	.307	511	88	157	**37**	0	22	102	22
Martinez, Domingo, Lions	.305	488	63	149	24	1	31	108	3
Sasaki, Makoto, Lions	.304	450	56	137	26	1	13	57	5
Donnels, Chris, Blue Wave	.302	384	55	116	25	1	17	67	0
Kokubo, Hiroki, Hawks	.302	527	88	159	37	3	36	**114**	4
Yoshinaga, Koichiro, Hawks	.300	443	57	133	21	0	29	73	0
Ueda, Yoshinori, Fighters	.300	360	41	108	23	0	6	39	7
Takagi, Taisei, Lions	.295	474	75	140	27	4	7	64	24
Taguchi, So, Blue Wave	.294	572	92	168	32	4	10	56	7
Omichi, Noriyoshi, Hawks	.293	441	55	129	17	2	6	46	1
Kataoka, Atsushi, Fighters	.286	514	67	147	28	2	17	67	3
Ide, Tatsuya, Fighters	.284	521	75	148	27	5	8	45	27
Mizuguchi, Eiji, Buffaloes	.284	388	54	110	16	2	7	50	10
Muto, Takashi, Buffaloes	.282	390	55	110	13	7	0	29	26
Ito, Tsutomu, Lions	.280	436	50	122	19	1	13	56	5
Carreon, Mark, Marines	.279	481	51	134	19	1	14	77	11
Otomo, Susumu, Lions	.278	460	71	128	21	7	5	45	31
Kaneko, Makoto, Fighters	.277	513	80	142	18	2	12	53	13
Brooks, Jerry, Fighters	.277	488	61	135	27	2	16	63	3
Wilson, Nigel, Fighters	.274	478	67	131	24	0	**37**	94	1
Hori, Koichi, Marines	.272	522	53	142	18	2	9	47	15
Neel, Troy, Blue Wave	.265	472	59	125	14	0	25	98	1
Ochiai, Hiromitsu, Fighters	.262	397	35	104	14	0	3	43	3
Suzuki, Takahisa, Buffaloes	.261	436	45	114	18	3	10	53	9
Kosaka, Makoto, Marines	.261	499	66	130	14	7	1	30	56

(Other Foreign Players)

Player	AVG	AB	R	H	2B	3B	HR	RBI	SB
Jennings, Doug, Blue Wave	.240	25	2	6	1	0	1	3	1
Pirkl, Greg, Hawks	.213	47	3	10	2	0	2	5	0
Pemberton, Rudy, Lions	.175	63	3	11	5	0	1	5	2
Bonnici, James, Blue Wave	.000	8	0	0	0	0	0	0	0

INDIVIDUAL PITCHING LEADERS

(Minimum 133 innings)

Player	W	L	ERA	G	SV	IP	H	BB	SO
#Kawamoto, Yasuyuki, Marines	6	6	1.96	49	**25**	73	57	24	67
Komiyama, Satoru, Marines	11	9	**2.49**	27	0	188	186	30	130
Okamoto, Akira, Buffaloes	10	6	2.82	30	0	147	138	50	84
Shiozaki, Tetsuya, Lions	12	7	2.90	27	0	174	157	49	108
Toyoda, Kiyoshi, Lions	10	6	2.93	23	0	151	128	54	86
Koike, Hideo, Buffaloes	**15**	6	2.96	27	0	183	137	96	136
Kuroki, Tomohiro, Marines	12	15	2.99	32	0	241	206	86	179
Nishiguchi, Fumiya, Lions	**15**	5	3.12	32	1	208	187	68	**192**
Hoshino, Nobuyuki, Blue Wave	14	10	3.24	29	0	203	194	54	121
Noda, Koji, Blue Wave	7	5	3.29	24	0	150	143	63	99
Kudo, Kimiyasu, Hawks	11	6	3.35	27	0	161	153	48	146
Ito, Takahide, Blue Wave	10	7	3.46	26	0	135	132	51	105
Shimoyanagi, Tsuyoshi, Fighters	9	4	3.49	65	0	147	140	62	136
Gross, Kip, Fighters	13	11	3.63	33	0	233	235	69	98
Takeda, Kazuhiro, Hawks	4	9	3.85	26	0	164	177	39	102
Yabuta, Yasuhiko, Marines	5	9	3.94	25	0	146	144	48	74
Takamura, Hiroshi, Buffaloes	8	9	4.76	23	0	146	171	61	95

(Other Foreign Players)

Player	W	L	ERA	G	SV	IP	H	BB	SO
Nichols, Rod, Hawks	0	0	3.00	3	0	3	3	1	0
Nunez, Jose, Hawks	1	2	3.71	24	1	34	35	7	26
Wishnevski, Rob, Lions	3	2	4.22	34	6	53	56	18	37
Fraser, Willie, Blue Wave	10	9	4.39	24	0	121	118	46	65
Givens, Brian, Lions	4	6	5.10	19	0	78	80	58	45
Ruffin, Johnny, Buffaloes	0	0	5.40	1	0	5	3	7	2
Dennis, Shane, Marines	0	3	5.45	14	0	33	23	29	36
Fyhrie, Mike, Marines	3	4	5.82	8	0	43	54	15	15
West, David, Hawks	8	5	6.38	19	0	92	105	62	63
Milacki, Bob, Buffaloes	0	2	7.30	6	0	25	37	19	9

Statistics in **boldface** indicate league leader
# Indicates league leader but non-qualifier

TAIWAN LEAGUES

Leagues stagger to finish line after scandal, expansion

BY JEFF WILSON

The greatest accomplishment in Taiwan professional baseball in 1997 was that the seasons were finished. A game-fixing scandal and the debut of a new league both threatened to stretch the local talent and the fan interest to the breaking point.

In September, 21 players and one assistant coach with ties to four teams in the Chinese Professional Baseball League were convicted in the game-fixing scandal. The scandal brought down some of the biggest stars in the league, including a former MVP, pitcher Kuo Chin-hsing, a home run champion, a batting champion and several former members of the national team.

It also contributed to the downfall of the league's secretary-general, Daniel Tu, who was relieved of his duties after the season. Falling attendance and difficulties in negotiating a cable television contract also contributed to Tu's ouster.

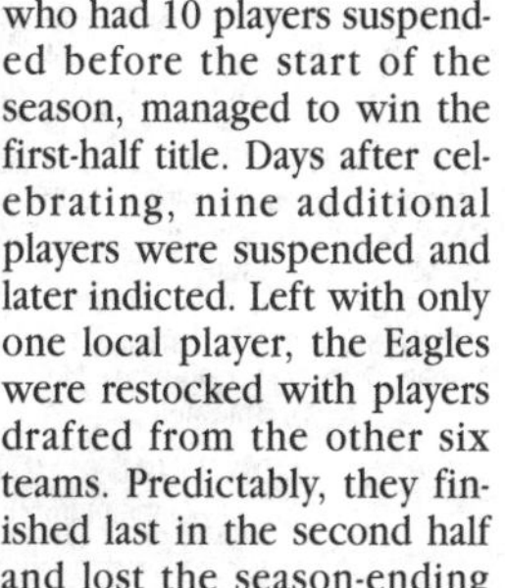

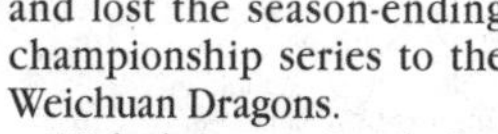

CPBL batting champ
Ted Wood

The China Times Eagles, who had 10 players suspended before the start of the season, managed to win the first-half title. Days after celebrating, nine additional players were suspended and later indicted. Left with only one local player, the Eagles were restocked with players drafted from the other six teams. Predictably, they finished last in the second half and lost the season-ending championship series to the Weichuan Dragons.

With their convicted players still under suspension pending appeals, the Eagles announced after the season that they were suspending operations for 1998.

The scandal also made headlines around the world in early August, when seven players—including four foreigners—were abducted at gunpoint and ordered to throw games by gangsters who had lost money on bets placed on a previous game.

The scandal likely hasn't seen its last victims. The presiding judge in the case turned over to prosecutors a list of additional players he thinks were involved in game-fixing from the 1996 season. The list included players now in both professional leagues.

The scandal overshadowed fine seasons for many of the import players. Weichuan closer Mike Garcia was named league MVP—the first foreigner to win the honor—based on his league-best 1.91 ERA and 27 save points. Outfielder Ted Wood of the Brother Elephants, a former San Francisco Giant and Montreal Expo, led the league in batting (.373) while setting records for RBIs (94) and hits (139).

The rival Taiwan Major League debuted with four teams. The new league raided the CPBL for some of the best local and import talent to play alongside rookies who showed considerable improvement over the season.

The Chia-nan Luka won the regular season, then outlasted the Taipei Gida in seven games to take the league title.

The Luka's Chen Yi-hsin, a two-time MVP in the CPBL, earned the TML award based on his 19-11 season. Otherwise, it was all foreigners leading the statistical categories.

Among the leaders, Taipei first baseman Sam Horn, a former Baltimore Oriole and Cleveland Indian, tied a Taiwan professional record with 31 home runs, while teammate Epy Guerrero hit a league-best .361. Eight-year Taiwan veteran Luis Iglesias led the TML in RBIs with 83 for Chia-nan.

In 1998, the TML looks to decrease the number of import players on its rosters from 11 to seven per team, and drop the number of foreign position players allowed on the field at the same time from four to three.

CHINESE PROFESSIONAL BASEBALL LEAGUE

STANDINGS

FIRST HALF	W	L	PCT	GB
China Times Eagles	30	16	.652	—
President Lions	28	16	.636	1
Brother Elephants	23	20	.535	5½
Mercury Tigers	22	22	.500	7
Sinon Bulls	20	26	.435	10
China Trust Whales	20	27	.426	10½
Weichuan Dragons	15	31	.326	15
SECOND HALF	**W**	**L**	**PCT**	**GB**
Weichuan Dragons	31	15	.674	—
President Lions	30	15	.667	½
Sinon Bulls	25	22	.532	6½
Mercury Tigers	24	22	.522	7
Brother Elephants	22	24	.478	9
China Trust Whales	19	29	.396	13
China Times Eagles	11	35	.239	20

INDIVIDUAL BATTING LEADERS
(Minimum 297 Plate Appearances)

	AVG	AB	R	H	2B	3B	HR	RBI	SB
Wood, Ted, Elephants	.373	373	84	139	32	5	23	94	5
Rodriguez, Boi, Lions	.360	314	83	113	22	1	27	77	5
Bell, Juan, Bulls	.356	371	85	132	27	3	16	73	22
Luo Min-ching, Lions	.336	348	47	117	19	2	13	70	3
Chimelis, Joel, Elephants	.334	341	59	114	21	0	7	42	7
Canale, George, Dragons	.331	335	62	111	21	2	20	71	2
Li Chu-ming, Elephants	.331	360	42	119	24	0	5	51	1
Mercedes, Rafaelito, Whales	.325	348	53	113	18	1	8	42	13
Roa, Hector, Lions	.317	398	81	126	30	3	12	51	14
Colon, Cris, Tigers	.315	343	55	108	20	3	11	48	2

(Remaining U.S. and Latin Players)

	AVG	AB	R	H	2B	3B	HR	RBI	SB
Francois, Manny, Dragons	.425	134	31	57	10	1	3	32	5
Villanueva, Hector, Eagles	.365	104	21	38	13	0	5	24	2
Cabrera, Francisco, Eagles	.331	260	31	86	18	1	4	40	2
Castleberry, Kevin, Bulls	.327	153	30	50	11	1	1	19	3
Quinones, Luis, Bulls	.324	108	18	35	12	0	2	16	2
Caraballo, Ramon, Lions	.324	105	23	34	8	3	1	16	8
Soto, Emison, Tigers	.316	155	30	49	17	0	7	23	1
Zambrano, Roberto, Whales	.315	111	17	35	8	0	11	33	0
Tatis, Bernie, Dragons	.313	383	72	120	22	3	5	40	71
Santana, Ruben, Eagles	.312	221	22	69	22	1	2	23	1
Oliva, Jose, Elephants	.311	273	56	85	11	0	25	81	0
Tokheim, Dave, Tigers	.304	112	15	34	4	1	2	12	2
Castillo, Juan, Whales	.301	292	37	88	19	2	3	35	10
Hernandez, Cesar, Lions	.296	358	64	106	20	4	19	64	23
Heffernan, Bert, Bulls	.293	215	38	63	6	3	4	26	4
Gordon, Keith, Tigers	.286	49	5	14	6	0	2	12	1
Afenir, Troy, Whales	.267	90	11	24	5	0	4	11	2
Guerrero, Juan, Eagles	.258	244	43	63	14	1	12	39	0
Gonzalez, Mauricio, Whales	.250	16	2	4	0	0	0	0	0
Zambrano, Eddie, Tigers	.231	78	9	18	2	0	3	6	1
Bernhart, Cesar, Eagles	.222	18	2	4	1	0	1	4	0
Chance, Tony, Tigers	.222	63	11	14	2	0	4	12	2
Yan, Julian, Whales	.209	67	5	14	2	0	2	5	3
Worthington, Craig, Whales	.100	20	1	2	0	0	0	0	0

INDIVIDUAL PITCHING LEADERS

(Minimum 96 Innings)

	W	L	ERA	G	SV	IP	H	BB	SO
Garcia, Mike, Dragons	7	4	1.89	50	20	104	87	29	128
Chen Hsien-chang, Elephants	9	2	2.23	26	0	109	113	31	75
Liu Yi-chuan, Tigers	8	8	2.41	51	10	145	138	35	115
Lemon, Don, Lions	10	7	2.80	39	4	154	143	42	81
Vasquez, Marcos, Lions	7	3	2.92	46	8	104	94	38	76
Wu Chun-liang, Lions	15	6	3.17	32	1	184	173	58	135
Weng Feng-yu, Tigers	9	5	3.22	23	0	123	125	28	100
Ali, Sam, Lions	5	3	3.22	27	4	131	118	58	67
Bencomo, Omar, Tigers	8	10	3.25	29	0	166	185	41	92
Huang Wen-po, Dragons	9	9	3.34	29	0	156	162	51	126

(Remaining U.S. and Latin Players)

	W	L	ERA	G	S	IP	H	BB	SO
Acosta, Roberto, Whales	0	0	0.00	2	0	1	2	1	0
Segura, Jose, Dragons	0	0	0.00	1	0	4	3	3	3
Santos, Henry, Tigers	0	1	1.80	4	0	10	11	7	2
Boze, Marshall, Bulls	4	3	1.94	23	5	51	48	22	44
Leon, Danilo, Eagles	3	2	2.01	52	15	76	54	28	66
Ozuna, Gabriel, Dragons	9	3	2.19	16	0	94	90	26	70
Dabney, Fred, Tigers	1	1	2.32	19	3	42	38	17	21
Rivera, Ben, Whales	5	5	2.51	49	19	86	59	46	112
Revenig, Todd, Dragons	6	2	2.85	12	0	53	55	11	37
Austin, James, Dragons	5	4	3.04	17	0	77	80	17	46
Wanke, Chuck, Lions	2	1	3.09	16	0	23	16	15	13
Lugo, Urbano, Tigers	1	2	3.21	11	4	33	27	10	18
Henry, Dwayne, Dragons	5	6	3.35	35	0	113	114	70	117
Martinez, Osvaldo, Bulls	14	7	3.39	41	1	104	155	79	132
Leon, Jose, Eagles	4	4	3.40	42	4	84	75	50	100
Martinez, Frankie, Bulls	1	9	3.43	51	10	86	81	39	49
Wagner, Hector, Whales	7	4	3.57	29	0	103	98	35	64
Bustillos, Albert, Elephants	9	8	3.63	24	0	119	120	48	87
Figueroa, Fernando, Tigers	7	7	3.64	21	0	112	102	56	66
Rivera, Lino, Tigers	9	8	3.64	37	8	138	138	54	87
Tapia, Jose, Lions	0	0	3.66	6	0	19	16	10	11
De los Santos, Mariano, Eagles	12	11	3.70	39	1	182	191	62	133
Burgos, Enrique, Elephants	7	7	3.75	34	4	144	143	67	177
Shephard, Keith, Elephants	2	2	3.76	15	1	38	29	22	50
Heredia, Julian, Whales	8	8	3.84	28	1	147	147	64	111
Montalvo, Rafael, Eagles	12	11	3.85	37	0	170	212	56	69
Hansen, Brent, Whales	6	7	3.88	22	0	97	103	43	63
Flynt, Will, Elephants	11	9	3.89	29	0	169	168	63	144
Solarte, Jose, Whales	3	3	3.98	15	1	40	39	14	22
Sanford, Mo, Elephants	2	0	3.99	23	0	47	42	25	39
Caridad, Ron, Whales	0	0	4.12	9	0	19	14	18	13
Brito, Mario, Elephants	1	6	4.21	28	8	62	59	27	58
Marshall, Randy, Bulls	1	2	4.23	11	1	38	44	22	33
Ventura, Cipriano, Whales	6	12	4.34	27	0	124	134	58	92
Johnstone, Joel, Dragons	1	4	4.35	21	0	62	76	34	52
Mejia, Delfino, Eagles	3	4	4.50	22	0	66	68	24	42
Knox, Kerry, Whales	2	3	4.62	50	0	1	59	21	35
Kiefer, Mark, Bulls	12	4	4.63	35	0	157	172	66	106
Soriano, Jose, Bulls	7	8	4.70	29	0	105	123	73	59
Slusarski, Joe, Bulls	2	4	4.94	25	2	71	76	24	31
Tranbarger, Mark, Tigers	1	1	5.09	7	0	23	31	9	11
Ganote, Joe, Dragons	2	5	5.16	8	0	45	50	22	25
Martino, Wilfredo, Whales	0	0	5.40	3	0	1	2	1	2
Martinez, Jose, Eagles	5	9	5.94	24	0	103	129	47	62
Perez, Gil, Dragons	1	3	6.00	18	0	39	50	19	22
Pierce, Jeff, Tigers	1	0	6.00	5	0	15	18	12	9
Zappelli, Mark, Eagles	2	8	6.05	18	0	74	100	41	58
DeJesus, Jose, Tigers	1	0	6.65	9	0	19	26	15	25
Petcka, Joe, Dragons	0	1	7.29	20	1	33	48	29	18
Fredrickson, Scott, Elephants	1	3	7.30	7	0	12	16	8	6
Hollinger, Adrian, Dragons	1	1	7.64	6	0	17	23	15	11
Murray, Matt, Elephants	0	0	9.00	1	0	2	3	1	2
Guilfoyle, Mike, Dragons	0	2	9.33	8	0	18	29	15	12
Gray, Dennis, Lions	0	2	18.00	2	0	3	4	6	5
Romano, Manuel, Eagles	0	0	108.0	1	0	1	6	2	0

TAIWAN MAJOR LEAGUE

STANDINGS

	W	L	Pct.	GB
Chia-nan Luka	53	42	.558	—
Taipei Gida	53	43	.552	½
Kao-ping Fala	42	51	.452	10
Taichung Agan	41	53	.436	11½

INDIVIDUAL BATTING LEADERS

(Minimum 278 Plate Appearances)

	AVG	AB	R	H	2B	3B	HR	RBI	SB
Guerrero, Epy, Taipei	.361	324	54	117	24	2	5	61	17
Lyden, Mitch, Taichung	.350	323	57	113	20	3	27	72	1
Strauss, Brad, Taipei/Chia-nan	.347	251	53	87	16	5	7	40	15
Li Yi-pao, Taipei	.344	270	40	93	19	2	2	41	7
Vatcher, Jim, Taipei	.327	352	83	115	25	1	15	57	11
Iglesias, Luis, Chia-nan	.326	341	53	111	22	3	19	83	55
Horn, Sam, Taipei	.313	288	62	90	14	0	31	76	2
Powell, Corey, Kao-ping	.307	361	63	111	21	2	25	60	7
Huang Shi-ming, Taipei	.303	264	36	80	23	1	3	36	12
Garcia, Leo, Taichung	.301	329	50	99	19	1	15	55	11

(Remaining U.S. and Latin Players)

	AVG	AB	R	H	2B	3B	HR	RBI	SB
Martinez, Julian, Taichung	.667	3	0	2	0	0	0	0	0
Tavarez, Ramon, Chia-nan	.348	115	16	40	8	2	1	22	4
Cockrell, Alan, Taipei	.324	176	29	57	10	0	11	32	1
Simmons, Nelson, Kao-ping	.301	308	35	90	14	0	8	42	1
Goldberg, Lonnie, Taichung	.288	375	64	108	17	2	8	35	41
Laureano, Frank, Kao-ping	.282	255	39	72	14	1	7	34	4
Gonzalez, Angel, Kao-ping	.282	255	36	72	12	0	9	21	7
Campusano, Sil, Chia-nan	.280	325	69	91	18	2	8	51	30
Gainer, Jay, Taichung	.274	219	25	60	9	2	9	29	3
O'Halloran, Greg, Taipei	.263	133	19	35	6	2	4	19	1
Massarelli, John, Chia-nan	.259	220	27	57	11	6	3	19	15
Nunez, Dimerson, Kao-ping	.241	29	2	7	0	0	0	1	0
Thomas, Keith, Chia-nan	.214	14	1	3	0	0	0	0	2

INDIVIDUAL PITCHING LEADERS

(Minimum 96 Innings)

	W	L	ERA	G	S	IP	H	BB	SO
Osuna, Al, Taichung	8	6	2.50	24	0	133	105	53	139
Mikkelsen, Linc, Taipei	17	12	2.70	34	0	233	212	81	187
Weber, Ben, Taipei	7	3	2.73	40	5	99	85	33	78
Chen Yi-hsin, Chia-nan	19	11	3.09	36	0	235	233	49	151
Cole, Victor, Kao-ping	6	10	3.34	27	1	145	132	75	153
Romanoli, Paul, Taichung	10	10	3.38	35	1	160	143	60	103
Picota, Len, Taipei	14	11	3.39	35	0	204	193	71	187
Mauser, Tim, Chia-nan	9	5	3.43	23	3	133	130	29	89
Gerstien, Ron, Kao-ping	7	6	3.45	25	5	140	134	62	99
LaPlante, Michel, Chia-nan	6	10	3.50	40	5	159	153	54	87

(Remaining U.S. and Latin Players)

	W	L	ERA	G	S	IP	H	BB	SO
Mintz, Steve, Chia-nan	1	0	0.73	9	3	12	8	7	8
Ettles, Mark, Chia-nan	0	0	1.69	10	1	16	19	6	10
Winkle, Ken, Kao-ping	6	6	2.50	30	6	50	50	24	47
Jones, Calvin, Taichung	7	5	3.04	50	22	91	75	36	108
August, Don, Kao-ping	10	12	3.51	29	0	205	209	47	110
Reyes, Pablo, Taichung	10	10	3.68	4	0	7	7	2	3
Mirabel, Carlos, Chia-nan	12	7	3.69	31	3	178	180	48	102
Compres, Fidel, Chia./Tai.	5	6	3.69	32	1	58	78	18	34
Wilson, Steve, Kao-ping	10	8	4.15	22	0	143	162	36	102
Taylor, Tom, Taipei	1	1	4.29	12	2	21	21	11	24
Vann, Brandy, Taipei	1	2	4.31	20	1	31	25	23	34
Santos, Jerry, Taichung	0	5	4.43	29	0	67	97	40	36
Eichhorn, Mark, Kao-ping	0	0	4.91	2	1	3	6	3	5
Horsman, Vince, Tai./Chia.	0	4	5.21	19	0	37	52	14	17
Liriano, Felix, Chia-nan	0	0	6.75	4	0	2	3	6	2
Castillo, Carlos, Chia-nan	0	1	7.11	6	2	6	13	2	4
Haas, Dave, Taipei/Taichung	0	0	7.71	9	0	18	32	7	7
Binversie, Brian, Taipei	0	0	8.10	5	0	6	11	3	3
Steinmetz, Earl, Taichung	1	2	9.82	7	0	11	18	8	6

Dodgers repeat in DSL; new Venezuela league opens

DOMINICAN SUMMER LEAGUE

In a showdown of the two Dodgers-affiliated clubs in the Dominican Summer League, the La Romana-based Dodgers defeated the Santo Domingo Dodgers 3-2 in the league's best-of-5 championship series.

It was the second straight title for the La Romana Dodgers and their fourth in six years. At 58-12, the Dodgers narrowly missed duplicating their record of the previous year (59-10).

Dodgers clubs went 1-2 in the league's regular season and, oddly, took turns at defeating the two Rangers-affiliated clubs in the first round of the playoffs. Only Los Angeles, Texas and Oakland fielded more than one DSL club in 1997. The Angels, Reds, Twins and White Sox did not participate at all.

La Romana, which won the San Pedro de Macoris Division by 19 games over the Blue Jays, was taken to the limit in both playoff rounds.

Ace lefthander Randey Dorame (8-0, 0.97), the league's pitcher of the year, failed to win a game in postseason play, pitching only a combined seven innings in two starts. But Orlando Suarez bailed Dorame out with a pair of complete-game victories.

STANDINGS

SANTO DOMINGO EAST	W	L	PCT	GB
Dodgers I	50	18	.735	—
Tigers	47	24	.662	4½
Marlins	41	30	.577	10½
Brewers	40	32	.556	12
Mariners	39	32	.549	12½
Athletics East	38	32	.543	13
Diamondbacks	32	39	.451	19½
Cardinals	28	43	.394	23½
Expos	19	50	.275	31½
Rockies	18	52	.257	33
SANTO DOMINGO WEST	**W**	**L**	**PCT**	**GB**
Rangers I	47	22	.681	—
Mets	41	27	.603	5½
Yankees	40	30	.571	7½
Athletics West	39	30	.565	8
Cubs	39	30	.565	8
Pirates	29	40	.420	18
Devil Rays	27	41	.397	19½
Padres	14	56	.200	33½
SAN PEDRO de MACORIS	**W**	**L**	**PCT**	**GB**
Dodgers II	58	12	.828	—
Blue Jays	40	32	.556	19
Astros	36	35	.507	22½
Braves	35	37	.486	24
Giants	30	40	.428	28
Red Sox	25	46	.352	33½
Orioles	24	46	.342	34
CIBAO	**W**	**L**	**PCT**	**GB**
Rangers II	49	23	.681	—
Indians	37	34	.521	11½
Royals	35	36	.493	13½
Phillies	22	50	.306	27

PLAYOFFS: Semifinals—Dodgers I defeated Rangers 1 2-1, and Dodgers II defeated Rangers II 2-0 in best-of-3 series. Finals—Dodgers II defeated Dodgers I 3-2 in best-of-5 series.

INDIVIDUAL BATTING LEADERS

(Minimum 170 Plate Appearances)

	AVG	AB	R	H	2B	3B	HR	RBI	SB
Rodriguez, Dio., Rangers II	.414	220	50	91	18	10	2	57	17
De Leon, Audes, Giants	.411	146	22	60	12	0	4	36	2
Ramirez, Frank, Dodgers II	.392	227	42	89	13	3	0	46	18
Vargas, Iankel, Tigers	.382	254	59	97	15	4	12	67	8
Santana, Pedro, Yankees	.378	201	47	76	13	4	7	54	4
Ramirez, Charles, Royals	.363	292	68	106	24	4	8	53	12
Beltre, Manuel, Yankees	.361	169	48	61	12	5	5	29	16
Guzman, Antonio, D'backs	.361	205	46	74	16	2	7	54	12
Martinez, Alejandro, Brewers	.360	239	50	86	17	3	9	67	10
Paulino, Waren, Yankees	.359	281	63	101	17	3	2	54	18
Medina, Luis, Cubs	.358	274	46	98	13	1	8	62	23
Rodriguez, Miguel, D'backs	.356	219	49	78	16	5	12	60	7
Mundo, Alberto, Braves	.355	222	44	79	7	6	1	36	11
Berroa, Cristian, Padres	.352	273	51	96	20	4	6	27	14
Gomez, Alexis, Royals	.351	248	51	87	12	9	0	42	9
Gomez, Richard, Tigers	.351	222	48	78	14	6	1	42	19
Santos, Jose, Yankees	.350	214	34	75	20	2	7	48	2
Ferrand, Francisco, Marlins	.349	275	57	96	25	5	6	51	13

INDIVIDUAL PITCHING LEADERS

(Minimum 50 Innings)

	W	L	ERA	G	SV	IP	H	BB	SO
Dorame, Randey, Dodgers II	8	0	0.97	12	0	65	33	11	69
Suarez, Orlando, Dodgers II	8	0	1.19	10	0	61	43	10	57
Colon, Jose, Indians	3	1	1.20	26	8	53	48	14	26
Ferreira, Ramon, Astros	1	2	1.21	41	16	52	42	21	38
Valdez, Fernando, Dodgers I	6	0	1.22	11	1	52	39	11	44
Alcantara, Albin, Cardinals	8	1	1.26	13	0	86	64	27	60
Ozoria, Jose, Rangers II	8	1	1.38	34	11	52	36	19	63
Lucena, Celis, Giants	4	7	1.45	17	0	112	85	35	103
Giron, Isabel, Blue Jays	9	4	1.63	14	0	99	64	19	109
Vega, Vigri, Blue Jays	5	1	1.67	9	0	54	27	17	40

VENEZUELAN SUMMER LEAGUE

The Dominican Summer League fielded 29 clubs in 1997, most in its 13-year history. The growing interest in the Caribbean spawned a new summer rookie league, the Venezuelan Summer League, which debuted with six clubs in 1997.

STANDINGS

	W	L	PCT	T	GB
Guacara 2	32	24	.567	4	—
San Joaquin 2	30	27	.525	3	2½
Maracay 2	30	28	.517	2	3
Maracay 1	28	27	.508	5	3½
San Joaquin 1	25	32	.442	3	7½
Guacara 1	24	31	.442	5	7½

PLAYOFFS: None.

INDIVIDUAL BATTING LEADERS

(Minimum 115 At-Bats)

	AVG	AB	R	H	2B	3B	HR	RBI	SB
Martinez, Victor, Mar. 1	.344	122	21	42	12	0	0	26	6
Salinas, Yilbert, Guacara 1	.338	130	21	44	4	0	7	22	1
Cornieles, Jefry, Mar. 2	.326	129	29	42	5	2	0	13	15
Villero, Armando, Gua. 2	.314	118	14	37	7	0	0	10	7
Ortega, Jose, SJ 2	.317	139	15	44	10	0	3	17	2
Hernandez, Orlando, Mar. 2	.297	158	23	47	4	6	1	29	6
Agly, Daniel, San Joaq. 1	.297	148	13	44	15	1	3	22	1
Jadagui, Carlos, SJ 2	.294	126	18	37	8	2	2	22	2

INDIVIDUAL PITCHING LEADERS

(Minimum 50 Innings)

	W	L	ERA	G	SV	IP	H	BB	SO
Rondon, Gabriel, Gua. 2	6	3	1.13	14	0	56	50	10	44
Gomez, Dio, Guacara 1	3	3	1.28	12	0	56	42	14	39
Mendez, Rafael, Guacara 2	6	2	1.81	13	1	60	44	27	36
Urdaneta, Lino, SJ 2	6	3	2.04	13	0	62	46	21	37

Winter Baseball

Dominican Republic's Aguilas proves players, not names, win baseball games

BY JOHN ROYSTER

If at first you don't succeed . . . try again with fewer resources?

Well, it's worked at least once. Aguilas of the Dominican Republic won the 1997 Caribbean World Series with a team of no-names, a year after it fielded a club laden with major leaguers and went 2-4 in the round-robin event.

LARRY GOREN
Tony Batista

The story actually goes back to 1995, when the Series was held in Puerto Rico and the San Juan Senators stormed to the title with a dream team lineup composed of players like Roberto Alomar, Carlos Baerga, Juan Gonzalez and Edgar Martinez.

Determined to even the score, the Dominicans fielded a similar all-star team when the Series shifted to their country in '96. But a lineup that included such major league stars as Julio Franco, Pedro Martinez, Jose Mesa and Raul Mondesi fell on its face.

The 1997 Aguilas team, featuring lesser lights such as Athletics shortstop Tony Batista and Red Sox outfielder Jesus Tavarez, almost met a similar fate in the Series, held in Hermosillo, Mexico. It lost its first two round-robin games before winning its last four and the title.

"No one gave us much of a chance coming in, and even less of one after the first two losses," said manager Mike Quade (Athletics), whose team was outscored 14-4 in its first two games. "This team took it on the chin but fought back. I'm proud of these guys and the way they overcame the adversity."

Aguilas beat Culiacan of Mexico, the defending champion, 4-3 in the title game. Batista, who had a tournament-high 13 RBIs, hit a three-run homer in the first inning, and Aguilas added another run in the sixth. It then held off a Culiacan rally that included an eighth-inning, two-run homer by tournament MVP Matt Stark.

MORRIS FOSTOFF
Matt Stark

"After the disappointments of the last two years, this tastes really sweet, especially since no one thought we had a chance," said Aguilas outfielder Luis Polonia.

With the Mexican team playing, the final game attracted an overflow crowd of 16,000 at Hector Espino Stadium, plus thousands more who didn't have tickets and tried to force their way in anyway. The onslaught forced police to lock the gates shortly after the start of the game, and hundreds of fans who did have tickets didn't get in until the seventh inning.

The tournament featured lots of home runs and high scores. The homers by Batista and Stark were the 47th and 48th of the 12-game tournament, breaking the record of 46. The old mark was set in 1990 in Miami's Orange Bowl, a football stadium with a ridiculously short, makeshift left-field fence. Stark hit four homers in six games.

The Puerto Rican entry, Mayaguez, became an early favorite when it won its first two games. The Indians had a pitching staff that featured seven major leaguers but even that well-fortified staff couldn't stem the tide of offense, and bullpen failures contributed heavily to a 2-4 last-place showing.

Culiacan and Magallanes of Venezuela each went 3-3 to tie for second.

1997 CARIBBEAN WORLD SERIES

Hermosillo, Mexico
Feb. 4-9, 1997

ROUND-ROBIN STANDINGS	W	L	PCT	GB
Dominican Republic (Aguilas)	4	2	.667	—
Mexico (Culiacan)	3	3	.500	1
Venezuela (Magallanes)	3	3	.500	1
Puerto Rico (Mayaguez)	2	4	.333	2

INDIVIDUAL BATTING LEADERS

(Minimum 16 Plate Appearances)

	AVG	AB	R	H	2B	3B	HR	RBI
Abreu, Bob, Venezuela	.588	17	5	10	2	0	1	5
Magallanes, Ever, Mexico	.526	19	7	10	0	0	1	2
Offerman, Jose, DR	.480	25	9	12	0	1	0	2
Sojo, Luis, Venezuela	.478	23	10	11	3	0	1	6
Tavarez, Jesus, DR	.421	19	10	8	0	0	0	0
Espinoza, Alvaro, Ven	.409	22	5	9	2	0	1	2
Hamelin, Bob, PR	.400	15	3	6	1	0	2	6
Batista, Tony, DR	.385	26	6	10	2	0	2	13
Alfonzo, Edgardo, Ven	.357	28	3	10	0	0	1	6
Garcia, Guillermo, DR	.348	23	3	8	2	0	3	8

INDIVIDUAL PITCHING LEADERS

(Minimum 5 Innings)

	W	L	ERA	G	SV	IP	H	BB	SO
Garcia, Ramon, Ven	1	0	0.00	1	0	8	6	2	6
Miranda, Julio, Mexico	1	0	0.00	4	0	5	3	1	3
Hernandez, Elvin, DR	0	0	1.29	2	0	7	3	3	3
Beltran, Rigo, Mexico	0	0	1.59	1	0	6	6	3	3
Heredia, Felix, DR	1	0	1.69	3	0	5	2	1	7
Rosado, Jose, PR	1	0	2.70	2	0	10	9	7	9
Hernandez, Martin, Mexico	1	1	3.18	2	0	11	12	4	2
Sirotka, Mike, DR	1	0	3.60	1	0	5	3	3	6
Higuera, Ted, Mexico	1	0	4.05	1	0	7	3	6	8
Parra, Jose, DR	0	1	5.40	2	0	8	9	6	11
Hernandez, Fernando, DR	0	0	5.40	2	0	5	9	1	3

ALL-TOURNAMENT TEAM: C—Guillermo Garcia, Dominican Republic. **1B**—Luis Raven, Venezuela. **2B**—Ever Magallanes, Mexico. **3B**—Edgardo Alfonso, Venezuela. **SS**—Luis Sojo, Venezuela. **OF**—Bob Abreu, Venezuela; Luis Garcia, Mexico; Armando Rios, Puerto Rico. **DH**—Matt Stark, Mexico. **P**—Ramon Garcia, Venezuela; Ted Higuera, Mexico.

Most Valuable Player—Matt Stark, Mexico.

1996-97 WINTER ALL-STAR TEAM

Selected by Baseball America

	Player, Club (League)	Organization	AVG	AB	R	H	2B	3B	HR	RBI	SB
C	Ivan Rodriguez, Caguas (Puerto Rico)	Rangers	.273	132	18	36	10	1	2	15	3
1B	Roberto Alomar, San Juan (Puerto Rico)	Orioles	.316	215	50	68	15	1	10	36	9
2B	Wilton Guerrero, Azucareros (Dom. Republic)	Dodgers	.336	214	28	72	7	5	0	20	10
3B	Kevin Orie, Phoenix (Arizona)	Cubs	.338	142	25	48	12	1	6	30	0
SS	Tony Batista, Aguilas (Dom. Republic)	Athletics	.320	244	33	78	15	0	8	45	4
OF	Darryl Brinkley, Mexicali (Mexico)	Padres	.339	339	56	115	15	3	7	40	33
	Richard Hidalgo, Magallanes (Venezuela)	Astros	.300	280	45	84	22	2	5	43	4
	Bubba Trammell, Peoria (Arizona)	Tigers	.328	177	30	58	11	2	7	41	2
DH	Brad Fullmer, Honolulu (Hawaii)	Expos	.333	177	37	59	12	3	6	41	3

	Player, Club (League)	Organization	W	L	ERA	G	SV	IP	H	BB	SO
P	Bartolo Colon, Aguilas (Dom. Republic)	Indians	6	1	0.89	14	0	61	41	21	57
	Omar Daal, Caracas (Venezuela)	Expos	10	5	1.77	18	0	127	100	31	89
	Marty Janzen, Lara (Venezuela)	Blue Jays	5	2	1.44	14	0	81	54	28	55
	Dan Hubbs, Azucareros (Dom. Republic)	Dodgers	9	0	1.66	17	0	87	71	15	58
RP	Oscar Henriquez, Magallanes (Venezuela)	Astros	3	2	2.25	36	16	40	22	16	40

PLAYER OF THE YEAR: Bartolo Colon, Aguilas (Dominican Republic).
MANAGER OF THE YEAR: Mike Quade, Aguilas (Dominican Republic).

Statistics include regular season, playoff and Caribbean World Series games.

PUERTO RICAN LEAGUE

It's a wonder the Puerto Rican League was ever able to crown one champion in 1996-97, what with all those ties everywhere.

Mayaguez and Santurce tied for the regular season championship. Arecibo and San Juan tied for fourth place and had to play an extra game to determine the fourth and final playoff entrant.

Mayaguez ended the madness in the playoffs, sweeping third-place Caguas in the semifinals and defeating San Juan in the finals.

First baseman Bob Hamelin (Tigers) was Mayaguez' hero in the finals, winning two games and tying another with clutch hits. The Indians' real strength was a deep bullpen fronted by Roberto Hernandez (White Sox) and Brian Bevil (Royals). But the bullpen faltered in the Caribbean Series, blowing two leads as Mayaguez went a disappointing 2-4.

Roberto Alomar

San Juan second baseman Roberto Alomar (Orioles) won his second straight league batting title and was a key player in the one-game playoff against Arecibo. His two-run homer in the first inning lifted the Senators to a 5-0 win.

First baseman Hector Villanueva powered Caguas into the playoffs with a league-leading 11 home runs. After a slow start with Santurce, he was traded to Caguas and promptly won his first game for the Criollos with a home run. That started a 10-game winning streak that moved the team from last place to first place.

Statistics in **boldface** indicate league leader.
#Indicates league leader but non-qualifier.

STANDINGS

REGULAR SEASON	W	L	PCT	GB
Santurce Crabbers	28	22	.560	—
Mayaguez Indians	28	22	.560	—
Caguas Criollos	27	23	.540	1
*San Juan Senators	26	25	.510	2½
Arecibo Wolves	25	26	.490	3½
Ponce Lions	17	33	.340	11

*Won one-game playoff

PLAYOFFS—Semifinals: Mayaguez defeated Caguas 4-0; San Juan defeated Santurce 4-0 in best-of-7 series. Finals: Mayaguez defeated San Juan 5-3 in best-of-9 series.

INDIVIDUAL BATTING LEADERS
(Minimum 146 Plate Appearances)

	AVG	AB	R	H	2B	3B	HR	RBI	SB
Alomar, Roberto, San Juan	**.347**	144	36	50	13	1	7	24	4
Garcia, Omar, Arecibo	.324	170	21	55	11	1	5	22	0
Vargas, Hector, Arecibo	.313	147	19	46	1	1	0	11	0
Rodriguez, Victor, Ponce	.312	170	14	53	3	2	0	13	5
Johnson, Russ, Santurce	.302	182	24	55	11	**3**	3	32	4
Glanville, Doug, Mayaguez	.289	194	31	**56**	4	**3**	2	18	8
Ledee, Ricky, San Juan	.287	136	19	39	2	**3**	7	24	3
Benitez, Yamil, Caguas	.284	183	26	52	**16**	1	4	31	4
Gomez, Leo, Santurce	.284	141	24	40	12	0	10	32	0
Crespo, Felipe, Caguas	.280	168	25	47	11	1	4	18	5
Hernandez, Jose, May.	.279	201	32	**56**	15	**3**	3	30	18
Vidro, Jose, Ponce	.265	166	16	44	9	0	5	28	1
McCracken, Quinton, SJ	.262	210	28	55	11	0	0	16	10
Rios, Armando, Mayaguez	.260	127	25	33	6	1	4	17	6
Valdes, Pedro, San Juan	.258	182	26	47	10	1	6	29	1
Jennings, Robin, Mayaguez	.252	147	16	37	5	0	2	17	2
Villanueva, Hector, San.-Cag.	.250	192	31	48	5	0	**11**	**35**	2
Mouton, James, Santurce	.250	180	**36**	45	9	0	0	14	**20**
Correa, Miguel, Ponce	.249	185	21	46	8	2	2	13	4
Munoz, Jose, Santurce	.249	173	26	43	8	0	1	12	10
Munoz, Pedro, Mayaguez	.245	155	14	38	9	0	2	21	0
Cruz, Jose, Santurce	.238	164	32	39	10	2	10	**35**	4
Diaz, Alex, Mayaguez	.235	136	17	32	4	1	4	19	10
Baez, Kevin, Caguas	.235	166	21	39	11	1	1	21	0
Rivera, Luis, Ponce-SJ	.235	132	15	31	7	1	2	12	0

INDIVIDUAL PITCHING LEADERS
(Minimum 43 Innings)

	W	L	ERA	G	SV	IP	H	BB	SO
Montalvo, Rafael, San Juan	**7**	1	**2.00**	16	0	67	59	18	16
Holt, Chris, Santurce	6	0	2.17	8	0	50	38	18	21
#Mahomes, Pat, Caguas	2	1	2.37	25	**15**	30	24	17	19
Patrick, Bronswell, Santurce	4	1	2.41	11	1	67	53	28	32
Gunderson, Eric, San Juan	5	2	2.56	15	0	70	69	15	41
Pace, Scotty, Caguas	2	2	2.70	17	1	47	45	21	13
Valera, Julio, Mayaguez	4	1	2.75	13	0	72	68	20	**42**

	W	L	ERA	G	SV	IP	H	BB	SO
Calero, Enrique, Mayaguez	2	1	2.87	13	0	47	43	16	33
Myers, Rodney, Mayaguez	3	3	2.89	8	0	44	42	19	19
Oliveras, Francisco, Caguas	5	3	2.97	13	0	73	62	25	28
Mendoza, Reynol, Ponce	0	6	3.53	11	0	64	66	28	36
Simons, Doug, San.-Ponce	3	3	3.74	11	0	53	58	21	22
Lorraine, Andrew, Santurce	4	3	3.90	10	0	58	58	14	32
Gandarillas, Gus, San Juan	5	4	3.91	13	0	69	62	30	25
Dunbar, Matt, San Juan	2	5	4.03	11	0	58	54	22	41
Orellano, Rafael, Caguas	3	3	4.29	10	0	57	49	21	32

DOMINICAN LEAGUE

Aguilas means Eagles in English, and the team with that name soared through the 1996-97 Dominican League season.

Santiago-based Aguilas won the league's regular season title, finished first in the round-robin playoff semifinals and then swept Escogido in the playoff finals.

Along the way, righthander Bartolo Colon (Indians) broke the league record for lowest ERA at 0.21, erasing the mark of Art Murray, who had a 0.57 ERA in 1955-56, the league's first season.

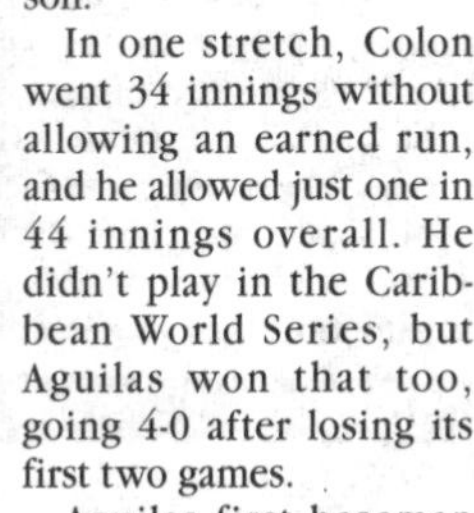

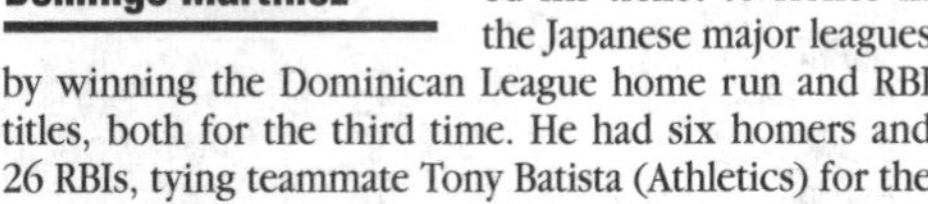

Domingo Martinez

In one stretch, Colon went 34 innings without allowing an earned run, and he allowed just one in 44 innings overall. He didn't play in the Caribbean World Series, but Aguilas won that too, going 4-0 after losing its first two games.

Aguilas first baseman Domingo Martinez punched his ticket to riches in the Japanese major leagues by winning the Dominican League home run and RBI titles, both for the third time. He had six homers and 26 RBIs, tying teammate Tony Batista (Athletics) for the latter honor. Batista was named league MVP.

Escogido reached the playoff finals after tying Azucareros for second place in the round robin, each with a 9-9 record. Escogido won a one-game playoff 7-2 in 14 innings. Outfielder Rudy Pemberton (Red Sox) keyed the rally with a three-run homer.

The season marked the entry of an expansion team, the Northeast Giants, based in San Francisco de Macoris. The new club gave the league six teams, and it managed to avoid last place in its first year, finishing fifth at 20-28.

STANDINGS

REGULAR SEASON	W	L	PCT	GB
Aguilas	32	16	.667	—
Escogido Lions	28	21	.571	4½
Azucareros	28	22	.560	5
Licey Tigers	25	23	.521	7
Northeast Giants	20	28	.417	12
Estrellas	13	36	.265	19½
PLAYOFFS	**W**	**L**	**PCT**	**GB**
Aguilas	12	6	.667	—
*Escogido	9	9	.500	3
Azucareros	9	9	.500	3
Licey	6	12	.333	6

*Won one-game playoff

Championship series: Aguilas defeated Escogido 4-0 in best-of-7 series.

INDIVIDUAL BATTING LEADERS

(Minimum 135 Plate Appearances)

	AVG	AB	R	H	2B	3B	HR	RBI	SB
Guerrero, Wilton, Azu	**.340**	153	21	**52**	6	**4**	0	16	9
Pemberton, Rudy, Esc.	.331	133	24	44	8	1	2	13	2
Cruz, Fausto, Northeast	.305	154	**28**	47	10	3	2	12	3
Batista, Tony, Aguilas	.295	156	22	46	**11**	0	4	**26**	2
Oliva, Jose, Estrellas	.286	126	16	36	10	0	5	25	0
Zinter, Alan, Northeast	.281	135	21	38	**11**	0	4	19	0
Garcia, Guillermo, Aguilas	.278	133	12	37	8	0	1	17	0
Herrera, Jose, Escogido	.274	146	24	40	6	2	4	20	4
Veras, Quilvio, Escogido	.273	121	21	33	5	2	1	19	5
Martinez, Manny, Licey	.270	126	21	34	10	1	0	9	7
Lee, Derek, Escogido	.257	144	17	37	7	0	3	20	2
Arias, Alex, Aguilas	.256	125	18	32	5	0	1	10	11
Pena, Geronimo, Licey	.255	137	20	35	4	1	3	20	1
Alexander, Manny, Estrellas	.252	131	19	33	4	1	1	9	9
Mercedes, Luis, Estrellas	.250	128	8	32	4	0	1	12	1
Tavarez, Jesus, Aguilas	.246	142	16	35	3	2	0	13	**18**
Felix, Junior, Azucareros	.243	140	17	34	8	0	2	18	0
Martinez, Domingo, Aguilas	.241	141	14	34	9	0	**6**	**26**	1
De la Cruz, Lorenzo, NE	.240	129	18	31	7	1	5	18	0
Tejada, Miguel, Aguilas	.237	135	14	32	3	2	3	21	4
Cedeno, Domingo, Azu	.235	136	14	32	3	**4**	0	10	2
Williams, Gerald, Estrellas	.233	129	16	30	4	1	2	7	6
#Bell, Juan, Azucareros	.225	151	17	34	**11**	0	2	16	2

INDIVIDUAL PITCHING LEADERS

(Minimum 40 Innings)

	W	L	ERA	G	SV	IP	H	BB	SO
Colon, Bartolo, Aguilas	4	1	**0.21**	10	0	44	24	16	39
Park, Chan Ho, Azucareros	2	2	1.35	8	0	40	27	18	32
Macey, Fausto, Escogido	2	1	1.39	10	0	45	40	12	34
Hubbs, Dan, Azucareros	**6**	0	1.94	13	0	60	54	11	43
Stull, Everett, Estrellas	2	4	1.94	10	0	56	35	26	**44**
Hollins, Stacy, Aguilas	5	1	2.00	9	0	45	38	22	25
Sirotka, Mike, Escogido	4	1	2.14	11	0	55	46	12	42
Brunson, Will, Azucareros	4	0	2.52	11	0	61	62	13	36
Torres, Salomon, Licey	3	2	2.98	9	0	48	50	17	30
Mercedes, Jose, Estrellas	1	4	3.12	11	0	58	62	16	28
Parra, Jose, Aguilas	4	3	3.23	10	0	47	49	15	33
Castillo, Marino, Northeast	5	1	3.59	13	1	48	43	17	34
Valdez, Efrain, Northeast	3	4	3.70	10	0	56	58	15	22
#Heredia, Felix, Escogido	1	1	4.35	21	**11**	21	15	4	19

VENEZUELAN LEAGUE

The Venezuelan League's two Caracas-based teams, the Caracas Lions and Magallanes Navigators, were on a collision course all season.

Magallanes finished one game ahead of Caracas for the regular season title in the Eastern Division, and the teams tied for first place in the round-robin playoff semifinals. The last team standing was Magallanes, which won the league title by beating the Lions in a final series that consistently drew large crowds.

Lara infielder Luis Sojo (Yankees) broke the record for hits in the playoffs, and his team didn't even advance to the finals. Sojo, a four-time league batting champion, went 27-for-66 in the round robin. Lara catcher Creighton Gubanich (Athletics) had five playoff home runs.

RODGER WOOD

Magglio Ordonez

Lara and Aragua finished 1-2 in the Western Division regular season race. Oriente and Zulia finished the regular season in a tie for the fifth (wild card) playoff spot, necessitating a one-game playoff. The game proved to be anticlimactic, as Oriente jumped to a 6-0 lead in the first inning and won 14-1.

Oriente, which finished a distant third to Caracas and Magallanes in the Eastern Division, featured the league MVP, outfielder Magglio Ordonez (White Sox). He won two-thirds of a triple crown, leading the league in home runs (seven) and RBIs (32). He went on to an equally fine season with Triple-A Nashville and finished the year in the big leagues.

Caracas lefty Omar Daal (Expos) was the league's best pitcher, winning nine regular season games in 12 starts.

STANDINGS

EAST	W	L	PCT	GB
Magallanes Navigators	33	17	.660	—
Caracas Lions	32	18	.640	1
*Oriente Caribbeans	25	28	.472	9½
La Guaira Sharks	16	34	.320	17
WEST	**W**	**L**	**PCT**	**GB**
Lara Cardinals	31	21	.596	—
Aragua Tigers	26	24	.520	4
Zulia Eagles	24	29	.453	7½
Occidente Pastora	18	34	.346	13

*Won one-game playoff

PLAYOFFS	W	L	PCT	GB
Caracas	12	4	.750	—
Magallanes	12	4	.750	—
Lara	9	7	.563	3
Oriente	4	12	.250	8
Aragua	3	13	.188	9

Championship Series: Magallanes defeated Caracas 4-1 in best-of-seven series.

INDIVIDUAL BATTING LEADERS

(Minimum 151 Plate Appearances)

	AVG	AB	R	H	2B	3B	HR	RBI	SB
Wilson, Desi, Occidente	**.349**	152	14	53	3	**3**	3	21	5
Alfonzo, Edgardo, Mag.	.340	156	24	53	10	1	1	23	3
Benard, Marvin, Magallanes	.313	134	30	42	9	0	2	24	12
Azocar, Oscar, Aragua	.305	154	23	47	7	2	0	21	0
Norman, Les, Oriente	.305	187	27	57	6	1	2	20	2
Centeno, Henri, Oriente	.304	135	19	41	5	0	1	18	0
Ordonez, Magglio, Oriente	.295	193	31	**57**	12	0	**7**	**32**	1
Amaro, Ruben, Zulia	.294	126	21	37	4	1	0	18	7
Perez, Robert, Lara	.293	191	**34**	56	8	1	5	22	4
Tinoco, Luis, Occidente	.288	132	9	38	4	0	1	14	3
Saffer, Jon, LaGuaira	.288	139	17	40	9	2	1	17	3
Ramirez, Alex, Lara	.286	147	10	42	6	2	1	23	2
Nava, Lipso, Zulia	.283	191	23	54	11	2	2	17	3
Abreu, Bob, Caracas	.282	156	33	44	10	2	1	26	9
Cedeno, Roger, Caracas	.282	156	27	44	6	2	0	11	**13**
Lewis, T.R., Caracas	.277	155	**34**	43	11	1	0	18	8
Hidalgo, Richard, Mag.	.276	181	30	50	**14**	2	3	28	2
Munoz, Orlando, Zulia	.265	147	19	39	2	0	0	12	5
Machado, Robert, Occidente	.265	170	12	45	13	1	3	17	3
Mendez, Jesus, Aragua	.265	155	14	41	6	0	0	13	0
Owens, Eric, Zulia	.261	176	24	46	6	2	4	17	8
Petagine, Roberto, Caracas	.254	118	22	30	7	0	1	19	0
#Cairo, Miguel, Lara	.230	187	20	43	4	2	0	12	**13**
#Rodriguez, Liu, Caracas	.211	133	16	28	2	**3**	0	15	4

INDIVIDUAL PITCHING LEADERS

(Minimum 45 Innings)

	W	L	ERA	G	SV	IP	H	BB	SO
Janzen, Marty, Lara	5	2	**1.40**	11	0	71	47	22	52
Daal, Omar, Caracas	**9**	1	1.49	12	0	84	68	21	64
Estrada, Horacio, Oriente	2	5	1.88	14	0	77	56	33	**66**
Pulido, Carlos, Magallanes	7	2	1.92	10	0	66	45	23	35
Whitten, Casey, Oriente	7	1	1.95	12	0	69	53	30	49
Garcia, Ramon, Magallanes	3	1	2.00	10	0	63	58	15	54
Armas, Antonio, Oriente	2	3	2.10	11	0	51	34	31	29
Herges, Matt, Caracas	3	2	2.14	14	1	59	54	28	40
Carrara, Giovanni, Lara	5	2	2.26	10	0	64	59	15	44
Villa, Jose, Occidente	4	2	2.60	22	1	52	45	21	38
Hurtado, Edwin, Lara	4	5	2.67	16	0	57	55	22	35
Lopez, Johan, Caracas	4	1	2.83	13	0	64	56	23	32
Haynes, Heath, Zulia	5	2	2.84	12	0	70	61	16	49
Jones, Bobby, LaGuaira	2	5	2.88	12	0	66	58	35	44
#Robinson, Ken, Lara	1	1	2.93	27	**12**	30	24	9	24

MEXICAN PACIFIC LEAGUE

Culiacan went just 16-16 in the first half of the Mexican Pacific League's split season, but dominated the league from that point on.

The Tomato Growers, who had won the Caribbean World Series the previous year, went 22-8 in the second half. They then beat Obregon, Los Mochis and Hermosillo in the playoffs and went all the way to the final game of the Caribbean Series again, this time losing to Aguilas of the Dominican Republic.

The team's top winner was former Anaheim Angels righthander Scott Lewis, who went 5-2 with a 1.94 ERA and won a memorable 13-inning game against Guasave. Lewis pitched 12 scoreless innings, allowing six hits. He won 1-0 when shortstop Benji Gil (Rangers) homered in the top of the 13th. Mercifully, Julio Cesar Miranda pitched the bottom of the 13th and picked up a save.

Hermosillo won the first-half title behind the hitting of first baseman Jose Tolentino, who finished the regular season with 22 doubles in just 217 at-bats. But the finals loss to Culiacan, in six games of a best-of-7 series, denied the Orange Growers a chance to play in the Caribbean Series on their home field.

Mexicali outfielder Darryl Brinkley (Padres), the 1996 Caribbean Series MVP for Culiacan, won the '97 batting title with a .369 average.

STANDINGS

REGULAR SEASON	W	L	PCT	GB
Aguilas	32	16	.667	—
Escogido Lions	28	21	.571	4½
Azucareros	28	22	.560	5
Licey Tigers	25	23	.521	7
Northeast Giants	20	28	.417	12
Estrellas	13	36	.265	19½
PLAYOFFS	**W**	**L**	**PCT**	**GB**
Aguilas	12	6	.667	—
*Escogido	9	9	.500	3
Azucareros	9	9	.500	3
Licey	6	12	.333	6

*Won one-game playoff

Championship Series: Aguilas defeated Escogido, 4-0, in best-of-7 series.

INDIVIDUAL BATTING LEADERS

(Minimum 138 Plate Appearances)

	AVG	AB	R	H	2B	3B	HR	RBI	SB
Brinkley, Darryl, Mexicali	**.369**	244	37	**90**	11	1	5	28	23
Riley, Marquis, Culiacan	.343	137	28	47	7	1	0	3	20
Tolentino, Jose, Herm.	.341	217	39	74	**22**	0	7	39	1
Valdez, Mario, Culiacan	.331	142	26	47	9	0	6	27	3
Myers, Rod, Los Mochis	.325	203	39	66	14	0	5	30	28
Tatis, Bernie, Obregon	.315	248	41	78	10	2	6	25	23
Garcia, Cornelio, Herm.	.313	224	40	70	8	2	1	20	17
Proctor, Brian, Mazatlan	.309	149	19	46	11	0	1	24	2
Seitzer, Brad, Guasave	.305	213	32	65	13	0	3	34	1
Valenzuela, Armando, Gua.	.301	153	25	46	4	0	0	8	6
Pough, Pork Chop, Navojoa	.296	152	20	45	8	1	7	30	0
Arredondo, Jesus, LM	.295	112	24	33	4	0	1	13	1
Ojeda, Miguel, Mazatlan	.294	218	24	64	13	1	4	20	2
Castaneda, Rafael, Nav.	.292	168	17	49	6	1	2	19	2
Carrillo, Matias, Mexicali	.291	223	33	65	8	1	8	32	7
Magallanes, Ever, Culiacan	.290	200	19	58	13	0	3	27	3
Garcia, Luis, Hermosillo	.290	221	27	64	13	0	4	32	6
Stairs, Matt, Navojoa	.289	190	29	55	8	0	8	29	2
Ball, Jeff, Hermosillo	.287	181	34	52	6	1	10	31	13
Arredondo, Luis, Hermosillo	.286	140	13	40	3	1	1	13	9
Nixon, Trot, Navojoa	.286	119	22	34	7	0	4	13	1
Sherman, Darrell, Culiacan	.283	166	29	47	4	3	0	7	16
Perez, Francisco, Mazatlan	.282	131	9	37	9	0	2	16	2

Saenz, Ricardo, Hermosillo	.282	124	16	35	6	0	2	22	3
Jimenez, Houston, Mexicali	.279	229	34	64	17	0	5	22	5
#Barron, Tony, Obregon	.275	218	31	60	10	0	**13**	43	6
#Spearman, Vernon, Navojoa	.269	234	38	63	6	1	0	15	**30**
#Martinez, Greg, Guasave	.252	242	40	61	3	**5**	0	13	23
#McDonald, Jason, LM	.247	219	**50**	54	8	0	6	24	29
#Pearson, Eddie, LM	.243	243	27	59	11	1	9	**47**	1
#Jimenez, Eduardo, Mex.	.210	181	36	38	5	0	**13**	41	2

INDIVIDUAL PITCHING LEADERS

(Minimum 41 Innings)

	W	L	ERA	G	SV	IP	H	BB	SO
Palacios, Vicente, Mexicali	5	1	**1.59**	11	0	74	51	32	46
Higuera, Ted, Los Mochis	5	2	1.72	10	0	52	46	26	29
Beatty, Blaine, Mazatlan	**9**	3	1.73	14	0	99	74	34	55
Purata, Julio, Guasave	4	6	1.78	13	0	91	74	54	46
Sauveur, Rich, Culiacan	4	2	1.80	7	0	45	39	15	17
Lewis, Scott, Culiacan	5	2	1.94	13	1	65	42	27	39
#Alvarez, Tavo, Obregon	3	3	2.02	29	16	35	30	27	24
Moore, Marcus, Hermosillo	1	2	2.53	23	1	43	18	38	47
Osuna, Roberto, Hermosillo	2	0	2.63	29	0	41	28	23	17
Reyes, Dennis, Los Mochis	2	5	2.70	**16**	0	80	59	58	48
Esquer, Mercedes, Guasave	6	2	2.92	11	0	74	62	38	45
Elvira, Narciso, Hermosillo	5	0	3.02	11	0	63	53	39	56
Gonzalez, Arturo, Navojoa	4	4	3.02	13	0	83	79	22	35
Moreno, Angel, Hermosillo	5	4	3.08	13	0	76	62	22	50
Rios, Jesus, Guasave	4	2	3.11	15	0	55	54	33	47
Quinones, Enrique, Culiacan	4	4	3.36	12	0	56	54	22	27
#Rodriguez, Raul, Guasave	5	4	3.42	14	0	97	90	39	**80**

AUSTRALIAN LEAGUE

The perennially strong Perth Heat had an unusually good year in 1996-97, dominating the Australian Baseball League from start to finish.

The Heat got off to a 27-5 start, cruised to the regular season title and took the playoff championship by beating the Brisbane Bandits 2-1 in a best-of-3 series.

Perhaps the most surprising thing was that Perth's finals opponent won a game. The Bandits took the second game 6-4, but self-destructed in the third and deciding game, committing seven errors in a 9-5 Perth win.

Star Milwaukee Brewers outfielder David Nilsson guided the Bandits to a playoff berth in his managing debut. The team got off to a poor start, but turned it around with plenty of help from Nilsson himself.

After recovering from knee surgery, Nilsson activated himself as a player at midseason and went 4-for-4 with a home run and a double in his first game.

Adelaide Giants first baseman Craig Watts also had a memorable single-game performance, becoming the first player in league history to hit grand slams in consecutive at-bats. The eight RBIs also were a league record for one game, and all of it came in an 11-1 win over Perth, no less.

STANDINGS

	W	L	PCT	GB
Perth Heat	40	20	.667	—
Adelaide Giants	36	23	.610	3½
Brisbane Bandits	33	27	.550	7
Sydney Blues	32	27	.542	7½
Gold Coast Cougars	31	28	.525	8½
Melbourne Monarchs	28	29	.491	10½
Hunter Eagles	18	40	.310	21
Melbourne Reds	17	41	.293	22

PLAYOFFS—Semifinals: Perth defeated Sydney, 2-0, and Brisbane defeated Adelaide, 2-1, in best-of-3 series. Finals: Perth defeated Brisbane, 2-1, in best-of-3 series.

INDIVIDUAL BATTING LEADERS

(Minimum 135 Plate Appearances)

	AVG	AB	R	H	2B	3B	HR	RBI	SB
Scott, Andrew, Adelaide	**.414**	181	44	**75**	12	1	5	37	12
Tunkin, Scott, Sydney	.385	192	47	74	6	3	10	34	2
Jelks, Greg, Perth	.375	144	48	54	6	2	11	38	4
White, Gary, Sydney	.358	204	35	73	11	0	14	41	3
McDonald, Grant, Brisbane	.354	164	32	58	9	1	6	28	3
Hewitt, Jason, Perth	.350	123	30	43	7	1	3	13	6
Hockey, Lydon, Monarchs	.345	165	21	57	11	0	2	23	1
Johnson, Ron, GC	.332	196	40	65	16	0	16	**63**	1
Jones, Sean, Perth	.329	170	35	56	6	1	12	45	2
Bradley, Chris, Hunter	.329	158	27	52	6	1	9	39	1
Kingman, Brendan, Sydney	.325	194	40	63	13	0	**21**	62	2
Gonzalez, Richard, Bris.	.323	186	41	60	8	1	15	54	4
Everingham, Matt, Sydney	.322	121	24	39	8	0	9	17	2
Butler, Rich, Sydney	.316	215	**58**	68	9	3	14	35	22
Byrne, Clayton, Perth	.316	206	41	65	12	0	15	48	6
Hockey, Jason, GC	.314	137	14	43	11	0	2	28	0
Buckley, Matthew, GC	.313	195	52	61	14	2	10	27	9
Vagg, Richard, Monarchs	.313	160	32	50	9	**5**	3	24	4
#Watts, Craig, Adelaide	.297	202	31	60	**17**	0	11	46	2
#Durrington, Trent, GC	.204	137	29	28	6	1	0	16	**24**

INDIVIDUAL PITCHING LEADERS

(Minimum 40 Innings)

	W	L	ERA	G	SV	IP	H	BB	SO
Bennett, Shayne, Adelaide	7	1	**2.06**	9	0	44	36	9	50
Resz, Greg, Reds	3	4	2.27	8	0	44	42	19	31
Wells, Robert, Perth	6	1	2.36	14	1	42	35	12	23
Wingrove, Leighton, Hunter	5	3	3.19	18	0	42	36	27	27
Spykstra, Dave, Adelaide	4	3	3.30	14	0	63	42	43	73
Reed, Brandon, Brisbane	**9**	6	3.33	17	0	97	95	20	54
Millwood, Kevin, Monarchs	8	5	3.44	16	0	89	72	40	92
Edmondson, Brian, Hunter	5	9	3.55	16	0	96	99	33	57
Challinor, John, Adelaide	8	6	3.65	19	0	69	74	17	45
Walters, Brett, Perth	2	3	3.68	11	0	44	37	22	38
Johnson, Mike, Sydney	8	4	3.69	17	0	105	89	38	**93**
Dale, Phil, Monarchs	**9**	7	3.70	16	0	105	106	16	85
Shepherd, Alvie, Perth	5	0	3.75	10	0	60	53	15	56

ARIZONA FALL LEAGUE

The Arizona Fall League was created to provide a springboard to major league success for young prospects. It sure worked for Kevin Orie.

Orie, playing for the Phoenix Desert Dogs, won the 1996 AFL batting title in the closest race in league history. He batted .3380 to edge Tempe first baseman Randall Simon (Braves), who finished at .3379.

Orie went on to win the Cubs' starting third-base job in spring training and held onto it with a solid if unspectacular 1997 season.

But Orie's Phoenix team finished just 25-25 and didn't win the league championship. That honor went to the Scottsdale Scorpions, who swept the Mesa Saguaros in two games in the playoffs. The Scorpions became the league's fifth different champion in five seasons.

Kevin Orie

Mesa had the strongest team during the regular season, finishing 28-22 and winning 10 straight at one point. Infielders Matt Howard (Yankees) and Donnie Sadler (Red Sox) led a speed-oriented club, with each reaching double figures in stolen bases and finishing in the top 10 in the league in batting.

Scottsdale closer Eric Ludwick (Cardinals) broke the league record for appearances with 29. The old record of 25 was shared by Kevin Rogers (1992) and Tom Wegmann (1993).

STANDINGS

NORTH	W	L	PCT	GB
Scottsdale Scorpions	27	24	.529	—
Peoria Javelinas	25	26	.490	2
Sun Cities Solar Sox	25	26	.490	2
SOUTH	**W**	**L**	**PCT**	**GB**
Mesa Saguaros	29	22	.569	—
Phoenix Desert Dogs	25	26	.490	4
Tempe Rafters	22	29	.429	7

Championship Series: Scottsdale defeated Mesa 2-0 in best-of-3 series.

INDIVIDUAL BATTING LEADERS
(Minimum 138 Plate Appearances)

	AVG	AB	R	H	2B	3B	HR	RBI	SB
Orie, Kevin, Phoenix	**.338**	142	25	48	12	1	6	30	0
Simon, Randall, Tempe	.338	145	17	49	13	1	1	23	3
Trammell, Bubba, Peoria	.328	177	**30**	**58**	11	2	**7**	**41**	2
Smith, Robert, Sun Cities	.325	151	25	49	10	1	6	26	3
Berblinger, Jeff, Scottsdale	.319	135	19	43	10	2	1	13	12
Aven, Bruce, Scottsdale	.316	114	18	36	10	1	5	19	4
Relaford, Desi, Peoria	.302	159	29	48	5	0	2	19	8
Nelson, Bry, Phoenix	.301	146	16	44	9	2	1	10	1
Howard, Matt, Mesa	.299	167	23	50	13	1	1	26	10
Sadler, Donnie, Mesa	.294	119	26	35	4	3	0	12	13
Lee, Derrek, Sun Cities	.292	192	22	56	12	4	2	22	5
Banks, Brian, Sun Cities	.288	153	21	44	8	2	5	20	1
Polcovich, Kevin, Mesa	.285	130	16	37	9	0	1	18	9
Milliard, Ralph, Tempe	.284	148	22	42	5	1	2	14	5
Stovall, DaRond, Mesa	.282	149	**30**	42	7	1	2	19	7
Sagmoen, Marc, Tempe	.282	149	25	42	5	0	5	23	1
McGuire, Ryan, Mesa	.280	132	16	37	4	1	3	20	3
Davis, Tommy, Phoenix	.280	132	13	37	9	0	1	25	1
Bell, Mike, Tempe	.280	161	23	45	12	1	5	23	0
Saunders, Chris, Peoria	.277	184	27	51	12	3	1	22	3
Grieve, Ben, Phoenix	.277	141	20	39	9	0	3	23	0
Ibanez, Raul, Peoria	.272	162	21	44	7	1	1	18	1
Wolff, Mike, Tempe	.265	147	18	39	5	1	4	18	2
Magee, Wendell, Peoria	.261	165	29	43	7	3	5	29	2
Luuloa, Keith, Tempe	.257	144	18	37	6	1	0	13	1
#Cradle, Rickey, Phoenix	.251	171	**30**	43	**14**	1	2	15	4
#Cromer, Brandon, Phx	.250	160	24	40	8	**5**	4	30	1
#Bartee, Kimera, SC	.223	179	23	40	5	**5**	0	14	14

INDIVIDUAL PITCHING LEADERS
(Minimum 41 Innings)

	W	L	ERA	G	SV	IP	H	BB	SO
King, Ray, Sun Cities	**4**	1	**1.90**	13	0	47	41	12	24
Carpenter, Chris, Phoenix	2	0	2.33	10	0	46	30	16	**43**
Meadows, Brian, Tempe	1	3	3.07	10	0	44	43	7	31
#Ludwick, Eric, Scottsdale	2	2	3.19	29	**17**	31	30	11	37
Carter, John, Peoria	1	5	3.27	11	0	44	47	19	28
Clemons, Chris, Tempe	1	2	3.38	10	0	43	42	12	33
Maeda, Katsuhiro, Mesa	2	2	3.40	11	0	50	51	17	35
Bunch, Mel, Sun Cities	3	3	3.40	12	0	42	41	14	41
Thomson, John, Peoria	**4**	1	3.53	11	0	51	37	13	39
Brownson, Mark, Peoria	2	1	3.95	12	1	41	40	7	46
Wright, Jaret, Scottsdale	1	1	4.10	10	0	42	31	26	37
Grzanich, Mike, Phoenix	3	2	4.37	10	0	45	44	13	25
Ray, Ken, Sun Cities	0	4	4.67	14	0	44	46	30	37
Lawrence, Sean, Mesa	1	2	5.36	11	0	49	66	8	34
Pett, Jose, Phoenix	1	4	6.75	11	0	43	55	12	34

HAWAII WINTER BASEBALL

Instead of holding their one-game playoff in 1996, Hawaii Winter Baseball officials could have just shown a videotape from 1995. The result was the same both times.

In both years, the Honolulu Sharks finished the regular season with the league's best record, only to lose to the Maui Stingrays in the playoff. This time the score was 6-4 as Maui took a 4-0 lead and held on.

Increased interest on the part of major league organizations brought the league the best group of prospects in its four-year history. Honolulu outfielder-first baseman Brad Fullmer (Expos) was a top attraction all season. He won the batting title at .333 and broke the league RBI record with 41. He even went 2-for-4 with an RBI in the Sharks' loss in the championship game.

Marlins outfielder and 1996 first-round pick Mark Kotsay concluded a whirlwind year by playing for Maui. He hit just .241 as fatigue set in: He had played all spring for Cal State Fullerton, then for the U.S. Olympic team, and then for 17 games with Class A Kane County.

MORRIS FOSTOFF

Brad Fullmer

The league held an all-star game for the first time, and it was a success at the gate. The attendance of 3,441 at Maui was a single-game league record, and more than a thousand of the fans were in standing room. The game was a nine-inning, 4-4 tie between a mainland team and a team of Asians and players with Hawaii ties.

STANDINGS

OUTRIGGER	W	L	PCT	GB
Honolulu Sharks	36	16	.692	—
West Oahu CaneFires	20	30	.400	15
VOLCANO	**W**	**L**	**PCT**	**GB**
Maui Stingrays	25	24	.510	—
Hilo Stars	19	30	.388	6

Championship Series: Maui defeated Honolulu 6-4 in one-game playoff.

INDIVIDUAL BATTING LEADERS
(Minimum 146 Plate Appearances)

	AVG	AB	R	H	2B	3B	HR	RBI	SB
Fullmer, Brad, Honolulu	**.333**	177	37	**59**	12	3	6	**41**	3
Blum, Geoff, Honolulu	.326	172	32	56	**13**	1	5	33	2
Bokemeier, Matt, WO	.318	179	25	57	7	2	0	16	5
Butler, Brent, Hilo	.310	155	18	48	8	0	1	21	2
Saito, Takayuki, Honolulu	.295	139	28	41	7	**4**	0	14	11
Gazarek, Marty, WO	.279	147	23	41	9	0	5	24	2
Hunter, Scott, Hilo	.275	149	21	41	7	1	2	19	15
Carr, Jeremy, Honolulu	.264	148	**39**	39	4	**4**	2	22	**19**
Rolison, Nate, Maui	.260	154	18	40	**13**	0	5	16	2
Hermansen, Chad, Hon.	.255	161	22	41	4	3	2	29	8
Inaba, Atsunori, West Oahu	.252	151	23	38	11	2	1	21	6
Derosso, Tony, Hilo	.252	151	21	38	10	3	4	29	7
Sanders, Anthony, Maui	.248	157	18	39	6	1	5	23	4
Kapler, Gabe, West Oahu	.247	182	28	45	12	3	**7**	20	4
Asche, Mike, Honolulu	.242	149	23	36	5	2	2	21	7
Kotsay, Mark, Maui	.241	133	21	32	8	3	2	12	7
Clyburn, Danny, Maui	.238	151	22	36	8	3	6	23	4
Johnson, Keith, Maui	.234	171	21	40	12	2	3	13	3
Smith, Matt, Honolulu	.226	137	14	31	7	3	3	18	1
Booty, Josh, Maui	.215	144	15	31	3	1	3	10	1

INDIVIDUAL PITCHING LEADERS
(Minimum 43 Innings)

	W	L	ERA	G	SV	IP	H	BB	SO
Teramae, Masao, Hon.	2	0	**1.50**	13	0	48	27	15	37
Okajima, Hideki, Hon.	**5**	1	2.00	10	0	45	30	17	**46**
Seaver, Mark, Maui	1	4	2.22	10	0	49	39	10	44
Takeuchi, Yoshiya, Hilo	3	0	2.60	10	0	45	47	16	32
Million, Doug, Maui	2	3	3.27	10	0	44	41	20	28
Ortiz, Russ, West Oahu	2	6	3.50	9	0	44	44	22	35
Pincavitch, Kevin, Maui	1	3	3.55	10	1	46	39	31	39
#Speier, Justin, West Oahu	1	2	3.72	18	**10**	19	18	2	16
Riggan, Jerrod, Hilo	0	3	3.74	10	0	43	42	17	40
Beaumont, Matt, Hilo	2	3	4.15	10	0	48	48	12	41

College Baseball

JEFF GOLDEN

Titles keep piling up
Louisiana State wins another College World Series

Louisiana State coach changes with times, brings home third championship in the 90s

BY JOHN MANUEL

If he's anything, Louisiana State coach Skip Bertman is flexible.

When he was an assistant at Miami, Bertman's philosophy was to win games with pitching and defense. He wasn't the type to sit back and wait for three-run homers.

But as the times changed and aluminum bats mutated into weapons of mass destruction, Bertman changed, too. As Louisiana State began its reign of dominance as college baseball's top program, it built its attack around power. Ten trips to Omaha in 12 seasons are enough to validate Bertman's change of heart.

How does he do it?
Skip Bertman

When Louisiana State won its third College World Series title in 1996, the Tigers hit a Southeastern Conference-record 131 home runs. But many of the stars of that team, including CWS hero Warren Morris, were gone.

So Bertman departed from another former tenet of his coaching philosophy.

"We usually center our recruiting around incoming freshmen," Bertman said. "But when we have a chance to get good junior-college talent, we will go that route."

Good junior-college talent? How about a College World Series MVP? How about a starting outfielder and DH, both parts of a catching platoon and the team's best pitcher in Omaha?

The Tigers rode the booming bats of shortstop Brandon Larson, the MVP in Omaha, outfielder Wes Davis, DH Danny Higgins, catchers Clint Earnhart and Conan Horton and the pitching of workhorse righthander Doug Thompson to its fourth national championship in the 1990s.

Larson set a national record for homers by a shortstop and SEC marks for homers and RBIs while hitting .381 with 40 homers and 118 RBIs. In Omaha, he set the tone for Louisiana State's undefeated run by drilling a line-drive shot over the Rosenblatt Stadium scoreboard against Rice righthander Matt Anderson, who became the first overall pick in the draft four days later.

Higgins had three RBIs in the championship game against Alabama, which had defeated Louisiana State in the SEC tournament title game. Davis clubbed 16 homers while Earnhart and Horton combined for 14.

The Tigers hit 188 homers in all in 1997, obliterating the NCAA record of 161 set by Brigham Young in 1988. They homered in each of their 70 games, believed to be an unprecedented accomplishment.

"It's changed a lot in the last five or six years," Bertman said. "Next year, you better get on the power train if you want to compete, at least until they change the alloy in the aluminum bats."

It would also serve teams well to jump on the Juco train. The Tigers weren't the only team in Omaha riding the strength of junior college transfers.

The Crimson Tide made it to the final in Omaha despite the absence of their best player, outfielder-lefthander Robert Vaz. MVP of the 1996 Junior College World Series, Vaz hit .400 with 22 homers for the Tide and went 4-1 with a 3.40 ERA and eight saves to key Alabama to its second consecutive trip to Omaha. Baseball America Coach of the Year Jim Wells fashioned a national contender around players like Vaz and righthander Pete Fischer, a transfer from the University of Maine.

For the second straight year, the Tide was ranked No. 1 by Baseball America going into the CWS. But Vaz broke his left foot when he stepped on a baseball during batting practice at the South II Regional championship game and was on crutches in Omaha.

Alabama's in-state SEC rival, Auburn, returned to Omaha for the second time in four years behind first-team All-American Tim Hudson, also a junior-college transfer. Hudson, an outfielder-righthander, hit .396 with 95 RBIs and was among the national leaders in wins, going 15-2, 2.97.

JEFF GOLDEN

Attracting attention
Brandon Larson

Mississippi State gave Omaha a distinctly Southeastern Conference flavor by also winning a regional, becoming the fourth team in the SEC West to make the trip. Junior lefthander Eric DuBose hurled two complete games in the Mideast Regional to lead the Bulldogs in what turned out to be coach Ron Polk's final season.

Double Trouble

Hudson and Vaz were the most visible two-way stars in college baseball in 1997, but the landscape was littered with an astonishing number of players who excelled at the plate and on the mound.

Florida's Brad Wilkerson was a third-team All-American in 1996 as a freshman and had an even better season in 1997, but his overall productivity left him a notch or two behind Hudson and Vaz.

The sophomore lefthander emerged as the Gators' best starting pitcher, going 9-4 with a 4.44 ERA and 89 strikeouts in 79 innings. At the plate, he continued to be coach Andy Lopez' top threat, setting a school record for home runs (23) while hitting .386.

Santa Clara senior Mike Frank, the West Coast Conference Player of the Year, led the Broncos within two wins of Omaha. Frank, a lefthander-outfielder, hit .405 with 80 RBIs while going 11-0 on the mound.

First baseman Lance Berkman and Anderson led Rice to its first CWS berth ever. While Anderson was the dominant closer in the country, Berkman drew headlines for his Mark McGwire-esque assault on one of college baseball's top records.

COLLEGE WORLD SERIES

Omaha, Nebraska
May 30-June 7, 1997

STANDINGS

BRACKET ONE	W	L	RF	RA
Louisiana State	4	0	41	24
Stanford	2	2	33	30
Auburn	1	2	17	20
Rice	0	2	5	15

Bracket One Final: Louisiana State 13, Stanford 9

BRACKET TWO	W	L	RF	RA
Alabama	4	2	35	34
Miami	2	2	21	20
Mississippi State	1	2	14	17
UCLA	0	2	8	14

Bracket Two Final: Alabama 8, Miami 2

CHAMPIONSHIP GAME: Louisiana State 13, Alabama 6

INDIVIDUAL BATTING LEADERS

(Minimum 12 At-Bats)

	AVG	AB	R	H	2B	3B	HR	RBI	SB
Bernhardt, Tom, LSU	.615	13	5	8	2	0	1	5	0
Pecci, Jay, Stanford	.588	17	6	10	0	0	0	3	0
Caruso, Joe, Alabama	.560	25	4	14	4	1	1	5	1
Furniss, Eddy, LSU	.533	15	8	8	1	0	1	4	0
Muth, Edmund, Stanford	.444	18	4	8	1	0	0	4	0
Michaels, Jason, Miami	.412	17	3	7	1	0	1	2	2
Koerner, Mike, LSU	.389	18	6	7	2	0	2	8	2
Gall, John, Stanford	.375	16	1	6	1	0	0	1	0
Lopez-Cao, Mike, Miami	.375	16	2	6	1	0	1	4	0
Larson, Brandon, LSU	.368	19	6	7	0	0	3	8	1

INDIVIDUAL PITCHING LEADERS

(Minimum 7 Innings)

	W	L	ERA	G	SV	IP	H	BB	SO
Austin, Jeff, Stanford	1	0	0.00	2	1	10	8	2	10
Reyes, Eddy, Miami	0	0	0.00	3	1	8	5	2	8
Kingrey, Jarrod, Alabama	2	0	1.38	4	1	13	12	9	10
Arteaga, J.D., Miami	0	1	3.18	2	0	11	15	2	7
DuBose, Eric, Miss. State	0	1	3.38	1	0	8	11	4	3

ALL-TOURNAMENT TEAM

C—Matt Frick, Alabama. **1B**—Eddy Furniss, Louisiana State. **2B**—Joe Caruso, Alabama. **3B**—Andy Phillips, Alabama. **SS**—Brandon Larson, Louisiana State. **OF**—Tom Bernhardt, Louisiana State; G.W. Keller, Alabama; Mike Koerner, Louisiana State. **DH**—Mark Peer, Alabama. **P**—Jeff Austin, Stanford; Jarrod Kingrey, Alabama.

Most Outstanding Player—Brandon Larson, ss, Louisiana State.

CHAMPIONSHIP GAME

Tigers 13, Crimson Tide 6

ALABAMA	ab	r	h	bi
Tidwell cf	5	2	2	0
Caruso 2b	4	1	3	4
Phillips 3b	5	0	1	0
Mohr rf	4	0	1	0
Keller lf	4	1	0	0
Frick c	5	1	1	0
Tucker 1b	4	0	1	2
Peer dh	4	1	1	0
Duncan ss	4	0	1	0
Totals	39	6	11	6

LSU	ab	r	h	bi
Higgins dh	4	1	2	3
Barbier 2b	5	1	1	0
Larson ss	6	1	2	3
Furniss 1b	5	1	3	0
Koerner cf	6	2	2	1
McClure 3b	3	1	0	0
Bernhardt rf	4	3	3	3
Witten rf	0	0	0	0
Davis lf	4	1	1	3
Earnhart c	2	0	0	0
Horton c	1	2	1	0
Totals	40	13	15	13

Alabama	002 200 020— 6
Louisiana State	630 002 11x—13

E—Caruso (10), Duncan (19), Henderson (3), McClure (4). **DP**—Alabama 1, Louisiana State 1. **LOB**—Alabama 9, Louisiana State 13. **2B**—Caruso (21), Phillips (25), Tucker (13), Peer (12), Bernhardt (7), Davis (7). **HR**—Caruso (15), Higgins (11), Bernhardt (17). **SB**—Caruso (13).

ALABAMA	ip	h	r	er	bb	so
Daniel L	⅔	5	5	4	0	0
Kingrey	3⅔	5	4	0	6	4
Henderson	2⅔	4	3	2	1	4
Hurst	1⅓	1	1	1	2	2

LSU	ip	h	r	er	bb	so
Coogan	4⅓	6	4	4	1	8
Thompson W	4⅓	5	2	2	1	7

WP—Coogan 3, Thompson. **PB**—Earnhart, Horton. **HBP**—Keller (by Coogan), McClure (by Henderson). **T**—3:15. **A**—24,401.

College Baseball

Berkman hit 41 homers, leaving him seven homers short of the record-setting 48 hit by Oklahoma State's Pete Incaviglia in 1985. Berkman also led the nation with 134 RBIs, second only to Incaviglia's 143.

In 1996, Louisiana State's Eddy Furniss, Illinois' Josh Klimek and Georgia Southern's Tommy Peterman shared the national lead with 26 home runs. In 1997, no fewer than 14 players equaled or bettered that mark.

Florida State's J.D. Drew, Baseball America's Player of the Year, hit 31 homers and stole 30 bases, becoming the first college player ever to reach the 30-30 plateau. Drew followed Anderson in the draft, going second overall to Philadelphia.

Other hitting feats:

■ Fordham senior outfielder Mike Marchiano, who attended the Bronx school on a football scholarship, turned to baseball as a sophomore and turned into a monster. After flirting with a .500 average for much of the 1997 season, Marchiano finished first in the nation in batting at .493 and added 29 homers and 85 RBIs.

■ Cal State Northridge shortstop Adam Kennedy had to settle for second in the batting race to Marchiano. Kennedy hit .482 with 26 homers and 99 RBIs and led the nation in hits (134) for the second consecutive year. Kennedy was drafted in the first round by the St. Louis Cardinals.

■ Hitting streaks popped up with numbing regularity.

Drew hit safely in a Florida State-record 34 straight games. Auburn catcher-first baseman Casey Dunn had a 31-game streak when he broke his hand in regional play and was lost for the season.

Junior second baseman Keith Ginter broke a Texas Tech record with a 29-game streak. Jacksonville senior first baseman Talmadge Nunnari set a Sun Belt Confer-

COLLEGE WORLD SERIES CHAMPIONS: 1947-97

Year	Champion	Coach	Record	Runner-Up	MVP
1947	California*	Clint Evans	31-10	Yale	None selected
1948	Southern California	Sam Barry	40-12	Yale	None selected
1949	Texas*	Bibb Falk	23-7	Wake Forest	Charles Teague, 2b, Wake Forest
1950	Texas	Bibb Falk	27-6	Washington State	Ray VanCleef, of, Rutgers
1951	Oklahoma*	Jack Baer	19-9	Tennessee	Sid Hatfield, 1b-p, Tennessee
1952	Holy Cross	Jack Berry	21-3	Missouri	Jim O'Neill, p, Holy Cross
1953	Michigan	Ray Fisher	21-9	Texas	J.L. Smith, p, Texas
1954	Missouri	Hi Simmons	22-4	Rollins	Tom Yewcic, c, Michigan State
1955	Wake Forest	Taylor Sanford	29-7	Western Michigan	Tom Borland, p, Oklahoma State
1956	Minnesota	Dick Siebert	33-9	Arizona	Jerry Thomas, p, Minnesota
1957	California*	George Wolfman	35-10	Penn State	Cal Emery, 1b-p, Penn State
1958	Southern California	Rod Dedeaux	35-7	Missouri	Bill Thom, p, Southern California
1959	Oklahoma State	Toby Greene	27-5	Arizona	Jim Dobson, 3b, Oklahoma State
1960	Minnesota	Dick Siebert	34-7	Southern California	John Erickson, 2b, Minnesota
1961	Southern California*	Rod Dedeaux	43-9	Oklahoma State	Littleton Fowler, p, Oklahoma State
1962	Michigan	Don Lund	31-13	Santa Clara	Bob Garibaldi, p, Santa Clara
1963	Southern California	Rod Dedeaux	37-16	Arizona	Bud Hollowell, c, Southern California
1964	Minnesota	Dick Siebert	31-12	Missouri	Joe Ferris, p, Maine
1965	Arizona State	Bobby Winkles	54-8	Ohio State	Sal Bando, 3b, Arizona State
1966	Ohio State	Marty Karow	27-6	Oklahoma State	Steve Arlin, p, Ohio State
1967	Arizona State	Bobby Winkles	53-12	Houston	Ron Davini, c, Arizona State
1968	Southern California*	Rod Dedeaux	45-14	Southern Illinois	Bill Seinsoth, 1b, Southern California
1969	Arizona State	Bobby Winkles	56-11	Tulsa	John Dolinsek, of, Arizona State
1970	Southern California	Rod Dedeaux	51-13	Florida State	Gene Ammann, p, Florida State
1971	Southern California	Rod Dedeaux	53-13	Southern Illinois	Jerry Tabb, 1b, Tulsa
1972	Southern California	Rod Dedeaux	50-13	Arizona State	Russ McQueen, p, Southern California
1973	Southern California*	Rod Dedeaux	51-11	Arizona State	Dave Winfield, of-p, Minnesota
1974	Southern California	Rod Dedeaux	50-20	Miami (Fla.)	George Milke, p, Southern California
1975	Texas	Cliff Gustafson	56-6	South Carolina	Mickey Reichenbach, 1b, Texas
1976	Arizona	Jerry Kindall	56-17	Eastern Michigan	Steve Powers, dh-p, Arizona
1977	Arizona State	Jim Brock	57-12	South Carolina	Bob Horner, 3b, Arizona State
1978	Southern California*	Rod Dedeaux	54-9	Arizona State	Rod Boxberger, p, Southern California
1979	Cal State Fullerton	Augie Garrido	60-14	Arkansas	Tony Hudson, p, Cal State Fullerton
1980	Arizona	Jerry Kindall	45-21	Hawaii	Terry Francona, of, Arizona
1981	Arizona State	Jim Brock	55-13	Oklahoma State	Stan Holmes, of, Arizona State
1982	Miami (Fla.)*	Ron Fraser	57-18	Wichita State	Dan Smith, p, Miami (Fla.)
1983	Texas*	Cliff Gustafson	66-14	Alabama	Calvin Schiraldi, p, Texas
1984	Cal State Fullerton	Augie Garrido	66-20	Texas	John Fishel, of, Cal State Fullerton
1985	Miami (Fla.)*	Ron Fraser	64-16	Texas	Greg Ellena, dh, Miami (Fla.)
1986	Arizona	Jerry Kindall	49-19	Florida State	Mike Senne, of, Arizona
1987	Stanford	Mark Marquess	53-17	Oklahoma State	Paul Carey, of, Stanford
1988	Stanford	Mark Marquess	46-23	Arizona State	Lee Plemel, p, Stanford
1989	Wichita State	Gene Stephenson	68-16	Texas	Greg Brummett, p, Wichita State
1990	Georgia	Steve Webber	52-19	Oklahoma State	Mike Rebhan, p, Georgia
1991	Louisiana State*	Skip Bertman	55-18	Wichita State	Gary Hymel, c, Louisiana State
1992	Pepperdine*	Andy Lopez	48-11	Cal State Fullerton	Phil Nevin, 3b, Cal State Fullerton
1993	Louisiana State	Skip Bertman	53-17	Wichita State	Todd Walker, 2b, Louisiana State
1994	Oklahoma*	Larry Cochell	50-17	Georgia Tech	Chip Glass, of, Oklahoma
1995	Cal State Fullerton*	Augie Garrido	57-9	Southern California	Mark Kotsay, of-lhp, Cal State Fullerton
1996	Louisiana State*	Skip Bertman	52-15	Miami (Fla.)	Pat Burrell, 3b, Miami
1997	Louisiana State*	Skip Bertman	57-13	Alabama	Brandon Larson, ss, Louisiana State

*Undefeated

ence mark with a 27-game string.

Putting Out The Fire

Amid all the hitting, there were enough good college pitchers around to get scouts excited, led by Rice's Anderson, who was selected by Detroit in the draft.

Many of the top pitchers worked on the West Coast. Junior lefthander Jim Parque, a member of the bronze-medal 1996 U.S. Olympic team, helped lead UCLA to its first CWS berth since 1969 by winning his first 10 decisions. Parque, a supplemental first-round pick of the Chicago White Sox, ended up 13-2 with a 2.97 ERA.

He was challenged for Pacific-10 South supremacy by Stanford junior righthander Kyle Peterson (11-2, 3.67), the conference's pitcher of the year and a first-round draft pick of the Milwaukee Brewers.

Pacific junior righthander Dan Reichert emerged from relative obscurity to become one of the nation's top hurlers. Reichert used a wicked slider to strike out 22 Washington State batters in an early-season game. He fanned 169 in 133 innings on the season and was drafted seventh overall by the Kansas City Royals.

Fresno State righthander Jeff Weaver was more of a known commodity coming into the season because he was an alumnus of the 1996 Olympic team. In Weaver's final outing of the year, he struck out an NCAA postseason record 21 against Texas A&M, giving him a national-high 181.

And for single-game feats, UC Santa Barbara freshman lefthander Barry Zito set an NCAA record with nine straight strikeouts in a 7-6 loss against Arizona State.

Northridge Slinks Out

In 1996, Cal State Northridge went 52-18, won the Western Athletic Conference title, came within two wins of its first trip to the College World Series and produced first-team All-America catcher Robert Fick. In 1997 the Matadors won 42 games and featured Kennedy, the first Matador drafted in the first round.

In 1998, Northridge will barely have a baseball team. In 1999, it won't.

The school voted June 11 to eliminate four sports to meet a tight budget and gender-equity requirements. Baseball was one of the four, making Northridge the 39th Division I school to drop baseball and the 11th in the 1990s.

"It's hard to believe," Fick said. "We've become a

NCAA TOURNAMENT

PLAY-IN SERIES

(Best-of-3)

Northeastern (America East) def. Bethune-Cookman (Mid-Eastern Athletic), 2-0

Harvard (Ivy) def. Army (Patriot), 2-1

Troy State (Mid-Continent) def. Detroit (Midwestern Collegiate), 2-0

Santa Clara (West Coast) def. Southern (Southwestern Athletic), 2-0

Marist (Northeast) def. Siena (Metro Atlantic), 2-0

REGIONALS

(Double elimination)

ATLANTIC

Site: Coral Gables, Fla.

Participants: No. 1 Miami (44-15, at large), No. 2 Florida (38-22, at large), No. 3 Arizona State (36-20, at large), No. 4 Florida International (42-19, at large), No. 5 St. John's (35-15, Big East), No. 6 Richmond (33-24, Colonial).

Champion: Miami (5-1).

Runner-Up: Arizona State (3-2).

Outstanding Player: Jason Michaels, of, Miami.

Attendance: 18,723.

CENTRAL

Site: Lubbock, Texas.

Participants: No. 1 Texas Tech (46-12, at large), No. 2 Rice (43-14, Western Athletic), No. 3 Clemson (40-21, at large), No. 4 Nevada (38-19, at large), No. 5 Southwest Missouri State (33-23, Missouri Valley), No. 6 Southwest Texas State (36-24, Southland).

Champion: Rice (4-0).

Runner-Up: Southwest Missouri State (2-2).

Outstanding Player: Lance Berkman, 1b, Rice.

Attendance: 22,957.

EAST

Site: Tallahassee, Fla.

Participants: No. 1 Florida State (46-15, Atlantic Coast), No. 2 Auburn (45-14, at large), No. 3 Central Florida (40-22, Trans America), No. 4 South Florida (37-22, at large), No. 5 Western Carolina (41-18, Southern), No. 6 Marist (32-17, Northeast).

Champion: Auburn (4-1).

Runner-Up: Florida State (4-2).

Outstanding Player: Tim Hudson, rhp-of, Auburn.

Attendance: 27,404.

MIDEAST

Site: Starkville, Miss.

Participants: No. 1 Georgia Tech (44-13, at large), No. 2 Mississippi State (41-18, at large), No. 3 Southwestern Louisiana (43-16, at large), No. 4 Washington (43-18, Pacific-10), No. 5 Ohio State (42-16, Big Ten), No. 6 Tennessee Tech (38-21, Ohio Valley).

Champion: Mississippi State (5-1).

Runner-Up: Washington (3-2).

Outstanding Player: Eric DuBose, lhp, Mississippi State.

Attendance: 59,378.

MIDWEST

Site: Stillwater, Okla.

Participants: No. 1 UCLA (40-18, at large), No. 2 Tennessee (41-17, at large), No. 3 Oklahoma State (43-17, at large), No. 4 Stetson (37-24, at large), No. 5 Ohio (43-16, Mid-American), No. 6 Harvard (33-14, Ivy).

Champion: UCLA (5-1).

Runner-Up: Oklahoma State (3-2).

Outstanding Player: Eric Valent, of, UCLA.

Attendance: 32,455.

SOUTH I

Site: Baton Rouge, La..

Participants: No. 1 Louisiana State (48-12, at large), No. 2 South Alabama (40-17, Sun Belt), No. 3 Oklahoma (39-18, Big 12), No. 4 Long Beach State (37-24, at large), No. 5 Houston (40-21, Conference USA), No. 6 UNC-Greensboro (44-15, Big South).

Champion: Louisiana State (5-1).

Runner-Up: South Alabama (3-2).

Outstanding Player: Trey McClure, 3b-2b, Louisiana State.

Attendance: 41,522.

SOUTH II

Site: Tuscaloosa, Ala.

Participants: No. 1 Alabama (48-12, Southeastern), No. 2 Southern California (39-18, at large), No. 3 North Carolina State (41-18, at large), No. 4 Wichita State (51-16, at large), No. 5 Virginia Tech (33-26, Atlantic 10), No. 6 Troy State (36-22, Mid-Continent).

Champion: Alabama (4-0).

Runner-Up: Southern California (3-2).

Outstanding Player: Jarrod Kingrey, rhp, Alabama.

Attendance: 26,656.

WEST

Site: Stanford, Calif.

Participants: No. 1 Stanford (39-18, at large), No. 2 Cal State Fullerton (38-22, Big West), No. 3 Texas A&M (30-20, at large), No. 4 Fresno State (37-26, at large), No. 5 Santa Clara (39-18, West Coast), No. 6 Northeastern (33-17, America East).

Champion: Stanford (4-0).

Runner-Up: Fresno State (3-2).

Outstanding Player: Josh Hochgesang, 3b, Stanford.

Attendance: 21,211.

Player of the Year

Drew forces admirers to speak in superlatives

J.D. Drew

Mike Martin relishes the question about as much as pitchers relished facing his star center fielder in 1997.

Is J.D. Drew the best player ever at Florida State?

"J.D. Drew is the best *hitter* I've seen at FSU, and I've been there half the years they've had baseball," said Martin, a Seminoles center fielder in the mid-1960s and their head coach since 1980. "There's been only one guy who could run better than him, and he's playing defensive back for the Dallas Cowboys. He has as strong an arm as anybody we've had in the program from the outfield.

"He's obviously the total package."

Press Martin, and he'll concede that he doesn't want to answer the question directly. He doesn't want to slight anybody. But it's Martin's own fault.

Drew hadn't played a game for the Seminoles before his coach said he had the potential to be the best player in the history of the program. Martin reiterated that point after Drew, as a freshman, became the first player to hit three home runs in a College World Series game.

Drew did nothing to hurt his case in three years in Tallahassee. He batted .391 with 69 home runs and 53 stolen bases in 200 games, setting nine school and eight Atlantic Coast Conference records. He also holds CWS marks for homers in a game, Series (four) and career (five).

He furthered his cause in 1997, winning Baseball America's College Player of the Year award. Drew hit .455 with 31 homers, 100 RBIs and 32 steals, scored 110 runs and even put together a 34-game hitting streak.

The 30-30 season was unprecedented in college baseball. Drew, who would much rather hunt or fish than talk about himself, isn't one to worry about personal accomplishments. But he did want to become college baseball's first 30-30 man.

"People asked me at the beginning of the year what my goals were, and I told them I just wanted to have quality at-bats," Drew said. "But once I found out the mark could be accomplished, I wanted to do it. As I got closer, the home runs were a little tougher to come by. I started to press a little bit."

Martin first noticed Drew at his baseball camp. Martin couldn't believe such a skinny kid could have so much power, and he told his assistants not to bother recruiting Drew because there was no way major league teams would let him get away.

But they did. The San Francisco Giants took him in the 20th round of the 1994 draft and tried to sway him with a late $100,000 offer. When Drew declined, saying he wanted to go to college to get bigger and stronger, the Giants' area scout asked, "How much bigger and stronger can you get?"

The answer was plenty. Drew cut his time in the 60-yard dash from 6.77 to 6.4 seconds. After being cut from the 1996 U.S. Olympic team, he spent the off-season lifting weights and bulked up his 6-foot-1 frame to 195 pounds.

When the draft came around again, Drew wasn't overlooked. He was the second player picked in the 1997 draft, but negotiations with the Philadelphia Phillies stalled quickly and Drew instead signed with the St. Paul Saints of the independent Northern League, hitting .341 with 18 homers.

Florida State may not ever really see another player like Drew. Just don't ask Mike Martin to admit it.

PREVIOUS WINNERS

1981—Mike Sodders, 3b, Arizona State
1982—Jeff Ledbetter, of-lhp, Florida State
1983—Dave Magadan, 1b, Alabama
1984—Oddibe McDowell, of, Arizona State
1985—Pete Incaviglia, of, Oklahoma State
1986—Casey Close, of, Michigan
1987—Robin Ventura, 3b, Oklahoma State
1988—John Olerud, 1b-lhp, Washington State
1989—Ben McDonald, rhp, Louisiana State
1990—Mike Kelly, of, Arizona State
1991—David McCarty, 1b, Stanford
1992—Phil Nevin, 3b, Cal State Fullerton
1993—Brooks Kieschnick, dh-rhp, Texas
1994—Jason Varitek, c, Georgia Tech
1995—Todd Helton, 1b-lhp, Tennessee
1996—Kris Benson, rhp, Clemson

school to be reckoned with, competing on the same level as the best schools with the most resources. For it all to end is frustrating and disappointing."

In July, state senator Cathie Wright engineered a $586,000 bailout of the school's athletic department, restoring baseball, volleyball, soccer and swimming to the school for one year. Coach Mike Batesole was scrambling to keep players on his team and opponents on his schedule.

New Hampshire, with a less storied history, also dropped baseball after 1997, going 17-22 in its last season. Among the school's baseball alumni was former big league righthander Rich Gale.

A more prolific producer of pro players, Miami-Dade Community College, also announced budget slashing affecting baseball. Previously, three Miami-Dade CC campuses–North, South and Wolfson–fielded teams, but the nation's largest junior college will now field only one team.

Among the Miami-Dade alumni are Hall of Famer Steve Carlton, Bucky Dent, Alex Fernandez and Mickey Rivers.

1997 COLLEGE ALL-AMERICA TEAM

Selected by Baseball America

FIRST TEAM

Pos.,	Player, School	YR	HT	WT	B-T	AVG	AB	R	H	2B	3B	HR	RBI	SB
C	Matthew LeCroy, Clemson	Jr.	6-3	220	R-R	.359	237	62	85	12	1	24	79	5
1B	Lance Berkman, Rice	Jr.	6-1	210	B-L	.431	255	109	110	22	4	41	134	8
2B	Tom Sergio, North Carolina State	Sr.	5-9	165	L-R	.412	243	85	100	14	4	16	68	18
3B	Troy Glaus, UCLA	Jr.	6-5	225	R-R	.409	264	100	108	15	1	34	91	10
OF	J.D. Drew, Florida State	Jr.	6-1	195	L-R	.455	233	110	106	15	5	31	100	32
OF	Jeremy Morris, Florida State	Sr.	6-2	200	R-R	.356	250	73	89	22	6	25	116	25
OF	Brad Wilkerson, Florida	So.	6-0	193	L-L	.386	236	82	91	15	3	23	76	11
DH	Pat Burrell, Miami (Fla.)	So.	6-4	220	R-R	.409	215	79	88	19	2	21	76	12
UT	Tim Hudson, Auburn	Sr.	6-0	160	R-R	.396	273	71	108	21	0	18	95	2

Pos.	Player, School	YR	HT	WT	B-T	W	L	ERA	G	SV	IP	H	BB	SO
P	Matt Anderson, Rice	Jr.	6-4	200	R-R	10	2	2.05	30	9	79	48	29	105
P	Jim Parque, UCLA	Jr.	5-11	165	L-L	13	2	3.08	19	0	120	117	63	119
P	Kyle Peterson, Stanford	Jr.	6-3	215	R-R	11	3	4.19	20	0	144	134	38	156
P	Dan Reichert, Pacific	Jr.	6-3	165	R-R	13	4	2.30	20	0	133	96	51	169
P	Jeff Weaver, Fresno State	So.	6-5	185	R-R	11	5	3.63	21	2	141	130	25	181
UT	Tim Hudson, Auburn	Sr.	6-0	160	R-R	15	2	2.97	22	0	118	87	50	165

SECOND TEAM

Pos.,	Player, School	YR	HT	WT	B-T	AVG	AB	R	H	2B	3B	HR	RBI	SB
C	Giuseppe Chiaramonte, Fresno State	Jr.	6-0	200	R-R	.341	267	72	91	16	5	26	72	6
1B	Joe Dillon, Texas Tech	Sr.	6-2	205	R-R	.393	229	80	90	20	3	33	89	19
2B	Keith Ginter, Texas Tech	Jr.	5-9	177	R-R	.426	249	93	106	24	2	17	77	29
3B	Andy Dominique, Nevada	Sr.	6-0	210	R-R	.357	241	80	86	14	0	30	96	6
SS	Kevin Nicholson, Stetson	Jr.	5-9	189	B-R	.415	229	76	95	23	4	17	71	24
OF	Mark Fischer, Georgia Tech	Jr.	6-2	200	R-R	.354	257	75	91	10	7	24	98	17
OF	Mike Marchiano, Fordham	Sr.	6-0	190	R-R	.493	207	91	102	21	2	29	85	22
OF	Dan McKinley, Arizona State	Jr.	6-0	185	L-R	.423	267	88	113	21	5	15	70	32
DH	Adam Kennedy, CS Northridge	Jr.	6-1	180	L-R	.482	278	96	134	32	5	26	99	22
UT	Mike Frank, Santa Clara	Sr.	6-3	195	L-L	.405	242	64	98	25	5	12	80	19

Pos.	Player, School	YR	HT	WT	B-T	W	L	ERA	G	SV	IP	H	BB	SO
P	Randy Choate, Florida State	Jr.	6-2	175	L-L	13	3	3.61	19	0	135	123	37	126
P	Chris Enochs, West Virginia	Jr.	6-3	210	R-R	12	1	3.03	15	0	95	92	21	86
P	Jason Gooding, Texas Tech	Jr.	6-0	195	L-L	11	0	3.57	16	0	116	111	31	137
P	Jason Navarro, Tulane	Jr.	6-4	230	L-L	12	2	2.00	17	0	112	81	37	135
P	Randy Wolf, Pepperdine	Jr.	6-0	185	L-L	9	4	1.79	17	1	121	100	25	128
UT	Mike Frank, Santa Clara	Sr.	6-3	195	L-L	11	0	2.69	15	0	74	59	23	73

THIRD TEAM

Pos.,	Player, School	YR	HT	WT	B-T	AVG	AB	R	H	2B	3B	HR	RBI	SB
C	Jason Grabowski, Connecticut	Jr.	6-3	185	L-R	.384	151	49	58	9	4	16	57	9
1B	Ross Gload, South Florida	Jr.	6-1	196	L-L	.399	248	85	99	25	1	18	80	8
2B	Harvey Hargrove, Sacramento State	Jr.	6-0	180	R-R	.361	219	49	79	8	0	26	62	11
3B	Rusty McNamara, Oklahoma State	Sr.	5-9	185	R-R	.387	282	80	109	25	5	24	93	10
SS	Kevin Miller, Washington	So.	6-1	200	R-R	.384	250	77	96	17	5	12	73	4
OF	Casey Child, Utah	Jr.	6-2	200	R-R	.408	255	86	104	24	3	31	97	27
OF	Jason Fitzgerald, Tulane	Jr.	6-1	187	L-L	.387	238	71	92	22	4	17	70	24
OF	Geofrey Tomlinson, Houston	Jr.	6-1	187	L-L	.427	248	74	106	29	3	16	67	25
DH	Jon Heinrichs, UCLA	Sr.	6-0	185	R-R	.358	299	92	107	28	2	28	79	16
UT	Roberto Vaz, Alabama	Jr.	5-9	190	L-L	.400	255	87	102	17	9	22	73	14

Pos.	Player, School	YR	HT	WT	B-T	W	L	ERA	G	SV	IP	H	BB	SO
P	Patrick Coogan, Louisiana State	Jr.	6-3	200	R-R	13	3	4.38	22	2	113	102	33	129
P	Robbie Morrison, Miami (Fla.)	So.	6-0	225	R-R	4	2	1.49	37	8	54	38	28	82
P	Jason Parsons, UNC Greensboro	Jr.	6-2	175	R-R	15	1	3.08	35	8	50	36	27	76
P	Trey Poland, SW Louisiana	Sr.	6-1	195	L-L	12	5	3.28	22	3	137	115	58	140
P	Kris Wilson, Georgia Tech	Jr.	6-4	227	R-R	12	2	3.10	19	2	118	114	30	103
UT	Roberto Vaz, Alabama	Jr.	5-9	190	L-L	4	1	3.40	22	8	50	35	27	52

Player of the Year: J.D. Drew, of, Florida State.
Coach of the Year: Skip Bertman, Louisiana State.
Freshman of the Year: Brian Roberts, ss, North Carolina.

Coach of the Year

One way or another, Alabama's Wells lays down the law

If everything had gone according to plan, Jim Wells would be practicing law and Sammy Dunn would be coaching at Alabama.

But Wells knew he wasn't cut out to be a lawyer, and Dunn decided he didn't want to coach the Crimson Tide. In his first three years in Tuscaloosa, Wells has taken the Alabama program from its greatest depths to its greatest heights. For that, he was named Baseball America's 1997 Coach of the Year.

Wells' father never saw this coming. A lawyer, he wanted his son to follow his career path. Wells was studying pre-law at Northwestern State when fate intervened in the summer of 1974.

He was 19 and back home working for the Bossier City, La., recreation department. Max Samford, who coached a team of 13- and 14-year-olds, needed an assistant after assistant his quit. He asked Wells for help.

"I really liked it. I always loved sports and I got the opportunity to do it," said Wells, whose playing career ended in high school. "I found I liked it and wanted to give it a try."

JEFF GOLDEN

Jim Wells

Though he later took the Law School Admission Test, Wells had found his destiny. After graduating, he got a job as a substitute teacher and continued coaching youth baseball.

When the head coach at Princeton Junior High in Haughton, La., was injured in an auto accident, Wells took his place in 1980. He began a successful five-year run at Shreveport's Loyola Prep in 1982, taking a team that hadn't made the playoffs in a decade to the state finals twice.

Good fortune smiled on him again when family friend Boots Garland was chatting with Skip Bertman, who was beginning to build a national power at Louisiana State. Bertman mentioned he had a vacancy for a graduate assistant and Garland suggested Wells, who soon was headed to Baton Rouge.

Wells coached hitting and outfield play for the Tigers from 1987-89--among his charges was a slugger named Joey Belle--before taking over the program at his alma mater in 1990. After enduring 12 straight losing seasons, Northwestern State won its first 20 games under Wells, who went 192-89 in five years with the Demons.

Northwestern State was playing in the 1994 Midwest I Regional at Oklahoma State when Wells learned that Alabama had hired Dunn, the coach at Vestavia Hills (Ala.) High, to replace Barry Shollenberger, who had been fired. When Dunn abruptly changed his mind, Crimson Tide athletic director Hootie Ingram called Bertman to ask about Wells. Bertman told him, "If you want to win, he's the guy."

Alabama was coming off a 21-35 season that included a 4-22 Southeastern Conference record, its worst ever. As he had at Loyola Prep and Northwestern State, Wells, 42, pulled off an immediate turnaround.

Alabama went 42-23 in 1995, winning the SEC Western Division tournament and coming within a game of reaching the College World Series. In 1996, the Tide went 50-19, took the SEC regular-season and tournament titles and finished fifth in Omaha. In 1997, Alabama went 56-14 to break the school record for victories for the second straight year, captured its third straight SEC tournament and reached the national championship game before losing 13-6 to Louisiana State.

"He's just an incredible, great coach," Bertman said. "Even I didn't think he could do it at that warp-like speed at Alabama. He's been magnificent."

—JIM CALLIS

PREVIOUS WINNERS

1981—Ron Fraser, Miami
1982—Gene Stephenson, Wichita State
1983—Barry Shollenberger, Alabama
1984—Augie Garrido, Cal State Fullerton
1985—Ron Polk, Mississippi State
1986—Skip Bertman, Louisiana State
Dave Snow, Loyola Marymount
1987—Mark Marquess, Stanford
1988—Jim Brock, Arizona State
1989—Dave Snow, Long Beach State
1990—Steve Webber, Georgia
1991—Jim Hendry, Creighton
1992—Andy Lopez, Pepperdine
1993—Gene Stephenson, Wichita State
1994—Jim Morris, Miami
1995—Rod Delmonico, Tennessee
1996—Skip Bertman, Louisiana State

Polk Bows Out

Ron Polk, who helped build the SEC into college baseball's most prolific conference along with Bertman, announced his retirement after the CWS. Polk, often at odds with the NCAA over scholarship limitations and gender-equity measures, never coached a losing team in 26 years at Georgia Southern and Mississippi State.

His career mark was 1,043-486 with six trips to Omaha. Among the big leaguers he managed were Will Clark, Rafael Palmeiro and John Tudor.

Polk was replaced by associate head coach Pat McMahon, who served as an assistant on Team USA over the summer of 1997. Among other college coaching changes:

■ Texas-Pan American coach Al Ogletree, who was the winningest active coach in Division I with a

Freshman of the Year

Ignored by recruiters, Roberts makes a name for himself

When Brian Roberts was 7, B.J. Surhoff was putting together the best offensive season in the history of North Carolina baseball.

Surhoff hit .399 with 14 homers and 57 RBIs in 1985, numbers that wouldn't raise too many eyebrows in this era of souped-up bats. He set school records with 77 runs and 98 hits, and the Milwaukee Brewers picked him first overall in that year's draft.

Roberts may not be Surhoff's equal as a pro prospect but no Tar Heels hitter ever has been as prolific.

Roberts, a 5-foot-9, 165-pound shortstop, smashed a single during the Atlantic Coast Conference tournament for his 99th hit, breaking Surhoff's single-season mark. Play was stopped and the Tar Heels' coaching staff, headed by Brian's father Mike, recovered the ball.

"I hadn't really been aware of any records until then," said Roberts, who used to play catch with Surhoff as a youngster. "I hadn't really looked around and been too aware of my stats, but that really dawned on me.

Brian Roberts

"To be put in a category with a player like B.J. Surhoff, wow. Breaking that record was really special. It was a special first year for me."

Special indeed. Roberts became Baseball America's 1997 Freshman of the Year after hitting .427 with eight homers and 44 RBIs. He set Tar Heels marks for average, hits (102), doubles (24) and stolen bases (47).

Roberts wasn't even the MVP on his Chapel Hill (N.C.) High team in 1996. He wasn't drafted, and he went downtown to play for his father only because no other schools offered him scholarships.

"Brian was always shoved to the background, whether it was because of his size or because he was my son and people just thought he would come play for me," his father said. "So his biggest obstacle to overcome was self-confidence."

The payoff was a season his father called one of the best he has seen in 20 years in coaching.

"The 47 steals, that's just amazing because it's hard to do," Mike Roberts said. "That's just Brian, nothing to do with aluminum bats or anything but his talent, his speed and his instincts.

"When you steal bases like that, you do more than just move up a base. You disrupt the pitcher, you disrupt the defense and you help your hitters."

Roberts complemented his season by making Team USA. He played second base, shortstop and third base while hitting .330 in a part-time role.

BA's 1997 Freshman All-America first team:

C—Eric Munson, Southern California (.336-13-50).

1B—Rich Park, Oklahoma (.304-6-49); **2B**—Blair Barbier, Louisiana State (.353-15-57); **3B**—Brant Ust, Notre Dame (.372-11-54); **SS**—Brian Roberts, North Carolina (.427-8-44, 47 SB).

OF—Kurt Keene, Tennessee (.368-13-58); Ryan Ludwick, Nevada-Las Vegas (.354-16-68); Edmund Muth, Stanford (.388-9-46).

DH—Josh Bard, Texas Tech (.359-13-69). **Util**—Vaughn Schill, Duke (388-4-31; 4-1, 4.05, 5 SV).

P—Jason Jennings, Baylor (3-4, 2.66); Ryan Mottl, Clemson (10-3, 4.72); Jeff Nichols, Rice (10-2, 3.42); Casey Rowe, Fresno State (8-1, 3.57); Alex Santos, Miami (9-3, 4.17).

—JOHN MANUEL

PREVIOUS WINNERS

1982—Cory Snyder, 3b, Brigham Young
1983—Rafael Palmeiro, of, Mississippi State
1984—Greg Swindell, lhp, Texas
1985—Jack McDowell, rhp, Stanford
Ron Wenrich, of, Georgia
1986—Robin Ventura, 3b, Oklahoma State
1987—Paul Carey, of, Stanford
1988—Kirk Dressendorfer, rhp, Texas
1989—Alex Fernandez, rhp, Miami
1990—Jeffrey Hammonds, of, Stanford
1991—Brooks Kieschnick, rhp-dh, Texas
1992—Todd Walker, 2b, Louisiana State
1993—Brett Laxton, rhp, Louisiana State
1994—R.A. Dickey, rhp, Tennessee
1995—Kyle Peterson, rhp, Stanford
1996—Pat Burrell, 3b, Miami

1,217-711 record, was replaced by longtime assistant Reggie Tredaway.

■ North Carolina coach Mike Roberts announced in August that 1998 would be his last year. The Tar Heels had their worst season ever in 1997, including a 6-18 mark in the ACC. New athletic director Dick Baddour did not immediately name a successor to Roberts, who has a record of 736-405 and two CWS trips.

■ Iowa's Duane Banks retired May 9 with a record of 901-585 in 30 seasons at Parsons State (Iowa) and Iowa.

■ Princeton hired former big leaguer Scott Bradley to replace Tom O'Connell. Bradley was mentioned as a possible replacement for Roberts at his alma mater.

■ East Carolina's Gary Overton resigned after going 427-237 in 13 years and was replaced by Keith Leclair, formerly head coach at Western Carolina.

■ Southern Mississippi's Hill Denson stepped down after 14 seasons and was replaced by assistant Corky Palmer.

■ Santa Clara's John Oldham retired after 13 seasons with the Broncos and was replaced by assistant Mike Cummins.

■ Coppin State replaced Jason Booker with two-time American League all-star outfielder Paul Blair. Blair's previous experience was with Fordham in 1983, where he went 14-19.

COLLEGE BASEBALL

NCAA DIVISION I LEADERS

TEAM BATTING

BATTING AVERAGE	G	AVG
Delaware	55	.365
Brigham Young	55	.363
Texas Tech	60	.352
Western Carolina	62	.351
Utah	58	.351
Massachusetts	47	.351
Ball State	59	.347
Oklahoma	59	.344
Canisius	37	.342
East Tennessee State	45	.342
Minnesota	54	.342

RUNS SCORED	G	R
Alabama	70	679
Louisiana State	70	673
Wichita State	69	654
Oklahoma State	65	653
Texas Tech	60	637
Florida State	67	635
Mississippi State	68	633
UCLA	67	631
Washington	66	624
Cal State Northridge	63	623

DOUBLES	G	2B
Texas Tech	60	185
Oklahoma State	65	179
Washington	66	176
Oklahoma	59	174
UCLA	67	173

TRIPLES	G	3B
Hawaii	56	36
Notre Dame	60	36
Oklahoma	59	35
Rice	63	35
Alabama	70	34

HOME RUNS	G	HR
Louisiana State	70	188
Alabama	70	160
Oklahoma State	65	149
UCLA	67	142
Utah	58	124
Rice	63	120
Florida State	67	114
Cal State Northridge	63	113
Texas Tech	60	108
Brigham Young	55	104

STOLEN BASES	G	SB	ATT
UNC Greensboro	62	169	209
Alcorn State	45	161	185
Florida State	67	160	202
Houston	63	152	186
Bethune-Cookman	55	151	189
Austin Peay	59	151	197
Miami (Fla.)	69	149	197
California	59	147	195
Indiana	55	130	173
Texas Tech	60	130	173

TEAM PITCHING

W-L PERCENTAGE	W	L	PCT
Delaware	45	10	.818
Louisiana State	57	13	.814
Alabama	56	14	.800
Texas Tech	46	14	.767
Oregon State	38	12	.755
Georgia Tech	46	15	.754
Jacksonville State	39	13	.750
Auburn	50	17	.746
Florida State	50	17	.746
Rice	47	16	.746

EARNED RUN AVERAGE	G	ERA
Arkansas State	53	3.14
San Diego	54	3.91
Miami (Fla.)	69	3.92
Delaware	55	4.01
Wichita State	69	4.01
Tulane	61	4.02
Jacksonville State	52	4.06
Florida International	63	4.08
Troy State	60	4.09
Oregon State	51	4.10

TEAM FIELDING

FIELDING AVERAGE	G	AVG
Pepperdine	59	.970
Ohio	61	.969
Florida	64	.968
Stanford	65	.967
Texas- Pan American	52	.967
Duke	58	.966
Harvard	50	.966
Purdue	55	.966
Alabama	70	.966
Louisiana State	70	.966

INDIVIDUAL BATTING

BATTING AVERAGE

(Minimum 125 At-Bats)

	AVG	G	AB	R	H	2B	3B	HR	RBI	BB	SO	SB
Mike Marchiano, Fordham	.493	53	207	91	102	21	2	29	85	45	20	22
Adam Kennedy, Cal St. Northridge	.482	63	278	96	134	32	5	26	99	31	21	22
Brian Nickerson, Dartmouth	.463	38	136	31	63	18	1	5	29	20	11	6
J.D. Drew, Florida State	.455	67	233	110	106	15	5	31	100	84	37	32
Talmadge Nunnari, Jacksonville	.450	54	200	68	90	23	4	10	61	44	23	22
Greg Ryan, East. Michigan	.447	54	197	56	88	25	1	9	56	29	14	5
Elvis Hernandez, Ill.-Chicago	.445	38	137	32	61	15	2	5	31	13	16	5
Dan Hummel, Seton Hall	.434	54	196	45	85	19	0	6	51	27	14	5
Brian August, Delaware	.432	54	199	72	86	26	1	20	82	36	19	2
Billy Rich, Connecticut	.432	47	190	61	82	20	1	13	55	27	32	6
Lance Berkman, Rice	.431	63	255	109	110	22	4	41	134	59	34	8
Joe DeMarco, Kansas	.429	56	224	64	96	16	3	2	28	34	20	34
Jason Trott, Ohio State	.429	49	140	40	60	11	0	4	30	25	10	5
Goefrey Tomlinson, Houston	.427	57	248	74	106	29	3	16	67	25	25	25
Brian Roberts, North Carolina	.427	60	239	63	102	24	1	8	44	38	17	47
LaMonte Collier, SE Missouri St.	.426	55	202	44	86	20	2	8	43	26	28	24
Keith Ginter, Texas Tech	.426	60	249	93	106	24	2	17	77	51	40	29
Jeremy Jackson, Arkansas	.425	56	221	57	94	18	8	9	72	16	35	12
Jason Murray, Ball State	.425	55	174	46	74	20	0	6	45	22	20	14
Darren Pulito, Delaware	.424	52	184	47	78	15	1	15	62	12	31	2
Dan McKinley, Arizona State	.423	61	267	88	113	21	5	15	70	28	31	32
Robert Gonzalez, New Mexico	.421	57	252	68	106	33	3	7	66	13	24	20
Todd Sears, Nebraska	.421	62	233	78	98	18	3	17	79	62	45	6
Brian Petrucci, Akron	.420	54	188	47	79	24	2	10	65	29	25	11
David Decker, Brigham Young	.420	47	169	63	71	14	0	5	48	30	16	6
David Kim, Seton Hall	.420	53	212	63	89	24	1	19	71	24	15	10
Ryan Bordenick, South Carolina	.419	56	229	81	96	18	2	13	87	38	43	2
Josh Patton, West. Kentucky	.419	52	191	42	80	22	3	6	46	26	19	4
Mike Colangelo, George Mason	.418	52	184	62	77	18	7	7	68	39	25	14
Jeff Guiel, Oklahoma State	.418	65	251	88	105	32	3	23	79	56	52	16
Justin Collins, Air Force	.417	42	127	37	53	14	1	11	44	21	15	3
Ryan Fleming, Dayton	.417	49	187	47	78	19	1	6	40	24	14	19
Mike Scioletti, Army	.415	41	130	47	54	15	4	12	67	40	11	5
Rick Southall, Portland State	.415	53	183	39	76	18	3	11	47	28	44	4
Doug Clark, Massachusetts	.415	47	183	51	76	12	1	11	60	24	26	20
Jason Meier, Ball State	.415	58	200	61	83	17	1	15	65	37	27	17
Kevin Nicholson, Stetson	.415	64	229	76	95	23	4	17	71	42	30	24
Chris Connally, Texas Christian	.414	51	198	71	82	16	2	23	72	26	33	12
Mike Perate, Villanova	.413	43	143	41	59	5	0	1	21	11	21	15
Scott Kidd, Cal Poly SLO	.412	58	255	71	105	21	2	14	66	31	54	6
Brian Issitt, Holy Cross	.412	36	136	32	56	12	2	0	21	13	18	7
Tom Sergio, North Carolina St.	.412	62	243	85	100	14	4	16	68	51	25	18
Earl Snyder, Hartford	.411	39	141	40	58	10	1	13	42	13	27	1
D.G. Nelson, Brigham Young	.411	54	197	65	81	14	1	22	81	22	41	5
Jason Michaels, Miami (Fla.)	.411	68	258	71	106	32	3	15	89	39	28	14
Lou Marchetti, Drexel	.409	51	171	47	70	12	0	13	74	26	23	4
Pat Burrell, Miami (Fla.)	.409	67	215	79	88	19	2	21	76	83	41	12
Heath Schesser, Kansas State	.409	56	237	70	97	20	8	16	85	33	25	7
Troy Glaus, UCLA	.409	67	264	100	108	15	1	34	91	57	52	10
Andrew Thompson, Mid. Tennessee	.409	53	176	38	72	9	0	13	42	37	19	0
Mike Pesci, Detroit	.409	47	176	53	72	14	1	16	46	15	26	1
Rob Farrell, Rhode Island	.409	43	154	51	63	17	3	12	56	20	33	21
Pat Magness, Wichita State	.409	52	137	31	56	9	0	7	37	23	15	1
Chris Briller, New York Tech	.408	46	169	41	69	14	2	4	37	25	16	13
Casey Child, Utah	.408	58	255	86	104	24	3	31	97	29	33	27
Matt Griswold, Virginia Tech	.408	62	211	49	86	14	4	13	69	49	36	8
Nolan Lofgren, East. Illinois	.407	46	162	40	66	10	1	8	37	18	22	11
Jose Miranda, CS Northridge	.407	63	247	80	98	16	2	25	90	49	30	14
Chad Shultz, Youngstown State	.406	46	165	41	67	10	4	2	36	19	22	4
Kevin Haverbusch, Maryland	.406	51	207	64	84	15	0	16	63	19	20	8
Mike Heidemann, Utah	.405	54	195	59	79	20	2	11	47	48	23	2
Troy Farnsworth, BYU	.405	39	148	53	60	12	0	6	34	12	23	3
Mike Frank, Santa Clara	.405	61	242	64	98	25	5	12	80	32	20	19
Spencer Oborn, Brigham Young	.403	55	186	60	75	16	3	15	75	27	28	21
Kevin Mench, Delaware	.403	55	211	71	85	19	5	19	67	17	25	8
Matt Ardizzone, Delaware	.403	54	226	56	91	25	6	4	32	3	18	7

RUNS SCORED	G	R
J.D. Drew, Florida State	67	110
Lance Berkman, Rice	63	109
Troy Glaus, UCLA	67	100
Adam Kennedy, CS North.	63	96
Eric Byrnes, UCLA	67	95
Keith Ginter, Texas Tech	60	93
John Heinrichs, UCLA	67	92
Mike Marchiano, Fordham	53	91
Chris Magruder, Washington	66	90
Billy Gasparino, Okla. State	65	89
Jeff Guiel, Oklahoma State	65	88
Dan McKinley, Arizona State	61	88
Scott Pratt, Utah	58	88
Eric Hinske, Arkansas	56	87
Roberto Vaz, Alabama	63	87
Casey Child, Utah	58	86
Matt Erickson, Arkansas	56	86
David Tidwell, Alabama	69	86
Scott Zech, Florida State	67	86

HITS	G	H
Adam Kennedy, CS Northridge	63	134
Dan McKinley, Arizona State	61	113
Lance Berkman, Rice	63	110
Brandon Larson, LSU	69	110
Francis Collins, Nebraska	62	109
Rusty McNamara, Okla. State	65	109
Dustin Carr, Houston	63	108
Troy Glaus, UCLA	67	108
Tim Hudson, Auburn	65	108
Jon Heinrichs, UCLA	67	107
J.D. Drew, Florida State	67	106
Keith Ginter, Texas Tech	60	106
Robert Gonzalez, New Mexico	57	106
Jason Michaels, Miami (Fla.)	68	106
Goefrey Tomlinson, Houston	57	106

SLUGGING PERCENTAGE

(Minimum 125 At-Bats)	G	PCT
Mike Marchiano, Fordham	53	1.034
Lance Berkman, Rice	63	1.031
J.D. Drew, Florida State	67	.961
Joe Dillon, Texas Tech	57	.939
Adam Kennedy, CS North.	63	.914
Casey Child, Utah	58	.890
Brian August, Delaware	54	.874
Mike Scioletti, Army	41	.869
Brandon Larson, LSU	69	.865
Chris Connally, Tx. Christian	51	.864

TOTAL BASES	G	TB
Lance Berkman, Rice	63	263
Adam Kennedy, CS North.	63	254
Brandon Larson, LSU	69	250
Casey Child, Utah	58	227
Troy Glaus, UCLA	67	227
J.D. Drew, Florida State	67	224
Jon Heinrichs, UCLA	67	223
Rusty McNamara, Okla. State	65	216
Joe Dillon, Texas Tech	57	215
Mike Marchiano, Fordham	53	214
Jeff Guiel, Oklahoma State	65	212
Roberto Vaz, Alabama	63	203
Jeremy Morris, Florida State	66	198
Eric Valent, UCLA	67	196
Giuseppe Chiaramonte, Fres. St.	68	195
Jose Miranda, CS Northridge	63	193
Bubba Crosby, Rice	63	192
Andy Dominique, Nevada	60	190
Ryan Lundquist, Arkansas	56	190

Adam Kennedy

Lance Berkman

DOUBLES	G	2B
Robert Gonzalez, New Mexico	57	33
Dustin Carr, Houston	63	32
Jeff Guiel, Oklahoma State	65	32
Adam Kennedy, CS Northridge	63	32
Jason Michaels, Miami (Fla.)	68	32
Kurt Bultmann, Clemson	60	31
Robert Berns, San Jose State	59	29
Jason Landreth, Texas Tech	56	29
Robb Quinlan, Minnesota	53	29
Bo Robinson, UNC Charlotte	57	29
Goefrey Tomlinson, Houston	57	29
Derek Feramisco, Fresno State	63	28
Jon Heinrichs, UCLA	67	28
Matt Erickson, Arkansas	56	27
Javier Flores, Oklahoma	58	27
Brian Shackelford, Oklahoma	58	27
Josh Adeeb, Vanderbilt	51	26
Brian August, Delaware	54	26
Bryan Besco, Michigan	55	26
Roby Brooks, Jack. State	52	26
Billy Gasparino, Okla. State	65	26
Ryan Lentz, Washington	65	26

TRIPLES	G	3B
Bubba Crosby, Rice	63	11
Adam Neubart, Rutgers	39	11
Dusty Rhodes, Illinois	58	9
Joe Schley, So. Illinois	55	9
Stewart Smothers, S.D. State	62	9
Roberto Vaz, Alabama	63	9

HOME RUNS	G	HR
Lance Berkman, Rice	63	41
Brandon Larson, LSU	69	40
Troy Glaus, UCLA	67	34
Joe Dillon, Texas Tech	57	33
Casey Child, Utah	58	31
J.D. Drew, Florida State	67	31
Andy Dominique, Nevada	60	30
Mike Marchiano, Fordham	53	29
Jon Heinrichs, UCLA	67	28
Eric Valent, UCLA	67	27
Giuseppe Chiaramonte, Fres. St.	68	26
Harvey Hargrove, CS Sac.	55	26
Adam Kennedy, CS Northridge	63	26
Jose Miranda, CS Northridge	63	25
Dustan Mohr, Alabama	68	25
Jeremy Morris, Florida State	66	25
Mark Fischer, Georgia Tech	61	24
Matthew LeCroy, Clemson	64	24
Ryan Lundquist, Arkansas	56	24
Rusty McNamara, Okla. State	65	24
Chris Connally, Tx. Christian	51	23
Jeff Guiel, Oklahoma State	65	23
Chad Sutter, Tulane	60	23
Brad Wilkerson, Florida	64	23
Jeremy Avery, Mercer	57	22
Bubba Crosby, Rice	63	22
Mike Koerner, Louisiana St.	69	22
D.G. Nelson, Brigham Young	54	22
J.J. Thomas, Georgia Tech	61	22
Roberto Vaz, Alabama	63	22

RUNS BATTED IN	G	RBI
Lance Berkman, Rice	63	134
Brandon Larson, LSU	69	118
Jeremy Morris, Florida State	66	116
J.D. Drew, Florida State	67	100
Adam Kennedy, CS Northridge	63	99
Mark Fischer, Georgia Tech	61	98
Casey Child, Utah	58	97
Andy Dominique, Nevada	60	96
Tim Hudson, Auburn	65	95
Rusty McNamara, Okla. State	65	93
Troy Glaus, UCLA	67	91
Eric Valent, UCLA	67	91
Joe Dillon, Texas Tech	57	90
Richard Lee, Mississippi St.	68	90
Jose Miranda, CS Northridge	63	90
Bubba Crosby, Rice	63	88
Ryan Bordenick, So. Carolina	56	87
Mike Marchiano, Fordham	53	85
Matt Pusey, Richmond	59	85
Heath Schesser, Kansas State	56	85
Ryan Upshaw, New Mexico St.	53	84

BASE ON BALLS	G	BB
J.D. Drew, Florida State	67	84
Pat Burrell, Miami (Fla.)	67	83
T.D. Hicks, Wright State	58	65
Jason Richards, Rice	61	65
Joel Williams, New Mexico St.	53	63
Brad Wilkerson, Florida	64	63

STRIKEOUTS	G	SO
J.J. Thomas, Georgia Tech	61	80
Aaron Jaworowski, Missouri	58	75
R.J. Radler, Cal Poly SLO	57	72
Benny Craig, Loyola Mary	60	70
Brent Magouirk, Mercer	58	69

TOUGHEST TO STRIKE OUT

(Minimum 125 At-Bats)	AB	SO	Ratio
Tom Stoudt, Lafayette	132	3	44.0
Jason Frushour, West Va.	171	5	34.2
Brian Poire, New Hamp.	117	4	29.3
Jack Wickersham, SW Texas	216	9	24.0
Matt Erickson, Arkansas	236	10	23.6

STOLEN BASES	G	SB	ATT
Clay Greene, Tennessee	59	54	63
Ryan Grimmett, Miami (Fla.)	62	53	67
Kent Brown, Austin Peay	59	50	65
Brian Harris, Indiana	54	50	59
Brian Roberts, No. Carolina	60	47	58
Kevin Fahy, Drexel	51	45	48
Nicky Phillips, UNC G'boro	60	45	50
Justin Love, Ball State	59	44	56
Brad Gorrie, Mass	46	43	47
Chris Magruder, Wash.	66	43	47
Mike Curry, So. Carolina	53	42	45
Tommy Lewis, NE La.	50	42	48
Dominic Pattie, UNC G'boro	62	41	49
Ned French, Stetson	62	40	44
Jason Maule, Cent. Conn.	36	39	44
Jason Tyner, Texas A&M	61	37	47
Giancarlo DiPrima, St. John's	52	36	41
Todd Donovan, Siena	50	36	44
David Eckstein, Florida	64	35	43
David Tidwell, Alabama	69	35	40
Travis Young, New Mexico	57	35	43

HIT BY PITCH	G	HBP
Andrew Slater, Richmond	56	33
Tony Hurtado, San Francisco	55	26
Clay Schwartz, Wis.-Milwaukee	57	26
David Eckstein, Florida	64	25
Corky Miller, Nevada	58	25

INDIVIDUAL PITCHING

EARNED RUN AVERAGE

(Minimum 60 Innings)

	W	L	ERA	G	GS	CG	SV	IP	H	R	ER	BB	SO
Sonny Garcia, Texas Southern	5	3	1.77	14	10	7	1	66	46	24	13	10	63
Randy Wolf, Pepperdine	9	4	1.79	17	16	7	1	121	100	35	24	25	128
Andy Smith, Bowling Green	9	3	1.85	16	14	8	0	87	69	26	18	16	79
Jay Akin, Arkansas State	8	5	1.96	18	12	7	2	110	87	32	24	28	77
Jason Navarro, Tulane	12	2	2.00	17	16	4	0	112	81	45	25	37	135
Tyson Taplin, Alcorn State	8	2	2.01	12	10	8	0	72	56	22	16	15	53
Eddie Reyes, Miami (Fla.)	8	2	2.04	43	0	0	2	71	53	26	16	26	79
Matt Anderson, Rice	10	2	2.05	30	0	0	9	79	48	27	18	29	105
Mark Newell, Oregon State	8	0	2.12	10	10	3	0	72	69	24	17	12	69
Eric Cammack, Lamar	5	5	2.15	26	1	0	8	63	41	23	15	20	89
Clay Eason, N.C. State	10	2	2.18	28	0	0	4	62	42	17	15	27	78
Geoff Geary, Oklahoma	4	3	2.20	32	0	0	8	61	47	18	15	28	63
Rich Perez, Yale	8	2	2.24	13	9	6	0	64	60	31	16	22	38
Matt Phillips, Delaware	9	0	2.25	14	11	7	2	76	59	24	19	38	68
Mark Mulder, Michigan State	7	2	2.26	20	7	4	4	68	66	22	17	12	56
Dan Reichert, Pacific	13	4	2.30	20	17	7	0	133	96	55	34	51	169
Mike Hughes, St. John's	8	4	2.30	14	12	7	0	86	62	33	22	29	79
Derek Adair, St. John's	9	2	2.32	17	12	6	1	85	65	27	22	24	71
Mark Barron, Marist	10	3	2.32	16	15	5	1	105	86	44	27	36	75
Damon Yee, Vanderbilt	4	2	2.33	22	4	1	1	66	56	23	17	22	69
Mark Maberry, Tennessee Tech	12	2	2.34	16	14	10	1	104	81	39	27	35	108
Andrew Duffell, Harvard	8	1	2.35	12	11	4	0	69	60	32	18	25	33
Josh Fogg, Florida	7	3	2.37	41	0	0	8	91	67	36	24	35	84
Thomas Ford, Hawaii-Hilo	2	5	2.39	12	12	2	1	67	59	40	23	44	58
Ray Cavanagh, Fla. International	9	2	2.49	25	3	1	4	80	67	28	22	30	82
Kevin Carlson, Navy	7	5	2.55	13	13	8	0	92	83	44	26	29	63
Mark Squire, Wright State	4	4	2.56	29	0	0	11	60	65	23	17	16	33
Jerry Lynde, Vermont	7	1	2.62	11	10	7	1	72	55	26	21	22	64
Chris Frey, Delaware	8	0	2.64	13	10	6	0	75	67	28	22	25	76
Chad Harville, Memphis	5	6	2.66	17	12	7	1	102	71	48	30	49	136
Mike Frank, Santa Clara	11	0	2.70	15	12	2	0	73	59	29	22	23	73
Ben Singer, Akron	7	3	2.75	13	12	1	0	72	68	29	22	26	43
Calvin Key, Arkansas State	6	4	2.80	14	12	2	0	80	74	34	25	26	64
Mark Vallecorsa, San Diego	3	4	2.86	14	8	3	0	63	65	28	20	16	32
Mike Hedman, Purdue	6	4	2.87	14	13	5	1	94	85	51	30	17	52
Ryan Mills, Arizona State	6	3	2.88	15	15	2	0	97	82	48	31	50	103
Eric Thompson, Ohio State	10	3	2.88	18	15	6	0	97	91	38	31	39	97

WINS	W	L
Jason Parsons, UNC G'boro	15	1
Tim Hudson, Auburn	15	2
Patrick Coogan, Louisiana State	14	3
Heath Henderson, Alabama	13	2
Jim Parque, UCLA	13	2
Randy Choate, Florida State	13	3
Dan Reichert, Pacific	13	4
Chris Enochs, West Virginia	12	1
Cody Robbins, SW Louisiana	12	1
Jason Navarro, Tulane	12	2
Brian Partenheimer, Indiana	12	2
Mark Maberry, Tennesse Tech	12	2
Kris Wilson, Georgia Tech	12	2
Doug Thompson, Louisiana St.	12	3
Louie Witte, Xavier	12	3
Trey Poland, SW Louisiana	12	5

LOSSES	W	L
Mark Bridges, Ark.-Little Rock	2	12
Jamie Burton, Southern Utah	1	11

APPEARANCES	G
Eddie Reyes, Miami (Fla.)	43
Tod Lee, Georgia Southern	42
Josh Fogg, Florida	41
Van Johnson, Mississippi State	39
Mike McDonald, Santa Clara	38

COMPLETE GAMES	GS	CG
Louie Witte, Xavier	15	12
Jonathan Coulombe, Davidson	13	10
Chris Enochs, West Virginia	14	10
Mark Maberry, Tenn. Tech	14	10
Mike Rawls, Bethune-Cook.	14	10
Brian Lawrence, NW State	15	10
Jeff Weaver, Fresno State	17	10

Jeff Weaver

SAVES	G	SV
Ara Petrosian, Long Beach State	35	15
Van Johnson, Miss. State	39	13
Marc Bluma, Wichita State	27	12
Mark Squire, Wright State	29	11
David Johnson, Kansas State	29	11
Jack Krawczyk, Southern Cal	33	11
Jon Schreiner, Wis.-Milwaukee	23	10
Tyler Steketee, Michigan	23	10
Jason Jennings, Baylor	27	10
Marques Davis, Oklahoma St.	30	10
Eric French, Texas	31	10
Mike McDonald, Santa Clara	38	10

Tim Hudson

INNINGS PITCHED	G	IP
Kyle Peterson, Stanford	20	144
Jason Norton, South Alabama	24	143
Jeff Weaver, Fresno State	21	141
Trey Poland, SW Louisiana	22	137
Eric Knott, Stetson	23	137
Randy Choate, Florida State	19	135
J.D. Arteaga, Miami (Fla.)	22	135
Dan Reichert, Pacific	20	133

BASES ON BALLS	IP	BB
Peter Moore, Temple	117	80
Daniel Wren, Howard	75	78
Rocky Biddle, Long Beach St.	105	74
Keith Wilson, Centenary	86	69
Matt McClendon, Florida	96	69

STRIKEOUTS	IP	SO
Jeff Weaver, Fresno State	141	181
Dan Reichert, Pacific	133	169
Tim Hudson, Auburn	118	165
Doug Thompson, LSU	124	158
Kyle Peterson, Stanford	144	156
Eric DuBose, Miss. State	119	145
Patrick Coogan, LSU	125	144
Jason Fawcett, Troy State	112	141
Trey Poland, SW Louisiana	137	140
Adam Pettyjohn, Fresno State	122	139
Jason Gooding, Texas Tech	116	137
Chad Harville, Memphis	102	136
Jason Navarro, Tulane	112	135
Rocky Biddle, Long Beach St.	105	134
Jason Norton, South Alabama	143	132
Marcus Jones, Long Beach St.	128	131
Randy Wolf, Pepperdine	121	128
Josh Gandy, Georgia	110	126
Randy Choate, Florida State	135	126
Jason Grilli, Seton Hall	81	125
Barry Zito, UC Santa Barbara	85	123
Eric Knott, Stetson	137	123
Bryan Hebson, Auburn	112	121
Peter Moore, Temple	117	120
Jim Parque, UCLA	120	119
Monty Ward, Texas Tech	86	117
Travis Easler, Char. Southern	109	117
David D'Amico, Mercer	120	117
Matt Wise, CS Fullerton	116	116
Brad Finken, Indiana State	109	115

STRIKEOUTS/9 INNINGS (Minimum 50 inninings)	IP	SO	AVG
Tod Lee, Georgia Southern	64	99	13.9
Jason Grilli, Seton Hall	81	125	13.8
Barry Zito, UCSB	85	123	13.0
Ryan Saylor, East. Ky.	68	98	12.9
Eric Cammack, Lamar	63	89	12.8
Tim Hudson, Auburn	118	165	12.5
Monty Ward, Texas Tech	86	117	12.2
Chad Harville, Memphis	102	136	12.0
Matt Anderson, Rice	79	105	12.0
Bryan Williamson, Jack. St.	66	87	11.9
Casey Fossum, Texas A&M	87	113	11.7

BASEBALL AMERICA'S COLLEGE TOP 25

BATTERS: 10 or more at-bats.
PITCHERS: 5 or more innings.
Boldface indicates selected in 1997 draft.

1. LOUISIANA STATE

Coach: Skip Bertman **Record:** 57-13

BATTING	AVG	AB	R	H	2B	3B	HR	RBI	SB
Larson, Brandon, ss	.381	289	82	110	16	2	40	118	9
Furniss, Eddy, 1b	.378	259	77	98	25	0	17	77	0
Barbier, Blair, 2b	.353	252	82	89	23	0	15	57	4
Koerner, Mike, of	.352	273	74	96	18	2	22	69	17
Bernhardt, Tom, of	.322	202	43	65	7	0	17	49	6
Higgins, Danny, dh-2b	.302	202	60	61	12	2	11	41	7
Cuntz, Casey, 3b	.287	164	40	47	8	1	11	33	1
Davis, Wes, of	.278	187	48	52	7	0	16	50	12
McClure, Trey, 3b-2b	.278	209	51	58	10	3	12	44	2
Witten, Jeremy, of	.277	47	21	13	3	1	3	11	4
Bennett, Bryon, of	.267	60	14	16	3	0	1	7	6
Horton, Conan, c	.255	110	24	28	3	0	5	24	1
Thibodeaux, Johnnie, 3b-p	.238	21	7	5	1	0	2	7	1
Earnhart, Clint, c	.233	90	20	21	6	0	6	20	1
Polozola, Keith, ss	.227	22	5	5	0	0	1	3	0
Cresse, Brad, c	.221	122	25	27	4	0	9	22	0

PITCHING	W	L	ERA	G	SV	IP	H	BB	SO
Albritton, Jason	0	0	3.45	15	1	16	12	12	21
Demouy, Chris	6	1	3.63	36	5	62	59	24	70
Guillory, Dan	1	0	3.79	24	1	36	39	8	36
Shipp, Kevin	4	1	4.10	11	0	53	56	10	56
Daugherty, Brian	4	0	4.37	34	1	47	45	10	42
Coogan, Patrick	14	3	4.46	25	3	125	114	36	144
Painich, Joey	9	2	4.52	22	1	78	81	27	72
Thompson, Doug	12	3	4.63	25	1	124	133	44	158
Berthelot, Eric	7	3	5.98	22	0	59	77	23	53
Leonardi, Antonio	0	0	9.20	12	0	15	25	8	23

2. ALABAMA

Coach: Jim Wells **Record:** 56-14

BATTING	AVG	AB	R	H	2B	3B	HR	RBI	SB
Vaz, Roberto, of-p	.400	255	87	102	17	9	22	73	14
Caruso, Joe, 2b	.378	259	64	98	21	3	15	76	12
Keller, G.W., dh-of	.369	249	62	92	14	3	21	68	5
Phillips, Andy, 3b	.366	279	68	102	25	3	15	65	5
Tidwell, David, of	.342	295	86	101	18	4	10	65	35
Mohr, Dustan, of	.337	249	68	84	19	0	25	79	1
Frick, Matt, c	.331	242	59	80	11	2	16	55	3
Watson, Brandon, dh	.327	55	15	18	5	0	0	13	0
Mote, David, 1b	.313	16	3	5	2	0	1	2	0
Peer, Mark, of	.307	75	23	23	6	0	4	16	0
Tucker, Robbie, 1b	.305	223	52	68	13	2	20	67	2
Chavers, Dan, ss	.290	31	10	9	0	2	0	5	0
Cox, Jayson, c	.279	43	12	12	2	0	3	7	0
Bounds, Drew, of	.274	62	22	17	1	2	5	13	0
Duncan, Nate, ss	.256	168	39	43	9	3	3	16	0
Davis, Heath, 2b	.190	21	7	4	0	1	0	1	0

PITCHING	W	L	ERA	G	SV	IP	H	BB	SO
Kingrey, Jarrod	10	1	3.16	33	4	88	83	38	76
Vaz, Roberto	4	1	3.40	22	8	50	35	27	52
Fisher, Pete	10	3	4.55	18	0	119	139	36	82
Henderson, Heath	13	2	4.63	22	1	124	139	37	104
Hurst, Doug	4	1	4.64	26	4	54	61	25	51
Eilers, Chris	1	1	4.67	10	0	17	27	4	13
Torres, Manny	5	0	5.27	13	0	56	63	15	43
Daniel, Michael	5	1	6.13	19	1	54	67	8	33
Bernard, Andy	4	4	6.65	18	1	47	59	10	40
Bernard, Matt	0	0	14.14	6	0	7	15	2	4

JEFF GOLDEN

Bellwether for No. 3 Miami
Pat Burrell batted .409 with 21 homers, 76 RBIs

3. MIAMI

Coach: Jim Morris **Record:** 51-18

BATTING	AVG	AB	R	H	2B	3B	HR	RBI	SB
Michaels, Jason, of	.411	258	71	106	32	3	15	89	14
Burrell, Pat, 3b	.409	215	79	88	19	2	21	76	12
Huff, Aubrey, 1b	.385	182	50	70	15	2	10	52	4
Jacomino, Mandy, of	.379	190	50	72	21	2	9	49	2
Grimmett, Ryan, of	.319	232	62	74	9	4	3	25	53
Lopez-Cao, Mike, c	.317	221	49	70	18	2	5	55	3
Alvarez, German, of-dh	.315	92	24	29	7	1	2	21	1
Saggese, Rick, of-dh	.296	115	19	34	6	0	3	20	1
Hill, Bobby, 2b-ss	.291	247	76	72	14	1	4	49	41
Esquival, Lale, 1b-dh	.279	129	27	36	6	0	7	33	3
Brewer, Brad, ss	.275	200	40	55	10	3	1	33	5
Walker, Mark, of	.266	109	20	29	8	1	2	21	7
Jacobson, Russ, c	.263	38	4	10	0	0	0	5	1
Gutierrez, Jimmy, 2b	.220	50	9	11	3	1	1	4	0
Cartaya, Oscar, ss	.200	55	9	11	0	1	2	9	0
Smith, Damar, of	.069	29	11	2	0	0	0	0	2

PITCHING	W	L	ERA	G	SV	IP	H	BB	SO
Morrison, Robbie	4	2	1.49	37	8	54	38	28	82
Reyes, Eddie	8	2	2.04	43	2	71	53	26	79
Petretta, Bob	0	0	2.31	18	0	12	13	6	11
Arteaga, J.D.	11	4	3.27	22	0	135	141	31	100
Santos, Alex	9	3	4.17	21	0	91	76	34	100
Spassoff, Darin	9	5	4.61	18	0	94	94	41	64
Ozias, Todd	4	1	4.93	22	1	38	41	21	31
Gil, David	5	0	5.13	15	1	54	55	30	52
Howell, Greg	0	1	5.95	13	0	20	27	7	15
Lopez-Cao, Andrew	0	0	6.30	15	0	10	11	9	5
Gutierrez, Lazaro	1	0	7.50	14	0	30	34	22	32

4. STANFORD

Coach: Mark Marquess **Record:** 45-20

BATTING	AVG	AB	R	H	2B	3B	HR	RBI	SB
Alvarado, Damien, c	.400	10	2	4	0	0	0	1	0
Muth, Edmund, of	.388	178	58	69	12	2	9	46	4
Gall, John, dh-1b	.376	258	49	97	18	0	8	59	3
Hochgesang, Josh, 3b	.365	263	59	96	22	2	17	77	9
Kilburg, Joe, 2b-of	.363	240	80	87	20	3	6	60	12
Schaeffer, Jon, c	.349	232	65	81	13	2	20	76	1
Pecci, Jay, ss	.320	231	46	74	13	0	3	31	7

	AVG	AB	R	H	2B	3B	HR	RBI	SB
Quaccia, Luke, 1b	.320	225	50	72	17	0	9	43	4
Clark, Chris, of	.311	219	38	68	11	1	9	44	8
Rizzo, Jeff, 3b	.306	36	6	11	3	0	0	5	0
Gerut, Jody, of	.305	249	66	76	15	1	9	63	13
Schrager, Tony, 2b	.289	142	36	41	6	0	7	18	4
Salter, John, c	.196	46	9	9	1	0	2	7	0
Day, Nick, of	.175	40	11	7	1	1	1	5	1
Chan, Stephen, of	.167	12	5	2	0	0	0	2	0

PITCHING	W	L	ERA	G	SV	IP	H	BB	SO
Cogan, Tony	7	4	3.63	36	4	72	61	21	51
Austin, Jeff	6	2	4.14	26	4	87	97	28	93
Newton, Cameron	1	0	4.15	7	1	9	6	5	7
Peterson, Kyle	11	3	4.19	20	0	144	134	38	156
Koons, Josh	4	3	4.31	22	1	48	42	22	35
Hoard, Brent	9	4	5.75	18	0	83	86	49	74
Hutchinson, Chad	8	4	5.76	19	0	106	102	68	114
Linville, Geoff	0	0	5.87	4	0	8	10	2	2
Harris, Adam	0	0	6.33	10	0	21	30	10	13
Fearnow, Brian	0	0	9.00	4	0	6	13	4	4

5. UCLA

Coach: Gary Adams **Record:** 45-21

BATTING	AVG	AB	R	H	2B	3B	HR	RBI	SB
Glaus, Troy, ss-3b	.409	264	100	108	15	1	34	91	10
Green, Jason, c	.394	33	10	13	3	0	0	9	1
Santora, Jack, ss	.389	90	14	35	2	2	2	17	1
Zamora, Pete, 1b-p	.379	240	46	91	19	1	16	74	1
Theodorou, Nick, 2b	.365	208	50	76	17	0	6	47	10
Heinrichs, Jon, of	.358	299	92	107	28	2	28	79	16
Valent, Eric, of	.339	274	74	93	16	3	27	91	3
Byrnes, Eric, of	.332	277	95	92	24	1	17	60	19
Hymes, Mike, of	.320	25	6	8	0	0	0	2	0
Matoian, Chad, dh-2b	.314	169	25	53	13	0	1	29	0
Nista, Brett, ss-1b	.311	122	24	38	7	0	4	25	3
Olson, Cassidy, 1b	.293	99	17	29	6	0	0	13	0
Pinto, Aldo, 3b	.289	128	22	37	8	0	1	14	0
Schult, Rob, 3b	.250	32	6	8	3	1	1	4	0
Jaramillo, Mike, c	.245	53	7	13	2	0	1	7	1
Cloud, Casey, c	.244	172	31	42	8	0	3	21	0
Roques, Ryan, of	.188	16	10	3	0	0	1	3	3
Valent, Royce, c	.118	17	1	2	1	0	0	3	0
Pieper, Billy, of	.091	11	0	1	0	0	0	1	0

PITCHING	W	L	ERA	G	SV	IP	H	BB	SO
Righetti, Tony	1	0	2.63	17	0	24	23	16	26
Jacquez, Tom	10	4	3.06	19	0	129	115	42	100
Parque, Jim	13	2	3.08	19	0	120	117	63	119
Henkel, Rob	3	3	3.67	34	2	42	37	19	49
Meyer, Jake	3	3	4.20	30	8	30	27	23	28
Zamora, Pete	6	2	5.06	17	2	100	121	33	73
St. George, Nick	1	0	5.14	11	0	21	28	7	9
Keller, Dan	3	5	5.66	19	0	56	76	34	22
Klein, Matt	2	0	6.50	15	0	18	25	11	7
Crecion, Gabe	1	2	7.01	11	0	26	31	18	16
Phillips, John	1	0	11.85	9	0	14	22	12	16
Thielemann, Al	0	0	13.50	6	0	10	19	4	8

6. AUBURN

Coach: Hal Baird **Record:** 50-17

BATTING	AVG	AB	R	H	2B	3B	HR	RBI	SB
Sullivan, Adam, of	.396	260	81	103	16	2	5	44	16
Hudson, Tim, of-p	.396	273	71	108	21	0	18	95	2
Macrory, Rob, 2b	.368	269	77	99	24	5	1	42	26
Dunn, Casey, c	.362	235	54	85	19	1	5	56	0
Reif, Derek, dh-of	.343	213	51	73	20	2	4	48	6
Etheredge, Josh, of	.342	234	79	80	16	2	20	82	6
Wandall, Chad, 3b	.318	233	51	74	11	1	10	55	4
Kersh, Jamie, 1b	.301	266	58	80	14	3	13	72	1
Kelly, Heath, ss	.288	233	48	67	13	1	4	41	5
Dearth, Tucker, of	.276	58	16	16	2	1	3	11	0
Hill, Harrel, 3b-ss	.263	38	6	10	1	0	0	8	0
Ross, David, c	.250	96	13	24	6	0	2	18	1

PITCHING	W	L	ERA	G	SV	IP	H	BB	SO
Hudson, Tim	15	2	2.97	22	0	118	87	50	165
Woodward, Finley	3	4	3.78	26	8	50	42	27	62
Dunham, Patrick	5	2	3.99	28	5	77	82	20	64
Knorst, Kevin	5	2	4.10	20	3	68	73	25	59
Hebson, Bryan	11	4	4.43	19	0	112	103	38	121
Hancock, Josh	2	0	4.75	13	0	30	34	15	32
Schoening, Brent	5	3	5.50	16	1	75	76	33	65
Jones, George	0	0	5.50	8	0	18	18	13	17

	W	L	ERA	G	SV	IP	H	BB	SO
Bean, Colter	1	0	6.65	14	0	22	22	12	23
Marriott, Alex	3	0	7.48	13	1	22	31	13	21

7. MISSISSIPPI STATE

Coach: Ron Polk **Record:** 47-21

BATTING	AVG	AB	R	H	2B	3B	HR	RBI	SB
McGrath, Ryan, c-of	.467	30	13	14	1	1	1	15	0
Sparkman, Sparky, of	.375	16	6	6	0	0	0	2	0
Lee, Richard, 1b	.362	276	71	100	14	3	19	90	2
Piatt, Adam, 3b	.361	244	71	88	17	2	17	69	7
Bryan, Brooks, of	.345	255	61	88	14	1	6	57	11
Chapman, Travis, 2b	.344	186	41	64	14	1	3	40	2
Scioneaux, Damian, of	.341	255	67	87	11	5	6	47	20
Thoms, Rusty, of	.338	204	50	69	10	2	4	31	5
Patton, Barry, c	.338	231	45	78	14	0	7	57	0
Terry, Brian, dh	.333	51	11	17	2	0	2	15	0
Dabbs, Dustin, dh-c	.320	122	28	39	3	0	4	27	2
Freeman, Brad, ss	.311	235	58	73	12	0	8	49	9
Wiese, Brian, dh-p	.303	99	22	30	7	0	1	24	2
Shumaker, Brad, ss-2b	.300	10	3	3	0	0	0	1	0
Power, Mark, of	.284	88	15	25	4	2	0	12	6
Clark, Scott, of	.278	18	6	5	1	0	1	5	0
Hauswald, Rob, 2b	.234	77	17	18	1	1	3	19	0
Peeples, Matt, ss-2b	.209	67	20	14	2	1	0	9	3

PITCHING	W	L	ERA	G	SV	IP	H	BB	SO
Thoms, Hank	5	0	2.81	23	1	51	53	14	55
Donovan, Kevin	3	2	4.19	12	0	19	17	5	25
Johnson, Van	5	4	4.21	39	13	83	80	14	90
Walters, Barry	0	0	4.24	16	0	17	22	12	21
DuBose, Eric	9	4	4.32	21	0	119	122	67	145
Reinike, Chris	3	3	4.91	21	2	66	75	38	69
Jackson, Jeremy	9	4	5.14	16	0	75	79	40	76
Ginter, Matt	2	0	6.23	17	0	43	57	14	61
Dilgard, Keith	6	1	6.25	15	0	72	90	24	64
Wiese, Brian	5	3	7.92	17	0	50	64	36	46

8. RICE

Coach: Wayne Graham **Record:** 47-16

BATTING	AVG	AB	R	H	2B	3B	HR	RBI	SB
Berkman, Lance, 1b	.431	255	109	110	22	4	41	134	8
Berg, Justin, c-dh	.386	215	40	83	10	3	13	59	6
Baker, Jacob, 3b	.362	232	52	84	9	3	12	51	5
Savarino, J.J., 2b-p	.357	28	11	10	0	0	0	6	1
Lorenz, Matt, dh	.353	17	6	6	0	0	1	7	0
Crosby, Bubba, of	.349	258	72	90	14	11	22	88	11
Cathey, Joseph, ss	.343	268	81	92	12	0	2	39	9
Herndon, Adam, of-p	.333	81	19	27	8	0	4	12	4
Richards, Jason, 2b	.314	229	76	72	14	4	9	37	6
Joseph, Kevin, p-ss	.300	10	3	3	1	0	1	3	0
Ford, Will, of	.300	233	51	70	10	6	9	59	12
McLaughlin, Tim, c	.288	160	20	46	4	1	0	29	2
Bates, Jeremy, 2b	.278	18	8	5	1	0	1	4	0
Mathews, Ryan, dh-3b	.275	102	24	28	4	0	2	17	2
Williams, Charles, of	.253	174	34	44	6	3	3	18	6

PITCHING	W	L	ERA	G	SV	IP	H	BB	SO
Anderson, Matt	10	2	2.05	30	9	79	48	29	105
Savarino, J.J.	0	0	2.25	9	0	12	9	9	8
Nichols, Jeff	10	2	3.42	21	1	108	104	31	71
Terrana, Peter	2	0	3.57	17	1	35	35	11	46
Ramos, Mario	9	3	5.09	23	1	111	127	49	91
Kurtz-Nicholl, Jesse	1	2	5.02	23	0	29	30	15	26
Bess, Stephen	3	3	6.23	14	0	48	52	31	45
Gwyn, Marc	8	0	6.49	24	0	61	64	37	60
Joseph, Kevin	3	2	6.30	15	1	40	46	29	34
Herndon, Adam	1	2	7.92	8	0	25	30	15	21

9. FLORIDA STATE

Coach: Mike Martin **Record:** 50-17

BATTING	AVG	AB	R	H	2B	3B	HR	RBI	SB
Drew, J.D., of	.455	233	110	106	15	5	31	100	32
Badeaux, Brooks, ss	.365	170	48	62	13	0	5	30	15
Morris, Jeremy, of	.356	250	73	89	22	6	25	116	25
Bonenberger, Jimmy, of	.333	12	4	4	0	0	2	4	1
Zech, Scott, 2b	.309	265	86	82	13	2	6	50	31
Zabala, Jose, 3b	.309	136	46	42	4	1	1	22	5
Mayfield, Henry, dh-c	.298	57	15	17	4	0	1	11	3
Salazar, Jeremy, c	.297	158	35	47	12	0	7	29	3
Sprague, Geoff, 3b-1b	.292	253	40	74	18	1	7	62	12

JEFF GOLDEN

All-around Arizona State star
Dan McKinley batted .423 with 15 homers, 70 RBIs

BATTING	AVG	AB	R	H	2B	3B	HR	RBI	SB
Henderson, Terry, dh-of	.289	114	27	33	8	1	6	26	6
Klosterman, Jeremiah, c	.289	135	25	39	7	1	5	24	1
Cox, Brian, of-1b	.264	125	30	33	6	0	2	14	13
Griggs, Reggie, dh-1b	.254	59	11	15	2	0	3	11	0
Cash, Kevin, ss-3b	.239	67	17	16	4	0	6	18	0
McCorkel, Shawn, of	.238	151	37	36	8	0	7	29	10
Woodward, Matt, 1b	.231	173	30	40	8	0	0	18	4

PITCHING	W	L	ERA	G	SV	IP	H	BB	SO
Diaz, Zach	3	4	3.26	30	5	69	66	19	68
Choate, Randy	13	3	3.61	19	0	135	123	37	126
Bentley, John	5	1	3.86	17	1	56	53	19	44
DiBlasi, Mike	2	1	3.86	21	2	28	22	23	31
Proctor, Scott	7	1	4.14	17	0	50	57	24	48
Chavez, Chris	4	1	4.24	27	6	74	76	42	78
Stanford, Matt	0	0	4.35	11	0	10	7	9	4
Niles, Randy	8	5	4.58	18	1	96	105	43	104
Howell, Chuck	8	1	5.18	21	1	83	100	17	70

10. SOUTHERN CALIFORNIA

Coach: Mike Gillepsie **Record:** 42-20

BATTING	AVG	AB	R	H	2B	3B	HR	RBI	SB
Hanoian, Greg, of	.429	119	28	51	10	0	1	30	7
Brown, Jason, of-c	.368	144	26	53	11	0	10	45	4
Rachels, Wes, 2b	.364	220	50	80	11	1	2	41	15
Gorr, Rob, of	.347	251	64	87	16	1	6	52	6
Munson, Eric, c-dh	.336	232	57	78	11	0	13	50	8
Ticehurst, Brad, of	.328	134	34	44	11	0	4	18	8
Mirizzi, Marc, ss	.325	277	53	90	21	0	5	37	6
Walbridge, Greg, 1b	.315	248	50	78	24	1	4	46	9
DePippo, Jeff, c	.310	87	24	27	6	0	1	9	8
Ensberg, Morgan, 3b	.306	235	60	72	17	1	8	44	14
Ponchak, Brian, dh	.282	124	21	35	9	0	6	30	3
Freitas, Jeremy, of	.277	137	28	38	9	1	7	35	5

PITCHING	W	L	ERA	G	SV	IP	H	BB	SO
Etherton, Seth	10	2	2.96	16	0	109	104	33	106
Krawczyk, Jack	2	3	3.20	33	11	39	29	3	26
Weibling, Mike	4	1	3.86	31	0	44	52	7	32
Immel, Steve	7	4	4.33	23	1	62	70	17	50
Jones, Craig	1	1	4.37	13	0	23	30	11	14
Flores, Randy	9	5	4.46	17	0	113	128	34	93
Penney, Mike	1	0	5.05	17	0	41	40	19	23
Henderson, Scott	8	4	5.82	18	0	73	93	19	43
Sanchez, Paul	0	0	6.55	18	0	22	31	15	27
Saenz, Jason	0	0	8.36	12	0	14	13	13	15

11. ARIZONA STATE

Coach: Pat Murphy **Record:** 39-22

BATTING	AVG	AB	R	H	2B	3B	HR	RBI	SB
McKinley, Dan, of	.423	267	88	113	21	5	15	70	32
Tillman, Kevin, 1b-dh	.386	83	19	32	5	1	2	22	0
Beinbrink, Andrew, 3b	.380	242	60	92	23	4	9	72	5
Bloomquist, Willie, ss-2b	.356	132	33	47	10	5	1	31	7
Leon, Richy, ss-p	.353	184	36	65	7	3	2	27	2
Gosewisch, Chip, c-2b	.348	112	21	39	10	1	0	19	4
Grijalva, Mike, 1b	.321	131	20	42	10	1	4	25	3
Kolb, Damien, dh	.316	19	4	6	1	0	0	3	1
Moreno, Mikel, of	.313	224	67	70	16	3	8	38	10
Arguelles, Rudy, of	.301	183	67	55	5	2	0	18	10
Halvorson, Greg, c	.295	183	31	54	23	0	10	49	1
Bradley, Ryan, p-1b	.278	18	6	5	0	0	1	5	0
Collins, Michael, ss	.277	148	30	41	5	1	1	14	2
Delucchi, Dustin, of-1b	.255	141	22	36	8	1	1	33	3
Cermak, Jeff, of-p	.238	63	12	15	3	1	2	11	1
Sitzman, Jay, of	.231	13	3	3	0	0	0	4	0
Tommasini, Kevin, of	.179	78	7	14	4	0	0	14	4
James, Brandon,1b	.133	15	4	2	1	0	0	2	0

PITCHING	W	L	ERA	G	SV	IP	H	BB	SO
Leon, Richy	1	1	2.01	17	2	31	28	10	31
Call, Colin	0	0	2.19	7	0	12	15	7	6
Mills, Ryan	6	3	2.88	15	0	97	82	50	103
Lowery, Phill	6	2	4.13	18	0	85	78	41	79
Gehrke, Jay	1	0	4.41	6	0	16	14	11	19
Bradley, Ryan	7	7	5.40	35	7	60	65	25	76
Cermak, Jeff	7	3	5.52	17	1	75	78	20	45
Verdugo, Jason	2	1	6.00	14	0	45	51	17	42
Byrd, Ben	6	2	6.29	20	2	54	63	22	40
Marietta, Ron	3	2	7.02	19	0	41	51	23	37
Bane, Jaymie	0	1	10.67	15	0	14	23	10	14
Vasquez, Tim	0	0	16.71	10	0	7	12	9	3

12. TEXAS TECH

Coach: Larry Hays **Record:** 46-14

BATTING	AVG	AB	R	H	2B	3B	HR	RBI	SB
Ginter, Keith, 2b	.426	249	93	106	24	2	17	77	29
Buckley, Brandon, c-3b	.418	98	23	41	9	0	2	26	0
Dillon, Joe, 1b-3b	.393	229	80	90	20	3	33	89	19
Landreth, Jason, of-dh	.379	203	72	77	29	1	9	66	20
Toro, Brandon, of	.376	229	69	86	25	4	10	51	26
Nadeau, Rick, of	.375	16	4	6	2	0	1	6	1
Bard, Josh, c	.359	231	60	83	23	0	13	69	0
Shuffield, Chris, 1b-of	.350	100	25	35	7	1	5	33	4
Smith, Joe, 3b-of	.327	52	12	17	1	0	1	9	0
Oliveras, Jess, ss	.325	169	57	55	15	1	6	40	5
Langen, Shane, of	.321	156	36	50	3	2	2	25	7
Rinehart, Jake, of	.313	16	13	9	1	0	0	3	1
Ayers, Carter, of-3b	.308	65	17	20	7	0	0	20	2
Huth, Jason, ss-2b	.271	221	49	60	12	7	5	43	14
Alvarez, Jose, 3b-of	.242	91	16	22	5	2	4	22	0
Barney, Cody, 3b	.200	10	0	2	0	0	0	0	0
Price, Duane, of	.167	24	10	4	1	0	0	3	2

PITCHING	W	L	ERA	G	SV	IP	H	BB	SO
Ulrich, Kirk	0	0	2.89	6	0	9	6	4	10
Gooding, Jason	11	0	3.49	16	0	116	111	31	137
Hooper, Jimmy	1	0	3.60	18	1	25	23	9	38
Ralston, Brad	3	3	3.65	28	7	57	50	36	72
Wright, Shane	10	2	3.90	15	0	90	108	10	65
Ward, Monty	9	4	4.07	16	0	86	87	29	117
Stewart, Zach	1	2	4.72	22	0	27	38	8	33
Smith, Joe	0	0	5.40	4	0	5	4	1	4
Therneau, David	6	0	5.56	13	0	45	47	10	58
Frush, Jimmy	5	3	6.99	20	0	46	62	20	49
Peck, Jeff	0	0	9.72	14	0	17	20	12	14

13. WASHINGTON

Coach: Ken Knutson **Record:** 46-20

BATTING	AVG	AB	R	H	2B	3B	HR	RBI	SB
Magruder, Chris, 2b-of	.400	260	90	104	19	2	8	54	43
Miller, Kevin, ss	.384	250	77	96	17	5	12	73	4
Soules, Ryan, 1b-dh	.383	235	63	90	23	2	12	67	3
Williamson, Bryan, of-p	.381	197	41	75	14	1	4	58	6
Na, Jim, of	.365	115	27	42	12	4	4	30	2
Woody, Dominic, c	.358	67	17	24	5	0	3	17	1
Erickson, Ed, 1b	.333	99	21	33	5	0	8	25	0
Woods, Kyle, of	.333	78	28	26	3	1	1	10	10
Lentz, Ryan, 3b	.327	251	58	82	26	2	9	69	3
Stefonick, Nick, of	.317	139	46	44	11	2	6	39	13
Bundy, Ryan, c	.311	193	45	60	17	1	6	40	14
Porter, Jamie, of	.292	209	61	61	11	5	4	30	16
Whitemarsh, Chris, 2b	.262	61	17	16	1	1	4	13	2

BATTING	AVG	AB	R	H	2B	3B	HR	RBI	SB
Nakagawa, Darin, 2b	.255	51	6	13	2	1	0	6	1
Orgill, Pete, dh	.239	88	10	21	6	0	3	19	0
Anderson, Rian, of	.211	19	9	4	0	0	1	3	0
Buck, Buddy, of	.195	41	5	8	3	0	0	6	0

PITCHING	W	L	ERA	G	SV	IP	H	BB	SO
Morrison, Cody	1	0	2.30	14	2	16	10	9	21
Sundby, Matt	3	0	2.81	11	0	26	23	13	21
Williamson, Bryan	4	2	2.89	22	6	44	34	24	49
Kringen, Jake	11	3	4.23	19	0	111	110	54	110
Hampton, Matt	7	1	4.40	17	0	76	91	31	52
Fowler, Blair	5	3	4.78	13	0	49	59	20	26
Lee, Wayne	1	0	4.87	17	0	20	17	7	17
Lynch, Jeff	4	5	5.45	17	1	74	91	26	47
Heaverlo, Jeff	7	4	6.43	16	0	91	108	30	88
Ferguson, Ken	0	0	7.94	12	2	17	18	14	14
Anderson, Travis	0	1	8.74	10	0	11	18	8	8
Hannah, Shawn	2	1	13.97	10	0	19	41	14	15

14. OKLAHOMA STATE

Coach: Tom Holliday **Record:** 46-19

BATTING	AVG	AB	R	H	2B	3B	HR	RBI	SB
Guiel, Jeff, of	.418	251	88	105	32	3	23	79	16
McNamara, Rusty, of-3b	.387	282	80	109	25	5	24	93	10
Lucca, Tony, 1b	.369	168	46	62	11	1	10	54	2
Folmar, Ryan, c-dh	.351	97	24	34	7	0	8	27	2
Kaup, Nathan, 3b	.345	87	17	30	6	0	2	28	0
Gasparino, Billy, 2b-ss	.336	265	89	89	26	4	18	62	21
Roossien, Tony, 3b	.328	174	41	57	11	1	12	54	5
Holliday, Josh, c	.323	223	68	72	21	1	14	60	0
Checotah, Sky, of	.321	28	17	9	2	2	0	4	8
McCullough, Jay, dh-1b	.309	97	25	30	7	0	9	26	0
Wood, Jamey, 1b	.309	94	19	29	4	1	6	22	0
Salhani, Ted, of	.304	148	46	45	5	1	13	42	11
Puffinbarger, Rusty, c	.282	78	22	22	6	0	4	15	1
Burton, Cory, 3b-ss	.277	119	22	33	6	1	1	14	5
Steelmon, Wyley, dh	.255	110	20	28	7	0	3	20	0
Nelson, Eric, ss	.175	80	21	14	3	0	0	8	7

PITCHING	W	L	ERA	G	SV	IP	H	BB	SO
Childers, Wakon	1	0	3.68	5	0	7	7	7	5
Adkins, Jon	11	4	4.62	18	0	117	115	30	82
Dreier, Thom	7	2	4.99	18	0	79	96	47	49
Hendrickson, Eric	3	1	5.03	20	0	34	38	27	20
Williamson, Scott	7	3	5.74	18	0	89	105	44	91
Davis, Marques	6	2	5.85	30	10	48	58	16	44
Nina, Elvin	2	0	5.97	22	0	29	43	14	28
Thomas, Brian	3	2	6.00	17	0	36	52	10	28
Maurer, Dave	3	3	7.02	22	0	58	72	24	57
Ortiz, Julio	2	0	7.04	5	0	8	10	4	3
Askew, Heath	1	0	7.48	11	0	22	34	14	13
Forsythe, Neil	0	1	9.19	19	0	32	51	20	11

15. SOUTH ALABAMA

Coach: Steve Kittrell **Record:** 43-19

BATTING	AVG	AB	R	H	2B	3B	HR	RBI	SB
Williamson, Casey, of	.500	16	7	8	2	0	0	2	2
Salvagio, Tom, 3b	.371	116	28	43	6	1	5	19	5
Curtis, Brey, of	.357	199	52	71	9	2	3	35	23
Choron, Joey, 2b	.348	253	58	88	17	2	21	73	4
Stacy, I.B., 1b	.341	226	59	77	19	1	15	62	7
Masino, Josh, of	.333	18	3	6	1	0	0	1	0
Taylor, Seth, ss	.325	114	27	37	10	0	3	32	6
Jackson, Brett, dh	.324	145	28	47	13	0	9	36	2
Whitehurst, Tom, of	.314	194	53	61	15	2	3	41	14
Sutley, Andy, of	.309	94	28	29	5	0	0	12	6
Smith, Eric, of	.308	143	28	44	5	0	5	26	2
Wiley, Terry, c	.302	215	33	65	11	0	6	36	6
Deason, Terrell, p-ss	.300	20	4	6	1	0	1	4	1
Granville, Earnie, of	.292	72	14	21	5	1	2	10	1
Touchstone, Brad, c	.231	26	4	6	3	0	0	4	0
Breazeale, Rob, ss-3b	.228	171	36	39	5	0	3	21	14
Bolton, Gabe, of	.228	57	7	13	2	0	2	9	0
Crain, Jason, 3b	.224	85	20	19	4	0	0	12	3

PITCHING	W	L	ERA	G	SV	IP	H	BB	SO
Nobles, Chris	0	0	2.16	7	0	8	10	7	4
Sparks, Stephen	11	1	3.73	19	0	101	104	46	84
Ramsden, Bryan	2	1	3.94	8	0	16	23	4	12
Fischer, Mike	5	3	3.96	29	9	64	60	17	68
Rayborn, Kenny	2	1	4.26	15	1	51	56	23	44
Norton, Jason	9	6	4.29	24	0	143	138	48	132
Nakamura, Mike	11	2	4.98	24	2	72	74	26	83

Over the top for Washington
Shortstop Kevin Miller drove in 73 runs

PITCHING	W	L	ERA	G	SV	IP	H	BB	SO
Deason, Terrell	3	4	5.27	21	1	56	69	29	46
Cooke, Peter	0	1	10.45	13	0	21	33	12	13
Driskell, Chris	0	0	12.71	2	0	6	11	1	2

16. FLORIDA

Coach: Andy Lopez **Record:** 40-24

BATTING	AVG	AB	R	H	2B	3B	HR	RBI	SB
Wilkerson, Brad, 1b-p	.386	236	82	91	15	3	23	76	11
Nicholson, Derek, of	.364	247	61	90	20	1	9	67	15
Haught, Brian, of	.357	182	34	65	8	5	9	44	15
Smith, Casey, c-of	.353	204	42	72	10	2	7	60	6
Eckstein, David, 2b	.341	276	85	94	18	3	8	34	35
Ellis, Mark, 3b	.326	267	67	87	16	3	11	45	9
Andre, Travis, 1b-dh	.313	83	15	26	4	0	2	20	0
Floyd, Mike, of	.300	30	5	9	3	1	0	5	1
Martin, Ty, ss	.291	213	30	62	12	1	2	27	8
Hazzard, Chuck, dh-1b	.283	226	46	64	9	1	5	36	6
Hudson, Josh, c-of	.256	121	20	31	6	1	3	18	2
Seroyer, Shane, c	.250	24	3	6	2	0	0	6	0
Edge, Dwight, of	.222	27	7	6	0	0	1	7	2
Ogle, Brian, of	.221	104	19	23	4	1	6	20	3
Medina, Octavio, c	.167	42	5	7	2	0	0	4	0
Rhine, Alan, 2b	.083	12	1	1	0	0	0	1	0

PITCHING	W	L	ERA	G	SV	IP	H	BB	SO
Fogg, Josh	7	3	2.37	41	8	91	67	35	84
Wilkerson, Brad	11	4	4.56	26	4	79	73	34	89
Knollin, Chris	5	0	5.37	27	2	65	71	21	58
Gray, Michael	3	3	5.58	27	0	71	103	13	86
Bond, Tommy	3	3	5.93	16	0	74	107	34	46
Rodriguez, Sergio	4	5	6.04	15	0	67	94	16	27
McClendon, Matt	7	6	6.49	20	0	96	117	49	68
Aulet, Charles	0	0	8.31	5	0	9	15	4	5
Fujinaga, Evan	0	0	9.00	I1	0	6	5	6	9
Varnes, Brian	0	0	9.31	5	0	10	15	6	10

17. GEORGIA TECH

Coach: Danny Hall **Record:** 46-15

BATTING	AVG	AB	R	H	2B	3B	HR	RBI	SB
Papetti, Todd, c	.357	28	3	10	1	0	1	2	0
Fischer, Mark, of	.354	257	75	91	10	7	24	98	17
Honeycutt, Heath, 3b-ss	.345	249	52	86	13	5	2	50	17
Leggett, Adam, 2b	.341	267	75	91	17	2	10	52	18
Hood, Jay, ss	.340	141	39	48	8	2	4	31	2
Prather, Scott, of-p	.333	204	56	68	13	0	9	62	4

BATTING	AVG	AB	R	H	2B	3B	HR	RBI	SB
Easterling, Adam, of	.327	217	61	71	9	2	3	26	17
McQueen, Eric, c	.316	206	47	65	7	3	8	46	11
Thomas, J.J., 1b-of	.304	237	70	72	13	1	22	70	9
Wilson, Kris, dh-1b	.299	241	45	72	14	1	5	43	3
Donaghey, Stephen, dh-3b	.292	113	23	33	4	0	3	19	0
Haney, Chris, c	.214	14	5	3	1	0	0	2	1
Overton, Jahmal, of	.188	16	2	3	0	1	0	2	0
Stuetzer, Ryan, 3b-of	.106	47	15	5	1	0	0	4	4

PITCHING	W	L	ERA	G	SV	IP	H	BB	SO
Crowder, Chuck	1	0	2.08	8	1	13	14	10	16
Wilson, Kris	12	2	3.12	19	2	118	114	30	103
Donaghey, Stephen	0	0	3.18	7	1	6	7	3	5
Elder, David	9	4	3.44	22	1	97	96	42	96
Young, Simon	0	0	4.44	19	0	24	27	15	26
Bien, Jeff	0	0	4.50	7	0	6	6	1	1
Wrigley, Jase	7	3	4.67	28	3	79	72	37	66
Yankosky, L.J.	8	3	5.03	19	2	77	79	43	51
Thieme, Rich	5	1	5.37	20	0	52	60	30	57
Prather, Scott	3	1	8.26	19	0	40	50	26	43
Aaron, Robert	1	1	10.38	19	1	26	31	26	20

18. LONG BEACH STATE

Coach: Dave Snow **Record:** 39-26

BATTING	AVG	AB	R	H	2B	3B	HR	RBI	SB
Sanchez, Toby, 1b-of	.402	219	51	88	23	1	13	54	6
Day, Paul, of	.348	233	50	81	13	4	5	42	10
Gonzalez, Izzy, 3b	.331	257	47	85	20	2	4	50	0
Martin, Casey, c	.323	217	40	70	17	0	9	50	2
Doherty, Steve, 2b	.304	237	40	72	15	1	3	45	3
Madison, Jaron, of	.304	138	32	42	11	0	0	18	6
Newkirk, J.J., of	.295	251	60	74	15	4	4	42	14
Lopez, Chuck, of	.290	186	30	54	5	2	2	34	6
Cowley, Keith, dh-1b	.281	135	29	38	2	1	6	28	0
Hyde, Brandon, c	.276	87	16	24	8	0	3	14	0
Vaughn, Lateef, ss	.268	231	38	62	9	0	1	18	11
Monroy, Sam, 2b-ss	.244	45	7	11	1	0	0	3	1
Redfox, Scott, 3b	.182	11	0	2	1	0	0	2	0
Depew, Boe, c	.174	23	3	4	0	0	0	1	0
Toomey, Chris, of	.160	25	3	4	1	0	0	2	0

PITCHING	W	L	ERA	G	SV	IP	H	BB	SO
Jones, Marcus	11	5	3.73	18	0	128	115	33	131
Petrosian, Ara	4	3	3.91	35	15	78	68	34	82
Thomas, Dan	0	0	4.00	16	0	18	20	12	12
Grant, Daryl	3	1	4.15	16	0	39	35	36	44
Biddle, Rocky	9	5	4.47	17	0	105	104	74	134
Cowley, Keith	0	0	5.21	6	0	19	16	2	13
Barrera, Iran	5	4	5.46	20	3	61	95	20	41
Gilich, Denny	5	5	7.47	20	0	59	78	23	40
Montgomery, Matt	2	2	7.78	29	0	42	61	26	40
Gallo, Mike	0	1	10.97	22	1	21	36	14	21

19. OKLAHOMA

Coach: Larry Cochell **Record:** 39-20

BATTING	AVG	AB	R	H	2B	3B	HR	RBI	SB
Bookout, Casey, 1b-dh	.387	212	58	82	19	0	16	66	3
Hart, Corey, 2b	.384	203	62	78	14	8	3	43	12
Shackelford, Brian, of-p	.384	224	66	86	27	1	16	70	4
Flores, Javier, c	.374	227	60	85	27	3	8	53	14
Noles, Jade, of	.371	35	9	13	3	1	2	10	0
Hill, Willy, of	.361	249	64	90	16	7	1	34	23
Wathan, Derek, ss	.357	255	52	91	20	7	1	21	16
Vidales, Jeremy, 3b	.348	23	4	8	3	0	0	6	0
Elsey, Justin, of	.333	141	28	47	9	2	8	34	8
Park, Richard, 1b-p	.304	184	30	56	16	2	6	49	2
Betts, Harold, c	.300	50	13	15	2	1	2	11	1
Mead, Chad, of-p	.296	71	10	21	3	0	2	11	1
Covitz, Hunter, ss	.286	14	4	4	1	0	0	5	0
Cochell, Chad, of	.250	20	9	5	1	1	0	5	2
Montenegro, Jose, 3b	.246	199	34	49	11	2	9	43	0
Pascucci, Val, 1b-p	.100	20	2	2	0	0	0	1	0

PITCHING	W	L	ERA	G	SV	IP	H	BB	SO
Geary, Geoff	4	3	2.20	32	8	61	47	28	63
Andra, Jeff	10	5	4.32	17	0	106	112	50	86
Olsen, Kevin	7	2	5.32	16	0	69	87	26	41
Shackelford, Brian	2	2	5.73	16	0	60	68	41	46
Amundson, Aron	0	3	6.14	11	1	15	20	10	4
McCurtain, Paul	0	0	6.70	25	3	47	56	30	38
Reyes, Thomas	1	0	6.75	14	2	15	17	11	10
Smith, Clint	3	1	6.92	14	0	40	44	39	34
Park, Richard	6	2	7.99	15	0	53	83	22	34
Pascucci, Val	3	0	8.42	18	1	31	46	11	30
Prather, Kendall	1	0	9.00	3	0	5	10	7	4
Fisher, Shayne	1	0	10.50	5	0	6	13	1	4
Mead, Chad	0	1	15.00	7	1	9	7	17	8

20. SOUTHWESTERN LOUISIANA

Coach: Tony Robichaux **Record:** 43-18

BATTING	AVG	AB	R	H	2B	3B	HR	RBI	SB
Aguirre, Oswaldo, 1b	.356	219	47	78	15	1	7	57	2
Cantrelle, Kevin, of	.346	191	42	66	15	2	8	54	7
Robinson, Jeff, 1b	.333	18	7	6	1	0	1	7	0
Hemme, Justin, dh	.332	187	35	62	16	2	12	49	1
Neyland, Jeremy, of	.310	84	18	26	1	5	2	14	6
Prejean, Neil, 2b	.308	39	8	12	0	0	1	8	1
Wilson, Zach, 2b	.306	196	56	60	13	4	3	19	6
Ryan, B.J., of-p	.306	147	27	45	9	1	4	26	2
Feehan, Steven, of	.300	130	36	39	5	0	2	14	10
Doucet, Brandon, of	.298	94	22	28	1	1	4	19	7
Poole, Shannon, c	.293	150	19	44	11	1	2	26	4
Stafford, Brett, 3b	.276	116	26	32	4	0	4	18	3
Calais, Ian, ss	.270	122	21	33	4	0	0	14	2
Fritz, Jim, 3b-c	.246	114	22	28	6	1	6	24	3
Goltry, Jason, ss	.242	91	9	22	3	0	2	16	0
Landry, Tony, of	.238	21	3	5	1	0	2	6	0
Bailey, Chad, of-p	.236	72	21	17	3	0	0	8	3
Minnick, Russell, of	.231	26	14	6	2	0	0	0	0
Cobb, Brannon, c	.231	13	2	3	0	0	1	3	0
Cabral, Angelo, c	.220	50	8	11	1	0	0	9	1

PITCHING	W	L	ERA	G	SV	IP	H	BB	SO
Poland, Trey	12	5	3.28	22	3	137	115	58	140
Robbins, Cody	12	1	3.73	15	0	101	112	24	73
Bailey, Chad	6	4	3.93	11	0	73	72	32	59
Devey, Philip	3	2	4.72	18	2	53	58	19	44
Landry, Tony	1	0	5.19	9	0	9	7	11	12
Ryan, B.J.	1	1	5.67	10	1	33	51	21	31
Masters, Dayne	1	0	5.73	10	0	22	26	10	20
Slaton, J.B.	4	1	6.60	13	0	44	51	23	27
Periou, Todd	2	4	8.13	9	0	31	47	19	18
Methvin, Cade	1	0	11.70	8	1	10	22	3	8

BILL SETLIFF

Two-way Florida star
Brad Wilkerson had 23 homers, 11 wins

21. NORTH CAROLINA STATE

Coach: Elliott Avent **Record:** 43-20

BATTING	AVG	AB	R	H	2B	3B	HR	RBI	SB
Sergio, Tom, 2b	.412	243	85	100	14	4	16	68	18
Weber, Jake, of	.391	253	72	99	23	6	9	68	16
Piercy, Brad, c-of	.356	191	44	68	11	3	6	47	10
Combs, Chris, of-1b	.337	255	64	86	12	0	17	76	14
Butler, Jeff, dh	.324	74	9	24	5	0	0	15	1
Postell, Matt, 3b-1b	.323	201	42	65	16	0	3	44	1
Lee, Craig, of	.321	134	31	43	3	4	7	32	5
Lawler, Scott, 1b-c	.308	185	43	57	8	1	9	43	0
Slaughter, Jimmy, of	.297	74	20	22	4	1	0	11	5
Smith, Jason, 2b	.295	44	10	13	1	0	0	4	0
Wolff, Stephen, 1b-dh	.288	125	32	36	6	0	6	27	1
Baker, Dustin, ss-p	.267	165	30	44	3	1	0	25	2
Figueroa, Luis, 1b	.265	98	22	26	7	0	1	16	1
Ballard, Josh, ss-3b	.202	84	20	17	0	0	1	10	6
Trexler, David, ss	.180	61	16	11	2	0	1	7	1
Ferguson, Andy, c	.156	32	8	5	1	0	0	4	1

PITCHING	W	L	ERA	G	SV	IP	H	BB	SO
Eason, Clay	10	2	2.18	28	4	62	42	27	78
Hughes, Whitney	0	0	3.24	6	0	8	9	7	8
Combs, Chris	2	2	3.45	14	3	16	17	6	22
Carter, Chris	0	0	3.57	15	0	18	14	11	11
Black, Brett	10	4	4.74	19	1	114	125	11	98
Jones, Brent	1	1	4.85	13	0	39	53	22	31
Ormond, Rodney	4	1	5.18	16	0	33	29	22	24
Scarce, Bubba	4	2	5.56	16	0	78	103	29	52
Baker, Dustin	2	2	5.89	11	1	37	38	16	24
Blackmon, Kurt	7	3	6.14	17	0	85	96	30	55
Hall, Jud	0	0	6.19	9	1	16	14	12	19
Dobson, Scott	2	1	8.49	10	0	23	20	22	26
Dorn, Grant	1	2	9.00	7	0	16	19	17	15
Gordon, Sean	0	0	9.95	6	0	6	4	12	8

22. SANTA CLARA

Coach: John Oldham **Record:** 41-20

BATTING	AVG	AB	R	H	2B	3B	HR	RBI	SB
Frank, Mike, of-p	.405	242	64	98	25	5	12	80	19
Chiaffredo, Paul, c	.352	236	49	83	23	1	16	65	3
Wheeler, Eliot, of	.343	35	6	12	2	1	0	4	0
Hughes, Todd, of	.337	202	61	68	8	7	1	32	18
Okimoto, Kevin, of	.333	177	35	59	10	0	6	52	2
Mott, Bill, of	.325	243	64	79	12	1	7	50	14
Frankel, Jeff, 2b	.278	151	25	42	8	0	1	18	0
Fairbairn, Liam, 2b-3b	.273	150	33	41	12	3	3	31	5
Fuqua, Aaron, 1b	.254	169	48	43	4	2	2	24	3
Cota, Gabe, 3b-ss	.254	209	44	53	8	1	6	30	3
Mensah, George, of	.226	31	6	7	1	0	0	0	4
Affrunti, Bernie, ss	.209	139	17	29	2	2	1	10	8
Wilkerson, Jason, c	.200	35	3	7	0	1	0	4	0
Hinn, Ryan, 2b	.167	12	1	2	0	0	0	1	0
Giannini, Matt, 1b	.156	32	1	5	1	0	0	4	0

PITCHING	W	L	ERA	G	SV	IP	H	BB	SO
Frank, Mike	11	0	2.69	15	0	74	59	23	73
Lanzetta, Tobin	8	3	3.03	19	0	116	104	30	106
Boyanich, Vince	5	4	3.36	14	0	59	47	27	52
Perry, Jeff	9	3	4.01	19	0	108	120	23	83
Crudale, Mike	2	6	4.97	11	0	54	62	28	44
McDonald, Mike	2	2	5.40	38	10	42	44	22	41
Bulich, Ryan	3	1	6.35	20	0	28	30	10	19
Rice, Peter	1	1	8.57	15	0	21	25	25	16
Henley, Kevin	0	0	14.21	7	0	6	11	11	7
Passalacqua, Jason	0	0	15.00	10	0	9	10	11	3

23. FRESNO STATE

Coach: Bob Bennett **Record:** 40-28

BATTING	AVG	AB	R	H	2B	3B	HR	RBI	SB
Williams. Mike, of	.354	79	16	28	2	0	0	6	1
Feramisco, Derek, of	.344	259	67	89	28	3	14	62	7
Hannah, Josh, of	.342	222	40	76	11	4	7	38	3
Chiaramonte, Giuseppe, c	.341	267	72	91	16	5	26	72	6
Dyt, Darren, of	.325	114	31	37	8	0	5	19	3
Levingston, Derrick, 1b	.311	254	35	79	24	0	5	53	0
da Luz, Craig, 3b	.283	240	32	68	14	4	6	42	1
Hook, Kevin, ss	.268	149	18	40	6	0	0	19	4
Pearse, Joe, 2b	.266	169	19	45	8	2	0	14	1
Rupcich, Larry, ss-2b	.266	154	25	41	5	0	0	15	3
Tafoya, Simon, of	.265	98	22	26	5	2	4	19	0
Prieto, Jeff, dh	.252	139	18	35	2	1	0	12	2
Aukerman, Carlos, of	.227	44	6	10	2	0	0	3	0
DeCanio, Jason, dh	.226	133	23	30	5	0	10	27	0
Gerber, Joe, of	.167	36	9	6	1	0	0	0	2
Howard, Keith, of	.161	31	5	5	0	0	0	4	0
Lopez, Oscar, ss	.154	13	3	2	0	0	0	0	0

PITCHING	W	L	ERA	G	SV	IP	H	BB	SO
Rowe, Casey	8	1	3.57	26	2	76	81	24	62
Pettyjohn, Adam	7	8	3.60	21	0	122	122	32	139
Weaver, Jeff	11	5	3.63	21	2	141	130	25	181
Griffin, Kirk	6	3	3.91	20	1	97	102	17	66
Tucker, Brad	3	3	4.42	16	0	57	70	37	39
Graham, Tom	4	3	5.04	27	1	55	62	14	65
Parantala, Mark	0	2	5.29	16	0	17	20	3	11
Goodrich, Randy	1	2	7.48	17	2	28	34	15	17

24. CAL STATE FULLERTON

Coach: George Horton **Record:** 39-24

BATTING	AVG	AB	R	H	2B	3B	HR	RBI	SB
Alviso, Jerome, ss	.391	225	59	88	18	0	2	43	14
Lamb, Mike, c-3b	.379	261	59	99	20	4	10	70	8
Ankrum, C.J., 1b	.359	234	60	84	14	4	2	43	11
Hill, Nakia, 2b	.357	196	43	70	12	4	7	40	7
Rowand, Aaron, of	.347	245	55	85	12	2	7	43	17
Chatham, Steve, of	.341	246	56	84	20	1	3	51	5
Fukuhara, Pete, of-dh	.320	178	42	57	12	2	6	32	10
Beck, Chris, of	.317	104	15	33	5	0	0	12	4
Johnson, Reed, of	.295	78	19	23	6	0	0	10	4
Owens, Ryan, 3b-2b	.291	151	29	44	17	2	1	34	9
Patterson, Craig, c	.286	35	4	10	1	1	1	9	0
Seal, Scott, dh-of	.283	152	32	43	15	1	5	31	3
Fullerton, Ryan, dh	.275	51	8	14	4	0	2	12	1
Hernandez, Jojo, of	.264	53	4	14	6	0	0	11	0
Phillips, Danny, 3b	.261	46	4	12	3	1	0	2	0
Halcovich, Gaby, ss	.192	26	8	5	1	0	0	2	4
Wright, Mike, c	.176	34	8	6	0	0	3	7	2

PITCHING	W	L	ERA	G	SV	IP	H	BB	SO
Greenlee, Mike	5	1	3.38	29	7	53	43	14	56
Wise, Matt	5	8	3.50	17	0	116	94	41	116
Tokarse, Brian	10	3	4.01	20	0	99	81	47	114
Spencer, Dustin	2	0	4.50	13	3	26	39	14	19
Duckworth, Brandon	8	1	4.93	20	3	80	92	39	88
Garner, Mike	2	1	5.15	24	0	51	59	28	39
Hild, Scott	4	4	5.66	18	0	56	72	29	30
Alkire, John	3	5	6.54	20	0	65	90	38	40
Baron, Tim	0	1	6.67	17	2	30	38	4	19

25. TENNESSEE

Coach: Rod Delmonico **Record:** 42-19

BATTING	AVG	AB	R	H	2B	3B	HR	RBI	SB
Evans, Jason, c	.391	64	18	25	4	0	4	19	0
Ross, Justin, of	.372	223	67	83	18	1	9	48	17
Keene, Kurt, ss-of	.368	223	57	82	23	3	13	58	4
Clabo, Jason, of	.357	157	29	56	13	3	4	26	8
Pickler, Jeff, 2b	.332	220	60	73	14	5	7	44	8
Folkers, Ken, 3b	.324	238	53	77	16	1	9	49	13
Moore, Baker, ss-2b	.317	167	28	53	12	1	1	28	0
Copley, Travis, 1b-dh	.316	215	46	68	19	2	9	53	1
Figueroa, Eduardo, 1b-of	.304	125	27	38	7	1	3	22	2
Anderson, Michael, c	.303	99	15	30	6	1	2	25	3
Cincera, Ron, ss	.293	123	29	36	2	3	8	28	1
Greene, Clay, of	.290	259	59	75	11	4	4	37	54
Coker, Shay, of	.263	19	9	5	1	0	0	1	4
Duckwiler, Justin, c	.261	92	14	24	3	0	5	15	1

PITCHING	W	L	ERA	G	SV	IP	H	BB	SO
Brummitt, Travis	1	0	3.00	11	0	15	14	10	18
Abell, Joe	2	0	3.32	20	0	41	42	19	41
Folkers, Ken	7	3	3.34	21	2	92	92	25	84
Ross, Justin	2	0	3.79	5	0	19	16	12	10
Hudson, Luke	6	2	4.12	14	0	83	74	43	77
Cosgrove, Michael	10	6	5.25	19	0	105	131	34	83
Marr, Jason	5	1	5.87	29	4	38	49	12	42
Myers, Mathew	6	3	6.13	16	0	62	88	24	40
Odom, Clark	1	4	6.39	28	2	49	53	22	36
Ruiz, John	2	0	7.94	9	0	17	27	5	8
Keene, Jack	0	0	9.18	10	0	17	23	16	7

CONFERENCE
Standings, Leaders

*Won conference tournament.
Boldface: NCAA regional participant/conference department leader.
#Conference department leader who is a non-qualifier

ATLANTIC COAST CONFERENCE

	Conference W	Conference L	Overall W	Overall L
Georgia Tech	19	4	46	15
***Florida State**	18	6	50	17
North Carolina State	15	8	43	20
Clemson	13	10	41	23
Wake Forest	10	13	37	20
Virginia	10	13	32	22
Duke	9	14	33	25
North Carolina	6	18	29	31
Maryland	5	19	22	32

ALL-CONFERENCE TEAM: C—Matthew LeCroy, Jr., Clemson. **1B**—J.J. Thomas, Jr., Georgia Tech. **2B**—Tom Sergio, Sr., North Carolina State. **3B**—Jeff Becker, So., Duke. **SS**—Brian Roberts, Fr., North Carolina. **OF**—J.D. Drew, Jr., Florida State; Jeremy Morris, Sr., Florida State; Jake Weber, Jr., North Carolina State. **DH**—Dave Lardieri, Sr., Wake Forest. **Util**—Vaughn Schill, Fr., Duke. **SP**—Randy Choate, Jr., Florida State; Ryan Mottl, Fr., Clemson; Kris Wilson, Jr., Georgia Tech. **RP**—Clay Eason, Sr., North Carolina State.

Player of the Year: J.D. Drew, Florida State. **Rookie of the Year:** Brian Roberts, North Carolina. **Coach of the Year:** Danny Hall, Georgia Tech.

ROBERT GURGANUS

Best in the ACC
J.D. Drew led ACC in four major categories

INDIVIDUAL BATTING LEADERS
(Minimum 125 At-Bats)

	AVG	AB	R	H	2B	3B	HR	RBI	SB
Drew, J.D., Fla. State	**.455**	233	**110**	**106**	15	5	**31**	100	32
Roberts, Brian, UNC	.427	239	63	102	24	1	8	44	**47**
Sergio, Tom, N.C. State	.412	243	85	100	14	4	16	68	19
Haverbusch, Kevin, Md.	.406	207	64	84	15	0	16	63	8
Weber, Jake, N.C. State	.391	253	72	99	23	6	9	68	16
Burnham, Gary, Clemson	.391	266	83	104	23	2	15	82	2
Schill, Vaughn, Duke	.388	240	59	93	16	3	4	31	3
Clemente, Joe, Maryland	.370	154	40	57	10	0	6	27	0
Badeaux, Brooks, Fla. State	.365	170	48	62	13	0	5	30	15
Lardieri, Dave, WF	.363	226	68	82	17	1	18	72	2
LeCroy, Matthew, Clemson	.359	237	62	85	12	1	24	79	5
Fletcher, Michael, Duke	.356	233	49	83	21	3	9	54	2
Piercy, Brad, N.C. State	.356	191	44	68	11	3	6	47	10
Morris, Jeremy, Fla. State	.356	250	73	89	22	6	25	**116**	25
Fischer, Mark, Ga. Tech	.354	257	75	91	10	**7**	24	98	17
Robinson, Adam, Virginia	.353	215	53	76	18	2	5	27	22
DeMoura, Eric, Clemson	.352	253	62	89	13	1	3	49	8
Bultmann, Kurt, Clemson	.348	253	69	88	**31**	1	16	61	3
Itzoe, Josh, Wake Forest	.347	236	72	82	11	2	11	41	4
Kinsman, Ted, Virginia	.347	176	41	61	6	0	2	25	17
Honeycutt, Heath, Ga. Tech	.345	249	52	86	13	5	2	50	17
Maluchnik, Gregg, Duke	.344	128	34	44	7	0	5	30	0
Leggett, Adam, Ga. Tech	.341	267	75	91	17	2	10	52	18
Hood, Jay, Ga. Tech	.340	141	39	48	8	2	4	31	2
Combs, Chris, N.C. State	.337	255	64	86	12	0	17	76	14
LaMarsh, Chris, UNC	.337	205	41	69	16	0	2	34	1
Gilleland, Ryan, Virginia	.335	218	44	73	19	2	8	52	9
Riepe, Andrew, WF	.335	179	34	60	11	1	6	40	1
Prather, Scott, Ga. Tech	.333	204	56	68	13	0	9	62	4
Easterling, Adam, Ga. Tech	.327	217	61	71	9	2	3	26	17
Galloway, John, Virginia	.326	215	47	70	14	4	9	56	11
Postell, Matt, N.C. State	.323	201	42	65	16	0	3	44	1
Malloy, Pat, Wake Forest	.322	205	57	66	13	2	17	67	8
Lopez, Javier, Virginia	.321	187	42	60	16	3	8	40	8
Lee, Craig, N.C. State	.321	134	31	43	3	4	7	32	5
Danosky, Ben, Wake Forest	.318	192	42	61	8	3	8	48	3
McQueen, Eric, Ga. Tech	.316	206	47	65	7	3	8	46	11
Becker, Jeff, Duke	.315	235	53	74	18	2	12	62	1
Palmieri, Jon, Wake Forest	.314	204	50	64	21	4	5	48	0
Sherlock, Brian, Virginia	.313	211	45	66	15	1	6	33	7
Marino, Larry, WF	.310	197	38	61	10	0	7	47	3
Zech, Scott, Fla. State	.309	265	86	82	13	2	6	50	31
Broome, Nathan, Clemson	.309	162	32	50	7	2	3	27	6
Zabala, Jose, Fla. State	.309	136	46	42	4	1	1	22	5
Lawler, Scott, N.C. State	.308	185	43	57	8	1	9	43	0
Goodroe, Randy, Duke	.307	137	26	42	5	1	0	16	8
Embler, Jason, Clemson	.305	269	70	82	17	0	14	56	3
#Chiou, Frankie, Duke	.286	206	50	59	9	**7**	6	36	5

INDIVIDUAL PITCHING LEADERS
(Minimum 50 innings)

	W	L	ERA	G	SV	IP	H	BB	SO
Eason, Clay, N.C. State	10	2	**2.18**	28	4	62	42	27	78
Cowie, Stephen, Duke	6	2	2.80	15	1	55	48	16	47
Wilson, Kris, Ga. Tech	12	2	3.12	19	2	118	114	30	103
Hendricks, John, WF	8	5	3.26	17	0	97	95	32	83
Diaz, Zach, Fla. State	3	4	3.26	30	5	69	67	19	68
Elder, David, Ga. Tech	9	4	3.44	22	1	97	96	42	96
Choate, Randy, Fla. State	**13**	3	3.61	19	0	135	123	37	**126**
Bentley, John, Fla. State	5	1	3.86	17	1	56	53	19	44
MacDougal, Mike, WF	6	4	4.12	18	2	92	87	38	85
Proctor, Scott, Fla. State	7	1	4.14	17	0	50	57	24	48
Dishman, Richard, Duke	4	2	4.21	17	0	73	71	35	86
Chavez, Chris, Fla. State	4	1	4.24	27	**6**	74	76	42	78
McAllister, Scott, UNC	3	5	4.38	18	2	76	78	39	58
Connor, Clayton, Duke	5	7	4.40	22	1	78	91	20	41
Nye, Rodney, UNC	8	1	4.58	20	1	57	57	18	51
Niles, Randy, Fla. State	8	5	4.58	18	1	96	105	43	104
Wrigley, Jase, Ga. Tech	7	3	4.67	28	3	79	72	37	66
Mottl, Ryan, Clemson	10	3	4.72	16	0	107	113	33	99
Black, Brett, N.C. State	10	4	4.74	19	1	114	125	11	98
Kennedy, Casey, Virginia	4	6	4.74	16	0	82	84	28	48
Yankosky, L.J., Ga. Tech	8	3	5.03	19	2	77	79	43	51
Browning, Skip, Clemson	6	6	5.11	17	0	76	85	32	59
Howell, Chuck, Fla. State	8	1	5.18	21	1	83	100	17	70
Zawatski, Geoff, Virginia	7	2	5.20	17	0	73	90	14	42
Thieme, Richard, Ga. Tech	5	1	5.37	20	0	52	60	30	57
Dupree, Brad, Duke	4	4	5.44	19	0	88	91	33	60
Agamennone, Brandon, Md.	3	8	5.52	15	0	93	97	19	88

AMERICA EAST CONFERENCE

	Conference W	Conference L	Overall W	Overall L
Delaware	19	3	45	10
Maine	16	8	24	27
Vermont	15	9	27	19
Drexel	13	10	28	22
***Northeastern**	12	12	33	19
Towson State	9	14	24	28
Hartford	7	16	16	23
Hofstra	7	16	14	28
New Hampshire	7	17	17	22

ALL-CONFERENCE TEAM: C—Lou Marchetti, So., Drexel. **1B**—John Riccio, Sr., Hartford. **2B**—Matt Ardizzone, Jr., Delaware. **3B**—Brian August, Jr., Delaware. **SS**—Dan Colunio, Sr., Delaware. **OF**—Kevin Mench, Fr., Delaware; Rex Turner, Jr., Maine; Joe Vuotto, Sr., Towson State. **DH**—Darren Pulito, Jr., Delaware. **P**—Garrett Quinn, Sr., Maine; Matt Phillips, Jr., Delaware.

Player of the Year: Brian August, Delaware. **Pitcher of the Year:** Garrett Quinn, Maine. **Rookie of the Year:** Kevin Mench, Delaware. **Coach of the Year:** Paul Kostacopoulos, Maine.

INDIVIDUAL BATTING LEADERS

(Minimum 100 At-Bats)

	AVG	AB	R	H	2B	3B	HR	RBI	SB
August, Brian, Delaware	**.432**	199	**72**	86	**26**	1	**20**	**82**	2
Pulito, Darren, Delaware	.424	184	47	78	15	1	15	62	2
Snyder, Earl, Hartford	.411	141	40	58	10	1	13	42	1
Marchetti, Lou, Drexel	.409	171	47	70	12	0	13	74	4
Mench, Kevin, Delaware	.403	211	71	85	19	5	19	67	8
Ardizzone, Matt, Delaware	.403	226	56	91	25	6	4	32	7
Agoglia, Nick, Towson	.402	164	46	66	13	2	5	25	3
Riccio, John, Hartford	.402	127	40	51	12	0	13	54	2
Biskupiak, Brian, Hartford	.392	130	34	51	9	2	6	26	5
Helkowski, Dennis, Drexel	.389	167	63	65	18	0	2	30	11
Sheedy, T.J., Maine	.388	178	56	69	11	1	2	28	6
Colunio, Dan, Delaware	.385	234	64	90	16	0	1	24	19
Mahony, Tim, Delaware	.385	208	53	80	19	2	14	71	0
Sperling, Matt, Drexel	.380	158	56	60	15	3	9	63	11
Daley, Tim, Northeastern	.372	188	52	70	13	2	15	59	2
#Joyce, Sean, Drexel	.314	169	39	53	12	**8**	4	44	5
#Fahy, Kevin, Drexel	.294	187	60	55	6	3	2	21	**45**

INDIVIDUAL PITCHING LEADERS

(Minimum 40 innings)

	W	L	ERA	G	SV	IP	H	BB	SO
Phillips, Matt, Delaware	**9**	0	**2.25**	14	2	76	59	38	68
Montalbano, Greg, North.	4	2	2.56	12	4	56	49	13	51
Lynde, Jerry, Vermont	7	1	2.62	11	1	72	55	22	64
Frey, Chris, Delaware	8	0	2.64	13	0	75	67	25	76
Stern, Dave, Delaware	8	3	3.13	13	0	72	65	29	69
Quinn, Garrett, Maine	**9**	3	3.28	15	1	82	80	21	**79**
Bonehill, Tim, Northeastern	4	4	3.32	9	0	62	64	24	56
Zack, Chris, Northeastern	6	5	3.60	12	1	75	82	18	19
McManus, Matt, North.	6	4	3.87	11	0	77	89	10	49
Burns, John, Northeastern	6	1	4.22	10	0	60	64	26	24
#Rogers, Kevin, New Hamp.	0	3	5.21	18	**8**	19	20	7	16
#Gellert, Scott, Delaware	3	1	5.25	23	**8**	48	54	12	46

ATLANTIC-10 CONFERENCE

	Conference W	Conference L	Overall W	Overall L
EAST				
Massachusetts	17	4	35	12
Fordham	12	9	34	19
St. Bonaventure	9	12	19	26
Temple	9	12	16	31
Rhode Island	6	15	14	28
St. Joseph's	4	17	14	35
WEST	**W**	**L**	**W**	**L**
Xavier	14	6	32	26
***Virginia Tech**	13	8	34	28
Dayton	12	9	21	28
Duquesne	12	9	17	32
George Washington	9	12	21	33
LaSalle	8	12	19	27

ALL-CONFERENCE TEAM: C—Jim Dallio, Jr., Xavier. **1B**—Rick Martinez, Sr., Temple. **2B**—Zach Swisher, So., Xavier. **3B**—Adam Correa, So, Massachusetts. **SS**—Kevin Kurilla, Sr., Virginia Tech. **OF**—Troy Allen, Jr., George Washington; Doug Clark, So., Massachusetts; Mike Marchiano, Sr., Fordham. **DH**—Jeff Rojik, Sr, Duquesne **P**—Denny Wagner, Jr., Virginia Tech; Louie Witte, So., Xavier.

Player of the Year: Mike Marchiano, Fordham. **Pitcher of the Year:** Louie Witte, Xavier. **Rookie of the Year:** B.J. Barns, Duquesne. **Coach of the Year:** John Morrey, Xavier.

INDIVIDUAL BATTING LEADERS

(Minimum 100 At-Bats)

	AVG	AB	R	H	2B	3B	HR	RBI	SB
Marchiano, Mike, Fordham	**.493**	207	**91**	**102**	**21**	2	**29**	**85**	22
Fleming, Ryan, Dayton	.417	187	47	78	19	1	6	40	19
Clark, Doug, Massachusetts	.415	183	51	76	12	1	11	60	20
Farrell, Rob, Rhode Island	.409	154	51	63	17	3	12	56	21
Griswold, Matt, Va. Tech	.408	211	49	86	14	4	13	69	8
Martinez, Rick, Temple	.389	144	39	56	7	1	17	56	8
Giglio, David, Mass.	.383	120	29	46	9	3	5	30	4
Gautreau, Pete, Mass	.374	174	49	65	5	3	11	46	26
Thiebaud, Tom, St. Bona.	.371	167	49	62	12	3	6	36	19
Lumia, Vince, Fordham	.369	157	47	58	10	0	10	30	11
Shiflett, Eric, Va. Tech	.369	214	54	79	16	2	4	40	2
Foutz, Chad, Va. Tech	.368	239	55	88	14	2	6	44	4
D'Auria, Mike, Fordham	.365	156	59	57	20	0	0	28	6
Rojik, Jeff, Duquesne	.364	154	25	56	11	2	5	27	1
Correa, Adam, Mass	.362	141	44	51	12	1	6	42	8
Gorrie, Brad, Mass	.361	180	63	65	10	1	9	40	**43**
Reynolds, Matt, Va. Tech	.356	194	49	69	11	0	10	45	9
Hampson, Rodd, Xavier	.352	210	42	74	18	1	6	40	5
Braunstein, Aaron, Mass	.351	168	47	59	13	1	14	49	1
Sposato, Mike, St. Joseph's	.348	115	26	40	2	1	1	16	13
Barns, B.J., Duquesne	.345	148	31	51	14	1	12	46	0
Munroe, Craig, Temple	.345	142	27	49	13	2	5	27	3
Dacey, Ryan, Ga. Wash.	.341	167	30	57	12	0	4	32	6
Samela, Brian, Mass	.338	142	37	48	13	0	8	35	3
Lanzilli, Kevin, RI	.337	101	27	34	6	3	1	25	6
#Martin, Randy, Va. Tech	.305	197	53	60	12	**5**	1	21	18
#Du Vall, Jason, Xavier	.279	179	36	50	8	**5**	3	30	14

INDIVIDUAL PITCHING LEADERS

(Minimum 40 innings)

	W	L	ERA	G	SV	IP	H	BB	SO
Witte, Louie, Xavier	**12**	3	**2.98**	21	3	124	116	27	107
Fleck, Will, La Salle	5	5	3.35	16	3	89	65	61	107
Davis, Jim, Duquesne	6	5	3.38	11	0	75	79	30	71
Sala, Steve, St. Joseph's	4	4	3.44	12	0	68	54	41	42
Moran, Chris, Fordham	4	1	3.86	15	1	40	47	18	24
Williams, Matt, Ga. Wash	7	5	4.16	17	0	89	86	44	74
Cooke, Bill, Massachusetts	6	2	4.22	11	1	60	65	11	37
Fisher, Mike, Duquesne	5	3	4.23	10	0	55	68	13	32
Moore, Peter, Temple	7	8	4.31	22	3	117	118	80	**120**
Zirkle, Todd, Virginia Tech	5	3	4.34	16	0	64	72	38	32
Wagner, Denny, Va. Tech	10	4	4.41	17	0	112	108	49	110
Hand, Jon, Virginia Tech	5	9	4.42	18	0	112	124	34	97
Baginski, Thomas, Ga. Wash	2	4	4.44	21	2	47	55	20	47
LaMattina, Ryan, St. Bona.	3	6	4.57	11	0	65	80	38	78
Bennett, Jason, Mass	9	2	4.58	14	2	79	87	20	47
Boser, Brock, Xavier	5	6	4.58	16	0	59	62	30	44
Barnsby, Scott, Mass	6	1	4.66	10	0	64	56	32	41
Cooke, Bill, Massachusetts	6	2	4.69	12	1	63	68	17	40
#Heitkamp, Brian, Dayton	3	3	6.70	23	5	43	57	23	34

BIG EAST CONFERENCE

	Conference W	Conference L	Overall W	Overall L
AMERICAN				
West Virginia	17	7	36	19
***St. John's**	16	7	35	17
Connecticut	11	13	27	20
Providence	10	15	26	23
Boston College	8	17	20	23
Pittsburgh	8	17	19	26
NATIONAL	**W**	**L**	**W**	**L**
Notre Dame	15	6	41	19
Rutgers	13	11	28	24
Seton Hall	13	11	32	22
Villanova	12	12	29	27
Georgetown	8	15	19	37

ALL-CONFERENCE TEAM: C—Jason Frushour, Sr., West Virginia. **1B**—Pete Zoccolillo, So., Rutgers. **2B**—Brant Ust, Fr., Notre Dame. **3B**—Craig Zimmerli, Jr., Seton Hall. **SS**—Giancarlo DiPrima, Jr., St. John's. **OF**—Randall Brooks, Sr., Notre Dame; David Kim, Jr., Seton Hall; Billy Rich, Jr., Connecticut. **DH**—Jeff Wagner, So., Notre Dame. **Util**—Angelo Ciminiello, So., Providence. **P**—Chris Enochs, Jr., West Virginia; Jason Grilli, Jr., Seton Hall; Mike Hughes, Jr., St. John's.

Player of the Year: David Kim, Seton Hall. **Pitcher of the Year:** Chris Enochs, West Virginia. **Rookie of the Year:** Brant Ust, Notre Dame. **Coach of the Year:** Greg Van Zant, West Virginia.

INDIVIDUAL BATTING LEADERS

(Minimum 100 At Bats)

	AVG	AB	R	H	2B	3B	HR	RBI	SB
Hummel, Dan, Seton Hall	**.434**	196	45	85	19	0	6	51	5
Rich Billy, Connecticut	.432	190	61	82	20	1	13	55	6
Kim, David, Seton Hall	.420	212	63	89	**24**	1	**19**	**71**	10
Perate, Mike, Villanova	.413	143	41	59	5	0	1	21	15
Zoccolillo, Pete, Rutgers	.396	192	58	76	20	2	7	44	4
Amrhein, Mike, ND	.394	231	**70**	**91**	13	3	14	**71**	0
Zimmerli, Craig, Seton Hall	.394	198	44	78	12	0	5	36	7
Zawalich Matt, Conn.	.386	145	48	56	5	1	12	38	2
Grabowski, Jason, Conn.	.384	151	49	58	9	4	16	57	9
Frushour, Jason, West Va.	.374	171	39	64	12	1	7	41	4
Wagner, Jeff, Notre Dame	.374	219	58	82	21	1	17	69	1
Ust, Brant, Notre Dame	.372	223	66	83	15	4	11	54	7
Williamson, Josh, West Va.	.368	220	62	81	20	1	6	36	12
Marciniak, Dave, Rutgers	.367	210	48	77	20	4	2	52	3
Neubart, Adam, Rutgers	.367	147	41	54	13	**11**	2	27	10
Villacres, Gary, St. John's	.367	109	19	40	7	1	2	22	9
Brooks, Randall, ND	.366	235	50	86	13	7	3	39	17
Brock, J.J., Notre Dame	.365	208	45	76	14	8	3	50	4
Greene, Allen, Notre Dame	.365	200	41	73	20	5	7	55	4
McNamee, Joe, West Va.	.365	192	46	70	7	0	15	56	7
DiPrima, Giancarlo, St.J	.362	213	51	77	9	1	0	23	**36**
McGowan, Sean, Bos Coll.	.360	172	37	62	14	1	12	55	0
Shank, Tom, Villanova	.358	120	22	43	8	0	2	19	0
Edgar, Jason, Connecticut	.357	196	67	70	13	2	16	47	12
Harrington, Mike, Prov.	.356	177	44	63	10	2	8	43	1
Taylor, Kirk, West Virginia	.356	202	53	72	14	3	16	48	14
Neyland, Matt, Villanova	.354	209	46	74	15	1	4	54	4
Rubino, Matt, West Va.	.354	189	41	67	10	0	5	38	11
Lobagh, Scott, Pittsburgh	.353	139	33	49	8	1	1	20	32
Friedholm, Scott, Prov.	.352	162	38	57	19	0	3	30	3
Delsignore, Chris, Pitt	.349	146	27	51	14	2	3	16	10
Wayne, Tyrone, St. John's	.349	175	38	61	13	4	9	54	6

INDIVIDUAL PITCHING LEADERS

(Minimum 40 innings)

	W	L	ERA	G	SV	IP	H	BB	SO
Hughes, Mike, St. John's	8	4	**2.30**	14	0	86	62	29	79
Adair, Derek, St. John's	9	2	2.32	17	1	85	65	24	71
Barton, Chris, Connecticut	4	4	2.86	13	0	57	54	30	43
Gangemi, Joe, Seton Hall	5	4	2.91	15	1	80	79	22	55
Enochs, Chris, West Va.	**12**	1	3.03	15	0	95	92	21	86
McKeown, Chris, Notre Dame	4	3	3.26	15	0	69	74	31	46
Mundy, Mike, Rutgers	5	5	3.57	14	0	76	90	14	34
Schmalz, Darin, Notre Dame	9	3	3.67	14	0	81	87	22	58
Kalita, Tim, Notre Dame	3	1	3.67	14	1	49	45	33	46
O'Brien, Jim, Providence	4	3	4.12	9	1	44	37	26	48
Rooney, Mike, St. John's	8	1	4.23	17	3	77	76	40	62
Gallick, Chris, Pittsburgh	4	3	4.27	16	1	65	79	17	63
Bibbo, Paul, Boston College	2	7	4.27	11	0	59	73	9	37
Culhane, Craig, Villanova	5	4	4.47	13	0	58	73	17	42
#Pines, Derek, Georgetown	2	0	4.56	19	**8**	24	24	12	23
Grilli, Jason, Seton Hall	6	4	4.65	16	1	81	61	34	**125**
Ridley, Brian, Seton Hall	8	3	4.79	14	0	73	81	28	57

BIG SOUTH CONFERENCE

	Conference W	Conference L	Overall W	Overall L
***UNC Greensboro**	18	3	45	17
Winthrop	14	7	27	29
Charleston Southern	12	8	21	36
Liberty	11	10	25	32
UNC Asheville	9	11	20	33
Radford	9	12	26	28
Coastal Carolina	5	16	23	31
Maryland-Baltimore County	5	16	12	35

ALL-CONFERENCE TEAM: C—David Benham, Jr., Liberty. **1B**—Chris Carr, Jr., Radford. **2B**—Dominic Pattie, Jr., UNC Greensboro. **3B**—Steve Mokan, UNC Greensboro. **SS**—Jeff Berman, Sr., UMBC. **OF**—Joe Colameco, Jr., Winthrop; Tony Costantino, Sr., Winthrop; Nicky Phillips, Sr., UNC Greensboro. **DH**—Billy Hillier, Jr., UNC Asheville. **P**—Mark Cisar, Jr., Charleston Southern; Jason Parsons, Jr., UNC Greensboro.

Player of the Year: Mark Cisar, Charleston Southern. **Rookie of the Year:** Scott Crandell, UMBC. **Coach of the Year:** Mike Gaski, UNC Greensboro.

INDIVIDUAL BATTING LEADERS

(Minimum 100 At-Bats)

	AVG	AB	R	H	2B	3B	HR	RBI	SB
Pattie, Dominic, UNCG	**.385**	260	**72**	**100**	19	1	5	37	41
Benham, David, Liberty	.384	198	35	76	12	1	7	40	1
Berman, Jeff, UMBC	.377	191	48	72	13	0	6	26	7
Phillips, Nicky, UNCG	.374	230	68	86	16	3	13	**72**	**45**
Cisar, Jeff, Winthrop	.370	219	55	81	11	1	**15**	61	4
Samatas, Jeremy, Co. Car.	.365	203	37	74	18	0	4	48	5
Carr, Chris, Radford	.363	168	38	61	12	1	8	30	6
Crandell, Scott, UMBC	.363	113	25	41	5	1	6	30	0
Tomshack, Steve, UMBC	.360	161	37	58	12	1	8	37	2
Dampeer, Kelly, Radford	.353	201	41	71	14	1	10	57	13
Dorsey, Todd, UMBC	.353	153	37	54	6	1	3	34	5
Vawter, Kenny, UNCG	.352	219	53	77	15	**5**	6	51	25
Vindich, Jason, Co. Carolina	.351	148	44	52	8	2	6	32	9
Mahoney, Bob, UMBC	.348	132	25	46	8	1	2	17	1
Marciante, Frank, Co. Car.	.345	110	20	38	5	0	4	22	1
Isidore, Jason, Co. Car.	.344	186	51	64	13	0	6	29	21
Faircloth, Chad, UNCA	.343	172	42	59	14	2	4	29	17
Schneider, Randy, UMBC	.342	184	40	63	14	1	8	32	0
Costantino, Tony, Winthrop	.338	204	64	69	17	1	1	21	33
Colameco, Joe, Winthrop	.338	210	46	71	12	2	10	48	19
#Wigginton, Ty, UNCA	.332	199	35	66	**20**	**5**	4	31	5

INDIVIDUAL PITCHING LEADERS

(Minimum 40 innings)

	W	L	ERA	G	SV	IP	H	BB	SO
Sundsmo, Aaron, Winthrop	3	5	**1.86**	28	4	48	39	15	46
Parsons, Jason, UNCG	**15**	1	3.08	35	**8**	105	92	36	90
Santa, Jeff, Winthrop	10	3	3.55	17	0	101	103	43	90
Anderson, Jason, Radford	7	8	3.64	16	0	106	98	40	93
Cisar, Mark, Char. South.	7	8	3.95	18	1	98	87	52	85
Easler, Travis, Char. South.	8	6	3.96	17	0	109	111	47	**117**
Moss, Sonny, UNCA	1	4	4.06	16	2	44	59	12	33
Manwiller, Tim, Radford	8	4	4.20	18	4	90	112	30	84
Miller, Benji, Liberty	7	2	4.20	17	0	71	58	44	59
Rask, Fred, UNC Asheville	3	7	4.40	22	1	92	110	32	85
Harrell, Brian, Liberty	5	3	4.43	18	0	61	67	17	47
Hillier, Billy, UNCA	4	3	4.47	11	0	48	57	21	38
Harrell, Tim, Liberty	5	5	4.52	19	0	82	68	59	76
Lambert, Ryan, Winthrop	7	2	4.53	15	0	60	75	35	30
White, Josh, UNCA	4	6	4.58	17	2	53	53	26	52

BIG TEN CONFERENCE

	Conference W	Conference L	Overall W	Overall L
Michigan	17	9	36	22
***Ohio State**	18	10	42	18
Purdue	17	11	30	25
Illinois	17	11	32	27
Minnesota	15	10	30	24
Penn State	12	14	29	24
Michigan State	12	16	26	28
Indiana	8	16	34	21
Northwestern	9	19	20	35
Iowa	7	16	17	30

ALL-CONFERENCE TEAM: C—Mike Kremblas, Jr., Ohio State. **1B**—Dan Seimetz, Jr., Ohio State. **2B**—Alex Eckelman, Sr., Ohio State. **3B**—Brian Mitchell, So., Iowa. **SS**—Mark Carek, Jr., Ohio State. **OF**—Jason Alcaraz, So., Michigan; Derek Besco, Jr., Michigan; Robb Quinlan, So., Minnesota. **DH**—Bill Bennett, Jr., Purdue. **SP**—Mike Diebolt, Sr., Minnesota; Justin Fry, So., Ohio State; Mike Hedman, Sr., Purdue; Mark Mulder, So., Michigan State. **RP**—Tyler Steketee, Jr., Michigan.

Player of the Year: Dan Seimetz, Ohio State. **Pitcher of the Year:** Justin Fry, Ohio State. **Freshman of the Year:** Mike Campo, Penn State. **Coach of the Year:** Geoff Zahn, Michigan.

INDIVIDUAL BATTING LEADERS

(Minimum 125 At-Bats)

	AVG	AB	R	H	2B	3B	HR	RBI	SB
Trott, Jason, Ohio State	**.429**	140	40	60	11	0	4	30	7
Besco, Derek, Michigan	.391	215	**65**	84	21	1	11	63	4
Grieco, Anthony, Purdue	.389	157	48	61	12	1	11	49	1
Seimetz, Dan, Ohio State	.385	226	64	**87**	25	0	19	**80**	0
Thompson, Patrick, North.	.379	140	25	53	6	1	4	29	2
Kremblas, Mike, Ohio State	.378	164	43	62	13	2	5	43	2
Baron, Brian, Northwestern	.375	184	34	69	12	1	1	34	9
Welter, Eric, Minnesota	.375	208	38	78	17	2	4	45	7
Selander, Craig, Minnesota	.372	156	38	58	10	2	10	47	6
Griffin, Ben, Minnesota	.364	140	45	51	13	0	3	25	7
Quinlan, Robb, Minnesota	.363	215	54	78	**29**	0	13	53	7
Hartley, Thomas, Mich St.	.359	184	37	66	17	2	3	33	7
Campo, Michael, Penn State	.357	126	40	45	6	2	10	27	4
Albrecht, Carl, Penn State	.356	180	41	64	15	3	10	52	0
Alcaraz, Jason, Michigan	.355	183	33	65	16	2	2	35	3
Nori, Micah, Indiana	.365	181	47	66	9	2	12	59	6
Kalczynski, Brian, Michigan	.350	217	41	76	16	3	4	49	11
Rothstein, Mike, Purdue	.346	191	35	66	9	3	8	41	4
Keeney, Bob, Minnesota	.344	154	33	53	8	5	7	30	6
Besco, Bryan, Michigan	.344	209	49	72	26	0	15	61	2
Cervenak, Mike, Michigan	.342	190	42	65	11	0	4	31	5
Rhodes, Dan, Illinois	.342	199	46	68	13	2	6	43	17
Eckelman, Alex, Ohio State	.341	226	53	77	16	1	17	67	3
Guse, Bryan, Minnesota	.339	180	37	61	6	3	5	29	9
Lockwood, Mike, Ohio St.	.338	213	55	72	16	2	1	28	13
Sadlowski, Jared, Penn St.	.337	184	40	62	16	1	12	46	3
McDermott, Phil, Minn.	.333	168	32	56	13	3	5	50	1
Patterson, Marty, Mich. St.	.331	191	39	60	10	3	12	47	5
Rodeheaver, Roger, Ind.	.330	179	51	59	14	0	7	40	6
Rhodes, Dusty, Illinois	.329	216	37	71	15	**9**	1	22	14
Harris, Brian, Indiana	.328	198	55	65	14	2	6	37	**50**
Bennett, Bill, Purdue	.327	162	27	53	7	2	6	38	4
Marquie, Craig, Illinois	.327	205	42	67	12	3	6	41	4
Middleton, Matt, Ohio State	.326	175	38	57	16	2	5	28	2
Beers, Adam, Penn State	.325	154	46	50	12	4	3	35	5
Deitrick, Jeremy, Penn St.	.325	160	46	52	11	2	10	35	4
McClure, Todd, Illinois	.325	237	52	77	16	4	5	38	9
#Mitchell, Brian, Iowa	.316	171	39	54	12	1	**20**	50	3

INDIVIDUAL PITCHING LEADERS

(Minimum 50 Innings)

	W	L	ERA	G	SV	IP	H	BB	SO
Zrust, Ted, Minnesota	6	2	**2.19**	23	4	53	46	22	41
Mulder, Mark, Mich. State	7	2	2.26	20	4	68	66	12	56
Hedman, Mike, Purdue	6	4	2.87	14	1	94	85	17	52
Thompson, Eric, Ohio State	10	3	2.88	18	0	97	91	39	97
#Steketee, Tyler, Michigan	2	0	3.32	23	**10**	41	31	20	42
Zidlicky, Tom, Illinois	6	2	3.52	19	1	64	69	13	48
Fry, Justin, Ohio State	10	3	3.58	16	0	118	132	31	101
Weber, Brett, Illinois	5	4	3.92	18	1	99	90	44	95
Murphy, Brian, Mich. State	5	4	3.93	12	0	89	107	30	56
Diebolt, Mike, Minnesota	7	4	3.99	14	0	90	83	37	**110**
Partenheimer, Brian, Ind.	**12**	2	4.15	19	1	100	104	27	72
Boyd, Kyle, Indiana	4	1	4.18	11	0	52	60	13	46
Hecht, Brian, Illinois	6	7	4.25	18	0	83	90	15	57
Wulf, Troy, Iowa	3	3	4.53	18	1	52	68	21	46
Rasmussen, Steve, Iowa	4	2	4.55	12	1	55	70	25	38
Fullenkamp, Kurt, Ohio State	7	1	4.57	14	0	61	64	14	32
Steinbach, Brian, Michigan	9	4	4.59	14	1	86	93	36	82
Cranson, Bryan, Michigan	6	3	4.67	17	0	52	56	34	33
Graft, Ryan, Indiana	6	5	4.91	18	2	70	69	20	48
Olejnik, Tom, Mich. State	3	6	5.00	13	0	76	90	23	47

BIG 12 CONFERENCE

	Conference W	Conference L	Overall W	Overall L
Texas Tech	23	7	46	14
Oklahoma State	21	9	46	19
Texas A&M	19	11	39	22
*Oklahoma	18	11	39	20
Baylor	18	12	32	23
Missouri	15	14	31	27
Texas	12	15	29	22
Kansas	12	18	31	25
Kansas State	10	20	30	24
Nebraska	7	23	27	35
Iowa State	6	21	21	31

ALL-CONFERENCE TEAM: C—Javier Flores, Sr., Oklahoma. **1B**—Joe Dillon, Sr., Texas Tech. **2B**—Keith Ginter, Jr., Texas Tech. **3B**—Rusty McNamara, Sr., Oklahoma State. **SS**—Heath Schesser, Jr., Kansas State. **OF**—Francis Collins, Jr., Nebraska; Jeff Guiel, Sr., Oklahoma State; Jason Tyner, So., Texas A&M. **DH**—Casey Bookout, So., Oklahoma. **Util**—Todd Sears, Jr., Nebraska. **SP**—Jason Gooding, Jr., Texas Tech; Kris Lambert, Sr., Baylor; Ryan Rupe, Jr., Texas A&M; Scott Williamson, Jr., Oklahoma State; Shane Wright, So., Texas Tech. **RP**—Geoff Geary, Jr., Oklahoma; Jason Jennings, Fr., Baylor.

Player of the Year: Joe Dillon, Texas Tech. **Freshman of the Year:** Josh Bard, Texas Tech. **Newcomer of the Year:** Keith Ginter, Texas Tech. **Coach of the Year:** Larry Hays, Texas Tech.

INDIVIDUAL BATTING LEADERS

(Minimum 125 At-Bats)

	AVG	AB	R	H	2B	3B	HR	RBI	SB
DeMarco, Joe, Kansas	**.429**	224	64	96	16	3	2	28	34
Ginter, Keith, Texas Tech	.426	249	**93**	106	24	2	17	77	29
Sears, Todd, Nebraska	.421	233	78	98	18	3	17	79	6
Guiel, Jeff, Oklahoma State	.418	251	88	105	**32**	3	23	79	16
Schesser, Heath, Kansas St.	.409	237	70	97	20	**8**	16	85	7
Dillon, Joe, Texas Tech	.393	229	80	90	20	3	**33**	89	19
Poepard, Scott, Kansas St.	.391	230	56	90	19	2	16	70	9
Bookout, Casey, Oklahoma	.387	212	58	82	19	0	15	66	3
McNamara, Rusty, Okla. St.	.387	282	80	**109**	25	5	24	**93**	10
Collins, Francis, Nebraska	.384	284	83	**109**	17	3	3	34	13
Hart, Corey, Oklahoma	.384	203	62	78	14	**8**	3	43	12
Shackelford, Brian, Okla.	.384	224	66	86	27	1	16	70	4
Landreth, Jason, T. Tech	.379	203	72	77	29	1	9	66	20
Harkrider, Kip, Texas	.376	202	54	76	17	5	5	43	12
Blair, James, Baylor	.376	218	54	82	8	3	10	51	18
Cridland, Mark, Texas	.376	165	40	62	10	3	9	53	6
Toro, Brandon, Texas Tech	.376	229	69	86	25	4	10	51	26
Flores, Javier, Oklahoma	.374	227	60	85	27	3	8	53	14
Johnson, David, Texas	.374	171	36	64	12	4	8	45	0
Wilmes, Aaron, Kansas	.373	150	24	56	10	1	5	39	1
Loeffler, Brett, Texas	.370	162	59	60	19	0	12	43	13
Tyner, Jason, Texas A&M	.370	270	57	100	11	2	0	27	**37**
Lucca, Tony, Okla. State	.369	168	46	62	11	1	10	54	2
Nelson, Eric, Baylor	.368	242	46	89	16	4	4	46	20
Juday, Andy, Kansas	.365	148	32	54	7	1	10	37	5
Hill, Willy, Oklahoma	.361	249	64	90	16	7	1	34	23
Uelmen, Bill, Iowa State	.360	186	43	67	11	7	13	42	0
Bard, Josh, Texas Tech	.359	231	60	83	23	0	13	69	0
Wathan, Derek, Oklahoma	.357	255	52	91	20	7	1	21	16
Sommerhauser, Eric, KS	.353	150	50	53	14	0	2	25	4
Topolski, Jon, Baylor	.353	238	69	84	13	6	11	46	13
Moore, Griffin, Missouri	.348	230	65	80	15	2	18	72	2
Hunter, Johnny, Texas A&M	.347	222	48	77	12	1	15	52	5
Stephens, Jason, A&M	.347	222	41	77	20	3	7	45	3
Headley, Justin, Kansas	.340	215	50	73	22	5	11	63	14
Dodson, Jeremy, Baylor	.337	169	43	57	12	3	15	46	3
Gasparino, Billy, Okla. State	.336	265	89	89	26	4	18	62	21
Senjem, Guye, Iowa State	.335	170	42	57	9	2	9	33	3
Leimbek, Shawn, Iowa	.335	209	43	70	11	2	5	46	1
Walrond, Les, Kansas	.335	182	37	61	15	1	6	37	3
Elsey, Justin, Oklahoma	.333	141	28	47	9	2	8	34	8
Terrell, Jeff, Missouri	.333	183	35	61	22	1	3	42	9
Roossien, Tony, Okla. State	.328	174	41	57	11	1	12	54	5
Fereday, Todd, Kansas St.	.327	211	54	69	14	6	11	54	21

INDIVIDUAL PITCHING LEADERS

(Minimum 50 Innings)

	W	L	ERA	G	SV	IP	H	BB	SO
Geary, Geoff, Oklahoma	4	3	**2.20**	32	8	61	47	28	63
Jennings, Jason, Baylor	3	5	2.90	27	10	50	34	22	79
Bergman, Brett, Baylor	7	3	3.25	22	2	55	54	26	40
Gooding, Jason, Texas Tech	**11**	0	3.49	16	0	116	111	31	**137**
Ralston, Brad, Texas Tech	3	3	3.65	28	7	57	50	36	72
Dunn, Scott, Texas	5	0	3.88	18	0	51	42	30	58
Wright, Shane, Texas Tech	10	2	3.90	15	0	90	108	10	65
Ward, Monty, Texas Tech	9	4	4.07	16	0	86	87	29	117
Rupe, Ryan, Texas A&M	8	2	4.28	12	0	80	93	25	63
Andra, Jeff, Oklahoma	10	5	4.32	17	0	106	112	50	86
Lambert, Kris, Baylor	8	6	4.35	19	0	110	111	36	104
Blank, Matt, Texas A&M	7	4	4.57	16	0	106	124	25	90
Adkins, Jon, Oklahoma State	**11**	4	4.62	18	0	117	115	30	82
Philbrick, Rusty, Kansas	3	1	4.71	19	0	57	57	20	36
Corson, Mark, Kansas	2	3	4.86	17	0	63	82	29	55
Adare, Kendal, Texas	5	3	4.87	17	0	89	100	25	65
Wingerd, Josh, Kansas	7	5	4.92	25	6	53	52	23	54
Dreier, Thom, Oklahoma State	7	2	4.99	18	0	79	96	47	49
Lyons, Tim, Kansas	3	4	5.23	16	0	64	59	42	62
Fossum, Casey, Texas A&M	3	5	5.28	23	5	87	89	49	113
#Johnson, David, Kansas State	2	3	5.28	29	**11**	29	24	27	29

BIG WEST CONFERENCE

	Conference		Overall	
NORTH	**W**	**L**	**W**	**L**
Nevada	20	10	39	21
Pacific	11	19	29	29
Sacramento State	8	22	16	39
New Mexico State	8	22	21	33
SOUTH	**W**	**L**	**W**	**L**
Long Beach State	22	8	39	26
***Cal State Fullerton**	21	9	39	24
Cal Poly San Luis Obispo	15	15	37	21
UC Santa Barbara	15	15	26	30

ALL-CONFERENCE TEAM: C—Mike Lamb, Jr., Cal State Fullerton. **1B**—Toby Sanchez, Jr., Long Beach State. **2B**—Harvey Hargrove, Jr., Sacramento State; Scott Kidd, Sr., Cal Poly San Luis Obispo. **3B**—Andy Dominique, Sr., Nevada. **SS**—Mike Young, Jr., UC Santa Barbara. **OF**—Gary Johnson, Jr., Nevada; Shane Rooney, Sr., Pacific; Ryan Upshaw, Sr., New Mexico State. **DH**—Marty Camacho, Sr., Cal Poly San Luis Obispo. **Util**—Jerome Alviso, Sr., Cal State Fullerton. **SP**—Marcus Jones, Jr., Long Beach State; Dan Reichert, Jr., Pacific; Matt Wise, Sr., Cal State Fullerton. **RP**—Mike Greenlee, Sr., Cal State Fullerton; Ara Petrosian, Jr., Long Beach State.

Player of the Year: Andy Dominique, Nevada. **Pitcher of the Year:** Dan Reichert, Pacific. **Coach of the Year:** Dave Snow, Long Beach State.

INDIVIDUAL BATTING LEADERS

(Minimum 125 At-Bats)

	AVG	AB	R	H	2B	3B	HR	RBI	SB
Kidd, Scott, Cal Poly SLO	**.412**	255	71	**105**	21	2	14	66	6
Sanchez, Toby, Long Beach	.402	219	51	88	23	1	13	54	6
Rooney, Shane, Pacific	.394	226	46	89	21	1	6	63	2
Alviso, Jeremy, CS Fullerton	.391	225	59	88	18	0	2	43	14
Upshaw, Ryan, NMS	.391	233	67	91	13	2	16	84	5
Booth, Jeremy, NMS	.389	198	49	77	15	0	15	64	1
Rohlmeier, Steve, SLO	.380	221	54	84	13	**5**	8	67	6
Lamb, Mike, CS Fullerton	.379	261	59	99	20	4	10	70	8
Story, Jason, New Mex. St.	.376	189	47	71	16	0	12	59	0
Willis, David, UCSB	.376	229	64	86	18	1	12	53	5
Harrell, Kenny, New Mex. St.	.372	188	49	70	15	**5**	10	47	9
Martin, Justin, Nevada	.365	148	36	54	4	4	0	20	16
Hargrove, Harvey, Sac. St.	.361	219	49	79	8	0	26	62	11
Young, Michael, UCSB	.359	237	62	85	16	3	12	55	6
Ankrum, C.J., CS Fullerton	.359	234	60	84	14	4	2	43	11
Wright, Brad, UCSB	.359	231	55	83	17	2	1	39	1
Smith, Cory, New Mex St.	.358	240	73	86	18	**5**	17	69	11
Uhlman, Jay, Nevada	.358	201	51	72	17	0	8	52	3
Dodder, Boyd, Cal Poly SLO	.358	179	50	64	12	2	16	55	1
Hanna, Tim, Nevada	.357	235	47	84	13	0	4	53	3
Hill, Nakia, CS Fullerton	.357	196	43	70	12	4	7	40	7
Dominique, Andy, Nevada	.357	241	80	86	14	0	**30**	**96**	6
Priess, Matt, Cal Poly SLO	.354	212	56	75	20	0	11	53	0
Hanseen, Tye, Pacific	.352	196	49	69	14	3	5	31	7
Balser, Justin, UCSB	.349	175	39	61	9	0	8	46	1
Day, Paul, Long Beach	.348	233	50	81	13	4	5	42	10
Rowand, Aaron, CS Full.	.347	245	55	85	12	2	7	43	17
Overbay, Lyle, Nevada	.342	260	57	89	18	4	7	67	7
Chatham, Steve, CS Full.	.341	246	56	84	20	1	3	51	5
Miller, Corky, Nevada	.337	199	67	67	10	1	13	47	2
Gemoll, Justin, UCSB	.337	205	34	69	10	1	5	39	5
Camacho, Marty, CPSLO	.335	158	31	53	9	2	14	45	1
Maier, Taber, Cal Poly SLO	.333	249	**81**	83	**25**	2	11	47	12
Walker, Joel, Sac. State	.333	183	34	61	16	1	8	48	2
Inglett, Joe, Nevada	.332	202	57	67	11	1	3	34	6
Williams, Joel, New Mex St.	.332	202	71	67	12	**5**	2	39	15
Gonalez, Izzy, Long Beach	.331	257	47	85	20	2	4	50	0
Radler, R.J., Cal Poly SLO	.327	220	41	72	11	2	9	51	1
Niheu, Eric, Pacific	.326	187	45	61	13	1	2	40	9
Johnson, Gary, Nevada	.323	248	62	80	19	2	12	70	6
Martin, Casey, LBS	.323	217	40	70	17	0	9	50	2
#Champagne, Andre, NMS	.286	196	41	56	7	1	3	33	**18**

INDIVIDUAL PITCHING LEADERS

(Minimum 50 Innings)

	W	L	ERA	G	SV	IP	H	BB	SO
Reichert, Dan, Pacific	**13**	4	**2.30**	20	0	133	96	51	**169**
Greenlee, Mike, CS Fullerton	5	1	3.38	29	7	53	43	14	56
Wise, Matt, CS Fullerton	5	8	3.50	17	0	116	94	41	116
Jones, Marcus, LBS	11	5	3.73	18	0	128	115	33	131
Petrosian, Ara, LBS	4	3	3.91	35	**15**	78	68	34	82
Tokarse, Brian, CS Fullerton	10	3	4.01	20	0	99	81	47	114
Biddle, Rocky, LBS	9	5	4.47	17	0	105	104	74	134
Church, Ryan, Nevada	6	5	4.74	17	1	80	92	35	48
Zirelli, Mike, Cal Poly SLO	10	6	4.85	18	1	119	147	33	69
Duckworth, Brandon, CS Full.	8	1	4.93	20	3	80	92	39	88
Husted, Brent, Nevada	8	1	5.02	15	0	90	107	39	64
Garner, Mike, CS Fullerton	2	1	5.15	24	0	51	59	28	39
Barrera, Iran, Long Beach	5	4	5.46	20	3	61	95	20	41
May, Kyle, Pacific	6	7	5.56	17	0	112	145	40	68
Hild, Scott, CS Fullerton	4	4	5.66	18	0	56	72	29	30
Bean, Seth, UCSB	5	9	5.68	21	0	101	133	31	72
Snowden, Chad, Cal Poly SLO	4	4	5.74	17	0	80	109	22	52

JEFF GOLDEN

Pacific's Dan Reichert
Led Big West with 169 strikeouts

COLONIAL ATHLETIC ASSOCIATION

	Conference		Overall	
	W	**L**	**W**	**L**
Virginia Commonwealth	15	4	32	23
Old Dominion	12	8	34	20
James Madison	10	10	31	26
George Mason	10	11	29	24
East Carolina	10	11	29	27
William & Mary	8	12	30	24
***Richmond**	8	12	34	26
UNC Wilmington	7	12	28	29

ALL-CONFERENCE TEAM: C—Cory Whitby, Jr., Virginia Commonwealth. **1B**—Matt Pusey, Sr., Richmond. **2B**—Trevor Haas, So., George Mason. **3B**—Ron Walker, Jr., Old Dominion. **SS**—Brandon Inge, So., Virginia Commonwealth. **OF**—Mike Colangelo, Jr., George Mason; Kevin Razler, So., James Madison; Steve Salargo, So., East Carolina. **DH**—Justin Lamber, Jr., Richmond. **LHSP**—Jesse James, Jr., Old Dominion. **RHSP**—Matt Burch, So., Virginia Commonwealth. **RP**—Brandon Inge, So., Virginia Commonwealth.

Player of the Year: Ron Walker, Old Dominion. **Rookie of the Year:** Brian Rogers, William & Mary. **Coach of the Year:** Paul Keyes, Virginia Commonwealth.

INDIVIDUAL BATTING LEADERS

(Minimum 125 At-Bats)

	AVG	AB	R	H	2B	3B	HR	RBI	SB
Colangelo, Mike, GM	**.418**	184	62	77	18	**7**	7	68	14
Pusey, Matt, Richmond	.401	252	66	**101**	**24**	0	15	**85**	2
Rogers, Brian, W&M	.380	192	42	73	16	1	8	48	3
Salargo, Steve, East Car.	.374	219	52	82	14	3	10	44	15
White, Greg, Jas. Madison	.372	223	53	83	**24**	2	9	51	12

	AVG	AB	R	H	2B	3B	HR	RBI	SB
Filson, Greg, George Mason	.370	154	20	57	12	1	3	36	3
Walker, Ron, Old Dominion	.366	183	**75**	67	14	2	**20**	64	6
Leek, Randy, W&M	.366	186	44	68	19	3	9	46	5
Haas, Trevor, GM	.363	190	57	69	9	1	5	31	11
Baksh, Ray, Jas. Madison	.362	210	37	76	**24**	1	5	52	3
Flaherty, Tim, East Car.	.361	194	51	70	16	1	**20**	52	5
Razler, Kevin, Jas. Madison	.358	215	52	77	14	2	10	52	16
Rigsby, Randy, East Car.	.356	216	58	77	17	1	11	55	17
Ashcraft, Jay, VC	.356	208	54	74	15	3	6	38	14
Williams, Derek, UNCW	.354	226	67	80	19	2	11	44	20
Gsell, Tony, Old Dominion	.351	228	61	80	16	4	10	52	16
Troilo, Joe, Old Dominion	.347	236	61	82	14	3	7	44	17
Inge, Brandon, VCU	.343	181	47	62	10	2	9	42	9
Pearson, Shawn, ODU	.341	138	44	47	7	6	1	16	17
Hoch, Corey, Jas. Madison	.329	228	57	75	18	2	8	48	14
Roach, Jason, UNCW	.327	226	45	74	14	2	13	63	4
#Wagler, John, Richmond	.310	213	70	66	13	1	5	38	**28**

INDIVIDUAL PITCHING LEADERS

(Minimum 50 innings)

	W	L	ERA	G	SV	IP	H	BB	SO
Brantley, Brian, Old Dominion	6	3	**3.14**	14	1	72	67	22	58
#Waligora, T.P., W&M	1	2	3.60	28	**9**	40	38	25	49
Roach, Jason, UNCW	4	3	3.63	16	1	79	75	29	68
James, Jesse, Old Dominion	8	2	3.92	14	0	99	113	24	94
Jernigan, Brooks, East Car.	8	8	4.07	20	2	113	112	44	**112**
Camp, Shawn, George Mason	5	5	4.16	14	0	84	85	34	78
Cocca, John, Old Dominion	5	5	4.28	14	0	74	80	28	64
Leek, Randy, William & Mary	6	4	4.42	17	0	92	105	10	77
Berryman, Chad, VCU	8	4	4.61	18	0	107	135	29	55
Adams, Jason, William & Mary	6	3	4.62	24	0	51	56	14	43
Bailey, David, Old Dominion	6	5	4.62	19	1	60	57	43	68
McGinn, Tom, George Mason	4	4	4.85	10	0	52	51	23	52
Burch, Matt, VCU	8	6	4.89	19	0	105	107	66	101
Preston, Bobbie, Richmond	5	3	4.98	21	1	90	92	25	60
Sams, Aaron, James Madison	6	5	4.98	17	3	69	85	22	62
Harper, Travis, Jas. Madison	8	3	4.99	15	0	88	88	39	85
Clark, Conrad, East Carolina	7	5	5.04	23	1	70	77	22	44
Huller, Mike, George Mason	2	4	5.04	18	0	50	44	44	43
Cook, Andy, William & Mary	**9**	3	5.14	18	0	75	74	25	53
Morris, Jason, Richmond	5	2	5.16	16	0	68	80	20	37
Hall, Brandon, UNCW	3	5	5.26	9	0	51	71	13	30
Payne, John, East Carolina	4	3	5.35	16	0	67	87	28	52
#Mazur, Bryan, UNCW	9	8	5.96	23	0	109	131	53	85

CONFERENCE USA

	Conference		Overall	
	W	L	W	L
Tulane	19	7	40	21
***Houston**	19	8	40	23
South Florida	18	8	39	24
Southern Mississippi	16	10	34	23
UNC Charlotte	14	12	30	26
Alabama-Birmingham	14	13	31	29
Louisville	11	15	23	32
Memphis	9	17	20	31
Saint Louis	8	19	21	30
Cincinnati	4	23	12	46

ALL-CONFERENCE TEAM: C—Chad Sutter, So., Tulane. **INF**—Dustin Carr, Sr., Houston; Jason Dellaero, Jr., South Florida; Ross Gload, Jr., South Florida; Keith Graffagnini, Jr., Tulane; Bo Robinson, Jr., UNC Charlotte. **OF**—Jeremy Albritton, So., Southern Mississippi; Jason Fitzgerald, Jr., Tulane; Kyle Logan, Sr., Southern Mississippi; Goefrey Tomlinson, Jr., Houston. **DH**—Cliff Wren, So., Southern Mississippi. **SP**—Chad Harville, Jr., Memphis; Jason Navarro, Jr., Tulane. **RP**—Luis Ramos, So., South Florida.

Most Valuable Player: Ross Gload, South Florida. **Pitcher of the Year:** Jason Navarro, Tulane. **Freshman of the Year:** Shane Nance, Houston. **Coach of the Year:** Rick Jones, Tulane.

INDIVIDUAL BATTING LEADERS

(Minimum 125 At-Bats)

	AVG	AB	R	H	2B	3B	HR	RBI	SB
Tomlinson, Goefrey, Hous.	**.427**	248	74	106	29	3	16	67	25
Schied, Jeremy, So. Miss.	.402	164	41	66	12	0	7	36	3
Gload, Ross, South Florida	.399	248	**85**	99	25	1	18	**80**	8
Carr, Dustin, Houston	.399	271	80	**108**	**32**	2	11	50	23
Robinson, Bo, UNCC	.395	228	54	90	29	4	7	53	6
Fitzgerald, Jason, Tulane	.387	238	71	92	16	4	20	79	21
Eaton, Bill, South Florida	.380	179	37	68	12	3	1	26	11
Harness, Dan, Ala.-Birm.	.379	261	63	99	14	0	3	35	8
DeLeon, Jorge, South Fla.	.370	243	41	90	16	2	4	53	8
Albritton, Jeremy, So. Miss.	.370	219	43	81	11	0	13	48	2
Carnes, Shayne, Ala.-Birm.	.369	236	51	87	14	0	11	49	9
Hughes, Brian, Tulane	.365	241	71	88	23	3	8	45	20
House, Craig, Memphis	.363	182	43	66	7	3	4	28	13
Cissell, Darin, St. Louis	.361	147	43	53	8	4	6	23	19
Wren, Cliff, So. Miss.	.357	207	50	74	11	0	12	39	3
Bredensteiner, Brett, StL	.356	202	51	72	12	**6**	18	63	6
Eberly, Rodney, Ala.-Birm.	.355	245	42	87	16	1	8	51	0
Hurst, Ryan, Ala.-Birm.	.353	184	31	65	10	0	5	31	1
Bennett, Kevin, Louisville	.353	190	38	67	12	1	6	41	3
Matan, James, UNCC	.351	225	48	79	19	1	11	57	3
Lynch, Sean, South Florida	.351	194	45	68	14	3	9	49	3
Gabris, Adam, St. Louis	.348	187	48	65	15	0	11	56	3
Diaz, Mike, South Florida	.347	236	64	82	10	5	4	30	10
Martin, Jared, So. Miss.	.341	214	44	73	15	2	6	40	9
Rhodes, Nick, UNCC	.330	221	49	73	17	1	3	22	21
Logan, Kyle, So. Miss.	.329	222	55	73	17	0	15	60	18
Diaco, Vinnie, UNCC	.329	146	21	48	5	1	0	13	12
Pursell, Mike, Tulane	.327	205	38	67	17	2	7	47	8
Dellaero, Jason, South Fla.	.324	247	67	80	16	5	20	74	4
Hesse, Chris, So. Miss.	.322	202	52	65	5	2	9	37	17
Berger, Matt, Louisville	.322	199	53	64	13	1	14	51	4
#Sutter, Chad, Tulane	.289	235	57	68	10	0	**23**	65	1
#Skrehot, Shaun, Houston	.285	246	48	70	9	2	5	41	**33**

INDIVIDUAL PITCHING LEADERS

(Minimum 50 Innings)

	W	L	ERA	G	SV	IP	H	BB	SO
Navarro, Jason, Tulane	**12**	2	**2.00**	17	0	112	81	37	135
#Ramos, Luis, South Florida	4	1	2.39	30	**8**	38	26	16	35
Harville, Chad, Memphis	5	6	2.66	17	1	102	71	49	**136**
Mason, Chris, Ala.-Birm.	4	2	3.29	31	**8**	66	75	7	57
Lontayo, Alex, Tulane	8	5	3.44	19	0	92	84	35	89
Berkowitz, Jared, Tulane	4	5	3.50	15	0	87	99	27	66
Glaser, Scott, South Florida	9	3	3.87	20	0	126	128	43	89
Gray, Mark, Ala.-Birm.	7	5	3.87	15	0	98	116	27	90
Bobbitt, Josh, Tulane	7	2	3.95	17	0	80	81	15	71
Ryan, Pat, South Florida	8	4	4.01	16	0	103	122	35	59
House, Craig, Memphis	2	4	4.09	18	5	51	39	23	54
Kirkland, Robb, Houston	7	3	4.11	17	1	61	64	12	55
Dickinson, Tighe, Ala.-Birm.	5	4	4.27	26	3	72	78	23	59
Dieudonne, Robert, Houston	4	4	4.42	30	6	55	49	22	54
Adams, Eric, Southern Miss.	8	4	4.50	18	0	82	97	35	56
Nance, Shane, Houston	7	6	4.53	17	0	103	94	52	106
McCrary, Scott, Ala.-Birm.	7	6	4.57	18	0	83	98	27	68
Parker, Brandon, So. Miss.	3	3	4.59	27	5	51	52	19	71
McKay, John, UNCC	5	6	4.74	20	3	74	72	44	85
Player, Brannon, UNCC	10	5	4.85	16	0	111	110	49	79
Stauffer, Scott, Louisville	8	4	4.88	17	0	103	130	22	77
Donnick, Dan, UNCC	6	3	5.00	23	1	81	96	32	49
Baker, Ryan, UNCC	4	4	5.01	21	2	88	93	45	58
Donohoo, Chris, Ala.-Birm.	2	5	5.22	23	2	59	69	35	50
Cantrelle, Heath, So. Miss.	7	6	5.24	20	0	101	126	31	86
Schaeffer, Michael, St. Louis	2	8	5.53	14	0	68	84	40	53

IVY LEAGUE

	Conference		Overall	
GEHRIG	W	L	W	L
Princeton	10	10	20	25
Penn	10	10	19	21
Cornell	7	13	13	26
Columbia	6	14	12	26
ROLFE	**W**	**L**	**W**	**L**
***Harvard**	18	2	34	16
Yale	16	4	24	19
Dartmouth	11	9	22	16
Brown	2	18	5	37

ALL-CONFERENCE TEAM: C—Eric Anderson, So., Dartmouth. **1B**—Peter Albers, Sr., Harvard. **2B**—Jason Wynn, Sr., Columbia. **3B**—Mike Conway, So., Dartmouth. **SS**—Brian Nickerson, Fr., Dartmouth. **OF**—Matthew Bird, Sr., Yale; Michael Hazen, Jr., Princeton; Brian Ralph, Jr., Harvard. **DH**—Travis Hunter, Sr., Columbia. **Util**—Armen Simonian, Jr., Penn. **SP**—Eric Gutshall, Jr., Yale; Frank Hogan, Sr., Harvard. **RP**—Dan Godfrey, Jr., Dartmouth.

Player of the Year: Brian Ralph, Harvard. **Pitcher of the Year:** Frank Hogan, Harvard. **Rookie of the Year:** Brian Nickerson, Dartmouth.

INDIVIDUAL BATTING LEADERS

(Minimum 100 At-Bats)

	AVG	AB	R	H	2B	3B	HR	RBI	SB
Nickerson, Brian, Dart.	**.463**	136	31	63	**18**	1	5	29	6
Nagata, Mark, Penn	.422	109	23	46	8	0	5	26	0
Conway, Michael, Dart.	.399	153	43	61	12	0	2	28	6
Ralph, Brian, Harvard	.390	164	**55**	**64**	15	2	6	36	**24**
Huling, Andrew, Harvard	.388	165	41	**64**	11	**4**	3	42	14
Spencer, Andrew, Dart.	.379	145	39	55	9	3	1	29	12
Hunter, Travis, Columbia	.377	146	34	55	15	0	**14**	**50**	0
Evans, Matt, Princeton	.377	146	29	55	15	1	6	38	3
Lawler, Jeff, Brown	.373	134	39	50	11	1	5	16	20
Farscht, Russ, Penn	.372	129	31	48	6	0	5	23	4
Hazen, Michael, Princeton	.368	152	27	56	11	1	2	38	17
Simonian, Armen, Penn	.365	104	23	38	11	0	1	18	0
Albers, Peter, Harvard	.364	162	37	59	16	1	8	46	11
Coyne, Tony, Yale	.359	131	24	47	12	0	2	32	2
Ivy, Brian, Yale	.355	138	28	49	9	1	1	28	10
Caggiano, Keith, Yale	.353	139	35	49	9	0	6	38	6
Bird, Matthew, Yale	.351	168	42	59	14	2	5	30	21
Dodge, David, Yale	.350	137	28	48	12	0	3	25	1

INDIVIDUAL PITCHING LEADERS

(Minimum 40 Innings)

	W	L	ERA	G	SV	IP	H	BB	SO
Perez, Rich, Yale	**8**	2	**2.24**	13	0	64	60	22	38
Duffell, Andrew, Harvard	**8**	1	2.35	12	0	69	60	25	33
Simonian, Armen, Penn	5	3	2.73	10	0	59	57	30	52
Gutshall, Eric, Yale	4	6	2.97	17	**6**	67	59	36	**82**
Volpp, Brian, Princeton	3	3	3.13	12	2	55	49	28	13
Hogan, Frank, Harvard	**8**	2	3.28	13	0	69	73	26	31
Jamieson, Donald, Harvard	5	3	3.36	18	5	67	69	23	31
Godfrey, Dan, Dartmouth	6	2	3.92	17	4	41	49	15	27
Tedeman, John, Princeton	3	2	4.53	13	0	48	41	23	28
Reddy, Sudha, Yale	6	2	4.58	11	0	55	60	20	28
Fischer, A.B., Penn	2	1	5.06	10	0	48	58	24	36
Brooks, Conor, Dartmouth	3	3	5.14	10	3	42	65	9	25
Killgoar, Tom, Princeton	5	4	5.40	10	0	50	58	19	40

METRO ATLANTIC CONFERENCE

	Conference		Overall	
NORTH	**W**	**L**	**W**	**L**
Niagara	11	7	17	21
*Siena	10	8	21	34
Le Moyne	10	8	16	23
Canisius	5	13	18	19
SOUTH	**W**	**L**	**W**	**L**
Fairfield	13	5	20	25
Iona	10	8	19	27
St. Peter's	7	11	10	27
Manhattan	6	12	11	28

MAAC North ALL-CONFERENCE TEAM: C—Daryl Besant, Jr., Canisius; Bill Kerry, Jr., Le Moyne. **1B**—Cameron Pelton, So., Le Moyne. **2B**—Mark Drablik, Jr., Niagara; Jason Kline, Sr., Canisius. **3B**—Vic Boccarosa, So., Le Moyne; Dave Marek, Jr., Siena. **SS**—Brian Przybysz, Sr., Canisius; Brian Spadafino, Jr., Niagara. **OF**—Todd Donovan, Fr., Siena; Aaron Mindel, So., Niagara; Jeremy Ross, Sr., Canisius. **DH**—Art Eastman, Sr., Canisius; Cory Pike, So., Niagara. **P**—Scott Cassidy, Jr., Le Moyne; Dennis Hogan, Sr., Siena.

Player of the Year: Aaron Mindel, Niagara. **Rookie of the Year:** Jack Kennedy, Le Moyne. **Coach of the Year:** Jim Mauro, Niagara.

MAAC South ALL-CONFERENCE TEAM: C—Kyran Connelly, Jr., Iona. **1B**—Elloid Alguila, Sr., Iona; Tom McDonough, So., Manhattan. **2B**—Adam Samuellan, Sr., Fairfield. **3B**—Brian Merkle, Jr., Iona. **SS**—Jeff Rowett, Jr., Manhattan. **OF**—Pat Callahan, Jr., Manhattan; Tom Lopusznick, Fr., Fairfield; John Penatello, Jr., Iona; Erik Zbranak, Jr., St. Peter's. **DH**—Jon Wilson, Sr., Fairfield. **P**—Rob Elinskas, Sr., Fairfield; Jeff Fortune, Sr., St. Peter's; Neil Longo, So., Manhattan.

Co-Players of the Year: Pat Callahan, Manhattan; Adam Samuelian, Fairfield. **Rookie of the Year:** Tom Lopusznick, Fairfield. **Coach of the Year:** John Slosar, Fairfield.

INDIVIDUAL BATTING LEADERS

(Minimum 100 At-Bats)

	AVG	AB	R	H	2B	3B	HR	RBI	SB
Ross, Jeremy, Canisius	**.400**	115	36	46	11	0	2	28	12
Callahan, Patrick, Man.	.381	113	22	43	8	1	5	28	6
Kline, Jason, Canisius	.378	127	36	48	12	1	9	32	7
Lucca, Mike, St. Peter's	.370	100	14	37	6	0	0	13	0
Mindel, Aaron, Niagara	.366	123	40	45	4	1	2	23	13
Marek, Dave, Siena	.364	112	21	48	9	1	4	36	5
Hennessy, Brian, Canisius	.355	124	33	44	9	0	3	27	10
Penatello, John, Iona	.354	164	**49**	58	12	3	8	37	19
Besant, Daryl, Canisius	.350	103	26	36	5	0	2	17	1
Connelly, Kyran, Iona	.349	146	42	51	9	2	4	34	2
Samuelian, Adam, Fairfield	.347	170	41	**59**	12	2	3	21	4
Alguila, Elloid, Iona	.346	130	23	45	**15**	1	8	38	0
Przybysz, Brian, Canisius	.340	103	20	35	5	0	2	26	0
Majewski, Ted, Canisius	.336	107	21	36	8	1	4	33	3
Zbranak, Erik, St. Peter's	.336	125	29	42	8	4	4	24	9
Kennedy, Jack, Le Moyne	.331	133	37	44	2	1	6	28	7
Rusinko, Andy, Niagara	.330	106	19	35	6	1	7	30	1
Olson, Drew, Le Moyne	.328	116	31	38	3	1	2	15	3
Felton, Cameron, LeMoyne	.328	128	23	42	4	1	5	28	0
Merkle, Brian, Iona	.327	165	35	54	13	0	**16**	42	1
#Ostrander, Mike, Siena	.316	155	32	49	9	5	5	**44**	3
#Wilson, Jon, Fairfield	.311	167	31	52	**15**	**5**	3	38	6
#Donovan, Todd, Siena	.306	173	38	53	5	4	3	18	**36**

INDIVIDUAL PITCHING LEADERS

(Minimum 40 Innings)

	W	L	ERA	G	SV	IP	H	BB	SO
Longo, Neil, Manhattan	5	4	**3.36**	12	0	70	67	9	47
Roberts, Mike, Siena	3	5	3.60	14	2	60	63	22	41
Fields, Dave, Siena	4	5	3.62	12	0	60	69	13	27
Elinskask, Rob, Fairfield	4	2	4.14	9	0	54	49	17	47
Moffitt, Mike, Iona	3	5	4.16	11	0	63	56	36	**68**
Hogan, Dennis, Siena	5	4	4.35	12	0	62	64	46	59
Wallace, Justin, Le Moyne	0	5	4.53	8	0	44	48	13	36
#Hennessy, Brian, Iona	1	2	4.58	20	**5**	39	35	32	35
Fortune, Jeff, St. Peter's	4	6	4.59	13	0	67	74	31	64
Cassidy, Scott, Le Moyne	3	3	4.78	10	0	49	47	13	36
Wyllie, Graham, Niagara	6	1	4.86	9	0	54	47	17	22
Wenzel, Bob, Fairfield	**7**	2	4.96	9	0	62	66	22	34

MID-AMERICAN CONFERENCE

	Conference		Overall	
	W	**L**	**W**	**L**
***Ohio**	22	9	43	18
Ball State	21	10	40	19
Kent	18	13	29	28
Miami (Ohio)	17	13	27	28
Eastern Michigan	17	14	29	25
Central Michigan	14	14	29	20
Akron	14	17	31	23
Bowling Green State	13	17	24	27
Toledo	9	20	18	33
Western Michigan	6	24	14	39

ALL-CONFERENCE TEAM: C—Brady Gick, Sr., Ohio. **1B**—Greg Ryan, So., Eastern Michigan. **2B**—Anthony Holyszko, So., Western Michigan. **3B**—Brian Dorrmann, Jr., Ball State. **SS**—Jason Murray, Sr., Ball State. **OF**—Brian Petrucci, Sr., Akron; Jason Meier, Sr., Ball State; Jason Graham, Sr., Ohio. **DH**—Bill Bronikowski, Sr., Toledo. **Util**—Jake Eye, Sr., Ohio. **SP**—Mark Rutherford, Sr., Eastern Michigan; Brian Schubmehl, Sr., Ohio; Bobby Sismondo, So., Ohio; Andy Smith, Sr., Bowling Green. **RP**—Tom Miller, Sr., Ohio.

Player of the Year: Greg Ryan, Eastern Michigan. **Pitcher of the Year:** Andy Smith, Bowling Green. **Freshman of the Year:** Larry Bigbie, Ball State. **Coach of the Year:** Joe Carbone, Ohio.

INDIVIDUAL BATTING LEADERS

(Minimum 100 At-Bats)

	AVG	AB	R	H	2B	3B	HR	RBI	SB
Ryan, Greg, East. Mich.	**.447**	197	56	**88**	**25**	1	9	56	5
Murray, Jason, Ball State	.425	174	46	74	20	0	6	45	14
Petrucci, Brian, Akron	.420	188	47	79	24	2	10	**65**	11
Meier, Jason, Ball State	.415	200	61	83	17	1	15	**65**	17
Graham, Jason, Ohio	.390	223	62	87	18	3	6	50	6
Rutherford, Mark, EMU	.388	170	40	66	16	0	11	48	3
Bronikowski, Bill, Toledo	.385	122	31	47	12	3	9	44	3
Peck, Tom, Miami	.373	193	52	72	12	1	6	31	10
Gick, Brady, Ohio	.365	181	37	66	16	2	10	56	2
Tyo, Brian, Cent. Michigan	.363	146	37	53	5	3	4	19	16
Jones, Greg, Cent. Mich.	.362	127	35	46	9	4	7	36	6
Holyszko, Anthony, WMU	.362	163	25	59	5	1	1	28	8
Eye, Jake, Ohio	.357	224	42	80	8	0	10	50	7
Cannon, Brian, Bowl. Green	.356	177	37	63	15	0	4	33	3
Haring, Brett, Cent. Mich.	.353	136	36	48	13	1	6	28	10

	AVG	AB	R	H	2B	3B	HR	RBI	SB
Fitzharris, Tim, Ball State	.352	193	49	68	12	2	5	33	1
Bechard, Jess, Kent	.351	202	44	71	15	1	4	44	10
Bigbie, Larry, Ball State	.349	189	49	66	6	4	5	42	21
Vokal, Todd, East. Mich.	.348	135	26	47	7	**5**	2	20	8
Henson, Jamie, Kent	.348	158	31	55	13	0	3	29	0
Love, Justin, Ball State	.346	205	**67**	71	11	4	5	43	**44**
Dorrmann, Brian, Ball State	.346	234	50	81	14	2	13	61	6
#Farris, Ed, Ball State	.313	208	55	65	**18**	3	18	63	0

INDIVIDUAL PITCHING LEADERS

(Minimum 40 Innings)

	W	L	ERA	G	SV	IP	H	BB	SO
Smith, Andy, Bowling Green	9	3	**1.85**	16	0	87	69	16	79
Singer, Ben, Akron	7	3	2.75	13	0	72	68	26	43
Taylor, Tim, Akron	3	2	2.96	11	0	49	51	23	32
Miller, Tom, Ohio	**11**	2	3.17	27	6	49	42	26	71
Hartman, Kory, Kent	2	3	3.40	21	**7**	42	37	20	39
Danner, Andy, Miami	6	7	3.51	18	1	105	97	37	73
#Guinan, Tim, Miami	2	3	3.54	25	**7**	28	27	11	26
Schubmehl, Brian, Ohio	10	0	3.62	22	2	67	63	41	58
Yoder, Dave, Akron	4	2	3.62	9	0	45	43	13	29
Miller, Brent, Cent. Mich.	3	3	3.63	12	0	42	44	14	26
Sismondo, Bobby, Ohio	**11**	2	3.65	15	0	101	99	26	**106**
Stanley, Bruce, Ball State	8	4	4.03	21	1	99	94	34	75
Skeefel, Adam, Ball State	6	5	4.18	18	0	52	61	15	40
Speicher, Matt, Ball State	3	2	4.30	25	4	46	46	24	39
Header, Jon, Akron	6	5	4.32	22	2	77	78	42	54
Rowland, Doug, Toledo	4	9	4.39	26	5	70	82	20	53
Skeeles, Mike, Kent	5	4	4.42	15	0	71	64	48	76
Rutherford, Mark, East. Mich.	9	3	4.48	14	0	74	71	26	51

MID-CONTINTENT CONFERENCE

	Conference		Overall	
EAST	**W**	**L**	**W**	**L**
*Troy State	8	6	36	24
C.W. Post	8	7	21	24
New York Tech	9	8	21	25
Pace	6	6	19	18
Central Connecticut State.	7	8	20	16
Youngstown State	8	11	29	21
WEST	**W**	**L**	**W**	**L**
Northeastern Illinois	16	7	29	29
Western Illinois	10	9	13	24
Chicago State	10	12	14	35
Valparaiso	6	14	20	31

EASTERN DIVISION ALL-CONFERENCE TEAM: C—Chad Shultz, Jr., Youngstown State. **1B**—Jamie Palmese, Sr., Central Connecticut. **2B**—Paul Marino, Sr., New York Tech. **3B**—Paul Tinelli, Sr., C.W. Post. **SS**—Kenny Krey, Jr., Troy State. **OF**—Danny Graham, Jr., Central Connecticut; Brian Hoffman, Jr., New York Tech; Bryan Kelly, Sr., Troy State. **DH**—Jorge Soto, Fr., Troy State. **Util**—Blake Bendett, Sr., C.W. Post. **SP**—Dean Cordova, Sr., Troy State; Jason Fawcett, Sr., Troy State; Shane Mead, Jr., Youngstown State. **RP**—Michael Riveles, So., Pace.

WESTERN DIVISION ALL-CONFERENCE TEAM: C—Tim Richardson, Sr., Western Illinois. **1B**—Chris Reehoff, Sr., Northeastern Illinois. **2B**—Brian Naese, Sr., Chicago State. **3B**—Matt Dunne, Sr., Northeastern Illinois. **SS**—Mark Binder, Jr., Chicago State. **OF**—Rob Hadrick, Sr., Valparaiso; Brian Hantosh, So., Northeastern Illinois; Jamie Sykes, Jr., Valparaiso. **DH**—Bob Kostuch, Jr., Northeastern Illinois. **Util**—Craig Majdecki, Jr., Chicago State. **SP**—Jay Kvasnicka, Jr., Northeastern Illinois; Mike Paskvan, Sr., Northeastern Illinois; Jamie Puorto, Sr., Northeastern Illinois. **RP**—Brian Sullivan, Sr., Northeastern Illinois.

Player of the Year: Bryan Kelly, Troy State. **Pitcher of the Year:** Jason Fawcett, Troy State. **Newcomer of the Year:** Mark Thomas, Youngstown State. **Coach of the Year:** John Mayotte, Troy State.

INDIVIDUAL BATTING LEADERS

(Minimum 100 At-Bats)

	AVG	AB	R	H	2B	3B	HR	RBI	SB
Richardson, Tim, West. Ill.	**.421**	107	27	45	12	1	6	31	2
Briller, Chris, NY Tech	.408	169	41	69	14	2	4	37	13
Shultz, Chad, Young. State	.406	165	41	67	10	4	2	36	4
McKenzie, Tim, Cent. Conn.	.390	100	22	39	10	0	3	25	0
Thomas, Mark, Young. St.	.389	157	49	61	11	2	0	24	14
Tinelli, Paul, C.W. Post	.382	170	40	65	10	2	9	42	7
Pruchnicki, Ken, Cent. Conn.	.381	126	31	48	10	0	2	35	2
Dunne, Matt, NE Illinois	.377	183	48	69	**22**	1	7	43	2
Hantosh, Brian, NE Illinois	.368	193	42	71	14	5	6	46	4
Hadrick, Rob, Valparaiso	.364	176	42	64	21	**7**	4	40	14
Kelly, Bryan, Troy State	.361	233	55	**84**	13	4	13	**69**	1
Harbold, Tom, Young. State	.361	183	44	66	14	1	4	43	2
Sykes, Jamie, Valparaiso	.354	130	27	46	9	4	7	41	10
Palmese, Jamie, Cent. Conn.	.354	127	40	45	9	1	**16**	54	2
Ciccone, Philip, Pace	.352	128	31	45	7	2	2	20	6
Rojas, Chris, New York Tech	.348	164	41	57	4	0	5	31	7
Maule, Jason, Cent. Conn.	.344	128	42	44	5	0	1	22	**39**
Reehoff, Chris, NE Illinois	.343	207	38	71	17	4	5	48	5
Urtnowski, Mike, C.W. Post	.340	153	29	52	12	0	7	35	0
Graham, Danny, Cent. Conn.	.339	115	40	39	9	1	8	40	3
Accardi, Bobby, Pace	.338	148	26	50	7	1	0	18	7
Jaworski, Jason, Pace	.336	116	26	39	11	2	2	26	1
Farcas, Ray, Young. State	.327	159	41	52	11	3	4	21	22
#Krey, Kenny, Troy State	.308	221	**56**	68	16	4	4	27	9
#Soto, Jorge, Troy State	.233	189	33	44	5	0	**16**	56	1

INDIVIDUAL PITCHING LEADERS

(Minimum 40 Innings)

	W	L	ERA	G	SV	IP	H	BB	SO
Hinson, B.T., Troy State	6	3	**3.16**	20	3	63	59	17	47
Mead, Shane, Young. State	2	4	3.26	12	2	49	68	14	54
Havrilla, Rick, Young. State	3	3	3.44	10	2	41	48	20	33
Sullivan, Brent, Pace	5	2	3.48	11	0	62	59	15	36
Fawcett, Jason, Troy State	**11**	3	3.61	17	0	112	96	49	**141**
Paskvan, Mike, NE Illinois	6	5	3.63	12	0	69	68	39	52
Sullivan, Brian, NE Illinois	3	3	3.64	30	**5**	42	40	15	53
#Walk, Jeremy, West. Illinois	1	2	3.68	14	**5**	22	26	5	15
Puorto, Jamie, NE Illinois	6	6	3.86	14	0	79	82	23	82
Wardle, Sean, Young. State	4	2	3.92	14	0	45	50	31	29
Powell, Donny, Chicago State	1	5	3.97	16	1	48	56	19	25
Cordova, Dean, Troy State	8	6	4.19	17	0	103	114	45	73
Scudder, John, Young. State	4	1	4.24	11	1	40	44	15	22
Pyles, Shawn, Troy State	2	5	4.29	17	0	63	51	38	80
Langford, Chris, Troy State	3	1	4.32	13	0	58	66	24	55
McKeon, Shane, NY Tech	5	4	4.33	15	1	54	54	36	23
Daggett, Barry, Young. State	6	4	4.37	12	0	58	60	24	47
Kelley, Brett, West. Illinois	1	2	4.54	12	0	42	52	14	18
Kvasnicka, Jay, NE Illinois	7	5	4.67	12	0	69	76	35	58
Caldwell, John, Young. State	2	4	4.85	17	0	61	81	23	41

MID-EASTERN CONFERENCE

	Conference		Overall	
NORTH	**W**	**L**	**W**	**L**
Howard	13	3	20	31
Coppin State	10	5	16	24
Delaware State	7	10	12	30
Maryland-Eastern Shore	3	15	8	36
SOUTH	**W**	**L**	**W**	**L**
Florida A&M	8	3	25	27
*Bethune-Cookman	5	5	21	33
North Carolina A&T	3	8	8	31

ALL-CONFERENCE TEAM: C—Keith Maxwell, Sr., Florida A&M. **INF**—Cecil Christwell, Jr., Coppin State; Toriano Gilbert, Sr., Bethune-Cookman; Jason Moore, Jr., North Carolina A&T; Chris Warren, So., Howard. **OF**—Danny Singletary, Sr., Coppin State; Wayne Slater, Jr., Bethune-Cookman; Herbert Wheat, Jr., Howard. **DH**—Terrance Johnson, Sr., Howard. **P**—Mike Rawls, Jr., Bethune-Cookman.

Player of the Year: Keith Maxwell, Florida A&M. **Rookie of the Year:** Eunique Johnson, Howard. **Coach of the Year:** Richard Skeel, Bethune-Cookman.

INDIVIDUAL BATTING LEADERS

(Minimum 100 At-Bats)

	AVG	AB	R	H	2B	3B	HR	RBI	SB
Johnson, Eunique, Howard	**.402**	179	45	**72**	**21**	4	1	52	4
Slater, Wayne, Beth.-Cook.	.393	163	49	64	13	5	1	35	**33**
Maxwell, Keith, Fla. A&M	.389	180	**52**	70	13	1	**15**	**62**	7
Hernandez, Johan, Howard	.359	184	39	66	13	2	3	40	3
Bell, Ruffin, Coppin State	.346	107	17	37	6	3	0	23	3
Averette, Robert, Fla. A&M	.344	128	25	44	10	3	3	29	4
Christwell, Cecil, Coppin St.	.338	136	28	46	9	0	2	20	2
Cobb, Floyd, Florida A&M	.329	152	47	50	3	2	0	21	9
Marsh, Mandell, UMES	.324	145	24	47	11	0	1	16	21
Mabrey, Izzy, Del. State	.323	127	37	41	7	2	3	21	11
Johnson, Terrance, Howard	.313	160	37	50	11	1	6	44	2
Easterling, Rodney, NC A&T	.311	106	12	33	3	0	1	7	3

Player	AVG	AB	R	H	2B	3B	HR	RBI	SB
Pisani, Brian, Coppin State	.308	117	35	36	10	1	5	25	2
Warren, Chris, Howard	.305	167	38	51	10	4	5	32	6
Moore, Jason, NC A&T	.303	119	32	36	4	1	11	28	2
#Wheat, Herbert, Howard	.262	202	44	53	13	**8**	3	36	24

INDIVIDUAL PITCHING LEADERS

(Minimum 40 Innings)

Player	W	L	ERA	G	SV	IP	H	BB	SO
Lewis, Derrick, Fla. A&M	5	6	**3.42**	12	0	76	74	60	80
Rawls, Mike, Bethune-Cook.	5	9	3.95	15	0	101	95	63	**105**
Averette, Robert, Fla. A&M	**7**	4	4.01	15	0	94	93	30	85
Burkindine, Larry, Del. State	3	3	4.89	8	0	50	41	32	43
Circo, Mark, Delaware State	5	2	5.14	8	0	42	53	23	27
Benton, Jared, Florida A&M	2	6	5.31	13	0	59	68	31	46
Davis, Rodney, Beth.-Cook.	**7**	7	5.46	17	0	93	106	56	63
Joswick, Mark, Del. State	2	6	5.71	12	1	65	69	60	42
#Burns, Nick, Coppin State	3	2	7.44	21	**3**	62	75	51	58

MIDWESTERN COLL. CONF.

	Conf. W	Conf. L	Overall W	Overall L
Wright State	16	8	31	28
*Detroit	15	9	27	24
Wisconsin-Milwaukee	13	11	28	30
Northern Illinois	12	12	22	29
Cleveland State	12	12	22	28
Butler	8	16	18	32
Illinois-Chicago	8	16	15	26

ALL-CONFERENCE TEAM: C—Bernie Pedersoli, Sr., Illinois-Chicago. **1B**—Eric Welsh, Jr., Northern Illinois. **2B**—Matt Bruner, Fr., Wright State. **3B**—Ed Gundry, Sr., Detroit. **SS**—Jason Gombos, So., Detroit. **OF**—Elvis Hernandez, Fr., Illinois-Chicago; T.D. Hicks, Sr., Wright State; Michael Pesci, Sr., Detroit. **DH**—Chad Sadowski, Fr., Wisconsin-Milwaukee. **Util**—Russ Gladish, Jr., Cleveland State. **P**—Terry Hayden, Sr., Detroit; Jason Henry, Jr., Illinois-Chicago.

Player of the Year: Michael Pesci, Illinois-Chicago. **Pitcher of the Year:** Jason Henry, Illinois-Chicago. **Newcomer of the Year:** Elvis Hernandez, Illinois-Chicago. **Coach of the Year:** Jerry Augustine, Wisconsin-Milwaukee.

INDIVIDUAL BATTING LEADERS

(Minimum 100 At-Bats)

Player	AVG	AB	R	H	2B	3B	HR	RBI	SB
Hernandez, Elvis, Ill.-Chi.	**.445**	137	32	61	15	2	5	31	5
Pesci, Mike, Detroit	.409	176	53	72	14	1	16	46	1
Gombos, Jason, Detroit	.389	167	38	65	9	2	6	31	5
Beam, Dusty, Wright State	.388	214	46	**83**	17	4	3	35	3
Gundry, Ed, Detroit	.388	178	51	69	11	1	**18**	**50**	4
Rodriguez, Joe, No. Illinois	.379	161	30	61	9	3	2	24	9
Matko, Andy, Wright State	.376	218	49	82	18	0	4	**50**	2
Gautcher, Brett, No. Illinois	.361	144	36	52	7	3	3	20	16
Gorta, Chris, Cleve. State	.361	169	31	61	13	3	5	26	2
Pedersoli, Bernie, Ill.-Chi.	.360	139	27	50	12	2	9	32	3
Horba, Dale, Cleve. State	.351	185	43	65	13	0	7	36	2
Poniewaz, Ken, Wis.-Mil.	.351	168	34	59	15	**6**	6	33	3
Welsh, Eric, NE Illinois	.349	166	38	68	14	1	11	44	10
O'Neill, Mike, No. Illinois	.342	190	50	65	11	1	2	40	10
Laird, Chuck, No. Illinois	.338	130	31	44	10	0	0	19	4
Rickon, Jim, Cleve. State	.337	169	36	57	8	0	9	43	1
O'Donovan, Ryan, Butler	.335	161	32	54	15	4	1	25	8
Maslowski, Mike, Butler	.335	185	35	62	**19**	2	3	29	11
Aspeslet, Preston, Cleve. St.	.335	161	37	54	8	0	5	28	3
#Hicks, T.D., Wright State	.295	176	**68**	52	14	1	3	20	13
#Stosik, Bill, Wright State	.293	198	37	58	11	1	0	18	**25**

INDIVIDUAL PITCHING LEADERS

(Minimum 40 Innings)

Player	W	L	ERA	G	SV	IP	H	BB	SO
Henry, Jason, Illinois-Chicago	3	3	**2.39**	13	2	53	51	18	45
Squire, Mark, Wright State	4	4	2.56	29	**11**	60	65	16	33
Schultz, Eric, Illinois-Chicago	6	2	3.05	11	0	59	60	14	60
Mroz, Gary, Detroit	4	2	3.35	9	0	43	46	20	32
Becker, Rob, Wis.-Mil.	6	6	3.60	13	0	90	76	25	54
Casper, Michael, Wis.-Mil.	5	6	3.69	15	0	78	97	25	41
Guler, Jeremy, Butler	4	6	4.28	15	0	80	102	29	41
Aseltine, Ryan, Ill.-Chicago	2	4	4.54	10	0	42	44	19	25
Clark, Matt, Wright State	2	4	5.00	11	0	54	83	18	21
Hillebrand, Joel, Detroit	4	3	5.00	12	0	72	80	33	58
#Sanford, Casey, Wright State	**7**	4	5.31	15	0	76	94	24	57
#McAnich, Sam, Wright State	6	4	5.54	16	0	76	85	22	**77**

MISSOURI VALLEY CONFERENCE

	Conference W	Conference L	Overall W	Overall L
Wichita State	21	7	51	18
Northern Iowa	18	8	32	23
***Southwest Missouri State**	16	10	35	25
Illinois State	18	13	29	26
Southern Illinois	13	15	23	32
Evansville	13	19	29	30
Creighton	10	15	27	27
Bradley	10	18	26	28
Indiana State	9	23	24	30

ALL-CONFERENCE TEAM: C—Lance Burkhart, Sr., Southwest Missouri State. **1B**—Brian Jergenson, Sr., Northern Iowa. **2B**—Chris Curry, Jr., Southwest Missouri State. **3B**—Tyler Turnquist, Jr., Illinois State. **SS**—Zach Sorensen, So., Wichita State. **OF**—Brian McMillin, So., Evansville; Aaron Pembroke, Jr., Evansville; Chad Saalfrank, Sr., Bradley. **DH**—Brad Benson, Jr., Southern Illinois. **Util**—Kevin Frederick, Jr., Creighton. **SP**—Rob Garola, Sr., Southwest Missouri State; Jason Krafft, Jr., Wichita State; David Parra, Jr., Northern Iowa. **RP**—Marc Bluma, So., Wichita State; Scott Geitz, Jr., Southwest Missouri State.

Player of the Year: Brian Jergenson, Northern Iowa. **Pitcher of the Year:** Rob Garola, Southwest Missouri State. **Freshman of the Year:** Jim Pecoraro, Southern Illinois. **Newcomer of the Year:** Brad Benson, Southern Illinois.

INDIVIDUAL BATTING LEADERS

(Minimum 125 At-Bats)

Player	AVG	AB	R	H	2B	3B	HR	RBI	SB
Magness, Pat, Wichita St.	**.409**	137	31	56	9	0	7	37	1
Preston, Brian, Wichita St.	.393	140	36	55	11	0	10	43	2
Hairston, Jerry, So. Illinois	.380	216	56	82	17	2	11	51	5
Hart, Jason, SW Missouri	.379	240	58	**91**	17	0	**20**	60	0
Benson, Brad, So. Illinois	.378	180	41	68	21	0	13	52	1
Jergenson, Brian, No. Iowa	.374	195	45	73	12	1	14	66	9
Knox, Ryan, Illinois State	.369	195	54	72	15	3	8	39	9
Sorensen, Zach, Wichita St.	.367	177	59	65	14	1	8	51	18
Provines, Kip, Indiana St.	.365	203	59	74	17	2	11	44	5
Pembroke, Aaron, Evan.	.360	236	52	85	19	4	0	38	**32**
Fogarty, Ben, Wichita State	.357	154	45	55	7	3	6	37	3
Reese, Nathan, Wichita St.	.352	210	46	74	19	1	12	63	0
Curry, Chris, SW Missouri	.352	230	44	81	18	3	13	53	3
Hooper, Kevin, Wichita St.	.348	233	67	81	11	3	0	35	18
Frederick, Kevin, Creighton	.346	188	48	65	10	3	12	37	3
Ryan, Jeff, Wichita State	.340	265	**85**	90	**25**	3	13	**77**	12
Saalfrank, Chad, Bradley	.337	181	38	61	16	1	6	24	13
Connors, Ryan, Evansville	.337	193	39	65	9	2	3	31	12
Jackson, Brandon, SW Mo.	.337	205	40	69	12	2	3	28	6
Burkhart, Lance, SW Mo.	.335	218	61	73	12	0	17	57	4
Hodges, Bobby, Evansville	.333	174	36	58	11	0	6	43	7
Sands, Jason, Illinois State	.333	219	51	73	7	6	3	41	8
Patrick, Matt, Wichita St.	.332	238	59	79	15	1	13	64	1
Abram, Aaron, Wichita St.	.331	139	33	46	9	1	1	21	0
Jones, Aaron, So. Illinois	.330	203	59	67	13	1	13	49	3
Dunham, Josh, Nor. Iowa	.328	131	21	43	6	2	1	11	7
Von Behren, Seth, Ill. State	.327	208	44	68	14	1	6	46	7
Turnquist, Tyler, Ill. State	.325	197	49	64	16	2	7	47	3
Pyfer, Jim, Illinois State	.324	210	47	68	12	2	1	29	11
Brownlee, Ryan, Evansville	.323	232	49	75	9	6	3	39	31
Mitchell, Todd, Illinois St.	.323	198	38	64	11	3	4	44	3
Cepicky, Matt, SW Mo.	.323	189	30	61	14	1	5	33	10
#Schley, Joe, So. Illinois	.291	223	51	65	9	**9**	2	26	10

INDIVIDUAL PITCHING LEADERS

(Minimum 50 Innings)

Player	W	L	ERA	G	SV	IP	H	BB	SO
Robertson, Nate, Wichita St.	5	0	**2.78**	17	0	58	49	27	52
Geitz, Scott, SW Missouri	7	2	2.97	22	5	76	63	35	60
Forystek, Brian, Illinois State	4	3	3.26	15	0	58	58	32	57
Bernhardt, Mark, Indiana St.	5	4	3.36	14	0	83	90	26	70
Bryan, Erich, Wichita State	3	0	3.40	20	0	50	35	23	42
Krafft, Jason, Wichita State	**10**	3	3.55	13	0	76	70	22	68
Frasor, Jason, So. Illinois	7	2	3.59	21	1	88	93	35	82
#Bluma, Marc, Wichita St.	2	5	3.63	27	**12**	40	37	8	30
Brown, Jeremy, Evansville	8	4	3.67	21	0	110	109	20	94
Pecoraro, Jim, So. Illinois	2	5	3.69	32	4	68	65	11	57
Thomas, Ben, Wichita State	7	1	3.74	14	0	84	81	27	70
Chaney, Drew, Bradley	3	2	3.74	10	0	55	60	23	39
Finken, Brad, Indiana State	7	5	3.81	16	1	109	116	28	**115**
Delatori, Keola, Illinois State	7	4	3.84	12	0	68	61	48	70

	W	L	ERA	G	SV	IP	H	BB	SO
Foral, Steve, Wichita State	**10**	7	3.93	20	0	110	117	36	104
Bauer, Greg, Wichita State	4	1	4.13	23	3	57	58	26	56
Garola, Rob, SW Missouri	9	5	4.33	19	0	87	90	30	59

NORTHEAST CONFERENCE

	Conference		Overall	
	W	L	W	L
***Marist**	14	7	32	19
Fairleigh Dickinson	14	7	23	24
Wagner	12	9	17	29
Rider	12	9	20	29
Monmouth	11	10	23	25
Long Island	10	11	17	21
St. Francis (N.Y.)	6	15	15	24
Mount St. Mary's	5	16	10	23

ALL-CONFERENCE TEAM: C—Jason Irizarry, Sr., Fairleigh Dickinson. **1B**—Mark Barron, Sr., Marist. **2B**—Mike Nazzaretto, So., Fairleigh Dickinson. **3B**—Joe McCullough, Jr., Monmouth; Ryan Pandolfini, Jr., Rider. **SS**—Jay Cevallos, So., Mount St. Mary's. **OF**—Eric Bardeguez, Jr., Long Island; Jeff Karpell, So., Fairleigh Dickinson; Will Vanjonack, So., Mount St. Mary's. **DH**—Duane Eason, Sr., Fairleigh Dickinson. **P**—Mark Barron, Sr., Marist; Jim Gordon, Sr., Rider.

Player of the Year: Mark Barron, Marist. **Pitcher of the Year:** Mark Nugent, Wagner. **Newcomer of the Year:** Dan Severino, Wagner. **Coach of the Year:** John Szefc, Marist.

INDIVIDUAL BATTING LEADERS

(Minimum 100 At-Bats)

	AVG	AB	R	H	2B	3B	HR	RBI	SB
Bardeguez, Eric, LIU	**.425**	120	32	51	7	3	7	29	4
DiDonna, Chris, St. Francis	.374	139	31	52	15	0	4	27	5
Eason, Duane, FDU	.367	158	41	58	11	1	9	36	4
Cevallos, Jay, Mt. St. Mary's	.364	107	22	39	5	0	4	14	3
Barron, Mark, Marist	.361	180	36	**65**	**22**	0	3	40	4
Pandolfini, Ryan, Rider	.358	165	32	59	15	2	5	36	11
Nazzaretto, Mike, FDU	.354	161	32	57	14	1	2	28	6
Mazzola, Tommy, Wagner	.347	173	47	60	10	2	8	34	7
McGowan, Jim, Marist	.337	169	25	57	9	1	5	41	0
Karpell, Jeff, FDU	.337	178	33	60	11	4	0	41	3
Vanjonack, Will, MSM.	.336	119	24	40	10	0	9	32	9
Dansky, Mike, Long Island	.336	137	32	46	13	2	3	30	4
Speckhardt, Michael, Marist	.335	176	44	59	8	3	6	42	14
Irizarry, Jason, FDU	.331	166	37	55	14	1	9	**46**	5
#Cervini, Anthony, Marist	.310	187	**57**	58	6	2	3	23	14
#Wenner, Michael, Rider	.308	201	32	62	13	**7**	3	34	11
#Francisco, Joe, Wagner	.284	141	35	40	9	1	4	17	**33**
#Battista, Frank, St. Francis	.270	126	28	34	7	0	**11**	33	10

INDIVIDUAL PITCHING LEADERS

(Minimum 40 Innings)

	W	L	ERA	G	SV	IP	H	BB	SO
Krajewski, Charlie, Monmouth	3	4	**2.29**	13	2	59	61	14	26
Barron, Mark, Marist	**10**	3	2.32	16	1	105	86	36	**75**
Liello, Tim, St. Francis	1	7	3.27	10	0	52	53	25	48
Nugent, Mark, Wagner	6	4	3.34	16	1	70	71	27	56
Moyer, Brian, Monmouth	4	2	3.53	10	0	51	48	34	47
Severino, Dan, Monmouth	4	5	3.61	12	1	62	68	24	47
Olore, Kevin, Marist	5	3	3.63	15	0	74	63	48	53
Gordon, Jim, Rider	6	2	3.82	11	0	66	60	31	53
Aragona, Joe, Monmouth	4	4	3.83	9	0	54	44	34	54
Webb, Chris, Marist	8	2	3.84	18	0	73	70	26	59
#Dawson, Dave, Monmouth	0	2	14.63	11	**4**	8	15	3	5

OHIO VALLEY CONFERENCE

	Conference		Overall	
	W	L	W	L
Middle Tennessee State	17	7	31	24
***Tennessee Tech**	17	7	39	23
Austin Peay State	14	10	28	31
Eastern Illinois	13	11	25	28
Southeast Missouri State	11	13	24	33
Morehead State	10	14	25	30
Eastern Kentucky	10	14	20	36
Murray State	8	16	24	30
Tennessee-Martin	8	16	15	30

ALL-CONFERENCE TEAM: C—Andrew Thompson, Sr., Middle Tennessee. **1B**—Clint Benhoff, Jr., Eastern Illinois. **2B**—LaMonte Collier, Sr., Southeast Missouri. **3B**—Jeremy Bonczynski, Sr., Tennessee Tech. **SS**—Clay Snellgrove, Sr., Middle Tennessee. **OF**—Kent Brown, Sr., Austin Peay; Sean Lyons, So., Eastern Illinois; Jeremy Owens, So., Middle Tennessee. **DH**—Mark Maberry, Sr., Tennessee Tech. **Util**—Aaron Sledd, Jr., Austin Peay. **P**—Mark Maberry, Sr., Tennessee Tech; Mike Moore, Jr., Tennessee Tech.

Player of the Year: Mark Maberry, Tennessee Tech. **Pitcher of the Year:** Mark Maberry, Tennessee Tech. **Coach of the Year:** David Mays, Tennessee Tech.

INDIVIDUAL BATTING LEADERS

(Minimum 100 At-Bats)

	AVG	AB	R	H	2B	3B	HR	RBI	SB
Collier, LaMonte, SE Mo.	**.426**	202	44	86	20	2	8	43	24
Thompson, Andrew, MT	.409	176	38	72	9	0	13	42	0
Lofgren, Nolan, E. Illinois	.407	162	40	66	10	1	8	37	11
Lyons, Sean, East. Illinois	.396	182	58	72	14	0	9	33	14
Snellgrove, Clay, Mid. Tenn.	.393	224	41	**88**	**21**	0	8	56	3
Brown, Kent, Austin Peay	.370	230	52	85	15	1	3	32	**50**
Quire, Jeremy, Murray St.	.363	190	42	69	9	1	11	46	11
Malone, Chad, Tenn. Tech	.363	215	**77**	78	16	2	5	26	8
Miller, Mike, SE Missouri	.359	170	33	61	14	0	7	59	0
Stone, Justin, E. Illinois	.359	145	35	52	9	1	2	23	12
Bonczynski, Jeremy, TT	.357	235	60	84	13	2	**20**	64	10
Sledd, Aaron, Austin Peay	.356	163	40	58	10	0	5	24	12
Doyle, Eddie, Murray St.	.355	186	54	66	17	4	6	33	7
Kelley, Donny, Murray St.	.355	141	22	50	12	0	4	35	2
Chinapen, Wayne, MT	.352	108	17	38	5	0	3	18	0
Dillard, Ryan, Middle Tenn.	.347	193	42	67	20	4	4	38	9
Owens, Jeremy, MT	.346	211	53	73	11	**5**	5	25	20
Browning, Ryan, Tenn. Tech	.346	185	44	64	9	1	0	21	5
Cox, Josh, Morehead State	.344	186	28	64	9	1	6	40	3
Maberry, Mark, Tenn. Tech	.344	221	44	76	10	3	17	**74**	9
Zink, Josh, Eastern Illinois	.342	193	51	66	9	2	9	40	8
Benhoff, Clint, E. Illinois	.341	173	32	59	11	1	10	44	1
Troy, Greg, Austin Peay	.340	144	39	49	8	2	5	27	14

INDIVIDUAL PITCHING LEADERS

(Minimum 40 Innings)

	W	L	ERA	G	SV	IP	H	BB	SO
#Witten, Joe, East. Kentucky	1	3	2.32	25	**7**	31	31	9	18
Maberry, Mark, Tenn. Tech	**12**	2	**2.34**	16	1	104	81	35	**108**
Moore, Mike, Tennessee Tech	8	1	3.15	16	1	74	66	29	79
Freytag, Billy, Murray State	5	3	3.19	22	4	54	51	19	43
Umbarger, Kurt, Murray State	4	6	3.79	14	0	71	74	27	62
Howard, Brad, Middle Tenn.	7	2	3.80	15	0	73	74	27	43
Hill, Jamie, Middle Tennessee	5	1	3.99	17	0	79	78	51	46
Bedwell, Ken, Middle Tenn.	3	4	4.05	16	3	40	44	11	22
Brooker, Jason, Tenn. Tech	2	2	4.30	15	1	46	49	22	46
Meyer, Chris, Tenn.-Martin	3	4	4.40	12	0	61	64	31	46
Carlton, Patrick, Morehead St.	1	5	4.54	18	4	75	88	44	66
Michel, David, SE Missouri	6	7	4.80	23	1	81	100	21	57
Bess, Eric, Eastern Kentucky	3	5	4.86	16	0	50	62	18	31
Saylor, Ryan, East. Kentucky	3	6	4.87	19	1	68	71	25	98

PACIFIC-10 CONFERENCE

	Conference		Overall	
NORTH	W	L	W	L
***Washington**	20	4	46	20
Oregon State	18	6	38	12
Washington State	7	17	13	42
Portland State	3	21	10	43

ALL-CONFERENCE TEAM: C—Ben Bertrand, Jr., Oregon State. **1B**—Ryan Soules, Jr. Washington. **2B**—Ryan McDonald, Sr., Oregon State; Scott Randall, Jr., Washington State. **3B**—Ryan Lipe, Jr., Oregon State. **SS**—Kevin Miller, So., Washington. **OF**—Chris Magruder, So., Washington; Jaime Porter, So., Washington; Rick Southall, So., Portland State; Jason Stranberg, Jr., Oregon State. **DH**—Mike Leone, Sr., Oregon State. **Util**—Bryan Williamson, So., Washington. **P**—Mike Boire, So., Oregon State; Andrew Checketts, Jr., Oregon State; Jake Kringen, Jr., Washington; Mark Newell, So., Oregon State.

Player of the Year: Kevin Miller, Washington. **Co-Coaches of the Year:** Pat Casey, Oregon State; Ken Knutson, Washington.

INDIVIDUAL BATTING LEADERS

(Minimum 100 At-Bats)

	AVG	AB	R	H	2B	3B	HR	RBI	SB
Southall, Rick, Port. State	**.415**	183	39	76	18	3	**11**	47	4
Magruder, Chris, Wash.	.400	260	**90**	**104**	19	2	8	54	**43**

	AVG	AB	R	H	2B	3B	HR	RBI	SB
Stranberg, Jason, Ore. State	.397	174	67	69	6	3	3	41	16
Miller, Kevin, Washington	.384	250	77	96	17	5	**12**	**73**	4
Soules, Ryan, Washington	.383	235	63	90	23	2	**12**	67	3
Williamson, Bryan, Wash.	.381	197	41	75	14	1	4	58	6
Na, Jim, Washington	.365	115	27	42	12	4	4	30	2
Bertrand, Ben, Oregon State	.365	170	52	62	10	4	10	49	1
Leone, Mike, Oregon State	.361	166	44	60	11	0	9	45	1
Curran, Steve, Wash. State	.350	163	30	57	6	0	5	42	0
Keith, Rusty, Portland State	.348	201	42	70	11	1	3	21	4
Lipe, Ryan, Oregon State	.345	200	46	69	9	0	7	54	8
Stevenson, Shawn, WSU	.345	203	41	70	9	2	2	26	8
Hattenburg, Ray, Wash. St.	.339	171	39	58	9	2	0	17	6
Randall, Scott, Wash. State	.337	172	47	58	10	4	1	22	17
Kelley, Casey, Wash. State	.331	148	32	49	11	0	**12**	36	1
Lentz, Ryan, Washington	.327	251	58	82	**26**	2	9	69	3
McDonald, Ryan, Oregon St.	.323	155	41	50	6	0	6	44	5
Vazquez, Abino, Oregon St.	.321	137	43	44	11	**7**	3	41	4

INDIVIDUAL PITCHING LEADERS

(Minimum 40 Innings)

	W	L	ERA	G	SV	IP	H	BB	SO
#Boire, Mike, Oregon State	0	0	1.29	16	**8**	21	22	2	18
Newell, Mark, Oregon State	8	0	**2.12**	10	0	72	69	12	69
Williamson, Bryan, Wash.	4	2	2.89	22	6	44	34	24	49
Checketts, Andrew, Oregon St.	7	4	3.33	12	1	68	66	23	63
Bowman, James, Oregon State	4	1	3.95	10	0	41	34	29	29
Kringen, Jake, Washington	**11**	3	4.23	19	0	111	110	54	**110**
Hampton, Matt, Washington	7	1	4.40	17	0	76	91	31	52
Fowler, Blair, Washington	5	3	4.78	13	0	49	59	20	26
Darling, Jesse, Portland State	1	3	5.18	21	0	40	44	28	32
Cook, B.R., Oregon State	2	3	5.23	9	0	43	45	18	32
Lynch, Jeff, Washington	4	5	5.45	17	1	74	91	26	47

PACIFIC-10 CONFERENCE

	Conference		Overall	
SOUTH	**W**	**L**	**W**	**L**
Stanford	21	9	45	20
UCLA	19	11	45	21
Southern California	17	13	42	20
Arizona State	16	14	39	22
Arizona	13	17	32	26
California	4	26	21	38

ALL-CONFERENCE TEAM: C—Eric Munson, Fr., Southern California; Jon Schaeffer, Jr., Stanford. **2B**—Wes Rachels, Jr., Southern California. **3B**—Andrew Beinbrink, So., Arizona State. **SS**—Troy Glaus, Jr., UCLA; Marc Mirizzi, Sr., Southern California; Brian Oliver, So., California. **OF**—Eric Byrnes, Jr., UCLA; Jody Gerut, So., Stanford; Jon Heinrichs, Sr., UCLA; Dan McKinley, Jr., Arizona State; Edmund Muth, Fr., Stanford; Eric Valent, So., UCLA. **Util**—Pete Zamora, Jr., UCLA. **P**—Seth Etherton, Jr., Southern California; Tom Jacquez, So., UCLA; Jim Parque, Jr., UCLA; Kyle Peterson, Jr., Stanford.

Player of the Year: Troy Glaus, UCLA. **Pitcher of the Year:** Kyle Peterson, Stanford. **Coach of the Year:** Mark Marquess, Stanford.

INDIVIDUAL BATTING LEADERS

(Minimum 125 At-Bats)

	AVG	AB	R	H	2B	3B	HR	RBI	SB
McKinley, Dan, Arizona St.	**.423**	267	88	**113**	21	5	15	70	**32**
Glaus, Troy, UCLA	.409	264	**100**	108	15	1	**34**	**91**	10
Rico, Diego, Arizona	.390	223	51	87	6	**8**	2	39	23
Muth, Edmund, Stanford	.388	178	58	69	12	2	9	46	4
Beinbrink, Andrew, ASU	.380	242	60	92	23	4	9	72	5
Zamora, Pete, UCLA	.379	240	46	91	19	1	16	74	1
Gall, John, Stanford	.376	258	49	97	18	0	8	59	3
Brown, Jason, USC	.368	144	26	53	11	0	10	45	4
Theodorou, Nick, UCLA	.365	208	50	76	17	0	6	47	10
Hochgesang, Josh, Stanford	.365	263	59	96	22	2	17	77	9
Oliver, Brian, California	.364	242	42	88	15	3	4	36	24
Rachels, Wes, USC	.364	220	50	80	11	1	2	41	15
Kilburg, Joe, Stanford	.363	240	80	87	20	3	8	50	12
Heinrichs, Jon, UCLA	.358	299	92	107	**28**	2	28	79	16
Bloomquist, Willie, Ariz. St.	.356	132	33	47	10	5	1	31	7
Leon, Richy, Arizona State	.353	184	36	65	7	3	2	27	2
Schaeffer, Jon, Stanford	.349	232	65	81	13	2	20	76	1
Mattern, Erik, Arizona	.348	184	41	64	19	2	4	30	9
Gorr, Robb, USC	.347	251	64	87	16	1	6	52	6
Furstenthal, John, Cal	.341	208	38	71	5	0	2	23	10
Valent, Eric, UCLA	.339	274	74	93	16	3	27	**91**	3
Munson, Eric, USC	.336	232	57	78	11	0	13	50	8
Byrnes, Eric, UCLA	.332	277	95	92	24	1	17	60	19
Corley, Kenny, Arizona	.332	223	56	74	22	1	12	55	5
Schmidt, Jim, California	.331	166	24	55	11	0	0	23	13
Ticehurst, Brad, USC	.328	134	34	44	11	0	4	18	8
King, Tom, Arizona	.326	129	20	42	16	0	2	25	2
Mirizzi, Marc, USC	.325	277	53	90	21	0	5	37	6
Grijalva, Mike, Arizona St.	.321	131	20	42	10	1	4	25	3
Pecci, Jay, Stanford	.320	231	46	74	13	0	3	31	7
Quaccia, Luke, Stanford	.320	225	50	72	17	0	9	43	4
Thrower, Jake, Arizona	.319	229	51	73	13	3	5	51	14
Porter, Colin, Arizona	.318	195	47	62	11	3	6	37	29
Walbridge, Greg, USC	.315	248	50	78	24	1	4	46	9
Matoian, Chad, UCLA	.314	169	25	53	13	0	1	29	0
Moreno, Mikel, Arizona St.	.313	224	67	70	16	3	8	38	10

INDIVIDUAL PITCHING LEADERS

(Minimum 50 Innings)

	W	L	ERA	G	SV	IP	H	BB	SO
Mills, Ryan, Arizona State	6	3	**2.88**	15	0	97	82	50	103
Etherton, Seth, USC	10	2	2.96	16	0	109	104	33	106
Jacquez, Tom, UCLA	10	4	3.06	19	0	129	115	42	100
Parque, Jim, UCLA	**13**	2	3.08	19	0	120	117	63	119
#Krawczyk, Jack, USC	2	3	3.20	33	**11**	39	29	3	26
Cuccias, Jon, California	2	0	3.38	33	3	51	62	15	28
Cogan, Tony, Stanford	7	4	3.63	36	4	72	61	21	51
Shabansky, Rob, Arizona	8	6	3.86	18	0	89	90	27	59
Lowery, Phill, Arizona State	6	2	4.13	18	0	85	78	41	79
Austin, Jeff, Stanford	5	2	4.14	25	4	87	97	28	93
Peterson, Kyle, Stanford	11	3	4.19	20	0	144	134	38	**156**
Immel, Steve, USC	7	4	4.33	23	1	62	70	17	50
Flores, Randy, USC	9	5	4.46	17	0	113	128	34	93
Quick, David, Arizona	4	0	4.65	14	0	50	62	18	42
Moskau, Ryan, Arizona	4	4	4.84	27	6	61	67	21	42
Zamora, Pete, UCLA	6	2	5.06	17	2	100	121	33	73
Johnson, James, Arizona	4	6	5.18	16	0	89	82	44	74
Bradley, Ryan, Arizona State	7	7	5.40	35	7	60	65	25	76
Shirley, Jon, California	2	7	5.47	17	1	82	106	34	54
Cermak, Jeff, Arizona State	7	3	5.52	17	1	75	78	20	45

PATRIOT LEAGUE

	Conference		Overall	
	W	**L**	**W**	**L**
*Army	15	5	26	20
Navy	12	6	19	27
Bucknell	10	10	25	24
Lehigh	9	11	18	24
Lafayette	7	12	11	26
Holy Cross	5	14	11	25

ALL-CONFERENCE TEAM: C—Pete Cann, Sr., Bucknell. **1B**—Ben Talbott, Sr., Lehigh. **2B**—Dave Apollon, Jr., Bucknell. **3B**—Brian Abell, Jr., Army; Tyler Prout, Fr., Bucknell. **SS**—Mike Scioletti, Jr., Army. **OF**—Alex Inclan, Sr., Bucknell; Brian Issitt, So., Holy Cross; Keith Treonze, So., Lehigh. **P**—Kevin Carlson, Sr., Navy; Scott Weiss, Jr., Army. **RP**—Pat Saxman, Sr., Army.

Player of the Year: Mike Scioletti, Army. **Pitcher of the Year:** Kevin Carlson, Navy. **Coach of the Year:** Dan Roberts, Army.

INDIVIDUAL BATTING LEADERS

(Minimum 100 At-Bats)

	AVG	AB	R	H	2B	3B	HR	RBI	SB
Scioletti, Mike, Army	**.415**	130	47	54	15	4	**12**	**67**	5
Issitt, Brian, Holy Cross	.412	136	32	56	12	2	0	21	7
Stoudt, Tom, Lafayette	.402	132	36	53	8	2	8	33	2
Talbott, Ben, Lehigh	.394	127	38	50	10	1	5	43	3
Treonze, Keith, Lehigh	.383	154	31	59	12	2	7	33	4
McGann, Ron, Holy Cross	.382	102	19	39	8	0	1	15	3
Osipower, Robert, Lafayette	.377	138	23	52	15	0	3	28	0
Power, Ben, Holy Cross	.375	128	22	48	8	0	6	26	1
Price, Bryan, Army	.372	183	**65**	**68**	13	2	2	31	13
Colley, Pad, Lafayette	.369	130	31	48	11	3	2	28	8
Rutkowski, Steve, Buck.	.362	174	33	63	7	2	3	30	0
Kirk, Chris, Army	.359	103	21	37	12	0	7	34	0
Souza, Darin, Army	.352	159	34	56	7	1	0	33	0
Prout, Tyler, Bucknell	.352	162	34	57	6	**8**	6	39	5
Sawyer, Matt, Army	.347	147	37	51	5	0	2	26	0
Apollon, Dave, Bucknell	.346	185	58	64	**16**	5	9	38	**27**
Inclan, Alex, Bucknell	.345	168	45	58	12	1	7	45	11
Lake, Toph, Navy	.344	154	29	53	9	4	1	29	3
D'Orazio, Joe, Bucknell	.336	128	33	43	12	3	5	32	1
Cann, Peter, Bucknell	.333	174	43	58	13	1	10	43	5

INDIVIDUAL PITCHING LEADERS

(Minimum 40 Innings)

	W	L	ERA	G	SV	IP	H	BB	SO
Carlson, Kevin, Navy	**7**	5	**2.55**	13	0	92	83	29	**63**
Groover, Shane, Navy	3	3	3.43	12	0	42	38	30	31
Heffernan, Kevin, Army	4	4	3.72	20	3	68	71	13	42
Eschleman, Joe, Lehigh	6	2	4.46	11	0	69	97	24	31
Kozink, Scott, Navy	5	2	4.53	12	0	54	60	23	43
McLemore, Tom, Navy	2	10	5.28	14	0	77	92	20	56
Kusko, Chad, Lehigh	4	5	5.37	9	0	52	67	25	27
Anders, Mike, Bucknell	5	7	5.55	14	0	71	93	19	55
Weiss, Scott, Army	4	4	5.78	15	0	62	83	27	49
Hoffman, Doug, Bucknell	4	2	5.98	13	1	44	30	12	10
#Junge, Eric, Bucknell	2	2	6.31	15	**6**	26	20	19	21

SOUTHEASTERN CONFERENCE

EAST	Conference W	Conference L	Overall W	Overall L
Florida	17	13	40	24
Tennessee	17	13	42	19
Vanderbilt	14	16	31	24
South Carolina	13	17	33	24
Kentucky	10	20	20	34
Georgia	8	22	28	27
WEST	**W**	**L**	**W**	**L**
Louisiana State	22	7	57	13
***Alabama**	20	9	56	14
Mississippi State	19	11	47	21
Auburn	17	12	50	17
Arkansas	15	14	36	20
Mississippi	6	24	22	31

ALL-CONFERENCE: C—Casey Dunn, So., Auburn. **1B**—Brad Wilkerson, So., Florida. **2B**—Joe Caruso, Sr., Alabama. **3B**—Matt Erickson, Jr., Arkansas. **SS**—Brandon Larson, Jr., Louisiana State. **OF**—Tim Hudson, Sr., Auburn; Jeremy Jackson, Jr., Arkansas; Ryan Lundquist, So., Arkansas; Roberto Vaz, Jr., Alabama. **DH**—Ryan Bordenick, Jr., South Carolina. **P**—Patrick Coogan, Jr., Louisiana State; Scott Downs, Jr., Kentucky; Tim Hudson, Sr., Auburn; Brett Jodie, So., South Carolina.

Player of the Year: Tim Hudson, Auburn.

INDIVIDUAL BATTING LEADERS

(Minimum 125 At-Bats)

	AVG	AB	R	H	2B	3B	HR	RBI	SB
Jackson, Jeremy, Arkansas	**.425**	221	57	94	18	8	9	72	17
Bordenick, Ryan, So. Car.	.419	229	81	96	18	2	13	87	2
Henderson, Brad, Miss.	.402	229	60	92	15	4	13	49	8
Vaz, Roberto, Alabama	.400	255	**87**	102	17	**9**	22	73	14
Erickson, Matt, Arkansas	.398	236	86	94	**27**	3	4	50	17
Lundquist, Ryan, Arkansas	.397	232	83	92	22	2	24	78	5
Sullivan, Adam, Auburn	.396	260	81	103	16	2	5	44	16
Hudson, Tim, Auburn	.396	273	71	108	21	0	18	95	2
Bledsoe, Hunter, Vandy	.389	193	46	75	14	1	6	49	10
Anthony, Aaron, Georgia	.387	217	52	84	24	0	13	58	5
Wilkerson, Brad, Florida	.386	236	82	91	15	3	23	76	11
Larson, Brandon, LSU	.381	289	82	**110**	16	2	**40**	**118**	9
Caruso, Joe, Alabama	.378	259	64	98	21	3	15	76	12
Furniss, Eddy, LSU	.378	259	77	98	25	0	17	77	0
Urquhart, Derick, So. Car.	.378	233	81	88	21	2	9	56	5
Ross, Justin, Tennessee	.372	223	67	83	18	1	9	48	17
Keller, G.W., Alabama	.369	249	62	92	14	3	21	68	5
Macrory, Rob, Auburn	.368	269	77	99	24	5	1	42	26
Keene, Kurt, Tennessee	.368	223	57	82	23	3	13	58	4
Adeeb, Josh, Vanderbilt	.367	221	53	81	26	0	9	50	16
Phillips, Andy, Alabama	.366	279	68	102	25	3	15	65	5
Nicholson, Derek, Florida	.364	247	61	90	20	1	9	67	15
Lee, Richard, Miss. State	.362	276	71	100	14	3	19	90	2
Curry, Mike, South Carolina	.362	221	77	80	14	5	8	51	42
Dunn, Casey, Auburn	.362	235	54	85	19	1	5	56	0
Piatt, Adam, Miss. State	.361	244	71	88	17	2	17	69	7
McConnell, Jason, Ark.	.359	251	71	90	23	5	3	44	21
Haught, Brian, Florida	.357	182	34	65	8	5	9	44	15
Clabo, Jason, Tennessee	.357	157	29	56	13	3	4	26	8
Everett, Adam, So. Car.	.356	236	82	84	10	5	8	52	16
Johnston, Clint, Vanderbilt	.354	195	53	69	17	1	15	52	4
Hinske, Eric, Arkansas	.353	232	**87**	82	18	2	17	76	8
Barbier, Blair, LSU	.353	252	82	89	23	0	15	57	4
Smith, Casey, Florida	.353	204	42	72	10	2	7	60	6
Koerner, Mike, LSU	.352	273	74	96	18	2	22	69	17
Eskra, Scott, Mississippi	.348	207	50	72	13	3	9	42	2
Stanton, Eric, South Car.	.345	226	54	78	18	0	14	69	3
Bryan, Brooks, Miss. State	.345	255	81	88	14	1	6	57	11
Chapman, Travis, Miss. St.	.344	186	41	64	14	1	3	40	2
Shannon, Lance, Georgia	.344	157	30	54	10	0	5	16	2
Reif, Derek, Auburn	.343	213	51	73	20	2	4	48	6
Tidwell, David, Alabama	.342	295	86	101	18	4	10	65	35
Etheredge, Josh, Auburn	.342	234	79	80	16	2	20	82	6
Scioneaux, Damian, MS	.341	255	67	87	11	5	6	47	20
Eckstein, David, Florida	.341	276	85	94	18	3	8	34	35
McNally, Dustin, Georgia	.339	236	42	80	14	2	1	38	20
Caldwell, Brent, Arkansas	.339	186	42	63	13	2	9	66	4
Loggins, Josh, Kentucky	.338	195	47	66	17	3	11	37	10
Thoms, Rusty, Miss. State	.338	204	50	69	10	2	4	31	5
Patton, Barry, Miss. State	.338	231	45	78	14	0	7	57	0
Mohr, Dustan, Alabama	.337	249	68	84	19	0	25	79	1
McGlone, Aaron, Kentucky	.335	170	33	57	9	0	7	29	3
Pickler, Jeff, Tennessee	.332	220	50	73	14	5	7	44	8
Frick, Matt, Alabama	.331	242	59	80	11	2	16	55	3
Ellis, Mark, Florida	.326	267	67	87	16	3	11	45	9
Folkers, Ken, Tennessee	.324	238	53	77	16	1	9	49	13
Eylar, Sean, Mississippi	.323	167	41	54	11	0	10	44	3
Bunch, Justin, Kentucky	.322	174	23	56	6	1	9	35	7
Bernhardt, Tom, LSU	.322	202	43	65	7	0	17	49	6
Streicher, Rob, So. Carolina	.321	224	45	72	11	1	16	70	3
Huisman, Jason, Mississippi	.321	209	46	67	13	3	7	37	1
Hightower, Etienne, So. Car.	.320	178	49	57	7	1	3	32	20
Tedesco, Jay, Kentucky	.320	200	45	64	13	1	8	43	4
Davis, Glenn, Vanderbilt	.319	216	52	69	9	2	18	64	7
Crawford, Chris, Georgia	.319	229	57	73	14	3	13	54	9
Clark, Chris, Arkansas	.318	179	45	57	17	4	6	41	17
Wandall, Chad, Auburn	.318	233	51	74	11	1	10	55	4
Moore, Baker, Tennessee	.317	167	28	53	12	1	1	28	0
Copley, Travis, Tennessee	.316	215	46	68	19	2	9	53	1
Farese, Jason, Vanderbilt	.312	202	46	63	12	0	18	52	7
Szwejbka, Ryan, So. Car.	.311	177	41	55	7	0	3	32	6
Freeman, Brad, Miss. State	.311	235	58	73	12	0	8	49	9
Kata, Matt, Vanderbilt	.310	203	48	63	7	2	1	22	6
Tucker, Robbie, Alabama	.305	223	52	68	13	2	20	67	2
Figueroa, Eduardo, Tenn.	.304	125	27	38	7	1	3	22	2
Voltz, Jude, Mississippi	.304	135	22	41	12	1	2	30	2
Dill, Justin, Vanderbilt	.303	175	41	53	10	0	10	42	1
Cheatle, David, Kentucky	.302	205	48	62	7	3	6	29	11
Higgins, Danny, LSU	.302	202	60	61	12	2	11	41	7
Kersh, Jamie, Auburn	.301	266	58	80	14	3	13	72	1
Meadows, Tydus, Vandy	.295	129	27	38	8	0	4	20	2
Martin, Ty, Florida	.291	213	30	62	12	1	2	27	8
Greene, Clay, Tennessee	.290	259	59	75	11	4	4	37	**54**

JEFF GOLDEN

Slow start, big finish

Eric DuBose pitched Mississippi State to Omaha

INDIVIDUAL PITCHING LEADERS

(Minimum 50 Innings)

	W	L	ERA	G	SV	IP	H	BB	SO
Yee, Damon, Vanderbilt	4	2	**2.33**	22	1	66	56	22	69
Fogg, Josh, Florida	7	3	2.37	41	8	91	67	35	84
Thoms, Hank, Miss. State	5	0	2.81	23	1	51	53	14	55
Hudson, Tim, Auburn	**15**	2	2.97	22	0	118	87	50	**165**
Kingrey, Jarrod, Alabama	10	1	3.16	33	4	88	83	38	76
Folkers, Ken, Tennessee	7	3	3.34	21	2	92	92	25	84
Vaz, Roberto, Alabama	4	1	3.40	22	8	50	35	27	52
Demouy, Chris, LSU	6	1	3.63	36	5	62	59	24	70
Woodward, Finley, Auburn	3	4	3.78	26	8	50	42	27	62
Dunham, Patrick, Auburn	5	2	3.99	28	5	77	82	20	64
Knorst, Kevin, Auburn	5	2	4.10	20	3	68	73	25	59
Shipp, Kevin, LSU	4	1	4.10	11	0	53	56	10	56
Hudson, Luke, Tennessee	6	2	4.12	14	0	83	74	43	77
Gandy, Josh, Georgia	8	8	4.17	20	0	110	115	62	126
Johnson, Van, Miss. State	5	4	4.21	39	**13**	83	80	14	90
Brand, Cliff, Georgia	3	2	4.27	12	0	53	62	13	41
Frachiseur, Zach, Georgia	7	8	4.27	17	0	116	120	42	106
DuBose, Eric, Mississippi State	9	4	4.32	21	0	119	122	67	145
Hebson, Bryan, Auburn	11	4	4.43	19	0	112	103	38	121
Jodie, Brett, South Carolina	8	4	4.44	15	0	107	125	32	84
Coogan, Patrick, LSU	14	3	4.46	25	3	125	114	36	144
Franks, Lance, Arkansas	7	2	4.52	28	8	74	83	27	75
Painich, Joey, LSU	9	2	4.52	22	1	78	81	27	72
Fisher, Pete, Alabama	10	3	4.55	18	0	119	139	36	82
Wilkerson, Brad, Florida	11	4	4.56	26	4	79	73	34	89
Henderson, Heath, Alabama	13	2	4.63	22	1	124	139	37	104
Thompson, Doug, LSU	12	3	4.63	25	1	124	133	44	158
Hurst, Doug, Alabama	4	1	4.64	26	4	54	61	25	51
Rogers, Brian, Arkansas	3	1	4.69	22	0	56	66	18	43
Poston, Jamie, South Carolina	4	3	4.78	18	1	53	64	19	43
Reinike, Chris, Miss. State	3	3	4.91	21	2	66	75	38	69
Tolbert, Lance, Mississippi	5	4	4.99	21	1	61	73	20	44
Downs, Scott, Kentucky	7	8	5.11	17	0	106	114	45	99
Jackson, Jeremy, Miss. State	9	4	5.14	16	0	75	79	40	76
Cosgrove, Michael, Tenn.	10	6	5.25	19	0	105	131	34	83
Torres, Manny, Alabama	5	0	5.27	13	0	56	63	15	43
Knollin, Chris, Florida	5	0	5.37	27	2	65	71	21	58
Duff, Matthew, Mississippi	2	3	5.45	27	2	68	65	32	45
Schoening, Brent, Auburn	5	3	5.50	16	1	75	76	33	65

SOUTHERN CONFERENCE

	Conference W	Conference L	Overall W	Overall L
***Western Carolina**	18	6	42	20
Georgia Southern	18	6	34	26
The Citadel	16	7	37	21
Furman	13	11	29	23
East Tennessee State	11	11	21	24
Davidson	8	15	18	34
Appalachian State	8	16	16	32
Virginia Military	6	13	13	35
Marshall	4	17	7	39

ALL-CONFERENCE TEAM: C—Michael Holder, Jr., Georgia Southern. 1B—Alex Tolbert, Sr., Western Carolina. **2B**—Bo Betchman, Sr., The Citadel. **3B**—A.J. Polichnowski, Sr., East Tennessee State. **SS**—Terrance Smalls, Jr., The Citadel. **OF**—Martin Barrow, Jr., Western Carolina; Kenny Osborne, Sr., Appalachian State; Jerry Simmons, Jr., The Citadel. **DH**—Britt Phelps, Sr., East Tennessee State. **P**—Tod Lee, Jr., Georgia Southern; Brian Rogers, So., The Citadel.

Player of the Year: Alex Tolbert, Western Carolina. **Pitcher of the Year:** Tod Lee, Georgia Southern. **Freshman of the Year:** Rodney Hancock, The Citadel. **Coach of the Year:** Keith LeClair, Western Carolina.

INDIVIDUAL BATTING LEADERS

(Minimum 100 At-Bats)

	AVG	AB	R	H	2B	3B	HR	RBI	SB
Bruce, Jeremy, West. Car.	**.401**	247	**82**	**99**	16	0	14	56	15
Polichnowski, A.J., ETSU	.399	183	52	73	17	1	11	51	2
Morrill, Jim, Furman	.390	182	45	71	12	3	9	53	7
McKay, Dave, West. Car.	.384	112	24	43	9	1	4	29	12
Barrow, Martin, West. Car.	.383	256	71	98	13	6	7	37	18
Jenkins, Jody, ETSU	.383	149	31	57	18	1	4	34	0
Moore, Chris, West. Car.	.370	257	69	95	17	5	10	65	5
Wagner, Ryan, ETSU	.366	202	51	74	14	2	1	19	9
Byrd, Jason, ETSU	.366	153	33	56	17	0	9	41	0
Hancock, Rodney, Citadel	.365	230	59	84	21	2	6	49	8
Osborne, Kenny, App. St.	.360	189	53	68	16	4	15	44	3
Carter, Shannon, ETSU	.358	148	38	53	8	4	4	36	11
Benner, Shane, ETSU	.358	123	34	44	8	3	5	27	2
Simmons, Jerry, Citadel	.357	230	71	82	17	3	14	68	23
Smalls, Terrence, Citadel	.353	249	70	88	12	2	2	32	**33**
Bissinger, D.J., Furman	.352	162	41	57	9	0	6	27	5
Cameron, Cliff, App. St.	.352	176	42	62	13	1	6	38	0
Ward, Frankie, West. Car.	.348	187	41	65	19	2	11	42	1
Phelps, Britt, ETSU	.348	161	34	56	15	0	10	47	0
Stillwell, Matt, West. Car.	.346	185	46	64	11	3	14	37	14
Burwell, J.P., West. Car.	.345	220	42	76	12	0	14	69	1
Tolbert, Alex, West. Car.	.345	220	71	76	15	1	**19**	69	6
#Butler, Ryan, Citadel	.335	224	48	75	**22**	0	12	68	1
#Walson, Steve, Ga. South.	.331	239	64	79	13	1	17	**77**	1
#Goodwin, Luke, Davidson	.327	196	58	64	13	**7**	10	47	16

INDIVIDUAL PITCHING LEADERS

(Minimum 40 Innings)

	W	L	ERA	G	SV	IP	H	BB	SO
Martin, Tom, Citadel	3	3	**3.25**	35	**7**	64	73	12	48
Rogers, Brian, Citadel	8	2	3.27	16	0	85	94	28	92
Lee, Tod, Georgia Southern	6	2	3.92	42	**7**	64	59	23	99
Cummings, Ryan, Ga. Southern	8	7	4.05	17	0	113	118	43	**104**
Noyce, David, Furman	4	6	4.17	19	2	83	92	22	62
Skidmore, Chris, ETSU	1	0	4.24	24	1	40	45	34	28
Rhine, Seth, Furman	7	2	4.26	18	0	70	66	35	39
Sauls, Clint, Georgia Southern	9	4	4.46	20	0	115	136	43	85
DiFelice, Mark, West. Car.	**10**	3	4.48	17	0	98	100	34	87
Williams, Matt, ETSU	4	1	4.53	24	2	44	54	6	37
Maxwell, Clark, West. Car.	9	2	4.56	19	1	103	83	51	102
Rowland, William, Furman	3	1	4.57	17	0	43	48	14	24
Davis, Kelvin, Ga. Southern	4	2	4.79	15	0	68	86	42	60
Wiley, Brian, The Citadel	8	3	5.04	15	0	80	72	41	95
Slade, Brandon, Furman	3	5	5.11	22	2	49	59	23	27
Foote, Ryan, Furman	1	3	5.44	21	2	46	44	30	37
Parker, Aaron, Ga. Southern	3	2	5.63	20	0	54	73	24	52
John III, Tommy, Furman	6	2	5.65	15	1	64	89	13	42
Fisher, Stephen, App. St.	2	3	5.74	33	6	58	59	31	44

SOUTHLAND CONFERENCE

	Conference W	Conference L	Overall W	Overall L
LOUISIANA	**W**	**L**	**W**	**L**
Northwestern State	19	9	35	22
NE Louisiana	17	11	33	21
McNeese State	11	19	19	32
Nicholls State	9	19	18	35
TEXAS	**W**	**L**	**W**	**L**
***SW Texas State**	18	11	38	26
Sam Houston St.	17	11	26	27
Texas-Arlington	12	17	22	35
Texas-San Antonio	12	18	20	36

ALL-CONFERENCE TEAM: C—Chad Spear, Jr., Southwest Texas State. **1B**—Ron Thames, Sr., Sam Houston State. **2B**—Robert Hewes, Sr., Northwestern State. **SS**—Rey Arrendondo, Jr., Southwest Texas. **OF**—Tommy Lewis, Sr., Northeast Louisiana; Corey Taylor, Jr., Northeast Louisiana; Matt Schnabel, Sr., Southwest Texas State. **DH**—Scott Duplantis, So., Nicholls State. **P**—Corey Ehlers, Sr., Southwest Texas State; Greg Kubes, So., Sam Houston State; Brian Lawrence, Jr., Northwestern State.

Players of the Year: Tommy Lewis, Northeast Lousiana; Chad Spear, Southwest Texas State. **Pitcher of the Year:** Greg Kubes, Sam Houston State. **Newcomer of the Year:** Josh Hoffpauir, Northwestern State. **Coach of the Year:** Dave Van Horn, Northwestern State.

INDIVIDUAL BATTING LEADERS

(Minimum 100 At-Bats)

	AVG	AB	R	H	2B	3B	HR	RBI	SB
Perret, Kevin, Nicholls St.	**.395**	205	50	**81**	15	4	8	40	4
Lewis, Tommy, NE La.	.393	163	62	64	9	2	4	37	**42**
Hewes, Robert, NW St.	.355	220	53	78	8	3	7	41	16
Ackel, David, NE Louisiana	.346	159	32	55	8	0	8	28	4
Taylor, Corey, NE Louisiana	.343	178	**64**	61	14	6	**12**	50	29
Schnabel, Matt, SW Texas	.340	235	61	80	14	2	9	50	7
Cotten, Nathan, Nicholls St.	.330	194	40	64	14	2	11	43	4
Zander, Bryan, NE La.	.325	157	31	51	5	3	4	37	8
Schmitz, Chris, McNeese	.321	168	31	54	8	**8**	6	38	9

Kopecky, Michael, UT-Arl.	.320	206	35	66	**20**	2	5	36	6
Hoffpauir, Josh, NW State	.318	214	43	68	11	6	2	29	7
Fikac, Jeremy, SW Texas	.316	193	49	61	6	2	9	42	15
Spear, Chad, SW Texas St.	.313	233	45	73	15	3	11	**52**	7
Wickersham, Jack, SWT	.310	216	43	67	12	3	0	23	14
Trahan, Mike, McNeese St.	.310	187	37	58	15	2	8	28	7
Nunn, Derek, NW State	.310	197	39	61	12	0	8	46	3
Arredondo, Ray, SW Texas	.308	221	31	68	15	1	1	35	8
Sims, Dan, Texas-Arlington	.306	147	18	45	6	1	1	22	7
Duplantis, Scott, Nicholls St.	.305	190	25	58	14	0	8	50	2

INDIVIDUAL PITCHING LEADERS

(Minimum 40 Innings)

	W	L	ERA	G	SV	IP	H	BB	SO
Harrald, Jonathan, Sam Hous.	4	4	**2.57**	24	4	42	37	13	34
Mondello, Peter, Nicholls State	3	2	2.70	23	2	43	38	16	34
Lawrence, Brian, NW State	8	5	3.02	17	0	102	99	24	75
Loland, D.J., NE Louisiana	**11**	2	3.14	17	0	86	87	38	94
Vistor, Dustin, Nicholls State	2	7	3.24	14	0	78	74	21	44
Ehlers, Corey, SW Texas	8	2	3.31	18	0	111	97	39	58
Arcement, Cody, Nicholls State	7	6	3.36	13	0	80	78	26	72
Fikac, Jeremy, SW Texas	4	1	3.38	8	1	45	40	17	38
Hermes, Kevin, Sam Houston	2	4	3.38	14	0	53	54	13	20
Kubes, Greg, Sam Houston	9	3	3.44	16	0	99	72	32	78
Brown, Chris, Northwestern St.	7	6	3.63	15	0	99	95	38	**110**
Balcer, David, Northwestern St.	8	3	3.67	23	1	76	78	18	45
McLendon, Pat, McNeese State	3	3	3.67	16	1	42	47	11	31
Lancaster, Roger, UT-Arl.	7	7	3.75	16	0	101	96	33	92
Davis, Allen, Northwestern St.	5	3	3.78	22	1	76	79	16	40
#Guidry, Quinn, Nicholls State	1	4	4.81	16	**6**	33	32	13	26

SWAC

	Conference		Overall	
EAST	**W**	**L**	**W**	**L**
Alcorn State	16	6	28	17
Jackson State	13	5	18	17
Alabama State	12	9	17	24
Mississippi Valley State.	1	22	4	30
WEST	**W**	**L**	**W**	**L**
*Southern	21	3	32	17
Grambling State	15	9	25	13
Texas Southern	9	13	16	21
Prairie View A&M	1	21	3	34

ALL-CONFERENCE TEAM: C—Alva Thompson, So., Southern. **1B**—Lincoln Williams, Jr., Southern. **2B**—Rickie Miller, Jr., Grambling State. **3B**—Tim Stephney, Sr., Alcorn State. **SS**—Schuyler Doakes, Jr., Jackson State. **OF**—Chris Chapman, Sr., Jackson State; Doug Smith, Sr., Southern; Gus Spencer, Sr., Alcorn State. **DH**—Chris Gatson, Sr., Grambling State. **P**—Sonny Garcia, Jr., Texas Southern; Rashaan Smith, So., Alabama State; Tyson Taplin, Sr., Alcorn State; Adam Toussaint, So., Southern.

Player of the Year: Schuyler Doakes, Jackson State. **Pitcher of the Year:** Adam Toussaint, Southern. **Freshman of the Year:** Dario Rosa, Alcorn State. **Newcomer of the Year:** Auntwan Riggins, Texas Southern. **Coach of the Year:** Roger Cador, Southern.

INDIVIDUAL BATTING LEADERS

(Minimum 100 At-Bats)

	AVG	AB	R	H	2B	3B	HR	RBI	SB
Mack, Torey, Alabama St.	**.429**	119	29	51	7	0	4	24	4
Stephney, Tim, Alcorn State	.400	150	42	**60**	**15**	3	6	**49**	15
Miller, Rickie, Grambling	.382	110	36	42	8	**6**	1	25	6
Banks, Antonio, Miss. Vall.	.375	120	19	45	14	2	0	24	1
Williams, Marcus, Ala. St.	.373	107	38	40	4	1	3	20	14
Kelley, Quirjara, Ala. St.	.368	106	40	39	8	0	3	24	10
Robinson, Robert, Tex. So.	.364	107	24	39	5	2	5	33	3
Bradberry, Herbert, Ala. St.	.348	109	20	38	5	0	6	33	4
Doakes, Schuyler, Jack. St.	.345	119	33	41	6	**6**	1	18	**30**
Riggins, Auntwan, Tex. So.	.341	129	40	44	8	**6**	5	24	21
Williams, Lincoln, Southern	.333	171	**45**	57	12	0	**8**	46	7
Rosa, Dario, Alcorn State	.331	160	39	53	8	5	2	39	20
Crossley, Brett, Alabama St.	.330	121	38	40	4	1	0	14	22
Credit, Andre, Alcorn State	.316	136	29	43	9	4	3	32	13
Witherspoon, Javier, South.	.313	150	36	47	13	3	2	29	9
Lacy, Ronnie, Alcorn State	.309	139	35	43	11	0	2	35	13
August, Marlon, Southern	.302	106	26	32	6	2	3	21	7
Kingdom, Eric, Alcorn State	.301	143	30	43	6	2	0	33	15

INDIVIDUAL PITCHING LEADERS

(Minimum 40 Innings)

	W	L	ERA	G	SV	IP	H	BB	SO
Garcia, Sonny, Texas Southern	5	3	**1.77**	14	1	66	46	10	**63**
Taplin, Tyson, Alcorn State	**8**	2	2.01	12	0	72	56	15	53
Charles, Donnie, Jackson State	3	2	2.85	11	1	41	33	21	31
Riley, Randall, Grambling	4	3	3.04	9	0	47	32	33	54
Washington, David, Grambling	5	2	3.59	10	0	58	53	26	32
Toussaint, Adam, Southern	6	0	3.89	10	0	42	42	14	34
Simons, Wendell, Southern	3	0	4.10	20	1	42	30	16	49
Smith, Rashaan, Alabama St.	7	1	4.67	12	0	62	57	27	53
Smith, Don, Jackson State	4	1	4.70	9	1	44	35	34	40
Hill, Terrence, Southern	6	5	4.79	13	0	62	59	35	44
Gauff, Lowell, Grambling State	5	3	4.85	10	0	46	35	24	36
Robinson, Marcus, Southern	5	2	4.94	12	0	51	55	11	47
#Lewis, Rickey, Miss. Valley	3	6	9.11	10	0	55	67	38	**63**

SUN BELT CONFERENCE

	Conf.		Overall	
	W	**L**	**W**	**L**
Southwestern Louisiana	22	5	43	18
***South Alabama**	15	10	43	19
Arkansas State	14	11	35	18
Louisiana Tech	15	12	26	30
Lamar	13	11	32	19
Texas-Pan American	14	12	30	22
Jacksonville	13	14	32	22
New Orleans	11	15	31	25
Western Kentucky	10	17	24	29
Arkansas-Little Rock	2	22	6	43

ALL-CONFERENCE TEAM: C—Erick Rosa, Sr., Western Kentucky. **1B**—Talmadge Nunnari, Sr., Jacksonville. **2B**—T.J. Soto, Fr., Louisiana Tech. **3B**—Josh Patton, Sr., Western Kentucky. **SS**—Matt Bryant, Sr., Arkansas State. **OF**—Kevin Cantrelle, Jr., Southwestern Louisiana; Brey Curtis, Sr., South Alabama; Bryan Droptini, Jr., Lamar. **DH**—Justin Hemme, Jr., Southwestern Louisiana. **SP**—Trey Poland, Sr., Southwestern Louisiana; Cody Robbins, Sr., Southwestern Louisiana. **RP**—Eric Cammack, Jr., Lamar.

Player of the Year: Talmadge Nunnari, Jacksonville. **Freshman of the Year:** T.J. Soto, Louisiana Tech. **Newcomer of the Year:** Trey Poland, Southwestern Louisiana. **Coach of the Year:** Tony Robichaux, Southwestern Louisiana.

INDIVIDUAL BATTING LEADERS

(Minimum 125 At-Bats)

	AVG	AB	R	H	2B	3B	HR	RBI	SB
Nunnari, Talmadge, Jack.	**.450**	200	**68**	**90**	**23**	4	10	61	22
Patton, Josh, West. Ky.	.419	191	42	80	22	3	6	46	4
Hecard, Lloyd, New Orleans	.380	192	56	73	13	4	7	37	4
Dean, Aaron, Lamar	.368	193	47	71	19	0	13	56	4
Bryant, Matt, Arkansas St.	.366	205	46	75	18	1	8	40	4
McIlwain, Mitch, La. Tech	.364	162	31	59	15	0	6	44	8
Avans, Chris, New Orleans	.363	204	51	74	18	1	10	52	4
New, Aaron, Arkansas St.	.358	176	37	63	17	2	10	43	2
Wilker, Buddy, New Orleans	.358	137	32	49	7	0	12	47	2
Curtis, Brey, So. Alabama	.357	199	52	71	9	2	3	35	23
Diggs, Ryan, Jacksonville	.357	199	49	71	17	1	5	39	4
Droptini, Bryan, Lamar	.357	185	58	66	17	1	9	35	17
Aguirre, Oswaldo, SW La.	.356	219	47	78	15	1	7	57	2
DellaCrosse, Ryan, Jax.	.353	167	30	59	8	2	1	30	6
Rosa, Erick, West. Kentucky	.353	184	30	65	16	1	8	57	0
Choron, Joey, So. Alabama	.348	253	58	88	17	2	**21**	**73**	4
Cabeceiras, Joey, UNO	.348	210	38	73	13	0	9	51	3
Cantrelle, Kevin, SW La.	.346	191	42	66	15	2	8	54	7
Stacy, I.B., South Alabama	.341	226	59	77	19	1	15	62	7
Ferguson, Lorenzo, WK	.339	186	58	63	14	**5**	8	35	14
Grice, Dan, West. Kentucky	.336	152	34	51	10	0	5	35	2
Bowman, Lloyd, Ark. St.	.333	195	42	65	16	2	6	30	3
Fowler, Justin, Arkansas St.	.333	180	34	60	16	2	9	34	1
Hemme, Justin, SW La.	.332	187	35	62	16	2	12	49	1
Layton, Blane, Jacksonville	.328	198	56	65	12	0	10	41	12
Rhoades, Todd, Ark. St.	.328	183	37	60	17	0	5	32	1
Torre, Frank, New Orleans	.325	169	28	55	14	1	10	42	3
Soto, T.J., Louisiana Tech	.325	203	44	66	19	0	13	45	8
#Miller, Matt, La. Tech	.253	170	42	43	6	1	0	14	**28**

INDIVIDUAL PITCHING LEADERS

(Minimum 50 Innings)

	W	L	ERA	G	SV	IP	H	BB	SO
Akin, Jay, Arkansas State	8	5	**1.96**	18	2	110	87	28	77
Cammack, Eric, Lamar	5	5	2.15	26	8	63	41	20	89
Key, Calvin, Arkansas State	6	4	2.80	14	0	80	74	26	64
Poland, Trey, SW La.	**12**	5	3.28	22	3	137	115	58	**140**
Trevino, Kiki, Texas-Pan Am	8	5	3.38	15	0	109	102	38	76
Kelley, Brent, Arkansas State	5	3	3.49	19	2	70	53	29	66
Faust, Jason, New Orleans	7	1	3.71	16	0	87	78	30	65

White, Wade, Lamar	5	5	3.72	22	1	77	69	26	88
Robbins, Cody, SW La.	**12**	1	3.73	15	0	101	112	24	73
Sparks, Stephen, So. Alabama	11	1	3.73	19	0	101	104	46	84
Stemle, Stephen, West. Ky.	7	4	3.89	16	0	88	87	35	89
Bailey, Chad, SW La.	6	4	3.93	11	0	73	72	32	59
Fischer, Mike, South Alabama	5	3	3.96	29	**9**	64	60	17	68
Benson, Jason, Arkansas State	7	4	3.98	15	0	72	78	15	56
Padilla, Juan, Jacksonville	7	2	4.07	13	1	60	60	16	53
Rayborn, Kenny, So. Alabama	2	1	4.26	15	1	51	56	23	44
Norton, Jason, South Alabama	9	6	4.29	24	0	143	138	48	132
Taylor, Wade, Jacksonville	3	2	4.63	18	1	68	89	23	52
Devey, Philip, SW Louisiana	3	2	4.72	18	2	53	58	19	44
Wilkins, Jason, La. Tech	8	8	4.81	21	0	103	123	19	85
Byrd, John, Jacksonville	5	3	4.88	14	0	76	69	36	57
Nakamura, Mike, So. Alabama	11	2	4.98	24	2	72	74	26	83

TRANSAMERICA CONFERENCE

	Conference		Overall	
EAST	**W**	**L**	**W**	**L**
Mercer	12	6	35	23
Georgia State	10	8	23	30
Campbell	7	11	17	40
Charleston	7	11	25	29
SOUTH	**W**	**L**	**W**	**L**
#Stetson	10	8	37	26
#Florida International	10	8	42	21
Florida Atlantic	8	9	32	24
***Central Florida**	7	10	40	24
WEST	**W**	**L**	**W**	**L**
Jacksonville State	14	4	39	13
Southeastern Louisiana	11	7	34	24
Samford	8	10	31	29
Centenary	3	15	11	39

ALL-CONFERENCE TEAM: C—Jim Morgan, Sr., Samford. **1B**—Mike Garner, Sr., Jacksonville State. **2B**—Roby Brooks, Sr., Jacksonville State. **3B**—Brian Batson, Sr., Charleston. **SS**—Kevin Nicholson, Jr., Stetson. **OF**—Jeremy Avery, Jr., Mercer; Ned French, So., Stetson; Ed Nodhturft, Sr., Southeastern Louisiana. **DH**—Brennan Hervey, Sr., Florida Atlantic. **SP**—J.R. Allen, Jr., Jacksonville State; Raul Garcia, So., Florida International. **RP**—Ray Cavanagh, Jr., Florida International.

Player of the Year: Kevin Nicholson, Stetson. **Coach of the Year:** Rudy Abbott, Jacksonville State.

INDIVIDUAL BATTING LEADERS
(Minimum 125 At-Bats)

	AVG	AB	R	H	2B	3B	HR	RBI	SB
Nicholson, Kevin, Stetson	**.415**	229	**76**	95	23	4	17	71	24
Brooks, Roby, Jack. St.	.401	187	62	75	**26**	4	9	59	12
Garner, Mike, Jack. St.	.396	212	56	84	23	3	19	**82**	1
Williamson, Pat, Cent. Fla.	.393	178	36	70	3	0	1	31	5
Kramer, Joe, Fla. Int.	.386	184	32	71	12	3	4	31	12
Avery, Jeremy, Mercer	.379	203	56	77	16	1	**22**	76	0
Berberich, Emmett, Stetson	.376	186	37	70	6	1	1	35	10
Nodhturft, Ed, SE Louisiana	.376	202	50	76	18	0	18	67	9
Lee, Monte, Charleston	.373	201	50	75	15	2	6	35	16
Ozarowski, Rich, Fla. Atl.	.373	185	46	69	20	0	11	46	3
Rogers, Ken, SE Louisiana	.369	217	48	80	16	3	6	44	3
Mortimer, Mark, Ga. State	.367	188	36	69	23	1	5	49	5
Souders, Brooks, Samford	.366	224	53	82	14	1	14	55	3
French, Ned, Stetson	.365	263	67	96	21	4	4	44	**40**
Diaz, Tony, Fla. Int.	.364	151	42	55	8	2	3	32	18
Florio, Jason, Mercer	.362	210	60	76	16	0	10	55	2
Riggs, Eric, Central Florida	.361	266	63	**96**	16	2	9	43	5
Corbitt, Mike, Campbell	.360	214	35	77	14	1	8	51	2
Connacher, Kevin, Fla. Atl.	.356	219	68	78	16	2	6	43	25
Higgins, Bert, Jack. St.	.356	191	48	68	14	2	0	33	4
Rodriguez, Jeff, Fla. Int.	.356	208	36	74	14	0	10	48	2
Johnson, Erik, Central Fla.	.348	221	43	77	17	4	6	42	5
Howell, Travis, Charleston	.348	187	48	65	10	1	9	35	10
Hervey, Brennan, Fla. Atl.	.346	179	45	62	11	0	16	61	3
Messner, Mike, Fla. Atl.	.345	177	31	61	14	0	1	32	0
Chrysler, Clint, Stetson	.344	180	31	62	13	2	1	32	3
Wease, Scott, Charleston	.343	178	43	61	21	0	8	47	0
Celli, Mick, Fla. Atlantic	.342	199	40	68	8	3	9	52	0
Vetter, Jason, Fla. Int.	.337	166	39	56	6	0	4	42	7
Serrano, Sammy, Stetson	.335	239	37	80	11	3	5	53	7
Buckley, Sean, Mercer	.333	189	41	63	9	0	3	17	5
#Marcano, Robert, Campbell	.278	180	39	50	13	**5**	4	24	7

INDIVIDUAL PITCHING LEADERS
(Minimum 50 innings)

	W	L	ERA	G	SV	IP	H	BB	SO
Barendregt, Jacob, Fla. Int.	4	2	**2.03**	10	0	53	37	17	50
Cavanagh, Ray, Fla. Int.	9	2	2.49	25	4	80	67	30	82
Allen, J.R., Jacksonville State	8	1	3.17	16	2	97	82	43	77
House, Jeff, Stetson	10	4	3.20	27	3	113	134	40	72
Garcia, Raul, Fla. Int.	**11**	2	3.34	19	0	116	105	41	108
Knott, Eric, Stetson	8	7	3.42	23	0	137	156	35	**123**
Collins, Ricky, Jacksonville St.	**11**	1	3.55	16	0	79	87	36	62
Held, Travis, Central Florida	6	2	3.72	18	0	102	102	39	110
Chrysler, Clint, Stetson	7	3	3.92	20	0	85	91	28	62
Greene, Ray, Campbell	4	3	3.93	23	0	50	46	28	34
Duke, Jason, SE Louisiana	6	3	4.02	15	0	69	67	44	58
Bellhorn, Todd, Central Florida	4	4	4.15	16	1	80	74	52	84
#Shives, Keith, Fla. Int.	0	1	4.15	18	**9**	17	18	6	13
Nebel, Jeff, Mercer	10	6	4.37	20	0	115	125	41	87
Dickinson, Rodney, Georgia St.	7	5	4.48	16	0	80	85	33	99
Lubozynski, Matt, Cent. Fla.	8	3	4.60	18	1	90	112	17	74
Parker, Matt, Mercer	4	2	4.60	25	5	59	60	34	58
D'Amico, David, Mercer	**11**	3	4.64	21	0	120	125	49	117
Maroth, Mike, Central Florida	4	4	4.73	24	3	72	77	33	65
Hinkson, Lee, Jack. State	10	2	4.90	17	0	83	87	37	62
Schmidt, George, Central Fla.	8	3	4.90	24	1	90	103	39	95
Williamson, Bryan, Jack. State	4	4	4.91	18	3	66	75	33	87
Duhon, Travis, SE Louisiana	7	4	4.99	17	0	83	82	33	40

WEST COAST CONFERENCE

	Conference		Overall	
	W	**L**	**W**	**L**
***Santa Clara**	23	5	41	20
Pepperdine	20	8	34	25
San Francisco	17	11	29	27
San Diego	13	15	25	27
Saint Mary's	12	16	21	34
Loyola Marymount	11	17	21	39
Portland	9	19	20	33
Gonzaga	7	21	19	33

ALL-CONFERENCE TEAM: C—Paul Chiaffredo, So., Santa Clara. **1B**—Tyler Ferrer, Jr., Pepperdine. **2B**—Jermaine Clark, Jr., San Francisco. **3B**—Mark Veronda, Sr., Loyola Marymount. **SS**—David Matranga, So., Pepperdine. **OF**—Mark Lopez, Jr., Pepperdine; Bill Mott, Jr., Santa Clara; Matt Riordan, Fr., Loyola Marymount. **DH**—Joe Sulentor, So., Loyola Marymount. **Util**—Mike Frank, Sr., Santa Clara. **P**—Tobin Lanzetta, Sr., Santa Clara; Bart Miadich, Jr., San Diego; Jeff Perry, Sr., Santa Clara; Randy Wolf, Jr., Pepperdine.

Player of the Year: Mike Frank, Santa Clara. **Pitcher of the Year:** Randy Wolf, Pepperdine. **Co-Freshmen of the Year:** Matt Riordan, Loyola Marymount; Steve Schenewerk, Pepperdine. **Coach of the Year:** John Oldham, Santa Clara.

INDIVIDUAL BATTING LEADERS
(Minimum 125 At-Bats)

	AVG	AB	R	H	2B	3B	HR	RBI	SB
Frank, Mike, Santa Clara	**.405**	242	**64**	**98**	**25**	5	12	**80**	19
Clark, Jermaine, San Fran.	.372	215	58	80	12	4	6	48	18
Sulentor, Joe, LMU	.369	157	21	58	10	1	3	28	4
Chiaffredo, Paul, Santa Clara	.352	236	49	83	23	1	16	65	3
Dougherty, Jeb, San Diego	.351	191	40	67	4	1	2	26	**21**
Riordan, Matt, LMU	.348	244	55	85	14	1	4	30	13
Lopez, Mark, Pepperdine	.340	215	36	73	18	2	7	45	10
Oder, Josh, Pepperdine	.338	216	47	73	19	1	1	41	1
Mazone, Brian, San Diego	.338	154	21	52	10	1	4	34	1
Hughes, Todd, Santa Clara	.337	202	61	68	8	**7**	1	32	18
Walsh, Pat, San Francisco	.336	131	30	44	7	0	1	19	8
Okimoto, Kevin, Santa Clara	.333	177	35	59	10	0	6	52	2
Hare, Brendan, Gonzaga	.330	200	48	66	10	0	4	31	3
Mott, Bill, Santa Clara	.325	243	**64**	79	12	1	7	50	14
Hurtado, Tony, USF	.321	196	47	63	13	2	4	28	8
Ferrer, Tyler, Pepperdine	.320	203	37	65	15	1	5	45	3
Veronda, Mark, LMU	.319	204	37	65	10	0	2	29	17
Reid, Rob, Pepperdine	.318	242	63	77	16	2	3	22	14
Marshall, Brad, USF	.318	217	48	69	11	2	10	38	15
Craig, Benny, LMU	.318	236	47	75	17	0	**17**	61	8
Murrell, Donnie, Gonzaga	.315	197	36	62	11	0	9	39	4
Nakamura, Troy, USF	.312	173	41	54	8	2	1	28	5
#Cosbey, Chris, Pepperdine	.279	215	46	60	7	**7**	3	29	12

INDIVIDUAL PITCHING LEADERS
(Minimum 50 Innings)

	W	L	ERA	G	SV	IP	H	BB	SO
Wolf, Randy, Pepperdine	9	4	**1.79**	17	1	121	100	25	**128**
Frank, Mike, Santa Clara	**11**	0	2.70	15	0	73	59	23	73
Workman, John, Pepperdine	4	5	2.84	22	3	51	46	13	32
Vallecorsa, Mark, San Diego	3	4	2.86	14	0	63	65	16	32
Miadich, Bart, San Diego	8	4	2.92	14	0	99	88	29	80
Lanzetta, Tobin, Santa Clara	8	3	3.03	19	0	116	104	30	106
Hazlett, Andy, Portland	2	4	3.05	13	2	80	59	17	69
Mazone, Brian, San Diego	7	6	3.25	15	0	97	94	36	65
Boyanich, Vince, Santa Clara	5	4	3.36	14	0	59	47	27	52
Hartman, Darren, Portland	7	5	3.52	14	0	79	73	35	57
Porter, Aaron, St. Mary's	3	6	3.89	17	0	88	88	32	66
Perry, Jeff, Santa Clara	9	3	4.01	19	0	108	120	23	83
Shibilo, Andy, Pepperdine	6	4	4.03	15	0	89	99	40	90
#McDonald, Mike, Santa Clara	2	2	5.40	38	**10**	42	44	22	41

WESTERN ATHLETIC CONFERENCE

	Conf.		Overall	
NORTH	**W**	**L**	**W**	**L**
Utah	22	8	36	21
Brigham Young	21	9	37	18
Air Force	6	24	13	37
Grand Canyon	5	25	13	43
SOUTH	**W**	**L**	**W**	**L**
***Rice**	20	9	47	16
Texas Christian	15	15	26	27
Nevada-Las Vegas	10	19	24	31
New Mexico	10	20	25	32
WEST	**W**	**L**	**W**	**L**
San Jose State	20	10	38	21
Fresno State	19	11	40	28
San Diego State	17	13	41	22
Hawaii	14	16	22	34

ALL-CONFERENCE TEAM: C—Giuseppe Chiaramonte, Jr., Fresno State. **1B**—Lance Berkman, Jr., Rice. **2B**—Travis Young, Sr., New Mexico. **3B**—Ryan Hankins, Jr., Nevada-Las Vegas. **SS**—Scott Pratt, So., Utah. **OF**—Casey Child, Jr., Utah; Chris Connally, Jr., Texas Christian; Bubba Crosby, So., Rice. **DH**—Justin Collins, Sr., Air Force. **SP**—Jeff Weaver, So., Fresno State. **RP**—Matt Anderson, Jr., Rice.

Player of the Year: Lance Berkman, Rice. **Freshman of the Year:** Jeff Stone, Brigham Young. **Coach of the Year:** Sam Piraro, San Jose State.

INDIVIDUAL BATTING LEADERS
(Minimum 125 At-Bats)

	AVG	AB	R	H	2B	3B	HR	RBI	SB
Berkman, Lance, Rice	**.431**	255	**109**	**110**	22	4	**41**	**134**	8
Gonzalez, Robert, NM	.421	252	68	106	**33**	3	7	66	20
Decker, David, BYU	.420	169	63	71	14	0	5	48	6
Collins, Justin, Air Force	.417	127	37	53	14	1	11	44	3
Connally, Chris, TCU	.414	198	71	82	16	2	23	72	12
Nelson, D.G., BYU	.411	197	65	81	14	1	22	81	5
Child, Casey, Utah	.408	255	86	104	24	3	31	97	27
Farnsworth, Troy, BYU	.405	148	53	60	12	0	6	34	3
Heidemann, Mike, Utah	.405	195	59	79	20	2	11	47	2
Oborn, Spencer, BYU	.403	186	60	75	16	3	15	75	21
Berns, Robert, San Jose St.	.399	233	72	93	29	5	14	81	4
Medeiros, Robert, Hawaii	.398	196	50	78	15	3	9	55	17
Hankins, Ryan, UNLV	.390	195	67	76	13	6	8	47	7
Huffman, Royce, TCU	.387	194	50	75	10	2	8	46	9
Berg, Justin, Rice	.386	215	40	83	10	3	13	59	6
Comeaux, Tavares, SDS	.375	152	32	57	10	2	3	33	10
Lopez, Oscar, San Diego St.	.374	155	37	58	10	3	2	28	7
Winget, Brad, BYU	.374	182	49	68	9	0	10	47	3
Spencer, Glen, BYU	.373	166	47	62	13	1	2	27	15
Pratt, Scott, Utah	.373	255	88	95	21	5	19	65	27
Alevras, Chad, New Mexico	.370	216	51	80	19	2	13	69	4
Young, Travis, New Mexico	.368	253	72	93	18	6	3	43	**35**
Pelaez, Alex, San Diego St.	.365	189	42	69	14	1	5	41	4
Atkinson, Dusty, Utah	.364	220	51	80	14	3	7	53	12
Forbush, Nate, Utah	.363	204	56	74	14	1	16	66	3
Baker, Jacob, Rice	.362	232	52	84	9	3	12	51	5
Koning, Bill, Grand Canyon	.360	175	36	63	18	0	9	42	4
Phillips, Jason, SDS	.360	200	38	72	19	3	4	43	8
Dowdell, Tyson, BYU	.358	179	58	64	10	1	14	61	1
Wood, Darren, TCU	.355	166	38	59	12	0	6	28	4
Lewis, Scott, San Jose State	.355	217	51	77	9	1	0	27	12
Ludwick, Ryan, UNLV	.354	229	50	81	14	5	16	68	4
Hammons, Ryan, SDS	.353	150	24	53	5	0	4	43	2
Bevins, Andy, San Diego St.	.352	227	57	80	18	3	10	53	6
Flint, Travis, Utah	.352	199	52	70	13	1	9	54	3
Stringham, Matt, BYU	.351	185	48	65	16	0	9	58	9
Williams, Dan, GC	.350	206	55	72	18	0	9	42	5
Crosby, Bubba, Rice	.349	258	72	0	14	**11**	22	88	11
James, Tony, San Jose St.	.348	210	48	73	15	1	5	48	6
Feramisco, Derek, FS	.344	259	67	89	28	3	14	62	7
Moulton, Thomas, NM	.344	154	28	53	8	2	8	34	0
Menke, Ben, Grand Canyon	.344	221	48	76	15	4	8	54	7
Cathey, Joseph, Rice	.343	268	81	92	12	0	2	39	9
Beggs, Ryan, New Mexico	.342	146	30	50	10	2	0	33	2
Dunn, Ryan, Texas Christian	.342	190	50	65	11	2	19	62	2
Hannah, Josh, Fresno State	.342	222	40	76	11	4	7	38	3
Chiaramonte, Giuseppe, FS	.341	267	72	91	16	5	26	72	6
Ashley, Steve, San Jose St.	.341	214	39	73	9	3	7	53	2

INDIVIDUAL PITCHING LEADERS
(Minimum 50 Innings)

	W	L	ERA	G	SV	IP	H	BB	SO
Anderson, Matt, Rice	10	2	**2.05**	30	9	79	48	29	105
McDermott, Ryan, San Jose St.	8	3	2.95	29	5	55	53	15	46
Wanders, Chad, San Diego St.	9	3	3.09	20	3	102	96	24	92
Baker, Jeff, San Jose State	4	2	3.20	26	2	51	47	12	52
Pamus, Javier, San Jose State	6	4	3.28	19	1	115	110	36	85
Nichols, Jeff, Rice	10	2	3.42	21	1	108	104	31	71
Rowe, Casey, Fresno State	8	1	3.57	26	2	76	81	24	62
Pettyjohn, Adam, Fresno State	7	8	3.61	21	0	122	122	32	139
Weaver, Jeff, Fresno State	**11**	5	3.63	21	0	141	130	25	**181**
Scott, Brian, San Diego State	8	4	3.77	17	0	93	93	33	98
Griffin, Kirk, Fresno State	6	3	3.91	20	1	97	102	17	66
Brunette, Justin, San Diego St.	6	4	3.92	18	0	78	93	19	85
Jimenez, Jason, SJS	6	4	4.05	16	0	96	96	33	90
Dufek, Jeff, San Diego State	2	1	4.26	34	**9**	51	51	24	65
Tucker, Brad, Fresno State	3	3	4.42	16	0	57	70	37	39
Meyer, David, Texas Christian	8	2	4.45	17	0	91	94	27	77
Carrieri, Steve, San Jose St.	4	3	4.55	19	0	65	83	19	57
#Stone, Jeff, Brigham Young	**11**	1	6.94	14	0	84	92	56	70

INDEPENDENTS

	Overall	
TEAM	**W**	**L**
Miami	51	18
Cal State Northridge	42	20
Oral Roberts	26	30
Hawaii-Hilo	17	30
Wofford	13	33
Southern Utah	8	37

INDIVIDUAL BATTING LEADERS
(Minimum 100 At-Bats)

	AVG	AB	R	H	2B	3B	HR	RBI	SB
Kennedy, Adam, CS North.	.482	278	96	134	32	5	26	99	22
Michaels, Jason, Miami	.411	258	71	106	32	3	15	89	14
Burrell, Pat, Miami	.409	215	79	88	19	2	21	76	12
Miranda, Jose, CS North.	.407	247	80	98	16	2	25	90	14
Sledge, Terrmel, CS North.	.392	232	84	91	16	5	8	53	6
Huff, Aubrey, Miami	.385	182	50	70	15	2	10	52	4
Jacomino, Mandy, Miami	.379	190	50	72	21	2	9	49	2
Pittman, Blue, Wofford	.357	140	20	50	11	0	3	16	5
Dinsmore, Brian, ORU	.356	202	44	72	11	0	8	36	10
Martinez, Cesar, CS North.	.350	234	55	82	18	2	5	48	4
Mattson, Keiki, Hawaii-Hilo	.349	166	43	58	16	2	6	28	11
Garrett, Justin, So. Utah	.344	160	36	55	5	1	3	30	8
Wilson, Andy, CS North.	.340	191	62	65	7	2	6	41	14
Newman, Chad, So. Utah	.338	142	24	48	5	0	8	38	3
Casper, Brett, Oral Roberts	.329	152	31	50	15	1	3	23	12

INDIVIDUAL PITCHING LEADERS
(Minimum 40 Innings)

	W	L	ERA	G	SV	IP	H	BB	SO
Morrison, Robbie, Miami	4	2	1.49	37	8	54	38	28	82
Reyes, Eddie, Miami	8	2	2.04	43	2	71	53	26	79
Ford, Thomas, Hawaii-Hilo	2	5	2.39	12	1	67	59	44	58
Flores, Benito, CS Northridge	11	3	3.09	22	2	116	120	36	105
Arteaga, J.D., Miami	11	4	3.27	22	0	135	141	31	100
Klomparens, Robbie, Wofford	4	7	3.77	15	1	88	96	36	76
Rice, Nathan, CS Northridge	5	5	3.98	17	0	72	67	28	65
Santos, Alex, Miami	9	3	4.17	21	0	91	76	34	100
Cole, Jason, CS Northridge	5	4	4.25	23	2	83	95	12	52
Yates, Tyler, Hawaii-Hilo	1	3	4.49	12	0	44	53	25	28

SMALL COLLEGES

Chico State, Southern Maine capture NCAA titles

DIVISION II

California's Chico State benefited from a pair of two-out, ninth-inning errors by Central Oklahoma to score the winning runs in a 13-12 victory to win the 1997 Division II World Series.

It was the first Division II title for Chico State (52-11). The Wildcats went undefeated in the tournament and rallied from a 5-0 deficit in the title game.

FINAL POLL

NCAA Division II	
1. Chico State, Calif.	52-11
2. Central Oklahoma	42-21
3. Tampa	46-16
4. Kennesaw State, Ga.	48-14
5. Florida Southern	44-12
6. Central Missouri State	39-13
7. Georgia Coll.	41-24
8. Mt. Olive, N.C.	38-10
9. So. Illinois-Edwardsville	37-19
10. Fort Hays State, Kan.	48-15

"To lose the national championship that way when you're so close is a bigger disappointment than I can describe," Central Oklahoma coach Wendell Simmons said.

Tampa catcher Angel Diaz was selected the tournament MVP although Tampa lost to Central Oklahoma in the semifinals. Diaz went 11-for-16 overall with five home runs and 17 RBIs in five games.

Chico State first baseman Steve Gotowala was named the Division II player of the year. Gotowala hit .418 with 20 homers and 97 RBIs. Lefthander Donnie Thomas, a ninth-round draft pick from defending champion Kennesaw State (Ga.), was the pitcher of the year. Thomas went 11-2 with a 1.83 ERA.

The most noteworthy individual performance belonged to Quinnipiac (Conn.) outfielder Tim Belcher. He set a Division II record with five grand slams while hitting .471 with 18 homers and 76 RBIs. He struck out just four times.

DIVISION III

Lefthander Jason Jensen, an 18th-round draft pick of the Arizona Diamondbacks, earned MVP honors as Southern Maine won its second Division III World Series title.

The Huskies (39-9), who previously won in 1991, bashed 20 hits in the championship game to beat top-seeded College of Wooster (Ohio), 15-1.

FINAL POLL

NCAA Division III	
1. Southern Maine	39-9
2. Wooster, Ohio	46-8
3. SUNY-Cortland	31-10
4. Carthage, Wis.	40-10
5. North Carolina Wesleyan	40-7
6. Wisconsin-Stevens Point	31-13
7. Bridgewater State, Mass.	29-11
8. Chapman, Calif.	31-16
9. William Paterson, N.J.	33-9
10. Allegheny, Pa.	40-8

Jensen took advantage of the offensive support to notch his fifth straight complete-game victory, including two in the tournament.

"I think the most satisfying thing will be seeing our team picture on the wall here, knowing we accomplished this together," Jensen said.

The championship came one year after a gambling scandal rocked the school, resulting in the suspensions of 11 players.

First baseman-lefthander Joe Thomas of Marietta (Ohio) was named player of the year for the second consecutive season. In 1996, Thomas starred at the plate, hitting .418 with 13 homers and 67 RBIs while going 4-3, 3.11 as a pitcher.

NAIA

Brewton-Parker (Ga.) College won its last 31 games, including five straight at the NAIA World Series, to capture its first national championship.

The top-seeded Barons (64-7), making their first trip to the World Series, beat 1995 champion Bellevue (Neb.) 8-4 in the deciding game.

"I guess everybody was right, we are the No. 1 team in the nation," coach Mike Robins said of his team, which finished the regular season ranked No. 1 in the NAIA. "We felt we were the best team here and wanted to prove it."

Third baseman Andy Kalcounos was the hitting star of the tournament, going 9-for-18 with three doubles, two home runs and 10 RBIs. His three-run, eighth-inning homer propelled the Barons to a 3-2 win over Cumberland (Tenn.) in a second-round game.

JUNIOR COLLEGE

On his way to becoming the first junior-college player picked in the first round of the draft since 1992, righthander Aaron Akin helped pitch Cowley County (Kan.) Community College to the National Junior College World Series title.

Cowley County got a three-run homer from tournament MVP Travis Hafner to stake it to a 4-2 win against heavily favored Seminole (Okla.), which had entered the 10-team double-elimination tournament with a 55-3 record. Akin pitched middle relief in the title game on one day of rest after beating Scottsdale (Ariz.) in the fifth round.

The Florida Marlins took Akin with the 12th overall selection in the draft. The last junior college player drafted in the first round was first baseman Eddie Pearson, the 24th overall pick of the Chicago White Sox in 1992.

It was a big draft year for junior college talent in 1997. The White Sox picked two JUCO players as supplemental first rounders. Righthander Kyle Kane of Saddleback (Calif.) went 33rd overall, while righthander Aaron Myette of Central Arizona went 43rd.

State co-player of the year Craig Kuzmic drove in three runs with a double and a home run to lead Cypress to a 7-4 win over Sacramento City College in the championship game of the California junior college tournament.

It was the third state title in the 1990s for Cypress, which was runner-up to Rancho Santiago in 1996.

SMALL COLLEGES

NCAA DIVISION II

WORLD SERIES

Site: Montgomery, Ala.

Participants: Adelphi, N.Y. (30-14); Central Missouri State (38-11); Central Oklahoma (39-19); Chico State, Calif. (48-11); Kennesaw, Ga, State (46-12); Slippery Rock, Pa. (30-19); Southern Illinois-Edwardsville (36-17); Tampa (42-14).

Champion: Chico State (4-0).

Runner-Up: Central Oklahoma (3-2).

Outstanding Player: Angel Diaz, c, Tampa.

ALL-AMERICA TEAM

Pos.	Player, School	Yr.	AVG	HR	RBI
C	Jerry Valdez, Fort Hays State (Kan.)	Sr.	.397	20	96
1B	Steve Gotowala, Chico State (Calif.)	Sr.	.418	20	97
2B	Ronnie Haring, Abilene Christian (Texas)	So.	.428	6	60
3B	Larry Satkowski, St. Joseph's (Ind.)	Sr.	.440	15	49
SS	Pat Cutshall, Mercyhurst (Pa.)	Sr.	.400	16	72
OF	Tim Belcher, Quinnipiac (Conn.)	Sr.	.471	18	76
OF	Jason Clark, UC Riverside	Sr.	.401	16	72
OF	Rich Gregory, Chico State (Calif.)	Jr.	.396	16	87
OF	Jay Nunley, North Florida	Sr.	.383	16	72
DH	Chris McClure, Mesa State (Colo.)	Sr.	.442	25	74
UT	Dan Esposito, Pittsburg State (Kan.)	Sr.	.460	13	71
		Yr.	**W**	**L**	**ERA**
SP	Greg Denly, Valdosta State (Ga.)	Sr.	8	0	2.04
SP	Josh Osborn, Chico State (Calif.)	Jr.	13	1	3.42
SP	Donnie Thomas, Kennesaw St. (Ga.)	Jr.	11	2	1.83
SP	Mike Valdes, Tampa	So.	13	1	3.76
RP	Pat McDonald, Indianapolis	Sr.	7	2	1.56

Player of the Year—Steve Gotowala, 1b, Chico State.

Pitcher of the Year—Donnie Thomas, lhp, Kennesaw State.

NATIONAL LEADERS

BATTING AVERAGE

(Minimum 125 At-Bats)

	AB	H	AVG
Tim Dubrule, West Texas A&M	207	101	.488
Chris Madsen, Assumption (Mass.)	125	60	.480
Jerod Hyde, Abilene Christian (Texas)	178	84	.472
Tim Belcher, Quinnipiac (Conn.)	140	66	.471
Dan Esposito, Pittsburg State (Kan.)	200	92	.460
Marco Randazzo, Lock Haven (Pa.)	153	70	.458
Tom Horny, Indianapolis	186	85	.457
Mike Moeller, Concordia (N.Y.)	163	74	.454
Rusty Clear, New Mexico Highlands	145	65	.448
Pat Koerner, Central Oklahoma	227	101	.445
Desmond Ray, Alabama A&M	151	67	.444
Angel Tejeda, Norfolk State (Va.)	140	62	.443

Department Leaders: Batting

Dept.	Player, School	G	Total
R	David Mallas, Chico State (Calif.)	59	94
H	Steve Gotowala, Chico State (Calif.)	59	108
TB	Steve Gotowala, Chico State (Calif.)	59	202
2B	Duke Baxter, North Florida	55	31
3B	Jon Visser, Grand Valley St. (Mich.)	48	11
	Jeff Stephens, SIU-Edwardsville	55	11
HR	Chris McClure, Mesa State (Colo.)	58	25
RBI	Jarred McAlvain, Cent. Oklahoma	63	104
SB	Paul Oelrich, St. Andrews (N.C.)	52	43

EARNED RUN AVERAGE

(Minimum 60 Innings)

	IP	ER	ERA
Mark Perec, New Hampshire Coll.	66	9	1.23
Ryan Kearney, Massachusetts-Lowell	78	14	1.62
Rich Drennen, Wingate (N.C.)	75	14	1.67
Donnie Thomas, Kennesaw St. (Ga.)	98	20	1.83
Greg Denly, Valdosta State (Ga.)	84	19	2.04
Shawn Austin, Florida Southern	100	23	2.06
Ryan Jackson, Florida Tech	96	22	2.07
Eric Hott, West Virginia Wesleyan	74	17	2.08

Department Leaders: Pitching

Dept.	Player, School	G	Total
W	Mike Valdes, Tampa	17	13
	Josh Osborn, Chico State (Calif.)	21	13
	John Hernandez, Chico State (Calif.)	24	13
	Jeremy Halpin, Francis Marion (S.C.)	16	13
	Donnie Bivins, Lynn (Fla.)	22	13
SV	Pat McDonald, Indianapolis	35	16
SO	Danny Lampley, Wingate (N.C.)	15	130

NCAA DIVISION III

WORLD SERIES

Site: Salem, Va.

Participants: Bridgewater, Mass., State (29-9); Carthage, Wis. (38-8); Chapman, Calif. (31-14); State U. of New York-Cortland (28-8); North Carolina Wesleyan (39-5); Southern Maine (35-8); Wisconsin-Stevens Point (29-8); Wooster, Ohio (42-6).

Champion: Southern Maine (4-1).

Runner-Up: Wooster (4-2).

Outstanding Player: Jason Jensen, lhp, Southern Maine.

ALL-AMERICA TEAM

Pos.	Player, School	Yr.	AVG	HR	RBI
C	Matt Jackson, Wooster (Ohio)	Sr.	.405	21	75
1B	Ryan Roder, St. John's (Minn.)	Sr.	.540	8	52
2B	Jason Henley, Southwestern (Texas)	Sr.	.389	6	39
3B	Mike Kowalewski, Illinois Benedictine	Sr.	.468	13	71
3B	Tony Miner, Southern Maine	Sr.	.397	14	64
SS	Cory Breyne, Aurora (Ill.)	Jr.	.486	13	68
OF	Tyler Laughery, Clare.-Mudd (Calif.)	Sr.	.388	13	60
OF	Joe Musgrove, Allegheny (Pa.)	Sr.	.444	16	72
OF	Jammes Rinne, Illinois Wesleyan	So.	.463	17	57
DH	Scott Baron, Aurora (Ill.)	Jr.	.447	16	61
UT	Joe Thomas, Marietta (Ohio)	Sr.	.415	3	36
		Yr.	**W**	**L**	**ERA**
P	Mike Abbruzzese, N.C. Wesleyan	So.	11	1	1.04
P	Jeff Hootselle, Mary Washington (Va.)	Sr.	11	1	1.18
P	Andy Kimball, Wisconsin-Oshkosh	Jr.	7	1	2.34
P	Bill Snyder, Rensselear (N.Y.)	Sr.	9	3	1.67
UT	Joe Thomas, Marietta (Ohio)	Sr.	11	1	2.14

Player of the Year—Joe Thomas, 1b-lhp, Marietta (Ohio).

NATIONAL LEADERS

BATTING AVERAGE

(Minimum 100 At-Bats)

	AB	H	AVG
Ryan Roder, St. John's (Minn.)	124	67	.540
Scott Feskanich, Case Reserve (Ohio)	108	56	.519
Landon Rathmann, Gust. Adolphus (Minn.)	105	53	.505
Frank Beckhorn, Kean (N.J.)	142	71	.500
Mark Mosier, Chicago	105	52	.495
Chris Batcheller, Washington & Lee (Va.)	104	51	.490
Cory Breyne, Aurora (Ill.)	175	85	.486
Colin Lydon, Framingham State (Mass.)	140	68	.486
Jason Zaremski, Emory (Ga.)	128	62	.484
Jon Cignetti, Babson (Mass.)	112	54	.482

Department Leaders: Batting

Dept.	Player, School	G	Total
R	Trevor Urban, Wooster (Ohio)	55	79
H	Travis Snyder, Wooster (Ohio)	55	94
TB	Travis Snyder, Wooster (Ohio)	55	168
2B	Scott Forbes, N.C. Wesleyan	47	27
3B	Four tied at		9
HR	Matt Jackson, Wooster (Ohio)	55	21
RBI	Matt Jackson, Wooster (Ohio)	55	75
SB	Kyle Schmidt, John Jay (N.Y.)	31	46

EARNED RUN AVERAGE

(Minimum 50 Innings)

	IP	ER	ERA
Mark Slavin, Moravian (Pa.)	54	3	0.50
Mike Abbruzzese, N.C. Wesleyan	104	12	1.04
Jeff Hootselle, Mary Washington (Va.)	106	14	1.18
Jeff Taglienti, Tufts (Mass.)	76	12	1.41
Ben Donay, Savannah (Ga.) Art & Design	48	8	1.49
Joe Ohm, Wis.-LaCrosse	57	10	1.57

Department Leaders: Pitching

Dept.	Player, School	G	Total
W	Bob Davies, Marietta (Ohio)	14	12
	Matt Rodgers, Wooster (Ohio)	20	12
SV	Chris Okolski, Old Westbury	19	12
SO	Jeff Hootselle, Mary Washington (Va.)	15	142

SMALL COLLEGES

NAIA

WORLD SERIES

Site: Sioux City, Iowa.

Participants: No. 1 Brewton-Parker, Ga. (59-7); No. 2 Southeastern Oklahoma (54-7); No. 3 Dallas Baptist (54-13); No. 4 Cumberland, Tenn. (48-11); No. 5 Mount Vernon Nazarene, Ohio (46-6); No. 6 California Baptist (36-13); No. 7 Bellevue, Neb. (40-14); No. 8 Dominican, N.Y. (38-11).

Champion: Brewton-Parker (5-0).

Runner-Up: Bellevue (3-2).

Outstanding Player: Andy Kalcounas, 3b, Brewton-Parker.

ALL-AMERICA TEAM

Pos.	Player, School	Yr.	AVG	HR	RBI
C	Marc Suarez, Cumberland (Tenn.)	Jr.	.381	27	79
C	Calvin Tanton, Briar Cliff (Iowa)	Jr.	.406	16	69
1B	Jason Kinchen, Brewton-Parker (Ga.)	Sr.	.476	30	125
2B	Travis Gray, Mt. Vernon Naz. (Ohio)	Sr.	.426	18	86
3B	Steve Green, Cumberland (Tenn.)	Sr.	.451	22	89
SS	Billy Romans, Birm.-Southern (Ala.)	Sr.	.381	14	78
OF	Tim Currens, Lindsey Wilson (Ky.)	Jr.	.395	19	84
OF	Steve Esquibol, Azusa Pacific	Sr.	.386	22	68
OF	Bucky Jacobsen, L-C State (Idaho)	Sr.	.354	22	73
OF	Jose Rijo-Berger, L-C State (Idaho)	Sr.	.392	13	67
DH	Raul Pujol, St. Thomas (Fla.)	Fr.	.400	8	61
UT	Nate Barnett, George Fox (Ore.)	So.	.459	11	69

Pos.	Player, School	Yr.	W	L	ERA
P	Carey Ammons, SE Oklahoma St.	So.	16	1	2.71
P	Mike Dutton, Cumberland (Tenn.)	Jr.	13	2	3.06
P	Levi Lacey, Albertson (Idaho)	Jr.	11	1	2.58
P	Hank Woodman, Brewton-Parker (Ga.)	Jr.	12	1	2.07

NATIONAL LEADERS

BATTING AVERAGE
(Minimum 100 At-Bats)

Player, School	AB	H	AVG
Eric Martin, Dominican (N.Y.)	170	86	.506
Pat Williams, Sterling (Kan.)	117	59	.504
Jamie Cancade, Minot State (N.D.)	101	50	.495
Joaquin Martinez, Lubbock Christian	186	89	.478
Clint Vaughn, Oklahoma Christian	172	82	.477
Jason Kinchen, Brewton-Parker (Ga.)	227	108	.476
Jason Knox, Kansas Newman	207	96	.464
Nate Barnett, George Fox (Ore.)	157	72	.459
Pat O'Sullivan, Freed-Hardeman (Tenn.)	171	78	.456
Brian Shipley, Urbana (Ohio)	147	67	.456

Department Leaders: Batting

Dept.	Player, School	G	Total
R	Adam Wein, Dominican (N.Y.)	52	87
H	Jason Kinchen, Brewton-Parker (Ga.)	71	108
TB	Jason Kinchen, Brewton-Parker (Ga.)	71	228
2B	Travis Flowers, Oklahoma City	64	31
3B	Jeremy Jones, MidAmer. Nazarene (Kan.)	44	13
	Chris Lothian, Dominican (N.Y.)	51	13
HR	Jason Kinchen, Brewton-Parker (Ga.)	71	30
RBI	Jason Kinchen, Brewton-Parker (Ga.)	71	125
SB	Eric Benevedez, Lubbock Christian	61	63

EARNED RUN AVERAGE
(Minimum 50 Innings)

Player, School	IP	ER	ERA
Dan Roman, Robert Morris (Ill.)	63	1	0.14
Scott DeKock, Aquinas (Mich.)	50	9	1.62
Brad Murray, Embry-Riddle (Fla.)	92	19	1.85
Curt Kvam, Midland Lutheran (Neb.)	58	12	1.86
John Urbanski, Bethel (Ind.)	94	20	1.91
Mike Corey, Willamette (Ore.)	95	21	2.00
Michael Hopper, Union (Tenn.)	85	19	2.02
Justin Royal, Pikeville (Ky.)	66	15	2.06

Department Leaders: Pitching

Dept.	Player, School	G	Total
W	Carey Ammons, SE Okla. State	17	16
SO	Carey Ammons, SE Okla. State	17	134

JUNIOR COLLEGE

Site: Grand Junction, Colo.

Participants: Allegany, Md. (40-7); Central Florida (35-16); Columbia State, Tenn. (39-16); Cowley County, Kan. (48-10); Hill, Texas (47-13); Indian Hills, Iowa (41-13); San Jacinto, Texas (39-24); Scottsdale, Ariz. (42-17); Seminole, Okla. (55-3); Wallace State, Ala. (43-12).

Champion: Cowley County (5-1).

Runner-Up: Seminole (4-2).

Outstanding Player: Travis Hafner, lhp-1b, Cowley County.

ALL-AMERICA TEAM

C—Todd Bell, Columbia State (Tenn.).

INF—Chaz Eiguren, Seward County (Kan.); Ryan Pond, Ricks (Idaho); John Summers, Trinidad State (Colo.); Sam Turner, Jackson State (Tenn.).

OF—Willie Eyre, Snow (Utah); Damione Merriman, Spartanburg Methodist (S.C.); Bruce Sutton, Seminole (Okla.). **DH**—Brian Justice, Walters State (Tenn.).

P—Aaron Akin, Cowley County (Kan.); Craig Lewis, Wallace State (Ala.); Aaron Myette, Central Arizona.

NATIONAL LEADERS

BATTING AVERAGE
(Minimum 100 At-Bats)

Player, School	AB	H	AVG
Ronnie Quintana, Crowder (Mo.)	145	75	.517
John Summers, Trinidad State (Colo.)	173	89	.514
Chaz Eiguren, Seward County (Kan.)	193	96	.497
Brian Justice, Walters State (Tenn.)	138	68	.493
Brian Fuess, Belleville Area (Ill.)	207	100	.483
Jeremiah Perez, Otero (Colo.)	170	81	.476
Travis Dawson, Belleville Area (Ill.)	212	100	.472
Billy Colome, Broward (Fla.)	135	63	.467

Department Leaders: Batting

Dept.	Player, School	G	Total
HR	Ryan Pond, Ricks (Idaho)	56	29
RBI	Ryan Pond, Ricks (Idaho)	56	101
SB	Juan Pierre, Galveston (Texas)	56	49

EARNED RUN AVERAGE
(Minimum 50 Innings)

Player, School	IP	ER	ERA
Roy Oswalt, Holmes (Miss.)	93	14	1.35
Dan Wheeler, Central Arizona	103	17	1.48
Rusty Rushing, Seminole (Okla.)	95	16	1.52
Aaron Myette, Central Arizona	97	18	1.66
Brett Kondro, Pensacola (Fla.)	57	11	1.74
Craig Lewis, Wallace (Ala.)	93	18	1.75

Department Leaders: Pitching

Dept.	Player, School	IP	Total
SV	Shane Henderson, Central Alabama	37	13
SO	Jason Russ, Central Florida	136	151

NJCAA DIVISION II

WORLD SERIES

Site: Millington, Tenn.

Participants: Brookdale (N.J.); Dundalk, Md.; Grand Rapids, Mich.; Iowa Central; Jefferson State (Ala.); Kankakee (Ill.); Northwest Mississippi, Redlands (Okla.).

Champion: Grand Rapids, Mich. (4-0).

Runner-Up: Iowa Central (3-2).

Outstanding Player: Scott Rath, of, Grand Rapids.

NJCAA DIVISION III

WORLD SERIES

Site: Batavia, N.Y.

Participants: Camden, N.J.; Cedar Valley, Texas.; Columbia-Greene, N.Y.; Joliet (Ill.); Madison Area Tech, Wis.; Norwalk, Conn.; Penn State-Beaver; Suffolk (West), N.Y.

Champion: Madison Area Tech (4-1).

Runner-Up: Cedar Valley (4-2).

Outstanding Player: Jim Shook, rhp, Columbia-Greene.

CALIFORNIA JUCOS

STATE CHAMPIONSHIP

Site: Fresno.

Participants: Cuesta (43-9); Cypress (38-11); Sacramento (36-9); Sequoias (38-11).

Champion: Cypress (3-0).

Runner-Up: Sacramento (2-2).

Most Valuable Players: Randy Case, 3b, Cypress; Scott Paeley, of, Cypress.

High School Baseball

HIGHSCHOOL

Tampa's Jesuit High adds national title to state success

BY STEPHEN BORELLI

The sign Tampa Jesuit High athletic director Sonny Hester and art teacher Roseanne Miller held high said it all.

Shortly after the Tigers drubbed Pasco High of Dade City 7-1 in the championship game and began celebrating their 1997 Florida Class 4-A title, the two greeted their team on the field with a banner that proclaimed Jesuit High "Baseball America's national champions."

The final votes weren't tallied yet, but that formality wasn't necessary. The Tigers had moved to the top of the Baseball America/National High School Baseball Coaches Association poll weeks earlier and closed their season with a 16-game winning streak.

THE TAMPA TRIBUNE

Celebrating in style
Members of Tampa's Jesuit High celebrate winning the Florida 4-A state title, which clinches a mythical national championship.

"We knew it was up to us not to overcoach them," said Jesuit coach John Crumbley, whose staff welcomed a core of 11 returning seniors. "We knew our kids had the savvy to carry us through."

Jesuit (32-3) reached the state final four a state-record sixth straight time. The Tigers previously won the title in 1994.

"We put the final four on our schedule expecting to get there," Crumbley said. "We have the mindset that if we work hard the entire season, then we can have a chance to play in the final four."

When the Tigers last mobbed each other after winning the state title in 1994, a skinny freshman on the junior varsity watched from the bleachers. Three years later, Geoff Goetz, a lanky 6 foot, 165-pound lefthander, had developed into the staff ace and the team's top hitter. As one of the nation's most prolific two-way performers, Goetz went 13-2 with a 0.68 ERA and 149 strikeouts in 83 innings. He also hit .486 with seven homers and a school-record 45 RBIs.

Goetz shook off flu symptoms to toss a five-hitter and go 3-for-4 with a bases-clearing double in the bottom of the sixth of the deciding game.

Two weeks later, the New York Mets took Goetz with the sixth overall pick in the 1997 draft and later signed him to a $1.7 million bonus. But that didn't make the national title any less sweet.

"It's a different great feeling," said Goetz, whose team lost in the state semifinals in 1996 and in the finals in 1995. "Last year when we lost, the seniors were all in tears. We've just been waiting so long. I'm sure I'll remember this for the rest of my life."

HIGH SCHOOL TOP 25

Baseball America's final 1997 Top 25, selected in conjunction with the National High School Baseball Coaches Association.

SCHOOL, CITY	W-L	Achievement
1. Jesuit HS, Tampa	32-3	State 4-A champion
2. Clovis (Calif.) HS	33-2	CIF sectional champion
3. George Washington HS, New York	44-2	N.Y.C. public school champion
4. Hamilton (Ohio) HS	29-2	State Division I champion
5. Rose HS, Greenville, N.C.	26-2	State 4-A champion
6. Iolani HS, Honolulu	31-2	State champion
7. Harrison County HS, Cynthiana, Ky.	40-1	State champion
8. St. Thomas Aquinas HS, Ft. Lauderdale	28-2	
9. Elk Grove (Calif.) HS	31-4	CIF sectional champion
10. Round Rock (Texas) HS	32-6	State 5-A champion
11. Duncanville (Texas) HS	34-4	
12. Archbishop Rummel HS, Metairie, La.	32-3	State 5-A champion
13. Westminster Christian HS, Miami	30-4	State 2-A champion
14. Esperanza HS, Anaheim	25-5	CIF sectional champion
15 The Woodlands HS, Conroe, Texas	26-4	
16. Brito Private HS, Miami	32-3	State 1-A champion
17. Christian Brothers HS, Memphis	35-5	State 3-A champion
18. Grossmont HS, La Mesa, Calif.	29-5	CIF sectional champion
19. Xaverian HS, Brooklyn	28-3	N.Y.C. private school champion
20. Chambersburg (Pa.) HS	21-3	
21. Eldorado HS, Albuquerque	23-2	State 4-A champion
22. Green Valley HS, Henderson, Nev.	30-3	State 4-A champion
23. Rochester (Mich.) HS	36-2	State Class A champion
24. Great Bridge HS, Chesapeake, Va.	23-3	
25. Cretin-Derham Hall HS, St. Paul, Minn.	22-2	State 2-A champion

Championship Rolls

Like Jesuit, several other national contenders put together long winning steaks.

No. 2 Clovis (Calif.) High reeled off 22 consecutive wins to finish at 33-2 and win the California Interscholastic Federation

High School Baseball

Player of the Year

Colorado's McDonald enjoys stellar two-sport high school career

It's no secret Darnell McDonald signed for $1.9 million two months after the Baltimore Orioles made him the 26th overall pick in the 1997 draft. We also know McDonald passed up an opportunity to play both baseball and football at the University of Texas.

But it's easy to lose sight of what McDonald actually did on the field at Cherry Creek High in Englewood, Colo. Amid all the hype, he had a remarkable high school career, leading to his selection as Baseball America's 1997 High School Player of the Year.

FRANK RAGSDALE

Darnell McDonald

McDonald led Cherry Creek High to three consecutive state titles in both baseball and football.

The two-time All-American center fielder hit .606 with 10 home runs, 35 RBIs and 18 stolen bases for the 19-3 Bruins. He went 13-for-17 with five homers and 15 RBIs in the playoffs. A year earlier, McDonald hit .581 with 15 home runs.

McDonald also rushed for a state-record 6,121 yards as a tailback at Cherry Creek and was one of the nation's most heavily recruited football players.

"You couldn't write a better story about a high school career," said McDonald, 18. "Whatever season it was, that was probably my favorite sport. Each year it became more fun. After each year, every team was out to beat us. It was more of a challenge."

John Quarton, the baseball coach at Denver's Mullen High, didn't see it that way.

"The one word I can use to describe Darnell out here is unchallenged," said Quarton, whose team lost to Cherry Creek 12-1 in the 1997 state semifinals. "This is the guy you love to hate. Even if you walk him, he'll still be on the pitcher's mind and on the coach's mind. He'll steal second and third, and plays a great center field."

You can see why Cherry Creek baseball coach Marc Johnson, who has been at the school since 1973 and has coached seven first-round picks in either high school or summer ball, dubs the 5-foot-10, 190-pound McDonald the most dominant athlete in Colorado prep history.

"He's a level ahead of all of them athletically," Johnson said. "I've had a lot of great players, and he's the real deal, no question about it."

—STEPHEN BORELLI

PREVIOUS WINNERS

1992—Preston Wilson, ss-rhp, Bamberg-Ehrhardt (S.C.) High
1993—Trot Nixon, of-lhp, New Hanover High, Wilmington, N.C.
1994—Doug Million, lhp, Sarasota (Fla.) High
1995—Ben Davis, c, Malvern (Pa.) Prep
1996—Matt White, rhp, Waynesboro (Pa.) Area High

Central section championship. California schools do not participate in state championships.

No. 3 George Washington High (44-2) closed with an 18-game winning streak to capture the New York City public school championship. No. 4 Hamilton (Ohio) High overcame a five-run deficit in the championship game to finish with 20 straight wins and its second state Division I crown. No. 5 Rose High (26-2) of Greenville, N.C., won its final 16 games to capture the North Carolina 4-A title.

Geoff Goetz

No. 6 Iolani High (31-2) of Honolulu, which won the Hawaii state championship for a second straight year, led a group of repeat champions. The most notable were No. 13-ranked Westminster Christian High (30-4) of Miami and unranked Cherry Creek High (19-3) of Englewood, Colo., which finished 1-2 in the nation a year earlier, and No. 22 Green Valley (30-3) of Henderson, Nev.

Westminster Christian, a two-time national champion, was a perfect 36-0 in 1996 and had a streak of 60 straight undefeated games (including one tie) over three seasons. But the Warriors lost three games in a week midway through the 1997 season and dropped out of national contention though they later rallied to successfully defend the Florida 2-A title.

Cherry Creek, led by national Player of the Year Darnell McDonald, won its third consecutive 5-A crown, while Green Valley, sporting a team batting average of .392 and a team ERA of 1.48, won its fifth straight Nevada 4-A title.

Atlanta Braves first-round pick Troy Cameron set a school career home run record with 30 as No. 8 St. Thomas Aquinas High (28-2) of Fort Lauderdale held the No. 1 spot for several weeks after it replaced Westminster Christian. Cameron, a shortstop, hit .475 with 14 homers, but the Raiders'

1997 HIGH SCHOOL ALL-AMERICA TEAM

Selected by Baseball America *Junior

FIRST TEAM

Pos.	Player, School	AVG	AB	R	H	2B	3B	HR	RBI	SB
C	Jayson Werth, Glenwood HS, Chatham, Ill.	.617	107	80	66	14	9	17	63	32
1B	Jack Cust, Immaculata HS, Flemington, N.J.	.592	76	61	45	9	7	15	51	14
INF	Troy Cameron, St. Thomas Aquinas HS, Fort Lauderdale	.475	80	45	38	6	0	14	36	9
	Michael Cuddyer, Great Bridge HS, Chesapeake, Va.	.500	70	41	35	10	2	6	30	11
	Jason Romano, Hillsborough HS, Tampa	.458	72	31	33	14	4	9	40	22
OF	Brett Caradonna, El Capitan HS, San Diego	.462	106	55	49	12	2	12	39	13
	Darnell McDonald, Cherry Creek HS, Englewood, Colo.	.606	66	37	40	8	1	10	35	18
	Vernon Wells, Bowie HS, Arlington, Texas	.565	69	39	39	10	2	7	20	19
DH	Chris Aguila, McQueen HS, Reno, Nev.	.580	119	76	69	18	5	29	81	19
UT	Geoff Goetz, Jesuit HS, Tampa	.486	109	26	53	15	4	7	45	4

Pos.	Player, School	W	L	ERA	G	SV	IP	H	BB	SO
P	Ryan Anderson, Divine Child HS, Dearborn, Mich.	5	3	0.94	10	2	59	10	41	148
	Rick Ankiel, Port St. Lucie (Fla.) HS	11	1	0.47	13	0	74	21	22	162
	Chad Cislak, Sabino HS, Tucson	14	0	1.19	19	4	100	51	22	152
	Jon Garland, Kennedy HS, Granada Hills, Calif.	9	3	1.21	13	0	81	52	18	111
	Chris Stowe, Chancellor HS, Fredericksburg, Va.	9	0	0.94	11	1	67	34	19	118
UT	Geoff Goetz, Jesuit HS, Tampa	13	2	0.68	19	1	83	35	46	149

SECOND TEAM

Pos.	Player, School	AVG	AB	R	H	2B	3B	HR	RBI	SB
C	Scott Ackerman, Oregon City (Ore.) HS	.618	85	32	53	12	1	9	44	13
1B	J.J. Davis, Baldwin Park (Calif.) HS	.532	77	29	41	7	2	9	29	7
INF	Aaron Capista, Joliet (Ill.) Catholic HS	.500	116	44	58	22	4	4	57	15
	Scott Hodges, Henry Clay HS, Lexington, Ky.	.474	97	47	46	13	2	15	33	13
	Chase Utley, Poly HS, Long Beach	.525	80	34	42	6	6	12	48	13
OF	Tyrell Godwin, East Bladen HS, Elizabethtown, N.C.	.459	61	27	28	7	2	3	27	12
	*Corey Patterson, Harrison HS, Kennesaw, Ga.	.437	103	42	45	4	3	2	19	47
	Vicente Rosario, George Washington HS, New York	.623	114	77	71	20	7	16	61	89
DH	Alvin Morrow, Kirkwood (Mo.) HS	.554	56	28	31	7	1	13	39	3
UT	Brian Gordon, Round Rock (Texas) HS	.310	126	38	39	5	6	7	31	9

Pos.	Player, School	W	L	ERA	G	SV	IP	H	BB	SO
P	Donnie Bridges, Oak Grove HS, Hattiesburg, Miss.	8	1	0.49	11	1	57	29	16	96
	Aaron Cook, Hamilton (Ohio) HS	10	0	1.23	15	0	79	48	24	101
	John Curtice, Great Bridge HS, Chesapeake, Va.	9	1	0.71	11	0	59	17	24	104
	Eric Glaser, Highlands HS, Fort Thomas, Ky.	10	1	0.68	14	1	72	33	11	139
	Shane Loux, Highland HS, Gilbert, Ariz.	11	2	1.15	14	0	85	50	22	111
UT	Brian Gordon, Round Rock (Texas) HS	14	0	1.44	15	0	97	63	23	130

season abruptly ended with a loss to nearby Port St. Lucie High in the Florida 5-A regional semifinals.

Twin First-Rounders

Michael Cuddyer and John Curtice once combined to record all 21 outs of a Little League game with strikeouts, but that no longer was their most remarkable joint accomplishment after the two Great Bridge High (Chesapeake, Va.) players became only the second pair of high school teammates to go in the first round of the same draft.

The Minnesota Twins chose Cuddyer, a shortstop-righthander, with the ninth overall pick. The Boston Red Sox took Curtice, a lefthander, with the 17th pick.

Rancho Cordova (Calif.) High was the first school to produce two first-rounders: shortstop Jerry Manuel and outfielder Mike Ondina in 1972.

"The odds of that happening are, I don't even think I could count them," Cuddyer said.

First-year Great Bridge coach Greg Jennings, who went from a career junior varsity coach to leading the No. 24-ranked team in the country, said he was just happy to be part of such a season.

"Scouts have already told me that this is a once-in-a-lifetime thing that you get two," Jennings said. "It's very seldom that you get one."

Viva Las Vegas

In his last game of the 1997 season, Reno (Nev.) McQueen High's Chris Aguila swung at pitches in the dirt and in his eyes.

His coach didn't mind.

"I just told him, 'Hey, with nobody on base, just go for it. Anything close, swing,' " McQueen coach Ed Lightner said. "It was probably the wrong thing to do, but hey, you're that close."

Aguila entered the Nevada Class 4-A final four game in Las Vegas against Silverado High (Las Vegas) with 29 home runs, which tied him for the national single-season record Shon Walker of Harrison County High (Cynthiana, Ky.) set in 1992.

He fell just short, literally. The righthanded-hitting Aguila went 0-for-2 with two walks in the 8-5 loss, but hit a fly ball to right in his final at-bat that the Silverado outfielder caught at the base of the wall. Aguila, a first-team All-American, later was drafted in the third round by the Florida Marlins. He hit .217 with one homer in 46 games in the Rookie-level Gulf Coast League in his professional debut.

Aguila, who started at pitcher, second base, shortstop and third base at different points during the 1997 season, hit .580 with 81 RBIs in 119 at-bats.

Amateur Baseball

AMATEUR BASEBALL

Cuba's travails highlight turbulent year internationally

BY JOHN MANUEL

For a non-Olympic year, 1997 proved to be an interesting one for amateur baseball.

International power and defending Olympic champion Cuba continued to lose players through defections and decided to back out of a series of exhibition games in the United States. It later lost a game in a major tournament for the first time since 1987.

Team USA had one of its stronger showings in a post-Olympic summer, finishing fourth at the Intercontinental Cup in Spain. But the youthful U.S. team, comprised entirely of college sophomores and freshmen, felt it should have done much better.

Players with previous professional experience also made their presence felt for the first time in 1997, the result of an International Baseball Association rule change that now allows pros to participate in international events, including the 2000 Olympics in Sydney, Australia.

A World Championships qualifying tournament scheduled for late September in Mexico City was supposed to be the first test for professionals from the U.S., Puerto Rico and the Dominican Republic, but the suspension of the tournament organizer and difficulty with player procurement after the tournament was delayed until October led to the pullout of most of the prominent nations. Cuba, Nicaragua, Panama and Puerto Rico pulled out of the qualifier first, and the U.S. followed suit.

The tournament, which was supposed to qualify four teams from the Americas for the 1998 World Championships in Italy, eventually was cancelled.

Intercontinental Flap

Team USA headed to Barcelona, Spain for the Intercontinental Cup, the year's major international competition, with what looked to be a full head of steam. The Americans had won seven straight games against barnstorming Australia before dropping their last exhibition to the Aussies before the tournament.

But Team USA wasn't properly prepared. A crucial eight-game tune-up series against Cuba was cancelled after two small bombs exploded at the Capri and National hotels in Havana on July 12–just two days before Cuba's scheduled arrival in the U.S. Cuban officials, who laid the blame for the bomb blasts on the U.S., said the safety of Cuban players was in doubt.

Also, a rash of defections and suspensions of top Cuban players, notably catcher Francisco Santiesteban (defector) and 1996 Olympic shortstop Eduardo Paret (suspension), hastened the Cubans' withdrawal from the series. More than a dozen Cubans have defected in the last three years.

Team USA general manager Mike Fiore stopped short of saying the U.S.-Cuba series would not resume in 1998, but said, "It's going to have a long-term effect on our relationship. This eliminates any type of trust factor, which was so fragile to begin with. Their word means nothing to me now."

In the short term, it eliminated a good test for Team USA prior to going to Barcelona. The U.S. faced Cuba twice in Spain, losing 4-1 and 7-1, but it was Australia that did in Team USA, winning a pair of extra-inning thrillers to place third. Australia, using a number of ex-pros, beat the U.S. 6-4 in 10 innings in the bronze-medal game.

TEAM USA '97

OVERALL STATISTICS

BATTING	AVG	AB	R	H	2B	3B	HR	RBI	SB	College	Class
Jason Tyner, dh-of	.434	129	31	56	8	0	0	17	11	Texas A&M	So.
*Jody Gerut, of	.429	7	4	3	0	1	1	2	0	Stanford	So.
Eric Munson, 1b-c	.393	112	30	44	6	0	6	28	3	Southern Cal	Fr.
Adam Everett, ss	.351	97	22	34	6	0	0	11	8	South Carolina	So.
Eric Valent, of	.345	119	24	41	10	3	7	34	1	UCLA	So.
Pat Burrell, 3b-1b	.343	99	33	34	9	1	12	42	3	Miami (Fla.)	So.
Chris Magruder, of	.336	113	31	38	7	0	4	27	5	Washington	So.
Brian Oliver, 2b	.333	96	21	32	6	0	1	10	7	California	So.
Brian Roberts, 3b-ss	.330	88	21	29	3	3	3	11	8	North Carolina	Fr.
Bubba Crosby, of	.322	121	31	39	9	2	8	28	6	Rice	So.
*Zach Sorensen, ss	.321	56	11	18	3	2	1	7	3	Wichita State	So.
Josh Bard, c	.305	59	7	18	2	0	0	9	1	Texas Tech	Fr.
David Matranga, 2b-ss	.282	39	7	11	2	1	2	8	1	Pepperdine	So.
Jason Hill, c	.281	57	12	16	3	0	2	19	3	California	So.
*Chad Sutter, c	.200	5	1	1	0	0	1	3	0	Tulane	So.
*Andrew Beinbrink, 3b	.167	6	2	1	0	0	0	0	0	Arizona State	So.
*Ryan Lundquist, of	.125	8	0	1	0	0	0	1	0	Arkansas	So.
Jason Jennings, p	.000	5	0	0	0	0	0	0	0	Baylor	Fr.
TOTALS	**.342**	**1216**	**288**	**416**	**74**	**13**	**48**	**257**	**60**		

PITCHING	W	L	ERA	G	SV	IP	H	BB	SO	College	Class
Adam Pettyjohn	3	0	2.48	12	0	33	31	9	36	Fresno State	So.
Monty Ward	3	0	2.55	9	0	35	31	14	43	Texas Tech	So.
Jeff Weaver	0	1	2.79	3	0	10	16	3	10	Fresno State	So.
Jason Jennings	0	1	3.00	11	0	18	16	12	17	Baylor	Fr.
*Nate Robertson	1	0	3.00	1	0	3	2	3	2	Wichita State	Fr.
Mike Fischer	0	0	3.43	12	1	21	15	9	19	South Alabama	So.
Jeff Austin	4	1	3.63	8	0	40	34	14	31	Stanford	So.
Greg Kubes	3	1	3.94	7	0	30	23	14	31	Sam Houston St.	So.
Casey Fossum	3	2	4.82	13	1	28	29	16	27	Texas A&M	Fr.
Robbie Morrison	1	2	5.03	13	2	20	23	9	32	Miami (Fla.)	So.
Ryan Mottl	2	2	6.21	5	0	15	17	14	13	Clemson	Fr.
*Chuck Crowder	1	1	6.46	5	0	15	17	14	13	Georgia Tech	So.
*Scott Sobkowiak	0	0	8.68	4	0	9	11	8	8	Northern Iowa	So.
*Mike MacDougal	0	1	11.57	1	0	2	3	4	3	Wake Forest	Fr.
TOTALS	**21**	**13**	**4.09**	**34**	**4**	**293**	**284**	**144**	**288**		

*Did not make final roster

MAJOR INTERNATIONAL TOURNAMENTS

INTERCONTINENTAL CUP

Barcelona, Spain
August 1-10, 1997

ROUND-ROBIN STANDINGS

	W	L	RF	RA
Cuba	7	0	61	13
Australia	6	1	68	32
Japan	4	3	46	26
United States	4	3	56	23
Nicaragua	4	3	38	33
Italy	2	5	18	43
France	1	6	19	64
Spain	0	7	13	85

GOLD MEDAL—Japan. **SILVER MEDAL**—Cuba. **BRONZE MEDAL**—Australia.

ALL-TOURNAMENT TEAM: C—Gary White, Australia. **1B**—Orestes Kindelan, Cuba. **2B**—Yosuke Takasu, Japan. **3B**—Paul Gonzales, Australia. **SS**—Omar Linares, Cuba. **OF**—Chris Magruder, United States; Yoshinobu Takahashi, Japan; Luis Ulacia, Cuba. **DH**—Greg Jelks, Australia. **LHP**—Akio Shimizu, Japan. **RHP**—Kohji Uehara, Japan.

Most Valuable Player—Paul Gonzales, 3b, Australia.

INDIVIDUAL BATTING LEADERS
ROUND ROBIN
(Minimum 16 At-Bats)

	AVG	AB	R	H	2B	3B	HR	RBI	SB
Paul Gonzalez, Aus	.600	20	7	12	3	0	4	16	1
Jason Tyner, USA	.484	31	7	15	2	0	0	6	2
Greg Jelks, Aus	.481	27	8	13	3	0	4	9	0
Yoshinobu Taka., Jap	.455	22	10	10	1	2	3	11	0
Orestes Kindelan, Cuba	.440	25	10	11	1	0	6	15	0
Eric Munson, USA	.440	25	8	11	2	0	1	9	1
Luis Ulacia, Cuba	.440	25	10	11	3	0	1	6	3
Yosuke Takasu, Japan	.429	21	3	9	2	0	0	4	0
Matt Buckley, Aus	.421	19	5	8	3	0	1	3	0
Chris Magruder, USA	.407	27	8	11	2	0	0	5	0
Omar Linares, Cuba	.400	20	7	8	1	0	1	7	2
Adam Burton, Aus	.375	24	10	9	3	1	0	2	0
Henry Roa, Nicaragua	.375	24	2	9	1	0	0	2	0
Takayuki Taka., Jap	.370	27	6	10	2	1	0	6	1
Andrew Scott, Aus	.367	30	7	11	1	0	1	5	0
Bayardo Davila, Nic	.364	22	4	8	2	0	0	8	1
Yobal Duenas, Cuba	.364	22	4	8	1	0	1	5	0
Gabriel Pierre, Cuba	.364	22	5	8	4	1	2	9	0
Jose Estrada, Cuba	.360	25	6	9	1	2	0	4	1
Gary White, Aus	.357	28	7	10	4	0	1	4	0
Clayton Byrne, Aus	.355	31	5	11	4	1	0	6	1
Adam Everett, USA	.350	20	4	7	0	0	0	2	0
Antonio Pacheco, Cuba	.346	26	4	9	4	0	1	5	0
Scott Tunkin, Aus	.333	24	5	8	0	0	0	4	0
Illuminati, Pierpaolo, Italy	.313	16	1	5	1	0	0	1	0

INDIVIDUAL PITCHING LEADERS
ROUND ROBIN
(Minimum 5 Innings)

	W	L	ERA	G	SV	IP	H	BB	SO
Kym Ashworth, Aus	1	0	0.00	1	0	5	5	4	4
Abel Madera, Cuba	2	0	0.00	2	0	6	1	1	7
Julio Raudez, Nic	1	0	0.00	1	0	7	5	0	9
Ciro Silvino, Cuba	1	0	0.00	2	0	11	3	0	14
Kohji Uehara, Japan	1	0	0.00	3	0	12	6	3	12
Monty Ward, USA	1	0	0.00	2	0	9	4	4	15
Pedro Lazo, Cuba	1	0	0.71	3	1	13	5	2	16
Diego Ricci, Italy	0	0	0.96	2	0	9	6	3	9
Jeff Austin, USA	1	0	1.29	1	0	7	2	1	9
Jeff Williams, Aus	1	0	1.29	1	0	7	2	1	10
Akio Shimizu, Japan	2	0	1.64	2	0	11	4	2	8
Alessandro Parri, Italy	0	0	1.80	2	0	5	4	3	1
Adam Pettyjohn, USA	0	0	1.80	3	0	5	3	1	7
Leonides Turcas, Cuba	0	0	1.80	2	0	5	5	1	3
Jose Contreras, Cuba	2	0	1.88	3	1	14	7	4	18
Phil Dale, Australia	0	0	2.31	2	0	12	10	5	5
Jeff Weaver, USA	0	1	2.79	3	0	10	16	3	10
Massimiliano Masin, Italy	1	0	2.92	2	0	12	11	8	10
Greg Kubes, USA	1	0	3.00	2	0	9	7	2	12
Syusei Ikezoe, Japan	0	0	3.18	3	0	6	4	3	7

WORLD JUNIOR CHAMPIONSHIP

Moncton, New Brunswick
August 8-16, 1997

ROUND-ROBIN STANDINGS

POOL A	W	L	RF	RA
Cuba	4	1	86	21
Canada	4	1	69	24
South Korea	4	1	69	35
Brazil	2	3	29	47
Russia	1	4	13	80
Czech Republic	0	5	9	68
POOL B	**W**	**L**	**RF**	**RA**
Chinese Taipei	4	0	35	17
United States	3	1	39	23
Australia	2	2	19	24
Venezuela	1	3	14	20
Netherlands	0	4	16	39

GOLD MEDAL—Cuba. **SILVER MEDAL**—Chinese Taipei. **BRONZE MEDAL**—Canada, United States (shared).

ALL-TOURNAMENT TEAM: C—Yosbany Peraza, Cuba. **1B**—Yoen Carlos Pedrosa, Cuba. **2B**—Cesar Kameoka, Brazil. **3B**—Mike Eskildsen, Canada. **SS**—Michel Enriquez, Cuba. **OF**—Bong Joong Keun, South Korea; Huang Long-Yi, Chinese Taipei; Serguey Perez, Cuba. **LHP**—Rick Ankiel, United States. **RHP**—Jason Mandryk, Canada.

Most Valuable Player—Bong Joong Keun, South Korea.

INDIVIDUAL BATTING LEADERS
ROUND ROBIN
(Minimum 15 Plate Appearances)

	AVG	AB	R	H	2B	3B	HR	RBI	SB
Austin Kearns, USA	.615	13	2	8	2	0	0	3	1
Hayden Chinn, Australia	.600	15	2	9	1	0	0	1	1
Chun-Ting Chu, CT	.600	15	8	9	2	2	1	3	1
Bong Joong Keun, Korea	.560	25	13	14	2	1	4	11	2
Trent Pratt, USA	.545	11	2	6	0	0	0	2	0
Josue Cabrera, Cuba	.533	15	10	8	2	0	1	6	0
Serguey Perez, Cuba	.522	23	12	12	5	2	1	9	0
Yosbany Peraza, Cuba	.500	24	10	12	0	0	3	9	0
Toby Barnett, Aus.	.500	12	4	6	1	0	1	3	1
Lee Hyun Gon, Korea	.480	25	9	12	1	1	3	10	0
Yuan-Chia Chen, CT	.455	11	3	5	1	0	1	3	1
Choi Hee Seop, Korea	.450	20	9	9	4	1	1	5	1
Lee Delfino, Canada	.444	18	10	8	1	1	2	10	0
Mike Eskildsen, Canada	.429	21	9	9	0	0	2	9	0
David Detienne, Canada	.429	14	6	6	0	0	0	2	0
Jan Stehlik, Czech	.429	14	3	6	1	0	0	1	0
Lee Smith, Canada	.429	14	6	6	1	0	0	6	0
Cesar Kameoka, Brazil	.421	19	5	8	2	0	0	3	1
Elson Nishimura, Brazil	.412	17	5	7	1	0	0	3	0
An Chi Yong, Korea	.409	22	6	9	2	1	1	6	2
Lee Jin Young, Korea	.409	22	6	9	3	0	0	7	3
Trent Kitsch, Canada	.409	22	6	9	0	1	3	16	0
Yoen Pedroso, Cuba	.391	23	11	9	0	0	4	12	0
Rick Ankiel, USA	.385	13	5	5	0	0	0	0	0
Wei-Lin Huang, CT	.385	13	6	5	0	0	1	5	0
Michel Enrique, Cuba	.381	21	8	8	0	0	3	4	0
Eliacer Valera, Cuba	.375	24	9	9	1	0	4	13	0

INDIVIDUAL PITCHING LEADERS
ROUND ROBIN
(Minimum 7 Innings)

	W	L	ERA	G	SV	IP	H	BB	SO
Chien-Ming Wang, CT	1	0	0.00	1	0	7	1	1	9
Chih-Cheng Chen, CT	1	0	0.00	3	0	9	8	1	6
Reggie LaPlante, Canada	1	0	0.00	1	0	7	6	1	10
Rodrigo Suzuki, Brazil	1	0	0.77	2	0	12	3	0	11
Manuel Alvarez, Venezuela	1	0	1.23	1	0	7	6	4	4
Cory Vance, USA	1	0	1.29	1	0	7	1	4	15
Jason Mandryk, Canada	1	0	2.00	1	0	9	6	2	8
Ricardo Imamura, Brazil	1	0	2.00	2	0	9	5	6	8
Alex Toropov, Russia	1	0	2.16	2	0	8	4	11	9
Luis Vasquez, Venezuela	0	0	3.00	2	0	9	7	0	9
Norberto Gonzalez, Cuba	1	1	3.24	2	0	8	7	3	4
Roman Bessonov, Russia	0	1	3.27	2	0	11	11	8	12
Jeon Yong Jong, Korea	1	0	3.38	1	0	8	9	3	5
Chad Cislak, USA	0	0	3.38	1	0	8	10	0	8

In all but one of its five losses in Spain, the U.S. offense sputtered. That surprised Team USA coach Bob Milano (University of California), who had faith in his team's bats.

"I'm very disappointed we finished fourth," Milano said. "After watching us play all summer, even though there were a tremendous number of players with pro experience on the other teams, I felt we had probably the second-best team there after Cuba."

Instead, the Cubans ended up second, losing to Japan 11-2 in the finals. The Japanese had 16 hits, including two homers, while all-tournament right-hander Kohji Uehara picked up the victory.

It was Cuba's first loss in a major international competition since the 1987 Pan American Games, a span of 134 games.

TEAM USA JUNIORS

OVERALL STATISTICS

BATTING	AVG	AB	R	H	2B	3B	HR	RBI	SB	High School	Class
Matt Riley, p	.800	5	2	4	1	0	0	1	0	Liberty Union HS, Oakley, Calif.	Sr.
Jason Hubbard, p	.750	4	1	3	1	0	0	0	0	White HS, Jacksonville, Fla.	Sr.
Paul French, p	.500	4	1	2	0	0	0	1	0	Northgate HS, Concord, Calif.	Jr.
Austin Kearns, 1b-p	.478	67	20	32	10	2	5	14	4	Lafayette HS, Lexington, Ky.	Jr.
Josh McKinley, 3b-2b	.408	49	14	20	4	0	4	17	5	Malvern Prep, Downingtown, Pa.	Jr.
Michael Cuddyer, ss	.397	68	24	27	6	2	7	26	6	Great Bridge HS, Chesapeake, Va.	Sr.
Rick Ankiel, of-p	.387	62	16	24	4	0	3	16	0	Port St. Lucie (Fla.) HS	Sr.
Matt Holliday, of	.387	62	22	24	10	0	3	19	8	Stillwater (Okla.) HS	Jr.
Trent Pratt, c	.383	47	10	18	5	0	0	12	4	Tooele (Utah) HS	Jr.
Seth Davidson, 2b	.338	77	25	26	11	1	1	13	11	University HS, San Diego	Sr.
Manny Crespo, of	.324	34	8	11	2	0	2	10	2	Westminster Christian HS, Miami	Sr.
Koyie Hill, 3b	.324	34	7	11	1	0	0	5	0	Eisenhower HS, Lawton, Ohio	Sr.
J.D. Closser, of-c	.394	34	11	10	2	0	2	5	4	Monroe HS, Alexandria, Ind.	Jr.
Jerry Laird, of-c	.289	76	15	22	5	0	1	13	6	La Quinta HS, Garden Grove, Calif.	Jr.
Chad Cislak, p	.250	8	1	2	1	0	0	2	0	Sabino HS, Tucson	Sr.
Cory Vance, p	.167	12	1	2	0	0	1	3	0	Butler HS, Vandalia, Ohio	Sr.
Will Rosellini, p	.000	5	0	0	0	0	0	1	0	Jesuit HS, Dallas	Sr.
Mike Smalley, p	.000	1	0	0	0	0	0	0	0	Bishop Moore HS, Maitland, Fla.	Sr.
TOTALS	**.367**	**649**	**178**	**238**	**63**	**5**	**29**	**158**	**50**		

PITCHING	W	L	ERA	G	SV	IP	H	BB	SO	High School	Class
Matt Holliday	0	0	0.00	1	0	2	0	0	2	Stillwater (Okla.) HS	Jr.
Cory Vance	4	1	1.55	5	0	29	16	9	44	Butler HS, Vandalia, Ohio	Sr.
Jason Hubbard	1	0	1.80	5	1	10	9	2	10	White HS, Jacksonville, Fla.	Sr.
Rick Ankiel	3	0	1.82	5	0	30	20	12	48	Port St. Lucie (Fla.) HS	Sr.
Mike Smalley	0	0	2.00	5	0	9	5	11	11	Bishop Moore HS, Maitland, Fla.	Sr.
Chad Cislak	3	0	2.14	5	0	21	16	8	28	Sabino HS, Tucson	Sr.
Matt Riley	1	1	3.09	5	1	12	15	7	14	Liberty Union HS, Oakley, Calif.	Sr.
Paul French	2	0	3.94	5	0	16	14	10	18	Northgate HS, Concord, Calif.	Jr.
Will Rosellini	2	1	4.15	7	1	17	17	5	16	Jesuit HS, Dallas	Sr.
Austin Kearns	0	0	5.40	3	0	10	10	8	19	Lafayette HS, Lexington, Ky.	Jr.
TOTALS	**16**	**3**	**2.60**	**19**	**3**	**156**	**122**	**72**	**210**		

JEFF GOLDEN

Miami's Pat Burrell
Leads Team USA with 12 homers, 42 RBIs

University of Miami third baseman Pat Burrell sparked Team USA's offense all summer, leading the team in home runs (12) and RBIs (42) while batting .343.

U.S. Juniors Win Bronze

Team USA's junior national team earned a bronze medal at the World Junior Championships in Moncton, New Brunswick when its third-place game with host Canada was rained out. It was the 17th straight World Junior medal for Team USA and second straight bronze.

The U.S., 16-3 on the summer, was relegated to the third-place game when it lost 8-4 to defending champion Cuba in the semifinals. Cuba won the tournament, defeating Chinese Taipei 7-3 in the championship game.

AL SOLOMON

Rich Ankiel

Three 1997 draftees, lefthanders Rick Ankiel and Cory Vance and shortstop Michael Cuddyer, were Team USA's mainstays.

Ankiel went 3-0 with a 1.82 ERA and later signed with the St. Louis Cardinals for $2.5 million, the largest bonus ever for a player signed by his draft team. Cuddyer signed with the Minnesota Twins for $1.85 million after leading Team USA in homers (seven) and RBIs (26).

Vance (4-1, 1.55), who lost to Cuba, was drafted in

AMATEUR/YOUTH CHAMPIONS 1997

INTERNATIONAL

LEAGUE (Age Group)	Site	Champion	Runner-Up
XIII Intercontinental Cup (open)	Barcelona, Spain	Japan	Cuba
AAA World Junior Championship (17-18)	Moncton, N.B.	Cuba	Chinese Taipei
AA World Youth Championship (15-16)	Chinese Taipei	Cuba	Chinese Taipei
AA Jr. Pan Am Games (14 & under)	Fairview Heights, Ill.	Brazil	Venezuela
AAA Jr. Pan Am Games (12 & under)	Santo Domingo, D.R.	Cuba	Dominican Republic

NATIONAL

LEAGUE (Age Group)	Site	Champion	Runner-Up
AAABA (21 and under)	Johnstown, Pa.	Prince William (Va.) Gators	Milford (Mass.) Town Team
American Legion (19 & under)	Rapid City, S.D.	Sanford, Fla.	Medford, Ore.
National Baseball Congress (open)	Wichita	Mat-Su, Alaska	Nevada, Mo.
USA Jr. Olympics (16 & under)	Fort Myers, Fla.	St. Petersburg PAL	Metro Dade (Fla.) PAL

AMATEUR ATHLETIC UNION (AAU)

HEADQUARTERS: Lake Buena Vista, Fla.

Event	Site	Champion	Runner-Up
9 & under	Sherwood, Ark.	Tampa Tarpons	San Diego Stars
10 & under	Kansas City, Mo.	River City (Fla.) Rhinos	Sun Valley Park (Calif.) Bombs
11 & under	Lake Buena Vista, Fla.	Knoxville (Tenn.) Stars	Yorba Linda (Calif.) Aztecs
12 & under	Burnsville, Minn.	Placentia (Calif.) Mustangs	Southern California Panthers
13 & under (90 foot)	Chickasha, Okla.	Connecticut Baseball Academy	Texas Titans
13 & under (80 foot)	Riverside, Calif.	Carson (Calif.) Reds	Valley (Calif.) White Sox
14 & under	Cocoa, Fla.	Encinitas (Calif.) Reds	Chet Lemon Juice, Lake Mary, Fla.
15 & under	Millington, Tenn.	Cucamonga (Calif.) Dodgers	Whittier (Calif.) Cardinals
16 & under	Charlotte, N.C.	East Cobb (Ga.) Astros	North California Angels
17 & under	Norman, Okla.	Texas Heat	Sacramento Capitals
18 & under	Lake Buena Vista, Fla.	Baton Rouge (La.) Red Sticks	Florida Express
20 & under	Fort Myers, Fla.	Baton Rouge (La.) Stars	Lee County, Fla.

AAU National Invitation Tournament

Event	Site	Champion	Runner-Up
10 & under	Moore, Okla.	Corona (Calif.) Yankees	Midwest City (Okla.) Slam
11 & under	Akron, Ohio	Chesterfield, Va., Cobras	Worcester, Mass., Heat
12 & under	Lake Buena Vista, Fla.	North Florida Hurricanes	Sarasota (Fla.) Sting Rays
14 & under	Lake Buena Vista, Fla.	Central Florida Bombers	South Texas Hitmen
15 & under	Sarasota, Fla.	Richmond, Va., Rockies	Charlotte, N.C., Renegades

AMERICAN AMATEUR BASEBALL CONGRESS (AABC)

HEADQUARTERS: Marshall, Mich.

Event	Site	Champion	Runner-Up
Roberto Clemente (8 & u.)	Wheatridge, Colo.	Dallas	Knoxville (Tenn.) Stars
Willie Mays (9-10)	Collierville, Tenn.	Dallas	Fajando, P.R.
Pee Wee Reese (11-12)	Toa Baja, P.R.	Potros, P.R.	Dallas
Sandy Koufax (13-14)	Jersey City, N.J.	Memphis Tigers	West Covina (Calif.) Dukes
Mickey Mantle (15-16)	McKinney, Texas	Orange County (Calif.) Stars	Nashville AFPC/Twitty City
Connie Mack (17-18)	Farmington, N.M.	Cincinnati Midland	Orange County (Calif.) Dodgers
Stan Musial (unlimited)	Battle Creek, Mich.	Puerto Rico	Grand Rapid (Mich.) Sullivans

BABE RUTH BASEBALL

HEADQUARTERS: Trenton, N.J.

Event	Site	Champion	Runner-Up
Bambino (11-12)	Altamonte Springs, Fla.	Brooklyn	Willamette Valley, Ore.
13 prep	Clifton Park, N.Y.	Oakland	South Shore, N.Y.
13-15	Longview, Wash.	Bakersfield, Calif.	Prince George's County, Md.
16	Springdale, Ark.	Satsuma, Ala.	South Shore, N.Y.
16-18	Jamestown, N.Y.	Antioch, Calif.	Weimer, Texas

CONTINENTAL AMATEUR BASEBALL ASSOCIATION (CABA)

HEADQUARTERS: Westerville, Ohio

Event	Site	Champion	Runner-Up
9 & under	Charles City, Iowa	East Cobb (Marietta, Ga.)	Houston
10 & under	Aurelia, Iowa	Honolulu Rainbows	Claremore (Okla.) Cardinals
11 & under	Tarkio, Mo.	Bayamon, P.R.	Miami Dream Team
12 & under	Omaha, Neb.	Rosemead (Calif.) Red Sox	San Juan (P.R.) Mariners
13 & under	Broken Arrow, Okla.	Palos Park (Ill.) Cougars	Topeka (Kan.) Orioles
14 & under	Dublin, Ohio	West Covina (Calif.) Dukes	Dallas Tornados
15 & under	Crystal Lake, Ill.	Maryland Little Orioles	Pensacola, Fla.
16 & under	Arlington, Texas	East Cobb (Ga.) Stallions	Fort Worth Blackhawks
High school age	Cleveland, Ohio	Fairfax, Va.	Miami
18 & under	Homestead, Fla.	Bayside (N.Y.) Yankees	East Cobb (Ga.) White Sox
College age	Glen Ellyn, Ill.	Wheaton (Ill.) White Sox	Melrose Park (Ill.) Indians
Unlimited age	Eau Claire, Wis.	Eau Claire, Wis.	Chicago Badgers

DIXIE BASEBALL

HEADQUARTERS: Montgomery, Ala.

Event	Site	Champion	Runner-Up
Youth (13 & under)	Bossier City, La.	Gonzales, La.	Phenix City, Ala.
Boys (13-14)	Covington, Ga.	Hartsville, S.C.	Bossier City, La.
Pre-Majors (15-16)	Enterprise, Ala.	Valdosta, Ga.	Bossier City, La.
Majors (15-18)	Lufkin, Texas	Montgomery, Ala.	Petal, Miss.

AMATEUR/YOUTH CHAMPIONS 1997

DIZZY DEAN BASEBALL

HEADQUARTERS: Hixson, Tenn.

Minor (9-10)	Athens, Tenn.	Baltimore	Meridian, Miss.
Freshman (11-12)	Eastridge, Tenn.	Baltimore	Slidell, La.
Sophomore (13-14)	Baton Rouge, La.	Pace, Fla.	Paris, Tenn.
Junior (15-16)	Boynton, Ga.	Mountain Brook, Ala.	Lynn Haven, Fla.
Senior (17-18)	Boynton, Ga.	Cincinnati	Boynton, Ga.

HAP DUMONT BASEBALL

HEADQUARTERS: Wichita

10 & under	Houston, Texas	Houston Indians	Southlake (Texas) Stars
11 & under	Harrison, Ark.	Texas Patriots (Houston)	Oklahoma Redhawks
12 & under	Casper, Wyom.	Edmond (Okla.) Bearcats	Jackson (Miss.) Diamondbacks
13 & under	Norman, Okla.	Kingwood (Texas) Sluggers	Topeka (Kan.) Jayhawks
14 & under	Harrison, Ark.	Tulsa Titans	Ohio Reds
16 & under	Brainerd, Minn.	Saddleridge (Mo.) Braves	League City (Texas) Aggies

LITTLE LEAGUE BASEBALL

HEADQUARTERS: Williamsport, Pa.

Little League (11-12)	Williamsport, Pa.	Guadalupe, Mexico	Mission Viejo, Calif.
Junior League (13)	Taylor, Mich.	Salem, N.H.	North Mission Viejo, Calif.
Senior League (13-15)	Kissimmee, Fla.	San Francisco, Venez.	Yucaipa, Calif.
Big League (16-18)	Fort Lauderdale, Fla.	Broward County, Fla.	Maracaibo, Venez.

NATIONAL AMATEUR BASEBALL FEDERATION (NABF)

HEADQUARTERS: Bowie, Md.

Freshman (12 & under)	Sylvania, Ohio	East Cobb (Ga.) Rangers	Oakland (Mich.) Sox
Sophomore (14 & under)	Miamisburg, Ohio	Oklahoma Sooners	Maryland Orioles
Junior (16 & under)	Northville, Mich.	Bayside (N.Y.) Yankees	East Cobb (Ga.) Rangers
High School	Hopkinsville, Ky.	Indiana Bulls	Suffolk County (N.Y.)
Senior (18 & under)	Evansville, Ind.	Bill Hood (La.)	Enon (Ohio) Warhawks
College (22 & under)	Rome, Ga.	Miami Valley (Ohio) Bulldogs	Mount Airy (Md.) Sharks
Major (open)	Louisville, Ky.	Troy (Mich.) Jetbox	Fairfield (Conn.) Sounders

POLICE ATHLETIC LEAGUE (PAL)

HEADQUARTERS: North Palm Beach, Fla.

16 & under	Niagara Falls, N.Y.	Metro Dade, Fla.	Lakeland, Fla.

PONY BASEBALL

HEADQUARTERS: Washington, Pa.

Mustang (9-10)	Irving, Texas	Houston Spring-Klein	San Diego North City
Bronco (11-12)	Monterey, Calif.	West Covina, Calif.	Tampa Forest Hills
Pony (13-14)	Washington, Pa.	Danville, Calif.	Hamilton, Ohio
Colt (15-16)	Lafayette, Ind.	Lutcher, La.	Levittown, P.R.
Palomino (17-18)	Greensboro, N.C.	Sylmar, Calif.	Carolina, P.R.

REVIVING BASEBALL IN INNERCITIES (RBI)

HEADQUARTERS: New York

Junior (13-15)	Denver	Miami	San Juan, P.R.
Senior (16-18)	Denver	San Juan, P.R.	Chicago

the 11th round by the Los Angeles Dodgers but chose to attend Georgia Tech.

The first USA Baseball-sanctioned youth (16 and under) national team finished fifth at the World Youth Championships in Chinese Tapiei. Cuba edged the host country, 5-4, in the gold-medal game.

Up In Arms

Fresno State righthander Jeff Weaver, who pitched impressively for Team USA in the 1996 Olympics, was the only Olympian to play for Team USA in 1997. A draft-eligible sophomore, Weaver was a second-round selection of the Chicago White Sox in the '97 draft and wasn't expected to be available for Team USA.

Jeff Weaver

Instead, Weaver and the White Sox never got together on a contract. Weaver pitched in the Cape Cod League to stay sharp for most of the summer before joining Team USA in Spain.

Weaver went 4-1 with a 1.31 ERA for Falmouth on the Cape, but Bourne lefthander Mark Mulder (Michigan State) graded out as that league's best professional prospect. Mulder went 5-2 with a 1.47 ERA.

Aside from Mulder, who throws in the low 90s with a solid four-pitch repertoire, Bourne also featured lefthander Chris Heck (St. Joseph's) and righthander Brian Rogers (The Citadel). All three are expected to be high-round picks in the 1998 draft.

Wareham beat Bourne in the Western Division playoffs and swept to the Cape Cod League title behind the slugging exploits of first baseman Carlos Pena (Northeastern), the league MVP. Pena, a Dominican native, led the league in home runs and RBIs.

Mining NBC Gold

The Mat-Su Miners became the 13th Alaska team in

Golden Spikes Award

Florida State's Drew meets lofty expectations

It's rare that a player can live up to expectations as well as Florida State's J.D. Drew, who earned the 1997 Golden Spikes Award, emblematic of excellence in amateur baseball.

Heralded as the nation's top player entering the season, the 6-foot-1, 195-pound outfielder did not disappoint in any way. He became the first player in college history to reach the 30-home run, 30-stolen base plateau. The Atlantic Coast Conference player of the year set or tied eight ACC and nine school records.

He had a 34-game hitting streak. He drew 84 walks while striking out 37 times. He dominated.

"I've never seen anybody have a better year than J.D. Drew had," Florida State coach Mike Martin said when it was over. "Consistency is paramount, and this is a guy who hits .455, scores 110 runs. That's mind-boggling to go with 100 RBIs, 31 home runs and 32 steals. That's something that may not ever really happen again."

Drew's postseason didn't hold as much success. Florida State failed to reach the College World Series for the first time in his three years and he was selected second overall in the June draft by the Philadelphia Phillies, but was embroiled in a contract dispute and had not signed by Nov. 1. He spent his summer playing for the St. Paul Saints of the independent Northern League.

Drew beat out eight other finalists, including Rice righthander Matt Anderson and first baseman Lance Berkman, Miami third baseman Pat Burrell, UCLA infielder Troy Glaus, Auburn righthander/outfielder Tim Hudson, Louisiana State shortstop Brandon Larson, Alabama outfielder/lefthander Roberto Vaz and Fresno State righthander Jeff Weaver.

Fort Pierce, Fla., lefthander Rick Ankiel, who signed for a draft-record $2.5 million bonus with the St. Louis Cardinals, topped off his 1997 season by being named USA Baseball's Junior Player of the Year.

Ankiel went 11-1 with a 0.46 ERA and 162 strikeouts in 74 innings at Port St. Lucie High, then led USA Baseball's junior national team to a bronze medal at the World Championships in Canada.

Ankiel tossed nine no-hitters during the high school season, then went 3-0 with a 1.82 ERA for Team USA.

ROBERT GURGANUS

J.D. Drew

PREVIOUS WINNERS

1978—Bob Horner, 3b, Arizona State
1979—Tim Wallach, 1b, Cal State Fullerton
1980—Terry Francona, of, Arizona
1981—Mike Fuentes, of, Florida State
1982—Augie Schmidt, ss, New Orleans
1983—Dave Magadan, 1b, Alabama
1984—Oddibe McDowell, of, Arizona State
1985—Will Clark, 1b, Mississippi State
1986—Mike Loynd, rhp, Florida State
1987—Jim Abbott, lhp, Michigan
1988—Robin Ventura, 3b, Oklahoma State
1989—Ben McDonald, rhp, Louisiana State
1990—Alex Fernandez, rhp, Miami-Dade CC South
1991—Mike Kelly, of, Arizona State
1992—Phil Nevin, 3b, Cal State Fullerton
1993—Darren Dreifort, rhp-dh, Wichita State
1994—Jason Varitek, c, Georgia Tech
1995—Mark Kotsay, of-lhp, Cal State Fullerton
1996—Travis Lee, 1b, San Diego State

28 years to win the annual National Baseball Congress World Series in Wichita. The Miners, who previously won the title in 1987, defeated the Jayhawk League's Nevada (Mo.) Griffons in the final, 10-9 in 10 innings.

Mat-Su had trailed by five runs in the game before rallying. The Miners won in the 10th when Mike Cervenak, who had tripled, scored on a single by University of Michigan teammate Derek Besco. Besco, whose twin brother played for Nevada, went 3-for-5 with two RBIs. It was the first time the twins had ever played against each other.

First baseman Ryan Soules (Washington) wasn't selected in the 1997 draft. With that as motivation, Soules emerged as the top player in the Alaska summer college leagues.

Soules, playing for the Alaska Goldpanners, hit .391 with 18 homers and 69 RBIs and was voted the Alaska player of the year.

South Of The Border

Forty years to the day after Mexico became the first international team to win the Little League (11-12) World Series, a team from Guadalupe, Mexico staged a stirring last-inning rally to beat Mission Viejo, Calif., 5-4 in the 1997 final.

Down 4-1 in the bottom of the sixth, the Mexicans rallied for four runs. Gabriel Alvarez' three-run homer broke up a no-hitter and tied the game. Three hitters later, Javier de Isla, who had walked, scored on Pablo Torres' single and center fielder Ashton White's error.

Traditional Little League power Chinese Taipei elected not to participate in Little League competition in 1997, citing the organization's stringent eligibility rules. Chinese Taipei had won 12 of the previous 23 championships, including four times in the 1990s.

Player Of The Year

Pitchers try to avoid Burrell

Third baseman Pat Burrell took his reputation as the most feared amateur hitter in the United States on the road in the summer of 1997.

As the defending NCAA batting champion, Burrell drew 83 walks in 67 games during the spring for the University of Miami while hitting .409 with 21 home runs.

Internationally, he was no less imposing. As the No. 3 hitter in the lineup for Team USA, Burrell drew 44 more walks in 33 games, giving him a combined 127 in 100 games for the year.

Pitchers from Cuba, Japan, Chinese Taipei and other international powers pitched around him often, but Burrell still hit .343 and led Team USA in both home runs (12) and RBIs (42) by wide margins. That led to his selection as Baseball America's 1997 Summer Player of the Year.

"Pat was our best hitter all summer," said Bob Milano, who coached Team USA to a fourth-place finish at the Intercontinental Cup in Spain. "Without him, we have an average or below-average year."

Burrell, 20, led Team USA to a 21-13 record. The powerful righthanded hitter joins a long list of future big leaguers who have won the award. His main competition came from Team USA teammates and players from the prestigious Cape Cod and Alaska summer college leagues.

Only players with college eligibility remaining are eligible for selection.

The complete Summer All-America first team:

C—Eric Munson, Team USA (Southern California), .393-6-28.

1B—Carlos Pena, Wareham, Cape Cod (Northeastern), .318-8-33. **2B**—Jason McConnell, Yarmouth-Dennis, Cape Cod (Arkansas), .345-0-9. **3B**—Pat Burrell, Team USA (Miami), .343-12-42. **SS**—Adam Everett, Team USA (South Carolina), .351-0-11.

OF—Bubba Crosby, Team USA (Rice), .322-8-28; Ryan Ludwick, Anchorage Glacier Pilots, Alaska Central (Nevada-Las Vegas), .372-22-60; Eric Valent, Team USA (UCLA), .345-7-34.

DH—Ryan Soules, Goldpanners, Alaska (Washington), .391-18-69. **Util**—Brian Wiese, Danville, Central Illinois (Mississippi State), .349-7-35; 2-0, 0.46, 6 Sv.

P—Jeff Austin, Team USA (Stanford), 4-1, 3.63; Brent Hoard, Harwich, Cape Cod (Stanford), 2-1, 0.72; Mark Mulder, Bourne, Cape Cod (Michigan State), 5-2, 1.47; Monty Ward, Team USA (Texas Tech), 3-0, 2.55; Jeff Weaver, Team USA/Falmouth, Cape Cod (Fresno State) 4-2, 1.72.

PREVIOUS WINNERS

1984—Will Clark, 1b, Team USA
Rafael Palmeiro, of, Hutchinson (Jayhawk)
1985—Jeff King, 3b, Team USA
Bob Zupcic, of, Liberal (Jayhawk)
1986—Jack Armstrong, rhp, Wareham (Cape Cod)
Mike Harkey, rhp, Fairbanks (Alaska)
1987—Cris Carpenter, rhp, Team USA
1988—Ty Griffin, 2b, Team USA
Robin Ventura, 3b, Team USA
1989—John Olerud, 1b-lhp, Palouse (Alaska)
1990—Calvin Murray, of, Anchorage Bucs (Alaska)
1991—Chris Roberts, of, Team USA
1992—Jeffrey Hammonds, of, Team USA
1993—Geoff Jenkins, of, Anchorage Bucs (Alaska)
1994—Steve Carver, 1b, Anchorage Glacier Pilots (Alaska)
1995—Travis Lee, 1b, Team USA
1996—Seth Greisinger, rhp, Team USA

COLLEGE SUMMER LEAGUES

NCAA-CERTIFIED

ATLANTIC COLLEGIATE LEAGUE

	W	L	PCT	GB
Quakertown Blazers	28	8	.778	—
Nassau Collegians	22	14	.611	6
Jersey Pilots	21	15	.583	7
Scranton/Wilkes-Barre Twins	20	16	.556	8
Metro New York Cadets	17	19	.472	11
Sussex Colonels	10	26	.278	18
West Deptford Storm	8	28	.222	20

PLAYOFFS: Jersey defeated Nassau 2-1 and Quakertown defeated Scranton/Wilkes-Barre 2-0 in best-of-3 semifinals. Jersey defeated Quakertown in a one-game final.

INDIVIDUAL BATTING LEADERS

(Minimum 100 Plate Appearances)

	AVG	AB	R	H	2B	3B	HR	RBI	SB
O'Brien, Michael, Jersey	.350	123	20	43	6	3	1	25	4
Villacres, Gary, Metro NY	.344	90	17	31	3	4	1	20	10
Domzalski, Jim, Scranton	.343	105	18	36	5	1	1	13	10
Sands, Dustin, Quakertown	.339	124	33	42	10	4	1	20	15
Goodwin, Luke, West Dept.	.330	103	11	34	4	0	1	11	7
Davies, Justin, Nassau	.328	119	36	39	3	1	1	12	25
Battista, Frank, Metro NY	.327	113	15	37	4	0	0	16	8
Karpell, Jeff, Jersey	.323	130	25	42	7	2	0	19	8
Grove, Augie, Quakertown	.322	121	22	39	12	3	1	33	0
Clark, Scott, Scranton	.320	100	19	32	8	1	1	19	10

INDIVIDUAL PITCHING LEADERS

(Minimum 35 Innings)

	W	L	ERA	G	SV	IP	H	BB	SO
Longo, Neil, Nassau	5	1	1.11	11	3	49	32	11	43
Olore, Kevin, Quakertown	1	1	1.64	13	5	44	36	19	43
Schroeder, Steve, Jersey	2	1	1.67	10	1	38	34	14	21
Schappi, Doug, Nassau	6	0	1.76	10	1	51	38	24	27
Esslinger, Cam, Jersey	3	2	1.81	13	2	40	20	17	63

CAPE COD LEAGUE

EAST	W	L	T	PCT	PTS
Harwich Mariners	22	22	0	.500	44
Chatham A's	22	22	0	.500	44
Brewster Whitecaps	22	22	0	.500	44
Yarmouth-Dennis Red Sox	19	25	0	.432	38
Orleans Cardinals	15	29	0	.341	30
WEST	**W**	**L**	**T**	**PCT**	**PTS**
Wareham Gatemen	28	16	0	.636	56
Bourne Braves	25	17	2	.595	52
Falmouth Commodores	24	20	0	.545	48
Cotuit Kettleers	21	21	2	.500	44
Hyannis Mets	19	23	2	.452	40

PLAYOFFS: Wareham defeated Bourne 2-0 and Harwich defeated Chatham 2-0 in best-of-3 semifinals. Wareham defeated Harwich 2-0 in best-of-3 final.

ALL-STAR TEAM: C—Jeff Wagner, Harwich (Notre Dame). **1B**—Carlos Pena, Wareham (Northeastern). **2B**—Jason McConnell, Yarmouth-Dennis (Arkansas). **3B**—Kevin Hodge, Wareham (Blinn, Texas, JC). **SS**—Brandon Inge, Bourne (Virginia Commonwealth). **OF**—Jody Gerut, Harwich (Stanford); Edmund Muth, Yarmouth-Dennis (Stanford); Jake Weber, Orleans (North Carolina State). **Util**—Rob Gorr, Brewster (Southern California). **SP**—Brent Hoard, Harwich (Stanford); Mark Mulder, Bourne (Michigan State); Bart Miadich, Cotuit (San Diego); Jeff Weaver, Falmouth (Fresno State). **RP**—Chris Aronson, Cotuit (George Mason).

Most Valuable Player: Carlos Pena, Wareham. **Pitcher of the Year:** Brent Hoard, Harwich.

KEN BABBITT

Out of nowhere

Northeastern's Carlos Pena emerged as Cape MVP

INDIVIDUAL BATTING LEADERS

(Minimum 119 Plate Appearances)

	AVG	AB	R	H	2B	3B	HR	RBI	SB
McConnell, Jason, Y-D	.345	145	29	50	4	3	0	9	19
Gerut, Jody, Harwich	.328	122	19	40	6	0	2	21	23
Pena, Carlos, Wareham	.318	154	25	49	9	1	8	33	8
Weber, Jake, Orleans	.318	151	31	48	9	1	6	23	22
Ross, Justin, Harwich	.307	140	28	43	12	1	1	19	13
Wagner, Jeff, Harwich	.295	132	8	39	6	0	2	19	1
Gorr, Robb, Brewster	.294	170	17	50	12	0	2	18	22
Waldren, Jeff, Falmouth	.294	119	14	35	5	0	3	18	2S
Ralph, Brian, Falmouth	.286	161	35	46	8	2	1	12	12
Johnson, Erik, Orleans	.286	147	9	42	7	1	4	20	3
Scheschuk, John, Cotuit	.283	152	21	43	4	0	7	27	2
Sledge, Terrmel, Brewster	.281	135	18	38	3	5	1	15	10
Mahoney, Sean, Chatham	.281	146	16	41	4	0	5	15	3
Muth, Edmund, Y-D	.280	157	35	44	8	2	6	28	20
Schrager, Tony, Y-D	.273	139	19	38	7	3	1	14	7
Mackiewitz, Mac, Bourne	.272	136	13	37	8	1	2	16	3
Trott, Jason, Harwich	.267	120	16	32	9	0	2	8	2
Fry, Ryan, Yar.-Dennis	.266	158	20	42	14	0	0	19	5
Inge, Brandon, Bourne	.265	151	22	40	14	0	5	19	9
Edgar, Jason, Falmouth	.264	140	16	37	6	1	3	16	4
Forbush, Nate, Falmouth	.264	125	15	33	8	0	3	15	1
Riggs, Eric, Bourne	.263	156	16	41	10	2	0	12	5
Quinlan, Robb, Cotuit	.262	145	15	38	9	0	2	23	3
Hankins, Ryan, Orleans	.262	126	14	33	10	0	1	16	2
Gall, John, Orleans	.261	138	15	36	7	0	1	14	7
Holst, Micah, Chatham	.254	114	19	29	5	1	1	7	7
Cortez, Sonny, Harwich	.254	130	13	33	11	1	3	23	2
Saggese, Rick, Hyannis	.253	146	14	37	11	1	2	20	2
Bush, Brian, Falmouth	.252	143	14	36	5	0	0	10	3
Ryan, Greg, Y-D	.250	140	17	35	4	1	0	9	3
Alcaraz, Jason, Y-D	.250	132	25	33	4	3	2	18	0
French, Ned, Wareham	.248	145	18	36	3	2	2	19	21
Tyson, Torre, Falmouth	.248	145	25	36	4	0	0	13	14
Bounds, Drew, Brewster	.247	154	21	38	5	1	5	20	12
Hart, Jason, Chatham	.246	138	11	34	5	0	1	16	1
Day, Nick, Cotuit	.243	107	18	26	4	0	1	14	4
Rowand, Aaron, Brewster	.242	161	23	39	7	2	7	29	8
Inglett, Joe, Chatham	.241	112	18	27	8	0	1	14	2

INDIVIDUAL PITCHING LEADERS

(Minimum 35 Innings)

	W	L	ERA	G	SV	IP	H	BB	SO
Hoard, Brent, Harwich	2	1	0.72	7	0	50	29	12	47
Penney, Mike, Chatham	4	5	1.24	11	1	72	42	26	61
Weaver, Jeff, Falmouth	4	1	1.31	8	1	48	25	7	53
Ralston, Brad, Hyannis	3	1	1.42	19	3	44	34	21	63
Miadich, Bart, Cotuit	5	2	1.44	10	0	75	48	32	89
Mulder, Mark, Bourne	5	2	1.47	15	1	73	48	11	64
Proctor, Scott, Hyannis	3	3	1.54	8	0	53	34	24	53
Noyce, David, Wareham	4	3	1.68	8	0	54	33	9	38
Fisher, Peter, Chatham	2	2	1.76	5	0	41	25	5	35
Bynum, Mike, Hyannis	4	4	1.78	10	0	76	48	34	75
Stine, Justin, Wareham	3	2	1.79	16	2	50	35	14	27
Santos, Alex, Hyannis	3	1	1.88	10	0	72	50	18	79
Wells, Kip, Brewster	5	6	1.92	14	0	52	36	14	49
Harber, Ryan, Wareham	2	3	1.99	13	1	41	37	21	48
Agamennone, Brandon, Ware	5	1	2.02	10	0	49	43	11	42
Bauer, Greg, Falmouth	3	3	2.06	19	8	35	19	21	33
White, Matt, Chatham	6	2	2.11	10	0	68	56	34	54
MacDougal, Mike, Cotuit	2	3	2.22	9	0	57	41	17	57
Keller, Dan, Orleans	3	2	2.31	8	0	51	46	14	40
Zito, Barry, Wareham	3	2	2.31	9	0	58	41	25	57
Burch, Matt, Bourne	2	3	2.49	11	2	51	37	32	45
Rogers, Brian, Bourne	3	3	2.54	12	0	74	60	26	81
Graham, Tom, Hyannis	1	5	2.61	7	0	48	44	11	37
Duckworth, Brandon, Brew	2	2	2.75	18	6	39	26	10	41
Balazentis, Bob, Harwich	3	1	2.76	6	0	42	29	11	28
Bobbitt, Josh, Cotuit	5	2	2.77	10	0	68	58	21	41
Rushing, Don, Y-D	5	3	2.78	11	0	65	40	38	83
Bess, Stephen, Orleans	3	5	2.93	11	0	61	47	24	61
Davidson, Chris, Orleans	2	4	2.95	11	1	58	45	16	51

CENTRAL ILLINOIS LEAGUE

FIRST	W	L	PCT	GB
Quincy	13	7	.650	—
Danville	11	7	.611	1
Springfield	8	10	.444	4
Twin City	8	10	.444	4
Decatur	6	12	.333	6

SECOND	W	L	PCT	GB
Danville	16	5	.762	—
Quincy	14	6	.700	1½
Springfield	11	11	.500	5½
Twin City	9	13	.409	7½
Decatur	3	18	.143	13

PLAYOFF TOURNAMENT: Danville 2-0, Quincy 1-1, Decatur 1-1, Springfield 0-1, Twin City 0-1.

ALL-STAR TEAM: C—Justin Beasley, Danville (Butler); Trey McClure, Danville (Louisiana State). **1B**—Jim Egan, Springfield (Minnesota); Les Graham, Quincy (Butler County, Kan., CC). **2B**—Joe Carlon, Twin City (Penn). **3B**—Blair Barbier, Danville (Louisiana State); Anthony Molina, Springfield (Evansville); Tyler Turnquist, Twin City (Illinois State). **SS**—Travis Chapman, Danville (Mississippi State). **OF**—Jeff Dunbar, Decatur (McKendree, Ill.); Scott Ellis, Quincy (Arkansas); Aaron Pembroke, Twin City (Evansville); Mike Pilger, Springfield (South Florida); Brian Weise, Danville (Mississippi State). **SP**—Chris Cabaj, Quincy (Ball State); Brian Laney, Danville (Indiana State); Tony Pena, Quincy (Lewis, Ill.); Chris Vaught, Danville (Bowling Green State); Tom Zidlicky, Quincy (Illinois). **RP**—J.T. Thomas, Quincy (Campbell); Brian Weise, Danville (Mississippi State).

Most Valuable Player: Travis Chapman, Danville. **Pitchers of the Year:** Brian Laney, Danville; Chris Vaught, Danville.

INDIVIDUAL BATTING LEADERS

(Minimum 106 Plate Appearances)

	AVG	AB	R	H	2B	3B	HR	RBI	SB
Chapman, Travis, Danville	.451	122	25	55	12	0	0	34	2
Graham, Les, Quincy	.361	155	23	56	11	0	5	35	5
Weise, Brian, Danville	.349	146	27	51	11	1	7	35	2
Pembroke, Aaron, TC	.342	152	30	52	5	1	1	9	10
Turnquist, Tyler, Twin City	.338	130	23	44	10	1	1	20	1
Dunbar, Jeff, Decatur	.336	119	22	40	6	3	1	15	4
Ellis, Scott, Quincy	.319	91	23	29	3	1	2	16	5
Egan, Jim, Springfield	.319	135	19	43	9	1	1	30	5
Barbier, Blair, Danville	.315	92	25	29	8	1	1	17	6
Molina, Anthony, Spring.	.304	148	17	45	8	2	3	20	7
Pilger, Mike, Springfield	.303	155	36	47	9	3	3	20	20
Nunn, Marc, Springfield	.297	128	11	38	9	2	0	20	2
McClure, Trey, Danville	.293	133	32	39	6	1	5	23	1
Beasley, Justin, Danville	.292	154	35	45	14	4	3	25	1
Koehlhoeffer, Aaron, TC	.291	158	18	46	8	0	2	30	0

INDIVIDUAL PITCHING LEADERS

(Minimum 40 Innings)

	W	L	ERA	G	SV	IP	H	BB	SO
Laney, Brian, Danville	7	0	1.46	11	1	62	42	20	50
Cabaj, Chris, Quincy	5	1	1.70	10	0	74	47	18	77
Pena, Tony, Quincy	4	1	1.86	13	3	48	45	17	26
Zidlicky, Tom, Quincy	6	3	2.02	11	0	76	63	20	53
Urban, Jeff, Quincy	2	2	2.04	11	1	57	54	12	49
Vaught, Chris, Danville	8	0	2.32	10	0	66	52	34	31
Wilderspin, Kirk, TC	3	3	2.65	8	0	68	53	33	47
Delatori, Keola, TC	4	4	2.71	9	0	63	53	48	68
Castelli, Bobby, Spring.	5	3	3.08	10	0	53	42	39	65
Winn, Matt, Springfield	1	3	3.17	9	1	48	47	28	32

GREAT LAKES LEAGUE

	W	L	PCT	GB
Grand Lake Mariners	30	10	.750	—
Columbus All-Americans	24	16	.600	6
Lima Locos	24	16	.600	6
Sandusky Bay Stars	18	22	.450	12
Central Ohio	16	24	.400	14
Lake County	8	32	.200	22

PLAYOFFS: Grand Lake defeated Sandusky 2-0 and Lima defeated Columbus 2-1 in best-of-3 semifinals. Grand Lake defeated Lima 2-0 in best-of-3 final.

ALL-STAR TEAM: C—Keith Carter, Lima (Vermont). **1B**—Dana Forsberg, Lima (Vermont). **2B**—Dominic Pattie, Columbus (UNC Greensboro). **3B**—Clint Fetzer, Grand Lake (Eastern Michigan). **SS**—Daryl Hallada, Grand Lake (Purdue). **OF**—Dan Seimetz, Columbus (Ohio State); Tyler Thompson, Grand Lake (Indiana State); Mark Tomsyck, Grand Lake (Purdue). **DH**—Roger Rodeheaver, Lima (Indiana). **P**—Matt Additon, Columbus (Clemson); Joe Cheney, Lima (Bowling Green); Tony Harden, Grand Lake (Indiana State); Jason Kelley, Grand Lake (Bowling Green).

Most Valuable Player: Keith Carter, Lima. **Pitcher of the Year:** Matt Additon, Columbus.

INDIVIDUAL BATTING LEADERS

(Minimum 100 Plate Appearances)

	AVG	AB	R	H	2B	3B	HR	RBI	SB
Seimetz, Dan, Columbus	.406	128	21	52	10	0	6	32	1
Spooner, Brent, LC	.378	127	11	48	7	0	2	24	0
Carter, Keith, Lima	.366	134	31	49	8	2	7	37	6
Tomsyk, Mark, Grand Lake	.365	104	24	38	7	3	3	15	22
Wazevich, Mark, LC	.359	103	22	37	9	1	0	8	5
Ludvigsen, Mark, Sandusky	.353	116	25	41	9	0	3	23	2
Weaver, Brent, Central Ohio	.346	81	12	28	4	0	0	10	0
Connors, Ryan, Lima	.344	122	25	42	7	1	1	25	7
Fetzer, Clint, Grand Lake	.337	86	16	29	11	0	0	14	7
Missler, Ryan, Columbus	.336	113	13	38	5	1	0	16	8

INDIVIDUAL PITCHING LEADERS

(Minimum 28 Innings)

	W	L	ERA	G	SV	IP	H	BB	SO
Kidd, Steven, Columbus	3	0	1.34	13	0	34	25	17	20
Harden, Tony, Grand Lake	6	0	1.60	7	0	45	37	11	32
Bernhardt, Mark, GL	5	1	1.67	11	1	43	43	10	25
Cummings, Jeremy, Lima	3	3	1.91	7	0	38	27	8	36
Murphy, Brian, Sandusky	3	2	2.25	7	0	44	30	9	38
Additon, Matt, Columbus	9	2	2.35	18	1	31	22	4	27
Header, Joe, Sandusky	5	1	2.47	11	1	51	47	22	53
Vogelmeyer, Phil, Columbus	2	3	2.56	10	0	39	31	10	24
Bay, Paul, Lake County	0	3	2.58	10	0	38	31	15	33
Yankosky, L.J., Columbus	2	0	2.70	7	1	37	29	14	35

NEW ENGLAND COLLEGIATE LEAGUE

	W	L	PCT	GB
Torrington Twisters	25	15	.625	—
Rhode Island Reds	22	18	.550	3
Middletown Giants	19	21	.475	6
Danbury Westerners	19	21	.475	6
Central Massachusetts Collegians	18	22	.450	7
Eastern Tides	17	23	.425	8

PLAYOFFS: Middletown defeated Rhode Island 2-0 and Torrington defeated Danbury 2-0 in best-of-3 semifinals. Middletown defeated Torrington 2-1 in best-of-3 final.

ALL-STAR TEAM: C—David Benham, Torrington (Liberty). **1B**—Jason Benham, Torrington (Liberty). **2B**—Jim Deschaine, Torrington (Brandeis) **3B**—Mike Dzurilla, Danbury (St John's). **SS**—David Forst, Torrington (Harvard). **OF**—Doug Clark, Middletown (Massachusetts); Alex Fernandez, Rhode Island (CC of Rhode Island); Peter Gautreau, Central Mass (Massachusetts). **DH**—Matt MacDonald, Rhode Island (Bowdoin, Mass.). **P**—Ryan Kearney, Torrington (Massachusetts-Lowell); Randy Leek, Danbury (William & Mary); Keith Surkont, Rhode Island (Williams, Mass.).

Most Valuable Player: David Benham, Torrington. **Pitcher of the Year:** Ryan Kearney, Torrington.

INDIVIDUAL BATTING LEADERS

(Minimum 108 Plate Appearances)

	AVG	AB	R	H	2B	3B	HR	RBI	SB
Deschaine, Jim, Torr.	.429	91	20	39	8	1	4	17	2
Marchetti, Lou, Eastern	.357	126	23	45	14	0	7	26	2
Dzurilla, Mike, Danbury	.355	110	29	39	8	1	5	23	12
Fernandez, Alex, RI	.342	114	16	39	9	0	3	24	2
Gautreau, Peter, CM	.323	133	27	43	5	2	5	23	19
Kidwell, Tom, Midd.	.319	113	17	36	3	1	3	21	1
Rikert, Wade, CM	.311	103	22	32	2	0	0	5	18
Benham, Jason, Torr.	.304	125	20	38	7	0	1	20	4
Sherrod, Justin, Torr.	.295	132	22	39	9	4	8	33	2
Gallaher, TT, Midd.	.293	140	28	41	6	2	1	12	24

INDIVIDUAL PITCHING LEADERS

(Minimum 32 Innings)

	W	L	ERA	G	SV	IP	H	BB	SO
Kearney, Ryan, Torrington	5	0	0.66	7	0	41	29	9	25
Cameron, Ryan, RI	5	1	1.66	19	7	38	21	18	52
Surkont, Keith, RI	5	2	1.93	9	1	56	45	11	42
Leek, Randy, Danbury	7	2	2.17	9	0	71	53	7	53
Berney, Scott, Middletown	5	5	2.17	10	0	62	60	26	37

NORTHEASTERN LEAGUE

EAST	W	L	PCT	GB
Utica Chiefs	29	13	.690	—
Little Falls Knickerbockers	25	17	.595	4
Schenectady Mohawks	23	19	.548	6
Rome Indians	15	27	.357	14
Binghamton Raptors	15	27	.357	14
WEST	**W**	**L**	**PCT**	**GB**
Ithaca Lakers	28	14	.667	—
Cortland Apples	24	18	.571	4
Geneva Knights	22	20	.524	6
Cohocton Red Wings	17	25	.405	11
Hornell Dodgers	12	30	.286	16

PLAYOFFS: Ithaca defeated Little Falls in sudden-death final.

INDIVIDUAL BATTING LEADERS

(Minimum 120 Plate Appearances)

	AVG	AB	R	H	2B	3B	HR	RBI	SB
Smalls, Terrance, Ithaca	.458	166	40	76	3	4	2	19	39
Lewis, Dave, Utica	.369	160	35	59	9	2	0	25	17
Rosamond, Mike, Ithaca	.357	157	24	56	6	5	5	29	14
Espy, Nate, Hornell	.345	142	15	49	13	3	2	36	0
Yaniszewski, Scott, Utica	.336	149	33	50	8	0	8	41	1
Schumaker, Shawn, LF	.336	149	27	50	6	1	2	21	8
Provines, Kip, Little Falls	.336	149	26	50	10	0	4	29	3
Constantino, Greg, Rome	.319	119	10	38	6	1	0	14	3
Whitby, Corey, Hornell	.315	130	40	41	4	3	1	12	23
Kazmarek, Robert, Cohocton	.311	103	21	32	4	1	2	15	5

INDIVIDUAL PITCHING LEADERS

(Minimum 45 Innings)

	W	L	ERA	G	SV	IP	H	BB	SO
Brand, Cliff, Little Falls	4	0	1.00	8	0	63	41	8	56
Mangrum, Micah, LF	5	2	1.07	9	0	59	52	23	54
Bearenger, Jared, Utica	7	0	1.76	8	0	46	32	6	39
Martinson, Dru, Hornell	4	3	1.84	7	0	54	32	13	34
Horney, Mike, Ithaca	5	1	2.12	8	0	51	37	25	55

NORTHWEST COLLEGIATE LEAGUE

FIRST	W	L	PCT	GB	SECOND	W	L	PCT	GB
Lobos	9	6	.600	—	Toros	12	6	.667	—
Ports	8	7	.533	1	Ports	9	6	.600	1½
Stars	8	7	.533	1	Dukes	8	6	.571	2
Bucks	7	7	.500	1½	Stars	8	7	.533	2½
Dukes	7	7	.500	1½	Lobos	7	11	.389	5
Toros	5	10	.333	4	Bucks	4	11	.267	6

PLAYOFFS: Lobos defeated Toros 2-1 in best-of-3 final.

INDIVIDUAL BATTING LEADERS

(Minimum 70 Plate Appearances)

	AVG	AB	R	H	2B	3B	HR	RBI	SB
Bertrand, Ben, Dukes	.475	61	17	29	7	0	3	17	1
Birley, Derek, Toros	.404	89	8	36	5	0	1	18	3
Meyer, Kevin, Ports	.390	82	24	32	8	2	0	18	15
Burnham, Jake, Bucks	.384	86	17	33	7	0	0	13	3
Rainwater, Travis, Lobos	.373	75	16	28	5	1	0	10	5
Beeler, Jeff, Bucks	.370	73	15	27	5	1	1	10	5
Maghan, Tim, Bucks	.370	92	20	34	5	0	0	16	2
Carlson, Scott, Ports	.366	82	22	30	7	1	0	17	25
Miller, Coy, Bucks	.364	77	10	28	3	0	0	8	9
Hollabaugh, Chad, Dukes	.354	65	14	23	5	0	2	19	3

INDIVIDUAL PITCHING LEADERS

(Minimum 25 Innings)

	W	L	ERA	G	SV	IP	H	BB	SO
Haij, Scott, Lobos	3	1	0.77	7	0	46	36	19	40
Faust, Ryan, Toros	6	3	1.50	11	0	65	49	20	48
Figueras, Torrey, Bucks	3	3	1.66	9	1	38	29	24	39
Romano, Kess, Stars	4	1	2.00	9	1	42	47	8	29
Westerholm, Jason, Stars	5	0	2.13	13	0	49	48	9	27

SAN DIEGO COLLEGIATE LEAGUE

FIRST HALF

AMERICAN	W	L	PCT	GB	NATIONAL	W	L	PCT	GB
Royals	11	4	.733	—	Cubs	8	5	.615	—
Indians	9	5	.643	1½	Mets	8	6	.571	½
Orioles	4	11	.267	7	Padres	2	11	.154	6

SECOND HALF

AMERICAN	W	L	PCT	GB	NATIONAL	W	L	PCT	GB
Royals	12	3	.800	—	Cubs	9	6	.600	—
Indians	8	7	.533	4	Mets	8	7	.533	1
Orioles	5	10	.333	7	Padres	3	12	.200	6

PLAYOFFS: Cubs defeated Mets in one-game semifinal. Cubs defeated Royals 2-1 in best-of-3 final.

INDIVIDUAL BATTING LEADERS

(Minimum 72 Plate Appearances)

	AVG	AB	R	H	2B	3B	HR	RBI	SB
Edmund, Max, Orioles	.458	83	15	38	4	1	1	21	1
Millwee, Matt, Royals	.457	81	26	37	4	2	1	21	2
Radwan, James, Royals	.424	85	16	36	6	1	2	23	0
Lopez, Oscar, Orioles	.405	79	17	32	3	0	0	11	3
Foulds, Kalin, Indians	.400	90	27	36	2	2	0	4	25
Olow, Adam, Mets	.379	66	17	25	4	4	0	12	8
Ramos, Javier, Padres	.375	72	16	27	0	0	0	6	2
Walker, Joel, Padres	.359	78	11	28	12	1	0	17	1
Sturgeon, Nolan, Mets	.357	84	15	30	3	2	0	18	4
States, Jason, Padres	.353	68	18	24	8	1	3	14	4

INDIVIDUAL PITCHING LEADERS

(Minimum 30 Innings)

	W	L	ERA	G	SV	IP	H	BB	SO
Lontayo, Alex, Indians	5	0	0.65	10	1	43	26	12	51
Burke, Kevin, Royals	1	1	1.12	20	7	31	25	14	40
Brown, Danny, Royals	5	2	1.70	10	0	37	36	18	31
Giese, Dan, Cubs	3	1	2.38	8	0	35	36	12	33
Rohn, Grady, Cubs	5	1	2.63	7	0	40	45	13	37

SHENANDOAH VALLEY LEAGUE

	W	L	PCT	GB
Staunton Braves	26	14	.650	—
New Market Rebels	23	17	.575	3
Winchester Royals	22	18	.550	4
Front Royal Cardinals	20	20	.500	6
Waynesboro Generals	16	24	.400	10
Harrisonburg Turks	13	27	.325	13

PLAYOFFS: BRACKET A—Winchester 4-2, Staunton 2-3, Waynesboro 2-3. BRACKET B—Front Royal 3-1, New Market 2-2, Harrisonburg 1-3. Winchester declared champion on basis of forfeit over Front Royal.

INDIVIDUAL BATTING LEADERS

(Minimum 100 Plate Appearances)

	AVG	AB	R	H	2B	3B	HR	RBI	SB
Rewers, Nate, Front Royal	.384	125	24	48	3	1	0	16	7
Rhodes, Dusty, Harr.	.361	166	24	60	9	4	1	22	11
Urquhart, Derick, Win.	.357	182	38	65	14	2	0	23	17
Anderson, E. J., Wayne.	.353	85	12	30	6	2	4	16	2
Salargo, Steve, Staunton	.340	153	26	52	6	5	1	25	13
Bronowicz, Scott, NM	.335	161	29	54	9	3	3	22	5
Sherlock, Brian, Staunton	.333	168	31	56	13	0	4	31	3
Pierre, Juan, Harr.	.332	187	45	62	9	3	1	17	40
Huff, Aubrey, Staunton	.330	100	23	33	8	0	10	32	4
Roper, Zack, Waynesboro	.327	168	28	55	12	0	1	18	7
Anthony, Jake, Harrisonburg	.327	107	21	35	7	1	3	20	1
McDonald, Bobby, Win.	.326	135	21	44	10	0	3	18	1
Dina, Allen, New Market	.322	146	27	47	3	4	4	23	12
Bush, Ron, New Market	.315	184	33	58	8	4	3	25	14
Deike, Mike, Wicchester	.309	162	33	50	9	1	8	26	7

INDIVIDUAL PITCHING LEADERS

(Minimum 30 Innings)

	W	L	ERA	G	SV	IP	H	BB	SO
Cisar, Mark, New Market	4	2	0.54	7	0	50	27	21	43
Rivera, Saul, New Market	4	1	0.69	5	0	39	17	14	52
Schmitt, Eric, Staunton	1	2	1.88	13	1	38	31	18	37
Zeckman, Dan, Waynesboro	5	2	2.39	12	0	87	85	22	66
Clark, Mark, Winchester	2	2	2.43	8	0	33	24	20	34
Brantley, Brian, Winchester	8	1	2.47	13	0	87	77	34	102
Kennedy, Casey, Staunton	8	3	2.48	12	0	69	65	10	58
Parsons, Jason, New Market	4	2	2.79	10	1	58	55	16	43
Spassoff, Darin, New Market	3	1	2.87	6	0	38	38	10	30
Easler, Travis, Waynesboro	1	3	2.90	7	0	31	28	16	29

NON-AFFILIATED LEAGUES

ALASKA LEAGUES

	League				Overall	
ALASKA	W	L	PCT	GB	W	L
Hawaii Island Movers	9	7	.563	—	—	—
Alaska Goldpanners	8	8	.500	1	38	18
Anchorage Bucs	7	9	.437	2	33	18

	League				Overall	
ALASKA CENTRAL	W	L	PCT	GB	W	L
Anchorage Glacier Pilots	25	16	.609	—	26	16
Kenai Peninsula Oilers	24	16	.600	½	29	18
Mat-Su Miners	24	17	.585	1	31	18

ALL-ALASKA TEAM: C—John Salter, Mat-Su (Stanford). **1B**—Ryan Soules, Goldpanners (Washington). **2B**—Royce Huffman, Bucs (Texas Christian). **3B**—Mike Cervenak, Mat-Su (Michigan). **SS**—J.J. Brock, Goldpanners (Notre Dame). **OF**—Darren Blakely, Goldpanners (Hawaii); Ryan Ludwick, Glacier Pilots (Nevada-Las Vegas); Brad Ticehurst, Bucs (Southern California). **DH**—Casey Bookout, Kenai (Oklahoma). **Util**—Jason Lane, Goldpanners (Southern California). **P**—Marc Bluma, Glacier Pilots (Wichita State); Craig Jones, Goldpanners (Southern California); Alex Shilliday, Kenai (Notre Dame); Jeremy Ward, Mat-Su (Wake Forest).

Player of the Year: Ryan Soules, Goldpanners.

INDIVIDUAL BATTING LEADERS

(Minimum 100 Plate Appearances)

	AVG	AB	R	H	2B	3B	HR	RBI	SB
Huffman, Royce, Bucs	.435	92	24	40	8	2	5	30	4
Mott, Bill, Bucs	.416	166	58	69	15	3	5	33	26
Ticehurst, Brad, Bucs	.415	171	65	71	14	3	15	68	36
Cervenak, Mike, Mat-Su	.398	226	69	90	16	4	10	43	10
Soules, Ryan, Alaska	.391	184	58	72	14	0	18	69	3
Mora, Adrian, Alaska	.386	88	19	34	8	1	0	11	5
Bookout, Casey, Kenai	.382	170	38	65	18	0	11	73	0
Ludwick, Ryan, Pilots	.375	160	44	60	14	0	19	53	3
Oder, Josh, Mat-Su	.357	196	49	70	14	0	5	43	15
Lane, Jason, Alaska	.355	200	54	71	13	3	11	47	4
Circuit, Chris, Mat-Su	.353	187	46	66	9	2	6	37	3
Brock, J.J., Alaska	.346	211	47	73	12	1	6	57	18
Riordan, Matt, Kenai	.346	185	43	64	14	1	3	24	11
Owens, Jeremy, Pilots	.345	142	49	49	8	1	6	22	5
Porter, Colin, Pilots	.345	145	34	50	13	1	9	40	9
Blakely, Darren, Alaska	.344	195	59	67	11	2	6	41	47
Beinbrink, Andrew, Bucs	.341	170	42	58	12	4	10	48	9
Walters, Bobby, Bucs	.339	165	36	56	11	4	5	28	17
Gamoll, Justin, Alaska	.333	183	60	61	15	1	5	34	8
Giles, Danny, Pilots	.327	156	30	51	7	0	5	23	1
Besco, Derek, Mat-Su	.325	194	47	63	21	3	7	46	10
Corley, Kenny, Bucs	.320	169	42	54	7	1	13	43	13
Depippo, Jeff, Mat-Su	.319	160	40	51	17	3	3	27	10
Pursell, Mike, Mat-Su	.317	142	29	45	6	1	5	29	2
Pico, Rory, Alaska	.308	107	28	33	6	1	0	11	4
Salter, John, Mat-Su	.308	172	31	53	11	0	6	48	4

INDIVIDUAL PITCHING LEADERS

(Minimum 32 Innings)

	W	L	ERA	G	SV	IP	H	BB	SO
Ward, Jeremy, Mat-Su	7	1	2.39	15	2	79	69	33	63
Jones, Craig, Alaska	8	3	2.43	13	0	78	68	30	64
Nichols, Jeff, Kenai	5	1	2.78	7	0	45	43	16	21
Shilliday, Alex, Kenai	9	0	2.82	12	0	83	75	20	70
Ho, Randon, Alaska	3	0	2.91	10	1	34	28	9	27
Krawczyk, Jack, Bucs	2	4	3.12	28	9	49	47	10	46
Ramos, Mario, Kenai	5	3	3.32	11	0	62	61	21	48

	W	L	ERA	G	SV	IP	H	BB	SO
Freeman, Wesley, Bucs	6	2	3.96	13	0	52	50	23	44
Thompson, Shawn, Bucs	6	0	4.01	12	0	65	59	22	49
Hendricks, John, Mat-Su	6	2	4.54	14	0	75	91	28	65
Wells, Jason, Pilots	4	1	4.63	9	0	47	52	23	39

CLARK GRIFFITH COLLEGIATE LEAGUE

FIRST	W	L	PCT	GB
Pr. Will.	15	5	.750	—
Arlington	13	7	.650	2
Reston	11	9	.550	4
Herndon	8	12	.400	7
S. Maryland	3	17	.150	12

SECOND	W	L	PCT	GB
Pr. Will.	17	3	.850	—
Arlington	15	4	.789	1½
Reston	7	12	.368	9½
S. Maryland	7	13	.350	10
Herndon	3	17	.150	14

PLAYOFFS: Prince William defeated Arlington in one-game final.

INDIVIDUAL BATTING LEADERS

(Minimum 85 At-Bats)

	AVG	AB	R	H	2B	3B	HR	RBI	SB
Turner, Jason, Arlington	.388	103	16	40	6	1	1	18	6
Magness, Pat, PW	.373	118	29	44	9	0	3	26	2
Guyton, Eric, PW	.328	125	30	41	10	4	4	32	2
Reynolds, Dusty, Arlington	.324	105	18	34	6	1	0	12	3
Kemmerer, Jon, Reston	.317	120	24	38	1	2	0	15	14
Huling, Andrew, Reston	.313	96	19	30	3	0	0	6	10
Crandell, Scott, SM	.308	120	14	37	9	1	1	14	1
Schoenhofer, Brian, PW	.306	111	31	34	8	3	1	17	8
Lambert, Tim, PW	.305	105	23	32	6	0	2	23	0
Hendricks, Ian, Arlington	.303	99	26	30	6	0	3	18	9

INDIVIDUAL PITCHING LEADERS

(Minimum 40 Innings)

	W	L	ERA	G	SV	IP	H	BB	SO
Steller, Mike, Arlington	5	1	0.87	6	0	41	21	4	35
Graham, Bobby, PW	6	2	1.44	11	1	56	35	22	70
Mazur, Bryan, Arlington	9	2	1.86	12	0	68	46	17	69
Baker, Ryan, SM	2	4	2.04	8	0	40	33	14	30
Fleming, Sean, Reston	2	2	2.41	6	0	41	42	11	33

COASTAL PLAIN LEAGUE

FIRST	W	L	PCT	GB
Raleigh	15	10	.600	—
Durham	15	10	.600	—
Rocky Mt.	14	11	.560	1
Outer Banks	14	11	.560	1
Wilmington	11	14	.440	4
Wilson	6	19	.240	9

SECOND	W	L	PCT	GB
Wilson	14	11	.560	—
Raleigh	14	11	.560	—
Durham	13	12	.520	1
Rocky Mt.	12	13	.480	2
Outer Banks	11	14	.440	3
Wilmington	11	14	.440	3

PLAYOFFS: Raleigh defeated Wilson 2-0 in best-of-3 final.

ALL-STAR TEAM: C—Gregg Maluchnik, Raleigh (Duke). **1B**—John Anderson, Outer Banks (Appalachian State). **2B**—Jeremy Cook, Raleigh (Southern Indiana). **3B**—Jeff Becker, Durham (Duke). **SS**—Greg Jones, Raleigh (Central Michigan). **OF**—Michael Fletcher, Durham (Duke); Rod Hall, Raleigh (Barton); Adam Poe, Raleigh (South Carolina). **SP**—Kurt Blackmon, Raleigh (North Carolina State); Chad Holland, Raleigh (Mount Olive). **RP**—Jeff Randall, Raleigh (Ball State).

Most Valuable Player: Michael Fletcher, Durham. **Pitcher of the Year:** Kurt Blackmon, Raleigh.

INDIVIDUAL BATTING LEADERS

(Minimum 135 Plate Appearances)

	AVG	AB	R	H	2B	3B	HR	RBI	SB
Anderson, John, OB	.316	171	30	54	12	1	7	40	0
Jones, Greg, Raleigh	.311	183	27	57	10	1	1	24	3
Fletcher, Michael, Durham	.310	174	32	54	13	3	2	32	16
Bledsoe, Hunter, OB	.308	172	32	53	11	1	1	14	4
Cook, Jeremy, Raleigh	.306	196	31	60	8	1	0	27	8
Becker, Jeff, Durham	.306	157	22	48	10	0	1	19	7
Folz, Jason, Rocky Mount	.303	142	26	43	2	0	0	26	6
Hammond, Joseph, Wilson	.302	192	24	58	9	2	1	13	2
Chapman, Billy, Wilson	.299	147	19	44	9	2	2	21	4
Filson, Greg, Rocky Mount	.291	196	33	57	9	2	1	21	7

INDIVIDUAL PITCHING LEADERS

(Minimum 40 Innings)

	W	L	ERA	G	SV	IP	H	BB	SO
Clark, Conrad, Raleigh	3	0	1.35	16	0	47	35	12	46
Blackmon, Kurt, Raleigh	7	0	1.66	13	0	65	55	14	72
Fields, Brian, Wilson	4	4	1.69	9	0	59	42	21	61
McGlone, Aaron, Durham	3	3	2.00	8	1	45	36	11	41
Cowie, Stephen, Durham	6	2	2.05	10	0	70	64	14	59

JAYHAWK LEAGUE

	W	L	PCT	GB
Nevada Griffons	28	12	.700	—
Liberal Bee Jays	22	18	.550	6
El Doroado Broncos	20	20	.500	8
Topeka Capitals	17	23	.425	11
Hays Larks	17	23	.425	11
Elkhart Dusters	16	24	.400	12

PLAYOFFS: None.

INDIVIDUAL BATTING LEADERS

(Minimum 100 At-Bats)

	AVG	AB	R	H	2B	3B	HR	RBI	SB
Hooper, Kevin, Liberal	.375	112	25	42	5	1	0	9	8
Bartolucci, Paul, Nevada	.368	125	23	46	7	2	0	16	7
McMillin, Brian, Nevada	.336	140	30	47	8	0	10	27	8
Heying, Scott, Hays	.336	140	32	47	7	1	2	16	9
Trosclair, Brent, Liberal	.322	143	21	46	5	2	1	12	4
Blue, Joey, El Dorado	.322	121	22	39	9	1	8	24	7
Schied, Jeremy, Nevada	.317	101	21	32	9	1	3	16	1
Juday, Andy, Hays	.315	108	14	34	8	3	0	15	1
Johnson, Reed, Topeka	.301	136	22	41	3	0	2	12	12
Nelson, Eric, Liberal	.297	145	18	43	10	3	2	27	1
Besco, Bryan, Nevada	.294	143	30	42	14	0	7	35	4
Juarez, Jeff, Nevada	.284	116	30	33	4	2	7	21	4
Moore, Jeff, Hays	.282	131	16	37	5	1	1	22	0
Hayes, Tim, El Dorado	.277	137	21	38	9	2	4	27	2
Barns, B.J., Hays	.275	138	21	38	6	3	1	20	4

INDIVIDUAL PITCHING LEADERS

(Minimum 30 Innings)

	W	L	ERA	G	SV	IP	H	BB	SO
Balcer, David, Liberal	5	1	0.94	10	2	38	25	9	24
McKeown, Chris, Nevada	5	2	1.40	7	0	39	28	15	29
Cox, Ryan, Nevada	4	0	1.45	6	0	31	25	5	20
Dickinson, Rodney, Hays	6	1	1.64	9	1	44	24	18	58
Therneau, David, Nevada	6	0	1.78	7	0	51	41	18	57
Hickman, Ben, Nevada	5	3	2.28	9	0	55	50	13	33
Zipser, Mike, Topeka	5	2	2.31	9	0	58	58	13	42
Traylor, Chris, El Dorado	3	2	2.38	8	0	53	38	22	38
Umbarger, Kurt, Hays	3	2	2.45	7	0	37	28	16	39
Clinton, Ray, Hays	2	1	2.65	6	0	37	29	8	26

NORTHWOODS LEAGUE

FIRST	W	L	PCT	GB
Rochester	22	10	.688	—
Kenosha	19	13	.594	3
Waterloo	18	14	.563	4
St. Cloud	17	15	.531	5
Manitowoc	12	20	.375	10
Wausau	8	24	.250	14

SECOND	W	L	PCT	GB
Waterloo	23	8	.742	—
Rochester	19	11	.633	3½
Kenosha	16	14	.533	6½
St. Cloud	16	15	.516	7
Manitowoc	9	22	.290	14
Wausau	9	22	.290	14

PLAYOFFS: Rochester defeated Waterloo 2-1 in best-of-3 final.

INDIVIDUAL BATTING LEADERS

(Minimum 162 Plate Appearances)

	AVG	AB	R	H	2B	3B	HR	RBI	SB
Carnes, Shayne, Waterloo	.395	258	60	102	20	1	9	52	9
Gripp, Ryan, Waterloo	.343	216	50	74	18	0	11	47	6
Cepicky, Matt, Waterloo	.342	243	43	83	18	3	10	53	6
Leimbek, Shawn, Roch.	.341	229	49	78	20	1	10	54	12
Curry, Chris, Waterloo	.339	236	61	80	11	3	5	31	8
Lotterhos, Chris, Wat.	.330	194	35	64	14	1	2	23	13
Burlage, Bob, St. Cloud	.327	147	23	48	13	0	8	30	0
Scanlon, Matt, St. Cloud	.323	198	38	64	10	3	4	29	5
Gibbons, Jay, Manitowoc	.318	245	50	78	12	2	17	68	6
Meliah, David, Kenosha	.306	222	44	68	22	2	2	28	8
Kehl, Chris, Rochester	.306	242	53	74	18	0	2	32	4

INDIVIDUAL PITCHING LEADERS

(Minimum 48 Innings)

	W	L	ERA	G	SV	IP	H	BB	SO
Verplancke, Jeff, Manitowoc	7	3	2.19	12	0	95	78	24	93
Heuring, Brad, Rochester	6	2	2.57	12	1	70	53	28	59
Bowman, Jeff, Kenosha	4	2	2.62	7	0	55	43	16	33
Parra, David, Waterloo	11	2	2.70	22	1	110	82	48	95
Sherrill, George, Kenosha	10	3	2.77	17	2	111	95	49	61

Amateur Draft

Signability becomes owners' watchword, but bonuses break draft records again in '97

BY ALLAN SIMPSON

Fearful of more fallout from a draft system that sprung leaks in 1996, major league teams took a cautious, more tempered approach to the selection of amateur talent in 1997.

In many cases players were chosen on the basis of signability, not ability. Several first-round picks reached verbal agreements before the draft, a condition of their being selected in that round. Others were passed over because their asking price was deemed too steep.

Still, bonuses reached record numbers in 1997.

Florida high school lefthander Rick Ankiel, selected 72nd overall by the Cardinals, established a new standard for a drafted player signing with the team that picked him by cutting a $2.5 million deal on Aug. 28. All teams passed on Ankiel in the first round because they couldn't get a handle on his bonus demands.

JEFF GOLDEN

Not acquainted with the dotted line
Matt Anderson proved reluctant to sign

Ankiel's record was expected to last only until the draft's first two picks agreed to terms. As of Nov. 1, 1997, Rice University righthander Matt Anderson and Florida State University outfielder J.D. Drew had yet to sign with Tigers and Phillies, respectively.

The Anderson and Drew cases were complicated by the fact that four draft picks from 1996 were declared free agents because of a loophole in contract-tendering procedures.

As a result, the four became eligible to offer their services to the highest bidder. Righthander Matt White landed the largest bonus, $10.2 million from the Devil Rays—roughly five times the amount No. 1 overall pick Kris Benson got weeks earlier from the Pirates. First baseman Travis Lee signed with the other expansion team, the Diamondbacks, for $10 million.

The Devil Rays and Diamondbacks, scheduled to begin play in 1998, signed all four free agents for bonuses totaling $29.275 million. With no player costs in 1996, they took advantage of a unique opportunity to stock their farm systems with top prospects, much to the dismay of many established clubs.

TOP 10 SIGNING BONUSES

DRAFTED PLAYERS

Player, Pos.	Club, Year (Round)	Bonus
1. Rick Ankiel, lhp	Cardinals '97 (2)	$2,500,000
2. Troy Glaus, 3b	Angels '97 (1)	2,250,000
3. Ryan Anderson, lhp	Mariners '97 (1)	2,175,000
4. Kris Benson, rhp	Pirates '96 (1)	2,000,000
5. Darnell McDonald, of	Orioles '97 (1)	1,900,000
6. Jason Grilli, rhp	Giants '97 (1)	1,875,000
7. Michael Cuddyer, ss	Twins '97 (1)	1,850,000
8. Geoff Goetz, lhp	Mets '97 (1)	1,700,000
9. Braden Looper, rhp	Cardinals '96 (1)	1,675,000
J.J. Davis, of-rhp	Pirates '97 (1)	1,675,000

FREE AGENTS (Amateurs only)

Player, Pos., Country	Club, Year	Bonus
1. Matt White, rhp, U.S.	Devil Rays '96	$10,200,000
2. Travis Lee, 1b, U.S.	Diamondbacks '96	10,000,000
3. Rolando Arrojo, rhp, Cuba	Devil Rays '97	7,000,000
4. John Patterson, rhp, U.S.	Diamondbacks '96	6,075,000
5. Bobby Seay, lhp, U.S.	Devil Rays '96	3,000,000
6. Livan Hernandez, rhp, Cuba	Marlins '96	2,500,000
7. Vladimir Nunez, rhp, Cuba	Diamondbacks '96	1,750,000
8. Jackson Melian, of, Venezuela	Yankees '96	1,600,000
9. Osvaldo Fernandez, rhp, Cuba	Giants '96	1,300,000
10. Larry Rodriguez, rhp, Cuba	Diamondbacks '96	1,250,000

Major League Baseball tightened legislation to make sure the situation wouldn't repeat itself in 1997. But in many ways, the damage had been done. Clubs were in the position of having to defend themselves against paying $10 million bonuses.

"Those were special circumstances involving expansion teams," Tigers general manager Randy Smith said. "Two million dollars is a lot of money. We're not interested in signing any of these players for $10 million. If we're going to spend that kind of money, we're going to spend it on a proven major leaguer, not on someone who is unproven."

But agent Scott Boras, who engineered White's windfall bonus, said the developments of 1996 prove conclusively that a draft system artificially stunts bonuses.

"What we've seen happen in the last two years, first internationally and then domestically, has given us a great barometer on the true worth of a select number of quality amateur players," Boras said. "The market has changed. I know from experience that

DRAFT '97 TOP 50 PICKS

Signing bonuses do not include college scholarships, incentive bonus plans or salaries from a major league contract.
*Highest level attained

Team. Player, Pos.	School	Hometown	Bonus	B'date	B-T	Ht.	Wt.	AVG	AB	H	HR	RBI	SB	'97 Assignment*
2. Phillies. J.D. Drew, of	Florida State U.	Hahira, Ga.	Unsigned	11-20-75	L-R	6-1	200	.455	233	106	31	100	32	St. Paul (Indep.)
3. Angels. Troy Glaus, 3b	UCLA	Oceanside, Calif.	$2,000,000	8-3-76	R-R	6-5	225	.409	264	108	34	91	10	Did Not Play
5. Blue Jays. Vernon Wells, of	Bowie HS	Arlington, Texas	1,600,000	12-08-78	R-R	6-0	195	.565	69	39	7	20	19	St. Catharines (A)
8. Pirates. J.J. Davis, of	Baldwin Park HS	Pomona, Calif.	1,675,000	10-25-78	R-R	6-6	230	.532	77	41	9	29	7	GCL Pirates (R)
9. Twins. Michael Cuddyer, 3b	Great Bridge HS	Chesapeake, Va.	1,850,000	3-27-79	R-R	6-3	195	.500	70	35	6	30	11	Did Not Play
14. Reds. Brandon Larson, ss	Louisiana State U.	San Antonio, Texas	1,330,000	5-24-76	R-R	5-11	190	.381	289	110	40	118	9	Chattanooga (AA)
15. White Sox. Jason Dellaero, ss	U. of South Florida	Brewster, N.Y.	1,056,000	12-17-76	B-R	6-2	195	.324	247	80	20	74	4	Hickory (A)
16. Astros. Lance Berkman, 1b	Rice U.	New Braunfels, Texas	1,000,000	2-10-76	B-L	6-1	205	.431	255	110	41	134	8	Kissimmee (A)
20. Cardinals. Adam Kennedy, ss	Cal State Northridge	Riverside, Calif.	650,000	1-10-76	L-R	6-1	180	.482	278	134	26	99	22	Prince William (A)
22. Orioles. Jayson Werth, c	Glenwood HS	Chatham, Ill.	885,000	5-20-79	R-R	6-5	191	.617	107	66	17	63	32	GCL Orioles (R)
24. Yankees. Tyrell Godwin, of	East Bladen HS	Council, N.C.	Did Not Sign	7-10-79	L-R	5-11	190	.459	61	28	3	27	12	Did Not Play
25. Dodgers. Glenn Davis, 1b	Vanderbilt U.	Aston, Pa.	825,000	11-25-75	B-L	6-1	205	.319	216	69	18	64	7	San Bernardino (A)
26. Orioles. Darnell McDonald, of	Cherry Creek HS	Englewood, Colo.	1,900,000	11-17-78	R-R	5-10	185	.606	66	40	10	35	18	Did Not Play
27. Padres. Kevin Nicholson, ss	Stetson U.	Surrey, B.C.	830,000	3-29-76	B-R	5-10	190	.415	229	95	17	71	24	Rancho Cucamonga (A)
29. Braves. Troy Cameron, ss	St. Thomas Aquinas HS	Fort Lauderdale, Fla.	825,000	8-31-78	B-R	5-11	185	.475	80	38	14	36	9	Danville (R)
30. Diamondbacks. Jack Cust, 1b	Immaculata HS	Flemington, N.J.	825,000	1-07-79	L-R	6-1	195	.592	76	45	15	51	14	AZL Diamondbacks (R)
32. Athletics. Nathan Haynes, of	Pinole Valley HS	Hercules, Calif.	525,000	9-07-79	L-L	5-10	170	.459	37	17	0	7	18	So. Oregon (A)
34. White Sox. Brett Caradonna, of	El Capitan HS	San Diego	497,500	12-03-78	L-R	6-0	185	.462	106	49	12	39	13	Bristol (R)
35. Red Sox. Mark Fischer, of	Georgia Tech	Marietta, Ga.	495,000	4-15-76	R-R	6-2	208	.354	257	91	24	98	17	Lowell (A)
36. Orioles. Ntema Ndungidi, of	Edouard Montpetit HS	Montreal	500,000	3-15-79	B-R	6-3	175		No high school team					GCL Orioles (R)
38. Expos. Scott Hodges, ss	Henry Clay HS	Lexington, Ky.	487,500	12-26-78	L-R	6-0	185	.474	97	46	15	33	13	GCL Expos (R)
39. Rangers. Jason Romano, 3b	Hillsborough HS	Tampa	600,000	6-24-79	R-R	6-0	185	.458	72	33	9	40	22	GCL Rangers (R)
41. Indians. Jason Fitzgerald, of	Tulane U.	Belle Chasse, La.	500,000	9-16-75	L-L	6-0	195	.387	238	92	20	79	21	Watertown (A)
45. Expos. Thomas Pittman, 1b	East St. John HS	Garyville, La.	475,000	11-02-79	R-R	6-4	260	.364	77	28	7	28	14	GCL Expos (R)
49. Giants. Dan McKinley, of	Arizona State U.	Chandler, Ariz.	390,000	5-15-76	L-R	6-0	180	.423	267	113	15	70	32	Did Not Play
50. Twins. Matthew LeCroy, c	Clemson U.	Belton, S.C.	775,000	12-13-75	R-R	6-2	220	.359	237	85	24	79	5	Did Not Play

Team. Player, Pos.	School	Hometown	Bonus	B'date	B-T	Ht.	Wt.	W	L	ERA	IP	H	BB	SO	'97 Assignment
1. Tigers. Matt Anderson, p	Rice U.	Louisville, Ky.	Unsigned	8-17-76	R-R	6-4	195	10	2	2.05	79	48	29	105	Did Not Play
4. Giants. Jason Grilli, p	Seton Hall U.	Baldwinsville, N.Y.	$1,875,000	11-11-76	R-R	6-5	185	6	4	4.65	81	61	34	125	Did Not Play
6. Mets. Geoff Goetz, p	Jesuit HS	Tampa	1,700,000	4-03-79	L-L	6-0	170	13	2	0.68	83	35	46	149	GCL Mets (R)
7. Royals. Dan Reichert, p	U. of the Pacific	Turlock, Calif.	1,450,000	7-12-76	R-R	6-3	165	11	4	2.30	133	96	51	169	Spokane (A)
10. Cubs. Jon Garland, p	Kennedy HS	Granada Hills, Calif.	1,325,000	9-27-79	R-R	6-5	200	9	3	1.21	81	52	18	111	AZL Cubs (R)
11. Athletics. Chris Enochs, p	West Virginia U.	Newell, W. Va.	1,204,000	10-11-75	R-R	6-3	210	12	1	3.03	95	92	21	86	Modesto (A)
12. Marlins. Aaron Akin, p	Cowley County (Kan.) CC	Manhattan, Kan.	1,050,000	6-13-77	L-R	6-2	190	12	0	2.03	93	66	26	102	GCL Marlins (R)
13. Brewers. Kyle Peterson, p	Stanford U.	Elkhorn, Neb.	1,400,000	4-09-76	R-R	6-3	210	11	3	4.19	144	134	38	156	Ogden (R)
17. Red Sox. John Curtice, p	Great Bridge HS	Chesapeake, Va.	975,000	11-01-79	L-L	6-4	210	9	1	0.71	59	17	24	104	GCL Red Sox (R)
18. Rockies. Mark Mangum, p	Kingwood HS	Kingwood, Texas	875,000	8-24-78	R-R	6-2	165	8	3	1.02	75	43	26	104	AZL Rockies (R)
19. Mariners. Ryan Anderson, p	Divine Child HS	Westland, Mich.	2,175,000	7-12-79	L-L	6-10	210	5	3	0.94	59	10	41	148	Did Not Play
21. Athletics. Eric DuBose, p	Mississippi State U.	Gilbertown, Ala.	860,000	5-15-76	L-L	6-3	215	9	4	4.32	119	122	67	145	Visalia (A)
23. Expos. Donnie Bridges, p	Oak Grove HS	Purvis, Miss.	870,000	12-10-78	R-R	6-4	195	8	1	0.49	57	29	16	96	GCL Expos (R)
28. Indians. Tim Drew, p	Lowndes County HS	Hahira, Ga.	1,600,000	8-31-78	R-R	6-2	200	4	2	0.43	32	14	11	62	Burlington (R)
31. Devil Rays. Jason Standridge, p	Hewitt Trussville HS	Birmingham, Ala.	700,000	11-09-78	R-R	6-4	205	9	1	2.19	51	28	19	72	GCL Devil Rays (R)
33. White Sox. Kyle Kane, p	Saddleback (Calif.) CC	Temecula, Calif.	537,500	2-04-76	L-R	6-3	205	2	0	0.36	25	10	10	26	Did Not Play
37. Expos. Chris Stowe, p	Chancellor HS	Fredericksburg, Va.	497,000	6-08-79	R-R	6-3	175	9	0	0.94	67	34	19	118	GCL Expos (R)
40. Yankees. Ryan Bradley, p	Arizona State U.	Chino Hills, Calif.	525,000	10-26-75	R-R	6-4	220	7	7	5.40	60	65	25	76	Oneonta (A)
42. Athletics. Denny Wagner, p	Virginia Tech	Castlewood, Va.	362,500	11-08-76	R-R	6-0	203	10	4	4.41	112	108	49	110	So. Oregon (A)
43. White Sox. Aaron Myette, p	Central Arizona JC	Surrey, B.C.	375,000	9-26-77	R-R	6-3	190	11	1	1.60	90	60	42	113	Hickory (A)
44. Expos. Bryan Hebson, p	Auburn U.	Phenix City, Ala.	435,000	3-12-76	R-R	6-6	210	11	4	4.43	112	103	38	121	Did Not Play
46. White Sox. Jim Parque, p	UCLA	La Crescenta, Calif.	345,500	2-08-76	L-L	5-11	165	13	2	3.08	120	117	63	119	Nashville (AAA)
47. Expos. T.J. Tucker, p	River Ridge HS	New Port Richey, Fla.	410,000	8-20-78	R-R	6-3	245	7	2	0.66	64	32	17	114	GCL Expos (R)
48. Expos. Shane Arthurs, p	Westmoore HS	Oklahoma City, Okla.	405,000	8-30-79	R-R	6-5	185	8	4	3.17	64	49	55	80	GCL Expos (R)

there are many teams willing to pay optimum dollars for a premium talent."

Eye Of The Storm

Drew, the consensus top player in the 1997 draft, was adamant that his rights were being stifled under a system that allowed him to negotiate with only one team.

He was represented by Boras, and set his price at a reported $10 million before the draft. He told every club not to draft him unless it was prepared to pay that amount, but the Phillies took him anyway with the No. 2 selection. Negotiations went nowhere for several months.

"We made it very clear to the Phillies the day before the draft, and even an hour before the draft, and they still picked me," said Drew, the '97 College Player of the Year. "We had things on the table that other teams would offer. And we let the Phillies know that if they weren't willing to match that, then don't draft us. There are other people that are willing to pay."

Phillies scouting director Mike Arbuckle was not deterred by Drew's hard-line stance.

"We viewed last year's situation as an aberration," Arbuckle said. "It does not set a new plateau in the draft."

Boras insisted that Drew's value was not established by what White got in 1996. Instead, Drew's market was set by offers other teams made before the draft.

"Our point is that J.D. would be signed and playing right now if he had been drafted by another team," Boras said. "There definitely were offers tendered to us by other teams.

"The true value of amateur players is now evident. It's very different this year. The draft once was seen as an evaluation structure. Now it's exposed as a barrier for keeping the premium talents from getting their true worth."

All along, the Phillies maintained a position that Benson's bonus was still the benchmark, no matter what happened in 1996.

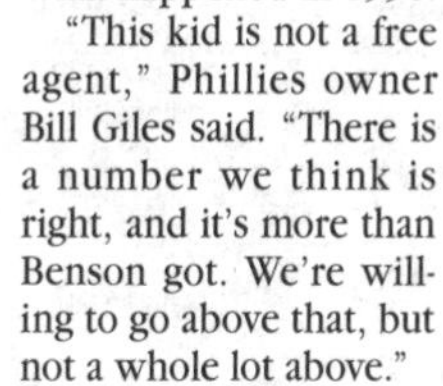
AL SOLOMON

Most costly, temporarily
Rick Ankiel

"This kid is not a free agent," Phillies owner Bill Giles said. "There is a number we think is right, and it's more than Benson got. We're willing to go above that, but not a whole lot above."

Drew sought to be declared a free agent on at least two occasions after he was drafted.

First, he filed a grievance contending the Phillies sent his contract to an incorrect address. It was mailed to his parents' home in Hahira, Ga., not his address in Tallahassee, Fla., and thus failed to reach him within the prescribed 15 days after his selection. An arbitrator ruled in favor of the Phillies.

A second grievance was filed in response to a rules change by Major League Baseball. It said that amateur players were defined as those who had not signed contracts with major league or National Association clubs.

LINDA CULLEN

A question of value
J.D. Drew took his bat to the Northern League

Drew muddied the waters when he signed with the independent Northern League's St. Paul Saints five weeks after being drafted by Philadelphia. He contended his signing with a professional team–albeit an independent team–meant he was not subject to rules as they applied to amateurs.

MLB changed some of its draft rules in the spring of 1997 to clarify its position in regard to amateurs, and said those changes didn't have to be bargained with the Players Association because they didn't alter the value of draft picks.

The union, though, contended that MLB changed its definition of an amateur player, a violation of the Basic Agreement. MLB termed it a clarification of Rule 60(i), not a change in the rule. A favorable ruling for Drew could make him a free agent in May 1998, when his exclusive rights would expire.

That would pave the way for other college and high school players to sign with an independent league team and gain free agency one year later, jeopardizing the very future of the draft.

Judging by how major league teams, competing in an open market, drove up the price on the four premium free agents in 1996, such a development could cost teams millions in bidding wars and probably force MLB to negotiate a new player-procurement system with the Players Association.

Tigers Focus On Anderson

The Tigers, who earned the No. 1 pick in 1997 because of their woeful 53-109 record a year earlier, focused their last-minute scouting efforts on four players: Anderson, Drew, lefthander Ryan Anderson and outfielder Darnell McDonald.

They settled on Matt Anderson, whose 98-mph fastball was the hardest in college baseball, because they believed he could make a contribution to the Tigers within a year or two in a position of need.

"For the past year, we've been wanting to build this organization around pitching and defense," Smith said. "We felt that Matt had the best arm in the draft. He has a terrific arm and terrific makeup."

The Tigers also chose Anderson, in part, because they thought he would be the easiest to sign of the four finalists.

"It doesn't make any sense to take a tremendous talent if he's not going to play professional baseball," Smith said. "You look at the risk versus the reward. The draft has come to that."

But Anderson was in no hurry to sign, preferring to wait until the market established itself.

The Tigers offered Anderson $2.2 million initially and increased that offer to $2.51 million—$10,000 more than Ankiel signed for. But Anderson refused all overtures from the Tigers, preferring to wait and see how Drew's negotiations with the Phillies unfolded. The Tigers proved just as stubborn.

"We're not going to go outside the marketplace to get a deal done," Smith said as negotiations reached a stalemate. "We're not sitting on a keg of money that we're holding back."

Depending on the outcome of the grievance filed on behalf of Drew, Anderson and Drew had until a week before the 1998 draft to sign or be thrown back into the pool. Normally, teams lose their rights to college players when they enroll in school in the fall, but Anderson kept his options open by choosing not to return to Rice.

Not Willing To Gamble

Unlike the Phillies, several clubs decided not to gamble in the first round. As a result, premier players like Ryan Anderson, McDonald and Ankiel were initially passed over.

Anderson was attractive to the Tigers because he was from the Detroit suburb of Dearborn, but he slid to 19th overall when the Tigers opted for the other Anderson. A 6-foot-10 lefthander, Ryan made it known he wanted to be drafted by Seattle. The Mariners obliged, though it took a bonus of $2.175 million to finally reel him in.

The younger Anderson was attracted to the Mariners in part because of the chance to one day pitch with his idol, Randy Johnson, another 6-foot-10 lefty.

"I wanted to go to Seattle if I wasn't drafted by the Tigers," Anderson said. "It will be a great thrill if I can play with Randy Johnson."

Ankiel ranked alongside Ryan Anderson as the premium high school pitchers in the draft, but he slipped out of the first round when reports had him asking for upwards of $5 million. He indicated he would attend the University of Miami if his bonus demands were not met.

The Cardinals played it safe in the first round by taking shortstop Adam Kennedy of Cal State Northridge with the 20th overall pick. They signed him for $650,000, the smallest bonus in the first round.

When their second-round pick came around and Ankiel was still on the table, St. Louis rolled the dice and took him.

"He should have been a first-round pick," Cardinals

NO. 1 DRAFT PICKS, 1965-97

Year	Club, Player, Pos.	School	Hometown	Highest Level (G*)	'97 Team	Bonus
1965	A's. Rick Monday, of	Arizona State U.	Santa Monica, Calif.	Majors (1,996)	Out of Baseball	$104,000
1966	Mets. Steve Chilcott, c	Antelope Valley HS	Lancaster, Calif.	Triple-A (2)	Out of Baseball	75,000
1967	Yankees. Ron Blomberg, 1b	Druid Hills HS	Atlanta	Majors (461)	Out of Baseball	75,000
1968	Mets. Tim Foli, ss	Notre Dame HS	Sherman Oaks, Calif.	Majors (1,696)	Out of Baseball	75,000
1969	Senators. Jeff Burroughs, of	Wilson HS	Long Beach, Calif.	Majors (1,689)	Out of Baseball	88,000
1970	Padres. Mike Ivie, c	Walker HS	Decatur, Ga.	Majors (857)	Out of Baseball	80,000
1971	White Sox. Danny Goodwin, c	Central HS	Peoria, Ill.	Majors (252)	Out of Baseball	DNS
1972	Padres. Dave Roberts, 3b	U. of Oregon	Corvallis, Ore.	Majors (709)	Out of Baseball	60,000
1973	Rangers. David Clyde, lhp	Westchester, HS	Houston	Majors (84)	Out of Baseball	125,000
1974	Padres. Bill Almon, ss	Brown U.	Warwick, R.I.	Majors (1,236)	Out of Baseball	90,000
1975	Angels. Danny Goodwin, c	Southern U.	Peoria, Ill.	Majors (252)	Out of Baseball	125,000
1976	Astros. Floyd Bannister, lhp	Arizona State U.	Seattle	Majors (431)	Out of Baseball	100,000
1977	White Sox. Harold Baines, of	St. Michaels HS	St. Michaels, Md.	Majors (2,463)	Wh. Sox/Orioles	40,000
1978	Braves. Bob Horner, 3b	Arizona State U.	Glendale, Ariz.	Majors (1,020)	Out of Baseball	175,000
1979	Mariners. Al Chambers, of	Harris HS	Harrisburg, Pa.	Majors (57)	Out of Baseball	60,000
1980	Mets. Darryl Strawberry, of	Crenshaw HS	Los Angeles	Majors (1,458)	Yankees	152,500
1981	Mariners. Mike Moore, rhp	Oral Roberts U.	Eakly, Okla.	Majors (450)	Out of Baseball	100,000
1982	Cubs. Shawon Dunston, ss	Jefferson HS	New York	Majors (1,352)	Cubs/Pirates	100,000
1983	Twins. Tim Belcher, rhp	Mt. Vernon Naz. Coll.	Sparta, Ohio	Majors (295)	Royals	DNS
1984	Mets. Shawn Abner, of	Mechanicsburg HS	Mechanicsburg, Pa.	Majors (392)	Out of Baseball	150,000
1985	Brewers. B.J. Surhoff, c	U. of North Carolina	Rye, N.Y.	Majors (1,392)	Orioles	150,000
1986	Pirates. Jeff King, 3b	U. of Arkansas	Colorado Springs	Majors (1,049)	Royals	160,000
1987	Mariners. Ken Griffey Jr., of	Moeller HS	Cincinnati	Majors (1,214)	Mariners	169,000
1988	Padres. Andy Benes, rhp	U. of Evansville	Evansville, Ind.	Majors (261)	Cardinals	235,000
1989	Orioles. Ben McDonald, rhp	Louisiana State U.	Denham Springs, La.	Majors (211)	Brewers	350,000
1990	Braves. Chipper Jones, ss	The Bolles School	Jacksonville	Majors (462)	Braves	275,000
1991	Yankees. Brien Taylor, lhp	East Carteret HS	Beaufort, N.C.	Double-A (27)	Yankees (A)	1,550,000
1992	Astros. Phil Nevin, 3b	Cal State Fullerton	Placentia, Calif.	Majors (178)	Tigers	700,000
1993	Mariners. Alex Rodriguez, ss	West. Christian HS	Miami	Majors (352)	Mariners	1,000,000
1994	Mets. Paul Wilson, rhp	Florida State U.	Orlando, Fla.	Majors (26)	Mets	1,550,000
1995	Angels. Darin Erstad, of	U. of Nebraska	Jamestown, N.D.	Majors (196)	Angels	1,575,000
1996	Kris Benson, rhp	Clemson U.	Kennesaw, Ga.	Double-A (14)	Pirates (AA)	2,000,000
1997	Matt Anderson, rhp	Rice U.	Louisville, Ky.	None	None	—

*No. of games at that level DNS—Did not sign

GM Walt Jocketty said. "We told him all along we would approach him like a first rounder."

The Cardinals applied little pressure on Ankiel. They allowed him to play for Team USA at the World Junior Championships in mid-August, then stepped up negotiations just as he was set to enroll in college.

McDonald, a football-baseball star, also established a high price for his services and lasted deep into the first round. The Orioles gambled the second of two first-round picks on him. He held out until the day before he was scheduled to attend the University of Texas to begin football practice.

ROBERT GURGANUS

Yankees lose in Carolina
Tyrell Godwin

The Yankees weren't as fortunate in their attempt to sign their first-round pick, outfielder Tyrell Godwin, who ended up at the University of North Carolina. It marked the first time in draft history that the Yankees failed to sign their first-round pick, and the first time since the Braves failed to sign righthander Chad Hutchinson in 1995 that any first-rounder went unsigned. Hutchinson has gone on to become a star quarterback at Stanford University.

In addition to being a standout baseball player, Godwin starred in football and in the classroom. His long-range goal was to become a doctor.

"I am flattered that Mr. (George) Steinbrenner and the Yankees selected me in the first round, but I do not feel it is the right time for me to begin a professional baseball career," Godwin said.

Godwin turned down a bonus of $1.9 million. While he had sought $2 million, most people close to the situation said this was one case that wasn't about money.

"Obviously it was not an economic decision," Yankees director of player development Mark Newman said. "The desire to play professional baseball was of lower priority to him."

It was not lost on Boras that teams approached the 1997 draft with a different agenda.

"The key to this draft was price-committing," Boras said. "Ankiel, (Ryan) Anderson and McDonald all were considered top five picks, but they got removed from the process. Teams are promoting average players to sign, and they're promoting greatness to go to college."

Conservative Approach

Several clubs didn't want to become bogged down in tedious negotiating, or risk losing their first-round pick altogether, and struck predraft deals. In many cases, a player was overdrafted to get him under contract for less than the going rate.

The Blue Jays were the first club to arrange such a deal. Selecting fifth and fearful of not getting a player they wanted for less than $2 million, the Jays agreed to terms with Texas high school outfielder Vernon Wells on a $1.6 million deal. They were rewarded when Wells played a full season at short-season St. Catharines and hit .307 with 10 home runs.

The Marlins and Rockies also signed their picks up front for well below the first-round average of $1.27 million.

The Royals thought they had a predraft deal worked out with righthander Dan Reichert, but he held out for a $1.415 million bonus.

While Godwin was the lone first-round pick not to sign–pending the unresolved status of Matt Anderson and Drew–43 players in the first 10 rounds did not sign, up from 26 in 1996.

The Twins, who lost first-round pick Travis Lee (No. 2 overall) to free agency a year earlier, went to the 11th hour to sign three high picks–first-rounder Michael Cuddyer, supplemental first-rounder Matthew LeCroy and second-rounder Mike Restovich. Cuddyer signed for $1.85 million, LeCroy for $775,000 and Restovich for $650,000.

LARRY GOREN

Tried to sign early
Troy Glaus

Cuddyer and lefthander John Curtice, the Red Sox' first-round pick, became only the second set of high school teammates drafted in the first round. The two, who played on the same teams since they were 7 years old, were teammates at Great Bridge High in Chesapeake, Va.

"Scouts have told me that this is a once-in-a-lifetime thing," Great Bridge coach Greg Jennings said. "It's very seldom you even get one first-round pick."

The only other time one high school had two first-round picks was in 1972, when Rancho Cordova (Calif.) High produced shortstop Jerry Manuel and outfielder Mike Ondina.

Glaus Deal Squashed

UCLA All-American third baseman Troy Glaus, the third pick in the draft, held out until mid-September before signing a $2.25 million bonus with the Angels, ending a cordial stalemate.

The commissioner's office earlier nixed a deal that provided for a flexible bonus, where the final amount would be tied to a percentage increase in first-round bonuses from 1996 to 1997. That arrangement was similar to a contract signed a year earlier by lefthander Nick Bierbrodt, Arizona's first-round pick. Bierbrodt signed quickly and ended up doubling the size of his original bonus when all first-round picks were finally signed.

Major league owners later voted to forbid flexible bonus amounts and vetoed Glaus' original $2 million deal.

All In The Family

While J.D. Drew struggled to get what he wanted from the Phillies, his younger brother Tim made out extremely well as the Indians' first-round pick. Cleveland paid a surprising $1.6 million to sign the younger Drew, the 28th overall pick and not even a consensus to go in the first round.

It was the first time in draft history that siblings had been selected in the first round of the same draft.

Drew's bonus was almost double the amount paid to the player selected before him, the Padres' Kevin Nicholson ($830,000), and right after him, the Braves' Troy Cameron ($825,000).

"We knew going in his bonus wasn't going to fall in line," said Indians first-year scouting director Lee MacPhail IV. "We knew we would have to make an aggressive offer. It's out of the ordinary. This being my first draft, I'm not proud that this signing will have a negative impact on the industry."

The bonus was stunning in another sense. Cleveland paid only $400,000, well below market value, to sign its first-round pick in 1996, first baseman Danny Peoples. He also was the 28th pick.

Threes Are Wild

With third-round picks, the Tigers and Dodgers each took a third brother from three-generation baseball families. Third baseman Matt Boone, grandson of Ray, son of Bob and younger brother of Bret and Aaron, was drafted by Detroit. Shortstop Ricky Bell, grandson of Gus, son of Buddy and younger brother of David and Mike, was chosen by Los Angeles. At the time, both fathers were managing in the big leagues, Buddy Bell with Detroit and Bob Boone with the Royals. The elder Boone was fired shortly after Matt was drafted . . . The Giants selected righthander Jason Grilli with the fourth overall pick. He's the son of ex-big leaguer and current Cardinals scout Steve Grilli . . . With their first pick, the Orioles took catcher Jayson Werth, the stepson of ex-big league catcher Dennis Werth and the grandson and nephew of Dick Schofield Sr. and Jr. . . . Darnell McDonald, the Orioles' other first-round pick, is the younger brother of Yankees outfield prospect Donzell McDonald . . . The Dodgers drafted first baseman Glenn Davis in the first round. He's the older brother of Padres catching prospect Ben Davis, the No. 2 overall pick in 1995 . . . The Yankees drafted catcher David Parrish, son of former all-star catcher Lance Parrish, in the 10th round. David Parrish decided to attend the University of Michigan . . . Felipe Alou Jr., son of the Expos manager, was drafted in the 12th round by the Angels.

Windfall Opportunity

Between them, the Expos and White Sox made 14 selections before the start of the second round. The clubs were granted three draft picks apiece for the loss of service-time free agents–players who gained the six years of service necessary to attain free agency by being credited with days lost to the 1994-95 player strike. The Expos were compensated for losing righthander Mel Rojas to the Cubs and outfielder Moises Alou to the Marlins, while the White Sox lost righthander Alex Fernandez to the Marlins. The Athletics also gained three bonus picks for losing shortstop Mike Bordick to the Orioles. One was the 21st pick overall (the position immediately ahead of Baltimore's first pick), effectively meaning the first round had 31 picks. Both the Expos and White Sox also gained a supplemental first-round pick for failing to sign their first rounder from the previous year . . . Canadians factored into the draft like never before. Shortstop Kevin Nicholson, chosen 27th overall by the Padres, became the first-ever Canadian claimed in the first round. He attended Stetson University but grew up in Surrey, British Columbia. Outfielder Ntema Ndungidi (36th overall, Orioles), born in Zaire and raised in Montreal, and righthander Aaron Myette (43rd overall, White Sox), another Surrey product who attended Central Arizona Junior College, were supplemental first-rounders . . . Six-foot-9 lefthander Mark Hendrickson was drafted in the 20th round by the Blue Jays, marking the sixth straight year he's been selected. That's the most a player has been drafted since the January phase of the draft was abolished in 1987. Hendrickson's main focus has been basketball. A second-round pick of the Philadelphia 76ers in 1996, Hendrickson averaged 2.9 points for the 76ers during the 1996-97 NBA season.

UNSIGNED PICKS

Players selected in the first 10 rounds of the 1997 draft who didn't sign, and the colleges they elected to attend:

Round, Club, Player, Pos.	College
1. Tigers. Matt Anderson, rhp	Not in school
Phillies. J. D. Drew, of	Not in school
Yankees. Tyrell Godwin, of	North Carolina
2. Royals. Dane Sardinha, c	Pepperdine
White Sox. Jeff Weaver, rhp	@Fresno State
Mariners. Patrick Boyd, of	Clemson
Dodgers. Chase Utley, ss	UCLA
#Dodgers. Steve Colyer, lhp	Meramec (Mo.) CC
3. Twins. Greg Withelder, lhp	Virginia
Astros. Scott Barrett, lhp	Texas
Orioles. Matt Riley, lhp	Sacramento CC
4. Giants. Kevin McGerry, rhp	St. John's
Astros. Eric Byrnes, of	@UCLA
Cardinals. Xavier Nady, ss	California
Expos. Ronte Langs, of	Gulf Coast (Fla.) CC
D'backs. Chase Voshell, ss	Wake Forest
5. Marlins. Paul Avery, lhp	Pepperdine
Astros. Derek Stanford, rhp	McLennan (Texas) CC
Padres. Tim Hummel, ss	Old Dominion
D'backs. Matt Riethmaier, rhp	Arkansas
6. Royals. Jason Anderson, rhp	Illinois
Red Sox. Kris Wilken, c	Houston
Orioles. Caleb Balbuena, rhp	Long Beach State
Braves. Brett Groves, ss	Florida State
7. Dodgers. Miles Durham, of	Texas Tech
8. Marlins. Clifton Lee, lhp	Meridian (Miss.) JC
Reds. Matt Borne, rhp	@Kentucky
9. Tigers. Bud Smith, lhp-of	Los Angeles Harbor JC
Phillies. Michael Schulte, rhp	Loyola Marymount
Giants. Todd Bellhorn, lhp	@Central Florida
Red Sox. Justin Wayne, rhp	Stanford
Mariners. Frank Corr, c	Stetson
Cardinals. Seth Etherton, rhp	@Southern Cal
Orioles. Logan Cuellar, rhp	SW Louisiana
Braves. Ryan Snare, lhp	North Carolina
D'backs. Justin Singleton, ss	Clemson
10. Giants. Joe Holland, lhp	Not in school
Blue Jays. Matt Bowser, 1b	Central Florida
Mets. Garrett Atkins, 3b	UCLA
Astros. Scott Fredericks, rhp	Arizona
Yankees. David Parrish, c	Michigan
Braves. Gary Loudon, rhp	@Shippensburg (Pa.) St.
Devil Rays. Dane Hutchens, rhp	McLennan (Texas) JC

#Supplemental second-round pick.
@College player returning to same school.

DRAFT '97

CLUB-BY-CLUB SELECTIONS

Boldface indicates player signed

ANAHEIM (3)

1. Troy Glaus, 3b, UCLA.
2. (Choice to Mariners—55th—as compensation for Type B free agent Dave Hollins).
3. Heath Timmerman, rhp, Northeastern Oklahoma A&M JC.
4. Joe Gangemi, lhp, Seton Hall U.
5. Michael Brunet, rhp, Pasco-Hernando (Fla.) CC.
6. Matt Wise, rhp, Cal State Fullerton.
7. Matt Garrick, c, Texas A&M U.
8. Ryan Cummings, rhp, Georgia Southern U.
9. Dwayne Dobson, rhp, U. of South Florida.
10. Steve Green, rhp, Fort Scott (Kan.) CC.
11. Brian Tokarse, rhp, Cal State Fullerton.
12. Felipe Alou Jr., of, Canada (Calif.) JC.
13. Doug Nickle, rhp, U. of California.
14. Adam Leggett, 2b, Georgia Tech.
15. Brent Wagler, rhp, Florida Southern Coll.
16. Casey Child, of, U. of Utah.
17. Keith Medosch, ss, U. of North Florida.
18. Michael O'Keefe, of, Notre Dame HS, Hamden, Conn.
19. Bo Donaldson, rhp, U. of Tampa.
20. Jaymie Bane, lhp, Arizona State U.
21. Mike Colangelo, of, George Mason U.
22. Steve Fish, rhp, U. of Nebraska.
23. Jake Brooks, rhp, Polk (Fla.) CC.
24. Ernie Miller, lhp, Methodist (N.C.) Coll.
25. Jeb Dougherty, of, U. of San Diego.
26. Tim Adams, 1b, U. of California-Davis.
27. David Walling, rhp, Grossmont (Calif.) JC.
28. Rogier Vandepohl, ss, Indian River (Fla.) CC.
29. Mike Condon, ss, Seton Hall U.
30. Oscar Betancourt, 3b, Cal Poly Pomona.
31. Steve Hagins, of, San Diego State U.
32. Ben Talbott, 3b, Lehigh U.
33. Eric Easton, rhp, East Lake HS, Tarpon Springs, Fla.
34. Peter Quittner, of, U. of San Francisco.
35. Graham McAllister, c-1b, Lyons (Kan.) HS.
36. Casey Martin, c, Long Beach State U.
37. Richard Stegbauer, c, Edison (Fla.) CC.
38. Scot Shields, rhp, Lincoln Memorial (Tenn.) U.
39. Ben Saxon, rhp, Chipola (Fla.) JC.
40. Jullian Harris, lhp, West Valley (Calif.) JC.
41. Josh Pearce, rhp, Centralia (Wash.) JC.
42. Jay Nunley, of, U. of North Florida.
43. Ryan Bast, ss-2b, Sierra (Calif.) JC.
44. Brad Brewer, ss, U. of Miami.
45. Wesley Crawford, lhp, Polk (Fla.) CC.
46. Matthew Steele, rhp, Chipola (Fla.) JC.
47. Jeff Kaita, rhp, Colfax HS, Applegate, Calif.
48. Aaron Porter, rhp, St. Mary's Coll.
49. Daniel Kerrigan, c, Manatee (Fla.) CC.
50. Sheldon Philip-Guide, of, Glendale (Calif.) CC.
51. William Hays, of, Garrett (Md.) CC.
52. Ben Margalski, c, Northwest HS, Highridge, Mo.
53. Steve Ahlers, ss, Livermore (Calif.) HS.
54. Shamar Cotton, rhp, Skyline HS, Oakland.
55. Brian Sullivan, lhp, Booker HS, Sarasota, Fla.
56. Gilberto Pichardo, of, South Shore HS, Brooklyn.
57. Ron Ricks, rhp, U. of West Florida.
58. Lamar Harvey, rhp, Fremont HS, Sunnyvale, Calif.
59. Jake Mapes, c, Hemet (Calif.) HS.
60. Alexis Acosta, ss, Polk (Fla.) CC.

ARIZONA (29)

1. Jack Cust, 1b, Immaculata HS, Flemington, N.J.
2. Jason Royer, rhp, Del City (Okla.) HS.
3. Jeffrey Brooks, 1b, Solanco HS, Quarryville, Pa.
4. Chase Voshell, ss, Milford (Ohio) HS.
5. Matt Riethmaier, rhp, Arkadelphia (Ark.) HS.
6. Mike Rooney, rhp, St. John's U.
7. Brian Gordon, of, Round Rock (Texas) HS.
8. Ron Calloway, of, Canada (Calif.) JC.
9. Justin Singleton, ss, St. Paul's HS, Lutherville, Md.
10. Casey Cuntz, ss, Louisiana State U.
11. Jamie Sykes, of, Valparaiso U.
12. Doug Kohl, rhp, Green Valley HS, Henderson, Nev.
13. Peter Nystrom, of, Dunedin (Fla.) HS.
14. Alvin Montilla, of, St. Raymond's HS, Bronx, N.Y.
15. Brian Fox, c, Grayson County (Texas) JC.
16. David Haverstick, rhp, Bethel (Ind.) Coll.
17. Steve Rowell, ss, Ridgewood HS, Kenner, La.
18. Jason Jensen, lhp, U. of Southern Maine.
19. Tony Hausladen, 1b, Saint Louis U.
20. Derek Michaelis, 1b, Midway HS, Waco, Texas.
21. Tutu Moye, ss, Rose HS, Greenville, N.C.
22. Keith Jones, 3b, Fullerton (Calif.) JC.
23. Jared Martin, ss, U. of Southern Mississippi.
24. Jason Martines, rhp, Siena Heights (Mich.) Coll.
25. Andrew Friedberg, lhp, Middleton (Wis.) HS.
26. Ben Mitchell, rhp, Horizon HS, Scottsdale, Ariz.
27. John Adams, of, Wichita State U.
28. Jared Hoerman, rhp, Eastern Oklahoma State JC.
29. Jeffrey Wilson, lhp, Elon (N.C.) Coll.
30. Daniel Hall, rhp, Plymouth (N.C.) HS.
31. Seth Tate, rhp, Wenatchee Valley (Wash.) CC.
32. Scott Abeyta, lhp, Contra Costa (Calif.) JC.
33. Lance Downing, 3b, Watson Chapel HS, Pine Bluff, Ark.
34. Phillip McKaig, rhp, Corona Del Sol HS, Tempe, Ariz.
35. Jeremy Quire, c, Murray State U.
36. Alex Cintron, ss, Mech Tech, Yabucoa, P.R.
37. Julio Guzman, of, Carson-Newman (Tenn.) Coll.
38. Charlie Jones, rhp, Florida Atlantic U.
39. Kelly Martin, rhp, Arcadia HS, Phoenix.
40. Wyley Steelmon, 1b, Oklahoma State U.
41. Jeremy Dameworth, of, Ramona (Calif.) HS.
42. Jason Scobie, rhp, Westwood HS, Austin.
43. Jamie Puorto, lhp, Northeastern Illinois U.
44. Jason Wiedmeyer, lhp, West Bend (Wis.) East HS.
45. Steve Doherty, 2b, Long Beach State U.
46. Chris Bloomer, rhp, Purdue U.
47. Jeff Santa, lhp, Winthrop U.
48. Bryce Terveen, c, JC of the Desert (Calif.).
49. John Meyers, rhp, Boswell HS, Dallas.
50. Thomas Murphy, rhp-ss, Charlotte (Fla.) HS.
51. George Dixon, of, Stamford (Conn.) Catholic HS.
52. Brandon Wells, lhp, Bagdad (Ariz.) HS.
53. Ronnie Goodwin, rhp, North Little Rock HS, Sherwood, Ark.
54. Aaron Rifkin, 1b, Etwanda HS, Fontana, Calif.
55. Stuart Hunt, lhp, Memorial HS, Edmond, Okla.
56. Samuel Mendoza, rhp, Highland HS, Gilbert, Ariz.
57. Anthony Denard, of, Laney (Calif.) JC.
58. Anthony Pena, rhp, Dallas Christian HS.
59. Ronald Corona, rhp, Victor Valley HS, Victorville, Calif.
60. Robert Pierce, 2b, Green Valley HS, Henderson, Nev.

ATLANTA (28)

1. Troy Cameron, ss, St. Thomas Aquinas HS, Fort Lauderdale.
2. Joey Nation, lhp, Putnam City HS, Oklahoma City.
3. Juan Velazquez, ss, Jose Campeche HS, San Lorenzo, P.R.
4. Cory Aldridge, of, Cooper HS, Abilene, Texas.
5. Horatio Ramirez, lhp, Inglewood (Calif.) HS.
6. Brett Groves, ss, Tampa Bay Tech HS.
7. Bry Ewen, c, Belton (Texas) HS.
8. Ryan Lehr, c-3b, Grossmont HS, La Mesa, Calif.
9. Ryan Snare, lhp, East Lake HS, Palm Harbor, Fla.
10. Gary Loudon, rhp, Shippensburg (Pa.) U.
11. Greg Strickland, of, Cumberland (Tenn.) U.
12. Manny Crespo, of, Westminster Christian HS, Miami.
13. Doug Dent, rhp, Citrus Heights, Calif.
14. Chris Frazier, rhp, Salado HS, Belton, Texas.
15. Jon Ciravolo, rhp, Kean (N.J.) Coll.
16. Jason Hairston, c, Washington State U.
17. Richard Thieme, lhp, Georgia Tech.
18. Brad Drew, lhp, Waterloo (Ontario) Collegiate Institute.
19. Stewart Smothers, of, San Diego State U.
20. Derrick Lewis, rhp, Florida A & M U.
21. Mike Roberts, rhp, Siena Coll.
22. Pat Schmidt, lhp, Bellefontaine (Ohio) HS.
23. Richard Dishman, rhp, Duke U.
24. Bill Scott, of, Bishop Alemany HS, Mission Hills, Calif.
25. Robert Porter, lhp, Southwest Mississippi CC.
26. Mark Burke, 1b, Portland State U.
27. Jason Bowers, lhp, Central Cabarrus HS, Concord, N.C.
28. Troy Allen, of, George Washington U.
29. John Wright, lhp, Walton HS, Defuniak Springs, Fla.
30. Tyler Kemhus, 3b, Oregon City HS.
31. David Lebejko, rhp, Central Connecticut State U.
32. Collin Wissen, of, Southwest Texas State U.
33. Craig Carter, ss, Lake Havasu (Ariz.) HS.
34. Patrick Hannaway, rhp, Monsignor Farrell HS, Staten Island, N.Y.

35. Jeremy Hale, rhp, Lafayette HS, St. Joseph, Mo.
36. Tim Lyons, rhp, U. of Kansas.
37. Mike Dolan, rhp, Chattahoochee (Fla.) HS.
38. Robert Medeiros, of, U. of Hawaii.
39. Sean Vann, of, Chaparral HS, Las Vegas.
40. Charlie Thames, rhp, Humble (Texas) HS.
41. Will Fleck, rhp, La Salle U.
42. Paul Shanklin, rhp, West Virginia State Coll.
43. Anthony Limbrick, of, Skyline HS, Oakland.
44. Matt Price, lhp, Greater Atlanta Christian HS, Norcross, Ga.
45. Justin Dansby, rhp, Eastern Oklahoma State JC.
46. Daniel Wright, of, Dixie HS, St. George, Utah.
47. Cameron Hardy, rhp, Lake City (Fla.) CC.
48. Prinz Milton, of, West Torrance (Calif.) HS.
49. Michael Gray, lhp, Cuesta (Calif.) JC.
50. Mike Robinson, rhp, Canby (Ore.) HS.
51. Jason Westemeir, 3b-rhp, Bishop Alemany HS, Mission Hills, Calif.
52. Tyler Shelton, ss, Hillsboro HS, Donnellson, Ill.
53. Robert Coley, c, Irwin County HS, Fitzgerald, Ga.
54. Travis Wessel, lhp, Morningside (Iowa) Coll.
55. Shannon Royal, lhp, Mariner HS, Fort Myers, Fla.
56. Greg Dukeman, rhp, Long Beach CC.
57. Anthony Purkiss, ss, Golden West HS, Visalia, Calif.
58. Jorge Guerrero, ss, Miller HS, Fontana, Calif.
59. Tony Piccotti, 1b, Capital HS., Boise, Idaho.
60. Tyler Vanpatten, 1b, Polk (Fla.) CC.
61. Travis Harrington, ss, Columbia HS, Lake City, Fla.
62. Jerel Johnson, 3b, McNair HS, Decatur, Ga.
63. Joey Alvarez, c, Temple (Texas) HS.
64. Lonnie Jaquez, c, Carlsbad (N.M.) HS.
65. Daniel Bell, of, Los Angeles CC.
66. Darryl Stephens, of, St. Pius X HS, Decatur, Ga.
67. Chris Carmichael, of, McNair HS, Decatur, Ga.
68. Adam Kepler, of, Riverwood HS, Atlanta.
69. Justin Echols, of, Thatcher (Ariz.) HS.

BALTIMORE (21)

1. Jayson Werth, c, Glenwood HS, Chatham, Ill.
1. Darnell McDonald, of, Cherry Creek HS, Englewood, Colo. (Choice from Yankees—26th—as compensation for Type A free agent David Wells).
1. Ntema Ndungidi, of, Edouard Montpetit HS, Montreal (Supplemental pick—36th—for loss of Wells).
2. Sean Douglass, rhp, Antelope Valley HS, Lancaster, Calif.
3. Matt Riley, lhp, Liberty Union HS, Oakley, Calif.
4. Shannon Carter, of, El Reno (Okla.) HS.
5. Richard Bauer, rhp, Treasure Valley (Ore.) CC.
6. Caleb Balbuena, rhp, Cuesta (Calif.) JC.
7. Ricky Casteel, rhp, Northeast Texas CC.
8. Jay Spurgeon, rhp, U. of Hawaii.
9. Logan Cuellar, rhp, Wharton County (Texas) JC.
10. David Zwirchitz, rhp, East HS, Appleton, Wis.
11. Jerry Hairston, ss, Southern Illinois U.
12. Darren Murphy, lhp, Grossmont (Calif.) JC.
13. Mack Haman, of, Coastal Carolina Coll.
14. Sean Jones, rhp, Barton HS, Hamilton, Ontario.
15. Jordan Romero, rhp, De Anza (Calif.) JC.
16. Cliff Wilson, 3b, Spartanburg Methodist (S.C.) JC.
17. Chris Thogersen, rhp, Newbury Park HS, Thousand Oaks, Calif.
18. Lance Surridge, rhp, UNC Greensboro.
19. Jason Ryba, rhp, Cuyahoga Heights HS, Brooklyn Heights, Ohio.
20. Joe Borchard, 1b, Camarillo (Calif.) HS.
21. Antoine Ide, of, Madison HS, Portland, Ore.
22. Juan Pacheco, ss, Rutgers U.
23. Tod Lee, c, Georgia Southern U.
24. Jason Taylor, of, Billy Ryan HS, Denton, Texas.
25. Roy Wells, rhp, Perry County Central HS, Hazard, Ky.
26. Daniel Carrasco, rhp, Pima (Ariz.) CC.
27. Brian Harper, of, Hershey (Pa.) HS.
28. Erick Eigenhuis, rhp-1b, Central Valley HS, Veradale, Wash.
29. Anthony Reed, rhp, Eisenhower HS, Walters, Okla.
30. Brian Schmitt, 1b, Monterey HS, Lubbock, Texas.
31. Terence Byron, 3b, St. Joseph HS, St. Croix, Virgin Islands.
32. Gavin Wright, of, Lufkin (Texas) HS.
33. Andrew Beal, lhp, Reidland HS, Paducah, Ky.
34. Matthew Schwager, rhp, Indian Hills (Iowa) CC.
35. Austin Bilke, 3b, Beaver Dam (Wis.) HS.
36. Juan Bonilla, c, Crestview (Fla.) HS.
37. Rodney Perry, of, Mater Dei HS, Irvine, Calif.
38. Sam Emerick, rhp, Lincoln Land (Ill.) CC.
39. William Duplissea, c, San Mateo (Calif.) JC.
40. Tommy Martin, ss, Hillsdale (Mich.) Coll.
41. Shawn Curtis, rhp, Lexington, Ky.

BOSTON (17)

1. John Curtice, lhp, Great Bridge HS, Chesapeake, Va.
1. Mark Fischer, of, Georgia Tech (Supplemental pick—35th—for loss of Type A free agent Roger Clemens).
2. Aaron Capista, ss, Joliet Catholic HS, Joliet, Ill. (Choice from Blue Jays—57th—as compensation for Clemens).
2. Eric Glaser, rhp, Highlands HS, Fort Thomas, Ky.
3. Travis Harper, rhp, James Madison U.
4. Ramon Santos, ss, Miguel Melendez HS, Cayey, P.R.
5. Greg Miller, lhp, Aurora HS, West Aurora, Ill.
6. Kris Wilken, c, Eldorado HS, Albuquerque.
7. Jeff Taglienti, rhp, Tufts (Mass.) U.
8. Andrew Hazlett, lhp, U. of Portland.
9. Justin Wayne, rhp, Punahou HS, Honolulu.
10. Marty McCleary, rhp, Mount Vernon Nazarene (Ohio) Coll.
11. Tom Miller, lhp, Ohio U.
12. Billy Rich, of, U. of Connecticut.
13. Charles Terni, ss, Montville HS, Uncasville, Conn.
14. Chad Alevras, c, U. of New Mexico.
15. Rick O'Dette, lhp, St. Joseph's U.
16. Jorge DeLeon, 3b, U. of South Florida.
17. Kenny Rayborn, rhp, U. of South Alabama.
18. Danny Haas, of, U of Louisville.
19. David Eckstein, 2b, U. of Florida.
20. Brian Partenheimer, lhp, U. of Indiana.
21. Joe Thomas, lhp, Marietta (Ohio) Coll.
22. Derek Rix, 1b, Florida CC.
23. Nate Bump, rhp, Penn State U.
24. Jason Fingers, rhp, Torrey Pines HS, San Diego.
25. Chris Domurat, c, Sandwich HS, Forestdale, Mass.
26. Heath McMurray, rhp, Splendora (Texas) HS.
27. Justin Fry, rhp, Ohio State U.
28. David Stickel, ss, Temple Heights HS, Tampa.
29. Ryan Yeager, ss, Port St. Joe (Fla.) HS.
30. Bret Prinz, rhp, Phoenix JC.
31. Matt Kamalsky, rhp, Somerset (Pa.) HS.
32. Robert Hardy, rhp, Countryside HS, Clearwater, Fla.
33. Patrick Santoro, ss, Fenwick HS, Elmwood Park, Ill.
34. Layne Meyer, rhp, Polk (Fla.) CC.
35. Jason Berni, rhp, Rancho Bernardo HS, San Diego.
36. Ryan Atkinson, rhp, Bellarmine Prep HS, San Jose.
37. Donovan Marbury, rhp, U. of Southern Mississippi.
38. Dennis Tankersley, rhp, St. Charles (Mo.) HS.
39. Shawn Weaver, rhp, Bald Eagle-Nittany HS, Loganton, Pa.
40. Chad Zaucha, of, Mount Pleasant (Pa.) HS.
41. Matthew Slagter, rhp, Jefferson HS, Tampa.
42. Scott Candelaria, ss, La Cueva HS, Albuquerque.
43. Nicholas Gray, ss, Florida HS, Tallahassee, Fla.
44. Todd Smith, 3b, Apopka (Fla.) HS.
45. Joseph Thurston, ss, Vallejo (Calif.) HS.

CHICAGO/AL (15)

1. Jason Dellaero, ss, U. of South Florida.
1. Kyle Kane, rhp, Saddleback (Calif.) CC (Supplemental pick—33rd—for loss of service-time free agent Alex Fernandez).
1. Brett Caradonna, of, El Capitan HS, San Diego (Supplemental pick—34th—for loss of Type A free agent Kevin Tapani).
1. Aaron Myette, rhp, Central Arizona JC (Supplemental pick—43rd—for loss of Fernandez).
1. Jim Parque, lhp, UCLA (Supplemental pick—46th—for loss of Fernandez).
1. Rocky Biddle, rhp, Long Beach State U. (Supplemental pick—51st—for failure to sign 1996 first-round pick Bobby Seay).
2. Jeff Weaver, rhp, Fresno State U. (Choice from Cubs—62nd—as compensation for Tapani).
2. (Choice to Indians—67th—as compensation for Type A free agent Albert Belle).
3. J.R. Mounts, of, Key West (Fla.) HS.
4. Curtis Whitley, lhp, Mount Olive (N.C.) Coll.
5. Pat Daneker, rhp, U. of Virginia.
6. Brian Scott, rhp, San Diego State U.
7. Jake Meyer, rhp, UCLA.
8. Tim Currens, rhp, Lindsey Wilson (Ky.) Coll.
9. Rolando Garza, ss, Coachella (Calif.) Valley HS.
10. Jamie Smith, rhp-c, Texas A&M U.
11. Kevin Connacher, 2b, Florida Atlantic U.
12. Andrew Jacobson, rhp, Alma (Mich.) Coll.
13. Ryan Hankins, 2b, U. of Nevada-Las Vegas.
14. Chad Durham, 2b-of, Surry (N.C.) CC.
15. Travis Rapp, c, U. of North Florida.
16. Adrean Acevedo, of, Miami-Dade CC Kendall.
17. Shawn Barksdale, rhp, Etowah HS, Gallant, Ala.
18. Tom Williams, rhp, Southern U.
19. Jason Bernard, rhp, Rutherford HS, Panama City, Fla.

20. Tyson Boston, 3b, Burlington-Edison HS, Burlington, Wash.
21. Jay Kvasnicka, rhp, Northeastern Illinois U.
22. Stuart Rohling, rhp, Northwest Shoals (Ala.) JC.
23. Matt Berger, 1b, U. of Louisville.
24. Cormac Joyce, lhp, Burke HS, Washingtonville, N.Y.
25. Eric Thompson, 1b, Gardner (Kan.) Edge HS.
26. Joshua Johnston, rhp, JC of Eastern Utah.
27. Anthony Garcia, c, Miami-Dade CC Wolfson.
28. Richardo Ramon, of, Miami Senior HS, Hialeah, Fla.
29. Matthew Goldsmith, rhp, Rockwall (Texas) HS.
30. Ray Goirgolzarri, 3b, Miami-Dade CC South.
31. Michael Mallonee, lhp, Southwestern (Calif.) JC.
32. Chadd Clarey, rhp, Des Moines Area (Iowa) CC.
33. Mark Floersch, rhp, New Trier HS, Winnetka, Ill.
34. Jason Moates, rhp, Central HS, Columbia, Tenn.
35. Nelson Carreno, c-of, Miami Christian HS.
36. Edward Scott, ss-of, Dominguez HS, Compton, Calif.
37. Kevin Provencher, rhp, Forest Hill HS, West Palm Beach, Fla.
38. John Newman, rhp-ss, Skyline HS, Idaho Falls.
39. Luis Suarez, ss, Miami-Dade CC North.
40. Darryll Rogue, rhp, Miami-Dade CC Kendall.
41. Michael Hill, 3b-of, Bentley (Mass.) Coll.
42. Richard Clover, rhp, Central Missouri State U.
43. Jeff Radziewicz, 1b, Easton (Md.) HS.
44. Matt Smith, lhp, Bishop Gorman HS, Las Vegas.
45. Jason Aspito, ss, Driscoll Catholic HS, Itasca, Ill.
46. Francisco De Armas, c, Southridge HS, Miami.
47. David Siemon, 3b, Forest Hill HS, West Palm Beach, Fla.
48. Jackie Pettigrew, rhp, Sperry HS, Skiatook, Okla.
49. J.J. Newkirk, of, Long Beach State U.
50. James Lunsford, c, Central HS, San Angelo, Texas.
51. Luke Albert, c, Chaminade Madonna Coll. HS, Hollywood, Fla.
52. Elio Borges, ss, Miami.

CHICAGO/NL (10)

1. Jon Garland, rhp, Kennedy HS, Granada Hills, Calif.
2. (Choice to White Sox—62nd—as compensation for Type A free agent Kevin Tapani).
3. Scott Downs, lhp, U. of Kentucky.
4. Nathan Teut, lhp, Iowa State U.
5. Jaisen Randolph, of, Hillsborough HS, Tampa.
6. Matt Mauck, 3b, Jasper (Ind.) HS.
7. Paul Vracar, rhp, Orchard Park HS, Stoney Creek, Ontario.
8. Ron Walker, 3b, Old Dominion U.
9. Gary Johnson, of, U. of Nevada
10. Mike Amrhein, c, U. of Notre Dame.
11. Michael Wuertz, rhp, Austin (Minn.) HS.
12. Randy Williams, lhp, Lamar U.
13. Tanner Ericksen, rhp, Bullard HS, Fresno.
14. Antwaan Randle, of, Thornton HS, Riverdale, Ill.
15. Tom Waligora, rhp, Coll. of William & Mary.
16. Matthew Magers, lhp, South Dakota State U.
17. Deon Eaddy, ss, Norfolk State U.
18. John Massey, c, Adamsville (Tenn.) HS.
19. Chris Piersoll, rhp, Fullerton (Calif.) JC.
20. Gerald Johnson, of, Atherton, Calif.
21. Kevin Waldrum, rhp, Millsap HS, Weatherford, Texas.
22. Cameron Likely, of, Port St. Joe (Fla.) HS.
23. Greg Jacobs, of, Cypress (Calif.) JC.
24. Kevin Hodge, ss, Blinn (Texas) JC.
25. Nathan Batts, lhp, Souhegan HS, Mont Vernon, N.H.
26. Michael Meyers, rhp, Black Hawk (Ill.) JC.
27. Michael Delano, lhp, Los Angeles CC.
28. Brad Love, lhp, Meridian (Miss.) CC.
29. Ryan Rupe, rhp, Texas A & M U.
30. George Arnott, c, Cabrillo (Calif.) JC.
31. Anthony Calabrese, ss, Brunswick HS, Riverside, Conn.
32. Andrew Perry, rhp, Claremont (Calif.) HS.
33. Ryan McKinley, rhp, Scottsdale (Ariz.) CC.
34. Chris Williamson, of-1b, Westfield HS, Houston.
35. Ken Conroy, rhp, East Gaston HS, Gastonia, N.C.
36. Todd Fereday, 3b, Kansas State U.
37. Brad Tucker, rhp, Fresno State U.
38. Clark Todd, c, Lufkin (Texas) HS.
39. Peter Selden, rhp, Holley (N.Y.) HS.
40. Robert Mitchell, lhp, Dixie Heights HS, Erlanger, Ky.
41. Jeff Duncan, of, Lamont HS, Frankfort, Ill.
42. Daren Bartula, rhp, McLennan (Texas) CC.
43. Josh Benedict, lhp, South Salem HS, Keizer, Ore.
44. John Halliday, 1b, Pasco-Hernando (Fla.) CC.
45. Tim Whitfield, rhp, Leland HS, San Jose.
46. Tom Bernhardt, of, Louisiana State U.
47. Mathew Bruback, rhp, Clements HS, Schertz, Texas.
48. John Janek, of, McLennan (Texas) CC.

JEFF GOLDEN

Cubs first-rounder
Jon Garland signed early, pitched well

49. Brad Hargreaves, c, Okaloosa-Walton (Fla.) CC.
50. Matt Gunderson, rhp, Walla Walla (Wash.) CC.
51. Coby Robinson, of, Enterprise State (Ala.) JC.
52. Lester Galer, rhp, Acalanes HS, Lafayette, Calif.
53. Jeremy Taylor, rhp, Ankeny (Iowa) HS.
54. Jeremy Smith, rhp, Cerro Coso (Calif.) CC.
55. Matthew Murphy, lhp, Wallace State (Ala.) CC.
56. Joshua Latimer, lhp, Kishwaukee (Ill.) JC.
57. Morey Aldrup, ss, La Quinta HS, Santa Ana, Calif.
58. Michael Joyce, lhp, Fitch HS, Groton, Conn.
59. Shane Kelly, of, Meridian (Miss.) CC.

CINCINNATI (14)

1. Brandon Larson, ss, Louisiana State U.
2. Travis Dawkins, ss, Newberry (S.C.) HS.
3. Thad Markray, 3b, Springhill (La.) HS.
4. Monte Roundtree, lhp, Rose HS, Greenville, N.C.
5. DeWayne Wise, of, Chapin (S.C.) HS.
6. Toby Sanchez, 1b, Long Beach State U.
7. Mike Frank, lhp-of, Santa Clara U.
8. Matt Borne, rhp, U. of Kentucky.
9. Scott Williamson, rhp, Oklahoma State U.
10. David Runk, rhp, Tussey Mountain HS, Saxton, Pa.
11. Clint Brewer, rhp, Blanchard HS, Dibble, Okla.
12. Dustin Robinson, rhp, Oklahoma Baptist U.
13. Fernando Rios, of, Glendale (Calif.) HS.
14. Daniel Timm, rhp, U. of Denver.
15. Braxton Whitehead, c-1b, U. of Southern Mississippi.
16. David Tidwell, of, U of Alabama.
17. Tye Levy, lhp, Juniata Valley HS, Alexandria, Pa.
18. Wesley Stumbo, rhp, Georgetown (Ky.) Coll.
19. Benny Craig, of, Loyola Marymount U.
20. Kevin Baderdeen, ss, Glen Oaks (Mich.) CC.
21. Robert Averett, rhp, Florida A & M U.
22. Eric Welsh, 1b, Northern Illinois U.
23. Brian Kirby, c, North Little Rock (Ark.) HS.
24. Terence Senegal, of, Comeaux HS, Lafayette, La.
25. Samone Peters, 1b, Mendocino (Calif.) CC.
26. Antjuan Mitchell, 1b, Mount Carmel HS, Chicago.
27. Josh Holbrook, c-1b, San Marcos (Calif.) HS.
28. Scott Sandusky, c, Texas A &M U.
29. Zadrian Brown, rhp, Midland Valley HS, Warrenville, S.C.
30. Marc Suarez, c, Cumberland (Tenn.) U.

31. Cody Stanley, rhp, Clark HS, San Antonio.
32. Todd Holt, of, Manchester HS, Chesterfield, Va.
33. Chad Rogers, rhp, Pine Forest HS, Pensacola, Fla.
34. Mke Bomar, lhp, Prairie HS, Brush Prairie, Wash.
35. John Whitesides, rhp, Santa Fe (Fla.) CC.
36. Jason Hubbard, lhp, White HS, Jacksonville.
37. Cade Allison, rhp, Odessa (Texas) JC.
38. Tim Godfrey, ss, Bacone (Okla) JC.
39. Brian Kennedy, c, North HS, Riverside, Calif.
40. Luis Munne, c, Miami Springs HS, Hialeah, Fla.

CLEVELAND (27)

1. Tim Drew, rhp, Lowndes County HS, Hahira, Ga.
1. Jason Fitzgerald, of, Tulane U. (Supplemental pick—41st—for loss of Type A free agent Albert Belle).
2. Edgar Cruz, c, Vocational Tech, Juncos, P.R. (Choice from White Sox—67th—as compensation for Belle).
2. Rob Vael, rhp, JC of Eastern Utah.
3. Rob Pugmire, rhp, Cascade HS, Snohomish, Wash.
4. Erick Thompson, of, Westover HS, Fayetteville, N.C.
5. Jonathan Hamilton, of-lhp, Ohlone (Calif.) JC.
6. Brian Benefield, 2b, Texas A&M U.
7. Mark Turnbow, rhp, Hardin County HS, Saltillo, Tenn.
8. Johnnie Wheeler, lhp, Connors State (Okla.) JC.
9. Dustan Mohr, of, U. of Alabama.
10. Joe Kilburg, 2b-of, Stanford U.
11. Daniel Jahn, lhp, Franklin HS, Seattle.
12. Brad Freeman, ss, Mississippi State U.
13. Chad Hawkins, rhp, Navarro (Texas) JC.
14. Mike Hughes, lhp, St. John's U.
15. Tyler Swinburnson, rhp, Oregon State U.
16. Denny New, lhp, Panola (Texas) JC.
17. Brian Shackelford, lhp, U. of Oklahoma.
18. Troy Silva, rhp, Lewis-Clark State (Idaho) Coll.
19. Devon Nicholson, rhp, Sacramento CC.
20. Nicholas Waak, rhp, Chugiak (Alaska) HS.
21. Erick Rosa, c, Western Kentucky U.
22. Kelly Dampeer, ss, Radford U.
23. Heath Bender, 1b, U. of Memphis.
24. Reggie Nelson, ss, Mission Bay HS, San Diego.
25. Ryan Upshaw, of, New Mexico State U.
26. Chris Jackson, c, Mountain Brook (Ala.) HS.
27. Todd Harding, 2b, Lane (Ore.) CC.
28. Derek Wigginton, of, Father Ryan HS, Antioch, Tenn.
29. Courtney Hall, rhp, Meadowdale HS, Edmonds, Wash.
30. Francis Paiso, lhp, Encinal HS, Alameda, Calif.
31. Brandon Smith, 1b, Canyon HS, Anaheim.
32. Jason Basil, c, St. Xavier HS, Westchester, Ohio.
33. Anthony Jackson, of, Wilde Lake HS, Ellicott City, Md.
34. Jon Rouwenhorst, lhp, Brethren Christian HS, Anaheim.
35. Kris McWhirter, rhp, Davidson Academy, Goodlettsville, Tenn.
36. Danny Borrell, lhp, Lee County HS, Sanford, N.C.
37. Ryan Satterwhite, c, Tate HS, Cantonment, Fla.
38. Austin Roberts, rhp, Elma (Wash.) HS.
39. Brandon Wheeler, rhp, Hillsborough (Fla.) CC.
40. Brandon Mauer, c, Lake Stevens HS, Everett, Wash.
41. Brad Drummond, rhp, Liberty HS, Renton, Wash.
42. Ryan Haley, 2b, U. of Central Oklahoma.
43. Danny Alvarez, rhp, Florida International U.
44. Joey Cole, rhp, Howard (Texas) JC.
45. Brian Seever, of, Sacramento CC.
46. Jeff Parker, rhp, Martin HS, Arlington, Texas.
47. Justin Hutton, c, Tyee HS, Tukwila, Wash.
48. Mark Hamilton, lhp, Panola (Texas) JC.
49. Richard Booth, of, Whiteville (N.C.) HS.
50. Darnell Sanders, 1b, Warrensville HS, Twinsburgh, Ohio.

COLORADO (18)

1. Mark Mangum, rhp, Kingwood (Texas) HS.
2. Aaron Cook, rhp, Hamilton (Ohio) HS.
3. Todd Sears, 1b, U. of Nebraska.
4. Chone Figgins, ss, Brandon (Fla.) HS.
5. Justin Miller, rhp, Los Angeles Harbor JC.
6. Sam Smith, ss, Jasper (Texas) HS.
7. Jake Kringen, lhp, U. of Washington.
8. Jeremy Jackson, of, U. of Arkansas.
9. Dave Johnson, rhp, Kansas State U.
10. Derrick Vargas, lhp, Chabot (Calif.) JC.
11. Agustin Sanchez, of, Luis Munoz Marin HS, Yauco, P.R.
12. Ryan Seifert, rhp, Iowa State U.
13. Roger Little, rhp, Perry Central HS, Hazard, Ky.
14. Jose Gonzales, c, Southeastern Louisiana U.
15. Rodney Little, rhp, Perry Central HS, Hazard, Ky.
16. Jason Franklin, 3b, Cumberland (Tenn.) U.
17. Jerome Alviso, ss, Cal State Fullerton.
18. Ara Petrosian, rhp, Long Beach State U.
19. Michael Johns, ss, Tulane U.
20. Mark Woodyard, 1b, Grand Bay (Ala.) HS.
21. Armando Gonzalez, rhp, Cerritos (Calif.) JC.
22. Kendall Rhodes, rhp, Angelina (Texas) JC.
23. Jacob Minter, 1b, Blanchet HS, Edmonds, Wash.
24. Melvin Rosario, of, Indian Hills (Iowa) CC.
25. Trevor Kitsch, c, Kelowna (British Columbia) HS.
26. Jeremy Schultz, rhp, Mason City (Iowa) HS.
27. Justin Lombardi, lhp, Coyle-Cassidy HS, Taunton, Mass.
28. Rocky Kirk, lhp, Viewmont HS, Casper, Wyo.
29. Dan Kelly, lhp, Okaloosa-Walton (Fla.) CC.
30. Jerome Easter, of, Mount Union (Pa.) HS.
31. Brian Putnam, rhp, Indianola (Miss.) HS.
32. Braxton Batson, lhp, Mississippi Gulf Coast JC.
33. Cody Trask, rhp, Riverside (Calif.) CC.
34. Mark Scates, of, Coeur D'Alene (Idaho) HS.
35. James McCoy, of, Miami-Dade CC Kendall.
36. Alfredo Amezaga, ss, Miami Senior HS.
37. Ronny Marmol, c, Southridge HS, Miami.
38. Ryan Price, rhp, Eastern New Mexico U.
39. Walcott Richardson, of, Dracut (Mass.) HS.
40. Brandon Roberson, rhp, Hill (Texas) JC.
41. Yamilke Ulloa, lhp, Hialeah (Fla.) HS.
42. Matthew Ortiz, c, Grossmont (Calif) JC.
43. Shaun Wooley, lhp, Rancho Santiago (Calif.) JC.
44. Chad Elliot, lhp, Rancho Santiago (Calif.) JC.
45. Casey Lopez, 3b, Los Altos (Calif.) HS.
46. Matthew Thomas, rhp, Weatherford (Texas) HS.
47. Bobby Bass, of, Livermore (Calif.) HS.

DETROIT (1)

1. Matt Anderson, rhp, Rice U.
2. Shane Loux, rhp, Highland HS, Gilbert, Ariz.
3. Matt Boone, 3b, Villa Park (Calif.) HS.
4. Alan Webb, lhp, Durango HS, Las Vegas.
5. Heath Schesser, ss, Kansas State U.
6. Chris Parker, c, Westlake HS, Westlake Village, Calif.
7. Mike Diebolt, lhp, U. of Minnesota.
8. Dan Lauterhahn, 2b, William Paterson (N.J.) Coll.
9. Bud Smith, of-lhp, St. John Bosco HS, Lakewood, Calif.
10. Rick Roberts, lhp, Forest Hills HS, Summerhill, Pa.
11. Leo Daigle, 1b, Monte Vista HS, Spring Valley, Calif.
12. Darrell Pender, of, Miami Northwestern HS.
13. John Alkire, rhp, Cal State Fullerton.
14. Brennan Hervey, 1b, Florida Atlantic U.
15. Jason Howard, rhp, Purdue U.
16. Alex Steele, of, SUNY Cortland.
17. Chris Curry, c, Meridian (Miss.) CC.
18. Ryan Grimmett, of, U. of Miami.
19. Jeremy Sassanella, c, DeKalb HS, Auburn, Ind.
20. Craig Johnson, rhp, Siena Coll.
21. Nelson Alvarez, 1b, North Rockland HS, Haverstraw, N.Y.
22. Mandy Jacomino, of, U. of Miami.
23. Kevin Mobley, rhp, Georgia Coll.
24. Doyle Washington, of, Inglewood (Calif.) HS.
25. Kelly Crosby, of, Wheaton (Ill.) Warrenville HS.
26. Maxim St. Pierre, c, Col de Levis HS, Montreal.
27. William Snyder, rhp, Rensselaer Polytechnic (N.Y.) Institute.
28. Jacob Schaffer, ss, Bradley U.
29. Joseph Hall, of, Artesia HS, Lynwood, Calif.
30. Richard Ozarowski, ss, Florida Atlantic U.
31. Scott Martines, 1b, Punahou HS, Honolulu.
32. Steve Rodriguez, of, East Los Angeles JC.
33. Joel Greene, lhp, William Penn (Iowa) Coll.
34. John Guilmet, rhp, Merrimack (Mass.) Coll.
35. Matthew Beck, rhp, Bradley U.
36. Brian Cole, ss, Meridian (Miss.) HS.
37. Antonio Hasbun, ss, Briarcliff HS, New York.
38. Curtis Wickwire, 1b, Clovis West HS, Fresno.
39. Bernie Pedersoli, c, U. of Illinois-Chicago.
40. Clark Parker, 2b, Cal State Northridge.
41. Matthew Altagen, 1b, University HS, Malibu, Calif.
42. Carlos Hernandez, rhp, Columbus HS, Bronx, N.Y.

FLORIDA (12)

1. Aaron Akin, rhp, Cowley County (Kan.) CC.
2. Jeff Bailey, c, Kelso (Wash.) HS.
3. Chris Aguila, 3b, McQueen HS, Reno, Nev.
4. Brandon Harper, c, Dallas Baptist U.
5. Paul Avery, lhp, Fresno CC.
6. Brian Reed, of, Green Valley HS, Henderson, Nev.

7. Matt Erickson, 3b, U. of Arkansas.
8. Clifton Lee, lhp, Benton (Ark.) HS.
9. Jon Heinrichs, of, UCLA.
10. Kelley Washington, ss, Shenandoah HS, Stephens City, Va.
11. Jesus Medrano, 2b, Bishop Amat HS, La Puente, Calif.
12. Javon Walker, of, St. Thomas More HS, Lafayette, La.
13. Ross Gload, 1b, U. of South Florida.
14. Wes Anderson, rhp, Pine Bluff (Ark.) HS.
15. Travis Bailey, ss, Palm Beach (Fla.) CC.
16. James Shook, rhp, Columbia-Greene (N.Y.) CC.
17. Rhodney Donaldson, of, Troy State U.
18. Drew Shields, rhp, Pima (Ariz.) CC.
19. Robert Garvin, rhp, St. Andrew's Parish HS, Charleston, S.C.
20. Howard Beard, of, Watkins HS, Laurel, Miss.
21. Eric Bernhardt, rhp, Pittsburg (Kan.) HS.
22. Alex Melconian, c, Seton Hall U.
23. Andres Torres, of, Miami-Dade (Fla.) CC Wolfson.
24. Jason Harrison, c, Allegany (Md.) CC.
25. Cory Lima, rhp, North Carolina A&T U.
26. Scott Henderson, rhp, U. of Southern California.
27. Matt Schnabel, of-1b, Southwest Texas State U.
28. James McGowan, rhp, Queensborough (N.Y.) CC.
29. Blair Forwler, rhp, U. of Washington.
30. Gaige Thomas, rhp, Brenham (Texas) HS.
31. Jason Farmer, rhp, Indio (Calif.) HS.
32. Bryant Hodges, rhp, Seminole HS, Donaldsonville, Ga.
33. Ronald Dorsey, of, Hammonton (N.J.) HS.
34. Chris Clark, of, U. of Arkansas.
35. Joshua Higgins, rhp, El Capitan HS, Santee, Calif.
36. Antwoine Anderson, lhp, Withrow HS, Cincinnati.
37. Chris Louwsma, ss, Seminole HS, Sanford, Fla.
38. Eric Abshor, of, Howard (Texas) JC.
39. Adam Spiker, 1b, Marina HS, Huntington Beach, Calif.
40. John Weis, lhp, Chipola (Fla.) JC.
41. Billy Nofsinger, rhp, King HS, Tampa.
42. Nicholas Carlson, rhp, Madison (Wis.) Area Tech JC.
43. Glen Myers, lhp, South Charleston (W.Va.) HS.
44. Esteben Elzy, c, Cochise County (Ariz.) CC.
45. Jimmy Barndollar, rhp, Pacifica HS, Garden Grove, Calif.
46. Michael Wenger, lhp, Potomac State (W.Va.) JC.
47. Michael Shumaker, 1b, Meyersdale (Pa.) Area HS.
48. Aaron Lough, c, Potomac State (W.Va.) JC.
49. Michael Nall, rhp, Schaumburg (Ill.) HS.
50. Kyle Jenkins, rhp, Deptford HS, Woodbury, N.J.
51. Frank Valois, of, Montgomery (Md.) JC.
52. Tim Strange, c, Eau Gallie HS, Melbourne, Fla.
53. Brian Middleton, rhp, Woodbury (N.J.) HS.
54. Adrian Earles, of, Austin East HS, Knoxville.
55. Nicholas Huntsman, rhp, Pleasant Grove (Utah) HS.
56. William Baber, 3b, Western Albemarle HS, Crozet, Va.
57. Michael Kalchuk, rhp, Broward (Fla.) CC.
58. Carl Lafferty, c, Pine Bluff (Ariz.) HS.

HOUSTON (16)

1. Lance Berkman, 1b, Rice U.
2. Camron Hahn, c, Male HS, Louisville.
3. Scott Barrett, lhp, Mayde Creek HS, Houston.
4. Eric Byrnes, of, UCLA.
5. Derek Stanford, rhp, Temple (Texas) HS.
6. Joe Messman, rhp, Oregon State U.
7. Rob Bystrowski, of, Sacramento CC.
8. Ryan Dunn, of, Texas Christian U.
9. Don Thomas, lhp, Kennesaw State (Ga.) Coll.
10. Scott Fredericks, rhp, Saguaro HS, Scottsdale, Ariz.
11. Javier Pamus, rhp, San Jose State U.
12. Peter Sullivan, rhp, Limestone (S.C.) Coll.
13. Barton Leahy, of, Ohio U.
14. Trey Hodges, rhp, Blinn (Texas) JC.
15. J.J. Thomas, 1b, Georgia Tech.
16. Jim Wallace, rhp, U. of North Carolina.
17. Pat Cutshall, ss, Mercyhurst (Pa.) Coll.
18. Simon Mitchell, of, West Seattle HS.
19. Brian Hecht, rhp, U. of Illinois.
20. Tim Redding, rhp, Monroe (N.Y.) CC.
21. Neal Maybin, of, Lake Howell HS, Castleberry, Fla.
22. Jason Alfaro, rhp, Hill (Texas) JC.
23. Kyle Logan, of-3b, U. of Southern Mississippi.
24. Tim Judd, rhp, Dixon (Calif.) HS.
25. Charlton Jimerson, of, Mount Eden HS, Hayward, Calif.
26. Jared Wood, rhp, St. Louis (Mo.) CC Meramec.
27. Derek Brewster, rhp, Carthage (Texas) HS.
28. Graham Travis, rhp, Ballard HS, Seattle.
29. Joe Cathey, ss, Rice U.
30. Chris Ross, rhp, Ringgold (Ga.) HS.
31. Kris Clute, ss, Killian HS, Miami.
32. Eric Armbruster, 1b, Central HS, Kalamazoo, Mich.
33. Lamont Matthews, of, Kiswaukee (Ill.) JC.
34. John Skinner, rhp, Chabot (Calif.) JC.
35. Kevin Marzion, rhp, Elk Grove (Calif.) HS.
36. Jason Dill, 1b, Charlotte HS, Punta Gorda, Fla.
37. Jerymane Beasley, of, Olympic (Wash.) JC.
38. John Colon, rhp, Molokai HS, Maunaloa, Hawaii.
39. Marcos Rios, c, Chabot (Calif.) JC.
40. Garreth Perry, c, Service HS, Anchorage, Alaska.

KANSAS CITY (7)

1. Dan Reichert, rhp, U. of the Pacific.
2. Dane Sardinha, c, Kamehameha HS, Kahuku, Hawaii.
3. Jeremy Affeldt, lhp, Northwest Christian HS, Spokane, Wash.
4. Goefrey Tomlinson, of, U. of Houston.
5. Jason Gooding, lhp, Texas Tech.
6. Jason Anderson, rhp, Danville (Ill.) HS.
7. Joe Dillon, 1b, Texas Tech.
8. Eric Yanz, rhp, Kansas State U.
9. Kris Wilson, rhp, Georgia Tech.
10. David Willis, 1b, UC Santa Barbara.
11. Joe Caruso, 2b, U. of Alabama.
12. Jason Gilfillan, rhp, Limestone (S.C.) Coll.
13. Ryan Douglass, rhp, Canevin Catholic HS, Pittsburgh.
14. Tony Mancha, rhp, Las Cruces (N.M.) HS.
15. Justin Pederson, rhp, U. of Minnesota.
16. Rolando Geigel, rhp, Georgina Vaquaro HS, Canovanas, P.R.
17. Justin Lamber, lhp, U. of Richmond.
18. Bruce Stanley, rhp, Ball State U.
19. Tarik Graham, of, Edgewater HS, Orlando.
20. Carlos Pagan, c, U. of Mobile (Ala.).
21. Rod Metzler, 2b, Purdue U.
22. James Woods, c, Muskegon (Mich.) HS.
23. Rickey Crutchley, lhp, Etowan HS, Acworth, Ga.
24. Cameron Tillis, of, Lurleen B. Wallace State (Ala.) CC.
25. Ryan Hutchison, rhp, Vincennes (Ind.) HS.
26. Michael Perkins, rhp, Charlotte HS, Punta Gorda, Fla.
27. Fontella Jones, rhp, Mississippi Gulf Coast JC.
28. Aaron Carter, rhp, St. Mary's (Texas) U.
29. David Ullery, c, Indiana State U.
30. Robert Balazentis, rhp, Mercyhurst (Pa.) Coll.
31. George Petticrew, rhp, Lakeside HS, Nine Mile, Wash.
32. Kyle Turner, lhp, Antioch (Calif.) HS.
33. Nelson Bellido, rhp, Brooklyn.
34. Freddie Fincher, c, Galveston (Texas) JC.
35. John Hale, rhp, Robert E. Lee HS, Midland, Texas.
36. Donny Davis, rhp, El Cerrito HS, San Pablo, Calif.
37. John Majors, rhp, Flomaton HS, Brewton, Ala.
38. John Raymer, rhp, West Orange-Stark HS, Orange, Texas.
39. Aaron Melebeck, ss, Galveston (Texas) JC.
40. Ken Thomas, c, Gloucester County (N.J.) JC.
41. Chris Sampson, ss, Lon Morris (Texas) JC.
42. Chris Tallman, of, Rancho Santiago (Calif.) JC.
43. Quentin Elder, rhp, Castlemont HS, Oakland.
44. Daniel Martinez, lhp, Sweetwater HS, National City, Calif.
45. Bret Halbert, lhp, Cypress (Calif.) JC.
46. Gary Schulz, lhp, Montgomery (Texas) HS.
47. Mark Villarreal, c, John Foster Dulles HS, Missouri City, Texas.
48. Matthew Williams, 3b, Millikan HS, Long Beach.
49. Carlos Spikes, of, North Florida Christian HS, Tallahassee, Fla.

LOS ANGELES (24)

1. Glenn Davis, 1b, Vanderbilt U.
2. Chase Utley, ss, Poly HS, Long Beach.
2. Steve Colyer, lhp, Fort Zumwalt South HS, St. Peters, Mo. (Supplemental pick—83rd—for loss of Type C free agent Delino DeShields).
3. Ricky Bell, ss, Moeller HS, Cincinnati.
4. John Hernandez, c, Nogales HS, La Puente, Calif.
5. Kip Harkrider, ss, U. of Texas.
6. Will McCrotty, c, Russellville (Ark.) HS.
7. Miles Durham, of, Cooper HS, Abilene, Texas.
8. Beau Parker, rhp, Prairie HS, Brush Prairie, Wash.
9. Jamie Goudie, ss, Hardaway HS, Columbus, Ga.
10. Joe Patterson, of, Ontario (Calif.) HS.
11. Cory Vance, lhp, Butler HS, Vandalia, Ohio.
12. David Lamberth, ss, Macon County HS, Montezuma, Ga.
13. Matt Bornyk, rhp, Esquimalt HS, Victoria, British Columbia.
14. Brent Husted, rhp, U. of Nevada.
15. David Mittauer, rhp, Dade Christian HS, Cooper City, Fla.
16. Scott Walter, c, Loyola HS, Manhattan Beach, Calif.
17. Chad Cislak, rhp, Sabino HS, Tucson.
18. Michael Balbuena, 3b, Key West (Fla.) HS.
19. Joel Allen, of, Glenns Ferry (Idaho) HS.
20. Peter Zamora, 1b-lhp, UCLA.

21. **Stephen Verigood, lhp, Spartanburg Methodist (S.C.) JC.**
22. **Matthew Montgomery, rhp, Long Beach State U.**
23. **Jared Moon, rhp, Redondo Union HS, Redondo Beach, Calif.**
24. **Michael Rawls, lhp, Bethune-Cookman (Fla.) Coll.**
25. David Detienne, 3b, Auburn Drive HS, Dartmouth, Nova Scotia.
26. **Bill Everly, rhp, West Virginia Wesleyan Coll.**
27. **Aaron Dean, 1b, Lamar U.**
28. **Richard Bell, lhp, California Lutheran U.**
29. **Darin Schmalz, rhp, U. of Notre Dame.**
30. Sam Lopez, ss, Dinuba (Calif.) HS.
31. **Wayne Slater, of, Bethune-Cookman (Fla.) Coll.**
32. Shaylar Hatch, rhp, Gilbert, Ariz.
33. Shaun Benzor, lhp, Redlands (Calif.) HS.
34. Blake McGinley, lhp, North HS, Bakersfield, Calif.
35. Adam Thomas, of, Hazel Park HS, Troy, Mich.
36. Jesus Feliciano, of, Academia HS, Bayamon, P.R.
37. Tyler Renwick, rhp, New Mexico JC.
38. Eliot Joyner, of, Mount San Antonio (Calif.) JC.
39. Jahseam George, lhp, Buchanan HS, Clovis, Calif.
40. John Nelson, ss, Denton (Texas) HS.
41. Ryan Beaver, rhp, Millikan HS, Long Beach.
42. **Carlos Orozco, of, Montgomery HS, San Diego.**
43. Michael Hernandez, lhp, Carson (Calif.) HS.
44. Graig Merritt, c, Pitt Meadows, British Columbia.
45. Shane Youman, lhp, New Iberia (La.) HS.
46. Ryan Kellner, c, Spartanburg Methodist (S.C.) JC.
47. Jean Emard, lhp, Edouard Montpetit HS, Montreal.
48. Luis DeJesus, c, Miguel De Cervantes, Bayamon, P.R.
49. **Lance Warren, c, Richmond Hill (Calif.) HS.**
50. Chris Howay, rhp, New Westminster (British Columbia) HS.
51. Eric Burris, 1b, Los Angeles Harbor JC.
52. Russell Ivory, of, Grossmont (Calif.) JC.
53. Ismael Garcia, 2b, Mount San Antonio (Calif.) JC.
54. Michael Ford, of, Elk Grove (Calif.) HS.
55. Melvin Anderson, 3b, North Iverville HS, Baton Rouge.
56. Reggie LaPlante, rhp, Edouard Montpetit, Montreal.
57. George Bailey, 3b, Indian River (Fla.) CC.
58. James Howard, rhp, Orange Park, Fla.
59. Joshua Ridgway, ss, Delta HS, Ladner, British Columbia.
60. Jason Ware, 1b, Long Beach CC.
61. Javier Gonzalez, rhp, Mount San Antonio (Calif.) JC.
62. Steve Holm, ss, McClatchy HS, Sacramento.
63. Cedric Herbert, rhp, Grayson County (Texas) JC.
64. Jeremy Loftice, rhp, Truett McConnell (Ga.) JC.
65. Luis Fontanez, c, Juana Colon HS, Bayamon, P.R.
66. John Castellano, c, Indian River (Fla.) CC.
67. Cory Stephen, c, Regina, Saskatchewan.
68. Matt Ybarra, c, Encinal HS, Alameda, Calif.
69. **Luis Medina, c, Bayamon, P.R.**
70. Ryan Withey, of, Seminole (Fla.) CC.

MILWAUKEE (13)

1. **Kyle Peterson, rhp, Stanford U.**
2. **Alvin Morrow, of, Kirkwood (Mo.) HS.**
3. **Jeff Deardorff, 3b, South Lake HS, Clermont, Fla.**
4. **Tommy Warren, of, Westchester HS, Inglewood, Calif.**
5. **Frank Candela, of, Peabody (Mass.) HS.**
6. **Jake Eye, rhp, Ohio U.**
7. **Bucky Jacobsen, of, Lewis-Clark State (Idaho) Coll.**
8. **Todd Incantalupo, lhp, Providence Coll.**
9. **Matt Childers, rhp, Westside HS, Augusta, Ga.**
10. **Chris Patton, ss, McClintock HS, Tempe, Ariz.**
11. **Jim Miller, rhp, Carthage (Wis.) Coll.**
12. **Kendall Guthrie, c, Northwood (Texas) Institute.**
13. Brent Kelley, rhp, Arkansas State U.
14. **Chris Rowan, 3b, Mount Vernon (N.Y.) HS.**
15. Romaro Miller, ss, Shannon (Miss.) HS.
16. **Andrew Cavanagh, rhp, Young Harris (Ga.) JC.**
17. **Mark Kirst, rhp, St. Norbert's (Wis.) Coll.**
18. **Jay Akin, lhp, Arkansas State U.**
19. **Shane Wooten, lhp, Birmingham-Southern Coll.**
20. Doug Clark, of, U. of Massachusetts.
21. Mark Cridland, of, U. of Texas.
22. Charles Manning, lhp, Winter Haven (Fla.) HS.
23. **Kevin Priebe, lhp, Bradley U.**
24. Robbie Baker, rhp, Blinn (Texas) JC.
25. Steve Beller, rhp, West Virginia U.
26. **Trad Sokol, lhp, Frederick (Md.) CC.**
27. **Brian Mallette, rhp, Columbus (Ga.) Coll.**
28. **Marty Patterson, c, Michigan State U.**
29. Alfred Corbeil, c, Plantation HS, Margate, Fla.
30. Brian Fields, lhp, East Carolina U.
31. **Chauncey Jones, rhp, Briar Cliff (Iowa) Coll.**
32. Gary McConnell, rhp, North Florida CC.
33. Arthur Garland, rhp, Magnolia HS, Anaheim.

JEFF GOLDEN

Brewers first-rounder
Kyle Peterson broke in with Rookie-level Ogden

34. James Igo, rhp, Galveston (Texas) JC.
35. Ryan Costello, lhp, Eastern HS, Voorhees, N.J.
36. **Chad Helmer, rhp, Florida Southern Coll.**
37. Landon Jacobsen, rhp, Howard HS, Canova, S.D.
38. Randy Rodriguez, lhp, Indian River (Fla.) CC.
39. **Joel Arroyo, rhp, Saint Leo (Fla.) Coll.**
40. **Robert Riggio, 3b, Lehman (N.Y.) Coll.**
41. Geoff Geary, rhp, Oklahoma U.
42. Justin Ames, lhp, Moorpark (Calif.) HS.
43. **Ryan Pearson, of, Troy State U.**
44. Marcos Quinones, rhp, Lee (Texas) JC.
45. **Nick Caiazzo, c, U. of Maine.**
46. Eric Tomlinson, of, Granbury (Texas) HS.
47. Jeff Savage, rhp, Palm Beach Gardens (Fla.) HS.
48. Oscar Ramirez, ss, Southridge HS, Miami.
49. Nick Quinn, of, Atlantic HS, Boynton Beach, Fla.
50. Jimmy Smith, of, Lake Mary HS, Longwood, Fla.
51. Jose Camilo, 2b, North Florida CC.
52. Michael Oiler, ss, Watertown (Wis.) HS.
53. Bennie Harris, of, Myers Park HS, Charlotte, N.C.

MINNESOTA (9)

1. **Michael Cuddyer, ss, Great Bridge HS, Chesapeake, Va.**

1\. **Matthew LeCroy, c, Clemson U.** (Supplemental pick—50th—for failure to sign 1996 first-round pick Travis Lee).

2. **Mike Restovich, of, Mayo HS, Rochester, Minn.**
3. Greg Withelder, lhp, Strath Haven HS, Wallingford, Pa.
4. **Bob Davies, lhp, Marietta (Ohio) Coll.**
5. **Peter Blake, lhp, Indianola (Iowa) HS.**
6. **Nate Melson, rhp, Rogers (Ark.) HS.**
7. **Matt Carnes, rhp, U. of Arkansas.**
8. **Ben Thomas, lhp, Wichita State U.**
9. **Jon Schaeffer, c, Stanford U.**
10. **Josh Gandy, lhp, U. of Georgia.**
11. **Matt Jurgena, rhp, Hastings (Neb.) Coll.**
12. **Lateef Vaughn, ss, Long Beach State U.**
13. **Marques Southward, of, Pasco Comprehensive HS, Dade City, Fla.**
14. Eddy Furniss, 1b, Louisiana State U.
15. Jake Weber, of, North Carolina State U.
16. Jordan Gerk, lhp, KLO HS, Kelowna, British Columbia.
17. Kevin Frederick, rhp-3b, Creighton U.
18. **Ray Underhill, rhp, Deland (Fla.) HS.**

19. Kevin Stuart, rhp, Golden West (Calif.) JC.
20. Billy Coleman, rhp, Western Michigan U.
21. Juan Romero, lhp, U. of Mobile.
22. Daniel Boyd, 3b, Pasco Comprehensive HS, Dade City, Fla.
23. Tim Sturdy, rhp, La Cueva HS, Albuquerque.
24. Creston Whitaker, of, Jesuit Collegiate HS, Dallas.
25. Adam Johnson, rhp, Torrey Pines HS, San Diego.
26. Dan Morris, lhp, Ayersville HS, Defiance, Ohio.
27. Daylan Holt, of, Mesquite (Texas) HS.
28. David Shank, rhp, Miramonte HS, Orinda, Calif.
29. Aaron Jaworowski, 1b, U. of Missouri.
30. Nate Stevens, ss, Keystone (Fla.) HS.
31. Mike Cosgrove, rhp, U. of Tennessee.
32. Trevor Mote, ss, Kingman (Ariz.) HS.
33. Nicholas Punto, ss, Saddleback (Calif.) CC.
34. Marques Tuiasosopo, 3b, Woodinville (Wash.) HS.
35. Craig Hawkins, rhp, Notre Dame HS, Burlington, Ontario.
36. Brian Fitts, rhp, Volunteer State (Tenn.) CC.
37. Patrick Stenger, rhp, St. Ignatius HS, Mentor, Ohio.
38. Bryant Melson, c, U. of North Florida.
39. Isaiah Haynes, of, Vanden HS, Fairfield, Calif.
40. Casey Fuller, lhp, Dixon (Calif.) HS.
41. Corey Richardson, of, Northeast Texas CC.
42. Russell Bratton, rhp, U. of Memphis.
43. Justin Smith, lhp, Seward County (Kan.) CC.
44. Josh Reese, rhp, Lincoln County HS, Fayetteville, Tenn.
45. Matt Booth, lhp, Henry Clay HS, Lexington, Ky.
46. Aaron Miller, lhp, Campbell U.
47. Joe Foote, rhp, Park View HS, Sterling, Va.
48. Jason McConnell, 2b, U. of Arkansas.
49. David Justice, ss, Washington HS, Pensacola, Fla.
50. Robert Bozied, c, Arvada (Colo.) West HS.
51. Clint Bailey, rhp, Chemainus, British Columbia.
52. Richard Durrett, 1b, El Paso (Texas) CC.
53. Shawn Stiffler, lhp, Somerset (Pa.) HS.

MONTREAL (22)

1. Donnie Bridges, rhp, Oak Grove HS, Hattiesburg, Miss.
1. Chris Stowe, rhp, Chancellor HS, Fredericksburg, Va. (Supplemental pick—37th—for loss of service-time free agent Mel Rojas).
1. Scott Hodges, ss, Henry Clay HS, Lexington, Ky. (Supplemental pick—38th—for loss of service-time free agent Moises Alou).
1. Bryan Hebson, rhp, Auburn U. (Supplemental pick—44th—for loss of Rojas).
1. Thomas Pittman, 1b, East St. John HS, Garyville, La. (Supplemental pick—45th—for loss of Alou).
1. T.J. Tucker, rhp, River Ridge HS, New Port Richey, Fla. (Supplemental pick—47th—for loss of Rojas).
1. Shane Arthurs, rhp, Westmoore HS, Oklahoma City (Supplemental pick—48th—for loss of Alou).
1. Tootie Myers, of, Petal (Miss.) HS (Supplemental pick—52nd—for failure to sign 1996 first-round pick John Patterson).
2. Kris Tetz, rhp, Lodi (Calif.) HS.
3. Josh Reding, ss, Rancho Santiago (Calif.) JC.
4. Ronte Langs, of, Whitehaven HS, Memphis.
5. Julio Perez, rhp, Brito Private HS, Miami.
6. Scott Ackerman, c, Oregon City HS.
7. Anthony Caracciolo, ss, Basic HS, Henderson, Nev.
8. Ryan Becks, lhp, West Valley (Calif.) JC.
9. Talmadge Nunnari, 1b, Jacksonville U.
10. Scott Strickland, rhp, U. of New Mexico.
11. Matt Blank, lhp, Texas A&M U.
12. Ryan Van Gilder, rhp, Mankato State (Minn.) U.
13. Luis Rivera, c, Florida Southern Coll.
14. Scott Zech, 2b, Florida State U.
15. Lance Burkhart, c-3b, Southwest Missouri State U.
16. Ryan Saylor, rhp, Eastern Kentucky U.
17. Spencer Nemer, rhp, Klein Forest HS, Houston.
18. Josh Merrigan, lhp, Vermillion (S.D.) HS.
19. Jonathan Boyett, 2b, Modesto (Calif.) JC.
20. Marcus Bell, rhp, Pace (Fla.) HS.
21. Ray Plummer, lhp, Point Loma Nazarene (Calif.) Coll.
22. Michael Edge, of, North Brunswick HS, Winnabow, N.C.
23. Matt Coleman, lhp, Centennial HS, Boring, Ore.
24. Tobin Lanzetta, rhp, Santa Clara U.
25. Shaun Poole, lhp, Hudson HS, Spring Hill, Fla.
26. Ralph Harrelson, rhp, Davis HS, Modesto, Calif.
27. Jason Hoffman, of, Ohlone (Calif.) JC.
28. Joseph Fretwell, rhp, Valencia (Fla.) CC.
29. Nathan Cook, 3b, Chabot (Calif.) JC.
30. Derek Smith, ss, Tulare (Calif.) Union HS.
31. Jeff Lincoln, rhp, American River (Calif.) JC.
32. Cory Vandegriff, ss, Halls HS, Knoxville.
33. Brandt Hayden, ss, South Salem (Ore.) HS
34. Joe Baldassano, rhp, Alta Loma (Calif.) HS.
35. Arthur Anderson, ss, East St. John HS, La Place, La.
36. Sam Anderson, c, Mesquite (Texas) HS.
37. David Vonah, 3b, Hoover HS, Fresno.
38. Edwin Gomez, of, Teodoro Aguilar Mora HS, Yabucoa, P.R.
39. James McKnight, c, Washington HS, Phoenix.
40. John White, c, Jacksonville U.
41. Luis Martinez, c, Jose Campeche HS, San Lorenzo, P.R.
42. Kevin Harmon, c, Palmdale HS, Acton, Calif.
43. Josh Laidlaw, of, Cheyenne HS, North Las Vegas.
44. Matthew Baird, of, Burlington, Ontario.
45. Mechel Elam, of, Eisenhower HS, San Bernardino, Calif.
46. Brian Oxley, ss, Los Medanos (Calif.) JC.
47. Matthew Cody, c, Woodlawn HS, Baton Rouge.
48. Chris Herman, ss, South Hills HS, Covina, Calif.
49. Dean Harper, c, Peoria, Ariz.

NEW YORK/AL (25)

1. Tyrell Godwin, of, East Bladen HS, Elizabethtown, N.C. (Choice from Rangers—24th—as compensation for Type A free agent John Wetteland).
1. (Choice to Orioles—26th—as compensation for Type A free agent David Wells).
1. Ryan Bradley, rhp, Arizona State U. (Supplemental pick—40th—for loss of Wetteland).
2. (Choice to Rangers—77th—as compensation for Type A free agent Mike Stanton).
2. Jason Henry, rhp, U. of Illinois-Chicago (Supplemental pick—84th—for loss of Type C free agent Jimmy Key).
3. Mike Knowles, rhp, Palatka (Fla.) HS.
4. Dion Washington, of, JC of Southern Idaho.
5. Randy Choate, lhp, Florida State U.
6. John Darjean, of, Dallas Baptist U.
7. Scott Wiggins, lhp, Northern Kentucky U.
8. Jeremy Morris, of, Florida State U.
9. Randy Flores, lhp, U. of Southern California.
10. David Parrish, c, Esperanza HS, Yorba Linda, Calif.
11. Cody Klein, lhp, Andrews (Texas) HS.
12. Ernie Villegas, of, Irving (Texas) HS.
13. Brian Tallet, lhp, Hill (Texas) JC.
14. Chris Wallace, rhp, Wright State U.
15. Marc Mirizzi, ss, U. of Southern California.
16. Matt Purkiss, 3b, U. of San Francisco.
17. Albert Jones, of, Pasco Comprehensive HS, Dade City, Fla.
18. Brian August, 3b, U. of Delaware.
19. Michael Shelley, lhp, Ashford (Ala.) HS.
20. Paul Manning, of, Hunting Hill HS, Red Deer, Alberta.
21. Bill Bronikowski, c, U. of Toledo.
22. Beau Hale, rhp, Little Cypress HS, Mauriceville, Texas.
23. David Langston, rhp, Ringgold (Ga.) HS.
24. Jack Koch, rhp, U. of Tampa.
25. Stanton Wood, rhp, El Camino (Calif.) JC.
26. Aaron Jones, 1b, Southern Illinois U.
27. Robert Fischer, ss, Lyons Township HS, LaGrange, Ill.
28. Adam Huddleston, 1b, Mississippi Gulf Coast JC.
29. Matt Vincent, lhp, Logan (Ill.) JC.
30. Keith Dunn, rhp, Grayson County (Texas) JC.
31. Digno Torres, of, Jaime Collazo HS, Morovis, P.R.
32. Brandon Davis, c, George County HS, Lucedale, Miss.
33. Carlos Arvizu, 1b, Tucson HS.
34. Jarrod Douglass, rhp, Briarcliff HS, Bayshore, N.Y.
35. Dustin Franklin, lhp, Odessa (Texas) JC.
36. Chris Parrish, c, Jackson State (Tenn.) CC.
37. Marshall McDougall, ss, Santa Fe (Fla.) CC.
38. James Kent, rhp, Motlow State (Tenn.) CC.
39. Jeremy Lyon, of, Donelson Christian Academy, Old Hickory, Tenn.
40. Michael Vento, of, New Mexico JC.
41. Chris Spurling, rhp, Sinclair (Ohio) CC.
42. Robert Mapp, lhp, Turner HS, Burneyville, Okla.
43. David Rodriguez, of, Southridge HS, Miami.
44. Andy Smith, rhp, Bowling Green State U.
45. Jason Halper, of, Columbia U.
46. Chad Conner, rhp, South Bend, Ind.
47. Matthew Berry, rhp, Christian HS, Lakeside, Calif.
48. Dylan Putnam, rhp, St. Mary's Prep, Ann Arbor, Mich.
49. Dan Seimetz, 1b, Ohio State U.
50. Blake Wilsford, 3b, Collierville (Tenn.) HS.
51. Chad Harris, rhp, Jasper (Texas) HS.
52. Anthony McNeal, 3b, Cosumnes River (Calif.) JC.
53. Robert Fletcher, c, Southland Academy, Americus, Ga.
54. Russ Chambliss, of, Washington (Mo.) U.
55. Aaron Heilman, rhp, Logansport (Ind.) HS.
56. Corey Ward, of, Dallas.
57. Mark Gilliam, 1b, Grundy County HS, Pelham, Texas.
58. Jeffrey Rossi, lhp, Skyline HS, Salt Lake City.
59. Adam Manley, of, Clover Park HS, Tacoma.

60. David Clark, of, Denham Springs (La.) HS.
61. Eric Rodriguez, rhp, Aureo Quiles HS, Guanica, P.R.
62. Paul Schlosser, 3b, McCoy HS, Medicine Hat, Alberta.
63. John Phillips, rhp, UCLA.
64. Nicolas Alvarez, rhp, Socorro HS, El Paso.
65. Javiier Sein, 1b, Palm Beach (Fla.) CC.
66. Nicholas Herz, c, Palomar (Calif.) JC.
67. Rodney Friar, c, Mount San Jacinto (Calif.) JC.
68. Scott Glaser, lhp, U. of South Florida.

NEW YORK/NL (6)

1. **Geoff Goetz, lhp, Jesuit HS, Tampa.**
2. **Tyler Walker, rhp, U. of California.**
3. **Cesar Crespo, ss, Notre Dame HS, Caguas, P.R.**
4. **Michael Yancy, of, Morse HS, San Diego.**
5. **Brian Jenkins, c, Port St. Joe (Fla.) HS.**
6. **Matt Lowe, rhp, Walhalla (S.C.) HS.**
7. **Robert Weslowski, rhp, Marcellus (N.Y.) Central HS.**
8. **Vicente Rosario, of, George Washington HS, New York.**
9. **Kenny Miller, ss, U. of Kentucky.**
10. Garrett Atkins, 3b, University HS, Irvine, Calif.
11. **John Mangieri, rhp, St. Francis Coll.**
12. **Nick Maness, rhp, North Moore HS, Robbins, N.C.**
13. **Eric Cammack, rhp, Lamar U.**
14. Craig Kuzmic, c, Cypress (Calif.) JC.
15. Jeremy Guthrie, rhp, Ashland (Ore.) HS.
16. **Mark Proctor, ss, Courtland HS, Fredericksburg, Va.**
17. **Bobby Hill, ss, Gainesville HS, Waldo, Fla.**
18. Dominic Rich, 2b, Line Mountain HS, Herndan, Pa.
19. **Nick Rains, of, John Carroll HS, Fort Pierce, Fla.**
20. **Jason Roach, 3b, UNC Wilmington.**
21. **Jason Brett, ss, South Georgia JC.**
22. Marcellus Presley, of, Hiram Johnson HS, Sacramento.
23. Seth Davidson, ss, University HS, San Diego.
24. **Jason Phillips, c, San Diego State U.**
25. James Mayfield, rhp, Jefferson State (Ala.) CC.
26. **J.D. Arteaga, lhp, U. of Miami.**
27. Matt Ardizzone, 2b, U. of Delaware.
28. Anthony Brown, of, DuPont HS, Hockessin, Del.
29. **Jose Rio-Berger, of, Lewis-Clark State (Idaho) Coll.**
30. **Jason Shuck, ss, Carl Albert State (Okla.) JC.**
31. **Randy Hamilton, lhp, Northern Kentucky U.**
32. **Jorge Santiago, ss, Marist Coll.**
33. **Shawn Mikkola, rhp, Largo (Fla.) HS.**
34. Barry Paulk, of, Southridge HS, Miami.
35. Miguel Miranda, ss, Academy HS, Rio Piedras, P.R.
36. Greg White, 1b, James Madison U.
37. Brandon Lyon, rhp, Taylorsville HS, Salt Lake City.
38. Barry Wichert, lhp, Seminole State (Okla.) JC.
39. Robert Scott, 2b, Cowley County (Kan.) CC.
40. Randy Keisler, lhp, Navarro (Texas) JC.
41. David Benham, c, Liberty U.
42. **David Lohrman, rhp, Rensselaer Polytechnic (N.Y.) Institute.**
43. David DeJesus, of, Manalapan (N.J.) HS.
44. Kevin Zaug, rhp, Carmel HS, Stormville, N.Y.
45. **Anthony Valentine, 2b, U. of New Hampshire.**
46. **Jason Bowring, 3b, Riverside (Calif.) CC.**
47. Tanner Brock, rhp, Lake Brantley HS, Altamonte Springs, Fla.
48. Matt Whitehead, rhp, Athens (Texas) HS.
49. Jeremy Jackson, lhp, Mississippi State U.
50. **Mark Maberry, rhp, Tennessee Tech.**
51. Elvin Cannon, of, Northland HS, Columbus, Ohio.
52. Mike Tonis, c, Elk Grove (Calif.) HS.
53. **Mathias Fafard, 3b, Indian River (Fla.) CC.**
54. Anthony Sutter, ss, Brookdale (N.J.) CC.
55. Brian Kuklick, rhp, Wake Forest U.
56. **Joshua Taylor, ss, Cowley County (Kan.) CC.**
57. **Clark Lambert, c, Lipscomb (Tenn.) U.**
58. Ryan Lamattina, lhp, St. Bonaventure U.

OAKLAND (11)

1. **Chris Enochs, rhp, West Virginia U.**
1. **Eric DuBose, lhp, Mississippi State U.** (Special compensation—21st—for loss of service-time free agent Mike Bordick).
1. **Nathan Haynes, of, Pinole Valley HS, Hercules, Calif.** (Supplemental pick—32nd—for loss of Bordick).
1. **Denny Wagner, rhp, Virginia Tech** (Supplemental pick—42nd—for loss of Bordick).
2. **Chad Harville, rhp, Memphis U.**
3. **Marcus Jones, rhp, Long Beach State U.**
4. **Jason Anderson, lhp, Radford U.**
5. **Andy Kimball, rhp, U. of Wisconsin-Oshkosh.**
6. **Tim Hudson, rhp, Auburn U.**
7. **Roberto Vaz, of, U. of Alabama.**
8. **Adam Piatt, 3b, Mississippi State U.**
9. **Jared Jensen, rhp, Brigham Young U.**
10. **Javier Flores, c, Oklahoma U.**
11. **Mike Koerner, of, Louisiana State U.**
12. **Adam Robinson, ss, U. of Virginia.**
13. Jonathan Winterrowd, rhp, Germantown (Tenn.) HS.
14. Ryan Drese, rhp, U. of California.
15. **Eric Meeks, rhp, West Orange HS, Orlando.**
16. **Jamie Porter, of, U. of Washington.**
17. **Elvin Nina, rhp, Oklahoma State U.**
18. **Mike Holmes, rhp, Wake Forest U.**
19. Josh Canales, ss, Carson (Calif.) HS.
20. **Randy Niles, rhp, Florida State U.**
21. **Brad Gorrie, ss, U. of Massachusetts.**
22. Forrest Johnson, c, Rialto (Calif.) HS.
23. **Gary Thomas, 3b-of, Vanderbilt Catholic HS, Houma, La.**
24. **Jeremy Crawford, lhp, Glenwood HS, Chatham, Ill.**
25. Ronnie Williams, of, Booker HS, Sarasota, Fla.
26. **David Waites, rhp, U. of New Mexico.**
27. **Miguel Declet, ss, Eloisa Pascual HS, Caguas, P.R.**
28. **Ed Farris, 1b, Ball State U.**
29. Stephen Murphy, rhp, Canada (Calif.) JC.
30. **Tim Manwiller, rhp, Radford U.**
31. Jonathan Weber, of, Los Angeles Harbor JC.
32. Tim Newman, rhp, Davis HS, Yakima, Wash.
33. Ian Perio, lhp, Laney (Calif.) JC.
34. Keith Foxton, of, Kirkwood (Iowa) CC.
35. Brandon Pack, c, Esperanza HS, Yorba Linda, Calif.
36. **Jason Faust, lhp, U. of New Orleans.**
37. Marshall Rubens, rhp, Del Campo HS, Citrus Heights, Calif.
38. Matt Carlock, rhp, Armijo HS, Suisun City, Calif.
39. Tony Dawson, rhp, Laney (Calif.) JC.
40. Will Lewis, of, Rialto HS, Adelanto, Calif.

PHILADELPHIA (2)

1. J.D. Drew, of, Florida State U.
2. **Randy Wolf, lhp, Pepperdine U.**
3. **Shomari Beverly, of, Encinal HS, Alameda, Calif.**
4. **Nick Marchant, of, Capital HS, Boise, Idaho.**
5. **Derrick Turnbow, rhp, Franklin (Tenn.) HS.**
6. **Tom Jacquez, lhp, UCLA.**
7. **Derek Adair, rhp, St. John's U.**
8. **Brian Harris, ss, Indiana U.**
9. Michael Schulte, rhp, Cleveland HS, Reseda, Calif.
10. **Bennie Bishop, of, Westchester HS, Inglewood, Calif.**
11. **Kevin Kurilla, ss, Virginia Tech.**
12. **Mark Rutherford, rhp, Eastern Michigan U.**
13. Lance Niekro, ss, Jenkins HS, Lakeland, Fla.
14. **Geoff Zawatski, rhp, U. of Virginia.**
15. **Troy Norrell, c, Navarro (Texas) JC.**
16. Brett Weber, rhp, U. of Illinois.
17. **Johnny Estrada, c-1b, JC of the Sequoias (Calif.).**
18. **Duane Johnson, of, Wooster HS, Reno, Nev.**
19. **Jimmy Frush, rhp, Texas Tech.**
20. **Jeff Terrell, 2b, U. of Missouri.**
21. **Rusty McNamara, of-3b, Oklahoma State U.**
22. **Gary Burnham, of, Clemson U.**
23. **Brett Black, rhp, North Carolina State U.**
24. **Pat Driscoll, lhp, U. of Nebraska.**
25. **Jerry Valdez, c, Fort Hays State (Kan.) U.**
26. **Andy Dominique, 3b, U. of Nevada.**
27. **Adam Walker, lhp, U. of Mississippi.**
28. **Kevin Shipp, rhp, Louisiana State U.**
29. **Chad Albaugh, rhp, William Penn (Iowa) Coll.**
30. Kevin Leighton, c, Brewster (N.Y.) HS.
31. **Mark Manbeck, rhp, U. of Houston.**
32. **Chris Humphries, rhp, U. of Nevada-Las Vegas.**
33. **Ed Fitzpatrick, c, Freed-Hardeman (Tenn.) U.**
34. **Lamonte Collier, ss, Southeast Missouri State U.**
35. **Calvin Key, rhp, Arkansas State U.**
36. **Jeff Hootselle, lhp, Mary Washington (Va.) Coll.**
37. **Uriel Casillas, ss, Cal State Los Angeles.**
38. **Clay Eason, rhp, North Carolina State U.**
39. **Peter Mondello, rhp, Nicholls State U.**
40. **Ryan Cody, c, Fort Vancouver (Wash.) HS.**
41. **Jim Fritz, c, U. of Southwestern Louisiana.**
42. John Marifan, lhp, Cerritos (Calif.) JC.
43. David Walther, 2b, De Smet Jesuit HS, St. Louis.
44. **Jonathan Bushman, of, Lindbergh HS, St. Louis.**

PITTSBURGH (8)

1. **J.J. Davis, 1b-rhp, Baldwin Park HS, Pomona, Calif.**
2. **Jose Nicolas, of, Westminster Christian HS, Miami.**
3. **John Grabow, lhp, San Gabriel (Calif.) HS.**
4. **Maurice Washington, of, Chaparral HS, Las Vegas.**

5. Chris Combs, rhp-of, North Carolina State U.
6. Andy Bausher, lhp, Kutztown (Pa.) U.
7. Korwin Dehaan, of, Morningside (Iowa) Coll.
8. Paul Stabile, lhp, Brookdale (N.J.) CC.
9. Michael Parkerson, lhp, Columbus (Ga.) HS.
10. Rico Washington, ss, Jones County HS, Gray, Ga.
11. Sam McConnell, lhp, Ball State U.
12. Jeff Leuenberger, rhp, Canyon HS, Anaheim.
13. Kris Lambert, lhp, Baylor U.
14. Ryan Carter, lhp, Beyer HS, Modesto, Calif.
15. Jason Moore, ss, Westminster Christian HS, Miami.
16. Jason Hardebeck, lhp, Carl Sandburg (Ill.) JC.
17. Chris Luttig, lhp, U. of Evansville.
18. Shawn Schumacher, c-3b, Panola (Texas) JC.
19. Andrew Jones, of, Mountain Point HS, Phoenix.
20. Kevin Haverbusch, ss-rhp, U. of Maryland.
21. Keith Maxwell, of-c, Florida A&M U.
22. Alex Tolbert, 1b, Western Carolina U.
23. Michael Smalley, lhp, Bishop Moore HS, Maitland, Fla.
24. Jeff Carlsen, rhp, North Kitsap HS, Poulsbo, Wash.
25. Jesse Daggett, c, JC of the Canyons (Calif.).
26. Michael Wiggs, ss, Mount Olive (N.C.) Coll.
27. Brad Guy, rhp, Cal State Los Angeles.
28. Matt Wood, rhp, Cary (N.C.) HS.
29. Ryan Earey, 3b, Laney HS, Wilmington, N.C.
30. Michael Gonzalez, lhp, San Jacinto (Texas) JC.
31. Jeff LaRoche, lhp, Blinn (Texas) JC.
32. Marcus Harris, lhp, Cabrillo HS, Lompoc, Calif.
33. William White, lhp, Benjamin Russell HS, Alexander City, Ala.
34. C.J. Steele, ss, Spiro (Okla.) HS.
35. Jamal Strong, of-ss, Citrus (Calif.) JC.
36. Jeff Phelps, ss, Kofa HS, Yuma, Ariz.
37. Chris Clark, of, Stanford U.
38. Mike Scarborough, of, U. of Texas.
39. Josh Newton, rhp, Springhill (La.) HS.
40. Peter Austin, of, Millsaps (Miss.) Coll.
41. Kevin Brown, 3b, North Fort Myers (Fla.) HS.
42. Derrick Lankford, 3b, Carson-Newman (Tenn.) Coll.
43. Brett Kaplan, of, U. of North Carolina.

ST. LOUIS (20)

1. Adam Kennedy, ss, Cal State Northridge.
2. Rick Ankiel, lhp, Port St. Lucie (Fla.) HS.
3. Patrick Coogan, rhp, Louisiana State U.
4. Xavier Nady, ss, Salinas (Calif.) HS.
5. Jason Navarro, lhp, Tulane U.
6. Bryan Rupert, c, Limestone (S.C.) Coll.
7. Joe Secoda, 2b, Rancho Santiago (Calif.) JC.
8. Jason Karnuth, rhp, Illinois State U.
9. Seth Etherton, rhp, U. of Southern California.
10. Finley Woodward, rhp, Auburn U.
11. Reynaldo Torres, 1b, Aurea Quiles HS, Guanica, P.R.
12. Aaron Gentry, ss, Berry (Ga.) Coll.
13. Derek Feramisco, of, Fresno State U.
14. Rob Macrory, 2b, Auburn U.
15. Jason Michaels, of, U. of Miami.
16. Jeremy Lambert, rhp, Kearns (Utah) HS.
17. Tim Davis, of, Atkinson County HS, Pearson, Ga.
18. David Kim, of, Seton Hall U.
19. Jeff Munster, rhp, Fresno CC.
20. Justin Brunette, lhp, San Diego State U.
21. Wes McCrotty, lhp, Russellville (Ark.) HS.
22. Tristan Jerue, rhp, U. of Georgia.
23. Chris Martine, c, George Mason U.
24. Jose Rodriguez, lhp, Florida International U.
25. Michael Huffaker, rhp, Birmingham-Southern Coll.
26. Craig Hopson, rhp, Boylan Catholic HS, Rockford, Ill.
27. Luke Quaccia, 1b, Stanford U.
28. Neal Arnold, rhp, U. of Nebraska-Kearney.
29. Derek Gooden, rhp, Brewton-Parker (Ga.) Coll.
30. Taber Maier, ss, Cal Poly San Luis Obispo.
31. Brady Gick, c, Ohio U.
32. Andy Kroneberger, 2b, Camarillo (Calif.) HS.
33. Blake Ledbetter, c, Bertrand, Mo.
34. Michael Speckhardt, of, Marist Coll.
35. Robert Vazquez, 3b, Westmar (Iowa) U.
36. Andy Bevins, of, San Diego State U.
37. Stephen Schaub, of, Cowley County (Kan.) CC.
38. Carl Gooden, of, MacArthur HS, Houston.
39. Remer McIntyre, of, Hillsborough HS, Tampa.
40. Scott Wilson, 3b-rhp, Tulane U.
41. Doug Gant, lhp, Central HS, Macon, Ga.
42. Jeremy Weinburg, 3b, Sonora HS, La Habra, Calif.
43. Cody Getz, lhp, Wooster HS, Reno, Nev.
44. William Eyre, rhp, Snow (Utah) JC.
45. Lionel Rogers, rhp, Fresno CC.
46. Josh Dorminy, 1b, Middle Georgia JC.

SAN DIEGO (26)

1. Kevin Nicholson, ss, Stetson U.
2. Ben Howard, rhp, Central Merry HS, Jackson, Tenn.
3. Jerry Darr, rhp, Glen Rose HS, Malvern, Ark.
4. Tony Lawrence, c, Louisiana Tech.
5. Tim Hummel, ss, Burke HS, Montgomery, N.Y.
6. Brittan Motley, of, Hickman Mills HS, Kansas City, Mo.
7. Douglas Young, rhp, Sierra (Calif.) JC.
8. Jason Dunaway, ss, Seward County (Kan.) CC.
9. Junior Herndon, rhp, Moffat County HS, Craig, Colo.
10. Tony Cosentino, c, West Torrance (Calif.) HS
11. David Maurer, lhp, Oklahoma State U.
12. Pat Ryan, rhp, U. of South Florida.
13. Brent Horsman, of, Solano (Calif.) CC.
14. Brian Dowell, rhp, Alvin (Texas) CC.
15. Kevin Burford, of, Rancho Santiago (Calif.) JC.
16. Shawn Camp, rhp, George Mason U.
17. Michael Tejada, c, Provo (Utah) HS.
18. Brandon Hemmings, of, Abraham Baldwin Agricultural (Ga.) JC.
19. Karl Ryden, of, Alvin (Texas) CC.
20. Jonathon Stone, 2b, Lodi (Calif.) HS.
21. Johnny Hunter, of, Texas A&M U.
22. Ricky Guttormson, rhp, Edmonds (Wash.) CC.
23. Scott Seal, 1b, Cal State Fullerton.
24. Clay Snellgrove, ss, Middle Tennessee State U.
25. Brian Jergenson, of-1b, U. of Northern Iowa.
26. Patrick Bourland, ss, Durango (Colo.) HS.
27. Ron French, c, Northgate HS, Concord, Calif.
28. Joe DeMarco, ss, U. of Kansas.
29. Shawn Garrett, ss, South Central HS, Kinmundy, Ill.
30. Todd Naff, rhp, St. Edwards (Texas) U.
31. Jon Oisseth, lhp, Kansas State U.
32. Ryan O'Donnell, c, Casa Grande (Ariz.) HS.
33. Chad Olszanski, ss, San Pasqual HS, Escondido, Calif.
34. Jason Rakers, 3b, Quincy (Ill.) U.
35. Bryan DeLeon, rhp, Trujillo Alto, P.R.
36. Dustin Viator, rhp, Nicholls State U.
37. Greg Bochy, rhp, Mount Carmel HS, Poway, Calif.
38. Josh France, c, Brophy Jesuit HS, Phoenix.
39. Jesse Curry, 1b, Gresham Union HS, Gresham, Ore.
40. Gus Ornstein, 1b, Michigan State U.
41. Ryan Quinn, 3b, Brother Rice HS, Chicago.
42. Bryce Trudeau, rhp, San Bernardino HS, Redlands, Calif.

SAN FRANCISCO (4)

1. Jason Grilli, rhp, Seton Hall U.
1. Dan McKinley, of, Arizona State U. (Supplemental pick—49th—for failure to sign 1996 first-round pick Matt White).
2. Scott Linebrink, rhp, Southwest Texas State U.
3. Jeff Andra, lhp, Oklahoma U.
4. Kevin McGerry, rhp, Father Judge HS, Philadelphia.
5. Giuseppe Chiaramonte, c, Fresno State U.
6. Kevin Joseph, rhp, Rice U.
7. Joe Farley, lhp, Capital HS, Olympia, Wash.
8. Brett Casper, of, Oral Roberts U.
9. Todd Bellhorn, lhp, U. of Central Florida.
10. Joe Holland, lhp, Bowling Green State U.
11. Travis Young, 2b, U. of New Mexico.
12. Jason Verdugo, rhp, Arizona State U.
13. C.J. Ankrum, 1b, Cal State Fullerton.
14. William Otero, ss, Ohio Dominican Coll.
15. Mike Byas, of, Southwest Missouri State U.
16. Tom Nielsen, lhp, Fordham U.
17. Scott Goodman, of, Cuesta (Calif.) JC.
18. Darin Cissell, of, Saint Louis U.
19. Nathan Rice, lhp, Cal State Northridge.
20. Jesse Travis, rhp, U. of Portland.
21. Paul Stryhas, 3b, Manatee (Fla.) CC.
22. Mark Hills, lhp, Chemeketa (Ore.) CC.
23. Bryan Guse, c, U. of Minnesota.
24. Will Malerich, lhp, Coll. of William & Mary.
25. Justin Lincoln, ss, Sarasota (Fla.) HS.
26. Todd Uzzell, rhp, El Paso (Texas) CC.
27. Shawn Austin, lhp, Florida Southern Coll.
28. George Crawford, of, Madison HS, Portland, Ore.
29. Zachary Wells, of, Diablo Valley (Calif.) JC.
30. Tim Flaherty, c, East Carolina U.
31. Clay Greene, 2b-of, U. of Tennessee.
32. Luis Santiago, rhp, Adolfo Rivera HS, Penuelas, P.R.

33. Mike Stevenson, rhp, Orange Coast (Calif.) JC.
34. Ty Burch, of, Cosumnes River (Calif.) JC.
35. Shawn Lindsey, of, Lower Columbia (Wash.) JC.
36. Dennis Anderson, c, Pima (Ariz.) CC.
37. Jonathan Storke, ss, Cuesta (Calif.) JC.
38. Lance Woodcock, ss, American River (Calif.) JC.
39. Justin Thurman, lhp, Blue Mountain (Ore.) CC.
40. Andy Neufeld, ss, Oviedo HS, Winter Springs, Fla.
41. Clifton Bowie, of, Alba HS, La Batre, Alberta.
42. John Tatum, c, Forest Hill HS, West Palm Beach, Fla.
43. Mark Mosier, 3b, U. of Chicago.
44. Jeremy Luster, 3b-1b, DeKalb (Ga.) JC.
45. Chad Faircloth, of, UNC Asheville.

SEATTLE (19)

1. Ryan Anderson, lhp, Divine Child HS, Westland, Mich.
2. Brandon Parker, rhp, U. of Southern Mississippi (Choice from Angels—55th—as compensation for Type B free agent Dave Hollins).
2. Patrick Boyd, of, Central Catholic HS, Clearwater, Fla.
3. Patrick Dunham, rhp, Auburn U.
4. Scott Prouty, rhp, Pekin HS, Marquette Heights, Ill.
5. Jermaine Clark, 2b, U. of San Francisco.
6. Harvey Hargrove, 2b, Sacramento State U.
7. Sam Walton, lhp, W.W. Samuel HS, Dallas.
8. Allan Simpson, rhp, Taft (Calif.) JC.
9. Frank Corr, c, Father Lopez HS, Deltona, Fla.
10. Peter Duprey, lhp, Forest HS, Ocala, Fla.
11. Cip Garcia, c, La Cueva HS, Rio Rancho, N.M.
12. Joel Pineiro, rhp, Edison (Fla.) CC.
13. Bret Soverel, rhp, Florida International U.
14. Peter Bauer, rhp, Paint Branch HS, Silver Springs, Md.
15. Richard Sundstrom, rhp, Cypress (Calif.) JC.
16. Danny Delgado, rhp, Monsignor Pace HS, Miami.
17. Clint Chrysler, lhp, Stetson U.
18. Ryan Oase, rhp-1b, Edmonds (Wash.) CC.
19. Jamie Clark, of, Brandon (Fla.) HS.
20. Mike Marchiano, of, Fordham U.
21. Emmanuel Ulloa, rhp, George Washington HS, Bronx, N.Y.
22. Hubert Parker, ss-2b, Eisenhower HS, Rialto, Calif.
23. Jim Abbott, rhp, Caledonia (Mich.) HS.
24. Jason Farren, rhp, Karns City (Pa.) Area HS.
25. Ryan Reynolds, 3b, The Woodlands (Texas) HS.
26. Glenn Murphy, lhp, Madison (Fla.) County HS.
27. John Gabaldon, rhp, La Cueva HS, Albuquerque.
28. Kirk Bolling, rhp, Saddleback (Calif.) CC.
29. Matt Huntingford, of, West Vancouver (British Columbia) HS.
30. Aaron Looper, rhp, Westark (Ark.) CC.
31. Matt Woodward, 1b, Florida State U.
32. Dave Garley, rhp, Glendale (Calif.) CC.
33. Cordell Lindsey, 3b, Blinn (Texas) JC.
34. Eric Mitchell, c, DuBois (Pa.) Area HS.
35. Israel Torres, lhp, Dominguez HS, Compton, Calif.
36. Brian Ferreira, of, Barron Collier HS, Naples, Fla.
37. Mario Jackson, of, Pasadena (Calif.) CC.
38. Ryan Webb, 3b, Citrus (Calif.) JC.
39. Brian Spottsville, ss, Compton (Calif.) HS.
40. Joseph Reyes, ss, Farmington (N.M.) HS.
41. Kaazim Summerville, of, Burlingame (Calif.) HS.
42. Andrew Padilla, ss, Highland HS, Bakersfield, Calif.
43. Bryan Krill, rhp, Rancho Santiago (Calif.) JC.
44. Peter Graham, rhp, Brookdale (N.J.) CC.
45. Shaun Stokes, rhp, Jefferson Township HS, Oak Ridge, N.J.
46. Barry Hawkins, rhp, Saddleback (Calif.) CC.
47. Thomas Cunningham, c, Leesburg (Fla.) HS.
48. Nick Padilla, rhp, St. Paul HS, Whittier, Calif.
49. Joe Barnes, of, Indian River (Fla.) CC.
50. Jonathan Brandt, rhp, Palo Alto (Calif.) HS.
51. Chris Silva, lhp, Queensborough (N.Y.) CC.
52. Shah Bobonis, rhp, Southridge HS, Miami.
53. Scott Starkey, lhp, Palomar (Calif.) JC.
54. Kie Polard, of, Crenshaw HS, Los Angeles.
55. D.J. Houlton, rhp, Servite HS, Yorba Linda, Calif.
56. Kevin Bice, rhp, Rancho Santiago (Calif.) JC.
57. Kyle Albright, of, Palomar (Calif.) JC.
58. Chris Mayberry, 3b, Saugus (Calif.) HS.
59. Jamel White, of, Antelope Valley (Calif.) JC.
60. Desmond Dailey, of, Eastern Arizona JC.

TAMPA BAY (30)

1. Jason Standridge, rhp, Hewitt Trussville HS, Trussville, Ala.
2. Kenny Kelly, of, Tampa Catholic HS.
3. Barrett Wright, rhp, Myers Park HS, Charlotte.
4. Todd Belitz, lhp, Washington State U.

MEL BAILEY

Mariners first-rounder
Ryan Anderson joins Randy Johnson with Seattle

5. Marquis Roberts, lhp-of, McLane HS, Fresno.
6. Doug Mansfield, of, Jacksonville HS, Sherwood, Ark.
7. Eddy Reyes, rhp, U. of Miami.
8. Jack Joffrion, ss, Lamar U.
9. Toby Hall, c, U. of Nevada-Las Vegas.
10. Carl Hutchens, rhp, Anderson HS, Austin.
11. Chris Wright, rhp, Cowley County (Kan.) CC.
12. Carlos Vazquez, c, Caribbean HS, Ponce, P.R.
13. Kevin Price, rhp, Bingham HS, Riverton, Utah.
14. Casey Davis, lhp, Boyd County HS, Ashland, Ky.
15. Jason Guerrero, ss, Pittsburg (Calif.) HS.
16. Lazaro Gutierrez, lhp, U. of Miami.
17. Chris Bootcheck, rhp, LaPorte (Ind.) HS.
18. Terry McCormick, lhp, Jesuit HS, Tampa.
19. Lavar Johnson, of, North Shore HS, Houston.
20. Matt Kaffel, rhp, Blinn (Texas) JC.
21. Damian Scioneaux, of, Mississippi State U.
22. Dustin Carr, 2b, U. of Houston.
23. Paul Hoover, ss, Kent U.
24. Travis Miller, of, Dallas Baptist U.
25. Josh Davis, rhp, Tallahassee (Fla.) CC.
26. Coty Cooper, rhp, Seward County (Kan.) CC.
27. Anthony Pigott, of, Elon (N.C.) Coll.
28. Jason Jiminez, lhp, San Jose State U.
29. Ryan Jorgensen, c, Kingwood (Tenn.) HS.
30. Jon Cummins, rhp, Indiana (Pa.) U.
31. Michael Meseberg, of, Royal HS, Othello, Wash.
32. Jeremy Murch, lhp, Sarasota (Fla.) HS.
33. Daniel Firlit, ss, Rend Lake (Ill.) JC.
34. Kris Ehmke, rhp, Thomas Stewart HS, Peterborough, Ontario.
35. Ben Peterson, rhp, East Lake HS, Tarpon Springs, Fla.
36. Chris Mason, rhp, U. of Alabama-Birmingham.
37. Heath McKoin, lhp, Watson Chapel HS, Pine Bluff, Ark.
38. Ryan Pandolfini, 1b, Rider U.
39. Jim Munroe, rhp, Servite HS, Orange, Calif.
40. David Cash, rhp, Davis HS, Modesto, Calif.
41. John Hutchens, rhp, Fort Gibson (Okla.) HS.
42. Lee Southard, rhp, Westmoore HS, Oklahoma City.
43. Nicholas Rhodes, c, Norwalk (Conn.) CC.
44. Alan Lowden, lhp, Hays HS, Kyle, Texas.
45. Adam Luczycky, rhp, Labette Community (Kan.) JC.

46. Marlyn Tisdale, rhp, Florida CC.
47. Fred Mitchell, of, Kathleen HS, Lakeland, Fla.
48. Josh Long, 3b, Northview HS, McDavid, Fla.
49. Jason Balkcom, rhp, Young Harris (Ga.) JC.
50. Chris Reynolds, rhp, North Lake (Texas) CC.
51. Ivar Wentzel, lhp, Flagler Palm Coast HS, Palm Coast, Fla.
52. Kyle Evans, rhp, Eldorado HS, Albuquerque.
53. Dustin McKey, of, John Carroll HS, Alabaster, Ala.
54. Alan Keller, c, Mendocino (Calif.) CC.
55. Tyler Tiesing, c, Butler County (Kan.) CC.
56. Nick Lyon, of, Monroe (Wash.) HS.
57. Jeremy Robinson, lhp, Okaloosa-Walton (Fla.) CC.
58. David Berry, c, Pearce HS, Richardson, Texas.
59. Cedric Razor, 2b, Pitt County (N.C.) CC.
60. Richard McCabe, rhp, Camden HS, St. Mary's, Ga.
61. Ron Brooks, rhp, Tallahassee (Fla.) CC.
62. Tavaris Keyes, rhp, Central HS, Fort Pierce, Fla.
63. Steve Gause, rhp, Jenkins HS, Lakeland, Fla.
64. Chris Wood, ss, Vanguard HS, Ocala, Fla.
65. Zachary Roper, 3b, Pasco-Hernando (Fla.) CC.
66. Ray Nevels, of, Sarasota (Fla.) HS.
67. Rafael Erazo, rhp, Labette Community (Kan.) JC.
68. Dusty Hall, ss, Lincoln HS, Gahanna, Ohio.
69. Heath Bell, rhp, Rancho Santiago (Calif.) JC.
70. Ken Baugh, rhp, Lamar HS, Houston.
71. Carlos Perez, 2b, Roosevelt HS, Brooklyn.
72. Julio Fortuna, rhp, Bushwick HS, Brooklyn.
73. John Gillespie, rhp, Lake Washington HS, Redmond, Wash.
74. Jarrod Reineke, rhp, Grove HS, Joplin, Mo.
75. Brian Brown, ss, Olney Central (Ill.) JC.
76. Brandon Brewer, rhp, Greely HS, Yarmouth, Maine.
77. Jeff Dragg, of, Covington HS, Madisonville, La.
78. Rob Meyers, rhp, De La Salle HS, Concord, Calif.
79. Jon Smith, lhp, Ferris HS, Nuevo, Calif.
80. Clint Kinsey, rhp, Allen County (Kan.) CC.
81. Jon Williams, c, Fox HS, Imperial, Mo.
82. Zach Lekse, ss, Sacramento CC.
83. Blake Williams, rhp, San Marcos (Texas) HS.
84. Mark Madsen, rhp, Quartz Hill HS, Lancaster, Calif.
85. Chad Ashlock, rhp, Seward County (Kan.) CC.
86. Bryan Edwards, rhp, Bowie HS, Austin.
87. Jon Benick, c, Greater Nanticoke HS, Glen Lyon, Pa.
88. Bart Carter, 1b, William Carey (Miss.) Coll.
89. Robbie Hammock, c, DeKalb (Ga.) JC.
90. William Harris, 2b-ss, Middle Georgia JC.
91. Beau Barcus, 3b, San Lorenzo HS, Ben Lomond, Calif.
92. Andy Baxter, ss, Unicoi County HS, Erwin, Tenn.

TEXAS (23)

1. (Choice to Yankees—24th—as compensation for Type A free agent John Wetteland).
1. Jason Romano, 3b, Hillsborough HS, Tampa (Supplemental pick—39th—for loss of Type A free agent Mike Stanton).
2. Jason Grabowski, c, U. of Connecticut.
2. Chris Tynan, rhp, Hudson's Bay HS, Vancouver, Wash. (Choice from Yankees—77th—as compensation for Stanton).
3. Brandon Warriax, ss, Purnell Swett HS, Pembroke, N.C.
4. David Elder, rhp, Georgia Tech.
5. Trey Poland, lhp, U. of Southwestern Louisiana.
6. Dan DeYoung, rhp, U. of Mississippi.
7. Mike Lamb, c, Cal State Fullerton.
8. Billy Diaz, rhp, Academia Adventista HS, Caguas, P.R.
9. Carlos Figueroa, lhp, Jose Lazaro HS, Carolina, P.R.
10. Kevin Harris, of, Tampa Bay Tech HS.
11. Tom Sergio, 2b, North Carolina State U.
12. Corey Wright, of, Workman HS, La Puente, Calif.
13. Robbie Milner, rhp, Deer Valley HS, Phoenix.
14. Jason Torres, c, John Carroll HS, Vero Beach, Fla.
15. Karl Jernigan, ss, Milton HS, Navarre, Fla.
16. Kevin Ruedi, rhp, Sacramento CC.
17. Geronimo Cruz, of, Alfred (N.Y.) U.
18. Jaime Bubela, of, Cypress Falls HS, Houston.
19. Travis Hughes, rhp, Cowley County (Kan.) CC.
20. Jay Signorelli, rhp, Lake Brantley HS, Altamonte Springs, Fla.
21. Jeff Ridenour, rhp, Southern Illinois U.-Edwardsville.
22. Curtis Gay, 1b, Cowley County (Kan.) CC.
23. Quenten Patterson, rhp, Blinn (Texas) JC.
24. Brian Shipp, ss, Central HS, Baton Rouge.
25. Alex Vazquez, of, Montgomery (Md.) JC.
26. David Lundberg, rhp, San Diego Mesa JC.
27. Tanner Herrick, 1b, Show Low (Ariz.) HS.
28. Mike Eskildsen, rhp, Maple Ridge (British Columbia) HS.
29. Jason Young, rhp, Berkeley (Calif.) HS.
30. Derek Hines, of, Yavapai (Ariz.) JC.
31. David Curtiss, ss, Havre (Mon.) HS.
32. Jeff Fields, c, Alamogordo (N.M.) HS.
33. Mitchell Jones, 3b, Utah Valley State JC.
34. Devon Younger, rhp, Meridian (Miss.) CC.
35. Kelley Gulledge, c, Mansfield HS, Arlington, Texas.
36. David Wigley, c, George C. Wallace (Ala.) CC.
37. Blakely Allen, rhp, Russell HS, Alexander City, Ala.
38. Jason Beitey, rhp, Olympic (Wash.) JC.
39. Peter Orr, ss, New Market HS, Hamilton, Ontario.
40. Craig Mosher, lhp, McRoberts HS, Richmond, British Columbia.
41. Josh Hawes, rhp, CC of Rhode Island.

TORONTO (5)

1. Vernon Wells, of, Bowie HS, Arlington, Texas.
2. (Choice to Red Sox—57th—as compensation for Type A free agent Roger Clemens).
3. Billy Brown, of, Florida Atlantic U.
4. Woody Heath, rhp, Green River (Wash.) CC.
5. Michael Young, ss, UC Santa Barbara.
6. Paul Chiaffredo, c, Santa Clara U.
7. Matt McClellan, rhp, Oakland (Mich.) U.
8. Joe Casey, rhp, Twin Valley HS, Elverson, Pa.
9. Carlos Ortiz, c, Loara HS, Anaheim.
10. Matt Bowser, 1b, Tarpon Springs HS, Palm Harbor, Fla.
11. Ron Bost, lhp, Central Cabarrus HS, Harrisburg, N.C.
12. Randy Eversgerd, rhp, Eastern Illinois U.
13. Travis Hubbel, rhp, East Glen Composite HS, Edmonton, Alberta.
14. Cameron Reimers, rhp, Sentinel HS, Missoula, Mon.
15. Colin Brackeen, lhp, St. Olaf (Minn.) Coll.
16. Dustin Seale, lhp, Safford (Ariz.) HS.
17. Brian Barnett, ss, Linfield (Ore.) Coll.
18. Matt Weimer, rhp, Penn State U.
19. Erik Lorenz, rhp, U. of Wisconsin-Whitewater.
20. Mark Hendricksen, lhp, Mount Vernon, Wash.
21. David Huggins, rhp, McNeese State U.
22. John Sneed, rhp, Texas A&M U.
23. Derek DeVaughan, rhp, Seminole State (Okla.) JC.
24. Anthony Salley, lhp, Wofford Coll.
25. Perfecto Gaud, lhp, Luis Munoz Marin HS, Yauco, P.R.
26. Floyd Mack, of, Mays HS, Fairburn, Ga.
27. Fred Smith, of, Volunteer State (Tenn.) CC.
28. Andrew Barrett, ss, Stadium HS, Tacoma.
29. Juan Santos, c-1b, Florida CC.
30. Tim Lacefield, rhp, Harding (Ark.) U.
31. Jermaine Davis, of, Chesnee (S.C.) HS.
32. Sean Green, rhp, Male HS, Louisville.
33. Taylor Smith, rhp, Green Valley HS, Henderson, Nev.
34. Jamie Jenkins, rhp, Hill HS, Miramachi, New Brunswick.
35. Josh Stevens, rhp, Jurupa Valley HS, Mira Loma, Calif.
36. Simon Stoner, rhp, Duchess Park HS, Prince George, British Columbia.
37. Jason Burkley, c-3b, Lexington (Ky.) Catholic HS.
38. Chivas Clark, of, Northeast HS, Macon, Ga.
39. Matt Easterday, 2b, Newton County HS, Covington, Ga.
40. Michael Ramsey, of, Columbus (Ga.) HS.
41. Patrick Versluis, rhp, Saddleback (Calif.) CC.
42. Andrew Beattie, ss, Pasco-Hernando (Fla.) CC.
43. Orlando Hudson, ss, Spartanburg Methodist (S.C.) JC.
44. Todd Thompson, rhp, Indian Hills (Iowa) CC.
45. Brandon Long, lhp, Central Alabama CC.
46. Brad Hawpe, lhp, Boswell HS, Fort Worth, Texas.
47. Jesus Lebron, of, Orlando.
48. David Siboda, rhp, Southeast Missouri State U.
49. Anthony Novelli, rhp, West Valley (Calif.) JC.
50. Michael Albert, ss, Grossmont (Calif.) JC.
51. Chad Schmidt, of, Blinn (Texas) JC.
52. Chad Qualls, rhp, Los Angeles Harbor JC.
53. Jeff Nettles, 3b, Palomar (Calif.) JC.
54. Craig Lariz, 1b, Indian River (Fla.) CC.
55. Rashard Casey, of, Penn State U.
56. Arlyn Dozier, of, Vermillion Catholic HS, Abbeville, La.
57. Travis Cole, rhp, Lakeridge HS, Lake Oswego, Ore.
58. William Traber, lhp, El Segundo (Calif.) HS.
59. Michael Willetts, rhp, Abraham Baldwin Agricultural (Ga.) JC.
60. Brandon Tellis, of, Charleston (Mis.) HS.
61. Gary Peete, of, Itawamba (Miss.) JC.
62. Matthew Dempsey, 1b, Cypress (Calif.) JC.
63. Charles Lawrence, of, Lakeside HS, Decatur, Ga.
64. Jeremiah Barnes, rhp, Downey (Calif.) HS.
65. William Wagner, of, Elmore County HS, Eclectic, Ala.
66. Cameron Newitt, rhp, Northwest Shoals (Ala.) JC.
67. Dave Steffler, rhp, Winthrop U.

Obituaries/Index

OBITUARIES

November 1996-October 1997

Cal Abrams, a former major league outfielder best remembered for being thrown out at the plate in the deciding game of the 1950 National League pennant race, died of a heart attack Feb. 25 in Fort Lauderdale. He was 72. In the final game of the 1950 season, he was thrown out at the plate by the Phillies' Richie Ashburn in the bottom of the ninth. Had Abrams scored, Brooklyn would have forced a one-game playoff.

Fred Anderson, owner of the California League's Modesto franchise, died March 24 in Sacramento. He was 72. Anderson died before the unveiling of the team's remodeled Joe Thurman Stadium, but not before he saved professional baseball in Modesto. In spite of middling enthusiasm from the city, Anderson kept the team there and eventually persuaded the city to pay for a renovation of Thurman Stadium, which opened in 1952.

Richie Ashburn, a Phillies broadcaster and Hall of Fame player, died of a heart attack Sept. 9 in New York, hours after broadcasting a Phillies-Mets game at Shea Stadium. He was 70. Ashburn also played for two years with the Cubs and for the Mets during their first season in 1962. Ashburn was part of the Philadelphia sportscape for 50 years as a Hall of Fame outfielder, a newspaper columnist and, for the last 35 years, a radio and television announcer.

JOHN KLEIN

Richie Ashburn

Harry Bardt, a member of the Dodgers board of directors, died Nov. 15 in Beverly Hills, Calif. He was 97. Bardt had been on the club's board since 1967. He also served as team treasurer from 1975-80. Bardt was known as "Banker to the Stars" during his career at Bank of America, which began in 1928.

Rex Barney, known more for his role as the Orioles public-address announcer than his six-season major league career as a pitcher, died Aug. 12 in Baltimore. He was 72. Barney, a righthander, spent parts of six seasons with the Brooklyn Dodgers from 1943-1950, compiling a 35-31, 4.33 career record. Barney spent more than 20 seasons as the Orioles' announcer. His trademark "Give that fan a contract," and "Thank youuuu," were staples at both Memorial Stadium and Camden Yards.

Tim Bishop, an outfielder for the Class A Capital City Bombers, was hit by a car and killed April 19 in Columbia, S.C. He was 22. Bishop, a 57th-round draft pick in 1994, was the Bombers' starting center fielder. He was hitting .204 and led the Bombers with seven stolen bases when he died.

Gene Brabender, who shares the record for wins by a pitcher on an expansion team, died Dec. 27 in Madison, Wis. He was 55. A righthander, Brabender went 35-43, 4.25 with the Orioles, Seattle Pilots and Brewers. In 1969, the Pilots' first and only year of existence, he went 13-14, 4.36.

Joe Branzell, the Rangers' area scout for Maryland and Virginia and a club employee since its founding as the Washington Senators in 1961, died of leukemia Sept. 28 in Washington. He was 78.

Ralph "Country" Brown, an outfielder who won two minor league batting titles, died Dec. 24 in Rome, Ga. He was 75. Brown led the Class C Florida International League in batting (.381) in 1946, and he followed up in 1947 by leading the South Atlantic League with a .356 average.

Bob "Sugar" Cain, best remembered for pitching to a midget, died of cancer April 7 in Cleveland. He was 72. A lefthander, Cain went 37-44, 4.50 in 140 games with the White Sox, Tigers and St. Louis Browns from 1949-53. Cain's claim to fame came Aug. 19, 1951, when Browns owner Bill Veeck sent 3-foot-7 Eddie Gaedel up as a pinch-hitter in the second game of a Browns-Tigers doubleheader. Cain walked Gaedel on four pitches.

Marino Castillo, a righthander for the Padres' Triple-A Las Vegas affiliate, died in a car crash in the Dominican Republic Sept. 14. He was 26.

Jack Kent Cooke, better known for his football and basketball pursuits but also instrumental in landing Toronto a major league franchise, died of a heart attack April 6 in Washington, D.C. He was 84. Cooke's first sports venture came in 1951, when he purchased the International League's Toronto Maple Leafs. His ownership is credited for paving the way for the Blue Jays, who began American League play in 1977.

Piper Davis, who had a long Negro Leagues and minor league playing career before becoming a scout for three organizations, died May 21 in Birmingham. He was 79. The versatile Davis played for the Birmingham Black Barons from 1942-50, managing the team in 1948 and '49.

Mike Diebolt, a lefthander for short-season Jamestown of the Tigers organization, died Sept. 5 in a car accident in suburban Cleveland. He was 22. During his final season (1997) at the University of Minnesota, Diebolt put together a 7-4, 3.99 record in which he had 110 strikeouts to break Dave Winfield's single-season school record.

Woody English, a shortstop/third baseman who played in the first All-Star Game and in two World Series for the Cubs, died Sept. 26 in Newark, Ohio. He was 90. The Cubs' captain for six years, English appeared in the 1933 All-Star Game and the 1929 and 1932 World Series.

Mat Erwin, a catcher for the Sioux Falls Canaries of the independent Northern League and a former Marlins farmhand, was shot and killed Sept. 12 in Sacramento. He was 24.

Hector Espino, the Mexican League's all-time home run leader, died of a heart attack Sept. 7 in Monterrey, Mexico. He was 58. Espino, a first baseman, played 24 seasons each in the Mexican League and winter Mexican Pacific League. He also played briefly for Triple-A Jacksonville. Espino's lifetime Mexican League average was .335 and he won five batting titles and played for seven teams, including 13 seasons with the Monterrey Sultans.

Curt Flood, whose challenge of baseball's reserve system altered the face of sports, died of throat cancer Jan. 20 in Los Angeles. He was 59. Flood, an outfielder who won seven Gold Gloves and made three All-Star Game appearances, is best remembered for his courtroom battle. He took his fight all the way to the U.S. Supreme Court, paving the way for baseball free agency. The Cardinals traded Flood to the Phillies in a seven-player deal in October 1969. By refusing to report to Philadelphia, he challenged baseball's reserve clause, which bound players to their teams indefinitely. Flood asked commissioner Bowie Kuhn to declare him a free agent but was turned down. Claiming that baseball was violating antitrust laws, Flood filed a lawsuit in January 1970. The case eventually reached the Supreme Court in 1972, with Flood losing the decision.

James Gentry, a righthander who spent parts of five seasons with the Detroit Tigers, died July 3 in Winston-Salem, N.C. He was 79. His career major league record was 13-17.

Irving Gordon, who wrote the "Who's On First" sketch for Abbott and Costello but was more noted as a songwriter, died Dec. 1 in Los Angeles. He was 81.

Fred Green, a reliever on the Pirates' 1960 World Series championship team, died of a heart attack Dec. 22 in Titusville, N.J. He was 62.

Luman Harris, who managed the Atlanta Braves to their first division title, died Nov. 11 in Pell City, Ala. He was 81. A righthander, Harris went 35-63, 4.16 with the Philadelphia Athletics and Washington Senators from 1941-47. Harris went 466-488 in parts of eight seasons managing Baltimore, Houston and Atlanta. The Braves won the National League West with a 93-69 record in 1969.

DIAMOND IMAGES

Doug Million

Buddy Hassett, a former big league first baseman, died Aug. 23 in Westwood, N.J. He was 85. Hassett batted .292-12-343 in 929 games with the Brooklyn Dodgers (1936-38), Boston Braves (1939-41) and Yankees (1942).

Joe Hauser, the only professional player with two 60-homer seasons, died July 11 in Sheboygan, Wis. He was 98. A first baseman, Hauser hit 63 homers in the International League in 1930 and 69 in the American Association in 1933, the sixth- and second-best single-season totals in pro history. He won five minor league home run crowns and ranks sixth all-time with 399 minor league homers. Hauser also played six seasons in the majors with the Philadelphia Athletics and Indians from 1922-29, batting .284-80-356 in 629 games.

Mark Holtz, a broadcaster for the Rangers, died Sept. 7 in Dallas of complications from a bone-marrow transplant for leukemia. He was 51. Holtz became the team's radio announcer in 1981, and he stayed in that job until 1994, when he took over as the team's television play-by-play announcer. Holtz was honored as Texas sportscaster of the year eight times and was elected to the Texas baseball hall of fame in 1990.

Art Hunt, who twice led the Pacific Coast League in home runs and RBIs, died Nov. 25 in Federal Way, Wash. He was 89. An outfielder, Hunt played in the minors from 1927-39. Playing for Seattle, he led the PCL with 30 homers in 1936 and with 39 in 1937.

Don Hutson, an NFL hall of fame wide receiver who had a brief minor league baseball career, died June 26 in Rancho Mirage, Calif. He was 84. Hutson played two years of minor league baseball as an outfielder and hit .301-7-61 with 41 steals in 194 games.

Billy Jurges, a former all-star shortstop, died March 3 in Clearwater, Fla. He was 88. Known as a slick fielder, Jurges hit .258-43-656 in 1,816 games with the Cubs and New York Giants from 1931-47.

Dwight Lowry, manager of the short-season New York-Penn League's Jamestown Jammers, died of heart failure July 10 in Jamestown, N.Y. He was 39. Lowry's 11-year playing career included four seasons in the major leagues, mostly as a reserve. He was a catcher for the 1984 World Series champion Tigers, and played his last major league game in 1988 with the Twins. He spent three seasons as manager at Class A Fayetteville before taking over at Jamestown in 1997.

Cliff Mapes, an outfielder who twice had "his" number retired by the Yankees, died Dec. 5 in Pryor, Okla. He was 74. Mapes batted .242-38-172 in 459 big league games from 1948-52. He wore No. 3 until the Yankees retired it in honor of Babe Ruth in 1948. He switched to No. 13 and then to No. 7, which became Mickey Mantle's number.

Phil "Babe" Marchildon, a former major league pitcher who was a prisoner of war in Germany during World War II, died of cancer Jan. 10 in Toronto. He was 83. A righthander, Marchildon went 68-75, 3.93 in 185 games with the Philadelphia Athletics and Red Sox in nine seasons from 1940-50.

Eddie Miller, a seven-time big league all-star, died July 31 in Lake Worth, Fla. He was 80. Miller, a shortstop, batted .238-97-640 in 1,510 games with the Reds (1936-37, 1943-47), Braves (1939-42), Phillies (1948-49) and Cardinals (1950).

Doug Million, a lefthander in the Rockies system, a first-round draft choice and Baseball America's 1994 High School Player of the Year, died of an asthma attack Sept. 24 in Mesa, Ariz. He was 21. The Rockies drafted Million, then a rail-thin 6-foot-4, out of Sarasota (Fla.) High. He signed for $905,000. After an impressive first pro season in the Rookie-level Arizona League (1-0, 2.50) and at short-season Bend (5-3, 2.34), Million put on 30 pounds over the winter and struggled to regain his old form.

Sam Narron, a former big league player and coach who appeared in two World Series, died of congestive heart failure Dec. 31 in Middlesex, N.C. He was 83. Narron played in the 1943 World Series for the Cardinals and later coached for the Pirates during their 1960 World Series championship season.

Charlie Neal, one of the heroes of the Dodgers' 1959 World Series championship, died Nov. 18 of heart failure in Dallas. He was 65. Neal, who took over for the retired Jackie Robinson at second base for the Dodgers, spent eight seasons in the majors from 1956-63, the first six with the Dodgers. He batted .259-87-391.

Jerry Neudecker, the last major league umpire to use a balloon chest protector, died of cancer Jan. 12 in Fort Walton Beach, Fla. He was 66. Neudecker was an American League umpire from 1965-86.

Don O'Riley, a former big league righthander, was shot and killed in a robbery May 2 in Kansas City, Mo. He was 52. O'Riley went 1-1, 6.17 in 27 games with the Royals from 1969-70.

Alejo Peralta, a member of the Mexican baseball hall of fame, died April 8 in Mexico City. He was 80. Peralta founded the Mexican League's Mexico City Tigers in 1955 and eventually became commissioner of the league.

George Pfister, who worked in baseball since 1939 as a player, manager, coach and Commissioner's Office staffer, died Aug. 14 in Somerset, N.J. He was 78. Pfister spent the last 23 years in the baseball operations department of Major League Baseball. He also worked as the Yankees' farm director from 1965-74. Pfister played one game for the Brooklyn Dodgers in 1941.

Chris Priest, a coach for the Will County Cheetahs of the independent Heartland League and a former Twins farmhand, died of cancer Oct. 4 in Plainfield, Ill. He was 25.

Eddie Sawyer, manager of the "Whiz Kids" Phillies team of 1950, died Sept. 22 in Phoenixville, Pa. He was 87. Sawyer, a former minor league player and manager, led the Phillies in two stints from 1948-1952 and 1958-1960.

Bill Sayles, who pitched in a demonstration game at the 1936 Berlin Olympics, died Nov. 20 in Lincoln City, Ore. He was 79. Sayles pitched in the Olympics while attending the University of Oregon. A righthander, he later would pitch in the big leagues, going 1-3, 5.61 in 28 games with the Red Sox (1939), New York Giants (1943) and Brooklyn Dodgers (1943).

Al Somers, credited with training more major league umpires than anyone else in the game's history, died Oct. 14. He was 92. Somers trained more than 70 big league umpires, according to one of his best students and friends, veteran National League umpire Harry Wendelstedt. Somers began umpiring in the minor leagues in 1940 and continued for 22 years.

Toni Stone, the first woman to play in the Negro American League, died Nov. 2 in Alameda, Calif. She was 75. Stone signed with the Indianapolis Clowns in 1953 after playing with the San Francisco Sea Lions and New Orleans Creoles, independent men's barnstorming teams.

Johnny Vander Meer, who gained a permanent place in baseball lore in 1938 by becoming the only major league pitcher to throw consecutive no-hitters, died Oct. 6 at age 82. Vander Meer, a Reds lefthander, pitched his first no-hitter on June 11, beating the Boston Braves 3-0. The game four days later was already notable as the first night game at Ebbets Field. When Vander Meer no-hit the Brooklyn Dodgers 6-0, he made it historic. He pitched for Cincinnati from 1937-49 except for two years during World War II. He finished up with the Cubs in 1950 and Indians in 1951. His career record was 119-121, 3.44.

Index

GENERAL INFORMATION